THIS EDITION WRITTEN AND RESEARCHED BY
Damian Harper,
Piera Chen, Chung Wah Chow, Megan Eaves, David Eimer, Tienlon Ho,
R... ...ayhew,

Contents

OPERA P977

CHINESE CUISINE P956

Contents

ON THE ROAD

HÚTÒNG, BĚIJĪNG P54
MATT MUNRO /GETTY IMAGES ©

Contents

Welcome to China

Whether it's your first visit or your twentieth, China is so big, so diverse and so fast-changing, it's always an adventure.

Breathtaking Antiquity

Let's face it: the world's oldest continuous civilisation is bound to pull an artefact or two out of its hat. There isn't history at every turn – three decades of perpetual development and socialist town-planning have taken their toll – but travel selectively in China and rich seams of antiquity await exploration. With tumble-down chunks of the Great Wall, mist-wreathed, temple-topped mountains, quaint villages, water towns and sublime Buddhist cave statues, China insists on a couple of requirements: a well-made pair of travelling shoes and a strong stomach for long-distance wayfaring.

Stupendous Scenery

Běijīng, Shànghǎi and Hong Kong are portraits of modern Chinese wherewithal and ambition, but it's the big outdoors that should top your list. From the placid mountain lakes of Tibet, the impassive deserts of Inner Mongolia to island-hopping in Hong Kong or cycling between fairy-tale karst pinnacles around Yángshuò, China's landscapes are beguiling. Swoon before the rice terraces of the south, size up some awesome sand dunes in Gānsù or trace the Great Wall as it meanders across mountain peaks, get lost in forests of bamboo, sail through dramatic river gorges or, when your energy fails you, flake out for a tan on a distant beach.

Cuisine

Treat yourself by trading your meagre local Chinatown menu for the lavish Middle Kingdom cookbook. Wolf down Peking duck, size up a sizzling lamb kebab in Kāifēng or gobble down a bowl of Lánzhōu noodles on the Silk Road. Spicy Húnán or Sìchuān dishes really raise the temperature but don't forget about what's cooking along China's frontier lands – always an excellent excuse to get off the beaten path. Culinary exploration is possibly the most enticing aspect of Middle Kingdom travel: you'll return with stimulated taste buds and much cherished gastronomic memories.

Diversity

China is vast. Off-the-scale massive. A riveting jumble of wildly differing dialects and climatic and topographical extremes, it's like several different countries rolled into one. Take your pick from the tossed-salad ethnic mix of the southwest, the yak-butter illuminated temples of Xiàhé, a journey along the dusty Silk Road, spending the night at Everest Base Camp or getting into your glad rags for a night on the Shànghǎi tiles. You're spoiled for choice: whether you're an urban traveller, hiker, cyclist, explorer, backpacker, irrepressible museum-goer or faddish foodie, China's diversity is second to none.

Why I Love China

By Damian Harper, Author

A passion for Chinese martial arts saw me enrolling for a four-year degree in modern and classical Chinese at university in London back in the 1990s. They were fun days, when travelling China was testing but exciting in equal measure. Must-see hotspots like Píngyáo were unheard of and Shànghǎi's Pǔdōng was a cocktail-free flatland. I could say it's the fantastic food, the awesome landscapes, the fun of train travel, the delightful people or pitching up in a small town I've never been to before, and I wouldn't be lying. But it's the Chinese language I still love most of all.

For more about our authors, see page 1056

Above: Night-time skyline, Shànghǎi (p186)

China

Silk Road
Camels, deserts and
vanished cities (p39)

Dūnhuáng
Silk Road oasis town (p845)

Jiǔzhàigōu National Park
Hiking in the beautiful wilds
of Sìchuān (p764)

Lhasa
The land of snows (p902)

Tiger Leaping Gorge
Stunning
Yúnnán scenery (p687)

Yuányáng Rice Terraces
For beautiful, iconic
views (p667)

RUSSIA

KAZAKHSTAN

TASHKENT

BISHKEK

KYRGYZSTAN

TAJIKISTAN

PAKISTAN

Yīníng

Ūrūmqi

Kuqa

Kashgar

Tashkùrgan

XĪNJIĀNG

MONGOLIA

Dūnhuáng

GĀNSÙ

Zhāngyè

Dégé

Qīnghǎi Hú

Xīníng

Xiàhé

Aldan Gol

Changtang
Nature
Preserve

QĪNGHǍI

Shílín

DELHI

Lake
Manusarovar

Milam
Glacier

TIBET

Siling-tso

Nam-
tso

Nagu Chu

SÌCHUĀN

NEPAL

Mt Everest
(8488m)

Lhasa

KATHMANDU

Thimphu
Valley

THIMPHU

BHUTAN

Zhōngdiàn
(Shangri-la)

Shíbǎoshān

Xiàguān
(Dàlǐ City)

Yangzi River

INDIA

BANGLADESH

DHAKA

MYANMAR
(BURMA)

Kūnmíng

YÚNNÁN

ELEVATION

6000m
5000m
4000m
3000m
2000m
1000m
500m
0

Jǐnghóng

Jǐngzhēn

20°N

NAY PYI
TAW

LAOS

Bay of
Bengal

THAILAND

85°E

90°E

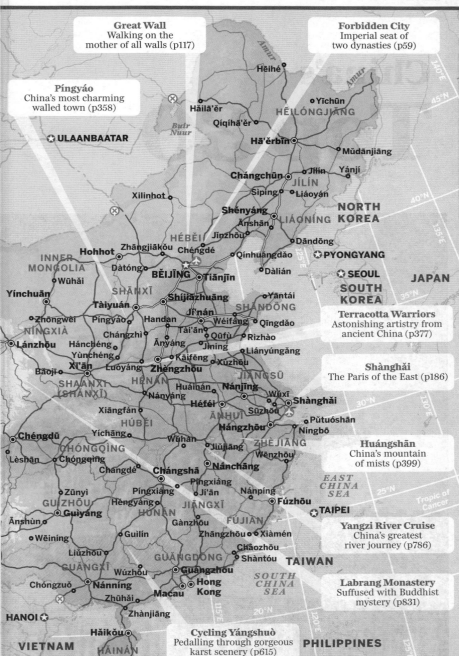

Great Wall
Walking on the mother of all walls (p117)

Forbidden City
Imperial seat of two dynasties (p59)

Píngyáo
China's most charming walled town (p358)

Terracotta Warriors
Astonishing artistry from ancient China (p377)

Shànghǎi
The Paris of the East (p186)

Huángshān
China's mountain of mists (p399)

Yangzi River Cruise
China's greatest river journey (p786)

Labrang Monastery
Suffused with Buddhist mystery (p831)

Cycling Yángshuò
Pedalling through gorgeous karst scenery (p615)

0 — 500 km
0 — 250 miles

China's
Top 30

Forbidden City

1 Not a city and no longer forbidden, Běijīng's enormous palace (p59) is the be-all-and-end-all of dynastic grandeur with its vast halls and splendid gates. No other place in China teems with so much history, legend and good old-fashioned imperial intrigue. You may get totally lost here but you'll always find something to write about on the first postcard you can lay your hands on. The complex also heads the list with one of China's most attractive admission prices and almost endless value-for-money sightseeing.

Great Wall

2 Spotting it from space is both tough and pointless: the only place you can truly put the Great Wall (p117) under your feet is in China. Select your Great Wall section according to taste: perfectly chiselled, dilapidated, stripped of its bricks, overrun with saplings, coiling splendidly into the hills or returning to dust. The fortification is a fitting symbol of those perennial Chinese traits: diligence, mass manpower, ambitious vision and engineering skill (coupled with a distrust of the neighbours).

ELIZABETH PHUNG / GETTY IMAGES ©

Tiger Leaping Gorge

3 Picture snowcapped mountains rising on either side of a gorge so deep that you can be 2km above the river rushing across the rocks far below. Then imagine winding up and down trails that pass through tiny farming villages, where you can rest while enjoying views so glorious they defy superlatives. Cutting through remote northwest Yúnnán for 16km, Tiger Leaping Gorge (p687) is a simply unmissable experience. Hikers returning from the gorge invariably give it glowing reviews.

Yangzi River

4 Snow melting from the world's 'third pole' – the high-altitude Tibet–Qīnghǎi plateau – is the source of China's mighty, life-giving Yangzi. The country's longest river, the Yangzi surges west–east across the nation before pouring into the Pacific Ocean. It reaches a crescendo with the Three Gorges, carved out throughout the millennia by the inexorable persistence of the powerful waters. The gorges are a magnificent spectacle and a Yangzi River cruise (p786) is a rare chance to hang up your travelling hat, take a seat and leisurely watch the drama unfold.

Top right: Little Three Gorges, Dàníng River (p787)

Shànghǎi

5 More than just a city, Shànghǎi (p186) is the country's neon-lit beacon of change, opportunity and sophistication. Its sights set squarely on the not-too-distant future, Shànghǎi offers a taste of all the superlatives China can dare to dream up, from the world's highest observation deck to its fastest commercially operating train. Whether you're just pulling in after an epic 44-hour train trip from Xīnjiāng or it's your first stop, you'll find plenty to indulge in here. Start with the Bund (p187), Shànghǎi's iconic riverfront area where it all began.

4

5

Mt Kailash, Western Tibet

6 Worshipped by more than a billion Buddhists and Hindus, Asia's most sacred mountain (p920) rises from the Barkha plain like a giant four-sided 6714m-high *chörten* (stupa). Throw in stunning Lake Manasarovar nearby and a basin that forms the source of four of Asia's greatest rivers, and it's clear that this place is special. Travel here to one of the world's most beautiful and remote corners brings a bonus: the three-day pilgrim path around the mountain erases the sins of a lifetime.

Hiking Lóngjǐ Rice Terraces

7 After a bumpy bus ride to northern Guǎngxī, you'll be dazzled by one of China's most archetypal landscapes: the splendidly named Lóngjǐ (Dragon's Backbone) Rice Terraces (p611). The region is a beguiling patchwork of minority villages, with layers of waterlogged terraces climbing the hillsides. You'll be enticed into a game of village-hopping. The invigorating walk between Píng'ān and Dàzhài villages offers the most spine-tingling views. Visit after the summer rains when the fields are glistening with reflections.

HIROYUKI NAGAOKA / GETTY IMAGES ©

KEREN SU / GETTY IMAGES ©

LARS RUECKER / GETTY IMAGES ©

SINO IMAGES / GETTY IMAGES ©

KYLIE MCLAUGHLIN / GETTY IMAGES ©

China's Cuisine

8 Say *zàijiàn* (goodbye) to that Chinatown schlock and *nǐhǎo* (hello) to a whole new world of food and flavour. For Peking duck and dumplings galore, Běijīng's a good place to start (p96), but you don't have to travel far to find that China truly is your oyster, from the liquid fire of a Chóngqìng hotpot to the dainty dim sum of Hong Kong. You'll see things you've never seen before, eat things you've never heard of and drink things that could lift a rocket into space.

Diāolóu in Kāipíng

9 If you only have time for one attraction in Guǎngdōng, Kāipíng's *diāolóu* (p567) should be it. Approximately 1800 outlandishly designed watchtowers and fortified residences are scattered higgledy-piggledy in the farmland in Kāipíng, a town not far from Guǎngzhōu. These sturdy bastions built in the early 20th century may not be what you'd typically expect in the Middle Kingdom, but they inspire awe with their fusion of foreign and domestic architectural styles. Greek, Roman, Gothic, Byzantine and baroque – you name it, they've got it.

French Concession, Shànghǎi

10 The French Concession (p198) is Shànghǎi sunny-side up, at its coolest, hippest and most alluring. Once home to the bulk of Shànghǎi's adventurers, revolutionaries, gangsters, prostitutes and writers – though ironically many of them weren't French – the former concession (also called Frenchtown) is the most graceful part of Pǔxī. The Paris of the East turns on its European charms to maximum effect here, where leafy streets and 1920s villas meet art deco apartment blocks, elegant restaurants and chic bars.

Huángshān & Hui Villages

11 Shrouded in mist and light rain more than 200 days a year, and maddeningly crowded most of the time, Huángshān (p399) has an appeal that attracts millions of annual visitors. Perhaps it's the barren landscape, or an otherworldly vibe on the mountain. Mist rolls in and out at will; spindly bent pines stick out like lone pins across sheer craggy granite faces. Not far from the base are the perfectly preserved Hui villages including Xīdì (p394) and Hóngcūn (p395). Unesco, Ang Lee and Zhang Yimou were captivated – you will be too. Above: Village of Hóngcūn

Hiking in Jiǔzhàigōu National Park

12 Strolling the forested valleys of Jiǔzhàigōu National Park (p764) – past bluer-than-blue lakes and small Tibetan villages in the shadow of snow-brushed mountains – was always a highlight of any trip to Sìchuān province, but an excellent new ecotourism scheme means travellers can now hike and even camp their way around this stunning part of southwest China. Guides speak English and all camping equipment is provided, so all you need to bring is your sense of adventure and a spare set of camera batteries. Top right: Rhinoceros Lake in Jiǔzhàigōu National Park

Terracotta Warriors

13 Standing silent guard over their emperor for more than 2000 years, the terracotta warriors (p377) are one of the most extraordinary archaeological discoveries ever made. It's not just that there are thousands of the life-sized figures lined up in battle formation; it's the fact that no two of them are alike – each one is animated with a distinct expression. This is an army, and one made up entirely of individuals; gazing at these skilfully sculpted faces brings the past alive with a unique intensity.

HAIBO BI / GETTY IMAGES ©

MERTEN SNIJDERS / GETTY IMAGES ©

The Lí River & Cycling Yángshuò

14 It's hard to exaggerate the beauty of Yángshuò and the Lí River area (p615), renowned for classic images of mossy-green, jagged limestone peaks providing a backdrop for weeping willows leaning over bubbling streams, wallowing water buffaloes and farmers sowing rice paddies. Ride a bamboo raft along the river and you'll understand why this rural landscape has inspired painters and poets for centuries.

Lhasa

15 The holy city of Lhasa (p902) is the perfect introduction to Tibet, and just arriving here can make the hairs stand up on the back of your neck. The prayer halls of the Potala Palace, Jokhang Temple and the monastic cities of Drepung and Sera are the big draws, but don't miss the less-visited chapels and pilgrim paths. The whitewashed alleys of the old town are the real heart of the Tibetan quarter, and you could spend hours here wandering around backstreet handicraft workshops, hidden temples and local teahouses.

Bottom: Sunrise over the Potala Palace (p903)

The Silk Road

16 There are other Silk Road cities in countries such as Uzbekistan and Turkmenistan, but it's in China where you get the feeling of stepping on the actual 'Silk Road', with its pervasive Muslim heritage and fragments from ancient Buddhist civilisations. Travel by bus and experience the route as ancient traders once did. Kashgar (p806) is the ultimate Silk Road town and remains a unique melting pot of peoples, but Hotan (p817) is equally special: a rough-and-tumble town still clinging to bygone days. Top right: Jiāyùguān Fort (p842), one of the Silk Road's defining sights

Píngyáo

17 Time-warped Píngyáo (p358) is a true gem: an intact, walled Chinese town with an unbroken sense of continuity to its Qing-dynasty heyday. Píngyáo ticks most of your China boxes with a flourish: imposing city walls, atmospheric alleys, ancient shopfronts, traditional courtyard houses, some excellent hotels, hospitable locals and all in a compact area. You can travel the length and breadth of China and not find another town like it. Step back in time and spend a few days here; it's unique.

Labrang Monastery

18 If you can't make it to Tibet, visit the Gānsù province town of Xiàhé, a more accessible part of the former Tibetan region of Amdo. One moment you are in Han China, the next you are virtually in Tibet. Here, Labrang Monastery (p831) attracts legions of Tibetan pilgrims who perambulate around the monastery's prayer-wheel-lined *kora* (pilgrim path). As a strong source of spiritual power, the monastery casts its spell far and wide, and with great hiking opportunities plus an intriguing ethnic mix, it's located in a fascinating corner of China.

Běijīng's Hútòng

19 To get under the skin of the capital, you need to lose yourself at least once in its enchanting, ancient alleyways (p79). *Hútòng* are Běijīng's heart and soul; it's in these alleys that crisscross the centre of the city that you'll discover the capital's unique street life. Despite its march into the 21st century, Běijīng's true charms – heavenly courtyard architecture, pinched lanes and a strong sense of community – are not high-rise. It's easy to find that out; just check into a courtyard hotel and true Běijīng will be right on your doorstep.

CHRISTIAN KOBER / GETTY IMAGES ©

YANN LAYMA / GETTY IMAGES ©

Yúngāng Caves

20 Buddhist art taken to sublime heights, these 5th-century caves (p351) house some of the most remarkable statues in all of China. Carved out of the harsh yellow earth of Shānxī and surrounded by superb frescoes, the statues inside the caves represent the highpoint of the Tuoba people's culture and draw on influences from as far away as Greece and Persia. Marvel at how the pigment clinging to some of them has miraculously survived 1500-odd years, and admire how sacred the statuary remains to followers of Buddhism.

Practise Taichi in Wǔdāng Shān

21 An ethereal form of moving meditation to some, an awesome arsenal of martial-arts techniques to others, taichi is quintessentially Chinese. Daily practice could add a decade or more to your lifespan or give you some handy moves for getting on those crowded buses. And it's not all slow-going: Chen style has snappy elements of Shàolín boxing and it'll give you a leg-busting workout. Join classes in the hills of Taoist Wǔdāng Shān (p438), the birthplace of taichi, and put some magic and mystery into your China adventure.

Yuányáng Rice Terraces

22 Hewn out of hills that stretch off into the far distance, the rice terraces of Yuányáng (p667) are testimony to the wonderfully intimate relationship the local Hani people have with the sublime landscape in which they live. Rising like giant steps, the intricate terraces are a stunning sight at any time of year. But when they are flooded in winter and the sun's rays are dancing off the water at sunrise or sunset, they're absolutely mesmerising and some of the most photogenic spectacles that China has to offer.

Cruising up Victoria Harbour

23 A buzzer sounds, you bolt for the gangplank. A whistle blows, your boat chugs forward. Beyond the waves, one of the world's most famous views unfolds – Hong Kong's skyscrapers in their steel and neon brilliance, against a backdrop of mountains. You're on the Star Ferry (p506), a legendary service that's been carrying passengers between Hong Kong Island and Kowloon Peninsula since the 19th century. Ten minutes later, a hemp rope is cast, then a bell rings, and you alight. At only HK$2, this is possibly the world's best-value cruise.

Grand Buddha, Lè Shān

24 You can read all the stats you like about Lè Shān's Grand Buddha statue (p737) – yes, its ears really are 7m long! – but until you descend the steps alongside the world's tallest Buddha statue and stand beside its feet, with its toenails at the same level as your eyes, you can't really comprehend just how vast it is. Still not impressed? Consider this, then: the huge stone statue was carved painstakingly into the riverside cliff face more than 1200 years ago.

Fújiàn Tǔlóu

25 Rising up in colonies from the hilly borderlands of Fújiàn and Guǎngdōng, the stupendous *tǔlóu* roundhouses house entire villages, even though occupant numbers are way down these days. The imposing and well-defended bastions of wood and earth – not all circular it must be added – can be most easily found in the Fújiàn counties of Nánjìng and Yǒngdìng (p291). Do the right thing and spend the night in one: this is a vanishing way of life, the pastoral setting is quite superb and the architecture is unique.

Tài Shān

26 A visit to China just isn't complete without scaling a sacred mountain or two, and antediluvian Tài Shān (p157) in Shāndōng province is the granddaddy of them all. Climb the Taoist mountain and you'll live to 100, they say, even if you feel you are going to drop dead with exhaustion on the gruelling Path of 18 Bends (lightweights can hitch a ride on the cable car instead). The views are outstanding and with Tài Shān's mountainous aspect in the east, summit sunrises are the order of the day.

Dūnhuáng

27 Where China starts transforming into a lunar desertscape in the far west, the handsome oasis town of Dūnhuáng (p845) is a natural staging post for dusty Silk Road explorers. Mountainous sand dunes swell outside town while Great Wall fragments lie scoured by abrasive desert winds, but it is the magnificent caves at Mògāo that truly dazzle. Mògāo is the cream of China's crop of Buddhist caves – its statues are ineffably sublime and some of the nation's most priceless cultural treasures.

© LOUIS MAZZATENTA / GETTY IMAGES ©

VIEW STOCK / GETTY IMAGES ©

FENG WEI PHOTOGRAPHY / GETTY IMAGES ©

YVES ANDRE / GETTY IMAGES ©

VINNYP IMAGES / ALAMY ©

Zhāngjiājiè

28 Claimed by some to be the inspiration behind Pandora's floating mountains in the hit film *Avatar*, Zhāngjiājiè's (p474) otherworldly rock towers do indeed seem like they come from another planet. Rising from the misty subtropical forests of northwest Húnán, more than 3,000 karst pinnacles form a landscape so surreal it is, arguably, unmatched by any other in China. Raft along a river, hike to your heart's content, or just spend hours filling up the memory card on your camera.

Fènghuáng

29 Houses perched precariously on stilts, ancestral halls, crumbling temples and gate towers set amid a warren of back alleys full of shops selling mysterious foods and medicines – it's enough on its own to make the ancient town of Fènghuáng (p478) an essential stop. Add in the seductive setting on either side of the Tuó River and the chance to stay at an inn right by the water, and you have one of the most evocative towns in the land.

Cycling Hǎinán

30 The same blue skies and balmy weather that make China's only tropical island (p587) ideal for a do-nothing holiday, make it superb for exploring on a bicycle (p593). Hit the east for picturesque rice-growing valleys, spectacular bays and some of Asia's finest beaches. And don't miss the sparsely populated central highlands, a densely forested region that's home to the island's original settlers, the Li and the Miao. Here, even the road more frequently taken is still not taken by many at all. Bottom right: Sānyà Bay (p598)

Need to Know

For more information, see Survival Guide (p991)

Currency
yuán (元; ¥)

Language
Mandarin, Cantonese

Visas
Needed for all visits to China except Hong Kong, Macau and 72-hour or under trips to Shànghǎi, Běijīng, Guǎngzhōu, Xī'ān, Guìlín, Chéngdū, Chóngqìng, Dàlián and Shěnyáng.

Money
ATMs in big cities and towns. Credit cards less widely used; always carry cash.

Mobile Phones
Inexpensive pay-as-you-go SIM cards can be bought locally for most mobile phones. Buying a local mobile phone is also cheap.

Time
GMT/UTC +8

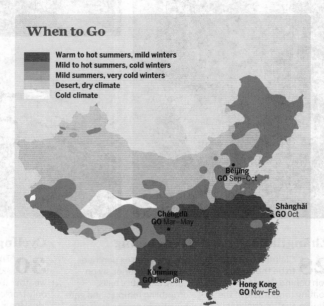

When to Go

Warm to hot summers, mild winters
Mild to hot summers, cold winters
Mild summers, very cold winters
Desert, dry climate
Cold climate

Běijīng
GO Sep–Oct

Shànghǎi
GO Oct

Chéngdū
GO Mar–May

Kūnmíng
GO Dec–Jan

Hong Kong
GO Nov–Feb

High Season (May–Aug)
➡ Prepare for summer downpours and crowds at traveller hot spots.

➡ Accommodation prices peak during the first week of the May holiday period.

Shoulder (Feb–Apr, Sep & Oct)
➡ Expect warmer days in spring, cooler days in autumn.

➡ In the north this is the optimal season, with fresh weather and clear skies.

➡ Accommodation prices peak during holidays in early October.

Low Season (Nov–Feb)
➡ Domestic tourism is at a low ebb, but things are busy and expensive for Chinese New Year.

➡ Weather is bitterly cold in the north and at altitude, and only warm in the far south.

Useful Websites

Lonely Planet (www.lonelyplanet.com/china) Destination information, hotel bookings, traveller forum and more.

Ctrip (www.english.ctrip.com) Hotel booking, air ticketing.

Sinocism (www.sinocism.com) An indispensable regular newsletter on China.

Chinasmack (www.chinasmack.com) Stories and videos.

Tea Leaf Nation (www.tealeafnation.com) Chinese social media pickings.

Popupchinese (www.popupchinese.com) Excellent podcasts (great for learning Chinese).

Important Numbers

Ambulance	☎120
Fire	☎119
Police	☎110
Country code (China/ Hong Kong/ Macau)	☎86/852/ 853
International access code	☎00
Directory assistance	☎114

Exchange Rates

Australia	A$1	¥5.3
Canada	C$1	¥5.4
Euro zone	€1	¥7.6
Hong Kong	HK$1	¥0.8
Japan	¥100	¥5.3
NZ	NZ$1	¥4.8
UK	UK£1	¥9.7
USA	US$1	¥6.1

For current exchange rates see www.xe.com.

Daily Costs

Budget: Less than ¥200

➡ Dorm Beds: ¥40–60

➡ Markets, street food: ¥40

➡ Internet, bike hire or other transport: ¥20

➡ Free museums

Midrange: ¥200–1000

➡ Double room in a midrange hotel: ¥200–600

➡ Lunch and dinner in local restaurants: ¥80–100

➡ Drinks in a bar: ¥60

➡ Taxis: ¥60

Top end: More than ¥1000

➡ Double room in a top-end hotel: ¥600 and up

➡ Lunch and dinner in excellent local or hotel restaurants: ¥300

➡ Top-end shopping: ¥300

➡ Two tickets to opera: ¥300

Opening Hours

China officially has a five-day working week. Saturday and Sunday are public holidays.

Banks, offices, government departments Monday to Friday 9am to 5pm or 6pm, some close for two hours midday. Many banks also open weekends.

Post offices usually daily.

Museums generally stay open on weekends; may shut one weekday.

Travel agencies usually daily.

Shops 10am to 10pm daily.

Internet cafes 24 hours (some only 8am to midnight).

Restaurants around 10.30am to 11pm; some shut between 2pm and 5pm or 6pm.

Bars open late afternoon, close around midnight.

Arriving in China

Běijīng Capital Airport (p1005) Airport Express train services run every 10 minutes. The Airport Bus runs to central Běijīng every 10 to 20 minutes. A taxi will cost ¥80 to ¥100.

Shànghǎi Pǔdōng International Airport (p1005) Maglev trains run every 20 minutes. Metro Line 2 links the airport with Hóngqiáo Airport. The Airport Bus runs every 15 to 25 minutes. A taxi to central Shànghǎi will cost ¥160.

Hong Kong International Airport (p1005) Airport Express trains run every 12 minutes. A taxi to Central will cost about HK$300.

Getting Around

Transport in China needs considerable pre-planning due to the distances involved and periodic shortages of tickets.

Air Affordable and excellent for long distances, but delays are common.

Train Very reasonably priced, apart from high-speed rail which is more expensive, and very efficient.

Bus Cheaper and slower than trains but crucial for remote destinations.

Car China is too large and there are too many restrictions to make this a viable option.

For much more on **getting around**, see p1008

First Time China

For more information, see Survival Guide (p991)

Checklist

➡ Check the validity of your passport

➡ Make any necessary bookings

➡ Secure your visa and additional permits well in advance

➡ Check the airline baggage restrictions

➡ Organise travel insurance

➡ Check if you can use your mobile/cellphone

➡ Work out your itinerary

➡ Inform your credit/debit card company

What to Pack

➡ Passport

➡ Credit card

➡ Phrasebook

➡ Money belt

➡ Travel plug

➡ Medical kit

➡ Insect repellent

➡ Mobile (cell) phone charger

➡ Sunscreen

➡ Sunhat and shades

➡ Waterproof clothing

➡ Torch

➡ Pocketknife

➡ Earplugs

Top Tips for Your Trip

➡ Be patient and understand that many things you take for granted – orderly queues, international levels of English ability, personal space – may not exist.

➡ Try to learn at least a few words of Chinese to help you interact better with local people.

➡ Treat China as an adventure, rather than purely as a holiday.

What to Wear

You can pretty much wear casual clothes throughout your entire journey in China, unless dining in a smart restaurant in Shànghǎi, Běijīng or Hong Kong, when you may need to dress less casually. In general, trousers (pants) and shirts or tees for guys, and dresses, skirts or trousers for women will serve you well nationwide; shorts and short sleeves are generally fine in summer, but don long trousers and long sleeves in the evenings to keep mosquitoes at bay. A sunhat can be invaluable. A thin waterproof coat and sturdy shoes are a good idea for all-weather hiking and sightseeing. Winter is a different ball game up north and especially at altitude: you'll need several layers, thick shirts, jerseys and warm coats, jackets, gloves, socks and a hat.

Sleeping

It's generally always a good idea to book your accommodation in advance, especially in the high season and when visiting big ticket destinations, such as Hángzhōu, at weekends. See p992 for more accommodation information.

➡ **Hotels** Range from two-star affairs with very limited English and simple rooms to international-level five-star towers and heritage hotels.

➡ **Hostels** Exist across China in growing numbers, usually offering both dorm beds and double rooms and dispensing useful travel advice.

➡ **Homesteads** In rural locations, you can often find double rooms in converted houses, with meals also provided.

Money

➜ **Credit Cards** Credit and debit cards are increasingly accepted in tourist towns and big cities, particularly Visa and MasterCard. Ask if bars and restaurants take cards before ordering.

➜ **ATMs** There are 24-hour ATMs available at Bank of China and ICBC branches.

➜ **Changing Money** You can change money at hotels, large branches of Bank of China, some department stores and international airports. Some towns don't have any money-changing facilities, so make sure you carry enough cash.

Bargaining

Haggling is standard procedure in markets and shops (outside of department stores and malls) where prices are not clearly marked. There's no harm in coming in really low, but remain polite at all times. In touristy markets in Shànghǎi and Běijīng, vendors can drop as low as 25% of the original price.

Tipping

Tipping is never expected at cheap and many mid-range restaurants. In general there is no need to tip if a service charge has already been added, so check. Hotel porters may expect a tip; taxi drivers do not.

Etiquette

China is a pretty relaxed country regarding etiquette, but there are a few things you need to be aware of:

➜ **Greetings & Goodbyes** Shake hands, but never kiss someone's cheek. Say 'Nǐhǎo' as you greet someone and 'Zàijiàn' to say goodbye.

➜ **Asking for Help** To ask for directions start by saying 'Qǐng wèn....' ('Can I ask...'); say 'Duìbuqǐ...' (sorry) to apologise.

➜ **Religion** Dress sensitively when visiting Buddhist (especially in Tibet) and Taoist temples, churches and mosques.

➜ **Eating & Drinking** Help fill your neighbour's plate or bowl at the dinner table; toast the host and others at the table; at the start of dinner, wait till toasting starts before drinking from your glass; offer your cigarettes around if you smoke; always offer to buy drinks in a bar but never fight over the drink/food tab if someone else wants to pay.

➜ **Gestures** Don't use too many hand movements or excessive body language.

Booking Ahead

Reserving a room, even if only for the first night of your stay, is the best way to ensure a smooth start to your trip. These phrases should see you through a call if English isn't spoken.

Hello	你好	Nǐhǎo
I would like to book a room	我想订房间	Wǒ xiǎng dìng fángjiān
a single room	单人间	dānrén jiān
a double room	双人间	shuāngrén jiān
My name is...	我叫...	Wǒ jiào...
from... to... (date)	从...到...	cóng... dào...
How much is it per night/person?	每天/个人多少钱？	Měi tiān/gè rén duōshǎo qián?
Thank you	谢谢你	Xièxie nǐ

Language

It is entirely possible to travel around China hardly hearing any English at all. Tourist industry employees across the land are more likely to speak English; in the big cities such as Shànghǎi, Běijīng and of course Hong Kong, English is more widely spoken and understood, but generally only among educated Chinese. In smaller towns and the countryside, English is often of little or no use (the vast majority of Chinese do not speak the language at all). For more, see the language chapter, p1023.

If You Like...

Imperial Architecture

Crumbling dynasties have deposited an imposing trail of antiquity across north China from vast imperial palaces to the noble ruins of the Great Wall and altars reserved for the emperor.

Forbidden City China's standout imperial residence in Běijīng, home to two dynasties of emperors and their concubines. (p59)

Summer Palace An epic demonstration of traditional Chinese aesthetics with all essential ingredients: hills, lakes, bridges, pavilions and temples. (p88)

Imperial Palace Manchu splendour in Shěnyáng within the former Manchurian heartland of Liáoníng province. (p304)

Xī'ān Shaanxi home of the Terracotta Warriors, an imposing Ming city wall and traces of the city's famous Tang apogee. (p380)

Chéngdé Summer bolt-hole of the Qing emperors, with palatial remains and a riveting brood of Tibetan-style temples. (p141)

Extremes

China has more than enough extremes to satisfy thrill-seekers, or just the plain inquisitive. From the world's highest mountain to its fastest trains and biggest Buddhist statues, take your pick from China's extremes.

Běihóngcūn China's northernmost village in Hēilóngjiāng, where winter temperatures can freeze mercury. (p340)

Turpan China's hottest spot and the world's second-lowest depression, where the thermometer has topped 48°C. (p813)

Grand Buddha, Lè Shān The world's tallest Buddha can make you feel truly Lilliputian. (p737)

Everest Base Camp Rise early for dramatic images of the world's highest mountain in the morning sun. (p917)

Shànghǎi Maglev The world's fastest commercially operating high-speed train. (p227)

Ancient Settlements

Traditional China can be glimpsed in its picturesque, ancient villages and towns. Ming- and Qing-dynasty architecture, narrow lanes and superlative *fēngshuǐ* combine in a pastoral aesthetic complemented by a relaxed rural tempo.

Píngyáo China's best-looking, best-preserved walled town – by a long shot – warrants thorough exploration. (p358)

Hóngcūn Within easy reach of Huángshān, this delightful Ānhuī village is a primer in the Huīzhōu style. (p395)

Wùyuán Take time off to village-hop in the gorgeous Jiāngxī countryside and dream of abandoning urban China for good. (p449)

Fújiàn Tǔlóu Explore the fortress-like earthen 'roundhouses' of Fújiàn, distinctive for their imposing enormity. (p291)

Xīnyè This effortlessly charming village is designed with an eye for traditional Chinese harmony and balance. (p274)

Urban Extravaganzas

Among China's most dynamic cities is Shànghǎi, where glittering skyscrapers overlook Maglev trains, and cashed-up consumers shop in chic malls, drink at elegant cocktail bars and dine at fashionable restaurants.

Shànghǎi The city that everyone – architects, fashionistas, cocktail connoisseurs, urban travellers – is talking about. (p186)

Hong Kong Poised between China and the West, the ex-British colony continues to plough its own lucrative furrow. (p489)

Kūnmíng Lake (p88), Summer Palace, Běijīng

Běijīng Engaging blend of ancient capital and modern metropolis in China's leading city. (p88)

Hángzhōu One of China's most attractive cities with the sublime and romantic West Lake at its heart. (p260)

Boat Trips

China is cut by some dramatic and breathtaking rivers, including the mighty Yangzi. Hop on a riverboat and ease into a totally different experience of China's landscapes.

Three Gorges China's most awesome river panorama. (p772)

Lí River The dreamlike karst landscapes of northeast Guǎngxī. (p260)

Star Ferry, Hong Kong The short but iconic ferry hop across Victoria Harbour from Tsim Sha Tsui. (p506)

Evening river cruise, Chóngqìng Before getting all misty on the Yangzi, experience Chóngqìng's nocturnal, neon performance. (p775)

Qīngyuǎn boat trip, Guǎngdōng Lazily float along the Běi River, past secluded Fēilái Temple and Fēixiá monastery. (p579)

Great Food

With its novel flavours, and unexpected aromas and tastes, China is a culinary travel adventure. Head west for zing, zest and spice, north for hearty and salty flavours, east for fresh and lightly flavoured seafood, and south for dim sum.

Peking duck Once bitten, forever smitten, and only in Běijīng. (p96)

Chóngqìng hotpot Sweat like never before over China's most volcanic culinary creation. (p777)

Xiǎolóngbāo Shànghǎi's bite-sized snack packs a lot of flavour (but watch out for the super-heated meat juice). (p227)

Dim Sum Head to Hong Kong for the very best in China's bite-size delicacies. (p515)

Museums

Urbanisation means that museum collections can be the clearest window onto China's past, and they are ubiquitous, covering everything from ethnic clothing to Běijīng tap water or Buddhist artefacts.

Palace Museum The official and highly prosaic name for the Forbidden City, China's supreme link to its dynastic past. (p59)

Shànghǎi Museum A dazzling collection of ceramics, paintings, calligraphy and much more at the heart of Shànghǎi. (p191)

Poly Art Museum Bronzes and Bodhisattvas in Běijīng. (p70)

Hong Kong Museum of History Entertaining, resourceful and informative. (p501)

Nánjīng Museum A lavish celebration of Chinese culture's big hitters, with astounding exhibitions. (p235)

Sacred China

From the esoteric mysteries of Tibetan Buddhism to the palpable magic of its holy Taoist mountains, to the disparate collection of Christian churches, mosques and shrines, China's sacred realm is the point at which the supernatural and natural worlds converge.

Pǔníng Temple, Chéngdé Be rendered speechless by China's largest wooden statue, a towering effigy of the Buddhist Goddess of Mercy. (p144)

Labrang Monastery Tap into the ineffable rhythms of south Gānsù's place of pilgrimage for legions of Tibetans. (p831)

Gyantse Kumbum An overwhelming sight and monumental experience, the nine-tiered *chörten* is Tibet's largest stupa. (p913)

Qīnglóng Dòng Climb through Taoist, Buddhist and Confucian realms in this cliffside labyrinth in riverside Zhènyuǎn. (p641)

Wǔdāng Shān Commune with the spirit of Taoist martial arts in the birthplace of taichi. (p436)

Hiking

Despite urban encroachment, China is one of the world's most geographically varied and largest nations, with stupendous hiking opportunities amid breathtaking scenery.

Tiger Leaping Gorge Yúnnán's best-known and most enticing hike is not for the faint-hearted. (p687)

Lóngjǐ Rice Terraces Work your way from Dàzhài to Píng'ān through some of China's most delicious scenery. (p611)

Wùyuán Follow the old postal roads from village to village in the drop-dead gorgeous Jiāngxī countryside. (p454)

Lángmùsì Excellent options in most directions from the charming monastic town on the Gānsù–Sìchuān border. (p836)

Ganden to Samye An 80km, four- to five-day high-altitude hike between these two Tibetan monasteries. (p918)

Ethnic Minorities

Han China hits the buffers around its far-reaching borderlands, where a colourful patchwork of ethnic minorities preserves distinct cultures, languages, architectural styles and livelihoods.

Tibet Explore this vast region in the west of China or jump aboard our itinerary through the easier-to-access regions outside the Tibetan heartland. (p897)

DéhāngThis Miao village in Húnán finds itself delightfully embedded in some breathtaking scenery. (p478)

Lìjiāng Yúnnán's famous home of the blue-clothed Naxi folk. (p711)

Kashgar Dusty Central Asian outpost and Uighur China's most famous town, on the far side of the Taklamakan Desert. (p813)

Stunning Scenery

You haven't really experienced China until you've had your socks blown off by one of its scenic marvels. China's man-made splendours have lent cities such as Shànghǎi head-turning cachet, but Mother Nature steals the show.

Yángshuò You've probably seen the karst topography before in picture-perfect photographs; now see the real thing. (p615)

Huángshān When suffused in their spectral mists, China's Yellow mountains enter a different dimension of beauty. (p399)

Jiǔzhàigōu National Park Turquoise lakes, waterfalls, snowcapped mountains and green forests: all this and more. (p764)

Chìshuǐ Trek past waterfalls and through ancient forests dating to the Jurassic. (p636)

Yuányáng Rice Terraces Be transfixed by the dazzling display of light and water. (p667)

Month by Month

TOP EVENTS

Monlam Great Prayer Festival, February or March

Naadam, July

Běijīng International Literary Festival, March

Spring Festival, January, February or March

Luòyáng Peony Festival, April

January

North China is a deep freeze but the south is far less bitter; preparations for the Chinese New Year get under way well in advance of the festival, which arrives any time between late January and March.

🎆 Spring Festival

The Chinese New Year is family-focused, with dining on dumplings and gift-giving of *hóngbāo* (red envelopes stuffed with money). Most families feast together on New Year's Eve, then China goes on a big week-long holiday. Expect fireworks, parades, temple fairs and lots of colour.

🎆 Hā'ěrbīn Ice & Snow Festival

Hēilóngjiāng's good-looking capital Hā'ěrbīn is all aglow with rainbow lights refracted through fanciful buildings and statues carved from blocks of ice. It's outrageously cold, but hey, this is the peak season.

⊙ Yuányáng Rice Terraces

The watery winter is the optimum season for the rice terraces' spectacular combination of liquid and light. Don't forget your camera, or your sense of wonder.

February

North China remains shockingly icy and dry but things are slowly warming up in Hong Kong and Macau. The Chinese New Year could well be firing on all cylinders, but sort out your tickets well in advance.

🎆 Monlam Great Prayer Festival

Held during two weeks from the third day of the Tibetan New Year and celebrated with spectacular processions (but not in Lhasa or the Tibetan Autonomous Region due to political tensions), with huge silk *thangka* (Tibetan sacred art) unveiled and, on the last day, a statue of the Maitreya Buddha conveyed around; catch it in Xiàhé.

🎆 Lantern Festival

Held 15 days after the spring festival, this celebration was traditionally a time when Chinese hung out highly decorated lanterns. Lantern-hung Píngyáo in Shānxī is an atmospheric place to soak up the festival (sometimes held in March).

March

China comes back to life after a long winter, although high-altitude parts of China remain glacial. The mercury climbs in Hong Kong and abrasive dust storms billow into Běijīng, scouring everything in their path. Admission prices are still low-season.

🎆 Běijīng Book Bash

Curl up with a good book at the Bookworm cafe for Běijīng's international literary festival, and lend an ear to lectures from international and domestic authors. Also earmark Shànghǎi for its international literary festival in the Bund-side Glamour Bar or the Man Hong Kong International Literary Festival.

◉ Fields of Yellow

Delve into the south Chinese countryside to be bowled over by a landscape saturated in bright yellow rapeseed. In some parts of China, such as lovely Wùyuán in Jiāngxī province, it's a real tourist draw.

April

Most of China is warm so it's a good time to be on the road, ahead of the May holiday period and before China's summer reaches its full power. The Chinese take several days off to pass the Qīngmíng festival, a traditional date for honouring their ancestors and now an official holiday period.

✳ A Good Soaking

Flush away the dirt, demons and sorrows of the old year and bring in the fresh at the Dai New Year, with its vast amount of water at the water-splashing festival in Xīshuāngbǎnnà. Taking an umbrella is pointless.

✳ Paean to Peonies

Wángchéng Park in Luòyáng bursts into full-coloured bloom with its peony festival: pop a flower garland on your head and join in the floral fun.

✳ Third Moon Festival

This Bai ethnic minority festival is another excellent reason to pitch up in the lovely north Yúnnán town of Dàlǐ. It's a week of horse racing, singing and merrymaking which begins on the 15th day of the third lunar month (usually April) and ends on the 21st. The origins of the fair lie in its commemoration of a fabled visit by Guanyin, the Buddhist Goddess of Mercy, to the Nanzhao kingdom.

◉ Formula One

Petrol heads and aficionados of speed, burnt rubber and hairpin bends flock to Shànghǎi for some serious motor racing at the track near Āntíng. Get your hotel room booked early: it's one of the most glamorous events on the Shànghǎi calendar.

May

China is in full bloom in mountain regions such as Sìchuān's Wòlóng Nature Reserve. The first four days of May sees China on vacation for one of the three big holiday periods, kicking off with Labour Day (1 May).

✳ Buddha's Birthday in Xiàhé

A fascinating time to enjoy the Tibetan charms of Gānsù province's Xiàhé, when Buddhist monks make charitable handouts to beggars and the streets throng with pilgrims. Buddha's Birthday is celebrated on the eighth day of the fourth lunar month, usually in May.

✳ Circling the Mountain Festival

On Pǎomǎ Shān, Kāngdìng's famous festival also celebrates the birthday of Sakyamuni, the historical Buddha, with a magnificent display of horse racing, wrestling and a street fair. Buddha's Birthday is celebrated on the eighth day of the fourth lunar month, which usually occurs in May.

✦ Great Wall Marathon

Experience the true meaning of pain (but get your Great Wall sightseeing done and dusted at the same time). Not for the infirm or unfit (or the cable car fraternity). See www.great-wall-marathon.com for more details.

June

Most of China is hot and getting hotter. Once-frozen areas, such as Jílín's Heaven Lake, are accessible – and nature springs instantly to life. The great China peak tourist season is cranking up around now.

✳ Festival of Aurora Borealis

The Northern Lights are sometimes visible from Mòhé in Hēilóngjiāng, in the ultra-far north of China not far from the Russian border. Even if you don't get to see the (often elusive) multicoloured glow, the June midnight sun is a memorable experience.

🎎 Dragon Boat Festival

Head to Zhènyuǎn or the nearest large river and catch all the water-borne drama of dragon boat racers in this celebration of one of China's most famous poets. The Chinese traditionally eat *zòngzi* (triangular glutinous rice dumplings wrapped in reed leaves).

🎎 Dhama Festival

This three-day festival in Gyantse in Tibet kicks off on 20 June for horse racing, wrestling, archery, yak races and more.

🎎 Shangri-la Horse Racing Festival

In mid- to late June, the north Yúnnán town of Shangri-la lets go of the reins with this celebration of horse racing, coupled with singing, dancing and merriment on the southeastern fringes of Tibet.

July

Typhoons can wreak havoc with travel itineraries down south, lashing the Guǎngdōng and Fújiàn coastlines. Plenty of rain sweeps across China: the 'plum rains' give Shànghǎi a big soaking, and the grasslands of Inner Mongolia and Qīnghǎi turn green.

🎎 Yùshù Horse Festival

This spectacular horse festival wasn't held for several years since the devastating 2010 Yùshù earthquake, but has galloped back to the high-altitude grasslands

of Qīnghǎi for equine fun and frolics, kicking off on 25 July.

🎎 Torch Festival, Dàlǐ

Held on the 24th day of the sixth lunar month (usually July), this festival is held throughout Yúnnán by the Bai and Yi minorities. Making for great photos, flaming torches are paraded at night through streets and fields, and go up outside shops around town.

🎎 Mongolian Merrymaking

Mongolian wrestling, horse racing, archery and more during the week-long Naadam festival on the grasslands of Inner Mongolia at the end of July, when the grass is at its summer greenest.

🍷 Dàlián International Beer Festival

Xīnghǎi Sq in the Liáoníng port city is steeped in the aroma of hops and ale and strewn with beer tents in this 12-day celebration of more than 400 international and Chinese beers from a plethora of breweries.

August

The temperature gauge of the 'three ovens' of the Yangzi region – Chóngqìng, Wǔhàn and Nánjīng – gets set to blow. Rainstorms hit Běijīng, which is usually way hotter than 40°C; so is Shànghǎi. So head uphill to Lúshān, Mògānshān, Huángshān or Guōliàngcūn.

🎎 Lǐtáng Horse Festival

Occasionally cancelled in recent years (restrictions on travel may suddenly appear) and also shrunk from one week to one day, this festival in West Sìchuān is a breathtaking display of Tibetan horsemanship, archery and more.

🍷 Qīngdǎo International Beer Festival

Slake that chronic summer thirst with a round of beers and devour a plate of mussels in Shāndōng's best-looking port town, a former German concession and home of the famous Tsingtao beer brand.

September

Come to Běijīng and stay put – September is part of the fleetingly lovely *tiāngāo qìshuǎng* ('the sky is high and the air is fresh') autumnal season – it's an event in itself. It's also a pleasant time to visit the rest of North China.

🎎 Tài Shān International Climbing Festival

Held annually since 1987, this festival at the sacred Taoist mountain of Tài Shān in Shāndōng draws hundreds of trail runners, mountain bikers, climbers and worshippers of all ages and abilities.

🎎 Mid-Autumn Festival

Also called the moon festival, locals celebrate by devouring daintily prepared moon cakes – stuffed with bean paste, egg yolk, walnuts and more. With a full moon, it's a romantic occasion for lovers and a special time for families. It's on the 15th day of the eighth lunar month.

✵ International Qiántáng River Tide Observing Festival

The most popular time to witness the surging river tides sweeping at up to 40km per hour along the Qiántáng River in Yánguān is during the mid-autumn festival, although you can catch the wall of water during the beginning and middle of every lunar month.

✵ Confucius' Birthday

Head to the Confucius Temple in Qūfù for the 28 September birthday celebrations of axiom-quipping philosopher, sage and patriarch Confucius.

October

The first week of October can be hellish if you're on the road: the National Day week-long holiday kicks off, so everywhere is swamped. Go mid-month instead, when everywhere is deserted.

✗ Hairy Crabs in Shànghǎi

Now's the time to sample delicious hairy crabs in Shànghǎi; they are at their best – male and female crabs eaten together with shots of lukewarm Shàoxīng rice wine – between October and December.

✵ Miao New Year

Load up with rice wine and get on down to Guìzhōu for the ethnic festivities in the very heart of the minority-rich southwest.

November

Most of China is getting pretty cold as tourist numbers drop and holidaymakers begin to flock south for sun and the last pockets of warmth.

☉ Surfing Hǎinán

Annual surfing competition in Shíméi Bay and Sun and Moon Bay in Hǎinán as the surfing season gets under way and hordes of Chinese flee the cold mainland for the warmer climes of the southern island.

Itineraries

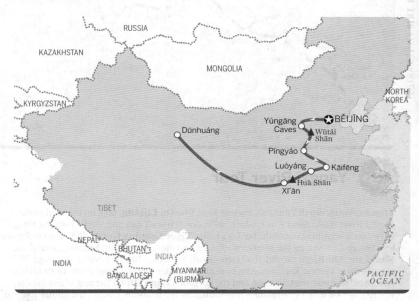

Northern Tour

4 WEEKS

Běijīng is fundamental to this tour, so you'll need at least five days to do the Forbidden City, size yourself up against the Great Wall, wander like royalty around the Summer Palace and lose your bearings within the city's *hútòng* (narrow alleyways). The splendour of the **Yúngāng Caves** outside Dàtóng should put you in a Buddhist mood, sharpened by a few nights on monastic **Wǔtái Shān**. We recommend a three-day stopover in **Píngyáo**, an age-old walled town you imagined China *should* look like. The historic walled city of **Kāifēng** in Hénán was the traditional home of China's small community of Chinese Jews and has some remarkable night markets; move on to **Luòyáng** and the Buddhist spectacle of the Lóngmén Caves and the Shàolín Temple, also within reach. Four days' sightseeing in **Xī'ān** brings you face-to-face with the Army of Terracotta Warriors and gives you time for the Taoist mountain of **Huà Shān**. Xī'ān traditionally marked the start of the Silk Road which you can follow through Gānsù province all the way to the oasis-town of **Dūnhuáng**, and beyond.

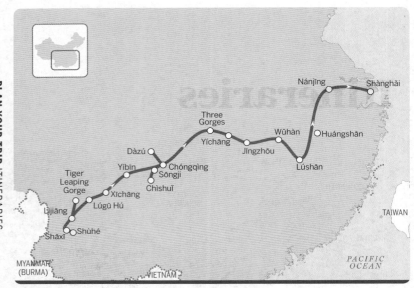

4 WEEKS Yangzi River Tour

After exploring north Yúnnán's ancient Naxi town of **Lìjiāng**, pick up the trail of the Jīnshā River (Gold Sand River, which spills down from Tibet and swells into the Yangzi River) on a breathtaking multiday hike along **Tiger Leaping Gorge**. Rest your worn-out legs before discovering the scattered villages and old towns around Lìjiāng, including **Shāxī** and **Shùhé** on the old Tea-Horse Road, and being blown away by the magnificent views of Yùlóng Xuěshān. Also consider (warmer months only) a trip from Lìjiāng northeast towards west Sìchuān and the gorgeous **Lúgū Hú** on the provincial border, where you can spend several days unwinding by the lakeside. During the winter months this entire area is snowbound, so you may have to fly on from Lìjiāng. An afternoon bus from Lúgū Hú runs to **Xīchāng** in Sìchuān, from where you can reach **Yíbīn** and then **Chóngqìng**; alternatively, return to Lìjiāng to fly to Chóngqìng, home of the spicy and searing Chóngqìng hotpot and gateway to the Three Gorges. Detour by bus to the stunning landscapes and natural beauty of **Chìshuǐ** on the Guìzhōu border to relax, unwind and explore the region before returning by bus to urban Chóngqìng. You'll need around three days in Chóngqìng for the sights in town and for a journey to the Buddhist Caves at **Dàzú** and a trip to the Yangzi River village of **Sōngjì** to keep a perspective on historic, rural China. Then hop on a cruise vessel or passenger boat (or even a bus followed by hydrofoil) to **Yíchāng** in Húběi through the magnificent **Three Gorges**. Journey from Yíchāng to the Yangzi River city of **Wǔhàn** via the walled town of **Jīngzhōu**, where it's worth spending the night. After two days in Wǔhàn, jump on a bus to **Lúshān** in Jiāngxī province, from where you can reach **Nánjīng** or make your way to **Huángshān** in the Yangzi River province of Ānhuī. Alternatively, travel direct to Nánjīng and thread your way to **Shànghǎi** via a delightful string of canal towns – Sūzhōu, Tónglǐ, Lùzhí and Zhūjiājiǎo. Explore Shànghǎi and consider launching into the East–South Rural Tour.

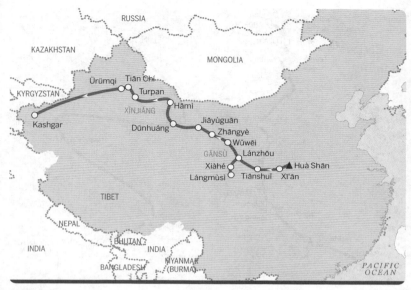

⑤ WEEKS Silk Road Tour

This breathtaking journey takes you along the ancient Silk Road. From the southernmost extents of the Silk Road at **Xī'ān**, discover one of imperial China's most iconic remains at the Army of Terracotta Warriors and, for a major workout, climb the precipitous Taoist mountain of **Huà Shān** – just don't look down. Back in Xī'ān, explore the Muslim Quarter to feast on local Hui specialities – one of the culinary high points of China travel – and climb atop the imposing city walls. Hop aboard the train to **Lánzhōu** but get off in southeast Gānsù at **Tiānshuǐ** for the remarkable Buddhist grottoes at verdant Màijī Shān. From Lánzhōu you have the option to disengage temporarily from the Silk Road to ramble along the fringes of the Tibetan world in the Buddhist monastic settlements of **Xiàhé** and **Lángmùsì**. The Hèxī Corridor draws you on to the ancient Great Wall outpost of **Jiāyùguān**, via the Silk Road stopover town of **Wǔwēi**, and the Great Buddha Temple with its outsize effigy of a reclining Sakyamuni in **Zhāngyè**. Stand on the wind-blasted ramparts of Jiāyùguān Fort, the last major stronghold of imperial China, and tramp alongside westerly remnants of the Great Wall. The delightful oasis outpost of **Dūnhuáng** is one of China's tidiest and most pleasant towns, with the mighty sand dunes of the Singing Sands Mountains pushing up from the south, a scattered array of sights in the surrounding desert and some excellent food. The town is also the hopping-off point for China's splendid hoard of Buddhist art, the spellbinding Mògāo Caves. From Dūnhuáng you can access the mighty northwestern Uighur province of Xīnjiāng via the melon-town of **Hāmì** before continuing to **Turpan** and **Ürümqi**; consider also spending the night in a yurt or camping on the shores of mountainous **Tiān Chí**. Thread your way through a string of Silk Road towns by rail to the Central Asian outpost of **Kashgar**, or reach the distant Uighur town via the Marco Polo–journeyed Southern Silk Road along the cusp of the Taklamakan Desert. From Kashgar, hatch exciting plans to conquer the Karakoram Hwy or, in the other direction, work out how to get back into China proper.

4 WEEKS Coastal China

From **Běijīng**, zip on the high-speed train to face-lifted **Tiānjīn** en route to the Ming-dynasty garrison town of **Shānhǎiguān** on the edge of Manchuria. Beyond the ancient port town of **Xīngchéng** and around the coast lies urbane **Dàlián**, where you can ponder trips to the North Korean border at **Dāndōng**, or the ferry crossing to **Yāntái** en route to a two-day sojourn around breezy **Qīngdǎo**, the eye-catching Shāndōng port city. Cashing in on dashing **Shànghǎi** is crucial – allow five to six days to tick off surrounding sights, including a trip to the cultured former southern Song dynasty capital of **Hángzhōu**. Work your way south around the coast to **Xiàmén** (Amoy) to capture some of the magic of **Gǔlàng Yǔ**, using the port town as a base to explore the roundhouses around **Yǒngdìng**. Conclude the tour feasting on dim sum and getting in step with the rhythms of **Hong Kong** before surrendering to the Portuguese lilt of **Macau**, or go further along the coast to the sleepy port town of **Běihǎi** in Guǎngxī and bounce over the sea in a boat to the volcanic island of **Wéizhōu**.

2 WEEKS Big Ticket Tour

After four days satiating yourself on **Běijīng's** mandatory highlights – the Forbidden City, Tiān'ānmén Square, the Summer Palace, the Great Wall and the city's charming *hútòng* (alleyways) – hop on the high-speed G-class train across north China from Běijīng West to **Xī'ān** to inspect the famed Terracotta Warriors, walk around the city's formidable Ming-dynasty walls and climb the granite peaks of Taoist **Huà Shān**. Then climb aboard the 11-hour overnight high-speed D-class sleeper to pulsating **Shànghǎi**, which pulls into town before 8am. After three days sightseeing, museum-going, shopping and sizing up the sizzling skyscrapers of Pǔdōng, detour for a day to the former southern Song-dynasty capital of **Hángzhōu**, before flying from either Hángzhōu or Shànghǎi to **Guìlín** for some of China's most serene and ageless panoramas, the breathtaking karst landscapes of **Yángshuò**. For a fitting and natural conclusion to your journey, fly straight from Guìlín to **Hong Kong**, or to Guǎngzhōu or Shēnzhèn to make your way south across the border to the former British territory. Squeeze in a day for exploring **Macau** to add a Portuguese complexion to your voyage.

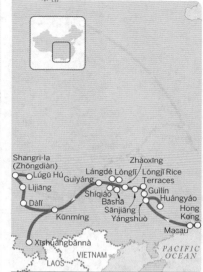

 ## East–Southwest Rural Tour
2 WEEKS

From **Shànghǎi**, head to **Zhūjiājiǎo** in the municipality's rural west to catch its canal-side charms; to further the canal-town mood, the water towns of Jiāngsū and north Zhèjiāng – including **Tónglǐ**, **Lùzhí** and **Wūzhèn** – are within easy reach. From either **Sūzhōu** or **Hángzhōu**, bus it to **Túnxī** in Ānhuī province to spend several days exploring the delightful ancient Huīzhōu villages of **Yīxiàn** and **Shèxiàn** and to scale gorgeous Huáng Shān. Bus it again across the border to Jiāngxī province for two or three days' fabulous hiking from village to village in the gorgeous rural landscape around **Wùyuán**. Take the bus to Nánchāng and then a high-speed train to Chángshā, the Húnán provincial capital, from where you can fly or take the train to the stunning karst panoramas of **Zhāngjiājiè**. Jump on a bus to the funky rivertown of **Fèng-huáng**, from where it's a hop, skip, and a bus-then-train jump via Huáihuà through the backdoor into Guìzhōu and the scenic riverside town of **Zhènyuǎn**. **Kǎilǐ** and the rest of the province lies beyond.

 ## Southwest China
3 WEEKS

Four days' wining and dining in **Hong Kong** and **Macau** should whet your appetite, before you head inland to **Guìlín** and three days' immersion in the dreamy karst landscape of **Yángshuò**. Join a local tour from Yángshuò to delightful **Huángyáo** before backtracking to Guìlín and journeying north to the **Lóngjǐ Rice Terraces** and the wind-and-rain bridges and ethnic hues of **Sānjiāng**. Creep over the border to explore the minority-rich villages of eastern Guìzhōu, including **Lángdé**, **Shíqiáo**, **Lónglǐ**, **Bāshā** and **Zhàoxīng**, before continuing to **Guìyáng** and on by train to the capital of Yúnnán province, **Kūnmíng**. Spend a few days in Kūnmíng before penetrating north Yúnnán to explore **Dàlǐ**, **Lìjiāng** and **Shangri-la (Zhōngdiàn)**. Consider exploring the border area with Sìchuān at the remote **Lúgū Hú**, from where you can head into Sìchuān. In the other direction, the fertile **Xīshuāngbǎnnà** region lies in the deep south of the province, where Yúnnán's Southeast Asian complexion comes to the fore. You will be rewarded with a profusion of ethnic villages and countless hiking opportunities around China's southwest borders.

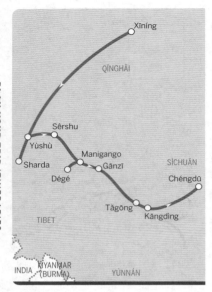

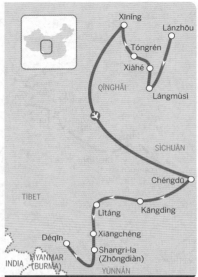

10 DAYS Qīnghǎi to Sìchuān

This colossal, rough-and-ready journey draws you through stunning landscapes from Xīníng to Chéngdū. The scenery is sublime but do this trip only in summer (it's too cold even in spring), and take cash and lots of food with you (you won't be able to change money). Prepare also for bus breakdowns, irregular transport connections, simple accommodation and high altitudes. The bus journey from **Xīníng** to **Sharda** in the former Tibetan kingdom of Nangchen, where monasteries and dramatic scenery await, takes 20 to 24 hours. From Sharda you can continue to Sìchuān via the Tibetan trading town of **Yùshù** (Jyekundo). You can also fly direct (or take the bus) from Xīníng to Yùshù to continue to Sìchuān from there, and you can stay in Yùshù as it has officially reopened after the 2010 earthquake. Buses from Yùshù run to **Sêrshu** (Shíqú Xiàn) in northwest Sìchuān, where bus connections run through some stunning scenery past **Manigango** (perhaps with a side trip to **Dégé**), the Tibetan town of **Gānzī** (check ahead to see it's open) and on past **Tǎgōng** to **Kāngdìng** (Dardo) along the Sìchuān–Tibet Hwy, from where you can head west in the direction of Tibet or east to **Chéngdū**.

3 WEEKS Tibet Fringes Tour

Travel permits are required for the Tibet Autonomous Region (TAR), a land periodically inaccessible to foreigners and an arduous undertaking at the best of times. This tour immerses you in more accessible areas. Only undertake the tour in the warmer summer months; other times can be dangerous. From **Lánzhōu** in Gānsù province, head southwest to **Lángmùsì** and **Xiàhé**, before passing by bus or taxi into Qīnghǎi via the monastery town of **Tóngrén**. Pick up a *thangka* (Tibetan sacred art) and continue by bus to **Xīníng**, then fly to **Chéngdū** in Sìchuān and take the bus to **Kāngdìng**, or fly to Kāngdìng via Chéngdū. The overland bus route from Xīníng to Kāngdìng is also possible via Yùshù in south Qīnghǎi. (Allow an extra week if taking this route.) Yùshù has officially reopened after the 2010 earthquake and transport connections are available. From Kāngdìng you can journey by bus west to the stupendous scenery around **Lǐtáng**, or travel south by minivan to **Xiāngchéng** and on to **Shangri-la (Zhōngdiàn)** and the gorgeous Tibetan region of north Yúnnán. From Shangri-la take a bus to high-altitude **Déqīn**, enveloped in gorgeous mountain scenery.

10 DAYS Northeast Tour

1 WEEK Běijīng to Mongolia

With **Běijīng** as a start point, hop on a train to stylish **Dàlián**, but plan to spend a few days exploring the historic walled coastal towns of **Shānhǎiguān** and **Xīngchéng** en route. You'll need several days for Dàlián's sights, including the historic port of **Lǚshùn** and an adorable coastline. Border watchers will be keen to get to **Dāndōng**, on the border with North Korea, for its peculiar frisson. Take a boat tour along the Yālù River, dine on North Korean food and visit Tiger Mountain Great Wall. Consider a trip by rail and bus to **Heaven Lake** in **Chángbái Shān** (the largest nature reserve in China) via **Tōnghuà**. Straddling the North Korea border, the volcanic lake is a stunning sight (only accessible mid-June to September). Alternatively, take the train to **Shěnyáng** and visit its Qing-dynasty Imperial Palace and the tomb of Huang Taiji, founder of the Qing dynasty. Hop on a bus or a train to **Hā'ěrbīn** to wonder at the city's Russian and Jewish ancestry. If you've really picked up momentum and can't stop, carry on to China's 'North Pole Village' to try to catch the aurora borealis in **Mòhé** or to bask in the summer's midnight sun.

After exhausting the superb sightseeing, and wining and dining choices, in **Běijīng**, jump aboard a train to **Hohhot** in Inner Mongolia where a late-July arrival should coincide with the Naadam festivities at Gegentala to the north, when the grasslands are turning green. Explore Hohhot's lamaseries and temples and make a trip to the grasslands outside town for a taste of the epic Inner Mongolian prairie. From Hohhot you can either take the train direct to **Ulaanbaatar** in Mongolia; or an alternative route to Mongolia is to first journey by bus from Hohhot to **Lánqí** and **Shàngdū** – vanished site of Kublai Khan's celebrated palace at Xanadu – and then on to **Hǎilā'ěr** in the far north of Inner Mongolia, towards the border with Mongolia and Russia. The grasslands outside Hǎilā'ěr are a real highlight, so consider spending the night under the stars in a yurt on the prairie. If you are Russia-bound, you can enter the country via the nearby trading town of **Mǎnzhōulǐ** on the border. Alternatively, jump aboard a flight to **Choibalsan** in eastern Mongolia.

JULY 1ST GLACIER

High up in the Qílián Shān range at 4300m, this glacier provides a cooling escape from the deserts of Gānsù. Avoid winter visits unless you're totally hardcore. (p844)

KHARA KHOTO

Hunt out this ruined and remote Tangut city in the northwest of the Badain Jaran Desert in Western Inner Mongolia. It was once buried by centuries of dust storms and today is embedded in a sublime landscape. (p876)

KAZAKHSTAN

TASHKENT

BISHKEK

UZBEKISTAN

KYRGYZSTAN

Yīníng

Ürümqi

TAJIKISTAN

Kuqa

XĪNJIĀNG

AFGHANISTAN

Kashgar

KHARA
KHOTO

Tashkurgan

Dūnhuáng

JULY 1ST
GLACIER

Zhāngyè

HIGHWAY 219

PAKISTAN

Xīníng

QĪNGHĂI

Shílín

Ali

INDIA

TIBET

TALAM KHANG
GUESTHOUSE

DELHI

NEPAL

Lhasa

KATHMANDU

SĪCHUĀN

THIMPHU

Zhōngdiàn
(Shangri-la)

HIGHWAY 219

The repaved Xīnjiāng–Tibet highway is China's remotest road and an awesome route through the largely uninhabited expanses of Aksai-Chin. (p816)

BHUTAN

INDIA

NÙ JIĀNG
VALLEY

Shíbǎoshān

BANGLADESH

Xiàguān
(Dàlǐ City)

Kūnmíng

DHAKA

MYANMAR
(BURMA)

YÚNNÁN

Bay of
Begal

Jīngzhèn

TALAM KHANG
GUESTHOUSE

This small, remote temple-stay in West Sìchuān matches rustic accommodation with a beautiful setting of snowcapped mountains and grasslands, a hot spring and the nearby monastery of Darjay Gompa. (p758)

NÙ JIĀNG VALLEY

This epic gorge in Yúnnán – pinched between Gāolígòng Shān, Myanmar, Tibet and Bìluó Shān – is the stunning habitat of a rich and vibrant diversity of fauna and flora. (p698)

LAOS

VIENTIANE

THAILAND

0   800 km
0   500 miles

GŬBĔIKŎU

The Coiled Dragon and Crouching Tiger Mountain are less-visited stretches of the Great Wall at Gŭbĕikŏu; off-the-beaten track but not too far from Bĕijīng. Perfect for day trips. (p119)

KOGURYO SITES

Scattered outside Jí'ān, the ruins, stone pyramids and tombs of the ancient Korean Koguryo kingdom dot a striking landscape of remote fields, terraces and green hills. (p325)

XĪNYÈ

A calm and unhurried portrait of geomantic harmony and architectural balance, the beautiful Zhèjiāng village of Xīnyè is a delightful retreat from the chaos of modern China. (p274)

CĀNGZHŌU'S IRON LION

Standing proud but battered (and missing the Buddhist statue that once rode it), Cāngzhōu's Iron Lion – China's oldest and largest cast iron sculpture – was devised to calm the seas in a distant corner of Héběi province. (p140)

Regions at a Glance

The high-altitude, far west of China, including Tibet, Qīnghǎi and west Sìchuān, gradually and unevenly levels out as it approaches the prosperous and well-watered canal-town provinces of Jiāngsū and Zhèjiāng, and the metropolis of Shànghǎi in the east. The lion's share of scenic marvels and hiking territory belongs to the mountainous interior of China, while in the mighty northwest, peaks and deserts meet in dramatic fashion. Minority culture is a speciality of the west and southwest, and of the remote border regions. Different cuisines range across the entire nation, from the hardy northeast to the warm jungles of the far southwest.

Běijīng

History
Temples
Food

Běijīng's imperial pedigree (and the Great Wall) assures it a rich vein of dynastic history, balanced by splendid seams of temple and *hútòng* (narrow alleyway) architecture. Wining and dining is a further attraction as the capital is home to a resourceful restaurant scene.

p54

Tiānjīn & Héběi

History
Temples
Outdoors

Tiānjīn's spruced-up foreign concession streetscapes echo stylish Shànghǎi, and some standout pagodas and temples can be found in Héběi, where the rural side of China – peppered with rustic village getaways – comes to the fore.

p127

Shāndōng

History
Mountains
Seaside

Shāndōng groans under the weight of its historical heavy-hitters: Confucius' revered home and tomb at Qūfù and sacred Tài Shān. Then, of course, there is the home of Tsingtao beer, Qīngdǎo, today a breezy, laid-back port city.

p151

Shànghǎi

Architecture
Food
Urban Style

Shànghǎi exudes a unique style unlike anywhere else in China. There's plenty to do, from nonstop shopping and skyscraper-hopping to standout art, fantastic eats and touring the city's elegant art deco heritage.

p186

Jiāngsū

Canal Towns
Outdoors
History

Jiāngsū is awash with cute-as-pie canal towns – from Tónglǐ to Sūzhōu – all reachable as day trips from neighbouring Shànghǎi. The provincial capital, Nánjīng, has history in spades, with its fabulous Ming wall and epic past as former national capital.

p231

Zhèjiāng

Canal Towns
Outdoors
Islands

Flushed with water and vaulted with bridges, the canal town of Wūzhèn is full of traditional charm. Hángzhōu is one of China's most appealing cities, while stunning pastoral escapes abound further south, including the gorgeous villages of Xīnyè and Zhūgě.

p258

Fújiàn

Architecture
Food
Islands

Fújiàn is Hakka heartland and home to the intriguing *tǔlóu* – massive packed stone, wood and mud structures once housing hundreds of families. Gǔlàng Yǔ, a tiny and hilly island off Xiàmén, is decorated with crumbling colonial villas, each one distinctive.

p281

Liáoníng

Festivals
History
Minority Culture

In history-rich Liáoníng, imperial relics contend with the legacy of Russian and Japanese colonialism. The North Korean border at Dāndōng is a sobering contrast to the wild beer festival at Dàlián.

p302

Jílín

Landscapes
Culture
Skiing

Boasting China's largest nature reserve, and a top ski destination, Jílín exerts a pull on the nature lover. On the trail of the exotic? Head to Jí'ān for the ruins of the ancient Korean Koguryo empire.

p320

Hēilóngjiāng

Festivals
Culture
Nature

Fire and ice are the highlights in this province where volcanic explosions have left one of China's most mesmerising landscapes, and the winter's bitter climate provides the raw materials for a spectacular ice sculpture festival.

p331

Shānxī

History
Culture
Mountains

Repository of one of China's most superlative Buddhist grottoes, Shānxī also brings you one of its most magical Buddhist mountains with Wǔtái Shān. History is on all sides: from the intact walled city of Píngyáo to the Hanging Monastery, a jaw-dropping, gravity-defying piece of temple architecture.

p346

Shaanxi

Historic Sites
Museums
Mountains

A treasure trove of archaeological sites is scattered across the plains surrounding Shaanxi's capital, Xī'ān, where there are museums galore. Blow off all that ancient dust with a trip to Huá Shān, one of China's five holy Taoist peaks.

p366

Ānhuī

Villages
Mountains
Outdoors

The amazing Unesco-listed Hui villages of Hóngcūn and Xīdì are some of China's best-preserved. But let's not forget that mountain, Huángshān. Its soaring granite peaks have inspired a legion of poets and painters.

p388

Hénán

History
Temples
Mountains

Hénán's overture of dynastic antiquity is balanced by some excellent mountain escapes and the quirky allure of Nánjiēcūn, China's last Maoist collective. The province's *wǔshù* (martial arts) credentials come no better: the Shàolín Temple is here.

p408

Húběi

Scenic Wonders
History
Rivers

Slashed by the mighty Yangzi River, history-rich Húběi is one of the gateways to the Three Gorges, but Taoist martial artists may find themselves mustering on Wǔdāng Shān, home of taichi and scenic views.

p428

Jiāngxī

Scenery
Mountains
Ancient Villages

Communists herald it as the mythic starting point of the Long March, but it's the spectacular mountain scenery and hiking trails past preserved villages and terraced fields that should pop Jiāngxī into your travel plans.

p442

Húnán

Ancient Towns
Minority Villages
Mountains

Home to one of China's most noteworthy ancient towns, Fènghuáng, as well as the sacred mountain of Héng Shān, the otherworldly karst peaks of Zhāngjiājiè, and secluded Miao and Dong villages.

p464

Hong Kong

Food
Shopping
Scenery

This culinary capital offers the best of China and beyond, while a seductive mix of vintage and cutting-edge fashion attracts armies of shoppers. Meanwhile, leafy mountains, shimmering waters, skyscrapers and tenements make an unlikely but poetic match.

p489

Macau

Food
Architecture
Casinos

Marrying flavours from five continents, Macanese cooking is as unique as the cityscape, where Taoist temples meet baroque churches on cobbled streets with Chinese names. It's also a billionaire's playground where casino-resorts and other luxuries vie for space.

p528

Guǎngdōng

Food
History
Architecture

A strong gastronomic culture offers travellers the chance to savour world-renowned Cantonese cuisine. Guǎngdōng's seafaring temperament has brought the region diverse, exotic architectural styles, including the World Heritage–listed watchtowers of Kāipíng.

p550

Hǎinán

Beaches
Cycling
Surfing

When it comes to golden-sand beaches and warm clear waters, this tropical island doesn't disappoint. An ideal cycling destination, Hǎinán attracts in-the-know adventurers with its good roads, balmy winters and varied landscape.

p587

Guǎngxī

Scenery
Outdoors
Cycling

Much famed for its out-of-this-world karst landscape, Guǎngxī offers adventure-loving travellers lush green valleys, charming folksy villages and countless walking, cycling and rafting opportunities.

p603

Guìzhōu

Festivals
Minority Villages
Waterfalls

With more than a third of the population made up of minorities, and more folk festivals than anywhere else in China, you can party here with the locals year-round. For nature lovers, there's an abundance of waterfalls; for old-town watchers, there's lovely Zhènyuǎn.

p630

Yúnnán

Ancient Towns
Mountains
Minority Villages

Yúnnán is the province that has it all: towering Hima-layan mountains, tropical jungle, sublime rice terraces and over half of China's minority groups. To top it off there's historic, little-visited villages like Nuòdèng and Hēijīng, gorgeous and ancient Lìjiāng, fantastic trekking and great food.

p652

Sìchuān

Mountains
Scenery
Cuisine

One province; three regions. Stay in central or southern Sìchuān for steamy bamboo forests and cute Ming-dynasty villages. Head north for stunning lakes set among alpine-esque mountain scenery. Venture west for remote Tibetan plateau grasslands and towering peaks.

p717

Chóngqìng

Cuisine
Ancient Villages
River Trips

A unique city with a unique location, hilly Chóngqìng hugs cliffs overlooking the Yangzi, bursts with old-China energy, offers some fascinating day trips and is home to hotpot – the spiciest dish on the planet.

p770

Xīnjiāng

History
Minority Culture
Nature

Bazaars, kebabs and camels are just a few of the icons that hint at your arrival in Central Asia. Ancient Silk Road towns include Tur-pan, Kashgar and Hotan, while hikers gravitate to Kanas Lake and the Tiān Shān range.

p792

Gānsù

**Silk Road
Tibetan Areas
Buddhism**

Gānsù is all about diversity: colourful Tibetan regions in the southwest, Inner Mongolia alongside the north, and a rich accumulation of Silk Road culture through the middle. Think deserts, mountains, Buddhist artefacts, camels, yaks, pilgrims and nomads.

p823

Níngxià

**History
Minority Culture
Activities**

In the designated homeland of the Hui, visit the great tombs of the Xixia, nomadic rock art and the enormous Buddhas of Xūmí Shān. For camel trekking or sliding down the sand dunes, head for the Tengger Desert.

p855

Inner Mongolia

**Remote Journeys
Food
Activities**

Ride a famed Mongolian horse at a yurt camp near Hohhot and Hǎilā'ěr and sit down to a Mongolian hotpot. Further-flung western Inner Mongolia is a hard-to-reach landscape of towering sand dunes, desert lakes and ancient sites.

p866

Qīnghǎi

**Monasteries
Scenery
Culture**

Vast and remote, the best parts of Qīnghǎi – way up on the Tibetan plateau – are for those who like their travel rough. Need a hot shower and a coffee every morning? If so, go somewhere else.

p880

Tibet

**Monasteries
Scenery
Culture**

The 'Roof of the World' is a stunningly beautiful high plateau of turquoise lakes, desert valleys and Himalayan peaks, dotted with monasteries, yaks and sacred Buddhist sites. Tight and ever-changing travel regulations can easily derail travel plans, though.

p897

Rickshaw ride, Běijīng (p75)

On the Road

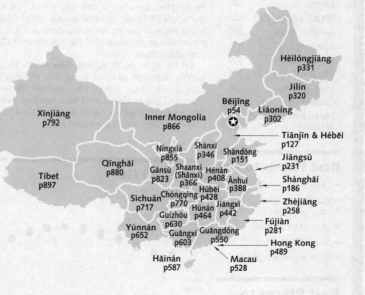

Běijīng

POP 21 MILLION / ☎ 010

Best Places to Eat

➡ Little Yúnnán (p97)

➡ Bǎihé Vegetarian Restaurant (p100)

➡ Zhāng Māma (p99)

➡ Duck de Chine (p102)

➡ Royal Icehouse (p103)

Best Places to Stay

➡ Courtyard 7 (p95)

➡ Graceland Yard (p96)

➡ Jǐngshān Garden Hotel (p93)

➡ Temple Hotel (p93)

Why Go?

Inextricably linked to past glories (and calamities) yet hurtling towards a power-charged future, Běijīng (北京), one of history's great cities, is as complex as it is compelling.

Few places on Earth can match the extraordinary historical panorama on display here – there are six Unesco World Heritage sites in this city alone, just one less than the whole of Egypt. But this is also where China's future is being shaped: Běijīng is the country's political nerve centre, a business powerhouse and the heartbeat of China's rapidly evolving cultural scene.

Yet for all its gusto, Běijīng dispenses with the persistent pace of Shànghǎi or Hong Kong. The remains of its historic *hútòng* (alleyways) still exude a unique village-within-a-city vibe, and it's in these most charming of neighbourhoods that locals shift down a gear and find time to sit out front, play chess and watch the world go by.

When to Go
Běijīng

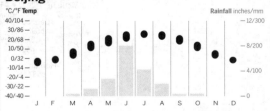

Sep–Oct Gorgeously fresh after the scorching summer, with blue skies and fewer tourists.

May Warming up after the winter freeze. Windy but usually dry and clear.

Dec–Feb Dry as a bone and brutally cold, but the streets are pleasantly quiet.

History

Although seeming to have presided over China since time immemorial, Běijīng (literally, Northern Capital) – positioned outside the central heartland of Chinese civilisation – only emerged as a cultural and political force that would shape the destiny of China with the 13th-century Mongol occupation of China.

Chinese historical sources identify the earliest settlements in these parts from 1045 BC. In later centuries Běijīng was successively occupied by foreign forces: it was established as an auxiliary capital under the Khitan, nomadic Mongolic people who formed China's Liao dynasty (AD 907–1125). Later the Jurchens, Tungusic people originally from the Siberian region, turned the city into their Jin-dynasty capital (1115–1234) during which time it was enclosed within fortified walls, accessed by eight gates.

But in 1215 the army of the great Mongol warrior Genghis Khan razed Běijīng, an event that was paradoxically to mark the city's transformation into a powerful national capital. Apart from the first 53 years of the Ming dynasty and 21 years of Nationalist rule in the 20th century, it has enjoyed this status to the present day.

The city came to be called Dàdū (大都; Great Capital), also assuming the Mongol name Khanbalik (the Khan's town). By 1279, under the rule of Kublai Khan, grandson of Genghis Khan, Dàdū was the capital of the largest empire the world has ever known.

The basic grid of present-day Běijīng was laid during the Ming dynasty, and Emperor Yongle (r 1403–24) is credited with being the true architect of the modern city. Much of Běijīng's grandest architecture, such as the Forbidden City and the iconic Hall of Prayer for Good Harvests in the Temple of Heaven Park, date from his reign.

The Manchus, who invaded China in the 17th century to establish the Qing dynasty, essentially preserved Běijīng's form. In the last 120 years of the Qing dynasty, though, Běijīng was subjected to power struggles, invasions and ensuing chaos. The list is long: the Anglo-French troops who in 1860 burnt the Old Summer Palace to the ground; the corrupt regime of Empress Dowager Cixi; the catastrophic Boxer Rebellion; the Japanese occupation of 1937; and the Nationalists. Each and every period left its undeniable mark, although the shape and symmetry of Běijīng was maintained.

Modern Běijīng came of age when, in January 1949, the People's Liberation Army (PLA) entered the city. On 1 October of that year Mao Zedong proclaimed a 'People's Republic' from the Gate of Heavenly Peace to an audience of some 500,000 citizens.

Like the emperors before them, the communists significantly altered the face of Běijīng. The *páilóu* (decorative archways) were destroyed and city blocks pulverised to widen major boulevards. From 1950 to 1952, the city's magnificent outer walls were levelled in the interests of traffic circulation. Soviet experts and technicians poured in, bringing their own Stalinesque touches.

The past quarter of a century has transformed Běijīng into a modern city, with skyscrapers, shopping malls and an ever-expanding subway system. The once flat skyline is now crenellated with vast apartment blocks and office buildings. Recent years have also seen a convincing beautification of Běijīng, from a toneless and unkempt city to a greener, cleaner and more pleasant place, albeit one heavily affected by ever-increasing pollution.

Sadly, as Běijīng continues to evolve, it is slowly shedding its links to the past. More than 4 million sq metres of old *hútòng* courtyards have been demolished since 1990; around 40% of the total area of the city centre. Preservation campaign groups have their work cut out to save what's left.

Climate

In winter, it's glacial outside (dipping as low as -20°C) and the northern winds cut like a knife through bean curd. But the air can be clear at this time and the city unusually

PRICE INDICATORS

The following price indicators refer to a standard twin room (sleeping) and a meal for one (eating).

Sleeping

$ less than ¥400
$$ ¥400 to ¥1000
$$$ more than ¥1000

Eating

$ less than ¥40
$$ ¥40 to ¥100
$$$ more than ¥100

Běijīng Highlights

❶ Hike your way along an unrestored 'wild' section of China's most famous icon, the **Great Wall** (p117)

❷ Marvel at the might and splendour of the **Forbidden City** (p59), the world's largest palace complex and home to 24 consecutive emperors of China

❸ Lose yourself in the city's warren of historic **hútòng** (alleyways), or follow our absorbing *hútòng* walking tour (p79)

❹ Wander around Běijīng's host of splendid royal parks, the highlight of which is the unmissable **Temple of Heaven Park** (p75)

❺ Enjoy a taste of imperial high life by wandering the sumptuous gardens, temples, pavilions and corridors of the **Summer Palace** (p88)

❻ Scoff **Peking duck** (p101), the capital's signature dish, in the restaurants where it originated

❼ Climb the magnificent **Drum Tower** (p70) or its charming counterpart, the **Bell Tower** (p70), and look over the grey-tiled rooftops in the alleys below

❽ Down a beer or catch some live music in one of Běijīng's **back-alley bars**. Jiāng Hú (p105) is a good place to start

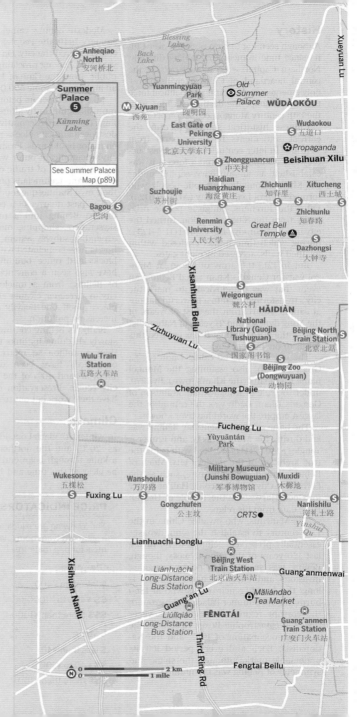

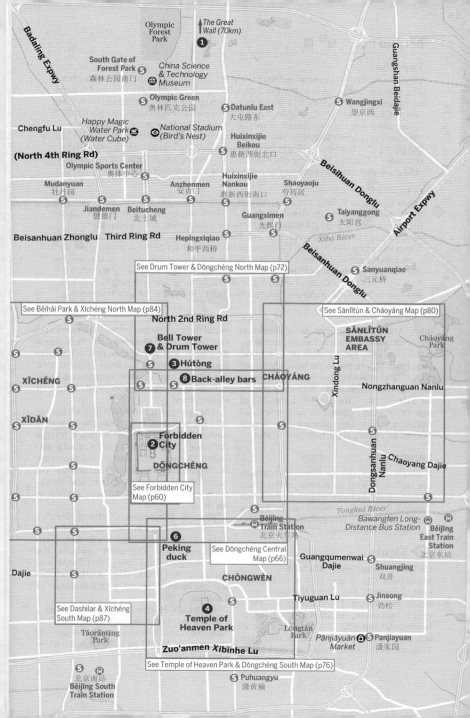

Olympic Forest Park

⓵ The Great Wall (70km)

Badaling Expwy

Guangshan Beidajie

South Gate of Forest Park
森林公园南门

China Science & Technology Museum

Chengfu Lu

Happy Magic Water Park
(Water Cube)

Olympic Green
奥林匹克公园

Datunlu East
大屯路东

Wangjingxi
望京西

National Stadium
(Bird's Nest)

Huixinxijie Beikou
惠新西街北口

(North 4th Ring Rd)

Olympic Sports Center
奥体中心

Mudanyuan
牡丹园

Anzhenmen
安贞门

Huixinxijie Nankou
惠新西街南口

Shaoyaoju
芍药居

Beisihuan Donglu

Jiandemen
健德门

Beitucheng
北土城

Guangximen
光熙门

Taiyanggong
太阳宫

Airport Expwy

Beisanhuan Zhonglu

Third Ring Rd

Hepingxiqiao
和平西桥

Xiba River

Beisanhuan Donglu

Sanyuanqiao
三元桥

See Drum Tower & Dōngchéng North Map (p72)

See Běihǎi Park & Xīchéng North Map (p84)

North 2nd Ring Rd

See Sānlǐtún & Cháoyáng Map (p80)

SĀNLǏTÚN EMBASSY AREA

Cháoyáng Park

Bell Tower & Drum Tower ⓻

XĪCHÉNG

Hútòng ⓷

Back-alley bars ⓼

CHÁOYÁNG

Nongzhanguan Nanlu

XĪDĀN

Xindong Lu

Forbidden City ⓶

DŌNGCHÉNG

Dongsanhuan Nanlu

Chaoyang Dajie

See Forbidden City Map (p60)

Tonghui River

Bǎijīng Train Station
北京火车站

Bawangfen Long-Distance Bus Station

Běijīng East Train Station
北京东站

Peking duck ⓺

See Dōngchéng Central Map (p66)

Guangqumenwai Dajie

Shuangjing
双井

Dajie

CHÓNGWÉN

Tiyuguan Lu

Jinsong
劲松

See Dashilar & Xīchéng South Map (p87)

Temple of Heaven Park ⓸

Lóngtán Park

Pānjiāyuán Market

Panjiayuan
潘家园

Táorántíng Park

Zuo'anmen Xibīnhe Lu

See Temple of Heaven Park & Dōngchéng South Map (p76)

Běijīng South Train Station
北京南站

Puhuangyu
蒲黄榆

BĚIJĪNG IN...

Two Days

Stroll around the incense smoke–filled courtyards of the Lama Temple (p71) before hopping over the road to the even more laid-back Confucius Temple (p73). Grab a coffee and lunch at Cafe Confucius (p102) before walking through the **hútòng alleys** to the ancient Drum and Bell Towers (p70) and finishing off the day with a meal in Dàlǐ Courtyard (p100).

Get up early to enjoy the Temple of Heaven Park (p75) at its magical, early morning best: filled with opera-singing locals rather than photo-snapping tourists. Grab lunch at Old Běijīng Zhájiàng Noodle King (p100) before walking via Tiān'ānmén Sq (p64) to the Forbidden City (p59). Finish the day by tucking into Běijīng's signature dish – roast duck – at China's most famous restaurant Quánjùdé Roast Duck Restaurant (p101).

Four Days

Follow the itinerary above, but save plenty of energy for the trip of a lifetime on day three: your journey to **The Great Wall** (p117). There are plenty of options, from a quick half-day jaunt at touristy **Bādálǐng** (p123) to a strenuous hike along wild, unrestored sections such as **Gǔběikǒu** (p119) or **Jiànkòu** (p120). **Mùtiányù** (p118) makes a good option for families. Pack a picnic and don't expect to get back to the city until nightfall.

Hop on the subway on day four to visit the Summer Palace (p88). You could spend the day here or make side trips to the Botanic Gardens (p90), Old Summer Palace (p88) or Fragrant Hills Park (p90), all of which are close. Return for an early evening meal so that you have time to catch a show – **Peking Opera** or **acrobatics** – on your final evening.

---

quiet. Arid spring is much more comfortable (unless there is a sand storm in town), but it only lasts for a month or so around May. From May onwards the mercury surges above 30°C, reaching the 40s in late summer. Sporadic downpours help clear the air for a day or two – this is often a smog-filled time of the year. Běijīng becomes cooler and clearer in autumn (end of September to early November), which is the best time to visit.

Language

Běijīnghuà (北京话), the Chinese spoken in the capital, is seen by purists as the finest variety of the Chinese language. Although standard Mandarin is based on the Běijīng dialect, the two are very different in both accent and colloquialisms.

⊙ Sights

Historic **Dōngchéng District** (东城区; Dōngchéng Qū) is the largest of Běijīng's central districts and by far the most interesting for visitors. For convenience, we've split it into north, central and south neighbourhoods. Dōngchéng Central has the lion's share of top-name sights, including the Forbidden City. A fascinating network of im-

perial *hútòng* (alleyways) fans out north and east from here. Dōngchéng North is also a fabulously historic, *hútòng*-rich neighbourhood, and arguably the most pleasant area in which to base yourself. Dōngchéng South is dominated by the wonderful Temple of Heaven Park.

Cháoyáng District (朝阳区; Cháoyáng Qū) sprawls east from Dōngchéng and is home to the majority of Běijīng's foreign embassies, as well as most of its expat population. The area lacks history and character, but it does contain some of the capital's best international restaurants, bars and shops, many of which are in the area known as Sānlǐtún.

West of Dōngchéng, **Xīchéng District** (西城区; Xīchéng Qū) has strong historical links. We've split it into north and south neighbourhoods. The north includes the city's lovely central lakes, at Hòuhǎi and within Běihǎi Park. The south includes the backpacker-central neighbourhood of Dashilar.

Outlying **Hǎidiàn District** (海淀区; Hǎidiàn Qū) is the capital's main university area, but it also includes some great day-trip destinations, including the hugely attractive Summer Palace.

⊙ Forbidden City & Dōngchéng Central

★ **Forbidden City**   HISTORIC SITE
(紫禁城; Zǐjìn Chéng; ☎ 010-8500 7114; www.dpm. org.cn; admission Nov-Mar ¥40, Apr-Oct ¥60, Clock Exhibition Hall ¥10, Hall of Jewellery ¥10, audio tour ¥40; ⊗ 8.30am-4pm May-Sep, 8.30am-3.30pm Oct-Apr, closed Mon; ⓢ Tian'anmen West or Tian'anmen East) Ringed by a 52m-wide moat at the very heart of Běijīng, the Forbidden City is China's largest and best-preserved collection of ancient buildings, and the largest palace complex in the world. So called because it was off limits for 500 years, when it was steeped in stultifying ritual and Byzantine regal protocol, the otherworldly palace was the reclusive home to two dynasties of imperial rule until the Republic overthrew the last Qing emperor.

Today, the Forbidden City is prosaically known as the Palace Museum (故宫博物馆; Gùgōng Bówùguǎn), although most Chinese people simply call it Gù Gōng (故宫; ancient palace).

In former ages the price for uninvited admission was instant execution; these days ¥40 or ¥60 will do. Allow yourself the best part of a day for exploration or several trips if you're an enthusiast.

Guides – many with mechanical English – mill about the entrance, but the automatically activated audio tours are cheaper (¥40; more than 40 languages) and more reliable. Restaurants, a cafe, toilets and even ATMs can be found within the palace grounds. Wheelchairs (¥500 deposit) are free to use, as are pushchairs/strollers (¥300 deposit).

ENTRANCE

Tourists must enter through **Meridian Gate** (午门; Wǔ Mén), a massive U-shaped portal at the south end of the complex, which in former times was reserved for the use of the emperor. Gongs and bells would sound imperial comings and goings, while lesser mortals used lesser gates: the military used the west gate, civilians the east gate. The emperor also reviewed his armies from here, passed judgement on prisoners, announced the new year's calendar and oversaw the flogging of troublesome ministers.

Through Meridian Gate, you enter an enormous courtyard, and cross the **Golden Stream** (金水; Jīn Shuǐ) – shaped to resemble a Tartar bow and spanned by five marble bridges – on your way to the magnificent **Gate of Supreme Harmony** (太和门; Tàihé Mén). This courtyard could hold an imperial audience of 100,000 people. For an idea of the size of the restoration challenge, note how the crumbling courtyard stones are stuffed with dry weeds, especially on the periphery.

FIRST SIDE GALLERIES

Before you pass through the Gate of Supreme Harmony to reach the Forbidden City's star attractions, veer off to the east and west of the huge courtyard to visit the Calligraphy and Painting Gallery inside the **Hall of Martial Valour** (武英殿; Wǔ Yīng Diàn) and the particularly good Ceramics Gallery, housed inside the creaking **Hall of Literary Glory** (文化殿; Wén Huà Diàn).

THREE GREAT HALLS

Raised on a three-tier marble terrace with balustrades are the Three Great Halls, the glorious heart of the Forbidden City. The recently restored **Hall of Supreme Harmony** (太和殿; Tàihé Diàn) is the most important and largest structure in the Forbidden City. Built in the 15th century and restored in the 17th century, it was used for ceremonial occasions, such as the emperor's birthday, the

---

DON'T MISS

CLOCK EXHIBITION HALL

The **Clock Exhibition Hall** (钟表馆; Zhōngbiǎo Guǎn; admission Y10; ⊗ 8.30am-4pm summer, 8.30am-3.30pm winter) is one of the unmissable highlights of the Forbidden City. Located in the **Hall for Ancestral Worship** (Fèngxiān Diàn) – just off to the right after the Three Great Halls – the exhibition contains an astonishing array of elaborate timepieces, many of which were gifts to the Qing emperors from overseas. Exquisitely wrought and fashioned with magnificently designed elephants and other creatures, they all display astonishing artfulness and attention to detail. Time your arrival for 11am or 2pm to see the **clock performance** in which choice timepieces strike the hour and give a display to wide-eyed children and adults.

Forbidden City

N
0 ____ 400 m
0 ____ 0.2 miles

Běihǎi Lake

Dashizuo Hutong

Jingshan Xijie

🎯 Jǐngshān
2 Park

● 36

Jingshan Qianjie 景山前街

Palace Moat

Palace Moat

Wusi Dajie
五四大街

@

Wenjin Jie
文津街

◉ 5

◉ 22

Imperial
Peace Hall

🏛 33
Well of
Concubine Zhen

🏛 25

Longevity &
Prosperity
Temple

🏛 19

🏛 15

◉ 18

◉ 14

◉ 20

Jǐngrèn
Hall

Hall of
Character
Cultivation

🏛 21

Beichizi Dajie

Qihelou Jie

Fúyòu
Temple

◉ 10

1 Forbidden
◉ City

Imperial
Supremacy
Hall

Restaurant ✕

Cafe

🍴 💲 🏛 4

Restaurant ✕

Heavenly
Purity Gate

32

◉ 17

◉ 12

◉ 11

✕ Restaurant

◉ 13

Golden
Stream

Hòngyì
Pavilion

🏛 9

◉ 7

🏛 8

Dōnghuá
Gate -
Exit Only

28

31

Gate of
Military
Prowess

Donghuamen Dajie

27

Pudusi Xixiang

Xīhuá Gate
- Closed

Xihe
Gate

Pǔdù
Temple

◉ 16

Pudusi Qianxiang

Cultural Workers Palace
northwest entrance

Rear
Hall

Duanku Hutong

Zhōngshān
Park

● 37

Middle
Hall

● 34

Nanchang Jie 南长街

3 🚽

39

23

30

Duān
Gate

◉ 24

Nanchizi Dajie 南池子大街

26

● 35

🚽 29

◉ 6

38 ●

🚽

Changpu
River Park

Bicycle
Stands

Xichang'an Jie 西长安街

Dongchang'an Jie

Tian'anmen
East
天安门东

💲

Tian'anmen
West
天安门西

Tiān'ānmén
Square

Forbidden City

nomination of military leaders and coronations. Inside the Hall of Supreme Harmony is a richly decorated **Dragon Throne** (龙椅; Lóngyǐ), from which the emperor would preside over trembling officials. The entire court had to touch the floor nine times with their foreheads (the custom known as kowtowing) in the emperor's presence. At the back of the throne is a carved Xumishan, the Buddhist paradise, signifying the throne's supremacy.

Behind the Hall of Supreme Harmony is the smaller **Hall of Middle Harmony** (中和殿; Zhōnghé Diàn), which was used as the emperor's transit lounge. Here he would make last-minute preparations, rehearse speeches and receive close ministers. On display are two Qing-dynasty sedan chairs, the emperor's mode of transport around the Forbidden City. The last of the Qing emperors, Puyi, used a bicycle and altered a few features of the palace grounds to make it easier to get around.

The third of the Great Halls is the **Hall of Preserving Harmony** (保和殿; Bǎohé Diàn), used for banquets and later for imperial examinations. The hall has no support pillars. To its rear is a 250-tonne marble imperial carriageway carved with dragons and clouds, which was transported into Běijīng on an ice path. The emperor used to be carried over this carriageway in his sedan chair as he ascended or descended the terrace. The outer housing surrounding the Three Great Halls was used for storing gold, silver, silks, carpets and other treasures.

A string of side halls on the eastern and western flanks of the Three Great Halls usually, but not always, house a series of excellent exhibitions, ranging from scientific instruments and articles of daily use to objects presented to the emperor by visiting dignitaries. One contains an interesting diorama of the whole complex.

LESSER CENTRAL HALLS

The basic configuration of the Three Great Halls is echoed by the next group of buildings. Smaller in scale, these buildings were more important in terms of real power, which in China traditionally lies at the back door.

The first structure is the **Palace of Heavenly Purity** (乾清宫; Qiánqīng Gōng), a residence of Ming and early Qing emperors, and

Forbidden City

WALKING TOUR

After entering through the imperious Meridian Gate, resist the temptation to dive straight into the star attractions and veer right for a peek at the excellent **Ceramics Gallery ❶** housed inside the creaking Hall of Literary Glory.

Walk back to the central complex and head through the magnificent Gate of Supreme Harmony towards the Three Great Halls: first, the largest – the **Hall of Supreme Harmony ❷**, followed by the **Hall of Middle Harmony ❸** and the **Hall of Preserving Harmony ❹**, behind which slopes the enormous Marble Imperial Carriageway.

Turn right here to visit the fascinating **Clock Exhibition Hall ❺** before entering the **Complete Palace of Peace & Longevity ❻**, a mini Forbidden City constructed along the eastern axis of the main complex. It includes the beautiful **Nine Dragon Screen ❼** and, to the north, a series of halls, housing some excellent exhibitions and known collectively as The Treasure Gallery. Don't miss the **Pavilion of Cheerful Melodies ❽**, a wonderful three-storey opera house.

Work your way to the far north of this section, then head west to the **Imperial Garden ❾**, with its ancient cypress trees and pretty pavilions, before exiting via the garden's West Gate (behind the Thousand Year Pavilion) to explore the **Western Palaces ❿**, an absorbing collection of courtyard homes where many of the emperors lived during their reign.

Exit this section at its southwest corner before turning back on yourself to walk north through the Gate of Heavenly Purity to see the three final Central Halls – the **Palace of Heavenly Purity ⓫**, the **Hall of Union ⓬** and the **Palace of Earthly Tranquility ⓭** – before leaving via the North Gate.

Water Vats
More than 300 copper and brass water vats dot the palace complex. They were used for fighting fires and in winter were prevented from freezing over by using thick quilts.

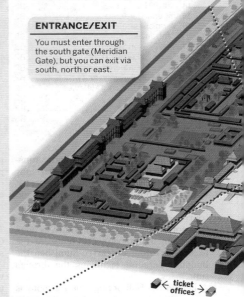

ENTRANCE/EXIT

You must enter through the south gate (Meridian Gate), but you can exit via south, north or east.

← ticket offices →

Guardian Lions
Pairs of lions guard important buildings. The male has a paw placed on a globe (representing the emperor's power over the world). The female has her paw on a baby lion (representing the emperor's fertility).

Kneeling Elephants
At the northern entrance of the Imperial Garden are two bronze elephants kneeling in an anatomically impossible fashion, which symbolise the power of the emperor; even elephants kowtowed before him.

Nine Dragon Screen
One of only three of its type left in China, this beautiful glazed dragon screen served to protect the Hall of Imperial Supremacy from evil spirits.

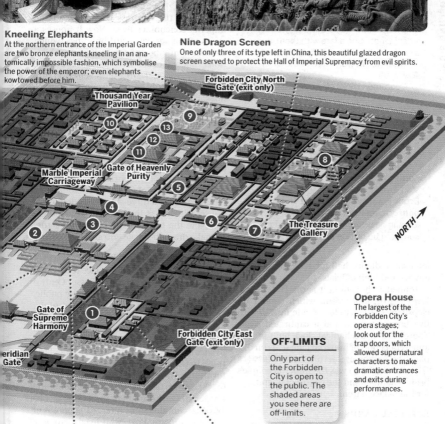

Forbidden City North Gate (exit only)

Thousand Year Pavilion

10
13
9
12
11
8

Gate of Heavenly Purity

Marble Imperial Carriageway

5
4
2
3
6
7

The Treasure Gallery

NORTH →

Gate of Supreme Harmony

1

Forbidden City East Gate (exit only)

eridian Gate

OFF-LIMITS
Only part of the Forbidden City is open to the public. The shaded areas you see here are off-limits.

Opera House
The largest of the Forbidden City's opera stages; look out for the trap doors, which allowed supernatural characters to make dramatic entrances and exits during performances.

Dragon-Head Spouts
More than a thousand dragon-head spouts encircle the raised marble platforms at the centre of the Forbidden City. They were – and still are – part of the drainage system.

Roof Guardians
The imperial dragon is at the tail of the procession, which is led by a figure riding a phoenix followed by a number of mythical beasts. The more beasts, the more important the building.

BEWARE THE RICKSHAW HUSTLERS!

Pushy rickshaw and taxi touts wait at the north gate of the Forbidden City to try to take advantage of weary visitors exiting the complex. It's always fun to take a rickshaw ride, but be very clear when negotiating a fare with them. As a guide, it should cost about ¥20 per rickshaw to get from here to the Drum Tower.

A common trick is for them to say 'three'. You think they mean three *yuán* (a bargain!). They insist later that they meant three hundred! It's probably best just to avoid them altogether by walking a few hundred metres in any direction, then hailing a passing cab.

Alternatively, turn left as you exit the north gate and walk to the nearby bus stop. From here, bus 124 goes to the Drum Tower, while buses 专1 and 专2 both do circuits of the Forbidden City, looping back south to Qiánmén, at the southern tip of Tiān'ānmén Sq.

later an audience hall for receiving foreign envoys and high officials.

Immediately behind it is the **Hall of Union** (交泰殿; Jiāotài Diàn), which contains a clepsydra – a water clock made in 1745 with five bronze vessels and a calibrated scale. There's also a mechanical clock built in 1797 and a collection of imperial jade seals on display. The **Palace of Earthly Tranquillity** (坤宁宫; Kūnníng Gōng) was the imperial couple's bridal chamber and the centre of operations for the palace harem.

IMPERIAL GARDEN

At the northern end of the Forbidden City is the **Imperial Garden** (御花园; Yù Huāyuán), a classical Chinese garden with 7000 sq metres of fine landscaping, including rockeries, walkways, pavilions and ancient cypresses. Before you reach the **Gate of Divine Prowess** (神武门; Shénwǔ Mén), the Forbidden City's north exit, and **Shùnzhēn Gate** (顺贞门; Shùnzhēn Mén), which leads to it, note the pair of bronze elephants whose front knees bend in an anatomically impossible fashion, signifying the power of the emperor; even elephants would kowtow before him.

COMPLETE PALACE OF PEACE & LONGEVITY

A mini Forbidden City, known as the **Complete Palace of Peace and Longevity** (宁寿全宫; Níng Shòu Quán Gōng) was built in the northeastern corner of the complex, mimicking the structure of the great halls of the central axis. During the Ming dynasty this was where the empress dowager and the imperial concubines lived. Now it houses a series of quieter courtyard buildings, which contain a number of fine museum exhibitions, known collectively as the **Treasure Gallery** (珍宝馆; Zhēn Bǎo Guǎn; admission ¥10).

The complex is entered from the south – not far from the Clock Exhibition Hall. Just inside the entrance, you'll find the beautiful glazed **Nine Dragon Screen** (九龙壁; Jiǔlóng Bì), one of only three of its type left in China.

Visitors then work their way north, exploring a number of peaceful halls and courtyards before being popped out at the **northern end** of the Forbidden City. Don't miss the **Pavilion of Cheerful Melodies** (音阁; Chàngyīn Gé), a three-storey wooden opera house, which was the palace's largest theatre. Note the trapdoors that allowed actors to make dramatic stage entrances.

WESTERN & EASTERN PALACES

About half a dozen smaller palace courtyards lie to the west and east of the Lesser Central Halls. They should all be open to the public, although at the time of research many of the eastern ones were closed for extensive renovation. It was in these smaller courtyard buildings that most of the emperors actually lived and many of the buildings, particularly those to the west, are decked out in imperial furniture. The **Hall of Mental Cultivation** (心殿; Yǎng Xīn Diàn) is a highlight, while the **Palace of Gathered Elegance** (储秀宫; Chǔ Xiù Gōng) contains some interesting photos of the last emperor Puyi, who lived here as a child ruler at the turn of the 20th century.

Tiān'ānmén Square   SQUARE
(天安门广场; Tiān'ānmén Guǎngchǎng; Map p66; ⑤ Tian'anmen West, Tian'anmen East or Qianmen) **FREE** Flanked by stern 1950s Soviet-style buildings and ringed by white perimeter fences, the world's largest public square (440,000 sq metres) is an immense flatland of paving stones at the heart of Běijīng. If you get up early, you can watch the flag-raising ceremony at sunrise, performed by a troop of People's Liberation Army (PLA) soldiers drilled to march at precisely 108 paces

per minute, 75cm per pace. The soldiers emerge through the Gate of Heavenly Peace to goosestep impeccably across Cháng'an Jiē; all traffic is halted. The same ceremony in reverse is performed at sunset.

Here one stands at the symbolic centre of the Chinese universe. The rectangular arrangement, flanked by halls to both east and west, to some extent echoes the layout of the Forbidden City: as such, the square employs a conventional plan that pays obeisance to traditional Chinese culture, but many of its ornaments and buildings are Soviet-inspired. Mao conceived the square to project the enormity of the Communist Party, and during the Cultural Revolution he reviewed parades of up to a million people here. The 'Tiān'ānmén Incident', in 1976, is the term given to the near-riot in the square that accompanied the death of Premier Zhou Enlai. Another million people jammed the square to pay their last respects to Mao in the same year. Most infamously, in 1989 the army forced prodemocracy demonstrators out of the square. Hundreds lost their lives in the surrounding streets, although contrary to widespread belief, it is unlikely that anyone was killed in the square itself.

Despite being a public place, the square remains more in the hands of the government than the people; it is monitored by closed circuit TV cameras, Segway-riding policemen and plain-clothes officers. The designated points of access, security checks on entry and twitchy mood cleave Tiān'ānmén Square from the city. A tangible atmosphere of restraint and authority reigns.

All this – plus the absence of anywhere to sit – means the square is hardly a place to chill out (don't whip out a guitar), but such is its iconic status that few people leave Běijīng without making a visit. In any case, there's more than enough space to stretch a leg and the view can be breathtaking, especially on a clear blue day or at nightfall when the area is illuminated.

Gate of Heavenly Peace   HISTORIC SITE
(天安门; Tiān'ānmén; admission ¥15, bag storage ¥2-6; ⊗8.30am-4.30pm; Ⓢ Tian'anmen West or Tian'anmen East) Hung with a vast likeness of Mao Zedong, and guarded by two pairs of Ming stone lions, the double-eaved Gate of Heavenly Peace, north of Tiān'ānmén Square, is a potent national symbol. Built in the 15th century and restored in the 17th century, the gate was formerly the largest of the four gates of the Imperial City Wall, and

it was from this gate that Mao proclaimed the People's Republic of China on 1 October 1949. Today's political coterie watches mass troop parades from here.

Climb the gate for excellent views of the square, and peek inside at the impressive beams and overdone paintwork; in all there are 60 gargantuan wooden pillars and 17 vast lamps suspended from the ceiling. Within the gate tower there is also a fascinating photographic history of the gate and Tiān'ānmén Square, although captions are in Chinese only.

There's no fee for walking through the gate, en route to the Forbidden City, but if you climb it you'll have to pay. The ticket office is on the north side of the gate. For Forbidden City tickets, keep walking about 600m further north.

Front Gate   HISTORIC SITE
(前门; Qián Mén; Map p66; admission ¥20, audio guide ¥20; ⊗9am-4pm Tue-Sun; Ⓢ Qianmen) Front Gate actually consists of two gates. The northernmost is the 40m-high Zhèngyáng Gate (正阳门城楼; Zhèngyáng Mén Chénglóu), which dates from the Ming dynasty and which was the largest of the nine gates of the Inner City Wall separating the inner, or Tartar (Manchu) city from the outer, or Chinese city. With the disappearance of the city walls, the gate sits out of context, but it can be climbed for decent views of the square and of Arrow Tower, immediately to the south.

Partially destroyed in the Boxer Rebellion around 1900, the gate was once flanked by two temples that have since vanished.

Inside the upper levels are some fascinating historical photographs, showing the area as it was at the beginning of the last century, before the city walls and many of the surrounding gates and temples were demolished. Explanatory captions are in English as well as Chinese.

Zhèngyáng Gate Arrow Tower (正阳门 箭楼; Zhèngyángmén Jiànlóu; Map p66), directly south, can't be climbed. It also dates from the Ming dynasty and was originally connected to Zhèngyáng Gate by a semicircular enceinte (demolished last century).

National Museum of China   MUSEUM
(中国国际博物馆; Zhōngguó Guójì Bówùguǎn; Map p66; en.chnmuseum.cn; Guangchangdongce Lu, Tiān'ānmén Sq; 天安门，广场东侧路; audio guide ¥30, cafe coffee from ¥20, tea from ¥10, pastries & sandwiches ¥10-20; ⊗9am-5pm Tue-Sun,

Dōngchéng Central

BĚIJĪNG

500 m
0.25 miles

CHÁOYÁNG

Dongsi
Shitiao

Chaoyangmen Beidajie

**Chaoyangmen Nandajie
(Second Ring Rd)**

Chaoyangmen

9

7

Dongsishitiao Lu

Chaoyangmen Beixiaojie

Dafangjia Hutong

18

Chaoyangmennei Dajie

26

Dongsi Liutiao

Baofang Hutong

20

Dongsi

22
Yanyue Hutong

Neiwubu Jie

10

Shijia Hutong

Zhangzizhonglu

Dongsi Beidajie 东四北大街 **Dongsi Beidajie** 东四北大街 Dongsi **Dongsi Nandajie**

Zhangzizhong Lu

Qianliang Hutong

**Chinese
Museum of Art**
中国美术馆

Dongsi Xidajie
东四西大街

Dengshikou Dajie

Wangfujing Dajie 王府井大街

31

Dengshikou Xijie

Meishuguan Houjie

Liangguochang

14

28

Chenguang Jie

Donghuangchenggen Beijie
东皇城根北街

38

Beiheyan Dajie 北河沿大街

Qihelou
Jie

Nanluoguxiang
南锣鼓巷

Shatanbei Jie

Wusi Dajie

24

Beichizi Dajie

Nianzi Hutong

Di'anmen Dongdajie

Sanyanjing
Hutong
三眼井胡同

23

32

Jingshan Dongjie

37

Huanghuamen Jie

19 15

29

Jingshan Qianjie 景山前街

Di'anmennei Dajie

Jingshan Houjie

33

Qiánhǎi
Lake

Beihai
North
北海北

30

Gongjian Hutong

Jingshan Xijie

39

See Forbidden City Map (p60)

Palace Moat

Di'anmen Xidajie

Běihǎi
Lake

北长街 Beichang Jie

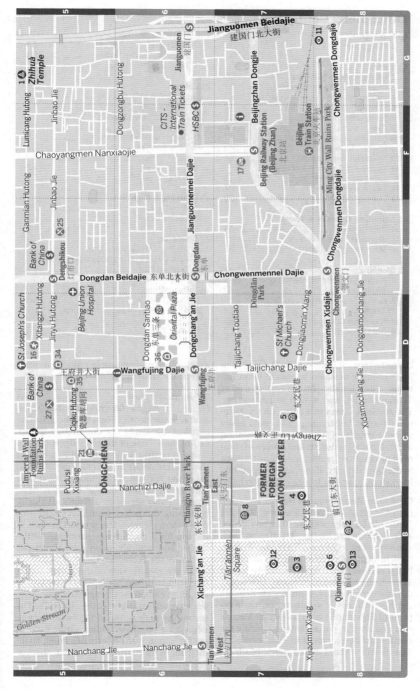

1 Zhihuà Temple

Lumicang Hutong

Ganmian Hutong

Jinbao Jie

Dongzongbu Hutong

Chaoyangmen Nanxiaojie

Bank of China

Dengshikou

25

Jinbao Jie

Jianguomen Beidajie
建国门北大街

Jianguomen
建国门

CITS - International
● Train Tickets

HSBC

Jianguomennei Dajie

Dongdan
东单

Beijingzhan Dongjie

i

Beijing Railway Station (Beijing Zhan)
北京站

Beijing
● Train Station
北京火车站

Chongwenmen Dongdajie

11

Ming City Wall Ruins Park

Chongwenmen Dongdajie

17

Dongdan Beidajie 东单北大街

St Joseph's Church

16

Xitangzi Hutong

Jinyu Hutong

34

Beijing Union Hospital

王府井大街 **Wangfujing Dajie**

Bank of China

27

Ciqiku Hutong
瓷器库胡同

35

Imperial Wall Foundation Ruins Park

Pudusi Xixiang

21

DŌNGCHÉNG

Nanchizi Dajie

Chángpu River Park

Tian'anmen East
天安门东

Dongdan Santiao
东单三条

Oriental Plaza

36

Chongwenmennei Dajie

Dongdan Park

Dongchang'an Jie

Taijichang Toutiao

St Michael's Church

Dongjiaomin Xiang

Taijichang Dajie

Wangfujing
王府井

5

Zhengyi Lu 正义路

8

FORMER FOREIGN LEGATION QUARTER

东交民巷

4

Chongwenmen Xidajie

Chongwenmen
崇文门

Dongdamochang Jie

Xidamochang Jie

Xichang'an Jie

东长安街 Tian'anmen West
天安门西

Nanchang Jie

Nanchang Jie

Tian'anmen Square

2

12

3

6

13

Qianmen
前门

前门东大街

Xijiaomin Xiang

Golden Stream

Dōngchéng Central

last entry 4pm; S Tian'anmen East) **FREE** Běijīng's premier museum is housed in an immense 1950s building on the eastern side of
Tiān'ānmén Sq, and is well worth visiting.
The **Ancient China** exhibition on the basement floor is outstanding. You could easily
spend a couple of hours in this exhibition
alone. It contains dozens and dozens of stunning pieces, from prehistoric China through
to the Qing dynasty, all displayed beautifully
in modern, spacious, low-lit exhibition halls.

Chairman Mao Memorial Hall MAUSOLEUM
(毛主席纪念堂; Máo Zhǔxí Jìniàntáng; Map p66;
Tiān'ānmén Sq; bag storage ¥2-10, camera storage
¥2-5; ☉ 7.30am-1pm Tue-Sun; S Tian'anmen West,
Tian'anmen East or Qianmen) **FREE** Mao Zedong
died in September 1976 and his memorial
hall was constructed on the southern side of
Tiān'ānmén Sq soon afterwards. This squat,
Soviet-inspired mausoleum lies on Běijīng's
north–south axis of symmetry on the footprint of Zhōnghuá Gate (Zhōnghuá Mén), a
vast and ancient portal flattened during the
communist development of Tiān'ānmén Sq.
Mao is still revered across much of China,

and you'll see some people reduced to tears
here at the sight of his mummified corpse.

★ **Jīngshān Park** PARK
(景山公园; Jǐngshān Gōngyuán; Jingshan Qianjie;
adult ¥2, in summer ¥5; ☉ 6am-9.30pm; S Tian'anmen West, then bus 5) The dominating feature
of Jīngshān – one of the city's finest parks –
is one of central Běijīng's few hills; a mound
that was created from the earth excavated to
make the Forbidden City moat. Called Coal
Hill by Westerners during Legation days,
Jīngshān also serves as a feng shui shield,
protecting the palace from evil spirits – or
dust storms – from the north. Clamber to
the top for a magnificent panorama of the
capital and princely views over the russet
roofing of the Forbidden City.

On the eastern side of the park a locust
tree stands in the place where the last of
the Ming emperors, Chongzhen, hung himself as rebels swarmed at the city walls. The
rest of the park is one of the best places in
Běijīng for people-watching. Come early to
see (or join in with) elderly folk going about
their morning routines of dancing, singing,
performing taichi or playing keepie-uppies

with oversized shuttlecocks. In April and May the park bursts into bloom with fabulously colourful peonies and tulips forming the focal point of a very popular flower fair (admission ¥10). The park has three gates: the **south** is directly opposite the Forbidden City's north gate (exit only), the **west** (Map p66) leads towards Běihǎi Park's east gate, while the **east gate** (Map p66) has a couple of nice cafes outside it.

★**Zhōngshān Park**   PARK
(中山公园; Zhōngshān Gōngyuán; adult ¥3, Spring Flower & Tulips Show ¥10; ☺6am-9pm; ⑤Tian'anmen West) Named after Sun Zhongshan (Sun Yatsen), the father of modern China, this peaceful park sits at the southwest corner of the Forbidden City and partly looks out onto the palace's moat (you can rent pedal-boats here) and towering walls. A refreshing prologue or conclusion to the magnificence of the Forbidden City, the park was formerly the sacred Ming-style Altar to the God of the Land and the God of Grain (Shèjìtán), where the emperor offered sacrifices. The **Square Altar** (wǔsè tǔ) remains, bordered on all sides by walls tiled in various colours.

Near the park's south entrance stands a towering dark-blue-tiled *páilóu* (traditional Chinese archway) with triple eaves that originally commemorated the German Foreign Minister Baron von Ketteler, killed by Boxers in 1900. Just off to the right (east) is the 100-year-old Láijīnyǔxuān Teahouse (p104). North of here, also in the eastern section of the park, is the Forbidden City Concert Hall (p105). As with Jǐngshān Park, April and May is a beautiful time to visit thanks to the hugely colourful Spring Flower and Tulips Show. The **northeast exit** of the park brings you out by Meridian Gate, from where you can enter the Forbidden City. The **south exit** brings you out near Tiān'ānmén Sq. There is also a **west gate**.

Workers Cultural Palace   PARK
(劳动人民文化宫; Láodòng Rénmín Wénhuà Gōng; ☑ tennis court 010-6512 2856; park entrance ¥2, tennis court per hr ¥80, Supreme Temple ¥10; ☺6.30am-7.30pm, tennis court 6am-11.30pm; ⑤Tian'anmen East) Despite the prosaic name and its location at the very heart of town, this reclusive park, between Tiān'ānmén Sq and the Forbidden City, is one of Běijīng's best-kept secrets. Few visitors divert here from their course towards the main gate of the Forbidden City, but this was the emperor's premier place of worship and contains

the **Supreme Temple** (太庙; Tài Miào; admission ¥10), with its beautifully carved interior roofing.

★**Zhìhuà Temple**   BUDDHIST TEMPLE
(智化寺; Zhìhuà Sì; Map p66; 5 Lumicang Hutong; adult ¥20, audio guide ¥10, Wed free; ☺8.30am-4.30pm, closed Mon; ⑤Jianguomen or Chaoyangmen) Běijīng's surviving temple brood has endured casual restoration that often buried authenticity. But this rickety nonactive temple, hidden down a rarely visited *hútòng,* is thick with the flavours of old Peking, having eluded the Dulux treatment that invariably precedes entrance fee inflation and stomping tour groups.

You won't find the coffered ceiling of the Zhìhuà Hall (it's in the USA), and the Four Heavenly Kings have vanished from Zhìhuà Gate (智化门; Zhìhuà Mén), but the **Scriptures Hall**, off to one side of the central courtyard, encases a unique, eight-sided, Ming-dynasty wooden library topped with a seated Buddha and a magnificently unrestored ceiling. The highlight, the **Ten Thousand Buddhas Hall** (万佛殿; Wànfó Diàn), is right at the back of the complex, and is an enticing two floors of miniature niche-borne Buddhist effigies and cabinets for the storage of sutras. Its entrance is dominated by three stunning, wood-carved deities (a 6m-tall Tathagata Buddha, flanked by Brahma and Indra). Unfortunately, visitors are no longer allowed to climb to the 2nd floor of this hall.

Try to time your visit to coincide with the free, 15-minute, **musical performance** which takes place in Zhìhuà Hall at 10am and 3pm each day. Performers use traditional Chinese instruments associated with Buddhist worship.

Note the surreal juxtaposition of this 15th-century temple with the swirling, space-age curves of the **Galaxy Soho** (Map p66) buildings, which now loom over this historic *hútòng* neighbourhood.

Former Foreign Legation Quarter   HISTORIC BUILDINGS
(租界区; Map p66; ⑤Chongwenmen, Qianmen or Wangfujing) The former Foreign Legation Quarter, where the 19th-century foreign powers flung up their embassies, schools, post offices and banks, lies east of Tiān'ānmén Sq. Apart from the Běijīng Police Museum, the **former French Post Office** (now a Sìchuān restaurant), and some of the Legation Quarter buildings (now high-end restaurants and members clubs), you can't enter

any of the buildings, but a stroll along the streets here (Dongjiaomin Xiang, Taijichang Dajie and Zhengyi Lu) gives you a hint of the area's former European flavour.

Poly Art Museum MUSEUM

(保利艺术博物馆; Bǎolì Yìshù Bówùguǎn; Map p66; ☑010-6500 8117; www.polymuseum.com; 9th fl, Poly Plaza, 14 Dongzhimen Nandajie; admission ¥20, audio guide ¥10; ◷9.30am-5pm, closed Sun; Ⓢ Dongsi Shitiao) This small but exquisite museum displays a glorious array of ancient bronzes from the Shang and Zhou dynasties, a magnificent high-water mark for bronze production. Check out the intricate scaling on the 'Zūn vessel in the shape of a Phoenix' (俪季凤鸟尊) or the 'Yǒu with Divine Faces' (神面卣), with its elephant head on the side of the vessel. The detailed animist patterns on the *Gangbo Yǒu* (椚柏卣) are similarly vivid and fascinating.

Shǐjiā Hútòng Museum MUSEUM

(史家胡同博物馆; Shǐjiā Hútòng Bówùguǎn; Map p66; 24 Shijia Hutong; 史家胡同24号; ◷9.30am-4.30pm Tue-Sun) FREE Housed in a pleasant, renovated double-courtyard, which used to be a local kindergarten, this small museum uses old photos, maps and artefacts, as well as some scale models, to explain the history of Shijia Hutong, and of Bĕijīng's *hútòng* districts in general. There are excellent English captions throughout, and the large-scale model of the whole local neighbourhood, with Shijia Hutong at its core, is particularly interesting to muse over.

◉ Drum Tower & Dōngchéng North

Drum Tower HISTORIC SITE

(鼓楼; Gǔlóu; Map p72; Gulou Dongdajie; admission ¥20, both towers through ticket ¥30; ◷9am-5pm, last tickets 4.40pm; Ⓢ Shichahai or Gulou Dajie) Along with the older-looking Bell Tower, which stands behind it, the magnificent red-painted Drum Tower used to be the city's official timekeeper, with drums and bells beaten and rung to mark the times of the day.

Originally built in 1272, the Drum Tower was once the heart of the Mongol capital of Dàdū, as Bĕijīng was then known. It was destroyed in a fire before a replacement was built, slightly to the east of the original location, in 1420. The current structure is a Qing-dynasty version of that 1420 tower.

You can climb the steep inner staircase for views of the grey-tiled rooftops in the sur-

rounding *hútòng* alleys. But you can't view the Bell Tower as the north-facing balcony has been closed. It's well worth climbing the tower, though, especially if you can time it to coincide with one of the regular drumming performances, which are played on reproductions of the 25 Ming-dynasty watch drums, which used to sound out across this part of the city. One of the original 25 drums, the **Night Watchman's Drum** (更鼓; Gēnggǔ), is also on display; dusty, battered and worn. Also on display is a replica of a Song-dynasty water clock, which was never actually used in the tower, but is interesting nonetheless.

The times of the **drumming performances**, which only last for a few minutes, are posted by the ticket office.

Bell Tower HISTORIC SITE

(钟楼; Zhōnglóu; Map p72; Gulou Dongdajie; admission ¥20, both towers through ticket ¥30; ◷9am-5pm, last tickets 4.40pm; Ⓢ Shichahai or Gulou Dajie) The more modest, grey-stone structure of the Bell Tower is arguably more charming than its resplendent other half, the Drum Tower, after which this area of Bĕijīng is named. It also has the added advantage of being able to view its sister tower from a balcony.

Along with the drums in the Drum Tower, the bells in the Bell Tower were used as Bĕijīng's official timekeepers throughout the Yuan, Ming and Qing dynasties, and on until 1924. The Bell Tower looks the older of the two, perhaps because it isn't painted. In fact both are of similar age. The Bell Tower was also built during the Mongol Yuan dynasty, in 1272, and was rebuild in the 1440s after being destroyed in a fire. This current structure was built in 1745.

Like the Drum Tower, the Bell Tower can also be climbed up an incredibly steep inner staircase. But the views from the top are even better here, partly because the structure is set back more deeply into the surrounding *hútòng,* and partly because you can get great photos of the Drum Tower from its viewing balcony. Marvel too at the huge, 600-year-old, 63-tonne bell suspended in the pleasantly unrestored interior. Note how Chinese bells have no clappers but are instead struck with a stout pole.

Inside the tower, on the ground floor (south side), is the **Bell Tower Tea House**, where you can sample a selection of Chinese teas (per person per hour ¥50) as well as buy tea and tea sets.

The Drum & Bell Sq, between the two towers, is a great people-watching area in which to while away some time even if you don't climb either of the two towers. There are a handful of excellent bars and cafes here too, some with rooftop views over the square. Both towers are lit up beautifully come evening. Note: the square was undergoing wholesale renovations at the time of research.

Lama Temple   BUDDHIST TEMPLE

(雍和宫; Yōnghé Gōng; Map p72; 28 Yonghegong Dajie; admission ¥25, English audio guide ¥50; ☉9am-4.30pm; ⑤Yonghegong-Lama Temple) This exceptional temple is a glittering attraction in Běijīng's Buddhist firmament. If you only have time for one temple (the Temple of Heaven isn't really a temple) make it this one, where riveting roofs, fabulous frescoes, magnificent decorative arches, tapestries, eye-popping carpentry, Tibetan prayer wheels, Tantric statues and a superb pair of Chinese lions mingle with dense clouds of incense.

The most renowned Tibetan Buddhist temple outside Tibet, the Lama Temple was converted to a lamasery in 1744 after serving as the former residence of Emperor Yong Zheng. Today the temple is an active place of worship, attracting pilgrims from afar, some of whom prostrate themselves in submission at full length within its halls.

Resplendent within the **Hall of the Wheel of the Law** (Fǎlún Diàn), the fourth hall you reach from the entrance, is a substantial bronze statue of a benign and smiling Tsong Khapa (1357–1419), founder of the Gelugpa or Yellow Hat sect, robed in yellow and illuminated by a skylight.

The fifth hall, the **Wànfú Pavilion** (Wànfú Gé), houses a magnificent 18m-high statue of the Maitreya Buddha in his Tibetan form, clothed in yellow satin and reputedly sculpted from a single block of sandalwood. Each of the Bodhisattva's toes is the size of a pillow. Behind the statue is the Vault of Avalokiteshvara, from where a diminutive and blue-faced statue of Guanyin peeks out. The Wànfú Pavilion is linked by an overhead walkway to the Yánsuí Pavilion (Yánsuí Gé), which encloses a huge lotus flower that revolves to reveal an effigy of the Longevity Buddha.

Don't miss the collection of bronze Tibetan Buddhist statues within the **Jiètái Lóu**, a small side hall. Most effigies date from the Qing dynasty, from languorous renditions of Green Tara and White Tara to exotic, Tantric pieces (such as Samvara) and figurines of the fierce-looking Mahakala. Also peruse the collection of Tibetan Buddhist ornaments within the **Bānchán Lóu**, another side hall, where an array of *dorje* (Tibetan sceptres), mandalas and Tantric figures are displayed

---

LOCAL KNOWLEDGE

AIRPOCALYPSE

Běijīng's air pollution has become notorious worldwide, but in 2013 it reached epic proportions. One week in January was dubbed 'Airpocalypse' after levels of pollution were described as the worst on record.

In that week, the measurement of the smallest, most dangerous type of particle matter (commonly known as PM2.5) reached more than 600 micrograms per sq metre, and at some monitoring stations was as high as 900. To put it in perspective, most cities in Europe and the US have average PM2.5 readings of less than 50, which is the level deemed 'good' by the US Environmental Protection Agency.

Běijīng's air isn't always terribly polluted, and travellers who arrive during spells of beautiful blue skies may well wonder what all the fuss is about, but the long-term stats do not bode well. Between April 2008 and March 2014, Běijīng experienced just 25 'good' days.

Travellers who are sensitive to pollution might want to consider buying a smog mask for their visit. You can find advice on which masks to buy on the excellent website **Air Quality Index China** (www.aqicn.org), which also publishes real-time pollution readings for Běijīng and other cities. Places in Běijīng that stock good-quality masks include **Torana Clean Air** (www.toranacleanair.com), which has two branches in the city. If you have kids in tow, you might want to buy their masks from home, as good-quality children's masks that fit properly are harder to find here.

Drum Tower & Dōngchéng North

Xibu River

Dong'erhuan (East 2nd Ring Rd)

二环 半

Liufang 柳芳 Ⓢ

North 2nd Ring Rd

Russian Embassy

Nánguàn Park

Hepingli Dongjie

Dongzhimen Beixiaojie

Hucheng River (City Moat)

North 2nd Ring Rd

Paoju Toutiao 炮局头条

Hepingli Beijie 和平里北街 Ⓢ

Hepingli

Beixinqiao Santiao Hutong 北新桥三条胡同

✕20

✕29 ⌂13

Hepingli Xijie

Ditán Park South Entrance

⌂6

Ditán Park

Yonghegong Dajie

Yonghegong Lama Temple 雍和宫

✕32

📷2

Guozijian Jie 国子监街

Fangjia Hutong 方家胡同 ⌂18

🏛3

⌂15 Wudaoying Hutong 五道营胡同

Andingmen 安定门

✕28

⌂37

⌂5 ⌂38

Ditán Park West Entrance

二环北路

Andingmenwai Dajie Ⓢ

Andingmennei Dajie 安定门内大街

Qingnián Hú Park Southeast Entrance

Qingnián Hú Park

✕22

Ande Lu

Beiluogu Xiang

📷44

北锣鼓巷

🛏46

净土胡同 Jingtu Hutong

🍴27

✕43

⌂36

Baochao Hutong

宝抄胡同

⌂19

✕11

Guloudajie Ⓢ

Gulouwai Dajie

Hucheng River (City Moat)

North 2nd Ring Rd

Cycle Rickshaw tours ticket office

🛏48

◉1

🛏39

Gulouwai Lu

Andeli Beijie

Jiugulouwai Dajie

✕31

Jiugulou Dajie 旧鼓楼大街

along with an impressive selection of ceremonial robes in silk and satin.

The street outside the temple entrance heaves with shops piled high with statues of Buddha, talismans, Buddhist charms, incense and keepsakes, picked over by a constant stream of pilgrims.

Confucius Temple & Imperial College

CONFUCIAN TEMPLE

(孔庙、国子监, Kǒng Miào & Guózǐjiàn; Map p72; 13 Guozijian Jie; admission ¥30, audio guide ¥30; ◷8.30am-5.30pm; ⑤Yonghegong-Lama Temple) An incense stick's toss away from the Lama Temple, China's second-largest Confucian temple has had a refit in recent years, but the almost otherworldly sense of detachment is seemingly impossible to shift. A mood of impassiveness reigns and the lack of worship reinforces a sensation that time has stood still. However, in its tranquillity and reserve, the temple can be a pleasant sanctuary from Běijīng's often congested streets – a haven of peace and quiet.

Antediluvian *bìxì* (mythical tortoise-like dragons) glare from repainted pavilions while lumpy and ossified ancient cypresses claw stiffly at the Běijīng air. There's a stone 'forest' of 190 stelae recording the 13 Confucian classics in 630,000 Chinese characters at the temple rear. Also inscribed on stelae are the names of successful candidates of the highest level of the official Confucian examination system.

Next to the Confucius Temple, but within the same grounds, stands the Imperial College, where the emperor expounded the Confucian classics to an audience of thousands of kneeling students, professors and court officials – an annual rite. Built by the grandson of Kublai Khan in 1306, the former college was the supreme academy during the Yuan, Ming and Qing dynasties. On the site is a marvellous, glazed, three-gate, single-eaved decorative archway called a *liúli páifāng* (glazed archway). The Biyong Hall beyond is a twin-roofed structure with yellow tiles surrounded by a moat and topped with a splendid gold knob. Its stupendous interior houses a vermillion and gold lectern.

Some of Běijīng's last remaining *páilóu* bravely survive in the tree-lined street outside (Guozijian Jie) and the entire area of *hútòng* here is now dotted with small cafes, cute restaurants and boutique shops, making it an ideal place to browse in low gear. At the western end of Guozijian Jie stands a

Drum Tower & Dōngchéng North

diminutive **Fire God Temple** (Huǒshén Miào; Map p72), built in 1802 and now occupied by Běijīng residents.

Nanluogu Xiang　　　　　　　　　STREET
(南锣鼓巷; Map p72; ⑤ Nanluoguxiang) Once neglected and ramshackle, strewn with spent coal briquettes in winter and silent bar the hacking coughs of shuffling old-timers and the jangling of bicycle bells, the funky north–south alleyway of Nanluogu Xiang (literally 'South Gong and Drum Alley', and roughly pronounced 'nan-law-goo-syang') has been undergoing evolution since 1999 when **Passby Bar** first threw open its doors, and was the subject of a complete makeover in 2006. Today, the alley is an insatiably bubbly strip of bars, wi-fi cafes, restaurants, hotels and trendy shops.

It is also a victim of its own success, though. Come here on a summer weekend to experience more people than you thought could possibly fit onto one street! With that in mind, don't miss exploring the quieter alleys, which fan out from the main lane and house Qing-dynasty courtyards as well as hidden cafes, shops, restaurants and bars.

Dìtán Park　　　　　　　　　　　PARK
(地坛公园, Dìtán Gōngyuán; Map p72; park admission ¥2, altar ¥5; ⊙ 6am-9pm; ⑤ Yonghegong-Lama Temple) Directly north of the Lama Temple, but cosmologically juxtaposed with the **Temple of Heaven** (Tiāntán), the **Altar of the Moon** (Yuètán), the **Altar of the Sun** (Rìtán) and the **Altar to the God of the Land and the God of Grain** (Shèjìtán), Dìtán is the Temple of the Earth. The park, site of imperial sacrifices to the Earth God, lacks the splendour of Temple of Heaven Park but is certainly worth a stroll if you've just been to nearby Lama Temple.

⊙ Temple of Heaven Park & Dōngchéng South

★ **Temple of Heaven Park**   PARK
(天坛公园; Tiāntán Gōngyuán; Map p76; ☑010-6701 2483; Tiantan Donglu; admission park/through ticket high season ¥15/35, low season ¥10/30, audio tour ¥40 (deposit ¥100); ☺park 6am-8pm, sights 8am-5.30pm Apr-Oct, park 6am-8pm, sights 8am-5pm Nov-Mar; ⑤Tiantandongmen) A tranquil oasis of peace and methodical Confucian design in one of China's busiest urban landscapes, the 267-hectare Temple of Heaven Park is absolutely unique. It originally served as a vast stage for solemn rites performed by the emperor of the time (known as the Son of Heaven), who prayed here for good harvests and sought divine clearance and atonement. Strictly speaking, it's an altar rather than a temple – so don't expect burning incense or worshippers.

Surrounded by a long wall and with a gate at each compass point, the arrangement is typical of Chinese parks, with the imperfections, bumps and wild irregularities of nature largely deleted and the harmonising hand of man accentuated in obsessively straight lines and regular arrangements. This effect is magnified by Confucian objectives, where the human intellect is imposed on the natural world, fashioning order and symmetry. The resulting balance and harmony have an almost haunting – but slightly claustrophobic – beauty. Police whir about in electric buggies as visitors stroll among old buildings, groves of ancient trees and birdsong. Around 4000 ancient, knotted cypresses (some 800 years old, their branches propped up on poles) poke towards the Běijīng skies within the grounds.

Seen from above, the temple halls are round and the bases square, in accordance with the notion 'Tiānyuán Dìfāng' (天圆地方) – 'Heaven is round, Earth is square'. Also observe that the northern rim of the park is semicircular, while its southern end is square. The traditional approach to the temple was from the south, via Zhāohēng Gate (昭亨门; Zhāohēng Mén); the north gate is an architectural afterthought.The highlight of the park, and an icon of Běijīng in its own right, is the **Hall of Prayer for Good Harvests** (祈年殿; Qínián Diàn; Map p76; admission ¥20), an astonishing structure with a triple-eaved purplish-blue umbrella roof mounted on a three-tiered marble terrace. The wooden pillars (made from Oregon fir) support the ceiling without nails or cement – for a building 38m high and 30m in diameter, that's quite an accomplishment. Embedded in the ceiling is a carved dragon, a symbol of the emperor. Built in 1420, the hall was reduced to carbon after being zapped by a lightning bolt during the reign of Guangxu in 1889; a faithful reproduction based on Ming architectural methods was erected the following year.

Continuing south along an elevated imperial pathway, you soon reach the octagonal **Imperial Vault of Heaven** (皇穹宇; Huáng Qióng Yǔ; Map p76), which was erected at the same time as the Round Altar, but with its shape echoing the lines of the Hall of Prayer for Good Harvests. The hall contained tablets of the emperor's ancestors, employed during winter solstice ceremonies.

Wrapped around the Imperial Vault of Heaven is **Echo Wall** (回音壁; Huíyīn Bì; Map p76). A whisper can travel clearly from one end to your friend's ear at the other – unless

TIME WILL TELL FOR THE DRUM AND BELL

Despite five years of opposition from local residents and heritage-preservation campaigners, controversial plans to redevelop the hútòng-rich neighbourhood surrounding the Drum & Bell Towers looked to be finally going ahead at the time of research.

The original plan to transform the area into the 'Běijīng Time Cultural City', complete with an underground mall, was, thankfully, scrapped. At the time of research, it was still unclear what the precise development plans were, but demolition had already begun.

The local district government was saying it wanted to restore the Drum & Bell Square to its 'original appearance' by using maps of the Qianlong period (18th century), though details remained vague. Although none of the buildings slated for demolition was more than 70 or 80 years old, critics argue that gentrifying the area to look like it did during its prosperous Qing-dynasty heyday would smack of inauthenticity. Perhaps most worrying is the very real chance that it will also tear the heart and soul out of the community in what has, for so many years, been one of the city's most charming residential neighbourhoods.

Temple of Heaven Park & Dōngchéng South

Temple of Heaven Park & Dōngchéng South

a cacophonous tour group joins in (get here early for this one).

Immediately south of Echo Wall, the 5m-high **Round Altar** (圜丘; Yuán Qiū; Map p76) was constructed in 1530 and rebuilt in 1740. Consisting of white marble arrayed in three tiers, its geometry revolves around

the imperial number nine. Odd numbers possess heavenly significance, with nine the largest single-digit odd number. Symbolising heaven, the top tier is a huge mosaic of nine rings, each composed of multiples of nine stones, so that the ninth ring equals 81 stones. The stairs and balustrades are similarly presented in multiples of nine. Sounds generated from the centre of the upper terrace undergo amplification from the marble balustrades (the acoustics can get noisy when crowds join in).

Off to the eastern side of the Hall of Prayer for Good Harvests, and with a green-tiled tow-tier roof, the **Animal Killing Pavilion** (Zǎishēng Tíng; Map p76) was the venue for the slaughter of sacrificial oxen, sheep, deer and other animals. Today it stands locked and passive but can be admired from the outside. Stretching out from here runs a **Long Corridor** (Cháng Láng; Map p76), where locals sit out and deal cards, listen to the radio, play keyboards, practise Peking opera, try dance moves and kick hacky-sacks. Just north of here is a large and very popular exercise park.

In the west of the park, sacrificial music was rehearsed at the **Divine Music Administration** (Shényuè Shǔ; Map p76), while wild cats inhabit the dry moat of the green-tiled **Fasting Palace** (Zhāi Gōng; Map p76).

Běijīng Railway Museum MUSEUM
(北京铁路博物馆; Běijīng Tiělù Bówùguǎn; Map p66; ☑010-6705 1638; 2a Qianmen Dongdajie; 前门大街2a号; admission ¥20; ◎9am-5pm Tue-Sun; ⑤Qianmen) Located in the historic former Qiánmén Railway Station, which once connected Běijīng to Tiānjīn, this museum offers an engaging history of the development of the capital and China's railway system, with plenty of photos and models. Its lack of space, though, means it doesn't have many actual trains, although there is a life-size model of the cab of one of China's high-speed trains to clamber into (¥10).

Běijīng Natural History Museum MUSEUM
(北京自然博物馆; Běijīng Zìrán Bówùguǎn; Map p76; ☑010-6702 7702; 126 Tianqiao Nandajie; admission ¥10; ◎9am-5pm Tue-Sun, last entry 4pm; ⑤Qianman or Tiantandongmen) The main entrance to this overblown, creeper-laden museum is hung with portraits of the great natural historians, including Darwin and Linnaeus. The contents range from dinosaur fossils and skeletons, includ-

---

BĚIJĪNG'S HÚTÒNG

Běijīng's medieval genotype is most discernible down the city's leafy *hútòng* (胡同; narrow alleyways). The spirit and soul of the city lives and breathes among these charming and ragged lanes where a warm sense of community and hospitality survives. Criss-crossing chunks of Běijīng within the Second Ring Rd, the *hútòng* link up into a huge and enchanting warren of one-storey dwellings and historic courtyard homes. Hundreds of *hútòng* survive but many have been swept aside in Běijīng's race to build a modern city. Identified by white plaques, historic homes are protected, but for many others a way of life hangs in a precarious balance.

After Genghis Khan's army reduced the city of Běijīng to rubble, the new city was redesigned with *hútòng*. By the Qing dynasty more than 2000 such passageways riddled the city, leaping to around 6000 by the 1950s; now the figure has drastically dwindled to somewhere above 1000. Today's *hútòng* universe is a hotchpotch of the old and the new: Qing-dynasty courtyards are scarred with socialist-era conversions and outhouses while others have been assiduously rebuilt.

Hútòng nearly all run east–west so that the main gate faces south, satisfying feng shui (wind/water) requirements. This south-facing aspect guarantees sunshine and protection from negative principles amassing in the north.

Old walled *sìhéyuàn* (courtyards) are the building blocks of this delightful universe. Many are still lived in and hum with activity. From spring to autumn, men collect outside their gates, drinking beer, playing chess, smoking and chewing the fat. Inside, scholar trees soar aloft, providing shade and a nesting ground for birds. Flocks of pigeons whirl through the Běijīng skies overhead, bred by locals and housed in coops often buried away within the *hútòng*.

More venerable courtyards are fronted by large, thick red doors, outside of which perch either a pair of Chinese lions or drum stones. To savour Běijīng's courtyard ambience, down a drink at Irresistible Cafe (p102) or Great Leap Brewing (p104), devour a meal at Dàlǐ Courtyard (p100) and sleep it all off at Courtyard 7 (p95). Alternatively, follow our leisurely Hútòng Walking Tour (p79).

Bike Běijīng (p91) does guided cycle tours of *hútòng* areas.

THE LOST CITY WALLS OF BĚIJĪNG

As Běijīng develops relentlessly, it's increasingly hard to believe that as recently as 40-odd years ago the capital was still surrounded by the city walls that protected it from invaders for over 500 years.

Two walls once guarded Běijīng: an outer wall and an inner wall. Now, nothing is left of the original outer wall, while only a few remnants of the inner city wall remain. Their absence is perhaps the most conspicuous chunk of lost heritage in Běijīng.

A few gateways survive (and a few more have been rebuilt from scratch), but the most notable epitaph to the walls is the **Ming City Wall Ruins Park** (明城墙遗址公园; Míng Chéngqiáng Yízhǐ Gōngyuán; Map p76; Chongwenmen Dongdajie; ⏰24hr; ⑤Chongwenmen). It runs next to a partly restored 2km stretch of the Ming inner-city wall, which rises to a height of around 15m.

The park extends to the **Southeast Corner Watchtower** (东南角楼、红门画廊; Dōngnán Jiǎolóu & Hóngmén Huàláng; Map p66; ☎010-6527 0574; admission ¥10; ⏰8am-5.30pm; ⑤Jianguomen or Chongwenmen), a splendid Ming-dynasty fortification, punctured with 144 archer's windows. The highly impressive interior has some staggering carpentry. On the 1st floor is the superb **Red Gate Gallery** (红门画廊; Hóngmén Huàláng; Map p76; ☎010-6525 1005; www.redgategallery.com; admission free; ⏰10am-5pm). An exhibition on the 2nd floor details the history of Běijīng's city gates and includes some fascinating old photographs. On top of the wall, off to one side of the watchtower, there's a small cafe serving coffee and snacks.

ing a *Mamenchisaurus jingyanensis* (a vast sauropod that once roamed China) to creepy-crawlies, an aquarium with Nemo-esque clown fish and an exhibition on the origins of life on earth.

◎ Sānlǐtún & Cháoyáng

Dōngyuè Temple   TAOIST TEMPLE

(东岳庙; Dōngyuè Miào; 141 Chaoyangmenwai Dajie; adult ¥10, with guide ¥40; ⏰7.30am-5.30pm Apr-Oct, 8.30am-4.30pm Nov-Mar, closed Mon year-round; ⑤Chaoyangmen or Dongdaqiao) Dedicated to the Eastern Peak (Tài Shān) of China's five Taoist mountains, the morbid Taoist shrine of Dōngyuè Temple is an unsettling, albeit fascinating, experience and one of the capital's most unique temples. An active place of worship tended by top-knotted Taoist monks, the temple's roots go all the way back to the Yuan dynasty. A visit here takes you into a world entirely at odds with the surrounding glass and steel high-rises.

Rìtán Park   PARK

(日坛公园; Rìtán Gōngyuán; Ritan Lu; admission free; ⏰6am-9pm; ⑤Chaoyangmen or Jianguomen) Meaning 'Altar of the Sun', Rìtán (pronounced 'rer-tan') is a real oasis in the heart of Běijīng's business district. Dating back to 1530 and one of a set of imperial parks which covered each compass point –

others include the Temple of Heaven and Temple of Earth (Dìtán Park) – the altar is now little more than a raised platform. But the surrounding park is beautifully landscaped and a great place to tune out from the surrounding mayhem.

Activities include dancing, singing, kite flying, rock climbing (¥25 per hour or ¥60 per day), table tennis and pond fishing (¥5 per hour). Otherwise, just stroll around and enjoy the flora, or head to one of the park's cafes; the standout one is **Stone Boat** (石舫咖啡; Shǐfǎng Kāfēi; ☎010-6501 9986; beers & coffee from ¥25, cocktails from ¥40; ⏰10am-10pm Apr-Oct, 10am-6pm Nov-Mar ; ⑤Jianguomen), located by a large pond artfully strewn with rocks.

CCTV Building   ARCHITECTURE

(央视大楼; Yāngshì Dàlóu; 32 Dongsanhuan Zhonglu; ⑤Jintaixizhao) Shaped like an enormous pair of trousers, and known locally as Dà Kùchǎ (大裤衩), or Big Underpants, the astonishing CCTV Tower is an architectural fantasy that appears to defy gravity. It's made possible by an unusual engineering design that creates a three-dimensional cranked loop, supported by an irregular grid on its surface. Designed by Rem Koolhaas and Ole Scheeren, the building is an audacious statement of modernity (despite its nickname) and a unique addition to the Běijīng skyline.

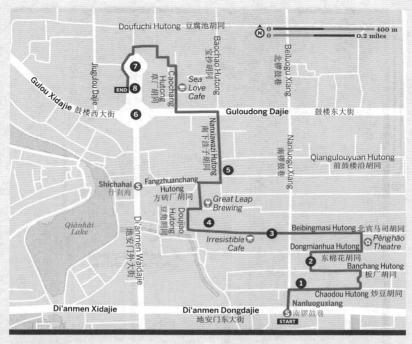

City Walk
Hútòng

START NANLUOGUXIANG SUBWAY STATION
END DRUM & BELL SQUARE
LENGTH 2KM; ONE HOUR

This leisurely stroll explores some of the historic alleyways that branch off Běijīng's most famous *hútòng*, Nanluogu Xiang.

Exit the subway station and turn right into Chaodou Hutong (炒豆胡同). Starting at No 77, the next few courtyards once made up the ❶ **former mansion of Seng Gelinqin**, a Qing-dynasty army general. Note the enormous *bǎogǔshí* (drum stones) at the entranceway to No 77, followed by more impressive gateways at Nos 75, 69, 67 and 63. After No 53 turn left up an unmarked winding alleyway then left onto Banchang Hutong (板厂胡同).

At No 19, turn right through an unusual ❷ **hallway gate**, a connecting passageway leading to Dongmianhua Hutong (东棉花胡同). Turn right here, then left down an unnamed alley, which is signposted to Pénghāo Theatre.

Turn left onto Beibingmasi Hutong (北兵马司胡同) and cross Nanluogu Xiang into historic ❸ **Mao'er Hutong** (帽儿胡同). Stop for a drink at Irresistible Cafe, or just admire the entranceways, if the gates are open, to the charming courtyards at Nos 5 and 11. Further on, No 37 was the ❹ **former home of Wan Rong**, who would later marry China's last emperor, Puyi.

Next, turn right down Doujiao Hutong (豆角胡同) and wind your way (past Great Leap Brewing) to Fangzhuanchang Hutong (方砖厂胡同) then Nanxiawazi Hutong (南下洼子胡同), with its small ❺ **fruit & veg street-market**, and continue north to Guloudong Dajie (鼓楼东大街). Turn left here and then, just before you reach the imperious red-painted ❻ **Drum Tower**, turn right into Caochang Hutong (草厂胡同). Continue down the lane beside Sea Love Cafe, then take the second left: you'll see the magnificent grey-brick ❼ **Bell Tower** in front of you. Follow this wonderfully winding alley (slated for redevelopment) to the back of the Bell Tower, then walk around the tower to see how the controversial plans to redevelop the ❽ **Drum & Bell Square** are going.

Sānlǐtún & Cháoyáng

0 — 1 km
0 — 0.5 miles

G
Cháoyáng Park

Dos Kolegas (2km)

26

F
8

Nongzhanguan Nanlu

Israeli Embassy (300m)
US Embassy (400m)

Liangmaqiao Lu

24

Liangmaqiao
练马桥

Liangma River

E

Xinyuan Nanlu

31

Sanlitun Dongliujie

SĀNLǏTÚN EMBASSY AREA

33

Agricultural Exhibition Center (Nongye Zhanlanguan)
农业展览馆

Dongsanhuan Beilu (East 3rd Ring Rd)

Tuanjiehu
团结湖

18

D

Sanlitun Xiwujie

30

23

Sanlitun Lu

27

Sanlitun Dongsanjie

22

Sanlitun Dongsilie

9

11

10

Nansanlitun Lu

Sanlitun Beije

5

13

16

Xindong Lu

15

Beijing Tourist Information Center 17

工人体育场东路

C

Xin Donglu

20

21

Dongzhimenwai Xiaojie

Zuojiazhuang Xijie

Chunxiu Lu

Xingfucun Lu

4

12

6

Gongrentiyuchang Beilu

Workers Stadium

B

Xiangheyuan Lu

Dongzhimenwai Xiele

Dongzhimenwai Dajie

7

Xinzhong Jie

CHÁOYÁNG

Dongzhong Jie

Gongrentiyuchang Xilu

Gongrentiyuchang

A

Xiba River

Dongzhimen Wai Bus Stand

Dongzhimen Transport Hub

Airport Express

Dongzhimen
东直门

Dong'erhuan (East 2nd Ring Rd)
东二环

Dongsi Shitiao
东四十条

1
2
3
4

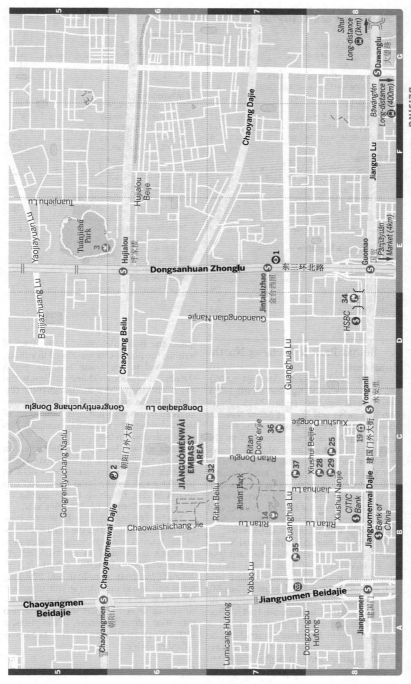

Sānlǐtún & Cháoyáng

⊙ Běihǎi Park & Xīchéng North

Běihǎi Park   PARK
(北海公园; Běihǎi Gōngyuán; Map p84; ☎010-6403 1102; admission high/low season ¥10/5, through ticket high/low season ¥20/15; ☉park 6am-9pm, sights until 5pm; ⑤Xisi or Nanluogu Xiang) Běihǎi Park, northwest of the Forbidden City (p59), is largely occupied by the North Sea (Běihǎi), a huge lake that freezes in winter and blooms with lotuses in summer. Old folk dance together outside temple halls and come twilight, young couples cuddle on benches. It's a restful place to stroll around, rent a rowing boat in summer and watch calligraphers practising characters on paving slabs with fat brushes and water.

The site is associated with Kublai Khan's palace, Běijīng's navel before the arrival of the Forbidden City. All that survives of the Khan's court is a large jar made of green jade in the Round City (团城; Tuánchéng; Map p84), near the southern entrance. Also within the Round City is the Chengguang Hall (Chéngguāng Diàn), where a white jade statue of Sakyamuni from Myanmar (Burma) can be found, its arm wounded by the allied forces that swarmed through Běijīng in 1900 to quash the Boxer Rebellion. At the time of writing, the Round City was closed to visitors.

Attached to the North Sea, the South (Nánhǎi) and Middle (Zhōnghǎi) Seas to the south lend their name to Zhōngnánhǎi (literally 'Middle and South Seas'), the heavily-guarded compound just over 1km south of the park where the Chinese Communist Party's top leadership live.

Topping Jade Islet (琼岛; Qióngdǎo) on the lake, the 36m-high Tibetan-style White Dagoba (白塔; Báitǎ; Map p84) was built in 1651 for a visit by the Dalai Lama, and was rebuilt in 1741. Climb up to the dagoba via the Yǒng'ān Temple (永安寺; Yǒng'ān Sì).

Xītiān Fánjìng (西天梵境; Western Paradise; Map p84), situated on the northern shore of the lake, is a lovely temple (admission to which is included in the park ticket). The nearby Nine Dragon Screen (九龙壁; Jiǔlóng Bì; Map p84), a 5m-high and 27m-long spirit wall, is a glimmering stretch of coloured glazed tiles depicting coiling dragons, similar to its counterpart in the Forbidden City. West, along the shore, is the pleasant Little Western Heaven (小西天; Xiǎo Xītiān), a further shrine.

WORTH A TRIP

798 ART DISTRICT

A vast area of disused factories built by the East Germans, **798 Art District** (798 艺术新区; Qī Jiǔ Bā Yìshù Qū; cnr Jiuxianqiao Lu & Jiuxianqiao Beilu; 酒仙桥路; ⊘ galleries 10am-6pm, most closed Mon; 🚌 403 or 909), also known as Dà Shānzi (大山子), is Běijīng's leading concentration of contemporary art galleries.

The industrial complex celebrates its proletarian roots in the communist heyday of the 1950s via retouched red Maoist slogans decorating gallery interiors and statues of burly, lantern-jawed workers dotting the lanes. The voluminous factory workshops are ideally suited to art galleries that require space for multimedia installations and other ambitious projects.

You could easily spend half a day wandering around the complex. Signboards with English-language maps on them dot the lanes.

Galleries

Some are more innovative than others. Highlights include the following:

BTAP (Ceramics Third St; ⊘ 10am-6pm Tue-Sun) One of 798's original galleries.

UCCA (798 Rd; ⊘ 10am-7pm Tue-Sun) A big-money gallery with exhibition halls, a funky shop and a small cinema screening films most days.

Pace (797 Rd; ⊘ 10am-6pm Tue-Sun) A wonderfully large space holding some top-quality exhibitions.

Galleria Continua (just south of 797 Rd; ⊘ 11am-6pm Tue-Sun) Long-established gallery that shows lots of foreign artists.

Eating & Drinking

Most places have fresh coffee, free wi-fi, Western food and English menus.

Happy Rooster (cnr 7 Star Rd & Ceramics First St; ⊘ 9.30am-9pm) Cheapest decent Chinese restaurant in 798. Has picture menu, plus coffee and wi-fi.

At Cafe (📞 010-5978 9943; 798 Rd; mains from ¥38; ⊘ 10am-midnight) 798's first cafe and still a popular hang-out for both artists and visitors. It serves Western standards like pasta and pizza, as well as good coffee (from ¥28). The outside terrace is fine for a drink in the evening.

Timezone 8 (📞 010-5978 9917; 798 Rd; mains from ¥55, sushi from ¥32; ⊘ 7am-2am) Cool cafe and the best spot to eat in 798, Timezone no longer has its attached bookshop but continues to pack people in with its huge sandwiches, burgers and all-day breakfasts, as well as a sushi bar. In the summer, the outside terrace gets jammed.

Getting There & Away

From Exit C of Dongzhimen subway station, take bus 909 (¥2) for about 6km northeast to Dashanzi Lukou Nan (大山子路口南), where you'll see the big red 798 sign. Buses run until 8.30pm.

A further extensive colony of art galleries can be found around 3km northeast of 798 Art District at **Cǎochǎngdì** (草场地). Bus 909 continues there.

⭐ **Hòuhǎi Lakes**　　　　　　LAKES
(后海; Hòuhǎi; Map p84; Ⓢ Shichahai, Nanluogu Xiang or Jishuitan) FREE Also known as Shíchàhǎi (什刹海) but mostly just referred to collectively as 'Hòuhǎi', the Hòuhǎi Lakes are comprised of three lakes: Qiánhǎi (Front Lake), Hòuhǎi (Back Lake) and Xīhǎi (West Lake). Together they are one of the capital's favourite outdoor spots, heaving with locals and out-of-towners in the sum-

mer especially, and providing some great people-spotting action.

During the day, senior citizens meander along, use the exercise machines scattered along the lakeshore, fish, fly kites or just sit and chew the fat. At night, the area turns into one of the more popular nightlife areas, as the restaurants, bars and cafes that surround the lakes spring into life. This is a night out, Chinese style, so be prepared for

Běihǎi Park & Xīchéng North

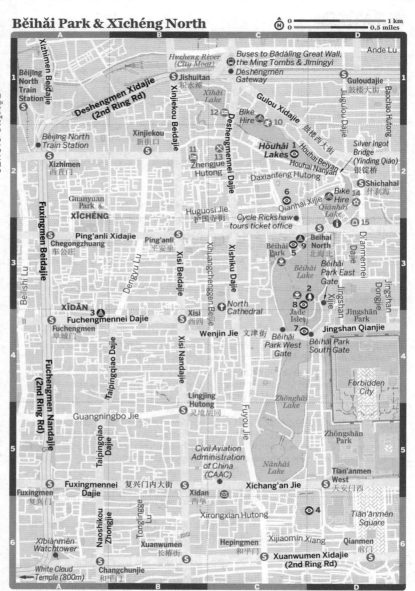

It's great fun, and even if you find parts of the lakes too hectic – **Silver Ingot Bridge** (银锭桥; Yíndìng Qiáo; Map p72) is a major bottleneck – it's easy enough to escape the crowds, by exploring the many *hútòng* that run both east and west of the lakes, or to just venture

neon lights galore, and plenty of karaoke being blasted out onto the surrounding lanes. Meanwhile, as the midday sun disappears, the lakes become a mass of pedalos circling round and round.

Běihǎi Park & Xīchéng North

BĚIJĪNG SIGHTS

further northwest towards the quieter Xīhǎi Lake. It's particularly good to cycle around and numerous places by the lakeshores hire out bikes by the hour (¥10 per hour, ¥200 deposit). There are many spots to rent pedalos too (¥80 per hour, ¥300 deposit), if you want to take to the water. Some locals swim in the lakes, even in midwinter!

The lakes look majestic in winter, when they freeze over and become the best place in Běijīng to ice skate (usually for around six weeks in January and February). Qiánhǎi Lake is most popular, although some people skate on Hòuhǎi Lake too; local vendors set themselves up with all the gear you need. You have to pay to enter the ice-skating area (weekday/weekend and evenings ¥15/¥20). If you want to rent ice skates and the like, you also have to buy a rental swipe card from kiosks by the entrance gates. The card will have a ¥200 deposit on it. You then get back any money you don't use. Skates (¥20 per day), chair sleds (¥20 per day), ice bikes (¥40 per hour) and even ice bumper cars (¥20 per 10 minutes) can all be rented. There is also a giant ice slide (¥5 per go).

**Prince Gong's
Residence**   HOUSE, HISTORIC BUILDING
(恭王府; Gōngwáng Fǔ; Map p84; ☑010-8328 8149; 14 Liuyin Jie; admission ¥40, tours incl short opera show & tea ceremony ¥70; ☉ 7.30am-4.30pm Mar-Oct, 8am-4pm Nov-Mar; ⑤ Ping'anli) Reputed to be the model for the mansion in Cao Xueqin's 18th-century classic *Dream of the Red Mansions,* the residence is one of Běijīng's largest private residential compounds. It remains one of the capital's more attractive retreats, decorated with rockeries, plants, pools, pavilions and elaborately carved gate-

ways, although it can get very crowded with tour groups.

★ **Capital Museum**   MUSEUM
(首都博物馆; Shǒudū Bówùguǎn; ☑010-6339 3339; www.capitalmuseum.org.cn; 16 Fuxingmenwai Dajie; ☉9am-5pm Tue-Sun; ⑤ Muxidi) **FREE**
Behind the riveting good looks of the Capital Museum are some first-rate galleries, including a mesmerising collection of ancient Buddhist statues and a lavish exhibition of Chinese porcelain. There is also an interesting chronological history of Běijīng, an exhibition that is dedicated to cultural relics of Peking opera, a fascinating Běijīng Folk Customs exhibition, and displays of ancient bronzes, jade, calligraphy and paintings.

Bring your passport for free entry. The small teahouse on the 2nd floor sells tea sets (from ¥500) as well as serving tea (from ¥15 per cup).

Come out of Exit C1 of Muxidi subway station (Line 1), and you'll soon see the museum on your right (200m).

**Miàoyīng Temple
White Dagoba**   BUDDHIST TEMPLE
(妙应寺白塔; Miàoyīng Sì Báitǎ; Map p84; ☑010-6616 0211; 171 Fuchengmennei Dajie; adult ¥20; ☉9am-5pm Tue-Sun; ⑤ Fuchengmen, then bus 13, 101, 102 or 103 to Baita Si) Originally built in 1271, the Miàoyīng Temple slumbers beneath its huge, distinctive, chalk-white Yuandynasty pagoda, which towers over the surrounding *hútòng.* It was, when it was built, the tallest structure in Dàdū (the Yuandynasty name for Běijīng), and even today it is the tallest Tibetan-style pagoda in China.

The temple has been under extensive renovation for some years, and was still closed at the time of research, but previous high-lights of a visit here included the diverse collection of Buddhist statuary: the Hall of the Great Enlightened One (大觉宝殿; Dàjué Bǎodiàn), for example, glittered splendidly with hundreds of Tibetan Buddhist effigies. After you finish here, exit the temple and wander the tangle of local alleyways for street-market action and earthy shades of *hútòng* life.

National Centre for the Performing Arts (NCPA) CONCERT HALL
(国家大剧院; Guójiā Dàjùyuàn; Map p84; ☑010-6655 0000; www.chncpa.org/ens; admission ¥30, concert tickets ¥100-400; ⊙9am-5pm Tue-Sun; ⑤Tian'anmen West) Critics have compared it to an egg (although it looks more like a massive mercury bead), while modernists love it to bits. The NCPA, also known as the National Grand Theatre, is a surreal location in which to catch a show.

Examine the bulbous interior, including the titanic steel ribbing of interior bolsters (each of the 148 bolsters weighs 8 tonnes), and tour the three halls. See the website for details on concerts.

👁 Dashilar & Xīchéng South

Dashilar HISTORIC SHOPPING STREET
(大栅栏; Dàzhàlan; Map p87; ⑤Qianmen) This centuries-old shopping street, also known as Dazhalan Jie, is just west of Qianmen Da-jie. While a misjudged makeover has sadly robbed it of much of its charm, many of the shops have been in business here for hundreds of years and still draw many locals. Some specialise in esoteric goods – ancient herbal remedies, handmade cloth shoes – and most make for intriguing window shopping.

Niújiē Mosque MOSQUE
(牛街礼拜寺; Niújiē Lǐbài Sì; ☑010-6353 2564; 88 Niu Jie; adult ¥10, admission for Muslims free; ⊙8.30am-sunset; ⑤Caishikou) Dating back to the 10th century and lively with worshippers on Fridays (it's closed to non-Muslims at prayer times), Běijīng's largest mosque is the centre of the community for the 10,000 or so Huí Chinese Muslims who live nearby. Look out for the **Building for Observing the Moon** (望月楼; Wàngyuèlóu), from where the lunar calendar was calculated.

Fǎyuán Temple BUDDHIST TEMPLE
(法源寺; Fǎyuán Sì; Map p87; 7 Fayuansi Qianjie; adult ¥5; ⊙8.30-4pm; ⑤Caishikou) Infused with an air of reverence and devotion, this lovely temple dates back to the 7th century. The temple follows the typical Buddhist layout, with drum and bell towers. Do hunt out the unusual **copper-cast Buddha**, seated atop four further Buddhas ensconced on a huge bulb of myriad effigies in the Pilu Hall (the fourth hall).

Xiānnóng Altar & Běijīng Ancient Architecture Museum MUSEUM
(先农坛、北京古代建筑博物馆; Xiānnóngtán & Běijīng Gǔdài Jiànzhù Bówùguǎn; Map p87;

WORTH A TRIP

WHITE CLOUD TEMPLE

Once the Taoist centre of northern China, **White Cloud Temple** (白云观; Báiyún Guàn; ☑010-6346 3887; 9 Baiyunguan Jie; adult ¥10; ⊙8.30am-4.30pm; ⑤Muxidi) was founded in AD 739, although most of the temple halls date from the Qing dynasty. It's a lively, huge and fascinating complex of shrines and courtyards, tended by Taoist monks with their hair gathered into topknots.

Near the temple entrance, worshippers rub a polished stone carving for good fortune. The halls at the temple, centre of operations for the Taoist Quanzhen School and abode of the China Taoist Association, are dedicated to a host of Taoist officials and marshals. The Hall of the Jade Emperor celebrates this most famous of Taoist deities, while Taoist housewives cluster earnestly at the Hall to the God of Wealth to divine their financial future. Depictions of the Taoist Hell festoon the walls of the Shrine Hall for the Saviour Worthy.

Drop by White Cloud Temple during the Spring Festival (Chinese New Year) and you will be rewarded with the spectacle of a magnificent temple fair (miàohuì).

The temple is about a 1km walk from Muxidi subway station (Line 1). Come out of Exit C1, walk past the Capital Museum, then turn right down Baiyun Lu. After crossing the canal, take the second left, down Baiyunguan Jie, and the temple will be on your left.

Dashilar & Xīchéng South

⊙ Sights
1 Dashilar D1
2 Fǎyuán Temple A3
3 Xiānnóng Altar & Bĕijīng Ancient
   Architecture Museum D4

🛏 Sleeping
4 Leo Courtyard C2
5 Qiánmén Hostel D1
6 Three-Legged Frog Hostel C2

⊗ Eating
7 Liú Family Noodles C2

✪ Entertainment
8 Húguǎng Guild Hall C3
9 Lao She Teahouse D1
10 Tiānqiáo Acrobatics Theatre D3

🛍 Shopping
11 Ruìfúxiáng D1
12 Yuèhǎixuān Musical Instrument
    Store C1

⊘ 010-6304 5608; 21 Dongjing Lu; admission ¥15; ⊙ 9am-4pm; ⑤ Taoranting) This altar – to the west of the Temple of Heaven – was the site of solemn imperial ceremonies and sacrificial offerings. Located within what is called the **Hall of Jupiter** (太岁殿; Tàisuì

Diàn) – the most magnificent surviving hall – is the excellent Bĕijīng Ancient Architecture Museum, which informatively narrates the elements of traditional Chinese building techniques.

◉ Summer Palace & Hǎidiàn

Summer Palace   HISTORIC SITE
(颐和园; Yíhé Yuán; Map p89; 19 Xinjian Gongmen; ticket ¥20, through ticket ¥50, audio guide ¥40; ⏱7am-7pm, sights 8am-5pm summer, 8.30am-4.30pm winter; ⓢ Xiyuan or Beigongmen) As mandatory a Běijīng sight as the Great Wall or the Forbidden City, the Summer Palace was the playground for emperors fleeing the suffocating summer torpor of the old imperial city. A marvel of design, the palace – with its huge lake and hilltop views – offers a pastoral escape into the landscapes of traditional Chinese painting. It merits an entire day's exploration, although a (high-paced) morning or afternoon exploring the temples, gardens, pavilions, bridges and corridors may suffice.

The domain had long been a royal garden before being considerably enlarged and embellished by Emperor Qianlong in the 18th century. He marshalled a 100,000-strong army of labourers to deepen and expand **Kūnmíng Lake** (昆明湖; Kūnmíng Hú), and reputedly surveyed imperial navy drills from a hilltop perch.

Anglo-French troops vandalised the palace during the Second Opium War (1856–60). Empress Dowager Cixi launched into a refit in 1888 with money earmarked for a modern navy; the marble boat at the northern edge of the lake was her only nautical, albeit quite unsinkable, concession. Foreign troops, angered by the Boxer Rebellion, had another go at torching the Summer Palace in 1900, prompting further restoration work. By 1949 the palace had once more fallen into disrepair, eliciting a major overhaul.

Glittering Kūnmíng Lake swallows up three-quarters of the park, overlooked by **Longevity Hill** (万寿山; Wànshòu Shān). The principal structure is the **Hall of Benevolence and Longevity** (仁寿殿; Rénshòu Diàn; Map p89), by the east gate, housing a hardwood throne and attached to a courtyard decorated with bronze animals, including the mythical *qílín* (a hybrid animal that only appeared on earth at times of harmony). Unfortunately, the hall is barricaded off so you will have to peer in.

An elegant stretch of woodwork along the northern shore, the **Long Corridor** (长廊; Cháng Láng; Map p89) is trimmed with a plethora of paintings, while the slopes and crest of Longevity Hill behind are adorned with Buddhist temples. Slung out uphill on a north–south axis, the **Buddhist Fragrance Pavilion** (佛香阁; Fóxiāng Gé; Map p89) and the **Cloud Dispelling Hall** (排云殿; Páiyún Diàn; Map p89) are linked by corridors. Crowning the peak is the **Buddhist Temple of the Sea of Wisdom** (智慧海; Zhìhuì Hǎi; Map p89) tiled with effigies of Buddha, many with obliterated heads.

Cixi's **marble boat** (清晏船; Qīngyuàn Chuán; Map p89) sits immobile on the north shore, south of some fine **Qing boathouses** (船坞; chuán wù; Map p89). When the lake is not frozen, you can traverse Kūnmíng Lake by ferry to **South Lake Island** (南湖岛; Nánhú Dǎo), where Cixi went to beseech the **Dragon King Temple** (龙王庙; Lóngwáng Miào; Map p89) for rain in times of drought. A graceful 17-arch bridge spans the 150m to the eastern shore of the lake. In warm weather, pedal boats are also available from the dock.

Try to do a circuit of the lake along the West Causeway to return along the east shore (or vice versa). It gets you away from the crowds, the views are gorgeous and it's a great cardiovascular workout. Based on the Su Causeway in Hángzhōu, and lined with willow and mulberry trees, the causeway kicks off just west of the boathouses. With its delightful hump, the grey and white marble Jade Belt Bridge dates from the reign of emperor Qianlong and crosses the point where the **Jade River** (Yùhé) enters the lake (when it flows).

Towards the North Palace Gate, **Sūzhōu Street** (苏州街; Suzhou Jie) is an entertaining and light-hearted diversion of riverside walkways, shops and eateries, which are designed to mimic the famous Jiāngsū canal town.

Old Summer Palace   HISTORIC SITE
(圆明园; Yuánmíng Yuán; 28 Qinghua Xilu; adult ¥10, through ticket ¥25, map ¥6; ⏱7am-6pm; ⓢ Yuanmingyuan) Located northwest of the city centre, the Old Summer Palace was laid out in the 12th century. The ever-capable Jesuits were later employed by Emperor Qianlong to fashion European-style palaces for the gardens, incorporating elaborate fountains and baroque statuary. In 1860, during the Second Opium War, British and French troops torched and looted the palace, an event forever inscribed in Chinese history books as a low point in China's humiliation by foreign powers.

Most of the wooden palace buildings were burned down in the process and little remains, but the hardier Jesuit-designed European Palace buildings were made of stone, and a melancholic tangle of broken columns

Summer Palace

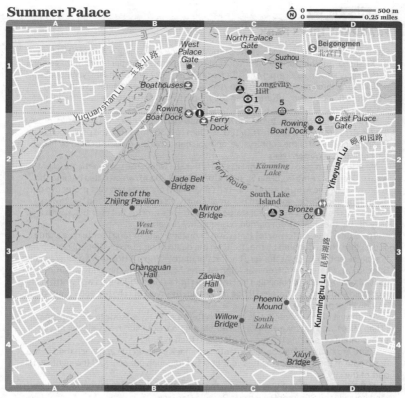

and marble chunks survives. Note: to see these remains, you need to buy the more expensive through ticket.

The subdued marble ruins of the **Palace Buildings Scenic Area** (Xīyánglóu Jǐngqū) can be mulled over in the **Eternal Spring Garden** (Chángchūn Yuán) in the northeast of the park, near the east gate. There were once more than 10 buildings here, designed by Giuseppe Castiglione and Michael Benoist. The buildings were only partially destroyed during the 1860 Anglo-French looting and the structures apparently remained usable for quite some time afterwards. However, the ruins were gradually picked over and carted away by local people all the way up to the 1970s.

The **Great Fountain Ruins** (Dàshuǐfǎ) are considered the best-preserved relics. Built in 1759, the main building was fronted by a lion-head fountain. Standing opposite is the **Guānshuǐfǎ**, five large stone screens

Summer Palace

⊙ Sights

embellished with European carvings of military flags, armour, swords and guns. The screens were discovered in the grounds of Peking University in the 1970s and later restored to their original positions. Just east of the Great Fountain Ruins stood a four-pillar archway, chunks of which remain.

WORTH A TRIP

FRAGRANT HILLS PARK

Easily within striking distance of the Summer Palace are Běijīng's Western Hills (西山; Xī Shān), another former villa-resort of the emperors. The part of Xī Shān closest to Běijīng is known as **Fragrant Hills Park** (香山公园; Xiāng Shān Gōngyuán; summer/winter ¥10/5, through ticket ¥15; ☺ 6am-7pm; ☐ 331, ⑤ Xiyuan or Yuanmingyuan, then). Běijīngers flock here in autumn when the maple leaves saturate the hillsides in great splashes of red.

Scramble up the slopes to the top of **Incense-Burner Peak** (Xiānglú Fēng), or take the **chairlift** (one way/return ¥60/120, 9.30am to 3.30pm). From the peak you get an all-embracing view of the countryside, and you can leave the crowds behind by hiking further into the Western Hills.

Near the north gate of Fragrant Hills Park, but still within the park, is the excellent **Azure Clouds Temple** (Bìyún Sì; adult ¥10; ☺ 8am-4.30pm), which dates back to the Yuán dynasty. The **Mountain Gate Hall** (Shānmén) contains two vast protective deities: Heng and Ha, beyond which is a small courtyard and the drum and bell towers, leading to a hall with a wonderful statue of Milefo – it's bronze, but coal-black with age. Only his big toe shines from numerous inquisitive fingers.

The **Sun Yatsen Memorial Hall** (Sūn Zhōngshān Jìniàn Táng) contains a statue and a glass coffin donated by the USSR on the death of Mr Sun (the Republic of China's first president) in 1925. At the very back is the marble **Vajra Throne Pagoda** (Jīngāng Bǎozuò Tǎ), where Sun Yatsen was interred after he died, before his body was moved to its final resting place in Nánjīng. The **Hall of Arhats** (Luóhàn Táng) is well worth visiting; it contains 500 *luóhàn* statues (those freed from the cycle of rebirth), each crafted with an individual personality.

Southwest of the Azure Clouds Temple is the Tibetan-style **Temple of Brilliance** (Zhāo Miào), and not far away is a glazed-tile pagoda. Both survived visits by foreign troops intent on sacking the area in 1860, and then in 1900.

There are dozens of cheap restaurants and snack stalls on the approach road to the north gate of the park, making this your best bet for lunch out of any of the sights in this part of the city.

At the time of writing it was expected that sometime after 2015 the subway will extend here via the Summer Palace and Botanic Gardens.

West of the Great Fountain Ruins are the vestiges of the **Hǎiyàntáng Reservoir** (Hǎiyàntáng Xùshuǐchí Táijī), where the water for the impressive fountains was stored in a tower and huge water-lifting devices were employed. The metal reservoir was commonly called the Tin Sea (Xīhǎi). Also known as the Water Clock, the **Hǎiyàntáng**, where 12 bronze human statues with animal heads jetted water for two hours in a 12-hour sequence, was constructed in 1759. The 12 animal heads from this apparatus ended up in collections abroad and Běijīng is attempting to retrieve them (four can now be seen at the Poly Art Museum). Just west of here is the **Fāngwàiguàn**, a building that was turned into a mosque for an imperial concubine. An artful reproduction of a former labyrinth called the **Garden of Yellow Flowers** is also nearby.

The palace gardens cover a huge area – 2.5km from east to west – so be prepared for some walking. Besides the ruins, there's the western section, the Perfection & Brightness Garden (Yuánmíng Yuán) and, in the southern compound, the 10,000 Springs Garden (Wànchūn Yuán).

Bus 331 goes from the south gate (which is by Exit B of Yuanmingyuan subway station) to the east gate of the Summer Palace before continuing to the Botanic Gardens and eventually terminating at Fragrant Hills Park.

Běijīng Botanic Gardens   GARDENS
(北京植物园; Běijīng Zhíwùyuán; adult ¥5, through ticket ¥50; ☺ 6am-8pm summer (last entry 7pm), 7.30am-5pm winter (last entry 4pm); ☐ 331, ⑤ Xiyuan or Yuanmingyuan, then) Exploding with blossom in spring, the well-tended Běijīng Botanic Gardens, set against the backdrop of the Western Hills and about 1km northeast

of Fragrant Hills Park, makes for a pleasant outing among bamboo fronds, pines, orchids, lilacs and China's most extensive botanic collection. Containing a rainforest house, the standout **Běijīng Botanical Gardens Conservatory** (Běijīng Zhíwùyuán Wēnshì; admission with through ticket; ⊙8am-4.30pm) bursts with 3000 different varieties of plants.

About a 15-minute walk from the front gate (follow the signs), but still within the grounds of the gardens, is **Sleeping Buddha Temple** (Wòfó Sì; adult ¥5, or entry with through ticket; ⊙8am-4.30pm summer, 8.30am-4pm winter). The temple, first built during the Tang dynasty, houses a huge reclining effigy of Sakyamuni weighing 54 tonnes; it's said to have 'enslaved 7000 people' in its casting. Sakyamuni is depicted on the cusp of death, before his entry into nirvana. On each side of Buddha are arrayed some sets of gargantuan shoes, gifts to Sakyamuni from various emperors in case he went for a stroll.

On the eastern side of the gardens is the **Cao Xueqin Memorial** (Cáo Xuěqín Jìniànguǎn; 39 Zhengbaiqi; ⊙8.30am-4.30pm summer, 9am-4pm winter) **FREE**, where Cao Xueqin lived in his latter years. Cao (1715–63) is credited with penning the classic *Dream of the Red Mansions*, a vast and prolix family saga set in the Qing period. Making a small buzz in the west of the gardens is the little **China Honey Bee Museum** (中国蜜蜂博物馆, Zhōngguó Mìfēng Bówùguǎn), open 8.30am to 4.30pm March to October.

🏃 Activities

Cycling

Běijīng is flat as a pancake and almost every road has a dedicated cycle lane, meaning cycling is easily the best way to see the city; it's especially fun to explore *hútòng* areas by bike. Most hostels rent bikes. There are also bike rental depots around the Hòuhǎi Lakes. Look out too for the city's **bike-sharing scheme**. Details of how to use it can be found on the very useful, independently created website www.beijingbikeshare.com.

Essentially, you need to take your passport, a ¥400 deposit and an ordinary Běijīng travel card (with at least ¥30 credit on it) to one of five bike-share kiosks (open 9.30 to 11.30am and 1.30pm to 4pm, Monday to Friday) in order to register. The two most handy kiosks are by Exit A of Dongzhimen subway station and by Exit A2 of Tiantandongmen subway station. Once registered, you can swipe your travel card to unlock any

bike any time at one of more than 100 bike stations scattered across the city, before returning it to any other bike station. The first hour is free. Subsequent hours are ¥1.

Bike Beijing   CYCLING
(康多自行车租赁, Kāngduō Zìxíngchē Zūlìn; Map p66; ☑010-6526 5857; www.bikebeijing.com; 34 Donghuangchenggen Nanjie; 东皇城根南街34号; ⊙9am-6pm; Ⓢ China Museum of Art) Rents a range of good-quality bikes, including mountain bikes (¥200), road bikes (¥400) and ordinary city bikes (¥100), and runs guided bike tours around the city (half-day tours from ¥300 per person) and beyond, including trips to the Great Wall (¥900 to ¥1800 per person).

Kite Flying

A quintessential Chinese pastime, kite flying is hugely popular in Běijīng. Top spots include the northeast portion of Temple of Heaven Park and the east gate of Dìtán Park. Sadly, you are no longer allowed to fly kites in Tiān'ānmén Sq.

Three Stone Kite Shop   KITES
(三石斋风筝; Sānshízhāi Fēngzhēng; Map p84; ☑010-8404 4505; 25 Di'anmen Xidajie; 地安门西大街甲25号; ⊙9am-9pm; Ⓢ Nanluogu Xiang) Kites by appointment to the former Qing emperors; the great-grandfather of the owner of this friendly store used to make the kites for the Chinese royal family. Most of the kites here are handmade and hand-painted, although the selection is limited these days, now that the owner uses half his shop to display other, admittedly attractive, souvenirs.

Massage

Dragonfly Therapeutic Retreat   MASSAGE TREATMENTS
(悠庭保健会所; Yōutíng Bǎojiàn Huìsuǒ; ☑010-6527 9368; www.dragonfly.net.cn; 60 Donghuamen Dajie, 东华门大街60号; ⊙11am-11pm; Ⓢ Tian'anmen East) Ideal for a foot massage after hours of walking around the Forbidden City, this popular boutique has a variety of treatments designed to help you de-stress. The two-hour Hangover Relief Massage (¥358) is self-explanatory, but for real pampering go for the Royal Delight (¥538), in which two masseurs get to work at the same time. A standard, hour-long body or foot massage costs ¥188.

Mào'ér Lǎolǐ Health Club   MASSAGE
(帽儿老李足疗保健馆; Mào'ér Lǎolǐ Zúliáo Bǎojiàn Guǎn; Map p72; 3 Mao'er Hutong; 帽儿胡同3号; ⊙11am-midnight) Located intriguingly

inside part of an old courtyard off historic Mao'er Hutong, this small massage parlour is great value. Half-hour foot massages are just ¥49, while one-hour full-body massages start from ¥89. They also provide cupping therapy (¥39) and, if you dare, Tibetan 'fire-dragon' therapy (¥59) – actual flames are used. Not much English spoken, but their massage menu has English translations.

The sign outside No 3 Mao'er Hutong is in Chinese only, but has the word 'massage' on it. Walk through the gateway, and continue on through a beautiful old carved gateway into the back courtyard where you'll find the place on your left.

Swimming

Locals swim daily in the Hòuhǎi Lakes (p83) – even in icy midwinter! If that's not clean enough for you, head to the outdoor leisure pools at **Qīngnián Hú Park** (青年湖公园; Qīngnián Hú Gōngyuán; Map p72; Qingnianhu Lu, off Andingmenwai Dajie, 安定门外大街，青年湖路; adult/child ¥40/30; ⏰6am-10pm May-Sep; **S**Andingmen), **Tuánjiéhú Park** or **Cháoyáng Park** (朝阳公园; Cháoyáng Gōngyuán).

Happy Magic Water Park SWIMMING
(水立方嬉水乐园; Shuǐlìfāng Xīshuǐ Lèyuán; Olympic Green, off Beichen Lu; 北辰路奥林匹克公园内; water park entrance adult/child ¥200/160, swimming only ¥50; ⏰10am-8pm; **S**Olympic Green) Unlike most of the 2008 Olympics venues, Běijīng's National Aquatics Centre, aka the Water Cube, has found a new lease of life post-Olympics. The otherworldly, bubble-like structure now houses Běijīng's largest indoor water park. It's a fave with children, who can negotiate neon plastic slides, tunnels, water jets and pools, all set alongside elaborate, surreal underwater styling.

Table Tennis

China's national sport can be played all over the capital at free-to-use, outdoor tables in parks, squares and housing estates. If you fancy being on the wrong end of a ping-pong thrashing, head to **Jīngshān Table Tennis Park** (东城全民健身第一园; Dōngchéng Quánmín Jiànshēn Dìyī Yuán; Map p66; Jingshan Houjie, 景山后街; ⏰6am-10pm; **S**Nanluoguxiang or Beihai North). **Hòuhǎi Exercise Park** (Map p84) also has tables. Pick up a cheap table tennis bat (paddle) on the 2nd floor of **Tiān Yì Goods Market** (天意商场; Tiānyì Shāngchǎng; Map p72; 158 Di'anmen Waidajie; 地安门外大街158号; ⏰9am-7.30pm; **S**Shichahai).

Courses

Chinese Language

Culture Yard LANGUAGE COURSES
(天井越洋; Tiānjǐng Yuèyáng; Map p72; ☑010-8404 4166; www.cultureyard.net; 10 Shique Hutong; 石雀胡同10号; ⏰10am-7pm, closed Sun; **S**Beixinqiao) Tucked away down a *hútòng*, this cultural centre focuses on Chinese classes. Its main program is a six-week course (¥3600), but you can tailor courses to suit your needs. Its 'Survival Chinese' course (four two-hour classes for ¥400) is ideal for tourists.

Martial Arts

Mǐlún Kungfu School MARTIAL ARTS
(北京弥纶传统武术学校; Běijīng Mǐlún Chuántǒng Wǔshù Xuéxiào; Map p66; ☑138 1170 6568; www.kungfuinchina.com; 33 Xitangzi Hutong; 西堂子胡同33号; per class ¥100, 8-class card ¥600; ⏰7-8.30pm Mon & Thu, 5-6.30pm Sat & Sun; **S**Dengshikou) Runs classes in various forms of traditional Chinese martial arts from a historic courtyard near Wángfǔjǐng shopping district. In summer, typically in August, classes are held in Rìtán Park. Has set-time drop-in classes, but can arrange individual schedules too. Instruction is in Chinese, but with an English translator.

Cuisine

Black Sesame Kitchen COOKING COURSES
(Map p72; ☑136 9147 4408; www.blacksesamekitchen.com; 3 Heizhima Hutong, off Nanluogu Xiang; 南锣鼓巷黑芝麻胡同3号) Runs popular cooking classes with a variety of recipes from across China. No sign; walk-in guests are not encouraged as this is a residential courtyard. Pre-booking essential. You can also eat here (set menu ¥300 per person) – it gets rave reviews – but again you must pre-book.

The Hutong CULTURAL CENTRE
(Map p72; ☑159 0104 6127; www.thehutong.com; 1 Jiudaowan Zhongxiang Hutong, off Shique Hutong; 北新桥石雀胡同九道弯中巷胡同1号; ⏰9am-9pm; **S**Beixinqiao) Hidden down a maze of alleys, this well-run cultural centre organises a variety of classes and tours, but the main speciality is Asian cuisine.

🛏 Sleeping

Hútòng-rich Dōngchéng North is Běijīng's most pleasant neighbourhood to stay in, although Dōngchéng Central has some great digs too. Dashilar, in Xīchéng South, is ground zero for budget backpackers, although there are good hostels throughout the capital.

Frustratingly, some of the very cheapest hotels do not accept foreigners.

If you want familiar Western-friendly luxury, international five-star hotel chains such as **Intercontinental** (www.ihg.com), **Hilton** (www.hilton.com), **Hyatt** (www.hyatt.com), **Westin** (www.starwoodhotels.com) and **Ritz-Carlton** (www.ritzcarlton.com) are well represented in Běijīng.

🛏 Forbidden City & Dōngchéng Central

Feel Inn   HOSTEL **$**
(非凡客栈; Fēifán Kèzhàn; Map p66; ☑010-139 1040 9166, 6528 7418; beijingfeelinn@gmail.com; 2 Ciqiku Hutong, off Nanheyan Dajie; 南河沿大街，磁器库胡同2号; dm ¥50-80, tw ¥240-300; ✹ @ 🛜) A small, understated hostel with a hidden, backstreet location, Feel Inn is tucked away amongst the alleys containing the little-known Pǔdù Temple, and yet is just a short walk from big-hitters such as the Forbidden City, Tiān'ānmén Sq and the shops on Wangfujing Dajie. Has simple, clean rooms, a small bar-restaurant, and wi-fi throughout.

Běijīng Saga International Youth Hostel   HOSTEL **$**
(北京实佳国际青年旅社; Běijīng Shíjiā Guójì Qīngnián Lǚshè; Map p66; ☑010-6527 2773; www.sagayouthhostelbeijing.cn; 9 Shijia Hutong, 史家胡同9号; dm ¥70, d with/without bathroom from ¥259/200, tr ¥319; ✹ @ 🛜; Ⓢ Dengshikou) Enjoying an interesting location on historic Shijia Hutong, this friendly hostel is a grey block, but inside compensates with some character and staff members are helpful towards travellers. Rooms are basic but well kept, and it has a decent restaurant-cum-bar. Rents bikes (¥50) and does Great Wall trips.

Běijīng City Central International Youth Hostel   HOSTEL **$**
(北京城市国际青年旅社; Běijīng Chéngshì Guójì Qīngnián Lǚshè; Map p66; ☑010-8511 5050, 010-6525 8066; www.centralhostel.com; 1 Beijingzhan Jie; 北京站街1号; 4-8 bed dm ¥60, s/d with shared bathroom ¥138/178, d ¥298-348; ⊗ ⊚ @ 🛜; Ⓢ Beijing Railway Station) The first youth hostel you hit after exiting Běijīng Train Station, this place is a decent choice if you can't be bothered to lug your heavy rucksack to nicer parts of the city. Rooms are pretty basic, but clean and spacious enough, and there's a large bar-cafe area with free wi-fi, internet terminals, pool tables and Western food.

★ Jǐngshān Garden Hotel   COURTYARD HOTEL **$$**
(景山花园酒店; Jǐngshān Huāyuán Jiǔdiàn; Map p66; ☑010-8404 7979; www.jingshangardenhotel.com; 68 Sanyanjing Hutong, off Jingshan Dongjie; 景山东街，三眼井胡同68号; r ¥650-750; ✹ @ 🛜) This delightful, unfussy, two-storey guesthouse has bright spacious rooms surrounding a large, peaceful, flower-filled courtyard. First-floor rooms are pricier, but brighter than the ground-floor ones, and some have views of Jǐngshān Park from their bathrooms. Walking down Sanyuanjing Hutong from the direction of Jǐngshān Park, turn right down the first alleyway, and the hotel is at the end.

City Walls Courtyard   HOSTEL **$$**
(城墙旅舍; Chéngqiáng Lǚshè; Map p66; ☑010-6402 7805; www.beijingcitywalls.com; 57 Nianzi Hutong, 碾子胡同57号; dm/s/tw ¥100/240/480; ✹ @ 🛜; Ⓢ Nanluoguxiang) This quiet hostel is on the pricey side for sure, but it's still an attractive choice because of its peaceful courtyard atmosphere and fabulous *hútòng* location – authentically hidden away from more touristy areas in one of the city's most historic neighbourhoods. All rooms have private bathrooms.

The maze of alleyways can be disorientating: from Jingshan Houjie, look for the *hútòng* opening just east of Jǐngshān Table Tennis Park. Walk up the *hútòng* and follow it around to the right and then left; the hostel is on the left-hand side.

Hulu Hotel   COURTYARD HOTEL **$$**
(壶庐宾馆; Húlú Bīnguǎn; Map p66; ☑010-6543 9229; www.thehuluhotel.com; 91 Yanyue Hutong, off Dongsi Nandajie; 东四南大街，演乐胡同91号; r ¥798, ¥898 & ¥1198) A stylish new addition to Běijīng's ever-growing brood of courtyard hotels, Hulu's converted *hútòng* space is minimalist throughout, with cool grey-painted wood beams, slate-tiled bathrooms and a cleverly renovated courtyard that combines its old-Běijīng roots with a modern, comfortable design. The atmosphere is laid-back, and the young staff speak excellent English. There are three grades of room (size increases with price), all of which have large double beds – no twins.

★ Temple Hotel   HERITAGE HOTEL **$$$**
(东景缘; Dōngjīng Yuán; Map p66; ☑010-8401 5680; www.thetemplehotel.com; 23 Shatan Beijie, off Wusi Dajie; 五四大街，沙滩北街23号; d ¥2000, ste ¥3000-4500) Unrivalled by anything else on the Běijīng hotel scene, this

unique heritage hotel forms part of a renovation project that was recognised by Unesco for its conservation efforts. A team spent five years renovating what was left of Zhìzhù Sì (智珠寺; Temple of Wisdom), a part-abandoned, 250-year-old Buddhist temple, and slowly transformed it into one of the most alluring places to stay in the capital.

★ **Côté Cour** COURTYARD HOTEL $$$

(北京演乐酒店; Běijīng Yǎnyuè Jiǔdiàn; Map p66; ☑010-6523 3958; www.hotelcotecourbj.com; 70 Yanyue Hutong, 演乐胡同70号; d/ste incl breakfast ¥1166/1995; ❋@☎; ⑤Dengshikou) With a calm, serene atmosphere and a lovely magnolia courtyard, this 14-room *hútòng* hotel makes a charming place to rest your head. The decor is exquisite – especially in the suite – and there's plenty of space to relax in the courtyard or on the extensive rooftop – perfect for a candle-lit evening drink.

🛏 Drum Tower & Dōngchéng North

Běijīng Downtown Backpackers HOSTEL $

(东堂客栈; Dōngtáng Kèzhàn; Map p72; ☑010-8400 2429; www.backpackingchina.com; 85 Nanluogu Xiang; 南锣鼓巷85号; dm ¥75-85, s ¥160, tw 160-210, ste ¥300; ❋@☎; ⑤Beixinqiao) Downtown Backpackers is Nanluogu Xiang's original youth hostel and it hasn't forgotten its roots. Rooms are basic, therefore cheap, but are kept clean and tidy, and staff members are fully plugged in to the needs of Western travellers. Rents bikes (per day ¥20) and runs recommended hiking trips to the Great Wall (¥280), plus a range of other city trips. Rates include breakfast.

Nostalgia Hotel HOTEL $

(时光漫步怀旧主题酒店; Shíguāng Mànbù Huáijiù Zhǔtí Jiǔdiàn; Map p72; ☑010-6403 2288; www.sgmbhotel.com; 46 Fangjia Hutong; 安定门内大街，方家胡同46号; r summer ¥388-408, winter ¥360-380) A good-value option if you don't fancy staying in a youth hostel, this funky hotel is housed in a small arts zone on trendy Fangjia Hutong. Rooms are dotted with retro knick-knacks, and have a different hand-painted mural in each. The bathrooms sparkle.

Staff on reception speak English, and there's lift access, but no restaurant. To find it, enter the small arts zone named after its address (46 Fangjia Hutong) and walk to the far left corner of the complex.

Confucius International Youth Hostel HÚTÒNG HOSTEL $

(雍圣轩青年酒店; Yōngshèngxuān Qīngnián Jiǔdiàn; Map p72; ☑010-6402 2082; 38 Wudaoying Hutong; 雍和宫大街，五道营胡同38号; dm/s/d/tw ¥80/120/138/158) One of the cheapest places that's open to foreigners in this area, Confucius has a handful of simple, no-frills rooms off a small, covered courtyard. No restaurant.

161 Lama Temple Courtyard Hotel COURTYARD HOTEL $$

(北京161酒店－雍和宫四合院店; Map p72; ☑8401 5027; beijing161lthotel@hotmail.com; 46 Beixinqiao Santiao; 北新桥三条46号; r ¥440 & ¥550) This hotel-cum-hostel, located on a *hútòng* which comes alive with restaurants in the evening, has 11 rooms, each themed on a different tourist sight in Běijīng. Rooms have a huge photo-mural to match their theme, and are small but spotless; the bathrooms likewise. The higher-category rooms come with a traditional wooden tea-drinking table, which can double up as an extra single bed.

There's a small cafe in reception and some cute courtyard seating.

★ **Orchid** COURTYARD HOTEL $$

(兰花宾馆; Lánhuā Bīnguǎn; Map p72; ☑8404 4818; www.theorchidbeijing.com; 65 Baochao Hutong; 鼓楼东大街宝钞胡同65号; d ¥700-1200; ❋@☎; ⑤Gulou Dajie) Opened by a Canadian guy and a Tibetan woman, this place may lack the history of other courtyard hotels, but it's been renovated into a beautiful space, with a peaceful courtyard and some rooftop seating with distant views of the Drum and Bell Towers. Rooms are doubles only, and are small, but are tastefully decorated and come with Apple TV home entertainment systems.

They also do Great Wall tours, and can organise taxis for city tours (half-/full day ¥400/600) or Great Wall trips (¥700). Hard to spot, the Orchid is down an unnamed, shoulder-width alleyway opposite Mr Shi's Dumplings.

★ **DùGé** COURTYARD HOTEL $$

(杜革四合院酒店; Dùgé Sìhéyuàn Jiǔdiàn; Map p72; ☑6445 7463; www.dugecourtyard.com; 26 Qianyuan Ensi Hutong; 交道口南大街前园恩寺胡同26号; r small/large ¥897/1817; ❋@☎; ⑤Nanluoguxiang or Beixinqiao) This 19th-century former residence was originally home to a Qīng-dynasty minister before being converted by a Belgian-Chinese couple into an exquisite designer courtyard hotel. Each of the six rooms is decorated uniquely with modern and artistic touches blended with overall themes of traditional China. Some of the wood furniture – four-poster beds, decorative Chinese screens – is beautiful.

Rooms are set around small, romantic, bamboo-lined courtyards, but space is at a premium – the small rooms really are small.

★ **Courtyard 7**   COURTYARD HOTEL **$$$**
(四合院酒店; Sìhéyuàn Jiǔdiàn; Map p72; ☎ 010-6406 0777; www.courtyard7.com; 7 Qiangulo‍uyuan Hutong, off Nanluogu Xiang; 鼓楼东大街南锣鼓巷前鼓楼苑胡同7号; r ¥900-1500; ✳ @; Ⓢ Nanluoguxiang) Immaculate rooms, decorated wiyh traditional Chinese furniture, face onto a series of different-sized, 400-year-old courtyards, which over the years have been home to government ministers, rich merchants and even an army general. Despite the historical narrative, rooms still come with modern comforts such as underfloor heating, broadband internet, wifi and cable TV.

The *hútòng* location – down a quiet alley, but very close to trendy Nanluogu Xiang – is also a winner. Breakfast included.

🏠 Temple of Heaven Park & Dōngchéng South

Emperor   HOTEL **$$$**
(皇家驿站; Huángjiā Yìzhàn; Map p76; ☎ 010-6701 7791; www.theemperor.com.cn; 87 Xianyukou St, Qianmen Commercial Centre; 前门商业区鲜鱼口街87号; r ¥1200; ✳ 🛜 ✉; Ⓢ Qianmen) Brand new, this modernist hotel comes with a spa and a roof-top pool that enables you to laze in the sun while enjoying fine views over nearby Tiān'ānmén Sq. The cool, all-white rooms aren't huge, but the price is reasonable for a hotel of this quality and the location is perfect. Service is attentive and the atmosphere laid-back.

🏠 Sānlǐtún & Cháoyáng

Sānlǐtún Youth Hostel   HOSTEL **$**
(三里屯青年旅馆; Sānlǐtún Qīngnián Lǚguǎn; ☎ 010-5190 9288; www.itisbeijing.com; Chunxiu Lu; 春秀路南口往北250米路东; 4/6 bed dm ¥80/70, d/tw with/without bathroom ¥280/220; ✳ @ 🛜; Ⓢ Dongsishitiao or Dongzhimen) Sānlǐtún's only decent youth hostel, this place has efficient, amiable staff and is always busy.

Rooms and dorms are functional and clean, although the shared bathrooms are a little pungent. Great Wall tours are available, as is bike hire (¥30 per day). There's an outdoor terrace for the summer and a good-value bar-restaurant area with a pool table.

Holiday Inn Express   HOTEL **$$**
(智选假日酒店; Zhìxuǎn Jiàrì Jiǔdiàn; ☎ 010-6416 9999; www.holidayinnexpress.com.cn; 1 Chunxiu Lu; 春秀路1号; r ¥598; ✳ @ 🛜; Ⓢ Dongsishitiao or Dongzhimen) There are 350 comfortable rooms at this well-located place with more personality than most chain hotels. Bright, pastel-coloured, clean rooms come with excellent beds (we love the big puffy pillows!). All are equipped with wide-screen TVs, free wi-fi and internet access via a cable. The lobby has Apple computers for the use of guests. Staff members are friendly and speak some English.

★ **Opposite House Hotel**   BOUTIQUE HOTEL **$$$**
(瑜舍; Yúshè; ☎ 010-6417 6688; www.theopposite‍house.com; Bldg 1, Village, 11 Sanlitun Lu; 三里屯路11号院1号楼; r ¥2300-3100; ⊜ ✳ ✉ 🛜; Ⓢ Tuanjiehu) With see-all open-plan bathrooms, American oak bath tubs, lovely mood lighting, underfloor heating, sliding doors, complimentary beers, TVs on extendable arms and a metal basin swimming pool, this trendy Swire-owned boutique hotel is top-drawer chic. The location is ideal for shopping, restaurants and drinking. No obvious sign. Just walk into the striking green glass cube of a building and ask.

🏠 Běihǎi Park & Xīchéng North

Sleepy Inn   HÚTÒNG HOSTEL **$**
(丽舍; Lì Shè; Map p84; ☎ 010-6406 9954; 103 Deshengmennei Dajie; 德胜门内大街103号; dm/tw ¥100/298; 🛜) Facilities aren't as good here as in other larger hostels, but the location by Xīhǎi Lake is lovely, and staff members are friendly. Rooms are simple but clean, there's bike rental and free wi-fi (although no computer terminals). Has a small cafe, but no restaurant. Heading south along Deshengmennei Dajie, turn right at the stone bridge (but don't cross it) and Sleepy Inn is on the right after 50m.

Red Lantern House   HÚTÒNG HOSTEL **$**
(仿古园; Fǎnggǔ Yuán; Map p84; ☎ 010-8328 5771; www.redlanternhouse.com; 5 Zhengjue Hutong; 正觉胡同 5号; 4-6 bed dm ¥85, d ¥220; ✳ @ 🛜; Ⓢ Jishuitan) Clean and simple rooms around a pleasant, covered courtyard, and a

fantastic, nontouristy, *hútòng* location make this welcoming hostel a sound choice. All rooms come with shared bathrooms. If you want private bathrooms, or if this place is full, ask to see its laid-back, but less charming sibling, Red Lantern House East Yard. It's a couple of minutes' walk away in an alley off Zhengjue Hutong, with doubles and triples for ¥330 and ¥420.

★ **Graceland Yard** COURTYARD HOTEL $$
(觉品酒店; Juepin Jiudian; Map p84; ☑159 1115 3219; www.graceland-yardhotel.com; 9 Zhengjue Hutong; 正觉胡同9号; s/d/tw/ste ¥599/699/799/1000, loft ¥899; @🏠) Graceland is an exquisitely renovated courtyard hotel, housed within the grounds of the abandoned, 500-year-old Zhèngjué Temple. Each of the eight rooms is slightly different – there are singles, doubles, twins, a couple of fabulous loft rooms and a suite – but each is decorated with style, using traditional Buddhist-themed furnishings. There's no restaurant – not even breakfast – but you're not short of eateries in the surrounding *hútòng*.

🛏 Dashilar & Xīchéng South

★ **Qiánmén Hostel** HOSTEL $
(前门客栈; Qiánmén Kèzhàn; Map p87; ☑010-6313 2369, 010-6313 2370; www.qianmenhostel. net; 33 Meishi Jie; 煤市街 33号; 6-8 bed dm ¥70, 4-bed dm ¥80, with/without bathroom d & tw ¥280/240, tr ¥380/300; ✳@🏠; Ⓢ Qianmen) A five-minute trot southwest of Tiān'ānmén Sq, this heritage hostel with a cool courtyard offers a relaxing environment with able staff. The rooms are simple and not big but, like the dorms, they are clean, as are the shared bathrooms, and all were being upgraded at the time of writing. There's a decent cafe to hang out in too.

Three-Legged Frog Hostel HOSTEL $
(京一会青年旅舍; Jīngyī Shí Qīngnián Lûshè; Map p87; ☑010-6304 0749; 3legs@threeleggedfroghostel.com; 27 Tieshu Xiejie; 铁树斜街 27号; 6-bed dm with bathroom ¥65, 10-bed dm ¥55, d & tw ¥220, tr ¥270, f ¥339; ✳🏠; Ⓢ Qianmen) The name is a mystery but the decent-sized six-bed dorms with bathrooms are an excellent deal, while the rooms are compact but clean. All are set around a cute courtyard that's pleasant in the summer. It has a helpful owner – it's geared to foreign travellers – and a communal area out front that does Western breakfasts and evening beers.

Leo Courtyard HOSTEL $
(上林宾馆; Shànglín Bīnguǎn; Map p87; ☑010-8316 6568; www.leohostel.com; 22 Shanxi Xiang, 陕西巷胡同 22号; 4-bed dm without bathroom ¥60, 8/10-bed dm with bathroom ¥55/60, d/tw ¥140/160, tr ¥180; ✳🏠; Ⓢ Qianmen) It's a superb, historic, warren of a building with a racy past featuring courtesans and the imperial elite, but like most courtyard hotels the rooms are a little old-fashioned and the dorms on the small side. However, the once-sleepy staff have upped their game and are now helpful and the bathrooms are clean. It's down an alley off Dazhalan Xijie.

🍴 Eating

Eating out will almost certainly be a highlight of your trip here. Běijīng has a staggering 60,000 restaurants, and between them they cater to all tastes and all budgets. True to its north China roots, Běijīng cuisine is warming, fatty and filling, with generous amounts of garlic finding their way into many dishes. The adventurous can sample some unusual stuff here – boiled tripe, tofu paste, sour soy milk... Just be sure to leave your table manners at home; Běijīngers like mealtimes to be raucous affairs, with plenty of drinking, smoking and shouting to accompany their hearty platters.

🍴 Forbidden City & Dōngchéng Central

★ **Crescent Moon Muslim Restaurant** XINJIANG $
(新疆弯弯月亮维吾尔穆斯林餐厅; Xīnjiāng Wānwányuèliàng Wéiwú'ěr Mùsīlín Cāntīng; Map p66; 16 Dongsi Liutiao Hutong; 东四六条胡同16号, 东四北大街; dishes from ¥18; ⏰11am-11pm; Ⓢ Dongsi Shitiao) You can find a Chinese Muslim restaurant on almost every street in Běijīng. Most are run by Huí Muslims, who are Hàn Chinese, rather than ethnic-minority Uighurs from the remote western province of Xīnjiāng. Crescent Moon is the real deal – owned and staffed by Uighurs, it attracts many Běijīng-based Uighurs and people from Central Asia, as well as a lot of Western expats.

It's more expensive than most other Xīnjiāng restaurants in Běijīng, but the food is consistently good, and it has an English menu. The speciality is the barbecued leg of lamb (¥128). The lamb skewers (¥6) are also delicious, and there's naan bread (¥5), homemade yoghurt (¥12) and plenty of noodle

LOCAL KNOWLEDGE

BĚIJĪNG MENU

The following are all classic Běijīng dishes, many of which you'll only find at places specialising in Běijīng cuisine. Try Zuǒ Lín Yòu Shè (p97), Yáojì Chǎogān (p98) or Bàodǔ Huáng (p101). Many roast duck restaurants will have some of the other Běijīng specialities as well as Peking duck.

Peking Duck (烤鸭; *kǎo yā*) Běijīng's most famous dish, the duck here is fattier but much more flavoursome than the roast duck typically served in Chinese restaurants in the West. Like back home, though, it also comes with pancakes, cucumber slices and plum sauce.

Zhá Jiàng Miàn (炸酱面) Very popular noodle dish found in many regions, but a favourite in Běijīng; thick wheat noodles with ground pork and cucumber shreds mixed together in a salty fermented soybean paste. Chilli oil (辣椒油; *làjiāo yóu*) is a popular optional extra.

Dàlián Huǒshāo (褡裢火烧) Finger-shaped fried dumplings with a savoury filling.

Má Dòufu (麻豆腐) Spicy tofu paste.

Zhá Guànchang (炸灌肠) Deep-fried crispy crackers served with a very strong garlic dip.

Chǎo Gānr (炒肝) Sautéed liver served in a gloopy (glutinous) soup.

Bào Dǔ (爆肚) Boiled tripe, usually lamb. Sometimes served in a seasoned broth.

Yáng Zá (羊杂) Similar to *bào dǔ*, but includes an assortment of sheep's innards, not just tripe, and is always served in a broth.

Ròu Bǐng (肉饼) Meat patty, usually filled with pork or beef, before being lightly fried.

Jiāo Quān (焦圈) Deep-fried dough rings, usually accompanied with a cup of *dòu zhī*.

Dòu Zhī (豆汁) Sour-tasting soy milk drink.

options (¥18 to¥25). You can also get Xīnjiāng tea (¥30 per pot), beer (¥15) and wine (¥95).

Zuǒ Lín Yòu Shè　　　　　　　　BEIJING **$**
(左邻右舍褡裢火烧; Map p66; 50 Meishuguan Houjie, 美术馆后街50号; dumplings per liǎng ¥6-7, dishes ¥10-30; ⊙11am-9.30pm; Ⓢ National Art Museum) This small, no-frills restaurant focuses on Běijīng cuisine. The speciality is *dàlián huǒshāo* (褡裢火烧), golden-fried finger-shaped dumplings stuffed with all manner of savoury fillings; we prefer the pork ones, but there are lamb, beef and veggie choices too. They are served by the *liǎng* (两), with one *liǎng* equal to three dumplings, and they prefer you to order at least two *liǎng* (二两; *èr liǎng*) of each filling to make it worth their while cooking a batch.

Other specialities include the pickled fish (酥鲫鱼; *sū jì yú*), the spicy tofu paste (麻豆腐; *má dòufu*) and the deep-fried pork balls (干炸丸子; *gān zhá wánzi*), while filling bowls of millet porridge (小米粥; *xiǎo mǐ zhōu*) are served up for free. No English sign (look for the wooden signboard), and no English spoken, but most parts of the menu have been translated into English.

Dōnghuámén Night Market　　STREET FOOD **$**
(东华门夜市; Dōnghuámén Yèshì; Map p66; Dong'anmen Dajie, 东安门大街; snacks ¥5-15; ⊙4-10pm; Ⓢ Wangfujing) A sight in itself, the bustling night market near Wangfujing Dajie is a veritable food zoo: lamb, beef and chicken skewers, corn on the cob, smelly *dòufu* (tofu), cicadas, grasshoppers, kidneys, quail eggs, snake, squid, fruit, porridge, fried pancakes, strawberry kebabs, bananas, Inner Mongolian cheese, stuffed eggplants, chicken hearts, pita bread stuffed with meat, shrimps – and that's just the start.

★ **Little Yúnnán**　　　　　　　　YUNNAN **$$**
(小云南; Xiǎo Yúnnán; Map p66; ☎6401 9498; 28 Donghuang Chenggen Beijie; 东皇城根北街28号; mains ¥20-60; ⊙10am-10pm) Run by young, friendly staff and housed in a cute courtyard conversion, Little Yúnnán is one of the more down-to-earth Yúnnán restaurants in Běijīng. The main room has a rustic feel to it, with wooden beams, flooring and furniture. The tables up in the eaves are fun, and there's also some seating in the small open-air courtyard by the entrance.

BĚIJĪNG EATING

GHOST STREET

For a close-up look at how Běijīngers treat their restaurants as party venues and not just places for a meal, take a trip to Ghost Street (簋街; Gui Jie; Map p72; S Beixinqiao).

This 1.4km strip of Dongzhimennei Dajie is home to over 150 restaurants. It never closes, making it one of Běijīng's most buzzing streets, and it's especially fun on Friday and Saturday nights. Most styles of Chinese cuisine are represented, but it's best known for its hotpot and spicy seafood restaurants.

The giant Xiǎo Yú Shān (小渔山; Map p72; 195 Dongzhimennei Dajie; 东直门内大街195号; ⊘10.30am-6am) is always jammed with people cracking open crayfish and shrimp. For classic Mongolian hotpot, try Little Sheep (小肥羊; Xiǎo Féi Yáng; Map p72; 209 Dongzhimennei Dajie; 东直门内大街209号; ⊘9am-4am), which sources its mutton from Inner Mongolia. For the spicier, Sìchuān version of hotpot, cross the road to Chóngqìng Kōngliàng Huǒguǒ (重庆孔亮火锅; Map p72; 218 Dongzhimennei Dajie, 东直门内大街218; pot from ¥35, dipping ingredients ¥7-20; ⊘9.30am-3am).

Sadly, Ghost Street's signature red lanterns, which for years lined both sides of the street, were torn down by local officials in 2014 – they were a fire risk, apparently.

Dishes include some classic southwest China ingredients, with some tea-infused creations as well as river fish, mushroom dishes and *là ròu* (腊肉; cured pork – south China's answer to bacon). They also serve Yúnnán rice wine and the province's local Dali Beer. Has an English sign and a well-translated English menu.

Mǎn Fú Lóu
MONGOLIAN, HOTPOT $$
(满福楼; Map p66; 38 Di'anmennei Dajie; 地安门内大街38号; raw ingredients ¥10-50; ⊘11am-10pm) This grand-looking but inexpensive 20-year-old hotpot restaurant serves up Mongolian hotpot – the nonspicy, lamb-based version which hails from the steppes, but has been adopted as a Běijīng speciality. Here each diner gets their own, mini, conical brass pot in which to boil their food. Choose the clear broth (*qīng tāng*; 清汤; ¥12), which isn't spicy, then pick portions of raw ingredients from the menu (in English and with photos).

Each person should also order a small bowl of sesame-paste dipping sauce (小料; *xiǎo liào*), which you dip your cooked food into before eating it. There should be a pot of chilli oil (辣椒油; *làjiāo yóu*) on your table (if not, ask for it), which can be mixed into the sesame paste to spice things up a bit.

Brian McKenna @ The Courtyard
FUSION $$$
(马克南四合轩; Mǎkènán Sìhéxuān; ☏010-6526 8883; www.bmktc.com; 95 Donghuamen Dajie; 东华门大街95号; set menus from ¥588; ⊘11.30am-2.30pm & 6-10pm; S Tian'anmen East or Dengshikou) This 10-year-old classic of the Běijīng fine-dining scene has been given a new lease of life by UK-born chef Brian McKenna. Courtyard still enjoys its peerless location, housed in a Qing-dynasty building beside the Forbidden City moat, but McKenna has revamped the interior (there are more tables with a view of the moat now) and the menu (with some innovative new creations, such as his chocolate terracotta warrior).

Běijīng Dàdǒng Roast Duck Restaurant
PEKING DUCK $$$
(北京大董烤鸭店; Běijīng Dàdǒng Kǎoyādiàn; Map p66; ☏010-8522 1111; 5th fl, Jinbao Pl, 88 Jinbao Jie, 东城区金宝街88号金宝汇购物中心5层; roast duck ¥268; ⊘10am-11pm; S Dengshikou) Ultramodern Dàdǒng sells itself on being the only restaurant that serves Peking duck with all the flavour of the classic imperial dish, but none of the fat – the leanest roast duck in the capital. For some it's hideously overpriced and far from authentic. For others it's the best roast duck restaurant in China.

✕ Drum Tower & Dōngchéng North

Yáojì Chǎogān
BEIJING $
(姚记炒肝店; Map p72; 311 Gulou Dongdajie; 鼓楼东大街311号; mains ¥8-20; ⊘6am-10.30pm; S Shichahai) Proper locals' joint, serving Běijīng dishes in a noisy, no-nonsense atmosphere. The house speciality is *chǎogān* (炒肝; pig's liver stew; ¥6 to ¥9). This is also a good place to try *zhá guànchang* (炸灌肠; garlic-topped deep-fried crackers; ¥6) and *má dòufu* (麻豆腐; spicy tofu paste; ¥10).

Its steamed pork dumplings (包子; *bāozi*; ¥3 for two) are excellent, and are perfect for breakfast with a bowl of *xiǎomǐ zhōu* (小米粥; millet porridge; ¥2) or locals' favourite *dòuzhī* (豆汁; soy milk; ¥2). It also does a decent bowl of Běijīng's best-known noodle dish, *zhájiàng miàn* (炸酱面; ¥12). No English menu or English sign.

Zhāng Māma
SICHUAN $

(张妈妈特色川味馆; Zhāng Māma Tèsè Chuānwèiguǎn; Map p72; 76 Jiaodaokou Nandajie, 交道口南大街76号; mains ¥10-20; ⏰10.30am-10.30pm; ⑤Beixinqiao) The original Zhāng Māma, on nearby Fensiting Hutong, was such a hit with Běijīngers they were forced to also open this new, larger branch with two floors. At the smaller, original branch you have to wait up to an hour for a table. Here, they've cut that down to about 15 minutes. It's worth the wait. This is arguably Běijīng's best-value Sìchuānese restaurant.

The speciality is *málà xiāngguō* (麻辣香锅; ¥48 to ¥58), a fiery, chilli-laced broth with either chicken (香锅鸡; *xiāngguō jī*), prawns (香锅虾; *xiāngguō xiā*) or ribs (香锅排骨; *xiāngguō páigǔ*) simmering away inside, and with a variety of vegetables added into the mix. One pot is enough for two or three people. Also worth trying here is the *dàndàn miàn* (担担面; spicy dry noodles; ¥8) and the rice meals; the classic being the *gōngbào jīdīng gàifàn* (宫爆鸡丁盖饭; spicy chicken with peanuts; ¥12), lip-tinglingly delicious thanks to the generous sprinkling of Sìchuān peppercorns. No English menu, so don't be shy about pointing to what fellow diners are eating. Chances are it'll be spicy, but delicious.

Yī Lóng Zhāi
XINJIANG $

(伊隆斋; Map p72; cnr Mao'er Hutong & Doujiao Hutong; 帽儿胡同和豆角胡同的路口; mains ¥15-30; ⏰11am-midnight; ⑤Shichahai) Bright and boisterous, this no-frills restaurant specialises in the Turkic-influenced cuisine of Xīnjiāng province, in west China. So expect lots of tasty lamb dishes. The *kǎo yáng tuǐ* (烤羊腿; grilled leg of lamb; ¥25) is excellent, as are the *yáng ròu chuàn* (羊肉串; lamb skewers; ¥3). There's also a good selection of noodle dishes (¥12 to ¥18) in the photo menu.

Another signature dish here is the *dà pán jī* (大盘鸡; literally, 'big plate chicken'; ¥70), which is enough to feed four or five hungry mouths, especially when the sauce is mopped up with some *kǎo náng* (烤馕; naan bread; ¥5). If there's only two or three of you, go for the small portion (*xiǎo pán jī*; 小盘鸡; ¥40), which is still massive. Has patio seating out front in summer.

Róng Tiān Sheep Spine
HOTPOT $

(容天土锅羊羯子馆; Róngtiān Tǔguō Yángjiézi Guǎn; Map p72; 8 Jingtu Hutong, off Beiluogu Xiang; 北锣鼓巷净土胡同8号; sheep spine per jīn ¥35, other ingredients ¥8-12; ⏰10.30am-10pm; ⑤Guloudajie) Hidden down a quiet *hútòng*, this locals' favourite serves mouthwateringly good sheep-spine hotpot. Order your sheep-spine chunks (普通羊蝎子; *pǔtōng yángxiēzi*) by the *jīn* (500g). Two jins' worth (二斤; *èr jīn*) is normally about right. They will then come ready-cooked in a boiling broth – the longer you leave them to simmer, the juicier they get. You then add other raw ingredients to cook in the broth like a standard Chinese hotpot.

Our favourite extras include sweet potato (红薯; *hóng shǔ*), tofu blocks (鲜豆腐; *xiān dòufu*), mushrooms (木耳; *mù'ěr*), Oriental radish (白萝卜; *bái luóbo*) and Chinese spinach (油麦菜; *yóu mài cài*). Complimentary fresh noodles are thrown in at the end, to soak up the juices. When you're ready for them, say '*fàng miàn*' (put the noodles in). No English sign or menu, and no English spoken.

Tàn Huā Lamb BBQ
BARBECUE $

(碳花烤羊腿; Tàn Huā Kǎo Yángtuǐ; Map p72; 63 Beixinqiao Santiao; 北新桥三条63号; lamb per jīn ¥52, side dishes ¥2-18; ⏰11am-midnight; ⑤Beixinqiao) Meat-loving Běijīngers flock to this raucous joint where you roast a leg of lamb on your own personal table-top barbecue spit before hacking away at the meatiest bits with a rudimentary, long-handled knife and fork. Tables spill out onto the lively *hútòng*, creating a party atmosphere of multibarbecue revelry.

Order your leg of lamb (羊腿; *yáng tuǐ*) by the *jīn* (500g). Three *jīn* (三斤; *sān jīn*) is enough for two or three people. You'll then be given a selection of free cold dishes as accompaniments, plus a cumin-based dry dip to roll your lamb slices in. Other popular side dishes include barbecued naan bread (烤馕; *kǎo náng*; ¥6), soy fried rice (酱油炒饭; *jiàng yóu chǎo fàn*; ¥10) and noodle-drop soup (疙瘩汤; *gēda tāng*; ¥12).

★ **Bǎihé Vegetarian Restaurant** CHINESE, VEGETARIAN $$

(百合素食; Bǎihé Sùshí; Map p72; 23 Caoyuan Hutong; 东直门内北小街草园胡同甲23号; mains ¥25-60, tea per cup/pot from ¥16/45; ⊙11am-10pm; S Dongzhimen or Beixinqiao) This peaceful, tastefully furnished, courtyard restaurant, which also serves as a delightful teahouse, has a wonderful air of serenity – it's not uncommon to see monks from nearby Lama Temple coming here for a pot of tea. The all-vegetarian menu (with English translations) includes imaginative mock-meat dishes as well as more conventional vegetable dishes and a range of tasty noodles.

With courteous service, this is one of Běijīng's more soothing dining experiences; and it's nonsmoking throughout. There's also a separate and extensive tea menu – customers are welcome to come here just to sample the tea. To get here, walk north on Dongzhimen Beixiaojie from the junction with Ghost St for 100m, then turn left into the first *hútòng*. The restaurant is on the right, although the sign is in Chinese only.

Stuff'd WESTERN $$

(塞; Sāi; Map p72; 9 Jianchang Hutong, off Guozijian Jie; 国子监街, 箭厂胡同9号; sausages ¥50, pies ¥60, pizza ¥60, home-brewed ale ¥40; ⊙11.30am-2.30pm & 6-10pm, closed Tue) Handmade sausages and home-brewed beer. What more could you want? This cute little sister branch of nearby Vineyard Cafe has a more rustic feel to it; almost like an English pub, only housed in a restored Chinese *píngfáng* (bungalow). Lunchtimes are all about the sausages and ale, but the evening menu also includes pies and pizza.

Xù Xiāng Zhāi Vegetarian Restaurant VEGETARIAN $$

(叙香斋; Xù Xiāng Zhāi; Map p72; 26 Guozijian Jie, 国子监街26号; buffet ¥68, mains ¥30-80; ⊙buffet 11.30am-2pm & 5.30-9pm, a la carte 1.30-3.30pm & 7.30-9pm; S Yonghegong Lama Temple) The lunchtime and early evening set-price buffet is very popular here, and good value. There's an elaborate selection of beautifully presented mock-meat creations, plus other standard vegetable dishes, representing vegetarian cuisine from across China. And it's all served in an elegant dining hall on the historic *hútòng* Guozijian Jie. The à la carte menu is in English and is also decent value.

Dàlǐ Courtyard YUNNAN $$$

(大理; Dàlǐ; Map p72; ☑010-8404 1430; 67 Xiaojingchang Hutong, Gulou Dongdajie; 鼓楼东大街小经厂胡同67号; set menu ¥150; ⊙noon-2pm & 6-10.30pm; S Andingmen) The charming *hútòng* setting in a restored courtyard makes this one of Běijīng's more pleasant places to eat, especially in summer (in winter they cover the courtyard with an unattractive temporary roof). It specialises in the subtle flavours of Yúnnán cuisine. There's no menu. Instead, you pay ¥150 (drinks are extra), and enjoy whatever inspires the chef that day. He rarely disappoints.

✖ Temple of Heaven Park & Dōngchéng South

Old Běijīng Zhájiàng Noodle King NOODLES $

(老北京炸酱面大王; Lǎo Běijīng Zhájiàng Miàn; Map p76; 56 Dongxinglong Jie; 东兴隆街56号; noodles from ¥18, other dishes from ¥28; ⊙10.45am-10pm; S Chongwenmen) Faux old-school Běijīng style – look for the two rickshaws parked outside the entrance – but always busy (especially at lunchtime) with locals sampling the signature noodles with bean paste sauce on offer here. The sauce, scallions and your choice of meat or vegie options come on the side and you mix them with the noodles.

★ **Lìqún Roast Duck Restaurant** PEKING DUCK $$$

(利群烤鸭店; Lìqún Kǎoyādiàn; Map p76; ☑010-6702 5681, 6705 5578; 11 Beixiangfeng Hutong; 前门东大街正义路南口北翔凤胡同11号; roast duck for 2/3 people ¥255/275; ⊙10am-10pm; S Qianmen) As you walk in to this compact courtyard restaurant, you're greeted by the fine sight of rows of ducks on hooks glowing in the ovens. The delectable duck on offer is so in demand that it's essential to call ahead to reserve both a bird and a table (otherwise, turn up off-peak and be prepared to wait an hour).

Inside, it's a little tatty (no prizes for the toilets) and service can be chaotic, but the food more than makes up for that. Buried away in east Qiánmén, the approach to the restaurant is through a maze of crumbling *hútòng* that have somehow survived total demolition; look for the duck signs pointing the way.

LOCAL KNOWLEDGE

PICNIC SUPPLIES

Western-style supermarkets are on the rise, but thankfully there are still some atmospheric food markets in Běijīng where you can stock up on fresh fruit and unusual snacks as you watch locals pick their favourite frogs and fish.

Rùndélì Food Market (润得立菜市场; Rùndélì Càishìchǎng; Map p84; 4 Sihuan Hutong, off Deshengmennei Dajie; 德胜门内大街四环胡同; ⏱7am-7pm), also known as Sihuán Market (四环市场; Sìhuán Shìchǎng), is close to the Hòuhǎi Lakes, while **Xīnmín Food Market** (新民菜市场; Xīnmín Càishìchǎng; Map p72; Jiugulou Waidajie, 就鼓楼外大街; ⏱5am-noon) is north of the Drum Tower.

Near Sānlǐtún, **Sānyuánlǐ Market** (三源里菜市场; Sānyuánlǐ Càishìchǎng; Shunyuan Jie; 朝阳区东三环顺源街; ⏱5am-7pm) has a great range of imported foodstuffs alongside all the usual Chinese favourites.

Qiánmén Quánjùdé Roast Duck Restaurant
PEKING DUCK $$$

(前门全聚德烤鸭店; Qiánmén Quánjùdé Kǎoyādiàn; Map p76; ☏010-6701 1379; 30 Qianmen Dajie; 前门大街30号; roast duck ¥296; ⏱11am-1.30pm & 4.30-8pm; Ⓢ Qianmen) The most popular branch of Běijīng's most famous destination for duck – check out the photos of everyone from Fidel Castro to Zhang Yimou. The duck, while not the best in town, is roasted in ovens fired by fruit-tree wood, which means the birds have a unique fragrance, as well as being juicy, if slightly fatty.

✖ Sānlǐtún & Cháoyáng

Bǎoyuán Dumpling Restaurant
DUMPLINGS $

(宝源饺子屋; Bǎoyuán Jiǎozi Wū; ☏010-6586 4967; 6 Maizidian Jie, 麦子店街6号; mains from ¥28, dumplings from ¥13; ⏱11.15am-10.15pm; Ⓢ Liangmaqiao or Agricultural Exhibition Centre) Fun for the kids – but also tasty enough for parents – this excellent dumplings restaurant dazzles diners with a huge selection of multicoloured jiǎozi (饺子; boiled dumplings), including many vegetarian options. The dough dyes are all natural (carrots make the orange; spinach the green) and only add to the flavour of the fillings; as good as any in Běijīng.

Dumplings are ordered and priced by the liǎng (about 50g). One liǎng gets you six dumplings. Not much English spoken, but there's an English sign and menu, and it's nonsmoking.

Bàodǔ Huáng
BEIJING $

(爆肚皇; 15 Dongzhimenwai Dajie; 东直门外大街15号; mains ¥18-35; ⏱11am-2pm & 5-9pm; Ⓢ Dongzhimen) Be prepared to queue at this no-nonsense apartment-block restaurant (look for the green sign with four yellow characters), where locals gobble and slurp their way through the authentic Běijīng-grub menu. The speciality is bàodǔ (爆肚; boiled lamb tripe; ¥18 or ¥35 depending on portion size). If you can't stomach that, then plump instead for a delicious niúròu dàcóng ròubǐng (牛肉大葱肉饼; beef and onion fried patty; ¥8).

The blanched vegetables are popular side dishes; choose from chǎo báicài (焯白菜; blanched cabbage; ¥6), chǎo fěnsī (焯粉丝; blanched glass noodles; ¥6) or chǎo dòng dòufu (焯冻豆腐; blanched tofu; ¥6). And if you haven't ordered a meat patty, grab a zhīma shāobing (芝麻烧饼; roasted sesame-seed bun; ¥1.5) instead. True Běijīngers will also nibble on jiāo quān (焦圈; deep-fried dough rings; ¥1), washed down with gulps of dòu zhī (豆汁; sour soy milk). But you may prefer to go for a bottle of píjiǔ (酒; local beer; ¥5). No English spoken, no English menu, no English sign.

Bocata
CAFE $

(☏6417 5291; 3 Sanlitun Lu, 三里屯北路3号; sandwiches from ¥28, coffee from ¥22; ⏱11.30am-midnight; ☏; Ⓢ Tuanjiehu) Great spot for lunch, especially in summer, located slap-bang in the middle of Sānlǐtún's bar street and opposite Běijīng's trendiest shopping area. As the name suggests, there's a Spanish/Mediterranean theme to the food, with Iberian ham and cheeses and decent salads (from ¥28), as well as great chips, but most punters go for the fine sandwiches on ciabatta.

The coffee, juices and smoothies go down a treat, too, and the large, tree-shaded terrace is very popular when the sun is out.

LOCAL KNOWLEDGE

HÚTÒNG CAFES

Scattered around the narrow lanes of Běijīng's *hútòng* neighbourhoods are dozens of cute, independently run cafes. Some are housed in converted courtyards. Most have free wi-fi, fresh coffee (from ¥20), Chinese tea, well-priced local beer (from ¥15) and a small selection of mostly Western food (dishes from ¥30). Here are some of our favourites:

Irresistible Cafe (诱惑咖啡厅; Yòu Huò Kāfēitīng; Map p72; 14 Mao'er Hutong; 帽儿胡同14号; ⊙11am-midnight, closed Mon & Tue; 🛜) Large courtyard. Czech beers. Good, healthy food.

Cafe Confucius (秀冠咖啡, Xiù Guàn Kāfēi; Map p72; 25 Guozijian Jie, 国子监街25号; ⊙8.30am-8.30pm; 🛜) Buddhist themed. Very friendly.

Other Place (Map p72; 1 Langjia Hutong; 朗家胡同1号; ⊙noon-midnight; 🛜) Cool staff. Cool tunes. Cool courtyard. No food.

Essence (萃饮咖啡; Cuìyǐn Kāfēi; Map p72; 47 Zhonglouwan Hutong, off Drum & Bell Sq; 钟鼓楼广场, 钟楼湾胡同47号; ⊙10am-10pm) Top-quality coffee. Small roof terrace with Drum Tower views.

Le Grenadier (石榴树下; Shíliushù Xià; Map p66; 7 Youqizuo Hutong, off Di'anmen Neidajie; 地安门内大街, 油漆作胡同7号; ⊙11am-9pm, closed Wed) Quiet location. Cheap coffee. Rooftop seating. French cuisine.

Three Trees Coffee (三棵树; Sān Kē Shù; Map p72; 89 Nanluogu Xiang; 南锣鼓巷89号; ⊙9.30am-10pm) Cosy bohemian retreat from Nanluogu Xiang's shopping frenzy.

Alley Coffee (寻常巷陌咖啡厅; Xúncháng Xiàngmò Kāfēi Tīng; Map p66; cnr Jingshan Dongjie & Shatan Houjie, 景山东街，沙滩后街61号; ⊙8.30am-11pm; 🛜; Ⓢ Nanluoguxiang or National Art Museum) Perfect for a coffee break after a visit to the Forbidden City or Jǐngshān Park, this cute, traveller-friendly courtyard cafe, diagonally opposite Jǐngshān Park's east gate, has friendly English-speaking staff and does fresh coffee (from ¥25), cold beer and a mix of Chinese and Western food, including breakfast fry-ups (until 11am). Also rents bikes (per day ¥50, deposit ¥600) and has free wi-fi.

Jīngzūn Peking Duck　　PEKING DUCK **$$**
(京尊烤鸭; Jīngzūn Kǎoyā; ☑010-6417 4075; 6 Chunxiu Lu; 春秀路6号; mains ¥36-96; ⊙11am-10pm; Ⓢ Dongzhimen or Dongsi Shitiao) Very popular place to sample Běijīng's signature dish. Not only is the bird here extremely good value at ¥128 including all the trimmings but, unusually for a roast duck restaurant, you can also sit outside on a wooden-decked terrace. There's also a big choice of dishes from across China, all decent, if you're not in the mood for duck.

Carmen　　SPANISH **$$**
(卡门; Kǎmén; ☑010-6417 8038; Nali Patio north side, 81 Sanlitun Lu; 三里屯路那里花园北外1层; mains from ¥70; ⊙noon-1am; Ⓢ Tuanjiehu) Běijīng's busiest tapas joint is a long, narrow space with tables hugging the walls. It's not the place for an intimate meal, but there's a great range of tapas, Spanish ham and cheeses and Mediterranean-inspired mains, including the huge paella (¥199), which can easily feed four. Strong wine list. It's around

the corner from the popular terrace courtyard Nali Patio.

There's live music from 7.30pm every night.

Bookworm　　CAFE **$$**
(书虫; Shūchóng; ☑010-6586 9507; www.beijingbookworm.com; Bldg 4, Nansanlitun Lu; 南三里屯路4号楼; mains from ¥60; ⊙9am-midnight; 🛜; Ⓢ Tuanjiehu) A combination of a bar, cafe, restaurant and library, the Bookworm is a Běijīng institution and one of the epicentres of the capital's cultural life. Much more than just an upmarket cafe, there are 16,000-plus books here you can browse while sipping your coffee. The food is reasonably priced, if uninspired, but there's a decent wine list.

Duck de Chine　　PEKING DUCK **$$$**
(全鸭季, Quányājì; ☑010-6521 2221; Courtyard 4, 1949, near Gongrentiyuchang Beilu; 工体北路四号院; mains ¥78-488; ⊙11am-2pm & 5.30-10.30pm; Ⓢ Tuanjiehu) Housed in a reconstructed industrial-style courtyard complex known as 1949, this very slick and stylish

operation incorporates both Chinese and French duck-roasting methods to produce some stand-out duck dishes, including a leaner version of the classic Peking roast duck (¥238). The mix of expats and moneyed locals who flock here argue it's the best bird in town.

The service is as good as it gets in Běijīng, while the wine list is lengthy and expensive. Alternatively, the pumpkin infused with sour plums makes a delicious accompaniment. Book ahead.

Běihǎi Park & Xīchéng North

★ **Royal Icehouse** SHANDONG $$
(皇家冰窖小院; Huángjiā Bīngjiào Xiǎoyuàn; Map p66; ☎010-6401 1358; 5 Gongjian Wuxiang, Gongjian Hutong; 恭俭胡同5巷5号; mains ¥30-60; ⊙11.30am-2pm & 5.30-9.30pm) Tucked away in the *hútòng* running alongside the east wall of Běihǎi Park, this intriguing restaurant is located inside one of the city's former royal ice houses – where, before the days of refrigeration, massive blocks of ice were stored for use in the imperial court during summer.

You can walk down into the underground ice cellars (which now keep the wine cool); look for the red arched door.

The main restaurant is decked out in old-Běijīng paraphernalia; look for the homemade *báijiǔ* (sorghum liquor) hanging in pig's bladders. The food is imperial cuisine, but with a heavy Shāndōng influence (the original chef was from Shāndōng province), so there is some crossover in dishes. All are very well done, though. The menu is in English. Specialities include: sautéed tofu with ham and pea, braised chicken in chilli sauce, and a dish called 'the fifth pot', which is a pork and vegetable stew. To find the restaurant, walk south down Gongjian Hutong from Di'anmen Xidajie, turn right into 5 Gongjian Wuxiang and you'll see it straight ahead of you.

Kǎo Ròu Jì CHINESE, MUSLIM $$
(烤肉季; Map p72; Qianhai Dongyan; 前海东沿银锭桥; mains ¥40-80; ⊙1st fl 11am-10pm, 2nd fl 11am-2pm & 5-8.30pm) They do good-value roast duck here (¥118), and a range of China-wide dishes, but it's the mutton that everyone comes for – and the lake views from the 2nd floor.

This place has been around for years (it featured in our very first edition of *Lonely Planet China,* in 1984), and its choice location, overlooking Qiánhǎi Lake, makes it as popular as ever. It's pricier than it should be, but the atmosphere is fun, and the English menu with photos makes ordering easy. Bag a table by the window on the 2nd floor (only open until 8.30pm), and order the roast mutton (¥98), a hot plate from heaven. If you're stuck for cash, fill up on freshly roasted sesame-seed buns (¥2 each), called 'sesame cakes' on the menu.

Dashilar & Xīchéng South

Liú Family Noodles NOODLES $
(刘家人刀削面; Liú Jiārén Dāoxiāomiàn; Map p87; 6 Tieshuxie Jie; 铁树斜街6号; noodles from ¥8; ⊙11am-3pm & 5-10pm; ⓢ Qianmen) A rarity in this area: a restaurant that welcomes foreigners without trying to overcharge them. On the contrary, the prices couldn't be much lower, while the friendly owner is keen to practise her (limited) English. Choose from a selection of tasty noodle and cold dishes. To find it, look for the black sign with 'Best Noodles in China' written in English.

🍷 Drinking & Nightlife

There are three or four top spots for a night out in Běijīng. **Sānlǐtún** (三里屯; Map p80), loud, brash and relatively expensive, is where expats and Chinese party-goers go when they want to drink all night long. Here you'll find the city's best cocktail bars, biggest night clubs and seediest dives. Head to Sanlitun Lu or the Workers Stadium.

Nanluogu Xiang (南锣鼓巷; Map p72) is far more laid-back than Sānlǐtún. This historic *hútòng,* and the network of lanes branching off it, houses smaller bars – some in converted courtyards – that are better for a drink and a chat rather than dancing. The city's coolest live-music venues are in this area too. Head to Nanluogu Xiang, Beiluogu Xiang, Baochao Hutong, or the square between the Drum & Bell Towers.

At **Hòuhǎi Lakes** (后海; Map p84) there's a noisy but undoubtedly fun strip of bars, located attractively on the banks of Hòuhǎi and Qiánhǎi Lakes and specialising in neon-lit guitar bars with karaoke on tap. More popular with Chinese drinkers than foreigners.

The once quiet residential lane of **Fangjia Hutong** (方家胡同; Map p72), just south of the Confucius Temple, has recently become another drinking hotspot with quirky, laid-back bars similar to those found in the Nanluogu Xiang area.

BEIJING DRINKING & NIGHTLIFE

TOP TEAHOUSES

Láijīnyǔxuān Teahouse (来今雨轩茶社; Láijīnyǔxuān Cháshè; inside Zhōngshān Park; 中山公园; Zhōngshān Gōngyuán; tea from ¥38 per cup; ⊘ 9am-9pm) This 100-year-old teahouse, set inside the grounds of Zhōngshān Park, has a large terrace in the east corner of the park and is a pleasant place to sample a cup of China's finest. A number of well-known writers, intellectuals and revolutionaries used to hang out here. These days it's mostly tourists, of course.

You'll pay around ¥180 to ¥380 for a pot, but you can get a cup for less than ¥40, which, as always, can be topped up with hot water as many times as you wish. The traditional Chinese biscuit-cakes (¥20 for four) are tasty accompaniments. English tea menu.

Tángrén Teahouse (唐人茶道听茶轩; Tángrén Chádàoyīn Cháxuān; Map p72; 15 Qianhai Nanyan; 前海南沿15号; tea from ¥40 per cup; ⊘ 9.30am-1am) Commanding fine views across Qiánhǎi Lake from its rooftop terrace, this cute teahouse is on a quieter stretch of the lake, away from the noisier bars, and is a delightful spot in which to sample Chinese tea.

Prices are high – you even have to pay extra for the spring water your tea is brewed in (from ¥10 per cup) – but the location, service and ambience compensate. The wooden decor is attractive, as is the tea menu – a bamboo scroll – which is translated into English. Teas are listed to the left of the tea type (oolong, green, black etc) they belong to.

Black-tea Tea Room (巷口红茶馆; Xiàngkǒu Hóngcháguǎn; Map p72; 65 Beiluogu Xiang; 北锣鼓巷65号; tea from ¥28 per cup; ⊘ 10am-10pm, closed Mon) Despite the name, this place does plenty of other Chinese teas besides black tea and is a welcoming little teahouse. The tea menu is translated into English, but one half of the couple who runs the place speaks some English so can talk you through things too. They also sell a small selection of teas and are happy for you to taste before you buy.

🍷 Drum Tower & Dōngchéng North

⭐ **Great Leap Brewing**   BAR, BREWERY
(大跃啤酒; Dàyuè Píjiǔ; Map p72; www.greatleap-brewing.com; 6 Doujiao Hutong; 豆角胡同6号; beer per pint ¥25-50; ⊘ 2pm-midnight; Ⓢ Shichahai) Běijīng's original microbrewery, this refreshingly simple courtyard bar, run by American beer enthusiast Carl Setzer, is housed in a hard-to-find, but beautifully renovated, 100-year-old Qing-dynasty courtyard and serves up a wonderful selection of unique ales made largely from locally sourced ingredients. Sip on familiar favourites such as pale ales and porters or choose from China-inspired tipples like Honey Ma, a brew made with lip-tingling Sìchuān peppercorns.

El Nido   BAR
(59号酒吧; Wǔshíjiǔ Hào Jiǔbā; Map p72; 59 Fangjia Hutong; 方家胡同59号; beers from ¥10; ⊘ 6pm-late; Ⓢ Andingmen) Friendly pint-sized bar, with more than 100 types of imported beer. There's no drinks menu; just dive into the fridge and pick out whichever bottles take your fancy. Prices for the foreign beers start at ¥30, while Harbin beer costs just ¥10 a bottle.

There's also some imported liquor, including a number of different types of absinthe.

There's some street-side seating out the front, but if it gets too packed (it really is tiny) then try walking up the road to No 46, where there's bunch of bars and cafes in a small cul-de-sac.

Zá Jiā   BAR
(杂家; Map p72; www.zajia.cc; Hóng Ēn Temple, Doufuchi Hutong; 豆腐池胡同宏恩观; ⊘ 1pm-2am; Ⓢ Guloudajie) Built into the entrance gate of Hóng Ēn Guàn (宏恩观), a 600-year-old former Taoist temple – most of which is now a household goods market – beautiful Zá Jiā is a cafe by day (coffee from ¥25), bar by night (beer from ¥20). The interior is as cool as it is unique, with split-level seating reaching up into the eaves, and the atmosphere is friendly and relaxed.

Mao Mao Chong Bar   BAR
(毛毛虫; Máo Máo Chóng; Map p72; 12 Banchang Hutong; 板厂胡同12号; beers from ¥35, cocktails ¥40-50; ⊘ 7pm-midnight, closed Mon & Tue; Ⓢ Nanluoguxiang) This small but lively expat favourite has a rustic interior, good-value cocktails and a no-smoking policy. Its pizzas (¥40 to ¥65) also get rave reviews.

Mài BAR
(麦; Map p72; 40 Beiluogu Xiang; 北锣鼓巷40号; cocktails from ¥45, beers from ¥30; ⊙6pm-2am; ⑤Guloudajie) This area's first proper cocktail bar, Mài is funky, friendly and housed in a beautifully renovated part of an old courtyard building. Most importantly, though, the manager mixes very good cocktails.

Mado BAR
(麻朵; Má Duǒ; Map p72; 60 Baochao Hutong; 宝抄胡同60号; beers from ¥15; ⊙summer 2pm-2am, winter 7pm-2am; ⑤Shichai or Gulou Dajie) Friendly, no-frills bar with good-priced drinks and a large roof terrace.

🍸 Sānlǐtún & Cháoyáng

Nali Patio BARS
(那里花园; Nàlǐ Huāyuán; off Sanlitun Lu, 三里屯路) Sānlǐtún's current drinking hotspot, Nali Patio is a small square surrounded and overlooked by clusters of hugely popular bars and restaurants. The big favourite is **Migas** (米家思; Mǐ Jiā Sī; ☑010-5208 6061; 6th fl Nali Patio, 81 Sanlitunbei Lu; 三里屯北路81号那里花园6层; beer from ¥30, cocktails from ¥60, mains from ¥98; ⊙noon-2.30pm & 6-10.30pm, bar 6pm-late; ☎; ⑤Tuanjiehu), a three-in-one venue which houses a good-quality Spanish restaurant, a cosy indoor bar and a wildly popular roof terrace bar. **Apothecary** (酒术; Jiǔ Shù; ☑010-5208 6040; www.apothecarychina.com; 3rd fl, Nali Patio, 81 Sanlitunbei Lu; 三里屯北路81号那里花园3层; cocktails from ¥65; ⊙6pm-late; ☎; ⑤Tuanjiehu) is Běijīng's best cocktail bar, while Saddle Cantina offers a decent pub vibe, and terrace seating. Most places are open from around midday until the early hours.

Just round the corner from Nali Patio, behind Saddle Cantina, is **First Floor** (壹楼; Yī Lóu; ☑010-6413 0587; ground fl, Tongli Studios, Sanlitun Houjie; 三里屯后街同里1层; beer from ¥20, cocktails from ¥40; ⊙10am-2am; ⑤Tuanjiehu), which is another popular pub-like venue, and **Tree** (树酒吧; Shù Jiǔbā; ☑010-6415 1954; 43 Sanlitun Beijie; 三里屯北街43号; beers from ¥20; ⊙10am-2am; ⑤Tuanjiehu), which does dozens of Belgian beers plus great pizza.

🍸 Běihǎi Park & Xīchéng North

Hòuhǎi Bar Strip BARS
(Map p72; Silver Ingot Bridge; 后海银锭桥; ⊙noon-late) For a peek at how moneyed Běijīngers party the night away, take a stroll around the neon-lit bars lining the lakes either side of Silver Ingot Bridge (银锭桥; Yíndìng Qiáo).

Fabulously located, and with roof terraces overlooking the lakes, these potentially peaceful drinking holes are transformed into noisy guitar bars and karaoke joints come evening, and fitted with speakers facing out onto the lakeshore. Inside, punters sing songs, play dice games or just down shots until they have to be carried home. All the bars are similar, so it's best just to walk around and see which one takes your fancy. Drinks prices start high, but can be negotiated. The further you walk away from Silver Ingot Bridge, the quieter the bars become.

☆ Entertainment

☆ Forbidden City & Dōngchéng Central

Forbidden City Concert Hall CLASSICAL MUSIC
(中山公园音乐堂; Zhōngshān Gōngyuán Yīnyuè Táng; ☑010-6559 8285; Zhongshan Park; 中山公园内; tickets ¥30-880; ⊙performances 7.30pm; ⑤Tian'anmen West) Located on the eastern side of Zhōngshān Park, this is a wonderfully romantic venue for performances of classical and traditional Chinese music. It's also the best acoustically.

☆ Drum Tower & Dōngchéng North

★ Jiāng Hú LIVE MUSIC
(江湖酒吧; Jiāng Hú Jiǔbā; Map p72; 7 Dongmianhua Hutong, 东棉花胡同7号; admission ¥30-50; ⊙7pm-2am, closed Mon; ⑤Nanluoguxiang) One of the coolest places to hear Chinese indie and rock bands, Jiāng Hú, run by a trombone-playing, music-loving manager, is housed in a small courtyard and packs in the

punters on a good night. Intimate, cool, and a decent spot for a drink in a courtyard, even when no bands are playing. Beers from ¥25.

Yúgōng Yíshān
LIVE MUSIC

(愚公移山; Map p72; ☑ 010-6404 2711; www.yugongyishan.com; 3-2 Zhangzizhong Lu, West Courtyard; 张自忠路3-2、号段祺瑞执政府旧址西院; admission from ¥50; ⊗ 7pm-2am; ⑤ Zhangzizhonglu) Reputedly one of the most haunted places in Běijīng, this historic building has been home to Qing-dynasty royalty, warlords and the occupying Japanese army in the 1930s. You could probably hear the ghosts screaming if it wasn't for the array of local and foreign bands, solo artists and DJs who take to the stage here every week.

Pénghāo Theatre
THEATRE

(蓬蒿剧场, Pénghāo Jùchǎng; Map p72; ☑ 010-6400 6452; www.penghaotheatre.com; in an alley beside 35 Dongmianhua Hutong; 东棉花胡同35号; tickets from ¥50; ⑤ Nanluoguxiang) Students from the nearby drama academy sometimes perform here, in this small informal nonprofit theatre, tucked away down a narrow, unnamed alleyway between Dongmianhua Hutong and Beibinmasi Hutong. The venue, which doubles as a cafe (drinks only), is enchanting, and has some lovely rooftop seating areas, shaded by a 200-year-old tree which slices through part of the building.

Performances are mostly modern drama, and are sometimes (but not always) held in English as well as Chinese. Check the website for details. Some English spoken.

☆ Sānlǐtún & Cháoyáng

★ Dos Kolegas
LIVE MUSIC

(两个好朋友; Liǎnggè Hǎo Péngyou; 21 Liangmaqiao Lu; 亮马桥路21号（汽车电影院内）; admission ¥30, beer from ¥15; ⊗ 8pm-2am Mon-Sat, 10am-9pm Sun; ☐ 909, ⑤ Liangmaqiao then) Tucked away to the side of Běijīng's drive-in cinema, a couple of kilometres northeast of Sānlǐtún, this fabulously bohemian venue has a large garden with patio seating and offers evening barbecues alongside some excellent live music. This is a great place to hear local bands (punk, rock, metal), especially in the summer when the whole gig moves outdoors.

☆ Běihǎi Park & Xīchéng North

★ East Shore Jazz Café
JAZZ

(东岸; Dōng'àn; Map p84; ☑ 010-8403 2131; 2 Shichahai Nanyan; 地安门外大街 什剎海南沿

2号楼2层, 地安门邮局西侧, 2nd fl; beers from ¥30, cocktails from ¥45; ⊗ 3pm-2am; ⑤ Shichahai) Cui Jian's saxophonist, whose quartet play here, opened this chilled venue just off Di'anmen Waidajie and next to Qiánhǎi Lake. It's a place to hear the best local jazz bands, with live performances from Wednesdays to Sundays (from 10pm), in a laid-back, comfortable atmosphere.

☆ Dashilar & Xīchéng South

Tiānqiáo Acrobatics Theatre
ACROBATICS

(天桥杂技剧场; Tiānqiáo Zájì Jùchǎng; Map p87; ☑ 010-6303 7449; 95 Tianqiao Shichang Lu Jie; 天桥市场街95号; tickets ¥180-380; ⊗ performances 5.30pm & 7.15pm; ⑤ Taranting) West of the Temple of Heaven Park, this 100-year-old theatre offers one of Běijīng's best acrobatic displays, a one-hour show performed by the Běijīng Acrobatic Troupe. Less touristy than the other venues, the theatre's small size means you can get very close to the action. The high-wire display is awesome. The entrance is down the eastern side of the building.

Húguǎng Guild Hall
PEKING OPERA

(湖广会馆; Húguǎng Huìguǎn; Map p87; ☑ 010-6351 8284; 3 Hufang Lu; 虎坊桥路3号; tickets ¥180-680, opera museum ¥10; ⊗ performances 8pm, opera museum 9am-5pm; ⑤ Caishikou) The most historic and atmospheric place in town for a night of Peking opera. The interior is magnificent, coloured in red, green and gold, and decked out with tables and a stone floor, while balconies surround the canopied stage. Opposite the theatre there's a tiny opera museum displaying operatic scores, old catalogues and other paraphernalia.

Lao She Teahouse
PERFORMING ARTS

(老舍茶馆; Lǎoshě Cháguǎn; Map p87; ☑ 010-6303 6830; www.laosheteahouse.com; 3rd fl, 3 Qianmen Xidajie; 前门西大街3号3层; evening tickets ¥180-380; ⊗ performances 7.50pm; ⑤ Qianmen) Lao She Teahouse, named after the celebrated writer, has daily and nightly shows, mostly in Chinese, which blend any number of traditional Chinese performing arts. The evening performances of Peking opera, folk art and music, acrobatics and magic (7.50pm to 9.20pm) are the most popular. But there are also tea ceremonies, frequent folk-music performances and daily shadow-puppet shows.

🔒 Shopping

With much of the nation's wealth concentrated in Běijīng, shopping has become a fa-

DON'T MISS

PĀNJIĀYUÁN MARKET

Hands down the best place in Běijīng to shop for *yìshù* (arts), *gōngyì* (crafts) and *gǔwán* (antiques) is **Pānjiāyuán Market** (潘家园古玩市场; Pānjiāyuán Gǔwán Shìchǎng; west of Panjiayuan Qiao; 潘家园桥西侧; ⏰8.30am-6pm Mon-Fri, 4.30am-6pm Sat & Sun; ⑤Panjiayuan). Some stalls open every day, but the market is at its biggest and most lively on weekends, when you can find everything from calligraphy, Cultural Revolution memorabilia and cigarette ad posters to Buddha heads, ceramics, Qing dynasty-style furniture and Tibetan carpets.

Pānjiāyuán hosts around 3000 dealers and up to 50,000 visitors a day, all scoping for treasures. The market is chaotic and can be difficult if you find crowds or hard bargaining intimidating. Make a few rounds to compare prices and weigh it up before forking out for something.

To get here, come out of Exit B at Panjiayuan subway station (Line 10), then walk west for 200m to find the main entrance to the market.

vourite pastime of the young and the rising middle class in recent years. Whether you're a diehard shopaholic or just a casual browser, you'll be spoiled for choice.

🏠 Forbidden City & Dōngchéng Central

Locals, out-of-towners and tourists haunt Wangfujing Dajie, a prestigious, partly pedestrianised shopping street that's been given a much-needed makeover in recent years and now sports some slick shopping malls, such as **Oriental Plaza** (东方广场; Dōngfāng Guǎngchǎng; Map p66; ☎010-8518 6363; 1 Dongchang'an Jie; 东长安街1号; ⏰10am-10.30pm; ⑤Wangfujing) and **Běijīng apm** (新东安广场; Xīndōng'ān Guǎngchǎng; Map p66; ⏰9am-10pm), as well as plenty of tacky souvenir outlets. You'll also find the well-stocked **Foreign Languages Bookstore** (外文书店; Wàiwén Shūdiàn; Map p66; 235 Wangfujing Dajie; 王府井大街235号; ⏰9.30am-9.30pm; ⑤Wangfujing) here.

⭐**Celadon Story** CERAMICS
(青瓷故事馆; Qīngcí Gùshi Guǎn; 49 Donghuamen Dajie; 东华门大街49号; ⏰10am-7pm) This lovely little porcelain shop sells exquisite examples of China's famous, jade-like, pale-green celadon porcelain. You can pick up small tea cups for ¥30. Whole tea sets start from around ¥300. Staff speak English and are unobtrusive. There are a couple of other tea shops along this stretch of road, selling tea, tea sets and other tea paraphernalia.

🏠 Drum Tower & Dōngchéng North

The wildly popular *hútòng* Nanluogu Xiang (p74), and the many lanes branching off it,

contain an eclectic mix of clothes and gifts, sold in trendy boutique shops. It can be a pleasant place to shop for souvenirs, but avoid summer weekends when the shopping frenzy reaches fever pitch and you can hardly walk down the street for the crowds.

🏠 Sānlǐtún & Cháoyáng

Cháoyáng district has some of the swankiest malls in town, many of which can be found in the eye-catching shopping zone known as **Sānlǐtún Village** (19 Sanlitun Lu; 三里屯路19号; ⏰10am-10pm; ⑤Tuanjiehu). The district is also home to two of the city's most popular (and crowded) multi-floor indoor clothing markets, the **Silk Market** (秀水市场; Xiùshuǐ Shìchǎng; 14 Dongdaqiao Lu; 东大桥路14号; ⏰9.30am-9pm; ⑤Yong'anli) and **Sānlǐtún Yashow Clothing Market** (三里屯雅秀服装市场; Sānlǐtún Yǎxiù Fúzhuāng Shìchǎng; 58 Gongrentiyuchang Beilu; 工体北路58号; ⏰10am-8.30pm; ⑤Tuanjiehu), both of which will test your bartering skills, and your patience, to the full.

🏠 Dashilar & Xīchéng South

Dashilar & Xīchéng South is one of the capital's most enjoyable neighbourhoods for shopping. Apart from Dashilar itself, Liulichang (meaning 'glazed-tile factory') is Běijīng's best-known antiques street, even if the goods on sale are largely fake.

⭐**Yuèhǎixuān Musical Instrument Store** MUSICAL INSTRUMENTS
(乐海轩门市部; Yuèhǎixuān Ménshìbù; Map p87; ☎010-6303 1472; 97 Liliuchang Dongjie; 琉璃厂东街97号; ⏰9.30am-6pm; ⑤Hepingmen) Fantastic, friendly emporium that specialises in traditional Chinese musical instruments, such as the zither-like *gǔzhēng* (some of which come with elaborate carvings on

WORTH A TRIP

MǍLIÁNDÀO TEA MARKET

The largest tea market in Běijīng, **Mǎliándào** (马连道茶城; Mǎliándào Cháchéng; ☑ 010-6334 3963; 11 Maliandao Lu; 马连道路11号; ⊘ 8.30am-6pm; Ⓢ Běijīng West Railway Station) is home to, if not all the tea in China, then an awful lot of it. Although it's mostly for wholesalers, this is a great place to wander for anyone interested in tea; the vendors are normally happy to let you sample some. The market is located 1km south of Běijīng West Train Station; walk south out of the subway station, turn left at the main road, then right onto Maliandao Lu.

them), the *èrhú* and *bǎnhú* (two-string Chinese violins), and *gǔ* (drums). It does great gongs and has many esoteric instruments from Tibet and Mongolia, too. It's on the eastern side of Liliuchang.

Ruìfúxiáng   SILK, CLOTHING
(瑞蚨祥丝绸店; Ruìfúxiáng Sīchóudiàn; Map p87; ☑ 010-6303 5313; 5 Dazhalan Jie; 大栅栏街5号; ⊘ 9.30am-8pm; Ⓢ Qianmen) Housed in a historic building on Dashilar, this is one of the best places in town to browse for silk. There's an incredible selection of Shāndōng silk, brocade and satin-silk. The silk starts at ¥168 a metre, although most of the fabric is more expensive. Ready-made, traditional Chinese clothing is sold on the 2nd floor.

Ruìfúxiáng also has an outlet in **Dianmenwai Dajie** (瑞蚨祥; Ruìfúxiáng; Map p72; 50 Di'anmen Waidajie; 地安门外大街50号; ⊘ 10am-8.30pm; Ⓢ Shichahai).

ⓘ Information

INTERNET ACCESS

Internet cafes (网吧; *wǎngbā*) are everywhere but rarely have English signs, so memorise the characters 网吧. They are generally open 24/7 and cost from ¥3 to ¥5 per hour. You must show your passport, and you may be photographed at the front desk. We've marked some internet cafes on our maps with the @ icon.

All hotels and hostels we've reviewed in this chapter provide internet access of some sort, and numerous bars, cafes and restaurants around Běijīng have free wi-fi.

MAPS

English-language maps of Běijīng can be grabbed for free at most big hotels and branches of the Běijīng Tourist Information Center, but the scale is sometimes too large to navigate accurately, especially in *hútòng* areas. The Foreign Languages Bookstore (p107) and other bookshops also have maps.

MEDICAL SERVICES

Pharmacies (药店; *yàodiàn*) are identified by a green cross and are widespread.

A consultation with a doctor in a private clinic will cost ¥500 and up, depending on where you go. It will cost ¥10 to ¥50 in a state hospital.

Běijīng Union Hospital (协和医院, Xiéhé Yīyuàn; Map p66; ☑ 010-6915 6699, emergency 010-6915 9180; 53 Dongdan Beidajie, Dōngchéng; ⊘ 24hr) A recommended hospital, open 24 hours and with a full range of facilities for inpatient and outpatient care, plus a pharmacy. Head for **International Medical Services** (国际医疗部, Guójì Yīliáo Bù; ☑ 010-6915 6699), a wing reserved for foreigners which has English-speaking staff and telephone receptionists.

Běijīng United Family Hospital (和睦家医疗, Hémùjiā Yīliáo; ☑ 4008 919191, 24hr emergency hotline 010-5927 7120; www.unitedfamilyhospitals.com; 2 Jiangtai Lu, Cháoyáng; ⊘ 24hr) Can provide alternative medical treatments, along with a comprehensive range of inpatient and outpatient care. There is a critical care unit. Emergency room staffed by expat physicians.

MONEY

ATMs (取款机; *qǔkuǎnjī*) taking international cards are in abundance, including at the airport. Carry cash at all times as credit cards are much less widely accepted than you'd expect.

Foreign currency and travellers cheques can be changed at large branches of most banks, at the airport and in top-end hotels.

For international money transfers, branches of **Western Union** (☑ 800 820 8668; www.westernunion.com) can be found at post offices across town.

Banks

Bank of China (中国银行, Zhōngguó Yínháng; Map p66; ☑ 010-6513 2214; 19 Dong'anmen Dajie, 东城区东安门大街19号, Dōngchéng District) By the Dōnghuámén Night Market, this is one of dozens of branches around Běijīng with money-changing facilities.

HSBC (汇丰银行, Huìfēng Yínháng; Map p66; ☑ 010-6526 0668, nationwide 800 820 8878; www.hsbc.com.cn; 1st fl, Block A, COFCO Plaza, 8 Jianguomennei Dajie, Dōngchéng; ⊘ 9am-5pm Mon-Fri, 10am-6pm Sat) One of 12 branches in the capital.

POST

Most **post offices** (邮局; yóujú) are open daily between 9am and 6pm. We've marked some on our Běijīng maps.

Letters and parcels marked 'Poste Restante, Běijīng Main Post Office' will arrive at the **International Post Office** (国际邮电局, Guójì Yóudiàn Jú; ☑ 010-6512 8114; Jianguomen Beidajie, Cháoyáng; ⊙ 8.30am-6pm).

Both outgoing and incoming packages will be opened and inspected. If you're sending a parcel, don't seal the package until you've had it inspected.

Express Mail Service (EMS; 快递; kuàidì) is available for registered deliveries to domestic and international destinations from most post offices. Prices are very reasonable. Alternatively, **FedEx** (Federal Express, 联邦快递, Liánbāng Kuàidì; ☑ 010-6438 5560, toll-free landline 800 988 1888, toll-free mobile phones 400 886 1888; www.fedex.com/cn; room 101, Tower C, Lonsdale Center, 5 Wanhong Lu, Cháoyáng, 朝阳区万红路5号蓝涛中心C座101; ⊙ 9am-9pm Mon-Sat) is near the CBD, and also has self-service counters in Kodak Express shops around town.

PUBLIC SECURITY BUREAU

PSB Main Office (北京公安局出入境管理处, Běijīngshì Gōng'ānjú Chūrùjìng Guǎnlǐchù; Map p72; ☑ 010-8402 0101, 010-8401 5292; 2 Andingmen Dongdajie, Dōngchéng; ⊙ 8.30am-4.30pm Mon-Sat) The Foreign Affairs Branch of the local PSB – the police force – handles visa extensions. The visa office is on the 2nd floor, accessed from the north second ring road. You can also apply for a residence permit here.

TOURIST INFORMATION

Hotels often have tourist information desks, but the best travel advice for independent travellers is usually dished out at youth hostels. **Běijīng Tourist Information Centers** (北京旅游咨询, Běijīng Lǚyóu Zīxún Fúwù Zhōngxīn; ⊙ 9am-5pm) have branches across town, including at **Běijīng train station** (Map p66; ☑ 010-6528 4848; 16 Laoqianju Hutong), **Capital Airport** (☑ 010-6459 8148; Terminal 3, Capital Airport), in **Cháoyáng** (北京旅游咨询服务中心, Běijīng Lǚyóu Zīxún Zhōngxīn; ☑ 010-6417 6656; Gongrentiyuchang Beilu), on **Wangfujing Dajie** (Map p66; 269 Wangfujing Dajie, 王府井大街269号, Wángfǔjǐng; ⊙ 9am-9pm) and at the **Hòuhǎi Lakes** (Map p84; 49 Di'anmenxi Dajie, 地安门西大街49号, Hòuhǎi Lakes). English skills are limited and information is basic, but you can grab free maps. The detailed map of the hútòng surrounding Hòuhǎi Lakes, which is given out at the Hòuhǎi branch, is particularly useful.

ⓘ Getting There & Away

As the nation's capital, getting to Běijīng is straightforward. Rail and air connections link the city to virtually every point in China, and fleets of buses head to abundant destinations from Běijīng. Using Běijīng as a starting point to explore the rest of the country makes perfect sense.

AIR

Běijīng's Capital Airport (p1005) has direct air connections to most major cities in the world and every major city in China. Prices vary depending on when you fly and when you book, but as a rough guide, expect to be able to find seats for between ¥600 and ¥1200 for any internal one-way flight from Běijīng.

If for some reason you can't get online, you can also purchase tickets in person at the **Civil Aviation Administration of China** (中国民航, Zhōngguó Mínháng, Aviation Bldg, 民航营业大厦, Mínháng Yíngyè Dàshà; Map p84; ☑ 010-6656 9118, domestic 010-6601 3336, international 010-6601 6667; 15 Xichang'an Jie; ⊙ 8.30am-6pm), close to Xidan subway station. Otherwise, check the following websites for good deals:

C-trip (www.ctrip.com)

eBookers (www.ebookers.com)

eLong (www.elong.net)

Travel Zen (www.travelzen.com)

BUS

Běijīng has numerous long-distance bus stations, including the following.

Bāwángfén Long-Distance Bus Station (八王坟长途客运站, Bāwángfén chángtú kèyùnzhàn; 17 Xidawang Lu) is in the east of town, 500m south of Dawanglu subway station. Destinations include:

Bāotóu 包头 ¥130 to ¥150, 12 hours, 6pm

Chángchūn 长春 ¥221, 12 hours, 9am, noon, 6pm and 9pm

Dàlián 大连 ¥211 to ¥276, 8½ hours, 11am, noon, 2pm and 10pm

Hā'ěrbīn 哈尔滨 ¥301, 14 hours, 6pm

Shěnyáng 沈阳 ¥165, nine hours, frequent (8am to 10pm)

Tiānjīn 天津 ¥40, two hours, 10am and 5pm

Sìhuì Long-Distance Bus Station (四惠长途汽车站, Sìhuì Chángtú Qìchēzhàn; ☑ 010-6557 4804; Jianguo Lu) is in the east of town, 200m east of Sihui subway station. Destinations include:

Bāotóu 包头 ¥130 to ¥150, 12 hours, 10.30am, 1.30pm and 2.30pm

Chéngdé 承德 ¥56 to ¥74, four hours, frequent (5.10am to 5.30pm)

Dāndōng 丹东 ¥180, 12 hours, one daily (4pm)

BUSES TO/FROM THE MONGOLIAN BORDER

Cheaper than the train and easier to snag tickets for, the sleeper bus to the Mongolian border at Èrlián (二连) is a viable budget option for overlanders heading to Mongolia.

Numerous buses (¥180, 12 hours) leave at around the same time (between 4pm and 5pm) from **Mùxīyuán Bus Station** (木樨园汽车站; Mùxīyuán qìchēzhàn; Dahongmen Lu; 大红门路); turn left out of Exit D of Liujiayuan subway station and keep walking straight for about 1km. Just before the road goes under Mùxīyuán Bridge, bear left, then left again down Dahongmen Lu (大红门路) and the bus station will be on your right after 500m. You can't pre-book tickets, but turning up anytime before 3pm should guarantee you a berth.

From Èrlián you can catch a bus (¥50, 1.30pm & 3pm) or a shared jeep or minivan (same price) over the border to Zamyn Uud, from where you can catch a train to Ulaanbaatar (5.35pm and, on some days, 9.25pm).

Arriving in Běijīng from the Mongolian border (usually in the early hours of the morning), buses will drop you near, but not in, Mùxīyuán Bus Station. From the drop-off, it's a 1.5km walk to Liujiayuan subway station; walk down the steps in front of you and turn right along the main highway. The first subway of the day is at 5.45am. If you need to take a taxi, avoid the black cabs that hustle passengers at the bus drop-off (they won't use meters), and hail a genuine blue-and-yellow painted taxi from the main road. At night, using the meter, it should cost around ¥40 to get to the Drum Tower from here.

Jìxiàn 蓟县 ¥19 to ¥24, two hours, frequent (5.10am to 7.30pm)

Liùlǐqiáo Long-Distance Bus Station (Liùlǐqiáo Chángtúzhàn; ☎ 010-8383 1716) is in the southwest of town, with its own subway stop. Destinations include:

Chéngdé 承德 ¥85, four hours, frequent (5.40am to 6.40pm)

Dàtóng 大同 ¥100 to ¥132, 4½ hours, frequent (7.10am to 6pm)

Héféi 合肥 ¥299, 13 hours, one daily (1.45pm)

Luòyáng 洛阳 ¥129 to ¥149, 10 hours, six daily (8.30am to 10pm)

Shíjiāzhuāng 石家庄 ¥75 to ¥90, 3½ hours, frequent (6.30am to 8.55pm)

Xiàmén 厦门 ¥479 to ¥519, 30 hours, two daily (11am and 11.30am)

Xī'ān 西安 ¥259, 12 hours, one daily (5.45pm)

Zhèngzhōu 郑州 ¥129 to ¥149, 8½ hours, nine daily (8.30am to 8.30pm)

TRAIN

When buying tickets at train stations, arm yourself with a few key Chinese phrases, or better still have a Chinese person write down what you want so you can show the ticket seller. Increasingly, ticket sellers at the three main stations speak a bit of English, but don't bank on it.

Many hotels and hostels can buy train tickets for you, for a commission, of course. Official **train ticket offices** (火车票代售处; huǒchēpiào dàishòuchù) are dotted around town and charge a very reasonable ¥10 commission per ticket. But although they have an English sign, English-language skills are usually nonexistent.

China DIY Travel (p1015) is transparent and reliable, and can pre-book train tickets for you, China-wide.

It's usually best to buy train tickets in advance, but if travelling on bullet trains to relatively nearby destinations such as Tiānjīn or Shíjiāzhuāng, you can simply turn up at the station and buy a ticket for the next most available train. You'll rarely have to wait more than an hour.

Běijīng has three major train stations for long-distance travel: Běijīng Train Station, Běijīng West Station and Běijīng South Station, all of which are connected to the subway system.

Běijīng Train Station (北京站; Běijīng Zhàn; ☎ 010-5101 9999) The most central of Běijīng's main stations is mainly for T-class trains (tèkuài), slow trains and trains bound for the northeast. Slower trains to Shànghǎi also leave from here. Most fast trains heading south now depart from Běijīng South Train Station or Běijīng West Train Station.

Approximate travel times and typical train fares (hard-sleeper unless indicated):

Dàlián 大连 Z-series train, soft-sleeper ¥372 to ¥388, 10½ hours (8.27pm)

Dàlián 大连 K-series, ¥239 to ¥255, 12 hours (8.06pm)

Dàtóng 大同 K-series, ¥99 to ¥107, six hours (frequent)

Hā'ěrbīn 哈尔滨 D-series, soft-seat ¥306, 10 hours (10.02am, 1.51pm and 3.15pm)

Hā'ěrbīn 哈尔滨 T-series, ¥261 to ¥279, 12 hours (6.18am, noon, 6.57pm and 9.23pm)

Jílín 吉林 T-series, ¥244 to ¥261, 12 hours (4.55pm)

Shànghǎi 上海 T-series, soft-sleeper ¥476 to ¥497, 14 hours (7.33pm)

Běijīng West Train Station (北京西站; Běijīng Xī Zhàn; ☑ 010-5182 6253) This gargantuan station accommodates fast Z-series trains, such as the following (fares are soft-sleeper unless indicated):

Chángshā 长沙 ¥504 to ¥527, 13 hours (6.01pm)

Fúzhōu 福州 ¥426 to ¥456, 20 hours (2.47pm)

Hànkǒu (Wǔhàn) 汉口 ¥407 to ¥427, 10 hours (8.49pm)

Lánzhōu 兰州 Z- and T-series, hard-sleeper ¥322 to ¥388, 17 hours (five trains daily)

Nánchāng 南昌 Hard-sleeper ¥296 to ¥407, 11½ hours (12.02pm, 2.06pm and 8.16pm)

Wǔchāng (Wǔhàn) 武昌 Hard-sleeper ¥261 to ¥279, 10 hours (8.55pm and 9.55pm)

Xī'ān 西安 Z- and T-series, hard-sleeper ¥254 to ¥288, 11 to 12 hours (eight trains daily)

Xī'ān 西安 G-series, 2nd-class seat ¥515, five to six hours (seven trains daily)

Kowloon (Hong Kong) 九龙 ¥584 to ¥611, 24 hours (train Q97, 1.08pm)

Other typical train fares for hard-sleeper tickets, and approximate travel times:

Chángshā 长沙 T- and K-series, ¥322 to ¥343, 14 hours (frequent)

Chéngdū 成都 T- and K-series, ¥389 to ¥486, 26 to 31 hours (9am, 11.08am, 6.29pm and 9.52pm)

Chóngqìng 重庆 T- and K-class trains, ¥389 to ¥456, 25 to 30 hours (five daily)

Guǎngzhōu 广州 T- and K-class trains, ¥426 to ¥456, 21 hours (five daily)

Guìyáng 贵阳 T- and K-series, ¥465 to ¥487, 29 hours (3.58pm and 4.57pm)

Kūnmíng 昆明 T-series, ¥536 to ¥575, 38 hours (6.26am and 4.31pm)

Shēnzhèn 深圳 T- and K-series, ¥434 to ¥464, 24 to 29 hours (8.12pm and 11.45pm)

Shíjiāzhuāng 石家庄 D-series, 2nd-class seat, ¥81 to ¥86, two hours (frequent)

Ūrümqi 乌鲁木齐 T-series, ¥536 to ¥585, 34 hours (10.01am and 3.18pm)

Xīníng 西宁 T-series, ¥353 to ¥428, 20 to 24 hours (11.56am, 4.37pm and 8pm)

Yíchāng 宜昌 K-series, ¥310 to ¥331, 21½ hours (11.11pm)

Běijīng South Station (北京南站; Běijīng Nán-zhàn) This ultra-modern station accommodates high-speed bullet trains to destinations such as Tiānjīn, Shànghǎi, Hángzhōu and Qīngdǎo.

Fúzhōu 福州 D-series, 2nd-class seat ¥765, 15 hours (8.13am)

Hángzhōu 杭州 G-series, 2nd-class seat ¥538 to ¥629, six hours (frequent)

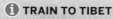

ⓘ TRAIN TO TIBET

For Lhasa (拉萨; Lāsà) in Tibet (西藏; Xīzàng), the T27 (hard-seat/hard-sleeper/soft-sleeper ¥360/763/1186, 44 hours) leaves Běijīng West at 8pm, taking just under two days. In the return direction, the T28 departs Lhasa at 1.48pm and arrives at Běijīng West at 8.19am. See p909 for more details.

Jǐ'nán 济南 G-series, 2nd-class seat ¥184 to ¥194, 1½ hours (frequent)

Nánjīng 南京 G-series, 2nd-class seat ¥445, four hours (frequent)

Qīngdǎo 青岛 G- and D-series, 2nd-class seat ¥249 to ¥314, five hours (frequent)

Shànghǎi (Hóngqiáo station) 上海虹桥 G-class trains, 2nd-class seat, ¥553, 5½ hours (frequent)

Sūzhōu 苏州 G-series, 2nd-class seat ¥523, five hours (frequent)

Tiānjīn 天津 C-series, ¥54 to ¥63, 30 minutes (frequent)

Běijīng North Station (北京北站; Běijīng Běizhàn; Map p84; ☑ 010-5186 6223) This small station is connected to Xizhimen subway station.

Hohhot 呼和浩特 K-series, hard-sleeper ¥129 to ¥136, nine hours (11.47pm)

Bādǎlíng Great Wall 八达岭 hard-seat ¥6, 75 minutes (frequent)

ⓘ Getting Around

TO/FROM CAPITAL AIRPORT

The **Airport Express** (机场快轨, jīchǎng kuàiguǐ; one way ¥25), also written as ABC (Airport Běijīng City), is quick and convenient and links Terminals 2 and 3 to Běijīng's subway system at Sanyuanqiao station (Line 10) and Dongzhimen station (Lines 2 and 13). Operating times are as follows: Terminal 3 (6.21am to 10.51pm), Terminal 2 (6.35am to 11.10pm), and Dongzhimen (6am to 10.30pm).

There are 11 different routes for the airport **shuttle bus** (机场巴士, jīchǎng bāshi; one way ¥15-24), including those listed here. They all leave from all three terminals and run from around 5am to midnight.

Line 1 To Fāngzhuāng (方庄), via Dàběiyáo (大北窑) for the CBD (国贸; guó mào)

Line 2 To Xīdàn (西单)

Line 3 To Běijīng Train Station (北京站; Běi-jīng Zhàn), via Dōngzhímén (东直门), Dōngsì Shítiáo (东四十条) and Cháoyángmén (朝阳门)

Line 7 To Běijīng West Train Station (西站; xī zhàn)

INTERNATIONAL TRAINS

Mongolia

Two direct weekly trains leave from Bĕijīng Train Station to the Mongolian capital of Ulaanbaatar (乌兰巴托; Wūlánbātuō): the **Trans-Mongolian Railway train K3** goes via Ulaanbaatar en route to Moscow, and leaves every Wednesday (hard-sleeper/soft-sleeper/deluxe ¥1222/1723/1883, 11.22am, 27 hours). Meanwhile the **K23** service has a train which leaves on Tuesdays (¥1222/1723/1883, 11.22am, 27 hours).

In the other direction, the **K4** leaves Ulaanbaatar at 7.15am on Tuesday and arrives in Bĕijīng at 11.40am on Wednesday. The **K24** departs from Ulaanbaatar at 7.15am on Thursday and reaches Bĕijīng the following day at 11.40pm.

Russia

The Trans-Siberian Railway runs from Bĕijīng to Moscow (莫斯科; Mòsīkē) via two routes: the **Trans-Mongolian Railway train K3** (¥3496/5114/5604; 11.22am) and the **Trans-Manchurian Railway train K19** (hard-sleeper/deluxe ¥3891/6044; 11pm). The K19 leaves Bĕijīng Train Station every Saturday at 11pm. It arrives in Moscow on Friday at 5.58pm.

The return **K20** leaves Moscow at 11.45pm on Saturday and arrives in Bĕijīng on Friday at 5.46am.

Vietnam

There are two weekly trains from Bĕijīng to Hanoi (河内; Hénèi). The **T5** (M2 in Vietnam) leaves Bĕijīng West Train Station at 3.57pm on Thursday and Sunday, arriving in Hanoi at 8.10am on Saturday and Wednesday.

In the other direction, the **T6** (M1 in Vietnam) leaves Hanoi at 6.30pm on Tuesday and Friday and arrives at Bĕijīng West at 12.07pm on Friday and Monday. Only soft-sleeper tickets (¥2081) are available.

North Korea

There are four weekly services to Pyongyang (平壤; Píngrǎng; hard-sleeper ¥1017, soft-sleeper ¥1476). The **K27** and **K28** both leave twice a week from Bĕijīng Train Station, meaning there's a train on Monday, Wednesday, Thursday and Saturday. Each train leaves at 5.27pm and arrives the following day at 7.30pm.

Return trains leave from Pyongyang at 10.10am on Monday, Wednesday, Thursday and Saturday and arrive the following day in Bĕijīng at 8.31am.

Visas, Tickets & Tours

Visas aren't available at these border crossings. Ensure you arrange yours beforehand.

You can only buy international tickets through travel agencies in Bĕijīng, not at train stations. For Mongolia, Russia and North Korea, buy tickets at the helpful office of the state-owned **CITS** (China International Travel Service, Zhōngguó Guójì Lǚxíngshè; Map p66; ☑ 010-6512 0507; 9 Jianguomennei Dajie, Bĕijīng International Hotel, Dōngchéng; ☉ 9am-noon & 1.30-5pm Mon-Fri, 9am-noon Sat & Sun), housed round the back of the left-hand side of the lobby of the Bĕijīng International Hotel (北京国际饭店; Bĕijīng Guójì Fàndiàn), one block north of Bĕijīng Train Station. Trans-Siberian/Mongolian/Manchurian tickets can be bought from home, using **Intourist Travel** (www.intourist.com), which has branches in the UK, the USA, Canada, Finland and Poland.

For Vietnam, buy tickets at the office of **CRTS** (China Railway Travel Service, 中国铁道旅行社, Zhōngguó Tiĕdào Lǚxíngshè; ☑ 010-5182 6541; 20 Beifengwo Lu, 北蜂窝路20号; ☉ 9am-4pm). There's no English sign, but it's opposite the easy-to-spot Tiānyòu Hotel (天佑大厦; Tiānyòu Dàxià). Walk straight out of Exit C1 of Military Museum subway station, take the first right and CRTS will be on your left (10 minutes).

For help with booking a tour to North Korea, Bĕijīng's leading tour company to the area is Koryo Tours (p1007).

Line 10 To Běijīng South Train Station (南站; nán zhàn)

Coach service to Tiānjīn (天津, ¥82, 2½ hours, 7am to 11pm hourly)

A **taxi** should cost ¥80 to ¥100 from the airport to the city centre, including the ¥10 airport expressway toll; bank on 40 minutes to one hour to get into town. Ignore unofficial drivers who may approach you as you exit customs and join the line for an official cab. When you get into the taxi, make sure the driver uses the meter (打表; *dǎ biǎo*). Have the name of your hotel written down in Chinese to show the driver. Very few drivers speak any English.

TO/FROM NÁNYUÀN AIRPORT

The very small **Nányuàn Airport** (南苑机场, Nányuàn Jīchǎng, NAY; ☐ 010-6797 8899; Jingbeixi Lu, Nányuàn Zhèn, Fēngtái District, 丰 台区南苑镇警备西路, 警备东路口) feels more like a provincial bus station than an airport, but it does service quite a few domestic routes. Airport facilities are limited to a few shops and snack stalls, and don't expect to hear much English.

The **shuttle bus** (机场巴士; jīchǎng bāshì) goes to Xīdàn (西单; ¥18, 1½ hours, 9am to last flight arrival) via Qiánmén (前门). You can pick up the subway at either destination.

A **taxi** is around ¥60 to the Tiān'ānmén Sq area. Ignore drivers who approach you. Use the taxi queue. Make sure the driver uses the meter (打表; *dǎ biǎo*).

SUBWAY

Massive and getting bigger every year, the **Běijīng subway system** (地铁, dìtiě; www.bjsubway.com; per trip ¥2; ◷ 6am-11pm) is modern, safe and easy to use. At the time of writing, plans had been announced to move from the current ¥2 flat fare to a distance-based pricing system, so fares may well have risen by the time you read this. Get hold of a **travel card** (交通一卡 通; jiāotōng yīkǎtōng; refundable deposit ¥20) if you don't fancy queuing for tickets each time you travel. If fares do go up, the card will get you a discount as eith all bus journeys within the municipality of Běijīng.

TAXI

Taxis (出租车; *chūzūchē*) are everywhere, although finding one can be a problem during rush hour, rainstorms and between 8pm and 10pm – prime time for people heading home after eating out.

Flag fall is ¥13 and lasts for 3km. After that it's ¥2 per kilometre. Drivers also add a ¥1 fuel surcharge. Rates increase slightly at night.

Drivers rarely speak any English so it's important to have the name and address of where you want to go written down in Chinese characters. Remember to keep your hotel's business card on you so you can get home at the end of the night.

TAKEN FOR A RIDE

A well-established illegal taxi operation at the airport attempts to lure weary travellers into a ¥300-plus ride to the city, so be on your guard. If anyone approaches you offering you a taxi ride, ignore them and join the official queue for a taxi outside.

Most Běijīng taxi drivers are honest and use the meter (打表; *dǎ biǎo*). If they refuse, get out and find another cab. The exception is for long, out-of-town trips to, say, the Great Wall, where prices are agreed (but not paid for!) beforehand.

CAR

The Vehicle Administration Office (p1010) on the 1st floor of Terminal 3 – look for the 'Traffic Police' sign – issues temporary driving licences for use in Běijīng municipality. Applicants must be between the ages of 18 and 70 and must hold a temporary Chinese visa (three months or less). The straightforward process takes about 30 minutes and costs ¥10. Once you have the licence, you can hire a car from **Hertz** (www.hertzchina.com), which has an office just along the corridor. Self-drive hire cars (自驾; zìjià) start from ¥230 per day (up to 150km per day), with a ¥10,000 deposit. A car-with-driver service (代驾; dàijià) is also available (from ¥660 per day).

BUS

Běijīng's buses (公共汽车; gōnggòng qìchē) have always been numerous and dirt cheap (from ¥1), but they're now easier to use for non-Chinese-speakers, with swipe cards, announcements in English, and bus stop signs written in pinyin as well as Chinese characters. Nevertheless, it's still a challenge to get from A to B successfully, and the buses are still as packed as ever, so you rarely see foreigners climbing aboard. At the time of writing, Běijīng's government had indicated that fares would rise in the near future.

If you use a travel card, you get 60% discount on all journeys. Useful routes:

2 Qianmen, north on Dongdan Beidajie, Dongsi Nandajie, Dongsi Beidajie, Lama Temple

5 Deshengmen, Di'anmen, Beihai Park, Xihuamen, Zhongshan Park, Qianmen

20 Běijīng South Train Station, Tianqiao, Dashilar, Tiān'ānmén Sq, Wangfujing, Dongdan, Běijīng Train Station

52 Běijīng West Train Station, Muxidi, Fuxingmen, Xidan, Gate of Heavenly Peace, Dongdan, Běijīng Train Station, Jianguomen

103 Běijīng Train Station, Dengshikou, China Art Gallery, Forbidden City (north entrance), Beihai Park, Fuchengmen, Běijīng Zoo

AROUND BĚIJĪNG

As well as the following, remember that a number of places covered in the Tiānjīn & Héběi chapter (p127) – including **Jìmíngyì**, **Cāngzhōu's Iron Lion**, and the city of **Tiānjīn** itself – are easy trips from Běijīng.

The Great Wall 长城

See for trips to the Great Wall from Běijīng (p117).

Ming Tombs 十三陵

The Unesco-protected Ming Tombs (十三陵; Shísān Líng) is the final resting place for 13 of the 16 Ming-dynasty emperors and makes for a fascinating half-day trip. The scattered tombs, each a huge temple-like complex guarding an enormous burial mound at its rear, back onto the southern slopes of Tiānshòu Mountain. Only three of the 13 tombs are open to the public, and only one has had its underground burial chambers excavated, but what you are able to see is impressive enough and leaves you wondering how many priceless treasures must still be buried here.

Cháng Líng (长陵; admission ¥50, audio guide ¥50), the resting place of the first of the 13 emperors to be buried here, contains the body of Emperor Yongle (1402–24), his wife and 16 concubines. It's the largest, most impressive and most important of the tombs. Seated upon a three-tiered marble terrace, the standout structure in this complex is the **Hall of Eminent Favours** (灵恩殿; Líng'ēn Diàn), containing a recent statue of Yongle, various artefacts excavated from Dìng Líng, and a breathtaking interior with vast *nán-mù* (cedar wood) columns. As with all three tombs here, you can climb the **Soul Tower** (明楼; Míng Lóu) at the back of the complex for fine views of the surrounding hills.

Dìng Líng (定陵; admission ¥65, audio guide ¥50), the resting place of Emperor Wanli (1572–1620) and his wife and concubines, is at first sight less impressive than Cháng Líng because many of the halls and gateways have been destroyed. It's the only tomb that has ever been opened, but many of the priceless artefacts were ruined after being left in a huge, unsealed storage room that leaked water. Other treasures – including the bodies of Emperor Wanli and his entourage – were looted and burned by Red Guards during the Cultural Revolution.

However, it is the only tomb where you can climb down into the vast but now empty burial chambers. The small **Museum of the Ming Tombs** (明十三陵博物馆; Míng Shísānlíng Bówùguǎn; free admission), just past the Dìng Líng ticket office, contains a few precious remaining artefacts, plus replicas of destroyed originals.

Zhāo Líng (昭陵; admission ¥35) is the smallest of the three, and many of its buildings are recent rebuilds. But it's much less visited than the other two and thus more peaceful; the **fortified wall** (宝成; *bǎo chéng*) surrounding the burial mound at the back is unusual in both its size and form. The tomb, which is the resting place of Emperor Longqing (1537–72), is located at the end of the small and eerily quiet village of Zhāolíng Cūn (昭陵村).

The road leading up to the tombs is a 7km stretch called **Spirit Way** (神道, Shéndào; admission ¥35), about 1km of which is a ticketed tourist sight. Commencing from the south with a triumphal triple archway, known as the **Great Palace Gate** (大宫门), the path passes through Stele Pavilion (碑亭), which contains a giant *bìxì* bearing the largest stele in China. From here, the site's famous guard of 12 sets of giant stone animals and officials ensues.

Eating

Ming Chang Ling Restaurant CHINESE $
(明长陵餐厅; Míng Cháng Líng Cāntīng; Cháng Líng Ming Tomb; ⏲8.30am-3pm) Simple, but clean restaurant, with an English menu, just beside the Cháng Líng ticket office.

❶ Getting There & Away

Běijīng's subway should reach here by 2015. Until then, bus 872 (¥9, one hour, 7.10am to 7.10pm) leaves from the north side of **Déshèngmén gateway** (德胜门) and passes all the sights, apart from Zhāo Líng, before terminating at Cháng Líng. Last bus back is at 6pm.

It's easy to bus-hop once you're here. Get off the 872 at Da Gong Men (大宫门) bus stop, and walk through the triple-arched Great Palace Gate (大宫门) that leads to the Spirit Way. After walking the length of Spirit Way, catch bus 67 from Hu Zhuang (胡庄) bus stop (the first bus stop on your right) to its terminus at Zhāo Líng (¥1); walk straight on through the village to find the tomb. Then, coming back the way you came, catch another 67, or walk (2km; left at the end of the road, then left again) to Dìng Líng, from where you can catch bus 314 to Cháng Líng (¥1).

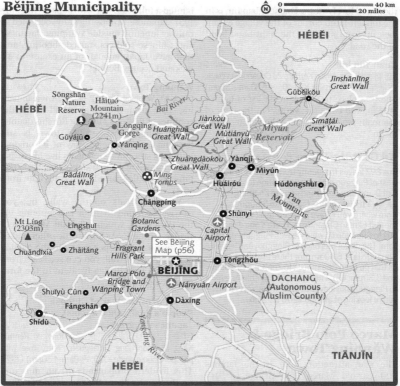

Chuāndĭxià　　爨底下

Nestled in a valley 90km west of Bĕijīng and overlooked by towering peaks is the Ming-dynasty village of Chuāndĭxià (entrance ¥35), a gorgeous cluster of historic courtyard homes with old-world charm. The backdrop is lovely: terraced orchards and fields with ancient houses and alleyways rising up the hillside. Two hours is more than enough to wander around the village because it's not big, but staying the night allows you to soak up its historic charms without the distraction of all those day-trippers.

There are Maoist slogans to track down and temples in the surrounding hills, but the main attraction here is the courtyard homes and the steps and alleyways that link them up. Many of the homes are from the Qing-dynasty, while others remain from Ming times. Some have been turned into small restaurants or guesthouses, meaning you can eat, drink tea or even stay the night in a 500-year-old Chinese courtyard.

🛏 Sleeping & Eating

Restaurant and guesthouse signs are clearly labelled in English, so places are easy to spot. Your best bet is to simply wander round and find what best suits you. Most restaurants have English menus. Specialities here include walnuts, apricots and roast leg of lamb.

Guchengbao Inn　　INN **$**
(古城堡客栈; Gǔ Chéngbǎo Kèzhàn; ☏136 9135 9255; r ¥100, with attached bathroom ¥120; mains ¥20-40) This 400-year-old building is perched high above much of the village and enjoys fine views from its terrace restaurant. Rooms are in the back courtyard and are basic but charming. Each room has a traditional stone *kàng* bed, which sleeps up to four people and can be fire-heated in winter.

The shared bathroom has no shower, but one new room comes with a small shower room and lovely views. Guchengbao Inn is in the top left-hand corner of the village as you look up from just past the right-hand bend in the road.

Cuan Yun Inn
INN $

(爨韵客栈, Chuànyùn Kèzhàn; 23 Chuāndǐxià Village, 爨底下村23号; mains ¥20-40; ⊙ 6.30am-8.30pm) The best place to sample roast leg of lamb (烤羊腿; *kǎo yáng tuǐ*; ¥200). On the right of the main road as you enter the village. Photo menu.

❶ Getting There & Away

Bus 892 leaves frequently from a bus stop 200m west of Pingguoyuan subway station (come out of Exit D and turn right) (斋堂; ¥16, two hours, 6.30am to 5.50pm), from where you'll have to take a taxi (¥20) for the last 6km to Chuāndǐxià. There's one direct bus to Chuāndǐxià, which leaves Pingguoyuan at 7am. The direct bus back to Pingguoyuan leaves Chuāndǐxià at 6.40am, but there are also two buses that go from Chuāndǐxià to Zhāitáng (9.30am and 3.30pm; ¥3). The last bus from Zhāitáng back to Pingguoyuan leaves at 5pm. If you miss that, you're looking at around ¥200 for a taxi.

Marco Polo Bridge & Wǎnpíng Town

The star attraction here is the famous 900-year-old Marco Polo Bridge (卢沟桥 Lúgōu Qiáo), but the unexpected bonus is the chance to see, at one end of the bridge, the enormous, war-torn, Ming-dynasty walls of the once heavily guarded Wǎnpíng Town (宛平城; Wǎnpíng Chéng).

Marco Polo Bridge
BRIDGE

(卢沟桥; Lúgōu Qiáo; ¥20; ⊙9am-6pm) Described by the great traveller himself, this 266m-long, multi-arched granite bridge is the oldest bridge in Běijīng and is decorated beautifully with 485 individually carved stone lions, each one different. Dating from 1189, it spans the Yǒngdìng River, and was once the main route into the city from the southwest.

Despite the praises of Marco Polo, the bridge wouldn't have rated more than a footnote in Chinese history were it not for the famed Marco Polo Bridge Incident, which ignited a full-scale war with Japan. On 7 July 1937 Japanese troops illegally occupied a railway junction outside Wǎnpíng. Japanese and Chinese soldiers started shooting, and that gave Japan enough of an excuse to attack and occupy Běijīng.

Wǎnpíng Town
CITY WALLS

(宛平城; Wǎnpíng Chéng) FREE An astonishing sight, given that you are still within the confines of Běijīng's 5th Ring Rd, this double-gated, Ming-dynasty walled town is still lived in today. Although few of its original buildings still stand (residents live in newish brick bungalows these days), its 2km-long, 6m-high, battle-scarred town walls date from 1640.

You can't walk on the walls, but you can walk around them or inside; enter via the West Gate, which is beside Marco Polo Bridge, or the East Gate, at the other end of the town's only proper road. On the outside of the southern wall, you can see scars from the Marco Polo Bridge Incident in the form of huge bullet holes.

Museum of the War of Chinese People's Resistance Against Japanese Aggression
MUSEUM

(中国人民抗日战争纪念馆; Zhōngguó Rénmín Kàng Rì Zhànzhēng Jìniànguǎn; entry free with passport, audio guide ¥120; ⊙9am-4.30pm) FREE This modern propaganda-driven museum, on the north side of the main road in Wǎnpíng Town, is dedicated to the July 7th Incident (as it's called here) and the ensuing war with Japan. Includes English captions.

❶ Getting There & Away

Bus 662 comes here from Changchunjie subway station (Line 2). Come out of Exit A1 and the bus stop is in front of you on the right. Get off the bus at Lu Gou Xin Qiao (卢沟新桥) bus stop (¥1, 30 minutes) then turn right, beside a petrol station, and bear left to follow the road to bridge and the West Gate (400m).

Dawayao subway station (Line 14) is about a 1km walk from the East Gate of Wǎnpíng Town. Come out of Exit A, turn left at the junction and walk alongside the highway for about 600m before turning right down Chengnei Jie (城内街), which leads to the walls.

The Great Wall

He who has not climbed the Great Wall is not a true man.
Mao Zedong

China's greatest engineering triumph and must-see sight, the Great Wall (万里长城; Wànlǐ Chángchéng) wriggles haphazardly from its scattered Manchurian remains in Liáoníng province to wind-scoured rubble in the Gobi desert and faint traces in the unforgiving sands of Xīnjiāng.

The most renowned and robust examples undulate majestically over the peaks and hills of Běijīng municipality – what we focus on here – but the Great Wall can be realistically visited in many other north China provinces.

Great Wall History

The 'original' wall was begun more than 2000 years ago during the Qin dynasty (221–207 BC), when China was unified under Emperor Qin Shi Huang. Separate walls that had been constructed by independent kingdoms to keep out marauding nomads were linked together. The effort required hundreds of thousands of workers – many of whom were political prisoners.

Ming engineers made determined efforts to revamp the eroding bastion, facing it with some 60 million cubic metres of bricks and stone slabs. This project took more than a century, and the cost in human effort and resources was phenomenal. The picture-postcard brick-clad modern-day manifestations of the Great Wall date from Ming times.

The wall occasionally served its impractical purpose but ultimately failed as an impenetrable line of defence. Genghis Khan dryly noted, 'The strength of a wall depends on the courage of those who defend it'. Sentries could be bribed. Despite the wall, the Mongol armies managed to impose foreign rule on China from 1279 to 1368, and again the bastion failed to prevent the Manchu armies from establishing two and a half centuries of non-Chinese rule over the Middle Kingdom. The wall did not even register with the 19th-century European 'barbarians' who simply arrived by sea, and by the time the Japanese invaded, it had been outflanked by new technologies (such as the aeroplane).

The wall was largely forgotten after that. Mao Zedong encouraged the use of the wall as a source of free building material, a habit that continues unofficially today. Without its cladding, lengthy sections have dissolved to dust and the barricade might have vanished entirely without the tourist industry.

Visiting the Wall

The heavily reconstructed section at Bādálǐng is the most touristy part of the Wall. Mùtiányù and Jīnshānlǐng are also restored sections. These can feel less than authentic, but have the advantage of being much more accessible (with cable cars, handrails etc). Huánghuā Chéng and Zhuàngdàokǒu are part-restored, part-'wild' and offer some short but challenging hikes. Unrestored sections of 'wild wall' include Gǔběikǒu and Jiànkòu, but there are many others. All of the above can be reached using public transport (you can even get to Bādálǐng by train!), although some people choose to hire a car to speed things up. Staying overnight by the Wall is recommended.

Tours run by hostels (¥250 to ¥300 per person), or by specialist tour companies (up to ¥1000 per person), are far preferable to those run by ordinary hotels or general travel companies, which often come with hidden extras, such as a side trip to the Ming Tombs or a gem factory. Most of the Běijīng hostels we've reviewed run decent Great Wall trips. The following reputable companies and associations run recommended trips to the Wall:

Bespoke Běijīng (www.bespokebeijing.com)

Great Wall Hiking (www.greatwallhiking.com)

China Hiking (www.chinahiking.cn)

Běijīng Hikers (www.beijinghikers.com)

Bike Běijīng (www.bikebeijing.com) For cycling trips.

Běijīng Sideways (www.beijingsideways.com) For trips in a motorbike sidecar.

Mùtiányù 慕田峪

Mùtiányù (慕田峪长城; Mùtiányù Chángchéng; adult/student ¥45/25; ⊙7am-6.30pm summer, 7.30am-5.30pm, winter) is a recently renovated stretch of wall, which sees a lot of tourists but is fairly easy to reach. It's also well set up for families.

Famed for its Ming-era guard towers and excellent views, this 3km-long section of wall is largely a recently restored Ming-dynasty structure that was built upon an earlier Northern Qi–dynasty edifice. With 26 watchtowers, the wall is impressive and manageable, and

The Great Wall

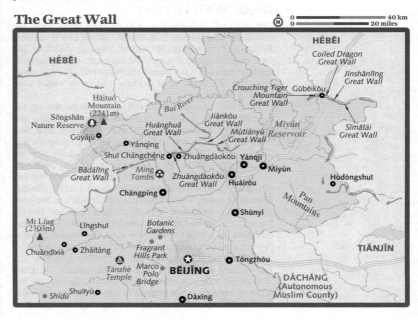

although it can get crowded, most souvenir hawking is reserved to the lower levels.

From the ticket office, there are three or four stepped pathways leading up to the wall, plus a **cable car** (缆车; *lǎn chē*; one-way/return ¥60/80, children half-price), a **chairlift** (索道; *suǒdào*; combined ticket with toboggan ¥80) – called a 'ropeway' on the signs here – and a **toboggan ride** (滑道 *huá dào*; one-way ¥60), making this ideal for those who can't manage too many steps or who have kids in tow.

🛏 Sleeping & Eating

Mùtiányù has a branch of **Subway** (just down from the car park). There are also lots of fruit and snacks stalls. Up by the main entrance is **Yì Sōng Lóu Restaurant** (翼松楼餐厅; Yì Sōng Lóu Cāntīng; mains ¥20-60; ⊙8.30am-5pm), which does OK Chinese food.

Brickyard Eco Retreat   GUESTHOUSE $$$
(瓦厂; Wǎ Chǎng; ☑ 010 6162 6506; www.brickyardatmutianyu.com; Běigōu Village, Huáiróu District; 怀柔区渤海镇北沟村; r ¥1480-1980, ste ¥3990; ❄🅿🛜) 🏊 A 1960s glazed-tile factory renovated into a beautiful guesthouse, sporting five lovingly restored rooms, each with views of the Great Wall. Rates include breakfast, use of a spa, and shuttle services to the Wall and surrounding villages. Brickyard is in Běigōu village (北沟村; Běigōu Cūn), about 2km from the Mùtiányù Great Wall. Reservations essential.

❶ Getting to Mùtiányù

Bus From Dongzhimen Wai Bus Stand (东直门外汽车站; Dōngzhíménwài Qìchēzhàn), bus 867 makes a special detour to Mùtiányù twice every morning (¥16, 2½ hours, 7am and 8.30am, 15 March to 15 November only) and returns from Mùtiányù twice each afternoon (2pm and 4pm).

Otherwise, go via Huáiróu: from Dongzhimen Transport Hub (东直门枢纽站; Dōngzhímén Shūniǔzhàn) take bus 916快 (the character is 'kuài', and means 'fast') to Huáiróu (¥12, one hour, 6.30am to 7.30pm). Get off at Mingzhu Guangchang (明珠广场) bus stop, then take the first right to find a bunch of minivans waiting to take passengers to Mùtiányù (per person ¥10 to ¥20, 30 minutes). After around 1pm, you'll probably have to charter your own van (¥60 one-way).

Return minivans start drying up around 6pm. The last 916快 back to Běijīng leaves Huáiróu at around 7pm. If you miss that, catch a taxi from Huáiróu to Shunyi subway station (顺义地铁站; Shùnyì Dìtiě Zhàn; about ¥100) on Line 15, or all the way back to Dōngzhímén (¥220).

TAXIS AND CAR HIRE

Miles Meng (☑137 1786 1403; www.beijingtourvan.blog.sohu.com)

Mr Sun (孙先生; Sūn Xiānsheng; ☑136 5109 3753) Only speaks Chinese but is very reliable and can find other drivers if he's busy. Does round trips to the Great Wall from ¥600.

Hertz (赫兹; Hèzī; ☑800 988 1336, 010 5739 2000; www.hertzchina.com; ⊙8am-8am Mon-Fri, 9am-6pm Sat & Sun)

Taxi Around ¥600 to ¥700 return day trip from Běijīng.

Warning! If taking bus 916快 to Huáiróu, ignore the tout who almost always gets on this bus at Nanhua Shichang bus stop and tries to lure foreign tourists onto an expensive minibus tour to the Great Wall. He sometimes wears a bus-driver shirt to aid the scam.

Gǔběikǒu   古北口

The historic, far-flung village of **Gǔběikǒu** was once an important, heavily guarded gateway into Běijīng from northeast China. The village, split into two sections by a ridge, with the Great Wall running along it and a small tunnel running through it, contains plenty of old courtyard homes and half a dozen small **temples** (¥20 combined ticket). Various stretches of the Wall meet in and around the village in a kind of Great Wall crossroads that gives you lots of hiking options. One short stony stretch of wall dates from the far-off Northern Qi dynasty (AD 550–77). The other stretches are Ming.

There are two main sections of Wall: the **Coiled Dragon** (蟠龙; Pán Lóng; admission ¥25), which runs along the ridge that cuts Gǔběikǒu Village in two and which eventually leads to Jīnshānlǐng Great Wall, and **Crouching Tiger Mountain** (卧虎山; Wò Hǔ Shān), on the other side of the Cháo Hé River (walk through the tunnel, cross the river bridge, and follow the steps you'll soon see on your right). Both make for fabulous hiking, although Crouching Tiger is extraordinarily steep.

🛏 Sleeping & Eating

All the tourist accommodation is in the recently redeveloped southern half of the village (before the Gǔběikǒu Tunnel), now called the **Folk Customs Village** (it's less twee than it sounds). Get off the bus immediately before the tunnel (if you miss the stop, you can walk back through the tunnel from the next stop), and walk through the archway on the right. There are dozens of **nóngjiāyuàn** (农家院; village guesthouses), so there's no need to book anything (unless you want to stay at Great Wall Box House). Just turn up and look for one you like. They all have English signage, but very little English is spoken. Expect to pay ¥80/120/150 for a single/double/triple occupancy in a simple room with bathroom. All guesthouses also do food (mains ¥20 to ¥40).

★ **Great Wall Box House** GUESTHOUSE $$
(团园客栈; Tuán Yuán Kèzhàn; ☑010 8105 1123; http://en.greatwallbox.com; No 18 Dongguan, Gŭběikǒu Village; 古北口镇东关甲18 号; weekday/weekend, incl dinner dm ¥180/200, s ¥200/220, tw ¥500/550) Run by a young, friendly, English-speaking Chinese couple called Joe and Sophie, this wonderful place is housed in a 100-year-old courtyard building that was an abandoned chessboard factory before being lovingly renovated by Joe. Rooms surround a long, well-tended garden-courtyard, and are large (the dorm is enormous), bright and spotlessly clean. Incredibly, a small, overgrown section of the Great Wall runs along one side of the property.

ⓘ Getting to Gŭběikǒu

Bus Take bus 980快 from Dongzhimen Transport Hub (东直门枢纽站; Dōngzhímén Shūniǔzhàn) to its terminus at Mìyún Bus Station (密云汽车站; Mìyún Qìchēzhàn; ¥15, 90 minutes, 6am to 7pm). The 快 (kuài) means fast. Come out of the bus station, cross the road and turn right to find the bus stop for bus 密25. The 密 (Mì) sands for Mìyún. Then take bus 密25 to Gŭběikǒu (¥9, 70 minutes). The last 密25 back to Mìyún leaves at 5.30pm. The last 980 back to Dongzhimen is at 7pm.

Taxi Around ¥1000 to ¥1200 return day trip from Bĕijīng.

Jiànkòu   箭扣

For stupefying hikes along perhaps Bĕijīng's most incomparable section of 'wild wall', head to the rear section of the **Jiànkòu Great Wall** (后箭扣长城; Hòu Jiànkòu Chángchéng), accessible from **Xīzhàzi village** (西栅子村; Xīzhàzi Cūn), via the town of Huáiróu. Tantalising panoramic views of the Great Wall spread out in either direction from here, as the crumbling brickwork meanders dramatically along a mountain ridge; the setting is truly sublime. This section of the wall is completely unrestored, so it is both dangerous and, strictly speaking, illegal to hike along it. Make sure you wear footwear with very good grip, and never attempt to traverse this section in the rain.

Xīzhàzi village is actually a collection of five hamlets (队; duì) strung out along a valley, to the left of which is a forested ridge, along the top of which runs the Great Wall. You can access the Wall from a number of points along this valley. If you're aiming to hike all the way to Mùtiányù Great Wall, turn left when you hit the Wall. The Wall here has various features that have been given names according to their appearance. They include the following: **Ox Horn** (牛角边; Niú Jiǎo Biān; 90-minute walk to Mùtiányù), which performs a great sweeping, 180-degree U-turn; **Sharp North Tower** (正北楼; Zheng Bei Lou; 3½ hours to Mùtiányù), which is the highest tower you can view to your left when standing in hamlet No 5; **Arrow Nock** (剪扣;

CAMPING AT THE GREAT WALL

Strictly speaking, camping on the Great Wall is not allowed. However, many people do it; some of the watchtowers make excellent bases for pitching tents or just laying down a sleeping bag. Remember: don't light fires and don't leave anything behind. You'll find fun places to camp at Zhuàngdàokǒu, Jiànkòu and Gŭběikǒu.

There are plenty of places to buy camping equipment in Bĕijīng, but one of the best in terms of quality and choice is **Sanfo** (三夫户外; Sānfū Hùwài; ☑010 6201 1333; www.sanfo. com; 3-4 Madian Nancun; 北三环中路马甸南村4之3－4号; ☺9am-9pm). There are branches across the city, but this location stands out because it has three outlets side by side, as well as a few smaller cheaper camping shops next door. Turn right out of Exit D of Jiandemen subway station (Line 10) and walk south for about 800m, then cross under the 3rd Ring Rd and the camping shops will be on your right.

Jiànkòu; six hours), a low pass in the ridge; and **Upward Flying Eagle** (鹰飞到仰; Yīngfēi Dàoyǎng; nine hours), consisting of three beacon towers, two of which (the wings) stand on the highest point of the mountain above the lower middle one (the eagle's head).

The H25 bus terminates at the end of the valley road, at Hamlet No 5 (五队; Wǔ Duì). From here you can access pathways to Upward Flying Eagle (beyond the village) and Arrow Nock (back towards hamlet No 4). Before the bus gets that far, though, it passes through a decorative archway at the entrance to the valley. Here you'll have to get out to buy an **entrance ticket** (¥25) to the scenic area. Hamlet No 1 (一队; Yī Duì) is just through this archway, to your left. You can walk from here to the Ox Horn in about 90 minutes.

🛏 Sleeping & Eating

Yáng Èr GUESTHOUSE $
(杨二; ☑ 010 6161 1794, 136 9307 0117; Xīzhàzi Village No 1; 西栅子村一队; r ¥100; ❄ 🛜) The first *nóngjiāyuàn* (农家院; farmers-style courtyard) you come to as you enter Hamlet No 1 of Xīzhàzi village. Rooms are set around a vegetable-patch courtyard, and are simple, but have private bathrooms. Food menu (mains ¥25 to ¥50) includes some photos. No English.

Zhào Shì Shān Jū GUESTHOUSE $
(赵氏山居; ☑ 010 6161 1762, 135 2054 9638; www.jkwall.com (Chinese only); r ¥100-220; ❄ 🛜) The last property in the valley (in Hamlet No 5 of Xīzhàzi village), this place is a favourite for Chinese hikers (not much English is spoken here). Has a large shaded terrace dining area with fine Great Wall views. Rooms are neat and clean and sleep two to four people. Most have attached bathrooms. Keep walking along the main road beyond where the bus terminates, and you'll see it up to your right. Food menu (mains ¥20 to ¥40) has photos.

❶ Getting to Jiànkòu

Bus Take bus 916快 from the Dongzhimen Transport Hub (东直门枢纽站; Dōngzhímén Shūniǔzhàn) to its teminus at Huáiróu Bus Station (怀柔汽车站; Huáiróu Qìchēzhàn; ¥12, 90 minutes, 6.30am to 7.30pm). Turn left out of the station, right at the crossroads and take bus 862 from the first bus stop to Yújiāyuán (于家园; ¥2; five stops), then take the H25 to Xīzhàzi (西栅子; ¥8, 70 minutes). Note, the H25 only runs twice a day; at 11.30am and 4.30pm.

The return H25 bus leaves Xīzhàzi at 6.30am and 1.15pm, so you can't do this in a day trip on public transport alone.
Taxi Around ¥700 to ¥900 return day trip from Běijīng. From Huáiróu to Xīzhàzi Village, expect to pay at least ¥120 one-way.

Zhuàngdàokǒu 撞道口

The small village of Zhuàngdàokǒu (撞道口) has access to a rarely visited, unrestored section of 'wild wall'. It's also possible to hike over to Huánghuā Chéng Great Wall (黄花城) on a restored section from here, although few people do this – surprising, considering how straightforward it is.

The bus should drop you off at the far end of Zhuàngdàokǒu village, where the road crosses a small stream. Pick up some water and snacks at the small shop near here, then turn right and follow the lane along the stream and up behind the houses until it meets a rocky pathway that leads up the Wall. Once at the Wall (20 minutes), turn right for the one-hour walk to Huánghuā Chéng, or left to commence a tough, two-hour hike along a crumbling stretch of shrub-covered Wall towards Shuǐ Chángchéng (水长城).

🛏 Sleeping & Eating

Zǎoxiāng Yard GUESTHOUSE $
(枣香庭院; Zǎoxiāng Tíngyuàn; ☑ 135 2208 3605; r ¥80-150) This modest guesthouse is housed in a 70-year-old courtyard building, which has some traditional features such as wooden window frames and paper window panes, as well as more recent add-ons such as a shower room and a dining area (you can also eat in the courtyard; English menu; mains ¥20 to ¥50). One room has a private bathroom. It's on your right on the main road, just before where the bus drops you off. There are three other guesthouses on the pathway leading up to the Great Wall.

❶ Getting to Zhuàngdàokǒu

Bus From Dongzhimen Transport Hub (东直门枢纽站; Dōngzhímén Shūniǔzhàn) take bus 916快 to Huáiróu (¥11, one hour, 6.30am to 7.30pm). Get off at Nanhuayuan Sanqu (南花园三区) bus stop, then walk straight ahead about 200m (crossing one road), until you get to the next bus stop, which is called Nanhuayuan Siqu (南花园四区). The H21 bus from here to Shuǐ Chángchéng (水长城) stops at Zhuàngdàokǒu (¥8, one hour, every 30 minutes until 6.30pm).

The last 916快 bus from Huáiróu back to Běijīng leaves Huáiróu at around 7pm.

Taxi Around ¥700 to ¥800 return day trip from Běijīng.

Jīnshānlǐng   金山岭

The **Jīnshānlǐng** (金山岭长城; Jīnshānlǐng Chángchéng; 📞0314 883 0222; summer/winter ¥65/55) section of the Great Wall is a completely restored stretch, but it's so far from Běijīng that it sees far fewer tourists than other fully restored sections. It contains some unusual features such as barrier walls (walls within the Wall), and each watchtower comes with an inscription, in English, detailing the historic significance of that part of the Wall. The landscape here can be drier and starker than at Jiànkǒu or even nearby Gǔběikǒu, but it's arguably more powerful, and it leaves you

in no doubt that this is remote territory. This is the finish point of an adventurous 6½-hour hike from Gǔběikǒu.

Hiking (in either direction) on the restored section of the Wall here is straightforward. There's an east gate and a west gate (about 2km apart), which means you can do a round trip (90 minutes) without backtracking; from the east gate, turn right at the Wall to find the west gate, then right again once back down on the road. If you need it, there's a **cable car** (缆车, lǎn chē; one way/return trip ¥30/50) by the west gate ticket office.

🍴 Eating

Beside the east gate entrance (东门; Dōngmén), is a hotel lobby–like **cafe** (coffee ¥30, beer ¥12, mains ¥20-60) with an English menu and friendly staff who do their best with limited English.

TOP GREAT WALL HIKES

Jiànkòu's Ox Horn to Mùtiányù

Two hours (plus one hour climb to the Wall) Unrivalled for pure wild-wall scenery, the Wall at Jiànkòu is very tough to negotiate. This short stretch, which passes through the 180-degree U-turn known as the Ox Horn, is equally hairy, but it soon links up with an easier, restored section at Mùtiányù. Access the Wall from Hamlet No 1 in Xīzhàzi Village (西栅子村一队; Xīzhàzi Cūn Yīduì; see p121). It takes an hour to reach the Wall from the village; from the sign that says 'this section of the Great Wall is not open to the public', follow a narrow dirt path uphill and through a lovely pine forest. When you reach a small clearing, go straight on (and down slightly), rather than up to the right. Later, when you hit the Wall, turn left. You'll climb up to and round the Ox Horn before descending (it's very slippery here) all the way to Mùtiányù where cable cars, toboggan rides and transport back to Běijīng await.

Zhuàngdàokǒu to Huánghuā Chéng

One hour (plus 20-minute climb to the Wall) A short hop rather than a hike, and on a mostly restored part of the Wall, but this comes with stunning views by a reservoir once you reach the summit of your climb. Access the Wall from Zhuàngdàokǒu Village. When you reach the Wall, turn right and keep going until you eventually descend to the main road by the reservoir. You can pick up buses, such as the H14, to Huáiróu from here (until 6pm).

Zhuàngdàokǒu to Shuǐ Chángchéng to Huánghuā Chéng

Two hours (plus 20-minute climb to the Wall) Climb up to the Wall from Zhuàngdàokǒu Village and turn left at the Wall to be rewarded with this dangerous but fabulous stretch of crumbling bastion. The Wall eventually splits at a corner tower; turn left. Then, soon after, you'll reach another tower from where you can see the reservoir far below you. Here the Wall crumbles down the mountain and is impassable. Instead of risking your life, take the path that leads down to your left, just before the tower. This path eventually links up with the Wall again, but you may as well follow it all the way down to the road from here, where you'll be able to catch the H21 bus back to Huáiróu from the lower one of the two large car parks.

The Coiled Dragon Loop

2½ hours This scenic but manageable hike starts and finishes in the town of Gǔběikǒu and follows a curling stretch of the Wall known as the Coiled Dragon. From the Folk Customs Vil-

❶ Getting to Jīnshānlǐng

Bus A direct bus takes you from Wangjing West subway station (Line 13) to a point about 30 minutes' walk from the Jīnshānlǐng east-gate ticket office. Come out of Exit C of the subway station and look over your right shoulder to see the red sign for the 'Tourist Bus to Jinshanling Great Wall' (金山岭长城旅游班车; Jīnshānlǐng Chángchéng lǚyóu bānchē), from where there are half-hourly buses to Jīnshānlǐng (¥32, 90 minutes, 7.30am-4pm). From the bus drop-off point (a service station on a highway), walk back under the highway and keep going for about 2km to the east-gate ticket office. Note, when you return (turn right out of the east gate area), the bus will pick up passengers from the same side of the highway it dropped you off at; not from the side which has a police station beside it. Last bus back leaves the service station at 4.20pm.

Taxi Around ¥1000 to ¥1200 return day trip from Běijīng.

Bādálǐng   八达岭

The mere mention of its name sends a shudder down the spine of hardcore Wall walkers, but **Bādálǐng** (八达岭长城; Bādálǐng Chángchéng; adult/student ¥45/25; ☺6am-7pm summer, 7am-6pm winter) is the easiest part of the Wall to get to (you can even get here by train!) and as such, if you are really pushed for time, this may be your only option. You'll have to put up with huge crowds of tourists, a lot of souvenir hawkers and a Wall that was completely renovated in the 1980s and so lacks a true sense of historical authenticity. The Bādálǐng Wall is highly photogenic, however, and has good tourist facilities (restaurants, disabled access, cable cars etc).

There is a **cable car** (缆车; lǎn chē; one-way/return ¥80/100) from the bottom of the west car park, and a **toboggan ride** (¥30;

lage (the southern half of Gǔběikǒu) walk up to the newly reconstructed **Gǔběikǒu Gate** (古北口关; Gǔběikǒu Guān), but turn right up a dirt track just before the gateway. You should start seeing yellow-painted blobs left over from a marathon that was run here; follow them. The first section of Wall you reach is a very rare stony stretch of **Northern Qi Dynasty Wall** (1500 years old!). It soon joins up with the Ming-dynasty bricked version, which you then continue to walk along (although at one stage, you need to follow yellow arrows down off the Wall to the left, before rejoining it later). Around 90 minutes after you set off, you should reach a big sweeping right-hand bend in the Wall (the coil), with three towers on top. The first and third of these towers are quite well preserved, with walls, windows and part of a roof (great for camping in). At the third tower (called **Jiangjun Tower**), turn left, skirting right around it, then walk down the steps before turning right at a point marked with a yellow 'X' (the marathon went straight on here). Follow this pathway all the way back to Gǔběikǒu (30 minutes), turning right when you reach the road.

Gǔběikǒu to Jīnshānlǐng

6½ hours This day-long adventure takes in some ancient stone Wall, some crumbling unrestored brick Wall and some picture-perfect, recently renovated Wall, as well as a 90-minute detour through the countryside. Bring plenty of water and enough food for lunch.

Follow the first part of our Coiled Dragon Loop hike, but instead of leaving the Wall just after **Jiangjun Tower**, continue along the Wall for another hour until you reach the impressive **24-window Tower** (there are only 15 windows left). Here, follow the yellow arrows off the Wall to avoid a military zone up ahead and walk down through the fields for about 25 minutes. Take the first right, at another yellow arrow, beside a vegetable plot, and climb the path back towards the Wall. After about half an hour you'll pass **Qing Yun Farmhouse**, where you may be able to buy food and drinks (but don't bank on it). It's a 25-minute climb up to the Wall from here (at the fork, the left path is easier). At the Wall, walk through the cute doorway to get up around the other side of the tower, then continue along the Wall to the restored section at Jīnshānlǐng. You'll have to buy a Jīnshānlǐng Wall entrance ticket (¥65) off a lady at **Xiliang Zhuandao Tower** from where it's about 30 minutes to **Little Jīnshān Tower** (for the path or cable car down to the west gate), or about 90 minutes to **East Tower with Five Holes** (for the path down to the east gate, from where it's a 30-minute walk to the bus back to Běijīng).

called a 'sliding car' on the signs here), which descends to the east car park. There is also disabled access. ATMs can be found in the west car park.

Eating

There are dozens of restaurants on the main drags leading up to the entrance to the Wall. Most are fast-food outlets or snack stalls. Just up from the west car park, between a KFC and a Subway, try **Yong He King** (永和大王; Yŏnghé Dàwáng; mains ¥15-30; ◷10am-9pm), for the Chinese version of fast food: rice meals, dumplings and noodles.

❶ Getting to Bādálǐng

Bus The 877 (¥12, one hour, 6am to 5pm) leaves for Bādálǐng from the northern side of the **Déshèngmén gateway** (德胜门), about 500m east of Jishuitan subway station. It goes to the east car park at Bādálǐng. From there, walk uphill a little, turn left through a covered souvenir-shop strip, then left again.

Taxi Expect to pay around ¥600 to ¥700 for a round trip.

Train Getting here by train is the cheapest and most enjoyable option. Bādálǐng train station is a 1km walk downhill from the west car park; come out of the train station and turn left. Morning trains (¥6, 70 to 80 minutes) leave from **Běijīng North Train Station** (北京北站; Běijīng Běizhàn), which is connected to Xizhimen subway station at the following times from Tuesday to Thursday: 6.12am, 8.34am, 10.57am and 12.42pm; and at the following times from Friday to Monday: 6.12am, 7.58am, 9.02am, 10.57am and 1.14pm and 1.35pm. Afternoon trains return at 1.40pm, 3.08pm, 5.30pm, 7.34pm and 9.33pm (Tuesday to Thursday); and at 1.40pm, 3.52pm, 4.14pm, 5.30pm, 8.06pm and 9.31pm (Friday to Monday).

1

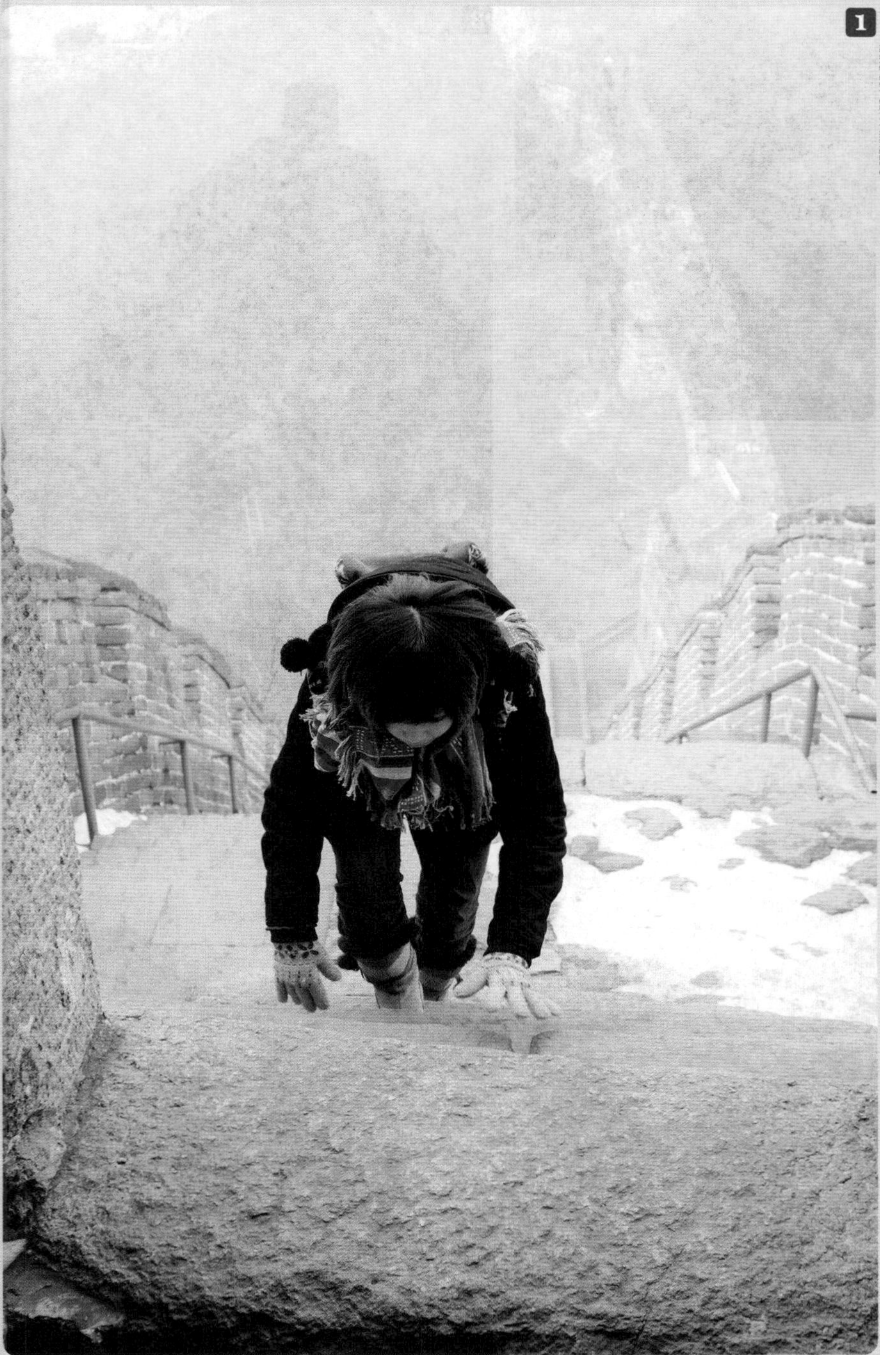

KANG-GG / GETTY IMAGES ©

DAVID ALLAN BRANDT / GETTY IMAGES ©

1. The Wall in winter
A woman climbing the Great Wall's snowy steps.

2. Kite runners
Children flying kites along the Wall.

3. Sunrise over the Wall
Morning sun lighting up two of the Wall's towers.

4. The Great Wall
Visitors to a stretch of the Wall just outside Běijīng.

Tiānjīn & Héběi

Best Architectural Beauties

➡ Lóngxīng Temple (p138)

➡ Pǔníng Temple (p144)

➡ Pǔtuózōngchéng Temple (p145)

➡ Jiǎo Shān Great Wall (p147)

➡ Jiǔménkǒu Great Wall (p149)

➡ Yújiācūn (p139)

Best Off the Beaten Track

➡ Yújiācūn (p139)

➡ Jìmíngyì (p149)

➡ Cāngzhōu's Iron Lion (p140)

➡ Zhàozhōu Bridge (p141)

Why Go?

Běijīng's breadbasket, Héběi (河北) is a slow-moving panorama of grazing sheep, brown earth and fields of corn and wheat. Cosmopolitan Tiānjīn (天津) may put on a dazzling show, but the true charms of this region are its time-worn, earthy textures and its deep-rooted historical narrative.

Héběi offers the ideal chance to disengage from Běijīng's modernity and frantic urban tempo, and experience a more timeless China without having to travel too far. Wander through ancient settlements and walled towns, skirt the wild edges of the former Manchuria and journey to the majestic 18th-century summer retreat of the Qing emperors in Chéngdé.

There are temples galore to explore, rarely visited stretches of the Great Wall and remote towns and villages whose ancient rhythms and rural seclusion make them the perfect retreats for those prepared to venture slightly off the beaten track.

When to Go
Tiānjīn

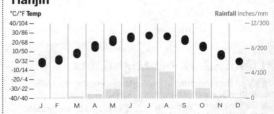

Feb It's bitterly cold, but Chinese New Year temple fairs in Zhèngdìng will warm your spirits.

Apr & May Héběi starts to thaw out after the big winter freeze. Comfortable temperatures.

Sep & Oct Autumn is Héběi's most pleasant season; not too hot, not too cold.

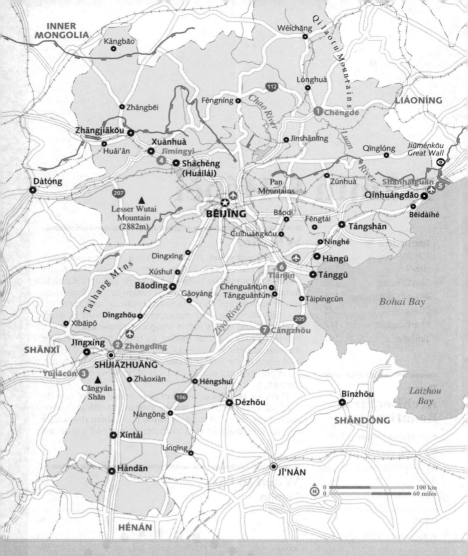

Tiānjīn & Héběi Highlights

① Visit the staggering collection of imperial buildings at the Qing-dynasty getaway of **Chéngdé** (p141)

② Explore the 1500-year-old Lóngxīng Temple in the pagoda-peppered town of **Zhèngdìng** (p138)

③ Step back in time as you walk the cobbled streets of the Ming-dynasty 'stone village' of **Yújiācūn** (p139)

④ Venture off the beaten track to the walled village of **Jīmíngyì** (p149), China's oldest surviving postal station

⑤ Hike some of the less-visited stretches of the Great Wall at the Ming garrison town of **Shānhǎiguān** (p135)

⑥ Sip Italian coffee and quaff a German beer or two in the European-inspired cityscape of laid-back **Tiānjīn** (p129)

⑦ Be one of the few tourists to hunt down the seemingly long-forgotten **Iron Lion of Cāngzhōu** (p140), China's oldest cast-iron sculpture

Language

Héběi is a Mandarin-speaking region, but areas furthest from Běijīng have pronounced regional accents and a distinctive argot.

ℹ Getting There & Around

Běijīng and Tiānjīn are the most convenient bases for exploring the province. Shíjiāzhuāng is also a well-connected transport hub. High-speed 'bullet' trains will whizz you between cities, but buses are best for reaching smaller towns and villages.

TIĀNJĪN 天津

🎵 022 / POP 9.8 MILLION

Forever being compared with Běijīng (if anything, it's more like Shànghǎi), the former foreign concession port of Tiānjīn is a large, booming, yet laid-back city, with a pleasant river promenade and some charming European-flavoured neighbourhoods. It's an easy day trip from the capital, but you may want a couple of days to explore the city properly.

History

Tiānjīn rose to prominence as a grain-storage point during the Mongol Yuan dynasty. The town found itself at the intersection of both inland and port navigation routes, and by the 15th century had become a walled garrison.

During the foreign concession era, the British and French settled in, joined by the Japanese, Germans, Austro-Hungarians, Italians and Belgians between 1895 and 1900. Each concession was a self-contained world, with its own prison, school, barracks and hospital. During the Boxer Rebellion, the foreign powers levelled the walls of the old Chinese city.

Tiānjīn was established as a municipality of China in 1927.

The Tángshān earthquake of 1976 killed nearly 24,000 people in the Tiānjīn area. The city was badly rocked, but escaped the devastation that virtually obliterated nearby Tángshān, where 240,000 people died.

◉ Sights

The grandiose vista that greets visitors as they exit Tiānjīn's Main Train Station signals the city's intent to rise even further. Facing you across **Liberation Bridge** (解放桥; Jiěfàng Qiáo) is a lengthy and ostentatious sweep of rebuilt red and orange Sino-

European pomposity in brick, splendidly illuminated at night. To the west the glittering, 337m-tall **Tiānjīn World Financial Centre** (金融大厦; Jīnróng Dàshà), a singularly bold statement of glass and steel, towers over the river.

◉ Treaty Port Area

South of the station across Liberation Bridge was the British concession. The rebuilt riverside facade is an impressive sight at night, but walk further south along Jiefang Beilu to see original, imposing, hundred-year-old European buildings, which once housed the city's international banks.

Buildings of note, all on Jiefang Beilu, include the former **French Municipal Administration Council Building** (原法国公议局大楼; Yuán Fǎguó Gōngyìjú Dàlóu; Jiefang Beilu), built in 1924; the **Sino-French Industrial and Commercial Bank** (中法工商银行; Zhōngfǎ Gōngshāng Yínháng), dating from 1932; the **Yokohama Specie Bank Ltd** (横滨正金银行; Héngbīn Zhèngjīn Yínháng), dating from 1926; the former **Qing Dynasty Post Office** (1878), the **Hong Kong & Shanghai Bank Building** and the **Jardine Matheson & Co Building**.

◉ Old Town

Originally enclosed by a wall, Tiānjīn's reconstructed old town centres on the rebuilt **Drum Tower** (鼓楼; Gǔ Lóu; Chengxiang Zhonglu; admission free, but must collect ticket from booth opposite; ⏰ 9-11.30am & 1.30-4.30pm) **FREE**, which houses some old photos of the area. Decorated with *páilóu* (ornate archways), the pedestrianised shopping street

Central Tiānjīn

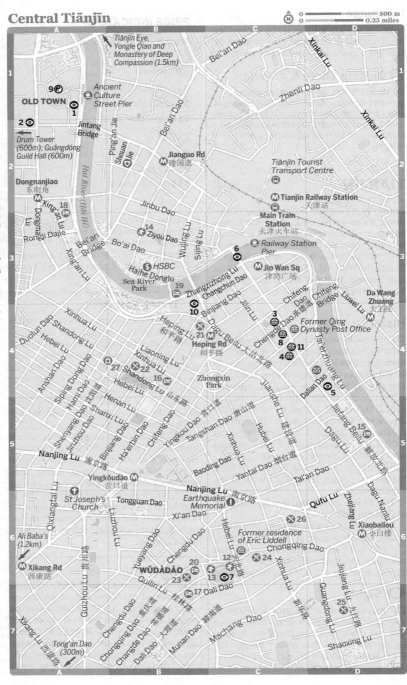

Central Tiānjīn

to the north of the Drum Tower is good for souvenirs.

Opposite the Drum Tower you'll find one of the few buildings of any genuine age in the 'old town': the **Guǎngdōng Guild Hall** (东会馆; Guǎngdōng Huìguǎn; 31 Nanmenli Dajie; admission ¥10; ◎9am-4.30pm), built in 1907. It's a lovely courtyard complex, centred on a beautiful, ornate, wooden hall which holds popular Peking opera performances on Sunday afternoons (¥20 to ¥50, 2.30 to 4pm). Don't miss poking your head into the back courtyard, with its fading murals by the south entrance. The historic (but also largely rebuilt) Confucius Temple is also nearby.

Between the **Confucius Temple** (文庙; Wén Miào; 1 Dongmennei Dajie; admission ¥30; ◎9am-4.30pm Tue-Sun) and the river is **Ancient Culture Street** (古文化街; Guwenhua Jie). Another largely rebuilt section of the old walled town, it's even better for shopping than the Drum Tower area, and is stuffed with vendors flogging Chinese calligraphy, paintings, tea sets, paper cuts and chops. Look out for the famous *Tiānjīn nírén* (天津泥人; chubby childlike clay figures that make cute souvenirs). The fascinating Toaist **Tiānhòu Temple** (天后宫; Tiānhòu Gōng; admission ¥10; ◎8.30am-4.30pm Tue-Sun), Tiānjīn's version of the shrine dedicated to the goddess of sailors that is found in every Chinese seaport, is also located here.

To get to the Drum Tower, walk north from Exit D of Gulou metro station. From the Drum Tower, turn right (east) for the Confucius Temple and the river.

◎ Wǔdàdào

The area of Wǔdàdào (五大道; Five Large Roads) is rich in the villas and pebble-dash former residences of the well-to-do of the early 20th century. Consisting of five roads in the south of the city – Machang Dao, Changde Dao, Munan Dao, Dali Dao and Chengdu Dao – the streetscapes are European, lined with charming houses dating from the 1920s and before.

The centrepiece is **Mínyuán Plaza** (民园广场; Mínyuán Guǎngchǎng; 83 Chongqing Dao; 重庆道83号) – rebuilt in 2012 on the site of a 90-year-old stadium, designed by former British Olympian Eric Liddell, who used to live and work in Tiānjīn (see p132).

◎ Other Sights

Monastery of Deep
Compassion   BUDDHIST TEMPLE
(大悲禅院; Dàbēi Chányuàn; 40 Tianwei Lu; admission ¥5; ◎9am-6.30pm Apr-Oct, 9am-5pm Nov-Mar) Tiānjīn's most important Buddhist temple – built in three stages from 1436 to 1734 – was always noted for its Sakya Hall (Shìjiā Bǎodiàn). Sadly, the hall seemed to be being entirely rebuilt when we were last here. The large hall behind it (also rebuilt) used to house a huge, golden multi-armed statue of Guanyin, whose eyes would follow

ERIC LIDDELL

Olympic champion, rugby international and devout Christian, Scotsman Eric Liddell is best known as the subject of the 1981 Oscar-winning film *Chariots of Fire*, but few know about his connection to Tiānjīn. He was born here in 1902 before being educated in Scotland and then embarking on a short but astonishing sporting career. He was capped seven times by the Scotland rugby union team and won gold in the 400m at the 1924 Paris Olympics. Famously, he pulled out of his favoured event – the 100m – because, as a Christian, he refused to run on a Sunday. A year later, he returned to Tiānjīn to follow his true passion as a Christian missionary, and he stayed in China until his death in 1945 in a Japanese internment camp in Shāndōng province. While in Tiānjīn, he lived at 38 Cambridge Rd (now Chongqing Dao; look for the plaque), and he helped build the Mínyuán Stadium, also in Cambridge Rd, in 1926. It's said that he based its design on Stamford Bridge (Chelsea Football Club's home ground and his favourite running track back in Britain). The stadium was demolished in 2012 before being reincarnated as Mínyuán Plaza (p131). It still has a running track (which is free to use), but the building itself is now a leisure and restaurant complex from where tourists can rent bicycles or hop on horse-drawn carriages for tours of the surrounding concession-era streets.

you around the hall. The statue has now been moved to the smaller Great Compassion Hall, in a side courtyard.

The monastery is close to the Tiānjīn Eye, on the east side of the river.

Tiānjīn Eye
FERRIS WHEEL

(天津之眼; Tiānjīn Zhī Yǎn; Yongle Qiao; adult/child ¥70/35; ⊙9.30am-9.30pm Tue-Sun, 5-9.30pm Mon) To get the city's transformation in perspective, or for a night-time angle on Tiānjīn, ride this huge Ferris wheel which straddles the Hǎi River.

🏃 Activities & Tours

Taking **cruise-boat tours** (per person day/evening ¥80/100) along the Hǎi River is very popular, especially at night. There are three main boat docks; by the **train station** (天津站码头; Tiānjīn Zhàn Mǎtóu; per person day/evening ¥80/100), by **Ancient Culture Street** (古文化街码头; Gǔwénhuà Jiē Mǎtóu) and by the **Tiānjīn Eye** (游船; yóu chuán; per person day/evening ¥80/100). Your boat will pass all three, but you'll only be allowed to get off at the one you got on at. The round trip takes about 50 minutes. Daytime boats leave hourly from 9am to 5pm. The two evening tours leave at 7.30pm and 8.30pm.

In summer, 45-minute **open-topped bus tours** (双层敞篷观光巴士; shuāngcéng chǎngpéng guānguāng bāshì; Marco Polo Sq, 马可波罗广场; per person ¥25) leave roughly hourly from Marco Polo Sq between 10am and 7pm. They pass a number of main sights, including the Old Town and the Tiānjīn Eye, before looping back to Marco Polo Sq.

The quiet, tree-lined streets of Wǔdàdào are ideal for cycling. You can **rent classic bicycles** (租自行车; zū zìxíngchē; Mínyuán Plaza; 民园广场; Mínyuán Guǎngchǎng; 1st hour free, after that ¥5 per 30 minutes, deposit ¥400; ⊙9am-8pm) from one corner of Mínyuán Plaza.

From another corner of Mínyuán Plaza, tourists can take 30-minute tours of the neighbourhood in **horse-drawn carriages** (马车; Mǎ Chē; Mínyuán Plaza, 民园广场; Mínyuán Guǎngchǎng; per person ¥50).

🛏 Sleeping

⭐ **Three Brothers Youth Hostel**
HOSTEL $

(戈萨国际青年旅舍; Gēsà Guójì Qīngniánlǔshè; ☑022 2723 9777; gesahostel@163.com; 141 Chongqing Dao, 重庆道141号; dm/s/d ¥80/138/238) Friendly hostel, with a laid-back atmosphere and a pleasant location right in the middle of historic Wǔdàdào. The small, covered front yard of the 90-year-old building has been turned into a cafe area, while simple but clean rooms are upstairs at the back. Take bus 951 from the Main Train Station and get off at Guilin Lu, which intersects Chongqing Dao.

Cloudy Bay Hostel
HOSTEL $

(云雾之湾; Yúnwù Zhīwān; ☑022 2723 0606; cloudybayhostel@hotmail.com; 120 Harbin Dao, 哈尔滨道120号; dm ¥60-100) Young and friendly, Cloudy Bay is housed in a four-storey building that's been renovated Greek-island-style – whitewashed walls, blue-paint trim, splashes of mosaic tiling. The theme carries over into the cool rooftop terrace (beers from ¥10), although stops short of Mediterranean views. Apart from one private room (¥480), all rooms are dorms, including a female-only dorm.

Orange Hotel
HOTEL **$$**

(桔子酒店; Júzi Jiǔdiàn; ☑ 022 2734 8333; www.orangehotel.com.cn; 7 Xing'an Lu 兴安路7号; d from ¥319, with river view from ¥339; ✳ 🛜) Good value with stylish, unfussy rooms, some of which have river views. Accessed from the rear, via an alley running off Xing'an Lu. Bicycles available to rent.

★ Astor Hotel
HOTEL **$$$**

(利顺德大饭店; Lìshùndé Dàfàndiàn; ☑ 022 2331 1688; www.luxurycollection.com/astor; 33 Tai'erzhuang Lu 台儿庄路33号; d ¥1035; ♻✳@🛜🏊) China's oldest foreign-run hotel, the Astor dates back to 1863, when it was opened by British missionary John Innocent. From the imposing, marbled lobby and solid wooden furniture, to the staff dressed in formal morning coats, there's an old school feel to the place that's hard to find elsewhere.

Make sure you ask for a room in the historic wing, rather than the modern wing, and you'll be rewarded with a four-poster bed, parquet flooring and bundles of charm. The fascinating **Astor House Museum** (admission ¥50) is free for guests.

★ Min Yuan 33
BOUTIQUE HOTEL **$$$**

(民园三三; Mínyuán Sānsān; ☑ 022 2331 1626; minyuan33.com; 31-33 Changde Dao; 常德道 31-33号; r ¥880-1300) Located in a beautifully renovated stretch of 100-year-old town houses, this Tiānjīn trendsetter has minimalist, all-white rooms with stripped-wood furniture and flooring, and tonnes of space.

The same owners run the Malaysian restaurant, **Cafe Sambal**, and the cosy cafe, **31 Cups**, both of which are next door.

St Regis Tiānjīn
HOTEL **$$$**

(天津瑞吉金融街酒店; Tiānjīn Ruìjí Jīnróngjiē Jiǔdiàn; ☑ 022 5830 9999; www.stregis.com/tianjin; 158 Zhangzizhong Lu, 张自忠路158号; d ¥1035-1298; ♻✳@🛜🏊) The last word in luxury in Tiānjīn. Rooms can be nabbed for as little as ¥700 through their website.

✗ Eating

Jīnfú Lóu
DUMPLINGS **$**

(金福楼; 143 Chongqing Dao; 重庆道143号; dumplings ¥3-4 each; ⏰7am-2pm; ✍) Simple, but clean dumplings joint run by a friendly guy who doesn't speak English, but does have an English menu. There's only five things on it, mind, and they're all dumplings (including veg options). No English sign, but it's next to the easy-to-spot Three Brothers Youth Hostel.

Shāguō Lǐ
PAN-CHINESE **$$**

(砂锅李; ☑ 022 2326 0075; 46 Jiujiang Lu; 九江路46号; dishes ¥30-80; ⏰11.30am-2.30pm & 5.30-8.30pm) Of all Tiānjīn's restaurants, this is the one the locals recommend. They flock here for the speciality pork spare ribs in a sweet barbecue sauce, so tender that they pull apart at the touch of a chopstick; the small portion (¥68) is easily enough for two people.

Gǒubùlǐ (Jīntǎ branch)
DUMPLINGS **$$**

(狗不理（金塔店）; 34 Dagu Beilu; 大沽北路 34号; mains ¥30-60; ⏰7.30-10am & 10.30am-9pm; ✍) Tiānjīn's most famous restaurant chain is a mixed bag. The trademark *bāozi* (steamed dumplings), including veg options, are big, juicy and delicious. They're also seriously overpriced (¥46 for eight). Prices for other dishes are more reasonable, but you can't come here without trying the dumplings. English menu with photos. The **main branch** (狗不理; 77 Shandong Lu; 山东路77号; dishes ¥26-70; ⏰9am-10pm) is walking distance from this one, but the staff are less friendly.

Qìng Wáng Fǔ Bistro
BISTRO **$$**

(庆王府庭悦咖啡花园; Qìngwángfǔ Tíngyuè Kāfēi Huāyuán; ☑ 022 5835 2500; www.qingwangfu.com; 55 Chongqing Dao; 重庆道55号; mains ¥50-150; ⏰11am-9pm (lunch menu 11am-2pm); ✍) Top-notch international cuisine served in the lush, lawned garden of the 1922 mansion, Qìng Wáng Fǔ. Lunchtime set menus are ¥68 and ¥98.

YY Beer House
THAI **$$**

(粤园泰餐厅; Yuèyuán Tàicāntīng; ☑ 137 5233 4520; 3 Aomen Lu; 澳门路3号; beer ¥30; ⏰11am-10pm) Despite the name, this cosy, atmospheric place is actually a Thai restaurant with a wide range of flavoursome dishes from the land of smiles. It does, though, have some craft beers too. It's tucked away down a quiet street behind Nanjing Lu.

🍸 Drinking

The rooftop terrace at Cloudy Bay Hostel (p132) is a decent place for a cheap drink.

SHI FAMILY COURTYARD

In Yángliǔqīng suburb, 20km west of central Tiānjīn, is the marvellous **Shi family residence** (石家大院; Shí Jiā Dàyuàn; 47 Yangliuqing Guyi Jie, 杨柳青估衣街 47号; admission ¥27; ⊙9am-5pm Apr-Oct, 9am-4.30pm Nov-Mar), a vast warren of courtyards and enclosed gardens.

Formerly belonging to a prosperous merchant family, the restored residence (originally built in 1875) contains a theatre and 278 rooms, some of which are furnished. Take bus 153 (¥2; 90 minutes) from Tiānjīn's West Train Station, which is on the metro.

Ali Baba's   BAR

(阿里巴巴; Ālǐ Bābā; Bldg 4, Weihua Nanli, off Tong'an Dao; 同安道卫华南里小区4号楼; beers from ¥10, mains ¥20-50; ⊙11am-3am) One of Tiānjīn's longest-running bars, this expat-friendly, slightly gritty, student hang-out has an unlikely location – hidden away in the middle of a housing estate – but is ever popular. Faintly bohemian, and somewhat eccentric, it's a fun place to drink into the early hours, and they do food too.

Come out of Exit A2 of Wujiayao subway station and walk north along Qixiangtai Lu for about 300m then turn left down Tong'an Dao. After passing the road called Wujiayao Si Haolu, take the first lane on your left, and Ali Baba's is up on the right. Alternatively, you can walk from Wǔdàdào (about 1.5km); walk southwest along Chengdu Dao then turn right up Tong'an Dao, from where it's a 600m walk to the left turn for the bar.

Shopping

Binjiang Dao, between Nanjing Lu and Dagu Beilu, is one huge long pedestrianised shopping strip. Nanjing Lu has more modern shopping malls, though.

In markets, look out for *Tiānjīn nírén* (天津泥人) – cute, chubby, childlike clay figures, which are the city's trademark souvenir. You can get them in Ancient Culture Street, as well as in the lobby of the main branch of the restaurant Gǒubùlǐ.

Shěnyángdào Antiques Market   MARKET

(沈阳道古物市场; Shěnyángdào Gǔwù Shìchǎng; cnr Shenyang Dao & Shandong Lu; ⊙8am-5pm) Best visited on Sunday, this antiques market is great for a rifle through its stamps, silver-ware, porcelain, clocks, Mao badges and Cultural Revolution memorabilia.

ℹ Information

A handful of 24-hour internet cafes can be found above the shops around the Main Train Station concourse. There are foreign-friendly ATMs inside and outside the station.

Bank of China (中国银行; Zhōngguó Yínháng; 80-82 Jiefang Beilu)

China Post (中国邮政; Zhōngguó Yóuzhèng; 153 Jiefang Beilu)

HSBC (汇丰银行; Huìfēng Yínháng; Ocean Hotel, 5 Yuanyang Guangchang) There's an HSBC ATM inside the International Building, at 75 Nanjing Lu.

Public Security Bureau (PSB; 公安局出入境管理局; Gōng'ānjú/Chūrùjìng Guǎnlǐjú; ☏022 2445 8825; 19 Shouan Jie)

Tiānjīn International SOS Clinic (天津国际紧急救援诊所; Tiānjīn Guójì Jǐnjí Jiùyuán Yīliáo Zhěnsuǒ; ☏022 2352 0143; Sheraton Tiānjīn Hotel, Zijinshan Lu) From Tianta metro station, walk southeast along Zijinshun Lu and the Sheraton is on your left after about 1km.

ℹ Getting There & Away

AIR

Tiānjīn Bīnhǎi International Airport (天津滨海国际机场; Tiānjīn Bīnhǎi Guójì Jīchǎng; ☏022 2490 2950) is 15km east of the city centre and has flights to all major cities in China, plus a few international destinations, including Singapore, Moscow and Seoul. Buy tickets through www.elong.net or www.english.ctrip.com.

BOAT

The nearest passenger port is the Tiānjīn International Cruise Home Port (p1010), 70km east of the city.

There's a ferry every other evening to Dàlián (大连; ¥260 to ¥880, 12 hours, 8pm) in Liáoníng province. It leaves on even numbers in the month (the return comes back on odd numbers). Boarding starts at 6pm. Tickets can be bought on the day of travel at the port.

There used to be a Thursday ferry to Incheon (仁川; Rénchuān; from ¥1300, 27 hours, 11am) in South Korea (韩国; Hánguó), but at the time of research this had been suspended. It should be up and running again by the time you read this, but not necessarily on a Thursday. The weekly ferry to Kōbe (神户; Shénhù) in Japan (日本; Rìběn) had been suspended indefinitely.

To get to the cruise port, take metro Line 9 to Citizen Plaza Station (市民广场; Shimin Guangchang; ¥11, one hour), then Bus 513 to the last stop (Dongjiang Youlun Mugang; 东疆游轮母港

¥2, 40 minutes, 7am to 5pm). The last bus back from the port is at 6pm.

BUS

Tiānjīn has a number of long-distance bus stations. Note, buses to Běijīng are few and far between these days, now that everyone uses the bullet train.

Tiānhuán Bus Station (天环客运站; Tiānhuán kèyùnzhàn; ☑ 022 2305 0530; cnr Hongqi Lu & Anshan Xidao), about 4km southwest of the centre, can be reached on local bus 50 from the Main Train Station; get off at *chuanranbing yiyuan* (传染病医院) bus stop:

Běijīng (Bāwángfén bus station) ¥40, two hours, twice daily (7am and 2pm)

Cāngzhōu ¥45, 1½ hours, every 40 minutes from 6.30am to 6.30pm

Jǐ'nán ¥120, five hours, one daily (10.20am)

Qīngdǎo ¥170, nine hours, one daily (8.30am)

Shànghǎi sleeper ¥300, 13 hours, one daily (6.30pm)

Xī'ān sleeper ¥300, 17 hours, every other day (3.30pm)

Tiānjīn West Bus Station (天津西站客运站, Tiānjīn Xīzhàn Kèyùnzhàn; ☑ 022 2732 1282; Xiqing Dao), about 1km west of the Tiānjīn Eye, uses West Railway Station (西站; *xī zhàn*) metro stop on Line 1:

Dàtóng ¥180, eight hours, one daily (8.30am)

Qínhuángdǎo (for Shānhǎiguān) ¥100, four hours, one daily at noon

Shíjiāzhuāng ¥130, five hours, hourly from 7.30am to 6.30pm

TRAIN

Tiānjīn has four train stations: Main, North, South and West, all of which are connected to the metro system. Most trains, including bullet trains to Běijīng, leave from Main Train Station. South Train Station is used for bullet trains to east-coast cities like Shànghǎi.

Bullet trains between here and Běijīng make day trips extremely feasible. No need to pre-book; just turn up and buy a ticket on the next available train. You rarely have to wait more than an hour (except on Sunday evenings). The last train back to Tiānjīn leaves Běijīng at 10.43pm.

Note, for some destinations, including Shíjiāzhuāng and Xī'ān, it can be quicker to take bullet trains from Běijīng.

From Main Train Station (天津站; Tiānjīn Zhàn) :

Běijīng C-class bullet ¥55, 30 minutes, every 10 minutes (6.17am to 10.53pm)

Qīngdǎo G-class bullet ¥266, 4½ hours, three daily (2.42pm, 3.50pm and 5.59pm)

Shànghǎi (Hóngqiáo Station) K/T-class hard-sleeper ¥290, 14 hours, three daily (8.33pm, 11.05pm and 11.17pm)

Shānhǎiguān G-class bullet ¥130, 1½ hours, 13 daily (7.30am to 5.30pm)

Shíjiāzhuāng hard seat ¥63, four to six hours, 15 daily (7am to 9.46pm)

Wǔhàn G-class bullet ¥493, seven hours, two daily (9.32am and 11.48am)

Xī'ān K-class hard sleeper ¥300, 18 hours, five daily (1.42am, 2.18am, 2.51am, 11.54am and 4.52pm)

From South Train Station (天津南站; Tiānjīn Nánzhàn):

Hángzhōu G-class bullet ¥495, 5½ hours, 10 daily (8.01am to 3.41pm)

Qīngdǎo D/G-class bullet ¥259, 4½ hours, six daily (7.46am to 2.20pm)

Shànghǎi (Hóngqiáo Station) G-class bullet ¥516, five hours, 20 daily (9am to 6pm)

❶ Getting Around

TO/FROM THE AIRPORT

The metro Line 2 extension to the airport was under construction at the time of research.

An airport shuttle bus (机场巴士; *jīchǎng bāshì*; ¥15, 40 minutes, every 30min 6am-7.30pm) leaves from the Tiānjīn Tourist Transport Centre (天津旅游集散中心; Tiānjīn Lǚyóujísàn Zhōngxīn), outside the north exit of the Main Train Station.

Taxis to the airport cost around ¥60.

PUBLIC TRANSPORT

Tiānjīn's easy-to-use metro (地铁; *dìtiě*) has four lines and runs from around 6.30am to 10pm. Ticket machines (tickets ¥2 to ¥5) have bilingual instructions.

Local buses (tickets ¥2 to ¥4) run from 5am to 11pm.

TAXI

Flag fall is ¥9 for the first 3km, then ¥1.70 per kilometre thereafter.

HÉBĚI

Shíjiāzhuāng   石家庄

☑ 0311 / POP 2.65 MILLION

An archetypal Chinese city, and the provincial capital of Héběi, Shíjiāzhuāng is a frantic, prosperous and sprawling railway-junction settlement with little sense of history. It does, however, make a comfortable base from which to explore gems such as Zhèngdìng and Yújiācūn.

Shíjiāzhuāng

Shíjiāzhuāng

◎ Sights

People's Square (人民广场; Rénmín Guǎng-chǎng) comes alive in the early morning (with legions of taichi practioners) and early evening (when group dancers descend en masse).

Héběi Provincial Museum　　MUSEUM
(河北省博物馆; Héběi Shěng Bówùguǎn; Zhong-shan Donglu; ⊙9am-5pm (last entry 4pm) Tue-Sun) **FREE** It's a colossus of a building; a shame that inside there are far more photos than there are exhibits. Worth a visit, nonetheless.

🛏 Sleeping

Like other cities in Héběi, foreigners are barred from staying in many of the cheaper hotels here.

Silver Spring Hotel　　HOTEL $
(银泉酒家; Yínquán Jiǔjiā; ☑0311 8598 5888; 12 Zhanqian Jie; 站前街12号; d from ¥198; 🕸@☎) Smart, good-value business hotel with welcoming staff and bright, modern rooms. You get good discounts if you buy a lifetime membership card (会员卡; huìyuán kǎ) for ¥28. Breakfast costs ¥18. Free wi-fi.

Huìwén Hotel　　HOTEL $$
(汇文大酒店; Huìwén Dàjiǔdiàn; ☑0311 8786 5818; 6 Zhanqian Jie; 站前街6号; s/tw from ¥358/480; 🕸@☎) This ageing hotel has a bit more character than Silver Spring, and the rooms are very spacious. Also has welcoming staff and wi-fi throughout. Rates include breakfast. After discounts, single and twin rooms go for as little as ¥208 and ¥258 respectively.

🍴 Eating & Drinking

A couple of cute, independently run **cafes** (Zhengdong Lu; 正东路; ⊙11am-10pm) on tree-lined Zhengdong Lu have proper coffee, cold beer and patio seating.

Tudari　　KOREAN $
(土大力; Tǔdàlì; 2 Jinqiao Beijie; mains ¥20-30; ⊙10am-11pm) A bustling, spotless Korean eatery that's open later than most Shí-jiāzhuāng restaurants. Tasty hotpots, including the ever-popular shíguō bànfàn (¥25; meat, rice, vegetables and egg served in a

clay pot), spicy salads and many different barbecued skewer options. Photo menu.

★ **Chéngdé Huìguǎn** HÉBĚI $$
(承德会馆; 12 Zhanqian Jie; 站前街12号; mains ¥20-60; ☉11am-2pm & 5.30-9pm) Specialising in northern Héběi cuisine, this fine place, just around the side of Silver Spring Hotel, is actually two restaurants in one. Ignore the slightly stuffy, posh one on the right and head instead to the more proletarian canteen-like restaurant on the left, where prices are more reasonable, but the food is just as good.

Has a photo menu with some handy Pinyin labelling.

ℹ Information

Bank of China (中国银行; Zhōngguó Yínháng; Jinqiao Beidajie) Round the back of Dōngfāng City Plaza Shopping Centre.

China Post (中国邮政; Zhōngguó Yóuzhèng; cnr Gongli Jie & Zhongshan Xilu; ☉8.30am-6pm)

Public Security Bureau (PSB; 公安局, Gōng'ānjú; 9 Yuhua Xilu; 裕华西路9号)

Tiānyǔ Wǎngbā (天宇网吧; per hour ¥3-5; ☉24hr) You'll need a Chinese ID card to get online, but staff will usually lend you one of theirs.

ℹ Getting There & Away

AIR

Shíjiāzhuāng's airport is 40km northeast of town, and has flights to all major cities in China.

BUS

Buses to Běijīng were fewer and slower than usual at the time of research, due to massive road reconstruction. They usually take four hours, and run at least hourly. The following are just some of the numerous services that leave from the **Long-Distance Bus Station** (石家庄客运总站, shíjiāzhuāng kèyùn zǒngzhàn; Zhanqian Jie):

Běijīng ¥83, five hours, three daily (8.55am, 10.15am and 12.15pm)

Chéngdé ¥160, seven hours, four daily (8am, 9.30am, 11.30am and 2.30pm)

Jì'nán ¥115, four hours, every 40 minutes (7.20am to 5.30pm)

Tiānjīn ¥130, four hours, every 40 minutes (7.30am to 6pm)

Bus services to Zhèngdìng and Zhàozhōu Bridge depart from the **South Bus Station** (南焦客运站, nánjiāo kèyùnzhàn; 🖀 0311 8657 3806), 6km southeast of the centre; to get there from central Shíjiāzhuāng, take bus 30 from outside the former train station on Jiěfàng Guǎngchǎng (解放广场; Liberation Square).

TRAIN

If you don't mind waiting an hour or so, there's no need to book for Běijīng; you'll just need to turn up at the station and buy a ticket.

Shíjiāzhuāng's new **train station** (火车站; huǒchēzhàn; Zhonghuanan Dajie; 中华南大街) is about 3km south of the more central former train station, which is no longer in operation; the area around the former train station is now known as **Jiěfàng Guǎngchǎng** (解放广场; Liberation Square). A few trains also stop at or depart from **Shíjiāzhuāng North Train Station** (石家庄北站; Shíjiāzhuāng Běizhàn; Taihua Jie; 泰华街).

To get to the town centre from the new train station, come out of the station's west entrance, turn left, and take bus 148 (¥1) two stops to changtu qichezhan (长途汽车站) bus stop.

Services, from the new train station unless otherwise stated:

Běijīng West G-class bullet ¥129, 1½ hours, every 30 minutes (6.30am to 10pm)

Chéngdé hard seat/sleeper ¥75/138, 10 hours, two daily (8.57am and 8.20pm)

Dàtóng hard seat/sleeper ¥90/164, six to 10 hours, three daily (3.53am, 4.56pm and 8.51pm, plus two daily from North Train Station at 1.59pm and 7.06pm)

Guǎngzhōu T-class hard-sleeper ¥400, 20 hours, six daily (12.14pm to 8.42pm)

Guǎngzhōu South (from North Train Station) G-class bullet ¥785, eight hours, seven daily 9.08am to 2.28pm)

Jì'nán K-class hard seat ¥47, 4½ hours, two daily (6.23am and 7.10am)

Luòyáng G-class bullet ¥250, 2½ hours, nine daily (8.28am to 5.30pm)

Luòyáng K-class hard seat/sleeper ¥75/138, 8½ hours, 11 daily (7.45pm to 1.22am)

Nánjīng Z-class hard sleeper ¥223, 8½ hours, one daily (10.35pm)

Shànghǎi Z-class hard sleeper ¥280, 11 hours, one daily (10.35pm)

Shānhǎiguān T-class hard seat/sleeper ¥81/148, seven hours, three daily (1.31am, 11.45am and 3.40pm)

Tiānjīn T/K-class hard seat ¥55, four to six hours, 20 daily (7.12am to 1.31am)

Xī'ān G-class bullet, ¥409, four hours, 12 daily (8.28am to 6.59pm)

Zhèngzhōu G-class bullet ¥190, two hours, every 15 minutes (8.20am to 9pm)

ℹ Getting Around

The Airport Bus (机场大巴; jīchǎng dàbā; ¥20, 90 minutes, 4.30am to 8.30pm) leaves every 30 minutes from the new train station; come out of the west entrance and turn right.

A taxi to the airport is about ¥150.

Shíjiāzhuāng's first metro line is due to open in 2017.

Around Shíjiāzhuāng

Zhèngdìng 正定

☎ 0311 / POP 130,300

Its streets littered with needy Taoist sooth-sayers and temple remains, the once walled town of Zhèngdìng is an appetising – albeit incomplete – slice of old China. From atop Zhèngdìng's reconstructed South Gate, you can see the silhouettes of four distinct pagodas jutting above the sleepy town. Affectionately known as the town of 'nine buildings, four pagodas, eight great temples and 24 golden archways', Zhèngdìng has tragically lost many of its standout buildings and archways – Píngyáo it isn't – but enough remains to lend the place an air of faded grandeur. And in Lóngxīng Temple, Zhèngdìng can lay claim to having one of the finest temples in northern China.

Zhèngdìng is an easy day trip from Shíjiāzhuāng.

◉ Sights

Bus 177 from Shíjiāzhuāng stops at all the sights, but you may as well start at the best of the lot – Lóngxīng Temple, aka Dàfó Temple – then slowly walk your way back to South Gate.

From Lóngxīng Temple turn right and walk about 500m to reach Tiānníng Temple (on your right). From here, continue along the same road then, at the crossroads, turn left down Yanzhao Nandajie to reach Kāiyuán Temple (on your right). From here, continue a little further south down Yanzhao Nandajie then turn left down Linji Lu to reach Línjì Temple. Walking further south on Yanzhao Nandajie, you'll soon reach Guǎnghuì Temple (on your left) and finally South Gate.

Opening hours are from 8am to 5.30pm.

★ Lóngxīng Temple BUDDHIST TEMPLE

(隆兴寺; 109 Zhongshan Donglu; admission ¥50) Considering its age – almost 1500 years old – we think this is one of the most impressive temples in northern China. It's certainly Zhèngdìng's star attraction.

More popularly known as Dàfó Temple (大佛寺; Dàfó Sì), or 'Big Buddhist Temple', the complex contains an astonishing array of Buddhist statuary, housed in some stunning temple halls.

The time-worn bridge out front constitutes a handsome historical prelude. Dating way back to AD 586, the temple has been much restored and stands divided from its spirit wall by Zhongshan Donglu.

You are greeted in the first hall by the jovial Milefo (the laughing Buddha). The four Heavenly Kings flanking him in pairs are disconcertingly vast.

Beyond the ruined Hall of Sakyamuni's Six Teachers is the Manichaean Hall, an astonishingly voluminous hall flagged in smoothed stone with amazing carpentry overhead, a huge gilded statue of Sakyamuni and delectable Ming frescoes (bring a torch) detailing Buddhist tales. At the rear of the hall is a distinctly male statue of the goddess Guanyin, seated in a lithe pose with one foot resting on her/his thigh (a posture known as *lalitásana*) and surrounded by *luóhàn* (disciples freed from the cycle of rebirth).

The Buddhist Altar behind houses an unusual bronze Ming-dynasty two-faced Buddha, gazing north and south. Signs say 'no touching' but it's evident that its fingers and thumb have been smoothed by legions of worshippers. There are two halls behind the Buddhist Altar. On the left is the Revolving Library Pavilion (Zhuānlúnzàng Gé), which contains a highly unusual revolving octagonal wooden bookcase for the storing of sutras, and some stele on the back of snarling *bìxì* (mythical tortoise-like dragons). Opposite stands the Pavilion of Kindness, containing a fabulous, 7.4m-high statue of Maitreya (the future Buddha), one hand aloft.

The immense Pavilion of Great Benevolence (大悲阁; Dàbēi Gé) contains Lóngxīng Temple's real drawcard: a 21.3m-tall, bronze colossus of Guanyin. Cast in AD 971 and sporting a third eye, the effigy is wonderful, standing on a magnificently carved base from the Northern Song. Examine the carvings which include myriad characters and musicians, including Buddhist angels and a woman blowing a conch.

Circumambulated by worshippers, the Hall of Vairocana at the rear of the complex contains a four-faced Buddha (the Buddha of four directions), crowned with another four-faced Buddha, upon which is supported a further set. The entire statue and its base contain 1072 statues of Buddha.

The **gardens** right at the back contain scattered temple remains, including some *very* old stele, plus a triple-arched stone *páilóu*, dating from 1591.

Tiānníng Temple
BUDDHIST TEMPLE

(天宁寺; Tiānníng Sì; Zhongshan Donglu; admission ¥15) The remains of this temple contain the 41m-high Tang-dynasty **Lofty Pagoda** (凌霄塔; Língxiāo Tǎ) – also called Mùtǎ or Wooden Pagoda. Originally dating from AD 779, the pagoda was restored in 1045, but is still in fine condition.

Kāiyuán Temple
BUDDHIST TEMPLE

(开元寺; Kāiyuán Sì; Yanzhao Nandajie; admission ¥20) This temple originally dates from AD 540 but was destroyed in 1966, the first year of the Cultural Revolution.

Little remains apart from a **Bell Tower** and its drawcard dirt-brown **Xūmí Pagoda** (须弥塔; Xūmí Tǎ). Dating from AD 636, this well-preserved and unfussy, nine-eaved structure is topped with a spire. Its round arched doors and carved stone doorway are particularly attractive, as are the carved figures on the base. You can enter a shrine at the bottom of the pagoda, but you can't climb up inside.

Also displayed, near the entrance, is a colossal stone **bìxì** – China's largest – with a vast chunk of its left flank missing (as well as the stele it would have once carried), and its head propped up on a plinth. Dating from the late Tang era, the creature was excavated in 2000 from a street in Zhèngdìng.

Línjì Temple
BUDDHIST TEMPLE

(临济寺; Línjì Sì; Linji Lu) `FREE` This active monastery is notable for its tall, elegant, carved brick **Chénglíng Pagoda** (澄灵塔; also called the Green Pagoda), topped with an elaborate lotus plinth plus ball and spire.

In the Tang dynasty, the temple was home to one of Chan (Zen) Buddhism's most eccentric and important teachers, Linji Yixuan, who penned the now famous words, 'If you meet the Buddha on the road, kill him!'

Guānghuì Temple
BUDDHIST TEMPLE

(广惠寺; Guānghuì Sì; Yanzhao Nandajie; admission ¥15) Nothing remains of this temple except **Huá Pagoda** (华塔; Huá Tǎ), dating from around AD 800. It's an unusual Indian-style pagoda decorated with lions, elephants, sea creatures and *púsà* (Bodhisattvas; those worthy of nirvana who remain on earth to help others attain enlightenment).

City Walls
HISTORIC SITE

(城墙; Chéngqiáng) Although not immediately obvious, Zhèngdìng was once a walled city. These days much of what remains of its 24km-long city wall is just an earthen mound, but at the southern end of Yanzhao Nandajie, **Chánglè Gate** (长乐门; Chánglè Mén; Yanzhao Nandajie; admission ¥15), also known as Nán Mén (South Gate), has been rebuilt to give you some idea of the city wall's former magnificence.

You can climb on top of the gateway, although more fun perhaps is to clamber up onto the earthen wall nearby and explore some of its original remains. The original wall (which dates back to the Northern Zhou; 557 to 581 AD) was made up of an outer wall (*yuèchéng*) and an inner wall (*nèichéng*), with enceintes (*wèngchéng*).

✗ Eating

There are plenty of dumplings joints along Yanzhao Nandajie (look for the steamer baskets piled high). Expect to pay less than ¥10 for one basket (一屉, yī tì), enough for two people, and a bowl of rice porridge (粥; zhōu), or a beer.

Also look out for *lǘ ròu huǒshāo* (驴肉火烧; donkey-meat pastry pockets), a Héběi speciality, and a delicious lunchtime snack.

ⓘ Information

There's an **ICBC** (ICBC; 工商银行; Gōngshāng Yínháng; cnr Zhongshan Donglu & Yanzhao Nandajie) with an ATM a couple of hundred metres past Tiānníng Temple.

ⓘ Getting There & Around

Zhèngdìng is an easy day trip from Shíjiāzhuāng. Take bus 30 (¥2) from beside the former train station to the south bus station (p137), then take bus 177 (¥2, one hour, 6.50am to 8.50pm), which passes through South Gate and the other temples before reaching Lóngxīng Temple (Dàfó Temple; 大佛寺; Dàfó Sì).

From Lóngxīng Temple, you can then walk to all the other temples before catching bus 177 back to Zhèngdìng from South Gate.

Yújiācūn
于家村

POP 1600

Also known as **Stone Village** (石头村; Shítou Cūn), and hidden in the hills near the Héběi–Shānxī border, is the peaceful little settlement of **Yújiācūn** (admission ¥20). Nearly everything, from the houses to furniture inside, was originally made of stone. As

OFF THE BEATEN TRACK

CĀNGZHŌU'S IRON LION

Battered and bruised, but still standing proud in a long-forgotten corner of southeast Héběi, **Cāngzhōu's Iron Lion** (沧州铁狮子; Cāngzhōu Tiě Shīzi; Cāngzhōu; admission ¥20) is the oldest and largest cast-iron sculpture in China. Cast way back in 953 AD, it weighs in at around 40 tonnes, and stands almost 6m tall, but unsurprisingly for a creature that is more than 1000 years old, it is a shadow of its former self. The lion lost its tail in the 17th century; its snout and belly were damaged in a storm 200 years later; and the bronze statue of the Bodhisattva Manjusri, which once sat on top of the lotus flower on its back, is thought to have been stolen many centuries ago.

Despite today being almost 100km from the coast, in ancient times Cāngzhōu was a large seaport, which suffered from flooding and tsunamis. The Iron Lion was built to protect the city from sea spirits, and was known back then as Zhèn Hǎi Hǒu (镇海吼), the Roaring Sea-calmer.

These days, it cuts a rather lonely figure, standing in an otherwise empty courtyard surrounded by farmland, 15km from the modern city of Cāngzhōu. But the site used to be the centrepoint of ancient Cāngzhōu, a walled settlement established in the far-off Han Dynasty (206 BC–220 AD). Incredibly, part of the **ancient city wall**, thought to have been built at the beginning of the Han dynasty – so more than 2200 years ago – can still be seen a short distance from here.

Your entrance ticket (¥20) comes with another ticket (¥10) for entry to a nearby courtyard, which looks like a temple, but is in fact just a small museum – called the **Iron Money Warehouse** (铁钱库; Tiě Qián Kù). It briefly details the history of ancient Cāngzhōu, although in Chinese only. However, the lane opposite the museum leads through farmland, and across a river to the southern section of the old, earthen city wall, 1.5km away. It's still around 5m tall here, and you can walk along it in places. It once stretched for almost 10km around the city.

You can make a day trip here from either Běijīng or Tiānjīn. High-speed trains to Cāngzhōu West Station (沧州西站; Cāngzhōu Xī Zhàn) run roughly half-hourly from Běijīng South Train Station (¥95, one hour, last train back 10.30pm) and roughly hourly from Tiānjīn South Train Station (¥40, 30 minutes, last train back 9pm). From Cāngzhōu West, take bus 16 to its terminus at Cāngzhōu Main Train Station (火车站; huǒchē zhàn; ¥2, 30 minutes), then bus 901 (¥3, 35 minutes). Tell the driver you want tiě shīzi (pronounced 'tee-air shur zuh') and he'll show you where to get off. Then follow the signposted lane beside the bus stop for about 1km and the Iron Lion will be on your right, with the Iron Money Storehouse museum on your left.

When you're on Bus 16, consider stopping off at the huge, brand-new **Cāngzhōu Museum** (博物馆; bówùguǎn; ⊙9am-4pm Tue-Sun) **FREE**, a couple of stops from Cāngzhōu West Train Station.

---

such, Yújiācūn is remarkably well preserved: bumpy little lanes lead past traditional Ming- and Qing-dynasty courtyard homes, old opera stages and tiny temples.

This is also a model Chinese clan village, where 95% of the inhabitants all share the same surname of Yu (于). One of the more unusual sights is inside the **Yu Ancestral Hall** (于氏宗祠; Yúshì Zōngcí), where you'll find the 24-generation family tree, reaching back over 500 years. There are five tapestries, one for the descendants of each of the original Yu sons who founded the village.

Another oddity is the three-storey **Qīngliáng Pavilion** (清凉阁; Qīngliáng Gé),

completed in 1581. Supposedly the work of one thoroughly crazed individual (Yu Xichun, who wanted to be able to see Běijīng from the top), it was, according to legend, built entirely at night, over a 16-year period, without the help of any other villagers. It was certainly built by an amateur architect: there's no foundation, and the building stones (in addition to not being sealed by mortar) are of wildly different sizes (some as large as 2m), giving it a higgledy-piggledy look that's quite uncommon in Chinese architecture.

Other buildings worth hunting down are the **Guānyīn Pavilion** (观音阁; Guānyīn Gé) and the **Zhēnwǔ Temple** (真武庙; Zhēnwǔ

Miào). Near the primary school is the **Stone Museum** (石头博物馆; Shítou Bówùguǎn) displaying local items made of stone.

Yújiācūn is dissected by a small village road, where the bus will drop you. The ticket office, the Stone Museum and Xīngshuǐ Yuàn guesthouse are to the right of the road; all the other sights we've mentioned are to the left.

You may have to get someone at the ticket office to open the sights you wish to see, as their doors are often padlocked.

🛏 Sleeping

Given the mission it took to get here, you'll want to stay the night – it's definitely worth it. As the sun sets, the sounds of village life – farmers chatting after a day in the fields, clucking hens, kids at play – are miles away from the raging pace of modern Chinese cities.

Xīngshuǐ Yuàn GUESTHOUSE **$**
(兴水院; ☑ 0311 8237 6517, 134 7311 0485; Yújiācūn; 于家村; per person ¥40) One of four or five *nóngjiā lè* (农家乐; village guesthouses) in Yújiācūn, this typically simple courtyard guesthouse has guest rooms in an old stone outhouse, although the main house itself is a white-tiled renovation. No English spoken, but a friendly welcome.

Meals in the courtyard cost around ¥10 to ¥20, depending on what you have. Dishes on offer include: *héle* (饸饹; buckwheat noodles with a preserved-vegetable sauce – a local speciality), *nóngjiā dòufu* (农家豆腐; village-style tofu) and *chǎo bènjīdàn* (炒笨鸡蛋; fried free-range eggs).

ℹ Getting There & Away

Prepare yourself for a three-hour, quadruple-bus mission. From Shíjiāzhuāng, take bus 17 (¥2) from Jiěfàng Guǎngchǎng (解放广场; Liberation Square) two stops to Xinbai Guangchang (新百广场) bus stop, then take bus 9 (¥2) to Xīwáng Bus Station (西王客运站; Xīwáng Kèyùnzhàn). From there, take one of the frequent buses to the small town of Jǐngxíng (井陉; ¥11, one hour, 6.30am to 7pm), from where you can catch a bus to Yújiācūn (¥7, one hour, 12 daily, 7.35am to 6.35pm).

Tell the driver on the Jǐngxíng bus that you want to go to Yújiācūn and he'll drop you by the place where the Yújiācūn buses leave from.

Note, the last bus back from Yújiācūn leaves at 3.30pm – all the more reason to stay the night.

Zhàozhōu Bridge 赵州桥

China's oldest-standing **bridge** (admission ¥40) has spanned the Jiǎo River (Jiǎo Hé) for 1400 years. In Zhàoxiàn County, about 40km southeast of Shíjiāzhuāng and 2km south of Zhàoxiàn town, this is the world's first segmental bridge (ie its arch is a segment of a circle, as opposed to a complete semicircle) and predates other bridges of its type throughout the world by 800 years. In fine condition, and now part of a riverside, landscaped park, it is 50.82m long and 9.6m wide, with a span of 37m. Twenty-two stone posts are topped with carvings of dragons and mythical creatures, with the centre slab featuring a magnificent *tāotiè* (an offspring of a dragon). The bridge is also known as 'Safe Crossing Bridge' (安济桥; Ānjì Qiáo).

To get here from Shíjiāzhuāng, take bus 30 from beside the former train station to south bus station (p137), then take a bus to Zhàoxiàn (赵县; ¥11, one hour, frequent). Get off at **Shí Tǎ** (石塔), a slim stone pagoda in the middle of the road, where you turn right to walk the final 2km, or take dinky local bus 2 (¥1). The last bus back to Shíjiāzhuāng swings past Shí Tǎ at about 7pm.

Chéngdé 承德

☑ 0314 / POP 479,703
Built on the banks of the Wǔliè River, and surrounded by forested hills, Chéngdé is a small, pleasant city which just happens to have an extraordinary history.

This was the summer playground of the Qing-dynasty emperors; beginning with Emperor Kangxi, the Qing Court would flee here to escape the torpid summer heat of the Forbidden City (and occasionally foreign armies) and to be closer to the hunting grounds of their northern homelands.

The Bìshǔ Shānzhuāng (Fleeing-the-Heat Mountain Villa) is a grand imperial palace and the walled enclosure it lies within houses China's largest regal gardens. Beyond the grounds is a remarkable collection of politically chosen temples, built to host dignitaries such as the sixth Panchen Lama. The Imperial Villa, the gardens and the eight temples are all, quite rightly, Unesco protected.

History

In 1703, when an expedition passed through the Chéngdé valley, Emperor Kangxi was so enamoured with the surroundings that he

Chéngdé

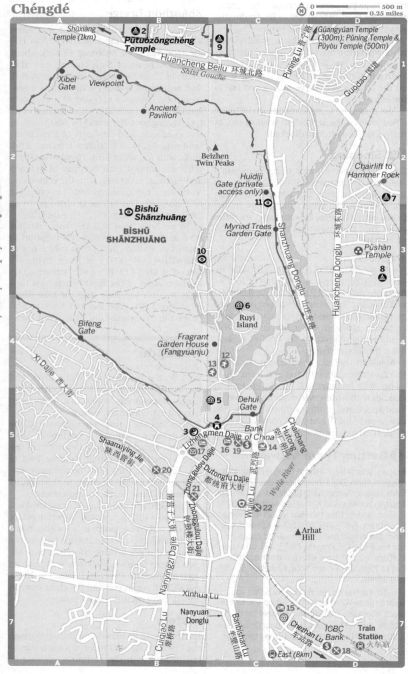

0   500 m
0   0.25 miles

Shūxiàng Temple (1km)

Pǔtuózōngchéng Temple

Guāngyuán Temple (300m); Pǔníng Temple & Pǔyòu Temple (500m)

Huancheng Beilu 环城北路
Shizi Gouche

Xibei Gate

Viewpoint

Ancient Pavilion

Beizhen Twin Peaks

Chairlift to Hammer Rock

Huidiji Gate (private access only)

Bishǔ Shānzhuāng

BISHǓ SHĀNZHUĀNG

Myriad Trees Garden Gate

Pùshàn Temple

Bifeng Gate

Ruyi Island

Fragrant Garden House (Fangyuanju)

Dehui Gate

Bank of China

Lizhengmen
Zhonggulou Dajie
Dutongfu Dajie 都统府大街

Xi Dajie 西大街

Shaanxiying Jie 陕西营街

Nanyingzi Dajie 南营子大街

Zhonggulou Dajie 钟鼓楼大街

Arhat Hill

Walie River

Chaichang Hutong 柴场胡同

Huancheng Donglu 环城东路

Shanzhuang Donglu 山庄东路

Guodao 国道

Puning Lu 普宁路

Wujie Lu 武烈路

Cuiqiao Lu 翠桥路

Banbishan Lu 半壁山路

Xinhua Lu

Nanyuan Donglu

Chezhan Lu 车站路

ICBC Bank

Train Station 火车站

East (8km)

Chéngdé

had a hunting lodge built, which gradually grew into the summer resort. Rèhé – or Jehol (Warm River; named after a hot spring here) – as Chéngdé was then known, grew in importance and the Qing court began to spend more time here, sometimes up to several months a year, with some 10,000 people accompanying the emperor on his seven-day expedition from Běijīng.

The emperors also convened here with the border tribes – undoubtedly more at ease here than in Běijīng – who posed the greatest threats to the Qing frontiers: the Mongols, Tibetans, Uighurs and, eventually, the Europeans. The resort reached its peak under Emperor Qianlong (1735–96), who commissioned many of the outlying temples to overawe visiting leaders.

Emperor Xianfeng died here in 1861, permanently warping Chéngdé's feng shui and tipping the Imperial Villa towards long-term decline.

⊙ Sights

★ **Bìshǔ Shānzhuāng** HISTORIC SITE
(避暑山庄; Imperial Villa; Lizhengmen Dajie; admission Apr-Oct ¥120, Nov-Mar ¥90; ⊗ palace 7am-6pm Apr-Oct, 8am-5.30pm Nov-Oct) The imperial summer resort is composed of a main palace complex and vast parklike gardens, all enclosed by a handsome 10km-long wall. The entrance price is steep (as it is with all the main sights here in Chéngdé), and it gets packed with tourists here in summer, but the splendid gardens provide ample opportunity to take a quiet walk away from the crowds.

A huge spirit wall shields the resort entrance at Lizhengmen Dajie. Through **Lìzhèng Gate** (丽正门; Lìzhèng Mén), the **Main Palace** (正宫; Zhèng Gōng) is a series of nine courtyards and five elegant, unpainted halls, with a rusticity complemented by towering pine trees. The wings in each courtyard have various exhibitions (porcelain, clothing, weaponry), and most of the halls are decked out in period furnishings.

The first hall is the refreshingly cool **Hall of Simplicity and Sincerity**, built of an aromatic cedar called *nánmù*, and displaying a carved throne draped in yellow silk. Other prominent halls include the emperor's study (Study of Four Knowledges) and living quarters (Hall of Refreshing Mists and Waves). On the left-hand side of the latter is the imperial bedroom. Two residential areas branch out from here: the empress dowager's **Pine Crane Palace** (松鹤斋; Sōnghè Zhāi), to the east, and the smaller **Western Apartments**, where the concubines (including a young Cixi) resided.

Exiting the Main Palace brings you to the gardens and forested hunting grounds, with landscapes borrowed from famous southern scenic areas in Hángzhōu, Sūzhōu and Jiāxīng, as well as the Mongolian grasslands.

The double-storey **Misty Rain Tower** (烟雨楼; Yānyǔ Lóu), on the northwestern side of the main lake, served as an imperial study. Further north is the **Wénjīn Pavilion** (文津阁; Wénjīn Gé), built in 1773. Don't miss the wonderfully elegant 250-year-old **Yǒngyòusì Pagoda** (永佑寺塔; Yǒngyòusì Tǎ), which soars above the fragments of its vanished temple in the northeast of the complex.

Most of the compound is taken up by lakes, hills, forests and plains. There are magnificent views of some of the outlying temples from the northern wall.

Just beyond the Main Palace is the start-point for **bus tours of the gardens** (环山车; huánshān chē; 1 hour, including 3 short stops; per person ¥50). Further on you'll find a place for **boat-rental** (出租小船; chūzū xiǎochuán; per hr ¥50-90, deposit ¥300).

Almost all of the forested section is closed from November to May because of fire hazard in the dry months, but fear not: you can still turn your legs to jelly wandering around the rest of the park.

Tourists can exit by any of the gates, but can only buy tickets to enter at Lìzhèng Gate.

Guāndì Temple
TAOIST TEMPLE

(关帝庙; Guāndì Miào; 18 Lizhengmen Dajie; admission ¥20; ☉7am-7pm Apr-Oct, 8am-5pm Nov-Oct) The heavily restored Taoist Guāndì Temple was first built during the reign of Yongzheng, in 1732. For years the temple housed residents but is again home to a band of Taoist monks, garbed in distinctive jackets and trousers, their long hair twisted into topknots. Note the original 300-year-old beamwork in the ceiling of the final hall.

◉ Eight Outer Temples

Skirting the northern and eastern walls of the Bìshǔ Shānzhuāng, the **Eight Outer Temples** (外八庙; wài bā miào) were, unusually, designed for diplomatic rather than spiritual reasons. Some were based on actual Tibetan Buddhist monasteries but the emphasis was on appearance: smaller temple buildings are sometimes solid, and the Tibetan facades (with painted windows) are often fronts for traditional Chinese temple interiors. The surviving temples and monasteries were all built between 1713 and 1780; the prominence given to Tibetan Buddhism was as much for the Mongols (fervent Lamaists) as the Tibetan leaders.

★ Pǔníng Temple
BUDDHIST TEMPLE

(普宁寺; Pǔníng Sì; Puningsi Lu; admission Apr-Oct ¥80, Nov-Mar ¥60; ☉8am-6pm Apr-Oct, 8.30am-5pm Nov-Mar) With its squeaking prayer wheels and the devotional intonations of its monks, Chéngdé's only active temple was built in 1755 in anticipation of Qianlong's victory over the western Mongol tribes in Xīnjiāng. Supposedly modelled on the earliest Tibetan Buddhist monastery (Samye), the first half of the temple is distinctly Chinese (with Tibetan buildings at the rear).

Enter the temple grounds to a stele pavilion with inscriptions by the Qianlong emperor in Chinese, Manchu, Mongol and Tibetan. The halls behind are arranged in typical Buddhist fashion, with the **Hall of Heavenly Kings** (天王殿; Tiānwáng Diàn) and beyond, the **Mahavira Hall** (大雄宝殿; Dàxióng Bǎodiàn), where three images of the Buddhas of the three generations are arrayed. Some very steep steps rise up behind (the temple is arranged on a mountainside) leading to a gate tower, which you can climb.

On the terrace at the top of the steps is the dwarfing **Mahayana Hall**. On either side are stupas and block-like Tibetan-style buildings, decorated with attractive water spouts. Some buildings have been converted to shops, while others are solid, serving a purely decorative purpose.

The mind-bogglingly vast gilded **statue of Guanyin** (the Buddhist Goddess of Mercy) towers within the Mahayana Hall. The effigy is astounding: over 22m high, it's the tallest of its kind in the world and radiates a powerful sense of divinity. Hewn from five different kinds of wood (pine, cypress, fir, elm and linden), Guanyin has 42 arms, with each palm bearing an eye and each hand holding instruments, skulls, lotuses and other Buddhist devices. Tibetan touches include the pair of hands in front of the goddess, below the two clasped in prayer, the right one of which holds a sceptre-like *dorje* (*vajra* in Sanskrit), a masculine symbol, and the left a *dril bu* (bell), a female symbol. On Guanyin's head sits the Teacher Longevity Buddha. To the right of the goddess stands a huge male guardian and disciple called Shàncái, opposite his female equivalent, Lóngnǚ (Dragon Girl). Unlike Guanyin, they are both coated in ancient and dusty pigments. On the wall on either side are hundreds of small effigies of Buddha.

Occasionally, tourists are allowed to climb up to the 1st-floor gallery for a closer inspection of Guanyin.

Housed within the grounds, on the east side, is the **Pǔyòu Temple** (普佑寺; Pǔyòu Sì; ☉8am-6pm). It is dilapidated and missing its main hall, but it has a plentiful contingent of merry gilded *luóhàn* in the side wings, although a fire in 1964 incinerated many of their confrères. The ticket price includes admission to Pǔyòu Temple.

Pǔníng Temple has a number of friendly lamas who manage their domain, so be quiet and respectful at all times.

Take bus 6 (¥1) from in front of Mountain Villa Hotel (p146).

★ **Pǔtuózōngchéng Temple** BUDDHIST TEMPLE
(普陀宗乘之庙; Pǔtuózōngchéng Zhīmiào; Shizigou Lu; admission Apr-Oct ¥80, Nov-Mar ¥60; ☉8am-6pm Apr-Oct, 8.30am-5pm Nov-Mar) Chéngdé's largest temple is a not-so-small replica of Lhasa's Potala Palace and houses the nebulous presence of Avalokiteshvara (Guanyin). A marvellous sight on a clear day, the temple's red walls stand out against its mountain backdrop. Enter to a huge stele pavilion, followed by a large triple archway topped with five small stupas in red, green, yellow, white and black.

Fronted by a collection of prayer wheels and flags, the Red Palace contains most of the main shrines and halls. Look out for the marvellous sandalwood pagodas in the front hall. Both are 19m tall and contain 2160 effigies of the Amitabha Buddha.

Among the many exhibits on view are displays of Tibetan Buddhist objects and instruments, including a *kapala* bowl, made from the skull of a young girl. The main hall is located at the very top, surrounded by several small pavilions and panoramic views.

The admission ticket includes the neighbouring Temple of Sumeru, Happiness and Longevity.

Bus 118 (¥1) goes here from in front of Mountain Villa Hotel (p146).

Temple of Sumeru, Happiness & Longevity BUDDHIST TEMPLE
(须弥福寿之庙; Xūmífúshòu Zhīmiào; Shizigou Lu; admission Apr-Oct ¥80, Nov-Mar ¥60; ☉8am-6pm Apr-Oct, 8.30am-5pm Nov-Mar) This huge temple was built in honour of the sixth Panchen Lama, who stayed here in 1781. Incorporating Tibetan and Chinese architectural elements, it's an imitation of the Panchen's home monastery Tashilhunpo in Shigatse, Tibet. Note the eight huge, glinting dragons (each said to weigh over 1000kg) that adorn the roof of the main hall.

The admission price includes entry to the neighbouring Pǔtuózōngchéng Temple.

Bus 118 (¥1) goes here from in front of Mountain Villa Hotel (p146).

Pǔlè Temple BUDDHIST TEMPLE
(普乐寺; Pǔlè Sì; admission incl Hammer Rock ¥50; ☉8am-5.30pm Apr-Oct, 8.30am-4.30pm Nov-Mar) This peaceful temple was built in 1776 for the visits of minority envoys (Kazakhs among them). At the rear of the temple is the unusual Round Pavilion, reminiscent of the Hall of Prayer for Good Harvests at Běijīng's Temple of Heaven Park. Inside is an enormous wooden mandala (a geometric representation of the universe).

It's a 30-minute walk to Hammer Rock (磬锤峰; Qìngchuí Fēng) from Pǔlè Temple – the club-shaped rock is visible for miles around and is said to resemble a kind of musical hammer. There is pleasant hiking and it offers commanding views of the area. If you don't fancy the hike, take the chairlift instead.

Bus 10 (¥1), from in front of Mountain Villa Hotel (p146), will take you to the chairlift (return ¥50) for Hammer Rock.

Guǎngyuán Temple BUDDHIST TEMPLE
(广缘寺; Guǎngyuán Sì) Unrestored and inaccessible, the temple's rounded doorway is blocked up with stones and its grounds are seemingly employed by the local farming community. The temple is a couple of hundred metres southeast of Pǔníng Temple. To get here, walk north up Puning Lu, turn right at Pǔníng Temple and continue for about 300m.

Pǔrén Temple BUDDHIST TEMPLE
(普仁寺; Pǔrén Sì) Built in 1713, this is the earliest temple in Chéngdé, but is not open to the public.

Shūxiàng Temple BUDDHIST TEMPLE
(殊像寺; Shūxiàng Sì) Surrounded by a low red wall, with its large halls rising on the hill behind and huge stone lions parked outside, this temple seems to be permanently closed. Just to the west of Shūxiàng Temple is a military zone which foreigners are not allowed to access, so don't go wandering around.

🏃 Activities

The west bank of the Wǔliè River has a popular promenade with plenty of shade, and makes for pleasant strolls. Locals meet at various spots along here for singing and dancing in the early evening.

There's an outdoor swimming pool (承德游泳馆; Chéngdé yóuyǒngguǎn; Wulie Lu; 武烈路; admission ¥30; ☉9am-5pm & 7-9pm) on Wulie Lu.

🛏 Sleeping

Yìyuán Bīnguǎn HOTEL $
(易园宾馆; ☑0314 589 1111; 7 Lizhengmen Dajie; 丽正门大街7号; r from ¥460) Rooms with and without a window can be had for ¥200 and ¥160 respectively, if you show enough disinterest. They are modern and functional, although the windowless ones are quite small.

TIĀNJĪN & HÉBĚI CHÉNGDÉ

Not much English spoken. Buses 13 and 29 come here from the train and bus stations.

Huilóng Hotel HOTEL **$$**
(会龙大厦酒店; Huìlóng Dàshà Jiǔdiàn; ☏ 0314 761 0360, 0314 252 8119; Huilong Plaza, Xinjuzhai, Chezhan Lu; 车站路新居宅会龙大厦; tw from ¥260; ✿ ✱ @ ⊛) Formerly Ming's Dynasty Hostel, this well-turned-out budget hotel is good value. It no longer has youth-hostel perks (common area, reliable travel advice), but some staff do speak English, and the rooms are very comfortable and well-equipped for the price (TV, wi-fi, modern bathroom).

Turn right out of the train station and it's a five-minute walk, or take bus 13, 24 or 29 from the east bus station.

Mountain Villa Hotel HOTEL **$$$**
(山庄宾馆, Shānzhuāng Bīnguǎn; ☏ 0314 209 5500; 11 Lizhengmen Dajie, 丽正门路11号; common/standard/deluxe ¥380/780/980; ✱ @) This huge hotel offers pole position for a trip to Bìshǔ Shānzhuāng. The standard and deluxe rooms are super smart, and are discounted to ¥580 and ¥680 respectively. The common-standard rooms are in a building out the back, but are tattier than cheaper rooms in other hotels.

Buses 13 and 29 link nearby Guāndì Temple with the train station and the east bus station.

✖ Eating

Chéngdé is famous for wild game – notably *lùròu* (venison) and *shānjī* (pheasant), a reminder of its past as an imperial hunting base, but don't expect to see too much on the menus these days. On summer nights, do as the locals do and head for Shaanxiying Jie where a busy night market on either side of the canal includes a number of stalls offering **shāokǎo** (skewers from ¥3; ⊙ 7-10pm), point-and-choose streetside barbecues. Just south of here, the **Tsingdao Beer Garden** (青岛啤酒花园; Qīngdǎo píjiǔ huāyuán) has food stalls as well as beer. There's also a **small beer garden** (skewers from ¥2; ⊙ noon-10pm) on the Wūliè River that does *shāokǎo* too.

★ **Dà Qīng Huā** DUMPLINGS **$**
(大清花; 241 Chezhan Lu; 车站路241号; mains from ¥20; ⊙ 10.30am-9.30pm; ✎) The finest dumpling house in Chéngdé, this excellent establishment has a big choice of juicy *jiǎozi* (boiled dumplings; ¥14 to ¥28 per serving) with some unusual fillings, including veg options and pan-fried dumplings. There's a

huge range of other dishes too – even some 'Emperor Dishes' such as venison.

The fresh, pinewood interior is a delight to eat in, and the English menu comes with photos too. There is **another branch** (大清花; Lizhengmen Dajie; mains from ¥20; ⊙ 10.30am-9.30pm) by Lìzhèng Gate.

❶ Information

Bank of China (中国银行; Zhōngguó Yínháng; 4 Dutongfu Dajie) Also on Xinsheng Lu and Lizhengmen Dajie; 24-hour ATMs.

China Post (中国邮政; Zhōngguó Yóuzhèng; cnr Lizhengmen Dajie & Dutongfu Dajie; ⊙ 8am-6pm)

ICBC Bank (Chezhan Lu)

Public Security Bureau (PSB, 公安局; Gōng'ānjú; ☏ 0314 202 2352; 9 Wulie Lu; ⊙ 8.30am-5pm Mon-Fri)

Xiàndài Internet Cafe (现代网吧; Xiàndài Wǎngbā; Chezhan Lu; per hr ¥3; ⊙ 24hr)

❶ Getting There & Away

BUS

Buses for Chéngdé leave Běijīng hourly from Liùlǐqiáo Bus Station (¥85, four hours, 5.40am to 6.40pm). From Chéngdé, they leave every half-hour for Běijīng (¥85, four hours, 6.20am to 6.40pm) from the train station car park.

Services from Chéngdé's **east bus station** (汽车东站; qìchē dōngzhàn), 8km south of town, include:

Běijīng ¥85, four hours, every 20 minutes (6am to 6pm)

Dàlián ¥224, 14 hours, one daily (3pm)

Qínhuángdǎo (for Shānhǎiguān) ¥110, three hours, six daily (7.30am, 8.05am, 8.30am, 10am, 1pm and 4pm)

Tiānjīn ¥120, six hours, three daily (6am, 8.50am and 2pm)

TRAIN

The three fastest trains from Běijīng Train Station (hard seat ¥35 to ¥40) take 4½ to five hours and leave at 7.56am, 12.20pm and 2.03pm. Return services leave Chéngdé at 5.45am, 7.45am and 7.15pm.

Shěnyáng hard seat ¥45-to ¥75, hard sleeper ¥96/145, 12/13 hours, two daily (7.02am and 5.31pm)

Shíjiāzhuāng hard seat/sleeper ¥75/138, nine/10 hours, two daily (1.13pm and 10.01pm)

❶ Getting Around

A taxi from the Train Station to the Bìshǔ Shānzhuāng should cost around ¥10.

Buses 13, 24 and 29 link east bus station with the train station; 13 and 29 carry on to Guāndì Temple.

Shānhǎiguān 山海关

☎ 0335 / POP 19,500

The drowsy walled town of Shānhǎiguān marks the point where the Great Wall snakes out of the hills to meet the sea.

Hugely popular with domestic tourists, Shānhǎiguān has, in recent years, sold some of its soul for a rebuild of the old town's central sections. The effect has been to render it more than a little sterile in places, although thankfully a few pockets of original buildings remain in the alleys running off the main streets.

Likewise, the ticketed sections of the Great Wall here have been heavily restored (and in some cases completely rebuilt), but there is still an accessible stretch of original earthen Great Wall here that can be explored.

History

Guarding the narrow plain leading to northeastern China, the Ming garrison town of Shānhǎiguān and its wall were developed to seal off the country from the Manchu, whose troublesome ancestors ruled northern China during the Jin dynasty (AD 1115–1234). This strategy succeeded until 1644, when Chinese rebels seized Běijīng and General Wu Sangui opted to invite the Manchu army through the impregnable pass to help suppress the uprising. The plan worked so well that the Manchus proceeded to take over the entire country and establish the Qing dynasty.

◉ Sights

Great Wall Museum   MUSEUM

(长城博物馆; Chángchéng Bówùguǎn; Diyiguan Lu; 第一关路; ⊙9am-4pm Tue-Sun) FREE This impressive museum provides a comprehensive history of the Wall in this region and includes interesting scale models of the walled town and surrounding Great Wall locations. Plenty of photos and artefacts, as well as OK English captions.

First Pass Under Heaven   HISTORIC SITE

(天下第一关; Tiānxià Dìyī Guān; cnr Dong Dajie & Diyiguan Lu; admission ¥50; ⊙7am-5.30pm) The town wall's east gate, which the Great Wall once linked up with on its way from the mountains down to the sea, has been tarted

Shānhǎiguān

◉ Sights

| 1 First Pass Under Heaven | B1 |
| 2 Great Wall Museum | B1 |

🛏 Sleeping

| 3 Jīngshān Hotel | A1 |
| 4 Shānhǎi Holiday Hotel | A1 |

🍴 Eating

| 5 Èrtiáo Xiǎoxiàng Jiǎoziguǎn | A1 |
| 6 Lánzhōu Zhèngzōng Niúròu Lāmiàn | A1 |

up for tourism. This was Shānhǎiguān's principal watchtower – two storeys with double eaves and 68 arrow-slit windows – and is a towering 13.7m high.

Several other watchtowers can also be seen and a *wèngchéng* (enceinte) extends out east from the wall. You can walk along a small stretch of the wall here.

★ Jiǎo Shān   GREAT WALL

(角山; admission ¥30, cable car one-way/return ¥10/20; ⊙7am-sunset) Albeit a heavily restored section of the Great Wall, Jiǎo Shān does nevertheless offer an excellent opportunity to hike up the Wall's first high peak; a telling vantage point over the narrow tongue of land below and one-time invasion route for northern armies. The views are fabulous on a clear day.

It's a steep 20-minute clamber from the base, or a cable car (索道; *suǒdào*) can yank you up. To leave behind the crowds, continue beyond the cable car station, to **Qīxián Monastery** (栖贤寺; Qīxián Sì) or even further to **Sweet Nectar Pavilion** (甘露亭; Gānlù Tíng).

Bus 5 (¥2) goes here from the train station, but it's an easy, 3km walk (or cycle) north of town. Just follow the road straight on from Shānhǎiguān's North Gate.

More fun than just following the road, though, is to approach Jiǎo Shān on an original, overgrown stretch of **earthen Great Wall**, which still creeps its way through farmland from Shānhǎiguān to Jiǎo Shān. Most of its Ming brickwork has long since been pillaged, but there's still a scattering of bricks, including a couple of collapsed watchtowers. To take this route, walk straight on from North Gate and then, after the bridge that goes underneath the highway, take the first right and follow the road for a couple of hundred metres. Turn left up the pathway beside the iron bridge and clamber up the wall beside you wherever you feel you're able to – there's at least one overgrown path that leads up to the top. You can walk on this earthen wall all the way Jiǎo Shān, where you'll have to clamber down to the ticket office to enter the restored section.

Old Dragon Head
GREAT WALL

(老龙头; Lǎolóngtóu; admission ¥60; ☼7.30am-6.30pm) Famous across China (although a little over-hyped if we're being honest), Old Dragon Head, 4km south of Shānhǎiguān, is where the Great Wall meets the sea. It's photogenic for sure, but bear in mind that what you see now was reconstructed in the late 1980s – the original wall crumbled away long ago.

It acts more like a small beach resort these days. In fact, you can jump in and actually swim around the Great Wall here. The water is filthy, though, so it's not surprising that the speedboat rides (¥80 per person) are more popular. Bus 25 (¥1) goes here from Shānhǎiguān's South Gate.

🛏 Sleeping

Local authorities have stipulated that almost all of the hotels in Shānhǎiguān are not allowed to accept foreigners these days. This includes all the cheap family-run guesthouses (旅馆; lǚguǎn) inside the town walls, which used to make staying here so much fun. Luckily, there are still a couple that do welcome foreign guests.

Jīngshān Hotel
HOTEL $

(景山宾馆; Jīngshān Bīnguǎn; ☎0335 513 2188/46; 1 Dong Dajie, 东大街1号; tw/tr from

¥220/240; ❋ ☎) The cheapest place in town that accepts foreigners, and it's decent value. Housed in a pleasant, reconstructed, two-storey courtyard complex, rooms are neat and comfortable and come with private bathrooms. There's wi-fi in the lobby. Not much English spoken.

Shānhǎi Holiday Hotel
HOTEL $$$

(山海假日酒店; Shānhǎi Jiàrì Jiǔdiàn; ☎0335 535 2888; www.shanhai-holiday.com; Bei Madao; 北马道; d & tw ¥880, discounted to ¥480; ❋@☎) A newly built, traditional-style four-star hotel with attractive rooms, pleasant staff, a restaurant and a bar.

🍴 Eating

Èrtiáo Xiǎoxiàng Jiǎoziguǎn
DUMPLINGS $

(二条小巷饺子馆; Ertiao Xiaoxiang, off Nan Dajie; 南大街二条小巷; dumplings per portion ¥20; ☼7am-7pm) Housed in a 200-year-old píngfáng (平房; bungalow), this small, family-run joint does delicious golden-fried dumplings (煎饺; jiānjiǎo) with a range of fillings, including pork and cabbage (白菜猪肉; báicài zhūròu), egg and chives (韭菜鸡蛋; jiǔcài jīdàn), pork and courgette (角瓜猪肉; jiǎoguā zhūròu), egg and courgette (角瓜鸡蛋; jiǎoguā jīdàn) and pork and fennel (茴香猪肉; huíxiāng zhūròu). No English, but a friendly welcome.

If walking south from the Drum Tower (p129), look for the sign saying '饺子馆' (meaning dumpling restaurant) pointing down the first alley on the left.

Lánzhōu Zhèngzōng Niúròu Lāmiàn
NOODLES $

(兰州正宗牛肉拉面; Nan Dajie; 南大街; noodles ¥8-20; ☼7am-9pm) Does a range of tasty noodle dishes, including: pulled noodles with beef (牛肉拉面; niúròu lāmiàn – the restaurant speciality), pulled noodles with lamb (羊肉拉面; yángròu lāmiàn), pulled noodles with Chinese cabbage (青菜拉面; qīngcài lāmiàn), pulled noodles with egg (鸡蛋拉面; jīdàn lāmiàn), braised beef noodles (红烧牛肉面; hóngshāo niúròumiàn) and knife-sliced beef fried noodles (牛肉炒刀削面; niúròu chǎo dāoxiāomiàn).

Has photos of much of the menu plastered across two walls. No English.

ℹ Information

Bank of China (中国银行; Zhōngguó Yínháng; Nanhai Xilu; ☼8.30am-5.30pm) Foreign exchange facility.

China Post (中国邮政; Zhōngguó Yóuzhèng; Nanhai Xilu; ☺8.30am-6pm)

Hēimǎ Chēxíng (黑马车行; 12-1 Nan Dajie; 南大街12-1号; ¥20 per day; ☺6am-7pm)

ICBC Bank (工行; Gōngháng; Nan Dajie)

Public Security Bureau (PSB, 公安局; Gōng'ānjú; ☑505 1163; Diyiguan Lu; 第一关路) Opposite the entrance to First Pass Under Heaven, on the corner of a small alleyway.

❶ Getting There & Around

There are a number of G- and D-class bullet trains (and many more slower ones) linking Běijīng and Shānhǎiguān (2½ hours, ¥93). Four leave from Běijīng Main Station between 7am and 10am. Another leaves Běijīng South at 8.42am. There are also three or four afternoon fast trains. Among the many trains going back to Běijīng, there are seven high-speed trains between 5pm and 9pm.

Alternatively, even more high-speed trains go from Běijīng to the nearby city of Qínhuángdǎo (秦皇岛; ¥90, two hours 20 minutes regularly from 7am to 9pm), 18km from Shānhǎiguān. Buses from Běijīng's Bāwángfén station also run to Qínhuángdǎo (¥110, four hours).

There's no long-distance bus station in Shānhǎiguān. Qínhuángdǎo's coach station, where the nearest long-distance buses arrive, is diagonally opposite its train station. From outside the train station, take bus 8 (¥1) a couple of stops to Ba San Dong Li (八三东里) bus stop, then take bus 33 (¥2, 30 minutes) to Shānhǎiguān's South Gate.

Buses leave Qínhuángdǎo's coach station for Běijīng's Bāwángfén station (¥110, four hours) at 7am, 8am, 9am, 10am, noon, 2pm and 3.30pm, and for Běijīng Capital Airport (¥140, 4½ hours) on the hour every hour from 5am to 3pm, and at 5pm. There are also numerous direct buses from Qínhuángdǎo to Chéngdé (¥110, three hours), although most of them leave before noon, and

there's one bus to Dàlián (¥150, 10am, seven hours).

Qínhuángdǎo's small airport has flights to Dàlián, Shànghǎi, Qīngdǎo and Xī'ān.

Taxis in Shānhǎiguān are ¥5 flag fall. Motor-rickshaws cost ¥2 to ¥3 for trips within town.

Jīmíngyì 鸡鸣驿

POP 1000

An ancient snapshot of China, the sleepy hamlet of Jīmíngyì is a delightful surprise to find amid the scruffy northern Héběi countryside. This walled town, establised during the Yuan dynasty (AD 1206–1368), is China's oldest surviving post station. It stands as an historic reminder of a system that endured for 2000 years and enabled the officials in the Forbidden City to keep in touch with their far-flung counterparts around China. Whipped by dust storms in the spring and with archaic, fading Mao-era slogans still visible on walls, Jīmíngyì sees few visitors and feels a long, long way from the gleaming capital – much further than the 140km distance would suggest.

During the Ming and Qing dynasties, this was a place of considerably more bustle and wealth, as evidenced in the numerous surviving temples and its town wall. Many of its courtyard houses remain too, albeit in dilapidated condition.

There has been a flurry of activity in Jīmíngyì recently, with the town walls and gates newly restored, as the local government attempts to boosts its appeal as a tourist destination. There is now also an admission fee (¥40), which you must pay if you want to gain access to any of the notable buildings.

JIǓMÉNKǑU GREAT WALL

In a mountain valley 15km north of Shānhǎiguān stretches the only section of the Great Wall ever built over water. Normally the wall stopped at rivers, as they were considered natural defence barriers on their own. At **Jiǔménkǒu Great Wall** (九门口长城; Jiǔménkǒu; admission ¥80), however, a 100m span supported by nine arches crosses the Jiǔjiāng River, which we can only guess flowed at a much faster and deeper rate than it does today (or else the arches would function more like open gates).

Much effort has gone into restoring this formidable-looking bridge and on both sides the wall continues its run up the steep, rocky hillsides. Heading left, you can quickly see where the wall remains unrestored on the opposite side. Sadly, access to this area is blocked but the distant sight of crumbling stone watchtowers truly drives home the terrible isolation that must have been felt by the guardians of frontier regions such as this.

No buses head to the wall from Shānhǎiguān. A taxi costs around ¥35 one-way – ask the ones gathered outside the **South Gate**. A return trip will cost more like ¥100 including waiting time.

◉ Sights

As well as the main sights, other small temples that can be visited include the **Temple of the God of Wealth** and the **Temple of the Dragon King** (龙王庙; Lóngwáng Miào). You will find the occasional *yǐngbì* (spirit wall) standing alone, its courtyard house demolished, and a few ancient stages. Adding to the time-capsule feel are the numerous slogans from the Cultural Revolution daubed on walls that seem to have been simply left to fade.

Confucius Temple   CONFUCIAN TEMPLE

(文昌宫; Wénchāng Gōng) Meandering along the baked-mud-wall warren of Jīmíngyì's courtyard houses takes you past scattered temples, including this simple Ming-dynasty temple which, like many Confucius temples, also doubled as a school.

Tàishān Temple   TEMPLE

(泰山行宫; Tàishān Xínggōng) This temple's simply stunning Qing murals, depicting popular myths (with the usual mix of Buddhist, Taoist and Confucian figures), were whitewashed – some say for protection – during the Cultural Revolution. A professor from Qīnghuá University helped to uncover them; you can still see streaks of white in places.

City Walls   HISTORIC SITE

(东门; Dōng Mén) Jīmíngyì's walls have been restored so you can now climb them and walk along the top of them. Ascend the **East Gate** for fine views of the town, surrounding fields and Jīmíng Mountain, which overlooks the town to the northwest. Across town is the **West Gate**; the **Temple of the Town Gods** (城隍庙; Chénghuáng Miào), overgrown with weeds and in ruins, stands nearby.

Temple of Eternal Tranquility   TEMPLE

(永宁寺; Yǒngníng Sì) The largest and oldest temple in the area sits atop **Jīmíng Mountain** (鸡鸣山; Jīmíng Shān), which overlooks the town to the northwest. It's still an active monastery and a large and lively festival is held here during April each year. It takes three to four hours to hike to the top from the town (the path is easier round the back of the mountain). A road goes about halfway up so you can sometimes thumb a lift for all but the last section.

🛏 Sleeping & Eating

It's possible to visit Jīmíngyì as a day trip from Běijīng, but spending the night allows you time to explore properly, and to enjoy the slower pace of rural life before returning to Běijīng's luxuries. There's a handful of restaurants and *nóngjiāyuàn* (农家院; village guesthouses) on Da Jie (大街), the road running east–west at the south end of town. Expect to pay ¥30 per bed and about the same for a meal. Bear in mind they eat a lot of donkey (驴肉; lǘ ròu) in these parts.

Bǎilè Kèzhàn   GUESTHOUSE $

(百乐客栈; ☑ 137 8533 9336; Da Jie; 大街; rooms ¥60-70) Simple but clean restaurant and village guesthouse on the south side of Da Jie, with small but tidy rooms off the tiny courtyard out the back. Has a common shower room. Look for the purple and pink signage.

The restaurant menu (mains ¥15 to ¥35) is in Chinese only. Specialities include *kělè jīchì* (可乐鸡翅; chicken wings marinated in coca-cola), *xiǎojī dùn yěmógu* (小鸡炖野蘑菇; stewed chicken with wild mushrooms) and *Guāntīng Hú Huóyú* (官厅湖活鱼; Guāntīng Lake fish). You'll also find standard dishes such as *zhájiàng miàn* (炸酱面; pork and beanpaste noodles), *xīhóngshì chǎojīdàn* (西红柿炒鸡蛋; scrambled eggs and tomatoes), *suānlà tǔdòusī* (酸辣土豆丝; shredded fried potato) and *jiācháng dòufu* (家常豆腐; homestyle tofu).

ℹ Getting There & Away

Jīmíngyì can be reached from the small mining town of Xià Huāyuán (下花园), 5km away. To get to Xià Huāyuán, take bus 880 (¥32, with travel card ¥24; 2½ hours) from beside Déshèngmén Gateway in Běijīng. Then take a minivan (per person ¥1.5) to the local bus station (汽车站; qìchēzhàn), then take the small bus to Shāchéng (沙城), which goes past Jīmíngyì (¥3, five minutes).

Bus 880 leaves from Déshèngmén Gateway on the half hour, every hour from 5.30am to 5.30pm. The return leaves Xià Huāyuán on the hour every hour from 5am to 5pm.

Three trains (10.40am, 2.37pm and 2.41pm) leave each day from Běijīng West Train Station to Xià Huāyuán. The cheapest and quickest is the 2.37pm (¥10, three hours).

Come out of Xià Huāyuán train station and turn right to walk to Jīmíngyì (4km) or flag down the Shāchéng bus (¥3).

There are four trains returning to Běijīng (7.09am, 8.41am, 10.17am and 4.44pm). The first goes to Běijīng North Station, the second to Běijīng Main, the other two to Běijīng West.

Shāndōng

POP 95.8 MILLION

Best Historical Sights

➜ Tài Shān (p157)

➜ Confucius Mansion (p165)

➜ Zhūjiāyù (p156)

➜ Pénglái Pavilion (p181)

Best Places for a Dip

➜ Shílǎorén Beach (p173)

➜ Wángfǔ Pool (p154)

➜ Nos 2 and 3 Bathing Beaches, Qīngdǎo (p173)

➜ No 1 Beach, Yāntái (p182)

Why Go?

Steeped in natural and supernatural allure, the Shāndōng (山东) peninsula on China's northeastern coast is the stuff of legends. Its captivating landscape – a fertile flood plain fed by rivers and underground springs, capped by granite peaks and framed in wild coastline – can't help but inspire wonder.

A lumpy-headed boy named Confucius was born here and grew up to develop a philosophy of virtue and ethics that would reach far beyond his lectures under an apricot tree. Three centuries later China's first emperor Qin Shi Huang would climb Tài Shān, Shāndōng's highest peak, to proclaim a unified empire in 219 BC.

But this place is more than its past. The energetic seaside city of Qīngdǎo ranks among the best places to live in Asia. This is Shāndōng's real draw: you can climb mountains, explore the legacies of kingdoms of old, and still have time to hit the beach.

When to Go

Qīngdǎo

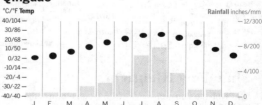

Jun–Aug Cool sea breezes and the beer festival make summer the time to explore Qīngdǎo.	**Sep & Oct** Sacred Tài Shān is gloriously shrouded in mist for just part (not all) of the day.	**Dec & Jan** Dress warmly and ascend Shāndōng's frosted peaks in the dry winter.

History

Shāndōng's tumultuous history is tied to the capricious temperament of the Yellow River, which crosses the peninsula before emptying into the Bo Sea. The 'Mother River' nurtured civilisation but when unhinged left death, disease and rebellion in its wake. After a long period of floods followed by economic depression and unrest, the river again devastated the Shāndōng plain in 1898.

Europeans had also arrived. After two German missionaries died in a peasant uprising in western Shāndōng in 1897, Germany readily seized Qīngdǎo, Britain forced a lease of Wēihǎi, and soon six other nations scrambled for concessions. These acts coupled with widespread famine emboldened a band of superstitious nationalists, and in the closing years of the 19th century, the Boxers rose out of Shāndōng, armed with magical spells and broadswords to lead a rebellion against the eight-nation alliance of Austria-Hungary, France, Germany, Italy, Japan, Russia, the UK and the USA. After foreign powers violently seized Běijīng in 1900, the Empress Cixi effectively surrendered and Boxer and other resistance leaders were executed. The Qing dynasty would soon collapse.

It was not until Japan's surrender in WWII that Shāndōng emerged from decades of war and recovered its cities. In 1955, engineers began an ambitious 50-year flood-control program, and 1959 marked Shāndōng's last catastrophic flood, though now China's economic boom threatens to suck the Yellow River dry.

Today Jǐ'nán, the provincial capital, and the prospering coastal cities of Yāntái and Wēihǎi, all play a supporting role to Qīngdǎo, the province's headliner.

Language

Standard Mandarin is the primary language spoken in Shāndōng, but regional varieties of northern Mandarin often pop up in casual conversation. The characteristic drawls of the three most common dialects,

Shāndōng Highlights

1 Climb the slopes of **Tài Shān** (p157), where stones speak the wisdom of millennia.

2 Chill in **Qīngdǎo** (p170) with a pitcher (or bag) of China's most famous beer.

3 Visit ancient **Qūfù**, (p164) hometown of the sage Confucius.

4 Be charmed by village life in venerable **Zhūjiāyù** (p156).

5 Hike **Láo Shān** (p179), with its magical springs.

6 Savour the ocean breezes in the port city of **Yāntái** (p180).

7 Discover the legends of immortals and pirates at **Pénglái Pavilion** (p181).

Jìlǔ (冀鲁), Zhōngyuán (中原) and Jiāoliáo (胶辽), are each distinctive.

ⓘ Getting There & Around

Shāndōng is linked to neighbouring and distant provinces by both bus and rail. Jǐ'nán is the transport hub, with rail connections to all major towns and cities in Shāndōng. The high-speed rail now links Jǐ'nán, Tàishān, Qūfù and Qīngdǎo to Běijīng and Shànghǎi. Buses also reach every corner of the province.

With South Korea and Japan just across the water, there are direct international flights through three airports – Jǐ'nán, Qīngdǎo and Yāntái. Ferries also sail from Qīngdǎo to South Korea (Incheon) and Japan (Shimonoseki), and from Yāntái to Incheon.

Jǐ'nán 济南

☑ 0531 / POP 3.5 MILLION

Jǐ'nán is Shāndōng's busy capital city, serving as the transit hub to other destinations around the province. On its surface, the city is in flux, but beneath the dusty construction and sprawl are 72 artesian springs, which gently roil in azure pools and flow steadily into Dàmíng Lake.

The train stations are to the west. The heart of the city, encircled by the Húchéng River, is tourist friendly, with shiny shopping districts on Quancheng Lu and Quancheng Sq.

◉ Sights

Thousand Buddha Mountain MOUNTAIN
(千佛山; Qiānfó Shān; 18 Jingshi Yilu; admission ¥30, cable car one way/return ¥20/30, luge ¥25/30; ⊙5am-9pm; ◻K51) Beginning in the Sui dynasty (581–618AD), the pious carved Buddhas into this mountain southeast of the city centre. The oldest are at **Xīnguóchán Temple** (兴国禅寺; admission ¥5; ⊙7.30am-4.30pm), the golden-roofed complex near the **cable car** and **luge** drop-off on the mountaintop. On the rare clear day looking south, you can spot Tài Shān, the anthill in the distance.

Jǐ'nán Museum MUSEUM
(济南博物馆; Jǐ'nán Bówùguǎn; ☑8295 9204; www.jnmuseum.com; 30 Jing Shiyilu; 经十一路30号; audio tour ¥10; ⊙8.30am-4pm Tue-Sun; ◻K51) FREE North of Thousand Buddha Mountain's main entrance, the Jǐ'nán Museum has a small, distinctive collection that includes paintings, calligraphy, ceramics, Buddhist figures from the Tang dynasty and a delightful boat carved from a walnut shell.

Shāndōng Museum MUSEUM
(山东博物馆; Shāndōng Bówùguǎn; ☑8505 8201; www.sdmuseum.com; 11899 Jingshi Lu; 经十路11899号; audio tour ¥30; ⊙9am-4pm Tue-Sun; ◻115, 202, 18) FREE The enormous new provincial museum – a 7km slog east of the city centre – surveys local culture from the mesolithic age to the present. Its collection began as one of the first organised museums in China in 1904. On display are oracle bones, Qi and Lu kingdom pottery, Han tomb murals and clothing worn by the Kong clan (Confucius' descendants).

Great Southern Mosque MOSQUE
(清真南大寺; Qīngzhēn Nán Dà Sì; 47 Yongchang Jie; ◻K50, 101) FREE Jǐ'nán's oldest mosque has stood in one form or another in the centre of town since 1295. Cover arms and remove hats before entering. A lively Hui (Muslim Chinese) neighbourhood is to the north.

Parks

Strolling among the swaying willows and quiet waterways of Jǐ'nán's particularly lovely parks is a pleasant escape from the urban din. The most central include the most famous of them all **Bàotū Spring** (趵突泉; Bàotū Quán; 1 Baotuquan Nanlu; admission ¥40; ◻K51); **Huánchéng Park** (环城公园; Huánchéng Gōngyuán; 2 Nanmen Jie) FREE where Black Tiger Spring empties into the old city moat, the Húchéng River; and **Five Dragon Pool** (五龙潭公园; Wǔlóngtán Gōngyuán; 18 Kuangshi Jie, 筐市街18号; admission ¥5; ◻5, 101), a serene study of local life, where elders paint calligraphy on the steps and kids chase the goldfish.

SHĀNDŌNG JǏ'NÁN

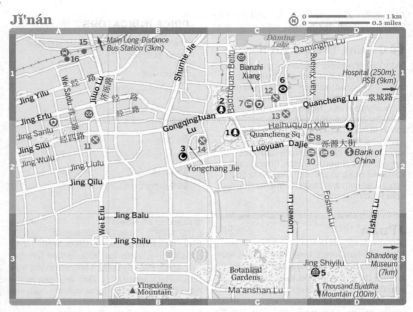

Jǐ'nán

⦿ Sights

⬤ Sleeping

⊗ Eating

ⓘ Transport

In a quiet alleyway off the walking street Furong Jie (turn right at the police stand), the neighbourhood comes to soak in spring-fed **Wángfǔ Pool** (王府池子; Wángfǔ Chízi) **FREE**. The waters are a brisk 18°C year round, so indulge frequently in barbecue and beer at one of the nearby stands.

All the springs eventually flow into **Dàmíng Lake** (大明湖; Dàmíng Hú; admission ¥30), the largest park with paddle boats, temples, and islands to explore.

🏃 Activities

Open-air, motorised **boats** (☎8690 5886; per stop ¥10; ◷every 20min 9am-5pm) circle clockwise around the lovely Húchéng River and the south side of Dàmíng Lake, making 10 stops at major sights including Bàotū Spring, Black Tiger Spring, Five Dragon Pool and Quancheng Sq, as well as rising and falling several storeys via two fascinating locks. It takes about 1½ hours for the full circuit.

🛏 Sleeping

Budget hotels with rooms for around ¥180 are clustered around the main train station, though not all cater to foreigners and rooms vary greatly. Look first.

Chéngběi Youth Hostel
HOSTEL **$**

(城北国际青年旅舍; Chéngběi Guójì Qīngnián Lǚshě; ☏8691 7661; w454488201@gmail.com; 111 Bianzhi Xiang, off Quancheng Lu; 鞭指巷111号; dm ¥40-45, d ¥120; ✳️🛜; 🚌3, 5, K50) In a town low on cheap rooms, this youth hostel in a small, converted courtyard residence is your best option. The dorms and common bathrooms are decent, but the one available double room is just a mattress on the ground. There's a small bar, solid travel advice, organised biking trips to interesting sites in and around Jǐ'nán, and hiking gear for rent.

To get here, follow the flow of traffic, turn right off Quancheng Lu down Bianzhi Xiang, a small alley, and at the police station turn left down an even smaller alley. The hostel is through the gate with the red horse.

Silver Plaza Quancheng Hotel
HOTEL **$$**

(银座泉城大酒店; Yínzuò Quánchéng Dàjiǔdiàn; ☏8629 1911; 2 Nanmen Jie; 南门大街2号; d/tr incl breakfast ¥360/385; ✆✳️@) You know this is a Chinese business hotel from the blinding Euro-style bling in the lobby. Professional staff and a prime spot overlooking Quancheng Sq make up for that and the compact rooms with stained tile ceilings. Shell out for an upgrade in the renovated B-wing.

Sofitel Silver Plaza
HOTEL **$$$**

(索菲特银座大饭店; Suǒfēitè Yínzuò Dàfàndiàn; ☏8981 1611; www.sofitel.com; 66 Luoyuan Dajie; 泺源大街66号; r from ¥612, plus 10% service charge; ✆✳️@🏊) The city's first five-star hotel is in the commercial district and is still the best option, though we wish standard rooms were as spacious as the lobby promises.

✖️ Eating

Jǐ'nán is a famed centre of Lǔ cuisine (see p958), characterised by bold flavours brought out by cooking over a high heat with plenty of oil and spices. Most of the best eating is had in the city's streets and alleys.

Fúróng Jie
STREET FOOD **$**

(芙蓉街; dishes from ¥10; 🚌3, 5, K50) Off Quancheng Lu's shopping strip, Fúróng Jie is a pedestrian alley crammed with restaurants and food stalls. **Fúshún Jūjiācháng Restaurant** (福顺居家常饭馆; Fúshùn Jūjiācháng Fànguǎn; ☏188 0640 9638; 112 Furong Jie; most dishes ¥8-28; ⏰9.30am-2.30pm & 5-10pm) is a popular stop, with all of Lǔ cuisine's greatest hits pictured on its menu.

Yīnhǔchí Jie
STREET FOOD **$**

(饮虎池街; dishes from ¥10) Evenings are smoky on Yīnhǔchí Jie in the Hui district near the Great Southern Mosque. Hawkers fan the flames of charcoal grills lining the street, roasting up all manner of *shāokǎo* (barbecue on a stick). They make crisp scallion pancakes and fresh noodles too.

Dàguān Gardens
STREET FOOD **$**

(大观园; Dàguān Yuán; Jing Silu; dishes from ¥10) About 1km south of the main train station is this dandified enclave of modern eateries. **Lǔxī'nán Flavor Restaurant** (鲁西南老牌坊; Lǔxī'nán Lǎopáifang; ☏8605 4567; 2 Daguan Yuan; dishes ¥28-98; ⏰11am-2.30pm & 5-10pm), inside the north gate, is the place for a refined take on Lǔ cuisine, such as sweet and spicy cabbage with glass noodles, or lamb (braised or sautéed), accompanied by sesame cakes – not rice. Chinese menu with pictures.

The alley nearby, **Wěi Èrlu** (纬二路), is a messy strip of noodle, *shāokǎo* and lamb soup carts (serving beer for ¥4!) that buzzes until late.

Seasons Mínghú
CANTONESE **$$**

(四季明湖; Sìjì Mínghú; ☏6666 9898; 7th fl, Parc66, 188 Quancheng Lu; mains from ¥38, dim sum from ¥18; ⏰11am-10pm) The dandy waiters at this elegant restaurant on the top of the Parc66 mall don gloves while serving southern Chinese classics, including dim sum, salt-baked chicken and durian cakes. Watch out when ordering fish, which can be priced up to ¥998 per *jīn* (600g)!

ℹ️ Information

ATMs (自动取款机; Zìdòng Qǔkuǎn Jī) Available in the lobbies of larger hotels like the Sofitel and Crowne Plaza. There are plenty of full-service banks around town.

Bank of China (中国银行; Zhōngguó Yínháng; 22 Luoyuan Dajie; ⏰9am-5pm Mon-Fri) Currency exchange/24-hour ATMs accepting foreign cards.

Public Security Bureau (PSB; 公安局; Gōng'ānjú; ☏8508 1000, visa inquiries ext 2459; 777 Shuhuaxi Lu; 舜华西路777号; ⏰9am-noon & 2-4.40pm Mon-Fri) About 9km or a ¥18 taxi ride east of the city centre.

Shāndōng Provincial Qiānfó Shān Hospital International Clinic (千佛山医院国际医疗中心; Qiānfó Shān Yīyuàn Guójì Yīliáo Zhōngxīn; ☏8926 8018, 8926 8017; www.sdhospital.com.cn; 16766 Jinshi Lu; ⏰8-11am & 2-5.30pm Mon-Fri) English and Japanese spoken. Take bus K51 or K68 to the Nánkǒu (南口) stop on Lishan Lu.

❶ Getting There & Away

AIR

Jǐ'nán's Yáoqiáng Airport is 40km from the city and connects to most major cities, with daily flights to Běijīng (¥769, one hour), Dàlián (¥502, one hour), Guǎngzhōu (¥897, 2½ hours), Hā'ěrbīn (¥523, two hours), Seoul (¥1034, one hour 40 minutes), Shànghǎi (¥612, 1½ hours), and Xī'ān (¥821, 1½ hours).

BUS

Jǐ'nán's most convenient station is the **main long-distance bus station** (长途总汽车站; Chángtú Zǒng Qìchē Zhàn; ☎ 8594 1472; 131 Jiluo Lu) about 3km north of the train station, though buses to destinations within the province also leave from the **bus station** (☎ 8830 3030; 22 Chezhan Jie) directly across from the train station.

Some buses departing regularly from the main long-distance bus station:

Běijīng ¥129, 5½ hours, six daily (9am, 10.40am, 12pm, 1.40pm, 2.20pm and 9pm)

Qīngdǎo ¥109, 4½ hours, hourly (7.20am to 8.30pm)

Qūfù ¥45, two hours, every 50 minutes (6.50am to 6pm)

Shànghǎi ¥266, 12 hours, four daily (9am, 3pm, 6pm and 8.30pm)

Tài'ān ¥25, two hours, every 30 minutes (6.45am to 6pm)

Tiānjīn ¥124, 4½ hours, three daily (10.50am, 1.40pm and 9pm)

Yāntái ¥167, 5½ hours, hourly (6.30am to 9.30pm)

TRAIN

Jǐ'nán is a major hub in the east China rail system and has several busy train stations. Most travellers can rely on the **main train station** (火车总站; huǒchē zǒng zhàn), a 4km ride on Bus 3 (¥2) from the city centre.

Lines at the station's ticket office can be slow. Ticket offices only charge ¥5 commission and are all around the train station square, including the **plane/train ticket office** (盛祥源航空铁路售票处; ☎ 8610 9666; Quánchéng Hotel lobby, 115 Chezhan Jie; commission ¥5; ⏰ plane 7.30am-10pm, train 8am-8pm) in the Quánchéng Hotel lobby. Chéngběi Youth Hostel (p155) can also book tickets.

Some express trains (second-/first-class seat) departing from the main train station:

Běijīng ¥195/330, two hours, frequently (7.15am to 8.02pm)

Qīngdǎo ¥120/145, two hours 40 minutes, every 10 minutes (7.20am to 8.20pm)

Qūfù ¥60/100, 40 minutes, four daily (7.26am, 9.22am, 11.09am and 7.08pm)

Shànghǎi ¥399/674, four hours, four daily (9.40am, 12.08pm, 4.37pm and 7.08pm)

Tài'ān ¥30/50, 24 minutes, five daily (7.26am, 9.40am, 12.08pm, 12.32pm and 5.22pm)

Wéifāng ¥65/80, one hour 20 minutes, every 20 minutes (7.20am to 8.20pm)

Some regular trains (seat/hard sleeper) departing:

Xī'ān ¥149/264, 13 to 18 hours, six daily (9.20am, 11.21am, 3.45pm, 5.04pm, 5.58pm and 10.35pm)

Yāntái ¥75/138, six to eight hours, five daily (1.27am, 6.43am, 7.39am, 11.02am and 3.50pm)

❶ Getting Around

TO/FROM THE AIRPORT

Airport shuttles (☎ 96888; adult ¥20; ⏰ hourly 6am-6pm) connect the main train station and the **Yùquán Simpson Hotel** (玉泉森信大酒店; Yùquán Sēnxìn Dàjiǔdiàn; Luoyuan Dajie) with Jǐ'nán's Yáoqiáng airport. The shuttle also runs directly to Tài'ān (¥80, two hours, five daily, 11.30am, 2pm, 4.30pm, 5.30pm and 8pm).

PUBLIC TRANSPORT

Bus 15 or 84 (¥1) connects the main long-distance bus station with the main train station. Bus K51 (¥2) runs from the main train station through the city centre and then south past Bàotū Spring Park to Thousand Buddha Mountain.

TAXI

Taxis cost ¥8 for the first 3km then ¥1.75 (slightly more at night) per kilometre thereafter.

Around Jǐ'nán

Zhūjiāyù   朱家峪

Eighty kilometres east of Jǐ'nán is one of Shāndōng's oldest hamlets, Zhūjiāyù (☎ 8380 8158; admission ¥40; ⏰ tickets 8am-5pm). Its intact structures mostly date back to the Ming and Qing dynasties, and many have been recently spruced up to serve as movie and soap-opera sets, but strolling the stone-paved streets is still a journey back in time.

Zhūjiāyù and its bucolic panoramas of rolling hills can be explored in an easy day trip. You can wander on your own, though there are official, Chinese-speaking guides (¥60) and eager long-time residents (¥30) ready to show you around. Posted maps are in English.

Ongoing updates have added a parking lot and official tourist centre, where you buy your ticket and, behind the centre, access the main gate. In a bid to get kids' attention away from their mobile phones, there is also a half-hour, immersive **movie experience** (incl entry ¥80; ⏰ 10am Mon-Fri, 10am & 2pm Sat & Sun) loosely based on the harrowing journeys of Shāndōng natives seeking opportunity.

Follow the Ming-dynasty, double-track ancient road (双轨古道; *shuāngguǐ gǔdào*) to the Qing-dynasty **Wénchāng Pavilion** (文昌阁; Wénchāng Gé), an arched gate topped by a single-roofed shrine where teachers would take new pupils to make offerings to Confucius before their first lesson. On your left is **Shānyīn Primary School** (山阴小学; Shānyīn Xiǎoxué), a series of halls and courtyards with exhibits on local life.

Walk on to see the many ancestral temples, including the **Zhu Family Ancestral Hall** (朱氏家祠; Zhūshì Jiācí), packed mudbrick homesteads, and quaint, arched *shíqiáo* (stone bridges). The **Kāngxī Overpass** (康熙双桥; Kāngxī Shuāng Qiáo) is one of the earliest examples in the world of such a traffic structure and dates from 1671. A further 30-minute climb past the last drystone walls of the village will take you to the gleaming white **Kuíxīng Pavilion** (魁星楼; Kuíxīng Lóu) crowning the hill.

The humble restaurants in the village cook up excellent fare from local ingredients. At **Lǎo Yī Mín Restaurant** (老农民菜馆; Lǎo Yī Mín Càiguǎn; ☎ 138 8498 9061; dishes ¥14-21), about 100m past the large Mao portrait, the genial owners take their dog hunting for wild rabbit (¥40 per *jīn*) and forage for fresh mushrooms and greens in the hills.

If you want to stay overnight, look for flags posting '农家乐' (*nóngjiālè*; a guesthouse or homestay). The basic but clean **Gǔcūn Inn** (古村酒家; Gǔcūn Jiǔjiā; ☎ 8380 8135; dm ¥30, d with bathroom ¥100; ☎) is set in a courtyard home with a spirit wall decorated with cranes and peacocks. The friendly owners also cook up meals (mains ¥15 to ¥38; English menu) using their garden-grown ingredients. Pass under the Kāngxī Overpass and take the low road at the split, then follow the bend to the left.

To get here from Jǐnán, catch bus K301 (¥14, 1½ hours, 7am to 6.30pm) to the Jìshī Xuéyuàn (技师学院) stop in front of a large technical college. From there catch bus 9 (¥1) to the large white gate marking the village drop-off. It's another 2km walk (locals offer lifts) to the tourist centre. Taxis from the college will go the whole way for ¥15. Returning to Jǐnán, reverse the process or flag down a bus across from the white gate on the main road. Buses back after 5pm are rare.

Tài'ān 泰安 & Tài Shān 泰山

📞 0538 / POP 1.1 MILLION

In China, where sacred mountains are a dime a dozen, the one that matters most is **Tài Shān** (泰山; www.taishangeopark.com; adult/student & senior Feb-Nov ¥127/60, Dec-Jan ¥102/50). Its fellow Unesco World Heritage Sites Éméi Shān and Huángshān may be higher and more photogenic, respectively, but Tài Shān has been worshipped since at least the 11th century BC. To scholars and poets, it is known as Dōng Yuè, the Eastern Great Mountain, one of China's five most sacred peaks.

Qin Shi Huang, the First Emperor, chose its summit to proclaim the unified kingdom of China in 219 BC. From its heights Confucius uttered the dictum 'The world is small'; Mao lumbered up and declared 'The east is red'. Seventy-one other emperors and countless figures also paid this mountain their respects. It inspired their poetry and prose inscribed in tablets, boulders, caves and cliffs all over the slopes. Pilgrims still make their way up the steps as a symbol of their devotion to Taoist and Buddhist teachings – and perhaps to earn a long life.

The gateway to Tài Shān's sacred slopes is the village of Tài'ān, which has had a tourist industry in full swing since before the Ming dynasty. In the 17th century, historian Zhang Dai described package tours that included choice of lodging (enormous inns with more than 20 kitchens and hundreds of servants, opera performers and courtesans), a post-summit congratulatory banquet, plus an optional sedan-chair upgrade (climbing tax not included).

Since you will need at least a full day to explore the mountain, spending the night in Tài'ān or at the summit is advised.

Autumn, when humidity is low, is the best time to visit; early October onwards has the clearest weather. In winter temperatures dip below freezing and many summit guesthouses have no hot water. Tourist season peaks from May to October. Definitely avoid holidays.

Tài'ān

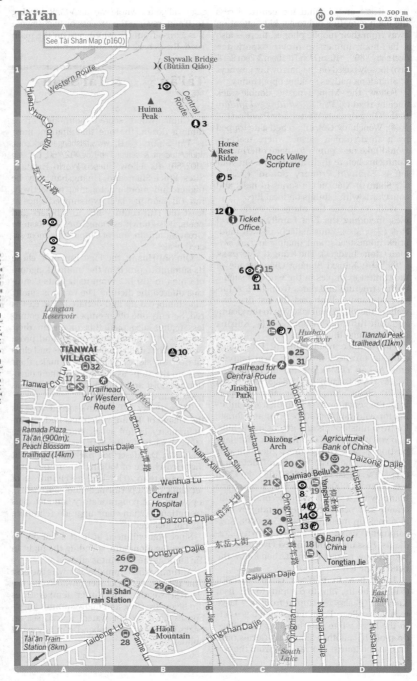

See Tài Shān Map (p160)

Skywalk Bridge
(Bùtiān Qiáo)

Western Route

Central Route

Huánshān Gōnglù

开山公路

Huíma Peak

Horse Rest Ridge

Rock Valley Scripture

Ticket Office

Longtan Reservoir

Hushan Reservoir

Tiānzhú Peak trailhead (11km)

TIĀNWÀI VILLAGE

Trailhead for Central Route

Tianwai Cūn Lu

Trailhead for Western Route

Nài River

Jinshān Park

Longtan Lu 北堂路

Naihe Xilu

Puzhao Silu

Jishan Lu

Dàizōng Arch

Hongmen Lu

Agricultural Bank of China

Ramada Plaza Tài'ān (900m);
Peach Blossom trailhead (14km)

Leigushi Dajie

Wenhua Lu

Central Hospital

Daizong Dajie 岱宗大街

Dongyue Dajie

东岳大街

Daimiao Beilu

Daizong Dajie

Yangsheng Jie 仰圣街

Hushan Lu

Qingnian Lu 青年路

青年路

Jiachang Jie

Caiyuan Dajie

Bank of China

Tongtian Jie

Tài Shān Train Station

Taidong Lu

Panhe Lu

Lingshan Dajie

Nanguan Dajie

Hushan Lu

Tài'ān Train Station (8km)

Hāolǐ Mountain

South Lake

East Lake

Tài'ān

⊚ Sights & Activities

Dài Temple TAOIST TEMPLE
(岱庙; Dài Miào; www.daimiao.cn/English; Daimiao Beijie Lu; adult/child ¥30/15; ⊙ 8am-6pm summer, to 5pm winter) This magnificent Taoist temple complex is where all Tài'ān roads lead, being the traditional first stop on the pilgrimage route up Tài Shān. The grounds are an impressive example of Song-dynasty (960–1127) temple construction with features of an imperial palace, though other structures stood here 1000 years before that.

Many visitors enter from the north through **Hòu Zài gate** (候载门), but entering from the south through **Zhèngyáng gate** (正阳门) allows you to follow the traditional passage through the main temple and up Hongmen Lu to the start of Tài Shān's central route ascent.

From the south end, two lions watch cars pass by on Dongyue Dajie, flanking the splendid *páifāng* (ornamental arch). Beyond this and the Zhèngyáng gate, **Yáocān Pavilion** (遥参亭; Yáocān Tíng; ⊙ 6.30am-6pm) contains a hall dedicated to deities including Bixia, the daughter of Tai Shan, who became the focus of worship by the 11th century, and Songzi Niangniang, her attendant to whom couples wanting children dutifully pay respects.

Between the buildings, the courtyards are filled with prized examples of poetry and imperial records. Fossilised-looking *bìxì* (the mythical tortoise son of the dragon), dating from the 12th century onward, carry stelae on their backs documenting everything from the civil exam process to emperors' birthdays. The Han Emperor Wudi himself is said to have planted some of the massive, twisting trees in the **Cypress Tree Pavilion** 2100 years ago.

The main hall is the colossal, twin-eaved, nine-bay-wide **Hall of Heavenly Blessing** (天贶殿; Tiānkuàng Diàn; shoe covers ¥1), which dates to AD 1009. The dark interior houses an exquisite, 62m-long Song-dynasty mural depicting Emperor Zhenzong as the Lord of Tài Shān, the god of longevity to whom the entire complex is dedicated. Before exiting, scale the walls over the Hòu Zài gate to see what's in store for your pilgrimage up the mountain.

⊚ Climbing Tài Shān

There are four routes up to the highest peak (1532m) that can be done on foot: **Central route**, historically the Emperor's Route, winds 8.9km from Dài Temple to the summit and gains 1400m in elevation; **Peach Blossom Park route** climbs 13km on the west side; and the least travelled 5.4km **Tiānzhú Peak route** goes up the back of the mountain from the east. **Western route** follows the 14km shuttle-bus route and converges with the Central route at the halfway point (Midway Gate to Heaven), from where it's another 3.5km up steep steps to the summit.

Tài Shān

Tài Shān

◎ Sights

1 Archway to Immortality	A1
2 Azure Clouds Temple	B1
3 Cloud Step Bridge	B2
4 Confucius Temple	A1
5 Five Great Pines	A2
6 God of Wealth Temple	B3
7 Jade Emperor Temple	B1
8 Midway Gate to Heaven	B3
9 North Gate to Heaven	B1
10 North Pointing Rock	B1
11 Opposing Pines Pavilion	A2
12 Path of 18 Bends	A2
13 Qīngdì Palace	B1
14 South Gate to Heaven	A1
15 Ten-Thousand Zhàng Tablet	B2
16 Zhǎnlǔ Terrace	B1

🛏 Sleeping

17 Nán Tiān Mén Bīnguǎn	A1
18 Shénqì Hotel	B1
19 Xiānjū Bīnguǎn	A1
20 Yùyèquán Hotel	B3

ℹ Transport

21 Main Cable Car	B3
22 Peach Blossom Park Cable Car	A1
23 Rear Rocky Recess Cable Car	B1

If this sounds like too much for your knees, cover the Western route by bus to Midway Gate to Heaven and then take the cable car to South Gate to Heaven near the summit. Reverse the journey or nab a bus to get back down.

Sights on the mountain close around 5pm. Weather can change suddenly and the summit gets very cold, windy and wet, so bring warm layers and rain gear. You can buy rain ponchos and, at the top, rent overcoats (¥30).

As with all Chinese mountain hikes, viewing the sunrise is an integral part of the experience. You can either do a night hike or, easier, stay overnight at one of the summit guesthouses to greet the first rays of dawn.

Central Route 中路

This has been the main route up the mountain since the 3rd century BC, and over the past two millennia a bewildering number of bridges, trees, rivers, gullies, inscriptions, caves, pavilions and temples have become famous sites in their own right. Although the central route is well paved, don't underestimate the challenge of its 7000 steps. Figure at least six hours from Dài Temple to get to the top.

Tài Shān functions as an outdoor museum of antiquities. Two of the most prized are **Rock Valley Scripture** (经石峪; Jīngshí Yù), in the first part of the climb, a massive inscription of a Buddhist text that was once hidden behind a waterfall, and **North Prayer Rock** (拱北石; Gǒngběi Shí), a huge boulder pointing skywards and a site of imperial sacrifices to heaven, at the summit.

Purists begin with a south–north perambulation through Dài Temple, 1.7km south of the actual ascent, in accordance with imperial tradition, but there is no shame in starting at the bus stop by **Guandi Temple** (关帝庙; Guāndì Miào; admission ¥10), the first of many dedicated to the Taoist protector of peace. Passing **First Gate of Heaven** (一天门; Yìtiān Mén) marks the start of the incline, though the **ticket office** (售票处; Shòupiào Chù; ☑806 6077; ⊙24hr) is still a way further at **Wànxiān Tower** (万仙楼). The **Red Gate Palace** (红门宫; Hóng Mén Gōng; admission ¥5; ⊙8am-5pm) is the first of a series of temples dedicated to Bìxia, the compassionate daughter of the god of Tài Shān. She wears a headdress adorned with phoenixes and is accompanied by nine attendants including the Goddesses of Children and of Eyesight.

Take a detour into the **Geoheritage Scenic Area** (地质园区; Dìzhí Yuánqū) for a look at unusual radial rock formations that mesmerised Confucius himself. Back on the main path is the Buddhist **Dǒumǔ Hall** (斗母宫; Dǒumǔ Gōng), first constructed in 1542 under the more magical name 'Dragon Spring Nunnery'. The back of the temple yard offers a quiet view of a triple waterfall, best seen in July and August. Prayers are written on the ribbons festooning the pines. Continue through the tunnel of cypresses known as **Cypress Cave** (柏洞; Bó Dòng) to **Balking Horse Ridge** (回马岭; Huímǎ Lǐng), which marks the point where Emperor Zhenzong had to dismount and continue by litter because his horse refused to go further.

The **Midway Gate to Heaven** (中天门; Zhōng Tiān Mén) marks the point where some travellers, seeing the stairway disappearing into the clouds, head for the cable car. Don't give up! Rest your legs, visit the small and smoky **God of Wealth Temple** (财神庙; Cáishén Miào) and stock up on snacks. (If you need them, 24-hour **first-aid stations** are at both the Midway and South Gate.)

If you decide to catch a ride, the **main cable car** (空中索道; kōngzhōng suǒdào; one way/return ¥100/200; ⏱7.30am-6.30pm 16 Apr-15 Oct, 8.30am-5pm 16 Oct-15 Apr) is a 15-minute ride to **Moon View Peak** (月观峰; Yuèguān Fēng) at the South Gate to Heaven. Be warned: peak season and weekend queues can take two hours. Also, the cable car stops when there is any risk of lightning.

If you continue on foot you'll come next to **Cloud Step Bridge** (云步桥; Yúnbù Qiáo), once a modest wooden bridge spanning a torrent of waterfalls, and the withered and wiry **Wǔdàfū Pine** (五大夫松; Wǔdàfū Sōng), under which Emperor Qin Shi Huang, overtaken by a violent storm, found shelter. Across the valley, each character carved in the **Ten-Thousand Zhàng Tablet** (万丈碑), dated 1748, measures 1m across.

You'll pass **Opposing Pines Pavilion** (对松亭; Duìsōng Tíng) and then finally reach the arduous **Path of 18 Bends** (十八盘; Shíbāpán), a 400m extremely steep ascent to the mountain's false summit; climbing it is performed in slow motion as legs turn to lead. If you have the energy, see if you can spot the small shrine dedicated to the Lord of Tài Shān's grandmother along the way. There is an alternate route to the Azure Clouds Temple here via another steep, narrow staircase to the right. If you continue on the main route, at the top is the **Archway to Immortality**

(升仙坊; Shēngxiān Fāng), once believed to bestow immortality on those dedicated enough to reach it. Emperors made sure to get off their huge litters and walk through.

The final stretch takes you to the **South Gate to Heaven** (南天门; Nán Tián Mén), the third celestial gate, which marks the beginning of the summit area. Bear right on Tian Jie, the main strip, and pass through the gate to reach the sublimely perched **Azure Clouds Temple** (碧霞祠; Bìxiá Cí; ⏱8am-5.15pm) FREE, dedicated to Bixia. The iron tiling of the temple buildings is intended to prevent damage by strong winds, and *chīwěn* (ornaments meant to protect against fire) decorate their bronze eaves.

You have to climb higher to get to the **Confucius Temple** (孔庙; Kǒng Miào), where statues of Confucius, Mencius, Zengzi and other Confucian luminaries are venerated. The Taoist **Qīngdì Palace** (青帝宫; Qīngdì Gōng) is right before the fog- and cloud-swathed **Jade Emperor Temple** (玉皇顶; Yùhuáng Dǐng), which stands at the summit, the highest point of the Tài Shān plateau. Inside is an effigy of the Jade Emperor, who governs all mortal realms.

The main sunrise vantage point is the **North Pointing Rock**; if you're lucky, visibility extends over 200km to the coast.

At the summit, you can see another side of the mountain by descending via the Tiānzhú Peak or Peach Blossom Park route.

Tiānzhú Peak Route 天烛峰景区

The route through the **Tiānzhú Peak Scenic Area** (Tiānzhú Fēng Jǐngqū) offers a chance to experience Tài Shān without crowds. It's mostly ancient pine forest, ruins and peaks back there, so consider combining it with the Central route for an entirely different view.

If you ascend this way, get an early start to the trailhead, which is 15km by bus 19 (¥2) from Tài Shān Train Station. The challenging climb itself can take five hours.

It's 5.4km from the trailhead to the **Rear Rocky Recess Cable Car** (后石坞索道; Hòu Shíwù suǒdào; ☏833 0765; one way ¥20; ⏱8.30am-4pm Apr-Oct, closed 16 Oct-15 Apr), which takes you from the back of the mountain to the **North Gate to Heaven** (北天门; Běi Tiānmén) cable-car stop (北天门索道站; Běi Tiānmén suǒdào zhàn) and views of Tiānzhú Peak – when it's running. Call in advance.

SHĀNDŌNG TÀI'ÀN & TÀI SHĀN

Peach Blossom Park Route
桃花源

A third route to the summit passes through a scenic valley of striking geological formations and trees that explode with colour in early spring and fall. It makes for an especially pleasant descent.

Near the South Gate to Heaven, take Peach Blossom Park **cable car** (桃花源索道; Táohuā Yuán suǒdào; ☑ 833 0763; one way/return ¥100/200; ⊙ 7.30am-5pm) down to Peach Blossom Valley. This cable car operates infrequently, so call ahead. From the cable car drop-off it is another 9km on foot or by bus (one way ¥30, departs when full 6am to 6pm and midnight to 2am) to reach the park exit and bus 16 back into town.

Western Route 西路

The most popular way to descend is by **bus** (one way ¥30; ⊙ 6am-6pm & midnight-2am peak, 7am-6pm off-peak) via the western route. These buses are also handy for night hikes up to catch the sunrise. They zip every 20 minutes (or when full) between Tiānwài Village and Midway Gate to Heaven, not stopping in between.

Walking the route is not always pleasant as the poorly marked footpath and road often intercept or coincide, but it rewards you with a variety of scenic orchards and pools. At the mountain's base, **Pervading Light Temple** (普照寺; Pǔzhào Sì; admission ¥5; ⊙ 8am-5.30pm) is a serene Buddhist temple dating from the Southern and Northern dynasties (420–589AD). The main attraction is **Black Dragon Pool** (黑龙潭; Hēilóng Tán), just below **Longevity Bridge** (长寿桥; Chángshòu Qiáo). The mythical pool is fed by a small waterfall and said to conceal grand carp palaces and herbs that turn humans into beasts.

✮✮ Festivals & Events

Trail runners and stair steppers converge to race up the Central route for the **International Climbing Festival** (www.zgjqdh.com/zt/tsgjdsj/index.shtml) every September.

🛏 Sleeping

🛏 Tài'ān

There are many midrange options in town, mostly clustered around the Tàishān train station. Ask for discounts.

Hóngmén International Youth Hostel HOSTEL $

(红门国际青年旅舍; Hóngmén Guójì Qīngnián Lǚshè; ☑ 808 6188; www.yhachina.com; 89 Hongmen Lu; 红门路89号; dm ¥45-65, s & d ¥188, tr ¥218; 🖳; 🚌 K3, K37) In a red courtyard building, formerly part of the Guandi Temple next door, this new hostel offers the best of all worlds – the mountain within a few steps, a cafe-bar and bright rooms with all necessary conveniences including wi-fi. The very knowledgeable staff organise night climbs and advise about how to take in the sights to the fullest.

Tàishān International Youth Hostel HOSTEL $

(太山国际青年旅舍; Tàishān Guójì Qīngnián Lǚshè; ☑ 628 5196; 65 Tongtian Jie; 通天街65号; dm ¥50-70, s & d ¥188; ❄@🖳; 🚌1, 4, 7, 8, 17) Tài'ān's first youth hostel has clean spartan rooms with pine furnishings and old propaganda posters. Bike rental, free laundry and a bar on the 4th floor make this a pleasant experience. Look for the pair of arches just off Tongtian Jie. Discounts get rooms down to ¥128.

Yùzuò Hotel HOTEL $$$

(御座宾馆; Yùzuò Bīnguǎn; ☑ 826 9999; www.yuzuo.cn; 50 Daimiao Beilu; 岱庙北路50号; s & d ¥780, ste ¥1680; ❄🖳; 🚌4, 6) This pretty hotel next to the Dài Temple's north gate was purposely kept to two storeys out of respect for its neighbour. Deluxe rooms are decked out imperial style; cheaper rooms are rather ordinary. The attached bakery and restaurants serve Taoist food (12 courses ¥168 per person). Discounts of 50% make this a good deal.

Ramada Plaza Tài'ān HOTEL $$$

(东尊华美达大酒店; Dōngzūn Huáměidá Dàjiǔdiàn; ☑ 836 8888; www.ramadaplazataian.com; 16 Yingsheng Donglu, 迎胜东路16号; s & d ¥1160-1400, ste ¥1960-3360; ⊖❄🖳✖; 🚌8) The town's first five-star hotel is in the northwest and has all the usual comforts plus fantastic views of the main attraction. Discounts of 40%.

🛏 On the Mountain

Look for signs posting 如家 (rújiā) or 宾馆 (bīnguǎn) at the summit area along Tian Jie for inns starting from ¥120 and going *way* up on weekends. Rates provided here don't apply to holiday periods, when they can triple. Try asking for discounts.

Yùyèquán Hotel HOTEL $$

(玉夜泉兵宾; ☑ 822 6740; Midway Gate to Heaven; s & d ¥200-300, ste ¥600; ✳) The only thing going at the Midway Gate to Heaven has drab but tidy rooms facing an indoor courtyard. Plenty of food options on the 1st floor and next door. Discounts of 50%.

Xiānjū Bīnguǎn HOTEL $$

(仙居宾馆; ☑ 823 9984; 5 Tian Jie; tw ¥100-360, d & tr ¥420-700; ✳) By the South Gate to Heaven, this two-star hotel has decent rooms. Some even have large windows overlooking greenery. Discounts of 30%.

Nán Tiān Mén Bīnguǎn HOTEL $$$

(南天门宾馆; ☑ 833 0988; 1 Tian Jie; d without/with bathroom ¥680-780/980, tr ¥880-980; ✳ @) Located smack bang before you turn onto Tian Jie, this is the easiest place to reach at the summit on weary legs. Rooms are a bit beaten up but still clean and airy. There's 24-hour hot water.

Shénqì Hotel HOTEL $$$

(神憩宾馆; Shénqì Bīnguǎn; ☑ 822 3866; fax 826 3816; s & d ¥1200-1800, ste ¥6000; ✳ @) The only hotel on the actual summit and prices reflect that. The priciest mountain-view, standard rooms have new everything and were the first on the mountain with hot water in the winter. The restaurant serves Taoist banquet fare (from ¥26).

🍴 Eating

There are three busy food streets in Tài'ān. The **night market** (yè shì; ⏱ 5.30pm-late) on the Nài River's east bank has many hotpot stalls. Pick your ingredients (thinly sliced meats, fish balls, vegetables, tofu etc) and take a seat at a low table. Meals cost about ¥28 and a large jug of beer is ¥8. Vendors on **Beǐxīn Snack Street** (北新小吃步行街; Beǐxīn Xiǎochī Bùxíng Jiē) set up carts for lunch (except Saturday) and dinner. Look for *mántóu* (馒头; steamed buns), various meats on skewers, fried chicken and more. Hawkers serve similar delights by the temple at **Dài Beǐ Market** (贷北市场; Dàiběi Shìchǎng), but expect tourist prices.

There is no food shortage on Tài Shān itself; the Central route is dotted with stalls and restaurants, with clusters at the cable cars. Prices rise as you do; expect to pay double the usual.

Ā Dōng de Shuǐjiāo CHINESE $

(阿东的水饺; ☑ 139 5489 8518; 31 Hongmen Lu; mains from ¥20; ⏱ 9am-10pm) This centrally lo-cated restaurant serves up northern Chinese staples including *shuǐjiǎo* (水饺; dumplings). There are a wide range of fillings including lamb (羊肉; *yángròu*; ¥34 per *jīn* – enough for two) and vegetarian tofu (豆腐; *dòufu*; ¥18 per *jīn*). The English menu is challenging, so be prepared to point.

Dōngzūn Court CHINESE $$

(东尊阁; Dōng Zūngé; ☑ 836 8222; 16 Yingsheng Donglu; mains from ¥28; ⏱ 11.30am-2.30pm & 5.30-8.30pm) This tablecloth affair at the Ramada Plaza has an entire room dedicated to live freshwater fish and shrimp (priced by the *jīn*) and freshly made spring-water bean curd (¥38).

ℹ️ Information

Agricultural Bank of China (22 Daizong Jie; ⏱ 8.30am-4pm Mon-Fri) Currency exchange and 24-hour ATM accepts foreign cards.

Bank of China (中国银行; Zhōngguó Yínháng; 116 Tongtian Jie; ⏱ 8.30am-4.30pm) Currency exchange and 24-hour ATM accepts foreign cards.

Central Hospital (中心医院; Zhōngxīn Yīyuàn; ☑ 822 4161; 29 Longtan Lu) Limited English.

China Post (中国邮政; Zhōngguó Yóuzhèng; 232 Daizong Dajie; ⏱ 8.30am-5.30pm)

Public Security Bureau (PSB; 公安局; Gōng'ānjú; ☑ 827 5264; cnr Dongyue Dajie & Qingnian Lu; ⏱ visa office 8.30am-noon & 1-5pm Mon-Fri, or by appointment) The visa office (出入境管理处) is on the east side of the shiny grey building.

ℹ️ Getting There & Away

Whether by road or track, most routes pass through Jǐ'nán, 80km north. Buses and trains are cheapest. Another option is picking up the **airport shuttle** (☑ 850 2600; 26 Hongmen Lu; adult ¥80; ⏱ 5.30am, 8.30am, 10am, 1.30pm, 4.40pm) in front of the Taishan Hotel; it connects to Jǐ'nán's Yáoqiáng airport, taking two hours.

Buy train and plane tickets at the Hongmen Lu **ticket office** (红门火车票代售点; ☑ 218 7989; 22 Hongmen Lu; commission ¥5; ⏱ 8am-6pm), or at the **ticket office** (火车票代售处, 空售票处; ☑ plane 218 3333, train 611 1111; 111 Qingnian Lu; ⏱ 8.30am-5.30pm) on Qingnian Lu. Hostels can help. Tickets sell out quickly so book early. Bear in mind that bus and train agents sometimes refer to Tài'ān and Tài Shān interchangeably.

BUS

The **long-distance bus station** (长途汽车站; chángtú qìchēzhàn; ☑ 218 8777; cnr Tài'shān Dalu & Longtan Lu), also known as the old station *(lǎo zhàn)*, is just south of the train station. Buses regularly depart for these destinations:

Jǐ'nán ¥27, 1½ hours, every 30 minutes (6.30am to 6pm)

Qīngdǎo ¥126, 5½ hours, five daily (6am, 8am, 8.40am, 2.30pm and 4pm)

Qūfù ¥23, one hour, every 30 minutes (7.20am to 5.20pm)

Wēihǎi ¥165, seven hours, two daily (7.20am and 9am)

Yāntái ¥150, six hours (7.20am)

TRAIN

Two train stations service this region. **Tài Shān Train Station** (泰山火车站; ☑ 688 7358; cnr Dongyue Dajie & Longtan Lu) is the most central, but express trains only pass through **Tài'ān Train Station** (泰安火车站; ☑ 138 0538 5950; Xingaotiezhan Lu), sometimes referred to as the new station *(xīn zhàn)*, 9km west of the town centre.

Some regular trains (seat/hard sleeper) departing from Tài Shān Train Station:

Jǐ'nán ¥13/64, one hour, frequent (24 hours)

Qīngdǎo ¥69/126, five to seven hours, hourly (12.28am to 2.52pm)

Qūfù ¥19/29, 1½ hours, two daily (6.05am and 10.50am)

Express trains (second-/first-class seat) departing from Tài'ān Train Station:

Běijīng ¥214/359, two hours, hourly (7.48am to 9.21pm)

Jǐ'nán ¥30/50, 18 minutes, frequent (7.48am to 10.14pm)

Nánjīng ¥254/429, 2½ hours, every 30 minutes (7.24am to 8.05pm)

Qīngdǎo ¥149/194, three hours, six daily (11.14am, 12.54pm, 3.10pm, 5.14pm, 5.46pm and 6.32pm)

Shànghǎi ¥374/634, 3½ hours, every 30 minutes (7.24am to 7.45pm)

ℹ Getting Around

Buses connect Tài Shān Train Station (p164) with access points to the mountain, mostly from 6.30am to 7.30pm during peak season and to 5.30pm otherwise.

Bus 3 (¥2) Runs until 11pm during peak season, going in one direction to the Central route trailhead and the other to Tiānwài Village (天外村; Tiānwài Cūn).

Bus 4 (¥2) Also runs until 11pm during peak season; runs to Dài Temple and around the town centre.

Bus 16 (¥2) Connects to Peach Blossom Valley.

Bus 19 (¥2, 50 minutes) Runs from Dongyue Dajie across from the Tài Shān Train Station to Tiānzhú Peak trailhead.

Taxis cost ¥6 to ¥7 for the first 3km and ¥1.50 (slightly more at night) per kilometre thereafter. It costs ¥12 from the Tài Shān Train Station or ¥26 from the Tài'ān Train Station to the Central route trailhead.

Frequent buses run up and down the mountain between Tiānwài Village and Midway Gate to Heaven. Cable cars reach the summit area from Midway Gate to Heaven, Peach Blossom Park and Rear Rocky Recess.

Qūfù 曲阜

☑ 0537 / POP 302,805

Home town of the great sage Confucius and his descendants the Kong clan, Qūfù is a testament to the importance of Confucian thought in imperial China to this day.

Viewing the main sights within the city walls of ancient Qūfù, a Unesco World Heritage Site, will take a full day.

⦿ Sights

The principal sights – Confucius Temple, Confucius Mansion and Confucius Forest – are known collectively as 'Sān Kǒng' ('Three Kongs'). The **main ticket office** (售票处; shòupiàochù) is on Shendao Lu just outside the Confucius Temple's main entrance. You can buy admission to the individual sights, but the **combination ticket** (per person ¥150), grants access to all three Confucius-related sights.

From 15 November to 15 February, admission to individual sights is ¥10 cheaper than listed (the combined ticket stays the same) and sights close about a half-hour earlier.

Confucius Temple   CONFUCIAN TEMPLE

(孔庙; Kǒng Miào; admission included in combination ticket or ¥90; ⊙8am-5.10pm) China's largest imperial building complex after the Forbidden City began as Confucius' three-room house. After his death in 478 BC, the Duke of the Lǔ state consecrated his simple abode as a temple. Everything in it, including his clothing, books, musical instruments and a carriage, was perfectly preserved. The house was rebuilt for the first time in AD 153, kicking off a series of expansions and renovations in subsequent centuries. By 1012, it had four courtyards and over 300 rooms. An imperial-palace-style wall was added. After a fire in 1499, it was rebuilt to its present scale.

Like shrines to Confucius throughout Asia, this is more museum than altar. Over 1000 stelae documenting imperial gifts and sacrifices from the Han dynasty onwards as well as treasured examples of calligraphy and stone reliefs are preserved on the grounds. Look for a *bìxì*, mythical tortoise, bearing the **Chéng Huà stele** (成化碑; Chénghuà bēi), dedicated by the Ming emperor in 1468, which praises Confucius in a particularly bold, formal hand. The characters are so perfect that copies were used to teach penmanship. The **Shèngjì Hall** (圣迹殿; Shèngjī Diàn) houses 120 famed Tang-dynasty paintings depicting Confucius' life immortalised as carvings.

The temple has nine courtyards arranged on a central axis. Halfway along rises the triple-eaved **Great Pavilion of the Constellation of Scholars** (奎文阁; Kuíwén Gé), an imposing Song-dynasty wooden structure. A series of gates and colossal, twin-eaved stele pavilions lead to the **Apricot Altar** (杏坛; Xìng Tǎn), which marks the spot where Confucius taught his students under an apricot tree.

The heart of the complex is the huge yellow-eaved **Dàchéng Hall** (大成殿; Dàchéng Diàn), which in its present form dates from 1724. Craftspeople carved the 10 dragon-coiled columns so expertly that they were covered with red silk when Emperor Qianlong visited, lest he feel that the Forbidden City's Hall of Supreme Harmony paled in comparison. Inside is a huge statue of Confucius resplendent on a throne. Above him are the characters for '*wànshì shībiǎo*', meaning 'model teacher for all ages'.

South of **Chóngshèng Hall** (崇圣祠; Chóngshèng Cí), which was once the site of the original family temple, the **Lǔ Wall** (鲁壁; Lǔ Bì) stands where Confucius' ninth generation descendant hid Confucius' writings in the walls of his house during Emperor Qin Shi Huang's book-burning campaign around 213 BC. The texts were uncovered during an attempt to raze the grounds in 154 BC, spurring new schools of Confucian scholarship and long debates over what Confucius really said.

Confucius Mansion   MUSEUM
(孔府; Kǒng Fǔ; admission included in combination ticket or ¥60; ⊙8am-5.15pm) Next to Confucius Temple is this maze of living quarters, halls, studies and more studies. The mansion buildings were moved from the temple grounds to the present site in 1377 and vastly expanded into 560 rooms in 1503. More remodelling followed, including reconstruction following a devastating fire in 1885.

The mansion was for centuries the most sumptuous private residence in China, thanks to imperial sponsorship and the Kong clan's rule, which included powers of taxation and execution, over Qūfù as an autonomous estate. They indulged in 180-course meals, and kept servants and consorts. Male heirs successively held the title of Duke Yan Sheng from the Song dynasty until 1935.

CONFUCIUS: THE FIRST TEACHER

Born into a world of violent upheaval, Confucius (551–479 BC) spent his life trying to stabilise society according to traditional ideals. By his own measure he failed, but over time he became one of the most influential thinkers the world has known. Confucius' ideals remain at the core of values in east Asia today.

Confucius was born Kong Qiu (孔丘), earning the honorific Kongfuzi (孔夫子), literally 'Master Kong', after becoming a teacher. His family was poor but of noble rank, and eventually he became an official in his home state of Lǔ (in present-day Shāndōng). At the age of 50, he put a plan into action to reform government that included routing corruption. This resulted in his exile, and he spent 13 years travelling from state to state, hoping to find a ruler who would put his ideas into practice. Eventually, he returned to his home town of Qūfù and spent the remainder of his life expounding the wisdom of the Six Classics (*The Book of Changes, Songs, Rites, History, Music* and the *Spring and Autumn Annals*). Taking on students from varied backgrounds, he believed that everyone, not just aristocracy, had a right to knowledge. This ideal became one of his greatest legacies.

Confucius' teachings were compiled by his disciples in *The Analects* (论语, *Lúnyǔ*), a collection of 497 aphorisms. Though he claimed to be merely transmitting the ideals of an ancient golden age, Confucius was in fact China's first humanist philosopher, upholding morality (humaneness, righteousness and virtue) and self-cultivation as the basis for social order. 'What you do not wish for yourself,' he said, 'do not do to others.'

Qūfù

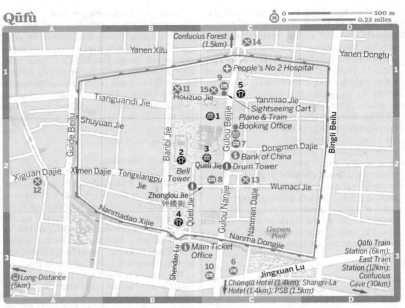

Qūfù

Sights

Sleeping

Eating

Confucius Mansion is built on an 'interrupted' north–south axis with administrative offices (taxes, edicts, rites, registration and examination halls) at the entrance (south) and private quarters at the back (north). The **Ceremonial Gate** (重光门; Chóngguāng Mén) was opened only when emperors dropped in. The central path passes a series of halls, including the **Great Hall** (大堂; Dà Táng) and **Nèizhái Gate** (内宅门; Nèizhái Mén), which separated the private and public parts of the residence and was guarded at all times.

The large *'shòu'* character (寿; longevity) within the single-eaved **Upper Front Chamber** (前上房; Qián Shàng Fáng) north of Nèizhái Gate was a gift from Qing Empress Cixi. The Duke lived in the two-storey **Front Chamber** (前堂楼; Qián Táng Lóu).

East just before the Nèizhái Gate is the **Tower of Refuge** (奎楼; Kuí Lóu), not open to visitors, where the Kong clan could gather if the peasants turned nasty. It has an iron-lined ceiling on the ground floor and a staircase that could be yanked up.

Confucius Forest　　　　CEMETERY
(孔林; Kǒng Lín; admission included in combination ticket or ¥40; ⏲ 8am-5.20pm) About 2km north of town on Lindao Lu is the peaceful Confucius Forest, a cemetery of pine and cypress covering 200 hectares bounded by a 10km-long wall. Confucius and more than 100,000 of his descendants have been buried here for the past 2000 years, a tradition still ongoing.

When Confucius died in 479 BC he was buried on the bank of the Si River beneath a simple marker. In the Western Han dynasty, Emperor Wudi deemed Confucianism the only worthy school of thought, and the

Tomb of Confucius (孔子墓; Kǒngzǐ Mù) became a place of pilgrimage. Today the tomb is a simple grass mound enclosed by a low wall and faced with a Ming-dynasty stele. Pairs of stone guardians stand at the ready. The sage's son and grandson are buried nearby, and scattered through the forest are dozens of temples and pavilions.

A slow walk through the parklike cemetery can take a couple of hours, though Confucius' tomb is just a 15-minute walk from the entrance (turn left after the carts). Open-air **shuttles** (one way/return ¥10/20) allow you to hop on and off in the forest.

Sightseeing carts (电动旅游车; diàndòng lǚyóu chē; cnr Houzuo Jie & Gulou Dajie; one way/return ¥10/15; ⊙7.40am-6pm) depart for the forest from the corner of Houzuo Jie and Gulou Dajie. Otherwise take a pedicab (¥10) or bus 1 (¥2) from Gulou Beijie. Walking takes about 30 minutes.

Yán Temple CONFUCIAN TEMPLE
(颜庙; Yán Miào; Yanmiao Jie; admission ¥50; ⊙8am-5.10pm; 🚍1, 3) This tranquil temple northeast of Confucius Mansion is dedicated to Confucius' beloved disciple Yan Hui, whose death at age 32 caused the understated Confucius 'excessive grief'. The main structure, **Fùshèng Hall** (复圣殿; Fùshèng Diàn), has a magnificent ceiling decorated with a dragon head motif. Outside a *bìxì* carries a stele that posthumously granted Yan the title of Duke of Yanguo (in both Han and Mongol script) in AD 1331.

⭐ Festivals & Events

Every morning at 8am, following a recitation, a costumed procession raucously walks up Shendao Lu from Jingxian Lu to the main gate to officially open the city.

Confucius Temple holds two major festivals a year: **Tomb Sweeping Day** (usually 5 April; celebrations may last all weekend) and the **Sage's Birthday** (28 September), both involving elaborate, costumed ceremonies. The city also comes alive with craftspeople, healers, acrobats and peddlers during annual fairs in the spring and autumn.

🛏 Sleeping

⭐**Qūfù International Youth Hostel** HOSTEL **$**
(曲阜国际青年旅舍; Qūfù Guójì Qīngnián Lǚshè; 📞441 8989; www.yhaqf.com; Gulou Beijie; 鼓楼北街北首路西; dm/tw/tr ¥45/128/158; ✳@🛜) The best deal in town, this friendly hostel at the north end of Gulou Beijie has rooms so clean you can smell the fresh linen. There's bike rental, ticket bookings and a cafe-bar (cocktails from ¥18) serving Chinese and Western fare. Dorms have four to eight beds and share a nice bathroom. Only fault? Hot water can be scarce in the mornings.

Fúyuàn Hotel HOTEL **$$**
(福苑酒店; Fúyuàn Jiǔdiàn; 📞138 6372 3660; 8 Gulou Beijie; incl breakfast s ¥198, d ¥208, tr ¥238; ✳🛜) Smack-bang in the middle of the old town, the courteous staff here make up for the worn edges. Go for the 2nd-floor rooms, and avoid the stuffy, windowless economy rooms. Discounts up to 40%.

Chūnqiū Hotel HOTEL **$$**
(春秋大酒店; Chūnqiū Dà Jiǔdiàn; 📞505 1888; www.chunqiuhotel.com; 13 Chunqiu Zhonglu; 春秋中路13号; incl breakfast r ¥298-398, ste ¥598; ⊜✳@) Just outside the old city walls, this subdued business hotel is a favourite of bureaucrats (government buildings are next door); you'll meet them in the morning breakfast buffet line. Rooms on the 7th floor and up have views of the park. Discounts available.

Quèlǐ Hotel HOTEL **$$$**
(阙里宾舍; Quèlǐ Bīnshè; 📞486 6400; www.quelihotel.com; 15 Zhonglou Jie; 钟楼街15号; incl breakfast s ¥398-598, d/ste ¥568/2288; ✳🛜) The four-star Quèlǐ was once the fanciest hotel in town. A recent refurb dusted off the fading photos of the visiting dignitaries

SHĀNDŌNG QŪFÙ

MAKING COPIES

For millennia, everything from imperial decrees to poetry, religious scriptures and maps were preserved by carving them into stone. This was done either as an inscription (yin-style) or a relief (yang-style). Copies were made by applying ink to the stone and pressing rice paper onto it, or by tamping a damp sheet of paper into the crevices and allowing it to dry, before patting ink onto the paper's surface. Over time, even stone would wear and the clearest, best-made prints became works of art themselves. Unfortunately, this prompted unscrupulous collectors to damage carvings to ensure they had the very best copy. These are the gouges and scratches you see in many of the most prized tablets and stelae.

HOME OF THE SECOND SAGE

Twenty-three kilometres south of Qūfù is **Zōuchéng** (邹城; also called Zōuxiàn, 邹县), where the revered Confucian scholar Mencius (孟子; Mengzi; c 372–289 BC) was born. Like Confucius, Mencius was raised by a single mother and grew up to travel the country trying to reform government. His belief that humanity is by nature good formed the core of all his teachings, including his call to overthrow self-serving rulers. Not surprisingly, his criticism made him unpopular among those in power, but a thousand years after his death Mencius' work was elevated a step below Confucius'.

Zōuchéng today is a relaxed town with fewer tourist hassles than Qūfú. Tickets (¥40) get you into the two adjacent main attractions and are sold at both. **Mencius Temple** (孟庙; Mèng Miào; incl Mencius Family Mansion ¥40; ⊙ 8am-5.50pm) originally dates to the Song dynasty and bears the marks of past anti-Confucian mood swings, though restoration is in progress. With few visitors around to cut in, you can stand in the shade of ancient gnarled cypresses and absorb the serene surroundings. The twin-roofed **Hall of the Second Sage** (亚圣殿; Yàshèng Diàn) looms in the centre of the grounds. A small shrine next to it is dedicated to Mencius' mother, the 'model for all mothers'. West of the temple, **Mencius Family Mansion** (孟府; Mèng Fǔ; incl Mencius Temple ¥40; ⊙ 8am-5.50pm) exhibits the family's living quarters, including teacups and bedding left by Mencius' 74th-generation descendant, who lived there into the 1940s.

Zōuchéng is any easy bus ride from Qūfù. Bus C609 (¥3, 35 minutes, 6.30am to 6.30pm) departs from Confucius Temple's main entrance and drops off at **Zōuchéng Museum** (邹城博物馆; ☎ 0537 525 3301; 56 Shunhe Lu; ⊙ 8.30am-5.30pm) **FREE**, less than a kilometre from the sights (just walk, keeping the river on your left).

on the walls, but some rooms are still nicer than others. Look first. Discounts of 20%.

Shangri-La Hotel HOTEL $$$
(香阁里拉大酒店; ☎ 505 8888; www.shangri-la.com; 3 Chunqiu Lu; incl breakfast r ¥805-1035, ste ¥2288; ❀❅☂❄) A luxury hotel fit for a major city but priced for a small one. Take advantage of the slick, top-end facilities, kids' activities and impressive buffets (no lines!) before it has to start cutting corners.

✖ Eating

The local speciality is Kong-family cuisine (孔家菜), which, despite its name, is the furthest thing from home cooking since it developed as a result of all the imperial-style banquets the family threw.

Restaurants skip the pageantry nowadays, but for still less formal fare visit the **street vendors** (特色小吃城; dishes from ¥2; ⊙ from 5pm) on the corner just outside the north city gate, or at the Wumaci Jie **night market** (夜市; yèshì; Wumaci Jie & Gulou Nanjie; snacks from ¥3, dishes from ¥9; ⊙ from 5pm). Vendors make noodles, grill skewers of meat, and serve *jiānbǐng guǒzi* (煎饼裹子; ¥3 to ¥5), a steaming parcel of egg, vegetables and chilli sauce wrapped in a pancake. Stalls displaying raw meat and produce cook it to order; just point at what you want. The

Muslim Quarter (Xiguan Dajie; 西关大街) outside the western gate is the place to feast on noodles and lamb.

Mù'ēn Lóu Halal Food & Drink MUSLIM $
(穆恩楼清真餐飲; Mùen Lóu, Qīngzhēn Cānyǐn; ☎ 448 3877; Houzuo Jie; mains ¥15-60; ⊙ 8.30am-1.30pm & 5-8.30pm) A friendly Hui family runs this simple place behind the Confucius Mansion, serving house specialities such as beef spiced with cumin, star anise and turmeric (南前牛肉片; *nánqián niúròu piàn*; ¥68) and tongue-numbing, spicy tofu (麻辣豆腐; *málà dòufu*; ¥12).

Yù Shū Fáng CHINESE $$$
(御书房; ☎ 441 9888; www.confuciusfood.com; 2nd fl, Houzuo Jie; banquet per person ¥138-500; ⊙ 11am-2pm & 5-8.30pm) 'Food can never be too good, and cooking can never be done too carefully', Confucius himself said. This restaurant of private rooms behind the Confucius Mansion takes this to heart, serving fine teas (铁观音; *tiě guānyīn*) from ¥38 per pot (壶) and Kong-family banquet meals (套餐; *tào cān*).

The most basic set involves six or so small cold dishes, followed by about 16 more hot dishes – from soup to vegetables, braised sea cucumber, spicy chicken and so on in quick succession. There's no English menu but ordering is easy (just pick a price). Reservations recommended, and some dishes can be ordered à la carte (from ¥38).

ℹ️ Information

ATMs accepting foreign cards are along and around Gulou Beijie. Internet cafes are often restricted to Chinese nationals. Try around Wumaci Jie (look for 网吧 signs; per hour ¥2 to ¥5), or surf at Qūfù International Youth Hostel.

Bank of China (中国银行; Zhōngguó Yínháng; 96 Dongmen Dajie; ☺ 8.30am-4.30pm) Foreign exchange and ATM.

China Post (中国邮政; Zhōngguó Yóuzhèng; Gulou Beijie; 鼓楼门分理处; ☺ 8am-6pm summer, 8.30am-5.30pm winter) Near the Drum Tower.

People's No 2 Hospital (第二人民医院; Dì'èr Rénmín Yīyuàn; ☑ 448 8120; 7 Gulou Beijie) Next to the Qūfù International Youth Hostel.

Public Security Bureau (PSB; 公安局; Gōng'ānjú; ☑ 443 0017; 1 Wuyutai Lu; 舞雩台路1号; ☺ 8.30am-noon & 2-6pm Mon-Fri) About 1.5km south of the city walls. Can help with initial paperwork for lost passports, but for more you'll have to go to Jīníng (济宁).

ℹ️ Getting There & Away

Buy plane and train tickets at the **booking office** (售票处; ☑ 150 5377 1869; commission ¥5; ☺ 8.30am-noon & 2-6pm) next to China Post. Qūfù International Youth Hostel also books tickets (¥15 to ¥20 commission).

AIR

Jīníng Qūfù Airport is 80km southwest of Qūfù's old town and connects to Běijīng (¥617, 1½ hours), Chéngdū (¥1167, two hours), Guǎngzhōu (¥877, 2½ hours), Shànghǎi (¥868, two hours), Xi'an (¥674, 55 minutes) and a handful of other cities. There are no direct buses from the airport to old town Qūfù. You have to transfer to a bus or taxi at the bus station in Jīníng (济宁) about 50km away, so flying into Jī'nán is about as convenient.

BUS

Qūfù's **long-distance bus station** (长途汽车站; chángtú qìchēzhàn; ☑ 441 2554; Yulong Lu & Yulan Lu; 裕隆路与玉兰路) is 3km west of the city walls. There is a **left luggage office** (¥2; ☺ 6am-6pm) available here.

Buses regularly depart for these destinations:

Jī'nán ¥44, three hours, every 30 minutes (7.30am to 6pm)

Qīngdǎo ¥134, five hours, five daily (8.30am, 9.30am, 1.30pm, 2.20pm and 4.40pm)

Tài'ān ¥23, 1½ hours, every 30 minutes

TRAIN

Trains are the most convenient transport. Catch express trains at the **East Train Station** (高铁 东火车站; ☑ 442 1571),12km east of the walled city. **Qūfù Train Station** (曲阜火车站; ☑ 442 1571; Dianlan Lu) is closest to the walled city (6km east), but only regular trains stop there. If tickets are sold out, try **Yǎnzhōu Train Station** (兖州火车站; ☑ 346 2965; Beiguan Jie), 16km west of Qūfù, which is on the Běijīng–Shànghǎi line and has more frequent regular trains.

Some express trains (second-/first-class seat) departing from East Train Station:

Běijīng ¥244/409, 2½ hours, frequently (7.26am to 9.01pm)

Jī'nán ¥60/100, 30 minutes, frequently (7.26am to 9.52pm)

Nánjīng ¥224/379, two hours, frequently (7.53am to 9.15pm)

Qīngdǎo ¥179/244, 3½ hours, five daily (9.11am, 2.49pm, 4.54pm, 5.25pm and 5.43pm)

Shànghǎi ¥344/584, 3½ hours, frequently (7.53am to 8.11pm)

Tiānjīn ¥190/320, two hours, hourly (7.26am to 7.22pm)

Some regular trains (seat/hard sleeper) departing from Qūfù Train Station:

Jī'nán ¥29/45, 2½ hours, three daily (8.08am, 5.22pm and 8.39pm)

Yāntái ¥72/139, 9½ hours, two daily (9.49am and 11.42pm)

ℹ️ Getting Around

Bus K01 connects the long-distance bus station to Qūfù's main gate (¥2) and the east train station (¥3). A taxi from within the walls is about ¥40 to the east train station and ¥20 to the long-distance bus station. Bus 1 (¥2) traverses the old town along Gulou Beijie to Confucius Forest.

Ubiquitous pedicabs (¥6 to ¥8 within Qūfù, ¥10 to ¥20 outside the walls) are the most pleasant way to get around. Take one (or a regular

---

CONFUCIUS SAYS...

➡ 'Our greatest glory is not in never failing but in rising every time we fall.'

➡ 'Real knowledge is to know the extent of one's ignorance.'

➡ 'Rotten wood cannot be carved, nor are dung walls plastered.'

➡ 'Study the past if you would divine the future.'

➡ 'We take greater pains to persuade others that we are happy than in endeavouring to think so ourselves.'

➡ 'He who wishes to secure the good of others has already secured his own.'

taxi) to the Qūfù train station, as there are no direct buses.

Minibuses (¥5 to ¥7) connect the main gate to Yánzhōu train station from 6.30am to 5.30pm; otherwise, a taxi costs about ¥50.

Tired ponies pull brightly decorated carts (¥50) from Queli Jie to the Confucius Forest.

Qīngdǎo 青岛

☑ 0532 / POP 3.5 MILLION

Offering a breath of fresh (ocean) air, Qīngdǎo is a rare modern city that has managed to preserve some of its past. Its blend of concession-era and modern architecture puts China's standard white-tile and blue-glass developments to shame. The winding cobbled streets and red-capped hillside villas are captivating. There is also plenty to enjoy in the city's diverse food scene, headlined by the ubiquitous hometown beer Tsingtao.

Qīngdǎo is rapidly expanding into a true multi-district city, but for now most of the fun is in or around Shì'nán district (市南区), the strip of land along the sea.

History

Before catching the acquisitive eye of Kaiser Wilhelm II, Qīngdǎo was a harbour and fishing village known for producing delicious sea salt. Its excellent strategic location was not lost on the Ming dynasty, which built a defensive battery – nor on the Germans who wrested it from them in 1897. China signed a 99-year concession, and it was during the next decade the future Tsingtao Brewery was opened, electric lighting installed, missions and a university established, and the railway to Jì'nán built.

In 1914 Japan seized control with a bombing assault on the city. When the Treaty of Versailles strengthened Japan's occupation in 1919, student demonstrations erupted in Běijīng and spread across the country in what became known as the May 4th Movement. After a period of domestic control, the Japanese took over again in 1938 and held on until the end of WWII.

In peacetime, Qīngdǎo became one of China's major ports and a flourishing centre of trade and manufacturing (home to both domestic and international brands). It seems to hold a permanent spot on the list of Asia's most liveable cities.

◉ Sights

Most sights in the Shì'nán district are squeezed into Old Town (the former concession area), with the train and bus stations, historic architecture and budget accommodation, and Bādàguān, a serene residential area of parks, spas and old villas.

East of Shandong Lu rises the modern city, with the central business district (CBD) to the north and the latest in retail and dining in Dōngbù, closer to the water to the south. Further east still is the developing Láo Shān (崂山区) district, anchored by the Municipal Museum, Grand Theatre and International Beer City (site of the annual International Beer Festival).

Governor's House Museum MUSEUM
(青岛德国总督楼旧址博物馆; Qīngdǎo Déguó Zǒngdū Lóu Jiùzhǐ Bówùguǎn; ☑8286 8838; 26 Longshan Lu; admission summer/winter ¥20/13, multilingual audio tour ¥10; ◷8.30am-5.30pm; ☐1, 221) East of Signal Hill Park stands one of Qīngdǎo's best examples of concession-era architecture – the former German governor's residence constructed in the style of a German palace. The building's interior is characteristic of Jugendstil, the German arm of art nouveau, with some German and Chinese furnishings of the era.

It was built in 1903 at a cost of 2,450,000 taels of silver by an indulgent governor, whom Kaiser Wilhelm II immediately sacked when he saw the bill. In 1957 Chairman Mao stayed here with his wife and kids on holiday. So did defence minister Lin Biao, who would later attempt to assassinate Mao.

St Michael's Cathedral CHURCH
(天主教堂; Tiānzhǔ Jiàotáng; ☑8286 5960; 15 Zhejiang Lu; admission ¥10; ◷8.30am-5pm Mon-Sat, 10am-5pm Sun; ☐1, 221, 367) Up a hill off Zhongshan Lu looms this grand Gothic- and Roman-style edifice. Completed in 1934, the church spires were supposed to be clock towers, but Chancellor Hitler cut funding of overseas projects and the plans were scrapped.

The church was badly damaged during the Cultural Revolution and the crosses capping its twin spires were torn off. Devout locals buried the crosses for safe keeping. In 2005, workers uncovered them while repairing pipes in the hills, and they have since been restored.

Tiānhòu Temple
TEMPLE

(天后宫; Tiānhòu Gōng; 19 Taiping Lu; 太平路19号; ⏰8am-6pm; 🚌25) **FREE** This small restored temple dedicated to the patron of seafarers has stood by the shore since 1467. The main hall contains a colourful statue of Tianhou, flanked by fearsome guardians. There is also **Dragon King Hall** (龙王殿; Lóngwáng Diàn), where a splayed pig lies before the ruler of oceans, and a shrine to the God of Wealth.

Protestant Church
CHURCH

(基督教堂; Jīdū Jiàotáng; 15 Jiangsu Lu; admission ¥10; ⏰8.30am-5.30pm; 🚌1, 221, 367) On a street of German buildings, this copper-capped church was designed by Curt Rothkegel and built in 1908. The interior is simple and Lutheran in its sparseness, apart from some carvings on the pillar cornices. You can climb up to inspect the clock mechanism (Bockenem 1909).

Huāshí Lóu
BUILDING

(花石楼; Huāshí Lóu; ☎8387 2168; 18 Huanghai Lu; admission ¥8.50; ⏰9am-6pm; 🚌26, 231, 604) This granite and marble villa built in 1930 was first the home of a Russian aristocrat, and later the German governor's hunting lodge. It is also known as the 'Chiang Kaishek Building', as the generalissimo secretly stayed here in 1947. While most of the rooms are closed, you can clamber up two narrow stairwells to the turret for a great view.

It's located on the east end of No 2 Bathing Beach at the southern tip of Zijingguan Lu in Bādàguān.

Tsingtao Beer Museum
BREWERY, MUSEUM

(青岛啤酒博物馆; Qīngdǎo Píjiǔ Bówùguǎn; ☎8383 3437; 56-1 Dengzhou Lu; admission ¥60, English guide ¥60; ⏰8.30am-6pm; 🚌1, 205, 221, 307, 308) For a self-serving introduction to China's iconic beer, head to the original and still operating brewery. On view are old photos, preserved brewery equipment and statistics, but there are also a few fascinating glimpses of the modern factory line. The aroma of hops is everywhere. Thankfully, you get to sample brews along the way.

After the tour, there's more to sip all along **Beer Street** just outside. If you're taking a bus, get off at the '15中' (shíwǔ zhōng) stop. A taxi from Old Town costs ¥15.

Little Qīngdǎo
LIGHTHOUSE, ISLAND

(小青岛; Xiǎo Qīngdǎo; 26 Qinyu Lu; admission summer/winter ¥15/10; ⏰7.30am-6.30pm; 🚌6, 26, 202, 231, 304) In the shape of a *qín* (a stringed instrument) jutting into Qīngdǎo Bay, this former island was connected to the mainland in the 1940s. The Germans built the white lighthouse in 1900 on the leafy promontory. It is an excellent spot for watching the city come to life in the morning, and there's free entry from 6am to official opening.

Chinese Navy Museum
MUSEUM

(中国海军博物馆; Zhōngguó Hǎijūn Bówùguǎn; ☎8286 6784; www.hjbwg.com; 8 Caiyang Lu; 菜阳路8号; admission ¥50; ⏰8.30am-5.30pm; 🚌26, 202, 501) Adjacent to Little Qīngdǎo lighthouse, this museum's main attractions are the rusty submarine and destroyer anchored in the harbour. There are also, of course, displays on Chinese naval history.

Municipal Museum
MUSEUM

(青岛市博物馆; Qīngdǎo Shì Bówùguǎn; ☎8889 6286; http://qingdaomuseum.com; 51 Meiling Lu; 梅岭路51号; ⏰9am-5pm, closed Mon; 🚌230, 321) **FREE** This massive collection of relics anchors the budding cultural zone about 13km east of Old Town in Láo Shān district. It has the usual broad span of exhibits expected in a big-city museum, ranging from the prehistoric to the industrial age. Collections of folk-art woodcuts and intriguing coins pressed with Kyrgyz script stand out.

🏖 Beaches

Qīngdǎo has very pleasant beaches, though they are sometimes afflicted with blue-green algae blooms and litter. Chinese beach culture is low-key, with men sporting the skimpy swimwear and women covering up – even under Spandex ski-masks. Swimming season (June to September) means hordes of sun-seekers fighting for towel space on weekends. Shark nets, lifeguards, lifeboat patrols and medical stations are on hand.

There are ways to enjoy the water without jumping in. If you give in to touts, 20-minute rides around the bay are ¥10 to ¥40, depending on the boat. Or stroll the **Bīnhǎi boardwalk** (滨海步行道; Bīnhǎi bùxíngdào), which stretches 30km along the city's shoreline.

No 6 Bathing Beach
BEACH

(第六海水浴场; Dì Liù Hǎishuǐ Yùchǎng; 🚌25, 202) Closest to the train station is the No 6 Bathing Beach, a short strip of sand and tidepools, next to **Zhàn Bridge** (栈桥; Zhàn Qiáo), a pier reaching into the bay. At its tip, the eight-sided **Huílán Pavilion** (回阑阁; Huílán Gé; 12 Taiping Lu; admission ¥4;

Qīngdǎo

500 m
0.25 miles

TAIDONG

Shandong Lu (1km); Central Business District (1km)

Ningxia Lu

Yan'an Sanlu 延安三路

Huāshí Lóu (300m)
Taidong Y'ilu

Culture Street (500m)

Dengzhou Lu 登州路

Yan'an Lu

15

29

SHIBEI DISTRICT

Huangtai Lu 黄台路

Rehe Lu 热河路

SHINAN DISTRICT

Qingdaoshan Park

Hongdao Lu

16

Café Yum (1km); Civil Aviation Building (airport shuttle) (1km); Dongbu District (2km); Marina City (4km); Jusco (4km); Shídàorén Beach (13km); Dàhédōng, Láo Shān (27km)

Villa Inn (150m)

Xiangganglu Xilu 香港西路

Dōnghǎi Xilu

Pushan Bay

No 2 Bathing Beach; Huāshí Lóu (300m)

Zhengyangguan Lu

10

13

17

Zhongshan Park

Wendeng Lu

Rongcheng Lu

Nanhai Lu 南海路

BADAGUAN

Fushan Lu

Qixia Lu

Yan Yilu

22

Huiquan Bay

Long-Distance Bus Station (2.3km)

Passenger Ferry Terminal (300m)

Jiaozhou Bay

Guantao Lu

Liaocheng Lu 聊城路

Jiangsu Lu

30

24

31

20

Jining Lu

Huangdao Lu

Zhifu Lu

27

26

25

23

28

33

12

35

32

Feicheng Lu 肥城路

Hubei Lu 湖北路

Dagu Lu 大沽路

Tianjin Lu 天津路

Train Station 火车站

Feixian Lu

Golden Sand Beach (15km)

Dáxué Lu 大学路

Longshan Lu

Signal Hill Park

2

11

19

9

8

14

21

Anhui Lu

Hunan Lu

Taiping Lu

Guanhaishan Park

Bank of China

OLD TOWN

Zhongshan Lu

Guangxi Lu

7

3

Zhan Bridge

Qingdao Bay

4

6

18

Laiyang Lu 莱阳路

Lu Xun Park

1

5

Qinyu Lu

34

Qīngdǎo

⊙ 8am-5pm) is constantly packed to the rafters. If the pavilion looks familiar, that's because it's on every Tsingtao beer label.

No 1 Bathing Beach
BEACH

(第一海水浴场; Dì Yī Hǎishuǐ Yùchǎng; 🚌304) South of tree-lined Bādàguān, No 1 Bathing Beach is a very popular spot, perhaps for its snack stalls and kiddie toy selection, but more likely for its muscle beach.

No 2 Bathing Beach
BEACH

(第二海水浴场; Dì Èr Hǎishuǐ Yùchǎng; 🚌214) Once reserved only for the likes of Mao and other state leaders, this sheltered cove just east of Bādàguān has calm waters good for a swim. Take bus 214 directly, or bus 26 to the Wǔshèngguān (武胜关) stop to first wander past the villas and sanitoriums scattered in Bādàguān's wooded headlands down to the sea.

No 3 Bathing Beach
BEACH

(第三海水浴场; Dì Sān Hǎishuǐ Yùchǎng; 🚌26, 202) On the eastern side of Tàipíng Cape in Bādàguān is this cove with dedicated swim lanes, paddle boats and gentle waves.

Shílǎorén Beach
BEACH

(石老人海水浴场; Shílǎorén Hǎishuǐ Yùchǎng; 🚌301) On the far east side of town in Láo Shān district, this 2.5km-long strip of clean sand is Qīngdǎo's largest and has the highest

waves in town (decent for bodyboarding). The 'Old Stone Man' from which the beach gets its name is the rocky outcrop to the east. Take bus 301 (¥2, 50 minutes) or taxi (¥45) from Old Town.

Parks

Within central Qīngdǎo, **Zhōngshān Park** (中山公园; Zhōngshān Gōngyuán; ⊙24hr; 🚌25, 26) is the crown jewel, a vast 69 hectares of lakes, gardens, walking paths and an amusement park for kids. It's the sight of lively festivals in the spring and summer. In the park's northeast rises hilly **Tàipíng Shān** (太平山; Tàipíng Shān) with a **cable car** (one way/return ¥60/80; ⊙7.30am-6.30pm) to the **TV Tower** (电视塔; Diànshì Tǎ; 🕿8361 2286; admission depending on view ¥50-100) at the top. The tower was under renovation when we visited. Also within the park is Qīngdǎo's largest temple, **Zhànshān Temple** (湛山寺; Zhànshān Sì; admission ¥10; ⊙8am-4pm), an active Buddhist sanctuary. When you get off the cable car at the temple, look for a round concrete dome on the right. This is the entrance to a bunker, which the Germans used as a wine cellar, and today houses a wine bar.

Many parks with ticket booths, including **Little Fish Hill** (小鱼山公园; Xiǎoyúshān Gōngyuán; 🕿8286 5645; 24 Fushanzi Lu; admission ¥10; ⊙6am-8pm) by No 1 Bathing Beach and **Signal Hill Park** (信号山; Xìnhào Shān;

A PRIVATE COLLECTION OF ANCIENT CARVINGS

Han Dynasty Brick Museum (崇汉轩汉画像砖博物馆; Chóng Hànxuān Hàn Huàxiàng Zhuān Bówùguǎn; ☑ 8861 6533, 158 6552 0097; http://zhangxinkuan.com; Binhai Dadao Kutao, inside 409 Hospital; 滨海大道枯桃409医院院内; adult/student ¥40/free; ◷ 8-11.30am & 2-5.30pm) Thirty years ago, Zhang Xinkuan was a young army officer laying a road in Hénán province when he noticed the huge granite slabs they were smashing into gravel were covered in exquisite carvings. Thus began his life's pursuit to save more than 5000 of these relics from the Han dynasty, now housed in his truly unique, private museum at the southwestern foot of Láo Shān.

Zhang put his entire life savings into finding these carvings, which document ancient Chinese life, mostly in backyards, kitchens and even pigsties in Hénán, Shāndōng, Shānxī, Jiāngsū and Sìchuān, where more than 2000 years ago they were made to decorate palaces, ancestral halls and tombs.

There are carvings of prancing deer, ladies in long flared skirts and hunters in Persian-style robes in five main galleries. Many have been captured as ink rubbings, which are available for purchase. Call ahead and the man himself might show you around.

Take bus 119 to the last stop, Taidong 1409 Hospital (台东一四零九医院), about an hour from downtown Qīngdǎo.

☑ 5872 5906; 16 Longshan Lu; viewing platform ¥15; ◷ 8.30am-5.30pm) in Old Town, are free to wander in after 6.30pm.

🎇 Festivals & Events

Lantern Festival NEW YEAR
The city glows at the end of the Chinese New Year/Spring Festival in February/March.

Cherry Blossom Festival CULTURAL
The cherry blossoms explode with colour in Zhōngshān Park around April.

International Beer Festival BEER
(www.qdbeer.cn) Draws more than three million tipplers every August.

International Sailing Week SPORTS
(www.qdsailing.org) Watch (or join) the regattas and windsurfing by the Olympic Sailing Center every August/September.

🛏 Sleeping

Old Town has excellent budget and midrange options. The CBD and Dōngbù have the top-end international chains but a lot less soul. Rates increase by as much as 30% in July and August.

★ **Wheat Youth Hostel** HOSTEL $$
(麦子青年旅社; Màizi Qīngnián Lǚshè; ☑ 8285 2121; www.qdmaizi.com; 35 Hebei Lu; 河北路35号; dm ¥80-100, r without/with bath ¥300/398; ❄ @ 🛜) The Maizis fell in love with backpacking and each other in western China, and this top-notch hostel (and an adorable daughter) is the result of their partnership.

It's in a beautiful, restored *lǐyuàn*, the courtyard apartments of 1920s Qīngdǎo, within a 10-minute walk of the train station. They designed this to provide all the services a weary traveller could possibly hope for.

Rooms are spotless with nostalgic details and creaky hardwood floors (if only there was more than one common shower room on busy mornings). There's a modern library and entertainment lounge, plus a bar where you can pick up good travel advice. Discounts of 50%.

YHA Old Observatory HOSTEL $
(奥博维特国际青年旅舍; Àobówéitè Guójì Qīngnián Lǚshè; ☑ 8282 2626; www.hostelqingdao.com; 21 Guanxiang Erlu; 观象二路21号; dm ¥80-90, r without/with bath from ¥398/428, discounted to ¥168/198; ❄ @ 🛜) Perched on a hill in a working observatory, this hostel has unbeatable views of the city and bay. Take them in with a drink in hand in the pleasant rooftop Sunset Lounge. Staff provide all the usual hostel services, plus they organise outings around town and Láo Shān. Comfort levels vary – some doubles have nicer bathrooms.

Renovations were about to begin when we visited. Book in advance.

Kǎiyuè Hostelling International HOSTEL $
(凯越国际青年旅馆; Kǎiyuè Guójì Qīngnián Lǚguǎn; ☑ 8284 5450; kaiyuehostel@126.com; 31 Jining Lu; 济宁路31号; dm ¥55-75, r without bath ¥70-150, with bath ¥100-300; ❄ 🛜) This hostel in a historic church at Sifang Lu and Jining Lu has a lively congregation. They come to

worship in the slick new bar and restaurant (Jinns' Café), which serves great pizza (from ¥55) and desserts on the ground floor. The rooms above need the equivalent revamp, though dorms are clean.

There's good travel advice, bike rental (¥10) and a free beer each night. Book in advance.

Héngshān No 5 Hostel HOSTEL $
(恒山路5号国际青年旅社; ☎8288 9888; http://hengshan5.com; 5 Hengshan Lu; 恒山路5号; dm/r ¥60/175; ❉@) On a short street south of the Governor's House Museum, this bright and cheery hostel in a white, three-storey mansion was once the servants' quarters. Beds and bunks are similar (tidy, pine frame, reasonably soft). In the garden, sunny Luka Garden Cafe & Bistro serves fantastic coffee and Kiwi fare, and feels like home on the patio.

Qīngdǎo International Youth Hotel HOTEL $$
(青岛国际青年旅舍; Qīngdǎo Guójì Qīngnián Lǚshè; ☎8286 5177; 7a Qixia Lu; 栖霞路7号甲; dm ¥80, r ¥450-600; ❉@☎; ☐31, 220, 312, 321) Despite the name, this place in Bādàguān feels more like a B&B. Rooms (and bathrooms) in this converted mansion are cavernous. There's some dust on the yesteryear charm, but there is a shared kitchen and discounts of 60%. Some English spoken.

Villa Inn BOUTIQUE HOTEL $$
(美墅假期酒店; Měishù Jiàqī Jiǔdiàn; ☎8387 8025; villainn@163.com; 21 Tianlin Huayuan, off Donghai Xilu; 东海西路2号天林花园21号楼乙; d from ¥300, breakfast ¥20; ❉☎; ☐312, 317) In a quiet enclave of ocean-side villas, this teeny 15-room hotel is great for couples. The luxe rooms each have one large bed only; the nicest look out at the ocean (¥900), though only the very top-floor room (¥1300) has a panoramic floor-to-ceiling window. No matter. The shore is just steps away. Discounts of 50%.

The hotel is a 10-minute walk to Donhai Xilu. Some English is spoken.

Sea View Garden Hotel HOTEL $$$
(海景花园大酒店; Hǎijǐng Huāyuán Dàjiǔdiàn; ☎8587 5777; 2 Zhanghua Lu; 彰花路2号; r ¥900-1700, ste from ¥1360; ❂❉☎; ☐231, 232) With all the five-star competition, this hotel on the water in Dōngbú distinguishes itself with beyond professional service. Refreshments, hot towels and even unsolicited delivery of homemade soup to ease a cough – we could get used to this, assuming our credit cards don't max out. Fortunately, the service

charge is already included and discounts up to 40% are available.

China Community Art & Culture HOTEL $$$
(老转村公社文华艺术酒店; Lǎozhuǎncūn Gōngshè Wénhuá Yìshù Jiǔdiàn; ☎8576 8776; 8 Minjiang Sanlu; 闽江三路8号; s from ¥288, d from ¥598, ste ¥1008; ☐228, 402, 604) With silk lanterns illuminating the hallways, ceramic bowls serving as sinks, wood-floor showers and antique furnishings, each sumptuously decorated room in this polished hotel in the heart of Dōngbù has the feel of a courtyard residence. There's a fantastic restaurant on premises. Discounts of 10%. Some English is spoken.

🍴 Eating

Qīngdǎo's kitchens have no problem satisfying all tastes. The waterfront area from No 6 to No 1 Bathing Beach is brimming with restaurants – priced for tourists. The **Dōngbù** neighbourhood of **Hong Kong Garden** (香港花园; Xiānggǎng Huāyuán; ☐222, 231) around Xianggang Zhonglu is jam-packed with hip, international eateries: Korean, Japanese, Thai, Italian and Russian are just some of the cuisines on offer.

For the staple local seafood, stick to the streets. The **Táidōng** neighbourhood between Taidong Yilu (台东一路) and Taidong Balu (台东八路) in Shìběi district (市北区) north of Old Town is packed with restaurants, street markets and carts. Take bus 2, 222 or 217. For the quintessential Qīngdǎo meal, buy a *jīn* of clams – in local-speak *gálá* (蛤蜊; from ¥18) – and take it to a street-side stall with '加功' (*jiā gōng*) on its sign. They'll cook up your catch for ¥5, and pour a bag of fresh Tsingtao beer for ¥8 more. (Pints and pitchers also available if you want to be fancy.)

Huángdǎo Market STREET FOOD $
(黄岛路市场; Huángdǎo Lù Shìchǎng; meals from ¥8; ⊙7am-late; ☐228, 231) In the heart of Old Town, this long-standing, frenetic street market is chock-a-block with vendors selling (depending on the time of day) squirming seafood, fried chicken, pancakes, fruit, soy milk...it's all cheap, so just stop when something catches your fancy. Nearby Zhifu Lu has sit-down, curbside joints (look for a '加功' – *jiā gōng* – sign) that will prepare whatever seafood you bring them for ¥5.

Firewood Court STREET FOOD $
(劈柴院; Pīcháiyuàn; meals from ¥14; ⊙6am-10pm; ☐2, 228) Off Zhongshan Lu, an arch-

way with a plaster motif '1902' leads to a vast warren of food stalls and the **Jiāngníng Assembly Hall** (江宁会馆), a long-time draw for renowned performers that still puts on musical acts. The whole place is rather done up, but at least that means prices are labelled and eateries have picture menus. Watch out for less-than-fresh offerings.

Chūn Hé Lóu
SHANDONG $

(春和楼; ☑8282 4346; 146-150 Zhongshan Lu; meals from ¥48; ◷11am-3.30pm & 5-9.30pm; ☒2, 228) This Lǔ cuisine institution, which was founded in 1891, makes legendary pot stickers (锅贴; *guōtiē*) and crispy, fragrant chicken (香酥鸡; *xiāngsū jī*). The top-floor tables have the most atmosphere and get the full attention of the chefs. Downstairs is a fast-food version and take-out counter for dumplings.

Mǎ Jiā Lāmiàn
NOODLES $

(马家拉面; 44 Gaomi Lu, near Yizhou Lu; noodles ¥8-14; ◷9am-11pm; ☒222, 308) This Old Town hole-in-the-wall isn't as done up as its neighbours, but the Hui family that runs it makes a variety of handmade noodles and skewers without shortcuts. You can taste the effort. The beef noodle soup (牛肉面; *niúròu miàn*) is savoury and good, but you can't go wrong and it's all cheap.

QĪNGDǍO'S MOST FAMOUS EXPORT

The beer of choice in Chinese restaurants around the world, Tsingtao is one of China's oldest and most respected brands. Established in 1903 by a joint German–British corporation, the Germania-Brauerei began as a microbrewery of sorts using spring water from nearby Láo Shān to brew a Pilsener Light and Munich Dark for homesick German troops. In 1914 the Japanese occupied Qīngdǎo and confiscated the plant, rechristening it Dai Nippon and increasing production to sell under the Tsingtao, Asahi and Kirin labels. In 1945 the Chinese took over and gave the brewery its current name. At first, only China's elite could afford to drink it, but advertisements touting Tsingtao as a health drink boosted its appeal ('It's not only harmless, it strengthens the body!'). In 2014 the world drank more than 181 million kegs of the golden brew.

Bottomless refills of soup and raw garlic or chilli sauce for accompaniment.

Wángjiě Shāokǎo
ROAST GRILL $

(王姐烧烤; 113 Zhongshan Lu; 中山路113号; skewers ¥3-12; ◷10am-9.30pm) Qīngdǎo's famous meat skewers will require your undivided attention. Join the throng outside this street-side stand gorging on lamb (羊肉; *yángròu*), cuttlefish (鱿鱼; *yóuyú*) and chicken hearts (鸡心; *jīxīn*), and toss your spent skewers in the bucket. There's a sit-down restaurant around the corner.

China Community Art & Culture
SHANDONG, SICHUANESE $$

(老转村公社文华艺术酒店; Lǎozhuǎncūn Gōngshè Wénhuá Yìshù Jiǔdiàn; ☑8077 6776; 8 Minjiang Sanlu; mains from ¥48, eight-course set meal ¥68; ◷11.30am-10pm; ☒228, 312) This lovely restaurant next to its namesake hotel is in a stylised Hakka roundhouse (the sort once mistaken by the CIA for missile silos). The kitchen turns out sophisticated regional cuisine from Shāndōng and Sìchuān. Everything from the mushrooms to water for the tea is locally sourced from Láo Shān.

Cafè Yum
INTERNATIONAL $$$

(☑8388 3838; 9 Xianggang Zhonglu; buffet breakfast/lunch/dinner ¥159/193/274; ◷6-10am, 11.30am-2.30pm & 5.30-9.30pm) All-you-can-eat buffets go on all day in the swish Shangri-La Hotel. They're pricey but the international spreads are a glutton's paradise. Did we mention the all-you-can-drink beer? Reservations recommended.

🍷 Drinking & Nightlife

Qīngdǎo wouldn't be Qīngdǎo without Tsingtao, the beer that bears its name. The first stop for any committed tipplers should probably be the many drinking holes along **Beer Street** (啤酒街; Píjiǔ Jiē; Dengzhou Lu; ☒221, 301), where you can sample the delicious dark, unfiltered *yuánjiāng* (原浆啤酒), which is hard to find elsewhere.

The youth hostel bars are pleasant, particularly **Sunset Lounge** on the top of YHA Old Observatory and **Jinns' Café** in Kǎiyuè Hostelling International. Check out our recommended websites (p177) for the latest.

Luka Garden Cafe & Bistro
CAFE

(路过花园咖啡; Lùguò Huāyuán Kāfēi; ☑185 0024 2021; http://lukagardencafe.com; 5 Hengshan Lu; ◷8.30am-9pm; 🛜) In a city where new coffee shops open up daily, here in the garden of Hengshan No 5 Hostel there's excellent java a-brewing (from ¥25). There's also food inspired by barista Matt's New Zealand roots, from legit meat pies (¥62) to fresh lamb chops (¥120) and fish and chips (¥52).

Club New York   BAR
(纽约吧; Niǔyuē Bā; ☎8573 9199; 2nd fl, 41 Xianggang Zhonglu; beer from ¥28; ☺7pm-2am; ☐208, 216) Despite the overpriced drinks, this expat favourite overflows with revellers and sports fans when there's a match on TV. Take advantage of happy hour, which is any time before 9.30pm and after midnight. There's a live band most nights (9pm to 1am) and an incongruously classy sushi bar (11.30am to 9pm) adjoining. Above the Overseas Chinese International Hotel lobby in Dōngbù.

Spark Café & Brewery   BAR, BREWERY
(咖啡酿酒厂; Kāfēi Niàngjiǔ Chǎng; ☎8578 2296; 35 Donghai Xilu, May 4th Sq; 东海西路35号, 五四广场) Grab a seat on a long wooden bench in this crowded watering hole on the east edge of the Municipal Government square. There's all manner of drinks – beer (including the house 'dark' and 'light' microbrews at ¥35 a pint), cocktails, coffee, tea and milkshakes. Sister restaurant the Diner brings over burgers and sausage platters (¥55 to ¥75).

☆ Entertainment

Broadway Cinemas   CINEMA
(百老汇影城; Bǎilǎohuì Yǐngchéng; www.b-cinema.cn; 88 Aomen Lu; 澳门路88号; tickets from ¥60) Domestic and Hollywood blockbusters on the 3rd floor of Marina City shopping mall in the CBD.

Qīngdǎo Grand Theatre   THEATRE
(青岛大剧院; Qīngdǎo Dàjùyuàn; ☎8066 5555; www.qingdaograndtheatre.com; 5 Yunling Lu; 云岭路5号; ☐230, 321) North of Shílǎorén in the Láo Shān district, the city's grand performing arts centre puts world-class theatre, music, dance, comedy and kiddie acts on its three stages.

🔒 Shopping

Qīngdǎo's main shopping drags are in Dōngbù, around Xianggang Zhonglu, but there are plenty of other places to spend.

Book City   BOOKS
(书城; Shū Chéng; 67 Xianggang Zhonglu at Yan'erdao Lu; ☺9am-7pm) Vast aisles of Chinese media and some in English.

Carrefour   DEPARTMENT STORE
(家乐福; Jiālèfú; ☎8584 5867; 21 Xianggang Zhonglu; 香港中路21号; ☺8.30am-10pm; ☐12, 26, 304) Massive general store at Nanjing Lu and Xianggang Zhonglu.

Culture Street   ANTIQUES
(文化路; Wénhuà Lù; Changle Lu btwn Lijin Lu & Huayang Lu; ☺8am-4pm) 'Antiques' and handicrafts sold in front of a tidy row of concession architecture north of Old Town. The most vendors come out on Saturday and Sunday.

Jímòlù Market   MALL
(即墨路小商品市场; Jímòlù Xiǎoshàngpǐn Shìchǎng; 45 Liaocheng Lu; ☺9am-5.30pm) A four-storey bargain bonanza north of Old Town. Pearls, fake Chanel, clothing, shoes, backpacks, jade, wigs – all for the haggling.

Jusco   DEPARTMENT STORE
(佳世客; Jiāshìkè; ☎8571 9630; 72 Xianggang Zhonglu; 香港中路72号; ☺8.30am-10pm; ☐33, 304) Food court and supermarket at Fuzhou Nanlu and Xianggang Zhonglu.

Marina City   MALL
(百丽广场; Bǎilì Guǎngchǎng; ☎6606 1177; 88 Aomen Lu; 澳门路88号; ☺10am-10pm) International brands plus an ice rink.

Parkson   MALL
(百盛; Bǎishèng; 44 Zhongshan Lu; 中山路44号; ☺8.30am-8.30pm Sun-Thu, to 10pm Fri & Sat) Multi-level shopping and a supermarket.

ℹ Information

ATMs are easy to find in Qīngdǎo.

Skip the travel agencies and consult with one of the city's excellent hostels for travel advice.

Useful websites include **That's Qingdao** (www.thatsqingdao.com) and **Red Star** (www.myredstar.com), an online entertainment guide and monthly magazine available in hostels, bars and foreign restaurants.

Bank of China (中国银行; Zhōngguó Yínháng; 68 Zhongshan Lu; 中山路68号; ☺9am-5pm Mon-Sat) On Zhongshan Lu at Feicheng Lu in Old Town. Also in the tower at the intersection of Fuzhou Nanlu and Xianggang Zhonglu in the CBD. Branches have currency exchange and 24-hour ATMs.

China Post (中国邮政; Zhōngguó Yóuzhèng) On the west edge of Táidōng (23-1 Taidong Yilu; ☺8.30am-6pm), north of Old Town. Also by the ICBC tower in the CBD (119 Nanjing Lu; ☺9am-5pm Mon-Fri, 9am-4.30pm Sat & Sun).

Public Security Bureau (PSB; 公安局; Gōng'ānjú; ☎general hotline 6657 0000, visa inquiries 6657 3250, ext 2860; 272 Ningxia Lu; 宁夏路272号; ◷ 9am-noon & 1.30-5pm Mon-Fri) Take bus 301 from the train station to the Xiāoyáo Lù (逍遥路) stop and cross the street to the terracotta-coloured building with the flag on top.

Qīngdǎo Municipal Hospital, International Clinic (青岛市立医院东院区国际门诊; Qīngdǎo Shìlì Yīyuàn Dōngyuàn Qū, Guójì Ménzhěn; ☑ emergency 8278 9120, international clinic 8593 7690, ext 2266; 5 Donghai Zhonglu; 东海西路5号; ◷ 7.30am-noon & 1.30-5pm Mon-Fri, by appointment Sat; ▣ 210, 317)

ⓘ Getting There & Away

A handy ticket office sells air, train and ferry tickets on the ground floor of the **Xīn Tiānqiáo Hotel** (青岛新天桥兵官售票处; Qīngdǎo Xīn Tiānqiáo Bīngguǎn Shòupiàochù; ☑ air & boat 8612 0222, train & bus 8612 0111; 47 Feicheng Lu; usual commission ¥5; ◷ 7.30am-9pm), near the train station. Otherwise, hostels can help.

AIR

Qīngdǎo's **Liúting International Airport** (☑ booking & flight status 8471 5139, hotline 96567; www.qdairport.com) is 30km north of the city. There are flights to most large cities in China, including daily services to Běijīng (¥710, 1¼ hours), Shànghǎi (¥440, 1¼ hours) and Hong Kong (¥1587, three hours). International flights include daily flights to Seoul (¥1035), Tokyo (¥2165) and four weekly flights to Osaka (¥1795).

Book tickets online with hostels' help, directly through the airport's hotline or via airline offices (many are on Xianggang Zhonglu).

BUS

Among Qīngdǎo's many bus stations, the **long-distance bus station** (长途汽车站; chángtú qìchēzhàn; ☑ 400 691 6916; 2 Wenzhou Lu) in the Sìfāng (四方区) district, north of most tourist sights, best serves most travellers. A limited number of buses also depart for provincial destinations, including Yāntái (¥83, four hours, hourly, 6am to 5.30pm), directly across from the train station.

Daily direct buses from the long-distance bus station:

Běijīng ¥218, 11 hours, five daily (6am to 8.10pm)

Hángzhōu ¥310, 12 hours, two daily (6pm and 6.30pm)

Héféi ¥276, 10 hours, three daily (8am, 5pm and 7.10pm)

Jǐ'nán ¥109, 4½ hours, every 30 minutes (6.50am to 6.30pm)

Qūfù ¥96, six hours, two daily (6.50am and 3.30pm)

Shànghǎi ¥298, 11 hours, hourly (5pm to 9pm)

Tài'ān ¥128, six hours, five daily (6am, 8.30am, 12.30pm, 2pm and 3.30pm)

Wēihǎi ¥104, four hours, every 40 minutes (6.30am to 6pm)

Yāntái ¥85, four hours, every 40 minutes (6am to 7pm)

TRAIN

All trains from Qīngdǎo pass through Jǐ'nán except for the direct Qīngdǎo to Yāntái and Wēihǎi trains. Buy tickets at the **train station** (☑ 9510 5175; 2 Tai'an Lu), which has a 24-hour ticket office on the hectic east side (be sure to bring your passport). The west side is less crowded. Booking offices around town collect a service charge, typically ¥5. Tickets tend to sell out early in peak season.

Express trains (second-/first-class seat) depart for:

Běijīng South ¥314/474, 4½ to five hours, 13 daily (5.32am to 5.07pm)

Jǐ'nán ¥117/140, 2½ to three hours, hourly (5.32am to 7.50pm)

Qūfù ¥179/244, three hours, three daily (6.23am, 8.31am and 4.21pm)

Shànghǎi ¥518/818, 6½ hours, four daily (6.55am, 9.26am, 1.55pm and 4.35pm)

Tài'ān ¥149/194, three hours, four daily (6.57am, 9.19am, 9.32am and 2.38pm)

Wéifāng ¥52/62, one hour, frequently (5.32am to 7.50pm)

Regular trains (seat/hard sleeper) depart for:

Jǐ'nán ¥55/106, five to six hours, every 30 minutes (6.39am to 7.32pm)

Tài Shān ¥69/126, 5½ to seven hours, eight daily (6.39am to 5.37pm)

Wéifāng ¥29/80, 2½ hours, 10 daily (6.39am to 7.19pm)

Xī'ān ¥190/334, 19 to 24 hours, three daily (9.48am, 10.56am and noon)

Yāntái ¥38/57, four hours, one daily (2.46pm)

ⓘ Getting Around

TO/FROM THE AIRPORT

Bright blue **airport shuttles** (机场巴士; jīchǎng bāshì; ☑ 8286 0977; tickets ¥20) follow three routes through town. Shuttles leave hourly from the train station's south lot and then **Airlines Hotel** (航空快线商务酒店; ☑ 96567; 77 Zhongshan Lu) in Old Town from 5.30am to 8.40pm; the **Civil Aviation Building** (民航大厦; 30 Xianggang Xilu) across from the Carrefour from 6am to 9pm; and the CBD's **Century Mandarin Hotel** (世纪文化酒店; 10 Haijiang Lu) from 6.45am to 4.45pm. A taxi to/from Shìnán district is ¥80 to ¥120.

BORDER CROSSING: QĪNGDǍO TO JAPAN & SOUTH KOREA

International boats cross the Yellow Sea from Qīngdǎo's **Passenger Ferry Terminal** (青岛港客运站; Qīngdǎogǎng kèyùnzhàn; ☑ 8282 5001; 6 Xinjiang Lu), a kilometre north of Old Town along Xinjiang Lu.

Orient Ferry (奥林汽船; ☑ 8387 1160, 8593 8919; www.orientferry.co.jp; Office, HiSense Plaza, 17 Donghai Xilu; 东海西路17号海信大厦1410室; incl breakfast dm ¥1340-1450, r from ¥1660, student tickets discounted by ¥200) sails twice weekly for Shimonoseki, Japan (下关; 36 hours, Monday and Thursday, check in by 3.30pm, departs 9pm), while **Weidong Ferry Company** (威东航运; ☑ 8280 3574; www.weidong.com; 4 Xinjiang Lu, next to Qīngdǎo Passenger Ferry Terminal; dm ¥750, r ¥890-1370) operates boats from Qīngdǎo to Incheon, South Korea (仁川; 18 hours, Monday, Wednesday and Friday, check in by 3pm, departs 5pm), as well as from Yāntái and Wēihǎi. The cheapest tickets are usually for spots on the floor in large carpeted rooms, so upgrade at least one level if you want privacy.

Buy advance or same-day tickets at the passenger ferry terminal and from some ticket offices like the Xīn Tiānqiáo Hotel (p178) around town. The ferry terminal also exacts a ¥30 exit fee per passenger.

PUBLIC TRANSPORT

From the train station, buses 26 and 501 head east past Zhōngshān Park and continue north on Nanjing Lu and east along Xianggang Lu, respectively. From the long-distance bus station, buses 210 and 362 go to Old Town and Shílǎorén, respectively. Bus 5 connects the long-distance bus and train stations. Bus 2 (¥15) goes west to Huángdǎo district. Most city buses cost ¥1 to ¥2, but onboard conductors issue tickets for further destinations. Plan your trip with www.qdjyjt.com (in Chinese).

For ocean sights, bus 304 (¥7, two hours, from 6.30am) picks up at the Zhàn Qiáo stop by No 6 Bathing Beach and stops at all the biggies, ending at Dàhédòng in Láo Shān.

Outside the train station, red double-decker **sightseeing buses** (one stop/unlimited ¥10/30, depart 8am onwards) also pass the sights along the water, going east to Shílǎorén or Láo Shān's various gates.

The first line of the highly anticipated underground metro, scheduled to open in late 2015, will ease some of Qīngdǎo's gridlock.

TAXI

Flag fall is ¥9 or ¥12 for the first 6km and then ¥2.10 (slightly more at night) per kilometre thereafter, plus a ¥1 fuel surcharge. If your driver takes detours, it's because many city streets are restricted from 7am to 10pm.

Láo Shān   崂山

A quick ride 28km east from Qīngdǎo, an arresting jumble of sun-bleached granite and hidden freshwater springs rises over the sea. It's easy to understand why Láo Shān (崂山; child, student & senior half price, park shuttle ¥40; ⊙ 7am-4.30pm) has attracted spiritual pilgrims throughout the centuries. It's a great place to recharge over a weekend today.

In his quest for immortality, Emperor Qin Shi Huang ascended these slopes (with the help of a litter party of course), and in the 5th century, Buddhist pilgrim Faxian landed here returning from India with a complete set of Buddhist scriptures. Láo Shān has its share of religious sites, but it is most steeped in Taoist tradition. Adepts of the Quanzhen sect, founded near Yāntái in the 12th century, cultivated themselves in hermitages scattered all over the mountain.

Paths wind past ancient temples (and ruins), bubbling springs trickling into azure pools, and inscriptions left by Chinese poets and German alpinists. For the most part, routes are paved but there are plenty of opportunities to off-road as well (look for red flags tied to branches marking trails).

There are a number of ways to enter the park. **Dàhédòng gate** to the south is the main one and the start of the picturesque hike to **Jùfēng** (巨峰; admission Apr-Oct ¥120, Nov-Mar ¥90), the highest point at 1133m above sea level. If you take the **cable car** (suǒ dào; one way/return ¥40/80) part way up the mountain, it's another four hours up steps past temples and a spring to the stone terrace at the peak and awe-inspiring views of mountains, sky and sea.

An easier route is the loop through **Běijiǔshuǐ Scenic Area** (北九水景区; admission Apr-Oct ¥130, Nov-Mar ¥100), a canyon area at the north end of the park, which is mostly flat and takes a couple of hours to traverse. The path winds beside and across clear, blue streams before reaching **Cháoyīn Waterfall** (潮音瀑), which in the wet season roars like the ocean tide. (In drier months, the water falls in pieces, hence its ancient name, Fish Scales Waterfall.)

On the east side, **Yǎngkǒu Scenic Area** (仰口景区; admission Apr-Oct ¥90, Nov-Mar ¥60) offers an opportunity to ascend by foot or **cable car** (one way/return ¥45/80) past wind- and water-carved granite. There's a 30m scramble in total darkness up a crevice to the top of **Looking for Heaven Cave** (觅天洞) and then upward still for views of the sea. The hike takes about three hours.

About halfway between Dàhédòng and Yǎngkǒu is Láo Shān's oldest and grandest temple, **Tàiqīng Palace** (太清宫; Tàiqīng Gōng; admission ¥30; ☉ closes 5.30pm), established by the first Song emperor around AD 960 to perform Taoist rites to protect the souls of the dead. Devotees in blue and white still live here, and many credit their good health to drinking from the **Spring of the Immortals** (神水泉), which feeds into the grounds. The massive ancient gingko, cedar and cypress trees also apparently benefit your health.

🛏 Sleeping & Eating

If you want to extend your stay, pick-your-own seafood restaurants and a range of guesthouses line the main road hugging the coast.

Yǎngkǒu Holiday Hotel HOSTEL $
(仰口度假宾馆; Yǎngkǒu Dùjià Bīnguǎn; ☎8282 2626, English 186 6394 2253; dm ¥50, r with private bath ¥150) The local branch of Qīngdǎo's Old Observatory youth hostel overlooks a picturesque fishing village. Staff are mostly hands-off but they sometimes organise off-trail hikes in the park. Rooms are spartan but reasonably comfortable. Big student groups often stay here. It's about 50m past the Yǎngkǒu gate, on the left across from the fishing harbour.

Abalone Island Hotel HOTEL $$
(鲍鱼岛酒店; Bàoyú Dǎo Jiǔdiàn; ☎130 6128 0055, 6770 3411; Shazi Kou, Liuqing River Village; 沙子口镇流清河村; r ¥280-380; ❀@) About 4km from the Dàhédòng gate on Láo Shān's south end, Abalone Island Hotel has a handful of simple rooms (some with ocean views) above an excellent seafood restaurant, which serves its namesake abalone. To get here, take local bus 104 or 113 to the Liúqīnghé (流清河总站) stop, then walk an-

other kilometre, keeping the ocean on your right. No English spoken.

Seagrass House BOUTIQUE HOTEL $$$
(海草房; ☑English 186 6394 2253; Quanxin He; 泉心河; r incl meals from ¥1200; ❀☎) Set in former rangers' quarters by a crystal clear stream and surrounded by mountains and sea, this little hotel is the most sophisticated option in the park. Rooms are elegantly rustic; some have plush mattresses set on *kàng* (炕), platforms heated on chilly nights. All meals are included and highlight Láo Shān-sourced ingredients.

There are also grass cabanas on the sandy beach nearby and, of course, mountains within easy reach. Take bus 106 or 618 to the Quánxīn Hé (泉心河) stop.

❶ Getting There & Away

From Qīngdǎo, red double-decker sightseeing buses (one stop/unlimited ¥10/30) stop at sights along the water going east to Yǎngkǒu (departing 8am to 3pm, returning 2pm to 3pm), and go directly to Dàhédòng (departing 9am to 3pm, returning 1pm to 5pm) and Běijiǔshuǐ (departing 8.40am, returning 3pm). Another option is bus 304 (¥7, two hours, from 6.30am), which picks up at the Zhàn Qiáo stop by No 6 Bathing Beach and ends at Dàhédòng. Private tour buses to Láo Shān (return from ¥40) ply Qīngdǎo's streets from 6am onwards but stop at 'sights' on the way to the mountain and back.

Private cars and taxis aren't allowed within park boundaries, but park shuttles (unlimited rides ¥40) at each gate cover the routes. There are also local buses (¥2).

Yāntái 烟台
☑ 0535 / POP 1.8 MILLION

The sleepy portside town of Yāntái somehow has one of the fastest-developing economies in China – no small feat in a country of exponential growth. It managed to court foreign investment in its high-tech industry while building itself into a popular beach resort. A new tunnel connects the old district of Zhīfú with the booming Láishān district to the southeast. For now, this is still a place where you can take things easy. With Pénglái Pavilion not far away, the town makes for a relaxing two-day sojourn.

History

Starting life as a defence outpost and fishing village, Yāntái's name literally means 'Smoke Terrace': wolf-dung fires were lit on the headlands during the Ming dynasty to warn villagers of Japanese marauders. Yāntái was thrust under the international spotlight in the late 19th century when the Qing government, reeling from defeat in the Opium War, signed over the city to the British and French, who established a treaty port here. The rest of the eight-nation alliance followed with outposts, which remained until the province was captured by the Japanese in WWII. After the war, China kept Yāntái's ports open for foreign trade.

◉ Sights

Yāntái Hill Park
PARK

(烟台山公园; Yāntáishān Gōngyuán; admission ¥50, lighthouse admission ¥10; ⊗ 7am-6pm) This quaint park of stone paths, leafy gardens and ocean vistas is also a museum of Western treaty port architecture.

Stroll by the former **American Consulate Building**, which retains some original interior features and contains an exhibit on Yāntái's port days. Nearby, the former **Yāntái Union Church** dates from 1875, and now serves as the office for a wedding-planning company. The former **British Consulate** overlooks the bay with its annexe surrounded by an overgrown English garden. At the top of the hill is the Ming-dynasty **Dragon King Temple**, which in 1860 was co-opted as military headquarters for French troops. Wolf-dung fires burned continuously along the smoke terrace above, beginning in the 14th-century reign of Emperor Hongwu. Behind the temple, the lighthouse houses a **maritime museum**. In the west of the park, the 1930s-built **Japanese Consulate** is an austere brick structure with a 'torture inquisition room'.

Yāntái Folk Custom Museum
MUSEUM

(烟台民俗博物馆; Yāntái Mínsú Bówùguǎn; 2 Yulan Jie; ⊗ 8.30-11.30am & 1.30-4.30pm; 🚌 43, 46) **FREE** It's really architecture on display at this museum, a guild hall built between 1884 and 1906 by arrivals from Fújiàn. In the centre of the courtyard is a spectacularly intricate, decorated gate. Supported by 22 pillars, it's adorned with hundreds of carved and painted figures, phoenixes and other beasties, depicting classic folk tales including *The Eight Immortals Crossing the Sea*.

The centerpiece is the **Hall of the Heavenly Goddess**, where the goddess Tianhou, the patron of seafarers, is surrounded by a set of tin instruments in the shapes of

SHĀNDŌNG YĀNTÁI

WORTH A TRIP

PÉNGLÁI PAVILION

About 75km northwest of Yāntái perched on a bluff overlooking the waves, the 1000-year-old **Pénglái Pavilion** (蓬莱阁; Pénglái Gé; admission ¥140; ⊗ 6.30am-6.30pm summer, to 5pm winter) is closely entwined with Chinese mythology and the Taoist legend of the *Eight Immortals Crossing the Sea*.

The route up to the pavilion passes the grounds of an ancient naval base and a series of temples. The pavilion itself is unassuming as its restored exterior is rather similar to surrounding structures. Inside is a collection of prized inscriptions left by famous visitors since the Song dynasty, and a beautiful modern rendering of the Eight Immortals by Zhou Jinyun. There are many versions of the story, but in this one the immortals, who came from different walks of life, shared drinks at the pavilion before crossing the Bo Sea using unique superpowers.

After the pavilion, zip across the bay by **cable car** (one way/return ¥30/50; ⊗ 8am-5.10pm) for cliffside walks overlooking the Bo and Yellow Seas. There are also **museums** (open 7.30am to 5.30pm) dedicated to ancient shipbuilding, regional relics and Qi Jiguang, a local-born Ming-dynasty general who battled pirates.

If you arrive after a heavy rain, keep an eye on the marine layer where mirages have appeared every few years. Long ago, this earned Pénglái a reputation as a gateway to immortal lands and compelled Emperor Qin Shi Huang to send ships in search of islands of immortality further east.

Pénglái is an easy day trip by bus from Yāntái (¥24, 1½ hours, frequently, 5.30am to 6.30pm), with the last returning at 7.30pm/6pm summer/winter. The bus station (166 Zhonglou Beilu) is a 15-minute walk to the park. Taxi drivers will go for ¥9 but sometimes stop elsewhere first.

Yāntái

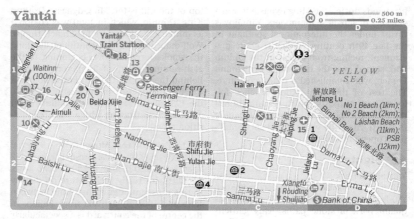

Yāntái

gourds and tiny mice, crawling dragons and dragon heads.

Yāntái Museum
MUSEUM

(烟台市博物馆; Yāntái Shì Bówùguǎn; ☏ 623 2976; 61 Nan Dajie; ⊗ 9am-4pm, closed Mon; 🚍 43, 46) **FREE** The sparkling new museum traces the historical development of the Jiāodōng peninsula, where Yāntái currently stands, from the prehistoric age and successive kingdoms to the present day. There's a display on the 'Shell Mound' culture (a glimpse at a neolithic civilisation's trash) and a wonderful collection of rare porcelain. English descriptions.

Changyu Wine Culture Museum
MUSEUM

(张裕酒文化博物馆; Zhāngyù Jiǔwénhuà Bówùguǎn; 56 Dama Lu; admission incl tasting ¥50; ⊗ 8am-5.30pm) The unexpected Changyu Wine Culture Museum introduc-

es the history of China's oldest and largest Western-style winery, which produces grape wines as well as brandy and a Chinese 'health liquor'.

Cheong Fatt-Tze, dubbed China's Rockfeller, founded the winery in 1894, after overhearing that Yāntái's climate might suit vineyards at a party at the French consulate. Tastings of Changyu's (so-so but improving) wines are in the atmospheric, old wine cellar.

⦿ Beaches

Bus 17 (¥2) conveniently runs along Yāntái's coastline passing a number of sandy strips and tide pools in between the main beaches that are worth jumping off for.

No 1 Beach
BEACH

(第一海水浴场; Dìyī Hǎishuǐ Yùchǎng; 🚍17) One of Yāntái's two main beaches, No 1 Beach is a long stretch of soft sand in a calm bay.

No 2 Beach
BEACH

(第二海水浴场; Dì'èr Hǎishuǐ Yùchǎng; 🖥17)
About 6km east of the old town, No 2 Beach
is rocky in parts but surrounded by lively
tide pools.

Láishān Beach
BEACH

(莱山海水浴场; Láishān Hǎishuǐ Yùchǎng; 🖥17)
This vast expanse of golden sand in the developing district 11km east of the old town
attracts clam diggers and sunbathers alike.
Get off at the Huánghǎi City Flower Garden
(黄海城市花园) stop.

🛏 Sleeping

Many hotels are clustered around the train
and bus stations where it's noisy and dull.
It's much more pleasant on the charming
old streets around Chaoyang Jie's north end.

Coast International Youth Hostel
HOSTEL $

(海岸国际青年旅舍; Hǎi'àn Guójì Qīngnián
Lůshě; 🖉623 0655, English 188 6550 0973; 41
Chaoyang Jie; 潮扬街41号; dm ¥50-60, s & d
¥198; ❄@🛜) Smack in the heart of Yāntái's
charming old town is this cheery, new hostel with a bright common room with wi-fi
and evening movies, a coffee bar and an
open kitchen. In between mixing drinks
and weekend barbecues, staff lead walking
tours of the neighbourhood and bike rides to
Yāngmǎ Island (bike rental ¥20), plus they
can help book tickets.

The dorms are clean, but management
also opens up some double rooms to backpackers at a discounted rate (¥90 per person). Discounts of 20% from November to
June. Some English spoken.

Shāndōng Machinery Hotel
HOTEL $$

(山东机械宾馆; Shāndōng Jīxiè Bīnguǎn; 🖉621
4561; 162 Jiefang Lu; 解放路162号; s & d ¥320-
480, ste ¥580; ❄🛜) With Korean and Japa-
nese restaurants, and an international tick-
eting office on the premises, staff here know
how to cater to non-Mandarin-speaking
guests. The Asian-decor rooms have nicer de-
tails (wooden soaking tubs) than the Western
ones, but all are way nicer than the building
exterior suggests. Discounts up to 30%. Look
for the 'SD MACH' sign on the rooftop.

Waitinn
HOTEL $$

(维特风尚酒店; Wéitè Fēngshàng Jiǔdiàn; 🖉212
0909; www.waitinn.com; 73 Beima Lu; 北马路73
号; tw & d ¥288-328, tr ¥358; ❄@) Opposite the
train station, this refurbished hotel is a decent place to, as it were, wait in. Rooms are
large, comfortable and equipped with flat-
screen TVs. Add breakfast for ¥15 and ask
for a discount. Another branch (🖉658 0909;
35 Qingnian Lu) is right by the bus station.

Golden Gulf Hotel
HOTEL $$$

(金海湾酒店; Jīnhǎiwān Jiǔdiàn; 🖉663 6999; fax
663 2699; 34 Haian Lu; 海安路34号; s & d incl
breakfast ¥990-1280; ❄🛜) The city's first five-
star hotel has a superb sea and parkside lo-
cation, and bright, well-maintained rooms.

🍴 Eating & Drinking

South of Yāntái Hill, the old town pedes-
trian streets branching off Chaoyang Jie
are crammed with vendors serving some
of the freshest seafood and tastiest street
food in these parts. There is also a range of
international restaurants, bars, cafes and
even an Irish pub or two, though some shut-
ter outside of summer.

DÀLIÁN–YĀNTÁI UNDERSEA TUNNEL

Two decades in the making, the blueprints are almost done for China's next epic infra-
structure project: a ¥220-billion tunnel 100ft under the bottom of the Bo Sea that will
trace Yāntái's coastline before curving north to Dàlián in Liáoníng province.

At 123km long, the Dàlián–Yāntái tunnel will be longer than the two previous re-
cord-holders – the Seikan Tunnel (between Honshu and Hokkaido in Japan) and the 'Chun-
nel' (between Britain and France) – combined. More importantly, it will cut a seven-hour
boat ride or a 1400km road trip down to a 40-minute high-speed-train ride or a quick drive,
linking China's north and south like never before.

The tunnel is actually three – one channel each for cars, trains and maintenance –
plus many more vertical ventilation pipes bored through the ocean floor. Building it will
rely on engineering that hasn't been tested before, and critics point out that the tunnel
could disturb two active fault lines. Architects counter with the argument that it will all be
accounted for in the plans. The tunnel is slated to open before 2020.

BORDER CROSSING: YĀNTÁI AND WĒIHǍI TO SOUTH KOREA

Shāndōng's coastline offers easy access to international cities across the Yellow Sea. Boats regularly depart from Yāntái's **Passenger Ferry Terminal** (烟台港客运站; Yāntái Gǎng Kèyùnzhàn; ☑ 624 2715; 155 Beima Lu) for Incheon, South Korea (仁川).

Weidong Ferry Company (威东航运; ☑ 660 3721; www.weidong.com; 155 Beima Lu, next to Yāntái Passenger Ferry Terminal) sails three times a week from Yāntái (16 hours, Monday, Wednesday and Friday, departs 6pm). Tickets sell out, so book in advance by phone or at the ticket office next to the ferry terminal. Plan to check in early, generally before 3pm, as customs and other inspections are required.

Weidong Ferry (威东航运; ☑ 0631 522 6173; 48 Haibin Beilu; 海滨北路48号, Wēihǎi; dm ¥750, r ¥890-1370) also sails from Wēihǎi (Tuesday, Thursday and Sunday, departs 7pm) from the **passenger ferry terminal** (威海港国际客运码头; Wēihǎi Gǎng Guójì Kèyùn Mǎtóu; ☑ 0631 523 6799; www.whport.com.cn; 288 Shū Gǎng Lù; 疏港路 (海埠路) 288号, Wēihǎi). Buses from Yāntái's long-distance main bus station (¥38) make the 70km drive to Wēihǎi's station every 25 minutes from 6am to 6pm, then you transfer to bus K01 for the 10km drive north to the ferry terminal.

There's a small cluster of snack **food stalls** (Nan Dajie; 南大街; snacks from ¥2; ◷ noon-9pm) along the park next to the Parkson department store in the heart of the shopping district, and a good variety of restaurants in the new, luxury **Joy City** (大悦城; 150 Beima Lu; ◷ 10am-10pm) shopping mall.

Xiāngfǔ Ròudīng Shuǐjiǎo   DUMPLINGS $
(乡府肉丁水饺; ☑ 155 0545 3700; Fulai Lijie; 福来里街(近烟台华侨小学西大门); mains from ¥20; ◷ 10.30am-2pm & 4.30-9pm; ☐ 6) At the south end of Fulai Lijie by the elementary school, this tiny restaurant draws foodies from afar with its speciality dumplings (shuǐjiǎo), particularly the ones filled with tender bàyú (鲅鱼; ¥28 per jīn, enough for two), a locally caught mackerel.

★ **Róngxiáng Hǎixiān**   SEAFOOD $$
(荣祥海鲜; ☑ 155 0663 3177; 25-1 Fumin Jie, at Haiguan Jie; 阜民街25-1号, 海关街; meals from ¥60; ◷ 11am-1pm & 5-8.40pm) At this perpetually packed local institution, the seafood is crawling/swimming/blinking in the back room where you put in your order. Quick-tongued staff toss out price per jīn and suggested cooking methods as you point – clams, ¥38, spicy (辣炒; làchǎo); crab, ¥38, ginger scallion (姜葱; jiāngcōng); abalone, ¥71, sautéed without chilli (清炒; qīng chǎo); and so on. Everything is in Chinese, so if intimidated, tell them your overall budget, point and just go with it. Then grab the first table you find.

❶ Information

Bank of China (中国银行; Zhōngguó Yínháng; 166 Jiefang Lu; 解放路166号) ATM accepts all cards. Full-service branch at Beima Lu and Dahaiyang Lu opens from 8.30am to 4.20pm.

China Post (中国邮政; Zhōngguó Yóuzhèng; Beima Lu & Dahaiyang Lu, across from train station; ◷ 8am-noon & 1-5pm) Another branch is at 28 Hai'an Jie.

Public Security Bureau (公安局; Gōng'ānjú; ☑ 629 7046; 7 Chang'an Jie; 长安路7号; ◷ 8-11.30am & 1.30-5pm Mon-Fri; ☐ 17) Office for entry-exit visas (出入境管理处) in Láishān district.

Yāntái Shān Hospital (烟台山医院; Yāntái Shān Yīyuàn; ☑ 660 2001; 91 Jiefang Lu) Chinese-speaking only.

❶ Getting There & Away

AIR

Yāntái **Láishān International Airport** (☑ 624 1330) is 20km south of town. Book tickets at the **Yāntái Traffic Tourism Group** (烟台交运国际旅行社; Yāntái Jiāoyùn Guójì Lǚxíngshè; ☑ 665 1110; Tōnghuì Hotel lobby, 67 Xi Dajie; 西大街67号, 通汇大酒店一楼; no commission; ◷ 8am-6pm) or the Civil Aviation Hotel **ticket centre** (烟台国际机场售票中心; Yāntái Guójì Jīchǎng Shòupiào Zhōngxīn; ☑ 658 3366; 78 Dahaiyang Lu; 大海阳路78号). Coast International Youth Hostel (p183) can also help.

There are regular flights to Běijīng (¥690, one hour), Shànghǎi (¥790, 1½ hours), Guǎngzhōu (¥1930, three hours), Seoul (¥1116, one hour) and Osaka (¥2388, 1½ hours).

Airport shuttles (机场巴士; ☑ 629 9146; tickets ¥10) run hourly from 6.15am to 8.45pm, arriving in about 30 minutes at **Tōnghuì Hotel** (通汇大酒店; Tōnghuì Dà Jiǔdiàn; 67 Xi Dajie; 西大街67号), a five-minute walk from the long-distance main bus station, and the Civil Aviation Hotel ticket centre to the south. The return ride departs from Tōnghuì Hotel every 20 minutes from 6am to 7pm, and from the Civil Aviation Hotel about hourly from 6am to 8.30pm.

BOAT

Purchase tickets for ferries to Dàlián (seat ¥180, bed ¥210 to ¥1200, seven hours, 7.45am, 9am, 12.40pm, 3.30pm, 8pm, 9.30pm and 11.30pm) at the **Yāntái Harbour Passenger Transit Terminal** (烟台港客运站; Yāntáigǎng Kèyùnzhàn; ☑ 650 6666; www.bohaiferry.com; 155 Beima Lu) or ticket offices east of the train station or in the bus station.

BUS

From the **long-distance main bus station** (长途总汽车站; chángtú zǒng qìchē zhàn; ☑ 666 6111; 86 Xi Dajie & Qingnian Lu) there are buses to numerous destinations:

Běijīng ¥246, 13 hours, one to two daily (8.45am and 3pm)

Jǐ'nán ¥175, 5½ hours, every 30 minutes (5am to 6pm)

Pénglái ¥24, 1½ hours, frequently (5.30am to 6.30pm)

Qīngdǎo ¥85, four hours, every 30 minutes (5am to 6pm)

Shànghǎi ¥308, 12 hours, one to two daily (5pm and 8.40pm)

Tiānjīn ¥198, 11 hours, one to two daily (10am and 7.30pm)

Wēihǎi ¥38, one hour, frequently (6am to 6pm)

TRAIN

Regular trains (seat/hard sleeper) depart from Yāntái **train station** (火车站; huǒchēzhàn; ☑ 9510 5175; Beima Lu) for:

Běijīng ¥129/231, 15 hours, one daily (11.25pm)

Jǐ'nán ¥75/138, 7½ hours, 10 daily (9.25am to 11pm)

Qīngdǎo ¥38/57, five hours, one daily (8.27am)

Shànghǎi ¥181/322, 21 hours, one daily (9.40am)

Xī'ān ¥198/349, 24 hours, one daily (3.15pm)

ⓘ Getting Around

Bus 17 runs along the coast from the train station and ferry terminal to the city's beaches. Bus 6 runs along Beima Lu from the old town to the bus station. Bus 10 reaches Láishān district's main streets.

Taxi flag fall is ¥8 for the first 6km and ¥1.80 (slightly more at night) per kilometre thereafter. It's about a ¥50 ride from the airport.

SHĀNDŌNG YĀNTÁI

Shànghǎi

☏ 021 / POP 24 MILLION

Best Places to Eat

→ Jian Guo 328 (p216)
→ Din Tai Fung (p219)
→ Lost Heaven (p214)
→ Fu 1039 (p218)
→ Commune Social (p218)

Best Places to Stay

→ Fairmont Peace Hotel (p211)
→ Urbn (p213)
→ Mandarin Oriental Pudong (p213)
→ Magnolia Bed & Breakfast (p212)
→ Le Tour Traveler's Rest (p213)

Why Go?

You can't see the Great Wall from space, but you'd have a job missing Shànghǎi (上海). One of the country's largest and most vibrant cities, Shànghǎi somehow typifies modern China while being unlike anywhere else in the land. Shànghǎi *is* real China, but – rather like Hong Kong or Macau – just not the China you had in mind.

This is a city of action, not ideas. You won't spot many Buddhist monks contemplating the dharma, oddball bohemians or wild-haired poets handing out flyers, but skyscrapers will form before your eyes. Shànghǎi best serves as an epilogue to your China experience: submit to its debutante charms after you've had your fill of dusty imperial palaces and bumpy 10-hour bus rides. From nonstop shopping to skyscraper-hopping to bullet-fast Maglev trains and glamorous cocktails – this is Shànghǎi.

When to Go
Shànghǎi

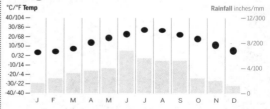

Feb Visit Yùyuán Gardens for the lantern festival, two weeks after Chinese New Year.

Apr & May March is chilly and 1 May is chaos, but otherwise spring is ideal.

Oct The optimal season: neither too hot nor too rainy.

History

As the gateway to the Yangzi River (Cháng Jiāng), Shànghǎi (the name means 'by the sea') has long been an ideal trading port. However, although it supported as many as 50,000 residents by the late 17th century, it wasn't until after the British opened their concession here in 1842 that modern Shànghǎi really came into being.

The British presence in Shànghǎi was soon followed by the French and Americans, and by 1853 Shànghǎi had overtaken all other Chinese ports. Built on the trade of opium, silk and tea, the city also lured the world's great houses of finance, which erected grand palaces of plenty. Shànghǎi also became a byword for exploitation and vice; its countless opium dens, gambling joints and brothels managed by gangs were at the heart of Shànghǎi life. Guarding it all were the American, French and Italian marines, British Tommies and Japanese bluejackets.

After Chiang Kaishek's coup against the communists in 1927, the Kuomintang cooperated with the foreign police and the Shànghǎi gangs, and with Chinese and foreign factory owners, to suppress labour unrest. Exploited in workhouse conditions, crippled by hunger and poverty, sold into slavery, excluded from the high life and the parks created by the foreigners, the poor of Shànghǎi had a voracious appetite for radical opinion. The Chinese Communist Party (CCP) was formed here in 1921 and, after numerous setbacks, 'liberated' the city in 1949.

The communists eradicated the slums, rehabilitated the city's hundreds of thousands of opium addicts, and eliminated child and slave labour. These were staggering achievements; but when the decadence went, so did the splendour. Shànghǎi became a colourless factory town and political hotbed, and was the power base of the infamous Gang of Four during the Cultural Revolution.

Shànghǎi's long slumber came to an abrupt end in 1990, with the announcement of plans to develop Pǔdōng, on the eastern side of the Huángpǔ River. Since then Shànghǎi's burgeoning economy, leadership and intrinsic self-confidence have put it miles ahead of other Chinese cities. Its bright lights and opportunities have branded Shànghǎi a Mecca for Chinese (and foreign) economic migrants. In 2010, 3600 people squeezed into every square kilometre, compared with 2588 per sq km in 2000 and by 2014, the city's population had leaped to a staggering 24 million. Over nine million migrants make Shànghǎi home, colouring the local complexion with a jumble of dialects, outlooks, lifestyles and cuisines.

Language

Spoken by more than 13 million people, the Shanghainese dialect (Shànghǎihuà in Mandarin) belongs to the Wú dialect. Fewer and fewer local people speak Shanghainese properly due to the spread of Mandarin, which virtually everyone speaks fluently.

Climate

Shànghǎi's winters are cold and damp while summers are hot, humid and sapping, with sudden epic rains. Try to catch the weather in between: April to mid-May is probably the best time to visit, along with autumn (late September to mid-November).

◉ Sights

Shànghǎi municipality covers a vast area, but the city proper is more modest. Broadly, central Shànghǎi cleaves into two zones: Pǔxī (浦西; west of the Huángpǔ River) and Pǔdōng (浦东; east of the Huángpǔ River). History, personality and charm are in Pǔxī, where you find the Bund (officially named East Zhongshan No 1 Rd), the former foreign concessions, the principal shopping districts, and Shànghǎi's trendiest bars, restaurants and nightclubs. Pǔdōng – the financial, skyscraper hub – is modern but charmless, with sights falling into the observation deck/skyscraper towers/museums bag.

◉ The Bund 外滩

The area around the Bund is the tourist centre of Shànghǎi and is the city's most famous mile. Extensively renovated **Yuanmingyuan Rd**, west of the north end of the Bund, is home to some art deco landmark architecture and further imposing concession-era buildings.

★**The Bund**   ARCHITECTURE
(外滩; Wàitān; Map p192; East Zhongshan No 1 Rd; 中山东一路; Ⓜ East Nanjing Rd) Symbolic of concession-era Shànghǎi, the **Bund (Wàitān)** was the city's Wall St, a place of feverish trading and fortunes made and lost. Originally a towpath for dragging barges of rice, the Bund (an Anglo-Indian term for the embankment of a muddy waterfront) was gradually transformed into a grandiose sweep of the most

Shànghǎi Highlights

❶ Stroll down the **Bund** (p187) promenade or raise an evening glass to phosphorescent Pǔdōng

❷ Load up on Chinese culture's greatest hits at the **Shànghǎi Museum** (p191)

❸ Admire the curvature of the earth from atop the **Shànghǎi Tower** (p203) or the **Shànghǎi World Financial Center** (p203)

❹ Catch up with the latest trends in contemporary Chinese art at the **Rockbund Art Museum** (p190)

❺ Weave through a forest of shoppers' elbows in the charming *shíkùmén* warren of **Tiánzǐfáng** (p224)

❻ Put on your best shoes and step out into the **French Concession** (p198)

❼ Plunge into the neon-lit swell of **East Nanjing Road** (p190)

❽ Dine at some of Shànghǎi's signature **Bund restaurants** (p214), all with showstopping views as standard

❾ Fathom the fantastic at Shànghǎi's most sacred shrine, the **Jade Buddha Temple** (p199)

❿ Eke out a quiet pocket and sit down within the **Yùyuán Gardens** (p195)

SHÀNGHǍI IN...

One Day

Rise with the sun for early morning riverside scenes on **the Bund** as the vast city stirs from its slumber. Then stroll down East Nanjing Rd to **People's Sq** and either the **Shàng-hǎi Museum** (p191) or the **Shànghǎi Urban Planning Exhibition Hall** (p191). After a dumpling lunch on Huanghe Rd food street, hop on the metro at People's Sq to shuttle east to Pǔdōng. Explore the fun and interactive **Shànghǎi History Museum** (p203) or contemplate the Bund from the breezy Riverside Promenade, then take high-speed lifts to some of the world's highest observation decks, in the **Shànghǎi Tower** (p203) or **Shànghǎi World Financial Center** (p203). Stomach rumbling? Time for dinner in the French Concession, followed by a nightcap on the Bund if you want to go full circle.

Two Days

Beat the crowds with an early start at the Old Town's **Yùyuán Gardens** before pok-ing around for souvenirs on Old St and wandering the alleyways. Make your next stop **Xīntiāndì** for lunch and a visit to the **Shíkùmén Open House Museum** (p198). Taxi it to **Tiánzǐfáng** for the afternoon, before another French Concession dinner. Caught a second wind? Catch the acrobats, hit the clubs or unwind with a traditional Chinese massage or some Shànghǎi jazz.

powerful banks and trading houses in Shàng-hǎi. The optimum activity here is to simply stroll, contrasting the bones of the past with the futuristic geometry of Pǔdōng's skyline.

The majority of art deco and neoclassical buildings here were built in the early 20th century and presented an imposing – if strikingly un-Chinese – view for those nos-ing by boat into the busy port city. Today it has emerged as a designer retail and res-taurant zone, and the city's most exclusive boutiques, restaurants and hotels see the Bund as the only place to be. Evening vis-its are rewarded by electric views of Pǔdōng and the illuminated grandeur of the Bund. Other options include taking a boat tour on the Huángpǔ River or relaxing at some fab-ulous bars and restaurants. Huángpǔ Park, at the north end of the promenade, features the modest Bund History Museum, which contains a collection of old photographs and maps.

East Nanjing Road   ARCHITECTURE

(南京东路; Nánjīng Dōnglù; Map p192; M East Nanjing Rd) Linking the Bund with People's Sq is East Nanjing Rd, once known as Nanking Rd. The first department stores in China opened here in the 1920s, when the modern machine-age – with its new products, au-tomobiles, art deco styling and newfangled ideas – was ushered in. A glowing forest of neon at night, it's no longer the cream of Shànghǎi shopping, but its pedestrian strip

remains one of the most famous and crowd-ed streets in China.

Shànghǎi's reputation as the country's most fashionable city was forged in part here, through the new styles and trends in-troduced in department stores such as the Sun Sun (1926), today the **Shànghǎi No 1 Food Store** (上海市第一食品商店; Shànghǎi Shì Dìyī Shípǐn Shāngdiàn; Map p192; 720 East Nan-jing Rd; 南京东路720号; M People's Sq), and the Sun Company (1936), now the **Shànghǎi No 1 Department Store** (上海市第一百货商店; Shànghǎi Shì Dìyī Bǎihuò Shāngdiàn; Map p192; 800 East Nanjing Rd; 南京东路800号; ⊘9.30am-10pm; M People's Sq). Today it's shops such as the vast **Apple Store** (Map p192; www.apple. com/cn; 300 East Nanjing Rd; 南京东路300号; ⊘10am-10pm; M East Nanjing Rd) that domi-nate the shopping landscape. The pedes-trianised section of the road is an assault course of fake-watch sellers, clinging pur-veyors of 'massagee' and English-speaking girls who encourage you to spend a king's ransom on cups of tea. Small 'train' tourist buses roll from one pedestrianised end to the other (¥5).

Rockbund Art Museum   MUSEUM

(上海外滩美术馆; Shànghǎi Wàitān Měishùguǎn; Map p192; www.rockbundartmuseum.org; 20 Huqiu Rd; 虎丘路20号; adult ¥15; ⊘10am-6pm Tue-Sun; M East Nanjing Rd) Housed in the former Royal Asiatic Society building (1933) – once Shànghǎi's first museum – this private space behind the Bund focuses on contemporary

Chinese art, with rotating exhibits year-round and no permanent collection. One of the city's top modern-art venues, the building's interior and exterior are both sublime. Check out the unique art deco eight-sided *bāguà* (trigram) windows at the front, a fetching synthesis of Western modernist styling and traditional Chinese design.

The interior is all textbook deco lines and curves, including the fine staircase. Head to the rooftop terrace for excellent views, despite the hulking form of the Peninsula hotel blocking out much of Lùjiāzuǐ. A cafe on the top floor dispenses free cups of tea.

Post Museum
MUSEUM
(邮政博物馆; Yóuzhèng Bówùguǎn; Map p192; 2nd fl, 250 North Suzhou Rd; 北苏州路250号2楼; ⏰9am-5pm Wed, Thu, Sat & Sun, last entry 4pm; Ⓜ Tiantong Rd) FREE This fascinating museum in the stunning Main Post Office building explores postal history in imperial China, which dates back to the 1st millennium BC. The system used an extensive pony express to relay messages; Marco Polo estimated there were 10,000 postal stations in 13th-century China. Check out the collection of pre- and post-Liberation stamps (1888–1978) in a special climate-controlled room; the 250cc Xingyue motorbikes used by postal workers to burn up and down Shànghǎi's roads; and a mechanised mail sorter.

Shanghai Gallery of Art
GALLERY
(外滩三号沪申画廊; Map p192; www.shanghaigalleryofart.com; 3rd fl, 3 on the Bund, 3 East Zhongshan No 1 Rd; 中山东一路三号三楼; ⏰11am-7pm; Ⓜ East Nanjing Rd) FREE Take the lift up to the 3rd floor of 3 on the Bund to this neat and minimalist art gallery for glimpses of current directions in highbrow and conceptual Chinese art. It's all bare concrete pillars, ventilation ducts and acres of wall space; there are a couple of divans where you can sit to admire the works on view.

👁 People's Square 人民广场

Once the site of the Shànghǎi Racecourse, People's Sq is the modern city's nerve centre. Overshadowed by the dramatic form of **Tomorrow Square** (明天广场; Míngtiān Guǎngchǎng; Map p192; 399 West Nanjing Rd; 南京西路399号; Ⓜ People's Sq), the open space is peppered with museums, performing arts venues, leafy People's Park and crowds.

★ Shànghǎi Museum
ART MUSEUM
(上海博物馆; Shànghǎi Bówùguǎn; Map p192; www.shanghaimuseum.net; 201 Renmin Ave; 人民大道201号; ⏰9am-5pm; Ⓜ People's Sq) FREE This must-see museum escorts you through the craft of millennia and the pages of Chinese history. It's home to one of the most impressive collections in the land: take your pick from the archaic green patinas of the Ancient Chinese Bronzes Gallery through to the silent solemnity of the Ancient Chinese Sculpture Gallery; from the exquisite beauty of the ceramics in the Zande Lou Gallery to the measured and timeless flourishes captured in the Chinese Calligraphy Gallery.

Chinese painting, seals, jade, Ming and Qing furniture, coins and ethnic costumes are also on offer, intelligently displayed in well-lit galleries. The building itself is designed to resemble the shape of an ancient Chinese *dǐng* (Chinese cauldron with three legs) vessel. Photography is permitted in some galleries and the audio guide is well worth the Y40 (deposit Y400 or your passport). The excellent museum shop sells postcards, a rich array of books, and faithful replicas of the museum's ceramics and other pieces. There are a few overpriced shops and teahouses inside the museum, as well as a snack bar, a cloakroom and an ATM. Expect to spend half, if not most of, a day here and note that the entrance is from East Yan'an Rd. Get here early as only 8000 people are allowed in daily.

Shànghǎi Urban Planning Exhibition Hall
MUSEUM
(上海城市规划展示馆; Shànghǎi Chéngshì Guīhuà Zhǎnshìguǎn; Map p192; 100 Renmin Ave, entrance

---

PRICE INDICATORS

The following price indicators are used in this region:

Sleeping

$ less than ¥500

$$ ¥500 to ¥1300

$$$ more than ¥1300

Eating

(based on meal)

$ less than ¥60

$$ ¥60 to ¥160

$$$ more than ¥160

The Bund & People's Square

See French Concession Map (p200)

Qipu Rd
N Fujian Rd
Tiantong Rd

Jinyuan Rd 晋元路
Wuzhen Rd

Qufu Rd
Ⓜ 曲阜路站
Qufu Rd

N Suzhou Rd 苏州北路
S Suzhou Rd 南苏州路
Xiamen Rd 厦门路

Guangfu Rd

Ⓜ **Xinzha Rd**
新闸路站

Xinzha Rd 新闸路

E Beijing Rd 北京东路

W Beijing Rd 北京西路

Middle Zhejiang Rd
Guizhou Rd
N Guangxi Rd

Fengyang Rd

⊗ 27
⊗ 37   ⊗ 28
Huanghe Rd

Fengyang Rd

🏛 53   🏛 54   17 🏤   61 ℹ
E Nanjing Rd 南京西路

🏛 Madame
Tussauds

Jiujiang Rd
Hankou Rd

25 🏤

**People's
Square**
人民广场站

**People's
Square**
人民广场站

33

Fuzhou Rd 福州路

Xinchang Rd

**People's
Park**
人民公园

**People's
Square**
人民广场站

48

SHÀNGHǍI

50 🔒

Fengyang Rd

⊗ 41   🏛 9   10 🏛

Middle Xizang Rd

Hubei Rd

N Chengdu Rd 成都北路

W Nanjing Rd 南京西路
◎ 11

N Huangpi Rd 黄陂北路

Jiangyin Rd
19 🏤   ⊗ 29   ⭐ 47

Renmin Ave 人民大道

**People's
Square**

35 ⊗

E Yan'an Rd

Weihai Rd

Wusheng Rd 武胜路

1 🏛 **Shànghǎi
Museum**

South Xizang Rd

18 🏤

52 🔒

⭐ 46

Dagu Rd

E Yan'an Rd 延安东路

S Huangpi Rd

Pu'an Rd
64 🏤
Middle Jinling Rd 金陵中路

Dashijie
大世界站
Ⓜ

**Middle
Huaihai Rd**

Liulin Rd

*Dongtai Rd
Antique Market (300m)*

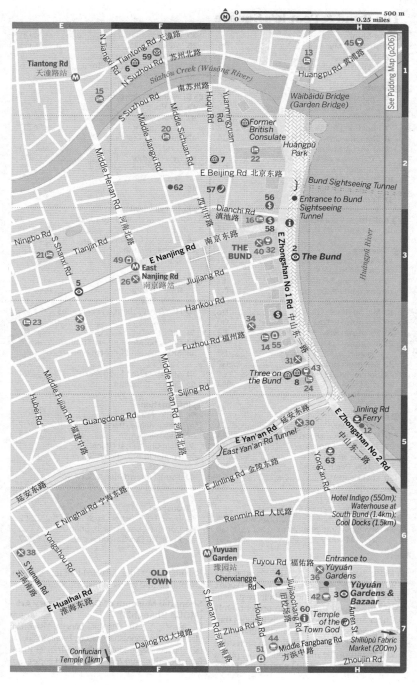

SHÀNGHĂI

0 — 500 m
0 — 0.25 miles

Tiantong Rd 天潼路

N Jiangxi Rd
N Suzhou Rd 苏州北路
6 59 Tiantong Rd 天潼路
45
13
Huangpu Rd 贵浦路

15

S Suzhou Rd
南苏州路
Sūzhōu Creek (Wúsōng River)

Middle Jiangxi Rd
Middle Sichuan Rd
Huqiu Rd
Yuanmingyuan Rd

Wàibáidù Bridge
(Garden Bridge)

20

Former British Consulate

Huángpǔ Park

7
22

E Beijing Rd 北京东路

Middle Henan Rd

62
57

Dianchi Rd 滇池路

56
Bund Sightseeing Tunnel

Ningbo Rd
S Shanxi Rd
Tianjin Rd
16
58

Entrance to Bund Sightseeing Tunnel

21
THE BUND
E Nanjing Rd

49
East Nanjing Rd
26 南京路站

E Zhongshan No 1 Rd 中山东一路

40 32
2
The Bund

Huángpǔ River

5

Jiujiang Rd

Hankou Rd

23
39

34

Fuzhou Rd 福州路

14 55

Sijing Rd

31
Three on the Bund
8
43
24

Hubei Rd
Middle Fujian Rd 福建中路
Middle Henan Rd 河南北路

Guangdong Rd

E Yan'an Rd 延安东路

30

Jinling Rd Ferry
12

E Zhongshan No 2 Rd 中山东二路

East Yan'an Rd Tunnel

E Jinling Rd 金陵东路

Yong'an Rd

Renmin Rd 人民路

Hotel Indigo (550m);
Waterhouse at South Bund (1.4km);
Cool Docks (1.5km)

63

38
Yongshou Rd
S Yunnan Rd 云南南路

E Huaihai Rd 淮海东路

Yuyuan Garden 豫园站

Fuyou Rd 福佑路

Entrance to Yuyuán Gardens
36

OLD TOWN
Chenxiangge Rd
4

Jiujiaochang Rd 旧校场路

Yùyuán Gardens & Bazaar

42
3

S Henan Rd 河南南路

Houjia Rd

60
Temple of the Town God

Anren St

Confucian Temple (1km)

Dajing Rd 大境路
Zihua Rd

44
51
Middle Fangbang Rd 方浜中路

Shíliùpù Fabric Market (200m)

Zhoujin Rd

See Pudong Map (p206)

The Bund & People's Square

on Middle Xizang Rd; 人民大道100号; adult ¥30; ◷9am-5pm Tue-Sun, last entry 4pm; Ⓜ People's Sq) Some cities romanticise their past; others promise good times in the present. Only in China are you expected to visit places that haven't even been built yet. The highlight here is the 3rd floor, where you'll find an incredible model layout of the megalopolis-to-be, plus a dizzying Virtual World 3-D wraparound tour.

Balancing out the forward-looking exhibits are photos and maps of historic Shànghǎi.

Shànghǎi Museum of Contemporary Art (MOCA Shànghǎi)   MUSEUM
(上海当代艺术馆; Shànghǎi Dāngdài Yìshùguǎn; Map p192; www.mocashanghai.org; People's Park; 人民公园; admission adult/student ¥50/25; ◷10am-6pm Mon-Thu, 9am-7pm Fri-Sun; Ⓜ People's Sq)

This nonprofit museum collection has an all-glass home to maximise natural sunlight when it cuts through the clouds, a tip-top location in People's Park and a fresh, invigorating approach to exhibiting contemporary artwork. Exhibits are temporary only; check the website to see what's on. On the top floor there's a funky restaurant and bar with a terrace.

Old Town & South Bund 南市

Known to locals as Nán Shì (Southern City), the Old Town is the most traditionally Chinese part of Shànghǎi, bar Qībǎo. Sections of the Old Town have been bulldozed over the past decade to make room for developments but tatty charm survives along the neighbourhood's narrow and pinched alleyways.

★ Yùyuán Gardens & Bazaar
GARDENS, BAZAAR

(豫园、豫园商城; Yùyuán & Yùyuán Shāngchéng; Map p192; Anren Jie; 安仁街; admission low/high season ¥30/40; ⊙8.30am-5.30pm, last entry at 5pm; Ⓜ Yuyuan Garden) With their shaded alcoves, glittering pools churning with fish, pavilions, pines sprouting wistfully from rockeries, and roving packs of Japanese tourists, these gardens are one of Shànghǎi's premier sights – but become overpoweringly crowded at weekends. The spring and summer blossoms bring a fragrant and floral aspect to the gardens, especially in the luxurious petals of its Magnolia grandiflora, Shànghǎi's flower. Other trees include the Luohan pine, bristling with thick needles, willows, gingkos, cherry trees and magnificent dawn redwoods.

The Pan family, rich Ming-dynasty officials, founded the gardens, which took 18 years (1559–77) to be nurtured into existence before bombardment during the Opium War in 1842. The gardens took another trashing during French reprisals for attacks on their nearby concession by Taiping rebels. Restored, they are a fine example of Ming garden design.

Next to the garden entrance is the Húxīntíng Teahouse (湖心亭; Húxīntíng; Map p192; tea upstairs/downstairs: Y50/35; ⊙8.30am-9.30pm), once part of the gardens and now one of the most famous teahouses in China.

The adjacent bazaar may be tacky, but it's good for a browse if you can handle the push and pull of the crowds and vendors. The nearby Taoist Temple of the Town God is also worth visiting. Just outside the bazaar is Old Street (老街; Lǎo Jiē; Map p192; Middle Fangbang Rd; 方浜中路; Ⓜ Yuyuan Garden) (老街; Lǎo Jiē), known more prosaically as Middle Fangbang Rd, a busy street lined with curio shops and teahouses.

Chénxiānggé Nunnery
BUDDHIST TEMPLE

(沉香阁; Chénxiāng Gé; Map p192; 29 Chenxiangge Rd; 沉香阁路29号; admission ¥10; ⊙7am-5pm; Ⓜ Yuyuan Garden) Sheltering a community of dark-brown-clothed nuns from the Chénhǎi (Sea of Dust) – what Buddhists call the mortal world, but which could equally refer to Shànghǎi's murky atmosphere – this lovely yellow-walled temple is a tranquil refuge. At the temple rear, the Guanyin Tower guides you upstairs to a glittering effigy of the male-looking goddess within a resplendent gilded cabinet.

Confucian Temple
CONFUCIAN TEMPLE

(文庙; Wén Miào; 215 Wenmiao Rd; 文庙路215号; adult/student ¥10/5; ⊙9am-5pm, last entry 4.30pm; Ⓜ Laoximen) A modest and charming retreat, this well-tended temple to Confucius is cultivated with maples, pines, magnolias and birdsong. The layout is typically Confucian, its few worshippers complemented by ancient and venerable trees, including a 300-year-old elm. The main hall for worshipping Confucius is Dàchéng Hall (大成殿; Dàchéng Diàn), complete with twin eaves and a statue of the sage outside.

Cool Docks
ARCHITECTURE

(老码头; Lǎomǎtou; www.thecooldocks.com; 479 South Zhongshan Rd; 中山南路479号; Ⓜ Xiaonanmen) The riverside Cool Docks consist of several shíkùmén (stone-gate houses) surrounded by red-brick warehouses, near (but not quite on) the waterfront. Now full of restaurants and bars and all lit up at night, the Cool Docks' isolated positioning (it lacks the central location and transport connections of Xīntiāndì in the French Concession) has

---

LOCAL KNOWLEDGE

CONFUCIUS TEMPLE BOOK MARKET

In line with Confucian championing of learning, a busy secondhand market of (largely Chinese language) books is held in the Confucius temple every Sunday morning (admission ¥1; 7.30am to 4pm). There are some genuine finds, if you can read Chinese.

The Bund

The best way to get acquainted with Shànghǎi is to take a stroll along the Bund. The waterfront was the seat of colonial power from the mid-19th century onward, and the city's landmark hotels, banks and trading houses all established themselves here, gradually replacing their original buildings with even grander constructions as the decades passed.

The Bund had its golden age in the 1920s and '30s before the turmoil of war and occupation brought an end to the high life enjoyed by Shànghǎi's foreign residents. Mothballed during the communist era, it's only in the past 15 years that the strip has sought to rekindle its past glory, restoring one heritage building after another. Today, it has become China's showcase lifestyle destination, and many of the landmarks here house designer restaurants, swish cocktail bars and the flagship stores of some of the world's most exclusive brands.

Once you've wandered the promenade and ogled at the Pǔdōng skyline opposite, return

Hongkong & Shanghai Bank Building (1923)
Head into this massive bank (◔9am-4.30pm Mon-Fri) to marvel at the beautiful mosaic ceiling, featuring the 12 zodiac signs and the world's (former) eight centres of finance.

North China Daily News Building (1924)
Known as the 'Old Lady of the Bund', the News ran from 1864 to 1951 as the main English-language newspaper in China. Look for the paper's motto above the central windows.

Russo-Chinese Bank Building (1902)

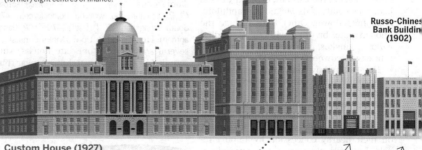

Custom House (1927)
One of the most important buildings on the Bund, Custom House was capped by the largest clock face in Asia and 'Big Ching', a bell modelled on London's Big Ben.

Former Bank of Communications (1947)

Bund Public Service Centre (2010)

TOP TIP

The promenade is open around the clock, but it's at its best in the early morning, when locals are out practising taichi, or in the early evening, when both sides of the river are lit up and the majesty of the waterfront is at its grandest.

to examine the Bund's magnificent facades in more detail and visit the interiors of those buildings open to the public.

This illustration shows the main sights along the Bund's central stretch, beginning near the intersection with East Nanjing Road. The Bund is 1km long and walking it should take around an hour. Head to the area south of the Hongkong & Shanghai Bank Building to find the biggest selection of prominent drinking and dining destinations.

FACT FILE

» Number of remaining heritage buildings on the Bund: 22

» Date the first foreign building on the Bund was constructed: 1851

» The year in which M on the Bund, the first high-profile Bund restaurant, opened: 1999

» Approximate number of wooden piles supporting the Fairmont Peace Hotel: 1600

Former Palace Hotel (1909)

Now known as the Swatch Art Peace Hotel (an artists' residence and gallery, with a top-floor restaurant and bar), this building hosted Sun Yatsen's 1911 victory celebration following his election as the first president of the Republic of China.

CHRISTOPHER PITTS

Bank of China (1942)

This unusual building was originally commissioned to be the tallest building in Shànghǎi, but, probably because of Victor Sassoon's influence, wound up being one metre shorter than its neighbour.

Former Bank of Taiwan (1927)

Former Chartered Bank Building (1923)

Reopened in 2004 as the upscale entertainment complex Bund 18, the building's top-floor Bar Rouge is one of the Bund's premier late-night destinations.

CHRISTOPHER PITTS

GREG ELMS/GETTY ©

Fairmont Peace Hotel (1929)

Originally built as the Cathay Hotel, this art deco masterpiece was *the* place to stay in Shànghǎi and the crown jewel in Sassoon's real estate empire.

hobbled ambitions. Although high-profile and trendy restaurant, bar and hotel openings have helped give it a much-needed lift, it remains an entertainment backwater.

Power Station of Art
GALLERY

(上海当代艺术博物馆; Shànghǎi Dāngdài Yìshù Bówùguǎn; Lane 20 Huayuangang Rd; ⊙9am-5pm Tue-Sun; Ⓜ South Xizang Rd) FREE Hosting the Shànghǎi Biennale, the Power Station of Art in the disused Nánshì Power Plant has seen some thought-provoking exhibitions. Check to see what is showing.

◉ French Concession 法租界

Once home to the bulk of Shànghǎi's adventurers, revolutionaries, gangsters, prostitutes and writers, the French Concession is the most graceful part of the city. The cream of Shànghǎi's old residential buildings and art deco apartment blocks, hotels and edifices are preserved here, while commercial Huaíhai Rd teems with shoppers.

★ Xīntiāndì
AREA

(新天地; Map p200; www.xintiandi.com; 2 blocks btw Taicang, Zizhong, Madang & South Huangpi Rds; 太仓路与马当路路口; Ⓜ South Huangpi Rd, Xintiandi) With its own namesake metro station, Xīntiāndì (新天地) has been a Shànghǎi icon for a decade or more. An upscale entertainment and shopping complex modelled on traditional alleyway (lòngtáng) homes, this was the first development in the city to prove that historic architecture makes big commercial sense. Elsewhere that might sound like a no-brainer, but in 21st-century China, where bulldozers were always on standby, it came as quite a revelation.

Well-heeled shoppers and al fresco diners keep things lively until late, and if you're looking for a memorable meal, to wet your whistle in a dapper bar or to browse through some of Shànghǎi's more fashionable boutiques, you're in the right spot. The heart of the complex, divided into a pedestrianised north and south block, consists of largely rebuilt traditional shíkùmén houses, brought bang up-to-date with a stylish modern spin. But while the layout suggests a flavour of yesteryear, you should not expect much in the cultural realm. Xīntiāndì doesn't deliver any of the lived-in charm of Tiánzǐfáng or the creaking, rickety simplicity of the Old Town. Beyond two worthwhile sights – the **Shikumen Open House Museum** (石库门屋里厢; Shíkùmén Wūlǐxiāng; Map p200; Xīntiāndì North Block, Bldg 25; 太仓路181弄新天地北里 25号楼; adult/child ¥20/10; ⊙10.30am-10.30pm; Ⓜ South Huangpi Rd, Xintiandi) and the Site of the 1st National Congress of the CCP – it's best for strolling the prettified alleyways and enjoying a summer evening over drinks or a meal.

★ Tiánzǐfáng
AREA

(田子坊; Map p200; www.tianzifang.cn; Taikang Rd; 泰康路; Ⓜ Dapuqiao) Xīntiāndì and Tiánzǐfáng (p198) are based on a similar idea – an entertainment complex housed within a warren of traditional lòngtáng – but when it comes to genuine charm and vibrancy, Tiánzǐfáng is the one that delivers. This community of design studios, wi-fi cafes and boutiques is the perfect antidote to Shànghǎi's oversized malls and intimidating skyscrapers. With some families still residing in neighbouring buildings, a community mood survives.

There are three main north–south lanes (Nos 210, 248, 274) criss-crossed by irregular east–west alleyways, which makes exploration slightly disorienting and fun. Among the art galleries is Beaugeste, a forward-thinking photography gallery (only open at the weekends, by appointment at other times). The real activity is shopping, and the recent explosion of creative start-ups makes for some interesting finds, from ethnic embroidery and hand-wrapped pu-erh (fermented dark tea) teas to retro communist dinnerware. Elsewhere, a growing band of cool cafes, restaurants and bars, such as Bell Bar, can sort out meals and drinks and take the weight off your feet.

Site of the 1st National Congress of the CCP
HISTORIC BUILDING

(中共一大会址纪念馆; Zhōnggòng Yīdàhuìzhǐ Jìniànguǎn; Map p200; Xīntiāndì North Block, 76 Xingye Rd; 兴业路76号; ⊙9am-5pm; Ⓜ South Huangpi Rd, Xintiandi) FREE On 23 July 1921 the Chinese Communist Party (CCP) was founded in this French Concession building (then 106 rue Wantz). In one fell swoop this fact transformed an unassuming shíkùmén block into one of Chinese communism's holiest shrines. Beyond the communist narcissism, there's little to see, although historians will enjoy ruminating on the site's historic momentousness.

Propaganda Poster Art Centre
GALLERY

(宣传画年画艺术中心; Shànghǎi Xuānchuánhuà Yìshù Zhōngxīn; Map p200; ☑6211 1845; Room B-OC, President Mansion, 868 Huashan Rd; 华山

路868号B-0C室; admission ¥20; ⊙10am-5pm; Ⓜ Shanghai Library) If phalanxes of red tractors, bumper harvests, muscled peasants and lantern-jawed proletariats fire you up, this small gallery in the bowels of a residential block should intoxicate. The collection of 3000 original posters from the 1950s, '60s and '70s – the golden age of Maoist poster production – will have you weak-kneed at the cartoon world of anti-US defiance.

The centre divides into a showroom and a shop selling posters and postcards. Once you find the main entrance, a guard will pop a small business card with a map on it into your hands and point you the way. Head around the back of the apartment blocks to Building B and take the lift to the basement. It's a good idea to phone ahead (they speak some English) before heading out here to make sure it's open. The exhibition rounds off with a collection of cigarette posters from the 1920s.

◉ West Nanjing Road & Jìng'ān
南京西路、静安

Lined with sharp top-end shopping malls, clusters of foreign offices and a dense crop of embassies and consulates, West Nanjing Rd is where Shànghǎi's streets are paved with gold, or at least Prada and Gucci.

But head north of West Nanjing Rd and you're plunged into a grittier and more absorbing section of Jìng'ān, which extends until reaching Shànghǎi Railway Station (p228).

★ Jade Buddha Temple BUDDHIST TEMPLE
(玉佛寺; Yùfó Sì; cnr Anyuan & Jiangning Rds; 安远路和江宁路街口; admission high/low season ¥20/10; ⊙8am-4.30pm; ☒19 from Broadway Mansions along Tiantong Rd, Ⓜ Changshou Rd) One of Shànghǎi's few active Buddhist monasteries, this temple was built between 1918 and 1928. The highlight is a transcendent Buddha crafted from pure jade, one of five shipped back to China by the monk Hui Gen at the turn of the 20th century. In February, during the Lunar New Year, the temple is very busy, as some 20,000 Chinese Buddhists throng to pray for prosperity.

Festooned with red lanterns, the first courtyard is located between the Hall of Heavenly Kings and the twin-eaved Great Treasure Hall, where worshippers pray to the past, present and future Buddhas. Also within the main hall are splendidly carved luóhàn (arhats), lashed to the walls with wires and a copper-coloured statue of Guanyin at the rear. Follow the right-hand corridor past the Hall of Heavenly Kings and the Guanyin Hall to arrive at the Jade Buddha Hall. The absolute centrepiece of the temple is the 1.9m-high pale green jade Buddha, seated upstairs. Photographs are not permitted. Near the Jade Buddha Hall downstairs are the Hall of Manjusri Bodhisattva, to whom students pray before exams, and the Hall of Ksitigarbha Bodhisattva, lord of the Buddhist underworld. Both halls stand before the Ancestral Hall. At the rear of the temple is the peaceful Jingyi Pool (净意潭; jìngyì tán) which swarms with Koi and multicoloured floating artificial lotus blooms, its floor glittering with coins.

A large vegetarian restaurant is attached to the temple around the corner.

★ M50 GALLERY
(M50创意产业集聚区; M50 Chuàngyì Chǎnyè Jíjùqū; 50 Moganshan Rd; 莫干山路50号; Ⓜ Shanghai Railway Station) FREE Edgier Běijīng still dominates the art scene, but swanky Shànghǎi's own gallery subculture is centred on this complex of industrial buildings down graffiti-splashed Moganshan Rd. Although the artists who originally established the M50 enclave are long gone, it's worth putting aside a half-day to poke around the galleries. There's a lot of mass-produced commercial prints, but there are also some challenging and innovative galleries. Most galleries are open from 10am to 6pm; some close on Monday.

The most established gallery here, **ShanghART** (Xiānggénà Huàláng; www.shanghartgallery.com; Bldg 16 & 18, M50; M50创意产业集聚区16和18号楼; Ⓜ Shanghai Railway Station) has a big, dramatic space to show the work of some of the 40 artists it represents. The forward-thinking and provocative **island6** focuses on collaborative works created in a studio behind the gallery; it has a smaller gallery on the first floor of building seven. Other notable galleries include **Other Gallery** (Bldg 9, M50; M50创意产业集聚区9号楼; Ⓜ Shanghai Railway Station) and **OFoto**, featuring China-related photography exhibitions. Across the street is **m97**, another innovative photography gallery. For paint and art materials, artists can drop by well-stocked **Espace Pébéo** (http://en.pebeo.com/Pebeo; 1st fl, Bldg 0, M50 Moganshan Rd; 莫干山路M50号0号楼1楼; ⊙9.30am-6pm; Ⓜ Shanghai Railway Station). For photo-developing courses and prints, pop into **Dark Room** (☑6276 9657; Rm 107, Bldg 17,

French Concession

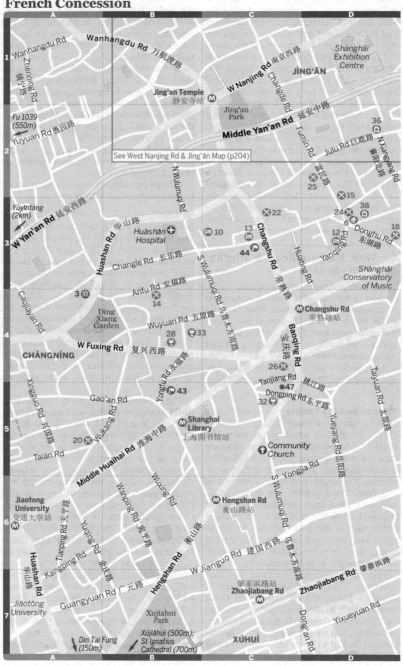

SHÀNGHÃI

Map labels:

Wanhangdu Rd
Wanhangdu Rd 万航渡路
Zhenning Rd 镇宁路
W Nanjing Rd 南京西路
JÌNG'ĀN
Shànghǎi Exhibition Centre
Fu 1039 (550m)
Jing'an Temple 静安寺站
Yuyuan Rd 愚园路
Jing'an Park
Changde Rd
Middle Yan'an Rd 延安中路
Furnin Rd 富民路
Julu Rd 巨鹿路
36
N Xiangyang Rd 襄阳北路
See West Nanjing Rd & Jìng'ān Map (p204)
Yúyìntáng (2km)
W Yan'an Rd 延安西路
N Wulumuqi Rd
25
15
22
24
38
6
Huashan Rd 华山路
Huàshān Hospital
10
13
Changshu Rd 常熟路
44
12
18
Donghu Rd 东湖路
Yanqing Rd
Changle Rd 长乐路
Shànghǎi Conservatory of Music
Caojiayan Rd
Anfu Rd 安福路
3
14
Huating Rd
Changshu Rd 常熟路站
Ding Xiang Garden
Wuyuan Rd 五原路
28
33
Baoqing Rd 宝庆路
CHÁNGNÍNG
W Fuxing Rd 复兴西路
Xingguo Rd 兴国路
Yongfu Rd 永福路
43
26
Taojiang Rd 桃江路
47
Dongping Rd 东平路
32
Taiyuan Rd 太原路
Gao'an Rd
Wukang Rd
20
Middle Huaihai Rd 淮海中路
Shanghai Library 上海图书馆站
Community Church
Yueyang Rd 岳阳路
Taian Rd
Jiaotong University 交通大学站
S Wulumuqi Rd 乌鲁木齐南路
Yongjia Rd
Tianping Rd 天平路
Kangping Rd
Yuqing Rd 余庆路
Wanping Rd 宛平路
Wuxing Rd
Hengshan Rd 衡山路站
Hengshan Rd
Huashan Rd 华山路
Jiāotōng University
Guangyuan Rd 广元路
Hengshan Rd
W Jianguo Rd 建国西路
S Wulumuqi Rd 乌鲁木齐南路
Zhaojiabang Rd 肇嘉浜路
Dong'an Rd
Yixueyuan Rd
Xujiahui Park
Din Tai Fung (150m)
Xújiāhuì (500m); St Ignatius Cathedral (700m)
Zhaojiabang Rd 肇家浜路站
XÚHUÌ

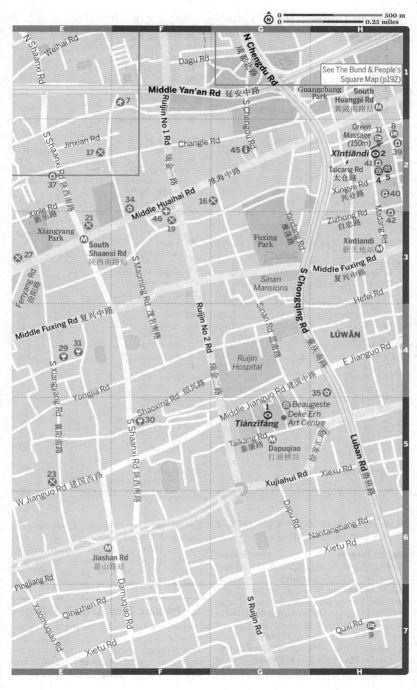

SHÀNGHǍI

French Concession

50 Moganshan Rd; M50创意产业集聚区17号楼 107室; Ⓜ Shanghai Railway Station).

Jing'ān Temple BUDDHIST TEMPLE
(静安寺; Jìng'ān Sì; Map p204; 1686-1688 West Nanjing Rd; 南京西路1686-1688号; admission ¥50; ⊗ 7.30am-5pm; Ⓜ Jing'an Temple) Its roof work an incongruous, shimmering mirage amid West Nanjing Rd's soaring skyscrapers, Jing'an Temple is a much-restored sacred portal to the Buddhist world that partially, at least, underpins this metropolis of 24 million souls. There are fewer devotees than at the neighbourhood's popular Jade Buddha Temple, but over a decade's restoration has fashioned a workable temple at the very heart of Shànghǎi. Its spectacular position among the district's soaring skyscrapers makes for eye-catching photos while the temple emits an air of reverence.

◎ Pǔdōng New Area 浦东新区

On the east side of the Huángpǔ River, the colossal concrete and steel Pǔdōng New Area (Pǔdōng Xīnqū) is best known for the skyscraper-stuffed skyline of Lùjiāzuǐ, one of China's most photographed panoramas. The best time to visit is at night when the neon effect is intoxicating and towers are lit up like TV screens. The next big-ticket Pǔdōng sight will be the **Shànghǎi Disney Resort**, due to open by early 2016.

★ **Shànghǎi World Financial Center** NOTABLE BUILDING
(上海环球金融中心; Shànghǎi Huánqiú Jīnróng Zhōngxīn; Map p206; ☑ 5878 0101; http://swfc-shanghai.com; 100 Century Ave; 世纪大道100号; observation deck adult 94th fl/94th, 97th & 100th fl ¥120/180, child under 140cm ¥60/90; ⓧ 8am-11pm, last entry 10pm; Ⓜ Lujiazui) Although trumped by the adjacent Shànghǎi Tower as the city's most stratospheric building, the awe-inspiring 492m-high Shànghǎi World Financial Center is an astonishing sight, even more so come nightfall when its 'bottle opener' top dances with lights. There are three observation decks here on levels 94, 97 and 100, with head-spinningly altitude-adjusted ticket prices and wow-factor elevators thrown in.

The top two (located at the bottom and top of the trapezoid) are known as Sky Walks. Whether it's debatable whether the top Sky Walk (474m) is the best spot for Shang-high views, though. The hexagonal space is bright and futuristic, and some of the floor is transparent glass, but the lack of a 360-degree sweep – windows only face west or east – detracts somewhat. But you get to look down on the top of the Jinmao, which might be worth the ticket price alone. A clear, smog-free day is imperative, so check the weather and pollution index up front.

If you want to make a meal (or a cocktail) of it, or if lines are long, you can sashay into restaurant/bar 100 Century Avenue on the 91st floor instead. Access to the observation deck is on the west side of the building off Dongtai Rd; access to the Park Hyatt is on the south side of the building.

★ **Shànghǎi Tower** NOTABLE BUILDING
(上海中心大厦; Shànghǎi Zhōngxīn Dàshà; Map p206; www.shanghaitower.com.cn; cnr Middle Yincheng & Huayuanshiqiao Rds; Ⓜ Lujiazui) China's tallest building dramatically twists skywards from the firmament of Lùjiāzuǐ. The 121-storey 632m-tall Gensler-designed Shànghǎi Tower topped out in August 2013 and was set to fully open in 2015. The spiral-shaped tower will house office space, entertainment venues, retail outlets, a conference center, a luxury hotel and 'sky lobbies'. The gently corkscrewing form – its nine interior cylin-

drical units wrapped in two glass skins – is the world's second-tallest building at the time of writing.

The twist is introduced by the outer skin of glass which swivels though 120 degrees as it rises, while atrium 'sky gardens' in the vertical spaces sandwiched between the two layers of glass open up a large volume of the tower to public use. The tower is sustainably designed: as well as providing insulation, the huge acreage of glass will vastly reduce electrical consumption through the use of sunlight. The tower's shape furthermore reduces wind loads by 24%, which generated a saving of US$58m in construction costs. Before the tower even went up, engineers were faced with building the 61,000 m^3 concrete mat that would support its colossal mass in the boggy land of Pǔdōng. Uppermost floors of the tower will be reserved for that obligatory Shànghǎi attraction – the world's highest skydeck above ground level – with passengers ferried skywards in the world's fastest lifts (40mph), designed by Mitsubishi (and the world's tallest single-lift elevator). Visitors will be able to gaze down on the both the Jinmao Tower and Shanghai World Finance Center below. A six-level luxury retail podium will fill the base of the tower.

Jīnmào Tower BUILDING
(金茂大厦; Jīnmào Dàshà; Map p206; ☑ 5047 5101; 88 Century Ave; 世纪大道88号; adult/student/child ¥120/90/60; ⓧ 8.30am-9.30pm; Ⓜ Lujiazui) Resembling an art deco take on a pagoda, this crystalline edifice is a beauty and by far the most attractive of the Shànghǎi World Financial Center (SWFC), Shànghǎi Tower, Jīnmào Tower triumvirate. It's essentially an office block with the high-altitude **Grand Hyatt** (金茂君悦大酒店; Jīnmào Jūnyuè Dàjiǔdiàn; Map p206; ☑ 5049 1234; www.shanghai.grand.hyatt.com; Jinmao Tower, 88 Century Ave; 世纪大道88号金茂大厦; d from ¥2000-2450; ✱ⓐⓢ; Ⓜ Lujiazu) renting space from the 53rd to 87th floors. You can zip up in the elevators to the 88th-floor **observation deck**, accessed from the separate podium building to the side of the main tower (aim for dusk for both day and night views).

Shànghǎi History Museum MUSEUM
(上海城市历史发展陈列馆; Shànghǎi Chéngshì Lìshǐ Fāzhǎn Chénlièguǎn; Map p206; ☑ 5879 8888; Oriental Pearl TV Tower basement; admission ¥35, English audio tour ¥30; ⓧ 8am-9.30pm; Ⓜ Lujiazui) The entire family will enjoy this informative museum with a fun presentation on

West Nanjing Rd & Jìng'ān

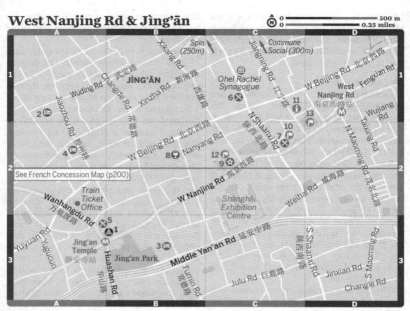

West Nanjing Rd & Jìng'ān

Sights
1 Jìng'ān Temple.................................B3

Sleeping
2 Le Tour Traveler's Rest.......................A1
3 Púlì...B3
4 Urbn...A2

Eating
5 Jen Dow Vegetarian Restaurant..........A3
6 Sumerian..C1
7 Wagas...C2

Drinking & Nightlife
8 Spot..B2

Entertainment
9 Shànghǎi Centre Theatre....................C2

Information
10 Australian Consulate........................C2
   Canadian Consulate.....................(see 12)
   Irish Consulate..........................(see 12)
11 Shànghǎi Cultural Information
   & Booking Centre..........................C1
12 UK Consulate.................................C2
13 US Consulate.................................D2

old Shànghǎi. Learn how the city prospered on the back of the cotton trade and junk transportation, when it was known as 'Little Sūzhōu'. Life-sized models of traditional shops are staffed by realistic waxworks, amid a wealth of historical detail, including a boundary stone from the International Settlement and one of the bronze lions that originally guarded the entrance to the HSBC bank on the Bund.

Oriental Pearl TV Tower BUILDING
(东方明珠广播电视塔; Dōngfāng Míngzhū Guǎng-bō Diànshì Tǎ; Map p206; ☏ 5879 1888; ⊙ 8am-10pm, revolving restaurant 11am-2pm & 5-9pm; Ⓜ Lujiazui) Love it or hate it, it's hard to be indifferent to this 468m-tall poured-concrete tripod tower, especially at night, when it dazzles. Sucking in streams of visitors, the Deng Xiaoping–era design is inadvertently retro, but socialism with Chinese characteristics was always cheesy back in the day. The highlight is the excellent Shànghǎi History Museum (p203), in the basement. You can queue up for views of Shànghǎi, but there are better views elsewhere and the long lines are matched by a tortuous ticketing system.

Boat tours on the Huángpǔ River operate from the **Pearl Dock** (明珠码头; Míngzhū Mǎtou; Map p206; 1 Century Ave; tickets ¥100), next to the tower.

Shànghǎi Science & Technology Museum
MUSEUM

(上海科技馆; Shànghǎi Kējìguǎn; ✆6862 2000; www.sstm.org.cn; 2000 Century Ave; 世纪大道2000号; adult/student/child under 1.3m ¥60/45/free; ⊙9am-5.15pm Tue-Sun, last tickets 4.30pm; Ⓜ Science & Technology Museum) You need to do a huge amount of walking to get about this seriously spaced-out museum but there are some fascinating exhibits, from relentless Rubik's-cube-solving robots to mechanical archers. There's even the chance to take penalty kicks against a computerised goalkeeper.

Riverside Promenade
WATERFRONT

(滨江大道; Bīnjiāng Dàdào; Map p206; ⊙6.30am-11pm; Ⓜ Lujiazui) Hands down the best stroll in Pǔdōng. The sections of promenade alongside Riverside Ave on the eastern bank of the Huángpǔ River offer splendid views to the Bund across the way. Choicely positioned cafes look out over the water.

Shànghǎi Ocean Aquarium
AQUARIUM

(上海海洋水族馆; Shànghǎi Hǎiyáng Shuǐzúguǎn; Map p206; ✆5877 9988; www.sh-aquarium.com; 1388 Lujiazui Ring Rd; 陆家嘴环路1388号; adult/child ¥160/110; ⊙9am-6pm, last tickets 5.30pm; Ⓜ Lujiazui) Education meets entertainment in this slick and intelligently designed aquarium that children will love. Join them on a tour through the aquatic environments from the Yangzi River to Australia, South America, the frigid ecosystems of the Antarctic and the flourishing marine life of coral reefs. The 155m-long underwater clear viewing tunnel has gobsmacking views. Feeding times for spotted seals, penguins and sharks are between 9.45am and 11.10am and 2.15pm and 3.40pm.

China Art Palace
MUSEUM

(中华艺术宫; Zhōnghuá Yìshùgōng; 205 Shangnan Rd; 上南路205号; ⊙9am-5pm Tue-Sun; Ⓜ China Art Museum) **FREE** This 160,000 sq metre five-floor modern-art museum has invigorating international exhibitions and the inverted red pyramid building is a modern icon of Shànghǎi; however, the permanent Chinese art collection is prosaic and there's lots of propaganda. Occasional quality surfaces, such as *Virgin*, (初潮的处女) by Xiang Jing, a moving, tender and comic sculptural work depicting awakening sexuality, while the Shànghǎi and Paris gallery looks absorbingly at the influence of impressionism on Shànghǎi art.

Captions are clumsily translated. From the Shanghai Power Station of Art, hop on bus 1213.

Mercedes-Benz Arena
ARENA

(梅赛德斯奔驰文化中心; Méisàidésī Bēnchí Wénhuà Zhōngxīn; www.mercedes-benzarena.com) Galactically styled UFO structure of an arena at 2010 World Expo site.

North Shànghǎi (Hóngkǒu)
虹口

Originally the American Settlement before the Japanese took over, Hóngkǒu welcomed thousands of Jewish refugees fleeing persecution.

★ Ohel Moishe Synagogue
MUSEUM

(摩西会堂; Móxī Huìtáng; 62 Changyang Rd; 长阳路62号; ⊙9am-5pm, last entry 4.30pm; Ⓜ Dalian Rd) This synagogue was built by the Russian Ashkenazi Jewish community in 1927 and lies in the heart of the 1940s Jewish ghetto. Today it houses the Shànghǎi Jewish Refugees Museum, a moving introduction to the lives of the approximately 20,000 Central European refugees who fled to Shànghǎi to escape the Nazis. Slip a pair of shower caps over your shoes to look at the synagogue itself (in the main building) and the exhibitions upstairs.

1933
HISTORIC BUILDING

(上海1933老场坊; Shànghǎi 1933 Lǎochǎngfáng; 10 Shajing Rd; 沙泾路10号; Ⓜ Hailun Rd) This vast concrete former abattoir is one of Shànghǎi's unique buildings, today converted to house boutiques, bars, shops and restaurants. An extraordinary place built around a central core, its structure is a maze of flared columns, sky-bridges (across which cattle would be led to slaughter), ramps, curved stairwells – and jostling photo opportunities. The shops are not of much interest, but a well-positioned branch of trendy Noodle Bull makes the most of its concrete setting.

Duolun Road Cultural Street
STREET

(多伦文化名人街; Duōlún Wénhuà Míngrén Jiē; Ⓜ Dongbaoxing Rd) This pleasantly restored but sleepy street of fine old houses, just off North Sichuan Rd, was once home to several of China's most famous writers (as well as several Kuomintang generals), when the road was known as Doulean Rd. Today it

Pǔdōng

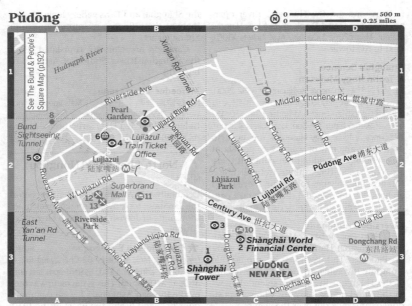

Pǔdōng

is lined with art-supply stores, curio and Burmese jade shops, galleries, teahouses and cafes. The main appeal of the street is its galleries and antique shops, including Dàshànghǎi (p225).

◉ Xújiāhuì & South Shànghǎi
徐家汇

Originally a Jesuit settlement dating back to the 17th century, Xújiāhuì today is more characterised by shopping malls, while south Shànghǎi sprawls to the Lónghuá Temple and Pagoda and beyond.

St Ignatius Cathedral   CHURCH
(徐家汇天主教堂; Xújiāhuì Tiānzhǔjiàotáng; ☑6438 4632; 158 Puxi Rd; 蒲西路158号; ◎9-11am & 1-4pm Mon-Sat, 2-4pm Sun; Ⓜ Xujiahui) The dignified twin-spired St Ignatius Cathedral (1904) is a major Xújiāhuì landmark. A long span of Gothic arches, its nave is ornamented on the outside with rows of menacing gargoyles; note how the church spires find reflection in much of the more recently built local architecture. The original stained glass was destroyed in the Cultural Revolution, but the vivid colours of the recent red, azure and purple replacements (with archaic Chinese inscriptions from the Bible) are outstanding.

SHÀNGHǍI FOR CHILDREN

Shànghǎi may not top most kids' holiday wish list, but the new **Shànghǎi Disney Resort** park in Pǔdōng, due to open in late 2015, will add an instant must-see attraction to the city. And the following sights will keep the family entertained.

➡ Observation deck at the Shànghǎi Tower (p203), Shànghǎi World Financial Center (p203) or Jīnmào Tower (p203)

➡ Shànghǎi History Museum (p203)

➡ Shànghǎi Ocean Aquarium (p205)

➡ Science & Technology Museum (p205)

➡ Acrobatics shows (p222)

➡ Bus tours (p208)

Note that, in general, 1.4m (4ft 7in) is the cut-off height for children's tickets. Children under 0.8m (2ft 7in) normally get in for free.

Lónghuá Temple & Pagoda BUDDHIST TEMPLE
(龙华寺、龙华塔; Lónghuá Sì & Lónghuá Tǎ; ✒6457 6327; 2853 Longhua Rd; 龙华路2853号; admission ¥10; ⏱7am-4.30pm; Ⓜ Longhua) Southeast from Xújiāhuì, Shànghǎi's oldest and largest monastery is named after the pipal tree (*lónghuá*) under which Buddha achieved enlightenment. The muchrenovated temple is said to date from the 10th century, its five main halls commencing with the **Laughing Buddha Hall**; note the four huge Heavenly Kings, each in charge of a compass point. The temple is particularly famed for its 6500kg bell, cast in 1894.

A large effigy of Sakyamuni seated on a lotus flower resides within the main hall – the **Great Treasure Hall**.

Other halls include the **Thousand Luóhàn Hall**, sheltering a huge legion of glittering arhat. Also within the temple is a vegetarian restaurant and a further imposing structure – the **Sānshèngbǎo Hall** – with a golden trinity of Buddhist statues.

Opposite the temple entrance rises the seven-storey, 44m-high **Lónghuá Pagoda**, originally built in AD 977. Sadly, visitors are not allowed to climb it.

The best time to visit is during the Lónghuá Temple Fair, in the third month of the lunar calendar (usually during April or May).

◉ West Shànghǎi

West Shànghǎi is mainly of interest for longterm expats and those on business, although the village of Qībǎo is worth a visit.

★ Qībǎo VILLAGE
(七宝; 2 Minzhu Rd, Mínháng district; 闵行区民主路2号; admission high/low season ¥45/30; ⏱sights 8.30am- 4.30pm; Ⓜ Qibao) When you tire of Shànghǎi's incessant quest for modernity, this tiny town is only a hop, skip and metro ride away. An ancient settlement that prospered during the Ming and Qing dynasties, it is littered with traditional historic architecture, threaded by small, busy alleyways and cut by a picturesque canal. If you can somehow blot out the crowds, Qībǎo brings you the flavours of old China along with huge doses of entertainment.

There are nine official sights included in the through ticket, though you can also skip the ticket and just pay ¥5 to ¥10 per sight as you go. The best of the bunch include the **Cotton Textile Mill**, the **Shadow Puppet Museum** (performances from 1pm to 3pm Wednesday and Sunday), **Zhou's Miniature Carving House** and the **Old Wine Shop** (still an active distillery and a good lunch spot). Half-hour **boat rides** along the canal slowly ferry passengers from Number One Bridge to Dōngtángtān (东塘滩) and back. Also worth ferreting out is the **Catholic Church** (天主教堂; 50 Nanjie), adjacent to a convent off Qibao Nanjie, south of the canal.

Wander along Bei Dajie north of the canal for souvenirs; Nan Dajie south of the canal is full of snacks and small eateries such as No 14, which sells sweet *tāngyuán* dumplings, and No 19, which is a rarely seen traditional teahouse.

Shànghǎi Railway Station

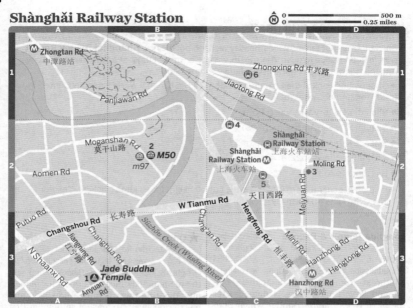

❧ Courses

Learn how to balance your yin and yang with the following courses.

The Kitchen At... COOKING COURSE
(☑ 6433 2700; www.thekitchenat.com; Ⓜ Changshu Rd) Great culinary school offering courses in regional Chinese and Western cuisines; good for both long-term residents and short-term visitors.

Lóngwǔ Kung Fu Center MARTIAL ARTS
(龙武功夫馆; Lóngwǔ Gōngfu Guǎn; Map p200; ☑ 6287 1528; www.longwukungfu.com; 1 South Maoming Rd; 茂名南路1号; 1-/2-/3-month lesson ¥100/450/700; Ⓜ South Shaanxi Rd) Hone your rusty Wing Chun *bong sao*, brush up on your Taekwondo *poomsae* or simply learn a few taichi moves to help slip aboard the bus at rush hour. The largest centre in the city, it also offers children's classes on weekend mornings and lessons in English.

☞ Tours

From boats to bikes to buses, organised tours offer a great introduction to Shànghǎi.

BOHDI BICYCLE TOUR
(☑ 5266 9013; www.bohdi.com.cn; tours ¥220) Night-time cycling tours on Tuesdays from March to November and trips around the region.

Huángpǔ River Cruise CRUISE

(黄浦江游览; Huángpǔ Jiāng Yóulǎn; Map p192; 219-239 East Zhongshan No 2 Rd; 中山东二路 219-239号; tickets ¥128; Ⓜ East Nanjing Rd) The Huángpǔ River offers intriguing views of the Bund, Pǔdōng and riverfront activity. The night cruises are arguably more scenic, though boat traffic during the day is more interesting – depending on when you go, you'll pass an enormous variety of craft, from freighters, bulk carriers and roll-on roll-off ships to sculling sampans and massive floating TV advertisements.

Most cruises last 90 minutes and include not one, but two trips up to the International Cruise Terminal and back.

Huángpǔ River Cruise (Pǔdōng) BOAT TOUR

(黄浦江游览船, Huángpǔjiāng Yóulǎnchuán; Map p206; Pearl Dock, 明珠码头; tickets ¥100; ⊙10am-1.30pm; Ⓜ Lujiazui) Forty-minute cruises departing hourly in Pǔdōng.

Insiders Experience DRIVING TOUR

(⊡138 1761 6975; www.insidersexperience.com; from ¥800) Fun motorcycle-sidecar tours of the city for up to two passengers, setting off from the Andaz in Xīntiāndì (but can pick up from anywhere, at extra cost).

Newman Tours TOUR

(新漫; Xīnmàn; ⊡138 1777 0229; www.newmantours.com; from ¥190) Bund tour, gangster tour, ancient Shànghǎi tour, ghost tour and a host of other informative and fun walking jaunts around the city. Also covers Hángzhōu and Sūzhōu.

Shànghǎi Sightseeing Buses BUS TOUR

(上海旅游集散中心, Shànghǎi Lǚyóu Jísàn Zhōngxīn; ⊡2409 5555; www.chinassbc.com; 2409 South Zhongshan No 2 Rd; ⊙6.30am-7pm; Ⓜ Caoxi Rd) Daily tours from Shànghǎi Stadium to nearby canal towns (eg Tónglǐ, Nánxún). Convenient but less fun than visiting on your own.

🎎 Festivals & Events

Lantern Festival CULTURAL

A colourful time to visit Yùyuán Gardens. People make *yuánxiāo* or *tāngyuán* (glutinous rice dumplings with sweet fillings) and some carry paper lanterns on the streets. The Lantern Festival (元宵节; *yuánxiāo jié*) falls on the 15th day of the first lunar month (usually in February/March).

Shànghǎi International Literary Festival LITERARY

(上海国际文学艺术节; Shànghǎi Guójì Wénxué Yìshù Jié) Held in March or April, this highly popular festival (上海国际文学艺术节; Shànghǎi Guójì Wénxué Yìshù Jié) for bibliophiles is staged in the Glamour Bar, with international and local authors in attendance.

Formula 1 SPORT

(www.formula1.com; 2000 Yining Rd, Jiādìng; Ⓜ Shanghai International Circuit, Line 11) The slick new Shànghǎi International Circuit hosts several high-profile motor-racing competitions, including the hotly contested Formula 1 in April.

Dragon Boat Festival SPORT

Celebrated on the fifth day of the fifth lunar month (23 June 2012, 12 June 2013, this festival (端午节; *Duānwǔ Jié*) sees dragon boats raced along Sūzhōu Creek and, more importantly for most, *zòngzi* (glutinous rice dumplings steamed in bamboo leaves) go on sale everywhere.

🛌 Sleeping

Shànghǎi's sleeping options are excellent at both ends of the spectrum, though quality in the midrange market remains patchy. In general, hotels fall into two main bags: luxury skyscraper hotels, historic old villa hotels, boutique hotels, Chinese chain hotels and hostels. There's a handful of B&Bs, though these are relatively scarce.

The most central neighbourhoods are the Bund and People's Sq. If you'd rather be based in a more residential area, consider the French Concession and Jìng'ān, where unique choices exist. Pǔdōng is perfect for panoramas and high-altitude rooms, with a price tag.

Discounts off rack rates are standard outside holiday periods. Four- and five-star hotels add a 10% or 15% service charge (sometimes negotiable).

🛏 The Bund & People's Square

★ Mingtown E-Tour Youth Hostel HOSTEL $

(明堂上海青年旅舍; Míngtáng Shànghǎi Qīngnián Lǚshè; Map p192; ⊡6327 7766; 57 Jiangyin Rd; 江阴路57号; dm ¥50, d without/with bathroom ¥160/260, tw ¥240; ✿@ 🛜; Ⓜ People's Sq) One of Shànghǎi's best youth hostels, E-tour has fine feng shui, a historic alleyway setting and pleasant rooms. But it's the tranquil courtyard with fish pond and the superb

GOING FOR A RIDE

Tickets for the handy hop-on, hop-off open-top **City Sightseeing Buses** (都市观光; Dūshì Guānguāng; ✆ 400 820 6222; www.springtour.com; tickets ¥30; ⏱ 9am-8.30pm summer, to 6pm winter) last 24 hours and are, besides touring Shànghǎi's highlights, a great way to get around the city centre and Pǔdōng. A recorded commentary runs in eight languages: just plug in your earphones (supplied). Buses have their own stops across central Shànghǎi, including the Bund, the Old Town and People's Sq. **Big Bus Tours** (上海观光车; Shànghǎi Guānguāngchē; ✆ 6351 5988; www.bigbustours.com; adult/child US$48/32) also operate hop-on, hop-off bus services, lassoing in the top sights along 22 stops across two routes. Tickets are valid for 48 hours and include a one-hour boat tour of the Huángpǔ River plus admission to the 88th-floor observation tower of the Jīnmào Tower.

split-level bar-restaurant with comfy sofas that really sell it, plus there's a free pool table and plenty of outdoor seating on wooden decking.

There are both women-only and mixed dorms.

Mingtown Nanjing Road Youth Hostel
HOSTEL $

(明堂上海南京路青年旅舍; Míngtáng Shànghǎi Nánjīng Lù Qīngnián Lǚshè; Map p192; ✆ 6322 0939; 258 Tianjin Rd; 天津路258号; dm ¥50, s ¥150, d ¥200-270, tr ¥250; ❋ @ 🛜; M East Nanjing Rd) This sociable and friendly Mingtown hostel is located halfway between the Bund and People's Sq, a short hop from the nearest metro station. The six-bed dorms each have a private bathroom, laminated wood flooring and simple particle-board decor; perks include laundry, a kitchen, ground-floor bar-restaurant, a DVD room and a pool table.

Mingtown Hiker Youth Hostel
HOSTEL $

(明堂上海旅行者青年旅馆; Míngtáng Shànghǎi Lǚxíngzhě Qīngnián Lǚguǎn; Map p192; ✆ 6329 7889; 450 Middle Jiangxi Rd; 江西中路450号; dm without/with window ¥50/55, s/d ¥160/220; ❋ @ 🛜; M East Nanjing Rd) This justifiably popular hostel is just a short stroll from the famous esplanade, on the southern corner of the grand old Hengfeng Building. It offers tidy four- and six-bed dorms with pine bunk beds and clean communal shower facilities, plus decent private rooms, including cheapies with shared bathrooms.

There's a pool table, movies, a bar-restaurant and a useful noticeboard in the lobby. Wi-fi in the lobby only.

Captain Hostel
HOSTEL $

(船长青年酒店; Chuánzhǎng Qīngnián Jiǔdiàn; Map p192; ✆ 6323 5053; 37 Fuzhou Rd; 福州路37号; dm ¥75, r from ¥358; ❋ @ 🛜; M East Nanjing Rd)

Despite being hands-down the least friendly youth hostel in Shànghǎi, this naval-themed backpackers' favourite still reels in punters with its fantastic location and decent rooftop bar. There's a microwave, washing machine and lobby cafe, but all bathrooms are communal. Wi-fi is in the communal area only.

Jinjiang Inn
HOSTEL $

(锦江之星; Jǐnjiāng Zhīxīng; Map p192; www.jinjianginns.com; 680 East Nanjing Rd; 南京东路680号; d from ¥300; ❋ @ 🛜; M People's Sq) Located in the former Shanghai Sincere Department Store (which opened in 1917), the erstwhile East Asia Hotel has been grabbed by the folk at Jinjiang Inn and re-presented with smartish rooms with showers. It's often booked out due to its prime location.

Marvel Hotel
HOTEL $$

(商悦青年会大酒店; Shāngyuè Qīngniánhuì Dàjiǔdiàn; Map p192; ✆ 3305 9999; www.marvelhotels.com.cn; 123 South Xizang Rd; 西藏南路123号; d ¥1080-1280, ste ¥1580; ❋ @ 🛜; M Dashijie) Occupying the former YMCA building (1931) just south of People's Sq, the Marvel is one of the city's better midrange hotels. Beyond the chintzy corridors, the brown and cream rooms offer a reassuring degree of style. The building resembles Běijīng's Southeast Corner Watchtower (although the blurb compares it to Qiánmén), with a traditional hammerbeam ceiling.

Sofitel Hyland Hotel
HOTEL $$

(索菲特海仑宾馆; Suǒfēitè Hǎilún Bīnguǎn; Map p192; ✆ 6351 5888; www.sofitel.com; 505 East Nanjing Rd; 南京东路505号; d ¥1150-2110; ❋ 🛜; M East Nanjing Rd) Rising up halfway along East Nanjing Rd, the Sofitel is a solid choice for those insisting on location without breaking the bank. The uncluttered and cool lobby area is dominated by open space and geometric lines. Standard rooms are rather dated, with a crisper and more modern finish in the executive rooms.

Facilities include a spa, two restaurants, a bar and a French bakery.

★ Fairmont Peace Hotel   HISTORIC HOTEL $$$

(费尔蒙和平饭店; Fèi'ěrmēng Hépíng Fàndiàn; Map p192; ☑ 6321 6888; www.fairmont.com; 20 East Nanjing Rd; 南京东路20号; d ¥2300-3800; ◉ ❄ ⬚ ⬚; Ⓜ East Nanjing Rd) If anywhere in town fully conveys swish 1930s Shànghǎi, it's the old Cathay, rising imperiously from the Bund. Renamed the Peace Hotel in the 1950s and reopened in 2010 after a protracted renovation, it's reaffirmed its position as one of the city's most iconic hotels. Rooms are decked out in art deco elegance, from light fixtures down to coffee tables.

The entire hotel is cast in the warm, subdued tints of a bygone era. Expect all the luxuries of a top-class establishment, though note that wi-fi and broadband access cost an extra ¥99 per day for guests. Standard rooms come without a view, deluxe rooms with a street view and suites with the coveted river view. The hotel is also home to a luxury spa, two upscale restaurants and several bars and cafes. Even if you're not staying here, it's worth popping in to admire the magnificent lobby (1929), or taking in an evening show at the jazz bar.

★ Peninsula Hotel   LUXURY HOTEL $$$

(半岛酒店; Bàndǎo Jiǔdiàn; Map p192; ☑ 2327 2888; www.peninsula.com; 32 East Zhongshan No 1 Rd; 中山东一路32号; d/ste ¥2800/5400; ❄ @ ⬚ ⬚; Ⓜ East Nanjing Rd) This spiffing hotel at the Bund's northern end combines art deco motifs with Shànghǎi modernity. It's a grade above many other market rivals, with TVs in the tub, well-equipped dressing rooms (with fingernail driers), valet boxes for dirty clothes, Nespresso machines and fabulous views across the river or out onto the gardens of the former British consulate. Lacquer fittings in rooms create a sumptuous, yet restrained, elegance.

★ Astor House Hotel   HISTORIC HOTEL $$$

(浦江饭店; Pǔjiāng Fàndiàn; Map p192; ☑ 6324 6388; www.astorhousehotel.com; 15 Huangpu Rd; 黄浦路15号; d/tw ¥1280-1680, 'celebrity' r ¥2080, ste ¥2800-4800; ❄ @ ⬚; Ⓜ Tiantong Rd) Stuffed with history (and perhaps a ghost or two), this august old-timer shakes up an impressive cocktail from select ingredients: a location just off the Bund; old-world, Shànghǎi-era charm; great discounts; and

colossal rooms. The original polished wooden floorboards, corridors and galleries pitch the mood somewhere between British public school and Victorian asylum.

Waldorf Astoria   LUXURY HOTEL $$$

(华尔道夫酒店; Huáěr Dàofū Jiǔdiàn; Map p192; ☑ 6322 9988; www.waldorfastoriashanghai.com; 2 East Zhongshan No 1 Rd; 中山东一路2号; d/ste ¥3100/4600; ❄ @ ⬚ ⬚; Ⓜ East Nanjing Rd) Grandly marking the southern end of the Bund is the former Shànghǎi Club (1910), once the Bund's most exclusive gentlemen's hang-out. The 20 original rooms here have been reconverted to house the Waldorf Astoria's premium suites, six of which look out onto the Huángpǔ River. Behind this heritage building is a new hotel tower, with 252 state-of-the-art rooms.

Yangtze Boutique Shanghai   BOUTIQUE HOTEL $$$

(朗廷扬子精品宾馆; Lǎngtíng Yángzǐ Jīngpǐn Bīnguǎn; Map p192; ☑ 6080 0800; www.theyangtzehotel.com; 740 Hankou Rd; 汉口路740号; d ¥1300-1800; ❄ ⬚; Ⓜ People's Sq) Originally built in the 1930s, this art deco gem has been splendidly refurbished. In addition to period decor, rooms feature deep baths, glass-walled bathrooms (with Venetian blinds) and even tiny balconies – a rarity in Shànghǎi. Check out the sumptuous stained-glass oblong and recessed skylight in the lobby, above a deco-style curved staircase.

The worn carpet in the foyer and on the stairs points to a high volume of traffic and the hotel is frequently booked out. The hammam and sauna in the fabulous Chuan spa are complimentary for guests; breakfast is served in the Italian restaurant, Ciao. Wi-fi costs extra.

Chai Living Residences   APARTMENT $$$

(Map p192; ☑ 5608 6051; www.chailiving.com; Embankment Bldg, 400 N Suzhou Rd; 苏州北路400号; 3 days/1 week/1 month apt from ¥3300/6000/13,500; ❄ ⬚; Ⓜ Tiantong Rd) If you need a stylish Shànghǎi address, you can't get much better than one of these 16 luxurious, beautifully appointed and individually styled apartments in the Embankment Building. The block is a living, breathing residential Shànghǎi block, and bumping into tenants merely adds authentic charm (although the grotty lift is a real shocker for some).

There's a minimum three-day stay – just enough time to fully savour the outstanding views (none lower than the fifth floor) and decor of each apartment, each with sound-proof

German windows. Apartments range from 40 to 200 sq metres, with daily maid service, underfloor heating, kitchens with Nespresso coffee machines and tantalising river views.

Old Town & South Bund

Waterhouse at South Bund BOUTIQUE HOTEL $$
(水舍时尚设计酒店; Shuǐshè Shíshàng Shèjì Jiǔdiàn; ☑6080 2988; www.waterhouseshanghai. com; 1-3 Maojiayuan Rd, Lane 479, South Zhongshan Rd; 中山南路479弄毛家园路1-3号; d ¥1100-2800; ❋⑤; MXiaonanmen) There are few cooler places to base yourself in Shànghǎi than this awfully trendy 19-room, four-storey South Bund converted 1930s warehouse right by the Cool Docks. Gazing out onto supreme views of Pǔdōng (or into the crisp courtyard), the Waterhouse's natty rooms (some with terrace) are swishly dressed. Service can be wanting, though, and it's isolated from the action.

Hotel Indigo HOTEL $$$
(英迪格酒店; Yīngdígé Jiǔdiàn; www.hotelindigo. com; 585 East Zhongshan No 2 Rd; 中山东二路585号; ❋⑤; MXiaonanmen) With its quirkily designed lobby – chairs like birdcages; tree branches trapped in cascades of glass jars; sheets of metal riveted to the wall; modish, sinuously shaped furniture; and funky ceiling lights – towering Hotel Indigo is a stylish South Bund choice. Chic and playful guestrooms are about colourful cushions and whimsical designs, with lovely rugs and spotless bathrooms.

Note that accommodation either looks out onto the Old Town (so-so) or the river (stellar). Service is very helpful and the infinity pool is a dream. Regular discounts tame prices by up to 60%.

French Concession

Blue Mountain Youth Hostel HOSTEL $
(蓝山国际青年旅舍; Lánshān Guójì Qīngnián Lǚshè; Map p200; ☑6304 3938; www.bmhostel. com; 2nd fl, Bldg 1, 1072 Quxi Rd, French Concession East; 瞿溪路1072号1号甲2楼; dm ¥50-65, d ¥130-200, tr ¥240, q ¥280; ❋@⑤; MLuban Rd) Although slightly out of the action, this excellent hostel is almost next door to Luban Rd metro station, so transport is sorted. Rooms are clean and simple with pine furniture and flooring, TV and kettle. There are women-only, men-only and mixed 4-to-8 bed dorms, and there's a wi-fi-enabled bar-

restaurant area with free pool table, free movie screenings and a kitchen with microwave.

★**Magnolia Bed & Breakfast** B&B $$
(Map p200; ☑138 1794 0848; www.magnoliabnbshanghai.com; 36 Yanqing Rd, French Concession West; 延庆路36号; r ¥702-1296; ❋@⑤; MChangshu Rd) Opened by Miranda Yao of the cooking school The Kitchen at... (p208), this cosy little five-room B&B is located in a 1927 French Concession home. It's Shànghǎi all the way, with an art deco starting point followed by comfort and stylish design. While rooms are on the small side, they are high-ceilinged and bright. It's a true labour of love.

There are discounts for stays of seven nights or more. There's no front desk, so phone ahead before visiting.

Quintet B&B $$
(Map p200; ☑6249 9088; www.quintet-shanghai. com; 808 Changle Rd, French Concession West; 长乐路808号; d incl breakfast ¥850-1200; ⊝❋⑤; MChangshu Rd) This chic B&B has six beautiful double rooms in a 1930s townhouse that's not short on character. Some of the rooms are small, but each is decorated with style, incorporating modern luxuries such as large-screen satellite TVs and laptop-sized safes, with more classic touches such as wood-stripped floorboards and deep porcelain bathtubs.

Staff members sometimes get a BBQ going on the roof terrace and there's an excellent restaurant on the ground floor. No sign – just buzz on the gate marked 808 and wait to be let in. Be aware there is no elevator.

Kevin's Old House B&B $$
(老时光酒店; Lǎoshíguāng Jiǔdiàn; Map p200; ☑6248 6800; www.kevinsoldhouse.com; No 4, Lane 946, Changle Rd, French Concession West; 长乐路946弄4号; ste ¥1180-1280; ❋⑤; MChangshu Rd) Housed in a secluded 1927 four-storey French Concession villa, this lovely boutique hotel is an elegant yet affordable place to stay. Six suites are spread throughout the house, each decorated with care, featuring wooden floorboards, traditional Chinese furniture, stylish artwork and a few antiques. There's an upright piano in the entrance. Suites usually go for around ¥950.

★**Langham Xīntiāndì** LUXURY HOTEL $$$
(新天地朗廷酒店; Xīntiāndì Lǎngtíng Jiǔdiàn; Map p200; ☑2330 2288; xintiandi.langhamhotels. com; 99 Madang Rd, French Concession East; 马当路99号; r/ste ¥1600/1840; ❋⑤❄; MSouth

Huangpi Rd) Xīntiāndì has become a magnet for luxury hotels, and they don't come much nicer than this one. Its 357 rooms all feature huge floor-to-ceiling windows, plenty of space to spread out in, and an attention to the minute details that make all the difference: Japanese-style wooden tubs in suites, heated bathroom floors, internet radio and white orchids.

Andaz
LUXURY HOTEL $$$

(安达仕酒店; Āndáshì Jiǔdiàn; Map p200; ☎2310 1234; http://shanghai.andaz.hyatt.com; 88 Songshan Rd, French Concession East; 嵩山路88号; r ¥1820-2820; ❄@🛜🛁; Ⓜ South Huangpi Rd) Housed in a tower with retro '70s style windows, this fab hotel's design-led lobby – a trendy pronouncement of metal latticework – suggests an art space, a sensation that persists when you hunt for the open-plan reception (it's on the right). Along curving corridors, guest-rooms are cool and modern, with sinks and bathtubs that glow in different colours and monumental flat-screen TVs.

🛏 West Nanjing Road & Jìng'ān

★ Le Tour Traveler's Rest
HOSTEL $

(乐途静安国际青年旅舍; Lètú Jìng'ān Guójì Qīngnián Lǔshè; Map p204; ☎6267 1912; www.letourshanghai.com; 319 Jiaozhou Rd; 胶州路319号; dm ¥70, d ¥260-280, tr/q ¥360/360; ❄@🛜; Ⓜ Changping Rd) Housed in a former towel factory, this fabulous youth hostel leaves most others out to dry. You'll pass a row of splendid *shíkùmén* (stone-gate houses) on your way down the alley to get here. The old-Shànghǎi textures continue once inside, with red-brick walls and reproduced stone gateways above doorways leading to simple but smart rooms and six-person dorms (shared bathrooms).

Double rooms are not very spacious, but they have flatscreen TVs and they're clean. Rooms are between ¥10 and ¥30 pricier on Fridays and Saturdays. The ground floor has a ping pong table, a pool table and wi-fi, all of which are free to use, and there's a fine rooftop bar-restaurant with outdoor seating. Bicycles can also be rented here.

Down an alley off Jiaozhou Rd.

Urbn
BOUTIQUE HOTEL $$$

(Map p204; ☎5153 4600; www.urbnhotels.com; 183 Jiaozhou Rd; 胶州路183号; r from ¥1500; ❄; Ⓜ Changping Rd) China's first carbon-neutral hotel not only incorporates recyclable materials and low-energy products where pos-

sible, it also calculates its complete carbon footprint – including staff commutes and delivery journeys – and off-sets it by donating money to environmentally friendly projects. Open-plan rooms are beautifully designed with low furniture and sunken living areas exuding space.

Púlì
LUXURY HOTEL $$$

(璞丽酒店; Púlì Jiǔdiàn; Map p204; ☎3203 9999; www.thepuli.com; 1 Changde Rd; 常德路1号; d from ¥3880; ❄🛜🛁; Ⓜ Jing'an Temple) With open-space rooms divided by hanging silk screens and an understated beige-and-mahogany colour scheme accentuated by the beauty of a few well-placed orchids, the Púlì is an exquisite choice. The Zen calm and gorgeous design of this 26-storey hotel make another strong case for stylish skyscrapers. Book ahead for discounts of up to 60%.

🛏 Pǔdōng New Area

★ Mandarin Oriental Pudong
HOTEL $$$

(上海浦东文华东方酒店; Shànghǎi Pǔdōng Wénhuá Dōngfāng Jiǔdiàn; Map p206; ☎2082 9908; www.mandarinoriental.com; 111 South Pudong Rd; 浦东南路111号; d from ¥3800; ❄@🛜🛁; Ⓜ Lujiazui) Slightly tucked away from the Lùjiāzuǐ five-star hotel melee in a sheltered riverside spot, the 362-room Mandarin Oriental is a visual feast, from the beautiful oval chandeliers in the lobby to the multicoloured glass murals (depicting forests) and gorgeous dining choices. All five-star expectations are naturally met, but it's the meticulous service that ices the cake.

Sumptuous rooms aside, there's a 24-hour pool and gym, spa and delicious views. The address may seem a bit stranded, but it's a short walk to the heart of Lùjiāzuǐ and there's a complimentary shuttle bus within the area.

Ritz-Carlton Shanghai Pudong
LUXURY HOTEL $$$

(上海浦东丽思卡尔顿酒店; Shànghǎi Pǔdōng Lìsī Kǎěrdùn Jiǔdiàn; Map p206; ☎2020 1888; www.ritzcarlton.com; Shànghǎi IFC, 8 Century Ave; 世纪大道8号; d from ¥2800; ❄@🛜🛁; Ⓜ Lujiazui) From the stingray-skin effect wallpaper in the lift to its exquisite accommodation and stunning al fresco bar, the deliciously styled 285-room Ritz-Carlton in the Shànghǎi IFC is a peach. The beautifully designed rooms – a blend of feminine colours, eye-catching art deco motifs, chic elegance and dramatic Bund-side views – are a stylistic triumph.

Park Hyatt LUXURY HOTEL $$$

(柏悦酒店; Bóyuè Jiǔdiàn; Map p206; ☑6888 1234; www.parkhyattshanghai.com; Shànghǎi World Financial Center, 100 Century Ave; 世纪大道100号 世界金融中心; d from ¥2500; ❄ @ 🛜 ✉; Ⓜ Lujiazui) Spanning the 79th to 93rd floors of the towering Shànghǎi World Financial Center, this soaring hotel sees Pǔdōng's huge buildings (bar the Shànghǎi Tower) dwarfing into Lego blocks as lobby views graze the tip of the Jinmao Tower. Smaller than the Grand Hyatt, it's a subdued but stylish 174-room affair with a deco slant, high-walled corridors of brown-fabric and grey-stone textures.

Rooms are luxurious, with nifty features (mist-free bathroom mirror containing a small TV screen, automatically opening toilet seats). All come with huge TVs, free wifi, free fresh coffee, deep bathtubs, leather chaise lounges, sumptuous beds and outrageously good views. Accessed from the south side of the tower.

✖ Eating

Shànghǎi cuisine itself is generally sweeter than other Chinese cuisines, and is heavy on fish and seafood. *Shēngjiān* (生煎; fried dumplings) and *xiǎolóngbāo* (小笼包; Shànghǎi's steamed dumpling) are copied everywhere else in China but are only true to form here. Make sure to reserve at fancier places.

✖ The Bund & People's Square

A Bund address is the crown jewels in Shànghǎi, luring international superchefs and cashed-up diners. While the settings are often spectacular and the views are knockout, there's less diversity and charm than in the French Concession. For a handy line up of affordable Asian restaurants a mere stone's throw from the waterfront, pop into **Hóngyī Plaza** (宏伊国际广场; Hóngyī Guójì Guǎngchǎng; Map p192; 299 East Nanjing Rd, 南京东路299号; meals from Y30; Ⓜ East Nanjing Rd).

Yúxìn Chuāncài SICHUANESE $

(渝信川菜; Map p192; ☑6361 1777; 5th fl, Huasheng Tower, 399 Jiujiang Rd; 九江路399号 华盛大厦5楼; dishes ¥20-98; ⏲11am-2.30pm & 5-9.30pm; 🛜; Ⓜ East Nanjing Rd) In the top league of Shànghǎi's best Sìchuān restaurants, Yúxìn is a dab hand in the arts of blistering chillies and numbing peppercorns. All-stars include the 'mouthwatering chicken' starter (口水鸡; *kǒushuǐ jī*), or opt for

the simply smoking spicy chicken (辣子鸡; *lazi jī*), the crispy camphor tea duck (half/whole ¥38/68) or catfish in chilli oil.

Shànghǎi Grandmother CHINESE $

(上海姥姥; Shànghǎi Lǎolao; Map p192; ☑6321 6613; 70 Fuzhou Rd; 福州路70号; dishes ¥25-55; ⏲10.30am-9.30pm; Ⓜ East Nanjing Rd) This packed eatery is within easy striking distance of the Bund and cooks up all manner of home-style dishes. You can't go wrong with the classics here: braised eggplant in soya sauce, Grandmother's braised pork, crispy duck, three-cup chicken and *mápó dòufu* (tofu and pork crumbs in a spicy sauce) rarely disappoint.

South Memory HUNANESE $

(望湘园; Wàng Xiāng Yuán; Map p192; ☑6360 2797; 6th fl, Hóngyī Plaza, 299 East Nanjing Rd; 南京东路299号宏伊国际广场6楼; dishes ¥29-88; Ⓜ East Nanjing Rd) This popular Húnán place is a chopstick's throw from the waterfront with a range of spicy drypots (served in a personal mini wok), including favourites such as bamboo shoots and smoked pork, and chicken and chestnuts. Also on the menu are other *xiāngcài* (Hunanese) classics (such as steamed pork served in a bamboo tube); it's absolutely jammed at lunchtime and only early birds get window seats.

Nánxiáng Steamed Bun Restaurant DUMPLINGS $

(南翔馒头店; Nánxiáng Mántou Diàn; Map p192; 2nd fl, 666 Fuzhou Rd; 福州路666号2楼; steamer 8 dumplings ¥25-50; Ⓜ People's Sq) This pleasant branch of Shànghǎi's most famous dumpling restaurant overlooks Fuzhou Rd and can be slightly less crowded than other branches.

★ Lost Heaven YUNNAN $$

(花马天堂; Huāmǎ Tiāntáng; Map p192; ☑6330 0967; www.lostheaven.com.cn; 17 East Yan'an Rd; 延安东路17号; dishes ¥50-210; ⏲noon-2pm & 5.30-10.30pm; Ⓜ East Nanjing Rd) Lost Heaven might not have the views that keep its rivals in business, but why go to the same old Western restaurants when you can get sophisticated Bai, Dai and Miao folk cuisine from China's mighty southwest? Specialities are flowers (banana and pomegranate), wild mushrooms, chillies, Burmese curries, Bai chicken and superb *pǔ'ěr* (pu-erh) teas, all served up in gorgeous Yúnnán-meets-Shànghǎi surrounds.

★ Mr & Mrs Bund　　　　FRENCH $$$
(Map p192; ☑ 6323 9898; www.mmbund.com; 6th fl, Bund 18, 18 East Zhongshan No 1 Rd; 中山东一路18号6楼; mains ¥150-800, 2-/3-course set lunch ¥200/250; ⏱ lunch 11.30am-2pm Mon-Fri, dinner 6-11pm Fri & Sat, 6-10.30pm Sun-Thu, night 10.30pm-2am Tue-Thu, 11pm-2am Fri & Sat; Ⓜ East Nanjing Rd) French chef Paul Pairet's casual eatery aims for a space that's considerably more playful than your average fine-dining Bund restaurant. The mix-and-match menu has a heavy French bistro slant, but reimagined and served up with Pairet's ingenious presentation. But it's not just the food you're here for: it's the postmidnight meals (discounted), the Bingo nights and the wonderfully wonky atmosphere. Reserve.

★ M on the Bund　　　　EUROPEAN $$$
(米氏西餐厅; Mǐshì Xīcāntīng; Map p192; ☑ 6350 9988; www.m-restaurantgroup.com/mbund/home.html; 7th fl, 20 Guangdong Rd; 广东路20号7楼; mains ¥128-288, 2-course set lunch ¥188, light lunch menu ¥118; Ⓜ East Nanjing Rd) M exudes a timelessness and level of sophistication that eclipses the razzle-dazzle of many other upscale Shànghǎi restaurants. The menu ain't radical, but that's the question it seems to ask you – is breaking new culinary ground really so crucial? Crispy suckling pig and a chicken tajine with saffron are, after all, simply delicious just the way they are.

The art deco dining room and 7th-floor terrace are equally gorgeous. Finish off with drinks in the Glamour Bar downstairs and reserve well in advance. It's also heavenly for a spot of afternoon tea (from ¥88 to ¥138).

Lobby, Peninsula　　　　BRITISH $$$
(上海半岛酒店; Map p192; http://shanghai.peninsula.com; 32 E Zhongshan No 1 Rd; 中山东一路32号; 1/2 persons ¥290/540; ⏱ 2-6pm; ☎; Ⓜ E Nanjing Rd) Afternoon heritage tea for smart/casually attired visitors in the sumptuous Peninsula lobby is a decadent delight, with gorgeously presented scones, macaroons, clotted cream, jam, cookies, tea (of course), and live piano tinklings. For ¥440, a glass of champers is thrown in.

In the evenings, a live jazz band takes over. You can dine here all day à la carte from 6am to midnight.

✕ Old Town & South Bund

Wúyuè Rénjiā　　　　NOODLES $
(吴越人家; Map p192; 234 Fuyou Rd; 福佑路234号; ⏱ 8am-9.30pm; Ⓜ Yuyuan Garden) Right

---

PEOPLE'S SQUARE FOOD STREETS

The following two streets are lined with an amazing variety of Chinese restaurants, each with its own speciality.

Huanghe Road Food Street (黄河路美食街; Huánghé Lù Měishí Jiē; Map p192; Ⓜ People's Square) With a prime central location near People's Park, Huanghe Rd covers all the bases from cheap lunches to late-night post-theatre snacks. Huanghe Rd is best for dumplings – get 'em fried at **Yang's** (小杨生煎馆; Xiǎoyáng Shēngjiān Guǎn; Map p192; 97 Huanghe Rd; 黄河路97号; 4 dumplings ¥6; ⏱ 6.30am-8.30pm; Ⓜ People's Sq) (No 97) or served up in bamboo steamers across the road at **Jiājiā Soup Dumplings** (佳家汤包; Jiājiā Tāngbāo; Map p192; 90 Huanghe Rd; 黄河路90号; ⏱ 7am-10pm).

Yunnan Road Food Street (云南路美食街; Yúnnán Lù Měishí Jiē; Map p192; Ⓜ Dashijie) Yunnan Rd has some great speciality restaurants and is just the spot for an authentic meal after museum hopping at People's Square. Look out for Shaanxi dumplings and noodles at No 15 and five-fragrance dim sum at **Wǔ Fāng Zhāi** (五芳斋; Map p192; 28 Yunnan Rd; 云南路28号; ⏱ 7am-10pm).

---

next to KFC north of the Yùyuán Gardens, this upstairs place doesn't look particularly appealing but it serves typical Old Town fare and it's a well-known family name in Shànghǎi. They serve up excellent and filling bowls of Sūzhōu noodles. Choose between tāng (soupy) and gān (dry) noodles; in either case, the flavouring comes on a side plate.

Try the noodles with meat and pickled vegetables (榨菜肉丝面; zhàcài ròusī miàn; ¥10;) or the spicy meat noodles in red oil (红油腊肉面; hóngyóu làròu miàn; ¥13;).

★ Kebabs on the Grille　　　　INDIAN $$
(☑ 6152 6567; No 8, Cool Docks, 505 South Zhongshan Rd; 中山南路505号老码头8号; mains ¥45-125, set lunch Mon-Fri ¥58; ⏱ 11am-10.30pm; Ⓜ Xiaonanmen) This immensely popular and busy Cool Docks restaurant is a genuine crowd-pleaser, and has alfresco seating by the pond outside. The Boti mutton (barbecued lamb pieces) is adorable. There's a delicious range of tandoori dishes, live table-top

grills, vegetarian choices, smooth and spicy daal options, plus an all-you-can-eat Sunday brunch (¥150). Another central branch can be found west of **People's Sq** (Map p192; ☑3315 0132; 227 North Huangpi Rd, inside Central Plaza; 黄陂北路227号; dishes ¥60-90, set lunch ¥48-58; Ⓜ People's Sq).

Char
STEAK $$$

(恰餐厅; Qià Cāntīng; ☑3302 9995; www. char-thebund.com; 29th-31st fl, Hotel Indigo, 585 East Zhongshan No 2 Rd; 中山东二路585号29-31楼; steaks from ¥438, burgers ¥298, mains from ¥188; ⊙6-10pm; 🛜; Ⓜ Xiaonanmen) Char has become a Shànghǎi steakhouse sensation. Park yourself on a sofa against the window or in a comfy chair facing Lùjiāzuǐ for optimum views. Or keep one eye on the open kitchen to see how your Tajima Wagyu rib-eye steak, grilled black cod or seafood tower is coming along. There's a choice of six different steak knives. Book ahead.

The views continue in spectacular fashion from the terrace of the supremely chilled-out upstairs **bar** (恰酒吧; Qià Jiǔbā; www. char-thebund.com; 30th fl, Hotel Indigo, 585 East Zhongshan No 2 Rd; 中山东二路585号30楼; ⊙5pm-1.30am Mon-Thu, to 2.30am Fri & Sat, 2pm-1am Sun; Ⓜ Xiaonanmen).

✖ French Concession

★ Jian Guo 328
SHANGHAINESE $

(Map p200; 328 West Jianguo Rd; 建国西路328号; mains from ¥12; ⊙11am-9.30pm; Ⓜ Jiashan Rd) Frequently rammed, this boisterous two-floor MSG-free spot tucked away on Jianguo Rd does a roaring trade on the back of fine Shànghǎi cuisine. You can't go wrong with the menu, but for pointers the deep-fried spare ribs feature succulent pork in a crispy coating while the eggplant in casserole is a rich, thick and thumb-raising choice, high on flavour.

★ Noodle Bull
NOODLES $

(狠牛面; Hěnniú Miàn; Map p200; ☑6170 1299; unit 3b, 291 Fumin Rd; 富民路291号3b室; noodles ¥28-35; ⊙11am-midnight; Ⓜ Changshu Rd, South Shaanxi Rd) Noodle Bull is the bees-knees: far cooler than your average street-corner noodle stand (minimalist concrete chic and funky bowls), inexpensive, and boy is that broth slurpable. It doesn't matter whether you go vegetarian or for the roasted beef noodles (¥38), it's a winner both ways. Vegetarians can zero in on the carrot-and-

cucumber-sprinkled sesame-paste noodles (¥32), which are divine.

★ Spicy Joint
SICHUANESE $

(辛香汇; Xīnxiānghuì; Map p200; ☑6470 2777; 3rd fl, K Wah Center, 1028 Middle Huaihai Rd; 淮海中路1028号嘉华中心3楼; dishes ¥12-60; ⊙11am-10pm; 🛜; Ⓜ South Shaanxi Rd) If you only go to one Sìchuān joint in town, make it this one, where the blistering heat is matched only by its scorching popularity. Dishes are inexpensive by the city's standards; favourites include massive bowls of spicy catfish in hot chilli oil, an addictive garlic-cucumber salad, smoked-tea duck and chilli-coated lamb chops.

Be forewarned that the wait can be excruciatingly long at peak times; you'll need a mobile number to secure a place in the queue.

Cha's
CANTONESE $

(查餐厅; Chá Cāntīng; Map p200; 30 Sinan Rd; 思南路30号; dishes ¥20-55; ⊙11am-1.30am; Ⓜ South Shaanxi Rd) This rammed Cantonese diner does its best to teleport you to 1950s Hong Kong, with old-style tiled floors, whirring ceiling fans and even an antique Coca-Cola ice box to set the scene. You'll need to wait to get a table, so use the time wisely and peruse the menu of classic comfort food (curries, sweet-and-sour pork) in advance.

Fortune Cookie
AMERICAN CHINESE $

(簽語餅; Qiānyǔ Bǐng; Map p200; ☑6093 3623; www.fortunecookieshanghai.com; 4th fl, 83 Changshu Rd; 常熟路83号4楼; mains from ¥36; ⊙11.30am-10pm Sun-Thu, to 11pm Fri & Sat; Ⓜ Changshu Rd) Selling coals to Newcastle and fridges to Eskimos was always high-risk, but Fortune Cookie's owners have cashed in on the nostalgic expat demand for Chinatown staples and the curiosity of Shànghǎi diners. Now you don't have to fly to the US to find Brooklyn *kung po* chicken, tofu chop suey, *moo shu* pork, orange chicken or sweet-and-sour pork.

Baker & Spice
CAFE $

(Map p200; 195 Anfu Rd; 安福路195号; mains from ¥40; ⊙6am-10.30pm; 🛜; Ⓜ Changshu Rd) Its wooden table a solitary slab of rustic wholesomeness, this bakery-cafe serves stuff the doctor did and didn't order, all lovingly presented: sandwiches on dense, fibre-rich bread; cellophane packed nuts; yoghurt cups; muffins; pain-au-chocolates; tarts; cakes; and sizeable vanilla custard Berliners. A couple of box tables are flung outside for sun-catching.

Fēngyù Shēngjiān DUMPLINGS $

(丰裕生煎; Map p200; 41 Ruijin No 2 Rd, cnr Nanchang Rd; 瑞金二路41号; mains from ¥5; ⊙6am-10pm; MSouth Shaanxi Rd) If you thought Shànghǎi dining was all white linen tablecloths, steaming hand towels and perfectly formed waitresses in cheongsam clutching gold-embossed menus, think again. Chow down on fine *xiǎolóngbāo* (dumplings; ¥6), *shēngjiān* (生煎; fried dumplings; ¥5) and *miàntiáo* (noodles; ¥8) with the hard-working proletariat at Fēngyù, where plastic trays, fixed furniture and zero English rule.

Pay at the entrance and join the queue.

★ **Dī Shuǐ Dòng** HUNANESE $$

(滴水洞; Map p200; ☑6253 2689; 2nd fl, 56 South Maoming Rd; 茂名南路56号2层; dishes ¥28-128; ⊙11am-12.30am; MSouth Shaanxi Rd) Until the chilled lagers arrive, the faint breeze from the spreading of the blue-and-white tablecloth by your waiter may be the last cooling sensation at Dī Shuǐ Dòng, a rustic upstairs shrine to the volcanic cuisine of Húnán. Loved by Shanghainese and expats in equal measure, dishes are ferried in by sprightly peasant-attired staff to tables stuffed with enthusiastic, red-faced diners.

ElEfante MEDITERRANEAN $$

(Map p200; ☑5404 8085; 20 Donghu Rd; 东湖路20号; ⊙11am-3pm & 6-10.30pm Tue-Sun; MSouth Shaanxi Rd) Willy Trullas Moreno's latest Shànghǎi creation sits squarely at the heart of the French Concession – in the same spot as his first venture – with a choice patio and romantic 1920s villa setting. It's tantalising Mediterranean menu with tapas-style dishes has pronounced Spanish and Italian inflections, and has local gastronomes buzzing.

Food Fusion MALAYSIAN $$

(融合; Rónghé; Map p200; 8th fl, Parkson Plaza, 918 Middle Huaihai Rd; 淮海中路918号百盛8楼; dishes ¥30-168, lunch sets from ¥38; ⊙10am-11pm; MSouth Shaanxi Rd) Up on the 8th floor of one of Huaihai Rd's numerous shopping malls you'll find this hopping Malaysian option. Join the thronging office workers filling the lift and ascend to aromas of coriander, star anise, nutmeg, cinnamon and ginger. Crowd-pleasing classics include *rendang* beef, chilli-flecked *laksa* (coconut curry noodle soup), chicken satay, fish curry, *roti canai* and Nyonya desserts.

Bǎoluó Jiǔlóu SHANGHAINESE $$

(保罗酒楼; Map p200; ☑6279 2827; 271 Fumin Rd; 富民路271号; dishes ¥58; ⊙11am-3am; MChangshu Rd, Jing'an Temple) Gather up some friends to join the Shanghainese at this expanded, highly popular Fumin Rd venue. It's a great place to get a feel for Shànghǎi's famous buzz. Try the excellent baked eel (保罗烤鳗; *bǎoluó kǎomán*) or pot-stewed crab and pork.

Ferguson Lane ITALIAN, FRENCH $$

(武康庭; Wǔkāng Tíng; Map p200; www.ferguson-lane.com.cn; 378 Wukang Rd; 武康路378号; mains ¥48-130; MShanghai Library, Jiaotong University) On those rare days when Shànghǎi's skies are cloud-free, the secluded Ferguson Lane courtyard fills up in the blink of an eye with sun-starved diners. There are several tempting options here, including the **Coffee Tree** (Map p200; Ferguson Lane, 376 Wukang Rd; 武康路376号; mains from ¥50; ⊙9am-10pm; 🖥; MShanghai Library), which features panini, pasta, salads and organic coffee, and **Farine** (Map p200; http://farine-bakery.com; Ferguson Lane, 378 Wukang Rd; 武康路378号1楼; ⊙7am-8pm; MShanghai Library, Jiaotong University), for breads and pastries.

Pho Real VIETNAMESE $$

(Map p200; 166 Fumin Rd; 富民路166号; noodles from ¥52, set lunch ¥60-70; ⊙11am-2pm & 5-10pm; MChangshu Rd, Jing'an Temple) This pint-sized eatery, overhung with woven fishing traps suspended from the ceiling, does a brisk trade in *pho* (beef noodle soup flavoured with mint, star anise and coriander), spring rolls and good-value set lunches. Round it all out with a chilled Saigon lager (¥40). It only seats about 20, with no reservations, so pitch up early and prepare to wait.

There's another branch at **1465 Fuxing Rd** (Map p200; ☑6437 2222; 1465 Fuxing Rd; 复兴中路1465号; ⊙11am-2pm & 6-10pm Mon-Fri, 11am-3.30pm & 6-10pm Sat-Sun; MChangshu Rd), which does take reservations.

Xībó CENTRAL ASIAN $$

(锡伯新疆餐厅; Xībó Xīnjiāng Cāntīng; Map p200; ☑5403 8330; www.xiboxinjiang.com; 3rd fl, 83 Changshu Rd; 常熟路83号3楼; mains ¥35-92; ⊙noon-2.30pm & 6pm-midnight; MChangshu Rd) Trust Shànghǎi to serve up a stylish Xīnjiāng joint, because this isn't the type of place you're likely to find out in China's wild northwest. But who's complaining? When you need a mutton fix, beef skewers or some spicy 'big plate chicken', Xībó will do you right (and the restaurant donates healthily to charities in West China).

Vedas
INDIAN $$

(Map p200; www.vedascuisine.com; 3rd fl, 83 Changshu Rd; 常熟路83号3楼; mains from ¥68; ⏱11.30am-2pm & 6-10.30pm; ▣; Ⓜ Changshu Rd) Vedas hides the sterility of its modern tower-block setting with good-looking woodwork, warm service and a generous menu of full-flavoured Indian dishes. The delightful Bombay prawn curry (¥88) is piquant and creamy in equal measure, while the basmati rice is cooked to perfection and arrives in steaming abundance.

West Nanjing Road & Jìng'ān

★ Jen Dow Vegetarian
Restaurant
CHINESE, VEGETARIAN $

(人道素菜小吃; Réndào Sùcài Xiǎochī; Map p204; 153 Yuyuan Rd; 愚园路153号; mains from ¥18; ⏱9am-midnight; ☑; Ⓜ Jing'an Temple) Your body is a temple, they say, so treat it with respect by dining at this fab ground-floor meat-free eatery slung out behind the Jing'an Temple. You can slurp up a vast, tasty bowl of noodles densely sprinkled with crisp and fresh mushroom, bamboo shoots, cabbage and carrots for a mere ¥18 – it's a meal in itself.

Also at hand are vegetarian hotpots and a host of other choices, plus egg tarts and other baked delicacies at the door. Order fast-food style from the counter. Upstairs, the smarter 2nd floor – with glass jars of herbs and dried grains lining the walls – is a civilised and tasty choice, and has a Chinese and Western menu. The blistering and salty *mápó dòufu* (tofu and pork crumbs in a spicy sauce) hits the Sìchuān nail squarely on the head, with mushrooms in place of meat, and the sizzling seafood bake with melted cheese is crisp and filling. Service is efficient; the only fly in the ointment is the Richard Clayderman musak.

The 3rd floor is smart self-service; 4th floor is exclusive set meals.

Sumerian
CAFE $

(Map p204; 415 North Shaanxi Rd; 陕西北路415号; mains from ¥20; ⏱7.30am-7.30pm; ☎; Ⓜ West Nanjing Rd) Run by a bright and sunny Californian and a sprightly Chinese, good-looking Sumerian packs a lot into a small space, with bagels, pumpkin soup, roasted vegetable salads, wraps and stand-out coffees (Mexican

Pluma Real Organic, Colombian Popayan decaf) on the menu.

Wagas
CAFE $

(沃歌斯; Wògēsī; Map p204; B11A, Citic Sq, 1168 West Nanjing Rd; 南京西路1168号中信泰富地下一层11A室; mains ¥48-60; ⏱7am-10pm; ☎; Ⓜ West Nanjing Rd) Express sandwiches are half-price before 10am weekdays; there are after-6pm deals; and you can hang out here for hours with your tablet and no one will shoo you away – need we say more? Hip Wagas is the best and most dependable of the local cafes, with chilled beats, tantalising wraps, salads and sandwiches, and prices displayed on an overhead blackboard menu.

★ Commune Social
TAPAS $$

(食社; Shíshè; www.communesocial.com; 511 Jiangning Rd; 江宁路511号; mains ¥58-398; ⏱noon-2.30pm & 6-10.30pm Tue-Fri, noon-3pm & 6-10.30pm Sat, till 3pm Sun; Ⓜ Changping Rd) Dividing neatly into upstairs cocktail bar with terrace, downstairs open-kitchen tapas bar and dessert bar, this natty Neri & Hu–designed Jason Atherton venture blends a stylish, yet relaxed, vibe with some sensational international dishes, exquisitely presented by chef Scott Melvin. It's the talk of the town, but has a no-reservations policy, so prepare to queue.

★ Fu 1039
SHANGHAINESE $$

(福一零三九; Fú Yào Líng Sān Jiǔ; ☑5237 1878; 1039 Yuyuan Rd; 愚园路1039号; dishes ¥60-108; Ⓜ Jiangsu Rd) Set in a three-storey 1913 villa, Fu attains an old-fashioned charm. Foodies who appreciate sophisticated surroundings and Shanghainese food on par with the decor, take note – Fu is a must. The succulent standards won't disappoint: the smoked fish starter and stewed pork in soy sauce are recommended, with the sautéed chicken and mango and the sweet-and-sour Mandarin fish a close second.

The entrance, down an alley and on the left, is unmarked and staff speak little English. There's a minimum charge of ¥200 per head here.

Pǔdōng New Area

★ South Beauty
SICHUANESE, CANTONESE $

(俏江南; Qiào Jiāngnán; Map p206; ☑5047 1817; 10th fl, Superbrand Mall, 168 West Lujiazui Rd; 陆家嘴西路168号正大广场10楼; dishes from ¥20; ⏱11am-10pm; Ⓜ Lujiazui) This smart restaurant with vermilion leather furniture and silky white table cloths on the 10th floor of the Superbrand Mall cooks up classic dishes from fiery Chóngqìng, Chéngdū and the south. The scorching boiled beef with hot pepper in chilli oil (¥48) opens the sweat pores, while the piquant *mápō dòufu* (¥38) arrives in a scarlet oily sauce. Divine.

Alternatively, if you don't like it hot, go for the delicious pan-fried scallion buns (¥26). Check the back pages of the menu for the cheaper dishes. You'll need to reserve for the coveted Bund-facing window seats on the terrace. Branches throughout Shànghǎi.

★**Bāguó Bùyī** SICHUANESE $
(巴國布衣; ☎3111 8055; Rm 110, 1368 Shibo Avenue; 世博大道1368号110室; mains from ¥35; Ⓜ China Art Palace) Pretty much the most authentic Sìchuān food in town is cooked up by the diligent chefs at this famous restaurant in the World Expo Site, originally founded in Chéngdū. With no concessions to the dainty Shànghǎi palate, prepare for a spicy firecracker of a meal. Make it an evening visit and catch the spectacularly lit Mercedes Benz Arena next door.

Sproutworks HEALTH FOOD $
(豆苗工坊; Dòumiáo Gōngfáng; Map p206; www.sproutworks.com.cn; B2-06-07, Superbrand Mall, 168 West Lujiazui Rd; 陆家嘴西路168号正大广场B2楼; mains from ¥35, lunch sets from ¥50; ⊙10am-10pm; Ⓜ Lujiazui) For a healthy recharge, Sproutworks offers a natural and earthy focus on fresh, wholesome food, in a clean-cut (but rather square) setting. Cleanse your insides with delicious smoothies; load up with brown rice, tasty soups and crisp, panini sandwiches; try freshly tossed salads, fresh juices, homemade desserts and lunch sets. Most dishes are pre-prepared so ready to go.

At the time of writing, a branch was about to open in Xīntiāndì.

🍴 North Shànghǎi (Hóngkǒu)

★**Guòyúan** HUNANESE $
(果园; 524 Dongjiangwan Rd; 东江湾路524号; mains from ¥18; ⊙11am-2pm & 5-10pm Mon-Fri, 11am-3pm & 5-10pm Sat & Sun; Ⓜ Hongkou Football Stadium) The cool lime-green tablecloths do little to tame the tempestuous flavours of this fantastic Húnán restaurant. The *tiěbǎn dòufu* (铁板豆腐; sizzling tofu platter; ¥30) here is a magnificent dish, but its fiery flavours are almost eclipsed by the enticing *xiāngwèi qiézibāo* (湘味茄子煲; Húnán

aubergine hotpot; ¥20) and the lovely *zīrán yángròu* (孜然羊肉; lamb with cumin; ¥32).

🍴 South Shànghǎi (Xújiāhuì)

★**Din Tai Fung** SHANGHAINESE $
(鼎泰丰; Dǐng Tài Fēng; ☎3469 1383; 5th fl, Grand Gateway 66; 港汇广场5楼; mains from ¥29; ⊙10.30am-9pm; Ⓜ Xujiahui) This brightly lit and busy Taiwan-owned restaurant chain may still be peddling its 'Top 10 restaurants of the world' mantra after a two-decades-old review in the *New York Times,* but it still delivers some absolutely scrummy Shànghǎi *xiǎolóngbāo* dumplings. Not cheap perhaps (five for ¥29, or 10 for ¥58), but they're worth every *jiǎo*.

Kota's Kitchen JAPANESE $
(烤串烧酒吧; Pītóushì Kǎochuànshāo Jiǔbā; ☎6481 2005; www.kotaskitchen.com; 2905 Xietu Rd; 斜土路2905号; mains from ¥35, skewers from ¥15; ⊙6pm-1am; Ⓜ Shanghai Stadium, Shanghai Indoor Stadium) This entertaining, funky, very welcoming and bijou Beatles-themed Japanese yakitori restaurant-bar cooks up some enticing grilled meat skewers, perfectly accompanied by a heady range of homemade *shochu* spirits. The effect is an enticing blend of 1960s musical nostalgia and Japanese culinary skill: book ahead.

🍷 Drinking & Nightlife

Shànghǎi is awash with watering holes, their fortunes cresting and falling with the vagaries of the latest vogue. Drinks are pricier here than in the rest of China, retailing from around ¥40 (beer) or ¥60 (cocktails) at most places, so happy-hour visits (typically 5pm to 8pm) can be crucial. There's a high turnover of clubs, so check listings websites and magazines for the latest.

The Bund & People's Square

★Long Bar
BAR

(廊吧; Láng Bā; Map p192; ☑ 6322 9988; 2 East Zhongshan No 1 Rd; 中山东一路2号; ⊙4pm-1am Mon-Sat, 2pm-1am Sun; ☎; Ⓜ East Nanjing Rd) For a taste of colonial-era Shànghǎi's elitist trappings, you'll do no better than the Long Bar. This was once the members-only Shànghǎi Club, whose most spectacular accoutrement was a 34m-long wooden bar. Foreign businessmen would sit here according to rank, comparing fortunes, with the taipans (foreign heads of business) closest to the view of the Bund.

★New Heights
BAR

(新视角; Xīn Shìjiǎo; Map p192; ☑ 6321 0909; 7th fl, Three on the Bund, 3 East Zhongshan No 1 Rd; 中山东一路3号7楼; ⊙11.30am-1.30am; Ⓜ East Nanjing Rd) The most amenable of the big Bund bars, this splendid roof terrace has the choicest angle on Pǔdōng's hypnotising neon performance. There's always a crowd, whether for coffee, cocktails or meals (set meals from ¥188).

★Bar Rouge
BAR

(Map p192; ☑ 021 6339 1199; 7th fl, Bund 18, 18 East Zhongshan No 1 Rd; 中山东一路18号7楼; ¥100 cover charge after 10pm Fri & Sat; ⊙6pm-late; Ⓜ East Nanjing Rd) Bar Rouge attracts a cashed-up party crowd who come for the fantastic views from the terrace and the all-night DJ parties. The lipstick-red decor is slick and the crowd is slicker, so ordinary mortals can sometimes struggle to get served on busy nights.

Sir Elly's Terrace
BAR

(艾利爵士露台; Map p192; 14th fl, The Peninsula Shanghai, 32 East No 1 Zhongshan Rd; 中山东一路32号外滩32号半岛酒店14楼; ⊙5pm-midnight Sun-Thu, to 1am Fri & Sat; ☎; Ⓜ East Nanjing Rd) Offering some of Shànghǎi's best cocktails,

---

PUB CRAWL SHANGHAI

Sign up to **Pub Crawl Shanghai** (http://pubcrawlshanghai.com; ¥150; ⊙9.30am Thu, Fri & Sat) to check out the city's bars and clubs.

---

shaken up with that winning ingredient: 270-degree views to Pǔdōng, over Suzhou Creek and down the Bund. Of course it's not cheap, but the views are priceless.

Barbarossa
BAR

(芭芭露莎会所; Bābālùshā Huìsuǒ; Map p192; www.barbarossa.com.cn; People's Park, 231 West Nanjing Rd; 南京西路231号人民公园内; ⊙11am-2am; ☎; Ⓜ People's Sq) Set back in People's Park alongside a pond, Barbarossa is all about escapism. Forget Shànghǎi, this is Morocco channeled by Hollywood set designers. The action gets steadily more intense as you ascend to the roof terrace, via the cushion-strewn 2nd floor, where the hordes puff on fruit-flavoured hookahs. At night, use the park entrance just east of the former Shànghǎi Raceclub building (上海跑马总会; Shànghǎi Pǎomǎ Zǒnghuì).

Old Town

Old Shanghai Teahouse
TEAHOUSE

(老上海茶馆; Lǎo Shànghǎi Cháguǎn; Map p192; ☑ 5382 1202; 385 Middle Fangbang Rd; 方浜中路385号; tea from ¥45; ⊙9am-9pm; Ⓜ Yuyuan Garden) A bit like the attic of an eccentric aunt, this wonderfully decrepit 2nd-floor teahouse, overlooking the throng of Old Street, is a temple to the 1930s, with music on scratched records, period typewriters, aged photos, an old fireplace, sewing machines, electric fans, an ancient fridge, oodles of charm and tea, of course.

French Concession

★Café des Stagiaires
BAR

(Map p200; www.cafestagiaires.com; 54-56 Yongkang Rd; 永康路54-56号; mains from ¥40; ⊙10am-midnight; ☎; Ⓜ South Shaanxi Rd) The best bar by far on buzzing Yongkang Rd, this hip oasis of Francophilia spills over with slightly zany Gallic charm. There's a coke bottle chandelier and a (French) geography lesson via the wine list: Languedoc, Provence, Côte du Rhône, Loire, Alsace, Bourgogne, Bordeaux and, bien sûr, Rest of the World. Each table is regularly stocked with addictive chilli peanuts.

If that's insufficient, sample the quality charcuterie, cheese and pizzas.

★Shelter
CLUB

(Map p200; 5 Yongfu Rd; 永福路5号; ⊙9pm-4am Wed-Sat; Ⓜ Shanghai Library) The darling of the underground crowd, Shelter is a converted bomb shelter where you can count on great music, cheap drinks and a nonexistent dress code. They bring in a fantastic line-up of international DJs and hip-hop artists; the large barely lit dance area is the place to be. Cover for big shows is usually around ¥30.

★**Boxing Cat Brewery** BREWERY
(拳击猫啤酒屋; Quánjīmāo Píjiǔwū; Map p200; www.boxingcatbrewery.com; 82 West Fuxing Rd; 复兴西路82号; ⊙5pm-2am Mon-Thu, 3pm-2am Fri, 10am-2am Sat & Sun; ⊛; Ⓜ Shanghai Library, Changshu Rd) A deservedly popular three-floor microbrewery, with a rotating line-up of fresh beers that range from the Standing 8 Pilsner to the Right Hook Helles. But that's not all – the omnipresent restaurateur Kelley Lee has paired Southern classics (gumbo) and sandwiches (Cali-Cajun chicken club) to go with the drinks. Come for a pint; stay for dinner.

Bell Bar BAR
(Map p200; bellbar.cn; Tiánzǐfáng, back door No 11, Lane 248, Taikang Rd; 泰康路248弄11号后门田子坊; ⊙11am-2am; ⊛; Ⓜ Dapuqiao) This eccentric, unconventional boho haven is a delightful Tiánzǐfáng hideaway, with creaking, narrow wooden stairs leading to a higgledy-piggledy array of rooms to the tucked-away attic slung out above. Expect hookah pipes, mismatched furniture, warped secondhand paperbacks and a small, secluded mezzanine for stowaways from the bedlam outside. It's in the second alley (Lane 248) on the right.

Dean's Bottle Shop BAR
(Map p200; 40 Yongkang Rd; 永康路40号; beers from ¥15; ⊙noon-10pm; Ⓜ South Shaanxi Rd) This well-priced nirvana for lovers of the grain (and, to a lesser extent, grape) has row upon row of imported bottled bliss – Moosehead lager, Old Rasputin, Young's double chocolate, Bombadier ale, pear cider – all at bargain prices. With more than enough labels to test even the most well-travelled palates, it's more shop than bar, but you can sit down.

It's a great start or concluding point to a trawl along the bars of Yongkang Rd. There's another shop on nearby **Shaoxing Rd** (Map p200; 37 Shaoxing Rd; 绍兴路37号; Ⓜ Dapuqiao).

Shànghǎi Brewery BREWERY
(Map p200; www.shanghaibrewery.com; 15 Dongping Rd; 东平路15号; ⊙10am-2am Sun-Thu, to 3am Fri & Sat; ⊛; Ⓜ Changshu Rd, Hengshan Rd) Hand-crafted microbrews, a big range of comfort food, pool tables and sports on TV...this massive two-storey hang-out might have it all. Well, it certainly has enough to

stand out on a strip already bursting with established names. Try the Czech-style People's Pilsner or the Hong Mei Amber Hefeweizen, which start at a mere ¥20 during happy hour (from 2pm to 8pm).

🍷 Jìng'ān

Spot BAR
(Map p204; ☎6247 3579; 331 Tongren Rd; 铜仁路331号; ⊙11am- late; ⊛; Ⓜ Jing'an Temple) The district's upscale watering hole, Spot offers two sections: dining (nonsmoking) and the bar (smoking). It's much slicker than the competition, with fluorescent-coloured chairs, a tank of moon jellyfish, fancy dining options plus live music. But when push comes to shove, it's still a sports bar, best for catching football and rugby matches in the middle of the night.

🍷 Pǔdōng New Area

★**Flair** BAR
(Map p206; 58th fl, Ritz-Carlton Shanghai Pudong, 8 Century Ave; 世纪大道8号58楼; cocktails ¥90; ⊙5am-2am; ⊛; Ⓜ Lujiazui) Wow your date with Shànghǎi's most intoxicating nocturnal visuals from the 58th floor of the Ritz-Carlton, where Flair nudges you that bit closer to the baubles of the Oriental Pearl TV Tower. If it's raining, you'll end up inside, but that's OK as the chilled-out interior is supercool and there's a minimum price (¥400) for sitting outside.

Cloud 9 BAR
(九重天酒廊; Jiǔchóngtiān Jiǔláng; Map p206; ☎5049 1234; 87th fl, Jinmao Tower, 88 Century Ave;

世纪大道88号金茂大厦87楼; wine from ¥65, cocktails ¥88; ☺5pm-1am Mon-Fri, 11am-2am Sat & Sun; Ⓜ Lujiazui) Watch day fade to night as the neon slowly flickers on. After an espresso martini or two, you'll probably find out what it means to be *shanghaied* (in the very best sense of the word). Access to Cloud 9 is through the lobby of the Grand Hyatt.

🍷 North Shànghǎi (Hóngkǒu)

★ Vue
BAR

(非常时髦; Fēicháng Shímáo; Map p192; 32nd & 33rd fl, Hyatt on the Bund, 199 Huangpu Rd; 外滩茂悦大酒店黄浦路199号32-33楼; ☺6pm-1am; Ⓜ Tiantong Rd) Extrasensory nocturnal views of the Bund and Pǔdōng from the Hyatt on the Bund with an outdoor Jacuzzi to go with your raised glasses of bubbly or Vue martinis (vodka and mango purée).

☆ Entertainment

There's something for most moods in Shànghǎi: opera, rock, hip-hop, techno, salsa and early-morning waltzes in People's Sq. None of it comes cheap, however (except for the waltzing, which is free).

Acrobatics

Shànghǎi Centre Theatre ACROBATICS

(上海商城剧院; Shànghǎi Shāngchéng Jùyuàn; Map p204; ☑6279 8948; Shànghǎi Centre, 1376 West Nanjing Rd; 南京西路1376号; tickets ¥180, ¥240 & ¥300; Ⓜ Jing'an Temple) The Shànghǎi Acrobatics Troupe has popular performances here most nights at 7.30pm. It's a short but fun show and is high on the to-do list of most first-time visitors. Buy tickets a couple of days in advance from the ticket office on the right-hand side at the entrance to the Shànghǎi Centre.

Shànghǎi Circus World ACROBATICS

(上海马戏城; Shànghǎi Mǎxìchéng; ☑6652 7501; www.era-shanghai.com/era/en/; 2266 Gonghexin Rd; 闸北区共和新路2266号; admission ¥120-600; Ⓜ Shanghai Circus World) Out on the far northern outskirts of town you'll find this impressive complex. The show – *Era: Intersection of Time* – combines awesome acrobatics with new-fangled multimedia elements. Shows start at 7.30pm. Tickets are available at the door, but booking ahead is advised.

Chinese Opera

Yifū Theatre CHINESE OPERA

(逸夫舞台; Yìfū Wǔtái; Map p192; ☑6322 5294; www.tianchan.com; 701 Fuzhou Rd; 人民广场福州路701号; tickets ¥30-280; Ⓜ People's Sq) One block east of People's Sq, this is the main opera theatre in town and recognisable by the huge opera mask above the entrance. The theatre presents a popular program of Běijīng, Kun and Yue (Shaoxing) opera. A Běijīng opera highlights show is performed several times a week at 1.30pm and 7.15pm; pick up a brochure at the ticket office.

Live Music

Yùyīntáng LIVE MUSIC

(育音堂; www.yytlive.com; 851 Kaixuan Rd; 凯旋路851号; ☺9pm-midnight Tue-Sun; Ⓜ West Yan'an Rd) Small enough to feel intimate, but big enough for a sometimes pulsating atmosphere, Yùyīntáng has long been one of the top places in the city to see live music. Any Shànghǎi rock band worth its amps plays here, but you can also catch groups on tour from other cities in China and beyond. Rock is the staple diet, but anything goes, from hard punk to gypsy jazz.

Fairmont Peace Hotel Jazz Bar JAZZ

(爵士吧; Juéshì Bā; Map p192; ☑6138 6883; 20 East Nanjing Rd; 南京东路20号费尔蒙和平饭店; ☺5.30pm-2am, live music from 7pm; Ⓜ East Najing Rd) Shànghǎi's most famous hotel features Shànghǎi's most famous jazz band, a septuagenarian sextet that's been churning out nostalgic covers such as 'Moon River' and 'Summertime' since the dawn of time. There's no admission fee, but you'll need to sink a drink from the bar (draught beer starts at ¥70, a White Lady is ¥Y98).

The original band takes the stage from 7pm to 9.45pm; to get the pulse moving, a 'sultry female vocalist' does her bit from 9.45pm.

MAO Livehouse LIVE MUSIC

(Map p200; www.mao-music.com; 3rd fl, 308 South Chongqing Rd; 重庆南路308号3楼; Ⓜ Dapuqiao) One of the city's best and largest music venues, MAO is a stalwart of the Shànghǎi music scene, with acts ranging from rock to pop to electronica. Check the website for schedules and ticket prices.

Classical Music & Theatre

Shànghǎi Grand Theatre
CLASSICAL MUSIC
(上海大剧院; Shànghǎi Dàjùyuàn; Map p192; ✆6386 8686; www.shgtheatre.com; 300 Renmin Ave; 人民广场人民大道300号; Ⓜ People's Sq) Shànghǎi's state-of-the-art concert venue hosts everything from Broadway musicals to symphonies, ballets, operas and performances by internationally acclaimed classical soloists. There are also traditional Chinese music performances here. Pick up a schedule at the ticket office.

Shànghǎi Concert Hall
CLASSICAL MUSIC
(上海音乐厅; Shànghǎi Yīnyuè Tīng; Map p192; ✆6386 2836; www.shanghaiconcerthall.org; 523 East Yan'an Rd; 人民广场延安东路523号; ¥80-480; Ⓜ People's Sq, Dashijie) A decade or so ago, the government shunted all 5650 tonnes of this classic 1930s building 66m away from busy East Yan'an Rd to a quieter park-side setting, a relocation that actually cost more than building a brand-new concert hall. It features smaller-scale concerts plus local and international soloists.

Cinemas

Cathay Theatre
CINEMA
(国泰电影院; Guótài Diànyǐngyuàn; Map p200; 870 Middle Huaihai Rd; 淮海中路870号; tickets from ¥40; Ⓜ South Shaanxi Rd) This 1932 art deco theatre is one of the cheaper and more centrally located French Concession cinemas. If you want to know if the film is in the original, ask if it's the *yuánbǎn* (原版) version.

🏠 Shopping

From mega-malls to independent boutiques and haute couture, Shànghǎi is once again at the forefront of Chinese fashion and design.

🏠 The Bund & People's Square

Shànghǎi Museum Art Store
GIFTS
(上海博物馆艺术品商店; Shànghǎi Bówùguǎn Yìshùpǐn Shāngdiàn; Map p192; 201 Renmin Ave; 人民大道201号; ⊙9.30am-5pm; Ⓜ People's Sq) Attached to the Shànghǎi Museum and entered from East Yan'an Rd, this store offers refreshing variety from the usual tourist tat. Apart from the excellent range of books on Chinese art and architecture, there's a good selection of quality cards, prints and slides. The annexe shop sells fine imitations of some of the museum's ceramic pieces, as well as scarves and bags.

🛈 TICKETS

Tickets for all of Shànghǎi's performing-arts events can be purchased at the venues where the performances take place. Tickets are also available from **Smart Ticket** (www.smartshanghai.com/smartticket) and the **Shànghǎi Cultural Information & Booking Centre** (上海文化信息票务中心; Shànghǎi Wénhuà Xìnxī Piàowù Zhōngxīn; Map p204; ✆6217 2426; www.culture.sh.cn; 272 Fengxian Rd; 奉贤路272号; ⊙9am-7pm; Ⓜ West Nanjing Rd), which is directly behind the Westgate Mall on West Nanjing Rd. It often has tickets available when other places have sold out.

There's another branch near **Xīntiāndì** (上海博物馆商店; Map p200; 123 Taicang Rd; 太仓路123号; ⊙11am-7pm; Ⓜ South Huangpi Rd).

Sūzhōu Cobblers
ACCESSORIES
(上海起想艺术品; Shànghǎi Qǐxiǎng Yìshùpǐn; Map p192; unit 101, 17 Fuzhou Rd; 福州路17号101室; ⊙10am-6.30pm; Ⓜ East Nanjing Rd) Right off the Bund, this cute boutique sells exquisite hand-embroidered silk slippers, bags, hats and clothing. Patterns and colours are based on the fashions of the 1930s, and as far as the owner, Huang Mengqi, is concerned, the products are one of a kind. Slippers start at ¥480 and the shop can make to order.

🏠 Old Town

Yùyuán Bazaar is a frantic sprawl of souvenir shops with some choice gift-giving ideas and quality handicrafts, from painted snuff bottles to paper and leather silhouette cuttings, delightful Chinese kites, embroidered paintings, and clever palm and finger paintings, but sadly the hard sell is off-putting. Shops along nearby Old Street (p195) are more ye olde, selling everything under the Shànghǎi sun from calligraphy to teapots, memorabilia, woodcuts, reproduction 1930s posters and surreal 3D dazzle photos of kittens.

Shíliùpù Fabric Market
FABRIC
(十六铺面料城; Shíliùpù Miànliào Chéng; ✆6330 1043; 2 Zhonghua Rd; 中华路2号; ⊙8.30am-6.30pm; Ⓜ Xiaonanmen) Having silk shirts, dresses and cashmere coats tailor-made for a song is one of Shànghǎi's great indulgences. This three-storey building, one of several fabric markets in

the city, is conveniently located near the Yùyuán Bazaar. It's a far cheaper source of silk than many shops, with prices no higher than ¥200 per metre.

Dongtai Road Antique Market   SOUVENIRS
(东台路古玩市场; Dōngtái Lù Gǔwán Shìchǎng; ☎5582 5254; Dongtai Rd; 东台路; ⊙9am-6pm; Ⓜ Laoximen) A block west of South Xizang Rd, this market street has more than 100 stalls strewn along both Dongtai Rd and Liuhekou Rd. It's a long sprawl of miniature terracotta warriors, Guanyin figures, imperial robes, walnut-faced *luóhàn* statues, twee lotus shoes, helicopter pilot helmets and Mao-era knick-knacks, but generally only recent stuff such as art deco (and later) ornaments are genuine.

🔒 French Concession

With boutiques on almost every corner, the French Concession is where it's at for shoppers.

⭐ **Tiánzǐfáng**   CLOTHING, SOUVENIRS
(田子坊; Map p200; Lane 210, Taikang Rd; 泰康路210弄; Ⓜ Dapuqiao) Burrow into the *lǐlòng* (alleys) here for a rewarding haul of creative boutiques, selling everything from hip jewellery and yak-wool scarves to retro communist dinnerware. **Shànghǎi 1936** (Map p200; Unit 110, No 3, Lane 210; ⊙10am-8pm; Ⓜ Dapuqiao) is the place to pick up a tailored *wàitào* (Chinese jacket) or *qípáo* (figure-hugging Chinese dress); it also has a nearby **men's store** (Map p200; Unit 910, No 9, Lane 210; ⊙10am-8pm; Ⓜ Dapuqiao).

Further along is **Harvest** (Map p200; Rm 18, Bldg 3, Lane 210, Taikang Rd, Tiánzǐfáng; 泰康路210弄3号楼118室田子坊; ⊙9.30am-8pm; Ⓜ Dapuqiao), which sells Miao embroidery from southwest China, and the courtyard at No 7, Lane 210 (aka the Yard): look for Himalayan

jewellery and tapestries at **Joma** (Map p200; Unit 6, No 7, Lane 210, Taikang Rd, Tiánzǐfáng; 泰康路210弄7号-6田子坊; Ⓜ Dapuqiao) and local fashion designers at **La Vie** (生; Shēng; Map p200; ☎6445 3585; Tiánzǐfáng, The Yard, No 7, Lane 210, Taikang Rd; 泰康路210弄7号13室; ⊙10.30am-8.30pm; Ⓜ Dapuqiao). For funky ceramics, cloisonné and lacquer, stop by excellent **Pilingpalang** (噼吟啪唧; Map p200; http://pilingpalang.com; No 220, Lane 210, Taikang Rd, Tiánzǐfáng; 泰康路210弄22号田子坊; ⊙10am-9pm; Ⓜ Dapuqiao). Pop into colourful **Link Shanghai** (搭界; Dàjiè; Map p200; www.olinksh.com; No 5, Lane 248, Taikang Rd, Tiánzǐfáng; 泰康路248弄5号田子坊; ⊙10.30am-9pm; Ⓜ Dapuqiao) for imaginative art work and books and **Shanghai Code** (上海密码; Shànghǎi Mìmǎ; Map p200; No 9, Lane 274, Taikang Rd, Tiánzǐfáng; 泰康路274弄9号田子坊; ⊙2.30-9.30pm; Ⓜ Dapuqiao) for vintage spectacle frames. You'll find 1960s propaganda prints and old calendar posters at **Unique Hill Gallery** (Map p200; www.uniquehillgallery.com; No 10, Lane 210, Taikang Rd, Tianzifang; 泰康路210弄10号田子坊; ⊙9am-10pm; Ⓜ Dapuqiao). The vibrant and colourful selection of crafts at **Esydragon** (Map p200; ☎021 6467 4818; No 51, Lane 210, Taikang Rd, Tiánzǐfáng; 泰康路210弄51号田子坊; Ⓜ Dapuqiao) makes for excellent gifts; **Zhēnchálín Tea** (臻茶林; Zhēnchálín; Map p200; No 13, Lane 210, Taikang Rd, Tiánzǐfáng; 泰康路210弄13号田子坊; ⊙10am-8.30pm; Ⓜ Dapuqiao) has Chinese herbal teas in nifty packaging. Other stand-out stores are **Chouchou Chic** (Map p200; No 5, Lane 248, Taikang Rd; 泰康路248弄5号; Ⓜ Dapuqiao) and **Urban Tribe** (Map p200; No 14, Lane 248, Taikang Rd; 泰康路248弄14号; Ⓜ Dapuqiao).

⭐ **Xīntiāndì**   CLOTHING, ACCESSORIES
(新天地; Map p200; www.xintiandi.com; 2 blocks btwn Taicang, Zizhong, Madang & South Huangpi Rds; 太仓路与马当路路口; Ⓜ South Huangpi Rd, Xintiandi) There are few bargains to be had at Xīntiāndì, but even window-shoppers can

---

ACUPRESSURE MASSAGE

Shànghǎi's midrange massage parlours are a must – for the price of a cocktail or three, you get your own set of PJs, some post-therapy tea and Chinese flute music to chill out with. Just don't expect the masseuses to be gentle. As they say: no pain, no gain. Reserve in advance. Beware of offers of massage along East Nanjing Rd, you could be fleeced.

Dragonfly (悠庭保健会所; Yōutíng Bǎojiàn Huìsuǒ; Map p200; ☎5403 9982; www.dragonfly.net.cn; 206 Xinle Road; 新乐路206号; massage per 60 mins ¥188; ⊙10am-2am; Ⓜ South Shaanxi Rd)

Green Massage (青籁养; Qīnglài Yǎngshén; ☎5386 0222; www.greenmassage.com.cn; 58 Taicang Rd; 太仓路58号; massages & spa treatments ¥198-318; ⊙10.30am-2am; Ⓜ South Huangpi Rd)

make a fun afternoon of it here. The North Block features embroidered accessories at **Annabel Lee** (安梨家居; Ānlí Jiājū; Map p200; Xīntiāndì North Block, Bldg 3; 太仓路181弄新天地北里3号楼; ⊙10.30am-10.30pm; Ⓜ South Huangpi Rd, Xintiandi), high-end fashion from **Shanghai Tang** (上海滩; Shànghǎi Tān; Map p200; Xīntiāndì North Block, Bldg 15; 太仓路181弄新天地北里15号楼; Ⓜ South Huangpi Rd) and home furnishings at **Simply Life** (逸品生活; Yìjú Shēnghuó; Map p200; ☑6387 5100; Xīntiāndì North Block, Unit 101, 159 Madang Rd; 马当路159号新天地北里101单元; ⊙10.30am-10pm; Ⓜ South Huangpi Rd, Xintiandi) and a few scattered souvenir shops. The South Block has not one, but two malls, including **Xīntiāndì Style** (新天地时尚; Xīntiāndì Shíshàng; Map p200; 245 Madang Rd; 马当路245号).

NuoMi CLOTHING
(糯米; Nuòmǐ; Map p200; www.nuomishanghai.com; 196 Xinle Rd; 新乐路196号; ⊙11am-10pm; Ⓜ Changshu Rd) This Shànghǎi-based label seems to do everything right: gorgeous dresses made from organic cotton, silk and bamboo; eye-catching jewellery fashioned from recycled materials; a sustainable business plan that gives back to the community; and even an irresistible line of kids' clothes.

Brocade Country HANDICRAFTS
(锦绣坊; Jǐnxiù Fǎng; Map p200; 616 Julu Rd; 巨鹿路616号; ⊙10am-7.30pm; Ⓜ South Shaanxi Rd) Peruse an exquisite collection of minority handicrafts from China's southwest, most of which are secondhand (ie not made for the tourist trade) and personally selected by the owner Liu Xiaolan, a Guìzhōu native. Items for sale include embroidered wall hangings (some of which were originally baby carriers), sashes, shoes and hats, as well as silver jewellery.

Garden Books BOOKS
(韬奋西文书局; Tāofèn Xīwén Shūjú; Map p200; 325 Changle Rd; 长乐路325号; ⊙10am-10pm; 🛜; Ⓜ South Shaanxi Rd) The ice-cream parlour occupies about as much space as its well-stocked bookshelves. For all those Penguin paperback, gelato-to-go moments.

🏠 Jīng'ān

⭐**Spin** CERAMICS
(旋; Xuán; 360 Kangding Rd; 康定路360号; ⊙11am-8pm; Ⓜ Changping Rd) High on creative flair, Spin brings Chinese ceramics up to speed with its oblong teacups, twisted sake sets and all manner of cool plates, chopstick

holders, and 'kung fu' and 'exploded pillar' vases. Pieces are never overbearing, but trendily lean towards the whimsical, geometric, thoughtful and elegantly fashionable.

Amy Lin's Pearls PEARLS
(艾敏林氏珍珠; Àimǐn Línshì Zhēnzhū; Map p192; Room 30, 3rd fl, 580 West Nanjing Rd; 南京西路580号3楼30号; ⊙10am-8pm; Ⓜ West Nanjing Rd) The most reliable retailer of pearls of all colours and sizes. Both freshwater pearls (from ¥80), including prized black Zhèjiāng pearls (from ¥3000), and saltwater pearls (from ¥200) are available here. The staff speak English and will string your selection for you. This place sells jade and jewellery, too.

Han City Fashion & Accessories Plaza CLOTHING
(韩城服饰礼品广场; Hánchéng Fúshì Lǐpǐn Guǎngchǎng; Map p192; 580 West Nanjing Rd; 南京西路580号; ⊙10am-10pm; Ⓜ West Nanjing Rd) This unassuming-looking building is a popular location to pick up knock-offs, with hundreds of stalls spread across four floors. Scavenge for bags, belts, jackets, shoes, suitcases, sunglasses, ties, T-shirts and electronics. Amy Lin's Pearls is located here. Prices can be inflated, so bargain hard.

🏠 Pǔdōng

⭐**AP Xīnyáng Fashion & Gifts Market** SOUVENIRS
(亚太新阳服饰礼品市场; Yàtài Xīnyáng Fúshì Lǐpǐn Shìchǎng; ⊙10am-8pm; Ⓜ Science & Technology Museum) This mammoth underground market by the Science & Technology Museum metro station is Shànghǎi's largest collection of shopping stalls. There's tons of merchandise and fakes, from suits to moccasins, glinting copy watches, Darth Vader toys, jackets, Lionel Messi football strips, T-shirts, Indian saris, Angry Birds bags, Bob Marley Bermuda shorts, Great Wall snow globes: everything under the sun.

🏠 Hóngkǒu & North Shànghǎi

Dàshànghǎi ANTIQUES
(大上海; 181 Duolun Rd; 多伦路181号; ⊙9am-5.30pm, to 6pm in summer; Ⓜ Dongbaoxing Rd) Explore keenly at this Duolun Rd shop, where shelves spill forth with all manner of historic collectables from pre-Liberation China; books and catalogues; 1950s maps of Běijīng and Shànghǎi; genuine posters and authentic memorabilia from the Cultural Revolution; black-and white-photos;

unopened matchboxes and cigarette packs from the 1960s; Republican-era lipsticks; toothbrushes and more.

ℹ️ Information

Free English and bilingual maps of Shànghǎi are available at airports, tourist information & service centres, bookshops and many hotels. Metro maps (地铁线路图; dìtiě xiànlùtú) are usually available at all stations.

INTERNET ACCESS

Internet cafes are scarce in touristy areas – it's more convenient to get online at your hotel or at a wi-fi hotspot. Otherwise, ask your hotel for the closest wǎngba (网吧; internet cafe) and take your passport; there are several around Shàng-hǎi Railway Station (p228).

MEDIA

Grab free copies of *That's Shanghai*, *City Week-end* and *Time Out Shanghai* for a plug into what's on in town.

MEDICAL SERVICES

Huashan Worldwide Medical Center (华山 医院国际医疗中心; Huáshān Yīyuàn Guójì Yīliáo Zhōngxīn; ☑ 6248 3986; www.sh-hwmc. com.cn; ⊗ 8am-10pm) Hospital treatment and outpatient consultations are available at the 8th-floor foreigners' clinic of Huàshān Hospital, with 24-hour emergency treatment on the 15th floor in building 6.

Parkway Health (以极佳医疗保健服务; Yǐjíjiā Yīliáo Bǎojiàn Fúwù; Unit 30, Mandarine City, 788 Hongxu Rd; 虹许路788号30室) Has seven locations around town. Offers comprehensive private medical care from internationally trained physicians and dentists. Members can access after-hours services and an emergency hotline.

Watson's (屈臣氏; Qūchénshì; Map p200; ☑ 6474 4775; 787 Middle Huaihai Rd; 淮海中路 787号) The Hong Kong pharmacy Watson's can be found in the basements of malls all over town (there's also a branch in Westgate Mall), mainly selling imported toiletries and a limited range of simple over-the-counter pharmaceuticals.

MONEY

Almost every hotel has money-changing counters. Most tourist hotels, upmarket restaurants and banks accept major credit cards. Twenty-four hour ATMs are everywhere; most accept major cards.

Bank of China (中国银行; Zhōngguó Yínháng; Map p192; The Bund; ⊗ 9am-noon & 1.30-4.30pm Mon-Fri, 9am-noon Sat) Right next to the Peace Hotel. Tends to get crowded, but is better organised than Chinese banks elsewhere around the country (it's worth a peek for its grand interior). Take a ticket and wait for your number. For credit-card advances, head to the furthest hall (counter No 2).

Citibank (花旗银行, Huāqí Yínháng; Map p192; The Bund; ⊗ 24hr; Ⓜ East Nanjing Rd) Useful ATM open 24 hours.

HSBC (Hongkong & Shanghai Bank; 汇丰银行; Huìfēng Yínháng) **Shànghǎi Centre** (Hongkong & Shanghai Bank; West Nanjing Rd); The Bund (Hongkong & Shanghai Bank; 15 East Zhong-shan No 1 Rd) Has ATMs in the above locations; also an ATM at Pǔdōng International Airport arrivals hall.

POST

Larger tourist hotels have post offices where you can mail letters and small packages – the most convenient option. China Post offices and post boxes are green. The **International Post Office** (中国邮政; Zhōngguó Yóuzhèng; Map p192; ☑ 6393 6666; 276 North Suzhou Rd; 苏州北 路276号; ⊗ 7am-10pm) is just north of Sūzhōu Creek.

PUBLIC SECURITY BUREAU

Public Security Bureau (PSB; 公安局; Gōng'ānjú; ☑ 2895 1900; 1500 Minsheng Rd; 民 生路1500号; ⊗ 9am-5pm Mon-Sat) Visa exten-sions in Shànghǎi are available from the PSB.

TELEPHONE

After Skype (www.skype.com) and Viber (www. viber.com), internet phone (IP) cards are the cheapest way to call internationally (¥1.80 per minute to the US), but may not work with some hotel phones. For mobile phone SIM cards, China Mobile shops are ubiquitous; cards can also be bought from newspaper kiosks with the China Mobile sign.

China Mobile (Bund) (中国移动通信; Zhōng-guó Yídòng Tōngxìn; Map p192; 21 Yuanmin-gyuan Rd; 圆明园路21号; ⊗ 8.30am-6.30pm; Ⓜ East Nanjing Rd) For sim cards, top-up credit and mobile phones.

TOURIST INFORMATION

Your hotel should be able to provide you with maps and most of the tourist information you re-quire. There are also numerous Tourist Informa-tion and Service Centres, which are conveniently located near major tourist sights. The standard of English varies from good to non-existent, but free maps and some information is available. Tourist Information Centres include: **The Bund** (旅游咨询服务中心; Lǚyóu Zīxún Fúwù Zhōngx-īn; Map p192; ☑ 6357 3718; 518 Jiujiang Rd; 九 江路518号; ⊗ 9.30am-8pm); **Jing'an** (旅游咨 询服务中心; Lǚyóu Zīxún Fúwù Zhōngxīn; Map p200; ☑ 5386 1882; 138 S Chengdu Rd; 成都南 路138号; ⊗ 9am-8.30pm); **Old Town** (旅游咨 询服务中心; Lǚyóu Zīxún Fúwù Zhōngxīn; Map p192; ☑ 6355 5032; 149 Jiujiaochang Rd; 旧校 场路149号; ⊗ 9am-7pm).

Shànghǎi Call Centre (☑ 962 288) This toll-free English-language hotline is possibly the most useful telephone number in Shànghǎi – it can even give your cab driver directions if you've got a mobile phone.

TRAVEL AGENCIES

CTrip (☑ 400 619 9999; http://english.ctrip.com) An excellent online agency, good for hotel and flight bookings.

eLong (☑ 400 617 1717; www.elong.net) Hotel and flight bookings.

STA Travel (☑ 2281 7723; www.statravel.com.cn; Room 1609, Shanghai Trade Tower, 188 Siping Rd; ⊙ 9.30am-6pm Mon-Fri, 9.30am-12.30pm Sat; Ⓜ Hailun Rd) Sells train and air tickets, and can issue international student identity cards.

WEBSITES

Lonely Planet (www.lonelyplanet.com/shanghai) Destination information, hotel bookings, traveller forum and more.

Time Out Shanghai (www.timeoutshanghai.com) Authoritative, in-the-know entertainment listings.

City Weekend (www.cityweekend.com.cn/shanghai) Comprehensive listings website of popular expat magazine. News stories can be weak.

Shanghaiist (www.shanghaiist.com) Excellent source for news and reviews.

Smart Shanghai (www.smartshanghai.com) Quality listings website with forum.

ⓘ Getting There & Away

With two airports, rail and air connections to places all over China, and buses to destinations in adjoining provinces and beyond, Shànghǎi's a handy springboard to the rest of the land.

AIR

Shànghǎi has international flight connections to most major cities.

All international flights (and a few domestic flights) operate out of **Pǔdōng International Airport** (PVG; 浦东国际机场; Pǔdōng Guójì Jīchǎng; ☑ 6834 1000, flight information 96990; www.shairport.com), with most (but not all) domestic flights operating out of Hóngqiáo Airport (p1005) on Shànghǎi's western outskirts. If you are making an onward domestic connection from Pǔdōng, it is essential that you find out whether the domestic flight leaves from Pǔdōng or Hóngqiáo, as the former takes *at least* an hour to reach.

Daily (usually several times) domestic flights connect Shànghǎi to major cities in China:

Běijīng ¥1300, 1½ hours

Chéngdū ¥1700, two hours and 20 minutes

Guǎngzhōu ¥1300, two hours

Guìlín ¥1250, two hours

Qīngdǎo ¥800, one hour

Xī'ān ¥1350, two hours

You can buy air tickets almost anywhere, including at major hotels, travel agencies and online websites such as ctrip.com and elong.net. Discounts of up to 40% are standard.

BOAT

Domestic boat tickets can be bought from the **domestic boat tickets shop** (Map p192; ☑ 6308 9822; 21 East Jinling Rd, 金陵东路21号; ⊙ 9am-6pm; Ⓜ East Nanjing Rd) on East Jinling Rd.

Overnight boats (¥139 to ¥499, 11½ hours) to **Pǔtuóshān** depart Monday, Wednesday and Friday at 7.30pm from the **Wúsōng Wharf** (吴淞码头, Wúsōng Mǎtou; Ⓜ Songbing Rd), almost at the mouth of the Yangzi River; to reach Wúsōng Wharf take metro Line 3 to Songbing Rd and then walk or hail a taxi.

BORDER CROSSING: GETTING TO JAPAN

The China-Japan International Ferry Company (中日国际轮渡有限公司; Zhōng-guó Guójì Lúndù Yǒuxiàn Gōngsī; ☑ 6595 6888, 6325 7642; www.chinajapanferry.com; 18th fl, Jin'an Bldg, 908 Dongdaming Rd, 东大明路908号金岸大厦; tickets from ¥1300, plus ¥150 fuel surcharge) has staggered departures weekly to either Osaka or Kobe in Japan on Saturdays at 12.30pm. The Shànghǎi International Ferry Company (上海国际轮渡; Shànghǎi Guójì Lúndù; ☑ 6595 8666; www.shanghai-ferry.co.jp/english/; 15th fl, Jin'an Bldg, 908 Dongdaming Rd; 东大明路908号金岸大厦; tickets from ¥1300, plus ¥150 fuel surcharge) has departures to Osaka on Tuesdays at 11am. Both ferry companies are located in the Jin'an Building (908 Dongdaming Rd; 东大明路908号金岸大厦), north of the Bund. Fares on all boats (44 hours) range from ¥1300 in an eight-bed dorm to ¥6500 in a deluxe twin cabin. Reservations are recommended in July and August. Passengers must be at the harbour three hours before departure to get through immigration. All vessels depart from the Shànghǎi Port International Cruise Terminal (上海港国际客运中心; Shànghǎi Gǎng Guójì Kèyùn Zhōngxīn; Gaoyang Rd; 高阳路).

A high-speed ferry service (¥258 to ¥352, three hours, 10.10am) to Pǔtuóshān departs daily from Xiǎo Yáng Shān (小洋山). A bus (price included in ferry ticket; two hours, departs at 8.15am) runs to Xiǎo Yáng Shān from the bus station by Nánpǔ Bridge (南浦大桥).

BUS

Shànghǎi has several long-distance bus stations, though given the traffic gridlock it's best to take the train when possible.

The vast **Shànghǎi south long-distance bus station** (上海长途客运南站; Shànghǎi Chángtú Kèyùn Nánzhàn; ☏ 5436 2835; www.ctnz.net; 666 Shilong Rd; Ⓜ Shanghai South Railway Station) serves cities in south China, including:

Hángzhōu (main bus station at Jiǔbǎo, Hángzhōu north bus station and Hángzhōu south bus station) ¥68, two hours, regular (7.10am to 7.20pm)

Nánjīng ¥96 to ¥105, four hours

Nánxún ¥47, 2½ hours, eight daily, take the bus for Húzhōu (湖州; 6.50am to 7.28pm)

Sūzhōu (south and north bus stations) ¥38, 1½ hours, regular (6.27am to 7.30pm)

Túnxī/Huáng Shān ¥135, six hours, nine daily

Wùyuán ¥210, five hours, two daily (9.32am & 6.52pm)

Wūzhèn ¥51, two hours, 11 daily (7.15am to 6.17pm)

Xītáng ¥36, 1½ hours, 20 daily

Xīn'ānjiāng ¥121, two daily (8.34am & 2.34pm)

Zhōuzhuāng ¥29, two daily (8.11am & 1.21pm)

The massive **Shànghǎi long-distance bus station** (上海长途汽车客运总站; Shànghǎi Chángtú Qìchē Kèyùn Zǒngzhàn; ☏ 6605 0000; www.kyzz.com.cn; 1666 Zhongxing Rd; 中兴路1666号; Ⓜ Shanghai Railway Station), north of Shànghǎi's train station, has buses to destinations as far away as Gānsù province and Inner Mongolia. Regular buses run to Sūzhōu (frequent) and Hángzhōu (frequent), as well as Nánjīng (12 daily) and Běijīng (¥311, 4pm). Although it appears close to the train station, it is a major pain to reach on foot. It's easiest to catch a cab here.

Shànghǎi Sightseeing Buses run to the canal towns outside Shànghǎi.

TRAIN

Many parts of the country can be reached by direct train from Shànghǎi. The city has three useful stations: the main **Shànghǎi Railway Station** (上海火车站; Shànghǎi Huǒchē Zhàn; ☏ 6317 9090; 385 Meiyuan Rd; Ⓜ Shanghai Railway Station), **Shànghǎi South Railway Station** (上海南站; Shànghǎi Nánzhàn; ☏ 9510 5123; 200 Zhaofeng Rd) and the newer **Hóngqiáo Railway Station** (上海虹桥站; Shànghǎi Hóngqiáo Zhàn; Ⓜ Hongqiao Railway Station) near Hóngqiáo Airport. Wherever you're going, make sure to get

your tickets as early as possible. If you're arriving in Shànghǎi, don't get off at **Shànghǎi West Railway Station** (上海西站; Shànghǎi Xīzhàn), which is inconvenient for travellers.

You can procure tickets at the station (generally stressful), via your hotel, travel agency (much easier but expect a commission charge), at train ticket offices around town, or using online ticketing providers, such as **China Highlights** (www.chinahighlights.com), which can deliver e-tickets by email.

At the main station there are two ticket halls (售票厅; shòupiàotīng): one in the main building (same-day tickets) and another on the east side of the square (advance tickets). One counter will have English speakers; you will need your passport to buy tickets. Hopelessly, the bilingual automated machines (自助售票处; zìzhù shòupiàochù) require Chinese ID.

Alternatively, tickets can be purchased for a small commission (¥5) from one of the numerous train ticket offices (火车票预售处; huǒchēpiào yùshòuchù) around town, such as: **Bund** (Map p192; 384 Middle Jiangxi Rd; 江西中路384号; ☺ 8am-8pm); and **French Concession** (Map p200; 12 Dongping Rd; ☺ 8am-noon & 1-6pm Mon-Fri, 9am-noon & 1-5.30pm Sat & Sun).

Prices and times listed following are always for the fastest train. Some trains leaving from Shànghǎi Railway Station:

Běijīng (D class) seat/sleeper ¥309/696, eight to 11½ hours, three daily

Chéngdū seat/hard sleeper ¥254/464, 35 hours, four daily

Hángzhōu (G class) 2nd/1st class ¥93/148, 1½ hours, four daily

Hong Kong hard/soft sleeper ¥471/732, 18½ hours, one daily (6.20pm)

Huángshān seat/hard sleeper ¥93/174, 11½ hours, two daily

Lhasa hard/soft sleeper ¥841/1310, 48 hours, one every other day (7.36pm)

Nánjīng (G class) 2nd/1st class ¥140/220, two hours, frequent

Sūzhōu (G class) 2nd/1st class ¥40/60, 30 minutes, frequent

Ürümqi hard/soft sleeper ¥695/1075, 44 hours, one daily (8.25pm)

Xī'ān North (D class) seat/sleeper ¥338/834, 16 to 20 hours, 10 daily

Some trains leaving from Shànghǎi South Train station:

Guìlín hard/soft sleeper ¥351/537, 22 hours, four daily

Hángzhōu ¥29, 2½ to three hours, frequent

Kūnmíng hard/soft sleeper ¥533/822, 38 hours, three daily

Yùshān (Sānqīng Shān) ¥130, six hours, six daily

Some trains leaving from Hóngqiáo Train Station:

Běijīng (G class) 2nd/1st class ¥553/933, 5½ hours, very regular (7am to 7.55pm)

Hángzhōu (G class) 2nd/1st class ¥73/117, one hour, very regular (6.20am to 10.36pm)

Qīngdǎo (G class) 2nd/1st class ¥518/818, 6½ hours, four daily

Shàoxīng North (G class) 2nd/1st class ¥92/150, 1½ hours, 10 daily

Sūzhōu (G class) 2nd/1st class seat ¥39/59, 30 minutes, regular

Sūzhōu North (G class) 2nd/1st class seat ¥34/64, 23 minutes, very regular

Xiàmén North (D class) 2nd/1st class ¥328/413, eight hours, 13 daily

Zhèngzhōu (D class) 2nd/1st class ¥236/379, seven hours, three daily

ⓘ Getting Around

The best way to get around Shànghǎi is the metro, which now reaches most places in the city, followed by cabs. Buses (¥2) are tricky to use unless you are a proficient Mandarin speaker. Whatever mode of transport you use, try to avoid rush hours between 8am and 9am, and 4.30pm and 6pm.

Walking from A to B, unless it's a short journey, is generally an exhausting and sometimes stressful experience.

TO/FROM THE AIRPORT

Pǔdōng International Airport handles most international flights and some domestic flights. There are four ways to get from the airport to the city: taxi, Maglev train, metro and bus.

Taxi rides into central Shànghǎi cost around ¥160 and take about an hour; to Hóngqiáo Airport costs around ¥200. Avoid monstrous overcharging by using the regular taxi rank outside the arrivals hall. Regular buses run to Sūzhōu (¥84, three hours) and Hángzhōu (¥100, three hours).

The bullet-fast and time-saving **Maglev** (磁浮列车; Cífú Lièchē; www.smtdc.com; economy one-way/return ¥50/80, with same-day air ticket ¥40, children under/over 1.2m free/half-price) train runs from Pǔdōng International Airport to its terminal in Pǔdōng in just eight minutes, from where you can transfer to the metro (Longyang Rd station) or take a taxi (¥40 to People's Sq). Economy single/return tickets cost ¥50/80, but show your same-day air ticket and it's ¥40 one way. Children under 1.2m travel free (taller kids are half-price). Trains depart every 20 minutes from roughly 6.45am to 9.40pm.

Metro Line 2 runs from Pǔdōng International Airport to Hóngqiáo Airport, passing through central Shànghǎi. It is convenient, though not for

TRANSPORT CARD

If you are going to be doing a lot of travelling in Shànghǎi, it's worth investing in a **transport card** (交通卡; jiāotōng kǎ), as it can save you queuing and finding change (but does not offer real savings to travellers). Sold at metro stations and some convenience stores, cards can be topped up with credit and used on the metro, most buses and in taxis. Credits are electronically deducted from the card as you swipe it over the sensor at metro turnstiles and near the door on buses; when paying your taxi fare, hand the card to the driver, who will swipe it for you. You'll need to pay a deposit of ¥20, which can be refunded at metro stations. One-day (¥18) and three-day metro (¥45) passes are also sold from information desks.

those in a hurry. From Pǔdōng Airport, it takes about 75 minutes to People's Sq (¥7) and 1¾ hours to Hóngqiáo Airport (¥8).

There are also numerous **airport buses**, which take between one and 1½ hours to run to their destinations in Pǔxī. Buses leave from the airport roughly every 15 to 25 minutes from 6.30am to 11pm; they go to the airport from roughly 5.30am to 9.30pm (bus 1 runs till 11pm). The most useful buses are airport bus 1 (¥30), linking Pǔdōng International Airport with Hóngqiáo Airport, and airport bus 2 (¥22), linking Pǔdōng International Airport with the Airport City Terminal on West Nanjing Rd, east of Jìng'ān Temple. Airport bus 5 (¥22) links Pǔdōng International Airport with Shànghǎi train station via People's Sq.

Hóngqiáo Airport is 18km from the Bund, a 30- to 60-minute trip. Most flights now arrive at Terminal 2, connected to the city centre via metro Lines 2 and 10 (30 minutes to People's Sq). Terminal 1 is connected to the centre of town by line 10; shuttle buses run regularly (6am to 11pm) between both terminals, taking 13 minutes. Airport bus 1 (¥30, 6am to 9.30pm) runs to Pǔdōng International Airport; bus 941 (¥6) links Hongqiao Airport with Shànghǎi main train station. Taxis cost ¥70 to ¥100 to central Shànghǎi.

PUBLIC TRANSPORT
Ferry

The Jinling Rd Ferry (金陵路轮渡站; Jīnlíng Lù Lúndù Zhàn) runs between the southern end of the Bund and the Dongchang Rd dock in Pǔdōng. Ferries (¥2) run roughly every 15 minutes from

7am to 10pm. The Fuxing Rd Ferry (复兴路轮渡站; Fùxīng Lù Lúndù Zhàn) runs from Fuxing Rd north of the Cool Docks in the South Bund to Dongchang Rd as well. Ferries (¥2) run every 10 to 20 minutes from around 5am to 11pm.

Metro

The Shànghǎi metro system, indicated by a red M, currently runs to 14 lines after huge expansion, with further lines and extensions under construction. Lines 1, 2 and 10 are the most useful for travellers. Single-fare tickets cost ¥3 to ¥10 depending on distance, sold from coin-and-note-operated bilingual automated machines (and from booths at some stations); keep your ticket until you exit.

Metro maps are available at most stations; the free tourist maps also have a small metro map printed on them.

TAXI

Shànghǎi's taxis are reasonably cheap, hassle-free and easy to flag down outside rush hour, although finding a cab during rainstorms is impossible. Flag fall is ¥14 (for the first 3km) and ¥18 at night (11pm to 5am).

Bāshì (巴士; ☑ 96840) Green-coloured Bāshì is one of Shànghǎi's major taxi companies.

Dàzhòng (大众; ☑ 96822) One of Shànghǎi's main taxi companies is the turquoise-coloured Dàzhòng.

Qiángshēng (强生; ☑ 6258 0000) Gold-coloured Qiángshēng taxis is one of the main taxi companies in Shànghǎi.

AROUND SHÀNGHǍI

The most popular day trips from Shànghǎi are to Hángzhōu (a quick zip away on the train) and Sūzhōu.

Zhūjiājiǎo 朱家角

Thirty kilometres west of Shànghǎi, Zhū-jiājiǎo (www.zhujiajiao.com/en; optional ticket incl entry to 4/8/9 sights ¥30/60/80) is easy to reach and charming – as long as your visit does not coincide with the arrival of phalanxes of tour buses.

What survives of this historic canal town today is a charming tableau of Ming- and Qing-dynasty alleys, bridges and gǔzhèn

(古镇; old town) architecture, its alleyways steeped in the aroma of chòu dòufu (stinky tofu).

On the west side of the recently built City God Temple bridge stands the **City God Temple** (城隍庙; Chénghuáng Miào; Caohe Jie, 漕河街; admission ¥10; ⊙7.30am-4pm), moved here in 1769 from its original location in Xuějiābāng. Further north along Caohe St (漕河街), running alongside the canal, is the **Yuánjīn Buddhist Temple** (圆津禅院; Yuánjīn Chányuàn; Caohe Jie, 漕河街; admission ¥5; ⊙8am-4pm) near the distinctive Tài'ān Bridge (泰安桥; Tài'ān Qiáo). Pop into the temple to climb the Qīnghuá Pavilion (清华阁; Qīnghuá Gé) at the rear, a towering hall visible from many parts of town.

Earmark a detour to the **Zhūjiājiǎo Catholic Church of Ascension** (朱家角耶稣升天堂; Zhūjiājiǎo Yēsū Shēngtiāntáng; 27 Caohe Jie, No 317 Alley, 漕河街27号317弄), a gorgeous church with its belfry rising in a detached tower by the rear gate. Also hunt down the **Qing Dynasty Post Office** (admission ¥5).

Of Zhūjiājiǎo's quaint ancient bridges, Fàngshēng Bridge (放生桥; Fàngshēng Qiáo) is the most photogenic, first built in 1571. Tour boats offer comprehensive tours from various points, including Fàngshēng Bridge. Tickets are ¥60/120 per boat for the short/long tour; speed boats (¥40) also run from the bridge.

Food sellers line Bei Dajie, flogging everything from pig's trotters to plump coconuts, while plentiful cafes have squeezed in along Caohe Jie, Xihu Jie and Donghu Jie. To overnight, a charming choice is the **Cǎo Táng Inn** (草堂客栈; Cǎotáng Kèzhàn; ☑ 021 5978 6442; 31 Dongjing Jie; 东井街31号; dm ¥100, d ¥300-320; ☀@🛜), not far from Fàngshēng Bridge. Book ahead.

To reach Zhūjiājiǎo, hop on the direct pink and white **Hùzhū Gāosù Kuàixiàn** bus (沪朱高速快线; ¥12, one hour, every 20 minutes from 6am to 10pm, less frequently in low season) from the **Pu'an Rd Bus Station** (普安路汽车站; Pǔ'an Lù Qìchē Zhàn; Map p214##; Pu'an Lu; 普安路; Dashijie) just south of People's Sq. Zhūjiājiǎo can also be reached from the bus station in Tónglǐ (¥15, 1½ hours).

Jiāngsū

POP 78.9 MILLION

Best Classical Gardens

➡ Garden of the Master of the Nets (p248)

➡ Humble Administrator's Garden (p245)

➡ Presidential Palace (p236)

Best Museums

➡ Nánjīng Museum (p235)

➡ Sūzhōu Museum (p244)

➡ Memorial Hall of the Nánjīng Massacre (p237)

Why Go?

A zip away from Shànghǎi, Jiāngsū (江苏) is an alluring and easy-to-manage region. The province, which owed its historical wealth to silk and salt production, boasts the Grand Canal as well as elaborate waterways that thread through the Yangzi River (Cháng Jiāng). It's known throughout China for its cute canal towns, enchanting gardens and sophisticated opera and folk arts.

The charms of the province are so well known that it has attracted domestic tourists in large numbers since the 1990s, much earlier than most other places in the country. Package tourists flock to Sūzhōu anytime of the year, and you're likely to be rubbing elbows with them in the gardens or any of the famous water towns. But don't be put off. Kick-start your day early, go slightly off the main streets, and you'll see the old-world charm and have the place to yourself. In the provincial capital and university town of Nánjīng there's a lot that remains relatively undiscovered by outsiders: Ming-dynasty heritage, leafy parks and fantastic museums.

When to Go

Nánjīng

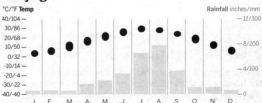

Mar & Apr Best time to visit the gardens when flowers bloom in early spring.	**Oct** Mist-shrouded vistas of gardens and canals in autumn.	**Dec** Snow-covered views of the pretty canal towns of Sūzhōu in winter.

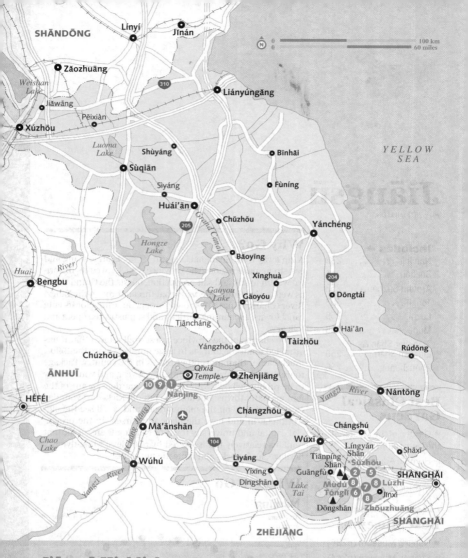

Jiāngsū Highlights

1 Get a grade A cultural fix at the **Nánjīng Museum** (p235)

2 Feast your eyes on the historical artefacts at **Sūzhōu Museum** (p244)

3 Indulge in the beauty of the **gardens of Sūzhōu** (p244)

4 Soak up the charms of yesteryear along Sūzhōu's **Píngjiāng Lù** (p248)

5 Enjoy tea-tasting and a traditional *pingtán* performance at Sūzhōu's **Pingtan Teahouse** (p252)

6 Lose yourself in the alleys and canals of **Tónglǐ** (p253)

7 Check out the fascinating **Chinese Sex Culture Museum** (p254)

8 Relax in the charming towns of **Lùzhí** (p255), **Mùdú** (p255) or **Zhōuzhuāng** (p256)

9 Get some highbrow culture at a **kūnqǔ opera performance** (p252)

10 Stroll around Nánjīng's scenic **Míng Xiàolíng Tomb** (p239)

History

Jiāngsū was a relative backwater until the Song dynasty (960–1279), when it emerged as an important commercial centre as trading routes were opened up by the Grand Canal. In particular, the south of the province flourished: the towns of Sūzhōu and Yángzhōu played an important role in silk production, overseen by a large mercantile class.

Prosperity continued through the Ming and Qing dynasties, and with the incursion of Westerners into China in the 1840s, southern Jiāngsū opened up to Western influence. During the catastrophic Taiping Rebellion (1851–64), the Taiping established Nánjīng as their quasi-Christian capital, naming it Tiānjīng (天京; Heavenly Capital).

Jiāngsū was also to play a strong political role in the 20th century when Nánjīng was established as the capital by the Nationalist Party until taken over by the communists in 1949, who moved the capital to Běijīng.

Today, proximity to Shànghǎi guarantees southern Jiāngsū a fast-growing economy and rapid development, although northern Jiāngsū still lags behind.

❶ Getting There & Around

Jiāngsū is well connected to all major cities in China. There are numerous flights daily from Nánjīng to points around the country, as well as frequent bus and train connections.

Jiāngsū has a comprehensive bus system that allows travellers to get around within the province without difficulty, but travelling by train is most straightforward.

Nánjīng   南京

▣ 025 / POP 6.5 MILLION

Many visitors only pass through Nánjīng (literally 'Southern Capital') when travelling from Shànghǎi to Běijīng (or vice versa), but the capital of Jiāngsū, lying on the lower stretches of the Yangzi River, boasts a surprisingly rich, impressive and extant historical heritage. The major attractions are the echoes of the city's brief, former glory as the nation's capital during its Ming-dynasty apogee and then as the capital of the Republic of China in the early years of the 20th century. A magnificent city wall still encloses most of the city, and elegant republican-era buildings dot the centre.

Nánjīng may sprawl today, but the atmosphere is both cultured and relaxed. This famous university town has wide, tree-lined boulevards, chic cafes and excellent museums, set in a beautiful landscape of lakes, forested parks and rivers. The city's pleasant *wutong* trees afford glorious shade on hot days and lend the city a leafy complexion, although summer temperatures are poleaxing.

History

During the Qin dynasty (221–207 BC), Nánjīng prospered as a major administrative centre. The city was razed during the Sui dynasty (AD 589–618) but later enjoyed some prosperity under the long-lived Tang dynasty, before slipping once more into obscurity.

In 1356 a peasant rebellion led by Zhu Yuanzhang against the Mongol Yuan dynasty was successful and in 1368 Nánjīng became capital under Zhu's Ming dynasty, but its glory was short-lived. In 1420 the third Ming emperor, Yongle, moved the capital back to Běijīng. From then on Nánjīng's fortunes variously rose and declined as a regional centre, but it wasn't until the 19th and 20th centuries that the city returned to the centre stage of Chinese history.

In the 19th century the Opium Wars brought the British to Nánjīng and it was here that the first of the 'unequal treaties' was signed, opening several Chinese ports to foreign trade, forcing China to pay a huge war indemnity, and officially ceding the island of Hong Kong to Britain. Just a few years later Nánjīng became the Taiping capital during the Taiping Rebellion, which succeeded in taking over most of southern China.

In 1864 the combined forces of the Qing army, the British army and various European and US mercenaries surrounded the city. They laid siege for seven months, before

---

PRICE INDICATORS

The following price indicators are used in this chapter:

Sleeping

$ less than ¥250

$$ ¥250 to ¥800

$$$ more than ¥800

Eating

$ less than ¥30

$$ ¥30 to ¥70

$$$ more than ¥70

Nánjīng

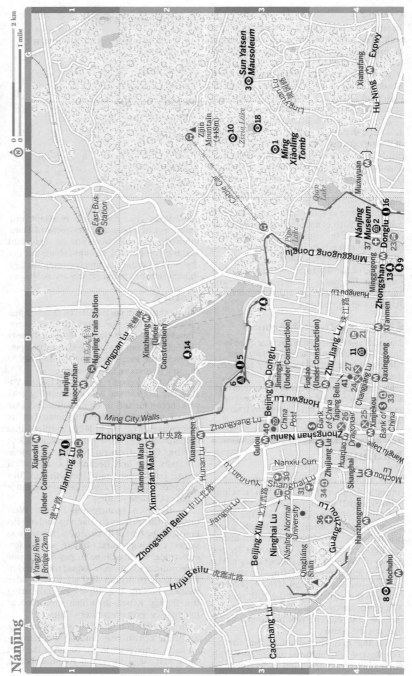

2 km
1 mile

Sun Yatsen
Mausoleum
3

Xiamafang
Hu-Ning Expwy

18
10
Zijin
Mountain
(448m)

1
Ming
Xiaoling Tomb

Muxuyuan

Cable Car

Quan Lake

Plpa Lake

Nánjīng Museum
37
2
16

East Bus
Station

Minggugong Donglu
Minggugong
Donglu 23
13
9

Xi'anmen

Longpan Lu 龙蟠路

Nanjing Train Station
南京火车站

Xinzhuang
(Under
Construction)

14

7

Huangpu Lu

Zhongshan

Daxinggong

Nanjing
Huochezhan
南京火车站

Ming City Walls

6
5

Donglu
Beijing
Jiming si
(Under Construction)

Fuqiao
(Under Construction)

Zhu Jiang Lu 珠江路

11

Changjiang Lu

Xinjiekou 33

Bank of
China

Xiaoshi

Jianning Lu
建宁路
(Under Construction)

17
39

Zhongyang Lu 中央路

Xuanwumen

Hunan Lu

Yunnan Lu

Gulou

China
Post

Zhongyang Lu

40

Zhongshan Nanlu

Bank
of China

Taiping Beilu

41 27

24
26
25

Huaqiao
Dragonair

Wangfu Dajie
Mochou Lu

Zhujiang Lu

Yangzi River
Bridge (2km)

Xinmofan Malu

Xinmofan Malu

Zhongshan Beilu 中山北路

Jiangsu Lu

Beijing Xilu 北京西路

Nanxiu Cun

Shanghai Lu

31

Ninghai Lu

Nanjing Normal
University

20

30

34

Shanghai
Lu

36

Guangzhou Lu 广州路

Hanzhongmen

Hujubeilu 虎踞北路

Qingliang Shan

Caochang Lu

Mochuhu
8

finally capturing it and slaughtering the Taiping defenders.

The Kuomintang made Nánjīng the capital of the Republic of China from 1928 to 1937. But in the face of advancing Japanese soldiers, the capital was moved to Chóngqìng in 1937. Nánjīng was again capital between 1945 and 1949, when the communists 'liberated' the city and made China their own.

⦿ Sights

◎ East Nánjīng

★ Nánjīng Museum   MUSEUM
(南京博物院, Nánjīng Bówùyuàn; 321 Zhongshan Donglu; 中山东路321号; ⊙9am-noon Mon, 9am-4pm Tue-Sun; Ⓜ Minggugong) FREE This fabulous museum had a massive and lavish expansion in 2013 with a brand new, dramatically modern exhibition block added next to its traditional, temple-style hall. All sleekly designed with lashings of marble and wood, alluring displays abound: from Jiāngsū landscape painting and ancient calligraphy (including sutra scrolls from Dūnhuáng) to sculpture (the Ming-dynasty carved wood Guanyin beneath the atrium is gorgeous) and much more. Look out for two magnificent Han-dynasty jade burial suits among treasures from a royal mausoleum.

On the 3rd floor, there's a spectacular selection of gold and copper Tibetan Buddha statues that belonged to the Qing emperors, as well as some extravagant clocks. Ceramics and Qing-dynasty furnishings round out a stunning collection. Several exhibition halls are temporary and will receive new collections down the line.

Ming Palace Ruins   PARK
(明故宫, Míng Gùgōng; Ⓜ Minggugong) The Ming Palace Ruins lie scattered around peaceful but maudlin Wǔcháomén Park (Wǔcháomén Gōngyuán; Zhongshan Donglu; ⊙6.30am-9.30pm) FREE. Built by Zhu Yuanzhang, the imperial palace was reportedly a magnificent structure and template for Běijīng's Forbidden City. Clamber atop the ruined Meridian Gate (Wǔ Mén), which once had huge walls jutting out at right angles from the main structure, along with watchtowers. Today the park is filled with locals practising ballroom dancing while saxophonists and other musicians gather in the resonant tunnels beneath the gate.

The ruins lend their name to the nearby metro station (Minggugong).

Nánjīng

Presidential Palace   HISTORIC BUILDING
(总统府, Zǒngtǒng Fǔ; 292 Changjiang Lu; 长江路 292号; admission ¥40; ⊙7.30am-5.30pm, to 6pm in summer; Ⓜ Daxinggong) After the Taiping took over Nánjīng, they built the **Mansion of the Heavenly King** (Tiānwáng Fǔ) on the foundations of a former Ming-dynasty palace. This magnificent palace did not survive the fall of the Taiping, but there is a reconstruction and a classical Ming garden, now known as the Presidential Palace. Other buildings on the site were used briefly as presidential offices by Sun Yatsen's government in 1912 and by the Kuomintang from 1927 to 1949.

⊙ **South Nánjīng**

Fūzǐ Temple   CONFUCIAN TEMPLE
(夫子庙, Fūzǐ Miào; Gongyuan Jie; admission ¥30; ⊙9am-10pm; Ⓜ Fuzimiao) The Confucian Fūzǐ Temple, in the south of the city in a pedestrian zone, was a centre of Confucian study

for more than 1500 years. But what you see here today are newly restored, late Qing-dynasty structures or wholly new buildings reconstructed in traditional style. Today the area surrounding Fūzǐ Temple has become Nánjīng's main shopping quarter and is particularly crowded. The whole area is lit up at night, adding to the kitsch ambience.

Tour boats (游船; *yóuchuán*) leave from the dock across from the temple itself for 30-minute day (¥60) and evening (¥80) trips along the Qínhuái River (秦淮河; Qínhuái Hé) between 9am and 10pm. From 2014, the area was due to be served by the Fuzimiao metro station on line 3.

**Imperial Examinations
History Museum**   MUSEUM
(江南贡院历史陈列馆, Jiāngnán Gòngyuàn Lìshǐ Chénlièguǎn; 1 Jinling Lu; admission ¥20; ⊙8.30am-10pm; Ⓜ Fuzimiao) Not far from the Fūzǐ Temple complex, this museum is a re-

cent reconstruction of the building where scholars once spent months – or years – in tiny cells studying Confucian classics in preparation for civil-service examinations. The exhibition provides valuable insights into the over-exacting culture of Confucian officialdom in dynastic China.

Taiping Heavenly Kingdom History Museum
MUSEUM
(太平天国历史博物馆, Tàipíng Tiānguó Lìshǐ Bówùguǎn; 128 Zhonghua Lu; 中华路128号; admission ¥30; ⊘8am-5pm; M Sanshan Jie) Hong Xiuquan, the Hakka leader of the Christian Taiping, had a palace built in Nánjīng (then named Tiānjīng or 'Heavenly Capital'), but the building was completely destroyed when Nánjīng was taken in 1864, after a long siege. This museum was originally a Ming-dynasty garden complex and housed Taiping officials. Displays of maps show the progress of the Taiping army, Taiping coins, weapons and texts that describe the radical Taiping laws on agrarian reform, social law and cultural policy.

West Nánjīng

Memorial Hall of the Nánjīng Massacre
MEMORIAL
(南京大屠杀纪念馆, Nánjīng Dàtúshā Jìniànguǎn; 418 Shuiximen Dajie; 水西门大街418号; ⊘8.30am-4.30pm Tue-Sun; M Yunjin Lu) FREE
In the city's southwestern suburbs, the unsettling exhibits in the Memorial Hall of the Nánjīng Massacre document the atrocities committed by Japanese soldiers against the civilian population during the occupation of Nánjīng in 1937. They include pictures of actual executions – many taken by Japanese army photographers – and a gruesome viewing hall built over a mass grave of massacre victims.

Detailed captions are in English, Japanese and Chinese, but the photographs, skeletons and displays tell their own haunting stories without words. At times it feels overwhelming but visitors might begin to fathom the link between the massacre and the identity of the city. Arrive early to beat the surge.

North Nánjīng

Jīmíng Temple
BUDDHIST TEMPLE
(鸡鸣寺; Jīmíng Sì; Jimingsi Lu; 鸡鸣寺路; admission ¥5; ⊘7.30am-5pm, to 5.30pm summer; M Jimingsi) Alongside the city's Ming walls and Xuánwǔ Lake (Xuánwǔ Hú) is Buddhist Jīmíng Temple, first built in AD 527 during the Three Kingdoms period and rebuilt many times since. The seven-storey-tall Yàoshīfó Pagoda (药师佛塔) offers views over Xuánwǔ Lake. Enter the base of the pagoda to the spectacle of hundreds of gold Buddha figures in cabinets. Walk up to the rear of the temple and out onto the city wall (admission ¥15; ⊘8am-4pm) for splendid jaunts along the overgrown ramparts (p238).

The temple also has a small shrine to the Indian monk and godfather to Shàolín boxing Bodhidharma (Damo), illustrated with a solitary shoe (p415). This temple is the most active in Nánjīng and is packed with worshippers during the Lunar New Year. By 2015 the temple will be served by its own namesake metro station (Jimingsi), on lines 3 and 4.

THE RAPE OF NÁNJĪNG

In 1937, with the Chinese army comparatively weak and underfunded and the Japanese army on the horizon, the invasion and occupation of Nánjīng appeared imminent. As it packed up and fled, the Chinese government encouraged the people of Nánjīng to stay, saying, 'all those who have blood and breath in them must feel that they wish to be broken as jade rather than remain whole as tile.' To reinforce this statement, the gates to the city were locked, trapping more than half a million citizens inside.

What followed in Nánjīng was six weeks of brutality to an extent unwitnessed in modern warfare. According to journalists and historians such as Iris Chang and Joshua Fogel, between 200,000 and 300,000 Chinese civilians were killed, either in group massacres or individual murders during Japan's occupation of Nánjīng. Within the first month, at least 20,000 women between the ages of 11 and 76 were raped. Women who attempted to refuse or children who interfered were often bayoneted or shot.

The Japanese, however, underestimated the Chinese. Instead of breaking the people's will, the invasion fuelled a sense of identity and determination. Those who did not die – broken as jade – survived to fight back.

Xuánwǔ Lake Park PARK
(玄武湖公园, Xuánwǔhú Gōngyuán; ⊗7am-9pm; Ⓜ Xuanwumen) FREE The vast lake within this lovely, verdant 530-hectare park – backing onto the towering city wall – is studded with five interconnected isles, scattered with bonsai gardens, camphor and cherry-blossom trees, temples and bamboo groves. The entire lake circuit is a whopping 9.5km jaunt. Alternatively, there are boat rides (¥70 per hour), pedalos (¥60 to ¥100 per hour) and buggy rides (¥12).

Yangzi River Bridge BRIDGE
(南京长江大桥, Nánjīng Chángjiāng Dàqiáo; ❒ 67, Ⓜ Shangyuanmen) Opened on 23 December 1968, the Yangzi River Bridge is one of the longest bridges in China – a double-decker with a 4.5km-long road on top and a train line below. Stirring socialist-realist sculptures can be seen on the approaches. Odds are that you'll cross the bridge if you take a train from the north. Probably the easiest way to get up on the bridge is to go through the Bridge Park (Dàqiáo Gōngyuán; Baotaqiao Dongjie, 宝塔桥东街; adult/child ¥12/10; ⊗7.30am-6.30pm; ❒ 67).

Catch bus 67 from Jiangsu Lu, northwest of the Drum Tower (鼓楼; Gǔlóu), to its terminus opposite the park. The nearest metro station will be Shangyuanmen, which was due to open in 2014.

MING CITY WALLS

Běijīng will be forever haunted by the 20th-century felling of its awe-inspiring city walls. Xī'ān's mighty Tang-dynasty wall – which was far, far larger than its current wall – is a mere memory. Even Shànghǎi's modest city wall came down in 1912.

The same story is repeated across China, but Nánjīng's fabulous surviving city wall is a constant reminder of the city's former glories. The wall may be overgrown, but this neglect – in a land where historical authenticity has too often courted destruction – has helped ensure its very survival.

The most absolute remnant of Nánjīng's Ming-dynasty apogee, the imposing five-storey Ming bastion, which measures over 35km, is the longest city wall ever built in the world. About two-thirds of it still stands.

Built between 1366 and 1393, by more than one million labourers, the layout of the wall is irregular, an exception to the usual square format of these times; it zigzags around Nánjīng's hills and rivers, accommodating the local landscape. Averaging 12m high and 7m wide at the top, the fortification was built of bricks supplied from five Chinese provinces. Each brick had stamped on it the place it came from, the overseer's name and rank, the brick maker's name and sometimes the date. This was to ensure that the bricks were well made; if they broke, they had to be replaced. Many of these stamps remain intact.

Some of the original 13 Ming city gates remain, including the Zhōngyāng Gate (中央门, Zhōngyāng Mén) in the north, Zhōngshān Gate (中山门; Zhōngshān Mén) in the east and Zhōnghuá Gate (中华门; Zhōnghuá Mén; admission ¥20; ⊗7am-9pm) in the south. The city gates were heavily fortified; built on the site of the old Tang-dynasty wall, Zhōnghuá Gate has four rows of gates, making it almost impregnable, and could house a garrison of 3000 soldiers in vaults in the front gate building. When walking through, observe the trough in either wall of the second gate, which held a vast stone gate that could be lowered into place. Horse ramps lead up the side to the wall and also note how the roads immediately north of the gate follow the circular line of the now missing enceinte (瓮城; wèngchéng), a further fortification.

You can climb onto the masonry for exploration at several points. Long walks extend along the wall from Zhōngshān Gate in the east of the city and it's quite common to see locals walking their dogs or taking post-dinner walks along the weathered path; there is no charge for climbing the wall here.

One of the best places to access the wall is from the rear of Jīmíng Temple (p237). Walk to Jiǔhuáshān Park off Taiping Beilu, looking out over huge Xuánwǔ Lake Park (玄武湖公园) and passing crumbling hillside pagodas along the way. Another access point is at Jiěfàng Gate (解放门; Jiěfàng Mén; admission ¥15; ⊗8.30am-6pm winter, 8am-6pm summer).

Zǐjīn Mountain　　　　紫金山

Dominating the eastern fringes of Nánjīng is Zǐjīn Mountain (紫金山; Zǐjīn Shān), or 'Purple-Gold Mountain', a heavily forested area of parks, and the site of most of Nánjīng's historical attractions – Sun Yatsen Mausoleum, Míng Xiàolíng Tomb, Línggǔ Temple Scenic Area, Plum Blossom Hill and the Botanic Gardens (植物园; Zhíwù Yuán). It's one of the coolest places to flee the steamy summer heat. Give yourself a day to explore it properly; discounts exist if tickets to various sights are purchased together.

★ Míng Xiàolíng Tomb　　　　TOMB

(明孝陵, Míng Xiàolíng; admission ¥70; ⏱8am-5.30pm, to 6.30pm summer; 🚍Y3, Ⓜ Muxuyuan) Zhu Yuanzhang (1328–98), the founding emperor of the Ming dynasty, was buried in the tomb of Míng Xiàolíng; he was the only Ming emperor buried outside Běijīng. The area surrounding the tomb is the Míng Xiàolíng Scenic Area (明孝陵风景区; Míng Xiàolíng Fēngjǐngqū). Near the entrance, Plum Blossom Hill (梅花山; Méihuā Shān) is delightfully garlanded with flowering plum blossoms in spring. A tree-lined pathway winds around pavilions and picnic grounds and ends at scenic Zǐxiá Lake (紫霞湖; Zǐxiá Hú; admission ¥10; ⏱6.30am-6pm), ideal for strolling.

The first section of this magnificent mausoleum is a 618m 'spirit path', lined with stone statues of lions, camels, elephants and horses that drive away evil spirits and guard the tomb. Among them lurks two mythical animals: a *xiè zhì*, which has a mane and a single horn on its head, and a *qílín*, which has a scaly body, a cow's tail, deer's hooves and one horn.

As you enter the first courtyard, a paved pathway leads to a pavilion housing several stelae. The next gate leads to a large courtyard with the Línghún Pagoda (Línghún Tǎ), a mammoth rectangular stone structure. Follow the crowds through a long uphill tunnel to a wall (which children and visitors clamber up!) and a huge earth tumulus (called the Soul Tower; 明楼; Mínglóu), beneath which is the unexcavated tomb vault of the emperor. On the wall are inscribed the characters '此山明太祖之墓' ('This hill is the tomb of the first Ming emperor').

A combo ticket for the tomb and the Línggǔ Temple Scenic Area is ¥100.

From Muxuyuan metro station (line 2), it's a 1.6km walk uphill. Bus Y3 from the city centre also takes you here.

★ Sun Yatsen Mausoleum　　　　MEMORIAL

(中山陵, Zhōngshān Líng; ⏱6.30am-6.30pm; 🚍9, Y1, Y2, Y3, Ⓜ Xiamafang) An astonishing sight, Sun Yatsen's tomb lies at the top of an enormous stone stairway – a breathless 392 steps. Reverentially referred to as *guófù* (国父; 'Father of the Nation'), Dr Sun is esteemed by both communists and Kuomintang. He died in Běijīng in 1925, and had wished to be buried in Nánjīng, no doubt with far less pomp than the Ming-style tomb his successors built for him. Within a year of his death, however, construction of this mausoleum began.

At the start of the path stands a dignified marble gateway, with a roof of blue-glazed tiles. The blue and white of the mausoleum symbolise the white sun on the blue background of the Kuomintang flag.

The crypt lies at the top of the steps at the rear of the memorial chamber. A tablet hanging across the threshold is inscribed with the 'Three Principles of the People', as formulated by Dr Sun: nationalism, democracy and people's livelihood. Inside is a statue of a seated Dr Sun. The walls are carved with the complete text of the 'Outline of Principles for the Establishment of the Nation' put forward by the Nationalist government. A prostrate marble statue of Dr Sun seals his copper coffin.

Buses 9, Y1, Y2 or Y3 go from the city centre to the Sun Yatsen Mausoleum. A shuttle bus (¥5) resembling a red steam train speeds from here to the Línggǔ Temple Scenic Area.

★ Línggǔ Temple Scenic Area　　　　BUDDHIST TEMPLE

(灵谷寺风景区, Línggǔ Sì Fēngjǐng Qū; admission ¥80; ⏱7am-6.30pm; 🚍Y2, Y3, Ⓜ Zhonglingjie) The large Ming Línggǔ Temple complex contains one of the most significant buildings in Nánjīng – the Beamless Hall (无梁殿; Wúliáng Diàn), built in 1381 entirely out of brick and stone and containing no beam supports. Buildings during the Ming dynasty were normally constructed of wood, but timber shortages meant that builders had to rely on brick. The structure has a vaulted ceiling and a large stone platform where Buddhist statues once sat.

A road runs on both sides of the hall and up two flights of steps to the graceful Pine Wind Pavilion (松风阁; Sōngfēng Gé), originally dedicated to Guanyin as part of Línggǔ Temple. The ochre-walled temple is home to the Dàbiàn Juétáng (大遍觉堂) memorial hall, dedicated to Xuan Zang (the Buddhist monk who travelled to India and brought back the Buddhist scriptures). Inside the memorial hall is a statue of the travelling monk, pen aloft, with a cabinet containing a golden model of a pagoda with part of Xuan Zang's skull within it. To his right is a model wooden pagoda, also within a cabinet.

Uphill to the rear of the temple is the colourful **Línggǔ Pagoda** (灵谷塔; Línggǔ Tǎ). This nine-storey, 60m-high, octagonal pagoda was finished in 1933 under the direction of a US architect, to remember those who died during the Kuomintang revolution. A vegetarian restaurant can be found nearby. Tour buses Y2 and Y3 run to the Línggǔ Temple from Nánjīng Train Station. Alternatively, take the metro to Zhonglingjie station, then hop on tour bus Y2 from a stop a short walk west. Bright red shuttle buses (¥5) resembling steam trains regularly connect the area to the Sun Yatsen Mausoleum.

★✦ Festivals & Events

Nánjīng International Plum Blossom Festival   CULTURAL
(梅花节, Méihuā Jié) Held yearly from the last Saturday of February to early March, this festival takes place on Plum Blossom Hill near the Míng Xiàolíng Tomb when the mountain bursts with pink and white blossoms.

🛏 Sleeping

Most of Nánjīng's accommodation is mid-range to top end in price. All rooms have broadband internet, and most places can help to book air and train tickets.

★ Nánjīng Time International Youth Hostel   HOSTEL $
(南京时光国际青年旅舍, Nánjīng Shíguāng Guójì Qīngnián Lǚshè; ☎ 8556 9053; www.yhachina.com; 6-5 Yongyuan, Méiyuán Xīncūn, 梅园新村雍园6-5号; dm ¥60, r ¥180-220; ❋ @; Ⓜ Xi'anmen) Time – for atmosphere alone it's the best in town – is in a republican-era mansion not far from the Presidential Palace. The salubrious neighbourhood guarantees you a good sleep at night. Dorms are spotless and the rooms have a simplistic charm. There's a lot of common area, including a relaxing rooftop terrace.

The hostel is hidden in an alley with lots of twists and turns in the Méiyuán Xīncūn district. Download a map from the hostel website for directions.

Nanjing Jasmine Youth Hostel   HOSTEL $
(南京国际青年旅社, Nánjīng Guójì Qīngnián Lǚshè; ☎ 8330 0517; 7 Hequnxincun, off Shanghai Lu; 上海路合群新村7号; dm ¥50-60, r ¥115-238; ❋ @ 🛜; ▢ 13, Ⓜ Zhujiang Lu) Staff are morose at this hostel, but the secluded location is good albeit a bit stranded for sightseers, tucked away down an alley off bar-strewn Shanghai Lu. From Nánjīng Train Station, take bus 13 to the Wǔtáishān Běizhàn (五台山北站) stop on Shanghai Lu and it's a few minutes walk west from there.

Orange Hotel (Dashiba)   HOTEL $$
(桔子酒店, Júzi Jiǔdiàn; ☎ 8696 8090; www.orangehotel.com.cn; 26 Dashiba Jie, 大石坝街26号; r ¥328-358; ❋ @) In a great riverside location, this reliable chain is big bang for the buck. The ultra-modern rooms, with good bedding and lighting, have every gizmo and gadget your computer, tablet or mobile phone might ever need. It's worth paying a bit extra for the rooms with river-facing balconies. Other pluses include complimentary fruit and free use of the hotel's bikes.

There's another handy branch right next to the old gate of Donghuamen in the east of town.

Orange Hotel (Donghuamen)   HOTEL $$
(桔子酒店, Júzi Jiǔdiàn; ☎ 6608 1122; 532-1 Zhongshan Donglu; 中山东路532-1号; r from ¥308; Ⓜ Minggugong) Handy branch of Orange Hotel right next to the old gate of Donghuamen and east of the Ming Palace Ruins on Zhongshan Donglu. Rooms are spick and span and the whole hotel presentation is stylish and cool. Free bike use for two hours. Breakfast is ¥15 per person.

★ Hilton Hotel   HOTEL $$$
(南京万达希尔顿酒店 Nánjīng Wàndá Xī'ěrdùn Jiǔdiàn; www3.hilton.com; 100 Jiangdong Zhonglu; 江东中路100号; d/ste ¥1209/2300; ❋ 🛜 ☎; Ⓜ Jiqingmen) This sleekly polished hotel, opening to a gargantuan marbled lobby with a huge calligraphic dedication and a vast and stylised depiction of Zǐjīn Mountain behind reception, is the town's best choice. Rooms are spacious and modern, there are three restaurants and service is tip-top. It's slightly out of the action in the southwest of town, but the metro is nearby.

Cheaper rooms are on the lower floors (beneath level 18).

✖ Eating

Main eating quarters include the Fūzǐ Temple complex and Shīziqiáo (狮子桥) off Hunan Lu, where you can find snack stands and small eateries. Near the Presidential Palace, **Nánjīng 1912** (cnr Taiping Beilu & Changjiang Lu; M Daxinggong) is a compound of shiny neon-lit bars, coffee houses and upscale chain restaurants. In the summer swelter, look no further than **Coco** (branches everywhere) for bubble tea (from ¥7).

★**Dàpái Dàng** JIĀNGSŪ $
(大牌档; 3rd fl, Deji Plaza, 18 Zhongshan Lu; 中山路18号德基广场3楼; mains from ¥16; ⊗11am-10.30pm; M Xinjiekou) This hectic and vast place, decorated like a Qing-dynasty eatery, with waiters scurrying around in period garb and lanterns hanging overhead, is deservedly packed out. There's a handy photo menu for ordering fried dumplings with pork, leek and mushroom (¥12 for three), sliced fish soup with preserved vegetables (¥46), Nánjīng fried noodles (¥16) and oodles of other tasty local dishes.

With eight branches in town, it's a big name in Nánjīng, but if you arrive during a busy period (such as weekends), you'll have to grab a ticket and wait in line.

Cafe 85°C CAFE $
(85度C咖啡店; Bāwǔdù C kāfēidiàn; 35 Taiping Beilu; coffee ¥10; ⊗9am-9pm; M Daxinggong) For cheap coffee, milk tea, bread and cakes on the go, come to this popular Taiwanese chain.

★**Element Fresh** CAFE $$
(新元素; Xīnyuánsù; www.elementfresh.com; 1st fl, IST Mall, 100 Zhongshan Nanlu; 中山南路100号艾尚天地1楼; mains from ¥48; ⊗11am-10.30pm Mon-Thu, 11am-11pm Fri, 9am-11pm Sat & Sun; 🛜; M Xinjiekou) This two-floor breath of fresh air in the trendy IST Mall gives the iffy Nánjīng cafe culture a good kick in the pants. Everything, from the delectable smoothies to the painted tea-candle shades, sleek design and snappy staff, is an unalloyed joy. There's homemade hummus (¥68), Laotian lettuce wraps (¥55), sandwiches, pasta, Asian classics and much more on the crisp, international menu.

Wagas CAFE $$
(沃歌斯; Wògēsī; A108, IST Mall, 100 Zhongshan Nanlu; 中山南路100号艾尚天地A108室; mains from ¥48; ⊗10am-10pm Mon-Fri, 8am-10pm Sat & Sun; 🛜; M Xinjiekou) With a trendy concrete floor

and attracting a similar tablet-toting crowd to Element Fresh next door, this branch of the hip Shànghǎi cafe can load you up with coffee, cakes, salads, smoothies, pasta and specials (chalked up on the wall).

Taj Mahal INDIAN $$
(cnr Moling Lu & Fengfu Lu; mains from ¥40; ⊗10.30am-3pm & 5-10.30pm; M Zhangfu Yuan) The Taj Mahal doesn't quite pull off its stab at a classy ambience (linen tablecloths), but the menu's a winner. The spiciness of the mutton vindaloo may be slightly moderated to suit lightweight local palates, but it's still delicious. Also on the menu are samosas (¥24), onion bhajia (¥26), seekh kebab (¥48), chicken tikka (¥45), naan (¥13) and a host of other choices.

Sculpting in Time WESTERN, CAFE $$
(雕刻时光; Diāokè Shíguāng; 32 Dashiba Jie; 大石坝街32号; mains ¥50; ⊗9am-11pm; M Fuzimiao) This charming and seriously spacious cafe is an appealing, relaxed spot with an outdoor terrace overlooking the river. With birdcage lampshades, soft music, cream curtains and comfy chairs, it's a favourite eating and drinking place for a cool but unpretentious crowd. The pastries and cakes make a good afternoon treat.

🍸 Drinking & Nightlife

Western-style drinking holes and sports bars congregate along Shanghai Lu.

★**Brewsell's** BAR
(www.brewsells.com; 77-1 Shanghai Lu; beers from ¥28; ⊗5pm-2am; M Zhujiang Lu) With well-priced Vedett (¥28) and La Chouffe on tap, Trappistes Rochefort, blue/red Chimay and other Belgian brews cooling down in the fridge, this small, specialist imported beer bar (named after 'Brussels') has expat ale fiends descending in droves for fine beer and table football. Free Belgian fries all night Saturday and offers other nights.

Nánjīng Time International Youth Hostel BAR
(南京时光国际青年旅舍; Nánjīng Shíguāng Guójì Qīngnián Lǚshè; 6-5 Yongyuan, Méiyuán Xīncūn, 梅园新村雍园6-5号; M Xi'anmen) Although primarily a hostel, the Nánjīng Time International Youth Hostel is also a charming choice for a beer, with sofas strewn with throws, small wooden tables, soft lighting, goldfish in bowls, potted plants and relaxing music.

Behind the Wall
BAR

(答案, Dá'àn; www.behindthewall-nanjing.com; 150 Shanghai Lu; pint ¥30; ☺6pm-1am; 🛜; ⓂGulou) Doubling as a Mexican restaurant, this atmospheric and time-worn bar divides into many beer-stained rooms, with a terrace for warmer months. There's draught beer, sangria and hypnotising live flamenco guitar performances in the evenings from a talented musician. It's literally 'behind the wall'.

Words Bar
BAR

(www.facebook.com/thewordsbar; 6-6 Yongyuan, Méiyuán Xīncūn; 梅园新村雍园6-6号; ☺7.30pm-3am; ⓂXi'anmen) Run by a Chinese-French two-man team, this colourful bar alongside the Nánjīng Time International Youth Hostel (p240) pairs a secluded location with a literary bent that fosters poetry nights, book readings, word games and other cultured pursuits.

☆ Entertainment

Lányuàn Theatre
CHINESE OPERA

(兰苑剧场, Lányuàn Jùchǎng; ☎8446 9284; 4 Cháotiāngong; ⓂShanghai Lu) *Kūnqǔ*, an extant form of Chinese opera originating from Jiāngsū, is staged here every Saturday evening. There are English subtitles and tickets are ¥80.

🛍 Shopping

The pedestrian area around **Fūzǐ Temple** has souvenirs, clothing, shoes and antiques for sale.

★ Librairie Avant-Garde
BOOKS

(先锋书店, Xiānfēng Shūdiàn; 173 Guangzhou Lu; ☺10am-9.30pm; ⓂShanghai Lu) Housed in a vast and disused bomb shelter, this astonishing indie bookshop has very few foreign-language books, but the underground ambience makes it a must for bibliophiles. With miles of books and a cavernous concrete floor, it's a Nánjīng cultural landmark, loved by students and literati for its sizeable collection of social science and humanities books. The shop also has a fine selection of postcards and handmade accessories, as well as a pleasant cafe and plenty of comfortable seating areas. Note the dominating black (Christian) cross as you go up the ramp. It's a 15-minute walk from Shanghai Lu metro station.

Foreign Languages Bookstore
BOOKS

(外文书店, Wàiwén Shūdiàn; 218 Zhongshan Donglu; ☺9am-7pm Mon-Thu, 9am-8pm Fri & Sat; ⓂD-axinggong) Novels are on the 2nd floor, where there's also a cafe.

ℹ Information

INTERNET RESOURCES

Nanjing Expats (www.nanjingexpat.com) Handy expat listings website.

MEDIA

Nanjing Expats (www.nanjingexpat.com) and **Map** (www.mapmagazine.com.cn) are handy expat listings magazines, available at restaurants and bars.

MEDICAL SERVICES

Jiāngsū People's Hospital (江苏省人民医院, Jiāngsū Shěng Rénmín Yīyuàn; ☎8371 8836; 300 Guangzhou Lu; ☺8am-noon & 2-5.30pm) Runs a clinic for expats and has English-speaking doctors available.

Nánjīng International SOS Clinic (南京国际 SOS 紧急救援诊所, Nánjīng Guójì SOS Jǐnjí Jiùyuán Zhěnsuǒ; ☎8480 2842, 24hr alarm centre 010 6462 9100; www.internationalsos. com.cn; Ground fl, Grand Metropark Hotel, 319 Zhongshan Donglu; ⓂMinggugong).

MONEY

Most bank ATMs are open 24 hours and take international cards. The banks listed below change major currency and travellers cheques.

Bank of China (中国银行, Zhōngguó Yínháng; 29 Hongwu Lu; ☺8am-5pm Mon-Fri, to 12.30pm Sat; ⓂXinjiekou) Handily located branch in the centre of town.

Bank of China (中国银行, Zhōngguó Yínháng; 3 Zhongshan Donglu; ☺8am-5pm Mon-Fri, to 12.30pm Sat; ⓂXinjiekou) Centrally located.

POST

China Post (中国邮政, Zhōngguó Yóuzhèng; 2 Zhongshan Nanlu; ☺8am-6.30pm; ⓂGulou) Postal services and international phone calls.

PUBLIC SECURITY BUREAU

Exit & Entry Administration Service Center (公安局出入境接待大厅, Gōng'ānjú Chūrùjìng Jiēdài Dàtīng; ☎8442 0018; cnr Fengfu Lu & Honggongci; ☺8.30am-5.30pm Mon-Fri, 9am-5pm Sat, 9am-noon & 2-5pm Sun; ⓂZhangfu Yuan)

TRAVEL AGENCIES

Most hotels have their own travel agencies and can book tickets for a service charge.

ℹ Getting There & Away

AIR

Nánjīng has regular air connections to all major Chinese cities. The main office for the **Civil Aviation Administration of China** (CAAC, 中国民航,

Zhōngguó Mínháng; ☑ 8449 9378; 50 Ruijin Lu) is near the terminus of bus 37, but you can also buy tickets at most top-end hotels.

Dragonair (港龙航空, Gǎnglóng Hángkōng; ☑ 8471 0181; Room 751-53, World Trade Centre, 2 Hanzhong Lu) has daily flights to Hong Kong.

BUS

Of Nánjīng's numerous long-distance bus stations, **Nánjīng Long-Distance Bus Station** (南京中央门长途汽车站; Nánjīng Zhōngyāng Chángtú Qìchēzhàn; ☑ 8533 1288; 1 Jianning Lu; 建宁路1号), aka Zhōngyángmén long-distance station, is the largest, located southwest of the wide-bridged intersection with Zhongyang Lu. Regular buses departing from here:

Hángzhōu ¥120, four hours

Héféi ¥53, 2½ hours

Shànghǎi ¥68, four hours

Sūzhōu ¥70, 2½ hours

Wúxī ¥57, two hours

Buses departing the **East Bus Station** (长途汽车东站; chángtú qìchē dōngzhàn):

Yángzhōu ¥38 1½ hours

Zhènjiāng ¥20, 1½ hours

From Nánjīng Train Station, take bus 13 north to Zhōngyángmén long-distance bus station. Bus 2 from Xīnjiēkǒu goes to the East Bus Station. A taxi from town will cost ¥20 to ¥25 to either station.

TRAIN

Nánjīng Train Station (☑ 8582 2222) is a major stop on the Běijīng–Shànghǎi train line. Heading eastward from Nánjīng, the line to Shànghǎi connects with Zhènjiāng, Wúxī and Sūzhōu. Many G and D trains depart or terminate at the **Nánjīng South Train Station** (南京南站; Nánjīng Nánzhàn), so check when you buy your ticket. G trains to Běijīng all depart from Nánjīng South Train Station.

Trains from Nánjīng Train Station in the north of town include:

Huángshān (Túnxī) hard/soft sleeper ¥108/159, six to eight hours, seven daily

Shànghǎi G train (main train station, Hongqiao and Shànghǎi), 2nd/1st class ¥140/220, 1½ to two hours, regular

Sūzhōu G train, 2nd/1st class ¥100/160, 80 minutes, regular

Yángzhōu hard/soft seat ¥17/28, 80 minutes, seven daily

Xī'ān North D train, 2nd-class seat/soft sleeper ¥279/685, eight hours, one daily (12.35am)

Trains leaving from Nánjīng South Train Station include:

Běijīng South G train, 2nd/1st class ¥444/749, 4½ hours, regular

Hángzhōu East 2nd/1st class ¥118/198, 1½ to two hours, regular

Xiàmén North D train, 2nd/1st class ¥360/484, nine to 11 hours, three daily

Try to get tickets via your hotel or at the **train ticket office** (火车票售票处, huǒchēpiào shòupiàochù; 2 Zhongshan Nanlu; ⊘ 8.30am-5pm) on the 3rd floor of the post office, or the **train ticket office** (35 Taiping Beilu; ⊘ 8am-11am & noon-5pm) on Taiping Beilu.

ⓘ Getting Around

TO/FROM THE AIRPORT

Buses (¥20; 90 mins) run to Nánjīng's Lùkǒu airport every 20 minutes between 5.40am and 9pm from the square east of Nánjīng Train Station. Most hotels have hourly shuttle buses to and from the airport. A taxi will cost around ¥130. From 2015, the S1 Airport Line express rail link will connect the airport with Nánjīng South Train Station (on Line 1).

PUBLIC TRANSPORT

Nánjīng has an efficient **metro system** that cuts through the city centre. Line 1 runs north–south and links both train stations. Line 2 goes east from Jīngtiānlù to Yóufāngqiáo in the west. Line 10 opened in 2014, connecting Andemen to Yushan Lu, and the new Airport Line is due to start running in 2015. Four other lines are under construction, also expected to commence service by 2015. Tickets are ¥2 to ¥5.

You can get to Xīnjiēkǒu, in the heart of town, by jumping on bus 13 from Nánjīng Train Station or from Zhōngyáng Gate. There are also tourist bus routes that visit many of the sights:

Bus Y1 Goes from Nánjīng Train Station and Nánjīng Long-Distance Bus Station through the city to the Sun Yatsen Mausoleum.

Bus Y2 Starts in the south at the Martyrs' Cemetery (烈士墓地; Lièshì Mùdì), passes Fūzǐ Temple and terminates halfway up Zǐjīn Mountain.

Bus Y3 Passes by Nánjīng Train Station en route to the Míng Xiàolíng Tomb and Línggǔ Temple.

Many local maps contain bus routes. Normal buses cost ¥1 and tourist buses cost ¥2.

TAXI

Taxi flagfall is ¥9 and it's ¥2.40 for each 3km thereafter. Trips to most destinations in the city are ¥10 to ¥14. Taxis are easy to flag down anywhere in the city; look out for spacious London-style cabs.

Around Nánjīng

Qīxiá Temple   BUDDHIST TEMPLE
(栖霞寺, Qīxiá Sì; admission Jan-Sep ¥25, Oct-Dec ¥40; ⊘7am-5.30pm) This temple on Qīxiá Mountain, 22km northeast of Nánjīng, was founded by the Buddhist monk Ming Seng-shao during the Southern Qi dynasty, and remains an active place of worship. Long one of China's most important monasteries, even today it's still one of its largest Buddhist seminaries. Relics believed to be part of the skull of Gautama Buddha were unveiled and interred here. The mountain's maple trees are a major draw in spring when the hills are splashed in crimson and bronze.

There are two main temple halls: the Maitreya Hall, with a statue of the Maitreya Buddha sitting cross-legged at the entrance, and the Vairocana Hall, housing a 5m-tall statue of the Vairocana Buddha.

Behind Qīxiá Temple is the Thousand Buddha Cliff (Qiānfó Yá). Several grottoes housing stone statues are carved into the hillside, the earliest of which dates as far back as the Qi dynasty (AD 479–502). There is also a small stone pagoda, Shělì Pagoda (舍利, Shělì Tǎ), which was built in AD 601 and rebuilt during the late Tang period. The upper part has engraved sutras and carvings of Buddha; around the base, each of the pagoda's eight sides depicts Sakyamuni.

Continue northwards to admire lovely views in the scenic area behind the temple. The steep path meanders via an array of pavilions and rocky outcrops: it's serene, so consider bringing lunch and spending time here.

Get to the temple from Nánjīng by public bus (南上, Nán Shàng, ¥2.50, one hour) from a stop by Nánjīng Train Station. When you get off the bus, you will be approached by motorcycle taxis that will offer to take you into the temple the 'back' way for ¥10. Be warned, it's an arduous hike up and down a large hill to the temple if you do this.

Sūzhōu   苏州

📂 0512 / POP 1.3 MILLION

Historically, Sūzhōu was synonymous with high culture and elegance, and generations of artists, scholars, writers and high society in China were drawn by its exquisite art forms and the delicate beauty of its gardens. Like all modern Chinese towns, Sūzhōu has unfortunately had to contend with the recent destruction of its heritage and its replacement with largely arbitrary chunks of modern architecture.

Having said that, the city still retains enough pockets of charm to warrant two to three days' exploration on foot or by bike. And the gardens, Sūzhōu's main attraction, are a symphonic combination of rocks, water, trees and pavilions that reflects the Chinese appreciation of balance and harmony. Adding to the charm are some excellent museums, surviving canal scenes, pagodas and humpbacked bridges (but don't expect much peace and quiet).

History

Dating back some 2500 years, Sūzhōu is one of the oldest towns in the Yangzi Basin. With the completion of the Grand Canal during the Sui dynasty, Sūzhōu began to flourish as a centre of shipping and grain storage, bustling with merchants and artisans.

By the 14th century, Sūzhōu had become China's leading silk-producing city. Aristocrats, pleasure seekers, famous scholars, actors and painters arrived, constructing villas and garden retreats.

The town's winning image as a 'Garden City' or a 'Venice of the East' drew from its medieval blend of woodblock guilds and embroidery societies, whitewashed housing, cobbled streets, tree-lined avenues and canals. The local women were considered the most beautiful in China, largely thanks to the mellifluous local accent, and the city was home to a variety of rich merchants and bookish scholars...no doubt drawn by the beautiful women.

In 1860 Taiping troops took the town without a blow and in 1896 Sūzhōu was opened to foreign trade, with Japanese and other international concessions. Since 1949 much of the historic city, including its city walls, has vanished.

◉ Sights

High-season prices listed apply from March to early May and September to October. Gardens and museums stop selling tickets 30 minutes before closing, and are best visited early in the mornings before crowds arrive. The gardens were not designed for tour groups, so don't expect too much zen-like tranquillity.

★ **Sūzhōu Museum**   MUSEUM
(苏州博物馆, Sūzhōu Bówùguǎn; 204 Dongbei Jie; 东北街204号; audioguides ¥30; ⊘9am-5pm; 🚇Y5) **FREE** An architectural triumph, this

THE GRAND CANAL

The world's longest canal, the Grand Canal (大运河; Dàyùnhé) once meandered for almost 1800km from Běijīng to Hángzhōu, and is a striking example of China's engineering prowess. Sections of the canal have been silted up for centuries and today perhaps half of it remains seasonally navigable.

The Grand Canal's construction spanned many centuries. The first 85km were completed in 495 BC, but the mammoth task of linking the Yellow River (Huáng Hé) and the Yangzi River (Cháng Jiāng) was undertaken between AD 605 and 609 by a massive conscripted labour force during Sui times. It was developed again during the Yuan dynasty (1271–1368). The canal enabled the government to capitalise on the growing wealth of the Yellow River Basin and to ship supplies from south to north.

The Jiāngnán section of the canal (Hángzhōu, Sūzhōu, Wúxī and Chángzhōu) is a skein of canals, rivers and branching lakes. There are boat rides along certain sections of the canal in Sūzhōu (p249) – with all the surrounding modernity, though, the grandness of the project seems to have all but faded.

IM Pei–designed museum is a modern interpretation of a Sūzhōu garden, a confluence of water, bamboo and clinical geometry. Inside is a fascinating array of jade, ceramics, wooden carvings, textiles and other displays, all with good English captions. Look out for the boxwood statue of Avalokiteshvara (Guanyin), dating from the republican period. No flip-flops.

Humble Administrator's Garden   GARDENS

(拙政园, Zhuōzhèng Yuán; 178 Dongbei Jie; 东北街178号; high/low season ¥70/50, audioguides free; ⏰ 7.30am-5.30pm) First built in 1509, this 5.2-hectare garden is clustered with water features, a museum, a teahouse and at least 10 pavilions such as 'the listening to the sound of rain' and 'the faraway looking' pavilions – hardly humble, we know. The largest of the gardens, it's often considered to be the most impressive. With zigzagging bridges, pavilions, bamboo groves and fragrant lotus ponds, it should be an ideal place for a leisurely stroll, but you'll be battling crowds for right of way.

North Temple Pagoda   PAGODA

(北寺塔, Běisì Tǎ; 1918 Renmin Lu; 人民路1918号; admission ¥25; ⏰ 7.45am-5pm) The tallest pagoda south of the Yangzi, the nine-storey North Temple Pagoda dominates the northern end of Renmin Lu. Part of Bào'ēn Temple (报恩寺; Bào'ēn Sì), you can climb the pagoda (塔; tǎ) for sweeping views of hazy modern-day Sūzhōu.

The complex goes back 1700 years and was originally a residence; the current reincarnation dates to the 17th century. Off to one side is Nánmù Guānyīn Hall (楠木观音殿; Nánmù Guānyīn Diàn), which was rebuilt in the Ming dynasty with some features imported from elsewhere.

The Chinese plaque outside the hall intones '一塵不染' ('spotless'), revealing Guanyin's state of unblemished purity. At the rear is a thoughtfully composed garden and rockery, with a teahouse. Within the temple compound is also the rather unusual Seven Buddha Hall.

Sūzhōu Silk Museum   MUSEUM

(苏州丝绸博物馆, Sūzhōu Sīchóu Bówùguǎn; 2001 Renmin Lu; 人民路2001号; ⏰ 9am-5pm; Ⓜ Sūzhōu Train Station) FREE By the 13th century Sūzhōu was the place for silk production and weaving, and the Sūzhōu Silk Museum houses fascinating exhibitions detailing the history of Sūzhōu's 4000-year-old silk industry. Exhibits include a section on silk-weaving techniques and silk fashion through the dynasties, and you can amble among mulberry shrubs outdoors. You can also see functioning looms and staff at work on, say, a large brocade.

Sūzhōu Art Museum   MUSEUM

(苏州美术馆 Sūzhōu Měishùguǎn; 2075 Renmin Lu; 人民路2075号; ⏰ 9am-5pm Tue-Sun; Ⓜ Sūzhōu Train Station) FREE There's a dazzling use of daylight and design in this brand new museum, creating a seemingly infinite white space hung with contemporary landscapes, calligraphy and modern art. The interior composition includes a lovely courtyard, sprouting bamboo. It's an element of a large complex that also includes the Sūzhōu Cultural Center and a theatre.

Sūzhōu

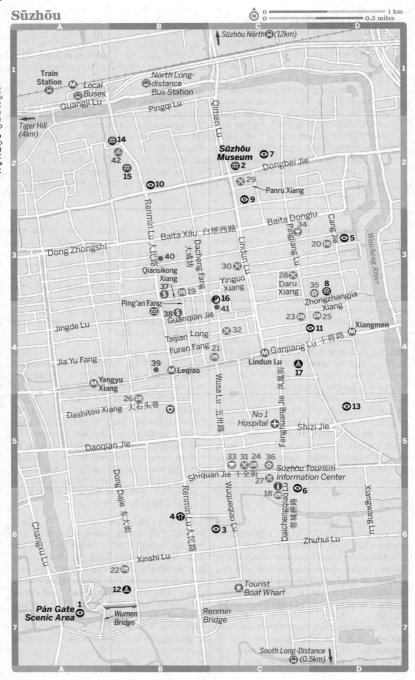

0 ———————— 1 km
0 ———————— 0.5 miles

Sūzhōu North (12km)

Train Station
Local Buses
Guangji Lu

North Long-distance Bus Station

Pingqi Lu

Qimen Lu

Tiger Hill (4km)

14
42
15

10

Sūzhōu Museum 2

7

Dongbei Jie

29
Panru Xiang

9

Baita Donglu
34

Cang Jie
20   5

Renmin Lu 人民路

Dong Zhongshi

Baita Xilu 白塔西路

Dacheng Fang 大成坊

Lindun Lu

Pingjiang Lu

Watcheng River

40
Qiaosikong Xiang
37   19
Ping'an Fang
38   Guanqian Jie

30

Yinguo Xiang

16
41

28
Daru Xiang

35   8

Zhongzhangjia Xiang

23   25

Jingde Lu

Jia Yu Fang

Taijian Long
Furen Fang

32

21

11   Xiangmen

Ganjiang Lu 干将路

39   Leqiao
Yangyu Xiang

Lindun Lu
17

Dashitou Xiang 大石头巷

26

Wusa Lu 五井路

No 1 Hospital
Shizi Jie

13

Daoqian Jie

Shiquan Jie 十全街

33 31 24 36

Sūzhōu Tourism Information Center

Fenghuang Jie 凤凰街

Daichengqiao Lu 带城桥路

27
18   6

Dong Dajie 东大街

Renmin Lu 人民路

Wuquqiao Lu

4
3

Changxu Lu

Xinshi Lu

Xiangwang Lu

Zhuhui Lu

22

12

Tourist Boat Wharf

Pán Gate Scenic Area
1
Wumen Bridge

Renmin Bridge

South Long-Distance (0.5km)

Sūzhōu

Lion's Grove Garden   GARDENS
(狮子林, Shīzi Lín; 23 Yuanlin Lu; high/low season ¥30/20; ⊙7.30am-5.30pm) Constructed in 1342 by the Buddhist monk Tianru to commemorate his master, who lived on Lion Cliff on Zhèjiāng's Tianmú Mountain, this garden's curiously shaped rocks were meant to resemble lions, protectors of the Buddhist faith. If the Humble Administrator's Garden was crowded, get ready to be pushed along by the tide of tourists here.

Temple of Mystery   TAOIST TEMPLE
(玄妙观, Xuánmiào Guàn; Guanqian Jie; 观前街; admission ¥10; ⊙7.30am-5pm; Ⓜ Lindun Lu or Leqiao) Lashed by electronic music from the shops alongside, the Taoist Temple of Mystery stands in what was once Sūzhōu's old bazaar, a rowdy entertainment district with travelling showmen, acrobats and actors. The temple dates from 1181 and is the sole surviving example of Song architecture in Sūzhōu. The complex contains several elaborately decorated halls, including the huge Sānqīng Diàn (三清殿; Three Purities Hall), which is supported by 60 pillars and capped by a double roof with upturned eaves.

The hall is home to three huge statues of Yuqing, Shangqing and Taiqing (the Three Purities); look out for the one-horned ox (独角神牛; dújiǎo shénniú) that conveyed Laozi on his travels; there are also shrines to Tianhou, clothed in a pink robe, and the Jade Emperor. Note the antique carved balustrade around the hall, which dates to the Five Dynasties period (10th century). The blank Wordless Stele stands just east of the hall. The first main hall of the temple now serves as a jewellery showroom.

Twin Pagodas   BUDDHIST TEMPLE, PAGODA
(双塔; Shuāng Tǎ; Dinghuisi Xiang; 定慧寺巷; admission ¥8; ⊙8am-4.30pm; Ⓜ Lindun Lu) Beautifully enhanced with flowering magnolias in spring, this delightful courtyard and former temple contains a pair of sublime pagodas. It's also home to the small Sūzhōu Ancient Stone Carving Art Museum.

Pingjiang Lu　　　　　　　　STREET

(平江路; Ⓜ Lindun Lu or Xiangmen) While most of the town canals have been sealed and paved into roads, the pedestrianised Pingjiang Lu offers clues to the Sūzhōu of yesteryear. On the eastern side of the city, this canal-side road has whitewashed local houses, many now converted to guesthouses, teahouses or trendy cafes selling overpriced beverages, sitting comfortably side-by-side. Duck down some of the side streets that jut out from the main path for a glimpse of slow-paced local life.

Along the main drag it's all rice wine, Tibetan trinkets, cigar sellers, fried potatoes, cake, dumplings and ice-cream vendors.

Kūnqǔ Opera Museum　　　　　MUSEUM

(昆曲博物馆; Kūnqǔ Bówùguǎn; 14 Zhongzhangjia Xiang; 中张家巷14号; ⊘8.30am-4pm) FREE Down a warren of narrow lanes, the small Kūnqǔ Opera Museum is dedicated to *kūnqǔ*, the opera style of the region. The beautiful old theatre houses a stage, musical instruments, costumes and photos of famous performers. It also puts on regular performances of *kūnqǔ*.

Couple's Garden　　　　　　GARDENS

(耦园; Ǒu Yuán; 6 Xiaoxinqiao Xiang; 小新桥巷6号; high/low season ¥20/15; ⊘8am-4.30pm; Ⓜ Xiangmen) The tranquil Couple's Garden is off the main tourist route and sees fewer visitors (a relative concept in China), though the gardens, pond and courtyards are quite lovely.

Soochow University　　　HISTORIC BUILDINGS

(苏州大学; Sūzhōu Dàxué; 1 Shizi Jie; 十梓街1号; Ⓜ Xiangmen) Before the communists took over, this college was China's oldest private university, founded by missionaries of the Methodist church in 1900. The university is still in operation and its beautiful old campus is accessible from the west gate (西门; *xīmén*) where you'll see **St Joseph Church**, built in 1881, standing right outside. Inside the leafy campus are ivy-clad colonial buildings, the most notable being the imposing **Clock Tower** and the **Laura Haygood Memorial Hall**.

The Xiangmen metro stop (exit 1) is next to the north gate of the campus, or bus 8 from the train station will drop you off at the west gate.

Garden of the Master of the Nets　GARDENS

(网师园; Wǎngshī) Off Shiquan Jie, this pocket-sized garden is considered one of Sūzhōu's best preserved. Laid out in the 12th century, it

went to seed and was later restored in the 18th century as part of the home of a retired official turned fisherman (hence the name). A striking feature is the use of space: the labyrinth of courtyards, with windows framing other parts of the garden, is ingeniously designed to give the illusion of a much larger area.

The central section is the main garden and the western section is an inner garden with a courtyard containing the master's study. Trivia nuts note: the Peony Study was used as the model for the Astor Court and Ming Garden in the Museum of Modern Art, New York.

There are two ways to the entry gate, with English signs and souvenir stalls marking the way: you can enter from the alley on Shiquan Jie, or via Kuojiatou Xiang (阔家头巷), an alley off Daichengqiao Lu.

Blue Wave Pavilion　　　　GARDENS

(沧浪亭; Cānglàng Tíng; Renmin Lu; 人民路; high/low season ¥20/15; ⊘7.30am-5pm) Originally the home of a prince, the oldest garden in Sūzhōu was first built in the 11th century, and has been repeatedly rebuilt since. Instead of attracting hordes of tourists, the wild, overgrown garden around the Blue Wave Pavilion is one of those where the locals actually go to chill and enjoy a leisurely stroll. Lacking a northern wall, the garden creates the illusion of space by borrowing scenes from the outside.

A double verandah leads along a canal from the front pavilion. From the outer path, you'll see green space inside and from the inner path you can see views of the water. Look out for a 'temple' whose dark walls are carved with the portraits of more than 500 sages, and the 'pure fragrance house' has some impressive furniture made from the gnarled roots of banyan trees.

Confucian Temple　　　CONFUCIAN TEMPLE

(文庙; Wénmiào; 613 Renmin Lu; 人民路613号; ⊘6.30am-4pm) FREE The restored Confucian Temple is a haven and place of solitude in a busy town, with several ancient gingkos (one is 830 years old) and rows of bonsai trees, plus a statue of the temperate sage. The highlight is the fabulous stelae carved during the Southern Song dynasty (1137–1279). One features a map of old Sūzhōu, detailing the canal system (much now paved over and blocked), old roads and the city walls.

There's also an astronomy stele from 1190 – one of the oldest astronomy charts in the world.

★ **Pán Gate Scenic Area**   LANDMARK

(盘门, Pán Mén; 1 Dong Dajie; admission Pán Gate only/with Ruìguāng Pagoda ¥25/31; ⊘7.30am-6pm; ⓠY2) This stretch of the city wall, straddling the outer moat in the southwest corner of the city has Sūzhōu's only remaining original coiled gate, Pán Gate, which dates from 1355. This overgrown double-walled **water gate** was used for controlling waterways, with defensive positions at the top. From the gate, you can view the exquisite arched **Wúmén Bridge** (Wúmén Qiáo) to the east, the long moat and the crumbling **Ruìguāng Pagoda** (瑞光塔; Ruìguāng Tǎ; Dong Dajie; admission ¥6), constructed in 1004.

The gate is also connected to 300m of the **ancient city wall**, which visitors can walk along, past old women harvesting dandelions. The gate also backs onto a delightful scenic area, dotted with old halls, bell towers, bridges, pavilions and a lake as well as the small **Wǔxiàng Temple** (Wǔxiàng Cí). It's far less crowded than Sūzhōu's gardens and in many ways, more attractive. To get here, take tourist bus Y2 or a taxi.

Garden to Linger In   GARDENS

(留园, Liú Yuán; 79 Liuyuan Lu; high/low season ¥40/30; ⊘7.30am-5pm; ⓠY1) One of the largest gardens in Sūzhōu, this 3-hectare plot was originally built in the Ming dynasty by a doctor as a relaxing place for his recovering patients. It's easy to see why the patients took to it: the winding corridors are inlaid with calligraphy from celebrated masters, their windows and doorways opening onto unusually shaped rockeries, ponds and dense clusters of bamboo. Stone tablets hang from the walls, inscribed by patients recording their impressions of the place.

The teahouse is a fantastic spot to recover from crowd overload. Order a cup of *lóngjǐng* (龙井; dragon well tea; ¥15) and relax. The garden is about 3km west of the city centre and can be reached on tourist bus Y1 from the train station or Renmin Lu.

West Garden Temple   BUDDHIST TEMPLE, GARDENS

(西园寺, Xīyuán Sì; Xiyuan Lu; 西园路; admission ¥25; ⊘8am-5pm; ⓠY1, Y3) This magnificent temple, with its mustard-yellow walls and gracefully curved eaves, was burnt to the ground during the Tàipíng Rebellion and rebuilt in the late 19th century. Greeting you as you enter the stunning **Arhat Hall** (罗汉堂; Luóhàn Táng) is an amazing four-faced and thousand-armed statue of Guanyin. Beyond lie mesmerising and slightly unnerving rows

of 500 glittering *luóhàn* (arhats; monks who have achieved enlightenment and passed to nirvana at death) statues, each unique and near life-size.

A vegetarian restaurant serves noodles. The temple is 400m west of the Garden to Linger In. Take Y1 or Y3 from the train station.

Tiger Hill   PARK

(虎丘山, Hǔqiū Shān; ☎6723 2305; Huqiu Lu; 虎丘路; high/low season ¥60/40; ⊘7.30am-6pm, to 5pm winter; ⓠY1, Y2) In the far northwest of town, Tiger Hill is popular with local tourists. The beacon drawing the visitors is the leaning **Cloud Rock Pagoda** (云岩塔; Yúnyán Tǎ) atop the hill. The octagonal seven-storey pagoda was built in the 10th century entirely of brick, an innovation in Chinese architecture at the time. It began tilting over 400 years ago, and today the highest point is displaced more than 2m from its original position.

The hill itself is artificial and is the final resting place of He Lu, founding father of Sūzhōu. He Lu died in the 6th century BC and myths have coalesced around him – he is said to have been buried with a collection of 3000 swords and be guarded by a white tiger. Tourist buses Y1 and Y2 from the train station go to Tiger Hill.

☞ Tours

Evening boat tours wind their way around the outer canal leaving nightly from 6pm to 8.30pm (¥120, 55 minutes, half-hourly). The trips, usually with *píngtán* (singing and storytelling art form sung in the Sūzhōu dialect) performance on board, are a great way to experience old Sūzhōu, passing Pán Gate and heading up to Chāng Gate (in the west of the city wall). Remember to bring bug repellent as the mosquitoes are tenacious. Tickets can be bought at the **Tourist Boat Wharf** (游船码头, Yóuchuán Mǎtóu) down the alley east of Rénmín Bridge, which shares the same quarters with the **Grand Canal Boats** (划船售票处, Huáchuán Shòupiàochù) ticket office. Buses 27 or 94 run to the wharf.

☆ Festivals & Events

Sūzhōu Silk Festival   CULTURAL

(丝绸节, Sīchóu Jié) Every September Sūzhōu hosts a silk festival. There are exhibitions devoted to silk history and production, and silk merchants get to show off their wares to crowds of thousands.

🛏 Sleeping

Hotels in general are terribly overpriced in Sūzhōu. Get ready to hone your bargaining skills.

★ Sūzhōu Mingtown Youth Hostel HOSTEL $

(苏州明堂青年旅舍, Sūzhōu Míngtáng Qīngnián Lǚshè; ☎6581 6869; 28 Pingjiang Lu, 平江路28号; 6-bed dm ¥50, r ¥125-185; ❈ @; M Xiangmen or Lindun Lu) A well-run youth hostel with a Thai sleeping Buddha at the door, a charming lobby and rooms and dorms with dark wooden 'antique' furniture. The only downside is that rooms aren't soundproof and hot water can misfire. There's free internet, free laundry, and bike rental. Rooms are around ¥20 pricier on Friday and Saturday.

Joya Youth Hostel HOSTEL $

(小雅国际青年旅舍, Xiǎoyǎ Guójì Qīngnián Lǚshè; ☎6755 1752; www.joyahostel.com; 1/21 Daxinqiao Xiang; 大新桥巷1/21号; dm/r ¥60/180; ☏; M Xiangmen) A lovely former residence (built in 1883), this tranquil place (set back from the main Pingjiang Lu drag) has Qing-dynasty charm, with floral lattice windows, many original wooden beams and a wisteria in the courtyard. Rooms are small, but have high ceilings and open out onto courtyards.

Sūzhōu Watertown Youth Hostel HOSTEL $

(苏州浮生四季国际青年旅舍, Sūzhōu Fúshēngsìjì Qīngnián Lǚshè; ☎65218885; www.watertownhostel.com; 7 Dashitou Xiang, Renmin Lu, 人民路大石头巷27号; 6-/4-bed dm ¥50/60, r ¥130-180; ❈ @; M Leqiao) Tucked away in an alley off Renmin Lu, this 200-year-old courtyard complex houses an OK hostel. Rooms on the 2nd floor are quieter while ground-floor rooms have better wi-fi reception. Dorms are compact but clean enough.

The cosy Sūzhōu-styled patio invites you to chill, and big bottles of Qīngdǎo are a mere ¥5. Another plus is that the airport bus station is just a stone's throw away.

Pod HOTEL $

(布丁酒店连锁, Bùdīng Jiǔdiàn Liánsuǒ; ☎6530 0767; www.podinns.com; 758 Shiquan Jie; 十全街758号; r from ¥199) Simple, clean and snappy, this place has vibrantly styled stack 'em high and rent 'em fast rooms with window and shower (but not much else) at the heart of things along busy Shiquan Jie.

★ Garden Hotel HOTEL $$$

(苏州南园宾馆, Sūzhōu Nányuán Bīnguǎn; ☎6778 6778; www.gardenhotelsuzhou.com; 99 Daichengqiao Lu; 带城桥路99号; r from ¥1558; ❀ @ ☏) Within huge, green grounds, the very popular and recently redone five-star Garden Hotel has lovely, spacious and attractively decorated accommodation. Washed over with Chinese instrumental *pípá* music, the lobby is a picture of Sūzhōu, with a clear pond, grey bricks and white walls. Serene stuff and an oasis of calm.

Hotel Soul HOTEL $$$

(苏哥李酒店, Sūgēlǐ Jiǔdiàn; ☎6777 0777; www.hotelsoul.com.cn; 27-33 Qiaosikong Xiang, 乔司空巷27-33号; d ¥1680; ❀ ☏) This 200-room, five-level Philippe Starck wannabe has a zappy foyer, sharp angles and neon blue lights, but little soul. It is, however, very good value and central. Rooms are huge and dapper, with textured wallpaper, plush beds and tones that make you want to order a martini. You can normally net rooms for ¥418, or ¥460 on Friday and Saturday.

Pan Pacific Sūzhōu HOTEL $$$

(苏州吴宫泛太平洋酒店, Sūzhōu Wúgōng Fàntàipíngyáng Dàjiǔdiàn; ☎6510 3388; www.panpacific.com/Suzhou; 259 Xinshi Lu, 新市路259号; d ¥1268; ❀ @) There's a kitschy feel to the exterior of this former Sheraton Hotel, which looks like a faux Forbidden City. But once you step into the lobby, you'll know this is truly five-star luxury. The 500-plus rooms are spacious and stylish, fitted with all the latest gadgets to make you happy. Services are simply impeccable.

A bonus is that guests get to enjoy free access to the adjacent Gán Gate Garden.

Píngjiāng Lodge BOUTIQUE HOTEL $$$

(苏州平江客栈, Sūzhōu Píngjiāng Kèzhàn; ☎6523 2888; www.pingjianglodge.com; 33 Niujia Xiang, 钮家巷33号; d ¥988-1588, ste ¥1888-2588; ❀ @; M Xiangmen or Lindun Lu) Capturing the whitewashed walls, canal-side Sūzhōu aesthetic, this 17th-century traditional courtyard building has well-kept gardens and 51 rooms bedecked in traditional furniture. Rooms at the pointy end are suites with split-level living spaces; standard rooms are a bit bashed and could do with new carpets. Staff speak (faltering) English. Discounts of up to 50% are available.

Marco Polo Suzhou
HOTEL $$$

(苏州玄妙马可波罗大酒店, Sūzhōu Xuán-miào Mǎkěbōluó Dàjiǔdiàn; ☑6801 9888; www.marcopolohotels.com; 818 Ganjiang Donglu, 干将东路818号; d/ste ¥950/2217; ✳@) Right in the heart of Sūzhōu, this former Sofitel has been rebranded and still makes the grade. Its 314 rooms are tailored to suit the needs of the business traveller. Leisure visitors also like the spacious rooms with modern furnishings. Discounts knock rooms down to around ¥500.

✖ Eating

Plentiful restaurants can be found along Guanqian Jie, especially down the road from the Temple of Mystery.

Yǎba Shēngjiān
DUMPLINGS $

(哑巴生煎; 12 Lindun Lu; dumplings eight for ¥12; ◷5.30am-6.30pm) With great clouds of steam rising from the kitchen, this 60-year-old institution mainly flogs noodles but its handmade *shēngjiān bāo* (生煎包; pan-fried dumplings), stuffed with juicy pork, are outstanding and flavour-packed. During lunch hours expect to queue for 30 minutes just to order! Protocol: get a ticket, join the line, snag a table and enjoy.

Head to the side for chilli oil and soy sauce. Watch out for the meat juice – it can fly. There's more room and a breeze through the window upstairs. No English menu.

Pingvon
TEAHOUSE $

(品芳, Pǐnfāng; 94 Pingjiang Lu; dishes from ¥6) A cute little teahouse perched beside one of Sūzhōu's most popular canal-side streets, Pingvon serves up excellent dumplings and delicate little morsels on small plates. The tearooms upstairs are more atmospheric. Try the pine nuts and pumpkin soup (¥6) and the crab *xiǎolóngbāo* (steamed dumplings; ¥10 a portion). Picture menu.

Zhūhóngxīng
NOODLES $

(朱鸿兴; Taijian Long; mains from ¥15; ◷6.45am-8.45pm; Ⓜ Lindun Lu) Popular with locals, this red-wood furniture bedecked eatery, with several branches across town, has a long history and wholesome, filling noodles – try the scrummy *xiàrén miàn* (虾仁面; noodles with baby shrimps) or the *xuěcài ròusīmiàn* (雪菜肉丝面; meat and vegetable noodles).

Wúmén Rénjiā
JIĀNGSŪ $$

(吴门人家; ☑6728 8041; 31 Panru Xiang; dishes from ¥30; ◷6.30-9.30am, 11am-1.30pm & 5-8.30pm) Hidden in a quiet alley north of Lion's Grove Garden, this lovely courtyard restaurant attracts a mix of locals and visitors for its subtly flavoured traditional Sūzhōu cooking. Service can sometimes be a bit slow, but the setting (with traditional Chinese music) is grade A. Reservations essential.

Try the stewed pork balls in brown sauce (¥30), *kungpao* chicken (spicy chicken with chilli and peanuts) or any of the plentiful seafood dishes.

Yàkèxī
UIGHUR $$

(亚克西酒楼, Yàkèxī Jiǔlóu; 768 Shiquan Jie, 十全街768号; mains ¥40; ◷10.30am-midnight) The Uighur kitsch atmosphere is entertaining and the Xīnjiāng staples – lamb kebabs (¥2.50), hot and spicy lamb soup (¥16) and *nang* bread (flatbread; ¥3) – all tasty. Round it off with a bottle of SinKiang beer (¥10) or a sour milk drink (¥8) and dream of Kashgar. No time to sit down? The lamb kebabs are grilled just outside.

Bistronomy
FRENCH $$$

(☑6572 5632; 711 Shiquan Jie; 十全街711号; mains from ¥88; ◷11.30am-2.30pm & 5.30-9.30pm Tue-Sun) With low-volume funky beats and two nifty and sleek floors, grey brick walls, drapes, spotlights and white linen tablecloths, this elegant restaurant is a choice stop on Shiquan Jie. Crowd-pullers include cheese fondue (¥118), rich and smooth onion soup (¥58) – in an over-the-top bowl – and braised rack of lamb served with gratin Dauphinois (¥148), and homemade cassoulet (¥138).

The homemade lasagne (¥88) is also excellent. You could go for the monster burger (3kg; ¥198) if you haven't eaten for a few days, or settle for pizzas (from ¥78).

⚫ Drinking & Nightlife

There are stacks of trendy cafe-bars scattered along Pingjiang Lu. The nightlife scene on Shiquan Jie is dying as most of the expats' watering holes have moved to the soulless Sūzhōu Industrial Park, 9km east of the centre of town (get there on the metro).

Locke Pub
BAR

(240 Pingjiang Lu; 平江路240号; ◷10am-midnight) Any place that plays Tom Waits is good in our book. This charming spot has ample space, comfy sofas, homemade ice cream, a whole wall of English books, hot whisky, Leffe,

Corona and Guinness, all set in a traditional building along Pingjiang Lu.

Bookworm CAFE, BAR
(老书虫, Lǎo Shūchóng; 77 Gunxiu Fang; 滚绣坊77号; ⊘9am-1am) Běijīng's Bookworm wormed its way down to Sūzhōu, although the book selection isn't as good as Běijīng's. The food is crowd-pleasing (lots of Western options) and the cold beers include Tsingtao and Erdinger. There are occasional events and books you can borrow or buy. Just off Shiquan Jie.

☆ Entertainment

Regular performances of *kūnqǔ* opera and *píngtán*, two of the exquisite performance arts sung in local dialects, are regularly scheduled at the following places.

Kūnqǔ Opera Museum CHINESE OPERA
(昆曲博物馆, Kūnqǔ Bówùguǎn; 14 Zhongzhangjia Xiang; 中张家巷14号; tickets ¥30) This place puts on performances of *kūnqǔ* at 2pm on Sundays.

Garden of the Master of the Nets MUSIC
(网师园, Wǎngshī Yuán; tickets ¥100) From March to November, music performances are held nightly from 7.30pm to 9.30pm for tourist groups at this garden. Don't expect anything too authentic.

Pingtan Teahouse TEAHOUSE
(评弹茶馆, Píngtán Cháguǎn; 2nd fl, 626 Shiquan Jie) *Píngtán* enthusiasts get together here to keep the traditions alive. The music usually starts between 8pm and 10pm. Order some tea (the speciality is Yúnnán *pu'er*; unlimited serves from ¥100), and pick songs (from ¥45; some lyrics have English translations) for the master to play.

Pingtan Museum PERFORMING ARTS
(评弹博物馆, Píngtán Bówùguǎn; 3 Zhongzhangjia Xiang; 中张家巷3号; admission ¥4, performance tickets ¥6; ⊘9.30am-noon & 3.30-5pm) Almost next to the Kūnqǔ Opera Museum is the Píngtán Museum, which puts on wonderful performances of *píngtán*, a singing and storytelling art form sung in the Sūzhōu dialect. Two-hour shows are at 1.30pm daily.

🛍 Shopping

Sūzhōu-style embroidery, calligraphy, paintings, sandalwood fans, writing brushes and silk underclothes are for sale nearly everywhere.

ℹ Information

Major tourist hotels have foreign-exchange counters.

Bank of China (中国银行, Zhōngguó Yínháng; 1450 Renmin Lu) Changes travellers cheques and foreign cash. There are ATMs that take international cards at most larger branches of the Bank of China.

China Post (中国邮政, Zhōngguó Yóuzhèng; cnr Renmin Lu & Jingde Lu) Centrally located.

Industrial & Commercial Bank of China (工商银行, Gōngshāng Yínháng; 222 Guanqian Jie) 24-hour ATM facilities.

No 1 Hospital (苏大附一院, Sūdà Fùyīyuàn; 96 Shizi Jie; 十梓街96号) At the heart of Sūzhōu.

Public Security Bureau (PSB, 公安局, Gōng'ānjú; ☑6522 5661, ext 20593; 1109 Renmin Lu) Can help with emergencies and visa problems. The visa office is about 200m down a lane called Dashitou Xiang.

Sūzhōu Tourism Information Center (苏州旅游咨询中心, Sūzhōu Lǚyóu Zīxún Zhōngxīn; ☑6530 5887; www.classicsuzhou.com; 101 Daichengqiao Lu; 带城桥路101号) This branch is just north of the Garden Hotel; there are several other branches in town including at bus stations. Can help with booking accommodation and tours.

ℹ Getting There & Away

AIR

Sūzhōu does not have an airport, but **China Eastern Airlines** (东方航空公司, Dōngfāng Hángkōng Gōngsī; ☑6522 2788; 115 Ganjiang Lu) can help with booking flights out of Shànghǎi. Buses leave here frequently between 6.20am and 4.50pm for Hóngqiáo Airport (¥53) and Pǔdōng International Airport (¥54) in Shànghǎi.

BUS

Sūzhōu has three long-distance bus stations and the two listed here are the most useful. Tickets for all buses can also be bought at the **Liánhé ticket centre** (联合售票处, Liánhé Shòupiàochù; ☑6520 6681; 1606 Renmin Lu; ⊘bus tickets 8.30-11.30am & 1-5pm, train tickets 7.30-11am & noon-5pm).

The principal station is the **north long-distance bus station** (汽车北站, Qìchē Běizhàn; ☑6577 6577; 29 Xihui Lu; 西汇路29号) at the northern end of Renmin Lu, next to the train station. Departures:

Hángzhōu ¥74, two hours, regular services

Nánjīng ¥72, 2½ hours, regular services

Tónglǐ ¥8, 30 minutes, every 30 minutes, 6am-7pm

Wūzhèn ¥36, 90 minutes, regular services, 8.15am-4.30pm

Zhōuzhuāng ¥16, one hour, every 40 minutes, 6.45am-5.50pm

The **south long-distance bus station** (汽车南站; Qìchē Nánzhàn; cnr Yingchun Lu & Nanhuan Donglu) has buses to the following:

Hángzhōu ¥74, two hours, every 20 minutes

Nánjīng ¥72, two hours, every 20 minutes

Shànghǎi ¥34, 1½ hours, every 30 minutes

Yángzhōu ¥76, two hours, hourly

TRAIN

Sūzhōu is on the Nánjīng–Shànghǎi express G line. Trains stop at either the more centrally located **Sūzhōu Train Station** (苏州站; Sūzhōu Zhàn) or the **Sūzhōu North Train Station** (苏州北站; Sūzhōu Běizhàn), 12km north of the city centre. Book train tickets on the 2nd floor of the Liánhé ticket centre. There's also a **ticket office** (Guanqian Jie; 观前街) along Guanqian Jie across from the Temple of Mystery and another (8am to 8pm) by the Confucian Temple. Another ticket office can be found on the other side of the road from the south long-distance bus station.

Běijīng South 2nd/1st class ¥524/884, five hours, 15 daily

Nánjīng 2nd/1st class ¥100/160, one hour, frequent

Shànghǎi 2nd/1st class ¥40/60, 25 minutes, frequent

Wúxī 2nd/1st class ¥20/30, 15 minutes, frequent

ⓘ Getting Around

BICYCLE

Sūzhōu could seriously do with a public bike hire scheme like Hángzhōu's, but you can rent a bike from most hostels. The **Yángyáng Bike Rental Shop** (洋洋车行, Yángyáng Chēháng; 2061 Renmin Lu; deposit ¥200, per day ¥25; ⊙7am-6pm), a short walk north of the Silk Museum, offers bike rentals.

PUBLIC TRANSPORT

Convenient tourist buses visit all sights and cost ¥2, passing by the train station.

Bus Y5 Goes around the western and eastern sides of the city and has a stop at Sūzhōu Museum.

Bus Y2 Travels from Tiger Hill, Pán Gate and along Shiquan Jie.

Buses Y1 & Y4 Run the length of Renmin Lu.

Bus 80 Runs between the two train stations.

Sūzhōu metro line 1 runs along Ganjiang Lu, connecting Mùdú in the southwest with Zhongnan Jie in the east and running through the Culture & Expo Centre and Times Square, in the Sūzhōu Industrial Park. Line 2 runs north–south from Sūzhōu North Station to Baodaiqiaonan in the south, via Sūzhōu Train Station. At present, the metro system is not terribly useful for visitors, but two more lines are under construction.

TAXI

Fares start at ¥10 and drivers generally use their meters. A trip from Guanqian Jie to the train station should cost around ¥15. From Sūzhōu North Train Station to downtown, the fare is around ¥50 to ¥60. Pedicabs hover around the tourist areas and can be persistent (¥5 for short rides is standard).

Around Sūzhōu

Sūzhōu's tourist brochures offer a mind-boggling array of sights around the town. Sadly, not all are great, and noteworthy ones are often overrun by tourists. Go early to avoid the crowds.

Tónglǐ   同里

☑ 0512

This lovely **Old Town** (老城区, Lǎochéngqū; ☑ 6333 1140; admission ¥100, free after 5.30pm), only 18km southeast of Sūzhōu, boasts rich, historical canal-side atmosphere and weather-beaten charm. Many of the buildings have kept their traditional facades, with stark whitewashed walls, black-tiled roofs, cobblestone pathways and willow-shaded canal views adding to a picturesque allure. The town is best explored the traditional way: aimlessly meandering along the canals and alleys until you get lost. A restrained carnival atmosphere reigns but the languorous tempo is frequently shredded by marauding tour groups that sweep in like cricket swarms, especially at weekends.

You can reach Tónglǐ from either Sūzhōu or Shànghǎi, but aim for a weekday visit.

The admission fee to the town includes access to the best sights, except the Chinese Sex Culture Museum.

◉ Sights

Gēnglè Táng   HISTORIC BUILDING

(耕乐堂; ⊙9am-5.30pm) There are three old residences in Tónglǐ that you'll pass at some point and the most pleasant is this elegant and composed Ming-dynasty estate with 52 halls spread out over five courtyards in the west of town. The buildings have been elaborately restored and redecorated with paintings, calligraphy and antique furniture while the black-brick faced paths, osmanthus trees and cooling corridors hung with traditional

Around Sūzhōu

Chinese *mǎdēng* lanterns conjure up an alluring charm.

Pearl Pagoda
PAGODA
(珍珠塔, Zhēnzhū Tǎ; ⊘ 9am-5.30pm) In the north of town, this compound dates from the Qing dynasty. Inside, you'll find a large residential complex decorated with Qing-era antiques, an ancestral hall, a garden and an opera stage. It gets its name from a tiny pagoda draped in pearls.

Tuìsī Garden
GARDENS
(退思园, Tuìsī Yuán; ⊘ 9am-5.30pm) This beautiful 19th-century garden in the east of the Old Town delightfully translates as the 'Withdraw and Reflect Garden', so named because it was a Qing government official's retirement home. The 'Tower of Fanning Delight' served as the living quarters, while the garden itself is a meditative portrait of pond water churning with koi, rockeries and pavilions, caressed by traditional Chinese music.

Chinese Sex Culture Museum
MUSEUM
(中华性文化博物馆, Zhōnghuá Xìngwénhuà Bówùguǎn; admission ¥20; ⊘ 9am-5.30pm) This private museum, located east of Tuìsī Garden, is quietly housed in a historic but disused girls' school campus and you won't miss it. Despite occasionally didactic and inaccurate pronouncements ('there were globally three abnormal sexual phenomena: prostitution, foot-binding and eunuchs'), it's fascinating, and ranges from the penal (sticks used to beat prostitutes, chastity belts) and the penile (Qing-dynasty dildos) to the innocent (small statues of the goddess of mercy) and the positively charming (porcelain figures of courting couples).

The setting – with a lovely garden and courtyard – is stunning.

☞ Tours

Slow-moving **six-person boats** (¥90 for 25 minutes) ply the waters of Tónglǐ's canal system. The boat trip on Tónglǐ Lake is free, though of no particular interest.

🛏 Sleeping & Eating

Guesthouses are plentiful, with basic rooms starting at about ¥100. Restaurants are everywhere, and food prices here are much higher than Sūzhōu. Some local dishes to try include *méigāncàishāoròu* (梅干菜烧肉; stewed meat with dried vegetables), *yínyúchǎodàn* (银鱼炒蛋; silver fish omelette) and *zhuàngyuángtí* (状元蹄; stewed pig's leg).

Tongli International Youth Hostel
HOSTEL $
(同里国际青年旅舍, Tónglǐ Guójì Qīngnián Lǚshè; ☑ 6333 9311; 10 Zhuhang Jie, 竹行街10号; dm ¥55, r from ¥110; ❋ @ 🛜) This youth hostel has two locations. The main one, slightly off Zhongchuan Beilu and near Zhongchuan Bridge, is 300m west of Zhèngfú Cǎotáng. With a charming wooden interior, rooms here have traditional furniture (some with four-poster beds), oozing old-China charm. The lobby area is attractive, decked out with international flags and sofas draped in throws.

The **alternative location** (234 Yuhang Jie; 鱼行街234号) beside Taiping Bridge has doubles (¥130) with shared bathroom only.

Zhèngfú Cǎotáng
BOUTIQUE HOTEL $$
(正福草堂, ☑ 6333 6358; www.zfct.net; 138 Mingqing Jie, 明清街138号; s/s/ste ¥480/680/1380; ❋ @ 🛜) *The* place to stay in town. Each one unique, the 14 deluxe rooms and suites are all aesthetically set with Qing-style furniture and antiques, with four-poster beds in some. Facilities like bathrooms and floor heating are ultra-modern.

Getting There & Around

From Sūzhōu, take a bus (¥8, 50 minutes, every 30 minutes) at the south or north long-distance bus station for Tónglǐ. Electric carts (¥5) run from beside the Tónglǐ bus station to the Old Town, or walk it in about 15 minutes.

Regular buses leave Tónglǐ bus station for Sūzhōu (¥8), Shànghǎi (¥32) and Zhōuzhuāng (¥6, 30 minutes). There is also one bus per day to Nánjīng (¥69) and Hángzhōu (¥51). For Zhōuzhuāng, you can also take public bus 263 (¥2).

Lùzhí   用直

This charming, minute canal town, only a 25km public bus trip east of Sūzhōu, is slightly less commercialised than others in the area. The entrance ticket of ¥78 can be skipped if you just want to wander the streets, alleys and bridges – you only have to pay if you enter the tourist sights (open 8am to 5pm), such as the **Wànshèng Rice Warehouse** (万盛米行; Wànshèng Mǐháng), the **Bǎoshèng Temple** (保圣寺; Bǎoshèng Sì) and a handful of museums, but these can be safely missed without diminishing its charm.

The humpbacked bridges are delightful. Check out the centuries-old **Jìnlì Bridge** (进利桥; Jìnlì Qiáo) and **Xīnglóng Bridge** (兴隆桥; Xīnglóng Qiáo). Half-hour **boat rides** (¥40) depart from several points, including **Yǒng'ān Bridge** (永安桥; Yǒng'ān Qiáo).

The **Lùzhí Cultural Park** (用直文化园), is a huge, faux Ming-dynasty complex filled with tourist shops and a couple of exhibition halls. Admission is free and the landscaped gardens, ponds, pavilions and an opera stage make it a nice area to amble.

To get to Lùzhí, take bus 518 from Sūzhōu Train Station (¥4, one hour, first/last bus 6am/8pm) or from the bus stop on Pingqi Lu (平齐路) to the last stop. When you get off, take the first right along Dasheng Lu (达圣路) to the decorative arch; crossing the bridge takes you into the back of the old town in five minutes. Hordes of pedicabs will descend upon you offering to take you to the main entrance. Pay no more than ¥5.

The last bus back from Lùzhí is at 7.30pm. If you want to continue to Shànghǎi from Lùzhí, buses (¥18, two hours) from the Lùzhí bus station run between 6.20am and 5pm.

Mùdú   木渎

Dating to the Ming dynasty, Mùdú was once the haunt of wealthy officials, intellectuals and artists, and even the Qing emperor Qianlong visited six times. Today, the village has been swallowed up by Sūzhōu's growing suburban sprawl. It's not as attractive as Jiāngsū's canal towns, but it's straightforward to reach.

The village is free if you merely want to soak up the atmosphere, as entrance fees are for the top sights alone, however they contain most of Mùdú's character and history.

Sights

Bǎngyǎn Mansion   HISTORIC BUILDING
(榜眼府第, Bǎngyǎn Fǔdì; Xiatang Jie; admission ¥10; ⊙ 8.30am-4.30pm; Ⓜ Mudu) This dignified complex was the home of the 19th-century writer and politician Feng Guifen. It has a rich collection of antique furniture and intricate carvings of stone, wood and brick – it often serves as a movie set. The surrounding garden is pretty, with lotus ponds, arched bridges and bamboo.

Hóngyǐn Mountain Villa   HISTORIC BUILDING
(虹饮山房, Hóngyǐn Shānfáng; Shantang Jie; admission ¥40; ⊙ 8.30am-4.30pm; Ⓜ Mudu) By far the most interesting place in Mùdú is this villa, with its elaborate opera stage, exhibits and even an imperial pier where Emperor Qianlong docked his boat. The stage in the centre hall is impressive; honoured guests were seated in front and the galleries along the sides of the hall were for women. The emperor was a frequent visitor and you can see his uncomfortable-looking imperial chair. Operas are still performed here on festival days.

Ancient Pine Garden   HISTORIC BUILDING
(古松园, Gǔsōngyuán; Shantang Jie; admission ¥20; ⊙ 8.30am-4.30pm; Ⓜ Mudu) In the middle of Shantang Jie is this courtyard complex known for its intricately carved beams. Look out for wooden impressions of officials, hats, phoenixes, flowers and other designs.

Yan Family Garden   HISTORIC BUILDING
(严家花园, Yánjiā Huāyuán; cnr Shantang Jie & Mingqing Jie; admission ¥40; ⊙ 8.30am-4.30pm; Ⓜ Mudu) This beautiful complex in the northwest corner of the village dates to the Ming dynasty and was once the home of a former magistrate. The garden, with its rockeries and a meandering lake, is divided into five sections by walls, with each section designed to invoke a season.

Míngyuè Temple
BUDDHIST TEMPLE

(明月古寺, Míngyuè Gǔsì; Shantang Jie; ⊘8.30am-4.30pm; Ⓜ Mudu) FREE This large and attractive temple originally dates to the 10th century, but has been mostly reconstructed (since last being largely destroyed during the Cultural Revolution). The 1000-arm, four-faced Guanyin statue is worth hunting down – notice the ruler she holds in one of her lower hands, among other ritual objects.

🕝 Tours

The most pleasurable way to experience Mùdú is along the canal by boat. You'll find a collection of traditional skiffs docked outside the Bǎngyǎn Mansion. A 10- to 15-minute boat ride is ¥10 per person (¥30 per boat minimum charge).

ℹ️ Getting There & Away

From Sūzhōu, take metro line 1 to Mùdú station then take exit 1 and hop on bus 2, 38 or 622 (all ¥1), 4km (four stops) away from the old town (木渎古镇站; Mùdú Gǔzhèn zhàn).

Tiānpíng Shān & Língyán Shān   天平山、灵岩山

Around 3km from Mùdú, scenic Tiānpíng Shān (天平山; Lingtian Lu; admission ¥25; ⊘7.30am-5pm) is a low, forested hill about 13km west of Sūzhōu. It's a wonderful place for hiking or just meandering along one of its many wooded trails. It's also famous for its medicinal spring waters.

Eleven kilometres southwest of Sūzhōu is Língyán Shān (灵岩山; Lingtian Lu; admission ¥20; ⊘8am-4.30pm winter, to 5pm summer), the 'Cliff of the Spirits' that was once the site of a palace where Emperor Qianlong stayed during his inspection tours of the Yangzi River valley. The mountain is today home to an active Buddhist monastery. The exhausting climb to the peak offers panoramic views of Sūzhōu. On the way up, take the path on the left for an exciting clamber over rough-hewn stone and paths.

Tourist bus 4 goes to Língyán Shān and Tiānpíng Shān from Sūzhōu's train station.

Zhōuzhuāng   周庄

Some 30km southeast of Sūzhōu, the 900-year-old water village of Zhōuzhuāng is the best known canal town in Jiāngsū. It is popular with tour groups, thanks to Chen Yifei, the late renowned Chinese painter whose works of the once idyllic village are its claim to fame.

It does, however, have considerable old-world charm. Get up early or take an evening stroll, before the crowds arrive or when they begin to thin out, to catch some of Zhōuzhuāng's architectural highlights. Admission to Zhōuzhuāng is ¥100 (access is free after 8pm). Make sure you get your photo digitally added to the ticket at purchase; this entitles you to a three-day pass.

👁️ Sights

Twin Bridges
BRIDGE

A total of 14 bridges grace Zhōuzhuāng, but the most attractive is this pair of Ming-dynasty bridges (双桥; Shuāngqiáo) gorgeously standing at the intersection of two waterways in the heart of this canal town. Shìdé Bridge (世德桥; Shìdé Qiáo) is a humpbacked bridge while the connecting Yǒngān Bridge (永安桥; Yǒngān Qiáo) is the one with a square arch. The bridges were depicted in Chen Yifei's *Memory of Hometown*, which shot the whole town to fame from the 1980s onwards.

It's fun to go under bridge after bridge by boat. There are loads of trips on offer, including an 80-minute boat ride (¥180 per boat; six people) from outside the international youth hostel.

Zhang's House
HISTORIC BUILDING

(张厅, Zhāngtīng; ⊘8am-7pm) To the south of the Twin Bridges, this beautiful 70-room, three-hall structure was built in the Ming era and bought by the Zhang clan in early Qing times as their residence. There's an opera stage to keep the ladies entertained (they were not supposed to leave home or seek entertainment outside). Also note the chairs in the magnificently named Hall of Jade Swallows. Unmarried women could only sit on those with a hollow seat back, symbolising that they had nobody to rely on!

Don't overlook the garden, where boats could drift straight up to the house to its own little wharf. Trek back to the road via the 'side lane', a long and narrow walkway for the servants.

Shen's House
HISTORIC BUILDING

(沈厅, Shěntīng; Nanshi Jie; 南市街; ⊘8am-7pm) Near Fù'ān Bridge, this property of the Shen clan is a lavish piece of Qing-style architecture boasting three halls and over 100 rooms. The first hall is particularly interesting, as it has a water gate and a wharf where the family moors their private boats. You can picture the compound entirely daubed in Maoist graffiti c 1969 (note the crudely smashed carvings above the doors).

You'll need a separate ticket (¥10) for the **Zǒumǎ Lóu** (走马楼; h8am-4.30pm) where a further six courtyards and 45 rooms await (a third of the entire building).

Quánfú Temple
BUDDHIST TEMPLE

(全福讲寺, Quánfú Jiǎngsì; ⊙8.30am-5.30pm) It's hard to miss this eye-catching amber-hued temple complex. The 'full fortune' temple was founded during the Song dynasty, but has been repeatedly rebuilt. The structure you see today is an incarnation from 1995, when a handful of halls and gardens were added to the mix. The setting is simply stunning, with willow-lined lakes that seethe with plump goldfish.

Sleeping & Eating

There is a handful of guesthouses in town. Expect to pay ¥80 for a basic room. With eateries at almost every corner, you won't starve, but avoid the local *āpó* tea (*āpó chá*; old woman's tea) which is extortionate. Sitting canal-side with a Zhōuzhuāng beer in the evening is the way to go.

Zhōuzhuāng International Youth Hostel
HOSTEL $

(周庄国际青年旅舍; ☑5720 4566; 86 Beishi Jie, 北市街86号; dm/s/d ¥45/120/140; ✳@🛜) Near an old opera stage, this efficient youth hostel occupies a converted courtyard. It has tidy rooms and a clean (but dim) dorm, and offers free laundry. The hostel owner is a barista, so enjoy a perfect brew in the ground-floor cafe. When it's slow, dorms go for ¥35; singles go for ¥100 and doubles for ¥120 on weekdays.

Zhèngfú Cǎotáng
BOUTIQUE HOTEL $$

(正福草堂; ☑5721 9333; www.zfct.net; 90 Zhongshi Jie, 中市街90号; d/ste ¥680/1080; ✳@🛜) This lovingly presented five-room boutique hotel – a converted historic residence, restored to within an inch of its life – combines antique furniture with top-notch facilities, wood flooring and a lovely courtyard to fashion the best hotel in Zhōuzhuāng.

ℹ Getting There & Around

From the north long-distance bus station in Sūzhōu, half-hourly buses (¥16, 1½ hours) leave for Zhōuzhuāng between 6.55am and 5.20pm. From the bus station in Zhōuzhuāng, turn left and walk till you see the bridge. Cross the bridge and you'll see the gated entrance to the village. The walk is about 20 minutes; a taxi should cost no more than ¥10. Local bus 263 (¥2) from Tónglǐ runs to Jiāngzé bus station, a 10-minute walk from Zhōuzhuāng. There are also buses from Jiāngzé bus station to Sūzhōu south long-distance bus station (¥13; first/last 6.33am/4.10pm) and Shànghǎi Hóngqiáo bus station. If you want to get to Hángzhōu, you will need to go back to Sūzhōu (frequent) or Tónglǐ (four a day).

Zhèjiāng

POP 55 MILLION

Best Escapes

➡ Mògānshān (p271)

➡ Pǔtuóshān (p276)

➡ Xīnyè (p275)

➡ Zhūgě (p275)

Best Places to Stay

➡ Le Passage Mohkan Shan (p272)

➡ Four Seasons Hotel Hángzhōu (p267)

➡ Mingtown Youth Hostel (p266)

➡ Hofang International Youth Hostel (p266)

Why Go?

Zhèjiāng's trump card is its handsome and much-visited capital, Hángzhōu. But while Hángzhōu – a quick zip away on the train from Shànghǎi – is the front-running highlight, Zhèjiāng (浙江) is no one-trick pony. There are the arched bridges and charming canal scenes of Wūzhèn, a water town that typifies the lushly irrigated north of Zhèjiāng with its sparkling web of rivers and canals. The Buddhist island of Pǔtuóshān is the best known of the thousands of islands dotting a ragged and fragmented shoreline while the mist- and tree-cloaked slopes of Mògānshān provide refreshing natural air-conditioning when the thermostat in Shànghǎi is set to blow in the steamy summer months. But it's Zhè-jiāng's ancient villages of Xīnyè (新叶) and Zhūgě which should demand your attention, for their unhurried portraits of traditional architecture and bucolic rhythms.

When to Go
Hángzhōu

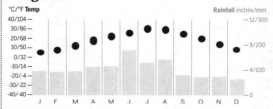

Late Mar–early May Spring sees low humidity and vegetation turning a brilliant green.

Aug & Sep Flee the simmering lowland heat to the cooler heights of Mògānshān.

Late Sep–mid-Nov Steal a march on winter and evade the sapping summer in Hángzhōu.

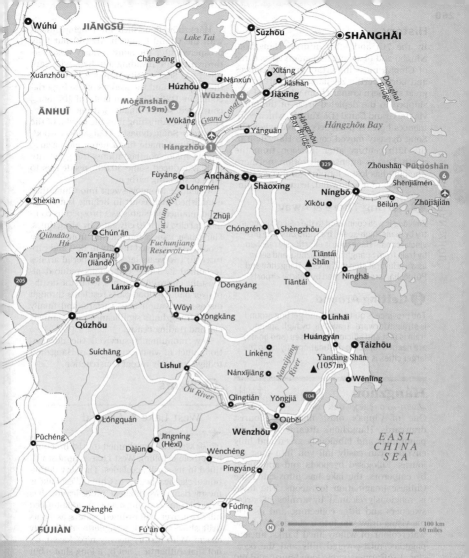

Zhèjiāng Highlights

1. Hop on a bike for a leisurely circuit of Hángzhōu's inimitable **West Lake** (p260)

2. Turn your back on urban China and explore the forested inclines of lush **Mògānshān** (p271)

3. Escape to the authentic village charms, ancient architecture and peaceful ponds of **Xīnyè** (p274)

4. Discover Zhèjiāng's picturesque canal-town culture at **Wūzhèn** (p272)

5. Fathom the ancient fēngshuǐ mysteries of **Zhūgě village** (p275)

6. Bounce over the waves to the sacred Buddhist island of **Pǔtuóshān** (p276)

History

By the 7th and 8th centuries Hángzhōu, Níngbō and Shàoxīng had emerged as three of China's most important trading centres and ports. Fertile Zhèjiāng was part of the great southern granary from which food was shipped to the depleted areas of the north via the Grand Canal (Dà Yùnhé), which commences here. Growth accelerated when the Song dynasty moved court to Hángzhōu in the 12th century after invasion from the north. Due to intense cultivation, northern Zhèjiāng has lost a lot of natural vegetation and much of it is now flat, featureless plain.

ℹ️ Getting There & Away

Zhèjiāng is well connected to the rest of the country by plane, high-speed train and bus. The provincial capital Hángzhōu is effortlessly reached by train from Shànghǎi and Sūzhōu, and serves as a useful first stop in Zhèjiāng. Hángzhōu and Pǔtuóshān are both served by nearby airports.

ℹ️ Getting Around

The province is quite small and getting around is straightforward. Travelling by high-speed train is fast and efficient but buses (and boats) are needed for some destinations; flying to the larger cities is also possible.

Hángzhōu   杭州

📞 0571 / POP 6.16 MILLION

One of China's most illustrious tourist drawcards, Hángzhōu's dreamy West Lake panoramas and fabulously green and hilly environs can easily lull you into long sojourns. Eulogised by poets and applauded by emperors, the lake has intoxicated the Chinese imagination for aeons. The town is religiously cleaned by armies of street sweepers and litter collectors, and its scenic vistas draw you into a classical Chinese watercolour of willow-lined banks, ancient pagodas, mist-covered hills and the occasional *shíkùmén* (stone gate house) and old *lǐlòng* (residential lane). Despite vast tourist cohorts, West Lake is a delight to explore, either on foot or by bike.

History

Hángzhōu's history dates to the start of the Qin dynasty (221 BC). Marco Polo passed through in the 13th century, calling Hángzhōu Kinsai and noting in astonishment that Hángzhōu had a circumference of 100 miles (161km), its waters vaulted by 12,000 bridges.

Hángzhōu flourished after being linked with the Grand Canal in AD 610 but fully prospered after the Song dynasty was overthrown by the invading Jurchen, who captured the Song capital Kāifēng, along with the emperor and the leaders of the imperial court, in 1126. The remnants of the Song court fled south, finally settling in Hángzhōu and establishing it as the capital of the Southern Song dynasty. Hángzhōu's wooden buildings made fire a perennial hazard; among major conflagrations, the great fire of 1237 reduced some 30,000 residences to piles of smoking carbon.

When the Mongols swept into China they established their court in Běijīng, but Hángzhōu retained its status as a prosperous commercial city. With 10 city gates by Ming times, Hángzhōu took a hammering from Taiping rebels, who besieged the city in 1861 and captured it; two years later the imperial armies reclaimed it. These campaigns reduced almost the entire city to ashes, led to the deaths of over half a million of its residents through disease, starvation and warfare, and finally ended Hángzhōu's significance as a commercial and trading centre.

Few monuments survived the devastation; much of what can be seen in Hángzhōu today is of fairly recent construction.

◉ Sights

◉ West Lake & Around

★ **West Lake**   LAKE

(西湖; Xīhú) The unashamed tourist brochure hyperbole extolling West Lake is almost justified in its shrill accolades. The very definition of classical beauty in China, West Lake is mesmerising. Methodical prettification has weaved some cunning magic: pagoda-topped hills rise over willow-lined waters as boats drift slowly through a vignette of leisurely charm. With history heavily repackaged, it's not that authentic – not by a long shot – but it's still a grade-A cover version of classical China.

Originally a lagoon adjoining the Qiántáng River, the lake didn't come into existence until the 8th century, when the governor of Hángzhōu had the marshy expanse dredged. As time passed, the lake's splendour was gradually cultivated: gardens were planted, pagodas built, and causeways and islands were constructed from dredged silt.

Celebrated poet Su Dongpo himself had a hand in the lake's development, constructing the **Sū Causeway** (苏堤; *Sūdī*) during his tenure as local governor in the 11th century. It wasn't an original idea – the poet-governor Bai Juyi had already constructed the **Bái Causeway** (白堤; *Báidī*) some 200 years earlier. Lined by willow, plum and peach trees, today the traffic-free causeways with their half-moon bridges make for restful outings.

Lashed to the northern shores by the Bái Causeway is **Gūshān Island** (孤山岛; *Gūshān Dǎo*), the largest island in the lake and the location of the **Zhèjiāng Provincial Museum** (浙江省博物馆; Zhèjiāng Shěng Bówùguǎn; 25 Gushan Lu; 孤山路25号; audioguide ¥10; ⊙9am-5pm Tue-Sun) **FREE** and **Zhōngshān Park** (中山公园; Zhōngshān Gōngyuán). The island's buildings and gardens were once the site of Emperor Qianlong's 18th-century holiday palace and gardens. Also on the island is the intriguing **Seal Engravers Society** (西泠印社; Xīlíng Yìnshè; ⊙9am-5.30pm) **FREE**, dedicated to the ancient art of carving the name seals (chops) that serve as personal signatures.

The northwest of the lake is fringed with the lovely **Qūyuàn Garden** (曲院风荷; Qūyuàn Fēnghé), a collection of gardens spread out over numerous islets and renowned for their fragrant spring lotus blossoms. Near Xīlíng Bridge (Xīlíng Qiáo) is **Su Xiaoxiao's Tomb** (苏小小墓; Sū Xiǎoxiào Mù), a 5th-century courtesan who died of grief while waiting for her lover to return. It's been said that her ghost haunts the area and the tinkle of the bells on her gown are audible at night.

The smaller island in the lake is **Xiǎoyíng Island** (小瀛洲; Xiǎoyíng Zhōu), where you can look over at **Three Pools Mirroring the Moon** (三潭印月; Sāntán Yìnyuè), three small towers in the water on the south side of the island; each has five holes that release shafts of candlelight on the night of the mid-autumn festival. From Lesser Yíngzhōu Island, you can gaze over to **Red Carp Pond** (花港观鱼; Huāgǎng Guānyú), home to a few thousand red carp.

Impromptu opera singing and other cultural activities may suddenly kick off around the lake, and if the weather's fine don't forget to earmark the east shore for sunset over West Lake photos. **Impression West Lake** is a spectacular evening performance on the lake waters near the Yue Fei Temple, usually starting at either 7.15pm or 7.45pm.

The best way to get around the lake is by bike (p270). Tourist buses Y1 and Y2 also run around West Lake.

Língyǐn Temple   BUDDHIST TEMPLE
(灵隐寺; Língyǐn Sì; Lingyin Lu; 灵隐路; grounds ¥35, grounds & temple ¥65; ⊙7am-5pm) Hángzhōu's most famous Buddhist temple, Língyǐn Temple, was built in AD 326 but has been destroyed and restored no fewer than 16 times. During the Five Dynasties (AD 907–960) about 3000 monks lived here. The Hall of the Four Heavenly Kings is astonishing, with its four vast guardians and an ornate cabinet housing Milefo (the future Buddha). The **Great Hall** contains a magnificent 20m-high statue of Siddhartha Gautama (Sakyamuni), sculpted from 24 blocks of camphor wood in 1956 and based on a Tang-dynasty original.

Behind the giant statue is a startling montage of Guanyin surrounded by 150 small figures, including multiple *luóhàn* (arhat), in a variety of poses. The earlier hall collapsed in 1949, crushing the Buddhist statues within, so it was rebuilt and the statue conceived. The Hall of the Medicine Buddha is beyond.

The walk up to the temple skirts the flanks of Fēilái Peak (*Fēilái Fēng*; Peak Flying from Afar), magically transported here from India according to legend. The Buddhist carvings (all 470 of them) lining the riverbanks and hillsides and tucked away inside grottoes date from the 10th to 14th centuries. To get a close-up view of the best carvings, including the famed 'laughing' Maitreya Buddha, follow the paths along the far (east) side of the stream.

Hángzhōu

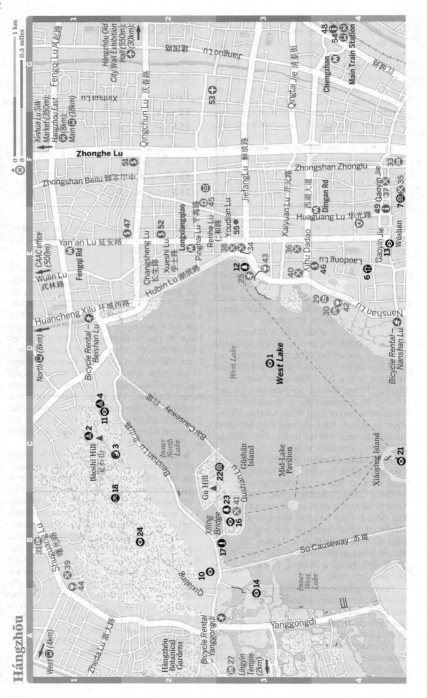

West Lake

West Lake

Mid-Lake Pavilion

Gushan Island

Gu Hill

Xiling Bridge

Gushan Island

Inner North Lake

Bai Causeway 白堤

Su Causeway 苏堤

Inner West Lake

Xiǎoyíng Island

Yanggongdi

Baoshi Hill 宝石山

Beishan Lu 北山路

Qixialing

Zhonghe Lu

Zhongshan Beilu 中山北路

Fengqi Rd

Yan'an Lu 延安路

Wulin Lu 武林路

Huancheng Xilu 环城西路

Zhonghe Lu

Changsheng Lu 长生路

Xueshi Lu 学士路

Hubin Lu 湖滨路

Longxiangqiao

Pinghai Lu 平海路

Renhe Lu 仁和路

Youdian Lu

Jiefang Lu 解放路

Zhongshan Zhonglu

Kaiyuan Lu 开元路

Huaguang Lu 华光路

Dingan Rd

Gaoyin Jie

Wùshān

Laodong Lu

Xihu Dadao

Nanshan Lu

Qingchun Lu 庆春路

Xinhua Lu

Fengqi Lu 风起路

Jianguo Lu

Qingtai Jie 清泰街

Chengzhàn

Main Train Station

Shuguang Lu 曙光路

Zheda Lu 浙大路

Hángzhōu Botanical Gardens

Lingyin Temple (2km)

Xinhua Lu Silk Market (350m); Hangzhou East (8km); Main (8km)

Hangzhou Old City Wall Exhibition Hall (550m); Main (30km)

CAAC office (500m)

Bicycle Rental – Beishan Lu

Bicycle Rental – Yanggongdi

Bicycle Rental – Nanshan Lu

West (4km)

North (8km)

1 km
0.5 miles

There are several other temples near Língyǐn Temple that can be explored, including Yǒngfú Temple and Tāoguāng Temple.

Behind Língyǐn Temple is the Northern Peak (*Běi Gāofēng*), which can be scaled by cable car (up/down/return ¥30/20/40). From the summit there are sweeping views across the lake and city.

Bus K7 and tourist bus Y2 (both from the train station), and tourist bus Y1 from the roads circling West Lake, go to the temple.

Léifēng Pagoda
PAGODA

(雷峰塔, Léifēng Tǎ; Nanshan Lu; 南山路; adult/child ¥40/20; ⊙8am-8.30pm Mar-Nov, 8am-5.30pm Dec-Feb) Topped with a golden spire, the eye-catching Léifēng Pagoda can be climbed for fine views of the lake. The original pagoda, built in AD 977, collapsed in 1924. During renovations in 2001, Buddhist scriptures written on silk were discovered in the foundations, along with other treasures.

Jìngcí Temple
BUDDHIST TEMPLE

(净慈寺, Jìngcí Sì; Nanshan Lu; 南山路; admission ¥10; ⊙6am-5.15pm summer, 6.30am-4.45pm winter) The serene yet monastically active Chan (Zen) Jìngcí Temple was originally built in AD 954 and is now fully restored. The splendid first hall contains the massive, foreboding Heavenly Kings and an elaborate red and gold case encapsulating Milefo (the future Buddha) and Weituo (protector of the Buddhist temples and teachings). The main hall – the **Great Treasure Hall** – contains a vast seated effigy of Sakyamuni (Buddha).

Hunt down the awesome 1000-arm Guanyin (千手观音) in the Guanyin Pavilion, with her huge fan of arms. The temple's enormous bronze bell is struck 108 times for prosperity on the eve of the Lunar New Year. There's a vegetarian restaurant attached.

Tàiziwān Park
PARK

(太子湾公园; Nanshan Lu; 南山路; ⊙24hr) This exquisite and serene park just south of the Sū Causeway off West Lake offers quiet walks among lush woodland, ponds, lakes, rose gardens and lawns along a wooden walkway. Just take off and explore. It's heavenly in spring, with gorgeous beds of tulips and daffodils and flowering trees.

Qīnghéfāng Old Street
STREET

(清河坊历史文化街; Qīnghéfāng Lìshǐ Wénhuà Jiē; Hefang Jie; 河坊街) At the south end of Zhongshan Zhonglu is this touristy, crowded and bustling pedestrian street, with makeshift puppet theatres, teahouses and gift and

Hángzhōu

curio stalls, selling everything from stone teapots to boxes of *lóngxūtáng* (龙须糖; dragon whiskers sweets), ginseng and silk. It's also home to several traditional medicine shops, including the **Húqìngyú Táng Chinese Medicine Museum** (中药博物馆; Zhōngyào Bówùguǎn; 95 Dajing Xiang; admission ¥10; ⊙8.30am-5pm), which is an actual dispensary and clinic.

Confucius Temple   CONFUCIAN TEMPLE
(文庙; Wénmiào; cnr Fuxue Xiang & Laodong Lu; ⊙9am-4.30pm Tue-Sun) **FREE** A repository of silence and calm, Hángzhōu's Confucius Temple is worth exploring for the main hall and the fabulous painted woodwork of its

beams and ceiling. Seated within are imposing figures of Confucius and other Confucian philosophers, including Mencius.

**Hángzhōu Old City Wall
Exhibition Hall**   MUSEUM
(杭州古城墙陈列馆; Hángzhōu Gǔchéngqiáng Chénlièguǎn; 1st fl, Qingchun Men, Qingchun Lu; 庆春路1号庆春门1楼; ⊙9am-4.30pm Wed-Mon) **FREE** Hángzhōu is famed for its lake, but the lake was a (glorious) appendage to a once-flourishing and magnificent city. The historic city of Hángzhōu – directly east of West Lake – has' vanished, its monumental city wall long gone. This exhibition hall within the reconstructed gate of Qingchun

Men celebrates the vanished bastion. For anyone keen to understand what Hángzhōu looked like until the early 20th century, there are photos and testaments to the old city (but no English).

The names of the city gates only survive in place names (such as Qingbo Men and Yongjin Men), but the old city of Hángzhōu (and its temples) has been buried beneath endless department stores and malls, leaving virtually nothing behind. This exhibition hall puts that tragic disappearance in its proper context.

Bus K212 from Yan'an Lu passes by.

Hángzhōu Botanical Garden　　GARDENS
(杭州植物园; Hángzhōu Zhíwùyuán; www.hzbg.cn; 1 Taoyuan Ling; 桃源岭1号; admission ¥10; ⊙7am-5.30pm) With huge tracts of towering bamboo, flowering magnolias and other delightful plants and trees, these vast gardens make for lovely walks to the northwest of West Lake. You can get here on bus K15, K28 or K82.

Mausoleum of General Yue Fei　　TEMPLE
(岳庙; Yuè Fēi Mù; Beishan Lu; admission ¥25; ⊙7am-6pm) This temple is more meaningful for Chinese patriots, rather than foreign visitors. Commander of the southern Song armies, General Yue Fei (1103–42) led successful battles against northern Jurchen invaders in the 12th century. Despite initial successes, he was recalled to the Song court, where he was executed, along with his son, after being deceived by the treacherous prime minister Qin Hui.

In 1163 Song emperor Gao Zong exonerated Yue Fei and had his corpse reburied at the present site.

◉ South of West Lake

The hills south of West Lake are a prime spot for walkers, cyclists and green tea connoisseurs.

China Silk Museum　　MUSEUM
(中国丝绸博物馆; Zhōngguó Sīchóu Bówùguǎn; 73-1 Yuhuangshan Lu; 玉皇山路73-1号; ⊙9am-5pm Tue-Sun, noon-5pm Mon) **FREE** This fascinating museum has excellent displays of silk samples, silk making techniques, a room of looms with workers, a textile conservation gallery where you can watch conservationists in action, a superb gallery devoted to silks from Dūnhuáng, silk embroideries and exhibitions on silkworm anatomy.

CRUISING WEST LAKE

Cruise boats (游船; yóuchuán; Hubin Lu; 湖滨路; 1½hr, incl entry to Three Pools adult/child ¥70/35; ⊙7am-4.45pm) shuttle frequently from four **No 1 Park** (公园; Yī Gōngyuán; Hubin Lu; 湖滨路) and three other points (Red Carp Pond, Zhōngshān Park and the Mausoleum of General Yue Fei) to the **Mid-Lake Pavilion** (湖心亭; Húxīn Tíng) and **Xiǎoyíng Island** (小瀛洲; Xiǎoyíng Zhōu). Trips take 1½ hours and depart every 20 minutes. Alternatively, hire one of the **six-person boats** (小船; xiǎo chuán; per person/boat or ¥80 /160) rowed by boatmen. Look for them along the causeways. **Paddle boats** (30 minutes, ¥15 plus ¥200 deposit) on the Bái Causeway are also available for hire.

China National Tea Museum　　MUSEUM
(中国茶叶博物馆; Zhōngguó Cháyè Bówùguǎn; http://english.teamuseum.cn; 88 Longjing Lu; 龙井路88号; ⊙8.30am-4.30pm Tue-Sun) **FREE** Not far into the hills of Hángzhōu, you'll begin to see fields of tea bushes planted in undulating rows, the setting for the China Tea Museum – 3.7 hectares of land dedicated to the art, cultivation and tasting of tea. Further up are several tea-producing villages, all of which harvest China's most famous variety of green tea, lóngjǐng (dragon well), named after the spring where the pattern in the water resembles a dragon.

You can enjoy one of Hángzhōu's most famous teas at the **Dragon Well Tea Village** (龙井问茶; Lóngjǐng Wènchá; ⊙8am-5.30pm), near the first pass.

Tourist bus Y3 or K27 will take you to the museum and the village.

Six Harmonies Pagoda　　PAGODA
(六和塔; Liùhé Tǎ; 16 Zhijiang Lu; 之江路; grounds ¥20, grounds & pagoda ¥30; ⊙6am-6.30pm) Three kilometres southwest of West Lake, an enormous rail and road bridge spans the Qiántáng River. Close by rears up the 60m-high octagonal Six Harmonies Pagoda, first built in AD 960. The stout pagoda also served as a lighthouse, and was said to possess magical powers to halt the 6.5m-high tidal bore that thunders up Qiántáng River. You can climb the pagoda, while behind stretches a charming walk through terraces dotted with sculptures, bells, shrines and inscriptions.

Take bus K4 or 504 from Nanshan Lu.

☞ Tours

Just about every midrange and top-end hotel in Hángzhōu offers tours to West Lake and the surrounding areas. Tours are also arranged by the Hángzhōu Tourist Information Centre (p269).

✯ Festivals & Events

The International Qiántáng River Tide Observing Festival (p271) takes place every autumn in Yánguān, outside Hángzhōu.

🛏 Sleeping

Book well ahead in the summer months, at weekends and during the busy holiday periods. Room prices at hostels and some hotels get a significant weekend hike.

Mingtown Youth Hostel　　　HOSTEL $
(明堂杭州国际青年旅社; Míngtáng Hángzhōu Guójì Qīngnián Lǚshè; ☏ 0571 8791 8948; 101-11 Nanshan Lu; 南山路101-11号; dm/s/d, ¥65/200/295; ✳ 🌐) With its pleasant lakeside location, this friendly and highly popular hostel is often booked out so reserve well ahead. It has a relaxing cafe/bar, offers ticket booking, internet access, rents bikes and camping gear and is attractively decked out with orchids.

Hofang International Youth Hostel　HOSTEL $
(荷方国际青年旅社; Héfāng Guójì Qīngnián Lǚshè; ☏ 0571 8706 3299; 67 Dajing Xiang; 大井巷67号; dm ¥50-60, s/tw/d/tr/q ¥138/208/168-238/260/300; ✳ @ 🌐) Pleasantly tucked away from the noise down a historic alley off Qīnghéfāng Old Street (p263), this hostel has an excellent location and exudes a pleasant and calm ambience, with attractive rooms, the cheapest of which come with tatami. Note that prices for non-dorm rooms go up by between ¥30 and ¥60 on Friday and Saturday.

Wúshānyì International Youth Hostel　　　HOSTEL $
(吴山驿国际青年旅社; Wúshānyì Guójì Qīngnián Lǚshè; ☏ 0571 8701 8790; 22 Zhongshan Zhonglu, 中山中路22号; dm ¥55, rm ¥158-178, d/tr/q ¥248-268/298/358; ✳ @ 🌐) With a healthy mix of Chinese and Western travellers, this quiet, unhurried and comfy hostel has clean rooms and excellent, helpful staff plus a charmingly tucked-away location off Qinghefang Jie (and not too far from West Lake either). There are female dorms available (¥65) and cheap attic tatami rooms. Note that prices for non-dorm rooms go up by at least ¥30 on Friday and Saturday.

BĂOSHÍ SHĀN WALK

For a manageable and breezy trek into the forested hills above West Lake, walk up a lane called Qixialing, immediately west of the **Yuè Fēi Temple** (岳庙; Yuè Miào; Beishan Lu; 北山路; admission ¥25; ⏲ 7.30am-5.30pm). The road initially runs past the temple's west wall to enter the shade of towering trees, with stone steps leading you up. At **Zǐyún Cave** the hill levels out and the road forks; take the right-hand fork towards the Bàopǔ Taoist Temple, 1km further, and the Bǎochù Pagoda. At the top of the steps, turn left and, passing the **Sunrise Terrace** (初阳台; Chūyáng Tái), again bear left. Down the steps, look out for the tiled roofs and yellow walls of the charming **Bàopǔ Taoist Temple** (抱朴道院; Bàopǔ Dàoyuàn; admission ¥5; ⏲ 6am-5pm) to your right; head right along a path to reach it. Come out of the temple's back entrance and turn left towards the Bǎochù Pagoda and, after hitting a confluence of three paths, take the middle track towards and up **Toad Hill** (蛤蟆峰; Hámá Fēng), which affords supreme views over the lake, before squeezing through a gap between huge boulders to meet the **Bǎochù Pagoda** (保俶塔; Bǎochù Tǎ) rising ahead. Restored many times, the seven-storey grey brick pagoda was last rebuilt in 1933, although its spire tumbled off in the 1990s. Continue on down and pass through a **páilou** (牌楼) – or decorative arch – erected during the Republic (with some of its characters scratched off) to a series of stone-carved **Ming-dynasty effigies**, all of which were vandalised in the tumultuous 1960s, save two effigies on the right. Turn left here and walk a short distance to some steps heading downhill to your right past the remarkable weathered remains of a colossal stone **Buddha** by the cliff-face (with square niches cut in him) – all that remains of the Big Buddha Temple (大佛寺; Dàfó Sì). Continue on down to Beishan Lu.

West Lake Youth Hostel HOSTEL $

(杭州过客青年旅社; Hángzhōu Guòkè Qīngnián Lǚshè; ☑ 0571 8702 7027; www.westlakehostel. com; 62-3 Nanshan Lu, 南山路62-3号; dm ¥50-55, s ¥170, tw ¥210-220; ❄ @) Set back off the road amid trees and foliage east of Jìngcí Temple, this is a good bet with decent rooms and a comfy lounge-bar area hung with lanterns, and a good sense of character and seclusion; reserve ahead. The kindergarten next door can be very noisy in the morning, especially when the brass bands kick in.

Rates rise between ¥20 and ¥40 at weekends. From the train station take bus Y2 and get off at the Chángqiáo (长桥) stop.

In Lake Youth Hostel HOSTEL $

(柳湖小筑青年旅社; Liǔhú Xiǎozhù Qīngnián Lǚshè; ☑ 0571 8682 6700; 5 Luyang Lu, 绿杨路5号; dm ¥70, tw & d ¥328-458; ❄ ☏) Well-located a few steps from West Lake off Nanshan Lu, this attractive choice is all Mediterranean arches and ochre shades, with a lovely plant-bedecked interior courtyard. Rooms have wood flooring and tall radiators. Six-person dorms (all with shower) are clean. There's a roof terrace for barbecues, a downstairs cafe and bar, and welcoming staff.

The cheapest doubles are a bit smaller and noisier than the others.

Four Seasons Hotel Hángzhōu HOTEL $$$

(杭州西子湖四季酒店; Hángzhōu Xīzihú Sìjì Jiǔdiàn; ☑ 0571 8829 8888; www.fourseasons. com/hangzhou; 5 Lingyin Lu, 灵隐路5号; d ¥3800, ste from ¥8200; ❄❄@☏☰) More of a resort than a hotel, the fabulous 78-room Four Seasons enjoys a seductive position in lush grounds next to West Lake. Low-storey buildings and villas echo traditional China, a sensation amplified by the osmanthus trees, ornamental shrubs, ponds and tranquillity.

Checking into the gorgeously appointed and very spacious ground-floor deluxe premier rooms throws in a garden. Rooms have lovely bathrooms, walk-in wardrobe and hugely inviting beds. The infinity pool alongside West Lake is a dream, as is the outstanding spa. Charges for wi-fi.

Tea Boutique Hotel HOTEL $$$

(杭州天伦精品酒店; Hángzhōu Tiānlún Jīngpǐn Jiǔdiàn; ☑ 0571 8799 9888; www.teaboutiquehotel.com; 124 Shuguang Lu, 曙光路124号; d from ¥1098, ste ¥2280; ❄❄@☏) The simple but effectively done wood-sculpted foyer area with its sinuously shaped reception is a presage to the lovely accommodation at this hotel where a Japanese-minimalist mood

holds sway among celadon teacups, muted colours and – interestingly for China – a Bible in each room.

Double-glazed windows roadside keep the traffic noise low while the wide corridors convey a sense of space the boutique label often lacks. Service is excellent and healthy discounts run between 20% and 40%.

Crystal Orange Hotel HOTEL $$$

(桔子水晶酒店; Júzi Shuǐjīng Jiǔdiàn; ☑ 0571 2887 8988; www.orangehotel.com; 122 Qingbo Jie, 清波街122号; tw/ste ¥788/1388; ❄@☏) Uncluttered and modern business hotel with a crisp and natty interior, Warhol prints in the lobby, glass lift and only four floors, but sadly no views of West Lake from the neat rooms. Discounts of 50%.

🍴 Eating

Hángzhōu's most popular restaurant street is **Gaoyin Jie**, parallel to Qīnghéfāng Old Street (p263), a long sprawl of restaurants brashly lit up like casinos at night.

★ Green Tea Restaurant HÁNGZHŌU $

(绿茶; Lǜchá; 250 Jiefang Lu, 解放路250号; mains from ¥20; ⏰10.30am-11pm; Ⓜ Longxiangqiao) Often packed, this excellent Hángzhōu restaurant has superb food. With a bare brick finish and decorated with rattan utensils and colourful flower-patterned cushions, the dining style is casual. The long paper menu (tick what you want) runs from salty and more-ish pea soup (¥18), to gorgeous eggplant claypot (¥20), lip-smacking Dōngpō Chicken (¥48) and beyond. Seven other branches in town.

★ Grandma's Kitchen HÁNGZHŌU $

(外婆家; Wàipójiā; 3 Hubin Lu; 湖滨路3号; mains ¥6-55; ⏰lunch & dinner; Ⓜ Longxiangqiao) Besieged by enthusiastic diners, this restaurant cooks up classic Hángzhōu favourites; try the *hóngshāo dōngpō ròu* (红烧东坡肉; braised pork), but prepare to wait for a table. There are several other branches in town.

Bì Fēng Táng CANTONESE $

(避风塘; 256 Jiefang Lu; 解放路256号; mains from ¥15; ⏰10am-9pm Sun-Thu, 10am-10pm Fri & Sat; Ⓜ Ding'an Rd or Longxiangqiao) The charcoal and silver piping on the seats is rather garish, but the dim sum is fabulous at this restaurant right in the action by West Lake. Canto classics include: roasted duck rice (¥26), steamed barbecue pork buns (¥20), fried dumplings (¥23), vegetable and mushroom buns (¥15) and deep fried bean curd stuffed with shrimp (¥25) – all lovely.

If the waiting staff hand you a menu tick sheet in Chinese, ask for the picture menu (图片菜单; *túpiàn càidān*).

Dōngyīshùn
MUSLIM $

(Dōngyīshùn; 101 Gaoyin Jie; 高银街101号; mains ¥12-50; ⊙11am-9pm) Specialising in food from China's Muslim Hui minority, this busy Gaoyin Jie spot has lamb kebabs (羊肉串; *yáng ròu chuàn;* ¥10 for four), roast mutton (¥40) and roast chicken (¥48) like all the others, but you'll also find hummus, falafel, cheese omelets (¥28) and even cheese spring rolls (¥22). There's a take-out hatch for kebabs and *náng* (flat bread). Picture menu.

Cafe de Origin
CAFE $

(瑞井; Ruìjǐng; 53 Dajing Xiang; 大井巷53号; mains from ¥15; ⊙11am-10pm Mon-Fri & 10am-midnight Sat & Sun; Ⓜ Dingan Rd) With a pleasant alfresco terrace upstairs and stylish downstairs cafe area, Origin is a good place to relax with a coffee, sink a beer or grab a snack (vegetarians and vegans also catered for).

Lǎomǎjiā Miànguǎn
MUSLIM $

(老马家面馆; 232 Nanshan Lu; 南山路232号; mains from ¥12; ⊙7am-10pm) Simple and popular Muslim restaurant stuffed into an old *shíkùmén* tenement building with a handful of tables and spot-on *niúròu lāmiàn* (牛肉拉面; beef noodles) and scrummy beef-filled *ròujiāmó* (肉夹馍; meat in a bun, with onion if you want). No English menu.

Carrefour
SUPERMARKET $

(家乐福; Jiālèfú; 135 Yan'an Lu; 延安路135号; ⊙9am-9pm) On Yan'an Lu in between Xihu Dadao and Kaiyuan Lu.

La Pedrera
SPANISH, TAPAS $$$

(巴特洛西班牙餐厅; Bātèluò Xībānyá Cāntīng; ☑0571 8886 6089; 4 Baishaquan, Shuguang Lu, 曙光路白沙泉4号; tapas from ¥30, meals ¥200; ⊙11am-11pm) This fine two-floor Spanish restaurant just off Shuguang Lu bar street has tapas diners in a whirl, paella-aficionados applauding and Spanish-wine fans gratified. Prices may take a sizeable bite out of your wallet, but the convivial atmosphere and assured menu prove popular and enjoyable.

Lóuwàilóu Restaurant
HĀNGZHŌU $$$

(楼外楼; Lóuwàilóu; ☑0571 8796 9023; 30 Gushan Lu; mains ¥30-200; ⊙10.30am-3.30pm & 4.30-8.45pm) Founded in 1838, this is Hángzhōu's most famous restaurant. The local speciality is *xīhú cùyú* (西湖醋鱼; sweet and sour

carp) and *dōngpō* pork, but there's a good choice of other well-priced standard dishes.

Drinking

For drinking, Shuguang Lu (曙光路), north of West Lake, is the place. For a comprehensive list of Hángzhōu bars and restaurants, grab a copy of *More – Hangzhou Entertainment Guide* (www.morehangzhou.com), available from bars and concierge desks at good hotels.

★ Maya Bar
BAR

(玛雅酒吧; Mǎyǎ Jiǔbā; 94 Baishaquan, Shuguang Lu; 曙光路白沙泉94号; ⊙10am-2am) Jim Morrison, Kurt Cobain, Mick Jagger, Bob Dylan, the Beatles and a mural of a shaman/spirit warrior look on approvingly from the walls of this darkly lit and rock-steady bar. Just as importantly, the drinks are seriously cheap; Tuesdays and Thursdays see Tsingtao and Tiger dropping to ¥10 a pint (¥20 at other times) and a DJ from 9.30pm.

Eudora Station
BAR

(亿多瑞站; Yìduōruìzhàn; 101-107 Nanshan Lu; 南山路101-107号; ⊙9am-2am) A fab location by West Lake, roof terrace aloft, outside seating, a strong menu and a sure-fire atmosphere conspire to make this welcoming watering hole a great choice. There's sports TV, live music, a ground-floor terrace, a good range of beers, and barbecues fire up on the roof terrace in the warmer months.

☆ Entertainment

JZ Club
CLUB

(黄楼; Huáng Lóu; ☑0571 8702 8298; www.jz-club.cc; 6 Liuying Lu, by 266 Nanshan Lu; 柳营路6号; ⊙7pm-2.30am) The folk that brought you JZ Club in Shànghǎi have the live jazz scene sewn up in Hángzhōu with this neat three-floor venue in a historic building near West Lake. There are three live jazz sets nightly, with music kicking off at 9pm (till midnight). There's no admission charge, but you'll need to reserve a seat on Fridays and Saturdays. Smokers get to go upstairs.

🛍 Shopping

Hángzhōu is famed for its tea, in particular *lóngjǐng* green tea, as well as silk, fans and, of all things, scissors. All of these crop up in the **Wúshān Lù night market** (吴山路夜市; Wúshān Lù Yèshì; Huixing Lu; 惠兴路), between Youdian Lu (邮电路) and Renhe Lu (仁和路), where fake ceramics jostle with ancient pewter tobacco pipes, Chairman Mao memorabilia, silk shirts and pirated CDs. Qīng-héfāng Old Street has loads of possibilities, from Chinese tiger pillows to taichi swords.

Xinhua Lu Silk Market   SILK
(新华路丝绸市场; Xīnhuá Lù Sīchóu Shìchǎng; Xinhua Lu; ⊙ 8am-5pm) For silk, try these shops strung out along the north of Xinhua Lu.

ℹ️ Information

INTERNET ACCESS

Twenty-four-hour internet cafes are in abundance around the main train station (typically ¥4 or ¥5 per hour); look for the neon signs '网吧'.

MEDICAL SERVICES

Zhèjiāng University First Affiliated Hospital
(浙江大学医学院附属第一医院; Zhèjiāng Dàxué Yīxuéyuàn Fùshǔ Dìyī Yīyuàn; ☑ 0571 8723 6114; 79 Qingchun Lu)

MONEY

Bank of China - Yanan Lu (中国银行, Zhōng-guó Yínháng; 320 Yanan Lu; 延安路320号; ⊙ 9am-5pm) A useful central branch with currency exchange.

Bank of China - Laodong Lu (中国银行, Zhōng-guó Yínháng; 177 Laodong Lu; ⊙ 9am-5pm) Offers currency exchange plus 24-hour ATM.

HSBC (汇丰银行; Huìfēng Yínháng; cnr Qing-chun Lu & Zhonghe Lu; ⊙ 9am-5pm) Has a 24-hour ATM.

Industrial & Commercial Bank of China (ICBC, 工商银行; Gōngshāng Yínháng; 300 Yan'an Lu) Has a 24-hour ATM.

POST

China Post (中国邮政; Zhōngguó Yóuzhèng; Renhe Lu; ⊙ 8.30am-6pm) Close to West Lake.

PUBLIC SECURITY BUREAU

Public Security Bureau (PSB; 公安局; Gōng'ānjú Bànzhèng Zhōngxīn; ☑ 0571 8728 0600; 35 Huaguang Lu; ⊙ 8.30am-noon & 2-5pm Mon-Fri) Can extend visas.

TOURIST INFORMATION

Asking at, or phoning up, your hostel or hotel for info can be very handy.

Hángzhōu Tourist Information Centre (杭州旅游咨询服务中心; Hángzhōu Lǚyóu Zīxún Fúwù Zhōngxīn; ☑ 0571 8797 8123; Léifēng Pagoda, Nanshan Lu; ⊙ 8am-5pm) Provides basic travel info, free maps and tours. Other branches include **Hángzhōu train station** and **10 Huaguang Lu**, just off Qīnghéfāng Old Street.

Tourist Complaint Hotline (☑ 0571 8796 9691) The Tourist Complaint Hotline can assist visitors with problems or issues during their stay.

Travellers Infoline (☑ 0571 96123) Helpful 24-hour information with English service from 6.30am to 9pm.

WEBSITES

Hángzhōu City Travel Committee (www.gotohz.com) has current information on events, restaurants and entertainment venues around the city. The news-oriented **Hángzhōu News** (www.hangzhou.com.cn/english) website also has travel info, and **More Hángzhōu** (www.morehangzhou.com) is a handy website with restaurant and nightlife reviews, forums and classifieds.

ℹ️ Getting There & Away

AIR

Hángzhōu has flights to all major Chinese cities (bar Shànghǎi) and international connections to Hong Kong, Macau, Tokyo, Singapore and other destinations. Several daily flights connect to Běijīng (¥1050) and Guǎngzhōu (¥960).

Most hotels will also book flights, generally with a ¥20 to ¥30 service charge. The **Civil Aviation Administration of China** (CAAC; 中国民航; Zhōngguó Mínháng; ☑ 0571 8666 8666; 390 Tiyuchang Lu; ⊙ 7.30am-8pm) office is in the north of town.

BUS

All four bus stations are outside the city centre; tickets can be conveniently bought for all stations from the **bus ticket office** (长途汽车售票处; Chángtú Qìchē Shòupiàochù; Chengzhan Lu; 城站路; ⊙ 6.30am-5pm) right off the exit from Hángzhōu's Main Train Station.

Buses leave Shànghǎi's South Station frequently for Hángzhōu's various bus stations (¥68, 2½ hours). Buses to Hángzhōu also run every 30 minutes between 10am and 9pm from Shànghǎi's Hóngqiáo airport (¥85, two hours). Regular buses also run to Hángzhōu from Shànghǎi's Pǔdōng International Airport (¥100, three hours).

Buses from the huge **Main Bus Station** (客运中心站; Kéyùn Zhōngxīn; ☑ 0571 8765 0678; Jiubao Zhijie; 九堡直街) at Jiǔbǎo, in the far northeast of Hángzhōu (and linked to the centre of town by metro, a taxi will cost around ¥60) include:

Huángshān (scenic zone) ¥98 to ¥110, four hours, five daily

Níngbō ¥62, two hours, regular

Shànghǎi ¥68, 2½ hours, regular

Sūzhōu ¥71, two hours, regular

Wūzhèn ¥27 to ¥30, one hour, 16 daily

Xīn'ānjiāng ¥35 ¥42 two hours, eight daily

Buses from the **South Bus Station** (汽车南站; Qìchē Nánzhàn; 407 Qiutao Lu):

Níngbō ¥62, two hours, every 20 minutes

Shàoxīng ¥25, one hour, every 20 minutes

Xīn'ānjiāng ¥57 two hours, eight daily

Zhūgě ¥58, two hours, 8.40am & 3.50pm

Buses from the **North Bus Station** (汽车北站; Qìchē Běizhàn; 766 Moganshan Lu):

Ānjí ¥27

Nánxún ¥40, 1½ hours, regular

Sūzhōu ¥72, two hours, regular

Tónglǐ ¥62, two hours, three daily

Wǔkāng ¥15, one hour, hourly

Buses from the **West Bus Station** (汽车西站; Qìchē Xīzhàn; 357 Tianmushan Lu) include:

Huángshān (scenic zone): ¥98 to ¥110, four hours, five daily

Wùyuán ¥129, 4½ hours, 9.20am & 1.40pm

Xīn'ānjiāng ¥57 two hours, every 30 minutes

Xīnyè ¥59, 2½ hours, 8.20am & 1.50pm

Zhūgě ¥58, two hours, 2.40pm

TRAIN

The easiest way to travel to Hángzhōu from Shànghǎi Hóngqiáo Train Station is on the high-speed G class train to **Hángzhōu Main Train Station** (杭州火车站; Hángzhōu Huǒchēzhàn; ☑ 0571 8762 2362; Chengzhan Lu; 城站路), east of West Lake. For Běijīng, the overnight Z10 (soft sleeper ¥537) departs Hángzhōu Main Train Station at 6.05pm, arriving at 7.40am, and the handy T32 (hard/soft sleeper ¥351/¥537) departs at 6.20pm, arriving at 10.21am. Most G class trains to Běijīng leave from Hángzhōu East Train Station.

G class trains running from the huge new **Hángzhōu East Train Station** (杭州东站; Hángzhōu Dōngzhàn; Dongning Lu; 东宁路), linked to the centre of town by metro, include:

Běijīng South 2nd/1st class ¥537/907, six hours, 12 daily

Shànghǎi Hóngqiáo Train Station 2nd/1st class ¥74/118, one hour, regular

Shàoxīng North 2nd/1st class ¥20/34, 20 minutes, regular

Sūzhōu 2nd/1st class ¥112/179, 1½ hours, three daily

Xiàmén North Train Station 2nd/1st class ¥306/402, 6½ hours, one daily

Wēnzhōu South Train Station 2nd/1st class ¥153/219, three hours, regular

Daily G class high-speed trains from Hángzhōu Main Train Station:

Běijīng South Train Station 2nd/1st class ¥629/1056, 6½ hours, two daily

Nánjīng South Train Station 2nd/1st class ¥119/200, two hours 20 minutes, five daily

Shànghǎi Hóngqiáo Train Station 2nd/1st class ¥78/124, 55 minutes, first/last 6.10am/8.26pm, regular

Sūzhōu 2nd/1st class ¥118 to ¥184, 1½ hours, two daily

Daily D class high-speed trains from Hángzhōu Main Train Station:

Shànghǎi Hóngqiáo Train Station 2nd/1st class ¥49/60, one hour 10 minutes, eight daily

Sūzhōu 2nd/1st class ¥75/91, two hours, two daily

A handy **train ticket office** (火车票售票处; Huǒchēpiào Shòupiàochù; 147 Huansha Lu; 浣纱路147号; ☺ 8am-5pm) is north of Jiefang Lu, just east of West Lake. Other offices are at **72 Baochu Lu** (near turning with Shengfu Lu) and **149 Tiyuchang Lu**. Train tickets are also available at certain China Post branches including 10 Desheng Lu and 60 Fengqi Lu. See the China by Train chapter (p1012) for ways of buying tickets on line.

ⓘ Getting Around

TO/FROM THE AIRPORT

Hángzhōu's airport is 30km from the city centre; taxi drivers ask around ¥100 to ¥130 for the trip. Shuttle buses (¥20, one hour) run every 15 minutes between 5.30am and 9pm from the CAAC office (also stopping at the train station).

BICYCLE

The best way to rent a bike is to use the **Hángzhōu Bike Hire Scheme** (☑ 0571 8533 1122; www.hzzxc.com.cn; credit /deposit ¥100/200; ☺ 6.30am-9pm Apr-Oct, 6am-9pm Nov-Mar). Stations (2700 in total) are dotted in large numbers around the city, in what is the world's largest network. Apply at one of the booths at numerous bike stations near West Lake; you will need your passport as ID. Fill in a form and you will receive a swipe card, then swipe the pad at one of the docking stations till you get a steady green light, free a bike and Bob's your uncle.

Return bikes to any other station (ensure the bike is properly docked before leaving it). The first hour on each bike is free, so if you switch bikes within the hour, the rides are free. The second hour on the same bike is ¥1, the third is ¥2 and after that it's ¥3 per hour. Your deposit and unused credit are refunded to you when you return your swipe card (check when it should be returned as this can vary). Note you cannot return bikes outside booth operating hours as the swipe units deactivate (you will be charged a whole night's rental).

Youth hostels also rent out bikes, but these are more expensive.

PUBLIC TRANSPORT
Bus

Hángzhōu has a clean, efficient bus system and getting around is easy (but roads are increasingly gridlocked). 'Y' buses are tourist buses; 'K' is simply an abbreviation of 'kōngtiáo' (air-con). Tickets are ¥2 to ¥5. The following are popular bus routes:

Bus K7 Usefully connects the Main Train Station to the western side of West Lake and Língyǐn Temple.

Tourist bus Y2 Goes from the Main Train Station, along Beishan Lu and up to Língyǐn Temple.

Tourist bus Y3 Travels around West Lake to the China Silk Museum, China National Tea Museum and Dragon Well Tea Village.

Bus K56 Travels from the East Bus Station to Yan'an Lu.

Buses 15 & K15 Connect the North Bus Station to the northwest area of West Lake.

Bus 188 Runs to the North Bus Station.

Metro

Hángzhōu's new metro line 1 (tickets ¥2 to ¥7; first/last train 6.06am/11.32pm), runs from the southeast of town, through the Main Train Station, the east side of West Lake and on to the East Train Station, the Main Bus Station and the northeast of town. It's not very useful for sightseeing around town. Line 2 is expected to start service in 2016, while other lines are planned.

TAXI

Metered Hyundai taxis are ubiquitous and start at ¥10; figure on around ¥20 to ¥25 from the main train station (queues can be horrendous though) to Hubin Lu.

Around Hángzhōu

Qiántáng River Tidal Bore
钱塘江潮

An often spectacular natural phenomenon occurs every month on Hángzhōu's Qiántáng River (钱塘江), when the highest tides of the lunar cycle dispatch a wall of water – sometimes almost 9m tall – thundering along the narrow mouth of the river from Hángzhōu Bay, at up to 40km per hour. Occasionally sweeping astonished sightseers away and luring bands of intrepid surfers, this awesome tidal bore (钱塘江潮; *qiántáng jiāngcháo*) is the world's largest and can be viewed from the riverbank in Hángzhōu, but one of the best places to witness the action is on the north side of the river at Yánguān (盐官), a delightful ancient town about 38km northeast of Hángzhōu.

The most popular viewing time is during the International Qiántáng River Tide Observing Festival, on the 18th day of the eighth month of the lunar calendar (the same day as the mid-autumn festival), which usually falls in September or October. You can however see it throughout the year when the highest tide occurs at the beginning and middle of each lunar month; access to the park in Yánguān for viewing the tide is ¥25. The Hángzhōu Tourist Information Centre (p269) can give you upcoming tide times. To make it a day trip, a through-ticket (¥100) is available in Yánguān to explore the charming historic temples and buildings of the town.

Take a bus (¥25, one hour, 6.30am to 6.50pm) from Hángzhōu's Main Bus Station to Hǎiníng (海宁) and change to bus 106 (¥8; 25 minutes) to Yánguān.

Mògānshān 莫干山
☑ 0572

A blessed release from the suffocating summer torpor roasting north Zhèjiāng, this delightful **hilltop resort** (admission ¥80) was developed by 19th-century Europeans from Shànghǎi and Hángzhōu. Refreshingly cool in summer and sometimes smothered in spectral fog, Mògānshān is famed for its scenic vistas, forested views, towering bamboo and stone villa architecture; the mountain remains a weekend bolt hole for expat *tàitai* (wives) fleeing the simmering lowland heat.

◎ Sights & Activities

The best way to enjoy Mògānshān is just to wander the winding forest paths and stone steps, taking in some of the architecture en route. There's Shànghǎi gangster **Du Yuesheng's old villa** (杜月笙别墅; *Dù Yuèshēng Biéshù*) – now serving as a hotel – Chiang Kaishek's lodge, a couple of churches (375 Moganshan and 419 Moganshan) and many other villas linked (sometimes tenuously) with the rich and famous, including the **house** (毛主席下榻处; *Máo Zhǔxí Xiàtàchù*; 126 Moganshan) where Chairman Mao rested his chubby limbs.

Apart from the gaunt villa architecture, more recent construction has flung up less attractive villas made of more regular blocks; the genuine older villas are made of irregularly shaped stone. Sadly, many of the original interiors have been ripped out, so much of the period charm is absent.

Containing **Tǎ Mountain** (塔山; *Tǎ Shān*) in the northwest, the **Dà Kēng Scenic Area** (大坑景区; *Dàkēng Jǐngqū*) is great for rambling.

🛏 Sleeping

Mògānshān is full of hotels of varying quality, most housed in crumbling villas; room prices peak at weekends (Friday to Sunday). If you come off-season (eg early spring) you can expect good rates, but be warned that many hotels either shut up shop or close for renovation over the winter.

⭐ **Le Passage Mohkan Shan**   HOTEL **$$$**
(莫干山里法国山居; Mògānshānlǐ Fǎguóshānjū; ☑0572 805 2958; www.lepassagemoganshan.com; Xiānrénkēng Tea Plantation, Zǐlíng Village, 紫岭村仙人坑茶厂; d/tr/q ¥4800/5800/6800; ❄🅰️♿) 🖊 Le Passage is a lovely and kid-friendly 38-room country-house hotel ensconced within a Mògānshān tea plantation. Rooms and bathrooms are big on period charm, with high ceilings. Rates are cheaper per night for a two-evening stay. Pick-up service from Shànghǎi (¥1300) and Hángzhōu (¥500) provided. There's a wine cellar, of course.

Mògānshān House 23   HOTEL **$$$**
(莫干山杭疗23号; Mògānshān Hángliáo 23 Hào; ☑0572 803 3822; www.moganshanhouse23.com; 23 Moganshan; 莫干山23号; d & tw weekday/weekend ¥900/1200; @🅰️) This restored villa bursts with period charm, from art deco–style sinks, black-and-white tiled bathroom floors, wooden floorboards and the original staircase to a lovely English kitchen. It's also kid friendly with a family room, baby chairs and swings in the garden. With only six rooms, book well in advance, especially for weekend stays (when it's a minimum two-night stay).

Breakfast is included in the room price. Also ask about the two other Mògānshān properties run by the same owners, House 2 (weekday/weekend d ¥650/975) and House 25 (weekday/weekend villa ¥1200/3600).

Naked Stables Private Reserve   VILLAS **$$$**
(☑021-6431 8901; www.nakedretreats.cn; 37 Shangxiazhuang, Lanshukeng Village, Fatou, 筏头乡兰树坑村上下庄37号; earth hut ¥2600, 2-/3-/4-room tree-top villas from ¥7200/9000/1200; ✳️@♿) 🖊 For unbridled escapism, head for these luxurious and beautifully situated mod-con-equipped tree-top villas and earth huts within a 24-hectare resort in Mògānshān; expect serene forest views, infinity pools, a spa and wellness centre, and heaps of eco brownie points.

🍴 Eating

Mògānshān Lodge   INTERNATIONAL **$$**
(马克的咖啡厅; Mǎkè de Kāfēitīng; ☑0572 803 3011; www.moganshanlodge.com; Songliang Shanzhuang, off Yinshan Jie; ⏰8.30am-11pm, Thu-Tue; 📶) This elegantly presented villa, up some steps from Yinshan Jie, does decent enough breakfasts, bacon sandwiches and lunches and coffee, but dinner's the main meal (phone ahead to find out what's the choice of the day) and travel advice is dispensed. Serves only coffee (no meals) on Tuesdays.

ℹ Information

The main village (Mògānshān Zhèn) is centred on Yinshan Jie (荫山街), where you will find the **China Post** (40 Moganshan; ⏰8.30-11am & 1-4pm), a branch of the PSB (opposite the post office) and several hotels.

ℹ Getting There & Away

Wǔkāng (武康; also known as also known as Déqīng; 德清) is the jumping-off point for Mògānshān. From Hángzhōu's north bus station, buses leave for Wǔkāng (¥15, one hour, every 30 minutes) from 6.20am to 7pm; in the other direction, buses run every 30 minutes from 6.30am till 7pm. Don't take a *sānlúnchē* (pedicab) as they will drop you at the foot of the mountain.

From Wǔkāng minivans run to the top of Mògānshān for around ¥80; a taxi will cost around ¥80 to ¥100. Buses from Shànghǎi South Bus Station run four times a day to Wǔkāng (¥63 to ¥75, four hours, 7.55am, 9.25am, 1.25pm and 2.55pm).

Wūzhèn 乌镇
☑0573

Like Zhōuzhuāng and other water towns in southern Jiāngsū, Wūzhèn's charming network of waterways and access to the Grand Canal once made it a prosperous place of trade and silk production.

🅞 Sights

With its old bridges, ancient temples, age-old residences, museums and canal-side Ming- and Qing-dynasty architecture, Wūzhèn (www.wuzhen.com.cn) is an appetising and photogenic if over-commercialised slice of old China. It's a lovely place to overnight, although you can easily make it a day trip from either Shànghǎi or Hángzhōu.

The old town is divided into two scenic areas: **Dōngzhà** (东栅; admission ¥100; ◷7am-5.30pm, till 6pm in summer) and **Xīzhà** (西栅; admission ¥120, after 5pm ¥80; ◷9am-10pm, till 10.30pm in summer); a combined ticket to visit the two areas costs ¥150. Buy your ticket at the **main visitor centre** (入口; Rùkǒu; Daqiao Lu; ◷8am-5.30pm), where a money exchange and an ATM can be found; you can also take a boat from here across the lake.

◎ Dōngzhà Scenic Zone

The main street of the Dōngzhà scenic zone, Dongda Jie (东大街), is a narrow path paved with stone slabs and flanked by wooden buildings and workshops embracing all trades from cloth dying to bamboo weaving and tobacco making. Most sights are open from 8am to 5pm. The Dōngzhà scenic zone is very hectic at weekends and during holiday periods.

Jiāngnán Wood Carving Museum   MUSEUM
(420 Dong Dajie; 东大街420号; ◷8am-5pm) This fascinating museum contains some outstanding specimens of wood carvings from the region.

Ancient Beds Museum   MUSEUM
(百床关; Bǎichuǎngguǎn; 212 Dong Dajie; 东大街212号; ◷8am-5pm) The Ancient Beds Museum has an intriguing collection of historic beds from the region.

Mao Dun's Former Residence   HISTORIC BUILDING
(茅盾故居; Máo Dùn Gùjū; Guanqian Jie; 观前街; ◷8am-5pm) Near the entrance to the Dōngzhà scenic zone, Mao Dun's Former Residence was the home of the revolutionary writer and author of *Spring Silkworms* and *Midnight*. His great-grandfather, a successful merchant, bought the house in 1885 and it's a fairly typical example from the late Qing dynasty.

Huìyuán Pawn House   HISTORIC BUILDING
(汇源当铺; Huìyuán Dàngpù; Changfeng Jie; ◷8am-5pm) The Huìyuán Pawn House was once a famous pawnshop that eventually expanded to branches in Shànghǎi.

◎ Xīzhà Scenic Zone

The Xīzhà scenic zone is far less packed and in general more pleasant and interesting than the crowded Dōngzhà scenic zone. Sights include ancestral halls, the **Indigo Fabric Workshop**, the **Zhàomíng Academy**, the **Black Pottery Workshop** and the **Yuèlǎo Temple**.

Chinese Footbinding Culture Museum   MUSEUM
(◷8am-5pm) FREE This fascinating museum charts the history of footbinding in China with examples of the shoes that constituted, as captions in the museum attest, to 'The Golden Lotus complex that was the freakish mentality of the males at that time'. Periodically banned, including a Taiping prohibition in the 19th century, footbinding was final abolished in the 20th century. Get the lowdown here.

White Lotus Pagoda   BUDDHIST
(白莲塔; Báilián Tǎ; Shenglian Sq; ◷8am-5pm) Climb up this towering pagoda at the west end of the Xīzhà scenic zone for excellent views over the Grand Canal.

☂ Activity

Dongshi River Boat Tours   BOATING
(Dōngzhì per person from ¥30, Xīzhà per person ¥60) Boats leave for trips along the Dongshi River to Xinghua Bridge from the Tourist Boat Quay near Wūzhèn Visitor Centre (p273).

🛏 Sleeping

Accommodation choices are principally in the Xīzhà scenic zone, including a youth hostel, B&Bs and inns.

Wūzhèn Guesthouse   GUESTHOUSE $
(☎0573 873 1666; 137 Xizha Jie; 西栅街137号; r from ¥300; ❊) In the Xīzhà scenic zone, this is a centralised collection of canal-side B&Bs along Xi Dajie and on the other side of the water, run by families where you are then given a well-presented room with air-con, telephone and bathroom. Non-river rooms are the cheapest. To identify accommodation, look for the characters 民宿.

Book at the entrance to the Xīzhà Scenic Zone or at No 137 Xi Dajie.

Wisteria Youth Hostel   HOSTEL $
(紫藤国际青年旅社; Zǐténg Guójì Qīngnián Lǚshè; ☎0573 8873 1088; 43 Sizuo Jie; 丝作街43号; 4-/6-/8-bed dm ¥100/80/60) This OK place has a lovely location on a lovely square opposite the Yida Silk Workshop on the far side of Renji Bridge, but only has dorm rooms. Wi-fi largely in lobby only.

☆ Entertainment

Regular live performances of shadow puppet shows (*píyǐngxì*) take place in the small **theatre** (皮影院院; Píyǐngxìyuàn; Xinghua Lu; ☉performances every 10min) off Xinghua Lu. **Martial arts performances** are held on a boat near the visitor centre (p273) every half and hour between 8.30am and 4.10pm.

❶ Getting There & Away

From Hángzhōu, buses (¥29, one hour, hourly from 6.35am to 6.15pm) run regularly to Wūzhèn from the Main Bus Station.

From Shànghǎi, buses (¥49, two hours, hourly 7am to 6pm) run from the Shànghǎi South Bus Station. Four buses (¥34) also run between Wūzhèn and Sūzhōu train station.

❶ Getting Around

From Wūzhèn bus station, bus 350 (¥2, 7am to 5.30pm) runs to both the Dōngzhà and Xīzhà scenic zones, or you can grab a *sānlúnchē* (¥10). A free shuttle bus runs (7.40am to 5.20pm) runs every 20 minutes between the Dōngzhà scenic zone and the Xīzhà scenic zone.

Xīn'ānjiāng 新安江

📋 0571 / TRANSPORT HUB

Also known as Jiàndé (建德) and arrayed along its namesake river of Xīn'ān Jiāng (新安江), this pleasant and modern town has little in the way of sights, but provides a gateway to the villages of Xīnyè and Zhūgě. It is famous among holidaying Chinese for the vast **Qiāndǎo Hú** (千岛湖; Thousand Island Lake), the more popular name for the Xīnānjiāng Reservoir, partitioned off from the town by a nearby dam. You can reach the nearest part of the reservoir by taxi for around ¥40 to ¥50.

🛏 Sleeping

Except for pricier places, most hotels in town don't accept foreigners and it's far more charming to overnight in either Xīnyè or Zhūgě.

Peninsula Kǎiháo Hotel　HOTEL **$$**
(半岛凯豪大酒店; Bàndǎo Kǎiháo Jiǔdiàn; 📋 0571 6418 5888; 668 Xin'an Donglu; 新安东路668号; d ¥880-1580, ste ¥2080-18888; ❈ @ 🛜) With the plushest rooms in town, this hotel is not far from the river in the east of Xīn'ānjiāng, but is away from the action. Lovely

rooms in the new wing, shabbier carpets in the older wing. Comfort all round and spacious bathrooms. Rooms can dip to ¥528.

Xīndōngfāng Hotel　HOTEL **$$**
(新东方商务大酒店; Xīndōngfāng Shāngwù Dàjiǔdiàn; 📋 0571 6411 0585; 427 Xin'an Donglu; 新安东路427号; s/d/ste ¥480/580-980/1280; ❈ @) This marbled hotel is an OK midrange choice with reasonable rooms, but a rather stranded location in the east of town.

✖ Eating

Night Market　MARKET
(Xin'an Lu; ☉4-10pm) For Xīnjiāng kebabs, seafood, hotpots and dumplings, head to the lively night market just north of Xīn'anjiāng's hopping **Old Square** (*Lǎo Guǎngchǎng*; 老广场) in between Kangle Lu (康乐路) and Caishi Lu (菜市路) off Xin'an Lu in the west of town.

❶ Information

Bank of China (130 Xin'an Lu; 新安路130号; ☉8.30am-4.30pm) For foreign exchange plus a 24hr ATM; by Wangjiang Lu.

China Post (中国邮政; Zhōngguó Yóuzhèng; cnr of Xin'an Lu and Fuqian Lu; 新安路和府前路的路口; ☉8am-5pm)

Jiàndé Tourist Information Center (建德旅游咨询中心; Jiàndé Lǚyóu Zīxún Zhōngxīn; 11 Xin'an Donglu; 新安东路11号; ☉8am-5.30pm, to 7.30pm summer) For tourist advice and tours.

❶ Getting There & Away

The blue **Main Bus Station** (新安江汽车站; Xīn'ānjiāng Qìchēzhàn; Fuqian Lu; 府前路) is at the heart of town, just south of the post office and the intersection with Xin'an Lu. There are seven buses daily (¥35, two hours) to Hángzhōu's Main Bus Station and two buses (¥126, 7.30am and 2.05pm, 4¼ hours) to Shànghǎi's Main Bus Station. There are also regular buses to the Hángzhōu South Bus Station (hourly, two hours) and West Bus Station (¥57, every 40 minutes, two hours) can be bought from the separate ticket office adjacent to the main ticket hall.

Buses (¥8, one hour, 7.20am to 5pm) to Xīnyè depart from the **South Bus Station** (汽车南站; Qìchē Nánzhàn; Baisha Lu; 白沙路), reachable on bus 2 (¥2) from the bus stop opposite the Main Bus Station on Fuqian Lu. There are also buses direct from Hángzhōu's West Bus Station to Qiāndǎohú (Y61), for trips to the lake.

Around Xīn'ānjiāng

Xīnyè 新叶

Cut with sparkling streams, centred on placid ponds and embraced by silent hills, the astonishingly picturesque village of **Xīnyè** (新叶; 8am-4pm; admission ¥68) is populated by families sharing the surname Ye (叶) and an abundance of free-roaming chickens. The village is laid out in accordance with the traditional five element (五行; *wǔ háng*) theory, so it's a balanced exercise in feng shui aesthetics. During spring, the village is framed by fields of bright yellow rapeseed. The admission fee covers all the village sights.

◉ Sights

A good place to start, the **Wénchāng Hall** (文昌阁; Wénchāng Gé; ⊙8am-4pm) contains a portrait of Confucius and an adjacent shrine (土地祠; *Tǔdì Cí*) to the village god (for good harvests); an effigy of the monkey god hides away in a further shrine upstairs. Smudged red Maoist slogans add their own narrative. The beautiful, white and elegant seven-storey, brick-built **Tuányún Pagoda** (抟云塔; Tuányún Tǎ; ⊙8am-4pm) right alongside is perhaps the definitive image of the village. Not far away, the **Xīshān Ancestral Temple** (西山祠堂; Xīshān Cítáng; ⊙8am-4pm) is a peach.

Next to the nearby rectangular Sìfāng Pond (四方塘; Sìfāng Táng), the huge white-washed **Jìnshì Hall** (进士堂; Jìnshì Táng; ⊙8am-4pm) encloses a cool, voluminous wooden interior.

The **Hall of Good Order** (有序堂; Yǒuxù Táng; ⊙8am-4pm) is central to the village; its front door does not open so its accessible side door faces out onto pyramid-shaped Dàofēng Mountain (道峰山; Dàofēng Shān), across the waters of half-moon shaped South Pond (南塘; Nántáng), from where eight alleys radiate out through the village. Originally built in 1290 and rebuilt during the Republic, the hall contains some astonishing wood carvings of a deer, small birds and a monkey in the trees. At the end of the day, sit just next to the pond and watch old folk gathering to chat.

The **Shuāngměi Hall** (双美堂; Shuāng-měi Táng; ⊙8am-4pm) is another lovely wood-panelled affair containing intricate and exquisite carvings above pillars. The

Chóngrén Temple (崇仁堂; Chóngrén Táng; ⊙8am-4pm) is charmingly located next to Half Moon Pond (半月塘; Bànyuè Táng).

🛏 Sleeping

Dàofēng Rénjiā Tǔcàiguǎn   GUESTHOUSE $
(稻丰人家土菜馆; ☎138 6810 1720; s/d ¥40/80) Not far from the bus drop off, this guesthouse is one of the few places you can stay in Xīnyè, with well-kept singles and doubles; it can cook up meals.

❶ Getting There & Away

There are two daily buses (¥8, one hour, 7.20am to 5pm) from Xīn'ānjiāng's South Bus Station.

There is also a direct bus service (¥59, two hours, 8.20am & 1.50pm) from Hángzhōu's West Bus Station.

The bus to Zhūgě (¥3.5, 30 minutes, four daily, 6.05am, 8.30am, 11.50am and 3.10pm) leaves from the drop off point for buses from Xīn'ānjiāng.

Zhūgě 诸葛

Zhūgě (诸葛; www.zhugevillage.cn; ¥100) is an astonishing village, traditionally designed according the *bāguà* (八卦; eight trigrams) of the i-Ching. It has a rather more commercialised feel than nearby Xīnyè, but remains a picturesque composition of traditional Chinese village architecture and meticulous feng shui planning.

◉ Sights

From the bus drop off, walk uphill along Gaolong Lu (高隆路) to the village and past the ticket collector; proceed downhill, round the corner and reach the lovely, huge Upper Pond (上塘; Shàng Táng) and the **Shòuchūn Hall** (寿春堂; Shòuchūn Táng; ⊙7.30am-5pm summer, 8am-4.30pm winter) – one of Zhūgě's 18 halls – itself a long sequence of chambers and courtyards alongside rectangular Lower Pond (下堂 or 夏堂; Xià Táng) and two further halls, the **Dàjīng Hall** (大经堂; Dàjīng Táng; ⊙7.30am-5pm summer, 8am-4.30pm winter) – housing a traditional Chinese medicine museum – and, up the steps, the **Yōngmù Hall** (雍睦堂; Yōngmù Táng; ⊙7.30am-5pm summer, 8am-4.30pm winter), a fine Ming dynasty hall with an eye-catching central stone door frame and an exhibition dedicated to local culture. Spot the black trigrams (八卦; bāguà) above some windows of whitewashed houses and stop by the old communist era **cinema** (电

影院; Diànyǐngyuàn; ☉ 7.30am-5pm summer, 8am-4.30pm winter) with its wooden seats, within the self-styled (and vacant) Tourist Reception Center. It's a snapshot of the 1960s.

Eight (the number mirroring the eight trigrams of the bāguà) lanes radiate from **Zhōng Pond** (钟池; Zhōng Chí) at the heart of the village. The fēng shuǐ symbol of the village, the circular pond resembles the Chinese twin-fish, yīn-yáng taiji diagram, half filled in and the other half occupied with water. Overlooking the water is the splendid **Dàgōng Hall** (大公堂; Dàgōng Táng; ☉ 7.30am-5pm summer, 8am-4.30pm winter), a huge, airy space with a pairing of huge black Chinese characters 武 ('Wǔ' or 'Martial') and 忠 ('Zhōng' or 'Loyal') on the walls outside. The memorial hall originally dates to the Yuan dynasty; note its two large and smooth drum stones. The **Prime Minister's Temple** (丞相祠堂; Chéng Xiàng Cítáng; ☉ 7.30am-5pm summer, 8am-4.30pm winter), an impressive and massive old hall with some splendid carved cross beams in the roof, is nearby.

🛏 Sleeping

Huāyuán Gōngyù　　　　　　HOTEL **$$**
(花园公寓; ☎ 0579 8860 0336; 48 Yitai Xiang; 義泰巷48号; r without bath ¥60, s/d ¥288/320) This quiet choice has an incredibly beautiful Chinese garden out back, decorated with osmanthus, camellias, other flowering trees, gingkos and potted plants and embellished with magnificent views over the rooftops of Zhūgě Cūn. Rooms are over two floors in an outside block; rooms upstairs are less damp. It's along an alley just up from Upper Pond.

✖ Eating

Restaurants are dotted around the village, but are squarely aimed at tourists. For fast-food style chicken and chips, head to **Kěndéqǐ** (肯德起; Gaolong Lu; 高଼路; set meal ¥11), shamelessly echoing the Chinese name for KFC.

❶ Information

Zhūgě has an **internet cafe** (10 Gaolong Lu; 高隆路10号; per hour ¥3; ☉ 24hr), a **post office** (中国邮政; Zhōngguó Yóuzhèng; Gaolong Lu; 高隆路; ☉ 8am-5pm) and a branch of **ICBC** (工商银行, Gōngshāng Yínháng; 60 Gaolong Lu; 高隆路60号) with a 24-hour ATM. For foreign exchange, you will need to go to the Bank of China (p274) in Xīn'ānjiāng.

❶ Getting There & Away

Buses from Xīnyè (¥3.50, 30 minutes) depart at 6.05am, 8.30am, 11.50am and 3.10pm; in the return direction, buses leave at 7.15am, 9.50am, 1.25pm and 4.45pm. The bus drop off is at the foot of Gaolong Lu.

Buses for Xīn'ānjiāng (¥10, one hour, eight daily) leave from the **bus station** (330 Guodao; 330 国道). To get to the bus station, walk down Gaolong Lu away from the village and turn right on to the main road; the bus station is as few minutes' walk away on the north side of the road. Buses run to **Hángzhōu** (¥50-60, two hours, 7am, 7.15am, 7.30am and 1.35pm), where you can connect to the national rail network.

From Hángzhōu South Bus Station, direct buses (¥58, two hours) to Zhūgě leave at 8.40am and 3.50pm; there's also a bus (¥58, two hours) to Zhūgě from Hángzhōu West Bus Station at 2.40pm.

Pǔtuóshān　　　　　普陀山

📇 0580

The lush and well-tended Buddhist island of Pǔtuóshān – the Zhōushān Archipelago's most celebrated isle – is the abode of Guanyin, the eternally compassionate Goddess of Mercy. One of China's four sacred Buddhist mountains, Pǔtuóshān is permeated with the aura of the goddess and the devotion of her worshippers. Endless boatloads of visitors, however, frequently upset the island's sacred balance, especially as access has improved in recent years. During holiday periods and weekends things can get rampant (aim for a midweek visit).

◎ Sights

A crippling **entrance fee** (summer/winter ¥160/140) is payable when you arrive; entry to some other sights is extra.

Images of Guanyin are ubiquitous and Pǔtuóshān's temples are all shrines for the merciful goddess. Besides the three main temples, you will stumble upon nunneries and monasteries everywhere you turn, while decorative archways may suddenly emerge from the sea mist.

The central part of the island is around Pǔjì Temple about 1km north of the ferry terminal, reachable by taking the roads leading east or west from the ferry terminal; either way takes about 20 minutes. Alternatively, minibuses from the ferry terminal run to Pǔjì Temple and to other points of the island.

Pǔtuóshān

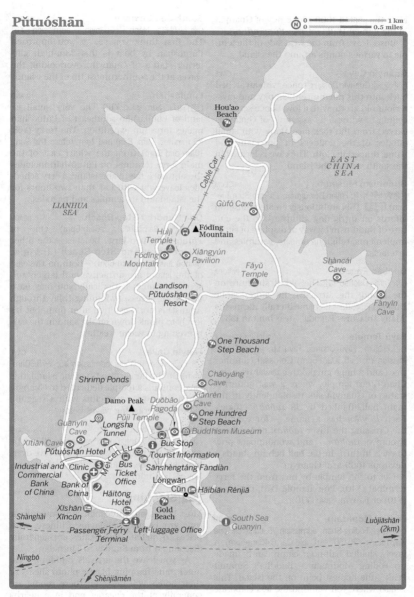

Pǔjì Temple

BUDDHIST TEMPLE

(普济禅寺; Pǔjì Sì; admission ¥5; ☺ 5.30am-6pm) Fronted by large ponds and overlooked by towering camphor trees and Luóhàn pines, this recently restored Chan (Zen) temple stands by the main square and dates to at least the 17th century. Beyond chubby Mile-fo sitting in a red, gold and green burnished cabinet in the Hall of Heavenly Kings, throngs of worshippers stand with flaming incense in front of the colossal main hall.

Note the seated 1000-arm effigy of Guanyin in the Pumen Hall (普门殿; *Pǔméndiàn*).

Buses leave from the west side of the temple to various points around the island.

Guānyīn Cave
CAVE

(观音洞; Guānyīn Dòng) Crouch with an arched back into this magnificent, smoky and mysterious old grotto with a low, bonce-scraping ceiling to witness its assembly of Guanyins carved from the rock face along with small effigies of the goddess in porcelain and stone, draped in cloth. The cave is located in the south west of the island.

Buddhism Museum
MUSEUM

(佛教博物馆; Fójiào Bówùguǎn; ⊘ 9am-3pm Tue-Sun) FREE This ambitiously created museum affords an intriguing glimpse into the culture of Buddhism by way of displays of ritual implements, religious objects, ceramics and artefacts.

Duōbǎo Pagoda
PAGODA

(多宝塔; Duōbǎo Tǎ) The oldest structure on the island, the attractive five-storey stone Duōbǎo Pagoda – its name literally means the 'Many Treasures Pagoda' – was built in 1334.

Fǎyǔ Temple
BUDDHIST TEMPLE

(法雨禅寺; Fǎyǔ Chánsì; Fayu Lu; 法雨路; admission ¥5; ⊘ 5.30am-6pm) Colossal camphor trees and a huge gingko tree tower over this Chan (Zen) temple, where a vast glittering statue of Guanyin sits resplendently in the main hall, flanked by 18 *luóhàn* effigies. Each *luóhàn* has a name – for example the Crossing the River *luóhàn* or the Long Eyebrows *luóhàn* – and worshippers pray to each in turn. In the hall behind stands a dextrous 1000-arm Guanyin.

Get to the temple by bus from the ferry terminal (¥10), Pǔjì Temple (¥5), cable car (¥10) or Fànyīn Cave (¥10).

Fódǐng Mountain
MOUNTAIN

(佛顶山; Fódǐng Shān; admission ¥5, cable car one way/return ¥30/50; ⊘ Cable Car 6.40am-5pm) A lovely, shaded half-hour climb can be made up Fódǐng Mountain – Buddha's Summit Peak – the highest point on the island. This is also where you will find the less elaborate Huìjì Temple (慧济禅寺, Huìjì Chánsì; admission ¥5; ⊘ 5.30am-6.30pm) In summer the climb is much cooler in the late afternoon; watch devout pilgrims and Buddhist nuns stop every three steps to either bow or kneel in supplication. The less motivated take the cable car.

The Xiāngyún Pavilion (香云亭; Xiāngyún Tíng) is a pleasant spot for a breather.

South Sea Guanyin
STATUE

(南海观音; Nánhǎi Guānyīn; admission ¥6) The first thing you see as you approach Pǔtuóshān by boat is this 33m-high glittering statue of Guanyin, overlooking the waves at the southernmost tip of the island.

Luòjiāshān
ISLAND

(洛伽山; admission ¥18) The very small island of Luòjiāshān southeast of Pǔtuóshān makes for a fun expedition. The ferry (¥68, 25 minutes, 7am, 8am and 1pm, return trip 9am, 10am and 3pm) from the wharf east of the main ferry terminal on Pǔtuóshān includes the entrance fee to the island. Ferry schedules leave you with less than two hours for the island and its temples and pagodas.

One Hundred Step Beach
BEACH

(百步沙; Bǎibùshā; ⊘ 6am-6pm) One of Pǔtuóshān's two large beaches – the other is One Thousand Step Beach (千步金沙; Qiānbù Jīnshā; ⊘ 6am-6pm) – both on the east of the island are attractive and largely unspoilt, although periodically you may have to pay for access; swimming (May through August) is not permitted after 6pm, but it's lovely to plonk down on the sand in the early evening in warm weather.

Fànyīn Cave
CAVE

(梵音洞; Fànyīn Dòng; admission ¥5; ⊘ 5.30am-6pm) On the far eastern tip of the island, this cave contains a temple dedicated to Guanyin perched between two cliffs with a seagull's view of the crashing waves below.

Cháoyáng Cave
CAVE

(朝阳洞; Cháoyáng Dòng; admission ¥12) The sound of the roaring waves in this cave overlooking the sea is said to imitate the chanting of the Buddha.

🛏 Sleeping

Most hotels on Pǔtuóshān aim squarely at tour groups and holidaying Chinese, with prices to match. Room rates are generally discounted from Sunday to Thursday.

As you leave the arrivals building, local hotel touts flapping plastic photo sheets of their hotels will descend; these rooms are generally at the cheaper end in a nearby village, not luxurious, but serviceable and more affordable than many other hotels on the island. Alternatively, turn left upon exiting the arrivals building and walk to the cheap guesthouses off Meicen Lu in Xīshān Xīncūn (西山新村), a short walk over the hill to the west from the ferry terminal. They are all very similar, with standard singles, twins and perhaps triples. Some hotels may not take foreigners, but others should (speaking Chinese helps); rooms go for around ¥100 to ¥150 on a weekday, but rise considerably at weekends; bargain for your room. Look for the characters '内有住宿', which means rooms are available. A similar assortment of guesthouses are in Lóngwān Cūn (龙湾村), around a fifteen minute walk east of the ferry terminal. Several of the larger hotels have shuttle buses to and from the pier.

Hǎibiān Rénjiā
GUESTHOUSE $

(海边人家; ☑ 0580 669 8035; 77, Bldg 34, Longwan Village; 龙湾村34幢77号; tw/d ¥180-420; 🛜) This very clean budget choice up the steps in Lóngwān Village and not far from Gold Beach in the southeast of the island has ten rooms with shower (including a sweet attic room with skylight) and a tip-top, clean ambience. There's no English spoken but the owners are hard-working and efficient. Seaview rooms are ¥260 during the week.

Landison Pǔtuóshān Resort
HOTEL $$$

(雷迪森广场酒店; Léidísēn Guǎngchǎng Jiǔdiàn; ☑ 0580 669 0666; www.landisonhotels.com; 115 Fayu Lu; 法雨路115号; tw & d ¥1588-2588, tr ¥3188, ste ¥3888-8888; ❄@☃) There's an elegant and unhurried charm about this place among the trees that does more than any other place on the island to create a relaxed and enjoyable tempo.

Pǔtuóshān Hotel
HOTEL $$$

(普陀山大酒店; Pǔtuóshān Dàjiǔdiàn; ☑ 0580 609 2828; www.putuoshanhotel.com; 93 Meicen Lu; 梅岑路93号; tw/d ¥1250-1700/1350-1700, ste ¥2900-5000; ❄@) Maximising its feng shui by backing onto a green hill, this is a fine choice with a pleasant and uncluttered feel, agreeable rooms and service to match. Discounts of up to 70% are regular midweek.

Sānshèngtáng Fàndiàn
HOTEL $$$

(三圣堂饭店; ☑ 0580 609 1277; 121 Miaozhuang Yanlu; 妙庄严路121号; d/tw ¥1000, tr ¥1300, q ¥1500, ste ¥1688; ❄) Often full, this traditional-style place is attractively set among trees off a small path near Pǔjì Temple. Rooms are rather musty but generally go for around ¥700 during the week.

🍴 Eating

Pǔtuóshān dining is largely seafood and hotel restaurants and therefore expensive, unless you choose noodle joints in the small villages of Xīshān Xīncūn (off Meicen Lu) and also in Lóngwān Cūn (龙湾村), in the southeast. There's a **vegetarian restaurant** (普济寺素菜馆; Pǔjìsì Sùcàiguǎn; breakfast ¥5, lunch & dinner ¥10; ⊙5.30am-7am, 10.30am-noon & 4.15-5.15pm) right by the Pǔjì Temple, serving great value meals. The other temples also have vegetarian kitchens.

ℹ️ Information

Bank of China (中国银行; Zhōngguó Yínháng; 85-7 Meicen Lu; 梅岑路; ⊙8-noon & 1.30-4.30pm) Forex currency exchange. ATMs (24-hour) taking international cards for the Bank of China and other banks are down the side of the block (which is called 'Financial Street').

China Mobile (中国移动; Zhōngguó Yídòng; Meicen Lu; 梅岑路; ⊙8am-5pm) For mobile phone SIM cards.

China Post (中国邮政; Zhōngguó Yóuzhèng; 124 Meicen Lu; 梅岑路; ⊙8am-5pm summer, 8am-4.30pm winter)

Clinic (诊所; Zhěnsuǒ; ☑ 0580 609 3102; Meicen Lu; 梅岑路; ⊙8am-5pm)

Industrial and Commercial Bank of China (ICBC; 工行; Gōngshāng Yínháng; 85-15 Meicen Lu; 梅岑路; ⊙8-11am & 2-5pm) Forex currency exchange.

Left-luggage Office (行李寄存; Xínglǐ Jìcúnchù; Matou; 码头; per large luggage piece ¥8; ⊙6.45am-4.30pm) At the ferry terminal.

Tourist Service Centre (旅游咨询中心; Lǚyóu Zīxún Zhōngxīn; ☑ 0580 609 4921; ⊙9am-6pm)

Yuánzhōu Internet Cafe (缘洲网吧; 8 Longsha Lu; 龙沙路8号; per hr ¥8; ⊙24hr) This place is the only internet cafe on the island, on the far side of the Lóngshā tunnel (walk through the tunnel just north of the Pǔtuóshān Hotel).

ℹ️ Getting There & Away

The construction of bridges lashing the principle islands of the Zhōushān archipelago to the mainland means you can largely make the trip here by bus from Shànghǎi or Hángzhōu.

Buses from **Hángzhōu's Main Bus Station** (¥88 to ¥98, regular, first/last 6am/6.15pm) arrive at Pǔtuó Chéngběi Bus Station (普陀城北车站; Pǔtuó Chéngběi Chēzhàn), from where shuttle buses run to Zhūjiājiān Dock (¥6, one hour, every 15 minutes, 9.40am-5.40pm). Buy tickets for the shuttle bus from the Zhōushān Pǔtuó Tourist Destination Service Center (舟山旅游目的地服务中心; Zhōushān Lǚyóu Mùdìdì Fúwù Zhōngxīn), adjacent to the Pǔtuó Chéngběi Bus Station. Bus 27 (¥3, one hour, 5.30am to 8pm) also runs to Zhūjiājiān Dock from the bus station. Buses also run from here to **Shànghǎi Nánpǔdàqiáo** (¥138, five hours, first/last bus 6.30am/6pm, regular) and **Shànghǎi South**

Bus Station (¥130, regular, 1st/last bus 5.50am/6.10pm). Bus 6 connects the wharf at Shěnjiāmén with Pǔtuó Chéngběi bus station, from where you can take a bus to Hángzhōu or Shànghǎi.

The shortest and fastest **ferry** crossing to Pǔtuóshān is from Zhūjiājiān Wharf (朱家尖 码头; Zhūjiājiān Mǎtou) on the neighbouring island of Zhūjiājiān. Fast boats (¥25, 7 minutes) from here leave every 30 minutes from 6.20am and 5.20pm, with single sailings afterwards at 5.35pm, 6.30pm, 7.30pm, 8.30pm and 9.50pm. Slower boats (¥22, 15 minutes) also run, but less frequently. Ferries (¥28, fast/slow 15/30 minutes) also cross to Pǔtuóshān from the wharf at Shěnjiāmén (沈家门) on the island of Zhōushān (舟山岛).

A more sedate way to journey is on the **night boat from Shànghǎi** that leaves for Pǔtuóshān from Wúsōng Wharf for the 12-hour voyage. Offering numerous grades of comfort from 4th class to special class, tickets cost ¥139 to ¥499; it's easy to upgrade (bǔpiào) once you're on board. From Shànghǎi, the boat leaves at 7.30pm on Monday, Wednesday and Friday, reaching Pǔtuóshān at around 8am. In the other direction, it leaves on Tuesday, Thursday and Saturday at 4pm (winter) or 4.40pm (summer), reaching Shànghǎi at around 6am.

A **fast boat** (¥260 to ¥352) departs Pǔtuóshān for the port of Xiǎo Yáng Shān (小洋山), south of Shànghǎi at 1.30pm, where passengers are then bused to Nánpǔ Bridge; the whole trip takes four hours. The daily ferry from Shànghǎi to Pǔtuóshān departs from Xiǎo Yáng Shān at 10.10am, connected to Nánpǔ Bridge (Nánpǔdàqiáo) in Shànghǎi with a bus that leaves at 8.15am. Tickets for both ferry and bus/ferry services are available at the travel agents from a shop at 21 East Jinling Rd in Shànghǎi.

On Pǔtuóshān, tickets for all of the above boats and buses can either be bought at the **ticket office** at the jetty/arrivals halls or from the office at 74 Meicen Lu, opposite the Pǔtuóshān Hotel.

The nearest **airport** is at Zhōushān (Pǔtuóshān) on the neighbouring island of Zhūjiājiān (朱家尖); get the ferry from the dock.

❶ Getting Around

Minibuses zip from the passenger ferry terminal to various points around the island, including Pǔjì Temple (¥5), One Thousand Step Beach (¥8), Fǎyǔ Temple (¥10) and the cable car station (¥10). There are more bus stations at Pǔjì Temple, Fǎyǔ Temple and other spots around the island serving the same and other destinations. If you're heading to Pǔjì Temple and the sights in the south of the island, walking is fine.

Fújiàn

POP 37.2 MILLION

Best Temples

➜ Nánpǔtuó Temple (p284)

➜ Kāiyuán Temple (p295)

➜ Guāndì Temple (p296)

Best Tǔlóu Clusters

➜ Tiánluókēng Tǔlóu Cluster (p292)

➜ Gāoběi Tǔlóu Cluster (p293)

➜ Hóngkēng Tǔlóu Cluster (p291)

➜ Yúnshuǐyáo Tǔlóu Cluster (p293)

Why Go?

The ancestral home to many overseas Chinese, Fújiàn (福建) on China's southern coast has a strong seafaring disposition and it used to be one of the windows that connected China to the outside world. Once a great emporium in Asia, its multicultural heritage still stands beautifully in Xiàmén and Quánzhōu, where you can glimpse the region's glorious maritime past.

Other standout attractions are the marvellous *tǔlóu* (roundhouses) in the southwest of the province. Rising like castles on rolling hills, these quirky buildings are Unesco World Heritage–listed. To the northwest, the hill station of Wǔyí Shān offers hiking opportunities aplenty.

The cheerful harbour city of Xiàmén is a welcoming first port of call. From here, you can hop over to the popular isle of Gǔlàng Yǔ, or venture to the intriguing Taiwanese outpost island of Kinmen.

When to Go
Xiàmén

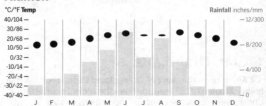

Mar & Apr Beat the summer heat with a springtime visit to the World Heritage–listed *tǔlóu*.

Jun & Sep Visit the breezy coast of Xiàmén and island-hop in summer or autumn.

Oct Low-season prices and clear mountain air coalesce in the rugged, lush Wǔyí Shān.

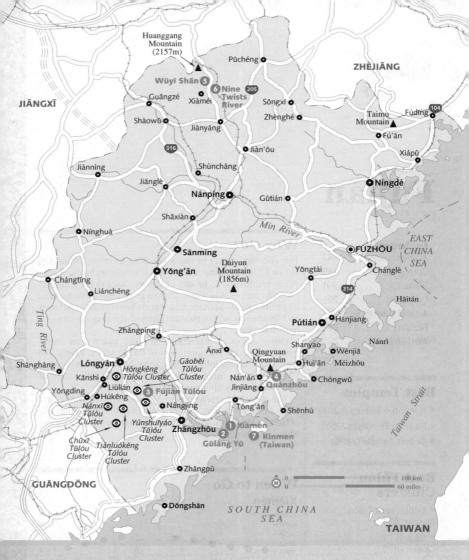

Fújiàn Highlights

1 Amble down the alleys in breezy **Xiàmén** (p283), one of China's most attractive cities

2 Dream of grand times long gone in **Gŭlàng Yŭ** (p289), an island packed with colourful colonial villas

3 Explore the region's World Heritage–listed, **Fújiàn Tŭlóu** (p291), massive, semi-enclosed earthen edifices that are the ancient equivalents of modern-day condos

4 Soak in the lingering traces of China's maritime past in **Quánzhōu** (p294)

5 Escape the heat of the plains at the picturesque hill station of **Wŭyí Shān** (p299)

6 Float on a raft down the **Nine Twists River** (p300) and look for boat-shaped coffins in cavities along the rock faces

7 Hop over to pretty **Kinmen** (p288), Taiwan's closest island outpost to China

History

The coastal region of Fújiàn, known in English as Fukien or Hokkien, has been part of the Chinese empire since the Qin dynasty (221–207 BC), when it was known as Min. Sea trade transformed the region from a frontier into one of the centres of the Chinese world. During the Song and Yuan dynasties the coastal city of Quánzhōu was one of the main ports on the maritime Silk Road, which transported not only silk but other textiles, precious stones, porcelain and a host of other valuables. The city was home to more than 100,000 Arab merchants, missionaries and travellers.

Despite a decline in the province's fortunes after the Ming dynasty restricted maritime commerce in the 15th century, the resourcefulness of the Fújiàn people proved itself in the numbers heading for Taiwan, Singapore, the Philippines, Malaysia and Indonesia. Overseas links that were forged continue today, contributing much to the modern character of the province.

Language

Fújiàn is one of the most linguistically diverse provinces in China. Locals speak variations of the Min dialect, which includes Taiwanese. Min is divided into various subgroups – you can expect to hear Southern Min (Mǐnnán Huà) in Xiàmén and Quánzhōu, and Eastern Min (Dōng Mǐn) in Fúzhōu. Using Mandarin is not a problem.

ℹ Getting There & Away

Fújiàn is well connected to the neighbouring provinces of Guǎngdōng and Jiāngxī by train and coastal highway. Xiàmén and Fúzhōu have airline connections to most of the country, including Hong Kong, and Taipei and Kaohsiung in Taiwan. Wǔyí Shān has flight connections to China's larger cities, including Běijīng, Shànghǎi and Hong Kong. The coastal freeway also goes all the way to Hong Kong from Xiàmén. The D class train links Xiàmén to Shànghǎi in eight hours.

ℹ Getting Around

For exploring the interior, D trains are more comfortable and safer than travelling by bus. Wǔyí Shān is linked to Fúzhōu, Quánzhōu and Xiàmén by train. There are also daily flights between Xiàmén and Wǔyí Shān.

Xiàmén 厦门

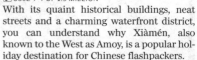

☑ 0592 / POP 1.9 MILLION

With its quaint historical buildings, neat streets and a charming waterfront district, you can understand why Xiàmén, also known to the West as Amoy, is a popular holiday destination for Chinese flashpackers.

The highlight of Xiàmén is to visit the tiny island of Gǔlàng Yǔ, once the old colonial roost of Europeans and Japanese. The seaside gardens, meandering alleys and beautiful colonial villas ooze an old-world charm rarely seen in Chinese cities.

History

Xiàmén was founded around the mid-14th century in the early years of the Ming dynasty, when the city walls were built and the town was established as a major seaport and commercial centre. In the 17th century it became a place of refuge for the Ming rulers fleeing the Manchu invaders. Xiàmén and nearby Kinmen (金门; Jīnmén) were bases for the Ming armies who, under the command of the general Koxinga, raised their anti-Manchu battle cry, 'resist the Qing and restore the Ming'.

The Portuguese arrived in the 16th century, followed by the British in the 17th century, and later by the French and the Dutch, all attempting, rather unsuccessfully, to establish Xiàmén as a trade port. The port was closed to foreigners in the 1750s and it was not until the Opium Wars that things began to change. In August 1841 a British naval force of 38 ships carrying artillery and soldiers sailed into Xiàmén harbour, forcing the port to open. Xiàmén then became one of the first treaty ports.

FÚJIÀN XIÀMÉN

PRICE INDICATORS

The following price indicators are used for this region:

Sleeping

$ less than ¥250

$$ ¥250 to ¥500

$$$ more than ¥500

Eating

$ less than ¥40

$$ ¥40 to ¥100

$$$ more than ¥100

Xiàmén & Gǔlàng Yǔ

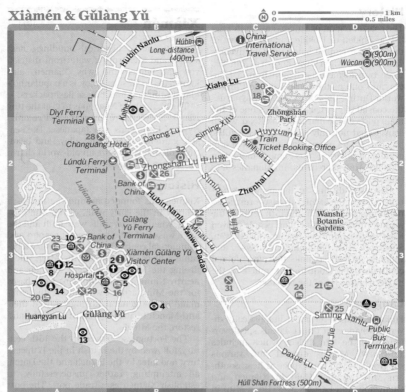

Japanese and Western powers followed soon after, establishing consulates and making Gǔlàng Yǔ a foreign enclave. Xiàmén was taken over by Japanese in 1938 and remained that way until 1945.

◉ Sights & Activities

The town of Xiàmén is on the island of the same name. It's connected to the mainland by a 5km-long causeway bearing a railway, a Bus Rapid Transit (BRT) line, road and footpath. The most absorbing part of Xiàmén is near the western (waterfront) district, directly opposite the small island of Gǔlàng Yǔ. This is the old area of town, known for its colonial architecture, parks and winding streets.

Nánpǔtuó Temple   BUDDHIST TEMPLE
(南普陀寺; Nánpǔtuó Sì; Siming Nanlu; ⊙8am-6pm) **FREE** This Buddhist temple complex

on the southern side of Xiàmén is one of the most famous temples among the Fujianese, and is also considered a pilgrimage site by dedicated followers from Southeast Asia. The temple has been repeatedly destroyed and rebuilt. Its latest incarnation dates to the early 20th century, and today it's an active and busy temple with chanting monks and worshippers lighting incense.

The temple is fronted by a huge lotus lake. In front of the courtyard is the twin-eaved Big Treasure Hall (Dàxióng Bǎodiàn), presided over by a trinity of Buddhas representing his past, present and future forms. Behind rises the eight-sided Hall of Great Compassion (Dàbēi Diàn), in which stands a golden 1000-armed statue of Guanyin, facing the four directions.

The temple has an excellent vegetarian restaurant in a shaded courtyard where you can dine in the company of resident,

Xiàmén & Gǔlàng Yǔ

FÚJIÀN XIÀMÉN

mobile-phone-toting monks. Round it all off with a hike up the steps behind the temple among the rocks and the shade of trees.

Take bus 1 from the train station or bus 21, 45, 48 or 503 from Zhongshan Lu to reach the temple.

Xiàmén University HISTORIC BUILDING
(厦门大学; Xiàmén Dàxué; 422 Siming Nanlu; ⊙museum open daily 9am-12.30pm & 1.30pm-5pm) FREE Next to Nánpǔtuó Temple and established with overseas Chinese funds, the university has beautiful republican-era buildings and an attractive lake. It's a good place for a pleasant stroll. The **anthropology museum** (人类学博物馆; Rénlèixué Bówùguǎn) in the campus boasts two large 'boat coffins' unearthed from a cliff in Wǔyí Shān. The campus entrance is next to the stop for bus 1.

Húlǐ Shān Fortress BUILDING
(胡里山炮台; Húlǐ Shān Pàotái; admission ¥25; ⊙7.30am-5.30pm) Across Daxue Lu, south of the university, is this gigantic German gun artillery built in 1894. You can rent binoculars to peer over the water to the Taiwanese-occupied island of Kinmen (金门; Jīnmén), formerly known as Quemoy and claimed by both mainland China and Taiwan.

Overseas Chinese Museum MUSEUM
(华侨博物馆; Huáqiáo Bówùguǎn; 73 Siming Nanlu; ⊙9.30am-4.30pm Tue-Sun) FREE An ambitious celebration of China's communities abroad, with dioramas, street scenes, photos and props.

Kāihé Lù Fish Market MARKET
(开禾路菜市场; Kāihélù Càishìchǎng; Kaihe Lu) In the old district of Xiàmén, this tiny but lively market sells various (weird) sea creatures to a backdrop of qílóu (骑楼; shophouses) and a church. Access from Xiahe Lu.

☞ Tours

China International Travel Service (p287; (CITS; 中国国际旅行社; Zhōngguó Guójì Lǚxíngshè) and many larger hotels can help with tours.

Apple Travel TRAVEL AGENCY
(☑505 3122; www.appletravel.cn; Shop 20, Guanren Lu) Pricey but can help arrange tours to attractions in Fújiàn such as Wǔyí Shān. Also organises English-speaking guides.

⚑ Festivals & Events

Xiàmén International Marathon   MARATHON

(厦门国际马拉松赛; Xiàmén Guójì Mǎlāsōng Sài; www.xmim.org) Held in January, this event draws local and international participants. Runners race around the coastal ring road that circles the island.

Dragon Boat Races   DRAGON BOATING

Held in Xiàmén at the Dragon Pool (龙舟池; Lóngzhōu Chí) in Jíměi (集美) every June, they are quite a sight.

⌂ Sleeping

Xiàmén is a popular, year-round destination in China, so making a reservation well in advance is essential. Hotels are clustered around the harbour and most are midrange, shading top end. Most places offer 40% discounts on weekdays.

Xiàmén International Youth Hostel   HOSTEL $

(厦门国际青年旅舍; Xiàmén Guójì Qīngnián Lǚshè; ☑ 208 2345; www.yhaxm.com; 41 Nanhua Lu, 南华路41号; dm from ¥60, s ¥95-160, d ¥160-240; ❋ @ �ি) With clean dorms and doubles, this famous hostel is run by an efficient and helpful staff. Reservations essential. Light meals are served in the attached cafe.

Xiàmén Locanda International Youth Hostel   HOSTEL $

(厦门卢卡国际青年旅舍; Xiàmén Lúkǎ Guójì Qīngnián Lǚshè; ☑ 208 2918; www.locandahostel.com; 35 Minzu Lu, 民族路35号; 4-bed/6-bed dm ¥60/55, s ¥208, d & tw ¥258; ❋ @) This friendly hostel can be easily identified by its ochre walls and a lovely courtyard. All rooms are clean and amber-hued. The dorms are compact, though.

Yue Hotel   BOUTIQUE HOTEL $$

(悦雅居酒店; Yuèyǎjū Jiǔdiàn; ☑ 206 7518; www.yuehotel.com; 21 Nanhua Lu, 南华路21号; r ¥340-560; ❋ @ �ি) Identifiable by two blocks of red-brick houses, this boutique hotel has a dozen well-presented rooms. Ask for one with a balcony. The hotel is just a stone's throw from Xiàmén University and Nánpǔtuó Temple.

Liángzhù Boutique Lifestyle Hotel   BOUTIQUE HOTEL $$

(良筑; Liángzhù; ☑ 207 1322; www.liangzhu22.com; 22 Huaxin Lu, 华新路22号; r ¥398-698; ❋ �ি) Tucked away in a tranquil neighbhourhood of 1950s mansions, this quaint old villa has eight chic rooms, every one of which is different. Breakfast is included. The hotel is a bit hard to find as the street numbers are not in sequential order. Look for the chocolate-coloured building not far from 32/HOW cafe (p287), or simply give the hotel a call.

Hotel Indigo Xiàmén Harbour   HOTEL $$$

(厦门海港英迪格酒店; Xiàmén Hǎigǎng Yīndígé Jiǔdiàn; ☑ 226 1666; www.hotelindigo.com; 16 Lujiang Dao, 鹭江道16号; d ¥2600-3600; ⊖ ❋ @) This chain hotel at the waterfront district has found a balance between funky and kitschy in its design and decor. Both business travellers and tourists will appreciate the central location and the generous number of rooms with sweeping harbour views. Staff are attentive. Discounts of around 50% are available.

Lùjiāng Harbourview Hotel   HOTEL $$$

(鹭江宾馆; Lùjiāng Bīnguǎn; ☑ 202 2922; www.lujiang-hotel.com; 54 Lujiang Dao, 鹭江道54号; s ¥670-730, sea-view d ¥929-1040; ❋ @) This 1950s structure has had a thorough revamp and is a great option for a little bit of luxury in the middle of the city. All rooms have modern facilities and quite tasteful furnishings that befit the hotel's four-star billing. The hotel is Xiàmén's landmark and all taxi drivers know where it is.

✗ Eating

Being a port city, Xiàmén is known for its fresh seafood, especially oysters and shrimps. The alleys on both sides of Zhongshan Lu teem with eateries of all shapes and sizes.

THE HEYDAY OF AMOY

When you are in Xiàmén, get a copy of *Old Xiamen, Cradle of Modern Chinese Business & Chinese Business Education*, edited by Dr Bill Brown, a long-time local resident from the US. The book explains in a most readable way how Xiàmén has historically played a vital role in fostering cultural interactions between the East and the West, and it also has a wonderful collection of old prints, news clips and literary extracts about the city dating back to as early as Marco Polo's time. The affordable paperback (¥30) is available in **Xinhua Bookshop** (新华书店; Xīnhuá shūdiàn; 155 Zhongshan Lu; ⊙ 9am-5pm).

Huángzéhé Peanut Soup Shop SNACKS $

(黄则和花生汤店; Huángzéhé Huāshēng Tāng-diàn; 22-24 Zhongshan Lu, 中山路20号; snacks ¥4-10; ⏱6.30am-10.30pm) Very popular restaurant with basic service and seating, famed for its delectably sweet *huāshēng tāng* (花生汤; peanut soup) and popular snacks including *hǎilìjiān* (海蛎煎; oyster omelette) and *zhūròu chuàn* (猪肉串; pork kebabs). You need to purchase coupons that you hand over when you order food.

Wūtáng Shāchámiàn NOODLES $

(乌糖沙茶面; 68 Minzu Lu, 民族路68号; noodles from ¥20; ⏱6.30am-1pm) This absolutely no-frills breakfast and early lunch joint serving excellent *shāchámiàn* (沙茶面; satay-inspired noodles) is a perennial local favourite. The ingredients can be customised but a typical bowl will include shellfish, meatballs and pig innards. Let your fingers do the talking.

The shop is identifiable by a long queue out front and the red and blue characters on the front panel.

Seaview Restaurant DIM SUM $$

(鹭江宾馆观海厅; Lùjiāng Bīnguǎn Guānhǎitīng; 7th fl, 54 Lujiang Dao; meals from ¥80; ⏱10am-10pm) What's better than sipping tea and enjoying freshly made dim sum on a sun-kissed terrace with sweeping harbour views? This rooftop restaurant in Lùjiāng Harbourview Hotel (p286) is a choice place to savour Fujianese street snacks in a comfy setting. No English dim sum menu, but you can pick what you want from the cooking stations.

Lucky Full City Seafood DIM SUM $$

(潮福城; Cháofú Chéng; 28 Hubin Beilu; dim sum from ¥14, meals from ¥70; ⏱10am-10pm) Priding itself on MSG-free dim sum and dishes, this extremely popular restaurant is where you'll have to try your luck or wait at least 30 minutes to get a table. Catch a taxi here: the driver will know where it is. It also has a branch (33 Lujiang Dao; ⏱8am-2.30am) 200m north of Lúndù ferry terminal.

32/HOW cafe CAFE $$

(Cherry 32 Cafe; 32 Huaxin Lu; coffee from ¥45; ⏱11am-11pm) This Taiwanese-owned cafe serves arguably the best coffee in town. The very delicate porcelains, the retro phones and clocks on the wall, together with the lovely courtyard, all evoke the mood of grandma's home.

NOT FOR THE SQUEAMISH!

Fancy aspic dishes, or some jelly with a difference? *Tǔsǔndòng* (土笋冻), or sandworm jelly, is one of the best loved appetisers in Fújiàn. The sandworms are boiled into a jelly mould and the crunchy end product, an aspic dish, is said to be rich in collagen. Locals love eating them with mustard, coriander leaves and turnip slices. You'll find the jelly sold in any street-food joints, but locals all recommend **Tiānhé Xīmén Tǔsǔndòng** (天河西门土笋冻; 33 Douxi Lu; snacks from ¥10; ⏱8am-10pm), near the west gate of Zhōngshān Park, for its sandworm jelly. If the idea of eating worms is too gross for you, the restaurant also serves delicious octopus and ark clams.

Dàfāng Sùcàiguǎn VEGETARIAN $$

(大方素菜馆; 209 3236; 3 Nanhua Lu; dishes ¥30-68; ⏱9am-9.30pm; ⚑) This cheerfully furnished vegetarian restaurant has a very wide range of delicious dishes including hotpots and mock meat.

🛍 Shopping

Zhongshan Lu is essentially a long shopping strip filled with souvenir shops and the latest fashion brands.

ℹ Information

Pickpockets operate around the popular areas in Xiàmén. This includes Zhongshan Lu and the ferry to/from Gǔlàng Yǔ.

Bank of China (中国银行; Zhōngguó Yínháng; 6 Zhongshan Lu) The 24-hour ATM accepts international cards.

China International Travel Service (CITS, 中国国际旅行社; Zhōngguó Guójì Lǚxíngshè; 335 Hexiang Xilu) There are several offices around town. The branch on Hexiang Xilu is recommended.

China Post (中国邮政; Zhōngguó Yóuzhèng; cnr Xinhua Lu & Zhongshan Lu) Telephone services available.

City Medical Consultancy (来福诊所; Láifú Zhěnsuǒ; 532 3168; 123 Xidi Villa Hubin Beilu; ⏱8am-5pm Mon-Fri, to noon Sat) English-speaking doctors; expat frequented. Telephone-operated 24 hours.

Public Security Bureau (PSB; 公安局; Gōng'ānjú; ☎226 2203; 45-47 Xinhua Lu) Opposite the main post and telephone office. The visa section (出入证管理处, *chūrùjing*

WORTH A TRIP

KINMEN, TAIWAN

If you have a multiple-entry China visa, it's worth making a detour to the island of Kinmen (金门; Jīnmén) in Taiwan. Lying only 2km off the coast of Xiàmén, this peaceful islet was once part of a five-decade political tug-of-war between the mainland and Taiwan, and was subjected to incessant bombings from the mainland throughout the 1950s and 1960s. It wasn't until 1993 that martial law was lifted and people living on this once off-limit frontier island were allowed to travel freely to and from the mainland and Taiwan.

Today, Kinmen is fairly developed and visitor-friendly. The former battlefields and military bunkers are now opened up for tourism. In addition to war relics, the island has tree-lined streets, lakes, a national park, colourful temples and a cluster of well-restored villages dating from the Ming and Qing dynasties, as well as Fújiàn-style houses (ironically, most of their counterparts back in Fújiàn have been demolished in the past 30 years). Attractions include **Juguang Tower** (莒光樓; Jǔguāng Lóu; ☉ 8am-10pm), built in 1952 to honour the fallen soldiers of Kinmen; the historical **Shuǐtóu Village** (水頭村; Shuǐtóu Cūn) and **Jhushan Village** (珠山村; Zhūshān Cūn); and the meandering alleys and market streets in **Kincheng** (金城; Jīnchéng), the largest city on Kinmen.

All these can be reached by bus from the ferry terminal and are ideal for a day trip. The size of Kinmen (153 sq km) suggests that a multi-day excursion is possible. It's rewarding to further venture to the cute **Lièyǔ Island** (列屿乡; Lièyǔ Xiāng), less than 2 sq km in area and a 10-minute boat ride from Kinmen.

Cycling is the best way to see both islands. Bikes can be borrowed free-of-charge for a maximum of three days from most visitor information centres, with a handy one in **Kincheng bus station**. Free maps are available in all visitor information centres.

Shuǐtóu and Jhushan villages have lots of B&Bs (民宿; mínsù), and we love **Qin Inn** (水頭一家親, Shuǐtóu Yījiāqīn; ☎ 0910-395 565; http://qininn.tumblr.com; 63-64 Shuitou Village, 水頭63-64號; s/d incl breakfast NT$1200/2400; ✳ 🛜). Booking ahead is a must. In Kincheng, **Urban@Farm House** (La Place; 那個地方; ☎ 886-82-328-337; www.laplace-kinmen.com; 6 Minsheng Lu; d NT$1700-2400), a 24-room boutique hotel located opposite the bus station, is the place to stay.

On Kinmen island, bus 7 links the ferry terminal with Shuǐtóu village and Kincheng, and bus 3 runs between Kincheng, Jhushan and the airport. Four tourist bus routes – each taking about three hours to complete – serve the island's major sights. Buy tickets at the tourist information centre adjacent to Kincheng bus station. Ferries to Lièyǔ Island depart from the dock diagonally opposite the ferry terminal every 30 minutes between 6.30am and 9pm.

Note that you need a multiple-entry China visa if you want to go back to Fújiàn. Otherwise you have to fly to Taipei or Kaohsiung to get one through a travel agent.

---

guǎnlǐchù; open 8.10am to 11.45am and 2.40pm to 5.15pm Monday to Saturday) is in the northeastern part of the building on Gongyuan Nanlu.
What's On Xiamen (www.whatsonxiamen.com) Up-to-date information on Xiàmén.

ℹ Getting There & Away

AIR

Air China, China Southern, Xiàmén Airlines and several other domestic airlines operate flights to/from Xiàmén to all major domestic airports in China. There are innumerable ticket offices around town, many of which are in the larger hotels.

There are international flights to/from Bangkok, Hong Kong, Jakarta, Kuala Lumpur, Los Angeles, Manila, Osaka, Penang, Singapore and Tokyo.

BOAT

Fast boats (¥10, 20 minutes) leave for the nearby coastal Fújiàn town of Zhāngzhōu (漳州) from the passenger ferry terminal (客运码头; kèyùn mǎtóu). Boats run every 15 minutes between 6.30am and 9.30pm. Boats to Kinmen (金门; Jīnmén), Taiwan (¥150, 30 minutes, hourly) leave from Wǔtōng ferry terminal (五通码头; Wǔtōng Mǎtóu) between 8am and 6.30pm.

BUS

There are three major bus stations in Xiàmén. **Húbīn long-distance bus station** (湖滨长途汽车站; Húbīn chángtú qìchēzhàn; 58 Hubin Nanlu) serves destinations south of Xiàmén and tickets can be bought two days in advance at the ticket booth in the local bus terminal adjacent to Xiàmén University at the end of Siming Nanlu.
Guǎngzhōu ¥227, nine hours, two daily

Lóngyán ¥75, three hours, eight daily

Nánjīng (in Fújiàn) ¥28, two hours, 11 daily

Yǒngdìng ¥75, four hours, nine daily

Wúcūn bus station (梧村汽车站; Wúcūn Qìchēzhàn; 925 Xiahe Lu), directly opposite Xiàmén's main train station, serves destinations north of the city, including Jìnjiāng (¥33, 1½ hours, every 20 minutes) and Quánzhōu (¥38, two hours, every 20 minutes). Note that buses to Fúzhōu (¥105, four hours, every 20 minutes) and Wǔyí Shān (¥191, nine hours, one daily, 9.30am) leave from the far-flung **Fānghú bus station** (枋湖客运中心; Fānghú Kèyùn Zhōngxīn).

TRAIN

Xiàmén's main train station is on Xiahe Lu. All trains stop at Xiàmén north station 25km north of the city centre. Tickets can be booked through the **train ticketing booth** (☑ 203 8565; cnr Xinhua Lu & Zhongshan Lu) behind the Gem Hotel (金后酒店; Jīnhòu Jiǔdiàn).

Fúzhōu ¥66 to ¥85, two hours

Hángzhōu ¥282 to ¥357, seven hours

Quánzhōu ¥21 to ¥25, 30 minutes

Shànghǎi ¥328 to ¥413, 7½ hours

Wǔyí Shān ¥144 to ¥223, 13½ hours

❶ Getting Around

TO/FROM THE AIRPORT

Xiàmén airport is 15km from the waterfront district. Taxis cost about ¥45. Bus 27 travels from the airport to Dìyī ferry terminal (but not vice versa). From the city centre, airport shuttle buses (¥10) leave from Chūnguāng Hotel, opposite the Lúndù ferry terminal.

PUBLIC TRANSPORT

Bus Rapid Transit (BRT) line 1 links the waterfront to both train stations via Xiahe Lu (¥1). Bus 19 runs to the train station from the ferry terminal (¥1). Buses to Xiàmén University leave from the train station (bus 1) and from the ferry terminal (bus 2). Taxis start at ¥8 plus ¥3 fuel surcharge.

Gǔlàng Yǔ　　　鼓浪屿

☑ 0592

The small island of Gǔlàng Yǔ is the trump card of Xiàmén. It's not hard to see why it attracts droves of visitors every day. Just a five-minute boat ride away, you'll find yourself on a breezy islet with warrens of backstreets, set in the architectural kaleidoscope of more than 1000 colonial villas and ancient banyan trees. The area near the ferry terminal tends to get very crowded, but the higher and further you go, the more you have the island to yourself.

The foreign community was well established on Gǔlàng Yǔ by the 1880s, with a daily English newspaper, churches, hospitals, post and telegraph offices, libraries, hotels and consulates. In 1903 the island was officially designated an International Foreign Settlement, and a municipal council with a police force of Sikhs was established to govern it. Today, memories of the settlement linger in the many charming colonial buildings and the sound of classical piano wafting from speakers (the island is nicknamed 'piano island' by the Chinese). Many of China's most celebrated musicians have come from Gǔlàng Yǔ, including the pianists Yu Feixing, Lin Junqing and Yin Chengzong.

The best way to enjoy the island is to wander along the streets, peeking into courtyards and down alleys to catch a glimpse of colonial mansions seasoned by local life before popping into one of the many cute cafes for a beer or milk tea.

BORDER CROSSINGS: GETTING TO TAIWAN

Ferries ply between Xiàmén and Kinmen (金门; Jīnmén) Island in Taiwan every 30 minutes between 8am and 6.30pm. You can catch the boat from Wǔtōng ferry terminal (五通码头; Wǔtōng Mǎtóu; Y160, 30 minutes), 8km east of Xiàmén's airport.

Tickets can only be bought an hour before departure time. In Kinmen, visas are issued on the spot for most nationalities. But you need a multiple-entry China visa if you want to return to Fújiàn.

Wǔtōng ferry terminal can only be reached by taxi. Expect to pay ¥20 to go from the airport to the terminal.

Rénmínbì is the only currency accepted in the money exchange counters in Kinmen's ferry terminal. From Kinmen, there are flights to other major cities in Taiwan.

Alternatively, you can catch a ferry (¥300, 90 minutes, 9.15am) from Fúzhōu's Mǎwěi ferry terminal (马尾码头; Mǎwěi Mǎtóu) to Taiwan's archipelago of Matzu (马祖; Mázǔ). From there, you'll find boats to Keelung and flights to other cities in Taiwan.

◉ Sights

Organ Museum
MUSEUM

(风琴博物馆; Fēngqín Bówùguǎn; 43 Guxin Lu, 鼓新路43号; admission ¥20; ⏱8.40am-5.30pm) Housed in the highly distinctive Bāguà Lóu (八卦楼) building is the Organ Museum, with a fantastic collection including a Norman & Beard organ from 1909.

Hàoyuè Garden
GARDENS

(皓月园; Hàoyuè Yuán; admission ¥15; ⏱6am-7pm) Hàoyuè Garden is a rocky outcrop containing an imposing statue of Koxingain full military dress.

Sunlight Rock Park
PARK

(日光岩公园; Rìguāng Yán Gōngyuán; admission ¥60; ⏱8am-7pm) Sunlight Rock (Rìguāng Yán), in Sunlight Rock Park, is the island's highest point at 93m. At the foot of Sunlight Rock is a large colonial building known as the Koxinga Memorial Hall (郑成功纪念馆 | Zhèngchénggōng Jìniànguǎn; ⏱8-11am & 2-5pm). Also in the park is Yīngxióng Hill (Yīngxióng Shān), near the memorial hall and connected via a free cable-car ride. It has an open-air aviary (admission free) with chattering egrets and parrots, and a terrible bird 'show'.

Shūzhuāng Garden
GARDENS

(菽庄花园; Shūzhuāng Huāyuán; admission ¥30; ⏱8.30am-6.30pm daily) The waterfront Shūzhuāng Garden on the southern end of the island is a lovely place to linger for a few hours. It has a small *pénzāi* (bonsai) garden and some delicate-looking pavilions. The piano theme is in full effect at the piano museum housed within the grounds. One piano has its original bill of sale from Melbourne at the turn of the 20th century.

Historic Buildings

Old colonial residences and consulates are tucked away in the maze of streets leading from the pier, particularly along Longtou Lu and the back lanes of Huayan Lu. Some of Gǔlàng Yǔ's buildings are deserted and tumbledown, with trees growing out of their sides, as residents cannot afford their upkeep.

Southeast of the pier you will see the two buildings of the former British Consulate (永顺卡斯特宾馆; Yǒngshùn Kǎsìtè Bīnguǎn; ☑206 0920; 14-16 Lujiao Lu; r ¥466), currently running as a hotel, above you, while further along at 1 Lujiao Lu is the cream-coloured former Japanese Bo'ai Hospital, built in 1936. Up the hill on a different part of Lujiao

Lu stands the red-brick former Japanese Consulate (日本领事馆; Rìběn lǐngshìguǎn; 26 Lujiao Lu), just before you reach the magnificent snow-white Ecclesia Catholica (鼓浪屿天主堂; Gǔlàngyǔ Tiānzhǔtáng; 34 Lujiao Lu), dating from 1917. The white building next to the church is the former Spanish Consulate (西班牙领事馆; Xībānyá lǐngshìguǎn). Just past the church on the left is the Huāng Róngyuǎn Villa (黄荣远堂; Huángróngyuǎn Táng; ☑257 0510; 32 Fujian Lu; admission ¥118; ⏱8.30am-5pm, seven shows daily) a marvellous pillared building, now the Puppet Art Centre. Other buildings worth looking at include the Protestant Sānyī Church (三一堂; Sānyī Táng; 67 Anhai Lu), a red-brick building with a classical portico and cruciform-shaped interior on the corner of Anhai Lu (安海路) and Yongchun Lu (永春路). Where Anhai Lu meets Bishan Lu (笔山路) is the former Law Court (1-3 Bishan Lu), now inhabited by local residents.

Doing a circuit of Bishan Lu will take you past a rarely visited part of the island. Guāncǎi Lóu (观彩楼; 6 Bishan Lu), a residence built in 1931, has a magnificently dilapidated interior with a wealth of original features. The building stands in stark contrast next to the immaculate Yìzú Shānzhuāng (亦足山庄; 9 Bishan Lu), a structure dating from the 1920s.

🛏 Sleeping

There's a plethora of accommodation choices in Gǔlàng Yǔ and most are overpriced. If you opt to stay here, and if you've got a lot of luggage, choose a hotel close to the ferry terminal, as cars aren't allowed on the island.

Gǔlàng Yǔ Lù Fēi International Youth Hostel
HOSTEL $

(鼓浪屿鹭飞国际青年旅舍; Gǔlàng Yǔ Lù Fēi Guójì Qīngnián Lǚshè; ☑208 2678; www.yhalf.cn; 20 Guxin Lu, 鼓新路20号; dm ¥65, s & d ¥260-380; ❄@🛜) Rooms are cute and sparklingly clean, and each has a theme. We love its pastel hues and wrought-iron beds. It's 400m west of the ferry terminal.

Yangtao Hotel
BOUTIQUE HOTEL $$

(杨桃院子; Yángtáo Yuànzi; ☑252 1333; www.yangtaohotel.com; 8 Anhai Lu, 安海路8号; r ¥398-698; ❄@🛜) An affordable luxury tucked away in the quieter part of Anhai Lu, this villa-turned-boutique hotel has 19 chic and comfortable rooms. There's a very pleasant courtyard that invites you to slow down for a lazy afternoon.

Miryam Boutique Hotel BOUTIQUE HOTEL $$$
(Miryam老别墅旅馆; Miryam Lǎo Biéshù Lǚguǎn;
206 2505; www.miryamhotel.com; 70 Huangyan
Lu, 晃岩路70号; r ¥688-1688; ❋ @ ⊛) Miryam
is located right below Sunlight Rock and is
housed in an opulent Victorian-era man-
sion. Rooms are ultra-spacious, with antique
bits and pieces of furniture to give them
character. The food served in the attached
restaurant is as dreamy as the surroundings.

✖ Eating

You'll find plenty of great places to eat, espe-
cially in the streets off Longtou Lu. Try the
shark fishballs and the Amoy pie (a sweet
filled pastry).

Lóngtóu Fishball SEAFOOD $
(龙头鱼丸店; Lóngtóu Yúwán Diàn; 183 Longtou
Lu; meals from ¥10; ⊙8.30am-8pm) Pull up a
bench and order some local specialities,
such as shark fishball noodles (鲨鱼丸粉
丝, shāyú wán fěnsī) or an oyster omelette
(海蛎煎, hǎilì jiān), in this nondescript yet
perennially popular place. Slurp it down and
order some more.

The Chu Family Coffee CAFE $$
(褚家园咖啡馆; Chǔjiāyuán Kāfēiguǎn; 206
3651; 15 Zhonghua Lu; meals from ¥60; ⊙11am-
9pm) Behind the red-brick wall is this sleek
cafe with a very nice, leafy alfresco area. Caf-
feine addicts can find their *real* cup of coffee
here. The tiramisu is a delight too.

❶ Information

There are various maps for sale (¥10) in cafes
and souvenir shops.
Bank of China (中国银行; Zhōngguó Yínháng;
2 Longtou Lu; ⊙9am-7pm) Forex and 24-hour
ATM.
China Post (中国邮政; Zhōngguó Yóuzhèng;
102 Longtou Lu; ⊙8.30am-5.30pm daily) Sells
stamps and postcards.
Hospital (Yīyuàn; 60 Fujian Lu) Has its own
miniature ambulance for the small roads.
Xiàmén Gǔlàng Yǔ Visitor Center (Xiàmén
Gǔlàng Yǔ Yóukè Zhōngxīn; Longtou Lu) Left
luggage ¥3 to ¥5.

❶ Getting There & Around

Ferries for the five-minute trip to Gǔlàng Yǔ
leave from **Lúndù ferry terminal** (轮渡) just
west of Xiàmén's Lùjiāng Harbourview Hotel.

The round-trip fare is ¥8 (getting on the upper
deck costs an additional ¥1). Boats run between
5.45am and midnight. Waterborne circuits of
the island can be done by boat (¥15), with departures every 30 minutes from the passenger
ferry terminal off Lujiang Lu between 7.40am
and 5pm.

Fújiàn Tǔlóu   福建土楼

☎ 0597 / POP 43,000
Scattered all over the pretty, rolling countryside in southwestern Fújiàn, the remarkable
tǔlóu (土楼) are vast, fortified earthen edifices that have been home to both the Hakka
and the Mǐnnán (Fujianese) people since the
year dot. Today, more than 30,000 survive,
many still inhabited and open to visitors.

Forty six *tǔlóu* were together given World
Heritage status by Unesco in 2008. Since
then, new roads have been added to link the
tǔlóu areas to the nearest counties and new
hotels have been erected. You'll see a con-
voy of tour buses bringing droves of visitors
to some of the most popular *tǔlóu* clusters,
but don't be deterred by that. The setting
and architectural structure of the *tǔlóu* are
simply stunning. If you venture off the beat-
en path, crowds thin out considerably and
some little-known or even nameless *tǔlóu*
are the most authentic reflection of rural life
in these packed-earth chateaux.

◉ Sights

The most notable of the 30,000-odd *tǔlóu* are
lumped into various clusters, and they are in
the vicinity of two main counties: Nánjìng (南
靖) and Yǒngdìng (永定). Only the three most
developed clusters: Hóngkēng, Tiánluókēng
and Yúnshuǐyáo are accessible by public
transport. However, bus services are neither
frequent nor punctual. Booking a tour or hiring a vehicle is recommended if you want to
venture off the beaten path and see more.

◉ Hóngkēng Tǔlóu
Cluster   洪坑土楼群

This cluster is 50km east of Yǒngdìng. From
Xiàmen, three buses (¥63, 3½ hours, 6.50am,
9.10am and 1pm) go directly to the cluster,
which is also known as Tǔlóu Mínsú Wén-
huàcūn (土楼民俗文化村). Admission is ¥90.

Zhènchéng Lóu   TǓLÓU
(振成楼) This most visited *tǔlóu* is a grandiose structure built in 1912, with two concentric circles and a total of 222 rooms. The
ancestral hall in the centre of the *tǔlóu* is
complete with Western-style pillars. The locals dub this *tǔlóu wángzǐ* (土楼王子), the
prince *tǔlóu*.

JUST WHAT IS A TǓLÓU?

Tǔlóu, literally mud houses, are outlandish, multi-storey, fortified mud structures built by the inhabitants of southwest Fújiàn to protect themselves from bandits and wild animals.

Tǔlóu were built along either a circular or square floor plan. The walls are made of rammed earth and glutinous rice, reinforced with strips of bamboo and wood chips. These structures are large enough to house entire clans, and they did, and still do! They are a grand exercise in communal living. The interior sections are enclosed by enormous peripheral structures that could accommodate hundreds of people. Nestled in the mud walls were bedrooms, wells, cooking areas and storehouses, circling a central courtyard. The later *tǔlóu* had stone firewalls and metal-covered doors to protect against blazes.

The compartmentalised nature of the building meant that these structures were the ancient equivalent of modern apartments. A typical layout would be the kitchens on the ground floor, storage on the next level and accommodation on the floors above this. Some *tǔlóu* have multiple buildings built in concentric rings within the main enclosure. These could be guest rooms and home schools. The centre is often an ancestral hall or a meeting hall used for events such as birthdays and weddings. For defence purposes, usually there is only one entrance for the entire *tǔlóu* and there are no windows on the first three storeys.

It was once believed that these earthen citadels were inhabited solely by the Hakka. They are the people who migrated from northwest China during the Jin dynasty (AD 265–314) to the south to escape persecution and famine, and they eventually settled in Jiāngxī, Fújiàn and Guǎngdōng. While most *tǔlóu* in the vicinity of Yǒngdìng County are inhabited by the Hakka, there are far more *tǔlóu* in other counties like Nánjìng and Huá'ān populated by the indigenous Mǐnnán (Fujianese) people. A key distinguishing feature between the Hakka and Mǐnnán *tǔlóu* is that the former has communal corridors and staircases as well as a central courtyard, while the latter *tǔlóu* puts more emphasis on privacy, for example each unit has its own staircases and patio.

No matter what type or shape of *tǔlóu* you're looking at, many of them are still inhabited by a single clan, and residents depend on a combination of tourism and farming for a living. The *tǔlóu* are surprisingly comfortable to live in, being '*dōng nuǎn, xià liáng*' (冬暖夏凉), or 'warm in winter and cool in summer'. These structures were built to last.

Kuíjù Lóu
TǓLÓU

(奎聚楼) Near Zhènchéng Lóu, this much older, square *tǔlóu* dates back to 1834.

Rúshēng Lóu
TǓLÓU

(如升楼) The smallest of the roundhouses, this late-19th-century, pea-sized *tǔlóu* has only one ring and 16 rooms.

Fúyù Lóu
TǓLÓU

(福裕楼) Along the river, this five-storey square *tǔlóu* boasts some wonderfully carved wooden beams and pillars. Rooms are available here from ¥100.

👁 Tiánluókēng Tǔlóu Cluster 田螺坑土楼群

A pilgrimage to the earthen castles is not complete if you miss Tiánluókēng (田螺坑), which is 37km northeast of Nánjìng and home to arguably the most picturesque cluster of *tǔlóu* in the region. The locals affectionately call the five noble buildings

'four dishes with one soup' because of their shapes: circular, square and oval.

There's one direct bus (¥47, 3½ hours) to the cluster from Xiàmén, leaving at 8.30am.

Make sure your driver, if you've hired one, takes you up the hill for a postcard-perfect view of Tiánluókēng.

Cluster admission, which includes entry to Yùchāng Lóu and Tǎxià village, is ¥100. A shuttle bus service (¥15) from the cluster's ticket office goes to the above two places, but the vehicle won't leave until it gets 10 passengers.

Yùchāng Lóu
TǓLÓU

(裕昌楼) The tallest roundhouse in Fújiàng, this vast five-floor structure has an observation tower to check for marauding bandits and 270 rooms. Interestingly, this 300-year-old property's pillars bend at an angle on the 3rd floor and at the opposite angle on the 5th floor, and each room and kitchen on the ground floor has its own well.

Tǎxià
VILLAGE

(塔下村) This delightful river settlement boasts several *tǔlóu*-converted guesthouses and it is a great base from which to explore the *tǔlóu* areas.

The highlight of the village is the **Zhang Ancestral Hall** (张氏家庙; Zhāngshì Jiāmiào; Tǎxià Village; ☺ 9am-5pm daily). It is surrounded by 23 elaborately carved spear-like stones, which celebrate the achievements of prominent villagers.

The bus station in Nánjìng runs six buses (¥17, 1½ hours) to the village between 8am and 5.30pm.

◉ Gāoběi Tǔlóu Cluster 高北土楼群

Cluster admission is ¥50.

Chéngqǐ Lóu
TǓLÓU

(承启楼) In the village of Gāoběi (高北), this 300-year-old *tǔlóu* has 400 rooms and once housed 1000 inhabitants. It's built with elaborate concentric rings, with circular passageways between them and a central shrine. It's one of the most iconic and photographed *tǔlóu* and it's no surprise that it has been dubbed the king *tǔlóu*.

Wǔyún Lóu
TǓLÓU

(五云楼) Deserted and rickety, this square building took on a slant after an earthquake in 1918.

Yíjīng Lóu
TǓLÓU

(遗经楼) The largest rectangular *tǔlóu* in Fújiàn. The crumbling structure has 281 rooms, two schools and 51 halls. Built in 1851.

◉ Yúnshuǐyáo Tǔlóu Cluster 云水谣土楼群

This cluster, 48km northeast of Nánjìng, is set in idyllic surrounds with rolling hills, verdant farms and babbling streams. Six buses leave from Nánjìng bus station (¥20; one hour) to Yúnshuǐyáo (云水谣) and seven leave from Nánjìng train station (¥25; one hour) between 8.30am and 5.25pm. Admission is ¥90.

Héguì Lóu
TǓLÓU

(和贵楼) This tallest rectangular *tǔlóu* in Fújiàn has five storeys and was built on a swamp. It boasts 120 rooms, a school, two wells, and a fortified courtyard in front of the entrance. The mammoth structure was built in 1732.

Huáiyuǎn Lóu
TǓLÓU

(怀远楼) This relatively young *tǔlóu* (built in 1909) has 136 equally sized rooms and a concentric ring that houses an ancestral hall and a school.

Chángjiào
VILLAGE

(长教村) Between the Héguì and Huáiyuǎn *tǔlóu* in the Yúnshuǐyáo Tǔlóu Cluster is this beautiful village (now also called Yúnshuǐyáo) where you can sip tea under the big banyan trees and watch water buffalo in the river. The village has a few guesthouses that offer rooms from ¥100.

◉ Chūxī Tǔlóu Cluster 初溪土楼群

This lesser-visited yet picturesque cluster is located 48km southeast of Yǒngdìng. Admission is ¥70.

Jíqìng Lóu
TǓLÓU

(集庆楼) This 600-year-old *tǔlóu* was built without using a single nail and is still pretty intact. It now houses an exhibition hall.

Yúqìng Lóu
TǓLÓU

(余庆楼) Built in 1729, this *tǔlóu* with two concentric wings is now a guesthouse.

Zhōngchuān Village
VILLAGE

(中川村; Zhōngchuān Cūn) This village, 17km northwest of the Chūxī Tǔlóu Cluster, is the ancestral home of the Burmese-Chinese businessman Aw Boon Haw, the inventor of the medicinal salve Tiger Balm and owner of the (in)famously quirky Haw Par Villa theme park in Singapore. Here, you'll find another **villa** (虎豹别墅; Hǔbào Biéshù; admission ¥30; ☺ 8am-5pm), but its scale and decor can't compete with its Singaporean (big) sister. More interesting is his family's **ancestral hall** (胡氏家庙; Húshì Jiāmiào) 100m behind the villa. The shrine, the spear-like pillars that celebrate the achievements of their family members, and the setting itself are spectacular.

◉ Nánxī Tǔlóu Cluster 南溪土楼群

Cluster admission is ¥70.

Huánjí Lóu
TǓLÓU

(环极楼) Sitting midway between Yǒngdìng and Nánjìng, this four-storey building is a huge roundhouse with inner concentric passages, tiled interior passages and a courtyard. It also sports a *huíyīnbì* (回音壁) – a wall that echoes and resonates to sharp sounds.

Some villagers may ask you for a 'sanitation fee'. It's not legal. Don't pay.

Yǎnxiāng Lóu
TǓLÓU

(衍香楼) This four-storey *tǔlóu* rises up beautifully next to a river, and is in the same direction as Huánjí Lóu *tǔlóu*.

Qìngyáng Lóu
TǓLÓU

(庆洋楼) Not far from Yǎnxiāng Lóu *tǔlóu*, this huge, rectangular, semi-decrepit structure was built between 1796 and 1820.

🛏 Sleeping & Eating

There are many hotels in Yǒngdìng and Nánjìng, but neither town is attractive. We recommend you base yourself in a *tǔlóu*, which will give you a glimpse of a vanishing dimension of life in China. Bring a flashlight and bug repellent. Most families can cook up meals for you. Expect to pay ¥150 for a two-person meal. Always ask the price before ordering.

Some *tǔlóu* have upgraded their rooms with modern facilities, but most are still very basic – a bed, a thermos of hot water and a fan. You might also find that the toilets are outside.

Most *tǔlóu* owners can also organise a pick-up from Yǒngdìng or Nánjìng and transport for touring the area.

Qìngdé Lóu
TǓLÓU $

(庆德楼; ☑ 777 1868, 89 0695 1868; www.qingde-lou.com; Tāxià Village; d ¥138-168; ❋ 🛜) The 30 rooms in this rectangular *tǔlóu* are modern, with air-con and wi-fi. A few rooms on the 2nd and 3rd floors have shared bathrooms only, but they are clean and comfy.

Fúyù Lóu Chángdì Inn
TǓLÓU $

(福裕楼常棣客栈; Fúyù Lóu Chángdì Kèzhàn; ☑ 553 2800, 37 9909 7962; www.fuyulou.net; Hóngkēng Tǔlóu Cluster; d incl breakfast ¥100-150; 🛜) Rooms are basic but comfy. Doubles come with with fan and TV. The owners are friendly and speak some English.

Défēng Lóu
TǓLÓU $

(德风楼; ☑ 775 6669, 180 5067 0878; nr the bridge to Yúnshuǐyáo Tǔlóu Cluster; d ¥128-158; ❋ 🛜) All rooms are now upgraded with ensuite bathrooms. This *tǔlóu* is conveniently located near the bridge to Yúnshuǐyáo and all buses stop in front of it. The *tǔlóu* is identifiable by a big red star above the entrance.

Tǔlóu Sunshine International Youth Hostel
HOSTEL $

(土楼沐浴阳光国际青年旅舍; Tǔlóu Mùyù Yángguāng Guójì Qīngnián Lǚshě; ☑ 777 1348; Tāxià Village; dm ¥40, d ¥130; @ 🛜) This HI-affiliated hostel has clean dorms and rooms. Carpool and bike rental can be arranged. Follow the HI signs after you get off the bus at Xueying bridge (雪英桥; Xuěyīng Qiáo) in the village.

ℹ Getting There & Away

BUS

From Xiàmén long-distance bus station (p288), take a bus headed to Nánjìng (¥32, two hours, 12 daily between 7am and 5.30pm). Upon arrival, you can either take the respective buses to some of the clusters, or hire a private vehicle to take you there.

Xiàmén has seven daily buses to Yǒngdìng (永定县; ¥75, four hours) from 7.10am to 4pm. From there, there are infrequent buses to Gāoběi Tǔlóu Cluster. Yǒngdìng can also be accessed by bus from Guǎngdōng and Lóngyán (¥20, one hour, regular).

TRAIN

Ten high-speed D trains link Xiàmén and Lóngyán via Nánjìng (¥27, 35 minutes) daily. Local buses 1 and 2 link the train and bus stations in Nánjìng.

ℹ Getting Around

The easiest way to see the *tǔlóu* is to book a tour, or hire a vehicle either from Xiàmén, Nánjìng or Yǒngdìng.

If you book a place to stay in one of the *tǔlóu*, most owners can help with transport and they usually arrange pick-up from Nánjìng or Yǒngdìng.

You'll find taxi drivers in Yǒngdìng and Nánjìng offering their services for around ¥400 a day (¥700 if you hire for two days), setting off early morning and returning late afternoon. Expect to see two clusters per day.

Amazing Fujian Tulou (www.amazingfujian-tulou.com) and **Discover Fujian** (discoverfujian. com) can organise English-speaking guided tours.

Quánzhōu
泉州

☑ 0595 / POP 934,500

Most people visit Quánzhōu as a day trip from Xiàmén, but we recommend you to spend a couple of days to take in the charm of this underrated city. This port city, an important stop on the maritime Silk Road back in the Song and Yuan dynasties, is actually an enchanting place to delve into for China's maritime past. Back in the 13th century, Marco Polo informed his readers that 'it is one of the two ports in the world with the biggest flow of merchandise'.

Though its heyday is long gone, much of Quánzhōu's impressive heritage has been preserved, and evidence of its multiculturalism, especially some fine lingering traces of a former Islamic presence, can still be detected among the city's residents and buildings.

◉ Sights

The centre of town lies between Zhongshan Nanlu, Zhongshan Zhonglu and Wenling Nanlu. This is where you'll find most of the tourist sights. The oldest part of town is to the west, where many narrow alleys and lanes, which still retain their traditional charm, are waiting to be explored.

Kāiyuán Temple
BUDDHIST TEMPLE

(开元寺; Kāiyuán Sì; 176 Xi Jie; admission ¥10; ⊙7.30am-7pm) In the northwest of the city is one of the oldest temples in Quánzhōu, dating back to AD 686. Surrounded by trees, Kāiyuán Temple is famed for its pair of rust coloured five-storey stone pagodas, stained with age and carved with figures, which date from the 13th century. Behind the eastern pagoda is a **museum** containing the enormous hull of a Song dynasty seagoing junk, which was excavated near Quánzhōu in 1974.

The temple's **Great Treasure Hall** (Dàxióng Bǎodiàn) and the hall behind are decorated with marvellous beams and brackets. The main courtyard is flanked by a row of wizened banyan trees; one is 800 years old! Take bus 2 (¥2) from Wenling Nanlu.

Maritime Museum
MUSEUM

(泉州海外交通史博物馆; Quánzhōu Hǎiwài Jiāotōngshǐ Bówùguǎn; Donghu Lu; ⊙8.30am-5.30pm Tue-Sun) **FREE** On the northeast side of town, this fabulous museum explains Quánzhōu's trading history, the development of Chinese shipbuilding and the kaleidoscope of religions in the port's heyday. The Religious Stone Hall and Islamic Culture Hall are highlights, boasting a beautiful collection of gravestones and reliefs of different religions dating from the Yuan dynasty. Take bus 7 or 203 and alight at Qiáoxiāng Tǐyùguǎn (侨乡体育馆).

Quánzhōu

FÚJIÀN QUÁNZHŌU

Qīngjìng Mosque
MOSQUE

(清净寺; Qīngjìng Sì; 108 Tumen Jie; admission ¥3; ⏱8am-5.30pm) Built by the Arabs in 1009 and restored in 1309, this stone edifice is one of China's only surviving mosques from the Song dynasty. Only a few sections (mainly walls) of the original building survive, largely in ruins. The adjacent mosque is a donation from the government of Saudi Arabia.

Língshān Islamic Cemetery
CEMETERY

(灵山伊斯兰教圣墓; Língshān Yīsīlán Shèngmù; cnr Donghu Lu & Lingshan Lu) Set at the foot of the mountain of Língshān, this leafy 'oasis' is truly a hidden gem in Quánzhōu and is one of the most intact historic cemeteries in China. Two of Mohammed's disciples are said to be buried here, and you'll also find some granite steles dated from the Míng dynasty. Take bus 7 or 203 and hop off at Shèngmùzhàn (圣墓站).

Guāndì Temple
TAOIST TEMPLE

(关帝庙, Guāndì Miào; Tumen Jie) **FREE** This smoky and magnificently carved temple is southeast of Qīngjìng Mosque. It's dedicated to Guan Yu, a Three Kingdoms general who was deified as the God of War. Inside the temple are statues of the god and wall panels that detail his life.

🎎 Festivals & Events

Lantern Festival
FESTIVAL

This festival is celebrated on the 15th day of the first lunar month. Streets in downtown Quánzhōu swell with people after dark, flashing their glow sticks or lanterns and marching to **Tiānhòu Temple** (天后宫; Tiānhòu Gōng; 1 Nanmen Tianhou Lu; ⏱9am-5pm) to pray for prosperity. Most pilgrims come here specifically to *qǐguī* (乞龟), that is to touch the gigantic 'rice turtle'. This effigy is created with bags of rice piled into the shape of a turtle, regarded as a sacred animal due to its longevity. The rice is given away to the crowds at the end of the festival.

🛏 Sleeping

There are plenty of nondescript midrange hotels along Wenling Nanlu heading north, as well as some decent accommodation near the old town.

54 Coffee Inn
GUESTHOUSE $

(泉州新街54咖啡客栈; Quánzhōu Xīnjiē Wǔshísì Kāfēi Kèzhàn; ☎2287 5167; 54 Xin Jie, 新街54号; dm ¥55, s & d ¥138-158; ❄@) This cosy guesthouse in a red-brick house has eight well-kept rooms and an inviting courtyard. It's good value but a little hard to find. The entrance to the unmarked Xin Jie is on Xi Jie, about 150m west of the intersection at Zhongshan Zhonglu. From there, walk north for another 150m and the guesthouse is to your right.

Tíhò Cafe & Hostel
HOSTEL $

(堤后咖啡客栈; Tíhòu Kāfēi Kèzhàn; ☎1865 9009 055, 2239 0800; caimj@126.com; 114 Tihou Lu, 堤后路114号; dm ¥50, s & d ¥108-158; ❄@) Located at the western edge of the old town of Quánzhōu is this cheery hostel-cum-cafe. The six-bed mixed dorm is small but clean, the rooms have no attached bathrooms but are cosy and relaxing. Catch bus 40 (westbound) from the long-distance bus station and alight at Línzhāngmén (临漳门). A taxi from the train station and the centre of town is around ¥20.

Quánzhōu Hotel
HOTEL $$$

(泉州酒店; Quánzhōu Jiǔdiàn; ☎2228 9958; www.quanzhouhotel.com; 22 Zhuangfu Xiang, 庄府巷22号; r from ¥800; ❄@) The real draw of this hotel is its good location in the heart of Quánzhōu's old town. Rooms in the old wing (东晖楼; Dōnghuī Lóu) are sparse, but rooms in the new wing (南馨楼; Nánxīn Lóu) are surprisingly comfy and modern, and the upgrade will only cost you a few more bucks.

The hotel is identifiable by its gaudy, faux-European palace exterior.

Wàndá Vista Quánzhōu
HOTEL $$$

(泉州万达文华酒店; Quánzhōu Wàndá Wènhuá Jiǔdiàn; ☎6829 8888; www.wandahotels.com; 719 Baozhou Lu, 宝洲路719号; d ¥1288-1588; ❄@🛜) Located at the southern edge of Quánzhōu city centre, this 322-room giant is arguably the best hotel in the city and is a favourite of many business travellers. Rooms on the upper floors have good views of Jìnjiāng River. Discounts of 30% available.

🍴 Eating & Drinking

You can find the usual noodle and rice dishes served in the back lanes around Kāiyuán Temple and also along the food street close to Wenling Nanlu. **New Overseas Chinese Village** west of Zhongshan Park and **Yuanhe 1916 Idea Land** on Xinmen Jie are two emerging nightlife areas, full of old-house-turned-cafes, bars and restaurants.

Lánshì Zhōnglóu
HAKKA $

(蓝氏钟楼肉粽; 9-21 Dong Jie; meals from ¥25; ⏰11am-9.30pm) Locals flock to this unpretentious joint for its famous glutinous rice dumplings. No English menu, but there are pictures of the dishes on the wall. The signature black rice dumplings (黑米粽; hēimǐzòng) and rice dumpling with yolk (蛋黄粽; dànhuángzòng) are recommended.

Ānjì Kèjiāwáng
HAKKA $$

(安记客家王; 461 Tumen Jie; meals from ¥50; ⏰11am-9pm) Excellent Hakka dishes are served here. Try the lovely *Kèjiā niàng dòufu* (客家酿豆腐; soft cubes of tofu impregnated with crumbs of pork) and the delectable barbequed pork (叉烧; Chāshāo).

Gǔcuò Cháfáng
TEA $$

(古厝茶坊; 44 Houcheng Xiang; tea ¥50-480, snacks from ¥20; ⏰9am-1am) This quaint teahouse in the alley behind the Guāndì Temple has a refreshing old-time courtyard ambience, paved with flagstones and laid out with traditional wooden halls and bamboo chairs.

ⓘ Information

Bank of China (中国银行; Zhōngguó Yínháng; 9-13 Jiuyi Jie; ⏰9am-5pm) Has a 24-hour ATM.

China Post (中国邮政; Zhōngguó Yóuzhèng; cnr Dong Jie & Nanjun Lu; ⏰8.30am-6pm) Sells stamps and postcards.

Public Security Bureau (PSB; 公安局; Gōng'ānjú; ☑2218 0323; 62 Dong Jie; ⏰visa section 8-11.30am & 2.30-5.30pm) You can extend your visa here.

Quánzhōu Xiéhé Hospital (Quánzhōu Xiéhé Yīyuàn; Tian'an Nanlu) In the southern part of town.

ⓘ Getting There & Around

BUS

Both **Quánzhōu bus station** (泉州汽车站; Quánzhōu Qìchēzhàn; cnr Wenling Nanlu & Quanxiu Jie) and the **long-distance bus station** (泉州客运中心站; Quánzhōu kèyùn zhōngxīnzhàn; cnr Quanxiu Jie & Pingshan Lu) further east along Quanxiu Jie have buses to the following destinations:

Guǎngzhōu ¥290, nine hours, five daily
Shēnzhèn ¥280, eight hours, four daily
Regular deluxe buses:
Fúzhōu ¥70, 3½ hours
Xiàmén ¥37, 1½ hours

Local bus 15 links both bus stations. Bus 2 goes from the bus station to Kāiyuán Temple. Taxi flag fall is ¥7, then ¥1.80 per kilometre.

TRAIN

D trains depart from the high-speed train station (高铁泉州站; Gāotiě Quánzhōu Zhàn), 15km from the town centre:

Fúzhōu ¥55, one hour, every 30 minutes
Shànghǎi ¥307, 8½ hours, 12 daily
Xiàmén ¥21, 45 minutes, every 30 minutes

Buses 17 and K1 run from the high-speed train station to Quánzhōu bus station and the long-distance bus station respectively, via Zhōnglóu (钟楼), the intersection of Zhongshan Zhonglu and Xijie. Bus 203 links the train station to Maritime Museum and Islamic Cemetery. A taxi from the centre of town to the train station costs ¥50. In town, train tickets can be bought at the Wenling Nanlu **ticket office** (铁路火车票代售点; Tiělù Huǒchēpiào Dàishòudiǎn; 166 Wenling Nanlu; ⏰9am-6pm) or from the **ticket office** (火车售票亭; Huǒchē Shòupiàotíng; 675 Quanxiu Jie; ⏰7am-6pm) just east of the long-distance bus station. There's a ¥5 booking fee.

Around Quánzhōu

Not far from Quánzhōu there are a few oft-overlooked sights worth exploring.

Chóngwǔ
崇武

One of the best-preserved city walls in China can be found in the ancient 'stone city' of **Chóngwǔ** (50km east of Quánzhōu; admission ¥46; ⏰7am-7pm daily). The granite walls date back to 1387, stretch over 2.5km and average 7m in height. Scattered around the walls are 1304 battlements and four gates into the city. The town wall was built by the Ming government as a frontline defence against marauding Japanese pirates, and it has survived the past 600 years remarkably well. You can also walk along the top of the wall at some points.

The ticket includes admission to the adjacent **Chóngwǔ Stone Arts Expo Park** (雕工艺博览园; Chóngwǔ Shídiāo Gōngyì Bólǎnyuán; admission included with entry to Chóngwǔ), which boasts a large park filled with 500 stone sculptures made by local crafts people, a small beach, a lighthouse and some seafood restaurants. You won't miss much if you skip it.

Frequent buses depart Quánzhōu's long-distance bus station (¥13, 1½ hours), taking you past arrays of stone statues (the area is famed for its stone-carving workshop) before ending up in Chóngwǔ. Motorbikes (¥5) will take you from the bus drop-off to the stone city.

Xúnpǔ Village 蟳埔村

The fishing village of Xúnpǔ, some 10km southeast of the city centre of Quánzhōu, was on the old trade route of the maritime Silk Road and was perhaps the Arabs' first port of call when they set foot in Quánzhōu during the Song dynasty. The village, now under encroaching urbanisation, is still fascinating and you'll find some old houses built with oyster shells behind the main road in the village. Meanwhile, the grannies still wear the flamboyant traditional head ornaments that they love to brag about.

The **Māzǔ Temple** (妈祖庙; Māzǔ Miào) on the knoll in the village is the local centre of worship. It's dedicated to the goddess of seafarers and turns very lively on the 29th day of the first lunar calendar month, the birthday of the protector. All the women in the village will turn out in traditional costumes to join in the annual Māzǔ procession.

A taxi ride from Quánzhōu bus station is about ¥25.

Cǎo'ān Manichaean Temple 草庵摩尼教寺

Perched on the hill of Huábiǎo, 19km south of Quánzhōu, this quirky **temple** (草庵摩尼教寺; Cǎo'ān Mónijiào Sì; Huábiǎo Hill, 19km south of Quánzhōu; admission ¥20; ⊙8am-6pm) is dedicated to Manichaeism, a religion originating in Persia in the third century, combining elements of Zoroastrian, Christian and Gnostic thought, which reached China in the 7th century.

The well-restored stone complex you see today is a rebuild dating to the Yuan dynasty (14th century). The most remarkable relic in the temple is the 'Buddha of Light', a sitting stone statue in the main hall, which is actually the prophet Mani, founder of Manichaeism, in a Buddhist disguise. Manichaeism was considered an illegal religion during the Song period and the religion had to operate in the guise of an esoteric Buddhist group. Take a closer look at the statue, and you'll find its hairstyle (straight instead of curly), hand gestures and colour combinations are distinctly different from most representations of the Buddha.

From the long-distance bus station in Quánzhōu, board a bus to Ānhǎi (安海; ¥11) and tell the driver to drop you off at Cǎo'ān Lùkǒu (草庵路口). Then look for the English signage saying Grass Temple and it's a 2km walk uphill. The road is not well-marked so taking a taxi is a recommended alternative. A taxi from Quánzhōu is around ¥60.

Ānxī 安溪

Mountainous Ānxī County, 66km northwest of Quánzhōu, is home to the famous *Tiě Guānyīn* (铁观音; Iron Buddha) tea, an oolong variety known for its thick fragrance and floral sweetness. Fifty-odd tea varieties from China, Taiwan and Japan are cultivated in the visitor-friendly, 11-acre **Ānxī Cháyè Dàguānyuán** (安溪茶叶大观园; Fengguan Shan, 安溪凤冠山; admission ¥5; ⊙7.30am-9pm). The theme park-like plantation also includes an oolong tea processing workshop, a museum and several temples.

The long-distance bus station in Quánzhōu has frequent buses to Ānxī (¥18, one hour). Ānxī Cháyè Dàguānyuán is 3km north of Ānxī bus station and motorbikes will take you there for ¥5.

Fúzhōu 福州

📋 0591 / TRANSPORT HUB

Fúzhōu, capital of Fújiàn, is one of the major transport hubs in southern China. You'll find flights, inter-city/-province trains and buses to most of the destinations you're likely to go to, especially the coastal provinces.

🛏 Sleeping

Fúzhōu accommodation falls mainly in the midrange and top-end categories. Many hotels offer discounts. If you're stranded in the city, there are some decent options near the train and bus stations.

Juchunyuan Inn Fuzhou   HOTEL $$
(福州聚春园驿馆; Fúzhōu Jùchūnyuán Yìguǎn; 📞6303 3888; 22 Gōng Xiàng, Sānfang Qīxiàng, 三坊七巷宫巷22号; d¥489-525; ⊖❉@🛜) A beautiful inn housed in a historic mansion in the pedestrianised Sānfáng Qīxiàn area. All 56 rooms are tastefully and modernly appointed.

Shangri-La Hotel   HOTEL $$$
(香格里拉大酒店; Xiānggélǐlā Dàjiǔdiàn; 📞8798 8888; www.shangri-la.com; 9 Xinquan Nanlu, 新权南路9号; d¥1250; ⊖❉@🛜🏊) Top-notch service is expected in every Shangri-La, and this classy tower at the heart of town overlooking Wuyi Sq is no exception. A cab from the south long-distance bus station is around ¥20.

✕ Eating

Sānfáng Qīxiàn (三坊七巷) is a popular dining and shopping area lined with Ming-style houses and lanterns.

You'll find small eateries on both sides of **Nanhou Jie** (南后街), the main street of the area. Take a cab and ask to be dropped off at the intersection of Yangqiao Donglu and Nanhou Jie. The fare is around ¥20 from the south long-distance bus station.

ℹ Getting There & Away

AIR

Fúzhōu airport is 45km southeast of the city centre and has daily flights to Běijīng (¥1550, 2½ hours), Guǎngzhōu (¥830, one hour), Shànghǎi (¥780, 70 minutes) and Hong Kong (¥1620, 80 minutes).

Airport buses leave from at least three locations in town: the Apollo Hotel (阿波罗大酒店; Ābōluó Dàjiǔdiàn; ¥25) on Wuyi Zhonglu, 400m north of the south long-distance bus station (¥20), has departures every 20 minutes between 5.30am and 10pm; the north long-distance bus station (¥25) near the North Rail Station has departures every hour between 6am and 8pm; the South Rail Station has departures every hour between 12pm and 5pm. The trip takes about an hour.

BUS

The **north long-distance bus station** (长途汽车北站; chángtú qìchē běizhàn; 317 Hualin Lu) is 400m south of the North Rail Station. Services include the following:

Guǎngzhōu ¥280, 12 hours, seven daily
Quánzhōu ¥70, two hours, regular
Shànghǎi ¥280, 10 hours, two daily
Wǔyí Shān ¥100, eight hours, 5.30pm
Xiàmén ¥105, 3½ hours, every 20 minutes

The **south long-distance bus station** (长途汽车南站; chángtú qìchē nánzhàn; cnr Guohuo Xilu & Wuyi Zhonglu) services the following destinations:

Guǎngzhōu ¥258, 13 to 15 hours, eight daily
Hong Kong ¥358, 15 hours, four daily
Shēnzhèn ¥260, 12 hours, five daily
Xiàmén ¥105, 3½ hours, every 15 minutes

TRAIN

Fúzhōu has a good network of trains to many major cities. D trains leave sometimes from the more centrally located **North Rail Station** (福州北站; Fúzhōu Běizhàn; 502 Hualin Lu) and more often from the **South Rail Station** (East of Lulei Village, Canshan District) (福州南站; Fúzhōu Nánzhàn) 17km southeast of the town centre:

Quánzhōu ¥55, one hour, every 30 minutes

Shànghǎi ¥261, 6½ hours, 16 daily
Xiàmén ¥81, 1½ hours, every 15 minutes

The North Rail Station also has 10 trains to Wǔyí Shān (¥47 to ¥147, 4½ to 6½ hours) daily and one direct G56 express to Běijīng (¥765, 10½ hours, 8am).

Wǔyí Shān 武夷山

📋 0599 / POP 230,000

With crisp climes and unspoilt scenery, Wǔyí Shān is a popular mountain retreat in the northwest corner of Fújiàn where many Chinese from the plains go to beat the heat. The rivers, waterfalls, mountains and protected forests combine to make it a great place for day hikes and short treks. Try to come midweek or in low season (November, March and April) and you might have the area to yourself. Avoid the area during heavy rain (especially during summer months) even if the hotels and tour organisers advise otherwise.

The scenic part lies on the west bank of Chóngyáng Stream (Chóngyáng Xī), and some accommodation is located along its shore. Most of the hotels are concentrated in the *dùjiàqū* (度假区; resort district) on the east side of the river. The main settlement is Wǔyí Shān city, about 10km to the northeast, with the train station and airport roughly halfway in between.

◉ Sights & Activities

Wǔyí Shān Scenic Area   MOUNTAIN PARK
(武夷宫; 1-/2-/3-day access ¥140/150/160; ⏱ 7am-5pm) The entrance to the area is at Wǔyí Gōng, about 200m south of the Wǔyí Mountain Villa. Trails within the scenic area connect all the major sites. Good walks include the 530m **Great King Peak** (大王峰; Dàwáng Fēng), accessed through the main entrance, and the 410m **Heavenly Tour Peak** (天游峰; Tiānyóu Fēng), where an entrance is reached by road up the Nine Twists River.

It's a moderate two-hour walk to Great King Peak among bamboo groves and steep-cut rock walls. The trail can be slippery and wet, so bring suitable shoes.

The walk to Heavenly Tour Peak is more scenic, with better views of the river and mountain peaks. But the path is also the most popular with tour groups. At the northern end of the scenic area, the **Water Curtain Cave** (水帘洞; Shuǐlián Dòng) is a cleft in the rock about one-third of the way up a 100m cliff face. In winter and autumn, water plunges over the top of the cliff, creating a curtain of spray.

Xiàméi

ANCIENT VILLAGE

(下梅; admission ¥60) This village dates to the Northern Song dynasty and boasts some spectacular Qing dynasty architecture from its heyday as a wealthy tea-trading centre.

Motorbikes in Wǔyí Shān city can take you to Xiàméi at ¥50 (roundtrip) for this 12km journey.

Wǔfū

ANCIENT VILLAGE

(五夫; admission ¥60) Sixty kilometres southeast of Wǔyí Shān Scenic Area, this 1700-year-old village got its fame as the hometown of Zhu Xi, a Confucian scholar in the Song dynasty. It's best visited when the lotus in the giant ponds, which are backdropped by some quaint Ming-era architecture, are in full bloom. Minibuses to Wǔfū (¥13, two hours) leave from the small bus station next to the long-distance bus station in Wǔyí Shān city.

Nine Twists River

BOAT TOUR

(九曲溪, Jiǔqū Xī; boat rides ¥130; ⊙7am-5pm) One of the highlights for visitors to Wǔyí Shān is floating down the river on **bamboo rafts** (zhúpái) fitted with rattan chairs. Departing from Xīngcūn (星村), a short bus ride west of the resort area, the trip down the river takes over an hour and brings you through some magnificent gorge scenery, with sheer rock cliffs and lush green vegetation.

One of the mysteries of Wǔyí Shān is the cavities, carved out of the rock faces at great heights, which once held boat-shaped coffins. Scientists have dated some of these artefacts back 3000 years. If you're taking a raft down the river, it's possible to see some remnants of these coffins on the west cliff face of the fourth meander, also known as Small Storing Place Peak (小藏山峰; Xiǎozàngshān Fēng).

🛏 Sleeping

Most of the accommodation in Wǔyí Shān is in the midrange category and most is overpriced unless you come here during low season. Hotels are mostly on the east side of the river, while family-run guesthouses and hostels are in the village of Lántāng on the relatively quieter west side. The village is 700m north of Wǔyí Mountain Villa.

Wǔyí Mountain

Dàwáng Peak Youth Hostel

HOSTEL $

(武夷山大王峰青年旅舍; Wǔyíshān Dàwángfēng Qīngnián Lǚshě; ☑520 9518; 46 Lantang Village, 兰汤村46号; dm ¥40, d ¥128-158; @🛜) The hostel is identifiable by a huge Che Guevara banner hanging on its façade. Rooms have a cosy feeling; dorms are small but clean. Most staff don't speak English. To get there, take bus 5, or pay about ¥30 to ¥40 for a taxi ride from the train station.

Liántiān Kè Boutique Hotel

HOTEL $$

(连天客精品酒店; Liántiān Kè Jīngpǐn Jiǔdiàn; ☑527 2799; Bldg A, Shuanglin Garden, Dawangfeng Lu, 大王峰路双利花园A栋; r ¥238-680; ❄@🛜) Best bang for your buck in the resort district on the east bank. Rooms are clean, modern and fairly new. Free airport/train-station pickups are provided if advance notice is given.

Wǔyí Mountain Villa

HOTEL $$$

(武夷山庄; Wǔyí Shānzhuāng; ☑525 1888; www.513villa.com; Wuyi Gong, 武夷宫; d ¥888-988, ste ¥1388-2888; ❄) Located at the foot of Great King Peak, the villa is considered by the Chinese to be the most prestigious place to stay in Wǔyí Shān. Some rooms are dated, but the views are fine. Discounts of 40% available.

🍴 Eating

Frogs, mushrooms, bamboo rice and bamboo shoots are the specialities of Wǔyí Shān's cuisine. In town, there are food stalls along the streets in the evening. As to be expected, restaurants are overpriced.

Wǒjiā Sīfángcài

FUJIANESE $$

(我家私房菜; ☑525 2758; Dawangfeng Lu; meals from ¥70; ⊙11am-10pm) This place is famed for using fresh, local produce, and getting a table is never easy, so book ahead. Try the braised chicken soup (清炖土鸡汤; *qīngdùn tǔjī tang*), stir-fried spare ribs with sweet potatoes (地瓜排骨; *dìguā páigǔ*) or sautéed black fungus with gingko (银杏木耳; *yínxìng mù'ěr*). The restaurant is 100m east of Xīnhuá Dàjiǔdiàn (新华大酒店).

ℹ Information

Chinese maps of the Wǔyí Shān area are available in bookshops and hotels in the resort district. There are some grubby internet cafes in the back alleys south of Wangfeng Lu (望峰路), charging ¥3 to ¥4 an hour.

Bank of China (中国银行; Zhōngguó Yínháng; Wujiu Lu; ☺9am-5pm) In Wǔyí Shān city, this branch has an ATM.

China International Travel Service (CITS; 中国国际旅行社; Zhōngguó Guójì Lǚxíngshè; ☑5134 666; Guolu Dalou, Sangu Jie; ☺9am-4pm Mon-Sat) The staff can arrange train tickets and tours.

❶ Getting There & Away

AIR

Wǔyí Shān has air links to several cities.
Běijīng ¥1350, two hours, two daily
Guǎngzhōu ¥890, 2½ hours, one daily
Shànghǎi ¥660, one hour, one daily
Xiàmén ¥720, 50 minutes, two daily

BUS

Buses run from the long-distance bus station in Wǔyí Shān city.

Fúzhōu ¥100, eight hours, two daily
Xiàmén regular/deluxe ¥191, nine hours, one daily

TRAIN

Direct trains go to Wǔyí Shān from Quánzhōu (¥148, 12 hours, hourly) and Xiàmén (¥149 to ¥232, 12 hours, hourly).

❶ Getting Around

Bus 6 links the long-distance bus station, the train station, the airport, the resort area and Wǔyí Mountain Villa.

The resort area is small enough for you to walk everywhere. Expect to pay about ¥15 for a motorised trishaw from the resort district to most of the scenic area entrances. A ride from the train station or airport to the resort district will cost ¥30.

FÚJIÀN WǓYÍ SHĀN

Liáoníng

POP 43.9 MILLION

Best Walks

➡ Dàlián's southwest coastline (p310)

➡ North Korean border (p315)

➡ Xīngchéng's beach (p318)

Best Historical Sites

➡ Imperial Palace (p304)

➡ North Tomb (p305)

➡ Tiger Mountain Great Wall (p316)

➡ Xīngchéng Old City (p318)

Why Go?

History and hedonism run side by side in Liáoníng (辽宁). Walled Ming-dynasty cities rub up against booming beach resorts, while imperial palaces sit in the centre of bustling modern cities. Nothing quite captures the fun and distinction, however, as much as seaside Dàlián with its golden coastline and summer beer festival (or is that bacchanalia?), and former battlegrounds where Russian and Japanese armies wrestled for control of the region in the early 20th century.

Outside of the major cities, Liáoníng is largely an expanse of farmland, forest and smokestack towns. The North Korean border runs alongside the province and is an intriguing area. It's as close as you can get to the Democratic People's Republic of Korea (DPRK) without actually going there...though you could go via tour from Dāndōng if you wanted to. Here, the large Korean population and easy mix of cultures provide a ready example that China is only a land of stereotypes if you never venture far into it.

When to Go
Dàlián

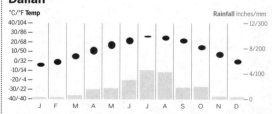

May & Jun Catch deals on a seaside hotel.	**Jun & Jul** Enjoy fresh cherries, mulberries and blueberries at roadside stands everywhere.	**Jul & Aug** Have fun at the Dàlián International Beer Festival.

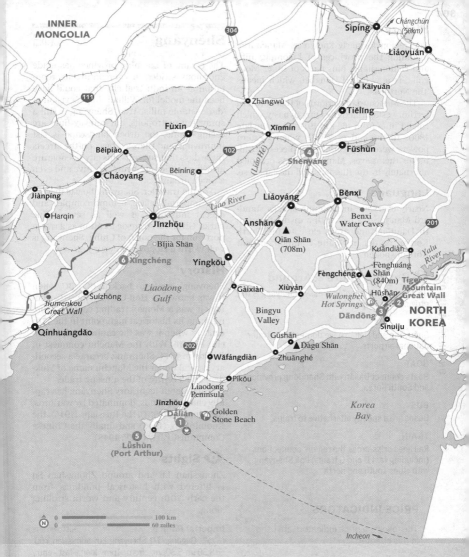

Liáoníng Highlights

1 Kick back in **Dàlián** (p308) and enjoy the beaches, coastal walkways and beer festival

2 Climb the easternmost stretch of the Great Wall at **Tiger Mountain Great Wall** (p316), near Dāndōng

3 Cruise the Yālù River close to North Korea and experience the mix of Korean and Chinese culture in **Dāndōng** (p314)

4 Explore the **tomb of Huang Taiji** (p305), founder of the Qing dynasty, in Shěnyáng

5 Wander the old battlefields and graves of **Lǚshùn** (p312), fought over by rival Japanese and Russian Empires

6 Laze on the beach and stroll the old walled city of historic, little-visited **Xīngchéng** (p318)

History

The region formerly known as Manchuria, including the provinces of Liáoníng, Jílín and Hēilóngjiāng, plus parts of Inner Mongolia, is now called Dōngběi, which means 'the Northeast'.

The Manchurian warlords of this northern territory established the Qing dynasty, which ruled China from 1644 to 1911. From the late 1800s to the end of WWII, when Western powers were busy carving up pieces of China for themselves, Manchuria was occupied alternately by the Russians and the Japanese.

Language

Nearly everyone in Liáoníng speaks standard Mandarin, albeit with a distinct accent. In Dāndōng and areas close to the North Korean border, it's quite common to hear Korean spoken.

❶ Getting There & Around

Getting around Liáoníng is easy. Shěnyáng is the province's transport hub.

AIR
Shěnyáng and Dàlián have domestic and international airports.

BOAT
Boats connect Dàlián with Shāndōng province and South Korea.

BUS
Buses are a speedy alternative to trains.

TRAIN
Rail lines criss-cross the region; connections (including fast D and G trains) link Shěnyáng with cities south and north.

PRICE INDICATORS

The following price indicators are used in this chapter:

Sleeping

$ less than ¥200

$$ ¥200 to ¥400

$$$ more than ¥400

Eating

$ less than ¥40

$$ ¥40 to ¥80

$$$ more than ¥80

Shěnyáng 沈阳

☑ 024 / POP 6.25 MILLION

The capital of Liáoníng province has made enormous strides in overcoming its reputation as an industrial city that could have been the model for William Blake's vision of 'dark satanic mills'. True, Shěnyáng is still a sprawling metropolis, but subway lines are easing traffic, the urban landscape is fast improving, and there's a buzz on the streets these days that suggests this city's people are growing confident, secure, positive and even a touch urbane.

For the traveller, Shěnyáng boasts its very own Imperial Palace, a tomb complex and decent museums, as well as several fine parks. Given its strategic location as a transport hub for the north of China, Shěnyáng is well worth a stopover on your journey.

History

Shěnyáng's roots go back to 300 BC, when it was known as Hou City. By the 11th century it was a Mongol trading centre, before reaching its historical high point in the 17th century when it was the capital of the Manchu empire. With the Manchu conquest of Běijīng in 1644, Shěnyáng became a secondary capital under the Manchu name of Mukden, and a centre of the ginseng trade.

Throughout its history Shěnyáng has rapidly changed hands, dominated by warlords, the Japanese (1931), the Russians (1945), the Kuomintang (1946) and finally the Chinese Communist Party (CCP; 1948).

⊙ Sights

Zhongshan Lu and around Zhongshan Sq is littered with historical buildings from the early 20th century and worth strolling along.

Imperial Palace   HISTORIC SITE
(故宫, Gùgōng; 171 Shenyang Lu; admission ¥60; ⊙8.30am-5.30pm, from 1pm Mon, last entry 4.45pm) This impressive palace complex resembles a small-scale Forbidden City. Constructed between 1625 and 1636 by Manchu emperor Nurhachi (1559–1626) and his son, Huang Taiji, the palace served as the residence of the Qing-dynasty rulers until 1644. The central courtyard buildings include ornate ceremonial halls and imperial living quarters, including a royal baby cradle.

In total, there are 114 buildings, not all of which are open to the public. Don't miss

Shěnyáng

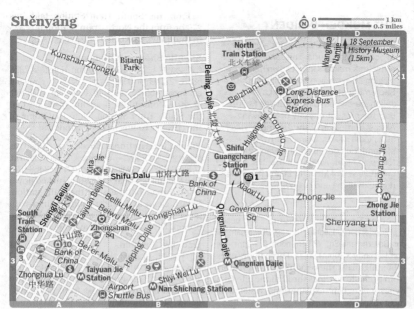

the double-eaved octagonal **Dàzhèng Hall** (at the rear of the complex), which has two gold dragons curled around the pillars at the entrance, a deep interior plafond ceiling and an elaborate throne, where Nurhachi's grandson, Emperor Shunzhi, was crowned. At **Chóngzhèng Hall**, the first large building as you enter, the beams over the entrance portico are all carved in the shape of five-fingered dragons.

Zhong Jie metro station (exit B) drops you off a few minutes north.

North Tomb HISTORIC SITE

(北陵, Běi Líng; 12 Taishan Lu; park/tombs ¥6/50; ⊙7am-6pm) Another Shěnyáng highlight is this extensive tomb complex, the burial place of Huang Taiji (1592–1643), founder of the Qing dynasty. The tomb's animal statues lead up to the central mound known as the Luminous Tomb (Zhāo Líng).

In many ways a better-preserved complex than the Imperial Palace, the tomb site is worth a few hours examining the dozens of buildings with their traditional architecture and ornamentation. **Lóng'ēn Hall** is a particularly fine structure – as you circumambulate the base observe the richness of traditional symbols (peonies, vases, lucky clouds) carved in relief.

The North Tomb sits a few kilometres north of town inside expansive **Běi Líng Park**. With its pine trees and large lake, the park is an excellent place to escape Shěnyáng's hubbub. Locals come here to promenade, sing or just kick back. Beiling Gongyuan metro station is directly outside the park.

THE MUKDEN INCIDENT

By 1931 Japan was looking for a pretext to occupy Manchuria. The Japanese army took matters into its own hands by staging an explosion on the night of 18 September at a tiny section of a Japanese-owned railway outside Mukden, the present-day city of Shěnyáng. Almost immediately, the Japanese attacked a nearby Chinese army garrison and then occupied Shěnyáng the following night. Within five months, they controlled all of Manchuria and ruled the region until the end of WWII.

Liáoníng Provincial Museum
MUSEUM

(辽宁省博物馆, Liáoníng Shěng Bówùguǎn; SE cnr Government Sq; ⏰ 9am-noon & 1-5pm, Tue-Sun, last entry 3.30pm) **FREE** Three floors of exhibits highlight the region's art and history, from prehistoric times through the late Qing dynasty. English explanations accompany most displays.

18 September History Museum
MUSEUM

(九一八历史博物馆, Jiǔ Yī Bā Lìshǐ Bówùguǎn; 46 Wanghua Nanjie; ⏰ 9am-5pm, Tue-Sun, last entry 4pm) **FREE** There's an obvious propagandic purpose to this museum, but the hundreds of photographs, sculptures, paintings and dioramas recreates a picture of China under Japanese rule. English captions are limited. Bus 325 from the North Train Station stops across the street. The museum is about 2km northeast from the town centre.

🛏 Sleeping

The main train station area is modern and vibrant, and near overloaded with shopping malls, restaurants and cafes of all stripes. With a metro station, it's also convenient for getting around town.

Sanpi Youth Hostel
HOSTEL $

(三皮青年旅社, Sānpí Qīngnián Lǔshè; ☎ 2251 1133; www.gjqnls.com; 21 Yalu Jiang Jie, 鸭绿江街21号; dm/tw with shared bathroom ¥55/110; ❄ @ 🛜) To the east of the North Tomb is this laid-back hostel akin to a best friend's basement suite in the suburbs. Which is a bit odd as it's on the 5th floor of an otherwise unpromising-looking building. The location's not great, but there's laundry and internet and the rooms are organised and clean.

From the South Train Station take bus 279 or from the North Train Station bus 325 to the Jiànyuàn Xiǎoqū (剑苑小区) stop.

Shěntiě Shěnzhàn Bīnguǎn
HOTEL $

(沈铁沈站宾馆, Railway Station Hotel; ☎ 2358 5888; 2 Shengli Dajie, 胜利大街2号; r without bathroom ¥60-80, tw with bathroom ¥138-168; ❄ @) A convenient if ageing place next to the South Train Station. Note that some of the cheaper rooms have no windows.

Vienna International Hotel
HOTEL $$

(维也纳国际酒店, Wéiyěnà Guójì Jiǔdiàn; ☎ 8360 8888; 58 Minzu Beijie; d & tw ¥468-576) The Vienna is a neat little hotel tucked down a small road 150m east of the train station. Smart, clean and bright rooms paired with good service make this a decent midrange option. Discounts of 40% available.

Liáoníng Bīnguǎn
HOTEL $$$

(辽宁宾馆, Liaoning Hotel; ☎ 2383 9104; 97 Zhongshan Lu, 中山路97号; r incl breakfast from ¥458; ❄ @) This grand dame dates back to 1927 and is perched across from Mao's statue at busy Zhongshan Sq. The Chairman himself stayed here and it retains many of its period details – the marbled lobby is particularly impressive as is the central stairwell. Rooms are comfortable but could use an update. The outdoor patio serves beer for when the sun deigns to shine. Discounts usually available.

🍴 Eating

Both the North and South Train Stations are cheap-restaurant zones. You'll also find lots of reasonably priced restaurants around the Imperial Palace. Most have picture menus. There's a Tesco supermarket near the Sanpi Youth Hostel.

★ Měijīn Hotpot
HOTPOT $$

(美津火锅, Měijīn Huǒguō; cnr Taiyuan Beijie & Bei Sanma Lu; ingredients ¥3-20; ⏰ 10.30am-2am) This popular hotpot chain teems with the energy of dozens of diners chowing down on everything from veggies to meat and noodles. Friendly staff can help explain ingredients on the incredibly diverse English menu.

Báiyù Chuànchéng
BARBECUE $$

(白玉串成; 85 Xita Jie; skewers ¥2-12; ⏰ 10am-midnight) It's hard not to get into the whole experience of charcoal grilling your own skewers of juicy meat and veg right at your table. If meat on a stick isn't to your liking, the rest of the street is rife with Korean restaurants.

Lăobiān Dumplings
DUMPLINGS $$

(老边饺子馆, Lăobiān Jiăoziguăn; 2nd fl, 208 Zhong Jie; dumplings ¥16-60; ⊙10am-10pm) Shěnyáng's most famous restaurant has been packing in the locals since 1829. It might be resting on its laurels a little but punters continue to flock here for the boiled, steamed and fried dumplings in an array of flavours: from abalone to cabbage and even curry.

The restaurant is on the 2nd floor of the Lăobiān Hotel, just across from the B1 exit of Zhong Jie metro station.

View & World Vegetarian Restaurant
VEGETARIAN $$

(宽巷子素菜馆, Kuān Xiàngzi Sùcàiguăn; 202 Shi-yi Wei Lu; dishes ¥10-168; ⊙10am-10.30pm;) Peking duck and meatballs are on the menu here, but there won't be any actual meat on your plate. Everything is meat-free at this classy nearly vegan paradise, which claims to be the only non-MSG restaurant in all of northeast China (an astonishing claim if true).

The restaurant is on one of Shěnyáng's busy eating streets and you'll find much to sample nearby, including real Peking duck, if you so desire.

Carrefour Supermarket
SUPERMARKET

(家乐福, Jiālèfú; Beizhan Lu) You can pack a picnic for your travels here or grab a quick bite from the decent food court. Beside the long-distance bus station.

Drinking & Nightlife

Stroller's
BAR

(流浪者餐厅, Liúlàngzhě Cāntīng; 36 Beiwu Jing Jie, 北五经街36号; drinks from ¥25, food ¥40-170; ⊙11.30am-late) This long-running atmospheric pub is popular with both locals and expats and has a decent imported beer selection and the usual pub grub. Take exit B of Nan Shichang metro station, cross the road and head up the side street 150m.

🏠 Shopping

Taiyuan Jie
SHOPPING STRIP

Near the South Train Station is Taiyuan Beijie, one of Shěnyáng's major shopping streets, with department stores and an extensive underground shopping street (mostly small clothing boutiques). Locals refer to it simply as Taiyuan Jie.

Zhong Jie
SHOPPING STRIP

This street, near the Imperial Palace, is another popular pedestrianised shopping zone that is now glossier than ever. It stretches across both sides of Chaoyang Jie. Expect malls with all manner of shops (local and international) and restaurants.

ℹ Information

ATMs can be found all over the city and around Zhongshan Sq.

Bank of China (中国银行; Zhōngguó Yínháng; 96 Zhonghua Lu) ATMs and currency exchange. There's another branch at Government Sq (253 Shifu Dalu)

Public Security Bureau (PSB, 公安局, Gōng'ānjú; ✆2253 4850; Zhongshan Sq) There's also a visa office opposite the entrance of the North Tomb.

ℹ Getting There & Away

Large hotels can help book airline and train tickets.

AIR

Shenyang Taoxian International Airport has flights to South Korea and Russia as well as the following domestic cities:

Běijīng ¥950, 1½ hours
Shànghǎi ¥1100, two hours

BUS

The **long-distance express bus station** (长途 汽车快速客运站, chángtú qìchē kuàisù kèyùn-zhàn; 120 Huibin Jie) is south of Beizhan Lu, about a five-minute walk from the North Train Station and next to the Carrefour Supermarket. Schedules are available at the information counter as you walk in. Buses service the following destinations:

Běijīng ¥129, eight hours, 9.10am, 10.10am, 12.40am and 7pm
Chángchūn ¥85, 4½ hours, seven per day (8.30am to 5pm)
Dàlián ¥100, five hours, hourly (7.40am to 6pm)
Dāndōng ¥84, 3½ hours, every 30 minutes (6am to 7pm)
Hā'ěrbīn ¥150, 6½ hours, 11am and 1.50pm
Xīngchéng ¥83, 4½ hours, 8.20am and 3pm

TRAIN

Shěnyáng's major train stations are the North and South Train Stations. Many trains arrive at one station, stop briefly, then travel to the next. It may be different when departing – always confirm which station you need. Buy sleeper or G/D train tickets (to Běijīng or Shànghǎi) as far

LIÁONÍNG SHĚNYÁNG

in advance as possible. Bus 262 runs between the North and South Train Stations, or take the metro.

South Station Trains

Báihé (for Chángbáishān) hard/soft sleeper ¥100/156, three daily (9.13am, 6.55pm and 8.18pm), 14 hours

Dàlián hard seat ¥57, four to seven hours

Dāndōng hard seat ¥44, five hours

Hā'ěrbīn hard seat ¥78, seven hours

Xīngchéng hard seat ¥54, four to five hours

North Station Trains

Běijīng (D train) ¥207, five hours, frequent

Běijīng hard seat/sleeper ¥96/180, 10 hours

Chángchūn (D/G train) ¥115/136, 2½/1½ hours

Dàlián (D/G train) ¥110/177, three/two hours

Hā'ěrbīn (D/G train) ¥161/245, 3/2½ hours

ⓘ Getting Around

TO/FROM THE AIRPORT

The airport is 25km south of the city. **Shuttle buses** (¥15.50, one hour, hourly) leave from an alley just before the intersection of Zhonghua Lu and Heping Dajie and from the North Train Station. Taxis cost ¥80.

BUS

Buses are cheap, frequent and cover the city, but the subway is easier to navigate.

SUBWAY

With only two lines (Line 1 running east–west and Line 2 running north–south) and one connecting station, Shěnyáng's clean and relaxed subway system is easy to figure out. There are stops at both the North and South Train Stations as well as the North Tomb and Zhong Jie (for the Imperial Palace). The average ride costs ¥2 to ¥4. Stations have public toilets.

TAXI

Taxi flagfall starts at ¥9.

Dàlián 大连

🖉 0411 / POP 6.69 MILLION

Perched on the Liáodōng Peninsula and bordering the Yellow Sea, Dàlián is one of the most relaxed and liveable cities in the northeast, if not all of China. Tree-lined hilly streets with manageable traffic and fresh air, a surfeit of early 20th-century architecture and an impressive coastline, complete with swimming beaches, are just some of its charms. Toss in a decent restaurant and

bar scene and serious shopping, and that frequent Dàlián epithet, the 'Hong Kong of the North', looks like more than just bluster.

Dàlián is a fine place to unwind for a few days. But after lazing on the beaches and strolling along the southwest coastline, pay a visit to the historic port town of Lǚshùn. The old battlefields and cemeteries offer a rare first-hand glimpse into some of the north's most turbulent days.

◉ Sights & Activities

Golden Stone Beach　　　　　BEACH
(金石滩; Jīnshí Tān) The coast around Golden Stone Beach, 50km north of the city, has been turned into a domestic tourism mecca with a number of theme parks and rock formations commanding inflated entrance fees. The long pebbly beach itself is free and quite pretty, set in a wide bay with distant headlands.

To get here take the light rail, known by the locals as Line 3 (轻轨三号线; Qīngguǐ Sānhàoxiàn), from the depot on the east side of Triumph Plaza, behind the Dàlián train station (¥8, 50 minutes). From the beach station it's a 10-minute walk to the beach, or catch a hop-on, hop-off tourist shuttle bus (¥20), which winds round the coast first before dropping you off at the beach. There's a visitor centre to the right of the train station as you exit, with English-speaking staff if you need help.

Zhongshan Sq　　　HISTORIC BUILDINGS
(中山广场, Zhōngshān Guǎngchǎng) This is Dàlián's hub, a 223m-wide square with 10 lanes radiating out from a central roundabout designed by the Russians in 1889. With the exception of the Dalian Financial Building, all the other grand structures hail from the early 20th century when Dàlián was under the control of the Japanese. Styles range from art deco to French Renaissance.

The **Dàlián Bīnguǎn**, a dignified hotel built in 1914 and called then the Dalian Yamato Hotel, appeared in the movie *The Last Emperor*.

🛏 Sleeping

Reservations are highly recommended in the summer months, when prices may be 50% more than listed below. The train station area has a number of budget hotels but it's a noisy, frenetic place. Touts will find you if you do need a room: rates start at ¥100 a night.

Dàlián

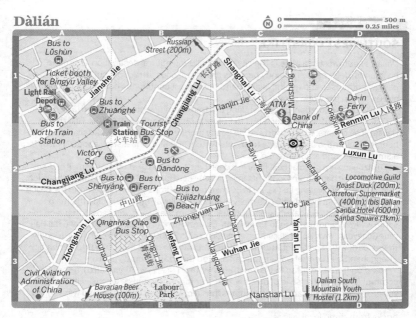

★ **Dàlián Noah's Ark Golden Beach Hostel** HOSTEL **$**

(大连挪亚方舟国际青年旅舍, Dàlián Nuóyà Fāngzhōu Guójì Qīngnián Lûshě; ☎ 3968 4088; www.yhachina.com/ls.php?id=339; 57 Binhai Xilu; dm with/without bathroom ¥85/80, d & tw ¥280; ☺ closed winter; @ ☎) There's nothing remotely biblical about the hostel: the architecture, a whitewashed edifice built against a hill and facing the sea, evokes Santorini. Rooms are simple but charming: consider staying in a greenhouse-type glasshouse at the top of the compound! The 2nd-level lounge area is a great spot to have a beer and stare out to sea. YHA membership required to stay here.

Getting here is tough; take bus 5 near the train station to Qīngníwā Qiáo (青泥洼桥) to the last stop. Walk ahead five minutes through a parking lot and down a slope towards Golden Sand Beach (金沙滩, Jīn Shā Tān), pay ¥2 entry and continue towards the seashore and follow it to the right. Pack light as it's a 1km walk. Note you have to pay the ¥2 entry daily if you go in and out of the area.

Dàlián South Mountain Youth Hostel HOSTEL **$**

(大连南山国际青年旅舍, Dàlián Nánshān Guójì Qīngnián Lûshě; ☎ 8263 1189; dlnanshan@126.com; 114 Mingze Jie, 明泽街114号; dm ¥75-85;

Dàlián

⊙ **Sights**
   1 Zhongshan Sq C2

⊟ **Sleeping**
   2 Aloft Dalian D2
   3 Hanting Express A1
   4 Home Inn D1

⊗ **Eating**
   5 Night Market B2
   6 Tiāntiān Yúgǎng D1

❋ @ ☎) Tucked away in a quiet hillside neighbourhood is this friendly little hostel with clean, comfortable dorms (but only two bathrooms!). Facilities include self-service laundry and kitchen, as well as computer use and wi-fi. The southwest coastline is a 15-minute bus ride away, numerous parks are within walking distance and the train station can be reached quickly by taxi (¥10).

If you want to catch a bus here contact the hostel for directions.

Ibis Dàlián Sanba Hotel HOTEL **$$**

(大连三八宜必思酒店, Dàlián Sānbā Yíbìsī Jiǔdiàn; ☎ 3986 5555; www.ibishotel.com.cn; 49 Wuwu Lu, 中山区五五路49号; d & tw ¥219; ❋ @) This business hotel is in a fantastic location

DON'T MISS

SOUTHWEST COASTLINE

Dàlián's southwest coastline is the city's most alluring natural destination. Dramatic headlands, deep bays and sandy beaches are the obvious attraction, but there are also parks, lighthouses and quaint villages, and the longest continuous boardwalk (reportedly at 20.9km) in the world joining them all.

Start your exploration either by taking the tram from downtown to **Xīnghǎi Sq** (星海广场, Xīnghǎi Guǎngchǎng), or a bus to **Fùjiāzhuāng Beach** (傅家庄海滩, Fùjiāzhuāng Hǎitān). The square, which sports some gaudy architecture, is the site of Dàlián's popular beer festival, and is a good place to people-watch, fly a kite or just stroll about. Nearby is a small beach and amusement park.

Fùjiāzhuāng is a popular beach set in a deep bay. Junks float just offshore, small broken islands dot the horizon, and loads of families come here for no other reason than to have fun. Bus 5 leaves from Jiefang Lu (¥1, 20 to 30 minutes) and drops you off across from the beach.

A very pleasant boardwalk (it's really a wooden walkway built alongside the main coastal road) joins Fùjiāzhuāng and Xīnghǎi Sq. From the beach you can continue on this same walkway another 8km to **Lǎohǔtān Ocean Park** (老虎滩海洋公园, Lǎohǔ Tān Hǎiyáng Gōngyuán; www.laohutan.com.cn; admission ¥210; ⊙7.30am-5.30pm), a family-friendly theme park with a polar aquarium. At Lǎohǔtān you can catch bus 30 (¥1) to Sanba or Zhongshan Sq in central Dàlián. You can also do the coastal route via taxi.

Head on from Lǎohǔtān to **Fisherman's Wharf** (渔人码头, Yúrén Mǎtóu), a seaside community built in the style of an early 20th-century American east coast village. The village makes a great backdrop for photos, has a row of pleasant coffee and wine shops, and features a perfect replica of the 1853 German Bremen Port Lighthouse, built with bricks from razed local villages.

surrounded by restaurants and markets, but is also a five-minute walk to parks and quiet tree-lined streets. Public buses connect the hotel to the train station and southwestern coast. Rooms are clean and modern and the English-speaking staff are fairly attentive. For best rates book online.

It's located just off Sanba Sq. A taxi from the train station here costs ¥12.

Hanting Express HOTEL $$
(汉庭快捷酒店, Hàntíng Kuàijié Jiǔdiàn; ☑6666 2888; 32 Yunyang Jie, 云阳街32号; r from ¥219; ❄@⊛) Just behind the train station, overlooking the light-rail square, is this tidy business hotel. The hotel entrance is to the back of the building away from the light-rail square.

⭐ **Aloft Dalian** HOTEL $$$
(大连雅乐轩酒店, Dàlián Yǎlèxuān Jiǔdiàn; ☑3907 1111; www.alofthotels.com/dalian; 18-1 Luxun Lu, 鲁迅路18-1号; r¥1720-2220; ❄@⊛) This brand-new swish hotel is borne aloft thanks to a hip charisma lacking in other international chain hotels. Its colourfully decorated rooms are large with good views and plush beds, and the staff are friendly to a fault. The in-house restaurant and lounge area are good too. Discounts tame rack rates to a more reasonable ¥600 range.

Home Inn HOTEL $$
(如家快捷酒店, Rújiā Kuàijié Jiǔdiàn; ☑8263 9977; www.homeinns.com; 102 Tianjin Jie, 天津街102号; d/tw ¥189/209; ❄@) With its brightly coloured and tidy little rooms, free broadband and in-house restaurant serving cheap but tasty dishes, this is a good choice for the city centre. Recently the square around the hotel has seen some impressive urban regeneration, with a fake but good 'old street' opening just 100m away with a number of high-end cafes and bars. There's also a continuous pedestrian-only street/night market extending all the way to the train station.

✗ Eating

There are plenty of small restaurants on the roads leading off Zhongshan Sq and Friendship Sq. Friendship Sq has numerous malls on it with food courts on the higher floors. The food court in the nearby underground mall in Victory Sq is a good place to eat too (dishes ¥10 to 20). Both sides of the plaza outside the train station are lined with fruit vendors and shops selling cheap *bāozi* (包子; steamed dumplings).

Night Market
MARKET $

(夜市, Yèshì) Stretching several blocks along Tianjin Jie from the train station to the Home Inn, this outdoor market, open during the evenings, offers outdoor venues to eat barbecued seafood with a beer. There's also a smaller (but better) market around Sanba Sq near the Carrefour Supermarket with outdoor barbecue stalls and seating, in addition to an abundance of fruit stands.

Handu Restaurant
KOREAN $$

(韩都, Hándū; 49-1 Wuwu Lu, 五五路49-1号; dishes ¥15-90; ⊙11am-10pm) Next door to the Ibis Hotel, this fabulous two-storey Korean restaurant decked out in luxe wood and granite fittings lets you barbecue your own meats at the table. There's also a selection of one-dish meals such as *bibimbap* (rice, vegetables and eggs served in a claypot) for those who don't wish to go the whole hog.

Locomotive Guild Roast Duck
ROAST DUCK $$$

(火车头果木烤鸭, Huǒchētóu Guǒmù Kǎoyā; 17 Luxun Lu; duck ¥197, dishes from ¥20; ⊙11am-2pm & 5-9pm) We're not sure what locomotives have to do with duck, but the birds here are roasted in a wood-fired oven to delicate crispness before being deftly sliced and presented by your table. Live seafood is also available for those who prefer fish over fowl. Picture menu available.

Tiāntiān Yúgǎng
SEAFOOD $$$

(天天鱼港; 10 Renmin Lu; dishes ¥22-99; ⊙11am-10pm) Choose your meal from the near museum-level variety of aquatic creatures at this upscale seafood restaurant. Most dishes are set out in refrigerated displays, making this a rare easy seafood-eating experience in China.

Carrefour Supermarket
SUPERMARKET

(家乐福, Jiālèfú; Luxun Lu; ⊙7.30am-9pm) Large supermarket with good selection of takeaway food and baked goods.

Drinking & Nightlife

Dàlián has the most happening bar and club scene of any city in the northeast. Check out *Focus on Dalian* (www.focusondalian.com) for the latest.

Bavarian Beer House
PUB

(53 Gao'erji Lu; ⊙11am-late) This upscale Bavarian beer pub serves a fantastic range of German beers, including several darks and whites on tap (¥35 for 0.5L). There is outdoor seating so you can enjoy the quiet neighbourhood atmosphere on Gao'erji Lu, and there's a selection of dishes if quenching your thirst builds up a hunger.

Shopping

There are malls all over Dàlián. Across from the train station there's an enormous underground shopping centre below Victory Sq. South of Victory Sq is a pedestrian plaza lined with upscale department stores. If tacky souvenirs are your thing, Dàlián's **Russian Street** (Tuanjie Jie), a pedestrianised street with some of the city's oldest buildings, is a good spot.

Information

There are ATMs all around town. Zhongshan Sq has a number of large bank branches including a **Bank of China** (中国银行, Zhōngguó Yínháng; 9 Zhongshan Sq), where you can change currency.

Dàlián Xpat (www.dalianxpat.com) An excellent source of English-language information about restaurants, bars and clubs in Dàlián.

Focus on Dalian (www.focusondalian.com) Bilingual site with good articles and restaurant and bar recommendations.

Getting There & Away

AIR

Dàlián International Airport is 12km from the city centre and well connected to most cities in China and the region. Tickets can be purchased at the **Civil Aviation Administration of China** (CAAC, 中国民航, Zhōngguó Mínháng; ☎8361 2888;

LIÁONÍNG DÀLIÁN

BEER MANIA

For 12 days from late July to early August, Dàlián stages the **Dàlián International Beer Festival**, its very own version of Munich's Oktoberfest. Beer companies from across China and around the world set up tents at the vast Xīnghǎi Sq, near the coast, and locals and visitors flock (more than two million in 2013) to sample the brews, gorge on barbecue and snacks from around China, listen to live music and generally make whoopee. Entrance tickets are a low ¥20 and in 2014 there were 30 beer vendors offering more than 400 brands for sampling. See the festivals page on the China Highlights (www.chinahighlights.com) website for the dates each year.

BORDER CROSSING: DÀLIÁN TO SOUTH KOREA

Da-in Ferry (☑ Dàlián 8270 5082, Incheon 032-891 7100, Seoul 822-3218 6500; www.dainferry.co.kr; 17th fl, 68 Renmin Lu, 人民路68号, 宏誉商业大厦17楼) The Korean-run Da-in Ferry to Incheon in South Korea departs from Dàlián on Monday, Wednesday and Friday at 4.30pm (¥980 to ¥1900, 16 hours).

Zhongshan Lu) or any of the travel offices nearby. In addition to the domestic destinations listed here, there are also flights to the Russian cities of Khabarovsk and Vladivostok; Hong Kong; and Tokyo.

Běijīng ¥600, 1½ hours
Hā'ěrbīn ¥900, 1½ hours

BOAT

There are several daily boats to Yāntái (¥180 to ¥500, five to eight hours) and Wēihǎi (¥190 to ¥500, seven to eight hours) in Shāndōng. Buy tickets at the passenger ferry terminal in the northeast of Dàlián or from one of the many counters in front of the train station. To the ferry terminal, take bus 13 (¥1) from the southeast corner of Shengli Guangchang and Zhongshan Lu near the train station.

BUS

Long-distance buses leave from various points around the train station. It can be tricky to find the correct ticket booths, and they do occasionally move.

Dāndōng 丹东; ¥100, four hours, nine daily, 6.20am to 2.30pm. Buses leave from stand No 2 on Shengli Guangchang just south of Changjiang Lu.

Lǚshùn 旅顺; ¥7, one hour, every 20 minutes. Buses leave from the back of the train station, across the square.

Shěnyáng 沈阳; ¥98, five hours, every two hours. Buses depart from south of Victory Sq.

Zhuānghé 庄河; ¥45, 2½ hours, frequent. Buses leave from in front of the ticket office on Jianshe Jie, the first street behind the train station.

TRAIN

Buy your ticket as early as possible. D and G trains leave from the north station. Get a bus (¥5, 30 minutes, regular) there from outside the Hanting Express behind the light-rail station.

Běijīng hard seat/sleeper ¥145/240, 10 to 12 hours

Běijīng (D/G train) ¥213/389, 6½/5½ hours

Chángchūn (G train) ¥300, three hours

Hā'ěrbīn (G train) ¥389, four hours
Shěnyáng (G train) ¥170, two hours

❶ Getting Around

Dàlián's central district is not large and can be covered on foot. A subway is under construction and will be ready in 2015 or so.

TO/FROM THE AIRPORT

A taxi to/from the city centre costs ¥30 to ¥60 depending on the time of day. No shuttle buses.

BUS

Buses are plentiful and stops have English signs explaining the route. There's a tourist bus (¥10, hourly, 8.30am to 4.30pm) in front of the train station. It does a hop-on, hop-off loop of the city and the southwestern coast.

TAXI

Fares start at ¥10; most trips are less than ¥20.

TRAM

Dàlián has a slow but stylish tram with two lines: the 201 and the 202 (¥1 to ¥2 each). No 201 runs past the train station on Changjiang Lu, while 202 runs out to the ocean and Xīnghǎi Sq (you must take 201 first and transfer).

Around Dàlián

Lǚshùn   旅顺

With its excellent port and strategic location on the northeast coast, Lǚshùn (formerly Port Arthur) was the focal point of both Russian and Japanese expansion in the late 19th and early 20th centuries. The bloody Russo-Japanese War (1904–05) finally saw the area fall under Japanese colonial rule, which would continue for the next 40 years.

Lǚshùn is worth a visit during any trip to Dàlián. While developers are piling on the high-rise apartments, Lǚshùn is still a relaxed town built on the hills. Most sites are related to military history, but there's an excellent museum on Liáoníng, as well as a number of scenic lookouts and parks.

As soon as you exit the bus station at Lǚshùn, taxis will cry out for your business. A few hours touring the sights will cost ¥150 (excluding ¥10 car parking fees at some sights). If the driver doesn't have one, pick up a bilingual English-Chinese map at the station newsstand to help you negotiate. We've listed the best sights here. Resist any attempts by taxi drivers to steer you towards sights with admission ¥100 upwards: they are overpriced and underwhelming.

Greater Dàlián

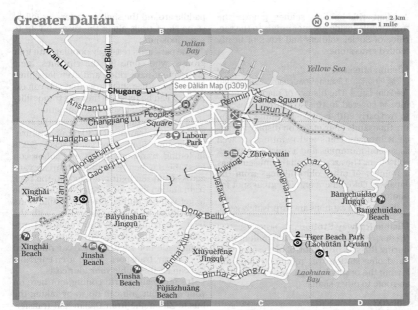

See Dàlián Map (p309)

Sights

★ **Lǚshùn Prison** HISTORIC SITE
(旅顺日俄监狱旧址博物馆, Lǚshùn Rì'é Jiānyù Jiùzhǐ Bówùguǎn; ☉ 9am-4.30pm, Tue-Sun, last entry 3.30pm) **FREE** Lǚshùn's best sight is a cluster of restored red-brick buildings which functioned as a prison from 1902 to 1945. It may have changed hands from the Russians to the Japanese, but its purpose remained unchanged: more than 450,000 prisoners came through its cells. Sombre displays, including an unearthed wooden-barrel coffin containing an executed inmate, paint a picture of a working early 20th-century jail.

English captions illuminate the plight of prisoners, torture methods, work camps and more.

Báiwáng Shān HISTORIC SITE
(白王山; admission ¥40) Head to the top of this hill opposite the bus station for panoramic views out to the bay and across the ever-expanding city. The phallic-shaped monument is **Báiwáng Shān Tǎ** (白王山塔), a pagoda erected by the Japanese in 1909 after they took Lǚshùn. Climb to the top up the stairs (made in the USA) for ¥10.

Greater Dàlián

◎ Sights
1 Fisherman's Wharf D3
2 Lǎohǔtān Ocean Park C3
3 Xīnghǎi Square A2

◎ Sleeping
4 Dàlián Noah's Ark Golden
   Beach Hostel A3
5 Dàlián South Mountain Youth
   Hostel C2
6 Ibis Dàlián Sanba Hotel C2

◎ Eating
7 Carrefour Supermarket C1
  Handu Restaurant .... (see 6)
  Locomotive Guild Roast
   Duck... (see 7)

◎ Drinking & Nightlife
8 Bavarian Beer House..........................B2

Soviet Martyrs Cemetery CEMETERY
(苏军烈士陵园, Sūjūn Lièshì Língyuán; ☉ 8.30am-4.30pm) **FREE** The largest cemetery in China for foreign-born nationals honours Soviet soldiers who died in the liberation of northeast China at the end of WWII, as well as pilots killed during the Korean War. Designed by Soviet advisers, the cemetery is heavy with communist-era iconography.

LIÁONÍNG AROUND DÀLIÁN

A giant rifle-holding soldier guards the front, while inside are memorials to the sacrifice of Soviet soldiers and rows of neatly tended gravestones.

Lǚshùn Museum   MUSEUM
(旅顺博物馆, Lǚshùn Bówùguǎn; ⊙9am-4pm Tue-Sun) FREE The history of Liáoníng province is covered in this stylish old museum in two early 20th-century buildings. Among the thousands of artefacts on display are ancient bronzes, coins and paintings, as well as several mummies and a quirky chopstick collection. The area around the museum has a number of other old buildings from the Japanese colonial era and is a great spot for photographs.

The English captions are surprisingly good.

Lǚshùn Railway Station   HISTORIC BUILDING
(旅顺火车站, Lǚshùn Huǒchēzhàn) Built in 1903 during Russia's brief control of the area, this handsome station was rebuilt in 2005 following the original design. It's worth a visit en route to other sights.

Hill 203   WAR MEMORIAL
(二0三景区, Èr Líng Sān Jǐngqū; admission ¥30) During the Russo-Japanese War, troops fought like wildcats for control of this strategic hill (when you get up the steep path to the top you'll see why). More than 5000 Russian and 10,000 Japanese soldiers lost their lives in the battle, which eventually went to the Japanese. Afterwards, the victors erected a 10m-high bullet-shaped memorial (constructed from shell casings) which, remarkably, still stands to this day.

ⓘ Getting There & Away

Buses to Lǚshùn (¥7, one hour) leave every 20 minutes from a stop across the square at the back of the Dàlián Train Station. Buy your ticket from the booth before lining up. Buses from both sides run from early morning to evening.

Bīngyù Valley   冰峪沟

If you can't travel south to Guìlín, **Bīngyù Valley** (Bīngyù Gōu; admission ¥168) offers a taste of what you're missing. About 250km northeast of Dàlián, the valley has tree-covered limestone cliffs set alongside a river; it's similar to Guìlín, if not nearly as dramatic. From the entrance a boat takes you along a brief stretch of the river, where rock formations rise steeply along the banks, before depositing you at a dock. From there, you can hire your own little boat or bamboo raft and paddle around the shallow waters, or follow some short trails along the river and up to some lookouts.

The park is increasingly popular with tour groups, who come for the zip lines, tame amusement-park rides, and even jet-skiing. Given the rather small area that you can explore, it can be tough to find any tranquillity in this otherwise lovely environment.

In summer, day tours run from the train station area, leaving at 7.30am and returning around 8pm. Buy your ticket (¥238 including transport, lunch and admission fees) the day before from the tourism vans across from the light-rail depot in the back train station area. Your hotel should be able to get you discounted rates. Note that tours sometimes do reverse itineraries (with the boat ride coming last) and you'll find precious little time alone. There are also (optional) add-ons such as cable-car rides and electric-car transport. These aren't terrible but can easily double your tour costs.

It's not really worth coming out here on your own, but you can do so by taking the bus to Zhuānghé from Dàlián and transferring to a bus headed to Bīngyù Gōu. Accommodation is available within the park, but is overpriced for what you get.

Dāndōng   丹东

☑ 0415 / POP 865,600

The principal gateway to North Korea (Cháoxiǎn) from China, Dāndōng has a buzz that's unusual for a Chinese city of its size. Separated from the Democratic People's Republic of Korea (DPRK) by the Yālù River (Yālù Jiāng), Dāndōng thrives on trade, both illegal and legal, with North Korea. It handles more than 50% of the DPRK's imports and exports and its increasing wealth means that there are now flashy malls stocking luxury brands and even a fast rail connection under construction.

For most visitors to Dāndōng, this is as close as they will get to the DPRK. While you can't see much, the contrast between Dāndōng's lively, built-up riverfront and the desolate stretch of land on the other side of the Yālù River speaks volumes about the dire state of the North Korean economy and the restrictions under which its people live.

Dāndōng is relatively compact and easy to walk around. The river is about 800m southeast of the train station, while the main shopping district is just east of the station.

Dāndōng

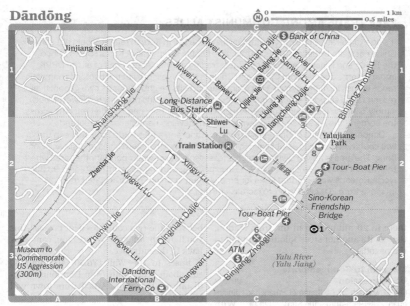

Sights & Activities

North Korean Border BORDER, PARK
(北朝鲜边界, Běi Cháoxiǎn Biānjiè) For views of the border, stroll along the riverfront **Yālù-jiāng Park** that faces the North Korean city of Sinuiju.

The area's most intriguing sight is the shrapnel-pockmarked **Broken Bridge** (鸭绿江断桥, Yālùjiāng Duànqiáo; admission ¥30; ☉7am-6.30pm). In 1950, during the Korean War, American troops 'accidentally' bombed the original steel-span bridge between the two countries. The North Koreans dismantled the bridge less than halfway across the river, leaving a row of support columns. You can wander along the remaining section and get within the distance of a good toss of a baseball to the North Korean shoreline. The Sino–Korean Friendship Bridge, the official border crossing between China and North Korea, is next to the old one, and trains and trucks rumble across it on a regular basis.

To get closer to North Korea, take a 30- to 40-minute **boat cruise** (观光船, Guānguāng Chuán; ☉7am-6pm) from the tour-boat piers on either side of the bridges. The large boats (¥60) are cheaper than the smaller speedboats (¥80), but you have to wait for the former to fill up with passengers (on average 30 minutes). In the summer you can sometimes

Dāndōng

Sights
1 Broken Bridge D3

Activities, Courses & Tours
2 Boat Cruise D2

Sleeping
3 Life's Business Hotel C1
4 Lǚyuàn Bīnguǎn C2
5 Zhong Lian Hotel C2

Eating
6 Sōngtáoyuán Fàndiàn C3
7 Tesco D1

Drinking & Nightlife
8 Peter's Coffee House D2

see kids splashing about in the river, as well as fishermen and the crews of the boats moored on the other side.

Jǐnjiāng Pagoda PAGODA
(锦江塔, Jǐnjiāng Tǎ) The highest point for miles, this pagoda sits atop Jǐnjiāng Shān in the park of the same name. The views across to North Korea are unparalleled and the park itself (a former military zone) is a well-tended expanse of forested slopes. You can take a taxi to the entrance or easily walk

LIÁONÍNG DĀNDŌNG

FREE TRADE AMONG COMMUNIST ALLIES

It's no exaggeration to say that without China, the North Korean regime would not survive. China has been trading with the Democratic People's Republic of Korea (DPRK) since the 1950s and is now the country's largest trading partner. Almost half of all the DPRK imports come directly from China, and China is the largest provider of humanitarian assistance to the Hermit Kingdom. That China supports its neighbour for its own geopolitical reasons is no surprise – that it does so for economic reasons probably is. However, put simply, Chinese leaders in the northern provinces insist they need market reforms across the border if they are to see their own long-term development plans fully realised.

Dāndōng is the hub of Sino–North Korean trade, and a free-trade zone between the two countries has been established in North Korea's northeastern cities of Rajin and Sŏnbong. The area is now known as Rason and is also a warm-water port. Another area where the two nations have made progress is in expanding working visas. In 2013 some 93,300 North Koreans were granted visas for employment in China. This translated to a 17% increase from 2012 and is set to increase further.

there in 20 minutes from the train station, though it's another steep kilometre uphill to the pagoda.

Museum to Commemorate US Aggression
MUSEUM

(抗美援朝纪念馆, Kàngměi Yuáncháo Jìniànguǎn; ⊙9am-4pm Tue-Sun) FREE With everything from statistics to shells, this comprehensive museum offers Chinese and North Korean perspectives on the war with the US-led UN forces (1950–53). There are good English captions here. The adjacent North Korean War Memorial Column was built 53m high, symbolising the year the Korean War ended. A taxi to the museum costs ¥10 from downtown.

Tiger Mountain Great Wall
GREAT WALL

(虎山长城, Hǔshān Chángchéng; admission ¥60, museum ¥10; ⊙8am-dusk) About 20km northeast of Dāndōng, this steep, restored stretch of the wall, known as Tiger Mountain Great Wall, was built during the Ming dynasty and runs parallel to the North Korean border. Unlike other sections of the wall, this one sees comparatively few tourists. The wall ends at a small museum with a few weapons, vases and wartime dioramas. You can buy tickets at the main entrance booth.

From here two routes loop back to the entrance. Heading straight ahead on the road is the easy way back, but there's nothing to see. It's better to climb back up the stairs a short way and look for a path on the right that drops then literally runs along the cliff face! There are some good scrambles and in 20 minutes or so you'll get to a point called Yībùkuà – 'one step across' – marking an extremely narrow part of the river

between the two countries. Not far past this you'll reach an area where you can walk back to the entrance.

Buses to the Wall (¥6.50, 40 minutes) run about every hour from Dāndōng's long-distance bus station. A taxi from town will cost ¥25 and you can usually flag a share taxi back for ¥10.

Speedboat Tours
BOAT TOURS

(快艇码头, Kuàitǐng Mǎtóu; per speedboat ¥180) About 23km northeast of Dāndōng is a small dock where you can board a speedboat (seats eight) for a thrilling 30-minute ride up the Yālù River. Close to shore, the driver will take you close to a portion of river where you are between two DPRK banks – the mainland on the left and a DPRK military-occupied island on the right.

Sidle up to waiting DPRK boatmen to buy local smokes, currency and alcohol (though it's cheaper in China!) before zipping back to shore. You can flag passing taxis at Tiger Mountain Great Wall (3km away) to ride up to the dock for ¥5. Alternatively, get a Dāndōng taxi to take you here directly.

🛏 Sleeping

There are many hotels in Dāndōng, most for around ¥200 a night. High-summer rates may be 30% to 50% more than the prices given here.

Lüyuàn Bīnguǎn
HOTEL $

(绿苑宾馆; ☎ 212 7777; fax 210 9888; cnr Shiwei Lu & Sanjing Jie, 三经街十纬路交界处; dm/s with shared bathroom ¥60/, d & tw with bathroom from ¥168; ❄ @) There are reasonable singles and three- and four-bed dorms at this long-running guesthouse on busy Shiwei Lu. The more expensive doubles and twins include internet connections.

Life's Business Hotel
HOTEL $$

(莱弗仕商务快捷酒店, Láifúshì Shāngwù Kuàijié Jiǔdiàn; ☎213 9555; www.lifeshotel.com; 29 Liuwei Lu, 六纬路29号; r ¥138-298; ❋ @) Life's is a smart business hotel popular with North Korean businessmen and within walking distance of the riverfront, restaurants and a Tesco supermarket. Rooms are tidy and comfortable with the ones on higher floors affording river views. Cheaper rooms have no windows.

Zhong Lian Hotel
HOTEL $$$

(中联大酒店, Zhōng Lián Dà Jiǔdiàn; ☎233 3333; www.zlhotel.com; 62 Binjiang Zhong Lu, 滨江中路 62号; d/tw incl breakfast ¥478/598; ❋ @ ⎙) Directly across from the Broken Bridge is this solid midrange option with large rooms, an even larger marble lobby (with wi-fi) and English-speaking staff. The pricier rooms offer great views of the bridge and river. Discounts available.

🍴 Eating & Drinking

On summer nights, the smoke from hundreds of barbecues drifts over Dāndōng as street corners become impromptu restaurants serving up fresh seafood and bottles of Yālù River beer, the refreshing local brew. One of the best places for barbecue is in the tents on the corner of Bawei Lu and Qijing Jie. More conventional restaurants, including a range of Korean, hotpot and DIY barbecue, as well as comfortable cafes where you can sip coffee and watch how the other half lives, line the riverfront on either side of the bridges. There's also a big Tesco (乐购; Lègòu; cnr Liuwei Lu & Sanjing Jie; ⎮8am-9.30pm) supermarket in the east part of town.

Sōngtāoyuán Fàndiàn
NORTH KOREAN $$

(松涛园饭店; Binjiang Zhonglu; dishes ¥10-78; ⎮11am-3pm & 5-10pm) A big part of the experience for many travellers to this region is eating at a North Korean restaurant with reputedly real North Korean waitresses. This locally recommended place sits appropriately enough just a few hundred metres from the Broken Bridge (directly beside SPR Coffee) and has a range of traditional dishes. There's a full picture menu to help you decide.

Peter's Coffee House
CAFE, WESTERN

(彼得咖啡室, Bǐde Kāfēi Shì; www.peterscoffeehouse.com; 103 Binjiang Zhong Lu; ⎮8am-10pm Mon-Sat, noon-10pm Sun; 🛜) Down by the riverfront is this friendly cafe run by a long-term Canadian expat family. In addition to its excellent coffee, Peter's serves milkshakes and sodas (¥25), authentic Western baked goods, a fine all-day breakfast (¥32), burgers and sandwiches. This is also the place to go for local information and restaurant recommendations.

ⓘ Information

Bank of China (中国银行, Zhōngguó Yínháng; 60 Jinshan Dajie) Has ATM and will change currency. Another ATM is closer to the river at 77-1 Binjiang Zhonglu.

Public Security Bureau (PSB, 公安局, Gōng'ānjú; ☎210 3138; 15 Jiangcheng Dajie)

ⓘ Getting There & Away

Dāndōng airport has infrequent flights to a few cities in China; most travellers arrive by bus or train.

BUS

The **long-distance bus station** (cnr Shiwei Lu & Jinshan Dajie) is near the train station.

Dàlián ¥100, 3½ hours, nine daily (6am to 2.50pm)

VISITING THE HERMIT KINGDOM

Most tours to the Democratic People's Republic of Korea (DPRK) start with a flight from Běijīng into Pyongyang, but Jílín and Liáoníng offer a more interesting alternative launching pad. You can visit the Special Economic Zone of Rason from Yánjí (p324) in Jílín province or consider taking a train from Dāndōng all the way to Pyongyang. The following tour agencies organise visas and offer trips designed for Westerners. Check the websites for costs and itineraries. Note that some travel restrictions apply to American and Japanese tourists.

Explore North Korea (www.explorenorthkorea.com) Dāndōng-based agency.

Koryo Tours (www.koryogroup.com) Large, long-running Běijīng-based agency.

Young Pioneer Tours (www.youngpioneertours.com) Offers alternative itineraries into Rason, Namyang, Hoeryong city and Onsong county.

BORDER CROSSING: DĀNDŌNG TO SOUTH KOREA

Dāndōng International Ferry Co (丹东国际航运有限公司; Dāndōng Guójì Hángyùn Yǒuxiàn Gōngsī; ☑ 315 2666; www.dandongferry.co.kr; cnr Xingwu Lu & Gangwan Lu; ☉ 8am-5pm) runs a boat to Incheon in South Korea on Tuesday and Thursday at 6pm and Sunday at 4pm (¥1010 to ¥1710, 16 hours). Buy tickets at the company's office on Xingwu Lu. A bus to the ferry terminal (¥20) leaves two hours before departure on the respective departure days from the train station.

Jí'ān ¥85, seven hours, 8.30am

Shěnyáng ¥82, three hours, every 30 minutes (5.10am to 6.30pm)

Tōnghuà ¥82, seven hours, 6.30am and 8.50am

TRAIN

The train station is in the centre of town. A lofty Mao statue greets arriving passengers.

Shěnyáng seat ¥24 to ¥44, four to five hours

Xīngchéng 兴城

☑ 0429 / POP 560,000

Despite having a bevy of talking points – it's one of only four Ming-dynasty cities to retain its complete outer walls, it has the oldest surviving temple in all of northeastern China and it's an up-and-coming beach resort – Xīngchéng has stayed well off the radar of most travellers. Yes, it's still a bit dusty and rough round the edges, but conditions are improving and historians and aficionados will have a field day here.

Xīngchéng's main drag is Xinghai Lu Er Duan (兴海路二段), where you'll find hotels, restaurants and a **Bank of China** (中国银行; Zhōngguó Yínháng) with a 24-hour ATM. From the train station head right, take the first left, and then a quick right to get onto Xinghai Lu Yi Duan. This merges into Er Duan (Section 2) in a kilometre.

◉ Sights & Activities

★ **Old City** HISTORIC SITE

(老城, Lǎo Chéng) FREE Standing like a miniature Píngyáo (albeit less polluted or glossy... in a good way), the walled city dates back to 1430 and is the principal reason to visit Xīngchéng. Modern Xīngchéng has grown up around it, but the Old City is still home to about 3000 people.

You can enter by any of the four gates, but the easiest one to find is the south gate (南门; nánmén), which is just off Xinghai Lu Er Duan. There are signs in English and Chinese pointing the way.

In addition to the **City Walls** (城墙, Chéngqiáng; admission ¥25; ☉ 8am-5pm), the **Drum Tower** (鼓楼, Gǔlóu; admission ¥20; ☉ 8am-5pm), which sits slap in the middle of the Old City, and the watchtower on the southeastern corner of the city are all intact. You can do a complete circuit of the walls in around an hour.

Also inside the Old City is the **Gao House** (将军府, Jiāngjūn Fǔ; admission ¥10; ☉ 8am-5pm), the former residence of General Gao Rulian, who was one of Xīngchéng's most famous sons. The impressive and well-maintained **Confucius Temple** (文庙, Wénmiào; admission ¥35; ☉ 8am-5pm), built in 1430, is reputedly the oldest temple in northeastern China. If you plan on seeing everything, buy the ¥100 pass that grants admission to every paid sight within the walled town.

Beach BEACH

(海滨浴场, Hǎibīn Yùchǎng) Xīngchéng's beach is pretty enough, with OK sands and calm waters, and is a good place to base yourself away from the messy, frenetic city.

At the entrance, look for a statue honouring **Juhua Nü** (the Chrysanthemum Woman). According to local legend, she changed herself into an island to protect Xīngchéng from a sea dragon. This island, **Júhuā Dǎo**, lies 9km off the coast and is home to a fishing community, a small beach and a couple of temples. Daily **ferries** (round trip/including Chinese-speaking guide and local transport ¥90/175; ☉ depart 8.30am, 10am, 11.30am, 2pm, 3pm & 4pm, return 1pm, 2.30pm, 3.30pm & 5pm) leave from the northern end of the beach, though frequency drops outside of summer.

At the time of research, the beach was undergoing massive upgrading, with new concrete paths and boardwalks being built. Bus 1 (¥1) travels from the bus station through Xinghai Lu to the beach (9km from the city centre) in about 30 minutes. A taxi to the area costs ¥15 to ¥20.

⌂ Sleeping

Cheap hotels around the train station won't accept foreigners. The beach is a good place to stay, with many of the larger hotels accepting foreigners. Note that rooms in ordinary beach hotels go for hundreds a night during the peak season.

Hǎiyì Holiday Hotel   HOTEL **$$$**
(海逸假日酒店, Hǎiyì Jiàrì Jiǔdiàn; ☏ 541 0000; 21 Haibin Lu; r & cabin ¥350-400; ❀ @) Set just off the beach, Hǎiyì has decent (if small) rooms and a good in-house restaurant. Better yet, stay in one of the cute cabins clustered under leafy trees. Off-peak discounts bring rooms to the ¥200 range. To get here, turn left when you hit the beach strip and walk 300m.

Jīn Zhǒng Zi Bīnguǎn   HOTEL **$$**
(金种子宾馆; ☏ 352 1111; 9 Xinghai Lu Yi Duan, 兴海路一段9号; r from ¥398; ❀ @) Right in the heart of the city on a busy intersection of Lu Yi Duan and Lu Er Duan, this hotel offers comfortable rooms, free broadband internet and a good attached restaurant (dishes from ¥16 to ¥36). With the standard discount a double goes for around ¥200.

Eating

Unsurprisingly, seafood is big here. Restaurants line the beachfront, where you can pick your crustacean or fish from the tanks. Prices vary according to the season so ask before eating. Most beach hotels have attached restaurants with picture menus and fair prices.

The restaurants in the listed hotels serve an excellent range of seafood, meat and vegetable dishes. The busy street leading from the South Gate to the main Lu Er Duan is lined with stalls serving noodles, barbecued meats and vegetables and plenty of beer. For less dusty environs, head to the food court on the 5th floor of the nearby **Happy Family Mall** (大家庭, Dàjiātíng; Lu Er Duan; dishes from ¥10; ⌚ 9.30am-8.30pm) where you'll find delicious hand-made *bāozi* and other Chinese staples.

❶ Getting There & Around

Xīngchéng is a frequent stop on the Běijīng–Hā'ěrbīn line. It can be easier to get a bus out than a train, but head to **Jǐnzhōu South Station** for comfortable D trains to major cities. Note that buses and trains from Xīngchéng go to the main station in Jǐnzhōu; there are buses (¥5, 30 minutes) to the South Station out front.

BUS
Xīngchéng's **bus station** (兴城市客运站; Xīngchéng shì kèyùn zhàn) is just to the left of the train station.
Běijīng ¥126, 9am
Jǐnzhōu ¥18, two hours, every 30 minutes (6.30am to 3.50pm)
Shānhǎiguān ¥26, two hours, 6.50am
Shěnyáng ¥81, 3½ hours, five daily

TRAIN
Běijīng seat/sleeper ¥64/122, six to seven hours, six daily
Jǐnzhōu seat ¥13, one hour, regular
Shānhǎiguān seat ¥19, 1½ hours, regular
Shěnyáng seat ¥47, four hours, regular

Jílín

POP 27.46 MILLION

Best Landscapes

➡ Heaven Lake (p323)

➡ Yánjí to Báihé (p326)

➡ Wandu Mountain City (p325)

Best Historical Sights

➡ Puppet Emperor's Palace (p327)

➡ Koguryo Sites (p325)

➡ Bānruò Temple (p328)

Why Go?

A flirty province, Jílín (吉林) teases with the ancient and the modern, the artificial and the supernatural. Travellers tired of great walls and imperial facades can explore Japanese-influenced architecture on the trail of the puppet emperor Puyi and the ruins of an ancient Korean kingdom. In fact, much of the far-eastern region comprises the little-known Korean Autonomous Prefecture, home to more than one million ethnic Koreans. Kimchi and cold noodles dominate the menu here and there's an easy acceptance of outsiders.

Although known for its motor cities and smokestack towns, Jílín is also a popular ski destination and boasts China's largest nature reserve. So go for the contrasts? No, go for the superlatives. Heaven Lake, a stunning, deep-blue volcanic crater lake within the country's largest reserve, is one of China's most mesmerising natural wonders. Yes, Jílín can be a little rough around the edges at times, but its rewards are pure polished jewels.

When to Go

Chángchūn

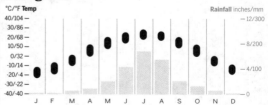

Jun–Sep
Best months to visit Chángbái Shān.

Jul & Aug
Countryside around the Korean Autonomous Prefecture at its most bucolic.

Nov–Mar
Ski season at Běidàhú Ski Resort.

Jílín Highlights

1 Visit China's largest nature reserve, **Chángbái Shān** (p322), with its waterfalls, birch forests and aptly named **Heaven Lake** (p323)

2 Hit the slopes at the **Běidàhú Ski Resort** (p325), one of China's premier skiing spots

3 Explore the mysterious remains of the ancient Koguryo kingdom in **Jí'ān** (p325), just across the Yālù River from North Korea

4 Go on the trail of Puyi, the last emperor of China, at the Imperial Palace of Manchu State in **Chángchūn** (p327)

5 See China's ethnic Korean culture in **Yánjí** (p324)

History

Korean kings once ruled parts of Jílín and the discovery of important relics from the ancient Koguryo kingdom (37 BC–AD 668) in the small southeastern city of Jí'ān has resulted in the area being designated a World Heritage Site by Unesco.

The Japanese occupation of Manchuria in the early 1930s pushed Jílín to the world's centre stage. Chángchūn became the capital of what the Japanese called Manchukuo, with Puyi (the last emperor of the Qing dynasty) given the role of figurehead of the puppet government. In 1944 the Russians wrested control of Jílín from the Japanese and, after stripping the area of its industrial base, handed the region back to Chinese control. For the next several years Jílín would pay a heavy price as one of the frontlines in the civil war between the Kuomintang and the Chinese Communist Party (CCP).

Jílín's border with North Korea has dominated the region's more recent history. As of 2012, there were an estimated 200,000 North Korean refugees in China. The Chinese government has not looked favourably on these migrants, refusing to grant them protected refugee status and has deported those discovered by the authorities.

Climate

Jílín is bitterly cold during its long winter, with heavy snow, freezing winds and temperatures as low as -20°C. In contrast, summer is pleasantly warm, especially along the coastal east, but short. Rainfall is moderate.

ℹ Getting There & Around

The rail and bus network connects all major cities and towns, but not many daily trains head east. The new airport connects Chángbái Shān with Chángchūn and other major Chinese cities.

Chángbái Shān   长白山

Chángbái Shān (Ever-White Mountains), China's largest nature reserve, covers 2100 sq km (densely forested) on the eastern edge of Jílín. By far the region's top attraction, the park's greenery and open space offers a very welcome contrast to Jílín's industrial cities.

The centrepiece of Chángbái Shān is the spellbinding Heaven Lake, whose white frozen surface melts into azure waters stretching across an outsized volcanic crater straddling the China–North Korea border come summer. Heaven Lake's beauty and mystical reputation, including its Loch Ness–style monster (guàiwu), lures visitors from all over China, as well as many South Kore-

ans. For the latter, the area is known as Mt Paekdu, or Paekdusan. North Korea claims that Kim Jung-il was born here (although he's believed to have entered the world in Khabarovsk, Russia).

At lower elevations, the park's forests are filled with white birch, Korean pines and hundreds of varieties of plants, including the much-prized Chángbái Shān ginseng. Above 2000m the landscape changes dramatically into a subalpine zone of short grasses and herbs. Giant patches of ice cover parts of the jagged peaks even in mid-June, and mountain streams rush down the treeless, rocky slopes. With the lake at an altitude of nearly 2200m, visitors should be prepared for lower temperatures. It might be sunny and hot when you enter the reserve, but at higher altitudes strong winds, rain and snow are possible.

Chángbái Shān has two main recreation areas: the northern slope (Běi Pō) and the western slope (Xī Pō), and the entrance areas are separated by 100km of road. Visitors to either area are limited to a few sights and a few short walks. Chángbái Shān is unfortunately geared towards Chinese tour groups rather than independent travellers, and a multibillion-yuán project has turned the western region into a luxury sightseeing zone – a Banff of sorts, with hot springs resorts, skiing and golf courses but little hiking or camping.

The Wanda International Ski Resort, about 15km from the local airport has 20 runs over two mountains with some decent hiking in summer. Certainly, the skiing is superlative in the winter. For more information about skiing in the area, see p341.

Though you can visit most of the year, the best time to see the crater (and be assured the roads are open) is from June to early September. Accommodation is widely available and most travellers stay in the respective scruffy gateway towns of Báihé and Sōngjiānghé.

PRICE INDICATORS

The following price indicators are used in this chapter:

Sleeping

$ less than ¥200

$$ ¥200 to ¥400

$$$ more than ¥400

Eating

$ less than ¥30

$$ ¥30 to ¥80

$$$ more than ¥80

Northern Slope   北坡

The views of Heaven Lake from the **northern slope** (Běi Pō; admission ¥125, transport fee ¥85; ⊙ 7am-6pm) are the best and most popular. The gateway town for this area, where travellers have to stay, is **Èrdào Báihé** (二道白河), generally known as Báihé. The town is undergoing heavy construction with roads and new buildings being upgraded to meet the increased tourist traffic.

You can see all the sights listed here in a day. Transport will drop you off at the flashy main entrance where you buy tickets before proceeding to queue for a tourist shuttle to the main transport junction/parking lot. From here you can catch a vehicle or the final 16km trek to Heaven Lake, or a shuttle to the Changhai waterfall and to the other sights listed. Unlimited park bus rides are all included in park's obligatory transportation fee, but the Heaven Lake vehicle is another ¥80 return.

◉ Sights & Activities

Heaven Lake   LAKE
(天池, Tiān Chí) This dormant crater lake, 13km in circumference, was formed around AD 969. It sits at an altitude of 2194m and is surrounded by rocky outcrops and 16 mountainous peaks. You can follow a fixed route that takes you around part of the crater lip with panoramic views of the lake below. Legend has it that the lake is home to a large, but shy, beastie that has the magical power to blur any photo taken of the creature.

Changbai Waterfall   WATERFALL
(长白瀑布, Chángbái Pùbù) From the bus stop, walk up to a small hot spring where you can soak your feet or buy delicious boiled eggs (cooked in the spring). Past that a 1km trail leads to the viewpoint for the magnificent 68m Changbai Waterfall. In the past you could follow the dramatic-looking caged trail beside the falls up the base of the Heaven Lake, but that route is now officially sealed. And don't bother trying to sneak in; park staff will quickly call you back.

If the 3.5km-long boardwalk running through birch forests from the falls to the Green Deep Pool area is open, it's worth the walk.

Small Heaven Lake   LAKE
(小天池, Xiǎo Tiān Chí) Grab a bus from the waterfall to Small Heaven Lake. Nowhere near the size or majesty of the main crater lake, this is instead a placid lake (or large pond) worth circuiting around. You could venture off into the surrounding forests for a short hike, but don't get lost and be careful not to cross into North Korea! A boardwalk takes you along a fissure stream to the Green Deep Pool.

Green Deep Pool   LAKE
(绿渊潭, Lǜ Yuān Tán) This large, aptly named pool of water, fed by the Changbai Waterfall, is 450m ahead of the Small Heaven Lake.

Cross the bus parking lot and head up the stairs to reach it. Buses run from the waterfall down to the main junction and the Underground Forest.

Underground Forest   FOREST
(地下森林, Dìxià Sēnlín) Lying between the park entrance and transport junction, this verdant woodland area, also known as the Dell Forest (谷底森林; Gǔdǐ Sēnlín), has a 3km boardwalk through the woods to the forest base and back. Allow at least 1½ hours for the walk. Buses run from here back to the junction and north gate.

🛏 Sleeping & Eating

Most people stay in Èrdào Báihé, about 20km north of the reserve. The town is divided into several distinct sections: the train station area, the modern Èrdào area with the government buildings and new hotels, the Báihé area with shops, and Chánggū where the Woodland Youth Hostel and cheap guesthouses are located.

The dusty main drag (Baishan Jie) is a few kilometres from the train station, and the riverside strip (Baihe Dajie) is gradually being turned into a modern luxury village. There's lodging and small restaurants in all areas. There are also overpriced restaurants inside the park.

A taxi from the train station into town costs ¥10. Taxi rides within town districts cost ¥5.

🛏 Èrdào Báihé

On your arrival at the train or bus station, touts for cheap guesthouses will likely approach. Many of these guesthouses can be found in the small lanes around town. Private rooms without bathroom go for ¥30 to ¥80. The more expensive rooms sometimes have their own computer.

Woodland Youth Hostel   HOSTEL $
(望松国际青年旅舍, Wàngsōng Guójì Qīngnián Lǚshè; ☎ 571 0800; cbs800@126.com; Wenhua Lu; dm/tw ¥50/220; ❊ @ 🛜) Set in a former hotel, the friendly Woodland offers same-sex dorms, clean twins and the usual hostel amenities such as a restaurant (dishes from ¥18 to 88), laundry, wi-fi and travel information. The hostel runs its own return shuttle to the North and Western slopes (¥30 and ¥80 respectively) and also sometimes offers overnight camping trips in the park.

To get here from the train or bus station, take a taxi (¥10) or ask about pick up.

⌷ Northern Slope

Lanjing Spa Holiday Inn HOTEL **$$$**
(蓝景温泉度假酒店, Lánjǐng Wēnquán Dùjià
Jiǔdiàn; ☑ 505 2222, 574 5555; r from ¥1702;
🌐 @) The top accommodation in the area,
this 200-room European-style lodge (with
obligatory touches of Chinese kitsch) is just
500m from the north gate entrance but qui-
etly secluded in a wooded setting off the
main road. In addition to multiple food and
beverage outlets, the inn features a high-
end hot spring spa with indoor and outdoor
facilities.

ⓘ Information

The **Bank of China** (中国银行, Zhōngguó Yín-
háng; Baishan Jie) is on the main street in Báihé
towards the end of town. It has an ATM.

ⓘ Getting There & Away

Public transport only goes as far as Báihé.

Buses leave from the **long-distance bus sta-
tion** (kèyùnzhàn). From the train station head to
the main road; the station is across and to the left.

Chángchūn ¥127, 6½ hours, 6.10am and 5pm
Sōngjiānghé ¥8, two hours, 9.10am, 12.30pm
and 2pm
Yánjí ¥46, 3½ hours, five daily

Trains from Báihé include the following:
Shěnyáng hard/soft sleeper ¥107/160, 14
hours, two daily (5.35pm and 7.10pm)
Sōngjiānghé seat ¥8, two hours, five daily
Tōnghuà hard seat/sleeper ¥24/58, six to
seven hours, four daily

ⓘ Getting Around

To get to the Northern Slope entrance, take the
return shuttle from the Woodland Youth Hostel
(¥30, departs 8am and returns 4.30pm). Taxis
charge ¥60 to ¥70 (per car) for the one-way trip
to the Northern Slope entrance. Returning, it's
usually easy to share a taxi back (per person
¥20) but not if you leave past 5.30pm.

Yánjí   延吉

☑ 0433 / POP 432,000

The relaxed and attractive capital of China's
Korean Autonomous Prefecture has one foot
across the nearby border with North Korea.
About a third of the population is ethnic Ko-
rean and it's common to both hear people
speaking Korean and to see Korean written
on official road signs.

The Bù'ěrhātōng River (布尔哈通河;
Bù'ěrhātōng Hé) that bisects the city has
pleasant parks and walkways running
alongside worth strolling along. ATMs are
all over the city including a 24-hour ATM at
the Industrial & Commercial Bank of China
(ICBC; 中国工商银行, Zhōnguó Gōngshāng
Yínháng) three blocks up from the train sta-
tion at the corner of Changbaishan Xīlu and
Zhanqian Jie.

The town is also a launching pad for tours
into Rason in North Korea. For more infor-
mation about visiting North Korea, see p317.

⌷ Sleeping & Eating

There are a few budget hotels around the
train station. Head to Guangming Lu near

THE WESTERN SLOPE

Chángbái Shān's **Western Slope** (西坡, Xī Pō; admission ¥125, transport fee ¥85; ☻ 7am-
6pm) offers much the same experience as the Northern Slope. The setup is fancier, but
as in the north you have little chance of getting away from the crowds here. Once again
the view from the crater is the main attraction, though the **Chángbái Shān Canyon**
(长白山大峡谷; Chángbái Shān Dàxiágǔ), a 200m-wide and 100m-deep gorge filled with
dramatic rock formations, is worth a look.

The Woodland Youth Hostel (p323) in Báihé has a return shuttle to the western slope
for ¥80. Taxis also run the route for ¥200 one way.

The gateway town for the western slope is dusty **Sōngjiānghé**, 40km to the north-
west, from where there are buses and trains to Tōnghuà and Shěnyáng. **Changbaishan
Airport**, halfway between the park and Sōngjiānghé, has flights to/from Shànghǎi
(¥1350, 2½ hours), Chángchún (¥1000, 45 minutes) and Běijīng (¥1330, two hours).

Sōngjiānghé offers midrange accommodation similar to Báihé, while closer to the
park a number of resorts have popped up in recent years, including **Days Hotel Land-
scape Resort** (蓝景戴斯度假酒店, Lánjǐngdàisī Dùjià Jiǔdiàn; ☑ 0433 633 7999; r from ¥850;
🌐 @ 🌐), a stylish lodge with a lobby fireplace, high-end eating and drinking venues, and
wood, glass and stone decor.

the corner of Renmin Lu for a busy pedestrian street with plenty of restaurants and a street market. Several cool Korean-run coffeeshops line Aidan Lu near the corner of Juzi Lu, a couple of doors down from the old bus station (老客运站, lǎo kèyùn zhàn). You can grab a decent sandwich and latte while surfing the net on the free wi-fi.

Baishan Hotel
HOTEL $$$

(白山大厦, Báishān Dàshà; ☎258 8888; www.baishan-hotel.com; 66 Youyi Lu, 友谊路66号; d & tw ¥888-1088; ✳@🛜) Seated just a stone's throw away from the river, the Baishan Hotel is an imposing piece of utilitarian architecture with large, comfortable rooms and friendly, efficient staff. The attached ground-floor restaurant has a large selection of excellent Korean and Chinese dishes (from ¥10). Ask for a river-facing room. Discounts knock prices down to the ¥400 range.

ℹ️ Getting There & Away

The train station and new bus station are south of the river, while the commercial district and old bus station are north. Taxi fares start at ¥5; most rides cost less than ¥10.

Buses to Chángchūn (¥116, 5½ hours, hourly, 6am to 5pm) leave from in front of the train station or **old bus station** (老客运站, lǎo kèyùn zhàn; Aidan Lu).

Yánjí's **new long-distance bus station** (新客运站; xīn kèyùn zhàn; 2319 Changbaishan Xilu) serves the following destinations:

Èrdào Báihé ¥45, four hours, six daily (6.40am to 2.30pm)

Húnchūn ¥30, two hours, every 30 minutes (7am to 3.50pm)

Mǔdānjiāng ¥73, five hours, three daily (6.30am, 9.50am, and 12.10pm)

Train service includes the following:

Chángchūn hard seat/sleeper ¥70/129, eight to nine hours, five daily

---

Jí'ān
集安

☎0435 / POP 240,000

This small city, just across the Yālù River from North Korea, was once part of the Koguryo (高句丽, Gāogōulì) kingdom, a Korean dynasty that ruled areas of northern China and the Korean peninsula from 37 BC to AD 668. Jí'ān's extensive Koguryo pyramids, ruins and tombs resulted in Unesco designating it a World Heritage Site in 2004. Archaeologists have unearthed remains of three cities plus some 40 tombs around

Jí'ān and the town of Huánrén (in Liáoníng province).

With a drive to capitalise on its Korean heritage's tourism potential, modern-day Jí'ān has transformed itself into one of northern China's more pleasant towns, with well-tended parks, leafy streets and a renovated riverfront area where you can gaze across to North Korea. Add in the town's mountain backdrop, excellent Korean food, friendly locals and scenic train or bus rides getting here, and it's a great little stopover on a loop through Dōngběi.

Summer evenings are lively in Jí'ān, both at the riverside and the park across from the hotel Cuìyuán Bīnguǎn, where live amateur performances of traditional song and dance are held most nights.

👁️ Sights

The main sights other than the river park are scattered on the outskirts of the city and you'll need to hire a taxi. Expect to pay at least ¥100 for a three-hour circuit. You'll need to negotiate further if you want to linger at the sights.

The **Koguryo sites** (🕐8am-5pm) are spread around the very lovely green hills surrounding Jí'ān. Despite their historical significance, most sites don't have a terrible amount of detail to examine. Many of the tombs are cairns – essentially heaps of stones piled above burial sites – while others are stone pyramids. But there is something magical about the open fields and high terraces they were constructed on that makes you want to linger. The most impressive site, Wandu Mountain City, needs two hours if you want to wander the expansive grounds.

A ¥100 ticket gets you into the four most important sites; you can also buy separate tickets for each sight for ¥30.

⭐ Wandu Mountain City
RUIN

(丸都山城, Wándū Shānchéng) First built in AD 3, the city became capital of the Koguryo kingdom in 209, after the fall of the first capital, Guonei city (on the site of present-day Jí'ān). There's little left of the original buildings, but the layout has been cleared and it's immensely enjoyable scrambling about the terraces and taking in the views that surely must have been a deciding factor in establishing the capital here.

Down on the plains below the city, on a large shelf above the river, sits Jí'ān's largest collection of giant stone cairns. Erected after the destruction of Wandu, this vast

THE LITTLE-KNOWN KOREAN AUTONOMOUS PREFECTURE

Ask people to list some of China's ethnic minorities and you will hear talk of Tibetans, Uighur, Mongolians, Hui and perhaps the Li or Dai. Mention that China also has almost two million ethnic Koreans, and that the majority live in their own autonomous prefecture along the North Korean border, and you'll likely get some astonished looks.

The **Yánbiān Korean Autonomous Prefecture** (延边朝鲜族自治州, Yánbiān Cháoxiānzú Zìzhìzhōu) is the only minority prefecture in the north of China. While established in 1955, in part as a reward for Koreans who fought on the side of the communists during the Civil War, the region has in fact been settled by Koreans since the 1880s. Today, street signs are officially bilingual, much of the population is bilingual (thanks to state-sponsored Korean-language schools), TV shows and newspapers are in Korean, and ethnic food is ubiquitous.

Over the past decades, however, the percentage of ethnic Koreans has dropped: from 60% in the 1950s to 38% today. In part this reflects the Chinese government's desire to stamp out any potential for irredentism (many Koreans refer to Yánbiān as the 'third Korea', after the South and North) by encouraging Han migrants. More positively, it seems to indicate that the well-educated ethnic population experiences little to no discrimination in seeking employment or advancement outside the prefecture. Yánbiān may occupy a quarter of all Jílín province (it's about half the size of South Korea), but the population is little more than two million, and opportunities are limited.

For those doing an extensive tour of northern China, consider looping up through Yánbiān as you go from Dāndōng or Chángbáishān to Hā'ěrbīn. The regional capital, Yánjí, is an attractive laid-back place, loaded with excellent Korean food, and the routes in and out run hour after hour through a bucolic landscape of corn fields, rolling forested hills and little brick villages.

cemetery for the city's noblemen is so far unaffected by mass tourism. The sight of the massive rock piles in fields of Spanish needle (*Bidens pilosa*) is probably the most photogenic in all Jí'ān.

Cemetery of Noblemen at Yushan TOMB

(禹山贵族墓地, Yǔshān Guìzú Mùdì) Scattered about a small gated park lie the stone crypts of various Koguryo-kingdom noblemen. You can enter and explore Tomb No 5 (wait for the guide) via a creepy descent underground. As your eyes adjust to the light in the chilly stone chamber, look for paintings of dragons, white tigers, black tortoises and lotus flowers on the walls and ceilings.

Hǎotàiwáng Stele TOMB

(好太王碑, Hǎotàiwáng Bēi) Inscribed with 1775 Chinese characters, the Hǎotàiwáng Stele, a 6m-tall stone slab that dates to AD 415, records the accomplishments of Koguryo king Tan De (374–412), known as Hǎotàiwáng. The surface is blackened from a botched restoration effort when it was re-discovered in 1877: to remove the moss covering the surface, locals smeared it with cow dung and set it alight. Tan De's tomb (labelled 'Tàiwáng Tomb') is on the same site.

Jiāngjūnfén (General's Tomb) TOMB

(将军坟) One of the largest pyramid-like structures in the region, the 12m-tall Jiāngjūnfén was built during the 4th century for a Koguryo ruler. The nearby smaller tomb is the resting place of a family member. The site is set among the hills 4km northeast of town.

Jí'ān Museum MUSEUM

(集安博物馆, Jí'ān Bówùguǎn; Jianshe Lu; admission ¥70, ¥35 if you show your ¥100 Koguryo ticket; ⊙8am-5.20pm Tue-Sun) The sleek but pricey museum sports a brown stone base and glass top with sails that open up like leaves. It features a small display of artefacts from the Koguryo era with good English captions. A lovely park with stone fountains, landscaped gardens, cobbled walkways, lotus ponds and statues is located just next to the museum.

Riverside Plaza WATERFRONT

This lively modern waterfront park features riverside decks where you can view North Korea across the Yālù River. You can also take a boat ride along the river (¥50, 40 minutes). The park is stretched out along Yanjiang Lu, south of the main Shengli Lu.

🛏 Sleeping & Eating

Head to the markets east and west of Liming Jie for fruit, dumplings, bread and barbecue. Tuanjie Lu (the parallel road north of Shengli Lu) is home to Chinese greasy spoons, while Liming Jie offers a number of hotpot and barbecue spots. Jianshe Lu near Shengli Lu has several clean Chinese fast-food joints.

Lùmíng Bīnguǎn   HOTEL **$**
(路明宾馆; ☑622 1293; 653 Shengli Lu, 胜利路653号; s/tw without bathroom ¥40/70, d with bathroom & incl breakfast ¥148-158; ✳@🛜) Friendly staff and well-kept rooms make this Jí'ān's best option. It's 500m east of the bus station on the north side of Shengli Lu just before you reach Liming Jie. Look for the English sign reading 'Guesthouse' above the entrance. Some rooms have their own computer.

ℹ Getting There & Around

The main routes to Jí'ān are via Tōnghuà and Báihé (the gateway to Chángbái Shān) to the north, and Shěnyáng and Dāndōng in Liáoníng province to the west and south. If you're travelling to Báihé by bus, you need to change in Tōnghuà. Don't bother with trains as only there's only one per day to Tōnghuà.

Shengli Lu runs east–west through town, with the **long-distance bus station** (客运站, kèyùn zhàn; Shengli Lu) at the west end. The main north–south road is Li Ming Jie, which ends at the river park. There's a Bank of China at the corner of Shengli Lu and Li Ming Jie with a 24-hour ATM. It's easy to get around on foot.

Bus service includes the following destinations:

Chángchūn ¥109, 5½ hours, two daily (6.25am and 2.50pm)

Dāndōng ¥85, six hours, two daily (7.30am and 9.20am)

Shěnyáng ¥98, six hours, two daily (6.20am and 11.20am)

Tōnghuà ¥28, two hours, hourly (5am to 5pm)

Báihé (via Tōnghuà) ¥76, six hours, 7.30am and 1.30pm

Běidàhú Ski Resort   北大湖滑雪场

Since it hosted the 2007 Asian Winter Games, **Běidàhú** (Běidàhú Huáxuěchǎng; 北大湖滑雪场; www.beidahuski.com) has established itself as one of China's premier ski resorts. Located in a tiny village 53km south of Jílín City, the resort has runs on two mountains ranging from beginner to advanced. Though it hasn't turned a profit since 2009, Běidàhú is seeing renewed investment resulting in an additional 10km of runs being added each year. For more on skiing here, including tour, transport and accommodation information, see **China Ski Tours** (www.chinaskitours.com).

Chángchūn   长春

☑0431 / POP 7.64 MILLION

The Japanese capital of Manchukuo between 1933 and 1945, Chángchūn was also the centre of the Chinese film industry in the 1950s and '60s. Visitors expecting a Hollywood-like backdrop of palm trees and beautiful people will be disappointed, though. Chángchūn is now better known as China's motor city, the largest automobile-manufacturing base in the country.

But for people on the trail of Puyi, China's last emperor, it's an essential stop. There are also a few historic buildings dating back to the early 20th century, mostly along and off Renmin Dajie.

Chángchūn sprawls from north to south. The long-distance bus station and the train station are at the north end of the city and surrounded by budget hotels. If you plan on more than an overnight in Chángchūn, however, the southern end is by far a more pleasant neighbourhood to stay in.

👁 Sights

⭐**Imperial Palace of the Manchu State**   MUSEUM
(Puppet Emperor's Palace, 伪满皇宫博物院, Wěimǎn Huánggōng Bówùyuàn; 5 Guangfu Lu; 光复北路5号; admission ¥80; ⊙8.30am-4.20pm, last entry 40min before closing) This is the former residence of Puyi, the Qing dynasty's final emperor. His study, bedroom, temple, his wife's quarters and opium den, as well as his concubine's rooms, have all been elaborately re-created. His American car is also on display, but it's the exhibition on his extraordinary life, told in part with a fantastic collection of photos, that is most enthralling. An English audio guide costs ¥20. A taxi from the train station here costs ¥7.

In 1908, at age two, Puyi became the 10th Qing emperor. His reign lasted just over three years, but he was allowed to remain in the Forbidden City until 1924. He subsequently lived in Tiānjīn until 1932, when the Japanese installed him at this palace as

Chángchūn

the 'puppet emperor' of Manchukuo. After Japan's defeat in 1945, Puyi was captured by Russian troops. In 1950 he was returned to China, where he spent 10 years in a re-education camp before ending his days as a gardener in Běijīng. Puyi died in 1967; his story later became the basis for the Bernardo Bertolucci film *The Last Emperor* (1987).

While you're here, look out for the swimming pool (Puyi never used it as an emperor was never allowed to show his body in public) and the dank underground air-raid shelter where he retreated with his family when the bombs fell.

Chángchūn World Sculpture Park SCULPTURE
(长春世界雕塑公园, Chángchūn Shìjiè Diāosù Gōngyuán; Renmin Dajie; 人民大街; ¥20; ☉8am-5pm; ☐66) Nestled amid 90 hectare of parklands in the far south of the city, the Chángchūn World Sculpture Park hosts an impressive array of sculptures from Chinese and international artists. The park is one of Chángchūn's unsung sights and worth sniffing out. A taxi from People's Sq will cost ¥25 to ¥30.

Bānruò Temple BUDDHIST TEMPLE
(般若寺, Bānruò Sì; 137 Changchun Lu; 长春路137 号; ☐281, 256) One of the largest Buddhist temples in northeast China, Bānruò is a lively

Chángchūn

place of worship for locals and pilgrims alike. After touring the inner grounds, wander the back alleys to observe the merchants peddling all manner of charms, statues, shrines and incense to the faithful.

Jìngyuètán National Forest Park
NATIONAL PARK

(净月潭国家森林公园, Jìngyuètán Guójiā Sēnlín Gōngyuán; admission ¥30; ⊙8.30am-5.30pm) This massive lakeside park on the southeast outskirts of Chángchūn encompasses more than 90 sq km and is a welcome break from the city. Established in 1934, it features well-tended gardens, pavilions, lookouts and a 20km round-the-lake bike path. Shuttle buses (¥10) take you to the dam, where you can take boat rides. At the front gate there are bike rentals (¥30 per hour).

Take the light rail from the station on Liaoning Lu (¥4, 55 minutes) to Jingyue Gongyuan Station.

🛏 Sleeping

There are half a dozen budget hotels within walking distance of the train station, with broadband-enabled rooms going for between ¥140 and ¥180.

Star Moon Fashion Inn
HOTEL $

(星月时尚酒店, Xīngyuè Shíshàng Jiǔdiàn; ☑8509 0555; www.starmoon.inn.com.cn; 1166 Longli Lu, 隆礼路1166号; d from ¥148; ❋@☎) For a grey industrial city, Chángchūn has its share of 'fashion inns' (hip hotels). This

modern hotel is in a good location near shops, restaurants and nightlife.

Home Inn
HOTEL $

(如家快捷酒店, Rújiā Kuàijié Jiǔdiàn; ☑8986 3000; 20 Changbai Lu, 长白路20号; r ¥159-209; ❂❋@) If you need a nonsmoking option near the train station, this branch of the well-run, spotlessly clean nationwide chain is a good choice. Rooms have broadband internet and there's also a computer in the lobby for guest use.

★ Sōngyuàn Hotel
HOTEL $$$

(松苑宾馆, Sōngyuàn Bīnguǎn; ☑8272 7001; www.songyuanhotel.com; 1169 Xinfa Lu, 新发路1169号; d & tw ¥498-998; ❋@☎) Nestled within its own park grounds, the Sōngyuàn was a former army commander's residence. Today, its heritage buildings now host tourists in plush, well-decorated rooms. Friendly staff and several good in-house restaurants (Japanese and international) seal the deal. The downside is a slightly inconvenient location. A taxi from the train station costs ¥7.

✖ Eating & Drinking

The area surrounding Tongzhi Jie between Longli Lu and Ziyou Lu is one of the most popular parts of Chángchūn and is packed with inexpensive restaurants, music and clothing shops. Tree-lined Xikang Lu (west of Tongzhi Jie) is now an unofficial cafe street. Most of the dozen or so cafes have wi-fi and offer sandwiches and other simple meals. Guilin Lu is lined with cheap eateries and snack stalls.

M+M
NOODLES $

(面面, Miàn Miàn; 2447 Tongzhi Jie; 同志街2447号; noodles ¥18-20; ⊙10am-10pm) You can slurp down your moreish noodles hot or cold, dry or in soup, with meat or without, at this popular 2nd-floor eatery overlooking busy Tongzhi Jie. Beer is ¥5.

Shinza Restaurant
KOREAN $$

(延边信子饭店, Yánbiān Xìnzǐ Fàndiàn; 728 Xikang Lu; 西康路728号; dishes ¥12-38; ⊙9am-midnight) This comfortable dining establishment offers Korean classics such as *shíguō bànfàn* (石锅拌饭; *bibimbap*; rice, vegetables and eggs served in a clay pot) as well as dumplings and filling cold noodle dishes. Korean beers are also available and there's a picture menu to help you order.

❶ Information

There are 24-hour ATMs all over town and in the north bus station.

Changchun Live (www.changchunlive.com) is a useful site started by long-term expats.

Civil Aviation Administration of China (CAAC, 中国民航, Zhōngguó Mínháng; ☎ 8298 8888; 480 Jiefang Dalu) For air tickets and shuttle buses to the airport. It's in the CAAC Hotel.

❶ Getting There & Away

AIR

Chángchūn Lóngjiā International Airport (长春龙嘉国际机场; Chǎngchūn Lóngjiā Guójì Jīchǎng) Has daily flights to major cities including Běijīng (¥900, two hours), Shànghǎi (¥1000, 2½ hours) and Chángbái Shān (¥1000, 1 hour).

BUS

The **long-distance bus station** (长途汽车站, chángtú qìchēzhàn; 226 Renmin Dajie) is two blocks south of the train station. Buses to Hā'ěrbīn leave from the **north bus station** (客运北站, kèyùn běi zhàn) behind the train station. Facing the station, head left and take the underpass just past the 24-hour KFC (not to be confused with the non-24-hour KFC to the right of the train station, or the two across the street).

Hā'ěrbīn ¥76, 3½ hours, 8.30am, 10am and noon

Yánjí ¥116, five hours, hourly, 7am to 5pm

Shěnyáng ¥83, 4½ hours, 10am and 2pm

TRAIN

Chángchūn's **main railway station** (长春火车站; Chángchūn huǒchē zhàn) serves the follow-ing destinations. Avoid getting tickets for Chángchūn's west station (xī zhàn), 13km out of town.

Běijīng (D train) seat ¥245, seven hours, eight daily

Běijīng hard seat/sleeper ¥133/245, nine to 14 hours, nine daily

Hā'ěrbīn (D train) seat ¥111, two hours, 8am and 1.50pm

Shěnyáng (G train) seat ¥144, 2½ hours, 17 daily

❶ Getting Around

TO/FROM THE AIRPORT

The airport is 20km east of the city centre, be-tween Chángchūn and Jílín. Shuttle buses to the airport (¥20, 50 minutes, every 30 minutes from 6am to 7pm) leave from the **CAAC Hotel** (民航宾馆, Mínháng Bīnguǎn; 480 Jiefang Dalu) on the east side of town. Taxi fares to the airport are ¥80 to ¥100 for the 40-minute trip.

BUS

Bus 6 follows Renmin Dajie from the **train station bus stop** all the way to the south part of town. Buses 62 and 362 travel from the train station to the Chongqing Lu and Tongzhi Jie shopping districts.

LIGHT RAIL & METRO

The **Chángchūn Light Rail** (长春轻轨; Chǎng-chūn Qīngguǐ; ⊗ 6.30am-9pm) service is only useful for getting to Jìngyuètán National Forest Park (p329). The station is just west of the train station. Subway lines are being laid but won't be ready for some years yet.

TAXI

Taxi fares start at ¥5.

Hēilóngjiāng

POP 38.3 MILLION

Best Landscapes

➡ Lǎohēi Shān (p343)
➡ Běijícūn (p345)
➡ Jìngpò Hú (p342)

Best Activities

➡ Ice and Snow Festival
(p336)
➡ Skiing (p341)
➡ Hiking in Wǔdàlián
Chí (p342)

Why Go?

Hēilóngjiāng (黑龙江) means Black Dragon River, and this particular coiling dragon is the separating line between China and Russia. Across the province a neighbourly influence is evident in architecture, food and even souvenirs. Capital Hā'ěrbīn's famed cobblestoned streets and European-style facades is ground zero for this hybrid experience.

Of course, it gets cold in China's northernmost province, sub-Arctic cold – but that frigid weather is put to good use in winter, the peak tourist season. Hā'ěrbīn hosts a world-renowned ice sculpture festival and the region has some of China's finest ski runs. It gets busy but it's worth swaddling yourself in layers and joining the crowds.

Outside the cities, Hēilóngjiāng is a rugged, beautiful landscape of forests, lakes, mountains and dormant volcanoes. From Mòhé, China's most northerly city, you can access the remote Běijícūn and Běihóngcūn for bragging rights to say you have stood at the very top of the Middle Kingdom.

When to Go
Hā'ěrbīn

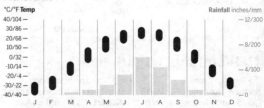

Jan Hā'ěrbīn hosts the Ice and Snow Festival.

Jun Mòhé holds the Northern Lights Festival.

Dec–Mar Ski season at Yàbùlì and Wǔdàlián Chí.

Hēilóngjiāng Highlights

1 Explore China's northernmost village of **Mòhé** (p345) while hoping to catch the elusive but spectacular aurora borealis

2 Brave the cold and join the crowds who flock to Hā'ěrbīn's world-famous **Ice and Snow Festival** (p336)

3 Walk the brick-lined streets of the historic **Dàolǐqū district** (p335) and explore Hā'ěrbīn's Russian and Jewish past

4 Hike to the top of a dormant volcano and through the lava fields of **Wǔdàlián Chí** (p342)

5 Ski and snowboard at **Yàbùlì** (p341), one of China's finest ski resorts

6 Go on the search for **rare cranes** (p344) in nature reserves across the north

History

Hēilóngjiāng forms the northernmost part of Dōngběi, the region formerly known as Manchuria. Its proximity to Russia has long meant strong historical and trade links with its northern neighbour. In the mid-19th century, Russia annexed parts of Hēilóngjiāng, while in 1897 Russian workers arrived to build a railway line linking Vladivostok with Hā'ěrbīn. By the 1920s well over 100,000 Russians resided in Hā'ěrbīn alone.

Hēilóngjiāng was occupied by the Japanese between 1931 and 1945. After the Chinese Communist Party (CCP) took power in 1949, relations with Russia grew steadily frostier, culminating in a brief border war in 1969. Sino-Russian ties have improved much in recent years and the two sides finally settled on the border in July 2008, after 40-odd years of negotiation.

Language

The vast majority of people in Hēilóngjiāng speak northeast Mandarin, which is the same as standard Mandarin, apart from the accent. You're also likely to hear a lot of Russian. In the far northwest, tiny numbers of the Oroqen, Daur, Ewenki and Hezhen ethnic minorities still speak their own languages. A handful of people can speak Manchu, once the dominant tongue of the region.

ⓘ Getting There & Around

Hā'ěrbīn is the logistical hub for the region and has extensive links with the rest of China. Buses are often a quicker way of getting around, rather than the slow local trains. If you're headed for Inner Mongolia, direct trains run from Hā'ěrbīn to the cities of Hǎilā'ěr and Mǎnzhōulǐ.

Hā'ěrbīn · 哈尔滨

📞 0451 / POP 4.59 MILLION

For a city of its size, Hā'ěrbīn (Harbin) is surprisingly easygoing. Cars (and even bicycles) are barred from Zhongyang Dajie, the main drag of the historic Dàolǐqū district, where most of Hā'ěrbīn's historical buildings can be found. The long riverfront also provides sanctuary for walkers, as does Sun Island on the other side.

The city's sights are as varied as the architectural styles on the old street. Temples, old churches and synagogues coexist, while deep in the southern suburbs a former Japanese germ-warfare base is a sobering reminder of less harmonious times. Hā'ěrbīn's rich Russian and Jewish heritage makes it worth visiting at any time of year, but winter is tops with the world-class ice sculpture festival turning the frosty riverfront, and other venues, into a multicoloured wonderland.

History

In 1896 Russia negotiated a contract to build a railway line from Vladivostok to both Hā'ěrbīn, then a small fishing village, and Dàlián (in Liáoníng province). The subsequent influx of Russian workers was followed by Russian Jews and then White Russians escaping the 1917 Russian Revolution.

These days, Hā'ěrbīn, whose name comes from a Manchu word meaning 'a place to dry fishing nets', is an ever-expanding, largely industrial city. While Chinese are the majority, foreign faces are still common on the streets.

◎ Sights

★ **Church of St Sophia**   CHURCH
(圣索菲亚教堂, Shèng Suǒfēiyà Jiàotáng; cnr Zhaolin Jie & Toulong Jie; admission ¥20; ⏰8.30am-5pm) The red-brick Russian Orthodox Church of St Sophia, with its distinctive green onion dome and roosting pigeons, is Hā'ěrbīn's most famous landmark. Built in 1907, the church has traded religion for photographs of Hā'ěrbīn from the early 1900s. Its unrestored interior and dusty chandeliers evokes a faded glamour of yesteryear.

The church is fronted by a large square replete with fountains and sketch artists, and is a popular spot for locals and tourists alike.

Stalin Park   PARK
(斯大林公园, Sīdàlín Gōngyuán) This tree-lined promenade, dotted with statues, historic

Hā'ěrbīn

buildings, playgrounds and cafes, runs along a 42km-long embankment built to curb the unruly Sōnghuā River and is a pleasant spot to escape the hubbub of the city. The **Flood Control Monument** (防洪胜利纪念塔; Fáng-hóng Shènglì Jìniàntǎ) from 1958 commemorates the thousands of people who died in years past when the river overflowed its banks.

Boats rides along the river and to/from Sun Island also depart from various points along the park.

Sun Island Park   PARK
(太阳岛公园, Tàiyángdǎo Gōngyuán; cable car one way/return ¥50/80; ⊘ cable car 8.30am-5pm) Across the river from Stalin Park is Sun Island Park, a 38-sq-km recreational zone with landscaped gardens, a 'water world', a 'Russian-style' town, and various small galleries and museums. It's a pleasant place to have a picnic, walk or bike (¥60 per hour), though as usual you need to pay extra to get into

many areas (too kitsch and not worth the money in our opinion).

Boat across (¥10 return) depart from one of many docks just north of the Flood Control Monument, or catch the nearby cable car.

★ **Siberian Tiger Park**   WILDLIFE RESERVE
(东北虎林园, Dōngběihǔ Línyuán; 88 Songbei Jie; 松北街88号; admission ¥100; ⊘ 8.30am-4.30pm, last tour 4pm; 🚍 13, 122) Here, visitors get the chance to see one of the world's rarest animals (and largest felines) up close via safari-style tour buses which do a circuit of the enclosures. Finish your visit by walking around large fenced spaces where tigers roam freely. The centre has successfully bred over 1000 cats and watching them play, sleep and mate is fascinating.

The park is 15km north of the city. A taxi from the city centre costs ¥30 to ¥40 one way. A tourist shuttle (¥10 return, hourly) leaves from the top of Tongjiang Jie (at the

Hā'ěrbīn

bus stop before the cable car to Sun Island) and does a loop to/from the park.

The squeamish should avoid buying (live!) chickens (¥60) and even cows (¥2800) to throw to the animals. Chinese visitors also take absolute pleasure in dangling strips of meat (¥20) for tigers to jump up and grab at. While the tigers live in decent conditions with plenty of space to roam, other animals including a lion and liger (a cross between a tiger and lion), live in less-than-stellar enclosures.

Japanese Germ Warfare Experimental Base
MUSEUM

(侵华日军第731部队遗址, Qīnhuá Rìjūn Dì 731 Bùduì Yízhǐ; Xinjiang Dajie; ⊗ 9-11am & 1-3.30pm Tue-Sun) FREE This museum is set in the notorious Japanese Germ Warfare Experimental Base (Division 731). Between 1939 and 1945, prisoners of war and civilians were frozen alive, subjected to vivisection or infected with bubonic plague, syphilis and other virulent diseases. Three to four thousand people died here in the most gruesome fashion. The museum includes photos, sculptures and exhibits of the equipment used by the Japanese. There are extensive English captions and an audio guide is available for ¥15.

The base is in the south of Hā'ěrbīn and takes an hour to get to by bus. In the alley

beside the Kunlun Hotel on Tielu Jie, catch bus 338 or 343 (¥2). Get off at the stop called Xinjiang Dajie. Walk back 500m along Xinjiang Dajie and look for the base on the left-hand side of the road. If you get lost, just ask the locals the way to 'Qī Sān Yī' (731).

Harbin Culture Park
AMUSEMENT PARK

(哈尔滨文化公园, Hā'ěrbīn Wénhuà Gōngyuán; Nantong Jie; admission ¥5, rides from ¥30; ⊗ 9am-5.30pm) If culture equals amusement, then the creators of this park have certainly ticked all the right boxes. The gigantic Ferris wheel offers panoramic views of the city and it's worth strolling around the grounds to see the locals having a great time. The park is in between the Temple of Bliss (p336) and the Confucius Temple (p336). Turn left after exiting the Temple of Bliss and enter the park past an atmospheric old Russian church.

Old Hā'ěrbīn

The **Dàolǐqū district**, in particular the brick-lined street of **Zhongyang Dajie**, is the most obvious legacy of Russia's involvement with Hā'ěrbīn. Now a pedestrian-only zone, the street is lined with buildings that date back to the early 20th century. Some are imposing, others distinctly dilapidated, but the mix of architectural styles is fascinating. Other nearby streets lined with handsome old buildings include **Shangzhi Dajie** and **Zhaolin Jie**.

Elsewhere in the city, **Hongjun Jie**, heading south from the train station, and **Dongdazhi Jie** also feature rows of stately old buildings, including a few churches. The latter street, and some of its arteries, also have the dubious reputation of sporting some heady postmodern Russian-style architecture of questionable taste.

In all of these areas, the city has erected plaques on the most worthy buildings giving short English and Chinese descriptions of the date of construction, the architect and the former usage.

Temples

A number of temples are within walking distance of each other in the Nángàng district. The first sits off a pedestrian-only street reachable by taxi from the Dàolǐqū district for ¥10. For the Confucius Temple, look for an arch down to the right at the start of the pedestrian street. Pass through this and then a second arch on the left. The temple is a 10-minute walk along Wen Miao Jie. You can also cut through the Harbin Culture Park (p335) after the Temple of Bliss en route to the Confucius Temple.

Temple of Bliss BUDDHIST TEMPLE
(极乐寺, Jílè Sì; 9 Dongdazhi Jie; 东大直街; admission ¥10; ⊙8.30am-4pm) Hēilóngjiāng's largest temple complex has an active Buddhist community in residence, giving it a genuine religious atmosphere despite the ticket sales. There are many large statues here, including Milefo (Maitreya, the Buddha yet-to-come) and the Sakyamuni Buddha. The **Seven-Tiered Buddhist Pagoda** (七级浮屠塔; Qījí Fútú Tǎ) dates from 1924. The entrance to the temple is on the left at the start of the pedestrian street.

Hā'ěrbīn Confucius Temple CONFUCIAN TEMPLE
(文庙, Wén Miào; 25 Wenmiao Jie; 文庙街25号; ⊙9am-3.30pm, closed Wed) FREE This peaceful temple complex was first built in 1929 and is said to be the largest Confucian temple in northeastern China. Most of what you see now, though, is from a recent restoration. The site also houses the fascinating **Minority Cultures Museum** replete with photos and artefacts focusing on indigenous tribes such as the Ewenki. You need a passport to enter.

From the main gate of the Harbin Culture Park, cross Nantong Dajie and head 1km southeast along Nanhai Lu. You will see the walls of the large compound. Follow it to get to round to the main entrance.

★ Festivals & Events

Harbin Ice & Snow Festival ICE SCULPTURE
(冰雪节, Bīngxuě Jié; ☑8625 0068; day/evening ticket ¥150/300; ⊙9.30am-9.30pm) Hā'ěrbīn's main claim to fame these days is this festival. Every winter, from December to February (officially the festival opens 5 January), Zhāolín Park (照林公园) and Sun Island Park (p334) become home to extraordinarily detailed, imaginative and downright wacky snow and ice sculptures. They range from huge recreations of iconic buildings, such as the Forbidden City and European ca-

THE GREAT CATS

As with many of the world's powerful wild creatures, size did not give the Amur (Siberian) tiger much of an advantage during the 20th century. The largest feline in the world, topping 300kg for males and capable of taking down a brown bear in a fair fight, was no match for the poachers, wars, revolutions, railway construction and economic development in its traditional territory in Russia, China and Korea. These days it's believed that fewer than 500 of the great cats still prowl the wilds of Russia. Perhaps 20 are divided between Hēilóngjiāng and Jílín provinces in China, and none are left in Korea.

It's a dismal figure, and in 1986 the Chinese government set about boosting numbers by establishing the world's largest tiger breeding centre (p334) in Hā'ěrbīn. Beginning with only eight tigers, the centre has been so successful that the worldwide number of Siberian tigers may now exceed 1000.

The majority of these are in captivity, which makes any wild sighting a cause for celebration. In April 2012 the figurative champagne flowed when an Amur tiger was captured on film for the first time in Wangqing Nature Reserve in Jílín province. Speculation had it that the cat was one of several that appeared in March in Húnchūn along the border with Russia. If true it may be evidence the cats are expanding their range south – back into traditional Chinese territory.

thedrals, to animals and interpretations of ancient legends. At night they're lit up with coloured lights to create a magical effect.

It might be mind-numbingly cold and the sun disappears mid-afternoon, but the festival, which also features figure-skating shows and a variety of winter sports, is Hā'ěrbīn's main tourist attraction – and prices jump accordingly.

The festival takes place in multiple locations. The main venue, Harbin Ice and Snow World, is on Sun Island. The Ice and Snow World exhibits are held in the west end of the island on the north bank of the Sōnghuā River. They are best seen at night, so note that the half-price daytime ticket (good from 9am to noon) does not grant admission to the venue at night.

The Ice Lantern Venue is held in Zhāolín Park and many consider it the least interesting venue. If you do go, go at night when the lanterns are lit.

Hotels and hostels also organise reasonably priced group transport to/from festival locations. Taxis are expensive and hard to flag down during the festival times but you can ride horse carriages, or even use your own feet: the Sun Island venues are actually reachable by crossing the frozen Sōnghuā River (plan on one to two hours). Note that prices for the festival have been skyrocketing recently so don't be surprised if they are even higher than quoted here.

🛏 Sleeping

The most convenient places to stay are along Zhongyang Dajie in the Dàolǐqū district or in one of the many hotels that surround the train station. During the Ice and Snow Festival expect hotel prices to go up by at least 20%.

Kazy International Youth Hostel HOSTEL $
(卡兹国际青年旅舍, Kǎzī Guójì Qīngnián Lǚshě; ☑8469 7113; kazyzcl@126.com; 27 Tongjiang Jie, 通将街27号; dm/s/tw with shared bathroom ¥50/60/80, d/tw with bathroom ¥180/160; 🛜; ▦13) It may have lost its enviable location in the Main Synagogue up the road, but this hostel still scores points for its cosy lounge area and friendly staff who are a great source of travel information for the city and province. The eight-bed dorms are better value than the musty (some are windowless) private rooms.

The hostel is popular with Chinese travellers, so book ahead. A taxi will cost you ¥12.

Ibis Hotel HOTEL $$
(宜必思酒店; Yíbìsī Jiǔdiàn; ☑8750 9999; www.ibis.com; 92 Zhaolin Jie; 兆麟街92号; d & tw ¥209; ▦@🛜) The spotless rooms and handy location, minutes up the road from the Church of St Sofia and Zhongyang Dajie, make up for the surly, unhelpful front-desk staff. Book online for deals with free (but unspectacular) breakfast.

Jīndì Bīnguǎn HOTEL $$
(金地宾馆; ☑8461 8013; 16 Dongfeng Jie, 东风街16号; s & d ¥218-298, tw ¥458; ▦@🛜) If you're looking for a river view on the cheap, then this is the place. The owners are friendly, rooms are spacious and there's wi-fi available, with computers in the more expensive twins. To get to the hotel, turn right at the very end of Zhongyang Dajie past the Gloria Plaza Hotel. Discounts of up to 30% available.

Hàolín Business Hotel HOTEL $$
(昊琳商务连锁酒店, Hàolín Shāngwù Liánsuǒ Jiǔdiàn; ☑8467 5555; 26 Tongjiang Jie, 通将街26号; d & tw ¥268-368; ▦@) In the centre of Jewish Hā'ěrbīn, a neighbourhood now loaded with restaurants and barbecue stalls at night, is this business-style express hotel with surprisingly comfortable rooms sporting high ceilings, bright interiors and good modern bathrooms. It's a two-minute walk to Zhongyang Dajie. Expect discounts of 30%.

Hàntíng Express HOTEL $$
(汉庭快捷酒店, Hàntíng Kuàijié Jiǔdiàn; ☑5180 1177; www.htinns.com; Huochezhan Guangchang Dian, 火车站广场店; d & tw ¥229-299; ▦@🛜) This tidy business-style hotel is to the right of the train station square (as you exit the station) on the 24th floor. The entrance is next to a KFC (one of many in the train station area). The wi-fi–enabled rooms are slightly pricey considering its cookie-cutter decor, but it's a handy location for those who need to catch the train.

★ Lungmen Grand Hotel HISTORIC HOTEL $$$
(龙门贵宾楼酒店, Lóngmén Guìbīn Lóu Jiǔdiàn; ☑8317 7777; 85 Hongjun Jie, 红军街85号; d/tw ¥580/680; ▦@) With its turn of the century old-world styling almost entirely intact (including the marble staircase, dark wood-panelled hallways and the copper revolving door), the Lungmen is one of the most atmospheric top-end options in town. Across from the train station, the hotel lobby opens onto Hongjun Jie and its rows of heritage buildings.

A quick walk up the street's wide pavements takes you into the shopping heart of Hā'ěrbīn. Discounts available.

Modern Hotel
HISTORIC HOTEL $$$

(马迭尔宾馆, Mǎdié'ěr Bīnguǎn; ☎8488 4000; www.madieer.cn; 89 Zhongyang Dajie, 中央大街89号; r incl breakfast from ¥980; ❄@🛜🛗) While hardly 'modern', this 1906 construction impressively features some of its original marble, blond-wood accents and art nouveau touches. Spend some time checking out the lobby bar's display of hotel memorabilia before retiring to (thankfully) modern rooms. Note that the entrance to the hotel is around the back. Discounts of up to 30% available.

🍴 Eating

Hā'ěrbīn dishes tend to be heavy, with thick stewlike concoctions commonly found on the picture menus of a thousand eateries. You'll also find delicious hotpot, barbecued meats and Russian dishes in the tourist areas. Zhongyang Dajie and its side alleys are full of small restaurants and bakeries. Tongjiang Jie has fruit stands, sit-down restaurants and an abundance of outdoor barbecue stalls (with ad hoc seating) set up in the evenings.

In summer, the streets off Zhongyang Dajie come alive with open-air food stalls and beer gardens, where you can sip a Hāpí (the local beer), while munching on squid on a stick, *yángròu chuàn* (lamb kebabs) and all the usual street snacks.

The year-round indoor **food market** (小吃城, Xiǎochī Chéng; 96 Zhongyang Dajie; ⏱8.30am-7.30pm) has stalls selling decent bread, smoked meats, sausages, wraps and fresh dishes, as well as nuts, cookies, fruits and sweets. It's a great place to grab a quick breakfast or to stock up on food for a long bus or train ride.

Just south of the market, on the opposite side of the street, look for the underground **Lóngjiāng Xiǎochī Jiē** (龙江小吃街; Zhongyang Dajie; dishes ¥8-15; ⏱9am-6pm), a clean modern food court with a range of inexpensive noodle and rice dishes, as well as kebabs.

★ Orient King of Eastern Dumplings
DUMPLINGS $

(东方饺子王, Dōngfāng Jiǎozi Wáng; 81 Zhongyang Dajie; 中央大街81号; dumpling plate ¥12-38; ⏱10.30am-9.30pm; 🛜) It's not just the cheap *jiǎozi* (饺子; stuffed dumplings) that are good at this always busy and ever-expanding chain restaurant: there are also plenty of tasty vegie

dishes and draft beer on tap. There's another location near the train station in the Kunlun Hotel. Picture menu available.

Láifùbiǎndàn Chóngqìng Xiǎo Miàn
SICHUAN $

(来负扁担重庆小面; 134-1 Youyi Lu; noodles ¥8-16; ⏱9am-10pm) A cute hole-in-the-wall eatery serving fiery Sìchuān noodles to a steady stream of customers. Pull up a rustic wooden chair and slurp down sweat-inducing *xiǎo miàn* (小面; spicy soup noodles) plain or with *niú ròu* (牛肉; beef). If you can't take the heat, order *qīng tāng* (清汤; clear soup noodles) instead. No one will notice... they're too busy eating!

Old Chang's Spring Rolls
SNACKS $

(老昌春饼, Lǎo Chāng Chūnbǐng; 180 Zhongyang Dajie; 中央大街180号; dishes ¥12-38; ⏱10.30am-9pm) At this well-known basement spring roll shop, order a set of roll skins (per roll ¥2), a few plates of meat and vegetable dishes, and then wrap your way to one enjoyable repast.

Katusha
RUSSIAN $$

(☎139 4566 6905; 261 Zhongyang Dajie; 中央大街261号; dishes ¥20-78; ⏱11am-9.30pm) A popular Russian-Western restaurant decked out in kitsch Chinese decor. Feast on a range of Russian and Western favourites such as borscht, blini and steak. Russian vodka and beer? Yes and yes. Located diagonally across from the Flood Control Monument (p334) next to the Jīndì Bīnguǎn.

Cafe Russia
RUSSIAN $$

(露西亚咖啡西餐厅, Lùxīyà Kāfēi Xī Cāntīng; 57 Xitoujiao; 西头到街57号; dishes ¥20-78; ⏱10am-midnight) Step back in time at this ivy-covered teahouse-cum-restaurant and cafe. Black-and-white photos illustrating Hā'ěrbīn's Russian past line the walls, while the old-school furniture and fireplace evoke a different era. Sadly, staff seem more interested in napping than serving their signature Russian fare such as borscht and *piroshki* (cabbage, potato and meat puffs). Russian vodka is available, too.

The restaurant is off Zhongyang Dajie in a little courtyard.

🍸 Drinking & Nightlife

Hā'ěrbīn has the usual collection of karaoke (KTV) joints. If communal singing isn't your bag, there are a few bars on and off Zhongyang Dajie and Tiandi Lu. Zhongyang Dajie and Stalin Park (p333) also have beer gardens in the summer with cheap drafts and

DON'T MISS

JEWISH HĀ'ĔRBĪN

The Jewish influence on Hā'ĕrbīn was surprisingly long lasting; the last original Jewish resident of the city died in 1985. In the 1920s Hā'ĕrbīn was home to some 20,000 Jews, the largest Jewish community in the Far East at the time. Tongjiang Jie was the centre of Jewish life in the city till the end of WWII, and many of the buildings on the street are from the early 20th century.

Hā'ĕrbīn New Synagogue (哈尔滨犹太新会堂, Hā'ĕrbīn Yóutài Xīnhuìtáng; 162 Jingwei Jie; 经纬街162号; admission ¥25; ⊙8.30am-5pm) This synagogue was built in 1921 by the city's Jewish community, the vast majority of whom had emigrated from Russia. Restored and converted into a museum in 2004, the 1st floor is an art gallery with pictures and photos of old Hā'ĕrbīn. The 2nd and 3rd floors feature photos and exhibits that tell the story of the history and rich cultural life of Hā'ĕrbīn's Jews.

Hā'ĕrbīn Main Synagogue (哈尔滨犹太会堂, Hā'ĕrbīn Yóutài Huìtáng; 82 Tongjiang Jie, Yóutài Jiùhuìtáng; 通江街82号) The beautiful old Main Synagogue, built in 1909, has been recently refurbished and has reopened as a concert venue with a small museum. Close by is the former Jewish Middle School.

Jewish Middle School (犹太中学, Yóutài Zhōngxué ; Tongjiang Jie; 通江街) This was the first Jewish middle school in the Far East and most recently housed a Korean school. It has since been immaculately restored as part of a shared compound with the original synagogue.

Turkish Mosque (土耳其清真寺, Tǔ'ĕrqí Qīngzhēn Sì; Tongjiang Jie; 通江街) Built in 1906, this mosque is no longer operating and is closed to visitors, but you can take a peek from the outside.

Huángshān Jewish Cemetery (皇山公墓, Huángshān Gōngmù) Located in the far eastern suburbs of Hā'ĕrbīn, this is the largest Jewish cemetery in East Asia. There are more than 600 graves here, all well maintained. A taxi here takes around 45 minutes and costs about ¥100.

plenty of snack food to enjoy as you watch sports on the big screens. Nightclubs come and go, so you're best off asking for the latest when you arrive.

Ming Tien   CAFE
(名典西餐, Míngdiǎn Xīcān; www.hrbmingdian.com; 214 Shangzhi Dajie; drinks ¥35-60; ⊙10am-9pm) For afternoon tea or coffee head to this slightly over-the-top cafe occupying two floors of a heritage building on Shangzhi Dajie. Enter via the subdued parlour, wind your way up the tree-enshrouding staircase and ease into a big brown leather booth with views of Zhāolín Park. There's an equally eclectic menu ranging from borscht to pizza if you get hungry.

🔒 Shopping

Shops along Zhongyang Dajie flog imitation Russian and Chinese souvenirs. But there are also department stores, boutiques and many Western clothes chains here. Souvenir shops selling Russian knick-knacks, dolls, binoculars and also vodka and other spirits can be found all over the city.

Locals head to Dongdazhi Jie for their shopping needs, as well as the Hóngbó Century Square (红博世纪广场, Hóngbó Shìjì Guǎngchǎng; ⊙6.30am-5pm), a huge subterranean shopping complex for men's and women's clothing.

ℹ Information

There are ATMs all over town. Most large hotels will also change money. Many midrange and top-end hotels have travel services that book tickets and arrange tours throughout the province.

Bank of China (中国银行, Zhōngguó Yínháng; Xi'er Daojie) Has a 24-hour ATM and will cash travellers cheques. Easy to spot on a side road as you walk up Zhongyang Dajie.

Harbin Modern Travel Company (哈尔滨马迭尔旅行社, Hā'ĕrbīn Mǎdié'ĕr Lǚxíngshè; 89 Zhongyang Dajie) This travel agency on the 2nd floor of the Modern Hotel offers one- and two-day ski trips to Yàbùlì and can handle flight tickets to Mòhé and other regions.

ℹ Getting There & Away

AIR
Harbin Taiping International Airport (哈尔滨太平国际机场, Hā'ĕrbīn Tàipíng Guójì Jīchǎng)

has flights to Russia and South Korea as well as the following domestic routes:

Běijīng ¥800, two hours

Dàlián ¥700, 1½ hours

Mòhé ¥1600, 3½ hours

BUS

The main **long-distance bus station** (长途客运站, chángtú kèyùn zhàn) is directly opposite the train station. Buy tickets on the 2nd floor.

Chángchūn ¥78, four hours, four daily (noon, 1pm, 2pm, 3pm and 4pm)

Mǔdānjiāng ¥70 & ¥96, 4½ hours, hourly from 8am to 5pm

Wǔdàlián Chí ¥91, five to six hours, three daily (9am, 11.30am and 1.30pm). The 1.30pm bus goes to the scenic area while the other two stop at Wǔdàlián Chí Shì, a ¥40 taxi ride from the scenic area.

Běi'ān ¥85 to ¥95, five hours, five daily (7.10am, 8.30am, 12.30pm, 2.20pm and 4.30pm)

Qíqíhǎěr ¥97, 3½ hours, six daily (8am, 9am, 10am, noon, 1pm and 2pm)

TRAIN

Hā'ěrbīn is a major rail transport hub with routes throughout the northeast and beyond. If you don't want to brave the lines in the **main station** (哈尔滨站, Hā'ěrbīn zhàn; 1 Tielu Jie, 铁路街1号), buy tickets at the nearby **train booking office** (铁路售票处, Tiělù Shòupiàochù; Tielu Jie; ⊙7am-9pm) to the left of Dico's (fast food restaurant). Note that the fast D and G trains leave from **Hā'ěrbīn West Station** (西站, Xīzhàn), 10km from town. A taxi will cost ¥30-40.

Běijīng hard seat/sleeper ¥159/293, 10 to 16 hours, eight daily

Běijīng (D train) seat ¥284, nine hours, four daily

Chángchūn (D/G train) seat ¥73/111, two/one hour, regular

Mòhé hard/soft sleeper ¥257/430, 21 hours, 7.44pm

Mǔdānjiāng hard seat/sleeper ¥52/100, five to seven hours, regular

Shěnyáng hard seat/sleeper ¥78/149, six to seven hours

Shěnyáng (D/G train) seat ¥161/245, three/two hours, five daily

ℹ️ Getting Around

TO/FROM THE AIRPORT

Hā'ěrbīn's airport is 46km from the city centre. From the airport, **shuttle buses** (¥20, one hour) will drop you at the railway station. To the airport, shuttles leave every 30 minutes from a stand just beside Dico's opposite the train station from 5.30am to 7.30pm. A taxi (¥100 to ¥125) takes 45 minutes to an hour.

PUBLIC TRANSPORT

Buses 101 and 103 run from the train station to Shangzhi Dajie, dropping you off at the north end of Zhongyang Dajie (the old street). Buses leave from a stop across the road and to the left as you exit the train station (where Chunshen Jie and Hongjun Jie meet).

Hā'ěrbīn's long-awaited metro has a single line that doesn't serve any of the tourist sights. Construction for further lines are underway.

TAXI

Taxis are fairly plentiful, though they fill up quickly when it's raining. Taxi flag-fall is ¥8.

Mǔdānjiāng 牡丹江

📞 0453 / POP 805,000

A pleasant and surprisingly small modern city surrounded by some lovely countryside, Mǔdānjiāng is the jumping-off point for nearby Jìngpò Hú (Mirror Lake) and the Underground Forest. Taiping Jie is the main drag in town and runs directly south (opposite) of the train station. There's a **Bank of China** (中国银行; Zhōngguó Yínháng) two blocks up with a 24-hour ATM.

🛏️ Sleeping & Eating

The train station area has a number of good hotels and there is no reason to look further into town. For budget accommodation head right as you exit the station. Just past the station square on Guanghua Jie runs a row of guesthouses. There are at least half a dozen to choose from, all offering similar prices and decent digs: dorm beds go for ¥30,

SKIING IN CHINA

China's ski industry has all the appearance of a success story. From 20,000 visits to the slopes in 1996, numbers have grown to around 15 million in 2012. There are now over 20 large resorts across the country in areas as diverse as Jílín, Hēilóngjiāng, Yúnnán and Héběi provinces, many of them also popular with foreigners and expats.

Building slopes and resorts has been easy: maintaining them while a ski culture develops has not been. In 2012 there was renewed hope, however, as another round of investment hit the industry. This time the focus would be on upping the luxury quotient, and also opening more runs and facilities for absolute beginners.

In China's north, the largest resorts are Jílín's **Běidàhú Ski Resort** (p327) and Hēilóngjiāng's **Yàbùlì Ski Resort** (亚布力滑雪中心, Yàbùlì Huáxuě Zhōngxīn; www.yabuliski. com) 200km southeast of Hā'ěrbīn. Yàbùlì was China's first destination ski resort, and remains the training centre for the Chinese Olympic ski team. Since 2009 the resort has expanded to cover two mountains and now has a good division of advanced, intermediate and beginner runs, as well as a four-star lodge that can reasonably cater to Western guests.

The latest slopes to be developed in the region are at Chángbái Shān on the China–North Korean border located about 15km from the new airport. At the **Wanda International Resort** (p322), you'll find 20 runs on two mountains as well as a luxury alpine village offering hotels, restaurants and private condos. Top-notch hotels in the area include the Sheraton and Westin chain of hotels. They offer guest pick-ups from the train station or airport.

Lift tickets in the north average around ¥500 per day on weekends, and a little less on weekdays. Clothing and equipment rental comes to another ¥140. For up-to-date information on all the major ski areas of China, as well as transport and tour advice, see the excellent **China Ski Tours** (www.chinaskitours.com).

rooms with shared bathroom for around ¥40 and rooms with their own bathroom (and sometimes even a computer) from ¥80.

There are plenty of cheap restaurants around as well, and also in the alleys off Qixing Jie, which intersects with Taiping Jie half a kilometre up from the train station. Dongyitiao Lu (off Qixing Jie) is a lively pedestrian-only street with a wide range of BBQ, noodle and snack venues open in the evening.

Home Inn
HOTEL $$

(如家快捷酒店, Rújiā Kuàijié Jiǔdiàn; ☑ 6911 1188; 651 Guanghua Jie, 光花街651号; r ¥129-179; ☀✿@🛜) Probably the best-value rooms around the train station are in this well-managed chain just to the right as you exit. Top floors are nonsmoking and very quiet despite the location.

★ Sunny Date International Hotel
HOTEL $$$

(禧禄达国际酒店, Xǐlùdá Guójì Jiǔdiàn; ☑ 6607 777; http://sunnydatehotel.com; cnr Guanghua Jie & Dongyitiao Lu; d & tw ¥598-798; ✿🛜) It's hard not to be impressed (or blinded) by the sunny opulence of the chandelier-lined lobby. Some rooms come equipped with a mah-

jong table but who cares as all the rooms are top notch with comfy beds, wi-fi and clean bathrooms. The gigantic attached bathhouse is equally opulent. Discounts bring rooms down to as low as ¥228...bargain!

The hotel is located 200m to the left opposite the road as you exit the station. It opens up to the busy Dongyitiao Lu pedestrian street.

Shuānglóng Jiǎozi Wáng
DUMPLINGS $

(双龙饺子王; cnr Qixing Jie & Taiping Jie; dumplings ¥12-38; ⏱ 9am-9pm) There's a wide selection of *jiǎozi* here, as well as the usual Dōngběi classics. As you turn left off Taiping Jie, the restaurant is the big glass building with the red signboard on the right. There's an English sign out front and a partial picture menu inside to help you order.

❶ Getting There & Away

BUS

Long-distance buses sometimes drop you off near the train station and depart from a long-distance station (客车站; *kè chēzhàn*) a few kilometres away on Xi Ping'an Jie. A taxi to the station costs ¥6.

Dōngjīng Chéng ¥18, 1¼ hours, half hourly

Hā'ěrbīn ¥70 & 96, 4½ hours, hourly (5.30am to 6pm)

Yánjí ¥72, five hours, 6.30am, 11.30am and 2pm

TRAIN

Mŭdānjiāng has rail connections:

Hā'ěrbīn hard seat/sleeper ¥52/100, five to seven hours, frequent services

Suífēnhé seat ¥20 to ¥30, four to five hours, four daily

Yánjí hard seat/sleeper ¥22/56, six hours, one daily (4.26pm)

Around Mŭdānjiāng

Jìngpò Hú

Formed on the bend of the Mŭdan River 5000 years ago by the falling lava of five volcanic explosions, Jìngpò Hú (镜泊湖, Mirror Lake; www.jingpohu.com.cn; admission ¥80), 110km south of Mŭdānjiāng, gets its name from the unusually clear reflections of the surrounding lush green forest in its pristine blue water.

Hugely popular in summer with Chinese daytrippers who come to paddle or picnic by the lakeside, it's a pleasant spot if you hike along the lake to escape the crowds. Shuttle buses (¥12 per trip) run to various sights, and ferries (¥100, 1½hours) make leisurely tours of the lake.

◉ Sights

Diàoshuǐlóu Waterfall   WATERFALL
(吊水楼瀑布, Diàoshuǐlóu Pùbù) One of the area's biggest attractions is this waterfall with a 12m drop and 300m span. During the rainy season (June to September), when Diàoshuǐlóu is in full throttle, it's a spectacular raging beauty, but during spring and autumn it's little more than a drizzle. You can walk to the waterfall from the north gate entrance in about five minutes. Just stay on the main road and follow the English signs.

Underground Forest   FOREST
(地下森林, Dìxià Sēnlín; admission ¥55, internal shuttle bus ¥30) Despite its name, the Underground Forest isn't below the earth; instead it has grown within volcano craters that erupted some 10,000 years ago. Hiking around the thick pine forest and several of the 10 craters takes about an hour.

The forest is 50km from Jìngpò Hú. Some day tours include it in their itinerary. Otherwise, you have to take a bus (¥40 return, one hour) from the north gate of Jìngpò, which

is doable but very tight if you only have a day at the lake.

🛏 Sleeping & Eating

It's pleasant to spend the night in the park and enjoy the lake when the crowds return to their hotels in Mŭdānjiāng.

Jìngpò Hú Shānzhuāng Jiǔdiàn   HOTEL $$
(镜泊湖山庄酒店; ☑ 627 0039, 139 0483 9459; r ¥480-580; ❈ @) This hotel sits just back from the water at the first lakeside drop-off point for the shuttle buses. Rooms are very modern, some with lake views and the hotel's restaurant has decent food (if a little overpriced). Discounts can knock prices down to the ¥240 range or less if you choose a room without a view.

❶ Getting There & Away

The easiest way to get to Jìngpò Hú is on the one-day tours that leave from the train station in Mŭdānjiāng from 6.30am to 7.30am. Tours cost ¥255 and include transport and admission. If offered, you can add an all-inclusive tour to the Underground Forest for an extra ¥115. Call ☑ 139 4533 1797 or book at a booth in front of the train station.

If you want to come here under your own steam, you can get a direct bus from the Mŭdānjiāng bus station (¥25, 2½ hours, 1.30pm & 2.30pm). If you want an earlier start from Mŭdānjiāng, first go to Dōngjīng Chéng (东京城, ¥15, 1½ hours, frequent) then change to a minibus (¥10, 40 to 60 minutes) to the lake. In the late afternoon you can try to get a seat on one of the tour buses directly back to Mŭdānjiāng from the lake (¥30) or head back again via Dōngjīng Chéng.

❶ Getting Around

The ticket centre for the lake is at the North Gate (Běimén). From here walk about five minutes to a car park for shuttle buses to the lake and ferry dock (get a ticket to the stop 'Jìngpò Shānzhuāng'; 镜泊山庄) and other sights (¥12 per ride). Diàoshuǐlóu Waterfall is just behind this car park.

Wŭdàlián Chí   五大连池

☑ 0456

Formed by a series of volcanic eruptions, the Wŭdàlián Chí nature reserve boasts one of northern China's most mesmerising landscapes. It's a genuine Lost World with vast fields of hardened lava, rivers of basalt, volcanic peaks, azure lakes and the odd little reed-lined pond. You could spend days exploring.

The last time the volcanoes erupted was in 1720, and the lava flow blocked the nearby North River (Běi Hé), forming the series of five interconnected lakes that give the area its name. Wǔdàlián Chí is about 250km northwest of Hā'ěrbīn, and in addition to the volcanic landscape is home to mineral springs that draw busloads of Chinese and Russian tourists to slurp the allegedly curative waters. So many Russians roll up that the town's street signs are in both Chinese and Russian.

There's no real town here, just a long, pleasant tree-lined street called Yaoquan Lu (药泉路). Everything you want is on a section that runs west of the bus station. The intersection of Yaoquan Lu and Shilong Lu (about 3km from the bus stop) is the main crossroad and is smack in the middle of the hotel area. Taxis make the trip from the bus station to the hotel area for ¥5 to ¥10.

Some travellers have started to base themselves in Wǔdàlián Chí Shì (五大连池市), a larger town about 20km away and where most buses drop you off from Hā'ěrbīn. Within a short walk of the bus station there are half a dozen hotels and plenty of restaurants. Unless you've got no other choice, it's worth making the effort to base yourself in Wǔdàlián Chí itself.

It's only really viable to visit Wǔdàlián Chí between May and October.

Sights & Activities

For a loop taking in the lakes, volcanoes and caves listed here, most people hire a taxi (¥150). If your time is short, just visit Lǎohēi Shān and you will get most of what the area has to offer.

★ Lǎohēi Shān   VOLCANO
(老黑山; admission ¥80 plus ¥25 shuttle fee; 7.30am-7pm May-Oct) It's a mostly uphill 1km stair climb to the summit of Lǎohēi Shān, one of the area's 14 volcanoes. Do a circuit of the crater lip for panoramic views of the lakes and other volcanoes dotting the landscape. Taxis drop you at the ticket booth from where park shuttle buses take you to a large car park. To the left is the trail up the mountain; to the right is a boardwalk to the aptly named Shí Hǎi (石海, Stone Sea), a magnificent lava field.

Back in the car park smaller green shuttle buses take you to Huǒshāo Shān (火烧山) and the end of the road at another collection of weirdly shaped lava stones. This stretch is one of Wǔdàlián Chí's most enchanting, with lava rock rivers, birch forests, grassy fields, ponds and more wide stretches of lava fields.

Lóngmén 'Stone Village'   LAVA FIELD
(龙门石寨, Lóngmén Shízhài; admission ¥50; 7am-6pm May-Oct) At this impressive lava field reminiscent of Middle Earth's Mordor (minus the orcs), walk through a forest of white and black birch trees on a network of boardwalks, with the lava rocks stretching away in the distance on both sides.

Sān Chí   LAKE
(三池; boat tour ¥80) Welcome to Third Lake, the largest of the five interconnected lakes that give rise to the region's name. Here, you can feel the wind whip through your hair on a zippy 40 minute boat ride across the still water.

Wēnbó Hú   LAVA FIELD
(温泊湖; admission ¥50; 7.30am-5.30pm) A long boardwalk takes visitors through a lava field dotted with ponds and informative interpretive boards explaining lava-related phenomenon such as fissures and, of course, the fields itself. The boardwalk ends at a small dock where you transfer to a boat for a slow putter down a reed-lined river. Your taxi will arrange to pick you from where the boat docks.

Běiyìnquán   MINERAL SPRING
(北饮泉; admission ¥30; 7.30am-5.30pm) Tourists and locals flock here to taste the supposedly curative mineral spring water that's piped out through installed taps. Some even use the water to wash their hair! Bring you own bottle and fill up on the good stuff (which tastes like metal-flavoured soda water) and stroll the pretty grounds.

Sleeping & Eating

Yaoquan Lu, the main east–west drag in Wǔdàlián Chí, has a dozen or more hotels operating from May to October. Some nice new hotels have opened about 500m up the road from the bus station.

For cheap ¥30 beds, contact Liu Jie (刘姐; 158 4687 3866). This friendly teacher has converted a brand-new apartment on the outskirts of town into a comfortable dorm/hostel. She will organise pick-up to/from the bus station as well as a taxi to see the local sights.

If your hotel doesn't have a restaurant, head to the local places on Guotu Jie, the street parallel to Yaoquan Lu in the area near the Quanshan New Holiday Inn or at the main intersection at Yaoquan and Shilong

CRANE COUNTRY

Northeastern China is home to several nature reserves established to protect endangered species of wild cranes. **Zhālóng Nature Reserve** (扎龙自然保护区, Zhālóng Zìrán Bǎohùqū; admission ¥60; ⊗ 8am-5.30pm) near Qíqíhā'ěr is the most accessible and most visited of these sanctuaries. The reserve is home to some 260 bird species, including several types of rare cranes. Four of the species that migrate here are on the endangered list: the extremely rare red-crowned crane, the white-naped crane, the Siberian crane and the hooded crane.

The reserve comprises some 2100 sq km of wetlands that are on a bird migration path extending from the Russian Arctic down into Southeast Asia. Hundreds of birds arrive in April and May, rear their young from June to August and depart in September and October. Unfortunately, a significant percentage of the birds you can see live are in captivity and are periodically released so that visitors can take photos.

The best time to visit Zhālóng is in spring. In summer the mosquitoes can be more plentiful than the birds – take repellent! To get to here, head to Qíqíhā'ěr and board bus 306 (¥20, 45 minutes, half-hourly) from Dàrùnfā (大润发) near Qíqíhā'ěr. Birds are released at 9.30am, 11am, 2pm and 3.30pm.

The **Xiànghǎi National Nature Reserve** (向海, Xiànghǎi Guójiā Zìrán Bǎohùqū), 310km west of Chángchūn in Jílín province, is on the migration path for Siberian cranes, and the rare red-crowned, white-naped and demoiselle cranes breed here. More than 160 bird species, including several of these cranes, have been identified at the **Horqin National Nature Reserve** (科尔沁, Kē'ěrqìn Guójiā Zìrán Bǎohùqū), which borders Xianghai in Inner Mongolia. The **Mòmògé National Nature Reserve** (莫莫格, Mòmògé Guójiā Zìrán Bǎohùqū) in northern Jílín province is also an important wetlands area and bird breeding site.

For more information about China's crane population and these nature reserves, contact the **International Crane Foundation** (www.savingcranes.org) or see the website of the **Siberian Crane Wetland Project** (www.scwp.info).

Lu. There are plenty of greasy-spoon choices (dishes ¥8 to ¥48), largely serving the same five types of local fish the area is famous for. You can also get cheap *jiǎozi*, noodles and BBQ. Several grocery stores sell fruit and imported snacks including real chocolate.

Quanshan New Holiday Inn HOTEL **$$**
(新泉山假日酒店; Xīnquánshān Jiàrì Jiǔdiàn; ☑ 722 6999; Yaoquan Lu; d & tw incl breakfast ¥368-690; ❇ @ 🖥) Unrelated to the Western Holiday Inn chain, this is actually a new Chinese-run hotel located 500m up the road from the bus station just off the main road. Modern rooms are fitted with plush carpets, large comfy beds and wi-fi. The cheaper rooms are windowless but just as comfortable. Discounts bring rooms down to ¥150 during the shoulder season.

★ **Wángmáolǘ Dòufu Měishí Diàn** DONGBEI **$$**
(王毛驴豆腐美食店; off Guotu Jie; dishes ¥22-58; ⊗ 11am-9.30pm) The locally made tofu is some of the best you'll probably taste in China. It's soft and delicate, and served in a variety of ways: with fish, vegies and such. If you can't decide, take your pick from the picture menu on the wall. It's located off Guotu Jie, the street parallel to the main drag where the Quanshan New Holiday Inn hotel is.

If you get lost, ask locals for directions; it's a famous restaurant.

❶ Information

There is an **ICBC** (工商银行, Gōngshāng Yínháng) ATM accepting foreign cards in Wǔdàlián Chí on Guotu Jie.

❶ Getting There & Away

BUS

Both Wǔdàlián Chí and Wǔdàlián Chí Shì have bus stations. Direct buses run from Hā'ěrbīn (¥91, six hours, three daily at 9am, 11.30am and 1.30pm). The 1.30pm bus terminates at Wǔdàlián Chí while the other two terminate at Wǔdàlián Chí Shì. A taxi the rest of the way will cost ¥40.

Buses leave for Hā'ěrbīn from Wǔdàlián Chí (¥91, six hours, 5.40am and 8.10am) and Wǔdàlián Chí Shì (6.50am and 9.30am). There are also buses to Hēihé and Běi'ān, the nearest train station, which has connections on to Hā'ěrbīn.

Russian Borderlands

Much of the remote northeastern border between China and Siberia follows the Black Dragon River (Hēilóng Jiāng), known to Russians as the Amur River. In this region it's possible to see Siberian forests and dwindling settlements of northern minorities, such as the Daur, Ewenki, Hezhen and Oroqen.

Major towns in the far north include Mòhé and Hēihé. On the eastern border, Suífēnhé is a gateway to Vladivostok.

Mòhé, Běijícūn (North Pole Village) & Běihóngcūn 漠河, 北极村, 北红村

📞 0457

The country's northernmost town, Mòhé, standing amid spindly pine forests and vast bogs, holds the record for the lowest plunge of the thermometer: -52.3°C, recorded in 1956. That same day in the southern extreme at Sānyà, a tropical beach paradise of azure waters and coconut palms, the temperature was likely in the high 20s.

Mòhé is one of China's most intriguing outliers, sharing not just a border with Russia, but architecture as well. In 1985 the town burned to the ground in a raging forest fire and when it came time to rebuild, Mòhé decided to redo the main streets in an imperial-era Russian style.

These days, Mòhé and the area is best known for its midnight sun, visible for as long as 22 hours during the annual Festival of Aurora Borealis (北极光节, Běijíguāng Jié), held in late June. Oddly, this is one of the few times you can see the northern lights, according to locals. Later in the summer, when there are more hours of darkness, the lights don't appear. Odds of seeing the aurora are fairly slim with the last spotting in 2012.

⊙ Sights

Běijícūn   VILLAGE

(北极村, North Pole Village; admission ¥60) Further north from Mòhé is Běijícūn, a sprawling village and recreation area on the banks of the Hēilóng Jiāng, separating China and Russia.

Běijícūn covers an area of forest, meadow-land and bog, with the occasional hamlet, log cabin and Russian-style structure dotting the pretty surroundings. If the mood strikes, you can stand at the top of a map of China that has been etched into a square. Step up on the podium and you are at the official 'most northerly point' one can be

within China's 9,671,018 sq km of land. One house has even been labelled China No 1 (中国最北一家), ie China's northernmost house. You can walk east along the river to a point where you can see a Russian village across the water.

Běihóngcūn   VILLAGE

(北红村) With Běijícūn on the tourist radar, intrepid travellers and enterprising locals have opened up a route to the even more northerly village of Běihóngcūn, 100km away. There's nowhere to go but back south here and while there's not much beyond wooden houses and swathes of farmland, it is a quiet, idyllic spot and lays claim to being China's real northernmost village.

From Běihóngcūn, you can push across to Hēilóng Jiāng Dìyī Wān (黑龙江第一弯), the first bend in the river. The 800+ steps to the viewing point is well worth the gorgeous panorama of the amazing horseshoe bend.

🛏 Sleeping & Eating

There are a number of cheap guesthouses and restaurants down the alleys off Fanrong Xiang in Mòhé. Fanrong Xiang is off Zhenxing Jie (the main street).

Mòhé International Youth Hostel   HOSTEL $

(漠河北极村驴友之家国际青年旅舍, Mòhé Běijícūn Lǘyóu Zhījiā Guójì Qīngnián Lǚshè; 📞 282 6326; dm ¥40, d & tw ¥110; ❄ 🛜) The best place to base yourself is at Běijícūn, where this cute farmhouse can organise onward transport to see Běihóngcūn and the other sights. Rooms are comfortable and you can get home-cooked meals from the attached kitchen. If you ring ahead, a car can pick you up from the train station or airport. You can also rent bicycles here for ¥5 per hour.

ℹ Getting There & Around

There are four flights a day from Hā'ěrbīn to Mòhé (¥1650, 2½ hours). Trains from Hā'ěrbīn (hard/soft sleeper ¥275/400, 7.44pm) take 21 hours to reach the northern town. Heading back, a train leaves at 4.45pm.

Mòhé's train station is about 2km from the centre of town and it costs ¥10 to get here by taxi. To/from the airport, taxis charge ¥20. Buses for Běijícūn (¥25, 1½ hours, 8am and 3pm) leave from Mòhé's bus station at the corner of Zhenxing and Zhonghua Jie. Return buses from Běijícūn depart at 6.40am and noon.

A good way to visit the area would be to hire a private car or taxi. Expect to pay around ¥350 per day; you can start your trip from Mòhé and do all the sights listed in a loop back.

Shānxī

POP 35.7 MILLION

Best Ancient Towns & Villages

➡ Píngyáo (p358)
➡ Guōyù (p365)
➡ Lǐjiāshān (p363)
➡ Qìkǒu (p363)

Best Temples

➡ Xiàntōng Temple (p354)
➡ Tǎyuàn Temple (p354)
➡ Huáyán Temple (p348)
➡ Hanging Monastery (p352)

Why Go?

Waist-deep in handsome history, Shānxī (山西) has a plethora of interesting sights but it unfortunately takes some patience to see through the pollution and coal dust that pervades much of the province. Most travellers start with the walled city of Píngyáo. Basing yourself here and jumping to Píngyáo's surrounding sights is practically all you need. You'll encounter time-worn temples, traditional Qing-dynasty courtyard architecture and some of the warmest people in the Middle Kingdom.

The mountain vastness of Wǔtái Shān, however, reveals Shānxī's other great source of magic, a Buddhist leaning that fashions classical monastic architecture, a disposition further concentrated in the astonishing Buddhist cave sculptures at Yúngāng and at the Hanging Monastery. Add in the time-warp walled village of Guōyù and the still-inhabited cave dwellings of Lǐjiāshān, and you could find yourself spending more time here than you had planned for.

When to Go
Dàtóng

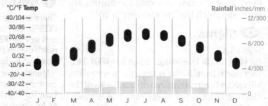

May Get a jump on the sapping summer months.

Late May–early Sep For trips to cooler, mountainous Wǔtái Shān.

Late Sep Enjoy the comfortable start of the lovely Shānxī autumn.

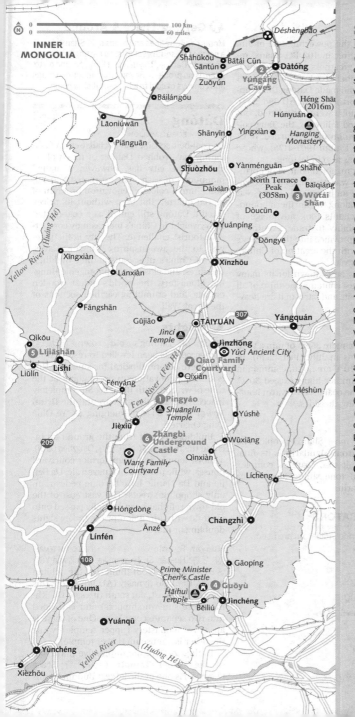

Shānxī Highlights

1 Wander the cobblestone ancient streets of time-warped **Píngyáo** (p358)

2 Discover the grandeur of the Buddhist statues at the **Yúngāng Caves** (p351)

3 Hang up your traveller's hat in the monastic enclave of **Wǔtái Shān** (p352)

4 Journey to the still-inhabited historical walled village of **Guōyù** (p365) in Shānxī's remote southeast

5 Experince 'old' China with an overnight stay at the Ming-dynasty cave village of **Lǐjiāshān** (p363)

6 Go subterranean at the fascinating **Zhāngbì Underground Castle** (p362)

7 Explore some of China's best-preserved courtyard architecture at the **Qiao Family Courtyard** (p357)

History

Though home to the powerful state of Jin, which split into three in 403 BC, Shānxī really only rose to greatness with the Tuoba, a clan of the Xianbei people from Mongolia and Manchuria who made Dàtóng their capital during the Northern Wei (AD 386–534). Eventually the Tuoba were assimilated, but as China weakened following the Tang collapse, the northern invaders returned; most notable were the Khitan (907–1125), whose western capital was also in Dàtóng.

After the Ming regained control of northern China, Shānxī was developed as a defensive outpost, with an inner and outer Great Wall constructed along the northern boundaries. Local merchants took advantage of the increased stability to trade, eventually transforming the province into the country's financial centre with the creation of China's first banks in Píngyáo.

Today Shānxī is best known for its many mines; the province contains one-third of all China's coal deposits and parts of it are heavily polluted.

Climate

Dry as dust, with a mere 35cm of rain a year. It only really rains in July (just 12cm). In Tàiyuán, lows of -10°C are not uncommon in January, while summer highs exceed 30°C. Avoid winter as the coal used to warm houses ends up blighting the skies.

Language

Jin is spoken by most Shānxī people. The main difference from Mandarin is its final glottal stop, but it also features complex grammar-induced tone shifts. Most locals also speak Mandarin.

PRICE INDICATORS

The following price indicators are used in this chapter:

Sleeping

$ less than ¥200

$$ ¥200 to ¥500

$$$ more than ¥500

Eating

$ less than ¥50

$$ ¥50 to ¥100

$$$ more than ¥100

ⓘ Getting There & Around

Modern railway lines and roads split Shānxī on a northeast–southwest axis, so getting from Běijīng to Dàtóng, Tàiyuán and Píngyáo, and on to Xī'ān, is no problem. Beyond that, mountain roads and convoys of coal trucks make it slow going.

Dàtóng 大同

☑ 0352 / POP 3.3 MILLION

Its coal-belt setting and socialist-era refashioning have robbed Dàtóng of much of its charm. The city has, however, ploughed mountains of cash – an estimated ¥50 billion – into a colossal renovation program of its old quarter. But even without its pricey facelift, Dàtóng still cuts it as a coal-dusted heavyweight in China's increasingly competitive tourist challenge. The city is the gateway to the awe-inspiring Yúngāng Caves, one of China's most outstanding Buddhist treasures, and close to the photogenic Hanging Monastery, the world's oldest wooden pagoda, and crumbling earthen sections of the Great Wall.

◎ Sights

Much of Dàtóng's **old town** (老城区; lǎochéngqū) has been levelled to restore what was there before. Illogical for sure, but this is China. Renovations were ongoing at the time of writing, with Red Flag Sq completely inaccessible and the area around the **Drum Tower** (鼓楼; Gǔ Lóu) emerging as 'Ye Olde Qing Quarter'.

Buildings rebuilt from the ground up include the **mosque** (清真大寺; Qīngzhēn Dà Sì), a Taoist temple and many former courtyard houses, while portions of Huayan Jie, Da Beijie and Da Nanjie have become pedestrian-only shopping streets. The vast cost of the old-town refit has been partially passed onto visitors, with admission prices to key sights doubling or more.

Huáyán Temple   BUDDHIST TEMPLE
(华严寺; Huáyán Sì; Huayan Jie; admission ¥80; ☉8am-6.30pm; 🚍38) Built by the Khitan during the Liao dynasty (AD 907–1125), this temple faces east, not south (it's said the Khitan were sun worshippers) and is divided into two separate complexes. One of these is an active monastery (upper temple), while the other is a museum (lower temple).

Dating to 1140, the impressive main hall of the **Upper Temple** (上华严寺; Shàng Huáyán Sì) is one of the largest Buddhist halls in China with Ming murals and Qing statues within. The rear hall of the **Lower Temple** (下华严寺; Xià Huáyán Sì) is the oldest building in Dàtóng (1038), containing some remarkable Liao-dynasty wooden sculptures. Side halls contain assorted relics from the Wei, Liao and Jin dynasties. Bus 38 runs here.

Nine Dragon Screen
WALL

(九龙壁, Jiǔlóng Bì; Da Dongjie; admission ¥10; 8am-6.30pm) With its nine beautiful multicoloured coiling dragons, this 45.5m-long, 8m-high and 2m-thick Ming-dynasty spirit wall was built in 1392. It's the largest glazed-tile wall in China and an amazing sight; the palace it once protected belonged to the 13th son of a Ming emperor and burnt down years ago.

China Sculpture Museum
GALLERY

(中国雕塑博物馆; Zhōngguó Diāosù Bówùguǎn; Da Beijie, 大北街; 8.30-11.30am & 2.30-5.30pm Tue-Sun) FREE This cavernous new museum, built within the northern gate section of the restored city walls, has seemingly endless corridors of excellent contemporary sculpture by Chinese and foreign artists. When you get tired of looking at busts, look out for uncovered sections of the original city walls.

Shànhuà Temple
BUDDHIST TEMPLE

(善化寺; Shànhuà Sì; Nansi Jie; admission ¥50; 8am-6pm) Originally constructed in AD 713, Shànhuà was rebuilt by the Jin. The grand wooden-bracketed rear hall contains five beautiful central Buddhas and expressive statues of celestial generals in the wings. Look for an impressive five-dragon screen out the front.

🛏 Sleeping

Fly By Knight Datong Highrise Hostel
HOSTEL $

(夜奔大同客栈; Yèbēn Dàtóng Kèzhàn; ☎130 4109 5935; datongfbk@gmail.com; 22nd fl, Unit 14, 15 Yingbin Xijie; 迎宾西街15号22楼14室 (桐城中央); dm ¥80-140, s & tw shared bathroom ¥150-180, d en suite ¥200; 🛜) China's (possibly) priciest hostel is housed within a modern apartment located 1.5km west of the old town. Neat Ikea-furnished bedrooms have been converted into dorms and private rooms. Bathrooms are clean and the English-speaking staff are friendly. The hostel is a ¥10 cab ride from the bus station and old town, and ¥15 from the train station.

Dàtóng

Dàtóng

Today Hotel
HOTEL $$

(今日商务酒店; Jīnrì Shāngwù Juǐdiàn; ☑537 9800; 1029 Weidu Dadao; 魏都大道1029号; d & tw ¥219; ❄ 🛜) This chain hotel located opposite the train station has large and spotless rooms with wooden-panelled flooring (no icky carpets), good bathrooms and is a great spot to decamp after you stumble out of the train station from an overnight journey. Get a room on the higher floor to escape the street noise.

★ Garden Hotel
HOTEL $$$

(花园大饭店; Huāyuán Dàfàndiàn; ☑586 5888; www.gardenhoteldatong.com; 59 Da Nanjie, 大南街59号; d & tw incl breakfast ¥1080-1380; ➰❄@🛜) The large impeccable rooms at this hotel feature goose-down quilts, carved rosewood bed frames, reproduction antique furnishings and superb bathrooms. It has an attractive atrium, Latin American and Chinese restaurants, plus excellent staff. The impressive breakfast spread includes good espresso coffee. Significant discounts (even in high season) knock prices as low as ¥310, making it one of the best-value hotels in China.

🍴 Eating

The Chinese restaurant at the Garden Hotel has a picture menu and serves excellent food. You'll also find plenty of restaurants and street stalls in the area near the Garden Hotel.

Dōngfāng Xiāo Miàn
NOODLES $

(East Wheat,; 东方削面; Yingze Jie; 迎泽街; noodles from ¥7; ⊙7am-10pm) Forgive the chainstore decor and bear the long queues and you'll soon be in noodle heaven. Steaming bowls of the humble Shānxī speciality is the star here; have it with pork, beef or lamb and pair it with a variety of side dishes such as sliced cucumbers. A beer will help top it all off.

If you're still hungry, you can grab charcoal-grilled lamb skewers (¥3) from the street stall just outside, come evening time.

Tónghé Dàfàndiàn
CHINESE $

(同和大饭店; Zhanqian Jie; dishes ¥16-40; ⊙11am-2pm & 6-9pm) This very popular, bright and cheery spot next to the Hongqi Hotel may look a little intimidating with its big round tables better suited to functions, but solo diners can also pull up a chair. There's a huge range of tasty, well-presented dishes on the picture menu, suiting all budgets.

Pick from a selection of dumplings, soups and vegie dishes, as well as the pricier fish and meat options.

🛈 Information

Agricultural Bank of China; ABC (中国农业银行; Zhōngguó Nóngyè Yínháng; Da Nanjie) ATM and money exchange.

Industrial and Commercial Bank of China; ICBC (工商银行; Gōngshāng Yínháng; Weidu Dadao)

China Post (中国邮政; Zhōngguó Yóuzhèng; Xinjian Beilu; ⊙8am-6.30pm)

Public Security Bureau (PSB; 公安局出入境接待处; Gōng'ānjú Chūrùjìng Jiēdàichù; ☑206 1833; 11 fl, Hualin Xintiandi, Weidu Dadao, 花林新天地, 11楼, 魏都大道; ⊙9am-noon & 3-5.30pm Mon-Fri)

🛈 Getting There & Away

AIR

Located 20km east of the city, Dàtóng's small airport has flights to Běijīng (¥450, one hour), Shànghǎi (¥1450, 2½ hours) and Guǎngzhōu (¥1650, 4½ hours). Buy tickets at www.ctrip.com or www.elong.net. No public transport goes to the airport. A taxi costs around ¥50.

BUS

Minibuses also run to some of the destinations listed below from outside the train station. Buses from the south bus station (新南站; xīnnán zhàn) located 9km from the train station:

Běijīng ¥128, four hours, hourly (7.10am to 4.10pm)

Mùtǎ ¥30, 1½ hours, hourly (7.30am to 7pm)

Tàiyuán ¥120, 3½ hours, every 20 minutes (6.50am to 7.30pm)

Wǔtái Shān ¥75, 3½ hours, two daily (8.30am, 9am and 2pm; summer only)

Buses from the **main bus station** (大同汽车站; dàtóng qìchēzhàn; ☑246 4464; Xinjian Nanlu):

Hanging Monastery ¥31, two hours, half-hourly (6.30am to 11am)

Hohhot ¥65, 3½ hours, hourly (7.20am to 4.20pm)

Jíníng (for **Déshèngbǎo**) ¥15, one hour, hourly (7.30am to 5.30pm)

TRAIN

Train departures from Dàtóng include the following:

Běijīng hard seat/sleeper ¥54/108, six hours, 11 daily

Hohhot hard seat ¥44, four hours, 16 daily

Píngyáo hard seat/sleeper ¥68/129, seven to eight hours, four daily

Tàiyuán hard seat/sleeper ¥46/101, six hours, seven daily

Xī'ān hard seat/sleeper ¥117/230, 16½ hours, one daily (4.40pm)

ℹ️ Getting Around

Bus routes are being readjusted owing to the massive construction all around town so expect changes. Buses 4 and 15 run from the train station to the main bus station. Bus 30 takes 30 minutes to run from the train station to the new south bus station. Buses 27 and 35 go to the old town from Weidu Dadao.

Taxi flagfall is ¥7.

Around Dàtóng

Yúngāng Caves

One of China's best examples of Buddhist cave art, the 5th-century **Yúngāng Caves** (Yúngāng Shíkū; ☑ 0352 302 6230; admission ¥150; ⊙ 8.30am-5.30pm summer) are impressive in scope. With 51,000 ancient statues, they put virtually everything else in the Shānxī shade. Carved by the Turkic-speaking Tuoba, the Yúngāng Caves drew their designs from Indian, Persian and even Greek influences that swept along the Silk Road. Work began in AD 460, continuing for 60 years before all 252 caves, the oldest collection of Buddhist carvings in China, had been completed.

Pass through the swanky visitors centre and a recreated temple before hitting the caves. At the time of writing, Caves 7 to 13 were shut for restoration. That still leaves 40 showcasing some of the most precious and elegant Buddhist artwork in China. Despite weathering, many of the statues at Yúngāng still retain their gorgeous pigment, unlike the slightly more recent statues at Lóngmén in Hénán. A number of the caves were once covered by wooden structures, but many of these are long gone, although Caves 5, 6, 7 and 8 are still fronted by wooden temples.

Some caves contain intricately carved square-shaped pagodas, while others depict the inside of temples, carved and painted to look as though made of wood. Frescoes are in abundance and there are graceful depictions of animals, birds and angels, some still brightly painted, and almost every cave contains the 1000-Buddha motif (tiny Buddhas seated in niches).

Eight of the caves contain enormous Buddha statues; the largest can be found in Cave 5, an outstanding 17m-high, seated effigy of Sakyamuni with a gilded face. The frescoes in this cave are badly scratched, but note the painted vaulted ceiling. Bursting with colour, Cave 6 is also stunning, resembling a set from an Indiana Jones epic with legions of Buddhist angels, Bodhisattvas and other figures. In the middle of the cave, a square block pagoda connects with the ceiling, with Buddhas on each side over two levels. Most foreign visitors are oblivious to the graffiti in bright red oil paint on the right-hand side of the main door frame within the cave, which reads 大同八中 (Dàtóng Bāzhōng; Datong No 8 Middle School), courtesy of pupils probably during the Cultural Revolution.

Caves 16 to 20 are the earliest caves at Yúngāng, carved under the supervision of monk Tanyao. Examine the exceptional quality of the carvings in Cave 18; some of the faces are perfectly presented. Cave 19 contains a vast 16.8m-high effigy of Sakyamuni. The Maitreya Buddha is a popular subject for Yúngāng's sculptors, for example in the vast seated forms in Cave 17 and Cave 13; the latter statue has been defaced with graffiti by workers from Hohhot and other miscreants.

Cave 20 is similar to the Losana Buddha Statue Cave (p420) at Lóngmén, originally depicting a trinity of Buddhas (the past, present and future Buddhas). The huge seated Buddha in the middle is the representative icon at Yúngāng, while the Buddha on the left has somehow vanished. Past the last set of caves is a new **museum** (⊙ 9.30am-4.50pm) detailing the Wei Kingdom.

Most of the caves come with good English captions, but there's also an audio guide in English (¥30 with ¥100 deposit). Note that photography is permitted in some caves but not in others.

To get here, take the 云冈 double decker bus (¥2, 45 minutes) from outside Dàtóng's train station to its terminus. Buses run every 10 to 15 minutes. A taxi from Dàtóng is ¥40 each way.

Great Wall 长城

The Great Wall (Chángchéng) is far less spectacular here than the restored sections found near Běijīng. Its Ming bricks – too useful for local farmers to leave alone – have all but disappeared, so just picture rammed earthen mounds, parts of which have crumbled away into nothing.

Déshèngbǎo   VILLAGE

(得胜堡) A good place to see some raw wall is little-visited Déshèngbǎo, a 16th-century walled fort almost on the border with Inner Mongolia that is now a small farming village. The fort's north and south gates are still standing, as are parts of its walls. Walk through the village (many of its houses are built out of Great Wall bricks) to the north gate and beyond it you'll see wild wall, 10m-high sections of it.

To get here, catch a minibus to Fēngzhèn (丰镇; ¥18, one hour) from beside Tónghé Dàfàndiàn opposite Dàtóng's train station. The bus will drop you at the turn-off for Déshèngbǎo, from where it's a 1km walk to the south gate. Heading back, return to the highway and flag down any Dàtóng-bound bus.

Hanging Monastery

Built precariously into the side of a cliff, the Buddhist **Hanging Monastery** (Xuánkōng Sì; admission ¥130; ⊙ 8am-7pm summer) is made all the more stunning by its long support stilts. The halls have been built along the contours of the cliff face, connected by rickety catwalks and narrow corridors, which can get very crowded in summer. It's a sight to behold, but we hear that the access up into the monastery itself might (understandably) eventually be closed owing to the large number of visitors. Get here soon.

Buses travel here from Dàtóng's main bus station (¥31, two hours). Most will transfer passengers to the monastery into a free taxi for the last 5km from Húnyuán (浑源). Heading back, you'll be stung for ¥20 for a taxi (per person) to Húnyuán. If you want to go on to Mùtǎ, there are frequent buses from Húnyuán (¥14, one hour), or shared taxis make the run from the monastery car park for ¥50 per person (when full).

Mùtǎ   木塔

Built in 1056, this impressive five-storey **tower** (admission ¥60; ⊙ 7.30am-7pm summer, 8am-5.30pm winter) is the world's oldest and tallest (67m) wooden pagoda. The clay Buddhist carvings it houses, including an 11m-high Sakyamuni on the 1st floor, are as old as the pagoda itself. Due to its fragile state, visitors can no longer climb the pagoda, but there are photos of the higher floors to the side of the pagoda.

Mùtǎ is located in unlovely Yìngxiàn (应县). Buses from Dàtóng's south bus station (¥30, two hours) run to its west bus station (西站; *xīzhàn*). From there, get public bus 1 (¥1) to Mùtǎ 2km up the road. Hourly buses return to Dàtóng until 6pm, or you can travel onto Tàiyuán (¥85, 3½ hours, last bus 2.30pm).

Wǔtái Shān   五台山

♪ 0350

The mountainous, monastic enclave of Wǔtái Shān (Five Terrace Mountains) is Buddhism's sacred northern range and the earthly abode of Manjusri (文殊; Wénshū), the Bodhisattva of Wisdom. Chinese students sitting the ferociously competitive *gāokǎo* (university entrance) exams troop here for a nod from the learned Bodhisattva, proffering incense alongside saffron-robed monks and octogenarian pilgrims.

While a powerful sense of the divine holds sway in Wǔtái Shān, some of the spiritual power is lost beneath the flashing LED lights hung from identikit buildings all selling the same spiritual trinkets. If you can look beyond that, the port-walled monasteries – the principal sources of spiritual power – are able to find further amplification in the sublime mountain scenery.

The forested slopes overlooking the town eventually give way to alpine meadows where you'll find more temples and great hiking possibilities. Wǔtái Shān is also famed for its mysterious rainbows, which can appear without rain and are said to contain shimmering mirages of Buddhist beings, creatures and temple halls.

There's a steep ¥218 entrance fee for the area – including a mandatory ¥50 'sightseeing bus' ticket (旅游观光车票; *lǚyóu guānguāng chēpiào*) for transport within the area, which is valid for three days. Some of the more popular temples charge an additional small entrance fee. Coming in, the bus will stop at a large visitors centre where you buy tickets and reboard after your tickets are checked. From the main bus station in Wǔtái Shān, you can jump on a free bus shuttle along the main road to get to different points. Note that your bus coming in might drop you behind the main town area from where you'll need to walk to the main drag.

Avoid Wǔtái Shān during the holiday periods and high-season weekends; temperatures

Wǔtái Shān

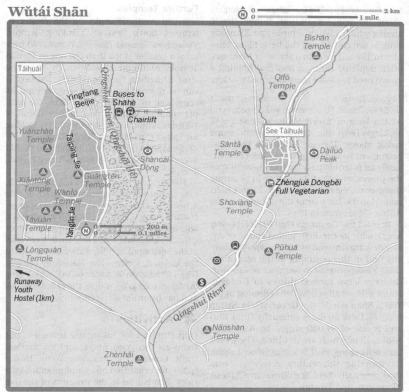

Táihuái

Yingfang Beijie

Buses to Shàhè

Chairlift

Yuánzhào Temple

Taiping Jie

Shàncái Dòng

Xiāntōng Temple

Guāngrén Temple

Wànfó Temple

Tǎyuàn Temple

Fangling Jie

Lóngquán Temple

Runaway Youth Hostel (1km)

Qingshui River (Qingshui He)

Qingshui River

Bǐshān Temple

Qīfó Temple

See Táihuái

Sāntǎ Temple

Dàiluó Peak

Zhèngjué Dōngběi Full Vegetarian

Shūxiàng Temple

Pǔhuà Temple

Nánshān Temple

Zhènhǎi Temple

are often below zero from October to March and roads can be impassable.

History

It's believed that by the 6th century there were already 200 temples in the area, although all but two were destroyed during the official persecution of Buddhism in the 9th century. During the Ming dynasty, Wǔtái Shān began attracting large numbers of Tibetan Buddhists (principally from Mongolia) for whom Manjusri holds special significance.

Climate

Wǔtái Shān is at high altitude and powerful blizzards can sweep in as late as May and as early as September. Winters are freezing with snowfall; the summer months are the most pleasant, but always pack a jacket, as well as suitable shoes or boots for rain, as temperatures fall at night. If you are climb-

ing up the peaks to see the sunrise, warm coats can be hired.

◉ Sights

Enclosed within a lush valley between the five main peaks is an elongated, unashamedly touristy town, called **Táihuái** (台怀) but which everyone simply calls Wǔtái Shān. It's here that you'll find the largest concentration of temples, as well as all the area's hotels and tourist facilities. The five main peaks are north (北台顶; *běitái dǐng*), east (东台顶; *dōngtái dǐng*), south (南台顶; *nántái dǐng*), west (西台顶; *xītái dǐng*) and central (中台顶; *zhōngtái dǐng*).

Táihuái Temple Cluster

More than 50 temples lie scattered in town and across the surrounding countryside, so knowing where to start can be a daunting prospect. Most travellers limit themselves to what is called the **Táihuái Temple**

Cluster (台怀寺庙群; Táihuái Sìmiàoqún), about 20 temples around Táihuái itself, among which Tǎyuàn Temple and Xiǎntōng Temple are considered the best. Many temples in Táihuái contain a statue of Manjusri, often depicted riding a lion and holding a sword used to cleave ignorance and illusion.

Tǎyuàn Temple
BUDDHIST TEMPLE

(塔院寺; Tǎyuàn Sì; admission ¥10; ⊙6am-6pm) At the base of **Spirit Vulture Peak** (灵鹫峰; Língjiù Fēng), the distinctive white stupa rising above, Tǎyuàn Temple is the most prominent landmark in Wǔtái Shān and virtually all pilgrims pass through here to spin the prayer wheels at its base or to prostrate themselves, even in the snow. Even Chairman Mao did his tour of duty, staying in the **Abbot Courtyard** in 1948.

Beyond the **Devaraja Hall** (Hall of Heavenly Kings), with its candlelit gilded statue of Avalokitesvara (instead of Milefo, who you usually find in this position), at the rear of the **Dàcí Yánshòu Hall** is an altar where worshippers leave canned drinks to Guanyin. Hung with small yellow bells chiming in the Wǔtái Shān winds, the **Great White Stupa** (大白塔; Dàbái Tǎ) dates originally from 1301 and is one of 84,000 stupas built by King Asoka, 19 of which are in China. The **Great Sutra-Keeping Hall** is a magnificent sight; its towering 9th-century revolving Sutra case originally held scriptures in Chinese, Mongolian and Tibetan.

Xiǎntōng Temple
BUDDHIST TEMPLE

(显通寺; Xiǎntōng Sì; ⊙6am-6pm) FREE Xiǎntōng Temple – the largest temple in town – was erected in AD 68 and was the first Buddhist temple in the area. It comprises more than 100 halls and rooms. The **Qiānbō Wénshū Hall** contains a 1000-armed, multifaced Wenshu, whose every palm supports a miniature Buddha. The squat brick **Beamless Hall** (无梁殿; Wúliáng Diàn) holds a miniature Yuan-dynasty pagoda, remarkable statues of contemplative monks meditating in the alcoves and a vast seated effigy of Wenshu.

Further on, up some steps is the blindingly beautiful **Golden Hall**, enveloped in a constellation of small Buddhas covering all the walls. Five metres high and weighing 50 tonnes, the metal hall was cast in 1606 before being gilded; it houses an effigy of Wenshu seated atop a lion.

Further Temples

You can continue exploring the cluster of temples north beyond Xiǎntōng Temple. **Yuánzhào Temple** (圆照寺; Yuánzhào Sì) contains a smaller stupa than the one at Tǎyuàn Temple. A 10-minute walk south down the road, **Shūxiàng Temple** (殊像寺; Shūxiàng Sì) can be reached up a steep slope beyond its spirit wall by the side of the road; the temple contains Wǔtái Shān's largest statue of Wenshu riding a lion. Before you go looking for Father Christmas at **Sāntǎ Temple** (三塔寺; Sāntǎ Sì) to the west of Táihuái, you should know the name actually means Three Pagoda Temple.

For great views of the town, you can trek, take a **chairlift** (one-way/return ¥50/85) or ride a horse (¥50 one-way) up to the temple on **Dàiluó Peak** (黛螺顶; Dàiluó Dǐng; admission ¥8), on the eastern side of Qīngshuǐ River (清水河; Qīngshuǐ Hé). For even better views of the surrounding hills, walk 2.5km south to the isolated, fortress-like **Nánshān Temple** (南山寺; Nánshān Sì; admission Y4), which sees far fewer tour groups than the other temples and has beautiful stone carvings.

🏃 Activities

Opportunities for hiking are immense, but there are no good maps, and no marked trails. Contact the Runaway Youth Hostel (p354) for organised hikes and moutain-bike rides. Roads lead to the summits of the five main peaks, so you could take a taxi up to one of them before hiking back into town using the road as a bearing. You can find minibuses at the big car park by the chairlift to Dàiluó Peak, which run to all five peaks for ¥350 (7.30am departure, return 5pm).

🛏 Sleeping

While the place is incredibly touristy, accommodation is fairly basic with most hostels identical in terms of pricing and standard. Touts can lead you to family-run hotels with decent rooms from ¥100. Find one that's close to the main road so you can easily get out to the temples.

★ **Runaway Youth Hostel**
HOSTEL $

(五台山Runaway国际青年旅舍; Runaway Guójì Qīngnián Lǚshè; %186 3604 2689, 654 9505; 648984355@qq.com; dm ¥50, d & tw ¥128-148; hclosed Oct-Apr; iW) The Húběi owner Zhou Jin is a passionate traveller who set up this hostel with his local wife in a quiet southwestern section of the mountain.

Enter via a cosy lounge area (equipped with an Xbox) that leads up to clean hotel-standard private rooms and rooftop bunk rooms, all en suite. Ask about organised hikes and mountain-bike rides, several to the peaks.

Call or email for latest directions. At the time of research, you had to take internal shuttle 4 from Zhēnhǎi Temple (镇海寺, Zhènhǎi Sì) to the terminal station (西线换乘区, Xīxiàn Huànchéng Qū). From here walk up the hill 100m and look for a YHA sign. The hostel is on the left.

Zhèngjué Dōngběi Full Vegetarian HOTEL $
(正觉东北全素斋; Zhèngjué Dōngběi Quán Sùzhāi; ☏ 875 3229; d & tw ¥160; ❉ 🛜) The owners of this vegetarian restaurant also run a tight set of rooms on the 2nd floor of the rear compound. Expect clean red-carpeted rooms, immaculate bathrooms, decent mountain views and extremely good food (dishes from ¥50) at the restaurant.

✕ Eating

Loads of small family-run restaurants are tucked away behind hotels and down small alleys off the main strip in Táihuái. *Táimó* (台蘑), the much-revered Wǔtái Shān mushroom, is the local treat and you will be steered towards it. Try *táimódùn jīkuài* (台蘑炖鸡块; *táimó* stewed chicken) or *táimódùn tǔ jī* (台蘑炖土鸡; *táimó* stewed wild chicken). Also look out for *táimódùn dòufu* (台蘑炖豆腐; *táimó* stewed tofu). Bear in mind, though, that *táimó* dishes are pricey (from ¥200!), and that there are plenty of other options available. Simple dishes such as noodles start at ¥15 and meat dishes from ¥40.

ⓘ Information

ATMs are found in the visitors centre and along the town's main road. You can pick up an OK tourist map (¥5) from many shops.
China Post (中国邮政; Zhōngguó Yóuzhèng; ⊙8am-7pm)

ⓘ Getting There & Away

BUS
Buses from Wǔtái Shān bus station (汽车站; qìchē zhàn; ☏ 654 3101):
Běijīng ¥145, five hours, 9am and 2pm
Dàtóng ¥75, four hours, three daily (8.30am, 1pm and 2pm, summer only)
Hanging Monastery ¥65, three hours, one daily (8.30am)

Tàiyuán ¥74, five hours, hourly (6.30am to 4pm)
Buses to Shāhé (¥25, 1½ hours, hourly, 8am to 5pm) leave from the car park by the chair lift to Dàiluó Peak.

TRAIN
The station known as Wǔtái Shān is actually 50km away in the town of Shāhé (砂河) from where you can get a minibus taxi the rest of the way from around ¥70. An example route and fare from Běijīng is: seat ¥50, six to seven hours, two daily.

Tàiyuán   太原
☏ 0351 / POP 4.2 MILLION
Most travellers pass through Shānxī's capital en route to Píngyáo, but the city has enough to keep you occupied for a day with its excellent museum and a few atmospheric temples.

⊙ Sights

Shānxī Museum MUSEUM
(山西博物馆; Shānxī Bówùguǎn; ☏ 878 9555; Binhe Xilu Zhongduan; ⊙9am-5pm Tue-Sun, last entry 4pm) FREE This top-class museum has three floors that walk you through all aspects of Shānxī culture, from prehistoric fossils to detailed local opera and architecture exhibits. All galleries are imaginatively displayed and some contain good English captions. Take bus 6 (¥1) from the train station, get off at Yìfén Qiaoxi (漪汾桥西) bus stop across the river and look for the inverted pyramid.

A new geology museum (shaped like a UFO) was being built next door at the time of research.

Twin Pagoda Temple/
Yǒngzuò Temple BUDDHIST TEMPLE
(双塔寺/永祚寺; Shuāngtǎ Sì/Yǒngzuò Sì; admission ¥30; ⊙8.30am-5.30pm) This gorgeous pair of namesake twin pagodas rises up south of the Nansha River in Tàiyuán's southeast. Not much of the temple itself is left but the area is well tended with shrubs and greenery; with the wind in their tinkling bells, the highlight brick pagodas are lovely. The 13-storey **Xuānwén Pagoda** (宣文塔; Xuānwén Tǎ) dates from the reign of Ming emperor Wanli and can be climbed.

The adjacent pagoda dates from the same period but cannot be climbed. Take bus 820 or 812 from the train station.

Tàiyuán

Tàiyuán

Chóngshàn Temple　　　BUDDHIST TEMPLE
(崇善寺; Chóngshàn Sì; Dilianggong Jie; admission ¥2; ☉8am-4.30pm) The double-eaved wooden hall in this Ming temple contains three magnificent statues: Samantabhadra (the Bodhisattva of Truth), Guanyin (the Goddess of Mercy with 1000 arms) and Manjusri (the Bodhisattva of Wisdom with 1000 alms bowls). The entrance is down an alley off Dilianggong Jie behind the **Confucius Temple** (文庙; Wén Miào; 3 Wenmiao Xiang; admission ¥30; ☉9am-5pm Tue-Sun), which still has its spirit wall standing guard, as well as a folk art museum.

🛏 Sleeping

There are guesthouses offering rooms from ¥50 on Yingze Nanjie. Touts will find you near the train station with offers of cheapies.

Tàiyuán Wànmíng Hotel　　　HOTEL $
(太原万明宾馆; Tàiyuán Wànmíng Bīnguǎn; ☑494 8888; 23 Wuyi Dongjie; 五一东街23号; tw ¥158-198; ⌘@) A blast from the past with its old-school *fúwùyuán* (attendants) on each floor, the rooms here are battered and noisy, but clean. There's a decent internet connection and an attached restaurant, while the location is fine for the train and main bus stations. Discounts of 10% available.

World Trade Hotel　　　HOTEL $$$
(山西国贸大饭店; Shānxī Guómào Dàfàndiàn; ☑868 8888; www.sxwtc.com; 69 Fuxi Jie; 府西街69号; d ¥1258-1578, ste ¥2478; ⊖⌘@🔓🛜⌘) Its marbled lobby a vast atrium-lit space slung between its two towers (named after and resembling New York's former World Trade Center), this dapper, efficient five-star hotel has the finest rooms and facilities in town, including a gym and spa. You need to pay extra for a view not looking straight into the neighbouring tower. Discounts of 25% available.

✕ Eating

Shānxī is famed for its noodles – including *dāoxiāo miàn* (刀削面; knife-pared noodles) and *lāmiàn* (拉面; hand-pulled noodles) – and vinegar, both in abundance in Tàiyuán. *Yángròu tāng* (羊肉汤; mutton soup) is lapped up by locals for breakfast.

Food Street

CHINESE $

(食品街; Shipin Jie; meals from ¥7; ⊙11am-2am) Head to this street lined with all manner of restaurants and outdoor *shāokǎo* (barbecue) places. You can get noodles here, of course, but also hotpot, dumplings and fried dishes. It gets lively late in the evening, when it's a good place for a beer and a bit of a chat with the locals. The street runs north off Zhonglou Jie; look for the Qing-era arch and go through it.

Tàiyuán Noodle House

NOODLES $

(太原面食店; Tàiyuán Miànshí Diàn; 5 Jiefang Lu; noodles ¥6-15; ⊙11am-9.30pm) Bustling locals' joint popular for Shānxī's famous vinegar/noodle combo. Classic forms (named after their shape, not ingredients) include *māo'ěrduo* (猫耳朵; cat's ears; ¥10) and *cuōyú* (搓鱼; rolled fish; ¥10). Garnishes include *ròuzhàjiàng* (肉炸酱; pork) and *yángròu* (羊肉; mutton). It also does *shāomài* (烧麦; ¥12). No English menu, but there are pictures.

SPAR Supermarket

SUPERMARKET $

(美特好; Měitèhǎo; Yingze Dajie; ⊙7.30am-10pm) Self-caterers can find most anything at this two-level supermarket opposite the train station.

★ Shānxī Huìguǎn

DONGBEI $$$

(山西会馆; 7 Tiyu Lu; 体育路北口7号; dishes ¥18-368; ⊙11am-9.30pm) Behind the imposing grey exterior is a refined restaurant serving quality northern Chinese cuisine. There's everything from hotpot to homemade tofu and of course, noodles, served by eager staff.

If you're lucky, you might be able to catch a noodle-making demonstration at dinner time. The picture menu has fairly accurate English translations. A taxi from the train station here costs ¥11.

ⓘ Information

Agricultural Bank of China (ABC; 中国农业银行; Zhōngguó Nóngyè Yínháng; Yingze Nanjie) ATM next to the Jǐnlín Oriental Hotel.

China Post (中国邮政; Zhōngguó Yóuzhèng; Yingze Dajie; ⊙8am-7pm) Opposite the train station.

Industrial & Commercial Bank of China (ICBC; 工商银行; Gōngshāng Yínháng; Yingze Dajie) ATM.

Public Security Bureau (PSB, 公安局, Gōng'ānjú; ☑895 5355; Wuyi Dongjie; ⊙8.30am-5.30pm Mon-Fri) Can extend visas.

ⓘ Getting There & Away

AIR

Shuttle buses to the airport (¥15, 40 minutes, hourly from 6am to 8.30pm) run from the side of the Sanjin International Hotel on Wuyi Guangchang. The airport is 15km southeast of downtown Tàiyuán; a taxi costs around ¥50.

Destinations include Běijīng (¥550), Hángzhōu (¥700), Hong Kong (¥1400), Kūnmíng (¥1440), Nánjīng (¥700), Shànghǎi (¥800) and Shēnzhèn (¥1190).

BUS

Tàiyuán's long-distance bus station (长途汽车站; *chángtú qìchēzhàn*) is 500m south of the

---

DON'T MISS

QIAO FAMILY COURTYARD

This 18th-century complex of courtyards at the Qiao Family Courtyard (乔家大院; Qiáojiā Dàyuàn; admission ¥72; ⊙8am-7pm) is one of the finest remaining examples of a traditional private residence in northern China. Once home to a celebrated merchant, it's an austere maze of doorways and courtyards that lead onto seemingly endless rooms (there are over 300 of them).

The complex is famous in China for being where Zhang Yimou's lush fifth-generation tragedy *Raise the Red Lantern* was filmed. Appropriately, there are red lanterns hanging everywhere, but there are also many fascinating exhibits of Qing-era furniture and clothes, as well as Shānxī opera costumes and props. Recently installed English signage helps understand Northern Chinese traditions and rites better.

The site is extremely popular with domestic tour groups so get here as early as you can. While the entrance is glossed up, and souvenir and food stalls surround the compound, the residence is still big enough to escape the crowds; you can step through one of the many doorways and they magically disperse.

To get here, catch any bus going to Qíxiàn (祁县; ¥23, 1½ hours) from Tàiyuán's Jiànnán bus station. Tell the driver where you're headed and they'll drop you at the main gate. You can also visit from Píngyáo (¥26, 45 minutes, every 30 minutes).

train station on Yingze Dajie. Buses travel to the following destinations:

Běijīng ¥146, seven hours, three daily (8.30am, 10.30am and 2.30pm)

Dàtóng ¥117, 3½ hours, every 20 minutes (7am to 7pm)

Shànghǎi ¥409, 17 hours, one daily (2.30pm)

Shíjiāzhuāng ¥65, 3½ hours, two daily (10.30am and 2.30pm)

Xī'ān ¥180, eight hours, five daily (8am to 6pm)

Zhèngzhōu ¥156, seven hours, five daily (7am to 5pm)

Buses from the Jiànnán bus station (建南站; Jiànnán zhàn), 3km south of the train station:

Jièxiū ¥42, two hours, half-hourly (7.40am to 6.40pm)

Jìnchéng ¥114, five hours, every 40 minutes (7am to 7pm)

Píngyáo ¥26, two hours, half-hourly (7.30am to 7.30pm)

Qíxiàn ¥23, two hours, half-hourly (7.30am to 7.30pm)

The east bus station (东客站; dōng kèzhàn) has buses to Wǔtái Shān ¥73, four to five hours, hourly, 6.40am to 6.30pm.

The west bus station (客运西站; kèyùn xīzhàn) has the following services:

Líshí ¥70, two hours, frequent (7am to 7.30pm)

Qìkǒu ¥79, four hours, one daily (10.30am)

TRAIN

At the time of writing, the area in front of the train station was undergoing massive renovations. Roads and bus routes might change. Sample routes from Tàiyuán Train Station (火车站; huǒchē zhàn):

Běijīng West G train ¥223, three hours, regular

Běijīng normal train seat/sleeper ¥80/150, eight to 12 hours, five daily

Dàtóng hard seat/sleeper ¥46/100, five to seven hours, eight daily

Jìnchéng hard seat/sleeper ¥48/108, seven hours, four daily

Píngyáo ¥18, 1½ hours, frequent

Wǔtái Shān ¥36, five hours, three daily

Xī'ān hard seat/sleeper ¥105/196, nine to 11 hours, nine daily

High-speed trains depart from the new **Tàiyuán South Train Station** (火车南站; Huǒchē Nán-zhàn), 8km south of the old train station in the Běiyíng (北营) district. The best way to get here is via taxi (¥20, 25 minutes) or bus 861 from the old station.

Běijīng West D/G train ¥145/270, 3½/three hours, 16 daily

Xī'ān North D train ¥155, 3½ hours, eight daily

Zhèngzhōu East G train ¥280, four hours, 10.35am

ⓘ Getting Around

Bus 1 (¥1) runs the length of Yingze Dajie. For the Jiànnán bus station and the west bus station, take bus 23 or 611 (¥1.50) from Yingze Dajie. For the east bus station take any bus (¥1.50) heading east from Wulongkou Jie. A taxi to Jiànnán bus station costs ¥13.

Taxi flagfall is ¥8.

Píngyáo   平遥

🕿 0354 / POP 502,000

Píngyáo is China's best-preserved ancient walled town and worth a visit if you're spending any time in Shānxī. Anyone with any China mileage under their belt will appreciate the town's age-old charms; charms squandered away – or forever lost – elsewhere across the Middle Kingdom. While other ancient 'ancient' cities in China will rustle together an unconvincing display of old city walls, sporadic temples or the occasional ragged alley thrust beneath an unsightly melange of white-tile architecture and greying apartment blocks, Píngyáo has managed to keep its beguiling narrative largely intact: red-lantern–hung lanes set against night-time silhouettes of imposing town walls, elegant courtyard architecture, ancient towers poking into the north China sky, and an entire brood of creaking temples and old buildings.

Píngyáo is also a living and breathing community where the 30,000-odd locals who reside in the old town hang laundry in courtyards, career down alleyways on bicycles, sun themselves in doorways or chew the fat with neighbours. Sadly, Píngyáo struggles to keep out much of the coal dust that pervades the province. Additionally, cars now throng everywhere apart from the pedestrian-only centre (radiating roughly one block out from Nan, Dong and Xi Dajie), destroying much of the old-world charm. Still, if you've been doing some hard travelling in the hinterlands, it's a great place to catch your breath and kick back for a few days, while Píngyáo is also a fine base for day trips to the Wang Family Courtyard and Zhāngbì Cūn and its 1400-year-old underground castle.

History

Already a thriving merchant town during the Ming dynasty, Píngyáo's ascendancy came in the Qing era when merchants created the country's first banks and cheques to facilitate the transfer of silver from one place to another. The city escaped the shocking reshaping much loved by communist town planners, and almost 4000 Ming- and Qing-dynasty residences remain within the city walls.

Sights & Activities

Bounded by an intact city wall, gates access the old town at various points in the east, west, north and south. The main drag is Nan Dajie (南大街), where you'll find guesthouses, restaurants, museums, temples and souvenir shops galore. If you have even the remotest interest in Chinese history, culture or architecture, you could easily spend a couple of days wandering the pinched lanes of Píngyáo, stumbling across hidden gems while ticking off all the well-known sights. It's free to walk the streets, but you must pay ¥150 to climb the city walls or enter any of the 18 buildings deemed historically significant. Tickets are valid for three days and can be purchased from near the gate openings. Opening hours for the sights are 8am to 7pm in summer and 8am to 6pm in winter.

City Walls
HISTORIC SITE

A good place to start your Píngyáo experience is the magnificent **city walls** (城墙; *chéng qiáng*), which date from 1370. At 10m high and more than 6km in circumference, they are punctuated by 72 watchtowers, each containing a paragraph from Sunzi's *The Art of War*.

Part of the southern wall, which collapsed in 2004, has been rebuilt, but the rest is original. Píngyáo's **city gates** (城门; chéngmén) are fascinating and are some of the best preserved in China; the **Lower West Gate** (Fèngyí Mén; Phoenix Appearing Gate) has a section of the original road, deeply grooved with the troughs left by cartwheels (also visible at the South Gate).

Rìshēngchāng Financial House Museum
MUSEUM

(日升昌; Rìshēngchāng; 38 Xi Dajie; 西大街38号; ⊙8am-7pm) Not to be missed, this museum began life as a humble dye shop in the late 18th century before its tremendous success as a business saw it transform into China's first draft bank (1823), eventually expanding to 57 branches nationwide. The museum has nearly 100 rooms, including offices, living quarters and a kitchen, as well as several old cheques.

Xiétóngqìng Draft Bank
MUSEUM

(协同庆票号, Xiétóngqìng Piàohào; Nan Dajie, 南大街; ⊙8am-7pm) First established in 1856,

this former bank had underground vaults protected by live-in guards. After checking out the courtyard displays, descend into the cool (literally) vaults and explore the cave-like rooms filled with stacks of faux gold and silver ingots.

Confucius Temple
CONFUCIAN TEMPLE

(文庙; Wén Miào; ⊙8am-7pm) Píngyáo's oldest surviving building is **Dàchéng Hall** (大成殿; Dàchéng Diàn), dating from 1163 and found in the Confucius Temple, a huge complex where bureaucrats-to-be came to take the imperial exams.

City Tower
TOWER

(市楼; Shì Lóu; Nan Dajie; ⊙8am-7pm) Snap a photo before passing under the tallest building in the old town en route to other sites. Sadly, you can no longer climb its stone steps for city views.

Qīngxū Guàn
TAOIST TEMPLE

(清虚观; Dong Dajie; ⊙8am-7pm) Shānxī dust has penetrated every crevice of the 10 halls that make up this impressive Taoist temple. But that only adds to its ancient aura; it dates back to the Tang dynasty.

Slogans
HISTORIC SITE

(153 Xi Dajie; ⊙8am-7pm) Pop into 153 Xi Dajie for two red-blooded slogans from the Cultural Revolution that have survived on buildings within the courtyard. The one on the left intones: 工业学大庆 ('Industry should learn from Dàqìng'); the rarer slogan on the right proclaims: 认真搞好斗批改 ('Earnestly undertake struggle, criticism and reform').

Nine Dragon Screen
MONUMENT

(九龙壁; Jiǔlóng Bì; Chenghuangmiao Jie) The old Píngyáo Theatre (大戏堂; Dàxìtáng) has now been converted into a hotel's banquet hall but is fronted by this magnificent stone wall.

Catholic Church
CHURCH

(天主堂; Tiānzhǔ Táng; 2 Anjia Jie) With a snow-white statue of the Virgin Mary outside, this historic, if dilapidated, church is the focal point for Píngyáo's Catholics.

Tours

Mr Deng, who runs the Harmony Guesthouse, gives reader-recommended day-long tours of the city for ¥150. He's a great source of local knowledge and can also point you towards some little-visited sites outside the town.

Píngyáo

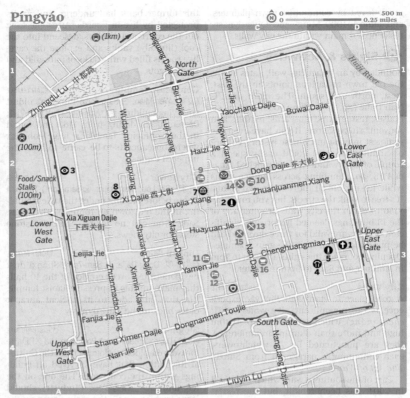

SHĀNXĪ PÍNGYÁO

🛏 Sleeping

Most of the old-town hotels are conversions of old courtyard homes, and finding a bed for the night is not hard. Píngyáo courtyards differ from their squarer Běijīng equivalents; courtyards in Píngyáo are 目字形, meaning 'shaped like the character 目', and are more rectangular in shape. Píngyáo hoteliers are increasingly tuned in to the needs of Western travellers, which means some English is spoken and they can make a passable Western breakfast. Most hotels and hostels will do pick-ups from the train or bus stations.

Upon arrival, touts will direct you to rooms with air-con, private bathrooms and wi-fi from ¥80. If you do take up this option, make sure your guesthouse isn't too far from the central section and don't be afraid to turn down the room. Píngyáo's hostels are surprisingly underwhelming considering the city's stature and popularity.

Zhèngjiā Kèzhàn COURTYARD HOTEL **$**
(郑家客栈; ☏ 568 4466; 68 Yamen Jie; 衙门街68号; dm ¥35-50, s ¥80, d from ¥140; ❀ @ 🛜) With two locations virtually next door to each other, head to the one closest to the Listen to the Rain Pavilion for decent doubles with *kàng* beds set around a very pleasant courtyard. The cramped but fresh and clean dorms are under the eaves at the neighbouring courtyard (which also has doubles) but the tiny bathrooms are dark.

There's a good communal area and it sees more Chinese travellers than the other guesthouses, making it a good place to meet the locals.

Yámén Youth Hostel HOSTEL **$**
(衙门官舍青年旅社; Yámén Guānshè Qīngnián Lǚshè; ☏ 568 3539; 69 Yamen Jie; 衙门街69号; dm ¥30-45, s ¥90, d from ¥140; ❀ @ 🛜) Set around a series of courtyards, rooms are larger than many in Píngyáo but rather done in; the bathrooms could do with an upgrade. Dorms

Píngyáo

under the eaves are clean, with OK showers and toilets downstairs. The staff are obliging and all the usual hostel favourites are here: DVD room, ticketing, laundry, free internet, wi-fi, bike hire, pool table and pick-up.

Déjūyuán Guesthouse   COURTYARD HOTEL $$
(德居源客栈, Déjūyuán Kèzhàn; ☎568 5266; www.pydjy.net; 43 Xi Dajie; 西大街43号; s ¥150, d & tw ¥280-488, ste ¥1480; ✳@☎) Very well-maintained rooms are set around two of the oldest courtyards in Píngyáo (400 years old) at this efficient and friendly place. The cheapest rooms are excellent value, while the suites are luxurious and come with tip-top bathrooms. Its restaurant is a fine place to try high-quality local dishes at reasonable prices. Staff can arrange train tickets and tours as well.

★ Jing's Residence   COURTYARD HOTEL $$$
(锦宅, Jǐn Zhái; ☎584 1000; www.jingsresidence.com; 16 Dong Dajie, 东大街16号; r ¥1500-3200; ✳@☎) With the super-hushed atmosphere that's unique to the most exclusive (and expensive) hotels, Jing's is a soothing blend of old Píngyáo and modern flair that's squarely aimed at upmarket Western travellers. At 260

years old the former home of a Qing-dynasty silk merchant is sleek and well finished with polished service from the English-speaking staff.

The themed courtyards are all picture-perfect, rooms are elegant and stylish (the vast upstairs suites have views over Píngyáo's rooftops), while the upstairs bar must be the most sophisticated in all of Shānxī. Its restaurant serves high-priced Western fusion cuisine. There are only 19 rooms here and it's essential to book ahead.

✕ Eating & Drinking

Most guesthouses can rustle up (Western or Chinese) breakfast, lunch and dinner. Píngyáo's lanes are stuffed with *xiǎochī guǎn* (小吃馆; hole-in-the-wall restaurants), almost all offering the same dishes at similar prices. For something cheaper and less touristy, head to Xia Xiguan Jie (下西关街) just outside the Lower West Gate, where food stalls offer different varieties of noodles from ¥5 and up, as well *ròujiāmó* (肉夹馍; fried pork or beef with green peppers in bread) and meat and vegie skewers.

Píngyáo doesn't have many worthwhile bars, but courtyard hotels provide virtually all you need: bottles of chilled beer and a gorgeous courtyard to sit in to watch the night sky.

Déjūyuán   SHANXI $
(Petit Resto; 德居源; 82 Nan Dajie; mains from ¥25; ⊙8.30am-10pm) Traveller friendly, but no worse for that, this welcoming and popular little restaurant has a simple and tasty menu (in English) of northern Chinese dishes, such as dumplings (¥15), as well as all the local faves. Try the famed Píngyáo beef (¥42) or the mountain noodles (¥12). Cold dishes start at ¥8.

★ Tiānyuánkuí Guesthouse   SHANXI $$
(天元奎客栈; Tiānyuánkuí Kèzhàn; ☎568 0069; 73 Nan Dajie; 南大街73号; dishes ¥10-68; ⊙8.30am-10pm; ☎) With warm wooden furnishing, friendly staff and free wi-fi, this restaurant has an easygoing vibe that invites travellers to linger over their meals. The English iPad menu has photos of the dishes – a range of traditional favourites such as Píngyáo beef sit next to the usual meat, veg and tofu offerings – making ordering a snap.

There are also comfortable rooms (from ¥400) in the rear courtyard compound.

Sakura Cafe
CAFE $$

(櫻花屋西餐酒吧; Yīnghuāwū Xīcān Jiǔbā; 6 Dong Dajie; dishes from ¥35, beers from ¥15; ⊙9.30am-midnight; 🛜) This dark and moody cafe-bar attracts both locals and foreigners with its daily food and drink specials. It does decent if pricey pizzas (from ¥55), burgers, as well as breakfast, coffee, beers and cocktails. There's another equally popular branch at 86 Nan Dajie.

Coffee by Shrew
CAFE

(池池咖啡管; Chíchí Kāfēiguǎn; 9 Chenghuang-miao Jie; coffee from ¥23, cakes ¥28, alcoholic drinks from ¥35; ⊙11am-9pm; 🛜) Behind its green doors is a cute-as-pie cafe serving Píngyáo's best espresso, lattes and single-origin brews in a warm setting lined with bookshelves and cosy seats. Come nighttime, swap caffeine for simple cocktails and start up a conversation with the Fujianese owner Shrew.

🛍 Shopping

Part of Píngyáo's charms lie in its peeling and weatherbeaten shopfronts, yet to be mercilessly restored. Nan Dajie is stuffed with wood-panelled shops selling Píngyáo snacks, knick-knacks, faux Cultural Revolution memorabilia, jade, shoes and slippers, and loads more. Look out for red and black Shānxī paper cuts, which make excellent presents.

ℹ Information

All guesthouses and hostels have internet and wi-fi access.

China Post (中国邮政; Zhōngguó Yóuzhèng; Xi Dajie; ⊙8am-6pm)

Industrial & Commercial Bank of China (ICBC; 工商银行; Gōngshāng Yínháng; Xia Xiguan Dajie) ATM

Public Security Bureau (PSB; 公安局; Gōng'ānjú; ☑563 5010; off Yamen Jie; ⊙8am-noon & 3-6pm Mon-Fri)

ℹ Getting There & Away

BUS

Píngyáo's **bus station** (汽车新站 | qìchēxīn-zhàn; ☑569 0011) has buses to Tàiyuán (¥26, two hours, frequent, 6.30am to 7.40pm), Líshí (¥44, two hours, 8.30am and 12.30pm), Cháng-zhì (¥79, three hours, 7.50am and 1.40pm) and the Qiao Family Courtyard (¥26, 45 minutes, half hourly).

TRAIN

Tickets for trains (especially to Xī'ān) are tough to get in summer, so book ahead. Your hotel/ hostel should be able to help. Trains depart for the following destinations:

Běijīng D train ¥161, 4½ hours, two daily

Dàtóng hard seat/sleeper ¥62/123, seven to eight hours, four daily

Tàiyuán ¥18, 1½ hours, frequent

Xī'ān D train ¥136, three hours, four daily

ℹ Getting Around

Píngyáo can be easily navigated on foot or bicycle (¥10 per day). Bike rental is available all over; most guesthouses offer it and there are many spots along Nan Dajie and Xi Dajie. Rickshaws run to the train and bus stations for ¥10.

Around Píngyáo

Most hostels and guesthouses will arrange transport to the surrounding sights. Day tours to the Wang Family Courtyard and Zhāngbì Underground Castle are ¥80 per person (excluding the admission price or food) and depart at 8.30pm, returning late afternoon. You can also hire a private car for ¥350 per day.

Shuānglín Temple
BUDDHIST TEMPLE

(双林寺; Shuānglín Sì; admission ¥40; ⊙8.30am-6.30pm) Within easy reach of Píngyáo, this Buddhist temple surrounded by cornfields, houses a number of rare, intricately carved Song and Yuan painted statues. Rebuilt in 1571, it's an impressive complex of halls and rather more authentic than many restored temples. The interiors of the Sakyamuni Hall and flanking buildings are especially exquisite. A rickshaw or taxi from town will cost ¥40 to ¥50 return, or you could cycle the 7km here (although expect to swallow coal-truck dust if you do).

Zhāngbì Underground Castle
CAVES

(Zhāngbì Gǔbǎo; admission ¥60; ⊙8am-6.30pm) This 1400-year-old network of **defence tunnels** are the oldest and longest series of such tunnels in all China. Built at the end of the Sui dynasty and stretching underground for 10km, they were never employed for their intended use against possible attack from Tang-dynasty invaders and subsequently fell into disrepair. Now, 1500m of tunnels on three levels have been restored. You descend as low as 26m in places and tour narrow and stooped subterranean passageways, which were once storage rooms, guardhouses and bedrooms.

Holes cut into the side of shafts leading to the surface indicate escape routes and places where the soldiers stood sentry to spy on would-be attackers. Chinese-speaking guides (included in the ticket price) are compulsory and essential; you don't want to get lost here.

The tour includes a visit to fascinating **Zhāngbì Cūn** (张壁村), a still-occupied Yuan-dynasty farming village above the tunnels. You can wander its cobblestoned streets and temples for free if you don't mind skipping the underground castle.

You can only get here on tour or by private car (per day ¥350). Check with your accommodation in Píngyáo.

Wang Family Courtyard   COURTYARD
(王家大院; Wángjiā Dàyuàn; admission Y66; ⊙8am-7pm) More castle than cosy home, this Qing-dynasty **former residence** is grand and has been very well maintained (note the wooden galleries still fronting many of the courtyard buildings). Its sheer size, though, means that the seemingly endless procession of courtyards (123 in all) becomes a little repetitive. It's easiest to join a tour or hire a car here. Four direct buses (¥17, one hour, 7.10am, 8.40am, 12.40pm and 4.20pm) leave from Píngyáo's bus station, returning at 10.50am, 12.30pm, 3.50pm and 5.20pm.

Behind the castle walls are interesting and still-occupied **cave dwellings** (窑洞; *yáodòng*), while in front of the complex is a Yuan-dynasty **Confucius Temple** (文庙; Wén Miào; admission ¥10), with a beautiful three-tiered wooden pagoda.

Qìkǒu   碛口

☑ 0358 / POP 32,000
Separated from neighbouring Shaanxi (Shǎnxī) province by the fast-flowing and muddy Yellow River (黄河; Huáng Hé), this tiny Ming River port found prosperity during its Qing heyday when hundreds of merchants lived here, only to lose it when the Japanese army arrived in 1938. It's well worth visiting for its evocative stone courtyards and cobbled pathways. All wind their way, eventually, up to the Black Dragon Temple, which overlooks the town.

Some of the houses have English captions revealing their former official roles, such as the pawnshop and chamber of commerce. The weekly market on Saturday is a good time to visit, when people from the surrounding villages arrive by tractor and electric cart for a day of shopping. Get here soon as there's a massive construction project in the main

town: a cluster of modern houses, a hotel and other tourist amenities are being built.

The main draw here, though, is the nearby ancient village of Lǐjiāshān, a seemingly long-forgotten settlement of hundreds of cave dwellings, some of which remain inhabited today (see p364).

◉ Sights

Lǐjiāshān   CAVES
(李家山) An absolute dream for travellers wanting to experience Shānxī's **cave houses** (窑洞; yáodòng), this remote, supremely peaceful 550-year-old village, hugging a hillside with terraces of crops running up it, has hundreds of cave dwellings scaling nine storeys. Once home to more than 600 families, most surnamed Li, today's population is around 45.

Almost all inhabitants are elderly: the local school, with caves for classrooms, no longer operates. Some of the stone paths and stairways that twist up the hill date from Ming times; note the rings on some walls that horses were tied to. These days, the village is popular with artists who have come to walk in the footsteps of the late Chinese painter Wu Guanzhong, a pioneer in modern Chinese painting who found inspiration here. The surrounding countryside offers ample opportunities for hikes and there are now several **homestays** (¥60 including meals) offering basic accommodation for those who wish to get away from it all. People here speak Jin, although most understand Mandarin.

To get here, cross the bridge by Qìkǒu's bus stop and follow the river for about 30 minutes until you see a blue sign indicating Lǐjiāshān. Walk on for about 100m and then take the road up the hill for another 30 minutes and you'll reach the old village. Local cars do a return run for ¥50 to ¥60. If you're planning on staying, you'll need to negotiate a rate or walk out.

Black Dragon Temple   TAOIST TEMPLE
(黑龙庙; Hēilóng Miào) They say the acoustics of this Ming Taoist temple, with wonderful views of the Yellow River, were so excellent that performances held on its stage were audible on the other side of the river in Shaanxi (Shǎnxī) province. Sadly, the stage is unused today. You can't miss the temple: from Qìkǒu's main road, head up any number of old cobbled pathways up the hill, via the odd courtyard or two.

CAVE DWELLINGS

People have been living in cave houses (窰洞; yáodòng) in Shānxī for almost 5000 years; it's believed that at one stage a quarter of the population lived underground. Shānxī's countryside is still littered with yáodòng, especially around the Yellow River area, and Lǐjiāshān is a wonderful example. These days most lie abandoned, but almost three million people in Shānxī (and around 30 million in total in China) still live in caves. And who can blame them? Compared to modern houses, they're cheaper, far better insulated against freezing winters and scorching summers, much more soundproof, while they also afford better protection from natural disasters such as earthquakes or forest fires. Furthermore, with far fewer building materials needed to construct them, they're a lot more environmentally friendly. So why isn't everyone living in them? Well, although most are now connected to the national grid, the vast majority of cave communities have no running water or sewerage system, turning simple daily tasks like washing or going to the toilet into a mission, and suddenly making even the ugliest tower block seem a whole lot more attractive.

🛏 Sleeping & Eating

Some locals offer clean beds (with an outhouse) for around ¥60. Restaurants line the road leading from the bus station towards Qìkǒu Kèzhàn and offer dishes from ¥15.

Qìkǒu Kèzhàn GUESTHOUSE $
(碛口客栈; ☑ 446 6188; d/tw/tr ¥188/218/388; @ 🛜) Overlooking the river in Qìkǒu, this historic (the Red Army used it as a base in WWII) and friendly place has comfortable and very large, yáodòng-style rooms (all with internet connections) with kàng beds set off two 300-year-old courtyards. Climb the stone stairs and there's a wonderful terrace with great views over the Yellow River.

It's a fine place to enjoy a beer, or the tasty meals cooked up here, under the starry sky. Discounts of 10% available.

ℹ Getting There & Away

One bus runs from Tàiyuán to Qìkǒu (¥79, four hours, 10.30am). If you miss it, or are coming from Píngyáo, you will have to go through Líshí (离石).

Regular buses go from Tàiyuán to Líshí (¥70, three hours, half-hourly from 7am to 7.30pm). There are two daily buses from Píngyáo (¥44, two hours, 8.30am and 12.30pm). From Líshí's long-distance bus station (长途汽车站; chángtú qìchēzhàn), take bus 5 (¥1, 25 minutes) to the Jìnián Běi (纪念北) crossroads where buses to Qìkǒu (¥20, 1½ hours, 7am to 7pm) depart.

There's one daily bus from Qìkǒu to Tàiyuán, but it leaves at 5.30am. There are hourly buses to Líshí from Qìkǒu until around 4pm. From Líshí, there are many buses back to Tàiyuán (¥70, from 7am to 8pm), two to Píngyáo (¥44, 8am and 1.40pm) and one to Xī'ān (¥180, eight hours, 11.30am).

Jìnchéng 晋城

☑ 0356 / POP 500,000

Jìnchéng has few sights, but this small, little-visited city is the launch pad for a historical adventure into Shānxī's southeast. The surrounding countryside hides some very impressive ancient architecture, making this a rewarding stop, particularly if you are continuing south into Hénán.

On Wenchang Dongjie you can find a branch of the Bank of China with an ATM (there are many more around town), and plenty of restaurants.

◉ Sights

Bǐfēng Temple BUDDHIST TEMPLE
(笔峰寺; Bǐfēng Sì; ⊙ 6am-6pm) FREE The only sight of note in Jìnchéng is Bǐfēng Temple, which sits atop a hill close to the train station. The temple itself is newly built but the nine-storey pagoda dates back to the Ming dynasty.

🛏 Sleeping

Most hotels in town are either overpriced or won't accept foreigners.

Sunshine Hotel HOTEL $$
(阳光大酒店; Yángguāng Dàjiǔdiàn; ☑ 222 9001; 568 Zezhou Lu, 泽州路568号; d & tw incl breakfast ¥398 & ¥498; ❄ @) Smart business hotel with clean rooms located just off Wenchang Dongjie. Discounts of 50% available.

ℹ Getting There & Around

Buses depart from the new east station (客运东站; kèyùn dōngzhàn). Destinations include

Tàiyuán (¥114, four hours, every 1½ hours, 6.30am to 6.30pm), Píngyáo (¥105, five hours, 7am, 8am and 9.30am), Zhèngzhōu (¥65, 1½ hours, half houly, 5.40am to 6.20pm), Luòyáng (¥50, hourly, 7.20am to 6pm), Xī'ān (¥179 to ¥196, seven hours, 8.30am and 10am) and Běijīng (¥261, 10 hours, 4pm).

The few trains that pass Jìnchéng shuttle between Tàiyuán (hard seat/sleeper ¥54/108, seven hours, four daily) and Zhèngzhōu (¥30, 3½ hours, three daily).

Buses 2, 3 and 19 (¥1) connect the train station with the east bus station. Bus 5 from the train station travels along the main Wenchang Dongjie. Taxi flagfall is ¥5.

Around Jìnchéng

Guōyù   郭峪古城

This atmospheric walled **village** (Guōyù Gǔchéng) is the highlight of a trip to this part of Shānxī. There's no entrance fee and no tourist nonsense (amazingly, many of the domestic tour groups skip the village); just the genuine charm of a historic and still-inhabited Ming-dynasty settlement.

The crumbling remains of this one-time fort's south gate and some of its old walls still stand sentry at the entrance to the village close to the road. Walk 200m and it's as if you've stepped back in time. Narrow alleys and stone streets run past courtyard houses, where the locals sit and chatter in their native dialect.

It's best to wander Guōyù aimlessly, but don't miss **Tāngdì Miào** (汤帝庙), a 600-year-old Taoist temple and the village's oldest building. Make sure to climb up to the stage, where there are two very rare Cultural Revolution–era paintings adorned with slogans exhorting the locals to work harder (the temple was a government building during that time). It's also worth looking inside the former courtyard residence of Minister Chen's grandfather at 1 Jingyang Beilu (景阳北路1号).

To get here, catch one of the frequent buses headed to Prime Minister Chen's Castle (¥15, 1½ hours, 6am to 6.30pm) from Jìnchéng's east station. Guōyù is a 10-minute walk south of the castle. Return transport is scarce, so it's best to take a minibus to the small town of Běiliú (北留; ¥5, 15 minutes), then catch an ordinary bus back to Jìnchéng (¥12).

Prime Minister
Chen's Castle   皇城相府

A beautifully preserved Ming-dynasty castle, the **Prime Minister Chen's Castle** (皇成相府, Huángchéng Xiàngfǔ; admission ¥100; ⊙8am-6.30pm) is the former residence of Chen Tingjing, prime minister under Emperor Kangxi in the late 17th century, and co-author of China's most famous dictionary. The Chen family rose to prominence as senior officials in the 16th century and the castle walls were originally constructed to keep revolting peasants out. There are now all the tourist trappings – souvenir sellers, flag-waving guides with microphones – but it remains an attractive maze of battlements, courtyards, gardens and stone archways.

Don't bother buying the pricier ¥120 ticket which includes entry to a nearby garden. Regular buses (¥15) run to the ticket office from Jìnchéng's east bus station. If there isn't a minibus back to Jìnchéng, get a minibus to the small town of Běiliú (北留; ¥3, 15 minutes) then catch an ordinary bus back to Jìnchéng (¥10).

Hǎihuì Temple   海会寺

This Buddhist **temple** (Hǎihuì Sì; admission ¥30), where Minister Chen studied, is dominated by its two magnificent brick pagodas. The 20m-high **Shělì Tǎ** (舍利塔) is almost 1100 years old. Towering above it, the octagonal **Rúlái Tǎ** (如来塔), built in 1558, can be climbed for an extra ¥10. To get here, take the bus to Prime Minister Chen's Castle but tell the driver you want to get off at Hǎihuì. To continue to the castle or Guōyù, flag a minibus from the main road (¥3).

Shaanxi (Shǎnxī)

POP 37.4 MILLION

Includes ➜

Best Historic Sites

➜ Army of Terracotta Warriors (p377)

➜ Tomb of Emperor Jingdi (p379)

➜ Big Goose Pagoda (p371)

➜ Yángjiālǐng Revolution Headquarters Site (p385)

Best Museums

➜ Forest of Stelae Museum (p369)

➜ Shaanxi History Museum (p371)

➜ Xiányáng City Museum (p379)

➜ Yán'ān Revolution Museum (p384)

Why Go?

Shaanxi (陕西) is where it all started for China. As the heartland of the Qin dynasty, whose warrior emperor united much of China for the first time, Shaanxi was the cradle of Chinese civilisation. Later on, Xī'ān was the beginning and end of the Silk Road and a buzzing, cosmopolitan capital long before anyone had heard of Běijīng.

Shaanxi's archaeological sites make it an essential destination. Around Xī'ān there's an excavated neolithic village and numerous royal graves; chief among them the tomb of Qin Shi Huang and his private Army of Terracotta Warriors. Shaanxi has its share of contemporary history too; the caves around Yán'ān were the Chinese Communist Party's (CCP) base in the 1930s and '40s.

Xī'ān is an emergent travellers hub, with good nightlife, museums, ancient pagodas and a fascinating Muslim Quarter. Set aside time to visit the rural areas, with fascinating villages barely touched by modern life and mountains that were once home to hermits and sages.

When to Go
Xī'ān

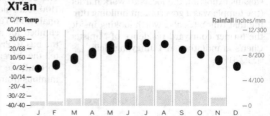

Apr & May Spring breezes and the ideal time to climb Huà Shān.

Sep & Oct The rain's stopped and it's still warm, so hit Xī'ān's sights.

Dec Avoid the crowds and maybe get the Terracotta Warriors all to yourself.

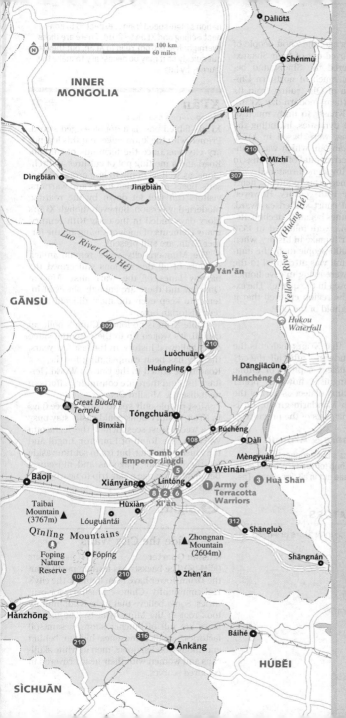

Shaanxi Highlights

1 See what an emperor takes with him to the grave at the extraordinary **Army of Terracotta Warriors** (p377)

2 Admire Xī'ān's distinctively named **Big Goose Pagoda** (p371), the centrepiece for a stunning sound and light show

3 Watch the sun rise over the Qínlǐng Mountains from atop Taoism's sacred western peak, **Huà Shān** (p380)

4 Explore the old town of **Hánchéng** (p382), a quaint quarter of buildings that date from the Yuan, Ming and Qing eras

5 Take a different look at China's past by gazing down on the enthralling excavations at the **Tomb of Emperor Jingdi** (p379)

6 Get lost wandering the backstreets of Xī'ān's ancient **Muslim Quarter** (p368)

7 Check out the **dugouts** (p385) where Mao Zedong lived in Yán'ān and the red tourists who flock to see it

8 Hop on a bike and ride atop Xī'ān's glorious **city walls** (p369), a pretty 14km loop of the city

History

Around 3000 years ago, the Zhou people of the Bronze Age moved out of their Shaanxi homeland, conquered the Shang and became dominant in much of northern China. Later the state of Qin, ruling from its capital Xiányáng (near modern-day Xī'ān), became the first dynasty to unify much of China. Subsequent dynasties, including the Han, Sui and Tang, were based in Xī'ān, then known as Cháng'ān, which was abandoned for the eastern capital of Luòyáng (in Hénán) whenever invaders threatened.

Shaanxi remained the political heart of China until the 10th century. However, when the imperial court shifted eastward, the province's fortunes began to decline. Rebellions and famine were followed in 1556 by the deadliest earthquake in history, when an estimated 830,000 people died (the unusually high death toll was attributed to the fact that millions were living in cave homes which easily collapsed in the quake). The extreme poverty of the region ensured that it was an early stronghold of the CCP.

Language

Locals like to joke that Xī'ān's dialect is the 'real' standard Mandarin – after all, the city was one of the ancient capitals of China. Those pedantic linguists, however, prefer to classify the Shaanxi dialect as part of the central Zhōngyuán Mandarin group. Jin is also spoken in some parts of the province.

ℹ️ Getting There & Around

Xī'ān has one of China's best-connected airports. Xī'ān is also a hub for road transport and mega-highways spread out in all directions. The nation's high-speed train is expected to connect Běijīng and Xī'ān by 2014. There are three overnight trains from Yúlín to Xī'ān, but they sell out quickly so it may be necessary to make this journey by bus.

Xī'ān 西安

✔️ 029 / POP 8.5 MILLION

Xī'ān's fabled past is a double-edged sword. Primed with the knowledge that this legendary city was once the terminus of the Silk Road and a melting pot of cultures and religions, as well as home to emperors, courtesans, poets, monks, merchants and warriors, visitors can feel let down by the roaring, modern-day version. But even though Xī'ān's glory days ended in the early 10th century, many elements of ancient Cháng'ān, the former Xī'ān, are still present.

The Ming-era city walls remain intact, vendors of all descriptions still crowd the narrow lanes of the warrenlike Muslim Quarter, and there are enough places of interest to keep even the most diligent amateur historian busy.

While Xī'ān is no longer China's political capital, it's woken up to the potential value of its hallowed history. In the last few years, the city has been campaigning for the Silk Road to be added to the Unesco World Heritage list, and there are continuing efforts to revitalise the Muslim Quarter.

Most people only spend two or three days in Xī'ān; history buffs could easily stay busy for a week. Must-sees include the Terracotta Warriors, the Tomb of Emperor Jingdi and the Muslim Quarter, but try to set time aside for the city walls, pagodas and museums. Better still, arrange a side trip to nearby Huà Shān or Hánchéng.

🔵 Sights

🔵 Inside the City Walls

Muslim Quarter   HISTORIC SITE
(回族区) The backstreets leading north from the Drum Tower have been home to the city's Hui community (Chinese Muslims) for centuries. Some believe that today's community took root in the Ming dynasty. The narrow lanes are full of butcher shops, sesame-oil factories, smaller mosques hidden behind enormous wooden doors, men in white skullcaps and women with their heads covered in coloured scarves.

It's a great place to wander and especially atmospheric at night. Good streets to stroll down are Xiyang Shi, Dapi Yuan and Damaishi Jie, which runs north off Xi Dajie through an interesting Islamic food market.

Great Mosque
MOSQUE

(清真大寺, Qīngzhēn Dàsì; Huajue Xiang, 化觉巷; admission Mar-Nov ¥25, Dec-Feb ¥15, Muslims free; ⊙8am-7.30pm Mar-Nov, to 5.30pm Dec-Feb) One of the largest mosques in China and a fascinating blend of Chinese and Islamic architecture. The present buildings are mostly Ming and Qing, though the mosque was founded in the 8th century. Arab influences extend from the central minaret (cleverly disguised as a pagoda) to the enormous turquoise-roofed Prayer Hall (not open to visitors) at the back of the complex, and elegant calligraphy gracing most entryways.

Facing west (towards Mecca) instead of the usual south, the mosque begins with a classic Chinese temple feature, the spirit wall, designed to keep demons at bay. The gardens, too, with their rocks, pagodas and archways are obviously Chinese, with the exception of the four palm trees at the entrance.

To get here, follow Xiyang Shi several minutes west and look for a small alley leading south past a gauntlet of souvenir stands.

Forest of Stelae Museum
MUSEUM

(碑林博物馆, Bēilín Bówùguǎn; www.beilin-museum.com; 15 Sanxue Jie, 三学街15号; admission Mar-Nov ¥75, Dec-Feb ¥50; ⊙8am-6.45pm Mar-Nov, to 5.45pm Dec-Feb, last admission 45min before closing) Housed in Xī'ān's Confucius Temple, this museum holds more than 1000 stone stelae (inscribed tablets), including the nine Confucian classics and some exemplary calligraphy. The highlight is the fantastic sculpture gallery (across from the gift shop), which contains animal guardians from the Tang dynasty, pictorial tomb stones and Buddhist statuary. To get to the museum, follow Shuyuan Xiang east from the South Gate.

The second gallery holds a Nestorian tablet (AD 781), the earliest recorded account of Christianity in China. (The Nestorians professed that Christ was both human and divine, for which they were booted out of the Church in 431.) The fourth gallery holds a collection of ancient maps and portraits, and is where rubbings (copies) are made, an interesting process to watch.

CITY WALLS

Xī'ān is one of the few cities in China where the old **city walls** (城墙, Chéngqiáng; admission ¥54; ⊙8am-8.30pm Apr-Oct, to 7pm Nov-Mar) are still standing. Built in 1370 during the Ming dynasty, the 12m-high walls are surrounded by a dry moat and form a rectangle with a perimeter of 14km.

Most sections have been restored or rebuilt, and it is now possible to walk the entirety of the walls in a leisurely four hours. English-speaking guides from the South Gate charge ¥80 per person. You can also cycle from the South Gate (bike hire ¥40 for 100 minutes, ¥200 deposit). Access ramps are located inside the major gates.

To get an idea of Xī'ān's former grandeur, consider this: the Tang city walls originally enclosed 83 sq km, an area seven times larger than today's city centre.

Bell Tower & Drum Tower
HISTORIC SITE

Now marooned on a traffic island, the **Bell Tower** (钟楼, Zhōng Lóu; admission ¥35, combined Drum Tower ticket ¥40; ⊙8.30am-9.30pm Mar-Oct, to 6.30pm Nov-Feb, last admission 30min before closing) sits at the heart of Xī'ān and originally held a large bell that was rung at dawn, while its alter ego, the **Drum Tower** (鼓楼, Gǔ Lóu; Beiyuanmen; admission ¥35, combined Bell Tower ticket ¥40; ⊙8.30am-9.30pm Mar-Oct, to 6.30pm Nov-Feb, last admission 30min before closing), marked nightfall. Both date from the 14th century but the Drum Tower was renovated in 1740 while the Bell Tower was moved and reconstructed in 1582 using the same beams and fixtures from where it stood two blocks west.

Musical performances, included in the ticket price, are held inside each at 9.10am, 10am, 11am, 3pm, 4pm and 5pm. Enter the Bell Tower through the underpass on the north side.

Folk House
HISTORIC SITE

(高家大院, Gāojiā Dàyuàn; 144 Beiyuanmen, 北院门144号; admission ¥15, with tea ¥20; ⊙8.30am-11pm) This well-rounded historic residence also serves as an art gallery, entertainment centre and teahouse. Originally the home of the Qing bureaucrat Gao Yuesong, it's a fine example of a courtyard home and has

SHAANXI (SHĂNXĪ) XĪ'ĀN

Xī'ān

Changle Lu

Yongle Lu

7

Zhongshan Gate

Huancheng Donglu

East Gate

Big Goose Pagoda & Dà Cí'ēn Temple (4km)

Dong Balu
Dong Qilu
Dong Liulu
Dong Wulu
Dong Silu
Dong Sanlu
Dong Erlu

24

Train Station
Long-Distance Bus Station

An Yuanmen
Huancheng Beilu

Xi Balu

China Eastern Geming Park

Beixin Jie北新街

Xi Wulu 西五路

Shangde Lu

Jiefang Lu

Heping Lu

Dong Xinjie
15

13
Dong Yilu

Dong Dajie
23

Shaanxi Grand Opera House (550m)

CITS; Tang Dynasty (2km); Little Goose Pagoda (12km); Shaanxi History Museum (3km); Xī'ān Museum (3km);

North Gate

Houzaimen

Juhuayuan Lu

Naxin Jie南新街

Nancheng Xiang南长巷

Xi Xinjie

10
11

Bank of China

18

Duanlumen

Shuyuan Xiang 书院巷
4
Dongmutou Shi 东木头市

20
Bank of China

Bei Dajie 北大街

Dapi Yuan

Zhonglou

Beiyuanmen

19

Lianhu Lu

Train Ticket Booth

Lianhu Park

花天大街

3
2

5

Beiguangji Jie

6

Nan Dajie 南大街

25
1

9

ATM

Advance Train Ticket Booth

14
12

South Gate

Yong Ningmen

水浒门路

Nanyuanmen

17

Defu Xiang 郭福巷

22

16
21

Xi Qilu

Xiyang Shi

Xi Dajie 西大街

Xiyang Shi

Damaishi Jie

Qianwei Jie

Huancheng Beilu

Honggang Jie

Shuncheng Nanlu Xiduan

Xiguan Zhengjie

West Gate

Huancheng Xilu 环城西路

Taibai Beilu

Daqing Lu

8

Airport Shuttle Bus

Xī'ān

◎ **Sights**

⏾ **Sleeping**

✕ **Eating**

◎ **Drinking & Nightlife**

✪ **Entertainment**

🛍 **Shopping**

ℹ **Information**

been tastefully restored. There are reception rooms, bedrooms, servants' quarters, an ancestral temple and a study (now the teahouse). Admission includes a tour that starts with an optional marionette or shadow-puppet demonstration (¥15).

As the complex currently belongs to the Shaanxi Artists Association, there's an art gallery here where you can pick up reasonably priced traditional Chinese art. Confusingly, despite the address, this place isn't at No 144, but is about 20m down the street.

◎ Outside the City Walls

Shaanxi History Museum　MUSEUM
(陕西历史博物馆, Shǎnxī Lìshǐ Bówùguǎn; 91 Xiaozhai Donglu, 小寨东路91号; ⏾ 8.30am-6pm Tue-Sun Apr-Oct, last admission 4.30pm, 9.30am-5pm Tue-Sun Nov-Mar, last admission 4pm) FREE Shaanxi's museum has plenty of overlap with Xī'ān's surrounding sights but makes for a comprehensive stroll through ancient Cháng'ān. Most exhibits include illuminating explanations in English. Look for the four original terracotta warrior statues on the ground floor. Go early and expect to queue for at least 30 minutes. Bring your passport to claim your free ticket.

The number of visitors is limited to 4000 per day (2500 tickets are distributed in the morning starting at 8.30am and another 1500 in the afternoon starting at 1.30pm). Take bus 610 from the Bell Tower or bus 701 from the South Gate.

In the Sui and Tang section there are unique murals depicting a polo match; and a series of painted pottery figurines with elaborate hairstyles and dress, including several bearded foreigners, musicians and braying camels.

Big Goose Pagoda　BUDDHIST TEMPLE
(大雁塔, Dàyàn Tǎ; Yanta Nanlu, 雁塔南路; admission to grounds ¥50, entry into pagoda ¥40; ⏾ 8am-7pm Apr-Oct, to 6pm Nov-Mar) This pagoda, Xī'ān's most famous landmark, 4km southeast of the South Gate, dominates the surrounding modern buildings. One of China's best examples of a Tang-style pagoda (squarish rather than round), it was completed in AD 652 to house the Buddhist sutras brought back from India by the monk Xuan Zang (p372). His travels inspired one of the best-known works of Chinese literature, *Journey to the West*.

Xuan spent the last 19 years of his life translating scriptures with a crack team of linguist monks; many of these translations are still used today.

Surrounding the pagoda is **Dà Cí'ēn Temple** (大慈恩寺, Dàcí'ēn Sì), one of the largest temples in Tang Cháng'ān. The buildings today date from the Qing dynasty. To the south of the pagoda is a newly developed open-air mall of shops, galleries, restaurants and public art; well-worth a wander. The area also includes a cinema and monorail.

Bus 610 from the Bell Tower and bus 609 from the South Gate drop you at the pagoda

MONKEY BUSINESS

Buddhist monk Xuan Zang's epic 17-year trip to India, via Central Asia and Afghanistan, in search of Buddhist enlightenment was fictionalised in *Journey to the West*, one of Chinese literature's most enduring texts. The Ming-dynasty novel gives the monk Xuan three disciples to protect him along the way, the best-loved of which is the Monkey King.

The novel, attributed to the poet Wu Cheng'en, has inspired many plays and TV shows, including the cult '70s series *Monkey*. More recently, the Gorillaz team of Damon Albarn and Jamie Hewlett collaborated with opera director Chen Shi-Zheng on a popular 2007 stage version, while a 2014 Steven Chow film had critics applauding its creative interpretation.

square; the entrance is on the south side. An evening fountain show is held on the square.

Xī'ān Museum MUSEUM
(西安博物馆, Xī'ān Bówùguǎn; www.xabwy.com; 76 Youyi Xilu, 友谊西路76号; ⊙ 8.30am-7pm Wed-Mon) FREE Housed in the pleasant grounds of the Jiànfú Temple is this museum featuring relics unearthed in Xī'ān over the years. There are some exquisite ceramics from the Han dynasty, as well as figurines, an exhibition of Ming-dynasty seals and jade artefacts. Don't miss the basement, where a large-scale model of ancient Xī'ān gives a good sense of the place in its former pomp and glory.

Also in the grounds is the **Little Goose Pagoda** (小雁塔, Xiǎoyàn Tǎ). The top of the pagoda was shaken off by an earthquake in the middle of the 16th century, but the rest of the 43m-high structure is intact. Jiànfú Temple was originally built in AD 684 to bless the afterlife of the late Emperor Gaozong. The pagoda, a rather delicate building of 15 progressively smaller tiers, was built from AD 707 to 709 and housed Buddhist scriptures brought back from India by the pilgrim Yi Jing. Admission to the grounds is free but climbing up the pagoda requires a ¥30 ticket. Bus 610 runs here from the Bell Tower; from the South Gate take bus 203.

Temple of the Eight Immortals TAOIST TEMPLE
(八仙庵, Bāxiān Ān; Yongle Lu, 永乐路; admission ¥3; ⊙ 7.30am-5.30pm Mar-Nov, 8am-5pm Dec-Feb)

Xī'ān's largest Taoist temple dates back to the Song dynasty and is still an active place of worship. Supposedly built on the site of an ancient wine shop, it was constructed to protect against subterranean divine thunder. Scenes from Taoist mythology are painted around the courtyard. Empress Cixi, the mother of the last emperor, stayed here in 1901 after fleeing Běijīng during the Boxer Rebellion. Bus 502 runs close by the temple (eastbound from Xi Xinjie).

The small antique market (p375) opposite is busiest on Sunday and Wednesday.

🛏 Sleeping

If you're arriving by air and have not yet booked accommodation, keep in mind that touts at the shuttle-bus drop-off (outside the Melody Hotel) can often get you discounted rooms at a wide selection of hotels.

All hostels in the city offer a similar range of services, including bike hire, internet, laundry, restaurant and travel services. Ask about free pick-up from the train station and book ahead at the most popular places. In low season (January to March) you can usually get 20% off at hostels.

Shūyuàn Youth Hostel HOSTEL $
(书院青年旅舍, Shūyuàn Qīngnián Lǚshè; ☑ 029 8728 0092; www.hostelxian.com; 2 Shuncheng Nan-lu Xiduan, 南门里顺城南路西段2号; dm ¥40-60, s/d ¥160/180; ❋ @ 🛜; Ⓜ Yong Ningmen) The longest-running hostel in Xī'ān, Shūyuàn is a converted residence with beautiful courtyards near the South Gate. The cafe serves excellent food and the lively bar in the basement (guests get a free beer voucher) is a popular locals/travellers meeting spot. Rooms are simple but clean and the staff is switched on to the needs of travellers.

The hostel is 20m west of the South Gate inside the city walls. Bus 603 to the main train station runs nearby.

Sahara Youth Inn HOSTEL $
(撒哈拉青年客栈, Sāhālā Qīngnián Kèzhàn; ☑ 029 8728 7631; http://site.douban.com/219529; 180 Beiyuanmen, 莲湖区北院门180号; dm ¥50-70, tw ¥150; 🛜; Ⓜ Zhonglou (Bell Tower)) You'd think staying smack bang in the Muslim Quarter would be noisy, but Sahara is set back around a quiet Chinese courtyard. The beds are firm but rooms are clean and peaceful, and really, you're here for the action outside, which you can see from the rooftop.

Xiāngzǐmén Youth Hostel HOSTEL $

(湘子门国际青年旅舍, Xiāngzǐmén Guójì Qīngnián Lǚshè; ☑029 6286 7888; www.yhaxian.com; 16 Xiangzimiao Jie, 南门里湘子庙街16号; dm ¥50, r ¥180-240; ❄@奈; Ⓜ Yong Ningmen) Set around a series of interconnected courtyards, this hostel is a big, sprawling place with an ever-busy pub known for its smoky and noisy atmosphere. Rooms are clean, modern and warm in winter but avoid the stuffy windowless basement rooms. Take bus 603 from opposite the train station to the South Gate and walk 100m west.

★ **Hàn Táng House** HOSTEL $$

(汉唐驿青年旅舍, Hàntáng Yì Qīngnián Lǚshè; ☑029 8738 9765; www.itisxian.com; 32 Nanchang Xiang, 南长巷32号; ◷dm/s/d/tr ¥60/168/268/338; ❄@奈; Ⓜ Zhonglou (Bell Tower)) A hybrid of sorts, this place has dorms and the vibe of a youth hostel but the look and feel of a three-star hotel. The spotless rooms are decked out with high-quality dark-wood furnishings, slab floors and some of the most comfortable beds in China. It's located down a residential street off Nanxin Jie.

A cafe with good Western food is on the ground floor. If Hàn Táng House is full, try its popular sister hostel, **Hàn Táng Inn** (汉唐驿, Hàntáng Yì; ☑029 8728 7772, 029 8723 1126; www.itisxian.com; 7 Nanchang Xiang, 南长巷7号; dm ¥40-50, s & d ¥160-200; ❄@奈), on the same street.

Jano's Backpackers HOSTEL $$

(杰诺庭院背包旅舍, Jíenuò Tíngyuàn Bèibāo Lǚshè; ☑029 8725 6656; www.xian-backpackers.com; 69 Shuncheng Nanlu Zhongduan, South Gate, 南门顺城南路中段69号; dm ¥50-60, r without bathroom ¥120, with bathroom ¥220-260, ste ¥320-390; ❄@奈; Ⓜ Yong Ningmen) Set in a little faux *hútòng* (narrow alleyway) with artist galleries and cafes nearby, Jano's is a pleasant place to escape bustling Xī'ān (though street-facing rooms get pub noise). Rooms are well-maintained and decorated in traditional style, including some with *kang* (heatable beds). Despite the name, it feels more like a small boutique hotel rather than a backpacker hang-out. Staff speak English.

Jǐnjiāng Inn HOTEL $$

(锦江之星, Jǐnjiāng Zhīxīng; ☑029 8745 2288; www.jj-xian.com; 110 Jiefang Lu, 解放路110号; d/tw/ste ¥189/219/249; ❄@; Ⓜ Zhonglou (Bell Tower)) By Xī'ān's standards, the prices are close to budget, but the clean and bright modern rooms, all with ADSL internet connections,

make this a better option than most three-star places in town. There's a cheap restaurant here, too.

Sofitel HOTEL $$$

(索菲特人民大厦, Suǒfēitè Rénmín Dàshà; ☑029 8792 8888; sofitel@renminsquare.com; 319 Dong Xinjie, 东新街319号; d/ste ¥1760/3150; ❄❄@奈; Ⓜ Zhonglou (Bell Tower)) Xī'ān's self-proclaimed 'six-star' hotel is undoubtedly the most luxurious choice in the city and has a soothing, hushed atmosphere. The bathrooms are top-notch. Cantonese, Japanese and Moroccan restaurants are on-site, as well as a South American–themed bar. Reception is in the east wing. Room rates change daily, so you can score a deal when business is slow.

Bell Tower Hotel HOTEL $$$

(西安钟楼饭店, Xī'ān Zhōnglóu Fàndiàn; ☑029 8760 0000; www.belltowerhtl.com; 110 Nan Dajie, 南大街110号; d ¥850-1080; ❄@; Ⓜ Zhonglou (Bell Tower)) Slap in the centre of downtown, this state-owned four-star place is comfortable and handy for the airport bus stop. Some rooms have a bird's-eye view of the Bell Tower and all are spacious and comfortable with cable TV and ADSL internet connections. Low-season discounts up to 30%.

✕ Eating

Hit the Muslim Quarter for tasty eating in Xī'ān. Common dishes here are *májiàng liángpí* (麻酱凉皮; cold noodles in sesame sauce), *fěnzhēngròu* (粉蒸肉; chopped mutton fried in a wok with ground wheat), the 'Chinese hamburger' *ròujiāmó* (肉夹馍; fried pork or beef in pitta bread, sometimes with green peppers and cumin), *càijiāmó* (菜夹馍; the vegetarian version of *ròujiāmó*) and the ubiquitous *ròuchuàn* (肉串; kebabs).

Best of all is the delicious *yángròu pàomó* (羊肉泡馍), a soup dish that involves crumbling a flat loaf of bread into a bowl and adding noodles, mutton and broth. You can also pick up mouth-watering desserts such as *huāshēnggāo* (花生糕; peanut cakes) and *shìbǐng* (柿饼; dried persimmons), which can be found at the market or in Muslim Quarter shops.

A good street to wander for a selection of more typically Chinese restaurants is Dongmutou Shi, east of Nan Dajie.

All the hostels serve up Western breakfasts and meals with varying degrees of success.

Sānjiěmèi Jiǎozi
DUMPLINGS $

(三姐妹饺子, Three Sisters Dumplings; ☎029 8725 2129; 140 Dongmutou Shi, 东木头市140号; dumplings ¥13-23; ⏰11am-2.30pm & 5-9.30pm) Weary diners with dumpling fatigue, let the rustic Three Sisters reinspire you with a twist on classics, well done. Try succulent carrot and lamb dumplings blanketed in crisp peanuts and fried chives. Or for vegetarians, the winning texture of dry and marinated tofu (yes, two types) with the zing of crunchy cilantro and a lashing of chilli. Picture menu.

Dǐng Dǐng Xiāng
CHINESE $

(顶顶香; 130 Nanyuanmen, 南院门130号; dishes ¥18-58; ⏰10am-10pm; 🚇) This is what modern Xī'ān is all about. A clean, cafe atmosphere over four floors with aspirational snaps of Europe in scattered picture frames on the walls while a lively well-dressed crowd peers down onto the street, drinking beer and eating Chinese classics such as hotpots with generous servings. The extensive English picture menu includes excellent veg options.

Muslim Family Restaurant
CHINESE, MUSLIM $

(回文人家; Huiwen Renjia; Beiyuanmen, 北院门; dishes ¥6-58; ⏰9am-10.30pm) Deep in the heart of the Muslim Quarter, this fine establishment serves all the classic Muslim dishes and quick dishes for solo travellers like soups and dumplings. There's no English sign so look out for the noodle chef in the open-air kitchen. Picture menu.

Lǎo Sūn Jiā
SHAANXI $$

(老孙家; ☎8240 3205; 5th fl, 364 Dong Dajie, 东大街364号5层; dishes ¥12-49; ⏰8am-9.30pm) Xī'ān's most famous, upmarket restaurant (with more than 100 years of history) is well known for its speciality dish – steaming bowls of *yángròu pàomó*. The catch here is that the patron is responsible for ripping up the bread before the chefs add the soup. The soup is an acquired taste for most people but the experience is fun.

Many other cold and hot dishes are on display to choose from, so you can just point if you don't speak Chinese. It's located on the 5th floor of a large black glass building.

Jamaica Blue
CAFE $$

(蓝色牙买加, Lánsè Yámǎijiā; 32 Nanchang Xiang, 南长巷32号; dishes ¥32-49; ⏰8am-11pm; 🛜) This Australia-based cafe has washed up in a little alley in Xī'ān, serving up excellent sandwiches, wraps, Western-style breakfast, pastas, desserts and reliable coffee. Has a friendly English-speaking staff, wi-fi, games and quasi-Irish pub atmosphere. Live music is played nightly from 9pm to 11pm.

Drinking & Nightlife

Xī'ān's nightlife options range from bars and clubs to cheesy but popular tourist shows.

The main bar strip is near the South Gate on leafy Defu Xiang – one of the most pleasant parts of Xī'ān to stroll through by day. The top end of the street has coffee shops and teahouses. The bars get more raucous the closer to the South Gate you get, but it's still fairly tame.

Clubs get going early in Xī'ān, in part because they're as much places to drink as to dance. They are free to get into, but expect to pay at least ¥30 for a beer. Most are located along or off Nan Dajie.

Old Henry's Bar
BAR

(老亨利酒吧, Lǎohēnglì Jiǔbā; 48 Defu Xiang, 德福巷48号; ⏰8pm-3am; 🔊) A small bar with a pub vibe and live music in the evenings. Always busy and has outside seating.

3 as 4 Bar
BAR

(甜糖酒吧, Tián Táng Jiǔbā; 12 Defu Xiang, 德福巷12号; drinks ¥20-55) A hidden world of low lighting and decor that resembles an antique-store boudoir. Extremely popular with Westerners for the pool table, the Chinese-inspired cocktails, TV/film projector and the larger-than-life Chinese owner, Samantha. It's 20m west of the intersection with Defu Xiang.

The Belgian
BAR

(比利时咖啡酒吧, Bǐlìshí Kāfēi Jiǔbā; 69 Shuncheng Nanlu, 顺城南路中段69号; ⏰7pm-3am) A laid-back Western-style bar stocked with around 40 types of imported Belgian beers and pub grub like burgers and fries. The little alley where it sits is developing as a pub street so it's fun to hang out on the patio and people-watch.

☆ Entertainment

Xī'ān has a number of dinner-dance shows, which are normally packed out with tour groups; reservations are recommended. They can be fun if you're in the mood for a bit of kitsch.

Fountain & Music Show
LIVE MUSIC

(Dayan Ta Bei Guangchang, 大雁塔北广场; ⏰9pm Mar-Nov, 8pm Dec-Feb) Some travellers enjoy spending the evening at the free fountain and music show on Big Goose Pagoda Sq; it's the largest such 'musical fountain' in Asia.

1+1
CLUB
(壹加壹俱乐部, Yījiāyī Jùlèbù; 2nd fl, Heping Yin-zuo Bldg, 118 Heping Lu, 和平银座二楼405号; ⏲7pm-late) The ever-popular 1+1 is a neon-lit maze of a place that pumps out slightly cheesy party tunes well into the early hours. Hip, it is not.

Tang Dynasty
DINNER SHOW
(唐乐宫, Tángyuè Gōng; ☎029 8782 2222; www.xiantangdynasty.com; 75 Chang'an Beilu, 长安北路75号; performance with/without dinner ¥500/220) The most famous dinner theatre in the city stages an over-the-top spectacle with Vegas-style costumes, traditional dance, live music and singing. It's dubbed into English.

Buses can take you to the theatre 1.5km directly south of the South Gate, or walk five minutes south of South Shaomen metro.

Shaanxi Grand Opera House
DINNER SHOW
(陕歌大剧院, Shǎngē Dàjùyuàn; ☎029 8785 3295; 165 Wenyi Beilu, 文艺北路165号; performance with/without dinner ¥298/198) Also known as the Tang Palace Dance Show, this is cheaper and less flashy than other dinner-dance shows in town. Wenyi Lu starts south of the city walls. You can get a better price by buying your ticket through a reputable hostel or hotel.

🛍 Shopping

Stay in Xī'ān for a couple of days and you'll be offered enough sets of miniature Terracotta Warriors to form your own army. A good place to search out gifts is the Muslim Quarter, where prices are generally cheaper than elsewhere.

Xiyang Shi is a narrow, crowded alley running east and west of the Great Mosque where Terracotta Warriors, Huxian farmer paintings, shadow puppets, lanterns, tea ware, Mao memorabilia and T-shirts are on offer.

Near the South Gate is the Qing-style Shuyuan Xiang, the main tree-lined strip for art supplies, paintings, calligraphy, paper cuts, brushes and fake rubbings from the Forest of Stelae Museum.

Northwest Antique Market
MARKET
(西北古玩城, Xīběi Gǔwán Chéng; Dong Xinjie (Shuncheng Donglu), 东新街 (顺城东路北段); ⏲10am-5.30pm) Serious shoppers should visit the Northwest Antique Market, by the Zhongshan Gate. This three-storey warren

of shops selling jade, seals, antiques and Mao memorabilia sees far fewer foreign faces than the Muslim Quarter. Dozing street sellers also display their wares south along Shuncheng Donglu (顺城东路北段).

Temple of the Eight Immortals Antique Market
MARKET
There's a small antique market by the Temple of the Eight Immortals on Sunday and Wednesday mornings.

ℹ Information

Pick up a copy of the widely available *Xi'an Traffic & Tourist Map* (¥12), a bilingual publication with listings and bus routes. It's available at the airport and some bookshops. Chinese-language maps with the bus routes are sold on the street for ¥5. Shūyuàn Youth Hostel has useful free maps with key bus routes. The English-language magazine *Xianese* (www.xianese.com) is available at some hotels and restaurants that cater to tourists.

All hostels and most hotels offer internet access, and a number of internet cafes (网吧, *wǎngbā*) can be found around the long-distance bus station.

In the event of an emergency, call ☎120.

Bank of China (中国银行, Zhōngguó Yínháng) Juhuayuan Lu (38 Juhuayuan Lu; ⏲8am-8pm); Nan Dajie (29 Nan Dajie; ⏲8am-6pm) You can exchange cash and travellers cheques and use the ATMs at both of these branches.

China International Travel Service (CITS, 中国国际旅行社, Zhōngguó Guójì Lǚxíngshè) Branch office (2nd fl, Bell Tower Hotel, 110 Nan Dajie, 南大街二楼110号; ⏲8am-8pm); Main office (www.chinabravo.com; 48 Chang'an Beilu, 长安北路48号; ⏲8am-9pm) The branch office at Bell Tower Hotel is best for organising tours but the better deals are usually with the hostels.

China Post (中国邮政, Zhōngguó Yóuzhèng; Bei Dajie; ⏲8am-8pm)

Public Security Bureau (PSB, 公安局, Gōng'ānjú; 2 Keji Lu; ⏲8.30am-noon & 2-6pm Mon-Fri) This is on the southeast corner of Xixie 7 Lu. Visa extensions take five working days. To get there from the Bell Tower, take bus K205 and get off at Xixie 7 Lu.

ℹ Getting There & Away

AIR
Xī'ān's Xiányáng Airport is one of China's best connected – you can fly to almost any major Chinese destination from here, as well as several international ones. Most hostels and hotels and all travel agencies sell airline tickets.

China Eastern Airlines (中国东方航空公司, Zhōngguó Dōngfāng Hángkōng; ☑ 029 8208 8707; 64 Xi Wulu; ⊙8am-9pm) Operates most flights to and from Xī'ān. Daily flights include Běijīng (¥840), Chéngdū (¥630), Guǎngzhōu (¥890), Shànghǎi (¥1260) and Ürümqi (¥2060). On the international front, China Eastern has flights from Xī'ān to Hong Kong (¥1640), Seoul, Bangkok, Tokyo and Nagoya.

BUS

The long-distance bus station (长途汽车站, chángtú qìchēzhàn) is opposite Xī'ān's train station. It's a chaotic place. Note that buses to Huà Shān (6am to 8pm) depart from in front of the train station.

Other bus stations around town where you may be dropped off include the **east bus station** (城东客运站, chéngdōng kèyùnzhàn; Changle Lu, 长乐路) and the **west bus station** (城西客运站, chéngxī kèyùnzhàn; Zaoyuan Donglu, 枣园东路). Both are located outside the Second Ring Rd. Bus K43 travels between the Bell Tower and the east bus station, and bus 103 travels between the train station and the west bus station. A taxi into the city from either bus station costs between ¥15 and ¥20.

Buses from Xī'ān's long-distance bus station:

Luòyáng ¥107.50, five hours (10am, noon, 1pm, 3pm)

Píngyáo ¥160, six hours (8am, 9.30am, 10.30am, 12.30pm, 4.30pm)

Zhèngzhōu ¥133, six hours, hourly (7am to 4pm)

Buses from Xī'ān's east bus station:

Hánchéng ¥69, four hours, half-hourly (8am to 6.30pm)

Huà Shān one way ¥40.50, two hours, hourly (7.30am to 7pm)

Yán'ān ¥92.50, five hours, every 40 minutes (8.30am to 5.35pm)

TRAIN

Xī'ān's main train station (huǒchē zhàn) is just outside the northern city walls. It's always busy so arrive early for your departure to account for queues and poor signage. Buy your onward tickets as soon as you arrive.

Most hotels and hostels can get you tickets (¥40 commission); there's also an **advance train ticket booking booth** (代售火车票, Dàishòu Huǒchēpiào; Nan Dajie; 南大街; ⊙8.50am-noon & 1.30-4.30pm) in the ICBC Bank's south entrance and another **train ticket booth** (代售火车票, Dàishòu Huǒchēpiào; 14 Lianhu Lu; 连湖路14号; ⊙9am-noon & 1.30-4.30pm, to 2.30pm Sat & Sun) at the ICBC north of the Muslim Quarter near Bei Da Jie metro. Much easier than the hectic crowds in the main ticket hall.

Xī'ān is well connected to the rest of the country. Deluxe Z trains run to/from Běijīng west (soft sleeper only ¥417, 11½ hours), leaving Xī'ān at 7.23pm and Běijīng at 9.24pm. Several express trains also make the journey (¥265, 12½ hours); departures begin late afternoon. The Z94 to Shànghǎi departs 5.12pm and arrives 7.42am (hard/soft sleeper ¥333/511, 14½ hours).

From Xī'ān's north train station (běi huǒchē zhàn) high-speed 'bullet' G trains zip to Běijīng west (1st/2nd class ¥826/517, 5½ hours, 10 daily), Luòyáng (1st/2nd class ¥203/169, 1½ hours), and Wǔhàn (1st/2nd class ¥516/430, four hours, nine daily), with Shànghǎi, Lánzhōu and other destinations starting in the next several years.

All prices listed below are for hard/soft sleeper tickets.

Chéngdū ¥195/302, 16½ hours

Chóngqìng ¥179/275, 11 hours

Guìlín ¥372/587, 28 hours

Lánzhōu ¥171/261, seven to nine hours

Luòyáng ¥101/156, five hours

Píngyáo ¥120/189, nine hours

Shànghǎi ¥312/490, 14 to 20 hours

Tàiyuán ¥179/275, nine to 12 hours

Ürümqi ¥466/737, 28 to 35 hours

Zhèngzhōu ¥137/205, six to eight hours

Within Shaanxi, there are five trains (including two night trains) to Yúlín (hard/soft sleeper ¥136/214, eight to 10 hours) via Yán'ān (hard/soft sleeper ¥97/147, three to five hours). Buy tickets in advance. There is also an early morning train to Hánchéng (¥33, 4½ hours).

ⓘ Getting Around

Xī'ān's Xiányáng Airport is about 40km northwest of Xī'ān. Shuttle buses run every 20 to 30 minutes from 5.40am to 8pm between the airport and the Melody Hotel (¥26, one hour). Taxis into the city charge over ¥100 on the meter.

If you're itching to try out the public buses, they go to all the major sights in and around the city. Bus 610 is a useful one: it passes the train station, then onto the Bell Tower, Little Goose Pagoda, Shaanxi History Museum and Big Goose Pagoda. Remember that packed buses are a pickpocket's paradise, so watch your wallet.

Taxi flagfall is ¥6. It can be very difficult to get a taxi in the late afternoon, when the drivers change shifts. If you can cope with the congested roads, bikes are a good alternative and can be hired at the youth hostels.

The Xī'ān metro system (西安地铁, Xī'ān dìtiě) started up in 2011 with Line 2, followed by Line 1 in 2013 and Line 3 planned for 2015. Rides cost ¥2 to ¥4 depending on distance. Useful stations on Line 2 include Běihuǒchē Zhàn (north train station) and Xiǎozhài (near the Shaanxi History Museum). Line 1 has a stop at the Bànpō Neolithic Village.

Around Xī'ān

The plains surrounding Xī'ān are strewn with early imperial tombs, many of which have not yet been excavated. But unless you have a particular fascination for burial sites, you can probably come away satisfied after visiting a couple of them. The Army of Terracotta Warriors is obviously the most famous site, but it's really worth the effort to get to the Tomb of Emperor Jingdi (see p379) as well.

Tourist buses run to almost all of the sites from in front of Xī'ān's main train station, with the notable exception of the Tomb of Emperor Jingdi.

◉ Sights

◉ East of Xī'ān

Army of Terracotta Warriors HISTORIC SITE
(兵马俑, Bīngmǎyǒng; www.bmy.com.cn; admission Mar-Nov ¥150, students ¥75, Dec-Feb ¥120, students ¥60; ⊙ 8.30am-5.30pm Mar-Nov, to 5pm Dec-Feb) The Terracotta Army isn't just Xī'ān's premier site, but one of the most famous archaeological finds in the world. This subterranean life-size army of thousands has silently stood guard over the soul of China's first unifier for more than two millennia. Either Qin Shi Huang was terrified of the vanquished spirits awaiting him in the afterlife, or, as most archaeologists believe, he expected his rule to continue in death as it had in life – whatever the case, the guardians of his tomb today offer some of the greatest insights we have into the world of ancient China.

The discovery of the army of warriors was entirely fortuitous. In 1974, peasants drilling a well uncovered an underground vault that eventually yielded thousands of terracotta soldiers and horses in battle formation. Throughout the years the site became so famous that many of its unusual attributes are now well known, in particular the fact that no two soldier's faces are alike.

The on-site theatre gives a useful primer on how the figures were sculpted. You could also employ a guide (¥150) or try the audio-guide (¥40, plus ¥200 deposit), although the latter is somewhat useless, being difficult to understand and not very compelling.

Then visit the site in reverse, which enables you to build up to the most impressive pit for a fitting finale.

Start with the smallest pit, Pit 3, containing 72 warriors and horses, which is believed to be the army headquarters due to the number of high-ranking officers unearthed here. It's interesting to note that the northern room would have been used to make sacrificial offerings before battle. In the next pit, Pit 2, containing around 1300 warriors and horses, you get to examine five of the soldiers up close: a kneeling archer, a standing archer, a cavalryman and his horse, a mid-ranking officer and a general. The level of detail is extraordinary: the expressions, hairstyles, armour and even the tread on the footwear are all unique.

The largest pit, Pit 1, is the most imposing. Housed in a building the size of an aircraft hangar, it is believed to contain 6000 warriors (only 2000 are on display) and horses, all facing east and ready for battle. The vanguard of three rows of archers (both crossbow and longbow) is followed by the main force of soldiers, who originally held spears, swords, dagger-axes and other longshaft weapons. The infantry were accompanied by 35 chariots, though these, made of wood, have long since disintegrated.

Almost as extraordinary as the soldiers is a pair of bronze chariots and horses unearthed just 20m west of the Tomb of Qin Shi Huang. These are now on display, together with some of the original weaponry and a mid-ranking officer you can see up close in the open air, in a small museum to the right upon entering the main entrance.

The Army of Terracotta Warriors is easily reached by public bus. From Xī'ān Train Station's eastern car park, take one of the air-conditioned green or blue, clearly English-labelled 'Terracotta Warriors' buses (¥8, one hour, every 10 minutes) to the last stop, which travels via Huáqīng Hot Springs and the Tomb of Qin Shi Huang. The car park for all vehicles is a 15-minute walk through souvenir stalls from the Terracotta Warriors site, with the ticket kiosk near the parking lot. Electric carts do the run for ¥5. If you want to eat here, go for the restaurants across from the car park. To get back to Xī'ān, buses leave from the parking lot.

Huáqīng Hot Springs HISTORIC SITE
(华清池, Huáqīng Chí; admission Mar-Nov ¥110, Dec-Feb ¥80, children under 1.2m free, cable car one way/return ¥45/70; ⊙ 7am-7pm Mar-Nov,

7.30am-6.30pm Dec-Feb) The natural hot springs in this park were once the favoured retreat of emperors and concubines during the Tang dynasty. It's now an obligatory stop for Chinese tour groups, who pose for photos in front of the elaborately restored pavilions and by the ornamental ponds. Thought a pretty place, it's not really worth the high admission price. You can, however, hike up to the **Taoist temple** on Black Horse Mountain (Lí Shān).

The temple is dedicated to Nuwa, who created the human race from clay and also patched up cracks in the sky. There's also a **cable car** to the temple, but note that the stop is outside the park, so you won't be able to get back in unless you buy another ticket.

Tomb of Qin Shi Huang   HISTORIC SITE
(秦始皇陵, Qín Shǐhuáng Líng; admission free with Terracotta Warrior ticket; ⊙ 8am-6pm Mar-Nov, to 5pm Dec-Feb) **FREE** In its time this tomb must have been one of the grandest mausoleums the world had ever seen. Historical accounts describe it as containing palaces filled with precious stones, underground rivers of flowing mercury and ingenious defences against intruders. The tomb reputedly took 38 years to complete, and required a workforce of 700,000 people. It is said that the artisans who built it were buried alive within, taking its secrets with them.

Archaeologists have yet to enter the tomb but probes and sensors have been sent inside. Levels of mercury inside exceed 100 times the normal occurring rate, which seems to substantiate some of the legends. Since little has been excavated there isn't much to see but you can climb the steps to the top of the mound for a fine view of the surrounding countryside.

The Terracotta Warriors bus from Xī'ān train station stops at the tomb, which is 2km west of the warriors.

Bànpō Neolithic Village   ANCIENT VILLAGE
(半坡博物馆, Bànpō Bówùguǎn; admission Mar-Nov ¥65, Dec-Feb ¥45; ⊙ 8am-6pm) Bànpō is the earliest example of the neolithic Yangshao culture, which is believed to have been matriarchal. It appears to have been occupied from 4500 BC until around 3750 BC. The excavated area is divided into three parts: a pottery manufacturing area, a residential area complete with moat, and a cemetery.

This village is of enormous importance for Chinese archaeological studies, but unless you're desperately interested in the subject it can be an underwhelming visitor experience.

There are two exhibition halls that feature some of the pottery, including strange shaped amphorae, discovered at the site.

The village is in the eastern suburbs of Xī'ān. Bus 105 (¥1) from the train station runs past (ask where to get off); it's also often included on tours.

◎ North & West of Xī'ān

Fǎmén Temple   BUDDHIST TEMPLE
(法门寺, Fǎmén Sì; admission Mar-Nov ¥120, Dec-Feb ¥90; ⊙ 8am-6pm) This temple dating back to the 2nd century AD was built to house parts of a sacred finger bone of the Buddha, presented to China by India's King Asoka. Although it may feel like a Cecil B DeMille Hollywood movie set, the older section is

WORTH A TRIP

TOMB OF EMPEROR JINGDI

The **Tomb of Emperor Jingdi** (汉阳陵, Hàn Yánglíng; admission Mar-Nov ¥90, Dec-Feb ¥65; ⊙8.30am-7pm Mar-Nov, to 6pm Dec-Feb), which is also referred to as the Han Jing Mausoleum, Liu Qi Mausoleum and Yangling Mausoleum, is easily Xī'ān's most underrated highlight. If you only have time for two sights, then it should be the Army of Terracotta Warriors and this impressive museum and tomb. Unlike the warriors, though, there are relatively few visitors here so you have the space to appreciate what you're seeing.

A Han-dynasty emperor influenced by Taoism, Jingdi (188–141 BC) based his rule upon the concept of *wúwéi* (nonaction or noninterference) and did much to improve the life of his subjects: he lowered taxes greatly, used diplomacy to cut back on unnecessary military expeditions and even reduced the punishment meted out to criminals. The contents of his tomb are particularly interesting, as they reveal more about daily life than martial preoccupations – a total contrast with the Terracotta Army.

The site has been divided into two sections: the museum and the excavation area. The **museum** holds a large display of expressive terracotta figurines (more than 50,000 were buried here), including eunuchs, servants, domesticated animals and even female cavalry on horseback. The figurines originally had movable wooden arms (now gone) and were dressed in colourful silk robes.

Inside the **tomb** are 21 narrow pits, some of which have been covered by a glass floor, allowing you to walk over the top of ongoing excavations and get a great view of the relics. In all, there are believed to be 81 burial pits here.

To get here, take Xī'ān metro Line 2 to the station Shitushuguan. Outside exit D take bus 4 (¥1) to the tomb, which leaves at 8.30am, 9.30am, 10.30am, noon, 1.30pm, 3pm, 4pm and 5pm, returning to the Xī'ān metro station at 9am, noon, 4pm and 5pm.

Alternatively, you can take a tour (around ¥160), usually arranged by the guesthouses. The tomb is 20 minutes from the airport, so makes an easy stop-off by taxi.

still worth a visit and you can join the queue of pilgrims who shuffle past the finger bone. The real reason to make the trip out here is the superb **museum** and its collection of Tang-dynasty treasures.

There are elaborate gold and silver boxes (stacked on top of one another to form pagodas) and tiny crystal and jade coffins that originally contained the four separated sections of the holy finger.

In 1981, after torrential rains had weakened the temple's ancient brick structure, the entire western side of its 12-storey pagoda collapsed. The subsequent restoration of the temple produced a sensational discovery. Below the pagoda in a sealed crypt were over 1000 sacrificial objects and royal offerings – all forgotten for over a millennium.

Sensing a cash cow, the local authorities began enlarging the temple complex and it now includes a sprawling modern section featuring a 1.6km-long walkway lined with 10 golden Buddhas, eccentric modern sculptures and outsized gates. Shuttle buses (¥20) are on hand to whisk the pious to the main temple, which is topped with an enormous replica of the box in which the finger bone was kept.

Other notable exhibits are ornate incense burners, glass cups and vases from the Roman Empire, statues, gold and silver offerings, and an excellent reproduced cross-section of the four-chamber crypt, which symbolised a tantric mandala (a geometric representation of the universe).

Fǎmén Temple is 115km northwest of Xī'ān. Tour bus 2 (¥25, 8am) from Xī'ān train station runs to the temple and returns to Xī'ān at 5pm. The temple is also generally included on Western Tours.

Xiányáng City Museum　　　MUSEUM
(咸阳市博物馆, Xiányáng Shì Bówùguǎn; Zhongshan Jie, 中山街; ⊙9am-5.30pm Tue-Sun) FREE More than 2000 years ago Xiányáng was the capital of the Qin dynasty. These days, it's just a dusty satellite of Xī'ān. Its chief attraction is this museum, which houses a remarkable collection of 3000 50cm-tall terracotta soldiers and horses, excavated from the tomb of Liu Bang, the first Han emperor, in 1965. Set in an attractive courtyard, the

museum also has bronze and jade exhibits and good English captions.

Show your passport for free entry. Buses run every 15 minutes to Xiányáng (¥8.50, one hour) from Xī'ān's long-distance bus station. Ask to be dropped off at the museum. To get back to Xī'ān, just flag down buses going in the opposite direction.

Imperial Tombs HISTORIC SITES

A large number of imperial tombs (皇陵, huáng líng) dot the Guānzhōng plain around Xī'ān. They are sometimes included on tours from Xī'ān, but most aren't so remarkable as to be destinations in themselves. By far the most impressive is the **Qián Tomb** (乾陵, Qián Líng; admission incl other imperial tombs Mar-Nov ¥45, Dec-Feb ¥25; ⊙8am-6pm), where China's only female emperor, Wu Zetian (AD 625–705), is buried with her husband Emperor Gaozong, whom she succeeded.

The long **Spirit Way** (神道, Shéndào; outdoor, paved path leading to the tomb) here is lined with enormous, lichen-encrusted sculptures of animals and officers of the imperial guard, culminating with 61 (now headless) statues of Chinese ethnic group leaders who attended the emperor's funeral. The mausoleum is 85km northwest of Xī'ān. Tour bus 2 (¥25, 8am) runs close to here from Xī'ān train station and returns in the late afternoon.

Nearby are the **tomb of Princess Yong Tai** (永泰幕, Yǒng Tài Mù) and the **tomb of Prince Zhang Huai** (章怀幕, Zhāng Huái Mù), both of whom fell foul of Empress Wu, before being posthumously rehabilitated. Other notable tombs are the **Zhao Tomb** (昭陵, Zhāo Líng), where the second Tang emperor or Taizhong is buried, and the **Mao Tomb** (茂陵, Mào Líng), the resting place of Wudi (156–87 BC), the most powerful of the Han emperors.

☞ Tours

One-day tours allow you to see all the sights around Xī'ān more quickly and conveniently than if you arranged one yourself. Itineraries differ somewhat, but there are two basic tours: an Eastern Tour and a Western Tour.

Most hostels run their own tours, but make sure you find out what is included (admission fees, lunch, English-speaking guide) and try to get an exact itinerary, or you could end up being herded through the Terracotta Warriors before you have a chance to get your camera out.

Eastern Tour

The Eastern Tour is the most popular as it includes the Army of Terracotta Warriors, as well as the Tomb of Qin Shi Huang, Bànpō Neolithic Village, Huáqīng Hot Springs and possibly the Big Goose Pagoda. Most travel agencies and hostels charge around ¥300 for an all-day, all-in excursion, including admission fees, lunch and guide, although sometimes the hostel tours skip Bànpō. Tours to the Terracotta Warriors only are also available at around ¥160.

It's perfectly possible to do a shortened version of the Eastern Tour by using the tourist buses or bus 306, all of which pass by Huáqīng Hot Springs, the Terracotta Warriors and the Tomb of Qin Shi Huang. If you decide to do this, start at the hot springs, then travel to Qin Shi Huang's tomb and end at the Terracotta Warriors.

Western Tour

The longer Western Tour includes the Xiányáng City Museum, some of the imperial tombs, and possibly also Fǎmén Temple and (if you insist) the Tomb of Emperor Jingdi. It's far less popular than the Eastern Tour and consequently you may have to wait a couple of days for your hostel or agency to organise enough people. It's also more expensive; expect to pay ¥600.

A tour of the Tomb of Emperor Jingdi, usually done by itself without any other sights, will cost around ¥160.

Huà Shān 华山

One of Taoism's five sacred mountains, the granite domes of Huà Shān used to be home to hermits and sages. These days, though, the trails that wind their way up to the five peaks are populated by droves of day trippers drawn by the dreamy scenery. And it is spectacular. There are knife-blade ridges and twisted pine trees clinging to ledges as you ascend, while the summits offer transcendent panoramas of green mountains and countryside stretching away to the horizon. Taoists hoping to find a quiet spot to contemplate life and the universe will be disappointed, but everyone else seems to revel in the tough climb and they're suitably elated once they reach the top. So forget all that spiritual malarkey and get walking.

◉ Sights & Activities

There are three ways up the mountain to the **North Peak** (北峰, Běi Fēng), the first of five summit peaks. Two of these options start from the eastern base of the mountain, at the North Peak cable-car terminus. The first option is handy if you don't fancy the climb: an Austrian-built **cable car** (one way/return ¥80/150; ⊙7am-7pm) will lift you to the North Peak in eight scenic minutes, though you may have to queue for over an hour at busy times.

The second option is to work your way to the North Peak under the cable-car route. This takes a sweaty two hours, and two sections of 50m or so are quite literally vertical, with nothing but a steel chain to grab onto and tiny chinks cut into the rock for footing. Not for nothing is this route called the 'Soldiers Path.'

The third option is the most popular, but it's still hard work. A 6km path leads to the North Peak from the village of Huà Shān, at the base of the mountain (the other side of the mountain from the cable car). It usually takes between three and five hours to reach the North Peak via this route. The first 4km up are pretty easy going, but after that it's all steep stairs.

The village at the trailhead is a good place to stock up on water and snacks; these are also available at shops on the trail but prices double and triple the further you head up the mountain. Curiously, you'll also see old ladies selling cotton gloves, the purpose of which becomes obvious at the steepest sections where you need to grab onto rusty chains for support.

If you want to carry on to the other peaks, then count on a minimum of eight hours in total from the base of Huà Shān. If you want to spare your knees, then another option is to take the cable car to the North Peak and then climb to the other peaks, before ending up back where you started. It takes about four hours to complete the circuit in this fashion and it's still fairly strenuous. In places, it can be a little nerve-racking, too. Huà Shān has a reputation for being dangerous, especially when the trails are crowded, or if it's wet or icy, so exercise caution.

But the scenery is sublime. Along **Blue Dragon Ridge** (苍龙岭, Cānglóng Lǐng), which connects the North Peak with the **East Peak** (东峰, Dōng Fēng), **South Peak** (南峰, Nán Fēng) and **West Peak** (西峰, Xī Fēng), the way has been cut along a narrow rock ridge with impressive sheer cliffs on either side.

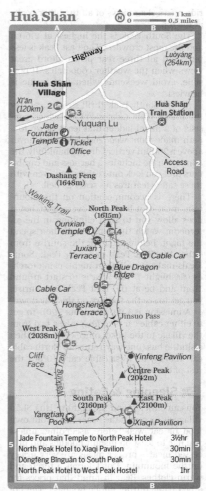

Huà Shān

🛏 Sleeping

A West Peak **cable car** (one way/return ¥140/280; ⊙7am-7pm) started operation in mid-2013. Less crowded than the North Peak cable car, the West Peak's 20-minute ride offers clear views of all the other peaks at the top.

The South Peak is the highest at 2160m and the most crowded. The East Peak is less busy, but all three rear peaks afford great views when the weather cooperates. If possible, avoid weekends when foot traffic is heaviest.

At the South Peak thrill-seekers can try the **Plank Walk** (admission ¥30), which consists of a metal ladder that leads down to a path made from wooden boards that hover above a 2000m vertical drop. Thankfully, the admission fee includes a harness and carabiners that you lock onto cables, but even with these safety features it's scary as hell.

There is accommodation on the mountain, most of it basic and overpriced, but it does allow you to start climbing in the afternoon, watch the sunset and then spend the night, before catching the sunrise from either the East Peak or South Peak. Some locals make the climb at night, using torches (flashlights). The idea is to start around 11pm and be at the East Peak for sunrise; you get to see the scenery on the way down.

Admission is ¥180 (students ¥90). To get to either cable car (suŏdào), take a taxi from the village to the ticket office (¥10) and then a shuttle bus (one way/return to North cable car ¥20/40, to West cable car ¥40/80) the rest of the way.

🛏 Sleeping & Eating

You can either spend the night in Huà Shān village or on one of the peaks. Take your own food or eat well before ascending, unless you like to feast on instant noodles and processed meat – proper meals are very pricey on the mountain. Don't forget a torch and warm clothes. Bear in mind that prices for a bed triple during public holidays. The hotels on the mountain are basic; there are no showers and only shared bathrooms.

In the village, there are a number of dingy, shabby hotels along Yuquan Lu, the road leading up to the trailhead, that offer beds from ¥50 upwards. Pretty much every shop has rooms and the owners will find you. There are smarter places on Yuquan Donglu.

Huáyuè Kuài Jié Jiŭdiàn HOTEL $
(华岳快捷酒店; ☑ 0913 436 8555; Yuquan Donglu, 玉泉路, Huà Shān village; s & d ¥150; ☜) Clean and simple rooms with OK bathrooms make this an obvious option for budget travellers. It's on Yuquan Lu at the bottom of the hill near the main intersection.

West Peak Hostel HOSTEL $
(西峰旅社, Xīfēng Lǚshè; dm ¥100) Rustic and basic, but also the friendliest place on the mountain. It shares its premises with an old Taoist temple.

Míngzhū Jiŭdiàn HOTEL $$
(明珠酒店; ☑ 0913-436 9899; Yuquan Donglu, 玉泉東路, Huà Shān village; s & d ¥238-281; ❉ ☜) Located in Huà Shān village at the main intersection, this Chinese two-star hotel has clean, modern rooms with wi-fi. Discounts of 30% available outside peak holiday travel times.

Dōngfēng Bīnguǎn HOTEL $$
(东峰宾馆; dm ¥150-220, tr/d ¥280/340) The top location on the East Peak for watching the sun come up also has the best restaurant.

Wǔyúnfēng Fàndiàn HOTEL $$
(五云峰饭店; dm ¥100-180, tr/d ¥220/300) This basic hotel is along the Black Dragon Ridge and on a hillside, not a peak. A good choice mostly if you're planning on doing a circuit of the rear peaks the next day, or want to catch the sunrise at the East or South Peak.

North Peak Hotel HOTEL $$
(北峰饭店, Běifēng Fàndiàn; ☑ 157 1913 6466; dm ¥100, d ¥260-280) The busiest of the peak hotels.

❶ Getting There & Away

From Xī'ān to Huà Shān, catch one of the private buses (¥36, two hours, 6am to 8pm) that depart when full from in front of Xī'ān train station. You'll be dropped off on Yuquan Lu, which is also where buses back to Xī'ān leave from 7.30am to 7pm. Coming from the east, try to talk your driver into dropping you at the Huà Shān highway exit if you can't find a direct bus. Don't pay more than ¥10 for a taxi into Huà Shān village. There are few buses (if any) going east from Huà Shān; pretty much everyone catches a taxi to the highway and then flags down buses headed for Yùnchéng, Tàiyuán or Luòyáng. If you can't read Chinese, try to find someone to help you out.

Hánchéng 韩城

☑ 0913 / POP 59,000

Hánchéng is best known for being the hometown of Sima Qian (145–90 BC), China's legendary historian and author of the *Shiji* (Records of the Grand Historian). Sima Qian chronicled different aspects of life in the Han dynasty and set about arranging the country's already distant past in its proper (Confucian) order. He was eventually castrated and imprisoned by Emperor Wudi, after having defended an unsuccessful general.

Hánchéng makes for a good side trip from Xī'ān. Built upon a hill, the new town (新城, *xīnchéng*) located at the top is dusty and unremarkable and is where you'll find hotels, banks and transport. But the more atmospheric old town (古城, *gǔchéng*) at the bottom of the hill boasts a handful of historic sights. The unique Ming-dynasty village of Dǎngjiācūn is 9km further east.

◉ Sights

Confucius & Chénghuáng Temples CONFUCIAN TEMPLE
In the heart of the old town, the tranquil **Confucius Temple** (文庙, Wén Miào; admission ¥15; ⊘8am-5.30pm) is the pick of the sights in Hánchéng itself. The weathered Yuan, Ming and Qing buildings give an understated sense of how long they have stood the test of time. They contrast with the dramatic towering cypress trees, half-moon pool and glazed dragon screens. The city museum holds peripheral exhibits in the wings.

At the back of the Confucius Temple is the **Chénghuáng Temple** (城隍庙, Chénghuáng Miào; admission ¥15; ⊘8am-5.30pm), in a lane lined with Ming-dynasty courtyard houses.

There has been a temple here since the Zhou dynasty, but the whole site has undergone extensive renovation in recent years. The main attraction is the **Sacrificing Hall**, with its intricate roof detail, where gifts were offered to the gods to protect the city.

Buying a ticket to either temple gets you into the other as well. Bus 102 (¥1) runs here from the southwest corner of Huanghe Dajie, close to the bus station. A taxi is ¥10.

Yuánjué Pagoda MONUMENT
(园觉寺塔, Yuánjué Sìtǎ; ⊘6am-6pm) Looming over the old town and dating back to the Tang dynasty, but rebuilt in 1958, this pagoda also acts as a memorial to Red Army soldiers killed fighting the KMT. It's impossible to climb the pagoda itself, but the steep ascent to it offers panoramic views over the old town. To get here, turn sharp right when leaving the Chénghuáng Temple and take the first major right you come to. The walk takes you through the most evocative part of the old town; exit the pagoda through the park on the other side and you're back in the new town.

Dǎngjiācūn HISTORIC SITE
(党家村; admission ¥40; ⊘7.30am-6.30pm) This perfectly preserved, 14th-century village nestles in a sheltered location in a loess valley. Once the home of the Dang clan, successful merchants who ferried timber and other goods across the Yellow River (黄河, Huáng Hé), it's since evolved into a quintessential farming community. The village is home to 125 grey-brick courtyard houses, which are notable for their carvings and mix of different architectural styles. The elegant six-storey tower is a **Confucian pagoda** (*Wénxīng gé*).

SHAANXI (SHĀNXĪ) HÁNCHÉNG

THE MAN BEHIND THE ARMY

Qin Shi Huang, China's first emperor, has gone down in history as the sort of tyrant who gives tyrants a bad name. It might be because he outlawed Confucianism, ordered almost all its written texts to be burnt and, according to legend, buried 460 of its top scholars alive.

Or perhaps it was his enslaving of hundreds of thousands of people to achieve his (admittedly monumental) accomplishments during his 36 years of rule (which began when he was just 13).

In recent years, there have been efforts by the China Communist Party (CCP) to rehabilitate him, by emphasising both his efforts to unify China and the far-sighted nature of his policies. A classic overachiever, he created an efficient, centralised government that became the model for later dynasties; he standardised measurements, currency and, most importantly, writing. He built over 6400km of new roads and canals and, of course, he conquered six major kingdoms before turning 40.

Nevertheless, he remains a hugely controversial figure in Chinese history, but also one whose presence permeates popular culture. The first emperor pops up in video games, in literature and on TV shows. He's also been the subject of films by both Chen Kaige and Zhang Yimou (*The Emperor and the Assassin* and *Hero*), while Jet Li played a thinly disguised version of him in the 2008 Hollywood blockbuster *The Mummy: Tomb of the Dragon Emperor*.

Unfortunately, many of the families have moved out and their homes are now exhibition showrooms, so the village feels a little lifeless. Still, it's worth a wander to explore the old alleys and admire the architecture.

Dǎngjiācūn is 9km northeast of Hánchéng. To get here, take a minibus (¥3, 20 minutes) from the bus station to the entrance road, from where it's a pleasant 2km walk through fields to the village. Otherwise, you can take a taxi from Hánchéng (¥35).

🛏 Sleeping

For something completely different, spend the night in Dǎngjiācūn, where basic dorm beds in some of the courtyard houses are available for ¥30. If a local doesn't approach you, just ask and you'll be pointed in the right direction. They also offer simple and cheap home cooking.

If you'd prefer to spend the night in town, try one of the following options.

Tiānyuán Bīnguǎn HOTEL $
(天园宾馆; ☑ 0913 529 9388; Longmen Dajie Beiduan, 龙门大街北段; s & d ¥120-130; ❄ @) A few doors down from the main bus station, this place has simple but perfectly functional rooms.

Yínhé Dàjiǔdiàn HOTEL $$
(银河大酒店; ☑ 0913 529 2555; Longmen Dajie Nanduan, 龙门大街南段; r ¥398; ❄ @) This is an upmarket option. From the bus station turn left and walk on the main road for about 10 minutes. Discounts of 30% are available.

ℹ Information

Bank of China (中国银行, Zhōngguó Yínháng; cnr Huanghe Dajie & Jinta Zhonglu; ⏱8am-6pm) There's a branch of the Bank of China close to the bus station that has a 24-hour ATM and will change cash.

ℹ Getting There & Away

Buses leave Xī'ān's east bus station for Hánchéng (¥68, three hours, seven daily) from 7am onwards. Buses back to Xī'ān run until 6.30pm. There are two buses per day to Huà Shān (¥40.50, two hours) at 7am and 12.30pm. There are also two daily buses to Yán'ān (¥79.50, eight hours) at 6.50am and 8am.

A middle-of-the-night train runs from Xī'ān to Hánchéng (¥33, 4½ hours) at 2.31am. From Hánchéng, the daily K610 train rumbles towards Běijīng (hard sleeper ¥238, 16 hours)

via Píngyáo (¥96, six hours) and Tàiyuán (¥115, eight hours), departing at 2.10pm.

Yán'ān 延安

☎ 0911 / POP 107,000

When the diminished communist armies pitched up here at the end of the Long March, it signalled the beginning of Yán'ān's brief period in the sun. For 12 years, from 1935 to 1947, this backwater town was the CCP headquarters, and it was in the surrounding caves that the party established much of the ideology that was put into practice during the Chinese revolution.

These days, Yán'ān's residents seem to be more interested in consumerism than communism; for a small place, there are a surprising number of shopping malls. But its livelihood is still tied to the CCP; endless tour groups of mostly middle-aged 'red tourists' pass through each year on the trail of Mao and his cohorts. Few foreigners make it here, so expect some attention.

⊙ Sights

Yán'ān Revolution Museum MUSEUM
(延安革命简史陈列馆, Yán'ān Gémìng Jiǎnshǐ Chénlièguǎn; Shengdi Lu; ⏱8.30am-5pm) FREE By far the most flash building in town is the **Yán'ān Revolutionary Memorial Hall** (延安革命纪念馆, Yán'ān Gémìng Jìniànguǎn), fronted by a statue of Mao and housing this museum. It offers an excellent, if obviously one-sided, account of the CCP's time in Yán'ān and the Sino-Japanese War. More English captions would be nice, but there are plenty of photos of the good old days and other exhibits that are self-explanatory. Bus 1 (¥1) runs here.

You can walk here in a few minutes southeast from the Wángjiāpíng Revolution Headquarters Site.

Wángjiāpíng Revolution Headquarters Site HISTORIC SITE
(王家坪革命旧址, Wángjiāpíng Gémìng Jiùzhǐ; Wangjiaping Lu; ⏱8am-5.30pm Mar-Nov, 8.30am-5pm Dec-Feb) FREE During an extended stay, the communist leadership moved around Yán'ān, resulting in numerous former headquarters sites. Adjacent to the Revolution Museum is the last site occupied by the communist leadership in Yán'ān. The improved living conditions at the site, houses rather than dugouts, indicate the way the CCP's fortunes were rising by the time it moved here.

Yángjiālíng Revolution Headquarters Site
HISTORIC SITE

(杨家岭革命旧址, Yángjiālíng Gémìng Jiùzhǐ; Yangjialing Lu; ⏱8am-6pm Mar-Nov, 8.30am-5pm Dec-Feb) **FREE** Perhaps the most interesting site, this is located 3km northwest of the town centre. Here you can see the assembly hall where the first central committee meetings were held, including the seventh national plenum, which formally confirmed Mao as the leader of the party and the revolution. It's fun watching the red tourists pose in old CCP uniforms in front of the podium.

Nearby are simple **dugouts** built into the loess earth where Mao Zedong, Zhu De, Zhou Enlai and other senior communist leaders lived, worked and wrote.

Zǎoyuán Revolution Headquarters Site
HISTORIC SITE

(枣园革命旧址, Zǎoyuán Gémìng Jiùzhǐ; Zaoyuan Lu, 枣园路; ⏱8am-6pm Mar-Nov, 8.30am-5pm Dec-Feb) **FREE** The Communist leadership took refuge here between 1943 and 1947, on land allocated by a wealthy merchant. The leafy grounds are perhaps the most attractive of the revolutionary sites. It is located 4km past the Yángjiālíng site.

Fènghuángshān Revolution Headquarters Site
HISTORIC SITE

(凤凰山革命旧址, Fènghuángshān Gémìng Jiùzhǐ; Fenghuangshanlu, 凤凰山路; ⏱8am-5pm Mar-Nov) This was the first site occupied by the communists after their move to Yán'ān, before being abandoned because it was too exposed to enemy aircraft fire. There's a photo exhibit about Norman Bethune, the Canadian doctor who became a hero in China for treating CCP casualties in the late 1930s. More accessible from town, this site is about 100m west of China Post.

Treasure Pagoda
PAGODA

(宝塔, Bǎo Tǎ; 宝塔山, Baota Shan; admission ¥65; ⏱6.30am-9pm Mar-Nov, to 8pm Dec-Feb) Yán'ān's most prominent landmark, Treasure Pagoda dates back to the Song dynasty. For an extra ¥10, you can climb the very narrow steps and ladders of the pagoda for an unrestricted view of the city.

Qīngliáng Mountain
PARK

(清凉山, Qīngliáng Shān; admission ¥31; ⏱8am-7pm Mar-Nov, to 5.30pm Dec-Feb) This was the birthplace of the CCP propaganda machine; *Xinhua* News Agency and the *Liberation Daily* started life here when the place was known as 'Information Mountain.' Now, it's a pleasant hillside park with good city views, some nice trails and a few sights, including **Ten Thousand Buddha Cave** (万佛洞, Wànfó Dòng) dug into the sandstone cliff beside the river. The cave has relatively intact Buddhist statues.

🛏 Sleeping & Eating

There are few budget options in Yán'ān. Most hotels, though, offer discounts. It's also not a gourmet's paradise, though the night market, just off the small square in the centre of town, is a fine spot for eating alfresco and meeting the locals. Try the very tasty handmade noodles.

Yàshèng Dàjiǔdiàn
HOTEL $$

(亚圣大酒店; ☎0911 266 6000; Erdaojie Zhongduan, 二道街中段; tw ¥328-368; ❄) Located in the centre of town, the rooms here are clean and comfortable, if a bit gloomy. There's a decent restaurant (dishes ¥14 to ¥40) on the top floor. Discounts of 40% are the norm.

Hǎishèng Jiǔdiàn
HOTEL $$$

(海盛酒店; ☎0911 821 3333; Daqiaojie, 大桥街; s/d ¥438/698; ❄@) This hotel has excellent rooms with computers and the price includes breakfast. In a town of overpriced hotels this is not a bad option, with rooms usually going for around ¥268. Discounts of 50% available outside peak travel times.

ℹ Information

Bank of China (中国银行, Zhōngguó Yínháng; Daqiao Jie; ⏱8am-5pm) On the corner of Daqiao Jie and Erdao Jie, this branch has a 24-hour ATM. There are other ATMs around town, too.

China Post (中国邮政, Zhōngguó Yóuzhèng; Yan'anshi Dajie, 延安市大街; ⏱9am-5pm) Post and telephone office.

Internet Cafe (网吧; Wǎngbā; Erdaojie Zhongduan, 二道街中段; per hr ¥3; ⏱24hr) On the 2nd floor, down an alley just to the left of the Yàshèng Dàjiǔdiàn.

ℹ Getting There & Away

BUS

From Xī'ān's east bus station (汽车东站, qìchē dōngzhàn), there are buses to Yán'ān (¥92.50, four hours) every 40 minutes from 8.30am to 5.35pm. The schedule back to Xī'ān is essentially the same. Buses arrive and depart from the south bus station (汽车南站, qìchē nánzhàn).

At Yán'ān's east bus station (汽车东站, qìchē dōngzhàn), there are buses to Yúlín (¥80, five hours) every 50 minutes from 7.25am to

SHAANXI (SHǍNXĪ) YÁN'ĀN

FROM FARM BOY TO EMPEROR

Li Zicheng enjoyed a remarkable rise from shepherd to sitting on the imperial throne and led the most successful of the many peasant rebellions that took place in the dying days of the Ming dynasty. Born in 1606, Li drew tens of thousands of followers in famine-racked, 1630s Shaanxi by advocating equal shares of land for all and no taxes. Having taken over large parts of Shaanxi, Shānxī and Hénán, Li and his army sacked Běijīng and, after the suicide of the last Ming emperor, Li proclaimed himself Emperor of the Shun dynasty in April 1644.

His reign was short-lived. Less than two months later, the invading Manchu forces defeated his army and Li retreated back to Shaanxi and subsequently to Húběi, where he either committed suicide or was killed in 1645. Four centuries later, Li's impeccable socialist credentials made him an ideal role model for the CCP, who continue to laud his exploits as an early revolutionary.

5.30pm. Local buses to Mǐzhī (¥53.50, four hours) depart at 9.15am, 1.10pm and 2.20pm.

Heading west, there are departures to Yínchuān in Níngxià (¥127, eight hours); buses leave at 8am, 9.30am and 10.30am, while sleepers leave at 4pm and 5.30pm. You can also get into Shānxī and Hénán from here.

TRAIN

Frequent high-speed trains to Xī'ān (hard/soft sleeper ¥96/146, three hours) started in 2013, making tickets easier to come by. A taxi from the train station into town costs ¥10.

ⓘ Getting Around

The Revolution Headquarters sites can be reached by taking bus 1, which runs along the road east of the river and then heads up Shengdi Lu. This bus starts at the train station. Bus 8 also passes by these places and can be caught from Da Bridge (大桥). The taxi flag fall is ¥5.

Yúlín   榆林

☑ 0912 / POP 92,000

Thanks to extensive coal mining and the discovery of natural gas fields nearby, this one-time garrison town on the fringes of Inner Mongolia's Mu Us Desert is booming. Despite all the construction, there's still enough of interest to make this a good place to break a trip if you're following the Great Wall or heading north on the trail of Genghis Khan.

⦿ Sights

Parts of the earthen city walls are still intact, while the main north–south pedestrian street in the elongated old town (divided into Beidajie and Nandajie) has several restored buildings, including a Bell Tower (钟楼, Zhōng Lóu) first erected in 1472 and destroyed several times (the current tower dates to the early 20th century). With several restaurants and antique shops, it's a nice street to wander at night, when it's lit by lanterns.

Seven kilometres north of the Yúlín bus station, on the outskirts of town, are some badly eroded sections of the Great Wall and a Ming-era four-storey beacon tower (镇北台, zhènběitái; admission ¥20; ☺7.30am-7.30pm) that dates to 1607. Bus 11 (¥1) runs here from Changcheng Nanlu, about 200m west of the main bus station.

🛏 Sleeping

Jiāyuán Shāngwù Bīnguǎn   HOTEL $
(嘉源商务宾馆; ☑0912 326 8958; 2nd fl, 5 Yuyang Zhonglu, 榆扬中路5号二楼; r ¥168) Five minutes' walk west from the main bus station, this cheapie has a filthy staircase but the rooms are OK. A massive internet cafe is located on the 2nd floor.

Jīnyù Hotel   HOTEL $$
(金域大酒店, Jīnyù Dàjiǔdiàn; ☑0912 233 3333; 6 Xinjian Nanlu, 新建南路6号; tw/d ¥238/268; ✳@) This midrange place has large comfortable rooms and cable internet access. It's across the street from the main train station. Discounts of 30% available.

ⓘ Getting There & Around

Taxis around town and to the train station will cost you ¥6.

AIR

There are several daily flights from Yúlín to Xī'ān (¥290).

BUS

Yúlín has two bus stations. If you get off the bus inside the town walls (near the south gate), you are at the **main (south) bus station** (汽车站, qìchē zhàn); the **regional (north) bus station** (客运站, kèyùn zhàn) is located 3.5km northwest on Yingbin Dadao.

The main bus station has regular buses to Xī'ān (¥170 to ¥181, seven to eight hours) from 7.25am to 7.30pm. You can also get frequent buses to Yán'ān (¥80, five hours, half-hourly) from 7.25am to 5pm, to Yínchuān (¥142, five to six hours, eight daily), and two daily buses to Tàiyuán (¥136, eight hours, 6.50am and 12.50pm).

The regional bus station has buses to Bāotóu in Inner Mongolia (¥94, four hours, hourly) and to Dàliǔtǎ (¥49, two hours, every 30 minutes), from where you can travel on to Dōngshèng. The buses to Dōngshèng pass by Genghis Khan's Mausoleum.

Bus 1 (¥1) runs between the two bus stations.

TRAIN

The train station is 4km west of the main bus station. There are trains to Xī'ān (hard/soft sleeper ¥145/223, nine to 10 hours, five daily) via Yán'ān, but sleeper tickets are pretty much impossible to grab on short notice.

Mǐzhǐ 米脂

☑ 0912

About 70km south of Yúlín, Mǐzhǐ is famous as the hometown of Li Zicheng, protocommunist and would-be emperor, as well as for the alleged beauty of its female residents.

Despite those twin draws, it's a sleepy place with a small Hui presence and way off the tourist circuit; you will be the sole foreigner in town and likely the only visitor of any description. Some of the local population still live in caves and homes carved out of the surrounding hillsides, while the small old quarter, with its narrow alleys and dilapidated courtyard homes, is a fascinating place to wander.

The principal sight, though, is the Li Zicheng Palace (李自成行宫, Lǐ Zichéng Xínggōng; Xinggong Lu, 行宫路; admission ¥20; ☉8am-5pm). This well-preserved and compact palace was built in 1643 at the height of Li's power. Set against a hillside, there's a statue of the man himself, as well as pavilions, which house exhibits about Li and notable Mǐzhǐ women, and a pagoda. There's also a fine theatre, where music performances and plays were held, sometimes for three days at a time, to celebrate Li's victories. To reach the palace, walk east on Xinggong Lu. It's a 10- to 15-minute walk from the bus station.

Turn left immediately after leaving the palace and you are in the heart of the old quarter of Mǐzhǐ. Many of the original, late-Ming-dynasty courtyard homes survive, albeit in a run-down condition.

ℹ Getting There & Away

Mǐzhǐ makes an easy day trip from Yúlín or you could stop here to/from Yán'ān. Frequent buses (¥20, two hours) run from Yúlín's main (south) bus station. Ask to get off at Jiulong Bridge (九龙桥, jiǔlóng qiáo), which is a little closer to the palace. Buses from Mǐzhǐ to Yán'ān (¥53.50, 3½ hours, three daily) depart at 7.40am, 8.20am and 1.30pm.

Ānhuī

POP 64.1 MILLION

Best Mountains

➡ Huángshān (p399)
➡ Jiǔhuá Shān (p404)
➡ Qíyún Shān (p393)

Best Villages

➡ Xīdì (p394)
➡ Hóngcūn (p395)
➡ Chéngkǎn (p397)

Why Go?

Well-preserved villages and fantastical mountain scapes are the principal draw for visitors to Ānhuī (安徽). The main attraction of this southern Huīzhōu region is unquestionably Huángshān, a jumble of sheer granite cliffs wrapped in cottony clouds that inspired an entire school of ink painting during the 17th and 18th centuries. But the often overlooked peaks of nearby Jiǔhuá Shān, where Buddhists bless the souls of the recently departed, are much quieter, with a hallowed aura that offers a strong contrast to Huángshān's stunning natural scenery.

At the foot of these ranges are strewn the ancient villages of Huīzhōu; their distinctive whitewashed walls and black-tiled roofs stand out against a verdant backdrop of green hills and terraced tea gardens. Ānhuī's lush mountains and slower pace of life are the perfect antidote to the brashness of China's larger cities.

When to Go

Túnxī

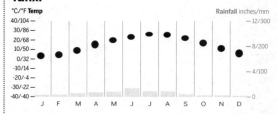

Mar Pack a camera to catch the flowering yellow rapeseed around Shèxiàn.

Oct Autumn days are best for climbing Huángshān.

Dec The snow-capped rooftops of Xīdì's Hui houses look a picture.

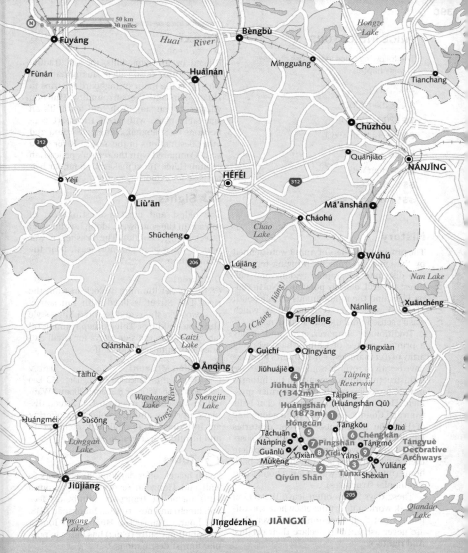

Ānhuī Highlights

① Catch the sunrise from the iconic Chinese mountain, **Huángshān** (p399)

② Explore the grottoes and dilapidated temples at Taoist **Qíyún Shān** (p393)

③ Soak up the Ming-dynasty vibe along Túnxī's **Old Street** (p390)

④ Join the Buddhist pilgrims at fog-shrouded **Jiǔhuá Shān** (p404)

⑤ Don't miss the World Heritage village of **Hóngcūn** (p395)

⑥ Eschew crowds and enjoy authentic village life at **Chéngkǎn** (p397)

⑦ Admire the palette of the colourful gateway to Shūguāngyù Hall in **Píngshān** (p395)

⑧ Seek out the **Pig's Heaven Inn** (p396) in Xīdì for a fantastic meal

⑨ Get your camera out at Shèxiàn's astonishing **Tángyuè Decorative Archways** (p399)

PRICE INDICATORS

The following price indicators are used in this chapter:

Sleeping

$ less than ¥200

$$ ¥200 to ¥550

$$$ more than ¥550

Eating

$ less than ¥25

$$ ¥26 to ¥60

$$$ more than ¥60

History

The provincial borders of Ānhuī were defined by the Qing government, bringing together two disparate geographic regions and cultures: the arid, densely populated North China Plain and the mountainous terrain south of the Yangzi River (Cháng Jiāng), which wasn't settled until the late Tang dynasty.

Traditionally impoverished and today a primary source of China's hard-working army of *āyí* (nannies), rural Ānhuī's fortunes have begun to reverse. Some say the massive infrastructure improvements to the hitherto remote areas are partly due to former president Hu Jintao, whose ancestral clan hails from Jìxī County. Hu comes from a long line of Huīzhōu merchants, who for centuries left home to do business or fill official posts elsewhere, but would never fail to complete their filial duty and send their profits back home (much of it by way of large homes and ceremonial structures).

These days locals often leave the region to seek work and fortune elsewhere (no different from their ancestors). However, they are never ashamed to declare their origins. And rightly so.

ⓘ Getting There & Away

The historic and tourist sights of Ānhuī gather in the south around the town of Túnxī and are easily accessible by bus, train or plane from Hángzhōu, Shànghǎi and Nánjīng, or any other part of China.

Túnxī 屯溪

☑ 0559 / POP 77,000

Ringed by low-lying hills, the old trading town of Túnxī (also called Huángshān Shì; 黄山市) is the main springboard for trips to Huángshān and the surrounding Huīzhōu villages. If you stay in the old town, it's an agreeable place with good transport connections to Shànghǎi, Nánjīng, Sūzhōu and other destinations in the Yangzi River delta area. Compared with the region's pedestrian capital, Héféi, Túnxī makes for a far, far better base for exploring southern Ānhuī.

⊙ Sights

The oldest and most interesting part of town is in the southwest, along bustling Old Street (老街, Lao Jie). The brasher, newer part of town is in the northeast, near the train station.

Old Street   STREET

(老街; Lao Jie) Running a block in from the river, Old Street is lined with fun souvenirs, wooden shops and restored Ming-style Huīzhōu buildings. Things keep running till late. Duck into the side alleys for small eateries and glimpses of local life.

Wàncuìlóu Museum   MUSEUM

(万粹楼博物馆, Wàncuìlóu Bówùguǎn; 143 Lao Jie; admission ¥50; ⊙8.30am-9.30pm) Wàncuìlóu Museum, located on Old Street, displays a private antiques collection, offering an introduction to Huīzhōu architecture and furniture over four floors.

ⓒ Tours

Youth hostels offer day-long village tours to Xīdì and Hóngcūn (expect to pay around ¥210 including transport, admission fees and lunch) and bus trips to Huángshān (¥18, one hour, 6.15am). The Huángshān Tourist Distribution Centre (p392) has buses to popular tourist destinations.

🛏 Sleeping

Old Street Hostel   HOSTEL $

(老街国际青年旅舍, Lǎojiē Guójì Qīngnián Lǚshè; ☑254 0386; www.hiourhostel.com; 266 Lao Jie, 老街266号; dm ¥45-50, tw ¥159-169, d/tr/f ¥139/199/219; ❇@✿) With a convenient location and decent rooms, this place clearly has an appeal that extends beyond

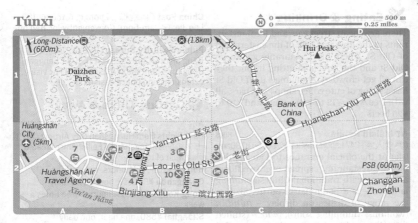

the backpacking crowd. The four-person dorms come with proper mattresses and private bathrooms, while the private rooms sport wood-lattice decor and flat-screen TVs. There's a cafe/bar on the 2nd floor, overlooking Lao Jie.

Reception and access is at the rear of a shop on Lao Jie. Staff speak English, and the manager is very helpful and efficient.

Ancient Town Youth Hostel HOSTEL $
(小镇国际青年旅舍, Xiǎozhèn Guójì Qīngnián Lǚshè; ☎252 2088; www.yhahs.com; 11 Sanma Lu, 三马路11号; dm ¥40-50, d & tw ¥148-198; ❄@🛜) Started by some former tour guides, this hostel ticks all the right boxes, with a well-stocked bar, movie room, good lounging areas, friendly and informative English-speaking staff, bike rental and organised tours. Dorms are spacious and comfy, while the cheapest of the (clean) twin rooms are lacking in natural light and quality varies, so check them first.

★**Hui Boutique Hotel** BOUTIQUE HOTEL $$
(黄山徽舍品酒店, Huángshān Huīshèpǐn Jiǔdiàn; ☎235 2003; 3 Lihong Xiang, 老街李洪巷3号; s/tw/d/f ¥450/450/570/690; ❄🛜) Tucked down an alley off Old St, this hotel blends boutique chic and traditional style with a restored Qing-dynasty building setting. Dark rooms are attractively decked out with antique furnishings and modern toilets, with 40% discounts online softening the tariff.

Harbour Inn & Bar HOTEL $$
(夜泊客栈, Yèbó Kèzhàn; ☎252 2179; 29 Zhongma Lu, 中马路29号; d & tw ¥200; ❄@🛜) We're not sure where to set sail from, but the rooms in this renovated traditional building in Túnxī's old town are a notch above the typical midrange options. Get a twin that overlooks the street or splash out for the deluxe room for a chance to sleep in a traditional wooden Chinese canopy bed. A bar is located downstairs, for when you get bored looking at the floral wallpaper and matching bed sheets in the rooms.

Túnxī Lodge HOTEL $$
(屯溪客栈, Túnxī Kèzhàn; ☎258 0388; 15 Lao Jie, 老街口15号; r ¥480-680; ❄@) At the western end of Lao Jie, this stylish hotel gets guests in the right mood with its Huīzhōu interior. The traditionally arrayed rooms have lovely wooden beds and clean, bright showers. There's a decent attached restaurant serving Chinese and Western cuisine. Discounts generally knock the cheapest doubles down to ¥290. Western breakfasts cost ¥25.

ÀNHUĪ TÚNXĪ

✖ Eating & Drinking

There are cheap street eats and local restaurants in the area just east of the eastern end of Old St. There are restaurants galore on Old St and the streets abutting it, but they can all get crowded. Zhongma Lu off Old St has a string of cute coffee shops and bars, all with free wi-fi, ¥12 to ¥20 coffees and ¥10 to ¥25 beers.

★ **Měishí Rénjiā** HUI $
(美食人家; 247 Lao Jie; dishes ¥7-60; ☺10.30am-late) At the official entrance to Lao Jie, this bustling restaurant – spread over two floors and hung with traditional Chinese *mǎdēng* lanterns – is a perennial favourite. Size up the range of dishes on display – *húndūn* (wontons; dumpling soup), *jiǎozi* (stuffed dumplings), *bāozi* (steamed buns stuffed with meat or vegetables), noodles, claypot and more – then have them cooked up.

A more expensive version is located next door.

Gāotāng Húndūn DUMPLINGS $
(高汤馄饨; 1 Haidi Xiang; húndūn ¥8-12; ☺10am-late) Duck down a little alley opposite 120 Lao Jie for warming bowls of *húndūn* made by a 12th-generation seller. The secret is in the superthin *húndūn* skins, meat minced from whole lean pork, and the tasty soup. No room on the skinny benches outside? Grab a seat in the owner's living room: it's set in an atmospheric Qing-era Hui home. Also sells *dà húndūn* (larger, vegie-filled dumplings).

Tóngjùlóu Huīcài HUIZHOU $$
(同聚楼徽菜; ☑257 2777; 216 Lao Jie; mains from ¥25) With a corner positioning at the heart of Lao Jie, this fun and boisterous restaurant is a great place for grabbing an outside seat, feasting on local Huīzhōu cuisine and watching the bustling street action. Platters are arrayed uncooked inside, so take a look and see what you fancy, order up, grab some beers and take a seat (but avoid the beggar's chicken, which is both expensive and meagre).

ℹ Information

Hostels have wi-fi and computers for internet (usually ¥4 per hour).
Bank of China (中国银行, Zhōngguó Yínháng; cnr Xin'an Beilu & Huangshan Xilu; ☺8am-5.30pm) Changes travellers cheques and major currencies; 24-hour ATM.

China Post (中国邮局, Zhōngguó Yóuqū; 183 Lao Jie; ☺8am-6pm) Conveniently located on Lao Jie.
Public Security Bureau (PSB, 公安局, Gōng'ānjú; ☑251 2929; 1st fl, 108 Changgan Donglu; ☺8am-noon & 2.30-5pm) For visa extensions and police assistance.

ℹ Getting There & Away

AIR

Daily flights from Huángshān City Airport (黄山市飞机场, Huángshānshì Fēijīchǎng), located 5km west of town:
Běijīng ¥1090, 2½ hours, two daily
Guǎngzhōu ¥960, 1½ hours, two daily
Hong Kong ¥2470, 1¾ hours, three times a week
Shànghǎi ¥580, one hour, one daily

You can buy tickets at the **Huángshān Air Travel Agency** (黄山航空旅游公司, Huángshān Hángkōng Lǚyóu Gōngsī; ☑251 7373; 1-1 Binjiang Xilu; ☺8am-5.30pm).

BUS

The **long-distance bus station** (客运总站, kèyùn zǒngzhàn; Qiyun Dadao) is roughly 2km west of the train station on the outskirts of town. Destinations include the following:
Hángzhōu ¥85, three hours, hourly (6.50am to 5.50pm)
Jǐngdézhèn ¥50, 3½ hours, three daily (9.15am, noon and 2.10pm)
Nánjīng ¥104, 5½ hours, three daily (7.25am, 12.10pm and 4.20pm)
Shànghǎi ¥132, five hours, 11 daily (last bus 6pm)
Sūzhōu ¥132, six hours, two daily (6am and 11am)
Wùyuán ¥34, two hours, three daily (8.10am, 9am and 12.30pm)

Within Ǎnhuī, buses go to these destinations:
Héféi ¥114, four hours, hourly (7.30am to 4pm)
Jiǔhuá Shān ¥63, 3½ hours, one daily (1.30pm)
Shèxiàn ¥6, 45 minutes, frequent services
Yīxiàn ¥12.50, one hour, frequent services (6am to 5pm)

Buses to Huángshān go to the main base at Tāngkǒu (¥18, one hour, frequent, 6am to 5pm) and on to the north entrance, Tàipíng (¥20, two hours). There are also minibuses to Tāngkǒu (¥18) from in front of the train station.

Inside the bus station (to the right as you enter) is the separate **Huángshān Tourist Distribution Centre** (黄山市旅游集散中心; Lǚyóu Jísàn Zhōngxīn; ☑252 4798; Qiyun Lu, 齐云

路; ☉7.30am-6pm) with special tourist buses to popular destinations. Return buses operate hourly from 8am to 4pm, with a break from noon to 1pm. Destinations include the following:

Hóngcūn ¥14.50, 1½ hours
Qíyún Shān ¥8.50, 40 minutes
Xīdì ¥12.50, one hour

TRAIN

Train connections are abysmal. Trains from Běijīng (¥181 to ¥510, 20 hours, 9.21am), Shànghǎi (¥110 to ¥265, 13 hours, 8.45pm and 10.06pm) and Nánjīng (¥70 to ¥159, six to 7½ hours, nine daily) stop at Túnxī (generally called Huángshān Shì; 黄山市). There is also a service to Jǐngdézhèn (¥25 to ¥115, three to five hours, 11 daily).

For better connections to southern destinations, first go to Yīngtán (鹰潭; ¥55 to ¥153, five to eight hours, nine daily) in Jiāngxī and change trains there.

❶ Getting Around

Taxi flag fall is ¥5; the 5km taxi ride to the airport costs about ¥30. Competition among pedicab drivers is fierce, so they are the cheapest way of getting around, costing approximately ¥4 for a trip to Old St from the train station area. Short rides start at ¥2. Bus 9 (¥1) runs between the bus station and train station; otherwise, a taxi should cost ¥7 to ¥10.

Around Túnxī

A 40-minute bus trip west of Túnxī brings you to the lush mountain panoramas of **Qíyún Shān** (齐云山; Qíyún Mountain; admission Mar-Nov ¥75, Dec-Feb ¥55; ☉8am-5pm Mon-Fri, 7.30am-5.30pm Sat & Sun). Long venerated by Taoists, the reddish sandstone rock provides a mountain home to the temples and the monks who tend to them, while mountain trails lead hikers through some stupendous scenery.

From the bus drop-off, cross the **Dēngfēng Bridge** (登封桥, Dēngfēng Qiáo) – dwelling on the luxuriant river views – and turn right through the village at the foot of the mountain for a 75-minute clamber up stone steps to the ticket office. Or ask the driver to drop you at the cable car (索道, suǒdào; up ¥26, down ¥14) station ahead and do the circuit in reverse.

Beyond the ticket office, the **Zhēnxiān Cave** (真仙洞府, Zhēnxiān Dòngfǔ) houses a complex of Taoist shrines in grottoes and niches gouged from the sandstone cliffs.

Further on, seated within the smoky interior of the vast and dilapidated **Xuán Tiān Tàisù Gōng** (玄天太素宫) is an effigy of Zhengwu Dadi, a Taoist deity. A further temple hall, the **Yùxū Gōng** (玉虚宫), is erected beneath the huge brow of a 200m-long sandstone cliff, enclosed around effigies of Zhengwu Dadi and Laotzu.

A charming village, **Qíyún Village** (齐云村, Qíyún Cūn), is seemingly plonked in the middle of the mountain range, its whitewashed buildings home to a variety of restaurants, souvenir stalls and friendly residents.

❶ Getting There & Away

Tourist buses run directly to Qíyún Shān (¥8.50, 40 minutes) from Túnxī's Huángshān Tourist Distribution Centre (p392), leaving hourly from 8am to 4pm. This bus can drop you at the Dēngfēng Bridge (登封桥; dēngfēng qiáo) or the cable-car station (索道; suǒdào). Otherwise, take any Yīxiàn-bound bus from Túnxī and ask the driver to stop at Qíyún Shān. Returning to Túnxī, wait at the side of the road for buses coming from Yīxiàn; however, note that the last bus from Yīxiàn to Túnxī departs at 5pm. The last tourist bus departs at 4pm.

Huīzhōu Villages

☑ 0559

The home of wealthy merchants who dealt in lumber, tea and salt – in addition to running a string of lucrative pawnshops throughout the empire – Huīzhōu was a double-edged sword: the inhabitants were often quite wealthy, but they were also mostly absent. At age 13, many young men were shunted out the door for the remainder of their lives to do business elsewhere, sometimes returning home only once per year. Rather than uproot their families and disrespect their ancestral clans, these merchants remained attached to the home towns they rarely saw, funnelling their profits into the construction of lavish residences and some of China's largest ancestral halls.

Consequently, the villages scattered throughout southern Ānhuī (also known as Wǎnnán; 皖南) and northern Jiāngxī are some of the country's loveliest, augmented by their lush surroundings of buckling earth, bamboo and pine forest, the silhouettes of stratified hills stacked away into the distance.

Western Villages (Yīxiàn) 黟县

Yīxiàn is home to the two most picturesque communities in Ānhuī: Xīdì and Hóngcūn. Even with soaring ticket prices and when spilling over with crowds (most of the time), these are, hands down, the most impressive sights in the Huīzhōu area.

◉ Sights

Xīdì
HISTORIC SITE

(西递; admission ¥104) Typical of the elegant Huīzhōu style, Xīdì's 124 surviving buildings reflect the wealth and prestige of the prosperous merchants who settled here. Its Unesco World Heritage Site status means Xīdì, located 54km northwest of Túnxī, enjoys a lucrative tourist economy, yet it remains a picturesque tableau of slender lanes, cream-coloured walls topped with horse-head gables, roofs capped with dark tiles, and doorways ornately decorated with carved lintels.

Dating to AD 1047, the village has for centuries been a stronghold of the Hu (胡) clan, descended from the eldest son of the last Tang emperor who fled here in the twilight years of the Tang dynasty.

Wander around the maze of flagstone lanes, examining lintel carvings above doorways decorated with vases, urns, animals, flowers and ornamental motifs, and try to avoid tripping over hordes of high-school artists consigning scenes of stone bridges spanning small streams to canvas.

Xīdì's magnificent three-tiered Ming-dynasty decorative arch, the **Húwénguāng Páifāng** (胡文光牌坊), at the entrance to the village, is an ostentatious symbol of Xīdì's former standing. Numerous other notable

HUĪZHŌU STYLE

Huīzhōu architecture is the most distinctive ingredient of the regional personality, representative of the merchant class that held sway in this region during the Ming and Qing dynasties. The residences of Yīxiàn and Shèxiàn are the most typical examples of Huīzhōu architecture, their whitewashed walls topped on each flank by horse-head gables, originally designed to prevent fire from travelling along a line of houses, and later evolving into decorative motifs. Strikingly capped with dark tiles, walls are often punctured by high, narrow windows, designed to protect the residence from thieves (and lonely wives from illicit temptations).

Exterior doorways, often overhung with decorative eaves and carved brick or stone lintels, are sometimes flanked by drum stones (鼓石, gǔshí) and lead onto interior courtyards delightfully illuminated by light wells (天井, tiānjǐng), rectangular openings in the roof. The doors are a talking point in themselves. It's said that an owner would spend 1000 taels of silver on the decorative archway and carvings but only four taels on the actual door!

Many Huīzhōu houses are furnished with intricately carved wood panels and extend to two floors, the upper floor supported on wooden columns. Even the furnishing holds much meaning. The main hall for taking visitors has several elements worth keeping an eye out for. You might notice semicircle half-tables against the walls: if the master of the house is in, the tables would be combined; if they are split, it's a subtle hint for male visitors to not intrude upon the wife. There might also be a mantelpiece where you will see a clock, vase and mirror. This symbolises peace and harmony in the house. The Chinese words for these items translate as: zhōng shēng (钟声; hourly chiming on clock), píng (平; harmony) and jìng (静; peace).

Another characteristic element of regional architecture is the obsession with decorative archways (牌坊, páifāng; or 牌楼, páilóu), which were constructed by imperial decree to honour an individual's outstanding achievement. Examples include becoming a high official (for men; páifāng) or leading a chaste life (for women; páilóu). Archways are common throughout China and don't always carry symbolic meaning, but in Huīzhōu they were of great importance because they gave the merchants – who occupied the bottom rung of the Confucian social ladder (under artisans, peasants and scholars) – much-desired social prestige. Roads were built to pass under a páifāng but around a páilóu, so that a man would never feel that his status was beneath that of a woman's. The most elaborate examples are the Tángyuè Decorative Archways outside Shèxiàn.

structures are open to inspection, including Díjí Hall (迪吉堂, Díjí Táng) and Zhuīmù Hall (追慕堂, Zhuīmù Táng), both on Dalu Jie (大路街). Jìng'ài Hall (敬爱堂, Jìng'ài Táng) is the town's largest building and was used for meetings, weddings and, of course, meting out punishment. Back in the day, women weren't allowed inside. Xīyuán (西园) is a small house known for its exquisite stone carvings on the windows. Unlike regular carvings, these are carved on both sides.

When you're done with the village, pop out on paths leading out to nearby hills where there are suitable spots for your picture-postcard panoramas of the village (though a mobile-phone tower blights the landscape). If you want to avoid the crowds, you'll have to start early or hang out late: tour groups start roaming around at 7am and only trickle out at 5pm or so.

Hóngcūn
VILLAGE

(宏村; admission ¥104) Dating to the southern Song dynasty, the delightful village and Unesco World Heritage Site of Hóngcūn, 11km northeast of Yìxiàn, has crescent-shaped Moon Pond (月沼, Yuè Zhǎo) at its heart and is encapsulated by South Lake (南湖, Nán Hú), West Stream (西溪, Xī Xī) and Léigǎng Mountain (雷岗山, Léigǎng Shān). Founding village elders of the Wang (汪) clan consulted a feng shui master and the village was remodelled to suggest an ox, with its still-functioning waterway system representing its entrails.

The village remains a charming and unhurried portrait of bridges, lakeside views, narrow alleys and traditional halls. Alleyway channels flush water through the village from West Stream to Moon Pond (the stomach of the ox) and from there on to South Lake, while signs guide visitors on a tour of the principal buildings. Lost? Just follow the water flow.

If the bridge at the entrance to the village looks familiar, it's because it featured in the opening scene from Ang Lee's *Crouching Tiger, Hidden Dragon*. The picturesque Moon Lake also features in the film. Built by a salt merchant, the Chéngzhì Hall (承志堂, Chéngzhì Táng; Shangshuizhen Lu, 上水圳路) dates from 1855 and has 28 rooms, adorned with fabulous woodcarvings, 2nd-floor balconies and light wells. Peepholes on top-floor railings are for girls to peek at boy visitors and the little alcove in the mah-jong room was used to hide the concubine. The now-faded gold-brushed carvings are said to have required 100 taels of the expensive stuff and took over four years to be completed.

Other notable buildings include the Hall of the Peach Garden (桃源居, Táoyuán Jū), with its elaborate carved wood panels, and the South Lake Academy (南湖书院, Nánhú Shūyuàn), which enjoys an enviable setting beside tranquil South Lake. Overlooking Moon Pond is a gathering of further halls, chief among which is the dignified Lèxù Hall (乐叙堂, Lèxù Táng), a hoary Ming antique from the first years of the 15th century. Turn up bamboo carvings, trinkets and a large selection of tea at the market west of Moon Pond. The busy square by Hóngjì Bridge (宏际桥, Hóngjì Qiáo) on the West Stream is shaded by two ancient trees (the 'horns' of the ox), a red poplar and a gingko. Léigǎng Mountain serves as the head of the ox.

Admission to the village includes a guide with limited English-speaking skills – you'll have to engage one at the main entrance in case you enter by the side gate.

Tǎchuān
VILLAGE

(塔川; admission ¥20) Only 3km northwest of Hóngcūn is the tiny little village of Tǎchuān, set at the base of a valley and famed for its stunning autumn scenery. Each year, the leaves on old-growth trees in and around the village change colours for anywhere between 10 to 30 days. The entire valley comes ablaze in shades of orange, green and brown, much to the delight of photographers.

On other days, the villagers eke out their living by planting rice and tea. From afar, the village looks like a pagoda (hence the name; the '*tǎ*' in Tǎchuān means 'pagoda') as it's built across the steps of foothills.

Píngshān
VILLAGE

(屏山; admission ¥50) Take a motorised pedicab (around ¥20) through the mulberry groves from Hóngcūn towards Xīdì to find this picturesque village, the streets of which are littered with young Chinese artists. Ancient, noteworthy halls include the Xiányì Táng (咸宜堂) with its terrifically decorated frontage and doorway. Sooner or later you'll encounter the overgrown and untouched Shūguāngyù Hall (舒光裕堂, Shūguāngyù Táng), its front gateway a colourful blaze of painted immortals, *luóhàn* (罗汉; arhats), lions and other characters. It's the sole painted *ménlóu* (门楼; gatehouse) in Huīzhōu.

Creep in if the door is open to a deep, inviting (and very cool in hot weather) chamber. Elsewhere in the village is the fabulous, rouge-coloured 900-year-old **Sāngū Miào** (三姑庙, Three Girls Temple) with two rectangular ponds where turtles swim blinking in the sun. In the temple's main hall are the Sānshèng Lóngnǚ (Three Sacred Dragon Girls) with 18 *luóhàn* in attendance. Other famous halls in the village include the **Chéngdào Hall** (成道堂, Chéngdào Táng) and the Ming dynasty **Shūqìngyú Hall** (舒庆余堂, Shūqìngyú Táng).

Nánpíng

VILLAGE

(南屏; admission ¥43) With a history of more than 1100 years, this intriguing and labyrinthine village, 5km to the west of Yīxiàn town, is famed as the setting of Zhang Yimou's 1989 tragedy *Judou* and, of course, scenes from *Crouching Tiger, Hidden Dragon*. Numerous ancient ancestral halls, clan shrines and merchant residences survive within Nánpíng's mazelike alleys, including the **Chéngshì Zōngcí** (程氏宗祠) and the **Yèshì Zōngcí** (叶氏宗祠).

The **Lǎo Yáng Jiā Rǎnfáng** (老杨家染坊) residence that served as the principal household of dyer Gongli and her rapacious husband in *Judou* remains cluttered with props, and faded stills from the film hang from the walls. Admission includes a guide with limited English-speaking skills.

Guānlù

VILLAGE

(关麓; admission ¥35) Around 8km west of Yīxiàn and further along the road beyond Nánpíng, this small village's drawcard sights are the fabulous households (八大家, Bādàjiā) of eight rich brothers. Each Qing-dynasty residence shares similar elegant Huīzhōu features, with light wells, interior courtyards, halls, carved wood panels and small gardens. Each an independent entity, the households are interconnected by doors and linked together into a systemic whole.

A distinctive aspect of the residences is their elegantly painted ceilings, the patterns and details of which survive. Admission includes a guide with limited English-speaking skills.

Mùkēng Zhúhǎi

FOREST

(木坑竹海; admission ¥30, zipline ¥40) A hike through Mùkēng's bamboo forest, 5km northeast of Hóngcūn, is an excellent diversion. Remember *Crouching Tiger, Hidden Dragon's* breathtaking bamboo-top fight scenes? Yep, they were filmed here. The two-hour circuit along a ridgeline leads past the top-heavy plumes of feathery bamboo, trickling streams and hillside tea gardens, past a small village where you can get a filling meal and a clean room with bathroom for ¥60 to ¥120, and eventually to a small hamlet. A zipline can take you down in 40 seconds.

🛏 Sleeping & Eating

Regulations mean you can't just pitch up and land homestay-style accommodation (住农家, *zhù nóngjiā*) in Xīdì and Hóngcūn. Each village has 'approved' accommodation for foreigners, most listed below. You can visit local homes to sample some excellent cooking – meals are generally around ¥20, unless you have a chicken slaughtered (土鸡, *tǔjī*), which will cost ¥50 to ¥100. Restaurants abound; in spring, succulent bamboo shoots (竹笋, *zhúsǔn*) figure prominently in many dishes.

XĪDÌ

Pig's Heaven Inn　　　　BOUTIQUE HOTEL **$$$**
(猪栏酒吧, Zhūlán Jiǔbā; ☏ 515 4555; http:// blog.sina.com.cn/zhulanjiuba; Renrang Li, 西递镇仁让里; d incl breakfast ¥460-560, ste ¥780-880; ✳🌐) This restored 400-year-old house in Xīdì has a study, two terraces and five distinctive rooms. Reservations are crucial (the entrance is unmarked) so book ahead; gourmet sleuths can seek it out for a fantastic lunch (dishes from ¥20) in the courtyard. This is a great place to just unwind for a day or three; grab one of their bicycles and get exploring.

The owners also have a larger, pricier property in Bìshān with doubles and villas (碧山; double from ¥600, villa ¥1200), several kilometres away. Transfers to both properties are available. Limited English.

Xīdì Travel Lodge　　　　HOTEL **$$$**
(西递行馆, Xīdì Xíngguǎn; ☏ 515 6999; 西递; d incl breakfast ¥368-738, ste ¥888-1290; ✳@) This can't-miss-it property, just behind the main gate to Xīdì village, is a sprawling multi building affair complete with comfortable rooms, its own restaurant and alfresco cafe. All rooms have modern showers, flat-screen TVs and faux antique furnishing, while some have balconies. Get a room facing the small tea garden.

The restaurant serves local fare (dishes ¥18 to ¥108) and there's cheap ¥10 beer at the cafe. Discounts of 30% available.

HÓNGCŪN

Old House Youth Hostel

HOSTEL **$**

(☑554 5888; Shanghshui Zhen, 上水圳; dm ¥55, d ¥268; 🛜) This very quiet and secluded youth hostel has a mere handful of doubles – finished in wood, with shower – so book up front. Dorms are upstairs and sleep four to six. It's tranquil and charming, and staff are welcoming and friendly and can book train and bus tickets.

Hóngdá Tíngyuàn

HOMESTAY **$**

(宏达庭院; ☑554 1262; 5 Shangshui Zhen, 上水圳5号; d/tr ¥160/200) The draw of this Hóngcūn home is the verdant courtyard filled with potted daphne, heavenly bamboo and other flowering shrubs, all set around a small pool and pavilion. Its rooms are unadorned, but the peaceful location in the upper part of the village is ideal. You can stop by for lunch (dishes from ¥20), space permitting. No English spoken.

★ Long Lane Inn

BOUTIQUE HOTEL **$$$**

(宏村一品更楼, Hóngcūn Yīpǐn Gēng Lóu; ☑554 2001; www.hcno-1.com; 1 Shangshui Zhen, 上水圳1号; r incl breakfast ¥380-1280; 🅿🛜) In a quiet corner of Hóngcūn, this 10-room Taiwanese-run boutique hotel is lovely. Choose between traditionally styled rooms with rosewood Chinese four-posted beds (or splash out for the suite with a cute garden and sunken bath) or simple tatami rooms, each one immaculate. Iris Hong, the owner, speaks good English and can help with travel plans and private-vehicle hire.

In-house meals are great too.

ℹ Getting There & Around

BUS

Tourist buses run directly to Xīdì (¥12.50, one hour) and on to Hóngcūn (¥14.50, 1½ hours) from Túnxī's Huángshān Tourist Distribution Centre (p392), leaving hourly from 8am to 4pm, with a break at noon. Otherwise, catch a local bus from the long-distance bus station to Yīxiàn (¥13, one hour, frequent, 6am to 5pm), the transport hub for public transport to the surrounding villages.

From Yīxiàn there are green minibuses (¥2 to ¥3, half-hourly, 7am to 5pm) to Xīdì (15 minutes), Nánpíng (15 minutes), Guānlù (20 minutes), Hóngcūn (20 minutes) and Píngshān (18 minutes). You will need to return to Yīxiàn to get between the different villages, with the exception of Nánpíng and Guānlù, which are both in the same direction. From Yīxiàn, it's possible to travel on to Tāngkǒu (¥18, one hour, four daily) for Huángshān, Qīngyáng (¥60, 2½ hours, three daily) for Jiǔhuáshān, Hángzhōu (¥91, one daily) and Shànghǎi (¥151, two daily).

BICYCLE

A great way to explore the surrounding countryside is on a bike (出租自行车, chūzū zìxíngchē; per four hours ¥5 to ¥15), found on the modern street opposite Hóngcūn's Hóngjì Bridge (宏济桥, Hóngjì Qiáo).

TAXI & PEDICAB

Taxis and pedicabs go to Xīdì (¥10), Píngshān (¥10), Hóngcūn (¥15), Nánpíng (¥20) and Guānlù (¥25) from Yīxiàn. Booking a pedicab to take you to all four villages from Yīxiàn can cost as little as ¥150 for the day, depending on your bargaining skills. A minivan for the day will cost ¥300 to ¥400. Most accommodation places can help with transport bookings. From Hóngcūn, get a pedicab to Tǎchuān (¥10), Mùkēng Zhúhǎi (¥15) and Píngshān (¥20). You'll need to negotiate for the driver to wait for you as returning pedicabs are rare.

Northern Villages

Rarely visited by individual travellers, the villages north of Túnxī can serve as a quieter antidote to the much-hyped and crowded towns to the west. A combined Chéngkǎn, Tāngmó, Shèxiàn Old Town, Tǎngyuè Decorative Archways and Qiánkǒu Ancient Houses ticket is available for ¥220.

◉ Sights

Chéngkǎn

VILLAGE

(呈坎; admission ¥107; ⊙8am-5pm) A real working community, Chéngkǎn presents a very different picture from its more affluent cousins in Shèxiàn – farmers walk through town with hoes slung over their shoulders, tea traders dump baskets of freshly picked leaves straight out onto the street, quacking ducks run amok in streams and the unmistakable odour of pig manure hangs in the air: a bona fide slice of life in rural China. Most visitors are here to see southern China's largest ancestral temple.

The **Luó Dōngshū Temple** (罗东舒祠, Luó Dōngshū Cí) is a massive wooden complex several courtyards deep that took 71 years (1539–1610) to build. It has a mixed bag of architectural styles, from Greco-Roman columns to Persian patterns on overhead beams. Look out for the three-storey **Yànyì Táng** (燕翼堂), nearly 600 years old; many residences are, however, in poor condition.

Tángmó
VILLAGE

(唐模; admission ¥80, incl electronic guide deposit ¥300; ◎8am-5pm) A narrow village extending 1km along a central canal, Tángmó originally dates to the late Tang dynasty. A pathway follows the waterway from the entrance at the east gate (东门, *dōng mén*) into the village, leading past the large **Tán'gàn Garden** (檀干园, Tán'gàn Yuán), modelled after Hángzhōu's West Lake. Here you'll enter the village proper, passing canalside Qing residences along **Shui Jie** (水街) before reaching the covered **Gāoyáng Bridge** (高阳桥, Gāoyáng Qiáo), built in 1733 and home to a small teahouse.

At the end of town is the **Shàngyì Ancestor Hall** (尚义堂, Shàngyì Táng), with 199 peony blossoms carved into the entrance beam. There's a string of traditional workshops and stalls near the east gate.

The public bus will probably drop you off at the west gate (meaning you'll see the sights listed above in reverse), but there should be onward transport of some kind to the east gate, or just backtrack.

🛈 Getting There & Around

A tourist bus from the Túnxī long-distance bus station stops at Tángmó (¥14, 1½ hours, every two hours), running from 8am to 4pm.

Getting to Chéngkǎn is slightly complicated. Start by taking a bus to Yánsì (岩寺; ¥4.50, 30 minutes, frequent) from the Túnxī long-distance bus station. From the Yánsì bus terminus, go to the town's north bus station (北站, běi zhàn) by public bus (¥1) or pedicab (¥4). From the north bus station, take another bus to Chéngkǎn (¥3.50, 20 minutes, hourly). You can also reach Tángmó (¥2.50, 20 minutes, hourly) from the north bus station in Yánsì.

Pedicabs also run from the Yánsì bus terminus to Chéngkǎn (¥30) or Tángmó (¥20). Decent bargainers can get one for a day for ¥80 to ¥100. To get between the villages on public transport, you'll need to return to Yánsì. Note that the last buses are at 5pm, and transport stops for an hour around noon.

Eastern Villages

Shèxiàn is a decent-sized provincial town with absorbing historic sights, while the neighbouring port of Yúliáng harbours an architectural heritage entirely different from the other Huīzhōu villages. A combined Chéngkǎn, Tángmó, Shèxiàn Old Town, Tángyuè Decorative Archways and Qiánkǒu Ancient Houses ticket is available for ¥220.

◉ Sights

Shèxiàn
VILLAGE

(歙县; admission incl entry to Yúliáng & Chinese-speaking guide ¥80, without entry to Yúliáng ¥60) Shèxiàn is 25km east of Túnxī and can be visited as a day trip. The town was formerly the grand centre of the Huīzhōu culture, serving as its capital. Today, the **Old Town** (徽州古城, Huīzhōu Gǔchéng) is the town's main sight. From the Shèxiàn bus station, cross the bridge over the river, hang right and go through a gate tower and along to **Yánghé Mén** (阳和门), a double-eaved gate tower constructed of wood.

Get your admission ticket and climb the gate to examine a Ming-dynasty stone *xièzhì* (獬豸; a legendary beast) and elevated views of the magnificent **Xǔguó Archway** (许国石坊, Xǔguó Shífáng) below. Fabulously decorated, this is China's sole surviving four-sided decorative archway, with 12 lions (18 in total if you count the cubs) seated on pedestals around it and a profusion of bas-relief carvings of other mythical creatures.

Continue in the same direction to reach the alleyway (on the left) to the old residential area of **Doushan Jie** (斗山街古民居, Dòushānjiē Gǔmínjū), a street of Huīzhōu houses, with several courtyard residences open to visitors and decorated with exquisitely carved lintels, beautiful interiors and occasional pairs of leaping-on blocks for mounting horses.

Local visitors don't receive the same rigorous ticket checks that foreign visitors do in and around the main gate. Wander around a bit and you'll find that there are also alleyways that lead into the old town.

Buses from Túnxī's long-distance bus station run regularly to Shèxiàn (¥6.50, 45 minutes, frequent).

Yúliáng
VILLAGE

(渔梁; admission ¥30) Little-visited Yúliáng is a historic riverine port village on the Liàn River (练江, Liàn Jiāng). The cobbled and picturesque alley of **Yuliang Jie** (渔梁街) houses former transfer stations for the wood, salt and tea that plied the river; the teashop at No 87 is an example. Note the firewalls separating the houses along the road. Examine the traditional Huīzhōu arrangement of the **Bāwèizǔ Museum** (巴慰祖纪念馆, Bāwèizǔ Jiniànguǎn), also on Yuliang Jie.

The **Lion Bridge** (狮子桥, Shīzǐ Qiáo) dates to the Tang dynasty, a time when the 138m-long granite **Yúliáng Dam** (渔梁

坝, Yúliáng Bà) across the river was first constructed. Observe how amazingly well built it is, with finely finished interlocking stones. Oarsman can take you on boats from the dam for excellent 20-minute return river trips (¥10 to ¥20).

There are rooms with lovely views at a small **inn** (☑ 0559-653 9731; 147 Yuliang Jie, 渔梁街147号; d with bathroom ¥50-60), and another similar **inn** (☑ 0559-653 8024; 145 Yuliang Jie, 渔梁街145号; d with bathroom ¥80-100) two doors along. Both serve meals with dishes starting at ¥15. The innkeepers will take you into the village if you book ahead.

To reach Yúliáng, take a pedicab (¥5) from Shèxiàn's bus station (by the bridge), or hop on bus 1, which runs to Yúliáng (¥1) from outside the bus station and also along the road opposite Shèxiàn Ancient City. The last bus back to Túnxī departs at 6pm.

Tángyuè Decorative Archways   MONUMENT
(棠樾牌坊群, Tángyuè Páifáng Qún; www.paifangqun.com; admission ¥130, incl Bào Family Garden; ☉ 7am-6pm summer, 7.30am-5.30pm winter) This astonishing row of seven elaborate, decorative stone arches is quite a bizarre sight, marching off in a slight curve from the village of Tángyuè towards the fields. The stone monuments form one of the most famous collections of memorial archways in the land. There's also the attached village to explore which contains several notable old halls and down the road, the beautifully laid-out **Bào Family Garden** is decorated with all manner of exquisite flowering plants and trees. It's a perfect spot for a tranquil breather.

The best way to get here is direct by tourist bus 4 from Shèxiàn, although it's possible to get here by bus (¥5) to the drop-off at Zhèngcūn Lùkǒu (郑村路口) from Túnxī and then transfer to tourist bus 4 (¥2) – or you can walk the remaining 1.5km.

Huángshān   黄山
☑ 0559

When its granite peaks and twisted pines are wreathed in spectral folds of mist, Huángshān's idyllic views easily nudge it into the select company of China's top 10, nay, top five, sights. Legions of poets and painters have drawn inspiration from Huángshān's iconic beauty. Yesterday's artists seeking an escape from the hustle and bustle of the temporal world have been replaced by crowds of tourists, who bring the hustle and bustle with them: the mountain is inundated with tourist traffic at points, so the magic can rapidly evaporate, especially during holiday periods and weekends. But Huángshān still rewards visitors with moments of tranquillity, and the unearthly views can be simply breathtaking.

Climate

Locals claim that it rains more than 200 days a year up on the mountain. Allow yourself several days and climb when the forecast is best. Spring (April to June) generally tends to be misty, which means you may be treated to some sublime scenery, but you're just as likely to encounter a dense fog that obscures everything except for a line of yellow ponchos extending up the trail. Summer (July to August) is the rainy season, though storms can blow through fairly quickly. Autumn (September to October) is generally considered to be the best travel period. Even at the height of summer, average temperatures rarely rise above 20°C at the summit, so come prepared.

◉ Sights & Activities

Buses from Túnxī drop you off in Tāngkǒu, the sprawling town at the foot of Huángshān. A base for climbers, this is the place to stock up on supplies (maps, raincoats, food, money), store your excess luggage and arrange onward transport. It's possible to spend time in Tāngkǒu, but unless you're on a tight budget, you might as well stay on the mountain.

Tāngkǒu consists of two main streets, the larger Feicui Lu – a strip of restaurants, supermarkets and hotels – and the more pleasant Yanxi Jie, which runs along the river perpendicular to Feicui Lu and is accessed by stairs leading down from the bridge.

Eastern Steps   HIKING
A medium-fast climb of the 7.5km eastern steps from Yúngǔ Station (890m) to **White Goose Ridge** (白鹅峰, Bái'é Fēng; 1770m) can be done in 2½ hours. The route is pleasant, but lacks the awesome geological scenery of the western steps. In spring wild azalea and weigela add gorgeous splashes of colour to the wooded slopes. Much of the climb is comfortably shaded and although it can be tiring, it's a doddle compared with the western steps.

Slow-moving porters use the eastern steps for ferrying up their massive, swaying

Huángshān

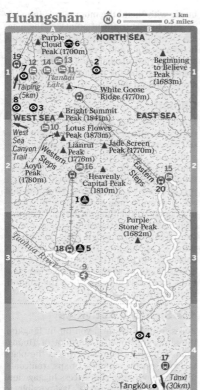

loads of food, drink and building materials, so considerable traffic plies the route. While clambering up, note the more ancient flight of steps that makes an occasional appearance alongside the newer set.

Purists can extend the eastern steps climb by several hours by starting at the **Front Gate** (黄山大门, Huángshān Dàmén) – also called the South Gate (南大门, Nán Dàmén) – where a stepped path crosses the road at several points before linking with the main eastern steps trail.

Western Steps   HIKING

The 15km western steps route has some stellar scenery, but it's twice as long and strenuous as the eastern steps, and much easier to enjoy if you're clambering down rather than gasping your way up. If you take the cable car up the mountain, just do this in reverse. The western steps descent begins at the **Flying Rock** (飞来石, Fēilái Shí), a boulder perched on an outcrop 30 minutes from

Běihǎi Hotel, and goes over **Bright Summit Peak** (光明顶, Guāngmíng Dǐng; 1841m), from where you can see **Áoyú Peak** (鳌鱼峰, Áoyú Fēng; 1780m), which resembles two turtles!

South of Áoyú Peak en route to Lotus Flower Peak, the descent funnels you down through a **Gleam of Sky** (一线天, Yīxiàn Tiān), a remarkably narrow chasm – a vertical split in the granite – pinching a huge rock suspended above the heads of climbers. Further on, **Lotus Flower Peak** (莲花峰, Liánhuā Fēng; 1873m) marks the highest point, but is occasionally sealed off, preventing ascents. **Liánruǐ Peak** (莲蕊峰, Liánruǐ Fēng; 1776m) is decorated with rocks whimsically named after animals, but save some energy for the much-coveted and staggering climb – 1321 steps in all – up **Heavenly Capital Peak** (天都峰, Tiāndū Fēng; 1810m) and the stunning views that unfold below. As elsewhere on the mountain, young lovers have padlocks engraved with their names up here and lash them for eternity to the chain railings. Access to Heavenly Capital Peak (and other peaks) is sometimes restricted for maintenance and repair, so keep those fingers crossed when you go!

Further below, the steps lead to **Bànshān Temple** (半山寺, Bànshān Sì) and below that, at the bottom of the steps, **Mercy Light Temple** (慈光阁, Cíguāng Gé). Huángshān is not one of China's sacred mountains, so little religious activity is evident. Mercy Light Temple is one of the few temples on the mountain whose temple halls survive, although they have been converted to more secular uses. The first hall now serves as the **Mt Huángshān Visitor Centre** (黄山游人中心, Huángshān Yóurén Zhōngxīn), where you can pore over a diorama of the mountain ranges.

From Mercy Light Temple, you can pick up a minibus back to Tāngkǒu (¥13) to find yourself some beer as a reward or continue walking to the hot springs area.

Huángshān Hot Springs HOT SPRINGS

(黄山温泉, Huángshān Wēnquán; adult/child ¥238/119; ☉10am-11pm) The hot springs area is the place to soak after the strenuous climb. It offers a mind-boggling variety of themed springs: soak in a coffee-infused pool or get heady in the wine- or alcohol-infused spring. There's also a pool with fish that nibble away dead skin on your feet. Follow it all up with a foot massage. Entry includes complimentary snacks and tea. Shuttle buses (¥11) run from Tāngkǒu to the Hot Springs.

West Sea Canyon HIKING

(西海大峡谷; Xīhǎi Dàxiágǔ) A strenuous and awe-inspiring 8.5km hike, the West Sea Canyon route descends into a gorge (Xīhǎi Dàxiágǔ) and has some impressively exposed stretches (it's not for those with vertigo), taking a minimum four hours to complete. You can access the canyon at either the northern entrance (near the Páiyúnlóu Hotel) or the southern entrance (near the Báiyún Hotel aka White Clouds Hotel).

A good option to start would be at the northern entrance. From there, you'll pass through some rock tunnels and exit onto the best bits of the gorge. Here, stone steps have been attached to the sheer side of the mountain – peer over the side for some serious butt-clenching views down. Don't worry, there are handrails. If you're pressed for

ÀNHUĪ HUÁNGSHĀN

ASCENDING & DESCENDING THE MOUNTAIN

Regardless of how you ascend **Huángshān** (admission Mar-Nov ¥230, Dec-Feb ¥150, child 1.2-1.4m ¥115, under 1.2m free), you will be stung by a dizzying entrance fee. You can pay at the eastern steps near the **Yúngǔ Station** (云谷站, Yúngǔ Zhàn; Eastern Steps) or at the **Mercy Light Temple Station** (慈光阁站, Cíguānggé zhàn; Western Steps), where the western steps begin. Shuttle buses (¥19) run to both places from Tāngkǒu.

Three basic routes will get you up to the summit: the short, hard way (eastern steps); the longer, harder way (western steps); and the very short, easy way (cable car). It's possible to do a 10-hour circuit going up the eastern steps and then down the western steps in one day, but you'll have to be slightly insane, in good shape and you'll definitely miss out on some of the more spectacular, hard-to-get-to areas.

A basic itinerary would be to take an early morning bus from Túnxī, climb the eastern steps, hike around the summit area, spend the night at the top, catch the sunrise and then hike back down the western steps the next day, giving you time to catch an afternoon bus back to Túnxī. Most travellers do opt to spend more than one night on the summit to explore all the various trails. Don't underestimate the hardship involved; the steep gradients and granite steps can wreak havoc on your knees, both going up and down.

Most sightseers are packed (and we mean *packed*) into the summit area above the upper cable car stations, consisting of a network of trails running between various peaks, so don't go expecting peace and quiet. The volume of visitors is mounting every year and paths are being widened at bottleneck points where scrums develop. The highlight of the climb for many independent travellers is the lesser-known West Sea Canyon hike, a more rugged, exposed section where most tour groups do not venture.

Make sure to bring enough water, food, warm clothing and rain gear before climbing. Bottled water and food prices increase the higher you go as porters (p402) carry everything up. As mountain paths are easy to follow and English signs plentiful, guides are unnecessary.

PORTERS ON THE MOUNTAIN

When climbing Huángshān, spare a thought for the long-suffering, muscular and sun-tanned porters (挑山工, tiāoshāngōng) who totter slowly uphill with all manner of goods from rice to water and building materials for the hotels and hawkers that populate the higher levels. They then descend with rubbish. Going up, they earn ¥1.8 per kg hauled aloft, downhill it's ¥1.5 per kg. They ferry around 100kg each trip (and only ascend once per day), balanced on two ends of a stout pole across their shoulder. Remember to give way to them on your way up (and down).

time or don't have the energy to stomach a long hike, do a figure-eight loop of **Ring Road 1** (一环上路口; Yīhuán Shàng Lùkǒu; West Sea Canyon) and **Ring Road 2** (二环上路口; Èrhuán Shàng Lùkǒu; West Sea Canyon), and head back to the northern entrance. Sure, you'll miss some stunning views across lonely, mist-encased peaks, but you'll also miss the knee-killing dip into the valley and the subsequent thigh-shuddering climb out to the southern entrance.

A new cable car (¥100) to this area opened in 2013, so the area has unfortunately become increasingly busier. Avoid this region in bad weather.

Huángshān Summit HIKING

Huángshān's summit is essentially one huge network of connecting trails and walks that meander up, down and across several different peaks. More than a few visitors spend several nights on the peak, and the North Sea (北海, Běihǎi) sunrise is a highlight for those staying overnight. **Refreshing Terrace** (清凉台, Qīngliáng Tái) is five minutes' walk from Běihǎi Hotel (p403) and attracts sunrise crowds. Lucky visitors are rewarded with the luminous spectacle of *yúnhǎi* (literally 'sea of clouds'): idyllic pools of mist that settle over the mountain, filling its chasms and valleys with fog.

The staggering and other-worldly views from the summit reach out over huge valleys of granite and enormous formations of rock, topped by gravity-defying slivers of stone and the gnarled forms of ubiquitous Huángshān pine trees (*Pinus taiwanensis*).

Many rocks have been christened with fanciful names by the Chinese, alluding to figures from religion and myth. **Beginning to Believe Peak** (始信峰, Shǐxìn Fēng; 1683m), with its jaw-dropping views, is a major bottleneck for photographers. En route to the North Sea, pause at the **Flower Blooming on a Brush Tip** (梦笔生花, Mèngbǐ Shēnghuā), a 1640m-high granite formation topped by a pine tree. Clamber up to **Purple Cloud Peak** (丹霞峰, Dānxiá Fēng; 1700m) for a long survey over the landscape and try to catch the sun as it descends in the west. Aficionados of rock formations should keep an eye out for the poetically named **Mobile Phone Rock** (手机石, Shǒujī Shí), located near the top of the western steps. Continue on to sights en route to the Western Steps.

🛏 Sleeping & Eating

Huángshān has clusters of hotels. Prices and availability vary according to season; book ahead for summit accommodation, especially so for dorms and at peak times. Prices for hotels tend to cost at least double what you'd pay in a non-mountain setting.

If you're on a tight budget, make sure to take plenty of food to the summit. You won't be able to get a hot meal there for under ¥50. Summit hotels usually offer warm jackets for sunrise watchers.

🏘 Tāngkǒu 汤口

Mediocre midrange hotels line Tāngkǒu's main strip, Feicui Lu; remember to look at rooms first and ask for discounts before committing. There are also a host of budget choices along Tiandu Lu. Restaurants cluster along Yanxi Jie, which runs along the river perpendicular to Feicui Lu.

Pine Ridge Lodge HOTEL **$**

(黄山天客山庄, Huángshān Tiānkè Shānzhuāng; ☏1377 761 8111; Scenic Area South Gate, 风景区南门; r incl breakfast ¥120-150; ❄) Wayne, the friendly English-speaking owner, likens it to a lodge in Aspen...in reality, the place isn't so much a ski lodge but a very decent midrange hotel. Book a cosy room in the charming outhouse for privacy. The in-house restaurant serves great local food. Rooms include return transfers to/from the Tāngkǒu bus station.

Zhōngruìhuáyì Hotel HOTEL **$$$**

(中瑞华艺大酒店, Zhōngruìhuáyì Dàjiǔdiàn; ☏556 6888, 556 8222; South Gate, 南大门; r from

¥780; ✳) This white four-star hotel on the west side of the river on the Huángshān access road has the most expensive and most pleasant rooms in Tāngkǒu. Staff can help with bus and flight bookings and there's a free shuttle bus to to the bus station.

🛏 On the Mountain

Yúngǔ Hotel   HOTEL $$$
(云谷山庄, Yúngǔ Shānzhuāng; ☑558 6444; s & d ¥580; ✳) With a lovely but inconveniently located setting looking out onto bamboo and forest, this traditionally styled hotel has fine, clean rooms, with 35% discounts frequently given. Walk down from the car park in front of the cable-car station.

Yùpínglóu Hotel   HOTEL $$$
(玉屏楼宾馆, Yùpínglóu Bīnguǎn; ☑558 2288; www.hsyplhotel.com; d/tw ¥1480/1680; ✳ @) A 10-minute walk from the Yùpíng cable car (go to your right), this four-star hotel is perched on a spectacular 1660m-high lookout just above the Welcoming Guest Pine Tree (迎客松, Yíngkèsōng). Aim for the doubles with the good views at the back, as some rooms have small windows with no views. Discounts bring doubles down to ¥880.

Báiyún Hotel   HOTEL $$$
(白云宾馆, Báiyún Bīnguǎn; ☑558 2708; dm ¥330, d/tr ¥1480/1680; ✳ @) Dorms come with TV and shower but are rather old and worn; doubles with private bathroom pass muster but the hotel is only an option if other places are booked out. No English sign, but well signposted in English as White Clouds Hotel. Discounts knock down dorms to around ¥200 and doubles to ¥980. Located on the Western Steps.

🛏 On the Summit 山顶

Huángshān visits should ideally include nights on the summit. Most hotel restaurants offer buffets (breakfast ¥60, lunch and dinner ¥100 to ¥140) plus a selection of standard dishes (fried rice ¥40), though getting service outside meal times can be tricky. Room prices rise on Saturday and Sunday, and are astronomical during major holiday periods.

Hotels in Tāngkǒu can arrange tents (帐篷, zhàngpéng; ¥180) for camping at selected points on the summit.

Shílín Hotel   HOTEL $$
(狮林饭店, Shílín Fàndiàn; ☑558 4040; www.shilin.com; dm with bathroom ¥300-360, d & tw from ¥1480; @) Cheaper rooms are devoid of views, but the pricier doubles are bright and clean. Eight- and 12-bed dorms are well-kept but cramped, with bunk beds and shared bathroom, but there are roomier quads; the block up the steps from the hotel has good views, as do some of the newer rooms in the main block and the villa behind. Doubles discount to around ¥1280.

Xīhǎi Hotel   HOTEL $$$
(西海饭店, Xīhǎi Fàndiàn; ☑558 8888; www.hsxihaihotel.cn; dm ¥330 d ¥1380-1680; ✳ @) Regular rooms are tired but clean with heating and hot water, but take a look at the doubles first, as some face inwards. Discounts knock dorms to ¥280 and doubles to ¥1280. A new 'five-star' block has been constructed, with plusher ¥1680 doubles. Located in the summit area near the Xīhǎi Reservoir.

Běihǎi Hotel   HOTEL $$$
(北海宾馆, Běihǎi Bīnguǎn; ☑558 2555; www.hsbeihaihotel.com; dm ¥360, d ¥1680; @ 🛜) Located north of White Goose Ridge, the four-star Běihǎi comes with professional service, money exchange, cafe and 30% discounts during the week. Larger doubles with private bathroom have older fittings than the smaller, better-fitted-out doubles (same price). There are ¥1280 doubles in the three-star compound on a hill across the main square. Although it's the best-located hotel, it's also the busiest and lacks charm.

Dorms can dip to ¥150 when it's quiet.

Páiyúnlóu Hotel   HOTEL $$$
(排云楼宾馆, Páiyúnlóu Bīnguǎn; ☑558 1558; dm/d/tr ¥360/1280/1680; @) With an excellent location near Tiānhǎi Lake (Tiānhǎi Hú) and the entrance to the West Sea Canyon, plus three-star comfort, this place is recommended for those who prefer a slightly more tranquil setting. None of the regular rooms have views, but the newer dorms are unobstructed and come with attached showers and TVs. Discounted dorms are ¥150 and doubles ¥680.

ℹ Information

TĀNGKǑU
Bank of China (中国银行, Zhōngguó Yínháng; Yanxi Jie, Tāngkǒu; ⊙8am-5pm) Southern end of Yanxi Jie.

Internet Cafe (网吧, wǎngbā; Tāngkǒu; per hr ¥3; ☺8am–midnight) On the west side of the river, 2nd floor.

Public Security Bureau (PSB, 公安局, Gōng'ānjú; ☑556 2311) Western end of the bridge.

ON THE MOUNTAIN

Most hotels on the mountain have internet access areas for guests and nonguests, with hourly rates of ¥15 to ¥20. Some have free wi-fi.

Bank of China (中国银行, Zhōngguó Yínháng; ☺8–11am & 2.30-5pm) Changes money and has ATM that accepts international cards. Opposite Běihǎi Hotel.

Police Station (派出所, pàichūsuǒ; ☑558 1388) Beside the bank.

🛈 Getting There & Away

Buses from Túnxī (aka Huángshān Shì) take around one hour to reach Tāngkǒu from either the long-distance bus station (¥18, one hour, frequent, 6am to 5pm) or the train station (¥18, departures when full, 6.30am to 5pm, may leave as late as 8pm in summer). Buses back to Túnxī from Tāngkǒu are plentiful, and can be flagged down on the road to Túnxī (¥18). The last bus back leaves at 5.30pm.

Tāngkǒu has two bus stations. When getting into Tāngkǒu, you will be dropped at the South Long-distance Station (南大门换乘分中心, Nándàmén Huànchéng Fēnzhōngxīn). When coming down the mountain, you may be dropped at the East Long-distance Bus Station (东岭换乘分中心, Dōnglǐng Huànchéng Fēnzhōngxīn) east of the town centre and within walking distance from Feicui Lu, the main street. Your hotel should be able to help with bookings and pick-up or transfers. Major destinations include:

Hángzhōu ¥100, 3½ hours, five daily

Héféi ¥90, four hours, four daily

Jiǔhuá Shān ¥55, 2½ hours, two daily (6.30am and 2.20pm)

Nánjīng ¥86, five hours, three daily

Shànghǎi ¥140, 6½ hours, four daily

Wǔhàn ¥190 to ¥220, nine hours, two daily (8.40am and 5.30pm)

Yīxiàn ¥13, one hour, four daily (stops at Hóngcūn and Xīdì)

🛈 Getting Around

SHUTTLE BUS

Official tourist shuttles run between the two long-distance bus stations in Tāngkǒu and the Hot Springs (¥11), Yúngǔ Station (¥19) and Mercy Light Temple Station (¥19), departing every 20 minutes from 6am to 5.30pm, though they usually wait until enough people are on board.

A taxi to the eastern or western steps will cost ¥50 and to the hot springs area ¥30.

CABLE CAR

Yúngǔ Cable Car (云谷索道, Yúngǔ Suǒdào; one way Mar-Nov ¥80, Dec-Feb ¥65; ☺7am-4.30pm) Shuttle buses (¥19) ferry visitors from Tāngkǒu to the cable car. Either arrive very early or late (if you're staying overnight) as long queues are the norm. The new cable-car station has shortened the three-hour queues to nothing more than 45 minutes.

Yùpíng Cable Car (玉屏索道, Yùpíng Suǒdào; one way 1 Mar-20 Nov ¥80, 1 Dec-29 Feb ¥65; ☺7am-4.30pm) Shuttle buses (¥19) run from Tāngkǒu to Mercy Light Temple, which is linked by the Yùpíng Cable Car to the area just below the Yùpínglóu Hotel.

Jiǔhuá Shān 九华山

☑0566

The Tang-dynasty Buddhists who determined Jiǔhuá Shān to be the earthly abode of the Bodhisattva Dizang (Ksitigarbha), Lord of the Underworld, chose well. Often shrouded in a fog that pours in through the windows of its cliff-side temples, Jiǔhuá Shān exudes an aura of otherworldliness, heightened by the devotion of those who come here to pray for the souls of the departed. At times, though, it can seem that the commerce that drives the religion – religious trinkets, good-luck charms and overpriced joss sticks – cheapens the effect. However, true believers brush it all off with their fervency. With its yellow-walled monasteries, flickering candles and the steady drone of Buddhist chanting emanating from pilgrims' MP3 players, the mountain is an entirely different experience from temporal Huángshān.

History

One of China's four Buddhist mountain ranges, Jiǔhuá Shān was made famous by the 8th-century Korean monk Kim Kiao Kak (Jin Qiaojue), who meditated here for 75 years and was posthumously proclaimed to be the reincarnation of Dizang. In temples, Dizang is generally depicted carrying a staff and a luminous jewel, used to guide souls through the darkness of hell.

🔾 Sights & Activities

Buses will let you off at Jiǔhuáshān Xīnqūzhàn (九华山新区站), the local bus terminus and main ticket office where you purchase your ticket for the mountain (p405). You'll also then need to buy a return shuttle bus ticket (¥50, 20 minutes, half-hourly) from the counters on the left of the admission-ticket windows. The shuttle bus goes to Jiǔhuájiē village, the main accommodation area that is about halfway up the mountain (or, as locals say, at roughly navel height in a giant Buddha's potbelly). The shuttle terminates at the bus station just before the gate (大门, dàmén) leading to the village, from where the main street (芙蓉路, Furong Lu) heads south past hotels and restaurants. The main square is on the right off Furong Lu as you proceed up the street.

Zhīyuán Temple
BUDDHIST TEMPLE

(祇园寺, Zhīyuán Sì; ⊙ 6.30am-8.30pm) FREE
Just past the village's main entrance on your left, worshippers hold sticks of incense to their foreheads and face the four directions at this enticingly esoteric yellow temple. Pilgrims can join chanting sessions in the evening.

Huàchéng Sì
BUDDHIST TEMPLE

(化成寺; ⊙ 6.30am-8.30pm) FREE The largest, most elaborate temple in town has ornately carved dragons serving as handrails up the main steps. The eaves and beams of the buildings are painted in every colour imaginable and the icing on the cake is the three huge golden Bodhisattvas that greet visitors: each one sits at least 25m tall and provides quite the setting come evening prayer time.

Jiǔhuá Shān Summit
HIKING

The real highlight is walking up the mountain alongside the pilgrims, following a trail (天台正顶) that passes waterfalls, streams and countless nunneries, temples and shrines. Jiǔhuá Shān (九华山; Jiǔhuá Mountain ; admission Mar-Nov ¥190, Dec-Feb ¥140) summit is on a mountain range behind the village. The hike up takes a leisurely four hours; count on about two to three hours to get back down to the village.

You can begin just after the village's main entrance, where a 30-minute hike up the ridge behind Zhīyuán Temple leads you to Bǎisuì Gōng (百岁宫; ⊙ 6am-5.30pm) FREE, an active temple built into the cliff in 1630 to consecrate the Buddhist monk Wu Xia, whose shrunken, embalmed body is coated in gold and sits shrivelled within an ornate glass cabinet in front of a row of pink lotus candles. If you don't feel like hiking, take the funicular (express/ordinary return ¥150/100, one way ¥55; ⊙ 7am-5.30pm) to the ridge.

From the top, walk south along the ridge past the Dōngyá Temple (东崖禅寺, Dōngyá Chánsì) to the Huíxiāng Pavilion (回香阁, Huíxiāng Gé), above which towers the seven-storey 10,000 Buddha Pagoda (万佛塔; Wàn Fó Tǎ; admission ¥10; ⊙ 6am-5.30pm), fashioned entirely from bronze and prettily lit at night. A western path leads to town, while the eastern one dips into a pleasant valley and continues past the Phoenix Pine (凤凰松, Fènghuáng Sōng) and the cable car station (one-way/return ¥75/140) to Tiāntái Peak (天台正顶, Tiāntái Zhèng Dǐng; 1304m). The two-hour walk to the summit is tough going, passing small temples and nunneries. The cable-car ride takes 15 minutes each way. Note that there's still a 1km walk up flights of stairs even if you take the cable car!

The summit is slightly damp, with mist shrouding the area. Within the faded Tiāntái Temple (天台寺, Tiāntái Sì) on Tiāntái Peak, a statue of the Dizang Buddha is seated within the Dìzàng Hall (地藏殿, Dìzàng Diàn), while from the magnificent 10,000 Buddha Hall (万佛楼, Wànfó Lóu) above, a huge enthroned statue of the Dizang Buddha gazes at the breathless masses mustering at his feet. The beams above your head glitter with rows of thousands of Buddhas.

There's another trail to your right before the main stairs to the Tiāntái Temple. This one leads you to one of the highest and quietest points of the mountain, Shíwáng Peak (十王峰, Shíwáng Fēng; 1344m), where you can stop and let the rolling fog sweep past.

An easier route is to take a bus (return trip included with the ¥50 bus ticket) from Jiǔhuájiē village up to the Phoenix Pine area to take the cable car. You can also walk to the summit in two hours from here. The bus option doesn't pass Bǎisuì Gōng.

🛏 Sleeping & Eating

There are a large number of hotels in Jiǔhuájiē village along Furong Lu. Outside of major holiday periods, most dorm beds go for ¥30, while basic twins can be had from ¥80. Prices often double on weekends and public holidays. Cheap guesthouses can be found along Jiuhua Lao Jie.

There are numerous restaurants in the village around the main square and along Furong Lu and Huacheng Lu, which serve local dishes (from ¥10 to ¥100). The Zhīyuán Temple serves good ¥8 vegetarian meals (5.30am, 10.40am and 4.40pm).

ĀNHUĪ JIǓHUÁ SHĀN

Food is plentiful on the way up; stop at one of the reasonable restaurants near the Phoenix Pine (about halfway up). Food costs rise the higher you climb.

Bǎisuìgōng Xiàyuàn Hotel HOTEL $$

(百岁宫下院, Bǎisuìgōng Xiàyuàn; ☑282 0588; r ¥360-1380; ❋❋) Pleasantly arranged around an old temple, this hotel has the right atmosphere and a good location. Standard rooms are just that – lino floors, small showers, but comfortable enough. It's right beside Jùlóng Hotel, opposite Zhīyuán Temple.

Jùlóng Hotel HOTEL $$$

(聚龙大酒店, Jùlóng Dàjiǔdiàn; ☑283 1368; Furong Lu, 芙蓉路; d & tw ¥1280-1480; ❋❋) The long-standing Jùlóng's recent facelift has resulted in quality rooms decked out with easy-on-the-eye hues of brown and gold. Flat-screen TVs, good bathrooms and friendly staff round out the experience. Discounts knock rooms down to ¥680 on weekdays, ¥880 on weekends. It's opposite Zhīyuán Temple, off Furong Lu after you enter the main gate.

Lóngquán Hotel HOTEL $$$

(龙泉饭店, Lóngquán Fàndiàn; ☑328 8888; Furong Lu; d & tw incl breakfast ¥780-880; ❋❋) Located at the end of Furong Lu, this corner hotel has compact but smartly renovated rooms. Comfy beds, modern showers that don't choke, Chinese cable TV and terrible breakfast. Don't pay rack rate: weekend discounts are 50% and soar to 70% on weekdays. Walk to the end of Furong Lu and it's on the right as the road curves.

Shàngkètáng Hotel HOTEL $$$

(上客堂, Shàngkètáng Bīnguǎn; ☑283 3888; Furong Lu; d & tw ¥1280; ❋❋) Keeping in tune with the mountain, this prime-located hotel has gone with a Buddhist theme. Rooms are splashed with rosewood furniture, flat-screen TVs and plush carpets (some rooms have a wet carpet smell though). Weekday discounts knock rooms down to ¥580, ¥780 on weekends. The in-house vegetarian restaurant (dishes from ¥22) is very good.

ⓘ Information

Bank of China (中国银行, Zhōngguó Yínháng; 65 Huacheng Lu; ⊙9am-5pm) Foreign exchange and 24-hour international ATM. West of the main square.

China Post (中国邮政, Zhōngguó Yóuzhèng; 58 Huacheng Lu; ⊙8am-5.30pm) Off the main square.

Jiǔhuáshān Red Cross Hospital (九华山红十字医院, Jiǔhuáshān Hóngshízì Yīyuàn; ☑283 1330) After the pond on Baima Xincun.

ⓘ Getting There & Away

Buses from Jiǔhuáshān Xīnqūzhàn (the bus terminus and main Jiǔhuá Shān ticket office) run to/from the following destinations:

Héféi ¥73, 3½ hours, 10 daily

Huángshān ¥60, three hours, one daily (7am)

Nánjīng ¥75, three hours, four daily (6.20am, 7.20am, 8.40am and 1pm)

Qīngyáng ¥7, 30 minutes, frequent services (6.30am to 5pm)

Shànghǎi ¥150, six hours, two daily (7am and 2pm)

Túnxī ¥60, 3½ hours, one daily (7am)

Wǔhàn ¥129, six hours, one daily (7am)

More frequent buses leave from nearby Qīngyáng:

Hángzhōu ¥85, five hours, hourly

Héféi ¥70, two to three hours, hourly

Huángshān ¥55, three hours, three daily (7.30am, 9.30am and 2pm)

Nánjīng ¥70, three hours, hourly

Shànghǎi ¥110, six hours, hourly

Túnxī ¥60, two hours, two daily (7.30am and 2pm)

Yīxiàn ¥60, 2½ hours, two daily (8.30am and 1.30pm)

ⓘ Getting Around

The ¥50 shuttle ticket includes four bus rides: from the main ticket office to Jiǔhuájiē village (the base for the mountain ascent), from the village to Phoenix Pine (cable-car station) and back to the village, and from the village back to the main ticket office (first bus 6am, last bus 5pm).

To get to Phoenix Pine, catch the bus (every 30 minutes or when full) from the bus station north of the main gate (cross the bridge on the right after the Jùlóng Hotel). On busy days you may need to queue for more than two hours for the cable car to/from the peak.

Héféi 合肥

TRANSPORT HUB

Best used as a transport hub to the rest of Ānhuī, the provincial capital is a friendly city with lively markets, pleasant lakes and parks but few attractions.

🛏 Sleeping & Eating

The city is awash with a range of hotels (but no hostels!). The area around the train station has Chinese budget- and midrange-category places (from ¥70; look for 宾馆, *bīnguǎn*) and the main commercial street of Changjiang Zhonglu is where you'll find the midrange hotel chains such as 7 Days, Home Inn and Hanting. For food, head to the pedestrianised Huaihe Lu Buxing Jie. The side streets have cheap eats and there's everything from fast-food chains to noodle shops. A night market sets up in the area too.

Green Tree Inn   HOTEL **$$**
(格林豪泰, Gélí'n Háotài; ☑ 6265 0988; www.998.com; 34 Hongxing Lu, 红星路34号; d ¥209; ✳ @) This reliable, modern midrange chain hotel offers compact, cheap and clean accommodation in a 24-room branch along a quiet residential street. There's food and shopping within walking distance.

Westin   HOTEL **$$$**
(合肥万达威斯汀酒店, Héféi Wàndáwēisītīng Jiǔdiàn; ☑ 6298 9888; www.westin.com/hefeibaohe; 150 Ma'anshan Lu, 马鞍山路150号; d ¥2800; ✳ @ ⚡) Among the best in town, with a full range of modern facilities including a fitness centre, swimming pool, spa, good restaurants and elegant and modern rooms, equipped with Westin's trademark Heavenly beds. There's a megamall across the street where you can shop at Gucci before watching an IMAX movie. Expect 35% discounts online.

ℹ Getting There & Away

AIR

The recently opened Héféi Xīnqiáo International Airport is 32km northwest of Héféi (the old airport has now shut). Bookings can be made at **China Eastern Airlines/Lanyu Travel** (东方航空售票处/兰宇旅行社, Dōngfāng Hángkōng Shòupiàochù; ☑ 262 9955; 158 Changjiang Zhonglu), situated next to the Húadū Hotel, and at the train station's ticket booking office.

Daily flights include the following:
Běijīng ¥1320, two hours
Guǎngzhōu ¥1030, two hours
Shànghǎi ¥590, one hour
Xiàmén ¥860, 1½ hours

BUS

Héféi has numerous bus stations for its relatively small size, but the following are the most useful.

The **Héféi long-distance bus station** (合肥长途汽车站, Héféi chángtú qìchēzhàn; 168 Mingguang Lu) has buses to numerous destinations in the surrounding provinces:
Hángzhōu ¥98 to ¥170, six hours, six daily
Nánjīng ¥35 to ¥55, 2½ hours, half-hourly
Shànghǎi ¥145, six hours, 25 daily
Wǔhàn ¥140, six hours, eight daily

Buses to Huángshān (¥60, four hours, half-hourly), Jiǔhuá Shān (¥88, 3½ hours, every 40 minutes) and Túnxī (¥110, four hours, regular) leave from the **tourist bus station** (旅游汽车站, lǚyóu qìchēzhàn; Zhanqian Jie) 500m west of train station.

The so-called **main bus station** (客运总站, kèyùn zǒngzhàn; Zhanqian Jie), just outside the train station, is for local buses only.

TRAIN

The train station is 4km northeast of the city centre. Express D and G trains:
Běijīng ¥428, 4½ hours, eight daily
Nánjīng ¥61, one hour, 27 daily
Shànghǎi Hóngqiáo ¥156 to ¥205, 3½ hours, regular
Wǔhàn ¥106, 2½ hours

Regular service destinations:
Běijīng ¥140 to ¥398, 10 to 16 hours, six daily
Shànghǎi ¥116 to ¥183, 6½ to 8½ hours, eight daily
Túnxī ¥66 to ¥162, six to seven hours, three daily

ℹ Getting Around

Metered taxis are cheap, starting at ¥6. Taking a taxi (¥100, 40 minutes) is the best way to the airport, 32km northwest of the city centre. Rides from the city to the train station should cost ¥10.

Hénán

POP 100 MILLION

Best Villages

➡ Guōliàngcūn (p421)
➡ Zhūxiān (p427)
➡ Nánjiēcūn (p413)

Best Historic Sites

➡ Shàolín Temple (p413)
➡ Kāifēng (p422)
➡ Luòyáng (p416)

Why Go?

Affluent Chinese roll their eyes at the mention of impoverished and land-locked Hénán (河南), yet the province's heritage takes us back to the earliest days of Chinese antiquity. Ancient capitals rose and fell in Hénán's north, where the capricious Yellow River (Huáng Hé) nourished the flowering of a great civilisation. Hénán is home to China's oldest surviving Buddhist temple and one of the country's most astonishing collections of Buddhist carvings, the Lóngmén Caves. There is also the Shàolín Temple, that legendary institution where the martial way and Buddhism found an unlikely but powerful alliance. Hénán's inability to catch up with the rest of the land perhaps helps explain why the unusual village of Nánjiēcūn still sees a future in Maoist collectivism. Hénán is also home to the excellent walled town of Kāifēng and the 1000-year-old craft of woodblock printing in Zhūxiān.

When to Go
Zhèngzhōu

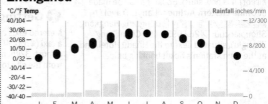

| **Apr** Wángchéng Park in Luòyáng is a blaze of floral colour during the peony festival. | **Jun** Trips to cool Guōliàngcūn up in the Ten Thousand Immortals Mountains. | **Sep & Oct** Catch the lovely and fleeting north China autumn. |

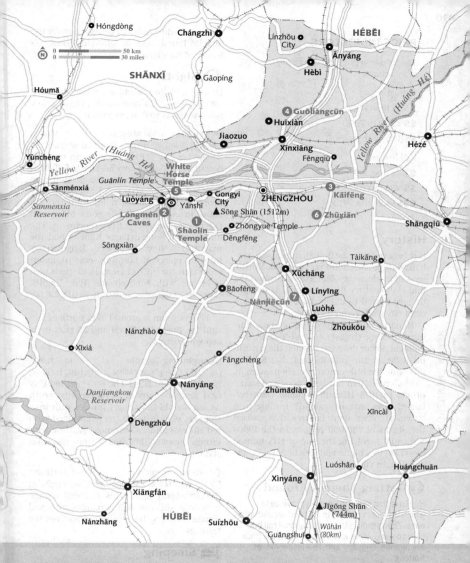

Hénán Highlights

1 Fathom the martial mysteries of Shàolín boxing at the **Shàolín Temple** (p413)

2 Seek enlightenment among the carved Bodhisattvas at the **Lóngmén Caves** (p419)

3 Take a trip back in time to **Kāifēng** (p422) and engage in some adventurous snacking at the night market

4 Hide away in cliff-top **Guōliàngcūn** (p421) – don't forget your sketchpad

5 Explore China's oldest Buddhist shrine: the **White Horse Temple** (p115) outside Luòyáng

6 Get acquainted with the ancient craft of Chinese woodblock printing in **Zhūxiān** (p413)

7 Rediscover communism with Chinese characteristics at **Nánjiēcūn** (p413)

PRICE INDICATORS

The following price indicators are used in this chapter:

Sleeping

$ less than ¥200

$$ ¥200 to ¥500

$$$ more than ¥500

Eating

$ less than ¥35

$$ ¥35 to ¥100

$$$ more than ¥100

History

It is believed that the first Shang capital, perhaps dating back 3800 years, was at Yǎnshī, west of modern-day Zhèngzhōu. Around the mid-14th century BC, the capital is thought to have moved to Zhèngzhōu, where its ancient city walls remain visible.

Hénán again occupied centre stage during the Song dynasty (AD 960–1279), but political power deserted it when the government fled south from its capital at Kāifēng following the 12th-century Jurchen invasion.

Modern Hénán has been poor and strife-prone. In 1975 Hénán's Bǎnqiáo Dam collapsed after massive rainfall, leading to a string of other dam failures that caused the deaths of 230,000 people. In the 1990s a scandal involving the sale of HIV-tainted blood led to a high incidence of AIDS in several Hénán villages.

ℹ Getting There & Around

Hénán is that rarity in China: a province in which travellers can get in, out and around with ease. Zhèngzhōu is the main regional rail hub; high speed G-class and D-class trains zip from Zhèngzhōu, Luòyáng and, to a lesser extent, Kāifēng.

Luòyáng has a small airport but Zhèngzhōu is the main hub for flying to/from Hénán.

Zhèngzhōu 郑州

☎ 0371 / POP 4.25 MILLION

The provincial Hénán capital of Zhèngzhōu is a rapidly modernising smog-filled metropolis with few relics from its ancient past (due to Japanese bombing in WWII). Zhèngzhōu can be largely zipped through, serving as a major transport hub and access point for the Shàolín Temple and the left-field Maoist collective of Nánjiēcūn.

◉ Sights

Despite a history reaching back to the earliest chapters of Chinese history, the city now has few sights to deter travellers.

Hénán Provincial Museum MUSEUM

(河南省博物馆; Hénán Shěng Bówùguǎn; 8 Nongye Lu; 农业路8号; English audio tour ¥20, deposit ¥200; ⊗9am-5pm Tue-Sun, to 5.30pm in summer) **FREE** The excellent collection here ranges from the artistry of Shang-dynasty bronzes, oracle bones, relics from the Yīn ruins in Ānyáng, to gorgeous Ming and Qing porcelain and pottery specimens. The dioramas of Song-dynasty Kāifēng and the magnificent, now obliterated, Tang-dynasty imperial palace at Luòyáng serve to underscore that the bulk of Hénán's glorious past is at one with Nineveh and Tyre. English captions. Take your passport as ID for admission.

The museum is around 2km north of Jinshui Lu. Buses 96, 61, 69 and 39 pass by; a taxi will cost ¥25.

Chénghuáng Temple TAOIST TEMPLE

(城隍庙I; Chénghuáng Miào; Shangcheng Lu; 商城路; ⊗9am-6pm) **FREE** The 600-year-old City God temple – any old Chinese city worth its salt should have one – bustles with worshippers who leave its trees festooned with red ribbons and its entrances swirling with incense smoke. Take bus 2 from the train station.

Confucius Temple CONFUCIAN TEMPLE

(文庙; Wén Miào; 24 Dong Dajie;, 东大街24号; ⊗8.30am-5pm) **FREE** This restored temple is replete with colourfully painted eves and ornate carvings. Take bus 60 or 85 from the train station.

🛏 Sleeping

There are cheap beds (¥60 to ¥150) at the numerous guesthouses (宾馆; bīnguǎn) around the train station, but they won't all take foreigners. More luxurious accommodation can be found on Jinshui Lu where chains such as Crowne Plaza and Holiday Inn reside.

Jǐnjiāng Inn MOTEL $$

(锦江之星; Jǐnjiāng Zhīxīng; ☎6693 2000; 77 Erma Lu; 二马路77号; d ¥229; ❋; Ⓜ Zhengzhou Railway Station) This modern and swish

Zhèngzhōu

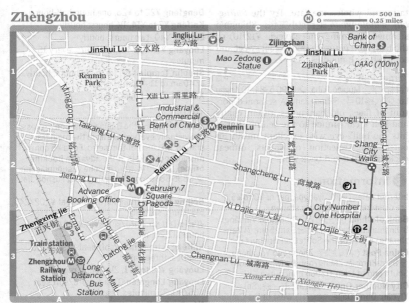

branch has crisp, sharp and well looked-after rooms (work desks, flat-screen TVs) in a block set back from the road.

Hilton Zhèngzhōu
HOTEL $$$

(希尔顿酒店; Xǐěrdùn Jiǔdiàn; ☑8996 0888; www3.hilton.com; 288 Jinshui Lu; 金水路288号; d/ste ¥1849/3746; ◉@☺☎☀; Ⓜ Yanzhuang) The best hotel in town by a fair distance, the new Hilton combines stylish elegance with a highly exacting level of service and a tempting range of five-star amenities and dining choices in a tower on Jinshui Lu. Rooms are contemporary, invitingly spacious and fully equipped.

✖ Eating & Drinking

Five hundred metres north of the train station is the busy February 7 Sq (二七广场; Èrqī Guáng Chǎng), also called Èrqī Sq, with nearby shops, restaurants and a night market. Look out for the large white pagoda.

Guāngcǎi Market
MARKET $

(光彩市场, Guāngcǎi Shìchǎng; btwn Erqi Lu & Renmin Lu; snacks ¥1-5; ⊗8am-9pm; Ⓜ Erqi Square) Gritty, maybe, but this crowded warren of food and clothes stalls in the block northeast of February 7 Sq is always packed. Try *málà tàng* (麻辣烫; spicy soup with skewered vegies and meat), *chūn juǎn* (春卷; spring rolls), *ròujiāmó* (肉夹馍; spicy meat in a bun), *càijiābǐng* (菜夹饼; vegetables in a bun), *guōtiē* (锅贴; fried dumplings) or *yángròu tāng* (羊肉汤; lamb soup).

There's also *bàokǎo xiān yóuyú* (爆烤鲜鱿鱼; fried squid kebabs), sweet *xìngrén chá* (杏仁茶; almond tea) and much more. Enter via Renmin Lu or Erqi Lu.

Hénán Shífǔ Chinese
HENAN $

(河南食府; ☑6622 2108; 25 Renmin Lu, 人民路25号; meals from ¥25; ⊗10am-2pm & 5-9.30pm; Ⓜ Renmin Lu) Tucked away in a courtyard off Renmin Lu, this well-known restaurant's photo menu is full of exotic-looking dishes, but turn to the rear pages for cheap, tasty and wholesome fare. Try the *Shàng-hǎi xiǎolóngbāo* (上海小笼包; Shànghǎi steamed dumplings; meat/vegie ¥12/10) or the tasty *lǐyú bèimiàn* (鲤鱼焙面; sweet and sour fish with noodles).

Target Pub
PUB

(目标酒吧; Mùbiāo Jiǔbā; ☑ 6590 5384; 10 Jingliu Lu; 经六路10号; ⊙ 5pm-3am) A seasoned portrait of flags, old banknotes, rattan chairs and half a car pinned to the ceiling, Target hits the bull's-eye with excellent music, an outstanding selection of spirits, offbeat cocktails and a laid-back vibe.

ⓘ Information

Internet cafes (网吧; *wǎngbā*; per hr ¥3 to ¥5) are clustered near the train station.

Bank of China (中国银行; Zhōngguó Yínháng; 8 Jinshui Lu; 金水路8号; ⊙ 9am-5pm; Ⓜ Yanzhuang) North of the Sofitel, on Jinshui Lu.

China Post (中国邮政; Zhōngguó Yóuzhèng; ⊙ 8am-8pm; Ⓜ Zhengzhou Railway Station) South end of train station concourse.

City Number One Hospital (市一院; Shì Yīyuàn; Dong Dajie; 东大街) West of the Confucius Temple.

Industrial & Commercial Bank of China (ICBC; 工商银行; Gōngshāng Yínháng; Renmin Lu; 人民路; Ⓜ Renmin Lu) Has a 24-hour ATM.

Public Security Bureau (PSB; 公安局出入境管理处; Gōng'ānjú Chūrùjìng Guǎnlǐchù; ☑ 6962 0350; 90 Huanghe Donglu, 黄河东路90号; ⊙ 8.30am-noon & 3-6.30pm Jun-Aug, 2-5.30pm Mon-Fri Sep-May) For visa extensions; take bus 135 or 114.

ⓘ Getting There & Away

AIR

Zhèngzhōu Airport is located 37km southeast of town. The **Civil Aviation Administration of China** (CAAC; 中国民航; Zhōngguó Mínháng; ☑ 6599 1111; 3 Jinshui Lu, at Dongmin Lu), east of the city centre, sells flight tickets, as does the **ticket office** (售票处, Shòupiàochù; ☑ 6677 7111) at the Zhèngzhōu Hotel; look for the sign that reads Zhèngzhōu Airport ticket office.

Flights include the following:

Běijīng ¥920, eight daily

Guǎngzhōu ¥1350, 11 daily

Guìlín ¥1250, one daily

Hong Kong ¥1460, one daily

Shànghǎi ¥800, 12 daily

Shēnzhèn ¥1410, nine daily

BUS

The long-distance bus station (长途汽车站, *chángtú qìchēzhàn*) is opposite the train station.

Dēngfēng ¥22 to ¥26, one hour, half-hourly

Kāifēng ¥7 to ¥14, 1½ hours, hourly

Línyǐng ¥40, two hours, hourly

Luòyáng ¥28 to ¥40, two hours, every 15 minutes

Shàolín Temple ¥27, 1½ to 2½ hours, hourly (7.40am to 11.40pm)

Xī'ān ¥127, six hours, hourly

TRAIN

Trains, including the Běijīng–Kowloon express, run virtually everywhere from the main train station, on Line 1 of the metro. For a ¥5 commission, get tickets at the **advance booking office** (火车预售票处, huǒchē yùshòupiàochù; ☑ 6835 6666; cnr Zhengxing Jie & Fushou Jie; ⊙ 8am-5pm).

Běijīng West D train, hard/soft seat ¥202/243, 5½ hours, six daily

Jǐ'nán D train, hard/soft seat ¥193/272, 5½ hours, 12.28pm

Kāifēng D train, hard/soft seat ¥19/24, 30 minutes, three daily

Luòyáng ¥18 to ¥71, 2½ hours, regular

Luòyáng Lóngmén G train, hard/soft seat ¥66/90, 35 minutes, regular

Nánjīng South D train, hard/soft seat ¥204/287, 5½ hours, three daily

Shànghǎi D train, hard/soft seat ¥238/381, 6½ hours, three daily

Xī'ān North G train, hard/soft seat ¥239/380, 2½ hours, regular

Accessible on Line 1 of the metro, the vast new Zhèngzhōu East Train Station (郑州东站, Zhèngzhōu Dōngzhàn) has high-speed G-class trains:

Běijīng West G train, hard/soft seat ¥309/504, 3½ hours, very regular

Luòyáng Lóngmén G train, hard/soft seat ¥66/90, 35 minutes, regular

Xī'ān North G train, hard/soft seat ¥239/380, 2½ hours, regular

ⓘ Getting Around

Buses for the airport (¥15, 70 minutes, hourly from 6.30am to 7pm) leave from the Zhèngzhōu Hotel (郑州大酒店, Zhèngzhōu Dàjiǔdiàn). A taxi costs around ¥100 and takes 40 minutes.

Bus 26 travels from the train station past 7 February Sq, along Renmin Lu and Jinshui Lu to the CAAC office. Local buses cost ¥1 to ¥2.

The east–west running Line 1 of the new metro runs through the train station, Erqi Sq, Renmin Lu and Zijingshan. The north–south Line 2 following Zijingshan Lu is under construction and is due to start service in 2015, while Line 5 will open in 2016 and Line 3 in 2018.

Taxi fares start at ¥8 (¥10 at night).

Nánjiēcūn 南街村

Nánjiēcūn VILLAGE

(南街村; www.nanjie cun.cn; admission ¥80)
South of Zhèngzhōu, Nánjiēcūn is China's
very last Maoist collective (gōngshè). There
are no Buddhist temples or mist-wreathed
mountain panoramas, but a trip to Nánjiēcūn is nonetheless one back in time: a
journey to the puritanical and revolutionary
China of the 1950s, when Chairman Mao
was becoming a supreme being, money was
yesterday's scene and the menace of karaoke
had yet to be prophesied by even the most
paranoid party faithful.

The first inkling you have arrived in an
entirely different world comes from the
roads: perfectly clean, willow tree-lined
streets run in straight lines with a kind of
austere socialist beauty, past noodle factories, schools and rows of identikit blocks of
workers' flats emblazoned with vermillion
communist slogans. There are hardly any
cars and no advertising billboards, but be-
atific portraits of Chairman Mao gaze down
on all.

From the main entrance, head along the
main drag, Yingsong Dadao (颖松大道), to
East is Red Square (东方红广场, Dōngfāng-
hóng Guǎngchǎng), where guards maintain a
24-hour vigil at the foot of a statue of Chairman Mao, and portraits of Marx, Engels, Stalin and Lenin (the original 'Gang of Four')
rise up on all four sides. The square is del-
uged in shrill propaganda broadcast from
speakers in true 1950s style, kicking off at
6.15am daily. A short stroll to the left brings
you to **Cháoyáng Gate Square** (朝阳门广
场, Cháoyángmén Guǎngchǎng) and the rebuilt,
traditional architecture of **Cháoyáng Gate**
(朝阳门, Cháoyáng Mén).

Once you look closer, however, you'll real-
ise that all is not well. Stroll to the edges of
the town and you'll see dilapidated buildings
with broken windows, and walk into a public toilet and you may find the taps locked.
But Nánjiēcūn is a welcome portrait of an
ideologically guided collective, whose cleanliness, order and quietness contrast with the
chaos and messiness of modern-day China.

ℹ️ Information

Tourist Service Centre (旅游接待处, Yóukè
Jiēdàichù; Yingsong Dadao; 颖松大道;
☉7.30am-5.30pm) Avoid the Tourist Service
Centre at the west end of Yingsong Dadao as
they'll ask you to buy an admission ticket for

¥80. If you do take up the offer, it comes with
a Chinese-speaking guide and a jaunt around
town on an electric cart.

ℹ️ Getting There & Away

From Zhèngzhōu bus station, buses (¥40, two
hours) run south every hour between 6.20am
and 6.20pm to the bus station at Línyǐng (临颍),
from where it's a ¥3 sānlúnchē (pedicab) journey
south to Nánjiēcūn.

Sōng Shān & Dēngfēng 嵩山、登封

☑ 0371

In Taoism, Sōng Shān is considered the central mountain (中岳; zhōngyuè) of the five
sacred peaks (五岳; wǔyuè), symbolising
earth (土; tǔ) among the five elements and
occupying the axis directly beneath heaven.
Despite this Taoist persuasion, the mountains are also home to one of China's most
famous and legendary Zen (禅; Chán) Buddhist temples: the inimitable Shàolín Temple. Two main mountain ranges crumple
the area, the 1494m-high **Tàishì Shān** (山)
and the 1512m-high **Shàoshì Shān** (少室
山) whose peaks compose Sōng Shān about
80km west of Zhèngzhōu. Both peaks can be
ascended.

At the foot of Tàishì Shān, 12km southeast of the Shàolín Temple and 74km from
Zhèngzhōu, sits the squat little town of
Dēngfēng. Tatty in parts, it is used by travellers as a base for trips to surrounding sights
or exploratory treks into the hills.

The main bus station is in the far east
of town. Most hotels and restaurants are
strung out on or near Zhongyue Dajie (中岳
大街), the main east–west street, and Shaolin Dadao (少林大道), parallel to the south.

⦿ Sights

Shàolín Temple BUDDHIST TEMPLE
(少林寺; Shàolín Sì; ☑ 6370 2503; admission ¥100;
☉7.30am-5.30pm) The largely rebuilt Shàolín
Temple is a commercialised victim of its
own incredible success. A frequent target
of war, the ancestral home of wǔshù (p414)
was last torched in 1928, and the surviving
halls – many of recent construction – are
today assailed by relentless waves of selfie-
shooting tour groups. The temple's claim to
fame, its dazzling gōngfū (kungfu) based
on the movements of animals, insects and
sometimes mythological figures, guarantees

WǓSHÙ OR GŌNGFÙ?

When planning to study Chinese martial arts, the first question you should ask is: shall I learn *Wǔshù* (武术) or *Gōngfu* (功夫)? There may be considerable overlap, but there are crucial differences. *Wǔshù* is a more recently created term strongly associated with athletic martial arts displays and competition-based martial arts patterns or forms. *Gōngfù* (kungfu) is more connected to the development of internal and more esoteric skills, rather than physical prowess or mainstream athleticism. If you are lucky enough to see a martial arts master break a piece of ceramic from a bowl and grind it to dust with his bare fingers, this is *gōngfù*, not *wǔshù*.

that martial arts clubs around the world make incessant pilgrimages.

A satisfying visit to the Shàolín Temple requires, rather than bestows, a Zen mentality (to handle the visiting hordes and the ticket prices). But if you explore away from the main areas, you could spend an entire day or two visiting smaller temples, climbing the surrounding peaks and eking out crumbs of solitude.

Coming through the main entrance, you'll pass several *wǔshù* schools. On the right, about 500m in, is a square showcasing impressive daily 30-minute outdoor martial arts performances. Next door is the **Wǔshù Training Centre**, also with shows featuring monks tumbling around and breaking sticks and metal bars over their heads.

The main temple itself is another 600m along. Many buildings such as the main **Dàxióng Hall** (大雄宝殿; Dàxióng Bǎodiàn; reconstructed in 1985) were levelled by fire in 1928. Although the temple seems to have been founded in approximately AD 500 (accounts vary), some halls only date back as far as 2004. Among the oldest structures at the temple are the decorative arches and stone lions, both outside the main gate.

At the rear, the **West Facing Hall** (西方圣人殿; Xīfāng Shēngrén Diàn) contains the famous depressions in the floor, apocryphally the result of generations of monks practising their stance work, and huge colour frescos. Always be on the lookout for the ubiquitous Damo (Bodhidharma), whose bearded Indian visage gazes sagaciously from stelae or peeks out from temple halls.

Across from the temple entrance, the **Arhat Hall** within the **Shífāng Chányuàn** (十方禅院) contains legions of crudely fashioned *luóhàn* (monks who have achieved enlightenment and passed to nirvana at death). The **Pagoda Forest** (少林塔林, Shàolín Tǎlín), a cemetery of 248 brick pagodas including the ashes of eminent monks, is well worth visiting if you get here ahead of the crowds. Sadly, where visitors were once allowed to wander among the pagodas, the area is now only viewable via a wooden fence circuit.

As you face the Shàolín Temple, paths on your left lead up **Wǔrǔ Peak** (五乳峰, Wǔrǔ Fēng). Flee the tourist din by heading towards the peak to see the **cave** (达摩洞, Dámó Dòng) where Damo (Bodhidharma) meditated for nine years; it's 4km uphill. From the base, you may spot the peak and the cave, marked by a large Bodhisattva figure. En route to the cave, detour to the **Chūzǔ Temple** (初祖庵; Chūzǔ Ān), a quiet and battered counterpoint to the main temple. Its main structure is the oldest wooden one in the province (c AD 1125).

At 1512m above sea level and reachable on the **Sōngyáng Cableway** (Sōngyáng Suǒdào; ¥60 return, 20 minutes), **Shàoshì Shān** (少室山) is the area's tallest peak. The area beyond the cable car is home to the peak and **Erzǔ Nunnery** (二祖庵, Erzǔ Ān; admission ¥2) with four wells where you can sample its various tasting waters (sour, sweet, peppery and bitter).

There's also a scenic trek to neighbouring **Sānhuángzhài** (三皇寨), taking about six hours return, covering 15km and going past craggy rock formations along a path that often hugs the cliff to the 782-step **Rope Bridge** (连天吊桥; Lián Tiān Diào Qiáo). To begin the hike, look for the small Chinese sign which leads to Sānhuángzhài. It's a long and hard-going hike, so for safety reasons, monks recommend trekking with a friend.

If you'd prefer an easier hike, use the **Shàolín Cableway** (少林索道; Shàolín Suǒdào; ¥60 return, 40 minutes) which conveys you to Sānhuángzhài. From there, it's a shorter hike to the bridge. Both cableways are just beyond the Pagoda Forest. Note that the bridge may be closed at times for repair or during inclement weather. Start hikes early, as you don't want to be caught out in the dark.

To reach the Shàolín Temple, take a bus (¥3, 15 minutes) from Dēngfēng's west bus station (西站; xīzhàn) on Zhongyue Dajie to the drop-off point, or bus 8 (¥2) from the old bus station. The temple compound office is across the road; buggies (¥10, from 8am to 6pm) run from here to the main temple entrance, or you can walk (20 minutes). Alternatively, take a minibus from either Luòyáng or Zhèngzhōu (¥20 to ¥27, 1½ to 2½ hours) to the drop-off. From the temple, return buses leave from the drop-off point (last bus at around 8pm). A taxi to the temple from Dēngfēng will cost ¥30 (unofficial fare, no meter).

Sōngyáng Academy ACADEMY

(嵩阳书院; Sōngyáng Shūyuàn; admission ¥30; ⏰7.30am-5.30pm) At the foot of Tàishì Shān sits one of China's oldest academies, the lush and well-tended Sōngyáng Academy, a building complex which dates to AD 484 and rises up the hill on a series of terraces. In the courtyard are two cypress trees believed to be around 4500 years old – and they're still alive!

Both bus 2 and bus 6 (¥1) from Dēngfēng run to the Sōngyáng Academy.

Mt Tàishì MOUNTAIN

(太室山; Tàishì Shān; admission ¥50; ⏰8am-6pm) A 2km walk from the Sōngyáng Academy, the attractive Sōngyuè Pagoda (嵩岳塔, Sōngyuè Tǎ; admission ¥40), built in AD 509, is China's oldest brick pagoda. Nearby is the Fǎwáng Temple (法王寺; Fǎwáng Sì), ringed by mountains and first established in AD 71. Most visitors, however, come here to ascend Mt Tàishì. To begin the climb, look for the large stone path just beyond the Sōngyáng Academy. The challenging climb up stone steps takes three to four hours (one way).

The 1470m-high Jùnjí Peak (峻极峰; Jùnjí Fēng) is little more than a viewing point.

Zhōngyuè Temple TAOIST

(中岳庙, Zhōngyuè Miào; admission ¥30; ⏰8am-6pm) A few kilometres east of Dēngfēng, the ancient and hoary Zhōngyuè Miào is a colossal active Taoist monastery complex that originally dates back to the 2nd century BC. The complex – embedded in a mountainous background, its monks garbed in traditional dress and sporting topknots – is less visited and exudes a more palpable air of reverence than its Buddhist sibling, the Shàolín Temple.

Besides attending the main hall dedicated to the Mountain God, walk through Huàsān Gate (化三门, Huàsān Mén) and expunge *pengju*, *pengzhi* and *pengjiao* – three pestilential insects that respectively inhabit the brain, tummy and feet. Drop by the four Iron Men of Song, rubbed by visitors to cure ailments and stop by the Sixty Gods Hall, where visitors pay respects to the God corresponding to their birth year. From Dēngfēng, take the green bus 2 along Zhongyue Dajie.

🛏 Sleeping & Eating

The stretch of Chonggao Lu (崇高路) around the Shàolín Travelers Hostel has eating options galore. You'll also find plenty of restaurants in town along Zhongyue Dajie (中岳大街) between Jiming Jie (鸡鸣街) and Songshan Lu (嵩山路) – a taxi will cost ¥5 to ¥7 from most hotels. At night, look for barbecue stalls set up outside restaurants. Local specialities are thickly cut handmade noodles in broth (烩面; *huì miàn*; ¥6 to ¥8) and barbecue lamb skewers (羊肉串; *yángròu chuàn*; ¥2).

BODHIDHARMA & HIS SOLE SHOE

Called Dámó (达摩) by the Chinese, Bodhidharma was a 5th-century Indian monk who travelled to the Shàolín Temple, bringing Chan (禅) Zen) Buddhism to China in the process. The monk is also traditionally revered for establishing the breathing and meditational exercises that lay the foundations of Shàolín Boxing. Bodhidharma's bearded, heavy-browed and serious expression can be seen in temples across China, especially Chan temples. Accomplishments and legends swarm around his name: he is said to have sat in a cave silently staring at a wall for nine years. Damo is also often depicted carrying a shoe on a stick. Folklore attests that he was spotted wandering in the Pamir Mountains holding a single shoe. When the news reached the Shàolín Temple, it caused consternation as Bodhidharma had previously passed away and was buried nearby. His grave was exhumed and discovered to contain nothing but a solitary shoe.

Shàolín Travelers Hostel   HOSTEL $

(旅行家青年旅舍, Lǚxíngjiā Qīngnián Lǚshè; ☎159 8188 3801, 6288 6799; www.shaolintravelershostel.hostel.com; 308 Chonggao Luxi, 崇高路西308号; dm ¥30-60, d ¥160; ❀@�) Roomy 10-bed dorms are basic with no lockers, but private rooms here are large with foam mattresses and an odd stone-slab decor, while the English-speaking owner can help with recommendations. It's a ¥7 taxi ride from the main bus station or take bus 1 (¥1) and stop along Shaoshi Lu (少室路).

Shàolín Hotel   HOTEL $$

(少林宾馆, Shàolín Bīnguǎn; ☎6016 1616; 66 Zhongyue Dajie, 中岳大街66号; d ¥300; ❀) Bright and cheery staff, good discounts and clean rooms make this neat and trim hotel a good choice. There's no English sign, so look for the four-storey white building east of Dicos (a fast-food restaurant) with the yellow and red sign. Take bus 1 from the main bus station or a ¥7 taxi ride. Discounts of 50%.

Shàolín International Hotel   HOTEL $$$

(少林国际大酒店, Shàolín Guójì Dàjiǔdiàn; ☎6285 6868; www.shaolinhotel.com; 20 Shaolin Dadao, 少林大道20号; d/ste ¥680/1328; ❀) Popular with visiting Chinese, this self-proclaimed four-star hotel is more like a smartish three-star, with scads of black Buicks parked outside. A taxi from the main bus station will cost ¥7. Discounts of 40%.

ℹ Information

Bank of China (中国银行; Zhōngguó Yínháng; ☺8am-5.30pm) 52 Zhongyue Dajie (☺9am-5pm Mon-Fri); 186 Shaolin Dadao (☺9am-noon & 2-5pm Mon-Fri) 24-hour ATM and foreign exchange.

China International Travel Service (CITS; 中国国际旅行社, Zhōngguó Guójì Lǚxíngshè; ☎6287 2137; Beihuan Lu Xiduan, 网吧) There are helpful, English-speaking staff at this branch of CITS.

China Post (中国邮政; Zhōngguó Yóuzhèng; cnr Zhongyue Dajie & Wangji Rd) Centrally located post office.

No 2 People's Hospital (第二人民医院; Dì'èr Rénmín Yīyuàn; ☎6289 9999; 189 Shaolin Dadao; 少林大道189号) On the main road.

ℹ Getting There & Around

The Dēngfēng bus station (总站; zǒng zhàn) is in the east of town; jump on bus 1 (¥1) to reach Zhongyue Dajie and the town centre. There's also a west bus station (西站, xī zhàn) which some buses head to after dropping people off at the main station. Buses to and from Zhèngzhōu (¥22, 1½ hours) and Luòyáng (¥20, two hours) run every 30 minutes from the main station. To purchase tickets for trains departing from Zhèngzhōu, go to the **train ticket office** (火车预售票处, huǒchē yùshòupiàochù; 72 Shaolin Dadao, 少林大道72号; ☺8am-6pm). Taxis are a cheap and easy way to get around. Fares start at ¥5 but use those with meters.

Luòyáng   洛阳

☒ 0379 / POP 1.4 MILLION

Access point for the incredible Lóngmén Caves outside town, Luòyáng was one of China's true dynastic citadels. The city was the prosperous capital of 13 dynasties, until the Northern Song dynasty shifted its capital east along the Yellow River to Kāifēng in the 10th century. The mighty Sui- and Tang-dynasty walls formed an imposing rectangle north and south of the Luò River, while worshippers flocked to 1300 Buddhist temples through the city. Luòyáng was once the very centre of the Chinese universe and the eastern capital of the resplendent Tang dynasty. Tragically, little remains of this glorious past: the heart of the magnificent Sui-dynasty palace complex was centred on the point where today's Zhongzhou Lu and Dingding Lu intersect in a frenzy of traffic.

⊙ Sights & Activities

★**Luòyáng Museum**   MUSEUM

(洛阳市博物馆, Luòyáng Shì Bówùguǎn; www.lymuseum.com; Nietai Lu, 聂泰路; audio tour ¥40; ☺9am-4.30pm Tue-Sun) FREE This huge new museum, situated out of the action south of the river, has exhilarating displays across two huge floors and is one of the few places to get ancient Luòyáng in any kind of perspective. There's an absorbing collection of Tang-dynasty three-colour *sāncǎi* porcelain and the city's rise is traced through dynastic pottery, bronzeware and other magnificent objects.

Take bus 77 (¥1) from the train station. A taxi from town will cost ¥20; getting a taxi from the museum can be hard without walking 10 minutes to the main road.

Old Town   HISTORIC SITE

(老城区; lǎochéngqū) Any Chinese city worth its salt has an old town. Luòyáng's is east of the rebuilt **Lìjīng Gate** (丽京门, Lìjīng Mén), where a maze of narrow and winding streets yield up old courtyard houses and the occasional creaking monument, including the old **Drum Tower** (鼓楼, Gǔ Lóu), rising up at

Luòyáng

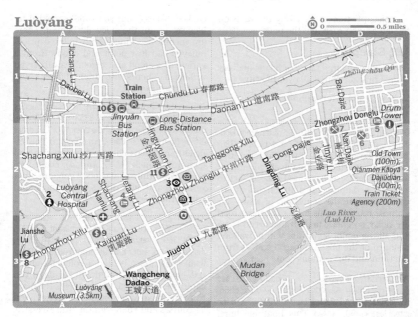

the east end of Dong Dajie (东大街), and the lovely brick **Wenfeng Pagoda** (文峰塔, Wénfēng Tǎ), originally built in the Song dynasty. The rest of Dong Dajie is a hubbub of local life, with hairdressers, noodle stalls and tradesmiths clustering within crumbling old houses.

Wángchéng Square   SQUARE, MUSEUM
(王城广场, Wángchéng Guángchǎng; Zhongzhou Zhonglu, 中州中路) This square is the meeting place for locals who come to play chess and cards under fluttering China flags, and is busy at night. Across Zhongzhou Zhonglu, a huge statue of six rearing horses marks the underground **Eastern Zhou Royal Horse & Carriage Museum** (周王城天子驾六博物馆, Zhōuwángchéng Tiānzi Jiàliù Bówùguǎn; Wangcheng Sq; admission ¥30; ☺ 9am-5pm winter, 8.30am-7pm summer). The principal draw is the unearthed remains of a former emperor's royal horses, buried alive when the emperor passed on.

Wángchéng Park   PARK
(王城公园, Wángchéng Gōngyuán; Zhongzhou Zhonglu; admission park ¥15, park & zoo ¥25, park, zoo & cable car ¥30, after 7pm ¥15, peony festival ¥55) One of Luòyáng's indispensable green lungs, this park is the site of the annual **peony festival**; held in April, the festival sees

the park flooded with colour, floral aficionados, photographers, girls with garlands on their heads and hawkers selling huge bouquets of flowers. Unfortunately, the park is home to a decrepit zoo for which you're forced to pay an admission charge. There's also an amusement park (rides ¥15 to ¥20).

Artists ply their trade along the walls on the left as your turn into the park.

🛏 Sleeping

Luòyáng has a large range of hotels in every budget bracket dotted all over the city.

Luòyáng Yijiā International Youth Hostel
HOSTEL $

(洛阳易家国际青年旅舍, Luòyáng Yijiā Guójì Qīngnián Lǚshè; ☑ 6351 2311; 329 Zhongzhou Donglu, 中洲东路329号; dm ¥45-55, d/tw ¥140/180; ❄ @ 🛜) Located in the busy old town, this hostel hits its stride with a lively communal area, bar and excellent food (pizzas ¥32 to ¥38). Six-bed dorms are a little tight but private rooms are the equivalent of a two-star Chinese room. Rooms facing the main road are noisy, so check first. Transport to town and all the major sights are within walking distance of the hostel. Buses 5 and 41 from the train and bus stations come past.

★ Christian's Hotel
BOUTIQUE HOTEL $$$

(克丽司汀酒店, Kèlisītīng Jiǔdiàn; ☑ 6326 6666; www.5xjd.com; 56 Jiefang Lu, 解放路56号; d inc Ibreakfast ¥1390; ❄ @) This boutique hotel scores points for its variety of rooms, each one with a kitchen and dining area, large plush beds, flat-screen TVs and mini-bar. Do you go for the room with the dark rich tones or the one with the white walls and circular bed? Regardless, you'll be thanking Christian each time you step into the room. Efficient staff rounds out the experience.

🍴 Eating

Luòyáng's famous 'water banquet' (水席; *shuǐxí*) resonates along China's culinary grapevine. The main dishes of this 24-course meal are soups served up with the speed of flowing water – hence the name.

A handy branch of the **Carrefour** (家乐福; *Jiālèfú*) supermarket can be found near the corner of Tanggong Xilu and Jiefang Lu in the **Today mall** (新都汇; *Xīndòuhuì*) where you can also find a wide variety of things to eat. The old town is also rife with everything from noodles to dumplings, hotpot and more.

Old Town Market
MARKET $

(南大街夜市, Nándàjiē yèshì; cnr Xi Dajie & Dong Dajie & north to Zhongzhou Donglu; ⊘5-10pm) This lively night market has a cornucopia of snacks from *yángròu chuàn* (羊肉串; lamb kebabs; ¥2) to super-sweet *zhī* (汁; juice; ¥3). Stalls on the left offer a wide range of

cooked dishes (from ¥8 to ¥58) served at tables set up on the sidewalk behind. There are menus in Chinese with marked prices but you can just point and choose from a variety of seafood and vegetables, all served wok-fried. There's also draught beer (生啤酒, *shēngpíjiǔ*; ¥5).

Qiánmén Kǎoyā Dàjiǔdiàn
PEKING DUCK $$

(前门烤鸭大酒店; ☑ 6395 3333; cnr Zhongzhou Donglu & Minzu Jie; half/whole duck ¥70/138, other dishes from ¥28; ⊘10am-2pm & 5-9pm) This efficient and smart choice serves up rich and tasty roast duck (烤鸭; *kǎoyā*), cooked by an army of white-clad chefs. There are other vegetable and meat dishes on the menu, but why bother?

Zhēn Bù Tóng Fàndiàn Chinese
HENAN $$

(真不同饭店, One of a Kind Restaurant; ☑ 6395 2609; 369 Zhongzhou Donglu, 中州中路369号; dishes ¥15-45, water banquet from ¥688; ⊘10am-9pm) Huge place behind a colourful green, red, blue and gold traditional facade. If you can rustle up a large group, this is the place to come to for a water-banquet experience; if 24 courses and ¥688 seems a little excessive, you can opt to pick individual dishes from the menu.

ℹ Information

Internet cafes (per hour ¥3) are scattered around the train station and sprinkled along nearby Jinguyuan Lu.

Bank of China (中国银行, Zhōngguó Yínháng; ⊘8am-4.30pm) Most branches have ATMs that take international cards. The Zhongzhou Xilu office exchanges travellers cheques. There's also a branch on the corner of Zhongzhou Lu and Shachang Nanlu. Another branch just west of the train station has foreign-exchange services.

China Post (中国邮政, Zhōngguó Yóuzhèng; Zhongzhou Zhonglu) East of Wángchéng Sq.

Industrial & Commercial Bank of China (ICBC, 工商银行, Gōngshāng yínháng; 228 Zhongzhou Zhonglu) Huge branch; foreign exchange and 24-hour ATM.

Luòyáng Central Hospital (洛阳市中心医院, Luòyáng Shì Zhōngxīn Yīyuàn; ☑ 6389 2222; 288 Zhongzhou Zhonglu) Works in cooperation with SOS International; also has a 24-hour pharmacy.

Public Security Bureau (PSB, 公安局, Gōng'ānjú; ☑ 6393 8397; cnr Kaixuan Lu & Tiyuchang Lu; ⊘8am-noon & 2-5.30pm Mon-Fri) The exit-entry department (出入境大厅, Chūrùjìng Dàtīng) is in the south building.

ℹ Getting There & Away

AIR

You would do better to fly into or out of Zhèngzhōu. Daily flights operate to Běijīng (¥860, 1½ hours), Shànghǎi (¥890, 1½ hours), Guǎngzhōu (¥1410) and other cities. Obtain tickets through hotels or Ctrip.

BUS

Regular departures from the **long-distance bus station** (一运汽车站, yīyùn qìchēzhàn; 51 Jinguyuan Lu), located diagonally across from the train station, include the following:

Dēngfēng ¥14, two hours, hourly (5.15am to 6.10pm)

Kāifēng ¥41, three hours, hourly

Shàolín Temple ¥19.50, 1½ hours, half-hourly (5.20am to 4pm)

Xī'ān ¥71 to ¥79, four hours, hourly (7am to 8.30pm)

Zhèngzhōu ¥24 to ¥30, 1½ hours, hourly

Buses to similar destinations also depart from the friendly and less frantic Jīnyuǎn bus station (锦远汽车站; Jīnyuǎn qìchēzhàn), just west of the train station.

TRAIN

Luòyáng's Luòyáng Lóngmén Station (洛阳龙门站, Lùòyáng Lóngmén Zhàn), over the river in the south of town, has D and G trains to Zhèngzhōu and Xī'ān. The regular train station (洛阳火车站, Luòyáng Huǒchē Zhàn) has regional and long-distance trains.

You can get tickets for a ¥5 commission from a **train ticket agency** (火车票代售处, Huǒchēpiàodàishòuchǔ; 249 Zhongzhou Donglu).

Regional destinations include Kāifēng (hard seat ¥35, three hours, regular) and Zhèngzhōu (hard seat ¥25, 1½ hours, regular).

Hard-sleeper destinations departing the regular train station:

Běijīng West seat/sleeper ¥106/196, nine hours, eight daily

Nánjīng seat/sleeper ¥112/315, eight to 12 hours, six daily

Shànghǎi seat/sleeper ¥153/263, 12 to 17 hours, five daily

Wǔhàn seat/sleeper ¥90/170, nine hours, regular

Zhèngzhōu 2nd/1st class ¥55/106, 40 minutes, 10 daily

From Luòyáng Lóngmén Station:

Běijīng West G train 2nd/1st class ¥368/589, four hours

Nánjīng D train 2nd/1st class ¥231/615, six hours, one daily

Shànghǎi D train 2nd/1st class ¥264/765, nine hours

Xī'ān North G train 2nd/1st class ¥175/280, two hours, regular

ℹ Getting Around

The airport is 12km north of the city. Bus 83 (¥1, 30 minutes) runs from the parking lot to the right as you exit the train station. A taxi from the train station costs about ¥35.

Buses 5 and 41 go to the Old Town from the train station, running via Wángchéng Sq. Buses 26, 28, 33, 65 and 66 run to Luòyáng Lóngmén Station. A taxi from town costs about ¥20.

Taxis are ¥5 at flag fall, making them good value and a more attractive option than taking motor-rickshaws, which will cost you around ¥4 from the train station to Wángchéng Sq.

Around Luòyáng

Lóngmén Caves 龙门石窟

The ravaged grottoes at Lóngmén constitute one of China's handful of surviving masterpieces of Buddhist rock carving. A Sutra in stone, the epic achievement of the **Lóngmén Caves** (龙门石窟, Lóngmén Shíkū; admission ¥120, English-speaking guide ¥150; ⏰ 7.30am-4.30pm & 7-10.30pm summer, 8am-4pm & 7-10.30pm winter) was commenced by chisellers from the Northern Wei dynasty, after the capital relocated here from Dàtóng in AD 494. During the next 200 years or so, more than 100,000 images and statues of Buddha and his disciples emerged from over a kilometre of limestone cliff wall along the Yī River (伊河, Yī Hé).

A disheartening amount of decapitation disfigures the statuary at this Unesco World Heritage Site. In the early 20th century, many effigies were beheaded by unscrupulous collectors or simply extracted whole, many ending up abroad in such institutions as the Metropolitan Museum of Art in New York, the Atkinson Museum in Kansas City and the Tokyo National Museum. A noticeboard at the site lists significant statues that are missing and their current whereabouts. Many statues have clearly just had their faces crudely bludgeoned off, vandalism that probably dates to the Cultural Revolution and earlier episodes of anti-Buddhist fervour. The elements have also intervened, wearing smooth the faces of many other statues.

The caves are scattered in a line on the west and east sides of the river. Most of the significant Buddhist carvings are on the west side, but a notable crop can also be admired after traversing the bridge to the east side. Admission also includes entry to a temple and garden on the east side. English captions are rudimentary despite the caves being a major tourist drawcard. Night-time illumination means aficionados can discover a different experience. Whether you visit in the day or night, allow your eyes to adjust to the light inside the caves for details to emerge.

The caves are 13km south of Luòyáng and can be reached by taxi (¥30) or bus 81 (¥1.50, 40 minutes) from the east side of Luòyáng's train station. The last bus 81 returns to Luòyáng at 8.50pm. Buses 53 and 60 also run to the caves.

From the west side, you can take a boat (¥20 to ¥25) back to the main entrance to get a riverside view of the grottoes. Note that you can't re-enter the west side once you leave. From the east side, electric carts (¥5 to ¥10) can take you back to the main entrance.

The major caves are listed below.

WEST SIDE

Three Bīnyáng Caves CAVE
(宾阳三洞, Bīnyáng Sān Dòng) Work began on the Three Bīnyáng Caves during the Northern Wei dynasty. Despite the completion of two of the caves during the Sui and Tang dynasties, statues here all display the benevolent expressions that characterised Northern Wei style. Traces of pigment remain within the three large grottoes and other small niches honeycomb the cliff walls. Nearby is the **Móyá Three Buddha Niche** (摩崖三佛龛, Móyá Sānfó Kān), with seven figures that date to the Tang dynasty.

Ten Thousand Buddha Cave CAVE
(万佛洞, Wànfó Dòng) South of Three Bīnyáng Caves, the Tang-dynasty Ten Thousand Buddha Cave dates from 680. In addition to its namesake galaxy of tiny bas-relief Buddhas, there is a fine effigy of the Amitabha Buddha. Note the red pigment on the ceiling.

Losana Buddha Statue Cave CAVE
(奉先寺; Fèngxiān Sì, Ancestor Worshipping Temple) The most physically imposing and magnificent of all the Lóngmén caves, this vast cave was carved during the Tang dynasty between 672 and 675; it contains the best examples of sculpture, despite evident weathering and vandalism. Nine principal figures dominate: the 17m-high seated central Buddha is said to be Losana, whose face is allegedly modelled

on Tang empress and Buddhist patron Wu Zetian, who funded its carving.

Tang figures tend to be more three-dimensional than the Northern Wei figures, while their expressions and poses also seem more natural. In contrast to the other-worldly effigies of the Northern Wei, many Tang figures possess a more fearsome ferocity and muscularity, most noticeable in the huge guardian figure in the north wall.

The final stretch of caves scattered along a maze-like set of stone steps have suffered the most damage and many grottoes are empty, so much so that staff sometimes discourage visitors from checking them out. There are gems to be found if you take the time to wander around. From the base, look up to see six pagodas carved at the top of the rock face.

EAST SIDE

When you have reached the last cave on the west side, cross the bridge and walk back north along the east side. The lovely **Thousand Arm & Thousand Eye Guanyin** (千手千眼观音龛 Qiānshǒu Qiānyǎn Guānyīn Kān) in Cave 2132 is a splendid bas-relief dating to the Tang dynasty, revealing the Goddess of Mercy framed in a huge fan of carved hands, each sporting an eye. Two Tang-dynasty guardian deities stand outside the sizeable **Lord Gāopíng Cave** (高平郡王洞, Gāopíng Jùnwáng Dòng). Further is the large **Reading Sutra Cave** (看经寺洞, Kàn Jīng Sìdòng), with a carved lotus on its ceiling and 29 *luóhàn* around the base of the walls. There is also a large **viewing terrace** for sizing up the Ancestor Worshipping Temple on the far side of the river.

Xiāngshān Temple BUDDHIST TEMPLE
(香山寺; Xiāngshān Sì) At the top of a steep flight of steps, this temple nestles against a hill. First built in AD 516 and repeatedly restored, it's filled with bronze Buddhist images. Look out for a stele with a poem written by Emperor Qianlong who visited and was moved to eulogise the temple's beauty. There's also a villa which once belonged to Chiang Kai-shek, built in 1936 to celebrate his 50th birthday.

Bai Juyi's Graveyard GARDEN, TOMB
This lovely garden is built around Tang-dynasty poet Bai Juyi's tomb (白居易墓地, Bái Jūyì Mùdì). It's a peaceful, leafy place to rest your tired feet. There's a cute alfresco teahouse inside where you can get tea (from ¥38), snacks and instant noodles.

White Horse Temple 白马寺

Although its original structures have all been replaced and older Buddhist shrines may have vanished, this active **monastery** (白马寺; Báimǎ Sì; admission ¥50; ☉7am-6pm) outside Luòyáng is regarded as China's first surviving Buddhist temple, originally dating from the 1st century AD. When two Han-dynasty court emissaries went in search of Buddhist scriptures, they encountered two Indian monks in Afghanistan; the monks returned to Luòyáng on two white horses carrying Buddhist sutras and statues. The impressed emperor built the temple to house the monks; it is also their resting place.

Ironically, the tombs are now overgrown and neglected and set off on the sides of the compound.

In the **Hall of the Heavenly Kings**, Mile-fo (the Laughing Buddha) laughs from within an intricately carved cabinet featuring more than 50 dragons writhing across the structure. Other buildings of note include the **Mahavira Hall** with its two-level carved wooden structure and the **Pilu Hall** at the very rear. Also look out for peony gardens in bloom come April and May. The stand-out **Qíyún Pagoda** (齐云塔, Qíyún Tǎ), an ancient five-tiered brick tower, is a pleasant five-minute walk through a garden and across a bridge.

The temple is 13km east of Luòyáng, around 40 minutes on bus 56 from the Xīguān (西关) stop. Bus 58 runs from Zhong-zhou Donglu in the old town also runs here.

Guōliàngcūn 郭亮村

☑ 0373 / POP 500

On its clifftop perch high up in the Wànxiān Shān (万仙山; Ten Thousand Immortals) Mountains in north Hénán, this delightful high-altitude stone hamlet was for centuries sheltered from the outside world by a combination of inaccessibility and anonymity. Guōliàngcūn shot to fame as the bucolic backdrop to a clutch of Chinese films, which firmly embedded the village in contemporary Chinese mythology.

Today, the village attracts legions of artists, who journey here to capture the unreal mountain scenery on paper and canvas. Joining them are weekend Chinese tourists who get disgorged by the busloads. For a true rustic mountaintop experience, come on a weekday when it's tranquil. New hotels

have sprung up at the village's foot, but the original dwellings – climbing the mountain slope – retain their simple, rustic charms. Long treks through the lovely scenery more than compensate for the hard slog of journeying here.

At 1700m above sea level and approximately 6°C colder than Zhèngzhōu, Guōliàngcūn is cool enough to be devoid of mosquitoes year-round (some locals say), but pack warm clothes for winter visits, which can be bone-numbing. Visiting in low season may seem odd advice, but come evening the village can be utterly tranquil, and moonlit nights are intoxicating. Pack a small torch as lights beyond the hotels are scarce.

Several kilometres before the village, you will be made to get off the bus to purchase an admission ticket (¥80) to the **Wànxiān Mountains Scenic Area**. There are no ATMs and nowhere to change money in Guōliàngcūn. A small **medical clinic** (☑671 0303) can be found in the village.

◉ Sights & Activities

All of the **village dwellings**, many hung with butter yellow *bàngzi* (sweetcorn cobs), are hewn from the same local stone that paves the slender alleyways, sculpts the bridges and fashions the picturesque gates of Guōliàngcūn. Walnut-faced old women peek from doorways and children scamper about, but locals are well used to outsiders.

You will have passed by the **Precipice Gallery** (绝壁长廊; Juébì Chángláng), also referred to on some signs as 'Long Corridor in the Cliffs' en route to the village, but back-track down for a closer perspective on these plunging cliffs, with dramatic views from the tunnel carved through the rock. Before this tunnel was built (between 1972 and 1978) by a local man called Shen Mingxin and others, the only way into the village was via the **Sky Ladder** (天梯; Tiān Tī), Ming-dynasty steps hewn from the local pink stone, with no guard rails but amazing views.

To get to the Sky Ladder, take the left fork of the road heading towards the tunnel and walk for 2.5km. Another 500m along the road takes you to the charming village of **Huītáo Zhài** (会逃寨), with its cliff-top cottages.

Over the bridge on the other side of the precipice from the village, walk past the small row of cottages almost on the edge of the cliff called **Yáshàng Rénjiā** (崖上人

家) and you can step onto a platform atop a pillar of rock for astonishing views into the canyon.

Head through the strip of street stalls, past the hotels to get to the start of a bracing 5km circuit through the mountain valley. From the end of the street, you can walk or take an electric cart (¥15 return) 1.3km to the starting point of the loop. Sadly, the mood of the area has been spoilt with the addition of several man-made oddities; a cable ride and a drain-like slide from the top of the mountain. If you start on the left-hand set of steps, you'll first pass the awe-inspiring curtain of rock above the **Shouting Spring** (喊泉; Hǎn Quán). According to local lore, its flow responds to the loudness of your whoops (it doesn't). You'll also pass the peaceful **Old Pool** (老潭; Lǎo Tán). Further along, you'll pass the **Red Dragon Cave** (红龙洞; Hónglóng Dòng), now closed, and after a few steep flights of stairs, the slide ride (¥30) and then the **White Dragon Cave** (白龙洞; Báilóng Dòng; admission ¥20). The last sight is a set of steps which lead up **Pearl Spring** (珍珠泉; Zhēnzhū Quán), a fissure in the mountain from which pours out cool, clear spring water. You can, of course, do the loop in the opposite direction (it's easier).

Once you've seen the big sights, get off the beaten trail and onto one of the small paths heading into the hills (such as the boulder-strewn brookside trail along the flank of Guōliàngcūn that leads further up into the mountain), but take water.

🛏 Sleeping & Eating

There are hotels galore in Guōliàngcūn though they offer identical two-star quality with hot showers and TVs (no toiletries or towels). There's a strip of hotels at the foot of the village and another strip on the precipice facing the tunnel. The latter has better views though you'll have to contend with roosters crowing at odd hours. Rooms cost ¥40 to ¥100 depending on size and orientation. Prices are a bit higher during the summer but negotiable in the low season and on weekdays. There are no restaurants, but hoteliers have kitchens and Chinese menus offering a wide variety of vegie and meat-based dishes, rice and noodles.

ℹ Getting There & Away

Reach Guōliàngcūn from Xīnxiāng (新乡), between Ānyáng and Zhèngzhōu. Fast trains run to Xīnxiāng from Zhèngzhōu (¥24, 45 minutes),

as do regular buses (¥14 to ¥21, 1½ hours). Exit Xīnxiāng Train Station, head straight ahead and take the first left and cross the road onto Ziyou Lu (自由路) to flag down buses to Huīxiàn (辉县; ¥6.50, 30 minutes, regular). The bus to Huīxiàn also departs from the bus station.

Five buses (¥12, one hour 40 minutes, first/last bus 7am/4.30pm) from Huīxiàn's bus station (辉县站; Huīxiàn zhàn) pass by the mountain road to Guōliàngcūn. Buses may have the characters for Guōliàng (郭亮) on the window, but may head straight to the final stop Nánpíng (南坪), a village beyond the base of the road to Guōliàngcūn, depending on passenger numbers. If the bus isn't going up the mountain, you can either ask to be dropped at the bottom of the Guōliàngcūn road and ask a local to bring you up the 4km steep winding road for a wallet-gouging ¥50 or head on to Nánpíng where there are green buses (¥15) that do a circuit to Guōliàngcūn. The green buses run regularly on the weekends but on weekdays will only go when there are enough passengers. The last bus leaves at 5.30pm.

In the other direction, Huīxiàn-bound minibuses (¥12) run from the bottom of the mountain road from Guōliàngcūn at 6.30am, 9am, noon, 1pm and 3pm. Guesthouse owners should be able to run you down to the drop-off point for around ¥40 if you spend the night in their lodgings. Otherwise, take the green bus to Nánpíng to catch a bus to Huīxiàn.

Kāifēng 开封

📶 0371 / POP 827,000

More than any other of Hénán's ancient capitals, Kāifēng today recalls its former grandeur. The walled town has character: you may have to squint a bit and sift the repro from its genuine historical narrative, but the city still offers up a riveting display of age-old charm, magnificent market food, relics from its long-vanished apogee and colourful chrysanthemums (the city flower; Kāifēng is also known as Júchéng, or 'Chrysanthemum Town'). One reason you won't see soaring skyscrapers is because buildings requiring deep foundations are prohibited, for fear of destroying the ancient northern Song-dynasty city below.

History

Once the prosperous capital of the Northern Song dynasty (960–1126), Kāifēng was established south of the Yellow River, but not far enough to escape the river's capricious wrath. After centuries of flooding, the city of the Northern Song largely lies buried 8m to

9m deep in hardened silt. Between 1194 and 1938 the city flooded 368 times, an average of once every two years.

Kāifēng was also the first city in China where Jewish merchants settled when they arrived, along the Silk Road, during the Song dynasty. A small Christian and Catholic community also lives in Kāifēng alongside a much larger local Muslim Hui community.

⊙ Sights

Most travellers should base themselves within the walls of the old town. For ancient Kāifēng architecture, wander along small streets off the main drag within the city walls, for old, tumbledown, one-storey buildings with misshapen tiled roofs.

Temple of the Chief Minister BUDDHIST TEMPLE (大相国寺; Dà Xiàngguó Sì; Ziyou Lu; 自由路; admission ¥30; ⊙8am-6.30pm) First founded in AD 555, this frequently rebuilt temple vanished along with Kāifēng in the early 1640s when rebels breached the Yellow River's dykes. During the Northern Song, the temple covered a massive 34 hectares and housed over 10,000 monks. The showstopper today is the mesmerising **Four-Faced Thousand Hand Thousand Eye Guanyin** (四面千手千眼观世音), towering within the octagonal **Arhat Hall** (罗汉殿, Luóhàn Diàn), beyond the **Hall of Tathagata** (大雄宝殿, Dàxióng Bǎodiàn).

Fifty-eight years in the carving, the 7m-tall gold-gilded, four-sided statue bristles with giant fans of 1048 arms, an eye upon each hand; the arhats themselves are presented with considerably less artistry. On the left of the **Hall of Tripitaka** (藏经楼, Cángjīng Lóu) is a small **hall** (大师堂, Dàshītáng) where a master calligrapher works and plies his craft (works from ¥100). A huge pagoda and hall has been constructed at the rear. Elsewhere in the temple you can divine your future by drawing straws (抽签, chōuqiān) or dine at the pleasant onsite vegetarian restaurant (素斋部, sùzhāibù). Don't overlook the first **Hall of the Revarajas** (天王殿, Tiānwáng Diàn), where the mission of chubby Milefo is proclaimed in the attendant Chinese: 'Big belly can endure all that is hard to endure in the world.'

Shānshǎngān Guild Hall GUILDHALL (山陕甘会馆, Shānshǎn'gān Huìguǎn; 85 Xufu Jie, 徐府街85号; admission ¥30; ⊙8.30am-6.30pm summer, 8.20am-5pm winter) This tiny, elaborately styled guildhall was built as a lodging and meeting place during the Qing dynasty by an association of merchants from Shānxi (山西), Shǎnxi (陕西; Shaanxi) and Gānsù (甘肃) provinces. Note the ornate carvings on the roofs, and delve into the exhibition on historic Kāifēng. Check out the fascinating diorama of the old Song city – with its palace in the centre of town – and compare it with a model of modern Kāifēng.

Also look out for the scale-model recreation of Zhang Zeduan's famed Qingming painting.

Iron Pagoda Park PARK (铁塔公园, Tiě Tǎ Gōngyuán; 210 Beimen Dajie, 北门大街210号; admission ¥50; ⊙7am-7pm) Rising up within Iron Pagoda Park is a magnificent 55m, 11th-century pagoda, a gorgeous, slender brick edifice wrapped in glazed rust-coloured tiles (hence the name); its narrow stairs are climbable for ¥30. Take bus 1 from Zhongshan Lu or a taxi will cost ¥10.

HÉNÁN KĀIFĒNG

ZHANG ZEDUAN'S MASTERPIECE

Now held in the Forbidden City and widely acknowledged as China's first shén (Godly) painting, *Along the River during the Qingming Festival* was completed by Zhang Zeduan (张择端) in the early 12th century. These days, you'll see it everywhere in Kāifēng. Museums and parks have it in carved wood and stone bas-relief, there are scale dioramas, souvenir posters, advertising (it's on the Kāifēng Hostel's poster) and even a historical theme park modelled on it.

The long 24.8cm x 528.7cm painting depicts life in a city which experts have attributed as Kāifēng. It's packed to the gills with details of the period: boats unloading goods at a harbour, an inn crowded with customers and children playing on the streets. As you would imagine, it offers valuable insight into the life and times of a large Song dynasty town. When the original is displayed in Běijīng, queues to see it last hours.

You can see versions at several places in Kāifēng including the Riverside Scenic Park, the scale diorama in the Shānshǎngān Guild Hall, the replica version in the museum and the paper cutting in Zhūxiān's Qīngzhēn Temple.

Kāifēng

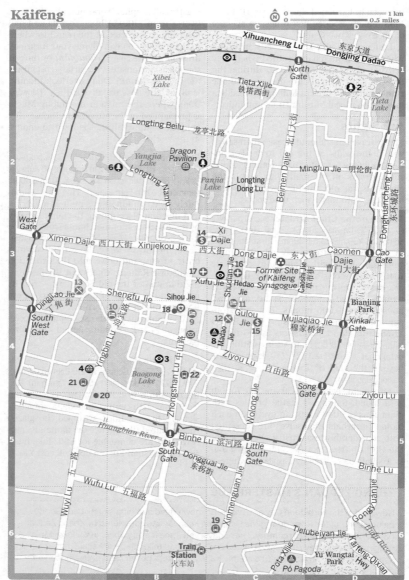

HÉNÁN KĀIFĒNG

Kāifēng Fǔ

HISTORIC SITE

(开封府; north side, Baogong East Lake; 包公湖北岸; admission ¥50; ⊙7am-7pm summer, 7.30am-5.30pm winter) Popular with Chinese tour groups, this reconstructed site of the government offices of the Northern Song next to Baogong Lake has theatricals commencing daily outside the gates at 9am – the doors are thrown open to costumed actors playing period scenes complete with cracking whips and the sound of gongs. They then retreat inside to continue the play (in Chi-

Kāifēng

nese). Drama aside, the site, encased within tall walls, is a recreation of Song imperial life, with buildings from ye olde times.

Kāifēng Museum
MUSEUM

(开封博物馆; Kāifēng Bówùguǎn; 26 Yingbin Lu, 迎宾路26号; ⊙9am-5pm Tue-Sun) **FREE** This museum has a modest collection of archaeological finds, woodblock prints and historical objects. The draw for most is two notable Jewish stelae on the 4th floor, managed by the **Kāifēng Institute for Research on the History of Chinese Jews** (☑ext 8010 393 2178), which costs ¥50 to see them. Buses 1, 4, 9, 16, 20 and 23 all travel past here.

Riverside Scenic Park Qīngmíng Garden
PARK

(清明上河园; Qīngmíng Shànghéyuán; Millennium City Park; Longting Nanlu, 龙亭南路; admission day/night ¥80/199; ⊙9am-6pm) High on historical kitsch, this theme park is a recreation of Zeduan's famous Qingming painting, brought to life with roving staff in Song-era costumes, cultural performances, folk art and music demonstrations. Despite the surfeit of souvenir stalls, there's fun to be had (there's a wedding ceremony and even a mock naval battle out on the lake). The night ticket allows entry during the day and a seat for a colourful night performance (8.10pm to 9.30pm) out on the lake.

Lóngtíng Park
PARK

(龙亭公园; Lóngtíng Gōngyuán; ☑566 0316; Zhongshan Lu, 中山路; admission summer/winter ¥40/35; ⊙7am-7pm) Site of the former imperial palace, this park is mostly lakes, into which hardy swimmers plunge in win-

ter. Reached by bridge, you can climb the namesake **Dragon Pavilion** (龙亭; Lóng Tíng) for town views. The spectacular Chrysanthemum Festival is held here in October, when admission prices go up.

City Walls
HISTORIC SITE

Kāifēng is ringed by a relatively intact, much-restored Qing-dynasty wall (城墙), which you can climb up at various points. Today's bastion was built on the foundations of the Song-dynasty **Inner Wall** (内城; Nèichéng). Encased with grey bricks, rear sections of the ramparts have been recently buttressed unattractively with concrete. Rising up outside was the mighty, now buried **Outer Wall** (外城; Wàichéng), a colossal construction containing 18 gates, which looped south of Pó Pagoda.

Former Site of Kāifēng Synagogue
RUIN

(开封犹太教堂遗址, Kāifēng Yóutài Jiàotáng Yízhǐ; Jiefang Rd Tujie Section, 解放路土街段) Sadly, nothing remains of the synagogue – finally swept away in mid-19th century floodwaters – except a well with an iron lid in the boiler room of the Kāifēng Traditional Chinese Medicine Hospital (开封中医院, Kāifēng Zhōngyīyuàn), which may allow you to examine it. The spirit of the synagogue lingers, however, in the name of the brick alley immediately south of the hospital – **Jiaojing Hutong** (教经胡同, Teaching the Torah Alley).

A local English-speaking guide (yisrael-kaifeng@hotmail.com) familiar with local Jewish history lives in the house with the blue sign. Send an email prior to visiting if

HÉNÁN KĀIFĒNG

you intend to engage her guide services or want an extended chat.

🛏 Sleeping

Kāifēng International Youth Hostel HOSTEL $
(开封国际青年旅舍, Kāifēng Guójì Qīngnián Lǚshè; ☑ 255 2888; 30 Yingbin Lu, 迎宾路30号; dm ¥50, s ¥120, d & tw ¥140; ❄ @ 🛜) With a good location on the edge of Baogong Lake, this hostel is an OK choice. Bunk-bed dorms have an ensuite shower and private rooms are comfy enough, but it's a largely average place. Bike rental costs ¥20 daily.

Jǐnjiāng Inn HOTEL $
(锦江之星; Jǐnjiāng Zhīxīng; ☑ 2399 6666; 88 Zhongshan Lu, 中山路88号; s & d ¥229/249; ❄ @) In a star location on the intersection of Zhongshan Lu, this chain hotel's branch ticks the right boxes: efficient staff, clean rooms, modern furnishing, flat-screen TVs and good plumbing.

Soluxe Hotel Kāifēng HOTEL $$$
(开封阳光酒店, Kāifēng Yángguāng Jiǔdiàn; ☑ 2595 8888; 41 Gulou Jie, 鼓楼街41号; s & d ¥518; ❄ @) The smart Soluxe Hotel offers compact but modern business-style rooms in shades of brown and white. Flat-screen TVs and PCs round out the features list. Discounts drop prices by 40%.

🍴 Eating & Drinking

Xīsī Square Night Market MARKET $
(西司广场夜市, Xīsī Guǎngchǎng Yèshì; Dingjiao Jie, 丁角街; snacks from ¥2, meal ¥20; ⏱ 6.30pm-late) Join the scrum weaving between stalls busy with red-faced popcorn sellers and hollering Hui Muslim chefs cooking up kebabs and *náng* bread. There are loads of vendors from whom you can buy cured meats, hearty *jiānbǐng guǒzi* (煎饼裹子; pancake with chopped onions), sweet potatoes, roast rabbit, *xiǎolóngbāo* (Shànghǎi-style dumplings), peanut cake (花生糕, *huāshēng gāo*), and cups of sugarcane juice.

Look for *yángròu kàngmó* (羊肉炕馍; lamb in a parcel of bread), a local Kāifēng Muslim speciality. Or opt for *yángròu chuàn* (羊肉串; lamb kebabs). Look out for noodle vendors who pull and twist fresh *niúròu lāmiàn* (牛肉拉面; noodles in beef broth).

Among the flames and clouds of steam erupting from the ovens slave vocal vendors of *xìngrén chá* (杏仁茶; almond tea), a sugary paste made from boiling water thickened with powdered almond, red berries, peanuts, sesame seeds and crystallised cherries. Take bus 24.

Gǔlóu Night Market MARKET $
(鼓楼夜市, Gǔlóu Yèshì; off Sihou Jie, 寺后街边; snacks from ¥2; ⏱ 6.30pm-late) Kāifēng's bustling night market is now all touristified. While the food is the same, it's now all faux antique tables and benches, and stalls housed in wooden huts. This hasn't stopped the locals from having a good time. Visit the Tsingtao stall serving jugs (壶, *hú*; ¥15 to ¥18) of draught lager (黄扎, *huáng zhā*), ale (红扎, *hóng zhā*) and stout (黑扎, *hēi zhā*).

East on Shudian Jie and around are more food stalls and others selling clothes, toys and books.

ℹ Information

The area around Zhongshan Lu has internet cafes, but at the time of research, you need local ID for surfing though some shops may let you get online for an hour or so.

Bank of China (中国银行, Zhōngguó Yínháng; cnr Xi Dajie & Zhongshan Lu) Has a 24-hour ATM.

China Construction Bank (中国建设银行, Zhōngguó Jiànshè Yínháng; Gulou Jie, 鼓楼街) Has a 24-hour ATM.

China Post (中国邮政, Zhōngguó Yóuzhèng; Ziyou Lu, 自由路; ⏱ 8am-5.30pm) West of the Temple of the Chief Minister.

Kāifēng No 1 People's Hospital (开封第一人民医院, Kāifēng Dìyī Rénmín Yīyuàn; ☑ 2567 1288; 85 Hedao Jie, 河道街85号) Located right in the heart of town.

Public Security Bureau (PSB, 公安局, Gōng'ānjú; ☑ 2595 8899; 86 Zhongshan Lu, 中山路86号; ⏱ 8.30am-noon & 2.30-6pm Mon-Fri) Visa renewals.

Zhāngzhòngjǐng Pharmacy (张仲景大药房, Zhāngzhòngjǐng Dàyàofáng; Xufu Jie, 徐府街; ⏱ 7.30am-10pm summer, 8am-9pm winter) Next to Shānshǎngān Guild Hall.

ℹ Getting There & Away

AIR

The nearest airport is at Zhèngzhōu. Tickets can be bought at the **IATA Air Ticket Office** (☑ 2595 5555; Zhongshan Lu) next to the PSB; two free daily buses (1½ hours, 8am and 2pm) run to Zhèngzhōu airport from here. There's also an airport shuttle from the corner of Gulou Jie and Jiefang Lu (¥40, 1½ hours, 10 daily, 5.30am to 6.4pm).

BUS

Buses run from the west long-distance bus station (长途汽车西站, *chángtú qìchē xīzhàn*):

Dēngfēng ¥35, three hours, two daily (9.30am and 1.20pm)

Luòyáng ¥41, three hours, two daily (9am and 2pm)

Xīnxiāng ¥30, two hours, six daily

Zhèngzhōu ¥7, 1½ hours, every 20 minutes (6.20am to 7.30pm)

Buses also leave from the south long-distance bus station (长途汽车南站, *chángtú qìchē nánzhàn*), opposite the train station:

Ānyáng ¥54, four hours, regular services

Luòyáng ¥57, three hours, hourly

Xīnxiāng ¥32, two hours, every 40 minutes

Zhèngzhōu ¥8, 1½ hours, every 15 minutes

TRAIN

The train station is located in the south of town, around 1km beyond the city walls. Buy tickets at the **railway ticket office** (火车票代售; Huǒchēpiào dàishòu; Yingbin Lu; ⊙8am-noon & 1.30-5.30pm) diagonally opposite the Kāifēng Hostel.

Běijīng West seat/sleeper ¥93/184, 12 hours

Luòyáng ¥30 to ¥84, 2½ hours, eight daily

Shànghǎi Hóngqiáo D train 2nd/1st class ¥232/371, six to seven hours, three daily

Xī'ān seat/sleeper ¥81/154, eight hours, regular

Zhèngzhōu ¥13 to ¥67, 45 minutes, frequently

❶ Getting Around

Zhongshan Lu is a good place to catch buses to most sights (¥1). Taxis (flag fall ¥5) are the best way to get about; a journey from the train station to Zhongshan Lu should cost ¥7. Avoid pedicabs as they frequently rip off tourists.

Zhūxiān Zhèn　朱仙镇

Twenty-three kilometres north of Kāifēng is Zhūxiān (Vermillion Immortal). Some say it's one of China's four 'ancient' towns – the other three are Hànkǒu (trade), Jǐngdézhèn (porcelain) and Fóshān (silk). Here, the 1000-year-old craft of woodblock printing (木板年画;*mùbǎn niánhuà*) continues to this day.

Families traditionally plaster their door fronts and houses with these prints (though many now use commercially printed ones) at the spring festival to usher in luck and prosperity for the year ahead. Five or so families have continued the craft. Sets of wooden blocks are painstakingly carved and each print requires anywhere from five to seven blocks, one for the base black outline and one for each other colour. Pigments (generally red, blue, yellow, black and green), made from natural materials such as seeds and plants, are then applied via handmade brushes onto rice paper. The outline in black is first printed, the paper left to dry and the process is repeated for each colour required. The prints feature Chinese characters from folklore, gods and others related to luck and blessings. These luridly coloured prints are embarrassingly cheap (¥5 to ¥30 for an A4/letter-size print to ¥100 for a print made from 150-year-old blocks).

Visit **Tiānchéng Niánhuà Lǎodiàn** (天成年画老店), 100m north of the Yuèfēi Temple. The artist and owner Mr Yin (尹) is a fifth-generation artisan, and his family has been in business for more than 200 years, 'excluding a period of 30 years or so because of the Cultural Revolution'. His work has been represented at the 2008 Běijīng Olympics and the 2010 Shànghǎi World Expo. You can pick up a beautifully bound book of prints with English explanations, housed in a wooden presentation box for ¥200 (if you're nice, he'll sell it for ¥180). There are several other workshops along the canal at the end of town.

Exploring the town further, you'll find two temples on the main drag: the **Yuèfēi Temple** (岳飞庙, Yuèfēi Miào; admission ¥20) and **Guānyǔ Temple** (关羽庙, Guānyǔ Miào; admission ¥1). Heading 700m or so south off the main road along a wide stone path, you'll get to the **Qīngzhēn Temple** (清真寺, Qīng Zhēn Sì) FREE. This is a mosque housed in a traditional Chinese temple compound with a pretty rose garden. On the wall is a paper-cut version of Zeduan's famed Qingming painting. Look for a stall featuring **elaborate paper-cutting art** by Mr Hu (胡).

Head to the Xiàngguó Sì bus station (相国寺汽车站) on Zhongshan Lu where buses (¥6, 45 minutes, every 12 minutes) run all the way to Zhūxiān. The last bus from Zhūxiān leaves at 5.50pm. You'll pass through a busy thoroughfare where you should get off.

Húběi

POP 61.8 MILLION

Best for Scenery

➡ Shénnóngjià (p439)
➡ Wǔdāng Shān (p437)
➡ Three Gorges Dam (p440)

Best for History

➡ Jīngzhōu (p435)
➡ Wǔdāng Shān (p437)
➡ Wǔhàn (p430)
➡ Húběi Provincial Museum (p430)

Why Go?

Vast hordes of travellers find themselves drifting into Húběi (湖北) through the magnificent Three Gorges, the precipitous geological marvel that begins in neighbouring Chóngqìng and concludes here. It's a once-in-a-lifetime trip which perfectly introduces Húběi's dramatic natural beauty.

Sliced by rivers (including, of course, the mighty Yangzi) and dappled with lakes, Húběi is largely lush and fertile, but its western regions are dominated by stunning mountain scenery. National parks such as Shénnóngjià are jaw-droppingly spectacular, while the sacred peaks of Wǔdāng Shān add pinches of Taoist mysticism to a sublime landscape.

Húběi's central location ensured it played a key role in Chinese history, with plenty of evidence around the ancient city of Jīngzhōu of the great Chu kingdom that ruled this part of China more than 2000 years ago. China's modern history, meanwhile, is woven into the fabric of Wǔhàn, Húběi's vast, battle-scarred capital city.

When to Go
Wǔhàn

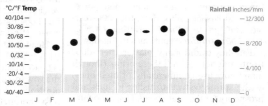

Mar & Apr Get in ahead of the draining Yangzi summer, but bring an umbrella.

Sep–Nov The stupefying summer heat has finally lifted.

Nov–Mar Wǔdāng Shān at its prettiest, snowiest best. Pack your thermals.

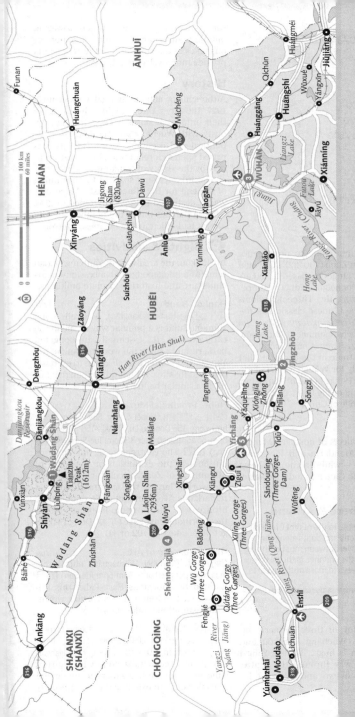

Húběi Highlights

① Study taichi where it all began, on the awe-inspiring mountain slopes of **Wǔdāng Shān** (p437).

② Explore the historic gates, city walls and ruined temples of ancient **Jīngzhōu** (p435).

③ Find a bar and knock back a beer in the riverside concession district of mighty **Wǔhàn** (p430).

④ Flee China's urban sprawl and camp out in the wilds of stunning **Shénnóngjià** (p439).

⑤ Go against the tourist tide and start your Three Gorges cruise in **Yíchāng** (p440) rather than Chóngqìng.

History

The Húběi area first came to prominence during the Eastern Zhou (700–221 BC), when the powerful Chu kingdom, based in today's Jīngzhōu, was at its height. Húběi again became pivotal during the Three Kingdoms (AD 220–280). The Chinese classic *The Romance of the Three Kingdoms (Sān Guó Yǎnyì)* makes much reference to Jīngzhōu. The mighty Yangzi River (Cháng Jiāng) ensured prosperous trade in the centuries that followed, especially for Wǔhàn, China's largest inland port and stage of the 1911 uprising, which led to the fall of the Qing and the creation of the Republic of China.

Language

Húběi has two dialects of northern Mandarin – southwest Mandarin and lower-mid Yangzi Mandarin – while in the southeast many people speak Gàn, a Mandarin dialect from Jiāngxī.

ℹ Getting There & Around

Húběi is well connected to the rest of China by high-speed rail, air, bus and boats along the Yangzi River. Rail travel between most of the big destinations within the province is the best way to go, with bus journeys to more outlying parts.

Wǔhàn 武汉

📱 027 / POP 4.26 MILLION

A gargantuan alloy of three formerly independent cities (Wǔchāng, Hànkǒu and Hànyáng), Wǔhàn is huge. But the Yangzi River thrusts its way through the centre, carving the city in two and allowing for some breathing space between towering buildings and gnarling traffic, while numerous lakes and a smattering of decent sights provide more welcome retreats.

History

Although not actually named Wǔhàn until 1927, the city's three mighty chunks trace their influential status back to the Han dynasty, with Wǔchāng and Hànkǒu vying for political and economic sway. The city was prised open to foreign trade in the 19th century by the Treaty of Nanking.

The 1911 uprising sparked the beginning of the end for the Qing dynasty. Much that wasn't destroyed then was flattened in 1944 when American forces fire-bombed the city after it had fallen under Japanese control.

◎ Sights & Activities

In Hànkǒu, the area west of Yanjiang Dadao remains a hodgepodge of concession-era architecture and historic consulate buildings.

Hànkǒu Bund   PARK
(汉口江滩; Hànkǒu Jiāngtān) A stroll along Hànkǒu Bund is a popular way to spend the early evening. It's essentially an elongated park, running along the western bank of the Yangzi, and is where locals come to exercise, chat and fly kites. It's not quite Shànghǎi but it's in a similar ballpark.

Húběi Provincial Museum   MUSEUM
(湖北省博物馆, Húběi Shěng Bówùguǎn; www. hbww.org; 156 Donghu Lu, 东湖路156号; ◎9am-5pm, no admission after 3.30pm, Tue-Sun; Ⓜ Dongting) **FREE** The centrepiece of this fabulous museum is the exhibition of the tomb of Marquis Yi of Zeng, which includes one of the world's largest musical instruments, a remarkable five-tonne set of 65 double-tone bronze bells. The museum is located beside the enormous East Lake (东湖, Dōng Hú). To get here, take bus 402 or 411.

Húběi Museum of Art   MUSEUM
(湖北美术馆, Húběi Měishùguǎn; http://en.hb-moa.com; Donghu Lu; ◎9am-5pm Tue-Sun) **FREE** Located by enormous East Lake, this impressive art museum stages regular worthwhile exhibitions. Take bus 402 or 411.

Guīyuán Temple   BUDDHIST TEMPLE
(归元寺, Guīyuán Sì; 20 Cuiweiheng Lu, 翠微横路20号; admission ¥10; ◎8am-5pm; Ⓜ Lanjianglu) Pass a large rectangular pond where turtles cling like shipwrecked sailors to two metal lotus flowers and examine the magnificently

burnished cabinet housing Milefo in the first hall. Also seek out this 350-year-old Buddhist temple's collection of more than 500 statues of enlightened disciples in the **Hall of Arhats** (罗汉堂, Luóhàn Táng). Completed in 1890, after nine years in the making, they remain in pristine condition.

In the **Mahasattva Pavilion** (大士阁, Dàshì Gé), the 2m-high Tang-dynasty tablet carved with an image of Guanyin holding a willow branch is impressive, and a jade Buddha resides in the **Sutra Storing Pavilion** (藏经阁, Cángjīng Gé). A vegetarian restaurant provides karmic sustenance. Buses 401 and 402 both go here.

Yellow Crane Tower　HISTORIC SITE
(黄鹤楼, Huánghè Lóu; Wuluo Lu, 武珞路; admission ¥80; ⊙7.30am-5.30pm, to 6.30pm in summer) Wǔhàn's magical dancing crane, immortalised in the 8th-century poetry of Cui Hao, has long flown, but the city's pride and joy remains perched atop Snake Hill. The tower has had its history rebuilt out of it since the original was constructed in AD 223, and today's beautiful five-storey, yellow-tiled version is a 1980s remake of the Qing tower that combusted in 1884. Buses 401, 402 and 411, and trolley buses 1 and 10, all go here.

Chángchūn Temple　TAOIST TEMPLE
(长春观, Chángchūn Guàn; ☑8280 1399; 269 Wuluo Lu, 武珞路269号; admission ¥10; ⊙8am-5pm) This charming Taoist temple dates back to the Han dynasty, although very recent restoration is evident. The **Hall of Supreme Purity** (太清殿, Tàiqīng Diàn), containing a white-bearded statue of Laotzu, is the centrepiece. Other halls lead up the steep steps behind it. There's a well-regarded vegetarian restaurant next door. Buses 411, 401 and 402 all go here.

Revolution of 1911 Museum　MUSEUM
(辛亥革命博物馆, Xīnhài Gémìng Bówùguǎn; Shouyi Guangchang (Uprising Square), 首义广场; ⊙9am-5pm Tue-Sun) **FREE** Housed in a dramatic, eye-catching red rock–like building, the Chinese Communist Party propaganda machine is in full tilt, but there are some interesting old photos.

East Lake　SWIMMING
(东湖游泳池, Dōnghú; Dōnghú Yóuyǒngchí; admission ¥10; ⊙9am-10pm) In summer, escape the sweltering city and head to this section of the vast East Lake, located in the east of Wǔchāng, which has been cordoned off for swimming. Take bus 402 to Donghu Donglu Youyongchi (东湖东路游泳池).

YELLOW CRANE TOWER BY CUI HAO

Penned in the 8th century by Tang dynasty luminary Cui Hao (崔颢), this poem recalls the departure of someone on the back of a yellow crane, possibly to become an immortal. The spot he left from is now occupied by a tower named after the bird.

黄鹤楼

昔人已乘黄鹤去，此地空余黄鹤楼。

黄鹤一去不复返，白云千载空悠悠。

晴川历历汉阳树，芳草萋萋鹦鹉洲。

日暮乡关何处是，烟波江上使人愁。

Yellow Crane Tower

A man of old left a long time ago on the Yellow Crane; this place is empty save for the Yellow Crane Tower.

Once the Yellow Crane left, it would never return; for a thousand years, the white clouds leisurely drifted.

The trees in Hànyáng are all arrayed by the clear river and the fragrant grasses grow luxuriously on Parrot Isle.

Where are the gates of my home at dusk? The mist and ripples on the river waters make me sad.

🛏 Sleeping

⭐**Pathfinder Youth Hostel**　HOSTEL **$**
(探路者国际青年旅社, Tànlùzhě Guójì Qīngnián Lǚshè; ☑8884 4092; yhawuhan@hotmail.com; 368 Zhongshan Lu, 中山路368号; dm ¥45-60, d/tr ¥160/210; ✴@�; ⓜPangxiejia) Wǔhàn's best budget option cultivates an art-warehouse feel where guests add graffiti to the walls. Pinewood-decorated rooms are smart and clean; bathrooms are small with squat loos (communal bathrooms have sit-down versions), but the rest of the place oozes space. There's wi-fi, travel advice, real coffee, bike rental and helpful, English-speaking staff.

Walk south from exit A2 of Pangxiejia (螃蟹岬) metro station along Zhongshan Lu, and it's on your right.

Wànkě Bīnguǎn　HOTEL **$**
(万可宾馆; ☑8271 9922; 315 Shengli Jie, 胜利街315号; r ¥158-178; ✴@; ⓜSanyang Lu) Wooden stairs and floorboards make this basic cheapie more stylish than most. It has a good location on the fringes of the pleasant

Wǔhàn

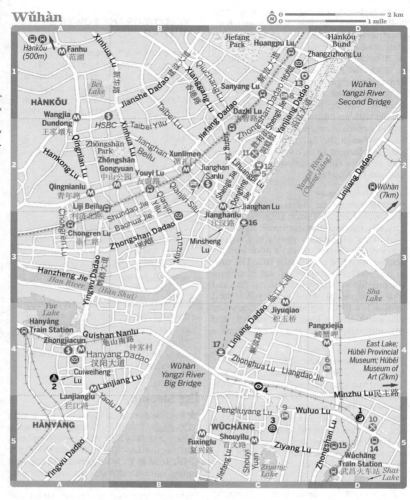

former concession area, and close to the river. Cheapest rooms have no window. No English sign; no English spoken (hence the unfortunate name). Discounts may apply.

Zhōng Huì Hotel HOTEL $$
(中惠宾馆, Zhōnghuì Bīnguǎn; ☑8805 9288; 188 Shouyi Xincun, 首义新村188号; d without/with window ¥208/228; ❋@; M Shouyilu) There are well-kept rooms with clean bathrooms at this Wǔchāng three-star choice. The cheapest rooms are smaller and have no windows, but are fine enough, and you'll have fun getting to them in the exterior brass lift. Rates

include breakfast. Some rooms have a computer. Others have internet connection. Discounts may apply.

Tomolo BOUTIQUE HOTEL $$$
(天美乐饭店, Tiānměilè Fàndiàn; ☑8275 7288; 56 Jianghan Sanlu, 江汉三路56号; r ¥698; ❋@☎; M Xunlimen) Tucked away in a lane off a modern pedestrianised shopping street, this excellent-value boutique hotel has a prime location and a natty finish throughout. Big rooms come with sofas, wide-screen TVs, internet access and lush carpets, while the bathrooms, complete with mosaic tiling and

Wŭhàn

power showers, are in pristine condition; staff make a real effort. Excellent discounts.

Marco Polo HOTEL **$$$**
(马哥孛罗酒店, Mǎgē Bóluó Jiǔdiàn; ☏ 8277 8888; www.marcopolohotels.com; 159 Yanjiang Dadao, 沿江大道159号; r from ¥897; Ⓜ Jianghanlu) The best-located five-star hotel in Wǔhàn, Marco Polo offers spacious and well-equipped rooms with sweeping views of the Yangzi River. It's backed by the tree-lined former concession area, which is dotted with bars, cafes and restaurants.

✖ Eating

In Hànkǒu, the alleyways north of Zhongshan Dadao, between Qianjin Yilu (前进一路) and Qianjin Silu (前进四路), are particularly lively. Jiqing Jie (吉庆街) has numerous *dàpáidǎng* (open-air food stalls or restaurants) selling seafood and duck, especially at the Dazhi Lu end. Cai'e Lu (蔡锷路) is littered with smoky *shāokǎo* (烧烤, barbecue).

In Wǔchāng, follow your nose to the hugely popular **Hùbù Xiàng Snack Street** (户部巷小吃; Hùbù Xiàng Xiǎochī).

Breakfast – called *guòzǎo* (过早) in Wǔhàn – is all about *règān miàn* (热干面; literally 'hot-dry noodles'; from ¥4).

Crown Bakery BAKERY **$**
(皇冠蛋糕, Huángguān Dàngāo; 345 Wuluo Lu, 武路路345号; cakes ¥2-5, drinks ¥5-12; ☺ 7am-9pm) Fabulously located in an old cruciform church built in 1907, with its original wood ceiling intact along with loads of portraits of Jesus, come here for the ambience, take

a seat in the apse to break bread and order egg tarts (¥4), tea, cappuccino or cakes.

★ Xiǎo Bèiké CHINESE **$$**
(小贝壳; 129 Dongting Jie, 洞庭街129号; mains ¥20-50; ☺ 9.30am-10.30pm) This stylish restaurant, with lovely tree-shaded terrace seating, offers an excellent range of pan-Chinese cuisine, with dishes from Húběi, Sìchuān and Chóngqìng featuring highly. It also does a number of fish dishes, including braised catfish and delicious scallops. No English sign; it's in the yellow building on the corner of Dongting Jie and Cai'e Lu (蔡锷路). English menu with photos.

Chángchūn Temple
Vegetarian Restaurant VEGETARIAN **$$**
(长春观素菜餐厅, Chángchūnguān Sùcài Cāntīng; 269 Wuluo Lu, 武路路269号; mains ¥20-50; ☺ 9am-8.30pm; ☑) Housed next door to the Chángchūn Temple, this place serves mock-meat creations but also cooks up fish dishes. Photo menu.

☷ Drinking & Nightlife

Hànkǒu is the place to go for a night out; Yanjiang Dadao (沿江大道) and its surrounding lanes are the best place to start. There are neon-tastic nightclubs towards the ferry port, while Lihuangpi Lu (黎黄陂路) is one of a number of lanes here with cutesy Western-style cafes.

York Teahouse BAR
(约克英式茶馆, Yuēkè Yīngshì Cháguǎn; ☏ 8279 1110; 162 Yanjiang Dadao; 沿江大道162号; ☺ 1pm-3am) Run by 'Mr Sugar' (Tang Xiansheng),

HÚBĚI WŬHÀN

this old-timer has been doing its thing on the riverfront for over a decade. Inside is a warren of rooms, but there's plenty of outdoor seating and occasional live music. Waiting staff speak English. Beers and coffee from ¥20.

Information

Most ATMs accept foreign cards. Internet cafes (网吧; *wǎngbā*) here may be reluctant to accept foreigners because they need to swipe a Chinese ID card to register users. All hotels listed here have internet access of some sort.

Public Security Bureau (PSB, 公安局, Gōng'ānjú; ☑ 8539 5351; 7 Zhangzizhong Lu, 张自忠路7号; ⊙ 8.30am-noon & 2.30-5.30pm) Can extend visas.

ⓘ Getting There & Away

AIR

Tiānhé International Airport (天河飞机场, Tiānhé Fēijīchǎng; ☑ 8581 8888) is 30km northwest of town, with daily direct flights to:

Běijīng ¥1440
Chéngdù ¥910
Guǎngzhōu ¥1230
Hong Kong ¥1480
Shànghǎi ¥1080
Xī'ān ¥920

Use www.elong.net or ctrip.com to book flights.

BUS

There are several long-distance bus stations, all of which run very similar services. In Hànkǒu, the main one is beside Hànkǒu Train Station. In Wǔchāng, the main two are Fùjiāpō long-distance bus station (傅家坡汽车客运站, *Fùjiāpō qìchē kèyùnzhàn*) and Hóngjī long-distance bus station (宏基长途汽车站, *Hóngjī chángtú qìchēzhàn*).

You can get buses to most major cities, even as far away as Shànghǎi and Běijīng. The following are sample services from Hóngjī long-distance bus station:

Jīngzhōu ¥75, three hours, every 45 minutes (7am to 8pm)
Mùyú (for Shénnóngjià) ¥150, eight hours, one daily (8.50am)
Shíyàn (for Wǔdāng Shān) ¥145, six hours, three daily (8.40am, 11.40am and 1.30pm)
Yíchāng ¥85 to ¥120, four hours, half-hourly (6.50am to 6pm)

TRAIN

Wǔhàn has three major train stations: Hànkǒu Train Station (汉口火车站, Hànkǒu Huǒchēzhàn), Wǔchāng Train Station (武昌火车站; *Wǔchāng Huǒchēzhàn*) and Wǔhàn Train

Station (武汉火车站; *Wǔhàn Huǒchēzhàn*), all of which should be linked up to the metro system by the time you read this. Services include:

Hànkǒu Station

Běijīng D train 2nd-/1st-class seat ¥267/333, 10 hours, two daily (8.06am and 9.05am)
Běijīng Z train hard/soft sleeper ¥263/411, 10 hours, two daily (8.24pm and 9.12pm)
Shànghǎi Hóngqiáo D train 2nd-/1st-class seat ¥264/316, six hours, 11 daily (7.05am to 5.23pm)
Wǔdāng Shān hard seat ¥70, six to seven hours, two daily (10.35am and 4pm)
Xī'ān D train 2nd-/1st-class seat ¥307/432, 7½ hours, one daily (9.15am)

Wǔchāng Station

Běijīng Z train hard/soft sleeper ¥263/411, 10 hours, two daily (9.03pm and 9.09pm)
Kūnmíng Hard/soft sleeper ¥380/600, 23 to 25 hours, five daily
Yíchāng Hard seat ¥54, five hours, four daily (7.36am, 11.26am, 12.10pm and 5.35pm)

Wǔhàn Station

Běijīng D train 2nd/1st class ¥267/333, 10 hours, one daily (11.57am)
Chángshā G train 2nd/1st class ¥165/265, 1½ hours, more than 40 daily (7am to 7.55pm)
Guǎngzhōu G train 2nd/1st class ¥464/739, four hours, more than 40 daily (7am to 7.55pm)
Shànghǎi Hóngqiáo G train, 2nd/1st class ¥303/428, five hours, two daily (1.35pm and 3.10pm)
Xī'ān North G train 2nd/1st class ¥458/733, 4½ hours, seven daily

ⓘ Getting Around

TO/FROM THE AIRPORT

Regular airport shuttle buses reach Hànkǒu Train Station (¥15, 45 minutes) and Fùjiāpō long-distance bus station (¥30, one hour). A taxi is about ¥100.

BUS

Bus 10 (¥1.50) Connects Hànkǒu and Wǔchāng Train Stations.

Bus 401 (¥2) From Hànyáng past Guīyuán Temple, Yellow Crane Tower and Chángchūn Temple to East Lake.

Bus 402 (¥2) From Wǔchāng Train Station to Chángchūn Temple and Yellow Crane Tower, then via Hànyáng to Yanjiang Dadao in Hànkǒu before returning over the river for the provincial museum and half a circuit of East Lake.

Bus 411 (¥1.50) Travels a more direct route from the museum to Yellow Crane Tower and Chángchūn Temple before carrying on to Hànkǒu Train Station.

FERRY

Ferries (¥1.50, 6.30am to 8pm) make swift daily crossings of the Yangzi between **Zhonghua Lu Dock** (中华路码头, Zhōnghuá Lù Mǎtóu) and **Wǔhàn Guān Dock** (武汉关码头, Wǔhàn Guān Mǎtóu).

METRO

Wǔhàn's fledgling metro system (地铁, *dìtiě*) includes Line 1, an overground light-rail line in Hànkǒu, and Lines 2 and 4, which tunnel under the river, linking the main train stations. Four more lines are under construction.

Jīngzhōu 荆州

☎ 0716 / POP 1.5 MILLION

Capital of the Chu kingdom during the Eastern Zhou, fantastic Jīngzhōu matches an ancient history with a homely small-town feel. One of China's few cities still ringed by an intact city wall, the town has clung onto some ancient temples, and boasts a noteworthy museum. The surrounding farmlands are dotted with several ancient burial sites, including Xióngjiā Zhǒng, the largest collection of Chu kingdom tombs ever discovered.

Sights

The walled section of Jīngzhōu is approximately 3.5km from east to west and 2.5km from north to south, with impressive city gates at each cardinal point, as well as several lesser gates. Passing through the wall at **New East Gate** (新东门, Xīn Dōngmén), as you will if you're on the bus from the main stations, you'll have Jingzhou Nanlu (荆州南路) stretching out in front of you, and you'll see the older **East Gate** (老东门, Lǎo Dōngmén) off to your right. Zhangjuzheng Jie (张居正街) leads away from East Gate and runs parallel to Jingzhou Nanlu.

Jīngzhōu Museum MUSEUM

(荆州博物馆, Jīngzhōu Bówùguǎn; Jingzhou Zhonglu, 荆州中路; audio tour ¥20, English tour guide ¥200; ⌚9am-5pm Tue-Sun) FREE This excellent museum next to Kāiyuán Temple showcases some wonderful artefacts unearthed from Chu tombs around the area. The highlight is the incredibly well-preserved 2000-year-old body of a man found in his tomb with ancient tools, clothing and even food; the airtight mud seal around his crypt helped preserve him. You can find him in one of the buildings around the large pond behind the main building. Take bus 12, 19 or 101 to the West Gate (西门, *Xīmén*), then backtrack 200m.

City Wall HISTORIC SITE

(城墙; Chéngqiáng) Jīngzhōu's original city wall was a tamped mud wall dating from the Eastern Han dynasty, later clad in stone during the Five Dynasties and Ten Kingdoms. The oldest surviving sections today, around **South Gate** (南门, Nánmén), are Song, but most dates to the Ming and Qing. The South Gate, with its enceinte (瓮城; *wèngchéng*) still attached, concocts flavours of medieval Jīngzhōu, swarming with Taoist soothsayers, outdoor hairdressers offering cutthroat shaves and vegetable sellers.

A similar carnival feel animates **East Gate** (老东门, Lǎo Dōngmén), which also has an enceinte and a fairground feel. You can walk on parts of the wall, sometimes for a small fee (¥7 to ¥27), but the best way to see it is to rent a bike and cycle around the outside (1½ hours) between the wall and the city moat. This path also makes a lovely walk.

Kāiyuán Temple TAOIST TEMPLE

(开元观, Kāiyuán Guàn; Jingzhou Zhonglu, 荆州中路) Explore the fascinating empty Taoist remains attached to the Jīngzhōu Museum.

Guāndì Temple TAOIST TEMPLE

(关帝庙, Guāndì Miào) Up the road from the South Gate, this historic Taoist temple originally dates to 1396.

Tiěnǚ Temple BUDDHIST TEMPLE

(铁女寺, Tiěnǚ Sì; off Jingbei Lu) Located in the north of town off Jingbei Lu, the name of this intriguing temple translates as the Iron Girl Temple.

Xuánmiào Temple TAOIST TEMPLE

(玄妙观, Xuánmiào Guàn; north of Jingbei Lu) This Taoist temple, just north of New North Gate (新北门, *xīnběimén*), literally translates as the 'Temple of Mystery'.

Confucian Temple CONFUCIAN TEMPLE

(文庙, Wén Miào; Jingzhou Zhonglu, 荆州中路) Now part of Shíyàn Zhōngxué (Experimental Middle School), it's a short walk east of the Jīngzhōu Museum. Smile sweetly to be let in.

Sleeping

Bāyī Bīnguǎn HOTEL $

(八一宾馆; ☎152 7248 2879; 14-4 Zhangju Zhengjie, 张居正街14-4号; r from ¥70; ❄📶) One of several cheap hotels on Zhangju Zhengjie, this renovated choice has newly decorated rooms, wi-fi and a good location 200m inside the older East Gate.

To get here, take bus 101 from either bus station and get off at the first stop after passing the East Gate. Walk back, take the first left, then left again down Zhangju Zhengjie and the hotel will be on your right.

Jiǔgē Holiday Hotel　　　　HOTEL $$
(九歌假日酒店, Jiǔgē Jiàrì Jiǔdiàn; ☑885 7777; 13 Jingzhou Nanlu, 荆州南路13号; r from ¥380; ✳@⑨) This decent midrange hotel, with large, comfortable, wi-fi–enabled rooms, a restaurant and a cafe, is located about 200m inside the New East Gate.

Take bus 101 from either bus station and get off after passing the East Gate. Keep walking straight and the hotel will be on your left after 200m.

✗ Eating

Come evening, locals head to the East Gate end of Zhangju Zhengjie for *shāokǎo*.

Bàyú Rénjiā　　　　HUBEI $$
(巴渝人家; New East Gate, Donghuan Lu, 东环路新东门外; mains ¥20-50; ⊙11am-9pm) Great location by the moat, outside New East Gate. Grab a table overlooking the city wall and moat and tuck into the restaurant speciality, *gānguō* (干锅), an iron pot of spicy delights, kept bubbling hot with a small candle burner. Varieties include chicken (干锅仔鸡, *gānguō zǐjī*; ¥38), bullfrog (干锅牛蛙, *gānguō niúwā*; ¥48) and tofu (干锅千叶豆腐, *gānguō qiānyè dòufu*; ¥32).

One pot is enough for two or three people with rice (米饭, *mǐfàn*), which is free. Exit New East Gate, cross the moat and the restaurant is on your right.

❶ Information

There are 24-hour internet cafes (网吧, *wǎngbā*) dotted around town.

China Construction Bank (中国建设银行, Zhōngguó Jiànshè Yínháng) Has a foreign-friendly ATM. Located between New East Gate and Jiǔgē Holiday Hotel.

❶ Getting There & Around

BICYCLE

The **bicycle rental place** (per hr/day ¥7/50) by East Gate is one of many around the walled section of the city.

BUS

You'll probably arrive at either Shāshì long-distance bus station (沙市长途汽车站, Shāshì chángtú qìchēzhàn) or Shāshì central bus station (沙市中心客运站, Shāshì zhōngxīn

kèyùnzhàn). Turn right out of either, walk to the first bus stop and take bus 101 (¥2) to East Gate (东门, *dōngmén*).

Buses from Shāshì long-distance bus station:
Wǔdāng Shān ¥120, five hours, two daily (7.45am and 1pm)
Wǔhàn ¥80, four hours, frequent (6.30am to 8pm)
Yíchāng ¥44, two hours, frequent (7am to 6pm)

TRAIN

Bus 49 (¥2) connects the train station (火车站, *huǒchē zhàn*) with the East Gate. D- and G-class trains (and slower trains) link Jīngzhōu with:
Shànghǎi Hóngqiáo 2nd/1st class ¥322/388, eight hours, five daily
Wǔhàn 2nd/1st class ¥60/70, 1½ hours, regular
Yíchāng East 2nd/1st class ¥25/30, 40 minutes, regular

Around Jīngzhōu

Xióngjiā Zhǒng　　　ARCHAEOLOGICAL SITE
(熊家冢; admission ¥30; ⊙9.30am-4.30pm) Forty kilometres north of Jīngzhōu, the 2300-year-old tombs of Xióngjiā Zhǒng are the source of a large collection of jade – on display at the Jīngzhōu Museum (p435) – while a fascinating and huge collection of skeletal horse and chariots in a section of the tomb in a hangerlike museum is open to visitors.

Buses (¥10, 70 minutes) leave hourly from the back of the bus station called Chǔdū Kèyùn Zhàn (楚都客运站) in Jīngzhōu. Bus 24 links this station with Jīnfèng Guǎngchǎng (金凤广场) bus stop, just outside East Gate (over the moat and turn left). A taxi will be at least ¥100 return.

Wǔdāng Shān　　　武当山

☑0719
Wǔdāng Shān may not be one of China's five sacred Taoist mountains but it's paradoxically known as the 'No 1 Taoist Mountain in the Middle Kingdom'. Sacrosanct in martial arts circles, it is acknowledged that 'in the north they esteem Shàolín, in the south they revere Wǔdāng'. The Unesco World Heritage Site of Wǔdāng Shān is the apocryphal birthplace of taichi, and possesses supernaturally good-looking vistas and an abundance of medicinal plants that naturally find their way into a panoply of Taoist medicinal potions. The mountain is also sadly over-

priced and overcommercialised, with new developments afoot, so expect the magic of Taoist chanting to be occasionally perforated by the squeal of buzz saws.

◉ Sights & Activities

The town's main road, Taihe Lu (太和路) – which at various sections is also labelled Taihe Donglu (太和东路, Taihe East) and Taihe Zhonglu (太和中路, Taihe Central) – runs east–west on its way up towards the main gate of the mountain. Everything of interest in town is either on or near this road and road numbers are clearly labelled. Buses often drop you at the junction by the main expressway, a 1km walk east of the town centre. From here, turn left to the mountain entrance (100m) or right into town.

You can buy Chinese (¥3) or English (¥8) maps at the main gate of the mountain.

Wǔdāng Museum of China   MUSEUM
(武当博物馆, Wǔdāng Bówùguǎn; Culture Sq, 文化广场; audio tour ¥20, deposit ¥200; ☉9-11.30am & 2.30-5pm) **FREE** This is a great opportunity to get a grip on Wǔdāng Shān history, lore and architecture. There's a whole pantheon of gods, including the eminent Zhenwu (patriarch of the mountain) and a section on Taoist medicine including the fundamentals of *nèidān Xué* (内丹学; internal alchemy). There are also some stunning bronze pieces.

The museum is down Bowuguan Lu (博物馆路), which leads to Culture Sq (Wenhua Guangchang).

Wǔdāng Shān   MOUNTAIN
(武当山; admission ¥140, bus ¥100, audio guide ¥30) Wǔdāng Shān attracts a diverse array of climbers, from Taoist nuns with knapsacks, porters shouldering paving slabs and sacks of rice, businessmen with laptops and bright-eyed octogenarians hopping along. It's a gruelling climb but the scenery is worth every step; plenty of Taoist temples line the route (where you can take contemplative breathers) and you'll see the occasional Taoist cairn or trees garlanded with scarlet ribbons weighed with small stones. On the way down, note how some pilgrims descend backwards!

To start your ascent, take bus 1 (¥1) or walk from Taihe Lu to the Main Gate (山门口, Shān Ménkǒu) and ticket office. The bus ticket (compulsory with your admission) gives you unlimited use of shuttle buses (from 6am to 6.30pm).

One bus – which often only leaves when it's full – runs to the start of the **cable car** (索道, suǒdào; up/down ¥50/45). For those who don't mind steps, take the bus to **South Cliff** (南岩, Nányán), where the trail to 1612m **Heavenly Pillar Peak** (天柱峰, Tiānzhù Fēng), the highest peak, begins. Consider disembarking early at the beautiful, turquoise-tiled **Purple Cloud Temple** (紫霄宫, Zǐxiāo Gōng; admission ¥20), from where a small stone path leads up to South Cliff (45 minutes). From South Cliff it's an energy-sapping, two-hour, 4km climb to the top.

The enchanting red-walled **Cháotiān Temple** (朝天宫, Cháotiān Gōng) is about halfway up, housing a statue of the Jade Emperor and standing on an old, moss-hewn stone base with 4m-high tombstones guarding its entrance. From here you have a choice of two ascent routes, via the 1.4km **Ming-dynasty route** (the older, Back Way) or the 1.8km **Qing-dynasty path** (the 'Hundred Stairs'). The shorter but more gruelling Ming route ascends via the Three Heaven's Gates, including the stupefying climb to the **Second Gate of Heaven** (二天门, Èrtiān Mén). You can climb by one route and descend by the other. Temple ruins, fallen trees, shocking inclines and steep steps misshapen by centuries of footslogging await you.

Near the top, beyond the cable-car exit, is the magnificent **Forbidden City** (紫禁城, Zǐjīn Chéng; admission ¥20) with its 2.5m-thick stone walls hugging the

THE BIRTH OF TAICHI

Zhang San Feng (张三丰), a semi-legendary Wǔdāng Shān monk from the 10th or 13th century (depending on what source you read), is reputed to be the founder of the martial art *tàijíquán* (literally 'Supreme Ultimate Boxing') or taichi. Zhang had grown dissatisfied with the 'hard' techniques of Shaolin boxing and searched for something 'softer' and more elusive. Sitting on his porch one day, he became inspired by a battle between a huge bird and a snake. The sinuous snake used flowing movements to evade the bird's attacks. The bird, exhausted, eventually gave up and flew away. Taichi is closely linked to Taoism, and many priests on Wǔdāng Shān practise some form of the art.

mountainside and balustrades festooned with lovers' locks. From here you can stagger to magnificent views from the **Golden Hall** (金殿, Jīn Diàn; admission ¥20), constructed entirely from bronze, dating from 1416 and in dire need of some buffing up. A small statue of Zhenwu – Ming emperor and Wŭdāng Shān's presiding Taoist deity – peeks out from within.

Courses

Wŭdāng Taoist Kungfu Academy SPORTS (武当道教功夫学院, Wŭdāng Dàojiào Gōngfu Xuéyuàn; ☑ 568 9185; www.wudang.org; Purple Cloud Temple; fees per day classes ¥300, accommodation ¥200-300, meals ¥80) Dozens of taichi schools pepper these parts, but this one has the edge for location, its qualities as a school and accessibility to foreigners. The setting is magical; in a large, secluded courtyard surrounded by pine trees halfway up the mountain. Classes, which follow a strict regime, are held either at the school or at various scenic spots on the mountain. For more information on taichi see p437.

At least one member of the admin staff speaks good English. You can sign up for anything from a few days to one year; the longer you study, the cheaper the rates. You'll have to find, and fund, your own way here the first time (it's down the steps to your left, just past Purple Cloud Temple; no English sign). After that, the school will arrange a pass for you so you can come and go without having to pay the hefty entrance fees to the mountain each time there. There are no classes on Wednesday afternoon or Thursday. Expect some 5.30am starts!

Sleeping

In Town

Xuán Yuè Hotel HOTEL $$ (玄岳饭店, Xuányuè Fàndiàn; ☑ 566 5111; 27 Yuxu Lu, 玉虚路27号; r from ¥380; ✳ @ ⧠) This smart, midrange hotel has comfortable rooms with clean bathrooms. It's on the corner of Yuxu Lu and Taihe Zhonglu and is accessed through an entranceway to the right of the one with the English sign for the hotel (the one with the English sign leads to the restaurant).

Shèngjǐngyuàn Bīnguǎn HOTEL $$ (圣景苑宾馆, ☑ 566 2118; 7 Taihe Zhonglu, 太和中路7号; r ¥288, discounted to ¥128; ✳ @ ⧠)

Simple, bright, pleasant rooms come with firm mattresses and spacious bathrooms. It's a couple of doors down from the Bank of China.

On the Mountain

There are about a dozen hotels and guesthouses by South Cliff. The cheapest rooms go for around ¥80, but bargain especially during the low season.

Nányán Hotel HOTEL $$$ (南岩大岳宾馆, Nányán Dàyuè Bīnguǎn; ☑ 568 9182; r ¥608; ✳ @) This revamped, smart hotel right by the bus stop at South Cliff has large, clean, comfortable rooms and welcoming staff. Discounts may apply.

Taichi Hotel HOTEL $$$ (太极会馆, Tàijí Huìguǎn; ☑ 568 9888; r ¥568, discounted to ¥348; ✳ @) The best-quality hotel on the mountain, although discounts aren't as good as elsewhere. Rooms with windows go for ¥348, and have fabulous mountain views. Rooms without windows are identical (apart from the views) but are generally not discounted. Internet connection for laptops is in all rooms. It's 200m downhill from the bus stop at South Cliff.

Eating

In town a few *shāokǎo* stalls set up every evening in an alley off Taihe Lu. Look for the neon-lit archway with the characters 鱼羊鲜, beside No 14.

On the mountain there are plenty of food options by South Cliff, although not many English menus.

Taìhé Xuánwǔ Dàjiǔdiàn CHINESE $$ (太和玄武大酒店; 8 Taihe Zhonglu, 太和路8号; mains ¥20-50; ☉ 6.30am-11.30pm) Large bustling restaurant with half its menu helpfully translated into English. Various regional cuisines are represented, from Sichuanese to Cantonese; even Běijīng roast duck! No English sign.

Entertainment

Wŭdāng Grand Theatre THEATRE (武当大剧院, Wŭdāng Dàjùyuàn; ☑ 506 2366; Culture Sq,, 文化广场; Wŭdāng Taichi Show tickets ¥200-280; ☉ Wŭdāng Taichi Show 8-9pm) Modern theatre opposite the Wŭdāng Museum of China. It hosts the **Wŭdāng Taichi Show** every Thursday, Friday and Saturday.

ℹ️ Information

Bank of China (中国银行, Zhōngguó Yínháng; 1 Taihe Zhonglu, 太和中路1号; ⏰ 8.30am-5.30pm) Foreign-friendly ATM and money-exchange facility.

Jísù Internet (极速网吧, Jísù Wăngbā; 2nd fl, 20 Taihe Lu, 太和路20号; per hr ¥3; ⏰ 24hr) Through a round archway. No English sign.

ℹ️ Getting There & Away

BUS

The new bus station (客运汽车站; kèyùn qìchēzhàn), 200m downhill from the expressway, is on the right of the road leading into town.

Jīngzhōu ¥120, five hours, one daily (9am)

Wǔhàn ¥150, five hours, two daily (8.30am and 11am)

Xī'ān ¥159, eight hours, one daily (8.30am)

Yíchāng ¥110, five hours, one daily (9.30am)

A fleet of small green buses shuttles between the two nearest train stations – Wǔdāngshān and Shíyàn (十堰; ¥15, one hour, 5.10am to 8pm) – via Liùlǐpíng (六里坪; ¥4, 20 minutes).

They leave from outside Tàihé Xuánwǔ Dàjiǔdiàn restaurant.

TRAIN

Wǔdāng Shān no longer has a train station, although the train station at Liùlǐpíng is often referred to as Wǔdāng Shān. You can buy train tickets from the **train ticket agency** (铁路客票代售, tiělù piàodàishòu; ⏰ 8.30am-6pm), beside Wǔdāng Shān's old train station on Chezhan Lu (车站路), a road opposite Tàihé Xuánwǔ Dàjiǔdiàn restaurant.

Liùlǐpíng (Wǔdāng Shān) trains:

Běijīng West Hard seat/hard sleeper ¥164/300, 19 to 22 hours, three daily

Chángshā Hard seat/hard sleeper ¥112/208, 14½ hours, one daily (7.58am)

Chéngdū Hard seat/hard sleeper ¥128/244, 11 to 18 hours, six daily

Shànghǎi South Hard seat/hard sleeper ¥192/351, 22 to 24 hours, three daily

Wǔhàn (Wǔchāng) Hard seat/hard sleeper ¥69/130, 6½ to 8½ hours, seven daily

Xī'ān Hard seat/hard sleeper ¥69/130, five to six hours, three daily

Xī'ān North Hard seat/hard sleeper ¥69/130, five to six hours, three daily

Xiāngyáng Hard seat/hard sleeper ¥24/78, two hours, regular (6am to 11.30pm)

Yíchāng East Hard seat/hard sleeper ¥55/109, three hours, one daily (4.23pm)

Shénnóngjià   神农架

🔊 0719

Famed for its medicinal plants and legendary ape-man (野人, yěrén), Shénnóngjià forms a significant chunk of the most spectacular region of Húběi province. Thickly forested peaks with part-exposed rock faces rise up dramatically from a small network of Yangzi River tributaries; the bus journey here alone will leave you gobsmacked.

Foreigners are only allowed into one of the four sections of the national park, at **Yāzikǒu** (鸭子口; admission ¥140), but the area is big enough for good walking and you can also camp here. Once inside the park, you can board shuttle buses (¥90) to various points of interest. Worth checking out are **Xiǎolóngtán** (小龙潭), about 10km from the entrance, and a good place to spot monkeys (Shénnóngjià is home to the rare golden snub-nosed monkey; 川金丝猴, chuān jīnsīhóu), and **Shénnóngdǐng** (神农顶), 20km from the entrance and the highest peak here (3105m). There's a camping area (¥30) at the base of Shénnóngdǐng, called **Shénnóngyíng** (神农营). Winter is bitterly cold and snow often blocks roads.

Yāzikǒu is accessed from **Mùyú** (木鱼), a small but well-developed tourist village about 14km down the mountain. All buses drop you in Mùyú.

🛏️ Sleeping & Eating

Shuānglín Hotel   HOTEL **$**
(双林酒店, Shuānglín Jiǔdiàn; 🔊 345 2803; 25 Muyu Lu; r from ¥88, with computer ¥128; ❄️ @) The modest Shuānglín Hotel, where buses drop you off, has tidy rooms and welcoming management, though there are flashier hotels, too. You can normally rent tents (帐篷, zhàngpeng; ¥100 to ¥200) once inside the park, or buy them (¥700 to ¥800) from a couple of camping shops in Mùyú.

Piān Qiáo Wān   CHINESE **$**
(偏桥湾; 53 Muyu Lu, 木鱼路53号; mains ¥20-40; ⏰ 10am-9pm) The coolest place to eat in Mùyú is Piān Qiáo Wān, which is accessed via a wobbly bridge and backs onto a small tea plantation (you can buy tea here). The menu is in Chinese only. Try the huíguō niúròu (回锅牛肉; spicy fried beef), the cháshùgū chǎolàròu (茶树菇炒腊肉; wild mushrooms and cured pork) or the xiānggū

ròusī (香菇肉丝; shiitake mushrooms with pork shreds).

Don't forget to leave room for the *qiáomài bǐng* (荞麦饼; flatbread made with buckwheat and wild herbs and served with a honey dip).

ℹ Information

The ICBC Bank at the top of Mùyú village has an ATM that accepts foreign cards. Internet cafes (网吧, *wǎngbā*) cost ¥4 per hour.

ℹ Getting There & Away

Buses leave from outside Shuānglín Hotel, where you can also buy tickets. Foreigners aren't allowed to continue north to Wǔdāng Shān from Mùyú.

Bādōng ¥55, three hours, one daily (9.30am)
Yíchāng ¥60, 2½ hours, five daily (7am to 3.30pm)

Shared minibuses to Yāzikǒu (per person ¥10) leave from the top end of Mùyú.

Yíchāng 宜昌

☑ 0717 / POP 4 MILLION

A young and vibrant city, Yíchāng lacks tourist sights but is on the map as a gateway to the magnificent Three Gorges.

◎ Sights

Three Gorges Dam ARCHITECTURE
(三峡大坝, Sānxiá Dàbà; admission ¥105) The huge Three Gorges Dam hulks away upstream. The world's largest dam due to its length (2.3km) rather than its height (101m), it isn't the most spectacular dam, but is worth a peek. You can't walk on it, but there's a tourist viewing area to the north. The view from the south is much the same, and free.

Take a bus from the long-distance station to Máopíng (茅坪; ¥15, 8.30am to 3pm), but get off at Bālù Chēzhàn (八路车战). Alternatively, bus 8 (¥20, one hour, 8am to 4pm) leaves from Yíchāng's East Train Station.

Day trips can also be taken by boat (¥280 including entrance fee and lunch) from the old ferry port (老码头; *lǎo mǎtóu*). They leave at 7.30am and return around 5pm. Buy tickets from Yangtze River International Travel at the port.

🛏 Sleeping

Yíchāng Hotel HOTEL $$
(宜昌饭店, Yíchāng Fàndiàn; ☑ 644 1616; 113 Dongshan Dadao, 东山大道113号; r from ¥288; ❉ @ 🛜) This jolly place complements an elegant foyer with large and pleasant rooms. English is limited but it's all smiles. Diagonally opposite the long-distance bus station. Wi-fi in the lobby only. Discounts may apply.

Yíling Hotel HOTEL $$$
(夷陵饭店, Yíling Fàndiàn; ☑ 886 7199; 41 Yunji Lu, 云集路41号; r from ¥528; ❉ @) Large bright rooms with laminated wood flooring. Well located close to the river and opposite a number of restaurants, bars and cafes. Discounts may apply. Take bus 4 from the old dock or bus 6 from the long-distance bus station; a taxi will cost ¥30.

🍴 Eating

Opposite Yíling Hotel there's a Korean restaurant called **Hánlìgōng Liàolǐ** (韩丽宫料理; ☑ 11am-9pm) with dishes, claypots and barbecues from ¥25; also a Western-style cafe. Both have English menus.

For something more local, hop on bus 2 or 6 (¥1) or into a taxi (¥7) to Běimén (北门), where you can eat *xiāo yè* (宵夜; literally 'midnight snacks') at a number of stalls and restaurants which spill out onto the streets each evening (5pm to 2am). You'll see skewers (串, *chuàn*), dumplings (饺子, *jiǎozi*) and noodles (面, *miàn*) as well as places doing barbecued fish (烤鱼, *kǎoyú*). Look out for the **pancake stall** making *fēi bǐng* (飞饼, 'flying pancakes'; ¥12 to ¥15); the banana ones (香蕉, *xiāngjiāo*) are delicious.

Xiǎo Hú Niú HUBEI $
(小胡牛; 73 Shangshu Xiang, Běimén; 北门尚书巷73号; ingredients ¥8-26; ☑ 4pm-2am) Our favourite restaurant in Běimén, this one specialises in a local beef hot plate called *xiǎo hú niú*; order that first, stipulating how spicy you want your beef (¥25 for 250g) or lamb (¥26 for 250g) – mild (微辣, *wēi là*), medium (中辣, *zhōng là*) or hot (麻辣, *mà là*) – before ordering other raw ingredients to fry with it on your hot plate.

Choices include *qīngjiāo* (青椒, green peppers), *xiānggū* (香菇, shiitake mushrooms), *tǔdòu piàn* (土豆片, potato slices) and *ǒu piàn* (藕片, lotus root slices).

ⓘ Information

There are plentiful 24-hour internet cafes (网吧, *wǎngbā;* per hr ¥3). Foreign-friendly ATMs are also everywhere.

ⓘ Getting There & Around

AIR

Daily flights from Three Gorges Airport (三峡 机场, *Sānxiá Jīchǎng*) include Běijīng (¥1300), Chéngdū (¥790), Guǎngzhōu (¥960), Shànghǎi (¥1080) and Xī'ān (¥840).

Airport shuttle buses (¥20, 50 minutes) run to and from the Qīngjiāng building (清江大 厦, *Qīngjiāng dàshà*), leaving two hours before outward bound flights and meeting all incoming flights. Flight tickets can be bought from the Air China office inside the Qīngjiāng building. Turn right out of Yíchāng Hotel and it's on your right after about 1km.

BUS

There are three main long-distance bus stations: Yíchāng long-distance bus station (长途汽车站, *chángtú qìchēzhàn*), plus ones at the east train station and the old ferry port. All are modern and well run, and offer very similar bus services. Services from the Yíchāng long-distance bus station include:

Jīngzhōu ¥40 to ¥65, two hours and 10 minutes, half-hourly (6.40am to 6.30pm)

Lǎoyíng (for Wǔdāng Shān) ¥130, six hours, regular (8am to 1pm)

Mùyú (for Shénnóngjià) ¥70, five hours, seven daily (7.45am to 3.30pm)

Wǔdāng Shān ¥130, six hours, two daily (8am and 12.20pm)

Wǔhàn (Wǔchāng) ¥78 to ¥110, 4½ hours, every hour (7am to 8pm)

TRAIN

Yíchāng's east train station (火车东站, *huǒchē dōngzhàn*) is now the station that almost all trains use. Train tickets (¥5 service charge) can also be bought at window 1 of Yíchāng long-distance bus station. Trains include:

Běijīng West G train 2nd/1st class ¥617/948, eight hours, 9.20am

Chéngdū D train 2nd/1st class ¥259/311, seven hours, nine per day (some to Chéngdū East)

Chóngqìng North D train 2nd/1st class ¥162/195, five hours, regular

Shànghǎi Hóngqiáo D train 2nd/1st class ¥349/420, eight hours, five daily

Wǔhàn D train 2nd/1st class ¥85/103, 2½ hours, regular

Xī'ān Hard sleeper ¥208, 11 hours, two daily (one to Xī'ān South)

Wǔdāng Shān Hard seat/hard sleeper ¥5 to ¥109, five hours, one daily (7.30pm)

PUBLIC TRANSPORT

Local buses cost ¥1. Useful routes for frequently running buses include:

Bus 4 Old ferry port (三码头, *sān mǎtóu*)– Yíling Hotel (夷陵饭店, *Yíling Fàndiàn*)–old train station (火车站, *huǒchē zhàn;* for Yíchāng Hotel or long-distance bus station).

Bus 6 Long-distance bus station (长途汽车 站, *chángtú qìchēzhàn;* for Yíchāng Hotel) to Běimén (北门).

Bus 9 East Train Station (火车东站, *huǒchē dōngzhàn*) to the long-distance bus station (长 途汽车站, *chángtú qìchēzhàn*).

Jiāngxī

POP 45.2 MILLION

Best Hiking

➡ Sānqīng Mountain (p453)
➡ Wùyuán (p454)
➡ Lúshān (p447)
➡ Wǔdāng Mountain (p456)
➡ Lónghǔ Mountain (p455)

Best Villages

➡ Lǐkēng (p451)
➡ Yáolǐ (p450)
➡ Guānkēng (p452)
➡ Xiǎoqǐ (p452)
➡ Sīxī & Yáncūn (p453)
➡ Luótiáncūn (p447)

Why Go?

An interconnected web of rivers, lakes and shimmering rice paddies, Jiāngxī (江西) is defined by its water. Farmers in ponchos and heavy boots till the fields in drizzling rain as snow-white herons whirl overhead, and off at the edges of the province, low-lying hills of tea plantations and pencil-thin pines give way to more substantial mountain ranges, seemingly shrouded in perpetual mist.

While not as remote as it used to be, Jiāngxī is still rarely visited by foreign tourists and can be just the spot if you're after something off the beaten track. Jǐngdézhèn will have porcelain enthusiasts going potty, while hikers will adore the hilltop trails around the northeastern mountains, but it's the irresistible countryside villages, their traditional architecture and their altogether slower pace of life which are the real highlight of a visit to this charming pocket of southeast China.

When to Go
Nánchāng

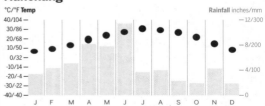

Mid-Mar Terraced rapeseed fields bloom in Wùyuán, drawing amateur photographers from across China.

Late May–early Jun Rhododendrons add splashes of pink to the Sānqīng Mountain canopy.

Sep–Nov Less rainfall and moderate temperatures; best time to visit Jiāngxī.

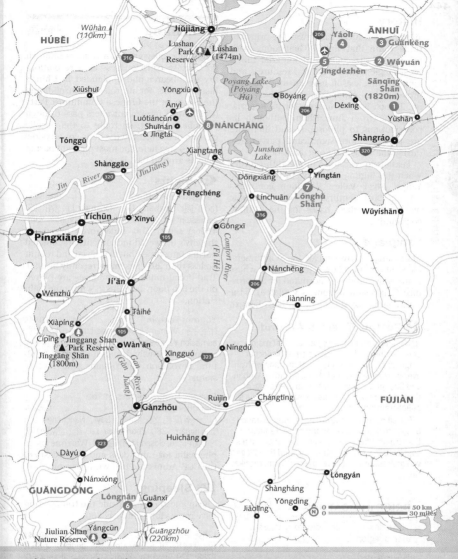

Jiāngxī Highlights

1 Look out over a forest of granite spires in **Sānqīng Mountain** (p453)

2 Rent a mountain bike and village-hop your way around the countryside of **Wùyuán** (p454)

3 Hike the ancient postal trail from the remote village of **Guānkēng** (p452)

4 Visit the ancient riverside village of **Yáolǐ** (p450)

5 Browse for tea sets in **Jǐngdézhèn** (p448), the porcelain capital of the world.

6 Explore Hakka country around **Lóngnán** (p456), where fortified villages and subtropical forest await

7 Discover a forgotten Taoist cultural centre at family-friendly **Lónghǔ Mountain** (p455)

8 Sample Jiāngxī's best restaurants (and treat yourself to some proper coffee) in the busy provincial capital, **Nánchāng** (p445)

History

Jiāngxī's Gan River Valley was the principal trade route that linked Guǎngdōng with the rest of the country in imperial times. Its strategic location, natural resources and long growing season have ensured that the province has always been relatively well off. Jiāngxī is most famous for its imperial porcelain (from Jǐngdézhèn), although its contributions to philosophy and literature are perhaps more significant, particularly during the Tang and Song dynasties.

Peasant unrest arose in the 19th century when the Taiping rebels swept through the Yangzi River Valley. Rebellion continued into the 20th century, and Jiāngxī became one of the earliest bases for the Chinese communists.

Language

Most Jiāngxī natives speak one of innumerable local variants of Gàn (赣), a dialect whose name is also used as a shorthand for the province. Gàn is similar (some say related) to the Hakka language, spoken in southern Jiāngxī.

❶ Getting There & Around

Nánchāng is connected by air to most major cities in China. There's also a small airport at Jǐngdézhèn. Bullet trains link Nánchāng with an ever-growing number of cities, including Wǔhàn and Shànghǎi. Wùyuán was also preparing, at the time of research, to be linked up to China's bullet-train network.

Travelling around the province, long-distance buses are usually quicker and more frequent than trains. Within towns and cities, local buses cost ¥1 (carry exact change). Around the villages, you may sometimes have to resort to motorbike taxis.

PRICE INDICATORS

The following price indicators are used in this region:

Sleeping

$ less than ¥100 (for a room)

$$ ¥100 to ¥300

$$$ more than ¥300

Eating

$ less than ¥30 (for a meal for one)

$$ ¥30 to ¥60

$$$ more than ¥60

Nánchāng 南昌

☎ 0791 / POP 2.5 MILLION

A bustling, busy city, Nánchāng is branded on Chinese consciousness as a revolutionary torchbearer and applauded in China's history books for its role in consolidating the power of the Chinese Communist Party (CCP). Most foreign travellers pass through without stopping, en route to the bucolic charms of Jiāngxī's marvellous countryside. If you do stay here, the most pleasant part of town is around Bāyī Park.

◉ Sights

Téngwáng Pavilion　　　　　MONUMENT

(腾王阁; Téngwáng Gé; Rongmen Lu; 榕门路; admission ¥50; ⊙7.30am-6.15pm summer, 8am-4.50pm winter) This nine-storey pagoda is the city's drawcard monument, first erected during Tang times, but destroyed and rebuilt no less than 29 times; most recently in 1989. Traditional music performances are played on the 6th floor. Take Bus 2内 from the train station.

Yòumín Temple　　　BUDDHIST TEMPLE

(佑民寺; Yòumín Sì; 181 Minde Lu; 民德路181号; admission ¥2; ⊙9am-5pm) This large, still-active temple was heavily damaged during the Cultural Revolution, but contains some notable statuary.

Former Headquarters of the Nánchāng Uprising　　　MUSEUM

(八一南昌起义纪念馆; Bāyī Nánchāng Qǐyì Jìniànguǎn; 380 Zhongshan Lu, 中山路380号; ⊙9am-5pm, closed Mon) **FREE** Wartime paraphernalia for rainy days and enthusiasts of the CCP. Admission free with passport.

⌂ Sleeping

Cheap guesthouses outside the train station have rooms for as little as ¥60.

Lìhú City Hotel　　　HOTEL $$

(丽湖城市酒店; Lìhú Chéngshì Jiǔdiàn; ☎8631 2288; 129 Supu Lu; 苏圃路129号; r from ¥160; ❀☎) One of a few hotels near Bāyī Park, Lìhú has large, modern rooms with smart furnishings and strong wi-fi. It's worth paying a few extra *kuài* for one of the rooms at the front, which are brighter and have park views. Take Bus 22 from the train station to Bayi Guangchangbei (八一广场北) bus stop, or Bus 212 from Xúfāng Bus Station to Zhongshanlu Dong (中山路东) bus stop.

Nánchāng

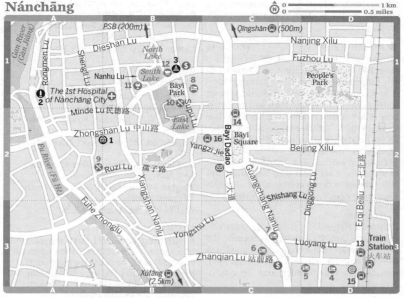

Nánchāng

⊙ Sights
1 Former Headquarters of the
Nánchāng Uprising B2
2 Téngwáng Pavilion A1
3 Yòumín Temple B1

🛏 Sleeping
4 7 Days Inn D3
5 7 Days Inn (older branch) D3
6 Galactic Classic International
Hotel C3
7 Galactic Peace Hotel C3
8 Líhú City Hotel B1

✕ Eating
9 Cháimǐ Yóuyán A2
10 Kǎlúnbì Kāfēi B1

● Drinking & Nightlife
11 Bossa Nova B1
12 Caffé Bene B1

● Transport
13 Airport Bus D3
14 Bayi Guangchangbei bus stop C2
15 Shuttle Bus for West Train Station D3
16 Zhongshanlu Dong bus stop C2

7 Days Inn HOTEL **$$**
(七天连锁酒店; Qītiān Liánsuǒ Jiǔdiàn; ☎8610
5088; www.7daysinn.cn; 19 Zhanqian Lu; 站前路19
号; r from ¥165; ❀@⑦) Well-run chain hotel
with clean rooms, reliable wi-fi and ¥7 Chi-
nese breakfasts. There's an older, slightly
cheaper **branch** further up the road.

**Galactic Classic
International Hotel** HOTEL **$$$**
(嘉莱特精典国际酒店; Jiālái tè Jīngdiǎn Guójì
Jiǔdiàn; ☎8828 1888; www.glthp.com; 2 Bayi
Dadao; 八一大道2号; r from ¥1288, discounted
to ¥699) Housed in an eye-catching modern
tower, this is the most luxurious hotel in the
train station area. Over the road, its older

sister, **Galactic Peace Hotel** (嘉莱特和平国
际酒店; Jiālái tè Hépíng Guójì Jiǔdiàn; ☎8611 1118;
www.glthp.com; 10 Guangchang Nanlu, 广场南路
10号; r from ¥1080, discounted to ¥498; ➌❀@
⑦✈), is a slightly cheaper option.

✕ Eating & Drinking

Cháimǐ Yóuyán JIANGXI **$**
(柴米油盐; 428 Ruzi Lu; 孺子路428号; mains
¥16-60; ⊙10am-2pm & 5-11pm) Dishes at
this clean, comfortable restaurant include
Jiāngxī specialties such as: *jiàng huáng niú
ròu* (酱黄牛肉; spicy stir-fried beef), *lǎo huǒ
mèn yā* (老火焖鸭; duck stew), *chì tāng
guì yú* 翅汤桂鱼; mandarin fish soup) and

tàn wēi zhǒu zi (炭煨肘子; barbecued pork shoulder). Has a clear photo menu with handy pinyin.

★ Kǎlúnbǐ Kāfēi
PAN ASIAN $$

(卡伦比咖啡; Inside Bāyī Park; 八一公园西门; mains ¥40-100; ☺ 9am-1.30am; 🛜) This modern cafe-restaurant, with a charming lakeside location inside Bāyī Park, does fresh coffee (¥40), Chinese tea (¥90) and imported beer (¥30) as well as good quality food. The steaks (¥100 to ¥200) are expensive. Instead, go for noodles (¥45) or one of the tasty casserole pots (¥50 to ¥60).

Pay a few extra *kuài* to upgrade your dish to a *tàocān*; a set meal with rice, soup and other small accompaniments. No English sign, but it does have an English menu.

Caffé Bene
CAFE

(1 Minde Lu; 民的路1号（佑民寺旁）; coffee ¥25; ☺ 10.30am-11pm; 🛜) Spacious branch of the stylish Korean coffee chain. Does good coffee plus a small selection of Western food, including Belgian waffles and ice cream. Free wi-fi.

Bossa Nova
BAR

(5 Nanhu Lu; 南湖路5号; beer from ¥15; ☺ 6pm-2am) Brazilian-owned, this is one of Nánchāng's friendliest bars. Hosts streetside Brazilian barbecues on Friday and Saturday evenings.

ℹ️ Information

There are 24-hour **internet cafes** by the train station. **ATMs** throughout Nánchāng accept foreign cards.

Bank of China (中国银行; Zhōngguó Yínháng; Zhanqian Xilu, 站前西路) Includes foreign exchange.

Public Security Bureau (PSB; 公安局; Gōng'ānjú; ☏ 8728 8493; 131 Yangming Lu, 阳明路131号; ☺ 8am-noon & 2.30-6pm)

The 1st Hospital of Nánchāng City (南昌市第一医院; Nánchāng Shì Dìyī Yīyuàn; ☏ 870 0989, 886 2288; 128 Xiangshan Beilu, 象山北路128号)

ℹ️ Getting There & Away

AIR
Chāngběi airport, 28km north of Nánchāng, has flights to all major Chinese cities as well as Bangkok and Singapore. Book tickets through www.ctrip.com.

BUS
Bus 89 links the train station with Xúfāng Bus Station. Bus 18 links the train station with Qīngshān Bus Station, which will eventually be connected to the metro.

Services from **Qīngshān Bus Station** (青山客运站; Qīngshān kèyùnzhàn):

Lúshān ¥55, 2½ hours, 8am, 9.30am & 10.40am

Wùyuán ¥102, 3½ hours, 8am, 10.25am, 12.40pm, 2.15pm & 4.25pm

Services from **Xúfāng Bus Station** (徐坊客运站; Xújiāfāng kèyùnzhàn):

Gànzhōu ¥120, 5½ hours, hourly, 7.20am-6.50pm

Jǐngdézhèn ¥83, three hours, hourly, 7am-7.30pm

Jiǔjiāng ¥37, two hours, every 40 minutes, 8am-7pm

Yīngtán ¥40, two hours, every 90 minutes, 7.45am-6.15pm

Yùshān ¥80, four hours, 2.40pm

TRAIN
An increasing number of bullet trains leave from Nánchāng's new West Train Station, which will eventually be connected to the metro. Until then, Shuttle Bus 1 (高铁巴士1号线; gāotiě bāshì yīhàoxiàn; ¥5, 45 minutes, half-hourly 6am-11pm) links the two train stations.

Services from **Nánchāng Train Station** (南昌火车站; Nánchāng Huǒchēzhàn):

Běijīng West Z-class hard sleeper ¥307, 11½ hours (7.55pm, 8.02pm)

Běijīng West K/T-class hard sleeper ¥307, 16 to 22 hours, eight daily

Gànzhōu K/T-class hard seat ¥63, four to six hours, 20 daily

Guǎngzhōu T/K-class hard sleeper ¥230 to ¥250, 11 to 13 hours, six daily

Hángzhōu East D-class bullet ¥190, five hours, four daily (8.10am, 8.58am, 1.18pm, 2.35pm)

Hángzhōu K-class hard sleeper ¥160 to ¥180, eight to 10 hours, 10 daily

Jǐngdézhèn K-class hard seat ¥41 to ¥47, 4½ hours, two daily (8.25am, 4.35pm)

Shànghǎi (Hóngqiáo) D-class bullet ¥240, 6½ hours, three daily (8.10am, 8.58am, 2.35pm)

Shànghǎi South K-class hard seat/sleeper ¥105/190, 10 to 14 hours, seven daily

Xī'ān T/K-class hard sleeper ¥270 to ¥320, 16 to 23 hours, five daily

Yùshān K-class hard seat ¥44, 4½ hours, seven daily

Services from **Nánchāng West Train Station** (南昌西站; Nánchāng Xīzhàn):

Běijīng West Z-class, hard sleeper ¥318, 12 hours, one daily (8.09pm)

Wǔhàn D-class bullet ¥100, 2½ to three hours, 13 daily (8.02am to 7.39pm)

ⓘ Getting Around

Line 1 of Nánchāng's new **metro** (地铁; *dìtiě*) should open in 2015, with Line 2 (connecting both train stations with Bāyī Sq) following soon after.

Airport buses (¥15, 50 minutes, every 20 minutes from 5.30am to 9pm) leave from the north side of the train station square. A taxi to the airport (机场; *jīchǎng*) costs around ¥100.

Around Nánchāng

The rarely visited, 1100-year-old village of Luótiáncūn (罗田村; admission ¥40), its uneven stone-flagged alleys etched with centuries of wear, provides a history-laden rural escape from urban Nánchāng.

A lazy amble around the village will take you through a tight maze of lanes, past hand-worked pumps, ancient wells, stone steps, scattering chickens, lazy water buffaloes and conical haystacks. Rudimentary walking-tour signs – 'visit and go ahead' – have been put up around this village, and its two siblings, and will point you towards the most notable old buildings. (Admission costs include entry to Shuǐnán and Jīngtái villages.)

A 1km-long flagstone path links Luótiáncūn with its sibling village, Shuǐnán (水南). A further 500m down the stone path (and across the road) is the forlorn village of Jīngtái (京台). Both also contain some wonderful old buildings.

Simple **guesthouses** (around ¥30 per person) are available in Luótiáncūn – ask for *zhùsù* (住宿, accommodation) – and there's a clutch of restaurants by the main square.

To get here, take Bus 22 (¥1) from Nánchāng train station to a bus stop called Bayi Qiao (八一桥; 30 minutes), then walk 400m straight ahead to catch Bus 136, from a bus stop underneath the flyover, to the small town of Ānyì (安义; ¥10, 90 minutes, frequent from 6am to 6pm). From Ānyì bus

JIĀNGXĪ AROUND NÁNCHĀNG

WORTH A TRIP

LÚSHĀN 庐山

A hilltop town with fresh air, cool temperatures and lovely mountain views, Lúshān has a long history; first as a Buddhist centre, then as a retreat for foreign missionaries and finally as a political conference base for the Chinese Communist Party. Sadly, almost all traces of its Buddhist past were destroyed during the Taiping Rebellion in the mid-19th century. Some 20th-century European-style villas still dot the hillsides, though. These days, however, most people come simply to escape the scorching summer heat of Nánchāng (it's particularly popular at weekends).

The walking up here is pleasant: there are plenty of viewpoints, some waterfalls and a few notable villas to head for. Buy a bilingual map (地图; *dìtú*; ¥6) in **Xīnhuá Bookshop** (新华书店; Xīnhuá Shūdiàn; 11 Guling Zhengjie), opposite the main square – called Jiēxīn Park (街心公园; Jiēxīn Gōngyuán) – and head off in whatever direction takes your fancy.

There are dozens of hotels up here, and even more restaurants. **Dàzìrán Youth Hostel** (大自然青年旅社; Dàzìrán Qīngnián Lǚshè; ☑ 0792 829 6327; www.yhalushan.com; 1 Hubei Lu, 湖北路1号; dm/d ¥50/180, weekends dm/d ¥70/260; ❄@☎) is the only youth hostel, though, and is worth pre-booking.

Getting There & Around

From Lúshān bus station, walk through the tunnel, then turn left to get to the main square (Jiēxīn Park). Continue past Xīnhuá Bookshop (on your left), then take the next left to reach Dàzìrán Youth Hostel (down to your right after 500m).

In summer, there are three direct buses to Lúshān from Nánchāng's Qīngshān Bus Station. Otherwise, you'll have to first go to the small city of Jiǔjiāng (九江) at the foot of the mountain, then catch a bus up to Lúshān (¥15.5, one hour, hourly 6.50am to 4.30pm) from there. The last bus back down to Jiǔjiāng from Lúshān is at 5pm.

Buses from **Jiǔjiāng Long-distance Bus Station** (九江长途汽车站; Jiǔjiāng chángtú qìchē zhàn):

Nánchāng ¥37, two hours, hourly until 7pm

Wǔhàn ¥100, 3½ hours, hourly until 5.30pm

Wùyuán ¥100, three hours, 8.30am, 11.50am and 2.30pm

station, where the 136 terminates, take a bus to nearby Shíbí (石鼻; ¥5; 30 minutes; half-hourly, 7am to 5.30pm), but tell the ticket seller on the bus that you want to go to Luótiáncūn. They will then sell you a bus ticket which is also valid for the final 5km-minibus ride to the village entrance. The last bus back to Nánchāng leaves Ānyì at 6.30pm.

Jĭngdézhèn 景德镇

The undisputed porcelain capital of China (and therefore the world), Jĭngdézhèn has been producing the finest-quality ceramics for more than 1700 years. The Imperial kilns have long been extinguished (although you can visit some), but Jĭngdézhèn still boasts a booming porcelain industry, including a thriving contemporary scene at the captivating arts district known as the Sculpture Factory.

Sights

★ Sculpture Factory ARTS CENTRE
(雕塑瓷厂; Diāosù Cíchǎng; 139 Xinchang Donglu; 新厂东路139号) This tree-lined street, and the pathways that branch off it, form a kind of porcelain-production arts district, which is a centre for contemporary ceramics in China. Some of the world's leading porcelain artists work and teach here and visitors can wander freely around the kilns, workshops and small factories as the latest masterpieces are being sculpted. This is also the most pleasant place in town to shop for ceramics, including tea sets.

While here, ceramics enthusiasts should pay a visit to the Pottery Workshop (乐天陶社; Lètiān Táoshè; ☑0798 844 0582; www.potteryworkshop.com.cn; inside the Sculpture Factory arts district; 雕塑瓷厂内; residencies incl accommodation & meals per week ¥2600). It runs highly regarded, month-long residency programmes for artists. Casual visitors can ask to look around. Staff speak English, and there's a pleasant cafe on site.

Bus 1, which runs along Zhushan Zhonglu in the centre of town, stops outside the south gate of the complex. Get off at Caojialing (曹家岭) bus stop then walk through the archway opposite.

Jĭngdézhèn Ancient Kiln MUSEUM
(古窑; Gǔyáo; Cidu Dadao; 瓷都大道; admission ¥95; ⊙8am-5pm) A bit like a living museum, this large, nicely landscaped site contains traditional porcelain-making equipment, including revived ancient kilns, and has teams of staff demonstrating how they were once used. Some of the buildings here date from Qing and Ming times, although have been largely rebuilt. Bus 5 runs here from the train station, via Zhushan Xilu.

🛏 Sleeping & Eating

★ Jĭngdézhèn International Youth Hostel HOSTEL $
(景德镇国际青年旅舍; Jĭngdézhèn Guójì Qīngniánlǚshè; ☑0798 844 9998, 0798 844 8886; jdzhostel@hotmail.com; south end of the Sculpture Factory, 139 Xinchangdong Lu; 新厂东路139号 (雕塑瓷厂前门门口内; dm ¥45-50, r ¥128-148) Located inside the Sculpture Factory arts district, about 3km east of the town centre, this is the only hostel in Jĭngdézhèn but is smart, clean and has English-speaking staff and a cafe. No website, but you can book through www.yhachina.com.

Jĭnjiāng Inn HOTEL $$
(锦江之星; Jĭnjiāng Zhīxīng; ☑0798 857 1111; www.jinjianginns.com, in Chinese only; 1 Zhushan Xilu; 珠山西路1号; r from ¥169; ❇🛜) Comfortable, well-run chain hotel overlooking Zhūshān Bridge (珠山大桥; Zhūshān Dàqiáo). Has attached restaurant. Bus 5 goes here from both the train station and the main bus station.

8 Dù Chúfáng JIANGXI $$
(八渡厨房; Bādù Chúfáng; 57 Guangchang Nanlu; 广场南路57号; mains ¥20-50; ⊙11am-9.30pm) Popular modern restaurant serving Jiāngxī specialities such as niúqi chōngtiān (牛气冲天; spicy beef claypot), xiāngcūn lǎodòufu (乡村老豆腐; village-style tofu) and hóngshāo huángyātou 红烧黄丫头; braised river fish). There are smaller, cheaper restaurants over the road, serving noodles and the like.

🛍 Shopping

Jĭnchānglì Porcelain Market MALL
(金昌利陶瓷大厦; Jĭnchānglì táocí dàshà; 2 Zhushan Zhonglu; 珠山中路2号; ⊙9am-6pm) This multi-storey shopping centre, specialising entirely in porcelain, isn't as pleasant a place to shop for ceramics as the Sculpture Factory, but it sure does stock a lot of tea sets!

ℹ Getting There and Away

AIR
There are daily flights to Běijīng and Shànghǎi. Book tickets though www.ctrip.com, or at the CITS office behind Jĭnjiāng Inn. The airport shut-

Jǐngdézhèn

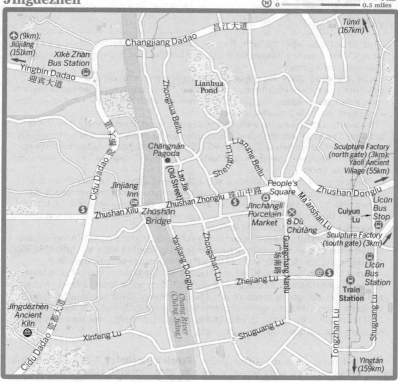

Jǐngdézhèn

tle bus (机场巴士; *jīchǎng bāshì*; ¥10) meets arriving flights and goes to the train station, via the bus station and People's Sq (人民广场, Rénmín Guǎngchǎng). A taxi costs at least ¥60.

BUS

Jǐngdézhèn's main bus station is called **Xīkè Zhàn** (西客站; Yingbin Dadao; 迎宾大道). Services include the following:

Nánchāng ¥85, three hours, hourly 6.50am to 7.30pm

Nánchāng Airport ¥60, three hours, every two hours, 6.50am to 5.50pm

Jiǔjiāng ¥56, 90 minutes, hourly 7.30am to 6.30pm

Wùyuán ¥30, one hour, 7.40am and 1.40pm

Yīngtán ¥61, 2½ hours, 7.40am, 9.15am, 1.20pm and 5pm

Yùshān ¥91, four hours, 8.20am

TRAIN

There's a train-ticket booking office beside Jǐnjiāng Inn. Services include the following:

Běijīng K-class hard sleeper ¥350, 23 hours, 5.54am

Huángshān K-class hard seat ¥25, three to four hours, three daytime trains (5.54am, 4.20pm and 5.44pm)

Nánchāng K-class hard seat ¥41 to ¥47, five hours, two daily (7.33am and 1.47pm)

Shànghǎi K-class hard sleeper ¥200, 17 hours, 5.44pm

Wùyuán 婺源

📞 0793 / POP 81,200

The countryside around Wùyuán is home to some of southeastern China's most immaculate views. Parcelled away in this hilly pocket is a scattered cluster of picturesque Huīzhōu villages, where old China remains preserved in enticing panoramas of ancient bridges, trickling streams and stone-flagged alleyways. For more on Huīzhōu villages, see p394.

WORTH A TRIP

YÁOLǏ 瑶里

Situated on the banks of the Yáohé River, and surrounded by forested hills and tea plantations, **Yáolǐ Ancient Village** (瑶里古镇; Yáolǐ Gǔzhèn), 90 minutes from Jǐngdézhèn, is a gorgeous rural getaway.

Like Jǐngdézhèn, Yáolǐ was one of China's original centres for porcelain production, and there's an ancient kiln site you can visit here. The village itself is made up of elegant, moss-hewn, stone-walled courtyard homes, many of which are still lived in, and wandering its tight, riverside pathways is a treat.

It's free to walk around the village but you need a ticket to enter any of the notable buildings. The ¥150 'through ticket' gives you access to all the sights, but better value is the ¥60 ticket, which gets you in to the village's four best sights, including the Ancient Kiln and the engaging **Chéng Ancestral Hall** (程民宗词; Chéngmín Zōngcí), where you can buy your ticket.

The **Ancient Kiln** (古窑; Gǔyáo) is about 3km beyond the village (away from Jǐngdézhèn); walk along the country road and you'll see the entrance on your right. It contains a collection of sights, all strung out along a riverside walk (give yourself at least an hour here). Don't miss the Song-dynasty 'dragon kiln' (龙窑; *lóngyáo*), which was built up a slope to increase the heat of the kiln's fire.

Simple restaurants, teahouses and family-run **guesthouses** (农家乐; *nóngjiālè*) are dotted around the village, including cute **Píngcháng Rénjia** (平常人家; ☎150 7980 8902; Yáolǐ Gǔzhèn; 瑶里古镇; r ¥80; ❄📶), to the left of the river as you enter the village.

Direct buses to Yáolǐ (¥14, 90 minutes) leave from Jǐngdézhèn's **Lǐcūn Bus Station** (李村车站; Lǐcūn Chēzhàn; Shuguang Lu; 曙光路) at 7.30am and 2.30pm, and return at 9am and 3.40pm. Alternatively, catch a bus to Éhú (鹅湖; every 20 minutes until 5pm) from the same station, then change for Yáolǐ (frequent). To get to Lǐcūn Bus Station, take Bus 1 to **Lǐcūn Bus Stop** (里村车站; Lǐcūn Chēzhàn; Cuiyun Lu; 翠云路), walk back on yourself, cross the junction and it will be on your right.

Despite lending its name to the entire area, Wùyuán itself is a fairly bog-standard town, but it has some comfortable hotels, and is where you can arrange bicycle hire for cycling trips into the countryside.

Wengong Beilu (文公北路), and its southern extension Wengong Nanlu (文公南路), is the main north–south drag.

Sleeping

Yíngdū Bīnguǎn HOTEL $
(迎都宾馆; ☎734 8620; 13 Wengong Nanlu, 文公南路13号; r ¥100; ❄@📶) Centrally located hotel in reasonable condition. Bus 1 to People's Hospital (Rénmín Yīyuàn).

Tiānmǎ Hotel HOTEL $$
(天马大酒店; Tiānmǎ Dàjiǔdiàn; ☎736 7123; www.wytm.cn; 119 Wengong Beilu, 文公北路119号; r from ¥628, discounted to ¥158; ❄@📶) This smart hotel, opposite Běizhàn (North Bus Station), is comfortable. Breakfast included.

Information

ATMs are plentiful in Wùyuán, but not in the villages, so load up with cash here.

People's Hospital (人民医院; Rénmín Yīyuàn; Wengong Nanlu) Bus 1 goes here.

Public Security Bureau (PSB; 公安局; Gōng'ānjú; 2 Huancheng Beilu; ⌚8-11.30am & 2.30-5.30pm) Bus 1 goes here.

Qǐháng Wǎngbā (启航网吧; Wengong Nanlu; per hr ¥3; ⌚24hr) Internet cafe; next to the People's Hospital.

Xīnhuá Bookstore (新华书店; Xīnhuá Shūdiàn; Tianyou Xilu; 天佑西路; ⌚8am-8pm) The **Wùyuán Tourist Map** (旅游交通图; *lǚyóu jiāotōng tú;* ¥6) sold here is in Chinese only, but includes a street map of Wùyuán town and a road map of the surrounding countryside. Very useful if you intend to cycle out to the villages. Bus 1 goes here, or walk downhill along Wengong Nanlu, bear left and it's on your left.

Getting There & Around

Local Bus 1 (¥1; 6am to 6pm), from Wùyuán Bus Station forecourt, goes to North Bus Station and People's Hospital before terminating at the new train station.

BUS

Wùyuán Bus Station (婺源汽车站; Wùyuán qìchēzhàn) is about 2km west of town. Bus services include the following:

Hángzhōu ¥140, 3½ hours, 9.10am, 1.30pm and 4.30pm

Jiǔjiāng ¥100, 2½ hours, 8.20am, 11.50am and 2.30pm

Nánchāng ¥111, 3½ hours, 8am, 10am, 12.10pm, 2pm and 5pm

Shànghǎi South ¥210, six hours, 9.50am and 10.30am

Sānqīng Mountain (east section) ¥32, 1½ hours, 11am

Túnxī ¥46, 2½ hours, 8.20am and 1.20pm

Yùshān ¥46, 2½ hours, 8.10am, 11am and 1.20pm

Services from the smaller **North Bus Station** (北站; Běizhàn) include the following:

Guānkēng ¥23, 2½ hours, 7am, 8.30am, 11am and 2.30pm

Lǐkēng ¥6, 20 minutes, half-hourly (6.30am to 5.20pm)

Lǐngjiǎo ¥20, 90 minutes, 8am, 9.20am, 10.30am, 1.30pm and 3.10pm

Qīnghuá (via Sīkǒu) ¥10, 30 minutes, half-hourly (7am to 5pm)

Xiǎoqī ¥15, one hour, hourly (6.30am to 3.30pm)

TRAIN

Wùyuán's new **train station** (火车站; huǒ-chēzhàn) was due to open sometime in 2015. It will form part of the high-speed rail line from Fúzhōu to Héféi, where it will connect with another high-speed line to Běijīng.

Around Wùyuán

Wùyuán has become a massively popular destination with domestic tourists in the past few years. Avoid public holidays and, if possible, weekends.

There are two main ticketing options: either a five-day pass (¥210), which grants you admission to 12 villages/scenic areas, or single tickets (¥60) at each village.

Lesser-known villages, such as Guānkēng, Lǐngjiǎo, Qìngyuán and Chángxī, are free to visit.

Pretty much every village will have accommodation (住宿; zhùsù) of some sort. Expect to pay around ¥30 to ¥40 per person per night, plus about the same for a meal.

ⓘ Getting Around

It's relatively easy to bus-hop your way from village to village if you stick to the more popular villages.

Buses, for example, shuttle between Wùyuán and Jiāngwān – via Lǐkēng and Wāngkǒu – every 20 minutes until 5pm. Likewise, there are frequent services along the Wùyuán-to-Qīnghuá road, via Sīkǒu.

If you're trying to get to a more remote village, then consider taking a motorbike taxi. Expect to pay around ¥20 for a 10km-ride.

The Villages

LǏKĒNG 李坑

Lǐkēng (admission ¥60) is the most picturesque village in the area (although the new elevated high-speed train line at one end does its best to spoil the scene). It enjoys a stupendous riverside setting, hung with lanterns, threaded by narrow alleys and tightly bound together by quaint bridges. Come nighttime, it's even more serene, with riverside lanes glowing softly under red lanterns and old-fashioned street lamps.

Lǐkēng's highly photogenic focal point hinges on the confluence of its two streams, traversed by the bump of the 300-year-old Tōngjì Bridge (通济桥; Tōngjì Qiáo) and signposted by the Shēnmíng Pavilion (申明亭; Shēnmíng Tíng), one of the village's signature sights, its wooden benches polished smooth with age.

Among the báicài (Chinese cabbage) draped from bamboo poles and chunks of cured meat hanging out in the air from crumbling, mildewed buildings, notable structures include the Patina House (铜录坊; Tónglù Fáng), erected during Qing times by a copper merchant, the rebuilt old stage (古戏台; gǔxìtái), where Chinese opera and performances are still held during festivals, and spirit walls erected on the riverbank to shield residents from the sound of cascading water.

Walk in any direction and you will hit the countryside.

Accommodation is easy to find; try the helpful Brook Hotel (小桥驿栈; Xiǎoqiáo Yìzhàn; ☑138 7032 7901, 138 7934 9519; limin608058@126.com; d ¥100; ❋ @ ☞) near Tōngjì Bridge, where young mum 'Linda' speaks some English, or the charming Guāngmíng Teahouse (光明茶楼; Guāngmíng Chálóu; ☑0793 737 0999; d ¥80; ❋ ☞), just beyond it, perched above the village stream. Guāngmíng Teahouse is a lovely spot for lunch (English menu; mains ¥12 to ¥40) even if you don't stay the night.

Around Wùyuán

Buses drop you off at the village turn-off, from where it's a five-minute walk to the ticket office.

Note, there are two Lǐkēng villages in the region. This one is smaller, so is sometimes called Xiǎo Lǐkēng (小李坑; Little Lǐkēng).

WĀNGKŎU 汪口

Less popular than some of the other ticketed villages, Wāngkǒu (admission ¥60), 9km northeast of Lǐkēng, enjoys a fine location beside a rushing weir at the confluence of two large rivers.

XIǍOQǏ 晓起

About 35km from Wùyuán, Xiǎoqǐ (admission ¥60) dates back to AD 787. There are actually two villages here: the larger, more touristy lower Xiǎoqǐ (下晓起; Xià Xiǎoqǐ) and the much quieter upper Xiǎoqǐ (上晓起; Shàng Xiǎoqǐ), where you'll find a fascinating old tea factory (传统生态茶作坊; chuántǒng shēngtài chá zuòfang). The two are linked by a timeworn, 500m-long stone pathway. Both parts of the village have accommodation.

GUĀNKĒNG 官坑

If you've had enough of the jostling tour groups, the isolated village of Guānkēng is a wonderful place to escape to. It doesn't have the architectural beauty of more famous villages here – although it is still highly attractive, nestled, as it is, in the pinch of two valleys – but unlike some other villages it is largely undeveloped and has never been repackaged for the tour bus crowd. This is also the start point of a wonderful three-hour hike to the equally quiet village of Lǐngjiǎo (see p454).

A few independent Chinese travellers come here, so there are a couple of guesthouses; riverside Guānkēng Fàndiàn (官坑饭店; ☎ 0793 725 9588; beside the arched bridge; per person ¥40; ✳ ☎) does good meals and has someone who speaks a little English. Lǚyǒu Zhījiā (驴友之家; ☎ 158 7936 4277; per person ¥20-40) has great views of the village from its rooftop.

Buses from here to Wùyuán (¥22, two hours) leave at 6am, 6.40am, 7.30am and 11am.

QĪNGHUÁ 清华

Qīnghuá is the largest and least-captivating place in Wùyuán, but it has restaurants, hotels, grocery stores and ATMs so can be a handy stop.

Laojie (老街; Old Street), which leads down to the 800-year-old Rainbow Bridge (彩虹桥; Cǎihóng Qiáo), is the town's most interesting street, and has a few simple guesthouses (客栈; kèzhàn). For something more comfortable try Qīnghuá Bīnguǎn (清华宾馆; ☎ 0793 724 2789; r ¥238, discounted to ¥120; ✳ ☎), the town's best hotel.

Buses leave from the turn-off into the town, and include the following:

Jǐngdézhèn ¥25, two hours, 7.20am, 8.30am and 2pm

Wùyuán (via Sīkǒu) ¥10, 30 minutes, half-hourly 6am to 5pm

Buses between Wùyuán and Lǐngjiǎo also stop here.

SĪXĪ & YÁNCŪN 思溪、延村

The village of Sīxī (admission including Yáncūn Village ¥60) is a delightful little place favoured by film crews, with the prow-shaped, covered wooden **Tóngjì Bridge** (通济桥; Tóngjì Qiáo) at its entrance, dating back to the 15th century. Follow the signs to the numerous Qing-dynasty residences, making sure not to miss the large **Jìngxù Hall** (敬序堂; Jìngxù Táng). A 15-minute walk back along the road, towards Sīkǒu, brings you to Yáncūn, Sīxī's more homely sibling, where you'll find yet more Qing architecture, plus the outstanding Go Home Hotel.

To get here, take any Wùyuán–Qīnghuá bus (¥3, 20 minutes) and get off at Sīkǒu (思口). Motorbikes will take you the rest of the way (¥5), or just walk (3km).

Go Home Hotel (归去来兮; Guīqù Láixī; ☎ 0793 733 5118; Yáncūn Village; 延村; r ¥328-1180; ✳☎), housed in a 270-year-old former residence in Yáncūn, is an immaculately renovated boutique hotel and is the most appealing place to stay in any of the villages around Wùyuán. Each room is different (ask to see them all), but decorated beautifully with period wooden furniture. Breakfast is free. Lunch and dinner cost ¥50 each. No website, but you can book a room through ctrip.com (search for Guiqulaixi Hotel).

Sānqīng Mountain 三清山

☑ 0793

Imagine a hiking trail built into a sheer rock face, looking out onto a forest of fantastical granite spires and a gorgeous canopy sprinkled with white rhododendron blooms. This is one of the many walks you can do at **Sānqīng Mountain** (三清山; Sānqīng Shān; www. sanqingshan.com.cn; adult/student ¥150/80), one of the most underrated national parks in eastern China.

CYCLING AROUND WÙYUÁN

Though you can reach most of Wùyuán's villages by bus, cycling gives you more freedom to village-hop around the surrounding countryside. Roads are in good nick and well signposted in pinyin as well as Chinese characters. You can pick up a Chinese map of the area from Xīnhuá Bookstore (p450).

One possible two- to three-day trip is the 130-km circuit from Wùyuán, passing Lǐkēng, Xiǎoqǐ and the Duànxīn Reservoir, before looping back to Wùyuán via Qīnghuá and Sīkǒu. Follow Wengong Beilu north out of Wùyuán to pick up signs to Lǐkēng.

How long the circuit takes you depends on how much time you spend in each village, but the total cycling time (not including side trips to villages such as Guānkēng and Lǐng-jiào (both 30 minutes from the main road)) is about seven or eight hours. You could do it in two days, but taking three days makes more sense.

Some roads are hilly, but the only really tough climb is the one-hour slog from Jiānglǐng up to the Duànxīn Reservoir.

Individual cycling times from Wùyuán to various villages:

➡ **Lǐkēng** one hour

➡ **Wāngkǒu** 90 minutes

➡ **Xiǎoqǐ** 2½ hours

➡ **Guānkēng** 4½ hours

➡ **Sīkǒu** one hour

➡ **Qīnghuá** 90 minutes

In Wùyuán, the following places rent bikes; don't forget to ask for a bike lock (车锁; chēsuǒ):

➡ **XDS Bikes** (喜德盛自行车; Xǐdéshèng Zìxíngchē; ☎ 187 2056 3868; 56 Wengong Beilu; 文公北路56号; ☉ 6.30am-10pm) This place rents brand new mountain bikes for ¥100 per day (deposit ¥1000). It is located down the hill from Tiānmǎ Hotel (p450).

➡ **Merida Bike Shop** (美利达自行车; Měilìdá Zìxíngchē; ☎ 0793 734 1818, 135 1703 3662; Liangli Shanlu; 凉笠山路 (二环路南段); ☉ 8.30am-9pm) Rents good-quality second-hand mountain bikes for ¥30 per day (deposit ¥500). Helpful staff. It is located a short walk downhill from Tiānmǎ Hotel (p450). Turn left at the crossroads, then second left.

WALKING WÙYUÁN'S ANCIENT POSTAL TRAILS

Many of Wùyuán's villages are linked by timeworn **postal roads** (驿道; *yìdào*) that today provide hikers with the perfect excuse to explore the area's gorgeous backcountry: imagine wild azalea, wisteria and iris blooms dotting steep hills cut by cascading streams and you're off to the right start.

Most trails are difficult to navigate without help from a local, but one fabulous 8km-long, three-hour trail linking the rarely visited villages of **Guānkēng** (官坑) and **Lǐngjiǎo** (岭脚) has bilingual signposts along its route, so can be done independently.

The path takes you up and over a pass, and has numerous steps, so is unfeasible if you've cycled out here.

Follow the hiking sign beside Guānkēng Fàndiàn, in Guānkēng village, and head straight upstream. After the second pavilion (near the top of the pass) turn left, then right immediately afterwards, to continue on the path to Lǐngjiǎo, from where you can catch a bus back to Wùyuán (¥20, 90 minutes, 7am, 11.30am and 1pm).

Unlike Huángshān, its more famous neighbour to the north, Sānqīng Mountain has a spiritual legacy and has been a place of retreat for Taoist adepts for centuries. The name Sānqīng means 'The Three Pure Ones', in reference to the three main peaks, believed to resemble Taoism's three most important deities. Views are spectacular in any season, reaching a climax when the rhododendrons bloom in late May.

There are enough trails that you could easily spend two days up here, though a long day hike is doable. There are two main access points: the southern section (南部; *nán bù*) and the eastern section (东部; *dōng bù*).

You can buy maps (¥5), or photograph ones on signboards.

◉ Sights & Activities

Nánqīng Garden   MOUNTAIN
(南清苑, Nánqīng Yuàn) Sānqīng Mountain's main summit area is known as the Nánqīng Garden, a looping trail that wends beneath strange pinnacles and connects the southern and eastern sections.

West Coast Trail   HIKING
(西海岸, Xī Hǎi'àn) The spectacularly exposed West Coast Trail was built into the cliff face at an average altitude of 1600m. This trail eventually leads to the secluded **Taoist Sānqīng Temple** (三清宫; Sānqīng Gōng), established during the Ming dynasty. It's one of the few Taoist temples in Jiāngxī to have survived the Cultural Revolution.

Sunshine Coast Trail   HIKING
(阳光岸, Yángguāng Àn) The Sunshine Coast Trail winds through a forest of ancient rhododendrons, sweet chestnut, bamboo, mag-

nolia and pine, and even features a glass-floored observation platform. There are lots of steps here; take it on the way back from the Taoist Sānqīng Temple.

🛏 Sleeping & Eating

You can sleep in three areas: on the summit, at the trailheads or in the town of Yùshān. Prices rise on weekends, when it's a good idea to reserve if you want to sleep at the trailheads or on the summit.

🛏 Yùshān

Fāngfāng Bīnguǎn   GUESTHOUSE $
(芳芳宾馆; ☑ 220 5890, 187 7931 6629; off Renmin Dadao, 人民大道日景现代城; s/d ¥60/90; ❄ @) The best of a few simple family-run guesthouses near the bus station. Left, then second left.

International Trade Hotel   HOTEL $$
(国贸大酒店; Guómào Dàjiǔdiàn; ☑ 0793 235 3922; Renmin Beilu, 人民北路（汽车站对面）; r ¥218, discounted to ¥198) Smart hotel with good-value, spacious rooms. Opposite the bus station.

Xīntíngjì Tǔcàiguǎn   JIANGXI $$
(新廷记土菜馆; Renmin Dadao; 日景现代城国际公寓126号; mains ¥20-50; ◷ 9am-9pm) Clean friendly restaurant with a clear photo menu and very tasty dishes. Specialties include *jīn-pái guōmèn tǔjī* (金牌锅焖土鸡; free-range chicken casserole), *xiǎochǎo huángniúròu* (小炒黄牛肉; spicy beef stir-fry) and *suìjiāo báiyù dòu* (碎椒白玉豆; a simple but tasty broad bean dish). Turn left out of the bus station and it's on your left just before the cross-roads.

At the Trailheads

There's at least a dozen hotels at both the eastern and southern trailheads.

Dìwáng Shānzhuāng HOTEL **$$**
(地王山庄; ☑ 213 7999; d from ¥280, discounted to ¥100) Convenient rooms at Sānqīng Mountain's eastern trailhead.

Nánqīng Kèzhàn GUESTHOUSE **$$**
(南清客栈; ☑ 138 7930 6267, 0793 218 0019; southern entrance; 三青山南部（索道站附近）; tw ¥160) Simple guesthouse near the cable car at Sānqīng Mountain's southern trailhead.

Sānqīngshān International Resort HOTEL **$$$**
(三清山国际度假酒店; Sānqīngshān Guójì Dùjià Jiǔdiàn; ☑ 223 3333; www.sqshotel.com; tw from ¥1988, discounted to ¥788; ☒) At the southern trailhead, this stylish hotel is Sānqīng Mountain's best.

On the Summit

Rìshàng Bīnguǎn HOTEL **$$$**
(日上宾馆; ☑ 218 9377; r from ¥480) One of several summit hotels; a 10-minute walk past the top of Sānqīng's southern chairlift.

Nǚshén Hotel HOTEL **$$$**
(女神酒店; Nǚshén Jiǔdiàn; ☑ 218 9366; r from ¥480) A 20-minute walk past the top of Sānqīng's eastern chairlift.

ⓘ Getting There & Away

Sānqīng Mountain is accessed via the town of Yùshān (玉山). The 11am bus from Wùyuán to Yùshān stops at Sānqīng Mountain (eastern section). The return to Wùyuán leaves at around 7pm.

BUS

Yùshān Bus Station (玉山汽车站; *Yùshān qìchēzhàn*) services:
Hángzhōu ¥105, four hours, 7.30am, 9am, 11.20am and 3.30pm
Nánchāng ¥80, four to five hours, 7.10am and 3pm
Shànghǎi ¥145, 5½ hours, 10am
Wùyuán ¥45, 2½ hours, 7.55am and 1.20pm

TRAIN

Local Bus 8 (¥1) links the train and bus stations, but is only hourly. A motor-rickshaw costs around ¥5. Destinations from **Yùshān train station** (玉山火车站; Yùshān huǒchēzhàn) include the following:

Hángzhōu K-class hard seat ¥52, four to five hours, four morning trains (6.47am, 6.54am, 7.05m and 8.38am)
Nánchāng K-class hard seat ¥44, four hours, four daytime trains (8.39am, 11.57am, 1.51pm and 3.47pm)
Shànghǎi South K-class hard seat/sleeper ¥75/138, seven hours, seven daily
Yīngtán K-class hard seat ¥24, two hours, six daytime trains (8.39am to 5.10pm)

ⓘ Getting Around

Buses (¥17, 80 minutes, 6.30am to 5.20pm) run from Yùshān bus station to the start of both the eastern section (东部) and southern section (南部) – make sure you specify your destination, as no buses link the two sections and they are at least 20km apart. The last buses back to Yùshān leave just after 4.30pm.

A **cable car** (三清山索道; Sānqīng Shān Suǒdào; one way/return ¥70/125) leaves from both sections. The eastern section cable car ride is more spectacular, but leaves you further from the West Coast Trail; if you're walking, the southern section is a much shorter hike. Note, you can use your return ticket on either cable car.

Estimated hiking times from the southern section trailhead:
➡ top of southern-section cable car: 1½ hours
➡ top of eastern-section cable car: three hours
➡ bottom of eastern-section cable car: five hours
➡ Nánqīng Garden loop and back: four hours

Lónghǔ Mountain 龙虎山

☑ 0701

Ideal for a family trip, Lónghǔ Mountain (龙虎山; Lónghǔ Shān) combines beautiful riverside scenery and a touch of Taoist history with raft rides, a miniature train and even a 4D cinema.

During the Song dynasty (AD960–1279) Lónghǔ Mountain became the centre of the emergent Zhèngyī sect, which claimed to represent the teachings of religious Taoism's founder, Zhang Daoling (AD34–156). Together with the Quánzhēn sect, Zhèngyī Taoism was one of the most prominent schools of Taoism in late imperial China, and there were once over 100 temples and monasteries here.

The Cultural Revolution may have wiped clean the physical traces of this past, but with a setting reminiscent of a landscape painting – a winding river, clusters of red sandstone peaks, grazing water buffaloes and solitary herons – this scenic area offers an easily packaged taste of the lush Jiāngxī countryside.

LÓNGNÁN (龙南)

In the deep south of Jiāngxī lies the rarely visited Hakka country, a region of lush hills peppered with fortified villages, unusually built in rectangular shapes, unlike the mostly circular tǔlóu (roundhouse) of Fújiàn. Although there are estimates of some 370 such dwellings in Lóngnán County, we've narrowed down the choices here to two relatively easy to access areas, both of which can be visited from the riverside town of Lóngnán.

Sights

Built in 1827 by Xu Mingjun, a wealthy lumber merchant, **Guānxī New Fort** (关西新围; Guānxī Xīn Wéi; admission ¥10) is the largest and most ornate fortified village in the county. The smaller, more run-down fort just behind it is known as *lǎo wéi* (old fort) and was built by Xu's father. Nearby is the **Hakka Wine Castle** (客家酒堡; Kèjiā Jiǔbǎo; admission ¥15, but rarely applied), built in 1836 by a rich wine producer. A bus from outside Xīnxìng Bīnguǎn in Binjiang Sq in Lóngnán runs to Guānxī (关西; ¥5.50, 40 minutes, every 45 minutes from 6.15am to 5.40pm), passing by the Hakka Wine Castle (¥3).

A number of crumbling old fortified villages lie in the vicinity of Yángcūn (杨村) town, including the fascinating, 350-year-old **Yànyì Wéi** (燕翼围; admission ¥10, but rarely applied), the tallest such residence in the county (four storeys). It's still lived in by villagers and you can climb all four storeys. Don't miss stopping off at the striking **Wǔdāng Mountain** (武当山; Wǔdāng Shān; admission ¥15; ☉8am-5.30pm), a group of weathered sandstone peaks (not to be confused with Húběi's more famous Wǔdāng Shān), which can be climbed (one hour) for fabulous views of the surrounding subtropical forest. To get to Yángcūn, take a bus (¥12.5, 1¼ hours, frequent) from the small bus station at 99 Longding Dadao (龙鼎大道99号) in Lóngnán. The bus passes Wǔdāng Mountain (one hour).

In Lóngnán, you can stay at **Xīnxìng Bīnguǎn** (新兴宾馆; ☎0797 353 6288; Binjiang Sq; d/tw ¥128/148, discounted to ¥70/90; ❄@✆), which overlooks Binjiang Sq.

If you're interested in exploring other traditional Hakka dwellings – or just fancy taking the back route into Guǎngdōng province – you can catch a bus from Lóngnán's long-distance bus station to Méizhōu (梅州; ¥80, 4 hours, 7.20am), where you'll find China's largest cluster of *wéilóngwū* (coiled-dragon houses). From there you can catch a bus on to Yǒngdìng, to see Fújiàn's famed *tǔlóu*.

Getting There & Around

Two direct trains to Lóngnán run from Nánchāng (hard seat ¥75, 7½ hours, 3.33pm and 3.47pm) while one runs from Guǎngzhōu East (hard seat ¥87, 5½ hours, 11.25am). Otherwise take a bus from Nánchāng to Gànzhōu (赣州; ¥120, 5½ hours, hourly, 7.20am to 6.50pm), where you can transfer to a Lóngnán bus (¥58, two hours, hourly until 6pm). The bus from Gànzhōu will stop at Lóngnán's long-distance bus station (长途汽车站; chángtú qìchēzhàn) before terminating at the small bus station at 99 Longding Dadao, which is 200m from Binjiang Sq (turn left).

Local Bus 1 (¥1) goes from the train station in Lóngnán, past the long-distance bus station and onto Binjiang Sq (滨江广场; Bīnjiāng Guǎngchǎng).

◉ Sights & Activities

The Lónghǔ Mountain scenic area encompasses 200 sq km, most of which is located along the eastern bank of the Lúxī River. Entrance costs ¥150, but most people buy the **combined ticket** (¥260), which includes admission to seven sites and a raft ride, as well as transport on miniature trains (main entrance to Zhèngyī Temple) and shuttle buses (from Zhèngyī Temple to the Residence of the Celestial Masters). To get the most out of your visit, narrow your sightseeing options to two main areas: the Residence of the Celestial Masters and Elephant's Trunk Hill.

At the main entrance are two small museums, the **Taoist Museum** (龙虎山道教博物馆; Lónghǔ Shān Dàojiào Bówùguǎn; ☉8am-5pm), with information in Chinese only, and the **Geology Museum** (龙虎山地质博物馆; Lónghǔ Shān Dìzhí Bówùguǎn; ☉8am-5pm), with detailed explanations of Lónghǔ Mountain's formation. The dinosaur-themed **4D-cinema** (电影院; Diànyǐngyuàn; ¥25) is above the ticket office.

Residence of the
Celestial Masters
TAOIST TEMPLE

(天师府; Tiānshī Fǔ) This is the largest and best-preserved temple in the area. It was originally built in the Song dynasty, thoroughly renovated in the Qing dynasty and then again in the 1990s. The oldest building still standing is the **Sanctuary of Triple Introspection** (三省堂; Sān Xǐng Táng), which dates to 1865. To get here, walk 15 minutes through old Shàngqīng village from the shuttle drop-off. Another 500m along Fuqian Jie (府前街) is an abandoned **Catholic church** (天主教堂; Tiānzhǔjiào Táng).

Located about 28km from Lónghǔ Mountain's main entrance.

Shàngqīng Palace
TAOIST TEMPLE

(大上清宫; Dà Shàngqīng Gōng) This temple complex was almost entirely destroyed by fire; only the entrance gate, first courtyard (with the drum and bell tower) and a few side halls remain. A mythic spot, Shàngqīng Palace is the alleged site of the residence of the first Celestial Master (Zhang Daoling).

Elephant's Trunk Hill
SCENIC AREA

(象鼻山; Xiàngbí Shān) Close to Lónghǔ Mountain's main entrance, this is the first stop you'll reach on the area's miniature train. Here you can hike a loop past rock formations and rebuilt temples, then descend to the river from where you'll be able to spy Lónghǔ Mountain's 2500-year-old **hanging coffins** (悬棺; xuán guān) on the opposite side of the bank.

🛏 Sleeping & Eating

Hotels and restaurants are conveniently based near the main entrance. There are also small restaurants inside the park, at Shàngqīng village.

Lónghǔ Shān Kèzhàn
GUESTHOUSE $

(龙虎山客栈; ☑665 9506; 39 Xianrencheng Lu; 仙人城路39号; r with/without air-con ¥80/60;

※ 🛜) One block back from the main entrance to Lónghǔ Mountain scenic area, this little guesthouse is clean and friendly.

Róngshèng Bīnguǎn
HOTEL $$

(荣盛宾馆; Róngshèng Bīnguǎn; ☑665 7666; 龙虎山新大门对面; tw from ¥168, discounted to ¥150; ※@🛜) Tasteful and surprisingly sophisticated, Róngshèng is opposite the Lónghǔ Mountain park entrance, on the corner.

ℹ Information

There are **internet cafes** (网吧; wǎngbā) and **ATMs** by the train station in Yīngtán.

ℹ Getting There & Around

Lónghǔ Mountain is near the small city of Yīngtán (鹰潭). To get to Lónghǔ Mountain from Yīngtán, take bus K2, which runs from the train station, past the bus station and on to the main entrance (¥3, 25 minutes, 6.15am to 7pm, every 15 minutes).

Services from **Yīngtán Train Station** (鹰潭火车站; Yīngtán huǒchēzhàn):

Hángzhōu D-class bullet, ¥148, four hours, five daily (9.17am to 3.42pm)

Hángzhōu T/K-class hard seat/sleeper ¥72/132, six to seven hours, 20 daily

Jǐngdézhèn K-class hard seat ¥24, three hours, four daytime trains (8.32am, 10.23am, 1.17pm and 2.52pm)

Nánchāng D-class bullet ¥43, one hour, four daily (1.02pm, 8.23pm, 9.27pm and 10.40pm)

Nánchāng K-class hard seat ¥24, two hours, 20 daily

Shànghǎi Hóngqiáo D-class bullet ¥195, 5½ hours, four daily (9.17am, 10.05am, 2.37pm and 3.42pm)

Shànghǎi South K-class hard seat/sleeper ¥94 to ¥168, eight to nine hours, 30 daily

Yùshān K-class hard seat ¥24, two hours, six daytime trains (6.27am to 5.56pm)

Services from **Yīngtán bus station** (鹰潭客运站; Yīngtán kèyùnzhàn):

Jǐngdézhèn ¥55, three hours, 7.40am, 8.40am, 12.40pm and 1.50pm

Nánchāng ¥42, two hours, hourly 7.30am to 6.15pm

Wùyuán ¥76, 3½ hours, 8.30am, 11.50am and 1.20pm

LUCA TETTONI / GETTY IMAGES ©

1. Dim sum and tea **2.** Sīchuānese *dàndan miàn*
3. Lamb hotpot, Hong Kong **4.** Steamed shrimp dumplings

THOMAS RUECKER / GETTY IMAGES ©

Cuisine

To the Chinese, food is life. Dining is the cherished high point of the daily social calendar and often the one occasion to stop work and fully relax. The only problem is knowing where to begin: the sheer variety on offer can have your head spinning and your tummy quivering.

Noodles

Marco Polo may have nicked the recipe to make spaghetti (so they say), but he didn't quite get the flavouring right. Noodles range across an exciting spectrum of taste, from the wincingly spicy *dàndan miàn* (spicy noodles) through to the supersalty *zhájiàng miàn (fried sauce noodles)*.

Dim Sum

Dim sum is steamed up across China, but like the Cantonese dialect, it's best left to the masters of the south to get it right. Hong Kong, Macau and Guǎngzhōu should be your first stops – they set the dim sum benchmark.

Dumplings

Set your compass north and northeast for the best *jiǎozi (*dumplings) – leek, pork, lamb, crabmeat wrapped in an envelope of dough. If you like them crispy, get them *guōtiē* (fried). Shànghǎi's interpretation is *xiǎolóngbāo* – scrummy and steamed.

Peking Duck

Purists insist you must be in Běijīng for true Peking duck roasted to an amber hue over fruit tree wood. You might as well take their advice as that's where you'll find the best Peking duck restaurants.

Hotpot

An all-weather meal, hotpot is ideal for banishing the bitter cold of a northern winter, while in steaming Chóngqìng old folk devour the spiciest variety in the height of summer.

KEREN SU / GETTY IMAGES ©

1. Ceremony Confucius Temple (p164), Qūfù **2.** Temple of Heaven Park (p75), Běijīng **3.** Jokhang Temple (p902), Lhasa **4.** Labrang Monastery (p831), Xiàhé

Temples

Divided between Buddhist, Taoist and Confucian faiths, China's temples are places of introspection, peace and absolution. Find them on mountain peaks, in caves, on side streets, hanging from cliffsides or occupying the epicentre of town, from Tibet to Běijīng and beyond.

Temple of Heaven, Běijīng

Not really a temple, but let's not quibble. Běijīng's Temple of Heaven was China's graceful place of worship for the Ming and Qing emperors, encapsulating the Confucian desire for symmetry and order, and harmony between heaven and earth.

Pǔníng Temple, Chéngdé

On a clear day this temple stands out against the hills around Chéngdé, while in the Mahayana Hall is the Guanyin statue, a 22m-high, multiarmed embodiment of Buddhist benevolence – this is perhaps China's most astonishing statue.

Confucius Temple, Qūfù

This is China's largest and most important Confucius Temple. The Shāndōng sage has had an immeasurable influence on the Chinese persona through the millennia – visit the town where it began and try to put his teachings in perspective.

Labrang Monastery, Xiàhé

If it's a hassle to rustle up a Tibet travel permit, pop down to this gargantuan Tibetan monastery in the scenic southwest corner of Gānsù. Its aura of devotion is amplified by the nonstop influx of Tibetan pilgrims and worshippers.

Jokhang Temple, Lhasa

Tibet's holiest place of worship, the Jokhang Temple in Lhasa is a place of pilgrimage for every Tibetan Buddhist at least once in their lifetime.

1. Mountain walkway, Huángshān (p399) 2. Yángshuò (p615)
3. Samye Monastery (p911), Tibet
4. Tiger Leaping Gorge (p687), Yúnnán Province

Hiking

If you're keen to escape the cities into the great outdoors, China's dramatic variety of landscapes is the perfect backdrop for bracing walks – whether island-hopping in Hong Kong, exploring the foothills of the Himalayas or trekking through gorges in Yúnnán province.

Huángshān, Ānhuī

Sooner or later you'll have to hike uphill, and where better than up China's most beautiful mountain. The steps may be punishing, but just focus on the scenery: even if the fabled mists are nowhere to be seen, the views are incredible.

Hong Kong's Outlying Islands & New Territories

A whopping 70% of Hong Kong is hiking territory, so fling off your Gucci loafers, lace up your hiking boots and go from island to island or make a break for the New Territories, where fantastic hiking trails await.

Ganden to Samye, Tibet

You'll need four to five days for this glorious high-altitude hike connecting two of Tibet's most splendid monasteries. The landscape is beautiful, but the trek requires preparation both physically and mentally, plus a Tibet travel permit.

Tiger Leaping Gorge, Yúnnán

The mother of all southwest China's treks, this magnificently named Yúnnán hike is at its most picturesque in early summer. It's not a walk in the park, so plan ahead and give yourself enough time.

Yángshuò, Guǎngxī

Yángshuò's karst topography is truly astonishing. Base yourself in town, give yourself three or four days, and walk your socks off (or hire a bike). Adventurous types can even try rock climbing.

Húnán

POPULATION 66 MILLION

Best Scenery

➜ Zhāngjiājiè (474)

➜ Héng Shān (p472)

➜ Yuèlù Mountain (p467)

➜ Déhāng's Liúshā Falls (p478)

Best for Chinese History

➜ Fènghuáng (p478)

➜ Hóngjiāng old town (p482)

➜ Mao's childhood home (p471)

➜ Chángshā's Old City Walls (p466)

Why Go?

Communist Party cadres might wax lyrical about the sacred standing of Húnán (湖南) in the annals of Chinese history, being as it is the birthplace of Mao Zedong, but it is Húnán's dramatic scenery that is the real draw.

A magnificent landscape of isolated mountain ranges and jagged, karst peaks covers more than 80% of the province. The most astonishing example is found at the phantasmagorical Zhāngjiājiè; one of China's most surreal national parks. Here, as in other parts of the province, geological marvels rise up majestically from green vales fed by tributaries in the fertile Yangzi River basin.

People have long made a home amid Húnán's natural wonders, taming the rocky slopes into terraces of lush fields, and their distinctive cultures live on in charming villages and towns, the most alluring being the historic riverside settlement of Fènghuáng.

When to Go
Chángshā

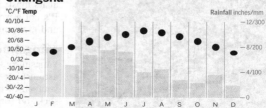

Apr & May After a chilly (though not freezing) winter, spring brings welcome warmth, and mountain flowers.

Sep & Oct Temperatures cool after a scorching summer. Autumnal leaves emblazon Zhāngjiājiè.

Dec–Feb Tour groups disappear from Fènghuáng. Zhāngjiājiè is sometimes brushed with snow.

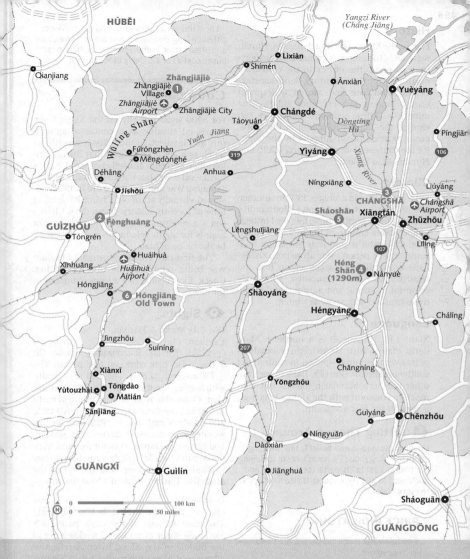

Húnán Highlights

① Hike among the otherworldly peaks of **Zhāngjiājiè** (p474), one of China's most spectacular national parks

② Settle in at a riverside guesthouse in ancient **Fènghuáng** (p478)

③ Sample authentic, chilli-laden *xiāng cài* (Húnán cuisine) in food-loving **Chángshā** (p466)

④ Ascend the sacred slopes of **Héng Shān** (p472)

⑤ Join the masses paying homage to Chairman Mao in **Sháoshān** (p470)

⑥ Wander the Qing-dynasty merchant streets of the rarely visited **Hóngjiāng old town** (p482)

History

During the Ming and Qing dynasties, Húnán was one of the empire's granaries, transporting vast quantities of rice to the embattled north. By the 19th century, land shortages and feudalism had caused widespread unrest among farmers and hill-dwelling minorities. These economic disparities galvanised the Taiping Rebellion in the 1850s, ensuring widespread support by the 1920s for the Chinese Communist Party (CCP) and Húnán's Mao Zedong.

Climate

Subtropical Húnán averages 28°C in summer, and 6°C during its brief winter. Monsoonlike rains fall from April to June, followed by high temperatures and humidity in July and August; Chángshā is positively scorching midsummer. The region's star attraction, Zhāngjiājiè, is beautiful during any season: lush and relatively cool during summer, stunningly colourful in spring and autumn, and sometimes brushed with snow in winter.

Language

Xiāng (湘; Hunanese) is a northern Mandarin dialect with six to eight subdialects of its own commonly spoken in central and southwest Húnán. Gàn (赣; Jiangxinese), another northern Mandarin dialect, but with much in common with the Hakka language, is used in the east and south.

ℹ️ Getting There & Around

Chángshā is loaded with bullet trains, heading south to Guǎngzhōu (2½ hours), north to Běijīng (six hours), east to Shànghǎi (seven hours) and northwest to Xī'ān (six hours). It also has flights to every major city.

PRICE INDICATORS

The following price indicators are used in this region:

Sleeping

$ less than ¥150 (for a room)

$$ ¥150 to ¥400

$$$ more than ¥400

Eating

$ less than ¥40 (for a meal for one)

$$ ¥40 to ¥80

$$$ more than ¥80

Local trains can get you around the province, although long-distance buses are more frequent and often faster. Within towns and cities, local buses cost ¥1 or ¥2. Carry exact change.

Chángshā   长沙

🎵 0731 / POP 2.5 MILLION

For 3000 years this city on the Xiāng River flourished steadily as a centre of agriculture and intellect. In the 1920s it was still so much as it always had been that British philosopher Bertrand Russell compared it to 'a mediaeval town', but not long after, the Sino–Japanese War and a massive fire in 1938 consumed virtually all of old Chángshā, leaving little of its early history. These days, Chángshā – a modern, energetic city – is known mainly for sights relating to a revolutionary by the name of Mao.

The first-rate Húnán Provincial Museum was being rebuilt at the time of writing. Check its website (www.hnmuseums.com) for news.

👁️ Sights

Old City Walls & Tiānxīn Pavilion   HISTORIC SITE

(古城墙，天心阁; Gǔchéngqiáng, Tiānxīn Gé; 3 Tianxin Lu; park admission free, pavilion ¥32; ⏰ 7.30am-6pm; 🚌 202) The old city walls, which once stretched for 9km around ancient Chángshā, were built of rammed earth in 202 BC, reinforced with stone in AD 1372, and finally demolished in 1928, save for this wonderfully imposing 250m-long section. You can enter Tiānxīn Park for free and wander around the old wall, but you have to pay to climb right up on top of it, and to visit the attractive Tiānxīn Pavilion which sits on top.

Orange Isle   PARK

(橘子洲, Júzi Zhōu; ⏰ 24hr; Ⓜ Juzizhou) FREE The most famous of the city's parks is a 5km-long sliver of an island smack-bang in the middle of the Xiāng River. A reflective 32-year-old Mao immortalised it in 'Changsha', probably his best regarded poem, after standing at its southern tip and looking west towards Yuèlù Mountain one autumn day. A towering granite bust of a youthful Chairman with flowing locks now stands at the spot – but faces in a new direction.

You can walk a circuit of the island on the pleasant riverside promenade, or catch a sightseeing electric trolley (¥20). You can also rent tandem bicycles (¥30 per hour) by the metro entrance.

Chángshā

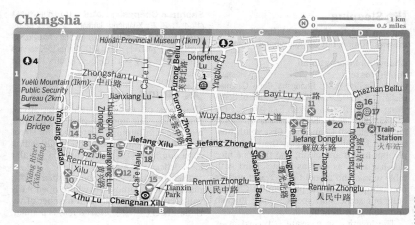

Yuèlù Mountain PARK

(岳麓山; Yuèlù Shān; Yueshan Lu; ⊙24hr; 🚍1, Ⓜ Yingwanzhen) **FREE** This large park on the slopes of Yuèlù Mountain makes a pleasant city break. You can climb to the top in less than an hour; or else go up on the **chairlift** (索道; suǒdào; up ¥30, return ¥50; ⊙9am-5pm), before whizzing back down on the **toboggan ride** (滑道; huá dào; ¥25; ⊙9am-5pm).

To get here, turn left out of Exit 3 of Yingwanzhen metro station, then turn right down Yueshan Lu and the entrance will soon be on your right. Bus 旅1 from the train station stops at the gate.

Chángshā Municipal Museum MUSEUM

(市博物馆; Shì Bówùguǎn; 538 Bayi Lu; ⊙9am-5pm Tue-Sun; Ⓜ Yingbin Road) **FREE** A colossal statue of Mao Zedong affably greets you at the entrance. It's the first clue that despite the paintings, ceramics and jade on display, this museum is really a shrine; note the huge portrait of a young Mao with shafts of light emanating from his head above the entrance.

The museum also houses the former site of the **Húnán CCP Committee** (中共湘区委员会旧址; Zhōng Gòng Xiāngqū Wěiyuánhuì Jiùzhǐ), where Mao lived from 1921 to 1923 while secretly running the local CCP.

Lièshì Park PARK

(烈士公园; Lièshì Gōngyuán; Yingpan Donglu; 营盘东路; ⊙ sunrise-sunset; 🚍136 from train station) **FREE** Tree-shaded and dotted with lakes, leafy Lièshì Park is very popular in the mornings for singing, dancing and taichi.

Chángshā

⊙ Sights

1 Chángshā Municipal Museum............B1
2 Lièshì Park C1
3 Old City Walls & Tiānxīn
   Pavilion.......................................B2
4 Orange Isle A1

🛏 Sleeping

5 Hàntíng Express.............................B2
6 Mini Hotel.....................................C2
7 Sheraton Chángshā Hotel B1

✖ Eating

8 Huǒgōngdiàn..................................A2
9 Huǒgōngdiàn (Wuyi Dadao
   branch).......................................C2
10 Lǎo Chángshā Lóngxiāguǎn A2
11 Sōnghuājiāng Jiǎoziguǎn..................D1

🍷 Drinking & Nightlife

12 Hualongchi Xiang...........................B2
13 Jiefang Xilu A2
14 Taiping Jie A2
15 Yìngshānlóu Cháguǎn B2

ⓘ Information

Bank of China ....(see 20)
16 China Post...................................D1
17 Internet Cafe...............................D1
18 Provincial People's Hospital.............B2

ⓘ Transport

Airport Shuttle Bus....................(see 20)
19 Bus Ticket Office..........................D1
20 Civil Aviation Administration
   of China....................................D2

HÚNÁN CHÁNGSHĀ

🛏 Sleeping

You can find basic rooms clustered around the train station, but you get what you pay for.

Chángshā International Youth Hostel
HOSTEL $

(长沙国际青年旅舍; Chángshā Guójì Qīngnián Lŭshè; ☎8299 0202; www.hnhostel.com; 61 Gongshang Xiang, 东风路下大陇工商巷61号; dm ¥40-45, s/d/tr ¥88/108/138; ⊛✳@🛜; 🖥136 from train station) Chángshā's first youth hostel, and still its best. Rooms here are simple, but bright and clean, and there's a nice cafe-bar area, as well as a back yard with table tennis and a pool table. Travel notices pinned up around the place are in Chinese only, but some staff speak a little English and are happy to help out.

The location is pleasant – tucked away down a quiet, tree-lined residential street – but out of the way. Take bus 136 from the train station and get off at Xiàdàlóng (下大陇) bus stop. Cross the road and you'll find Gongshang Xiang behind the shops, running parallel to the main road. From Xiàdàlóng bus stop, buses 112 and 901 go to Jiefang Xilu.

Its sister hostel – **Yuèlù Mountain International Youth Hostel** (岳麓山国际青年旅舍; Yuèlù Shān Guójì Qīngniánlŭshè; ☎8536 8418; 50 Xinmin Lu, 新民路50号; dm/s/d ¥40/98/128; 🖥1, Ⓜ Yingwanzhen) – isn't as nice, but is OK if this place is full. It's on Xinmin Lu, which is opposite the entrance to Yuèlù Mountain.

Hàntíng Express
HOTEL $

(汉庭快捷酒店; Hàntíng Kuàijié Jiŭdiàn; ☎567 1155; 147 Jiefang Xilu; 解放西路147号; r ¥219-259, with shared bathroom ¥99; ✳@🛜) If you want to be close to the action come evening, then consider this cheap hotel chain where small rooms without windows, and with shared (but clean) shower rooms, go for ¥99. Normal, well-appointed twins and doubles with private bathrooms cost upwards of ¥200.

Mini Hotel
BOUTIQUE HOTEL $$

(觅你酒店; Mìnĭ Jiŭdiàn; ☎8273 3999; www.mini2008.com; 79 Wuyi Dadao, 五一大道79号; r inc breakfast ¥286-486; ✳@🛜) With an owner who's nuts about Mini Coopers, this funky car-themed establishment is the closest thing to a boutique hotel in Chángshā. Run by young cheerful staff, the hotel is dotted with toy-sized Minis, and has a real one in the lobby. Rooms are modern yet understated, and each has its own computer.

Sheraton Chángshā Hotel
LUXURY HOTEL $$$

(喜来登酒店; Xǐláidēng Jiŭdiàn; ☎8488 8888; www.starwoodhotels.com; 478 Furong Zhonglu, 芙蓉中路一段478号; r from ¥1000 plus 15% service charge; ⊛✳@🛜) The best luxury hotel in the city.

🍴 Eating

The lanes off the major shopping street, Huangxing Lu, and on and around the nightlife hub Taiping Jie, are good for street food. Follow your nose to the stalls selling chòu dòufu (臭豆腐; stinky tofu), a popular local delicacy.

Breakfast here is all about mĭfĕn (米粉; rice noodles). Almost anywhere open early will serve them, usually in a number of varieties; beef (牛肉粉; niúròu fĕn) is popular.

★ Lăo Chángshā Lóngxiāguǎn
HUNAN $

(老长沙龙虾管; 72 Xiangjiang Zhonglu; 湘江中路二段72号; mains ¥10-30, crayfish ¥58-98; ⏱5.30pm-3am) A cavernous warehouselike dining hall with a raucous atmosphere, this is the most enjoyable place to sample one of Chángshā's signature dishes: lóngxiā (龙虾; spicy crayfish). You'll probably have to wait for a table, so grab a number, and a cold beer, and wait on a stool outside, before diving into the chilli-laced action.

The crayfish options – printed along the top of the tick-list menu – are as follows: Chángshā kŏuwèi xiā (长沙口味虾; ordinary), Chángshā zhēngxiā (长沙蒸虾; steamed) and Chángshā yóubào xiā (长沙油爆虾; deep-fried). All are huge ¥98-portions; enough for three or four people to share. Alternatively, try the slightly smaller kăo xiāwěi (烤虾尾; barbecued crayfish-tail skewers; ¥58), about right for two to share.

The rest of the menu is split into four columns; a ¥10 column, a ¥20 column, a ¥30 column and a drinks column. ¥10 dishes include: kōngxīncài (空心菜; water spinach); lăo Chángshā chòudòufu (老长沙臭豆腐; traditional Chángshā stinky tofu), which isn't all that stinky here; and kŏuwèi dòusŭn (口味豆笋; bamboo shoots). ¥20 dishes include lăo Chángshā suōluó (老长沙唆螺; traditional Chángshā spicy snails).

The only downside is that it charges you for using the tissues (¥2) and the tableware (¥1) – bit cheeky really.

Sōnghuājiāng Jiăoziguǎn
DUMPLINGS $

(松花江饺子馆; 102 Wuyi Dadao; dumplings from ¥10, mains ¥30-60; ⏱9am-9.30pm) If you need a break from chillies, this bustling eatery specialises in the mellow cuisine of northern China. *Jiǎozi* (饺子; dumplings) are the specialty and come in many varieties, including: *báicài zhūròu* (白菜猪肉; pork and cabbage), *jiǔcài zhūròu* (韭菜猪肉; pork and chives), *xīhóngshì jīdàn* (西红柿鸡蛋; egg and tomato) and *húluóbo jīdàn* (胡萝卜鸡蛋; carrot and egg). Other dishes come with photos on the menu.

The dumplings are priced by the *liǎng* (两; 50g), which gets you six dumplings. You must order at least two *liǎng* (*èr liǎng*) of each type of dumpling.

⭐ **Huǒgōngdiàn**   HUNAN $$
(火宫殿; ☑ 8581 4228; 127 Pozi Jie; dishes ¥5-78; ⊘ 6am-2am) There's a great buzz at this landmark eatery, established in 1747 and set in and around a small templelike courtyard. In 1958 Mao tried the housemade *chòu dòufu* (臭豆腐), and praised it as both 'stinky and delicious'. The *xiǎo chī* (小吃; snacks) menu is for those eating in the courtyard and off to one side. The *Xiāngcài* (湘菜; Húnán cuisine) menu is for those seated in the back room.

Dishes to look out for include *Máojiā hóngshāoròu* (毛家红烧肉; Mao-style braised pork; ¥98, taster portion ¥15), *làjiāo chǎoròu* (辣椒炒肉; pork fried with chillies; ¥28) and *qīngtāng miàn* (清汤面; nonspicy vegetable soup noodles; ¥18).

The **Wuyi Dadao branch** (火宫殿（五一大道店; 93 Wuyi Dadao; 五一大道93号; ⊘ 11am-2pm & 5pm-2am), near the train station, is less atmospheric, but slightly cheaper and has a photo menu.

🍷 Drinking & Entertainment

Chángshā comes alive after dark. A good place to start the night is Taiping Jie (太平街), a cobbled pedestrianised street between Wuyi Dadao and Jiefang Xilu. One of Chángshā's oldest surviving streets, it has a mix of bars, cafes, boutiques and souvenir shops. From here, it's a short walk around the corner to Jiefang Xilu (解放西路), Chángshā's club central with all manner of karaoke (KTV) joints and discos. There are no covers but drinks are expensive.

There's another busy enclave of bars down an ancient alley off the shopping strip Huangxing Zhonglu. Turn down the alley marked Dagudao Xiang (大古道巷) and walk 100m to Hualongchi Xiang (化龙池巷).

Yìngshānlóu Cháguǎn   TEAHOUSE
(映山楼茶馆; in Tianxin Park; 天心公园; tea per cup ¥18-88, per pot ¥88-288; main dishes ¥30-60; ⊘ 8am-11pm) This lovely three-storey teahouse is hidden away inside Tiānxīn Park, right beside the entrance to the Old City Wall & Tiānxīn Pavilion. The building actually straddles part of the ancient wall, and you can sit beside it, on the tree-shaded terrace.

The tea menu is in Chinese, although each tea category – green, black, oolong etc – is written in English, so you at least know what type of tea you're ordering. Some teas are priced per *bēi* (杯; cup); others per *hú* (壶; pot). As always, you can fill up your cup or pot with hot water as often as you like.

This is also a nice quiet spot for lunch. Again the menu is in Chinese only, but recommendations include *píngguǒ jǐyú* (平锅鲫鱼; pan-fried carp; ¥38), *jiàng xiāngròu* (酱香肉; very spicy pork stew; ¥48), *qīngjiāo chǎoròu* (青椒炒肉; pork fried with slightly spicy peppers; ¥32) and *jiāngcōng chǎo mù'ěr* (姜葱炒木耳; mushroom fried with onion and ginger; ¥28).

ℹ️ Information

ATMs all over town take foreign cards. The train station area is densely populated with 24-hour internet cafes. Look for the large '网吧' signs.

Bank of China (中国银行, Zhōngguó Yínháng; 43 Wuyi Dadao) By the Civil Aviation Hotel. Has an exchange.

China Post (中国邮政; Zhōngguó Yóuzhèng; 460 Chezhan Lu; ⊘ 9am-5pm) By the train station.

HSBC ATM (汇丰银行; Huìfēng Yínháng; 159 Shaoshan Lu) Twenty-four-hour ATM in Dolton Hotel lobby.

Provincial People's Hospital (省人民医院; Shěng Rénmín Yīyuàn; ☑ 8227 8120; 61 Jiefang Xilu; 解放西路61号)

Public Security Bureau (PSB; 公安局; Gōng'ānjú; ☑ 8887 8741; 2 Fenglin Yilu; 枫林一路2号) For visa extensions, go to this PSB about 2km west of the river. Yingwanzhen metro station is closest.

ℹ️ Getting There & Away

AIR

Chángshā's **Huánghuā International Airport** (黄花国际机场; Huánghuā Guójì Jīchǎng; ☑ 8479 8777; www.hncaac.com) has flights to pretty much every city in China plus services to Bangkok, Seoul, Phnom Penh and Singapore. Also has daily local flights to Huáihuà (¥800, one hour) and Zhāngjiājiè (¥950, one hour).

Book tickets through www.elong.net or www.ctrip.com, or at the **Civil Aviation Administration of China** (CAAC; 中国民航售票处, Zhōng-guó Mínháng Shòupiàochù; ☑ 8411 2222; 49 Wuyi Dadao; 五一大道49号; ⊙ 8.30am-5.30pm) near the train station.

BUS

Chángshā has multiple bus stations, but most travellers use south bus station (take Bus 107 or 7 from the train station, or Bus 16 from south train station) or west bus station (at Wang-chengpo metro station). Long-distance buses also leave from both train stations.

Buy tickets at the bus stations, or at the **bus ticket office** (长途汽车售票处; Chángtú Qìchē Shòupiào Chù) in the train station square.

Services from south bus station (汽车南站, qìchē nánzhàn):

Héng Shān ¥46, three hours, hourly 8am to 5.20pm

Héngyáng ¥60, two hours, hourly 7.50am to 6.20pm

Huáihuà ¥150, six hours, hourly 8.30am to 4pm

Sháoshān ¥34, 1½ hours, half-hourly 8am to 5.30pm

Services from west bus station (汽车西站; qìchē xīzhàn):

Fènghuáng ¥140, five hours, two daily (9am and 3.40pm)

Guǎngzhōu sleeper ¥210, 12 hours, four daily (2.30pm, 5.30pm, 6.30pm and 6.40pm)

Guìlín ¥140, seven hours, 12.30pm

Nánchāng ¥126, five hours, two daily (8.30am and 3.30pm)

Shànghǎi sleeper ¥360, 16 hours, 5pm

Zhāngjiājiè ¥120, four hours, hourly 7.50am to 7pm

TRAIN

Both train stations are connected to the metro. Bullet trains leave from Chángshā South.

Services from Chángshā Train Station (长沙火车站; Chángshā Huǒchēzhàn):

Běijīng T-class hard seat/sleeper ¥190/334, 14 hours, 10 daily

Guǎngzhōu T/K-class hard seat/sleeper ¥98/176, seven to eight hours, 30 daily

Huáihuà T/K-class hard seat/sleeper ¥72/132, seven hours, 15 daily

Jíshǒu T/K-class hard seat/sleeper ¥56/124, seven to nine hours, five daily

Shànghǎi D-class bullet ¥258, seven hours, 10.35am

Shànghǎi K-class hard seat/sleeper ¥149/264, 15 hours, three daily (6.36pm, 7.19pm and 12.37am)

Wǔhàn K-class hard seat ¥54, four hours, 10 daily

Zhāngjiājiè T/K-class hard seat/sleeper ¥55/116, 5½ hours, seven daily

Services from Chángshā South Train Station (长沙南站; Chángshā Nánzhàn):

Běijīng West G-class bullet ¥650, six to seven hours, 10 daily (7.30am to 4pm)

Guǎngzhōu South G-class bullet ¥314, 2½ hours, every 10 minutes (7am to 9.20pm)

Shànghǎi G-class bullet ¥470, seven hours, 1.28pm

Shēnzhèn G-class bullet ¥390, 2½ hours, half-hourly 7am to 7.30pm

Xī'ān G-class bullet ¥590, six hours, nine daily (8.10am to 4.32pm)

Wǔhàn G-class bullet ¥165, 1½ hours, half-hourly 7.30am to 9.50pm

ⓘ Getting Around

TO/FROM THE AIRPORT

The airport is 26km from the city centre. Airport shuttle buses (机场巴士; jīchǎng bāshì; ¥16.50, 40 minutes) depart from the CAAC office near the train station, every 15 minutes between 5.20am and 10.30pm, and take 40 minutes.

Local Bus 114 (¥3, 70 minutes, 6.30am to 6.30pm) also links the train station to the airport.

A taxi from the city centre is about ¥90.

The eagerly anticipated **Maglev** (磁浮; cífú; magnetic levitation train) is due to start operating in 2016 and will whoosh passengers from the airport to South Train Station in just 10 minutes.

PUBLIC TRANSPORT

Handy Line 2 of Chángshā's new **metro** (地铁; dìtiě; tickets ¥2 to ¥5) goes from South Train Station to Chángshā Train Station then along Wuyi Dadao to Orange Isle and on to west bus station.

Local buses cost ¥1 or ¥2 per trip. Carry exact change.

Sháoshān   韶山

☑ 0732

More than three million people make the pilgrimage each year to Mao Zedong's home town, a pretty hamlet frozen in time 130km southwest of Chángshā. The swarms of young and old drop something to the tune of ¥1.8 billion annually. Mao statues alone are such big business that each must pass inspection by no fewer than five experts checking for features, expression, hairstyle, costume and posture. The 6m-high bronze statue of Mao erected in 1993 in Mao Zedong Sq is considered a model example.

⊙ Sights

Shāoshān has two parts: the modern town with the train and bus stations, and the original village about 5km away, where all the sights are clustered. Only a handful of the popular sights have a genuine connection to Mao.

The minibus from town will drop you on the main road by the village, a few hundred metres from Mao's former residence; cross the small river to the left of the road. You'll then see **Mao Zedong Square** (with its Mao statue) to your right, but turn left to reach Mao's former residence.

Former Residence of Mao Zedong
HISTORIC SITE

(毛泽东故居; Máo Zédōng Gùjū; ⊙8.30am-5pm) **FREE** Surrounded by lotus ponds and rice paddies, this modest mudbrick house is like millions of other country homes except that Mao was born here in 1893. By most accounts, his childhood was relatively normal, though he tried to run away at age 10. He returned briefly in 1921 as a young revolutionary. On view are some original furnishings, photos of Mao's parents and a small barn. No photography inside.

MAO: THE GREAT HELMSMAN

Mao Zedong was born in the village of Sháoshān in 1893, the son of 'wealthy' peasants. Mao worked beside his father on the 8-hectare family farm from age six and was married by 14.

At 16, he convinced his father to let him attend middle school in Chángshā. In the city, Mao discovered Sun Yatsen's revolutionary secret society. When the Qing dynasty collapsed that year, Mao joined the republican army but soon quit, thinking the revolution was over.

At the Húnán County No 1 Teachers' Training School, Mao began following the Soviet socialism movement. He put an ad in a Chángshā newspaper 'inviting young men interested in patriotic work to contact me', and among those who responded were Liu Shaoqi, who would become president of the People's Republic of China (PRC), and Xiao Chen, who would be a founding member of the Chinese Communist Party (CCP).

Mao graduated in 1918 and went to work as an assistant librarian at Peking University, where he befriended more future major CCP figures. By the time he returned to teach in Chángshā, Mao was active in communist politics. Unlike orthodox Marxists, Mao saw peasants as the lifeblood of the revolution. The CCP was formed in 1921, and soon included unions of peasants, workers and students.

In April 1927, following Kuomintang leader Chiang Kaishek's attack on communists, Mao was tasked with organising what became the 'Autumn Harvest Uprising'. Mao's army scaled Jīnggāng Shān, on the border with Jiāngxī province, to embark on a guerrilla war. The campaign continued until the Long March in October 1934, a 9600km retreat from which Mao emerged the CCP leader.

Mao forged a fragile alliance with the Kuomintang to expel the Japanese, and from 1936 to 1948 the two sides engaged in betrayals, conducting a civil war simultaneously with WWII. Mao's troops eventually won, and the PRC was established 1 October 1949.

As chairman of the PRC, Mao embarked on radical campaigns to repair his war-ravaged country. In the mid-1950s he began to implement peasant-based and decentralised socialist developments. The outcome was the ill-fated Great Leap Forward and later the chaos of the Cultural Revolution.

China saw significant gains in education, women's rights, and average life expectancy under Mao's rule; however, by most estimates between 40 and 70 million people died during that era of change. Five years after Mao's death, Deng Xiaoping famously announced Mao had been 70% right and 30% wrong in an effort, some say, to tear down Mao's cult of personality. Yet today, Mao remains revered as the man who united the country, and he is still commonly referred to as the 'Great Leader', 'Great Teacher' and 'supremely beloved Chairman'. His image hangs everywhere – in schools, taxis and living rooms – but as a symbol of exactly what is the question with which China now grapples.

Nán'àn School
HISTORIC SITE

(南岸私塾, Nán'àn Sīshú; ⊙8.30am-5pm) FREE
Mao began his education in this simple
country school, next door to his childhood
home.

Mao Zedong Memorial Museum
MUSEUM

(毛泽东同志纪念馆, Máo Zédōng Tóngzhì Jìniànguǎn; ⊙9am-4.30pm) FREE Exiting Mao's
home, turn left and walk straight on to Mao
Zedong Sq where, on your left, you'll see the
entrance to this museum. It portrays Mao's
life through paintings and old photos and
has decent English captions.

Exiting from the back of the museum,
you'll see the **Relic Hall of Mao Zedong**
(毛泽东遗物馆; Máo Zédōng Yíwùguǎn; ⊙9am-
4.30pm) FREE in front of you. This more
modern museum includes everyday artefacts used by Mao, clothing he wore, plus
more photos from his life, and also has good
English captions. Turn left as you exit here
to get back to Mao Zedong Square.

🛏 Sleeping & Eating

Máo Jiā Fàndiàn
HUNAN $$

(毛家饭店; Sháoshān Village; 韶山; mains ¥20-
60; ⊙6am-9pm) The best-known restaurant
in the village was opened in 1987 by the
business-savvy octogenarian Madam Tang,
who used to live in the house opposite Mao,
but who now owns a restaurant empire
with more than 300 outlets worldwide. *Máo
Zédōng hóngshāoròu* (毛泽东红烧肉; Mao's
favourite braised pork belly; ¥58) takes pride
of place as first dish on the menu.

Other dishes worth sampling include:
duò jiāo yútóu (剁椒鱼头; spicy steamed
fish head; ¥58), *chòudòufu* (臭豆腐; smelly
tofu; ¥28) and *qiézi dòujiǎo* (茄子豆角;
fried aubergine with green beans; ¥22).

The adjacent **hotel** (毛家饭店; ☎0731
5568 5132; r from ¥180) has huge rooms facing
onto an overgrown courtyard, but most visit
Sháoshān on a day trip.

ℹ Getting There & Around

Buses from Chángshā terminate at Sháoshān
bus station (韶山汽车站; Sháoshān qìchēzhàn),
where minibuses (¥2.50 one way; ¥10 hop-on,
hop-off) wait to take passengers to the village,
5km away. They then shuttle between the sights,
but it's nicer just to walk around once you're
there.

The last bus back to Chángshā is at 5.30pm.

There's one daily train to Sháoshān (¥10, two
hours 40 minutes) from Chángshā Train Station

at 6.35am. The return leaves at 4.48pm. Tickets
are easy to get, and the train isn't crowded.

At weekends, an extra, faster train (¥10, one
hour 40 minutes) is put into service. It leaves
Chángshā Train Station at 9.15am, returning at
2.38pm. Again, tickets are easy to buy.

Héng Shān
衡山

📋 0734

About 130km south of Chángshā rises the
southernmost of China's five sacred Tao-
ist mountains, to which emperors came to
make sacrifices to heaven and earth. The
ancients called it Nányuè (南岳; Southern
Mountain), a name it now shares with the
town at its base. The imperial visits left a
legacy of Taoist temples and ancient inscrip-
tions scattered amid gushing waterfalls,
dense pine forests and terraced fields cut
from lush canyons. Bring extra layers, as the
weather can turn quickly and the summit is
often cold and wet.

👁 Sights & Activities

Héng Shān
MOUNTAIN

Seventy-two peaks spanning 400km com-
prise Héng Shān, but most visitors focus on
Zhùróng Peak (祝融峰; Zhùróng Fēng; admis-
sion ¥120), rising 1290m above sea level.

The lung-busting, 13km ascent up wind-
ing paths, steep staircases and, in places, a
road busy with tourist shuttle buses, takes
around four hours one way, although it can
fill the best part of a day if you take in the
many temples en route. Alternatively, tourist
buses, or a combination of bus and cable car,
can take you almost the whole way up.

If you want to take the bus, buy the *chē
piào* (车票; bus ticket; ¥80 return, including
cable car), along with your *mén piào* (门票;
entrance ticket; ¥120) on the 2nd floor of
the modern **tourist centre** (旅客服务中心;
Lǚkè Fúwù Zhōngxīn; Yanshou Lu; ⊙7am-5.30pm),
where you can also store luggage (¥10 per
bag) and pick up a free leaflet with a *dìtú*
(地图; map) on it. Buses depart directly from
here to the mountain's **halfway point** (半山
亭; Bànshān Tíng; 15 minutes). From there,
you can either take the five-minute cable car
ride to **Nántiānmén** (南天门), or change
to another bus. From Nántiānmén, it's a
30-minute hike to Zhùróng Peak.

Note, the mountain is open 24 hours,
but the buses and cable car only run until
around 6pm.

If you decide to hike up the mountain (a wise choice, as you miss most of the temples if you take the bus), it's nicer to start up the tree-lined road 300m east of the tourist centre marked by the stone **Shènglì Archway** (胜利坊; Shènglì Fāng). This road leads to another entrance, where you can pay admission, and then to a tranquil path that winds 5km past lakes, waterfalls and streams in **Fànyīn Valley** (梵音谷; Fànyīn Gǔ) to almost the cable-car departure point at **Bànshān Tíng**. Along the way, you can stop to see the colourful figures of Taoist and Buddhist scripture on display in **Shénzhōu Temple** (Shénzhōu Zǔmiào), the grand and dignified **Nányuè Martyrs Memorial Hall** (南岳忠烈祠; Nányuè Zhōngliècí), dedicated to the anti-Japanese resistance, and a **stele** inscribed with a dedication from Kuomintang leader Chiang Kaishek celebrating the pine forest. Before you jump on the cable car, take a break and reconsider at **Xuándōu Guàn** (玄都观), an active Taoist temple. The couplet carved at the entry reminds weary climbers that the path of righteousness is long, so don't give up halfway through!

The next 4.5km up to Nántiānmén frequently takes the busy road and scattered staircases, but there are plenty more inspiring temples along the way. Once you reach Nántiānmén, it's a chilly (outside of July and August) 30-minute ascent to the peak – you can rent coats (¥20) by the cable-car station.

At the top is **Zhù Róng Palace** (祝融殿; Zhù Róng Diàn), an iron-tiled, stone structure built for Zhu Rong, an ancient official who devised a method of striking stones to create sparks. After his death, he became revered as the god of fire.

Nányuè Temple
TAOIST, BUDDHIST TEMPLE
(南岳大庙; Nányuè Dàmiào; admission ¥60; ⏰7.30am-5.30pm) This sprawling Taoist and Buddhist temple was moved from Héng Shān summit to its foot in the Sui dynasty and then rebuilt many times, most recently in the Qing dynasty. Each carved panel in the main pavilion's balustrade tells a legend of one of Héng Shān's peaks. Its north gate is opposite the tourist centre.

Zhùshèng Temple
BUDDHIST TEMPLE
(祝圣寺, Zhùshèng Sì; 67 Dong Jie; ⏰5am-6pm) **FREE** A 10-minute walk east of Nányuè Temple, this Zen Buddhist temple, with an attractive stone-carved entrance, dates back to the Tang dynasty. Outside, on Dong Jie, you can

watch carpenters making wooden Buddha statues for the various temples in town.

Dàshàn Chán Temple
MONASTERY
(大善禅寺; Dàshàn Chánsì; Zhurong Beilu; ⏰7.30am-6pm) **FREE** This active Taoist nunnery is on the west side of Nányuè.

Giant
BICYCLE RENTAL
(捷安特; Jié'āntè; ☑138 7562 9725; 231 Heng Shan Lu; 衡山路231号; bike rental per hr/day ¥15/80, deposit ¥1000; ⏰8.30am-9pm) If you fancy cycling up a holy Taoist mountain, these guys can fix you up with a decent mountain bike. You can ride all the way to the summit at Zhùróng Peak – there are three routes. If that sounds too much like hard work, simply take off into the surrounding countryside for a few hours before asking your way back to Nányuè 'nan yoo-weh').

The Giant shop is near *páifāng*, diagonally opposite Bank of China.

🛏 Sleeping & Eating

The cheapest hotels are found near Nányuè Bus Station. On the lower slopes of the mountain, basic hotels line the road at various places.

Nányuè has more than its share of restaurants. Try Zhurong Lu, the road Nányuè Telecom Hotel is on. Food on the mountain is costlier, although the vegetarian meals at Zǔshī Temple are decent value.

🛏 In Town

Auspicious Margin Hotel
HOTEL $
(吉缘宾馆; Jíyuán Bīnguǎn; ☑187 1149 7187; 338 Hengshan Lu; 衡山路338号; r ¥70-100; ✳@🛜) Opposite the bus station, this simple hotel has a variety of rooms, all with air-con, TV and bathroom.

Nányuè Telecom Hotel
HOTEL $$
(南岳电信兵官; ☑567 8888; 173 Zhurong Lu, 祝融路173号; r from ¥438, discounted to ¥238; ✳@🛜) This large hotel has comfortable, smart twins and doubles, going for ¥238 when we were here. Has a decent restaurant too. Turn right out of the bus station, left through the *páifāng* (decorative stone archway) and it's on your left.

🛏 On the Mountain

Zǔshī Temple
GUESTHOUSE $$
(祖师殿, Zǔshī Diàn; ☑189 7476 3290; near Nántiānmén; d ¥348; @) The rooms in this Taoist temple are spartan, but the views

are magic. Vegetarian rice meals (¥20 per plate) are served up throughout the day. It's a five-minute walk from the cable car station by Nántiānmén; turn left as you exit the cable car.

Wàngrì Tái Jiēdàizhàn HOTEL $$
(望日台接待站; ☑ 566 3188; Wàngrì Tái; r from ¥300) The mountain's highest accommodation, this place is just a 10-minute walk below Zhùróng Peak (up to your right as you are climbing), and has small but modern rooms with air-con/heaters, TV and bathroom. Does food (mains ¥30 to ¥60). Doesn't do internet.

❶ Information

Turn right out of the main bus station to reach the *páifāng* (牌坊), a stone archway, and a focal point in town. Just past *páifāng*, on your left, is a branch of **Bank of China** (中国银行, Zhōngguó Yínháng; 270 Hengshan Lu; ⏰ 9am-5pm) with currency exchange and a 24-hour ATM. Opposite the bank is a 24-hour **internet cafe** (网吧; wǎng-bā; per hr ¥3).

Walk through the *páifāng* to reach the tourist centre (1km; follow signs for Zhùróng Peak) and the town's temples, all of which are also signposted.

❶ Getting There & Around

Buses from Chángshā arrive at Nányuè Bus Station, which has 12 buses a day back to Chángshā (¥48, three hours, 7am to 4pm).

Bullet trains from Chángshā South Station (¥65, 30 minutes, 7.25am to 9.20pm) stop at Héng Shān West Station (衡山西站; Héng Shān Xīzhàn), 10km from Nányuè town centre. Local buses wait at the train station car park to take passengers to Nányuè (¥6). They will drop you at a small local bus station, called Zhōngxīn Zhàn (中心站), which is diagonally opposite the main Nányuè bus station (南岳汽车站; Nányuè Qìchēzhàn).

Returning to Chángshā, bullet trains leave Héng Shān West Station roughly half-hourly from 9.14am to 9.54pm. You can buy tickets at a train ticket office (火车票代售; huǒchē piàodàishòu; 167 Zhurong Lu; 祝融路167号; commission per ticket ¥5; ⏰ 7.40am-9pm) near the *páifāng*; walk through the *páifāng*, and it's on your left.

Zhāngjiājiè   张家界

☑ 0744

Avatar director James Cameron never mentioned Zhāngjiājiè as the inspiration to the floating mountains on Pandora (although that hasn't stopped China's tourism industry from promoting the supposed connection), but the incredible collection of karst pinnacles in this unique national park do indeed resemble a scene from another world, especially when the early-morning mountain mist rolls in around them.

Rising from the subtropical and temperate forests of northwest Húnán, Zhāngjiājiè has a concentration of quartzite-sandstone formations found nowhere else in the world. Some 243 peaks and more than 3000 karst pinnacles and spires dominate the scenery in this Unesco-protected park. It is truly one of the most remarkable landscapes in China.

For thousands of years, this was a remote land known mainly to three minority groups: Tujia, Miao and Bai. Today more than 20 million visitors annually come to the park. It is also home to more than 3000 distinct plant species as well as diverse fauna. You'll see lots of macaques on the main trails (remember, they are wild so don't feed them), while endangered species such as the Chinese giant salamander, Chinese water deer and the elusive clouded leopard (only their tracks have been seen) lurk deep in the park.

❖ Sights

◉ The National Park

The national park's official name is the **Wǔlíngyuán Scenic & Historic Interest Area** (武陵源风景区; Wǔlíngyuán Fēngjǐngqū; ; adult/student ¥245/160), but almost everyone refers to it simply as Zhāngjiājiè, the name of one section of the park.

Zhāngjiājiè is also the name of the city (张家界市; Zhāngjiājiè shì) 30km south of the park, and the village (张家界村; Zhāngjiājiè cūn) by the 'Forest Park' entrance.

The park, covering a vast 264 sq km, is divided into three main areas: the Zhāngjiājiè, Tiānzǐ Shān and Suǒxī Valley scenic areas.

There are access points on all sides of the park, but most enter from the south, passing through Zhāngjiājiè village to the **Zhāngjiājiè National Park entrance** (张家界公园门票站; Zhāngjiājiè Gōngyuán *ménpiàozhàn*), more commonly called **Forest Park** (森林公园; Sēnlín Gōngyuán). Otherwise, many enter from the east through the less spectacular **Wǔlíngyuán entrance** (武陵源门票站; Wǔlíngyuán *ménpiàozhàn*).

Zhāngjiājiè

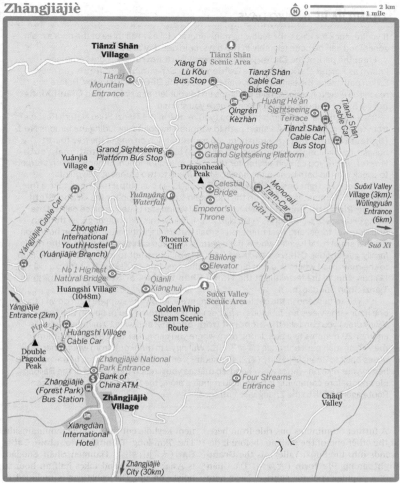

0 ___ 2 km
0 ___ 1 mile

Tiānzǐ Shān Village

Tiānzǐ Mountain Entrance

Tiānzǐ Shān Scenic Area

Xiāng Dà Lù Kǒu Bus Stop

Tiānzǐ Shān Cable Car Bus Stop

Huáng Hé'àn Sightseeing Terrace

Qíngrén Kèzhàn

Tiānzǐ Shān Cable Car Bus Stop

Tiānzǐ Shān Cable Car

Yuánjiā Village

Grand Sightseeing Platform Bus Stop

One Dangerous Step

Grand Sightseeing Platform

Dragonhead Peak

Celestial Bridge

Monorail Tram-Car

Suǒxī Valley Village (3km); Wǔlíngyuán Entrance (6km)

Yuányáng Waterfall

Emperor's Throne

Gān Xī

Suǒ Xī

Yángjiājiè Cable Car

Zhōngtiān International Youth Hostel (Yuánjiājiè Branch)

Phoenix Cliff

Bǎilóng Elevator

No 1 Highest Natural Bridge

Huángshí Village (1048m)

Qiānlǐ Xiānghuì

Suǒxī Valley Scenic Area

Yángjiājiè Entrance (2km)

Pípá Xī

Huángshí Village Cable Car

Golden Whip Stream Scenic Route

Double Pagoda Peak

Zhāngjiājiè National Park Entrance

Bank of China ATM

Four Streams Entrance

Zhāngjiājiè (Forest Park) Bus Station

Zhāngjiājiè Village

Cháqí Valley

Xiāngdiàn International Hotel

Zhāngjiājiè City (30km)

Zhāngjiājiè Scenic Area
NATIONAL PARK

From the 'Forest Park' entrance, there is an early opportunity for a bird's-eye view of the karst towers from Huángshí Village (黄石寨; Huángshí Zhài), a 3km loop on a plateau 1048m up. It's a two-hour slog up 3878 stone steps, or a half-hour by electric bus (free), then cable car (one way ¥65).

Back on the canyon floor, the Golden Whip Stream Scenic Route (金鞭溪精品游览线; Jīnbiānxī Jīngpǐn Yóulǎnxiàn) is a flat path meandering 5.7km east along its namesake stream to the Báilóng Elevator (白龙天梯; Báilóng Tiāntī; ¥72 one way), a cliff-side lift rising 335m in under two minutes to the Tiānzǐ Shān section of the park. There are steps up the cliff as well (one hour).

Tiānzǐ Shān Scenic Area
NATIONAL PARK

This area is on top of the plateau, and hence enjoys most of the park's more spectacular (and busiest) viewpoints. Touring here means manoeuvring around particularly large crowds (and waiting in long lines for buses), but the vistas are worth it; not least the No 1 Highest Natural Bridge (天下第一桥; Tiānxiàdìyī Qiáo), a remarkable stone structure spanning two peaks, 357m above the canyon floor.

ZHĀNGJIĀJIÈ IN TWO DAYS

If you're stuck for ideas, the following mini-itinerary takes in all three of the park's main zones, and can be done leisurely in two days, or in one day at a push.

Enter the park at the **Zhāngjiājiè National Park entrance**, more commonly known as **Forest Park**. Follow the **Golden Whip Stream Scenic Route**, an easy 5.7km path along the canyon floor, which leads to the **Bǎilóng Elevator**. Before you reach the elevator, though, take the steps up to your left at a point called **Qiānlǐ Xiānghuì** (千里相会), about one hour from where you started.

It's a tough one-hour climb to the top (you're now in the Tiānzǐ Shān Nature Reserve), from where you can follow a short path to various viewpoints, including the famous **No 1 Highest Natural Bridge**. From here you can either hop on one of the free tourist buses, or walk along the main road (20 minutes) to **Zhōngtiān International Youth Hostel**, where you can either stop for the night, or just for lunch. Either way, don't forget to check out the path behind the hostel, which leads to two stunning viewpoints.

The hostel is right beside **Wàng Qiáo Tái** (望桥台) bus stop. From here, take a free bus about 30 minutes further up the mountain to the bus stop for the **Grand Sightseeing Platform**, and find a rarely taken trail which starts near a place called **One Dangerous Step** (一步难行; Yī Bù Nán Xíng). Follow this cliff-hugging trail through dripping-wet forest and past numerous small waterfalls, until, after about an hour, you reach a small rural hamlet where, if it's getting late, you can stay the night in the rustic family guesthouse **Qíngrén Kèzhàn** (情人客栈). Or turn left to follow the lane back up to the main road where you can pick up another free bus, at **Xiāng Dà Lù Kǒu** (湘大路口) bus stop, to the terminus at the **Tiānzǐ Shān Cable-Car Station** (天子山索道站; Tiānzǐ Shān Suǒdàozhàn).

It's ¥67 to descend in the cable car. Alternatively, follow the stepped path down (about one hour – the views are fabulous in places). At the bottom (you're now in the Suǒxī Valley area) you can take the **monorail tram-car** (¥52 one way, 10 minutes) or walk another 20 minutes to a bus depot, from where you can either take a free bus 10km to the Wǔlíngyuán park entrance (武陵源门口; Wǔlíngyuán ménkǒu), from where there are buses back to Zhāngjiājiè City (¥12, 45 minutes), or turn right to get back to the path you began your hike on – after a few hundred metres you'll reach the bottom of the Bǎilóng Elevator before continuing for about 90 minutes along the Golden Whip Stream Scenic Route again, back to the Zhāngjiājiè entrance.

A further 30-minutes bus ride from here, at the other end of the plateau (before it descends into the Suǒxī Valley), is the **Grand Sightseeing Platform** (大观台; Dà Guān Tái), a popular spot for sunrise. Near here is a collection of other fine viewpoints, including **Celestial Bridge** (仙人桥; xiānrén qiáo) and **Emperor's Throne** (天子座; Tiānzǐ Zuò). A *suǒdào* (索道; cable car; one way ¥67) can take you down into the Suǒxī Valley, or you can hike down then take a cute **monorail tram-car** (电车; *diànchē*, one way ¥52) along a short stretch of the valley.

◉ Zhāngjiājiè City

Tiānmén Mountain   MOUNTAIN
(天门山; Tiānmén Shān; admission ¥258; ⊙8am-4.30pm) Visible from anywhere in Zhāngjiājiè city, this distinctive mountain range features **Tiānmén Dòng** (天门洞), a promi-

nent keyhole cut through the mountainside. The 7km-long **Tiānmén Mountain Cable Car** (天门山索道; Tiānmén Shān Suǒdào) is Asia's longest, and takes half an hour to hoist you up. The cable car is included in your entrance ticket. Once at the top, a riveting 60m, glass plank road a short walk from the upper cable station will test your belief in human engineering.

It's a 10-minute walk to the cable-car station from Zhāngjiājiè's central bus station; Turn left at the bus station, take the second left, then left again at the roundabout.

🏃 Activities

With more than 40 limestone caves hidden along the banks of the Suǒxī River and the southeast side of Tiānzǐ Shān, the region offers ample opportunities to **raft** (漂流; *piāoliú*) and tour **caves**.

Zhōngtiān International Youth Hostel in Zhāngjiājiè City runs numerous one- and two-day tours, including a number of rafting trips (per person ¥200 to ¥500).

🛏 Sleeping & Eating

There are hotels just outside all the main entrances to the park, although, naturally, they cost more than hotels in Zhāngjiājiè City. Inside the park itself, family-run *kèzhàn* (客栈; guesthouses) are dotted along the main road in the Tiānzǐ Shān area. Expect to pay ¥50 to ¥100 for a room. Every guesthouse will also do meals (around ¥30). Snack stalls and restaurant shacks line all the main hiking trails around the park.

🛏 Zhāngjiājiè City 张家界市

Zhōngtiān International Youth Hostel HOSTEL $

(中天国际青年旅舍; Zhōngtiān Guójì Qīngnián Lûshè; ☑ 832 1678; www.zjjzthostel.com; 4th fl, Zhōngtiān Bldg, cnr Ziwu Lu & Beizheng Lu; 子午路和北正路街角, 中天大厦4楼; dm from ¥40, tw & d from ¥128; ❄@🛜) Despite the location in an anonymous office block, this pleasant hostel has a rooftop garden, a small bar and restaurant, and cosy rooms. Helpful staff speak some English, and the claypot rice meals (¥15 to ¥20) are delicious.

You can store luggage here for free, or have it delivered to the branch inside the park for ¥20. It also runs a range of day trips, including rafting. To get here, take bus 6 (¥2) from outside Zhāngjiājiè central bus station to Lieshi Gongyuan (烈士公园) bus stop, then take bus 3 (¥2) to Beizheng Lu (北正路) and the Zhōngtiān Building will be up on your left.

BM Guesthouse HOTEL $

(北门客栈; Běimén Kèzhàn; ☑ 218 6777; in an alley off Beizheng Jie; 北正街永定医院对面; r ¥100; ❄@🛜) This tidy, modern hotel has clean, comfortable rooms that come with a computer terminal as well as wi-fi access. A better deal than the private rooms at Zhōngtiān Youth Hostel, but no English spoken, and no restaurant. The hotel is in an alley, set back off Beizheng Jie (also called Beizheng Lu), between Nos 331 and 349. Take a bus to Beizheng Lu bus stop, then walk downhill slightly and it's on the right.

🛏 Zhāngjiājiè Village 张家界村

Xiāngdiàn International Hotel HOTEL $$$

(湘电国际酒店, Xiāngdiàn Guójì Jiǔdiàn; ☑ 571 2999; r from ¥1080; ☺❄@) A five-minute walk from the park entrance, this elegant four-star hotel has smart rooms set around courtyard gardens, courteous staff, and great discounts. Standard rooms went for ¥468 when we were here; and for ¥498 with a mountain view.

🛏 The National Park

Zhōngtiān International Youth Hostel (Yuánjiājiè branch) HOSTEL $

(中天国际青年旅舍，袁家界店; Zhōngtiān Guójì Qīngniánlûshè, Yuánjiājièdiàn; ☑ 0744 571 3568; Wang Qiao Tai bus stop, Yuánjiājiè; 望桥台袁家界; dm ¥50, r from ¥150) Not as good as the branch in Zhāngjiājiè City, this quiet hostel is still an excellent option within the park. Rooms are a bit musty (everywhere's musty up here!), but are clean and tidy. Not much English spoken, but the food menu (mains ¥15 to ¥30), and notices around the hostel, are all in English.

A path behind the hostel leads to two stunning viewpoints, while about 50m beyond the hostel are steps leading down into the canyon below.

The easiest and quickest way to get here is to enter the park through the Tiānzǐ Shān entrance (天子山门票站; Tiānzǐshān *ménpiàozhàn*) then take the free bus to Wang Qiao Tai (望桥台) bus stop; about 40 minutes. You can also get here from the Zhāngjiājiè entrance.

Qíngrén Kèzhàn GUESTHOUSE $

(情人客栈; ☑ 189 0744 1378; Xiangda Lukou bus stop, Tianzi Shan area; 天子山，湘大路口; r ¥80) Remote, rustic, family-run guesthouse, with simple rooms, home-cooked meals and farmyard animals running around the courtyard. No English spoken. Easiest way to get here is to take a free bus from the Tiānzǐ Shān park entrance to Xiangda Lukou (湘大路口) bus stop, not far before the Tiānzǐ Shān cable-car station.

ℹ Information

In Zhāngjiājiè City, tree-lined Beizheng Lu (北正路; also known as Beizheng Jie, 北正街) has everything you need: accommodation, restaurants, snack stalls, pharmacies, ATMs, internet cafes, bars tucked away down alleys, and a side-

HÚNÁN ZHĀNGJIĀJIĒ

DÉHĀNG 德夯

Set against a backdrop of forested peaks, the once utterly charming Miao village of Déhāng (admission ¥100) has been tarted up for tourism these days and lacks authenticity, but it still offers the chance to take some relatively short and easy-to-follow hikes into the stunning countryside. Bilingual signs and map-boards around the main square (where the bus terminates) show you the way to the various trailheads, including one which leads to the 216m-tall Liúshā Falls (流沙瀑布; Liúshā Pùbù), one of China's tallest waterfalls.

There are plenty of guesthouses and restaurants around the main square and along the river. The most attractive is the simple Jiēlóngqiáo Inn (接龙桥客店, Jiēlóngqiáo Kèdiàn; ☑ 135 1743 0915; r ¥50-70), overlooking the arched Jiēlóng Bridge (接龙桥; Jiēlóng Qiáo).

Déhāng is accessed from the town of Jíshǒu (吉首). Buses to Déhāng (¥8, 45 minutes) leave frequently from outside Jíshǒu train station.

You can catch frequent buses to Fènghuáng (¥22, one hour, 7.30am to 7pm) and Zhāngjiājiè (¥45, three hours, 8am to 5pm) from Jíshǒu bus station. Local bus 3 (¥2) links Jíshǒu's train and bus stations.

street food market. See Zhōngtiān International Youth Hostel for details on how to get here.

Bilingual dìtú (地图; maps) of the national park and Zhāngjiājiè City are available at ticket offices and hotels and hostels for ¥5.

ⓘ Getting There & Away

AIR

There are flights to Běijīng, Chángshā, Chóngqìng, Guǎngzhōu, Shànghǎi and Xī'ān. Use www.english.ctrip.com for bookings.

BUS

Buses leave from central bus station (中心汽车站; zhōngxīn qìchēzhàn), right beside Zhāngjiājiè train station. As well as those listed here there are also daily sleeper buses to cities such as Běijīng, Shànghǎi, Wǔhàn and Xī'ān.

Chángshā ¥97, four hours, at least hourly 7am to 7pm

Fènghuáng ¥78, four hours, 8.30am, 9.30am, 12.30pm, 2.30pm, 3.30pm and 5.20pm

Jíshǒu ¥52, two hours, hourly 7am to 5pm

TRAIN

The train station (火车站; huǒchēzhàn) is beside central bus station. Note, Huáihuà trains also stop at Jíshǒu (¥20, two hours).

Běijīng hard sleeper ¥350 to ¥390, 24 to 26 hours, two daily (12.45pm and 5.54pm)

Chángshā hard seat ¥48 to ¥84, six hours, seven daily between 1.16pm and 6.54pm

Huáihuà hard seat ¥38, three to four hours, nine daily between 8.03am and 7.12pm

Yíchāng hard seat ¥39 to ¥44, five hours, three daily (4.09am, 9.15am and 4.40pm)

ⓘ Getting Around

The airport (机场; jīchǎng) is 6km southwest of Zhāngjiājiè City and about 40km from the Zhāngjiājiè National Park entrance; a taxi from the airport costs about ¥100 to the park. To get to the airport from the city, take local Bus 4 (¥2, 5.30am to 8.30pm) from outside the Tiānmén Mountain Cable Car.

Shuttle buses travel every 10 minutes from Zhāngjiājiè central bus station to the three main park entrances: Zhāngjiājiè (better known as Forest Park; 森林公园; Sēnlín Gōngyuán; ¥10, 45 minutes), Wǔlíngyuán (武陵源; ¥12, one hour) and Tiānzǐ Shān (¥13, one hour, less frequent). Once inside the park, all buses are free with your park ticket, but other transport (cable car, elevator, monorail tram-car) costs extra, typically around ¥70 per ride.

A taxi from the city to Forest Park entrance costs around ¥120.

Fènghuáng 凤凰
☑ 0743

Fènghuáng was once a frontier town, marking the boundary between the Han civilisations of the central plains and the Miao (苗), Tujia (土家) and Dong (侗) minorities of the southwest mountains. Protective walls went up in the Ming dynasty, but despite the implications Fènghuáng prospered as a centre of trade and cultural exchange. Its diverse residents built a breathtaking riverside settlement of winding alleys, temples and rickety stilt houses, which these days attract tourists by the bucketload.

Fènghuáng

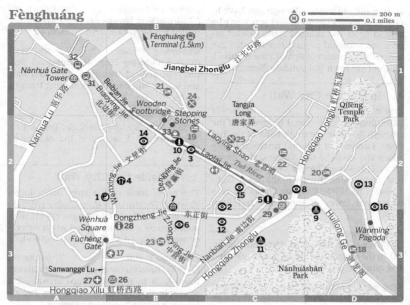

HÚNÁN FÈNGHUÁNG

Fènghuáng

◎ Sights
1 Cháoyáng Temple.................................A2
2 Chóngdé Hall......................................C2
3 City Wall..B2
4 Confucian Temple..............................B2
5 East Gate Tower.................................C2
6 Former Home of Shěn Cóngwén.........B3
7 Gǔchéng Museum...............................B2
8 Hóng Bridge.......................................C2
9 Jiāngxīn Buddhist Temple...................D3
10 North Gate Tower...............................B2
11 Three Kings Temple............................C3
12 Tiānhòu Temple..................................C3
13 Wànshòu Temple................................D2
14 Xióng Xī Líng Former Residence..........B2
15 Yáng Family Ancestral Hall.................C2
16 Yíngxī Gate..D2

◎ Activities, Courses & Tours
17 Mountain Bike Hire.............................B3

◎ Sleeping
18 A Good Year..D3
19 Běiyīmén Lǚshè..................................B2

20 Fènghuáng Zhōngtiān
   International Youth Hostel...................D2
21 Love Hotel..B1
22 Phoenix Jiāngtiān Holiday
   Village...C2
23 Shí'èr Hào Shíguāng...........................B3

◎ Eating
24 Miss Yang Restaurant.........................B1
25 Soul Cafe...C2

◎ Information
26 China Post..B3
27 Kāimíng Pharmacy..............................A3
28 Tourism Administrative Bureau
   of Fènghuáng.....................................B3
29 Train Ticket Booking Office.................C3
30 Xīndōnglì Internet Cafe......................C2

◎ Transport
31 Bus 1 to Fènghuáng Bus
   Terminal..A1
32 Bus 2 to Tǔqiáolóng Bus Station..........A1
33 North Gate Boat Dock.........................B2

◎ Sights

Wandering aimlessly is the best way to experience the charms of the **old town** (古城; *gǔchéng*). The back alleys are a trove of shops, temples, ancestral halls and courtyard homes.

The *tōngpiào* (通票; through ticket; ¥148) gains you three-day access to the old town, plus entrance to all the major sights and a half-hour boat trip on the river. It is possible to avoid buying the ticket and still wander around the old town, although you have to pick your routes carefully, and you won't be able to enter the ticketed sights. Ticket offices are scattered around town. Sights are generally open 8am to 6pm. Come nightfall, much of old town is dazzlingly illuminated.

◎ Inside the City Wall

City Wall   HISTORIC SITE
(城墙; Chéngqiáng) Restored fragments of the city wall lie along the south bank of the Tuó River. Carvings of fish and mythical beasts adorn the eaves of the **North Gate Tower** (北门城楼; Běimén Chénglóu), one of four original main gates. Another, the **East Gate Tower** (东门城楼; Dōngmén Chénglóu), is a twin-eaved tower of sandstone and fired brick.

Hóng Bridge   BRIDGE
(虹桥; Hóng Qiáo; through ticket for upstairs galleries) In the style of the Dòng minority's wind and rain bridges.

Yáng Family Ancestral Hall   HISTORIC SITE
(杨家祠堂; Yángjiā Cítáng; admission with through ticket) West of East Gate Tower. Built in 1836, its exterior is covered with slogans from the Cultural Revolution.

Xióng Xī Líng Former Residence HISTORIC SITE
(熊希龄故居; Xióng Xī Líng Gùjū; admission with through ticket) The home of a former premier and finance minister.

Jiāngxīn Buddhist Temple   BUDDHIST TEMPLE
(江心禅寺; Jiāngxīn Chánsì) Secreted away on Huilong Ge, a narrow alley.

Three Kings Temple   BUDDHIST TEMPLE
(三皇庙; Sānhuáng Miào) Great views of town, colourfully carved dragons, and thousands of lucky charms, await up stone steps.

Tiānhòu Temple   TEMPLE
(天后宫; Tiānhòu Gōng) Off Dongzheng Jie, dedicated to the patron of seafarers.

Former Home of Shěn Cóngwén HISTORIC SITE
(沈从文故居; Shěn Cóngwén Gùjū; admission with through ticket) The famous modern novelist was born here in 1902. (His tomb is east of town.)

Chóngdé Hall   HISTORIC SITE
(崇德堂; Chóngdé Táng; admission with through ticket) The town's wealthiest resident, Pei Shoulu's personal collection of antiques is on display in his former residence on Shijialong.

Confucian Temple   CONFUCIAN TEMPLE
(文庙; Wén Miào; Wenxing Jie) This 18th-century walled temple is now a middle school.

Cháoyáng Temple   TAOIST TEMPLE
(朝阳宫; Cháoyáng Gōng; 41 Wenxing Jie) Features an ancient theatrical stage and hall, and is now home to a silver-forging training centre.

Gǔchéng Museum   MUSEUM
(古城博物馆; Gǔchéng Bówùguǎn; Dengying Jie; ◎6.30am-6pm) A survey of the old town's history.

◎ Outside the City Wall

The north bank of the river offers lovely views of Fènghuáng's *diàojiǎolóu* (吊脚楼; stilt houses). Cross by *tiàoyán* (跳岩; stepping stones) – best navigated when sober – or *mùtóu qiáo* (木头桥; wooden footbridge).

Wànshòu Temple   HISTORIC SITE
(万寿宫; Wànshòu Gōng; admission with through ticket) Built in 1755 by Jiāngxī arrivals, this assembly hall north of Wànmíng Pagoda houses a minority-culture museum.

Yíngxī Gate   GATE
(迎曦门; Yíngxī Mén) Dates from 1807.

Southern Great Wall   ARCHITECTURE
(南方长城; Nánfāng Chángchéng; admission ¥45) The Ming-dynasty defensive wall, 13km from town, once stretched to Guìzhōu province. Take bus 2 from Nánhuá Gate to its terminus at Tǔqiáolǒng bus station (土桥垅车站; Tǔqiáolǒng *chēzhàn*), from where you can catch a bus here.

Huángsī Bridge Old Town   VILLAGE
(黄丝桥古城; Huángsī Qiáo Gǔchéng; admission ¥20) A Tang-dynasty military outpost 25km from town. The Southern Great Wall bus continues to here.

🏃 Activities

You can rent **mountain bikes** (☑137 8933 6467; 1 Tuanjieqiao; 团结桥1号; half-/full day ¥40/60, deposit ¥200 plus passport copy) with helmet and bike lock from Dōngfāng Wēinísī Jiǔdiàn (东方威尼斯酒店), a small hotel just outside Fùchéng Gate. It takes about one hour to cycle to Southern Great Wall; head west along Hongqiao Xilu, turn left at the roundabout, onto Tuqiao Lu (土桥路), and keep going. Huángsī Bridge Old Town is 10km further, on the same road.

HÚNÁN FÈNGHUÁNG

🛏 Sleeping

Fènghuáng is full of *kèzhàn* (客栈; guest-houses).

A Good Year   GUESTHOUSE $
(一年好时光; Yì Nián Hǎo Shíguāng; ☎322 2026; 91 Huilong Ge, 迴龙阁91号; r ¥100-130; ❄ 🛜) There are just 10 rooms in this sweet, wood-framed inn on the river; all have balconies, showers and TVs but six have fantastic river views (¥130). Air-con is ¥20 extra.

Love Hotel   GUESTHOUSE $
(鸟巢旅店; Niǎocháo Lǔdiàn; ☎326 6722, 135 7430 8830; 116 Laoying Shao; 老营哨116号; r ¥120; ❄ @ 🛜) Despite rooms and bathrooms being small, it's hard not to love this cutesy boutique guesthouse. Each room is different, and although one takes the 'love' theme a bit too far (heart-shaped bed, anyone?), most are decked out like bedrooms in a countryside cottage and open out onto little communal terraces. Each has a computer and wi-fi. No river views.

Fènghuáng Zhōngtiān
International Youth Hostel   HOSTEL $
(凤凰中天国际青年旅馆; Fènghuáng Zhōngtiān Guójì Qīngnián Lǚguǎn; ☎326 0546; yhaphoenix@163.com; 11 Shawan; 沙湾11号; dm ¥35-50, r from ¥135; ❄ @ 🛜) Accessed through a 100-year-old wooden doorway, Fènghuáng's branch of the Zhōngtiān brood has character as well as location, and is run by a friendly old guy. He doesn't speak English, but other staff do. Rooms are small and simple, but some have river views.

Shí'èr Hào Shíguāng   HOSTEL $
(十二号时光国际青年旅舍; ☎0743 350 0302, 137 6210 6759; 12 Zhongying Jie; 中营街12号; dm ¥47, r without/with bathroom ¥118/148; ❄ @ 🛜) Friendly, laid-back hostel with a quiet, back-alley location on historic Zhongying Jie.

Běiyìmén Lǚshè   GUESTHOUSE $$
(北一门旅舍; ☎366 6508, 153 0743 8250; 32 Laoying Shao; 老营哨32号; d ¥288 & ¥388; ❄ @ 🛜) Recently renovated, this modern guesthouse has seven tastefully decorated rooms with balconies overlooking the river. Very comfortable, though bathrooms are small.

Phoenix Jiāngtiān Holiday Village HOTEL $$$
(凤凰江天旅游度假村; Fènghuáng Jiāngtiān Lǚyóu Dùjiàcūn; ☎326 1998; Jiangtian Sq, 虹桥路江天广场; r from ¥588; ❄ @ 🛜) The only proper hotel by the old town, Phoenix has decent, good-sized rooms, but bathrooms are small and there are no river views. Rooms can be discounted to ¥288.

🍴 Eating & Drinking

Fènghuáng has plenty of cheap, tasty street food – everything from kebabs to spicy *dòufu* (tofu) and cooling bowls of *liángfěn* (jellies made from grasses or starchy roots). Look out for evening *shāokǎo* (street barbecues) on the north side of Hóng Bridge.

Bars wake up with a shout at nightfall along Lǎoyíng Shào (老营哨) and along both sides of the river.

Soul Cafe   ITALIAN $$
(亦素咖啡; Yìsù Kāfēi; 18 Laoying Shao; mains ¥35-65; ⏲8am-midnight; 🛜) This upmarket cafe serves proper coffee (from ¥25), pizza (¥50 to ¥65) and pasta (¥35), as well as Italian ice cream, imported wines and Cuban cigars. Lovely riverside location with balcony seating to boot.

Miss Yang Restaurant   HUNAN $$
(杨小姐的餐厅; Yángxiǎojiede Cāntīng; 45 Laoying Shao; 老营哨45号; mains ¥30-80; ⏲11am-9pm) Specialising in local cuisine, particularly that of the Miao and the Tujia people, this intimate restaurant serves some truly tasty delights, including Fènghuáng's most famous dish, *Fènghuáng xuèbāyā* (凤凰血粑鸭; duck-blood cakes). Trust us: it's much nicer than it sounds.

It also does a delicious Taiwanese chicken stew called *sān bēi jī* (三杯鸡), and its *là ròu* (腊肉; cured pork) dishes are superb – it has four types. Also worth trying is the *tǔdòu fěn* (土豆粉), a rice-noodle dish from neighbouring Guìzhōu province. The only downside here are the expensive beers (¥15 to ¥35). Photo menu.

ℹ Information

The main bank branches are on Nanhua Lu.

China Post (中国邮政; Zhōngguó Yóuzhèng; cnr Sanwangge Lu & Hongqiao Zhonglu; ⏲8am-5.30pm)

Kāimíng Pharmacy (开明大药房; Kāimíng Dàyàofáng; Hongqiao Xilu; ⏲7.30am-10.30pm) Opposite the post office.

New People's Hospital (新人民医院; Xīn Rénmín Yīyuàn; ☎322 1199; Hongqiao Xilu) Southwest of town at the Jiensu Lu intersection.

Tourism Administrative Bureau of Fènghuáng (凤凰旅游中心; Fènghuáng Lǚyóu Zhōngxīn; ☎322 8365; ⏲6.30am-6pm) Off Wénhuà Sq.

Xīndònglì Internet Cafe (新动力网吧; Xīndònglì Wǎngbā; 2nd fl, Jianshe Lu; per hr ¥3; ⏰24hr) Beside Hóng Bridge.

ℹ️ Getting There & Around

Buses from **Fènghuáng Bus Terminal** (凤凰汽车客运总站; Fènghuáng Qìchē Kèyùn Zǒngzhàn) include the following:

Chángshā ¥140, five hours, hourly 7am to 5pm

Huáihuà ¥40, three hours, hourly 8am to 6pm

Jíshǒu ¥22, one hour, frequent 6.30am to 7.30pm

Zhāngjiājiè ¥80, 4½ hours, hourly 8.30am to 5pm

If you're heading to Guìzhōu province, there are frequent buses to Tóngrén (铜仁; ¥25, 1½ hours, 8am to 4.30pm), from where you can change for Zhènyuǎn.

Local Bus 1 goes from Fènghuáng Bus Terminal to Nánhuá Gate Tower.

There's no train station in Fènghuáng, but you can book tickets at the **train ticket booking office** (火车代票处; Huǒchē Dàipiàochù;; ☎322 2410; Hongqiao Zhonglu; ⏰8am-10pm) south of Hóng Bridge.

Hóngjiāng Old Town 洪江古商城

☎0745 / POP 60,783

This little-known town boasts an extraordinary history as a Qing-dynasty financial and trading centre, due to its fortuitous location at the confluence of the Yuán (沅江; Yuán Jiāng) and Wū (巫水; Wū Shuǐ) Rivers. At one time it was the main opium-distribution hub in southwest China. Dating as far back as the Northern Song dynasty, the surrounding city is mostly modern now, but the past lives on in the remarkable **old town** (古商城; *gǔshāngchéng*), which is still home to a few thousand people.

👁 Sights

The old town can be visited in half a day. It spreads in a maze of alleys running uphill from Yuanjiang Lu (沅江路) – a road running close to the river bank – but can be accessed from all sides.

There's an official **ticket office** (admission ¥120; ⏰8am-5pm) marked with red lanterns in an alley off Yuanjiang Lu. Admission includes guided two-hour tours in Chinese. You need not pay admission if you enter via any of the other alleys connecting to the main roads, but you won't be allowed into the notable buildings without a ticket.

The old town undulates in a higgledy-piggledy, often steep, maze of narrow stone-flagged alleys and lanes. Many of the less important buildings remain in a charming state of dilapidation. English and Chinese signposts point the way to the more notable buildings, most of which have been fully restored. These include the tax office, an opium shop, a brothel, a newspaper office, ancestral halls, and courtyard homes of prominent merchants. Most are of the *yìnzǐwū* (窨子屋) style, characterised by a series of adjoining courtyards, high exterior walls and concave roofs.

🛏 Sleeping & Eating

Hóngjiāng Hotel   HOTEL **$**
(洪江大酒店, Hóngjiāng Dàjiǔdiàn; ☎766 2999; 308 Xinmin Lu, 新民路308号; r from ¥168; ❄️@🛜) This ageing hotel with large rooms is well maintained and comfortable. Rooms can be discounted to ¥118. The alley opposite, between 225 and 227 Xinmin Lu, leads into the old town. While here pull up a stool and grab a bowl of *mǐfěn* (米粉; ¥5), Hóngjiāng's specialty rice noodles. The hotel is a few hundred metres uphill from the ticket office. The bus from Huáihuà passes here before terminating by the ticket office.

ℹ️ Information

Bank of China (中国银行; Zhōngguó Yínháng; 318 Xinmin Lu) Next to Hóngjiāng Hotel.

ℹ️ Getting There & Away

Don't confuse Hóngjiāng old town with Hóngjiāng city (洪江市; Hóngjiāng Shì), the town on the railway 30km west. The old town is most easily reached via the town of Huáihuà (怀化).

Buses from Huáihuà:

Chángshā ¥150, four hours, frequent 7.30am to 6.20pm

Fènghuáng ¥40, one hour, frequent 7am to 5.30pm

Hóngjiāng old town ¥25, 90 minutes, half-hourly 6.30am to 6pm

Buses to and from Fènghuáng use Huáihuà west bus station (汽车西站; Qìchē Xīzhàn), which is walking distance from Huáihuà train station (turn left out of the bus station, then second left at the roundabout).

Buses to and from Chángshā and Hóngjiāng old town use Huáihuà south bus station (汽车南站; Qìchē Nánzhàn).

Local bus 12 links Huáihuà's train station and south bus station.

Buses back to Huáihuà (6.30am to 6pm) from Hóngjiāng old town leave from opposite the ticket office.

1. Chinese opera (p977)
This art form has a continuous history stretching back 900 years.

1. West Lake (p260), Hángzhōu
The lake was created in the 8th century by Hángzhōu's governor.

2. Grand Buddha (p737), Lè Shān
The 1200-year-old statue, carved from the cliffs, is 71m tall.

3. Yùyuán Gardens (p195), Shànghǎi
Created in the 16th century, these gardens are a prime example of Ming landscape design.

4. Zhuang woman (p946)
A woman from the Zhuang ethnic minority group drying chillies.

1. Giant panda cub (p984)
These elusive animals are best seen in the wild in Sìchuān province.

2. Lóngjǐ Rice Terraces (p611)
The terraces are best visited after the summer rains in May.

3. Jade Market (p503), Hong Kong
All varieties and grades of jade are available here.

4. Lìjiāng (p678)
The city's maze-like Old Town was made a Unesco World Heritage Site in 1997.

THOMAS JANISCH / GETTY IMAGES ©

MAISANT / GETTY IMAGES ©

DAVID MCINTYRE / GETTY IMAGES ©

1. Jīndǐng (Golden Summit) Temple (p735)
This golden elephant forms part of a 48m-tall statue of Samantabhadra.

Hong Kong

📞 852 / POP 7 MILLION

Best Places to Eat

➡ Luk Yu Tea House (p516)

➡ 22 Ships (p516)

➡ Kowloon Tang (p518)

➡ Yè Shanghai (p518)

➡ Little Bao (p516)

Best Places to Stay

➡ Peninsula Hong Kong (p513)

➡ Tai O Heritage Hotel (p515)

➡ Mira Moon (p511)

➡ Helena May (p510)

➡ Upper House (p512)

Why Go?

Like a shot of adrenalin, Hong Kong quickens the pulse. Skyscrapers march up jungle-clad slopes by day and blaze neon by night across a harbour criss-crossed by freighters and motor junks. Above streets teeming with traffic, five-star hotels stand next to ageing tenement blocks.

The very acme of luxury can be yours, though enjoying the city need not cost the earth. The HK$2 ride across the harbour must be one of the world's best-value cruises. A meander through a market offers similarly cheap thrills. You can also escape the crowds – just head for one of the city's many country parks.

It's also a city that lives to eat, offering diners the very best of China and beyond. Hong Kong, above all, rewards those who grab experience by the scruff of the neck, who'll try that jellyfish, explore half-deserted villages or stroll beaches far from neon and steel.

When to Go

Hong Kong

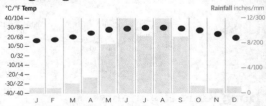

°C/°F Temp — Rainfall inches/mm

Mar–May Asia's top film festival, rugby and deities' birthdays beckon beyond a sea of umbrellas.

Jun–Sep Get hot (beach, new wardrobe), get wet (dragon boat, beer): antidotes to sultry summers.

Nov–Feb Hills by day, arts festival by night, celebrate Chinese New Year under Christmas lights.

Hong Kong Highlights

1 Crossing Victoria Harbour on the legendary **Star Ferry** (p506).

2 Taking the steep ascent to Victoria Peak on the **Peak Tram** (p493).

3 Eating yum cha under whirling fans at **Luk Yu Tea House** (p516).

4 Soaking up the incensed air at **Man Mo Temple** (p493).

5 Feeling the chug of the world's last **double-decker trams**.

6 Indulging in the visual feast of **Tsim Sha Tsui East Promenade** (p500).

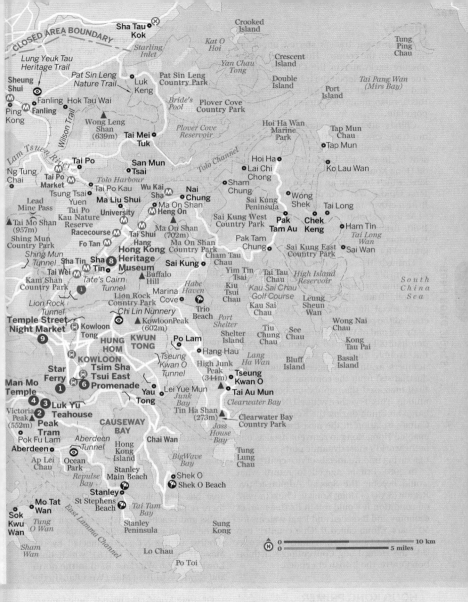

7 Losing yourself in a walled village on the **Ping Shan Heritage Trail** (p505).

8 Getting some context for it all at the **Hong Kong Heritage Museum** (p506).

9 Taking in the indigenous sights, sounds and smells of the **Temple Street Night Market** (p503).

10 Paying your respects to the magnificent Big Buddha at **Po Lin Monastery** (p507).

History

Until European traders started importing opium into the country, Hong Kong was an obscure backwater in the Chinese empire. The British developed the trade aggressively and by the start of the 19th century traded this 'foreign mud' for Chinese tea, silk and porcelain.

China's attempts to stamp out the opium trade gave the British the pretext they needed for military action. Gunboats were sent in. In 1841 the Union flag was hoisted on Hong Kong Island and the Treaty of Nanking, which brought an end to the so-called First Opium War, ceded the island to the British crown 'in perpetuity.'

At the end of the Second Opium War in 1860, Britain took possession of Kowloon Peninsula, and in 1898 a 99-year lease was granted for the New Territories.

Through the 20th century Hong Kong grew in fits and starts. Waves of refugees fled China for Hong Kong during times of turmoil. Trade flourished as did British expat social life, until the Japanese army crashed the party in 1941.

By the end of WWII Hong Kong's population had fallen from 1.6 million to 610,000. But trouble in China soon swelled the numbers again as refugees (including industrialists) from the communist victory in 1949 increased the population beyond two million. This, together with a UN trade embargo on China during the Korean War and China's isolation in the next three decades, enabled Hong Kong to reinvent itself as one of the world's most dynamic ports and manufacturing and financial-service centres.

In 1984 Britain agreed to return what would become the Special Administrative Region (SAR) of Hong Kong to China in 1997, on condition it would retain its free-market economy and its social and legal systems for 50 years. China called it 'One country, two systems.' On 1 July 1997, in pouring rain, outside the Hong Kong Convention & Exhibition Centre, the British era ended.

In the years that followed, Hong Kong weathered major storms – an economic downturn, the outbreak of the SARS virus and a nagging mistrust of the government.

In March 2012, Leung Chun-ying, a former property surveyor, became Hong Kong's fourth chief executive. Though a seemingly more decisive man than his predecessors, Leung's unsubstantiated 'red' connections have many Hong Kongers worried, something not helped by spiralling living costs and China's treatment of its dissidents.

Pro-democracy protesters took over the streets of downtown Hong Kong in September 2014, demanding free elections. Demonstrations continued until mid-December, with Beijing refusing to budge.

Language

Almost 95% of all Hong Kongers are Cantonese-speaking Chinese, though Putonghua (Mandarin) is increasingly used. Visitors should have few problems, however, because English is widely spoken and the street signs are bilingual, as are most restaurant menus. Written Chinese in Hong Kong uses traditional Chinese characters, which tend to be more complicated than the simplified Chinese used on the mainland.

Sights

Hong Kong comprises four main areas: Hong Kong Island, Kowloon, the New Territories (NT) and the Outlying Islands. Most sights are distributed in the northwestern part of Hong Kong Island, southern Kowloon Peninsula and throughout the NT.

More than 70% of Hong Kong is mountains and forests, most of it in the NT. The area has seen plenty of urbanisation, but there remain traditional villages, mountain walks and beaches, all within an hour or so of the urban area by public transport. The suburbs in the NT are connected by the Mass Transit Railway (MTR), which links Kowloon to Lo Wu (East Rail) in the north and Kowloon to Tuen Mun (West Rail) in the west.

Of Hong Kong's 234 islands, only Lantau, Cheung Chau, Lamma and Peng Chau have easy access by ferry.

Admission charges for children and seniors at many sights are roughly half the regular price.

HONG KONG PRIMER

Partly owing to its British colonial past, Hong Kong's political and economic systems are still significantly different from those of mainland China. Prices in this chapter are quoted in Hong Kong dollars (HK$).

◉ Hong Kong Island

Central is where high finance meets haute couture, and mega deals are closed in towering skyscrapers. To the west is historically rich – and increasingly hip – Sheung Wan, while Admiralty with its few but excellent offerings lies to the east. The 800m-long **Central–Mid-Levels Escalator** (Map p494; ⊙ down 6-10am, up 10.30am-midnight), which begins on Queen's Rd Central and finishes at Conduit Rd, is useful for negotiating the slopes of Sheung Wan.

East of Admiralty is Wan Chai which features skyscrapers in the north and old neighbourhoods in the south. Neon-clad Causeway Bay lies to the east.

Peak Tram   TRAM

(Map p494; ☑ 2522 0922; www.thepeak.com.hk; Lower Terminus 33 Garden Rd, Central; one-way/return adult HK$28/40, seniors over 65 & child 3-11yr HK$11/18; ⊙ 7am-midnight) The Peak Tram is not really a tram but a cable-hauled funicular railway that has been scaling the 396m ascent to the highest point on Hong Kong Island since 1888. It is thus the oldest form of public transport in the territory.

The Peak Tram runs every 10 to 15 minutes from 7am to midnight. Octopus cards can be used.

HSBC Building   BUILDING

(滙豐銀行總行大廈; Map p494; www.hsbc.com.hk/1/2/about/home/unique-headquarters; 1 Queen's Rd Central, Central; ⊙ escalator 9am-4.30pm Mon-Fri, 9am-12.30pm Sat; M Central, exit K) FREE Make sure you have a close-up look at the stunning headquarters of what is now HSBC (formerly the Hongkong & Shanghai Bank) headquarters, designed by British architect Sir Norman Foster in 1985. The building is a masterpiece of precision, sophistication and innovation. And so it should be. On completion in 1985 it was the world's most expensive building (it cost upward of US$1 billion).

★ Man Mo Temple   TAOIST TEMPLE

(文武廟; Map p494; ☑ 2540 0350; 124-126 Hollywood Rd, Sheung Wan; ⊙ 8am-6pm; ☐ 26) FREE One of Hong Kong's oldest temples and a declared monument, atmospheric Man Mo Temple is dedicated to the gods of literature ('Man'), holding a writing brush, and of war ('Mo'), wielding a sword. Built in 1847 during the Qing dynasty by wealthy Chinese merchants, it was, besides a place of worship, a court of arbitration for local disputes when trust was thin between the Chinese and the colonialists. Oaths taken at this Taoist temple (often accompanied by the ritual beheading of a rooster) were accepted by the colonial government.

Outside the main entrance are four gilt plaques on poles that used to be carried around at processions. Two describe the gods being worshipped inside, one requests silence and a show of respect within the temple's grounds, and the last warns menstruating women to keep out of the main hall. Inside the temple are two 19th-century sedan chairs with elaborate carvings, used to carry the two gods during festivals.

Lending the temple its beguiling and smoky air are rows of large earth-coloured spirals suspended from the roof, like strange fungi in an upside-down garden. These are incense coils burned as offerings by worshippers.

Off to the side is Lit Shing Kung, the 'saints' palace', a place of worship for other Buddhist and Taoist deities. Another hall, Kung Sor ('public meeting place'), used to serve as a court of justice to settle disputes among the Chinese community before the modern judicial system was introduced. A couplet at the entrance urges those entering to leave their selfish interests and prejudices outside. Fortune-tellers beckon from inside.

Asia Society Hong Kong
Centre   HISTORIC BUILDING, GALLERY

(亞洲協會香港中心, Hong Kong Jockey Club Former Explosives Magazine; Map p494; ☑ 2103 9511; www.asiasociety.org/hong-kong; 9 Justice Dr, Admiralty; ⊙ gallery 11am-5pm Tue-Sun, to 8pm last Thu of month; M Admiralty, exit F) An architectural feat, this magnificent site integrates 19th-century British military buildings, including a couple of explosives magazines, and transforms them into an exhibition gallery, a multipurpose theatre, an excellent restaurant and a bookshop, all open to the public. The architects Tod Williams and Billie Tsien eschewed bold statements for a subdued design that deferred to history and the natural shape of the land. The result is a horizontally oriented site that offers an uplifting contrast to the skyscrapers nearby. Experience it with a meal at AMMO (p516).

Dr Sun Yat-Sen
Museum   HISTORIC BUILDING, MUSEUM

(孫中山紀念館; Map p494; ☑ 2367 6373; http://hk.drsunyatsen.museum; 7 Castle Rd,

Sheung Wan, Central & Admiralty

Western Harbour Crossing

TurboJet

Hong Kong–Macau
Ferry Terminal

West Fire Service St

Chung Kong Rd

Connaught Rd West

Courtyard by
Marriott Hong Kong (650m)

Des Voeux Rd West

Tramway

Wilmer St

Ko Shing St

Queen St

New Market St

Wing Lok St

Bonham Strand West

22

Pier Rd

Sheung Wan

Man Wa La

Tramway

CTS Express Coach

Gilman

59

Morrison St

17

Queen's Rd West

Hollywood Road Park

Possession St

SHEUNG WAN

Bonham Strand East

Wing Lok St

Wing Wo St

55

Gilman's Bazaar

Wing Kut St

King George V
Memorial Park

New St

Wa La

Sai St

Lok Ku Rd

Cleverly St

Burd St

Jervois St

Dragonair

Hospital Rd

Po Yan St

Pound La

Tung St

Sai St

Hiller St

Queen's Rd Central

Gough St

30

Jubilee St

High St

Bonham Rd

Blake Garden

Tai Ping Shan St

Po Hing Fong

Man Mo
Temple

2

Hollywood Rd

Aberdeen St

Peel St

35

Stanley St

Park Rd

Breezy Path

Ladder St

Bridges St

Wing Lee St

Shing Wong St

Staunton St

38

45 47

Graham St

Gage St

Wellington St

Caine Rd

31

Lyndhurst Tce

39

6

Conduit Rd

Castle Rd

12

Seymour Rd

7

46 SOHO

60

5 42

Wyndham St

Robinson Rd

MID-LEVELS

Elgin St

29

Prince's Tce

Shelley St

Central-Midlevels Escalator

Old Bailey St

Old Chancery La

Arbuthnot Rd

Glenealy

21

Mosque St

11

Mosque Jct

8

18

Glenealy Lower

Albert Rd

Pok Fu Lam
Country
Park

Hornsey Rd

Glenealy

Robinson Rd

Old Peak Rd

Victoria Peak
(552m)

Lugard Rd

Mt Austine Rd

THE PEAK

Tregunter Path

May Rd

Brewin Path

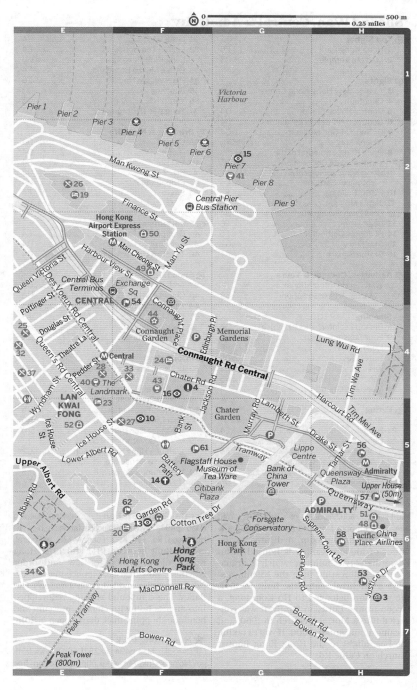

Sheung Wan, Central & Admiralty

Mid-Levels; adult/concession HK$10/5, Wed free; ◷10am-6pm Mon-Wed & Fri, to 7pm Sat & Sun; ▣3B) The museum, dedicated to the father of modern China, is housed in an Edwardian-style building, which is arguably more interesting than the solemn displays of archival materials. Built in 1914, the mansion belonged to Ho Kom-tong, a tycoon from a Eurasian family. It was converted into a Mormon church in 1960, and became a museum in 2006. If you're taking the bus, alight at the Hong Kong Baptist Church on Caine Rd.

Central Police Station   HISTORIC BUILDING
(Map p494; www.centralpolicestation.org.hk; 10 Hollywood Rd, Lan Kwai Fong; ▣26, Ⓜ Central, exit D2) Built between 1841 and 1919, Hong Kong's oldest symbol of law and order is this now-disused, police-magistracy-prison complex modelled on London's Old Bailey. The compound is being redeveloped into an arts hub with cinema, museum and boutique shopping mall, due to open in 2016.

★ **Hong Kong Park**   PARK
(香港公園; Map p494; ☑2521 5041; www.lcsd. gov.hk/parks/hkp/en/index.php; 19 Cotton Tree

Dr, Admiralty; ◷park 6am-11pm; 🍴; Ⓜ Admiralty, exit C1) **FREE** Designed to look anything but natural, Hong Kong Park is one of the most unusual parks in the world, emphasising artificial creations such as its fountain plaza, conservatory, waterfall, indoor games hall, playground, taichi garden, viewing tower, museum and arts centre. For all its artifice, the 8-hectare park is beautiful in its own weird way and, with a wall of skyscrapers on one side and mountains on the other, makes for some dramatic photographs.

Hong Kong Zoological & Botanical Gardens
PARK
(香港動植物公園; Map p494; www.lcsd.gov.hk/ parks; Albany Rd, Central; ◷terrace gardens 5am-10pm, greenhouse 9am-4.30pm; 🍴; ▢3B, 12) **FREE** Built in the Victorian era, this garden has a welcoming collection of fountains, sculptures and greenhouses, plus a zoo and some fabulous aviaries. Along with exotic vegetation, some 160 species of bird reside here. The zoo is surprisingly comprehensive, and is also one of the world's leading centres for the captive breeding of endangered species. Albany Rd divides the gardens, with the plants and aviaries to the east, close to Garden Rd, and most of the animals to the west.

Statue Square
SQUARE
(皇后像廣場; Map p494; Edinburgh Pl, Central; Ⓜ Central, exit K) This leisurely square used to house effigies of British royalty. Now it pays tribute to a single sovereign – the founder of HSBC. In the northern area (reached via an underpass) is the **Cenotaph** (和平紀念碑; Map p494; Chater Rd), built in 1923 as a memorial to Hong Kong residents killed during the two world wars. On the south side of Chater Rd, Statue Sq has a pleasant collection of fountains and seating areas, with tiling that's strangely reminiscent of a 1980s municipal washroom.

Old Wan Chai
VILLAGE
The area around Queen's Rd E (Wan Chai metro station, exit A3) is filled with pockets of local culture that are best explored on foot.

The historic **Blue House** (72-74A Stone Nullah Lane) is a prewar building with cast-iron Spanish balconies reminiscent of those found in New Orleans. Conservationists love it; tenants loathe it (old Bluesy's loos don't flush!). **Old Wan Chai Post Office** (舊灣仔郵政局; 221 Queen's Rd E, Wan Chai; ◷10am-5pm Wed-Mon; ▢6, 6A) is Hong Kong's oldest

post-office building. The area sandwiched by Queen's Rd E and Johnston Rd is a lively outdoor bazaar. **Wan Chai Market** (◷7.30am-7pm) vendors flaunt their wares on Cross St and Stone Nullah Lane. **Tai Yuen St** has goldfish, plastic flowers and granny underwear but is best known for its toy shops selling collectibles such as clockwork tin.

Pak Tai Temple
TAOIST TEMPLE
(北帝廟; 2 Lung On St, Wan Chai; ◷8am-5pm; Ⓜ Wan Chai, exit A3) A short stroll up Stone Nullah Lane takes you to a majestic Taoist temple built in 1863 to honour a god of the sea, Pak Tai. The temple – the largest on Hong Kong Island – is impressive. The main hall contains a 3m-tall copper likeness of Pak Tai cast in the Ming dynasty.

Victoria Park
PARK
(維多利亞公園; www.lcsd.gov.hk/en/ls_park. php; Causeway Rd, Causeway Bay; ◷6am or 7am-

HONG KONG

Wan Chai & Causeway Bay

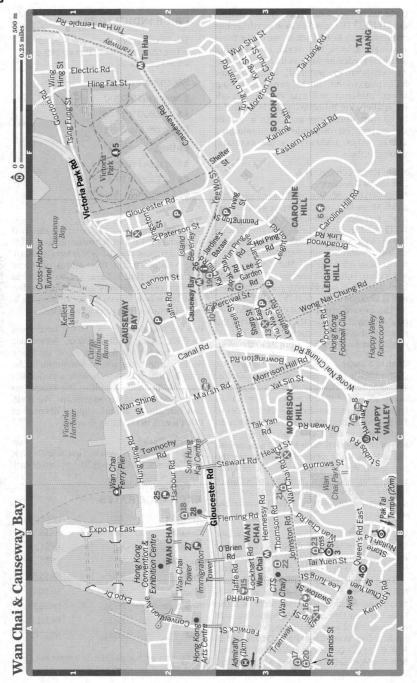

Wan Chai & Causeway Bay

11pm; Ⓜ Tin Hau, exit B) **FREE** Victoria Park is the biggest patch of public greenery on Hong Kong Island. The best time to go is on a weekday morning, when it becomes a forest of people practising the slow-motion choreography of taichi. The park becomes a flower market a few days before the Chinese New Year. It's also worth a visit during the Mid-Autumn Festival, when people turn out en masse carrying lanterns.

St John's Cathedral CHURCH
(聖約翰座堂; Map p494; ☎ 2523 4157; www. stjohnscathedral.org.hk; 4-8 Garden Rd, Central; ⊙ 7am-6pm; ☐ 12A, 40, 40M, Ⓜ Central, exit K) **FREE** Services have been held at this Anglican cathedral since it opened in 1849, with the exception of 1944, when the Japanese army used it as a social club. It suffered heavy damage during WWII, and the front doors were subsequently remade using timber salvaged from HMS *Tamar*, a British warship that guarded Victoria Harbour. You walk on sacred ground in more ways than one here: it is the only piece of freehold land in Hong Kong. Enter from Battery Path.

Khalsa Diwan Sikh Temple SIKH TEMPLE
(☎ 2572 4459; www.khalsadiwan.com; 371 Queen's Rd E, Wan Chai; ⊙ 4am-9pm; ☐ 10 from Central) Sitting quietly between a busy road and a cemetery is Hong Kong's largest Sikh temple, a descendant of a small original built in 1901 by Sikh members of the British army. The temple welcomes people of any faith, caste or colour to join in its services. Sunday prayer (9am to 1.30pm) sees some 1000 believers and nonbelievers in collective worship (fewer at the daily prayers, 6am to 8.30am and 6.30pm to 8pm).

Jamia Mosque MOSQUE
(些利街清真寺; Map p494; ☎ 2523 7743; 30 Shelley St, Mid-Levels) Also called Lascar Mosque, Hong Kong's oldest mosque was erected in 1849. Non-Muslims can only admire the facade from the terrace out front. Jamia Mosque is accessible by the Central–Mid-Levels Escalator.

Ohel Leah Synagogue SYNAGOGUE
(莉亞堂; Map p494; ☎ 2589 2621; www.ohelleah. org; 70 Robinson Rd, Mid-Levels; ⊙ by appointment only 10.30am-7pm Mon-Thu, services 7am Mon-Fri, 6pm Mon-Thu; ☐ 3B, 23) This Moorish Romantic temple, completed in 1902, is named after Leah Gubbay Sassoon, the matriarch of a philanthropic Sephardic Jewish family. It's Hong Kong's earliest synagogue. Be sure to bring ID if you plan on visiting the sumptuous interior.

Stanley VILLAGE
This crowd-pleaser is best visited on weekdays. **Stanley Market** (赤柱市集; Stanley Village Rd; ⊙ 9am-6pm; ☐ 6, 6A, 6X or 260) is a maze of alleyways that has bargain clothing (haggling a must!). **Stanley Main Beach** is for beach-bumming and windsurfing. With graves dating back to 1841, **Stanley Military**

HONG KONG IN...

One Day

Catch a tram up to **Victoria Peak** (p493) for great views of the city, stopping for lunch in **Central** on the way down. Head to **Man Mo Temple** (p493) for a taste of history before boarding the **Star Ferry** (p506) to Kowloon. Enjoy the views along **Tsim Sha Tsui East Promenade** as you stroll over to the **Hong Kong Museum of History**. Dine on ultraluxe Cantonese cuisine (think seafood) at **Boss** (p517) in Central. After dinner, take the MTR to Soho for drinks at **Club 71** (p520).

Two Days

In addition to the above, you could go to **Aberdeen** for a boat ride, then seafood and shopping. After dark, head to the **Temple Street Night Market** (p503) for sightseeing, shopping and street food. If you're still game, check out the Yau Ma Tei **Wholesale Fruit Market** (油麻地果欄; Map p501; cnr Shek Lung St & Reclamation St, Yau Ma Tei; ⊙2-6am; ⓜYau Ma Tei, exit B2).

Cemetery (赤柱軍人墳場; ☑2557 3498; Wong Ma Kok Rd; ⊙8am-5pm; ☐14, 6A), 500m south of the market, is worth a visit.

Aberdeen
VILLAGE

Aberdeen's main attraction is the typhoon shelter it shares with sleepy **Ap Lei Chau** (☑Ap Lei Chau), where the sampans of Hong Kong's boat-dwelling fisherfolk used to moor. On weekday evenings, you may spot dragon boat teams practising here. The best way to see the area is by sampan. A half-hour tour of the typhoon shelter costs about HK$55 per person. Embark from **Aberdeen Promenade**.

Repulse Bay
BEACH

(淺水灣; ☐6, 6A, 6X, 260) The long beach with tawny sand at Repulse Bay is visited by Chinese tourist groups year-round and, needless to say, gets packed on weekends in summer. It's a good place if you like people-watching. The beach has showers and changing rooms and shade trees at the roadside, but the water is pretty murky.

Ocean Park
AMUSEMENT PARK

(☑3923 2323; www.oceanpark.com.hk; Ocean Park Rd; adult/child 3-11yr HK$320/160; ⊙10am-7.30pm; ☑; ☐629 from Admiralty, ☐973 from Tsim Sha Tsui, ☐6A, 6X, 70, 75 from Central, ☐72, 72A, 92 from Causeway Bay) It may have to compete with the natural crowd-pulling powers of Disneyland on Lantau, but for many Ocean Park remains the top theme park in Hong Kong. The park's constant expansion and addition of new rides and thrills, as well as the presence of four giant pandas plus two very cute, rare red pandas – all

gifts from the mainland – has kept this a must-visit for families.

Shek O Beach
BEACH

(☐9 from Shau Kei Wan MTR station, exit A3) Shek O beach has a large expanse of sand, shady trees to the rear, showers, changing facilities and lockers for rent.

◉ Kowloon

Tsim Sha Tsui, known for its variety of dining and shopping options, is Hong Kong's most eclectic district, with the glamorous only a stone's throw from the pedestrian, and a population comprising Chinese, South Asians, Africans, Filipinos and Europeans.

To the north, buzzing with local life, is down-at-heel **Yau Ma Tei**. Traffic- and pedestrian-choked **Mong Kok** is the world's most densely populated place.

★ Tsim Sha Tsui East Promenade
HARBOUR

(尖沙嘴東部海濱花園; Map p502; Salisbury Rd, Tsim Sha Tsui; ⓜTsim Sha Tsui, exit E) One of the finest city skylines in the world has to be that of Hong Kong Island, and the promenade here is one of the best ways to get an uninterrupted view. It's a lovely place to stroll around during the day, but it really comes into its own in the evening, during the nightly **Symphony of Lights** (⊙8-8.20pm), a spectacular sound-and-light show involving 44 buildings on the Hong Kong Island skyline. The new Deck 'n Beer bar located here is a great spot to have an alfresco, waterside drink (weather permitting).

Yau Ma Tei

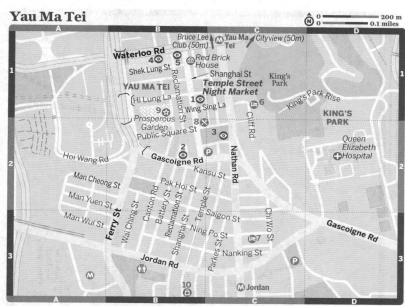

Hong Kong Museum of History   MUSEUM
(香港歷史博物館; Map p502; ☎2724 9042;
http://hk.history.museum; 100 Chatham Rd
South, Tsim Sha Tsui; adult/concession HK$10/5,
Wed free; ◷10am-6pm Mon & Wed-Sat, to 7pm
Sun; ♿; MTsim Sha Tsui, exit B2) For a whis-
tle-stop overview of the territory's archaeology, ethnography, and natural and local
history, this museum is well worth a visit,
not only to learn more about the subject
but also to understand how Hong Kong
presents its stories to the world. 'The Hong
Kong Story' takes visitors on a fascinating
walk through the territory's past via eight
galleries, starting with the natural environment and prehistoric Hong Kong – about
6000 years ago, give or take a lunar year –
and ending with the territory's return to
China in 1997.

**Former Marine Police
Headquarters**   HISTORIC BUILDING
(前水警總部; Map p502; ☎2926 8000, tour reservation 2926 1881; www.1881heritage.com; 2A
Canton Rd, Tsim Sha Tsui; ◷10am-10pm; ⚓Star
Ferry, MEast Tsim Sha Tsui, exit L6) FREE Built
in 1884, this gorgeous Victorian complex,
is one of Hong Kong's four oldest government buildings. It was used continuously
by the Hong Kong Marine Police except
during WWII when the Japanese navy

Yau Ma Tei

◉ **Top Sights**

◉ **Sights**

🛏 **Sleeping**

🍴 **Eating**

🎭 **Entertainment**

🛍 **Shopping**

took over. The complex is now a nakedly
commercial property called 'Heritage 1881'.
Some of the old structures are still here,
including stables, pigeon houses and bomb
shelter. Why 1881? Because '4' has a similar
pronunciation to 'death' in Chinese, and
the developer was superstitious.

Kowloon

HONG KONG

500 m
0.25 miles

HUNG HOM
Hung Hom

Hung Hom Bypass

Cross-Harbour Tunnel

Cheong Wan Rd

Hong Chong Rd

Yuk Choi Rd

Cheong Wan Rd

Concordia Plaza

Science Museum

Chinachem Golden Plaza

TSIM SHA TSUI EAST

Salisbury Rd

Victoria Harbour

Energy Plaza

Chatham Rd South

Granville Rd

Centenary Gardens

East Tsim Sha Tsui (KCR East Rail) Terminus

Mody Rd

Wing On Plaza

Tsim Sha Tsui East Waterfront Podium Garden

Tsim Sha Tsui East Promenade

Austin Rd

Hillwood Rd

Austin Ave

Observatory Rd

Kimberley Rd

Kimberley St

Granville Rd

Carnarvon Rd

Cameron Rd

Prat Ave

Hart Ave

Hanoi Rd

Minden Ave

Minden Row

Avenue of the Stars

Nathan Rd

Chinese Garden

Kowloon Park

TSIM SHA TSUI

Haiphong Rd

Humphreys Ave

Carnarvon Rd

Cornwall Ave

Tsim Sha Tsui

Lock Rd

Hankow Rd

Ashley Rd

Salisbury Gardens

Salisbury Rd

Minden Row

Kowloon Park Dr

Peking Rd

Eternal East Cross Border Coach

Middle Rd

Former KCR Clock Tower

Canton Rd

HARBOUR CITY

China Hong Kong City

China Ferry Terminal

Ocean Terminal

Cathay Pacific Airways

Star Ferry Terminal

Star Bus Terminal

Star Ferry Pier

1 Ritz Carlton Hong Kong, Ozone, Tin Lung Heen (200m); Elements, Kowloon Tang (350m)

Kowloon

HONG KONG SIGHTS

St Andrew's Anglican Church CHURCH
(聖安德烈堂; Map p502; ☎2367 1478; www.
standrews.org.hk; 138 Nathan Rd, Tsim Sha Tsui;
☺7.30am-10.30pm, church 8.30am-5.30pm; ⓂT-
sim Sha Tsui, exit B1) Sitting atop a knoll, next
to the Former Kowloon British School, is a
charming building in English Gothic style
that houses Kowloon's oldest Protestant
church. St Andrew's was built in 1905 in
granite and red brick to serve Kowloon's
Protestant population; it was turned into a
Shinto shrine during the Japanese occupation. Nearby you'll see the handsome former
vicarage with columned balconies (c 1909).
Enter from the eastern side of Nathan Rd via
steps or a slope.

Hong Kong Museum of Art MUSEUM
(香港藝術館; Map p502; ☎2721 0116; http://
hk.art.museum; 10 Salisbury Rd, Tsim Sha Tsui;
adult/concession HK$10/5, Wed free; ☺10am-6pm
Mon-Fri, to 7pm Sat & Sun; ⛴Star Ferry, ⓂEast
Tsim Sha Tsui, exit J) This excellent museum
has seven galleries spread over six floors, exhibiting Chinese antiquities, fine art, historical pictures and contemporary Hong Kong
art. Highlights include the Xubaizhi collection of painting and calligraphy, contempo-

rary works, and ceramics and other antiques
from China. Audio guides are available for
HK$10. Refer to the tour schedule in the lob-
by for free English-language tours.

★ Temple Street Night Market MARKET
(廟街夜市; Map p501; Yau Ma Tei; ☺6-11pm;
ⓂYau Ma Tei, exit C) The liveliest night market in Hong Kong, Temple St extends from
Man Ming Lane in the north to Nanking St
in the south and is cut in two by the Tin Hau
temple complex. While you may find better
bargains further north in New Kowloon,
and certainly over the border in Shēnzhèn,
it is still a good place to go for the bustling
atmosphere and the smells and tastes on offer from the *dai pai dong* (open-air street
stall) food.

Jade Market MARKET
(玉器市場; Map p501; Battery St & Kansu St, Yau
Ma Tei; ☺10am-6pm; ⓂYau Ma Tei, exit C) The
covered Jade Market, split into two parts
by Battery St, has hundreds of stalls selling
all varieties and grades of jade. But unless
you really know your nephrite from your
jadeite, it's not wise to buy expensive pieces
here.

Tin Hau Temple
TEMPLE

(天后廟; Map p501; ☑ 2385 0759; www.ctc.org. hk; cnr Temple St & Public Square St, Yau Ma Tei; ⊗ 8am-5pm; M Yau Ma Tei, exit C) This large, incense-filled sanctuary built in the 19th century is one of Hong Kong's most famous Tin Hau (Goddess of the Sea) temples. The public square out front is Yau Ma Tei's communal heart where fishermen once laid out their hemp ropes to sun next to Chinese banyans that today shade chess players and elderly men. Yau Ma Tei Police Station is a listed blue-and-white structure one block to the east along Public Square St.

★ Yuen Po Street Bird Garden & Flower Market
PARK, MARKET

(園圃街雀鳥花園, 花墟; Yuen Po St & Boundary St, Mong Kok; ⊗ 7am-8pm; M Prince Edward, exit B1) In this enchanting corner of Mong Kok, you will find a handful of old men out 'walking' their caged songbirds. Stick around long enough and you should see birds being fed squirming caterpillars with chopsticks. There are also feathered creatures for sale, along with elaborate cages carved from teak. Adjacent to the garden is the **flower market** (Flower Market Rd), which theoretically keeps the same hours, but only gets busy after 10am.

Chi Lin Nunnery
BUDDHIST NUNNERY

(志蓮淨苑; ☑ 2354 1888; www.chilin.org; 5 Chi Lin Dr, Diamond Hill; ⊗ nunnery 9am-4.30pm, garden 6.30am-7pm; M Diamond Hill, exit C2) **FREE** One of the most beautiful and arrestingly built environments in Hong Kong, this large Buddhist complex, originally dating from the 1930s, was rebuilt completely of wood (and not a single nail) in the style of the Tang dynasty in 1998. It is a serene place, with lotus ponds, immaculate bonsai tea plants and bougainvillea, and silent nuns delivering offerings of fruit and rice to Buddha and arhats (Buddhist disciples freed from the cycle of birth and death) or chanting behind intricately carved screens.

Sik Sik Yuen Wong Tai Sin Temple
TEMPLE

(嗇色園黃大仙祠; ☑ 2327 8141, 2351 5640; www.siksikyuen.org.hk; 2, Chuk Yuen Village, Wong Tai Sin; donation HK$2; ⊗ 7am-5.30pm; M Wong Tai Sin, exit B2) An explosion of colourful pillars, roofs, latticework, flowers and incense, this busy temple is a destination for all walks of Hong Kong society, from pensioners and businesspeople to parents and young professionals.

Some come simply to pray, others to divine the future with *chìm* – bamboo 'fortune sticks' that are shaken out of a box on to the ground and then read by a fortune-teller (they're available free from the left of the main temple).

Middle Road Children's Playground
PARK

(中間道兒童遊樂場; Map p502; Middle Rd, Tsim Sha Tsui; ⊗ 7am-11pm; ⊕; M East Tsim Sha Tsui, exit K) Accessible via a sweep of stairs from Chatham Rd South, this hidden gem atop the East Tsim Sha Tsui MTR station has play facilities, shaded seating and views of the waterfront. On weekdays it's the quiet backyard playground of the residents nearby, but on weekends it's filled with children and picnickers of as many ethnicities as there are ways to go down a slide (if you're eight).

Signal Hill Garden & Blackhead Point Tower
PARK

(訊號山公園和訊號塔; Map p502; Minden Row, Tsim Sha Tsui; ⊗ tower 9-11am & 4-6pm; M East Tsim Sha Tsui, exit K) The views from the top of this knoll are quite spectacular, and if it were the 1900s the ships in the harbour might be returning your gaze – a copper ball in the handsome Edwardian-style tower was dropped at 1pm daily so seafarers could adjust their chronometers. The garden is perched above the Middle Road Children's Playground. Enter from Minden Row (Mody Rd).

Kowloon Park
PARK

(九龍公園; Map p502; www.lcsd.gov.hk; Nathan & Austin Rds, Tsim Sha Tsui; ⊗ 6am-midnight; ⊕; M Tsim Sha Tsui, exit C2) Built on the site of a barracks for Indian soldiers in the colonial army, Kowloon Park is an oasis of greenery and a refreshing escape from the hustle and bustle of Tsim Sha Tsui. Pathways and walls criss-cross the grass, birds hop around in cages, and ancient banyan trees dot the landscape. In the morning the older set practise taichi amid the serene surrounds, and on Sunday afternoon Kung Fu Corner stages martial arts displays.

Jockey Club Creative Arts Centre
ARTS CENTRE

(賽馬會創意藝術中心; JCCAC; www.jccac.org. hk; 30 Pak Tin St, Shek Kip Mei; ⊗ 10am-10pm; M Shek Kip Mei, exit C) Over 150 artists have moved into these factory premises that used to churn out shoes and watches. Many studios are closed on weekdays, but you can visit the breezy communal areas, the cafes and the shops with regular opening hours.

Fook Tak Ancient Temple TEMPLE
(福德古廟; Map p502; 30 Haiphong Rd, Tsim Sha Tsui; ⏰6am-8pm; Ⓜ Tsim Sha Tsui, exit C2) Tsim Sha Tsui's only temple is a smoke-filled hole in the wall with a hot tin roof. Little is known about its ancestry except that it was built as a shrine in the Qing dynasty and renovated in 1900. Before WWII, worshippers of its Earth God were the coolies from Kowloon Wharf nearby, where the **Ocean Terminal** (Map p502; www.oceanterminal.com.hk; Salisbury Rd, Tsim Sha Tsui; ⏰10am-9pm; 🚢 Star Ferry, Ⓜ East Tsim Sha Tsui, exit J) now stands. Today most incense offerers are octogenarians – the temple specialises in longevity.

Kowloon Mosque & Islamic Centre MOSQUE
(九龍清真寺; Map p502; ☎2724 0095; http://kowloonmosque.com; 105 Nathan Rd, Tsim Sha Tsui; ⏰5am-10pm; Ⓜ Tsim Sha Tsui, exit C2) This structure, with its dome and carved marble, is Hong Kong's largest mosque. It serves the territory's 70,000-odd Muslims, more than half of whom are Chinese, and accommodates up to 3000 worshippers. The mosque was originally established to serve the Indian Muslim troops of the British army who were stationed at what is now Kowloon Park. Muslims are welcome to attend services, but non-Muslims should ask permission to enter. Remember to remove your footwear.

⊙ New Territories

Occupying 747 sq km of Hong Kong's land mass, the New Territories is a combination of housing estates and unspoiled rural areas.

The New Towns of Tsuen Wan, Tuen Mun, Fanling, Sheung Shui, Tai Po and Sha Tin are all worth visiting for their temples and museums. They are accessible via their eponymous MTR stations, and Tuen Mun is served by the Light Rail network.

Yuen Long boasts Hong Kong's most historical walled villages and a world-class nature reserve. It's on both the West Rail and the Light Rail Transit networks.

The Sai Kung Peninsula is great for hiking, sailing and seafood. The New Territories' best beaches are here.

★ Mai Po Nature Reserve NATURE RESERVE
(米埔自然保護區; ☎2471 3480; www.wwf.org.hk; Mai Po, Sin Tin, Yuen Long; admission HK$120; ⏰9am-5pm; 🚌76K from Sheung Shui East Rail or Yuen Long West Rail station) The 270-hectare nature reserve includes the **Mai Po Visitor Centre** (☎2471 8272) at the north

eastern end, where you must register; the **Mai Po Education Centre** (☎2482 0369) to the south, with displays on the history and ecology of the wetland and Deep Bay; floating boardwalks and trails through the mangroves and mud flats; and a dozen hides (towers or huts from where you can watch birds up close without being observed). Disconcertingly, the cityscape of Shēnzhèn looms to the north.

Ping Shan Heritage Trail HERITAGE WALK
(屏山文物徑; ☎2617 1959; ⏰ancestral halls 9am-1pm & 2-5pm, Tsui Sing Lau 9am-1pm & 2-5pm, closed Tue; Ⓜ West Rail Tin Shui Wai, exit E) Hong Kong's first ever heritage trail features historic buildings belonging to the Tangs, the first and the most powerful of the 'Five Clans'. Highlights of the 1km trail include Hong Kong's oldest **pagoda** (Tsui Sing Lau) a magnificent **ancestral hall**, a temple, a study hall, a well and a **gallery** inside an old police station that was built by the British as much to monitor the coastline as to keep an eye on the clan.

Lung Yeuk Tau Heritage Trail HERITAGE WALK
(龍躍頭文物徑; 🚌54K) This 4.5km-long trail northeast of Fanling meanders through five relatively well-preserved walled villages and, like the village of Ping Shan, they are home to the Tang clan. The most attractive of the lot is the oldest (800 years) but most intact **Lo Wai**, identifiable by its 1m-thick fortified wall. Unfortunately, it's not open to the public. Admire the exterior, before carrying on to the more welcoming villages of **Tung Kok Wai** to the northeast and **Sun Wai** towards the northern end of the trail.

Kat Hing Wai VILLAGE
(吉慶圍; 🚌64K) This tiny village is 500 years old and was walled during the early years of the Ming dynasty (1368–1644). It contains just one main street, off which a host of dark and narrow alleyways lead. There are quite a few new buildings and retiled older ones

THE STAR FERRY

You can't say you've 'done' Hong Kong until you've taken a ride on a **Star Ferry** (天星小輪; Map p494; ☎2367 7065; www.starferry.com.hk; adult HK$2.50-3.40, child HK$1.50-2.10; ⊙every 6-12min, 6.30am-11.30pm; Ⓜ Hong Kong, exit A2), that legendary fleet of electric-diesel vessels with names like *Morning Star* and *Twinkling Star*. At any time of the day, the HK$2.50 ride, with its riveting views of skyscrapers and jungle-clad hills, must be one of the world's best-value cruises. The Star Ferry crosses the harbour between Central and Tsim Sha Tsui, and Wan Chai and Tsim Sha Tsui. At the end of the 10-minute journey, a hemp rope is cast and caught with a billhook, the way it was in 1888 when the first boat docked.

The Star Ferry was founded by Dorabjee Nowrojee, a Parsee from Bombay. Parsees believe in Zoroastrianism, and the five-pointed star on the Star Ferry logo is an ancient Zoroastrian symbol – in fact the same as the one followed by the Three Magi (who may have been Zoroastrian pilgrims) to Bethlehem in the Christmas tale.

Zoroastrians consider fire a medium through which spiritual wisdom is gained, and water is considered the source of that wisdom. No wonder that on an overcast day, the only stars you'll see over Victoria Harbour are those of the Star Ferry.

in the village. A small temple stands at the end of the street. Visitors are asked to make a donation when they enter the village; put the money in the coin slot by the entrance.

Tai Po Market MARKET
(大埔街市; Fu Shin St; ⊙6am-8pm; Ⓜ Tai Wo) Not to be confused with the East Rail station of the same name, this street-long outdoor wet market is one of the most winning in the New Territories. Feast your eyes on a rainbow of fruits and vegetables, tables lined with dried seafood, old ladies hawking glutinous Hakka rice cakes, and stalls selling fresh aloe and sugar-cane juices.

★ Hong Kong Wetland Park PARK
(香港濕地公園; ☎3152 2666; www.wetlandpark. gov.hk; Wetland Park Rd, Tin Shui Wai; adult/concession HK$30/15; ⊙10am-5pm Wed-Mon; ♿; ☒ line 705, 706) This 60-hectare ecological park is a window on the wetland ecosystems of northwest New Territories. The natural trails, bird hides and viewing platforms make it a handy and excellent spot for birdwatching. The futuristic grass-covered headquarters houses interesting galleries (including one on tropical swamps), a film theatre, a cafe and a viewing gallery. If you have binoculars then bring them; otherwise be prepared to wait to use the fixed points in the viewing galleries and hides.

Fung Ying Sin Temple TAOIST TEMPLE
(☎2669 9186; 66 Pak Wo Rd, Fanling; ⊙8am-6pm, restaurant 10am-5pm; Ⓜ Fanling) This huge Taoist temple complex opposite the Fanling East Rail station has wonderful exterior murals of Taoist immortals and the Chinese

zodiac, an orchard terrace, a herbal clinic and a **vegetarian restaurant** (ground and 1st floors, Bldg A7). Most important are the dozen ancestral halls behind the main temple, where the ashes of the departed are deposited in niche urns.

★ Hong Kong Heritage Museum MUSEUM
(香港文化博物館; ☎2180 8188; www.heritage museum.gov.hk; 1 Man Lam Rd; adult/concession HK$10/5, Wed free; ⊙10am-6pm Mon & Wed-Sat, to 7pm Sun; ♿; Ⓜ Che Kung Temple) Southwest of Sha Tin town centre, this spacious, high-quality museum gives a peek into local history and culture. Highlights include a **children's area** with interactive play zones; the **New Territories Heritage Hall** with mock-ups of traditional minority villages; the **Cantonese Opera Heritage Hall**, where you can watch old operas with English subtitles; and an elegant **gallery** of Chinese art. Lately, the big draw is a semipermanent **Bruce Lee exhibit**, with some 600 items of the Kung Fu star's memorabilia on display until 2018.

Tsing Shan Monastery BUDDHIST MONASTERY
(青山禪院; ☎2461 8050; Tsing Shan Monastery Path; ⊙24hr; ☒ line 610, 615, 615P) Also known as Castle Peak Monastery, this temple complex perched on the hill of Castle Peak is the oldest in Hong Kong. Founded by Reverend Pui To (literally, 'travelling in a cup') 1500 years ago, the complex you see today was rebuilt in 1926. Check out shrines and temples for different saints and Bodhisattvas, including one to Pui To in a grotto, as you ascend the hill. Some of these have slid into dilapidation; nonetheless they're imbued with a spooky charm.

★ 10,000 Buddhas Monastery
BUDDHIST MONASTERY

(萬佛寺; ☎2691 1067; ⊙10am-5pm; Ⓜ Sha Tin, exit B) **FREE** This quirky temple about 500m northwest of Sha Tin station is worth the uphill hike to visit. Built in the 1950s, the complex actually contains more than 10,000 Buddhas. Some 12,800 miniature statues line the walls of the main temple and dozens of life-sized golden statues of Buddha's followers flank the steep steps leading to the monastery complex. There are several temples and pavilions split over two levels, as well as a nine-storey pagoda.

Hoi Ha Wan Marine Park
MARINE PARK

(海下灣; ☎hotline 1823; Hoi Ha; 🚐green minibus 7) A rewarding 6km walk in the area starts from the village of Hoi Ha (literally 'Under the Sea'), now part of the Hoi Ha Wan Marine Park, a 260-hectare protected area blocked off by concrete booms from the Tolo Channel and closed to fishing vessels. It's one of the few places in Hong Kong waters where coral still grows in abundance and is a favourite with snorkellers and kayakers.

⊙ Outlying Islands

Lantau is the largest island in Hong Kong and is ideal for a multiday excursion to explore its trails and villages and to enjoy the beaches. Mui Wo is the arrival point for ferries from Central, and Tung Chung is connected by MTR.

Laid-back **Lamma** has decent beaches, excellent walks and a cluster of restaurants in **Yung Shue Wan** and **Sok Kwu Wan**. A fun day involves taking the ferry to Yung Shue Wan, walking the easy 90-minute trail to Sok Kwu Wan and settling in for lunch at one of the seafood restaurants beside the water.

Dumbbell-shaped **Cheung Chau**, with a harbour filled with fishing boats, a windsurfing centre, several temples and some waterfront restaurants, also makes a fun day out. Not far away is **Peng Chau**, the smallest and most traditional of the easily accessible islands.

★ Po Lin Monastery & Big Buddha
BUDDHIST MONASTERY

(寶蓮禪寺; ☎2985 5248; Lantau; ⊙9am-6pm) Po Lin is a huge Buddhist monastery and temple complex that was built in 1924. Today it seems more of a tourist honeypot than a religious retreat, attracting hundreds of thousands of visitors a year and still being expanded. Most of the buildings you'll see on arrival are new, with the older, simpler ones tucked away behind them.

★ Tai O
VILLAGE

(🚐1 from Mui Wo, 11 from Tung Chung, 21 from Ngong Ping) On weekends, droves of visitors trek to the far-flung west coast of Lantau to see a fascinating way of life. Here in Tai O, historical home to the Tanka boat people, life is all about the sea. Houses are built on stilts above the ocean, sampans ply the dark-green waterways, and elderly residents still dry seafood on traditional straw mats and make the village's celebrated shrimp paste.

Hong Kong Disneyland
AMUSEMENT PARK

(香港迪士尼樂園; ☎183 0830; http://park. hongkongdisneyland.com; adult/child HK$499/355; ⊙10am-8pm Mon-Fri, to 9pm Sat & Sun; 🅿; Ⓜ Disney Resort Station) Ever since it claimed Hong Kong in 2005, Disneyland has served as a rite of passage for the flocks of Asian tourists who come daily to steal a glimpse of one of America's most famous cultural exports. It's divided into seven areas – Main Street USA, Tomorrowland, Fantasyland, Adventureland, Toy Story Land, Mystic Point, and Grizzly Gulch – but it's still quite tiny compared to the US version, and most of the attractions are geared to families with small children.

Most of the rides are appropriate for all but the smallest kids. Highlights include the goofy-scary tour through the Mystic Manor, and classics like 'It's a Small World' and the Mad Hatter teacups. Adrenalin junkies have only a few true thrills – the whipping-through-utter-darkness Space Mountain roller coaster in Tomorrowland, the Big Grizzly Mountain coaster in Grizzly Gulch, and the stomach-dropping RC Racer half-pipe coaster in Toy Story Land. The Iron Man Experience 3D motion simulator is slated to open in 2016.

While most of Hong Kong Disney is essentially a scaled-down version of the American Disneyland, there are a number of nods to Chinese culture. Disney consulted a feng shui master when building the park, and ended up moving the entrance 12 degrees to avoid *chi* slipping into the ocean. The lucky number eight is repeated throughout the park (the Western mining town of Grizzly Gulch was said to be founded on 8 August 1888), and Canto-pop singer Jacky Cheung is the park's official spokesperson.

The hungry will never be far from a snack or a sit-down meal, whether Eastern (dried

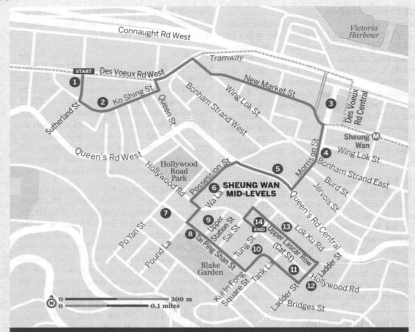

Walking Tour
Sheung Wan

START SUTHERLAND ST STOP OF KENNE-DY TOWN TRAM
END HOLLYWOOD RD
LENGTH 2.5KM; ONE HOUR

A walk through Sheung Wan will lead you down the memory lane of Hong Kong's past. Begin the tour at the Sutherland St stop of the Kennedy Town–bound tram. Have a look at Des Voeux Rd West's ❶ **dried seafood shops**, then turn up Ko Shing St, where there are ❷ **herbal medicine wholesalers**. 'Medicinal' items on display range from deer antlers to cordyceps, a kind of of fungus that lives parasitically by eating insect's brains. At the end of the street, walk northeast along Des Voeux Rd West and turn right onto New Market St, where you'll find ❸ **Western Market**. Walk south along this street past Bonham Strand, which is lined with ❹ **gin-seng root sellers**, and turn right on Queen's Rd Central. To the right you'll pass ❺ **traditional shops** selling bird's nests (for soup) and paper funeral offerings (for the dead).

Cross Queen's Rd Central and turn left onto ❻ **Possession Street**, where the British flag was first planted in 1841.

Climbing Pound Lane to where it meets Tai Ping Shan St, look right to see ❼ **Pak Sing Ancestral Hall**, then turn left to find ❽ **Kwun Yam Temple** and ❾ **Tai Sui Temple**. The center of a late-19th-century outbreak of black plague, the whole Tai Ping Shan St area is thought by many Hong Kongers to be haunted by unhappy ghosts who died far from home. But that hasn't kept the hipsters away – the neighborhood is home to an increasing number of cool shops and cafes.

A bit further on, turn left into Square St, where you'll pass ❿ **Cloth Haven**, a weaving workshop, and ⓫ **funeral shops**. Turn left into Ladder St and you'll see ⓬ **Man Mo Temple** (p493). Descend Ladder St to Upper Lascar Row, home of the ⓭ **Cat Street bazaar**. Go down the length of Cat St, then turn left into Lok Ku Rd. Another left takes you to ⓮ **Hollywood Road**, with its antique shops and art galleries.

squid, fish balls on a stick, dim sum) or Western (burgers, cotton candy, muffins). And you'll certainly never be far from a souvenir shop.

There's a parade daily through Main Street at 3.30pm, and a music, light and fireworks show centred on Sleeping Beauty's Castle nightly at 8pm. As in any Disney theme park, costumed characters wander around ready to be greeted by excited children.

Disneyland is linked by rail with the MTR at Sunny Bay station on the Tung Chung line; passengers just cross the platform to board the dedicated train for Disneyland Resort station and the theme park. Journey times from Central/Kowloon/Tsing Yi stations are 24/21/10 minutes respectively.

🏃 Activities

The Hong Kong Tourism Board (p525) offers a range of fun and free activities, from feng shui classes through sunset cruises to taichi sessions. For a list of what's on, visit www.discoverhongkong.com. The Map Publications Centre (香港地圖銷售處) sells excellent maps detailing hiking and cycling trails; buy online (www.landsd.gov.hk) or at major post offices. Sporting buffs should contact the **South China Athletic Association** (南華體育會; ☏ 2577 6932; www.scaa.org.hk; 88 Caroline Hill Rd, 5th fl, South China Sports Complex, Causeway Bay; visitor membership per month HK$60; ⌨31), which has facilities for any number of sports. Another handy website is www.hkoutdoors.com.

Martial Arts

Wan Kei Ho International Martial Arts Association MARTIAL ARTS
(尹圻灝國際武術總會; Map p494; ☏ 2544 1368, 9506 0075; www.kungfuwan.com; 304 Des Voeux Rd Central, 3rd fl, Yue's House, Sheung Wan; ⏰10am-8pm Mon-Fri, 9am-1pm Sat & Sun; Ⓜ Sheung Wan, exit A) English-speaking Master Wan teaches northern Shaolin Kung Fu to a wide following of locals and foreigners. Classes are offered in the evenings from Monday to Thursday. Depending on how many classes you take, the monthly fees may range from HK$300 to HK$1400.

Hiking

Hong Kong is an excellent place to hike and the numerous trails on offer are all very attractive. The four main ones are **MacLehose Trail**, **Wilson Trail**, **Lantau Trail** and **Hong Kong Trail**. For more information check out www.hkwalkers.net.

HONG KONG'S BEST HIKES

Hong Kong has some of Asia's most impressive hiking trails, some of them just a few minutes from the high-rises of Central. Here are a few of the best spots:

Dragon's Back A popular see-the-sea ramble that undulates from central Hong Kong Island to the somnolent village of Shek O.

Lamma Island Family Trail Take a gentle 4km hike across the leafy island to the embrace of waterside seafood restaurants.

Hong Kong Cemetery Wander through this hilly, overgrown, deeply atmospheric resting place of Hong Kong's good and naughty.

Pok Fu Lam Reservoir to the Peak A picturesque ascent past dense forests, waterfalls and military ruins.

Tai Mo Shan Several hiking trails thread up and around Hong Kong's tallest mountain.

Cycling

Cycle tracks in Hong Kong are located predominantly in the New Territories, running from Sha Tin through Tai Po to Tai Mei Tuk.

Bikes can be rented from **Wong Kei** (☏ 2662 5200; Ting Kok Rd, Tai Mei Tuk) and **Friendly Bike Shop** (老友記單車; ☏ 2984 2278; Shop B, 13 Mui Wo Ferry Pier Rd, Lantau; per day HK$30; ⏰10am-7pm Mon-Fri, to 8pm Sat & Sun).

Online resources include **Agriculture, Fisheries & Conservation Department** (www.afcd.gov.hk) and **Crazy Guy on a Bike** (www.crazyguyonabike.com/doc/hongkong).

Golf

The **Hong Kong Golf Club** (www.hkgolfclub.org) welcomes nonmembers on weekdays at its **Fanling** (☏ 2670 1211; Lot No 1, Fan Kam Rd, Sheung Shui; Ⓜ Fanling) and **Deep Water Bay** (☏ 2812 7070; 19 Island Rd, Deep Water Bay; ⌨6, 6A) venues.

Jockey Club Kau Sai Chau Public Golf Course GOLF
(☏ 2791 3388; www.kscgolf.org.hk/index-e.asp; Kau Sai Chau, Sai Kung) The territory's only public golf course. A ferry departs for Kau Sai Chau (every 20 minutes from 6.40am to 7pm weekdays, 6.40am to 9pm Friday to Sunday) from the pier near the Wai Man Rd car park.

☞ Tours

Star Ferry (p506) runs a 60-minute Harbour Tour (HK$80 to HK$200) covering calling points at Tsim Sha Tsui, Central and Wan Chai. Get tickets at the piers.

Tours run by the Hong Kong Tourism Board:

HKTB Island Tour   BUS TOUR
(half-/full day HK$350/490) Includes Man Mo Temple, the Peak, Aberdeen, Repulse Bay and Stanley Market.

Hong Kong Dolphinwatch   CRUISE
(香港海豚觀察; Map p502; ☑2984 1414; www.hkdolphinwatch.com; 15th fl, Middle Block, 1528A Star House, 3 Salisbury Rd, Tsim Sha Tsui; adult/child HK$420/210; ☺cruises Wed, Fri & Sun) Hong Kong Dolphinwatch was founded in 1995 to raise awareness of Hong Kong's wonderful pink dolphins and promote responsible ecotourism. It offers 2½-hour cruises to see them in their natural habitat every Wednesday, Friday and Sunday year-round (adult/child HK$420/210). About 97% of the cruises result in the sighting of at least one dolphin; if none are spotted, passengers are offered a free trip.

✲ Festivals & Events

Western and Chinese culture combine to create an interesting mix of cultural events and about 20 public holidays. However, determining the exact times can be tricky: some follow the Chinese lunar calendar, so the dates change each year. For a full schedule with exact dates see www.discoverhongkong.com.

Hong Kong Arts Festival   PERFORMING ARTS
(www.hk.artsfestival.org) February to March.

**Man Hong Kong International
Literary Festival**   LITERATURE
(www.festival.org.hk) March.

Hong Kong International Film Festival FILM
(www.hkiff.org.hk) March to April.

Le French May Arts Festival   CULTURAL
April to May.

**Tin Hau Festival & Buddha's
Birthday**   CULTURAL
April or May.

Cheung Chau Bun Festival   FOOD
(www.cheungchau.org) April or May

Art Basel Hong Kong   ART
(hongkong.artbasel.com) May.

International Dragon Boat Races   SPORTS
(www.hkdba.com.hk) May to June.

Summer International Film Festival FILM
(www.hkiff.org.hk) August to September.

**Hong Kong International
Jazz Festival**   MUSIC
(http://hkja.org/blog) November.

Clockenflap Outdoor Music Festival MUSIC
(www.clockenflap.com)

🛌 Sleeping

Hong Kong offers the full gamut of accommodation, from cell-like spaces to palatial suites in some of the world's finest hotels. Compared with those in other cities in China, rooms are relatively expensive, though they can still be cheaper than their US or European counterparts. The rates listed here are the rack rates.

Most hotels are on Hong Kong Island between Central and Causeway Bay, and either side of Nathan Rd in Kowloon, where you'll also find the largest range of budget places. All hotels and some budget places add 13% in taxes to the listed rates.

Prices fall sharply outside the peak seasons, particularly in the midrange and top-end categories, when you can get discounts of up to 50% if you book online.

High seasons are March to early May, October to November and Chinese New Year (late January or February). Check the exact dates on www.discoverhongkong.com.

Unless specified otherwise, all rooms listed here have private bathrooms and airconditioning. Almost all places offer broadband and/or wi-fi access, as well as computers for guests' use. All hotels that are midrange and above, and some budget places, have nonsmoking floors, or are nonsmoking.

🛌 Hong Kong Island

Most of Hong Kong Island's top-end hotels are in Central and Admiralty, while Wan Chai and Sheung Wan cater to the midrange market. Causeway Bay has quite a few budget guesthouses that are a step up (in both price and quality) from their Tsim Sha Tsui counterparts.

★**Helena May**   HOTEL $
(梅夫人婦女會主樓; Map p494; ☑2522 6766; www.helenamay.com; 35 Garden Rd, Central; s/d HK$510/670, studios per month HK$15,520-20,230; ▣23) If you like the peninsula's colo-

nial setting but not its price tag, this grand dame could be your cup of tea. Founded in 1916 as a social club for single European women in the territory, the **Helena May** (梅夫人婦女會主樓; Map p494; ☑ 2522 6766; www.helenamay.com; 35 Garden Rd, Central; ☐ 23) is now a private club for women of all nationalities and a hotel with 43 creaky but charming rooms.

Rooms in the main building are women's-only with shared bathrooms, while the rent-by-month studios in an adjacent building are also open to men. You must be 18 or above to stay at the Helena May. The building is a stone's throw from the Peak Tram Terminus and the Zoological & Botanical Gardens.

YesInn
HOSTEL $

(☑ 2213 4567; www.yesinn.com; 472 Hennessy Rd, 2nd fl, Nan Yip Bldg, Causeway Bay; dm HK$159-469, r HK$199-459; M Causeway Bay, exit F2) This funky, vibrant hostel attracts backpackers from all over the world, as evidenced by their signatures on the building's chalkboard-paint ceiling. There are both single-sex and mixed dorms, as well as private rooms, all brightly painted. The small reception area is made up for by the excellent roof deck, sometimes the site of hostel-sponsored barbecues.

The hostel entrance is at the side of the building on the corner. Private rooms are in a building across the street. The neon, shopping and late-night sushi of Causeway Bay are a two-minute walk. YesInn has sister hostels in Fortress Hill and Kowloon.

Bishop Lei International House
HOTEL $

(宏基國際賓館; Map p494; ☑ 2868 0828; www.bishopleihtl.com.hk; 4 Robinson Rd, Mid-Levels; s/d/ste from $650/700/1250; @※; ☐ 23, 40) This hotel in residential Mid-Levels, though out of the way, provides a lot of bang for your buck. It boasts good service, a swimming pool, a gym and proximity to the Zoological & Botanical Gardens. The standard single and double rooms are small. It's worth paying a little more for the larger, harbour-facing rooms, which offer good views of the skyline and the cathedral from high up. Buses to Central and Wan Chai stop in front of the hotel.

Cosmo
BOUTIQUE HOTEL $

(☑ 3552 8388; www.cosmohotel.com.hk; 375-377 Queen's Rd E, Wan Chai; r/ste from HK$650/1000; ☺☎; M Causeway Bay, exit A) Aiming for boutiquey ambience, this good-value hotel on the quiet side of Wan Chai has lovely rooms done up in cool whites and grays with modish pops of bright orange. The cheaper rooms have frosted-glass windows, so no view. Not to be confused with its pricier sister hotel, the **Cosmopolitan** (香港麗都酒店; ☑ 3552 1111; www.cosmopolitanhotel.com.hk; 387-397 Queen's Rd E, Wan Chai; r/ste from HK$900/1800; @☎; M Causeway Bay, exit A), just down the block.

★ Mira Moon
BOUTIQUE HOTEL $$

(☑ 2643 8888; www.miramoonhotel.com; 388 Jaffe Rd, Wan Chai; r HK$1400-3000; ☎; M Wan Chai, exit A1) ✈ The new kid on the block is also the coolest. Decor at this 91-room boutique hotel riffs on the Chinese fairy tale of the Moon Goddess and the Jade Rabbit – stylized rabbit wall art, oversized Chinese lanterns, graphic peony floor mosaics. For all its hipness, the hotel's staff are warm and helpful, and the architecture is ecofriendly to boot.

It's all about the details here. Freestanding bathtubs in the 'Half Moon' and 'Full Moon' rooms are to die for, while the more budget-friendly 'New Moon' rooms offer walk-in showers. All rooms come with a phone, which guests can take with them for free 3G and local and international calls. There's free soy milk and soda in the minifridge, and the room's iPad connects to the TV. Amenities include a 24-hour gym, a Spanish-Chinese fusion tapas restaurant, and (naturally) a house DJ.

★ T Hotel
HOTEL $$

(T酒店; ☑ 3717 7388; www.vtc.edu.hk/thotel; 145 Pokfulam Rd, VTC Pokfulam Complex, Pok Fu Lam; r from HK$900; @☎※; ☐ 7, 91 from Central, 973 from Tsim Sha Tsui) Ah, we almost don't want to tell you about this gem on the island! The 30-room T, perched high in the serene neighbourhood of Po Fu Lam, is entirely run by students of the local hospitality training institute. The young trainees are attentive, cheerful and very eager to hone their skills. Rooms are sparkling and spacious, and offer ocean or mountain views.

The food and beverage outlets, run by the famous culinary school in the complex, provide excellent Chinese and Western meals.

Ibis
HOTEL $$

(上環宜必思酒店; Map p494; ☑ 2252 2929; www.ibishotel.com; 18-30 Des Voeux Rd W, Sheung Wan; r from HK$950; @; ☐ 5B from Central) The 550-room Ibis offers a more affordable option in an expensive part of town. The rooms and facilities are decent, but do not expect luxury. The highlight here is the warm service by staff dressed perpetually in polo tees and a smile which lends the hotel a relaxing, resortlike flair. Prices are in the hundreds if you book online.

★**Upper House** BOUTIQUE HOTEL $$$
(☎2918 1838; www.upperhouse.com; 88 Queensway, Pacific Pl, Admiralty; r/ste from HK$4500/12,000; @☎; MAdmiralty, exit F) Every corner of this boutique hotel spells Zen-like serenity – the understated lobby, the sleek eco-minded rooms, the elegant sculptures, the warm and discreet service and the manicured lawn where guests can join free yoga classes. Other pluses include a free and 'bottomless' minibar, and easy access to the Admiralty MTR station.

Guests of the Upper House can pay to use the pool facilities of nearby hotels. This is a superb alternative to luxury options in Central and Admiralty, if you don't mind fewer luxuries.

★**Four Seasons** HOTEL $$$
(四季酒店; Map p494; ☎3196 8888; www.fourseasons.com/hongkong; 8 Finance St, Central; r HK$4800-8100, ste HK$9800-65,000; @☎☀; MHong Kong, exit F) The Four Seasons arguably edges into top place on the island for its amazing views, pristine service, and its location close to the Star Ferry Pier, Hong Kong station, and Sheung Wan. Also on offer are palatial rooms, a glorious pool and spa complex, and award-winning restaurants **Caprice** (Map p494; ☎3196 8888; www.fourseasons.com/hongkong; Four Seasons Hotel, 8 Finance St, Central; set lunch/dinner from HK$540/1740; ◷noon-2.30pm & 6-10.30pm; ☎; MHong Kong, exit E1) and Lung King Heen (p517).

Mandarin Oriental HOTEL $$$
(文華東方酒店; Map p494; ☎2522 0111; www.mandarinoriental.com/hongkong/; 5 Connaught Rd, Central; r HK$5300-7400, ste HK$8000-65,000; @☎☀; MCentral, exit J3) The venerable Mandarin has historically set the standard in Asia and continues to be a contender for the top spot, despite competition from the likes of the Four Seasons. The styling, service, food and atmosphere are stellar throughout and there's a sense of gracious, old-world charm. The sleek **Landmark Oriental** (Map p494; ☎2132 0088; www.mandarinoriental.com/landmark; 15 Queen's Rd, Central; r HK$3500-6800, ste HK$9300-45,000; @☎☀), just across the way, offers modern luxury, but with a business vibe.

Hotel LKF HOTEL $$$
(隆堡蘭桂坊酒店; Map p494; ☎3518 9688; www.hotel-lkf.com.hk; 33 Wyndham St, Central; r HK$2600-6000, ste from HK$10,000; @☎; MCentral, exit D2) Located on the upper, flatter section of Wydham St, Hotel LKF is arguably the best gateway to the Lan Kwai Fong action, but is far enough above it not to be disturbed by it. It has high-tech rooms in muted tones and they brim with all the trimmings you'll need: fluffy bathrobes, espresso machines and free bedtime milk and cookies. There's a plush spa and yoga studio in the building.

Courtyard by Marriott Hong Kong BUSINESS HOTEL $$$
(香港萬怡酒店; ☎3717 8888; www.marriott.com/hotels/travel/hkgcy-courtyard-hong-kong; 167 Connaught Rd W; r HK$1300-3000, ste from HK$2600; @☎; ⌕5, 5B from Central) This hotel juggles luxury with limited space, and it works. Most rooms offer harbour views and are smartly decorated with modern furnishings. The plump beds and high-thread-count sheets guarantee you a good night's sleep. Service is impeccable. There's an Airbus stop across the street.

🛏 Kowloon

Kowloon has an incredible array of accommodation: from the Peninsula, the 'grand dame' of hotels, to its infamous neighbour, Chungking Mansions, plus plenty in between.

Hop Inn on Hankow HOSTEL $
(Map p502; ☎2881 7331; www.hopinn.hk; 19-21 Hankow Rd, flat A, 2nd fl, Hanyee Bldg, Tsim Sha Tsui; s HK$410-530, d & tw HK$520-790, tr HK$650-980, q HK$1020-1200; @☎; MTsim Sha Tsui, exit C1) This nonsmoking hostel has a youthful vibe and nine spotless and dainty rooms, each sporting illustrations by a different Hong Kong artist. The rooms without windows are quieter than the ones that have them. The other branch, **Hop Inn on Carnarvon** (Map p502; ☎2881 7331; www.hopinn.hk; 33-35 Carnarvon Rd, 9th fl, James S Lee Mansion, Tsim Sha Tsui; s HK$410-530, d & tw HK$520-790, tr HK$650-980, q HK$1020-1200; ☎; MTsim Sha Tsui, exit A2), has newer rooms in an older building. Both branches offer free in-room wi-fi and will help to organise China visas.

Nic & Trig's GUESTHOUSE $
(☎6333 5352; rooms@nostalgic.org; 703 Shanghai St, Mong Kok; r from HK$400; ☎; MPrince Ed-

ward, exit C1) Run by a friendly hipster couple, this place inside a 'walk-up' tenement building (c 1957) has atmospheric rooms inspired by retro Hong Kong. Toilet and shower areas are shared; provisions are basic. If you need anything, just ask. The owners are happy to give you restaurant and sightseeing tips. Email and they will tell you how to get there.

★ **Madera Hong Kong** BOUTIQUE HOTEL $$
(木的地酒店; Map p501; ☑2121 9888; www.hotelmadera.com.hk; 1-9 Cheong Lok St, Yau Ma Tei; r HK$1200-4000, ste HK$4200-$9000; Ⓜ Jordan, exit B1) A spirited addition to Kowloon's mid-range options, Madera is close to the Temple Street Night Market (p503) and the Jordan MTR station. The decent-sized rooms come in neutral tones accented with the bold, vibrant colours of Spanish aesthetics. Madera (meaning 'wood') also has a ladies' floor, a hypo-allergenic floor, and a tiny but adequate gym room.

★ **Salisbury** HOTEL $$
(香港基督教青年會; Map p502; ☑2268 7888; www.ymcahk.org.hk; 41 Salisbury Rd, Tsim Sha Tsui; dm HK$300, s/d/ste from HK$1000/1200/2200; @📶♿; Ⓜ Tsim Sha Tsui, exit E) If you can manage to book a room at this fabulously located place, you'll be rewarded with professional service and excellent exercise facilities. Rooms and suites are comfortable but simple, so keep your eyes on the harbour: that view would cost you five times as much at the Peninsula next door. The dormitory rooms are a bonus but restrictions apply.

The four-bed dorm rooms are meant for short-stay travellers, hence no one can stay there more than seven consecutive nights and walk-in guests aren't accepted if they've been in Hong Kong for more than seven days; check-in is at 2pm. The same restrictions do not apply to the other rooms of the Salisbury. Sports enthusiasts will love it here – the hotel has a 25m swimming pool, a fitness centre, and a climbing wall. The 7th floor is the smoking floor.

BP International Hotel HOTEL $$
(龍堡國際酒店; Map p502; ☑2376 1111; www.bpih.com.hk; 8 Austin Rd, Tsim Sha Tsui; r/ste from HK$1900/6500; @📶; Ⓜ Jordan, exit C) This enormous hotel overlooks Kowloon Park (p504). The rooms are of a reasonable standard and some of the more expensive ones have good harbour views. The family rooms have bunk beds, which is good if you're travelling with kids. Haggle before you book: depending on the season and day of the week, prices are often reduced by 50%.

Caritas Bianchi Lodge GUESTHOUSE $$
(明愛白英奇賓館; Map p501; ☑2388 1111; www.caritas-chs.org.hk/eng/bianchi_lodge.asp; 4 Cliff Rd, Yau Ma Tei; s HK$1350, d & tw HK$1600, f HK$2100; 📶; Ⓜ Yau Ma Tei, exit D) This 90-room guesthouse run by a Catholic NGO is just off Nathan Rd (and a stone's throw from Yau Ma Tei MTR station), but the rear rooms are quiet and some have views of King's Park. All rooms are clean The wait for lifts can be long, especially at night. Breakfast is included in the rates.

★ **Peninsula Hong Kong** HOTEL $$$
(香港半島酒店; Map p502; ☑2920 2888; www.peninsula.com; Salisbury Rd, Tsim Sha Tsui; r/ste from HK$4080/7880; @📶♿; Ⓜ Tsim Sha Tsui, exit E) Lording it over the southern tip of Kowloon, Hong Kong's finest hotel exudes colonial elegance. Your dilemma will be how to get here: landing on the rooftop helipad or arriving in one of the hotel's 14-strong fleet of Rolls Royce Phantoms. Some 300 classic European-style rooms sport wi-fi, CD and DVD players, as well as marble bathrooms.

Many rooms in the 20-storey annexe also offer spectacular harbour views; in the original building you'll have to make do with the glorious interiors. There's a top-notch spa and swimming pool, and **Gaddi's** (Map p502; ☑2696 6763; www.peninsula.com/Hong_Kong; 19-21 Salisbury Rd, 1st fl, the Peninsula, Tsim Sha Tsui; set lunch/dinner HK$500/2000; ⏱noon-2.30pm;

MECCA OF CHEAP SLEEPS

Chungking Mansions (重慶大廈; CKM; Map p502; 36-44 Nathan Rd, Tsim Sha Tsui; Ⓜ Tsim Sha Tsui, exit F) has been synonymous with budget accommodation in Hong Kong for decades. The crumbling block on Nathan Rd is stacked with the city's cheapest hostels and guesthouses. Rooms are usually minuscule and service rudimentary. But standards have risen in recent years and several guesthouses positively sparkle with new fittings. Even the lifts have been upgraded, though they're still painfully slow.

Mirador Mansion (美麗都大廈; Map p502; 54-64 Nathan Rd, Tsim Sha Tsui; Ⓜ Tsim Sha Tsui, exit D2), its neighbour just up the street, also has a fair number of cheap sleeps.

& 7-10.30pm; M Tsim Sha Tsui, exit E) is one of the best French restaurants in town.

★ Hyatt Regency Tsim Sha Tsui HOTEL $$$

(尖沙咀凱悅酒店; Map p502; 📞 23111234; http://hongkong.tsimshatsui.hyatt.com; 18 Hanoi Rd, Tsim Sha Tsui; s/d/ste from HK$1200/4200/3600; @ 🛜 ⊠; M Tsim Sha Tsui, exit D2) Top marks to this classic that exudes understated elegance and composure. Rooms are plush and relatively spacious with those on the upper floors commanding views over the city. Black-and-white photos of Tsim Sha Tsui add a thoughtful touch to the decor. The lobby gets crowded at times, but the helpful and resourceful staff will put you back at ease.

Hotel Icon HOTEL $$$

(唯港薈; Map p502; 📞 3400 1000; www.hotel-icon.com; 17 Science Museum Rd, Tsim Sha Tsui; r HK$2200-4100, ste HK$3000-6500; @ 🛜 ⊠; M East Tsim Sha Tsui, exit P1) The rooms at this teaching hotel of a local university are modern and spacious, and the service is warm. Icon is a 10-minute walk from the MTR and there's a shuttle service to the more central parts of Tsim Sha Tsui. Not all rooms have harbour views and children are not allowed into the terrace lounge, but overall, it's great value for money.

Ritz-Carlton Hong Kong HOTEL $$$

(麗思卡爾頓酒店; 📞 2263 2263; www.ritzcarl-ton.com; 1 Austin Rd W, Tsim Sha Tsui; r HK$7200-9900, ste from HK$13,000; 🛜 ⊠; M Kowloon, exit C1 or D1) Sitting on Kowloon Station, this out-of-the-way luxury hotel is the tallest hotel on earth (lobby's on the 103rd floor). And to echo the theme of excess, the decor is over-the-top with imposing furniture and a superfluity of shiny surfaces; the service is stellar; Tin Lung Heen (p518) serves top-notch Chinese food, and the views on a clear day are mindblowing.

Cityview HOTEL $$$

(城景國際; 📞 2771 9111; www.thecityview.com.hk; 23 Waterloo Rd, Yau Ma Tei; d/tr HK$1880/2280, ste from HK$3080; @ 🛜 ⊠; M Yau Ma Tei, exit A2) All 413 rooms at this YMCA-affiliated hotel are clean and smart, featuring mellow colour tones and stylish fabrics. The service is also impeccable. The hotel occupies a quiet corner between Yau Ma Tei and Mong Kok. It's a short stroll from Yau Ma Tei Theatre (p117) and the Yau Ma Tei Wholesale Fruit Market (p500).

🛏 New Territories

Good-value accommodation in the New Territories is sparse, but there are both official and independent hostels, usually in remote areas. The **Country & Marine Parks Authority** (www.afcd.gov.hk) maintains 40 no-frills campsites in the New Territories. Visit the website and click on 'Country & Marine Parks.'

Pilgrim's Hall HOSTEL $

(📞 2691 2739; www.tfssu.org/pilgrim.html; 33 Tao Fong Shan Rd; s/d with shared bathroom HK$260/400; 🚈 Sha Tin, exit B) This Lutheran Church–affiliated hostel provides a nice escape from the city as it's set on a peaceful hillside above the town. To get here, take the MTR East Rail to Sha Tin station, leave via exit B and walk down the ramp, passing a series of old village houses on the left. To the left of these houses is a set of steps signposted 'To Fung Shan'. Follow the path all the way to the top and you'll see Pilgrim's Hall. The walk should take around 20 minutes. A taxi from the nearest MTR station in Sha Tin will cost around HK$20. The canteen serves simple and healthy meals (booking required).

Bradbury Jockey Club Youth Hostel HOSTEL $

(📞 2662 5123; www.yha.org.hk; 66 Tai Mei Tuk Rd; dm members under/over 18yr HK$65/95, d/q members HK$290/420; 🚌 75K) This is the HKYHA's flagship hostel in the New Territories and is open daily year-round. Bradbury is next to the northern tip of the Plover Cove Reservoir dam wall, a few hundred metres south of Tai Mei Tuk. To get here take bus 75K (or 275R on Sundays and public holidays) from Tai Po Market KCR East station to the Tai Mei Tuk bus terminus. The hostel is on the road leading to the reservoir.

Hyatt Regency Hong Kong HOTEL $$$

(📞 3723 1234; www.hongkong.shatin.hyatt.com; 18 Chak Cheung St; r HK$2500-3000, ste HK$3500-12,500; 🚈 University) This is the plushest sleeping option as you head out towards the border with China. Views of Tolo Harbour or the rolling hills of Sha Tin can be seen in most rooms. It's a five-minute walk from University East Rail station.

🛏 Outlying Islands

Lantau, Lamma and Cheung Chau all have decent accommodation with a holiday vibe. For campers, the **Country & Marine Parks**

Authority (☎1823; www.afcd.gov.hk) maintains 11 sites on Lantau. Camping is prohibited on Hong Kong beaches.

Bali Holiday Resort
HOTEL $

(☎2982 4580; www.lammabali.com; 8 Main St, Yung Shue Wan; r Sun-Fri HK$300-750, Sat & holidays HK$700-1400; ☞; ☒Yung Shue Wan) Near the ferry in Yung Shue Wan, Bali has basic, pleasant, tile-floored rooms with TVs and fridges, as well as family apartments. The nicest are the upper-floor rooms with balconies. Wi-fi available on the patio.

★Tai O Heritage Hotel
BOUTIQUE HOTEL $$

(大澳文物酒店; www.taioheritagehotel.com; Shek Tsai Po St, Tai O; r HK$1900-2500; @☞☒; ☐1 from Mui Wo, 11 from Tung Chung, 21 from Ngong Ping) Housed in a century-old former police station, this is Lantau's newest hotel. All nine rooms are handsomely furnished in a contemporary style, offering top-of-the-line comfort. Our favourite is the inspector-office-turned–Sea Tiger Room, the smallest digs (24 sq metres) but with picture windows ushering in the sea breeze.

Espace Elastique
B&B $$

(歸田園居; ☎2985 7002; www.espaceelastique.com.hk; 57 Kat Hing St, Tai O; r Sun-Thu HK$500-1400, Fri & Sat HK$540-1700; @☞☒; ☐1 from Mui Wo, 11 from Tung Chung, 21 from Ngong Ping) This cosy four-room B&B is one of the best-kept gems on Lantau. All rooms are tastefully decorated; the 2nd-floor double room with a balcony overlooking the main Tai O waterway gets booked up quickly. The friendly owner Veronica provides multilingual travel advice, plus a hearty breakfast in the cafe. The jacuzzi on the rooftop is a delight.

✗ Eating

One of the world's greatest food cities, Hong Kong offers culinary excitement whether you're spending HK$20 on a bowl of noodles or megabucks on haute cuisine.

The best of China is well represented, be it Cantonese, Shanghainese, Northern or Sichuanese. What's more, the international fare on offer – French, Italian, Spanish, Japanese, Thai, Indian, fusion – is the finest and most diverse in all of China.

Hong Kong is an expensive place to dine by regional Chinese standards, but cheaper than Sydney, London or New York, and with more consistent quality of food and service than most eateries in mainland China.

At most of the eateries listed here, reservations are strongly advised, especially for dinner.

✗ Hong Kong Island

The island's best range of cuisines is in Central, Sheung Wan and Wan Chai.

★Delicious Kitchen
SHANGHAINESE $

(☎2577 7720; 9-11B Cleveland St, Causeway Bay; meals HK$40-100; ☉11am-11pm; Ⓜ Causeway Bay, exit E) The Shanghainese rice cooked with shredded Chinese cabbage is so good at this *cha chaan teng* (tea cafe) that fashionistas are tripping over themselves to land a table here. It's best with the legendary honey-glazed pork chop. Fat, veggie-stuffed wontons and perfectly crispy fried tofu are also winners.

Lin Heung Teahouse
DIM SUM, CANTONESE $

(蓮香; Map p494; ☎2544 4556; 160-164 Wellington St, Sheung Wan; lunch/dinner from HK$60/120; ☉6am-11pm; ☐26, Ⓜ Sheung Wan, exit E1) This 80-year-old restaurant, packed with older men reading newspapers and extended families, has decent dim sum (until 5pm) and old-school Cantonese dishes. The grandfather-like waiters still wear traditional white tunics over black trousers, and pour tea from huge brass kettles. Tables are shared at this no-frills place, giving a feel of community even for first-timers.

Sing Kee
DAI PAI DONG $

(盛記; Map p494; ☎2541 5678; 9-10 Stanley St, Soho; meals HK$200; ☉11am-3pm & 6-11pm daily; ☝; Ⓜ Central, exit D2) In the fine-dining enclave of Soho, finding a good and cheap meal can be tricky. Sing Kee, one of the few surviving *dai pai dong* (food stalls) in the area, has withstood the tide of gentrification, and still retains a working-class, laugh-out-loud character. There's no signage. Look for the crammed tables at the end of Stanley St.

Life Cafe
VEGETARIAN, INTERNATIONAL $

(Map p494; ☎2810 9777; www.lifecafe.com.hk; 10 Shelley St, Soho; meals HK$100; ☉noon-10pm; ☞☝; Ⓜ Central, exit D1) Right next to the Central–Mid-Levels Escalator, Life is a vegetarian's dream, serving organic vegan salads, guilt-free desserts, and tasty dishes free of gluten, wheat, onion, garlic – you name it – over three floors stylishly decked out in reclaimed teak and recycled copper-domed lamps. The ground-floor counter has goodies to take away.

★ **Luk Yu Tea House** CANTONESE, DIM SUM $$
(陸羽茶室; Map p494; ☑2523 5464; 24-26 Stanley St, Lan Kwai Fong; meals HK$300; ☺7am-10pm, dim sum to 5.30pm; ☒; ⓂCentral, exit D2) This gorgeous teahouse (c 1933), known for its masterful cooking and Eastern art-deco decor, was the haunt of opera artists, writers and painters (including the creator of one exorbitant ink-and-brush image gracing a wall), who came to give recitals and discuss the national fate. Today some of the waiters who served the tousled glamourati will pour your tea in the same pleasantly irreverent manner.

★ **22 Ships** TAPAS $$
(☑2555 0722; www.22ships.hk; 22 Ship St, Wan Chai; tapas HK$68-178; ☺noon-3pm & 6-11pm; ⓂWan Chai, exit B2) The star of the recent crop of new tapas restaurants to open in Hong Kong, this tiny, trendy spot is packed from open to close. But the long wait (the restaurant doesn't take reservations) is worth it for exquisite, playful small plates by much-buzzed-about young British chef Jason Atherton.

Molecular gastronomy techniques are on display in dishes like crispy fish skin with dollops of foamy cod mousse and the house sangria with powdered raspberry. Others, like a special of beef cheeks on toast with anchovy butter, are pure luxe comfort food.

★ **Little Bao** ASIAN FUSION $$
(Map p494; ☑2194 0202; www.little-bao.com; 66 Staunton St, Sheung Wan; meals HK$200-500; ☺6-11pm Mon-Sat; ⓂCentral, exit D2) A trendy diner that wows with its *bao* (Chinese buns) – snow-white orbs crammed with juicy meat and slathered with a palette of Asian condiments. The signature pork-belly *bao* comes with hoisin ketchup, sesame dressing, and a leek and *shiso* salad. If spot-on flavours and full-on sauces appeal, go early – they don't take reservations.

Megan's Kitchen CANTONESE, HOTPOT $$
(☑2866 8305; www.meganskitchen.com; 165-171 Wan Chai Rd, 5th fl, Lucky Centre, Wan Chai; hotpot per person HK$200-300; ☺noon-3pm & 6-11.30pm; ⓂWan Chai, exit A3) Broth choices like Thai-flavored tom yum and 'lobster borsch' make for a modern twist on the classic hotpot experience at Megan's, though standbys like spicy Sichuan soup are just as good. The vast menu of items to dip runs the gamut from the standard (mushrooms, fish slices, tofu) to the avant-garde (don't miss the fabulous rainbow cuttlefish balls).

Like all hotpot restaurants, Megan's is best visited with a crowd of at least four. Subdivided hotpots mean you can sample up to three broths, so the more the merrier. Call ahead for reservations, especially on weekends.

AMMO EUROPEAN $$
(Map p494; ☑2537 9888; www.ammo.com.hk; 9 Justice Dr, Asia Society Hong Kong Centre, Admiralty; meals HK$200-400; ☺noon-midnight Sun-Thu, to 1am Fri & Sat; ⓂAdmiralty, exit F) Awash in a coppery light the colour of bullets, this sleek glass-walled cafe at the Asia Society Hong Kong Centre (p493) features chandeliers and copper panels evoking the site's past as an explosives magazine. The excellent menu is well thought out and pricey, with a selection of mostly Italian mains, preceded by tapas available at cocktail hour. Bookings essential.

Yardbird JAPANESE $$
(Map p494; ☑2547 9273; www.yardbirdrestaurant.com; 33-35 Bridges St, Sheung Wan; meals HK$300; ☺6pm-midnight Mon-Sat; ☐26) Yardbird is a hipster's ode to the chicken. Every part of the cluck-cluck, from thigh to gizzard, is seasoned, impaled with a stick then grilled, yakitori style. The resulting skewers are flavourful with just the right consistency. The highly popular eatery doesn't take reservations, so sample the sakes at the convivial bar area while you wait for a table.

Pure Veggie House VEGETARIAN, CHINESE $$
(Map p494; ☑2525 0556; 51 Garden Rd, 3rd fl, Coda Plaza; meals HK$200-400; ☺11am-10pm; ☒; ⓂAdmiralty, then bus 12A) This Buddhist restaurant goes way beyond the usual tofu-n-broccoli to serve innovative, exquisitely presented vegetarian dishes: sauteed lily bulb, fried rice with black truffle and pine nuts, seaweed-wrapped tofu rolls. Excellent all-veggie dim sum will please even dedicated carnivores. The tranquil setting resembles a rustic inn.

Yung Kee Restaurant CANTONESE, DIM SUM $$
(鏞記; Map p494; ☑2522 1624; 32-40 Wellington St, Lan Kwai Fong; lunch HK$150-400, dinner from HK$450; ☺11am-10.30pm; ☒; ⓂCentral, exit D2) The roast goose here, made from fowl raised in the restaurant's own farm and roasted in coal-fired ovens, has been the talk of the town since 1942. Celebrities and well-to-dos are regulars at this well-illuminated and welcoming place, and its lunch dim sum is popular with the Central workforce.

Irori
JAPANESE $$

(酒處; ☎2838 5939; Yiu Wa St, 2nd fl, Bartlock Centre, Causeway Bay; lunch/dinner from HK$150/300; ◷noon-3pm & 6-11pm; Ⓜ Causeway Bay, exit A) Irori's versatile kitchen turns out raw and cooked delicacies of an equally impressive standard. Seasonal fish is flown in regularly from Japan, and carefully crafted into sushi and sashimi. To warm the stomach between cold dishes, there's a creative selection of tasty tidbits, such as fried beef roll and yakitori.

★ Lung King Heen
CANTONESE, DIM SUM $$$

(龍景軒; Map p494; ☎3196 8888; www.fourseasons.com/hongkong; 8 Finance St, Four Seasons Hotel, Central; set lunch/dinner HK$500/1560; ◷noon-2.30pm & 6-10.30pm; ☎; Ⓜ Hong Kong, exit E1) The world's first Chinese restaurant to receive three stars from the Michelin people, still retains them. The Cantonese food, though by no means peerless in Hong Kong, is excellent in both taste and presentation, and when combined with the harbour views and the impeccable service, provides a truly stellar dining experience. The signature steamed lobster and scallop dumplings sell out early.

★ Boss
CANTONESE $$$

(波士廳; Map p494; ☎2155 0552; www.theboss1.com; Basement, 58-62 Queen's Rd Central, Central; meals from HK$500; ◷11.30am-midnight Mon-Sat, from 11am Sun; ☎; Ⓜ Central, exit D2) Awarded one Michelin star, the Boss is a perfectionist. Flawless service, austere modern decor, and a meticulous kitchen point to high expectations being imposed. The old-school Cantonese dishes are impressive, notably the deep-fried chicken pieces with home-fermented shrimp paste, and the baked-crab casserole. Dim sum, made with first-rate ingredients, is available at lunch.

Otto e Mezzo Bombana
ITALIAN $$$

(Map p494; ☎2537 8859; www.ottoemezzobombana.com; Shop 202, Landmark Alexandra, 18 Chater Rd, Central; lunch/dinner from HK$700/1380; ◷noon-2.30pm & 6.30-10.30pm Mon-Sat; ☎; Ⓜ Central, exit H) Asia's only Italian restaurant with three Michelin stars lives up to its reputation, and Chef Bombana is here, sleeves rolled, to see that it does. 'Eight and a Half' is the place for white truffles, being the host of the local bid for these pungent diamonds. To eat here though you'll need the tenacity of a truffle hound – book two months ahead.

L'Atelier de Joël Robuchon
MODERN FRENCH $$$

(Map p494; ☎2166 9000; www.robuchon.com; 15 Queen's Rd Central, Shop 401, Landmark, Central; lunch HK$450-1900, dinner HK$800-2000; ◷noon-2.30pm & 6.30-10.30pm; ☎; Ⓜ Central, exit G) One-third of celebrity chef Joel de Robuchon's Michelin-crowned wonder in Hong Kong, this red-and-black workshop has a tantalising list of tapas (from HK$350) and a 70-page wine list. If you prefer something more formal, visit Le Jardin in the next room. Le Salon de The, one floor down, has the best sandwiches and pastries in town for dine-in or take away.

⊗ Kowloon

There's plenty of choice in both cuisine and budget, especially in Tsim Sha Tsui. More local places can be found further north.

Woodlands
INDIAN, VEGETARIAN $

(活蘭印度素食; Map p502; ☎2369 3718; 62 Mody Rd, Upper ground fl, 16 & 17 Wing On Plaza, Tsim Sha Tsui; meals HK$70-180; ◷noon-3.30pm & 6.30-10.30pm; ☑⚕; Ⓜ East Tsim Sha Tsui, exit P1) Located above a department store, good old Woodlands offers excellent-value Indian vegetarian food to compatriots and the odd local. Dithering gluttons should order the thali meal, which is served on a round metal plate with 10 tiny dishes, a dessert and bread.

Chicken HOF & Soju Korean
KOREAN $

(李家, Map p502; ☎2375 8080; Kimberley Rd, G/F, 84 Kam Kok Mansion, Tsim Sha Tsui; meals from HK$150; ◷5pm-4am; Ⓜ Jordan, exit D) This place with darkened windows may look dodgy from the outside, but in fact it's a Korean gastropub with a friendly owner who'll holler a greeting when customers enter. The excellent fried chicken, made with a light and crispy batter, comes in five versions. Traditional fare like Korean barbecue is also available. Whatever you order, steer clear of the pupa soup. Ours tasted so musty, we thought we were eating a library.

Mido Café
CAFE $

(美都餐室; Map p501; ☎2384 6402; 63 Temple St; meals HK$40-90; ◷9am-10pm; Ⓜ Yau Ma Tei, exit B2) This retro *cha chaan tang* (1950), with mosaic tiles and metal latticework, stands astride a street corner that comes to life at sundown. Ascend to the upper floor and take a seat next to a wall of iron-framed windows overlooking Tin Hau Temple (p504) – atmosphere is what makes it Kowloon's most famous tea cafe, despite passable food and service.

Ziafat MIDDLE EASTERN, INDIAN $
(Map p502; ☑ 2312 1015; 81 Nathan Rd, 6th fl, Harilela Mansion, Tsim Sha Tsui; meal HK$80-200; ⊙ noon-midnight; ☑; M Tsim Sha Tsui, exit R) This halal restaurant serves up decent Arabic and Indian fare like falafel, lentil soup, kebabs and curries. It's in a weary, post-WWII building alongside budget guesthouses, but the restaurant is clean, quiet and humbly furnished with Arabic art. You can also smoke shisha here.

★ **Great Beef Hot Pot** HOTPOT $$
(禾牛薈火焗館; Map p502; ☑ 3997 3369; 48 Cameron Rd, 1st & 2nd fl, China Insurance Bldg, Tsim Sha Tsui; meals HK$350-600; ⊙ 5.30pm-2am; M Tsim Sha Tsui, exit B3) Indecisive gluttons will scream at the mind-blowing hotpot choices here – 200 ingredients (the majority fresh or homemade; HK$25–270), 20 kinds of broth (from clam soup to fancy herbal concoctions; HK$68–468), and an embarrassment of condiments (all-you-can-dip)! There's no escaping the menu either, the lights are too bright! Now onto the sashimi options... Booking essential.

★ **Yè Shanghai** SHANGHAINESE, DIM SUM $$
(夜上海; Map p502; ☑ 2376 3322; www.elite-concepts.com; Canton Rd, 6th fl, Marco Polo Hotel, Harbour City, Tsim Sha Tsui; meals HK$400-800; ⊙ 11.30am-2.30pm & 6-10.30pm; ☑; M Tsim Sha Tsui, exit C2) The name means 'Shànghǎi Nights'. Dark woods and subtle lighting inspired by 1920s Shànghǎi fill the air with romance. The modern Shanghainese dishes are also exquisite. The only exception to this Jiāngnán harmony is the Cantonese dim sum being served at lunch, though that too is wonderful. Sophisticated Yè Shanghai has one Michelin star.

Kowloon Tang CHINESE, DIM SUM $$
(九龍廳; ☑ 2811 9398; www.kowloontang.com; 1 Austin Rd W, Shop R002-003, Civic Square, 3rd fl, roof deck, Elements Mall; meals HK$300-2000; ⊙ noon-10.30pm; ☑; M Kowloon, exit U3) Sophisticated Kowloon Tang serves impeccable Cantonese dishes, including a few Dong Guan classics, a laudable Peking duck, and an impressive selection of Western-style desserts in an art deco–inspired setting, reminiscent of its cousin across the harbour, Island Tang (港島廳; Map p494; ☑ 2526 8798; www.islandtang.com; 9 Queen's Rd Central, Shop 222, Galleria, Central; set lunch from HK$308, dinner from HK$400; ⊙ noon-2.30pm & 6-10.30pm; ☎; M Central, exit D1).

Din Tai Fung TAIWANESE, NOODLES $$
(鼎泰豐; Map p502; ☑ 2730 6928; www.dintaifung.com.hk; 30 Canton Rd, Shop 130, 3rd fl, Silvercord, Tsim Sha Tsui; meals HK$120-300; ⊙ 11.30am-10.30pm; ☑; M Tsim Sha Tsui, exit C1) Whether it's comfort food or a carb fix you're craving, the juicy Shanghai dumplings and hearty Northern-style noodles at this Taiwanese chain will do the trick. Queues are the norm and it doesn't take reservations, but service is excellent. DTF has one Michelin star.

Typhoon Shelter Hing Kee Restaurant CANTONESE $$
(避風塘興記; Map p502; ☑ 2722 0022; 180 Nathan Rd, 1st fl Bowa House, Tsim Sha Tsui; meals HK$380-1200; ⊙ 6pm-5am; M Jordan, exit D) This celebrity haunt is run by a feisty fisherman's daughter who's known for her brilliant dishes prepared the way they were on sampans. The signature crabs smothered in a mountain of fried garlic are a wonder to taste and behold. The service can be a little edgy. Be sure you know the price of every dish before you order.

Spring Deer NORTHERN CHINESE $$
(鹿鳴春飯店; Map p502; ☑ 2366 4012; 42 Mody Rd, 1st fl, Tsim Sha Tsui; meals HK$80-500; ⊙ noon-3pm & 6-11pm; M East Tsim Sha Tsui, exit N2) Hong Kong's most authentic Northern-style roasted lamb is served here. Even better known is the Peking duck, which is very good. That said, the service can be about as welcoming as a Běijīng winter, c 1967. Booking is essential.

Dong Lai Shun CHINESE $$
(東來順; Map p502; ☑ 2733 2020; www.rghk.com.hk; 69 Mody Rd, B2, the Royal Garden, Tsim Sha Tsui; meals HK$250-1500; ⊙ 11.30am-2.30pm & 6-10.30pm; ☎; M East Tsim Sha Tsui, exit P2) Besides superbly executed Northern Chinese dishes, the phonebook of a menu here also features Shanghainese, Sichuanese and Cantonese favourites. But Dong Lai Shun is best known for its mutton hotpot, which involves dunking paper-thin slices of mutton into boiling water and eating it with sesame sauce. The atmosphere is a little formal but the service is warm.

Tin Lung Heen CANTONESE $$$
(天龍軒; ☑ 2263 2270; www.ritzcarlton.com/hongkong; 1 Austin Rd W, 102nd fl, Ritz-Carlton Hong Kong, International Commerce Centre; meals HK$400-1700; ⊙ noon-2.30pm & 6-10.30pm; M Kowloon, exit U3) Though the decor is im-

posing – Xi Jinping could walk in any minute and feel at home – the service is personable and we were floored by the views. The signature *char siu* made with Spanish Iberico pork is the priciest plate of barbecue in town, but also the most succulent. Do not ask for a window seat if you suffer from vertigo.

Fook Lam Moon CANTONESE, DIM SUM $$$
(福臨門; Map p502; ☎ 2366 0286; www.fooklammoon-grp.com; 53-59 Kimberley Rd, Shop 8, 1st fl, Tsim Sha Tsui; meals HK$400-2000; ⊙11.30am-2.30pm & 6-10.30pm; ⓂTsim Sha Tsui, exit B1) Locals call FLM 'celebrities' canteen'. But even if you're not rich and famous, FLM will treat you as if you were. The huge menu contains costly items such as abalone which would shoot your bill up to at least HK$1000 per head. But no one will snub you if you stick to the dim sum (from HK$60 a basket), which is divine and available only at lunch.

🍴 New Territories

Cuisines are less diverse here than Kowloon and Hong Kong but this area has an abundance of seafood and local eateries.

Ho To Tai Noodle Shop CANTONESE $
(好到底麵家; ☎ 2476 2495; 67 Fau Tsoi St; wonton noodles HK$23; ⊙8am-8pm; ⓇTai Tong Rd Light Rail station) This 60-year-old Yuen Long institution is one of the world's cheapest Michelin restaurants. It is best known for the fresh Cantonese egg noodles and shrimp roe noodles that it churns out daily. Foodies from all corners come to slurp the delightful wonton noodles. An English menu is available at the cashier. The haunt is a three-minute walk south of Tai Tong Rd Light Rail station.

Dai Wing Wah HAKKA $
(大榮華酒樓; 2nd fl, Koon Wong Mansion, 2-6 On Ning Rd; dim sum HK$16, dishes from HK$70; ⊙6am-midnight; ⓇTai Tong Rd Light Rail station) The brainchild of celebrated chef Leung Man-to, Dai Wing Wah is most famous for its walled-village dishes. Leung sources local ingredients from small farms and food producers whenever possible, and complements them with his innovations in cooking. Must-eats include lemon-steamed grey mullet, smoked oysters and Malay sponge cake.

Honeymoon Dessert DESSERTS $
(滿記甜品; ☎ 2792 4991; 9, 10A, B&C Po Tung Rd; per person HK$30; ⊙1pm-2.45am; ▣1) This

SELF-CATERING

Hong Kong's two main supermarket chains **Park'nShop** (www.parknshop.com) and **Wellcome** (www.wellcome.com.hk) have so many outlets you're bound to run into a few. The gourmet **city'super** (Map p502; www.citysuper.com.hk; Shop 3001, Gateway Arcade, 25-27 Canton Rd, Harbour City Level 3, Tsim Sha Tsui; ⊙10am-10pm) has attractive but expensive produce; there's a branch in the IFC Mall (p522).

shop specialising in Chinese desserts such as sweet walnut soup and durian pudding is so successful that it has branches all over China and in Indonesia, not to mention some 20 locations in Hong Kong.

★**Yue Kee Roasted Goose Restaurant** CANTONESE $$
(裕記大飯店; ☎ 2491 0105; www.yuekee.com.hk/en; 9 Sham Hong Rd, Sham Tseng; meals HK$100-200; ⊙11am-11pm; ▣minibus 302 from Tai Wo Hau MTR) In an alley lined with roast-goose restaurants, 54-year-old Yue Kee is king. Order gorgeous plates of coppery-skinned charcoal-roasted goose (half is plenty for four people) and sample house specialities like soy-braised goose web (feet), garlic-fried goose kidneys, and spicy goose intestines. If that's not your speed, there are plenty of standard Cantonese dishes on offer. English menu.

Sha Tin 18 CANTONESE, NORTHERN CHINESE $$
(沙田18; ☎ 3723 1234; www.hongkong.shatin.hyatt.com; 18 Chak Cheung St, Hyatt Regency Hong Kong; meals HK$300-500; ⊙11.30am-3pm & 5.30-10.30pm; ⓂUniversity) The Peking duck (whole HK$538, half HK$328) here has put this hotel restaurant, adjacent to the campus of the Chinese University, in the gastronomic spotlight since its opening in 2009. Book your prized fowl 24 hours in advance. Tantalise your taste buds in two ways – pancakes with the crispy skin, and wok-fried minced duck with iceberg lettuce. The restaurant also boasts a tempting dessert counter.

🍴 Outlying Islands

Lamma boasts the biggest choices in Yung Shue Wan and Sok Kwu Wan. There are also some decent choices on Lantau and fewer on Cheung Chau.

★ Mavericks
BURGERS, INTERNATIONAL **$**

(☑5402 4154; Pui O beach; meals from HK$100; ☺5.30-11.30pm Fri, 11.30am-11.30pm Sat & Sun; ☐1 from Mui Wo) Sunburned beachgoers gather for house-made sausages and burgers on artisan buns at this hip new surf-themed weekend spot, right on the water in Pui O. Many of the veggies are grown on the restaurant's own farm, the meat and dairy used are hormone free, and menus are printed on recycled bamboo paper. Wash your meal down with a locally brewed Young Master Ale.

Bookworm Cafe
CAFE, VEGETARIAN **$**

(南島書蟲; ☑2982 4838; 79 Main St, Yung Shue Wan; meals from HK$80; ☺9am-9pm Fri-Wed; ⛴Yung Shue Wan) Veggie foodies are in heaven at Bookworm, the grand-daddy of Hong Kong's healthy and eco-conscious dining scene. Tasty dishes include the dhal and salad combo, goat's cheese sandwich and shepherdess pie, which all pair well with the carefully selected organic wines. The cafe is also a secondhand bookshop.

♟ Drinking

Lan Kwai Fong in Central is synonymous with nightlife in Hong Kong, attracting everyone from expat and Chinese suits to travellers. In general, watering holes in Wan Chai are cheaper and more relaxed (some say seedier), though sleek new spots have been fast emerging around Star St. Drinking places in Kowloon tend to attract more locals. Most places offer discounts on drinks during happy hour, usually from late afternoon to early evening – 4pm to 8pm, say – but times vary from place to place.

⬚ Hong Kong Island

★ Club 71
BAR

(Map p494; 67 Hollywood Rd, Basement, Soho; ☺3pm-2am Mon-Sat, 6pm-1am Sun, happy hour 3-9pm; ☐26, MCentral, exit D1) This friendly bar with a bohemian vibe is named after a protest march on 1 July 2003. It's a favourite haunt of local artists and activists who come for the beer and music jamming sessions. In the garden out front, revolutionaries plotted to overthrow the Qing dynasty a hundred years ago. Enter from the alley next to 69 Hollywood.

★ Pawn
BAR

(www.thepawn.com.hk; 62 Johnston Rd, Wan Chai; ☺11am-2am, to midnight Sun; MWan Chai, exit A3) This handsome three-storey establishment used to be a row of tenement houses and the century-old Woo Cheong pawn shop. Now it's occupied by a restaurant and a bar. The slouchy sofas with space to sprawl, shabby-chic interiors designed by a filmmaker, plus great little terrace spaces overlooking the tram tracks, make this an ideal location to sample a great selection of lagers, bitters and wine.

Sevva
COCKTAIL BAR

(Map p494; ☑2537 1388; www.sevva.hk; 10 Chater Rd, 25th fl, Prince's Bldg, Central; ☺noon-midnight Mon-Thu, to 2am Fri & Sat; ☎; MCentral, exit H) If there was a million-dollar view in Hong Kong, it'd be the one from the balcony of ultrastylish Sevva – skyscrapers so close you can see their arteries of steel, with the harbour and Kowloon in the distance. At night it takes your breath away. To get there though, you have to overcome expensive drinks and patchy service.

Globe
PUB

(Map p494; ☑2543 1941; www.theglobe.com.hk; 45-53 Graham St, Soho; ☺10am-2am, happy hour 9am-8pm; MCentral, exit D1) Besides an impressive list of 150 imported beers, including 13 on tap, the Globe serves T8, the first cask-conditioned ale brewed in Hong Kong. Occupying an enviable 370 sq metres, the bar has a huge dining area with long wooden tables and comfortable banquettes.

Pier 7
BAR

(Map p494; ☑2167 8377; www.cafedecogroup. com; Shop M, Roof Viewing Deck, Central Pier 7, Star Ferry Terminal, Central; ☺9am-midnight, happy hour 6-9pm; ☎; MHong Kong, exit A1) Sitting atop the Star Ferry terminal, Pier 7 has a large outdoor terrace with views of neighbouring skyscrapers, the hills of Kowloon and a sliver of the harbour. It's an unpretentious spot for a quiet premovie (or postdinner) drink and some light refreshments. On random weekends there are reggae DJs in the house and the vibe turns shaggy.

MO Bar
BAR

(Map p494; ☑2132 0077; 15 Queen's Rd Central, Landmark, Central; ☺7am-1.30am; ☎; MCentral, exit D1) If you want to imbibe in quiet or to catch up with a chat, the swish MO Bar, attached to the Mandarin's swanky outpost at the Landmark, offers peace, soft lighting, and a first-rate drinks list of wines and cocktails.

Executive Bar LOUNGE

(☑ 2893 2080; 3 Yiu Wa St, 7th fl, Bartlock Centre, Causeway Bay; ⊗ 5pm-1am Mon-Sat; Ⓜ Causeway Bay, exit A) You won't be served if you just turn up at this clubby, masculine bar high above Causeway Bay – it's by appointment only. Odd perhaps, but worth the trip if you are serious about whisky and bourbon. Several-dozen varieties are served here, in large brandy balloons with large orbs of ice hand-chipped by the Japanese proprietor to maximise the tasting experience.

Delaney's BAR, PUB

(www.delaneys.com.hk; 18 Luard Rd, ground & 1st fl, One Capital Place, Wan Chai; ⊗ noon-3am, happy hour noon-9pm; Ⓜ Wan Chai, exit C) At this immensely popular Irish watering hole you can choose between the black-and-white-tiled pub on the ground floor and a sports bar and restaurant on the 1st floor. The food is good and plentiful; the kitchen allegedly goes through 400kg of potatoes a week.

🛑 Kowloon

★ Butler COCKTAIL BAR

(Map p502; ☑ 2724 3828; 30 Mody Rd, 5th fl, Mody House, Tsim Sha Tsui; cover HK$200, snacks HK$30; ⊗ 6.30pm-3am Mon-Fri, to 2am Sat & Sun; Ⓜ East Tsim Sha Tsui, exit N2) A cocktail and whisky heaven hidden in the residential part of Tsim Sha Tsui (TST). You can flip through its whisky magazines as you watch bartender Uchida create magical concoctions with the flair and precision of a master mixologist in Ginza. We loved the cocktails made from fresh citruses. A discreet and welcome addition to the TST drinking scene.

Ozone BAR

(☑ 2263 2263; www.ritzcarlton.com; 1 Austin Rd, 118th fl, ICC, Tsim Sha Tsui; ⊗ 5pm-1am Mon-Wed, to 2am Thu, to 3am Fri, 3pm-3am Sat, noon-midnight Sun; ☎; Ⓜ Kowloon, exit U3) Ozone is the highest bar in Asia. The imaginative interiors, created to evoke a cyberesque Garden of Eden, have pillars resembling chocolate fountains in a hurricane and a myriad of refracted glass and colour-changing illuminations. Equally dizzying is the wine list, with the most expensive bottle selling for over HK$150,000. Offers potential for a once-in-a-lifetime experience, in more ways than one.

Ned Kelly's Last Stand PUB

(Map p502; ☑ 2376 0562; 11A Ashley Rd, Tsim Sha Tsui; ⊗ 11.30am-2am, happy hour 11.30am-9pm; Ⓜ Tsim Sha Tsui, exit L5) Named after a gun-toting Australian bushranger, Ned's is one of Hong Kong's oldest pubs. Most of the expat regulars here (and there are many) are drawn to the laid-back atmosphere and the Dixieland jazz band that plays and cracks jokes between songs. The bar is filled with old posters, rugby shirts and Oz-related paraphernalia.

Tapas Bar BAR

(Map p502; ☑ 2733 8756; www.shangri-la.com; 64 Mody Rd, Lobby, Kowloon Shangri-La, Tsim Sha Tsui; ⊗ 3.30pm-1am Mon-Fri, from noon Sat & Sun; ☎; Ⓜ East Tsim Sha Tsui, exit P1) An intimate vibe and bistro-style decor make this a good place to unwind over champagne, tapas and the sports channel after a day of sightseeing. A table in the alfresco area will let you smoke and take in harbour views, visible beyond a river of cars.

★ Entertainment

Hong Kongers work hard and play harder. To find out what's on, pick up a copy of *HK Magazine* (http://hk-magazine.com), an entertainment listings magazine. It's free, appears on Friday and can be found in restaurants, bars and hotels. For more comprehensive listings buy the fortnightly *Time Out* (www.timeout.com.hk) from newsstands. Also worth checking out is the freebie *bc magazine* (www.bcmagazine.net).

The main ticket providers, **Urbtix** (☑ 2734 9009; www.urbtix.hk; ⊗ 10am-8pm), **Cityline** (☑ 2317 6666; www.cityline.com.hk) and **Hong Kong Ticketing** (☑ 3128 8288; www.hkticketing.com; ⊗ 10am-8pm), have among them tickets to every major event in Hong Kong. Book online or by phone.

Cinema

Tickets can be bought through Cityline (for mainstream films) and Urbtix (for alternative screenings). If you're into art-house films, don't miss **Broadway Cinematheque** (百老匯電影中心; Map p501; ☑ 2388 3188; 3 Public Square St, Ground fl, Prosperous Gardens, Yau Ma Tei; Ⓜ Yau Ma Tei, exit C).

Cantonese Opera

Hong Kong is one of the best places to watch Cantonese opera. **Sunbeam Theatre** (新光戲院; ☑ 2856 0161, 2563 2959; www.sunbeamtheatre.com/hk; 423 King's Rd, Kiu Fai Mansion, North Point; Ⓜ North Point, exit A4) and Yau Ma Tei Theatre (p117) are dedicated to the art form. You can book through Urbtix or Cityline.

Live Music

★ Street Music Concerts
LIVE MUSIC

(☎2582 0280; www.kungmusic.hk; Wan Chai) **FREE** Don't miss one of the free outdoor gigs thrown by eclectic musician Kung Chi-sing. One Saturday a month, the musician holds a concert outside the Hong Kong Arts Centre (6.30pm to 9pm). The exciting line-ups have included anything from indie rock, punk and jazz to Cantonese opera and Mozart. It's excellent, professional-quality music performed in an electrifying atmosphere. There are also performances at the Blue House (p497) on the second Thursday of the month (7.30pm to 9.30pm). Check the website for dates.

★ Peel Fresco
JAZZ

(Map p494; ☎2540 2046; www.peelfresco.com; 49 Peel St, Soho; ☉5pm-late Mon-Sat; 🚌13, 26, 40M) Charming Peel Fresco has live jazz six nights a week, with local and overseas acts performing on a small but spectacular stage next to teetering faux-Renaissance paintings. The action starts around 9.30pm, but go at 9pm to secure a seat.

Grappa's Cellar
LIVE MUSIC

(Map p494; ☎2521 2322; www.elgrande.com.hk/ outlets/HongKong/GrappasCellar; 1 Connaught Pl, Central; ☉9pm-late; 🚇Hong Kong, exit B2) For at least two weekends a month, this subterranean Italian restaurant morphs into a jazz or rock-music venue – chequered tablecloths and all. Call or visit the website for event and ticketing details.

Gay & Lesbian Venues

For the latest, try Utopia Asia (www.utopia-asia.com/hkbars.htm), Gay HK (www.gayhk.com) or the free, monthly magazine *Dim Sum* (www.dimsum-hk.com).

Hong Kong's premier lesbian organisation, Les Peches (☎9101 8001; lespechesinfo@ yahoo.com) has monthly events for lesbians, bisexual women and their friends.

ⓘ SMOKING BAN

In Hong Kong, smoking is banned in all restaurants, bars, shopping malls and museums – even at beaches and public parks – but you can light up in 'alfresco' areas. Some bars, however, risk getting fined to attract more customers during nonpeak hours. You'll know which ones they are by the ashtray they nonchalantly place on your table.

Propaganda
GAY CLUB

(Map p494; ☎2868 1316; 1 Hollywood Rd, lower ground fl, Central; ☉9pm-4am Tue-Thu, to 6am Fri & Sat, happy hour 9pm-1.30am Tue-Thu; 🚇Central, exit D2) Hong Kong's default gay dance club and meat market; cover charge (HK$120 to HK$160) applies on Friday and Saturday. Enter from Ezra's Lane.

T:ME
GAY BAR

(Map p494; ☎2332 6565; www.time-bar.com; 65 Hollywood Rd; ☉6pm-2am Mon-Sat; 🚇Central, exit D1) A small and chic gay bar located in a back alley off Hollywood Rd, close to Club 71; drinks are a bit on the pricey side but it has happy hour throughout the week.

🛍 Shopping

It's not the bargain destination it was, but Hong Kong is crammed with retail space, making it a delight for shoppers. If you prefer everything under one roof, some of the sleeker options are: IFC Mall (Map p494; ☎2295 3308; www.ifc.com.hk; 8 Finance St; 🚇Hong Kong, exit F), Pacific Place (太古廣場; Map p494; ☎2844 8988; www.pacificplace.com. hk; 88 Queensway, Admiralty; 🚇Admiralty, exit F), Elements (圓方; www.elementshk.com; 1 Austin Rd W, West Kowloon; ☉11am-9pm; 🚇Kowloon, exit U3) and the enormous Harbour City (Map p502; www.harbourcity.com.hk; 3-9 Canton Rd; 🚇Tsim Sha Tsui, exit C1).

If you're looking for antiques and curios, Central's Hollywood Rd should be your first stop, while cheaper Cat St, also in Central, specialises in younger (ie retro) items such as Mao paraphernalia.

For cheap attire, browse at Jardine's Bazaar (渣甸街) in Causeway Bay, Johnston Rd in Wan Chai or the Tung Choi Street Market (通菜街, 女人街, Ladies' Market; Tung Choi St; ☉noon-11.30pm; 🚇Mong Kok, exit D3) in Mong Kok, Kowloon.

Hong Kong is one of the best places in Asia to buy English-language books, and the city's computer malls have some of the lowest prices on earth. Similarly, there are some fantastic camera stores, though most are *not* on Nathan Rd in Tsim Sha Tsui.

🛍 Hong Kong Island

Central and Causeway Bay are the main shopping districts on Hong Kong Island. For cheap souvenirs, try the faux antiques vendors on Cat St or the street markets in Wan Chai.

Horizon Plaza　　　FACTORY OUTLETS
(新海怡廣場; 2 Lee Wing St, Ap Lei Chau, Aberdeen; ◎10am-7pm; 🚌90 from Exchange Sq in Central) Tucked away on the southern coast of Ap Lei Chau, this enormous outlet, in a converted factory building, boasts more than 150 shops over 28 storeys. Most locals come here to buy furniture, but you'll also find Alexander McQueens on offer and Jimmy Choos at knock-down prices.

Arch Angel Antiques　　　ANTIQUES
(Map p494; 📞2851 6848; 53-55 Hollywood Rd, Lan Kwai Fong; ◎9.30am-6.30pm Mon-Sat, to 6pm Sun; 🚌26) Though the specialities are ancient porcelain and tombware, Arch Angel packs a lot more into its three floors: it has everything from mah-jong sets and terracotta horses to palatial furniture.

★**Shanghai Tang**　　　CLOTHING, HOMEWARES
(上海灘; Map p494; 📞2525 7333; www.shanghaitang.com; 1 Duddell St, Shanghai Tang Mansion, Central; ◎10.30am-8pm; Ⓜ Central, exit D1) This elegant four-level store is the place to go if you fancy a body-hugging *qipao* (cheongsam) with a modern twist, a Chinese-style clutch or a lime-green mandarin jacket. Custom tailoring is available; it takes two weeks to a month and requires a fitting. Shanghai Tang also stocks cushions, picture frames, teapots, even mah-jong tile sets, designed in a modern chinoiserie style.

Fook Ming Tong Tea Shop　　　FOOD, DRINK
(福茗堂; Map p494; 📞2295 0368; www.fookmingtong.com; 8 Finance St, Shop 3006, Podium Level 3, IFC Mall, Central; ◎10.30am-8pm Mon-Sat, 11am-8pm Sun; Ⓜ Central, exit A) Tea-making accoutrements and carefully chosen teas of various ages and grades are available here, from gunpowder to Nanyan Ti Guan Yin Crown Grade – costing anything from HK$10 to HK$9000 per 100g.

Chinese Arts & Crafts　　　DEPARTMENT STORE
(Map p494; 88 Queensway, Shop 220, Pacific Place, Admiralty; ◎10am-9pm; Ⓜ Admiralty, exit F) Mainland-owned CAC is probably the best place in Hong Kong to buy quality jade, porcelain chopsticks and other pricey Chinese crafts; it's positively an Aladdin's cave of souvenirs. On Hong Kong Island there are also branches in **Central** (Map p498; 📞2901 0338; 59 Queen's Rd, ground fl, Asia Standard Tower; Ⓜ Admiralty, exit F) and **Wan Chai** (Map p498; 28 Harbour Rd, 2nd Causeway Centre; Ⓜ Wan Chai, exit A5).

★**Wan Chai Computer Centre**　　　ELECTRONICS
(灣仔電腦城; Map p498; 130-138 Hennessy Rd, 1st fl, Southorn Centre, Wan Chai; ◎10am-8pm Mon-Sat; Ⓜ Wan Chai, exit B2) This gleaming, beeping warren of tiny shops is a safe bet for anything digital and electronic.

★**Kapok**　　　CLOTHING, ACCESSORIES
(Map p498; 📞2549 9254; www.ka-pok.com; 5 St Francis Yard, Wan Chai; ◎11am-8pm, to 6pm Sun; Ⓜ Admiralty, exit F) In the hip Star St area, this boutique has a fastidiously edited selection of luxe-cool local and international clothing and accessory labels. Look for the new line of Kapok-label made-in-HK men's shirts, and graphic Mischa handbags by local designer Michelle Lai. The sister boutique is around the corner at 3 Sun St.

Kung Fu Supplies　　　SPORTS
(功夫用品公司; Map p498; 📞2891 1912; www.kungfu.com/hk; 188-192 Johnston Rd, Room 6a, 6th fl, Chuen Fung House, Wan Chai; ◎Mon-Sat; 🚌6, 6A, 6X) If you need to stock up on martial-arts accessories, including uniforms, nunchaku and safety weapons for practice, or just want to thumb through a decent collection of books and DVDs, this is the place to go. The staff here are very helpful.

★**Eslite**　　　BOOKS
(Map p498; 📞3419 6789; 500 Hennessy Rd, Causeway Bay, Hysan Place, 8/f-10/f; ◎10am-11pm Sun-Thu, to 2am Fri & Sat; Ⓜ Causeway Bay, exit F2) You could spend an entire evening inside this swank three-floor Taiwanese bookshop (literally – it's open till 2am on weekends), which features a massive collection of English and Chinese books and magazines, a shop selling gorgeous stationary and leather-bound journals, a cafe, a bubble-tea counter, and a huge kids toy and book section.

Yiu Fung Store　　　FOOD
(么鳳; Map p498; 3 Foo Ming St, Causeway Bay; ◎11am-10pm; Ⓜ Causeway Bay, exit A) Hong Kong's most famous store (c 1960s) for Chinese pickles and preserved fruit features sour plum, liquorice-flavoured lemon, tangerine peel, pickled papaya and dried longan. Just before the lunar New Year, it's crammed with shoppers.

🔒 Kowloon

Shopping in Kowloon is a mix of the down at heel and the glamorous; you can find just about anything – especially in Tsim Sha Tsui.

Premier Jewellery
JEWELLERY

(愛寶珠寶有限公司; Map p502; ☑2368 0003; 50 Nathan Rd, Shop G14-15, Ground fl, Holiday Inn Golden Mile Shopping Mall, Tsim Sha Tsui; ⊗10am-7.30pm Mon-Sat, to 4pm Sun; Ⓜ Tsim Sha Tsui, exit G) This third-generation family firm is directed by a qualified gemmologist and is one of our favourite places to shop. The range isn't huge but if you're looking for something particular, give Premier Jewellery a day's notice and a selection will be ready in time for your arrival. Staff can also help you design your own piece.

Initial
CLOTHING

(Map p502; www.initialfashion.com; 48 Cameron Rd, Shop 2, Tsim Sha Tsui; ⊗11.30am-11.30pm; Ⓜ Tsim Sha Tsui, exit B2) This attractive shop and cafe carries stylish, multifunctional urbanwear with European and Japanese influences. The clothes created by local designers are complemented by imported shoes, bags and costume jewellery.

Ap Liu Street Flea Market
MARKET

(鴨寮街; Ap Liu St, btwn Nam Cheong & Yen Chow Sts, Sham Shui Po; ⊗noon-midnight; Ⓜ Sham Shui Po, exit A1) A geek's heaven, this flea market specialises in all things digital and electronic. The market spills over into Pei Ho St.

Swindon Books
BOOKS

(Map p502; ☑2366 8001; 13-15 Lock Rd, Tsim Sha Tsui; ⊗9am-6pm Mon-Fri, to 1pm Sat; Ⓜ Tsim Sha Tsui, exit A1) This is one of the best 'real' (as opposed to 'supermarket') bookshops. An excellent range and knowledgable staff. Strong on local books and history in particular.

Rise Shopping Arcade
CLOTHING

(利時商場; Map p502; www.rise-hk.com; 5-11 Granville Circuit, Tsim Sha Tsui; ⊗3-9pm; Ⓜ Tsim Sha Tsui, exit B2) Bursting the seams of this minimall is cheap streetwear from Hong Kong, Korea and Japan, with a few knockoffs chucked in for good measure. Patience and a good eye could land you purchases fit for a Vogue photo shoot. It's best visited between 4pm and 8.30pm when most of the shops are open.

Bruce Lee Club
SOUVENIRS

(李小龍會; ☑2771 7093; www.bruceleeclub.com; 530 Nathan Rd, Shop 160-161, In's Point, Mong Kok; ⊗1-9pm; Ⓜ Yau Ma Tei, exit A1) Founded by Bruce Lee's fans, this mini-museum and souvenir shop has action figures, toys, movie products and other memorabilia related to the kung fu icon.

★Chan Wah Kee Cutlery Store
HOMEWARES

(陳華記刀莊; Map p501; ☑2730 4091; Temple St, 278D, Yau Ma Tei; ⊗11am-6pm, closed Wed; Ⓜ Jordan, exit C2) At this humble shop, 80-year-old Mr Chan, one of Asia's few remaining master knife-sharpeners, uses nine different stones to grind each blade, and alternates between water and oil. If you bring him your blade, he charges between HK$100 and HK$600 with a three-month wait. But if you buy from him, and he has a great selection, he'll do it there and then. Prices range from HK$200 for a small paring knife to around HK$2000 for a Shun knife.

ⓘ Information

EMERGENCY

Fire, Police & Ambulance (☑999)

INTERNET ACCESS

Internet cafes are hard to come by, but wi-fi is widely available. It's free at Hong Kong International Airport, and at parks, public libraries, sports centres, museums, cooked-food markets, community halls and government premises listed at www.gov.hk/en/theme/wifi/location. Some chain restaurants offer free wi-fi with purchase.

A one-hour PCCW wi-fi pass is available at Hong Kong Tourist Board (HKTB) visitor centres. A 3G rechargeable SIM card (from HK$48) will connect your phone to the internet and these are available at PCCW and SmarTone shops; PCCW provides some 10,000 wi-fi hot spots. Check service plans at www.pccwwifi.com.

MEDIA

Local and Asian editions of printed newspapers and journals available locally include the *South China Morning Post*, *The Standard*, *HK Magazine*, *BC Magazine*, *Time Out*, *USA Today*, *International Herald Tribune*, *Financial Times* and *Wall Street Journal Asia*.

English-language TV (terrestrial) and radio include TVB Pearl, ATV World, BBC World Service, RTHK 3 and 4.

MEDICAL SERVICES

Medical care is of a high standard in Hong Kong, though private hospital care is costly.

Hospitals with 24-hour emergency services:

Matilda International Hospital (明德國際醫院; ☑2849 0111; 41 Mt Kellett Rd, The Peak) Private hospital.

Prince of Wales Hospital (威爾斯親王醫院; ☑2632 2211; 30-32 Ngan Shing St, Sha Tin) Public hospital.

Queen Elizabeth Hospital (伊利沙伯醫院; Map p501; ☑ 2958 8888; 30 Gascoigne Rd, Yau Ma Tei) Public hospital in Kowloon.

MONEY

ATMs are available throughout Hong Kong, including at the airport. Most are available 24 hours. Banks have the best exchange rates, but some levy commissions of HK$50 or more per transaction. Opening hours are 9am to 4.30pm or 5.30pm Monday to Friday, 9am to 12.30pm Saturday.

Licensed moneychangers are abundant in tourist districts, the ground floor of Chungking Mansions (p513) and at **Wing Hoi Money Exchange** (Map p502; G/F, Shop No 9b, Mirador Mansion, 58 Nathan Rd, Tsim Sha Tsui; ⌚ 8.30am-8.30pm Mon-Sat, to 7pm Sun). Rates at the airport are poor.

POST

Hong Kong Post (☑ 2921 2222; www.hongkong-post.com) offices:

General Post Office (中央郵政局; Map p494; 2 Connaught Pl, Central; ⌚ 8am-6pm Mon-Sat, 9am-5pm Sun) On Hong Kong Island, the General Post Office is just west of the Star Ferry pier.

Tsim Sha Tsui Post Office (尖沙咀郵政局; Map p502; ground & 1st fl, Hermes House, 10 Middle Rd, Tsim Sha Tsui; ⌚ 9am-6pm Mon-Sat, to 2pm Sun) In Kowloon, the Tsim Sha Tsui Post Office is just east of the southern end of Nathan Rd.

TELEPHONE

All phone numbers have eight digits (except ☑ 800 toll-free numbers) and no area codes. Local calls are free on private phones and cost HK$1 for five minutes on pay phones.

A phonecard, available at convenience stores, will let you make international direct-dial calls. A SIM card (from HK$50) with prepaid call time will connect you to the local mobile phone network.

TOURIST INFORMATION

Hong Kong Tourism Board (香港旅遊發展局, HKTB; ☑ visitor hotline 2508 1234; www.discoverhongkong.com; ⌚ hotline 9am-6pm) runs a website, visitor hotline and several visitor information and service centres:

Hong Kong International Airport HKTB Centres (Chek Lap Kok; ⌚ 7am-11pm) There are centres in Halls A and B on the arrivals level in Terminal 1 and the E2 transfer area.

Hong Kong Island HKTB Centre (港島旅客諮詢及服務中心; Peak Piazza; ⌚ 9am-9pm)

Kowloon HKTB Centre (香港旅遊發展局; Map p502; Star Ferry Concourse, Tsim Sha Tsui; ⌚ 8am-8pm)

Lo Wu HKTB Centre (羅湖旅客諮詢及服務中心; 2nd fl, Arrival Hall, Lo Wu Terminal Bldg; ⌚ 8am-6pm) At the border to mainland China.

TRAVEL AGENCIES

China Travel Service (中國旅行社, CTS; Map p494; ☑ 2522 0450; www.ctshk.com; 77 Queen's Rd, Ground fl, China Travel Bldg; ⌚ 9am-6pm Mon-Fri, 9am-7.30pm Mon-Sat, 9.30am-5pm Sun)

WEBSITES

Discover Hong Kong (www.discoverhongkong.com) A good general resource if you're seeking inspiration with lots of pictures.
Lonely Planet (www.lonelyplanet.com/hong-kong) Destination information, bookings, traveller forum and more.

Getting There & Away

AIR

Over 100 airlines operate between Hong Kong International Airport (p1005) and some 160 destinations around the world. Fares are relatively low and you can find quite a number of discounted tickets.

That said, bargain airfares between Hong Kong and mainland China are few, as the government regulates the prices. The volume of business travellers and Chinese tourists is enormous, so book well in advance. If you're prepared to travel to Guǎngzhōu or Shēnzhèn, in Guǎngdōng province, you can find much cheaper flights. Shēnzhèn airport has flights to just about everywhere in China (see www.elong.net).

Airline offices in Hong Kong:

Air China (☑ 3970 9000; www.airchina.hk)
Cathay Pacific Airways (CX; Map p502; ☑ 2747 1888; www.cathaypacific.com) Hong Kong's major international airline has flights to 20 cities in mainland China.
China Airlines (Map p494; ☑ 2868 2299; www.china-airlines.com)
China Southern (www.cs-air.com)
Dragonair (KA; Map p494; ☑ 3193 3888; www.dragonair.com) Owned by Cathay Pacific, Dragonair specialises in regional flights and flies to 20-plus cities in mainland China.
Hong Kong Airlines (HX; ☑ 3151 1888; www.hongkongairlines.com) Cheaper airline that specialises in regional routes, including 17 cities in mainland China.

BOAT

Regular ferries link the **China Ferry Terminal** (中港碼頭; Map p502; China Hong Kong City, 33 Canton Rd, Tsim Sha Tsui) in Kowloon and the **Hong Kong–Macau Ferry Terminal** (Map p494; Shun Tak Centre, 200 Connaught Rd, Sheung Wan) on Hong Kong Island with towns and cities on the Pearl River delta – but not central

Guǎngzhōu or Shēnzhèn. You'll find left-luggage lockers (HK$20 to HK$30 per hour) in both terminals.

Chu Kong Passenger Transportation Co (2858 3876; www.cksp.com.hk) provides regularly scheduled ferries to Zhūhǎi (HK$200, 70 minutes), Zhōngshān (HK$230, 1½ hours), Shùndé (HK$240, two hours), Zhàoqìng (HK$220, four hours) and Shékǒu (HK$140, one hour).

BUS

You can reach virtually any major destination in Guǎngdōng province by bus (HK$100 to HK$220):

CTS Express Coach (Map p494; 2764 9803; http://ctsbus.hkcts.com)

Trans-Island Limousine Service (3193 9333; www.trans-island.com.hk) Mainland destinations from Hong Kong include Dōngguǎn, Fóshān, Guǎngzhōu, Huìzhōu, Kāipíng, Shēnzhèn's Bǎoān airport and Zhōngshān.

TRAIN

For schedules and ticket prices, see www.mtr.com.hk.

Immigration formalities at Hung Hom train station must be completed before boarding, including checking your visa for China; arrive at the station 45 minutes before departure.

Tickets can be booked at CTS, East Rail stations in Hung Hom, Mong Kok, Kowloon Tong and Sha Tin, and MTR Travel at Admiralty Station; tickets booked with credit card by phone (2947 7888) must be collected at least one hour before departure.

Destinations include:

Guǎngzhōu, Shànghǎi, Běijīng, Zhàoqìng Daily from Hung Hom station (HK$190 to HK$1191).

Shēnzhèn The East Rail train takes you to Lo Wu or Lok Ma Chau; from Shēnzhèn you can take a local train or bus to Guǎngzhōu and beyond.

ⓘ Getting Around

Hong Kong's public transport system is fast, convenient, relatively inexpensive and easy to use with the Octopus card payment system.

TO/FROM THE AIRPORT

The **Airport Express** (2881 8888; www.mtr.com.hk; HK$100/90/60 per 24/21/13min from Central, Kowloon and Tsing Yi) is the fastest and costliest public route to the airport; most airlines allow Airport Express passengers to check in at Central or Kowloon stations between 5.30am and 12.30am one day to 90 minutes before departure; at Hong Kong International Airport there is a **left-luggage office** (2261 0110; Level 3, Terminal 2; per hr/day HK$12/140; ⏲ 5.30am-1.30am).

Bus fares to the airport are HK$21 to HK$45. See 'Transport' on the www.hkairport.com website for details.

A taxi to Central is about HK$300 plus luggage charge of HK$5 per item.

BICYCLE

In quiet areas of the Outlying Islands or New Territories, a bike can be a lovely way of getting around. Some convenience stores in rural villages or beach areas rent out bikes; don't even think of taking one into the city.

CAR & MOTORCYCLE

Driving in Hong Kong isn't for the faint-hearted. But if you are determined to see Hong Kong under your own steam, try **Avis** (2890 6988; www.avis.com.hk; 183 Queen's Rd E, Hopewell Centre, Wan Chai; Ⓜ Wan Chai, exit B2), which has Honda Civics with unlimited kilometres. An international driving license is required.

PUBLIC TRANSPORT
Bus

On Hong Kong Island the most important bus stations are the bus terminus in Central and the one at Admiralty. From these stations you can catch buses to Aberdeen, Repulse Bay, Stanley and other destinations on the southern side of Hong Kong Island. In Kowloon the Star Ferry bus terminal has buses heading up Nathan Rd and to the Hung Hom train station.

The bus system runs from 5.30/6am to midnight/12.30am and will get you almost anywhere. Fares start at $2.50 and exact change or an Octopus card is required. The HKTB has leaflets on major bus routes.

Public Light Bus

Better known as 'minibuses,' these 16-seaters come in two varieties:

OCTOPUS CARD

Octopus Card (2266 2222; www.octopuscards.com) This rechargeable 'smart card' is valid on the Mass Transit Railway (MTR) and most forms of public transport in Hong Kong. It also allows you to make purchases at retail outlets across the territory (such as convenience stores and supermarkets). The card costs HK$150 (HK$70 for children and seniors), which includes a HK$50 refundable deposit and HK$100 worth of travel. Octopus fares are about 5% cheaper than ordinary fares on the MTR. You can buy one and recharge at any MTR station.

With red roof/stripe Fares cost HK$2 to HK$22; supplement bus services. Get on or off almost anywhere – just yell *'ni do, m gói'* (here, please); Octopus card accepted on certain routes.

With green roof/stripe Operate on more than 350 set routes and make designated stops; Octopus card accepted on all routes.

Ferry

The cross-harbour Star Ferry (p506) operates on two routes: Central–Tsim Sha Tsui and Wan Chai–Tsim Sha Tsui.

For ferries to the Outlying Islands, see schedules at ferry piers and ferry company websites, or ask for a pocket-sized timetable. Most ferries depart from the Outlying Islands Piers close to the IFC building in Central. The main companies are:

Train

The **Mass Transit Railway** (MTR; ☑ 2881 8888; www.mtr.com.hk; fares HK$4-25) runs 10 lines; buy tickets or use the Octopus card (slightly cheaper). Once past the turnstile, you must complete the journey within 150 minutes.

The MTR also runs overland services on two main lines and two smaller lines, offering transport to the New Territories:

East Rail From Hung Hom station in Kowloon to Lo Wu and Lok Ma Chau (HK$36 to HK$48),

gateway to Shēnzhèn; a spur runs from Tai Wai to Wu Kai Sha.

Light Rail Fares cost HK$4.10 to HK$6.50; routes in western New Territories between Tuen Mun and Yuen Long, and feeds the West Rail.

West Rail From Hung Hom station to Tuen Mun (HK$20) via Yuen Long.

There are left-luggage lockers at major MTR train stations, including Hung Hom station.

Tram

Hong Kong's century-old **trams** (☑ 2548 7102; www.hktramways.com; fares HK$2.30) represent the only all double-decker wooden-sided tram fleet in the world. They operate on six overlapping routes running east–west along the northern side of Hong Kong Island.

TAXI

Hong Kong is served by taxis of three colours:

Blue Serving Lantau; HK$17 flag fall, then HK$1.40 for every 200m.

Green Serving the New Territories; HK$18.50 flag fall, then HK$1.40 for every 200m.

Red Serving Hong Kong Island and Kowloon; HK$22 flag fall for the first 2km, then HK$1.60 for every additional 200m.

HKIA TO CHINA THE FAST WAY

Airport Express

Hong Kong's convenient Airport Express check-in counters allow you to check in your luggage from downtown Hong Kong as early as 24 hours before your flight. There's one in the MTR's Hong Kong Station and one in Kowloon Station.

Bus

You can head straight from Hong Kong International Airport (HKIA) to Macau and airports in Shēnzhèn and Guǎngzhōu. The following companies (all with counters at HKIA Terminal 2) have buses going to points in southern China (Fóshān HK$230, Guǎngzhōu HK$250 and Shēnzhèn airport HK$130):

CTS Express Coach

Eternal East Cross Border Coach (Map p502; ☑ 3760 0888, 3412 6677; 4-6 Hankow Rd, 13th fl, Kai Seng Commercial Centre; ⊘7am-8pm)

Trans-Island Limousine Service

Ferry

Chu Kong Passenger Transportation Co Has ferries from HKIA to Shēnzhèn airport (HK$220, 40 minutes, eight daily, 10.15am to 6.30pm) and to Macau, Shékǒu, Dōngguǎn, Zhūhǎi and Zhōngshān.

You can also head straight from the airport to other Pearl River delta cities by ferry: **Skypier** (☑ 2215 3232) A fast ferry service that links HKIA with Macau and six Pearl River delta destinations. Travellers can board ferries without clearing Hong Kong customs and immigration. Book a ticket prior to boarding from ticketing desks located in the transfer area at Arrivals (Level 5, near to immigration counters).

TurboJet (Map p494; ☑ 2859 3333; www.turbojet.com.hk) Has services to Macau (HK$159, one hour, eight daily, 10am to 10pm).

Macau

☎ 853 / POP 556,783

Best Places to Eat

➡ A Petisqueira (p544)
➡ Antonio (p545)
➡ Guincho a Galera (p545)
➡ Clube Militar de Macau (p545)

Best Sights

➡ Ruins of the Church of St Paul (p529)
➡ Guia Fort (p537)
➡ Mandarin's House (p533)
➡ St Lazarus Church District (p533)

Why Go?

The Chinese people have stood up and they're off to Macau. Chairman Mao (who coined the first half of that sentence) must be spinning faster than a roulette wheel in his crystal coffin. Mainlanders can't get enough of this once Portuguese-administered backwater-turned-gambling-megaresort.

Such has been its explosive growth since 2002 that it is commonplace to refer to Macau as the Vegas of the East. It might be more appropriate to put that the other way round, since Macau has eclipsed its American rival in gambling income. And there are many other things that Macau does better. Beyond the gaming halls, it offers cobblestoned streets punctuated with Chinese temples and baroque churches, pockets of natural greenery, and a historic centre of Unesco World Heritage status.

Macau's unique history has also created a one-of-a-kind cuisine that celebrates the marriage of European, Latin American, African and Asian flavours.

When to Go
Macau

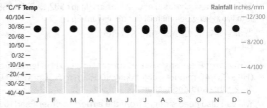

Mar–May Celebrate the arts, a sea goddess and a dragon as mist hangs over the harbour.

Jun–Sep Days in the shade of temples and dragon boats; nights aglow with fireworks.

Oct–Feb Music and Grand Prix in a high-octane run-up to Christmas and New Year.

History

Portuguese galleons first visited southern China to trade in the early 16th century, and in 1557, as a reward for clearing out pirates, they obtained a leasehold for Macau. The first Portuguese governor of Macau was appointed in 1680, and as trade with China grew, so did Macau. However, after the Opium Wars between the Chinese and the British, and the subsequent establishment of Hong Kong, Macau went into a long decline.

In 1999, under the Sino–Portuguese Joint Declaration, Macau was returned to China and designated a Special Administrative Region (SAR). Like Hong Kong, the pact ensures Macau a 'high degree of autonomy' in all matters (except defence and foreign affairs) for 50 years. The handover, however, did not change Macau socially and economically as much as the termination of the gambling monopoly in 2001. Casinos mushroomed, redefining the city's skyline, and tourists from mainland China surged, fattening up the city's coffers.

Yet the revenue boost, coupled with government policies (or the lack thereof), also led to income inequality and a labour shortage. Macau residents are also increasingly critical of their chief executive's pro-Beijing stance. In May 2014 thousands in the formerly placid city took to the streets to protest Chief Executive Fernando Chui, who was reelected three months later.

Language

Cantonese and Portuguese are the official languages of Macau, though few people actually speak Portuguese. English and Mandarin are reasonably well understood, though the former is harder to find here than in Hong Kong.

◉ Sights

For a small place (just 29 sq km), Macau is packed with important cultural and historical sights, including eight squares and 22 historic buildings, which have collectively been named the Historic Centre of Macau World Heritage Site by Unesco. Most of the sights are on the peninsula. At many of these sites, seniors aged over 60 years and children 11 years or under are admitted free.

◉ Central Macau Peninsula

Running from Avenida da Praia Grande to the Inner Harbour, Avenida de Almeida

MACAU SIGHTS

Macau Highlights

❶ Get context for your impressions at the **Macau Museum** (p533)

❷ Explore the ethereal ruins of the very symbol of Macau at the **Church of St Paul** (p529)

❸ Sample Macau's unique cuisine at **Alfonso III** (p545)

❹ Lose yourself in mazelike spaces at **Lou Lim Ioc Garden** (p538) and the **Mandarin's House** (p533)

❺ Take the cable car to handsome **Guia Fort** (p537) and its gorgeous chapel

❻ Mingle with artists on the cobbled paths of the charming **St Lazarus district** (p533)

Ribeiro – or San Ma Lo (新馬路; New Thoroughfare) in Cantonese – is the peninsula's main thoroughfare and home to the charming **Largo do Senado** (Map p534), a black-and-white tiled square close to major sights.

★ **Ruins of the Church of St Paul**   RUIN
(大三巴牌坊; Ruínas de Igreja de São Paulo; Map p530; Travessa de São Paulo; admission free; 🚌 8A,

Macau Peninsula

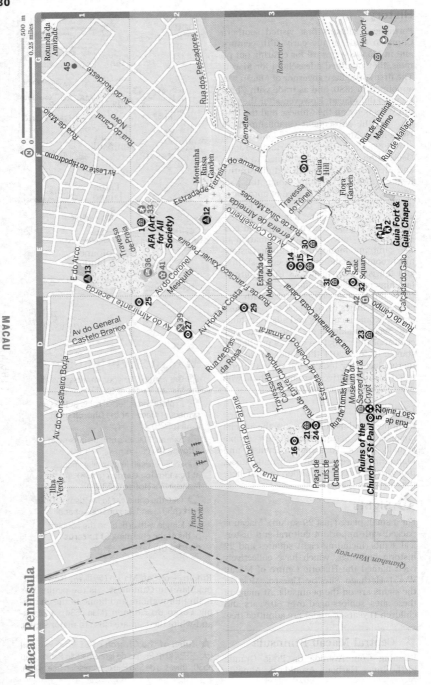

0 — 500 m
0 — 0.25 miles

Rotunda da Amizade

45

Av do Nordeste

Av Leste do Hipódromo

Rua de Maio

Rua do Canal Novo

Reservoir

Rua dos Pescadores

Heliport
46

Cemetery

Rua de Terminal Marítimo

Rua de Mallaca

Montanha Russa Garden

Estrada de Ferreira do amaral

10
Guia Hill
Flora Garden

1
AFA (Art 33 for All Society)

12

Travessa de Praia

Travessa de Túnel

11
12
Guia Fort & Guia Chapel

Estrada de Ferreira de Almeida

Av do Conselheiro Ferreira de Almeida

Rua de Silva Mendes

E do Arco

36

13

Av do Coronel Mesquita

41

30

14
15
17

Estrada de Adolfo de Loureiro

Tap Seac Square

Calçada do Gaio

Av do Almirante Lacerda

25

Rua de Francisco Xavier Pereira

31

32

42

Av do General Castelo Branco

39

27

Av Horta e Costa

29

Rua de Tomás da Rosa

Rua do Campo

Ilha Verde

Av do Conselheiro Borja

Rua da Ribeira do Patane

Rua de Bras da Rosa

Rua de Coelho do Amaral

Rua do Almirante Costa Cabral

23

Travessada Corda

Rua de Entena Carnaros

Estrada de Coelho do Amaral

Rua de Tomás Vieira

Museum of Sacred Art & Crypt

16

21
24

Praça de Luís de Camões

5
22
Rua de São Paulo

Ruins of the Church of St Paul

Inner Harbour

Qianshan Waterway

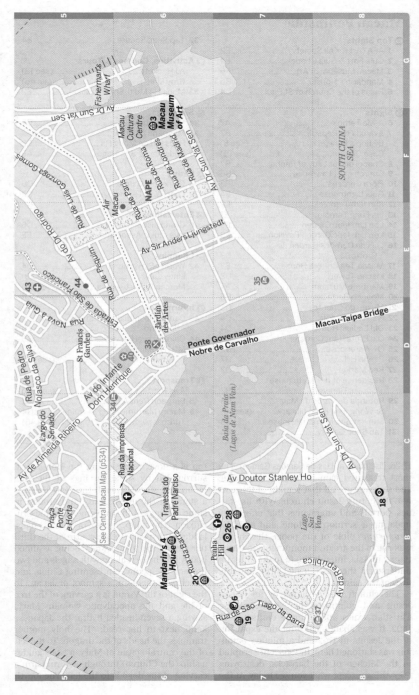

MACAU

Fisherman's Wharf

Av Dr Sun Yat Sen

Macau Cultural Centre

Macau Museum of Art 3

NAPE

Rua de Roma
Rua de Londres
Rua de Madrid

Av Dr Sun Yat Sen

SOUTH CHINA SEA

Air Macau

Rua de Paris

Rua do Rodrigo

Av do Dr Rodrigo

Rua de Luis Gonzaga Gomes

Av Sir Anders Ljungstedt

Rua de Pequim

43

44

Estrada de São Francisco

Rua Nova à Guia

Jardim des Artes

35

38

Ponte Governador Nobre de Carvalho

Macau-Taipa Bridge

St Francis Garden

40

Av do Infante Dom Henrique

Rua de Pedro Nolasco da Silva

34

Baía da Praia (Lagos de Nam Van)

Av Dr Sun Yat Sen

Rua da Imprensa Nacional

Largo do Almeida Ribeiro

Av de Almeida Senado

See Central Macau Map (p534)

9

Av Doutor Stanley Ho

Travessa do Padré Narciso

Praça Ponte e Horta

8
26 28
7

18

Lago Sai Van

Mandarin's House 4

Rua da Barra

Penha Hill

20

Av da República

6
19

37

Rua de São Tiago da Barra

Macau Peninsula

17, 26, disembark at Luís de Camões Garden) The most treasured icon in Macau, the facade and stairway are all that remain of this early-17th-century Jesuit church. With its statues, portals and engravings that effectively make up a 'sermon in stone' and a *Biblia pauperum* (Bible of the poor), the church was one of the greatest monuments to Christianity in Asia, intended to help the illiterate understand the Passion of Christ and the lives of the saints.

The church was designed by an Italian Jesuit and completed by early Japanese Christian exiles and Chinese craftsmen in 1602. It was abandoned after the expulsion of the Jesuits in 1762 and a military battalion was stationed here. In 1835 a fire erupted in the kitchen of the barracks, destroying everything, except what you see today. At the top is a dove, representing the Holy Spirit, surrounded by stone carvings of the sun, moon and stars. Beneath the Holy Spirit is a statue of the infant Jesus, and around it, stone carvings of the implements of the Crucifixion (the whip, crown of thorns, nails, ladder and spear). In the centre of the third tier stands the Virgin Mary being assumed bodily into heaven along with angels and two flowers: the peony, representing China, and the chrysanthemum, a symbol of Japan. To the right of the Virgin is a carving of the tree of life and the apocalyptic woman (Mary) slaying a seven-headed hydra; the Japanese kanji next to her read: 'The holy mother tramples the heads of the dragon'. To the left of the central statue of Mary, a 'star' guides a ship (the Church) through a storm (sin); a carving of the devil is to the left. The fourth tier has statues of four Jesuit doctors of the church: (From left) Blessed Francisco de Borja; St Ignatius Loyola, the founder of the order; St Francis Xavier, the apostle of the Far East; and Blessed Luís Gonzaga.

Monte Fort
FORT

(大炮台; Fortaleza do Monte; Map p534; ⏱7am-7pm; 🚌7, 8, disembark at Social Welfare Bureau) Just east of the ruins, Monte Fort was built by the Jesuits between 1617 and 1626 as part of the College of the Mother of God. Barracks and storehouses were designed to allow the fort to survive a two-year siege, but the cannons were fired only once, during the aborted attempt by the Dutch to invade Macau in 1622. Now the ones on the south side are trained at the gaudy Grand Lisboa Casino like an accusing finger.

Macau Museum
MUSEUM

(澳門博物館; Museu de Macau; Map p534; ☑2835 7911; www.macaumuseum.gov.mo; 112 Praceta do Museu de Macau; admission MOP$15, 15th of month free; ⏱10am-5.30pm Tue-Sun; 🚌7, 8, disembark at Social Welfare Bureau) This interesting museum inside Monte Fort will give you a taste of Macau's history. The 1st floor introduces the territory's early history and includes an elaborate section on Macau's religions. Highlights of the 2nd floor include a recreated firecracker factory and a recorded reading in the local dialect by Macanese poet José dos Santos Ferreira (1919–93). The top floor focuses on new architecture and urban-development plans.

★ Mandarin's House
HISTORIC BUILDING

(鄭家大屋; Caso do Mandarim; Map p530; ☑2896 8820; www.wh.mo/mandarinhouse; 10 Travessa de Antonio da Silva; ⏱10am-5.30pm Thu-Tue; 🚌28B, 18) FREE Built around 1869, the Mandarin's House, with over 60 rooms, was the ancestral home of Zheng Guanying, an influential author-merchant whose readers had included emperors, Dr Sun Yatsen and Chairman Mao. The compound features a moon gate, tranquil courtyards, exquisite rooms and a main hall with French windows, all arranged in that labyrinthine style typical of certain Chinese period buildings.

★ St Lazarus Church District
AREA

(瘋堂斜巷; Calcada da Igreja de Sao Lazaro; Map p534; www.cipa.org.mo; 🚌7, 8) A lovely neighbourhood with colonial-style houses and cobbled streets. Designers and independents like to gather here, setting up shop and organising artsy events, such as the weekly Sun Never Left – Public Art Performance (p546). **Tai Fung Tong Art House** (大瘋堂藝舍; Map p534; ☑2835 3537; 7 Calcada de Sao Lazaro; ⏱2-6pm Tue-Sun; 🚌7, 8), **G32** (Map p534; ☑2834 6626; 32 Rua de Sao Miguel; ⏱free guided tours 2.30-5pm Sat & Sun; 🚌7, 8) and the Old Ladies' House are also here.

Old Ladies' House
HISTORIC BUILDING

(仁慈堂婆仔屋; Albergue da Santa Casa da Misericórdia; Albergue SCM; Map p530; ☑2852 2550; www.albcreativelab.com; 8 Calcada da Igreja de Sao Lazaro; ⏱noon-7pm Wed-Mon; 🚌7, 8) The Old Ladies' House was a shelter for Portuguese refugees from Shànghǎi in WWII, and later a home for elderly women. It's now run by an art organisation, Albergue SCM, which organises cultural events here. The two yellow colonial-style buildings sit in a poetic courtyard with magnificent old camphor trees. Fashion boutique Lines Lab (p547) and Portuguese grocery shop Mercearia Portuguesa (p547) are here.

Church of St Dominic
CHURCH

(玫瑰堂; Igreja de São Domingos; Map p534; Largo de São Domingos; ⏱10am-6pm; 🚌3, 6, 26A) Northeast of Largo do Senado, this baroque church with a beautiful altar and a timber roof was founded by three Spanish Dominican priests from Acapulco, Mexico, in the 16th century, though the current structure dates to the 17th century. It was here, in 1822, that the first Portuguese newspaper was published on Chinese soil. The former bell tower now houses the **Treasury of Sacred Art** (聖物寶庫; Tresouro de Arte Sacra; Map p534; ⏱10am-6pm) FREE, an Aladdin's cave of ecclesiastical art and liturgical objects exhibited on three floors.

Lou Kau Mansion
HISTORIC BUILDING

(盧家大屋; Casa de Lou Kau; Map p534; ☑8399 6699; 7 Travessa da Sé; ⏱10am-5.30pm Tue-Sun; 🚌3, 4, 6A, 8A, 19, 33) FREE Built around 1889, this Cantonese-style mansion with southern European elements belonged to merchant Lou Wa Sio (aka Lou Kau), who also commissioned the Lou Lim Ioc Garden (p538).

MACAU PRIMER

Macau's political and economic systems, like Hong Kong's, are still significantly different from those of mainland China. The term 'Macanese' refers specifically to people of mainly Portuguese descent who were born in Macau, or their traditions.

MACAU SIGHTS

Central Macau

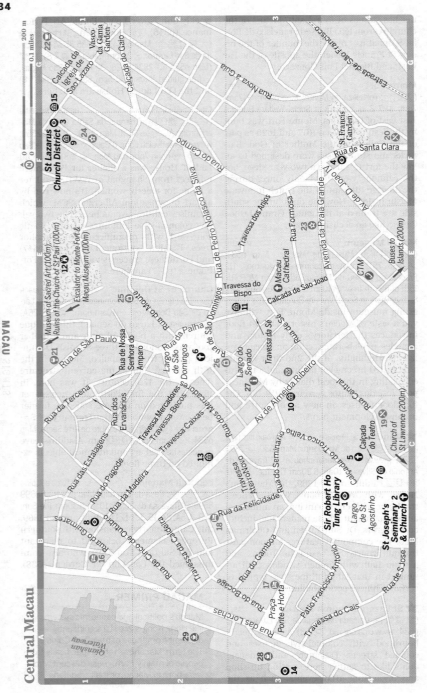

MACAU

Qianshan Waterway

200 m
0.1 miles

St Lazarus Church District

Calçada da Igreja de São Lazaro

22

15

3

9

24

Vasco da Gama Garden

Calçada do Gato

Rua Nova à Guia

Estrada de São Francisco

St Francis Garden

20

Rua de Santa Clara

4

Av de D. João

Avenida da Praia Grande

Rua Formosa

23

Rua de Pedro Nolasco da Silva

Travessa dos Anjos

Rua do Campo

Museum of Sacred Art (100m);
Ruins of the Church of St Paul (100m)

Escalator to Monte Fort &
Macau Museum (100m)

12

21

Rua de São Paulo

Rua da Tercena

Rua dos Ervanários

Rua de Nossa Senhora do Amparo

Rua da Palha

Rua do Monte

25

Rua de São Domingos

Travessa do Bispo

11

Macau Cathedral

Calçada de São João

Av de Almeida Ribeiro

CTM

Buses to Islands (200m)

Largo de São Domingos

6

26

Rua de São Domingos

Travessa da Sé

Rua da Sé

Largo do Senado

27

10

Rua Central

Rua da Madeira

Travessa Mercadores

Travessa Becos

Travessa Caixas

Rua dos Mercadores

Calçada do Tronco Velho

Calçada do Teatro

19

Church of St Lawrence (200m)

Rua da Estalagens

Rua do Pagode

Travessa Aterro Novo

Rua do Seminário

13

5

7

Sir Robert Ho Tung Library

1

Largo de St Agostinho

2

St Joseph's Seminary & Church

Rua da Felicidade

18

Rua de Chico de Outubro

8

16

Travessa da Caldeira

Rua do Gamboa

Rua Francisco Antonio

Patio Francisco Antonio

Rua de S. José

Rua do Borage

17

Praça Ponte e Horta

Rua das Lorchas

Travessa do Cais

29

28

14

Central Macau

Behind the grey facade, an intriguing maze of open and semi-enclosed spaces blurs the line between inside and outside. The flower-and-bird motif on the roof can also be found in the Mandarin's House and A-Ma Temple. Free guided **tours** in Chinese on weekends (from 10am to 7pm).

★ St Joseph's Seminary & Church   CHURCH
(聖若瑟修院及聖堂; Capela do Seminario Sao Jose; Map p534; Rua do Seminario; ⊙church 10am-5pm; 🚍9, 16, 18, 28B) St Joseph's, which falls outside the tourist circuit, is one of Macau's most beautiful models of tropicalised baroque architecture. Consecrated in 1758 as part of the Jesuit seminary (not open to the public), it features a white and yellow facade, a scalloped entrance canopy (European) and the oldest dome, albeit a shallow one, ever built in China. The most interesting feature, however, is the roof that features Chinese materials and building styles.

Leal Senado   HISTORIC BUILDING
(民政總署大樓; Map p534; 📞2857 2233; 163 Avenida de Almeida Ribeiro; ⊙9am-9pm Tue-Sun; 🚍3, 6, 26A, 18A, 33, disembark at Almeida Ribeiro) Facing Largo do Senado is Macau's most important historical building, the 18th-century

'Loyal Senate', which houses the Instituto para os Assuntos Cívicos e Municipais (IACM; Civic and Municipal Affairs Bureau). It is so-named because the body sitting here refused to recognise Spain's sovereignty during the 60 years that it occupied Portugal. In 1654, a dozen years after Portuguese sovereignty was re-established, King João IV ordered a heraldic inscription to be placed inside the entrance hall, which can still be seen today.

Inside the entrance hall is the **IACM Temporary Exhibition Gallery** (民政總署臨時展覽廳; Map p534; 📞8988 4100; 163 Avenida de Almeida Ribeiro; ⊙9am-9pm Tue-Sun; 🚍3, 6, 26A, 18A, 33, disembark at Almeida Ribeiro) **FREE**. On the 1st floor is the **Senate Library** (民政總署圖書館; Map p534; 📞2857 2233; ⊙1-7pm Tue-Sat; 🚍3, 6, 26A, 18A, 33, disembark at Almeida Ribeiro) **FREE**, which has a collection of some 18,500 books, and wonderful carved wooden furnishings and panelled walls.

Na Tcha Temple   TEMPLE
(哪吒廟; Map p530; 6 Calçada de Sao Paulo; ⊙8am-5pm; 🚍3, 4, 6A, 8A, 18A, 19) There's no better symbol of Macau's cultural diversity than Na Tcha Temple, sitting quietly beside a major Christian monument – the Ruins of the Church of St Paul. Built around 1888, it's

dedicated to the child god of war to halt the plague occurring at that time. The wall outside, often said to be a section of Macau's old city walls, in fact belonged to the former St Paul's College located at the ruins.

Ox Warehouse
ARTS CENTRE

(牛房倉庫; Armazem de Boi; Map p530; ☑2853 0026; http://oxwarehouse.blogspot.com; cnr Avenida do Coronel Mesquita & Avenida do Almirante Lacerda; ⊙noon-7pm Wed-Mon; ☐4, 5, 25, 26A, 33) This atmospheric former slaughterhouse is run by a nonprofit that hosts contemporary exhibitions, workshops and performances by local and visiting artists. Much of the work is engagingly experiential. Even if nothing's on, the architecture of the old buildings here makes it worthwhile to come for a peek.

★ AFA (Art for All Society)
GALLERY

(全藝社, Map p530; ☑2836 6064; www.afamacau.com; 3rd fl, Edificio da Fabrica de Baterias N E National, 52 Estrada da Areia Preta; ⊙noon-7pm Mon-Sat; ☐8, 8A, 18A, 7) Macau's best contemporary art can be seen at this nonprofit gallery, which has taken Macau's art worldwide and holds monthly solo exhibitions by Macau's top artists. AFA is near the Mong Há Multi-Sport Pavilion (望廈體育館; Map p530). Disembark from the bus at Rua da Barca or Rua de Francisco Xavier Pereira. Alternatively, it's a 20-minute walk from Largo do Senado.

Pawnshop Museum
HISTORIC BUILDING

(典當業展示館; Espaço Patrimonial – Uma Casa de Penhores Tradicional; Map p534; ☑2892 1811; 396 Avenida de Almeida Ribeiro; admission MOP$5; ⊙10.30am-7pm, closed 1st Mon of month; ☐2, 3, 7, 26A) This museum housed inside the former Tak Seng On ('virtue and success') pawnshop offers an atmospheric glimpse into Macau's

---

EXCHANGE RATES

Australia	A$1	MOP$6.47
Canada	C$1	MOP$6.75
China	¥1	MOP$1.28
Euro zone	€1	MOP$9.44
Hong Kong	HK$1	MOP$1.03
Japan	¥1	MOP$0.07
New Zealand	NZ$1	MOP$6.22
UK	UK£1	MOP$12.04
USA	US$1	MOP$7.99

For current exchange rates see www.xe.com.

pawnshop business, which dates to the Qing dynasty. Built in 1917, it comprises an office, a lobby and an eight-storey, fortress-like tower. On display is equipment from the original establishment, safes where goods were stored and financial records.

◉ Southern Macau Peninsula

The southern Macau Peninsula features a number of old colonial houses and baroque churches that are best visited on foot.

Church of St Augustine
CHURCH

(聖奧斯定教堂; Igreja de Santo Agostinho; Map p534; No 2, Largo de St Agostinho; ⊙10am-6pm; ☐3, 4, 6, 26A) The foundations of this church date from 1586 when it was established by Spanish Augustinians, but the present structure was built in 1814. The high altar has a statue of Christ bearing the cross, which is carried through the streets during the Procession of the Passion of Our Lord on the first Saturday of Lent, followed by thousands of devotees.

Dom Pedro V Theatre
HISTORIC BUILDING

(崗頂劇院; Teatro Dom Pedro V; Map p534; ☑2893 9646; Calçada do Teatro, Largo de St Agostinho; ⊙10am-6pm Wed-Mon; ☐3, 4, 6A, 8A, 19) Opposite the Church of St Augustine, Dom Pedro V, a colonnaded, neoclassical theatre in green and white, is the oldest (1858) Western-style theatre in China, and remains an important cultural venue for the Macanese community.

Church of St Lawrence
CHURCH

(聖老楞佐教堂; Igreja de São Lourenço; Map p530; Rua de São Lourenço; ⊙10am-5pm Tue-Sun, 1-2pm Mon; ☐9, 16, 18, 28B) One of Macau's three oldest churches, St Lawrence was originally constructed of wood in the 1560s, then rebuilt in stone in the early 19th century. The neoclassical church has a magnificent painted ceiling and one of its towers once served as an ecclesiastical prison. Enter from Rua da Imprensa Nacional.

★ Macau Museum of Art
MUSEUM

(澳門藝術博物館; Museu de Arte de Macau; Map p530; ☑8791 9814; www.mam.gov.mo; Macau Cultural Centre, Avenida Xian Xing Hai; adult/child MOP$5/2, Sun free; ⊙10am-6.30pm Tue-Sun; ☐1A, 8, 12, 23) This excellent five-storey museum has well-curated displays of art created in Macau and China, including paintings by Western artists like George Chinnery, who lived in the enclave. Other highlights are ceramics and stoneware excavated in Macau, Ming- and Qing-dynasty calligraphy from Guǎngdōng, ceramic statues from Shíwān (Guǎngdōng) and seal carvings. The museum also features 19th-century Western historical paintings from all over Asia, and contemporary Macanese art.

Avenida da República   AREA
(Map p530; ☐6, 9, 16) Avenida da República, along the northwest shore of Sai Van Lake, is Macau's oldest Portuguese quarter. There are several grand colonial villas not open to the public here. The former Bela Vista Hotel, one of the most-storied hotels in Asia, is now the **Residence of the Portuguese Consul-General** (葡國駐澳門領事官邸; Consulado-Geral de Portugal em Macau; Map p530; Rua do Boa Vista). Nearby is the ornate **Santa Sancha Palace**, once the home of Macau's Portuguese governors, and now used to accommodate state guests. Not too far away are beautiful, abandoned art deco–inspired buildings.

A-Ma Temple   TAOIST TEMPLE
(媽閣廟; Templo de A-Ma; Map p530; Rua de São Tiago da Barra; ☺7am-6pm; ☐1, 2, 5, 6B, 7) A-Ma Temple was probably already standing when the Portuguese arrived, although the present structure may date from the 16th century. It was here that fisherfolk once came to replenish supplies and pray for fair weather. A-Ma, aka Tin Hau, is the goddess of the sea, from which the name Macau is derived. It's believed that when the Portuguese asked the name of the place, they were told 'A-Ma Gau' (A-Ma Bay). In modern Cantonese, 'Macau' (Ou Mun) means 'gateway of the bay'.

Penha Hill   AREA
(西望洋山; Colina da Penha; Map p530; ☐6, 9, 16) Towering above the colonial villas along Avenida da República is Penha Hill, the most tranquil and least-visited area of the peninsula. From here you'll get excellent views of the central area of Macau. Atop the hill is **Bishop's Palace** (主教府; Map p530), built in 1837 and a residence for bishops (not open to the public), and the **Chapel of Our Lady of Penha** (主教山小堂; Ermida de Nossa Senhora da Penha; Map p530; ☺9am-5.30pm; ☐6B, 9, 16, 28B), once a place of pilgrimage for sailors.

Moorish Barracks   HISTORIC BUILDING
(Map p530; Calcada da Barra, Barra Hill; ☐18, 28) These former barracks (c 1874) were designed by an Italian in a neoclassical style inspired by Moorish architecture, to accommodate Muslim Indian policemen from Goa. The confusion of Muslims with Moors was due to the fact that dated Cantonese refers to Indians as 'moh loh cha' and 'moh loh' is a transliteration of 'Moorish'. You can't enter the building, now occupied by the Macau Maritime Administration. Turn right as you leave A-Ma Temple; a 10-minute uphill walk will take you here.

Maritime Museum   MUSEUM
(海事博物館; Museu Marítimo; Map p530; ☑2859 5481; www.museumaritimo.gov.mo; 1 Largo do Pagode da Barra; adult MOP$3-10, child free; ☺10am-5.30pm Wed-Mon; ☐1, 2, 5, 6B, 7, 10) The highlights here are the interactive displays detailing the maritime histories of Portugal and China, the artefacts from Macau's seafaring past, and the mock-ups of boats (including the long, narrow dragon boats used during the Dragon Boat Festival) and a Hakka fishing village.

◉ Northern Macau Peninsula

The northern peninsula is quite a good area to just wander around in. The historic **Three Lamps** (三盞燈; saam jaan dang) district is known for its Southeast Asian – particularly Burmese – influences. It begins at **Rotunda de Caros da Maia** (Map p530) and sprawls over several square blocks.

★ Guia Fort & Guia Chapel   FORT, CHURCH
(東望洋炮台及聖母雪地殿聖堂; Fortaleza da Guia e Capela de Guia; Map p530; ☺chapel 9am-5.30pm; ☐2, 2A, 6A, 12, 17, 18, Flora Garden stop) As the highest point on the peninsula, Guia Fort affords panoramic views of the city and, when the air is clear, across to the islands

PRICE INDICATORS
The following price indicators are quoted in patacas (MOP$). Note that prices for eating are per meal.

Sleeping
$ less than MOP$700
$$ MOP$700 to MOP$2000
$$$ more than MOP$2000

Eating
$ less than MOP$200
$$ MOP$200 to MOP$400
$$$ more than MOP$400

and China. At the top is the stunning Chapel of Our Lady of Guia, built in 1622 and retaining almost 100% of its original features, including some of Asia's most valuable frescoes. Next to it stands the oldest modern **lighthouse** (旅遊局東望洋燈塔分局; Map p530; ☑ 2856 9808; ⏱ 9am-1pm & 2.15-5.30pm) on the China coast – an attractive 15m-tall structure that is closed to the public.

You could walk up, but it's easier to take the Guia cable car that runs from the entrance of **Flora Gardens** (Jardim da Flora; Map p530; Travessa do Túnel; ⏱ 7.30am-8.30pm), Macau's largest public park.

Lou Lim Ieoc Garden GARDENS
(盧廉若公園; Jardim Lou Lim Ieoc; Map p530; 10 Estrada de Adolfo de Loureiro; ⏱ 6am-9pm; ⬜ 2, 2A, 5, 9, 9A, 12, 16) Locals come to this lovely Suzhou-style garden to practise taichi, play Chinese music or simply to relax among its lotus ponds and bamboo groves. The Victorian-style **Lou Lim Ieoc Garden Pavilion** (盧廉若公園; Pavilhão do Jardim de Lou Lim Ieoc; Map p530; ☑ 8988 4100; 10 Estrada de Adolfo Loureiro; ⏱ 9am-7pm Tue-Sun; ⬜ 2, 2A, 5, 9, 9A, 12, 16) was where the Lou family received guests, including Dr Sun Yatsen, and is now used for exhibitions. Adjacent to the garden is the **Macao Tea Culture House** (澳門茶文化館; Caultura do Chá em Macau; Map p530; ☑ 2882 7103; Lou Lim Ieoc Garden, Avenida do Conselheiro Ferreira de Almeida; admission free; ⏱ 9am-7pm Tue-Sun; ⬜ 2, 2A, 5, 9, 9A, 12, 16), displaying Chinese tea-drinking culture with exhibits of teapots and paintings related to the coveted drink.

Luís de Camões Garden & Grotto GARDENS
(白鴿巢公園; Jardim e Gruta de Luís de Camões; Map p530; Praça de Luís de Camões; ⏱ 6am-10pm; ⬜ 8A, 17, 26) This relaxing garden with dappled meandering paths is dedicated to the one-eyed poet Luís de Camões (1524–80), who is said to have written part of his epic *Os Lusíadas* in Macau, though there is little evidence that he ever reached the city. You'll see a bronze bust (c 1886) of the man here. The wooded garden attracts a fair number of chess players, bird owners and Chinese shuttlecock kickers. The Sr Wong Ieng Kuan Library is also here.

Kun Iam Temple BUDDHIST TEMPLE
(觀音廟; Templo de Kun Iam; Map p530; 2 Avenida do Coronel Mesquita; ⏱ 7am-5.30pm; ⬜ 1A,

MACAU'S INNER BEAUTIES

Lovely Libraries
Macau's libraries show how tiny proportions can be beautiful.

Sir Robert Ho Tung Library (何東圖書館; Map p534; 3 Largo de St Agostinho; ⏱ 10am-7pm Mon-Sat, 11am-7pm Sun; ⬜ 9, 16, 18) A stunner comprising a 19th-century villa and a glass-and-steel extension rising above a back garden, with Piranesi-like bridges shooting out between the two.

Chinese Reading Room (八角亭圖書館; Map p534; Rua de Santa Clara; ⏱ 9am-noon & 7pm-midnight; ⬜ 2A, 6A, 7A, 8) A former drinks booth, known as 'Octagonal Pavilion' (c 1926) in Chinese.

Sr Wong Ieng Kuan Library (白鴿巢公園黃營均圖書館, Map p530; Praça de Luís de Camões; ☑ 2895 3075; ⏱ 8am-8pm Tue-Sun) An oasis of calm between a boulder (which juts into its interior) and a banyan tree (which frames its entrance) in the Luís de Camões Garden.

Coloane Library (路環圖書館; Map p542; Rua de Cinco de Outubro, Coloane; ⏱ 1-7pm Mon-Sat; ⬜ 21A, 25, 26A) A mini Grecian temple c 1917 with a pediment and too-fat columns.

Modernist Marvels

Pier 8 (8號碼頭; Map p534; Rua do Dr Lourenco Pereira Marquez; ⬜ 5, 7) A fine example of Chinese modernism in grey, 50 paces south from Macau Masters Hotel; best views are from the **South Sampan Pier** (南艄板碼頭; Map p534) next door.

East Asia Hotel (東亞酒店; Map p534; cnr Rua do Guimares & Rua da Madeira; ⬜ 5, 7) Has Chinese art deco in mint green; it's a little shabby and very chic.

Red Market (紅街市大樓, Mercado Almirante Lacerda; Map p530; cnr Avenida do Almirante Lacerda & Avenida Horta e Costa; ⏱ 7.30am-7.30pm; ⬜ 23, 32) Another art deco edifice that houses a wet market.

10, 18A, stop Travessa de Venceslau de Morais) Macau's oldest temple was founded in the 13th century, but the present structures date back to 1627. Its roofs are embellished with porcelain figurines and its halls are lavishly decorated. Inside the main one stands the likeness of Kun Iam, the Goddess of Mercy; to the left of the altar is a statue of a bearded arhat rumoured to represent Marco Polo. The first Sino-American treaty was signed at a round stone table in the temple's terraced gardens in 1844.

Lin Fung Temple
BUDDHIST TEMPLE

(蓮峰廟; Lin Fung Miu; Map p530; Avenida do Almirante Lacerda; ⊙7am-5pm; ☐1A, 8, 8A, 10, 28B) Dedicated to Kun Iam, the Goddess of Mercy, this Temple of the Lotus was built in 1592, but underwent several reconstructions from the 17th century. It used to host mandarins from Guǎngdōng province when they visited Macau. The most famous of these imperial visitors was Commissioner Lin Zexu, who was charged with stamping out the opium trade.

Tap Seac Gallery
GALLERY

(塔石藝文館; Galeria Tap Seac; Map p530; www. macauart.net/ts; 95 Avenida Conselheiro Ferreira de Almeida; ⊙10am-7pm Tue-Sun; ☐) One of a handful of 1920s houses surrounding Tap Seac Sq, this building features a European-style facade and Moorish arched doors. The gallery inside hosts excellent contemporary art exhibitions. The original patio in the middle of the house has been kept, which creates a light-filled, relaxing setting.

Macau Tower
LANDMARK

(澳門旅遊塔; Torre de Macau; Map p530; ☑2893 3339; www.macautower.com.mo; Largo da Torre de Macau; adult/child observation deck MOP$135/70; ⊙10am-9pm Mon-Fri, 9am-9pm Sat & Sun; ☐9A, 18, 23, 26, 32) At 338m, Macau Tower looms above the narrow isthmus of land southeast of Avenida da República. You can stay put on the **observation decks** on the 58th and 61st floors, or challenge yourself to a bungee jump or some other form of extreme sport.

Tap Seac Square
SQUARE

(塔石廣場; Praca do Tap Seac; Map p530; ☐7, 8) This beautiful square surrounded by important historic buildings from the 1920s (Cultural Affairs Bureau, Tap Seac Health Centre, Central Library, Library for Macau's Historical Archives, Tap Seac Gallery) was

---

MACAU IN ONE DAY

Start in the **Largo do Senado** and wander up to the Ruins of the Church of St Paul (p529). Spend an hour or so in the Macau Museum (p533) to give it all some context. Have lunch at Clube Militar de Macau (p545), before getting a feel for Macau's living history as you wander back through the tiny streets towards the Inner Harbour port and A-Ma Temple (p537). Jump on a bus to sleepy **Coloane Village**. Take an easy stroll around here and bus it back to Taipa for some sight-seeing and dinner at the lovely Antonio (p545). Then head for the gaudy magnificence of the Grand Lisboa casino (p546), before sautering over to Macau Soul (p545) for wine and jazz.

---

designed by Macanese architect Carlos Marreiros. Marreiros also created the Tap Seac Health Centre, a contemporary interpretation of Macau's neoclassical buildings.

Sun Yat Sen Memorial House
MUSEUM

(國父紀念館; Casa Memorativa de Doutor Sun Yat Sen; Map p530; ☑2857 4064; 1 Rua de Silva Mendes; ⊙10am-5pm Wed-Mon; ☐2, 2A, 5, 9, 9A, 12) **FREE** This mock-Moorish house (c 1910) commemorates Dr Sun Yatsen's (1866–1925) brief stay in Macau where he gathered support to overthrow the Qing dynasty. You'll see documents and personal belongings of the 'Father of the Chinese Republic'. Interestingly, Sun himself never lived in the house, though it was built by his son, and his first wife Lu Muzhen lived here until she died in 1952.

Casa Garden
HISTORIC BUILDING

(東方基金會會址; Map p530; 13 Praça de Luís de Camões; ⊙garden 9.30am-6pm daily, gallery open only during exhibitions 9.30am-6pm Mon-Fri; ☐8A, 17, 26) Sitting quietly east of the Luís de Camões Garden is this beautiful colonial villa built in 1770. It was the headquarters of the British East India Company when it was based in Macau in the early 19th century. Today it's the headquarters of the Oriental Foundation, and includes a gallery, **Museu do Oriente** (東方基金會博物館; Map p530; 13 Praça de Luís de Camões; ⊙during exhibitions 9.30am-6pm Mon-Fri; ☐8A, 17, 26), that mounts interesting art exhibitions.

Old Protestant Cemetery
CEMETERY

(基督教墳場, Antigo Cemitério Protestante; Map p530; 15 Praça de Luís de Camões; ⊙8.30am-5.30pm; ☐8A,17,26) As church law forbade the burial of non-Catholics on hallowed ground, this cemetery was established in 1821 as the last resting place of (mostly Anglophone) Protestants. Among those interred here are Irish-born artist George Chinnery (1774–1852), and Robert Morrison (1782–1834), the first Protestant missionary to China and author of the first Chinese-English dictionary.

⊙ The Islands

Connected to the Macau mainland by three bridges and joined together by an ever-growing area of reclaimed land called Cotai, the islands of Coloane and, to a lesser extent, Taipa are oases of calm and greenery. By contrast, the Cotai Strip is development central, with megacasinos sprouting up.

⊙ Taipa

Traditionally an island of duck farms and boat yards, Taipa (冰仔) is rapidly becoming urbanised. But a parade of baroque churches, temples, overgrown esplanades and lethargic settlements means it's still possible to experience the traditional charms of the island.

Taipa Village
VILLAGE

(Map p541; ☐22, 26, 33) The historical part of Taipa is best preserved in this village in the south of the island. With a tidy sprawl of traditional Chinese shops and some excellent restaurants, the village is punctuated by colonial villas, churches and temples. Avenida da Praia, a tree-lined esplanade with wrought-iron benches, is perfect for a leisurely stroll.

Taipa Houses-Museum
MUSEUM

(龍環葡韻住宅式博物館, Casa Museum da Taipa; Map p541; ☑2882 7103; Avenida da Praia, Carmo Zone; adult/student/child & senior MOP$5/2/free, Sun free; ⊙10am-5.30pm Tue-Sun; ☐11, 15, 22, 28A, 30, 33, 34) The pastel-coloured villas (c 1921) here were the summer residences of wealthy Macanese. House of the Regions of Portugal showcases Portuguese costumes. House of the Islands looks at the history of Taipa and Coloane, with displays on traditional industries, such as fishing and the manufacture of fireworks. Macanese House offers a snapshot of life in the early 20th century.

Church of Our Lady of Carmel
CHURCH

(Igreja de Nossa Senhora de Carmo; Map p541; Rue da Restauração; ☐22, 28A, 26) Built in 1885, this pretty church stands on a hill overlooking the harbour, scenic Taipa village and the pastel-coloured Taipa Houses-Museum.

Pak Tai Temple
TAOIST TEMPLE

(Map p541; Rua do Regedor; ☐22, 28A, 26) Pak Tai Temple sits quietly in a breezy square framed by old trees. It is dedicated to a martial deity – the Taoist God (Tai) of the North (Pak) – who defeated the Demon King who was terrorising the universe. A pair of Chinese lions guards the entrance to the temple. On the third day of the third lunar month each year, Cantonese opera performances take place here.

⊙ Coloane

A haven for pirates until the start of the 20th century, Coloane (路環), is the only part of Macau that doesn't seem to be changing at a head-spinning rate. All buses stop at the roundabout in Coloane Village.

Chapel of St Francis Xavier
CHURCH

(聖方濟各教堂, Capela de São Francisco Xavier; Map p542; Rua do Caetano, Largo Eduardo Marques; ⊙10am-8pm; ☐15, 21A, 25, 26A) This chapel built in 1928 contains paintings of the infant Christ with a Chinese Madonna, and other reminders of Christianity and colonialism in Asia. It's a quirky place painted in yellow and embellished with red lanterns. In front of the chapel are a monument and fountain surrounded by four cannonballs that commemorate the successful (and final) routing of pirates in 1910.

Tam Kong Temple
TAOIST TEMPLE

(譚公廟, Map p542; Avenida de Cinco de Outubro, Largo Tam Kong Miu; ⊙8.30am-5.30pm; ☐15, 21A, 25, 26A) This temple is dedicated to Tam Kung, a Taoist god of seafarers. Inside the main altar is a long whale bone carved into a model of a dragon boat. To the left of the main altar is a path leading to the roof, which has views of the village and waterfront.

A-Ma Statue & Temple
MEMORIAL

(媽祖像及媽閣廟, Estátua da Deusa A-Ma; Estrada do Alto de Coloane; ⊙temple 8am-7.30pm) Atop Alto de Coloane (176m), this 20m-high white jade statue of the goddess who gave Macau its name was erected in 1998. It's the best part of a touristy 'cultural village' that

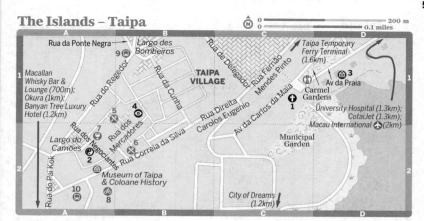

also features **Tian Hou Temple**. A free bus runs from the A-Ma ornamental entrance gate (媽祖文化村石牌坊) on Estrada de Seac Pai Van (bus 21A, 25, 50) half-hourly from 8am to 6pm. You can also reach both by following the Coloane Trail (Trilho de Coloane) from Seac Pai Van Park.

🏃 Activities

While Macau is no adventure paradise, it offers a taste of everything from spectator sport to extreme sport. For more ways to get those endorphins flowing, visit www.iacm. gov.mo (click 'facilities').

AJ Hackett   ADVENTURE SPORTS
(Map p530; ✆8988 8656; http://macau.aj hackett.com) New Zealand–based AJ Hackett organises all kinds of adventure climbs up and around the Macau Tower.

Cycling
Cycling is a great way to see Taipa and Coloane. Taipa has two cycling trails. Taipa Grande Trail (bus 21A, 26, 28A) can be accessed via a paved road off Estrada Colonel Nicolau de Mesquita, near the United Chinese Cemetery. Taipa Pequena Trail (bus 21A, 33, 35) is reachable by way of Estrada Lou Lim Ieok, behind the Regency Hotel.

A store (有記士多) on 11 Rua dos Negotiantes, near Pak Tai Temple and two shops up from Old Taipa Tavern, has bikes for rent at MOP$20 per hour; it's open from 9am to 7pm. Dang Rang (東榮單車行), on Rua do Meio in Coloane, does the same. Cycling across the Macau–Taipa bridges is prohibited.

👉 Tours

Quality Tours, coach trips organised by the Macau Government Tourist Office (MGTO) and tendered to such agents as **Gray Line** (Map p530; ✆2833 6611; Room 1015, Ground fl, Macau Ferry Terminal; adult/child 3-11yr MOP$118/108), take about 10 hours.

🎊 Festivals & Events

The blend of Cantonese and Portuguese culture and religious occasions creates an unusual and intriguing succession of holidays and festivals in Macau; Chinese festivals usually fall on dates in the lunar calendar.

**The Script Road & Macau
Literary Festival**   LITERATURE
(✆6207 2294; www.thescriptroad.org) Ten brilliant days of literary events in March.

The Islands – Coloane

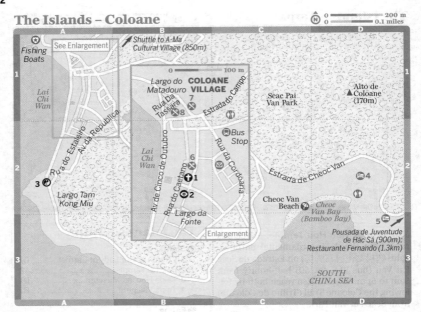

Macau Arts Festival   ART
(www.icm.gov.mo/fam) Music, dance and theatre troupes; takes place in May.

**Procession of Our Lady
of Fatima**   RELIGIOUS
Takes place in May.

Feast of the Drunken Dragon   CULTURAL
Features a dragon dance performed by drunken men; held in May or June.

Macau Formula 3 Grand Prix   SPORTS
(📞2855 5555; www.macau.grandprix.gov.mo) Macau's biggest sporting event of the year is held in the third week of November.

🛏 Sleeping

Most of Macau's hotels are aimed at moneyed visitors rather than budget travellers.

For those with the cash, there are world-class options. Rates shoot up on Friday or Saturday, while during the week you can find some incredible deals at travel agencies, hotel websites and specialist sites such as www.macau.com, and booths at Hong Kong's **Shun Tak Centre** (200 Connaught Rd, Sheung Wan), from where the Macau ferries depart, and the arrivals hall of the Macau Ferry Terminal.

Rooms listed here have air-conditioning and a bathroom, unless otherwise stated. Most midrange and top-end hotels have shuttle buses from the ferry terminal.

🛏 Macau Peninsula

Cheap guesthouses occupy central Macau, on and around Rua das Lorchas and Avenida de Almeida Ribeiro, with options aplenty on Rua da Felicidade (Street of Happiness), whose shuttered terraces were once Macau's main red-light district (scenes from Indiana Jones and the Temple of Doom were shot here). The top-end casino-hotels generally occupy the southeast and centre of town.

Ole London Hotel INN $
(澳萊英京酒店; Map p534; ☑2893 7761; 4-6 Praça de Ponte e Horta; d MOP$420-500; ❈@⍢; ⛼2,7,10A) A stone's throw from the Inner Harbour, this place has smart, clean rooms. They are small, but given its location and rates you can't really complain. Bigger discounts apply if you book via www.macau.com.

San Va Hospedaria GUESTHOUSE $
(新華大旅店; Map p534; ☑reservations 8210 0193, 2857 3701; www.sanvahotel.com; 65-67 Rua da Felicidade; d $190-220, tw $320-360, tr $380; ⛼3, 6, 26A) Built in 1873, San Va, with its green partitions and retro tiles, is about the cheapest and most atmospheric lodging in town: Wong Kar-wai filmed parts of *2046* here. However it's also very basic, with shared bathrooms and no air-conditioning (just fans).

⭐**Pousada de Mong Há** INN $$
(澳門望廈迎賓館; Map p530; ☑2851 5222; www.ift.edu.mo; Colina de Mong Há; r MOP$700-1300, ste MOP$1300-1800; ⍟❈@⍢; ⛼5, 22, 25) Sitting atop Mong Há Hill near the ruins of a fort built in 1849 is this Portuguese-style inn run by students at the Institute for Tourism Studies. Rooms are well appointed, with some having computers, and the service is attentive. Rates include breakfast. Discounts of 25% to 40% midweek and off season.

⭐**5Footway Inn** INN $$
(五步廊旅舍; Map p534; www.5footwayinn.com; 8 Rua de Constantino Brito; d & tw MOP$700, tr MOP$900; ⍟❈⍢; ⛼1, 2, 10, 5, 7) Converted from a love motel, this Singapore-owned accommodation has 23 small clean rooms, vibrant paintings in communal areas and excellent English-speaking staff. Rates include a self-service breakfast. It's opposite the Sofitel Macau at Ponte 16, which means you can take the latter's free shuttle buses to and from the ferry terminal.

Hotel Sintra HOTEL $$
(澳門新麗華酒店; Map p530; ☑2871 0111; www.hotelsintra.com; Avenida de Do João IV; r MOP$1500-2000, ste from MOP$2500; ❈⍢; ⛼3, 11, 22) Spotless rooms and professional flair make this centrally located three-star hotel a great-value option. Our only complaints are the slow-moving lift and the massive LED

screen of the Grand Emperor Hotel nearby, which is visible from some rooms. Discounts of up to 50% midweek.

Mandarin Oriental HOTEL $$$
(文華東方; Map p530; ☑8805 8888; www.mandarinoriental.com/macau; Avenida Dr Sun Yat Sen, Novos Aterros do Porto Exterior; r MOP$2088-4000, ste MOP$4788-6588; ⍟❈@⍢⛾) A great high-end option, the Mandarin has everything associated with the brand – elegance, superlative service, comfortable rooms and excellent facilities. Though relatively small, it's a refreshing contrast to the glitzy casino hotels.

Pousada de São Tiago HISTORIC HOTEL $$$
(聖地牙哥古堡; Map p530; ☑2837 8111; www.saotiago.com.mo; Fortaleza de São Tiago da Barra, Avenida de São Tiago da Barra; ste MOP$3000-5400; ⍟❈@⍢⛾; ⛼6, 9, 28B) Built into the ruins of the 17th-century Barra Fort, the landmark São Tiago is the most romantic place to stay in Macau. No other hotel has such a rich history. All 12 rooms are elegantly furnished suites. Discounts of up to 35% off season. The restaurant La Paloma is here.

🛏 The Islands

Taipa is changing fast, with several high-end international hotel chains opening up along the Cotai Strip. Coloane offers some great budget options, including two HI-affiliated hostels.

Pousada de Juventude de Cheoc Van HOSTEL $
(Map p542; ☑2888 2024; www.dsej.gov.mo; Rua de António Francisco, Coloane; dm/tw/q from MOP$100/160/120; ❈⍢; ⛼21A, 25, 26A) This government-run, beachside hostel is excellent value, but conditions apply. You'll need to book three months in advance and own an International Youth Card, International Youth Hostel Card or similar. It's closed to tourists in July and August. More details on the website.

Pousada de Juventude de Hác Sá HOSTEL $
(☑2888 2701/2; www.dsej.gov.mo; Rua de Hác Sá Long Chao Kok, Coloane; dm Sun-Fri MOP$50-80, Sat additional MOP$20-40; ❈⍢; ⛼21A, 25, 26A) Similar deal as the Cheoc Van, but with more beds and recreation space. It's 400m uphill from the beach on Rua de Hác Sá Long Chao Kok. Showers and toilets are shared, though its website says otherwise.

LOCAL KNOWLEDGE

COLOANE'S STILT HOUSES

Macau was a fishing village before gambling was legalised in the mid-19th century. Now the only vestiges of that idyllic past are found in Coloane.

Along the coastline, on Rua dos Navegantes in Coloane's old fishing village, there are a few stilt houses and shipyards. These huts of colourful corrugated metal, extending like chunky chopsticks out into the harbour, were once landing spots for houseboats. A couple have been turned into dried seafood shops, such as Loja de Peixe Tong Kei (棠記魚舖) at Largo do Cais, the square just off the charming old pier of Coloane.

From the square, take the slope to the right of the Servicos de Alfangega building. After two minutes, you'll see the cavernous cadaver of a shipyard on stilts.

Pousada de Coloane   HOTEL $$
(Map p542; ☑ 2882 2143; www.hotelpcoloane.com.mo; Estrada de Cheoc Van, Coloane; r from MOP$750; @ ☒; ☐ 21A, 25) This 30-room hotel with its Portuguese-style rooms (all with balconies and sea views) is great value, though some rooms are better maintained than others. And the location above Cheoc Van beach is about as chilled as you'll find. Rates drop considerably during midweek. Discounts of 20% to 40% off season.

Grand Hyatt Macau   HOTEL $$$
(☑ 8868 1234; http://macau.grand.hyatt.com; City of Dreams, Estrada do Istmo, Cotai; r MOP$1300-3200, ste from MOP$2300; ☺ ☒ @ ☎ ☒; ☐ 35, 50) The most tasteful of the casino hotels on the Cotai Strip, the Grand Hyatt is part of the City of Dreams complex. The massive rooms come with glass-and-marble showers, bath-tubs and a full battery of technology.

Banyan Tree Luxury Hotel   HOTEL $$$
(☑ 8883 8833; www.banyantree.com/en/macau; Galaxy, Avenida Marginal Flor de Lotus, Cotai; ste MOP$2880-63,800, villas MOP$23,600-35,100; ☐ 25, 25X) One of two hotels at the new Galaxy Macau, this extravagant resort re-creates tropical-style luxury in Macau. All 10 villas come with private gardens and swimming pools, while the suites have huge baths set by the window. If you need more pampering, there's a spa with state-of-the-art facilities. Slightly more affordable than Banyan Tree is the other hotel at the Galaxy, Okura (www.ho-

telokuramacau.com; Avenida Marginal Flor de Lotus, Cotai; r MOP$2200-5600, ste MOP$3000-20,000), which offers luxury with a Japanese twist.

✗ Eating

Browse a typically Macanese menu and you'll find an enticing stew of influences from Chinese and Asian cuisines, as well as from those of former Portuguese colonies in Africa, India and Latin America. Coconut, tamarind, chilli, jaggery (palm sugar) and shrimp paste can all feature. A famous Macanese speciality is *galinha africana* (African chicken), made with coconut, garlic and chillies. Other Macanese favourites include *casquinha* (stuffed crab), *minchi* (minced meat cooked with potatoes, onions and spices) and *serradura,* a milk pudding.

You'll find Portuguese dishes here too; popular ones include *salada de bacalhau* (dried salted cod salad), *arroz de pato* (rice with duck confit) and *leitão assado no forno* (roast suckling pig). While Macau's Chinese cuisine is excellent, most people come here to sample Macanese or Portuguese food.

★ **A Petisqueira**   PORTUGUESE $
(葡國美食天地; Map p541; ☑ 2882 5354; 15 Rua de São João, Taipa; meals MOP$150-500; ☺ 12.30-2.15pm & 6.45-10pm Tue-Sun; ☒; ☐ 22, 28A) 'The Snackery' is an amicable place with myriad Portuguese choices set in an obscure alley. It serves its own *queijo fresca da casa* (homemade cheese). Try the bacalao five ways, and baked seafood with rice.

Lung Wah Tea House   CANTONESE $
(龍華茶樓; Map p530; ☑ 2857 4456; http://lungwahteahouse.com; 3 Rua Norte do Mercado Aim-Lacerda; dim sum from MOP$14, tea MOP$10, meals MOP$50-180; ☺ 7am-2pm; ☒; ☐ 23, 32) There's grace in the retro furniture and the casual way it's thrown together in this airy Cantonese teahouse (c 1963). Take a booth by the windows overlooking the Red Market where the teahouse buys its produce every day. There's no English menu; just point and take. Lung Wah sells a fine array of Chinese teas.

Café Nga Tim   MACANESE $
(雅憩花園餐廳; Map p542; Rua do Caetano, Coloane; mains MOP$70-200; ☺ noon-1am; ☒; ☐ 21A, 25, 26A) We love the Chinese-Portuguese food, the small-town atmosphere, the view of the Chapel of St Francis Xavier, the prices and the owner – a guitar- and *èrhú*-strumming ex-policeman named Feeling Wong.

Lord Stow's Bakery
BAKERY $

(澳門安德魯餅店; Map p542; 1 Rua da Tassara; ☉7am-10pm Thu-Tue, to 7pm Wed) Though the celebrated English baker Andrew Stow passed away, his cafe (9 Largo do Matadouro) and Lord Stow's Bakery keep his memory well alive by serving his renowned *pastéis de nata*, a warm egg-custard tart (MOP$6) and cheesecake (MOP$14) in unusual flavours, including black sesame and green tea.

⭐ Clube Militar de Macau
PORTUGUESE $$

(陸軍俱樂部; Map p534; ☑2871 4000; www.clubemilitardemacau.net; 975 Avenida da Praia Grande; meals MOP$150-400; ☉1.45-2.30pm & 7-10.30pm Mon-Fri, noon-2.30pm & 7-10pm Sat & Sun; ☐6, 28C) Housed in a distinguished colonial building, with fans spinning lazily above, the Military Club takes you back in time to a slower and quieter Macau. The simple and delicious Portuguese fare is complemented by an excellent selection of wine and cheese from Portugal. The MOP$153 buffet is excellent value. Reservations are required for dinner and weekend lunches.

Alfonso III
PORTUGUESE $$

(亞豐素三世餐廳; Map p534; ☑2858 6272; 11a Rua Central; meals MOP$300; ☉11.30am-2.30pm & 6-9.30pm; 📶; ☐3, 6, 26A) A short stroll southwest of Leal Senado is this tiny, family-run restaurant that has won a well-deserved reputation among Macau's Portuguese community. Service is patchy, but no one seems to mind. Tables are often in short supply, so phone ahead.

Restaurante Fernando
PORTUGUESE $$

(法蘭度餐廳; ☑2888 2264; 9 Hác Sá beach, Coloane; meals MOP$150-270; ☉noon-9.30pm; 📶; ☐21A, 25, 26A) Possibly Coloane's most famous restaurant, Fernando's easy-breezy atmosphere makes it perfect for a protracted seafood lunch by the sea, as its devoted customers would agree. The bar stays open till midnight.

⭐ António
PORTUGUESE $$$

(安東尼奧; Map p541; ☑2899 9998; www.antoniomacau.com; 7 Rua dos Clerigos, Taipa; meals MOP$350-1200; ☉noon-10.30pm; ☐22, 26) The cosy mahogany-framed dining room, the meticulously thought-out menu and the entertaining chef, António Coelho, all make this the go-to place for traditional Portuguese food. If you can only try one Portuguese restaurant in Macau, make it this one.

⭐ Guincho a Galera
PORTUGUESE $$$

(葡国餐廳; Map p530; ☑8803 7676; 3rd fl, Hotel Lisboa, 2-4 Avenida de Lisboa; meals MOP$550-1800; ☉noon-2.30pm & 6.30-10.30pm; ☐3, 10) The international branch of Portugal's famous Fortaleza do Guincho, this luxuriously decorated restaurant brings Portuguese haute cuisine to Macau. The menu features well-executed classical dishes, with a couple of Macanese additions. Set meals are available at lunch (from MOP$300) and dinner (from MOP$600).

Espaco Lisboa
PORTUGUESE, MACANESE $$$

(里斯本地帶; Map p542; ☑2888 2226; 8 Rua das Gaivotas, Coloane; meals MOP$250-800; ☉noon-3pm & 6.30-10pm Thu & Sun-Tue, noon-10.30pm Fri & Sat; 📶; ☐21A, 25, 26A) The home-style dishes here are good, but what makes this two-storey restaurant in Coloane village unique is the combination of Portugal-inspired decor and a Chinese village house; in other words, the space *('espaco')*.

🍷 Drinking

Macau's unique and atmospheric drinking places are far removed from the glitz of the Outer Harbour.

⭐ Macallan Whisky Bar & Lounge
BAR

(☑8883 2221; www.galaxymacau.com; 203, 2nd fl, Galaxy Hotel, Cotai; ☉5pm-1am Mon-Thu, to 2am Fri & Sat; ☐25, 25X) Macau's best whisky bar is a traditional affair featuring oak panels, Jacobean rugs and a real fireplace. The 400-plus whisky labels include representatives from Ireland, France, Sweden and India, and a 1963 Glenmorangie.

⭐ Macau Soul
BAR

(澳感廊; Map p534; ☑2836 5182; www.macausoul.com; 31a Rua de São Paulo; ☉3-10pm Sun, Mon & Thu, to midnight Fri & Sat; ☐8A, 17, 26) An elegant haven in wood and stained glass, where twice a month a jazz band plays to a packed audience. On most nights though, Thelonious Monk fills the air as customers chat with the owners and dither over their 430 Portuguese wines. Opening hours vary; phone ahead.

Club Cubic
CLUB

(☑6638 4999; www.cubic-cod.com; 2105-02, Level 2, City of Dreams, Estrada do Istmo, Cotai; ☉11.30pm-6am Mon-Sat; ☐50, 35) The massive and flashy Club Cubic at the Hard Rock Hotel has themed rooms and a large disco ball. There are DJs mixing a variety of tunes,

BRIGHT LIGHTS, SIN CITY

Gargantuan monuments in all forms of postmodern kitsch have taken over Macau's seafront. There are close to 40 casinos in Macau, their total gaming revenue surpassing all of the world's major gambling jurisdictions combined.

Table games are the staple at casinos here – mostly baccarat, then roulette and a dice game called *dai sai* (big small). You'll hardly hear any whooping and clunking – slot machines make up only 5% of total casino winnings (versus Vegas' 60%). Drunks are also hard to come by, as Chinese players believe that booze dulls their skill. Over 80% of gamblers and 95% of high rollers come from mainland China. The latter play inside members-only rooms where the total amount wagered on any given day can exceed a country's GDP.

For recreational players, the only thing to watch out for is harassment by tip hustlers – scam artists who hang around tables acting like your new best friend. They may steal your chips, nag you for a cut or try to take you to a casino that'll tip them for bringing clients. Casinos are open 24 hours. To enter, you must be 18 years or older and properly dressed.

MACAU ENTERTAINMENT

including hip hop, techno and Korean pop, pumped out of the club's top-notch sound system.

★ **Single Origin** CAFE
(單品; Map p534; ☎6698 7475; www.single-origincoffee.com; 19 Rua de Abreu Nunes; coffees MOP$35; ☺11.30am-8pm Mon-Sat, 2-7pm Sun; ☏; ☐2, 4, 7, 7A, 8) This airy corner cafe, opened by coffee professional Keith Fong, makes a mean shot of espresso. You can choose your poison from a daily selection of 10 beans from various regions. If you can't decide, the well-trained barristas are more than happy to help.

Old Taipa Tavern PUB
(好客鄉村餐廳; Map p541; 21 Rua dos Negociantes, Taipa; ☏; ☐22, 28A, 26) A location near the Pak Tai Temple makes laid-back OTT a sublime spot to watch the comings and goings in the centre of Taipa village.

☆ Entertainment

Macau's nightlife may be dominated by the ever-expanding casino scene, but a number of interesting live-music venues have also sprung up about town. For entertainment/cultural events listings, check out the bimonthly *CCM+* and monthly *Destination Macau* available for free at MGTO outlets and larger hotels.

★ **Live Music Association** LIVE MUSIC
(LMA; 現場音樂協會; Map p530; www.lmamacau.com; 11b San Mei Industrial Bldg, 50 Avenida do Coronel Mesquita; ☐3, 9, 12, 25, 32) The go-to place for indie music in Macau, this excellent dive inside an industrial building has hosted local and overseas acts, including Cold Cave, Buddhistson, Mio Myo and Pet Conspiracy. See the website for what's on. Macau indie bands to watch out for include **WhyOceans** (www.whyoceans.com) and **Turtle Giant** (www.turtlegiant.com).

Sun Never Left – Public Art Performance LIVE MUSIC
(黃昏小叙-街頭藝術表演; Map p534; www.cipa.org.mo; Rua de Sao Roque; ☺3-6pm Sat & Sun; ☝; ☐7, 8) Every weekend, artists at St Lazarus Church District set up shop on the picturesque Rua de Sao Roque, selling art and handicrafts. Buy coffee from a nearby cafe and sip it as you browse and enjoy the live music.

Grand Lisboa Casino CASINO
(新葡京; Map p530; ☎2838 2828; Avenida de Lisboa, Macau Peninsula; ☐3, 10) The only Macau-born casino, the plush Grand Lisboa, with its flaming-torch-shaped tower and glowing bulb exterior, has become the landmark by which people navigate the peninsula's streets.

House of Dancing Water THEATRE
(水舞間; ☎8868 6688; http://thehouseofdancingwater.com; City of Dreams, Estrada do Istmo, Cotai; tickets MOP$580-980; ☐50, 35) 'The House of Dancing Water', Macau's most expensively made show, is a breathtaking melange of stunts, acrobatics and theatre designed by Franco Dragone, the former director of Cirque du Soleil. The magic revolves around a cobalt pool the size of several Olympic-sized swimming pools, over, around, into and under which a cast of 80 perform hair-raising stunts dressed in glorious costumes.

Rui Cunha Foundation CULTURAL CENTRE
(官樂怡基金會; Fundacao Rui Cunha; Map p534; ☎2892 3288; http://ruicunha.org; 749 Avenida da

Praia Grande; ⊙ gallery 10am-7pm; 🚍 2A, 6A, 7A, 8) From its airy venue in the heart of the peninsula, this foundation promotes the Macau identity through a thoughtfully curated series of art exhibitions, literary readings and recitals. These are held alongside thought-provoking seminars on Macau's legal and social systems.

🔒 Shopping

Browsing through the shops in the old city, specifically on crumbly Rua dos Ervanários and Rua de Nossa Senhora do Amparo near the Ruins of St Paul, can be a great experience. You can also look for antiques or replicas at shops on or near Rua de São Paulo, Rua das Estalagens and Rua de São António. Rua de Madeira and Rua dos Mercadores, which lead up to Rua da Tercena and its flea market, have stores selling mah jong tiles and bird cages.

Mercearia Portuguesa   FOOD
(Map p530; ☑ 2856 2708; www.merceariaportuguesa.com; 8 Calçada da Igreja de São Lazaro; ⊙ 1-9pm Mon-Fri, noon-9pm Sat & Sun; 🚍 7, 8) The charming Portuguese corner shop opened by a film director and actress has a small but well-curated selection of provisions, which includes honey, chinaware, wooden toys and jewellery from Portugal, gorgeously packaged and reasonably priced.

Futura Classica   BEAUTY
(Map p534; ☑ 2835 8378; www.futuraclassica.com; 1A, Calcada da Rocha; ⊙ noon-8pm; 🚍 3, 6, 18A, 26A, 33) This dizzyingly sweet-smelling shop is the Asian distributor of Claus Porto, a Portuguese brand of luxury soap and beauty products. It's a great place to shop for souvenirs. Prices range from MOP$50 to MOP$1000.

Pinto Livros   BOOKS
(邊度有書; Map p534; http://blog.roodo.com/pintolivros; 1a Veng Heng Bldg, 31 Largo do Senado; ⊙ 11.30am-11pm; 🚍 3, 6, 26A) This upstairs reading room overlooking Largo do Senado has a good selection of titles in art and culture, a few esoteric CDs and two resident cats.

Lines Lab   CLOTHING
(Map p530; www.lineslab.com; Shop A3, 8 Calçada da Igreja de São Lazaro; ⊙ 1-8pm Tue-Sun; 🚍 7, 8) Two Lisbon-trained designers opened this boutique in the Old Ladies' House art space and created edgy Macau-inspired clothes and bags for it.

Worker Playground   CLOTHING
(Map p530; ☑ 2875 7511; Ground fl, Edificio Cheung Seng, 83A Avenida do Conselheiro Ferreira de Almeida; ⊙ 3-10pm; 🚍) Worker Playground makes solid-quality baseball jackets, biker pants and fashionably androgynous garments for men and women. The brand pays tribute to the old Workers' Stadium, a nostalgic landmark that was razed to make way for the Grand Lisboa Casino.

ℹ Information

The Macau Government Tourist Office (MGTO) distributes the excellent (and free) *Macau Tourist Map*, with tourist sights and streets labelled in Portuguese and Chinese.

EMERGENCY

Visitors can utilise a dedicated **24-hour emergency hotline** (☑ 112) for tourists. **Police, fire and ambulance** can be reached by dialling ☑ 999.

INTERNET ACCESS

You can access free public wi-fi in select government premises, tourist hot spots and public areas daily from 8am to 1am the following day. See www.wifi.gov.mo for details.

Most cafes and hotels in Macau have free wi-fi.

You can also buy prepaid phonecards from CTM, ranging from MOP$50 to MOP$130, to enjoy mobile broadband; or buy a mobile broadband pass for unlimited internet access for one day (MOP$120) or five days (MOP$220).

MACAU'S SWORD MASTER

One of Macau's most accomplished artists and former director of the Macau Museum, Antonio Conceição Júnior (aka Antonio Cejunior) custom designs blades (www.arscives.com/bladesign) inspired by Macau, mythology and the modern world.

The charismatic Antonio has designed Eastern and Western swords, as well as hybrids such as one featuring a Western-style blade with a guard inspired by the Harley Davidson wheel. Antonio does not manufacture the swords himself, but he will recommend North American bladesmiths. Interested parties should email Antonio at antonio.cejunior@gmail.com. Expect about two weeks for the design and a designer's fee of US$3000.

MEDICAL SERVICES

Centro Hospitalar Conde Saõ Januário (山頂醫院, Map p530; ☑ 2831 3731; Estrada do Visconde de São Januário) Southwest of Guia Fort.

University Hospital (☑ 2882 1838; www.uh.org.mo; Block H, Macau University of Science & Technology, Avenida Wai Long, Taipa; ☺ 9am-9pm Mon-Sat, to 5pm Sun) Western and Chinese medical services available.

MONEY

ATMs are everywhere. Most allow you to choose between patacas and Hong Kong dollars.

You can change cash and travellers cheques at the banks (open 9am to 5pm, Monday to Friday, to 1pm Sat) lining Avenida da Praia Grande and Avenida de Almeida Ribeiro.

Hong Kong dollars are accepted everywhere in Macau, but your change will be returned in patacas, especially at smaller establishments.

POST

Correios de Macau, Macau's postal system, is efficient and inexpensive.

The **main post office** (郵政總局; Map p534; ☑ 2832 3666; 126 Avenida de Almeida Ribeiro; ☺ 9am-6pm Mon-Fri, to 1pm Sat) faces Largo do Senado. There are other post offices in Macau Peninsula, including a Macau ferry terminal branch (Map p530; ☑ 2872 8079; Macau Ferry Terminal; ☺ 10am-7pm Mon-Sat).

EMS Speedpost is available at the main post office. Other companies can also arrange express forwarding.

TELEPHONE

Local calls are free from private phones and most hotel telephones; calls from public payphones cost MOP$1 for five minutes. Dial ☑ 101 for International Directory Assistance or ☑ 181 for Local Directory Assistance.

Phonecards

Prepaid International Direct Dialling (IDD) and local phonecards can be used in most mobile phones. You can purchase them from CTM stores or the ferry terminal for MOP$50.

TOURIST INFORMATION

MGTO has themed leaflets on Macau's sights and bilingual maps at its outlets.

MGTO – Hong Kong Branch (澳門政府旅遊局旅客詢問處 - 香港分行; ☑ 2857 2287; 200 Connaught Rd Central, 336-337 Shun Tak Centre; ☺ 9am-1pm & 2-6pm) The Hong Kong branch of the Macau Government Tourist Office.

Tourist office (Map p534; ☑ 2831 5566, tourism hotline 2833 3000; www.macautourism.gov.mo; Edificio 'Hot Line', 12o andar, 335-341 Alameda Dr Carlos d'Assumpcao; ☺ 9am-1pm & 2.30-5.35pm Mon-Fri)

MGTO-Macau Ferry Terminal (旅遊局外港碼頭分局; Map p530; ☑ 8790 7039; ☺ 9am-10pm)

TRAVEL AGENCIES

China Travel Service (CTS; 中國旅行社; Zhōngguó Lǚxíngshè; Map p530; ☑ 2870 0888; www.cts.com.mo; Nam Kwong Bldg, 207 Avenida do Dr Rodrigo Rodrigues; ☺ 9am-6pm) China visas (MOP$285 plus photos) are available to most passport holders in one day.

USEFUL WEBSITES

Macau Cultural Affairs Bureau (www.icm.gov.mo) Macau's cultural offerings month-by-month.

ⓘ Getting There & Away

Macau is connected to limited destinations in Asia by air. If you are coming from outside Asia, your best option is to fly to Hong Kong International Airport (p1005) and take a ferry to Macau without going through Hong Kong customs.

AIR

Macau International Airport (☑ 2886 1111; www.macau-airport.com) is located on Taipa Island, 20 minutes from the city centre. There are requent services to destinations including Bangkok, Chiang Mai, Kaohsiung, Kuala Lumpur, Manila, Osaka, Seoul, Singapore, Taipei and Tokyo. There are also regular flights to Běijīng, Hángzhōu, Nánjīng, Níngbō, Shànghǎi and Xiàmén and less frequent flights to Chéngdū, Chóngqìng, Fúzhōu and Wǔhàn.

Sky Shuttle (☑ in Hong Kong 2108 9898; www.skyshuttlehk.com) runs a 15-minute helicopter shuttle between Macau and Hong Kong up to 27 times daily.

BOAT

Macau's **main ferry terminal** (外港客運碼頭; Terminal Maritimo de Passageiros do Porto Exterior; Map p530; Outer Harbour, Macau) is located on the eastern side of the peninsula, with services to mainland China and Hong Kong. **TurboJet** (Map p530; ☑ bookings 852-2921 6688, in Hong Kong 790 7039, information 852-2859 3333; www.turbojet.com.hk) has departures daily to Shékǒu, in Shēnzhèn (MOP$210, one hour, 10 between 9.45am and 8.45pm). It also has departures to Shēnzhèn airport (MOP$210, one hour, five from 11.30am to 7.30pm), and to Nánshà, near Guǎngzhōu (MOP$180, two between 10.45am and 4.15pm).

Macau is linked directly to Hong Kong International Airport by TurboJet, which has eight ferries operating between 10am and 10pm. It costs MOP$233/178/126 per adult/child/infant and takes 45 minutes. However, note that this ferry service is for transit passengers only. It is not available for passengers originating in Hong Kong.

CotaiJet (☑ 2885 0595; www.cotaijet.com.mo) Every half-hour from 7am to 1am; runs between Taipa Ferry Terminal and Hong Kong's Hong Kong–Macau Ferry Terminal. A feeder shuttle bus service drops off at destinations on the Cotai Strip. Check the website for services to Hong Kong International Airport.

Yuet Tung Shipping Co (粵通船務有限公司; Map p534; ☑ 2893 9944, 2877 4478; www. ytmacau.com; Point 11A Inner Harbour, Inner Harbour Ferry Terminal) Has ferries connecting Macau's Taipa temporary ferry terminal (MOP$155, 1½ hours, 11am, 2pm, 7pm) with Shékŏu. Ferries also leave from Macau maritime ferry terminal (MOP$12, every half-hour, 8am to 4.15pm) for Wanzai of Zhūhǎi.

BUS

There are two gateways to Guǎngdōng from Macau. One is the Border Gate at the border with Zhūhǎi (p579); the other is the Cotai Frontier Post at the end of the Lotus Bridge in Cotai. Travellers are required to have the same documents as when entering China from elsewhere.

Border Gate Bus (Portas de Cerco; ☺7am–midnight) Take bus 3, 5 or 9 and walk across.

Cotai Frontier Post (☺ 9am-8pm) On the causeway linking Taipa and Coloane; allows visitors to cross Lotus Bridge by shuttle bus (HK$3) to Zhūhǎi; buses 15, 21, 25 and 26 drop you off at the crossing.

Kee Kwan Motor Rd Co (歧關車路有限公司; ☑ 2893 3888; Underground bus terminal near Border Gate; ☺7.15am-9pm) Has buses going to Guǎngzhōu (MOP$80, four hours, every 15 minutes from 8am to 9.40pm) and to Zhōngshān (MOP$23, 90 minutes, every 20 minutes from 8am to 8pm).

Macau International Airport Bus Terminal (☑ 2888 1228) Buses to Guǎngzhōu and Dōng-guǎn (both MOP$155, four hours).

ⓘ Getting Around

TO/FROM THE AIRPORT

Take buses 21 and 26 from the airport to Coloane. Bus 21 goes from the airport to A-Ma Temple.

Airport Bus AP1 Airport to Macau Ferry Terminal and Border Gate; stops at major hotels en route. Runs every 15 minutes from 7am to midnight. Extra charge of MOP$3 for each large piece of luggage.

Airport Buses MT1 and MT2 Airport to Praça de Ferreira do Amaral near Casino Lisboa (p546). Runs from 7am to 10am, then 4pm to 8pm.

Taxi Airport to town centre (MOP$60, 20 minutes).

BICYCLE

Bikes can be rented (Map p541) in Taipa Village. You are not allowed to cross the Macau–Taipa bridges on a bicycle.

CAR

Avis Rent A Car (Map p530; ☑ 2872 6571; www.avis.com.mo; Room 1022, Ground fl, Macau Maritime Ferry Terminal; ☺10am–1pm & 2-4pm) Hires out cars for MOP$700 to MOP$1400 per day; with chauffeur from MOP$300 per hour, 20% more on weekends.

Burgeon Rent A Car (Map p530; ☑ 2828 3399; www.burgeonrentacar.com; Shops O, P & Q, Block 2, La Baie Du Noble, Avenida Do Nordeste) Hires out Kia cars from MOP$190/270/390 for 6/11/24 hours; with chauffeur from MOP$160 per hour, minimum two hours.

PUBLIC TRANSPORT

Routes Macau has about 50 public bus and minibus routes running from 6am to midnight. Fares range from MOP$3.20 to MOP$6.40.

Destinations Displayed in Portuguese and Chinese.

Information For info on routes and fares, see **Macau Transmac Bus Co** (☑ 2827 1122; www. transmac.com.mo), **Macau TCM Bus** (www. tcm.com.mo) and **Reolian** (☑ 2877 7888; www. reolian.com.mo). The *Macau Tourist Map*, available at MGTO outlets, has a list of bus routes.

Useful services Buses 3 and 3A (between ferry terminal and city centre); buses 3 and 5 (to the Border Gate); and bus 12 (from ferry terminal, past Hotel Lisboa to Lou Lim Ioc Garden and Kun Iam Temple). Buses 21, 21A, 25 and 26A go to Taipa and Coloane.

TAXI

Language Not many taxi drivers speak English, so it can help to have your destination written in Chinese.

Cost Flag fall is MOP$15 (first 1.6km); then it's MOP$1.50 for each additional 230m.

Surcharge MOP$5/2 surcharge to Coloane from Macau Peninsula/Taipa; MOP$5 surcharge for journeys from the airport; large bags cost an extra MOP$3.

Handy numbers Call ☑ 2851 9519 or ☑ 2893 9939 for yellow radio taxis.

Guǎngdōng

POP 93 MILLION

Best for History

➜ New Guǎngdōng Museum (p552)

➜ Mausoleum of the Nányuè King (p556)

➜ Zǔmiào (p566)

➜ Whampoa Military Academy (p553)

Best Views

➜ Zìlì (p567)

➜ Yúyìn Mountain Villa (p566)

➜ Nánlíng National Forest Park (p550)

➜ Dīnghú Shān Reserve (p572)

➜ Lover's Road (p579)

Why Go?

Guǎngdōng's unique culture and natural beauty fly under the radar and have yet to be discovered by many travellers, so you may have a plethora of sublime sights (not to mention great dim sum) all to yourself.

Northern Guǎngdōng (广东) is home to some wild and wondrous landscapes. In the blue pine forests of Nánlíng, the music of waterfalls and windswept trees boomerangs in your direction. If it's Unesco-crowned heritage you're after, Kāipíng's flamboyant watchtowers and the stylised poses of Cantonese opera will leave you riveted. What's all the fuss about Hakka and Chiuchow cultures? Well, find out in Méizhōu and Cháozhōu.

Historically Guǎngdōng was the starting point of the Maritime Silk Road and the birthplace of revolution. On the scenic byways of the Pearl River delta, you'll uncover the glory of China's revolutionary past. While on the surf-beaten beaches of Hǎilíng Island, an ancient shipwreck and its treasures await.

When to Go
Guǎngzhōu

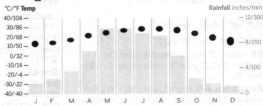

| Apr–Jun Verdant paddy fields against the built wonders of Kāipíng and Méizhōu. | Jul–Sep Blue pines and stained-glass windows offer respite from summer. | Oct–Dec The typhoons and heat are gone; this is the best time to visit. |

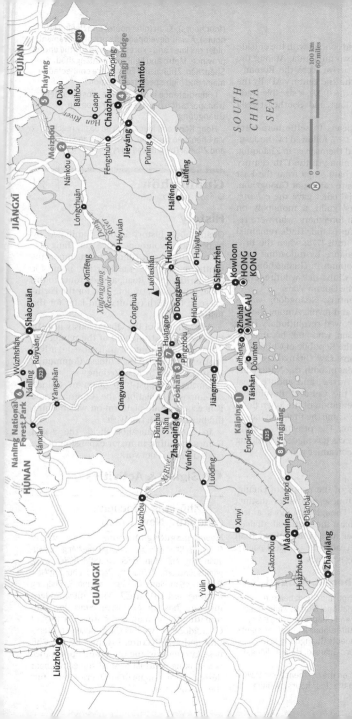

Guǎngdōng Highlights

1 Climb dramatic Unesco-crowned watchtowers at **Kāipíng** (p567)

2 Be awed by the crouching dragons of the Hakka architecture at **Méizhōu** (p584)

3 Visit **Fóshān** (p566), the hometown of two martial arts legends

4 Cross the majestic **Guǎngjì Bridge** (p582) with its 18 boats and 24 piers

5 Be mesmerised by the labyrinthine streets and storied mansions of old towns such as **Cháyáng** (p585)

6 After a day's hike, fall asleep to the whispered symphony of an ancient forest in **Nánlíng National Forest Park** (p574)

7 Lunch in a garden-restaurant in **Guǎngzhōu** (p552) while listening to an operatic aria

8 Visit silken beaches and an 800-year-old shipwreck in **Yángjiāng** (p569)

History

Guǎngdōng has had contact with the outside world for nearly two millennia. Among the first outsiders to arrive were the Romans, who appeared in the 2nd century AD. By the Tang dynasty (AD 618–907), a sizeable trade with the Middle East and Southeast Asia had developed.

The first Europeans to settle here were the Portuguese in 1557, followed by the Jesuits who established themselves in Zhàoqìng. The British came along in the 17th century and by 1685 merchant ships from the East India Company were calling at Guǎngzhōu. In 1757 an imperial edict gave the *cohong*, a local merchants' guild, a monopoly on China's trade with foreigners, who were restricted to Shāmiàn Island. Trade remained in China's favour until 1773, when the British shifted the balance by unloading 1000 chests of Bengal opium in Guǎngzhōu. Addiction spread in China like wildfire, eventually leading to the Opium Wars.

In the 19th century, Guǎngdōng was a hotbed of reform and revolt. Among the political elites who sowed revolutionary ideas here was Sun Yatsen, who later became the first president of the Republic of China.

The 20th century saw Guǎngdōng serve as the headquarters of both the Nationalist and Communist Parties, and endure great suffering during the Cultural Revolution. After the implementation of the 'open door' policy in 1978, it became the first province to embrace capitalism. The province's continued economic success has made it a leading export centre for consumer goods.

Language

The vast majority of the people of Guǎngdōng speak Cantonese, a dialect distinct from Mandarin. Though it enjoys a less exalted status than the national dialect, Cantonese is older and better suited than Mandarin for the reading of classical poetry, according to many scholars.

❶ Getting There & Around

Airports at Guǎngzhōu and Shēnzhèn run domestic and international flights, while those at Zhūhǎi, Méizhōu and Cháozhōu bring every major city within a three-hour flight of the sights. High-speed rail connects Guǎngdōng to its provincial neighbours Guǎngxī, Húnán, Jiāngxī and Fújiàn.

The fastest trains on the northeast–southwest axis head for Nánchāng (four hours), Wǔhàn (four hours), Xī'ān (nine hours) and Běijīng (10 hours). A well-developed network of convenient, older rail lines and expressways spans the entire province. Metro and light rail in Guǎngzhōu, Shēnzhèn, Zhūhǎi and Fóshān are connected to major and high-speed train stations.

Long-distance buses are the most frequent transportation between major areas in Guǎngdōng.

Hong Kong and Macau can be easily reached via Shēnzhèn (by train, metro, bus and ferry) and Zhūhǎi (by bus and ferry).

Guǎngzhōu 广州

🎵 020 / POP 12 MILLION

History

Guǎngzhōu's history is one dominated by trade and revolution. Since the Tang dynasty, it had been China's most important southern port and the starting point for the Maritime Silk Road, a trade route to the West. It became a trading post for the Portuguese in the 16th century, and later for the British.

After the fall of the Qing dynasty in 1911, the city was a stronghold of the republican forces led by Sun Yatsen and, subsequently, a centre of activity of the Chinese Communist Party (CCP) led by Mao Zedong.

During the post-1949 years of China's self-imposed isolation, the Canton Trade Fair was the only platform on which China did business with the West.

In 2010 Guǎngzhōu held the Asian Games, resulting in major expansion of the city's transport network.

◉ Sights & Activities

⊙ Zhūjiāng Xīnchéng (Zhūjiāng New Town)

New Guǎngdōng Museum   MUSEUM
(广东省博物馆新馆; Guǎngdōngshěng Bówùguǎn Xīnguǎn; Map p558; ☑ 3804 6886; www.gdmuseum.com; 2 Zhujiang Donglu, Zhūjiāng New Town; ⊙ 9am-4pm Tue-Sun; Ⓜ Line 3, Zhūjiāng Xīnchéng, exit B1) **FREE** This ultramodern museum has an extensive collection illuminating the human and natural history of Guǎngdōng, as well as Cantonese art, literature and architecture. Inspired by the Chinese lacquer box, the museum's appearance is a striking contrast against the curvilinear design of the Guǎngzhōu Opera House further to the west.

Guăngzhōu Opera House BUILDING
(广州大剧院; Guăngzhōu dà jù yuàn; Map p558; ☑ tour bookings 3839 9847, 3839 2666; www. chgoh.org; 1 Zhujiang Xilu; admission ¥30, tours in English per person ¥200; ⊙ 9am-4.30pm, closed Mon, tours 10am, 11am, 2pm, 3pm & 4pm; M Line 3, Zhūjiāng Xīnchéng, exit B1) Authored by architect Zaha Hadid, southern China's biggest performance venue has transformed the area with its other-worldly appearance. With futuristic glass panels knitted together to form subtle curves, it's been described as pebbles on the bed of the Pearl River. To enter, you have to join one of five 45-minute daily tours. Tours in English require booking a day in advance. The visit will allow you to see the ethereal opera hall with its 4200 LED lights and floor planks from Russia, as well as the state-of-the-art rehearsal studios.

◎ Hăizhū District

Memorial Museum of Generalissimo Sun Yatsen's Mansion HISTORIC SITE
(孙中山大元帅府; Sūn Zhōngshān Dàyuánshuài Fŭ; Map p554; ☑ 8901 2366; www.dyshf.com; 18 Dongsha Jie, Fangzhi Lu; ⊙ 9am-4.30pm Tue-Sun; M Line 2, Shì Èrgōng) FREE Sun Yatsen lived in this restored mansion when he established governments in Guăngzhōu in 1917 and 1923. The beautiful complex comprises two Victorian-style buildings housing displays on the history of Guăngzhōu in the revolutionary era, as well as Sun's living quarters. A cab from Shāmiàn Island costs about ¥40, and from Shì Èrgōng station, about ¥20.

Memorial Hall of the Lĭngnán School of Painting MUSEUM
(岭南画派纪念馆; Lĭngnán Huàpài Jìniànguăn; ☑ 8401 7167; www.lingnans.org; 257 Changgang Donglu; ⊙ 9am-5pm Tue-Sun; M Xiăo Găng, exit A) FREE This small but excellent museum on the leafy campus of the Guăngzhōu Academy of Fine Arts (广州美术学院; Guăngzhōu Mĕishù Xuéyuàn) pays tribute to the founders of the Lĭngnán school of painting, such as Gao Jianfu, and shows the colourful ink and brush works of contemporary artists versed in the Lĭngnán style.

◎ Lìwān District

★ **Chén Clan Ancestral Hall** HISTORIC SITE
(陈家祠; Chénjiā Cí; Map p554; ☑ 8181 4559; 34 Enlong Li, Zhongshan Qilu; admission ¥10; ⊙ 8.30am-5.00pm; M Line 1, Chénjiācí, exit D) An all-in-one ancestral shrine, Confucian school

and 'chamber of commerce' for the Chen clan, this compound was built in 1894 by the residents of 72 villages in Guăngdōng, where the Chen lineage is predominant. There are 19 buildings in the traditional Lĭngnán style, all featuring exquisite carvings, statues and paintings, and decorated with ornate scrollwork throughout.

◎ Islands

★ **Shāmiàn Island** HISTORIC SITE
(沙面岛; Shāmiàn Dăo; Map p554; M Line 1, Huángshā) To the southwest of Guăngzhōu is the dappled oasis of Shāmiàn Island. It was acquired as a foreign concession in 1859 after the two Opium Wars. Shamian Dajie, the main boulevard, is a gentle stretch of gardens dotted by old houses, cafes and galleries. The **Church of Our Lady of Lourdes** (天主教露德圣母堂; Tiānzhŭjiào Lùdé Shèngmŭ Táng; Map p554; 14 Shamian Dajie; ⊙ 8am-6pm; M Line 1, Huángshā), built by the French in 1892, is on the eastern end.

Whampoa Military Academy MUSEUM
(黄埔军校; Huángpŭ Jūnxiào; ☑ 8820 1082; ⊙ 9am-5pm Tue-Sun; M Line 2, Chìgăng, exit C1) FREE This academy on Chángzhōu Island (长洲岛; Chángzhōu Dăo) was founded in 1924 by the Kuomintang to train military elites for both the Kuomintang and the Communist Party. Many of the graduates went on to fight in important conflicts and civil wars. The present structure has a museum dedicated to the revolutionary history of modern China. After leaving the metro, board bus 262 on Xingang Zhonglu to Xīnzhōu Pier (新洲码头; Xīnzhōu Mătou). Ferries (¥2) to the academy depart every hour from 7.40am to 7.40pm.

Guǎngzhōu

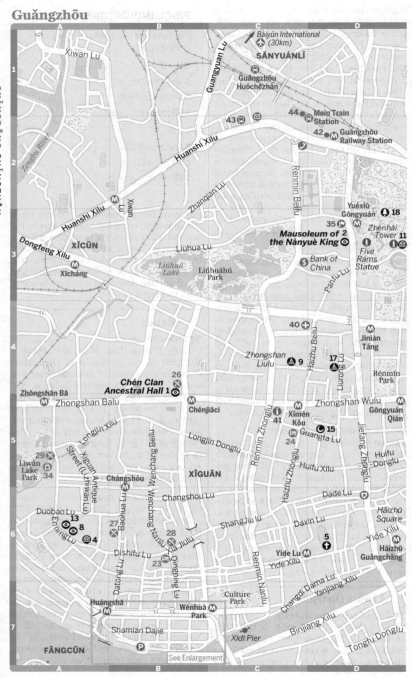

Báiyún International (30km)

SĀNYUÁNLǏ

Guangyuan Lu

Xiwan Lu

Guǎngzhōu Huǒchēzhàn

43

44 Main Train Station

42 Guǎngzhōu Railway Station

Zengbu River

Huanshi Xilu

Renmin Beilu

Huanshi Xilu

Xiwan

Zhanqian Lu

Yuèxiù Gōngyuán

35

Zhènhǎi Tower 11

18

Mausoleum of the Nányuè King

2

Dongfeng Xilu

XĪCŪN

Liuhua Lu

Bank of China

Five Rams Statue

Xīcháng

Liúhuā Lake

Liúhuāhú Park

Panfu Lu

40

Jìniàn Táng

Zhongshan Liulu

9

17

Rénmín Park

Haizhu Beilu

Chén Clan Ancestral Hall

26

1

Liurong Lu

Zhōngshān Bā

Zhongshan Balu

Chénjiācí

Zhongshan Wulu

Gōngyuán Qián

41

Xīmén Kǒu

Renmin Zhonglu

Jiefang Zhonglu

Longjin Xilu

Longjin Donglu

24

15 Guangta Lu

Huifu Donglu

Haizhu Zhonglu

Huifu Xilu

Lìwān Lake Park

29

34

Xiguan Antique Street (Lìzhīwan Lu)

XĪGUĀN

Changshou Lu

Dade Lu

Chángshòu

W Wenchang Beilu

Baohua Lu

Shangjiu lu

Daxin Lu

Hǎizhū Square

Duobao Lu

13

8

27

28

Enning Lu

4

Dishifu Lu

Datong Lu

Xia Jiulu

Qingping Lu

Renmin Nanlu

Yide Lu

5

Yide Xilu

Hǎizhū Guǎngchǎng

23

Yide Xilu

Huángshā

Culture Park

Wénhuà Park

Changdi Dama Lu

Yanjiang Xilu

FĀNGCŪN

Shamian Dajie

Xīdī Pier

Binjiang Xilu

Tongfu Donglu

See Enlargement

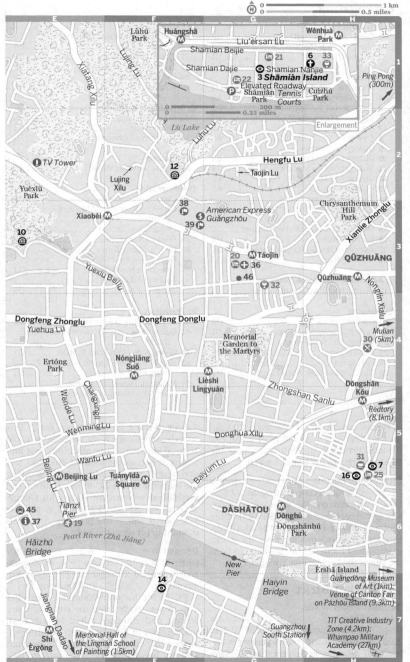

0   1 km
Ⓝ
0   0.5 miles

Lúhú
Park
Huángshā Ⓜ
Liu'èrsan Lù
Wénhuà
Park Ⓜ
Shamian Beijie
🖿 21   6 ✚   33
Xiatang Xilu
Shamian Dajie
Shamian Nanjie ◉
22   **3 Shāmiàn Island**
Elevated Roadway
Ping Pong
(300m)
Lujing Lu
Ⓟ   Shāmiàn   Tennis   Cuìzhú
Park   Courts   Park
0   500 m
0   0.25 miles
Enlargement

Lùhú Lake
Lùhú Lu

❶ TV Tower
Hengfu Lu
Lujing
Xilu
12 🏛
Taojin Lu

Yuèxiù
Park
Chrysanthemum
Hill
Park
Xíaoběi Ⓜ
38 🖿
American Express
Guǎngzhōu
39 🖿
Xianlie Zhonglu
10 🏛
QŪZHUĀNG
Yuexiu Beilu
20 ◉ Táojīn
🖿➕ 36
● 46
🖿 32
Qūzhuāng Ⓜ
Nonglin Xialu
Dongfeng Zhonglu
Dongfeng Donglu
Yuehua Lu
Mulian
30 (5km)
🗙
Memorial
Garden to
the Martyrs
Ertóng
Park
Nóngjiǎng
Suǒ
Dōngshān
Kǒu
Changxing Li
Lièshì
Língyuán
Zhongshan Sanlu
Redtory
(8.1km)
Wende Lu
Wenming Lu
Donghua Xilu
Wanfu Lu
31
16 ◉ 🖿 25
Beijing Lu
Beijing Lu Ⓜ
Tuányīdà Ⓜ
Square
Baiyun Lu
🖿 45
Tiānzǐ
Pier
❶ 37
❸ 19
DÀSHÀTOU Ⓜ
Dōnghú Ⓜ
Pearl River (Zhū Jiāng)
Dōngshānhú
Park
Hǎizhū
Bridge
Jiangnan Dadao
New Pier
 Èrshā Island →
Guǎngdōng Museum
of Art (1km);
Venue of Canton Fair
on Pázhōu Island (9.3km)
Haiyin
Bridge
14 ◉
Shí
Èrgōng Ⓜ
Memorial Hall of
the Lingnán School
of Painting (1.5km)
Guangzhou
South Station
TIT Creative Industry
Zone (4.2km);
Whampoa Military
Academy (27km)

Guǎngzhōu

Ferries leave from the pier every 20 minutes between the rush hours of 7.50am to 9.30am. Private boats will also make the 10-minute trip to the island for ¥40.

Guǎngdōng Museum of Art MUSEUM
(广东美术馆; Guǎngdōng Měishùguǎn; ☎8735 1468; www.gdmoa.org; 38 Yanyu Lu; admission ¥15; ◎9am-5pm Tue-Sun; 📵89, 194, 131A) At the southern end of Èrshā Island (Èrshā Dǎo), this worthy museum showcases the works of important Cantonese artists and has been the site of the Guǎngzhōu Triennale.

◎ Yuèxiù District

★ Mausoleum of the Nányuè King MAUSOLEUM
(南越王墓; Nányuèwáng Mù; Map p554; ☎3618 2920; www.gznywmuseum.org/nanyuewang/index. html; 867 Jiefang Beilu; admission ¥12; ◎9am-

4.45pm; Ⓜ Line 2, Yuèxiù Gōngyuán, exit E) This superb mausoleum from the 2000-year-old Nányuè kingdom is one of China's best museums. It houses the tomb of Zhao Mo, second king of Nányuè, who was sent south by the emperor in 214 BC to quell unrest and established a sovereign state with Guǎngzhōu as its capital. Don't miss Zhao Mo's jade burial suit – the precious stone was thought to preserve the body.

Dōngshān HISTORIC SITE
(东山区; Dōngshān Qū; Map p554; Ⓜ Dōngshān Kǒu) Tree-lined Xinhepu Lu (新河浦路), Xuguyuan Lu (恤孤院路) and Peizheng Lu (培正路) in the historic Dōngshān area offer a welcome respite from the city. There are schools and churches raised by American missionaries in the 1900s, and exquisite villas commissioned by overseas Chinese and military bigwigs of the Kuomintang. Take

the metro to Dōngshān Kǒu station. From exit A, walk south along Shuqian Lu and follow the signs.

The most beautifully restored building is the three-storey Kuí Garden (p560), built in 1922 by an overseas Chinese in America. **Spring Garden** (春园; Chūnyuán; Map p554; 24 Xinhepu Lu; ⊘9.30am-5pm) **FREE** was the former headquarters of the central committee of the Chinese Communist Party in 1923.

Yuèxiù Park
PARK

(越秀公园; Yuèxiù Gōngyuán; Map p554; ✆8666 1950; 988 Jiefang Beilu; ⊘6am-9pm; M Line 2, Yuèxiù Gōngyuán) A statue of the symbol of Guǎngzhōu – the five rams (五羊) that supposedly carried the five immortals who founded the city – stands guard at this park. On a hilltop is red-walled Zhènhǎi Tower (镇海楼; Zhènhǎi Lóu), built in 1380 as a watchtower to keep out pirates. The tower is home to the excellent **Guǎngzhōu City Museum** (广州市博物馆; Guǎngzhōushì Bówùguǎn; Map p554; ✆8355 0627; www.guangzhoumuseum.cn/en/main.asp; admission ¥10; ⊘9am-5pm; M Line 2, Yuèxiù Gōngyuán), which traces the city's history from the Neolithic period. To the east is **Guǎngzhōu Art Gallery** (广州美术馆; Guǎngzhōu Měishùguǎn; Map p554; Yuèxiù Park), which has embroidery, ivory carvings and other displays on the city's trading history with the West.

Guǎngzhōu Museum of Art
MUSEUM

(广州艺术博物院; Guǎngzhōu Yìshù Bówùyuàn; Map p554; ✆8365 9337; www.gzam.com.cn; 13 Luhu Lu; ⊘9am-5pm Tue-Fri, 9.30am-4.30pm Sat & Sun; 🚌10, 84, 109, 297, 808, M Line 5, Xiǎoběi) **FREE** This massive museum has an extensive collection of Chinese art that ranges from the ancient to the contemporary. The emphasis is on calligraphic works and paintings, especially those created in the Lǐngnán area. Rare Tibetan tapestries are displayed on the top floor.

Temple of the Six Banyan Trees
BUDDHIST TEMPLE

(六榕寺; Liùróng Sì; Map p554; ✆8339 2843; 87 Liurong Lu; admission ¥5, pagoda ¥10; ⊘8am-5pm; 🚌56) This Buddhist temple was built in AD 537 to enshrine Buddhist relics brought over from India; they were placed in the octagonal **Decorated Pagoda** (Huā Tǎ). The temple was given its current name by the exiled poet Su Dongbo in 1099, who waxed lyrical over the (now gone) banyans in the courtyard. You can see the characters 'six banyans' (liùróng) that he wrote above the gates.

Many prominent monks taught here, including Bodhidharma, the founder of Zen Buddhism. The temple opens at 6.30am on the first and 15th day of the lunar month.

Guǎngxiào Temple
BUDDHIST TEMPLE

(光孝寺; Guǎngxiào Sì; Map p554; ✆8108 7421; 109 Guangxiao Lu; admission ¥5; ⊘6am-5.30pm; M Line 1, Xīmén Kǒu) 'Bright Filial Piety Temple' is the oldest temple in Guǎngzhōu, dating back to the 4th century. By the time of the Tang dynasty it was well established as a centre of Buddhist learning in southern China. Bodhidharma, the founder of Zen Buddhism, taught here. Most of the current buildings date from the 19th century, including a main hall with double eaves and a 10m-tall Buddha statue.

Mosque Dedicated to the Prophet
MOSQUE

(怀圣寺; Huáishèng Sì; Map p554; ✆8333 3593; 56 Guangta Lu; ⊘daybreak to sundown; M Line 1, Xīmén Kǒu) The original building is believed to be founded here in 627 by Abu Waqas, an uncle of the prophet Mohammed. The present mosque dates from the Qing dynasty.

Cathedral of the Sacred Heart
CHURCH

(石室教堂; Shíshì Jiàotáng; Map p554; 368 Yide Lu; M Line 2, Hǎizhū Guǎngchǎng) The French were granted permission to build this impressive twin-spired Roman Catholic cathedral after the second Opium War, between 1863 and 1888. It features a neo-Gothic style and is constructed entirely of granite, with massive towers reaching a height of 48m.

Guǎngzhōu Star Cruises Company
CRUISE

(广州之星游轮有限公司; Guǎngzhōu Zhīxīng Yóulún Yǒuxiàn Gōngsī; Map p554; ✆8333 2222; cruises ¥48-88; ⊘6pm-11pm) The Guǎngzhōu Star Cruises Company has eight two-hour evening cruises on the Pearl River. Boats leave from the **Tiānzì Pier** (Tiānzì Mǎtou; Beijing Lu), just east of Hǎizhū Bridge (Hǎizhū Qiáo; catch metro line 2 from Hǎizhū Guǎngchǎng station), and head down the river as far as Èrshā Island (Èrshā Dǎo) before turning back.

⊙ Tiānhé District

Redtory
VILLAGE

(红砖厂; Hóngzhuān Chǎng; ✆8557 8470; www.redtory.com.cn/english/redtory.htm; 128 Yuancun Sihenglu; 员村四横路128号; ⊘6am-midnight; M Line 3, Yúncūn, exit B) The Bauhaus structures of Guǎngdōng Canned Food Factory (c 1958)

East Guǎngzhōu

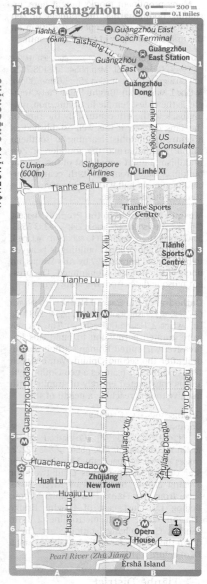

ately behind the one you're on. About 200m down the alley, turn left into a dirt road.

🎊 Festivals & Events

Canton Trade Fair   TRADE FAIR

(Zhōngguó Chūkǒu Shāngpǐn Jiāoyì Huì; ☑ 2608 8888; www.cantonfair.org.cn) The 15-day Canton Trade Fair is held twice yearly, usually in April and October, on Pázhōu Island south of the Pearl River in Guǎngzhōu.

🛏 Sleeping

Guǎngzhōu has few good choices in the budget and lower midrange, but plenty of excellent top-end and upper-midrange hotels. During the Canton Trade Fair (usually in April and October), prices go up. All hotels offer wi-fi and air-conditioning.

🛏 Hǎi Zhū, Yuèxiù & Tiānhé Districts

Lazy Gaga   HOSTEL $

(春田家家; Chūntián Jiājiā; Map p554; ☑ 8192 3232, 8192 3199; www.gagahostel.com; 215 Haizhu Zhonglu; 海珠中路215号; dm ¥55-65, d & tw ¥168-198, tr ¥225; M Xīménkǒu, exit B) Only five minutes' walk from the metro, Lazy Gaga has 45 cheerful rooms and homey communal areas enlivened by colourful walls and furniture. Guests can have free use of the spotless kitchen; and the pleasant staff members are up for a chat when they're not busy. In-room lockers come thoughtfully embedded with chargers for mobile devices.

Old Canton Youth Hostel   HOSTEL $

(广州古粤东山青年旅舍; Guǎng Zhōu Gǔyuè Dōngshān Qīngnián Lǚshè; Map p554; ☑ 8730 4485; 22 Xuguyuan Lu; 恤孤院路22号; dm ¥50, s with bathroom ¥120-150, d without bathroom ¥150; ✳ @ 🛜; M Dōngshānkǒu, exit F) Located close to Kuí Garden in the leafy Dōngshān area (东山) of Yuèxiù (越秀) District, this hostel is a good budget option. Rooms are clean and come with free wi-fi.

are now stuffed with the galleries, bookshoptores and cafes of Redtory art village. The art is only so-so, but the dated architecture and the old factory equipment on display make a visit worthwhile. Turn right from the metro exit and make your way to the alley immedi-

★ **Garden Hotel** HOTEL $$$

(花园酒店; Huāyuán Jiǔdiàn; Map p554; ☑ 8333 8989; www.thegardenhotel.com.cn; 368 Huanshi Donglu; 环市东路368号; r/ste from ¥3200/5200; ❋@🛜❄; Ⓜ Line 5, Táojīn) One of the most popular luxury hotels in Guǎngzhōu with waterfalls and lovely gardens in the lobby and on the 4th floor. The rooms are just as classy. Bookings essential.

Holiday Inn HOTEL $$$

(假日酒; Jiàrì Jiǔdiàn; Map p554; ☑ 8138 0088; www.holidayinn.com.cn; 188 Dishifu Lu; 第十甫路188号; r ¥1680-2790, ste ¥2980-6888; ➖❋@🛜❄; Ⓜ Chángshòu Lù) Don't be distracted by the chaotic street outside. Holiday Inn has everything you'd associate with the name: reliable service, and clean, comfortable rooms with a few luxuries. Huge discounts are available, too.

Mulian BOUTIQUE HOTEL $$$

(广州木莲庄酒店; Guǎngzhōu Mùliánzhuāng Jiǔdiàn; ☑ 8353 8888; www.themulian.com; 715 Jinsui Lu; 金穗路715号; r ¥868-1068, ste ¥1168; ❋🛜; Ⓜ Táncūn, exit D) If you don't mind windowless rooms (which is 90% of the rooms here), the Mulian is perfect for a getaway: the soundproofing is seamless; the decor is exotically Thai; there are a host of gadgets to keep you entertained indoors; and there's free afternoon tea when you get hungry.

The metro exit sits at the junction between Huacheng Dadao (花城大道) and Machanglu (马场路). Turn right into the latter. Walk for 10 minutes, turn left into Jinsui Lu (金穗路). You'll see the entrance to a residential community. The hotel is on the left about 100m from the entrance.

🛏 Shāmiàn Island

Shāmiàn Island is by far the quietest and most attractive area to stay in Guǎngzhōu.

Guǎngzhōu Youth Hostel HOSTEL $

(广东鹅潭宾馆; Guǎngdōng Étán Bīnguǎn; Map p554; ☑ 8121 8298; www1.gzyhostel.com; 2 Shamian Sijie; 沙面四街2号; dm/s/tr ¥60/240/390, d ¥260-320; @) For the cheapest beds on Shāmiàn Island, head to this nondescript hostel. Backpacker ambience is nonexistent, but rooms are moderately clean.

Guǎngdōng Victory Hotel HOTEL $$$

(胜利宾馆; Shènglì Bīnguǎn; Map p554; ☑ 8121 6688; www.vhotel.com; 53 & 54 Shamian Beijie; 沙面北街53、54号; r from ¥800, tr ¥1180, ste ¥1380-3880; ❋@🛜) There are two branches of the Victory Hotel on Shāmiàn Island: an older one at 54 Shamian Beijie (enter from 10 Shamian Sijie) and a newer wing (胜利宾馆 (新楼)) at 52 Shamian Nanjie. Both offer decent value for money.

🍴 Eating

Guǎngzhōu is home to some excellent Cantonese restaurants. Dim sum (点心; diǎnxīn), or yum cha (饮茶; yǐnchá; tea drinking), may be the best-known form of Cantonese cuisine to foreigners, but in fact noodles, congee and desserts are equally popular locally.

Chén Tiānjì CANTONESE $

(陈添记; Map p554; ☑ 8182 8774; 59 Baohua Lu; dishes ¥7-32; ⏱ 9.30am-10.30pm; Ⓜ Chángshòu Lù) This old hole-in-the-wall serves three things – crunchy blanched fish skin (鱼皮; yúpí) tossed with peanuts and parsley; sampan congee (艇仔粥; tǐngzǎi zhōu); and rice-flour rolls (肠粉; chángfěn). At 59 Baohua Lu, turn into an alley; it's the second eatery.

★ **Guǎngzhōu Restaurant** DIM SUM $

(广州酒家; Guǎngzhōu Jiǔjiā; Map p554; 2 Wenchang Nanlu; 文昌南路2号; dim dum per portion ¥7.5-23; ⏱ 7am-11pm; Ⓜ Chángshòu Lù) A large, traditional yum cha restaurant that offers an exquisite selection of teas (¥8 to ¥50 per person) to go with its well-made dim sum. Tables and dining spaces are dispersed around a beautiful interior garden in the atrium. Go early: by 8.30am all the tables with views are taken.

Chén Clan Ancestral Hall Food Stalls CANTONESE $

(陈家祠大排档; Chénjiācí Dàipáidàng; Map p554; Enlong Li, Zhongshan Qilu; per person ¥40-60; ⏱ from 7pm; Ⓜ Line 1, Chénjiācí, exit D) Locals munch on grilled oysters (烤生蠔; kǎoshēngháo), pepper salt shrimp (椒盐虾; jiāoyánxiā) and stir-fried crab (炒蟹; chǎoxiè) at the outdoor food stalls that come into being every evening in an alley next to Chén Clan Ancestral Hall (p553). It's clean by food-stall standards.

★ **Pànxī Restaurant** DIM SUM $$

(泮溪酒家; Pànxī Jiǔjiā; Map p554; ☑ 8172 1328; 151 Longjin Xilu; dishes from ¥40; ⏱ 7.30am-midnight; Ⓜ Chángshòu Lù) Set in a majestic garden and embracing another one within its walls, Pànxī is the most representative of Guǎngzhōu's garden-restaurants. Corridors and courtyards are brought together to give the effect of 'every step, a vista' (一步一景). Elderly diners are known to get up and sing

ĒNNING LÙ

If you like history, a stroll down century-old Ēnning Lù (恩宁路; Ēnning Rd ; Map p554; ⓂChángshòu Lù) can be rewarding. Located in the area known traditionally as Xīguān (西关), the western gate and commercial hub of old Canton, it retains a few cultural relics, despite earnest urban-renewal efforts.

Bāhé Academy (八和会馆; Bāhé Huìguǎn; Map p554; 117 Enning Lu) Bāhé Academy was a guild hall for Cantonese opera practitioners. The original institution opened in 1889 to provide lodging and other services to opera troupes. It's now a meeting place for retired artists. Bāhé is not open to the public, but you can see the original 3m-tall wooden door from 1889, the only item that survived a bombing by the Japanese in 1937. It was used during the Great Leap Forward as a parking plank for 4-tonne vehicles, and clearly survived that as well.

Luányú Táng (鸾舆堂; Map p554; ⊙10am-3pm) Luányú Táng is a 200-year-old union for actors playing martial and acrobatic roles in Cantonese opera. The union still gives theatrical martial-arts training to children, and members come for opera 'jamming' sessions. It's the second-last unit along a small lane off Yongqing Erxiang (永庆二巷), off Ēnning Lù.

Birthday of the Fire God (⊙28th day of the 9th lunar month) Every year on the birthday of the Fire God, usually around November, Bāhé Academy guild hall throws a banquet for the opera industry. From early morning, you'll hear gongs and drums, and ceremonies are performed at Luányú Táng. Hundreds show up for the daylong feasting that takes place both indoors and on the pavement. According to legend, the Fire God (华光师傅; Huáguāng Shīfu) was sent by the heavenly emperor to burn down an opera house that was making too much noise. But the god was so moved by the performance that he asked the audience to burn incense instead to fool the emperor. People involved in opera believe that the Fire God protects them from fire, poverty, tricky negotiations and other mishaps to which those from the grassroots, like themselves, are prone.

Ancestral Home of Bruce Lee (Map p554) The last unit along a small lane off Yongqing Erxiang (永庆二巷), which runs off Ēnning Lù, was the ancestral home of Bruce Lee, the kung-fu icon, whose father Li Haiquan (李海泉) was a Cantonese opera actor. There's now a wall in its place, but if you retrace your steps out of the two alleys, turn right and head up Ēnning Lù, you'll pass the gates of a school. In the right corner, just past the entrance, you can see the shuttered house.

an operatic aria or two when the mood is right. You'll need to queue for a table after 8.30am.

Wilber's EUROPEAN $$
(Map p554; ☑3761 1101; www.wilber.com.cn; 62 Zhusigang Ermalu; mains ¥30-180; ⊙11am-4pm & 5-9pm; ☎; ⓂDōngshān Kǒu) Hidden on the edge of Yuèxiù District, gay-friendly Wilber's gets top marks for drinks and atmosphere, and the food is not far behind. You can munch on cold cuts and mini burgers at the bar, or opt for seafood risotto and pan-fried scallops in the restaurant. Look for the restored colonial villa with whitewashed walls and a patio.

🍷 Drinking

Guǎngzhōu's party hub is Zhūjiāng Pátí (珠江琶醍), a strip of land by the river that is the site of the massive Zhūjiāng Brewery (though by the time you read this, the brew-

ery should have relocated). Abandoned facilities now throb with trendy bars and clubs. With the brewery still visibly in operation, it's the city's most surreal (and boozy) party place. Upmarket Yánjiāng Lù Bar St is also worth a visit.

★Kuí Garden CAFE
(逵园; Kuí Yuán; Map p554; ☑8765 9746; 9 Xuguyuan Lu; 恤孤院路9号; ⊙10am-midnight; ⓂLine 1, Dōngshānkǒu, exit F) From its location inside the gorgeous Kuí Garden in the historic Dōngshān area, this cafe serves decent coffee and canapes during the day and morphs into a bar at night. Stylish, warm-toned seating areas occupy the rooms of the original residence. Built in 1922, the house is famous for its Western architectural features that include colonnaded verandahs and a portico.

There's a small exhibition space on the ground floor and a light-flooded shop on the top floor that is breathtaking to look at but doesn't sell much. Both the gallery and the shop close at 10pm.

Sun's
LOUNGE

(☎8977 9056; www.sunsgz.com; B25-26 Yuejiang Xilu; ⏰7am-2am Sun-Thu, to 5am Fri & Sat; 🚌779, 765) The best of the lot in Zhūjiāng Pátí (珠江琶醍), Sun's lets you sip cocktails on couches by the river or dance to electronic music. It's the final stop on Bus 765.

Paddy Field
PUB

(Map p554; ☎8360 1379; 38 Hua Le Lu, 2nd fl, Central Plaza; ⏰11.30am-2.30pm & 4.30pm-2am Mon-Fri, 11.30am-2am Sat & Sun; Ⓜ Táojīn, exit A) An old name in the city's drinking scene, this Irish pub is frequented for its top-notch beer and jovial atmosphere.

Shāmiàn Clubhouse
BAR

(沙面会馆; Shāmiàn Huìguǎn; Map p554; Shamian Dajie; ⏰11am-11pm; ☏; Ⓜ Huángshā) The 'Red Mansion' (c 1907), once known as 'Shāmiàn's grandest mansion', fuses features of British colonial architecture such as colonnades and louvre windows with the Lǐngnán fondness for skylights. It has a small, clubby bar with long teak flooring.

☆ Entertainment

Your best resource for entertainment in Guǎngzhōu is www.gzstuff.com.

★191 Space
LIVE MUSIC

(191Space 音乐主题酒吧; 191 Space Yīnlè Zhǔtí Jiǔba; Map p558; ☎8737 9375; www.191space.com; 191 Guangzhou Dadao Zhonglu; 广州大道中路191号; ⏰8pm-2am; Ⓜ Line 5, Wǔyángcūn, exit A) Two steps from the metro exit, this is a throbbing dive that features live indie gigs from China and overseas every weekend.

Ping Pong
LIVE MUSIC

(乒乓空间; Pīngpāng Kōngjiān; ☎2829 6306; 60 Xianlie Donghenglu, Starhouse 60; ⏰6pm-2am) This bohemian place is where you'll find live music, theatrical performances and art exhibitions. It's hard to find, though. Tell the taxi driver to drop you at the rear entrance of Xīnghǎi Conservatory (星海音乐学院后门), Xīnghǎi Yīnyuè Xuéyuàn Hòumén) and make sure they haven't taken you to Xīnghǎi Concert Hall on Èrshā Island!

T Union
LIVE MUSIC

(凸空间; Tū Kōng Jiān; Map p558; ☎3659 7623; http://weibo.com/uniontutu; G/F, 361-365 Guangzhou Dadaozhong; 广州大道中路361-365号;

Ⓜ Yángjī, exit B) A rustic-looking cafe that hosts performances by local and overseas acts. The genre tends towards modern folk and singer-songwriter, but postrock and heavy metal have been featured too. It's next to a 7 Days Inn.

Fei Live House
LIVE MUSIC

(飞; Fēi; Unit B4, 128 Yuancun Sihenglu, Redtory; Ⓜ Line 3, Yúncūn, exit B) A new live-music space with an awesome sound system that just opened inside Redtory art village.

C Union
LIVE MUSIC

(喜窝; Xǐwō; ☎3584 0144; 115 Shuiyin Lu; ⏰7pm-2am) Unpretentious C Union hosts a good mix of bands playing jazz, R&B and reggae. It's behind the Chéngshìhuì (城市会) building, in the Yuèxiù District. Only accessible by taxi.

Guǎngzhōu Opera House
THEATRE

(广州大剧院; Guǎngzhōu Dàjùyuàn; Map p558; ☎3839 2666, 3839 2888; http://gzdjy.org; 1 Zhujiang Xilu; ⏰9am-4.30pm, closed Mon; Ⓜ Line 3, Zhūjiāng Xīnchéng, exit B1) Guǎngdōng's premier performance venue.

🔒 Shopping

TIT Creative Industry Zone
CLOTHING

(TIT 创意园; TIT Chuàngyì Yuán; 397 Xingang Zhonglu; ⏰10am-7pm; Ⓜ Kècūn, exit A) This fashion village on the leafy site of a communist-era textile factory has boutiques selling a variety of locally designed clothing – office wear, modern Chinese garments, European brand lookalikes, and gauzy, lacy ultragirly dresses. There are also a couple of trendy cafes. Turn left from the metro exit and walk for five minutes.

Xīguān Antique Street
ANTIQUES

(西关古玩城; Xīguān Gǔwánchéng; Map p554; Lizhiwan Lu; Ⓜ Line 5, Zhōngshān Bālù) This street sells everything from ceramic teapots to Tibetan rugs. Even if you're not in the mood to load up your pack with ceramic vases, it's a wonderful place in which to browse. Note that most artefacts here are known to be fakes.

Fāng Suǒ Commune
BOOKS

(方所; Fāngsuǒ; ☎3868 2327; MU35, Tai Koo Hui, 383 Tianhe Lu; ⏰10am-10pm; Ⓜ Line 1, Shípáiqiáo) Occupying some 2000 sq metres in a classy mall, this elegant bookstore also sells (pricey) clothes, homewares and coffee. There are more than 90,000 titles, mostly Chinese, including books from Taiwan.

LĬNGNÁN CULTURE

Lĭngnán (岭南), literally 'South of the Ranges', refers to that region to the south of the five mountain ranges that separate the Yangzi River (central China) from the Pearl River (southern China). Traditionally Lĭngnán encompassed several provinces, but today it's become almost synonymous with Guăngdōng.

The term Lĭngnán was traditionally used by men of letters on the Yangzi side as a polite reference to the boonies, where 'mountains were tall and emperors out of sight'. These northerners regarded their southern cousins as less robust (physically and morally), more romantic and less civilised. But being far-flung had its benefits. Lĭngnán offered refuge to people not tolerated by the Middle Kingdom; and played host in various diasporas in Chinese history to migrants from the north, such as the Hakka in Méizhōu. This also explains why some Cantonese words are closer in pronunciation to the ancient speech of the Chinese.

Culturally Lĭngnán was a hybrid and a late bloomer that often went on to reverse-influence the rest of the country. Its development was also fuelled by the ideas of the revolution to end feudalism. Boundaries between refined and pedestrian are relaxed and there's an open-mindedness towards modernity. For a long time in the Qing dynasty, Guăngzhōu was the only legal port for trade between China and the world. Interactions with the outside world infused the local culture with the foreign and the modern. Some of the most important political thinkers in modern China came from Lĭngnán, such as Kang Youwe and Sun Yatsen.

Lĭngnán culture is an important part of Cantonese culture and it manifests itself most notably in food, art and architecture, and Cantonese opera.

Lĭngnán School of Painting (1900–50)

The Lĭngnán painters were an influential lot who ushered in a national movement in art in the first half of the 20th century.

Traditionally, Chinese painters were literati well versed in calligraphy, poetry and Confucian classics. These scholar-artists would later become imperial bureaucrats, and as they were often stationed somewhere far away from home, they expressed their nostalgia by recreating the landscapes of their childhood villages from memory.

The founding masters of the Lĭngnán School of Painting, however, studied abroad, where they were exposed to Japanese and European art. China, during the Qing dynasty, was being carved up by Western powers. Sharing the ideals of the revolutionaries, these artists devoted themselves to a revolution in art by combining traditional techniques with elements of Western and Japanese realist painting.

The New National Painting, as it came to be called, featured a bolder use of colours, more realism and a stronger sense of perspective – a style that was more accessible to the citizenry of China's new republic than the literati painting of the past.

You can see Lĭngnán paintings at the Guăngdōng Museum of Art (p556) and Memorial Hall of the Lĭngnán School of Painting (p553).

Lĭngnán Architecture

The Lĭngnán school of architecture is one of three major schools of modern Chinese architecture, alongside the Bĕijīng and Shànghăi schools. It was founded in the 1950s, though earlier structures exhibiting a distinctive local style had existed since the late Ming dynasty (1600s). The features of the Lĭngnán school are lucidity, openness and an organic incorporation of nature into built environments.

ANCIENT

Examples of this style of architecture include schools, ancestral halls and temples of the Ming and Qing dynasties. The Chen Clan Academy in Guăngzhōu and Zŭmiào in Fóshān are prime illustrations of this style.

Vernacular Lĭngnán-style houses are more decorative than their austere northern cousins. The 'wok-handle' houses (锅耳屋; guǒ'ěr wū) in Líchá Village near Zhàoqing have distinctive wok-handle-shaped roofs that also serve to prevent the spread of fire. You'll also see in Líchá Village bas-relief sculpting and paintings (浮雕彩画; fúdiāo căihuà), intricate and colourful, above windows or doors, portraying classical tales, birds, flowers and landscapes.

MODERN

An excellent example of this style of architecture, appearing in the late Qing dynasty, are the Xīguān houses on Ěnníng Lù (p560) in Guǎngzhōu, with their grey bricks and stained-glass windows. These windows were products of the marriage between Manchurian windows (洲窗; *mǎnzhoū chuāng*), simple contraptions consisting of paper overlaid with wood and coloured glass introduced to Guǎngzhōu by Westerners. It's said that when a foreign merchant presented the empress dowager with a bead of coloured glass, she was so dazzled by its beauty that she reciprocated with a pearl. Pànxī Restaurant in Guǎngzhōu and Yúyìn Mountain Villa have Manchurian windows embedded with coloured glass.

Another example of modern Lǐngnán architecture are shophouses with arcades (骑楼; *qílóu*) on the ground floor, a style that evolved from the arcades of southern Europe. You see them in Cháyáng Old Town in Méizhōu and Chìkǎn in Kāipíng.

CONTEMPORARY

The garden-restaurants and garden-hotels that proliferated between the 1950s and 1990s are examples of contemporary architecture. Guǎngzhōu's Garden Hotel, Guǎngzhōu Restaurant and Pànxī Restaurant all contain elaborate indoor gardens complete with trees and waterfalls, and make use of glass to blur the boundary between built and natural environments.

These indoor Edens were fashioned after the private Lǐngnán-style gardens of wealthy families, such as Liáng Garden in Fóshān, which together with the imperial gardens of Peking and the scholars' gardens of Jiāngnán, constituted the three main types of Chinese gardens. Thanks to these architects, the privilege of having gardens in the interior was now available to all.

Cantonese Opera

Cantonese opera is a regional form of Chinese opera that evolved from theatrical forms of the north and neighbouring regions. Like Peking opera, it involves music, singing, martial arts, acrobatics and acting. There's elaborate face painting, glamorous period costumes and, for some of the roles, high-pitched falsetto singing. But compared to its northern cousin, it tends to feature more scholars than warriors in its tales of courtship and romance.

You don't have to understand or even like Cantonese opera to appreciate it as an important aspect of Cantonese culture – there's no shortage of related attractions, such as Bāhé Academy and Luányú Táng in Guǎngzhōu, a festival, and a props speciality shop in Cháozhōu.

If you do decide to catch a show at Culture Park in Guǎngzhōu, those exotic strains could years later become the key that unlocks your memory of your travels in China.

Cantonese Cuisine

There's a saying 'Good food is in Guǎngzhōu' (食在广州; shí zài Guǎngzhōu). Regional bias aside, Cantonese food is very good. The most influential of the eight major regional cuisines of China, it's known for complex cooking methods, an obsession with freshness and the use of a wide range of ingredients.

Many Cantonese dishes depend on quick cooking over high heat – these require skills (versus patience over a stew) that are less common in other regional cuisines. Cantonese chefs are also masters at making new techniques sizzle in their language. Dishes such as sweet-and-sour pork, crab shell au gratin and tempura-style prawns show an open-mindedness to foreign ideas.

When it comes to haute cuisine, even northern cooks would acknowledge the superiority of their Cantonese colleagues in making the best of expensive items such as abalone. Also, much of the costliest marine life to grace the Cantonese table, such as deep-sea fish and large prawns, simply don't grow in inland rivers.

ℹ Information

Good maps of Guǎngzhōu in both English and Chinese can be found at news-stands and bookshops.

EMERGENCY
Ambulance (☏120)
Fire (☏119)
Police (☏110)

INTERNET ACCESS
Most hotels provide free broadband internet access. Free wi-fi is available at all Guǎngdōng branches of Starbucks, Fairwood (大快活; Dàkuàihuó) and Cafe de Coral (大家乐; Dàjiālè).

MEDICAL SERVICES
Can-Am International Medical Centre (加美国际医疗中心; Jiāměi Guójì Yīliáo Zhōngxīn; Map p554; ☏8386 6988; www.canamhealthcare.com; 5th fl, Garden Tower, Garden Hotel, 368 Huanshi Donglu) Has English-speaking doctors, but you'll need to call ahead.
Guǎngzhōu First Municipal People's Hospital (广州第一人民医院; Guǎngzhōu Dìyī Rénmín Yīyuàn; Map p554; ☏8104 8888; 1 Panfu Lu) Medical clinic for foreigners on the 1st floor.

MONEY
ATMs are available – most 24 hours – throughout Guǎngzhōu.
American Express Guǎngzhōu (美国运通广州; Měiguó Yùntōng Guǎngzhōu; Map p554; ☏8331 1611; fax 8331 1616; Room 1004, Main Tower, Guǎngdōng International Hotel, 339 Huanshi Donglu; ☺9am-5.30pm Mon-Fri) Cashes and sells Amex travellers cheques.
Bank of China (中国银行; Zhōngguó Yínháng; Map p554; ☏8334 0998; 686 Renmin Beilu; ☺9am-5.30pm Mon-Fri, to 4pm Sat & Sun) Most branches change travellers cheques.

POST
China Post (中国邮政; Zhōngguó Yóuzhèng; Map p554; 151 Huanshi Xilu; ☺8am-8pm) Located next to the train station.

TELEPHONE
China Telecom (中国电信; Zhōngguó Diànxìn; Map p554; ☏10000; 196 Huanshi Xilu; ☺9am-6pm) Main branch is opposite the train station (eastern side of Renmin Beilu).

TOURIST INFORMATION
Tourism Administration of Guǎngzhōu (Map p554; www.visitgz.com; 325 Zhongshan Liulu) Has 19 tourist information centres, including at the airport, at the train station and at 325 Zhongshan Liulu (open from 9am to 6pm).
Tourist Complaint Hotline (☏8666 6666)

TRAVEL AGENCIES
Most hotels offer travel services that, for a small charge, can help you book tickets and tours.
China Travel Service (CTS; 广州中国旅行社; Zhōngguó Lǚxíngshè; Map p554; ☏8333 6888; 8 Qiaoguang Lu; ☺8.30am-6pm Mon-Fri, 9am-5pm Sat & Sun) Located next to Hotel Landmark Canton (华厦大酒店; Huáxià Dàjiǔdiàn).

WEBSITES
Delta Bridges Guǎngzhōu (www.deltabridges.com/users/guangzhou) Listings of events around town.
Guǎngzhōu Stuff (www.gzstuff.com) Entertainment listings, forums and classifieds.
Life of Guǎngzhōu (www.lifeofguangzhou.com) Yellow pages for visitors and expats.

ℹ Getting There & Away

AIR
China Southern Airlines (中国南方航空; Zhōngguó Nánfāng Hángkōng; Map p554; ☏95539; www.cs-air.com; 181 Huanshi Xilu; ☺24hr) Frequent flights to major cities in China include Guìlín (¥660), Shànghǎi (¥1280) and Běijīng (¥1700); also numerous international destinations.

BUS
Guǎngzhōu has many long-distance bus stations with services to destinations in Guǎngdōng, southern Fújiàn, eastern Guǎngxī and further afield. There are frequent buses to Fóshān (¥20, 45 minutes), Kāipíng (¥56, two hours), Shēnzhèn (¥60, two hours) and Zhūhǎi (¥60, two hours) from Tiānhé bus station, Fāngcūn bus station, Guǎngzhōu East coach terminal and Guǎngdōng long-distance bus station.

Other destinations:
Cháozhōu ¥170 to ¥180, six hours, hourly from Tiānhé station
Guìlín ¥160, 10 hours, eight daily from Guǎngdōng long-distance bus station (8.30am to 11.30pm)
Hǎikǒu ¥250 to ¥280, 12 hours, seven daily from Guǎngdōng long-distance bus station
Nánníng ¥180, 10 hours, five daily from Guǎngdōng long-distance bus station
Qīngyuǎn ¥30 to ¥40, 1½ hours, every half-hour from Tiānhé station
Shàntóu ¥180 to ¥200, five hours, every 30 minutes from Tiānhé station
Sháoguān ¥70 to ¥80, four hours, every 45 minutes from Guǎngdōng long-distance bus station
Xiàmén ¥220, nine hours, every 45 minutes from Tiānhé station
Zhàoqìng ¥35 to ¥50, 1½ hours, every 15 minutes from Tiānhé station

Deluxe buses ply the Guăngzhōu–Shēnzhèn freeway to Hong Kong, which is the easiest route to travel. Buses (from ¥100 to ¥110, 3½ hours) to Hong Kong and its airport leave from Hotel Landmark Canton near Hăizhū Sq station or China Hotel a Marriott hotel near Yuèxiù Park station every 30 minutes.

Buses through Zhūhăi to Macau (¥75, every hour, 2½ hours) leave frequently from Tiānhé station (7.40am to 8pm).

Tiānhé Bus Station (天河客运站; Tiānhé Kèyùnzhàn; ☎ 3708-5070; www.tianhebus. com; Yanling Lu; 燕玲路; Ⓜ Tiānhé Kèyùnzhàn) Most frequent departures to destinations in Guăngdōng; accessible by metro.

Fāngcūn Bus Station (芳村客运站; Fāngcūn Kèyùnzhàn; ☎ 3708 5070; www.fangcunbus. com; Huadi Dadao; 华地大道; Ⓜ Kēngkŏu) Accessible by metro (Kēngkŏu station).

Guăngzhōu East Coach Terminal (广州东站汽车客运站; Guăngzhōu Dōngzhàn Kèyùnzhàn; Map p558; Linhe Xilu) Behind Guăngzhōu East Station. Good for destinations within Guăngdōng; departures aren't as frequent as from other stations.

Guăngdōng Long-Distance Bus Station (广东省汽车客运站; Guăngdōng Shěng Qìchē Kèyùnzhàn; Map p554; Huanshi Xilu) To the left of the Guăngzhōu Railway Station (metro). There's a smaller long-distance bus station (Guăngzhōu Shìqìchēzhàn) over the footbridge.

TRAIN

Guăngzhōu's three major train stations serve destinations all over China. China Travel Service, next to Hotel Landmark Canton, books train tickets up to five days in advance for ¥10 to ¥20.

From **Guăngzhōu Main Train Station** (广州火车总站; Guăngzhōu Zhàn; Map p554; Huanshi Xilu; Ⓜ Line 2, Guăngzhōu Huŏchēzhàn):

Lhasa ¥818, 54 hours, one every two days (11.46pm)

Sháoguān ¥38, 2½ hours, frequent services

Zhàoqìng ¥19 to ¥42, two hours, 14 daily

High-speed trains leave from **Guăngzhōu South Station** (广州火车南站; Guăngzhōu Nánzhàn; Shibi, Pānyú) in Pānyú:

Chángshā ¥314, 2½ hours, frequent

Qīngyuăn ¥40, 25 minutes, frequent

Sháoguān ¥104, 50 minutes, frequent

Shēnzhèn North Station ¥75, 45 minutes

Wŭhàn ¥464, four hours, frequent

Light rail goes to Zhūhăi (¥34, one hour).

To get to Guăngzhōu South Station, take metro line 2 from the main train station (¥6, 34 minutes) or one of the South Station Express buses (南站快线; Nánzhàn Kuàixiàn) that leave from Tianhe Sports Centre metro station, Garden Hotel and Hotel Landmark Canton (¥14, 45 minutes).

From **Guăngzhōu East station** (广州火车东站; Guăngzhōu Dōngzhàn; Map p558; Ⓜ Line 1, Guăngzhōu Dōngzhàn):

Běijīng ¥250 to ¥450, 22 hours, one daily (4.11pm)

Shànghăi ¥220 to ¥380, 16 hours, one daily (6.06pm)

The station is used more for bullet trains to Shēnzhèn (¥80, 1½ hours, every 15 minutes, 6.15am to 10.32pm) and a dozen direct trains to Hong Kong (¥190, HK$190, two hours, 8.19am to 9.32pm).

ℹ Getting Around

Greater Guăngzhōu extends some 20km east to west and north to south. The metro is the speediest way to get around.

TO/FROM THE AIRPORT

Báiyún International Airport (☎ 020-3606 6999; www.baiyunairport.com) is 28km north of the city. Airport shuttle buses (¥17 to ¥32, 35 to 70 minutes, every 20 to 30 minutes, 5am to 11pm) leave from half-a-dozen locations, including Garden Hotel and Tiānhé bus station. A taxi to/from the airport will cost about ¥150.

Metro line 2 links the airport's south terminal (Airport South station; Jīchǎng Nán) and Guăngzhōu East station. The ride takes 40 minutes (¥7, from 6.10am to 11pm).

BUS

Guăngzhōu has a large network of motor buses and bus rapid transport (BRT; ¥2).

METRO

Guăngzhōu has 10 metro lines in full service, all with free maps available. Operating hours are approximately from 6.20am to 11.30pm and fares cost from ¥2 to ¥14.

Transit passes (羊城通; *yáng chéng tōng*) are available at metro stations from ¥70 (deposit ¥20 included). The deposit is refundable at designated stations, including Tiyu Xilu and Gōngyuán Qián. This pass can be used on all public transport, including yellow taxis. There are also one-day (¥20) and three-day (¥50) metro passes. Both allow unlimited use within the specified period and do not require a deposit.

TAXI

Taxis are abundant but demand is high. Peak hours are from 8am to 9am, and around lunch and dinner. Yellow or red cabs are driven by local drivers; others by migrant drivers who may not know the city well. Flag fall is ¥10 for the first 2.5km; ¥2.6 for every additional kilometre, with a ¥1 fuel surcharge.

Around Guǎngzhōu

★ **Yúyìn Mountain Villa** GARDENS
(馀荫山房; Yúyīn Shānfáng; ☑ 3482 2187; Náncūn, Pānyú; adult/child ¥18/9; ☉ 8am-6pm; Ⓜ Line 1, Dàshí, exit A) One of Guǎngdōng's four famous classical gardens, this graceful property was built in 1871 by an official of the Qing court. It incorporates the landscaping styles of Sūzhōu and Hángzhōu, and the features of Lǐngnán architecture. The result is a photogenic collection of pavilions, terraces, halls, bridges and lakes. It also has a dessert shop selling ginger milk curd (姜汁撞奶, *jiāngzhī zhuàngnǎi*).

The Waterside Pavilion commands a different vista on each of its eight sides; the Deep Willow Room features ancient art and coloured 'Manchu' windows (满洲窗; *mǎnzhōu chuāng*) aka 'four-season windows' (四季窗; *sìjì chuāng*), which create an illusion of changing seasons by altering the hue of the outside scenery.

Turn left when you leave the metro. There's a stop for the Route 8 feeder bus to Qīxīnggǎng Gōngyuán (七星岗公园; ¥2). Disembark at Nánshān Gōngyuán (南山公园), the 20th stop, after half an hour. Cross to the opposite and leafy side of the road. Bus 30 (¥2) from the stop there takes you to the entrance of Yúyìn Mountain Villa just one stop away.

Fóshān 佛山

☑ 0757 / POP SIX MILLION

An hour-long bus ride will take day trippers from Guǎngzhōu to this city. Fóshān (佛山; literally 'Buddha Hill') was famous for its ceramics in the Ming dynasty. Today, it's better known as the birthplace of two kung fu icons, Wong Fei Hung and Ip Man.

◉ Sights

Zǔmiào TAOIST TEMPLE
(祖庙; ☑ 8229 3723; www.fszumiao.com; 21 Zumiao Lu; admission ¥20, combo with Ancient Nánfēng Kiln ¥35; ☉ 8.30am-5.30pm; Ⓜ Zǔmiào, exit A) The 11th-century Zǔmiào temple is believed to be the site where Cantonese opera flourished. The art is still performed today during festivals to entertain the gods, and the tourists. Sharing the complex are a Confucius temple (c1911) and memorial halls dedicated to Wong Fei Hung (aka Huang Fei Hong) and Ip Man.

There are daily performances of kung fu (10am, 2pm and 3pm) and lion dance (10.30am, 2.30pm and 3.30pm). The temple runs martial-arts classes for children every summer. Call ☑ 8222 1680 for details.

Liáng Garden GARDENS
(梁园; Liáng Yuán; ☑ 8224 1279; Songfeng Lu; admission ¥10; ☉ 8.30am-5.30pm; 🚍 205, 212) This tranquil residence of a family that produced painters and calligraphers was built during the Qing dynasty. Designed in a Lǐngnán style, it delights with ponds, willow-lined pathways and, in summer, trees heavy with wax apple and jackfruit. Like Yúyìn Mountain Villa near Guǎngzhōu, it's one of the four great classical gardens. Liáng Garden is north of Rénshòu Temple and 300m north of the Bank of China (中国银行; Zhōngguó Yínháng).

Nánfēng Ancient Kiln KILN
(南风古灶; Nánfēng Gǔzào; ☑ 8271 1798; 6 Gaomiao Lu, Shíwān; admission ¥25; ☉ 9am-5.30pm; 🚍 137) Shíwān (石湾), 2km from downtown Fóshān, was once China's most important ceramics production centre. Much of the Ming-dynasty pottery you see at museums comes from here (those in shops nearby, however, are mass-produced copies). Two

---

THE MAKING OF A NATIONAL LEGEND

Fóshān-born Wong Fei Hung (1847–1924) is one of China's best-known folk heroes. Although a consummate *gōngfū* (kung fu) master in his lifetime, he didn't become widely known until his story was merged with fiction in countless movies made since 1949, most by Hong Kong directors, such as Hark Tsui's *Once Upon a Time in China*, starring Jet Li. Sadly, Wong spent his later years in desolation, after his son was murdered and his martial-arts school was destroyed by fire. Regardless, an astonishing 106 movies (and counting!) have celebrated this son of Fóshān, resulting in the world's longest movie series and the creation of a national legend.

Another Fóshān hero, Ip Man (1893–1972) rose to fame as a Wing Chun master at the outset of WWII. He fled to Hong Kong in 1949 and founded the first Wing Chun school. His most famous student was Bruce Lee. Ip Man was immortalised by Wong Kar-wai's award-winning *The Grandmaster* and a series of semibiographical movies starring Donnie Yen.

ancient 'dragon kilns' of more than 30m length are set in this lovely complex with meandering stone-paved paths.

Rénshòu Temple
BUDDHIST TEMPLE

(仁寿寺; Rénshòu Sì; ☑ 8225 3053; 9 Zumiao Lu; ⊙ 8am-5pm; ☐ 1, 2B, 5, 11) This former Ming monastery remains an active place of worship today. Inside, you'll find a pagoda built in 1656, and the **Fóshān Folk Arts Studio**, featuring pretty paper-cut art.

Fóshān Lǐngnán Tiāndì
HISTORIC BUILDING

(Tiandi Lu, Chánchéng Qū; ⊙ 11am-9pm; ☐ 101, 105) A photogenic collection of restored medicinal shops, Chinese liquor stores and old villas that are occupied by swanky boutiques, upmarket eateries and trendy bars.

✖ Eating

Healthy Buddha Vegetarian
CANTONESE, VEGETARIAN $

(健康菩提素食; Jiànkāng Pútí Sùshí; ☑ 8230 2836; mains ¥18-35; ⊙ lunch & dinner; ☑; ☐ 1, 2b, 5, 10, 11) This vegetarian restaurant on the property of Rénshòu Temple offers great value for money.

Yīngjì Noodle Shop
NOODLES $

(应记面家; Yīngjì Miànjiā; ☑ 3171 2533; 116 Lianhua Lu; 莲花路116号; noodles ¥5-10; ⊙ 7am-11pm) This excellent noodle shop opposite Liánhuā Supermarket (莲花超市; Liánhuā Chāoshì) is the go-to place in Fóshān for noodles with shrimp wonton (鲜虾云吞面; *xiānxiā yúntūnmiàn*).

Shùndé Double Layer Milk Pudding
DESSERT

(顺德双皮奶; Shùndé Shuāngpínǎi; 31 Zumiao Lu; 祖庙路31号; ¥10-25; ⊙ 9.30am-10pm summer, to 9.30pm winter; Ⓜ Zūmiào, exit A) This dessert shop sells the popular southern Chinese dessert 'double layer' milk pudding, so-called because of the layer of milk skin on the surface. It can be eaten hot or cold.

☆ Entertainment

AD Livehouse
LIVE MUSIC

(西元 Livehouse; Xīyuán Livehouse; ☑ 139 2991 1129; Bldg 5, Xijie, Poly Canal Plaza, Denghu Xilu, Nánhǎi District; 水岸长廊, 南海区, 灯湖西路, 保利水岸西街5栋1号; ⊙ 8.30am-2am; 🐓) This large and out-of-the-way bar with a hardcore sound system has live music from 10pm every night. Performances are usually by a local band, but every month or so overseas acts feature in various genres. A cab from downtown Fóshān costs less than ¥35.

ℹ Getting There & Around

Buses leave from **Fóshān bus station** (佛山汽车站; Fóshān Shěng Qìchēzhàn; Fenjiang Zhonglu), 400m south of the train station:

Shēnzhèn ¥75 to ¥90, 2½ hours, every 30 minutes

Zhūhǎi ¥70, three hours, every 30 to 60 minutes

Trains go to Guǎngzhōu (¥9 to ¥24, 30 minutes, 21 daily).

The metro runs between Guǎngzhōu and Fóshān on the Guǎngfó line (¥6, 30 minutes). There's a direct express train to Hong Kong (¥210, 2½ hours, 4.13pm) and at 10.42pm from Kowloon.

Buses 101 and 134 (¥2) link the train station to Zūmiào and Shíwān. Taxis start at ¥8 for the first 2km; ¥2.6 for every addition 1km.

Kāipíng
开平

☑ 0750 / POP 680,000

Kāipíng (开平), 140km southwest of Guǎngzhōu, is home to one of the most arresting human-constructed attractions in Guǎngdōng – the Unesco-crowned *diāolóu* (碉楼), eccentric watchtowers featuring a fusion of Eastern and Western architectural styles. Out of the approximately 3000 original *diāolóu*, only 1833 remain.

Downtown Kāipíng is pleasant, especially the section near the Tánjiāng River (谭江), where you'll see people fishing next to mango and wampee trees. Kāipíng is also the home of many overseas Chinese. Currently, 720,000 people from the county are living overseas – 40,000 more than its local population.

◎ Sights

A combo ticket for seven sights, including Lì Garden and the villages of Zìlì, Jīnjiānglì and Mǎjiānglóng, costs ¥180. It's only available at Lì Garden and Zìlì village. The price for just Lì Garden and one village is ¥150. A village alone costs from ¥50 to ¥80. Some towers charge an extra ¥5 to ¥10 to let you in.

★ Zìlì
VILLAGE

(自力村; Zìlì Cūn; ⊙ 8.30am-5.30pm) Zìlì, 11km west of Kāipíng, has the largest collection of *diāolóu* historic watchtowers, though only a few of the 15 are open to the public. The most stunning is **Míngshí Lóu** (铭石楼), which has a verandah with Ionic columns and a hexagonal pavilion on its roof. It appeared in the film *Let the Bullets Fly*. **Yúnhuàn Lóu** (云幻楼) has four towers known as 'swallow nests', each with embrasures, cobblestones and a water cannon.

Next to the village is Fang Clan's Dēng Lóu (方氏灯楼), aka Light Tower, because of its powerful searchlight. Admission is free.

Jĭnjiānglĭ Historic Village
VILLAGE

(锦江里; Jĭnjiānglĭ Cūn; ⏰ 9am-5pm) The highlights in this village, 20km south of Kāipíng, are the privately run **Ruìshí Lóu** (瑞石楼; admission ¥20) and **Shēngfēng Lóu** (升峰楼). The former (c 1923) is Kāipíng's tallest *diāolóu* and comprises nine storeys, topped off with a Byzantine-style roof and a Roman dome. The latter is one of very few *diāolóu* that had a European architect.

In nearby Nánxìng village, Nánxìng Xié Lóu watchtower tilts severely to one side, with its central axis over 2m off-centre.

Lì Garden
HISTORIC SITE

(立园; Lì Yuán; ⏰ 8.30am-5.30pm) About 15 minutes by taxi from Kāipíng, Lì Garden has a fortified mansion built in 1936 by a wealthy Chinese American. The interiors featuring Italianate motifs, and the gardens with their artificial canals, footbridges and dappled pathways, are delightful.

Diāolóu watchtowers here include the oldest of the historic towers, **Yínglóng Lóu** (迎龙楼), found in Sānménlĭ village (三门里), and the fortified villas of **Mǎjiànglóng** (马降龙; Mǎjiànglóng) village.

Chìkǎn
VILLAGE

The charming old town of Chìkǎn (赤坎), 10km southwest of Kāipíng, has streets of shophouses with arcades on the ground floor flanking the Tánjiāng River (潭江). These distinctive *qílóu* (骑楼) buildings were built by overseas Cantonese merchants in the 1920s. Bus 6 from Yìcí bus station takes you to Chìkǎn.

Fēngcǎi Hall
HISTORIC SITE

(风采堂; Fēngcǎi Táng; admission ¥5; ⏰ 9am-4.30pm) Not a typical ancestral hall, this compound built in 1906 retains an exquisite southern Chinese architectural style, but with Western elements eccentrically blended. The complex is hidden inside a school 1.5km south of Chángshā bus station. Bus 2 from either Chángshā or Yìcí bus stations takes you to Fēngcǎi Zhōngxué (风采中学).

🛏 Sleeping & Eating

Staying overnight in Kāipíng allows you to give its sights the attention they deserve.

Many villagers in Zìlì village serve rustic dishes cooked with home-grown ingredients inside their homes. Popular items include free-range chicken (走地鸡; zǒudìjī) for ¥28 a catty (斤; jīn), and rice cooked with baby eel (黄鳝饭; huángshàn fàn; ¥70).

Pan Tower Hotel
HOTEL $

(潭江半岛酒店; Tánjiāng Bàndǎo Jiǔdiàn; ☎ 233 3333; www.pantower.com; 2 Zhongyin Lu; 中银路

KĀIPÍNG'S BIZARRE TOWERS

Scattered across Kāipíng's 20km periphery are *diāolóu* – multistorey watchtowers and fortified residences displaying a flamboyant mix of European, Chinese and Moorish architectural styles. The majority were built in the early 20th century by villagers who made a fortune working as coolies overseas. They brought home fanciful architectural ideas they'd seen in real life and on postcards, and built the towers as fortresses to protect their families from bandits, flooding and Japanese troops.

The oldest *diāolóu* were communal watchtowers built by several families in a village. Each family was allocated a room within the citadel, where all its male members would go to spend the night to avoid being kidnapped by bandits. These narrow towers had sturdy walls, iron gates and ports for defence and observation. The youngest *diāolóu* were also watchtowers, but ones equipped with searchlight and alarm. They are located at the entrances to villages.

More than 60% of *diāolóu*, however, combined residential functions with defence. Constructed by a single family, they were spacious and featured a mix of decorative motifs. As the builders had no exposure to European architectural traditions, they took liberties with proportions, resulting in outlandish buildings that seem to have leapt out of an American folk-art painting or a Miyazaki cartoon.

These structures sustain a towerlike form for the first few floors, then, like stoic folk who have not forgotten to dream, let loose a riot of arches and balustrades, Egyptian columns, domes, cupolas, corner turrets, Chinese gables and Grecian urns.

PIGLETS FOR SALE

The mid-19th century saw Guǎngdōng in a state of despair, stalked by famine and revolt. Meanwhile, slavery was outlawed in most Western countries, creating a need to recruit cheap labour for the exploitation of the New World. Conditions were ripe for many unskilled workers from Táishān (where Kāipíng was located) to seek opportunities for a better life overseas. Disingenuous recruiters promised good pay and working conditions, but in reality the workers were made to work as coolies under deplorable conditions on the sugar-cane fields of South America, on farms in Southeast Asia, and in gold mining and rail construction in North America. The coolie trade was known in Cantonese as *maai ju jai* – 'selling piglets'.

Of the nine million Chinese workers who left home in the mid-19th to early 20th centuries, many died, but a handful made a fortune, becoming wealthy 'overseas Chinese', a powerful community that often brought home exotic ideas that were assimilated into the local culture.

2号; r ¥800-1800, ste ¥1800-2400; ❊ @) *The* place to stay in Kāipíng. It's on an islet on the Tánjiāng River and only accessible by taxi (¥12 from Chángshā bus station, five minutes away). Offers discounts of 50% to 60%.

Tribe of Diāomín   HOTEL $
(碉民部落; Diāomín Bùluò; ✆261 6222; 126 Henan Lu, Chìkǎn; 赤坎镇河南路126号; dm per person ¥50, r ¥110-300; ☎) An old building right by Tánjiāng River in Chìkǎn has been turned into a pleasant backpacker hostel by a bicycle club. You can rent one of the 100-plus bikes for a full day of sightseeing for ¥50 to ¥80.

Wilson Hotel   HOTEL $$
(威尔逊酒店; Wēi'ěrxùn Jiǔdiàn; ✆220 8888; www.wilsonhotel.com.cn; 70 Musha Rd; 幕沙路70号; r ¥620-880; ❊@☎) A centrally located hotel inside a shopping mall, Wilson has 146 neat, spacious and slightly outmoded guest rooms. It offers good value if you don't mind the human traffic from the mall. It's a 15-minute walk from Yìcí and Chángshā bus stations, or a ¥7 motorcycle taxi ride.

Cháojiāngchūn Restaurant   CHINESE $$
(潮江春酒楼; Cháojiāngchūn Jiǔlóu; ✆221 9963; 114 Guangming Lu; mains ¥25-90; ◷11am-10.30pm) This excellent restaurant serves the local speciality – braised wild-grown goose (狗仔鹅; *gǒuzǎi é*). The steamed tofu with shredded taro and ground pork (肉碎芋丝蒸豆腐; *ròusuì yùsī zhēng dòufu*) and salt-baked chicken (手撕鸡; *shǒusījī*) are also delicious.

ⓘ Getting There & Around

Kāipíng has two bus stations (www.bus.ko.com.cn) that are linked by local buses 7 and 13: **Yìcí bus station** (义祠汽车总站; Yìcí zǒngzhàn;

✆221 3126; Mucun Lu) and **Chángshā bus station** (长沙汽车站; Chángshā qìchēzhàn; ✆233 3442; Xijao Lu). Both run frequent services:

Guǎngzhōu ¥60, 2½ hours, every 40 minutes (6.30am to 7.30pm)

Hong Kong HK$150, four hours, three to four times daily

Shēnzhèn ¥90, three to 3½ hours, every 45 minutes (7.30am to 7.30pm)

Zhūhǎi ¥50 to ¥70, 2½ to three hours, every 40 minutes (7am to 7.43pm)

From both Yìcí and Chángshā bus stations, local buses (from ¥2 to ¥5) go to Chìkǎn and some of the historic *diāolóu* watchtowers. But as the *diāolóu* are scattered over several counties, your best bet is to hire a taxi for the day. A full day costs around ¥600, but you can negotiate.

Yángjiāng   阳江
✆0662 / POP 2.4 MILLION

Yángjiāng is a city on the southwestern coast of Guǎngdōng. While downtown Yángjiāng is unexciting, picturesque Hǎilíng Island (海陵岛; Hǎilíng Dǎo), located 50km or an hour's drive away, is home to the Maritime Silk Road Museum and some of the finest beaches in the province.

If money is not an issue, stay on Hǎilíng Island – in the up-and-coming resort area near the museum or in lively Zhápō (闸坡) resort town. Downtown Yángjiāng, though, has the cheapest sleeping options.

⊙ Sights

Maritime Silk Road
Museum of Guǎngdōng   MUSEUM
(广东海上丝绸之路博物馆; Guǎngdōng Hǎishàng Sīchóu Zhīlù Bówùguǎn; ✆368 1111; www.msrmuseum.com; admission ¥80, free English

audioguide; ⊙9am-5pm, closed 1st & 2nd Mar & Nov) Sitting right on Shílǐ Yíntān (十里银滩) beach, this museum is purpose-built to house an 800-year-old Song-dynasty shipwreck that was wholly salvaged near the island. The remains of the 30m-long merchant vessel (南海一号; *Nanhai No 1*), and much of the 70,000 pieces of merchandise on board, now rest in a sealed glass tank. The displays are supplemented by temporary exhibitions of treasures from dynastic China.

The ship is believed to have been headed for the Middle East or Africa when it sank. The wreckage has significant archaeological value, though only a few hundred pieces of the porcelain, gold and copper treasures have been put on display. Excavation is being carried out in phases.

Shílǐ Yíntān
BEACH

(十里银滩; southern shore of Hǎilíng Island, Jiāngchéng District; 江城区海陵岛南面; ⊙8am-7pm, 6.30am-6pm summer) Literally '10 miles of silver beach', this is the most beautiful and the longest stretch of coastline in the area. It's where you'll find the Maritime Silk Road Museum of Guǎngdōng.

Dàjiǎowān
BEACH

(大角湾; ⊙ 8am-7pm, 6.30am-6pm summer) A ¥50 ticket gives you two days' unlimited entry to the centrally located Dàjiǎowān beach in the lively Zhápō (闸坡) area. Tickets to the beach are also sold at a water world at Dàjiǎowān, but they're good for only a day. Lockers and showering facilities are available for ¥10 and ¥5 respectively. It's 10 minutes away from beautiful Shílǐ Yíntān beach on Hǎilíng Island by pedicab.

🛏 Sleeping & Eating

Zhápō on Hǎilíng Island has plenty of seafood restaurants that are all quite similar. Pick out what you want from the tanks, agree on the price, and it'll be cooked for you. Generally, seafood items cost from ¥28 to ¥230 per 500g/1 *catty*; nonseafood dishes go for between ¥20 and ¥90. Most eateries pay drivers commission for bringing customers – it's better to choose a restaurant yourself.

7 Days Inn
HOTEL $

(7天连锁酒店; Qītiān Liánsuǒ Jiǔdiàn; ☑321 7888; www.7daysinn.cn; 37 Dongfeng Erlu, Yángjiāng; 阳江市, 东风二路37号; r ¥140-195; 🛜) Located in Yángjiāng, this place has cheerful rooms, and wi-fi in the lobby.

Jīnhǎilì Hotel
HOTEL $$

(金海利大酒店; Jīnhǎilì Dàjiǔdiàn; ☑389 6688; fax 389 5599; 23 Haibin Lu, Zhápō Town; 闸坡市海滨路23号; r ¥260-320) This affordable option in the upmarket Zhápō area has a gloomy lobby and big decent rooms (it's a designated host for government officials). In July and August prices go up by 30% on Fridays and double on Saturdays.

Hǎilíng Crowne Plaza
HOTEL $$$

(海陵岛皇冠假日酒店, Hǎilíngdǎo Huángguān Jiàrì Jiǔdiàn; ☑386 8888; www.ihg.com/crowneplaza; Shílǐ Silver Beach; 十里银滩; ¥2628-3800; 🅿❄@🛜🏊) The most luxurious place to stay in Yángjiāng offers 313 top-notch rooms, its own stretch of beach, a spa, swimming pools, BBQs and child-minding services. In July and August expect to share all of the above with hordes of moneyed local tourists who follow rules of etiquette that may be different from yours. Packages and off-season discounts are often available.

ⓘ Getting There & Away

Yángjiāng's **main bus station** (阳江汽车客运总站; Yángjiāng qìchē kèyùn zǒngzhàn; ☑316 9999; Xiping Belu) has direct services to the following:

Fóshān ¥95, three hours, six daily (8.30am to 4.50pm)

Guǎngzhōu ¥65 to ¥93, 3½ hours, frequent (6.05am to 7.20pm)

Hong Kong ¥170 to ¥260, six hours, four daily (8am to 5pm)

Shēnzhèn ¥120, four to five hours, 14 daily (8am to 8.30pm)

Zhūhǎi ¥90, 3½ to four hours, frequent (8am to 7.30pm)

No 2 bus station (阳江二运汽车站; Yángjiāng èr yùn qì chē zhàn; ☑342 9168; 666 Shiwan Beilu) has daily direct services to the following:

Guǎngzhōu ¥85, three hours, frequent (6.10am to 7pm)

Kāipíng ¥50, two hours, five daily (8.20am to 4.40pm)

Shēnzhèn ¥135, four hours, 11 daily (7.40am to 8.30pm)

Kāiping's Yìcí bus station has two buses daily (from 12.55pm and 5.15pm) to Yángjiāng's main bus station and six (from 8.45am to 4.10pm) to its No 2 station (¥36).

ⓘ Getting Around

Local buses run every 20 minutes to Zhápō from No 2 station (¥13, one hour, 6.30am to 9pm) and the main station (6am to 9.30pm, one hour, ¥13 to ¥20).

Zhápò and the museum area on Hǎilíng Island are connected by pedicabs (¥10 to ¥15, 10 minutes). A taxi from downtown Yángjiāng to the Maritime Silk Road Museum of Guǎngdōng costs ¥100 (one hour).

Zhàoqìng 肇庆

📍 0758 / POP 3.9 MILLION

Bordered by lakes and limestone formations, the leisurely town of Zhàoqìng in western Guǎngdōng province was where Jesuit Mateo Ricci first set foot in China in 1583.

👁 Sights

Seven Star Crags Park PARK
(七星岩公园; Qīxīng Yán Gōngyuán; 📞 230 2838; admission ¥78; ⏱ 8am-5.30pm) The landscape of limestone hills, grottoes and willow-graced lakes in this massive park is beautiful, so it's a pity the authorities try so hard – the caves are illuminated like nightclubs and boat rides cost extra (¥15 to ¥60). The easiest way to navigate between sights is to use the battery-operated carts (¥15 to ¥30 per person).

Plum Monastery Buddhist BUDDHIST TEMPLE
(梅庵; Méiàn; 📞 283 3284; Mei'an Lu, Duānzhōu Qū; ⏱ 8.30am-4pm) This dignified temple is dedicated to the Father of Chinese Zen Buddhism – Master Huineng (六祖慧能), who was said to be fond of plum blossoms. Born in Zhàoqìng during the Tang dynasty, Master Huineng planted plum trees all over the hillside during a sojourn here, and dug a well (look for the one with petals carved into its parapet) to irrigate them.

The temple's plum trees bloom between winter and spring. A pedicab from downtown Zhàoqìng costs ¥20.

City Walls HISTORIC SITE
Zhàoqìng's city walls (古城; Gǔ Chéng) were built during several periods – the lowest part with large mud bricks are Song dynasty; above that is Ming; then a Qing extension featuring smaller bricks. Anything above that was built yesterday. Interestingly, there are alleyways and dwellings at the top. The **River View Tower** and **Cloud-Draped Tower** here are only open for dignitaries.

🍴 Sleeping & Eating

Shānshuǐ Trends Hotel BUSINESS HOTEL $$
(山水时尚酒店; Shānshuǐ Shíshàng Jiǔdiàn; 📞 285 9999; 36 Xijiang Beilu; 西江北路36号;

d/tw ¥168-308, tr from ¥338, ste, from ¥438; ❄ ✴ @ ☎) A decent option for the price and location, if you don't mind slightly thin walls (pray for a quiet neighbour) and small TV screens. There are more than 200 rooms in this hotel adjacent to a shopping centre.

Bōhǎilóu CHINESE $
(波海楼; 📞 230 2708; Xinghu Xilu; dim sum ¥6-32; ⏱ 11.30am-1.30pm & 5.30-7.30pm) This restaurant with lake views serves Zhàoqìng delicacies such as sticky rice dumplings (裹蒸粽; guǒzhēngzòng), containing beans, pork, chestnuts and egg yolk, and fox nuts buns (芡实包; cìshí bāo). It's a 10-minute walk from the western entrance of Seven Star Crags Park. Bus 19 (¥2) from the entrance passes here (波海楼; Bōhǎilóu).

Kuàihuolín Restaurant CANTONESE $$
(快活林食家; Kuàihuolín Shíjiā; 📞 285 1332; Xijiang Beilu; 西江北路, 水果市场侧; ⏱ 11am-2.30pm, 5pm-2am) if you're hankering for seafood, this restaurant near a fruit market will overwhelm with its options. It's wildly popular and, at peak times, can get slightly chaotic. But the food is great. We recommend the broiled shrimp (白灼沙虾; báizhuó shāxiā; ¥24) and the fish soup with tofu and parsley (芫茜豆腐黄骨鱼汤; yánqiàn dòufu huánggǔyú tāng; ¥37). Chinese picture menu.

ℹ Information

Bank of China (中国银行; Zhōngguó Yínháng; Duanzhou Wulu; ⏱ 9am-5pm Mon-Sat)

China Post (中国邮政; Zhōngguó Yóuzhèng; Jianshe Sanlu; ⏱ 9am-8pm)

China Travel Service (CTS; 肇庆中国旅行社; Zhàoqing Zhōngguó Lǚxíngshè; 📞 226 8090; Duanzhou Wulu; ⏱ 8am-9pm)

ℹ Getting There & Away

BUS

The **main bus station** (肇庆汽车客运总站; Zhàoqing Qìchē Kèyùn Zǒngzhàn; 📞 223 5173; Duanzhou Silu) runs frequent services to the following:

Guǎngzhōu ¥55, 1½ hours, frequent (6.30am to 9.30pm)

Shēnzhèn ¥100, three hours, frequent (7.30am to 7.30pm)

Zhūhǎi ¥100, four hours, 13 daily (7.40am to 6.30pm)

The **east bus station** (肇庆城东客运站; Zhàoqing Chèngdōng Kèyùnzhàn; 📞 271 8474; Duanzhou Sanlu), 1.5km east of the main bus station, has services to Kāipíng (¥55, 2½ hours).

Zhàoqìng

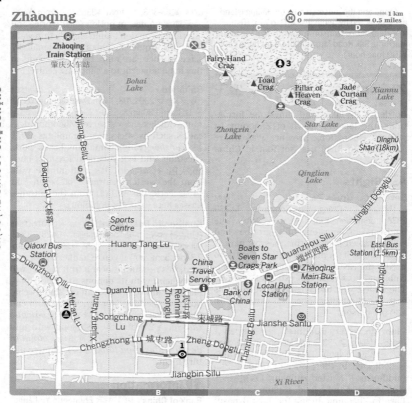

Zhàoqìng

◉ Sights
1 City Walls B4
2 Plum Monastery Buddhist A4
3 Seven Star Crags Park C1

🛏 Sleeping
4 Shānshuǐ Trends Hotel A3

🍽 Eating
5 Bǒhǎilóu B1
6 Kuàihuólín Restaurant A2

TRAIN

The fastest train to Guǎngzhōu (¥17 to ¥26, every 30 minutes) takes two hours. The direct express train to Hong Kong (HK$235, four hours) departs at 3.10pm.

⊙ Getting Around

Bus 12 links the train station (¥2, every 10 minutes) and main bus station with the ferry pier.

A taxi to the train station from the centre costs about ¥15.

Around Zhàoqìng

Dǐnghú Shān   鼎湖山

The reserve of Dǐnghú Shān, northeast of Zhàoqìng, offers great walks among lush vegetation, rare trees and roaring waterfalls, and makes for a relaxing day trip.

Bus 21 (¥2) goes to Dǐnghú Shān from the local bus station in Zhàoqìng.

Dǐnghú Shān Reserve   NATURE RESERVE
(鼎湖山自然保护区; Dǐnghúshān Zìrán Bǎohù Qū; ☑262 2510; 21 Paifang Lu; admission ¥78; ☉8am-6pm) The 11.3-sq-km Dǐnghú Shān Reserve lies 18km northeast of Zhàoqìng. A boat (¥35) will ferry you to a butterfly reserve on a tiny wooded island on Dǐng Lake (Dǐnghú). From there, a guide will take you

on an hour-long hike through a scenic forest with ponds and waterfalls, to emerge near Băodǐng Garden (宝鼎园; Băodǐng Yuán), which has the world's largest *dǐng,* a three-legged ceremonial cauldron. Battery-operated carts (¥20) are useful for navigating the reserve.

Qìngyún Temple (庆云寺; Qìngyún Sì) may look a little gaudy, but the site was built in 1636, making it one of Guǎngdōng's four oldest temples (广东四大名刹; *guǎngdōng sì dà míngshā*). What's more, it's surrounded by towering ancient banyans, and it's where you'll find a great vegetarian restaurant.

★ Qìngyún Vegetarian Restaurant

VEGETARIAN $$

(庆云寺斋堂, Qìngyúnsì Zhāitáng; ☑ 262 1585; mains ¥38-135; ⏰ 8am-2pm & 5-7pm; 🍴) An excellent but pricey eatery in Dǐnghú Shān Reserve that serves the famous Dǐnghú Vegetarian Dish (鼎湖上素; Dǐnghú Shàngsù; ¥68), supposedly an invention by monks around here. It also does an exceptional sweet-and-sour pork (糖醋咕噜肉; *tángcù gūlúròu;* ¥50) with fried winter melon, no less.

Things to note: when servers give you tea, make sure it's regular tea (普通茶; pǔtōngchá; ¥3 per person) and not exotic varieties that will inflate your bill by ¥30 to ¥100; snacks left at your table also cost money.

Bāguà Villages 八卦村

Two villages, exceptional for their shape and feng shui, make great excursions from Zhàoqìng. These '*bāguà* villages' (Bāguà Cūn) are designed according to *bāguà,* an octagon-shaped Taoist symbol with eight trigrams representing different phases in life.

Líchá Village

VILLAGE

(黎槎村; Líchá Cūn; admission ¥25; ⏰ 8.15am-5.30pm) At 700-year-old Líchá village, 21km east of Zhàoqìng, houses, many with wok-handle roofs and bas-relief sculptures, radiate from a taichi (a symbol of yin and yang) on a central terrace, turning the village into a maze. Most residents have emigrated to Australia; only the elders remain. Bus 315 (¥10, 40 minutes) leaves for Líchá from behind Qiáoxī bus station in Zhàoqìng every 15 minutes.

Xiǎngǎng Village

VILLAGE

Fifteen kilometres southeast of downtown Zhàoqìng, Xiǎngǎng village (蚬岗村; Xiǎngǎng Cūn), founded in the Ming dynasty, is a large and lively '*bāguà*' village, and has a market at its entrance. Its 16 ancestral halls, some opulent, only open on the first and 15th day of the lunar month. Board bus 308 (¥10, one hour) at Qiáoxī bus station in Zhàoqìng to get here.

Qīngyuǎn 清远

☑ 0763 / POP 3.7 MILLION

The industrial town of Qīngyuǎn is where to set off for a scenic jaunt down the Běijiāng River (北江). The secluded temple in Fēilái and the monastery in Fēixiá are the main attractions. Four-hour cruises (¥380 to ¥600 for the whole boat, depending on size) leave from Qīngyuǎn's Wǔyī dock (五一码头; Wǔyī Mǎtóu).

You can buy seafood from the floating market at Fēixiá and your boatman will cook it for you at no extra charge. Make sure you do so after sightseeing. Boat operators are known to return produce to vendors in exchange for cheaper versions, when you're not looking.

◉ Sights

Fēilái

BUDDHIST TEMPLE

(飞来; admission ¥15) Cruise along the Běijiāng River from Qīngyuǎn's Wǔyī dock, heading past ancient pagodas to the Buddhist temple complex of Fēilái. Though it has been around for more than 1400 years, the complex was destroyed by a landslide in 1997 and subsequently rebuilt. The mountain-top pavilion offers terrific views of the river gorge below.

Fēixiá

MONASTERY

(飞霞; admission ¥50; ⏰ 7.30am-5.30pm) The admission fee to the monastery at Fēixiá, 4km upstream from Fēilái, includes an eight-minute ride (every 15 minutes) to the Taoist relics uphill. Cángxiá Ancient Cave (藏霞古洞; c 1863) is a maze of whispering shadows, abandoned courtyards and crumbling alleys connected by arboured paths. Further up, there is a pagoda; further down, a nunnery.

❶ Getting There & Around

To visit Fēilái and Fēixiá on a day trip from Guǎngzhōu, catch one of the 10 high-speed trains from Guǎngzhōu South Station that stop in Qīngyuǎn (¥25 to ¥40, 30 minutes). On arrival, it's a 15-minute walk to Qīngyuǎn's Wǔyī dock. Turn right as you leave the station.

Buses run every 25 minutes from Guǎngzhōu's long-distance bus stations (¥37 to ¥42, 70 to 80 minutes, 6.30am to 9pm).

Nánlǐng National Forest Park 南岭国家森林公园

📞 0751 / POP 2000

Lying 285km north of Guǎngzhōu, the Nánlǐng (Southern Mountains) ranges stretch from Guǎngxī to Jiāngxī provinces, separating the Pearl River from the Yangzi River.

The range in Guǎngdōng, home to the only ancient forests in the province, is a reserve for old-growth blue pines, a species unique to this part of Guǎngdōng.

🏃 Activities

Come here with your walking boots. There are four trails, most of which can be completed under three hours.

The Nánlǐng National Forest Park entrance is at the southern end of the village of Wúzhǐshān (五指山), which is small enough to cover on foot. Farmers nearby do their weekly shopping and stock clearance at Wúzhǐshān's lively Sunday market. Staying in Orange House here will give you access to the park the next day. Just get your ticket and receipt stamped at the hotel.

From Wúzhǐshān it's 6km to the start of the trails to Pùbù Chángláng waterfalls and Water Valley, and another 6km to Little Yellow Mountain. The best way is to hire a car from Wúzhǐshān. For between ¥350 and ¥500 you can hire one for the whole day. The driver can drop you at one end of the trail and wait for you at the other. A one-way trip to the lower entrance of the trail to Little Yellow Mountain costs ¥120.

Water Valley   HIKING
The easiest of the four walks through Nánlǐng National Forest Park, this 6km trail follows a stream and leads you through the steep-sided gorges and crystalline pools of Water Valley (亲水谷; Qīnshuǐgǔ).

Pùbù Chángláng   HIKING
This short but more interesting 3.5km trail (瀑布长廊; Pùbù Chángláng) through Nánlǐng National Forest Park takes you past roaring waterfalls.

Little Yellow Mountain   HIKING
The 12km-long trail through Nánlǐng National Forest Park to Little Yellow Mountain (小黄山; Xiǎo Huángshān) is a challenging

hike through a forest of blue pines. The view of rolling mountain ranges from the crest (1608m) is spectacular.

Shíkēngkōng   HIKING
The longest (28km) and most difficult of the four trails through Nánlǐng National Park is the No 4 Trail (四号林道; Sìhào Líndào) to Shíkēngkōng (石坑空). At 1902m, Shíkēngkōng is the highest peak in Guǎngdōng and straddles the boundary between Guǎngdōng and Húnán.

🛏 Sleeping & Eating

As camping inside Nánlǐng National Forest Park is prohibited, the only option is to stay in Wúzhǐshān. There are a couple of zhāodàisuǒ (招待所; basic lodgings), where you can get a room from ¥90.

Orange House   BOUTIQUE HOTEL $$
(橙屋; Chéngwū; 📞 523 2929; www.ctrip.com; d ¥398-489, Ranger House tr ¥198; ❄ @) A cheery boutique hotel with 32 comfortable but slightly musty rooms. The hotel also manages an air-con-free Ranger House (林舍; Línshè) behind Orange House. Discounts of 30% to 40% via www.ctrip.com. It can arrange transportation to and from the park.

Feng's Kitchen   CANTONESE $
(冯家菜; Féngjiācài; 📞 138 2799 2107; mains ¥10-40; ⏰ 7am-8.30pm) A farmer restaurant that cures its own meat and grows its own vegetables (¥10 per plate). Reservations necessary. Mr Feng can arrange for car hire of any duration.

ℹ Getting There & Away

BUS
Sháoguān (韶关) is your gateway to Nánlǐng. Buses (¥70 to ¥90, 3½ hours) leave Guǎngzhōu's long-distance bus stations for Sháoguān's Xīhé bus station every hour (6.50am to 8.30pm).

If you miss the bus to Wúzhǐshān, catch a bus to Rǔyuán (乳源; ¥10, one hour, every 15 minutes). From Rǔyuán, three buses to Wúzhǐshān (¥10) leave at 9am, 12.45pm and 4.30pm, or you can hire a taxi (¥80).

In Wúzhǐshān, buses to Sháoguān leave at 7.30am, 12.30pm and 3.30pm.

TRAIN
High-speed trains (¥105, one hour) leave from Guǎngzhōu South station for Sháoguān train station (韶关高铁站; Sháoguān Gāotiézhàn). From there, board bus 22 and get off at **Xīhé bus station** (西河汽车站; Xīhé qìchēzhàn; 📞 875

4176; Gongye Donglu). Buses to Wúzhìshān (¥20, two hours) depart at 8am, 11.45am and 3.30pm.

Guǎngzhōu's main train station has trains that stop over at **Sháoguān East station** (韶 关东站; Sháoguān Dōngzhàn; ¥38, 2½ hours). Buses to Wúzhìshān leave at 7.45am, 11.15am and 3.15pm.

Shēnzhèn   深圳

☏ 0755 / POP 10.5 MILLION

One of China's wealthiest cities and a Special Economic Zone (SEZ), Shēnzhèn draws a mix of business people, investors and migrant workers to its golden gates. It's also a useful transport hub to other parts of China.

You can buy a five-day Shēnzhèn-only visa (¥160 for most nationalities, ¥469 for Brits; cash only) at the **Luóhú border** (Lo Wu; ☉ 9am-10.30pm), Huánggǎng and Shékǒu. US citizens must buy a visa in advance in Macau or Hong Kong.

◉ Sights

Shēnzhèn Museum   MUSEUM
(深圳博物馆新馆; Shēnzhèn Bówùguǎn Xīnguǎn; ☏ 8201 3036; www.shenzhenmuseum.com.cn; East Gate, Block A, Citizens' Centre, Fuzhong Sanlu, Fútián District; ☉ 10am-6pm Tue-Sun; Ⓜ Line 4, Shìmín Zhōngxīn, exit B) **FREE** The hulking Shēnzhèn Museum provides a solid introduction to Shēnzhèn's short yet dynamic history of social transformation, both before and after the implementation of Deng Xiaoping's policies of reform. Highlights include propaganda art popular in the 1940s and the colourful scale models in the folk culture hall.

★ **OCT-LOFT**   ARTS CENTRE
(华侨城创意文化园; Huáqiáochéng Chuàngyì Wénhuàyuán; ☏ 2691 1976; Enping Jie, Huáqiáochéng, Nánshān District; ☉ 10am-5.30pm; Ⓜ Qiáochéngdōng, exit A) The sprawling OCT-LOFT complex, converted from fashionably austere communist-era factories, is one of the best places to see contemporary art in Shēnzhèn, and makes for a wonderful browse-as-you-stroll experience. Large exhibition spaces and private galleries – many closed on Mondays – are complemented by chilled-out cafes (not to mention the ubiquitous Starbucks), restaurants with exposed ventilation ducts, quirky fashion boutiques, a gem of a bookstore, and the obligatory 'lifestyle' outlets.

Turn right as you exit the metro station and follow the signs.

OCT Art & Design Gallery   GALLERY
(华美术馆; Huá Měishùguǎn; ☏ 3399 3111; www.oct-and.com; 9009 Shennan Lu; adult/child ¥15/8; ☉ 10am-5.30pm Tue-Sun; Ⓜ Huáqiáochéng, exit C) The bare interiors of this former warehouse are filled with the works of excellent mainland and international graphic designers. Exhibits change frequently. It's a glass-encased steel structure adjacent to Hé Xiāngníng Art Gallery.

Hé Xiāngníng Art Gallery   GALLERY
(何香凝美術館; Héxiāngníng Měishúguǎn; ☏ 2660 4540; www.hxnart.com; 9013 Shennan Lu; ☉ 9.30am-4.30pm Tue-Sun; Ⓜ Huáqiáochéng, exit C) **FREE** The esoteric permanent collection here features Japanese-influenced Chinese water paintings by He Xiangning (1878–1972), the late master of modern Chinese art and well-known revolutionary. These are complemented by temporary exhibits that range from avant-garde Chinese art to Western works of an experimental nature. The gallery is one metro stop from OCT-Loft.

🛏 Sleeping

Hotels in Shēnzhèn regularly slash up to 50% off the regular rack rates on weekdays, though you should ask for a discount at any time.

★ **Shēnzhèn Loft Youth Hostel**   HOSTEL $
(深圳侨城旅友国际青年旅舍; Shēnzhèn Qiáochéng Lǚyǒu Guójì Qīngnián Lǚshè; ☏ 8609 5773; www.yhachina.com; 7 Xiangshan Dongjie, OCT-LOFT, Huáqiáochéng, Nánshān district; 南山区，华侨城香山东街7号; dm/d/ste from ¥65/200/370; ❀✳@☎; Ⓜ Qiáochéngdōng, exit A) Located in a tranquil part of OCT-LOFT, near the junction of Enping Jie and Xiangshan Dongjie, this immaculate YHA hostel has over 50 private rooms, all with showers, and dormitory-type accommodation with shared bathrooms. The staff are well trained and helpful. There's wi-fi in the lobby only.

New Melbourne Hostel   HOSTEL $
(墨尔本一家; Mò'ěrběn Yìjiā; ☏ 158 2076 6520; 1435113378@qq.com; Unit 1801, Lìjǐng Dàshà, 1008 Hongling Zhonglu; 红岭中路1008 号，荔景大厦1801室; dm from ¥70; ❀✳@☎; Ⓜ Dàjùyuàn, exit B) Three spotless dormitory rooms (two women's, one men's) with a total of 18 bed spaces, run by John, the well-mannered English-speaking owner. Some rooms overlook a river and a park. The building is a 10-minute stroll on Hongling Zhonglu from the metro station.

Shēnzhèn

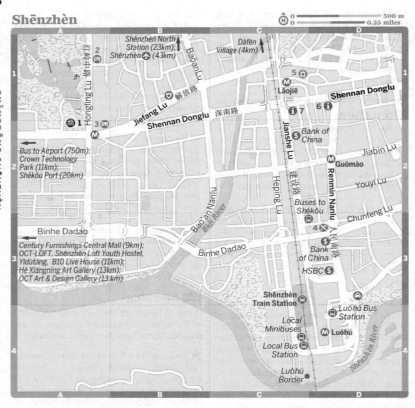

Shēnzhèn

**Shēnzhèn Vision
Fashion Hotel**   BOUTIQUE HOTEL $$
(深圳视界风尚酒店; Shēnzhèn Shìjiè Fēngshàng
Jiǔdiàn; ☑2558 2888; www.visionfashionhotel.

com; 5018 Shennan Donglu; 深南东路5018号; d
¥486-1880; ✳@☎; MDàjùyuàn, exit B) Inside a
theatre complex is this boutique hotel fea-
turing eclectic designs in its rooms. Some
are chic, some bizarre. Its prime location
and quiet environment make it a very good
choice. Discounts of 50% to 70% available.

✕ Eating

Laurel   DIM SUM, CANTONESE $
(丹桂轩; Dānguìxuān; ☑8232 3668; Renmin Nan-
lu; 人民南路; dim sum ¥8-28, dishes ¥40-180;
☺7am-11pm) An excellent modern dim sum
restaurant on the 5th floor of Luóhú Com-
mercial City. Tables are a little close together,
but the environment is pleasant and service
is warm.

♟ Drinking & Entertainment

The free *That's PRD* (http://online.
thatsmags.com/city/shenzhen) has monthly
events listings.

Yīdùtáng
BAR

(一渡堂; ☎ 8610 6046; Enping Lu, Block F3, OCT-LOFT, Huáqiáochéng, Nánshān District; ☉ 11.30am-2am; Ⓜ Qiáochéngdōng, exit A) International and local indie bands play almost every night after 10pm at this warehouse-turned-bohemian-haunt in OCT-LOFT. It's a pleasant place with large glass panes, a soaring ceiling (from which chandeliers hang) and velvet armchairs placed next to brick walls. During the day, it's an upmarket cafe.

B10 Live House
LIVE MUSIC

(☎ 8633 7602; Shantou Jie, northern section, OCT-LOFT, Huáqiáochéng, Nánshān District; Ⓜ Qiáochéngdōng, exit A) A huge warehouse-turned-cultural space that morphs into a live house when there are no exhibitions going on. It's located on the north side of the Block B10 in the northern section of OCT-LOFT.

Brown Sugar
LIVE MUSIC

(红糖罐子; Hóngtáng Guànzi; www.hongtangguan. com; Tairan Jiulu, Fútián District, Ground fl, Block 2, Huángguān Kējì Yuán; tickets ¥40-120; ☉ 2pm-midnight Sun-Thu, to 2am Fri & Sat; Ⓜ Chēgōngmiào, exit C) Sandwiched between a garage and a hair salon near the entrance of Crown Technology Park (皇冠科技園, Huángguān Kējìyuán), this loft-like bar is where local and foreign indie bands play every weekend from 9pm. Run by young musicians, it sports eclectic furniture and paintings displayed on bare concrete walls.

At the metro exit, turn right and walk to the end of the road, then make a left. You should see the park entrance on your right after two minutes.

🛍 Shopping

Die-hard shoppers won't leave Shēnzhèn empty-handed, though the quality may vary. Remember to bargain!

Dàfēn Village
ARTS, CRAFTS

(大芬村; Dàfēncūn; ☎ 8473 2633; www.dafenvillage online.com; Dafen, Buji, Lónggǎng District) A real eye-opener: 600 studios-cum-stores, churning out thousands of copies of Rembrandt, Renoir and Picasso paintings every week, and some original work. Prices start from ¥300. It's also a good place to stock up on art supplies, with prices about 50% cheaper than in downtown Shēnzhèn. Bus 306 from Shēnzhèn's Luóhú station takes you to the village in about an hour. A taxi ride costs around ¥80.

INDIE MUSIC FESTIVALS

Shēnzhèn's indie music scene is rocking. **Strawberry Music Festival** (草莓音乐节; Cǎoméi Yīnyuè Jié; www.modernsky. com; ☉ May) and **Midi Music Festival** (谜笛音乐节; Midí Yīnyuè Jié; www.midifestival.com) have had Shēnzhèn editions since 2013–14. Both events feature the strongest bands from China, Taiwan and Hong Kong performing for three days. Midi takes place at the end of the year and Strawberry is usually in May.

⭐ Old Heaven Books
BOOKS

(旧天堂书店; Jiùtiāntáng Shūdiàn; ☎ 8614 8090; oldheavenbooks@gmail.com; Room 120, Block A5, northern section, OCT-LOFT, Huáqiáochéng, Nánshān District; ☉ 11am-10pm; Ⓜ Qiáochéngdōng, exit A) A delicious bookstore specialising in cultural and academic titles, which also doubles up as music store (vinyl anyone?). Gigs sometimes take place in the adjoining cafe. Located in the northern section of OCT-LOFT, it's up the street perpendicular to B10 Live House, on the left-hand side.

Century Furnishings Central Mall
HOMEWARES

(世纪中心家居广场; Shìjìzhōngxīn Jiājūguǎng Cháng; ☎ 8371 0111; www.sz-sjzx.com; Shennan Dadao, west of Xiāngmì Hú Water Park, Fútián District; ☉ 9.30am-8pm Mon-Fri, to 8.30pm Sat & Sun; Ⓜ Chēgōngmiào, exit A) This mall has a whopping 30,000 sq metres of retail space for homewares. There are three main zones. A and B sell mainly tiles, and bathroom and shower gadgets; C – the most popular among leisure shoppers – is all about lamps. A cab from Shēnzhèn's Luóhú station costs about ¥40.

Dōngmén Market
MARKET

(东门市场; Dōngmén Shìchǎng; ☉ 10am-10pm; Ⓜ Lǎojiē, exit A) A chaotic market popular for tailored suits, skirts, curtains and bedding. Be careful of pickpockets.

ℹ Information

Bank of China (中国银行分行; Zhōngguó Yínháng; 2022 Jianshe Lu; ☉ 9am-5.30pm Mon-Fri, to 4pm Sat & Sun) You can use either Chinese rénmínbì (or yuán, abbreviated '¥') or Hong Kong dollars in Shēnzhèn, but the rise of the rénmínbì makes Hong Kong dollars less desired.

China Travel Service (CTS, 深圳中国旅行社; Zhōngguó Lǚxíngshè; ☑ 8228 7644; 3023 Renmin Nanlu; ◷ 9am-6pm)

Great Land International Travel Service (巨邦国际旅行社; Jùbāng Guójì Lǚxíngshè; ☑ 2515 5555; 3rd fl, Jùntíng Hotel, 3085 Shennan Donglu; ◷ 10am-6pm) Good for air tickets.

HSBC (汇丰银行; Huìfēng Yínháng; Ground fl, Shangri-La Hotel, 1002 Jianshe Lu; 香格里拉大酒店, Xiānggélǐlā Dàjiǔdiàn; ◷ 9am-5pm Mon-Fri, 10am-6pm Sat)

Public Security Bureau (PSB; 公安局; Gōng'ānjú; ☑ 2446 3999; 4018 Jiefang Lu)

SZ Party (www.shenzhenparty.com) For current events in Shēnzhèn.

❶ Getting There & Away

AIR

Shēnzhèn Airport (深圳宝安国际机场; Shēnzhèn Bǎoān Guójì Jīchǎng; ☑ 2345 6789; http://eng.szairport.com) Shēnzhèn airport has flights to most major destinations around China.

BOAT

Shékǒu Port (☑ 2669 1213) has services to Hong Kong:

Hong Kong International Airport ¥260, 30 minutes, 14 daily (7.45am to 9pm)

Hong Kong–Macau Ferry Terminal, Central ¥120, one hour, six daily (7.45am, 10.15am, 11.45am, 2.15pm, 4.45pm and 7.15pm)

To Macau:

Macau Maritime Ferry Terminal ¥190, one hour, 11 daily (8.15am to 7.30pm)

Taipa Temporary Ferry Terminal ¥190, one hour, seven daily (9.30am-7pm)

To Zhūhǎi:

Jiǔzhōu Port ¥150, one hour, every 30 minutes (7.30am to 8.30pm)

Fúyǒng ferry terminal (Fúyǒng Kèyùnzhàn; ☑ 2345 5388) in Shēnzhèn airport runs ferries to Hong Kong and Macau:

Macau Maritime Ferry Terminal ¥222, 80 minutes, seven daily (8.15am to 6pm)

Sky Pier, Hong Kong International Airport ¥295, 40 minutes, four daily (8.35am, 11.30am, 3.30pm and 6.30pm)

BUS

Regular intercity buses leave from **Luóhú bus station** (罗湖汽车站; Luóhú Qìchēzhàn; ☑ 8232 1670):

Cháozhōu ¥150, 5½ hours, three daily (8.30am, 1.40pm and 8pm)

Guǎngzhōu ¥50 to ¥70, two hours, every 20 minutes (7am to 10pm)

Shàntóu ¥130 to ¥170, four to five hours, every 30 minutes (7.20am to 9.40pm)

Xiàmén ¥220 to ¥240, eight hours, six daily (9.30am, 11am, 7.30pm, 8.30pm, 9.30pm and 9.50pm)

TRAIN

Services to Guǎngzhōu and Hong Kong leave from Luóhú train station to Guǎngzhōu East station (¥80, 1½ hours); and from Shēnzhèn North station (深圳北站; Shēnzhèn Běizhàn) in Lónghuá to Guǎngzhōu South station (¥80, 40 minutes). The Mass Transit Railway (MTR) links Shēnzhèn with Hong Kong.

❶ Getting Around

TO/FROM THE AIRPORT

Shēnzhèn's airport, 36km west of the city, is connected to Luóhú by metro line 1 (¥9, 70 minutes). A taxi costs ¥180 to ¥200. Airport bus departures are from **Huálián Mansion** (华联大厦, Huálián Dàshà; Shennan Zhonglu; ☐ 101, Ⓜ Kēxué Guǎn, exit B2) and cost ¥20 (40 minutes, every 15 minutes, 5am to 9pm), and Luóhú train station in Luóhú (¥20, one hour, every 15 minutes, 7am to 10pm). Buses leave from the local bus station west of the train station.

PUBLIC TRANSPORT

Shēnzhèn has a good public transport network, with five metro lines (¥2 to ¥11). Transit passes (深圳通; Shēnzhèn Tōng) can be bought in metro stations and are good for all except taxis. Bus and minibus fares cost ¥2 to ¥10.

TAXI

Flag fall costs ¥12.50 (from 11pm to 6am ¥16), plus ¥4 fuel surcharge and ¥2.40 every additional kilometre.

Around Shēnzhèn

Dàpéng Fortress   VILLAGE
(大鹏所城; Dàpéng Suǒchéng; ☑ 0755-8431 5618; Dàpéng Town, Lónggǎng District; adult/student & senior ¥20/10; ◷ 10am-6pm) This walled town and lively village built 600 years ago lies on Shēnzhèn's eastern edge. Stately mansions, fortress gates and ornate temples from the Ming and Qing dynasties are the main attractions. Board bus 360 at Yínhú bus station or near China Regency Hotel on Sungang Lu. The journey takes about 90 minutes. At Dàpéng bus station (Dàpéng zǒngzhàn; 大鹏总站), change to bus 966. A taxi from Luóhú costs ¥190.

★**Guānlán Original Printmaking Base**   VILLAGE
(观澜版画原创产业基地; Guānlán Bǎnhuà Yuánchuàng Chǎnyè Jīde; ☑ 2978 2510; www.guanlan-prints.com/en/; Dàshuǐtián, Niúhú, Bǎo'ān District;

📖 312, M258, M285, M288, M338, M339 to Guānlán Printmaking Base stop, 📖 B650, B768, B769, E4 to Guānlán jiēdàobàn zhàn (观澜街道办站) At this 300-year-old village, rows of quaint black-and-white houses exuding a modest, functional elegance unique to Hakka architecture are occupied by the workshops and galleries of printmaking artists from China and overseas. The village, with its tree-lined paths and lotus ponds, is open all day, but the galleries keep different hours. The journey from downtown Shēnzhèn takes about 1½ hours.

Zhūhăi 珠海

📞 0756 / POP 1.6 MILLION

Zhūhăi is close enough to Macau for a day trip. It's laid-back, and the driving isn't too maniacal. Gǒngběi in the south is the main tourist district. Ferries connecting to Hong Kong, Shēnzhèn and Guǎngdōng stop at Jídàin in the northeast.

Visas (¥168 for most nationalities, ¥469 for Brits) valid for three days are available at the border (8.30am to 12.15pm, 1pm to 6.15pm, and 7pm to 10.30pm). US citizens must buy a visa in advance in Macau or Hong Kong.

👁 Sights

Lover's Road STREET

This balmy promenade (情侣路; Qínglǔ Lù) starts at Gǒngběi (拱北), at the border with Macau, and sweeps north for 28km along the coast, passing some of Zhūhăi's most coveted real estate. The section near Tángjiā Public Garden is the most beautiful. There are kite and bicycle rentals along the way, and snack booths at night.

Tángjiā Public Garden GARDENS

(唐家共乐园; Tángjiā Gònglèyuán; 📞 338 8896; Eling, Tángjiāwān; adult/student ¥10/5; ⏰ 8.30am-5.30pm) Thirteen kilometres north of Zhūhăi is the labyrinthine town of Tángjiāwān (唐家

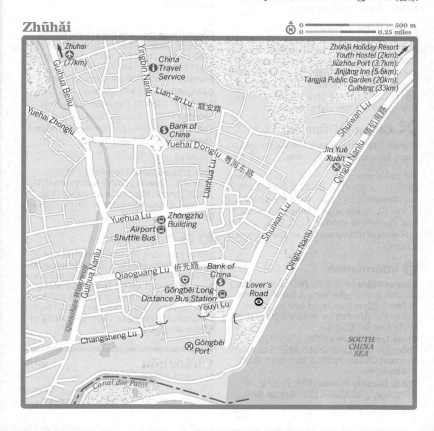

湾), where you'll find the former estate of the first premier of the Republic of China, Tong Shaoyi. It's now a garden with old-growth and rare trees. From Zhūhǎi take the K3, 3A, 69 or 3 bus (40 minutes) at the bus stop near the junction of Fenghuang Nanlu and Dongfeng Lu, and exit at Tángjiā Shìchǎngzhàn (唐家市场站; Tangjia Market station).

🛏 Sleeping

There's little demand for budget accommodation as very few travellers stay in Zhūhǎi.

Jǐnjiāng Inn INN $
(锦江之星; Jǐnjiāng Zhīxīng; ☑ 221 9899; 1058 Fenghuang Nanlu; 凤凰南路1058号; r ¥220-450; ☀ �ⓢ) The best of several branches in Zhūhǎi, this one is 50m from Lover's Rd, and 300m from Wānzǎishā Sq (湾仔沙广场; Wānzǐshā Guǎngchǎng). Rooms are bright and clean though those facing the street can be a tad noisy. Not all staff members speak English, but they're helpful and courteous. A reliable and affordable option.

Zhūhǎi Holiday Resort Youth Hostel HOSTEL $
(国际青年学生旅馆; Guójì Qīngnián Xuéshēng Lǚguǎn; ☑ 333 3838; www.zhuhai-holitel.com; 9 Shihua Donglu; 石花东路9号; dm ¥60; ☐ 99) Hidden away inside the Zhūhǎi Holiday Resort (珠海度假村; Zhūhǎi Dùjiàcūn) in Jídà, this hostel has two eight-bed dorms.

🍴 Eating & Drinking

Gǒngběi, near the Macau border, has restaurants, bars and street hawkers.

Jīn Yuè Xuān DIM SUM $$
(金悦轩; ☑ 813 3133; 1st-3rd fl, Block B, 265 Rihua Commercial Sq, Qinglu Nanlu; meals ¥100-130; ☺ 9am-10pm) For some of the best dim sum and Cantonese cuisine in Zhūhǎi, head to this elegant restaurant before 11am to secure a table.

❶ Information

Bank of China (中国银行; Zhōngguó Yínháng) Gǒngběi (cnr Yingbin Nanlu & Yuehai Donglu; ☺ 9am-5.30pm Mon-Fri, to 4pm Sat & Sun); Lianhua Lu (Lianhua Lu; ☺ 9am-5.30pm Mon-Fri, to 4pm Sat & Sun).
China Travel Service (CTS; 中国旅行社; Zhōngguó Lǚxíngshè; ☑ 889 9228; 2nd fl, Overseas Chinese Hotel, 2016 Yingbin Nanlu; ☺ 8am-8pm)
Public Security Bureau (PSB; 公安局; Gōng'ānjú; ☑ 888 5277; 1038 Yingbin Nanlu)

❶ Getting There & Away

AIR
Zhūhǎi Airport (☑ 777 8888; www.zhairport.com) serves various destinations in China, including Běijīng (¥1950), Shànghǎi (¥1400) and Chéngdū (¥1460).

BOAT
Hong Kong–bound jetcats leave from **Jiǔzhōu Port** (九州港; Jiǔzhōu Gǎng; ☑ 333 3359):
China Ferry Terminal, Kowloon ¥175, 70 minutes, six daily (8am to 5pm)
Hong Kong International Airport ¥290, one hour, four daily (9.30am, 12.40pm, 3.30pm and 6.30pm)
Hong Kong–Macau Ferry Terminal, Central ¥175, 70 minutes, nine daily (9am to 9.30pm)

Ferries leave Jiǔzhōu Port for Shēnzhèn's port of Shékǒu (¥150, one hour, every half-hour, 8am to 9.30pm); ferries leave Shékǒu for Jiǔzhōu Harbour every half-hour (7.30am to 9.30pm).

Local buses 3, 4, 12, 23, 25 and 26 go to Jiǔzhōu Port.

BUS
Gǒngběi long-distance bus station (拱北长途汽车站; Gǒngběi chángtú qìchēzhàn; ☑ 888 5218; Lianhua Lu) at Gǒngběi Port runs regular buses between 6am and 9.30pm.
Fóshān ¥55 to ¥70, three hours, 10 daily
Guǎngzhōu ¥55 to ¥70, 2½ hours, frequent
Kāipíng ¥40 to ¥75, three hours, four daily
Shàntóu ¥180, 6½ hours, two daily
Shēnzhèn ¥75, three hours, every 30 minutes
Zhàoqìng ¥65, 4½ hours, 10 daily

LIGHT RAIL
Guǎngzhōu–Zhūhǎi Light Rail (广珠城轨; ☑ 9510 5105) serves Zhūhǎi North station (珠海北站) and Guǎngzhōu South station (¥36, 70 minutes). Zhūhǎi North station can be reached by buses K1, 3A and 65.

❶ Getting Around

Zhūhǎi's airport, 43km southwest of the centre, runs a shuttle service (¥25, 50 to 70 minutes) to the city centre (every 30 minutes, 6am to 9.30pm) from Jiǔzhōu Port and the **Zhōngzhū Building** (Zhōngzhū Dàshà; cnr Yuehua Lu & Yingbin Nanlu). A taxi to the centre costs about ¥150. Flag fall for taxis is ¥10 for the first 3km, then ¥0.60 for each additional 250m.

Cháozhōu 潮州

☑ 0768 / POP 2.7 MILLION

Charming Cháozhōu was once a thriving trading and cultural hub in southern Chi-

Cháozhōu

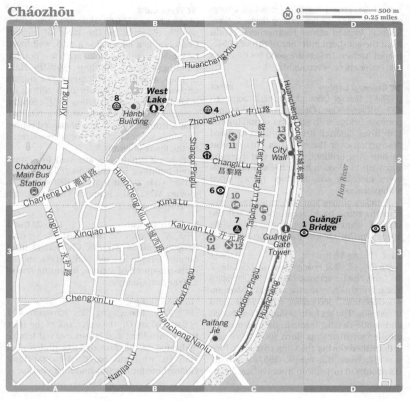

Cháozhōu

na, rivalling Guǎngzhōu. Today, it still preserves its distinct dialect, cuisine and opera. Cháozhōu is best appreciated at a leisurely pace, so do consider spending a night here.

Paifang Jie (牌坊街; Street of Memorial Arches), running 1948m from north to south in the old quarter, has signage to the main sights and is a good place to orient yourself.

It's made up of Taiping Lu (太平路; 1742m) and Dongmen Jie (东门街; 206m).

◎ Sights

Sights abound in Cháozhōu but admission charges can add up. Before you go sightseeing, buy a combo ticket (¥80) from **Jīnlóng**

Travel Service (金龙旅行社; Jīnlóng Lǚxíngshè; ☎ 222 1437; 39 Huangcheng Nanlu; ⊙ 9am-5.30pm), located across Huangcheng Nanlu from the southern entrance of Street of Memorial Arches. Tickets are good for two days and cover six or seven sights.

★ Guăngjĭ Bridge
BRIDGE

(广济桥; Guǎngjǐ Qiáo; ☎ 222 2683; admission ¥50; ⊙ 10am-5.30pm) Originally a 12th-century pontoon bridge with 86 boats straddling the Hán River, Guǎngjǐ Bridge suffered repeated destruction over the centuries. The current version is a brilliant, faux-ancient passageway with 18 wooden boats hooked up afresh every morning and 24 stone piers topped with pagodas.

A ticket allows you one crossing. If you want to come back, remember to tell the staff 'I want to come back' (我要回来; 'wǒyào huílai') before leaving the bridge.

Jīluè Huáng Temple
TEMPLE

(己略黄公祠; Jīluè Huánggōngcí; ☎ 225 1318; 2 Tie Xiang, Yian Lu; admission ¥10; ⊙ 8.30am-5pm) The highlights here are the ancient Cháozhōu woodcarvings decorating the walls and thresholds. The art form is famous for its rich and subtle details, intricate designs and exquisite craftsmanship. Born 1000 years ago, it flourished during the Qing dynasty, which was also when this temple (1887) was built. It's about ¥10 by pedicab from Paifang Jie.

★ West Lake
PARK

(西湖; Xīhú; ☎ 222 0731; Huancheng Xilu; admission ¥8; ⊙ 8am-11pm) The moat of ancient Cháozhōu is a lake inside a park well loved by locals. Around the lake are a few notable buildings. Hánbì Building (涵碧楼; Hánbì Lóu) served as a military office during antiwarlord expeditions in 1925. Sitting on a knoll is Phoenix Building (凤楼; Fènglóu; admission ¥5; ⊙ 6am-6pm), with its bird-like shape, iron moon gate, gourd-shaped ceiling openings, and quirky interior spaces formed by the fowl's anatomy.

Phoenix Building is attached to a shuttered building, Sìwàng Lóu (四望楼), in a period style reminiscent of 1970s kung fu movies. West Lake is about ¥10 by pedicab from Paifang Jie.

Kāiyuán Temple
BUDDHIST TEMPLE

(开元寺; Kāiyuán Sì; admission ¥5; ⊙ 6am-5.30pm) Built in AD 738, Cháozhōu's most famous temple has old bodhi trees and an embarrassment of statues, including one of a 1000-arm Guanyin.

Hánwén Temple
TEMPLE

(韩文公祠; Hánwéngōng Cí; admission ¥20; ⊙ 8am-5.30pm) On the east bank of the Hán, this is the oldest and best-preserved temple dedicated to the Tang-dynasty philosopher Han Yu, who was banished to 'far-flung' Guăngdōng for his anti-Buddhist views.

WORTH A TRIP

SHÀNTÓU

If you like history, the industrial town of Shàntóu (汕头) has a couple of interesting sights on its outskirts that can be covered on a day trip from Cháozhōu.

Buses run from Cháozhōu (¥13, one hour, 13 daily, 7am to 6.40pm). Shàntóu's main bus station and CTS bus station run buses every 30 minutes to an hour to Cháozhōu (¥17, one hour, 8.20am to 4.10pm); Guǎngzhōu (¥90 to ¥150, 5½ hours, 7am to 11pm); Méizhōu (¥60, 2½ hours, 6am and 5pm); and Shēnzhèn (¥100, five hours, 6.20am to 10pm).

Cultural Revolution Museum (文革博物馆; Wéngé Bówùguǎn; admission ¥10; ⊙ 9.30am-5.30pm) The only museum in China that honours the victims of the Cultural Revolution sits atop Tǎshān Park (塔山风景区; Tǎshānfēngjǐngqū). 25km north of Shàntóu's city centre. Names and inscriptions are engraved on the walls. Take eastbound bus 102 from the long-distance bus station to Tǎshān Lùkǒu (塔山路口). After the 45-minute ride, cross the road and walk 800m to the entrance, then another 3.5km uphill (take the path on the left).

Chen Cihong Memorial Home (陈慈黉故居; Chén Cíhóng Gùjū; admission ¥30; ⊙ 8am-5.30pm) This attractive complex was built by a businessman who made his fortune in Thailand in the 19th century. He had the region's best raw materials shipped here and assembled in imaginative ways that incorporated Asian, Western and Moorish motifs. Board the northbound bus 103 from People's Sq (eastern edge) in Shàntóu. The hour-long ride will cost you ¥6.

Emperor Xu's
Son-in-Law's Mansion   HISTORIC BUILDING

(许驸马府; Xǔfùmǎ Fǔ; ☑ 225 0021; 4 Dong-fucheng, Putao Xiang, Zhongshan Lu, Xiāngqiáo District; admission ¥20; ⏰8am-5pm) This breezy mansion originally built in 1064 retains some of the ancient stonework and wall coverings. The high door saddles, unique to southern China, were used to protect doors from humidity. The antechamber was used to keep coffins.

Confucian Academy   CONFUCIAN TEMPLE, GARDENS

(海阳县儒学宫; Hǎiyángxiàn Rúxué Gōng; cnr Changli Lu & Wenxing Lu, Xiāngqiáo District; admission ¥10; ⏰8am-5pm) This 4000-sq-metre compound has lily ponds teeming with koi and a main temple dedicated to Confucius that is supported by 48 pillars.

🛏 Sleeping

Zàiyáng Inn   HOTEL $

(载阳客栈; Zàiyáng Kèzhàn; ☑ 223 1272; www.czdafudi.com; 15 Zaiyang Xiang, Taiping Lu; 太平路, 载阳巷15号; r ¥128-368; 🛜) This classy Qing-style inn with graceful courtyards and antique woodcarvings (that were smothered in lime during the Cultural Revolution to prevent looting) is *the* place to stay in Cháozhōu. Rooms are small, but clean and very quiet. Prices more than double during holidays. Located in an alley off Paifang Jie; ¥10 by pedicab from the main bus station (汽车总站).

Chéngfǔ Inn   HOTEL $

(城府客栈; Chéngfǔ Kèzhàn; ☑ 222 8585; 9 Fensi Houxiang, Taiping Lu; 太平路, 分司后巷9号; r ¥158-220) Located in an old building inside an alley off Paifang Jie, Chengu Inn offers decent accommodation and opportunities to meet fellow travellers. Rooms on the ground floor can be noisy. It's ¥10 by pedicab from the main bus station (汽车总站).

🍴 Eating & Drinking

Food is generally good in Cháozhōu. On Paifang Jie, you'll find China's best beef balls with noodles (牛丸粉; *niúwán fěn*) and oyster omelette (蚝烙; *háolào*). **Hú Róng Quán** (⏰8am-late), which has three branches close to each other, sells pastries and sweet soups. There are also a number of trendy cafes, all offering free wi-fi.

★ Liánhuā Vegetarian   CHINESE, VEGETARIAN $

(莲华素食府; Liánhuā Sùshífǔ; ☑ 223 8033; 9 Kaiyuan Sq; mains ¥15-30; ⏰11am-2.30pm & 5.30-9.30pm; 🥢) An excellent vegetarian restaurant opposite Kāiyuán Temple. The menu also features Cháozhōu specialities, including the delightful desserts on the last page.

★ Zhèng's Private Kitchen   CHINESE $$

(郑厨私房菜; Zhèngchú Sīfángcài; ☑ 399 1310; 1 Shangdong Pinglu; 上东平路1号; per person ¥50-100; ⏰lunch & dinner) A new private kitchen that whips up impressive Cháozhōu-style seafood dishes. Ask a Mandarin- or Cantonese-speaking friend to call and book at least a day in advance. Also tell them your budget per person; and if you don't want shark's fin, a speciality here, say so too. It's in the first lane opposite Shàngshuǐmén Gate Tower (上水门城楼; Shàngshuǐmén Chénglóu). Walk down the lane until you see the stairs.

🛍 Shopping

Cháozhōu Opera
Costumes & Props   SOUVENIRS

(吉元戏剧歌舞用品; ☑ 222 6041; 12 Kaiyuan Lu; ⏰9am-10.30pm) Diagonally across the road from Kāiyuán Temple is this tiny shop that makes gowns, headdresses, swords, sedans and shoes for the Cháozhōu opera stage.

ℹ Getting There & Away

BUS

Services from Cháozhōu's **main bus station** (潮州汽车总站; Cháozhōu qìchē zǒngzhàn; ☑ 220 2552; 2 Chaofeng Lu):

Guǎngzhōu ¥110 to ¥170, 5½ hours, eight daily (8am to 11.55pm)

Méizhōu ¥55, two hours, two daily (8.30am and 3pm)

Ráopíng ¥17, one hour, 13 daily (6.30am to 6.30pm)

Shànghǎi ¥380, 20 hours, one daily, (2.45pm)

Shàntóu ¥13, one hour, 13 daily (7am to 6.40pm)

Shēnzhèn ¥120 to ¥140, five hours, five daily (8am to 11pm)

Xiàmén ¥100, 3½ hours, four daily (7am to 2.20pm)

Zhūhǎi ¥140, 9½ hours, two daily (8.30am and 9.10pm)

TRAIN

Services from Cháozhōu's train station, 8km west of the centre:

Guǎngzhōu ¥91 to ¥167, seven hours, two daily (8.41am and 12.45pm)

Shàntóu ¥9, 35 minutes, three daily (7.45am, 3.30pm, 6.53pm)

Around Cháozhōu

Located in Ráopíng (饶平), 53km from downtown Cháozhōu, is China's largest octagonal Hakka earthen house, **Dàoyùnlóu** (道韵楼; admission ¥20; ⊙ 8.30am-5.30pm). Six hundred villagers once resided in this stunning complex built in 1587; now only 100 remain. Ascend to the upper floors from unit 18 to admire the views and frescoes.

Buses to Ráopíng (¥20, one hour) leave from the Cháozhōu main bus station. Change to a bus to the village of Sānráo (三饶; ¥11), another 50km away. From there, motor-rickshaws will take you to Dàoyùnlóu (¥5, 10 minutes).

Méizhōu   梅州

☑ 0753 / POP FIVE MILLION

Méizhōu, populated by the Hakka (Kèjiā in Mandarin; 客家) people, is home to China's largest cluster of 'coiled dragon houses' or *wéilóngwū* (围龙屋). Specific to the Hakka, these are dwellings arranged in a horseshoe shape evocative of a dragon napping at the foot of a mountain. You'll also see *tǔlóu* (roundhouses) dotting the fields like mysterious flying saucers, and a jumble of other architectural treasures.

⦿ Sights

Hakka Park   PARK, MUSEUM
(客家公园; Kèjiā Gōngyuán; Dongshan Dadao; 东山大道; ⊙ Xiānqín Bldg 8.30am-5.10pm, Dáfū Bldg 8.30-11.30am & 2-5.30pm; 🚌1, 6) Pebbled paths and a willow-fringed pond make this small park on the north bank of the Méijiāng River a delight to stroll around in. The **Hakka Museum** (客家博物馆; Kèjiā Bówùguǎn; Dongshan Dadao; ⊙ 9am-5.10pm, closed Mon; 🚌1, 6) FREE here offers a quick warm-up to the culture of Hakkaland, and there are a couple of interesting 1930s buildings: Xiānqín Building (先勤楼; Xiānqínlóu), a courtyard-style Hakka house; and the East–West hybrid Dáfū Building (達夫樓; Dáfūlóu), which evokes a pseudo-Western train terminal drawn by Japanese cartoonist Miyazaki.

Nánkǒu Village   VILLAGE
(南口; Nánkǒu) This quiet village about 16km west of Méizhōu is where you'll see fine examples of *wéilóngwū* (围龙屋) dwellings nestled between paddy fields and the hills like dragons in repose. If you make your way to the back of Dōnghuā Lú (東華盧)

and Déxīn Táng (德馨堂), you'll see rooms arranged in a semicircle on an undulating slope, like the coiled body of a dragon. Another of the old houses, Nánhuá Yòulú (南华又庐) charges an admission of ¥10.

Bus 9 from the Méizhōu's local bus terminal and buses to Xìngníng (兴宁; ¥10, every 20 minutes) from Méizhōu's main bus station go to Nánkǒu. Once you get off, walk 1km to the village entrance. The last bus back leaves at 4.30pm. A taxi ride costs around ¥35.

Méizhōu Old Street   STREET
(梅州老街; Méizhōu Lǎojiē; Lingfeng Lu) Méizhōu's sleepy Old Street covers four blocks on Lingfeng Lu. There's not much to see by way of building design, but there are traditional industries that cannot be found elsewhere producing fishing implements, funereal and wedding accessories, and more. Walk through the vehicular passage in the brown building opposite Huáqiáo Dàxià (華僑大厦) at 12 Jiangbian Lu (江边路) and you'll see it.

🛏 Sleeping & Eating

Royal Classic Hotel   HOTEL **$$**
(皇家名典酒店; Huángjiā Míngdiǎn Jiǔdiàn; ☑ 867 7777; www.hjmd-hotel.com; 35 Dongmen Lu; 東門路35号; r ¥118-1288, ste ¥1888-2888) This glitzy Hong Kong–owned hotel has clean, quiet rooms, with wide, comfortable beds. Lifts can only be activated with guestroom card-keys, which makes it feel safe. The extravagant breakfast buffet (at ¥50 per person) in the revolving restaurant offers a good selection of local delicacies. Rates are often 30% to 50% of those posted.

★ **Dàbù Handmade Noodles**   NOODLES **$**
(大埔手工面馆; Dàbù Shǒugōng Miànguǎn; 15 Bingfang Dadao; noodles ¥4-15, soup ¥5; ⊙ 6.30am-2pm & 5pm-2am;) This neighbourhood shop whips up al dente Hakka tossed noodles (腌面; *yānmiàn*) and pig innards soup (三及第湯; *sānjídì tāng*), The strands also come stir-fried (炒面; *chǎomiàn*). Bus 4, which runs from Méizhōu train station, a 15-minute walk away, stops here. Disembark at Méiyuán Xīncūn (梅园新村). It's on your left.

Chéngdé Lóu Coiled Dragon House Restaurant   CHINESE, HAKKA **$**
(承德楼圍龍屋酒家; Chéngdélóu Wéilóngwū Jiǔjiā; ☑ 233 1315; Fuqi Lu; mains ¥33-120) From inside a mazelike 19th-century Hakka local, this atmospheric eatery serves local dishes such as salt-baked chicken (盐局鸡; *yánjú*

jī; ¥88/58) and pork braised with preserved vegetables (梅菜扣肉; *méicài kòuròu;* ¥48). The manager speaks English. A taxi here from Méizhōu centre costs ¥15.

🛈 Getting There & Away

AIR

Méizhōu's airport, 4km south of town, has flights to Guǎngzhōu (¥700, daily) and Hong Kong (¥1000, Mondays and Fridays).

BUS

Méizhōu has two bus stations: the **main bus station** (粤运汽车总站; Yuèyùn Qìchē Zǒngzhàn; ☑ 222 2427; Meizhou Dadao), north of the river, and **Jiāngnán bus station** (江南汽车站; Jiāngnán qìchēzhàn; ☑ 226 9568; Binfang Dadao) to the south. Most buses to Méizhōu drop you off at the former.

Cháozhōu ¥54, 2½ hours, two daily (10.40am and 3.30pm)

Cháyáng ¥25, three daily (5.45am, 7am and 11.10am)

Guǎngzhōu ¥100, five hours, 15 daily (7am to 10.30pm)

Hong Kong ¥200, eight hours, two daily (7.40am and 2.40pm)

Shàntóu ¥60, 2½ hours, 13 daily (8am to 5.20pm)

Shēnzhèn ¥100, six hours, five daily (8.30am, 10am, 11.20am, 1.40pm and 4.30pm)

Yǒngdìng ¥49, three hours, two daily (6am and 12.45pm)

TRAIN

The train station, south of town, has four daily trains to Guǎngzhōu (¥78 to ¥117, 12.12am, 8.40am, 3.25pm and 10.59pm) and three daily trains to Yǒngdìng (¥19 to ¥32, 12.01am, 2.41am and 1.52pm).

🛈 Getting Around

A taxi ride into Méizhōu town centre from the airport, 4km south, costs about ¥15.

Bus 6 links the airport and train station to both bus stations. Anywhere within the city by taxi should cost no more than ¥15.

Most sights are scattered in different villages, and almost inaccessible by public transport. It makes more sense to hire a taxi for a day. Expect to pay about ¥450.

Dàbù 大埔

Dàbù sits on the border with Fújiàn, in the easternmost part of Guǎngdōng, about 89km from downtown Méizhōu. It's encircled by mountains and rivers, which means beauti-ful natural scenery and nicely preserved old towns. You can stay in downtown Dàbù and make day trips to surrounding areas.

🍴 Sleeping & Eating

There are rooms for ¥80 upwards with air-con on Wanxiang Dadao (畹香大道), about 240m from the bus station.

Ruìjīn Hotel HOTEL $$$
(瑞锦酒店; Ruìjīn Jiǔdiàn; ☑ 518 5688; www.ruijin -hotel.com; 2nd St, Long Shan, Neihuan Xilu; 内环西路龙山二街; r ¥888-988, ste ¥1688-1988; ✱@🛜⊠) Large, plush rooms and an attractive swimming pool make this a great place to stay. Discounts are often available. The hotel is a 20-minute walk from Dàbù bus station (大埔汽车客运站, Dàbù Qìchē Kèyùn Zhàn). Turn left at the hotel entrance and walk several blocks up until you reach a T-junction, then left and you'll see the station.

Dàbù Gourmet Street HAKKA
(大埔美食街; Dàbù Měishí Jiē; Huliao Tongyen Lu; ⊙8am-5pm) Littered with tiny eateries, Huliao Tongyen Lu, built in the Qing dynasty, is known as Dàbù Gourmet Street. Comb it (it's only 330m) for Dàbù and Hakka snacks such as pancakes (薄饼; *báobǐng*) and bamboo-shoot dumplings (笋板; *sǔnbǎn*).

🛈 Getting There & Around

Méizhōu has buses to Dàbù from Jiāngnán bus station at 2.30pm and 4.30pm (¥22).

Buses head daily from Dàbù to the following:

Cháozhōu ¥67, three hours, 157km, one daily (8.10am)

Cháyáng ¥5, 30 minutes, two daily (5pm, 5.30pm)

Guǎngzhōu ¥233, 6½ hours, 535km, eight daily (7.30am, 8am, 8.40am, 9am, 1.10pm, 6.30pm, 7pm, 7.30pm)

Méizhōu ¥13, one hour, frequent

Shàntóu ¥78, three hours, 163km, one daily (7.40am)

Shēnzhèn ¥221, six hours, 505km, five daily (8.20am, 9am, 1.30pm, 2.50pm, 3.30pm)

Xiàmén ¥103, 4½ hours, 243km, one daily (6.40am)

Cháyáng Old Town 茶阳古镇

People still take long siestas in lazy Cháyáng (Cháyáng Gǔzhèn), 27km from downtown Dàbù County. Its old streets (老街; *lǎojiē*) with pillared arcades are nice to lose yourself in for a couple of hours.

Memorial Arch of the Father and Son Graduates
MONUMENT

(父子进士牌坊; FùzǐJìnshì Páifāng; Dàpu High School, Xueqian Jie; 学前街,大埔中学) This handsome granite edifice from 1610 stands before a school. The arch was set up by the Ming government to commemorate a father and son who both became successful candidates in the imperial exams.

Soviet Department Store Building
HISTORIC BUILDING

(百货大樓; Bǎihuò Dàlóu; Shengli Lu) This weather-beaten, three-storey building on Shengli Lu (胜利路) just opposite Cháyáng Guesthouse (茶陽賓館; Cháyáng Bīnguǎn) was a department store built in the 1950s with Soviet funds. Patches of yellow paint still cling onto its facade, and you can make out Mao-era slogans on its red pillars.

If you walk along the river and cross the bridge, then go straight, turn left and walk to the end of the road, you'll see the stunning Xuán Lú (旋盧) villa.

★ Xuán Villa
HISTORIC BUILDING

(旋庐; Xuánlú; 115 Dahua Lu; 大华路115号) Foreboding and beautiful Xuán Villa was built in 1936 by a wealthy Malaysian Chinese who was a member of a secret society tied to Sun Yatsen. Parts of the building doubled up as an air-raid shelter. If the owners let you in, you'll see crumbling but elegant staircases and sweeping balconies with views of tea fields.

ℹ️ Getting There & Around

Buses run from Cháyáng to Méizhōu every half hour from 7.10am to 6pm.

Bǎihóu Old Town

Scenic Bǎihóu (百侯), Dàbù's closest town to Méizhōu, is known for its Qing dynasty buildings. These were the stately residences and public spaces of the Yang (楊) family, a family known for the number of scholars and government officials it nurtured. Bǎihóu literally means 'a hundred noblemen'.

Buildings with a flamboyant hybrid style tend to cluster around the southern end, while ancestral halls and village houses are in the north. Between them are winding paths, peanut vines, longan and wampi trees, and a huge lily pond.

Hǎiyuán Building
HISTORIC BUILDING

An eye-catching early 20th-century mansion, the Hǎiyuán Inn (海源客栈, Hǎiyuán Kèzhàn) combines Southeast Asian features, Western details and the attributes of a hakka (走马楼; zǒumǎ lóu), a two-storey residence with a wide wooden corridor that keeps the rooms safe and dry.

Zhàoqìng Hall
HISTORIC BUILDING

(肇庆堂; Zhàoqìng Táng; admission ¥15; ⊙8.30am-noon, 2-5pm) Inhabited by the third and fourth generations of the founder, a pharmaceutical merchant, this balmy courtyard residence (c 1914) features stone, wood and ceramic carvings, and stained-glass windows from Italy. The stately two-storey structure in front of it was the study quarters of the younger members of the family.

Qīnán Villa
HISTORIC BUILDING

Lack of upkeep and old age (early 18th century) means Qīnán Villa (企南軒; Qīnán Xuān) looks a bit like a princeling-turned-pauper. The stone carvings around its elegant arches and the terraces fringed with urn-shaped balusters are now overgrown with black moss and weed. The villa was built as a study with 27 rooms in the early decades of the Qing dynasty.

ℹ️ Getting There & Around

All southbound buses from Dàbù pass through Bǎihóu (¥5). Tell the driver you want to get off at Bǎihóu Tourist Area (百侯旅游區; Bǎihóu Lǚyóu Qū). From Dàbù, it's 20 minutes (11km).

Huā'è Lóu
花萼楼

The 400-year-old 'house of calyx' (admission ¥10), 20km south of Méizhōu, is the largest circular earthen castle in Guǎngdōng. It comes complete with three rings and stone walls more than 1m thick. There's no public transport to Huā'è Lóu. A taxi from Dàbù costs ¥100 and takes about an hour.

Hǎinán

POP 8.9 MILLION

Best Beaches

➡ Sānyà Bay (p598)

➡ Yàlóng Bay (p599)

➡ Bó'áo (p596)

➡ Hòuhǎi (p599)

Best Activities

➡ Climb Wǔzhǐshān (p594) & Seven Fairy Mountain (p595)

➡ Cycle the Central Highlands (p593)

➡ Xīncūn fishing harbour (p601)

➡ Hǎinán Museum (p590)

➡ Hǎikǒu Volcanic Cluster Geopark (p592)

Why Go?

China's largest tropical island boasts all the balmy weather, coconut palms and gold-sand beaches you could ask for. Down at Sānyà it's see-and-be-seen on the boardwalks or escape altogether at some of Asia's top luxury resorts. Thatched huts and banana pancakes haven't popped up anywhere yet, but there's a whiff of hipness coming from the east coast beachside towns, and the budding surf scene is helping to spread the gospel of chill out.

Money is pouring into Hǎinán (海南) these days to ramp up the luxury quotient. You can cruise on the high-speed rail, but cycling is still the better way to get around. When you've had enough of a lathering on the coast, the cool central highlands are an ideal place to be on two wheels. The good roads, knockout mountain views, and concentration of Li and Miao, the island's first settlers, give the region an appealing distinction from the lowlands.

When to Go
Sānyà

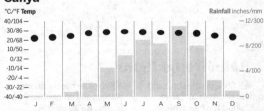

Apr–Oct Low season is hot, hot, hot but ideal for hotel bargains.

Nov–Mar Cool dry months are perfect for cycling under the blue South China sky.

Nov–Jan Winter winds blow in the island's best surfing season.

History

Until the economic boom of the last 30 years, Hăinán had been a backwater of the Chinese empire since the first Han settlements appeared on the coast almost 2000 years ago. Largely ignored by a series of dynasties, Hăinán was known as the 'tail of the dragon,' 'the gate of hell' and a place best used as a repository for occasional high-profile exiles such as the poet Su Dongpo and the official Hai Rui.

More recently, China's first communist cell was formed here in the 1920s, and the island was heavily bombarded and then occupied by the Japanese during WWII. Li and Han Chinese guerrillas waged an effective campaign to harass the Japanese forces but the retaliation was brutal – the Japanese executed a third of the island's male population.

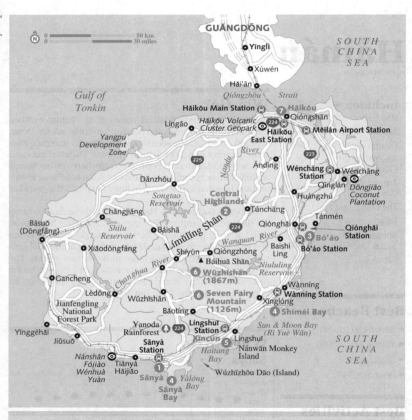

Hăinán Highlights

① Soak up the sun, sand and cocktails at **Sānyà**, China's top beach resort (p598)

② Cycle the **Central Highlands** (p593), home of the Li and Miao

③ Explore the traditional villages and empty beaches around **Bó'áo** (p596)

④ Surf China's best waves at **Sānyà Bay** (p598) and **Shímĕi Bay** (p598)

⑤ Wander a classic fishing port at **Xīncūn** (p601)

⑥ Climb **Wǔzhǐshān** (p594) and **Seven Fairy Mountain** (p595), the most famous peaks on Hăinán

⑦ Enjoy seafood at markets all over the island including **Bănqiáo Road Seafood Market** (p591) in Hăikŏu

Even today resentment over Japanese atrocities lingers among the younger generation.

In 1988 Hǎinán was taken away from Guǎngdōng and established as its own province and Special Economic Zone (SEZ). After years of fits and starts, development is now focused on turning tropical Hǎinán into an 'international tourism island' by 2020. What this really means, besides developing every beach, and building more golf courses and mega-transport projects (such as a high-speed rail service round the island, a cruise ship terminal and even a spaceport), is not entirely clear.

Climate

The weather on Hǎinán is largely warm in autumn and winter, and hot and humid in spring and summer. The mountains are always cooler than the coast, and the north is cooler than the south. Hǎinán is hit by at least one typhoon a year, usually between May and October.

Language

Hǎinánese is a broad term for the baker's dozen local dialects of Hǎinán Mǐn (it's known by many other names), most of which are also spoken in Guǎngdōng. While the Li and Miao can usually speak Mandarin, they prefer to use their own languages.

ℹ Getting Around

Getting around most of Hǎinán is both cheap and easy. Hǎikǒu and Sānyà are linked by three main highways: the eastern expressway along the coast (only 3½ hours by bus); the central and much slower highway via Wǔzhǐshān; and the less popular western expressway. The main roads are great, bus services comfortable and departures regular.

A high-speed rail system runs from Hǎikǒu to Sānyà along the east coast. Tickets cost only slightly more than buses, but most stations are not centrally located.

Hǎikǒu　　　　海口

📞 0898 / POP 2 MILLION

Hǎikǒu means 'Mouth of the Sea', and while sea trade remains relatively important, the buzzing provincial capital at the northern tip of Hǎinán is most notable for its booming construction. New and restarted projects are everywhere.

While poor in actual sights, Hǎikǒu makes a good base for exploring the north of the island. There are some decent beaches a short

bike or bus ride away, the air is fresh and clean (though worsening yearly because of traffic), and some visitors find themselves quite satisfied just hanging out here for a few days.

Travellers tend to stay around Hǎikǒu Park or north of the river on Hǎidiàn Island (海甸岛, Hǎidiàn Dǎo). These are both older, less flashy neighbourhoods (especially compared with the western sections of the city), but all your life-support systems, including banks, food and travel agents, can be found here.

To the northwest are the main railway station, port area and the city's beach zone. The main bus station and high-speed rail terminal are in the southeast of town. The airport is about 25km to the east.

◎ Sights & Activities

A few kilometres west of the city centre is a long stretch of sandy beaches. Take bus 37 (¥2) from Értóng Park and get off anywhere; alternatively, rent a bike in town. Cycling Hǎidiàn Island is also rewarding; look for news of the completion of a network of routes out to reservoirs and the Hǎikǒu Volcanic Cluster Geopark.

Hǎikǒu Old Town　　　　NEIGHBOURHOOD

(海口老街; Hǎikǒu Lǎo Jiē; Bo'ai Beilu) The streets around Bo'ai Beilu are a looking glass into Hǎikǒu's French colonial past, with cobblestone blocks of porticoed row houses – some restored, some charmingly decayed. Though still a work in progress, 'Old Town' aims to be a dining and shopping destination, and some cute cafes, bookshops, and markets hawking handicrafts and spices have popped up recently. Amateur photographers will delight in the atmosphere here, especially down the funky un-rehabbed alleys.

Hăikŏu

0 —— 500 m
0 —— 0.25 miles

Giant Bicycle (500m)

Hăikŏu

Hăinán Museum MUSEUM
(海南省博物馆; Hăinán Shěng Bówùguǎn; 68 Guoxing Dadao; ⊙9am-5pm Tue-Sun) FREE This modern colossus of a building should be your first stop when you arrive in Hăinán. The displays on ethnic minorities, as well as Hăinán's 20th-century history, which included fierce resistance against the Japanese and later Nationalists, are particularly informative (and in English, too!).

The museum is about 2km southeast of Hăikŏu Park, along the river. Buses 43 and 48 from downtown stop outside the museum. A taxi will cost around ¥30.

Five Officials Memorial Temple TEMPLE
(五公祠; Wǔgōng Cí; 169 Haifu Dadao; adult/child ¥20/17; ⊙8am-6pm) This atmospherically decaying Ming temple and surrounding gardens are dedicated to five officials who were banished to Hăinán in earlier times. Famous Song-dynasty poet, Su Dongpo, also banished to Hăinán, is commemorated here as well.

The temple is about 2km southeast of Hăikŏu Park. Grab a taxi for about ¥30.

🛏 Sleeping

Unlike in the more seasonal Sānyà, prices in Hăikŏu tend to be greatly discounted from the published rates pretty much year-round. Only during major holidays might you get a rude shock.

★**Hăikŏu Banana Youth Hostel** HOSTEL $
(海口巴纳纳国际青年旅舍; Hăikŏu Bānànà Qīngnián Lǚshè; ☑0898 6628 6780; www.haikouhostel.com; 3 Dong, 6 Bieshu Liyuan Xiaoqu, 21 Renmin Dadao; 海甸岛人民大道21号梨园小区6号别墅3栋; dm/s/tw/tr ¥50/90/130/160; ❄@✿) The digs of choice for international budget travellers, the simple, friendly Banana Hostel is tucked away down a quiet residential alley. Staff speak English, and amenities include laundry, internet and common areas, as well as a super-informative bulletin board and website.

Bicycle rentals range from day-trip beaters (per day ¥20) to solid Giant mountain bikes for multiday trips (per day ¥50; book in advance).

Hăinán Mínháng Bīnguǎn HOTEL $
(海南民航宾馆; Hăinán Civil Aviation Hotel; ☑0898 6650 6888; www.mhbghotel.com; 9 Haixiu Donglu; r from ¥190; ❄@) The hotel isn't setting any trends, but the inoffensive modern decor offers a cosy environment to unwind. There's an attached restaurant and the surrounding zone is loaded with cheap eateries. As a bonus, the airport shuttle bus (¥15) starts and ends here. Also known as the 'Green Hotel'.

Golden Sea View Hotel HOTEL $$
(黄金海景大酒店; Huángjīn Hǎijīng Dà Jiǔdiàn; ☑ 0898 6851 9988; www.goldenhotel.com.cn; 67 Binhai Dajie; r from ¥350) With discounts of 40% to 50%, rooms in this well-run three-

star hotel are priced similarly to those stuck deep in the city. The Sea View, however, sits across from a large park at the start of the beaches to the west of town. The hotel's revolving restaurant has excellent views over Hǎikǒu and the ocean, and is well regarded for its breakfast buffet.

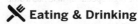 Eating & Drinking

A lot of evening eating is done in the refreshingly cool outdoors on practically every major street. Haixiu Donglu on the south side of Hǎikǒu Park is chock-a-block full of cheap food stalls and fast-food joints. On the corner of Haidian 3 Donglu and Renmin Dadao you'll find a stack of cafes, fruit stalls, supermarkets and restaurants with picture menus. Haidian 2 Donglu is one long row of barbecue stalls at night with tables set up from Renmin Dadao to Heping Beilu.

★ **Hǎikǒu Qílóu Snack Street** MARKET $
(海口骑楼小街; Hǎikǒu Qílóu Xiǎo Jiē; cnr Datong Lu & Jiefang Lu; snacks from ¥6) This marvellous colonial arcade contains dozens of snack shops surrounding a massive open interior. Buy a prepaid plastic card at the window on the right of the entrance, then use that to pay for your snacks – you can refund the unused amount later. Local treats on offer include coconut rice served in the shell, plates of cockles, and dumplings of all sorts.

On weekends and busy nights, expect opera and other traditional performances on the stage in the open atrium. There's plenty of seating.

Directly to the left of the Qílóu building, a traditional covered alley sells snacks (cash-only) like cumin-roasted corn and Muslim-style meat-stuffed pastries in a slightly less touristy setting.

Bǎnqiáo Road Seafood Market SEAFOOD, MARKET $$
(板桥路海鲜市场; Bǎnqiáo Lù Hǎixiān Shìchǎng; Banqiao Lu; 板桥路; meals per person from ¥50) For a fresh seafood dinner with lots of noise, smoke and toasting, head to the hectare of tables at the Bǎnqiáo Road Seafood Market, known island-wide. It's best to go with a group; prices average ¥50 per person (not including beer). A taxi to the market from downtown costs ¥15.

Banqiao Lu is about 3km south of the city centre.

Hépíng Road Bar Street BAR
(和平大道; Heping Beilu; ⏰ noon-late) Various (often short-lived) bars and open air pubs line Heping Road in Hǎidiàn Island, all of which tend to be more casual than the KTV bars found elsewhere on Hǎinán. Look for the highest concentration a few blocks north of the river.

ℹ️ Information

The annually published *Hǎinán Island Guide Map* (¥6) has a good city map of Hǎikǒu, which includes a map of all of Hǎinán Island on the back in addition to smaller maps of Sānyà and Bó'áo.
Xīnhuá Bookstore (新华书店; Xīnhuá Shūdiàn; 10 Jiefang Xilu; ⏰ 9am-10pm) has good maps if you are biking.

Many cafes around Guomao and Jinlong Lu have wi-fi.

Bank of China (中国银行; Zhōngguó Yínháng; Datong Lu) Changes money and travellers cheques. ATM outlets are plentiful around town.

HĂINÁN FARE

There is a huge variety of Chinese cuisine available in Hǎinán. Fresh fruit and vegies are available everywhere, and, unlike much of China, they are grown under blue skies and in red soil mostly free from industrial contamination. There are myriad seafood dishes available, but most of them use imported or locally farmed fish and crustaceans.

Don't forget to try Hǎinán's own famous four dishes.

Dōngshān mutton (东山羊; *dōngshān yáng*) A black-wool mountain goat fed camellias and orchids, and stewed, roasted or cooked in coconut milk, or used in soups.

Hélè crab (和乐蟹; *hélè xiè*) Juicy crab, usually steamed but also roasted, from Hélè near Wànnìng; it's best eaten in autumn.

Jiājī duck (加积鸭; *jiājī yā*) To-die-for roast duck from Jiājī (the alternative name for Qiónghǎi).

Wénchāng chicken (文昌鸡; *wénchāng jī*) Most famous of all and originally cooked up in coastal Wénchāng, this is succulent chicken raised on a diet of rice and peanuts.

❶ Getting There & Away

AIR

Hăikŏu's **Mĕilán Airport** (www.mlairport.com) is well connected to most of China's major cities, including Hong Kong and Macau, with international flights to Bangkok, Singapore, Kuala Lumpur and Taipei. Low-season one-way domestic fares are cheap. Destinations include Bĕijīng, Guăngzhōu and Shànghǎi.

BUS

Xiùyīng Harbour Station (海口秀英港客运站, Hăikŏu Xiùyīnggǎng Kèyùn Zhàn) is far to the west of town. To get here, catch bus 37 from Értóng Park. A taxi costs about ¥25 from downtown. Destinations include:

Guăngzhōu ¥290, 10 hours, hourly

Guìlín ¥280, 15 hours, hourly

Buses from the **south bus station** (汽车南站; 32 Nanhai Dadao), 3km south of downtown, go to:

Qióngzhōng ¥38, three hours via the central highway, hourly

Sānyà ¥80, 3½ hours, every 20 minutes

Wŭzhǐshān ¥80, four hours via the east highway, hourly

Buses from the **east bus station** (汽车东站; 148 Haifu Lu), 1.5km south of downtown, go to:

Qiónghǎi ¥30, 1½ hours, frequent

Sānyà ¥80, 3½ hours

Wénchāng ¥20, 1½ hours, frequent

TRAIN

Hăikŏu Railway Station, the main train station, is far west of the city. Bus 37 (¥2) connects the train station and Értóng Park. Bus 40 (¥2) connects the southern part of the city with the train station.

Trains to/from Guăngzhōu (hard/soft sleeper ¥192/296, 12 hours, five daily between 11.36am and 23.55pm) are shunted onto a ferry to cross the Qióngzhōu Strait. Buy tickets (¥5 service fee) at the train station or from the dedicated counter at **China Southern Airlines** (中国南方航空; Zhōngguó Nánfāng Hángkōng; 9 Haixiu Donglu).

HIGH-SPEED TRAIN

Running from Hăikŏu to Sānyà via the east coast, the new high-speed rail stops in Hăikŏu at the main train station (Hăikŏu Railway Station) to the west of the city, the east train station (Hăikŏu East Railway Station) and Mĕilán Airport. Note that many trains don't go all the way to Hăikŏu Railway Station. Services:

Qiónghǎi ¥45, one hour, irregular schedule

Sānyà ¥99, two hours, frequent

❶ Getting Around

TO/FROM THE AIRPORT

Mĕilán Airport is 25km southeast of the city centre. A shuttle bus (¥15, every 30 minutes) runs to/from Hăinán Mínháng Bīnguǎn in downtown. A taxi costs around ¥80 (negotiated price) to downtown. The high-speed rail also has a stop at the airport.

PUBLIC TRANSPORT

Hăikŏu's centre is easy to walk around. The bus system (¥1 to ¥2) is decent, though it often takes transfers to get around.

TAXI

Taxis charge ¥10 for the first 3km. They're easy to spot, but difficult to catch on large roads because of roadside barriers.

Around Hăikŏu

❷ Sights

Hăikŏu Volcanic Cluster Geopark   VOLCANO (雷琼世界地质公园; Léiqióng Shìjiè Dìzhì Gōngyuán; Shíshān Town; admission ¥60; ☺10am-5pm) While this geopark encompasses about 108 sq km of rural countryside, the main attraction here is a corny tourist park surrounding a (genuinely cool) extinct volcano cone. Make haste past the snack stands and gift kiosks to descend the stairs winding down into the lushly vegetated crater, which feels more like a cave. Then climb back up for luscious views of the countryside all the way to the sea.

The geopark entrance is about 18km west of Hăikŏu. To get here, first take a taxi to the T-intersection of Xiuying Xiaojie and Xiuying Dadao (秀英小街、秀英大道) and then catch one of the frequent minibuses (¥4, 30 minutes) to Shíshān County (石山镇, Shíshān Zhèn) from the bus stop on the far side of Xiuying Dadao. A taxi to the park costs ¥60.

Mĕi Shè Village   HISTORIC SITE (美社村; Mĕi Shè Cūn) Photogenic Mĕi Shè was built out of the rough grey volcanic stone so prevalent in this part of Hăinán. Wander the quiet back alleys and gawp at the castle-like five-storey gun tower in the centre of town. It was built in the 1920s to protect the village from bandits.

A taxi (about ¥60 from Hăikŏu) is the best way to get here, unless you've got a bike and a very good map. It's a 15-minute drive from the Hăikŏu Volcanic Cluster Geopark entrance.

CYCLING HĂINÁN

Hăinán is a great destination for recreational touring. You're rarely more than an hour from a village with food and water, and never more than a few hours from a town with a decent hotel. At the same time, you'll find most of your riding is out in nature or through pretty farming valleys, not urban sprawl. Preparation time for a tour can be minimal.

Some popular routes include the following:

Hăidiàn Island Plenty of fishing villages and rural landscapes and so close to Hăikŏu.

North Coast Ride alongside kilometre after kilometre of sand beaches and down side routes into the interior.

Wénchāng County Ride 100km out to Dōngjiāo Coconut Plantation and spend the night at a quiet beachside cabin. The next day head to Tónggŭ Lĭng, one of Hăinán's best undeveloped beaches.

The most popular multiday ride is the 250km journey from Hăikŏu to Wŭzhĭshān and on to Sānyà. The highway has a good shoulder most of the way, and allows for endless side trips up small country roads and stops in tiny villages. After a day riding through the lush Túnchāng County valley, the route climbs into some fine hill country around **Shíyùn** (什运). The village, 32km southwest of Qióngzhōng, sits on a grassy shelf above a river and is worth a look around. Local cyclists recommend the 42km side trip from here up a wooded canyon to **Báishā** (白沙). The major towns in this area are **Túnchāng** (屯昌) and **Qióngzhōng** (琼中), the latter a major settlement for the Miao.

After Shíyùn you can look forward to a long climb (at least 10km), followed by a long fast descent into Wŭzhĭshān. If you are continuing on to Sānyà, the road is one long, steep downhill after the turn-off to Băotíng.

If you're not bringing your own wheels, you can rent decent-quality mountain bikes at Hăikŏu Banana Youth Hostel (p590) for ¥50 a day. Check out the hostel's website for detailed information on cycling Hăinán. There's also a **Giant Bicycles** (☑6865 5598; www.hncycling.com; 26 Jinmao Xilu; 金贸西路26号; bike rentals per day ¥50-100) shop in Hăikŏu that does rentals. It's worth noting that people in Hăinán call bikes *dānchē*.

Dōngjiāo Coconut Plantation BEACH, VILLAGE (东郊椰林; Dōngjiāo Yēlín) This coconut farming community takes up a big chunk of Wénchāng County on the northeast coast. Cool, palm-lined lanes wind through traditional villages where locals harvest coconuts and snooze in hammocks. At the shore, kilometres of long (though somewhat scrubby and gnat-ridden) beaches hardly see a tourist all year long.

For a very intrepid solo traveller, a few days of biking through the plantation would be a fine adventure. For the rest of us, hiring a car to explore the area as a day trip from Hăinán is the best bet. Plan on packing your own food (though villagers would be happy to feed you a simple lunch if communication allows), or subsisting on coconuts.

From Hăikŏu's east train station catch a high-speed train to Wénchāng (¥30, 30 minutes, hourly). Then catch bus 6 (¥2) to the Xinhua Chu Dian stop (about five minutes' ride), cross the street and catch a bus on to Jiànhuáshān (建华山; ¥8.50), the last stop. The beach is just ahead through the gate

of the Hăinán Prima Resort, the area's only accommodation.

Central Highlands

☑ 0898

Hăinán's reputation rests on its tropical beaches, but for many travellers it's in this region of dark green mountains and terraced rice-growing valleys that they make genuine contact with the island's culture.

Until recently, Han Chinese had left almost no footprint here, and even today visible signs of Chinese culture, such as temples or shrines, are very rarely seen. Instead, the region is predominantly Li and Miao – minority ethnic groups who have lived a relatively primitive subsistence existence for most of their time on the island. Indeed, groups of Li living as hunter-gatherers were found in the mountainous interior of Hăinán as recently as the 1930s. Today, they are by far the poorest people on Hăinán.

Travelling in the region is easy, as a decent bus system links major and minor towns.

THE LI & MIAO

There are some 39 ethnic groups on Hăinán, of which four are the main minorities. These include the first settlers of the island, the Li and Miao (H'mong), who today are found mostly in the forested areas covering the Límǔlǐng Shān (Mother of the Lí Mountain) range that stretches down the centre of the island. The Li probably migrated to Hăinán from Fújiàn 3000 years ago and today they number more than one million.

Despite a long history of rebellion against the Chinese, the Li aided communist guerrillas on the island during the war with the Japanese. Perhaps for this reason the island's centre was made an 'autonomous' region in 1952 after the communist takeover. The region hereafter would be self-governing, giving the marginalised Li and Miao communities a degree of control. That situation, however, proved short-lived after newly empowered local politicians were done in for corruption and money-wasting.

Like the Li, the Miao spread from southern China and now can be found across northern Vietnam, Laos and Thailand. There are some 60,000 Miao living on Hăinán today, occupying some of the most rugged terrain on the island.

Most buses from Hăikŏu reach Wǔzhǐshān in a few hours via the east coast highway. If you want to ply the central highway, head first to Qióngzhōng and from there catch a bus onward to Wǔzhǐshān. Cycling is also a great way to get around this region.

Wǔzhǐshān City (Tōngshí)
五指山市（通什）

Once called Tōngzhá or Tōngshí, Wǔzhǐshān Shì was renamed after the famous nearby mountain, the highest point on the island and a symbol of Hăinán. Though the size of a large town, Wǔzhǐshān is actually China's smallest city, having been given such status when it became the capital of the short-lived Li and Miao Autonomous Prefecture back in the 1980s.

Most travellers here are heading out to climb the mountain, or using the town as a base for exploring the region. There are several ATMs in Wǔzhǐshān, so get cash before heading out of town.

🛏 Sleeping & Eating

There are cheap restaurants all around the bus station area (50 Haiyu Beilu), as well as countless fruit stalls, bakeries and cafes. Barbecue stalls are set up in the evenings all around town. Off Buxing Jie, the wide riverside promenade with more than 1km of old spreading banyan trees, sit rows of *lǎobà chá* (places selling coffee and snacks), teahouses and barbecue joints.

Hóngyè Hotel HOTEL $
(鸿业大酒店; Hóngyè Dàjiǔdiàn; ☑ 3862 1111; 1 Nonglin Lu; 农林路; r from ¥135) Convenient to the bus station (just turn left out of the station and walk to the traffic circle, then turn right), this newish modern business hotel has clean, comfortable rooms at excellent price points. No English.

Zhèngzōng Lánzhōu Lāmiàn NOODLES $
(正宗兰州拉面; Authentic Lanzhou Noodles; Haiyu Lu; 海榆路; dishes ¥7-15; ⊙ 6.30am-10pm) Across from the bus station, this Hui Muslim restaurant sells a wide range of cheap but excellent noodle and lamb dishes. Try the *gānbànmiàn* (干伴面; ¥8), a kind of stir-fried spaghetti bolognaise with hand-pulled noodles.

ℹ Getting There & Away

The bus station is on the town's main thoroughfare, on the northeast side of the river. Buses from Wǔzhǐshān include the following:

Bǎotíng ¥9, 40 minutes, hourly
Hăikŏu ¥90, four hours, seven daily
Qióngzhōng ¥30, two hours, hourly
Sānyà ¥23, 1½ hours, frequent
Shuǐmǎn ¥8, one hour, hourly

Around Wǔzhǐshān City

Wǔzhǐshān (Five Finger Mountain) 五指山

The mountain (五指山; Five Finger Mountain; admission ¥50; ⊙ 24hr) after which Wǔzhǐshān is named rises 1867m out of the centre of Hăinán in a reserve 30km northeast of the city. As the highest peak in the land, it's naturally steeped in local lore: the five peaks, for example, are said to represent the Li people's five most powerful gods. Despite the name, however, from most angles the summit looks like a single volcanic peak or a cleft hoof. It's a great area for hiking. A good time to visit is on the third day of the third month of the lunar calendar, when lots of Miao people gather for an annual festival.

The reserve is the source of the Wànquán (万泉河) and Chānghuà (昌化江) Rivers and protects a mixed forest containing 6.5% of all vascular plant species in China. It's a rich (though threatened) ecosystem and receives the highest rainfall in Hǎinán. Average humidity is more than 90% and the mountaintop is often shrouded in fog and mist.

It's pretty much an all-day event to get out here and climb the mountain, so leave as early as possible if you hope to enjoy clear views from the peak. Most people can reach the top of the first finger (the second is highest) in three hours. The path is clear but very steep and includes a number of ladder climbs further up. Coming down is not much faster than going up, so give yourself six to eight hours.

Wǔzhǐshān sits about 4km from the village of Shuǐmǎn (水满). There is no fixed schedule to Shuǐmǎn but buses (¥8, one hour, 35km) run about every hour. In Wǔzhǐshān, buy your ticket on the bus, which leaves across the street from the station front. Make sure to get a bus going to Shuǐmǎn via Nánshèng.

In Shuǐmǎn, motorcycle taxis will take you the remaining 4km for ¥15. The last bus back to Wǔzhǐshān leaves Shuǐmǎn around 6pm.

Qī Xiān Lǐng (Seven Fairy Mountain)　七仙岭

About 39km southeast of Wǔzhǐshān lies the small and conspicuously orderly Li town of Bǎotíng (保亭). While that orderliness may strike you as noteworthy after a few weeks spent travelling in China, the main reason to come here is to climb the 1126m Seven Fairy Mountain (七仙岭温泉国家森林公园; Qī Xiān Lǐng Wēnquán Guójiā Sēnlín Gōngyuán; admission ¥48), comprising an eye-catching ridge of jagged spearlike crags. The area is perhaps more famous among Chinese, however, for the hot-spring resorts popping up in the tropical forest.

The mountain entrance and hot springs area are 9km off the main road from Bǎotíng in what is ostensibly now a national hot springs and forest park. Tickets (¥42) to climb the Seven Fairy Mountain can be purchased at the park office at the start of the 2.4km long trail, though at the time of writing the park administration was in flux and admission was free. It's three hours to the top and back along a stepped path through a dense, healthy rainforest buzzing with bird and insect life. The final 100m climb to the peak runs up a pitted slope with chains and railings in place to aid your near-vertical climb. The views from the top are worth the effort.

There are frequent buses to Bǎotíng from Wǔzhǐshān (¥9, 40 minutes) and also Sānyà (¥22, 1½ hours). From Bǎotíng's bus station, catch a motorcycle (¥30) to the national park entrance. Make sure not to catch a motorcycle with a side car as they lack the power to make it the last 4km from the hot springs area up to the trailhead.

🛏 Sleeping

Narada Resort　RESORT $$$
(君澜度假酒店; Jūnlán Dùjià Jiǔdiàn; ☑0898 8388 8888; www.hainanparadise.com; Qīxiānlíng Hot Springs National Forest Park; r from ¥617) At the foot of Seven Fairy Mountain, the Narada is an elegant surprise in the middle of the peaceful (though increasingly developed) rainforest. The 222 bright, airy rooms are done up in wood with ethnic minority art; the manicured grounds drip with fruit trees. Most guests come to soak in the many hot tubs, some spiked with different healing herbs and teas.

The East Coast

☑0898

Hǎinán's east coast is a series of spectacular palm-lined beaches, long bays and headlands most of which are, unfortunately, not usually visible from the main roads, not even at bicycle level. With the best beaches developed or being developed, there is little reason to make a special trip out here (to Bó'áo being the exception) unless you are surfing or wish to stay at a resort. Biking or motorcycling is another story, however, as there are endless small villages and rural roads to explore and even a few near-deserted bays.

In the past, the east coast was the centre of Han settlement. If you are coming from the highlands you will start to notice temples, gravesites, shrines and other signs of Chinese culture dotting the landscape.

Bó'áo 博鳌

This attractive little coastal town at the confluence of three rivers is famous as the site of the Bó'áo Forum for Asia (BFA), an annual April meet-up of top-level officials, academics and economists exclusively from the Asia region. For cyclists, Bó'áo is a natural stop along the coast, offering good accommodation and food. For all travellers, it's an unpretentious little beach town (with a usually deserted beach), surrounded by some of the prettiest countryside on Hăinán.

Like much of Hăinán, or China for that matter, during the past few years Bó'áo has been under the spell of the construction fairy, and in the north of town luxury villas and resorts continue to pop up. Officially Bó'áo is starting to cover a large area, but the 'downtown' blocks, where most travellers both stay and eat are tiny, in essence being two streets that intersect at a T-junction: Haibin Lu (海滨路) runs north–south and Zhaobo Lu (朝博路) runs east–west. The beach is a five-minute walk from here.

Avoid planning a trip to Bó'áo either during the forum or the week before as the town is pretty much closed off under the scrutiny of high-level security (there are even warships in the harbour).

◉ Sights & Activities

Despite hosting the BFA every year, and despite over-construction giving parts of town the look of a small Dubai, Bó'áo is still a rather rural place. Even a few blocks from the main junction are small villages of stone and brick buildings where locals dry rice in the middle of the lanes, and burn incense in small shrines to their local folk deities. Some good examples are **Dà Lù Pō Village** (大路坡村; Dà Lù Pō Cūn) and **Nánqiáng Village** (南强村; Nánqiáng Cūn) off the main road about 2km west of the downtown junction. About 20km northeast of Bó'áo look for the little fishing village of **Tánmén** (潭门), where the local multicoloured wooden junks are made and repaired.

Bó'áo Beach   BEACH
Bó'áo's beach is a few hundred metres east of the main road. Head south down Haibin Lu, turn left at the Jinjiang Hot Spring Hotel and follow the road as it swings right to drop you off at a Chinese temple. The river hits the sea here and a long thin sandbar at the mouth is (for very dubious reasons – go ahead and ask the locals) a popular place to boat out to.

If you plan to swim, head at least 500m north to avoid dangerous currents.

Cài Family Former Residence   HISTORIC SITE
(蔡家宅; Càijiā Zhái) For a rewarding half-day trip, grab a bike, or rent a motorcycle taxi (¥50), and head to this sprawling old mansion built in 1934 by several brothers who made their fortune in the Indonesian rubber industry. The building was abandoned in 1937 after the Japanese invaded Hăinán, and later became a guerrilla outpost for resistance fighters. In 2006 it was declared a heritage site and these days you can wander around inside for a look if the caretaker is about.

To reach the house, head west out of town and when the road ends at a junction turn left (south) and cross two long bridges. Head right after crossing the second bridge at the English sign. In a couple of blocks stay left and enjoy a sumptuous ride through green fields and collections of handsome old and new houses alongside the road. It's about 5km from town.

Bó'áo Temple   BUDDHIST MONASTERY
(东方文化苑; Dōngfāng Wénhuàyuàn) This modern Buddhist temple complex is not being maintained well, but it's still worth a visit to see the enormous statue of the many-armed and many-headed Guanyin, the stunning pagoda, and the views over the delta which show just how pretty and rural Bó'áo can still be.

A motorcycle taxi costs ¥10 from the centre of Bó'áo. You can easily walk the 3km back to town and take in some of the traditional villages along the way.

🛏 Sleeping

Měiwénměiyă International
Youth Hostel   HOSTEL $
(美文美雅青年旅社; Měiwén Měiyǎ Qīngnián Lǚshè; ☎ 0898 3222 7222; Měiyǎ Village, Bó'áo Town, Qionghai; 琼海市博鳌镇美雅村; dm ¥30) This bamboo-shrouded hamlet a stone's throw from downtown Bó'áo is trying to make a go of being an 'ecovillage'. The very rustic set-up at this hostel includes spartan dorms with bunk beds and mosquito nets, and a spot for camping. Don't expect to see any other travellers unless there's a group cycling trip passing through.

Bó'áo Golden Coast Hot Spring Hotel
RESORT $$$

(琼海博鳌金海岸温泉大酒店; Qiónghǎi Bó'áo Jīnhǎi'àn Wēnquán Dàjiǔdiàn; ☑0898 6277 8888; 8 Jinhai'an Dadao, Bó'áo; 博鳌金海岸大道8号; r from $450) One of the more classically resort-y options in town, this sprawling complex has more than 300 rooms, an enormous pool, manicured lawns, and several restaurants and bars. In the off-season (most of the year), it's great value.

✗ Eating

Because of its international status as the site of the BFA, the town has a good range of Chinese restaurants dedicated to regional cuisine (Hui Muslim, Húnán and Sìchuān are just the start) as well as plenty of barbe-cue stalls that set up in the evenings. You'll see English signs out the front and even some English or picture menus within. On the main streets there are grocery stores, and abundant fruit stands.

Around 4pm each day head north about 150m from the main intersection on Haibin Lu and look for stalls on either side of the road near the Hainan Bank selling succulent Jiājī duck (加积鸭; *Jiājī yā*; ¥10 for a leg), a Hǎinán speciality. Don't be tardy as it sells out quickly.

Colourful Noodles
VEGETARIAN, NOODLES $

(七彩面馆; Qīcǎi Miànguǎn; Zhaobo Lu; dishes ¥13-15; ⊘8am-late; ☑) Though a few meat dishes are on offer at this warm family-run place, it's otherwise a true vegetarian set-up serving vegie-flavoured noodle dishes, as well as dumplings, fresh fruit and juices. To get here, head west along Zhaobo Lu almost to the end of the two-storey row of white-washed buildings.

★ Sea Story
SEAFOOD, CAFE $$

(海的故事; Hǎide Gùshì; dishes ¥18-38; ⊘9.30am-1am; ☎) The ocean-facing Sea Story has an open driftwood frame with a funky beachcomber design: an old wood fishing junk even sits as the centrepiece inside the lobby. Outside, the breezy deck is an ideal spot for cocktails or an extended lunch or dinner. Loud music, karaoke and other in-trusive noises or activities are banned. Sea Story is about 1km north from the temple along the seaside lane.

Áozhuāng Hǎixiān Chéng
SEAFOOD $$

(熬庄海鲜城; dishes ¥60; ⊘6pm-late) For seafood, head north out of town to this col-lection of seaside cafes, which are famous across the island. Just choose and then point to what you want cooked up but make sure to ask the price before sitting down. Restau-rants open around 9.30am and close when the last customers leave. You can walk here on the main road, or better yet along the seaside lane starting at the Matsu Temple, in about 30 minutes.

🍷 Drinking & Nightlife

The beach road leading north from down-town has been redeveloped into a 'Seaside Bar Street' lined with spanking-new wine bars and cafes. Unless it's BFA season, you'll probably have the views to yourself.

★ Lǎo Wood Coffee Rest Area
CAFE

(老房子; Lǎo Fángzi; 61 Haibin Lu; drinks from ¥18; ⊘9am-2am; ☎) The owner of this cafe, a local dancer and art administrator, literally had an old traditional stone house taken apart and reassembled on Bó'áo's coastal street to make his dream of opening a stylish cafe come true. The inside is chock-full of antiques and *objets d'art*, while in front is a sculpture-filled garden dotted with cafe tables.

ℹ Information

You can buy high-speed train tickets from **Yuantong International Travel Agency** (64 Haibin Lu; ⊘8am-10pm) about 200m north of the main intersection across from an ABC Bank. In the same area is a **Bank of China** (中国银行, Zhōngguó Yínháng) with an ATM. A decent map

---

of the Bó'áo area can be found at the bottom of the general *Hăinán Island Guide Map*.

❶ Getting There & Away

HIGH-SPEED TRAIN

The nearest station to Bó'áo is actually Qiónghăi and from there you'll need to catch a taxi (¥40) the rest of the way. Alternatively, catch bus 6 or 7 outside the train station to Qiónghăi East Bus Station (琼海东站) and then take a minibus the rest of the way (see p598).

Hăikŏu ¥45, one hour, hourly

Sānyà ¥53, one hour, hourly

BUS

From Hăikŏu's east bus station catch a bus to the main station in Qiónghăi (琼海; ¥26, 1½ hours, 102km) then cross the street to the Kentucky Fried Chicken side, and look for the bus stop just down the road to the left. Catch minibus 2 to Bó'áo (¥4, 30 minutes, frequent). Passengers get dropped off at the main junction in Bó'áo.

Shímĕi Bay & Sun & Moon Bay
石梅湾、日月湾

Shímĕi Bay (Shímĕi Wān) and Sun and Moon Bay (Rì Yuè Wān) are among the most stunning stretches of coastline on Hăinán. Development of major resorts is proceeding apace but the beaches are still open to the public and offer some of China's best surfing waves, especially from November to January. Some hostels and hotels in Sānyà offer day trips to the bays and you can ride out to them if you are biking the east coast.

Sānyà   三亚

☑ 0898 / POP 685,400

China's premier beach community claims to be the 'Hawaii of China', but 'Moscow on the South China Sea' is more like it. The modern, hyper-developed resort city has such a steady influx of Russian vacationers these days that almost all signs are in Cyrillic as well as Chinese. Middle-class Chinese families are increasingly drawn to Sānyà's golden shores as well, which means the beaches are just as full at night as they are during the day (due to the Chinese aversion to sunburn).

While the full 40km or so of coastline dedicated to tourism is usually referred to as Sānyà, the region is actually made up of three distinct zones. Sānyà Bay is home to the bustling city centre and a long stretch of beach and hotels aimed at locals and mainland holidaymakers. Busy, cheerfully tacky Dàdōnghăi Bay, about 3km southeast, beyond the Lùhuítóu Peninsula, is where most Western travellers stay. A further 15km east, at exclusive Yàlóng Bay, the beach is first-rate, as is the line of plush international resorts.

You'll find the bus station in the Sānyà Bay area on Jiefang Lu, the main drag. This road morphs into Yuya Lu as it heads into Dàdōnghăi Bay and Yàlóng Bay.

❂ Sights & Activities

Unsurprisingly for a beach resort, the vast majority of things to see and do revolve around sand, sea, shopping and after-hours entertainment. Strolling along the river fronts is pleasant in the cool evenings. Banyan trees shade the boulevards, healthy-looking mangroves line the shore, and a modern glitzy skyline dominates the background.

If you want to scuba or snorkel, May to August, before typhoon season, is the best time though locals will tell you honestly that there is not that much to see in the water. Surfing is possible year-round if you alternate between Dàdōnghăi, Hòuhăi and nearby Sun and Moon Bay.

Be aware that although beaches often have lifeguards they may not be properly trained.

Sānyà Bay   BEACH

(三亚湾; Sānyà Wān) The long sandy strip off the city centre at Sānyà Bay is the most relaxed of the three main beaches, where you'll find crowds of mostly mainland Chinese tourists kicking back, laughing, playing and having a beachy old time. In little covered areas locals play music, sing, engage in conspiracy, write characters in the sand, and so on. There's a long pathway for strolling in the cool evenings, and if the tide is out a little you can walk on the sand for many kilometres. In the evenings it's fun to watch the lights on Phoenix Island (the awesome cruise-ship terminal) turn on.

Dàdōnghăi Bay   BEACH

(大东海湾; Dàdōnghăi Wān) Dàdōnghăi Bay sports a wider beach than Sānyà and has a shaded boardwalk running along most of its length. The setting, in a deep blue bay with rocky headlands, is simply gorgeous but it does get busy here. At night, half the crowd

Dàdōnghǎi (Sānyà)

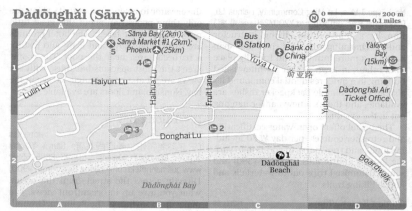

is knocking back beers and eating crabs at the boardwalk restaurants, while the other half is still bobbing in the sea under the light of the moon.

Yàlóng Bay   BEACH

(亚龙湾; Yàlóng Wān; Asian Dragon Bay; ⊙6.30am-6.30pm) Yàlóng Bay is more attractive and less crowded than Sānyà's other beaches, though with fewer shops and vendors budgeters might want to bring their own food and water. It offers a wide range of activities, including jet-skiing, banana boats, snorkelling and diving.

China's beaches are theoretically open to everyone but at Yàlóng Bay there can be a quasi-official fee if you're not staying at one of the beachfront resorts. To avoid any sporadically enforced, quasi-official beach entry fees, walk through one of the hotels rather than entering the beach from the main square. No one will bother you.

Hòuhǎi Beach   BEACH

(后海) Hòuhǎi, a crescent-shaped sandy beach about 45 minutes northeast out of Dàdōnghǎi, is popular with those looking to get away from the crowds (though ironically it lies in the southern reach of Hǎitáng Bay where the scale of development must be believed). Sānyà-based hostels take people here to surf and scuba while Chinese tourists are shuttled to the pier for a boat ride out to Wúzhīzhōu Island (蜈支洲岛).

Bus 28 from the main road in Dàdōnghǎi (¥11) takes you to the beach. There's a small village here with plenty of small restaurants and fruit stands.

Dàdōnghǎi (Sānyà)

◉ Sights

1 Dàdōnghǎi Bay................................C2

⬤ Sleeping

2 Golden Beach Villa.........................C2
3 Resort Intime..................................B2
4 Sānyà Backpackers........................B1

✖ Eating

5 Casa Mia Italian Restaurant..........B1

Sānyà Market #1   MARKET

(Jiefang Lu, Sānyà; ⊙11am-2am) Sānyà's most popular market practically writhes with life – vendors hawking cheap jewellery, frozen fruit treats and women's underwear, teenage tourists jostling to play rickety arcade games, old women pushing through the crowds with pails of crabs. Things really heat up after dark.

🛏 Sleeping

A glut of hotel rooms makes even luxury resorts affordable in Sānyà. Dàdōnghǎi Bay is the place to head for midrange and budget lodgings catering to the international set. The top-end resorts are off the beach at Yàlóng Bay, in a private area of palm-lined roads and landscaped grounds. Outside peak periods 30% to 60% discounts are common everywhere.

🏠 Dàdōnghǎi Bay

★ Sānyà Backpackers   HOSTEL **$**

(三亚背包度假屋; Sānyà Bēibāo Dùjià Wū; ☎0898 8821 3963; www.sanyabackpackers.com;

No 1 Type 1 Villa, Lu Ming Community, Haihua Lu, Dàdōnghǎi Bay; dm ¥75, s/d ¥200/240; ❇@🛜) Run by a Singaporean diving instructor and his charming wife, this spick-and-span hostel is a more intimate and friendly place than others in town. Set in a whitewashed building in a quiet residential compound it's also an oasis. Simple backpacker dishes are available, and there's a new bar for hanging out in the evenings.

The hostel offers open-water certification and refresher courses (per day ¥500 including lunch and transport), in addition to surfing lessons and rentals (per day ¥380) and some customised trips out to waterfalls and jungle hiking trails.

Golden Beach Villa — HOTEL $$
(金沙滩海景度假别墅; Jīn Shātān Hǎijǐng Dùjià Biéshù; ☑ 0898 8821 2220; www.jinshatan888.com; 21 Haihua Lu; r from ¥360; ❇) Despite the address, the front office and the suites are actually on Donghai Lu facing the beach. Rooms, which are enclosed in a walled-off garden, face the sea, and the upper floors have excellent views. Despite being so close to the seaside action this is a fairly quiet part of Dàdōnghǎi.

Resort Intime — RESORT $$$
(湘投银泰度假酒店; Xiāngtóu Yíntài Dùjià Jiǔdiàn; ☑ 0898 8821 0888; www.resortintime.com; Dàdōnghǎi Bay; r from ¥768; 🚳❇@🖥) It feels a bit like you are entering a busy bus terminal when you walk in the lobby and head up the elevator to reception, but that's about the only thing pedestrian about this great little resort right by the beach. The hotel grounds are surprisingly large and leafy, and feature a barbecue area near the pool. The rooms aren't the most spacious but those with sea views are set at a perfect angle to take in the bay. Nonsmoking floors are available.

Yàlóng Bay

Hotel Pullman — HOTEL $$$
(三亚湾海居铂尔曼度假酒店; Sānyà Wānhǎi Jūbó'ěr Màndùjià Jiǔdiàn; ☑ 0898 8855 5588; www.pullmanhotels.com; Yàlóng Bay; r from ¥900) Directly across the street from the ocean, what you give up in oceanfront views, you make up in savings at the Pullman. Ground-floor rooms have 'swim up' entrances to the pool, which surrounds an emerald interior courtyard. Kids will dig the water-slide area. Don't expect five-star luxury, just solid mid-range value and comfort.

Ritz-Carlton — RESORT $$$
(☑ 0898 8898 8888; www.ritzcarlton.com; Yàlóng Bay; r from ¥1800) While some of Yàlóng Bay's palatial resorts can feel a bit ghost town-y due to Sānyà's overbuilding, the Ritz is always abuzz. Well-heeled matrons sip tea on the grand patio, princelings splash down water slides in the kids' pool, and young couples lie on the wide, sugar-white beach. Rooms are large and airy, all white linen and elegant mahogany.

HITTING THE WAVES ON HĀINÁN

Surfing is slowly gaining a following in China, and Hǎinán is without question the centre of that budding scene. While the majority of people out on the waters are still Westerners, the number of Chinese trying the sport grows each year. Conditions are never going to make this the next Indonesia, but every level, from beginner to advanced, can find suitable waves. In recognition of the growing interest, two annual competitions are now held each year in the Shímǎi Bay and Sun and Moon Bay area: the **Hǎinán Surf Open**, in November, organised by Brendon Sheradon's **Surfing Hǎinán** (冲浪海南; Chōnglàng Hǎinán; www.surfinghainan.com); and the **Hǎinán Classic**, in January, sponsored by ASP (the Association of Surfing Professionals).

If you want to try your hand at the sport, Dàdōnghǎi and Hòuhǎi get decent waves from May to September and are suitable for absolute novices (especially quiet Hòuhǎi). Shímǎi Bay and Sun and Moon Bay are prime from November to January but it's possible to surf all year. With up to five breaks, the area is suitable for all levels; advanced surfers can try their luck on the Ghost Hotel waves. Unlike further south, Shímǎi Bay and Sun and Moon Bay get a bit chilly and overcast in the winter months, so light wetsuits are recommended.

You can find rentals and basic lessons in Sānyà at Sānyà Backpackers (p599), but if you want professional instruction contact Surfing Hǎinán, which offers two-hour lessons for ¥400 and rentals for ¥100 per day. It also has wetsuits for rent at ¥50 per day.

WORTH A TRIP

COLOURFUL FISHING PORT OF XĪNCŪN

This classic south seas fishing port (新村; Xīncūn) is one of the most authentic, and authentically picturesque, destinations on Hăinán. Among the hubbub, clutter, filth and flotsam of a typical fishing port float hundreds of painted wooden ships in a deep blue tropical bay ringed with emerald green hills. Fish dry on the docks, women weave nets, men weld old scraps of metal together, and a whole community thrives, including the hundreds of families who live on permanent floating houseboats across the bay.

Most people come to this area simply to see the rather dull **Nánwān Monkey Islet** (南湾猴岛, Nánwān Hóudǎo) across the bay and reached by China's longest **gondola** (return incl admission ¥163; ⊘8am-4.50pm, last gondola 4.20pm). Some 1000 macaque monkeys (*Macaca mulatta*) live on the hilly islet, and while most of the area is now off limits to tourists, monkeys are still made to perform for visitors in a depressing spectacle of chains, whips and too-small cages.

If you just want to see the monkeys and ride the gondola the best way is to go on a tour from Sānyà. Otherwise, to visit the fishing port, catch a bus 79km from Sānyà to Língshuǐ (陵水; ¥20, 1½ hours, hourly). In Língshuǐ, after leaving the station's main exit, cross the road and head right. Walk a few blocks and catch a minibus in front of the Bank of China to Xīncūn (¥3, 40 minutes). In Xīncūn, catch a motorcycle taxi or walk the 1km to the harbour.

✖ Eating

The entire beachfront at Dàdōnghǎi is one long strip of restaurants, bars and cafes, most of which are overpriced and not terribly good, even if the overall atmosphere is cool, shady and scenic. At night, Haihua Lu is lined with restaurants featuring outdoor seating for barbecue and seafood.

When ordering seafood, be sure to settle on price beforehand – Sānyà has had some fairly infamous restaurant scams.

Yingjie Eatery CHINESE $
(147 Xinmin Lu; dishes from ¥40; ⊘noon-10pm) Buy live seafood at the nearby market and have it cooked up fresh with garlic, soy sauce or whatever you desire at this friendly little local eatery in Sānyà town. There's very little English spoken, so plan on either bringing a friend to translate or doing a lot of pointing.

★**Casa Mia Italian Restaurant** ITALIAN $$
(卡萨米亚意大利餐厅; Kǎsà Mǐyà Yìdàlì Cāntīng; Resort Intime, Dàdōnghǎi; mains ¥48-100; 🕿) A jaded traveller might pooh-pooh the thought of finding top-notch Italian in a Chinese resort town. They'd be wrong. Casa Mia has truly divine pizzas, pastas (try the special seafood linguine) and classics like veal scallopini. The inside dining area is a bit cramped and bright, so choose to sit outside by the fountain. The wine list is nothing to sneeze at either.

Baan Rim Nam Antara THAI $$
(🗗 0898 8888 5088; http://sanya.anantara.com; Anantara Sanya Resort, Sānyà Bay; dishes ¥98-268) Dine on Thai classics like curried crab, green papaya salad and basil pork at this hushed and elegant restaurant in the Antara, a spa-like resort all done up in mirrors and dark wood. Service is extremely friendly. If it's not too hot, opt to sit on the patio.

🍷 Drinking & Nightlife

Most of the after-hours fun is in Sānyà and Dàdōnghǎi Bay. There's a bar and karaoke TV (KTV) street on Yuya Lu near the river.

★**Dolphin Sports Bar & Grill** PUB
(🗗 0898 8821 5700; www.sanyadolphin.com; 99 Yuya Lu, Dàdōnghǎi; ⊘11am-2am) International tourists and expats mingle with locals at this always-packed Western-style pub. Wash down a (very good) cheeseburger with a pint while watching football on the multiple TVs, or wait until after 10pm, when the live music starts up and the crowd really gets rolling. Friendly servers speak impeccable English.

Club M2 NIGHTCLUB
(🗗 0898 7685 8711; www.clubmj.cn; Times Coast Bar Street; Jiu Ba Jie; ⊘8pm-3am) You've got to dress the part to get into M2, one of the swankier clubs on Sānyà's bar row – think lots of hair gel/high heels/skinny suits/mini-dresses. Chinese big shots wheel and deal by the bar, while the younger crowd dances to ear-splitting EDM.

ℹ Information

There is the full gamut of internet cafes (Chinese ID required), banks, travel agencies etc in Sānyà city as well as Dàdōnghǎi Bay. Wi-fi is widely available in restaurants and cafes.

Bank of China (中国银行; Zhōngguó Yínháng; Yuya Lu, Dàdōnghǎi; ⊙9am-5pm) Changes travellers cheques and has an ATM.

ℹ Getting There & Away

AIR

Sānyà's **Phoenix Airport** (www.sanyaairport. com) has international flights to Singapore, Hong Kong, Malaysia, Thailand, Taiwan and Japan, plus Běijīng, Guǎngzhōu and Shànghǎi.

BUS

Frequent buses and minibuses to most parts of Hǎinán depart from the **long-distance bus station** (三亚汽车站; Sānyà Qìchēzhàn; Jiefang Lu; 解放路), in busy central Sānyà.

Bǎotíng ¥25, 1½ hours, hourly

Hǎikǒu ¥80, 3½ hours, regular services

Língshuǐ ¥20, 1½ hours, hourly

Wànníng ¥30, two hours, hourly

Wǔzhǐshān ¥25, two hours, regular services

HIGH-SPEED TRAIN

Tickets can be purchased in Dàdōnghǎi from the **air ticket office** (蓝色海航空售票中心; Yuya Lu) two bus stops east of Summer Mall (the stop is called Bayi Zhongxue). You can also order tickets online (at least a week in advance) from **Apple Travel** (www.appletravel .cn/china-trains).

Hǎikǒu ¥99, two hours, frequent

Qiónghǎi ¥49, one hour, hourly

ℹ Getting Around

Phoenix Airport is 25km from Dàdōnghǎi Bay. Shuttle bus 8 (¥5, one hour) leaves for the airport from Yuya Lu. A taxi costs ¥60 to ¥70. The high-speed train station is far out of town. Bus 4 (¥1) runs there from Dàdōnghǎi but takes over an hour. A taxi will cost ¥40 for a 20-minute ride.

Buses 2 and 8 (¥1, frequent) travel from Sānyà bus station to Dàdōnghǎi Bay.

From Dàdōnghǎi Bay to Yàlóng Bay, catch bus 15 (¥5).

Taxis charge ¥8 for the first 2km. A taxi from Sānyà to Dàdōnghǎi Bay costs ¥10 to ¥15, and from Dàdōnghǎi Bay to Yàlóng Bay it's ¥60.

Guǎngxī

POP 51 MILLION

Best Non-Karst Sights

➡ Lóngjǐ Rice Terraces (p611)

➡ Chéngyángqiáo Scenic Area (p614)

➡ Tōnglíng Grand Canyon (p628)

Best Mountain Scenery

➡ Bājiǎozhài National Geopark (p611)

➡ Tiānmén Mountain National Park (p611)

➡ Lèyè Geopark (p629)

➡ Yángshuò (615)

Why Go?

Tell someone you're heading to Guǎngxī (广西) and they'll seethe with envy, imagining you cycling and bamboo-rafting under the famous karst peaks of Yángshuò, or hiking between ethnic villages in the lofty Lóngjǐ Rice Terraces. You'll also be taking selfies in front of the dramatic Dānxiá landscape (a type of landform) at Tiānmén Mountain and Bājiǎozhài National Geopark, and getting sprayed by the waterfall of Détiān or splashed by live seafood in Běihǎi's Vietnamese quarter.

What's more, you'll be contemplating the 2000-year-old Huāshān Cliff Murals from a boat, getting your feet massaged by the cobblestones of Dàxū Ancient Town, and comparing the poetry of the Dòng villages at Chéngyáng to the beauty of Kyoto in Japan.

After you've had your fill of wonders above ground, you'll be plunging into the subterranean forests of Lèyè and soaking your feet in the underground streams of Tōnglíng Grand Canyon. Tell them all that and they're bound to hop on the next flight to Guìlín or Nánníng.

When to Go
Guìlín

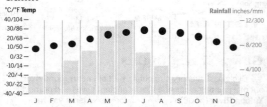

| **Apr & May** Karst peaks in Guìlín and Yángshuò don emerald robes. | **Jun–Sep** Rains turn rice terraces into mirrors and fatten waterfalls. | **Sep & Oct** The gulf breeze caresses your face as you stroll on Wéizhōu Island. |

Guăngxī Highlights

① Cycle past scenery straight out of a painting alongside the **Yùlóng River** (p608)

② Trek among stilt houses and fields at **Lóngjǐ Rice Terraces** (p611)

③ Visit the Chéngyáng Wind & Rain Bridge and drum towers of the artistic Dòng people in **Sānjiāng** (p614)

④ Let underground rivers, ancient caves and primeval forests whisper you their secrets at **Tōnglíng Grand Canyon** (p628)

⑤ Watch the drama of Dānxiá geology unfold as you explore **Bājiăozhài National Geopark** (p611)

⑥ Be awestruck by massive sinkholes and their caverns at **Lèyè Geopark** (p629)

⑦ Enjoy the rustic pleasures of 1000-year-old **Dàxū Ancient Town** (p610)

⑧ Revisit the charms of Yángshuò as it would have been 15 years ago in **Xìngpíng** (p618)

History

In 214 BC a Qin-dynasty army attempted to assimilate the Zhuàng people, living in what is now called Guǎngxī, into their newly formed Chinese empire. But while the eastern and southern parts submitted, the western extremes remained largely controlled by hill-tribe chieftains.

Major tribal uprisings occurred in the 19th century, the most significant being the Taiping Rebellion (1850–64), which became one of the bloodiest civil wars in human history.

Communist bases were set up in Guǎngxī following the 1929 Bǎisè Uprising led by Deng Xiaoping, although they were eventually destroyed by Kuomintang forces. Much of Guǎngxī fell briefly under Japanese rule following the highly destructive WWII invasions.

Today the Zhuàng, China's largest minority group, makes up 32% of Guǎngxī's population, which led to the province being reconstituted in 1955 as the Guǎngxī Zhuang Autonomous Region. As well as Zhuang, Miao and Yao, Guǎngxī is home to significant numbers of Dong people.

Language

Travellers with a grasp of Mandarin (Pǔtōnghuà) will have few problems navigating Guǎngxī's vast sea of languages. Cantonese (Guǎngdōnghuà), known as Báihuà in these parts, is the language of choice in Nánníng, Píngxiáng and Dàxīn, but most people also understand Mandarin. Visitors will also hear a number of minority languages being spoken, including Zhuang, Dong and Yao.

ℹ Getting There & Around

Airports at Guìlín and Nánníng run domestic flights of three hours or less to every major city, as well as international flights mainly to destinations in Southeast Asia, such as Thailand, Vietnam, Malaysia and Singapore.

A well-developed network of convenient rail lines and expressways spans the province, taking you to every corner in four hours.

High-speed rail, centred in Nánníng, connects Guǎngxī to provincial neighbours including Guǎngdōng, Guìzhōu, Húnán and Yúnnán. The fastest trains reach Guǎngzhōu (three hours), Guìyáng (five hours) and Běijīng (13 hours).

Long-distance buses are the most frequent form of transportation between major cities in Guǎngxī and neighbouring provinces.

Guìlín 桂林

☑ 0773 / POP 5,189,562

Guìlín was China's first city to develop tourism after 1949. For decades, children's textbooks proclaimed 'Guìlín's landscape is the best under heaven' (桂林山水甲天下). It was the darling of Chinese politicians, the star city proudly presented to visiting dignitaries. Today Guìlín's natural endowments still amaze, yet, thanks to imperfect urban planning, there is a pervasive feeling that the city is past its prime.

No matter where you're going in Guǎngxī, you're likely to spend a night or two here – Guìlín is a convenient base to plan trips to the rest of the province. It's clean and modern, with a high percentage of English-speaking locals, but you'll have to put up with touts and high admission fees to sights.

◉ Sights

Guìlín's sights are built around scraggly karst peaks that dot the bustling city. Some, owing to exorbitant admission prices, can be skipped. A ride down the magical Lí River (漓江; Lí Jiāng) and a stroll around tranquil Róng and Shān Lakes offer pleasing, wallet-friendly alternatives.

City Wall   GATE, LAKE

On the northern shore of **Róng Lake** (榕湖; Róng Hú) and strikingly illuminated at night, the **South Gate** (南门; Nán Mén) is the only surviving section of the original Song-dynasty city wall (城墙; chéng qiáng). The area is abuzz with activity and is a good place to watch locals practising taichi, calligraphy and dancing.

PRICE INDICATORS

The following price indicators are used in this chapter:

Sleeping

$ less than ¥150

$$ ¥150 to ¥400

$$$ more than ¥400

Eating

$ less than ¥40

$$ ¥40 to ¥100

$$$ more than ¥100

Guìlín

About 1km north of Folded Brocade Hill (叠彩山; Diécăi Shān) is the partly reconstructed **East Gate** (东镇门; Dōngzhèn Mén), flanked by crumbling sections of the original wall. To reach the East Gate, take bus 1 or 2 and get off at the Dōngzhèn Lù stop, then turn right down the road of the same name. Alternatively, it's a short walk or cycle north along the river bank, just east of the entrance to Folded Brocade Hill.

Sun & Moon Twin Pagodas
PAGODA

(日月双塔; Rìyuè Shuāng Tǎ; admission ¥45; ⊙8am-10.30pm) Elegantly embellishing the scenery of **Shān Lake** (杉湖; Shān Hú), the Sun and Moon Twin Pagodas, beautifully illuminated at night, are the highlight of a stroll around Guìlín's two central lakes. The octagonal, seven-storey Moon Pagoda (月塔; Yuè Tǎ) is connected by an underwater tunnel to the 41m-high Sun Pagoda (日塔; Rì Tǎ), one of the few pagodas with a lift.

Solitary Beauty Peak
PARK

(独秀峰; Dúxiù Fēng; 1 Wangcheng; 王城1号; admission ¥130; ⊙7.30am-6pm; ☐1, 2) This park is a peaceful, leafy retreat from the city centre. The entrance fee for the famous lone pinnacle includes admission to an underwhelming 14th-century Ming prince's mansion (oversold as a 'palace'). The 152m peak affords fine views of Guìlín.

🏃 Activities

Swimming in the Lí River is popular in summer.

👉 Tours

The popular **Lí River trip** from Guìlín to Yángshuò lasts about 4½ hours and includes a wonderfully scenic boat trip to Yángshuò, lunch and a bus ride back to Guìlín. Expect to pay ¥350 to ¥450 for a boat with an English-speaking guide. There's also the **Two Rivers Four Lakes** (二江四湖; Èr Jiāng

Guìlín

Sì Hú) boat ride around Guìlín that does a loop of the Lí River and the city's lakes. Prices vary from ¥150 to ¥340 for 90 minutes, depending on the time of day (it costs more at night). Pretty much every Guìlín hotel and tourist information service centre can arrange these two tours.

🛏 Sleeping

This Old Place Hostel HOSTEL $
(老地方国际青年旅舍; Lǎodìfāng Gúojì Qīngnián Lǚshè; ☑ 281 3598; www.topxingping.com; 2 Yiwu Lu; 翊武路2号; dm from ¥40, d ¥140-160, tr ¥220-320; ❄ @ 🛜) This hostel with an enviable position facing Róng Lake is a 10-minute walk to the main eating and shopping areas. Three-bed dorms are single beds with an en suite; regular rooms have a similar, though more spacious, arrangement. A taxi here from the train or bus station costs about ¥10.

Ming Palace International Youth Hostel HOSTEL $
(桂林王城青年旅舍; Guìlín Wángchéng Qīngnián Lǚshè; ☑ 283 6888; mingpalace123@hotmail.com; 10 Donghua Lu; 东华路10号, 中华小学旁; dm ¥40, d ¥120-160, tr ¥180; ❄ ✳ @ 🛜; 🚌 99, 100 from South Guilin bus station) An affordable and well-located option with large, dimly illuminated rooms. Some were being renovated at the time of writing, and, according to the helpful staff, rates may go up. Disembark from the bus at Lèqún Lùkǒu (乐群路口), turn right at the first crossing, walk on, passing two arches, and then you'll see the hostel. A taxi from the airport costs ¥130.

Riverside Hostel INN $$
(九龙商务旅游酒店; Jiǔlóng Shāngwù Lǚyóu Jiǔdiàn; ☑ 258 0215; www.guilin-hostel.com; 6 Zhumu Xiang, Nánmén Qiáo; 南门桥竹木巷6号; s & d ¥150-300; ✳ @ 🛜) This cosy inn by the Táohuā River (桃花江) comes highly recommended by travellers (especially couples) for its attentive staff and pleasant rooms. Advance booking is essential.

★**White House** BOUTIQUE HOTEL $$$
(白公馆; Bái Gōngguǎn; ☑ 899 9888; www.glb-gg.com; Bldg 4, 16 Ronghu Beilu; 榕湖北路16号4栋; d ¥1380-1780, ste ¥2380; ❄ ✳ @ 🛜) The White House is decked out in all manner of art deco–inspired trappings to honour the building it's in – part of the former residence of General Bai Chongxi (白崇禧), a powerful regional Guǎngxī warlord and father of the Taiwanese writer Kenneth Pai Hsien-yung (白先勇). The spacious guest rooms are lavishly appointed, featuring, among other luxuries, a minispa and high-thread-count bedding.

Photos of General Bai (literally 'white') and his era grace the corridors, and vintage artefacts are displayed in the lobby. The hotel is ¥12 by cab from the main bus station, and ¥120 from the airport.

🍴 Eating

Local specialities include Guìlín rice noodles (桂林米粉; *Guìlín mǐfěn*), beer duck (啤酒鸭; *píjiǔ yā*) and snails (田螺; *tiánluó*). The pedestrianised Zhengyang Lu and its surrounding lanes are the busiest dining areas.

Chóngshàn Rice Noodle Shop NOODLES $
(崇善米粉店; Chóngshàn Mǐfěn Diàn; ☑ 282 6036; 5 Yiren Lu, near junction with Zhengyang Lu, Qixing District; noodles ¥3-5; ⊙ 6.30am-midnight) Wildly popular Guìlín noodle shop with

GUĂNGXĪ GUÌLÍN

branches all over town. Order at the front, take your docket to the cook and retrieve your food from a window. The slippery rice noodles come with a variety of ingredients, but the Guìlín speciality (also the tastiest) is with stewed vegetables (卤菜粉; *lŭcài fěn*).

Lǎo Chén Jì
NOODLES $

(老陈记; Zhengyang Lu; dishes ¥6-15; ⊙10am-midnight) Here's a twist on the local noodles...they are served with horse meat (马肉米粉; *mǎròumífěn*). If you like them boring, there's beef (牛肉; *niúròu*) and pork (猪肉; *zhūròu*) too.

★ Céngsān Jiāwèiguǎn
GUANGXI $$

(曾三家味馆; ☑ 286 3781; 10 Xinyi Lu, near junction with Xicheng Lu; dishes ¥20-158; ⊙11am-2pm & 5-9pm) A modern restaurant jam-packed with middle-class locals who come for the generously plated wild boar, rabbit and cured meat dishes. If you prefer tamer flavours, there are other great options in the phone book of a menu. For weekend dinner, go before 6.15pm to snag a table. Smoking is allowed inside the restaurant. Chinese picture menu.

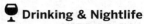

Drinking & Nightlife

Guìlín's streets are dotted with trendy cafes: Zhengyang Lu has a short stretch of bars with outdoor seating, while Binjiang Lu has a slew of cute drinking spots, most with free wi-fi.

Róng Coffee
CAFE

(榕咖啡; Róng Kāfēi; Bldg 5, Rónghú Hotel, 16 Ronghu Beilu; coffee & tea ¥18-188, cake ¥24-28; ⊙1-11pm; 🖂) Looking like a greenhouse with colourful armchairs, this peaceful cafe by the picturesque Róng Lake offers a lovely getaway. It's even got a tiny garden with a couple of tables and a garden swing.

Shopping

Guìlín Night Market
MARKET

(夜市; Yèshì; Zhongshan Zhonglu; 中山中路; ⊙from 7pm) For souvenirs, check out Guìlín's night market, which runs along Zhongshan Zhonglu from Ronghu Beilu to Sanduo Lu.

GREAT GUĂNGXĪ BIKE RIDES

Ancient Village Pursuit

Guìlín to Jiāngtóuzhōu (25km, three hours) This countryside spin takes you to the village of Jiāngtóuzhōu. From the west gate of Guìlín's Solitary Beauty Peak, head north along Zhongshan Beilu for 1km, then turn left onto Huancheng Beiyilu (环城北一路) before taking the first right. Keep cycling north until you leave the town of Dìngjiāng Zhèn (定江镇), then continue along the country lane for about 15km. When the road forks, bear right towards Tánxià Zhèn (潭下镇). At the Tánxià Zhèn junction, turn left then follow signs to Jiǔwū (九屋). Jiāngtóuzhōu is down a track on the right, just past Jiǔwū.

Yùlóng River Loop

Yángshuò to Dragon Bridge & back (20km round trip, four hours) Follow the Yùlóng River past rice paddies and fish farms to the 600-year-old Dragon Bridge (遇龙桥; Yùlóng Qiáo). From Yángshuò, cycle along Pantao Lu and take the first main road on the left after the Farmers Trading Market. Continue straight, past the hospital and through the village of Jìmǎ (骥马), before following the road round to the right to reach the start of a bumpy track. Follow this all the way to Dragon Bridge. After the crossing, follow another track south for around 8km until it becomes a small, paved road, which eventually stops at the river's edge. Take a bamboo raft across the river (¥5), then turn left off a small paved road down a tiny pathway, which leads you back to Jìmǎ village road.

Lí Valley Boat 'n' Bike Combo

Yángshuò to Xìngpíng & back (15km boat ride, 20km cycle, half-day) Combine a river cruise from Yángshuò to Xìngpíng with a bike ride back along the glorious Lí Valley. Put your bike on a bamboo raft (¥170 to ¥250, 1½ hours), then sit back and enjoy the views to the village of Xìngpíng. From here, cycle south, following the trail past the villages of Gǔpí Zhài (古皮寨), Qiáotóu Pù (桥头铺) and Dòngxīn (洞心) before reaching Fúlì (福利), 4km east of Yángshuò. Just past Fúlì take your bike on a ferry (¥5) across the Lí River, then continue past Dùtóu (渡头) and back to Yángshuò, crossing the river once more, this time over a bridge.

Bird Flower Market MARKET

(花鸟市场; Huāniǎo Shìchǎng; ⏰8am-5pm Sat & Sun; 🚌51) This local flea market has everything from electronics to vintage magazines, calligraphy brushes, dogs and, of course, birds and flowers.

ℹ️ Information

Buy a map of Guìlín (桂林地图; *Guìlín dìtú*) from bookshops or kiosks (¥7).

Bank of China (中国银行; Zhōngguó Yínháng) Branches on Zhongshan Nanlu (near the main bus station) and Jiefang Donglu change money, give credit-card advances and have 24-hour ATMs.

China International Travel Service (CITS; 中国国际旅行社; Zhōngguó Guójì Lǚxíngshè; www.guilintrav.com; Binjiang Lu) Helpful staff.

Guìlín Tourist Information Service Centre (桂林旅游咨询服务中心; Guìlín Lǚyóu Zīxún Fúwù Zhōngxīn; ☎280 0318; South Gate, Ronghu Beilu; ⏰8am-10pm) These helpful centres dot the city. There's a good one by the South Gate on Róng Lake.

People's Hospital (人民医院; Rénmín Yīyuàn; 70 Wenming Lu) This large, well-equipped hospital is a designated International SOS service provider, and the teaching hospital of several universities in Guǎngxī.

Public Security Bureau (PSB; 公安局; Gōng'ānjú; ☎582 3492; 16 Shijiayan Lu; ⏰8.30am-noon & 3-6pm Mon-Fri) Visa extensions. Located by Xiǎodōng River and 500m south of the Seven Stars Park. A taxi from downtown will cost around ¥18.

ℹ️ Getting There & Away

AIR

Air tickets can be bought from the **Civil Aviation Administration of China** (CAAC; 中国民航; Zhōngguó Mínháng; ☎384 7252; cnr Shanghai Lu & Anxin Beilu; ⏰7.30am-8.30pm). Direct flights include Běijīng (¥1800), Chéngdū (¥920), Chóngqìng (¥676), Hǎikǒu (¥10,140), Guǎngzhōu (¥860), Hong Kong (Xiānggǎng; ¥1819), Kūnmíng (¥600), Shànghǎi (¥1600) and Xī'ān (¥1090).

International destinations include Seoul, Korea (Hànchéng; ¥2000), and Osaka, Japan (Dàbǎn; ¥3200).

BUS

Guìlín's **main bus station** (桂林汽车客运总站; Guìlín Qìchē Kèyùn Zǒngzhàn; ☎386 2358; 65 Zhongshan Nanlu; 🚌3, 9, 10, 11, 16, 25, 51, 88, 91, 99) has regular buses to the following destinations:

Běihǎi ¥190, seven hours, three daily (8.30am, 9.20am and 9pm)

Guǎngzhōu ¥180, 9½ hours, eight daily

Huángyáo ¥60, five hours, three daily (9.10am, 1.10pm and 2.20pm)

Lóngshèng (for Lóngjǐ Rice Terraces) ¥40, two hours, five daily (8am, 8.30am, 9.30am, 1pm and 3pm)

Nánníng ¥120 to ¥140, five hours, every 15 minutes

Sānjiāng ¥43, four hours, hourly

Shēnzhèn ¥270, 12 hours, two daily (6pm and 9.20pm)

Yángshuò ¥24, 1½ hours, every 15-20 minutes

Both the main bus station and **North bus station** (桂林汽车客北站; Guìlín Qìchē Běizhàn; 76 Beichen Lu; 🚌18, 32, 99, 100) have buses to Zīyuán (¥13 to ¥26, every 20 minutes 6.40am to 6pm).

Buses to Lóngjǐ Rice Terraces also depart from **Qíntán Bus Station** (琴潭汽车站; Qíntán Qìchē Zhàn; 31 Cuizhu Lu, Xiangshan; 🚌2, 12, 26, 32, 85, 91) (¥24 to ¥29, two hours, every 40 minutes 6.10am to 7pm).

TRAIN

Few trains start in Guìlín, which means it's often tough to find tickets, so get them a few days in advance. Most trains leave from Guìlín Station (桂林站; Guìlín Zhàn), but some may leave from Guìlín north train station (桂林北站; Guìlín Běizhàn), 9km north of the city centre.

Direct services include the following:

Běijīng ¥446, 23 hours, four daily (1.57am, 1.05pm, 3.40pm and 6.55pm)

Běijīng West G train ¥806, 10 hours, one daily (7.47am)

Chóngqìng ¥280, 19 hours, two daily (12.38pm and 12.58pm)

Guǎngzhōu ¥230, 12 hours, two daily (6.28pm and 9.18pm)

Kūnmíng ¥310, 18½ to 24 hours, three daily (9.50am, 10.09am and 3.23pm)

Nánníng ¥130, six hours, regular

Shànghǎi ¥360, 22 hours, four daily (11.58am, 3pm, 5.13pm and 7.11pm)

Xī'ān ¥390, 27 hours, one daily (5.49pm)

ℹ️ Getting Around

TO/FROM THE AIRPORT

Guìlín's Liǎngjiāng International Airport (两江国际机场; Liǎngjiāng Guójì Jīchǎng) is 30km west of the city. Half-hourly shuttle buses (¥20) run from the CAAC office between 6.30am and 9pm. From the airport, shuttle buses meet every arrival. A taxi costs about ¥120 (40 minutes).

BICYCLE

Guìlín's sights are all within cycling distance. Many hostels rent out bicycles (about ¥20 per day). For decent bikes, head to **Ride Giant**

(捷安特自行车; Jié'āntè Zìxíngchē; ☑ 286 1286; 16 Jiefang Donglu; 解放东路16号; per day ¥30, deposit ¥500; ☺ 9am-8.30pm).

BUS

Buses numbered 51 to 58 are all free but run very infrequently. Regular buses cost ¥1 to ¥2. The following are the most useful:

Bus 2 Runs past Elephant Trunk Hill and Folded Brocade Hill.

Bus 51 Starts at the train station and heads north along the length of Zhongshan Lu to the Bird Flower Market and beyond.

Bus 58 Goes to Elephant Trunk Hill, Seven Stars Park, Wave-Subduing Hill, Folded Brocade Hill and Reed Flute Cave.

Around Guìlín

There are many ancient towns and old villages around Guìlín that make for a refreshing day trip.

Dàxū Ancient Town 大墟古镇

One of the four greatest ancient market towns in Guǎngxī, Dàxū (literally, 'big market') was founded in AD 200. The town's dusty streets run alongside the Lí River for 2km, flanked by one- and two-storey houses. Some of these are 'home offices' from which herbalists, barbers, cobblers and traditional craftspeople ply their trade. It's a leisurely place where doors are left open, children and chickens run freely, and corn is dried on the crooked banisters of an old stone bridge.

◉ Sights

Guǎngchāng Museum   MUSEUM, HISTORIC BUILDING
(广昌博物馆; Guǎngchāng Bówùguǎn; 66 Minzhu Lu) The opulent residence of Dàxū's wealthiest family, the Gaos (高), will soon be turned into a museum, according to the new owner. The house and its courtyards are lavishly embellished with ornate carvings and expensive classical furniture. Renovations were underway at the time of writing.

✗ Eating

★ Ancient Town Fish Restaurant   SEAFOOD $$
(古镇鱼餐厅; Gǔzhèn Yú Cāntīng; ☑ 635 2299; 69 Minzhu Lu; dishes ¥28-58; ☺ 11.30am-3pm & 6-8.30pm) The kitchen of this excellent rustic place has cured pork hanging on white-tiled walls, fish swimming in tubs, and baskets of vegetables plucked from their plot. Some-

times the staff will let you go into the kitchen and choose your meal. Look for the door with a red sign that says 古镇旅社 (Gǔzhèn Lǚshè). Go through the lobby into a courtyard and you'll see the restaurant.

ⓘ Getting There & Away

The town is 15km from Guìlín. Buses headed for Guānyán (冠岩) stop at Dàxū Zhèn (大圩镇). They depart from Guìlín's main bus station every 30 minutes from 7.30am to 4.30pm. The 40-minute ride costs ¥4.50.

Jiāngtóuzhōu 江头洲

The 1000-year-old village of Jiāngtóuzhōu is tucked away among farmland 32km north of Guìlín. There's an unmistakable rustic charm, with cobblestone alleyways and weathered homes from the Ming and Qing dynasties, where blocks of tofu are laid out to set in the courtyards. Tourists have to pay a ¥20 admission fee to the village.

The residents are descendants of the philosopher Zhou Dunyi (周敦颐) who is famed for his essay on virtue, 'Love of the Water-Lily'. The flower is a decorative motif throughout the village and inside the **ancestral hall**.

Jiāngtóuzhōu is a two- to three-hour bike ride from Guìlín. Alternatively, take an orange minibus on the stretch of Zhongshan Beilu near Guìlín North Train Station to Língchuān (灵川; ¥3, 40 minutes). Get off at Tánxià Lùkǒu (潭下路口), zip across the road and change to a bus to Jiǔwū (九屋; ¥4, 45 minutes), from where it's a 15-minute walk to the village. Buses stop running around 5.30pm.

Zīyuán & Around 资源

About 107km north of Guìlín, Zīyuán County (资源), built around the pristine Zī River, is a gateway to some geological gems of Dānxiá (丹霞) topography, such as Bājiǎozhài National Geopark and Tiānmén Mountain National Park.

The town of Zīyuán is a good place to base yourself to explore these two sites. **Chéngyuán Hotel** (盛源大酒店; Chéngyuán Dàjiǔdiàn; Chéngběi Kāifāqū, near County Government Headquarters; 城北开发区, 近县政府总部; r from ¥320; ☺ ✲ ☺) offers plush lodgings.

On the way up to the Bājiǎozhài car park, you'll pass a few farm restaurants. The chicken hotpot (土鸡火锅; *tǔjī huǒguō*), made with freshly slaughtered free-range fowl and just-picked vegetables, is divine.

⊙ Sights

★ Bājiǎozhài National Geopark
NATIONAL PARK

(八角寨; Bājiǎozhài; Meixi Xiang Fúzhú Village; 梅溪乡,福竹村; admission ¥80) This park is named after eight Dānxiá stone peaks that lie near the border with Húnán. Round, isolated, featuring ringlike troughs and leaning 45 degrees in the same direction, they resemble snails sunning themselves after the rain. The trail winds past steep cliffs, collapsed boulders, plunging gorges and bamboo forests.

From the car park, hike up to Jiànglóng Monastery (降龙寺; Jiánglóng Sì). After descending for 15 minutes, you'll see a junction near a snack shop. Bear left for an hour to Longtou Xiang (龙头香), from where, on a fine day, you can see the eight peaks that gave the area its name. Another 10 minutes takes you back to the car park.

Tiānmén Mountain National Park
MOUNTAIN

(天门山景区; Tiānmén Shān Jǐngqū; adult/child ¥60/30, cable car one-way/return ¥60/120; ⊙9am-5pm, cable car 9.30am-4pm) Tiānmén Mountain is home to proud cliffs, sharp ravines and dramatic waterfalls of Dānxiá topography, but also lush subtropical foliage, clusters of ash-brown dwellings and crumbling roadside shrines. There are multiple viewing spots along hiking trails in the park, including a U-shaped deck with a transparent floor. If you have time, there are boats to take you for a ride down the lovely Zī River for ¥130 to ¥258 (per boat).

❶ Getting There & Around

Buses leave Guìlín's main bus station and Guìlín North Bus Station for Zīyuán every 20 minutes from 6.40am to 6pm. Tickets are ¥13 to ¥26 for the three-hour ride.

From downtown Zīyuán, you can hire a car to Tiānmén Mountain, 30 minutes away, for ¥120, or to Bājiǎozhài National Geopark, 45 minutes away, for ¥150. The driver will wait for you to hike. If you do both places on the same day, it's ¥200, but you'll need to start off early (say, at 7am) and spend no more than four hours at each destination. A car directly from Guìlín will set you back ¥600 to ¥700.

Lóngjǐ Rice Terraces
龙脊梯田

☑ 0773

This part of Guǎngxī is famous for its breathtaking vistas of terraced paddy fields cascading in swirls down into a valley. For hundreds of years, the paddy fields remained unknown to travellers, then everything changed in the 1990s when a photographer named Li Yashi (李亚石) moved here. His images of the scenery amazed the world and put Lóngjǐ (literally 'Dragon's Back') firmly on the tourist trail.

You'll find the most spectacular views around the villages of Píng'ān (平安), a sprawling Zhuàng settlement; the more remote Dàzhài (大寨), a mesmerising Yáo village; and Tiántóuzhài (田头寨), which sits atop a mountain.

Being the earliest to open to tourism, Píng'ān has the best facilities but is less visually sublime than Dàzhài and Tiántóuzhài, which would move even hardened cynics. That said, tourism is picking up at these two villages and a cable-car service now connects their main viewing points (for ¥70 or ¥120 round trip).

As hiking is a way of life here, bring a day pack and leave your luggage in Guìlín or in the main ticket office. Otherwise villagers will carry your bags up for ¥50 apiece. There's nowhere here to change money.

The best time to visit Lóngjǐ is after the summer rains in May, which leave the fields glistening with reflections. The fields turn golden just before harvesting (October) and become snow-white in winter (December). Avoid early spring (March), when the mountains are shrouded in mist.

⊙ Sights & Activities

You can take a number of short **walks** from each village to the fabulous viewing points. These are numbered and clearly marked by signs. The three- to four-hour trek between the villages of Dàzhài and Píng'ān is highly recommended. Get a local to guide you for ¥100 or ask directions often along the way, as there are almost no signposts for this hike.

Lóngjǐ Rice Terraces
RICE TERRACE

(龙脊梯田; Lóngjǐ Tītián; adult ¥80) These are the clear standouts in the area. Rising to 1000m, they are an amazing feat of farm engineering on hills dotted with minority villages. The oldest field is over 700 years old; you pass it just before making your ascent to Dàzhài.

🛏 Sleeping & Eating

You can stay in traditional wooden homes for ¥30 to ¥40 a night (per bed). Nearly all guesthouses offer food, and most restaurants have English menus; dishes cost between ¥16 and ¥100.

ETHNIC CUSTOMS & FOLKLORE

The Zhuàng are China's most numerous ethnic minority and they're indigenous to Guăngxī. The Yáo were refugees from Shāndōng province who fled here in dynastic China. The cultures of both are filled with legends and traditions often as vibrant as their garments.

Traditional Dress

Yáo women are distinguished by their colourful costumes and long, shiny hair. Mothers wear it in a thick bun over the forehead. Women with hair coiled on top of their heads like a turban are married but childless. Heavy silver earrings and pink tunics are sported by the unmarried, and patterned tunics by older women. Zhuàng women, on the other hand, have simple hairdos, and wear plain tunics over wide, often dark-coloured pants.

Customs

The eating of dog meat, sometimes practised in Guăngxī, stops short of the Yáo hearth. This is because Pánhù (盘瓠), the Yáo totem, is a mythological dog who was given the hand of the princess by the emperor to reward his bravery. The Yáo believe that Pánhù, aka King Pan (盘王), was their first ancestor.

Up until the 1970s, young people of the mountainous Yáo and Zhuàng found romantic partners by yodelling. If they were in the fields and someone's singing pleased their ears, they sang back. Intermarriage between the two ethnic groups was forbidden by tradition up until the late 1980s. Occasionally a Zhuàng man may have been permitted to take a Yáo wife, but exceptions were never made for the women.

Legend

Viewing point number 2 in Dàzhài – Seven Stars Chase the Moon (七星追月; Qīxīng Zhuī Yuè), comprising seven terraced knolls developed in the early days – is also known as 'dead man's mound' (死人包; sǐrén bāo). According to one legend, a Yáo girl married her Zhuàng lover, and secretly set up house here. But her clansmen tracked them down and killed her husband. He was buried on the spot. The widow left the village for many years, then stole back one night to pay respects at her husband's grave. She was discovered and killed by a band of Yáo men. As she breathed her last, lightning struck, electrocuting her murderers. No one dared to touch the corpses and they eventually turned into knolls.

Festivals

One of the biggest Yáo festivals is the **Clothes Drying Festival** (晒衣节; Shàiyī Jié), which falls on the sixth day of the sixth lunar month. On that day, the women lay out all their traditional costumes under the sun. This serves the dual purpose of disinfection and allowing the ladies to show off. If it rains, they take their fashion spread indoors, leaving the door open. In the evening, from 7.30pm to 9.30pm, the villagers light a thousand torches by the fields and set off fireworks.

During the **Ghost Festival** (鬼节; Guǐ Jié), celebrated on the eighth day of the fourth lunar month, the Yáo and Zhuàng eat 'rice of seven colours' (七彩饭; qīcǎi fàn), which consists of white glutinous rice, and rice dyed naturally with maple (black), amaranth (red), sweet vernal-grass (yellow) and a kind of berry (blue); and artificially with purple and green dyes. Some say the practice is a tribute to their forefathers – the colours represent the generations before them. Others say the colours stand for different crops, and the practice is a prayer for an abundant harvest. There are also variations with five colours and eight colours.

The 14th day of the fifth month is **Memorial Day of Fighting the Japanese** (打日军纪念日; Dǎ Rìjūn Jìniàn Rì) for some Yáo villages. Two men (volunteers) carrying a red flag are chased from field to field and beaten up by children under the age of 11. (The age limit was set after the violence got out of hand.) The gang of people sets off early in the morning after paying their respects and slaughtering a pig in a temple. Every time they pass a field, the owners feed everyone wine and rice dumplings. For their blood and sweat, the two men receive a rooster, some pork and ¥36. A village banquet wraps up the day.

Oil tea – fried tea leaves brewed and drunk with rice puffs and peanuts – is consumed for breakfast, as is egg in sweet wine (甜酒鸡蛋; *tián jiǔ jīdàn*), heated rice wine into which an egg is dropped. Another common dish is *zhútǒng fàn* (竹筒饭), glutinous rice baked inside bamboo sticks.

🛏 Píng'ān

Lìqíng Hotel　　　　　　　　　　　HOTEL **$**
(丽晴饭店; Lìqíng Fàndiàn; ☏138 7835 2092; www.liqinghotel.com; d ¥100, tw ¥120-200, tr ¥280, ste ¥398; ❄@🛜) This excellent-value hotel offers simple, comfortable rooms with different feature combos to suit different wallets. The friendly, English-speaking staff will explain the details. Lìqíng is a 20-minute climb from the village parking lot; villagers will carry your bags for ¥40 apiece.

Lóngjǐ Holiday Hotel　　　　　　　INN **$$**
(龙脊假日酒店; Lóngjǐ Jiàrì Jiǔdiàn; ☏758 3545, 134 5731 8219; www.ljjrjd.com; d/ste ¥299/520; ❄@🛜) This cosy place, run by a pleasant Zhuàng woman and her brother, has spacious rooms with sharp colour coordination and a display of Zhuàng artefacts. All rooms come with balconies, great views and wi-fi.

🛏 Dàzhài

Minority Cafe & Inn　　　　　GUESTHOUSE **$**
(龙脊咖啡店; Lóngjǐ Kāfēidiàn; ☏758 5605; r ¥100) Perched above Dàzhài village on the trail leading up to Tiántóuzhài, this small guesthouse has a terrace. It's about a 20-minute walk (1km) uphill from the village's main gate.

Dragon's Den Hostel　　　　　　　HOSTEL **$**
(大寨青年旅舍; Dàzhài Qīngnián Lǘshè; ☏182 7838 7610, 758 5780; www.dragonsdenhostel.com; Tiántóu Zhāi, Dàzhài Village; 龙脊梯田大寨村田头摘; dm ¥30-35, r ¥90-120; ♨❄) This youth hostel has a cosy lounge with a children's library. All rooms with views have sit-down toilets and air-conditioning; the rest have squatting latrines and the cool night breeze. 'Dorms' are actually spacious triples. It's a 40-minute climb from Dàzhài. When you see Mr Liao Cafe & Bar, turn right and go another 150m.

⭐ Panorama House Hotel　　　　HOTEL **$$**
(全景楼大酒店; Quánjǐnglóu Dàjiǔdiàn; ☏758 5688, 136 1786 9898, 130 7764 6291; www.quanjinglou.com; scenic spot no 1, Lóngjǐ Terrace; 龙脊金坑大寨瑶族梯田1号景观点; s ¥180, d ¥308-398, tr ¥498, ste ¥488-688, extra bed ¥120; ❄🛜)

There's much to be said for this 100-room brick-and-concrete hotel near the summit of Dàzhài: it has a bird's-eye view of the fields, the rooms are sparkling, the restaurant is good (though pricey), and there are swings on the balconies. Ask for a room facing east.

🛏 Tiántóuzhài

Méijǐnglóu　　　　　　　　　　　　INN **$**
(美景楼; ☏758 5678; r ¥120-150; ❄@) This welcoming guesthouse is located above Tiántóuzhài. Rooms at the front have unobstructed views to the fields. After you leave Tiántóuzhài village, take the path up to the right. From there it's another 800m. There are steps leading up to the entrance.

🔒 Shopping

You'll find women peddling clothes and handicrafts with ethnic prints in the villages. Though attractive, most of these are little different from goods sold in other touristy areas in Guǎngxī.

Red Bean Handicrafts Workshop　　　　　　　　　HANDICRAFTS
(红豆手工艺作坊; Hóngdòu Shǒugōngyì Zuōfang; Píng'ān Village) This attractive shop about a 30-minute uphill walk from the Píng'ān car park sells traditional handicrafts (straw shoes, silver jewellery, slippers, bracelets, earrings and scarves) that are a cut above the souvenirs you see elsewhere.

ℹ Getting There & Away

Hotels in Dàzhài and Tiántóuzhài arrange direct shuttle services from Dàzhài to Guìlín (10am, 1pm and 4pm), and from Guìlín to Dàzhài (8am, 10.30am and 2pm) for their guests. The price is ¥50 per person. They also take other passengers if seats are available. Reservations are a must. All hotels in Píng'ān provide a similar service.

For public transport, head to Guìlín's Qíntán Bus Station (p609) via public bus 1. From there, take a bus to Lóngshèng (龙胜; ¥24 to ¥35, 1½ hours, every 40 minutes 7am to 7pm) and ask to get off at Hépíng (和平). From the road junction (or the ticket office three minutes' walk away), minibuses trundle between Lóngshèng and the rice terraces, stopping to pick up passengers to Dàzhài (¥9, one hour, every 30 minutes 7am to 5pm) and Píng'ān (¥7, 30 minutes, every 20 minutes to one hour 7am to 5pm).

Guìlín's main bus station (p609) also has buses to Dàzhài and Lóngjǐ (Píng'ān; ¥50, three hours, 8.30am, 9am and 2pm). Renting a car from Guìlín to here is about ¥400.

Six buses run daily between Lóngshèng and Píng'an (¥7, one hour, 7.30am, 9am, 11am, 1pm, 3pm and 5pm).

To continue to Sānjiāng you have to catch a bus from Lóngshèng bus station.

Sānjiāng 三江

☎ 0772 / POP 367,707

Sānjiāng is a convenient springboard to the ethereal Dòng villages and their architectural wonders in **Chéngyángqiáo Scenic Area** (程阳桥景区; Chéngyángqiáo Jǐngqū; admission ¥60). The best way to take in the area's natural and manmade beauty is by walking among the fields. Each hamlet has a distinctive-looking drum tower and a stage on which tables are set up for mahjong games. The homes are simple one- or two-storey cabins made of chocolate-toned cedar bark that exude an ancient grace evocative of Kyoto. The Dòng are known for their exquisite carpentry and you can certainly see why.

The late-afternoon sun and the yellow light bulbs that come on at dusk lend the villages a mesmerising mood – these are the best times to visit. At night electricity outages are not uncommon, so bring a torch with you.

There are lots of simple eateries here, serving breakfast for ¥5 and dishes for ¥15 to ¥80.

◉ Sights

★**Chéngyáng Wind & Rain Bridge**   BRIDGE
(程阳桥; Chéngyángqiáo; admission ¥60) The grandest of over 100 nail-less wind-and-rain bridges in the area, this photogenic black-and-white structure (78m) was built from

BRIDE'S HOMECOMING

On the third day of the Lunar New Year, the Dòng villages are ablaze with Bride's Homecoming (送新娘; Sòng Xīnniáng) festivities. Dòng weddings usually take place at the New Year, and on the third day, the women return home for a visit. The grooms and their kin will carry a slaughtered pig, rice cakes and other edible gifts in processions accompanying the brides to their maternal homes. Each procession is led by men who set off firecrackers to 'clear' the path, with the bride bringing up the rear. The night before, you'll see villagers cooking up a storm.

cedar and stone over 12 years in the 1910s. It features towers with upturned eaves, pavilions where people gather to socialise or take shelter from the elements, and a sweeping corridor with handrails and benches – a picture of pure poetry.

★**Drum Towers**   TOWER
A drum tower (鼓楼; Gǔlóu) resembles a flamboyant, multi-eaved pagoda plonked on a rectangular pavilion. The taller ones are built entirely of cedar. Donate a few coins as you enter, and look up at the receding beams and the scalelike tiles. Some towers have a fire pit. Once the social and religious heart of the village, they're now colonised by old men watching TV and playing ping pong.

▣ Sleeping

Lóngfèng Hotel   INN $
(龙凤客栈; Lóngfèng Kèzhàn; ☎189 7727 8037, 858 2619; www.lfhotel.net; d ¥90, tr ¥110-120; @☎) This conveniently located place with a nice cafe has 15 basic rooms with wi-fi. Look for the waterwheel at the entrance.

Dòng Village Hotel   INN $$
(程阳桥侗家宾馆; Chéngyángqiáo Dòngjiā Bīnguǎn; ☎858 2421; www.donghotel.com; d/tr ¥200/250; ❀❀☎) An inn run Michael Yang, who speaks English and can give sightseeing suggestions. Rooms have balconies, air-con and bathrooms. Pray for quiet neighbours – the walls are thin. It's immediately on your left after the bridge crossing.

❶ Getting There & Around

Most buses go to/from Sānjiāng's east bus station (河东车站; hédōng chēzhàn), but buses to Chéngyáng bridge go from the west bus station (河西车站; héxī chēzhàn), a 10-minute walk (about 500m, or a ¥4 pedicab ride) across the river. To reach the west bus station, turn right from the east bus station, right again over the river and right once more after you cross the river.

For Chéngyáng bridge, take the half-hourly bus bound for Línxī (林溪) from Sānjiāng west bus station (¥7, 30 minutes, 7.30am to 5.30pm). If you miss the last bus, private minivans to Línxī wait on the main road outside the west bus station. The fare is the same but they won't leave until they're full. It's ¥50 to have the minivan to yourself.

Guìlín has trains to Sānjiāng (¥63, 6¼ hours, 1.25pm and 7.40pm) and buses (¥27, 155km, five hours, 6am, 6.30am, 7.10am, 7.40am, 8.40am, 1.30pm, 2.45pm and 4.30pm) daily. There are 21 buses daily from Lóngshèng to Sānjiāng (¥15, 65km, three hours, 6.30am to 6pm).

Yángshuò 阳朔

☑ 0773 / POP 308,296

Seasoned travellers to Guǎngxī used to make Yángshuò their base, but many of these veterans now gripe about Yángshuò's lack of authenticity – 'too many tourists', they complain. And they're right: the town, once peaceful, is now a collage of Chinese tour groups, bewildered Westerners, pole-dancing bars, bad traffic and the glue that binds any tourist hot spot together – touts.

Outside of town, though, the karst landscape is surreal. Take a bamboo-raft ride or cycle through the dreamy valleys and you'll see.

Yángshuò is one of China's more family-friendly destinations, with English-speaking locals, well set-up hostels and food for the finicky.

◉ Sights

Bilián Peak · MOUNTAIN
(碧莲峰; Bìlián Fēng; admission ¥30) Located in the southeastern corner of town, this is Yángshuò's main peak; it's also the most accessible (it can be climbed in half an hour). Because it has a flat northern face that is supposed to resemble an ancient bronze mirror, it is also called Bronze Mirror Peak (Tóngjìng Fēng). The peak rises up next to the Lí River, in the Mountain Water Garden (Shānshuǐ Yuán); look for the sign that says 山水园.

🏃 Activities

Yángshuò is one of the hottest climbing destinations in Asia. There are eight major peaks in regular use, already providing more than 250 bolted climbs. **Insight Adventures Yángshuò** (☑ 881 1033; www.insight-adventures.com; 12 Fu Rong Lu; ⏰ 9am-9pm) offers guided climbs, while **Bike Asia** (☑ 882 6521; www.bikeasia.com; 42 Guihua Lu; 桂花路42号; ⏰ 9am-6pm) hires out bicycles, and offer maps and English-speaking guides.

🛏 Sleeping

Yángshuò teems with hotels run by English-speaking staff, and all provide internet access. While the Xijie neighbourhood has abundant options, some of the best lodgings are on the outskirts.

★ **Green Forest Hostel** · HOSTEL $
(瓦舍; Wǎshě; ☑ 888 2686; greenforest_yangshuo@yahoo.com; 3rd fl, Zone A, Business St, Chéngzhòngchéng, Diecui Lu; 叠翠路, 城中城, 城南商业街A区3楼; dm/r ¥40/200; ❂ @ ☎) This hostel's

attractiveness is highlighted by the rundown building it's in. Rooms have earth-toned furnishings; communal areas are flooded in natural light. From the bus station, turn right and walk along Diecui Lu, past Guihua Lu. At the junction with Chengzhong Lu, turn right and look for 99 Shopping Centre (99超市).

Phoenix Pagoda Fonglou Retreat · BOUTIQUE HOTEL $$
(凤楼岁月; Fènglóu Suìyuè; ☑ 180 7730 5230, 877 8458; www.fonglou.com; 98 Fènglóu Village, Gāotián Town; 高田镇, 凤楼村98号; d & tw ¥320-380, ste ¥560; ☺ ❂ @ ☎) The 12 rooms here have wide balconies overlooking the hills, furniture made from local materials, wi-fi and no TV. Meals are served on the scenic rooftop patio. The Taiwanese owner Jerry has tips on hiking and biking. It's a ¥40 taxi ride from downtown Yángshuò.

C Source West Street Residence · HOTEL $$
(禧朔源西街公馆; Xǐshuòyuán Xījiēgōngguǎn; ☑ 882 9489; 79 Xijie; 西街79号; r ¥298-398, ste ¥558-658; ❂ @ ☎) This 268-year-old building on heaving Xijie was once a Taoist temple and then a French-owned private club. The rooms of the hotel occupying it are quiet, with ancient China-inspired decor in a modern setting. Service can be a tad impersonal.

River View Hotel · HOTEL $$
(望江楼酒店; Wàngjiānglóu Jiǔdiàn; ☑ 882 2688; www.riverview.com.cn; 11 Binjiang Lu; 滨江路11号; r ¥360-680; ❂ @ ☎) If you prefer staying downtown but want to avoid the crowds, this good-value hotel is a decent bet. The balcony rooms overlook the Lí River and are somewhat old-fashioned but decent. The street below can be noisy so ask for a room on the 3rd or 4th floor.

★ **Secret Garden** · BOUTIQUE HOTEL $$$
(秘密花园酒店; Mìmì Huāyuán Jiǔdiàn; ☑ 877 1932, 138 0773 5773; www.yangshuosecretgarden.com; Jiuxian Village; 旧县村; r ¥420-460, ste ¥560-580; ❂ @ ☎) A South African designer nicknamed 'Crazy One' by the locals has turned a cluster of Ming-dynasty houses in the village of Jìuxiàn into a gorgeous Western-style boutique hotel with 18 rooms. A taxi to town from here costs ¥50.

★ **Tea Cozy Hotel** · BOUTIQUE HOTEL $$$
(水云阁; Shuǐyún Gé; ☑ 135 0783 9490, 881 6158; www.yangshuoteacozy.com; 212 Báishā Zhèn, Xiàtáng Village; 白沙镇下塘村212号; r ¥480, ste ¥528-880; ❂ @ ☎) What makes Tea Cozy a true winner is not the 12 wonderful,

Yángshuò

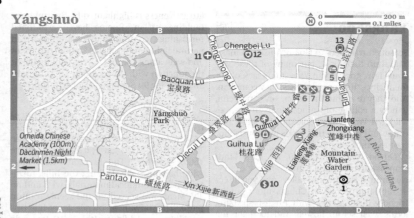

Yángshuò

ethnic-style balcony rooms, but the exceptional service by the English-speaking staff. Also laudable are the culinary skills of the restaurant staff (mains ¥18 to ¥108). The hotel has shuttle buses daily to Yángshuò and back, or you can take a taxi for ¥30.

🍴 Eating & Drinking

Local specialities include stuffed snails (田螺酿; *tiánluóniàng*) and beer fish (啤酒鱼; *píjiǔyú*). The fish with the least bones are *jiàngǔyú* (剑骨鱼) and the bigger and cheaper *máogǔyú* (毛骨鱼). Almost all restaurants have English menus.

You can find anything from wood-fired pizza to that most famous of fast foods around Xijie. Just off Xijie is where you might find German beer gardens sitting alongside generic Western-style cafes.

Lǎojiāxiāng Shāguōfàn GUANGXI $
(老家香砂锅饭; 3 Guifa Lu, near junction with Diecui Lu; dishes ¥10-28; ⊙9am-11pm) A small shop with tables spilling onto a busy street, serving hearty, reasonably priced meals. There's a huge selection of claypot rice dishes (砂锅饭; *shāguōfàn*), including vegetarian options, and beer fish (啤酒鱼, *píjiǔyú*; ¥28 to ¥68 per kilo). It's the third shop on the left as you turn from Diecui Lu into Guifa Lu. Look for the black-and-white awning.

Dàcūnmén Night Market MARKET $
(大村门夜市; Dàcūnmén Yèshì; Pantao Lu; ⊙5pm-late) This night market is a culture-filled slice of nontourist Yángshuò life. Watch locals sniffing out the best spices, haggling over snails or tucking into a dog hotpot. It's a 30-minute walk from Xijie. After you pass the petrol station on Pantao Lu, the market is behind the fire station on the left.

★ Pure Lotus

Vegetarian Restaurant   CHINESE, VEGETARIAN **$$**
(暗香蔬影素菜馆; Ànxiāng Shūyǐng Sùcàiguǎn;
☑881 8995; www.yangshuomagnolia.com/pure
lotus.htm; 7 Diecui Lu; dishes ¥18-48; ☺10am-
10.30pm; ❄☑ℳ) A Zen-like atmosphere cre-
ated by Buddhist music, antique furniture
and a cast of quiet, industrious staff pre-
pares you for an innovative vegetarian meal.

River View

Hotel Restaurant   GUANGXI, WESTERN **$$**
(望江楼餐厅; Wàngjiānglóu Cāntīng; 11 Binjiang
Lu; dishes ¥15-80; ☺8.30am-8.30pm; ❄☑)
Just a street removed from traffic-choked
Diecui Lu, this place offers good food, quiet
surrounds and attractive prices, with river
views to boot. There's an English menu with
pizzas and sandwiches, and a Chinese one
with all the usual suspects, well executed.

Kaya

  BAR
(☑186 7735 0084; 31 Xianqian Jie, beside
Shuāngyuè Bridge; drinks ¥20-50, cover charge
¥30-40; ☺8pm-3am) Bars that do not play
pop or hire pole dancers have a hard time
surviving in Yángshuò, which makes this
place a slight anomaly. Kaya has monthly
reggae performances, and a DJ on weekends playing bass and dubstep. The rest of
the time, the artist owner has Bob Marley
on loop.

☆ Entertainment

Impressions Liú Sānjiě   PERFORMING ARTS
(印象刘三姐; Yìnxiàng Liú Sānjiě; ☑881 7783;
tickets ¥200-680; ☺7.30-8.30pm & 9.30-10.30pm)
The busiest show in town is directed by filmmaker Zhang Yìmou, who also directed the
opening ceremony at the Běijīng Olympics
and acclaimed films such as *Raise the Red
Lantern*. Six hundred performers take to the
Lí River each night with 12 illuminated karst
peaks serving as a backdrop. Book at your
hotel for discounts and transport to/from
the venue (1.5km from town).

🛍 Shopping

Souvenir shops run the length of Xijie, while
stalls set up daily along Binjiang Lu. You'll
find silk scarves, knitted shoes and all manner
of other goods here. Bargain your socks off.

Qiúhuáng

  CLOTHING
(求皇; 111 Guihua Lu; clothing ¥50-3000; ☺noon-
11pm) Fine-looking modern clothing with an
ethnic twist for men and women. The owner
is a designer from Yúnnán's Tibetan region.

❶ Information

Travel agencies are all over town. Backpacker-
oriented cafes and most hotels can often dispense
good advice. Shop around for the best deals.

Touts are a constant nuisance in Yángshuò, but
with a greater percentage of English speakers
than in most places in China there's little need for
their services. Fend them off firmly but politely.

Bank of China (中国银行; Zhōngguó Yínháng;
Xijie; 西街; ☺9am-5pm) Foreign exchange and
24-hour ATM for international cards.

People's Hospital (人民医院; Rénmín Yīyuàn;
26 Chengzhong Lu) English-speaking doctors
available.

Public Security Bureau (PSB; 公安局;
Gōng'ānjú; Chengbei Lu; ☺8am-noon & 3-6pm
summer, 2.30-5.30pm winter) Has several
fluent English speakers. Doesn't issue visa
extensions. It's 100m east of People's Hospital.

❶ Getting There & Away

AIR

The closest airport is in Guìlín. Your hotel should
be able to organise taxi rides directly to the
airport (about ¥240, one hour).

BUS

Yángshuò has two bus stations: **Shímǎ South
Station** (石马南站; Shímǎ Nánzhàn; Courtyard
of the Agriculture Mechanisation Management
Bureau, 321 Guodao, 国道321号, 农业机械化管
理局) and **Dàcūnmén North Station** (大村门北
站; Dàcūnmén Běizhàn; fishery market next to
Dàcūnmén Provincial Government Service
Centre, Qingquan Lu, 大村门开发区清泉路,大
村门县政务服务中心,水产批发市场处).

Direct bus links:

Guǎngzhōu ¥120, seven hours, five daily
(10.20am, noon, 8pm, 9.30pm and 10.30pm)

Guìlín ¥20, one hour, every 15 to 20 minutes
(6.45am to 8.30pm)

Nánníng ¥166, 6½ hours, three daily (8.40am,
11.30am and 3.30pm)

Shēnzhèn ¥180, eight hours, seven daily
(1.30am, 12.30pm, 1.30pm, 3pm, 8.30pm,
9.30pm and 10.30pm)

Xìngpíng ¥8, one hour, every 15 minutes
(6.30am to 6pm)

Yángdī ¥9.50, one hour, every 20 minutes
(7am to 6pm)

The bus from Guìlín to Huángyáo only stops in
Yángshuò (¥50, two hours, one daily) erratically,
so check before purchasing tickets.

TRAIN

Yángshuò has no train station, but train tickets
for services from Guìlín and Nánníng can be
bought from hotels and travel agencies around
town. Expect to pay ¥50 commission.

ⓘ Getting Around

Most places in town can be reached by pedicab for under ¥20. Bicycles can be rented at almost all hostels and from streetside outlets for ¥10 to ¥25 per day. A deposit of ¥200 to ¥500 is standard, but don't hand over your passport. For better-quality bikes, head to Bike Asia (p615).

Around Yángshuò

The countryside of Yángshuò offers weeks of exploration by bike, boat, foot or any combination thereof. Scenes that inspired generations of Chinese painters are the standard here: wallowing water buffalo and farmers tending their crops against a backdrop of limestone peaks. Some of the villages come alive on **market days**, which operate on a three-, six- and nine-day monthly cycle.

Xìngpíng & Around   兴坪

Some say Xìngpíng is the Yángshuò of 15 years ago before the latter became a honeypot, for better or worse. This 1750-year-old town is certainly attractive; the landscape you see when you disembark from the raft is printed on the back of the ¥20 banknote.

A bus from Yángshuò to Xìngpíng takes 40 minutes (¥7, every 15 minutes, 6am to 7pm).

Around Yángshuò

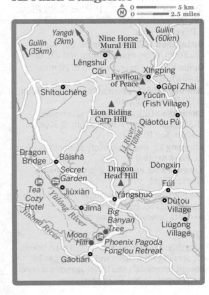

◎ Sights

Xìngpíng Ancient Stage   HISTORIC SITE
(兴平古戏台; Xìngpíng Gǔ Xìtái; ⊙9am-5pm)
FREE The highlight of Xìngpíng's old street is this well-preserved opera stage from the Qing dynasty. You can see intricate carvings depicting operatic scenes, and slash marks made by prop weaponry on the pillars. If you want to take pictures, an old man will collect a ¥1 donation from you. The trendy-looking Master Cafe has recently opened in the same compound.

Fish Village   VILLAGE
(鱼村; Yúcūn; admission ¥10, 'Clinton' house ¥1)
You can hike the mountain behind Xìngpíng, past pomelo and orange groves, to sleepy Fish Village. Miraculously untouched during the Sino-Japanese War and the Cultural Revolution, the 400-year-old village has friendly residents and vernacular houses similar to those at Xìngpíng. It was visited by Bill Clinton in the 1990s, something it still takes pride in today.

A bamboo raft back to Xìngpíng or Yángshuò costs ¥200 to ¥300.

🛏 Sleeping & Eating

★**This Old Place**   HOSTEL **$**
(老地方; Lǎo Dìfang; ☏870 2887; www.topxingping.com; 5 Rongtan Lu; 榕潭街5号; dm ¥50-80, s ¥100-120, d ¥140-380; ❄@🛜) This hostel has a nice backpacker vibe, 42 solid rooms, and a living room with a wood-fire oven that makes delicious pizzas (¥32 to ¥46). The south-facing rooms in the new wing are the best. The hostel operators can suggest plenty of itineraries for guests.

Old Neighbourhood   CHINESE **$$**
(老街坊餐吧; Lǎojiēfāng Cānbā; ☏870 1808, 137 3739 6512; 12 Xingjie; dishes ¥15-120; ⊙8am-10.30pm) Old Neighbourhood's owner is a cook from northeastern China who's lived in Guǎngdōng, so dishes from these and other regions all figure on the menu. Of particular note are the dumplings (饺子; jiǎozi) and the stuffed duck (莲子鸭; liánzǐ yā), which requires three hours' pre-ordering.

This Old Place Cafe   CHINESE, WESTERN **$$**
(老地方; Lǎo Dìfang; ☏870 2901; 46 Laojie; mains ¥18-88; ⊙8am-8pm; ❄🛜) Affiliated with This Old Place hostel, this pretty cafe serves sandwiches and pizzas alongside Guǎngxī dishes. It's a popular place as evidenced by the number of customers' notes plastered on its brick walls.

Yùlóng River 遇龙河

The scenery along this smaller, quieter river (Yùlóng Hé) about 6km southwest of Yángshuò is breathtaking.

Tell the boatperson you want to visit the fairy-tale-like **Dragon Bridge** (遇龙桥; Yùlóng Qiáo), about 10km upstream. This 600-year-old stone arched structure overhung with old gnarly trees is among Guǎngxī's largest, and comes with crooked steps and leaning parapets.

You can also get here by taking the bus to Jīnbǎo (金宝); get off at Dragon Bridge (¥6, 35 minutes), just after Báishā (白沙).

Liúgōng Cūn 留公村

The quiet 400-year-old village of Liúgōng (Liúgōng Cūn), 13km from Yángshuò, was a trading hub on the Lí River during the Ming and Qing dynasties. Traces of its former affluence are visible in the handsome buildings (the walls of some still blush with slogans painted during the Cultural Revolution). You can stroll from the village to the hills behind it, where the only things punctuating the silence are cockerels and murmurs of the past.

◉ Sights

Déyuè Building HISTORIC BUILDING
(得月楼; Déyuè Lóu) Once among Lí River's most beautiful buildings, Déyuè now stands weather-beaten by the river. Residents say it used to be an opera house, and on performance nights music would reverberate over the moonlit water. An exquisite four-cornered pavilion sits on the rooftop.

From the village pier, a 90-minute raft ride to Yángshuò costs ¥200 per person (¥260 for two).

✗ Eating

Liúgōng Gǔpú Farmer Restaurant GUANGXI $$
(留公古朴农家饭; Liúgōng Gǔpú Nóngjiāfàn; ☏ 892 3581, 136 6946 2263; mains ¥16-98; ◷ 7am-late) All visitors to Liúgōng come here for fresh river fish, local fowl and homemade tofu. On national holidays, it's colonised by local tourists; book ahead. The restaurant also rents out kayaks (¥60 per day).

❶ Getting There & Away

To cycle there, take Kangzhan Lu (抗戰路) in Yángshuò until the roundabout. Bear

THE LEGEND OF THE CARP

In Liúgōng Cūn, the **House of Two Lions** (双狮门户; Shuāngshī Ménhù), the former home of Yángshuò's richest man, has a bulge over a 1-sq-metre area of its living-room floor. According to legend, the bulge is the gill of a carp (a symbol of abundance), and it would protrude every morning then flatten in the afternoon. However, on the advice of an ill-intentioned feng-shui master, the owner removed the soil from under the spot where the bulge was. This killed the carp – whose gill protruded one last time, creating a permanent bulge – and ruined the family.

Mr Li, a descendant, still lives here and he may let you in. It's a 30-second walk down the first alley that leads west away from the river, past Liúgōng Gǔpú Farmer Restaurant. It's the one with wooden doors and steps, just before the concrete building with red lanterns.

left, passing traffic lights and entering the new Shima Lu (石馬路). After crossing the bridge, you'll see Aishān Village (矮山村). At the junction, look for signage for Pǔyì (普益). Take the concrete road that heads in that direction. After a curve, continue for another 4km, passing other villages. At a road junction with small shops including a motorcycle-repair shop, you'll see signage for Liúgōng Village. Another 5km on a concrete road brings you to a hill close to the roadside and then a rusty sign pointing to the village.

Huángyáo 黄姚

☏ 0774
Huángyáo is one of China's most high-profile villages, with many movies filmed here; *The Painted Veil*, starring Edward Norton, is possibly the most well known.

Bucolic charm permeates the lovingly preserved 900-year-old village, though roving tour groups take some of the shine off. Still, there's plenty on its eight streets to ensure the ¥100 entry fee is well spent, including two massive 500-year-old Chinese banyans that have wound their way up from the river's edge.

Huángyáo is famous for its condiments and chilli salsa, which you'll see and smell everywhere.

🛏 Sleeping & Eating

Yuánfāngde Jiā INN $
(远方的家; ☎672 2792, 133 7703 6002;
Yfdj13377036002@163.com; 94 Liyu Jie; 鲤鱼街94
号; r ¥138-168, ste ¥228; 🛜) Two floors of small
but adequate rooms connected by a creaky
wooden staircase. It's on a busy street just
before you reach Dàilóng Bridge (带龙桥;
Dàilóng Qiáo).

★Heterotopias Clan BOUTIQUE HOTEL $$
(异托邦会馆; Yìtuōbāng Huìguǎn; ☎181 7679
6519; heterotopias@126.com; 49 Anle Jie; 安乐街
49号; r ¥250-350; ⊖❀@🛜) With its cultured
air and eight elegant rooms, Heterotopias
sits inside an old courtyard complex. The
owners are intellectual types and the hotel's
white walls and minimalist aesthetic showcase their literary collection and paintings
by their artist friends to great effect.

★Dàilóng Farmer Restaurant GUANGXI $
(带龙桥龙家饭庄; Dàilóngqiáo Lóngjiā Fàn-
zhuāng; ☎131 0054 9638; Zhongxing Jie, at the
start of Dàilóng Bridge; mains ¥15-80; ⊙11am-
8pm) Rarely does a famous eatery (it's been
featured countless times by the media) up-
hold its culinary excellence, and its boss, its
modesty, so well. But that's precisely why
patrons keep returning to feast on steamed
spare ribs (豆豉蒸排骨; dòuchǐ zhēng
páigǔ), stuffed tofu (豆腐酿; dòufu niàng)
and other deliciousness on the river bank.
Mr Liang speaks English too.

❶ Getting There & Away

There are two direct buses daily from Guìlín
(¥60, three hours, 8.30am and 1.30pm). The
return buses from Huángyáo leave at 2pm and
8pm, though the service is erratic, meaning you
may have to take a bus to Hèzhōu (贺州; ¥18,
two hours) and change to a Guìlín service (¥60
to ¥80, 2½ to four hours). Joining a local tour
from Yángshuò (arriving at 11am and departing
at 4.30pm) costs ¥198.

Nánníng   南宁
☎0771 / POP 7.1 MILLION

Like many provincial capitals in China, Nánníng is a bog-standard city with few sights
of note. But it's a fairly relaxing place to recharge your batteries before leaving for, or
returning from, Vietnam. Nánníng's metro
system will be completed in phases in 2016,
and is expected to improve the city's traffic.

👁 Sights & Activities

Guǎngxī Museum MUSEUM
(广西博物馆; Guǎngxī Bówùguǎn; www.gxmuse-
um.com; cnr Minzu Dadao & Gucheng Lu; ⊙9am-
4.30pm Tue-Sun; 🚌6) FREE A fairly interesting
museum showcasing Qing ceramics, art and
calligraphy with Guǎngxī characteristics,
and the customs of ethnic minorities. The
collection of ancient copper drums is one
of China's best. The traditional handicrafts
shop (广西传统工艺展示馆) on the ground
floor has great souvenirs.

South Lake Park PARK
(南湖名树博览园; Nánhú Míngshù Bólǎnyuán;
🚌12, 25, 33, 46, 220) FREE This 193-hectare
park has dozens of species of trees including
some rare ones, but you don't have to be a
botanist to enjoy it. The setting is lovely and
some of the foliage is simply interesting to
look at, or read a book under. There are also
lawns to nap on and a lake to stroll around
and watch the locals fish.

Get off the bus at South Lake South Sq (南
湖南广场; Nánhú Nánguǎngchǎng).

🛏 Sleeping

There's a cluster of budget hotels around the
train station, displaying the price of their
cheapest discounted rooms on signs in the
windows. Prices are ¥60 upwards.

Green Forest Hostel HOSTEL $
(瓦舍; Wǎshě; ☎281 3977; greenforest_nanning@
yahoo.com; 3rd fl, 3 Jiefang Lu, near Minsheng
Buxingjie, 解放路3号3楼, 近民生步行街; dm
¥50-60, d¥138; ⊖❀@🛜; 🚌6, 8, 32, 41) Like its
newer Yángshuò branch, this hostel is located in an old building. The rooms are highly
liveable despite the slightly musty-smelling
corridors. Get off the bus at Cháoyáng Sq
(朝阳广场; Cháoyáng Guǎngchǎng), walk on
for 10m, and you'll see the pedestrianised
Minsheng Buxingjie.

Lotusland Hostel HOSTEL $
(荷逸居 琅东客运站; Héyì Jū Lángdōng Kèyùnzhàn; ☎677 3664; newlotuslandhostel@163.com;
155 Minzu Dadao; 民族大道155号; d/tw ¥70/120;
❀@🛜) A spiffy fit out and clean rooms
make this hostel close to the Lángdōng
long-distance bus station a good choice.

Wànxīng Hotel HOTEL $$$
(万兴酒店; Wànxīng Jiǔdiàn; ☎238 1000; www.
nnwxhotel.com; unit 1, 42 Beining Jie; 北宁街42-1
号; d ¥438-788, tr/ste ¥888/1688; ❀@🛜) One
of those seemingly characterless urban ho-

tels that turn out to be very good. The guest rooms are very comfortable though not large, and the service is exceptional.

✗ Eating

Zhongshan Lu is jam-packed with eateries selling squid kebabs, grilled oysters, roasted pigeon, crocodile skewers, *chòu dòufu* (臭豆腐; stinky tofu) and noodles of all persuasions. Street food costs ¥5 to ¥10 and a seafood dish at a restaurant starts at ¥25.

★ Gānjiājiè Lemon Duck
GUANGXI $$
(甘家界牌柠檬鸭; Gānjiājiè Pái Níngméngyā; ☑ 585 5585; www.ganjiajie.com; 12 Yuanhu Lu; mains ¥30-68; ⊙ 10am-9.30pm) The star here is the flavourful lemon duck (柠檬鸭; *níngméngyā*), a Nánníng dish that cooks the fowl with pickled lemon peel, ginger, garlic and chilli. You can choose from two types of quack-quack; we recommend the more tender cherry duck (樱桃谷鸭; *yīngtáo gǔyā*).

Líyǔ Cūn
GUANGXI $$
(漓雨村; ☑ 283 6800; 131 Minsheng Lu, near junction with Jiefang Lu; mains ¥35-58) Hearty Guìlín specialities are the highlights of this bustling place with a faux-rustic interior, including good beer fish (干蒸剑骨鱼; *gānzhēng jiàngǔyú*) and fried pork knuckle (鸿运招财手; *hóngyùn zhāocáishǒu*). Service can be careless. It's a three-minute walk to Green Forest Hostel.

Āmóu Delicious Eats
GUANGXI $$
(阿谋美食; Āmóu Měishí; Gucheng Lu; mains ¥28-98; ⊙ 9am-9pm; ✱) Unique and flavourful ethnic dishes served on a photogenic wind-and-rain bridge or in a dining room, both in the compound of the Guǎngxī Museum. We liked the spare ribs and green-pea mush (壮乡绿茸骨; *zhuàngxiāng lǜróng gǔ*) and fried pork belly dipped in rice wine (么佬族乳香肉饼甜酒; *melǎozú rǔxiāng ròubǐng tiánjiǔ*).

🍷 Drinking & Nightlife

You can find plenty of bars on Jiangbei Dadao (江北大道).

Interesting Tavern
BAR
(意酒馆; Yì Jiǔguǎn; ☑ 186 7708 9179; 8 Jiangbei Dadao; beer from ¥260; ⊙ 7pm-4am; ☐ 27, 35, 71) This watering hole is decorated like a bar in Lìjiāng, Yúnnán, with old ship wood and artefacts from Lìjiāng. Local and Lìjiāng bands croon mellow tunes from 10pm to 1am, and there's a good variety of imported beer.

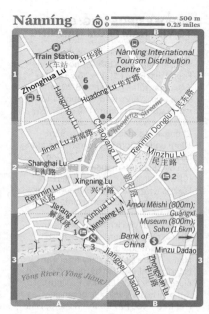

Nánníng

Soho
CLUB
(苏荷; Sūhé; ☑ 530 8111; www.sohobar.com.cn; 18 Xinghu Lu Beiyi Li; beer from ¥280; ⊙ 8pm-6am) White-collar Nánníngers love this place with pounding pop music, dizzying lights and over-the-top modern baroque decor.

☆ Entertainment

★ King of Live
LIVE MUSIC
(侯朋友现场; Hóupéngyǒu Xiànchǎng; car park of Mínghú Bldg, 171 Mingxiu Donglu, 明秀东路171号,

BORDER CROSSING: GETTING TO VIETNAM FROM NÁNNÍNG

There are seven daily buses to Hanoi (Hénèi, Vietnam; ¥150, 7½ hours) via Friendship Pass (友谊关; Yŏuyì Guān). Two departures (8am and 8.20am) leave from Nánníng International Tourism Distribution Centre (南宁国际旅游集散中心; Nánníng Guójì Lǚyóu Jísàn Zhōngxīn), and four (8.40am, 9am, 10am and 1.40pm) leave from Lángdōng bus station. One bus (¥158, 7.30am) run by **China International Travel Service** (CITS; 中国国际旅行社; Zhōngguó Guójì Lǚxíngshè; 🖂 232 3330; 76 Chaoyang Lu; ⏰7am-11pm) leaves from Nánfāng Hotel (南方酒店; Nánfāng Jiǔdiàn).

Note that you'll have to get off and walk across the border at Friendship Pass before boarding another bus to Hanoi. There's also a daily train from Nánníng train station to Hanoi (1st/2nd class ¥248/160, 11 hours, 6.20pm).

Local hostels will help organise visas (for free – you pay for the visa only) and transport (¥30 to ¥50 fee).

接近跟北湖路交叉路口，明湖大厦停车场) Nánníng's only 'live house' (live-music venue) sees indie bands from China and overseas doing three to 10 gigs a month. It's inside a building's car park in the pleasant but out-of-the-way university neighbourhood of Xīxiāngtáng (西乡塘). The building is next to a teacher-training school (师范学院明秀校). Enter below the fast-food shop Sānpǐnwáng (三品王). Check the Douban or Weibo websites for the venue's line-up.

ℹ Information

The useful *Street Map of Nanning* (南宁街道图; Nánníng Jiēdào Tú; ¥5), in English and Chinese, can be found at bookshops and kiosks around town.

Bank of China (中国银行; Zhōngguó Yínháng; Chaoyang Lu; ⏰9am-5pm Mon-Fri) Changes travellers cheques and gives credit-card advances. Other Bank of China branches around town have 24-hour ATMs that accept international cards.

China International Travel Service (CITS; 中国国际旅行社; Zhōngguó Guójì Lǚxíngshè; 🖂 232 3330; 76 Chaoyang Lu; ⏰7am-11pm) Has some English-speaking staff, issues one-month Vietnam visas (¥420) and sells bus tickets to Hanoi (Hénèi; ¥150).

Public Security Bureau (PSB; 公安局; Gōng'ānjú; 🖂 289 1260; 10 Xiuling Lu Xierli; 秀灵路西二里10号; ⏰9am-4.30pm Mon-Fri) Located 2km north of the train station, off Xiuling Lu (秀灵路).

ℹ Getting There & Away

AIR

Direct daily flights from Nánníng include Běijīng (¥1800), Shànghǎi (¥1550), Xī'ān (¥1800), Kūnmíng (¥780), Guǎngzhōu (¥660) and Hong Kong (¥1880). You can also fly to a number of other countries in Asia, including Vietnam (Yuènán; ¥1950).

The **Civil Aviation Administration of China** (CAAC; 中国民航; Zhōngguó Mínháng; 🖂 243 1459; 82 Chaoyang Lu; ⏰24hr) sells tickets.

BUS

The main **Lángdōng long-distance bus station** (琅东客运站; Lángdōng Kèyùnzhàn; 🖂 550 8333; east end of Minzu Dadao; 民族大道东端; 🚌 6, 25, 42, 76, 90, 98, 206, 603, 701, 704), 5km east of the city centre, has high-speed, direct buses to pretty much everywhere, although you may be dropped at one of the other bus stations, also on the outskirts, when arriving. There's a downtown ticketing office on Chaoyang Lu near CAAC.

Běihǎi ¥65, three hours, every 10 to 20 minutes (7am to 10pm)

Guǎngzhōu ¥160 to ¥220, nine hours, 15 daily (8am to 11pm)

Guìlín ¥80 to ¥140, 4½ hours, every 15 to 30 minutes (7.30am to 10pm)

Píngxiáng ¥70, 2½ hours, 16 daily (7.30am to 8.30pm)

There is one direct bus daily to Détiān Waterfall (Détiān Pùbù; ¥50, 3½ hours, 7.40am). Other daily routes include Chóngqìng, Chéngdū, Hǎinán Dǎo, Shànghǎi and Hong Kong (Xiānggǎng).

TRAIN

Following are some daily services:

Běihǎi ¥38 to ¥50, three hours, two daily (12.55pm and 1.40pm)

Běijīng West ¥280, 27 hours, two daily (8am and 10.30am)

Chéngdū ¥199, 36½ hours, one daily (7.38pm)

Chóngqìng ¥162, 27 hours, one daily (12.50pm)

Guǎngzhōu ¥96 to ¥115, 11½ to 14 hours, three daily (12.27am, 5.12am and 6.50pm)

Guìlín ¥60 to ¥1180, 4½ to 6½ hours, over 20 daily

Shànghǎi ¥199 to ¥231, 28 to 31 hours, two daily (6am and 9am)

Xī'ān ¥227, 33 hours, one daily (11.20am)

Two daily trains go to Píngxiáng (¥15 to ¥17, 3½ to 5½ hours, 7.40am and 11.45am) near the Vietnam border. Both stop at Chóngzuǒ (¥9 to ¥10, two to three hours) and Níngmíng (¥11 to ¥13, 2½ to four hours), but only the slow one stops at Píngxiáng's north train station.

Booth 16 in the train station sells international tickets to Hanoi.

ⓘ Getting Around

Buses 6 and 213 run the length of Chaoyang Lu and Minzu Dadao until around 11pm (¥2 per ride). A taxi ride from Lángdōng bus station to downtown is around ¥40. Taxis start at ¥7 and short pedicab rides cost ¥5.

The twice-hourly airport shuttle bus (¥20, 40 minutes, 5.30am to 10.30pm) leaves from the CAAC office. A taxi to the airport is about ¥120.

Yángměi 扬美

A rambling bus ride 25km west of Nánníng takes you to this former market town (admission ¥10) on the Yōng River (邕江; Yōng Jiāng). Yángměi was founded a millennium ago and flourished in the 17th century, earning the nickname 'Little Nánníng'.

Most of Yángměi's inhabitants were migrants from Shāndōng, with a small percentage from Guǎngdōng. Hybridity is reflected in its buildings, which feature both the sturdy solemnity of Shāndōng vernacular architecture, and the penchant for embellishment of the softer southern style.

Spend a couple of hours wandering the cobbled streets, munching on fried fish (from ¥2), steamed rice rolls (¥4) and local starfruit (¥5 a catty) as you walk. The pace is slow and you're free to peep into the musty Ming- and Qing-dynasty homes.

Buses leave from behind Huátiān Guójì (华天国际), an office-block building at 202 Huaqiang Lu (华强路), just west of Nánníng's train station. Departures and returns are from 8.30am to 4.30pm (¥15, two hours, hourly). The last bus gets packed so arrive early for a seat.

Běihǎi 北海

📍 0779 / POP 1.5 MILLION

Běihǎi (literally 'North Sea') is famed among Chinese tourists for its Silver Beach, dubbed 'number one beach on earth' in tourism brochures (it's not). More charming though is the old quarter, where you'll find colonnaded streets and colonial-era architecture that's escaped the demolition ball.

◉ Sights & Activities

Silver Beach　　　　　BEACH
(银滩; Yíntān) A long stretch of silvery-yellow sand with apparently clean water, about 8km south of the city centre. Take bus 3 (¥1.50) from the central bus station.

Former British Consulate Building　　　HISTORIC BUILDING
(英国领事馆旧址; Yīngguó Lǐngshìguǎn Jiùzhǐ; Beihai No 1 Middle School, 1 Beihai Lu) Běihǎi's first consulate of a Western country is a whitewashed edifice built in 1885 that now sits inside an elite school. The guard will let you in for a peek if you're nice.

THE CHARMING STREETS OF OLD BĚIHǍI

Běihǎi's old streets (老街; lǎojiē) usually refer to Zhongshan Lu (中山路) and Zhuhai Lu (珠海路), which were part of old Běihǎi's trading hub, but are now home to sleepy residences of the city's older population. Built a century ago, the streets spread from west to east and are flanked by recently restored 19th-century qílóu buildings (arcade houses) housing an alarming number of pearl shops.

Start your stroll at the western end of Zhuhai Lu. Look for the small white arch inscribed with the Chinese characters 升平街 (Shengping Jie), the road's former name. This street has been paved over and offers visitors an atmospheric, albeit slightly contrived, walk.

Former Post Office (大清邮政北海分局旧址; Dàqīng Yóuzhèng Běihǎi Fēnjú Jiùzhǐ; cnr Zhongshan Donglu & Haiguan Lu; ⊙9am–noon & 2.30–5.30pm Wed-Sun) Dating from 1896, this attractive edifice now serves as a tiny museum devoted to relics of the Qing-dynasty postal system. No English captions, nor photos allowed indoors.

Maruichi Drugstore (丸一药房; Wányī Yàofáng; 📍203 9169; 104 Zhuhai Zhonglu; ⊙8.30-11.30am & 3-5.30pm) This site was disguised as a pharmacy that allowed the Japanese to carry out espionage activities in the 1930s. It's now a tiny national security museum. No English captions.

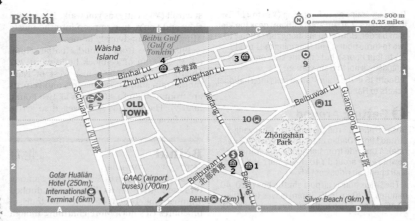

Běihǎi

Sights

Sleeping

Eating

Information

Transport

Former German Consulate Building HISTORIC BUILDING

(德国领事馆旧址; Déguó Lǐngshìguǎn Jiùzhǐ; 2 Beijing Lu) Across the street from the Former British Consulate Building, next to Yínruì Hotel (银瑞大酒店), is this charming two-storey yellow structure built in 1905.

🛏 Sleeping

From the central bus station, cross Sichuan Lu (四川路) to reach Běihǎi's cheapest accommodation on Huoshaochuang Wuxiang (火烧床五巷). This small alley off Beibuwan Xilu is jam-packed with zhāodàisuǒ (招待所), simple guesthouses offering doubles and twins from ¥35.

Backpacker Inn INN $$

(老道精舍; Lǎodào Jīngshě; 🕿 203 0605; www.backpacker-china.com; 165 Haizhu Xilu; 海珠西路165号; s ¥158, d ¥188-208, tw ¥388-588; ❄ 🛜) This place on the western end of one of Běihǎi's lesser-known old streets, Haizhu Xilu, has 13 spiffy rooms with upholstered bay windows that make for relaxed reading.

Gofar Huālián Hotel HOTEL $$

(国发花联酒店; Guófā Huālián Jiǔdiàn; 🕿 308 7888; Beibuwan Xilu; 北部湾西路; d/tw ¥258/358; ❄ @) A midrange hotel close to the central bus station and shopping action. Spacious doubles/twins drop to ¥120/150 during the low season, offering good value if you can put up with blaring karaoke music. Turn left from the bus station and walk 700m.

Bavaria City Hotel HOTEL $$$

(巴伐利亚酒店; Bāfálìyà Jiǔdiàn; 🕿 223 7000; reservation@bavariahotel.net; 338 Xinan Dadao, Hǎichéng District, 海城区, 西南大道338号; r ¥438, ste ¥647-736; ⊝ ❄ @ 🛜) A plush option in a new quarter close to the high-speed train station (¥15 by cab or a 25-minute walk), Bavaria offers clean, bright and quiet rooms. You can flag down pedicabs outside the hotel, or the thoughtful staff will find you a taxi – just give them 10 minutes.

🍴 Eating

The old town is full of stalls selling steamed rice rolls (粉卷; fěnjuǎn) and shrimp pancakes (虾饼; xiābǐng). Overseas Town is your best bet for reasonably priced seafood.

★ **Kieu Viet Vietnam**
Banh Cuon VIETNAMESE **$**
(侨越越南卷粉汤粉; Qiáoyuè Yuènán Juǎnfěn Tāngfěn; 1 & 2 Fengsheng Jie, Overseas Town, 侨港镇, 丰盛街1号2号商铺; rice rolls ¥1.50-2.50; ☺7am-1am) Piping hot steamed rice rolls (粉卷; fěnjuǎn) made fresh.

Old Town Coffee, Bar & Restaurant CAFE **$**
(老道咖啡; Lǎodào Kāfēi; ☑203 1828; www.backpacker-china.com; 155 Zhuhai Lu; 珠海路155号; snacks ¥16-35, mains ¥25-30, drinks ¥28-45; ☺9am-1.30am; ☏) At the western end of the old street Haizhu Lu is this moody cafe (flickering candles, bricks exposed in the right places) inside a 19th-century building. The ground floor is open all day, and the upper floors morph into a bar at night.

Aunty Li's Shrimp Pancakes GUANGXI **$**
(李姨虾饼店; Lǐyí Xiābǐng Diàn; 110 Haizhu Lu; pancakes ¥3; ☺8am-6pm) Dried shrimp pancakes (虾饼; xiābǐng) are a delicacy here and nobody does them better than this hawker stall opposite Běihǎi Christ Church.

★ **Overseas Town**
Restaurant SEAFOOD, VIETNAMESE **$$**
(侨港镇瘦佬大排档; Qiáogǎngzhèn Shòulǎo Dàpáidàng; ☑388 2086; 7-8 Hongmian Lu, Overseas Town; 侨港镇, 红棉路7-8号; fish per catty ¥60-120, shrimp per catty ¥50-150, clams from ¥38; ☺10.30am-10.30pm) Take your pick from the tanks of aquatic life near the entrance and tell the staff how you'd like it cooked, making sure you know the prices before committing. The pan-fried squid (香煎小鱿鱼; xiāngjiān xiǎoyóuyú) is exceptional. If you're coming from Gangkou Lu (港口路),

go south, turn left into Qiaoxing Lu (侨兴路), then right into Hongmian Lu.

From Binhai Lu (滨海路), go west and turn left into Qiaobei Lu (侨北路). Walk to the end, turn right into Qiaoxing Lu (侨兴路), then left into Hongmian Lu.

ℹ Information

Industrial Commercial Bank of China (CBC; 中国工商银行; Zhōngguó Gōngshāng Yínháng) Has a 24-hour ATM for international cards.

Public Security Bureau (PSB; 公安局; Gōng'ānjú; 213 Zhongshan Donglu; ☺8am-noon & 2.30-5.30pm, 3-6pm summer) At the eastern end of the old town; can extend visas.

ℹ Getting There & Away

AIR
There are daily flights to Běijīng (¥2010) and Shànghǎi (¥1700). The airport is 21km northeast of the town centre.

BOAT
The international ferry terminal (国际客运码头; guójì kèyùn mǎtou) is on the road to Silver Beach (bus 3; ¥1.50). Three ferries leave daily for the volcanic island of Wéizhōu (¥120 to ¥240, 1½ hours, 8.30am, 11.15am and 4pm). Ferries return to Běihǎi at 9.45am, 2.30pm and 5.15pm. Services double on the weekend.

BUS
Direct bus routes include Nánníng (¥65, three hours, every 30 minutes 7am to 9.30pm) and Guìlín (¥180, seven hours, seven daily).

TRAIN
Two trains leave daily to Nánníng from Běihǎi Train Station (¥40 to ¥60, three hours, 9.24am and 11.50am). Tickets to onward destinations

---

LOCAL KNOWLEDGE

CHOW DOWN IN OVERSEAS TOWN

Běihǎi is the place to feast on fresh seafood – it's excellent and abundant. Yet at the most visible seafood eateries, especially those near Silver Beach, customers pay through the nose for a plate of squid. This is because cab and pedicab drivers get a cut for bringing customers to these places – up to 50% of the bill! With that kind of incentive, some drivers will try to lure you to eateries that pay them. Insist on going elsewhere and they may feign ignorance of the location, or take you to their pet eatery and pretend it's the one you're after.

But there are exceptions to the rule. Seafood restaurants that don't overcharge can be found in Overseas Town (侨港镇; Qiáogǎng Zhèn), 4km away from Silver Beach. OT was established in 1979 to settle Vietnamese Chinese refugees who had arrived near the shores of Běihǎi. Most of the arrivals were fishermen who brought their unique mix of Chinese and Vietnamese culture to the area.

So ask a driver to take you to Overseas Town (without mentioning a restaurant), then walk to your destination. The whole town is only 1.1 sq km.

can be bought from the **train station ticket office** (⊘ 8.10am–noon & 2–5pm) for a ¥5 fee.

Express trains from Nánníng (about ¥70, 1½ hours, 10.35am and 2.55pm) arrive at the new Běihǎi Express Train Station (北海高铁火车站) on Zhanbei Lu (站北路).

ⓘ Getting Around

TO/FROM THE AIRPORT

Airport shuttle buses (¥10, 30 minutes) leave from outside the **Civil Aviation Administration of China** (CAAC; 中国民航; Zhōngguó Mínháng; ☑ 303 3757; Beibuwan Xilu; 北部湾西路; ⊘ 8am–10pm), a few hundred metres beyond Huo-shaochuang Wuxiang, and connect with every flight. Flight tickets can also be bought here.

BUS

There are two main bus stations: a central long-distance one (客运总站; kèyùn zǒngzhàn) on Beibuwan Lu (北部湾路) and a newer, inconveniently located one (北海南珠汽车站; Běihǎi nánzhū qìchē zhàn). Most buses drop you at the latter station. You'll need to take public bus 15 (¥1.50) to Beibuwan Lu or a taxi (¥25).

From the central bus station, bus 2 (¥1.50) goes to the train station.

PEDICAB & MOTORCYCLE TAXI

There are three-wheeled pedicabs and motorcycle taxis. You can get to most places in town, including to Silver Beach, for ¥5 to ¥20.

Wéizhōu Island 涸洲岛

China's largest volcanic island Wéizhōu (6.5km long) makes for a relaxing day trip from Běihǎi, 124km away, if you like dormant volcanic scenery, water sports and religious architecture. You can pay for the entry ticket (¥90 per person) and buy a map (¥3) at the Běihǎi pier. The island's growing popularity with Chinese tourists has meant new surcharges and sometimes less-than-honest operators.

The main settlement of **Nánwān Port** (南湾港; Nánwān Gǎng) is 5km south of the pier. The waters around Wéizhōu contain some of the most diverse coral communities in the area; ask in Nánwān Port about motorboat rides and diving opportunities, though instructions will be in Chinese. If you're not into water sports, skip the beaches.

The entry ticket includes admission to the **Mouth of the Volcano** (火山口; Huǒshān Kǒu), a site marked by a pile of black rocks and one of the highlights along a seafront boardwalk that snakes past wave-sculpted

caverns and animal shapes that were molten lava several millennia ago.

The star of the island by far, however, is the Catholic church in the northeastern part.

⊙ Sights

★ Wéizhōu Catholic Church   CHURCH

(涸洲天主堂; Wéizhōu Tiānzhǔ Táng; Shèngtáng; 盛塘) This baby was built in 1835 in a neo-Gothic style with coral and volcanic rocks from the seabed, and looks quite formidable despite its modest size. As it looms into view behind hawkers and tour vans, your mouth drops a little.

The church was constructed by French missionaries for followers who had fled here to escape ethnic conflict in Guǎngdōng. It was damaged during the Cultural Revolution and rebuilt with donations from the wife of former premier Zhou Enlai, and a Catholic priest in Hong Kong. The lovely garden sports a 125-year-old mango tree. Outside the church are hawkers selling noodles and delicious coconut buns (椰子包; yēzi bāo; ¥2).

ⓘ Getting There & Around

To get from the ferry pier to Nánwān Port, it's ¥15 by pedicab. Consider hiring a pedicab (roughly ¥120 for four to five hours), a van (¥150) or a sightseeing cart (¥220) to save time. Drivers from the same operator may take turns chauffeuring you around, so make sure no one owes you change before you let them out of your sight.

Tickets for boats to Wéizhōu Island can be purchased from the international ferry terminal in Běihǎi.

Huāshān Cliff Murals 花山岩画

The enigmatic Huā Mountain Cliff Murals (Huāshān Shíhuà), 2000-year-old rock paintings of people and animals on sheer cliff faces, are the reason many people come to Guǎngxī. For several years, conservation works have been carried out on the murals and portions of the cliff are covered by scaffolding, as China applies for the site's inclusion on the UN World Heritage list in 2016.

The red-painted murals are believed to be the work of ancestors of the Zhuàng, who refer to Huā Mountain as *pay laiz* (mountain with colourful paintings) but why they were painted remains a mystery. For an idea of scale, the largest of 1900 distinguishable images is 3m tall.

The crudely drawn figures are barefoot and shown in silhouette. Many have hands raised and knees bent, accompanied by pictures of drums and animals – features that suggest celebration of harvest or victory.

The admission fee (¥80) includes a two-hour boat ride on a spectacular section of the Zuǒ River (左江; Zuǒ Jiāng) past ducks and fallen cliff faces. The boat leaves at 10am and 2pm; outside these times, you can hire a private boat; it's ¥300 to ¥500 for 90 minutes to three hours, depending on the type of boat used.

The only way to see this ancient wonder is by boat from the village of Pānlóng (攀龙), commonly known as Huāshān Shānzhài (花山山寨). The cliffs are in Níngmíng (宁明), a county between Nánníng and Píngxiáng.

❶ Getting There & Away

Trains and buses that run between Nánníng and Píngxiáng stop at Níngmíng (宁明). From the train or bus station, take a pedicab (¥30 to ¥50, 40 minutes) to Huāshān Shānzhài (花山山寨).

Regular buses leave Níngmíng for Píngxiáng (¥12, one hour), Chóngzuǒ (¥20, 1½ hours) and Nánníng (¥65, three hours); the last buses leave at 6.30pm, 6pm and 7.50pm, respectively.

Trains to Píngxiáng leave at 10.57am (¥62, 55 minutes) and 4.44pm (¥38, one hour 13 minutes). Trains to Chóngzuǒ (slow/fast ¥38/46, 1½ hours/one hour) and Nánníng (¥46/72, four hours 40 minutes/three hours) leave at 9.50am (slow train) and 1.07pm (fast train).

Píngxiáng 凭祥

📞 0771 / POP 110,000

Guǎngxī's gateway to Vietnam (越南; Yuènán) is a market town with a dusty, end-of-the-world feel.

◉ Sights

Friendship Pass Scenic Area PARK
(友誼關景区; Yǒuyìguān Jǐngqū; admission ¥42; ⊙8am-8pm) The Chinese side of the Sino-Vietnamese border is an attractive park sprinkled with old buildings. These include the virile-looking Friendship Pass Tower, rebuilt in 1957 on the original 2000-year-old site with battlements and ramparts.

⬓ Sleeping

On Beida Lu (北大路) bare hotels with aircon and internet ranging from ¥50 to ¥150. Look for the characters 宾馆 (bīnguǎn).

Xiáng City Hotel HOTEL $$
(祥城国际大酒店; Xiángchéng Guójì Dàjiǔdiàn; 📞802 2666; www.xc-hotel.com; 2 Beida Lu; 北大路2号; r/ste ¥260/538; ❈🞢) One of the more comfortable places to stay in Píngxiáng.

❶ information

Turn right from the bus station's front entrance onto Yingxing Lu (银兴路) to find the Bank of China (中国银行; Zhōngguó Yínháng) and some internet cafes (网吧; wǎngbā). Turning left from the station will take you to rice and noodle stalls.

GUĂNGXĪ PÍNGXIÁNG

BORDER CROSSING: GETTING TO/FROM VIETNAM FROM PÍNGXIÁNG

The Friendship Pass (友谊关; Yǒuyì Guān) border is about 18km south of Píngxiáng on the Chinese side, and several kilometres from the obscure town of Dong Dang on the Vietnamese side; the nearest Vietnamese city (Liàngshān; Lang Son in Vietnamese) is 18km away. The border is open from 8am to 8pm Chinese time (China is one hour ahead of Vietnam), but some travellers have reported that passports aren't always stamped after 4.30pm.

To get to the border crossing, take a pedicab or taxi (about ¥40) from Píngxiáng. From there it's a 600m walk to the Vietnamese border post. Onward transport to Hanoi, located 164km southwest of the border, is by bus or train via Lang Son.

If you're heading into China from Friendship Pass, catch a minibus to Píngxiáng bus station, from where there are regular onward buses to Nánníng and beyond. A word of caution: though train tickets to China are more expensive in Hanoi, it isn't advisable to walk across the border from Dong Dang and buy the ticket on the Chinese side. Dong Dang is several kilometres from Friendship Pass, and you'll need someone to take you by motorbike. If going by train, buy a ticket from Hanoi to Píngxiáng, and then in Píngxiáng, buy a ticket to Nánníng or beyond.

There are still reports of Lonely Planet's China being confiscated by border officials at Friendship Pass. We advise copying vital information and putting a cover over your guidebook just in case. Note that all bags are searched as you walk into the train station. Once you leave Píngxiáng, you won't have a problem.

❶ Getting There & Away

Regular buses depart from Píngxiáng bus station for Níngmíng (¥12, one hour) until 7pm, for Chóngzuǒ (¥33, 80 minutes) until 6.40pm, and for Nánníng (¥80, three hours) until 8pm.

Trains leave for Níngmíng (¥62) and Nánníng (¥78, 3½ hours) from Píngxiáng Station (凭祥站; Píngxiáng Zhàn) from 10.25am. The train station is 3km south of the bus station and pedicabs (about ¥5) link the two.

Détiān Waterfall   德天瀑布

☑ 0771

The picturesque **Détiān Waterfall** (Détiān Pùbù; Ban Gioc Waterfall; ☑ 261 2482; www.detian. com; admission ¥80) belongs to Chūnguī River (春归河, Chūnguīhé), which flows between China and Vietnam. The river is only 30m across in this upstream section, which means that folks on both sides can see each other going about their business. Some border residents make a living by smuggling. It's not uncommon around here to hear someone comment how poor the Vietnamese look, then, in the same breath, gush over their trucks ('So much sturdier than ours!') and their goods of herbs, coffee and perfume.

It's not grand like Niagara Falls, it's still quite a beauty. There's the added buzz of being surrounded by karst peaks and being able to legally cross the Vietnamese border at the 53rd mere stone – tourists like to take photos of themselves stepping into what's officially Vietnamese territory. The falls drop in three stages to create cascades and small pools. Swimming is not allowed, but bamboo rafts (¥30) will take you up to the spray.

After visiting the waterfall, follow the signs to the **53rd mere stone**. After running the gauntlet of Chinese souvenir stalls, you'll hit a market of Vietnamese traders hawking snacks and smokes, and the weathered stone marking the border.

Outside the entrance gates, there are guesthouses offering doubles with air-con for about ¥80, and eateries from ¥10-a-bowl noodle shops to restaurants (¥35 per person).

❶ Getting There & Away

Unless you catch the one direct bus, which departs from Nánníng's International Tourism Distribution Centre (one way/return ¥50/90, 3½ hours, 7.40am) and stops en route at Lángdōng bus station (8.30am), you will have to come via Dàxīn (大新) from Nánníng. At Dàxīn, switch to a bus headed to Détiān (德天; ¥20, two hours, hourly); a cab costs ¥110.

The last bus leaves for Dàxīn around 5.30pm. There are regular buses from Dàxīn to Nánníng (¥55, 2½ hours) until 8.30pm. The direct bus from the falls to Nánníng leaves at 3.30pm.

Tōnglíng Grand Canyon   通灵大峡谷

Some 30km from Détiān Waterfall in Bǎisè city (百色市), Jìngxī County (靖西县), **Tōnglíng Grand Canyon** (Tōnglíng Dàxiá Gǔ; ☑ 618 0076; www.tonglinggu.com; admission ¥90; ◑ 8am-5pm) is like a beautiful wound on the land's surface, offering virgin forests and geological drama over a 1000m by 200m area. As you make your way down from the entrance in the north, you'll understand why it's named Tōnglíng – 'connected to the spiritual world'.

Follow flights of narrow stairs that zigzag precariously down to a large cavern, with flickering bulbs and the roar of an underground river your only guides. From there, you venture (or your eyes do) through a thick tropical forest into gorges wild and wonderful, and past vaulted cliffs with hanging stalactites, more subterranean rivers and dramatic waterfalls that end in crystal pools framed by boulders.

You can walk around some of the waterfalls into the cool, otherworldly caves beyond. But you can't go near the tallest one, which has a drop of 170m and a splash of up to hundreds of metres in the summer.

From the canyon's exit, you can walk 30 minutes uphill to the car park, where your hired car will be waiting for you. Alternatively, vans can take you for ¥5. There are buses from Jìngxī south bus station that make the hour-long trip (¥10) to the canyon every 20 to 30 minutes until 7pm. Look for those headed for Húrùn town (湖润镇; Húrùnzhèn).

❶ Getting There & Away

Buses depart from Nánníng north station for Jìngxī every 20 minutes. Nánníng's Lángdōng bus station runs tour buses to Dàxīn (大新) that stop at the canyon.

Lèyè   乐业

☑ 0776

Guǎngxī's highest county is perched on the western edge of the province, and makes a good springboard to underground caves, primeval forests and natural sinkholes.

⊙ Sights & Activities

Peaceful and compact Lèyè belongs to Bǎisè city (百色市), which also administers Jìngxī County where Tōnglíng Grand Canyon is located. Allow a day or two to visit the area's impressive sights.

You can buy a combo ticket for the two sinkholes of Lèyè Geopark (乐业世界地质公园; Lèyè Shìjiè Dìzhì Gōngyuán; ⊙ 8.30am-5pm) and the Lotus Cave (¥158); just for the sinkholes (¥118); or for Dàshíwéi Sinkhole and the Lotus Cave (¥128). Every 20 to 30 minutes, between 8am and 4.30pm, a bus leaves Lèyè for Dàshíwéi Sinkhole. Catch it at a large temporary car park diagonally opposite the People's Hospital (人民医院; Rénmín Yīyuàn). The car park is accessible via a small alley. The 30-minute ride costs ¥4.30. There's no bus to Chuāntóng Sinkhole, but if you go to Dàshíwéi Sinkhole, the staff can arrange a driver to take you there and back to the city centre for ¥80 to ¥100 a car (seats four).

★ Chuāntóng Sinkhole   CAVE
(穿同天坑; Chuāntóng Tiānkēng; Lèyè Geopark; ⊙ to 5.30pm) A two-hour hike takes you past limestone caves, primeval vegetation and an underground river. You can trek to the sinkhole's bottom via an ethereal-looking cavern with a hole in its roof. On sunny days at noon, a shaft of light passes through the hole onto the cavern floor.

Dàshíwéi Sinkhole   CAVE
(大石围天坑; Dàshíwéi Tiānkēng; Lèyè Geopark; admission ¥98; ⊙ 8am-5.30pm) From the ticket office here, you're transferred to an electric cart for a 20-minute ride to what resembles a deep meteor crater. Follow the path to one of three viewing platforms at the top for cloud-level views of karst ranges.

Luómèi Lotus Cave   CAVE
(罗妹莲花洞; Luómèi Liánhuā Dòng; Tongle Lu; admission ¥80; ⊙ 8am-5pm) This 970m-long cave, once an underground river, shelters the world's largest collection of lotus-shaped limestone formations, illuminated (too ambitiously) by colourful lights. The cave is 200m north of the bus station.

🛏 Sleeping & Eating

There are noodle shops and hotels along Xingle Lu (兴乐路), a ¥7 pedicab ride from the train station. Rooms start at ¥75 and come with air-con and en suite bathrooms. From Xingle Lu, it's a ¥5 ride or a 10-minute walk west towards Tongle Zhonglu (同乐中路), where you'll find vendors selling snacks and fruit.

City Comfort Inn   HOTEL $$
(城市便捷酒店; Chéngshì Biànjié Jiǔdiàn; ✆ 255 9888; www.cc9d.com; unit 1, Bldg 4, Lètiān Gardens District, 乐天花园小区第4栋1单元; r ¥166-199) Small, bright and comfortable rooms in a small hotel next to Mínzú Middle School (民族中学).

ⓘ Getting There & Around

There are four daily buses from Nánníng (¥135, six hours). The main station is on the southern end of Tongle Lu (同乐路) and the town is 1km to the north.

Détiān's Húrùn Town Bus Station (湖润镇客运汽车站; Húrùnzhèn Kèyùn Qìchēzhàn) runs buses to Jìngxī (靖西) every 20 minutes (¥10); Jìngxī has frequent buses to Bǎisè (¥55, 3½ hours).

Regular daily buses depart from Lèyè for the following destinations:

Bǎisè (the regional hub where you can connect to southern destinations such as Dàxīn and Guǎngdōng) ¥55, three to four hours, 12.30pm to 8pm

Nánníng ¥140, seven hours (9am, 12.40pm, 7pm and 9.50pm)

The easiest way to see the sights in Lèyè is to hire a pedicab for the day (¥180 to ¥250). Ask the driver: *Bāochē yìtiān yào duō shǎo?* (包车一天要多少? How much is it to hire your car with chauffeur service for a day?) Short rides cost about ¥7.

SKY PITS

Sinkholes, known as 天坑 (*tiānkēng*), literally 'sky pits' in Chinese, are depressions in the land caused by the collapse of the surface layer. This happens when bedrock made of a soluble substance such as limestone is eroded by underground water, forming caves that may eventually collapse from the surface. Some sinkholes have openings into the caves below or to underground rivers. Some are carpeted by primeval forests.

Guìzhōu

POP 34.7 MILLION

Best Views

➡ Yúnjiù Temple (p648)

➡ Huángguǒshù Falls (p646)

➡ Shízhàngdòng Waterfall (p650)

➡ Tiāntáishān (p648)

Best Historic Towns & Villages

➡ Zhènyuǎn (p641)

➡ Yúnshān (p648)

➡ Zhàoxīng (p112)

➡ Tiānlóng (p647)

Why Go?

Little-visited Guìzhōu (贵州) has always been the least fashionable southwest China province. A much-quoted proverb describes it as a place 'without three *lǐ* of flat land, three days of fine weather, or three cents to rub together'. Ouch!

Certainly, pockets of Guìzhōu are desperately poor and not for nothing do expats refer to it as 'Greyzhōu'. The upside is that there's plenty of elbow room out in the simply stunning countryside, a sublime mix of undulating hills and carpets of forest, riven with rivers tumbling into magnificent waterfalls and down into spooky-thrilling karst cave networks.

As big a draw as the landscapes is Guìzhōu's extraordinary human mosaic. Around 37% of the province's population consists of more than 18 ethnic minorities. They all contribute to Guìzhōu's social-butterfly calendar, which enjoys more folk festivals than any other province in China, and those parties more than make up for the weather.

When to Go
Guìyáng

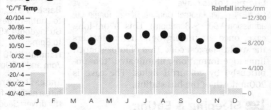

Jan Brave the chill for the wondrous sight of thousands of rare birds wintering at Cǎohǎi Lake.

Jun Hope for some summer sunshine as you village-hop around the southeast.

Oct & Nov See in the Miao New Year in Xījiāng with gallons of rice wine.

Guìzhōu Highlights

① Spend a week village-hopping around **Kǎilǐ** (p636)

② Party with the locals at one of the thousand-odd **festivals** held in Guìzhōu each year (p636)

③ Get off the beaten track in the prehistoric fern forests around **Chìshuǐ** (p649)

④ Head underground at **Zhījīn Cave** (p118), the largest cavern in China

⑤ Soak yourself in the mists at the thundering **Huángguǒshù Falls** (p646), China's largest waterfall

⑥ Escape the madding crowds and get up close with rare black cranes at remote **Cǎohǎi Lake** (p648)

⑦ Amble in low gear around the charming old town of **Zhènyuǎn** (p641), on either bank of the Wǔyáng River

PRICE INDICATORS

The following price indicators have been used for this region:

Sleeping

$ less than ¥200

$$ ¥200 to ¥400

$$$ more than ¥400

Eating

$ less than ¥50

$$ ¥50 to ¥100

$$$ more than ¥100

History

Chinese rulers set up an administration in this area as far back as the Han dynasty (206 BC–AD 220), but it was merely an attempt to maintain some measure of control over Guìzhōu's non-Han tribes.

It wasn't until the Sino-Japanese war, when the Kuomintang made Chóngqìng their wartime capital, that the development of Guìzhōu began. Most of this activity ceased at the end of WWII and industrialisation of the area wasn't revived until the Chinese Communist Party (CCP) began construction of the railways.

Despite an expanding mining industry, Guìzhōu's GDP per capita remains the lowest in all China.

Language

Mandarin Chinese is spoken by the Han majority, although with a distinctive local accent. Thai and Lao are spoken by some, and Miao-Yao (Hmong-mien) dialects by the Miao and Yao.

ℹ Getting There & Away

You can fly to more than 40 destinations within China from Guìyáng Lóngdòngbǎo International Airport, including all major Chinese cities plus direct flights to Taipei in Taiwan.

Guìyáng and Chóngqìng are linked by an expressway. Another expressway links Guìyáng with Kūnmíng, via Huángguǒshù Falls. Yúnnán is also accessible – less comfortably – by bus via Wēiníng in the west. Reach Guǎngxī through Cóngjiāng in the southeastern part of the province from Guǎngxī.

Major roads within the province have been upgraded, cutting journey times dramatically.

However, secondary roads in the northeast, west and southeast are often poor.

Sleepers to Chéngdū, Kūnmíng and Guìlín are popular. Guìyáng is due to be linked by high-speed rail with Chéngdū, Guìlín, Lèshān and Guǎngzhōu by 2015. You can enter Guìzhōu by train from Húnán through the back door from Huáihuà to Zhènyuǎn.

ℹ Getting Around

Buses are useful for much of Guìzhōu, but the train is very handy for Kǎilǐ, Zhènyuǎn, the east of the province and major cities. New expressways access the more remote western areas of the province, while the train now runs to Wēiníng in the far west too. Roads between smaller cities and villages remain a work in progress – and there are many mountains and hills out there to wind around – so bring bags of patience.

CENTRAL GUÌZHŌU

The capital city, Guìyáng, dominates the central portion of the province.

Guìyáng   贵阳

▣ 0851 / POP 3 MILLION

Guìzhōu's capital serves as a jumping-off point to Ānshùn and its surrounding sights, Huángguǒshù Falls, Kǎilǐ, Zhènyuǎn and other destinations in the province.

◉ Sights

Hóngfú Temple   BUDDHIST TEMPLE

(弘福寺; Hóngfú Sì; admission ¥2, cable car up/down ¥15/20; ⊙7am-6pm, cable car 9am-5pm) Located in **Qiánlíng Park** (黔灵公园; Qiánlíng Gōngyuán; admission ¥5; ⊙24hr) in the north of the city, Hóngfú Temple is perched near the top of 1300m Qiánlíng Shān and dates back to the 17th century. It's an easy 40-minute walk to the temple, or there's a **cable car**. The monastery has a vegetarian restaurant in the rear courtyard. From the train station area, take bus 2.

◉ Other Sights

Walk north across the river, turn right onto Yangming Lu, cross a roundabout, descend to the river and follow it to the triple-roofed **Jiàxiù Pavilion** (甲秀楼; Jiàxiù Lóu; ⊙8.30am-6.30pm) **FREE**, which is Guìyáng's most famous landmark.

Across the river stands **Cuìwēi Gōngyuán** (翠微公园; ⊙8am-11pm) FREE, an erstwhile Ming-dynasty temple which has picturesque pavilions and some pricey Miao souvenirs.

Backtrack across the bridge and walk north along Wenchang Beilu to another Ming-dynasty speciality: **Wénchāng Pavilion** (文昌阁; Wénchāng Gé), restored along with the city walls.

There are always plenty of locals lounging around, chatting and snacking here.

☞ Tours

Organised tours (in Chinese) to Huángguǒshù Falls and Lónggōng Caves leave daily from a special tourist bus station (旅游客运站; lǚyóu kèyùnzhàn) opposite Qiánlíng Park. Many hotels also organise day tours, with fewer tours (if at all) in the low season.

🛏 Sleeping

Motel 168   HOTEL **$**
(莫泰酒店; Mòtài Jiǔdiàn 168; ☑0851 1010 2020; www.motel168.com; 2 Shengfu Lu; 省府路2号; tw & d ¥199; ❋🛜) Bland, but clean and modern rooms slap in the middle of town, close to restaurants and shops. The 2nd-floor **One Cafe** is a surprisingly cool teahouse–coffee shop–bar.

Hàntíng Express   HOTEL **$$**
(汉庭连锁酒店; Hàntíng Liánsuǒ Jiǔdiàn; ☑0851 855 1888; www.htinns.com; 372 Jiefang Lu; 解放路372号; tw & d ¥219-239; ❋@🛜) Efficient and clean hotel with decent rooms. Free coffee awaits guests in the lounge, there are three internet terminals and a lift. Walk north up Zunyi Lu and turn left along Jiefang Lu; it's on the far side of the road.

Sheraton Hotel   HOTEL **$$$**
(喜来登贵航酒店; Xǐláidēng Guìháng Jiǔdiàn; ☑0851 588 8280; www.sheraton.com/guiyang; 49 Zhonghua Nanlu; 中华南路49号; d/ste ¥2488/4888; ⊖❋@🛜🏊) Sitting astride a central intersection like a colossus, the rooms here are Guìyáng's top digs. Huge, comfy beds, as well as a spa, gym, pool, and Western and Chinese restaurants. English-speaking staff too; a rarity in this town. Discounts of 50% are routinely available.

🍴 Eating & Drinking

North of the train station and Jiefang Lu, Zunyi Xiang (遵义巷) is a lively and busy food street of hotpot, Sichuan and Jiāchángcài restaurants. It shuts around 10pm.

Sìhéyuàn   GUIZHOU **$**
(四合院; ☑0851 682 5419; Qianling Xilu; mains from ¥15; ⊙noon-9.30pm) Every Guìyáng local knows this place – a rowdy, riotous and labyrinthine spot with very tasty local dishes. Perfunctory service, no English menu. It's tough to find – walk west along Qianling Xilu off Zhonghua Beilu and look for a church with a red cross atop it on the right; the restaurant is down a small alley opposite the church.

★ **Kǎilǐ Sour Fish Restaurant**   MIAO **$$**
(老凯俚酸汤鱼; Lǎo Kǎilǐ Suāntāngyú; ☑0851 584 3665; 55 Shengfu Lu; mains from ¥38; ⊙11.30am-10pm) Locals come here for the best suāntāngyú (酸汤鱼; sour fish soup) in town. A Miao delicacy that's Guìzhōu's most famous dish; fish are chopped up or dumped whole in a bubbling hotpot. Fling in vegies of your choice and you're all set. Look for the Miao waitresses standing guard outside in traditional costume.

Tree Kitchen   GUIZHOU **$$**
(树厨; Shù Chú; ☑0851 582 6853; next door to Novotel Hotel; 诺富特酒店旁; dishes from ¥28; ⊙10.30am-9.30pm) Hip for Guìyáng, this cool place in an old courtyard home has only 36 dishes on offer. All are good and offer a fusion-like take on local dishes. Try the barbecued beef and leeks (火烧葱香牛肉; huǒshāo cōng xiāng niúròu) or the pork and sliced potato (软哨土豆片; ruǎnshào túdòupián). Book ahead here.

Hobo's   BAR
(☑150 0851 2834; 11 Shangyu Jia Xiang; 上余家巷11号; cocktails from ¥45; ⊙7pm-2am) The only cocktail bar in Guìyáng – no beer here. The bartenders were trained in Japan and really know their stuff. Reasonably priced drinks, a fine collection of single malts as well and an amenable crowd. It's tucked down an alley off Qianlong Donglu's buzzing bar strip.

ℹ Information

At the time of writing, internet cafes in Guìyáng were not accepting foreigners. Some places may let you log on using one of the staff's ID cards, but don't count on it.

Bank of China (中国银行; Zhōngguó Yínháng; near cnr Dusi Lu & Zhonghua Nanlu; ⊙9am-5pm) Has an ATM and offers all services you need. Other branches can be found on the corner of Wenchang Beilu and Yan'an Donglu, and on Zunyi Lu near Renmin Sq.

Public Security Bureau (PSB; 公安局; ☑0851 590 4509; Daying Lu; ⊙8.30am-noon & 2.30-

Guìyáng

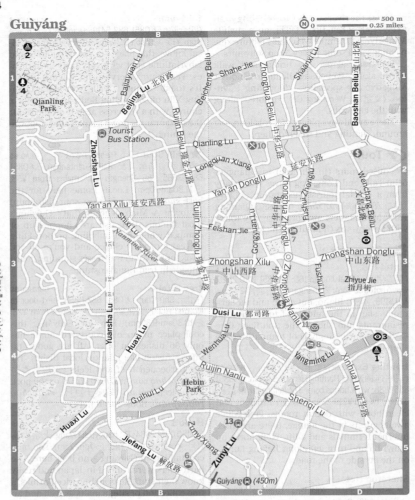

5pm Mon-Fri) The staff don't see many foreigners here, but they seem pleasant enough.

❶ Getting There & Around

AIR

Guìyáng Lóngdòngbǎo International Airport is around 10km east of the city. Destinations include:

Běijīng ¥1363, two hours 50 minutes, 10 daily

Shànghǎi ¥964, two hours 15 minutes, 10 daily

Guǎngzhōu ¥853, 1½ hours, nine daily

Chéngdū ¥719, 70 minutes, nine daily

Xī'ān ¥799, one hour 45 minutes, eight daily

Kūnmíng ¥355, 70 minutes, eight daily

Hong Kong ¥1797, 95 minutes, one daily

The **Civil Aviation Administration of China** (CAAC; 中国民航; Zhōngguó Mínháng; 264 Zunyi Lu; ☺8am-7pm) is around 1km north of the train station, on the corner with Qingyun Lu; airport buses depart every 30 minutes from the CAAC office (¥10, 20 minutes, 8am to 7pm). A taxi from the airport will cost around ¥60.

BUS

The Jīnyáng long-distance bus station (金阳客运站; Jīnyáng kèyùnzhàn) is in the western suburbs on Jinyang Nanlu, a long haul from central Guìyáng. Take bus 219 (¥2, 6.30am to

Guìyáng

10pm) from the train station; a taxi will cost ¥45. Destinations include the following:

Ānshùn ¥35, 1½ hours, every 20 minutes (7am to 9pm)

Huángguǒshù ¥55, 2½ hours, every 40 minutes (7.40am to 12.45pm)

Wēiníng ¥128, six hours, two daily (9am and 12.30pm)

For Kǎilǐ (¥60, 2½ hours, every 20 to 30 minutes, 7am to 9pm) and Cóngjiāng (¥150, seven hours, 9am, 11am and 3pm), head to the east bus station (东客运站; Dōng Kèyùnzhàn) on the eastern outskirts of town. Bus 229 (¥2) runs here from the train station. A taxi is ¥25 to ¥30.

TAXI

Taxi flagfall is ¥9; late at night it increases to ¥10.

TRAIN

Guìyáng's train station is useful for reaching Kǎilǐ, Ānshùn, Wēiníng and Zhènyuǎn. Destinations include the following (prices are for hard sleeper berths):

Ānshùn (seat) ¥16, 1½ hours, 27 daily (4.20am to 11.59pm)

Cǎohǎi (for Wēiníng) (seat) ¥50, four to eight hours, eight daily (11.30am to 6.01pm)

Chéngdū ¥223, 11 to 20 hours, seven daily (12.16am to 8.11pm)

Chóngqìng ¥143, nine to 12 hours, eight daily (12.16am to 10.05pm)

Guǎngzhōu ¥306, 19 to 22 hours, five daily (8.09am to 4.16pm)

Kǎilǐ (seat) ¥29, two to three hours, 27 daily (2.23am to 11pm)

Kūnmíng ¥156, seven to 10 hours, 16 daily (4.20am to 11.59pm)

Zhènyuǎn (seat) ¥41, three to four hours, 16 daily (2.39am to 9pm)

Qīngyán 青岩

With its winding, stone-flagged streets and restored city walls, **Qīngyán** (admission ¥10, through ticket ¥80) makes a pleasant diversion from modern Guìyáng. A former Ming-era military outpost dating back to 1378, Qīngyán was once a traffic hub between the southwest provinces, leaving the village with Taoist temples and Buddhist monasteries rubbing up against Christian churches and menacing watchtowers.

Some of the places of worship are still active; make sure to visit the tranquil **Yíngxiáng Temple** (迎祥寺; Yíngxiáng Sì), on a side street populated by fortune tellers, and to compare the current, minimalist **Catholic Church** (天主教堂; Tiānzhǔ Jiàotáng) with the now disused but much more impressive 19th-century original. Note that you don't need the through ticket to see the major sights, but you do need it to access some places in town.

Qīngyán is about 30km south of Guìyáng and makes an easy day trip. Bus 210 runs here from the left-hand side of Hébīn Park (¥2, one hour 15 minutes, every 30 minutes from 6.30am). At the time of writing, surrounding construction meant buses were stopping 5km short of Qīngyán, where you transfer onto a smaller bus (¥3) that drops you a five-minute walk from the ticket office.

EASTERN GUÌZHŌU

More than a dozen minority groups live in the gorgeous misty hills and river valleys east of Kǎilǐ; this area is truly a rare window on a typical life in China. Sure, some villages have been discovered big time, but there are still places to lose yourself here. Booming country markets and festivals are held almost weekly.

China's largest Miao village, Xījiāng, and the Dong village of Zhàoxīng, in the southeast, are particularly popular. If you have time, consider visiting them as part of the back-door route into Guǎngxī. Outside Kǎilǐ there are no places to change money, so bring plenty of renminbi with you.

Kǎilǐ 凯里

📱 0855 / POP 153,000

About 195km east of Guìyáng, Kǎilǐ is an expanding town that makes a good base for visiting minority villages or planning a backdoor trip into Guǎngxī or Húnán.

🔍 Sights & Activities

Check out the **Minorities Museum** (贵州民族博物馆; Guìzhōu Mínzú Bówùguǎn; Ningbo Lu; ⏱9am-4.30pm) **FREE** in the south of town, which has some displays of minority clothing and artefacts.

Wu Min, also known as Louisa, a local Miao woman, runs **treks** to remote Miao and Dong villages that come highly recommended. She can also organise homestays, as well as arrange for visitors to study the Miao and Dong languages and learn local dances. She speaks good English. Contact her via email at wuminlouisa@gmail.com or on 📱 158 8583 5852.

🎊 Festivals & Events

Markets and festivals are one of Guìzhōu's major attractions, and their profusion around Kǎilǐ makes this sleepy town the best place to base yourself for exploring them.

🛏 Sleeping

C'est La Vie Hotel HOTEL $$
(斯拉威酒店; Sī Lā Wēi Jiǔdiàn; 📱 0855 823 9111; www.klslw.com; 44 Yingpan Donglu; 营盘东路44号; tw/d ¥228/248; ❄🛜) New hotel with efficient staff, comfortable and sizeable rooms and a handy location close to the bus station. By far the best-value choice in town, while the attached restaurant (picture menu) is a solid and reasonably priced spot to eat.

New Century Hotel HOTEL $$
(新世纪大酒店; Xīnshìjì Dàjiǔdiàn; 📱 0855 826 0333; 1 Shaoshan Nanlu; 韶山南路1号; tw/d ¥210/200; ❄@🛜) Decent-sized rooms, if a little scuffed, comfy beds and a good central location. Avoid the noisy ones at the front. Wi-fi and ADSL internet in the rooms.

Yíngpánpō Mínzú Bīnguǎn HOTEL $$
(营盘坡民族宾馆; 📱 0855 382 7779; 53 Yingpan Donglu; 营盘东路53号; tw ¥288; ❄) This old-school, government-run place has reasonable rooms in a pleasant, secluded location with a lovely garden decorated with *Magnolia grandiflora*. Discounts of around 30% are common. No internet or wi-fi.

🍴 Eating

Kǎilǐ's streets are lined with some fantastic snack stalls. Savoury crepes, potato patties, barbecues, tofu grills, noodles, hotpot, *shuǐjiǎo* (boiled dumplings) and wonton soup overflow at reasonable prices. Look out for *guōtiēdiàn* (锅贴店; dumpling snack restaurants), which sell scrummy *guōtiē* (锅贴; fried dumplings) and Shànghǎi-style *xiǎolóngbāo;* there are several on Wenhua Beilu, including a tasty outfit just north of the long-distance bus station.

Also make tracks for the **night market** (夜市; Yèshì; off Beijing Donglu; ⏱5pm-2am), which is packed with locals and open till the wee hours.

Lǐxiǎng Miànshídiàn NOODLES $
(理想面食店; Wenhua Nanlu; dishes from ¥7; ⏱7am-7.30pm) This friendly eatery, with blue plastic furniture, serves simple dishes such as spare ribs soup (¥7) as well as tasty noodles, and is handy for a morning meal or coffee prior to village-hopping.

CELEBRATING WITH THE LOCALS, GUÌZHŌU-STYLE

Minority celebrations are lively events that can last for days at a time, and often include singing, dancing, horse racing and buffalo fighting.

One of the biggest is the **lúshēng festival**, held in either spring or autumn, depending on the village. The *lúshēng* is a reed instrument used by the Miao people. Other important festivals include the dragon boat festival (p642), **hill-leaping festival** and **'sharing the sister's meal festival'** (equivalent to Valentine's Day in the West). The **Miao new year** is celebrated on the first four days of the 10th lunar month in Kǎilǐ, Guàdīng, Zhōuxī and other Miao areas. The **fertility festival** is celebrated only every 13 years (the next one's due in 2016).

All minority festivals follow the lunar calendar and so dates vary from year to year. They will also vary from village to village and shaman to shaman. CITS in Kǎilǐ can provide you with a list of local festivals.

❶ Information

Every other shop in Kǎilǐ is a chemist.

Bank of China (中国银行; Zhōngguó Yínháng; Shaoshan Nanlu; ⊙9am-5pm) This main branch has all services and an ATM. A second branch on Beijing Donglu will also change cash. Many other ATMs around town accept foreign cards.

Bóyǔ Internet Cafe (博宇网吧; wǎngbā; Wenhua Beilu; per hr ¥3; ⊙24hr) One of a number of internet cafes on Wenhua Beilu, the staff here will normally log you in on one of their ID cards.

China International Travel Service (CITS; 中国国际旅行社; Zhōngguó Guójì Lǚxíngshè; ☑ 0855 822 2506; 53 Yingpan Donglu; ⊙9am-5.30pm) Tucked just behind Yingpan Donglu, CITS has the most up-to-date information on minority villages, festivals, markets and organised tours. Staff are helpful, with some English spoken.

Kǎilǐ People's Hospital (Kǎilǐshì Dìyī Rénmín Yīyuàn; 28 Yingpan Xilu) The best place in town for medical care.

Post Office (中国邮政; Zhōngguó Yóuzhèng; cnr Shaoshan Beilu & Beijing Donglu; ⊙9am-6pm) You can send mail overseas from here.

Public Security Bureau (PSB; 公安局; Gōng'ānjú; ☑ 0855 853 6113; Beijing Donglu; ⊙8.30-11.30am & 2.30-5.30pm Mon-Fri) Deals with all passport and visa enquiries.

❶ Getting There & Away

AIR

For departures from Guìyáng Lóngdòngbǎo International Airport, airport buses (¥60, 2½ hours, 7am to 6pm) leave regularly from the **airport office** (☑ 0855 836 3868; 73 Jinjing Lu; ⊙8am-7pm), where you can also check-in before your flight. You can also buy air tickets here.

BUS

Kǎilǐ's **long-distance bus station** (长途客运站; Chángtú Kèyùnzhàn; ☑ 0855 825 1025; Wenhua Beilu) has departures to most destinations.

Cóngjiāng ¥110, five hours, five daily (9am to 4pm)

Guìyáng ¥60, three hours, every 20 minutes (7am to 8pm)

Jǐnpíng (锦屏; for Lónglǐ) ¥91, four hours, 10 daily (8am to 4pm)

Léishān ¥14, 50 minutes, every 25 minutes (7.25am to 7pm)

Lípíng ¥137, five hours, eight daily (7.40am to 4.30pm)

Mǎjiāng ¥17, one hour, hourly (8.20am to 5.50pm)

Róngjiāng ¥77 to ¥90, 4½ hours, every 40 minutes (7.20am to 6.20pm)

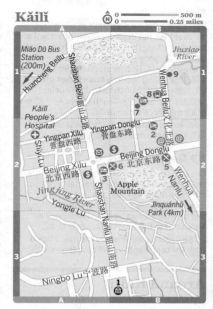

Kǎilǐ

	0	500 m
	0	0.25 miles

Kǎilǐ

◎ Sights
1 Minorities Museum...............................B3

◎ Sleeping
2 C'est La Vie Hotel................................B2
3 New Century Hotel..............................A2
4 Yíngpánpō Mínzú Bīnguǎn.................B1

◎ Eating
5 Lǐxiǎng Miànshídiàn...........................B2
6 Night Market.......................................B2

❶ Information
7 China International Travel
   Service... B1

❶ Transport
8 Long-Distance Bus Station B1
9 Train Ticket Office B1

Xījiāng ¥15.50, 80 minutes, hourly (8.40am to 5.40pm)

Zhènyuǎn ¥35, two hours, six daily (8.30am to 4pm)

For Chóng'ān (¥13, one hour, every 20 minutes, 6.40am to 6pm) and Huángpíng (¥20, one hour, every 20 minutes, 6.40am to 6pm) head to the **Miáo Dū Bus Station** (苗都客运站; Miáo Dū Kèyùnzhàn) on Huangcheng Beilu.

TRAIN

Kǎilǐ's train station is a couple of kilometres north of town but departures are infrequent and the service slow (but cheap), apart from regular trains to Guìyáng (¥28, two to three hours), Zhènyuǎn (¥14, 1½ hours) and Huáihuà (¥21 to ¥42, four hours). A handy **train ticket office** (火车票代售处; Huǒchēpiào dàishòuchù; ☑ 0855 381 7920; 38 Wenhua Beilu; ⊙ 8.30am-6.30pm) is on Wenhua Beilu.

For longer distances, it's worth stopping in Guìyáng to secure a reservation.

ℹ️ Getting Around

Bus fares cost ¥1 in Kǎilǐ and almost all of the buses departing from the train station follow the same route: up Qingjiang Lu, past the long-distance bus station, along Beijing Donglu and down Shaoshan Nanlu to the Minorities Museum. For the train station, take bus 2.

Taxi flagfall is ¥6. A taxi to the train station from the centre of town will cost around ¥10.

Around Kǎilǐ

If you are village-hopping into Guǎngxī, plan on spending about a week. Note that some of these villages charge entrance fees. An extraordinary number of markets are held in the villages surrounding Kǎilǐ. Check with the CITS in Kǎilǐ for the latest information.

Xījiāng   西江

Snugly ensconced in the pretty Léigōng Hills, **Xījiāng** (西江; admission ¥100) is thought to be the largest Miao village (its full name in Chinese is 西江千户苗寨; Xījiāng Qiānhù Miáozhài – Xījiāng 1000-Household Miao Village) and is famous for its embroidery and silver ornaments (the Miao believe that silver can dispel evil spirits). Now firmly embedded on the tourist trail, commercialisation has cheapened its allure but it still flings together a pastoral picture of paddies, wooden *diàojiǎolóu* (traditional handcrafted houses), water buffalo and mists.

From the ticket office, buses (¥5) run to the village itself. The tourist infrastructure runs to a performance square, English signposts, souvenir shops, an ATM taking foreign cards (sometimes) and even a few cafes with wi-fi. Head to the western side of the village for a more authentic experience. Come evening, when the day trippers have disappeared, the village reverts to a more traditional pace of life.

When the sun obliges, Xījiāng is lovely. Head away from the village on paths that weave through rice paddies, sidestepping farmers and water buffalo, and recharge your soul in the surrounding hills. A lovely **trek** is the 50-minute hike past terraced fields and rice paddies over the hills to Kāijué Miao Village (开觉苗寨; Kāijué Miáozhài) and Kāijué Waterfall (开觉瀑布; Kāijué Pùbù) a bit further beyond.

There's also a three-day **trek** from Xījiāng to Páiyáng (排羊), a Miao village north of Xījiāng. This trail winds its way through some remote minority villages and lush scenery. You will probably find accommodation with locals en route, but you shouldn't expect it so come prepared to sleep under the stars. Also ask about the largely uphill 27km trek from Xījiāng to gorgeous Léigōngpíng through a lushly green and forested landscape; you can continue on to Léishān from Léigōngpíng.

Many families in Xījiāng offer rooms from ¥50 and there are an increasing number of guesthouses. The **Miao Family Guesthouse** (苗寨人家; Miáo Zhài Rénjiā; ☑ 0855 334 8688; tw ¥188) has clean, comfortable rooms with hot water. It's across the river on the eastern side of the village. Quite a hefty walk to the top of the village is rewarded with excellent views from the undisturbed **Gǔzàngtóujiā** (鼓藏头家; ☑ 136 3809 5568; r ¥50-100), where clean and fresh wooden rooms occupy a traditional building opposite the historic Gǔzàngtáng, an ancestral home which houses drums used in festivals. It's run by an old man who speaks nary a word of English.

From Kǎilǐ, buses run hourly between 8.40am and 5.40pm. There are hourly buses back to Kǎilǐ from 8.30am to 5.30pm. Alternatively, heading south and east towards Guǎngxī, there are regular buses to Léishān (¥11, 1½ hours, 6.30am to 5.40pm), from where you can head south towards Róngjiāng (榕江). There are also two buses a day to Guìyáng's East Bus Station (¥80, four hours, 9am and 3pm).

Lángdé   郎德

Superb extant Miao architecture and cobbled pathways naturally draw loads of tour buses for elaborate singing, dancing and reed flute performances in this village. But the commercialisation can't overcome the wondrousness of the locals. There's a terrific 15km **trail** along the Bālā River that will take you through several Miao villages.

About 20km outside Kǎilǐ, buses pass by Lángdé (¥11) on the way to Léishān. The village is 2km from the main road. Getting away, head out on the street and flag down a bus back to Kǎilǐ.

Léishān 雷山

This village is usually used as a transit point, but you can also head to **Léigōng Shān** (雷公山; Léigōng Mountain; admission ¥100), at 2178m, which offers some interesting hiking opportunities and some charming settlements, including the attractive Miao village of Wūdōngzhài. Other nearby Miao villages include Páikǎ (Páikǎ Miáozhài), around 3km south of Léishān, where *lúshēng* bamboo and reed musical instruments have been handmade for centuries. Either walk or hop on a Dàtáng-bound bus (¥3) from Léishān bus station. The road from Léishān continues towards Róngjiāng. From Kǎilǐ, there are numerous buses to Léishān (¥14, one hour).

Shíqiáo 石桥

Shíqiáo means 'stone bridge' and you'll know why when you spy the lovely ones in this beautiful Miao town southwest of Kǎilǐ. This town was also famed for its handmade paper, which can still be seen.

To reach Shíqiáo, take any bus to Léishān and change there.

Mátáng 麻塘

This village around 20km from Kǎilǐ is home to the Gejia. Officially classified as a subgroup of the Miao minority, the Gejia have different customs, dress and language, and are renowned batik artisans; their traditional dress often features batik and embroidery. Mátáng has been dolled up for tourism – the inevitable performance square has materialised – and the women hawkers can be persistent. A worthwhile 30-minute walk from Mátáng brings you to the village of Shílóngzhài, populated by another sub-branch of the Miao called the Xijia.

Mátáng is 2km from the main road and buses regularly run past the drop-off point in the direction of Chóng'ān (¥7) and Kǎilǐ (¥9). Just stand on the side of the road and flag down anything that comes your way.

Lónglǐ 隆里

Stranded in splendid isolation amid fields and rice paddies near the Húnán border, **Lónglǐ** is a former garrison town populated by the descendants of Han soldiers sent to protect the empire from the pesky Miao. One of the province's 'eco-museums' (read, real-live village), it's fascinating for its extant architecture.

Enter via the East Gate (Dōngmén) and savour its warren of narrow cobblestone streets – you'll only need about an hour – and mostly wooden houses, lovely courtyards,

GUIZHOU AROUND KǍILǏ

TRADITIONAL GARMENTS

The assortment of clothing among Guìzhōu's minorities provides travellers with a daily visual feast. Clothes are as much a social and ethnic denominator as pure decoration. They also indicate whether or not a woman is married, and provide clues to a woman's wealth and skills at weaving and embroidery.

Many women in remote areas still weave their own hemp and cotton cloth. Some families, especially in Dong areas, still ferment their own indigo paste as well, and you will see this for sale in traditional markets. Women will often not attend festivals in the rain for fear that the dyes in their fabrics will run. Methods of producing indigo are greatly treasured and kept secret, but are increasingly threatened by the introduction of artificial chemical dyes.

Embroidery is central to minority costume and is a tradition passed down from mother to daughter. Designs include many important symbols and references to myths and history. Birds, fish and a variety of dragon motifs are popular. The highest quality work is often reserved for baby carriers, and many young girls work on these as they approach marrying age. Older women will often spend hundreds of hours embroidering their own funeral clothes.

Costumes move with the times. In larger towns, Miao women often substitute their embroidered smocks with a good woolly jumper (sweater) and their headdresses look suspiciously like mass-produced pink and yellow Chinese towels.

pavilions, temples and town walls. The surrounding area looks prime for bike exploration, as well.

Just outside the old town, **Lóngli Gǔchéng Jiǔdiàn** (隆里古城酒店; ☎ 0855-718 0018, 136 3855 4888; tw ¥80) offers basic rooms with squat toilets.

Coming from Kǎilǐ is rather arduous as there's no direct bus. First take a bus to Jǐnpíng (锦屏; ¥91), then switch to another bus (¥16, 1½ hours, half-hourly or so from 7.30am to around 5pm) to Lóngli.

Bāshā   岜沙

Visiting historic **Bāshā** (岜沙; admission ¥60) is like stepping back in time to the Tang or Song eras. The local men wear period clothes with daggers secured to their belts and, when not farming, hunt with antique rifles. Meanwhile, the women parade in full Miao rig with their hair twisted in a curl on top of their heads.

Quite why Bāshā is stuck in a timewarp is a mystery, as it's only 7.5km from very modern Cóngjiāng (从江). Not even the locals can explain why they've retained their ancient customs so well. Nor is Bāshā undiscovered. A collection of six hamlets that sprawls across a beautiful valley, Chinese–English signs point the way to the various places of interest. It's best seen during a festival, even if that means more visitors, because most of the year the men are out in the fields during the day. But at any time, the surrounding countryside is superb. You might also be able to arrange a hunting trip with the men.

You can find very rudimentary rooms for ¥30. By far the nicest place to stay is the family-run **Gǔfēngzhài Qīngnián Lǚguǎn** (古风寨青年旅馆; ☎ 138 8554 9720; dm ¥50, tw/d ¥128/168; @ 🛜). Walk down the path to the left of the village square to find it. Alternatively, you can spend the night in Cóngjiāng. The **Zhèng Péng Bīnguǎn** (正鹏宾馆; ☎ 0855 641 2757; tw ¥120; ❄ 🛜) has spacious, clean rooms (but squat toilets) and wi-fi and is across the road from the bus station.

A few orange and grey minibuses run between Cóngjiāng and Bāshā early in the morning and late in the afternoon (¥5). Otherwise, you'll have to take a taxi (it's a very steep walk up to the village). The return trip should cost ¥60; you'll need the driver to wait for you.

Zhàoxīng   肇兴

Perhaps the quintessential Dong village and packed with traditional wooden structures, several wind and rain bridges and four remarkable drum towers, **Zhàoxīng** (admission ¥100) is no longer the little-known paradise it once was. Its sheer uniqueness makes for a powerful draw, and the locals are certainly not complaining about the increase in visitors.

Yet, the essential, amazing nature of Zhàoxīng hasn't changed. Yes, the restaurants on the main street have English menus, which is just as well as they eat rat (老鼠肉; lǎoshǔ ròu) in these parts, and there are now any number of quasi-inns and guesthouses offering rooms from ¥50. But away from the main street, Zhàoxīng remains a working farming village, where most people still speak only their native Dong language and are extremely welcoming. The tour groups might swoop in, but Zhàoxīng remains a very easy place to while away a few days.

Nearby, too, are mostly tourist-free Dong villages. Hike west out of Zhàoxīng from the bus station for an hour, up a steep hill and past some splendid rice terraces, and you're in equally friendly **Jītáng** (基塘), which has its own drum tower. Head the other way out of Zhàoxīng through the fields and two hours later you reach **Táng'ān** (堂安), a village so essentially Dong it's been named a living museum.

The **Wàngjiāng Lóu Hostel** (望江楼客栈; Wàngjiānglóu Kèzhàn; ☎ 0855 613 0269; tw & d ¥100; ❄ @ 🛜) isn't a hostel but a family-run place by the river with fresh and clean wooden rooms featuring hot showers and sit-down toilets. The most upmarket digs in the village can be found at the **Zhàoxīng Bīnguǎn** (肇兴宾馆; ☎ 0855 613 0899; tw & d ¥228-398; ❄ 🛜), where rooms are spotless, with tiny gleaming bathrooms. It's a tour-group haunt, so it's often booked out.

Getting here from Kǎilǐ is a slog. First you have to travel to Cóngjiāng (¥110, 4½ hours, five daily from 9am to 4pm) and then change for a bus to Zhàoxīng (¥19, two hours, 7.50am and 1pm). From Líping (黎平), there are five buses daily (¥25, 3½ hours, 8.20am to 2.50pm).

Heading out of Zhàoxīng, there are two morning buses (¥19, 7.30am and noon) to Cóngjiāng. If you're heading to Sānjiāng (三江) in Guǎngxī, you'll need to change buses in Líping (¥25, four daily, 7.20am, 9am, 10am and 1pm) or Cóngjiāng, where there are frequent buses to Guìlín (¥82) too.

Zhènyuǎn   镇远

☑ 0855 / POP 60,000

Plunging into the far east of Guìzhōu from Kǎilǐ to Zhènyuǎn, the train traverses an astonishing panorama of surging peaks and hills densely cloaked with trees. The delightful riverine town of Zhènyuǎn sits picturesquely astride the Wuyang River (Wǔyáng Hé), pinched between towering cliffs and peaks. A former outpost on the trade route from Yúnnán to Húnán, Zhènyuǎn is largely off the Western traveller radar and the old town is a delightful place for a few days temple hunting before framing the enchanting night-time river scenes through your hotel window.

⊙ Sights

Qīnglóng Dòng   TEMPLE
(青龙洞; Green Dragon Cave; admission ¥60; ⊙ 7.30am-6pm) Across the river from the old town, the epic vertical warren of temples, grottoes, corridors and caves of Qīnglóng Dòng rises up against **Zhōnghé Mountain** (中和山; Zhōnghéshān). Flooded with lights at night, it forms a sublime backdrop to the town. Put aside a good hour for exploration: it's a labyrinth and there's a lot to see, including some choice panoramas.

The intriguing complex was commenced in the Ming dynasty, its temples dedicated to the three faiths of Buddhism, Taoism and Confucianism. At the far entrance to **Zhōngyuán Cave** (中元洞; Zhōngyuán Dòng) is a stone table allegedly used by the eccentric founder of taichi, Zhang Sanfeng. The exterior of the splendid **Wànshòu Gōng** (万寿宫) – once the Jiāngxī Guildhall – is still bedecked with slogans, its interior a prime example of *jiāngnán*-style architecture with delightful woodcarvings. The unruffled Jade Emperor presides over everything – and some fine views – from the **Yùhuáng Gé** (玉皇阁; Jade Emperor Pavilion), his namesake pavilion at the top. Watch out when walking, as some of the stone steps are super slippery.

Zhùshèng Bridge   BRIDGE
Zhènyuǎn's old **bridge** (祝圣桥; Zhùshèng Qiáo), a gorgeous and robust span of arches topped with a three-storey **pavilion**, is an impressive sight, leading visitors across the

water to Qīnglóng Dòng. River views along the river from the bridge at night are serene, with Qīnglóng Dòng splendidly lit up.

Sifangjing Xiang   ALLEY
(四方井巷) Four old and well-preserved alleys lead north away from the river: Sifangjing Xiang, Fuxing Xiang, Renshou Xiang and Chongzikou Xiang. Wander along Sifangjing Xiang and peek at its namesake **Sìfāngjǐng** (Four Directions Well), with its three deities overlooking the water, capped with red cloths. Note the magnificently made stone steps of this alley and the gorgeous old residences, a picture at night when they're dressed with red lanterns.

Miáojiāng Great Wall   WALL
(苗疆长城; Miáojiāng Chángchéng; Miao Border Great Wall; admission ¥30) There's an energetic half-hour climb past the **Four Officials Temple** (四官殿; Sìguān Diàn) to the top of **Shípíng Shān** (石屏山) above town to the remains of this **wall**. Get up really early or leave it late in the day and you could get a jump on ticket collectors. Undulating across peaks, the wall is quite substantial and glorious views range over town.

Tán Gōngguǎn   HISTORIC BUILDING
(谭公馆) Just north of Wuyanghe Bridge (Wǔyánghé Dàqiáo), the splendid Tán Gōngguǎn (谭公馆) is sadly shut, inaccessible and unrestored. Festooned with Mao-era slogans, the building is a remarkably solid piece of historic architecture and remains unconverted. Note the carvings on the door pillars.

⊙ Other Sights

The small **Fire God Temple** (炎帝宫; Yándì Gōng) backs onto the green cliffs, housing the fearsome deities Yandi and the fiery-faced Huoshen (Fire God). Now pretty much a block of flats from the 1960s, little remains of the **Confucius Temple** (文庙; Wénmiào; Shuncheng Jie) save its main facade and the Lǐ Mén (Gate of Rites). The **Zhènyuǎn Museum** (镇远展览馆; Zhènyuǎn Zhǎnlǎnguǎn; ⊙ 8.30am-5.30pm) FREE displays items relating to the history of the town. The old **city walls** on the south side of the Wuyang River have been restored and you can walk a considerable way along them towards the train station. The **Tiānhòu Temple** (天后宫; Tiānhòu Gōng) – a temple dedicated to the goddess Tianhou – can be found along Minzhu Jie to the west of the old town. It's worth hunting

Zhènyuǎn

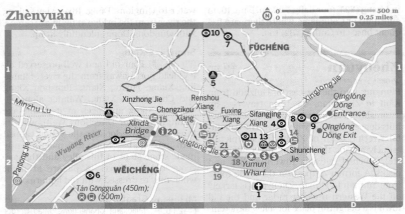

Zhènyuǎn

out the welcoming **Catholic Church** (天主教堂; Tiānzhǔ Jiàotáng) south of the river. Further along the road from the church, the compound and watchtowers of **Hépíng Cūn** (和平村; ⊙8.30am-5.30pm) was Kuomintang HQ during the war against Japan.

ⓖ Tours

Buy tickets for the riverborne cruises (¥80 for 35 minutes, 8.30am to 9.30pm) at the office next to **Yumun Wharf** (禹门码头; Yǔmén Mǎtóu), identified by the decorative arch. Travel agents line Xinglong Jie; you should also be able to book tours through your hotel.

✲ Festivals & Events

On the fifth day of the fifth lunar month **dragon boat festival** races churn the waters of the Wuyang River. In the high season, **dragon boat races** take place most Saturdays at around 1pm from Xīndà Bridge (新大桥; Xīn Dàqiáo).

🛏 Sleeping

There are rooms everywhere in the old town. Don't expect any spoken English. Rooms south of the river get the amplified sound of trains rumbling by. Ask for discounts.

Liúhúlán Jiǔdiàn HOTEL $
(刘胡兰酒店; ☏0855 572 0586; Xinglong Jie; 兴隆街; r ¥180-260; ❄@🛜) This handy hotel has clean, decent-sized rooms overlooking the river, some with big sliding windows and terraces, although there are no sit-down toilets. Note that locals pronounce this place 'Liufulan'. Regular discounts bring room prices down to ¥130.

Deyin Hotel
HOTEL $

(德音驿站; Déyīn Yìzhàn; ☑ 0855 217 0888; 70 Xingzhong Jie; 新中街70号; tw & d ¥168-188; ✻ 🛜) Brand-new, modern digs with great beds and nice bathrooms. The top-floor rooms have river views.

Dàhéguān Hotel
HOTEL $$

(大河关宾馆; Dàhéguān Bīnguǎn; ☑ 0855 571 0188; Shuncheng Jie; 顺城街; tw & d ¥268-469; ✻ 🛜) Rather swish for Zhènyuǎn, this place on the corner comes with attractive rooms with proper bathrooms and comfy beds, all set around a wooden courtyard. Discounts of 25% are normally available.

Héjiā Dàyuàn Kèzhàn
HOTEL $$

(何家大院客栈; ☑ 0855 572 3770; Chongzikou Xiang; 冲子口巷 8 号; tw/d ¥388/428; ✻ 🛜) Just refurbished, this traditional courtyard hotel has pleasant rooms in a lovely old property tucked away up an alley away from the river. Discounts should be available.

🍴 Eating & Drinking

The main drag is full of restaurants, many of them aimed at tourists. Look out for local men wielding hefty wooden mallets to pound *mùchuí xiāngsū*, a kind of sweet, crispy and brittle biscuit made from walnut, sesame seeds, sugar and honey (it's delicious). A handful of places along Xinglong Jie sell cheap plates of fried *jiǎozi* (stuffed dumplings). A few bars dotted along Xinglong Jie see local bands step up on stage to an audience of largely empty tables.

Gǔchéng Zhēngjiǎo
DUMPLINGS $

(古城蒸饺; Xinglong Jie; 兴隆街; mains ¥9; ⊙noon-2am) Right next to Yumun Wharf, this very simple restaurant does lovely *jiānjiǎo* (fried dumplings) and is a cheap place for a beer.

Man Man's Little Space Café
CAFE

(漫漫的小宇宙; Mànmàn dē Xiǎoyǔzhòu; 41 Zhou Dajie; 周大街41号; dishes from ¥18) Amiable, easygoing place for a coffee or evening beer right by the river. Also does a few small Chinese dishes. Look for the yellow lantern

ℹ️ Information

Agricultural Bank of China (农业银行; Nóngyè Yínháng; Xinglong Jie; ⊙9am-5pm) ATM taking foreign cards; opposite Zhènyuǎn Museum.

Industrial and Commercial Bank of China (ICBC; 工商银行; Gōngshāng Yínháng; Xinglong Jie; ⊙9am-5pm) ATM taking foreign cards.

Post Office (中国邮政; Xinglong Jie; ⊙9am-6pm) You can send mail overseas from here.

Public Security Bureau (PSB; 公安局; Gōng'ānjú; Xinglong Jie; ⊙8.30-11.30am & 2.30-5.30pm) Across from Yumun Pier.

Shénzhōu Internet Cafe (神舟网吧; Shénzhōu wǎngbā; per hr ¥3; ⊙24hr) On south side of the Xīndà Bridge by the wall.

Xīnshíkōng Internet Cafe (新时空网吧; Xīnshíkōng wǎngbā; Panlong Jie; per hr ¥3; ⊙24hr) Internet cafe.

Zhènyuǎn Tourist & Information Centre (镇远旅游咨询服务中心; Zhènyuǎn Lǚyóu Zīxún Fúwù Zhōngxīn; Xinzhong Jie; ⊙8am-8pm) Good for maps of Zhènyuǎn.

ℹ️ Getting There & Around

A **ferry** (¥1; ⊙6am-7.30pm) can punt you across the river.

The best way to reach Zhènyuǎn from Guìyáng is by train (the tracks thunder south of the old town). The train station (huǒchēzhàn) is on the south of the river in the southwest of town, not far from Wuyanghe Bridge (Wǔyánghé Dàqiáo). A taxi to the old town from the train station is ¥5. It's a good 20-minute walk to the old town from the train station, so either book your ticket out of Zhènyuǎn when you arrive or ask your hotel owner to book one for you (they will need to take your passport, however). You can book tickets more than three days in advance at the post office for a commission (¥15). Trains from Zhènyuǎn include the following:

Ānshùn ¥54, 5½ hours, five daily (6.30am to 3.45pm)

Guìyáng ¥41, 3¾ hours, regular

Huáihuà ¥29, 2½ hours, regular

Kǎilǐ ¥15, 1¼ hours, regular

Yùpíng ¥13, one hour, regular

The bus station (chángtú qìchēzhàn) is opposite the train station.

Bàojīng ¥13, three daily (10.20am, 12.30pm and 3.20pm)

Kǎilǐ ¥21, six daily (8.30am to 4.30pm)

Tóngrén ¥55, two daily (11am and 3pm)

Around Zhènyuǎn

Tiěxī Gorge
铁溪

A trip to the pleasant **Tiěxī Gorge** (admission ¥50) offers the chance to plunge along rocky trails shaded by overhanging trees. Make sure not to miss **Dragon Pool** (龙潭; Lóngtán) and **Jīguān Mountain** (鸡冠岭; Jīguān Lǐng). Food vendors are scattered along the two and half hour route to the mountain, ensuring you won't go hungry. Reach the gorge by buggy (¥6, 20 minutes) from the western end of Zhusheng Bridge in Zhènyuǎn; vehicles depart when full.

Bàojīng 报京

Although a January 2014 fire destroyed around 100 homes in this Dong minority village, most will have been rebuilt by the time you visit. A few examples of fine *diàojiǎolóu* architecture remain. Located 40km from Zhènyuǎn, the village is also known for the **seed sowing festival** (播种 节; *bōzhǒngjié*). Held on the third day of the third lunar month, it's a lively celebration of dancing and courtship rituals. Three buses (¥13, 10.20am, 12.30pm and 3.20pm) run to Bàojīng daily from the bus station in Zhènyuǎn.

WESTERN GUÌZHŌU

Birds, caves and waterfalls are the main attractions of this region. Outside Ānshùn, the thundering Huángguǒshù Falls is Guìzhōu's premier tourist attraction, while Zhījīn Cave is one of the largest in the world. Way out west, the town of Wēiníng has one of China's top birdwatching locations in Cǎohǎi Lake, and also offers a backdoor route into Yúnnán.

Ānshùn 安顺

☑ 0853 / POP 763,313

Once a centre for tea and opium trading, Ānshùn remains the commercial hub of western Guìzhōu and is now most famous as a producer of batik, kitchen knives and the lethal Ānjiǔ brand of alcohol. Once a marvellous historical city ringed by a town wall, the city's heritage has largely vanished and it's the surrounding sights that are the real draws.

◎ Sights

A modest chunk of the former **Ānshùn city walls** (安顺城墙遗址; Ānshùn chéngqiáng yízhǐ) stands opposite the Fènghuángshān Dàjiǔdiàn on Tashan Donglu, where a revealing photo on the wall depicts Ānshùn during Republican days, before the advent of concrete, road widening and socialist aesthetics.

Fǔwén Miào CONFUCIAN TEMPLE

(府文庙; admission ¥10; ☉7.30am-midnight) Check out this charming Confucian temple in the north of town with some stunningly intricate cloud-scrolling carvings on the twin stone pillars before the main hall.

Dōnglín Temple BUDDHIST TEMPLE

(东林寺; Dōnglín Sì; ☉8am-5pm) FREE The resident Buddhist monks welcome visitors warmly to this temple, built in AD 1405 (during the Ming dynasty) and restored in 1668.

Lóngwáng Miào BUDDHIST TEMPLE

(龙王庙; ☉7.30am-5.30pm) FREE A working Buddhist temple, just off Zhonghua Beilu.

⌂ Sleeping

If your Chinese is up to it, try one of the guesthouses *(lǚguǎn)* in the train station area for a cheap room.

Péngchéng Bīnguǎn HOTEL $

(鹏程宾馆; ☑0853 372 2555; 10 Ma'anshan Lu; 马鞍山路10号; d ¥80-120; ❄@☎) A cut above its competitors close to the train station – less noisy with modern, compact rooms and wi-fi. It's near the top of Maan Shan Lu. No English sign: look for four white characters on a yellow background.

Xīxiùshān Bīnguǎn HOTEL $$

(西秀山宾馆; ☑0853 333 7888; 63 Zhonghua Nanlu; 中华南路63号; s, d & tw ¥288-388; ❄@☎) Pleasingly different, rooms here are set back from the road with a garden in the main courtyard at the rear. Rooms are clean, large and comfortable. Singles are discounted by 50%, but are smaller and older and don't come with wi-fi or ADSL internet.

Fènghuángshān Dàjiǔdiàn HOTEL $$

(凤凰山大酒店; Golden Phoenix Mountain Hotel; ☑0853 322 5724; 58 Tashan Donglu; 塔山东路 58号; tw & d ¥228; ❄@☎) There's loads of brass and faded marble here, bathrooms are cramped and rooms have seen better days, but the staff are pleasant enough and there's wi-fi. Look for the building with two lions standing guard outside. Discounts of around 30% are normally available.

✗ Eating

Local speciality *qiáoliángfěn* (乔凉粉) is a spicy dish made from buckwheat noodles and preserved bean curd. A good on-the-run snack is *chōngchōng gāo* (冲冲糕), a cake made from steamed sticky rice with sesame and walnut seeds and sliced wax gourd. Also look out for plates of fried potatoes, hawked at the roadside, which taste like chips; locals call them *yángyù*. There are hotpot places on Nan Shui Lu close to the night market.

By far the best place to eat is the **night market** (安顺夜市; Ānshùn Yèshì; Gufu Jie; ⏰5pm-late). It's the most happening spot in Ānshùn, with the locals crowding out the many food tents and stalls that set up here. The speciality is barbecued fish (*kǎoyú),* while Uighur chefs, snails sizzling up in woks and proudly displayed pigs' trotters fill out the picture.

Liúyìshǒu Kǎoyú   SEAFOOD **$**
(留一手烤鱼; Hongqi Lu; 红旗路; fish per jīn from ¥30; ⏰6pm-late) Packed during night-market hours, when the restaurant fills its premises on Hongqi Lu and spills onto tables flung out on Gufu Jie, this heaving eatery specialises in tasty grilled fish. It's best to dine as a group, as fish weights start at around three *jīn*.

❶ Information

Bank of China (中国银行; Zhōngguó Yínháng; cnr Tashan Xilu & Zhonghua Nanlu; ⏰9am-5pm) Offers all services and has an ATM. There are many other ATMs around town.

Post Office (中国邮政; Zhōngguó Yóuzhèng; cnr Zhonghua Nanlu & Tashan Donglu) Look for it tucked next to the China Telecom building.

❶ Getting There & Around

The north bus station (客车北站; kèchē běizhàn) has buses (¥34, three hours, every 20 minutes, 7am to 6pm) to Zhījīn town (for Zhījīn Cave). Almost every other bus now leaves from the new **east bus station** (东客运站; dōng kèyùnzhàn), 10km east of the centre. Bus 16 (¥1) runs here from Zhonghua Nanlu opposite the Xīxiùshān Bīnguǎn. A taxi is ¥25 to ¥30.

Guìyáng ¥35, 1½ hours, every 20 minutes (7.10am to 7.10pm)

Huángguǒshù ¥20, one hour, every 20 minutes (7.20am to 7pm)

Kūnmíng sleeper ¥150, 10 hours, four daily (9am, 10.40am, 1pm and 4pm)

Lónggōng Caves ¥10, 40 minutes, every 30 minutes (7.30am to 6pm)

Píngbà ¥15, 40 minutes, every 30 minutes (7.30am to 6.30pm)

Shuǐchéng ¥60, 3½ hours, every 50 minutes (8.20am to 4.40pm)

Wēiníng ¥90, five to six hours, one daily (10am)

Yúnfēng ¥5, 40 minutes, every 30 minutes (7.30am to 6pm)

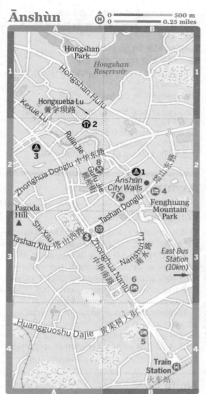

Ānshùn

⊚ **Sights**
1 Dōnglín Temple.....................................B2
2 Fūwén Miào...A2
3 Lóngwáng Miào....................................A2

⌂ **Sleeping**
4 Fènghuángshān Dàjiǔdiàn..................B2
5 Péngchéng Bīnguǎn...........................B4
6 Xīxiùshān Bīnguǎn..............................B3

⊗ **Eating**
7 Ānshùn Night Market..........................B2
8 Liúyìshǒu Kǎoyú.................................A2

Most trains from the train station (huǒchēzhàn) heading east stop in Guìyáng (¥15, 1½ hours, regular). It is still hard to get sleeper reservations for trains from here; pick them up in Guìyáng instead. There's a train ticket office a few hundred metres north of the train station on Zhonghua Nanlu.

Destinations include the following:

Cǎohǎi (for Wēiníng) ¥37, three to five hours, eight daily

Guìyáng ¥15, 1½ hours, regular

Kǎilǐ ¥43, four hours, nine daily

Kūnmíng ¥75 (seat), ¥133 (hard sleeper), eight to 10 hours

Liùpánshuǐ ¥24, 2½ hours, regular

Bus 1 zips around town from the train station and up Tashan Donglu. Bus 2 travels between the train station and the north bus station. Bus 16 runs from Zhonghua Nanlu to the east bus station. Buses cost ¥1. Taxi flagfall is ¥6.

Around Ānshùn

Lónggōng Caves　龙宫洞

The vast **cave** (Lónggōng Dòng; Dragon Palace; admission ¥120; ☺8.30am-5.30pm) network snakes through 20 hills. While some travellers enjoy drifting through the caves on rowboats with their subdued guides, others find the whole experience – coloured lights, cheesy music, tour groups – kitschy.

Lónggōng is 23km south of Ānshùn and an easy day trip from there. Local buses (¥10, 40 minutes) depart every 30 minutes from Ānshùn's east bus station from 7.30am. Returning, buses leave until about 5pm.

Zhījīn Cave　织金洞

As the largest cave in China, and one of the biggest in the entire world at 10km long and up to 150m high, **Zhījīn Cave** (Zhījīn Dòng; admission ¥135; ☺8.30am-5.30pm) gets tourist accolades. *Lord of the Rings* has been used to describe the abstract landscape of spectacular shapes and spirals, often cathedral-like, reaching from the floor to the ceiling.

Tickets to the cave, which is 15km outside Zhījīn and 125km north of Ānshùn, include a compulsory 2½-hour Chinese-only tour (minimum 10 people). The tour covers some 6km of the cave, up steep, slippery steps at times, and there are English captions at the main points along the way. Solo travellers visiting outside peak summer months or Chinese holidays should be prepared for what can be a tedious wait for enough people to roll up to form a group.

A long day trip from Ānshùn is possible, but you need to be on an early bus to Zhījīn (¥34, three hours, from 7am), from Ānshùn's north bus station. Once there, hop in a taxi (¥4) to the local bus station on Yuping Jie

and catch one of the minibuses that leave regularly for the cave entrance (¥8, 50 minutes). Returning from the caves, buses leave regularly. The last bus back to Ānshùn heads out of Zhījīn at 5.30pm.

From Guìyáng, regular buses (return ¥110, four hours) depart every 30 minutes to Zhījīn from the long-distance bus station from 6.30am in the morning until 5.20pm.

Huángguǒshù Falls　黄果树大瀑布

Disgorging from endless buses, a friendly invasion of frenetic tourists from all over China come to see the 77.8m-tall, 81m-wide **Huángguǒshù Falls** (Huángguǒshù Dàpùbù; Yellow Fruit Tree Falls; admission Mar-Oct ¥180, Nov-Feb ¥160; ☺7.30am-6pm), making this Guìzhōu's number-one natural attraction. From May to October in particular, these falls really rock the local landscape with their cacophony, while rainbows from the mist dance about **Rhinoceros Pool** below and colourful peacocks show off their dazzling plumage.

The cascades are actually part of a 450-sq-km cave and karst complex discovered when engineers explored the area in the 1980s to gauge the region's hydroelectric potential. Although there are paths around the falls, the entire area is vast and sights so spread out you'll really need to board one of the **sightseeing cars** (guānguāngchē; ¥50). They link the main areas, which include **Dǒupōtáng Waterfall**, **Lúosītān Waterfall**, **Tiānxīng Qiáo Scenic Zone** and the **Main Waterfall Scenic Zone**. Hiring a cab from the entrance for a tour will cost around ¥100 or expect to pay around ¥20 for a single journey.

In the main waterfall area, don't miss groping your way through the dripping natural corridor in the rock face of the 134m-long **Water Curtain Cave** (水帘洞; Shuǐlián Dòng), behind the waterfall.

Going underground into the colossal caves within the geological **Tiānxīng Qiáo Scenic Zone** (天星桥景区; Tiānxīng Qiáo Jǐngqū) is a quite awe-inspiring sideshow, especially if you do not have time for the Lónggōng or Zhījīn Caves.

You can do Huángguǒshù Falls in a day trip from Guìyáng at a push, while it's an easy one from Ānshùn. There are accommodation options everywhere in Huángguǒshù village, but there is little need to overnight.

From Ānshùn, buses (¥20, one hour, 7.20am to 7pm) run every 30 minutes from

> **WORTH A TRIP**
>
> ## FÀNJÌNGSHĀN
>
> Accessed via the gateway town of Tóngrén in the northeast of Guìzhōu, the 2572m-high Buddhist-named mountain of **Fànjìngshān** (梵净山; ¥110) is a must for fans of Buddhist culture, nature lovers or those en route to Húnán or Chóngqìng from Zhènyuǎn or Kǎilǐ. The reserve provides a home to more than half the province's protected plants and two-thirds of its animals, including the very rare (and even more rarely glimpsed) golden monkey (jīnsīhóu).
>
> To reach the mountain, hop on a bus (¥21, hourly, 7.30am to 5.30pm, 40 minutes) to Jiāngkǒu (江口) from Tóngrén's main bus station. From Jiāngkǒu, buses (¥9, 50 minutes, hourly, 6am to 6pm) run close to the ticket office. You could climb the mountain, but it is a marathon on the legs so most people take the **cable car** (one way/return ¥90/160), which takes 20 minutes to ascend the mountain from where you can climb to the summit (金顶; jīndǐng).
>
> Spring and autumn are the best seasons to visit Fànjìngshān, but check on the weather before you go as it is often fogged out; clear days are rewarded with spectacular views. Bear in mind, too, that the animals here are very retiring. There are a number of restaurants and serviceable hotels on the approach to the ticket office. Ignore listed prices. You should be able to snag a room for ¥80 to ¥100. Try the **Bù Chà Qián Shān-zhuāng** (不差钱山庄; ☑ 138 8567 4067; 100m from entrance gate; 梵净山大门入口100米处; tw ¥388; ☎).
>
> From Zhènyuǎn, there are two daily buses to Tóngrén (¥55, 11am and 3pm). Otherwise, take a train (¥12.50) to Yùpíng, cross the road from the train station to the bus station and jump on a bus to Tóngrén (¥26, two hours). Other buses from Tóngrén's bus station run to Huáihuà (¥55, three daily), Kǎilǐ (¥80, six daily) and Guìyáng (¥140, eight daily). Trains run southeast from Tóngrén to Huáihuà and north to Chóngqìng and Chéngdū.

the east bus station. There are seven buses a day from Guìyáng to Huángguǒshù (¥55, 2½ hours, every 40 minutes from 7.40am to 12.45pm) from the long-distance bus station on Jinyang Nanlu. The last bus returns to Guìyáng at 4pm.

Tiānlóng & Tiāntáishān 天龙、天台山

You only need around a couple of hours to explore this delightful village cut with a sparkling stream not far outside Ānshùn. **Tiānlóng** (admission ¥35, through ticket ¥50) is a well-preserved **Túnpǔ village** (屯堡), its settlements erected by Ming-dynasty garrison troops posted here during the reign of Hongwu to help quell local uprisings and consolidate control. Coming from the middle and lower reaches of the Yangzi River, the soldiers brought their customs and language with them. Han descendants of these 14th-century soldiers live in Tiānlóng today, and the women are notable for their turquoise tops with embroidered hems. Gorgeous-looking embroideries are on sale everywhere (bargain hard), while local women sit sewing small and exceptionally colourful embroidered shoes, in all sizes.

Complementing its dry stonewalls and narrow alleyways, the architectural highlight of the village is the **Tiānlóng Xuétáng** (天龙学堂), an impressive and distinctive building. The **Sānjiào Temple** (三教寺; Sānjiào Sì) is a creakingly dilapidated shrine dedicated to Taoism, Confucianism and Buddhism. Short performances of dìxì – an ancient form of local drama – are regularly held in the **Yǎnwǔtáng** (演武堂) throughout the day.

Other local idiosyncrasies include distinct colloquialisms: the local expression for a thief is a yèmāozi (night cat). A couple of kèzhàn (inns) in the village can put you up for the night for around ¥70, a delightful option for a bucolic evening. To reach Tiānlóng, hop on a bus for Píngbà (平坝; ¥15, 40 minutes, every 30 minutes, 7.30am to 6.30pm) from Ānshùn's east bus station and at the drop-off, change to the bus for Tiānlóng (¥4, 20 minutes).

Around a 20-minute walk from Tiānlóng, the astonishing temple of **Wǔlóng Sì** (伍龙寺) emerges surreally from the summit of **Tiāntáishān** (admission ¥20), a bit like Colditz Castle. A refreshing hike through the trees takes you to the summit, where you can explore the various rooms of the temple. In a hall at the rear, a figure of Guanyin lithely sits, illuminated by a guttering candle; a further hall displays exhibits relating to local *dìxì* theatre. Afterwards, climb to the Dàyuètái terrace to gaze out over the glorious countryside.

When descending from the temple keep an eye out for a small shrine along a narrow trail where a statue of one of the 18 *luóhàn* sits grumpily all alone. His skinny frame is the result of generosity in giving food to others; he also bestows good fortune on all. Further below rises a 21m-high and 500-year-old gingko tree, festooned with ribbons, while other trails disappear into the trees.

Yúnfēng Bāzhài 云峰八寨

Yúnfēng Bāzhài is a scattering of traditional villages about 20km northeast of Ānshùn. Introduced by the mildly interesting **Tunpu Culture Museum** (屯堡文化博物馆; Túnpǔ Wénhuà Bówùguǎn; through ticket ¥50; ⊗8am-6pm), which serves as the point of entry, the village of Yúnshān (云山), at the top of a steep set of steps from the road a 15-minute walk from the museum, is a gem. Hung with bright yellow dried corncobs and red lanterns, protected by a wall and a main gate and overlooked by the Yúnjiù Shān (Cloud Vulture Mountain), the settlement is a charming and unruffled portrait of rural Guìzhōu. At the heart of the almost deserted village stands the rickety **Money God Temple** (Cáishén Miào), opposite an ancient pavilion.

If you want to spend the night, a couple of *kèzhàn* can put you up in basic rooms for around ¥50. Whatever you do, don't miss the chance to walk up to **Yúnjiù Temple** (云鹫寺; Yúnjiù Sì) at the top of Yúnjiù Shān for some of the most extraordinary views in Guìzhōu. You can walk virtually all around the top of the temple for a sublime and unparalleled panorama of fields and peaks ranging off into the distance. In spring, flowering bright yellow rapeseed plants *(yóucàihuā)* add vibrant splashes of colour.

From Yúnshān it's a 15-minute walk along the road to the village of **Běnzhài** (本寨), also at the foot of Yúnjiù Shān. With its old pinched alleyways, high walls, carved wood lintels, stone lions and ancient courtyard residences, Běnzhài is brim-full of history.

To reach Yúnfēng Bāzhài, take a bus (¥5, 40 minutes, every 25 minutes, 7am to 6pm) from Ānshùn's east bus station. The last bus from Yúnfēng Bāzhài to Ānshùn leaves at 6.20pm, passing through Běnzhài. Coming from Tiānlóng, hop on a bus from the main road to Qīyǎnqiáo (七眼桥; ¥5, 20 minutes) and then take a motorbike (¥10) for the 10-minute journey to the museum and the villages.

Wēiníng 威宁

🕽 0857 / POP 57,000

A dusty, scrappy but surprisingly busy town, Wēiníng is one of the top spots in the world for that most sedate of hobbies, birdwatching. The jewel-like Cǎohǎi Lake sits close to the city centre and draws twitchers to observe wintering migratory birds, especially the rare black-necked crane. Called 'Sun City' by Chinese for its abundant rays, and historically an important route linking north Yúnnán and Sìchuān, Wēiníng is home to a large population of Hui (Muslim), Miao and Yi; a big market held every three or four days sees the town thronged with people from the surrounding minority villages.

⦿ Sights & Activities

Cǎohǎi Lake LAKE

(草海湖; Cǎohǎi Hú; Grass Sea Lake) Guìzhōu's largest highland lake and southwest China's most significant wetland, Cǎohǎi Lake draws some 180 or so protected bird species, including black-necked cranes, black and white storks, golden and imperial eagles, white-tailed sea eagles, Eurasian cranes and white spoonbills. The prime time to see them is from November to March.

The lake has a fragile history, having been drained during both the Great Leap Forward and the Cultural Revolution in hopes of producing farmland. It didn't work and the lake was refilled in 1980. Government tinkering with water levels in ensuing years impacted on the local environment and villagers' livelihoods; officials have since enlisted locals to help with the lake's protection in an effort to remedy both problems. The 20-sq-km freshwater wetland has been a national nature reserve since 1992, but many environmental problems remain.

Lovely trails explore much of the lake, but the best way for a close-up of the birds is to cruise around the lake on a punt. Buy tickets at the **ticket office** (per boat 1/2/3hr

¥120/240/360; ☉8.30am-5.30pm) at the end of the path leading to the lake, rather than from the touts lurking nearby.

To get to the lake it's a 45-minute walk southwest of central Wēiníng or a 10-minute taxi ride (¥6).

🛏 Sleeping & Eating

For budget rooms, try the bus station area and nearby Jianshe Donglu, where you should be able to net a room for around ¥100.

With a large population of Hui, Muslim *yángròu fěn* (lamb rice noodles) and *niúròu fěn* (beef rice noodles) places are all over town, especially around the bus station area. A local delicacy is dragonfly lava, consumed fried.

Cǎohǎi Jiàrì Jiǔdiàn　　　　HOTEL $$
(草海假日酒店; ☏0857 623 1881; Caohai Lu; 草海路; tw ¥358-388; ❋🅿) Right by the lake, rooms here are big and comfortably furnished, if old-fashioned, and service has improved markedly. It's still not worth the price, but discounts (of 50% to 60%) when the twitchers aren't in town make things more tolerable. Some rooms have lake views and all have wi-fi.

ℹ Information

There's no place to change money in Wēiníng. A couple of branches of the ICBC, including one on Jianshe Donglu close to the bus station, take foreign cards, but bring extra cash just in case. Opposite the bus station, above the China Mobile shop, there's an **internet cafe** (per hr ¥3; ☉24hr).

ℹ Getting There & Away

Wēiníng has a near-new train station 6km west of the town centre, connecting it to points east in Guìzhōu and Kūnmíng in Yúnnán. Sleeper tickets, though, are virtually impossible to buy here. Note that the station's official name is Cǎohǎi (草海).

Wēiníng is a seven-hour bus ride from Guìyáng (¥130, 9am and 11am). You can also get here from Ānshùn's east bus station. First take a bus to Shuǐchéng (水城; ¥60, 3½ hours, every 50 minutes from 8.20am to 4.40pm), then transfer to a Wēiníng-bound bus (¥35, two hours, hourly from 7.45am). Note that Shuǐchéng is also referred to as Liùpánshuǐ (六盘水).

Leaving Wēiníng, you can backtrack to Guìyáng, or take a bus south to Xuānwēi in Yúnnán (¥65, five to six hours, eight daily, 7.30am to 4pm), where you can transfer to a bus for Kūnmíng. From Wēiníng, there is also a daily direct bus to Kūnmíng (¥130, 10 hours, 12.30pm).

Alternatively, take a bus to Zhāotōng (¥45, three hours, three daily, 8.30am, 1.40pm and 3.30pm), from where you can hop over to Xīchāng in southern Sìchuān and connect with the Kūnmíng–Chéngdū train line.

Taxi flagfall is ¥6. Taxis charge a flat ¥15 to go to the train station.

NORTHERN GUÌZHŌU

This is where things get a bit wild. Few foreigners venture north of Guìyáng; those that do will find that already incomprehensible accents get broader, roads more rugged and a stray *lǎowài* (foreigner) can stop the traffic. Way up on the Sìchuān border, Chìshuǐ and its surrounding valleys, waterfalls and national parks are still virgin territory for western travellers, and utterly gorgeous. It's a good-looking and little-travelled route into southern Sìchuān.

Chìshuǐ　　　　赤水

☏0852 / POP 50,000

Plonked on the border with Sìchuān, Chìshuǐ was once a riverine node for the transport of salt. Some 230 million years before that this was all ocean and today it's the gateway to some of the least-seen natural delights in the southwest. Just outside town are deep gorges and valleys flanked by towering cliffs hewn out of red sandstone – a World Heritage–listed feature known as *dānxiá* – a profusion of waterfalls, as well as luxuriant bamboo and fern forests that date to the Jurassic era.

While the locals are extremely friendly, there's nothing of intrinsic interest in Chìshuǐ itself, but it's the logical base for exploring the surrounding sights. The town sits on the east bank of the Chìshuǐ River (Chìshuǐ Hé). Cross the town's main bridge (Chìshuǐ Dàqiáo) to the other side and you're in Jiǔzhī (九支) in Sìchuān.

Note that you cannot change money in either Chìshuǐ or Jiǔzhī, so bring extra cash with you.

🛏 Sleeping

Chìshuǐ Hotel　　　　HOTEL $
(赤水大酒店; Chìshuǐ Dàjiǔdiàn; ☏0852 282 1334; 106 Xinei Huanlu; 西内环路106号; tw & d ¥220; ❋@🅿) On the corner of Renmin Xilu, this new hotel comes with modern and spacious rooms (some with computers) and wi-fi, although the beds are hard. Expect discounts of 30% to 40% (ask if one isn't offered).

Chìshuǐ Yuán Bīnguǎn HOTEL $$
(赤水源宾馆; ☑ 0852 288 7798; 18 Renmin Bei-
lu; 人民北路18号; tw & d ¥388-588; ❄@❂) A
short walk from the bus station, this hotel is
the town stalwart and remains popular with
tour groups. Rooms are large and perfectly
fine, if rather old-fashioned, with plain bath-
rooms. Significant discounts (50% and up)
are available if it's not booked out. ADSL in-
ternet in the rooms, wi-fi in the lobby.

Zhōngyuè Dàjiǔdiàn HOTEL $$$
(中悦大酒店; ☑ 0852 282 3888; 22 Nanzheng
Jie; 南正街22号; tw & d ¥628-768; ❄@❂) The
posh option in town. A slick operation with
comfy rooms, proper showers and helpful
staff, although they seem a little alarmed by
foreigners. Discounts (30%), even in summer. Wi-fi in the lobby and ADSL internet
in the rooms.

🍴 Eating

Popular restaurants are scattered in the area
around Hebin Zhonglu, near the Chìshuǐ River, where there are also simple outdoor bars
for an evening beer. The main drag of Renmin Xilu has hole-in-the-wall eateries serving noodle and rice dishes, dumplings and
the ever-present pigs' trotters. There are also
street-food stalls, supermarkets and a few
hotpot places scattered along Renmin Beilu.

ℹ Information

There's a brand-new branch of the **Industrial
and Commercial Bank** (ICBC; 工商银行; Gōngshāng Yínháng; Hongjun Dadao; ⊙9am-5pm)
with an ATM on Hongjun Dadao, off Renmin Xilu.
Another ATM on the corner of Renmin Xilu and
Renmin Beilu should also take foreign cards. A
couple of internet cafes are in this vicinity too.
The post office is on Nanzheng Jie.

ℹ Getting There & Around

Chìshuǐ's **bus station** (旅游车站; Lǚyóu
Chēzhàn) is on Nan Jiao Lu on the riverfront opposite Sìchuān, a ¥5 cab ride from Renmin Xilu.
Buses for very local destinations leave from next
door to it. Destinations include the following:

Chéngdū ¥120, five hours, three daily (7.50am,
9.30am and 3pm)

Chóngqìng ¥90, five hours, seven daily (6am
to 5pm)

Guìyáng ¥163, 5½ hours, three daily (7.30am,
9.30am and 3pm)

Jīnshāgōu ¥12, 1½ hours, hourly (6am to 5pm)

Shízhàngdòng ¥12, 1½ hours, nine daily
(6.50am to 4.30pm)

Sìdònggōu ¥8, 30 minutes, hourly (7am to
5pm)

Zūnyì ¥115, four hours, four daily (6.50am to
11.15am)

Taxi flagfall is ¥4.

Around Chìshuǐ

It's hard to imagine a more dramatic landscape. The locals claim the region has 4000
waterfalls, and some are spectacular, but
everywhere you look they're gushing into
the rivers that run red from the colour of
the earth (Chìshuǐ means 'red water') and
which cut through valleys and gorges covered in lush foliage. As if that wasn't enough,
there are huge forests of bamboo and alsophila plants, giant ferns that date back
200 million years and were once the food of
dinosaurs.

As sights are scattered, consider hiring a
taxi or minibus to scoop them all up. Expect
to pay ¥300 to ¥400 per day, depending on
your bargaining skills. To see the waterfalls
at their fullest and loudest, come during the
rainy season (May to October).

Shízhàngdòng Waterfall

A mere metre or so shorter than the much
better-known, and visited, Huángguǒshù
Falls, the 76m-high **Shízhàngdòng Waterfall** (十丈洞瀑布; Shízhàngdòng Pùbù; admission
¥40; ⊙8am-4pm) explodes in a sea of spray as
it it plunges. You can stand 100m away and
still get drenched if the wind is right.

About 40km from Chìshuǐ, nine buses
a day (¥12, 1½ hours) run here starting at
6.50am. The bus will drop you in Shízhàngdòng village, from where it's a short walk to
the ticket office.

From there, it's a 30- to 40-minute walk
up a hard road to the turn-off to the waterfall, or you can ride there on a buggy (one-
way/return ¥10/20). Another, more pleasant
walk, stretches to the falls on the other side
of the river. Doing the complete circuit takes
three to four hours. Try to visit before noon
during the low season as a hydroelectric
dam upriver slows the water after that time.
The waterfall is also known as Chìshuǐ Waterfall (Chìshuǐ Dàpùbù).

Yànziyán National Forest Park

Yànziyán National Forest Park (Yànziyán Guójiā Sēnlín Gōngyuán; admission ¥25; ☺8am-5pm) is famed for its *dānxiá* (red rock) formations. An attractive hike cuts through the trees to an imposing red *dānxiá* cliff face featuring an impressive cascade. It's around 9km from the Shízhàngdòng Waterfall; the bus to the waterfall from Chìshuǐ passes by the park.

Sìdònggōu 四洞沟

This 4.5km long **valley** (四洞沟谷; Sìdònggōu Gǔ; admission ¥30; ☺8am-5pm) around 15km from Chìshuǐ is forested with ancient ferns, as well as being dotted with gushing cataracts. Paths follow both sides of a river, as minifalls gush down over them, and take you past four 'proper' waterfalls. The biggest and most impressive is the last one, the 60m-high **White Dragon Pond Waterfall** (Báilóngtán Pùbù). The cool thing here is that you can get really close to the falls, including being able to walk behind one. It takes about three hours to do the circuit, although there are plenty of trails leading off the main paths that will provide fun and games for intrepid hikers.

Sìdònggōu is the most touristy of Chìshuǐ's sights, but still not overly crowded, even in summer. Buses run here from Chìshuǐ's bus station (¥8, 30 minutes) hourly from 7am and return on the same schedule. Buses to Sìdònggōu from Chìshuǐ also pass by the town of **Dàtóng** (大同), which has an attractive and historic old town (*gǔzhèn*) quarter.

Jīnshāgōu Nature Reserve 金沙沟自然保护区

By far the least-visited of the sights in the area, this reserve (Jīnshāgōu Zìrán Bǎohùqū) was established to protect the alsophila ferns that grow in abundance here. It's also the site of a bamboo forest, known as the **Bamboo Sea** (竹海; Zhúhǎi; admission ¥25; ☺8am-5pm), where you can trek through the trees in almost total isolation. The paths get very slippery when wet and mosquitoes are everywhere, so come armed with repellent.

To get here, catch the buses heading to Jīnshāgōu village (¥12, 1½ hours). From there, you'll have to negotiate with the locals for a motorbike or minibus ride to the park entrance, which is another 20 minutes away. Expect to pay ¥30 to ¥40 each way. Make sure to arrange a pick-up for your return; very little transport hangs around the park.

Red Rock Gorge 红石野谷

Also known as Yángjiāyán, **Red Rock Gorge** (红石野谷; Hóngshí Yěgǔ; admission ¥30; ☺8am-5pm) is dotted with small waterfalls that make for a vivid contrast with the red sandstone *dānxiá* cliffs. There are impressive photo opportunities here, particularly if the sun is shining, when the red earth really stands out.

Minibuses make the 16km journey here from the local bus station next door to the main bus station (¥6, 40 minutes, five daily from 8am to 4.30pm).

Yúnnán

POP 46.3 MILLION

Best Hikes

➜ Tiger Leaping Gorge (p687)

➜ Nù Jiāng Valley (p698)

➜ Xīshuāngbǎnnà Minority Villages (p706)

➜ Yǔbēng Village (p697)

➜ Cāng Shān (p675)

Best Natural Sights

➜ Lúgū Hú (p690)

➜ Báishuǐtái (p689)

➜ Yùlóng Xuěshān (p686)

➜ Swallow's Cavern (p667)

➜ Kawa Karpo (697)

Why Go?

Yúnnán (云南) is perhaps the most diverse province in all China, both in its extraordinary mix of peoples and in the splendour of its landscapes. That combination of superlative sights and different ethnic groups has made Yúnnán *the* trendiest destination for China's exploding domestic tourist industry.

More than half of the country's minority groups reside here, providing a glimpse into China's hugely varied mix of humanity. Then there's the eye-catching contrasts of the land itself: dense jungle sliced by the Mekong River in the south, soul-recharging glimpses of the sun over rice terraces in the southeastern regions, and snow-capped mountains as you edge towards Tibet.

With everything from laid-back villages and spa resorts to mountain treks and excellent cycling routes, Yúnnán appeals to all tastes. Transportation links are good so getting around is a breeze but you'll need time to see it all: whatever time you've set aside for Yúnnán, double it.

When to Go
Kūnmíng

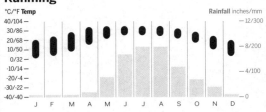

Apr Prepare to get soaked in Xīshuāngbǎnnà during the Dai water-splashing festival.

Jul & Aug Head for the mountains and glaciers around Déqīn.

Dec & Jan Escape China's winter chill and head for Kūnmíng, the city of eternal spring.

Yúnnán Highlights

① Gaze over the magical **Yuányáng Rice Terraces** (p667)

② Test your legs and lungs trekking **Tiger Leaping Gorge** (p687)

③ Marvel at the peaks (and glacier) around **Déqīn** (p696)

④ Step off the tourist trail in the ancient village of **Hēijǐng** (p664)

⑤ Hike to minority villages in the jungle of **Xīshuāngbǎnnà** (p706)

⑥ Kick back in the cafes and bars of **Dàlǐ** (p670)

⑦ Laze around the shores of stunning **Lúgū Hú** (p690)

⑧ See how time has stood still in the former Tea-Horse Trail oasis of **Shāxī** (p677)

⑨ Get way off the map in **Nù Jiāng Valley** (p698)

⑩ Check out the classic architecture in **Jiànshuǐ** (p665)

History

With its remote location, harsh terrain and diverse ethnic make-up, Yúnnán was once considered a backward place populated by barbarians.

The early Han emperors held tentative imperial power over the southwest and forged southern Silk Road trade routes to Myanmar (Burma). From the 7th to mid-13th centuries, though, two independent kingdoms, the Nanzhao and Dàlǐ, ruled and dominated the trade routes from China to India and Myanmar.

It wasn't until the Mongols swept through that the southwest was integrated into the Chinese empire as Yúnnán. Even so, it remained an isolated frontier region, more closely aligned with Southeast Asia than China.

Yúnnán is still a strategic jumping-off point to China's neighbours. Despite its geographical isolation, much of the province has modernised rapidly in recent years.

Language

Many different dialects are spoken in Yúnnán. Most belong either to the Tibeto-Burman family (eg the Naxi language) or the Sino-Tibetan family (eg the Lisu language).

ⓘ Getting There & Around

Kūnmíng's newish airport is the fourth largest and seventh busiest in China and has daily flights to most cities, as well as to an increasing amount of international destinations. Lìjiāng is also well-connected to a number of Chinese cities, while Dàlǐ and Jǐnghóng have many more flights than before.

In the past it was possible to travel by cargo boat from Jǐnghóng to Thailand. However, recent security threats have mostly stopped passenger travel on boats.

Expressways link Kūnmíng with Dàlǐ, east to Guìzhōu and Guǎngxī, southwest past Bǎoshān to Ruìlì and past Jǐnghóng to the Laos border. An expressway is also being built from Kūnmíng to Hékǒu on the Vietnam border and beyond to Hanoi.

Railways link Yúnnán to Guìzhōu, Guǎngxī, Sìchuān and beyond. In Yúnnán itself, development of the railways has been slower than elsewhere, due mostly to topographical interference. Trains link Dàlǐ and Lìjiāng and, by the time you read this, the line onward to Shangri-la should be open.

CENTRAL YÚNNÁN

Kūnmíng   昆明

♪ 0871 / POP 3.58 MILLION

Kūnmíng has long been regarded as one of China's most liveable cities. Known as the 'Spring City' for its equable climate, it remains a very pleasant place to kick back for a few days. For visitors who haven't succumbed to the laid-back attitude displayed by the locals, there are plenty of temples and national parks nearby (including the legendary Stone Forest) to keep you busy.

Of course, like other Chinese cities, the face of Kūnmíng is constantly changing and many old neighbourhoods have been torn down to make way for shopping malls. And the traffic jams that were unknown a few years ago, are now a regular occurrence. Yet, the essentially easy-going nature of Kūnmíng is, thankfully, still the same.

History

The region of Kūnmíng has been inhabited for 2000 years, but it wasn't until WWII that the city really began to expand, when factories were established and refugees, fleeing from the Japanese, started to pour in from eastern China. As the end point of the famous Burma Road, a 1000km-long haul from Lashio in Myanmar, the city played a key role in the Sino-Japanese war. Renmin Xilu marks the tail end of the road.

Following the war the city returned to being overlooked and isolated. When China opened to the West, however, tourists noticed the province, and Kūnmíng used its gateway status to the rest of Yúnnán to become one of the loveliest cities in southwest China.

◉ Sights

Yuántōng Temple   BUDDHIST TEMPLE

(圆通寺; Yuántōng Sì; Yuantong Jie; admission ¥6, surrounding park ¥10; ⊗5.30am-5pm) This temple is the largest Buddhist complex in Kūnmíng and a draw for both pilgrims and locals. It's more than 1000 years old, but has been refurbished many times. To the rear, a hall has been added, with a statue of Sakyamuni, a gift from Thailand's king.

Green Lake Park   PARK

(翠湖公园; Cuìhú Gōngyuán; Cuihu Nanlu; ⊗6am-10pm) Come here to people-watch, practise taichi or just hang with the locals and stroll. The roads along the park are lined with wannabe trendy cafes, teahouses and shops. In November everyone in the city awaits the return of the local favourites, red-beaked seagulls; it's a treat watching people, er, 'flock' to the park when the first one shows up.

Yúnnán Provincial Museum
MUSEUM

(云南省博物馆; Yúnnán Shěng Bówùguǎn; 118 Wuyi Lu; ⊙9am-4.30pm Tue-Sun) FREE Set inside a 1950s-era building, Yúnnán's provincial museum has been upgraded and its interior is sparkling throughout. There are reasonable exhibitions on Diān Chí (Lake Dian) prehistoric and early cultures but the highlight is the section on Yúnnán's minorities, with excellent displays of ethnic costumes and musical instruments.

Chuàng Kù
GALLERY

(创库艺术主题社区; Loft; 101 Xiba Lu) West of downtown in a disused factory area known as Chuàng Kù, you'll find a small number of galleries and cafes featuring modern Chinese artists and photographers. **Yuánshēng Art Space** (源生坊; Yuánshēngfáng; ☑6419 5697; 101 Xiba Lu; ⊙2.30-8.30pm) is a gallery-bar-restaurant-theatre that focuses on the province's ethnic groups. The cornerstone of sorts is **TCG Nordica** (诺地卡; Nuòdìkǎ; ☑411 4691; 101 Xiba Lu; ⊙5-11.30pm Mon, 11.30am-11pm Tue-Sat, noon-4pm Sun), best described as a gallery-exhibition hall-cultural centre – with, oddly, a restaurant serving Scandinavian and Chinese food.

Not many taxi drivers know this place as The Loft; ask to go to 101 Xiba Lu.

West Pagoda
PAGODA

(西寺塔; Xīsì Tǎ; Dongsi Jie; ⊙9am-5pm) FREE This Tang pagoda can't be climbed, nor is the temple complex open, but it is a good spot for people-watching with all manner of tea-drinking and mah-jong games going on.

East Pagoda
PAGODA

(东寺塔; Dōngsì Tǎ; 63 Shulin Jie; ⊙9am-5pm) FREE The East Pagoda is a Tang structure that was, according to Chinese sources, destroyed by an earthquake (Western sources say it was destroyed by the Muslim revolt in the mid-19th century). It's now a hang-out for senior citizens.

Nánchéng Mosque
MOSQUE

(南城清真古寺; Nánchéng Qīngzhēn Gǔsì; 51 Zhengyi Lu) Originally built more than 400 years ago, this mosque was ripped down in 1997 in order to build a larger version, which looks vaguely like a bad Las Vegas casino. And sadly, that's now about it for the area's once-thriving Muslim neighbourhood (torn down in toto in 2007).

🛏 Sleeping

Kūnmíng Upland Youth Hostel
HOSTEL $

(昆明倾城青年旅社; Kūnmíng Qīngchéng Qīngnián Lǚshè; ☑6337 8910; uplandhostel@gmail.com; 92 Huashan Xilu; 华山西路92号; dm ¥45, r ¥138-218; @ 🛜) This place aims to impress with its sharp red and black decor, sizeable bar and inside and outdoor communal areas. Rooms have wood furnishings and dorms come with big lockers and power outlets. It has helpful English-speaking staff and a handy location near Green Lake.

It's just off Huashan Xilu on a little alley called Dameiyuan Xiang (大梅园巷), near the back entrance of the landmark Green Lake Hotel.

Hump Hostel
HOSTEL $

(驼峰客栈; Tuófēng Kèzhàn; ☑6364 0359; www.thehumphostel.com; Jinmabiji Sq, Jinbi Lu; 金碧路金马碧鸡广场; dm ¥40-55, tw or d with/without bathroom ¥165/110; @ 🛜) You'll hear about Kūnmíng's most notorious hostel long before you arrive. Students, socialites and party animals love the place due to its close proximity to dozens of bars, karaoke joints and restaurants. Bring some earplugs as all this activity could keep you up at night. The hostel itself has clean and big dorms; some of the private rooms lack windows.

Bike hire is ¥30 a day and the hostel's own bar and terrace are popular spots for late-night carousing.

PRICE INDICATORS

The following price indicators are used in this chapter:

Sleeping

$ less than ¥160

$$ ¥160 to ¥300

$$$ more than ¥300

Eating

$ less than ¥40

$$ ¥40 to ¥60

$$$ more than ¥60

Kūnmíng

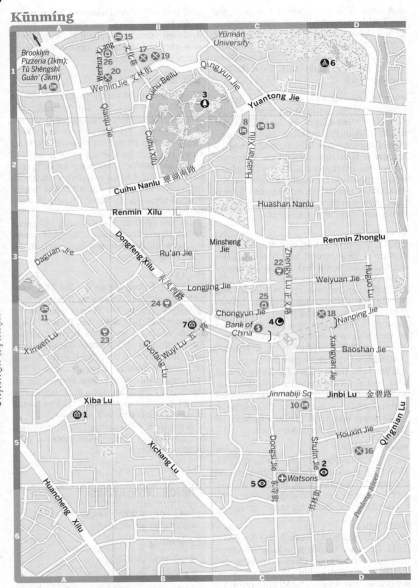

Brooklyn
Pizzeria (1km);
Tǔ Shēngshí
Guǎn' (3km)

Yúnnán
University

Wenhua Xiang

Wenlin Jie 文林街

Cuihu Beilu

Qingyun Jie

Yuantong Jie

Cuihu Xilu

Qianju Jie

Huashan Xilu

Cuihu Nanlu 翠湖南路

Huashan Nanlu

Renmin Xilu

Daguan Jie

Dongfeng Xilu 东风西路

Ru'an Jie

Minsheng Jie

Zhengyi Lu 正义路

Renmin Zhonglu

Weiyuan Jie

Huguo Lu

Longjing Jie

Chongyun Jie

Nanping Jie

Xinwen Lu

Guofang Lu

Wuyi Lu 五一路

Bank of
China

Xiangyan Jie

Baoshan Jie

Xiba Lu

Jinmabiji Sq

Jinbi Lu 金碧路

Houxin Jie

Qingnian Lu

Xichang Lu

Dongsi Jie

Shulin Jie

Watsons

Panlong River

Huancheng Xilu

**Kūnmíng Cloudland
Youth Hostel**   HOSTEL $

(昆明大脚氏青年旅社; Kūnmíng Dàjiǎoshì Qīngnián Lǚshè; ☑6440 3777; www.cloudlandhostel.
com; 23 Zhuantang Lu; 篆塘路23号; dm ¥35-40, r

¥138-198; @☎) This long-established hostel
attracts a steady flow of Western and Chinese travellers. Rooms and dorms are clean
and well furnished and there's a cute roof
terrace, although the communal areas are

Kūnmíng

⭐ **Lost Garden Guesthouse**　　GUESTHOUSE $$

(一丘田园客栈; Yìqiū Tiányuán Kèzhàn; ☏ 6511 1127; www.lostgardenguesthouse.com; 7 Yiqiu Tian, 一丘田7号; 4-/6-bed dm ¥45/50, d & tw ¥148-260; ❀ 🛜) A relaxing oasis amid white-brick apartment blocks, this boutique guesthouse has nouveau Dàlǐ decor with wood furniture, antiques, pleasant lounge and roof terrace. The cafe serves surprisingly good Western meals. It's tricky to locate: start by walking up the little alley to the right of Green Lake Hotel, take the first left and look for the sign pointing left.

Ask for a room towards the back; there is a noisy school across the road.

smallish. It's located on a hard-to-spot alley off Xichang Lu. To get here from the train station or long-distance bus station, take city bus 64 and get off at Yúnnán Rìbàoshè Zhàn (云南日报社站).

YÚNNÁN KŪNMÍNG

Hanting Express

HOTEL $$

(汉庭快捷酒店; Hàntíng Kuàijié Jiǔdiàn; ☑400 812 1121; www.htinns.com; 277 Beijing Lu; 北京路 277号; tw/d ¥209/219; ❋ @ ☎; S Tangzixiang) Handily located budget chain hotel with compact but modern and clean rooms. You won't hear any English spoken, but it's close to the subway, the train station and the centre of town. To get here, walk south of the Tangzixiang subway stop (line 2) for 200m.

Green Lake Hotel

HOTEL $$$

(翠湖宾馆; Cuìhú Bīnguǎn; ☑6515 8888; www. greenlakehotel.com; 6 Cuihu Nanlu; 翠湖南路6号; r from ¥2277; ❂❋@☎☎) Proud but subdued, this gentle giant of Kūnmíng *hôtellerie* history has a fabulous location, opposite Green Park, and has kept up with modernity, doing so tastefully and with top-notch service. The panorama from the top floors is worth the price alone. Discounts of 30% to 50% are often available, and there are Chinese and Western restaurants on site.

Te Yun Hotel

HOTEL $$$

(特运酒店; Tè Yùn Jiǔdiàn; ☑6809 0999; 40 Longxiang Jie; 龙翔街40号; d & tw ¥688; ❋@☎) A Chinese-style midrange hotel; big rooms with decent beds and bathrooms, a useful location close to restaurants and bars, and routine 50% discounts make it an attractive choice. Wi-fi in the lobby only, but there's ADSL internet in the rooms, and the staff are helpful despite limited English. It's set back from the road.

Kūnmíng Hotel

HOTEL $$$

(昆明饭店; Kūnmíng Fàndiàn; ☑6316 2063; www. kunminghotel.com; 52 Dongfeng Donglu; 东风东 路52号; d & tw ¥780; ❂❋@☎) In business since the 1950s, this city landmark has gone through extensive renovations and posits itself as a five-star hotel. It's not the Ritz but it does have professional staff and comfortable rooms, which are a good deal with the 30% discounts sometimes given. It offers a free airport shuttle and wi-fi is available in the lobby.

Yúndà Bīnguǎn

HOTEL $$$

(云大宾馆; Yúnnán University Hotel; ☑6503 4179; Wenhua Xiang; 文化巷; d & tw ¥398-598; ❋@☎) Conveniently close to the restaurant and bar hub of Wenhua Xiang and Wenlin Jie, the Yúndà's rooms are not exciting but do the job. The hotel is divided into two, with the cheaper rooms in the wing across the road from the main entrance. Regular 50% discounts bring it into the mid-range price category.

✖ Eating

Kūnmíng is home to all of Yúnnán's fabulous foods. Regional specialities are *qìguōjī* (汽锅鸡; herb-infused chicken cooked in an earthenware steam pot and imbued with medicinal properties depending on the spices used – *chóngcǎo*; 虫草; caterpillar fungus, or pseudo-ginseng, is one), *xuānwēi huǒtuǐ* (宣威火腿; Yúnnán ham), *guòqiáo mǐxiàn* (过桥米线; across-the-bridge noodles), *rǔbǐng* (乳饼; goat's cheese) and various Muslim beef and mutton dishes.

For all manner of foreign restaurants, including Indian, Korean and Japanese, head to Wenhua Xiang. For self-catering, try **Carrefour Supermarket** (家乐福超级市场; Jiālèfú; Nanping Jie), a branch of the popular French chain.

ACROSS-THE-BRIDGE NOODLES

Yúnnán's best-known dish is 'across-the-bridge noodles' (过桥米线; *guòqiáo mǐxiàn*). You are provided with a bowl of very hot soup (stewed with chicken, duck and spare ribs) on which a thin layer of oil is floating, along with a side dish of raw pork slivers (in classier places this might be chicken or fish), vegetables and egg, and a bowl of rice noodles. Diners place all of the ingredients quickly into the soup bowl, where they are cooked by the steamy broth. Prices generally vary from ¥15 to ¥25, depending on the side dishes. It's usually worth getting these, because with only one or two condiments the soup lacks zest.

It is said the dish was created by a woman married to an imperial scholar. He decamped to an isolated island to study and she got creative with the hot meals she brought to him every day after crossing the bridge. This noodle dish was by far the most popular and was christened 'across-the-bridge noodles' in honour of her daily commute.

Hóng Dòu Yuán
YUNNAN $

(红豆圆; ☑6539 2020; 142 Wenlin Jie; dishes from ¥18; ☉11am-9pm) An old-school Chinese eatery, with a duck-your-head stairway and plastic-film-covered tables, this is a real locals' hang-out on cosmopolitan Wenlin Jie. The food is excellent and will draw you back. Try regional specialities like the *táozá rǔbǐng* (fried goat's cheese and Yúnnán ham) and *liáng bái ròu* (peppery, tangy beef). Picture menu.

Zhènxīng Fàndiàn
YUNNAN $

(振兴饭店; Yúnnán Typical Local Food Restaurant; ☑316 6221; cnr Baita Lu & Dongfeng Donglu; dishes from ¥10; ☉24hr) There's always a queue of hungry locals waiting to eat here. It offers a reliable introduction to Kūnmíng fare, especially for *guòqiáo mǐxiàn* (¥18), and is handy for late-night eats. Pay upfront at the desk where the grumpy middle-aged ladies sit.

★1910 La Gare du Sud
YUNNAN $$

(火车南站; Huǒchē Nánzhàn; ☑6316 9486; 8 Houxin Jie; 后新街8号; dishes from ¥12; ☉11am-9pm) Offering Yúnnán specialities in a pleasant neo-colonial-style atmosphere, this place is now a fave with both expats – it's the kind of place foreign students take their parents when they come to visit – and cashed-up locals. It's hidden down an alley off Chongshan Lu, south of Jinbi Lu. Call ahead for instructions on how to get here.

Tǔ Shēngshí Guǎn
YUNNAN $$

(土生食馆; ☑6542 0010; District B, Jinding 1919, 15 Jindingshan Beilu; 金鼎山北路15号金鼎1919 B区; dishes ¥20-48; ☉10am-9pm) Located on the ground floor of a converted warehouse a couple of kilometres northwest of the city centre, this family-run place uses strictly organic ingredients for its selection of favourite local dishes. The vegies and homemade tofu are outstanding, and the atmosphere relaxed; there's a pleasant outside area. No English spoken, but there is an English menu.

Salvador's
WESTERN $$

(萨尔瓦多咖啡馆; Sà'ěrwǎduō kāfēiguǎn; ☑6536 3525; 76 Wenhua Xiang; 文化巷76号; sandwiches from ¥24, mains from ¥30; ☉9am-11.30pm; ☎) Always busy with travellers and foreign students, Salvador's is now a Kūnmíng staple. With a Mexican/Mediterranean food theme, as well as solid breakfasts, good coffee and a decent range of teas, it caters for all hours of the day. In the evening you can hang around the bar and watch as Kūnmíng's beautiful people parade along Wenhua Xiang.

Brooklyn Pizzeria
WESTERN $$

(布鲁克林批萨店; Bùlǔkèlín Pīsàdiàn; ☑6533 3243; 6-8, Bldg 12 Banzhucuiyuan, 11 Hongshan Donglu; 虹山东路11号版筑翠园12栋6-8商铺; pizzas from ¥45; ☉noon-11pm Thu-Tue; ☎) A big selection of stone-oven pizzas, as well as excellent New York–style grinder and Philly cheese steak sandwiches, are on offer here, as well as lots of foreign beers. It's just northwest of the centre of town, in a rapidly expanding area of new restaurants and bars.

Tell your taxi to head for Banzhucuiyuan and then walk east from the McDonald's for 100m or so.

As You Like
WESTERN $$

(有佳面包店; Yǒujiā Miànbāo Diàn; ☑6541 1715; 5 Tianjundian Xiang, off Wenlin Jie; pizzas from ¥32, salads from ¥15; ☉11am-10.30pm Tue-Sun; ☎) Cute cubbyhole cafe/restaurant that's all-vegetarian. Staff make excellent pizza, salads and sandwiches, all from local organic produce. It's an adventure to find: as you walk east on Wenlin Jie (coming from Wenhua Xiang) take the first left up the narrow alley after the Dune Cafe.

🍷 Drinking & Nightlife

Foreigners congregate in the bars on and around Wenhua Xiang, while Jinmabiji Sq is home to many Chinese-style bars and karaoke joints. The Kūndū Night Market area is also a club and bar zone.

Mask
BAR

(脸谱酒吧; Liǎnpǔ jiǔbā; 14 Kūndū Night Market; beers from ¥15; ☉8pm-late) In the heart of the Kūndū Night Market area, and jammed on weekends when there are DJs, the Mask is popular with expat and local students. It offers a fair range of domestic and foreign beers. During the week, it's more relaxed and a decent spot for a quiet drink.

Alei
BAR

(☑836 9099; Bldg A1, Zhengyifang, 3 Qianwang Jie; 正义坊A1栋 钱王街3号; cocktails from ¥50; ☉5pm-midnight; ☎) The only genuine cocktail bar in Kūnmíng, Alei is a large, low-lit, modern space that has proved a hit with upwardly mobile locals. The bartenders know their trade and there's nightly live music of one form or another.

FLOWER & BIRD MARKET

The **Flower & Bird Market** (花鸟市场, Huāniǎo Shìchǎng; Tongdao Jie), also known as *lǎo jiē* (old street), has shrunk dramatically in recent years and is now ominously hemmed in by encroaching modernity. Nor are flowers and birds the main draw here any more. Instead, strollers peruse stalls chock-full of jewellery, endless curios, knick-knacks and doodahs (the contents of someone's back hall often enough), some occasionally fine rugs and handmade clothing, and a hell of a lot of weird stuff.

One block west of the intersection of Guanghua Jie and the pedestrian-only Zhengyi Lu sits **Fú Lín Táng** (福林堂), the city's oldest pharmacy, which has been dishing out the *sānqì* (the legendary Yúnnánese cure-all root mixed into tea; around ¥160 per gram) since 1857.

Moondog BAR

(月亮狗; Yuèliàng Gǒu; 138-5 Wacang Nanlu; beers from ¥15; ☺6pm-late) An expat-Chinese run dive bar that attracts a mixed crowd of expats and locals. Fine collection of whiskies (from ¥50) and live music or occasional DJs.

🛍 Shopping

Yúnnán specialities are marble and batik from Dàlǐ, jade from Ruìlì, minority embroidery, musical instruments and spotted-brass utensils.

Some functional items that make good souvenirs include large bamboo water pipes for smoking angel-haired Yúnnán tobacco; and local herbal medicines, such as Yúnnán Báiyào (Yúnnán White Medicine), which is a blend of more than 100 herbs and is highly prized by Chinese throughout the world.

Yúnnánese tea is an excellent buy and comes in several varieties, from bowl-shaped bricks of smoked green tea called *tuóchá*, which have been around since at least Marco Polo's time, to leafy black tea that rivals some of India's best.

Tiānfú Famous Teas DRINK

(天福茗茶; Tiānfú Míngchá; cnr Shangyi Jie & Beijing Lu; ☺8.30am-10.30pm) This place offers most types of teas grown in Yúnnán, including the famed *pǔ'ěr* tea.

Mandarin Books & CDs BOOKS

(五华书苑; Wǔhuá Shūyuàn; 52 Wenhua Xiang; ☺9am-10pm) Good spot for guidebooks, novels and a selection of travel writing in English and other languages, as well as books on Yúnnán itself.

ℹ Information

For any and all information on the city, check out www.gokunming.com (it also covers parts of the rest of Yúnnán).

Maps (¥8) are available from the train/bus station areas and in hotels, but they're not much use to non-Chinese speakers.

DANGERS & ANNOYANCES

Although Kūnmíng's reputation as one of China's safest cities was dented by a March 2014 attack on passengers at the train station by restive Uighurs that left 29 people dead, foreigners have little to fear here. As always, take special precautions against pickpockets at and around the train and long-distance bus stations. There have been a number of victims who've been drugged and robbed on overnight sleeper buses.

INTERNET ACCESS

Every hotel and cafe frequented by travellers offers internet (网吧) and/or wi-fi, usually for free. The city has many internet cafes, charging ¥3 to ¥4 per hour.

MEDICAL SERVICES

Richland International Hospital (瑞奇德国际医院; Ruìqídé Guójì Yīyuàn; ☎6574 1988; Beijing Lu) Most of the doctors are Chinese but English is spoken here. Standards are generally good and prices are reasonable (consultations start from ¥30). It's on the bottom three floors of the Shàngdū International building; Yanchang Xian extension near Jinxing Flyover. A taxi ride from the city centre costs around ¥20.

Watsons (屈臣士; Qū Chén Shì; Dongsi Jie; ☺9am-10pm) Western cosmetics and basic medicines. Other branches around town.

Yán'ān Hospital (延安医院; Yán'ān Yīyuàn; ☎317 7499, ext 311; 1st fl, block 6, Renmin Donglu) Has a foreigners' clinic.

MONEY

Many ATMs around town should accept international cards.

Bank of China (中国银行; Zhōngguó Yínháng; 448 Renmin Donglu; ☺9am-noon & 2-5pm) All necessary services and has an ATM.

POST

China Post (国际邮局; Zhōngguó Yóuzhèng; 223 Beijing Lu) The main international office has poste restante and parcel service (per letter ¥3, ID required). It is also the city's Express Mail Service (EMS) and Western Union agent. Another branch on Dongfeng Donglu.

TOURIST INFORMATION

Many of the backpacker hotels and some of the cafes can assist with travel queries.

You can complain about, or report, dodgy tourist operations via the **Tourist Complaint & Consultative Telephone** (316 4961).

VISA EXTENSIONS

Public Security Bureau (PSB; 公安局; Gōng'ānjú; 6301 7878; 399 Beijing Lu; 9-11.30am & 1-5pm Mon-Fri) To visit the givers of visa extensions, head southeast off Government Sq (Dōngfēng Guǎngchǎng; 东风广场) to the corner of Shangyi Jie and Beijing Lu. Another office (571 7001; Jinxing Lu) is off Erhuan Beilu in northern Kūnmíng; take bus 3, 25 or 57.

ℹ️ Getting There & Away

AIR

Kūnmíng's airport has direct services to/from North America, Europe and Australia. International flights to Asian cities include Bangkok (¥1555), Hong Kong (¥1447), Vientiane (¥1575), Yangon (¥1865) and Kuala Lumpur (¥1598).

China Eastern Airlines/Civil Aviation Administration of China (CAAC; Zhōngguó Mínháng; 28 Tuodong Lu; 8.30am-7.30pm) issues tickets for any Chinese airline but the office only offers discounts on certain flights.

Daily flights from Kūnmíng go to most major cities across China, including Běijīng (¥1455), Guǎngzhōu (¥1007) and Shànghǎi (¥1208). There are regional services to Lhasa in Tibet (¥1960) and within Yúnnán, including Bǎoshān (¥726), Lìjiāng (¥570), Xiàguān/Dàlǐ (¥1130).

BUS

Kūnmíng's five bus stations are located on the outskirts of the city. The following buses depart from the south bus station (彩云北路南客运站; cǎiyún běilù nán kèyùnzhàn):

Jiànshuǐ ¥83, 3½ hours, every 30 minutes (7.30am to 8.30pm)

Jǐnghóng ¥165, eight hours, every 30 minutes (8am to 8.10pm)

Yuányáng ¥136, seven hours, three daily (10.20am, 12.30pm and 7pm)

The following buses depart from the west bus station (马街西客运站; mǎjiē xī kèyùnzhàn):

Bǎoshān ¥181 to ¥207, nine hours, every hour (8.30am to 8.20pm)

Chǔxióng ¥48, two to three hours, every 20 minutes (7am to 7.20pm)

Dàlǐ ¥138, four to five hours, every 20 minutes (7.20am to 8pm)

Lìjiāng ¥102, nine hours, seven daily (8.50am to 8.30pm)

Ruìlì ¥261, 12 to 14 hours, 10 daily (8.30am to 9pm)

Shangri-la ¥243, 12 hours, seven daily (8.30am to 8.30pm)

Téngchōng ¥235, 11 hours, seven daily (9am to 9pm)

The following buses depart from the **east bus station** (白沙河东客运站; báishāhé dōng kèyùnzhàn):

Hékǒu ¥147, eight hours, six daily (9.40am to 7.30pm)

Shílín ¥37, two hours, every 30 minutes (7am to 7.30pm).

BORDER CROSSING: GETTING TO LAOS & VIETNAM

Getting to Laos

A daily bus from Kūnmíng to Vientiane (¥587) leaves from the south bus station, at 6pm, reaching its destination 30 hours later. Alternatively, take a bus to Móhān on the border with Laos; these depart at 12.20pm and 8pm, cost ¥243 to ¥378 and take about 14 hours.

Getting to Vietnam

Apart from getting on a plane, the only way to get to Vietnam from Kūnmíng for now is by bus. Six buses (9.40am to 7.30pm) run daily from Kūnmíng's east bus station to the border town of Hékǒu (¥147).

Official proceedings at this border crossing can be frustrating (and officials have been known to confiscate Lonely Planet guides because they show Taiwan as a different country to China). Just keep your cool.

On the Chinese side, the border checkpoint is technically open from 8am to 11pm, but don't bank on anything after 6pm. Set your watch when you cross the border: the time in China is one hour later than in Vietnam. Visas are unobtainable at the border crossing.

Allow plenty of time to get to the bus stations (60 to 90 minutes). Line 2 of the subway runs to the south bus station, as does bus 154 from the train station. Bus 80 runs to the west bus station from the train station, while bus 60 goes to the east bus station, which is also on the subway network. A taxi will cost ¥40 to ¥50.

TRAIN
You can buy train tickets up to 10 days in advance. The following prices are for hard-sleeper, middle berths on the fastest train:

Běijīng ¥555
Chéngdū ¥263
Guǎngzhōu ¥349
Guìyáng ¥156
Liùpánshuǐ ¥114
Shànghǎi ¥515
Xī'ān ¥383

Within Yúnnán, eight daily trains run to Dàlǐ (seat ¥64, hard sleeper ¥102, six to seven hours, 4.41am to 5.56pm). Book ahead, as it is a popular route.

Six trains run daily to Lìjiāng (seat ¥89, hard sleeper ¥147, nine hours, 9.47am to 11pm).

❶ Getting Around
The first of Kūnmíng's subway lines has opened, with others under construction. Fares range from ¥2 to ¥4 and trains run 6.30am to 11pm. For now, the most useful stops include the train station and south bus station, as well as Government Sq (Dongfeng Guangchang) in the centre of town.

TO/FROM THE AIRPORT
Kūnmíng's airport is located 25km northeast of the city. Airport buses (¥25) run to and from it every 30 minutes from six different locations, the most convenient being the train station, north and west bus stations and the Kūnmíng Hotel. The subway should have been extended to reach the airport by the time you read this. Watch out for the unofficial taxi touts who will approach you after you exit customs. Always take an official cab. Taxis charge a flat ¥120 to the airport and around ¥100 into town.

BICYCLE
Some hostels rent out bikes for around ¥30 per day.

BUS
Bus 63 runs from the east bus station to the main train station. Bus 2 runs from the train station to Government Sq (Dongfeng Guangchang) and then past the west bus station. Fares range from ¥1 to ¥4. The main city buses have no conductors and require exact change.

Around Kūnmíng

There are some grand sights within a 15km radius of Kūnmíng, but getting to most of them is time-consuming and you'll find the majority of them extremely crowded (weekdays are best to avoid the crowds).

If you don't have much time, the Bamboo Temple (Qióngzhú Sì) and Xī Shān (Western Hills) are the most interesting. Both have decent transport connections. Diān Chí (Lake Dian) has terrific circular-tour possibilities of its own.

Bamboo Temple   筇竹寺
Bamboo Temple   BUDDHIST TEMPLE
(Qióngzhú Sì; admission ¥40; ☺8am-7pm) This serene temple (no photos allowed inside) is definitely one to be visited by sculptors as much as by those interested in temple collecting. Raised during the Tang dynasty, it was rebuilt in the 19th century by master Sichuanese sculptor Li Guangxiu and his apprentices, who fashioned 500 luóhàn (arhats or noble ones) in a fascinating mishmash of superb realism and head-scratching exaggerated surrealism.

Li and his mates pretty much went gonzo in their excruciating, eight-year attempt to perfectly represent human existence in statuary. How about the 70-odd surfing Buddhas, riding the waves on a variety of mounts – blue dogs, giant crabs, shrimp, turtles and unicorns? And this is cool: count the arhats one by one to the right until you reach your age – that is the one that best details your inner self.

So lifelike are the sculptures that they were considered in bad taste by Li Guangxiu's contemporaries (some of whom no doubt appeared in caricature), and upon the project's completion he disappeared into thin air.

The temple is about 12km northwest of Kūnmíng. Take bus 2 to Huáng tǔ pō, from where shared minivans (¥10 per person) run to the temple.

Diān Chí   滇池

The shoreline of Diān Chí (Lake Dian), located to the south of Kūnmíng, is dotted with settlements, farms and fishing enterprises. The western side is hilly, while the eastern side is flat country. The southern end of the lake, particularly towards the southeast, is industrial.

The lake is elongated – about 40km from north to south – and covers an area of 300 sq km. Plying the waters are *fānchuán* (pirate-sized junks with bamboo-battened canvas sails).

The area around the lake is mainly for scenic touring and hiking, and there are some fabulous aerial views from the ridges at Dragon Gate in Xī Shān.

Xī Shān 西山

This cool, forested mountain range on the western side of Diān Chí makes for a great day trip from Kūnmíng. The range is full of walking trails (some very steep sections), quiet temples, gates and lovely forests. But avoid the weekends when Kūnmíngers come here in droves.

It's a steepish approach from the north side. The hike to Dragon Gate takes 2½ hours, though most people take a connecting bus to the top section.

Alternatively, it is possible to cycle to the hills from the city centre in about an hour – to vary the trip, consider doing the return route across the dikes of upper Diān Chí.

A through ticket (通票; *tōngpiào*) for all the sights on the mountain and the bus costs ¥100.

◉ Sights

Huátíng Temple BUDDHIST TEMPLE
(华亭寺; Huátíng Sì; admission ¥25; ⊙8am-6pm)
At the foot of the climb, about 15km from Kūnmíng, is Huátíng Temple, a country temple of the Nanzhao kingdom believed to have been constructed in the 11th century. It's one of the largest in the province and its numerous halls are decorated with arhats. A combined ¥25 ticket allows admission here and to Tàihuá Temple.

Tàihuá Temple BUDDHIST TEMPLE
(太华寺; Tàihuá Sì; admission ¥25; ⊙8am-6pm)
The road from Huátíng Temple winds 2km up to the Ming-dynasty Tàihuá Temple. The temple courtyard houses a fine collection of flowering trees, including magnolias and camellias.

A combined ¥25 ticket will get you into both temples.

Sānqīng Gé TAOIST TEMPLE
Near the top of the mountain, Sānqīng Gé (三清阁; Sānqīng Temple) was a country vil-

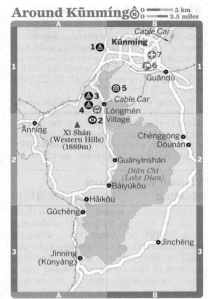

Around Kūnmíng

0 —— 5 km
0 —— 2.5 miles

la of a Yuan-dynasty prince, and was later turned into a temple dedicated to the three main Taoist deities (*sānqīng* refers to the highest level of Taoist 'enlightenment').

From near here you can catch a **chairlift** (one way/return ¥25/40) if you want to skip the final ascent to the summit.

Dragon Gate HISTORIC SITE
(龙门; Lóng Mén; admission ¥40) Close to the top of the mountain is Dragon Gate, a group of grottoes, sculptures, corridors and pavilions that were hacked from the cliff between 1781 and 1835 by a Taoist monk and coworkers, who must have been hanging up here by their fingertips.

ℹ Getting There & Away

Take bus 54 (¥1) from the corner of Renmin Zhonglu and Zhengyi Lu in Kūnmíng to its terminus at Mián Shān Chē Chǎng (眠山车场), and then change to bus 6 (¥1), which will take you to the foot of the hills. Buses run up Xī Shān itself to Sānqīng Gé (one way/return ¥12.50/25, every 15 minutes, 8.10am to 6.10pm).

Returning, you could take the cable car across to Hǎigēng Park for ¥40. From here, take the 94 bus or a taxi for the 3km or so to the Yúnnán Nationalities Village, opposite the Yúnnán Minorities Museum, where you can catch bus 44 (¥2, 40 minutes) to Kūnmíng's main train station.

Yúnnán Nationalities Museum   云南民族博物馆

On the northeast corner of Diān Chí (Lake Dian), the **Yúnnán Nationalities Museum** (云南民族博物馆; Yúnnán Mínzú Bówùguǎn; www.ynnmuseum.com; ◷9am-4.20pm Tue-Sun) **FREE** is reputedly the largest minorities museum in China, even if it doesn't have a whole lot on display. But the ground-floor exhibition of costumes is comprehensive and comes with proper English captions.

Across the road is the **Yúnnán Nationalities Village** (云南民族村; Yúnnán Mínzú Cūn; admission ¥90; ◷8.30am-9.30pm). Here you can walk through a tacky re-creation of an old Kūnmíng street to reach the 'village', where all-smiling, all-dancing minorities perform for mostly domestic tour groups. Skip it and head to Xīshuāngbǎnnà for the real thing instead.

Buses 44 (¥2) runs to both the museum and village from the main train station.

Shílín   石林

☑ 0871

A conglomeration of utterly bizarre but stunning karst geology and a hell of a lot of tourists, **Shílín** (石林; Stone Forest; admission ¥175), about 120km southeast of Kūnmíng, is equal parts tourist trap and natural wonderland. A massive collection of grey limestone pillars split and eroded by wind and rainwater (the tallest reaches 30m high), the place was, according to legend, created by immortals who smashed a mountain into a labyrinth for lovers seeking privacy.

Yes, it's packed to the gills, every single rock is affixed with a cheesy poetic moniker, Sani women can be persistent in sales, and it's all pricey as hell. Yet, idyllic, secluded walks are within 2km of the centre and by

sunset or moonlight Shílín becomes otherworldly. To avoid the crowds, arrive early and avoid weekends.

Sani song and dance evenings are organised when there are enough tourists. Shows normally start at around 8pm at a stage next to the minor stone forest but there are sometimes extra performances. There are also Sani performances at the same location during the day between 2pm and 3pm.

Shílín can easily be visited as a day trip from Kūnmíng, and it doesn't have much in the way of budget accommodation. But if you want to stay the night, the rooms at the **Shílín Hēisōngyán Jiǔdiàn** (石林黑松岩酒店; ☑6771 1088; tw/d ¥280/380; ✿) are quiet and have good views over Shílín, double rooms regularly get knocked down to ¥180.

Near the main entrance is a cluster of restaurants and snack bars that are open from dawn to dusk. Check all prices before you order, as overcharging is not uncommon.

During the July/August **torch festival**, wrestling, bullfighting, singing and dancing are held at a natural outdoor amphitheatre by Hidden Lake, south of Shílín.

Buses to Shílín (¥37, two hours, every 30 minutes, 7am to 7.30pm) leave from Kūnmíng's east bus station.

Hēijǐng   黑井

☑ 0878

Time-warped **Hēijǐng** (admission ¥30) has been known for salt production for centuries and is still an important producer of the 'white gold', as well as home to a sizeable Hui Muslim community. Hēijǐng has retained much of its period architecture and is a great place to wander for a day or two, marvelling at the old gates, temples and shady narrow alleys. The village makes a fine stopping-off point if you want to take the route less-travelled between Dàlǐ and Kūnmíng.

A small tourist information office near the first bridge can point the way to the various sights.

◎ Sights & Activities

The admission fee at the main gate (a few kilometres before the village) includes admission to **Dàlóng Cí** (大龙祠; the clan meeting hall) and **Gǔyán Fáng** (古盐坊; an old salt-production facility). The latter offers brief descriptions of the history of salt production, although none in English. You can find it by walking east from the village for about 15 minutes. A few old salt wells can also be inspected, look out for the **Black Cow Well** (黑牛井; Hēiniú Jǐng), just south of Dàlóng Cí.

Should you tire of salty attractions just take a stroll around some of the back alleys and admire the temples, gates and old homes. Hēijīng is especially magical at night, when the day trippers disappear and the village reverts to its natural sleepy state.

There's pleasant **walking** to be done in the hills behind the town too. An obvious path leads up to **Feilai Temple** (飞来寺; Fēilái Sì), then along the ridge line past some tombs before descending to the village. Plan on two to three hours for this walk.

🛏 Sleeping & Eating

Locals will approach you offering basic beds from ¥30. Meals are extra, but there are a few restaurants and *shāokǎo* (barbecue) places in the village.

Wang Family Courtyard   INN **$**
(王家大院; Wángjiā Dàyuàn; ☑ 489 0506; r ¥60-80; @) One of the best-value guesthouses in all Yúnnán, the rooms at this family-run place are big and bright enough and the more expensive have working ADSL internet connections. Bathrooms are simpler (squat toilets), but the courtyard is perfect for star-gazing come nightfall.

Wu Family Courtyard   INN **$$**
(武家大院; Wǔjiā Dàyuàn; ☑ 489 0358; s/tw ¥180/280; 🖘) The best-known and most comfortable place in town was once owned by local salt magnate Wu Weiyang, who was summarily executed by communist forces in 1949. Single rooms are cramped but the twins are large and all are set around a very attractive courtyard. It's worth a visit even if you don't stay here.

ℹ Getting There & Away

Getting to Hēijīng is tricky. The best option is local train 6162 (¥11.50, four hours), departing Kūnmíng at 9.10am and arriving at 1pm. The train stops a couple of kilometres from the village but horse-drawn buggies (¥3 per person) meet the train to make the journey here. Going the other way, train 6161 departs at 1.34pm and reaches Kūnmíng at 5.30pm.

The alternative is to take the bus from Kūnmíng or Dàlǐ to the county capital Chǔxióng (楚雄). From Chǔxióng's main bus station, take a taxi (¥7) to the east bus station (东站), where there are buses to Hēijīng (¥14) every hour between 9am and 3.50pm. From Hēijīng, buses to Chǔxióng leave from outside the market at the end of the village from 7am to 2.30pm.

Jiànshuǐ   建水
☑ 0873 / POP 17,400

Jiànshuǐ is a charming town of old buildings, an enormous Confucian temple, a cave laden with swallows, and some of the best steam-pot cooking and barbecue you'll find in Yúnnán. The architecture is constantly being 'facelifted', but still retains much of its distinct character, and the locals, who are a mix of Han, Hui and Yi, are extremely friendly.

Known in ancient times as Bùtóu or Bādiàn (巴甸), Jiànshuǐ's history dates back to the Western Jin period, when it was under the auspices of the Ningzhou kingdom. It was handed around to other authorities until its most important days as part of the Tonghai Military Command of the Nanzhao kingdom. The Yuan dynasty established what would eventually become the contemporary town.

⊙ Sights

Classic architecture surrounds you in Jiànshuǐ, and not just in the old-style back alleys. Virtually every main street has a historically significant traditional structure. The architecture here is especially intriguing because of the obvious mixture of central plains and local styles. Many old buildings, despite official decrees positing them as state treasures, have been co-opted for other purposes and the trick – and the great fun – is trying to find them.

Note that you can buy a ¥133 **through ticket** (通票; *tōngpiào*) that gets you into the Confucian Temple, the Zhu Family Garden and Swallow's Cavern. It's on sale at any of those places.

Confucian Temple   CONFUCIAN TEMPLE
(文庙; Wénmiào; Lin'an Lu; admission ¥60; ⊙ 6.30am-8pm) Jiànshuǐ's most famous temple was modelled after the temple in Confucius' hometown of Qūfù (Shāndōng province) and finished in 1285; it covers 7.5 hectares and is the third-largest Confucian temple in China. (Some locals employ a flurry of Byzantine mathematics to prove it's the largest; either way, Xué Lake, around which it sits, uses the Chinese word for 'sea' in its name!)

The temple operated as a school for nearly 750 years and its academic credentials were such that more than half of all Yúnnán's successful candidates in imperial examinations during this period came from Jiànshuǐ. Many of the names of buildings in Jiànshuǐ use the ideogram wén, or 'literacy'.

Zhu Family Garden   HISTORIC SITE

(朱家花园; Zhūjiā Huāyuán; Hanlin Jie; admission ¥50; ◷ 8am-8pm) This spacious 20,000-sq-metre complex, a fascinating example of Qing-era one-upping-the-Joneses, comprises ancestral buildings, family homes, ponds and lovely gardens, and took 30 years to build. The Zhu family made its name through its mill and tavern, and dabbled in everything from tin in Gèjiù to opium in Hong Kong, eventually falling victim to the political chaos following the 1911 revolution.

Cháoyáng Gate   HISTORIC SITE

(朝阳搂; Cháoyáng Lóu; FREE) Being refurbished at the time of writing, Cháoyáng Gate is an imposing Ming edifice that guards the entrance to the old town. Modelled on the Yellow Crane Tower (p431) in Wǔhàn and the Yuèyáng Tower located at Dòngtíng Lake (洞庭湖, Dòngtíng Hú) in Húnán, it bears more than a passing resemblance to the Gate of Heavenly Peace in Běijīng.

Zhǐlín Sì   BUDDHIST MONASTERY

(指林寺; ◷ 6am-midnight) FREE The largest preserved wooden structure in Yúnnán, this monastery was built during the latter stages of the Yuan dynasty; its distinctive design feature is the brackets between columns and crossbeams.

🛏 Sleeping

Jiànshuǐ International
Youth Hostel   HOSTEL $

(建水国际青年旅舍; Jiànshuǐ Guójì Qīngnián Lûshè; ☑ 765 2451; yhajianshui@yahoo.com; 253 Lin'an Lu; 临安路253号; dm/d/tw ¥25/60/90; @ 🜁) Recently relocated, this place has basic but bearable dorms and rooms with reasonable bathrooms. No English spoken but the staff are affable. To find it, walk 30m past the Confucian Temple and turn down an alley on the left-hand side of the road by 253 Lin'an Lu.

Huáqīng Jiǔdiàn   HOTEL $$

(华清酒店; ☑ 766 6166; 46 Hanlin Jie; 翰林街46号; d & tw ¥298; ❄ @ 🜁) Decorated in a neo-Qing-dynasty style, the rooms here are a fair size and some come with small terraces. Discounts of 40% are standard and the staff are friendly. There's a downstairs teahouse too. It's close to the Cháoyáng Gate at the entrance to the old town.

Lín'ān Inn   INN $$$

(临安客栈; Lín'ān Kèzhàn; ☑ 765 5866; 32 Hanlin Jie; 翰林街32号; d & tw ¥328; ❄ @ 🜁) In a prime location in the heart of the old town and with well-kept rooms, the biggest draw here is the great communal courtyard which is very pleasant for a beer in the evening. Regular discounts bring prices under ¥200 and they rent bikes for ¥30 per day.

🍴 Eating

Jiànshuǐ is legendary for its qìguō (汽锅), a stew made in the county's famed earthenware pots and often infused with medicinal herbs. The cook may make use of the local speciality, cǎoyá (草牙; grass sprouts), also known as elephant's tooth grass root, which tastes like bamboo. Only found in Jiànshuǐ County, it's often used in broth or fried with liver or pork. Vegetarians might find a place that will substitute tofu. Expect to pay ¥40 per pot. You'll also find places serving delicious liáng miàn (cold rice noodles served with sesame paste and tofu balls cooked on a grill).

Then there's glorious Jiànshuǐ barbecue (建水烧烤; Jiànshuǐ shāokǎo). Tons of cubbyhole restaurants are filled with braziers roasting meats, vegies, tofu and perhaps goat's cheese. A perfect night out is a roasted meal under the Jiànshuǐ stars with friends. Head to Hanlin Jie and Lin'an Lu and the alleys off it for both restaurants and barbecue places.

ℹ Information

There are plenty of ATMs around town that take foreign cards.

Internet cafe (山城网吧; Wǎngbā; per hour ¥3; ◷ 24hr) On Hanlin Jie next to Huáqīng Jiǔdiàn.

ℹ Getting There & Away

Jiànshuǐ has a couple of bus stations. The main one is 3km north of Cháoyáng Gate. For very local destinations, you need to head to the second small (regional) bus station a few minutes' walk west at the corner of Chaoyang Beilu and Beizheng Jie.

From the main station, there are buses continually leaving for Nánshà (new town) in Yuányáng (¥30, 2½ hours). For Xīnjiē and the rice terraces, there is one daily bus (¥43, four hours, 11.34am).

Frequent buses head to Kūnmíng (¥73, every 25 minutes, three to four hours, 7am to 7.35pm). Hékǒu-bound travellers have four buses to choose from (¥72 to ¥77, five hours, 6.40am, 7.26am, 8.10am and 10.53am). Sleepers to Jǐnghóng (¥175, 12 hours) depart at 1.30pm and 4.30pm.

Around Jiànshuǐ

Swallow's Cavern 燕子洞

A freak of nature and ornithology, **Swallow's Cavern** (Yànzǐ Dòng; admission ¥80; ⊙9am-5pm) is halfway between Jiànshuǐ and Gèjiù. The karst formations (the largest in Asia) are a lure, but what you'll want to see are the hundreds of thousands of swallows flying around in spring and summer. The cave is split into two – one high and dry, the other low and wet. The higher cave is so large that a three-storey pavilion and a tree fit inside.

Plank walkways link up; the Lú River runs through the lower cave for about 8km and you can tour the caverns in 'dragon-boats'.

There's no direct bus, but the ones bound for Méngzì, Kāiyuán or Gèjiù which don't take the expressway pass the cavern (¥10, one hour).

Twin Dragon Bridge 双龙桥

This bridge (Shuānglóng Qiáo; 双龙桥) across the confluence of the Lú and Tàchōng Rivers is 5km from the western edge of town. One of the 10 oldest in China, the bridge features 17 arches, so many that it took two periods of the Qing dynasty to complete the project. To get here, take minibus 4 from Jiànshuǐ's second bus station (¥2). Note that you have to ask the driver to tell you where to get off and then point you in the right direction.

Bus 4 continues to Huánglóng Sì (黄龙寺), a small temple.

Yuányáng Rice Terraces 元阳梯田

☏ 0873 / POP 22,700

Picture hilltop villages, the only things visible above rolling fog and cloud banks, an artist's palette of colours at sunrise and sunset, spirit-recharging treks through centuries-old rice-covered hills, with a few water buffalo eyeing you contentedly nearby. Yes, it's hard not to become indulgent when describing these *tītián* (rice terraces), hewn from the rolling topography by the Hani throughout the centuries. They cover roughly 12,500 hectares and are one of Yúnnán's most stunning sights.

Yuányáng is actually split into two: Nánshà, the new town, and Xīnjiē, the old town an hour's bus ride up a nearby hill. Either can be labelled Yuányáng, depending what map you use. Xīnjiē is the one you want, so make sure you get off there.

Xīnjiē 新街

Xīnjiē is a bit grubby, but makes a useful base. The bus station is a minute's walk from Titian Sq, the town's hub.

⊙ Sights & Activities

The terraces around dozens of outlying villages have their own special characteristics, often changing with the daylight. Bilingual maps are available at all hotels in town. Bear in mind that the *tītián* are at their most extraordinary in winter when they are flooded with water which the light bounces off in spectacular fashion. Avoid visiting at Chinese public holidays, when prices for minibuses go sky-high (¥600 and more per day).

Duōyīshù (多依树), about 25km from Xīnjiē, has the most awesome sunrises and is the one you should not miss. **Quánfúzhuāng** (全福庄) is a less-crowded alternative and has easy access down to the terraces. For sunsets, **Bàdá** (坝达) and **Měngpǐn** (勐品), also known as **Lǎohǔzuǐ** (老虎嘴), can be mesmerising. A combined ¥100 ticket gets you access to Duōyīshù, Bádá, Quánfúzhuāng and Měngpǐn/Lǎohǔzuǐ.

Buses run to all the villages from the bus station, but you are much better off arranging your own transport, or hooking up with other travellers to split the cost of a sunrise/sunset drive. Minibuses and motor-rickshaws congregate around Yúntī Shùnjié Dàjiǔdiàn and on the street west of the bus station. Expect to pay ¥400 to ¥500 in peak season for a minibus. Less comfortable motor-rickshaws can be got for ¥250.

Several **markets** are worth visiting; check with your accommodation for the latest information.

Yuányáng Rice Terraces

Map Distances

Xīnjiē to Nánshā	30km
Xīnjiē to Lóngshùbà	4km
Xīnjiē to Qīngkǒu	6km
Xīnjiē to Měngpǐn/Lǎohǔzuǐ	18km
Xīnjiē to Bàdá	16km
Xīnjiē to Duōyīshù	25km

🛏 Sleeping & Eating

There are a number of places around the bus station where rooms can be found for ¥40 and up. Restaurants surround Titian Sq. Try **Liù Jūn Fàndiàn** (六军饭店; dishes from ¥12; ⊙8am-10pm), on the corner of the square closest to the bus station.

Increasing numbers of travellers are now basing themselves in much more picturesque **Pǔgāolǎo** (普高老) in Duōyīshù (多依树), an hour by bus from Xīnjiē, where the rice terraces are all around you. The village has spawned many guesthouses but there's still only one restaurant (eat where you stay).

Timeless Hostel Yuanyang   HOSTEL **$**
(久居元阳青年旅舍; Jiǔ Jū Yuányáng Qīngnián Lǚshè; ☑153 6837 6718; yuanyang.timeless@gmail.com; 6-bed dm ¥35, d & tw ¥120; @🛜) New hostel in the heart of Duōyīshù's Pǔgāolǎo village, with fresh dorms and rooms, a roof terrace with decent views, an amenable communal area and English-speaking staff. Bikes can be hired for ¥30 per day and staff can offer advice on potential hiking routes, as well as organise transport to other villages.

Sunny Guesthouse   GUESTHOUSE **$**
(多依树阳光客栈; Duōyīshù Yángguāng Kèzhàn; ☑159 8737 1311; sunny_guesthouse@163.com; 10-bed dm ¥40, d ¥120-160) Great views of the rice terraces from the roof at this guesthouse, which has a collection of basic rooms (cold in the winter), with both shared and private bathrooms, some overlooking the terraces. It's a 10-minute walk through Pǔgāolǎo village to find it.

Yǐngyǒuliàn Jiǔdiàn   HOTEL **$**
(影友恋酒店; ☑159 8737 4367; caihumei2006@163.com; r ¥40-80; 🛜) In Xīnjiē and basic (the price is a clue), but some rooms have Western toilets and the wi-fi connection is strong. Owner Belinda speaks good English and is helpful when it comes to arranging transport to the outlying villages. To get here, walk up the road from the bus station for five minutes and it's on your left.

Yúntī Shùnjié Dàjiǔdiàn   HOTEL **$$**
(云梯顺捷大酒店; ☑562 1588; Xīnjiē; d & tw ¥298; 🛜) Just off Titian Sq in Xīnjiē and a few minutes from the bus station, this place has clean, compact and comfortable rooms, discounted by 50% or more outside high season. Wi-fi is only available in the lobby.

ℹ Information

There are a couple of internet cafes (网吧, *wǎngbā*; ¥3 per hour) off Titian Sq near Yúntī Shùnjié Dàjiǔdiàn.

Agricultural Bank of China (中国农业银行; Zhōngguó Nóngyè Yínháng) Has an ATM that sometimes takes foreign cards: don't rely on it. To find it, head down the stairs by the entrance to Yúntī Shùnjié Dàjiǔdiàn and walk on for a couple of minutes; it's on the left-hand side.

ℹ Getting There & Around

There are three buses daily from Kūnmíng to Yuányáng (¥136, seven hours, 10.20am, 12.30pm and 7pm); these return at 9.05am, 12.30pm and 6.30pm. Other destinations include Hékǒu (¥58, four hours) at 7.30am and 10am.

To forge on to Xīshuāngbǎnnà, catch any of the frequent buses to Nánshà (¥10, one hour), where there's a daily bus to Jǐnghóng at 4pm (¥150, eight hours). Alternatively, you can backtrack to Jiànshuǐ (¥43, four hours, six daily from 10.20am to 4.30pm) and catch one of the Jǐnghóng sleepers (¥175, 1.30pm and 4.30pm).

From Xīnjiē, local buses leave when full to Duōyīshù's Pǔgāolǎo village for ¥15.

Xiàguān   下关

☑0872 / POP 158,000
TRANSPORT HUB

Xiàguān, on the southwest shore of Ěrhǎi Hú (Erhai Lake), serves as a transport hub for travellers headed to Dàlǐ, a few kilometres further up the highway. Confusingly, Xiàguān is sometimes referred to as Dàlǐ (大理) on tickets, maps and buses. There is no reason to stay in Xiàguān and you only need to come here to catch a bus or train.

ℹ️ Information

Bank of China (中国银行; Zhōngguó Yínháng; Jianshe Donglu) Changes money and travellers cheques, and has an ATM that accepts all major credit cards.

Public Security Bureau (PSB; 公安局; Gōng'ānjú; ☑ 214 2149; Tai'an Lu; ☺ 8-11am & 2-5pm Mon-Fri) Handles all visa extensions for Xiàguān and Dàlǐ. Take bus 8 from Dàlǐ and ask to get off at the Shi Ji Middle School (世纪中学; Shìjì Zhōngxué).

ℹ️ Getting There & Away

AIR

Xiàguān's **airport** is 15km from the town centre. Buy air tickets online or at an agency in Old Dàlǐ. No public buses run to the airport; taxis will cost ¥50 from Xiàguān or ¥100 from Dàlǐ. Five flights daily leave for Kūnmíng (¥782) and two to Xīshuāngbǎnnà (¥991).

BUS

Xiàguān has no fewer than five bus stations. The Dàlǐ express bus station (*kuàisù kèyùnzhàn*) is on Nan Jian Lu. The second main station used by travellers is Xīngshèng bus station (also called *gāo kuài kèyùnzhàn*), located down the road from the express bus station. To find it, walk out of the express bus station, turn right and walk downhill, cross the big intersection to Xingsheng Lu and walk for 100m. The third station of interest is the north bus station (*běi kèyùnzhàn*) on Dali Lu, which is reached by bus 8 (¥2) or a ¥10 taxi ride.

Remember that when departing, the easiest way to Kūnmíng or Lìjiāng is to get a bus from Old Dàlǐ. The following departures are from the Dàlǐ express bus station:

Chǔxióng ¥74, 2½ hours, every 40 minutes (7.10am to 6.40pm)

Kūnmíng ¥115, four to five hours, every 30 minutes (7.50am to 7pm)

Liùkù ¥83, five hours, five buses (7.40am to 12.30pm)

The following departures are from the Xīngshèng bus station (*gāo kuài kèyùnzhàn*):

Bǎoshān ¥65, 2½ hours, every 40 minutes (7.50am to 7.20pm)

Jǐnghóng ¥200, 16 hours, two daily (9am and 11am)

Kūnmíng ¥145, four to five hours, every 30 minutes (7.20am to 7.30pm)

Lìjiāng ¥87, three to four hours, five daily (8.30am to 7pm)

Mángshì (Lùxī) ¥118, six to eight hours, three daily (10am, 11.30am and 1pm)

Ruìlì ¥147, eight hours, three daily (8.30am, 3pm and 8pm)

Téngchōng ¥132, six hours, three daily (10am, 1pm and 7.30pm)

Yúnlóng (Nuòdèng) ¥42, three hours, 14 daily (7.30am to 4.30pm)

Departures from the north bus station (*běi kèyùnzhàn*) include the following:

Jiànchuān (for Shāxī) ¥33, three hours, every 15 minutes (6.25am to 6.50pm)

Shangri-la (Zhōngdiàn) ¥100, seven hours, every 30 minutes (6.30am to noon)

If you want to head to Jǐnghóng (¥218, 15 hours, 8.20am and 9.40am), you need the east bus station (*dōng kèyùnzhàn*) by the train station, which also serves destinations on the east side of Ěrhǎi Hú such as Shuānglǎng and Wāsè.

For Wēishān, you must go to the southwest bus station (*xī nán kèyùnzhàn*).

Buses to Old Dàlǐ (¥3, 35 minutes) leave from outside the Xīngshèng bus station. Bus 8 (¥3, 35 minutes) runs from the train station to the centre of Xiàguān to Dàlǐ's West Gate. If you want to be sure, ask for Dàlǐ *gǔchéng* (Dali old city).

Tickets for nearly all destinations can be booked in Dàlǐ and this is often the easiest way to do it as it will save you a trip to Xiàguān (although you will pay a small service fee).

TRAIN

There are eight **trains** daily from Kūnmíng's main train station (hard seat/sleeper ¥68/111, six to seven hours, 4.41am to 5.56pm). Returning to Kūnmíng, there are seven daily trains (1.18am to 5.45pm). There are trains daily to Lìjiāng (¥37, two hours) at 5.52am, 7.18am and 5.01pm.

Wēishān 巍山

☑ 0872 / POP 20,700

Some 55km or so south of Xiàguān, Wēishān is the heart of a region populated by Hui and Yi. It was once the nucleus of the powerful Nanzhao kingdom, and from here the Hui rebel Du Wenxiu led an army in revolt against the Qing in the 19th century. Today, it's an attractive small town of narrow streets lined with wooden houses, with drum towers at strategic points and a lovely backdrop of the surrounding hills.

The town's central point is the unmistakable **Gǒngcháng Tower** (拱长楼; Gǒngcháng Lóu). South from Gǒngcháng Lóu you'll come first to **Xīnggǒng Tower** (星拱楼; Xīnggǒng Lóu) and then on the right-hand side of the street to **Mēnghuà Old Home** (蒙化老家; Mēnghuà Lǎojiā; admission ¥8; ☺ 8.30am-9pm), the town's best-preserved slice of architecture.

Línyè Bīnguǎn (林业宾馆; 612 0761; 24 Xi Xin Jie; 西新街24号; s ¥60, tw ¥80-100; ❋ ☎) is not far from Gǒngcháng Lóu and has big and comfortable rooms. It's a ¥5 ride from the bus station in a motor-rickshaw.

The only restaurants in the town are cubbyhole eateries. Head north or south of Gǒngcháng Lóu to find most of them. You may see people indulging in a local Yi speciality, baked tea.

Xiàguān's south bus station has buses to Wēishān (¥16, 1½ hours, every 20 to 30 minutes, 6.20am to 6pm). They return to Xiàguān from 6.30am.

Wēibǎo Shān   巍宝山

Eminently worthy **Wēibǎo Shān** (Wēibǎo Mountain; admission ¥60), about 10km south of Wēishān, has a relatively easy hike to its peak at around 2500m. During the Ming and Qing dynasties it was the zenith of China's Taoism, and you'll find some superb Taoist murals; the most significant are at **Wénchéng Gōng** (文昌宫; Wénchéng Palace; No 3 on the entrance ticket) and **Chángchún Cave** (长春洞; Chángchún Dòng; No 1 on the entrance ticket). Birders in particular love the mountain; the entire county is a node on an international birding flyway.

There are no buses here. Head to the street running east of Gǒngcháng Lóu in Wēishān to pick up a microvan to the mountain. Expect to pay ¥80 to ¥100 for the round trip; you'll need the driver to wait for you.

Dàlǐ   大理

 0872 / POP 40,000

Dàlǐ, the original backpacker hang-out in Yúnnán, was once *the* place to chill, with its stunning location sandwiched between mountains and Ěrhǎi Hú (Erhai Lake). Loafing here for a couple of weeks was an essential part of the Yúnnán experience.

In recent years, domestic tourists have discovered Dàlǐ in a big way and the scene has changed accordingly. Instead of dreadlocked Westerners, it's young Chinese who walk around with flowers in their hair. Still, Dàlǐ has not been overwhelmed by visitors like nearby Lìjiāng and remains a reasonably relaxed destination, with the local Bai population very much part of daily life.

Surrounding Dàlǐ there are fascinating possibilities for exploring, especially by bicycle and in the mountains above the lake, or you can do what travellers have done for years – eat, drink and make merry.

History

Dàlǐ lies on the western edge of Ěrhǎi Hú at an altitude of 1900m, with a backdrop of the imposing 4000m-tall Cāng Shān (Green Mountains). For much of the five centuries in which Yúnnán governed its own affairs, Dàlǐ was the centre of operations, and the old city retains a historical atmosphere that is hard to come by in other parts of China.

The main inhabitants of the region are the Bai, who number about 1.5 million and are thought to have settled the area some 3000 years ago. In the early 8th century they succeeded in defeating the Tang imperial army before establishing the Nanzhao kingdom, which lasted until the Mongol hordes arrived in the mid-13th century.

◉ Sights & Activities

Three Pagodas   PAGODA

(三塔寺; Sān Tǎ Sì; adult incl Chóngshèng Temple ¥121; ☉7am-7pm) Absolutely *the* symbol of the town/region, these pagodas, a 2km walk north of the north gate, are among the oldest standing structures in southwestern China. The tallest of the three, **Qiānxún Pagoda**, has 16 tiers that reach a height of 70m. It was originally erected in the mid-9th century by engineers from Xī'ān. It is flanked by two smaller 10-tiered pagodas, each of which are 42m high.

While the price is cheeky considering you can't go inside the pagodas, **Chóngshèng Temple** (Chóngshèng Sì) behind them has been restored and converted into a relatively worthy museum.

Dàlǐ Museum   MUSEUM

(大理博物馆; Dàlǐ Shì Bówùguǎn; Fuxing Lu; ☉8am-5.30pm) **FREE** The museum houses a small collection of archaeological pieces relating to Bai history, including some fine figurines. English descriptions are lacking.

Catholic Church   CHURCH

(off Renmin Lu) It's worth checking out Dàlǐ's Catholic Church. Dating back to 1927, it's a unique mix of Bai-style architecture and classic European church design. Mass is held here every Sunday at 9.30am.

Dàlǐ

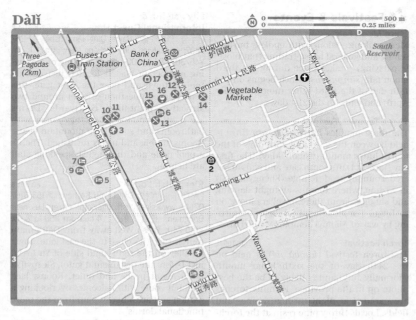

Dàlǐ

Climb Dàlǐ　　　　ROCK CLIMBING

(📞131 5064 4701; info@climbdali.com; 20 Renmin Lu) This outfit runs active adventures around Dàlǐ, including rock climbing, mountaineering, kayaking and rafting trips. Contact Adam Kritzer.

Rice & Friends　　　　COOKING COURSE

(📞151 2526 4065; www.riceandfriends.com) Recommended cooking school that includes trips to markets to purchase ingredients and tips on preparation, as well as cooking classes.

☞ Tours

China Minority Travel　　　　CULTURAL TOUR

(📞138 8723 5264; chinaminoritytravel@gmail.com) Henriette, a Dutch expat, can offer a long list of trips, including tours to Muslim and Yi minority markets as well as through remote areas of Yúnnán and Guìzhōu.

Zouba Tours　　　　BICYCLE TOUR, HIKING

(📞136 9877 9374; www.zoubatours.com) Bike tours and treks to the less-visited parts of Yúnnán.

✿ Festivals & Events

Third Moon Fair   CULTURAL
Merrymaking – along with endless buying, selling and general horse-trading (but mostly partying) – takes place during the third moon fair (*sānyuè jié*), which begins on the 15th day of the third lunar month (usually April) and ends on the 21st day.

Three Temples Festival   CULTURAL
The three temples festival (*ràosān líng*) is held between the 23rd and 25th days of the fourth lunar month (usually May). The first day starts at Dàlǐ's south gate and ends at Sacred Fountainhead Temple (Shèngyuán Sì) in Xīzhōu, where there is all-night dancing and singing. From there, revellers move on to Jīnguì Temple (Jīnguì Sì), before returning by way of Mǎjiǔyì Temple (Mǎjiǔyì Sì).

Torch Festival   CULTURAL
The torch festival (*huǒbǎ jié*) is held on the 24th day of the sixth lunar month (normally July) and is likely to be the best photo op in the province. Flaming torches are paraded at night through homes and fields. Locals throw pine resin at the torches causing minor explosions everywhere. According to one local guesthouse owner, 'it's total madness'.

🛏 Sleeping

There's heaps of accommodation in Dàlǐ, but the popular places fill up quickly during peak summer months.

★ Jade Emu   HOSTEL $
(金玉缘中澳国际青年旅舍; Jīnyùyuán Zhōng'ào Guójì Qīngnián Lǚshè; ☑267 7311; www.jade-emu.com; West Gate Village; 西门村; 4-bed dm with bathroom ¥40, 6-bed dm without/with bathroom ¥25/35, d & tw ¥150-180; @🛜) Smack in the shadow of Cāng Shān (a five-minute walk from the old town), the Jade Emu sets the standard for hostels in Dàlǐ and elsewhere with its attention to detail. There's an in-house VPN for access to social media sites banned in China, while the dorm beds are more comfortable than most and the staff efficient and friendly.

Private rooms are spacious, clean and well maintained. Staff also arrange tours and bus tickets. Around the corner, sister establishment Jade Roo copes with the overflow of travellers with similar rooms, while next door is its own cafe-cum-bookshop and new restaurant La Dolce Vita.

Lily Pad Inn & International Guest House   HOSTEL $
(百合青年旅舍; Bǎihé Qīngnián Lǚshě; ☑267 7807; www.lilyinn.com; Xīchéng Mén; 西城门; dm ¥45/30, d & tw ¥100-180; @🛜) One of a growing number of hostels located just outside the old town and near the west gate, this cool, relaxed guesthouse is set around two attractive, plant-filled courtyards. Dorms are a little cramped, but they come with bathrooms and some have mountain views. Rooms are big and nicely furnished. There's a pool table and the English-speaking staff are helpful.

Sleepyfish Lodge   HOSTEL $
(大理乐游客栈; Dàlǐ Lèyóu Kèzhàn; ☑153 3167 0214; www.sleepyfishlodge.com; Yu'er Lu, near Dongmen; 玉洱路东门; 4-bed dm ¥50, d & tw ¥180-240; @🛜) Well away from Dàlǐ's main tourist strip (it's close to the east gate, down an alley off the right-hand side of Yu Er Lu just before the ornamental gate), Sleepyfish is all about peace and quiet. Rooms lack TVs, but come with balconies overlooking a garden and are a big step up from the more functional dorms.

Bike hire is available from ¥25 a day; you may need one as it's a good 20-minute walk to the centre of town.

Five Elements   HOSTEL $
(五行国际客栈; Wǔ Xíng Guójì Kèzhàn; ☑130 9985 0360; www.5elementschina.com; West Gate Village; 西门村; dm ¥40/30, d & tw ¥120; @🛜) This place has a popular following with backpackers, thanks to the low prices and friendly vibe. Dorms lack lockers but are reasonably sized, while the private rooms are a decent deal for the price. There's a nice courtyard and garden where the manager grows organic vegies. Tours and tickets can be booked and bike hire is ¥30 per day.

Four Seasons International Youth Hostel   HOSTEL $
(春夏秋冬国际青年旅舍; Chūn Xià Qiūdōng Guójì Qīngnián Lǚshě; ☑267 1668; dicxqd@hotmail.com; 26 Renmin Lu; 人民路26号; dm/d/tw ¥40/150/180; @🛜) Located in the heart of Dàlǐ, this hostel sees far more Chinese travellers than foreigners. Rooms are big, clean and well maintained, with beds raised off the floor, and the communal area spreads into an attractive garden. Dorms are less spacious but you're just steps away from cafes and restaurants. Wi-fi in the lobby, ADSL internet in the rooms.

Jim's Tibetan Hotel   HOTEL **$$**
(吉姆和平酒店; Jímǔ Hépíng Jiǔdiàn; ☑267 7824; www.china-travel.nl; 13 Yuxiu Lu; 玉秀路13号; s/d ¥300; ❄@🛇) The rooms here are some of the most distinctive in Dàlǐ, coming with Tibetan motifs and packed with antique Chinese furniture. The bathrooms too are a cut above the competition, while there's a garden, rooftop terrace, restaurant and bar. Travel services and tours can be booked.

✖ Eating

Bai food makes use of local flora and fauna – many of which are unrecognisable! Province-wide, *ěr kuài* (饵块) are flattened and toasted rice 'cakes' with an assortment of toppings (or plain). *Rǔshàn* (乳扇; 'milk fan') may not sound appetising, but this 'aired' yoghurt/milk mixture (it ends up as a long, thin sheet) is a local speciality and is often fried or melted atop other foods. This is distinct from *rǔbǐng* (goat's cheese). Given Ěrhǎi Hú's proximity, try *shāguō yú* (沙锅鱼), a claypot fish casserole/stew made from salted Ěrhǎi Hú carp – and, as a Bai touch, magnolia petals. Local tastes also ensure that when ordering beef the fat-to-meat ratio is typically 50:50.

Good Panda   YUNNAN **$**
(妙香园; Miàoxiāng Yuán; 81 Renmin Lu; 人民路81号; dishes from ¥18; ⏱9am-10pm) Surrounded by Western-style restaurants, this is a more local joint and a good introduction to classic Dàlǐ dishes like sizzling beef (*tiěbǎn niúròu*) and crispy carp (*jiànchuān gānshāo yú*), plus Yúnnán and Sìchuān food. There's a limited English menu, but you can point at the vegetables that look best. The patio is an excellent spot for people-watching.

Lovely Lotus
Delicious Vegetarian   CHINESE, VEGETARIAN **$**
(爱莲说素膳; Ài Lián Shuō Sùshàn; ☑533 7737; B2, Jiulongju, west side of Fuxing Lu; 复兴路西侧九隆居B2号; buffet ¥20; ⏱11.30am-1.30pm & 6-8pm; 🌱) There's no menu here; instead you choose from a tempting buffet of all-vegetarian dishes. It's very popular at lunchtimes and there's a small outside area to eat at. It's just off Boai Lu on the right-hand side of a forecourt.

Sweet Tooth   CAFE **$**
(甜点屋; Tiándiǎn Wū; ☑266 3830; 52 Boai Lu; cakes from ¥25, sandwiches from ¥28; ⏱8.30am-10.30pm; 🛇) Owned and run by a culinary-

arts graduate, Sweet Tooth's homemade ice cream and desserts are simply inspiring. There's also fine coffee, proper English tea and healthy fruit and yoghurt shakes. As an added bonus, profits from the cafe benefit the hearing impaired.

Duan's Kitchen   YUNNAN **$$**
(小段厨房; Xiǎoduàn Chúfáng; ☑153 0872 7919; 12 Renmin Lu; 人民路12号; dishes from ¥20; ⏱11am-2pm & 5.30-9pm) Cosy and cute courtyard restaurant at the far eastern end of Renmin Lu which sees a lot of Chinese travellers. The dishes are an interpretation of Bai cuisine rather than 100% the real deal, but the ingredients are absolutely local.

Bakery No. 88   WESTERN **$$**
(88号西点店; Bāshíbā Hào Xīdiǎndiàn; ☑267 9129; 17 Renmin Lu; 人民路17号; sandwiches from ¥25; ⏱8.30am-10pm; 🛇) Spread across two floors and with a small garden, this smoke-free haven of tranquillity has excellent sandwiches, pastas and soups, all prepared with local produce, as well as fine breads and cakes.

Méizi Jǐng   YUNNAN **$$**
(梅子井; ☑267 1578; 130 Renmin Lu; 人民路130号; dishes from ¥15; ⏱11am-9pm) This charmingly authentic Bai restaurant is composed of three grey-brick courtyards each containing small seating nooks where you can feast on traditional local cuisine. The nonsensical English menu includes a few mystery dishes ('Sewing kit fried lily', anyone?), but the 'braised chicken' or 'wild mushroom' dishes are both fine starting points. It's tucked off Renmin Lu opposite the vegetable market.

Birdbar Cafe   JAPANESE **$$**
(鸟吧咖啡馆; Niǎoba Kāfēi Guǎn; ☑250 1902; 20 Renmin Lu; 人民路20号; breakfast ¥38, sushi from ¥38; ⏱10am-8.30pm Tue-Sun; 🛇) There's a great, sun-filled upstairs area to lounge in over a coffee, tea or beer, while the menu is an intriguing take on Japanese cuisine. The breakfasts are an especially good deal, as are the set dinners (¥68).

🍷 Drinking & Nightlife

The Western-style restaurants double as bars.

Bad Monkey   BAR
(坏猴子; Huài Hóuzi; Renmin Lu; beers from ¥15; ⏱9am-late) The eternally happening, Brit-run Bad Monkey brews its own strong

ales (from ¥25), has regular live music and endless drink specials. There's also average pub grub (pizzas, burgers and shepherd's pie) and Sunday roast for ¥45 (including a glass of wine).

Sun Island BAR
(324 Renmin Lu; 人民路324号; beers from ¥12; ☺3pm-late) Courtyard bar with a sound selection of foreign beers, a pool table and a laid-back vibe. It's on the right-hand side of Renmin Lu going towards the east gate.

🛍 Shopping

Dàlǐ is famous for its marble blue and white batik printed on cotton and silk.

The centre of town has a profusion of clothes shops. Most shopkeepers can also make clothes to your specifications – which will likely come as a relief when you see how small some of the items of ready-made clothing are.

A few more-or-less useful maps (¥8) can be picked up at hostels and restaurants around town. You can also find them at **Mandarin Books & CDs** (五华书苑; Wǔhuá Shūyuàn; Huguo Lu; ☺9.30am-9.30pm), along with guidebooks and novels in Chinese, English, French and German.

❶ Information

On hikes around Cāng Shān there have been several reports of robbery of solo walkers. On the overnight sleeper bus from Kūnmíng, a bag is often pinched or razored. Bags in the luggage hold are also not safe.

All hostels and many hotels offer travel advice, arrange tours and book tickets for onward travel. There are also numerous travel agencies and cafes that will book bus tickets and offer all manner of tours. They can be expensive unless you can get a group together.

A couple of internet cafes can be found on Renmin Lu (¥3 per hour).

Note that there is a **Public Security Bureau** (PSB; 公安局; Gōng'ānjú; 🕾214 2149; Dàlǐ Rd, Xiàguān; ☺8-11am & 2-5pm Mon-Fri) in Dàlǐ, though visas cannot be renewed here; you have to go to Xiàguān.

Bank of China (中国银行; Zhōngguó Yínháng; Fuxing Lu) Changes cash and travellers cheques, and has an ATM that accepts all major credit cards.

China Post (中国邮政; Zhōngguó Yóuzhèng; cnr Fuxing Lu & Huguo Lu; ☺8am-8pm) You can make international calls here.

❶ Getting There & Away

The golden rule: most buses advertised to Dàlǐ actually go to Xiàguān. Coming from Lìjiāng, Xiàguān-bound buses stop at the eastern end of Dàlǐ to let passengers off before continuing on to the Xīngshèng bus station.

From Kūnmíng's west bus station there are numerous buses to Dàlǐ (¥138, four to five hours, every 20 minutes from 7.20am to 8pm). Heading north, it's easiest to pick up a bus on the roads outside the west and east gates: buy your ticket in advance from your guesthouse or a travel agent and they'll make sure you get on the right one. (You could hail one yourself to save a surcharge but you're not guaranteed a seat.)

From the old town (near West Gate Village) you can catch a 30-seat bus to Kūnmíng for ¥110, departing 9am, 10.30am, 11.30am, 1.30pm and 4.30pm.

Buses run regularly to Shāpíng (¥10), Xǐzhōu (¥6) and other local destinations from outside the west gate.

❶ Getting Around

From Dàlǐ, a taxi to Xiàguān airport takes 45 minutes and costs around ¥100; to Xiàguān's train station it costs ¥50.

Bikes are the best way to get around and can be hired at numerous places from ¥20 to ¥30 per day.

Buses (¥3, 30 minutes, marked 大理) run between the old town and Xiàguān from as early as 6.30am; wait along the highway and flag one down. Bus 8 runs between Dàlǐ and central Xiàguān (¥2, 30 minutes) on the way to the train station every 15 minutes from 6.30am.

Around Dàlǐ

Travellers have a **market** to go to nearly every day of the week. Every Monday at **Shāpíng** (沙坪), about 30km north of Dàlǐ, there is a colourful Bai market (Shāpíng Gǎnjí). From 10am to 2.30pm you can buy everything from food products and clothing to jewellery and local batik.

Regular buses to Shāpíng (¥10, one hour) leave from just outside the west gate. By bike, it will take about two hours at a good clip.

Markets also take place in **Shuānglíang** (双廊; Tuesday), **Shābā** (沙坝; Wednesday), **Yòusuǒ** (右所; Friday morning, the largest in Yúnnán) and **Jiāngwěi** (江尾; Saturday). **Xǐzhōu** (喜州) and **Zhōuchéng** (州城) have daily morning and afternoon markets, respectively. **Wāsè** (挖色) also has a popular market every five days with trading from

9am to 4.30pm. Thanks to the lack of boats, travellers now have to slog to Xiàguān's east bus station for buses to Wāsè (¥20).

Many cafes and hotels in Dàlǐ offer tours or can arrange transportation to these markets for around ¥150 for a half-day.

Ěrhǎi Hú 洱海湖

Ěrhǎi Hú (or 'Ear-Shaped' Lake) dominates the local psyche. The seventh-biggest freshwater lake in China, it sits at 1973m above sea level and covers 250 sq km; it's also dotted with trails perfect for bike rides and villages to visit. It's a 50-minute walk, a 15-minute bus ride or a 10-minute downhill zip on a bike from Dàlǐ.

◉ Sights & Activities

Cáicūn (才村), a pleasant little village east of Dàlǐ (¥1.50 on bus 2), is the nexus of lake transport. Sadly, putt-putt local ferries are a distant memory. All boat travel is now on 'official' vessels. Expect to pay ¥180 for a three-hour trip.

On the east side of the lake the beautiful lakeside town of **Shuānglǎng** (双廊) is now extremely popular with domestic tourists. The town is a labyrinth of winding old alleys and traditional homes sitting on a little peninsula that juts into the lake. Just offshore is **Nánzhào Customs Island** (南诏风情岛; Nánzhào Fēngqíng Dǎo), which has gardens; parks; a 17.5m-tall marble statue of Avalokiteshvara (Chenresig), aka Guanyin; and a hotel. Boats to the island cost ¥50, the price includes admission.

The other east-side highlight, close to Wāsè, is **Pǔtuó Dǎo** (普陀岛; Pǔtuó Island) and **Lesser Pǔtuó Temple** (小普陀寺; Xiǎopǔtuó Sì), set on an extremely photogenic rocky outcrop.

Roads encircle the lake so it is possible to do a loop (or partial loop) of the lake by **mountain bike**. A bike path goes from Cáicūn to Tǎo Yuán Port, which makes a great day trip (but most travellers turn around at Xīzhōu, 喜洲). Some hard-core cyclists continue right around the lake (the full loop is around 98km). The lack of boats means you're looking at an overnight stay or an extremely long ride in one day.

🛏 Sleeping

There are several guesthouses in Shuānglǎng, including the **Sky & Sea Lodge** (海地生活; Hǎidì Shēnghuó; ☑ 0872-246

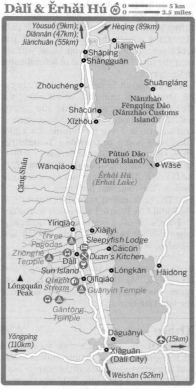

Dàlǐ & Ěrhǎi Hú

1762; www.skysealodge.org; 8-bed dm ¥40, d & tw ¥120-300; 🛜), with excellent lake views. You can't take a taxi here so you'll have to walk about 10 to 15 minutes through the village, ask locals to point the way.

Cāng Shān 苍山

This range of gorgeous peaks rises imposingly above Dàlǐ and offers the best legwork in the area. Most travellers head first for **Zhōnghé Temple** (中和寺; Zhōnghé Sì), on the side of **Zhōnghé Shān** (中和山; Zhōnghé Mountain; admission ¥30; ⏰8am-6pm). At the temple, be careful of imposter monks passing out incense and then demanding ¥200 for a blessing.

You can hike up the mountain, a sweaty two to three hours for those in moderately good shape (but note the warning that there have been several reports of robbery of solo walkers). Walk about 200m north of the **chairlift** (¥60 return) base to the riverbed. Follow the left bank for about 50m and walk through the cemetery, then follow the path zigzagging under the chairlift. When you reach some stone steps, you know you are near the top. This is but one of several paths to the temple.

Branching out from either side of Zhōnghé Temple is a trail that winds along the face of the mountains, taking you in and out of steep, lush valleys and past streams and waterfalls. From the temple, it's a nice 11km walk south to **Gǎntōng Temple** (感通寺; Gǎntōng Sì), **Qīngbì Stream** (清碧溪; Qīngbì Xī) and/or **Guānyīn Temple** (观音堂; Guānyīn Táng), from where you can continue to the road and pick up a Dàlǐ-bound bus. The path, called **Jade Belt Road** (玉带路; Yùdài Lù), is paved and easily walkable.

There's also a **cable car** (one way/return ¥50/80) between Qīngbì Stream and Gǎntōng Temple.

Alternatively, take the new **cable car** (return ¥230) up to the **Horse Washing Pond** (洗马潭; Xǐ Mǎ Tán), high in the mountain range, where Kublai Khan set up his base in the late 13th century.

Xǐzhōu   喜洲

A trip to the old town of Xǐzhōu for a look at its well-preserved Bai architecture is lovely, and some travellers now make it their base. You can catch a local bus (¥6) from the west gate in Dàlǐ, but a bicycle trip is also a good idea.

Walk through the market to find the old town and the American-run **Linden Centre** (喜林苑; Xǐ Lín Yuàn; ☑ 245 2988; www.linden -centre.com; 5 Chengbei; d/ste incl breakfast ¥980/1480; @ ⑤), a traditional home turned boutique hotel with 15 rooms that come with antique furniture and modern bathrooms. But there are other places in the village where you can find a room for ¥80.

From here, the interesting town of **Zhōuchéng** (州城) is 7km further north; it too has basic accommodation.

Nuòdèng   诺邓

☑ 0872

This anachronistic hamlet, oft-lauded as the 'thousand-year-old' village, has one of the highest concentrations of Bai in Yúnnán and some of the best-preserved buildings in the entire province. Nuòdèng has managed to maintain traditional village life, with ponies and donkeys clomping up the steep flagstone streets past traditional mudbrick buildings with ornate gates, many of which date back to the Ming and Qing dynasties, making it a delightful place to kick back for a while.

◉ Sights

After crossing the bridge at the bottom of the village you'll see one of the original **salt wells**, located inside a wooden shed. The town is built upon a steep hill and winding up through the alleys you'll reach an impressive **Confucian Temple** (孔庙; Kǒngmiào), which today serves as the village primary school (check out the detailed frescoes still visible on the ceiling). Further uphill is the picturesque 16th-century **Yuhuang Pavillion** (玉皇阁; Yùhuáng Gé).

Village life is centred on the small **market square**; a good place to catch some sun and gab with the local elders.

On the way to Nuòdèng village from Yúnlóng, the **Bi River** is forced by the surrounding hills into a serpentine roll that from above looks remarkably like a yin-yang symbol, or **Tàijítú** (太极图). You won't notice this natural phenomenon from ground level; you need to go up to a viewing platform on the nearby hill. The road to the pavilion is 7km of endless switchbacks, a tedious and tiring hike, or you could hire a rickshaw to take you there for ¥20.

⌕ Sleeping & Eating

Good Life Hostel   HOSTEL **$**
(古道坊客栈; Gǔdàofāng Kèzhàn; ☑ 572 3526; 292970620@qq.com; 4-bed dm ¥40, d without/with bathroom ¥120/160; ⑤) Converted courtyard home with compact but clean rooms and friendly staff. To find it, head for the stone steps leading uphill from the bridge where rickshaws arrive and depart, and follow the signs. Staff can cook simple Chinese dishes too.

Fùjiǎ Liúfāngyuàn   INN **$**
(复甲留方苑; ☑ 572 3466; dm/d & tw ¥30/80) Big rooms at this family-run guesthouse set around a lush garden of bougainvillea. It's right at the top of the village; call ahead and they'll come and meet you.

Yán Quán Nóngjiā   YUNNAN **$$$**
(盐泉农家; ☑ 552 5111; dishes from ¥36; ⊙ 11am-7.30pm) The one genuine restaurant in the village is also one of the most famous in all Yúnnán, having being featured on the hit

Chinese TV cooking show *A Bite of China*. People come from far and wide to sample *huǒtuǐ* (火腿), a slightly salty cured ham that is the local speciality. Prices are accordingly expensive, but the food tastes great.

ℹ️ Getting There & Away

Buses (¥42, three hours, 14 daily from 7.30am to 4.30pm) leave from Xiàguān's Xīngshèng bus station to the county seat Yúnlóng (云龙), from where you can take a three-wheel rickshaw (¥20 to ¥25) the final 7km to Nuòdèng. Buses back to Xiàguān leave on a similar schedule, the final departure is at 4pm. Heading to and from Liùkù, catch the hourly buses that run to and from Lánpíng (兰坪) between 8am and 1pm (¥46).

Shāxī   沙溪

📲 0872

The tiny hamlet of Shāxī, 120km northwest of Dàlǐ, is a hugely evocative throwback to the days of the Tea-Horse Roads. You can almost hear the clippety-clop of horses' hooves and shouts of traders.

Shāxī is one of only three surviving caravan oases from the old Tea-Horse Roads that stretched from Yúnnán to India. It's by far the best preserved and the only one with a surviving market (held on Fridays).

The village's wooden houses, courtyards and narrow, winding streets make it a popular location for period Chinese movies and TV shows (and day trippers), but this is still a wonderfully sleepy place where nightlife means sitting out under the canopy of stars and listening to the frogs croaking in the rice paddies.

👁️ Sights

Sideng Jie (寺登街) is the ancient town street leading off the main road. It's about 300m downhill to the multifrescoed Xīngjiào Sì (兴教寺; Xīngjiào Temple; admission ¥20; ⏰8.30am-5.30pm), the only Ming-dynasty Bai Buddhist temple. On the opposite side of the courtyard is the Three Terraced Pavilion (魁星阁; Kuíxīnggé), which has a prominent theatrical stage (古戏台; *gǔxìtái*), something of a rarity in rural Yúnnán. There is a small museum here, ask the guard at the temple for the key. The absolute highlight, however, is the Ōuyáng Courtyard (欧阳大院; Ōuyáng Dàyuàn), a superb example of three-in-one Bai folk architecture in which one wall protected three yards/residences. Sadly, most of it is currently closed to the public, although you can poke your head inside for a quick look.

Exit the east gate and head south along the Huì River (惠江; Huì Jiāng) for five minutes, cross the ancient Yùjīn Qiáo (玉津桥; Yùjīn Bridge), and you're walking the same trail as the horse caravans. If you look hard enough, you'll still be able to see hoofprints etched into the rock, or so the locals claim.

YÚNNÁN SHĀXĪ

THE TEA-HORSE ROAD

Less well known than the Silk Road, but equally important in terms of trade and the movement of ideas, people and religions, the Tea-Horse Road (茶马古道; Chámǎgǔdào) linked southwest China with India via Tibet. A series of caravan routes, rather than a single road, which also went through parts of Sìchuān, Myanmar (Burma), Laos and Nepal, the trails started deep in the jungle of Xīshuāngbǎnnà. They then headed north through Dàlǐ and Lìjiāng and into the thin air of the Himalayan mountains on the way to the Tibetan capital Lhasa, before turning south to India and Myanmar.

Although archaeological finds indicate that stretches of the different routes were in use thousands of years ago, the road really began life in the Tang dynasty (AD 618–907). An increased appetite for tea in Tibet led to an arrangement with the Chinese imperial court to barter Yúnnán tea for the prized horses ridden by Tibetan warriors. By the Song dynasty (AD 960–1279), 20,000 horses a year were coming down the road to China, while in 1661 alone some 1.5 million kilos of tea headed to Tibet.

Sugar and salt were also carried by the caravans of horses, mules and yaks. Buddhist monks, Christian missionaries and foreign armies utilised the trails as well to move between Myanmar, India and China. In the 18th century the Chinese stopped trading for Tibetan horses and the road went into a slow decline. Its final glory days came during WWII, when it was a vital conduit for supplies from India for the allied troops fighting the Japanese in China. The advent of peace and the communist takeover of 1949 put an end to the road.

Otherwise, the main activity around town is walking. The guesthouses in town have maps that can get you started and keep you busy for days.

🛏 Sleeping & Eating

Basic beds are available along Sideng Jie from ¥50.

Horsepen 46　　　　　　　　　INN $
(马圈46客栈; Mǎjuàn Sìshíliù Kèzhàn; ☑ 472 2299; www.horsepen46.com; 46 Sideng Jie; 寺登街46号; dm ¥30, r ¥60-120; @ ☎) In-demand guesthouse with cute, compact rooms surrounding a sunny little courtyard. There's a laid-back traveller vibe here with daily communal dinners (¥20). There's also bike hire (¥20 per day) and the helpful English-speaking staff can organise hikes in the area. It's tucked away to the right of the stage in the village square.

Tea and Horse
Caravan Trail Inn　　　　　　INN $
(古道客栈; Gǔdào Kèzhàn; ☑ 472 1051; 83 Sideng Jie; 寺登街83号; d & tw ¥120-200; ☎) There are a couple of cheap rooms without bathrooms (¥60) at this friendly place, but the more expensive ones are a significant step up and come with comfy beds and decent bathrooms, as well as being set around a pleasant garden.

★ Old Theatre Inn　　　GUESTHOUSE $$$
(戏台会馆; Xìtái Huìguǎn; ☑ 472 2296; reservations@shaxichina.com; Duànjiādēng Village; 段家登; r incl breakfast ¥460; @ ☎) This boutique guesthouse has been lovingly restored out of a 200-year-old Chinese theatre and inn. There are only five very comfortable rooms here, all with photogenic views towards the nearby mountains; book ahead. It's located 3km north of Shāxī; you can rent a bike here (¥20) to get around.

Bàn Xián Jū　　　　　　　YUNNAN $
(半闲居; Sideng Jie; 寺登街; dishes from ¥20; ☺9am-10pm) On the corner of the village square, this courtyard restaurant attracts both locals and travellers with its small but authentic range of Bai dishes, as well as Yúnnánese fare.

Hungry Buddha　　　　　　ITALIAN $$
(大嘴佛; Dàzuǐ Fó; dishes from ¥40; ☺9.30am-9pm Wed-Sun) Quite the most sophisticated eatery in town, with a mouth-watering menu utilising locally produced ingredients.

Great homemade cheese, pasta and pizza, as well as a fine breakfast. Proper wine list too.

ℹ Getting There & Away

From Jiànchuān (剑川), minivans (¥10, one hour) run to and from Shāxī. Moving on you'll have to backtrack to Jiànchuān. There are frequent buses to Dàlǐ (¥42) between 6.30am and 6pm. To Lìjiāng (¥20) there are buses at 8am, 9.30am, 11.30am, 1.30pm and 3.30pm. Buses to Kūnmíng (¥160) leave at 9.30am and 2pm, and to Shangri-la (¥53) at 9am and 10am.

NORTHWEST YÚNNÁN

Lìjiāng　　　　　　　　丽江
☑ 0888 / POP (OLD TOWN) 40,000

How popular is this timelocked place? Lìjiāng's maze of cobbled streets, rickety (or rickety-looking, given gentrification) wooden buildings and gushing canals suck in over *eight million* people a year. So thick are the crowds in the narrow alleys that it can feel like that they've all arrived at the same time.

But remember the 80/20 rule: 80% of the tourists will be in 20% of the places. Get up early enough and you can often beat the crowds. And when they do appear, that's the cue to hop on a bike and cycle out to one of the nearby villages.

A Unesco World Heritage Site since 1997, Lìjiāng is a city of two halves: the old town and the very modern new town. The old town is where you'll be spending your time and it's a jumble of lanes that twist and turn. If you get lost (and most do), head upstream and you'll make your way back to the main square.

◉ Sights

Note that a ¥80 'protection fee', allegedly for old-town preservation projects, is sold at most guesthouses and provides free entry to Black Dragon Pool. Proof of payment of this fee is required at some other sites, such as Jade Dragon Snow Mountain.

Old Town　　　　　　　HISTORIC SITE
(古城) The old town is centred around the busy and touristy **Old Market Square** (四方街; Sìfāng Jiē). The surrounding lanes are dissected by a web of artery-like canals that once brought the city's drinking water from Yuquan Spring, on the far outskirts of what is now Black Dragon Pool Park. Several wells

and pools are still in use around town (but hard to find). Where there are three pools, these were designated into pools for drinking, washing clothes and washing vegetables.

A famous example of these is the **White Horse Dragon Pool** (白马龙潭; Báimǎlóng Tán; ⊙7am-10pm) in the deep south of the old town, where you can still see the odd local washing their vegies after buying them in the market.

Now acting as sentinel of sorts for the town, the **Looking at the Past Pavillion** (望古楼; Wànggǔ Lóu; admission ¥50, free with town entrance ticket; ⊙7.30am-7pm) has a unique design using dozens of four-storey pillars – culled from northern Yúnnán old-growth forests.

A must-see is **Zhongyi Market** (忠义市场; Zhōngyì Shìchǎng; ⊙6am-5pm) where locals sell produce, copper items and livestock. If you are craving a slice of old Lìjiāng, this is where you'll find it.

Black Dragon Pool Park   PARK
(黑龙潭公园; Hēilóngtán Gōngyuán; Xin Dajie; admission free with town entrance ticket; ⊙7am-7pm) On the northern edge of town is the Black Dragon Pool Park; its view of **Yùlóng Xuěshān** (Jade Dragon Snow Mountain) is the most obligatory photo shoot in southwestern China. The **Dōngbā Research Institute** (东巴文化研究室; Dōngbā Wénhuà Yánjiūshì; ⊙8am-5pm Mon-Fri) is part of a renovated complex on the hillside here. You can see Naxi cultural artefacts and scrolls featuring a unique pictograph script.

Trails lead up **Xiàng Shān** (Elephant Hill) to a dilapidated gazebo and then across a spiny ridge past a communications centre and back down the other side, making a nice morning hike, but note that there have been reports of solo women travellers being robbed in this area.

The **Museum of Naxi Dongba Culture** (纳西东巴文化博物馆; Nàxī Dōngbā Wénhuà Bówùguǎn; ⊙9am-5pm) is at the park's northern entrance and is a decent introduction to traditional Naxi lifestyle and religion, complete with good English captions.

Note that the pool has dried up in recent years and without water some visitors are disappointed with this site; ask at your accommodation first if the pool has water before deciding whether or not to visit.

Mu Family Mansion   HISTORIC SITE
(木氏土司府; Mùshì Tǔsīfǔ; admission ¥60; ⊙8.30am-5.30pm) The former home of a Naxi chieftain, the Mu Family Mansion was heavily renovated (more like built from scratch) after the devastating earthquake that struck Lìjiāng in 1996. Mediocre captions do a poor job of introducing the Mu family but many travellers find the beautiful grounds reason enough to visit.

☞ Tours

There are dozens of tour operators in the old town, but these largely cater to tour groups. Your best bet is to book trips through your accommodation.

THE NAXI

Lìjiāng has been the homeland of the 286,000-strong Naxi (纳西; also spelt Nakhi and Nahi) minority for about the last 1400 years. The Naxi descend from ethnically Tibetan Qiang tribes and lived until recently in matrilineal families. Since local rulers were always male it wasn't truly matriarchal, but women still seemed to run the show.

The Naxi matriarchs maintained their hold over the men with flexible arrangements for love affairs. The *azhu* (friend) system allowed a couple to become lovers without setting up joint residence. Both partners would continue to live in their respective homes; the boyfriend would spend the nights at his girlfriend's house but return to live and work at his mother's house during the day. Any children born to the couple belonged to the woman, who was responsible for bringing them up. The man provided support, but once the relationship was over, so was the support. Children lived with their mothers and no special effort was made to recognise paternity. Women inherited all property and disputes were adjudicated by female elders.

There are strong matriarchal influences in the Naxi language. Nouns enlarge their meaning when the word for 'female' is added; conversely, the addition of the word for 'male' will decrease the meaning. For example, 'stone' plus 'female' conveys the idea of a boulder; 'stone' plus 'male' conveys the idea of a pebble.

YÚNNÁN LÌJIĀNG

Lìjiāng

500 m
0.25 miles

Timeless Hostel
(200m)

Jinhong Lu

Wuyi Jie

Chongren Xiang

**OLD
TOWN**

Bank of
China

Qiyi Jie 七一街

● 2

Dong Dajie

Xinhua Jie

● 4

7

Yu
River

Bank of China

Yuyuan Lu

Buses to
Yùlóng
Xuěshān

Mao Square ●

Xin Dajie ●

Main Entrance
to the Old Town

Waterwheel

● 5

Bus 6 to
Báishā
Village

民主路 Minzhu Lu

● 1

Shīzi Shān
(Lion Hill)

Long-Distance
(600m)

Long-Distance

Fuhui Lu 福慧路

Shangri-la Dadao

NEW TOWN

Express Bus
Station

CAAC ●

Enlargement

Wenzhi Xiang

9

18
16

10

6
17

Jinhong Lu

**OLD
TOWN**

Wuyi Jie

11

Chongren Xiang

12

Qiyi Jie 七一街

Bank of China

8

14

13

Xinyi Jie

Jishi Xiang

Mishi Xiang

19

15

3 ●

Xinhua Jie

Dong Dajie

Yu River

Xinhua Jie

200 m
0.1 miles

Lìjiāng

Keith Lyons   TOUR
(☑ 137 6900 1439; keithalyons@gmail.com) A Lìjiāng-based guide, Keith Lyons runs tours and treks that specialise in the area outside Lìjiāng.

Insiders   DRIVING TOUR
(☑ 138 1761 6975; www.insidersexperience.com) If you fancy seeing Lìjiāng's environs from the sidecar of a vintage Chinese motorbike, Insiders runs tours from its base in nearby Báishā.

🎊 Festivals & Events

Fertility Festival   CULTURAL
The 13th day of the third moon (late March or early April) is the traditional day to hold this festival.

Torch Festival   CULTURAL
July brings the torch festival (Huǒbǎ Jié), also celebrated by the Bai in the Dàlǐ region and the Yi all over the southwest. The origin of this festival can be traced back to the Nanzhao kingdom, when the wife of a man burned to death by the king eluded the romantic entreaties of the monarch by leaping into a fire.

These days, flaming torches are paraded through the streets to much merriment.

🛏 Sleeping

There are well over a thousand places to stay in the old town, with more appearing all the time. Many have less than 10 rooms. In peak seasons (especially holidays), prices double (or more).

★ Timeless Hostel   HOSTEL $
(久居元阳青年旅舍; Jiǔ Jū Yuányáng Qīngnián Lǚshě; ☑ 517 4626; lijiang.timeless@gmail.com; 63 Wenming Xiang, Wuyi Jie, Yishang; 义尚村五一街文明巷63号; 4-/8-bed dm ¥45/40, d & tw ¥140-160; @ ☎) Formerly known as the Panba, this amiable hostel at the quieter eastern end of Wuyi Jie has the best dorms in town: large with en suite bathrooms and big lockers, as well as clean private rooms with shared balconies. The solicitous staff are pleasant and the attached restaurant and bar are good for both meals and hanging out.

Bicycles can be hired for ¥40 a day and all the usual tickets and tours can be arranged.

Garden Inn   GUESTHOUSE $
(丽江文庙国际客栈; Lìjiāng Wénmiào Guójì Kèzhàn; ☑ 151 0887 3494; www.mayhostel.wix.com/gardeninn; 7 Wenmiao Xiang, Beimen Jie; 文庙巷7号, 北门街; dm ¥35, d & tw ¥140-300; ❄@☎) Just relocated higher up in the old town (so the views are better), this popular backpacker hostel is set around an attractive courtyard garden. All dorms come with their own bathrooms, and there's a range of private rooms. There's a decent communal area too, and the helpful staff can arrange tours or rent you a bike (¥40 per day).

Mama Naxi's Guesthouse   GUESTHOUSE $
(古城香格韵客栈; Gǔchéng Xiānggéyùn Kèzhàn; ☑ 510 7713; mamanaxi@hotmail.com; 4-/6-bed dm ¥40/36, d & tw ¥100-180; @☎) The energetic Mama operates two guesthouses near each other, named '1' and '3'. Head to '3' (70 Wangjia Zhuang Lane) for cramped dorms, clean standard rooms, information-gathering, socialising and cheap eats. It's a bit loud when a Naxi wedding is taking place at the next-door wedding hall. '1' (78 Wangjia Zhuang Lane) is dorm free and more peaceful.

YÚNNÁN LÌJIĀNG

Lijiang International Youth Hostel HOSTEL $
(丽江老谢车马店; Lìjiāng Lǎoxiè Chēmǎdiàn; ✆ 518 0124; Maying130@126.com; 44 Mishi Xiang, Xinyi Jie; 新义街密士巷44号; 12-/8-/4-bed dm ¥35/55/40, d & tw ¥138-168; @ 🛜) This hostel sees mostly domestic travellers – not much English is spoken – but dorms and rooms are reasonably sized and priced, if uninspired. No bike hire but there's a good bar/communal area.

⭐ **Blossom Hill Joyland** BOUTIQUE HOTEL $$$
(花间堂; Huājiān Táng; ✆ 4000 767 123; www.blossomhillinn.com; 55 Wenhua Xiang, Wuyi Jie; 五一街文华巷55号; d & tw ¥880-1586; ❋ 🛜) There are only 18 rooms, all individually decorated in very tasteful and comfortable fashion, at this boutique inn in the heart of the old town. Bathrooms are modern and large, while each room comes with its own collection of antiques and wood furnishings. Staff are helpful and there's a small common area with a library. It's essential to book ahead.

Crowne Plaza Lijiang HOTEL $$$
(丽江和府假日酒店; Lìjiāng Héfǔ Jiàrì Jiǔdiàn; ✆ 558 8888; www.crowneplaza.cn; 276 Xianghe Lu; 祥和路276号; d/ste ¥1553/3370; @ 🛜 ⛲) The best hotel in the old town, a magical space with lofty ceilings, little gardens and epic views of the Jade Dragon Mountain. The bathrooms are the finest in town, the beds huge and comfy. Other amenities include two restaurants, a swimming pool, day spa and children's play room. Discounts of 25% are sometimes available.

Zen Garden Hotel HOTEL $$$
(瑞和园酒店; Ruìhé Yuán Jiǔdiàn; ✆ 518 9799; www.zengardenhotel.com; 36 Xingren Lane, Wuyi Jie; 五一街兴仁下段36号; d/ste ¥500/1200; @ 🛜) As befits its name, this is a serene, hushed establishment. Run by a Naxi teacher and decorated with help from her artist brother, the furniture and design in the communal areas is tremendous, while the rooms have been recently upgraded and come with top bathrooms.

🍴 Eating

There are many, many eateries around the old town, and almost every menu will have both Chinese and Western dishes.

Bābā is the Lìjiāng local speciality – thick flatbreads of wheat, served plain or stuffed with meat, vegetables or sweets. There are always several 'Naxi' items on menus, including the famous 'Naxi omelette' and 'Naxi sandwich' (goat's cheese, tomato and fried egg between two pieces of local *bābā*). Try locally produced *qīng méi jiǔ*, a plum-based wine with a 500-year history – it tastes like a semisweet sherry.

⭐ **Tiāntiān Xiān** YUNNAN $
(天天鲜; ✆ 518 4933; 47 Wangjiazhuang Xiang, Wuyi Jie; 五一街王家庄巷47号; dishes from ¥14; ⌚ noon-9pm) Locals flock here for the superb, signature grilled fish and chicken and soybean-paste dishes (get here before 7pm or it will have run out). But all the great-value Naxi specialities on offer are fantastic. No English spoken, but there is an English menu. To find it, look for the three characters with 'Daily Fresh' written in English underneath them.

Tiān Hé Cāntīng YUNNAN $
(天和餐厅; ✆ 139 8887 6492; 139 Wuyi Jie; dishes from ¥18; ⌚ 7am-11pm) It's hard to find a neighbourhood-style restaurant in the old town, or one that doesn't also serve Western food, but this very solid, family-run place hits the spot with a mix of Naxi dishes and Chinese staples like dumplings, hotpots and *gōng bǎo jī dīng* (a chicken, peanut and chilli-flavoured dish).

Sakura Good Food Square YUNNAN $
(樱花美食广场; Yīnghuā Méishí Guángchǎng; Qiyi Jie; snacks from ¥10; ⌚ 10am-late) Snackers should not miss the open-air food mar-

---

NAXI SCRIPT

The Naxi created a written language more than 1000 years ago using an extraordinary system of pictographs – the only hieroglyphic language still in use. The most famous Naxi text is the Dongba classic *Creation*, and ancient copies of it and other texts can still be found in Lìjiāng, as well as in the archives of some US universities. The Dongba were Naxi shamans who were caretakers of the written language and mediators between the Naxi and the spirit world.

The Dongba religion, itself an off-shoot of Tibet's pre-Buddhist Bon religion, eventually developed into an amalgam of Tibetan Buddhism, Islam and Taoism.

Useful phrases in the Naxi language are *nuar lala* (hello) and *jiu bai sai* (thank you).

ket where vendors sell appetising bite-size treats, some of which are native to Lìjiāng. Try the *Nàxī kǎo qiézì* (纳西烤茄子; Naxi grilled eggplant) served in a boat-shaped crust, *tǔ dòu bǐng* (土豆饼; Naxi potato pancake) and *Nàxī kǎolà cháng* (纳西烤腊肠; Naxi grilled, salty sausage) made with pork, fat and pepper.

For dessert, try the delightful *Nàxī nuomi tuán* (纳西糯米团), a sticky rice ball stuffed with either *hóngdòushā* (红豆沙; red bean), *shūcài* (蔬菜; vegetable) or *ròu* (肉; meat).

Āmāyì Nàxī Snacks
YUNNAN $$

(阿妈意纳西饮食院; Āmāyì Nàxī Yǐnshí Yuàn; ☑ 530 9588; Wuyi Jie; dishes from ¥28; ☺ 11am-9.30pm) The name doesn't do justice to the small but select and very authentic selection of Naxi cuisine on offer at this calm courtyard restaurant. There are fantastic mushroom dishes, as well as *zhútǒng fàn*, rice that comes packed in bamboo. It's down an alley off Wuyi Jie, close to the Stone Bridge.

N's Kitchen
WESTERN $$

(二楼小厨; Èrlóu Xiǎochú; ☑ 512 0060; 17 Jishan Xiang, Xinyi Jie; breakfast from ¥20, mains from ¥25; ☺ 9am-10pm; 🕿) Clamber up the steep stairs for one of the best breakfasts in town, a monster burger and fine Yúnnán coffee. It's a good source of travel info too and can arrange bus tickets.

Lamu's House of Tibet
TIBETAN $$

(西藏屋西餐馆; Xīzàngwū Xīcāntīng; ☑ 511 5776; 56 Xinyi Jie; dishes from ¥20; ☺ 7am-midnight; 🕿) Friendly Lamu has been serving up smiles and hearty Tibetan and international fare for more than a decade. Ascend the little wooden staircase to the 2nd-floor dining area, a great spot for people-watching, and try the excellent Naxiburger, a pasta or steak. There's also a good selection of paperback books to thumb through.

🍺 Drinking

Xinhua Jie, just off Old Market Sq, is packed out with Chinese-style drinking dens.

Stone the Crows
BAR

(134-2 Wenzhi Xiang; beers from ¥15; ☺ 2pm-late) Worth checking out is this Irish-owned, endearingly ramshackle bar with a good range of local and foreign beers and a mixed crowd of locals and Westerners. It gets going later rather than earlier.

KEEPING THE GOOD FORTUNE

An interesting local historical tidbit has it that the original Naxi chieftain, whose former home is the Mu Family Mansion, would not allow the old town to be girdled by a city wall because drawing a box around the Chinese character of his family name would change the character from *mù* (木; wood) to *kùn* (困; surrounded, or hard-pressed).

☆ Entertainment

Nàxī Orchestra
LIVE MUSIC

(纳西古乐会; Nàxī Gǔyuè Huì, Nàxī Music Academy; Xinhua Jie; 新华街; tickets ¥120-160; ☺ performances 8pm) Attending a performance of this orchestra inside a beautiful building in the old town is a good way to spend an evening in Lìjiāng. Not only are all two dozen or so members Naxi, but they play a type of Taoist temple music (known as *dòngjīng*) that has been lost elsewhere in China.

The pieces they perform are said to be faithful renditions of music from the Han, Song and Tang dynasties, and are played on original instruments.

ℹ️ Information

Crowded, narrow streets are a pickpocket's heaven. Solo women travellers have been mugged when walking alone at night in isolated areas. Xiàng Shān (Elephant Hill) in Black Dragon Pool Park (Hēilóngtán Gōngyuán) has been the site of quite a few robberies.

Lìjiāng's cafes and backpacker inns are your best source of information on the area. There are no internet cafes in the old town, but all hostels and hotels have internet access and/or wi-fi, as do virtually all the cafes in town.

Bank of China (中国银行; Zhōngguó Yínháng; Yuyuan Lu; ☺ 9am-5pm) This branch has an ATM and is convenient for the old town. There are many ATMs in the old town too.

China Post (中国邮政; Zhōngguó Yóuzhèng; Minzhu Lu; ☺ 8am-8pm) In the old town just north of Old Market Sq.

Public Security Bureau (PSB; 公安局; Gōng'ānjú; ☑ 518 8437; 110 Taihe Jie, Xianghelicheng District; ☺ 8.30-11.30am & 2.30-5.30pm Mon-Fri) Reputedly speedy with visa extensions. Located on the west side of the Government Building. A taxi here will cost ¥15 from the city centre.

YÚNNÁN LÌJIĀNG

ℹ Getting There & Away

AIR

Lìjiāng's airport is 28km east of town. Tickets can be booked at **CAAC** (中国民航; Zhōngguó Mínháng; cnr Fuhui Lu & Shangrila Dadao; ☺ 8.30am-9pm). Most hotels in the old town also offer an air-ticket booking service.

From Lìjiāng there are oodles of daily flights to Kūnmíng (¥580), as well as daily flights to the following:

Běijīng ¥1985
Chéngdū ¥823
Chóngqìng ¥710
Guǎngzhōu ¥1600
Shànghǎi ¥1825
Shēnzhèn ¥1555
Xīshuāngbǎnnà ¥879

BUS

The main long-distance bus station (客运站; kèyùnzhàn) is south of the old town; to get here, take bus 8 or 11 (¥1; the latter is faster) from along Minzhu Lu.

Chéngdū ¥326, 24 hours, one daily (1pm)
Jiànchuān ¥23, two to three hours, five daily (8.20am to 4pm)
Kūnmíng ¥232, eight to nine hours, eight buses daily (9am to 6.30pm)
Lúgū Hú ¥100, nine hours, two daily (8.30am and 9am)
Nínglàng ¥56, five hours, 11 daily (9.10am to 4.10pm)
Pānzhīhuā ¥99, eight hours, nine daily (7.10am to 4pm)
Qiáotóu ¥29, two hours, two daily (8.30am and 9am); Lìjiāng to Shangri-la buses also stop here.
Shangri-la ¥63 to ¥72, five hours, every 30 minutes (7.30am to 3.30pm)
Xiàguān ¥63 to ¥80, three hours, every 30 minutes (7.10am to 7pm)
Xīshuāngbǎnnà ¥276, 18 hours, one daily (7.30am)

In the north of town, the **express bus station** (高快客运站; Gāo kuài kèyùnzhàn; Shangrila Dadao) is where many of the above bus services originate, but it's usually more convenient to catch your bus from the long-distance bus station.

TRAIN

There are six trains daily to Dàlǐ (¥34, two hours, 7.39am to 10.55pm) and eight trains to Kūnmíng (hard sleeper ¥147, nine hours, 7.39am to 11.20pm). Trains to Shangri-la should be running by the time you read this.

ℹ Getting Around

Buses to the airport (¥20) leave from outside the CAAC office from 6.30am to 10pm.

Taxi flagfall is ¥8, although you will struggle to get drivers to use their meters. Taxis are not allowed into the old town. Bike hire is available at most hostels (¥40 per day).

Around Lìjiāng

It is possible to see most of Lìjiāng's environs on your own, but a few agencies in Lìjiāng, such as Keith Lyons, offer half- or full-day tours, starting from ¥200, plus fees.

There are a number of monasteries around Lìjiāng, all Tibetan in origin and belonging to the Karmapa (Red Hat) sect. Most were extensively damaged during the Cultural Revolution and there's not much monastic activity nowadays.

Jade Peak Monastery (玉峰寺; Yùfēng Sì; admission ¥30) is on a hillside about 5km past Báishā. The last 3km of the track requires a steep climb. The monastery sits at the foot of Yùlóng Xuěshān (5500m) and was established in 1756. The monastery's main attraction nowadays is the **Camellia Tree of 10,000 Blossoms** (Wànduǒ Shānchá). Ten thousand might be something of an exaggeration, but locals claim that the tree produces at least 4000 blossoms between February and April. A monk on the grounds risked his life to keep the tree secretly watered during the Cultural Revolution.

Lìjiāng is also famed for its **temple frescoes**, most of which were painted during the 15th and 16th centuries by Tibetan, Naxi, Bai and Han artists; many were restored during the later Qing dynasty. They depict various Taoist, Chinese and Tibetan Buddhist themes and can be found on the interior walls of temples in the area. Keep in mind that the Cultural Revolution did lots of ravaging here. Frescoes can be found in Báishā and on the interior walls of **Dàjué Palace** (Dàjué Gōng) in the village of Lóngquán.

Báishā   白沙

By far, the most serene spot around Lìjiāng, Báishā is a small village near several old temples and makes a great day trip by bike. Alternatively, it's an ideal spot for lazing and cycling the surrounding area for a day or two.

JOSEPH ROCK

Yúnnán has always been a hunting ground for famous, foreign plant-hunters such as Kingdon Ward and Joseph Rock (1884–1962). Rock lived in Lìjiāng between 1922 and 1949, becoming the world's leading expert on Naxi culture and local botany.

Born in Austria, the withdrawn autodidact lerarned eight languages, including Sanskrit. After becoming the world's foremost authority on Hawaiian flora, the US Department of Agriculture, Harvard University and later *National Geographic* (he was their famed 'man in China') sponsored Rock's trips to collect flora for medicinal research. He devoted much of his life to studying Naxi culture, which he feared was being extinguished by the dominant Han culture.

Rock sent more than 80,000 plant specimens from China – two were named after him – along with 1600 birds and 60 mammals. His caravans stretched for half a mile, and included dozens of servants, including a cook trained in Austrian cuisine, a portable darkroom, trains of pack horses, and hundreds of mercenaries for protection against bandits, not to mention the gold dinner service and collapsible bath tub.

Rock lived in Yùhú village (called Nguluko when he was there), outside Lìjiāng. Many of his possessions are now local family heirlooms.

The *Ancient Nakhi Kingdom of Southwest China* (1947) is Joseph Rock's definitive work. Immediately prior to his death, his Naxi dictionary was finally prepared for publishing.

Located on the plain north of Lìjiāng, Báishā was the capital of the Naxi kingdom until Kublai Khan made it part of his Yuan empire (1271–1368).

⊙ Sights

The 'star' attraction of Báishā is **Dr Ho Shi Xiu**, a legendary herbalist who was propelled to fame by the travel writer Bruce Chatwin when he mythologised him in a 1986 *New Yorker* story as the 'Taoist physician in the Jade Dragon Mountains of Lìjiāng'.

A sprightly 92 at the time of writing and still treating the ill every day with herbs collected from the nearby mountains, Dr Ho is very chatty (he speaks English, German and Japanese) and is happy to regale visitors with the secrets of good health and longevity.

There are a couple of **frescoes** worth seeing in town and the surrounding area. The best can be found in Báishā's **Dàbǎojī Palace**, and at the neighbouring **Liúlí Temple** (琉璃殿; Liúlí Diàn) and **Dàdìng Gé** (大定阁). Note that you'll have to show the ¥80 Lìjiāng town-entrance ticket to gain access to the palace.

🛏 Sleeping & Eating

There are a few places to stay in the village. The laidback **Baisha There International Youth Hostel** (白沙那里青年旅舍; Báishā Nálǐ Qīngnián Lǚshè; ☑534 0550; www.yhachina.

com; dm ¥40, d & tw ¥168-198; @⊙) is down a lane left off the main street, past Dr Ho's.

On the same street as Dr Ho you'll find a number of small cafes and restaurants including **Country Road Café** (☑133 6888 0272; Xiāng Cūn Lù; dishes from ¥12; ⊙7.30am-7pm; ⊙), a rustic cafe with Western, Chinese and Naxi dishes. The owner Rosey and her sister Lucy speak good English and are a reliable source of travel information.

ℹ Getting There & Away

Báishā is a one-hour bike ride from Lìjiāng. Otherwise, take the bus 8 (¥1) from Minzhu Lu, near the pedestrian bridge, to Xiangshan Lu opposite the market and change to bus 6 (¥1). It returns to Lìjiāng regularly.

Shùhé Old Town 束河古城

Marginally more tranquil than Lìjiāng, Shùhé Old Town (Shùhé Gǔchéng) is attracting both increasing numbers of travellers and day trippers. A former staging post on the Tea-Horse Road that's just 4km from Lìjiāng, Shùhé can be visited in a day, or makes a less frenetic alternative base for exploring the region.

⊙ Sights

Although there's little in the way of sights, the cobblestoned alleys and streets south of its **main square** are very picturesque and

Around Lìjiāng

more peaceful at night than Lìjiāng. Head for the **original section of town**, which is sandwiched between the Jiŭdīng and Qīnglóng Rivers and nestles beneath the foothills of Yùlóng Xuěshān. The first part of town, identified by a large Chinese-style gate, is actually completely new (though it looks old), built for the purposes of tourism in the early 2000s (this section of town is actually owned by a private company).

Sleeping & Eating

There are many guesthouses, cafes and restaurants scattered around Shùhé. The big and busy **K2 Hostel** (K2国际青年旅舍; K2 Guójì Qīngnián Lǚshè; ☑ 513 0110; www.k2yha.com; 1 Guailiu Xiang, Kangpu Lu; 康普路拐柳巷1号; dm ¥35-50, d & tw ¥158; @ ☎) is very popular with Chinese travellers. The dorms are a bit cramped but there is a large communal area. To get here, don't enter the town's main gate, but take the road to the right, which leads on to Kangpu Lu after five minutes. More upmarket is the **Sleepy Inn** (丽舍客栈; Lìshè Kèzhàn; ☑ 6401 0235; 8 Qinglong Lu; 青龙路8号; d & tw ¥268; ☎), which has comfortable rooms with balconies set around a courtyard. Reach it by crossing the bridge over the Qīnglóng River and walking 100m west on Qinglong Lu.

ⓘ Getting There & Away

Getting to Shùhé is easy from Lìjiāng, with regular minivans (¥3) running from Shangrila Dadao, close to the junction with Fuhui Lu.

Yùlóng Xuěshān 玉龙雪山

Also known as Mt Satseto, **Yùlóng Xuěshān** (玉龙雪山; Jade Dragon Snow Mountain; adult ¥105, protection fee ¥80) soars to some 5500m. Its peak was first climbed in 1963 by a research team from Běijīng and now, at some 35km from Lìjiāng, it is regularly mobbed by hordes of Chinese tour groups and travellers, especially in the summer.

Buses from Lìjiāng arrive at a parking area where you can purchase tickets for the various cable cars and chairlifts that ascend the mountain. This is also where the **Impression Lijiang** (admission ¥190-260; ☺ daily 1pm) show is held, a mega song-and-dance performance. Note that if you are going to the performance you will also have to pay the park admission fees. Close to the parking area is **Dry Sea Meadow** (干海子; Gànhǎizi), a good spot for photographing the mountain.

A **cable car** (¥185) ascends the mountain to an elevation of 4506m; from here you can walk up another 200m to a viewing point to see the glacier near the peak. It can often get chilly near the top so bring warm clothes. You will also have to pay ¥20 for the bus ticket to the base of the cable car.

Back down at the parking lot you can switch to a bus that goes to **Blue Moon Lake** (蓝月湖; Lányuè Hǔ) and **White Water River** (白水河; Bái Shuǐ Hé), where a walking trail leads along the river up to the lake (the round-trip walk takes about 90 minutes). The cable-car bus ticket is also good for the bus to the lake.

A 10-minute drive past Blue Moon Lake is **Yak Meadow** (牦牛坪; Máoniúpíng), where a **chairlift** (¥60, plus bus ticket ¥20) pulls visitors up to an altitude of 3500m.

In summer, when crowds for the cable car are long (up to two hours' wait), most travellers just do the trip to the lake and Yak Meadow.

Minibuses (¥30) leave from opposite Mao Sq. Returning to Lìjiāng, buses leave fairly regularly but check with your driver to find out what time the last bus will depart.

Tiger Leaping Gorge 虎跳峡

☏ 0887

Gingerly stepping along a trail swept with scree to allow an old fellow with a donkey to pass; resting atop a rock, exhausted, looking up to see the fading sunlight dance between snow-shrouded peaks, then down to see the lingering rays dancing on the rippling waters a thousand metres away; feeling utterly exhilarated. That pretty much sums up **Tiger Leaping Gorge** (虎跳峡; Hǔtiào Xiá; admission ¥65), the unmissable trek of southwest China.

One of the deepest gorges in the world, it measures 16km long and is a giddy 3900m from the waters of the Jīnshā River (Jīnshā Jiāng) to the snowcapped mountains of Hābā Shān (Hābā Mountain) to the west and Yùlóng Xuěshān to the east, and, despite the odd danger, it's gorgeous almost every single step of the way.

The gorge hike is not to be taken lightly. Even for those in good physical shape, it's a workout and can certainly wreck the knees. The path constricts and crumbles and is alarmingly narrow in places, making it sometimes dangerous. When it's raining (especially in July and August), landslides and swollen waterfalls can block the paths, in particular on the low road. (The best time to come is May and the start of June, when the hills are afire with plant and flower life.)

A few people – including a handful of foreign travellers – have died in the gorge. During the past decade, there have also been cases of travellers being assaulted on the trail. As always, it's safer in all ways not to do the hike alone.

Check with cafes and lodgings in Lìjiāng or Qiáotóu for trail and weather updates. Most have fairly detailed gorge maps; just remember they're not to scale and are occasionally out of date.

Make sure you bring plenty of water on this hike – 2L to 3L is ideal – as well as plenty of sunscreen and lip balm.

🏃 Activities

There are two trails: the higher (the older route) and the lower, which follows the new road and is best avoided, unless you enjoy being enveloped in clouds of dust from passing tour buses and 4WDs. While the scenery is stunning wherever you are in the gorge, it's absolutely sublime from the high trail. Make sure you don't get too distracted by all that beauty, though, and so miss the arrows that help you avoid getting lost on the trail.

From the ticket office, it's six hours to Běndìwān, eight hours to Middle Gorge (Tina's Guesthouse) or nine hours to Walnut Garden. It's much more fun, and a lot less exhausting, to do the trek over two days. By stopping overnight at one of the many guesthouses along the way, you'll have the time to appreciate the magnificent vistas on offer at almost every turn of the trail.

Ponies can be hired (their owners will find you) to take you to the gorge's highest point for ¥200; it's not uncommon to see three generations of a family together, with the oldies on horseback and the young ones panting on foot behind them.

The following route starts at Jane's Guesthouse. Walk away from **Qiáotóu** (桥头), past the school, for five minutes or so, then head up the paved road branching to the left; there's an arrow to guide you. After about 2.5km on the road the gorge trail proper starts and the serious climbing begins.

Note that locals may try and hit you up for an additional 'fee' at this point, which they will claim is reward for them keeping the trail litter-free.

Tiger Leaping Gorge

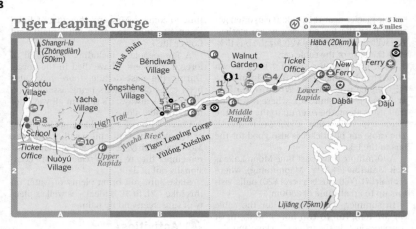

Tiger Leaping Gorge

The toughest section of the trek comes after **Nuòyú** (诺余) village, when the trail winds through the 28 agonising bends, or turns, that lead to the highest point of the gorge. Count on five hours at normal pace to get through here and to reach **Yāchà** (牙叉) village.

It's a relatively straightforward walk on to **Běndìwān** (本地湾). About 1½ hours on from here, you begin the descent to the road on slippery, poor paths. Watch your step here; if you twist an ankle, it's a long hop down.

After the path meets the road at Tina's Guesthouse, there's a good detour that leads down 40 minutes to the middle rapids and **Tiger Leaping Stone**, where a tiger is once said to have leapt across the Yangzi, thus giving the gorge its name. Locals charge ¥10 to go down the path. At the bottom of this insanely steep trail locals charge another ¥10 for one viewpoint

but another spot is free. From one of the lower rest points another trail (¥10) heads downstream for a one-hour walk to **Walnut Garden** (核桃园).

Most hikers stop at Tina's, have lunch, and head back to Qiáotóu. Those continuing to Walnut Garden can take the trail along the river or use an alternative trail that keeps high where the path descends to Tina's, crosses a stream and a 'bamboo forest' before descending into Walnut Garden. If you are deciding where to spend the night, Walnut Garden is more attractive than Tina's.

🛏 Sleeping & Eating

🍽 Qiáotóu

Jane's Guesthouse GUESTHOUSE $
(峡谷行客栈; Xiágǔ Xíng Kèzhàn; ☎880 6570; 4-bed dm ¥30, d or tw without/with bathroom ¥60/120; @🛜) This friendly place with tidy, clean rooms is where many people start their trek. The breakfasts here make for good walking fuel and it has left-luggage facilities (¥5 a bag).

🍽 In the Gorge

The following list of accommodation options along the way (listed in the order that you'll come to them) is not exhaustive. In the unlikely event that everywhere is full, basic rooms will be available with a local. We've never heard of anyone who had to sleep rough in the gorge.

All the guesthouses double as restaurants and shops, where you can pick up bottled water and snacks along the way.

Naxi Family Guesthouse GUESTHOUSE $
(纳西雅阁; Nàxī Kèzhàn; ☑880 6928; dm ¥30, d & tw ¥120; @ ☎) Taking your time to spend a night here instead of double-timing it to Walnut Garden isn't a bad idea. It's an incredibly friendly, well-run place (organic vegies and wines), set around a pleasant courtyard.

Tea Horse Guesthouse GUESTHOUSE $
(茶马客栈; Chámǎ Kèzhàn; ☑139 8870 7922; dm ¥35, d & tw ¥150) Just after Yāchà village, this ever-expanding place has a new restaurant – which makes a good lunch stop – as well as a small spa and massage parlour where aching limbs can be eased.

Come Inn GUESTHOUSE $
(下一客栈; Xiàyī Kèzhàn; ☑181 8385 3151; 4-bed dm ¥50, d & tw ¥200) Huge dorms with bathrooms and sliding doors that open out onto a vast wooden terrace with super views are on offer at this brand-new guesthouse near the entrance to Běndìwān village. Private rooms are in tip-top condition.

Halfway Guesthouse GUESTHOUSE $$
(中途客栈; Zhōngtú Kèzhàn; ☑139 8870 0522; Běndìwān; dm ¥40, d & tw ¥120-200) Once a simple home to a guy collecting medicinal herbs ,and his family, this is now a busy-busy operation. The vistas here are awe-inspiring and perhaps the best of any lodging in the gorge; the view from the communal toilets is worth the price of a bed alone.

Tina's Guesthouse GUESTHOUSE $
(中峡旅店; Zhōngxiá Lǚdiàn; ☑820 2258; 2625441148@qq.com; dm ¥30, d & tw ¥120-280; @ ☎) Almost like a package-holiday operation, with travellers funneled to and from the gorge, Tina's lacks the charm of its competitors. But it's efficiently run, has plenty of beds and the location is perfect for those too knackered to make it to Walnut Garden. Pricier rooms have excellent views. There are daily buses from here to Lìjiāng and Shangri-la (¥55, 3.30pm).

Sean's Spring Guesthouse GUESTHOUSE $$
(山泉客栈; Shānquán Kèzhàn; ☑820 2223, 158 9436 7846; www.tigerleappinggorge.com; r ¥60-80, with bathroom ¥160-380; @ ☎) One of the original guesthouses on the trail, and still the spot for lively evenings, the eponymous Sean is a true character and one of the few locals seriously concerned with the gorge's environmental well-being. There are 28 rooms here, including a couple of cheapies, and the best have great views of Yùlóng Xuěshān.

Chateau de Woody GUESTHOUSE $
(山白脸旅馆; Shānbáiliǎn Lǚguǎn; ☑139 8871 2705; sgrlwoody@163.com; dm ¥30, d & tw ¥60-180) This old-school gorge guesthouse has rooms with good views and modern bathrooms that are a decent deal. Across the road, the less-attractive modern extension has the cheapest rooms.

❶ Getting There & Away

From Lìjiāng's long-distance bus station there are two direct buses a day to Qiáotóu (¥29, 2¼ hours, 8.30am and 9am). Otherwise, catch any bus to Shangri-la (¥40, 2¼ hours, every 40 minutes, 7.30am to 3.30pm) and get off at Qiáotóu.

Most travellers get a minivan (¥35) to the start of the walking track, organised through their guesthouse in Lìjiāng. The minivan can deliver extra luggage to the guesthouse of your choice (usually Tina's or Jane's).

Returning to Lìjiāng from Qiáotóu, buses start passing through from Shangri-la at around 10am. The last one rolls through at around 8pm. The last bus to Shangri-la passes through at around 5.30pm. Tina's Guesthouse also organises one bus a day to both Lìjiāng and Shangri-la.

At the time of writing, there were no buses to Báishuǐtái from Lìjiāng. There are three buses a day from Shangri-la to Báishuǐtái (¥24, three hours, 9.10am, 9.20am & 2pm).

Tiger Leaping Gorge to Báishuǐtái

An adventurous add-on to the gorge trek is to continue north all the way to Hābā (哈巴) village and the limestone terraces of Báishuǐtái (白水台; admission ¥35). This turns it into a four-day trek from Qiáotóu and from here you can travel on to Shangri-la. From Walnut Garden to Hābā, via Jiāngbiān (江边), is a seven- to eight-hour walk. From here to the Yi village of Sānbà (三坝), close to Báishuǐtái, is about the same, following trails. You could just follow the road and hitch with the occasional truck or tractor, but it's longer and less scenic.

The best way would be to hire a guide in Walnut Garden (for ¥400 to ¥500 per day for an English-speaker). A horse will cost ¥250 per day extra. The turn-off to Hābā starts 6km down the road from Walnut Garden, up the hill where you see 'Welcome to Tibet Guesthouse' painted on the retaining wall.

In Hābā most people stay at the **Hābā Snow Mountain Inn** (哈巴雪山客栈; Hābā Xuěshān Kèzhàn; ☏ 088 7886 6596; dm ¥30, d & tw ¥80-150; @), which has older dorms and new double rooms. The enthusiastic host can organise guides to lead you up **Hābā Mountain** (哈巴山, Hābā Shān), a two-day trek, or to **Black Lake** (黑海, Hēi Hǎi), a nine-hour round-trip hike. Note that locals now charge a ¥200 'protection fee' per person for access to the mountain, supposedly going towards conservation efforts.

From Tina's to Sānbà there is a daily bus at 1.30pm (¥47, three hours), but it sometimes doesn't run due to the road being blocked. From Sānbà to Shangri-la there is also a daily bus (¥50, three hours) at noon. Minivans frequently ply these routes so flagging down a ride isn't too tough.

If you plan to hike the route alone, assume you'll need all provisions and equipment for extremes of weather. Ask for local advice before setting out.

Lúgū Hú 泸沽湖

☏ 0888

Straddling the remote Yúnnán–Sìchuān border, this **lake** (admission ¥100) is an absolutely idyllic place, even with the rise in domestic tourism. The ascent to the lake, which sits at 2690m, is via a spectacular switchback road and the first sight of the 50-sq-km body of water, surrounded by lushly forested slopes, will take your breath away.

Villages are scattered around the outskirts of the lake, with **Luòshuǐ** (洛水) the biggest and most developed, and the one where the bus will drop you. As well as guesthouses and restaurants, and a few cafes with English menus and Western food, there are the inevitable souvenir shops. Nevertheless, it's hardly a boomtown, with the dominant night-time sound being the lapping of the lake.

Most travellers move quickly to **Lǐgé** (里格), 9km further up the road, tucked into a bay on the northwestern shore of the lake. Although guesthouses make up most of the place, along with restaurants serving succulent, but pricey, barbecue, the sights and nights here are lovely. If you want a less touristy experience, then you need to keep village-hopping around the lake to the Sìchuān side. At the moment, top votes for alternative locations are **Luòwǎ** (洛瓦) and **Wǔzhīluó** (五支罗).

The area is home to several Tibetan, Yi and Mosu (a Naxi subgroup) villages. The Mosu are the last practising matriarchal society in the world and many other Naxi customs lost in Lìjiāng are still in evidence here.

The best times to visit the lake are April to May, and September to October, when the weather is dry and mild. It's usually snowbound during the winter months.

◉ Sights

Mosu Folk Custom Museum   MUSEUM
(摩俗民族博物馆; Mósú Mínzú Bówùguǎn; Luòshuǐ; admission ¥60; ⊘ 8.30am-5.30pm) This museum in Luòshuǐ is set within the traditional home of a wealthy Mosu family, and the obligatory guide will explain how the matriarchal society functions. There is also an interesting collection of photos taken by Joseph Rock in the 1920s. The entrance fee is normally discounted by 50%.

Zhāmǎ Temple   MONASTERY
(扎美寺; Zhāmǎ Si; admission by donation) On the outskirts of Yǒngníng, this is a Tibetan monastery with at least 20 lamas in residence. Admission is free, but a donation is expected. A private minivan costs ¥20 per person for the half-hour ride.

◉ Activities

From Luòshuǐ and Lǐgé you can punt about with local Mosu by dugout canoe – known by the Mosu as 'pig troughs' (zhūcáo). Expect to head for **Lǐwùbǐ Dǎo** (里务比岛), the largest island (and throw a stone into Sìchuān). The second-largest island is **Hēiwǎé Dǎo** (黑瓦俄岛). Boat-trip prices vary wildly. If you're in a group, it's around ¥30 per person. But if it's a quiet time, you should be able to get a ride on your own for ¥50.

Bikes (per day ¥30) and scooters (per day ¥100 to ¥150) can be hired along the lakeshore at Luòshuǐ and Lǐgé.

🛏 Sleeping & Eating

Hotels and guesthouses line the lakeside in Luòshuǐ and Lǐgé, with basic rooms available for around ¥80. Many have attached restaurants that serve traditional Mosu foods, including preserved pig's fat and salted sour fish – the latter being somewhat tastier than the former. Of the two places, Lǐgé is really the place to go for fantastic barbecue.

Lao Shay Youth Hostel
HOSTEL **$**

(老谢车马店; Lǎoxiè Chēmǎdiàn; ☑588 1555; www.laoshay.com; Lǐgé; 4-bed dm ¥45, r ¥78-218; @ 🛜) Still the best spot for cheap digs in Lǐgé, with a prime location smack in the middle of the village. The best rooms have balconies and lake views, the cheapest share bathrooms. Dorms have lockers and are in reasonable condition. Enthusiastic staff. Bike hire is ¥40 per day.

Húsī Teahouse
HOSTEL **$**

(湖思茶屋; Húsī Cháwū; ☑588 6960; husihostel@gmail.com; Luòshuǐ; 6-bed dm ¥35, d & tw ¥98-288; @ 🛜) The granddaddy of all Lúgū Hú backpacker joints, this place in Luòshuǐ is a multistorey complex of dorms and private rooms, the more expensive with excellent lake views. There is a big lounge with computers and a restaurant serving Chinese food and average Western meals. The English-speaking staff are helpful.

Yǎsé Dábā Lǚxíngzhě Zhījiā
HOTEL **$$$**

(雅瑟达吧旅行者之家; ☑588 1196; ligemosuo@126.com; Lǐgé; d ¥420-460; @ 🛜) Stuck out on a little promontory at the edge of Lǐgé, all the rooms here come with decent views, but the ones on the 2nd floor are tremendous. They're a little overpriced but the bathrooms are a cut above the rest in the village. In the attached restaurant, try Lúgū Hú fish (泸沽湖鱼; *lúgū hú yú*) or sausage (香肠; *xiāngcháng*).

Zhāxī Cāntīng
BARBECUE **$$**

(扎西餐厅; ☑588 1055; Lǐgé; dishes from ¥30; ⏱5pm-midnight) Lively restaurant and barbecue joint that's good for the local speciality, Mosuo pork (¥50). You'll see the pigs being roasted whole outside, where you can sit near the lake.

🛈 Getting There & Away

Lìjiāng's express bus station has two direct buses a day to the lake (¥100, seven hours, 8.30am and 9am), but buy your ticket at least one day in advance as it's frequently sold out. Note too that it often takes nine or 10 hours to get to the lake for various road-related reasons.

For Lǐgé you'll have to change for a minibus in Luòshuǐ (¥20 per person), or hire a bike.

Leaving Luòshuǐ, there are two daily buses to Lìjiāng at 10am and 10.30am. Again, tickets should be bought at least a day in advance. You can also catch one of the regular minivans to Nínglàng (宁蒗; ¥30, four hours), from where there are plenty of buses to Lìjiāng.

For Sìchuān, there's a daily bus at 2pm to Xīchāng (西昌; ¥110, nine hours).

Shangri-la (Zhōngdiàn) 香格里拉(中甸)
☑0887 / POP 120,000

Shangri-la, previously known as Zhōngdiàn (and also known in Tibetan as 'Gyalthang'), is where you begin to breathe in the Tibetan world. That's if you can breathe at all, given its altitude (3200m).

Home to one of Yúnnán's most rewarding monasteries, Shangri-la is also the last stop in Yúnnán before a rough five- or six-day journey to Chéngdū via the Tibetan townships and rugged terrain of western Sìchuān.

Shangri-la is divided into two distinct sections: the much larger modern side of town and the old quarter. A devastating fire in January 2014 sent much of the old town up in smoke and the area now resembles a bomb site as it is being rebuilt. It's a work in progress, so expect changes when you arrive.

But even with most of the old town gone, Shangri-la remains an intriguing destination thanks to its blend of Tibetan and Han Chinese culture. The surrounding area, too, is simply delightful with its mix of mountains, meadows and lakes.

Plan your visit for between March or April and October. During winter the city practically shuts down and transportation is often halted completely by snowstorms.

In mid- to late June, the town hosts a **horse-racing festival** that sees several days of dancing, singing, eating and, of course, horse racing. Accommodation is tight at this time.

👁 Sights

Shangri-la is a wonderful place for getting off the beaten track, with plenty of trekking and horse-riding opportunities, as well as little-visited monasteries and villages. However, the remote sights are difficult to reach independently given the lack of public transport.

Ganden Sumtseling Gompa
MONASTERY

(松赞林寺; Sōngzànlín Sì; admission ¥115; ⏱7am-7pm) About an hour's walk north of town is this 300-year-old Tibetan monastery complex with around 600 monks. Extensive rebuilding has robbed the monastery of some

Shangri-la (Zhōngdiàn)

of its charm, but it remains the most important in southwest China and is definitely worth the visit. Bus 3 runs here from anywhere along Changzheng Lu (¥1). From the main gate where the tickets are sold you can catch a tourist bus to the monastery.

If you don't mind hiking its possible to visit for free by walking to the left side of the ticket office, up the hill parallel to the paved road and down to a lake with the monastery on the other side (a 30-minute walk).

Old Town   HISTORIC SITE
A few streets survived the 2014 fire and retain the mix of cobbled lanes and renovated wooden buildings that characterised the old town. Worth a visit is **Guīshān Sì** (龟山寺; Guīshān Temple), which is home to a handful of monks who conduct morning prayers. Next to it is **Zhùangjīn Tǒng**, the world's biggest prayer wheel standing at 21m high and containing 100,000 small prayer wheels. At least six people are needed to make it spin.

On the far side of Guīshān Sì is the **Shangri-la Thangka Academy** (唐卡学会; Tángkǎ Xuéhuì; ☑ 888 1612; www.thangkaacademy. com; 31 Jinlong Jie), where *thangka* (Tibetan sacred art) master Lobsang Khudup trains young monks in painting and Buddhist philosophy. The academy also offers classes for tourists, costing ¥200 per day; a real bargain considering the price includes room and board.

Bǎijī Sì   BUDDHIST TEMPLE
(百鸡寺; 100 Chickens Temple) FREE For the best views over Shangri-la, head to this delightfully named and little-visited temple. The temple has three monks inside and dozens of chickens wandering around outside. To get here, walk along the narrow paths behind Kersang's Relay Station, past the deserted temple, continue uphill and you'll see it on the left.

Tours

Khampa Caravan   TOUR
(康巴商道探险旅行社; Kāngbā Shāngdào Tànxiǎn Lǚxíngshè; ☑ 828 8648; www.khampacaravan. com; 2nd flr, cnr Dawa Lu & Changzheng Lu; ☺ 9am-noon & 2-5.30pm Mon-Fri, 9am-noon Sat) Tibetan-run, this well-established outfit organises some excellent treks and overland journeys, inside Tibet too, that get good feedback. The company also runs a lot of sustainable development programs within Tibetan communities. See www.shangrilaassociation.org for more details.

Haiwei Trails TOUR
(☑139 8875 6540; www.haiweitrails.com) Has a good philosophy towards local sustainable tourism, and over a decade of experience running treks and trips.

🛏 Sleeping

With so many guesthouses destroyed in the fire, good places to stay are at a premium, although that will change in the future. Cheap digs (¥60 a room) can be found around the bus station and the square off Dawa Lu at the edge of the old town.

Despite Shangri-la's often glacial night temperatures, many guesthouses are neither heated nor have 24-hour hot water. Most dorms in town are fairly basic too.

★ Kevin's Trekker Inn GUESTHOUSE $
(龙门客栈; Lóngmén Kèzhàn; ☑822 8178; www.kevintrekkerinn.com; 138 Dawa Lu; 达娃路138号; d & tw ¥120-300; @🛜) Kevin, a Yúnnánese Bai, and his wife Becky are charming, and a great source of local knowledge. Their guesthouse has a cosy lounge and rooms that range from the cheap and boxy, to the very comfortable, with good bathrooms and views over the old town (or what's left of it). It's located just off Dawa Lu behind the Long Xiang Inn.

Kersang's Relay Station INN $
(格桑藏驿; Gésāng Zàng Yì; ☑822 3118; kersangs@yahoo.com; 1 Yamenlang, Jinlong Jie; 衙门廊1号、金龙街; dm ¥50, d & tw ¥180-240; @🛜) This friendly, Tibetan-run place, popular with Western travellers, survived the fire by the skin of its teeth and now overlooks the devastated old town. Rooms are cosy with modern bathrooms and come with much-needed electric blankets. There's a cool terrace, communal lounge and pleasant staff.

Dragoncloud Guesthouse GUESTHOUSE $
(龙行客栈; Lóngxíng Kèzhàn; ☑828 9250; www.dragoncloud.cn; 94 Beimen Jie, Jiantang Zhen; 建塘镇北门街94号; dm ¥50, d & tw ¥120-165; @🛜) Set around a courtyard, the dorms are spacious if rudimentary, while the standard rooms come with modern bathrooms. There are a few more basic doubles that are cheaper. During bouts of chill, you'll love the fireplace in the common area, which also has a pool table.

Arro Khampa Hotel BOUTIQUE HOTEL $$$
(阿若康巴-南索达庄园; Aruòkāngbā Nánsuǒdá Zhuāngyuán; ☑8881007; www.zinchospitality.com; 15 Jinlong Jie; 金龙街15号; d ¥1080; 🅿🛜) Hushed boutique hotel with very swish rooms set around a stone-flagged courtyard. Excellent beds and bathrooms, and the underfloor heating keeps everything toasty-warm. There's a restaurant offering Chinese and Tibetan dishes on site. Efficient staff. Nonsmoking too.

🍴 Eating & Drinking

Shangri-la's eating options include Tibetan, Chinese, Indian and Western food.

★ Rebgong TIBETAN $
(热贡艺人阁; Règòng Yìrén Gé; ☑182 8882 0252; 9-2 Juelang Lu; 觉廊路9-2号; dishes from ¥25; ⏱11am-9pm) Excellent joint for Tibetan eats. The house speciality is yak-meat hotpot, but if you're not in a group then the *mómo* (馍馍; Tibetan dumplings), which come in meat or vegie versions, or the spicy yak-meat pizza are good alternatives. To find it, look for the small sign and walk through the forecourt to where two pine-fresh rooms await you.

Kailash TIBETAN, CHINESE $
(格拉夏餐吧; Gélāxià Cānba; ☑822 5505; 20 Beimen Ji; 北门街20号; dishes from ¥15; ⏱10am-9pm) Reliable, family-run courtyard restaurant with a strategically located stove to keep the place warm. The dishes are a mix of Tibetan and Chinese, with the odd Indian-themed one. This is a good place to sample yak meat, stir-fried or in a hotpot, as well as some of the local vegies that are unique to the area.

Compass WESTERN $$
(舒灯库乐; Shūdēng kùlè; ☑822 3638; 50 Shangye Jie; 商业街50号; dishes from ¥35; ⏱8.30am-9.30pm; 🛜) Bustling spot for a fine breakfast, and the tastiest Western food in town. Steaks, pasta, pizzas and kebabs are all available, as well as a few generic Asian dishes. Great cakes and coffee, and it's nonsmoking too. It's an ideal place to take a break from sightseeing.

Tara Gallery Café & Bar TIBETAN, INDIAN $$
(☑822 6128; House 29 Old Town; dishes from ¥25; ⏱10am-10pm) This upmarket restaurant, bar and cafe (and art gallery) is a tasteful, thoughtfully designed space, and includes a plant-filled 2nd-floor terrace. The menu is a tantalising mix of Tibetan, Indian and Yúnnán dishes; the seven-course Indian set meal (¥95) is a feast. It's also a relaxing spot for a coffee or an evening drink. The owner, Utara, is very friendly.

SHANGRI-LA: UP IN SMOKE

On 11 January 2014, much of Shangri-la's old town went up in flames, reducing the city's prime tourist attraction to a pile of smoking ashes.

The fire was caused by an electrical fault in a guesthouse. Once it took hold, the old town – a tightly packed warren of narrow, twisting lanes and wooden houses – had no chance. Some 260 buildings, including 40 guesthouses, were destroyed.

Thankfully, no one died in the inferno, a result of the fire services ordering an immediate evacuation of the area. Less impressive was the fact that their fire engines turned up without any water, resulting in them having to turn around and head to the nearest river to fill up.

For many locals, the fire was an accident waiting to happen. Ever since Chinese 'experts' announced in 1997 that the city of Zhōngdiàn and the surrounding area was the fabled Shangri-la of James Hilton's best-selling 1933 novel *Lost Horizon,* and so renamed it, the city had expanded at a pace that far outstripped its infrastructure.

Water shortages were common, while a lack of planning ensured the old town was nothing more than a fire trap, with locals opening shops, guesthouses and restaurants on top of each other to cash in on the tourism boom prompted by the re-naming of Zhōngdiàn.

Rebuilding is under way, but it will take three or four years for a new 'old town' to emerge.

Hilton's novel – likely inspired by articles written by the famed northwest Yúnnán explorer Joseph Rock – tells the story of four travellers who are hijacked and taken to a mountain utopia whose residents can live for over 150 years. In contrast, the 'real' Shangri-la lasted a mere 17.

Raven BAR
(乌鸦酒吧; Wūyā Jiǔbā; 9a Cangfang Jie; 仓房街 9a号; beers from ¥15; ⊙noon-late; 🛜) Relocated since the fire, but still in the old town, this comfy and compact 2nd-floor bar is owned by a Londoner and has a decent range of local and foreign beers (including Yúnnán-brewed craft ales).

🛍 Shopping

Dropenling HANDICRAFTS
(卓番林; Zhuó fān lín; ☎823 2292; www.tibet-craft.com; 18 Cengfang Lu; 达娃路18号; ⊙10am-8.30pm) Wide array of Tibetan handicrafts made for Western tastes, including bags, cushions, toys and ornaments.

**Yunnan Mountain
Handicraft Center** HANDICRAFTS
(云南山地手工艺品中心; Yúnnán Shāndì Shǒugōng Yìpǐn Zhōngxīn; ☎822 7742; www.ymhf shangrila.com; 1 Jinlong Jie; 金龙街1号) Fairtrade handicraft shop that sells locally produced products including pottery, clothing, jewellery, carpets, Nixi black pottery and more.

ℹ Information

Altitude sickness can be a problem here and most travellers need a couple of days to acclimatise.

There are no internet cafes in the old town, but all hostels and hotels and most cafes have wi-fi or internet.

Bank of China (中国银行; Zhōngguó Yínháng; Heping Lu) Has a 24-hour ATM and changes US dollars.

ℹ Getting There & Away

Note that some bus tickets refer to Shangri-la as Zhōngdiàn.

AIR

There are six flights daily to Kūnmíng (¥1188), two flights to Chéngdū (¥1028), and a daily flight to Lhasa (¥2480) in peak season. Flights for other domestic destinations also leave from the airport but are completely irregular and destinations change from week to week. You can enquire about your destination or buy tickets at **CAAC** (中国民航; Zhōngguó Mínháng; Wenming Jie). If booking online, you need to type in 'Diqing' for the airport name.

BUS

Following destinations from Shangri-la:
Báishuǐtái ¥24, three hours, three daily (9.10am, 9.20am and 2pm)
Dàochéng ¥109, 11 hours, one daily (7.30am)
Déqīn ¥67, four to five hours, four daily (8.20am, 9.20am, noon and 2.30pm)
Dōngwàng ¥50, seven to eight hours, one daily (7.30am)

Kūnmíng ¥237 to ¥256, 12 hours, four daily (8.30am, 9.30am, 5pm and 7pm)
Lìjiāng ¥66, five hours, every 30 minutes (7.30am to 6pm)
Xiàguān ¥75 to ¥100, seven hours, every 30 minutes (7am to noon, then 6.30pm)
Xiāngchéng ¥85, eight hours, one daily (8am)

If you're up for the bus-hopping trek to Chéngdū, in Sìchuān, you're looking at a minimum of three to four days' travel (often five to six) at some very high altitudes – you'll need warm clothes. Note that for political reasons this road may be closed at any time of the year (if the ticket seller at the bus station says, 'Come back tomorrow', it's closed indefinitely for sure).

If you can get a ticket, the first stage of the trip is to Xiāngchéng in Sìchuān. From Xiāngchéng, your next destination is Lǐtáng, though if roads are bad you may be forced to stay overnight in Dàochéng. From Lǐtáng, it's on to Kāngdìng, from where you can make your way west towards Chéngdū.

Note that roads out of Shangri-la can be temporarily blocked by snow at any time from November to March. Bring a flexible itinerary.

TRAIN
A railway is being built from Lìjiāng to Shangri-la and is expected to be finished sometime in 2015.

ⓘ Getting Around
Bikes can be hired on Beimen Jie from ¥20 a day.

TO/FROM THE AIRPORT
The airport is 5km from town and is sometimes referred to as Díqìng or Deqen – there is currently no airport at Déqīn. A taxi or minivan between the airport and Shangri-la will cost between

GETTING TO TIBET
At the time of writing, it was not possible to enter Tibet overland from Shangri-la, or anywhere in Yúnnán. If you're tempted to try and sneak in, then think again. There were at least 11 checkpoints operating on the road between Shangri-la and Lhasa in 2014; you will be caught, fined, detained and escorted to Chéngdū by the police.

You can fly to Lhasa from Shangri-la, but flights are cheaper from elsewhere (Kūnmíng and Chéngdū) and you'll need to be part of an organised group with all the necessary permits. By far the best people to talk to about Tibet travel in Shangri-la are Khampa Caravan (p692).

¥30 and ¥50. Otherwise, try to call your hotel to arrange a pick-up.

TO/FROM THE BUS STATION
From outside the bus station take local bus 1 (¥1) to the old town (古城, gǔchéng). The bus station is 2km north of the old town, straight up Changzheng Lu.

Around Shangri-la
Around Shangri-la are any number of sights: mountains, meadows, ponds, *chörten* (Tibetan stupas), waiting to be explored. Just note that virtually everywhere has or will have a pricey admission fee.

Nàpà Hǎi 纳帕海
Some 7km northwest of Shangri-la you'll find the seasonal **Nàpà Hǎi** (Nàpà Lake; admission ¥60), in a large meadow. Between September and March it attracts a myriad of rare species, including the black-necked crane. Outside of these months, the lake dries up and you can see large numbers of yaks and cattle grazing on the meadow.

Tiānshēng Bridge 天生桥
Approximately 15km southeast of Shangri-la is the **Tiānshēng Bridge** (Tiānshēng Qiáo; admission ¥20, hot springs ¥100; ◷9am-11pm). Local Tibetans believe that the sulphur-rich water can cure any number of skin ailments and other health issues. There is a co-ed swimming pool and a natural sauna (inside a cave) that is divided into male and female sections. It's possible to cycle here in about two hours or you could take a taxi (¥100 round trip).

Great Treasure Temple 大宝寺
Another 10km past the hot spring at Tiānshēng Bridge is the **Great Treasure Temple** (Dàbǎo Sì; admission ¥5), one of the oldest Buddhist temples in Yúnnán.

Emerald Pagoda Lake 碧塔海
Also known as Pǔdácuò (普达错), a Mandarinised-version of its Tibetan name, **Emerald Pagoda Lake** (Bìtǎ Hǎi; admission ¥258) is 25km east of Shangri-la. The bus to Sānbà can drop you along the highway. From there, it's 8km down a trail (a half-hour by pony), and while the ticket price is laughably steep, there are other (free) trails to the lake. A bike

is useful for finding them; taxis will drop you at the ticket office.

Pony trips can be arranged at the lake. An intriguing sight in summer are the comatose fish that float unconscious for several minutes in the lake after feasting on azalea petals.

The whopping entrance fee is also due to the inclusion of Shŭdū Hú, another lake approximately 10km to the north. The name means 'Place Where Milk is Found' in Tibetan because its pastures are reputedly the most fertile in northwestern Yúnnán.

Getting to the lake(s) is tricky. You usually have to catch the bus to Sānbà, get off at the turn-off and hitch. Getting back you can wait (sometimes interminably) for a bus or hike to one of the entrances or main road and look out for taxis – but there may be none. A taxi will cost around ¥300 to ¥400 for the return trip, including Shŭdū Hú.

Báishuǐtái
TERRACE

(白水台; admission ¥35) Báishuǐtái is a limestone deposit plateau 108km southeast of Shangri-la, with some breathtaking scenery and Tibetan villages en route. For good reason it has become probably the most popular backdoor route between Lìjiāng and Shangri-la. The terraces – think of those in Pamukkale in Turkey or Huánglóng in Sìchuān – are lovely, but can be tough to access if rainfall has made trails slippery.

From Shangri-la there are three daily buses to Báishuǐtái (¥24, three hours). One adventurous option is to hike or hitch all the way from Báishuǐtái to Tiger Leaping Gorge. A taxi from Shangri-la is ¥600.

A couple of guesthouses at the nearby towns of Báidì and Sānbà have rooms with beds from ¥50.

Déqīn
德钦

☑ 0887 / POP 60,100

Mellifluously named Déqīn (that last syllable seems to ring, doesn't it?) lies in some of the most ruggedly gorgeous scenery in China. Snuggly cloud-high at an average altitude of 3550m, it rests in the near embrace of one of China's most magical mountains, Kawa Karpo (梅里雪山; often referred to as Méilí Xuěshān). At 6740m, it is Yúnnán's highest peak and straddles the Yúnnán–Tibet border.

A true border town, Déqīn is one of Yúnnán's last outposts before Tibet, but from here you could also practically hike east to Sìchuān or southwest to Myanmar. Díqìng Prefecture was so isolated that it was never really controlled by anyone until the PLA (People's Liberation Army) arrived in force in 1957.

More than 80% of locals are Tibetan, though a dozen other minorities also live here, including one of the few settlements of non-Hui Muslims in China. The town, though, is seriously unattractive and a little rough – the local police impose a midnight curfew. Confusingly, Déqīn is the name of the city and county; both are incorporated by the Díqìng Tibetan Autonomous Prefecture (迪庆藏族自治州).

Most people make immediate tracks for Fēilái Sì. Either catch one of the minivans (¥10 per person) that hang around the main street, or take a taxi (¥40). The daily 3pm bus to Xīdāng also stops at Fēilái Sì (¥10, one hour).

For Shangri-la, four daily buses leave from Déqīn's small bus station on the main street (¥67, four to five hours, 8.30am, 9.30am, noon and 2.40pm). There is also a daily bus to Lìjiāng (¥189, 10 hours, 7.30am) and to Kūnmíng (¥268, 18 hours, 1pm).

Around Déqīn

The main reason to come to Déqīn is to spend time in the valleys below Kawa Karpo. Most access is on foot, so you'll need at least three or four days to make the most of your journey.

Note that entry to the sights requires buying a Meili Snow Mountain National Park (梅里雪山国家公园; Měilǐ Xuěshān Guó Jiā Gōng Yuǎn; admission ¥150-230) entrance ticket. There are three ticket options: one includes three observation points and the glacier (¥228), another ticket is the same three observation points and Yùběng village (¥230), and the third is just three observation points (¥150).

If you want to go to the glacier and Yùběng village you should buy the full ticket plus a ¥85 supplement for the village. A student card nets a 50% discount.

Fēilái Sì
飞来寺

Approximately 10km southwest of Déqīn is the small but interesting Tibetan Fēilái Sì

(飞来寺; Fēilái Temple; entry by donation), or Naka Zhashi (or Trashi) Gompa in Tibetan, devoted to the spirit of Kawa Karpo. There's no charge but leave a donation. No photos are allowed inside the tiny hall.

Everyone comes here for the sublime **views** – particularly the sunrises – of the Méilǐ Xuěshān range, including 6740m-high Kawa Karpo (also known as Méilǐ Xuěshān or Tàizi Shān) and the even more beautiful peak to the south, 6054m-high Miacimu (神女; Shénnǚ in Chinese), whose spirit is the female counterpart of Kawa Karpo.

Joseph Rock described Miacimu as 'the most glorious peak my eyes were ever privileged to see...like a castle of a dream, an ice palace of a fairy tale'. Locals come here to burn juniper incense to the wrathful spirit of the mountain.

Sadly, the weather often as not does not cooperate, shrouding the peaks in mist. October/November is your best shot at a sunrise photo op. A ticket office near the platform sells tickets for Fēilái Sì and other sites.

The 'town' is actually just an ugly, expanding strip of concrete shops, hotels and restaurants along the main road. Across the road, the government has unsportingly set up a wall, blocking the view of the mountains (just walk downhill 200m for the same view).

Most backpackers stay at **Feeling Village Youth Hostel** (觉色滇乡国际青年旅舍; Juésè Diānxiāng Guójì Qīngnián Lǚshè; ☑ 0887-841 6133; juesedianxiang@163.com; dm ¥30-40, d & tw ¥120-170; @ 🛜), which has cheerful English-speaking staff, simple but clean rooms with electric blankets, and hot water in the evenings. It's set back from the main road; look for the sign turning right up the little alley at the bottom of the village.

On the main road, the **Zàng Jí Wáng Shāngwù Jiǔdiàn** (藏吉王商务酒店; ☑ 0887 841 6998; d & tw ¥256; 🛜) has comfortable rooms with huge windows and spectacular

YŪBĒNG & KAWA KARPO HIKES

The principal reason to visit Déqīn is the chance to hike to the foot of Kawa Karpo. The main destination is **Yǔbēng** (雨崩) village, from where you can make day hikes to mountain meadows, lakes and the fabulous **Yǔbēng Waterfall** (雨崩神瀑; Yǔbēng Shénpù).

The five-hour trek to Yǔbēng starts at the **Xīdāng** (西当) hot spring, about 3km past Xīdāng village. The drive from Fēilái Sì takes one hour and 40 minutes and a taxi will cost ¥180. You could also hike all the way here from Fēilái Sì using local roads and paths. Another possibility is the 3pm bus from Déqīn to Xīdāng (¥20), which stops in Fēilái Sì. There is a ¥5 entrance fee for Yǔbēng but when you show your receipt at your guesthouse you'll get ¥5 discount off your bill.

Yǔbēng consists of two sections. You first arrive in 'Upper Yǔbēng', which contains most guesthouses, then the trail continues another 1km to 'Lower Yǔbēng'.

Lobsang Trekker Lodge (藏巴乐之家; Zàngbālè Zhījiā; ☑ 139 8879 7053; http://lobsangtrekkerlodge.webs.com; dm ¥30, d & tw ¥200-300), in Upper Yǔbēng, is a popular place that offers meals, comfortable rooms, modern bathrooms and good traveller info (English is spoken here). Also in Upper Yǔbēng is the much more basic **Yak Butter Inn** (酥油茶客栈; Sūyóuchá Kèzhàn; ☑ 182 8884 0453; dm ¥35-40), which has knowledgeable staff.

From Yǔbēng village, loads of treks lie out here. It's a three- to four-hour trip on foot or horseback to the waterfall. Or, you could head south to a picturesque lake (it's around 4350m high and not easy to find, so take a guide). Guides cost around ¥200 per day. Supplies (food and water) are pricey in Yǔbēng so stock up in Fēilái Sì.

Leaving the village, trekkers will often hike to **Nínóng** (尼农) village by the Mekong River, a four- to five-hour hike that definitely requires a guide (and a good sense of balance as it's very steep in some sections). If you are prone to vertigo, head back to Xīdāng instead. Arrange a pick-up in Nínóng or ask around for a taxi; if you are stuck walk 6km to Xīdāng where there is more transport.

Then there's the legendary Kawa Karpo *kora*, a 12-day pilgrim circumambulation of Méilǐ Xuěshān. However, half of it is in the Tibetan Autonomous Region, so you'll need a permit to do it, and you'll definitely need a guide.

mountain views. Prices are regularly discounted by 20%.

Restaurants on the main road serve pricy Chinese and Western meals.

To get here from Déqīn a taxi will cost you ¥40, or take a minivan (¥10 per person).

Míngyǒng Glacier 明永冰川

Tumbling off the side of Kawa Karpo peak is the 12km-long **Míngyǒng Glacier** (Míngyǒng Bīngchuān; admission ¥228). At over 13 sq km, it is not only the lowest glacier in China (around 2200m high) but also an oddity – a monsoon marine glacier, which basically translates as having an ecosystem that couldn't possibly be more diverse: tundra, taiga, broadleaf forest and meadow.

The mountain has been a pilgrimage site for centuries and you'll still meet a few Tibetan pilgrims, some of whom circumambulate the mountain over seven days in autumn. Surrounding villages are known as 'heaven villages' because of the dense fog that hangs about in spring and summer.

The trail to the glacier leads up from Míngyǒng's central square. After 70 minutes of steady uphill walking you will reach the Tibetan **Tàizǐ Miào** (太子庙), a small temple where there are snack and drink stalls. A further 30 minutes along the trail is **Lotus Temple** (莲花庙; Liánhuā Miào), which offers fantastic views of the glacier framed by prayer flags and *chörten*. Horses can also be hired to go up to the glacier (¥200).

If you're coming from Yǔběng, you could also hike to Míngyǒng from Xīdāng in around three hours if you hoof it.

Míngyǒng village consists of only a couple hotels, restaurants and shops. You can overnight in the simple **Renqin Hotel** (仁钦酒店; Rénqín Jiǔdiàn; ☎ 139 8871 4330; dm/d ¥25/100; @ ☎), which also serves meals.

From Déqīn, private minibuses to Míngyǒng leave regularly from the bridge near the market at the top end of town (¥20 per person), or hire your own for ¥120.

The road from Déqīn descends into the dramatic Mekong Gorge. Six kilometres before Míngyǒng the road crosses the Mekong River and branches off to Xīdāng. Nearby is a small temple, the **Bǎishūlín Miào**, and a *chörten*. There is a checkpoint here where you will need to show your national-park ticket.

NÙ JIĀNG VALLEY

The 320km-long Nù Jiāng Valley (怒江大峡谷) is one of Yúnnán's best-kept secrets. The Nù Jiāng (known as the Salween in Myanmar; its name in Chinese means 'Raging River') is the second-longest river in Southeast Asia and one of only two undammed rivers in China, as well as being a Unesco World Heritage Site.

Sandwiched between the Gāolígòng Shān and Myanmar to the west, Tibet to the north and the imposing Bìluó Shān to the east, the gorge holds nearly a quarter of China's flora and fauna species, and half of China's endangered species. The valley also has a mix of Han, Nu, Lisu, Drung and Tibetan nationalities, and even the odd Burmese trader. And it's simply stunning – all of it.

Getting here is a pain. On a map, it seems a stone's throw from Déqīn in the province's northwest. Nope. All traffic enters via the Bǎoshān region. Once here, you trundle eight hours up the valley, marvelling at the scenery, and then head back the way you came. Plans have been announced to blast a road from Gòngshān in the northern part of the valley to Déqīn, and another from the village of Bīngzhōngluò even further north into Tibet. Given the immense topographical challenges, these plans are a long way off. Sadly, though, it seems likely that the river will be dammed in the next few years. Get here before that happens.

Liùkù 六库

☎ 0886 / POP 17,800
TRANSPORT HUB

Liùkù is the lively, pleasant capital of the prefecture. Divided by the Nù Jiāng River, it's the main transport hub of the region, although it's of little intrinsic interest. You will likely have to register with a police checkpoint about 5km before entering the town.

🛏 Sleeping & Eating

There are a few scruffy cheapies on Chuancheng Lu in the centre of town where rooms can be got from ¥80.

To eat, head to the riverbank, south of Renmin Lu, where loads of outdoor restaurants cook great barbecued fish.

Nùjiāng Géruì
Shāngwù Jiǔdiàn HOTEL $$$
(怒江格瑞商务酒店; ☎ 388 8885; 123 Chuancheng Lu; 穿城路123号; d & tw ¥488;

✱☎) Routine discounts of 70% bring this solid midrange place into the budget category. It has modern showers and comfortable rooms, although it can get a bit busy at night when a gaggle of scantily clad 'hostesses' stand by the door to welcome punters to karaoke upstairs. After crossing the bridge it's one block uphill from Renmin Lu.

ℹ Information

Bank of China (中国银行; Zhōngguó Yínháng) Located uphill from the bus station.

Internet cafe (网吧; Wǎngbā; per hr ¥4) There is an internet cafe near the main pedestrian bridge, in a little shopping mall, opposite the Shèng Bǎo Lù Hotel.

ℹ Getting There & Away

The bus station is located south of downtown and across the river (a ¥15 taxi ride).

Bǎoshān ¥52, three to four hours, eight daily (8am to 4.30pm)

Bǐngzhōngluò ¥81, nine hours, one daily (8.20am)

Fúgòng ¥40, four hours, nine daily (7.20am to 4.20pm)

Gòngshān ¥71, eight hours, eight daily (7am to 1pm)

Kūnmíng ¥201, 11 to 12 hours, seven daily (8.30am to 7pm)

Téngchōng ¥66, six hours, three daily (8am, 10am and 11am)

Xiàguān ¥83, four to five hours, 10 daily (8am to 7pm)

Fúgòng 副攻

Hemmed in by steep cliffs on all sides, Fúgòng offers some of the best scenery in the valley and has a large Lisu population, even if the town itself is unremarkable. Fúgòng is roughly halfway up the valley and the best place to break your journey if it's late.

The **Fúgòng Bīnguǎn** (副攻宾馆; ☎301 7013; d & tw ¥188; ✱☎) is across the road from the bus station. Its big rooms are routinely discounted to ¥100.

There are twice-hourly buses to Liùkù (¥40, four hours) between 7.20am and 4.20pm. For Bǐngzhōngluò you'll have to wait for the bus from Liùkù to pass by, which happens around noon. Otherwise, buses to Gòngshān (¥33, seven daily) start running at 10.30am. Your best bet for a quick getaway to Gòngshān is to take a shared minivan for ¥40. They start running from 7.30am outside the bus station.

Bǐngzhōngluò 丙中洛

☑ 0886

The main reason to come to the Nù Jiāng Valley is to visit this isolated, friendly **village** (adult/student ¥100/50), set in a beautiful, wide and fertile bowl. Just 35km south of Tibet and close to Myanmar, it's a great base for hikes into the surrounding mountains and valleys. The area is at its best in spring and early autumn. Don't even think about coming in the winter.

⚑ Activities

Potential **short hops** include heading south along the main road for 2km to the impressive 'first bend' of the Nù Jiāng River, or north along a track more than 15km long that passes a 19th-century church and several villages (the road starts by heading downhill from Road to Tibet Guesthouse).

Longer three- or four-day treks include heading to the Tibetan village of **Dímáluò** (迪麻洛) and then onto the village of **Yǒnzhī** (永芝). From Yǒnzhī it's another two hours' walk to the main road, from where you can hitch a ride to Déqīn. It is a demanding trek that can really only be done from late May until September as the 3800m pass is too difficult to cross in heavy snow.

A guide is pretty much essential. Tibetan trek leader Aluo comes highly recommended. He's based at Road to Tibet Guesthouse, although he's often away on treks so email him first (aluo_luosang@hotmail.com). Treks usually cost around ¥250 per day. Note that there are no villages en route to Yǒnzhī so you'll need to carry all your own food and sleep in basic huts along the way (porters can be hired for around ¥100 per day).

Another pricier option is Peter, a Lemao guide, who offers treks for ¥350 a day. He speaks good English, although some travellers report he doesn't always deliver what he promises. You can find him at **Nù Jiāng Baini Travel** (☎139 8853 9641; yangindali@yahoo.co.uk) on the main street, where he also rents out mountain bikes for ¥80 a day.

🛏 Sleeping & Eating

Road to Tibet Guesthouse GUESTHOUSE $
(☑358 1168, 189 0886 1299; wanliwwang@hotmail.com; dm/s ¥70/120, d & tw ¥160-260; ☎) Most backpackers end up at this place, set on the street heading downhill from the main road. Beds are hard but it's a clean place with some English spoken and 50%

discounts a lot of the time. The owner, Aluo, also has a simple guesthouse in his home village of Dímáluò, a good destination for a day hike.

Yù Dòng Bīnguǎn   HOTEL **$$**
(玉洞宾馆; ☑ 358 1285; d & tw ¥180; ☏) With standard 30% discounts, well-maintained rooms and reasonable beds, this is actually a good budget option. The rooms at the back have fine views of the valley.

❶ Information

All hotels in town have wi-fi and Peter has internet access at Nù Jiāng Baini Travel for ¥3 per hour.

There is a brand-new ATM that allegedly takes foreign cards. Don't rely on it.

❶ Getting There & Away

There is one direct bus a day from Liùkù to Bīng-zhōngluò (¥81, nine hours, 7am). It returns from opposite Yù Dòng Bīnguǎn at 8am. Otherwise, take a bus to Gòngshān (¥12, one hour), where there are eight buses daily to Liùkù (¥76, eight hours, 7.30am to 12.10pm).

Dúlóng Valley   独龙江

Separated from the Nù Jiāng Valley by the high Gāolígòng Shān range and only reached by road in 1999, the Dúlóng Valley is one of the remotest valleys in China and is home to the 5000-strong Dulong ethnic group. The Dúlóng River actually flows out of China into Myanmar, where it eventually joins the Irrawaddy.

Although the road into the valley has been upgraded, no buses run here. Minivans make the four-hour, 96km trip infrequently (¥100 per person, or hire one for ¥600). There are a couple of hotels in the county capital **Kǒngdāng** (孔当) where you can find rooms for ¥80 to ¥100.

The main road in the valley itself is now paved south towards the border with Myanmar and north towards Tibet, but there are no hotels or restaurants and hardly any cars outside Kǒngdāng. Strong cyclists will have a field day here, but bring your own tent and food.

It might be possible to find a bed in a village (most are close to the main road), but bear in mind that the Dulong people are very shy and you won't hear much Mandarin, let alone English, here.

BĂOSHĀN REGION

Scrunched up against Myanmar and bisected by the wild Nù Jiāng, the Bǎoshān region (保山) is a varied landscape that includes thick forests, dormant volcanoes and hot springs.

The eponymous capital is unremarkable; lovely Téngchōng (and its environs) is where it's at. The Téngchōng area is peppered with minority groups whose villages lie in and around the ancient fire mountains.

As early as the 4th and 5th centuries BC (two centuries before the northern routes through central Asia were established), the Bǎoshān area was an important stop on the southern Silk Road – the Sìchuān–India route. The area did not come under Chinese control until the Han dynasty. In 1277 a huge battle was waged in the region between the 12,000 troops of Kublai Khan and 60,000 Burmese soldiers and their 2000 elephants. The Mongols won and went on to take Bagan.

Téngchōng   腾冲

☑ 0875

With 20 volcanoes in the vicinity, lots of hot springs and great trekking potential, there's plenty to explore in this neck of the woods. And the city itself is a bit of an oddity – one of the few places in China that, though much of the old architecture has been demolished, remains a pleasant place to hang out, with oodles of green space (you can actually smell the flowers!) and a friendly, low-key populace.

❂ Sights & Activities

Much of the old-time architecture is now gone, but some OK places for a random wander are still to be found. Téngchōng's proximity to Myanmar means there are many jade and teak shops around town.

Walking along Fengshan Lu from Feicui Lu, the first side street on the left has a **small produce market** (产品市场; Chǎnpǐn Shìchǎng). Further down on the right is a large, covered **jade market** (珠宝玉器交易中心; Zhūbǎo Yùqì Jiāoyì Zhōngxīn), where you can sometimes see the carving process. Walk east along Yingjiang Xilu and you will come across a larger **produce market** (大产品市场; Dà Chǎnpǐn Shìchǎng) on your right.

Téngchōng

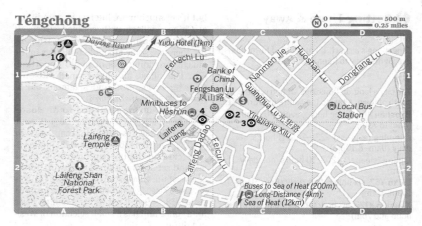

YÚNNÁN TÉNGCHŌNG

Diéshuǐ Waterfall   WATERFALL
(叠水瀑布; Diéshuǐ Pùbù; admission ¥20) In the western suburbs of town, beside the **Xiānlè Temple** (仙乐寺; Xiānlè Sì), this is a good place for a picnic. The area makes a nice destination for a bike ride and you could easily combine it with a trip to **Héshùn** (和顺), a picturesque village 4km outside Téngchōng.

Láifēng Shān National Forest Park   PARK
(来凤山国家森林公园; Láifēng Shān Guójiā Sēnlín Gōngyuán; ⊙8am-7pm) **FREE** On the western edge of town, walk through lush pine forests of this park to **Láifēng Temple** (来凤寺; Láifēng Sì) or make the sweaty hike up to the summit, where a pagoda offers fine views.

🛏 Sleeping & Eating

There's no shortage of places to stay; bargain hard at any hotel.

There are many hole-in-the-wall eateries and barbecue places along Feicui Lu and elsewhere around town. At night, food stalls are set up in the centre of town off Fengshan Lu.

Xīnghuá Dàjiǔdiàn   HOTEL $
(兴华大酒店; ☑5132688; 7 Tuanpo Xiaoqu; 团坡小区7号; d & tw ¥120; ❋@🛜) It's been around a while, and there are alarming, tiger-pattern carpets here, but the rooms themselves are clean, if a little old-fashioned. The location is handy in what is a spread-out town. There's wi-fi in the lobby, ADSL internet in the rooms.

Yudu Hotel   HOTEL $$
(玉都大酒店; Yùdū Dàjiǔdiàn; ☑513 8666; 15 Tengyue Lu; 腾越路15号; d & tw ¥978; ❋🛜) Rooms at this very comfortable, professionally run place are routinely discounted by a whopping 70%, making them a great deal. Don't expect to hear any English, though. It's about 500m north of Xīnghuá Dàjiǔdiàn.

ⓘ Information

Bank of China (中国银行; Zhōngguó Yínháng; cnr Fengshan Lu & Yingjiang Xilu) Has a 24-hour ATM and will change cash and travellers cheques. There are other ATMs around town that take foreign cards too.

China Post (国际邮局; Zhōngguó Yóuzhèng; Fengshan Lu) Serves as post and telephone office.

Internet cafe (网吧; wǎngbā; 100m north of Xīnghuá Dàjiǔdiàn; per hour ¥3) At the time of writing, internet cafes in Tèngchōng were not admitting foreigners.

Public Security Bureau (PSB; 公安局; Gōng'ānjú; Yingjiang Xilu; ⊙8.30-11.30am & 2.30-5.30pm Mon-Fri) Can help with visa extensions.

ⓘ Getting There & Away

AIR

Téngchōng's airport, 12km south of town, has five flights daily to Kūnmíng (¥1187).

BUS

The city's long-distance bus station is in the south of town. A taxi to the centre of town is ¥15.

Bǎoshān ¥63, three hours, every 40 minutes (8am to 7pm)

Kūnmíng (express) ¥231–248, 11 hours, six daily (9am–8.10pm)

Lìjiāng (sleeper) ¥203, 10 hours, one daily (7pm)

Liùkù ¥62, six hours, four daily (8am, 9am, 10am, 11am)

Xiàguān ¥125, six hours, three daily (10.30am, noon and 7pm)

Téngchōng's local bus station (客运站; *kèyùn zhàn*) is on Dongfang Lu.

Mángshì ¥42, two to three hours, 10 daily (8am to 4.30pm)

Ruìlì ¥80, four hours, nine daily (7.50am to 3.50pm)

Buses to local destinations north of Téngchōng, such as Mǎzhàn, Gùdōng, Ruìdián, Diántán or Zìzhì, leave from a forecourt on the corner of Huoshan Lu and Guaijinlou Xiang in the northeast of town.

ⓘ Getting Around

Minivans run to the airport from the junction of Feicui Lu and Rehai Lu (¥20 per person). Bus 2 runs from the town centre to the long-distance bus station (¥1). Taxis charge ¥6 to hop round town.

Around Téngchōng

Getting out to the sights around Téngchōng is a bit tricky. Catching buses part of the way and hiking is one possibility, hiring a taxi for the day (¥300) is another.

Some highlights of the region are the traditional villages that are scattered between Téngchōng and Yúnfēng Shān (Cloudy Peak Mountain). The relatively plentiful public transport along this route means that you can jump on and off minibuses to go exploring as the whim takes you.

Héshùn 和顺

Southwest of Téngchōng, **Héshùn** (和顺; admission ¥80; ⊙ 8am-7.30pm) has been set aside as a retirement village for overseas Chinese,

but it's of much more interest as a traditional Chinese village with cobbled streets. It sees an increasing number of day trippers, but there are some great old buildings in the village, providing lots of photo opportunities. The village also has a small **museum** (博物馆; *bówùguǎn*) and a famous old **library** (图书馆; *túshūguǎn*).

The **Héshùn International Youth Hostel** (和顺国际青年旅舍; Téngchōng Guójì Qīngnián Lǚshè; ☑ 515 8398; hsyha123@163.com; Cunjiawan; 寸家湾; 4-bed dm ¥35-40, d & tw ¥128) in the village (close to the big banyan tree) is pleasant and set around a small courtyard. In the centre of the village, the **Lanna Cafe** (兰纳咖啡; Lánnà Kāfēi; ☑ 136 2586 2709; coffee from ¥23, dishes ¥38; ⊙ 9am-10pm; 📶) is a chilled place for a coffee and has a small selection of Western dishes.

From Téngchōng bus 6 (¥1) goes to Héshùn from Feicui Lu, or you can take a minibus (¥3) from the corner of Feicui Lu and Laifeng Xiang.

Yúnfēng Shān 云峰山

A Taoist mountain dotted with 17th-century temples and monastic retreats, **Yúnfēng Shān** (云峰山; admission ¥80) is 47km north of Téngchōng. It's possible to take a **cable car** (one way/return ¥90/160) close to the top, from where it's a 20-minute walk to **Dàxióng Bǎodiàn** (大雄宝殿), a temple at the summit. **Lǔzǔ Diàn** (鲁祖殿), the temple second from the top, serves up solid vegetarian food at lunchtime. It's a quick walk down but it can be hard on the knees. You can walk up the mountain in about 2½ hours.

To get to the mountain, go to Huoshan Lu in Téngchōng and catch a bus to Gùdōng (¥15), and then a microbus from there to the turn-off (¥10). From the turn-off you have to hitch, or you could take the lovely walk past the village of **Hépíng** (和平) to the pretty villages just before the mountain. From the parking lot a golf cart (¥5) takes you to the entrance. Hiring a vehicle from Téngchōng for the return trip will cost about ¥300 to ¥350.

Volcanoes

Téngchōng County is renowned for its volcanoes, and although they have been behaving themselves for many centuries, the seismic and geothermal activity in the area indicates that they won't always continue to do so. The closest volcano to Téngchōng is **Mǎ'ān**

Shān (马鞍山; Saddle Mountain), around 5km to the northwest. It's just south of the main road to Yíngjiāng.

Around 22km to the north of town, near the village of Mǎzhàn, is the most accessible cluster of volcanoes (admission ¥60). The main central volcano is known as Dàkōng Shān (大空山; Big Empty Hill), which pretty much sums it up, and to the left of it is the black crater of Hēikōng Shān (黑空山; Black Empty Hill). You can haul yourself up the steps for views of the surrounding lava fields (long dormant).

To get here from Téngchōng, take a Gùdōng-bound bus (¥15) from Huoshan Lu. From Mǎzhàn town, it's a 10-minute walk or you can take a motor-tricycle (¥5) to the volcano area. Once you are in the area there is a fair bit of walking to get between the sights, or you can hitch rides.

Sea of Heat   热海

The intriguingly named Sea of Heat (热海; Rèhǎi; admission ¥60, pool access ¥268; ⊙8am-9pm) is a steamy cluster of hot springs, geysers and streams (but no actual sea, per se). Located about 12km southwest of Téngchōng, it's essentially an upmarket resort, with a few outdoor springs, a nice warmwater swimming pool along with indoor baths. Even if you don't pay the steep price to enter the pools it's possible to just wander along the stone paths admiring the geothermal activity. Some of the springs here reach temperatures of 102°C (don't swim in these ones!).

The rooms at the Yǎng Shēng Gé (养生阁; ☑586 9700; www.chinaspa.cn; d & tw ¥1960, ste ¥3600; 🖳) all come with their very own mini-spa complete with water piped from the hot springs. It's close to the ticket office.

Note that it's possible to buy a combined ticket (¥100) for both the Sea of Heat and the Mǎzhàn volcanoes here.

Bus 2 (¥3) leaves Téngchōng from Rehai Lu, 200m south of the junction with Feicui Lu, for the Sea of Heat.

DÉHÓNG PREFECTURE

Déhóng Prefecture (德宏州; Déhóng Zhōu and Jingpo Autonomous Prefecture) juts into Myanmar in the far west of Yúnnán. Once a backwater of backwaters, from the late 1980s the region saw tourists flock in to experience its raucous border atmosphere.

That's dimmed quite a bit and most Chinese tourists in Déhóng are here for the trade from Myanmar that comes through Ruìlì and Wǎndīng; Burmese jade is the most desired commodity and countless other items are spirited over the border.

The most obvious minority groups in Déhóng are the Burmese (who are normally dressed in their traditional saronglike *longyi*), Dai and Jingpo (known in Myanmar as the Kachin), a minority group long engaged in armed struggle against the Myanmar government.

Ruìlì   瑞丽

☑0692

Back in the 1980s this border town was a notorious haven for drug and gem smugglers, prostitution and various other iniquities. The government cleaned it up in the 1990s (on the surface anyway) and today you're more likely to stumble into a shopping mall than a den of thieves. Still, Ruìlì has an edge to it, thanks to a thriving gem market operated largely by Burmese traders. And with its palm-tree-lined streets, bicycle rickshaws and steamy climate, it has a distinctly laidback, Southeast Asian feel.

The minority villages nearby are also good reason to come and it's worth getting a bicycle and heading out to explore. Another draw for travellers is Myanmar, which lies only a few kilometres away. Though individual tourists are not allowed to cross freely, organising permits to take you through the sensitive border area is becoming easier.

◉ Sights

Think atmosphere rather than aesthetics. The huge market (市场; shìchǎng) in the west of town is one of the most colourful and fun in Yúnnán; a real swirl of ethnicities, including Dai, Jingpo, Han and Burmese, as well as the odd Bangladeshi and Pakistani trader. Get here in the morning, when the stalls are lined with Burmese smokes, tofu wrapped in banana leaves, dodgy pharmaceuticals from Thailand, clothes, you name it. It's also a good place to grab lunch at one of the many snack stalls.

Also great for people-watching is Ruìlì's ever-expanding jade market (珠宝街; zhūbǎo jiē), the centre of town in all senses. Burmese jade sellers run most of the shops here and for a while you may even forget you are still in China.

Ruìlì

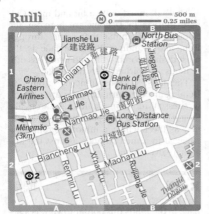

Ruìlì

Sights

Sleeping

Eating

Sleeping

There are many hotels in Ruìlì, with cheap rooms (¥80) available along Nanmao Jie near the bus station.

Bāshí Jiǔdiàn HOTEL $

(巴石酒店; ☑ 412 9088; cnr Renmin Lu & Nanmao Jie; 南卯街; d & tw ¥100-120; 🌐 🛜) The once-sleepy staff are now on their toes, while the rooms have been given a much-needed upgrade and are now clean. Beds remain a little lumpy.

Míngruì Hotel HOTEL $$

(明瑞宾馆; Míngruì Bīnguǎn; ☑ 410 8666; 98 Nanmao Jie; 南卯街98号; d & tw ¥268; 🌐 🛜) Big, bright and clean rooms – normally discounted by 60% – and a handy location close to the bus station make this a good-value choice. Staff are friendly. Strong wi-fi connection. From the bus station, it's just down an alley off the right-hand side of Nanmao Jie.

Ruìlì Bīnguǎn HOTEL $$$

(瑞丽宾馆; ☑ 410 0888; 25 Jianshe Lu; 建设路 25号; d & tw ¥520; 🌐 @ 🛜) This place, garishly painted orange and gold, is perhaps the best value in town for comfort and facilities, with regular 50% discounts. Wood-panelled rooms have ADSL internet and there is wi-fi in the lobby. The staff are amenable and can sell maps (¥10) of town and the surrounding area.

Eating & Drinking

Street stalls set up all over town come nightfall; just follow your nose.

★ Bo Bo's Cold Drinks Shop CAFE $

(步步冷饮店; Bùbù Lěngyǐndiàn; Xi'nan Lu; dishes from ¥12; ⏱ 9am-midnight; 🛜) Busy from early to late, the *longyi*-clad Burmese waiters at this Ruìlì institution hustle as they serve up fantastic fruit juices, Burmese-style milky tea, ice cream and cakes, as well as simple but tasty rice and noodle dishes. Head to the 2nd-floor terrace for an evening beer and wi-fi.

Huáfēng Market MARKET $

(华丰市场; Huáfēng Shìchǎng; off Jiegang Lu; ⏱ 6pm-late) An outdoor food court that thrives once darkness descends; come here for Burmese and Chinese food, including superb barbecue dishes. The food is all on display, so just pick and point.

Information

Bank of China (中国银行; Zhōngguó Yínháng; Nanmao Jie) Provides all the usual services and will cash travellers cheques for US dollars if you're headed to Myanmar. There are other ATMs around town that take foreign cards. You can also change/find US dollars at the jade market.

China Post (国际邮局; Zhōngguó Yóuzhèng; cnr Mengmao Lu & Renmin Lu) Despite (or perhaps because of?) its border location, sending any kind of package abroad from this post and telephone office is difficult, if not impossible.

Internet cafe (网吧; wǎngbā; cnr Nanmao Jie & Jiegang Lu; per hour ¥4; ⏱ 24hr) At the time of writing, foreigners weren't allowed to use Ruìlì's internet cafes.

Public Security Bureau (PSB; 公安局; Gōng'ānjú; Jianshe Lu; ⏱ 8.30-11.30am & 2.30-5.30pm) Come here for visa extensions.

ℹ️ Getting There & Away

An expressway from Bǎoshān to Ruìlì was being built at the time of writing, which will link Ruìlì to Xiàguān and on to Kūnmíng. The first five hours or so out of Ruìlì are still on older roads that pass through villages (and checkpoints), then you get on the highway for a speedy finish to Xiàguān.

AIR

Daily flights come from Kūnmíng via Mángshì, a two-hour drive away. You can buy tickets at **China Eastern Airlines** (东方航空公司; Dōngfāng Hángkōng Gōngsī; 🗹 411 1111; Renmin Lu; ⊙8am-10pm). Shuttle taxis leave daily from the office, three hours before scheduled flights (¥70).

BUS

Ruìlì has a long-distance bus station (长途客运站; *chángtú kèyùn zhàn*) in the centre of town and a north bus station (汽车北站; *qìchē běizhàn*), really more of a forecourt, at the top of Jiegang Lu. Head to the north bus station if you're trying to get to Mángshì (¥35, last bus 6pm – they leave when full) or Zhāngfēng (¥15, one hour); for everything else, you're better off going to the long-distance station.

Bǎoshān ¥90, six to seven hours, every 40 minutes (6.30am to 4pm)

Jǐnghóng ¥417, 22 hours, one daily (10am)

Kūnmíng ¥294 to ¥310, 14 hours, six daily (8.30am to 7pm)

Téngchōng ¥82, four to five hours, every 40 minutes (7.10am to 12.20pm)

Xiàguān ¥150 to ¥170, nine to 10 hours, two daily (9am and 7pm)

For local destinations, minibuses and buses leave from the left of the main bus station, or you can just flag one down in the street. Destinations include Wǎndīng (¥15) and the village of Nóngdǎo (¥8).

ℹ️ Getting Around

The most interesting day trips require a bicycle. Ask at your accommodation about the best place to rent one.

A flat rate for a taxi ride inside the city should be ¥6, and up for negotiation from there. There are also cheaper motor and cycle rickshaws.

Around Ruìlì

Most of the sights around Ruìlì can be explored by bicycle. It's worth making detours down the narrow paths leading off the main roads to visit minority villages. The people are friendly, and there are lots of photo opportunities. The *Tourism and Traffic Map*

of *Ruìlì*, available from the Xīnhuá bookshop on Renmin Lu, shows major roads and villages.

The shortest ride is to turn left at the corner north of China Post and continue out of Ruìlì into the little village of Měngmǎo. There are half a dozen Shan temples scattered about; the fun is in finding them.

Golden Duck Pagoda

In the outskirts of town to the southwest, on the main road, **Golden Duck Pagoda** (弄安金鸭塔; Nòng'ān Jīnyā Tǎ) is an attractive stupa set in a temple courtyard. It was established to mark the arrival of a pair of golden ducks that brought good fortune to what was previously an uninhabited marshy area.

Temples

Just past Golden Duck Pagoda is a crossroads and a small wooden temple. The road to the right (west) leads to the villages of **Jiěxiàng** (姐相) and **Nóngdǎo** (弄岛), and on the way are a number of small temples, villages and stupas. None are spectacular but the village life is interesting and there are often small markets near the temples.

The first major Dai temple is **Hǎnshā Zhuāng Temple** (喊沙奘寺; Hǎnshā Zhuāng Sì), a fine wooden structure with a few resident monks. It's set a little off the road and a green tourism sign marks the turn-off. The surrounding Dai village is interesting.

A few kilometres further on is **One Village Two Countries** (一寨两国寺; Yīzhài Liǎngguó; admission ¥20; ⊙9am-6pm), a low-tourist attraction where you can stand on the border between China and Myanmar. It's rather tacky – Kayan women show off their brass neck rings – but borderholics will be satisfied.

Another 20 minutes or so further down the road, look out for a blue-and-gold-roofed traditional building on the right side of the road. Turn right here and follow the narrow paved road through the fields to **Léizhuāngxiāng** (雷装相), Ruìlì's oldest stupa, dating back to the middle of the Tang dynasty.

Jiěgào Border Checkpoint 姐告边检点

On land jutting into Myanmar, Jiěgào is the main checkpoint for a steady stream of cross-border traffic. It's a bustling place,

BORDER CROSSING: GETTING TO MYANMAR (BURMA)

At the time of writing it was not possible for third-country nationals to travel across the border at Jiěgào. The only way to go is by air from Kūnmíng. Visas are available at the embassy in Běijīng or in Kūnmíng at the Myanmar consulate (p997). In Kūnmíng visas cost ¥235, take three days to process and are good for a maximum 28-day visit

At the time of writing there were two daily flights to Yangon from Kūnmíng on Air China and China Eastern Airlines for ¥1835 and one daily to Mandalay for ¥2335.

with plenty of traders doing last-minute shopping in the many shops and goods outlets. Tourists saunter right up to the border and snap photos in front of the large entry gate. It remains busy well into the night.

To get here, continue straight ahead from Golden Duck Pagoda, cross the Myanmar bridge over Ruìlì Jiāng and you will come to Jiěgào, about 7km from Ruìlì.

Shared red taxis (¥5) with signs for Jiěgào (姐告) drive around the centre of Ruìlì from dawn until late at night.

Golden Pagoda 姐勒金塔

A few kilometres east of Ruìlì on the road to Wǎndīng is the Golden Pagoda (Jiělè Jīntǎ), a fine structure that dates back 200 years.

XĪSHUĀNGBǍNNÀ REGION

North of Myanmar and Laos, Xīshuāngbǎnnà is the Chinese approximation of the original Thai name of Sip Sawng Panna (12 Rice-Growing Districts). The Xīshuāngbǎnnà region (西双版纳), better known as Bǎnnà, has become China's mini-Thailand, attracting tourists looking for sunshine, water-splashing festivals and epic jungle treks.

But Xīshuāngbǎnnà is big enough that it rarely feels overwhelmed by visitors and even the expanding capital, Jǐnghóng, is still basically an overgrown town.

Environment

Xīshuāngbǎnnà has myriad plant and animal species, although recent scientific studies have shown the tropical rainforest areas of Bǎnnà are now acutely endangered. The jungle areas that remain contain a handful of tigers, leopards and golden-haired monkeys. The number of elephants has doubled to 250, up 100% from the early 1980s; the government now offers compensation to villagers whose crops have been destroyed by elephants, or who assist in wildlife conservation. In 1998 the government banned the hunting or processing of animals, but poaching is notoriously hard to control.

People

About one-third of the million-strong population of this region are Dai; another third or so are Han Chinese and the rest are a conglomerate of minorities that include the Hani, Lisu and Yao, as well as lesser-known hill tribes such as the Aini (a subgroup of the Hani), Jinuo, Bulang, Lahu and Wa.

Xīshuāngbǎnnà Dai Autonomous Prefecture, as it is known officially, is subdivided into the three counties of Jǐnghóng, Měnghǎi and Měnglà.

Climate

The region has two seasons: wet and dry. The wet season is between June and August, when it rains ferociously, although not every day and only in short bursts. From September to February there is less rainfall, but thick fog descends during the late evening and doesn't lift until 10am or even later.

November to March sees temperatures average about 19°C. The hottest months of the year are from April to September, when you can expect an average of 25°C.

✵ Festivals & Events

During festivals, booking same-day airline tickets to Jǐnghóng can be extremely difficult. Hotels in Jǐnghóng town are booked solid and prices usually triple. Most people end up commuting from a nearby Dai village. Festivities take place all over Xīshuāngbǎnnà, so you might be lucky further away from Jǐnghóng.

Tanpa Festival CULTURAL
In February, young boys are sent to the local temple for initiation as novice monks.

Tan Jing Festival
CULTURAL

Held between February and March, this festival's participants honour Buddhist texts housed in local temples.

Water-Splashing Festival
CULTURAL

Held in mid-April, the same time as it is celebrated in Thailand and Laos, the three-day water-splashing festival washes away the dirt, sorrow and demons of the old year and brings in the happiness of the new. Jǐnghóng celebrates it from 13 to 15 April but dates in the surrounding villages vary. The actual splashing only occurs on the last day. Foreigners earn special attention, so prepare to be drenched all day.

Closed-Door Festival
CULTURAL

The farming season, July to October, is the time for the closed-door festival (傣族关门节), when marriages or festivals are banned. Traditionally, this is also the time of year that men aged 20 or older are ordained as monks for a period of time. The season ends with the **Open-Door Festival**, when everyone lets their hair down again to celebrate the harvest.

Tan Ta Festival
CULTURAL

This festival is held during a 10-day period in October or November, with temple ceremonies, rocket launches from special towers and hot-air balloons. The rockets, which often contain lucky amulets, blast into the sky; those who find the amulets are assured of good luck.

Jǐnghóng   景洪

🕿 0691 / POP 520,000

Jǐnghóng – the 'City of Dawn' in local Dai language – is the capital of Xīshuāngbǎnnà Prefecture, but don't take that too seriously. While many Chinese from more frigid regions are buying holiday homes here – and the new apartment blocks are sprawling down both sides of the Mekong River (known as the Láncāng in China), which bisects the city – it's still a perfect representation of laid-back Bǎnnà. And everything from the food to the weather has more in common with Southeast Asia than China.

In the summer, the low season, prepare yourself for searing heat and a sapping humidity that puts the entire city into extended slow motion. If you've acclimatised to higher and nippier elevations in Yúnnán, you'll probably find yourself needing lots of midday siestas. During the winter months, though, the temperature is just perfect.

Xīshuāngbǎnnà

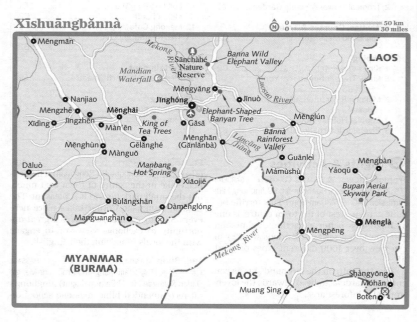

Jǐnghóng

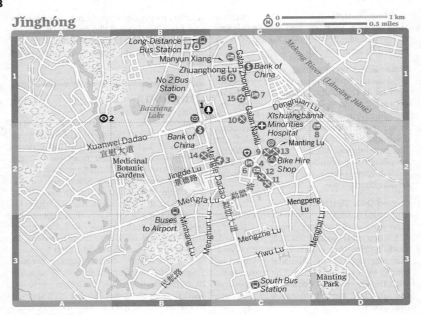

Jǐnghóng

◉ Sights
1 Peacock Lake Park B1
2 Tropical Flower & Plants Garden A1

⊕ Activities, Courses & Tours
3 Tàijí Blind Massage C2

🛏 Sleeping
4 King Land Hotel C2
5 Many Trees International Youth
   Hostel C1
6 Mekong River International Youth
   Hostel C2
7 Popular Holiday Hotel C1
8 Riverside International Hostel D2

⊗ Eating
9 Bǎnnà Cafe C2
10 Luō Luó Bīng Wū C1
11 Měiměi Café C2
12 Mekong Café C2
13 Thai Restaurant C2
14 YDN B2

⊕ Entertainment
15 Měngbālā Nàxī Arts Theatre C1

🛍 Shopping
16 Jade Market C1
17 Market B1

◉ Sights & Activities

Tropical Flower & Plants Garden   GARDENS
(热带花卉园; Rèdài Huāhuìyuán; 99 Jinghong Xilu;
admission ¥40; ⊙ 7.30am-6pm) This terrific botanic garden, west of the town centre, is one
of Jǐnghóng's better attractions. Admission
gets you into a series of gardens where you
can view over 1000 different types of plant
life.

Take the path on the left-hand side as you
enter the gardens to head towards the lovely
tropical rainforest area.

Peacock Lake Park   PARK
(孔雀湖公园; Kǒngquè Hú Gōngyuán) The artificial lake in the centre of town isn't much,
but the small park next to it is pleasant. The
English Language Corner takes place here
every Sunday evening, so this is a great opportunity to exchange views or to engage
with the locals practising their English.

Tàijí Blind Massage   MASSAGE
(太极盲人按摩; Taijí Mángrén Ànmó; cnr Mengle
Dadao & Jingde Lu; ⊙ 9am-midnight) Jǐnghóng's
oft-recommended blind massage school of-

fers hour-long massages for ¥60. Staff are extremely kind and travellers give it terrific reports. Head down the lane off Mengle Dadao and climb the stairs on your left up to the 2nd floor.

🛏 Sleeping

Manting Lu is lined with cheapies, where you can find bearable rooms from ¥50. Outside of festival season, big discounts are normally on offer all over town.

Riverside International Hostel   HOSTEL **$**
(西双版纳囍居国际青年旅舍; Xīshuāngbǎnnà Xǐjū Guójì Qīngnián Lǚshě; ☎ 219 5611; lim711@ foxmail.com; 15f, Bldg 1, Xishuang Shi'er Cheng, next to Green Eastern Hotel; 西双十贰城国际公馆1栋15楼，格林东方酒店旁; 4-/8-bed dm ¥45/40, d & tw ¥158-188; ☀ @ 🛜) Despite its location in a new tower block, this is the best hostel in Jǐnghóng. The private rooms are bright, fresh and large and many come with great Mekong River views. The dorms are spacious too and have little balconies and lockers. There's a big communal area and helpful staff, and bikes can be hired for ¥30 a day.

To find it, look for the two tower blocks beyond the performance square off Menghai Lu and head for the right-hand one.

**Many Trees
International Youth Hostel**   HOSTEL **$**
(曼丽翠国际青年旅舍; Mànlìcuì Guójì Qīngnián Lǚshě; ☎ 212 6210; manytreesyha@gmail.com; 5 Manyun Xiang; 嘎兰中路曼允巷5号; 4-bed dm ¥40-45, d & tw ¥98-108; ☀ @ 🛜) Dorms here have superthin mattresses – a theme of Jǐnghóng's hostels – but come with lockers and en suite bathrooms. The twins and doubles are a bit tatty but the price is right. There's wi-fi throughout and a cosy communal area. It's down an alley off Galan Zhonglu.

**Mekong River
International Youth Hostel**   HOSTEL **$**
(湄公河国际青年旅舍; Méigōng Hé Guójì Qīngnián Lǚshě; ☎ 229 8000; mekongyha@gmail.com; 6 Menglong Lu; 勐龙路6号景兰国际幢; 6-bed dm ¥40, d & tw ¥138-168; ☀ @ 🛜) This centrally located hostel has a utilitarian feel, but it makes a very convenient base. Dorms are cramped and lack lockers, but the private rooms are reasonable. It sees more Chinese travellers than Westerners, but some English is spoken.

King Land Hotel   HOTEL **$$$**
(鲸兰大酒店; Jīnglán Jiǔdiàn; ☎ 216 9999; 6 Jingde Lu; 景德路6号; d & tw ¥980-1580; ☀ @ 🛜 🖥) Sporting two enormous elephants

---

HIKING IN XĪSHUĀNGBǍNNÀ

Hikes around Xīshuāngbǎnnà used to be among the best in China – you'd be invited into a local's home to eat, sleep and drink *mǐjiǔ* (rice wine). Growing numbers of visitors have changed this in many places, while encroaching rubber and banana plantations – some wags now refer to the region as Xīshuāngbanana – are having an increasingly deleterious effect on the environment.

It's still possible to find villages that see very few foreigners and remain pristine, but they are remote. But you can't expect to roll up in Jǐnghóng and the next day be in a village that hasn't seen a Westerner before. Or automatically expect a welcome mat and a free lunch because you're a foreigner.

If you do get invited into someone's home, try to establish whether payment is expected. If it's not, leave an offering or modest gift (ask at the backpacker cafes to find out what's considered appropriate), even though the family may insist on nothing.

Also take care before heading off. It's a jungle out there, so go prepared, and make sure somebody knows where you are and when you should return. In the rainy season you'll need to be equipped with proper hiking shoes and waterproof gear. At any time you'll need water purification tablets, bottled water or a water bottle able to hold boiled water, as well as snacks and sunscreen.

Seriously consider taking a guide. You won't hear much Mandarin on the trail, let alone any English. Expect to pay around ¥300 per day.

Both the Mekong Café (p711) and the Bǎnnà Cafe (p711) in Jǐnghóng can arrange treks and guides. The nearby Měiměi Café (p711) doesn't organise treks but does have lots of details in binders so you can find your own way.

MINORITY GROUPS OF XĪSHUĀNGBǍNNÀ

The Dai (傣族) are Hinayana Buddhists (as opposed to China's majority Mahayana Buddhists) who first appeared 2000 years ago in the Yangzi Valley and were subsequently driven south to here by the Mongol invasion of the 13th century. The common dress for Dai women is a straw hat or towel-wrap headdress, a tight, short blouse in a bright colour, and a printed sarong with a belt of silver links. Some Dai men tattoo their bodies with animal designs, and betel-nut chewing is popular. The Dai language is quite similar to Lao and northern Thai dialects. Some Dai phrases include *douzao li* (hello), *yindi* (thank you) and *goihan* (goodbye).

The Jinuo people (基诺族), sometimes known as the Youle, were officially 'discovered' as a minority in 1979 and are among the smallest groups – numbering between 12,000 and 18,000. They call themselves 'those who respect the uncle' and are thought to possibly have descended from the Qiang. The women wear a white cowl, a cotton tunic with bright horizontal stripes and a tubular black skirt. Earlobe decoration is an elaborate custom – the larger the hole and the more flowers it can contain, the more beautiful the woman is considered. Teeth are sometimes painted black with the sap of the lacquer tree, for both beauty and to protect from teeth decay.

The Bulang people (布朗族) live mainly in the Bùlǎng, Xīdìng and Bādá mountains of Xīshuāngbǎnnà. They keep to the hills farming cotton, sugar cane and *pǔ'ěr* tea, one of Yúnnán's most famous exports. Men traditionally tattoo their arms, legs, chests and stomachs while women wear vibrant headdresses decorated with flowers.

The Hani (哈尼族, also known in adjacent countries as the Akha) are closely related to the Yi as a part of the Tibeto-Burman group; the language is Sino-Tibetan but uses Han characters for the written form. They are mostly famed for their river-valley rice terraces, especially in the Red River valley, between the Āiláo and Wúliàng Shān, where they cultivate rice, corn and the occasional poppy. Hani women (especially the Aini, a subgroup of the Hani) wear headdresses of beads, feathers, coins and silver rings, some of which are decorated with French (Vietnamese), Burmese and Indian coins from the turn of the century.

at its entrance, this is one of Jǐnghóng's unmistakable landmarks. It has a supercentral location, four-star standard rooms and a swimming pool. Rooms are routinely discounted by 60% out of season and it accepts Western credit cards.

Popular Holiday Hotel HOTEL $$$
(假日时尚酒店; Jiàrì Shíshàng Jiǔdiàn; ☑ 213 9001; 104 Galan Zhonglu; 嘎兰中路104号; d & tw ¥558; ❉ @ ☎) Standing out from the three-star pack by virtue of its light, clean and modern rooms, many of which come with computers, the optimistic name of this place is justified. Ask for a room at the back for peace and quiet at night. Ignore the listed prices; you should be able to get a room for ¥120 outside of festival time.

✖ Eating

The Dai restaurants along Menghai Lu, Mengpeng Lu and Menghun Lu are where you'll find the locals and the most authentic and tastiest food in town (as well as at

the food stalls that pop up all over town at night).

Dai dishes include barbecued fish, eel or beef cooked with lemongrass or served with peanut and tomato sauce. Vegetarians can order roast bamboo shoots prepared in the same fashion. Other specialities include fried river moss (better than it sounds and excellent with beer), spicy bamboo-shoot soup and *shāokǎo* (skewers of meat wrapped in banana leaves and grilled over wood fires).

Luō Luō Bīng Wū NOODLES $
(啰啰冰屋; 96 Xuanwei Dadao; 宣威大道96号; dishes from ¥12; ⊙ 6.30am-10pm) A buzzing local spot, Jǐnghóngers flock here for the cheap and tasty rice-noodle and fried-rice dishes, as well as fruit juices, shakes and Taiwanese-style shaved-ice desserts that are perfect for cooling off. There's also an open-air area out back.

Thai Restaurant THAI $
(泰国餐厅; Tàiguó Cāntīng; ☑ 216 1758; 193 Manting Lu; 曼听路193号; dishes ¥12-40; ⊙ 10am-9.30pm) If you're not making the trek

overland to Southeast Asia, get your Thai fix at this ever-reliable open-air restaurant. It's not the most upmarket Thai place in town, but it's certainly the busiest and there's a huge range of dishes to choose from.

YDN   YUNNAN, BURMESE $
(椰德纳; Yēdénà; ☑ 214 1640; 3/F, Shawan International Plaza, 39 Mengle Dadao; 勐泐大道39号莎湾商业广场3楼; dishes from ¥12; ⊙ 8am-midnight) There's a big picture menu here of tasty, decently priced local dishes, but the cuisine-curious will be more interested in the reasonably authentic Burmese curries and salads also on offer here. It's on the 3rd floor of a shopping mall.

Bǎnnà Cafe   WESTERN $
(版纳咖啡; Bǎnnà Kāfēi; ☑ 216 0970; 1 Manting Lu; 曼听路1号; breakfast from ¥22, dishes from ¥25; ⊙ 9am-11pm; 🛜) A good place for breakfast, this friendly, Akha-owned cafe also has a small terrace that is ideal for a sundowner or late-evening libation while watching the world go by. Staff can also arrange treks and guides.

Měiměi Café   WESTERN $$
(美美咖啡; Měiměi Kāfēi; ☑ 216 1221; www.meimei-cafe.com; 107-108 Menglong Lu; 勐龙路107-108号; dishes from ¥25; ⊙ 8am-1am; 🛜) You'll find it and you'll eat here. This is the original of all the Western-style cafes in town and still the best, thanks to its menu of steaks, burgers, sandwiches, pizza and pasta, and foreigner-friendly Chinese and Thai dishes. Good range of local and foreign beers and proper coffee and juices too. Owner Orchid is a great source of local info.

Mekong Cafe   WESTERN $$
(湄公咖啡; Méigōng Kāfēi; ☑ 216 2395; 104 Menglong Lu; 勐龙路104号; dishes from ¥26; ⊙ 8am-2am; 🛜) French-owned, the Mekong is a long-time presence and serves up a wide-ranging mix of Western, Japanese and Chinese food. The steaks (¥74) and pizzas (from ¥38) are decent. It has the best wine list in town, as well as many foreign ales. There's an outdoor area out back and it's a reliable source of trekking info too.

☆ Entertainment

Měngbālā Nàxī Arts Theatre   THEATRE
(蒙巴拉纳西艺术宫; Měngbālā Nàxī Yìshùgōng; Galan Zhonglu; tickets ¥200; ⊙ 8pm & 9.40pm) Wildly popular with tour groups, this theatre has nightly song and dance shows.

🛍 Shopping

Market groupies can head to the fabulous fish and produce **market** (市场; Shìchǎng; Minhang Lu) next to the long-distance bus station. The nearby **Jade Market** (玉市场; Yù Shìchǎng; Zhuanghong Lu) features lots of Burmese hawking their goods alongside locals, and is fun for people-watching as well as shopping.

❶ Information

Every once in a while we get reports from travellers who have been drugged and then robbed on the Kūnmíng–Jǐnghóng bus trip. Be friendly but aware, accept nothing, and never leave your stuff unattended when you hop off for a break.

Bank of China (中国银行; Zhōngguó Yínháng; Xuanwei Dadao) Changes travellers cheques and foreign currency, and has an ATM machine. There are other branches on Galan Zhonglu and Minhang Lu.

China Post (国际邮局; Zhōngguó Yóuzhèng; cnr Mengle Dadao & Xuanwei Dadao; ⊙ 9am-6pm) You can send mail overseas from here.

Internet cafe (网吧; wǎngbā; Manting Lu; per hour ¥3; ⊙ 24hr) One of a number of internet cafes along this street.

Public Security Bureau (PSB; 公安局; Gōng'ānjú; 13 Jingde Lu; ⊙ 8-11.30am & 3-5.30pm Mon-Fri) Has a fairly speedy visa-extension service.

Xīshuāngbǎnnà Minorities Hospital (西双版纳民族医院; Xīshuāngbǎnnà Mínzú Yīyuàn; ☑ 213 0123; Galan Nanlu) The best bet for having an English-speaker available.

ETIQUETTE IN DAI TEMPLES

Around Dai temples the same rules apply as elsewhere: dress appropriately (no sleeveless tops or shorts); take off shoes before entering; don't take photos of monks or the inside of temples without permission; leave a donation if you do take any shots and consider leaving a token donation even if you don't – unlike in Thailand, these Buddhists receive no government assistance. It is polite to *wai* (clasp your hands together in a prayerlike greeting) the monks and remember to never rub anyone's head, raise yourself higher than a Buddha figure or point your feet at anyone. (This last point applies to secular buildings too. If you stay the night in a Dai household, it is good form to sleep with your feet pointing towards the door.)

BǍNNÀ BORDER CHECKPOINTS

At the time of writing, normally sleepy Bǎnnà was a hive of police activity, especially along the borders with Laos and Myanmar. The reason for this is the increase in the number of Uighurs – the restive Muslim ethnic-minority group native to far-off Xīnjiāng Province – attempting to flee China across what are normally the country's most porous frontiers.

Any bus or car travelling close to the borders will be stopped at any number of checkpoints and the IDs of all passengers scrutinised. It is absolutely essential for all travellers to carry their passports with them when journeying around the border areas. The police will be unimpressed if you have no proof of who you are and where you are from.

Gǎnlǎnbà ¥18, 40 minutes, every 20 minutes (7.40am to 6pm)

Měnghǎi ¥17, 50 minutes, every 20 minutes (7am to 7pm)

Měnglà ¥50, 2½ hours, every 30 minutes (7am to 6pm)

Měnglún ¥20, 1½ hours, every 20 minutes (7am to 6pm)

Měngyǎng ¥10, 40 minutes, every 30 minutes (7am to 6pm)

Sānchàhé ¥15, one hour, 10 daily (8am to 5pm)

Sīmáo ¥55, two hours, every 30 minutes (6.30am to 7pm)

For Měnghùn, take any bus to Měnghǎi and change there.

For buses to Dàměnglóng, head to the south bus station (客运南站; *kèyùn nánzhàn*), which also has departures to Kūnmíng.

If you want to get to the Yuányáng Rice Terraces, there is normally a daily bus from the long-distance bus station to Nánshà (¥150, eight hours), where you can catch a bus onto Xīnjiē. You could also take a bus from here to Jiànshuǐ and then catch a bus to Yuányáng.

ⓘ Getting There & Away

AIR

There are several daily flights to Kūnmíng (¥730) but in April (when the water-splashing festival is held) you'll need to book tickets several days in advance to get in or out.

There are also daily flights to Dàlǐ (¥978) and Lìjiāng (¥570), as well as increasing numbers of flights that connect with cities across China via Kūnmíng. Lao Airlines has one flight a week to Luang Prabang in Laos on Sunday (¥870). Travel agents all over town sell air tickets, or book online. Note that Jǐnghóng's airport is known as Xīshuāngbǎnnà.

BUS

The **long-distance bus station** (长途客运站; Chángtú kèyùnzhàn; Minhang Lu) serves the following destinations and also has a daily bus to Luang Nam Tha in Laos (¥70, seven hours, 10.40am).

Jiànshuǐ ¥178, 12 hours, two daily (9.30am and 10.30am)

Kūnmíng ¥219 to ¥252, eight hours, seven daily (8.30am to 10pm)

Lìjiāng ¥276, 18 hours, one daily (9.30am)

Ruìlì ¥417, 22 to 24 hours, one daily (9am)

Xiàguān ¥220, 12 hours, two daily (8.30am and 10am)

If you want to explore Xīshuāngbǎnnà, go to the No 2 bus station (第二客运站; Dì'èr kèyùnzhàn), also known as the Bǎnnà bus station.

ⓘ Getting Around

Bus 1 (¥2) runs to the airport, 5km south of the city, from a stop on Mengla Lu near the corner with Minhang Lu. A taxi will cost around ¥25 but expect to be hit up for much more during festivals.

Jǐnghóng is small enough that you can walk to most destinations, but a bike makes life easier and can be rented through most accommodation for ¥25 to ¥30 a day or from the **bike hire shop** (◷ 8.30am-10pm) on Manting Lu.

A taxi anywhere in town costs ¥7.

Around Jǐnghóng

Trekking (or busing) to the endless minority villages is the draw here. You could spend weeks doing so, but even with limited time most destinations in Xīshuāngbǎnnà are only two or three hours away by bus. Note that to get to the most isolated villages, you'll often first have to take the bus to a primary (and uninteresting) village and stay overnight there, since only one bus per day – if that – travels to the tinier villages.

Market addicts can rejoice – it's an artist's palette of colours in outlying villages. The most popular markets are the Thursday market in Xīdìng, then Měnghùn, followed by Měnghǎi.

Take note: it can feel like every second village begins with the prefix 'Meng' and it isn't unheard of for travellers to end up at the wrong village entirely because of communication problems. It's a good idea to have your destination written down in script before you head off.

Sānchàhé Nature Reserve 三岔河自然保护区

This nature reserve (Sānchàhé Zìrán Bǎohùqū), 48km north of Jǐnghóng, is one of five enormous forest reserves in southern Yúnnán. It has an area of nearly 1.5 million hectares; seriously, treat it with respect – you get off-trail here, you won't be found. The madding crowds head for **Bǎnnà Wild Elephant Valley** (版纳野象谷; Bǎnnà Yěxiànggǔ; admission ¥65), named after the 50 or so wild elephants that live in the valley. The elephants are very retiring, and rare are the travellers who have actually seen any of them. You will see monkeys, though, and it's worth a visit if you want to see something of the local forest. A 2km-long **cable car** (one way/return ¥50/70) runs over the treetops from the main entrance into the heart of the park, as does an elevated walkway.

There is no accommodation in the park; it's best to stay in Jǐnghóng. There are 10 buses daily to Sānchàhé (¥15, one hour, 8am to 5pm).

Měngyǎng 勐养

The much photographed **Elephant-Shaped Banyan Tree** (象形榕树; Xiàngxíng Róngshù) is the reason most people visit Měngyǎng, 34km northeast of Jǐnghóng on the road to Sīmáo. It's also a centre for the Hani, Floral-Belt Dai and Lahu, one of the poorest minorities in the region.

From Měngyǎng it's another 19km southeast to Jīnuò (基诺), which is home base for the Jinuo minority.

Měnghǎn (Gǎnlǎnbà) 勐罕(橄榄坝)

A few years ago, Měnghǎn (or Gǎnlǎnbà as it's sometimes referred to) was a grand destination – you'd bike here and chill. Sadly, much of the main attraction – the lovely, friendly, somnolent village itself – has basically been roped off as a quasi-minority theme park with tour buses, cacophonic dancing – the usual. That said, the environs of the village are still wondrous.

◎ Sights

Dai Minority Park   VILLAGE
(傣族园; Dàizúyuán; ☑ 250 4099; Manting Lu; admission ¥65) This was once the part of town that everyone in this region came to experience – especially for its classic temples and Dai families hosting visitors in their traditional homes. (It's now the aforementioned 'theme park'.) Tourists can spend the night in villagers' homes and partake in water-splashing 'festivals' twice a day. Despite the artificial nature of it all, some people love the experience.

For wonderful scenery along rivers and rice paddies, travellers recommend heading to the south of town, crossing the Mekong by ferry (¥2) and then heading left (east). The last ferry returns at 7pm.

⌦ Sleeping & Eating

Beds in a Dai home within the park will cost between ¥50 and ¥60 per person. Food is extra. Beds are traditional Dai mats and are usually very comfortable. Most homes will also have showers for you. Restaurants inside the park are pricey and firmly aimed at tour groups.

BORDER CROSSING: GETTING TO THAILAND

Until late 2011, it was possible to travel by cargo boat to Chiang Saen in northern Thailand; the journey took around 24 hours. However, piracy and drug-related violence has largely put an end to that adventurous route south. At the time of writing, the only way to reach Thailand directly was to fly from Kūnmíng. However, you could ask about hitching a ride on a cargo boat. They leave from Guānleì (关累), about 75km southeast of Jǐnhóng. The Mekong Cafe (p711) can sometimes arrange a ride. If you get one, expect to pay ¥1200 per person for the trip. Alternatively, head into Laos and then skip over the Thai border.

BORDER CROSSING: GETTING TO LAOS

On-the-spot visas for Laos can be obtained at the border. The price will depend on your nationality (generally US$35 to US$40). You can also pick one up at the Lao Consulate (p997) in Jǐnghóng, which is on the other side of the river on the edge of town. A taxi here will cost ¥15.

The **Chinese checkpoint** (☎069 1812 2684; ⏰8am-5.30pm) is generally not much of an ordeal. Don't forget that Laos is an hour behind China.

A daily bus runs to Luang Nam Tha in Laos from Jǐnghóng (¥70, seven hours, 10.40am). Along with the daily bus to Vientiane from Kūnmíng (¥587, 30 hours, 6pm), it stops at Měnglà, but you're not guaranteed a seat.

No matter what anyone says, there should be no 'charge' to cross. Once your passport is stamped (double-check all stamps), you can jump on a motor-rickshaw to take you 3km into Laos for around ¥5. Whatever you do, go early, in case things wrap up early on either side. There are guesthouses on both the Chinese and Lao sides; people generally change money on the Lao side.

ℹ Getting There & Away

Buses to Měnghǎn leave from Jǐnghóng's No 2 bus station (¥18, every 20 minutes, 7.40am to 6pm). Note that at the time of writing, roadworks meant buses were taking a more circuitous route and the journey time was two hours. From Měnghǎn's bus station, there are buses back to Jǐnghóng (¥18) every 20 minutes. The last bus leaves at 7.30pm. There's also one bus a day to Kūnmíng (¥250, nine hours, 6.30pm).

If there are no roadworks, it is possible to cycle from Jǐnghóng to Měnghǎn in a brisk two hours or a leisurely three hours, but the traffic is heavy.

Měnglún 勐伦

East of Měnghǎn, Měnglún sports the **Tropical Plant Gardens** (热带植物园; Rèdài Zhíwùyuán; admission ¥104; ⏰7.30am-midnight). The gardens are gorgeous and get some high marks from visitors. To get here, turn left out of the bus station and then take the first left. Follow the road downhill and bear right and you'll reach the ticket office, which is just before a footbridge across the Mekong.

Your best bet for a clean bed in town is the **Chūnlín Bīnguǎn** (春林宾馆; ☎069 1871 5681; tw ¥60; ❄), which is close to the gardens' entrance.

From Jǐnghóng's No 2 bus station there are buses to Měnglún (¥20, 75 minutes, every 20 minutes, 7am to 6pm). From Měnglún, there are buses to Měnglà (¥26, 2½ hours, every 20 minutes, 8am to 6pm) and Jǐnghóng (¥20, 75 minutes, every 20 minutes, 6.30am to 6pm).

Měnglà 勐腊

Měnglà is the last (or first) main city for travellers headed to/from Laos. It has a few palm-tree-lined streets and some garish orange-coloured buildings designed with local architecture in mind, but little in the way of sights. Depending on bus condition/road traffic/arrival time, you may be stuck here for the night (the border is another 45km away). If you need a hotel, try **Jīnqiáo Dàjiǔdiàn** (金桥大酒店; ☎069 1812 4946; d & tw ¥40-80; ❄📶), convenient for the north bus station just up the hill.

Měnglà has two bus stations. The northern long-distance bus station has buses to Kūnmíng (¥290, two or three buses daily, 8.30am to 11.30am). The No 2 bus station is in the southern part of town.

Bus services from Měnglà's No 2 station include the following:

Jǐnghóng ¥50, every 30 minutes (6.30am to 6pm)

Měnglún ¥26, every 20 minutes (7am to 7pm)

Móhān ¥15, every 20 minutes (8am to 6pm)

Dàměnglóng 大勐龙

Dàměnglóng (just the latter two characters, 'Měnglóng', are written on buses) is a scrappy place with drowsy folks lolling about the dusty streets. Sights include some decent pagodas, but mostly you're here to traipse or bike through endless villages (ask about bike hire at Huá Jié Bīnguǎn). Bear in mind that new rubber plantations here have made the countryside less pristine than it once was.

About 55km south of Jǐnghóng and a few kilometres from the Myanmar border, the border-crossing point (not open for foreigners) with Myanmar has been designated as the entry point for a planned highway linking Thailand, Myanmar and China, which should really liven things up around here if it ever gets built.

◉ Sights

White Bamboo Shoot Pagoda PAGODA
(曼飞龙塔; Mànfēilóng Tǎ; admission ¥10) Surrounded by jungle (watch out for stray snakes!), this pagoda dates back to 1204 and is Dàměnglóng's premier attraction. According to legend, the pagoda's temple was built on the location of a hallowed footprint left behind by the Sakyamuni Buddha, who is said to have visited Xīshuāngbǎnnà. If you have an interest in ancient footprints, you can look for it in a niche below one of the nine stupas. The temple has been extensively renovated in recent years.

If you're in the area in late October or early November, check the precise dates of the Tan Ta Festival. At this time, White Bamboo Shoot Pagoda is host to hundreds of locals whose celebrations include dancing, rockets and fireworks, paper balloons and so on.

The pagoda is easy to get to: just walk back along the main road towards Jǐnghóng for 2km until you reach a small village with a temple on your left. From here there's a path up the hill; it's about a 20-minute walk. There's often no one around to collect the entry fee. A motor-rickshaw from Dàměnglóng is ¥10.

Black Pagoda PAGODA
(黑塔; Hēi Tǎ; FREE) Just above the centre of town is a Dai monastery with a steep path beside it leading up to the Black Pagoda – you'll notice it when entering Dàměnglóng. The pagoda itself is actually gold, not black. Take a stroll up and have a chat with the few monks in residence. The views of Dàměnglóng and surrounding countryside are more interesting than the temple itself.

🛏 Sleeping & Eating

There are simple Dai barbecue places scattered around the village. Try the ones close to the Black Pagoda.

Huá Jié Bīnguǎn HOTEL $
(华杰宾馆; ☎069 1274 2588; d & tw ¥60; ❋) Not very prepossessing, but the best option in town. To get here, turn right out of the bus station, then left up the hill and it's on the left-hand side, set back from the road.

❶ Getting There & Away

Buses to Dàměnglóng (¥16, 90 minutes, every 20 minutes, 6.30am to 6.30pm) leave from Jǐnghóng's south bus station. Remember, the 'Da' character is sometimes not displayed. Buses for the return trip run on the same schedule.

Měnghǎi 勐海

This modern town is another potential base for exploring the countryside, although it's not as pleasant a place as Jǐnghóng. Grab a bike and head north for the most interesting pagodas and villages.

If you're passing through Měnghǎi, it's worth visiting the huge daily produce market that attracts members of the hill tribes. The best way to find it is to follow the early-morning crowds.

Buses run from Jǐnghóng's No 2 bus station to Měnghǎi (¥17, 45 minutes, every 20 minutes, 7am to 7pm). They return every 20 minutes or so too.

Měnghùn 勐混

This quiet little village, about 26km southwest of Měnghǎi, has a colourful Saturday market. The town begins buzzing around 7am and the action lingers on through to midday. The swirl of hill-tribe members alone, with the women sporting fancy leggings, headdresses, earrings and bracelets, makes the trip worthwhile. Some travellers love it, while others decry the 'foreignisation' of locals.

There are several guesthouses, though none are remarkable. For ¥50 you get a double with bathroom and TV, but no air-con.

To get here, take any bus to Měnghǎi from the No 2 bus station in Jǐnghóng and then change for a minivan (¥7) or any bus heading through Měnghùn (¥4).

Xīdìng 西定

This sleepy hillside hamlet comes alive every Thursday for its weekly market (⊙7am to 11am), one of the best in the region. At other times you'll find Xīdìng almost deserted. If you want to see the market at its most interesting, you'll really have to get here the night before. Beds in the village are available for ¥50; their owners will find you.

To get here by public transport you can catch one of the two direct buses from Měnghǎi (¥12, 10.30am and 3pm); going the other way you can catch the bus back to Měnghǎi at 8am and 12.30pm. There are also twice-daily buses from Xīdìng to Měnghùn (¥11, 7.20am and 1pm). If you miss the bus you can always get a ride on a motorbike (¥30), a spectacular if hair-raising experience.

Jǐngzhēn 景真

In the village of Jǐngzhēn, about 14km west of Měnghǎi, is the Octagonal Pavilion (八角亭; Bājiǎo Tíng; admission ¥10; ☺8am-6pm), first built in 1701. The original structure was severely damaged during the Cultural Revolution but renovated in 1978 and the ornate decoration is still impressive. The temple also operates as a monastic school. The paintings on the wall of the temple depict scenes from the Jataka, the life history of Buddha.

Frequent buses from Měnghǎi's bus station go via Jǐngzhēn (¥10, 30 minutes).

Sìchuān

POP 80.8 MILLION

Best Hiking

➡ Yàdīng Nature Reserve (p756)

➡ Jiǔzhàigōu National Park (p764)

➡ Sōngpān (p760)

➡ Tǎgōng (p749)

Best History & Culture

➡ Chéngdū (p721)

➡ Dégé (p754)

➡ Sèdá (p751)

➡ Dānbā (p748)

➡ Luòbiāo (p744)

Why Go?

It's fitting that an ancient form of opera and magic called *biànliǎn* (face-changing) originated here, for Sìchuān (四川) is a land of many guises.

Capital Chéngdū shows a modern face, but just beyond its bustling ring roads you'll find a more traditional landscape of mist-shrouded, sacred mountains, and a countryside scattered with ancient villages and cliffs of carved Buddhas. Central Sìchuān is also home to the giant panda, the most famous face in China.

To the north, the visage changes again into a fairyland of alpine valleys and blue-green lakes. Sìchuān's Tibetan face appears as you venture west. This is Kham, one of the former Tibetan prefectures: a vast landscape of plateau grasslands and glacial mountains where Tibetan culture still thrives and you're certain to have your most challenging, yet most magical, experiences.

When to Go

Chéngdū

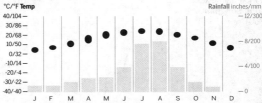

°C/°F **Temp**
Rainfall inches/mm

Mar–May Prime time for Chéngdū. Not too humid, little rain and peach blossoms.

Jul–Aug In the west, the warm grasslands bloom in technicolor.

Aug–Oct The turquoise lakes to the north offer secluded camping amid stunning autumn leaves.

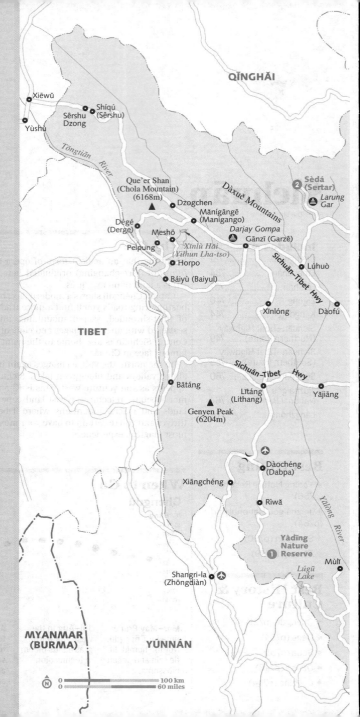

Sìchuān Highlights

1 Make the pilgrimage trek around the stunning holy mountains of **Yàdīng Nature Reserve** (p756)

2 Chat with monks and nuns in training at Sèdá's massive **Buddhist institution** (p751)

3 Rise with the sun on the forested slopes of **Éméi Shān** (p734)

4 Meet China's cuddly national icon at Chéngdū's **Giant Panda Breeding Research Base** (p721)

5 Camp in Jiǔzhàigōu's alpine valley through the park's **ecotourism program** (p764)

6 Break bread with Tibetan nomads on **Tǎgōng**'s (p749) grasslands

7 Peer over the toenails of the world's largest **Buddha statue** (p737) in Lè Shān

8 Discover salt and dinosaurs in **Zìgòng** (p740)

9 Horse trek to the mountain lakes around **Sōngpān** (p760)

QĪNGHǍI

Xiēwǔ

Shíqú (Sêrshu)

Sêrshu Dzong

Yùshù

Tōngtiān River

Que'er Shan (Chola Mountain) (6168m)

Dzogchen

Dàxuě Mountains

Sèdá (Sertar)

Larung Gar

Dégé (Derge)

Meshö

Pelpung

Mǎnígāngē (Manigango)

Darjay Gompa

Gānzī (Garzê)

Xīnlù Hǎi (Yilhun Lha-tso)

Horpo

Báiyù (Baiyul)

Sìchuān-Tibet Hwy

Lúhuò

Xīnlóng

Dàofú

TIBET

Sìchuān-Tibet Hwy

Bātáng

Lǐtáng (Lithang)

Yǎjiāng

Genyen Peak (6204m)

Dàochéng (Dabpa)

Xiāngchéng

Rìwǎ

Yàlóng River

Yàdīng Nature Reserve

Mùlǐ

Lúgū Lake

Shangri-la (Zhōngdiàn)

MYANMAR (BURMA)

YÚNNÁN

N

0 — 100 km
0 — 60 miles

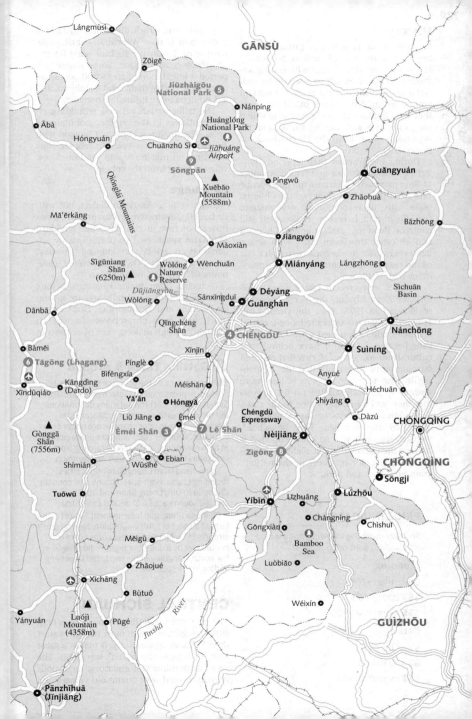

History

Sìchuān's early history was turbulent. The region was the site of various breakaway kingdoms, ever skirmishing with central authority, but it was finally wrested under control and established as the capital of the Qin empire in the 3rd century BC. It was here that the kingdom of Shu (a name by which the province is still known) ruled as an independent state during the Three Kingdoms period (AD 220–80).

During the Warring States period (475–221 BC), local governor and famed engineer Li Bing managed to harness the flood-prone Mín River (岷江; Mín Jiāng) on the Chuānxī plain with his revolutionary weir system; the Dūjiāngyàn Irrigation Project still still controls flooding, and supplies Chéngdū and 49 other provincial cities with water, 2200 years after it was constructed! It's one of the reasons the Sìchuān basin is synonymous with fertile soil.

Another more recent factor was the efforts of Zhao Ziyang, the Party Secretary of Sìchuān in 1975. After the Great Leap Forward, when an estimated one-tenth of Sìchuān's population died of starvation, Ziyang became the driving force behind agricultural and economic reforms that restored farming output. He reinstated the 'Responsibility System', whereby plots of land were granted to farming families on the proviso that they sold a quota of crops to the state. Any additional profits or losses would be borne by the families. This household-focused approach was so successful that it became the national model. Sìchuān continues to be a major producer of the nation's grain, soybeans and pork.

Catastrophe struck the region on 12 May 2008, when the Wènchuān earthquake measuring 7.9 on the Richter scale hit the province's central region. Some sources reported it killed more than 88,000 people, as many as 10,000 of them school children, and left millions more injured or homeless.

The trillion-yuan aid and rebuilding effort continues in the remote, mountainous areas. The main road linking Chéngdū with Jiǔzhàigōu took four years to reopen. Now travellers on that route will see brand-new villages rising from the rubble.

Language

Sichuanese is a Mandarin dialect, but with its fast clip, distinctive syntax, and five tones instead of four, it can challenge standard Mandarin speakers. Two phrases easily understood are *yàodé* (pronounced 'yow-day', meaning 'yes' or 'OK') and *méidé* (pronounced 'may-day', meaning 'no').

Sìchuān's other major languages belong to the Tibeto-Burman family and are spoken by Tibetans and Yí minorities. Don't expect much help from phrasebooks. In western Sìchuān, Tibetan dialects vary from town to town.

ⓘ Getting There & Around

Chéngdū serves as the province's transit hub. Smooth expressways to eastern and southern Sìchuān make short trips of many destinations, but heading north or west is a different story. Many roads are in poor shape or are under construction. Weather conditions are unpredictable at high elevations, and hazards ranging from landslides to overturned semis are common.

Trains head from Chéngdū to major cities, including Lhasa. High-speed trains now connect Chéngdū to Qīngchéng Shān and Dūjiāngyàn, and will soon reach Lè Shān and Éméi Shān.

Chéngdū Shuāngliú International Airport is the largest airport in southwest China. Several small airports in Sìchuān's furthest corners are connected to it by a one-hour flight — Jiǔzhàigōu in the north, Kāngdìng in the west, and Dàochéng-Yàdīng in the southwest.

CENTRAL SÌCHUĀN

The province's friendly and modern capital city, Chéngdū, is where most travellers start their Sìchuān explorations. It makes a great base for trips to the region's top sights. The area surrounding this emerging metropolis remains dotted with quaint old villages and

---

PRICE INDICATORS

We have used the following price indicators to represent price ranges:

Sleeping

$ less than ¥200

$$ ¥200 to ¥600

$$$ more than ¥600

Eating

$ less than ¥30

$$ ¥30 to ¥50

$$$ more than ¥50

farmsteads. Nearby, rise the lush, forested peaks of Éméi Shān, the cliffs of Lè Shān with an ancient Buddha (the world's largest), and, hidden in the bamboo thickets, pandas; practically impossible to see in the wild, they are easy to spot in area reserves.

Chéngdū 成都

028 / POP 14.2 MILLION

On the face of it, Chéngdū should be a drag. It's flat, with no distinguishing natural features. The weather is grey and drizzly much of the year. The traffic is alarming. Yet somehow everyone comes away satisfied. Perhaps it's the truly fabulous food, and the laid-back local folk. Or it could be the relaxing teahouse culture. Maybe it's the lively nightlife? Then there are the pandas, of course. Who knows?

As the transport hub for the whole region, most travellers in China's southwest will be fortunate enough to pass through and find out for themselves.

◎ Sights

★ Giant Panda Breeding Research Base
WILDLIFE RESERVE

(大熊猫繁育基地; Dàxióngmāo Fányù Jīdì; ☎028 8351 0033; www.panda.org.cn; 1375 Xiongmao Dadao; adult/student ¥58/29; ⊙8am-5.30pm) One of Chéngdū's most popular attractions, this reserve, 18km north of the city centre, is the easiest way to glimpse Sìchuān's famous residents outside of a zoo. The enclosures here are large and well maintained. Home to nearly 120 giant and 76 red pandas, the base focuses on getting these shy creatures to breed.

March to May is the 'falling in love period' (wink wink). If you visit in autumn or winter, you may see tiny newborns in the nursery.

Try to visit in the morning, when the pandas are most active. Feeding takes place around 9.30am, although you'll see them eating in the late afternoon, too. They spend most of their afternoons sleeping, particularly during the height of midsummer, when they sometimes disappear into their (air-conditioned) living quarters.

Catch bus 49 (¥2, 40 minutes) and transfer at Zhāojué Hénglù stop (昭觉横路站) to bus 87 or 198 (¥2, 20 minutes) to the Panda Base stop (熊猫基地站, Xióngmāo Jīdì). Alternatively, from the north train station take bus 9 (¥2, 60 minutes) to the Zoo stop (动物园站, Dòngwùyuán) and switch to 198 (¥2, 20 min-

utes). Hostels run trips here, too. Metro line 3 will run directly here when it is completed.

Wénshū Temple
BUDDHIST TEMPLE

&(文殊院; Wénshū Yuàn; Renmin Zhonglu; ⊙8am-10.50pm; 1) FREE This Tang-dynasty monastery is dedicated to Wenshu (Manjushri), the Bodhisattva of Wisdom, and is Chéngdū's largest and best-preserved Buddhist temple. The air is heavy with incense and the low murmur of chanting; despite frequent crowds of worshippers, there's still a sense of serenity and solitude.

The temple's popular **vegetarian restaurant** (文殊院素宴厅; Wénshūyuàn Sùyàn Tīng; Wénshū Temple, Renmin Zhonglu; dishes ¥12-48; ⊙10.30am-8.30pm) and teahouse were closed for renovations when we visited. The 'old' neighbourhood streets surrounding the temple are crowded with teahouses, snack stalls and shops; touristy, yes, but fun to wander.

Jīnshā Site Museum
MUSEUM

(金沙遗址博物馆; Jīnshā Yízhǐ Bówùguǎn; www.jinshasitemuseum.com; 227 Qingyang Dadao; admission ¥80; ⊙8am-5.30pm) In 2001 archaeologists made a historic discovery in Chéngdū's western suburbs: they unearthed a major site containing ruins of the 3000-year-old Shu kingdom. This excellent, expansive museum includes the excavation site and beautiful displays of many of the uncovered objects, which were created between 1200 and 600 BC.

Like the discoveries further outside the city at Sānxīngduī (p731), the 6000 or so relics include both functional and decorative items, from pottery and tools to jade artefacts, stone carvings and ornate gold masks. A large number of elephant tusks were also unearthed here.

Take bus 901 from Xīnnánmén bus station, or metro line 2 to Yinpintianxia (一品天下).

Tomb of Wáng Jiàn
TOMB

(王建墓; Wángjiàn Mù; 10 Yongling Lu; 永陵路10号; admission ¥20; ⊙8am-6pm; 54, 30) Built for Wang Jian (847–918), a general who rose to power following the collapse of the Tang dynasty to rule as emperor of the Shu kingdom, this above-ground tomb, the only one excavated in China so far, was pillaged just once, sometime after the subsequent collapse of the Shu.

The tomb is decorated with carvings of 24 musicians and dancers all playing different instruments and is considered to be the best surviving record of Tang-dynasty court entertainment; the statue at the back

Chéngdū

0 — 2 km
0 — 1 mile

Zhāojué Sì (3km); Giant Panda Breeding Research Base (12km)

North Train Station
北火车站

Intercity Trains
Ticket Office
Train Ticket Office

Bei Erhuan Lu 北二环路

North Train Station Bus Station

North Railway Station
火车北站

Renmin North Road
人民北路

10

Bei Erhuan Lu
北二环路

1 Huanlu Bei 4 Duan
一环路北四段

Běimén Bus Station

12

Sha River

Hongxing Lu

Xing Hui Rd West
星辉西路

Jiefang Lu 解放路

23

17

Renmin Beilu
人民北路

Brocade River (Jinjiang)

Bank of China

Wenwu Road
文殊院

6

26

19

8

Bei Dajie 北大街

Xinhua Dadao

Taishengbei Lu

Shuwa Beijie

Renmin Zhonglu

9

Bank of China

22

Xi-Yulong Jie

Luomashi
骡马市

Tianzuo Jie

Dongchenggen Jie

Qinglong Jie

Changshun Zhongjie

16

Xi'r Dajie

Shang to nerun Lu

Kuan Xiangzi

28

34

Zhai

Xiaotong Xiang 小通巷

Xiangzi

Tonghuimen
通惠门

Shi'er Qiao Lu

Qintai Lu

1

41

Xi'an Lu

5

Xi Yihuan Lu 永陵路

Yingmenkou Lu

Yongling Lu

Shawan Lu 沙湾路

Qingyang Dadao

Chengdu University of Traditional Chinese Medicine
中医学院

Jinsha Museum (2km)

Qinghua Jie

Chadianzi (5km)

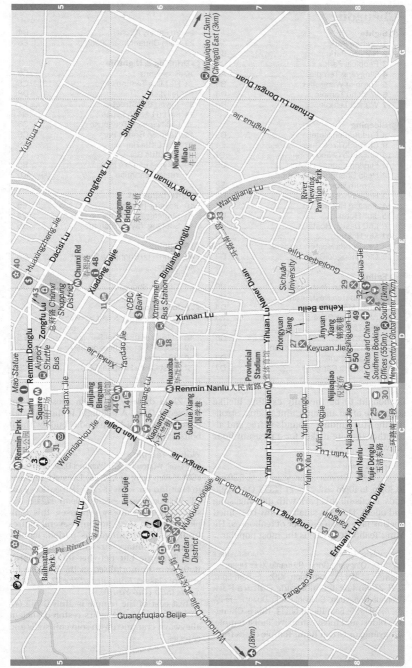

Wǔguìqiáo (1.5km);
Chéngdū East (3km)

Erhuan Lu Dongsi Duan

Niúwàng
Miào 牛王庙

Jinghua Jie

Shuǐnianhe Lu

Dong Yihuan Lu

Yushua Lu

Dongfeng Lu

Wangjiang Lu

Huaxingzheng Jie

Dacisi Lu

Dongmen
Bridge
东门大桥 M

River
Viewing
Pavilion Park

Chunxi Rd
春熙路

40

Renmin Donglu

Zongfu Lu
总府路 /43 $

Chunxi
Shopping
District

Xiadong Dajie

33

Yihuan Lu Naner Duan

Sìchuān
University

Guojiaqiao Xijie

Kehua Jie

Mao Statue

Renmin Donglu

1

Airport
Shuttle
Bus

ICBC
Bank

Xīnnánmén
Bus Station Binjiang Donglu

11

Xinnan Lu

Kehua Beilu

29

32
24

49

Renmin Park
人民公园

Tianfu
Square
天府广场

Xinhai Jie

Yandao Jie

18

Zhongyuan
Xiang

Jinyuan
Xiang
锦苑巷

27

Keyuan Jie 路

Lingshiguan Lu

50

Shanxi Jie

Jinjiang
Binguan
锦江宾馆

44

14

Huaxiba
华西坝 M

Renmin Nanlu 人民南路

Provincial
Stadium
省体育馆

3

31

35

36

Xiaojiazhu Jie
小天竺街

Guoxue Xiang
国学巷

51

Nan Dajie

Wenmiaohou Jie

Nijiaqiao
倪家桥

Nijiaqiao Jie

30

25

Yulin Donglu

Yihuan Lu Nansan Duan

Yulin Nanlu
玉洁南路

Yulin Donglu

38

Yulin Lu

Yulin Xilu

Yujie Donglu

Jinli Lu

Jinli Gujie

15

23 46

7

2

20

13

45

Wǔhòucí Donglie

Tibetan
District

Jianxi Jie

Ximian Qiao Jie

Yongfeng Lu

Fangqin
Jie

37

Erhuan Lu Nansan Duan

42

39

Pu River (Fǔ Hé)

4

Bǎihuātán Park

Wǔhòucí Dàjie 武侯祠大街

Guangfuqiao Beijie

Fangcao Jie

(18km)

Air China and China
Southern Booking
Offices (550m); South (1km);
New Century Global Center (7km)

Chéngdū

is thought to be the only existing lifelike sculpture of an ancient Chinese king. Strolling the surrounding grounds is free and altogether the site makes for a pleasant hour or two.

People's Park   PARK
(人民公园; Rénmín Gōngyuán; ◷ 6.30am-10.30pm, to 10pm winter; Ⓜ 2) **FREE** On weekends, locals fill this park with dancing, song and taichi. There's a small, willow-tree–lined boating lake and a number of teahouses: Hè Míng Teahouse (p727) is the most popular.

Qīngyáng Temple   TAOIST TEMPLE
(青羊宫; Qīngyáng Gōng; 9 Huanlu Xi Er Duan; 一环路西二段9号; admission ¥10; ◷ 8am-5pm; ☐ 11, 27, 45) Located alongside **Culture Park** (Wénhuà Gōngyuán; 9 Huanlu Xi Er Duan; 一环路西二段9号; ◷ 6am-10pm) **FREE**, this is Chéngdū's oldest and most extensive Taoist temple. Qīngyáng, or Green Ram, Temple dates from

the Zhou dynasty, although most of what you see is Qing. A highlight is the unusually squat, eight-sided pagoda, built without bolts or pegs.

Wǔhóu Temple   BUDDHIST TEMPLE
(武侯祠; Wǔhóu Cí; 231 Wuhouci Dajie; admission ¥60; ◷ 8am-6pm; ☐ 1, 21, 26) Located adjacent to **Nánjiāo Park** (南郊公园; Nánjiāo Gōngyuán; 235 Wuhouci Dajie; ◷ 6am-7.30pm) **FREE** and surrounded by mossy cypresses, this temple (rebuilt in 1672) honours several figures from the Three Kingdoms period, namely legendary military strategist Zhuge Liang and Emperor Liu Bei (his tomb is here). Both were immortalised in the Chinese literature classic, *Romance of the Three Kingdoms (Sān Guó Yǎnyì)*.

Just east of the temple is **Jǐnlǐ Gǔjiē** (锦里古街), one of Chéngdū's restored ancient alleyways, crammed with souvenir stalls and eateries.

🛏 Sleeping

★ Hello Chéngdū International Youth Hostel
HOSTEL $

(老实青年旅舍; Lǎosòng Qīngnián Lǔshě; ☑ 028 8196 7573, 028 8335 5322; www.gogosc.com; 211 Huanlu Bei 4 Duan; 一环路北四段211号; dm from ¥40, s without/with bathroom ¥90/120, d from ¥140, ste ¥210; ☻❉@❆; 🚌 28, 34) Once one of the best hostels in China, nevermind Chéngdū, this place has lost some of its finesse in recent years. It's still a nice space, though, sprawled around two garden courtyards, good for kids and adults to laze about. Rooms are clean and simple, and facilities are what you'd expect from a top-class hostel.

There's a solid bar and cafe, bike rental (from ¥10), a DVD library, and ready travel advice.

Loft Design Hostel
HOSTEL $

(四号工厂青年旅馆; Sìhào Gōngchǎng Qīngnián Lǔguǎn; ☑ 028 8626 5770; www.lofthostel.com; 4 Xiaotong Xiang off Zhongtongren Lu; 中通仁路, 小桶巷4号; dm ¥50-60, s/d from ¥180/300; ❉@❆; 🚌 48, 54, 341) Chic boutique meets trendy hostel in this converted printing factory, with its pretty cafe and bar, exposed brick and arty vibe. The front desk at this hostel for grown-ups offers solid travel advice plus a decent cocktail selection. Dorms are small but the deluxe private rooms are spacious. The main downfall: wi-fi is only in the common spaces.

Mix Hostel
HOSTEL $

(驴友记青年旅舍; Lǔyǒujì Qīngnián Lǔshè; ☑ 028 8322 2271; www.mixhostel.com; 23 Ren Jia Wan, Xinghui Lu West; 星辉西路任家湾23号; dm ¥35-50, s ¥88, d/tr from ¥98/130; ❉@❆; 🚌 16, 55) Mix exudes a laid-back, backpacker vibe. It's not particularly central but is only a short walk from the Renmin Beilu metro stop, so it's easy to plug yourself into the action. There's a good cafe, wi-fi (lobby area mostly), bike rental (¥20), and trustworthy travel advice. Shared bathrooms only.

Flipflop Lounge Hostel
HOSTEL $

(拖板鞋青年旅舍; Tuō Bǎnxié Qīngnián Lǔshě; ☑ 028 6250 0185; www.chengduhostel.com; 98 Dongsheng Jie; 东升街98号; dm ¥35-45, s/d/tr ¥140/170/200; ❉@❆; 🚌 1, 2, 55) This very lively hostel offers travellers all the usual services plus a few rare gifts – a pool table, decent water pressure in the communal showers, and experienced help when filing for permits and booking tours to Tibet. Rooms are slightly more expensive than

other hostels, but you're paying for the 10-minute walk to the Chunxi Lu shopping district (p729) and metro station.

Mrs Panda Hostel
HOSTEL $

(熊猫夫人青年旅舍; Xióngmāo Fūrén Qīngnián Lǔshě; ☑ 028 8705 5315; mrspandahostel@hotmail. com; 6 Linjiang Zhonglu; 临江中路6号; dm ¥40-50, r without bathroom ¥90, with bathroom ¥170-210; ❉@❆; 🚌 55, 76, 16) New owners have spruced up the beloved Traffic Inn hostel with a panda theme. Rooms with shared bathrooms remain the best value thanks to the spotless shared showers and toilets. Close to Xīnnánmén bus station, this is extremely convenient for day trips.

Chéngdū Free Guys
HOSTEL $

(闲人国际青年旅舍; Xiánrén Guójì Qīngnián Lǔshě; ☑ 028 8666 6478, 180 8486 6478; www. freeguyshostel.com; 55 Dongjiaochang Jie; 东较场街55号; dm ¥25-35, r without ¥80-135, with bathroom ¥120-160; ❉❆; 🚌 28, 101) A solid choice for those needing a cheap, clean bed and decent shower. There's not much by way of frills in this windowless maze of rooms, but the chill guys (and gals) managing the comfortable bar and library on the 2nd floor pour cold beers.

BuddhaZen Hotel
HOTEL $$

(圆和圆佛禅客栈; Yuán Hé Yuán Fú Chán Kèzhàn; 0和0; ☑ 028 8692 9898; www.buddhazenhotel. com; B6-6 Wenshufang; 青羊区文殊坊B6-6号, near Wenshu Temple; incl breakfast s & d from ¥495, ste from ¥788; ❉@❆; Ⓜ 1) Set in a tranquil courtyard building, this boutique hotel blends traditional decor with modern comforts and a taste of Buddhist philosophy. You can ponder life sipping tea on your private balcony, circling the sand garden, or soaking in a wooden tub at the spa. It's so nice here that you're bound to forget your suffering long enough to enjoy a vegetarian meal (mains from ¥30) in the silk-adorned downstairs restaurant. Limited English.

Jǐnlǐ Hotel
HOTEL $$

(锦里客栈; Jǐnlǐ Kèzhàn; ☑ 028 6631 1335; www. cdjinli.com; 231 Wuhouci Dajie, 11 Zhangwu Jie; 武侯祠大街章武街11号; s/d/ste ¥398/518/618; ❉❆; 🚌 1, 21, 26) If you don't mind the tourists swarming Jinli Gujie by Wǔhóu Temple, this upmarket inn set in two courtyard-style buildings is a nice place to stay. Rooms mix traditional Chinese wooden furnishings with modern touches such as puffy white duvets and wide-screen TVs. The two standard rooms do not have wi-fi.

Holly's Hostel
HOSTEL $$

(九龙鼎青年客栈; Jiǔlóngdǐng Qīngnián Kèzhàn; ☑ 028 8555 7349, 028 8554 8131; hollyhostelcn@ yahoo.com; 246 Wuhouci Dajie; 武侯祠大街246号; dm ¥40-55, d ¥260-280; ✳@🛜; 🖳27, 45) Prepare for trips out west by plugging yourself in to Chéngdū's small Tibetan district, which surrounds this cute and friendly hostel. Holly's has clean, basic rooms plus wi-fi, bike rentals (¥20) and a nice rooftop cafe (Western and Chinese mains ¥10 to ¥50). They can also help with permits to Lhasa. Discounted doubles go for as low as ¥120.

Chéngdū Grand Hotel
HOTEL $$

(成都大酒店; Chéngdū Dàjiǔdiàn; ☑ 028 8317 3888; www.cdgrandhotel.com; 29 North Renmin; 人民北路二段29号; d & tw ¥400-580, discounted to ¥240-280; ✳@; 🖳1, 27, Ⓜ1) This 23-storey old-school hotel with decent, internet-enabled rooms is a comfortable choice near the north train station.

Jǐnjiāng Hotel
HOTEL $$$

(锦江宾馆; Jǐnjiāng Bīnguǎn; ☑ 028 8550 6550; www.jjhotel.com; 80 Renmin Nanlu, 2nd Section; 人民南路二段80号; r from ¥1099; ✳@🛜✉; 🖳1, 57, Ⓜ1) At nine storeys, Jǐnjiāng was Sìchuān's first five-star hotel and the tallest building in Chéngdū until the late 1970s. There are more luxurious options now, but this one retains a charm that the chains lack, from the courteous and polished bell hops to the Michelin-level chef helming Jinyue French Restaurant.

Old Chéngdū Club
HOTEL $$$

(成都会馆; Chéngdū Huìguǎn; ☑ 028 8695 6688; www.oldchengduclub.com.cn; 28 Wuyuegong Jie; 五吴宫街28号; s/d/tr from ¥380/580/780; ✳@) On Wénshū Temple's doorstep, the Ming dynasty–style courtyard buildings and luxurious rooms of this hotel are decorated with lovely Chinese furnishings and artwork. It's worth upgrading to the bright and sumptuous rooms in the main building. Limited English.

✗ Eating

With the highest density of restaurants and teahouses of any city in the world, and the first city in Asia to be named a Unesco City of Gastronomy, your most memorable Chéngdū moments are likely to involve food.

One popular speciality is *chuànchuàn xiāng* (串串香), the skewer version of the famous Chóngqìng hotpot (火锅; huǒguō), that is just as spicy. First, choose the broth – usually either *hóng guō* (红锅; spicy) or *yuānyang guō* (鸳鸯锅; half-spicy, half-not) – then your meats, vegetables and whatnot. Skewers generally cost ¥1; platters ¥2. There are restaurants specialising in this quintessential local eating experience all over the city.

Several monasteries, including Wénshū Temple, have popular vegetarian restaurants (dishes from ¥12) that are generally open only for lunch.

Yángyáng Cānguǎn
SICHUANESE $

(杨杨餐馆; ☑ 028 8523 1394; 32 Jinyuan Xiang; 锦苑巷32号; mains ¥15-50; ⏱11.30am-2pm & 5-9pm; 🍽) The go-to for good-quality, tasty and inexpensive Sichuanese cooking. The Chinese menu (中文菜单; zhōngwén càidān) has photos and prices, but the English menu (英文菜单; yīngwén càidān) has neither, so ask for both. The spicy Guìzhōu chicken (贵州鸡; Guìzhōu jī; ¥38) is a good start.

Arè Tibetan Restaurant
TIBETAN $

(啊热藏餐老店; Arè Zángcān Lǎo Diàn; ☑ 028 8551 0112; 3 Wuhouci Dongjie; mains from ¥13; ⏱8.30am-10pm; 🍽) Choose from a delicious array of Tibetan staples from *tsampa* (roasted barley flour; ¥20) to *thugpa* (noodles in soup; ¥13 to ¥16), *momo* (dumplings; ¥20) and yak butter tea (¥18 to ¥25). Their newer, less quaint location (啊热藏餐店; Arè Zángcān Diàn; ☑ 028 8557 0877; 234 Wuhouci Dajie; ⏱8.30am-10pm), just across from Wǔhóu Temple (p724), has fast counter service and a dining room upstairs. English, picture menus.

★ Yùlín Chuànchuàn Xiāng
HOTPOT $$

(玉林串串香; 2-3 Kehua Jie; 科华街2677号; broth ¥20-25, skewers short/long ¥0.20/1.50, sauce from ¥2; ⏱10.30am-2am) Sìchuān University's hungry students crowd this lively branch of the popular chain, which specialises in *chuànchuàn xiāng* (串串香). Pick your broth, then load up on skewers from the refrigerated back room to cook up at your table. Staff will tally the damage at the end of your meal. There's another smaller branch in the city's southside.

Chén Mápó Dòufu
SICHUANESE $$

(陈麻婆豆腐; ☑ 028 8674 3889; 197 Xi Yulong Jie; 西玉龙街197号; mains ¥22-58; ⏱11.30am-2.30pm & 5.30-9pm; 🍽) The plush flagship of this famous chain is a great place to experience *mápó dòufu* (麻婆豆腐; small/large ¥12/20) – soft, house bean curd with a fiery sauce of garlic, minced beef, fermented soybean, chilli oil and Sìchuān pepper. It's one of Sìchuān's most famous dishes and is this restaurant's speciality. Nonspicy choices, too.

Huì Zhī Fèng
BARBECUE **$$**

(惠之凤; ☑181 1302 5306; Blue Caribbean Plaza, cnr Kehua Beilu & Kehua Jie, 科华北路143号蓝色加勒比广场; mains ¥39-58; ⊙11am-2am; ⑩) A satisfying place to fill up before (or between) drinks on Kehua Jie. There are tables outside or seats around the *tiĕ băn* (铁板) to watch the chef sear your order to perfection. A highlight is the seared bacon-wrapped mushrooms (铁板培根卷; *péigēn juăn;* ¥25). Two dishes per person is usually enough.

Yu Family Kitchen
MODERN CHINESE **$$$**

(喻家厨房; Yù Jiā Chúfáng; ☑ 028 8669 1975; 43 Zhai Xiangzi near Xia Tongren Lu; 下同仁路, 窄巷子43号; set menu per person ¥660, with 4 or more guests ¥330; ⊙noon-2pm & 5-9pm) Pioneering the next phase of Chinese cuisine, Chef Yu Bo dazzles with a set menu that begins with 16 intricate cold dishes followed by many more courses of ever-changing, meticulously prepared seasonal dishes – some traditional and many you've never seen before. By reservation only. With all the acclaim and just six private rooms, call early.

Sultan
MIDDLE EASTERN **$$$**

(苏坦土耳其餐吧; Sūtăn Tŭĕrqí Cānba; ☑028 8555 4780; 5 Fanghua Jie; 芳华街25号附12号; mains from ¥50; ⊙11am-11pm; ⑩⑩) Crowd-pleasing fare from the western reaches of the Silk Road, including lamb kebabs, hummus, house-made yoghurt, Turkish coffee and warm naan. Hook into the free wi-fi outside on the patio, or into a sheesha pipe (¥50) in a private room piled with cushions.

Chóngqìng Bāyé
CHINESE **$$$**

(重庆巴爺; ☑ 028 6820 8243; www.cqbaye.com; 2nd fl,cnr Jiefang Lu & Zhangjia Xiang; 解放路二段张家巷口, 二楼; mains ¥12-28, pots small/medium/large ¥88/118/148; ⊙9.30am-11pm) This *gānguō* (干锅, 'dry pot') specialist serves sizzling concoctions in very hot iron pots. Our favourites include *chāoji huānlà xiā* (超级欢辣虾; shrimp), *zhúsŭn jībāo* (竹笋鸡煲; chicken and bamboo shoots), *xiānglà páigŭ* (香辣排骨; pork ribs) and *xiānglà yāchún* (香辣鸭唇; duck beak). With rice (米饭; *mĭfàn*), a small pot is enough for two or three; a ¥38 pot (单人的; *dānrénde*) is plenty for one. The menu also includes regular Sichuanese dishes, or head upstairs for standard (with broth) hotpot (from ¥50 per person). Finish with the *mĭjiŭ tāngyuán* (米酒汤圆; sweet glutinous rice balls; ¥10).

 Drinking

Sìchuān does teahouses better than anywhere else in China. The art of tea – the brewing, serving and savouring – dates back 3000 years, and teahouses have long been the centres of neighbourhood social life. In Chéngdū, they are as they always have been – people gossip, play cards, watch opera, get haircuts and even have their ears cleaned! Try a Sìchuān-grown green tea like *máofēng* (毛峰), which uses tender, downy tea leaves, and *zhúyèqīng* (竹叶青), which looks like tiny bamboo leaves.

Today you'll find crowded teahouses all over the city, particularly in parks and temple grounds. There are also pleasant ones along the river banks. Tea is generally served by the cup (¥20 to ¥40) and is topped up for free as often as you like.

There are plenty of options for the harder stuff too, including raucous **Jiŭyăn Bar Street** (九眼酒吧街; Jiŭyăn Jiŭbā Jiē), a neon strip of bars and clubs on the Jìn Jiāng, and the cluster of comparatively subdued watering holes by **Nánmén Bridge** (南门桥; Nánmén Qiáo).

For the latest on Chéngdū's nightlife, pick up copies of *Hello Chengdu* or *More Chengdu* (www.morechengdu.com), or check out www.gochengdoo.com/en.

Hè Míng Teahouse
TEAHOUSE

(鹤鸣茶馆; Hèmíng Cháguăn; People's Park; tea ¥12-30; ⊙6am-9pm) Always lively is this century-old spot, which is most pleasant for whiling away an afternoon with a bottomless cup of tea. Neat tea-pouring performances happen on Saturdays from 2pm to 3pm. Ear cleanings (¥20) are available daily.

Kǎi Lú Lǎo Zháiyuàn
TEAHOUSE

(恺庐老宅院; ☑ 180 3041 6632; 11 Kuan Xiangzi; 宽巷子11号; from ¥35 a cup; ☉ 10am-11pm) For 200 years one of the city's most venerable teahouses has been tucked away in a peaceful courtyard behind a stone archway off the otherwise frenetic Kuan Alley.

New Little Bar
LIVE MUSIC

(小酒馆(芳沁店); Xiǎo Jiǔguǎn (Fāngqìn Diàn); ☑ 028 8515 8790; site.douban.com/littlebar; 47 Yongfeng Lu & Fangqin Jie; 永丰路47号丰尚玉林商务港1楼附1号5号, 芳沁街; beer from ¥15, cocktails from ¥25; ☉ 6pm-2am) This small pub-like venue is *the* place in Chéngdū to catch live local bands. Bands play most Fridays and Saturdays, and occasional weekdays, usually from 8pm. Live music carries a cover charge of around ¥15, depending on who's playing. Check online for the schedule.

Old Little Bar
BAR

(小酒馆(玉林店); Xiǎo Jiǔguǎn (Yùlín Diàn); ☑ 028 8556 8552; 55 Yulin Xilu; 玉林西路55号; beer from ¥15, cocktails from ¥25; ☉ 6pm-2.30am) The former epicentre of Chéngdū's rock scene no longer puts on live performances, but it's still a chill place to hang out with beer- and music-loving locals.

Bookworm
CAFE

(老书虫; Lǎo Shūchóng; ☑ 028 8552 0177; www.chengdubookworm.com; 2-7 Yujie Dongjie, 28 Renmin Nanlu; 人民南路28号、玉洁东街2-7号; mains ¥35-95; ☉ 9am-1am) This hopping bookstore-cafe, like its branches in Běijīng and Sūzhōu, is a gathering place for expats and a pleasant spot for a beer or coffee (from ¥25). It also serves decent Western food. You can buy or borrow from the English-language section, or stop by for author talks, live music and other events. Check the website for the schedule.

Lǎo Nánmén Teahouse
TEAHOUSE

(老南门茶苑; Lǎo Nánmén Cháyuàn; Binjiang Xi Lu; 滨江西路; tea per cup ¥10-38; ☉ noon-11pm summer, to 7pm rest of year) This pocket-sized riverside tea garden stays open late for the summer crowds. Just under the bridge beside a rushing weir, it's a pleasant local favourite that serves all the usual teas and snacks. No English menu.

Sǎnhuā Lóu/Yè Píjiǔ
TEAHOUSE, BEER GARDEN

(散花楼/夜啤酒; 1 Qingyang Zhengjie; 青羊正街1号; tea per cup ¥15-50, beer ¥10-40; ☉ 8am-2am) Housed in a four-storey red pagoda, this teahouse overlooking the river and the other

teahouses in Bǎihuātán Park (百花潭公园) turns into a beer garden come 7pm, complete with football on the projection screen and small bites (¥10 to ¥30) to wash down with a bottle or five.

Jellyfish
BAR

(海母酒吧; Hǎi Mǔ Jiǔbā; ☑ 152 0833 3220; 2nd fl, Blue Caribbean Plaza, cnr Kehua Beilu & Kehua Jie; 科华北路143号蓝色加勒比广场2楼; cocktails from ¥25; ☉ 7.30pm-2.30am, to 4am weekends) This cocktail bar turns into a hotbed of awkward dance-floor international relations when the DJs spin late nights. Gawk while enjoying a six cocktail flight with bar snacks (¥488) from your banquette or, better yet, join in. Happy hour goes from midnight to 1am, and ladies drink free on Thursday nights.

☆ Entertainment

Chéngdū is the birthplace of Sìchuān opera, which dates back more than 250 years. Besides glass-shattering songs, performances feature slapstick, martial arts, men singing as women, acrobatics and even fire breathing. An undoubted highlight is *biànliǎn* (变脸; face changing) where performers change character in a blink by swapping masks, manipulating face paint, and other prestidigitation.

Shǔfēng Yǎyùn Teahouse
SÌCHUĀN OPERA

(蜀风雅韵; Shǔfēng Yǎyùn; ☑ 028 8776 4530; www.shufengyayun.net; inside Culture Park; tickets ¥140-320; ☉ ticket office 3-9.30pm, nightly shows at 8pm) This famous century-old theatre and teahouse puts on excellent 1½-hour shows that include music, puppetry and Sìchuān opera's famed fire breathing and face changing. Come at around 7.30pm to watch performers putting on their elaborate make-up and costumes. For ¥50 to ¥100, kids (and adults) can try on garb and have a costume artist paint their face.

Ignore the newer venue just outside the park's east gate, which offers showings for very large tour groups. Buy tickets from the red ticket booth outside the park's east gate or either theatre.

Jīnjiāng Theatre
SÌCHUĀN OPERA

(锦江剧场; Jīnjiāng Jùchǎng; ☑ 028 8666 6891; 54 Huaxingzheng Jie; 华兴正街54号; tickets ¥150-280; ☉ 8-9.10pm) Mixed-performance shows are held daily at this renowned opera theatre. The adjoining Yuèlái Teahouse (悦来茶楼; Yuèlái Chálóu; 54 Huaxingzheng Jie; 华兴

正街54号; tea from ¥12, tickets for shows ¥20-40; ⊙8.30am-5pm), a local favourite, holds wonderfully informal performances on its small stage on Saturdays from 2pm to 4.30pm.

🛍 Shopping

Fancy-pants shopping centres dot the city with the highest concentration around **Chunxi Lu** (春熙路; Metro 2), the pedestrian street area east of Tianfu Sq.

On the south end of town sprawls the monstrous **New Century Global Center** (新世纪环球中心; Xīn Shìjì Huánqiú Zhōngxīn; ☑ 028 6273 2888; 1700 Tianfu Bei Dadao; Ⓜ1 to Jincheng Square), the world's largest mall with 511,000 sq metres of consumption possibilities, as well as a faux-seaside town complete with beach, waves and 24-hour sunshine.

For a more traditional option, try the small shops in the **Tibetan neighbourhood** (藏族用品一条街; Zàngzú Yòngpǐn Yītiáo Jiē) southeast of Wǔhóu Temple, which sell prayer flags, colourful scarves, beads and brass goods.

Sanfo OUTDOOR EQUIPMENT
(三夫户外; Sānfū Hùwài; www.sanfo.com; 243 Wuhouci Dajie; 武侯词大街243号; ⊙10am-8.30pm) Outdoor clothing and camping equipment are a brisk business in Chéngdū, as many people head to Tibet or the western mountains. Quality varies and fakes abound, but this place has good-quality gear. Another large branch is at **32 Renmin Nanlu** (人民南路32号) by Nijiaqiao metro station.

ℹ Information

MEDICAL SERVICES

Global Doctor Chéngdū Clinic (环球医生; Huánqiú Yīshēng; ☑ 028 8528 3660, 24hr helpline 139 8225 6966; www.globaldoctor. com.au; 2nd fl, 9-11 Lippo Tower, 62 Kehua Beilu; 科华北路62号力宝大厦2层9-11号; consultation ¥840, after-hours visit ¥1050, house call ¥1700; ⊙9am-6pm Mon-Fri) English- and Chinese-speaking doctors and a 24-hour emergency line.

West China Hospital SCU (四川大学华西医院; Sìchuān Dàxué Huáxī Yīyuàn; ☑24hr emergency assistance in Chinese & English ☑ 028 8542 2761, ☑ for appointment 028 8542 2408; http://eng.cd120.com; 37 Guoxue Xiang; 国学巷37号) This hospital complex is China's largest and is among the most well-regarded. Foreigners should head for the International Hospital, where doctors and some staff members speak English. Note, some treatments without qualifying insurance may require a deposit.

MONEY

Most ATMs accept foreign cards.

Bank of China (中国银行; Zhōngguó Yínháng; 35 Renmin Zhonglu, 2nd Section; 人民中路二段35号; ⊙8.30am-5.30pm Mon-Fri, to 5pm Sat & Sun) Changes money and travellers cheques, and offers cash advances on credit cards.

VISAS

Chéngdū Entry & Exit Service Centre (成都市出入境接待中心; Chéngdūshì Chūrùjìng Jiēdài Zhōngxīn; ☑ 028 8640 7067; www. chengdu.gov.cn; 2 Renmin Xilu; 人民西路2号; ⊙9am-noon & 1-5pm Mon-Fri, to 4pm Sat) Visa extensions (five working days), residence permits, and paperwork for lost passports on the 3rd floor. In the building behind the Mao statue's right hand.

TRAVEL AGENCIES

Skip the gazillion Chinese travel agencies around town and head to the travel desk at one of Chéngdū's many excellent hostels. You can book anything from Giant Panda Base visits to full-blown multiweek camping excursions across western Sìchuān into Tibet.

ℹ Getting There & Away

AIR

You can fly directly to Chéngdū Shuāngliú International Airport from nearly any other major Chinese city in less than three hours. There are also direct international flights from Amsterdam, Bangkok, Doha, Frankfurt, Kathmandu, Kuala Lumpur, London, Melbourne, Mumbai, San Francisco, Seoul, Singapore and Tokyo.

Many travellers fly from here to Lhasa (¥892 to ¥1286, prepare for palpable oxygen deprivation). Flights to destinations within Sìchuān include Kāngdìng (¥470 to ¥923), Jiǔzhàigōu (¥830 to ¥1239) and Dàochéng-Yàdīng (¥701 to ¥1468).

Many hostels can book tickets.

Air China Chéngdū Booking Office (国航世界中心; Guóháng Shìjiè Zhōngxīn; ☑nationwide bookings 95583; 1 Hangkong Lu; 人民南路四段航空路1号; ⊙8.30am-5.30pm) By Tongzilin metro station, on the north side of Hangkong Lu.

China Southern Airlines (中国南方航空; Zhōngguó Nánfāng Hángkōng; ☑ 028 8666 3618; www.csair.com; 45 Renmin Nanlu 4th Section, New Hope Tower, 15th fl; 人民南路四段45号新希望大厦15室; ⊙8.30am-5.30pm) Near Tongzilin metro station, just south of Hangkong Lu.

BUS

The main bus station for tourists is **Xīnnánmén** (南门汽车站; Xīnnánmén Qìchēzhàn; ⊙24hr) (officially the central tourist station, 旅游客运中心). Two other useful stations are Chádiànzi

(店子) and Běimén (北门). Be prepared to be dropped at any one of these (and other) bus stations when arriving in Chéngdū. If you end up at Shíyángchǎng bus station (石羊场公交站), local bus 28 (¥2) connects it to Xīnnánmén and Běimén bus stations, as well as the north train station. Buses also depart directly from the airport (双流客运站) for Lè Shān, Yǎ'ān, Yíbīn and Zìgòng.

Destinations from Xīnnánmén Station

Bamboo Sea ¥90 to ¥101, five hours, two daily (9.10am, 3.30pm)

Éméi Shān ¥41, 2½ hours, every 20 minutes from 6.40am to 7.20pm

Guǎnghàn (for Sānxīngduī) ¥14, two hours, two daily (8.30am, 3pm)

Hóngyǎ (for Liǔ Jiāng) ¥38, two hours, every 45 minutes from 7.40am to 5.40pm

Jiǔzhàigōu ¥128 to ¥138, 10 hours, six daily (from 7.10am to 8.40pm). Extra morning buses run in July and August. Note that these buses pass Sōngpān (eight hours), but you may have to pay the full fare even if you get off at Sōngpān.

Kāngdìng ¥117 to ¥127, seven hours, hourly from 7am to 2pm

Lè Shān ¥49, two hours, every 20 minutes from 7.20am to 7.35pm

Pínglè ¥20 to ¥24, two hours, approximately hourly from 8.10am to 6.20pm

Yǎ'ān (for Bìfēngxiá) ¥44, two hours, every 40 minutes from 7.30am to 7.30pm

Western Destinations from Chádiànzi Station

Dānbā ¥79, eight hours, one daily (6.30am). Weather permitting; often cancelled from January to April.

Sèdá ¥158, 15 hours, two daily (6.35am, 8am)

Sōngpān ¥86, seven hours, three daily (6.30am, 7.30am, 9.30am)

Destinations from Běimén Station

Lángzhōng ¥90 to ¥100, five hours, eight daily (8.30am to 3.30pm)

Yíbīn ¥80, four hours, two daily (9am, 3pm)

Zìgòng ¥60, three hours, departs when full from 7am to 7.20pm

TRAIN

Chéngdū's two main train stations are Chéngdū North Train Station (火车北站; huǒchē běizhàn) and the newer Chéngdū East Train Station (火车东站; huǒchē dōngzhàn), both of which connect directly to the metro.

Hotels, hostels and **CYTS** (中国青年旅行社; ☏ 028 6599 9955; www.cytstours.com; 63 Xiadong Dajie; 下东大街63号; ⏰ 8.30am-9pm) can book tickets, usually for a ¥5 fee.

Destinations from North Train Station

The north station ticket office is in the separate building on your right as you approach the station. Buy high-speed train tickets at the adjacent intercity trains ticket office (城际列车售票处; chéngjì lièchē shòupiàochù).

Chóngqìng (D class) 2nd/1st class ¥97/116, two hours, seven daily (7.41am to 7.11pm)

Éméi Town seat ¥24, 2½ hours, eight daily (6.40am to 7.39pm)

Kūnmíng seat/hard sleeper ¥139/247, 18 to 22 hours, six daily (8.42am to 7.04pm)

Lè Shān seat/hard sleeper ¥22/73, 2½ hours, two daily (6.40am, 5.55pm)

Lhasa hard/soft sleeper ¥689/1101, 43 hours, one daily (8.45pm)

Qīngchéng Shān (D class) seat ¥15, 45 minutes, six daily (9.01am to 8.44pm)

Xī'ān seat/hard sleeper ¥112/200, 13 to 17 hours, 11 daily (7.39am to 10.30pm)

Yíbīn seat/hard sleeper ¥51/102, six to 7½ hours, seven daily (8.30am to 11.37pm)

Zìgòng seat/hard sleeper ¥41/92, five hours, seven daily (8.31am to 11.48pm)

Destinations from East Train Station

Daily D-class trains depart from the east train station for the following:

Chóngqìng 2nd/1st class ¥97/116, two hours, frequently (7am to 8.53pm)

Wǔhàn 2nd/1st class ¥344/413, 10 hours, seven daily (7am to 10.07am)

ⓘ TRAVELLING INTO KHAM

For trips west into Kham, groups might consider booking an SUV (越野车; yuèyě chē) with a driver. Given the high cost of petrol and the challenging road conditions, rates are generally high, starting at ¥850 per day including tolls and petrol, but excluding food and sleeping costs for the driver. Add at least an additional ¥150 per day if the driver speaks English or Tibetan.

Most of Chéngdū's hotels and hostels can assist with finding a reliable, properly insured driver. Before embarking, settle on the itinerary, fee and what it covers, and what happens should the car break down or some other unpredictable, trip-altering problem arise.

ℹ Getting Around

TO/FROM THE AIRPORT

Shuāngliú Airport is 18km west of the city. **Airport shuttle buses** (机场大巴; Jīchǎng Dàbā; www.cdairport.com; ¥10; ☉ 6am-10pm, varies by route) cover four routes, reaching all corners of the city. Route 1 is the most direct to the city centre, stopping in front of the Jīnjiāng Hotel on Renmin Nanlu, from where you can catch the metro. Route 2 reaches the south train station (which also has a metro connection), and then stops frequently along Renmin Lu to the north train station.

A taxi will cost ¥70 to ¥90. Most guesthouses offer airport pick-up services for slightly more.

BICYCLE

Chéngdū is nice and flat with designated biking lanes, although the traffic can be a strain on cyclists. Youth hostels rent out bikes for around ¥20 per day. Always lock it up.

BUS

You can get almost anywhere in Chéngdū by bus, as long as you can decipher the labyrinthine routes. Stops are marked in Chinese and English and some post route maps. Fares within the city are usually ¥2.

Useful routes:

Bus 1 City centre–Běimén bus station–Wǔhóu Temple

Bus 28 Shíyángchǎng bus station–Xīnnánmén bus station–Běimén bus station–north train station

Bus 16 North train station–Renmin Lus–South train station

Bus 82 Chádiànzi bus station–Jīnshā Site Museum (stop is 青羊大道口站)–Wǔhóu Temple–Xīnnánmén bus station

Bus 81 Mao statue–Qīngyáng Temple

Bus 69 North train station bus station–Zhāojué Sì bus station

Tourist Bus 87 Zhāojué Sì bus station–Giant Panda Breeding Research Base

Tourist Bus 60 Traffic Inn–Giant Panda Breeding Research Base

METRO

Line 1 links the north and south train stations, running the length of Renmin Lu and beyond. East–west running Line 2 links Chéngdū East Train Station with the city centre, meeting Line 1 at Tianfu Sq before continuing west to Chádiànzì bus station.

Line 3, which will run to the Giant Panda Breeding Research Base and Xīnnánmén bus station, and Line 4, for the new Chéngdū West Train Station, will be completed in 2015.

Rides cost ¥2 to ¥6 depending on the distance covered. Stations have bilingual signs, maps and ticket machines.

TAXI

Taxis are ¥8 (¥9 from 11pm to 6am) for the first 2km, then ¥1.90 (¥2.20 at night) per kilometre thereafter.

Around Chéngdū

Sānxīngduī   三星堆

The **Sānxīngduī Museum** (三星堆博物馆; Sānxīngduī Bówùguǎn; ☑ 028 565 1526; www.sxd.cn; 133 Xi'an Lu, Guǎnghàn; admission ¥80, audio guide ¥10; ☉ 8.30am-6pm, last entry 5pm), 40km north of Chéngdū in Guǎnghàn (广汉), exhibits relics of the Shu kingdom, a cradle of Chinese civilisation dating from 1200 BC to 1100 BC. Some archaeologists regard these artefacts, which include stunningly crafted, angular and stylised bronze masks, as even more important than Xī'ān's Terracotta Warriors. Art and archaeology buffs will need at least a half day here.

Throughout the 20th century, farmers around Guǎnghàn continually unearthed intriguing pottery shards and dirt-encrusted jade carvings when digging wells and tilling their fields. However, war and lack of funds prevented anyone from investigating these finds. Finally, in 1986, archaeologists launched a full-scale excavation and made a startling discovery when they unearthed the site of a major city dating back to the neolithic age in the upper reaches of the Yangzi River (Cháng Jiāng). It was previously believed that the oldest civilisations were concentrated around the Yellow River (Huáng Hé).

Buses to the site depart Chéngdū's Xīnnánmén bus station (¥15, 1½ hours, six daily, from 8.30am to 3pm). Alternatively, buses from Chéngdū's Zhāojué Sì station (¥12, 1½ hours, 7am to 8pm) head to Guǎnghàn's tourist bus station (广汉客运中心); from there, transfer to local bus 6 (¥2, from 7am to 6pm) for the remaining 10km to the site.

A bus from the site back to Zhāojué Sì station (7km northeast of Chéngdū centre) leaves at 4.10pm; otherwise buses depart the tourist bus station for Xīnnánmén every 10 minutes (¥16, from 6.40am to 6.50pm).

Dūjiāngyàn   都江堰

Two Unesco World Heritage Sites in Dūjiāngyàn, 60km northwest of Chéngdū, make for separate, very full day trips.

◉ Sights

Dūjiāngyàn Irrigation Project   HISTORIC SITE

(都江堰水利工程; Dūjiāngyàn Shuǐlì Gōngchéng; admission ¥90, shuttle to Yùlěi Pavilion ¥10; ⊙8am-6pm) This system of channels, floodgates and weirs, constructed in the 3rd century BC, is the oldest and only surviving non-dam irrigation system in the world. Still in use, this feat of engineering is in a beautifully scenic area with forested hills, ancient temples, hilltop pagodas and coursing waters.

To tame the devastating floods caused by the fast-flowing Mín Jiāng, the region's magistrate Li Bing set a crew of tens of thousands to work. Using sausage-shaped bamboo baskets filled with stones they reshaped the river bends and also cut a 20m-wide channel through Yùlěi Shān. Since gunpowder had yet to be invented, they used fire and water to crack the mountain's hard rock.

Numerous teahouses and restaurants on either side of the decorative South Bridge (南桥; Nán Qiáo), near the park entrance, are good for a bite.

Every 5 April, catch elaborately costumed re-enactments of the building process, ceremonial sacrifices, and elegies sung to Li Bing at the Water Releasing Festival.

Qīngchéng Shān   MOUNTAIN

(青城山; Azure City Mountain; Dūjiāngyàn; admission ¥90) Covered in lush, dripping forests, the sacred mountain of Qīngchéng Shān has been a Taoist spiritual centre for more than 2000 years. Its beautiful trails are lined with ginkgo, plum and palm, and there are caves, pavilions and centuries-old wooden temples to explore.

Visitors can experience two sides of the mountain. The main entrance is on the mountain's front side (前山, Qián Shān), and leads to paths that wind past 11 important Taoist sites. Those interested in hiking will prefer the back entrance (后山, Hòu Shān), accessed 15km northwest. In either case, to actually enjoy the views, avoid major holidays when hordes of tourists arrive to pay tribute to their ancestors.

➡ Qián Shān

The trails here lead to a summit of only 1600m, a relatively easy climb — four hours up and down, even easier via the cable car (one way/return ¥35/60). Snack stands are scattered along the mountain trails.

If you want to stay the night, a few temples on Qián Shān welcome guests, including the fabulous Shàngqīng Temple (上清宫; Shàngqīng Gōng; r from ¥50), a Qing-dynasty rebuild of the original Jin-dynasty temple set in the forest near the top of the mountain; it has a restaurant (dishes ¥18 to ¥45) and teahouse (tea from ¥5). The cheapest rooms are reserved for pilgrims, but you may be able to land one if business is slow.

➡ Hòu Shān

The back of the mountain has 20km of rugged pathways – expect a six-hour hike to the summit, where you'll find Báiyún Temple (白云寺, Báiyún Sì); the cable car (¥30) will shave a couple of hours off the hike. You can find basic guesthouses (客栈, kèzhàn) at both Yòuyī Village (又一村, Yòuyī Cūn), less than halfway up the mountain, and near the top at Báiyún Ancient Village (白云古寨; Báiyún Gǔzhài).

❶ Getting There & Away

There are two separate high-speed rail routes from Chéngdū's north train station to the Dūjiāngyàn sites.

For the Dūjiāngyàn Irrigation Project, take an early train to Líduī (离堆公园; Líduī Gōngyuán; ¥15, 40 minutes, 6.30am, 8.32am and 11.12am); from there, take bus 4 (¥2, 15 minutes) to the last stop (离堆公园; Líduī Gōngyuán).

For Qīngchéng Shān, take the train to Qīngchéng Shān (¥15, 45 minutes, 6.53am, 7.29am, 9.01am, 10.45am, 11.45am and 12.51am). Don't get off at the stop before this, which is confusingly called Dūjiāngyàn. Pick up bus 101 (¥2, 10 minutes) to the main gate (Qián Shān), or take a tourist bus (中巴车; ¥10, 35 minutes) to Hòu Shān. Tourist buses leave when full and pass the main gate en route, but only stop for passengers if there are spare seats.

Bus 101 (¥2, 40 minutes) also connects the Líduī stop with Qīngchéng Shān's main gate.

The last trains back to Chéngdū depart at 10.56pm from Líduī and 9.45pm from Qīngchéng Shān.

Yǎ'ān   雅安

Established in prime forest in Yǎ'ān in 2003 for research purposes rather than tourism, the mission of the Yǎ'ān Bìfēngxiá Panda Base (雅安碧峰峡大熊猫基地; Bìfēngxiá Dàxióngmāo Jīdì; ☑083 5231 8145; www.china-panda.org.cn; admission ¥118, shuttle ¥15; ⊙8.30-11.30am & 1.30-4.30pm, kindergarten feeding 3.20pm) expanded in 2008, following the earthquake that severely damaged its sister reserve, Wòlóng (卧龙自然保护区; Wòlóng Zìrán Bǎohùqū). Though Wòlóng continues to do ground-breaking work, it is closed indefinitely to the public. Bìfēngxiá is now home to 80 pandas, some of which may someday be returned to the wild.

It's a treat to glimpse any one of the 1600 surviving pandas in the world, but with bustling Chéngdū 150km east, you can get a real sense of their natural habitat here. Cubs in the 'panda kindergarten' climb high into the trees in their reasonably pleasant enclosures. Humans can hike along a forested river gorge with waterfalls and stunning scenery surrounding the main attraction.

The panda centre is 3km from the ticket office in the main car park where the minibus drops its passengers. Turn left out of the ticket office then take the free lift (请云梯; qǐngyúntī) 50 storeys down to the foot of the gorge. From here you can walk on to catch the free bus or cross the bridge to hike. On foot, it takes about two hours to reach the centre, slightly longer if you picnic or stop at snack stalls along the way. (Skip the regular zoo nearby.)

You can enjoy Bǐfēngxiá as an easy day trip from Chéngdū or stay longer for the **volunteer program** (www.pandaclub.cn). Those aged 12 and up can sign on for a minimum one day of work (with time to explore the park) sweeping pens, prepping food and even feeding the pandas. The cost is ¥200 per day, plus a one-time ¥150 uniform fee, and volunteers must cover their own costs such as food, lodging and park entry.

Those staying overnight can sleep in the park at **Xiǎoxītiān Mínlǚcūn** (小西天民旅村; ☏ 135 5155 6417; r without/with sit-down toilet ¥80/100; ✸🛈), a basic guesthouse at the end of the gorge hike just before you reach the panda centre. A handful of guesthouses and restaurants are also by the entrance.

🛈 Getting There & Around

Buses from Chéngdū (¥114) terminate at Yǎ'ān's Xīmén bus station (西门车站; xīmén chēzhàn), but for Bǐfēngxiá, get off before this at the tourist bus station (旅游车站; lǚyóu chēzhàn), where minibuses (¥5) wait to take you the final 18km to the Panda Base. The last bus back to Chéngdū from the tourist bus station leaves at 6.30pm.

From Yǎ'ān's Xīmén bus station, you can head on to various other destinations:

Éméi Town ¥50, 2½ hours, four daily (8.30am, 10am, 12.10pm, 2pm)

Kāngdìng ¥100, 4½ hours, three daily (8am, 10am, 1pm)

Lè Shān ¥55, 2½ hours, seven daily (8.30am to 6pm)

A pedicab between Yǎ'ān's two bus stations costs ¥8.

Liǔ Jiāng   柳江

The charming pastoral setting is the main attraction of this riverside village nestled in central Sìchuān's countryside. The **old town** (古镇; gǔzhèn), with its narrow alleyways, wooden courtyard buildings and ancient banyan trees, straddles both sides of the Yángcūn River (杨村河; Yángcūn Hé) in a picture-perfect scene. For now at least, the reconstruction and sales tactics remain more palatable here than in other 'fixed-up' old towns.

This is a great spot for a lazy lunch or a dip in the river. If you want to stay the night, near the plank bridge (板板桥), the century-old **Wàngjiāng Kèzhàn** (望江客栈; ☏ 159 8432 8196; 38 Liujiang Jie; 柳江街38号; r ¥60-80) has creaky wooden floorboards and simple rooms with shared bathrooms and river views. You can have tea (from ¥20) or locally grown dishes (¥10 to ¥50) on the pleasant terrace. Downriver by the jumping stones (跳磴桥), **Shuǐ Mù Shí Kōng** (水木时空; ☏ 028 3752 7789; s/d ¥140/160; ✸🛈) offers slightly more upscale rooms with river views.

There's some excellent walking to be done in the surrounding countryside. Look for wooden signboards in the old town with maps in Chinese of walking trails. One option is the 3.5km uphill hike to **Hóujiā Shānzhài** (侯家山寨), marked by a wooden archway off the main driving road on the opposite side of the river from where the buses drop off. Once you've found that, follow the road up. Near the top is **Tiàowàng Wǎwū** (眺望瓦屋; ☏ 130 8838 1221; 两河4号，柳江镇; r ¥100, meals ¥20-80), a renovated courtyard guesthouse, run by the friendly Liu family, with simple rooms and fabulous views. They'll feed you tea and noodle (面; miàn) or rice (饭; fàn) dishes all made from ingredients grown in their hillside gardens. A minibus from the old town is about ¥30.

To reach Liǔ Jiāng, take a bus from Chéngdū's Xīnnánmén bus station to Hóngyǎ (洪雅; ¥60, 2½ hours, every half hour from 5.30am to 6pm), then change for Liǔ Jiāng (¥9, 45 minutes, every 15 minutes until 5.30pm). The last bus from Hóngyǎ to Chéngdū is at 5pm. There are also regular buses from Hóngyǎ to Éméi Shān, Lè Shān and Yǎ'ān.

Émči Shān 峨眉山

0833

A cool, misty retreat from Sìchuān basin's usual heat, stunning 3099m Émči Shān (峨眉山; 028 552 3646; adult/student & senior ¥185/90, winter ¥110/55; 6am-6pm) is one of China's four sacred Buddhist Mountains (the others being Pǔtuó Shān, Wǔtái Shān and Jiǔhuá Shān). A farmer built the first Buddhist temple near its summit in the 1st century CE, marking Buddhism's arrival in the Eastern world.

Later adorned with brass tiling engraved with Tibetan script and, in 1614, named Huázáng Temple (华藏寺), that first temple stood at Jīn Dǐng until it was gutted by fire in 1972. It was restored in 1989. Many of the more than 150 temples on the mountain suffered similar fates, or were looted, over the centuries. Some 30 have been maintained and restored in various degrees over the years. Wànnián Temple, the oldest surviving temple, clocks in at a respectable 1100 years.

In addition to its rich cultural heritage, the mountain stands on the edge of the eastern Himalayan highlands and is home to a diverse range of plants and animals. Together with nearby Lè Shān, Émči Shān is on Unesco's list of World Heritage Sites.

The entry ticket gives you access to most sites on the mountain but does not include rides on the three buses to the main routes up. Most rewarding is walking the whole way, starting from Bàoguó Temple, but most opt to ride to Wànnián depot, because of its easy access to the **cable car** (¥65 up, ¥45 to ¥55 down; 6am to 6pm), or to Wǔxiǎngǎng depot, which is an easy walk to poetic Qīngyīn Pavilion and other important sights. The Léidòngpíng bus drops off closest to the summit. Regardless of your starting point, getting a feel for the place takes at least a full day, ideally two. Wander the wooden temples, meet the macaques demanding tribute for safe passage, then find shelter in a monastery guesthouse and wake up in time to welcome the sun. The early morning light refracting in the cool mist has been heralded since ancient times as Buddha's Halo.

When to Go

The best time to visit is June to October, when the mist burns off by early afternoon. Epic crowds arrive in July and August. Avoid national holidays, of course.

Snowfall generally begins around November on the upper slopes. In winter you can rent crampons to deal with ice and snow. Expect rain and mist throughout the year.

Average temperatures:

	JAN	APR	JUL	OCT
Émči town	7°C	21°C	26°C	17°C
Summit	-6°C	4°C	12°C	4°C

◉ Sights

Bàoguó Temple BUDDHIST MONASTERY

(报国寺; Bàoguó Sì; Declare Nation Temple; admission ¥8; 7am-7.30pm) Constructed in the 16th century, this temple (550m) features beautiful gardens of rare plants, as well as a 3.5m-high porcelain Buddha dating back to 1415, which is housed near the Sutra Library. This is not included in the Émči Shān entrance ticket. You can stay in a basic guesthouse (p736) or the five-star hotel on the premises.

Fúhǔ Temple BUDDHIST MONASTERY

(伏虎寺; Fúhǔ Sì; Crouching Tiger Monastery; admission ¥6) Located about 1km from Bàoguó Temple, Fúhǔ Temple (630m) is hidden deep within the forest. It houses a 7m-high copper pagoda inscribed with Buddhist images and texts. Not included in the Émči Shān entrance ticket.

Xiānfēng Temple BUDDHIST MONASTERY

(仙峰寺; Xiānfēng Sì; Immortal Peak Monastery) Somewhat off the beaten track, this carefully tended monastery (1752m) is backed by rugged cliffs and surrounded by fantastic scenery.

Qīngyīn Pavilion BUDDHIST TEMPLE

(清音阁; Qīngyīn Gé) Named 'Pure Sound Pavilion' after the soothing sounds of the waters coursing around rock formations, this temple (710m) is built on an outcrop in the middle of a fast-flowing stream. Rest in one of the small pavilions here while you appreciate the natural 'music'.

Monkey Zone WILDLIFE RESERVE

Between Qīngyīn Pavilion and Hóngchūn Píng (Venerable Trees Terrace) you will encounter the mountain's infamous monkeys. Unfortunately, those before you have teased this merry band into grabby monsters. Rangers are usually on hand to help if things get out of hand, but avoid extended eye contact (a sign of aggression), put away any food and drinks when approaching, and keep bags closed.

Émei Shān

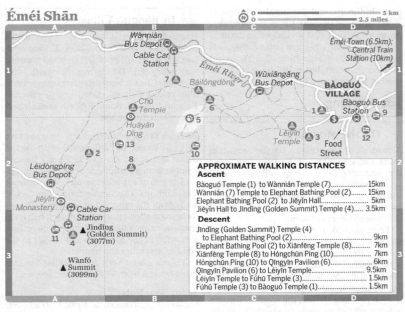

APPROXIMATE WALKING DISTANCES
Ascent

Bàoguó Temple (1) to Wànnián Temple (7)	15km
Wànnián (7) Temple to Elephant Bathing Pool (2)	15km
Elephant Bathing Pool (2) to Jiēyǐn Hall	5km
Jiēyǐn Hall to Jīndǐng (Golden Summit) Temple (4)	3.5km

Descent

Jīndǐng (Golden Summit) Temple (4) to Elephant Bathing Pool (2)	9km
Elephant Bathing Pool (2) to Xiānfēng Temple (8)	7km
Xiānfēng Temple (8) to Hóngchūn Píng (10)	7km
Hóngchūn Píng (10) to Qīngyīn Pavilion (6)	6km
Qīngyīn Pavilion (6) to Léiyīn Temple	9.5km
Léiyīn Temple to Fúhǔ Temple (3)	1.5km
Fúhǔ Temple (3) to Bàoguó Temple (1)	1.5km

Émei Shān

◎ Sights

1	Bàoguó Temple	D1
2	Elephant Bathing Pool	A2
3	Fúhǔ Temple	D2
4	Jīndǐng (Golden Summit) Temple	A3
5	Monkey Zone	B2
6	Qīngyīn Pavilion	C1
7	Wànnián Temple	B1
8	Xiānfēng Temple	B2

⊜ Sleeping

	Bàoguó Temple Guesthouse	(see 1)
9	Happy Hotel	D1
10	Hóngchūn Píng	B2
11	Jīndǐng Dàjiǔdiàn	A3
12	Teddy Bear Hotel	D2
	Xiānfēng Temple	(see 8)
13	Yùxiān Temple	B2

Wànnián Temple   BUDDHIST MONASTERY
(万年寺; Wànnián Sì; Long Life Monastery; admission ¥10) Reconstructed in the 9th century, Wànnián Temple (1020m) is the oldest surviving Émei temple. It's dedicated to the man on the white elephant, the Bodhisattva Puxian (also known as Samantabhadra), the Buddhist Lord of Truth and patron of the mountain. This 8.5m-high statue cast in copper and bronze dates from AD 980 and weighs an estimated 62,000kg. If you can manage to rub the elephant's hind leg, good luck will be cast upon you.

The statue is housed in Brick Hall, a domed building with small stupas on it – it was the only building left unharmed in a 1945 fire.

Elephant Bathing Pool   BUDDHIST MONASTERY
(洗象池; Xǐxiàng Chí) According to legend, Elephant Bathing Pool (2070m) is where Puxian flew his elephant in for a nice scrub, but today there's not much of a pool to speak of. Being almost at the crossroads of both major trails, the temple here is sometimes crowded with pilgrims.

Jīndǐng (Golden Summit)
Temple   BUDDHIST TEMPLE
(金顶寺; Jīndǐng Sì) This magnificent temple is at the **Golden Summit** (Jīn Dǐng; 3077m), commonly referred to as the mountain's highest peak. The temple is a striking modern renovation, covered with glazed tiles and surrounded by white marble balustrades. In front, the prominent 48m-tall golden statue

of multidimensional Samantabhadra (十方普贤; Shífāng Pǔxián) honours mountain protector Puxian, and was added in 2006.

The mountain's highest point (3099m) is actually nearby Wànfó Dǐng (Ten Thousand Buddha Summit), but it has been closed to visitors for some years now.

🛏 Sleeping

🛏 On the Mountain

Almost all of the temples on the mountain (with the exception of Jīndǐng Temple at the summit) offer cheap dormitory-style accommodation with shared bathrooms but usually no showers. Some also have guesthouse-quality private rooms with private bathrooms for a premium.

There are also standard hotels on the mountain, mostly by the **cable car stations**. **Jīndǐng Dàjiǔdiàn** (金顶大酒店; ☑0833 509 8088, 0833 509 8077; r from ¥980, discounted to ¥780; ❋🛜) is to the right of the Jīn Dǐng cable car exit and is a convenient launch pad for catching the sunrise. You can reach it on foot in about 9½ hours from the base of the mountain or 30 minutes from the summit.

Xiānfēng Temple MONASTERY $
(仙峰寺; Xiānfēng Sì; ☑189 8131 0142; dm & tw without bathroom ¥50-240, tw with bathroom ¥600; 🛜) This remote temple hidden in a forest backed by rugged cliffs has a good range of rooms, from dorms to pricey twins with showers. There's even wi-fi in the common space. Approximate walking time from base/summit is about six/four hours.

Hóngchún Píng MONASTERY $
(洪椿坪; ☑083 3509 9043; dm ¥50, tw ¥60-130; 🛜) The smartest temple accommodation on the mountain is at a comfortable 1120m. Rooms are simple, with wi-fi and shared bathrooms. Approximate walking time from base/summit is three/six hours.

Yùxiān Temple MONASTERY $
(遇仙寺; Yùxiān Sì; dm/tw from ¥50/240) At 1680m the views from this small temple are stunning. Choose from basic dorms to private twins. It is very remote here, which can either feel glorious or eerie, depending on your travel style. Approximate walking time from base/summit is seven/three hours.

🛏 In Bàoguó Village

Happy Hotel HOTEL $
(幸福树酒店; Xìngfú Shù Jiǔdiàn; 31 Bàoguó Village, 4th group, 报国村4组31号; r incl breakfast from ¥188; 🛜) This straightforward, very tidy hotel has a surprisingly good, reasonably priced Chinese restaurant (a rarity in Bàoguó Village). Some English spoken and there's bike rental, too.

Bàoguó Temple Guesthouse MONASTERY $
(报国寺; Bàoguó Sì; ☑0833 559 2822; Declare Nation Temple; dm ¥15-30, r ¥200; ❋) Bàoguó Temple is an atmospheric and accessible option if you want a monastery stay without the climb up. The simple rooms are tucked away from the crowded public areas. There's a common shower area and dining hall (vegetarian meals ¥10). Check in (Chinese spoken only) at the guest counter (客堂) to the right as you enter the temple.

There's also a very un-Buddhist five-star hotel (rooms from ¥1300) on the premises.

Teddy Bear Hotel HOSTEL $$
(玩具熊酒店; Wánjùxióng Jiǔdiàn; ☑0833 559 0135; manager 138 9068 1961; www.teddybear.com.cn; 43 Baoguo Lu, next to bus station; dm ¥40, r ¥80-260; ❋@🛜) If you can get past the theme (bears, bears, everywhere), this very clean backpacker hotel offers nice rooms and English-speaking staff that provides solid, hostel-style travel services plus decent coffee and Western food. The left-luggage service is free, as are walking sticks, crampons, maps and pick-up from Éméi town (call Andy, the manager). You can even indulge in an in-room massage (50 minutes for ¥60) when you make it back down the mountain. For a good night's sleep, avoid rooms overlooking the Bàoguó bus station next door and perhaps shell out for the downright sumptuous, Chinese-themed rooms on the 4th floor.

🍴 Eating

On the mountain, most temples have small dining halls, and you're never very far from a trailside food stall selling simple dishes, instant noodles (方便面; fāngbiàn miàn), tea and snacks. In Bàoguó Village, restaurants and supermarkets abound. **Haochi Jie** (好吃街; Food St) is crammed with places to eat, many with outdoor seating. The menus contain various Sichuanese dishes (¥15 to ¥40) and have English translations.

ℹ Information

Agricultural Bank of China (农业银行; Nóngyè Yínháng; ⊙9am-5pm) Has a foreign-exchange desk and a foreign-card–friendly ATM. The ATM by Bàoguó bus station also accepts foreign cards.

ℹ Getting There & Away

The town of Éméi (峨眉山市; Éméi Shān Shì) is the transport hub and lies 6.5km east of the park entrance. Most buses terminate at Éméi Shān central station (峨眉山客运中心; Éméi Shān kèyùn zhōngxīn), directly opposite Éméi Railway Station (峨眉火车站; Éméi Huǒchēzhàn). If you ask, some drivers will go all the way to the more convenient Bàoguó Village bus station (报国汽车站) – which confusingly is also known as the Éméi Shān tourist bus station (峨眉山旅游客运中心; Éméi Shān lǚyóu kèyùn zhōngxīn) – for ¥10 more.

A taxi from Éméi Town to Bàoguó Village is about ¥25. Many guesthouses will pick you up if you arrange it with them in advance. Local bus 8 (¥1) connects the Éméi Town station with the park entrance.

BUS

While it's not possible to travel directly to Bàoguó from most long-distance destinations, some long-distance buses do leave from Bàoguó:

Chéngdū ¥50, 2½ hours, frequent services from 8am to 6pm

Chóngqìng ¥140, six hours, 8.30am

Lè Shān ¥11, 45 minutes, every 20 minutes from 8am to 5pm

Buses from Éméi Shān central station to:

Kāngdìng ¥120, seven hours, 9.50am

Yǎ'ān ¥51, three hours, four daily (7.45am, 9.30am, 12.30pm and 2.20pm)

Zìgòng ¥51, three hours, frequently from 7.40am to 5.10pm

TRAIN

Chéngdū K ¥24, 2½ hours, seven daily (3.16am to 10.25am, then 6.36pm and 9.15pm)

Kūnmíng K seat/hard sleeper ¥124/223, 17 hours, four daily (3.23pm, 4.37pm, 5.19pm and 9.42pm)

Lè Shān K ¥8, 16 minutes, three daily (7.27am, 10.25am and 6.36pm)

Xī'ān K hard/soft sleeper ¥231/364, 20 hours, 10.25am

ℹ Getting Around

Buses from **Bàoguó bus station** travel to three depots on the mountain: Wǔxiǎngǎng (五显冈; 30 minutes, round trip ¥40), about a 20-minute walk below Qīngyīn Pavilion; Wànnián (万年; 45

minutes; round trip ¥40), below Wànnián Temple; and Léidòngpíng (雷洞坪; 1½ hours, round trip ¥90), a few minutes' walk from Jīn Dǐng cable car. If you return via a different depot, you may have to pay a small surcharge.

Buses run frequently from around 6am to 5pm (7am to 4pm in winter). The last buses head down the mountain at 6pm (5pm in winter).

Lè Shān 乐山

☑ 0833 / POP 678,752

With fingernails bigger than the average human, the world's largest ancient Buddha draws plenty of tourists to this relaxed riverside town. This Unesco World Heritage Site is an easy day trip from Chéngdū or stopover en route to or from Éméi Shān.

◉ Sights

Grand Buddha BUDDHIST STATUE

(大佛; Dàfó; adult ¥90, student & senior ¥50; ⊙7.30am-6.30pm Apr-early Oct, 8am-5.30pm early Oct-Mar) Lè Shān's serene, 1200-year-old Grand Buddha sits in repose, carved from a cliff face overlooking the confluence of three busy rivers: the Dàdù, Mín and Qīngyì. The Buddhist monk Haitong conceived the project in AD 713, hoping that Buddha would protect the boats and calm the lethal currents.

It was 90 years after Haitong's death that the project was completed, but afterwards the river waters obeyed. Believers credited Buddha's grace; cynics pointed to the construction process, in which piles of surplus rocks reshaped the rivers and changed the currents.

At 71m tall, he is indeed grand. His shoulders span 28m, and each of his big toes is 8.5m long. His ears are 7m. Their length symbolises wisdom and the conscious abandonment of materialism. It is said that heavy gold baubles left Siddartha's earlobes elongated even after he was no longer weighed down by material things.

Inside the body, hidden from view, is a water-drainage system to prevent weathering, although the statues is showing its age and soil erosion is an ongoing problem.

To fully appreciate this Buddha's magnitude, get an up-close look at his head, then descend the steep, winding stairway for the Lilliputian view. Avoid visiting on weekends and holidays, when traffic on the staircase can come to a complete standstill.

Admission also includes access to a number of caves and temples on the grounds, though they are a decent hike from the main attraction. **Máhàoyá Tombs Museum** (麻

Lè Shān

Lè Shān

◎ Sights

⊙ Activities, Courses & Tours

⊜ Sleeping

⊗ Eating

浩崖墓博物馆; Máhàoyámù Bówùguǎn) has a modest collection of tombs and burial artefacts dating from the Eastern Han dynasty

(AD 25–220). **Wūyóu Temple** (乌尤寺; Wūyóu Sì), like the Buddha, dates from the Tang dynasty, and has Ming and Qing renovations. This monastery contains calligraphy and artefacts, with the highlights in the Luóhàn Hall – 1000 terracotta *arhat* (Buddhist celestial beings, similar to angels) displaying an incredible variety of postures and facial expressions – no two are alike. Also inside is a fantastic statue of Avalokiteshvara (Guanyin), the Goddess of Mercy.

A separate park (not included in the Grand Buddha admission), the **Oriental Buddha Capital** (东方佛都; Dōngfāng Fódū; admission ¥80; ◻3, 13), houses a collection of 3000 Buddha statues and figurines from across Asia, including a 170m-long reclining Buddha, one of the world's longest. There is an entrance near the Grand Buddha's South Gate; otherwise exit and take bus 3 or 13 (¥1) to the Oriental Buddha Capital (东方佛都, Dōngfāng Fódū) stop. The entrance is further than it looks on the park maps.

⟨F⟩ Tours

Tour boats (游船; yóuchuán; 20-minute round trip ¥70, kids under 12 free; ⊙7.30am-6.30pm Apr-Oct, from 8am winter) leave regularly from **Lè Shān dock** (乐山港; Lè Shān gǎng), passing by the cliffs for views of Dàfó, revealing two guardians in the cliff side that are not visible from land. The ride is short and otherwise unexciting.

Mr Yang TOURS

(☑0833 211 2046, 159 8438 2528; richardyang-min@163.com; 186 Baita Jie, 2nd fl, Apt 1; per person ¥200) Affable Mr Yang has been guiding foreign tourists around Lè Shān since the 1970s. His hearing is going but his expertise is not. Email him to make arrangements. His signature half-day tour includes a calligraphy demonstration, an old-town stroll and a visit to a villager's home. Transport, lunch and his services as an English-speaking guide are included. He can also book tickets.

🛏 Sleeping

The choices in town, unfortunately, are mostly large hotels devoid of personality and priced for tourists. Stay in Éméi Shān, if you can.

Jiāzhōu Hotel HOTEL **$$**

(嘉州宾馆; Jiāzhōu Bīnguǎn; ☑0833 213 9888; 85 Baita Jie; 白塔街85号; r incl breakfast from ¥360; ❋❀🐾) Rooms aren't as grand as the lobby suggests, but this place is more upmarket than most and makes for a comfortable stay. Even some of the cheaper rooms have river views.

Jīntáoyuán Dàjiǔdiàn HOTEL $$
(金桃源大酒店; ☑ 0833 210 7666; 136 Binjiang Lu; 滨江路南段136号; d ¥158-218; ✳@🕸) Smart, clean and across the street from the river. The river-view rooms are a good deal at ¥188. No English sign.

🍴 Eating

The best food by day and night is found on the streets. Stalls also line the riverbank, but to eat like a local, head to Baita Jie (白塔街) where you can try all manner of simmering stews (沙锅; *shāguō*; from ¥18), or gorge on cool yet spicy *bàng bàng chicken* (棒棒鸡; *bàng bàng jī*; from ¥20). Zhanggong Qiao Jie (张公桥街) has a small night market and many restaurants to choose from.

Zhao Family Crispy Duck BARBECUE $
(赵记油烫甜皮鸭; ☑ 0833 211 4196; 169 Xincun Jie & Renmin Nanlu; 新村街169号(人民南路与新村街交界处); meal ¥20; ⊙10am-6pm) Foodies flock to this tiny barbecue stand for its speciality – sweet, crispy roast duck (*jīn* ¥22). The draw is the skin, which is best described as duck candy, a miraculously ungreasy bite of heaven. Eat it while it's hot – in the middle of the sidewalk with your bare hands, if necessary. Look for the sign 'Zhaoyazi, 赵鸭子'.

Xiàogōngzuǐ Bàbā SICHUANESE $
(肖公嘴巴吧; Binhe Lu; 滨河路; mains from ¥15; ⊙9am-midnight; 🎐) One of a cluster of cafe-restaurants with terrace seating on the riverbank, this place is perfect for tea (from ¥15) or fresh coffee (from ¥25) during the day, or a riverside beer (from ¥10) come evening. Choose from barbecue skewers (from ¥1.5) and Sichuanese main courses. To get to the riverbank, walk down the steps from the road.

ℹ️ Information

People's Hospital (人民医院; Rénmín Yīyuàn; ☑ 0833 211 9310, after-hours emergencies 0833 211 9328; www.leshan-hospital.com.cn; 222 Baita Jie) Has some English-speaking doctors. Pharmacies cluster around the entrance.
Public Security Bureau (PSB; 省公安厅外事科; Gōng'ānjú; ☑ 0833 518 2555; http://lsscrj. gotoip1.com; 548 Fenghuang Lu Zhongduan, 3rd fl; 凤凰路中段548号; ⊙9am-noon & 1-5pm Mon-Fri) Visa extensions in five days. Take bus 6 (¥1) from the centre.

ℹ️ Getting There & Away

BUS

Lè Shān has three main bus stations, all within 5km of each other. Buses from Chéngdū's Xīnnánmén station usually arrive at Xiàobà bus station (肖坝车站; Xiàobà chēzhàn), the main tourist station. The central bus station (乐山客运中心车站; Lè Shān kèyùn zhōngxīn chēzhàn) and Liányùn bus station (联运车站; Liányùn chēzhàn) are also useful.

Note, if you're heading to Éméi Shān, it's a better option to use Xiàobà bus station, as buses from there go all the way to Bàoguó station (¥11, 45 minutes, every 30 minutes from 7.30am to 5pm).

Other services from Xiàobà bus station include:

Chéngdū ¥47, two hours, every 30 minutes from 7am to 7pm
Chóngqìng ¥138, six hours, 10.40am
Éméi town ¥8, 30 minutes, every 30 minutes from 7.30am to 6pm
Yǎ'ān ¥54, 2½ hours (9.50am, 2pm and 4.10pm)
Zìgòng ¥42, three hours, hourly from 8.30am to 5.10pm

TRAIN

The new 37-minute high-speed rail link from Chéngdū to Lè Shān may be ready by the time you read this.

ℹ️ Getting Around

BUS

Local buses cost ¥1. Some handy routes:
Bus 13 Xiàobà bus station–town centre–Oriental Buddha Capital–Grand Buddha–Wūyóu Temple
Bus 1 Xiàobà bus station–Jiāzhōu Hotel–town centre–Liányùn bus station
Bus 6 Xiàobà bus station–town centre–Public Security Bureau
Bus 9 Central bus station–town centre–Lè Shān dock

SOUTHERN SÌCHUĀN

Not often on the radar of foreign tourists, steamy southern Sìchuān is for those who enjoy digging into history. There are dinosaur fossils, ancient cliff-face hanging coffins, and lush bamboo forests to explore. It's also home to some stellar teahouses.

Zìgòng 自贡

📞 0813 / POP 666,204

This intriguing riverside city has been an important centre of Chinese salt production for almost 2000 years. Remnants of that industry make up part of an unconventional list of sights that includes the world's deepest traditional salt well and Asia's first dinosaur museum. Zìgòng is also the undisputed king of Sìchuān teahouses, so there's plenty of opportunity to just put your feet up for a day.

◎ Sights

Zìgòng has exploded into a sprawling city, but travellers will spend most of their time in the ancient district on the north side of the Fǔxī River (釜溪河; Fǔxī Hé), which cuts through the centre of town.

Salt Industry History Museum   MUSEUM
(盐业历史博物馆; Yányè Lìshǐ Bówùguǎn; 89 Dongxing Si; 东兴寺89号; admission ¥22; ⊙8.30am-5pm; 🚌1, 3, 11, 33, 35) Housed in an ornate 270-year-old guildhall, this unique museum documents the course of the region's salt industry, which dates to the 1st century CE. Salt, a vital ingredient of life, was at one time valued more than gold, and by the late 19th century industrious salt merchants had turned Zìgòng into a leading industrial centre.

The museum tells the story through old photographs (some with English captions) and a modest collection of exhibits demonstrating how the extraction process developed; though the building itself, built by Shaanxi salt merchants in 1736, with its tranquil stone courtyards, beautiful woodcarvings and swooping eaves, sometimes steals the show.

To get here from Róngguāng Business Hotel, walk down the hill and turn left onto Jiefang Lu (解放路). The museum will be on your right after about 500m.

Shēnhǎi Salt Well   HISTORIC SITE
(桑海井; Shēnhǎi Jǐng; 📞0813 510 6214; 289 Da'an Jie; 大安街289号; admission ¥22; ⊙8.30am-5.30pm) This fascinating museum is also a working salt mine. Its 1001m-deep artesian salt well was the world's deepest well when it was built in 1835 and it remains the deepest salt well ever made using percussion drilling, a technique invented here and later applied throughout the world.

Many pieces of original equipment, including a 20m-high wooden derrick that towers above the tiny, 20cm-wide mouth of the well, are still intact. On the 2nd floor of the salt house, rows of cauldrons bubble away day and night over fires powered by natural gas, the mine's other product, until only fluffy white piles of glistening salt remain.

There are excellent English captions explaining the process, from how bamboo was once used to siphon brine from beneath the earth to how soymilk is added to clarify it. Bags of the salt (from ¥3) are sold from the window to the right when you exit.

Take bus 5 or 35 (¥1, 10 minutes) from opposite the Róngguāng Business Hotel. Bus 35 continues to the Dinosaur Museum.

Dinosaur Museum   MUSEUM
(恐龙馆; Kǒnglóng Guǎn; 📞0813 580 1235; www.zdm.cn/en; 238 Dashan Pu, Da'an District; 大安区大山铺238号; admission ¥42, movie ¥25; ⊙8.30am-5pm; 🚌35) Built on top of the Dashanpu excavation site, which has one of the world's largest concentrations of dinosaur fossils, this museum has a fine collection of reassembled skeletons, as well as partially excavated fossil pits.

The first publicised finds here were made in 1972. The huge numbers of fossils, mostly dating from the rarely seen early and middle Jurassic periods, baffled archaeologists at first. It is now believed that floods swept them here en masse. Budding paleontologists will appreciate the *Huayangosaurus taibaii*, the most primitive and complete stegosaur ever discovered, as well as the incredibly rare skin fossil specimens on display. A kid-friendly movie screens at 10am, 11am, 2.30pm and 3.30pm daily.

Take bus 35 (¥1, 25 minutes) from opposite Róngguāng Business Hotel.

🛏 Sleeping

Róngguāng Business Hotel   HOTEL $$
(荣光商务酒店; Róngguāng Shāngwù Jiǔdiàn; 📞0813 211 9999; 25 Ziyou Lu; 自由路25号; r incl breakfast ¥100-258; ❄@) Large, clean rooms, friendly staff, free-to-use computers on the 4th floor and a free buffet breakfast distinguish this hotel from others in this prime location. Take bus 1 or 35 from the bus station, or bus 34 from the train station.

Xióngfēi Holiday Hotel   HOTEL $$$
(雄飞假日酒店; Xióngfēi Jiàrì Jiǔdiàn; 📞0813 211 8888; 193 Jiefang Lu; 解放路193号; r incl breakfast from ¥960, discounted to ¥389; ❄@🛜) This large, upmarket hotel is within close reach of Zìgòng's riverside sights.

✕ Eating & Drinking

Evenings here are all about *shāokǎo* (烧烤, barbecue skewers; ¥1 to ¥4), with stalls spilling onto the pavement. Most of them set up from around 7pm. Zìgòng locals love their rabbit meat (兔子肉; *tùzi ròu*) and some stalls cook up various rabbit parts. Our favourite sets up in front of the Bank of China on Ziyou Lu. There are also cheap noodle and steamed dumpling (包子) stands along the **walking street** (商业步行街; ⏰7am-9pm).

Běifāng Wèi
DUMPLINGS $
(北方味; 70 Jiefang Lu; mains from ¥18; ⏰8am-8pm) For a break from fiery Sìchuān cuisine, try this generally packed Northern-style *shuǐjiǎo* (水饺) restaurant. Lamb (羊, *yáng*), vegetable (菜, *cài*), chicken (鸡, *jī*) and seafood (海鲜, *hǎixiān*) *shuǐjiǎo* are ¥18 to ¥48 per half *jīn* (good for one).

★ Huánhóu Palace
TEAHOUSE
(桓侯宫; Huánhóu Gōng; Zhonghua Lu; 中华路; tea ¥5-8; ⏰7am-9pm) This teahouse is located inside an 1868 butchers' guildhall. Its dramatic stone facade opens up into a tree-shaded courtyard with an old stone stage framed on all sides by beautiful wooden carvings. The antique dealers who share the space generally don't cut into the tranquillity — unless you make eye contact.

It's on your left as you walk towards the salt museum from the hotels.

★ Wàngyé Temple
TEAHOUSE
(王爷庙; Wángyé Miào; 3 Binjiang Lu; 滨江路3号; tea ¥5-20; ⏰8.30am-11pm; 🚍3, 11, 33) Housed within the ochre walls of a 100-year-old guildhall of boatmen and merchants, this lively teahouse (officially 临江茶楼; Línjiāng Chálóu) is one of the neatest in Sìchuān.

Perched above the Fùxī, it sits opposite the still-active Fǎzàng Temple (法藏寺; Fǎzàng Sì). The pair were built to ensure safe passage for boats transporting salt downstream. Everyone in the industry came here to make sacrifices to Wangye, the protector of boatmen and sailors. Now locals gather here to banter, play cards and admire the river view. From the hotels, walk down to the river, turn left and follow the river for about 750m.

ℹ Information

Bank of China (中国银行; Zhōngguó Yínháng; Ziyou Lu) Foreign-card–friendly ATMs.

ℹ Getting There & Around

To get to the hotels, walk out of the bus station, turn right and walk 200m to the first bus stop. Then take bus 1 or 35 (¥1) four stops to the Shízì Kǒu (十字口) stop. The hotels are down the hill and across the road. From the train station, which is on the east end of town, take bus 34 (¥1) to Bīnjiāng Lù (滨江路) bus stop. From there, walk back 200m and turn left up Ziyou Lu.

BUS

Destinations from the main **bus station** (客运总站; 817 Dangui Dajie; 丹桂大街817号) include:

Chéngdū ¥65, 3½ hours, about hourly from 6.30am to 7.50pm

Chóngqìng ¥95, four hours, hourly from 6.20am to 6pm

Éméi Shān ¥52, 3½ hours, four daily (9.20am, 11.50am, 2.50pm and 4pm)

Lè Shān ¥45, three hours, hourly from 8am to 5.30pm

Yíbīn ¥28, one hour, every 40 minutes from 7.10am to 6.20pm

TRAIN

Chéngdū K ¥41, five hours, seven daily (1.38am to 10.07am)

Kūnmíng K seat/hard sleeper ¥115/206, 17 hours, two daily (2.12pm and 7.48pm)

Yíbīn K ¥13, two hours, eight daily from 4.30am to 9.44pm

Yíbīn
宜宾

📞0831 / POP 549,650

Where the Mín and Jīnshā converge to become the mighty Yangzi River, Yíbīn has stood as a town of great strategic military importance throughout history. Today it's a relatively modern, mid-sized city, making it a convenient travel hub for trips to old town Lǐzhuāng, the Bamboo Sea and Luòbiǎo's hanging coffins.

The city is easily explored on foot. Turn right out of Jīngmào Hotel, and right again to reach the **river confluence**, accessed through the reconstructed **Shuǐ Dōng Mén** (水东门; East Water Gate), which has a teahouse on top of it. Further down and off to the right is a genuinely old city-wall **gateway**, plus remnants of the original **ancient city wall**, leading towards a modern public square where locals dance in the evening. Up from the square are more city-wall remains with **Guanying Jie** (冠英街), a street of courtyard homes, dating from the Qing dynasty.

In the middle of the action, the no-frills, clean **Jīngmào Hotel** (经贸宾馆; Jīngmào Bīnguǎn; ☑ 0831 513 7222; 108 Minzhu Lu; 民主路 108号; tw ¥160-180; ✱ @ ⏦) is a bargain when it offers discounts of up to 20%. There are foreign-card–friendly ATMs by Xùfǔ Shāng-chéng (叙府商场) bus stop.

There's a lively **night market** (东街; Dong Jie) with stalls serving *diǎndiǎn xiāng màocài* (点点香冒菜; skewers boiled in a spicy sauce). Turn left out of Jīngmào Hotel and Dong Jie is on your left. In the daytime, look for *ránmiàn* (燃面), a spicy, fried noodle dish that is a local favourite.

ℹ Getting There & Around

BUS

Most travellers arrive at Gāokè bus station (高客 站; Gāokè zhàn). To get to the town centre from here, take bus 22 (¥2, 15 minutes) into town and get off at the Xùfǔ Shāngchéng (叙府 商城) stop on Renmin Lu (人民路). Turn right at the light; Jīngmào Hotel will be on your left.

Continue on bus 4 to get to Nánkè bus station (南客站; Nánkè zhàn) for buses to Lǐzhuāng (¥4, 35 minutes, every 15 minutes), the Bamboo Sea (竹海; Zhúhǎi; ¥22, 1½ hours, 8am, 9.30am, 10am, 11.30am and 4.30pm) and Luòbiāo (¥33, three hours, 2pm).

Travellers may find the nearby cities of Cháng-níng (长宁) and Gǒngxiàn (珙县) have more direct buses to the Bamboo Sea and Luòbiāo.

Buses from Gāokè bus station include the following:

Chángníng ¥15, one hour, frequent services

Chéngdū ¥100, four hours, frequent services from 7.20am to 7pm

Chóngqìng ¥110, four hours, frequent services from 7.10am to 7pm

Gǒngxiàn ¥17, 1½ hours, frequent services

Lè Shān ¥62, four hours, hourly from 8.20am to 5.30pm

Zìgòng ¥28, one hour, frequent services from 7.30am to 7pm

TRAIN

Bus 11 (¥1) links the train station with Gāokè bus station (or it's a 10-minute walk between the two) and passes by the end of Renmin Lu. Trains leaving from Yíbīn Train Station (火车站; huǒchē zhàn) include:

Chéngdū K ¥51, 6½ to eight hours, seven daily from 3.06am to 11.59pm

Kūnmíng K seat/hard sleeper ¥105/190, 15 hours, three daily (4.20pm, 7.54pm and 9.15pm)

Zìgòng K ¥13, 1½ hours, nine daily from 3.06am to 11.59pm

Bamboo Sea 蜀南竹海

Swaths of swaying bamboo, well-marked walking trails and a handful of charming lakes and waterfalls make south Sìchuān's **Shǔnán Zhúhǎi National Park** (蜀南竹 海国家公园; Shǔnán Zhúhǎi Guójiā Gōngyuán; Apr-31 Oct ¥112, Nov-31 Mar ¥60, shuttle van ¥10) a worthwhile detour. There are more than 30 types of bamboo across this 120-sq-km national park and the scenery is gorgeous enough to have attracted many a TV and film director. Bamboo is an especially fast-growing grass that can shoot up nearly a metre in 24 hours. In May, in between the downpours, you can actually hear the pops and wiggles as new shoots spring up.

◉ Sights & Activities

The villages of Wànlǐng (万岭), at the west gate, and Wànlǐ (万里), near the east gate, are the main settlements inside the park. It's about an 11km hike from one to the other if you follow the road the whole way.

Two cable cars (索道; *suǒdào*) ease the journey considerably, and are a great way to see the forest from another angle. The **Guānguāng cable car** (观光索道; Guānguāng Suǒdào; one way/return ¥30/40; ⏲ 8am-5pm) near Wànlǐng takes you on a 25-minute ride over a stunning forest. There's a pleasant, one-hour streamside walk that loops around the forest just past the cable car entrance.

The second cable car, **Dàxiágǔ** (大峡谷 索道; Dàxiágǔ Suǒdào; one way/return ¥20/30; ⏲ 8.30am-5.30pm), is to the right as you exit the first. The 10-minute ride traverses a dramatic gorge and ends in another scenic area with two lakes. From here, Sānhé Jiè (三合 界) is a nearby junction where you can find accommodation, or pass it and continue on to Wànlǐ village another few kilometres away.

Two waterfalls near Wànlǐ are worth a look. To get to **Rainbow Falls** (七彩飞瀑; Qīcǎi Fēipù), either follow the lake by the village or turn right before it and walk about 1km along the road to the signposted main gate. Onward to **Clear Dragon Falls** (清龙瀑 布; Qīnglóng Pùbù), usually serene as it's off the maps, although you may have to pay ¥10 to an enterprising old man to see it.

✖ Eating & Sleeping

Most settle in a hotel in Wànlǐng or Wàn-lǐ. For a more tranquil escape, walk 1km beyond Wànlǐ to **Zhúyùn Shānzhuāng**

WORTH A TRIP

LǏZHUĀNG 李庄

On a quiet bend of the Yangzi, 19km east of Yíbīn, sits the remote village of Lǐzhuāng, just as it has for two millennia. Its ramshackle rooftops, crooked alleyways and peeling woodwork date back to the Ming and Qing dynasties and offer visitors a rare glimpse of a disappearing age.

The old town covers just a few sq km, with all the main sights between the bus stop and the river. Entry to the main temples and courtyard residences requires a ticket, but visitors are free to amble the streets and tranquil riverside.

Among the important sights is **Xízi Xiàng** (席子巷), a narrow lane named for the craftsman who wove grass sleeping mats here. The two-storey, wooden houses on either side are characteristic of architecture from 400 years ago, with wide eaves that nearly touch their neighbours. To the east, a towering gate welcomes you at the **Jade Buddha Temple** (玉佛寺), built by Fújiàn arrivals in 1845. By the river on Bingjiang Lu, the windows of the 200-year-old **Zhang Family Ancestral Hall** (张家祠) are adorned with 50 pairs of intricately carved red-crowned cranes. Between 1937 and 1942, the hall and the **Huīguāng Temple** (蕙光寺), the architectural masterpiece downriver, secreted many of China's most precious cultural relics. Villagers gave refuge to scholars and thousands of works of art, literature, history and science during the Japanese invasion.

Lǐzhuāng deserves a day of exploration. Refuel on local specialties such as *ránmiàn* (燃面; spicy noodles; from ¥7) and *báiròu* (白肉; paper-thin slices of seasoned pork with garlic sauce; ¥25 to ¥40) on **Zhèng Jiē** (正街). **Wàng Jiāng Lóu** (望江楼; ☑0831 244 2729, 153 7827 1187; 顺河路94号, 94 Shunhe Lu, aka Binjiang Lu; s/d/tr ¥60/80/100; ✹📶) has tidy rooms (the rooftop ones are nicest) by the river.

Buses travel between here and Yíbīn's Nánkè bus station frequently (¥4, 35 minutes). From the bus stop, head towards the river for the old town.

(竹韵山庄; ☑0831 497 9001, 138 9092 5673; r from ¥100), opposite Rainbow Falls main gate (look for the sign 'Waterfall Rural Inn'). These spotless rooms in a rustic bamboo-framed house overlook a lovely bank of Qīnglóng Lake. In Wànlǐng, the friendly Yang family keeps a tidy, basic guesthouse called **Jīngxīn Yuán Yījiālè** (晶鑫园农家乐; Joan's Guesthouse; ☑139 9091 1705, English 135 4771 7196; www.snzhjourney.com; west gate, 200m past the small bridge; 小桥广场往观云亭方向前行200米左手边; r ¥120-160; ✹📶).

All guesthouses and hotels serve food, which is generally pretty good. Try dishes with *zhúsǔn* (竹笋), tender bamboo shoots, and the various local fungi that propagate at their roots.

ⓘ Getting There & Around

Ask for a free map when you buy your ticket. There are also detailed maps with English posted throughout the park. All the main sights are signposted, too.

Motorbike taxis can take you between the two main villages (around ¥50, 45 minutes) if you decide not to walk.

BUS

Buses into the park stop at the west gate to allow you to get off and buy your entrance ticket, before passing through Wànlǐng and then terminating at Wànlǐ. There are two direct buses from Wànlǐ to Yíbīn (¥25, two hours, 7am and 1pm). Both pass Wànlǐng (30 minutes) and, if you ask, will drop you at the junction for Chángníng (one hour), where you can change for Gōngxiàn to get to Luòbiāo. Smaller local buses shuttle every 15 minutes between Wànlǐng and Chángníng (¥6, 7am to 6pm).

WESTERN SÌCHUĀN

West of Chéngdū, green tea becomes butter tea, gentle rolling hills morph into jagged snowy peaks and *nǐ hǎo!* gives way to *tashi-delek!* This is the Garzê Tibetan Autonomous Prefecture, a territory that corresponds roughly with the Kham (in Chinese 康巴; Kāngbā), one of old Tibet's three traditional provinces. It is home to more than a dozen distinct Tibetan tribes, the largest being the Khampas, who historically are fierce warriors and horsemen.

SÌCHUĀN'S MYSTERIOUS HANGING COFFINS

Travellers looking to get off the beaten track should make time for **Luòbiǎo** (洛表镇), a small town in the southeast corner of Sìchuān, that is home to one of the province's most mysterious sights: the hanging coffins (悬棺, *xuánguān*) of the ancient Bo (僰人).

The origins of the Bo kingdom more than 3000 years ago and its disappearance by the 16th century continue to baffle archaeologists. One theory is that they are distant relatives of the Tǔjiā minority, who still inhabit the Three Gorges area. We do know that the Bo were keen horsemen with a sharp social hierarchy. Recovered adult skeletons indicate the Bo knocked out their back teeth while still alive, although exactly why they practised this custom is unknown.

Almost everything we know about the Bo has been gleaned from their burial sites, the remaining coffins that rest balanced on wooden stakes hammered into the side of cliffs, and the fading, primitive paintings alongside them.

Sights

Luòbiǎo Hanging Coffins (僰人悬棺景区, Bó Ren Xuánguān Jǐngqū; Luòbiǎo; entry & museum admission ¥20; ⊗ 8am-dark) There are hanging coffins found in other parts of China, but there are more in Luòbiǎo than anywhere else and they are reasonably accessible. At one time there were more than 300 hanging coffins, although a third have fallen to the ground as their support stakes have rotted away over the past 600 years.

There's a small, free museum just inside the site entrance with old photos, burial artefacts and a coffin. About 100m further is a large cluster of coffins on the cliff. Steps lead up to a better vantage point and a huge cave. About 2km further is another impressive grouping right by the road, though there are many others to be spotted in the surrounding cliffs.

The area is at its most photogenic first thing in the morning as the sun rises opposite the cliffs, so consider arriving the evening before and staying the night.

To get to the coffin site, turn left out of the small Luòbiǎo bus station and walk (45 minutes); take the right fork at the black stele dedicated to Bo (心花园). Or you can catch a motorcycle taxi (¥30) to the entrance.

Each season brings its own rugged beauty. In May many remote towns and monasteries can feel abandoned as villagers head out to harvest *byar rtswa dgun bu* (虫草, *chóngcǎo*), a medicinal caterpillar fungus that grows on the alpine slopes.

Western Sìchuān endures up to 200 freezing days per year, but summer days can be blistering. This, combined with the high altitude, can leave new arrivals vulnerable to bad sunburn and altitude sickness. Pack layers and take a couple of days to acclimatise when you arrive.

Kāngdìng 康定

♪ 0836 / POP 110,000

Coming from the Chéngdū area, there are two main gateways into Tibetan Sìchuān. One is Dānbā, but far more popular is Kāngdìng (known in Tibet as Dartsendo or Dardo), the capital of the Garzê Tibetan Autonomous Prefecture. Set in a steep river valley at the confluence of the raging Zhéduō and Yǎlā Rivers (the Dar and Tse in Tibetan), Kāngdìng offers an easy introduction to Tibetan culture and elevations above 2500m.

This town has long stood as a trading centre between the Tibetan and Han, with sizeable Hui and Qiang minority populations also part of the mix. You'll find elements of all of these cultures represented here. Snow-white Gònggā Shān stands sentinel to the south, one of nearly two dozen peaks over 6000m within a few hours' drive of town.

◉ Sights & Activities

Small mountains loom over Kāngdìng and make for pleasant day hikes. Several monasteries are scattered around town.

Guōdá Shān   MOUNTAIN
(郭达山; Zhedra Rawo) Guōdá Shān looms large at the eastern end of town and takes a full day to climb up and down. From the peak (1500m) you can take in the breathtaking glaciers to the south.

Sleeping

Bóxiānjū Bīnguǎn (僰仙居宾馆; ☑ 083 1441 0169; Luobiao Chezhan Jie; r without/with computer ¥60/70; ✳ @ ☎) Two doors down from the bus station is a friendly hotel with basic rooms. Some overlook the surrounding farms and mountains. Soap and air-con remote upon request.

Getting There & Away

One of the reasons this place is so rarely visited is that it's a pain to reach. Roads wind through small towns (only some picturesque), and are either in rough shape or under construction.

Buses run directly from Yíbīn (宜宾) to Luòbiǎo (¥35, five hours, 10.30am, 2pm and 3.30pm), heading back to Yíbīn twice in the morning (¥35, 6.50am and 10am). From Chángníng (长宁; ¥20, one hour, frequent services from 6.20am to 6.20pm), you must transfer at the grim coal-mining town of Gǒngxiàn (珙县; ¥30, 2½ hours, every half hour from 6am to 5.30pm).

To continue into Guìzhōu province, take a bus from Luòbiǎo to Xúnchǎng (巡场; ¥22, 2½ hours, every half hour from 6am to 5pm) where there are regular buses across the border to Lóngtóu (龙头; ¥10, two hours, every 40 minutes from 6am to 5pm); from there it's an easy transfer to Guìyáng (贵阳). For Yúnnán province, buses depart Luòbiǎo's Sānchà Lù bus lot (三叉路; ¥35, three hours, hourly from 6am to 5.30pm); in Wēixìn you can change for Kūnmíng.

Ticket Office (售票处; ☑ 135 0819 5096; Chezhan Jie, behind the black stele with the flame; 车站街虎儿花园处; tickets ¥2-5, from shuttle service ¥10; ⊘ 6am-7.30pm) Books bus tickets around Sìchuān and into Guìzhōu and Yúnnán. They'll also shuttle you to connecting stations, if necessary, for reasonable fees. Chinese only spoken.

Pǎomǎ Shān   MOUNTAIN

(跑马山; Dentok Rawo; admission ¥50) Pǎomǎ Shān is the famed mountain of the 'Kāngdìng Qíng Gē' (Kangding Love Song), one of China's most enduring folk songs. It's an easy ascent on foot or take the **cable car** (索道; suǒdào; one way/return ¥30/45; ⊘ 8.30am-6pm) halfway up for excellent views of the town and surrounding peaks and valleys. You have to pay to go all the way up the stepped path, past ribbons of prayer flags and **Pǎomǎ Sì** (跑马寺; Dentok Lhakang; admission ¥50), or just loop north and descend another way.

Gānzī Prefecture Tibetan Cultural Heritage Museum   MUSEUM

(甘孜藏族自治州非物质文化遗产博物馆; ☑ 0836 2811 1312; 36 Xiangyang Jie; ⊘ 8.30am-5:30pm) By the Pǎomǎ Shān cable car entrance, behind the building with the big red 'om', this *bēng kē*-style (崩柯) structure (three-storey structures with split log and packed earth walls) houses exhibits surveying the Kham's rich heritage from the garb of

regional tribes to *thangka* (sacred paintings), and a sky burial horn fashioned from a teenage girl's femur.

Make time for a Tibetan lunch and dinner, served in the traditional kitchen (¥50 per person).

Nánwú Sì   BUDDHIST TEMPLE

(南无寺; Lhamo Tse; Lucheng Nanlu; 炉城南路; ⊘ dawn-5pm) Nánwú Temple belongs to the Gelugpa (Yellow Hat) sect of Tibetan Buddhism and is the most active monastery in the area. Walk south along the main road, cross the river and keep going for about 200m until you see a small sign ('南無寺') for the monastery on your right. Follow the road uphill to the gold-capped roofs.

Jīngāng Sì   BUDDHIST TEMPLE

(金刚寺; Dordrak Lhakang; Lucheng Nanlu; 炉城南路) About 100m past Nánwú Temple along the main road is this 400-year-old Nyingma (Red Hat sect) monastery. Turn right at the sign for Sally's Cafe Chiruman Youth Hostel.

Kāngdìng (Dartsendo)

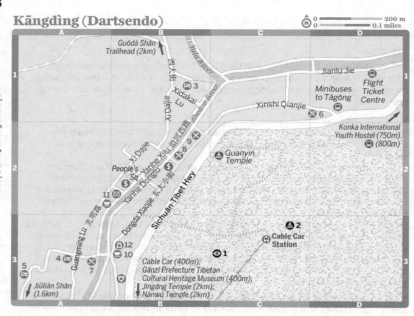

Kāngdìng (Dartsendo)

Gònggā Shān MOUNTAIN

(贡嘎山; Minyak Konka) The trailhead for the nine-day pilgrims' circuit of holy Gònggā Shān (7556m) is a half-hour drive from Kāngdìng. Many hostel staff can advise you on how to approach the trek, and rent out camping equipment. We recommend finding a guide with horses through Zhilam Hostel.

⚡ Festivals & Events

Circling the Mountain Festival RELIGIOUS

(转山节; Zhuǎnshānjié) Kāngdìng's biggest annual festival takes place on Pǎomǎ Shān (p745) on the eighth day of the fourth lunar month (normally in May) to commemorate the birthday of the Historical Buddha, Sakyamuni. White and blue Tibetan tents cover the hillside and there's wrestling, horse racing and visitors from all over western Sìchuān.

🛏 Sleeping

★**Zhilam Hostel** HOSTEL $

(汇道客栈; Huìdào Kèzhàn; ☑0836 283 1100; www.zhilamhostel.com; 72 Bái Tǔkǎn Cūn Lu; 白土坎村路72号; dm/r from ¥40/260; @ 🎧) Run by an American family, this fabulous, kid-friendly, hillside hostel is a comfortable base in Kāngdìng. They provide all manner of top-end hostel services, from camping-gear rental to good Western food and travel advice. It's a winding 10-minute walk uphill by the road that passes Yǒngzhū Hotel.

Zhilam is also a reliable resource for wilderness adventures. Resident Tibetan guide Patru doesn't speak English, but is experienced with guiding foreigners around the Gònggā Shān circuit (from ¥300 per day, not including horse fees).

Konka International Youth Hostel
HOSTEL $

(贡嘎国际青年旅舍; Gònggā Guójì Qīngnián Lûshè; ☑ 0836 281 7788; G318, Dongguan Xingcheng, 3rd fl; dm ¥35-40, s/d ¥150/170; @ 🛜) The most convenient option for bus travellers, this pleasant hostel offers all the usual services, plus they can help with self-guided excursions into the mountains. They even loan out outdoor gear. From June through November, beds in rooftop tents go for ¥25. Lively communal dinners include vegetarian options (¥18 to ¥24 per person). Just 50m to the left of the bus station.

Dēngbā Hostel
HOSTEL $

(登巴国际青年旅舍; ☑ 0836 2877 377; 88 Xida Jie; 西大街88号; dm ¥70, r with private bathroom ¥120-150; @ 🛜) This is a worn but welcoming hostel with small rooms in an alley off Xi Dajie.

Yōngzhū Hotel
GUESTHOUSE $

(拥珠驿栈; Yōngzhū Yìzhàn; ☑ 0836 283 2381, 159 8373 8188; dm ¥35-45, r ¥160-200; 🛜) Hidden in a lane near Ānjué Sì, this simple guesthouse has rooms built around an inner atrium decorated with colourful Tibetan flourishes.

🍴 Eating & Drinking

Stock up on trail snacks at the **market** (德惠超市; Déhuì Chāoshì; Neijie Shang Ye, off Dongda Jie; ⊙ 8am-10pm) in the Liu Liu Cheng shopping complex. On mild evenings, **barbecue stalls** set up around the northeast corner of People's Sq.

For a sit-down meal, the Tibetan Cultural Heritage Museum (p745) offers a unique experience with dishes cooked over a traditional iron stove.

Mágē Miàn
NOODLES $

(麻哥面; Yanhe Xilu; noodles ¥7-12; ⊙24hr) A solid late-night option, the speciality here is *ma'gē miàn* (麻哥面), house noodles topped with a spicy mince-meat sauce in small (一两; *yīliǎng;* ¥9), medium (二两; *èr liǎng;* ¥10) or large (三两; *sānliǎng;* ¥12).

Ā'Rè Tibetan Restaurant
TIBETAN $$

(阿热藏餐; Ā'rè Zàngcān; ☑ 0836 669 6777; Xinshi Qianjie; 新市前街; mains from ¥18; ⊙9am-10pm; 🍴) This reliable standby serves tasty soups, *tsampa,* and lamb- and yak-meat dishes, including a whole yak hoof, if that sort of thing takes your fancy.

Taste of Tibet
TIBETAN $$

(葩姆名卡; Pama Linka; ☑ 0836 699 9999; off Yanhe Donglu; 水井电梯公离; mains from ¥38; ⊙9.30am-late) This upscale arrival offers a refined take on Tibetan fare in a rustic dining room decorated with a fine collection of traditional nomad tools. The chef sources ingredients from the Kham — from Xīndūqiáo's fragrant barley (青稞) to tender yak from Shíqú. Live music (and enthusiastic smoking) starts at 7pm.

Mǎlāyà Tibetan Restaurant
TIBETAN $$

(玛拉亚藏餐; Mǎlāyà Zàngcān; ☑ 0836 287 7111; Yanhe Donglu; 沿河东路; dishes from ¥18; ⊙11am-11pm; 🍴) Friendly restaurant-cum-teahouse serving authentic Tibetan dishes. If you need inspiration, try the yak meat burger (meat stew topped with flatbread; ¥68) or the very filling curry (beef and potato on rice; ¥18). Located on the 6th floor above the fast-food joint **Dico** (德克士).

Tibetan Culture Dew
TEAHOUSE

(西藏雨; Xīzàng Yǔ; Yanhe Xilu; 沿河西路; snacks ¥2-18, tea & beer ¥15; ⊙10am-11pm) Hang out with the sipping, snacking locals at this lovely teahouse with a rustic stone and wood interior decorated with colourful Tibetan prayer flags.

Himalayan Coffee
CAFE

(☑ 0836 281 8887; 13 Neijie Shang Ye, off Dongda Jie; coffee ¥25, mains from ¥18; ⊙10am-11pm; 🛜) The only spot for actual pour-over coffee in all of the Kham, this cafe near the big yak sculpture is a veritable oasis for the caffeine-deprived. Wraps, pizza, house-baked pastries and wi-fi satisfy other common traveller cravings – though at homeland prices.

⭐ Entertainment

At 7pm, there's one place you must go: every evening dozens, if not hundreds, of locals descend on People's Sq for a get-together of dancing and calisthenics.

ℹ️ Information

Agricultural Bank of China ATM (自动柜员机; Zìdòng Guìyuán Jī; Yanhe Xilu) One of several around town that takes foreign cards.

Public Security Bureau (PSB; 公安局; Gōng'ānjú; ☑ 0836 281 1415; 232 Dongda Xiaojie; 东大街232号; ⊙8.30am-noon & 2.30-5.30pm) Visa-extension service in three working days. First-time extensions only.

LOAD UP WITH CASH

At the time of research it was impossible to change money or travellers cheques, get advances on credit cards or use ATMs with foreign bank cards anywhere in western Sìchuān apart from Kāngdìng. Larger towns such as Xīndūqiáo and Gānzī have a branch of the Agricultural Bank of China that usually accept foreign cards, but in others, despite the Visa signs, expect rejection.

ⓘ Getting There & Away

AIR

Kāngdìng Airport is 43km west of town and has daily flights to Chéngdū (¥700, 11.30am) and four weekly flights to Chóngqìng (¥751, 8.35am Sunday, Monday, Wednesday and Friday).

Buy tickets online or from the **flight ticket centre** (机场售票中心; Jīchǎng Shòupiào Zhōngxīn; ☑ 0836 287 1111; in the Airport Hotel, 28 Jianlu Jie; 箭炉街28号, 康定机场兵官; ⊗ 8.30am-5.30pm), which sometimes has tickets discounted by ¥100 or so. Pick up the airport shuttle (¥35, 1½ hours) in front of the Airport Hotel at 8.30am. Shuttles from the airport (¥50) arrive here at around 1pm.

BUS

The bus station is a 10-minute walk from the centre of town (taxi ¥7). Shared minibuses to all destinations listed here leave from outside the bus station.

Rides to Tǎgōng (¥50 to ¥80) and Gānzī (around ¥200) also leave from the walking street, Xinshi Qianjie. Remember: private hire – *bāochē* (包车); shared vehicle – *pīnchē* (拼车).

Báiyù ¥192, 20 hours, 6am (stops overnight in Gānzī; book the day before)

Chéngdū ¥120 to ¥140, eight hours, hourly from 6am to 11pm

Dānbā ¥45, three hours, two daily (6am, 6.30am)

Dàochéng ¥162.50, 12 hours, two daily (both at 6am)

Dégé ¥202, 16 hours, one daily (6.45am, layover in Gānzī)

Gānzī ¥129, 11 hours, two daily (6.30am, 9am)

Lǐtáng ¥97, eight hours, three daily (6am, 7am, 9am)

Yǎ'ān ¥68, 4½ hours, about every hour from 6am to 4pm

Dānbā 丹巴

☑ 0836 / POP 58,200

Dusty Dānbā (known as Rongtrak in Tibet; 1893m) straddles a dramatic gorge near the confluence of three rivers, and makes an interesting alternative to Kāngdìng as a gateway into or out of western Sìchuān.

The town itself is not very exciting, but in the surrounding hills are clusters of picturesque Jiāróng Tibetan and Qiāng villages with ancient watchtowers and welcoming homestays.

◉ Sights

Qiāng Watchtowers RUIN
(羌族碉楼; Qiāngzú diāolóu) The 30m- to 60m-high ancient stone towers scattered throughout the villages overlooking the Dàdù River were built by the Qiāng between 700 and 1200 years ago. Some enterprising families have opened theirs up to those travellers (¥10 to ¥20) who are willing to climb log ladders 6m up to the entrance.

Household towers were signs of status, and were used to store precious goods (and family members during wartime). Village towers were taller, built for conducting religious rituals, demarcating borders and passing smoke signals. In wartime, they were used to launch assaults against Tibetan marauders and the Qing army.

Jiǎjū Zàngzhài VILLAGE
(甲居藏寨; adult/student ¥30/15) Of all the pretty villages in the hills around here, Dānbā's pride and joy is Jiǎjū, 12km northwest of town and perched at the top of a multiswitchback track that winds its way up a steep river gorge. With its fruit trees, charming Tibetan stone houses and homestays, Jiǎjū's quaint architecture will suck in travellers for a day or two. To get here, take a shared minivan (¥10) from the Bāměi end of Dānbā. A private taxi costs about ¥50 one way.

Suōpō VILLAGE
(梭坡) Dānbā's nearest village with watchtowers is a 30-minute walk along the river. An enterprising family has rebuilt the wooden base levels of a tower next to their home. Visitors can climb up the inside from their rooftop (¥15). Don't worry about finding them. They, or a 'friend' of theirs, will find you.

To get to Suōpō, turn left out of Zháxī Zhuōkāng Backpackers Hostel and follow the river. Turn down the track beside the small police station, then cross the suspension bridge and keep walking up to the village. Look for stone steps under some large trees up to your left, just after you reach the village's first couple of buildings. These steps lead to the nearest towers.

Zhōnglù

VILLAGE

(中路; admission ¥20) Comparatively remote Zhōnglù is a popular village for homestays, and a good base for wandering through the countryside. It's 13km from town. Take a taxi (¥80).

🛏 Sleeping

Zháxī Zhuōkāng
Backpackers Hostel

HOSTEL **$**

(扎西卓康青年旅舍; Zháxī Zhuōkāng Qīngnián Lǚshè; ☑139 9046 4961, 0836 352 1806; 35 Sanchahe Nanlu; 三岔河南路35号; dm ¥25-30, tw without/with bathroom ¥80/100; @ 🛜) Traveller central in Dānbā proper, the friendly management can arrange minibus rides (with advance notice) and extended treks to natural springs and remote villages off the tourist map. Rooms are decidedly average but tidy, and there are free internet terminals and wi-fi. Some English is spoken.

It's a 25-minute walk from the bus station (keep the river on your left, and follow it as it curves right), or a ¥6 taxi ride.

Liǎngkē Shù

HOMESTAY **$**

(两棵树; ☑135 6868 5278; Jiǎjū Zàngzhài; dm incl meals ¥60) One of a number of stone houses that have been converted into a homestay, excellent Liǎngkē Shù has simple dorms decorated with Tibetan furniture, a pleasant central courtyard and stunning views. The owner can arrange trips into the fabulous surrounding countryside.

Village Hotel

GUESTHOUSE **$**

(东坡藏家; Dōngpō Zángjiā; ☑135 5850 9707; Zhōnglù; r incl meals without/with bathroom ¥80/90; 🛜) Spend a night or two in this converted white-stone and crimson-timber house, so that you have time to partake in the multi-course meals and wander the surrounding countryside. If you're lucky, Mr Dōngpō, the family patriarch, will show you his collection of clothing, weapons and ancient relics.

Don't miss climbing up to the ancient altar (经堂) in the crumbling watchtower, which dates back 700 years. If you want to climb higher, neighbours have restored theirs to safely accommodate visitors.

🍴 Eating & Drinking

In town, small restaurants by the bus station open early for breakfast noodles (面; *miàn*) or dumplings (小龙包子; *xiǎolóng bāozi*), but the best eating is to be done in the homestays and guesthouses.

Ask at Zháxī Zhuōkāng Backpackers Hostel for recommendations.

ℹ Getting There & Away

For Tǎgōng, take a minibus (¥60, three hours) from the west end of town, via Bāměi (¥40, two hours). Bus destinations include:

Chéngdū ¥115, eight hours, two daily (6.30am and 10am)

Gānzī ¥101, nine hours, 6.50am

Kāngdìng ¥48, five hours, two daily (6.30am and 3pm)

Sìchuān–Tibet Highway (Northern Route)

The famous Sìchuān–Tibet Hwy splits in two just west of Kāngdìng. The northern route is 300km longer than the southern route, and is generally less travelled. Following it, you'll traverse high-plateau grasslands and numerous Tibetan settlements, often attached to a local monastery.

Making it to the other side of Chola Mountain (雀儿山; Què'ér Shān) requires negotiating a 5050m narrow pass – the highest this side of Lhasa – that takes you to Dégé and the border with the Tibet Autonomous Region (西藏; Xīzàng). You can continue on this route north into Qīnghǎi province via Shíqú. From Gānzī, you can hook back up with the southern route via Xīnlóng.

Come here prepared. Bring warm clothing; it can be frigid at these elevations even in midsummer. Remember that bus services can be unreliable – this is no place to be in a hurry.

Tǎgōng

塔公

☑0836 / POP 8984

The Tibetan village of Tǎgōng (Lhagang; 3700m) and its surrounding grasslands offer plenty of excuses to linger.

On the road from Kāngdìng is a sea of mani stones carved (and spray-painted) with ༀ་མ་ནི་པདྨེ་ཧཱུྃ (*om mani padme hum*), the mantra of Buddha's path. Explore this terrain on horseback or foot, sip real yak butter tea, then fall asleep in tents under the stars.

⊙ Sights

Lhagang Monastery　BUDDHIST MONASTERY
(塔公寺; Tǎgōng Sì; admission ¥20) The story goes that when Princess Wencheng, the Chinese bride-to-be of Tibetan king Songtsen Gampo, was on her way to Lhasa in AD 640, a precious statue of Jowo Sakyamuni Buddha toppled off one of the carts in her entourage. A replica of the statue was carved on the spot where it landed and a temple built around it.

That replica is now in the hall on the right. The original, which is the most revered Buddha image in all of Tibet, is housed in Lhasa's Jokhang Temple. Also make note of the beautiful 1000-armed Chenresig (Avalokiteshvara) in the hall to the left, and the impressive collection of over 100 *chörtens* (Tibetan stupas) behind the monastery.

You can also visit the Sakya Monastic School across the river; exit the monastery and walk straight down the main road, turn right at the police station, cross the bridge and walk another 800m. Monks in training sit face-to-face on cushions, debating Buddhist texts. In seven years, they will be able to join the others in Lhagang.

🏃 Activities

Horse riding (per person per day 1/2/3 people ¥420/310/290) and guided **grassland hikes** (per person per day ¥200) can be arranged through Khampa Cafe & Arts Centre (p750). It's an extra ¥60 per person with meals and accommodation. They rent out camping equipment (tent per day ¥30) and mountain bikes (per day ¥40).

You can also hike out into the grasslands on your own. One popular option is the two-hour hike south to **Ser Gyergo** (和平法会; Hépíng Fǎhuì), the largest nunnery in the area – ask at **Khampa Cafe** (☑136 8449 3301; http://definitelynomadic.com) for directions.

🎉 Festivals & Events

Tǎgōng holds an annual **horse-racing festival** (*sàimǎhuì*) during the fifth lunar month (usually early July).

🛏 Sleeping & Eating

The three most popular places to stay are in a row to the left of Lhagang Monastery, along one side of the main square. All transport drops passengers here.

★**Khampa Cafe & Arts Centre**　GUESTHOUSE $
(☑136 8449 3301; http://definitelynomadic.com; r ¥100-200; ☎) Angela, an American, and her Tibetan husband, Djarga, run the most comfortable place to stay in Tǎgōng. There is just one shared bathroom, but the bedrooms are spacious, tasteful and exceptionally clean. The top-floor cafe (open 8.30am to 11pm, dishes ¥15 to ¥70) is also the best hang-out in town, with great food and advice on hiking, camping etc. Angela can also arrange very cool Tibetan homestays out in the grasslands, as well as multiday horse treks. Wi-fi is available in one corner downstairs.

Jya Drolma and Gayla's Guesthouse　GUESTHOUSE $
(☑0836 286 6056; dm ¥25, tw without bathroom ¥60) Bedrooms here – even the dorms – are a riot of golds, reds and blues, with elaborately painted ceilings and walls. There are common toilets on each floor and one shower with 24-hour hot water. Some English is spoken.

Snowland Guesthouse　GUESTHOUSE $
(雪城旅社; Xuěchéng Lǚshè; ☑0836 286 6098; tagongsally@yahoo.com; dm from ¥20, s/d ¥50/80) 🅿 This long-standing backpacker hang-out is the cheapest option for budget travellers. Rooms are basic, but you'll get a decent night's sleep. The attached **Sally's Kham Restaurant** (yak burger ¥22; ☉8am-10pm) serves a selection of Tibetan, Chinese and Western standards. No English.

ℹ Getting There & Around

For destinations north, take a shared minivan to Bāměi (八美; ¥20, one hour), where you'll have your pick of minivans to places such as Dānbā (¥30, two hours) and Gānzī (¥50 to ¥70, seven hours). For Gānzī, you can also try to snag a seat on the bus from Kāngdìng, which passes the square at around 9am, or arrange a shared minivan (¥100 to ¥150).

To get to Lǐtáng, take a shared minivan to Xīndūqiáo (新都桥; ¥13, one hour), where you can flag down the Kāngdìng–Lǐtáng bus (¥64, seven hours), which passes there at around 9am, or take a shared minivan the whole way (¥150).

To head back east, the Gānzī–Kāngdìng bus (¥40, two hours) passes the square at around 9am but is often full. Take a shared minivan (¥50 to ¥70), but note, you might struggle to find fellow passengers after 10am.

For close destinations, rent motorbikes in town (per day from ¥100).

Sèdá 色达

Sèdá (Sertar), home to the largest Buddhist academy in the world, offers an incredible glimpse into the life of monks and nuns.

◉ Sights & Activities

Larung Gar Five Sciences Buddhist Academy
BUDDHIST MONASTERY

(喇荣五明佛学院; Lǎróng Wǔmíng Fó Xuéyuàn) Of all the Buddhist sights in western Sìchuān, there is none as striking as Larung Gar. The future of Tibetan Buddhism is contained here in this school, the largest of its kind in the world, cradled in a valley some 170km northeast of Gānzī. Some 10,000 students study here, dedicated for the next six to 13 years to serious monastic study.

Larung Gar was founded in 1980 by 30 disciples gathering at their charismatic leader Khenpo Jikphun's modest home. Many more soon arrived. Today the two main halls that anchor the valley floor – the **nunnery** (女金室; *nǚjīn shì*) distinguished with three *darchen* (flag poles) in front, and the massive main **monastery** (大金室; *dàjīn shì*) – are thoroughly surrounded by a hive of subsidiary chapels and low-slung living quarters that blanket the valley in crimson. Devoted pilgrims climb to the ridge to prostrate before a huge *chörten* and walk the *kora* (holy path) spinning prayer wheels.

Most of the classes in Buddhist philosophy, history and discourse are taught in Tibetan, even though the students are a mix of Tibetan, Han and other minorities from across China and as far away as Singapore. You can observe students engaging in lively debates at 5pm in the monastery.

Monks- and nuns-in-training live separate lives, only gathering in the monastery hall for scripture readings. Living quarters are divided by a high wall, and they even cook their meals in designated areas. At around 11am, you can watch monks cooking for 3000 in giant woks outside, next to the monastery.

Sky Burial (Jhator)
CEREMONY

(天葬; Tiān zàng; ⏱1-2.30pm) **FREE** There is no more stark a contrast between Tibetan and Western religion than in the ceremonies surrounding death. Early Tibetan kings were buried, and the holy are still cremated and their ashes enshrined in *chörten*. But where soft earth and kindling are rare resources, ordinary Tibetans are honored through *jhator*. On a hill 1km north of Larung Gar, visitors can view this extraordinary funerary rite firsthand.

Bodies of the deceased arrive having already undergone rituals over the preceding three days. A lama has recited prayers from the *Book of the Dead* to help the soul on its journey to rebirth. The body arrives wrapped in cloth, which *rogyapas* (designated caretakers) remove to cut the hair and break up the body with a large knife. It is believed the soul has already departed when the vultures descend. To confront death openly and without fear is to watch these massive birds tear at the flesh. Through all of this, there is no open mourning by loved ones. This final act of compassion to return the deceased back to earth evokes a sober joy.

If you're wondering, yes, watching these rites is controversial. Under pressure from the tourist industry, this once private ritual now takes place next to some hideous, amusement-park Buddhist iconography. It's hard to strike a balance between sanctity and gawking, so if you do attend, never take photos, never point, and stay in the roped-off viewing area, 100m away from the deceased.

⌘ Sleeping & Eating

There are a handful of simple restaurants and small shops around the main halls of Larung Gar. Up on the ridge, **Lǐróng Bīngguǎn** (喇荣兵馆; ☎189 4283 6579; dm from ¥35, s/d ¥160/180) serves buffet meals and is a decent (but chilly) sleeping option on the school grounds.

There is a crowded strip of businesses just outside the monastery, but better options with wi-fi and 24-hour hot water overlook the walking street (步行街; Bùxíngjiē)

ROUGH ROADS

The roads in western Sìchuān are notoriously bad, and many sections have been reduced to mud and gravel as part of an ongoing resurfacing project. Travel times are sometimes double what they could be and, after heavy rain, some stretches are impassable. Ask hostels in the area for the latest travel time information.

EATING TIBETAN

ENGLISH	TIBETAN PRONUNCIATION	TIBETAN SCRIPT	CHINESE PRONUNCIATION	CHINESE SCRIPT
Butter tea	bo-cha	ཆོད་ཇ།	sūyóu chá	酥油茶
Noodles	thuk-pa	ཐུག་པ།	zàngmiàn	藏面
Rice, potato and yak-meat stew	shemdre	ན་འབྲས།	gālí niúròu fàn	咖喱牛肉饭
Roasted barley flour	tsampa	ཙམ་པ།	zānbā	糌粑
Tibetan yoghurt	sho	ཞོ།	suānnǎi	酸奶
Yak-meat dumplings	sha-momo	ན་མོག་མོག	niúròu bāozi	牛肉包子
Vegetable dumplings	tse-momo	ཚལ་མོག་མོག	sùcài bāozi	素菜包子

in Sèdá Xiàn (色达县), 20km northwest. **Zàngyuán Bīngguǎn** (藏缘兵官; ☑083 6852 2188; Buxing Jie, Sèdá County; 色达县步行街; r without/with bathroom ¥120/160; 🛜) has a fantastic Tibetan teahouse downstairs.

A gaggle of friendly ladies keep **Shūshì Bīngguǎn** (舒适兵馆; ☑083 6852 1850; Buxing Jie, Sèdá County; 色达县步行街; r without/with bathroom ¥158/248) particularly tidy. Your hotel may ask you to register in person at the PSB (派出所, *pàichūsuǒ*) on one end of the walking street.

ℹ Getting There & Around

Minibuses arrive and drop-off at the big parking lot halfway up the hill on the Larung Gar grounds. A ride to the Sèdá Xiàn walking street or the Sky Burial site is about ¥10 with other passengers, ¥70 private. Minibuses to and from Gānzī (¥70 to ¥100, 4½ hours) arrive and depart from here as well.

From Sèdá Xiàn, regular buses to Chéngdū (¥239) and Kāngdìng (¥53) depart at around 6am from the east end of town, less than 1km from the walking street.

Gānzī 甘孜

🎵 0836 / POP 68,523

It's easy to spend a couple of days in the lively market town of Gānzī (Garzê) exploring the beautiful countryside, which is scattered with Tibetan villages and large monasteries surrounded by snowcapped mountains. Photo opportunities abound, especially from late July to October, when the grassland is an impossible green accented with wildflowers in bloom.

◉ Sights & Activities

Garzê Gompa BUDDHIST TEMPLE

(甘孜寺; Gānzī Sì; admission ¥20) North of the town's Tibetan quarter is the region's largest monastery, dating back more than 500 years and glimmering with gold. Encased on the walls of the main hall are hundreds of small golden Sakyamunis. In a smaller hall just west is an awe-inspiring statue of Jampa (Maitreya or Future Buddha), dressed in a giant silk robe. Catch fantastic views from the rooftop.

The monastery is a 25- to 30-minute walk from the bus station. Turn left out of the station and just keep going.

Róngbō Hot Springs HOT SPRING

(绒播温泉; Róngbō Wēnquán; per r ¥50; ⊙6am-midnight) Perfect after a day of hiking in the hills, Gānzī's hot springs are a short walk past the turn-off for Hotel Himalaya. When you see the road Xinqu Lu (新区路) on your left, turn right down the alley opposite and follow it downhill towards the sulphur smell. Each room is private with a large soaking tub. Towels (浴巾; *yùjīn*) are available for ¥10.

🛏 Sleeping & Eating

Eateries offering the promise of a full stomach on ¥20 or less abound along Dongda Jie and Chuanzang Lu. The colourful teahouses offer an excellent range of Tibetan dishes beyond just tea.

Hotel Himalaya HOTEL $

(喜马拉雅宾馆; Xǐmǎlāyǎ Bīnguǎn; ☑ 0836 752 1878; 13 Dongda Jie; 东大街13号; r ¥150) Run by a Gānzī local who happens to speak German, this is the most comfortable place in town. Rooms are large, bright and come with attached bathrooms featuring sit-down toilets and hot-water showers. Turn left out of the bus station, then take the first right up Chuanzang Lu. Dongda Jie is on your left after a couple of hundred metres.

Hóng Fú Guesthouse
GUESTHOUSE $

(鸿福旅馆; Hóngfú Lǔguǎn; ☑ 0836 752 5330; 49 Chuanzang Lu; 川藏路49号; per bed ¥40) In a traditional Tibetan wooden building on the main drag, Hóng Fú has straightforward twin rooms, shared toilets and one cramped shower, but, as the owners say, the hot springs are just up the road.

Turn left out of the bus station, take the first left and you'll soon see a sign on your right for Long Da Guesthouse (same prices; not as good). Walk towards that and you'll see Hóng Fú just before it, on your left.

Jīntàiyáng Bīnguǎn
HOTEL $

(金太阳宾馆; ☑ 0836 752 2444; Chuanzang Lu at Shizimen; 川藏路 (狮子门); r ¥150-180, discounted to ¥100; ☎) If you need wi-fi, this standard midrange hotel does the trick. Turn left out of the bus station, take the first right and it's on your left through the police station archway. No English sign.

❶ Getting There & Away

Minivans congregate outside the bus station and head to:

Dégé ¥160, six to seven hours
Lǐtáng ¥120, six to seven hours
Mǎnígāngē ¥50, two to three hours

Scheduled bus services run to the following destinations:

Chéngdū ¥226, 18 hours, 6.30am
Dānbā ¥101, nine hours, 6.30am
Kāngdìng ¥117 and ¥129, 11 hours, two daily, both at 6.30am)
Shíqú ¥96, six hours, every other day (6.30am)

Mǎnígāngē
马尼干戈

☑ 0836

There's not much going on in Mǎnígāngē (Manigango), a rough two-street transit town halfway between Gānzī and Dégé. The surrounding hills do offer wonderful hiking opportunities, though. The vast monastery and school, Dzogchen Gompa (竹庆寺; Zhú Qìng Sì) an important seat of the Nyingma (Red Hat sect), is also within striking distance, on the road north to Yùshù.

🛏 Sleeping & Eating

Fēnglíngdù Kèzhàn
GUESTHOUSE $

(风陵渡客栈; ☑ 150 0248 8791; beds ¥30; ☎) Lorna, the friendly owner from Liáoníng speaks some English, and keeps her few rooms spic-and-span. Both dorm and private rooms are priced by the bed and have a nice travellers' vibe thanks to all the young Chinese backpackers. No showers, but you can request a bucket of hot water.

It's 200m down from the Manigange Pani Hotel (where the buses drop you). Look for the 'Guesthouse' sign on the left.

Mǎnígāngē Pàni Hotel
HOTEL $

(马尼干戈怕尼酒店; Mǎnígāngē Pàni Jiǔdiàn; ☑ 0836 822 2788; 317国道; dm from ¥30, tw without bathroom ¥130, with bathroom ¥150-200) This OK hotel is the town's centre of gravity, with its parking lot serving as the unofficial bus station and its restaurant (mains ¥25 to ¥40, open 7am to 10pm) a popular lunch stop for passing cyclists.

❶ Getting There & Away

A daily bus to Dégé (¥50, three to four hours) passes through Mǎnígāngē between 7am and 8.40am, but is often full. Going the other way, there are usually empty seats on the Gānzī-bound bus (¥50, three to four hours), which passes by at 7am to 8am. Catch both from Mǎnígāngē Pàni Hotel.

Minibuses congregate at the east end of town at the crossroads of the main drag (G317) and the road north to Yùshù (S217). They head to Gānzī (¥40), Dégé (¥60) or Shíqú (¥80) when full. A bus from Gānzī to Shíqú (¥70, seven hours) also passes by here at around 8.30am.

Xīnlù Hǎi
新路海

Xīnlù Hǎi
LAKE

(新路海; Yilhun Lha-tso; admission ¥20) It is said King Gesar's beloved concubine Zhumu was so taken by these stunning turquoise-blue waters that her heart fell in. This now holy glacial lake, 13km southwest of Mǎnígāngē, is still awe inspiring.

The water is frigidly cold and the surface freezes solid from September through to March. Take it in by hiking among the *chörten* and *mani* stones, beneath snow-capped Chola Mountain, which feeds this lake, to the west.

You can walk a couple of hours up the foothills on the left side of the lake for more breathtaking views and possible glimpses of white-lipped deer (白唇鹿; báichúnlù).

You can also ride horses led by guides (from ¥100). Camping is frowned upon – though some self-sufficient travellers have slept in the caves without trouble. In summer, you may run into local monks setting up colourful tents.

To get here, take a Dégé-bound minibus (¥20 to ¥40), hitch a ride or hike (turn right out of Mǎnígāngē Pàní Hotel and keep going for two hours). The lake is a five-minute walk from the main road, along a signposted track. Minivans (¥20) wait to take you back to Mǎnígāngē.

Dégé
德格

📞 0836 / POP 58,600

Your bumpy bus ride just got bumpier. Dégé (Derge) is cut off from the rest of western Sìchuān by the towering Chola Mountain (雀儿山; Que'er Shan, 6168m); to get here from the east, you have to endure a highly uncomfortable, harrowing, five-hour ride by dirt track over the 5050m-high Chola Pass. At the highest point, Buddhists on board throw coloured prayer papers out the window and chant mantras that you can only hope will help carry you all to safety.

Unless you've secured the rare permit to enter the Chamdo prefecture of Tibet proper (西藏, Xīzàng), the main reason to make the arduous trek out here is to see Dégé's famous printing monastery, one of this region's premier sights.

◎ Sights

The printing press is in the centre of town, but further along the road up the hill beyond it, you'll reach the huge, reconstructed **Gonchen (Dégé) Monastery**, which has stood here in various forms for a millennium. High in the mountains to the south and east are several other monasteries, including Pelpung Gompa, Dzongsar Gompa and Pewar Gompa.

⭐ **Bakong Scripture Printing Press & Monastery**   BUDDHIST MONASTERY, HISTORIC SITE
(德格印经院; Dégé Yìnjīngyuàn; www.dege-parkhang.org; admission ¥50; ⊙ 8.30am-noon & 2-6.30pm) This fascinating 1792 monastery houses one of western Sìchuān's star attractions: an ongoing printing operation that still uses traditional woodblock printing methods and maintains more than 320,000 scripture plates, an astonishing 70% of Tibet's literary heritage.

The wood blocks are engraved with scriptures from all of the Tibetan Buddhist orders, as well as Bön (苯教), a religion that predates the arrival of Buddhism in Tibet. These ancient writings cover astronomy, geography, music, medicine and Buddhist classics, including two of the most important Tibetan sutras. A set of 555 woodblock plates, written in Hindi, Sanskrit and Tibetan, describes the history of Indian Buddhism and is the only surviving copy in the world.

Within the monastery, dozens of workers produce more than 2500 prints each day, as ink, paper and blocks fly through the workers' hands at lightning speed. In a side room, you'll find the senior printers making larger and more complex prints of Tibetan gods on paper and coloured cloth.

You can also examine storage chambers, paper-cutting rooms and the main hall of the monastery itself, protected from fire and earthquakes by the guardian goddess Drölma (Tara). There are some nice murals in the two ground-floor chapels, so bring a torch.

You aren't allowed to take photos of the library shelves or the main hall, but ask the printers if it is OK to snap away as they meditatively fill customers' orders.

To get here, turn right out of the bus station, then left over the bridge and keep walking up the hill.

🛏 Sleeping & Eating

There are guesthouse and food options, including cheap noodle shops, clustered near the bus station.

Héxié Hotel   HOTEL $
(和谐旅馆; Héxié Lǔguǎn; 📞 0836 822 6111; 67 Chamashang Jie; 茶马上街67号; dm/tw ¥50/80; 🛜) This friendly Tibetan-run hotel has a homely feel. Spacious carpeted rooms come with comfy beds, clean sheets and even warm duvets. There's also occasional wi-fi and shared bathrooms with 24-hour hotwater showers. Turn left out of the bus station; it's a few hundred metres on your left.

Dégé Hotel   HOTEL $$
(德格宾馆; Dégé Bīnguǎn; 📞 822 6666; 11 Gesa'er Dajie; 格萨尔大街11号; r from ¥380, discounted to ¥180; ✳🛜) This standard, reliable hotel is in a big building by the river, near the bus station. All rooms have private bathrooms and some even have nice mountain views. Turn left out of the bus station, cross the bridge, and follow the signs to turn right down the lane into the hotel courtyard.

Kāngbā Zàngcān TIBETAN $

(康巴藏餐; ☎139 9049 9866; Chamashang Jie; 茶马上街; dishes ¥20-30; ☺9am-10pm) This Tibetan teahouse serves authentic Tibetan food, plus tea and beer. There's no menu, but here's a sample of what's on offer: yak pancakes (牛肉饼; *niúròu bǐng*; ¥30), yak-meat *momos* (¥2 per dumpling), *thukpa* (¥15), *tsampa* (¥10) and butter tea (from ¥15). No English is spoken. Turn left out of the bus station; it's on your right, on the 2nd floor.

Jiàng Hóng Relay Station CAFE $

(绛红驿站; Jiàng Hóng Yìzhàn; 3 Bagong Jie; 巴宫街3号; ☺10am-midnight; ☎) This little cafe serves small snacks such as chicken wings and fries (from ¥15), OK coffee (¥30), and has cushy sofas. The owner lets out the *very* basic upstairs rooms (expect cloth-covered windows, very low ceilings, and a sink in the hall) for ¥50 a night. It's on your left on the road up the hill to the Bakong monastery.

⊙ Getting There & Away

Just one daily eastbound bus leaves from here at 7am, heading for Kāngdìng (¥182 to ¥201, next-day arrival) via Mǎnígāngē (¥36 to ¥39, 4½ hours), Gānzī (¥64 to ¥70, six hours) and Lúhuò (炉霍, ¥115 to ¥127, 7½ hours), where it stops for the night. Otherwise, there are minivans to Gānzī (¥100), Báiyù (¥80) and Mǎnígāngē (¥60).

Foreigners are not allowed to take public transport west from here into Tibet proper.

Sìchuān–Tibet Highway (Southern Route)

Travel along the southern route of the Sìchuān–Tibet Hwy takes you through vast grasslands dotted with alpine lakes, Tibetan block homes and abundant, contentedly grazing yaks. Majestic peaks seem to touch the sky.

Journeying along this 2140km route is slightly easier than taking the northern route, but it's still not for the faint-hearted; settlements are remote and high altitude is a factor as much as ever. Warm clothing and sunscreen are a must. However, as the Kāngdìng–Lǐtáng–Xiāngchéng–Shangri-la journey has become a popular route into Yúnnán province, road conditions have vastly improved.

The new, very high, Dàochéng-Yàdīng Airport puts everything in closer reach, but those who opt for the one-hour flight from Chéngdū should make sure to set aside a couple of days to acclimatise.

Lǐtáng 理塘

☎0836 / POP 51,300

At a dizzying altitude of 4014m, Lǐtáng (Lithang) is one of the highest settlements on earth. Its scenery will certainly leave you breathless, and getting out to see it – whether on horse, motorbike or foot – calls for spending at least a couple of days here.

For Tibetans, Lǐtáng occupies another exalted space as the birthplace of holy men, including the seventh and 10th Dalai Lamas and many revered lamas. Their birthplace and the town's large monastery, Chöde Gompa, draw devoted pilgrims from afar.

⊙ Sights & Activities

Former Residence of the 7th Dalai Lama BUDDHIST TEMPLE

(仁康古屋; Rénkāng gǔwū; Renkang Gujie, off Genie Lu; 仁康古街, 格聂路; ☺visitors 8am-7pm) Kelzang Gyatso (1708–57), the 7th Dalai Lama, was born in the basement of this house during a period of intense political struggle. Eventually growing into a visionary leader, under his rule Tibet established a national archive, instituted civil-service training programs, and formalised the Tibetan government structure. The house, built in the 16th century, is Lǐtáng's best preserved temple.

Not all Tibetans shared the belief he was the reincarnate; to escape the ongoing civil war, the Dalai Lama was raised and educated largely in exile. Qing Emperor Kangxi issued a proclamation affirming his identity, and in 1720 sent his son and troops to install the Dalai Lama to power in Lhasa. Mongol uprisings, rebellions and several coups later, the Dalai Lama gained the support of the clergy and the people.

The main house is a series of rooms crowded with devotees lost in prayer and displays of sacred relics of the Dalai Lama and the 13 other lamas born here. You may have to ask to see his actual birthplace, which is behind a door to the left of the entrance.

To get here, walk along Xinfu Xilu (辛附西路) towards Báitǎ Gōngyuán. Turn down the lane marked Renkang Gujie (仁康古街), which is on your right, before Chengxihe Lu (城河西路北二段).

Chöde Gompa BUDDHIST MONASTERY

(长青春科尔寺; Chángqīngchūn Kē'ěr Sì) At the north end of town, the large Chöde Gompa is a Tibetan monastery that was built for the third Dalai Lama. Inside there is a statue of

Sakyamuni, believed to have been carried from Lhasa by foot. Don't miss climbing onto the roof of the main hall on the far right for great views of the Tibetan homes leading up to the monastery, as well as the grasslands and mountains beyond. Monks climb up here to sound the *dungchen* (long horns).

To get here from the post office, turn left at the end of Tuanjie Lu, then take the first right and keep walking north.

Báitǎ Gōngyuán
CHÖRTEN

(白塔公园) Circle Báitǎ Gōngyuán with the worshippers as they recite mantras and spin the massive prayer wheels, or join the locals just hanging out in the surrounding park. Turn left out of the bus station and just keep walking.

 Activities

Hiking opportunities abound north of town and further afield.

You can trace the steps of the two-day *kora* around Zhāgā Shénshān (扎嘎神山), a holy mountain a three-hour hike south of town. You'll need a tent. For help, talk to Mr Zheng at Tiān Tiān Restaurant (p758). Me-

dok at Potala Inn (p757) can also organise horse trekking (from ¥180).

There are **hot springs** (温泉; wēnquán; admission per person from ¥20) to soak in post-adventure. From Báitǎ Gōngyuán, keep hiking west for about 5km until you see a steaming creek. Skip the bathhouses right by the road; the nicer options are just over the hill.

Lǐtáng has a secluded **sky burial** (天葬; Tiān zàng) site in the hills behind Chöde Gompa. You must have the permission of the monastery to attend, so ask Mr Zheng or your guesthouse to help make the arrangements. If you do attend a sky burial, always remember exactly what you are watching and treat the rites, and all those involved, with the utmost respect.

🎎 Festivals & Events

Unfortunately, one of the biggest and most colourful Tibetan festivals, the Lǐtáng Horse Festival, which is usually held over several days from 1 August, hasn't happened in recent years. A series of smaller horse races from the end of July through August have been held instead. Check with your guesthouse for details.

YÀDĪNG NATURE RESERVE

The magnificent **Yàdīng Nature Reserve** (亚丁风景区, Yàdīng Fēngjǐngqū; ☑ 0836 572 2666; admission incl shuttle bus ¥270; ⊙ 7.30am-6.30pm), 140km south of Dàochéng, centres around three sacred snowcapped mountains, a holy trinity encircled by forested valleys, crystal-clear rivers and glacier-fed lakes. These are, quite simply, some of the most stunning landscapes you'll ever see. There are opportunities to hike, ride and camp here.

Locals have worshipped these mountains for more than 800 years. The three peaks – Chenresig (compassion), Chana Dorje (power) and Jampelyang (wisdom) – represent bodhisattvas in Tibetan Buddhism. Even for nonbelievers, walking the 35km *kora* (holy hike; 转山) around the highest peak, Chenresig (仙乃日; Xiānnǎiri), which tops out at 6032m, can be a hugely meaningful experience.

The clockwise circuit around Chenresig begins at **Lóngtóng Bà** (龙同坝) and takes at least 12 hours of serious hiking. To avoid one very long day, many use the campsites located about two-thirds round, near **Tiānpíng Chéng** (天平称). You have to bring all your own gear and supplies. (Though you'll pass locals living in simple stone huts, under park rules they are not supposed to take you in.) Remember to keep the mountain on your right, and to always take the right-hand turn when there's a choice of paths. There is a longer, four-day, 110km hike that adds a circuit around 5958m **Chana Dorje** (夏郎多吉; Xiàláng Duōjí), which begins and ends at the same place as the *kora*.

These hiking trails are all around 4000m above sea level, so acclimatise properly and pack for a serious expedition before you set off. Guides are available for hire at Lóngtóng Bà.

If you don't have the time (or energy) for a full circuit, there are buses and electric carts to shorter hikes. Take the shuttle bus from the ticket office into the park, to the small settlement of **Lóngtóng Bà**. From here hike 3km to the 800-year-old **Chonggu Monastery**

🛏 Sleeping

Potala Inn
HOSTEL $

(布达拉大酒店; Bùdálā Dàjiǔdiàn; ☑ 0836 532 2533, English 135 6867 7588; dm/tw ¥25/120, tr without bathroom ¥60; @ 🛜) Medok, a warm, English-speaking Tibetan, runs this large backpackers hostel, which has a mixed bag of rooms ranging from basic dorms to Tibetan-style twins with private bathrooms. Some are much nicer than others, so look first. For organising hiking trips, horse trekking, sky burial viewings or anything else in the area, Medok is the best in town.

There's free internet and wi-fi on the 1st and 2nd floors, and a pleasant cafe and bar. Turn left from the bus station and it's on the right, set back from the main street.

Lǐtáng Summer International Youth Hostel
HOSTEL $

(理塘的夏天国际青年旅舍; Lǐtáng de Xiàtiān Guójì Qīngnián Lǚshě; ☑ 180 1579 1574; 47 Ping'an Lu; 平安路47号; dm ¥35-40, r ¥160, ste ¥260) This lively youth hostel has the most cheerful rooms in town with colourful, warm bedding and a service demeanour to match. Hike this mountain? Find this unmapped route? Make me breakfast (¥10)? They'll make it happen. Except there's no English spoken. Turn left out of the bus station, and then left again down Ping'an Lu.

Night of Grassland
GUESTHOUSE $

(草原之夜; Cǎoyuán Zhīyè; ☑ 0836 532 2655, 189 9047 3777; dm from ¥35, r ¥130-200; 🛜) Smart twin rooms with wi-fi and private bathrooms are set around a garden courtyard. The upgrades have nifty oxygen machines for the O_2 deprived. It's popular with groups road-tripping in the summer, so call ahead (although little English spoken). Turn left out of the bus station, then left after the Potala Inn turn-off.

Peace Guest House
HOTEL $

(和平宾馆; Hépíng Bīnguǎn; ☑ 136 8449 3036; Chenghe Xilu; 城河西路; dm ¥25-30, d without/with bathroom ¥100/120, tr ¥150; @ 🛜) The private rooms, with a choice of wood veneer or colourful Tibetan decor, are clean and a real bargain. The dorms and shared bathrooms are another story. A revamped restaurant was in the works when we visited. Turn right out of the bus station and walk 50m up the hill.

(古寺; Chōnggǔ Sì), where you can pick up **electric carts** (one-way/return ¥50/80, 6km, 20 minutes) into the **Luòróng Grassland** (洛绒牛场; Luòróng Niúchǎng), which offers incredible views of the trinity and is as far as most tourists go.

It's worth continuing another 5km (three hours) to **Milk Lake** (牛奶海; Níunǎi Hǎi) and stunning **Five-Colour Lake** (五色海; Wǔsè Hǎi). You can also ride guided mules (one-way/return ¥200/300) for this segment, but keep in mind, even on four legs, the return journey takes 5½ hours on a steep, rocky trail. Riders must dismount multiple times to scramble alongside their ride for about a kilometre.

There are guesthouses and places to eat in **Yàdīng village** (亚丁村) and Lóngtóng Bà. To get an early start on the *kora*, try **Drolma's Youth Hostel** (卓姆民居青年旅舍; Zhuōmǔ Mínjū Qīngnián Lǚshě; ☑ 133 3079 0284, 0836 572 1069; tent ¥30, dm ¥40-50, r ¥120; 🛜) in Yàdīng village, which has a friendly backpacker vibe and the most pleasant rooms around. From the shuttle bus stop, take a few steps back up the hill and then follow the small road to the last Tibetan house on the right.

The best times to visit the reserve are May to June and September to early October.

Getting There & Away

Take a shared minibus (per person ¥50, 2½ hours) from Dàochéng to the small town of **Rìwǎ** (日瓦), where you buy tickets for the reserve. The ticket includes a mandatory ¥120 shuttle-bus fee, so take the park shuttle bus the last 32km into the park; it stops first in Yàdīng village and then 3km later at Lóngtóng Bà.

To get back to Dàochéng, catch the shuttle back to Rìwǎ, and then a minibus (¥50, 10am, 2pm and 5pm) back to Dàochéng.

DON'T MISS

DARJAY GOMPA 大金寺

Travellers sick of dusty market towns and only seeing gorgeous scenery through bus windows will enjoy two days exploring the grasslands around one of Gānzī prefecture's most venerated monasteries, **Darjay Gompa** (大金寺; Dà Jīn Sì), 30km west of Gānzī on the road to Dégé.

Talam Khang (大金寺旅馆, Dàjīn Sì Lǚguǎn; ☑ 187 8366 2272; Gānzī; camping & dm ¥50, d/tw ¥100/200) is a small temple, a short walk from Darjay Gompa, with snowcapped mountains to one side, and rolling grasslands and a river to the other. Three friendly monks welcome guests to share their mudbrick and wood-framed living quarters. Beds are carpeted benches, and rooms are similarly rustic and full of character. The monks cook up vegetarian noodle dishes (¥10 to ¥15) upon request.

To get to the temple from Darjay Gompa, exit from the monastery's back gate and walk about 15 minutes along the dirt road. Walk towards the white stupa furthest on the left, keeping the grassland villages on your right. You'll see the temple as you come over the hill.

It costs around ¥40 to get here from Gānzī in a shared minivan, at least ¥60 in a private taxi. Hitching is another option.

Lítáng International Youth Guesthouse HOTEL $
(理塘国际青年大酒店; Lítáng Guójì Qīngnián Dàjiǔdiàn; ☑ 0836 532 4666, English 135 6867 7588; Chengdong He Lu; 城东河路; dm ¥20-35, s & d ¥120-130) Under the same management as Potala Inn, this place has basic twins and doubles with attached bathrooms and offers travel advice and tours. The ¥10 upgrade gets you a sit-down toilet. Take the next right after the Potala Inn turn-off.

✖ Eating

★ Tiān Tiān Restaurant CHINESE, WESTERN $
(天天饮食; Tiāntiān Yǐnshí; ☑ 135 4146 7941; 108 Xingfu Donglu; 幸福东路108号; mains ¥15-35; ⊙ 9am-11pm; ◉) Long-standing travellers' haven run by ever-friendly, English-speaking ace chef, Mr Zheng. The food is a good mix of Chinese, Tibetan and Western cuisines; there's also coffee and delicious *tǔdòu bǐng* (土豆饼; potato pancakes; ¥20), as well as expert travel advice. Turn left out of the bus station and Tiān Tiān is about 600m along, on the left.

Tibetan Special Dishes TIBETAN $
(藏人家特餐; Zàngrénjiā Tècān; ☑ 182 8367 0582; 18 Xingfu Donglu; 幸福东路18号; mains from ¥20; ⊙ 8am-10pm; ◉) For authentic Tibetan food, try this simple place run by a friendly family from Tǎgōng. He doesn't speak English but has an English menu. Turn left out of the bus station. Tibetan Special Dishes is about 500m on the left.

❶ Information

China Post (中国邮政; Zhōngguó Yóuzhèng; Tuanjie Lu; ⊙ 9-11.30am & 2-5.30pm) Turn left out of the bus station, then right at the main roundabout crossroads.

❶ Getting There & Away

It's normally easy to bag Kāngdìng or Xīndūqiáo bus tickets but otherwise, buses are often full by the time they reach Lítáng. Minivans (around ¥40 more expensive than buses) loiter outside the bus station to save the day. The quickest way north to Gānzī (¥110, around five hours) is by minivan via Xīnlóng. No scheduled buses run this route.

Buses go to the following:

Bātáng ¥63, 3½ hours, around 3pm

Dàochéng ¥48, four hours, around 1.30pm

Kāngdìng ¥87, eight hours, 6.30am

Xiāngchéng ¥66, five hours, two daily (around 1.30pm and 3pm)

Xīndūqiáo ¥63, six hours, 6.30am

Dàochéng 稻城

☑ 0836 / POP 32,300

Although the small town centre is modernized these days, Dàochéng (Dabpa; 3750m) still packs bags of rural charm and makes a lovely base for exploring magnificent Yàdīng Nature Reserve (p756). After Yàdīng, you can fill another couple of days here, walking or cycling around boulder-strewn wetlands, hills, and barley fields, which are scattered with Tibetan monasteries. Fall is particularly beautiful, when a blaze of red leaves and grass electrifies the landscape.

🛏 Sleeping

Given the size of this town, there is a surprising number of decent options. Dexi Jie (德西街), a quiet lane just to the left of the bus station, has a number of good choices.

Drolma's Guesthouse HOSTEL $
(📞 136 8449 1026; zhuomarenjia@163.com; 50 Dexi Jie; dm ¥30-40, r without/with bathroom ¥80/120; 🛜) The best place to stay in town is this Tibetan-style house tucked behind a big gate on Dexi Jie. The English-speaking manager runs a neat, comfortable ship and can advise on hiking routes in Yàdīng and beyond. There's coffee, laundry (¥10), bike rental (¥20), and organised trips to nearby Rúbùzhákǎ (茹布扎卡) hot springs (¥40).

Yàdīng Backpackers Hostel HOSTEL $
(亚丁人社区国际青年旅舍; Yàdīng Rén Shèqū Guójì Qīngnián Lûshě; 📞 136 1813 7066; www.yading.net; 58 Dexi Jie; dm ¥40-50, tw ¥180; @ 🛜) Small rooms are set around the courtyard of a pretty Tibetan blockhouse (first right off Dexi Jie).

Dé Jí Zàng Jiā Kèzhàn GUESTHOUSE $
(德吉藏家客栈; 📞 135 4715 2157, 0836 773 5781; 6 Dexi Jie; dm ¥20-40, tw ¥180; @ 🛜) The dorm beds in this Tibetan blockhouse are the cheapest in town at ¥20. Wi-fi is only in the common areas.

Péng Sōng Cuò HOTEL $
(彭松措; 📞 0836 572 8581; Xingfu Lu; 幸福路; dm ¥30-40, r ¥120-160; 🛜) The rooms in this new Tibetan-style house by the river are either standard hotel rooms with private, modern bathrooms, or rustic wood cabins. All have wi-fi. Turn left out of the bus station, walk past Dexi Jie and the police station, then turn left onto Xingfu Lu.

🍴 Eating

The town is small enough to wander into something tasty. E Chu Jie (俄初街; make two right turns out of the bus station) is a walking street with dependable noodle (¥10 to ¥12) and barbecue (¥1.50 to ¥4 per stick) establishments. Street vendors set up along the main drags of Gongga Jie and Gongba Lu.

ℹ Getting There & Away

Two buses leave daily at 6am. One goes to Chéngdū (¥239, 20 hours), via Lǐtáng (¥60, three hours) and Kāngdìng (¥135, 10 hours); the other goes southwest to Shangri-la (Zhōngdiàn; ¥114, 10 hours) in Yúnnán province, via Xiāngchéng (three hours). You can buy tickets from 2pm the day before, although you cannot buy tickets to Lǐtáng or Xiāngchéng until the morning the bus leaves. Minibuses (per person ¥80) are more common for these two destinations.

Minibuses are the only option for Yàdīng Nature Reserve (¥50, three hours).

The new Dàochéng-Yàdīng Airport, 43km north, has daily flights to Chéngdū (¥1180, one hour, 8.55am) and thrice-weekly flights to Chóngqìng (¥1550, 8.50am Tuesday, Thursday and Saturday). Airport shuttle buses (¥30, 50 minutes, 6am and 6.15am) leave from Gongga Lu. Turn left out of the bus station and keep walking for about 1km. Shuttles wait by the tall, new building on the right.

Xiāngchéng 乡城

📞 0836
The little valley town of Xiāngchéng (Chaktreng; 3180m) is a good spot to break your journey into or out of Yúnnán province. It benefits from a microclimate that keeps temperatures here slightly warmer than everywhere else around it, making it a particularly comfortable stop.

The ornate **Sampeling monastery** (桑披岭寺; Sāngpīlíng Sì; admission ¥15) at the top end of town commands fine views of the surroundings. There are also quiet lanes of beautiful, high-walled Tibetan houses off the main road. Turn left out of the bus station, then take a right at the Delei Hotel (德勒大酒店) down Nainai Zhong Jie (奶奶仲街).

Lāmǔ Bīnguǎn (拉姆宾馆; 📞 158 8405 2619; r without/with bathroom ¥60/100) has a few very basic rooms, some with great views, in a white Tibetan-style house down the hill, across from the bus station. **Seven Lake Hotel** (七湖宾馆; Qīhú Bīnguǎn; 📞 0836 582 5059; 114 Xiangbala Nanlu; 香巴拉南路114号; r without/with bathroom ¥50/80, tr ¥120; 🛜), past the bus station on the left, has four storeys of simple rooms with wi-fi.

Further up the main street, on the left before the town square, a northern couple cooks up their hometown style of dumplings (水饺; shuǐjiǎo; ¥15 per half jīn) at **Hēilóngjiāng Dōngběi Jiǎozi** (黑龙江东北饺子; 📞 182 8362 6582; 9 Sangpi Jie; 桑披街9号; dishes from ¥10; ⏰ 8.30am-9pm). A half jīn (bàn jīn) is plenty for one. So is a killer bowl of bànmiàn (干拌面; mince-meat dry noodles; ¥10 to ¥12).

❶ Getting There & Away

Two buses leave daily at 6am. One goes south to Shangri-la (Zhōngdiàn; ¥87, eight hours); the other goes to Kāngdìng (¥154, 12 hours). Note tickets to Lǐtáng are not sold on the Kāngdìng-bound bus, even though it's en route; take a shared minivan instead (¥80, 4½ hours).

There are also buses to Dàochéng (¥50, three hours, 6am and 3.30pm). A shared minivan to Dàochéng is around ¥80.

NORTHERN SÌCHUĀN

Hiking, or even camping, in the stunning Jiǔzhàigōu National Park or heading out on horseback around Sōngpān are how most travellers experience the carpets of alpine forest, swaths of grasslands, icy lakes and snow-topped mountains of northern Sìchuān. You can also travel north from here into Gānsù, Shaanxi or even Qīnghǎi, or loop around towards western Sìchuān via Dānbā.

Note that banks in this region cannot change foreign currency.

Sōngpān   松潘

📳 0837 / POP 71,650

Horse trekking into the woods and mountains is the main attraction of this laid-back, historic town, a holdover from its role as a major trading centre on the Tea Horse Road (茶马路). The hiking is also good, so there's a healthy backpacker population to swap travel tales with.

In midwinter (December to March) Sōngpān slows down, and some businesses close; however, even in the cold, horse trekking is still possible.

◉ Sights

Old Town   HISTORIC SITE
(古镇; Gǔzhè) Sōngpān's old town is full of cranes and jackhammers, part of a major initiative to add more top-end guesthouses and eateries. Parts of the city and rebuilt city wall may be less than a decade old, but its borders are still marked by ancient gates.

The gates are original Ming-dynasty structures going back some 600 years. Note the horse carvings at the foot of the two south gates, half swallowed by the ever-rising road. The only original part of the old wall is by the rebuilt West Gate, which overlooks the town from its hillside perch.

Two wooden covered bridges – Gǔsōng Qiáo (古松桥) and Yìngyuè Qiáo (映月桥) – the bases of which are very old, span the Mín River. On the western side of the river is Guānyīn Gé (观音阁), a small temple near the start of a hillside trail that offers good views over Sōngpān.

✷ Activities

One of the most popular ways to experience the alpine forests and lakes surrounding Sōngpān is by signing on for a horse trek. Many people rate this experience as a highlight of their travels in this region. Guides lead you through otherwise unseen territory to remote campsites aboard not-so-big, very tame horses. Food and gear are all provided.

One of the most popular routes is a three- or four-day trek through unspoilt scenery to Ice Mountain (雪宝顶; Xuěbǎodǐng), a spectacular peak. A three-day trek to Qīcáng Valley (七藏沟; Qīcáng Gōu), recently opened to camping, passes several technicolor lakes.

The nearby hills are wonderfully good for hiking. One option is to hike around one hour up to the only remaining part of the original town wall, by the West Gate. There are three paths up: one starts beside the stream north of North Gate; another leads up the hill from the west end of Gulou Jie; while a third is accessed via Guānyīn Gé. Another option is to hike for about two hours to Shàngníbā Monastery (上泥巴寺庙; Shàngníbā Sìmiào) in the eastern hills.

Shùnjiāng Horse Treks   HORSE RIDING
(顺江旅游马队; Shùnjiāng Lǚyóu Mǎduì; 📳153 0904 6777, 0837 723 1064; Shunjiang Beilu; 顺江北路; per person per day ¥220-320) The most established union of guides in town has been leading tourists, foreign and domestic, on horse treks for years. You can tailor trips from one to five days. Expect limited English-language skills.

Rates are all-inclusive of gear, horses and two meals. Your guides take care of setting up tents and cooking, unless you want to. The only additional charges are park entry fees for some of the trips (you are told of these before you set out), and tips, should you be inclined.

The majority of travellers seem happy with their services, but we do sometimes receive reports of guides careless about environmental impact. Also, some travellers have had trouble getting refunds, particularly when the weather turned bad, which

Sōngpān

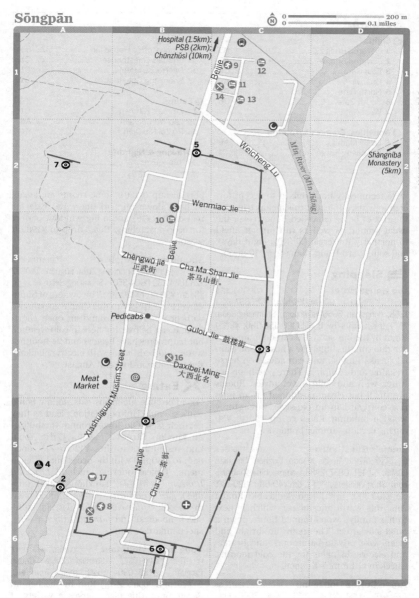

Hospital (1.5km);
PSB (2km);
Chūnzhǔsì (10km)

Beijie

Weicheng Lu

Mǐn River (Mǐn Jiāng)

Shàngníbā
Monastery
(5km)

Wenmiao Jie

Beijie

Zhèngwǔ jie
正武街

Cha Ma Shan Jie
茶马山街

Pedicabs

Gulou Jie 鼓楼街

Xiashuǐguan Muslim Street

Meat
Market

Daxibei Ming
大西北名

Nanjie

Cha Jie 茶街

it often does. If you don't speak Chinese or Tibetan, we recommend booking through local and Chéngdū hostels, which will help you negotiate details, such as the terms for a refund.

Qíqílè Mǎduì   HORSE RIDING
(骑奇乐马队; ☎ 0837 723 4138, 135 6879 2936; per day per person ¥220) If you speak Chinese, you may want to inquire at this well-run outfitter, although as of this writing, they

were technically not licensed to accept foreign tourists. (Officially, this means trips run the risk of being cancelled.) They cover the usual ground as well as run further afield to northerly Ruò'ěrgài (若尔盖; eight days), and southward Hóng Yuán (红原; 10 days).

🛏 Sleeping

Old House Hotel　　　　　GUESTHOUSE $
(松山古韵客栈; Gǔyùn Kèzhàn; ☑0837 723 1368; dongshan_6666@sina.com; Shunjiang Beilu; 顺江北路; dm/s/tw/tr ¥35/120/150/180; @ 🛜) Right by the bus station, a can-do mum-and-son duo run this hotel like a hostel. Son Daniel speaks English and can advise on horse trekking and camping. There's 24-hour hot water, wi-fi and solid travel advice. Rooms are small but clean, positioned off an interior courtyard in an old-style, three-storey wooden building. Rates go up ¥50 to ¥80 during certain summer holidays.

Emma's Guesthouse　　　GUESTHOUSE $
(小区欧洲青年旅舍; Xiǎoqū Ōuzhōu Qīngnián Lǚshě; ☑131 0837 2888; emmachina@hotmail.com; Shùn Village; 顺江村; dm ¥40-60, r ¥120-180, ste ¥200-300; ❄🛜) Knowledgeable Emma runs this warm guesthouse, which is next to her family's wood-framed house down a quiet side street. The rooms are bright and clean with private bathrooms, and heaters and electric blankets for the cold months. Check in at Emma's Kitchen.

Amdo Coffee House Inn　　　HOTEL $$
(安多房子咖啡客栈; ☑139 9041 7006, English 135 1596 0964; Beijie, North Gate; s/d with shared bathroom from ¥248; ⊖🛜) In this stylish wooden structure inside the old town's north gate, management is still working out the kinks. Hot water is elusive and staff speak little English, but at least there's airport pickup (¥120). Some rooms are small, so head downstairs to the wired cafe for real coffee (¥18) and a big window, perfect for people watching. Rates drop to ¥198 off season.

Shùnjiāng Guesthouse　　　GUESTHOUSE $
(顺江自助旅馆; Shùnjiāng Zizhù Lǚguǎn; ☑0837 723 1064, 139 0904 3501; Shunjiang Beilu; 顺江北路; dm ¥30-40, r ¥120; 🛜) The owners of Shùnjiāng Horse Treks run this simple guesthouse with decent rooms around an open courtyard. It can be freezing here in cold weather, but bathrooms have heaters and 24-hour hot water, and beds come with electric blankets. Rates double in July and August.

🍴 Eating

For affordable, delicious eats, follow Sōngpān's sizeable Huí population's lead as they get their fix in Old Town around **Xiashuiguan Muslim Street** (下水關清真街). You'll find restaurants (dishes ¥12 to ¥15; open 8am to 9.30pm) with the occasional English menu. Typical offerings include *Lánzhōu lāmiàn* (兰州拉面; Lánzhōu pulled noodles), *gān bànmiàn* (干拌面; minced-meat dry noodles), *dāoxiāo miàn* (刀削面; knife-sliced noodles) and *yángzá tāng* (羊杂汤; sheep innards soup).

Song in the Mountain　　CHINESE, WESTERN $
(山里子之歌川菜馆; Shānlizǐ Zhīgē Chuān Càiguǎn; ☑189 0904 3640; mains from ¥10; ⊙7.30am-11.30pm; 🍴🖥) Run by the helpful Sarah Yang, this place serves a variety of simple Western and Chinese dishes at reasonable prices.

★ Emma's Kitchen　　　CAFE, PIZZA $$
(小欧洲西咖啡餐厅; Xiǎo Ōuzhōu Xī Kāfēi Cāntīng; ☑131 0837 2888, 0837 723 1088; em-

machina@hotmail.com; Shunjiang Beilu; mains ¥18-58; ⊙8am-midnight; 🛜📶) Sōngpān's main travellers' hang-out is this laid-back cafe with wi-fi and fresh coffee (from ¥16), pizza and other Western fare, along with a number of Chinese dishes. Emma is exceedingly knowledgeable and can sort out almost anything from laundry to tickets to picnic lunches for your horse trek. She also has leads on mountain-biking tours (from ¥220).

This is where you check-in for Emma's Guesthouse (p762).

Rǔ Zǎi Niú Diǎn
HOTPOT $$
(乳崽牛点; ☑0837 725 3555; Daxibei Ming Snack St; 大西北名小吃一条街; pot from ¥88, fixings ¥6-30) A soothing meal after a long trek into the grasslands. Start with a pot of the house speciality, a unique, nonspicy tomato-based soup, and then add your choice of fixings: thinly sliced beef (鲜牛肉; xiān niúròu), chicken wings (鸡翅; jīchì), cabbage (大白菜; dà báicài), winter melon (冬瓜; dōngguā) and bamboo shoots (竹荪; zhú sūn) are all possibilities. It's in Old Town near the east gate.

🍷 Drinking

Along the Mín River (岷江; Mín Jiāng), on the southern edge of town, are several small teahouses (tea from ¥5; open 8am to 6pm) where you can while away the afternoon with the locals.

Lǎo Wū Càiyuán
TEAHOUSE
(老屋菜园; tea from ¥5, dishes from ¥8; ⊙8am-11pm) Through an unassuming archway near the east end of Yìng Yuè Qiáo is this buzzing courtyard teahouse, a local favourite. The house special, spicy liángfěn (凉粉; ¥8), made of mung bean and potato starch, won the prize for being the best in the region.

ℹ️ Information

It is not possible to change foreign currency in Sōngpān.

Agricultural Bank of China (中国农业银行; Nóngyè Yínháng; Shunjiang Beilu) Foreign-card–friendly ATM.

Public Security Bureau (PSB; 公安局; Gōng'ānjú; ☑0837 723 3778; 新区; ⊙8.30am-noon & 3-6pm) Take a ¥10 taxi from Old Town to get here in the new district (新区). Can usually renew visas in one day.

ℹ️ Getting There & Around

AIR
There's no public transport between Sōngpān and the Jiǔhuáng Airport. A taxi should be around ¥100 (¥150 at night).

BUS
Buses leaving Sōngpān bus station (客运站; kèyùnzhàn) include:

Chéngdū ¥124, 7½ hours, three daily (6am, 6.30am and 7am)

Dūjiāngyàn ¥107, 6½ hours, 7.20am

Huánglóng National Park ¥32, two hours, three daily (6am, 7am and 1.50pm)

Jiǔzhàigōu ¥46, 2½ hours, two daily (9am and 1pm)

Zöigě ¥51, three hours, two daily (10am and 2.30pm)

PEDICAB
Pedallers wait on the west end of Gulou Jie (鼓楼街) to give rides generally starting at ¥5.

THE ROAD TO GĀNSÙ

Those heading north into Gānsù province will need to bus-hop their way from Sōngpān. First stop is Zöigě (若尔盖; Ruò'ěrgài), a small, remote Tibetan town, with a distinct frontier feel. The grasslands here burst into life with wildflowers in late summer, and it's possible to arrange horse treks, although facilities are more rustic than those in Sōngpān, and English-language skills are rare.

Shǔguāng Bīnguǎn (曙光宾馆; ☑083 7229 2988; Shuguang Jie; r without/with bathroom ¥120/160) is known for its decent rooms, some with private bathrooms. Turn left out of the bus station and walk 100m. There are plenty of eating options on Shuguang Jie.

Zöigě buses go to Sōngpān (¥51, three hours, 10am and 2.30pm) and Lángmùsì (郎木寺; ¥20, two hours, 2.30pm), an enchanting monastery town straddling the Sìchuān–Gānsù border. From Lángmùsì you can catch onward transport towards Lánzhōu. Buses can be sporadic, especially when snow renders roads impassable. Zöigě is at 3500m and temperatures can plummet suddenly.

Jiǔzhàigōu National Park 九寨沟风景名胜区

📞 0837 / POP 62,000

Jiǔzhàigōu National Park (Jiǔzhàigōu Fēngjǐng Míngshèngqū; 九寨沟风景名胜区; 📞 0837 773 9753; www.jiuzhai.com; admission incl bus adult/concession 1 May–15 Nov ¥310/200, 16 Nov–31 Apr ¥170/130; ⏰ 7am-7pm May–mid-Nov, 8am-6pm mid-Nov–Apr, last tickets 3hr before closing), an enchanting Unesco World Heritage Site, is one of Sìchuān's star attractions. More than two million people visit annually to gawk at its famous bluer-than-blue lakes, rushing waterfalls and deep woodlands backlit by snowy mountain ranges. The park's major sites are easily accessed on foot, via kilometres of well-maintained boardwalk trails, or by bus. There are even opportunities to camp (p765).

The best time to visit is September through to November, when you're most likely to have clear skies and (particularly in October) blazing autumn colours to contrast with the turquoise lakes. Summer is the busiest, and also rainiest, time. Spring can be cold but still pleasant, and winter, if you're prepared for frigid temperatures, brings dramatically frosted trees and frozen-in-place waterfalls.

Jiǔzhàigōu means 'Nine Village Valley' and refers to the nine Tibetan villages scattered in the parklands. According to Tibetan legend, Jiǔzhàigōu was created when a jealous devil caused the goddess Wunosemo to drop her magic mirror, a present from her lover the warlord god, Dage. The mirror dropped to the ground and shattered into 114 shimmering turquoise lakes.

Seniors (70 and over) and kids get in free, but are required to purchase ¥10 visitor insurance. A ¥90 hop-on, hop-off bus fee is automatically included in admission for all visitors.

⊙ Sights

There are a number of lakes and waterfalls in the area worth visiting. The main road follows **Zéchǎwā River** (Zéchǎwā Hé) up Shùzhēng Valley, as it runs past **Héyè Village** (Héyè Cūn) to **Sparkling Lake** (火花海; Huǒhuā Hǎi), the first in a series of lakes filled by the **Shùzhēng Waterfall** (树正瀑布; Shùzhēng Pùbù).

A walking trail begins north of Sparkling Lake and runs along the eastern edge of the river up to **Nuòrìlǎng Waterfall** (诺日朗瀑布; Nuòrìlǎng Pùbù). Here, the road branches in two, with the eastern road leading to **Long Lake** (长海; Cháng Hǎi) and **Five-Coloured Pool** (五彩池; Wǔcǎi Chí); and the western road leading to **Swan Lake** (天鹅海; Tiān'é Hǎi).

The western route has a greater concentration of attractions, most of which are accessible from the quiet forest trail leading from **Mirror Lake** (镜海; Jìnghǎi) to **Panda Lake** (熊猫海; Xióngmāo Hǎi). Views from this trail are particularly fantastic, especially those of the waterfall known as **Pearl Shoals** (珍珠滩瀑布; Zhēnzhūtán Pùbù).

The eastern route is almost better done by bus as the narrow road sees a great deal of traffic and there are fewer 'sights'. Never-

---

ℹ HOW TO 'DO' JIŬZHÀIGŌU

➡ **Start early** Get to the park entrance just a few minutes after opening. The early jam will have cleared up, and you'll still avoid the crush of late-rising tour groups.

➡ **Go up first** Since the most spectacular scenery is in the park's upper reaches, you'll see the highlights first if you take the bus to the top, then walk or ride down. Head first to either Long Lake or Grass Lake, work your way down to the Nuòrìlǎng junction, then go up the other fork. Later in the day you can see the lakes between Nuòrìlǎng and the entrance.

➡ **Get off the bus** Trails run throughout the park; by walking, you'll steer clear of the biggest crowds. The walking trails are generally on the opposite side of the lakes from the road, so you'll have more peace and quiet, too. If you have just a day, though, buses are required to see both routes.

➡ **Pack a lunch** Dining options inside the park are limited and expensive. If you bring your own food, you can picnic away from the hordes.

➡ **Take it easy** Site elevations veer from 2140m to 3060m, which is tough if you're not acclimated.

theless, the two lakes at the far end, Long Lake and Five-Coloured Pool, are well worth a visit.

It's about 14km from the park entrance to Nuòrìlǎng Waterfall; a further 17.5km along the western road to Swan Lake; then another couple of kilometres on to the Virgin Forest, which is as far as the road goes. On the eastern route, it's about 18km from Nuòrìlǎng Waterfall to Long Lake.

Zhārú Temple (Zaru Gompa) BUDDHIST TEMPLE
(扎如寺; Zhārú Sì) The first official sight inside the park proper is the Tibetan Zhārú Temple in the Zhārú Valley. The park bus doesn't stop here, but it's only a short walk from the ticket office; turn left at the first fork off the main road.

🏃 Activities

As part of the park's **ecotourism program** (九寨扎如沟生态旅游; Jiǔzhài Zhārú Gōu Zhēngtài Lǚyóu; ☑0837 773 7070; zharu.jiuzhai. com; Héyè Guesthouse, 2nd fl; 荷叶迎宾馆二楼; 1-/2-/3-day from ¥560/1320/1960) visitors can now hike and even camp inside the Zhārú Valley, just east of the main tourist valley. Prices include English-speaking guides, all camping equipment and main meals (although you may want to bring along some fruit and snacks), but exclude the park entrance fee. The multiday hikes include time to visit the main park without a guide after your hike. To have access to such unspoiled and hallowed land is an extremely rare opportunity in China and numbers are strictly limited, so it's highly advisable to email or phone ahead, especially if you want to camp. The program office is on the 2nd floor of the Jiǔzhàigōu Administration Héyè Guesthouse, the white hotel to the right of the park entrance.

There are other great **hiking** opportunities all over this area, although not in the national park itself. One option is to hike around the hills near Zhuo Ma's homestay (p766); Zhuo Ma can advise you on good routes. She also arranges short **horse treks** (two hours, ¥180) from the village, and helps run two- to three-hour **Tibetan cookery classes** (per person including a meal ¥150) at Ābù Lǚzī restaurant (p766).

🛏 Sleeping

There's an almost endless supply of hotels around Péngfēng Village (彭丰村; Péngfēng Cūn), the area near the park entrance, so

don't worry if the place you had your heart set on is full.

★ **Zhuo Ma's**   HOMESTAY $

(卓玛; Zhuómǎ; 🕿135 6878 3012; www.zhuomaji-uzhaigou.hostel.com; per person ¥200) A genuine Tibetan homestay, this pretty wood cabin in a tiny village about 10km up the valley from the main park has six simple rooms and a wonderfully accommodating family. There's a common bathroom with shower, and prices include three meals and pick-up from the bus station (otherwise it's around ¥60 in a taxi).

The lovely Zhuo Ma speaks some English and is usually on hand to welcome foreign guests. Her mother (amma) is the host and cooks the meals. If you're coming from Sōngpān you could ask the driver to drop you on the main road at Shàng Sì Village (上寺; Shàng Sì Zhài). Zhuo Ma's is about a 15-minute walk uphill from there. Any problems, just call Zhuo Ma.

Angelie Hotel   HOSTEL $

(三嘉宾馆; Sānxī Bīnguǎn; dm from ¥35, r from ¥200, discounted to ¥100) More hostel than hotel, the friendly, English-speaking staff here organise Huánglóng tours (¥120), cook up Eastern and Western food, and book tickets: all the usual hostel stuff in a hotel-ish setting. Dorms are stand-alone rooms on top of the roof, which offers incredible views of the mountains. From the park entrance, cross the street, turn left and walk about 400m.

Jiǔzhài Rénjiā Youth Hostel   HOSTEL $

(九寨人家青年旅舍; Jiǔzhài Rénjiā Qīngnián Lǚshè; 🕿0837 777 4455, some English 189 0904 4443; www.jzrjhostel.com; Péngfēng Village; dm

TIBET'S NO-GO REGIONS

Foreigners are forbidden from travelling individually overland from Sìchuān into Tibet proper (西藏, Xīzàng) as Tibet's far eastern prefecture of Chamdo (昌都地区, Chāngdū Dìqū), which borders Sìchuān, is usually off limits. During March (a time of holy celebrations and politically sensitive anniversaries), Tibet is often completely closed to foreigners. This closure has extended to Sìchuān's Ābà and Gānzī prefectures though not in recent years. Hostels keep up with the latest information, or check the China and Tibet branches of Lonely Planet's online forum, **Thorn Tree** (www.lonelyplanet.com/thorntree).

¥40, s from ¥190, discounted to ¥80; 🕿) There are five or so run-of-the-mill youth hostels within 100m of each other in Péngfēng Village. This one is furthest from the park entrance (a 15-minute walk), but has a good vibe with friendly staff. Call ahead for a ride from the bus station.

Jiǔzhàigōu Grand Hotel   HOTEL $$$

(九寨沟贵楼饭店; Jiǔzhàigōu Guìbīnlóu Fàndiàn; 🕿0837 773 9066, 0837 773 5555; r incl breakfast from ¥696, discounted to ¥460) You can't beat the location, just beside the park entrance gate. The rooms themselves are fairly midrange, but they're large and many have views of either the mountains or the stream that runs alongside the hotel.

🍴 Eating & Drinking

Péngfēng Village is crammed with Sichuanese restaurants. If you're willing to catch a cab, there's a strip of small places with a bit more atmosphere (and drink options) along the pleasant riverside, Bianbian Jie (边边街).

Inside the park you can buy pricey snacks and drinks. There is also a restaurant (also pricey) at the **Nuòrìlǎng junction** (诺日朗). Some hostels can pack a lunch for you.

★ **Ābù Lǔzī**   TIBETAN $$

(阿布镥孜藏餐; Ābù Lǔzī Fēngqíng Zàngcānba; 🕿135 6878 3012; www.abuluzi.com; Péngfēng Village; dishes from ¥39; ⊙11am-11pm, 📶) The nicest Tibetan restaurant in Jiǔzhàigōu, this excellent establishment is run by the same family behind Zhuo Ma's homestay (Zhuo Ma's brother, Ke Zhu, is a trained chef). There's an extensive menu of delicious Tibetan dishes, and some Western ones as well. They also run Tibetan cookery classes (per person ¥150).

Star Cafe   CAFE

(太白楼西餐酒吧; Tàibái Lóu Xīcān Jiǔbà; 🕿0837 773 9839; 23 Bianbian Jie; 边边街23号; mains ¥20-48; ⊙11.30am-midnight; 🕿) A chill hangout, Star Cafe has a decent selection of fresh coffee (from ¥25), beer (from ¥15) and wine, plus a range of international dishes from the most common tourist nationalities. There's free wi-fi and patio seating by the river.

Ā Mī Luō Luō   BAR

(阿咪罗罗; 🕿187 8375 7666; 11 Bian Bian Jie; beer from ¥30, dishes from ¥40; ⊙9.30pm-midnight) This dimly lit bar by the river has an international selection of brews to wash down Tibetan bites and Western bar snacks.

WORTH A TRIP

HUÁNGLÓNG NATIONAL PARK

A trip to Huánglóng National Park (黄龙景区, Huánglóng Jǐngqū; ☑ 083 7724 9166; www.huanglong.com; adult/student & senior ¥200/110, cable car ¥80; ⊗ admission 8am-5pm) is essentially a five-hour, moderate hike up and down one small valley. The valley, however, is stunning, with exquisite terraces of coloured limestone ponds in blues, greens, oranges, yellows and white. The best time to come is May to October, ideally during mild July and August. At this elevation (3600m), always bring a jacket.

With smaller crowds than Jiǔzhàigōu, Huánglóng is certainly worth the trip. To see the whole park, walk 800m to the cable car (8am to 5.30pm), which drops you in a deep forest. The path leads you up a few kilometres to the start of the main sights, and then down again to the entrance, some 8km of long ascents and descents in all.

By the park entrance is a visitor centre with restaurant, teahouse and luggage check. Pack a picnic as bottled water costs ¥10 in the park. There are also a few expensive tour-group hotels nearby, but most people day trip it from Sōngpān or Jiǔzhàigōu.

To get here, two daily buses depart Jiǔzhàigōu (¥48, three hours, 7am and 7.30am); travellers arriving on morning flights can take an airport shuttle (¥100, 1½ hours) directly to Huánglóng, where you'll wait for four hours before departing for Jiǔzhàigōu. There's also one return bus to Jiǔzhàigōu (¥45, 3pm) and a minibus (¥120, departs when full) by the visitors centre. To get to Sōngpān, take the Jiǔzhàigōu bus and ask the driver to drop you at Chuānzhǔ Sì (川主寺; one hour), where you can catch a shared taxi to Sōngpān (¥60).

❶ Information

An **ATM** (自动柜员机, Zìdòng Guìyuán Jī) at the park entrance accepts foreign cards, as does the China Construction Bank (near the bus station) and Agricultural Bank of China (in Péngfēng Village), where you can also change cash.

The park has an informative multilanguage website at www.jiuzhai.com. The visitors centre by the park entrance is less helpful.

❶ Getting There & Around

AIR

More than a dozen daily flights link Chéngdū with Jiǔzhàigōu Airport (officially, Jiǔhuáng Airport), which is located in Chuānzhǔ Sì (川主寺), a small town closer to Sōngpān than Jiǔzhàigōu. Direct flights include Běijīng, Shànghǎi, Hángzhōu, Chóngqìng, Kūnmíng and Xī'ān.

Shuttle buses to Jiǔzhàigōu (¥50, 1½ hours) meet arriving flights and drop off at Mènghuàn Jiǔzhài parking lot (梦幻九寨停车场; Mènghuàn Jiǔzhài tíngchē chǎng), 4km west of the park entrance. A taxi from there costs about ¥10.

A taxi all the way from the airport is pricey during peak season – about ¥300 (over ¥500 after 11pm). Many hotels and hostels offer pick-up services for about the same price.

BUS

Jiǔzhàigōu central bus station (九寨沟口客运中心汽车站; gōu kǒu zhàn) is just 2km east of the park entrance. Some buses arrive at Jiǔzhàigōu

Xiàn's station (九寨沟县), 40km away. A taxi from Jiǔzhàigōu Xiàn to Péngfēng Village costs ¥40 to ¥100, depending on season and time of day. Note, you can travel to western Sìchuān, via Dānbā, without having to go via Chéngdū.

Selected buses departing Jiǔzhàigōu central bus station:

Chéngdū ¥149, 10 hours, four daily (6am, 7am, 8am and 10am)

Chóngqìng ¥230, 12 hours, 7.30am

Guǎngyuán ¥93, eight hours, 6.30am

Huánglóng National Park ¥48, three hours, two daily (7am and 7.30am)

Sōngpān ¥38, two hours, 7.30am

TAXI

Taxis ply the streets and don't use meters. Generally, rides within Péngfēng Village and to the central bus station cost ¥10.

Lángzhōng 阆中

☑ 0817 / POP 242,535

An endless sea of black-tile roofs with waves of swooping eaves, flagstone streets lined with tiny shops, and temples atop hills of mist overlooking the river. It's all here in the town of Lángzhōng, Sìchuān's capital city during the Qing dynasty and now home to the province's largest grouping of extant traditional architecture.

◉ Sights

Old Town   HISTORIC SITE
(古镇; Gǔzhèn) Base yourself in old town Lángzhōng, the main attraction. Most will be happy enough not buying a ticket, instead wandering the alleys and studying the architecture, which is a blend of northern *táiliáng* (抬梁; pillars and beams) and southern *chuāndòu* (穿斗; through joint) styles that allow for a variety of dramatic roof shapes.

Don't miss Zhāng Fēi Temple (张飞庙; Zhāngfēi Miào; Xi Jie; 西街; admission ¥50), the tomb of local boy Zhang Fei, a legendary general during the kingdom of Shu, who administered the kingdom from here. The Fēng Shuǐ Museum (风水馆; Fēngshuǐ Guǎn; Dadong Jie; 大东街; admission ¥30) includes a model of the town, illustrating its feng shui–guided design. A helpful English-speaking guide is sometimes available here. Gòng Yuàn (贡院; Xuedao Jie; 学道街; admission ¥45) is among the best-preserved imperial examination halls in China.

For bird's-eye views of the town's rooftops and lanes, climb to the top of one of the three towers: Huáguāng Lóu (华光楼; 21 Dadong Jie; admission ¥15), just past the Fēng Shuǐ Museum and rebuilt in 1867; Zhōngtiān Lóu (中天楼; Wumiao Jie; admission ¥15), a 2006 rebuild on the way to Zhāng Fēi Temple; or South Gate (南门楼; Nánmén Lóu) FREE, a 2010 rebuild on Nan Jie, a street running parallel to Dadong Jie.

At any of the sights, you can buy a combination ticket (¥130, including shuttle to Jīnpíng Hill), which admits you to all of the above attractions as well as to a pagoda on Jīnpíng Hill (锦屏山). Sights are open from 8am to 6pm.

Grand Buddha Temple   HISTORIC SITE
(大佛寺; Dàfó Sì; admission ¥10) There's also some good exploring to be done across the river, south of the old town. At the foot of one hill, and among other Buddhist statuary and caves, sits the sedate-looking Grand Buddha. From the old town, walk down to the river, turn left and keep going past the second road bridge. Then cross the river on a small passenger boat (¥3).

🛏 Sleeping

There are dozens of renovated courtyard guesthouses in Old Town. Look for signs saying 客栈 (*kèzhàn;* guesthouse) or 住宿 (*zhùsù;* lodgings).

THE WAY TO XĪ'ĀN

Those on their way to Xī'ān from Jiǔzhàigōu can take the most direct overland route via the mid-sized town of Guǎngyuán (广元) on the main Chéngdū–Xī'ān train line.

China's only female emperor, Wu Zetian, was born in Guǎngyuán during the Tang dynasty. Huángzé Temple (皇泽寺, Huángzé Sì; adult/student ¥50/25; ⊗8am-6pm), with its pavilions and a thousand carvings, is dedicated to her. Further north on the east bank of the Jiālíng River, Qiānfú Cliff (千佛崖摩崖造像, Qiānfú Yá Móyá Aàoxiàng; adult/student ¥50/25; ⊗8am-6pm) is a honeycomb of more than 7000 grotto carvings dating back 1500 years.

Guǎngyuán's train and long-distance bus station (途汽车客运站) are adjacent. If you need to stay the night, to the right of the train station exit, Tiānzhào Hotel (天曌马瑞卡酒店, Tiānzhào Mǎruìkǎ Jiǔdiàn; ☑083 9366 8888; 212 Jinlun Nanlu, 金轮南路212号; r from ¥168; ❀@❀) has smart rooms. Huángzé Temple is about 750m beyond the hotel. Qiānfú Cliff is a walkable 4km northeast of the town, near the river's east bank.

Selected Buses from Guǎngyuán

Chéngdū ¥118, four hours, frequently from 6.30am to 9pm

Jiǔzhàigōu ¥80, 8½ hours, 6am and 4.10pm

Lángzhōng ¥60, three hours, five daily (7.40am, 8.30am, 10am, 12.30pm and 2.30pm)

Xī'ān ¥160, six hours, every 30 minutes from 6am to 5.30pm

Selected Trains from Guǎngyuán

Chéngdū K ¥47, five hours, very frequently from 12.16am to 10.55pm

Xī'ān K ¥75, 10 hours, 10 daily from 12.05am to 11.12pm

★ **Tiānyī Youth Hotel**   GUESTHOUSE **$**
(天一青年旅舍; Tiānyī Qīngnián Lǚshè; ☑0817 622 5501; 100 Dadong Jie; 大东街100号; r without bathroom ¥98-138, with bathroom ¥168-238; ✳@�) If you want to improve your geomancy, settle into this beautiful courtyard inn beside the Fēng Shuǐ Museum. The nice twin rooms are each inspired by a particular feng-shui element: earth, wood, fire, metal or water. The shared-bathroom twins and doubles are more simple, but are crisp and clean with lots of natural wood. Some have simple bedrolls (褥子; *rùzi*).

Ancient Hotel   HOTEL **$$**
(杜家客栈; Dùjiā Kèzhàn; ☑0817 622 4436; 63 Xiaxin Jie; 下新街63号; r from ¥480, discounted to ¥198; ✳@) The nicest rooms in this large wooden building with multiple courtyards are set around a back courtyard with an open-air stage (performances Friday and Saturday, 8pm to 10pm), and go for ¥295. Turn right off Dadong Jie just before the Huáguāng Lóu tower.

Lee's Courtyard   HOTEL **$$$**
(李家大院; Lǐjiā Dàyuàn; ☑0817 623 6500; 47 Wumiao Jie; 武庙街47号; r from ¥688, discounted to ¥410; ✳�) This is the most upscale option in Old Town, with lux bedding, fully equipped bathrooms and private balconies. After recent renovations, this ancient courtyard hotel, built in 1506, sparkles like a five-star hotel and is priced to match.

🍴 Eating

Popular local fare includes *zhāngfēi niúròu* (张飞牛肉; preserved water-buffalo beef; from ¥25 per packet), which makes a great road-trip snack. Eateries abound throughout Old Town.

Zhēng Zīwèi   NOODLES **$**
(筝滋味; 6 Shanghua Jie; 上华街6号; noodles ¥8-12; ⊙8am-10pm, to 8pm winter) This small, friendly noodle joint is run by Grace, an English teacher and zither (筝; *zhēng*) player, and her cook husband. No English menu, but Grace can help. If she's teaching or performing when you visit, just go for *niúròu*

miàn (牛肉面; beef noodles), with either *hóng tāng* (红汤; spicy soup) or *zhāngfēi* (张飞; more of a stew).

Shanghua Jie is a continuation of Dadong Jie; this place is just up from the Huáguāng Lóu tower.

☆ Entertainment

North Sìchuān Shadow Puppetry   THEATRE
(川北皮影; Chuānběi Píyǐng; ☑0817 623 8668; 67 Wumiao Jie; 武庙街67号; tickets ¥20; ⊙10am-9.30pm) A fifth-generation family of puppeteers put on fun, informal 20-minute performances of north Sìchuān shadow puppetry in a tiny, open-air courtyard. Shows are performed for audiences of two or more. It's a couple of doors from Lee's Courtyard.

ℹ Information

You can pick up **street maps** (地图; dìtú; ¥5) at some shops in the Old Town or at some tourist sights. Multilingual signs and maps are posted throughout the Old Town streets.

Bank of China ATM (cnr Dadong Jie & Neidong Jie) At the top end of Dadong Jie; accepts foreign cards.

ℹ Getting There & Away

Buses from Chéngdū's Běimén bus station arrive at Lángzhōng's main bus station (客运中心汽车站, kèyùn zhōngxīn qìchēzhàn), which also serves Chóngqìng (¥107, five hours, hourly from 7am to 3pm). Buses returning to Chéngdū (¥98, four hours) leave frequently between 6.40am and 5.30pm.

Lángzhōng also has a smaller bus station, Bāshíjiǔ Duì (89队), which serves Guǎngyuán (¥60, three hours, 8am, 9am, 10am, 1pm and 2pm), from where you can catch trains north to Xī'ān or buses west to Jiǔzhàigōu. Local bus 89队 (Bāshíjiǔ Duì; ¥2, 20 minutes) connects the two stations via the Old Town (ask to get off at Huáguāng Lóu, then walk up towards the tower for Dadong Jie).

From the Bāshíjiǔ Duì bus station, it's easiest just to walk to the Old Town. Turn left out of the station; after a couple of blocks turn right onto Tianshanggong Jie (天上宫街) and keep walking straight. Dadong Jie will be on your left. Wumiao Jie will be straight on.

Chóngqìng

POP 28.8 MILLION

Best for History

→ Dàzú Buddhist Caves (p783)

→ Fishing Town Fortress (p781)

→ Chóngqìng's city gates (p773)

Best for Scenery

→ Three Gorges (p772)

→ Wǔlóng County National Geology Park (p782)

→ Zhōngshān (p785)

Why Go?

Chóngqìng (重庆) municipality may be a relatively recent creation, having been carved out of Sìchuān province in 1997, but with its eponymous city driving the economy of western China, it's now one of the most important regions in the whole country. And, despite its new name, the area it covers has played a significant role throughout Chinese history and remains a place of great natural beauty.

Thanks to the mighty Yangzi River (Cháng Jiāng), which powers its way through here, this region has long been one of strategic military importance. The river was responsible for creating one of China's greatest natural wonders, the magnificent Three Gorges.

Humans have left their indelible mark as well, with a panoply of ancient Buddhist sculptures, dozens of seemingly lost-in-time villages and, of course, the -megalopolis that is Chóngqìng: one of the fastest-growing, buzzing cities in all China.

When to Go
Chóngqìng

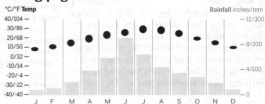

| Apr & May Winter chill has lifted; full force of summer sweat box yet to arrive, but still rainy. | Jul & Aug It's hot; temperatures top 40°C and Chóngqìng City resembles a steam bath. | Sep & Oct Manageable temperatures; a good time to explore the countryside. |

Chóngqìng Highlights

1 Shift down a gear or two as you float past the awe-inspiring Three Gorges on a **Yangzi River Cruise** (p776)

2 Gasp in wonder at the exquisite ancient artwork of the **Dàzú Buddhist Caves** (p783)

3 Explore the wild waterfalls and Karst formations of

Wǔlóng County National Geology Park (p782)

4 Tuck into the world's most mouth-numbing hotpot at **Mǎngzi** (p778)

5 Wander the cobblestones, or chill in a teahouse in the village of **Sōngji** (p785)

6 See traditional wooden stilt

housing in the ancient riverside village of **Zhōngshān** (p785)

7 Hike the ruins of **Fishing Town Fortress** (p781), one of China's greatest battlefields

8 Pull up a stool and sample the delights of **shāokǎo** (p777), Chóngqìng's no-nonsense streetside barbeques

History

Stone tools unearthed along the Yangzi River valleys show that humans lived in this region two million years ago. The ancient Ba kingdom ruled from here more than 2000 years before subsequent Qin, Sui and Southern Song dynasty rulers took over. From 1938 to 1945, Chóngqìng City (previously known as Chungking) became the Kuomintang's wartime capital. It was here that representatives of the Chinese Communist Party (CCP), including Zhou Enlai, acted as 'liaisons' between the Kuomintang and the communists headquartered at Yán'ān, in Shaanxi province.

Refugees from all over China flooded into the city during WWII. More followed when the construction of the Three Gorges Dam displaced more than one million people.

In 1997 Chóngqìng separated from Sìchuān province and became a municipality under the direct control of the central government.

The city was the backdrop for one of modern China's biggest political scandals in 2012 when Gu Kailai, the wife of Chóngqìng's Communist Party boss Bo Xilai, was convicted of murdering British businessman Neil Heywood. Allegations of corruption, extortion and espionage surrounded the case, as well as rumours that Běijīng was unhappy with Bo's populist policies and wanted him out of the

way. Both Bo and his wife were sentenced to lengthy prison terms.

Language

In addition to standard Mandarin Chinese, Chóngqìng residents also speak Sichuanese. It's a Mandarin dialect, but pronunciation is different enough that it's often difficult for those who speak standard Chinese to understand. Two words visitors will often hear are *yàodé* (pronounced 'yow-day', meaning 'yes' or 'ok') and *méidé* (pronounced 'may-day', meaning 'no').

Chóngqìng City 重庆市

🎵 023 / POP 6.7 MILLION

There's a frontier town vibe to Chóngqìng City, one of the most booming metropolises on earth. Despite a history that dates back to the ancient Ba kingdom (as well as being China's de facto capital during WWII) this former walled fortress has a distinctly brash feel.

Sprawling down both banks of the Yangzi River for miles – with further development ongoing – very little remains of old Chóngqìng. Yet the city has a unique energy that makes it a fascinating place and the locals are some of the most welcoming in all China. The gritty docks, too, are a permanent reminder of how

Chóngqìng City

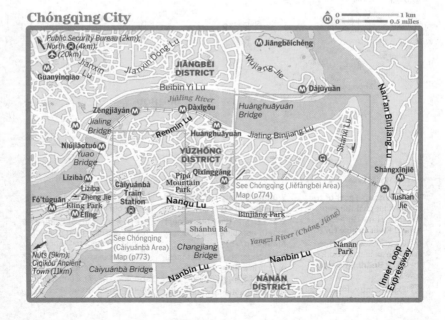

Chóngqìng's fortunes have long been tied to the river that flows through it.

Chóngqìng is sometimes mistakenly referred to as the most populous city in the world. It isn't. Figures for the whole municipality's population are close to 30 million but, for now anyway, the city of Chóngqìng itself has just under seven million inhabitants.

◉ Sights & Activities

Arhat Temple
BUDDHIST TEMPLE

(罗汉寺; Luóhàn Sì; Map p774; Luohan Si Jie; 罗汉寺街; admission ¥10; ⊗7am-5pm; Ⓜ Xiǎoshízi) Built around 1000 years ago, this still-active temple is now sandwiched between skyscrapers. A notable feature is the corridor flanked by intricate rock carvings found just after you enter the complex, but the main attraction here is **Arhat Hall** (罗汉堂; Luóhàn Táng), off to your right just after the corridor, which contains 500 terracotta *arhats* (a Buddhist term for those who have achieved enlightenment and who pass to nirvana at death).

Húguǎng Guild Hall
MUSEUM

(湖广会馆; Húguǎng Huìguǎn; Map p774; ☑6393 0287; Dongshuimen Zhengjie; 东水门正街; admission ¥30; ⊗9am-5pm; Ⓜ Xiǎoshízi) You could spend several hours poking around the beautifully restored buildings in this gorgeous museum complex, which once served as a community headquarters for immigrants from the Hú (Húnán and Húběi) and Guǎng (Guǎngdōng and Guǎngxī) provinces, who arrived in Chóngqìng several hundred years ago. There are rooms filled with artwork and furniture, a **temple**, a **teahouse** and several stages for Chinese **opera performances**.

Free-to-watch rehearsals of Yuèjù (an operatic style originating from Zhèjiāng province) and Jīngjù (Běijīng Opera) are held every Sunday, usually between 3pm and 6pm.

At the time of research, nearby construction meant that access to the Hall was via a dizzying series of steps to the right of the Dōngshuǐmén Bridge. Keep asking the way.

Ancient City Gates
RUIN

(古城门; Gǔchéngmén) Sadly, only fragments remain of Chóngqìng's once magnificent Ming dynasty city wall, which stretched 8km around the Jiěfàngbēi peninsula and was more than 30m tall in places. Of the 17 gates that punctuated the wall before demolition began in 1927, two are still standing. The charming, moss-hewn **Dōngshuǐ Mén** (东水门; Map p774) is on a pathway beside the

Chóngqìng (Càiyuánbà Area)

◎ Sights
1 Three Gorges Museum A1

✸ Eating
Made in Kitchen .... (see 1)

ℹ Information
2 Global Doctor Chóngqìng Clinic A2

ℹ Transport
3 Airport Shuttle Bus A1
4 Càiyuánbà Bus Station A3
5 Escalator A3

Yangtze River Hostel. Larger, and partly restored is **Tōngyuán Mén** (通远门; Map p774; Ⓜ Qixingang, exit 1), a short walk from Qīxīnggǎng metro station.

You can walk along the wall for a short stretch at both locations. If you're interested in seeing how the wall once encircled the old city, look for the carved map of ancient Chóngqìng on the **public square at Cháotiānmén** (朝天门广场; Cháotiānmén Guǎngchǎng; Map p774), itself once a city gate.

Cíqìkǒu Ancient Town
OLD TOWN

(磁器口古镇; Cíqìkǒu Gǔzhèn; Ⓜ Cíqìkǒu, exit 1) The opportunity to snatch a glimpse of old Chóngqìng makes it worth riding out to this

Chóngqìng (Jiěfàngbēi Area)

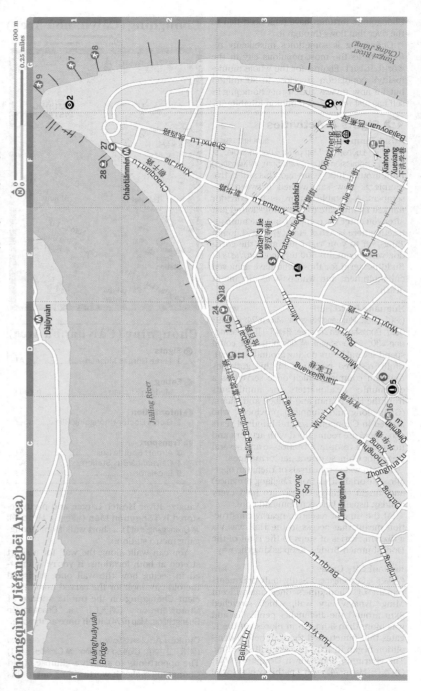

500 m
0.25 miles

Huánghuāyuán Bridge

Dàjùyuán

Jialing River

Jialing Binjiang Lu 嘉陵滨江路

Jialing River (Chang Jiang)
Yangzi River

17

3

4

15

Xiahong Xuexiang 下洪学巷

Baijiayuan

Dongzheng Jie

Xi-San Jie 西三街

10

Shanxi Lu 陕西路

Xinyi Jie 新义街

Xinhua Lu 新华路

Luohan Si Jie 罗汉寺街

Datong Jie 打铜街 Xiǎoshìzi

1

Muzhu Lu

Bayi Lu

Wuyi Lu 五一路

Chāotiānmén

Chaoijan Lu 朝千路

27

28

18

24

14

11

Cāngbáilù 苍白路

Jianglaixiang

Linjiang Lu

Wusi Lu

Minzu Lu

Zhonghua Lu

Zhonghua Xiang 中华巷

Qingnian Lu

16

5

Zourong Sq

Linjiāngmén

Datong Lu

Beidu Lu

Lujiang Lu

Hua Yi Lu

Beiqu Lu

part of town, on the Jiālíng River west of the centre. Through the archway that is the entrance to the town, most of the buildings – many dating to the late Ming dynasty – have been restored, and the main drag can feel like a carnival, especially on weekends, but away from the central street, a living, working village remains.

You can easily lose yourself in its narrow lanes, peeking into homes and tiny storefronts. And there's plenty to eat here, both in the alleys and overlooking the river. It's also worth poking your head inside **Bǎolún Sì** (宝轮寺; admission ¥5; ⊙7am-6pm), one of Cíqìkǒu's only remaining temples. Its main building is more than 1000 years old. The alley the temple is on, Heng Jie (横街), is one of the most pleasant places to explore, and contains a string of cute cafes with wi-fi.

Three Gorges Museum   MUSEUM
(三峡博物馆; Sānxiá Bówùguǎn; Map p773; 236 Renmin Lu; ⊙9am-4pm Tue-Sun; Ⓜ Zēngjiāyán, exit A) **FREE** This sleek museum showcases the history of settlement in the Chóngqìng region. There's the inevitable exhibition on the Three Gorges, including a model of the dam, as well as clothing and artwork relating to southwest China's minority groups. Some exhibits have better English captions than others.

🏃 Activities

Yangzi River Cable Car   CABLE CAR
(长江索道; Chángjiāng Suǒdào; Map p774; one-way ¥10; ⊙7am-10pm; Ⓜ Xiǎoshízì, exit 5) A ride on the creaky old Yangzi River cable car is slightly disconcerting, but gives you a wonderful bird's-eye view of the murky waters and the cityscape beyond. It drops you off near the riverside bar and restaurant strip on Nan'an Binjiang Lu.

City River Cruises

Chóngqìng looks best from the water, especially at night when the city flashes with neon. The so-called two-river cruises last for 60 to 90 minutes, leaving every afternoon (2pm to 3pm) and evening (7pm to 8pm) from Cháotiānmén Dock, and can be a fun way of getting an alternative view of this unique metropolis.

There are a number of boats offering the same service. The difference in prices reflects the quality and age of the boats. **Cháotiāngōng** (朝天宫; Map p774; evening cruise ¥136), **Cháotiānmén** (朝天门; Map p774;

Chóngqìng (Jiěfàngbēi Area)

evening cruise ¥148) and **Jīnbì Huánggōng** (金碧皇宫; Map p774; evening cruise ¥148) were the three most popular at time of research. Although there are cruises every day, not all boats run daily. The boats have no English signs and very little English is spoken. You can eat on board, although menus are in Chinese only and the food is pretty expensive (dishes ¥30 to ¥80). Prices listed are for evening cruises, which are much more popular (and more worthwhile). Expect to get tickets for as little as ¥40 to ¥50 for an afternoon cruise. Buy your tickets from the end of the jetty leading to the boat in question, or at any number of ticket sellers around town.

⚑ Tours

While it is possible to **cruise the Yangzi River** (p786) in either direction, Chóngqìng is the most popular spot to start your trip along the river, mainly because of its proximity to the mighty Three Gorges. Both luxury and ordinary cruises depart daily and tickets for them are sold at travel agencies all over town. It's best to book a day or two ahead and, if possible, avoid Chinese public holidays when the boats get very crowded.

🛏 Sleeping

★ Green Forest Hostel HOSTEL $
(瓦舍; Wǎshě; Map p774; ☑ 6310 4270; chongqing-greenforest@gmail.com; 4/F, Yuya Bldg, 7 Zhongxing Lu; 中兴路7号渝亚大厦4楼; dm/s/d/tw/tr ¥55/148/180/220/270; ✳@🛜; Ⓜ Jiàochǎngkǒu, exit 4) The office block location may lack the character of its sibling the Yangzi River Hostel, but this new place has bigger, better and brighter dorms and rooms, all with bathrooms. There's also an excellent, spacious cafe-communal area, efficient, pleasant staff and a very handy location, close to restaurants, shops and bars.

Yangtze River Hostel HOSTEL $
(玺院青年旅舍; Xǐyuàn Qīngnián Lǚshè; Map p774; ☑ 6310 4208; yangtzeriverhostelreception@gmail.com; 80 Changbin Lu; 朝天门长滨路80号; dm ¥35-50, tw & d ¥200; ✳@🛜; Ⓜ Xiǎoshízi) Overlooking the river and backing onto one of the remaining stretches of Chóngqìng's ancient city wall, this friendly, well-run hostel is a smart choice if you don't mind climbing steps to walk into town (there are few eating options in the immediate area). Dorms are spacious and some come with bathrooms, while private rooms are bright and clean, if compact.

There's a pool table and a restaurant-cafe in the lobby area. Staff provide reliable travel advice without giving it the hard sell, making this a good place to book your Yangzi River cruises.

Sunrise Míngqīng Hostel   COURTYARD HOTEL **$**
(尚悦明清客栈; Shàngyuè Míngqīng Kèzhàn; Map p774; ☑ 6393 1579; www.srising.com; 23 Xiahong Xuexiang (down steps from 26 Jiefang Donglu); 下洪学巷23号 (解放东路26中对面); dm ¥69, tw & d ¥369,; ❋ @ ⦿; M Xiǎoshízí) Facing the western wall of Húguǎng Guild Hall, this renovated Qing dynasty courtyard hotel isn't a true hostel – there's no restaurant or cafe – but remains an atmospheric place to stay. Rooms are beautifully decorated but, like all courtyard places, they are dark and small. It can also be accessed by climbing the steep alley just to the west of Húguǎng Guild Hall.

Deck 88 Hostel   HOSTEL **$**
(桃亭国际青年旅舍; Táotíng Guójì Qīngnián Lǚshè; Map p774; ☑ 6281 7796; 88 Jiabin Lu; 嘉滨路88号; dm/s/tw/d ¥50/150/210/200; ❋ @ ⦿; M Xiǎoshízí) New hostel right on the riverfront that sees more Chinese travellers than foreigners. Dorms are poky, but the private rooms are a decent deal for this part of town. Staff are friendly, although there's not much English spoken, and there's an amenable communal area with a bar. To get here, take the lift at the Hóngyádòng complex on Cangbai Lu down to the ground floor, turn left and walk for 75 metres.

Hóngyádòng Dàjiǔdiàn   HOTEL **$$**
(洪崖洞大酒店; Map p774; ☑ 6399 2888; 56 Cangbai Lu; 沧白路56号; tw & d from ¥650; ❋ @ ⦿; M Xiǎoshízí) This huge complex – built in faux Chóngqìng stilt-house style – hugs the cliff side overlooking the Jiālíng River and comes with restaurants, bars, shopping streets and this comfortable hotel with welcoming staff. Rooms are big and well maintained, some with balconies and river views. Reception is on the 11th floor of the complex. Discounts (up to 30%) are generally available.

Xīnhuá Hotel   HOTEL **$$**
(新华酒店; Xīnhuá Jiǔdiàn; Map p774; ☑ 6355 7777; 9 Qingnian Lu; 青年路9号; tw from ¥828; ❋ @ ⦿; M Jiàochǎngkǒu) Elegant, low-lit interior with spacious, well-equipped rooms (TV, fridge, safe) but smallish bathrooms. Some English spoken. A stone's throw from Liberation Monument so about as central as it gets. Routine 40% discounts make it a fair choice.

Harbour Plaza   HOTEL **$$$**
(重庆海逸酒店; Chóngqìng Hǎiyì Jiǔdiàn; Map p774; ☑ 6370 0888; www.harbour-plaza.com; Wuyi Lu; 五一路; tw & d from ¥1500; ❋ @ ⦿ ⦿; M Jiàochǎngkǒu) Smart and large rooms at this centrally located and popular hotel. All come with wide-screen TV, fridge and safe. Wi-fi throughout and proper bathrooms. English spoken and the travel desk on the 3rd floor can help with Yangzi River cruises. Up to 50% discounts are often available.

✖ Eating

Chóngqìng is all about hotpot (火锅; huǒguō): a fiery cauldron of head-burning làjiāo (辣椒; chillies) and mouth-numbing huājiāo (花椒; Sìchuān peppers) into which is dipped deliciously fresh ingredients, from vegetables and tofu to all types of fish and meat. It's a dish best sampled with a group. Indeed, hotpot restaurants tend to be among the liveliest you'll find.

As well as the local noodle dishes, another great thing to sample in Chóngqìng is shāokǎo (烧烤; barbeque skewers), the perfect point-and-eat street food. Just choose your skewers, hand them over and wait for them to come back spiced and grilled. Select from dòufu pí (豆腐皮; tofu skin), xiǎo mántou (小馒头; mini steamed rolls), niángāo (年糕; sticky rice cake), qiézi (茄子; eggplant/aubergine), and jiǔcài (韭菜; leek) among other ingredients.

Shāokǎo barbeque spots are found all over the city. Most shāokǎo places in Chóngqìng also do bowls of pigs brain (脑花; nǎohuā) as a side dish. We dare you.

Zhào'èr Huǒguō
HOTPOT $

(赵二火锅; Map p774; ☎ 6671 1569; 128 Jiefang Donglu, 3rd fl; 解放东路128号世纪龙门大厦三楼; dipping ingredients ¥4-25; ⏱ 11am-2pm & 5.30pm-midnight) Highly popular, Zhào'èr's hotpot is rightly lauded. There are various options: the nine-sectioned pot (九宫锅; *jiǔgōng guō*) allows you to separate the flavours of your raw ingredients (ideal if one of you is vegetarian), although the broth is shared; while the two-sectioned *yuānyang guō* (鸳鸯锅) has a clear broth that is separated completely from the spicy one.

You may be asked if you want your broth spicy (红的; *hóngde*) or clear (青的; *qīngde*) and therefore spiceless. Assuming you opt for spicy, we highly advise you plump for mild! As well as all the usual hotpot raw ingredients, the speciality here is fresh lamb tripe (鲜毛肚; *xiān máodǔ*). The water spinach (空心菜; *kōngxīn cài*) is also particularly good.

No English sign or menu. Look for the archway with yellow characters against a red backdrop and walk up the stairs to the left.

Mǎngzi
HOTPOT $

(莽子老火锅; Mǎngzi Lǎo Huǒguō; Map p774; ☎ 6371 8492; Zhongxing Lu, 10 Wangyeshibao; 中兴路王爷石堡10号; dipping ingredients ¥6-26; ⏱ 11am-2am) A real locals' fave with some of the tastiest (and spiciest) hotpot in town. You sit on wooden benches around your table and bubbling broth. Expect to see male diners with their shirts off, beer bottles close to hand. It's just up the alley at the end of Qingnian Lu in the midst of the flower market on the left-hand side.

Look for two red characters on a yellow sign. No English menu, but the friendly staff will do their best to assist.

Uncle
CANTONESE $

(表叔; Biǎo Shū; Map p774; ☎ 6326 5050; Riyueguang Zhongxin Sq, 89 Minquan Lu; 民权路89号日月光中心广场; dishes ¥26-49; ⏱ 11am-11pm; Ⓜ Jiàochǎngkǒu) If your body needs a break from Chóngqìng's fiery chillies, head to this Guǎngzhōu restaurant chain, modelled on a type of Hong Kong teahouse-cum-canteen. It's young, friendly, brightly lit and serves a good variety of tasty Cantonese dishes – lots of soups as well as noodle and rice meals.

Portions are hearty, meaning most dishes are meals in themselves. It's at the back of a public square, under the giant TV screen. Nonsmoking, too.

Liúyīshǒu Huǒguō
HOTPOT $

(刘一手火锅; Map p774; ☎ 6161 8555; 46 Cangbai Lu, 3rd fl; 沧白路46号南国丽景大厦3楼; dipping ingredients ¥5-28; ⏱ 10am-midnight; Ⓜ Xiǎoshízì) The hotpot here is decent enough, and the atmosphere is congenial, but the real attraction is the view; you dine as you gaze out across the Jiālíng River. You'll be pushed to find a river-view table at peak eating times, so perhaps come earlier or later than you'd usually eat. Take the lift to the right of Motel 168.

CHÓNGQÌNG NOODLES

Chóngqìngers are particularly fond of noodles and you'll find noodle joints all over the region. They rarely have English menus or signs – just look for the character 面 (*miàn*; noodles) and you're good to go.

Specialities here include *xiǎomiàn* (小面) or *málà xiǎomiàn* (麻辣小面) – often eaten for breakfast despite being very spicy – and *liángmiàn* (凉面), which are delicious despite being served cold. Noodles in Chóngqìng are served by the *liǎng* (两; 50g). Two-*liǎng* (二两; *èr liǎng*) or three-*liǎng* (三两; *sān liǎng*) portions are most common. Expect to pay between ¥6 and ¥10 for a bowl. Remember: *wǒ néng chī làde* (I can handle spicy food); *bù yào tài là* (not too spicy, please).

Menu Decoder

➧ *málà xiǎomiàn* (麻辣小面; spicy noodles)

➧ *liángmiàn* (凉面; cold noodles)

➧ *niúròu miàn* (牛肉面; beef noodles)

➧ *jīdàn miàn* (鸡蛋面; egg noodles)

➧ *suānlà fěn* (酸辣粉; tangy glass noodles)

➧ *féicháng miàn* (肥肠面; pig intestine noodles)

HOTPOT MENU

The best hotpot restaurants are entirely local affairs so you have about as much chance of finding an English menu as you have of being able to eat the thing without your nose running. (Do not underestimate a hotpot's bite. This part of China is renowned for fiery food, and it doesn't come spicier than hotpot.)

As with many dishes in Chóngqìng, the first thing to establish when ordering hotpot is how hot you want it – *bù là* (不辣; not spicy, but in Chóngqìng this will still be spicy), *wēi là* (微辣; mildly spicy), *zhōng là* (中辣; medium spicy), *zuì là* (最辣; very spicy) and *jiā má jiā là* (加麻加辣; extra, extra spicy).

Then you'll be given a menu checklist of raw ingredients that you will later cook in your pot. Here are some of our favourites for you to look out for on the menu:

➡ *yángròu juǎn* (羊肉卷; wafer-thin lamb slices)

➡ *féi niúròu* (肥牛肉; beef slices)

➡ *xiān máodǔ* (鲜毛肚; fresh tripe, usually lamb)

➡ *xiān yācháng* (鲜鸭肠; strips of duck intestine)

➡ *lǎo dòufu* (老豆腐; tofu slabs)

➡ *ǒu piàn* (藕片; slices of lotus root)

➡ *xiān huánghuā* (鲜黄花; chrysanthemum stalks)

➡ *tǔ dòu* (土豆; potato slices)

➡ *bái cài* (白菜; cabbage leaves)

➡ *mù'ěr* (木耳; mushroom)

➡ *kōngxīn cài;* (空心菜; water spinach)

★ **Zēng Lǎo Yāo Yú Zhuāng**   HOTPOT $$
(曾老幺鱼庄; Map p774; ☑ 6392 4315; Changbin Lu; 长滨路 (洞子邮亭鲫鱼); ⊙24hr) Outside, it's a seething mass of people crowded around tables. Inside, it's even more packed as you descend into a former bomb shelter – white-tiled walls and a rock roof. This Chóngqìng institution is a unique, utilitarian dining experience, with all stratum of society in search of the signature fish dish (鲫鱼; *jìyú;* carp) and the simply sublime spare ribs (排骨; *páigǔ*).

As always, it's best to eat in a group and be prepared to wait for a table. But it never closes, so you can roll up anytime. No English menu, so point at what others are eating. Every taxi driver in town knows this place.

Xiǎo Bīn Lōu   CHONGQING $$
(小滨楼; Map p774; ☑ 6383 8858; Riyueguang Zhongxin Sq, 4/F, 89 Minquan Lu; 民权路89号日月光中心广场4层; set menu ¥50-78; ⊙11.30am-2pm, 5.30-8.30pm) A gentle introduction to Chóngqìng cuisine, especially good for the spice-averse. Choose from a selection of small-sized dishes on display, or better still go for one of the set menus, either six or eight dishes. It's on the fourth floor of a shopping mall, but the interior is a spacious approximation of an old Chóngqìng eatery.

Made in Kitchen   ASIAN, WESTERN $$$
(厨房制造, Chúfáng Zhìzào; Map p773; ☑ 6363 6228; Three Gorges Museum, 236 Renmin Lu, 人民路236号三峡博物馆; dishes from ¥48; ⊙11am-10pm; Ⓜ Zēngjiāyán) It's an unpreposseing approach through a dimly lit underpass, but this is a swish, stylish restaurant with tip-top service. The menu spans Asia – sushi and Thai dishes as well as Chinese – and it's also a fine place for a Western steak (¥198). Decent wine list too.

Located underneath the Three Gorges Museum, the entrance is down to the left as you face the museum entrance.

🍷 Drinking & Nightlife

As well as the places listed below, there are a string of riverside bars (酒吧; *jiǔbā*), cafes and restaurants on **Nan'an Binjiang Lu** (南岸滨江路); take the cable car over the Yangzi, then walk down to the river and turn left. From there, walk 15 minutes along the river or hop on any bus for one stop. Note: the cable car stops running at 10pm.

THE TOUGHEST PORTERS IN CHINA

Ever since the first Chóngqìngers couldn't bear the thought of carrying their buckets of water from the river up to their cliff-side homes, there's been a need for a special kind of porter. A porter who can lift more than his body weight and lug that load up and down hills all day long. A porter who can't use a trolley like in other cities, or a bike or a rickshaw, but instead works on foot using only the cheapest of tools: a bamboo pole – or 'bangbang' – and a length of rope.

Known as the Bangbang Army, these porters have been bearing the city's weights on their shoulders for hundreds of years, but their numbers really exploded in the 1990s when the government began resettling millions who lived along the Yangzi River. Many came from the countryside with little education and no relevant skills, and soon became part of the 100,000-strong workforce.

'Bangbang' porters earn around ¥50 per day to work in one of China's hottest, hilliest cities, lugging heavy loads up and down steep hills, although you'll also see them carrying people's shopping home on the subway.

Despite the wealth that's been pumped into the city in recent years (just look across the river at the Grand Theatre), the Bangbang Army continues to be an integral feature of Chóngqìng and porters are especially plentiful in the area close to the docks.

Dé Yī Shì Jiè (得以世界) is a public square surrounded by tacky bars, karaoke joints and the city's biggest nightclubs.

For traditional **teahouses**, head to Cíqìkǒu Ancient Town and look for signs for 茶园 (cháyuán; tea garden).

★ Cici Park   BAR
(西西公园; Xīxī Gōngyuán; Map p774; 1/F Hong-yadong, Jiabin Lu; 洪崖洞, 嘉滨路; beer from ¥15; ⊙5pm-late; ⓂXiāoshízì) The most amenable bar in Chóngqìng, Cici's has a very chilled vibe and bohemian furnishings. Beers are affordable, mixers start at ¥30 and sometimes there are DJs and live music. It attracts a mixed crowd of both locals and expats, some of whom like to roll their own cigarettes.

Nuts   LIVE MUSIC
(坚果俱乐部; Jiānguǒ Jùlèbù; ☑8810 1647; www.douban.com/host/nutsclub; Shazhong Lu, Shapingba district; 沙坪坝区沙中路; beers from ¥15; ⊙7pm-2am; ⓂShāpíngbà, exit 2) Fabulous, pint-sized club that's *the* place to catch live music. Local bands take to the stage every weekend, but it also hosts any act of note passing through town. It's right by Chóngqìng University so gets a decent crowd in. Live music carries a ¥30 cover charge.

You can walk here from Shāpíngbà metro station in 20 minutes. Take exit 2, walk through the Three Gorges Square, then straight along Hanyu Lu (汉榆路), then left down Shazhong Lu (沙中路) and it's on the right-hand side.

The Harp Irish Pub   BAR
(竖琴爱尔兰酒吧; Shùqín Àiěrlán Jiǔbā; ☑6880 0136; Chóngqìng Tiāndì; 化龙桥重庆天地; draught beers from ¥35; ⊙3pm-1am; ☎) Not much to do with the Emerald Isle, but by far the best spot in town to catch live sport, especially the English Premier League, NBA and NFL. Strong selection of foreign brews and decent pub grub: fish and chips, pizzas, burgers and salads, as well as reasonable Mexican dishes. Also has a pool table and is nonsmoking.

It's located in a new complex of bars and restaurants a ¥25 taxi ride from the centre. There's another, smaller branch on the ninth floor of the Hóngyádòng complex (p780).

Chóngqìng Sìchuān Opera House   THEATRE
(重庆市川剧院; Chóngqìngshì Chuānjùyuàn; Map p774; ☑6371 0153; 76 Jintang Jie; 金汤街76号; tickets ¥20; ⊙2pm) Holds a 2½-hour performance of Sìchuān opera every Saturday afternoon.

🛍 Shopping

For top-name brands, head to the glitzy shopping malls around the **Liberation Monument** (解放碑; Jiěfàngbēi; Map p774). For souvenirs, try the unashamedly touristy 3rd floor of **Hóngyádòng** (洪崖洞; Map p774; 56 Cangbai Lu, 沧白路56号; ⊙9am-10pm; ⓂXiāoshízì), below the hotel of the same name, or head to Cíqìkǒu Ancient Town.

ℹ Information

INTERNET ACCESS

There are internet cafes (网吧, wǎngbā; per hour ¥3) all over the city, including three or four by Càiyuánbà Bus Station.

MEDICAL SERVICES

24-Hour Pharmacy (药店; Yàodiàn; Map p774; 63 Minquan Lu; 民权路63号; ⊗24hr; Ⓜ Jiàochǎngkǒu) Western medicine, ground floor; Chinese medicine, 1st floor.

Global Doctor Chóngqìng Clinic (环球医生重庆诊所; Huánqiú Yīshēng Chóngqìng Zhěnsuǒ; Map p773; ✍ 8903 8837; Suite 701, 7th fl, Office Tower, Hilton Hotel, 139 Zhongshan Sanlu; 中山三路139号希尔顿酒店商务楼7层701室; ⊗9am-5pm Mon-Fri) A 24-hour emergency service is available by dialling the general clinic number.

MONEY

ATMs are everywhere, and most accept foreign cards.

HSBC (汇丰银行; Huìfēng Yínháng; Map p774; Minquan Lu; 民权路; ⊗9am-5pm Mon-Fri; Ⓜ Jiàochǎngkǒu) Has a money-exchange facility.

ICBC (Industrial & Commercial Bank of China; Gōngshāng Yínháng; 工商银行; Map p774; Minzu Lu; 民族路; ⊗9am-6pm; Ⓜ Jiàochǎngkǒu) On Minzu Lu beside the Liberation Monument. Has a dedicated money-exchange facility.

POST & TELEPHONE

China Post (中国邮政; Zhōngguó Yóuzhèng; Map p774; Minquan Lu; 民权路; ⊗9am-6pm; Ⓜ Jiàochǎngkǒu) You can top up your Chinese phone and buy SIM cards at the China Mobile store (open 9am to 9pm) on the 1st floor.

TRAVEL AGENCIES

Yangtze River (p776) and Green Forest (p776) hostels can arrange tours of all types (including Three Gorges cruises) and have better English-language speakers than the travel agencies and ticket offices around town. They charge minimal commission.

Harbour Plaza Travel Centre (海逸旅游中心; Hǎiyì Lǚyóu Zhōngxīn; Map p774; ✍ 6373 5664; 3rd fl, Harbour Plaza, Wuyi Lu; ⊗8am-10pm; Ⓜ Jiàochǎngkǒu) Staff here are helpful, speak English and can book air tickets and arrange Three Gorges cruises.

VISAS

Public Security Bureau (PSB; 公安局; Gōng'ānjú; ✍ 6396 1994; 555 Huanglong Lu; 黄龙路555号; ⊗9am-noon & 2-5pm; Ⓜ Tángjiā Yuànzi, exit 2) Extends visas. Accessed from Ziwei Zhilu (紫薇支路). Take metro Line 3 to Tángjiā Yuànzi (唐家院子). Leave from exit 2, go up the escalator, turn left then first right, then keep going until you see the large building with flags on your right (10 minutes).

CHÓNGQÌNG CHÓNGQÌNG CITY

WORTH A TRIP

FISHING TOWN FORTRESS

Fishing Town Fortress (钓鱼城; Diàoyú Chéng; admission ¥80; ⊗8.30am-6pm) Famed throughout China for being one of the great ancient battlefields, this 700-year-old fortress is surrounded by rushing rivers on three sides and perched on top of a 300m-tall rocky mountain. This was the last stand of the Southern Song dynasty and famously, in the 13th century, the fortress withstood the mighty Mongol armies for an incredible 36 years, during which time an estimated 200 battles were fought here.

The fortress was protected by an 8km-long, 30m-tall double wall, punctuated with eight gate towers. Much of the outer wall and all the main gates remain today; some partly restored, others crumbling away. There is little here in terms of facilities (bring a picnic) but it's a fascinating and peaceful place to walk around; narrow stone pathways lead you through the forest, past Buddhist rock carvings, gravestones, bamboo groves, ponds, caves, the wall and its gateways and some fabulous lookout points. Sights not to miss include the serene, 11m-long, 1000-year-old Sleeping Buddha (卧佛; Wòfó), cut into the overhang of a cliff, Hùguó Temple (护国寺; Hùguó Sì), dating from the Tang dynasty, although largely rebuilt, and the Imperial Cave (黄洞; Huángdòng), an ancient drainage passage with steps leading down to it, clinging to the outside of the fort wall.

To reach the fortress, take a bus from Chóngqìng to Héchuān. Alternatively, numerous trains run from Chóngqìng North train station (¥12.50, 40 minutes) to Héchuān. There are no direct buses to the fortress. A taxi from the train station should be ¥25; from the bus station ¥10. The last bus back to Chóngqìng from Héchuān is at 6pm.

WORTH A TRIP

WŬLÓNG COUNTY NATIONAL GEOLOGY PARK

Head a couple of hours southeast of Chóngqìng City and you enter a dramatic landscape where deep ravines cut through the thickly-forested hills, while waterfalls plunge into mighty rivers, and jagged limestone Karst formations rise up towards the sky. Mostly off the map for foreign travellers, the **Wŭlóng County National Geology Park** (武隆国家地质公园; Wŭlóng Guójiā Dìzhí Gōngyuán) is a fantastic place to experience the area's wild scenery.

A vast area of natural beauty, the park contain any number of attractions – endless caves, giant canyons and many waterfalls – the unmissable one is the **Three Natural Bridges** (天生三桥; Tiānshēng Sān Qiáo; admission ¥135). Towering above huge, hollowed-out karst formations, these natural bridges (you don't walk across them) are the highest in the world and utterly unique; you won't see anything like them anywhere else on the planet.

Unfortunately, visiting the park as an independent traveller is difficult. While there are regular buses to the unremarkable town of Wŭlóng from Chóngqìng's Sìgōnglǐ Bus Station, the park is 22km northeast of there and you'll need a taxi to reach it. You'll also require private transport to get around the park, which is massive. Each site too, has a separate (and pricey) admission ticket, while the restaurants and hotels scattered around the park are also expensive.

The best way to visit is on a day tour. Expect to pay ¥350 to ¥400 (bring your passport), which will include transport, lunch and admission to the Three Natural Bridges. The tours include at least one other sight in the park, normally **Lóngshuǐ Canyon** (龙水峡; Lóngshuǐ Xiá), a very deep gorge off which waterfalls tumble (take an umbrella!). Yangtze River and Green Forest hostels can arrange tours.

ℹ️ Getting There & Away

AIR

Chóngqìng's Jiāngběi Airport (重庆江北飞机场) is 25km north of the city centre, and connected to the metro system. As always, it's easiest to book online. Try www.ctrip.com or www.elong.net. Alternatively, buy tickets at the **China International Travel Service** (CITS; 中国国际旅行社; Zhōngguó Guójì Lǚxíngshè; ☑ 6383 9777; 8th fl, 151 Zourong Lu; 邹容路151号; ⊙ 9.30am-5.30pm Mon-Fri). Some English is spoken. Because of the high-speed rail link, there are no longer flights between Chóngqìng and Chéngdū. Direct flights include:

Běijīng ¥988, 2½ hours
Kūnmíng ¥531, 70 minutes
Shànghǎi ¥790, 2½ hours
Xī'ān ¥453, 90 minutes
Wǔhàn ¥603, 90 minutes

BOAT

Chóngqìng is the starting point for hugely popular cruises down the Yangzi River through the magnificent Three Gorges (p786).

BUS

Chóngqìng has several long-distance bus stations, but most buses use **Càiyuánbà Bus Station** (菜园坝汽车站; Càiyuánbà Qìchēzhàn; Map p773; Ⓜ Liǎnglùkǒu) beside the main (old) train station.

Destinations include:

Chéngdū 成都, Sìchuān (¥88 to ¥98, four hours, every hour, 7.40am to 6.30pm)

Chìshuǐ 赤水, Guìzhōu (¥65 to ¥70, 4½ hours, six daily, 7.40am to 6.30pm)

Dàzú 大足 (¥36 to ¥43, 2½ hours, every 30 minutes, 7am to 7pm)

Héchuān 合川 (¥29, 90 minutes, every 30 minutes, 6.30am to 8.30pm)

Sōngji 松溉 (¥41, two hours, one daily, 1.20pm)

Wànzhōu 万州 (¥111, 3½ hours, five daily from 8am to 5.30pm)

Yíbīn 宜宾, Sìchuān (¥97 to ¥115, three to four hours, every 30 minutes, 6.45am to 8.30pm)

Yǒngchuān 永川 (¥32, 90 minutes, every 20 minutes, 8.30am to 9.20pm)

Buses for **Jiāngjīn** 江津 (¥24, 70 minutes, every 30 minutes, 7am to 9pm) and **Fèngjié** 奉节 (¥160, four to five hours, hourly, 7.30am to 8.30pm), where you can catch the Three Gorges hydrofoil or ferry, leave from Lóngtóusì Bus Station (龙头寺汽车站; Lóngtóusì Qìchēzhàn), which is on metro Line 3 (station name: 龙头寺; Lóngtóusì).

For **Wǔlóng** 武隆 (¥60, three hours, every 40 minutes, 7.30am to 7.40pm), you need the Sìgōnglǐ Bus Station (四公里汽车站; Sìgōnglǐ Qìchēzhàn), which is on metro Line 3 (station name: 四公里; Sìgōnglǐ).

TRAIN

New, faster trains, including the D class 'bullet' train to and from Chéngdū, use Chóngqìng's new **North Station** (重庆北站; Chóngqìng Běizhàn; Kūnlún Dàdào; 昆仑大道), but some others, such as the train to **Kūnmíng** use the older train station at Càiyuánbà (菜园坝).

Destinations include:

Běijīng West 北京西 (hard sleeper ¥393, 23 to 31 hours, five daily, 11.34am to 11.40pm)

Chéngdū East 成都东 (hard seat from ¥46, two to 2½ hours, 20 daily, 6.49am to 7.51pm)

Guìlín 桂林 (hard sleeper ¥270, 20 hours, one daily, 8.35pm)

Kūnmíng 昆明 (hard sleeper ¥252, 18 to 19 hours, three daily, 9.24am, 2.12pm and 6.32pm)

Shànghǎi 上海 (hard sleeper from ¥421, 28 to 40 hours, three daily, 8.02am, 1.10pm and 4.29pm)

Wǔhàn 武汉 (hard sleeper from ¥206, 15 hours, three daily, 2.15pm, 6.18pm and 7.28pm)

Xī'ān 西安 (hard sleeper from ¥184, 10 to 11 hours, three daily, 10.05am, 12.45pm and 5.26pm)

🛈 Getting Around

AIRPORT

Metro Line 3 goes from the airport (机场; jīchǎng) into town (¥7, 45 minutes, 6.22am to 10.30pm). Note, the metro is signposted as 'Light Rail' (轻轨; qīngguǐ) at the airport.

The **airport shuttle bus** (机场大巴, Jīchǎng Dàbā; Map p773; ¥15, 45 minutes) meets all arriving planes and takes you to Meizhuanxiao Jie (美专校街), a small road off Zhongshan Sanlu (中山三路), via a couple of stops in the north of the city. Bus 461 goes from Zhongshan Sanlu to Cháotiānmén (朝天门). To get to the metro, turn left onto Zhongshan Sanlu and go straight over the large roundabout. Niújiǎotuó (牛角沱) station will be on your left.

Shuttle buses going to the airport run from 6am to 8pm.

A taxi is ¥60 to ¥70.

BUS

Local bus fares are ¥1 or ¥2. Useful routes:

Bus 105 North Train Station–Línjiāngmén (near Liberation Monument)

Bus 120 Cháotiānmén–Càiyuánbà Train Station

Bus 141 North Train Station–Cháotiānmén

Bus 419 North Train Station–Càiyuánbà Train Station

Bus 461 Cháotiānmén–Zhongshan Sanlu (for airport bus)

Bus 462 Zhongshan Sanlu (airport bus)–Liberation Monument

METRO

Chóngqìng's part-underground, part-overground **metro system** (轨道; Guǐdào; per trip ¥2-10; ⏱ 6.30am-11.30pm) has four lines and links the Jiěfàngbēi peninsula with many parts of the city, including the airport and the two train stations. Fares are ¥2 to ¥10 and trains run 6.30am to 11.30pm. Signs are bilingual but, unhelpfully, the metro map is in Chinese characters only (although stops are marked in pinyin on the maps on the trains).

The metro station for Càiyuánbà Train Station is called Liǎnglùkǒu (两路口) and is accessed via one of the world's longest **escalators** (大扶梯; dà fútī; Map p773; ¥2).

TAXI

Taxi flagfall is ¥10. A taxi from Jiěfàngbēi to Nuts (p780) should cost around ¥45.

Dàzú Buddhist Caves 大足石窟

The superb rock carvings of Dàzú (Dàzú Shíkū) are a Unesco World Heritage site and one of China's four great Buddhist cave sculpture sites, along with those at Dūnhuáng, Luòyáng and Dàtóng. The Dàzú sculptures are the most recent of the four, but the artwork here is arguably the best and in better condition.

Scattered over roughly 40 sites are thousands of cliff carvings and statues (with Buddhist, Taoist and Confucian influences), dating from the Tang dynasty (9th century) to the Song dynasty (13th century). The main groupings are at Treasured Summit Hill and North Hill.

👁 Sights

Treasured Summit Hill ARCHAEOLOGICAL SITE
(宝顶山; Bǎodǐng Shān; admission ¥135, combination ticket with North Hill ¥170; ⏱ 8.30am-6pm) Of all the stunning sculptures here, which are believed to have been carved between 1174 and 1252, the centrepiece is a 31m-long, 5m-high reclining Buddha depicted entering nirvana, with the torso sunk into the cliff face. Next to the Buddha, protected by a temple, is a mesmerising gold Avalokiteshvara (or Guanyin, the Goddess of Mercy). Her 1007 individual arms fan out around her, entwined and reaching for the skies. Each hand has an eye, the symbol of wisdom.

Treasured Summit Hill differs from other cave sites in that it incorporates some of the area's natural features – a sculpture next to the reclining Buddha, for example, makes use of an underground spring. At the time of writing, some of the sculptures were undergoing renovation.

The site is about 15km northeast of Dàzú town and is accessed by bus (¥3, 20 minutes, every 30 minutes, until 7pm) that leave from Dōngguānzhàn bus stop. Dàzú has two bus stations; old and new. Buses from Chóngqìng drop you at Dàzú's old bus station (老站; *lǎozhàn*). Buses from Chéngdū drop you at Dàzú's new bus station (新站; *xīnzhàn*). From either, take bus 101 (¥1) or a ¥7 taxi to get to Dōngguānzhàn bus stop.

Once at the site, it's a 10- to 15-minute walk from where the bus drops you off to the entrance to the sculptures. Buses returning from Treasured Summit Hill run until 6pm.

North Hill   ARCHAEOLOGICAL SITE
(北山; Běi Shān; admission ¥90, combination ticket with Treasured Hill Summit ¥170; ⊙8.30am-6pm; 📷) This site, originally a military camp, contains some of the region's earliest carvings. The dark niches hold several hundred statues. Some are in poor condition, but it is still well worth a visit. It's about a 30-minute hike – including many steps – from Dàzú town; turn left out of the old bus station and keep asking the way. It's ¥20 in a taxi.

South Hill   ARCHAEOLOGICAL SITE
(南山; Nán Shān; admission ¥20; ⊙8.30am-6pm) This modest site really only has one set of carvings, but makes a nice appetiser before you delve into the main courses at North Hill and Treasured Summit Hill. It's behind the old bus station and takes around 15 minutes to walk to. It's ¥10 in a taxi.

Stone Gate Hill & Stone Seal Hill   ARCHAEOLOGICAL SITE
If you're really into Buddhist rock carvings, try to get out to the rarely visited sculptures at **Stone Gate Hill** (石门山; Shímén Shān), 19km southeast of Dàzú, or those at **Stone Seal Hill** (石篆山; Shízhuàn Shān), 20km southwest of town. You'll have to take a taxi.

Buddha Vaironcana Cave   CAVE
(毗卢洞; Pílú Dòng) The truly adventurous might like to catch a bus to the tiny town of Shíyáng (石羊), which has a little-seen collection of Song dynasty Buddhist rock carvings.

Buses to Shíyáng, just over the border in Sìchuān province, leave from Dàzú's old bus station. When you get there, keep asking for Pílú Dòng (毗卢洞); it's walking distance. From Shíyáng, you can continue by bus to Chéngdū.

🛏 Sleeping

Most cheapies in Dàzú won't accept foreigners. Try the **Fragrant Begonia Hotel** (海棠香国酒店; Hǎitáng Xiāngguó Jiǔdiàn; ☎023 4372 1189; 35-37 Yihuan Zhonglu; 一环中路35-37号; tw & d ¥298; 🌀). To find it, turn right out of Dàzú's old bus station, walk 100 metres, then turn right onto Yihuan Zhonglu and it's on the right-hand side.

ℹ Getting There & Away

Buses from Dàzú old station:
Chóngqìng (¥35-43, 2½ hours, every 30 minutes, 6.30am to 6.30pm)
Shíyáng (¥12, one hour, every 40 minutes, 7.20am to 5.40pm)
Yǒngchuān, for Sōngjì (¥22, 90 minutes, every 30 minutes, 7.10am to 5.40pm)

Buses from Dàzú new station:
Chéngdū (¥102, four hours, five daily, 7.15am to 9.50pm)
Lèshān (¥102, 4½ hours, one daily, 7.20am)
Zìgòng (¥52, 3½ hours, two daily, 8am and 1.30pm)

STILT HOUSES

Once a striking feature of the Chóngqìng skyline, stilt houses (吊脚楼; *diàojiǎo lóu*) were, in many ways, the predecessor to the modern skyscraper; sprawling vertically rather than horizontally to save space. Their design also served to keep family units in close quarters despite the uneven terrain of hilly Chóngqìng. They were built on a bamboo or fir frame that was fitted into bore holes drilled into the mountainside, and their thin walls were stuffed with straw and coated with mud to allow for cooling ventilation in a city that swelters in summer.

Modernisation has turned stilt housing into a symbol of poverty and as a result it has all but disappeared in the city itself, with the last remaining stilt houses in the centre slated for demolition at the time of research. But many survive in the villages around Chóngqìng municipality, with some fine examples in the alleyways of Sōngjì and especially by the river in Zhōngshān.

Zhōngshān 中山

Chóngqìng's once-ubiquitous stilt houses have all but disappeared from the city itself, but visit this gorgeous riverside village and you'll find plenty of them to gawp at. The **old town** (古镇; gǔzhèn) is essentially one long street lined with wooden homes on stilts above the riverbank. Walk down to the river and look up at the houses to see their support structures. You can also hike along the other side of the river.

🛏 Sleeping & Eating

Restaurants (dishes ¥18 to ¥60) and teahouses are plentiful and there are at least half a dozen guesthouses (rooms ¥30 to ¥100); look for signs saying 住宿 (zhùsù; lodgings). Most are small but clean and the more expensive rooms have their own bathrooms and cracking river views.

If you're stuck for choice, try the guesthouse run by Mrs Zhao – **Zhào Shìkè** (赵世客; ☏ 138 8320 9407; r ¥30-80) **FREE**. She doesn't speak English but is welcoming. A couple of doors down **Yì Xiān Lóu** (逸仙楼; dishes ¥8-60) does decent food (no English menu). Look for gǔzhèn lǎolàròu (古镇老腊肉; cured pork fried with green chillies; ¥35), héshuǐ dòufu (河水豆腐; river water tofu; ¥7) and yě cài (野菜; a type of spinach grown in the hills here; literally 'wild veg'; ¥10).

🛍 Shopping

Most residents have turned their front rooms into storefronts. While some hawk souvenir trinkets, others sell locally made products such as chilli sauce or jugs of rice wine. Popular snacks include squares of smoked tofu (烟熏豆腐; yānxūn dòufu; ¥2) and sweet doughy rice cakes filled with ground nuts.

ℹ Getting There & Away

To get here from Chóngqìng, change buses at Jiāngjīn (江津), from where buses leave for Zhōngshān (¥15, one hour 45 minutes, roughly every 30 minutes from 6.30am to 4.45pm). The last bus back to Jiāngjīn is at 4.20pm. The last bus from Jiāngjīn back to Chóngqìng is at 7pm. You can also head south into Guìzhōu province from Jiāngjīn, via Zūnyì (遵义; ¥107, 3½ hours, 8.40am and 2pm), or north to the caves at Dàzú (大足; ¥51, two hours, 7.30am and 2.10pm).

Sōngji 松溉

Winding cobblestone alleyways housing temples, teahouses, old gateways and some wonderful courtyard homes dominate this still-lived-in Ming dynasty village on the banks of the Yangzi River. Sōngji is a genuine community, rather than just a tourist destination, and sees very few foreigners, making it a great place to wander.

To guide yourself around the lanes, take a photo of the large wooden bilingual map at the entrance to the old town, just down towards the river from where the bus drops you.

⊙ Sights

Chén Family Compound　　　HOUSE
(陈家大院; Chén Jiā Dàyuàn; admission ¥1) If you're looking for a focus, seek out the historic home of the village's most prominent family. This sprawling structure once contained more than 100 rooms. What remains of the compound is much smaller, but its walls are extensively decorated with family photos and memorabilia. Actress/director Joan Chen (known in China as Chén Chōng), who starred in Bernardo Bertolucci's *The Last Emperor* and Ang Lee's *Lust, Caution*, is the most famous family member.

Dōngyù Temple　　　BUDDHIST TEMPLE
(东狱庙; Dōngyù Miào) On a bluff above the river, about a 20-minute walk from the old town, is this temple, home to a 9.5m-tall Buddha and some gruesome dioramas depicting various hells (impaling, scalding, having your tongue ripped out).

🛏 Sleeping & Eating

Sōngshān Bīnguǎn　　　HOTEL $
(松山宾馆; ☏ 023-4954 6078; tw/d ¥100/120; ❄) Clean rooms, some with river views, in a quiet location. No internet access.

Gǔzhèn Jiǔdàwǎn　　　CHINESE $
(古镇九大碗; dishes ¥20-50; ⊙9am-8pm) This nicely renovated old courtyard has been turned into a restaurant-cum-teahouse and offers reasonably priced dishes.

ℹ Getting There & Away

There's one direct bus from Chóngqìng (¥41, two hours, 1.20pm). Otherwise, catch a bus to Yǒngchuān (¥32), from where buses to Sōngji (¥10, 70 minutes) leave every 20 to 30 minutes. The last bus back to Yǒngchuān leaves Sōngji at about 5.30pm. The last bus from Yǒngchuān to Chóngqìng leaves at 6.50pm.

Cruising the Yangzi

Why Go?

Taking a boat down the Yangzi River – China's longest and most scenic waterway – is all about the journey rather than the destination. It isn't just an escape from marathon train journeys and agonising bus rides, but a chance to kickback as an astonishing panorama slides by at a sedate pace which allows time for contemplation and relaxation. Cruising the Yangzi is a truly unique experience, one that gets you up close with mostly domestic travellers allowing time for real interaction. Jump aboard.

When to Go

Dec–Mar The low season; rates are cheaper and the journey is more serene.

Apr & May The best weather, but the highest prices and rowdiest crowds.

Oct & Nov Cooler climes but the crowds are back.

The Three Gorges

Few river panoramas inspire as much awe as the Three Gorges (三峡, Sānxiá). Well-travelled Tang dynasty poets and men of letters have gone weak-kneed before them. Voluble emperors and hard-boiled communist party VIPs have been rendered speechless. Flotillas of sightseers have mega-pixelled their way from Chóngqìng to Yíchāng. For as long as many Yangzi boat hands can remember, the Three Gorges have been a member of the prestigious China Tour triumvirate, rubbing shoulders with the Terracotta Warriors and the Great Wall.

Yet the gorges these days get mixed press. Some travellers have their socks well and truly blown off; others arrive in Yíchāng scratching their heads and wondering what all the fuss was about. The route's natural scenery is certainly far more dramatic than its historical sights, often crammed with historical allusions obscure to all but Chinese minds.

Yangzi River (Cháng Jiāng)

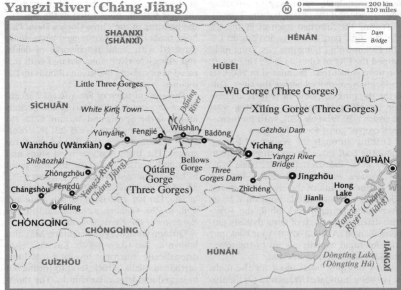

Temples along the way can be crowded, while uniform riverine towns and settlements are modern-looking rather than twee and charming. To some, the gorges' dramatic appearance can become rather repetitive, especially overlong Xīlíng Gorge (Xīlíng Xiá). The reservoir built up behind the Three Gorges Dam – a body of water almost the length of England – has certainly taken its toll as much moreof the gorges is now inundated.

But if you don't expect to swoon at every bend in the river, journeying downriver is a stimulating and relaxing adventure, not least because of the change of pace and perspective.

The River

The journey puts you adrift on China's mightiest – and the world's third-longest – river, the gushing 6300km Yangzi River (长江; Cháng Jiāng). Starting life as trickles of snow melt in the Tánggŭlā Shān of southwestern Qīnghǎi, the river then spills from Tibet, swells through seven Chinese provinces, sucks in water from hundreds of tributaries and rolls powerfully into the Pacific Ocean north of Shànghǎi.

THE ROUTE

Apocryphally the handiwork of the Great Yu, a legendary architect of the river, the gorges – Qútáng, Wū and Xīlíng – commence just east of Fèngjié in Chóngqìng province and level out west of Yíchāng in Húběi province, a distance of around 200km. The principal route for those cruising the Yangzi River is therefore between the cities of Chóngqìng and Yíchāng.

The route can be travelled in either direction, but most passengers journey downstream from Chóngqìng. Travelling upstream does ensure a less crowded boat, but somehow feels less dramatic.

If you buy your ticket from an agency, ensure you're not charged upfront for the sights along the way, as you may not want to visit them all. Some of the sights are underwhelming and entrance fees are as steep as the surrounding inclines. The only ticket truly worth buying in advance is for the popular and worthwhile Little Three Gorges tour, which is often full.

Chóngqìng to Wànzhōu 重庆-万州

The initial stretch is slow-going and unremarkable, although the dismal view of factories gradually gives way to attractive countryside and the occasional small town.

Passing the drowned town of Fúlíng (涪陵), the first port of call is at Fēngdū (丰都), 170km from Chóngqìng city. Long nicknamed the City of Ghosts (鬼城; Guǐchéng), the town is just that: inundated in 2009, its residents were moved across the river. This is the stepping-off point for crowds to clamber up **Míng Mountain** (名山; Míng Shān; admission ¥120, cable car ¥20), with its theme-park crop of ghost-focused temples.

Drifting through the county of Zhōngzhōu, the boat takes around three hours to arrive at **Shíbǎozhài** (石宝寨; Stone Treasure Stockade; admission ¥50; ☺8am-4pm) on the northern bank of the river. A 12-storey, 56m-high wooden pagoda built on a huge, river-water-encircled rock bluff, the structure dates to the reign of Qing dynasty emperor Kangxi (AD1662–1722). Your boat may stop for rapid expeditions up to the tower and for climbs into its interior.

Most morning boats moor for the night at partially inundated **Wànzhōu** (万州; also called Wànxiàn). Travellers aiming to get from A to B as fast as possible while taking in the gorges can skip the Chóngqìng to Wànzhōu section by hopping on a 3½ hour bus and then taking either the hydrofoil or a passenger ship from the Wànzhōu jetty.

Wànzhōu to Yíchāng 万州-宜昌

Boats departing from Wànzhōu soon pass the relocated **Zhāng Fēi Temple** (张飞庙; Zhāngfēi Miào; admission ¥40). Quick disembarkations can be made here, allowing a visit to the ancient but much-restored temple which was moved 20 miles upstream in 2002 and now sits opposite **Yúnyáng** (云阳). A modern, utilitarian and unremarkable town strung out along the northern bank

of the river, Yúnyáng is typical of many of the new settlements created in the wake of the building of the Three Gorges Dam. Past here, boats drift on past ragged islets, some carpeted with small patchworks of fields, and alongside riverbanks striated with terraced slopes, rising like green ribbons up the inclines.

The ancient town of **Fèngjié** (奉节), capital of the state of Kui during the periods known as the 'Spring and Autumn' (722–481 BC) and 'Warring States' (475–221 BC), overlooks Qútáng Gorge, the first of the three gorges. The town – where most ships and hydrofoils berth – is also the entrance point to half-submerged **White King Town** (白帝城; Báidìchéng; admission ¥120), where the King of Shu, Liu Bei, entrusted his son and kingdom to Zhu Geliang, as chronicled in *The Romance of the Three Kingdoms*.

Qútáng Gorge (瞿塘峡; Qútáng Xiá), also known as Kui Gorge (夔峡; Kuí Xiá), rises dramatically into view, towering into huge vertiginous slabs of rock, its cliffs jutting out in jagged and triangular chunks. The shortest and narrowest of the three gorges, 8km-long Qútáng Gorge is over almost as abruptly as it starts, but is considered by many to be the most awe-inspiring. The gorge offers a dizzying perspective onto huge strata despite having some of its power robbed by the rising waters. On the northern bank is **Bellows Gorge** (风箱峡; Fēngxiāng Xiá), where nine coffins were discovered, possibly placed here by an ancient tribe.

After Qútáng Gorge the terrain folds into a 20km stretch of low-lying land before boats pull in at the riverside town of **Wūshān** (巫山), situated high above the river. Most boats stop at Wūshān for five to six hours so passengers can transfer to smaller boats for trips along the **Little Three Gorges** (小三峡; Xiǎo Sānxiá; tickets ¥200) on the Dàníng River (大宁河; Dàníng Hé). The landscape is gorgeous and you're right up close to it;

THE EFFECTS OF THE THREE GORGES DAM

The dwarfing chasms of rock, sculpted over aeons by the irresistible volume of water, are the Yangzi River's most fabled stretch. Yet the construction of the controversial and record-breaking Three Gorges Dam (三峡大坝; Sānxiá Dàbà) cloaked the gorges in as much uncertainty as their famous mists: have the gorges been humbled or can they somehow shrug off the rising waters?

In brief, the gorges have been undoubtedly affected by the rising waters. The peaks are not as towering as they once were, nor are the flooded chasms through which boats travel as narrow and pinched. The effect is more evident to seasoned boat hands or repeat visitors. For first-timers the gorges still put on a dramatic show.

FAST FACTS

➡ The Three Gorges Dam is the world's largest artificial generator of electric power from a renewable source.

➡ The Three Gorges Dam is designed to withstand an earthquake of 7 on the Richter scale.

➡ Plans for the Three Gorges Dam date from 1919, when Sun Yatsen (Sun Zhongshan) saw its huge potential for power generation.

➡ The Yangzi River will deposit more than 500 million tonnes of silt every year into the reservoir behind the dam.

➡ An estimated one-third of China's population live in the Yangzi River basin. The river delta generates not just electricity, but around 20% of China's GDP.

➡ Hundreds of catastrophic floods have been caused by the Yangzi River, including the disastrous inundation of 1931, in which an estimated 145,000 people died.

---

many travellers insist that the narrow gorges are more impressive than their larger namesakes. Some tours include a 40 minute ride on local fishing boats here too.

Back on the Yangzi River, boats pull away from Wūshān to enter the penultimate Wū Gorge, under a bright-red bridge. Some of the cultivated fields on the slopes overhanging the river reach almost illogical angles.

Wū Gorge (巫峡; Wū Xiá) – the Gorge of Witches – is stunning, cloaked in green and carpeted in shrubs, its sides frequently disappearing into ethereal layers of mist. About 40km in length, its towering cliffs are topped by sharp, jagged peaks on the northern bank. A total of 12 peaks cluster on either side, including **Goddess Peak** (神女峰; Shénnǚ Fēng) and **Peak of the Immortals** (集仙峰; Jíxiān Fēng). If you're fortunate, you'll catch the sunrise over Goddess Peak.

Boats continue floating eastward out of Wū Gorge and into Húběi province, along a 45km section before reaching the last of the three gorges. At this time, many boats offer the option of a two hour trip on motorised dragon boats along **Jiǔwǎn Stream** (九畹溪; Jiǔwǎn Xī) and nearby tributaries of the Yangzi. Some travellers enjoy the experience, although the scenery isn't as inspiring as that of the Little Three Gorges.

At 80km, **Xīlíng Gorge** (西陵峡; Xīlíng Xiá) is the longest and perhaps least spectacular gorge; sections of the gorge in the west have been submerged. Note the slow-moving cargo vessels, including long freight ships loaded with mounds of coal, ploughing downriver to Shànghǎi. The gorge was traditionally the most hazardous, where hidden shoals and reefs routinely holed vessels, but it has long been tamed,

even though river traffic slows when the fog reduces visibility.

Apart from a few of the top-end luxury cruises, tour boats no longer pass through the monumental **Three Gorges Dam**, although many tours offer the option of a visit to the dam by bus. The passenger ferries and hydrofoils tend to finish (or begin) their journey at **Tàipíng Creek Port** (太平溪港; Tàipíngxī Gǎng), upstream from the dam. From here, two types of shuttle bus wait to take you into Yíchāng (one hour). One is free and takes you to the old ferry port (老码头; lǎo mǎtóu) in the centre of town. The other costs ¥10 and drops you at Yíchāng East Train Station (火车东站; Huǒchē Dōngzhàn). Ordinary tourist boats tend to use **Máopíng Port** (茅坪港; Máopíng Gǎng), from where you can at least see the dam, and which is also connected to Yíchāng via shuttle buses.

BOATS

There are four categories of boats: luxury cruises, tourist boats, passenger ships and hydrofoil.

Luxury Cruises   豪华游轮

The most luxurious passage is on international-standard cruise ships (háohuá yóulún), where maximum comfort and visibility accompany a leisurely agenda. Trips normally depart Chóngqìng mid-evening and include shore visits to all the major sights (Three Gorges Dam, Little Three Gorges etc), allowing time to tour the attractions (often secondary to the scenery). Cabins have air-con, TV (perhaps satellite), fridge/minibar and sometimes more. These

BEST TOP-END CRUISES

Viking River Cruises (www.vikingriver-cruises.com; from $6337) Very luxurious cruise, offering five-day cruises from Chóngqìng to Wǔhàn, as part of a larger 13-day tour of China. Complete tour from US$6337.

Century Cruises (www.centuryriver-cruises.com) Claims to be the most luxurious cruise service on the Yangzi. Ships are new, service is first class and facilities are top notch. Chóngqìng to Yíchāng tickets booked through Harbour Plaza Travel Centre start at US$650.

Victoria Cruises (www.victoriacruises.com; from US$980) Comfortable four-day trips between Chóngqìng and Yíchāng. Older boats than some other operators, but has excellent English-speaking guides. From US$980, through Harbour Plaza Travel Centre.

vessels are aimed specifically at Western tourists and are ideal for travellers with time, money and negligible Chinese skills. The average duration for such a cruise is three nights and three to four days.

Tourist Boats 普通游轮

Typically departing from Chóngqìng at around 9pm, ordinary tourist cruise ships (pǔtōng yóulún) usually take just under 40 hours to reach Yíchāng (including three nights on board). Some boats stop at all the sights; others stop at just a few. They are less professional than the luxury tour cruises and are squarely aimed at domestic travellers (Chinese food, little spoken English).

Expect early starts: the public-address system starts going off after 6am. Cabins in all classes are fairly basic – hard beds in 2nd and 3rd class – but come with AC and a TV and usually have a small attached bathroom with a shower (although that doesn't mean hot water). Many travellers now book packages that take you first by bus from Chóngqìng to Wànzhōu, where you board a vessel for the rest of the trip. This reduces the journey by one night.

In theory, you can buy tickets on the day of travel, but booking one or two days in advance is recommended. Fares vary, although not by much, depending whether you buy your ticket from a hostel, agency or direct from the ticket hall, so it's worth shopping around to check. If buying a ticket through an agent, ensure you know exactly what the price includes. Note that the following prices include admission to the most popular stops along the way (including the Little Three Gorges):

Special class (特等; tèděng) ¥1780, two-bed cabin

1st class (一等; yīděng) ¥1440, two-bed cabin

2nd class (二等; èrděng) ¥1150, four-bed cabin

3rd class (三等; sānděng) ¥1000, six-bed cabin

Passenger Ships 客船

Straightforward passenger ships (kè chuán) are cheap, but can be disappointing because you sail through two of the gorges in the dead of night. Stops are frequent, but hasty, and they pass by the tourist sights. Journeys between Chóngqìng and Yíchāng take around 36 hours; between Fèngjié and Yíchāng, around 12 hours. Toilets are shared, and soon get pretty grotty. There are no showers, but there are sinks and power sockets in the twin cabins (as well as TVs, which usually don't work). Meals on board are decent and cheap but there is no choice of dishes, so take along your own food and drinks in case you don't like what's on offer.

Eastbound boats leave Chóngqìng at 10pm and Fèngjié at 9pm. For westbound journeys, shuttle buses, which connect with the boats, leave Yíchāng's old ferry port at 7.30pm; the boat leaves at 9pm. Tickets can usually be bought on the day of travel.

Chóngqìng to Yíchāng fares:

1st class (一等; yīděng) ¥884, twin cabin

2nd class (二等; èrděng) ¥534, twin cabin

3rd class (三等; sānděng) ¥367, four- to six-bed dorm

4th class (四等; sìděng) ¥224, eight-bed dorm

Fèngjié to Yíchāng fares:

1st class ¥343

2nd class ¥212

3rd class ¥147

4th class ¥119

Hydrofoil 快艇

Yangzi River hydrofoils (kuài tǐng) are a dying breed. There are now just three per day and they only run between Fèngjié and Yíchāng. Buses, though, connect Fèngjié with Chóngqìng (¥160, five hours, hourly, 7.30am to

Xīnjiāng

POP 21.8 MILLION

Includes ➡

Best Bazaars

➡ Sunday market (p817), Hotan

➡ Livestock market (p807), Kashgar

➡ Sunday bazaar (p805), Kuqa

➡ Sunday market (p816), Yarkand

Best Off the Beaten Track

➡ Shipton's Arch (p809)

➡ Horse trek to Hémù in Kanas Lake Nature Reserve (p821)

➡ Hiking around Muztagh Ata (p813)

➡ Bezeklik Caves (p804)

Why Go?

In this far-flung and restive frontier province, Central Asian culture is very much alive: from the irresistible smell of tea-house kebabs, to the bustle of bazaars and markets, to the sound of the call to prayer from the neighbourhood mosque. Xīnjiāng is China's Uighur homeland, but for a thousand years it was also a portal and stronghold for Buddhism in the Middle Kingdom. Outside Silk Road oasis towns the legacy of this remains in stunning cave art, and the ruins of ancient cities and monasteries. The awesomeness of Xīnjiāng's environment is an equal draw for travellers, from the scorching sands of the Taklamakan Desert to the cool forests and lakes of the Tiān Shān (Heavenly Mountains). In short, a journey to Chinese Turkestan rewards as an exploration of China's past, its unsettled multicultural present, or simply as an adventure into one of the most sublime landscapes on earth.

When to Go
Ürümqi

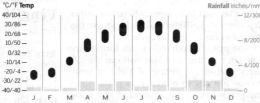

°C/°F Temp — Rainfall inches/mm

Mar Nauryz (New Year) festivals held in Kazakh and Kyrgyz villages.

Aug Celebrate the grape-harvest festival in Turpan.

Sep Autumnal colours at Kanas Lake and Hémù.

8.30pm) so this is still a quick and reasonably convenient way of seeing the Three Gorges.

Hydrofoils are passenger vessels and are not geared towards tourists, so there's no outside seating. Visibility is OK (albeit through perspex windows), but if you stand by the door you can get a good view. Food and refreshments are served on board, but are nothing special. Hydrofoils make regular but very brief stops at towns along the river for embarkation and disembarkation.

At the time of research, times of departure and prices for tickets bought at the relevant port's official ticket office were as follows (note, the Yíchāng times of departure are for the free shuttle buses which leave from Yíchāng's old port before connecting with the hydrofoils which leave from a newer port 45km upstream):

Yíchāng to Fèngjié ¥245, four to five hours (7.20am, 9.50am and 1.20pm)

Fèngjié to Yíchāng ¥235, four to five hours (8.30am, 11am and 2pm)

If you get stuck for the night in Fèngjié, **Fènggǎng Bīnguǎn** (奉港宾馆; ☏023 5683 4333; tw & d from ¥80), attached to the ferry port, has large clean rooms, some with river views. It's run by a friendly family, but no English is spoken; no English sign.

TICKETS

In Chóngqìng or Yíchāng, most hotels, hostels and travel agents can sell you a trip on either the luxury cruise ships or the ordinary tourist boats. In either city, passenger ferry tickets have to be bought at the ferry port ticket halls, which also sell ordinary tourist boat tickets. For the hydrofoil, you can buy westbound tickets in Yíchāng from the Three Gorges Tourist Centre at the old ferry port. Eastbound tickets must be bought at the ticket hall in Fèngjié, where the hydrofoil starts its journey. You can no longer buy hydrofoil tickets in Chóngqìng.

The price of your ticket will include the one-hour shuttle bus ride to/from the old ferry port in the centre of Yíchāng from/to one of the two newer ferry ports, about 45km upstream, where almost all boats now leave from or terminate at.

Chóngqìng

The **Yangtze River Hostel** (p776) mostly sells tickets for the ordinary tourist boats, but can arrange luxury cruises too. Helpful

and excellent English skills. The Harbour Plaza Travel Centre (p781) specialises in luxury cruises, but also sells ordinary tourist boat tickets. Staff are friendly and speak OK English. The Chóngqìng Ferry Port Ticket Hall is the cheapest place to buy ordinary tourist boat tickets, and the only place that sells passenger ferry tickets; no English is spoken.

Yíchāng

China International Travel Service TOURS (CITS; 中国国际旅行社; Zhōngguó Guójì Lǚxíngshè; ☏0717 625 3088; Yunji Lu; ⏱8am-6pm) Sells luxury cruises to Chóngqìng (from ¥2800) and tourist boat tickets to Chóngqìng (¥880 to ¥900), but not hydrofoil tickets. Some English spoken.

Three Gorges Tourist Centre FERRY TICKETS (三峡游客中心; Sānxiá Yóukè Zhōngxīn; ☏0717 696 6116; Yanjiang Dadao, 沿江大道; ⏱7am-8pm) Commission-free, so cheaper than CITS. Sells hydrofoil tickets to Fèngjié (¥245) plus passenger ferry tickets to various destinations between Yíchāng and Chóngqìng. Minimal English spoken, but staff members are helpful. Enter the modern tourist centre (no English sign) and head to the ticket counters at the far right of the building.

Yangtze River International Travel FERRY TICKETS (宜昌长江国际旅行社; Yíchāng Chángjiāng Guójì Lǚxíngshè; ☏0717 692 1808; ⏱7am-8pm) Marginally cheaper than CITS for ordinary tourist-boat tickets to Chóngqìng (from ¥890). Also sells luxury cruises. Housed inside the Three Gorges Tourist Centre, but has a separate desk beside the passenger-boat ticket counters.

Fèngjié

Fèngjié Ferry Port Ticket Hall (奉节港售票厅; Fèngjié Gǎng Shòupiàotīng) sells passenger ferry tickets in either direction, plus hydrofoil tickets to Yíchāng (¥235). Don't expect to be able to board tourist boats from here because tickets are usually sold out in Chóngqìng or Yíchāng.

Wǔhàn

The Pathfinder Youth Hostel (p431) sells tickets for westbound trips from Yíchāng, which include the bus from Wǔhàn to Yíchāng.

History

By the end of the 2nd century BC the expanding Han dynasty had pushed its borders west into what is now Xīnjiāng. Military garrisons protected the fledgling trade routes, as silk flowed out of the empire in return for the strong Ferghana horses needed to fight nomadic incursions from the north. Chinese imperial rule waxed and waned over the centuries, shrinking after the collapse of the Han and reasserting itself during the 7th-century Tang, though central control was tenuous at best. A Uighur kingdom based at Khocho thrived from the 8th century and oversaw the Central Asian people's transformation from nomads to farmers and from Manichaeans to Buddhists.

It was during Kharakhanid rule in the 10th to 12th centuries that Islam took hold in Xīnjiāng. In 1219, Yīlí (Ili), Hotan and Kashgar fell to the Mongols and their various successors controlled the whole of Central

Xīnjiāng Highlights

1 Follow the footprints of Marco Polo along the **southern Silk Road** (p814)

2 Stay overnight in a yurt and marvel at the dramatic mountain scenery of the **Karakoram Highway** (p812)

3 Explore the ancient ruins, such as **Jiāohé** (p803), near the laid-back oasis town of Turpan

4 Haggle for a fat-tailed sheep at the Sunday livestock market at **Kashgar** (p807)

5 Explore the story of Buddhism and Central Asian silk in **Hotan** (p817)

6 Pause on the northern Silk Road at **Kuqa** (p805), for its authentic bazaar and nearby Buddhist ruins

Asia until the mid-18th century, when the Manchu army marched into Kashgar.

In 1865 a Kokandi officer named Yaqub Beg seized Kashgaria, proclaimed a short-lived independent Turkestan, and made diplomatic contacts with Britain and Russia. The Manchu army eventually returned and two decades later Kashgaria was formally incorporated into China's newly created Xīnjiāng (New Frontier) province. With the fall of the Qing dynasty in 1911, Xīnjiāng came under the chaotic and violent rule of a succession of Muslim and Chinese warlords, over whom the Kuomintang (the Nationalist Party) had very little control. In the 1930s and 1940s there was an attempt in both Kashgar and Ili to establish an independent state of Eastern Turkestan, but both were short-lived.

Since 1949, the Chinese government's main social goal in Xīnjiāng has been to keep a lid on ethnic separatism, dilute local culture, and flood the region with Han Chinese. Economically, the 'Develop the West' campaign has used the region's oil resources to ramp up the local economy. But this has led to an increase in Han settlers, which has exacerbated ethnic tensions. In a telling statistic, Uighurs once composed 90% of Xīnjiāng's population; today they make up less than 50%.

In 2008, street protests and bomb attacks rocked the province, and in 2009, communal violence between Han and Uighur civilians in downtown Ürümqi led to around 200 deaths and 1700 injuries, according to Chinese police reports.

Violence also wracked 2014. First, a March attack by knife-wielding assailants (blamed on Uighur separatists) at a train station in Kūnmíng, Yúnnán province saw 29 killed and 143 injured. The next month, two attackers stabbed people at the Ürümqi train station before setting off vest explosives. A few weeks later, a suicide car and bomb attack on a market in Ürümqi ended with 31 killed and 90 injured. The Chinese authorities cracked down hard with a campaign against terrorism, which was expected to last until at least summer 2015.

Heightened security in airports, railways and subways was felt across the country. Pictures of passengers waiting in epically long lines to enter the Běijīng subway made international news, as did several mass public 'trials' that summer, including one before a 7000-person audience in a stadium in Yīníng. Hundreds of Uighurs were sentenced to long jail terms, and dozens executed.

More violence came in July in Yarkand but, by then, Xīnjiāng was under heavy media control and details of what happened are murky. The Chinese government took a week to announce that 96 people had been killed following a knife attack on a police station. Exiled Uighur groups claimed the violence began after government forces suppressed protesters angry over Ramadan restrictions, and that the deaths numbered in the thousands.

Whatever the truth, as long as Uighur resentment is fuelled by what they view as economic marginalisation, cultural restrictions, ethnic discrimination and outright oppression, violence looks likely to continue in the restive province.

Climate

Xīnjiāng's climate is one of extremes. Turpan is the hottest spot in the country – up to 47°C in summer (June to August), when the Tarim

---

DANGERS & ANNOYANCES

The increased unrest and terrorism that hit in Xīnjiāng in 2014 had not, at the time of writing, resulted in the type of massive clampdown seen in Tibet after the 2008 riots. But it was by no means business as usual. In addition to paying close attention to your safety in transport stations, crowded public areas and government offices (in particular, police stations), there are a few things to be aware of. As of the summer of 2014, you will need a passport to buy long-distance bus tickets. Some city buses also ban the carrying of cigarette lighters, water and yogurt. There was also a push to ban beards, typically worn by Uigher men, from public transport. Note too that fewer hotels are now authorised to take foreigners, and many hotels no longer have available internet connections. We hadn't heard of any new regional closures, but many popular markets in large cities (such as Ürümqi) were closed and were expected to remain closed for at least the entire duration the government's new anti-terrorism campaign, slated to last into summer 2015. In short, expect the adage 'things change' to apply to this region much more than usual.

WHICH TIME IS IT?

Making an appointment in Xīnjiāng is not just a matter of asking what time, but also 'which time?' All of China officially runs on Běijīng time (*Běijīng shíjiān*). Xīnjiāng, several time zones removed from Běijīng, however, runs duelling clocks: while the Chinese tend to stick to the official Běijīng time, the locals set their clocks to unofficial Xīnjiāng time (*Xīnjiāng shíjiān*), two hours behind Běijīng time. Thus 9am Běijīng time is 7am Xīnjiāng time. Most government-run services, such as banks, post offices, bus stations and airlines, run on Běijīng time, generally operating from 10am to 1.30pm and from 4pm to 8pm to cater to the time difference. Unless otherwise stated, we use Běijīng time in this chapter.

and Jungar Basins aren't much cooler. As daunting as the heat may seem, spring (April and May) is not a particularly good time to visit, with frequent sandstorms making travel difficult and dust clouds obscuring the landscape. Winters (November to March) see the mercury plummet below 0°C throughout the province, although March is a good time to catch some festivals. Late May through June and September through October (especially) are the best times to visit.

Language

Uighur, the lingua franca of Xīnjiāng, is part of the Turkic language family and thus fairly similar to other regional languages, such as Uzbek, Kazakh and Kyrgyz. The one exception is Tajik, which is related to Persian.

The Han Chinese in Xīnjiāng don't speak Uighur. Vice versa, many Uighurs can't, or won't, speak Mandarin. However, learning Mandarin is now mandatory in Uighur-language schools (but not the other way round), and Mandarin is exclusively used in universities. Nominally this is to provide more economic opportunities to the Uighurs, but resistance to Sinicisation, and its effects on Uighur culture and traditions, is steadfast.

ℹ Getting There & Away

You can fly between Xīnjiāng and most Chinese domestic cities, Central Asia and a couple of cities further afield, including Moscow and Tehran.

There are overland border crossings with Pakistan (Khunjerab Pass), Kyrgyzstan (Irkeshtam and Torugart Passes) and Kazakhstan (Korgas, Ālāshānkŏu, Tăchéng and Jímùnǎi). The Qolma Pass to Tajikistan may conceivably open to foreign travel in the coming years. All of these border crossings are by bus, except Ālāshānkŏu, China's only rail link to Central Asia.

Heading back into mainland China, the obvious route is the train following the Silk Road through Gānsù. More rugged approaches are the mountain roads from Charklik to Qīnghǎi, and Karghilik to Ali (Tibet).

ℹ Getting Around

The railway from Gānsù splits near Turpan, with one branch heading west through Ürümqi to Yīníng and Kazakhstan, and the other going southwest to Kashgar and Hotan. In 2015 high-speed rail was slated to link Ürümqi (and towns in between) to Lánzhōu in Gānsù.

Distances are large in Xīnjiāng and buses are often sleepers. On-board entertainment usually includes kung fu film marathons cranked to the hilt. Shared taxis run along many of the bus routes, taking up to half as long again, and costing twice as much as buses. Shared taxis only depart when full.

Flying around the province can save a lot of time and tickets are often discounted by up to 60%. Flights are sometimes cancelled for lack of passengers or due to bad weather.

CENTRAL XĪNJIĀNG

Bounded by deserts and mountain ranges, much of present-day Central Xīnjiāng would have been completely familiar to Silk Road traders on the Northern Route to Kashgar. Today the largest and most important city in the region is Ürümqi, though for travellers the ancient cities around Turpan, the Tianshan mountains, and the Buddha caves of Kuqa are the bigger draws.

Ürümqi (Wūlŭmùqí)   乌鲁木齐

☑ 0991 / POP 3.1 MILLION

Ürümqi's more than three million urban residents live in a city that sprawls 20km across a fertile plain in the shadow of the Tiān Shān mountains. High-rise apartments and tower blocks form a modern skyline that will soon dash any thoughts of spotting wandering camels and ancient caravanserais.

Ürümqi

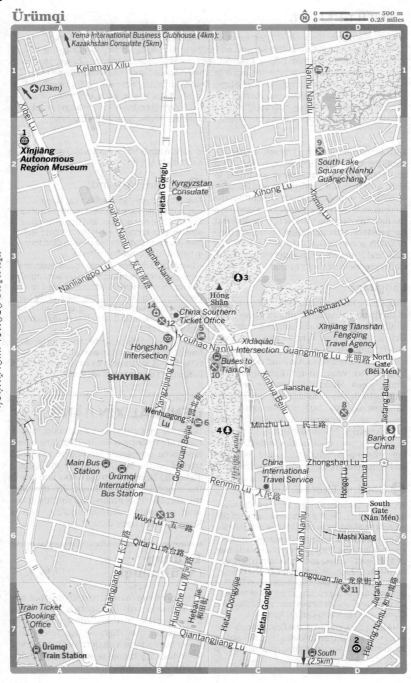

0 — 500 m
0 — 0.25 miles

Yema International Business Clubhouse (4km);
Kazakhstan Consulate (5km)

Kelamayi Xilu

Xibei Lu

(13km)

1
Xīnjiāng Autonomous Region Museum

Youhao Nanlu

Nanliangpo Lu

Hetan Gonglu

Binhe Nanlu

Kyrgyzstan Consulate

Xihong Lu

Nanhu Nanlu

7

9
South Lake Square (Nánhú Guāngchǎng)

Xinmin Lu

Hóng Shān

3

Hongshan Lu

14
China Southern Ticket Office

12

5

Xīnjiāng Tiānshān Fēngqíng Travel Agency

Hóngshān Intersection

Youhao Nanlu

Xīdàqiáo Intersection

Guangming Lu 光明路

North Gate (Běi Mén)

SHAYIBAK

Buses to Tian Chi

10

Xinhua Beilu

Jianshe Lu

8

Jiefang Beilu

Wenhuagong Lu

6

4

Minzhu Lu 民主路

Bank of China

S

Main Bus Station

Ürümqi International Bus Station

Yangzijiang Lu 扬子江路

Gongyuan Beijie

Hebing Canal

China International Travel Service

Zhongshan Lu

Hongli Lu

Wenhua Lu

Renmin Lu 人民路

South Gate (Nán Mén)

13
Wuyi Lu 五一路

Qitai Lu 奇台路

Xinhua Nanlu

Mashi Xiang

Changjiang Lu 长江路

Huanghe Lu 黄河路

Hetan Jie 和田街

Hetan Dongjie

Hetan Gonglu

Longquan Jie 龙泉街

11

Jiefang Nanlu

Heping Nanlu 和平南路

Train Ticket Booking Office

Ürümqi Train Station

Qiantangjiang Lu

South (2.5km)

2

Ürümqi

As a fast-growing Central Asian hub (high-speed rail is expected to reach the city by 2015) the city does business with traders from Běijīng to Baku and plays host to an exotic mix of people. Cyrillic signs and fragrant corner kebab stands add a Central Asian feel, though in reality over 75% of Ürümqi's inhabitants are Han Chinese.

Ürümqi is not a historic city, but the provincial museum is excellent and there are some interesting Uighur districts. If you find yourself hanging around for a Kazakh or Kyrgyz visa, consider a side trip to Turpan or Hami.

◎ Sights & Activities

★ Xīnjiāng Autonomous
Region Museum   MUSEUM
(新疆自治区博物馆; Xīnjiāng Zìzhìqū Bówùguǎn; 132 Xibei Lu; ⊙10am-6pm Tue-Sun) **FREE** Xīnjiāng's massive provincial museum is a must for Silk Road aficionados. The highlight is the locally famous 'Loulan Beauty', one of the 3800-year-old desert-mummified bodies of Indo-European ancestry that became symbols of Uighur independence in the 1990s. Other exhibits include some amazing silk and sculpture from Astana and an introduction to all of the province's minorities. From the Hóngshān Intersection, take bus 7 for four stops and ask to get off at the museum *(bówùguǎn)*.

Èrdàoqiáo Market   BAZAAR
(二道桥市场; Èrdàoqiáo Shìchǎng; Jiefang Nanlu) The Èrdàoqiáo Market and nearby International Bazaar (Guójì Dàbāzhá) have undergone extensive 'redevelopment' in recent years and are now aimed more at Chinese tour groups than Uighur traders. Planted in the bazaar is a replica of the Kalon Minaret

from Bukhara in Uzbekistan (though the 12th-century original doesn't have an elevator inside it). The surrounding streets are worth a stroll for their Uighur markets and snack stalls.

Hóngshān Park   PARK
(红山公园; Hóngshān Gōngyuán; admission ¥10; ⊙dawn-dusk) More of an amusement park, but with good city views, particularly from the 18th-century hilltop pagoda. The main southern entrance is to the north of the Xīdàqiáo Intersection.

People's Park   PARK
(人民公园; Rénmín Gōngyuán; admission ¥5; ⊙7.30am-dusk) A green oasis, with north and south entrances.

🛏 Sleeping

Màitián International
Youth Hostel   HOSTEL $
(麦田国际青年旅舍; Màitián Guójì Qīngnián Lǚshě; ☑459 1488; www.xjmaitian.net; 726 Youhao Nanlu; 友好南路726号; dm ¥45-55, r ¥160; @ 🛜) On the east side of the Parkson Shopping Mall, centrally located Màitián has simple doubles and dorms, some with private bathrooms, and a pleasant common area–bar. The shared bathrooms are pretty grotty, but the rooms do get a regular cleaning. Book ahead in summer. Private rooms are discounted from November to mid-April.

White Birch International
Youth Hostel   HOSTEL $
(白桦林国际青年旅舍; Báihuàlín Guójì Qīngnián Lǚshě; ☑488 1428; www.yhaxinjiang.com; 186 Nanhu Nanlu; 南湖南路186号; dm ¥40-50, d ¥120; @ 🛜) The English-speaking staff at this hostel are usually friendly and can help organise trips and onward transport. It's a bit out

PRICE INDICATORS

The following price indicators are used in this region:

Sleeping

$ less than ¥170 (for a room)

$$ ¥170 to ¥280

$$$ more than ¥280

Eating

$ less than ¥20 (for a meal for one)

$$ ¥20 to ¥35

$$$ more than ¥35

of the centre but rooms are modern, and there's laundry and a nearby park. Email for bus directions or arrange an airport pickup. From the train station a taxi is around ¥15.

Super 8 HOTEL $$

(速8酒店; Sùbā Jiǔdiàn; ☏ 559 0666; www.super8.com.cn; 140 Gongyuan Beijie; 公园北街140号; tw ¥218-228; ❈ 🕸) Quietly located behind People's Park, this is the best of the budget chain hotels, representing good value with its ultra-neat rooms, modern bathrooms and free Chinese-style breakfast.

Yěmǎ International Business Clubhouse HOTEL $$$

(野马国际商务会馆; Yěmǎ Guójì Shāngwù Huìguǎn; ☏ 768 8888; 158 Kunming Lu; 昆明路158号; tw incl breakfast ¥598-698; ❈ @) This elegant and surprisingly stylish modern hotel has an art gallery, wine bar and restaurant, mixing traditional Chinese design with urban chic. It even has its own zoo out the back with rare animals including Przewalski horses (wild horses indigenous to Central Asia). There is a range of rooms, from less expensive Japanese-style doubles to larger rooms in the main tower. The hotel is located north of the city, next to the Kazakhstan Consulate.

🍴 Eating & Drinking

Wǔyī Night Market MARKET

(五一夜市; Wǔyī Yèshì; Wuyi Lu) This animated night market was closed at the time of writing as part of the government's campaign against terrorism. It was well known for its shish kebabs and handmade noodles, so check its status when in town.

Carrefour SUPERMARKET $

(加乐福; Jiālèfú) The branches of this French supermarket chain, notably in Èrdàoqiáo Market (p797) and near White Birch International Youth Hostel, are good for produce and both have excellent-value cafeterias.

Tiānfǔ Zhēngcài SHANGHAINESE $$

(天府蒸菜; ☏ 773 0076; 17 Lanxiuyuan Xijie; 揽秀园西街; mains ¥15-40; ⊙11am-11pm) A cosy and friendly neighbourhood place just northwest of the Hóngshān Intersection, featuring tasty eastern Chinese dishes. Try the Shanghai-style braised meatballs (hóngshāo shīzi tóu; 红烧狮子头) or tiger-skin peppers with braised eggplant (hǔpí làzi shāoqiézi; 虎皮辣子烧茄子). It's down a side alley.

May Flower UIGHUR $$$

(五月花; Wǔyuèhuā; 153 Longquan Jie; meals ¥25-55; ⊙11am-midnight) Though part of a chain this place is still recommended for delicious Uighur cuisine. Try the specialty, polo (rice pilaf; zhuāfàn), along with a few sticks of shish kebab and a glass of pomegranate juice, then sit back and enjoy the traditional live music (8pm).

Aroma EUROPEAN $$$

(啊诺玛西餐厅; Ā'nuòmǎ Xīcāntīng; 196 Jianshe Lu; meals ¥40-100; ⊙noon-midnight) A Maltese chef who somehow washed up in Ürümqi runs this cosy and warm bistro. Pizzas, pastas and risottos are local favourites, or sink your teeth into a tasty steak. Most of the ingredients are either home-grown or home-made. It's opposite the Laiyuan Hotel.

Fubar PUB FOOD $$$

(福吧; Fúbā; 40 Gongyuan Beijie; beer ¥25-35, mains ¥35-65; ⊙11am-4am; 🕸) This well-known, long-running expat watering hole recently changed hands. In addition to a good selection of imported beers, and classic pub grub such as pizzas and burgers, you'll find some Spanish fare. Young expat teachers and volunteers congregate here, making this a good place to get the skinny on activities around Ürümqi. Fubar is on a street of bars and clubs if you want to make a big night of it.

🔒 Shopping

Navigate the Outdoors OUTDOOR EQUIPMENT

(畅行户外用品店; Chàngxíng Hùwài Yòngpǐn Diàn; ☏ 453-0938; 437 Youhao Nanlu) Almost directly opposite the China Southern Airlines Hotel, this small shop rents camping gear such as tents (per day ¥15), sleeping bags (per day ¥10) and sleeping pads (per day ¥5).

ℹ Information

Bank of China (中国银行; Zhōngguó Yínháng; cnr Jiefang Beilu & Dongfeng Lu; ⊙10am-6.30pm Mon-Fri, 11am-3.30pm Sat & Sun) Can handle most transactions and has an ATM (and at other branches).

China International Travel Service (CITS; 中国国际旅行社; Zhōngguó Guójì Lǚxíngshè; ☑ 282 1428; www.xinjiangtour.com; 33 Renmin Lu; ⊙10am-7.30pm Mon-Fri) This office runs standard tours around the province and can supply a driver and English-speaking guide.

China Post (中国邮政; Zhōngguó Yóuzhèng; Hóngshān Intersection; ⊙10am-10pm) The main branch handles all international parcels.

Public Security Bureau (PSB; 公安局; Gōng'ānjú; ☑ 281 0452, ext 3456; Kelamayi Donglu; ⊙10am-1.30pm & 4-6pm Mon-Fri) You should be able to renew a visa here but it might take two weeks.

Xīnjiāng Tiānshān Fēngqíng Travel Agency (新疆天山风情旅行社; Xīnjiāng Tiānshān Fēngqíng Lǚxíngshè; ☑883-9406; Bógédá Bīnguǎn, 253 Guangming Lu) For trips to Kanas Lake.

ℹ Getting There & Away

AIR

International flights include Almaty (Kazakhstan), Bishkek and Osh (Kyrgyzstan), Baku (Azerbaijan), Tbilisi (Georgia), Istanbul (Turkey), Islamabad (Pakistan), Moscow (Russia), Dushanbe (Tajikistan), Tashkent (Uzbekistan) and Tehran (Iran). Some of these are seasonal and many are suspended without warning.

You can get to Ürümqi from almost anywhere in China. Destinations within Xīnjiāng include Altay (Àlètài), Hotan (Hétián), Kashgar (Kàshí), Kuqa (Kùchē), Tǎchéng and Yīníng. **China Southern** (南方航空收票处; Nánfāng Hángkōng Shòupiàochù; http://skypearl.csair.com/cn/; 576 Youhao Nanlu) has the most flights to and around Xīnjiāng, with a central booking office in the Southern Airlines Pearl International Hotel.

BUS

Two long-distance bus stations in Ürümqi serve northern and southern destinations. The **main bus station** (碾子沟长途汽车站; Niǎnzigōu Chángtú Qìchēzhàn; Heilongjiang Lu) has sleeper buses to the following:

Bù'ěrjīn ¥178 to ¥188, 12 hours, three daily (11.15am, 8.10pm and 8.40pm)

Hāmì ¥150 to ¥160, seven hours, three daily (11am, 1pm and 8pm)

Yīníng ¥178 to ¥188, 11 to 12 hours, almost hourly (8.30am to 9pm)

BRT bus 1 runs from the train station to Hóngshān, passing Heilongjiang Lu on the way. Bus 44 or 906 pass directly in front of the bus station.

The **south bus station** (nánjiāo kèyùnzhàn) has frequent departures to the following:

XINJIANG ÜRÜMQI (WÙLǓMÙQÍ)

BORDER CROSSING: GETTING TO KAZAKHSTAN

If you have a Kazakhstan visa, you can go to Almaty in Kazakhstan by the daily 7pm bus (upper/lower bunk ¥440/460, 24 hours) departing from Ürümqi International Bus Station (乌鲁木齐国际运输汽车站; Wūlǔmùqí Guójì Yùnshū Qìchēzhàn; ☑ 587 8637), behind the main bus station. Expect delays of several hours at the Korgas customs posts. A longer but more pleasant trip is to break the journey in Yīníng.

Trains currently depart Ürümqi twice weekly for Almaty, Kazakhstan (K9795, via Ālāshānkǒu) on Monday and Saturday at midnight. The journey takes a slow 32 hours, six of which are spent at Chinese and Kazakh customs. Tickets cost ¥804 to ¥829.

There is also a Monday service (9797) to the Kazakh capital of Astana leaving at midnight. Tickets cost ¥1094.

Tickets can only be purchased in the lobby of the Yà'ōu Jiǔdiàn (next to the train station), at the booking office (往阿拉木图火车票售票处; wǎng ālāmùtú huǒchēpiào shòupiàochù; ⊙10am-1pm & 3.30-6pm Sat, Mon, Wed & Thu). The booking office regulations are worth noting. Monday you buy same-day train tickets. Wednesday and Thursday you buy tickets for the next Saturday and Monday. Saturday you buy same-day tickets and tickets for next Monday.

At the time of research you could get a 30-day tourist visa at the Kazakhstan Consulate (哈萨克斯坦共和国驻; Hāsàkè Sītǎn Gònghéguó Zhù; ☑369-1444; 216 Kunming Lu; ⊙9am-1pm Mon-Fri) in Ürümqi. Visas take five days to be issued, cost US$25 and you need one passport photo and copy of your passport and China visa. Visas generally specify your entry date into Kazakhstan. Show up early to apply and don't expect the consulate to pick up the phone if you call. If possible apply for a visa in Beijing or your home country.

Hotan ¥370 to ¥390, 24 hours, every 30 minutes in the afternoon only (crossing the Taklamakan Desert)

Kashgar ¥260 to ¥280, 24 hours, every 40 minutes in the afternoon only

Kuqa ¥145 to ¥220, 12 to 13 hours, every 30 minutes in the afternoon only

Turpan ¥45, 2½ hours, every 20 minutes

There is also a once-daily bus that travels to Cherchen (¥320 to ¥340, 22 to 24 hours) on the southern Silk Road, departing at 7pm. A seat in a private car to Turpan costs ¥85 and takes around two hours.

Bus 51 or 7 will get you to the south bus station from Hóngshān Intersection. BRT (Bus Rapid Transit) bus 3 will get you here from the South Lake Square (via People's Sq).

TRAIN

Ürümqi is expected to be connected to China's high-speed rail network by 2015. The following are regular train routes and schedules with hard/soft sleeper ticket prices:

Běijīng ¥575/887, 33 to 41 hours, two daily (10.35am and 5.33pm)

Dūnhuáng (via Liǔyuán) ¥214/325, 8½ to 10 hours, frequent

Hāmì ¥148/223, 5½ to 7½ hours, frequent

Kashgar ¥343/724 24 to 30 hours, three daily (8.43am, 9.17am and 11.51am)

Kuqa ¥123-214/210-325, 14 to 19 hours, four daily (8.43am, 9.17am, 11.51am and 9.21pm)

Yīníng ¥150/233, 10 hours, four daily (two at 8.50pm, 10.20pm and 11.17pm)

ⓘ Getting Around

The airport is 16km northwest of the centre; a taxi costs about ¥40 to ¥50. An airport bus (¥10) runs straight south through town via Hóngshān Intersection to the train station every 30 minutes. In the city centre, an airport shuttle (¥15, free for China Southern passengers) leaves from the Southern Airlines Pearl International Hotel every 30 minutes starting at 7.30am. You'll need to arrive 10 minutes early to get a seat.

A subway system was under construction at the time of writing and as this is expected to disrupt bus lines for years to come, regard the following as mere guidelines.

The fastest and most useful buses are the BRT expresses, which dodge traffic by having their very own bus lanes. BRT 1 runs from the railway station to Hóngshān Intersection and then north up Beijing Nanlu. BRT 3 runs from the south bus station to People's Sq and the South Lake Sq. Fares are a flat ¥1. See www.chinabrt.org for a route map.

Other useful buses (¥1) include bus 7, which runs up Xinhua Lu from the southern bus station through the Xīdàqiáo and Hóngshān Intersections, and bus 52 from the train station to Hóngshān Intersection.

Tiān Chí 天池

The rugged Tianshan range was well known to travellers along the northern Silk Road, who had to traverse its southern edge if they had any hope of making progress. Modern travellers have it easy and plan trips into the mountains themselves, especially to the stunning Tiān Chí. This high-altitude lake is extremely popular these days (and getting more and more developed for mass Chinese tourism), but you can still ditch most of the crowds, who either stick to the paved paths on the northern end or ride overpriced boats across the lake. Stay overnight to get a few hours of quiet in the morning before the tour buses arrive.

◉ Sights

Tiān Chí Lake LAKE

(Heaven Lake; 天池; admission ¥100) Two thousand metres up in the Tiān Shān range is Tiān Chí, a small, long, steely-blue lake nestled below the view-grabbing 5445m **Peak of God** (博格达峰; Bógédá Fēng). Scattered across the alpine pine and spruce-covered slopes are Kazakh yurts and lots of sheep. It was a paradise described in Vikram Seth's wonderful travelogue *From Heaven Lake*; and still is for some.

There are dirt roads, boardwalks and trails at Tiān Chí to various peaks, or it's seven hours hiking around the lake (if the whole system is open, which it may not be anymore). For an easy walk try the path up to **Little Heavenly East Lake** (东小天池, Dōng Xiǎo Tiānchí). There are also temples to explore on both the east and west shores, though many travellers are turned off by the commercial nature of these.

⌂ Sleeping

In late May, Kazakhs set up yurts around the lake for tourists at ¥50 to ¥80 per person in a shared yurt for up to 10 people; English-speaking **Rashit** (☎138 9964 1550; www.rashityurt.com; twin ¥150, with meals ¥200) is a popular host for backpackers and can arrange for a car to pick you up at the ticket booth. The yurt owners sometimes require ID, so make sure to bring your passport. Alternatively, you can camp at the lake but do so away from the main areas. Regardless of the temperature in Ürümqi, take warm clothes and rain gear, as the weather can be unpredictable. Also don't forget to bring your own water and food if you plan to go hiking for any length of time.

ℹ Getting There & Around

Tourist buses to Tiān Chí main gate leave Ürümqi around 9am from the north gate of People's Park, and return around 6pm. Most stop at major hotels to pick up passengers before leaving town. In the low season they may not run at all. The return fare is ¥50 and the trip takes about 2½ hours one way. Expect to stop at the usual tourist shopping traps along the way.

From the main gate (where you purchase a ticket), all travellers must take the park's own bus (¥90, every 10 to 15 minutes) for the 30-minute ride to another parking lot, which itself is still 1km before the lake. You can walk from the final lot or take a shuttle (¥10).

Turpan 吐鲁番

☎ 0995 / POP 273,400

Turpan (Tǔlǔfān) is China's Death Valley. At 154m below sea level, it's the second-lowest depression in the world and the hottest spot in China. In July and August temperatures soar above 40°C, forcing the local population and visiting tourists into a state of semi-torpor.

Despite the heat, the ground water and fertile soil of the Turpan depression has made this a veritable oasis in the desert, evidenced by the nearby centuries-old remains of ancient cities, imperial garrisons and Buddhist caves.

Though the Turpan area has been inhabited for thousands of years, and was once an important oasis on the northern Silk Road, ruled and coveted by the Xiongnu, Han, Tiele, Tibetans and Uighurs, the new town is a fairly recent creation; the historic sites are scattered in the surrounding basin. Still, there is mellow vibe to the place, and recovering from a day's sightseeing over a cold Xinjiang beer under the grape vines on a warm summer evening is one of the joys of travelling through the province.

◎ Sights

Emin Minaret ISLAMIC SITE
(额敏塔; Émǐn Tǎ; admission ¥50; ⊗9am-8pm) Built to honor Turpan general Emin Hoja, this splendid 44m-high mud-brick structure, built 1777–78, is the tallest minaret in China.

Also known as Sūgōng Tǎ after Emin's son Suleiman, who oversaw its construction, its bowling pin shape is decorated with an interesting mix of geometrical and floral patterns: the former reflect traditional Islamic design, the latter Chinese. You can no longer climb the interior steps of the minaret itself but the rest of the grounds, including the adjacent mosque, are open.

Biking or strolling the 3km to get there is half the fun. The dusty, tree-lined Uighur streets give a fascinating glimpse into old Turpan.

Turpan Museum MUSEUM
(吐鲁番博物馆; Tǔlǔfān Bówùguǎn; ⊗10am-7pm Tue-Sun) FREE Xīnjiāng's second-largest museum houses a rich collection of relics recovered from archaeological sites across the Turpan Basin, including dinosaur fossils and a couple of local mummies. Pop in here before signing up for a tour; the photos of nearby sites might help you decide which ones to visit.

🛏 Sleeping

Turpan White Camel Youth Hostel HOSTEL $
(吐鲁番白驼青年旅舍; Tǔlǔfān Bái Tuó Qīngnián Lǚshě; ☑156 0995 5676, 866 0556; www.turpan-whitecamel.hostel.com; 55 Bezeklik Lu; 柏孜克勒克路55号; dm/d Y¥50/100; ❀@◉) In an alley behind the Bezeklik Hotel is Turpan's one and only hostel. Rooms are bare but clean and there's wi-fi and bike rental (per day ¥30).

Tiānhé Bīnguǎn HOTEL $
(天和宾馆; ☑862 6999; 969 Laocheng Lu; tw ¥168; ❀@) The spacious, modern and clean rooms are good value, though you might have to gently persuade them to take foreigners.

Tǔlǔfān Bīnguǎn HOTEL $$
(吐鲁番宾馆; ☑856 8888; tlfbg@126.com; 2 Qingnian Nanlu; 青年南路2号; tw incl breakfast ¥280; ❀@) The white-tile exterior of the old-school Turpan Hotel is uninspiring, but things improve when you enter the Arabian Nights–style lobby. Bike hire (per hour ¥5) and internet access are bonuses.

★ Turpan Silk Road Lodge BOUTIQUE HOTEL $$$
(吐鲁番市丝绸之路公寓; Tǔlǔfānshì Sīchóu Zhīlù Gōngyù; ☑856 8333; https://silkroadlodges.com; Munar Lu; r with breakfast ¥680; ❀@◉) One of the very few boutique hotels in Xīnjiāng, Silk Road is set in a grape orchard

Turpan

⊙ Sights
1 Turpan Museum.................................B2

⊜ Sleeping
2 Tiānhé Bīnguǎn A2
3 Tǔlǔfān Bīnguǎn B2
4 Turpan White Camel Youth
   Hostel B1
5 Xīzhōu Dàjiǔdiàn B1

⊗ Eating
6 Gaochang Lu Night Market A2
7 Hanzada Restaurant A2
   John's Information Café .... (see 3)

across from Emin Minaret. Though the rooms feature a flat international-chain-hotel design, the rooftop views over the fields and low rising desert hills make this a unique and peaceful retreat.

Xīzhōu Dàjiǔdiàn   HOTEL $$$
(西州大酒店; ☑855 3666; 8 Qingnian Beilu; 青年北路8号; tw incl breakfast ¥320; ❉🛜) A clean and friendly option, with an ugly pink-and-white exterior.

✕ Eating

The string of restaurants that set up tables under the vine trellises on **Qingnian Lu** are a fine place to savour a cold drink and bowl of *laghman* (pulled noodles; ¥15).

Gaochang Lu Night Market   MARKET $
(高昌路夜市; Gāochāng Lù Yèshi; Gaochang Lu; dishes from ¥10; ⊙7pm-midnight) Come dusk dozens of stalls set up shop by the foun-

tains to the west of the main central square. Grab a cold beer and choose from fried fish, *shāguō* (沙果; casseroles), goat's feet soup and cumin-scented kebabs. Due to construction on Gaochang Lu the market can be a bit difficult to find, and noisy when there. Check out the area around the southern end of the Bazaar, near the new long-distance bus station.

John's Information Café   INTERNATIONAL $
(☑150 2626 8966; Qingnian Nanlu; dishes from ¥12; ⊙7.30am-11pm, May-Oct) This backpacker refuge has a quiet location in the backyard of the Tǔlǔfān Bīnguǎn (p801). Western and Chinese dishes are offered and the ice-cream sundae is a treat in Turpan's blistering heat. There is little in the way of traveller information but it does have bike rental (per hour ¥5).

Hanzada Restaurant   UIGHUR $$
(韩扎达豪华餐厅; Hánzádá Háohuá Cāntīng; Gaochang Lu; mains ¥15-40) Popular with locals for its ornate Central Asian decor (think painted alabaster and chintzy chandeliers) and diner-style booths. The picture menu helps sort out the noodles from the *polo* (pilau rice) and *dàpánjī* (大盘鸡; Huí-style spicy chicken, potatoes and peppers), all of which are excellent.

ⓘ Information

Bank of China (中国银行; Zhōngguó Yínháng; Laocheng Lu; ⊙9.30am-12.30pm & 4.30-7.30pm) Changes cash and travellers cheques.
Public Security Bureau (PSB; 公安局; Gōng'ānjú; Gaochang Lu) North of the city centre; will likely refer you to the capital for visa extensions.

ⓘ Getting There & Away

The nearest train station is at Dàhéyán (大河沿), 54km north of Turpan. Even the new high-speed rail station (which should open late 2014) is out there. You can buy tickets in Turpan at the **train booking office** (火车售票处; Huǒchē Shòupiàochù; Laocheng Xilu; commission ¥5; ⊙9am-1pm, 3.30-8pm), located inside a China Mobile office with the sign '中国铁通 China TieTong' above. There are three trains a day to Kashgar (hard/soft sleeper ¥317/484, 23 hours) departing at 10.42am, 11.14am and 1.50pm.

From the **long-distance bus station** (长途汽车站; Chángtú Qìchēzhàn; Chun Shu Lu; 椿树路), which is in Turpan, minibuses to Dàhéyán (¥11, 1½ hours) run approximately every 40 minutes.

Buses to Ürümqi (¥45, 3½ hours) run every 20 minutes. There is one daily sleeper bus at 4pm to Kashgar (¥292 to ¥320, 23 hours). A bus to Hāmì (¥89, six hours) departs in the morning (check at the station for the exact schedule). For Dūnhuáng (¥161, 11 hours) in Gānsù take afternoon sleeper bus (again, check in person for the schedule).

❶ Getting Around

Public transport around Turpan is by taxi (flag fall at ¥5), minibus or bicycle. Bicycles (about ¥5 per hour), available from John's Information Café (p802) and White Camel Youth Hostel (p801), are convenient for the town and the Emin Minaret.

Around Turpan

Most of Turpan's surrounding sights are fascinating, but some can be skipped if time is tight. Turpan's long-distance bus station has buses to a couple of the spots, but it won't save you much. The easiest way to see the sights is on a customised day tour. Several travellers have recommended English-speaking **Tahir** (☑150 2626 1388; tahirtour8@yahoo.com) who offers both an English speaking driver service and a non-English service. A full day tour costs ¥380 to ¥480 per car. Contact Tahir by email first to ensure he is available and to discuss what you want to see. You'll be gone for the day, so don't underestimate the desert heat. Essential survival gear includes a water bottle, sunscreen, sunglasses and a hat.

You can bypass the **Astana Graves** (阿斯塔那古墓区; Āsītǎnà Gǔmùqū; admission ¥20), since the most interesting finds of this imperial cemetery are in museums in Ürümqi and Turpan. Some travellers enjoy the **Karez System** (坎儿井; Kǎn'érjǐng; admission Y30), a museum dedicated to the uniquely Central Asian–style irrigation system that includes hundreds of kilometres of above and underground canals, wells and reservoirs (much of it still working). **Aydingkul Lake** (艾丁湖, Àidīng Hú; admission ¥10), the second-lowest lake in the world and the hottest place in China, has dried in recent decades and now is mostly a muddy, salt-encrusted flat. But many people still enjoy the views.

Near Bezeklik Caves and Tuyoq are the **Flaming Mountains** (火焰山, Huǒyàn Shān; admission ¥40), which appear midday like multicoloured tongues of fire. The Flaming Mountains were immortalised in the Chinese classic *Journey to the West*, when Sun Wukong (the Monkey King) used his magic fan to extinguish the blaze. There's no need to pay the entry fee, as you can see the mountains anywhere on the roadside from Hāmì or Gāochāng.

Jiāohé Ruins 交河故城

Also called Yarkhoto, **Jiāohé** (交河故城, Jiāohé Gù Chéng; admission ¥40) was established by the Chinese as a garrison town during the Han dynasty. It's one of the world's largest (6500 residents once lived here), oldest (1600 years old) and best-preserved ancient cities, inspiring with its scale, setting, and palpable historical atmosphere. Get an overview of the site at the central governor's complex then continue along the main road past a large monastery to a 'stupa grove' with a 10m-tall pagoda surrounded by 100 smaller pagoda bases.

The ruins are 8km west of Turpan. Take bus 101 (¥1) to its terminal station Yǎ'er Xiāng (亚尔乡) and then a minibus (¥2) or taxi (¥15). It's also possible to cycle here from Turpan.

Tuyoq 吐峪沟

Set in a green valley fringed by the Flaming Mountains, the mud-constructed village **Tuyoq** (吐峪沟; Tǔyùgōu; admission ¥30) offers a glimpse of traditional Uighur life and architecture. Tuyoq has been a pilgrimage site for Muslims for centuries: the devout claim that seven trips here equal one trip to Mecca. On the hillside above the village (near the road) is the **Hojamu Tomb** (admission ¥20), a *mazar* (a tomb of a saint or holy notable that often functions as a pilgrims' destination), said to hold the first Uighur to convert to Islam.

Any Uighur planning a pilgrimage to Mecca is expected to stop here beforehand.

Up the gorge look for a series of Buddhist caves dating back to the 3rd century AD (thus the earliest discovered Buddhist caves in Xīnjiāng). The caves may still be closed, however, so check before heading out.

Don't leave town without trying some of the locally produced mulberry juice or dried berries, available near the tomb entrance.

Tuyoq is often looped into a tour with the Flaming Mountains and Bezeklik Caves.

Gāochāng (Khocho) Ruins

Originally settled in the 1st century BC, Gāochāng (高昌故城; Gāochāng Gù Chéng; admission ¥40) rose to power in the 7th century during the Tang dynasty. Also known as Khocho, or sometimes Karakhoja, Gāochāng became the Uighur capital in AD 850 and was a major staging post on the Silk Road until it burnt in the 14th century.

Texts in classical Uighur, Sanskrit, Chinese and Tibetan have all been unearthed here, as well as evidence of a Nestorian church and a significant Manichaean community. Manichaeanism was a major dualistic Persian religion widespread in the east and west between the 3rd and 7th centuries (St Augustine was once a Manichaean).

Though the earthen city walls, once 12m thick, are clearly visible, not much else is left standing other than a large Buddhist monastery in the southwest. To the north, adjacent to an adobe pagoda, is a two-storey structure (half underground), purportedly the ancient palace.

Bezeklik Caves

The Bezeklik Cave Complex (柏孜克里克千佛洞; Bózīkèlīkè Qiānfó Dòng; admission ¥20), which dates from the 6th to 14th century, has a fine location in a mesmerising desert landscape. Bezeklik means 'Place of Paintings' in Uighur and the murals painted in the 11th century represented a high point in Uighur Buddhist art. Sadly the site is now famous for having most of its distinctive cave art cut out of the rock face by German, Japanese and British teams in the early 20th century.

Even more sad is that many of these did not survive WWII bombings. Today, only photographic remains exist for many masterpieces but there is still enough at the original site to make the trip out worthwhile. Most travellers also simply enjoy the chance to walk around a major historical complex without the usual crowds.

Hāmì (Kumul)　哈密

☏ 0902 / POP 365,000

Hāmì, with its famously sweet melons, was a much-anticipated stop on the Silk Road for ancient travellers. It's still worth a break today. There are enough sights to keep you busy for a day and the town is a convenient halfway point between Turpan and Dūnhuáng.

A Bank of China (中国银行; Zhōngguó Yínháng; Guangchang Beilu) is located just north of the main square (Shídài Guǎngchǎng).

◉ Sights

The main sights are located together, near the main bus station and 5km south of the train station; a taxi between the two is about ¥10.

Hāmì Kings Mausoleum　　　TOMB
(哈密王陵; Hāmì Wánglíng; Huancheng Lu; admission ¥40; ◉9.30am-8pm) The main site in Hāmì is this peaceful complex of tombs containing the nine generations of Hāmì kings who ruled the region from 1697 to 1930. The green-tiled main tomb is of the seventh king Muhammed Bixir, with family members and government ministers housed in Mongolian-style buildings to the side.

Hāmì Museum　　　MUSEUM
(哈密博物馆; Hāmì Bówùguǎn; Huancheng Lu; ◉9.30am-7pm Tue-Sun) FREE Across from the Hāmì Kings Mausoleum, this mildly interesting museum spotlights mummies and dinosaurs found in the region, including a cool fossilised nest of dinosaur eggs.

Kumul Muqam Heritage Centre　　　MUSEUM
(哈密木卡姆传承中心; Hāmì Mùkǎmǔ Chuánchéng Zhōngxīn; admission ¥15; ◉9am-1pm & 4-7pm) This eye-catching building focuses specifically on *muqam*, the classical form of Uighur music.

🛌 Sleeping

Jiǔchóngtiān Bīnguǎn　　　HOTEL $$
(九重天宾馆; ☏231 5656; 4 Tianshan Beilu; d ¥158-168; ✳@) Clean and fresh rooms, some with computers. With your back to the train station, it's 50m straight ahead, on the right.

ℹ Getting There & Away

A high-speed rail station should open in late 2014 (tests of the line began in the summer) in Hāmì connecting it with Ürümqi and Turpan in the west and Dūnhuáng in the east. This will be by far the fastest way to travel between these regions. Use Hāmì's other name, Kumul, when doing rail searches.

There are also frequent regular trains in the morning (less frequent in the afternoon) to Ürümqi (hard seat/sleeper ¥78/148, six hours).

Long-distance buses depart from the **south bus station** (南郊客运站; nánjiāo kèyùnzhàn), located 200m east of the Hāmì Kings Mausoleum.

Dūnhuáng ¥65, 8.30am and 4pm

Turpan ¥60, six hours, 9.30am

Ürümqi ¥80 to ¥90, nine hours, 11am, 1pm and 8pm

Local bus No 3 runs from the train station to the south bus station and museum via the central bus station.

Kuqa 库车

☑ 0997 / POP 68,100

Part of an excellent triangular itinerary with Kashgar and Hotan, Kuqa (Kùchē) is well worth a couple of days for its interesting bazaars and excursions to the surrounding desert ruins.

The once thriving city-state, known as Qiuci, was a major centre of Buddhism and was famed in Tang-era China for its music and dancers. Kumarajiva (AD 344–413), the first great translator of Buddhist sutras from Sanskrit into Chinese, was born here to an Indian father and Qiuci princess, before later being abducted to central China to manage translations of the Buddhist canon. When the 7th-century monk Xuan Zang passed through nearby Subashi, he recorded that two enormous 30m-high Buddha statues flanked Kuqa's western gate, and that the nearby monasteries held over 5000 monks.

The bus station is east of the town centre on Tianshan Lu, and the train station is a further 5km southeast.

◎ Sights

Qiuci Palace MUSEUM

(库车王府; Kùchē Wángfǔ; Linjilu Jie; 林基路街; admission ¥60; ⊙9am-8.30pm) Located in the old town, 3.5km west of the centre, is the newly restored (ie rebuilt) Qiuci Palace, the residence of the kings of Qiuci until the early 20th century. The museum has a good collection of Buddhist frescoes, some from the nearby Kumtura and Simsim caves, and there are human remains from the surrounding desert ruins. Behind the museum, the ancestral hall displays the history of the Qiuci kings and photos of the life of the last king, Dawud Mahsut, now an elderly local party official.

Nearby is an impressive section of Qing-dynasty city wall.

Sunday Bazaar MARKET

(老成巴扎; Lǎochéng Bāzā) Every Sunday a large bazaar is held about 2.5km west of the modern town, next to a bridge over the Kuqa River on Renmin Lu. It doesn't quite rival Kashgar's, but you won't find any tour buses here. A small livestock market also takes place here on Fridays.

Rasta Mosque MOSQUE

(热斯坦清真寺; Rèsītǎn Qīngzhēn Sì) The charming Rasta Mosque, near Kuqa's Sunday Bazaar, draws a throng of worshippers at Friday lunchtime. North of here, through the old town, is the large but less animated **Great Mosque** (清真大寺; Qīngzhēn Dàsì; admission ¥15), built in 1931 on the site of a 16th-century original.

Maulana Ashiddin Mazar TOMB

(默拉纳额什丁麻扎; Mòlānà Éshídīng Mázā) This timeless green-tiled mosque and tomb of a 13th-century Arabian missionary is surrounded by a sea of graves and overflows with worshippers at Friday lunchtime prayers. It's a 10-minute walk from the Kùchē Bīnguǎn, along mulberry-tree-lined Wenhua Lu.

🛏 Sleeping & Eating

Jiāotōng Bīnguǎn HOTEL $

(交通宾馆; Traffic Hotel; ☑712 2682; 194 Tianshan Lu; 天山路194号; tw ¥160; ❋🛜) Located next to the bus station, this place has a range of acceptable rooms. There's wi-fi in the lobby.

Kùchē Bīnguǎn HOTEL $$

(库车宾馆; ☑712 2901; 17 Jiefang Beilu; tw with breakfast ¥258; ❋🛜) Kuqa's main hotel has fresh rooms with plush carpets in the new block and scruffier but acceptable rooms in the quiet old block. It's located near the city centre. Catch a taxi here.

★**Uchar Darvaza Bazaar** MARKET $

(乌恰农贷市场; Wūqià Nónghuò Shìchǎng) The best place for Uighur food is this street at the junction of Tianshan Zhonglu and Youyi Lu. Kebabs, noodles and *samsas* (baked mutton pies) are all served hot and fresh, though our favourites are the chicken kebabs served with sombrero-sized local nan. Some stalls start to close at 9pm, others only set up from 10pm.

ℹ Information

Bank of China (中国银行; Zhōngguó Yínháng; 25 Wenhua Lu; ⊙9.30am-6.30pm Mon-Fri) Wenhua Lu has several Bank of Chinas. Travellers cheques are not accepted.

ⓘ Getting There & Away

The new airport, 35km west of the city, has daily flights to Ürümqi (¥550). A taxi there costs ¥30.

The bus station has a variety of sleepers heading east.

Aksu ¥65, four hours, hourly. At Aksu you can connect to Kashgar.

Hotan ¥192, eight hours, one daily at noo

Kashgar ¥150, 16 hours. You may have to wait for a sleeper from Ürümqi to pass and hope that it has berths.

Ürümqi ¥207 to ¥262, 12 hours, seven per day (one at noon, the others in the evening)

The train station is southeast of the centre. A taxi costs ¥10.

Kashgar hard/soft sleeper ¥182/275, 10 hours, three daily (12.40am, 6.59am and 11.23pm)

Ürümqi hard/soft sleeper ¥214/325, 15 to 19 hours, four daily (7.14am, 7.13pm, 8.43pm and 10.18pm)

ⓘ Getting Around

Taxi rides are a standard ¥5 per trip, with pedicabs, tractors and donkey carts around half this.

Around Kuqa

Kizil Thousand Buddha Caves

Seventy-five kilometres northwest of Kuqa are the Kizil Thousand Buddha Caves (克孜尔千佛洞; Kèzī'ěr Qiānfó Dòng; admission ¥55; ☉ daylight), the largest Buddhist cave art site in Xīnjiāng. The interior murals date from the 3rd to the 8th centuries and as ancient Kuqa was an ethnically diverse place, artisans were inspired by Afghanisti, Persian and Indian motifs and styles. The heavy use of blue pigment in middle-period murals is a Persian influence, for example. Only the last phase shows any Chinese influence.

The caves are generally built the same way, with two chambers and a central niche. The front vaulted chamber roof contains murals of the Buddha's past lives (so-called *jataka* tales) and, unique to Kizil, the pictures are framed in diamond-shaped patterns. There are 236 caves at Kizil, but only a handful are open to the public. Several were stripped by German archaeologist Albert Von le Coq, while the others have been defaced by both Muslims and Red Guards.

The caves are 75km from Kuqa. A return taxi will cost around ¥200 to ¥300 and takes 90 minutes each way. Add on stops in Sūbāshí and the 13.5m-tall Han-dynasty **watchtower** (烽火台; fēnghuǒtái; admission ¥15) at Kizilgah if you can't bargain down a lower price.

Sūbāshí Ruins 苏巴什故城

Sūbāshí (苏巴什故城; admission ¥25; ☉ daylight) was a Buddhist complex that thrived from the 3rd to the 13th centuries. It's less visited than other ancient cities in Xīnjiāng, but with its starkly beautiful desert setting, is a highlight for many travellers in the region. Most people visit the west complex, with its large central *vihara* (monastery) and two large pagodas, but the dramatic eastern complex across the Kuqa River is worth the hike.

A return taxi to Sūbāshí, 23km northeast of Kuqa, costs about ¥80 to ¥100; you'll need to pay extra waiting time if you want to visit the eastern ruins.

SOUTHWEST XĪNJIĀNG – KASHGARIA

The Uighurs' heartland is Kashgaria, the rough-but-mellifluous-sounding historical name for the western Tarim Basin. Consisting of a ring of oases lined with poplar trees, it was a major Silk Road hub and has bristled with activity for more than 2000 years, with the weekly bazaars remaining the centre of life here to this day.

Kashgar 喀什

☑ 0998 / POP 350,000

Locked away in the westernmost corner of China, physically closer to Tehran and Damascus than to Běijīng, Kashgar (Kāshí) has been the epicentre of regional trade and cultural exchange for more than two millennia.

In recent years modernity has swept through Kashgar like a sandstorm. The roads, rail and planes that now connect the city to the rest of China have brought waves of Han migrant workers and huge swaths of the old city have been bulldozed in the name of economic 'progress'.

Yet, in the face of these changes, the spirit of Kashgar lives on. Uighur craftsmen and artisans still hammer and chisel away in side alleys, traders haggle over deals in the boisterous bazaars and donkey carts still trundle their way through the suburbs. And the Sunday livestock market is the real deal, no matter how many tour buses roll up.

So soak it in for a few days, eat a few kebabs, chat with the local carpet sellers, visit the holiest sites in Xīnjiāng and prepare your trip along the southern Silk Road to Hotan, over the Torugart or Irkeshtam Passes to Kyrgyzstan or south along the stunning Karakoram Hwy to Pakistan.

◎ Sights

★ Grand (Sunday) Bazaar MARKET

(大巴扎; Dàbāzhā; Yengi Bazaar; Aizirete Lu, 艾孜热特路; ☉daily) Kashgar's main bazaar is open every day but really kicks it up a gear on Sunday. Step carefully through the jam-packed entrance and allow your five senses to guide you through the market; the pungent smell of cumin, the sight of scorpions in a jar, the sound of *muqam* music from tinny radios, the taste of hot *samsas* and the feel of soft sheepskin caps are seductive, and overwhelming.

A section on the northern side of the market contains everything of interest to foreign visitors, including the spice market, musical instruments, fur caps, kitschy souvenirs and carpets. A taxi to the market is ¥5 to ¥10.

Sunday Livestock Market MARKET

(动物市场, Dòngwù Shìchǎng, Mal Bazaar; ☉8am-6pm Sun) No visit to Kashgar is complete without a trip to the Livestock Market, which takes place once a week on Sunday. The day begins with Uighur farmers and herders trekking into the city from nearby villages. By lunchtime just about every sellable sheep, camel, horse, cow and donkey within 50km has been squeezed through the bazaar gates. It's dusty, smelly and crowded, and most people find it wonderful, though the treatment of the animals often leaves something to be desired.

Trading at the market is swift and boisterous between the old traders; animals are carefully inspected and haggling is done with finger motions. Keep an ear out for the phrase '*Bosh-bosh!*' ('Coming through!') or you risk being ploughed over by a cartload of fat-tailed sheep.

In 2012 the market relocated to the northeastern suburbs. A taxi here costs ¥20 to ¥25; it's a good idea to pay it to wait for your return. Alternatively take bus 23 from the Sunday Bazaar. Tour buses usually arrive in the morning, so consider an early afternoon visit. A few simple stalls offer hot *samsas* if you get peckish.

If you miss the Sunday Market, don't despair: there are plenty of other markets in Xīnjiāng to visit. Try the Sunday market in Hotan or Kuqa, the Monday market in Upal or the Tuesday market in Charbagh.

Abakh Hoja (Afaq Khoja) Mausoleum TOMB

(香妃墓; Xiāngfēimù, Abakh Hoja Maziri; admission ¥30; ☉daylight) On the northeastern outskirts of town is the Abakh Hoja Mausoleum, a 3-hectare complex built by the Khoja family who ruled the region in the 17th and 18th centuries. Widely considered the holiest Muslim site in Xīnjiāng, it's a major pilgrimage destination and a beautiful piece of Islamic architecture well worth a long lingering visit.

Founded as a religious school by Yusuf Khoja, the mausoleum was built in 1640 with further halls and mosques being added over the next three centuries. In addition to housing the remains of Yusuf, dozens of Khoja family members are interned here. These include Yusuf's son Abakh Hoja, a famed 17th-century Sufi and political leader (and after who the mausoleum is named), and according to legend, Iparhan, Abakh Hoja's granddaughter.

Known to the Chinese as Xiang Fei, the 'Fragrant Concubine' of the Emperor Qianlong, Iparhan remains a potent symbol of the Chinese-Uighur divide. To the Han, she was the beloved but homesick concubine of the Emperor and thus a symbol of national unity. To the Uighur she was a resistance leader (or the wife of one) who was captured and taken to Beijing where she died (and was likely buried) broken-hearted, or was killed by the Emperor's mother.

The mausoleum complex has an irregular design so all the mosques face Mecca at a slightly different angle. South are the main stone gate, with its striking blue tiles, and the High and Low Mosques. These mosques form a typical pairing in Uighur religious architecture and are known as summer and winter mosques: their open-sided and closed structures, respectively, allow for prayer during the different seasons. Note the wooden and painted columns here, carved in 1926, with their *muqarnas* capitals (a traditional Persian design likened to hanging stalactites).

The Great Mosque is in the west of the complex, while the small Green Mosque (which also has summer and winter halls) is in the north. The domed mausoleum, the tallest structure in the complex, is east, and is

Kashgar

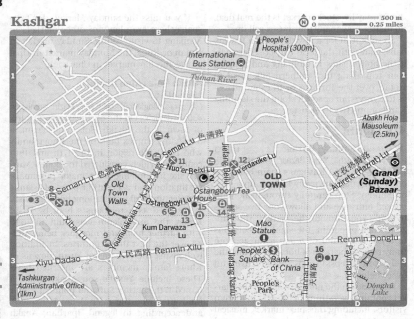

Kashgar

surrounded by a graveyard wall with four colourful towers in the corners. The most striking feature, however, are the mismatched exterior tiles, the result of piecemeal repairs over the years. A taxi here is ¥10 to ¥15.

Old Town
OLD TOWN

The Chinese government spent the past two decades knocking the Old Town down, block by block, and building a replacement. Many travellers still enjoy exploring the new areas but to see some of the last remaining alleys check out the neighborhood near Donghai Lake in the east part of the city. Sprawling on both sides of Jiefang Lu there are also alleys lined with Uighur workshops and adobe houses right out of an early-20th-century picture book.

Where they exist, houses range in age from 50 to 500 years old and the lanes twist haphazardly through neighbourhoods where Kashgaris have lived and worked for centuries. It's a great place for strolling, peeking through gates, chatting up the locals and admiring the craftsmen as they bang on tin and chase copper.

Traditional houses in Kashgar, rarely more than two-stories high, are built with poplar timber and mud bricks. Walls are very thick but usually unadorned on the outside. The inner courtyards and balconies, however, are decorated with woodcarvings and hangings.

At the eastern end of Seman Lu stands a 10m-high section of the Old Town walls, which are at least 500 years old.

Id Kah Mosque   MOSQUE
(艾提尕尔清真寺; Ài Tígǎ'ěr Qīngzhēn Sì; Id Kah Sq; admission ¥30) The yellow-tiled Id Kah Mosque, which dates from 1442, is the spiritual and physical heart of the city. Enormous (it's the largest mosque in China), its courtyard and gardens can hold 20,000 people during the annual Qurban Baiyram. Also known as Eid, or Id, celebrations they fall in September for the next few years.

Non-Muslims may enter, but not during prayer time. Dress modestly, including a headscarf for women. Take off your shoes if entering carpeted areas and be discreet when taking photos.

The stalls outside the mosque are a good place to pick up a striped *khalat* (cloak) or traditional Uighur *doppi* (skullcap).

Shipton's Arch
(Tushuk Tagh)   NATURAL LANDMARK
This natural rock arch (the Uighur name means 'mountain with a hole in it') is reputedly the tallest on earth. The first Westerner to describe it was the British mountaineer and last British consul-general in Kashgar, Eric Shipton, during his visit to the region in 1947. Successive expeditions attempted to find it without success until a team from *National Geographic* rediscovered the arch in 2000. The arch, located 80km northwest of Kashgar, is a half-day excursion from Kashgar.

The first part of the trip involves an hour's drive towards the Irkeshtam Pass, followed by another 20km ride and then a 30-minute hike. At times you'll be scrambling through the narrowest part of the gorge over small ladders. Kashgar-based tour operators can arrange a day trip with guide for ¥600 to ¥800 per car plus ¥400 for the guide. Bring sturdy shoes, a fleece, snacks and water.

Mor Pagoda   RUIN
(莫尔佛塔; Mù'ěr Fótǎ; admission ¥15; ☉ daylight) At the end of a 45km drive northeast of town are the ruins of Ha Noi, a Tang-dynasty town built in the 7th century and abandoned in the 12th century. Little remains apart from an enigmatic pyramid-like structure and the impressive four-tiered Mor Pagoda. A round-trip taxi, including waiting time, costs ¥100 to ¥150.

☞ Tours

Popular tours include four-day treks around Muztagh Ata, overnighting in tents, yurts or villages, as well as overnight camel tours into the dunes fringing the Taklamakan Desert around Davakul Lake or Yarkand. For a real challenge, consider biking the Karakoram Hwy.

Ablimit 'Elvis' Ghopar   TOUR
(☑ 138 9913 6195; elvisablimit@yahoo.com) Local English-speaking Uighur carpet dealer Elvis organises city-wide cultural trips, with a special emphasis on Uighur classical music and the Kashgar carpet market. Find him at the Saqiya Teahouse near Id Gah Mosque.

Old Road Tours   TOUR
(☑ 220 4012, 138 9913 2103; www.oldroadtours. com; 337 Seman Lu) One of the best, run by Abdul Wahab and operating out of the Sèmǎn Bīnguǎn. Can arrange trekking at Muz Tagh Ata, homestays in Turpan villages and Yining, overnighting in the desert, and overnight camel tours in the Taklimakan desert.

Uighur Tours   TOUR
(☑ 298 1073; www.kashgartours.com; 144 Seman Lu) Ali Tash runs this recommended agency based in the Chini Bagh Hotel. It offers tours and treks of Karakul lake and Muztagh Ata, camel treks in the Taklimakan desert, and even UIghur cooking lessons.

🛏 Sleeping

Accommodation can be tighter on the days preceding the Sunday Market.

★ Pamir Youth Hostel   HOSTEL $
(喀什帕米尔青年旅舍; Kāshí Pàmǐ'ěr Qīng-nián Lǔshě; ☑ 282-3376, 180-9985-1967; www. pamirhostel.com/en; 3f Id Kah Bazaar District 7, Section A; dm ¥40-50, d without bathroom ¥150; ❄ 🛜) With an outdoor terrace that overlooks the beautiful Id Kah Mosque, this hostel has quickly become a popular base for explor-

ing the city and its historical surroundings. Dorm rooms are basic but include individual lockers and free wi-fi. To find Pamir look for the green dome just north of the mosque.

Kashgar Old Town Youth Hostel HOSTEL $
(喀什老城青年旅舍; Kāshí Lǎochéng Qīngnián Lǚshè; ☎282 3262; www.pamirinn.com; 233 Ostangboyi Lu (Wusitangboyi Lu), 吾斯塘博依路233号; tw without bathroom ¥100-120, tw with breakfast ¥160; @🛜) Nestled in the old city, this atmospheric place is set around a courtyard where overlanders hang out on *shyrdaks* (Kyrgyz-style felt carpets), swapping stories and travel info. The rooms are bare, the toilets simple and the beds are rock hard, but staff speak English and there's cheap laundry and free internet access.

Sahar Hotel BUDGET HOTEL $
(色哈尔宾馆; Sèhā'ěr Bīnguǎn; ☎258 1122; 348 Seman Lu; tw ¥70; 🛜) A friendly but dowdy hotel whose customers are mostly Pakistani, Tajik and Uighur traders. The hotel offers some of the cheapest ensuite rooms available to foreigners, with wi-fi, though they are pretty simple. Rooms on the 3rd floor are best.

Chini Bagh Hotel HOTEL $$
(其尼瓦克宾馆; Qíníwǎkè Bīnguǎn; ☎298 2103; 144 Seman Lu; tw with breakfast ¥288-328; ✴@🛜) The Chini Bagh, immortalised in William Dalrymple's travelogue *In Xanadu*, is located on the grounds of the former British consulate (1901–51). The central location is convenient for the Old Town. Visit the Chinese restaurant behind the north block to see the old consulate building.

Eden Hotel HOTEL $$
(海尔巴格大饭店; Hǎiěrbāgé Dàfàndiàn; ☎266 4444; 148 Seman Lu; tr with breakfast ¥188; 🛜) The quiet rooms and excellent location of this midrange hotel make it good value. The staff speak some English and there's an excellent attached Turkish restaurant.

Yambu Hotel HOTEL $$
(金座大饭店; Jīnzuò Dàfàndiàn; ☎258 8888; 198 Renmin Xilu; d ¥238; ✴@) A good bet for affordable, modern and spacious midrange comfort but check a couple of rooms as standards vary. As ever, the back rooms are quietest.

✗ Eating

Kashgar is one of the best places in Xīnjiāng to try the full gamut of Uighur food.

★ Ōu'ěr Dáxīkè Night Market MARKET $
(欧尔达稀克夜市; Ōu'ěr Dáxīkè Yèshì; Ou'er Daxike Lu; meals from ¥10; ⊙8pm-midnight Xīnjiāng time) The night market across Jiefang Beilu from the Id Kah Mosque is a great place to sample local fare. Among the goodies are fried fish, chickpeas, kebabs, fried dumplings known as *hoshan* and bubbling vats of goat's head soup. Top off a meal with a glass of tart pomegranate juice or freshly churned vanilla-scented ice cream.

Karakorum Café CAFE $$
(87 Seman Lu; mains ¥20-48; ⊙10.30am-10.30pm; 🛜) Smart-looking but slightly sterile cafe serving Western-style breakfasts, sandwiches, desserts and coffee (¥10 to ¥28) in an oasis of delicious quiet.

Altun Orda UIGHUR $$
(金噢尔达饮食; Jīn'ào'ěrdà Yǐnshí; Xibei Lu; dishes from ¥25; ⊙8am-10pm) Perfect for a celebration or last Kashgar meal, Altun Orda is a sumptuously decorated Uighur restaurant famous for its roasted mutton (¥78), *gosh nan* (meat pie) and *mirizlig samsa* (pastry with raisins and almonds). There are branches across Xīnjiāng.

John's Cafe INTERNATIONAL $$
(约翰中西餐厅; Yuēhàn Zhōngxī Cāntīng; www.johncafe.net; 337 Seman Lu; mains from ¥20; ⊙May-Oct; 🛜) This is a popular backpacker hang-out, offering both Western (pricey) and Chinese (cheaper) dishes. Management also arranges local tours.

🔒 Shopping

For serious shopping go to the Old Town, ready to bargain. Kum Darwaza Lu is a good starting point. The Grand Bazaar has a decent selection but prices tend to be higher. Hats, teapot sets, copper- and brassware, kebab skewers and Uighur knives are among the best souvenirs.

Grand (Sunday) Bazaar MARKET
(大巴扎; Dàbāzhā; Aizirete Lu; ⊙daily) Most carpet dealers display their wares at the Market pavilion. The rugs here are made of everything from silk to synthetics and finding traditional designs can be difficult. The brightly coloured felt Kyrgyz-style *shyrdaks* are a good buy.

Ahmed Carpet Shop   HOMEWARES
(☎ 283 1557; 49 Kum Darwaza Lu) Ahmed and his son run this Old Town carpet shop, offering a good selection of antique and new carpets, *gilims* and *shyrdaks* from across Central Asia.

**Uighur Musical
Instrument Factory**   MUSICAL INSTRUMENTS
(272 Kum Darwaza Lu) You'll find long-necked stringed instruments here running the gamut from souvenirs to collectors' items. If any traditional performances are on, owner Mohammed will know where to find them. There are several places with the same name on the same street.

Ilhas Supermarket   SUPERMARKET
(伊合拉斯超市; Yīhélāsī Chāoshì; Jiefang Beilu; ⊘10am-midnight) An excellent choice of Turkish and Central Asian goods underneath the Id Kah plaza.

❶ Dangers & Annoyances

Travellers have lost money or passports to pickpockets at the Sunday Market, so keep yours tucked away.

Kashgar is the most conservative corner of Xīnjiāng and the one place where you will see women's faces obscured by headscarves or veils. Some foreign women walking the streets alone have been sexually harassed. It is wise for women travellers to dress as would be appropriate in any Muslim country, covering arms and legs.

UIGHUR FOOD

Uighur cuisine includes all the trusty Central Asian standbys, such as kebabs, *polo* (pilau rice) and *chuchura* (dumplings), but has benefited from Chinese influence to make it the most enjoyable region of Central Asia in which to eat.

Uighurs boast endless varieties of *laghman* (pulled noodles; *lāmiàn* in Chinese), though the usual topping is a combination of mutton, peppers, tomatoes, eggplant and garlic shoots. *Suoman* are torn noodle squares fried with tomatoes, peppers, garlic and meat, with *suoman goshsiz* the vegetarian variety. *Suoman* can be quite spicy, so ask for *lazasiz* (without peppers) if you prefer a milder version.

Kebabs are another staple and are of a much better standard than the ropey *shashlyk* of the Central Asian republics. *Jiger* (liver) kebabs are the low-fat variety. *Tonor* kebabs are larger and baked in an oven *tonor* (tandoori) style. True kebab connoisseurs insist on *kovurgah kebab* or *bel kebab*, made from rib and waist meat respectively. Most are flavoured with *zir* (cumin).

Nan (breads) are a favourite staple and irresistible when straight out of the oven and sprinkled with poppy seeds, sesame seeds or fennel. They make a great plate for a round of kebabs, especially the Hotanese variety, which are more than 2ft wide. Most Uighur restaurants serve small cartons of delicious *ketik* (yoghurt) to accompany your meal.

Other snacks include *serik ash* (yellow, meatless noodles), *nokot* (chickpeas), *pintang* (meat and vegetable soup) and *gang pan* (rice with vegetables and meat). *Opke* is a broth of bobbing goat's heads and coiled, stuffed intestines.

Samsas (baked mutton dumplings) are available everywhere, but the meat-to-fat ratio varies wildly. Hotan and Kashgar offer huge meat pies called *daman* or *gosh girde*.

For dessert try *morozhenoe* (vanilla ice cream churned in iced wooden barrels), *kharsen meghriz* (fried dough balls filled with sugar, raisins and walnuts, also known as *chiker koimak*) or *dogh* (sometimes known as *doghap*), a delicious mix of shaved ice, syrup, yoghurt and iced water. As with all ice-based food, try the latter at your own risk. *Tangzaza* are triangles of glutinous rice wrapped in bamboo leaves covered in syrup.

Anyone with a sweet tooth should look for carts selling *matang* (walnut fruit loaf), and *sokmak*, a delicious paste of walnuts, raisins, almonds and sugar, sold by the 500g jar (¥20 to ¥30) at honey and nut stalls. It's fine to ask for a free sample.

Xīnjiāng is justly famous for its fruit, whether it be *uruk* (apricots), *uzum* (grapes), *tawuz* (watermelon), *khoghun* (sweet melon) or *yimish* (raisins). The best grapes come from Turpan; the sweetest melons from Hāmì. Markets groan with the stuff from July to September.

Meals are washed down with *kok chai* (green tea), often laced with nutmeg or rose petals. The one local beer worth going out of your way for is bottled Xinjiang Black Beer, a dark lager-style brew.

ℹ Information

Bank of China (中国银行; Zhōngguó Yínháng; People's Sq; ⊙ 9.30am-1.30pm & 4-7pm) Changes travellers cheques and cash, and has a 24-hour ATM. You can also sell yuan back into US dollars at the foreign-exchange desk if you have exchange receipts; this is a good idea if you are headed to Tashkurgan, where the bank hours are erratic.

People's Hospital (人民医院; Rénmín Yīyuàn; Jiefang Beilu) North of the river.

Public Security Bureau (PSB; 公安局; Gōng'ānjú; 111 Youmulakexia Lu; ⊙ 9.30am-1.30pm & 4-8pm) Visa extensions take three to four days, dependent on the political climate.

ℹ Getting There & Away

It's imperative when you buy tickets in Kashgar to verify 'which time' the ticket is for. It should be Běijīng time, but this isn't always the case.

Note that in 2014, heightened security meant there were a number of new checkpoints on the roads and bus journeys could be 50% longer than scheduled. It's best to take the train whenever possible.

Over a dozen daily flights depart for Ürümqi (¥1100).

Domestic buses use the **long-distance bus station** (地区客运站, Dìqū Kèyùnzhàn; Tiannan Lu):

Hotan ¥132 to ¥145, seven to 10 hours, every 1½ hours

Karghilik ¥52 to ¥65, four hours, frequent

Tashkurgan (on the Karakorum Hwy) ¥55, six hours, two per day (9.30am and 10am)

Yarkand ¥39 to ¥47, three hours, frequent

Yengisar ¥17, 1½ hours, frequent

Faster shared taxis also run to all these places for twice the bus fare; a ticket office just inside the entrance sells tickets.

Sleeper buses depart from the **international bus station** (国际汽车站; Guójì Qìchēzhàn; Jiefang Beilu):

Ürümqi ¥265 to ¥280, 24 hours, eight buses per day between 9am and 10pm

Kuqa ¥260 12 hours, three per day (11am, 4pm and 7pm)

Ürümqi hard sleeper ¥182-342, soft sleeper ¥338-527, 25 to 31 hours, three daily (8.01am, 12.52pm and 9.41pm)

Hotan hard seat/sleeper ¥33/77, seven hours, one per day (9.21am)

There are also trains to **Yengisar** (two hours), **Yarkand** (four hours), and **Karghilik** (5½ hours).

You can buy tickets from the **train booking office** (火车售票处; Huǒchē Shòupiàochù; Tiannan Lu; commission ¥5; ⊙ 9.30am-1pm & 3-8pm) at the long-distance bus station.

ℹ Getting Around

The airport is 13km northeast of the town centre. A taxi costs ¥15 to ¥20 but drivers often ask for double this. Bus 2 (¥1) goes directly to the airport from People's Sq and Id Kah Mosque.

Giant Bike Shop (捷安特自行车; Jié'āntè Zìxíngchē; ☑ 640 1616; 37 Jiankang Lu) rents bikes for ¥50 per day. It's located 1.5km south of town opposite the Three Fortune Hotel (三运宾馆; Sānyùn Bīnguǎn). Kashgar Old Town Youth Hostel (p810) also rents bikes (per day ¥40).

Useful bus routes are Buses 2 (Jiefang Lu north to the international bus station and the airport), 9 (international bus station to the Chini Bagh Hotel and Sèmǎn Bīnguǎn), 20 (China Post to Abakh Hoja Tomb) and 28 (Id Kah Mosque to the train station). The fare is ¥1.

Taxis are metered and the flag fall is ¥5. Nowhere in town should cost more than ¥15.

Karakoram Highway 中巴公路

The Karakoram Hwy (KKH; Zhōngbā Gōnglù) over the Khunjerab Pass (4800m) is one of the world's most spectacular roads and China's gateway to Pakistan. For centuries this route was used by caravans plodding down the Silk Road. Khunjerab means 'valley of blood' – local bandits used to take advantage of the terrain to slaughter merchants and plunder caravans.

Facilities en route are being gradually improved, but take warm clothing, food and drink on board with you – once stowed on the bus roof it will be unavailable on the journey. Check the state of the highway well ahead of time.

Within China, many travellers head up the highway at least to Tashkurgan. It's possible to do a day trip to Karakul Lake and back but it's much better to spend a night or two up in these gorgeous mountains camping and trekking. Some travellers also hire bikes in Kashgar: get a lift up to Tashkurgan and cycle back for an exciting three-day journey.

During times of political tension foreigners need a permit from a travel agent to get past the checkpoint at Ghez. Check in advance with a Kashgar travel agency.

Kashgar to Tashkurgan

Travelling up the KKH to Tashkurgan is a highlight of Kashgaria. The journey begins with a one-hour drive through the Kashgar oasis to **Upal** (Wùpà'ěr in Chinese), where most vehicles stop for breakfast, especially during the interesting Monday market. The renovated **Tomb of Mahmud Kashgari** (admission ¥30), a beloved local 11th-century scholar, traveller and writer, is a potential excursion but it's far from unmissable. The tomb is about 2.5km from the market on the edge of Upal hill.

Two hours from Kashgar you enter the canyon of the Ghez River (Ghez Darya in Uighur), with its dramatic claret-red sandstone walls. Ghez itself is a major checkpoint; photographing soldiers or buildings is strictly prohibited. At the top of the canyon, 3½ hours above the plain, you pop out into a huge wet plateau ringed with mountains of sand, part of the Sarikol Pamir, and aptly called Kumtagh (Sand Mountain) by locals.

Soon Kongur Mountain (Gōnggé'ěr Shān; 7719m) rises up on the left side of the road, followed by heavily glaciered Muztagh Ata (Mùshìtǎgé Shān; 7546m). The main stopping point for views is **Karakul Lake**, a glittering mirror of glacial peaks 194km from Kashgar. From here you can hike into the hills or circumnavigate the lake. Old Road Tours (p809) can organise four- to 11-day trekking tours around the lake to Subash village or the Muztagh Ata base camp (4500m), overnighting in tents, villages and Kyrgyz yurts along the way. The trek includes food, permits, guide and even a camel to haul your gear.

The journey climbs to a pass offering fine views, then meanders through high mountain pastures dotted with grazing camels and yaks, before passing the turn-off to the Qolma Pass (currently closed to foreigners). The final

---

BORDER CROSSING: GETTING TO KYRGYZSTAN, PAKISTAN & TAJIKISTAN

To Kyrgyzstan

There are two passes into Kyrgyzstan: the Torugart Pass, which leads to Naryn and then Bishkek in the north; and the Irkeshtam Pass, which goes to Osh in the south. Getting to Osh (¥570, two days) is straightforward, with a sleeper bus leaving Kashgar's international bus station (p812) at 9am on Monday and Friday. You can also hire a car through a Kashgar agency, though no special permits or guide are needed for this route.

Crossing the Torugart requires more red tape, for which you will need a travel agency's help. You will also need to have pre-arranged transport on the Kyrgyz side, which travel agents can arrange with their contacts in Naryn or Bishkek. Old Road Tours (p809) in Kashgar runs trip to Naryn and back nearly every day. It usually only needs a day or two to arrange permits.

Kyrgyzstan visas are available from the consulate in Ürümqi. Bring one passport photo and a copy of your passport and visa and arrive early because the consulate is only open for two hours a day.

To Pakistan

Buses to/from Sost (¥270, two days) in Pakistan leave Kashgar's international bus station (p812) daily at noon. However, if there are fewer than 10 passengers the bus may not depart until the following day. The 500km trip stops overnight at Tashkurgan, where customs procedures are conducted. You can also hire a car from one of the tour outfits in Kashgar though this will be considerably more expensive.

Officially, the border opens daily between 1 May and 31 October. However, the border can open late or close early depending on conditions at the Khunjerab Pass, and may close on weekends. The Chinese customs and immigration formalities are done at Tashkurgan (technically 3km down the road towards Pakistan). Then it's 126km to the last checkpost at Khunjerab Pass, the actual border, where your documents are checked again before you head into Pakistan. Pakistan immigration formalities are performed at Sost. Pakistani visas are no longer available to tourists on arrival (and visas are difficult to get in Běijīng), so the safest option is to arrive in China with a visa obtained in your home country. Check the current situation as this could change.

To Tajikistan

The 4362m Qolma (Kulma) Pass linking Kashgar with Murghab (via Tashkurgan) opened in 2004 to local traders. As of 2014 it was still closed to foreign travellers.

major town on the Chinese side is **Tashkurgan** at 3600m. You could easily kill a couple of hours wandering the streets and visiting the small museum at the **Folk Culture Centre** (admission ¥30; ⊘10am-5pm) at the central crossroads (marked by the eagle statue).

On the outskirts of town, close to the river, is **Tashkurgan Fort** (石头城; Shítóuchéng; admission ¥30), whose 1400-year-old stone (*tash*) fortifications (*kurgan*) give the town its name. The ruins were one of the filming locations for the movie *Kite Runner*. The boggy valley below is dotted with Tajik yurts in summer and offers some spectacular views back towards the fort.

Some travellers head up to the Khunjerab Pass for a photo opportunity on the actual Pakistan–China border. Note that you need a border permit (available in Kashgar) and a guide, which most tour agencies can arrange.

🛏 Sleeping

Jiāotōng Bīnguǎn　　　　　　　HOTEL $
(交通宾馆; ☎0998-342 1192; tw ¥120-140; ☎) The bus station hotel has fresh and modern twins. Bus passengers en route to Sost generally overnight here.

Crown Inn　　　　　　　　　HOTEL $$$
(皇冠大酒店; Huángguān Dàjiǔdiàn; ☎0998-342 2888; www.crowninntashkorgan.com; 1 Pami'er Lu; d/tw with breakfast ¥630; @☎) This plush Singaporean-run hotel offers comfortable, bright rooms and a good though pricey restaurant. Internet was cut off by the government in 2014.

❶ Getting There & Away

From Kashgar two daily buses run to Tashkurgan from the long-distance bus station, leaving at 9.30am and 10am (¥55, six hours). Shared taxis also depart from the city's **Tashkurgan Administration Office** (塔什库尔干办事处; Tǎshíkù'ěrgān Bànshìchù; 166 Xiyu Dadao Lu; 西域大道166号), in the west of town.

From Kashgar it's 118km to the Ghez checkpoint, 194km to Karakul Lake, 283km to Tashkurgan and 380km to the Pakistani border.

SOUTHERN SILK ROAD

The Silk Road east of Kashgar splits into two threads in the face of the Taklamakan Desert, the second-largest sandy desert in the world. The northern thread follows the modern road and railway to Kuqa and Turpan. The southern road charts a more remote course between desert sands and the towering Pamir and Kunlun mountain ranges.

This off-the-grid journey takes you far into the modern Uighur heartland, as well as deep into the ancient multi-ethic heritage of the region. You're as likely to come across a centuries-old tiled mosque as the ruins of a Buddhist pagoda from the 4th century.

It's possible to visit the southern towns as a multiday trip from Kashgar before crossing the Taklamakan Desert to Ürümqi, or as part of a rugged backdoor route into Tibet or Qīnghǎi.

Yengisar　　　英吉沙

The tiny town of Yengisar (Yīngjíshā) is synonymous with knife production. A lesser-known but more sensitive fact is it's the birthplace of the Uighur's icon of nationalism, Isa Yusuf Alptekin (1901–95), the leader of the First East Turkestan Republic in Kashgar, who died in exile in Istanbul.

There are dozens of knife shops here, most of them strung along the highway; ask for the 'knife factories' (小刀厂; *xiǎodāochǎng* in Chinese; *pichak chilik karakhana* in Uighur). Each worker makes the blade, handle and inlays himself, using only the most basic of tools. To get there from the main bus station, hop in a taxi (¥5) for the 3km trip to the knife shops. They are right on the main road, so you'd even pass them on the way to Yarkand. Note that knives are prohibited in check-in luggage, so you'll have to ship them home.

Buses pass through the town regularly en route between Yarkand (¥28, 1½ hours) and Kashgar (¥13, 1½ hours).

Yarkand　　　莎车

At the end of a major trade route from British India, over the Karakoram Pass from Leh, Yarkand (Shāchē) was for centuries an important caravan town and regional centre for the trade in cashmere wool. This traditional and conservative town is worth a stop, though be aware that Yarkand was the site of a still opaque violent protest on 28 July 2014, which led to 96 official deaths; the WUC (World Uyghur Congress) claim it was more than 2000. At the time of writing many hotels were not accepting foreigners and most had had their internet cut off. It's

THE SILK ROAD

Nomadic trading routes across Asia and Europe had existed for thousands of years but what we now call the Silk Road, an intercontinental network connecting the East and West, began to take shape in the 2nd century BC. At the time, the Mediterranean had already been linked to Central Asia by Alexander the Great (and his Roman successors), and China, in its need to defend itself from marauding Xiongnu, was about to do its part.

In 138 BC the Emperor Wudi sent envoy Zhang Qian to negotiate an alliance with the Yuezhi, a Central Asian people being driven west by the Xiongnu. On his return (after much hardship which included being kidnapped twice) Zhang piqued the emperor's interest with tales of wealthy neighbouring kingdoms, powerful horses, and trade of Chinese goods, including silk, that had already reached these regions. Over the next two centuries the Han experienced endless setbacks as they sought to defeat the Xiongnu and secure safe passage from Gānsù through Xīnjiāng, but eventually formal trade with Central Asia was established.

Owing as much to continuous political instability as geographical challenges, there was never any one route that goods travelled along, much less a road; the name Silk Road in fact was coined in 1877 by German geographer Ferdinand von Richtofen. The loose, fragile and often dangerous network of ancient times had its Chinese start in Cháng'ān (modern Xī'ān) and from there proceeded up the Héxī Corridor to Dūnhuáng. At this great oasis town it split north and south to circumvent the unforgiving Taklamakan desert. The routes then met again at Kashgar, where they once more split to cross the high, snowy Pamirs, Karakorum and Tiān Shān Mountains to connect with Samarkand (and eventually Iran and Constantinople), India and the Russian Volga.

Despite the distances that goods could reach, almost all trade was small scale and local: large caravan teams were rare unless travelling as official envoys, and goods were seldom carried more than a few hundred kilometres by any one group. An average day's journey was 15km to 20km and traders often made lengthy stops at oasis towns to plan their next stage.

In addition to silk, which was often used as currency, goods included spices, nuts, fruit, metals, leather products, chemicals, glass, paper, precious gems, gold, ivory, porcelain and exotic animals including the powerful Ferghana horse much prized by the Chinese. It was the exchange of ideas, technology and culture, however, that is the true legacy of the Silk Road.

Buddhism entered China via the Silk Road, and later allowed Chinese monks to travel to Gandhara and India for direct study and the gathering of primary texts. In copying Buddhist cave art, which originated in India, the Chinese created some of the finest examples in locations such as Mogao and Kizil. Going the other direction, fine Chinese tri-colored pottery had influence across Central Asia, the Middle East and Europe.

The heyday of Silk Road trade began in the 6th century under the stable but militarily strong Tang Dynasty. Cháng'ān became one of the most cosmopolitan capitals in the world, with an estimated 5000 foreigners, including Indians, Turks, Iranians, Japanese and Koreans permanently settled there. Trade declined and then stabilised under Mongolian rule of China, but by the 14th century sea routes were supplanting the slow and still dangerous overland routes. By the 16th century the Silk Road network had reverted to obscure local trading and never recovered its former importance.

In June 2014, at the behest of China, Kirghistan and Kyrgyzstan, UNESCO listed the 5000km Tiān Shān Corridor of the Silk Road as World Heritage. The designation highlights not just the obvious pagodas, palaces, cave art and remains of the Great Wall (including beacon towers and forts), but also the caravanserai and way stations that provided relief and lodging for traders. Hopefully in the coming years the listing will encourage more conservation and research into one of the world's 'preeminent long-distance communication networks' and not be seen as a license for unfettered tourist development.

best to check conditions in Kashgar before heading out here.

Modern Yarkand is split into a Chinese New Town and a Uighur Old Town to its east. Take a right upon exiting the bus station to get to the main avenue. Once there, take another right and flag down any public bus, which will take you past the **Shāchē Bīnguǎn** (莎车宾馆), 1km east of the bus station; the Old Town and the Altun Mosque complex are 1km further.

Yarkand has a **Sunday Market** a block north of the Altun Mosque, though it's considerably smaller than those of Kashgar or Hotan.

Sights

Altun Mosque Complex MOSQUE, CEMETERY
(阿勒屯清真寺; Ālètún Qīngzhēn Sì) Yarkand's main sights are clustered around its charming central 18th-century mosque. Next to the mosque in the modern square is the **Mausoleum of Ammanisahan** (admission ¥15), commemorating a 16th-century local Uighur queen and musician famed for her work collecting Uighur *muqam* music. Behind the tomb is the central **mazar** (tomb) of her husband Sultan Sayid Khan, the founder of the Yarkand dynasty of rulers (1514–1682).

The surrounding sprawling cemetery is home to several other impressive shrines, with white flags marking the graves of *pir* (holy men). There are normally groups of elderly Uighurs praying here.

Yarkand Old Town NEIGHBOURHOOD
In the Old Town to the east of the Altun Mosque craftsmen still work their wares with ball-peen hammers and grindstones and several workshops churn out traditional Uighur instruments. To get here take the dirt lane headed east, just south of the Altun Sq, and keep going. Eventually you'll link up with Laocheng Lu and can return west back to the New Town. We've heard of police stopping travellers from photographing in this area so exercise caution.

Sleeping & Eating

There are several good restaurants by Altun Sq with traditional Uighur food and decor.

Xīnshèng Bīnguǎn HOTEL $$
(新盛宾馆; 852 7555; 4 Xincheng Lu, 新城路4号; tw¥218) This place has clean and modern rooms. It's on the main road, just beside the gates of the Shāchē Bīnguǎn.

Getting There & Away

Buses leave half-hourly to Kashgar (¥40, three hours), Yengisar (¥34, 1½ hours) and Karghilik (¥12, 1½ hours). Four buses daily take the expressway to Hotan (¥58, five hours), and six leave for Ürümqi (¥310 to ¥340, 25 hours). Faster shared taxis also depart when full to Kashgar, Yengisar and Karghilik.

Karghilik 叶城

Karghilik (Yèchéng) is of importance to travellers as the springboard to the fantastically remote Hwy 219, the Xīnjiāng–Tibet highway that leads to Ngari (Ali) in far west Tibet.

The main attraction in town is the 15th-century **Friday Mosque** (Jama Masjid) and the surrounding adobe-walled backstreets of the Old Town.

The town of **Charbagh**, located 10 minutes' drive towards Yarkand, has a large market on Tuesday.

Sleeping & Eating

The PSB limits foreigners to staying at either Jiāotōng Bīnguǎn or Qiáogēlǐfēng Dēngshān Bīnguǎn.

There are busy Uighur eateries outside the Friday Mosque and 24-hour food stalls across from the bus station.

Jiāotōng Bīnguǎn HOTEL $
(交通宾馆; 728-5540; 1 Jiatong Lu; tw¥125;) Try to get rooms in the quieter and cleaner back block.

Qiáogēlǐfēng Dēngshān Bīnguǎn HOTEL $$
(乔戈里峰登山宾馆; 748 5000; 9180 Línggōnglǐ, 零公里9180号; r¥30-190;) The 'K2 Hotel' is an OK place to stay but the location isn't great if you're only passing through. It's 6km from the bus station; a taxi here will cost ¥10 to ¥15.

Getting There & Away

Buses to Yarkand (¥15) and Kashgar (¥53, four hours) leave every 30 minutes or one hour from 10am until 8.30pm. During the same period, every two hours there is a bus to Hotan (¥53, five hours), or take a faster shared taxi.

The newly paved 1100km road to Ali, in western Tibet, branches off from the main Kashgar–Hotan road 6km east of Karghilik. The only way to (legally) take the highway is by organising a Land Cruiser tour with an agent in Lhasa. See Lonely Planet's *Tibet* guide for details.

Hotan 和田

☑ 0903 / POP 166,000

This oasis town (and its surrounding basin) has a long and illustrious history intimately tied to the Silk Road. Hotan (Hétián, also Khotan, especially when refering to the ancient kingdom: 224 BC to 1006 AD) sat at the junction of the southern Silk Road and trade routes into India. With its relatively abundant water supplied from the nearby Kunlun Mountains, it became the largest settlement in western Xīnjiāng and boasted steady trade, and more importantly, facilitated cultural and technological exchanges.

New religions entered Xīnjiāng (and China) first through Hotan, and as with Buddhism (which arrived around 84 BC), they became well established. In fact, the Khotan Kingdom was a center for Buddhist translation and study, and famous Chinese monks such as Faxian and Xuan Zang who passed through in the 5th and 7th centuries, respectively, commented favorably on the wealth and size of Khotan's Buddhist community. In 1006 Khotan was conquered by the Muslim Karakhanids and slowly Islam became the dominant cultural force. In the 13th century Marco Polo reported that the entire population followed the new religion.

Hotan has also long been known as the epicentre of the central Asian and Chinese jade trade. Locally unearthed jade artefacts have been dated to around 5000 BC and it is believed that Hotan attracted Chinese traders along the Jade Road even before they headed westward to open up the Silk Road. In 5th century AD the Hotanese were also the first non-Han to learn the secret of Chinese silkmaking, and later established themselves as the region's foremost carpet weavers.

Today Hotan is a modern city, with a largely Uighur population, but it still has some fascinating old neighbourhoods and markets and retains a cultural authenticity that is increasingly hard to find in Kashgar.

Beijing Xilu is the main east–west axis running past the enormous main square (Tuánjié Guǎngchǎng), with its paternalistic statue of Mao looking down on an under-sized Uighur craftsman.

◎ Sights

★ Hotan Sunday Market   MARKET
(星期天市场; Xīngqítiān Shìchǎng) Hotan's most popular attraction is its weekly Sunday

market. The covered market bustles every day of the week but on Sundays it swamps the northeast part of town, reaching fever pitch between noon and 2pm Xīnjiāng time. The most interesting parts are the *doppi* (skullcap) bazaar, the colourful *atlas* (tie-dyed, handwoven silk) cloth to the right of the main entrance and the *gilim* (carpet) bazaar, across the road. Nearby Juma Lu (加买路) is filled with traditional medicine and spice shops.

The small but authentic Sunday livestock bazaar is about 2km further east, near the Jade Dragon Kashgar River on Donghuan Beilu.

Carpet Factory   HANDICRAFTS
(地毯厂; Dìtǎn Chǎng; ⊙10am-7pm) FREE On the eastern bank of the Jade Dragon Kashgar River is this large factory (*gilim karakhana* in Uighur). It's primarily set up for group visits but you can look around the various halls when open. Even with up to 10 weavers, 1 sq m of wool carpet takes 20 days to complete.

Jíyà Silk Workshop   HANDICRAFTS
(丝绸手工工艺; Sīchóu Shǒugōng Gōngyì; ⊙10am-7.30pm) Northeast of Hotan is the small town of Jíyà (吉亚乡), a traditional centre for silk production. Visitors can wander the recently renovated workshop (*atlas karakhana* in Uighur) to see how the silk is spun from silk cocoons, then dyed and woven, all using traditional methods. A return trip by taxi to the workshop, taking in the carpet factory, costs ¥100. Buses run frequently to Jíyà from Hotan's east bus station.

Melikawat Ruins   RUIN
(玛利克瓦特古城; Mǎlìkèwǎtè Gǔchéng; admission ¥10) The deserts around Hotan are peppered with the faint remains of abandoned cities. The most interesting are those of Melikawat, 25km south of town, a Tang-dynasty settlement with wind-eroded walls,

Hotan

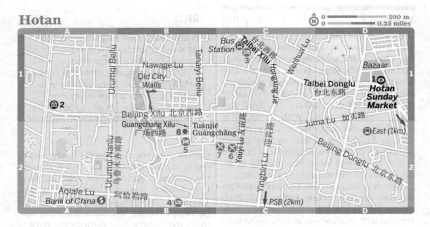

Buddhist stupas and the remains of pottery kilns. Some scholars believe Melikawat was a capital city of the Yutian state (206 BC–907 AD), an Indo-European civilisation that thrived during the height of the Silk Road. A taxi should cost about ¥100 to Melikawat.

Rawaq (Rawak) Stupa   ARCHAEOLOGICAL SITE
This 9m-tall ruin is the largest of the southern Silk Road stupas yet discovered. Built between the 3rd and 5th centuries for a wealthy Khotanese monastery, it might have been visited by the Chinese monk Faxian in 401AD on his way to India. It was certainly explored by archeologist Aurel Stein, who excavated the site in 1901, and declared it a magnificent ruin. Stein's original work also uncovered 91 large Buddhist statues (now all sadly gone).

Rawaq is about 50km north of Hotan. You'll need to buy a ticket in advance to visit (expect to pay several hundred rénmínbì for this). Contact the **Cultural Department** (Wénhuàjú; ☎ 0903-618 2018) at Hotan Museum for information on this and other specialised archaeological sites.

Hotan Cultural Museum   MUSEUM
(和田博物馆; Hétián Bówùguǎn; Beijing Xilu; ◎ 9.45am-1pm & 4-7.30pm, closed Wed) FREE
West of the centre is the regional museum. The main attractions are a fine painted wooden coffin and two 1500-year-old Indo-European mummies unearthed from the nearby Imam Musa Kazim Cemetery. There are also some fascinating finds from ancient Niya, including a large wooden pillar, a 2000-year-old bow and arrow and wooden tablets engraved with Indian-influenced Kharoshthi script.

Mazar of Imam Asim   TOMB
A few kilometres beyond Jíyà lies the tomb complex of Imam Asim (Tomb of Four Imams). It's a popular pilgrimage site, particularly during May, and you'll likely see groups of Uighurs praying and chanting at the desert shrine, which is slowly being engulfed by the Taklamakan Desert.

The best day to visit is Thursday, when a pilgrim market springs up by the roadside, about 2km before the tomb, and buses run direct to the site from Hotan's east bus station. At other times buses to Jíyà drop you 3km from the site, from where you should be able to hire a motorised cart.

🛏 Sleeping

Jiāotōng Bīnguǎn HOTEL $
(交通宾馆; ☑ 203 2700; Taibei Xilu; 台北西路; d with/without bathroom ¥140/120; ❄ 🕾) The bus station hotel is worn out and overpriced but it's the only real budget option. The shared bathrooms are awful.

Tarim Hotel HOTEL $$
(塔里木大饭店; Tǎlǐmù Dàfàndiàn; ☑ 206 7777; 135 Aqiale Xilu; 阿恰勒西路135号; r incl breakfast ¥218; ❄ @) New four-star hotel with fresh, modern rooms, some with computers (add ¥20), that make it the best-value midrange choice. It's a block southwest of the main square.

Yùdū Dàjiǔdiàn HOTEL $$
(玉都大酒店; ☑ 202 3456; 11 Guangchang Xilu; 广场西路11号; tw/d ¥198/238; ❄) The three-star 'Jade Capital' has spacious and modern rooms, with a useful location on the west side of the main square. You can buy air tickets in the lobby.

🍴 Eating

Uighur Night Market MARKET $
(维族人夜市; Wéizúrén Yèshì; Guangchang Donglu; ⊙ 7pm-midnight) On the southeast corner of the square; a good place to grab such goodies as *tonur kebab* (whole roast sheep) and *chuchvara* (meat dumplings in broth), topped off with sweet *tangzaza* (sticky rice with syrup and yoghurt).

Marco's Dream Cafe CAFE $
(马克驿站; Mǎkè Yìzhàn; www.marcodreamcafe.blogspot.com; 57 Youyi Lu; mains ¥18-30; ⊙ 1.30-9.30pm Tue-Sun) This Malaysian-run restaurant serves a nice range of Southeast Asian dishes, including curried chicken, plus cakes and coffee. The friendly English-speaking owners can provide excellent travel advice.

ℹ Information

Bank of China (中国银行; Zhōngguó Yínháng; cnr Urumqi Nanlu & Aqiale Lu; ⊙ 9.30am-1.30pm & 4-8pm Mon-Fri) Cashes travellers cheques, and has a 24-hour ATM in the southwest of town.

Southern Silk Road Travel Information Center (☑ 137 7929 1939; www.southernsilkroadtour.com; 11 Guangchang Xi Lu) Local guide Kurbanjan runs private day and multiday tours along the southern Silk Road.

ℹ Getting There & Away

There are about a dozen flights daily between Hotan and Ürümqi (¥1500). The airport is 10km southwest of town.

There are two bus stations in Hotan. From the **main bus station** (客运站; kèyùnzhàn; Taibei Xilu):
Kashgar ¥128, seven to 10 hours, every 1½ hours from 9.30am to 10.30pm. Buses to Kashgar also stop at **Karghilik** (¥52, five hours) and **Yarkand** (¥71, six hours).
Kuqa ¥168 to ¥185, eight hours, two daily departs at 2pm and 8pm
Ürümqi ¥257 to ¥387, 25 hours, hourly from 9.30am to 10.30pm. Buses head straight across the desert on one of two cross-desert highways.

Shared taxis also run to Karghilik (¥90), Yarkand (¥120) and Kashgar (¥200).

East bus station (东郊客运站; dōngjiāo kèyùnzhàn), 2km east of downtown:
Cherchen ¥124 to ¥160, 10 hours
Niya ¥63, four hours

The railway line from Kashgar reached Hotan in 2011.
Kashgar hard seat/sleeper ¥33/77, eight hours, one daily at 1.36pm
Ürümqi hard/soft sleeper ¥239/411, 32 hours

Cherchen 且末

☑ 0996 / POP 53,000

The next major stop along the southern Silk Road after Hotan is Cherchen (Qiěmò), 580km away via the townships of Keriya (于田; Yútián) and Niya (民丰; Mínfēng). The road initially passes the towering Kunlun Mountains that mark the border with Tibet to the south, before crossing impressive sand dunes and then stony desert for the last 300km.

A taxi/cart from Cherchen bus station to the centre of town costs ¥10/3.

To visit the main sights outside Cherchen go first to the Cherchen Museum, as you need to take a guide with you to unlock the gates. Guides can also help arrange a taxi.

👁 Sights

Cherchen Museum MUSEUM
(且末县博物馆; Qiěmò Xiàn Bówùguǎn; ⊙ 9.30am-1.30pm & 4-7.30pm) **FREE** Relics from Cherchen's main sights are on display at this new regional museum, alongside displays ranging from yetis in the Altun Tagh mountains to the travels of explorer Sven Hedin. It's in the northwest of town, by the huge new government square.

Toghraklek Manor
HISTORIC BUILDING

(托乎拉克庄园; Tuōhūlākè Zhuāngyuán; admission ¥20) Cherchen's main sight is this fine example of early-20th-century Kashgarian architecture, built in 1911 for a local warlord. It's 2.5km west of town.

Zaghunluq Ancient Mummy Tomb
TOMB

(扎滚鲁克古墓群景点; Zāgǔnlǔkè Gǔmùqún Jǐngdiǎn; admission ¥30) This 2600-year-old tomb contains a dozen or so naturally mummified bodies, still sporting shreds of colourful clothing. The site is a further 4km west of the Toghraklek Manor, on the edge of the desert. Figure on ¥50 for a taxi to both sites.

🛏 Sleeping

Hóngzǎo Shāngwù Bīnguǎn
HOTEL $

(红枣商务宾馆; ☎ 761 1888; Aita Lu; 埃塔路; r ¥110-120; ❄@🛜) Clean, fresh and spacious rooms next to the bazaar, though some bathrooms are cleaner than others. The pricier rooms come with computers.

Kūnyù Bīnguǎn
HOTEL $

(昆玉宾馆; ☎ 762 6555; Tuanjie Beilu; tw ¥100) Decent option next to the central town square.

ℹ Getting There & Away

There are sleeper buses to Ürümqi (¥280 to ¥300, 16 hours) and a 10am and 7pm bus to Korla (¥170, six hours); both of these go via the Cross-Desert Hwy.

The bus to Hotan (¥127 to Y177, 10 hours) leaves at 10am and is normally a sleeper bus.

A daily 10am bus (¥61, four hours) continues 350km east to Charklik.

Charklik
若羌

Charklik (Ruòqiāng; not to be confused with Karghilik further west) is a soulless, modern Chinese city, but there are several ancient ruined cities nearby. The most famous is remote Lóulán (楼兰), located some 260km northeast of Charklik, but you'll probably have to join a very pricey group tour to visit as permits can run into the thousands of dollars. The ruined fortress and stupa of Miran (米兰) is closer, located just 7km southeast of the modern town of Miran (which is 85km northwest of Charklik). Permits are more reasonable, being a few hundred rénmínbì for a group. Contact CITS (www.xinjiangtour.com) in Ürümqi for help with the paperwork.

If you get stuck in town, there are hotels near the bus station.

From Charklik you can complete the Taklamakan loop by taking a bus to Korla. Alternatively, you can continue east over the mountains to Golmud in Qīnghǎi on a daily sleeper bus.

NORTHERN XĪNJIĀNG

This region of thick evergreen forests, rushing rivers and isolated mountain ranges is historically home to pastoral nomads. It was closed to foreigners until the 1990s, due to the proximity of the sensitive Russian, Mongolian and Kazakhstan borders.

Bù'ěrjīn
布尔津

☎ 0906 / POP 60,000

Bù'ěrjīn, 620km north of Ürümqi, marks the end of the desert-like Jungar Basin and the beginning of the lusher sub-Siberian birch forests and mountains to the north. The town's population is mainly Kazakh, but there are also Russians, Han, Uighurs and Tuvans.

If you have some time to kill, stroll to the southern limits of town to the Erqis (Irtysh) River, where dozens of stone *balbals* (Turkic grave markers) line the river embankment. From here the river flows eventually into the Arctic Ocean; the only major river in China to do so. In summer you'll be confronted with swarms of biting insects around dusk, so stock up on insect repellent.

🛏 Sleeping & Eating

Hotel rates peak between July and September and are heavily discounted at other times.

Burqin Tourist Hotel
HOTEL $$$

(布尔津旅游宾馆; Bù'ěrjīn Lǚyóu Bīnguǎn; ☎ 651 0099; 4 Wolongwan Xilu; 卧龙湾西路4号; d¥260-460; ⊙May-Nov; 🛜) Large, dependable hotel with two-, three- and four-star blocks.

Bù'ěrjīn Night Market
MARKET $

(河提夜市; Hétí Yèshì; Hebin Lu; mains from ¥10; ⊙7pm-midnight) Specialising in grilled fish, fresh yoghurt and *kvas* (a yeasty brew popular in Russia), this riverside night market makes for very atmospheric dining. To find it, walk south on Youyifeng Lu and keep going until the street dead ends: it's on the right.

ℹ Getting There & Away

Nearby Altay has an airport with year-round daily flights to/from Ürümqi (¥1290).

There are both day (¥180, 10 hours) and night buses (¥183, 12 hours) to Ürümqi. Hourly buses run to Altay (Ālètài; ¥24, 1½ hours) between 10am and 7pm. Two buses a day run to Jímùnǎi (¥20, two hours) on the border with Kazakhstan at 11am and noon.

Faster shared taxis run from outside the bus station to Ürümqi and Altay.

There are no direct trains to Bù'ěrjīn. The closest station is Běitún (北屯), from where you have to catch a shared taxis or bus the final 90km. Make sure to buy your return train tickets in advance.

Kanas Lake Nature Reserve 哈纳斯湖自然保护区

Stunning Kanas Lake is a long finger of water nestled in the southernmost reaches of the Siberian taiga ecosystem, pinched in between Mongolia, Russia and Kazakhstan. Most of the local inhabitants are Kazakh or Tuvan. Chinese tourists (and the occasional foreigner) descend on the place like locusts in summer, but with a little effort it's just about possible to escape the crowds. Many come hoping for a cameo by the Kanas Lake Monster, China's Nessie, who has long figured in stories around yurt campfires to scare the kids. She appears every year or two, bringing loads of journalists and conspiracy hounds.

The whole area is only accessible from mid-May to mid-October, with ice and snow making transport difficult at other times. The gorgeous autumn colours peak around mid-September.

◎ Sights & Activities

About 160km from Bù'ěrjīn the road comes to an end at Jiǎdēngyù, basically a collection of hotels near the entrance to the **Kanas Lake Nature Reserve** (Kānàsī Hú Zìrán Bǎohùqū; 喀纳斯湖自然保护区; admission ¥150). Buy a ticket and board a tourist bus (per person ¥90, unlimited rides), which carries you 16km up the canyon to a tourist base.

At the tourist base you can change buses to take you the final 2km to Kanas Lake. From the final stop it's a five-minute walk to the lake. At the lakeshore you can take a speedboat ride, walk along a long boardwalk along the shore, walk downstream from the dock along the river, or hike to the lookout point **Guānyú Pavilion** (观鱼亭; Guānyú Tíng; 2030m). You can also explore the Tuvan village in the park, go on white-water-rafting

trips (¥200) and horse rides (per hour ¥30 to ¥60). It's even possible to take an overnight horse trek to the **valley of Hémù** (禾木), 70km southeast of Kanas Lake, via Karakol (Black Lake, or Héi Hú). Check with the youth hostel in Hémù.

☞ Tours

Xīnjiāng Tiānshān Fēngqíng Travel Agency (p799) in Ürümqi offers a four-day tour of the lake for ¥900. This includes return transport from Ürümqi, a park entrance ticket, and lodging. This company operates some of the facilities and activities in the park, including the rafting and boating trips.

🛏 Sleeping & Eating

There are homestays and hotels at Jiǎdēngyù, and in the park at the tourist base and Tuvan. In Hémù, stay at the **AHA International Youth Hostel** (阿哈国际青年旅社; Āhā Guójì Qīngnián Lǚshè; ☎1380-995 5505; www.yhakanas.com; dm/d ¥100/380; ☎), a rustic wood-cabin hostel and comfortable base for exploring the village and nearby mountains.

ℹ Getting There & Away

Kanas airport, 50km south of the reserve, has flights to and from Ürümqi (¥1403, one hour) in July and August only. From here taxis will take you the rest of the way to the reserve.

There is no public bus to the main gate at Jiǎdēngyù from Bù'ěrjīn. Buses to Hémù leave from Jiǎdēngyù but are sporadic (email the hostel in Hémù for the latest).

Share taxis do run to/from Bù'ěrjīn and Jiǎdēngyù, though outside summer it may be hard to find a ride. Taxi drivers will look for you at Bù'ěrjīn's bus station.

Yīníng 伊宁

☎ 0999 / POP 430,000

Located on the historic border between the Chinese and Russian empires, Yīníng (Yīli, or Gulja) has long been subject to a tug-of-war between the two sides. The city was occupied by Russian troops between 1872 and 1881, and in 1962 there were major Sino-Soviet clashes along the Ili River (Yīlí Hé). There are no unmissable sights here but it's a pleasant, untouristed stop on route to Sayram Lake or Kazakhstan.

In 2014 the stadium in Yīníng was the site of a mass trial in which 55 Uighurs were charged with terrorist activities. At least one death sentence was handed down. A similar mass trial was held in 1997 and is the subject of Nick Holdstead's *The Tree That Bleeds*.

The bus station is 3km from the centre at the northwest end of Jiefang Lu, the main thoroughfare through town.

◉ Sights

People's Square
SQUARE

(Rénmín Guǎngchǎng) The heart of the city is People's Sq, a popular place to fly kites. The south side is lined with ice cream, fruit and kebab stands.

Shǎnxī Mosque
MOSQUE

(陕西大寺; Shǎnxī Dàsì; Shengli Nan Lu) South of the People's Sq is the Uighur Old Town and the 260-year-old Shǎnxī Mosque, as well as workshops making traditional-style leather Uighur boots.

Baytullah Mosque
MOSQUE

(拜图拉清真寺; Bàitúlā Qīngzhēnsì) From the Old Town, head through backstreets west to Jiefang Nanlu and the Baytullah Mosque.

⊫ Sleeping & Eating

Just to the south of town is a line of open-air restaurants where you can sit and watch the mighty Ili River (Ili Daria in Uighur, Yīlì Hé in Chinese) slide by over a bottle of honey-flavoured *kvass* (a fermented drink made from rye bread).

V8 Shāngwù Jiǔdiàn
HOTEL $

(V8 商务酒店; ☎ 819 8555; Jiefang Lu, 解放西路 460号; d ¥148; ✳ @ ☎) The new bus station hotel offers immaculate and excellent-value rooms with flat-screen TVs, internet-enabled computers and gold-coloured carpets.

Yīlì Bīnguǎn
HOTEL $$

(伊犁宾馆; ☎ 802 3799; www.yilibinguan.com; 8 Yingbin Lu, 迎宾路8号; tw ¥228-268; ✳ @) Yili's

former Soviet consulate is full of character and super-quiet if not booked out by a group of Maotai-slurping visiting party officials. A bust of Lenin greets you at the entrance, beyond which is a forest of chirping birds and 1950s Russian dachas. The restaurant offers fancy Western-style meals and quiet internet access.

ⓘ Getting There & Away

From the **main bus station** (长途客运站; chángtú kèyùnzhàn) on Jiefang Xi Lu there are hourly buses to Ürümqi (¥165 to ¥180, nine to 12 hours) from 8.30am to 2pm, and three evening sleepers. There are also hourly buses to Bólè (博乐) for Sayram Lake (¥60, four hours from 10.50am to 3.50pm). Buses also run frequently for the Kazakh border at Korgas and once a day to Almaty in Kazakhstan itself. You must have a Kazakhstan visa if you wish to enter the country.

There are five daily trains to Ürümqi (hard/soft sleeper ¥150/233, 10 to 12 hours). The station is 8km northwest of the city centre.

There are a dozen daily flights to Ürümqi (¥1300). The airport is 5km north of town.

Sayram Lake　　塞里木湖

Vast Sayram Lake (塞里木湖; Sàilǐmù Hú), 120km north of Yīníng and 90km west of Bólè, is an excellent spot to get a taste of the Tiān Shān range (Tengri Tagh in Kazakh). The lake is especially colourful during June and July, when the alpine flowers are in full bloom. In the height of summer there are Kazakh yurts scattered around the lake willing to take boarders.

By bus, Sayram Lake is two hours from Bólè or three hours from Yīníng; any bus passing between the two cities can drop you by the lake. Coming from Yīníng, the last section of road is a spectacular series of mountain bridges and tunnels.

Gānsù

POP 26.4 MILLION

Best Landscapes

➡ Yǎdān National Park (p850)

➡ Singing Sands Mountain (p850)

➡ Road to Bǐnglíng Sì (p828)

➡ Gǎnjiā Grasslands (p835)

➡ Lángmùsì (p836)

Best Buddhist Sites

➡ Mògāo Caves (p848)

➡ Zhāngyè Great Buddha Temple (p840)

➡ Bǐnglíng Sì (p828)

➡ Labrang Monastery (p831)

➡ Màijī Shān (p852)

Why Go?

Synonymous with the Silk Road, the slender province of Gānsù (甘肃) flows east to west along the Héxī Corridor, the gap through which all manner of goods once streamed from China to Central Asia. The constant flow of commerce left Buddhist statues, beacon towers, forts, chunks of the Great Wall and ancient trading towns in its wake.

Gānsù offers an entrancingly rich cultural and geographic diversity. Historians immerse themselves in Silk Road lore, art aficionados swoon before the wealth of Buddhist paintings and sculptures, while adventurers hike to glaciers, ride camels through the desert and tread along paths well worn by Tibetan nomads. The ethnic diversity is equally astonishing: in Línxià, the local Hui Muslims act as though the Silk Road lives on; in Xiàhé and Lángmùsì a pronounced Tibetan disposition holds sway, while other minority groups such as the Bao'an and Dongxiang join in the colourful minority patchwork.

When to Go

Lánzhōu

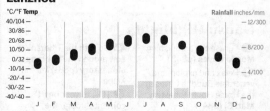

Feb & Mar Join the Tibetan pilgrims for the magnificent Monlam Festival in Xiàhé.

Apr & May Before the full heat of summer switches on.

Sep & Oct For crisp northern Gānsù autumnal colours, blue skies and cooler climes.

History

Although the Qin dynasty had a toehold on eastern Gānsù, the first significant push west along the Héxī Corridor came with the Han dynasty. An imperial envoy, Chang Ch'ien, was dispatched to seek trading partners and returned with detailed reports of Central Asia and the route that would become known as the Silk Road. The Han extended the Great Wall through the Héxī Corridor, expanding their empire in the process. As trade along the Silk Road grew, so did the small way stations set up along its

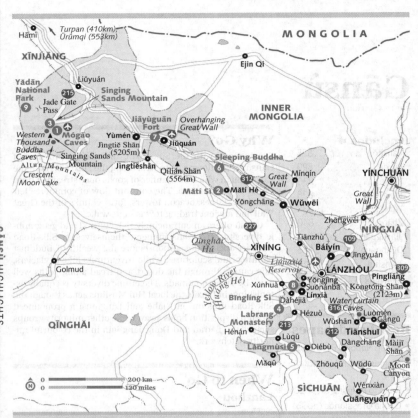

Gānsù Highlights

❶ Peruse the astonishing **Mògāo Caves** (p848)

❷ Relax and explore the venerable Buddha Caves at the Horse Hoof Monastery, **Mǎtí Sì** (p841)

❸ Camp beneath the stars amid the vast dunes of the **Singing Sands Mountain** (p850) near Dūnhuáng

❹ Go with the Tibetan flow around the **Labrang Monastery** (p831) *kora* in Xiàhé

❺ Hike to your heart's content through the fantastic scenery around **Lángmùsì** (p836)

❻ Stand head-to-head with the vast **Sleeping Buddha** (p840) of Zhāngyè

❼ Feel the Gobi wind in your hair as you stand on the ramparts of **Jiāyùguān Fort** (p842) in Jiāyùguān

❽ Ride through a mesmerising terraced landscape on the road to **Bǐnglíng Sì** (p828)

❾ Walk in a dried-out desert lake and witness the setting sun melt over the dunes at **Yádān National Park** (p850)

route; these grew into towns and cities that form the major population centres of modern Gānsù. The stream of traders from lands east and west also left their mark in the incredible diversity of modern Gānsù. The Buddhist grottoes at Mògāo, Màijī Shān and elsewhere are testament to the great flourishing of religious and artistic schools along the Silk Road.

The mixing of cultures in Gānsù eventually led to serious tensions, which culminated in the Muslim rebellions of 1862 to 1877. The conflict left millions dead and virtually wiped out Gānsù's Muslim population. Ethnic tensions have never really left the province as the pro-Tibetan demonstrations in Xiàhé in 2008 and 2012 illustrate.

Though remote from the investment banks and manufacturing hubs along the east coast of China, Gānsù is not a poor province. Gross Domestic Product has been growing at a higher rate than the already blistering national average and massive investments in wind energy are fuelling the transformation of both the natural and urban landscapes.

Climate

Gānsù rarely sees any rain outside of the southern regions, and dust storms can whip up, particularly in the spring, so it's good to come prepared with face masks and even antibiotic eye drops. Winters are nippy from November to March. Summer temperatures in the desert regions can top 40°C.

Language

Gānsù has its own group of regional Chinese dialects, loosely known as Gansuhua (part of the northwestern Lanyin Mandarin family). On the borders of Qīnghǎi and Sìchuān there is a significant Tibetan population speaking the Tibetan Amdo dialect.

ℹ Getting There & Around

Lánzhōu has flights around the country; other airports such as Dūnhuáng, Jiāyùguān and outside Xiàhé only have a handful of flights to major cities, with fewer flights in the winter.

Both trains and buses are handy for connecting the province's Silk Road sights. For southern Gānsù you are largely at the mercy of (sometimes painfully slow) buses.

LÁNZHŌU & SOUTHERN GĀNSÙ

Lánzhōu is a major transportation hub employed by most travellers as a springboard for elsewhere. The Tibetan-inhabited areas around Xiàhé and Lángmùsì are the principal enticements – perfect stopovers for overlanders heading to or from Sìchuān.

Lánzhōu   兰州

☑ 0931 / POPULATION 2.17 MILLION

Roughly at China's cartographic bullseye, Gānsù's elongated capital marks the halfway point for overlanders trekking across the country. Growing up on a strategic stretch of the Yellow River (*Huáng Hé*), and sitting between competing Chinese and Central Asian empires, Lánzhōu frequently changed hands. Trapped between mountains, modern Lánzhōu has frequent bad-air days when a grey sun sets anaemically over a hazy city.

The city sprawls in an inelegant east–west concrete melange for over 20km along the southern banks of the Yellow River. There are some attractive neighbourhoods along the northwest, and a pleasant riverside promenade, but most travellers will spend their time around the train station, home to an assortment of hotels and eateries.

◉ Sights

Gānsù Provincial Museum   MUSEUM
(甘肃省博物馆; Gānsù Shěng Bówùguǎn; Xijin Xilu; ⊙9am-5pm Tue-Sun) **FREE** This museum has an intriguing collection of Silk Road artefacts with English descriptions, including inscribed Han-dynasty wooden tablets used to relay messages along the Silk Road, and dinosaur skeletons.

The graceful Eastern Han (25 BC–AD 220) bronze horse galloping upon the back of a swallow is known as the 'Flying Horse of Wǔwēi'. Unearthed at Léitái, it has been proudly reproduced across northwestern China. Bring your passport for admission.

Take bus 1 (¥1, 40 mins) here from Lánzhōu train station.

White Pagoda Temple   BUDDHIST TEMPLE
(白塔寺; Báitǎ Sì; White Pagoda Park; Binhe Zhonglu, 白塔山宾河中路; cable car up/down/return ¥35/25/45) **FREE** This temple, built during the Yuan dynasty (AD 1206–1368) for a fallen Tibetan monk, stands in **White Pagoda Park**

Lánzhōu

Lánzhōu

(白塔山, Báitǎ Shān; Binhe Zhonglu, 宾河中路;
◎6.30am-8.30pm) on the northern bank of the
Yellow River and provides city and river views.

Enter from a gate on the north side of
Zhōngshān Bridge and walk or catch a cable
car (closed in winter) on the south side a few
blocks to the east. Bus 34 from the train station drops you off near the cable car.

White Cloud Temple
TAOIST

(白云观, Báiyún Guān; Binhe Zhonglu, 宾河中
路; ◎7am-6.30pm) **FREE** This largely rebuilt

Qing-dynasty Taoist temple is an oasis of reverential calm at the heart of the city.

Water Wheels   HISTORIC SITE

(水车园; Shuǐchē Yuán; Binhe Donglu, 宾河东路; admission ¥6; ⊙8am-6pm, to 8pm summer) Lánzhōu is the only city centre that the Yellow River flows through and these massive wooden copies of irrigation devices give a taste of what once lined the banks. A few kilometres east, look for a larger collection of about a dozen wheels (兰州水车博览园, Lánzhōu Shuǐchē Bólǎn Yuán; 4 Binhe Zhonglu, 宾河中路4号; admission ¥10; ⊙8am-10pm).

🛏 Sleeping

Most budget hostels around the train station won't accept foreigners (or are too dreary to recommend) and throughout the city even many midrange places are off limits to foreigners, including some nationwide chains.

Huálián Bīnguǎn   HOTEL $$

(华联宾馆; ☑0931 499 2109; www.lzhlbg.com; 7-9 Tianshui Nanlu, 天水南路7-9号; d/tw ¥319/399; ❋🛜) This 360-room mammoth has comfortable rooms with wi-fi, a restaurant, mini-gym and travel agency. The staff are friendly, but you'll have to put up with some traffic noise if you get a lower floor. The hotel is conveniently located opposite the train station, from where you can read the English sign 'Lanzhou Mansions'. Expect discounts of 50%.

Jǐnjiāng Inn   HOTEL $$

(锦江之星; Jǐnjiāng Zhīxīng; ☑0931 861 7333; 182 Tianshui Nanlu, 天水南路182号; tw ¥229-289; ❋🛜) Neat and tidy express business-style hotel around 1km north of the train station with unfussy, compact and well-maintained rooms and snappy service.

JJ Sun Hotel   HOTEL $$$

(锦江阳光酒店; Jǐnjiāng Yángguāng Jiǔdiàn; ☑0931 880 5511; 589 Donggang Xilu, 东岗西路589号; tw/d ¥800/900; ❋@) This good four-star choice has well-groomed, spacious and affordable rooms. There's a pleasant wood-panelled restaurant on the 2nd floor. Discounts of 40% are usual.

🍴 Eating

Lánzhōu enjoys nationwide fame (take that as you will) for its niúròumiàn (牛肉面; beef noodle soup) that's spicy enough to make you snort. A handy phrase is 'bùyào làjiāo' (不要辣椒; without chillies). There are plen-ty of places to try the dish on Huochezhan Donglu (left as you exit the train station) and Tianshui Nanlu north of the station. These streets are also lined with restaurants serving dumplings and noodle dishes. Most have picture menus.

Hezheng Lu Night Market   MARKET $

(和政路夜市场; Hézhèng Lù Yèshìchǎng; Hezheng Lu, 和政路) This bustling ramshackle market, extending from Tianshui Nanlu to Pingliang Lu, is terrific for savouring the flavours of the northwest. The mix of Hui, Han and Uighur stalls offer everything from goat's head soup to steamed snails, ròujiābǐng (肉夹饼; mutton served inside a 'pocket' of flat bread), lamb dishes seasoned with cumin, dàpán jī (大盘鸡; large plate of spicy chicken, noodles and potatoes), dumplings, spare-rib noodles and more.

Néngrénjù   HOTPOT $$

(能仁聚; 216 Tianshui Nanlu; hotpot starting at ¥35; ⊙11am-10pm) At this tasty Běijīng-style shùan yángròu (涮羊肉; traditional lamb hotpot) the pot of broth costs ¥25, after which you can add sliced mutton (¥30), greens (¥10) and various other dishes. The restaurant is about 100m past the intersection with Minzhu Lu.

🛍 Shopping

Chénghuáng Miào   ANTIQUES

(城隍庙; City God Temple; 202 Zhangye Lu; ⊙9am-6pm daily) The gods would probably not approve, but this former house of Taoist worship has been turned into one of Lánzhōu's best shopping venues. Vendors sell everything from Mao kitsch to tea sets, beautiful pottery, woodwork and antiquities. The temple is set back on the north side of Zhangye Lu (pedestrian-only) 500m east of Zhongshan Lu.

ℹ Information

Bank of China (中国银行; Zhōngguó Yínháng; Tianshui Lu; ⊙8.30am-noon & 2.30-5.30pm Mon-Fri) Has an ATM and changes travellers cheques on the 2nd floor.

Internet Cafe (网吧; Wǎngbā; 11-13 Tianshui Nanlu, 天水南路11-13号; per hr ¥3; ⊙24hr) On the 2nd floor, to the right of Huálián Bīnguǎn.

Public Security Bureau (PSB; 公安局; Gōng'ānjú; ☑0931 871 8610; 482 Wudu Lu; ⊙8.30-11.30am & 2.30-5.30pm Mon-Fri) The foreign-affairs branch is on the 2nd floor. Visa extensions take several days; one photo required.

THE BUDDHA CAVES & POTATO TERRACES OF BĬNGLÍNG SÌ

With its relative inaccessibility, **Bĭnglíng Sì** (炳灵寺; ☑ 0930 887 9057; admission ¥50; ☺8am-6pm; closed Dec-Mar) is one of the few Buddhist grottoes in China to have survived the tumultuous 20th century unscathed. Which is a good thing, as during a period spanning 1600 years, sculptors dangling from ropes carved 183 niches and sculptures into the porous rock of steep canyon walls. Today the cliffs are isolated by the waters of the Liújiāxiá Reservoir (劉家峽水庫; Liújiāxiá Shuǐkù) on the Yellow River and hemmed in by a ring of dramatic rock citadels. The cave art can't compare to Dūnhuáng, but the setting, few tourists and the remarkable terraced landscapes you pass getting here make Bĭnglíng Sì an unmissable day trip from Lánzhōu.

The star is the 27m-high seated **statue of Maitreya**, the future Buddha, but some of the smaller, sway-hipped Bodhisattvas and guardians, bearing an obvious Indian influence, are equally exquisite.

As you loop around past the Maitreya cave, consider hiking 2.5km further up the impressive canyon to a small **Tibetan monastery**. There might also be jeeps running the route.

You can visit Bĭnglíng Sì as a day trip from Lánzhōu or en route to Línxià. Take a boat or taxi from the town of Liújiāxiá. Frequent buses from Lánzhōu's west bus station (¥20, 2½ hours) run to Liújiāxiá and will drop you off a short walk from the boat ticket office (1km before Liújiāxiá itself) or at the town's main bus station, where you can hire a taxi. Try to catch the earliest buses possible from Lánzhōu (starting at 7am) to avoid getting stuck on the way back. The last return bus to Lánzhōu leaves at 6.30pm.

A covered speedboat (seating up to eight people) costs ¥700 for the one-hour journey. The boat ticket office is good at hooking up independent travellers with small groups; expect to pay around ¥150 per person in this case.

Surprisingly, the much more scenic route to the caves is by taxi (¥250 return). Out of Liújiāxiá, the road runs high into the rugged hills above the reservoir, and for 90 minutes you will twist and turn, dip and rise through a wonderland of potato-growing terraces laddering and layering every slope, mound, outcrop and ravine. The final descent to the green-blue reservoir, with its craggy backdrop, is sublime.

If heading to Línxià after the caves, there are frequent buses from the station at Liújiāxiá.

Western Travel Agency (西部旅行社; Xībù Lǚxíngshè; ☑ 0931 882 0529; 486 Donggang Xilu; ☺8am-6pm daily) On the 2nd floor of the west wing of Lánzhōu Fàndiàn at the corner of Donggang Xilu and Tianshui Nanlu. Offers tours around Lánzhōu (as far south as Xiàhé) and ticket bookings.

❶ Getting There & Away

AIR

Lánzhōu has flights to Běijīng (¥1460), Dūnhuáng (¥1466), Jiāyùguān (¥1576), Kūnmíng (¥1902), Shànghǎi (¥1750) and Xī'ān (¥480).
Gānsù Airport Booking Office (甘肃机场售 票中心; Gānsù Jīchǎng Shòupiào Zhōngxīn; ☑ 0931 888 9666; 616 Donggang Xilu; ☺8.30am-6pm) Can book all air tickets at discounted prices.

BUS

Lánzhōu has several bus stations, all with departures for Xīníng. The **main long-distance bus station** (长途车站; Chángtú Chēzhàn; Pingliang

Lu) is just a ticket office, outside which you catch a shuttle bus 30 minutes before departure for the **east bus station** (汽车东站; Qìchē Dōngzhàn; ☑ 0931 841 8411; Pingliang Lu). Most bus journeys back into Lánzhōu end up at the east bus station; if you want to rough it on a sleeper to Zhāngyè or Jiāyùguān, buy a ticket directly at that station.

A bus station 150m east of the train station on Huochezhan Donglu offers most of the same routes as the main long-distance and east bus stations.

For journeys to the south of Gānsù you must head to the **south bus station** (汽车南站; Qìchē Nánzhàn; Langongping Lu). A taxi from the train station costs ¥35 and takes 45 minutes. Touts from the bus station charge ¥7 for a seat in shared minivans to Lánzhōu train station, departing when full.

From the main long-distance bus station:
Píngliáng ¥125, five hours, hourly (7am to 6pm)
Tiānshuǐ ¥84, four hours, every 30 minutes (7am to 6pm)

Xīníng ¥59, three hours, every 30 minutes (7.10am to 8.10pm)

Yínchuān ¥124, six hours, seven per day (7am to 8pm)

The following services depart from the south bus station. Frustratingly tickets can only be purchased there, though can be bought just before departure:

Hézuò ¥74, four hours, every 20 minutes (8am to 5pm)

Lángmùsì ¥121, eight hours, two daily (8.40am and 9.40am)

Línxià ¥35, three hours, every 30 minutes (7am to 7pm)

Xiàhé ¥76.50, 3½ hours, five daily (7am to 3pm)

The **west bus station** (汽车西站; Qìchē Xīzhàn; Xijin Xilu) has frequent departures to Liújiāxiá (¥19.50, 2½ hours, 7am to 6pm), if you are heading to Bǐnglíng Sì.

Hidden off the main street, the **Tiānshuǐ bus station** (天水汽车站; Tiānshuǐ Qìchēzhàn; Tianshui Lu) has buses for eastern Gānsù, including Luòmén (¥55, four hours, hourly). To find the station, look for a large WC sign and turn right into the narrow alley.

TRAIN

Lánzhōu is the major rail link for trains heading to and from western China. In summer buy your onward tickets a couple of days in advance to guarantee a sleeper berth. For Xīníng, you may be better off taking a bus, as the service is more frequent and Xīníng's train station has temporarily moved to the outskirts of town (the main railway station is expected to reopen in late 2014). For Dūnhuáng make sure to get a train to the town itself and not Liǔyuán, a time-wasting 180km away.

There are frequent trains to the following:

Dūnhuáng hard/soft sleeper ¥244/398, 13 hours (two per day direct to Dūnhuáng at 5.50pm and 7.10pm; the rest go to Liǔyuán)

Jiāyùguān hard/soft seat ¥103/160, seven to eight hours; hard/soft sleeper ¥179/275, 11 hours

Ürümqi hard/soft sleeper ¥396/598, 24 hours

Wǔwēi hard/soft seat ¥44/72, 3½ hours

Xī'ān hard/soft sleeper ¥164/252, eight to nine hours

Zhāngyè hard/soft seat ¥76/119, five to six hours

Zhōngwèi seat/hard sleeper ¥48/127, five to six hours

ⓘ Getting Around

Lánzhōu's streets are filled with vehicles these days and traffic jams are common. Give yourself plenty of time to get around, especially if you have a morning bus or train to catch. The airport is 70km north of the city. Airport buses leave hourly from 5.30am to 7pm in front of **China Eastern Airlines** (东方航空公司; Dōngfāng Hángkōng Gōngsī; ☏ 0931 882 1964; 586 Donggang Xilu). The trip costs ¥30 and takes 60 minutes. A taxi costs around ¥150 though you might be able to find a shared taxi across the street from where the airport buses leave.

Useful bus routes:

Buses 1 and 6 From the train station to the west bus station via Xiguan Shizi.

Bus 111 From Zhongshan Lu (at the Xiguan Shizi stop; 去汽车南站的111路公交车) to the south bus station.

Buses 7 and 10 From the train station up the length of Tianshui Nanlu before heading west and east, respectively.

Public buses cost ¥1; taxis are ¥7 for the first 3km. There is no bus from the train station to the south bus station, so you are better off taking a taxi for ¥35 for 45 minutes.

Línxià 临夏

☏ 0930 / POP 198,600 / TRANSPORT HUB

Known as the 'Little Mecca of China', this stronghold of Chinese Islam is filled with over 100 mosques and the descendants of ancient Silk Road Muslims. Línxià is mostly used by travellers (and monks) to break up the trip to or from Xiàhé, or points in Qīnghǎi.

🛏 Sleeping & Eating

As you walk out of the bus station onto Jiefang Lu, you'll find both sides of the street lined with small noodle restaurants and decent budget hotels all asking around ¥68 to ¥88 for a room without a bathroom and ¥158 to ¥188 for one with.

About 1km north of the train station (head right as you exit), on the west of Zhōngxīn Guǎngchǎng (中心广场) look for a night market with rows of vendors selling lamb kebabs (¥1 each) and *shā guō* (砂锅; mini hotpots; ¥10).

Jīnhé Bīnguǎn　　　　　　　　　　HOTEL **$**
(☏ 0930 631 1301; Qianheyan Xilu; tw with bathroom ¥138-168; 🅿 🖭) In this alcohol-free hotel, rooms sport a relaxed modern design with just a few carpet stains to spoil the effect. From the south bus station exit, turn right and walk 300m to the first big intersection. Cross and turn left down Qianheyan Xilu for 50m.

MINORITY COMMUNITIES AROUND LÍNXIÀ

Spilling over a ridge high above Línxià and home to both Hui and Dongxiang minorities, the little market town of **Suǒnánbà** (锁南坝; population 12,000) has a single street that's a hive of activity, with locals trading livestock and occasional shepherds shooing flocks about.

The town is sometimes also called Dōngxiāng (东乡) after the surrounding county. The Dongxiang people speak an Altaic language and are believed to be descendants of 13th-century immigrants from Central Asia, moved forcibly to China after Kublai Khan's Middle East conquest.

Dàhéjiā (大河家; population 4500), with sweeping views over the Yellow River, towering red cliffs and (in summer) verdant green terraces, is equally a kaleidoscope of colour. The surrounding area is home to a significant population of Bao'an (保安族), Muslims who speak a Mongolic language. The Bao'an are famed for producing knives and share cultural traits with the Hui and Dongxiang. Their Mongol roots come out during summer festivals, when it is possible to see displays of wrestling and horse riding.

To Suǒnánbà, frequent minibuses (¥7, one hour) head up on the pleasant journey past terraced fields from Línxià's east bus station.

You can visit Dàhéjiā when travelling on the road between Línxià and Xīníng. Most buses between the two will stop here. From Línxià you can also catch a frequent minibus (¥25, three hours) from the station called chéngjiāo qìchē zhàn (城郊汽车站) on the outskirts of town.

ⓘ Information

Bank of China (中国银行, Zhōngguó Yínháng; Jiefang Lu; ⏲ 8.30am-5pm Mon-Fri) is 400m up Jiefang Lu to the right as you exit the south bus station. There's a 24-hour ATM here and you can change travellers cheques.

ⓘ Getting There & Away

Línxià has three long-distance bus stations: south (南站; nánzhàn), west (西站; xīzhàn) and east (东站; dōngzhàn). You may be dropped off at the west bus station but it is of little use otherwise. Bus 6 links the south and the west bus stations; a taxi between the two costs ¥5.

From the **east bus station** there are frequent buses to Dōngxiāng (¥7, one hour) and Liújiāxiá (¥16, three hours).

From the **south bus station** there are frequent buses to Hézuò (¥31, two hours), Lánzhōu (¥35, three hours) and Xiàhé (¥32, 2½ hours; 6.30am to 5pm), and one daily to Xīníng (¥64, eight hours; 6am).

One interesting side route is to the Mèngdá Nature Reserve in Qīnghǎi. The fastest way here is a bus to Dàhéjiā (¥7, one hour) from Línxià's **east bus station**, followed by a taxi for the last 15km.

If you're on the slow road to Qīnghǎi, buses to Xúnhuà (¥50, 3½ hours, 8am to 3.30pm) leave every hour or two from a courtyard behind the Tiānhé Fàndiàn (天河饭店) hotel. To get here, walk about 300m from the south bus station (turning right as you exit) to the first intersection and then turn right and walk 350m to the hotel. From Xúnhuà you'll find onward transport to Xīníng or Tóngrén.

Xiàhé   夏河

☑ 0941 / POP 70,000

The alluring monastic town of Xiàhé attracts an astonishing band of visitors: backpack-laden students, insatiable wanderers, shaven-headed Buddhist nuns, Tibetan nomads in their most colourful finery, camera-toting tour groups and dusty, itinerant beggars. Most visitors are rural Tibetans, whose purpose is to pray, prostrate themselves and seek spiritual fulfilment at holy Labrang Monastery (拉卜楞寺; Lābǔléng Sì).

In a beautiful mountain valley at 2920m above sea level, Xiàhé has a certain rhythm about it and visitors quickly tap into its fluid motions. The rising sun sends pilgrims out to circle the 3km kora (pilgrim path) that rings the monastery. Crimson-clad monks shuffle into the temples to chant morning prayers. It's easy to get swept up in the action, but some of the best moments come as you set your own pace, wandering about town or in the splendid encircling mountains.

The Xiàhé area was long part of the Tibetan region of Amdo. As a microcosm of southwestern Gānsù, the three principal ethnic groups are represented here. In rough terms, Xiàhé's population is 65% Tibetan, 25% Han and 10% Hui. Labrang Monastery marks the division between Xiàhé's mainly Han and Hui Chinese eastern quarter and the scruffy Tibetan village to the west.

Xiàhé

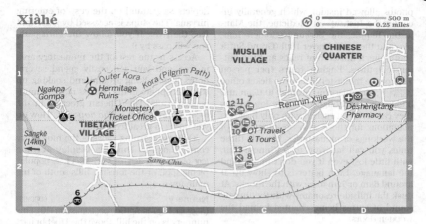

Despite Xiàhé's ostensible tranquillity, these ethnic groups don't necessarily mix peacefully. The Tibetan community maintains a strong solidarity with their brethren on the plateau, and demonstrations and rioting here in the wake of riots in Lhasa led to the region being closed for nearly two years in 2008, and for a few months at the end of 2012.

Sights

Labrang Monastery   BUDDHIST
(拉卜楞寺; Lābǔléng Sì; Renmin Xijie; tour ¥40) With its endless squeaking prayer wheels (3km in total length), hawks circling overhead and the throb of Tibetan longhorns resonating from the surrounding hills, Labrang is a monastery town unto itself. Many of the chapel halls are illuminated in a yellow glow by yak-butter lamps, their strong-smelling fuel scooped out from voluminous tubs.

Even if Tibet is not on your itinerary, the monastery sufficiently conveys the esoteric mystique of its devout persuasions, leaving indelible impressions of a deeply sacred domain.

In addition to the chapels, residences, golden-roofed temple halls and living quarters for the monks, Labrang is also home to six *tratsang* (monastic colleges or institutes), exploring esoteric Buddhism, theology, medicine, astrology and law.

Labrang Monastery was founded in 1709 by Ngagong Tsunde (E'angzongzhe in Chinese), the first-generation Jamyang (a line of reincarnated Rinpoches or living Buddhas ranking third in importance after the Dalai and Panchen lamas), from nearby Gānjiā.

Xiàhé

◉ Sights
1	Barkhang	B1
2	Gòngtáng Chörten	A2
3	Hall of Hayagriva	B2
4	Labrang Monastery	B1
5	Nunnery	A1
6	Thangka Display Terrace	A2

🛏 Sleeping
7	Labrang Baoma Hotel	C1
8	Labrang Red Rock International Hostel	C2
9	Overseas Tibetan Hotel	C2
10	Tara Guesthouse	C2
11	White Stupa Hotel	C1

✴ Eating
12	Gesar Restaurant	C1
13	Nirvana Restaurant & Bar	C2

The monastery is one of the six major Tibetan monasteries of the Gelugpa order (Yellow Hat sect of Tibetan Buddhism). The others are Ganden, Sera and Drepung monasteries near Lhasa; Tashilhunpo Monastery in Shigatse; and Kumbum (Tǎ'ěr Sì) near Xīníng, Qīnghǎi.

At its peak, Labrang housed nearly 4000 monks, but their ranks greatly declined during the Cultural Revolution. Modern Labrang is again such a popular destination for young disciples that numbers are currently capped at 1800 monks, drawn from Qīnghǎi, Gānsù, Sìchuān and Inner Mongolia.

➜ Main Buildings
The only way to visit the interior of the most important buildings is with a tour (no

photos allowed inside), which generally includes the Institute of Medicine, the Manjushri Temple, the Serkung (Golden Temple) and the main Prayer Hall (Grand Sutra Hall), plus a museum of relics and yak-butter sculptures. English **tours** (per person ¥40) of the monastery leave the ticket office (售票处; shòupiàochù) around 10.15am and 3.15pm, and although they give lots to see, they can feel a bit rushed with only basic explanations for those with no knowledge of the workings of monasteries. Outside those times you can latch on to a Chinese tour, with little lost even if you don't understand the language. Even better is to show up at around 6am or 7am to be with the monks. At dusk the hillside resonates with the throaty sound of sutras being chanted behind the wooden doors.

➡ **Other Buildings**

The rest of the monastery can be explored by walking the *kora*. Although many of the temple halls are padlocked shut, there are a couple of separate smaller chapels you can visit, though they can often be closed for unexplained reasons. Some charge admission.

The three-storey **Barkhang** (Labrang Monastery, Renmin Xijie; admission ¥10) is the monastery's traditional printing press. With rows upon rows of more than 20,000 wood blocks for printing, it's well worth a visit, and photos are allowed. The Barkhang is off the main road down a small side lane. Ask your guide for the latest opening hours.

The **Hall of Hayagriva** (马头明王殿; Mǎtóu Míngwáng Diàn, Hall of Horsehead Buddha; Labrang Monastery, Renmin Xijie; admission ¥10), destroyed during the Cultural Revolution, was reopened in 2007. A repository of vivid and bright murals, the hall also encapsulates a startlingly fierce 12m-high effigy of Hayagriva – a wrathful manifestation of the usually calm Avalokiteshvara (Guanyin) – with six arms and three faces. The hall is down a side lane almost directly across from the lane to the Barkhang.

With an interior splashed with murals and illuminated by a combination of yak-butter lamps and electric light bulbs by the thousand, the 31m-tall **Gòngtáng Chörten** (贡唐宝塔; Gòngtáng Bǎotǎ, Gòngtáng Stupa; Labrang Monastery, Renmin Xijie; admission ¥20) is a perennial favourite with visitors. Head up to the roof for landscape views. At the rear of the golden *chörten* (Tibetan stupa) look for a **Sleeping Buddha** (卧佛; Wòfó), which depicts Sakyamuni on the cusp of entering nirvana. The stupa is accessed by gates that face the river. If you follow the *kora* path, you will pass by it.

Access to the rest of the monastery area is free, and you can easily spend several hours just walking around and soaking up the atmosphere in the endless maze of mud-packed walls. The Tibetan greeting in the local Amdo dialect is *Cho day mo?* ('How do you do?') – a great icebreaker.

The best morning views of the monastery come from the **Thangka Display Terrace** (cnr of Jiujialu & Renmin Xijie) **FREE**, a popular picnic spot, or the forested hills south of the main town.

Nunnery   BUDDHIST
(尼姑庵, Nígū'ān, Ani Gompa; admission ¥10) This nunnery is on the hill above the Tibetan part of town. The higher *kora* path begins just to the left of here.

👉 Tours

Losang at OT Travels & Tours and the staff at Tara Guesthouse are both excellent resources for information and tours of the surrounding area.

🎆 Festivals & Events

Festivals are central to the calendar for both the devotional monks and the nomads who stream into town from the grasslands in multicoloured splendour. Tibetans use a lunar calendar, so dates for individual festivals vary from year to year.

Monlam Festival   RELIGIOUS
(Great Prayer Festival) This festival starts three days after the Tibetan New Year, which is usually in February or early March, with significant days accompanied by spectacular processions and prayer assemblies. Monlam Festival finishes with a creative display of monk-sculpted butter lanterns lighting up the 15th evening (and full moon) of the New Year.

On the morning of the 13th day of the New Year, more than 100 monks carry a huge *thangka* (sacred painting on cloth) of the Buddha, measuring more than 30m by 20m, and unfurl it on the hill facing the monastery. On the 14th day there is an all-day session of Cham dances performed by 35 masked dancers, with Yama, the lord of death, playing the leading role. On the 16th day the Maitreya statue is paraded around the monastery.

GĀNSÙ XIÀHÉ

WALK LIKE A TIBETAN

Following the 3km *kora* (pilgrim path) encircling Labrang Monastery is perhaps the best approach to grasping its layout, scale and significance. The *kora* is lined with long rows of squeaking prayer wheels, whitewashed *chörtens* (Tibetan stupas) and chapels. Tibetan pilgrims with beads in their hands and sunhats on their heads, old folk, mothers with babies and children, shabby nomads and more walk in meditative fashion clockwise along the path (called *zhuǎnjìngdào*, 'scripture-turning way' in Chinese), rotating prayer wheels as they go. Look also for the tiny meditation cells on the northern hillside.

For a short hike, the more strenuous outer *kora* path takes about an hour and climbs high above the monastery. To reach the start, head past the monastery's western edges and about one block into the Tibetan village look for a large signpost (in Tibetan but it's the only one around) on the right. Follow the alley up, and make your way to the ridge, where you wind steeply uphill to a collection of prayer flags and the ruins of a hermitage. The views of the monastery open up as you go along. At the end of the ridge there's a steep descent into town.

🛏 Sleeping

Overseas Tibetan Hotel HOTEL $
(华侨饭店; Huáqiáo Fàndiàn; ☏0941 712 2642; www.overseastibetanhotel.com; 77 Renmin Xijie; 人民西街77号; dm ¥50, d ¥200-300; ☏) A well-run and bustling place, mid-2014 saw the final renovations of the guesthouse including wi-fi that reaches every corner, and solar power to ensure 24/7 hot water. The modern doubles are the best value in town with clean enclosed showers (proper glass doors!), flat-screen TVs and the cushiest thick mattresses in Xiàhé. Discounts of 20% in quiet periods.

This hotel is owned by Losang, an energetic, likeable Tibetan with faultless English and in touch with the wants of travellers. Services include bike rental (¥20 per day), laundry, a travel agency and the Everest Cafe with Western set breakfasts with yak yoghurt (¥30).

Labrang Red Rock International Hostel HOSTEL $
(拉卜楞红石国际青年旅馆; Lābǔléng Hóngshí Guójì Qíngnián Lǚguǎn; ☏0941 712 3698; 253 Yagetang; 雅鸽搪253号; dm ¥45, d ¥140; ☏) This Tibetan-themed, quiet hostel has pine-wood rooms, solar-powered hot showers, a restaurant-bar, and a beautiful display of *thangka*. Doubles are clean with futon style beds, and YHA card holders get a discount. To get here, walk past the Tara Guesthouse on Yagetang, turn left and left again at the last street before the river. Look for the prayer flags outside.

Tara Guesthouse GUESTHOUSE $
(卓玛旅社; Zhuōmǎ Lǚshè; ☏0941 712 1274; 268 Yagetang; 雅鸽搪268号; dm ¥15, s/tw without bathroom ¥30-40/¥60-100, d with bathroom ¥180; ☏) This long-established budget place is run by monks from Sìchuān and has extremely frugal dorms, small, comfortable *kàng* rooms (shared shower room, no phone), and larger doubles with private bathrooms. English is spoken at the front desk. The attached restaurant serves some of the best *mómo* (Tibetan dumplings; ¥15) around and is popular with monks for the many vegetarian options.

Labrang Baoma Hotel HOTEL $$
(拉卜楞宝马宾馆; Lābǔléng Bǎomǎ Bīnguǎn; ☏0941 712 1078; www.labranghotel.com; 77 Renmin Xijie; 人民西街77号; 5-bed dm ¥35, r from ¥480; @) Pleasant and vibrantly colourful hotel with friendly staff, nice interior, Tibetan-style courtyard and comfortable en suite doubles. Discounts of 50% are common.

White Stupa Hotel HOTEL $$
(曲登嘎布宾馆; Qūdēng Gǎbù Bīnguǎn; ☏0941 712 2866; Renmin Xijie; 人民西街; d/tw ¥168/300; @) This friendly place has clean, if scruffy, bright rooms with en suite bathrooms. Expect discounts of 20%.

🍴 Eating & Drinking

For those of you who can't make it to Tibet, Xiàhé provides an opportunity to develop an appetite for the flavours of the Land of Snows, whether it's *mómo, tsampa* (a porridge of roasted barley flour), yak-milk yoghurt or throat-warming glasses of the local firewater. Most hotels and guesthouses have their own attached restaurants, and it seems the entire 2nd floor of the main street is all eateries; finding an English menu in this crowd is not hard.

GĀNSÙ XIÀHÉ

★ Gesar Restaurant TIBETAN $

(cnr Renmin Xijie & Tengzhilu; dishes ¥12-35; ⏱ 7am-8pm daily) This simple, family-run restaurant takes care to bring out tasty dishes with very fresh ingredients (the yoghurt is the best around). There's a long selection of vegetarian dishes, as well as stews, traditional Tibetan staples such as vegetarian *mómo* (¥3), *tsampa* and fried bread, and a decent à la carte Western breakfast menu.

Nirvana Restaurant & Bar TIBETAN, CAFE $

(德古园; Déguyuán; ☎ 0941 718 1702; 247 Yagetang; 雅鸽塘247号; dishes ¥15-35; ⏱ 9am-10pm; ❄ 🛜) Travellers wanting authentic Tibetan and Western dishes congregate here for a large helping of yak stew with potatoes (¥35), simple pizza, fresh espresso and travel advice with the English-speaking Tibetan-Dutch couple who own the restaurant. The welcoming, casual vibe makes leaving Nirvana difficult, as does the long wine and spirits menu.

🛍 Shopping

Xiàhé is an excellent place to look for Tibetan handicrafts, so why not don a cowboy hat or a Tibetan trilby, enshroud yourself in a *chuba* (Tibetan cloak), light up some juniper incense, wrap your head in a furry yellow monk's hat, jump into a pair of monk's boots, flap a prayer flag or shell out for brocaded silks, *thangka*, Tibetan-style tents or a silver teapot? Stacks of handicraft shops line the upper part of the main road, before the monastery walls, and some painting shops are found off the lower *kora* route alongside the river.

ℹ Information

Internet cafes around town require Chinese ID, though some will allow you to use their ID. Ask at hostels for nearby internet access.

China Post (中国邮政; Zhōngguó Yóuzhèng; 8 Renimn Xijie; ⏱ 8am-6pm)

Déshèngtáng Pharmacy (德盛堂药店; Déshèngtáng Yàodiàn; 14 Renmin Xijie; ⏱ 9.30am-9pm daily) Western, Chinese and Tibetan medicine; just west of China Post.

Industrial & Commercial Bank of China (ICBC; 工商银行; Gōngshāng Yínháng; 98 Nanxiahe Jie, 南下河街98号; ⏱ 8.30am-4pm daily) Has an ATM and changes US dollars but not travellers cheques.

OT Travels & Tours (☎ 1390 9419 888; amdolosahe@hotmail.com; 77 Renmin Xijie, 人民西街77号; ⏱ 8am-9pm daily) This reliable travel agency at the Overseas Tibetan Hotel can arrange cars and guides to nearby sights, and also specialises in overland tours from Lánzhōu, Xīníng and Chéngdū to Xiàhé.

ℹ Getting There & Away

Trains don't run to Xiàhé, but it's regularly serviced by bus. Most travellers head on to either Lánzhōu or Sìchuān; the road less travelled takes you over the mountains to Tóngrén in Qīnghǎi.

AIR

The **Gānnán Xiàhé Airport** (code GXH; Gānnán Xiàhé Jīchǎng; 甘南夏河机场) opened in early 2014 with flights to Xī'ān (¥1130), dodging the uninspiring Lánzhōu-Xiàhé bus journey, and Lhasa (¥1760), with Běijīng and Chéngdū to come. Book flights online in English at ctrip.com. There is no airport bus, but OT Travels & Tours can arrange a private 1hr taxi to the airport for ¥400.

BUS

The following bus services depart from Xiàhé:

Hézuò ¥21.50, one hour, every 30 minutes (6.10am to 5.20pm)

Lángmùsì ¥72.50, 3½ hours, one daily (7.40am)

Lánzhōu ¥77, 3½ hours, four daily (6.30am, 7.30am, 8.30am and 2.30pm)

Línxià ¥32, two hours, every 30 minutes (6am to 5.25pm)

Tóngrén ¥32, 2½ hours, one daily (7.30am)

Xīníng ¥79, seven hours, one daily (6.10am)

If you can't get a direct ticket to/from Lánzhōu, take a bus to Línxià or Hézuò and change there. If you are heading to Xīníng, note that buses run there every 40 minutes from Tóngrén.

ℹ Getting Around

Hotels and restaurants rent out bikes for ¥30 per day. Taxis cost ¥1 to ¥2 per seat for a short trip around town, including to the bus station and monastery. Leaving the bus station, turn right for a 1km walk to town.

Around Xiàhé

Sāngkē Grasslands 桑科草原

Expanses of open grassland dotted with Tibetans and their grazing yak herds highlight a trip to the village of **Sāngkē** (桑科), 14km from Xiàhé. Development has turned the area into a small circus, complete with touristy horse rides and fake tourist yurts, but there is good hiking in the nearby hills and you can keep going to more distant and pristine grasslands in the direction of Amchog. You can cycle up to Sāngkē in about one hour. A taxi costs ¥50 return. The grasslands are lushest in summer.

Gānjiā Grasslands 甘加草原

The Gānjiā Grasslands (*Gānjiā Cǎoyuán*), 34km from Xiàhé, aren't as pretty as at nearby Sāngkē, but there is more to explore. From Xiàhé the bumpy road crosses the Naren-Ka pass (impassable after long rains) before quickly descending into wide grasslands dotted with herds of sheep and backed by ever-more dramatic mountain scenery. Past Gānjiā Xiàn village, a side road climbs 12km to **Nekhang** (白石崖溶洞; Báishí Yá Róng dòng; admission ¥30), a cave complex where pilgrims lower themselves down ropes and ladders into two sacred underground chambers. A Dutch traveller fell to his death here in 2006, and to prevent the same fate we advise avoiding this place.

Just up the road from the caves is **Trakkar Gompa** (白石崖寺; Báishíyá Sì; admission ¥30), a monastery of 90 monks set against a stunning backdrop of vertical rock formations. From Trakkar it's a short drive to the 2000-year-old Han-dynasty village of **Bājiǎo** (八角; Karnang in Tibetan; admission ¥25). The remarkable 12-sided walls here still shelter a small living community. From the village it's a short 5km diversion to the renovated **Tseway Gompa** (佐海寺; Zuǒhǎi Sì; admission ¥30), one of the few Bön monasteries in Gānsù. Make sure you circumnavigate any holy site counterclockwise in the Bön fashion. There are great views of Bājiǎo from the ridge behind the monastery.

A four- to five-hour return trip to the Gānjiā Grasslands costs around ¥180 for a taxi from Xiàhé. If you want an English-speaking driver and guide (which will cost more), contact OT Travels & Tours (p834).

HIKING

It's possible to hike over several days from the Gānjiā Grasslands to 4636m-high **Dálǐjiā Shān** (达里加山; Dálǐjiā Mountain), but you will need to be well equipped. Summer is the best season for such treks as you have more daylight hours, wildflowers and warmer weather. There are also treks between Tibetan villages and around **Dàowéi Tibetan Village** (道帏藏族乡; Dàowéi Zàngzú Xiāng; also called *Guru*).

OT Travels & Tours (p834) in Xiàhé can advise on these and other trips and arrange a car for four people for ¥400 per day and an English-speaking guide (for another ¥400); they can also arrange fun camping trips for overnighting on the grasslands.

Hézuò 合作

📞 0941 / POP 76,000

The booming regional capital of Gānnán (甘南) prefecture, Hézuò is a transit point for travellers plying the excellent overland route between Gānsù and Sìchuān provinces. The city is also the sight of the incredible Milarepa Palace, a bewitching Tibetan temple ranging spectacularly over nine floors.

Hézuò is a fairly compact town, with a large public square (文化广场; Wenhua Guangchang) roughly halfway between the two bus stations. You'll find banks with ATMs around the square. Most taxi rides around town cost ¥2.

👁 Sights

Milarepa Palace Buddhist Temple BUDDHIST (九层佛阁; Sekhar Gutok, Jiǔcéng Fógé; admission ¥20; ⏰7am-6pm) About 2km from the bus station along the main road towards Xiàhé is this towering temple, ringed by prayer wheels. Resembling a boutique hotel, Milarepa is odd in the Tibetan world in that different spiritual leaders from varying sects are worshipped on each floor. The town's main monastery, **Tso Gompa** (合作寺, Hézuò Sì, Hézuò Monastery; Nawulu, 那吾路; ⏰8am-6pm) **FREE**, is next door. A taxi here costs ¥2 to ¥3 from the central main bus station.

The Milarepa's ground-floor is a powerful spectacle: a galaxy of Bodhisattvas, Buddhist statues and yak-butter lamps illuminating celestial figures. Climb upstairs to a further rich display of lamas and living Buddhas. More deities muster on the 4th floor and an unsettling array of fearsome, turquoise tantric effigies awaits on the 6th floor. The 8th floor houses effigies of Sakyamuni and Guanyin, with views over the hills and town.

🛏 Sleeping & Eating

With Xiàhé just an hour to the north there is little reason to stay here, and cheap hotels are loath to take foreigners. If you get stuck, the **Gānnán Fàndiàn** (甘南饭店; 📞 0941 821 4733; Maqu Xilu, 玛曲西路; tw ¥180-260, discounts of 20%; ❄@) has decent, clean and bright doubles with shower and internet; it's on the southwest corner of the public square.

There are restaurants around the public square, and also around the bus stations. Across the road from the entrance to the central bus station, look for a **Muslim restaurant** (opposite the central bus station; dishes ¥4-10; ⏱ 8am-8pm daily) with a picture menu outside. Try the *gānbǎnmiàn* (干板面; ¥10), a type of spaghetti bolognese with hand-pulled noodles.

❶ Getting There & Away

Hézuò is where buses from Zōigě (Ruò'ěrgài), in Sìchuān, and Lángmùsì and Xiàhé meet. There is a train booking office just outside the central bus station (though no trains pass through here).

Services from the **central bus station** (长途汽车站; Chángtú Qìchēzhàn; Nawulu, 那吾路):
Lánzhōu ¥74, four hours, every 30 minutes
Línxià ¥30, 1½ hours, every 30 minutes
Xiàhé ¥14.50, 1½ hours, every 30 minutes

From the **south bus station** (汽车南站; Qìchē Nánzhàn; cnr Zhuoni Donglu & Tongqin Jie, 卓尼东路通钦街):
Lángmùsì ¥33 to ¥50, three hours, three daily (7am, 10.20am and 12.20pm)
Zōigě ¥78, 3½ hours, one daily (7.30am)

A taxi between the two bus stations costs ¥2 per person, or take bus 1 (¥1).

Lángmùsì 郎木寺

📞 0941 · POP 3000

Straddling the border between Sìchuān and Gānsù is Lángmùsì (Taktsang Lhamo in Tibetan), an expanding and modernising alpine Amdo Tibetan village nestled among steep grassy meadows, evergreen forests of slender pine trees brushing the sky, crumbling stupas, piles of *mani* stones and snow-clad peaks. Lovely and moist compared to the lowlands, Lángmùsì is a delightful place, surrounded by countless red and white monastery buildings, flapping prayer flags and the mesmerising sound of monks chanting at twilight.

The White Dragon River (白龙江; Báilóng Jiāng) divides the town in two and the Sìchuān side has quickly become the far nicer part to stay in. From where the bus drops you off on the scruffy main street, walk up the road about three blocks and then turn left. The well-paved street runs a few blocks up to the Kerti monastery and is lined with a range of hostels, hotels, eateries and souvenir shops.

◉ Sights

Kerti Gompa BUDDHIST
(格尔底寺, Géěrdǐ Sì; admission valid 2 days ¥30; ⏱ 6.30-8am, 11am-1pm & 6-8pm) Rising up on the Sìchuān side of White Dragon River is this monastery – otherwise dubbed the Sìchuān Monastery – built in 1413, home to around 700 monks, and composed of five temples and colleges. Try your luck catching a glimpse of student monks in class (from a respectful distance) by visiting the monastery in the morning (6.30am to 8am and 11am to 1pm) or late afternoon (6pm to 8pm).

A short walk from the monastery stand small pavilions built over a brook whose waters power a round-the-clock revolving of prayer wheels housed inside – the ultimate in holiness! Just across from the entrance is a small **Hui Muslim village** with yellow houses and central mosque.

Serti Gompa BUDDHIST
(赛赤寺, Sàichì Sì; admission ¥30; ⏱ 6.30-8am, 11am-1pm & 6-8pm) This small monastery with golden- and silver-roofed halls dates from 1748 stands on the Gānsù side of White Dragon River and is simply referred to as the Gānsù Monastery. The best chance of seeing sky burials is in the morning (6.30am to 8am and 11am to 1pm) and late afternoon (6pm to 8pm). At all times of day the views are lovely from up here.

🏃 Activities

Hiking
Bountiful hiking opportunities radiate in almost every direction. For reasonably priced guides for all-day or overnight treks, including to **Huágàishén Shān** (华盖神山; 4200m), all the horse-trekking companies and hostels in town can offer a local guide.

Southwest of Kerti Gompa is **Namo Gorge** (纳摩大峡谷; Nàmó Dàxiágǔ), which makes for a superlative two- to three-hour (return) hike. The gorge contains several sacred grottoes, one dedicated to the Tibetan goddess Palden Lhamo, the other is the stone-tablet labelled **Fairy Cave** (仙女洞; Xiānnǚ Dòng), where monks sometimes chant inside, which gives the town its Tibetan name (*lángmù* meaning fairy). Cross rickety bridges flung over the gushing stream, trek past piles of *mani* stones and prayer flags, and hike on into a splendid ravine. After about 30 minutes of clambering over rocks you reach a grassy plain surrounded by towering peaks.

Another popular trek is the hike along the White Dragon River to the river's source (白龙江源头; *Báilóng Jiāng Yuántóu*), where Chinese hikers go in search of *chóngcǎo* (虫草), a coveted herb used in Chinese medicine.

A lovely walk heads out over the hills along a narrow paved road from the stupa at Serti Gompa (you must pay admission to pass through) to the small village of Jíkēhé Cūn (吉科合村). This hike can be combined with the hike to the White Dragon River source. When you reach the village, simply follow the loop and then head down a dirt path towards the valley below. Watch out for local dogs.

For some glorious open views over Xiàhé, trek up the coxcomb-like Red Stone Mountain (红石崖; Hóngshí Yá). To start, turn right one street down (heading out of Lángmùsì) past the intersection where the bus drops you off.

Horse Trekking

The mountain trails around Lángmùsì offer spectacular riding opportunities. There are two outfits in town offering similar one- to four-day treks overnighting at nomads' tents and with the option of climbing nearby peaks along the way. Both companies have English-speaking staff and are good sources of travel information.

Lángmùsì Tibetan Horse Trekking   HORSE RIDING
(✆ 0941 667 1504; www.langmusi.net; ⏰ 8am-10pm) This established, officially licensed outfit offers horse hire per day for ¥300 for a single traveller; ¥220 for two or more. In addition to guide, food and sleeping bags, trips include a package on nomad culture.

Wind Horse Trekking   HORSE RIDING
(郎木寺白戊马队; Lángmùsì Báiwù Mǎduì; ✆ 151 0944 1588; ⏰ 8am-8pm) Offers horse-riding packages starting at ¥180 per day (bring your own sleeping bag). Opposite the China Telecom office on the main road of Lángmùsì.

Biking

Lángmùsì is worth exploring on two wheels for serious cyclists. The many dirt tracks snaking into the hills, Red Stone Mountain and the source of the White Dragon River all make for hard steep work. Two distant lakes, both around 40km from town on quiet, flat highways, are popular destinations. Lángmùsì Tibetan Horse Trekking can help

with bike tours and also rents bikes (¥60 to ¥80 per day).

⚜ Festivals & Events

If you are in the area in late July, head out to Mǎqǔ (玛曲) to see the annual horse races. The dates change each year, so try contacting the Lángmùsì Bīnguǎn hotel (p837) to find out when it is being held. Mǎqǔ is 67km west of Lángmùsì. Travellers cafes and hotels in Lángmùsì can arrange transport to the town.

🛏 Sleeping

Tibetan Barley Youth Hostel   HOSTEL $
(藏地青稞国际青年旅舍; Zàngdé Qīngkē Guójì Qīngnián Lǔshè; ☎ mobile 134 3879 8688; dm ¥40-45, d/tw with shower ¥220; ☎) This hostel has clean, colourful rooms, some with sunny rooftop views, and a homely bar-lounge with Chinese meals and cushion seating. Comanager Yezi speaks good French and English, is full of travel information, can arrange tours and has even drawn a useful Lángmùsì map. To get here, go straight ahead from the bus dropoff, cross the river and turn left.

Lángmùsì Bīnguǎn   HOTEL $
(郎木寺宾馆; ✆ 0941 667 1086; tibetanyakboy@yahoo.co.uk; dm ¥30, d/tw with shower ¥160-180) Just up the side road from where the bus drops you off is this friendly English-speaking place with basic three-bed dorms and clean en suite rooms that show a bit wear and tear. The courtyard rooms are quietest. Discounts of 30%.

Yǒng Zhōng Hotel   HOTEL $$
(永忠宾馆, Yǒngzhōng Bīnguǎn; ✆ 0941 667 1032; tw ¥180-220; ❋@) On the Sìchuān side of town, just down from Kerti Gompa (p836), is this pleasant family-run hotel with small, bright, modern rooms, all with air-con and 24-hour hot water. There's also a free computer with internet downstairs in the shoe shop where you access the hotel. Expect discounts of 30%.

Lángmùsì Hotel   HOTEL $$$
(朗木寺大酒店, Lángmùsì Dà Jiǔdiàn; ✆ 0941 667 1555; langmusihotel@yahoo.com.cn; d ¥666-699, tr ¥700) This friendly four-storey hotel is the most upscale in Lángmùsì and offers very pleasant, clean and spacious rooms in either standard or Tibetan styling. It's on the road towards Kerti Gompa (p836), literally across from the ticket booth. Discounts of up to 70%.

Eating

Practically every backpacker-oriented guesthouse and hostel has its own attached restaurant-bar serving a combination of Western, Tibetan and Chinese dishes. On the Sìchuān side of town you'll find a dozen pleasant small restaurants serving Sìchuānese, Yúnnánese and Tibetan dishes. For cheap noodles, head to the Muslim restaurants across from the entrance to Kerti Gompa.

**Happy Homemade
Yunnan Taste**   YUNNANESE $
(源自原位; Yuánzì Yuánwèi; dishes ¥10-18; ⊗10am-10pm; ⑨) The Yúnnánese folk at this family-run restaurant are infectiously happy. Sample the strong home-made *báijiǔ* (Chinese spirit) and you might be too. Popular with Chinese travellers for the *guòqiáo mǐxiàn* (Yúnnánese hot pot) and huge servings of classics such as *yúxiāng qiézi* (red-pepper stewed eggplant). Located just north of the east side of main street.

★ **Black Tent Cafe**   TIBETAN, CAFE $$
(黑帐蓬咖啡, Hēi Zhàngpeng Kāfēi; dishes ¥25-50; ⊗8am-10pm; ⑨) Great service, a Tibetan-style interior, rooftop seating and a good little menu offering Western and Tibetan dishes are just some of the highlights of this 2nd-floor cafe run by the folks at Lángmùsì Tibetan Horse Trekking (p837). Our only complaint is the price of beer: ¥12 for a small can! The cafe is just up the side street from the intersection where the bus drops you off (off the west side of main street).

ⓘ Information

There is nowhere to change money and no ATMs that accept foreign cards. Wi-fi is widely available at hostels and cafes. The **Public Security Bureau** (PSB; 公安局; Gōng'ānjú) is just down from the Lángmùsì Hotel.

ⓘ Getting There & Away

There's one daily bus to Zōigě (Ruò'ěrgài; ¥25, 2½ hours) at 6.30am which arrives with time to connect with the bus to Sōngpān. There are two to three daily buses to Hézuò (¥50, three hours), departing at 6.30am (summer only), 7.20am and noon. Take the one direct bus to Xiàhé (¥72, 3½ hours) at 2pm, or change in Hézuò for frequent buses. Note that while there is a daily bus from Lánzhōu to Lángmùsì, there is no return bus. For the latest schedule see www.langmusi.net.

HÉXĪ CORRIDOR

Bound by the Qílián Shān range to the south and the Mǎzōng (Horse's Mane) and Lóngshǒu (Dragon's Head) ranges to the north, the narrow strip of land that is Héxī Corridor (河西走廊; Héxī Zǒuláng), around which the province is formed, was once the sole western passage in and out of the Middle Kingdom.

Wǔwēi   武威
☑ 0935 / POP 509,000

Wǔwēi stands at the strategic eastern end of the Héxī Corridor. It was from here, two millennia ago, that the emperors of China launched their expeditionary forces into the unknown west, eventually leading them to Jiāyùguān and beyond. Temples, tombs and traditional gates hint at Wǔwēi's Silk Road past, while the rapidly modernising city has some pleasant squares and pedestrian streets.

Wǔwēi is compact enough that with the exception of Hǎizàng Temple you can walk to all the sights in an afternoon. Most travellers base themselves in the southern part of town near the rebuilt South Gate (南门). The city's main square, Wénhuà Guǎngchǎng (文化广场), is about 1km directly north of the gate on Bei Dajie.

◉ Sights

The following sights are written in the order you would approach them starting from the South Gate.

Confucius Temple   CONFUCIAN TEMPLE
(文庙,Wénmiào; cnr Xin Qingnianxiang & Wenmiao-lu, 新青年巷文庙路; admission ¥30; ⊗8am-6pm) This Ming-era temple is divided into Confucian Temple and Wénchāng Hall sections. Both display some fine examples of traditional architecture. Head east from the South Gate along pleasant Mingqing Fanggu Wenhua Jie to the square at the end (about 600m).

There is also an important stele featuring the extinct Xīxià language carved into one side and a Chinese translation on the other: a sort of Rosetta stone allowing researchers to understand the once unintelligible Xīxià texts. The stele is now housed in a small **museum** (free with temple ticket) on the left side of the square as you exit the temple.

Kumarajiva Pagoda
BUDDHIST PAGODA

(罗什寺塔, Luóshísì Tǎ; cnr Gonghejie & Bei Dajie; ⊘8am-6pm daily) FREE Located 400m north of Wǔwēi's main square (文化广场; *Wénhuà Guǎngchǎng*), on Bei Dajie, this pagoda dates from AD 488 and is surrounded by a tranquil complex of both unpainted and colourful wooden temples with old folk gossiping under trees. Dedicated to the great translator of Buddhist sutras (whose tongue was buried beneath the pagoda), the pagoda was toppled during the great earthquake in 1927 and rebuilt.

Léitái Sì
HISTORIC SITE

(雷台寺; Lei Tai Dong Lu; admission ¥50; ⊘8am-6pm) The pride and joy of the city, the bronze **Flying Horse of Wǔwēi** (飞马) was discovered here in 1969 and is the unofficial symbol of Gānsù. It was found in a secret tomb beneath this temple, built on top of steep earthen ramparts. The Flying Horse is now displayed in the Gānsù Provincial Museum (p825).

The site is 1.2km north of Wǔwēi; turn right at Lei Tai Dong Lu. Note that you'll need your passport to enter.

While it's a thrill to explore a 2000-year-old tomb, there is precious little inside.

Hǎizàng Temple
BUDDHIST

(海藏寺, Hǎizàng Sì; Haizang Park; admission ¥10; ⊘6am-6pm) A fascinating active monastery with a minute pavilion to the right of the entrance containing a **well** whose 'magic waters' (神水; *shénshuǐ*) are said to connect by subterranean streams to a Holy Lake (圣湖; Shènghú) in the Potala Palace in Lhasa. Drinking the water is said to cure myriad ailments. A short trip on bus 3 (¥2) or taxi (¥15 to ¥20) outside town takes you to the entrance of shabby **Haizang park** (admission ¥2), with the temple out back.

The **Three Sages Hall** (Sānshèng Diàn) contains a 'hermaphroditic Guanyin'. Dating to the Ming dynasty, the raised **Wúliàng Palace** (Wúliàng Diàn) was once used to store sutras but now houses a reclining Buddha in a glass cabinet.

🛏 Sleeping & Eating

The best place to situate yourself is around the South Gate. Mingqing Fanggu Wenhua Jie (or simply Mingqing Jie) extends east from the gate and is an attractive street lined with restaurants, coffee shops and a KTV (karaoke) or two.

THE BIG BUDDHA OF TIĀN TĪSHĀN

It's hard to appreciate how massive the 15m-high Shakyamuni Buddha statue at **Tiāntīshān Grottoes** (天梯山石窟; Tiāntīshān Shíkū; Dengshan village; admission ¥10; ⊘8am-6pm daily) is until you are at its truck-sized feet and peering up at its outstretched hand emerging from the cliff face. These 1600-year-old carvings stand majestically in the open air, not hidden in dark caves, so snap away.

The similarly ancient murals (tigers, black dragons) are worth a look amongst the 17 caves, along with some scroll paintings, but most relics have been whisked off to Dūnhuáng, so the Buddha is the real star.

The grottoes are 50km south of Wǔwēi. From Wǔwēi bus station, ask for the Tiāntīshān minibus (¥12, 3.5 hours, every 30 minutes). You'll be dropped off at Zhōnglù (钟路), from where it's a short taxi ride (¥10) to the grottoes.

Wǔwēi Nánchéngmén Bīnguǎn
HOTEL $

(武威南城门宾馆; ☑0935 231 9999; 62 Nan Dajie; tr without bathroom ¥108, d/tw with bathroom ¥138/158; 🅿) Almost touching the northwest side of the South Gate is this friendly hotel with small rooms with wear and tear but sporting disproportionally spacious bathrooms. Mention whether you prefer street views or a quiet inner room. The hotel entrance is down a short alley. Discounts of 15% to 20%.

Zǐyúngé Hotel
HOTEL $$

(紫云阁酒店; Zǐyúngé Jiǔdiàn; ☑0935 225 3888; Mingqing Fanggu Wenhua Jie; 明清仿古文化街; s/d/tr ¥198/280/218; ❋@) Just east of the South Gate, this great hotel has bright, comfortable and spacious rooms with showers and new furnishings. Wi-fi only in lobby. You can often net a standard double for around ¥140.

Korean Special Seafood & Hotpot
KOREAN, HOTPOT $

(韩国特别特海鲜火锅面; Hánguó Tèbié Tèhǎixiān Huǒguōmiàn; ☑186 9350 7234; Xinqingnian Alley, 新青年巷; dishes ¥10-22; ⊘9am-9pm) This modern restaurant breaks the monotony of dumplings with seafood *okonomiyaki* (Japanese pancake), cooked-at-your-table hotpots (¥56) with kimchi, and sushi on its large picture menu. Pass north through the South Gate and take the first right two blocks till the corner with Huiguan Alley (会馆巷). Look for the long black sign with yellow script.

ⓘ Information

There's a **Bank of China** (中国银行 | Zhōngguó Yínháng; Buxing Shangye Jie; 步行商业街) on the west end of the pedestrian shopping street where you can change money. There's also a branch with a 24-hour ATM behind the Zǐyúngé Hotel (p839). Internet cafes in Wǔwēi require Chinese ID.

ⓘ Getting There & Around

BUS

Express buses run from the long-distance bus station (长途汽车站; *chángtú qìchē zhàn*), 1.5km southwest of Wénhuà Guǎngchǎng to Jiāyùguān, Lánzhōu and Zhāngyè, though trains are faster and cheaper still.

TRAIN

The station is 3.5km southwest of Wénhuà Guǎngchǎng; the two are connected by buses 1 and 2 (¥1) or taxi (¥10). Taxis rides around town are around ¥4 to ¥7. There are frequent trains to the following:

Dūnhuáng hard/soft sleeper ¥195/302, 10 hours (two per day directly to Dūnhuáng at 9.21pm and 10.46pm; other trains drop you off at Liǔyuán)

Jiāyùguān hard/soft seat ¥70/108, five to six hours, six daily

Lánzhōu hard/soft seat ¥47/72, 3½ hours, every 20-30 minutes

Zhāngyè hard/soft seat ¥41/61, three hours, every 20-30 minutes

Zhōngwèi seat/hard sleeper ¥40.5/86.5, three to four hours, seven daily

To pre-purchase tickets, cross the square opposite the Confucius Temple (cnr of Xin Qingnianxiang & Wenmiaolu; 新青年巷文庙路) to the **train booking office** (火车票代售点).

Zhāngyè　　张掖

☑ 0936 / POP 260,000

Most people use this mid-size Silk Road town as a jumping-off base for the unique cliff temples at nearby Mǎtí Sì. But budget at least the afternoon here. There's a colossal Buddha ensconced inside one of China's best preserved wooden temples that deserves an extended visit.

The main road through town (as far as the traveller is concerned) is divided into Xi (West) Dajie and Dong (East) Dajie, depending which direction it radiates from the drum tower. Jianfu Jie intersects with Xi Dajie a few blocks from the drum tower and heading north takes you to a pleasant eating street while south leads to the Great Buddha Temple and Wooden Pagoda.

◎ Sights

★ **Great Buddha Temple**　　BUDDHIST TEMPLE
(大佛寺, Dàfó Sì; ☑ 0936 821 9671; off Jianfu Jie; admission ¥41; ◎8am-6pm) Originally dating to 1098 (Western Xia dynasty), this behemoth contains an astonishing 35m-long sleeping Buddha – China's largest of this variety – surrounded by mouldering clay arhats (Buddhists who have achieved enlightenment) and Qing-dynasty murals. Until the 1960s, small children would clamber into the huge Buddha and play around inside his tummy.

From Xi Dajie head south about 1km.

This is one of the few wooden structures from this era still standing in China and there is a wealth of traditional symbols to examine. Even the unrestored exterior is fascinating and there's an impressive white clay stupa (土塔; *tǔ tǎ*) dating from the Ming dynasty.

Wooden Pagoda　　PAGODA
(木塔, Mùtǎ; cnr Xianfu Jie & Minzhu Xijie; admission ¥5; ◎8am-noon & 2.30-6pm) In the town's main square stands this brick and wooden pagoda. Though first built in AD 528, the present structure is a thorough reconstruction from 1926.

🛌 Sleeping & Eating

For meals, head 300m west of the drum tower and look for Mingqing Jie (明清街), an alley of faux-Qing architecture lined with dozens of clean, friendly restaurants with picture menus. There is also a food court on the northeast side of the drum tower beside the China Construction Bank.

Huáyì Bīnguǎn　　HOTEL $
(华谊宾馆; ☑ 0936 824 2118; Dong Dajie; d without/with bathroom ¥40/90; ❀ @) Surprisingly clean and tidy budget hotel with rooms showing minimum wear and tear. In-room broadband is a definite bonus, as is the location just east of the drum tower. Look for the stone lions guarding the entrance.

Gānzhōu Hotel HOTEL **$$**

(甘州宾馆, Gānzhōu Bīnguǎn; ☑ 0936 888 8822; 373 Nan Dajie; d & tw ¥399; ❀ ◐) A solid if entirely generic midrange hotel with bright modern rooms, courteous staff and a good location just 150m south of the drum tower. Discounts of up to 50% make this a great choice.

ⓘ Information

There's an **internet cafe** (网吧; wǎngbā; 3rd fl, 403 Nan Dajie; per hr ¥3; ◷ 8am-late) on the southwest corner of the drum tower intersection. The **Bank of China** (中国银行; Zhōngguó Yínháng; Dong Dajie; ◷ 8.30am-noon & 2.30-5pm Mon-Fri) can change travellers cheques and has a 24-hour ATM.

ⓘ Getting There & Around

BUS

The town has three bus stations, in the south, east and west. The **west bus station** (西站, Xī Zhàn; ☑ 0936 821 0597; 347 Xihuanlu, 西环路) has the most frequent departures. Destinations include Xīníng, Golmud, Jiāyùguān, Lánzhōu, Dūnhuáng and Wǔwēi, though it's faster and cheaper to take a train.

From any of the bus stations to the hotels costs ¥4 to ¥5. Bus 4 runs past the west bus station from Dong or Xi Dajie.

TRAIN

The **train booking office** (12 Oushi Jie, 欧式街 12号; ◷ 8am-6pm) is near a Marco Polo statue (the great explorer spent a year in town). To get here walk west of the drum tower and turn right (north) at Oushi Jie.

Dūnhuáng hard/soft sleeper ¥145/223, 7½ hours (two daily at 12.19am and 2.04am; day trains all go to Liǔyuán)

Jiāyùguān hard/soft seat ¥38/57, two to three hours, every 10-30 minutes

Lánzhōu hard/soft seat ¥76/119, six to seven hours, every 20 minutes

Wǔwēi seat/hard sleeper ¥41/92, three to four hours, every 20-30 minutes

The station is 7km northeast of the city centre. A taxi will cost ¥10, or take bus 1 (¥1).

Mǎtí Sì 马蹄寺

Carved into the cliff sides in foothills of the grand Qílián Mountains (Qílián Shān), the venerable Buddhist grottoes of Mǎtí Sì make for a fine short getaway from the hectic small towns along the Héxī Corridor. There's excellent hiking in the nearby hills, and a

WORTH A TRIP

THE RAINBOW ROCKS OF ZHĀNGYÈ

Multicoloured rock formations, known in China as **Dānxiá rocks** (张掖丹霞; Zhāngyè Dānxiá), gained a bit of attention after six well-known formations in the south were inscribed as Unesco World Heritage sites. If you are hiring a taxi to go to Mǎtí Sì, consider taking a side trip to Zhāngyè's spectacularly colourful examples. The swirling rainbow palette and the scale of the formations is astonishing.

From Zhāngyè a taxi to both Mǎtí Sì and the rocks will cost around ¥200.

decent range of simple accommodation and food in the nearby village from May to September. Come in July to see the mountain valleys carpeted in blue wildflowers.

◉ Sights & Activities

Mǎtí Sì CAVE, BUDDHIST

(马蹄寺) Mǎtí Sì translates as Horse Hoof Monastery, a reference to when a heavenly horse left a hoof imprint in a grotto. Between the 5th and 14th centuries a series of caves were almost as miraculously built in sheer sandstone cliffs and filled with carvings, temples and meditation rooms. The caves are reached via twisting staircases, balconies, narrow passages and platforms that will leave your head spinning.

Mǎtí Sì is 65km north of Zhāngyè, and one or both of the main caves may be closed outside of May to September.

The grottoes are not in one area but spread over many sections. The most accessible are the **Thousand Buddhas Caves** (千佛洞石窟, Qiān Fó Dòng Shíkū; admission ¥35) just past the entrance gate to the scenic area. Within this complex is the **Pǔguāng Temple** where you'll find the relic of the horse foot imprint. The **Mǎtí Sì North Caves** (马蹄寺 北洞, Mǎtísì Běi Dòng; admission ¥35) are just above the village (2km up the road from the Thousand Buddhas Caves). Other collections of grottoes are scattered about the cliff faces, as are utilitarian caves that were formerly used as dwellings by local people.

Hiking

There are several good day hikes around Mǎtí Sì, including the five-hour loop through pine forest and talus fields to the **Línsōng**

Waterfall (临松瀑布; Línsōng Pùbù) and back down past **Sword Split Stone** (剑劈石; Jiànpīshí). For unrivalled panoramas, take the steep ascent of the ridge starting across from the white *chörten* just above the village at Sānshísāntiān Shíkū (三十三天石窟).

Horse Riding

Horse riding is a popular activity. Prices are fixed at ¥200 for a four-hour ride. Note it costs ¥20 just to enter into the general village/grotto scenic area.

🛏 Sleeping & Eating

If you're adequately prepared for camping, some overnight trips are possible. The tiny village also has several basic guesthouses. Call **Mr Hua** (☏ 130 859 2081; tw ¥60) to book at a friendly family-run place and arrange a pick-up at Mǎtí Hé. Decent meals can be had at a couple of village restaurants or head up into the fields towards the mountains to one of several large comfortable tents serving Tibetan-style fare (including butter-milk tea and *tsampa*).

⊙ Getting There & Away

Buses leave every 30 minutes from Zhāngyè's south bus station for the crossroads village of Mǎtí Hé (马蹄河; ¥9.50, 1½ hours, 6.40am to 5.40pm), from where you can catch a minibus or taxi (¥30) for the final 7km or so.

Direct buses to Mǎtí Sì depart from Zhāngyè's south bus station at 7.35am, 8.25am and 9.15am from May to September. The last bus back to Mǎtí Hé or Zhāngyè leaves before 5pm. Check with locals on the exact time.

A one-way taxi from Zhāngyè will cost around ¥80.

Jiāyùguān & Around

嘉峪关

✓ 0937 / POP 170,000

You approach Jiāyùguān through the forbidding lunar landscape of north Gānsù. It's a fitting setting, as Jiāyùguān marks the symbolic end of the Great Wall, the western gateway of China proper and, for imperial Chinese, the beginning of the back of beyond. One of the defining points of the Silk Road, a Ming-dynasty fort was erected here in 1372 and Jiāyùguān came to be colloquially known as the 'mouth' of China, while the narrow Héxī Corridor, leading back towards the *nèidì* (inner lands), was dubbed the 'throat'.

You'll need plenty of imagination to conjure up visions of the Silk Road, as modern Jiāyùguān is a city of straight roads and identikit blocks, almost as if airlifted into position from North Korea. But the Jiāyùguān Fort is an essential part of Silk Road lore and most certainly worth a visit.

⊙ Sights

With the exception of the Wèi Jìn Tombs, all the sites are covered by the entrance ticket to the Jiāyùguān Fort; admission fees quoted for individual sites are for entry without admission to the fort. A taxi to all the sights (including the tombs), which are all outside town, is likely to cost ¥200 for the half-day. A taxi to cover just to the sites covered by the fort ticket will cost ¥100 to ¥150 depending on how long you stay to look at things.

Jiāyùguān Fort   FORT

(嘉峪关城楼; Jiāyùguān Chénglóu; Xinhua Nanlu; admission ¥120; ⊙ 8am-6pm) One of the classic images of western China, the fort guards the pass between the snowcapped Qílián Shān peaks and the Hēi Shān (Black Mountains) of the Mǎzōng Shān range.

Built in 1372, it was christened the 'Impregnable Defile Under Heaven'. Although the Chinese often controlled territory far beyond the Jiāyùguān area, this was the last major stronghold of imperial China – the end of the 'civilised world', beyond which lay only desert demons and the barbarian armies of Central Asia.

Towards the eastern end of the fort is the **Gate of Enlightenment** (光化楼; Guānghuá Lóu) and in the west is the **Gate of Conciliation** (柔远楼; Róuyuǎn Lóu), from where exiled poets, ministers, criminals and soldiers would have ridden off into oblivion. Each gate dates from 1506 and has 17m-high towers with upturned flying eaves and double gates that would have been used to trap invading armies. On the inside are horse lanes leading up to the top of the inner wall. On the west-facing side of the Gate of Enlightenment are the shadowy remains of **slogans** praising Chairman Mao, blasted by the desert winds. A further prolix quote from Mao stands out in yellow paint on the south wall of **Wénchāng Pavilion** (文昌阁; Wénchāng Gé).

Near the fort entrance gate is the excellent **Jiāyùguān Museum of the Great Wall** (Xinhua Nanlu; ⊙ 8.30am-6pm), with photos, artefacts, maps, Silk Road exhibits and models to show just how the fort and wall crossed the land.

Overhanging Great Wall
HISTORIC SITE

(悬壁长城, Xuánbì Chángchéng; 3904-4646 Xinhua Beilu; admission ¥21; ⊙8.30am-8pm, to 6pm winter) Running north from Jiāyùguān Fort, this section of wall is believed to have been first constructed in 1539, though this reconstruction dates from 1987. It's quite an energetic hike up to excellent views of the desert and the glittering snowcapped peaks in the distance. The wall is about 9km north of the fort.

First Beacon Platform of the Great Wall
HISTORIC SITE

(长城第一墩, Chángchéng Dìyī Dūn; Lianhuo Gaosu; admission ¥20; ⊙8.30am-8pm, to 6pm winter) Atop a 56m-high cliff overlooking the Tǎolài River south of Jiāyùguān, the remains of this beacon platform are a disappointing pile of dirt, but the views over the river and bare rock gorge are impressive and you can walk alongside attached vestiges of Ming-era Great Wall. Your driver will likely drop you off 150m away at a **subterranean viewing platform**, labelled the 'Underground Valley'.

Wèi Jin Tombs
TOMB

(新城魏晋墓, Xīnchéng Wèijìnmù; admission ¥31; ⊙8.30am-7.30pm) These tombs date from approximately AD 220–420 (the Wei and Western Jin periods) and contain extraordinarily fresh brick wall paintings (some ineptly retouched) depicting scenes from everyday life, from making tea to picking mulberries for silk production. There are thousands of tombs in the desert 20km east of Jiāyùguān, but only one is currently open to visitors, that of a husband and wife.

The small museum is also worth a look and the only area where photos are permitted. A taxi here from central Jiāyùguān will cost around ¥70 so it's worth paying a little more (¥100) to also visit Yěmáwān Bǎo Yízhǐ (野麻湾堡遗址), a former walled town with dramatically crumbling remains. Nearby are some unrestored sections of the Great Wall dotting farm fields and free to access.

Sleeping

Jīnyè Bīnguǎn
HOTEL $

(金叶宾馆, ☑0937 620 1333; 12 Lanxin Xilu, 兰新西路12号; d/tw without/with shower ¥138/200; ✳) The en-suite rooms are a bit of a tight squeeze but overall good value at this hotel with a useful location by the bus station. The cheapest rooms are a bit tatty and the shared bathrooms could be cleaner. Expect discounts of 40%.

Jiāyùguān

🛏 **Sleeping**

1 Jiāyùguān Hotel	A1
2 Jīnyè Bīnguǎn	A2
3 Kānghūi Hotel	A1

🍴 **Eating**

4 Jìngtiě Xiǎochīchéng	B2
5 Yuàn Zhōng Yuàn Restaurant	A2

ℹ **Information**

6 People's No 1 Hospital	B2

ℹ **Transport**

7 Train Booking Office	B2

Kānghūi Hotel
HOTEL $$

(康辉宾馆, Kānghūi Bīnguǎn; ☑0937 620 3456; 1599 Xinhua Zhonglu; 新华中路1599号; tw/tr ¥208/288; ✳@🛜) Wide windows, high ceilings and very spacious rooms (and bathrooms) are highlights at this tidy business hotel in the centre of town. Renovations finished in 2013 yet prices remained the same, making its excellent location on the tree-lined street hard to beat. Discounts of 30% are typical.

Jiāyùguān Hotel
HOTEL $$$

(嘉峪关宾馆; ☑0937 620 1588; 1 Xinhua Beilu, 新华北路1号; d/tw from ¥669/768; ✳@🛜) Rooms here are modern with heavy accents on the brown woods and faux marble. Most include a Chinese breakfast and computers with broadband. Other services include a restaurant serving Western-style food, a spa, travel agent and attentive staff. Conveniently located on the pleasant tree-lined shopping boulevarde of Xinhua Zhonglu. Discounts of 30% to 60% are common.

JULY 1ST GLACIER

July 1st Glacier (七一冰川; Qīyī Bīngchuān; admission ¥101) About 90km southwest of Jiāyùguān, this glacier sits high in the Qílián Shān range at 4300m. Hikers can walk a 5km trail alongside the glacier. Icy winter weather grinds transport to a halt from November to March. In summer it's a great place to come to escape the heat of the desert below, but if you come in the spring or autumn it can be a cold and forbidding place – the glacier fills the rocky valley and there is little life up here. Global warming is having an effect on the glacier, which has retreated 50m in recent years.

It is reached via the train to the iron-ore town of Jìngtiěshān (镜铁山; Y10), departing from Jiāyùguān's Luhua train station at 8am. It's a scenic three-hour train trip to Jìngtiěshān, where you can hire a taxi to the glacier (return Y120, 20km).

You could theoretically do this in one day, but it's better to stay the night in Jìngtiěshān, where there is a cheap and basic hostel (zhāodàisuǒ). This will leave you with enough time the next morning to hire a taxi up to Tiān'é Hú (return Y50) and the Tibetan village of Qíqīng. Return trains depart around 1.46pm from Jìngtiěshān. A return taxi to the glacier from Jiāyùguān costs around Y400 (nine hours).

✖ Eating

For breakfast ask or look around for small shops selling *bāozi* (包子; steamed meat- or veg-filled buns) and *dòujiāng* (豆浆; soya milk).

Fùqiáng Market   MARKET **$**
(富强市场, Fùqiáng Shìchǎng; 14 Xinhua Beilu; ⊙10am-9pm) For a fast, hot meal in the evenings, especially barbecued lamb washed down with beer, try the food stalls at this market, north of the traffic circle.

Jìngtiě Xiǎochīchéng   MARKET **$**
(镜铁小吃城, Jìngtiě Market; Xinhua Zhonglu; ⊙10am-10pm) At this busy market load up on lamb kebabs, *ròujiāmó* (肉夹馍), wonton soup, dumplings, roast duck and more.

Yuàn Zhōng Yuàn Restaurant   SICHUANESE **$$**
(苑中苑酒店, Yuànzhōngyuàn Jiǔdiàn; Jingtie Shangchang; dishes ¥12-48; ⊙9am-9pm) Directly across from the bus station on the far side of a small park is this pleasant Sìchuān restaurant nice enough for a first date. Try its *gōngbǎo jīdīng* (宫保鸡丁; spicy chicken and peanuts), *tiěbǎn dòufu* (铁板豆腐; fried tofu) or a *yúxiāng ròusī* (鱼香肉丝; stir-fried pork and vegetable strips).

❶ Information

The **Bank of China** (中国银行 | Zhōngguó Yínháng; 33-41 Xinhua Zhonglu; ⊙9.30am-5.30pm Mon-Fri, 10am-4pm Sat & Sun) south of the Lanxin Xilu intersection has an ATM and can change money. There's a large **post office** (Xinhua Zhonglu; ⊙8am-6pm) which can send packages internationally. Look for an **internet cafe** (网络, wǎngbā; Lanxin Xilu; per hr ¥3; ⊙24hr) beside the bus station.

❶ Getting There & Away

Jiāyùguān has an airport with flights to Běijīng, Shànghǎi and Lánzhōu but most people arrive by bus or train.

BUS

Doubling as a billiards hall, Jiāyùguān's **bus station** (汽车站; Qìchēzhàn; Lanxin Xilu) is by a busy four-way junction on Lanxin Xilu, next to the main budget hotels. It is cheaper and quicker to take a train, but bus destinations include Dūnhuáng, Lánzhōu, Wǔwēi and Zhāngyè.

TRAIN

Direct trains to Dūnhuáng are labelled as such. Beware of the more frequently scheduled trains to Liǔyuán – a lengthy 180km away from Dūnhuáng.

Dūnhuáng seat/hard sleeper ¥55/118, five hours.

Lánzhōu hard/soft seat ¥103/160, seven to eight hours; hard/soft sleeper ¥179/275, nine hours.

Ürümqi hard/soft sleeper ¥246/384, 15 hours
Wǔwēi seat/hard sleeper ¥69/126, four to six hours.

Zhāngyè hard/soft seat ¥38/57, two to three hours.

Purchase tickets at the **train booking office** (火车站售票处, Huǒchēzhàn Shòupiàochù; 28 Xinhua Zhonglu; ⊙8am-noon & 1-4pm Mon-Fri, to 3.30pm Sat & Sun) near the People's No 1 Hospital, next to the China Construction Bank. Note that you can't buy tickets here for Jìngtiěshān (for the July 1st Glacier) but must purchase these directly at the station.

Jiāyùguān's **train station** (火车站) is south-west of the town centre. Bus 1 runs here from Xinhua Zhonglu (¥1). A taxi costs ¥10.

❶ Getting Around

Bus 1 (¥1) runs from the train station to the bus station. A taxi to the airport (25 minutes) costs ¥50.

Dūnhuáng   敦煌

📱 0937 / POP 187,000

The fertile Dūnhuáng oasis has long been a refuge for weary Silk Road travellers. Most visitors stayed long enough only to swap a camel and have a feed; but some settled down and built the forts, towers and magnificent cave temples that are now scattered over the surrounding area. These sites, along with some dwarfing sand dunes and desert-scapes, make Dūnhuáng a magnificent place to visit.

Despite its remoteness, per capita income in Dūnhuáng is among the highest in China, thanks to a push into wind and solar energy production. The town is now thoroughly modern, but there's no doubt it has maintained its distinctive ambience of a desert sanctuary. With clean tree-lined streets, slow-moving traffic, bustling markets, budget hotels, cafes and souvenir shops, it has remained as much an oasis for the weary traveller as ever.

◉ Sights

Though relatively small, Dūnhuáng is a great walking town with wide sidewalks and endless narrow alleys opening up into squares, markets and the lives of ordinary citizens. The riverside is worth a visit if only to see if you are brave enough to cross to the platforms in the middle of the stream.

Dūnhuáng Museum   MUSEUM

(敦煌博物馆, Dūnhuáng Bówùguǎn; 📱 0937 882 2981; Mingshan Lu; ⊙8am-6.30pm) **FREE** Outside of town on the road to Singing Sands Mountain (p850) is this sparkling museum that takes you on an artefact-rich journey through the Dūnhuáng area (from prehistoric to Qing-dynasty times) via hallways designed to make you feel as if you were in a cave. You can easily walk here in 15 minutes from the centre of town. Bring your passport for admission.

🛏 Sleeping

Competition among Dūnhuáng's hotels is fierce, and you should get significant discounts (50% or more) outside of summer.

There are a dozen or so smaller business-type hotels along Mingshan and Yang-guan Zhonglu. They tend to be around ¥200 in the off-season and ¥300 to ¥400 in the height of summer.

★ Dune Guesthouse   HOSTEL $

(月泉山庄青年旅舍, Yuèquán Shānzhuāng Qīngnián Lǚshè; 📱138 9376 3029; dhzhzh@163.com; Sha Sheng Botanical Garden, 沙山沙生植物园; dm ¥30, r & cabins with shared bathroom ¥100) Near the base of the Singing Sands Mountain (p850) and surrounded by flowering gardens and grapevines, this chilled-out backpackers' retreat is superbly located with fruit trees and a courtyard. A taxi here is ¥15, or catch minibus 3 from Shazhou Nanlu to the terminus, then walk back towards town, taking the first left past the vines, following the signs.

The guesthouse is run by the folks at Charley Johng's Cafe (p846), so make enquiries there first.

Shazhouyi International Youth Hostel   HOSTEL $

(敦煌沙州驿国际青年旅舍; Dūnhuáng Shāzhōuyì Guójì Qīngnián Lǚshè; 📱0937 880 8800; shazhouyiyha@gmail.com; 8 Qilian Lu, 祁连路8号（北辰市场对面）; dm ¥45-55, d ¥180; [P][⊛][❋][⊚]) This hostel is plant- and light-filled, inviting you to lounge and plan one of the offered tours. Dorm beds are comfy with modern shared bathrooms. Doubles are bright and spacious. The street is traffic heavy but has cheap eats, with the Shāzhōu Night Market (p847) a 10-minute walk away through a leafy park. English spoken.

Free shuttle bus from train station.

Mògāo Hotel   HOTEL $$

(莫高宾馆, Mògāo Bīnguǎn; 📱0937 885 1777; 12 Mingshan Lu; 鸣山路12号; d/tw from ¥308/428; [❋][@][⊚]) With its excellent location near restaurants and shops, this is one of the better options for the single traveller who wants a private room. There's in-room broadband and wi-fi in the lobby. Off-season the smaller doubles go for around ¥188.

Fēitiān Bīnguǎn   HOTEL $$

(飞天宾馆; 📱0937 882 2337; www.fttravel.cn; 22 Mingshan Lu, 鸣山路22号; d/tw ¥428/458; [❋][@]) This long-standing two-star hotel has

Dūnhuáng

Dūnhuáng

😴 Sleeping
1 Fēitiān Bīnguǎn B4
2 Mògāo Hotel B3
3 Shazhouyi International Youth
   Hostel A1

🍽 Eating
4 Bǔ Jì Lú Ròu Huáng Miànguǎn C3
5 Charley Johng's Cafe B3
6 Shāzhōu Night Market D2

🍸 Drinking & Nightlife
7 Brown Sugar Cafe...............................D3

🎭 Entertainment
8 Dūnhuáng Theatre..............................C2

a good location on one of Dūnhuáng's major streets. Rooms are small but tidy and well lit. Discounts of 50%.

Silk Road Dūnhuáng Hotel HOTEL $$$
(敦煌山庄, Dūnhuáng Shānzhuāng; ☑ 0937 888 2088; www.dunhuangresort.com; Dunyue Lu, 敦月路; dm ¥80, d ¥350-1200; 🌐@🌐) This four-star resort is tastefully designed with Central Asian rugs, a cool stone floor and Chinese antiques. The hotel's rooftop restaurant has without doubt the best outdoor perch in Dūnhuáng. A taxi from town costs ¥10, or take minibus 3 (¥1). Discounts of 20% to 40%.

🍴 Eating

There are restaurants large and small all over Dūnhuáng, many with English or picture menus. For *niúròu miàn* (牛肉面; beef noodles) head to any of a number of restaurants along Xiyu Lu.

Charley Johng's Cafe BREAKFAST, CHINESE $
(风味餐馆, Fēngwèi Cānguǎn; ☑ 0937 388 2411; Mingshan Lu; dishes ¥6-36; ⊙8am-10pm) Tasty Western-style breakfast items including

scrambled eggs, muesli with yoghurt, and pancakes are available all day either à la carte or as a set. There are also sandwiches, and a host of Chinese dishes such as stir-fries and dumplings. It also offers tours and good traveller information.

★ **Zhāixīng Gé** CHINESE, INTERNATIONAL **$$**
(摘星阁, Silk Road Dūnhuáng Hotel; Dunyue Lu; dishes ¥18-38; ⊙7am-1pm & 4.30pm-midnight) Part of the Silk Road Dūnhuáng Hotel, this superb rooftop restaurant is ideal for a meal (the Western buffet breakfast is well regarded by travellers) or a sundowner gazing out over the golden sand dunes with someone you love. Dishes do not cost much more than places in town. Try the Uighur bread or the surprisingly good thick-crust pizza.

Shāzhōu Night Market MARKET **$$**
(沙洲夜市, Shāzhōu Yèshì; btwn Yangguan Donglu & Xiyu Lu; ⊙morning-late) Extending from Yangguan Lu south to Xiyu, this market is both a place to eat and to socialise, night and day. Off Yanguang Donglu are dozens of well-organised stalls with English signs: expect Sìchuān, Korean noodles, dumplings, claypot, barbecue including *ròujiāmó* (肉夹馍) and Lánzhōu noodles. Also look out for cooling cups of *xìngpíshuǐ* (杏皮水; apricot juice; ¥5).

There is also an open-air seating area nearby with singing, music bands and roast lamb by the platter or skewer. Along with the seated areas along Fanggu Shangye Yitao Jie, this is the most expensive place to eat barbecued meat. For a better deal try the alleys radiating east.

Bǔ Jì Lú Ròu Huáng Miànguǎn NOODLES **$$**
(卜记驴肉黄面馆; Shazhou Nanlu; dishes ¥12-38; set meals from ¥60; ⊙10am-10pm) Donkey meat with yellow noodles is a local speciality and this is one popular place to try it. Donkey tastes like roast beef and set meals are served with noodle dishes topped with tofu. There's a picture menu.

🍷 Drinking

The alley behind the mosque has a row of stylish cafes that also serve as bars in the evening. In summer the Silk Road Dūnhuáng Hotel hosts a **beer garden** at the entrance to the grounds, while their stylish rooftop **Zhāixīng Gé** (Dunyue Lu, 敦月路; ⊙4.30pm-midnight) offers peerless views over the desert to go with a beer or a glass of local red wine.

Brown Sugar Cafe CAFE
(黑糖咖啡, Hēitáng Kāfēi; ☑0937 881 7111; 28 Tianma Jie; 天马街28号; tea ¥25-38, bottle of wine ¥78-198; ⊙1pm-midnight; 🛜) This three-level cafe mixes modern with crafty decor and cafe classics with a Dūnhuáng twist. Try one of the 11 varieties of fresh-leaf Chinese teas to balance out a sweet black-rice muffin. Things turn smoky at night when fashionable locals come to sip beer and Mògāo wine.

☆ Entertainment

There are often night-time opera and other music performances in the square behind the mosque. This is also a good place to go if you have children, as there are several large free play areas.

Dūnhuáng Theatre (敦煌大剧院; Dūnhuáng Dàjùyuàn; Yangguan Zhonglu) hosts **Dūnhuáng Goddess** (敦煌神女, Dūnhuáng Shénnǚ; tickets ¥220; ⊙8.30pm), an 80-minute acrobatic dramatisation of stories on the walls of the Mògāo Caves. English subtitles are provided.

ℹ️ Information

Ask at any hostel or Charley Johng's Cafe for tourist info; they can also help with tours from camel rides to overnight camping excursions. The north end of Mingshan Lu has stores for camping, hiking, camera and luggage needs. Wi-fi is widely available in cafes and hotel rooms, and there's an **internet cafe** (网吧, wǎngbā; cnr Mingshan Lu & Xiyu Lu; per hr ¥3; ⊙24hr).

Bank of China (中国银行, Zhōngguó Yínháng; Yangguan Zhonglu; ⊙8am-noon & 2-6pm Mon-Fri) Has a 24-hour ATM and changes travellers cheques.

Fēitiān Travel Service (飞天旅行社, Fēitiān Lǚxíngshè, Fēitiān Bīnguǎn; ☑138 3070 6288, 0937 885 2318; Mingshan Lu) Can arrange buses to Mògāo, local tours and car rental.

China Post (Yangguan Donglu; ⊙8.30am-6pm daily) Sells stamps and delivers packages internationally.

Public Security Bureau (PSB; 公安局; Gōng'ānjú; ☑0937 886 2071; Yangguan Zhonglu; ⊙8am-noon & 3-6.30pm Mon-Fri) Two days needed for visa extension.

ℹ️ Getting There & Away

AIR

Apart from November to March, when there are only flights to/from Lánzhōu and Xī'ān, there are regular flights to/from Běijīng (¥1880), Lánzhōu (¥1466), Shànghǎi (¥2460), Ūrümqi (¥710) and Xī'ān (¥1160).

Seats can be booked at the air ticket office in the lobby of the Yóuzhèng Bīnguǎn hotel (邮政宾馆), on Yangguan Donglu west of China Post.

BUS

Dūnhuáng's **bus station** (长途汽车站; Zhǎngtú Qìchēzhàn; ☑ 0937 885 3746; Xiyu Lu; ⊗ 7am-8pm daily) is a ten-minute walk from the mosque. Buses go to Jiāyùguān and Lánzhōu (though trains are cheaper and faster), as well as:

Golmud ¥99, nine hours, two daily (9am and 7.30pm)

Liǔyuán (柳园) ¥20, eight per day (7.30am to 6.30pm)

Ürümqi ¥198, 14 hours, one daily (7pm), sleeper. May stop in Turpan.

TRAIN

Dūnhuáng's station is 10km east of town, but for some destinations, such as Běijīng West and Ürümqi, you'll have to leave from Liǔyuán station, a crazy 180km away.

Jiāyùguān seat/hard sleeper ¥58/163, 5 hours (two per day at 9.30am and 6.58pm)

Lánzhōu hard/soft sleeper ¥246/383, 14 hours (two per day at 9.32am and 6.58pm; more trains leave from Liǔyuán Station)

Turpan (from Liǔyuán Station) hard/soft sleeper ¥164/252, eight to nine hours

Ürümqi (from Liǔyuán Station) hard/soft sleeper ¥195/302, 11 hours

For tickets to Ürümqi head to the **train booking office** (铁路售票处, Tiělù Shòupiàochù; ☑ 0937 595 9592; Yangguan Lu; ⊗ 8.30am-8pm). For Lánzhōu or Jiāyùguān, head to the **train booking office** (火车票发售点, Huǒchē Piào Fāshòu Diǎn; Tianma Jie; ⊗ 8am-noon & 1-4pm, to 8pm

summer) behind the mosque. Both charge a ¥5 commission.

ⓘ Getting Around

Dūnhuáng's airport is 13km east of town; a taxi into town costs ¥30 and takes 20 minutes. The train station is on the same road as the airport and costs a similar amount. Bus 1 runs to the train station from the stand at Mingshan Lu from 7.30am to 9pm.

If you are heading to Liǔyuán train station (for trains to Ürümqi), catch a bus or shared taxi (per person ¥45) from the front of the bus station on Sanwei Lu. Give yourself at least three hours to get to Liǔyuán station (including waiting for the taxi to fill up with other passengers).

Taxis around town start at ¥5.

You can rent bikes from travellers' cafes for ¥5 per hour. Getting to some of the outlying sights by bike is possible, but hard work at the height of summer.

Around Dūnhuáng

Most people visit the Mògāo Caves in the morning, followed by the Míngshā Shān sand dunes in the late afternoon to catch the sunset. Note that it can be above 40°C in the desert during the summer so go prepared with water, a sunhat and snacks.

⊙ Sights

Mògāo Caves

The Mògāo Caves (莫高窟; Mògāo Kū; low/high season ¥100/180; ⊗ 8.15am-6pm May-Oct, 9.15am-5.30pm Nov-Apr, tickets sold till 1hr before

---

THE WINDY ROAD TO A CLEANER CHINA

The road from Jiāyùguān to Dūnhuáng will likely impress you as much for the stark desert landscape as the endless spinning turbines. Once the cradle of China's oil industry, this windswept northern region has become the site of nearly two dozen energy farms and 5000 (and growing) individual turbines. At the industry centre in Jiǔquán (southeast of Jiāyùguān) dozens of companies are cranking out several thousand more each year.

The pace of change has been breathtaking. From 2006 to 2010, the wind industry experienced triple-digit growth and construction began on 10GW wind farms in Gānsù (1GW is the capacity of a large coal or nuclear power plant), Xīnjiāng, Inner Mongolia, Jílín and Héběi.

Rapid progress has brought hiccups. Installed capacity has far outpaced the rate at which it can be absorbed by the national electric grid. And while China became the world's largest wind farm market by 2013, it also overtook the US as the largest emitter of greenhouse gases. By 2020, coal production will add another 1000GW of capacity (which incredibly is the current total capacity of the US).

Yet the blades won't stop churning. The green light was given in 2014 to construct wind farms in Jiāngsū with a whopping 300GW total capacity! Long-term projections have wind potentially accounting for up to one-third of all capacity by 2050. With an equally strong push into solar, hydro and nuclear, China's electrical production could one day become among the cleanest in the world.

closing) are, simply put, one of the greatest repositories of Buddhist art in the world. At its peak, the site housed 18 monasteries, more than 1400 monks and nuns, and countless artists, translators and calligraphers.

Excellent English-speaking guides are available (and included in the admission price) at 9am, noon and 2pm, and you should be able to arrange tours in other languages as well.

Wealthy traders and important officials were the primary donors responsible for creating new caves, as caravans made the long detour past Mògāo to pray or give thanks for a safe journey through the treacherous wastelands to the west.

The traditional date ascribed to the founding of the first cave is AD 366. The caves fell into disuse after the collapse of the Yuan dynasty and were largely forgotten until the early 20th century, when they were 'rediscovered' by a string of foreign explorers.

Entrance to the caves is strictly controlled – it's impossible to visit them on your own. The general admission ticket grants you a two-hour tour (display great interest at the start as your guide has the discretion to make this longer) of around 10 caves, including the infamous Library Cave (cave 17) and a related exhibit containing rare fragments of manuscripts in classical Uighur and Manichean.

Of the 492 caves, 20 'open' caves are rotated fairly regularly, so recommendations are useless, but tours always include the two big Buddhas, 34.5m and 26m tall. It's also possible to visit some of the more unusual caves for ¥100 to ¥500 per cave.

Photography is strictly prohibited everywhere within the fenced-off caves area. And if it's raining or snowing or there's a sand storm, the caves will be closed.

After the tour it's well worth visiting the Dūnhuáng Research Centre, where eight more caves, each representative of a different period, have been flawlessly reproduced, along with selected murals. The 15-minute video on the paintings in cave 254 is also worth watching.

If you have a special interest in the site, check out the International Dūnhuáng Project (http://idp.bl.uk), an online database of digitised manuscripts from the Library Cave at Mògāo.

The Mògāo Caves are 25km (30 minutes) southeast from Dūnhuáng. A green minibus (one way ¥8) leaves every 30 minutes from 8am to 5pm from outside Charley Johng's Cafe (p846); buses return every 30 minutes 9am to 6pm to Shāzhōu Night Market's (p847) north end. A return taxi costs ¥100 to ¥150 for a day, or try finding a taxi willing to take you back to Dūnhuáng from the caves for ¥40.

Some people ride out to the caves on a bicycle, but be warned that half the ride is through total desert – hot work in summer.

Northern Wei, Western Wei & Northern Zhou Caves CAVE, BUDDHIST

These, the earliest of the Mògāo Caves, are distinctly Indian in style and iconography. All contain a central pillar, representing a stupa (symbolically containing the ashes of the Buddha), which the devout would circle in prayer. Paint was derived from malachite (green), cinnabar (red) and lapis lazuli (blue), expensive minerals imported from Central Asia.

The art of this period is characterised by its attempt to depict the spirituality of those who had transcended the material world through their asceticism. The Wei statues are slim, ethereal figures with finely chiselled features and comparatively large heads. The Northern Zhou figures have ghostly white eyes.

Sui Caves CAVE, BUDDHIST

The Sui dynasty (AD 581–618) was short-lived and very much a transition between the Wei and Tang periods. This can be seen in the Sui caves at Mògāo: the graceful Indian curves in the Buddha and Bodhisattva figures start to give way to the more rigid style of Chinese sculpture.

The Sui dynasty began when a general of Chinese or mixed Chinese–Tuoba origin usurped the throne of the northern Zhou dynasty and reunited northern and southern China for the first time in 360 years.

Tang Caves CAVE, BUDDHIST

The Tang dynasty (AD 618–907) was Mògāo's high point. Painting and sculpture techniques became much more refined, and some important aesthetic developments, notably the sex change (from male to female) of Guanyin and the flying *apsaras,* took place. The beautiful murals depicting the Buddhist Western Paradise offer rare insights into the court life, music, dress and architecture of Tang China.

Some 230 caves were carved during the religiously diverse Tang dynasty, including two impressive grottoes containing enor-

GĀNSÙ AROUND DŪNHUÁNG

mous, seated Buddha figures. Originally open to the elements, the statue of Maitreya in cave 96 (believed to represent Empress Wu Zetian, who used Buddhism to consolidate her power) is a towering 34.5m tall, making it the world's third-largest Buddha. The Buddhas were carved from the top down using scaffolding, the anchor holes of which are still visible.

Post-Tang Caves
CAVE, BUDDHIST

Following the Tang dynasty, the economy around Dūnhuáng went into decline, and the luxury and vigour typical of Tang painting began to be replaced by simpler drawing techniques and flatter figures. The mysterious Western Xia kingdom, which controlled most of Gānsù from 983 to 1227, made a number of additions to the caves at Mògāo and began to introduce Tibetan influences.

Singing Sands Mountain & Crescent Moon Lake

Six kilometres south of Dūnhuáng at Singing Sands Mountain (鸣沙山; Míngshā Shān; admission ¥120; ☉6am-9pm), the desert meets the oasis in most spectacular fashion. From the dunes it's easy to see how Dūnhuáng gained its moniker 'Shāzhōu' (Town of Sand). The view across the undulating desert sands and green poplar trees below is awesome.

You can bike to the dunes in 20 minutes. Minibus 3 (¥1) shuttles between Dūnhuáng and the dunes from 7.30am to 9pm, departing from Mingshan Lu. A taxi costs ¥20 one way.

The climb to the top of the dunes – the highest peak swells to 1715m – is sweaty work, but worth it. Rent a pair of bright orange shoe protectors (防沙靴; fángshāxuē; ¥10) or just shake your shoes out later.

At the base of the colossal dunes is a famous yet underwhelming pond, **Crescent Moon Lake** (Yuèyáquán). The dunes are a no-holds-barred tourist playpen, with camel rides (per person ¥80) as well as dune buggies, 'dune surfing' (sand sliding), paragliding (jumping off the dunes with a chute on your back) and even microlighting. But it's not hard to hike away to enjoy the dunes in peace.

Hostels in Dūnhuáng offer overnight camel trips to the dunes from ¥400 per person. There are also five- to eight-day expeditions out to the Jade Gate Pass, Liǔyuán and even as far as Lop Nor in the deserts of Xīnjiāng.

Yǎdān National Park & Jade Gate Pass

Yǎdān National Park
DESERT

(雅丹国家地质公园, Yǎdān Guójiā Dìzhì Gōngyuán; incl tour ¥80) The weird, eroded desert landscape of Yǎdān National Park is 180km northwest of Dūnhuáng, in the middle of the Gobi Desert's awesome nothingness. A former lake bed that eroded in spectacular fashion some 12,000 years ago, the strange rock formations provided the backdrop to the last scenes of Zhang Yimou's film *Hero*. The desert landscape is dramatic, but you can only tour the site on a group minibus, so there's little scope to explore on your own.

SILK ROAD RAIDERS

In 1900 the self-appointed guardian of the Mògāo Caves (p848), Wang Yuanlu, discovered a hidden library filled with tens of thousands of immaculately preserved manuscripts and paintings, dating as far back as AD 406.

It's hard to describe the exact magnitude of the discovery, but stuffed into the tiny room were texts in rare Central Asian languages, military reports, music scores, medical prescriptions, Confucian and Taoist classics, and Buddhist sutras copied by some of the greatest names in Chinese calligraphy – not to mention the oldest printed book in existence, the *Diamond Sutra* (AD 868). In short, it was an incalculable amount of original source material regarding Chinese, Central Asian and Buddhist history.

Word of the discovery quickly spread and Wang Yuanlu, suddenly the most popular bloke in town, was courted by rival archaeologists Auriel Stein and Paul Pelliot, among others. Following much pressure to sell the cache, Wang Yuanlu finally relented and parted with an enormous hoard of treasure. During his watch close to 20,000 of the cave's priceless manuscripts were whisked off to Europe for the paltry sum of £220.

Today, Chinese intellectuals bitter at the sacking of the caves deride Stein, Pelliot and other 'foreign devils' for making off with a national treasure. Defenders of the explorers point out that had the items been left alone they may have been lost during the ensuing civil war or the Cultural Revolution.

To get to Yǎdān you have to pass through (and buy a ticket to) the Jade Gate Pass. The best way to get here is to take one of two daily **minibus tours** (per person for 7am departure ¥76, for 2pm departure ¥86), which you can book through Charley Johng's Cafe (p846) or Dune Guesthouse (p845). Shazhouyi International Youth Hostel (p845) has similar (per person departing 12:30pm ¥85). Tour prices don't include entrance fees. The 10- to 12-hour tours include a stop at the Jade Gate Pass and the **Western Thousand Buddha Caves** (西千佛洞; Xī Qiānfó Dòng; admission ¥40; ◷7am-5.30pm), 35km west of Dūnhuáng, where there are 16 caves hidden in the cliff face of the Dǎng Hé gorge, ranging from the Northern Wèi to the Tang dynasties. Take an afternoon departure to witness a glorious desert sunset.

Jade Gate Pass   HISTORIC SITE
(玉门关; Yùmén Guān; admission ¥50) The Jade Gate Pass and the **South Pass** (阳关; Yáng Guān), 78km west of Dūnhuáng, were originally military stations, part of the Han dynasty series of beacon towers that extended to the garrison town of Lóula'n in Xīnjiāng.

Admission includes entry to a small museum (with scraps of Silk Road **silk**); a nearby section of Han-dynasty **Great Wall** (101 BC), impressive for its antiquity and lack of restoration; and the ruined city walls of **Hécāng Chéng**, 15km down a side road.

For caravans travelling westward, the Jade Gate marked the beginning of the northern route to Turpan, while the South Pass was the start of the southern route through Miran. The Jade Gate derived its name from the important traffic in Khotanese jade.

Yúlín Grottoes

Yúlín Grottoes   CAVE, BUDDHIST
(榆林窟; Yúlín Kū; ◷9am-5pm, to 6pm summer, last ticket 1hr before closing) About 180km south of Dūnhuáng, the 40-plus caves of the Yúlín Grottoes face each other across a narrow canyon. It's intriguing to observe the original carved interior tunnels that formerly connected the caves. The interior art spans a 1500-year period, from the Northern Wèi to the Qing dynasty. Many show a distinctive Tibetan influence.

The only way to get out here is to rent a minivan (¥400) for the half-day. Excellent English guides are available on-site for ¥15.

While the art at the Mògāo Caves (p848) is considered higher quality, the frescoes here are better preserved; there is little of the oxidation and thickening of painted lines so prevalent at Mògāo.

EASTERN GĀNSÙ

Most travellers speed through eastern Gānsù, catching mere glimpses from the train window as they shuttle between Lánzhōu and Xī'ān. This is a shame because the area contains some spectacular Silk Road remnants and dramatic grottoes at Màijī Shān to rival the Mògāo Caves.

Tiānshuǐ   天水

☑ 0938 / POP 450,000
Tiānshuǐ's splendid Buddhist caves at nearby Màijī Shān entice a consistent flow of visitors to this otherwise bland provincial town. Or is that two towns? Modern Tiānshuǐ is actually two very separate districts 15km apart: there is the railhead sprawl, known as Màijī Qū (麦积区; formerly *Běidào*), and the central commercial area to the west, known as Qínzhōu Qū (秦州区), where you'll arrive if coming in by bus. The two sections are lashed together by a long freeway that runs through a hilly corridor.

◎ Sights

Tiānshuǐ's main draw are the grottoes at Màijī Shān, 35km south of the train station. Within walking distance of the Tiānshuǐ Dàjiǔdiàn hotel are two temples worth checking out if you have time to kill.

Fúxī Temple   BUDDHIST TEMPLE
(伏羲庙; Fúxī Miào; off Jiefang Lu, Qínchéng; admission ¥30; ◷8am-6pm) This Ming-dynasty temple was founded in 1483 in honour of Fúxī, the father and emperor of all Chinese people. The Tiānshuǐ resident's semi-naked statue is in the main hall, along with traditional symbols such as bats, dragons and peonies. The hall ceiling's original paintings of the 64 hexagrams (varying combinations of the eight trigrams used in the *I Ching*) have uncanny similarities to computer binary language. It's worth visiting just for the 1000-year-old cypress tree in the tranquil gardens.

Yùquán Temple — TAOIST

(玉泉观, Yùquán Guàn; Renmin Xilu, Qínchéng; adult/student ¥20/10; ⏱ 8am-6pm, to 8pm summer) Ascending in layers up the hillside above Qínchéng, this Taoist temple has been a place of worship since the Tang dynasty. Most of the buildings have been restored in recent decades, but this is still a pleasant, green and rambling shrine with a number of ancient cypress trees.

🛏 Sleeping

Tiānshuǐ has plenty of accommodation options in both parts of town – Màijī Qū, the district around the railway, and Qínzhōu Qū, the central commercial area 15km to the west.

Tiānshuǐ Dàjiǔdiàn — HOTEL $

(☎ 0938 828 9999; 1 Qinzhou Dazhong Nanlu; r ¥130) This popular hotel is a solid choice in Qínzhōu Qū district. The bus to Màijī Shān is just 200m south and restaurants abound. Standard ensuite rooms are usually discounted up to 40%.

New Leaf Inn — HOTEL $

(辛叶酒店, Xīn Yè Jiǔdiàn; ☎ 0938 261 8808; Longchang Lu; 陇昌路; d & tw ¥138; ❀ @ ☎) This small business hotel has clean bright rooms with Ikea-style furnishings. The hotel is about 200m east (left as you exit) of the train station on the far side of Longchang Lu in Màijī Qū district.

✗ Eating

Tiānshuǐ is famed for its *miànpí* (面皮) noodles, which can be found everywhere. In Qínzhōu, good claypot, Sìchuān and noodle snack stalls, as well as fruit and nut sellers can be found around the Tiānshuǐ Dàjiǔdiàn hotel.

Tasty *ròujiāmó* (肉夹馍) and other fine snack food in Màijī Qū fill Erma Lu, a pedestrian mall two blocks directly south of the train station.

One place to try is **Běidào Qīngzhēn Lǎozìhào Niúròu Miànguǎn** (北道清真老字号牛肉面馆; Erma Lu; dishes ¥4-12; ⏱ 24hr). Get a ticket from the kiosk out front and collect your beef noodles (*niúròumiàn*) and flatbread (*shāobǐng*) from the kitchen window. Point to side dishes of spicy cabbage and other cold vegetables. There's no English sign, but it's nearly opposite an ICBC bank.

ℹ Information

There's a **Bank of China** (中国银行, Zhōngguó Yínháng; Longchang Lu; ⏱ 8.30am-noon & 2.30-5.30pm) with a 24-hour ATM three blocks directly south from the train station almost at the river. An **internet cafe** (网吧; wǎngbā; Longchanglu; per hr ¥2.50; ⏱ 24hr) can be found on the 2nd floor of the Wànhuì Zhāodàisuǒ guesthouse in Màijī Qū.

ℹ Getting There & Away

BUS

Buses leave from the long-distance bus station in Qínzhōu for:

Gāngǔ ¥15, 1½ hours, every 15 minutes

Huīxiàn ¥35, three hours, hourly (7.20am to 6pm)

Lánzhōu ¥74, four hours, every 20 minutes (7.20am to 7pm)

Línxià ¥99, seven hours, one daily (6.30am)

Luòmén ¥25, two hours, three daily (7am, 11am and 2.30pm)

Píngliáng ¥65, five hours, hourly (7am to 3pm)

TRAIN

Tiānshuǐ is on the Xī'ān–Lánzhōu rail line; there are dozens of daily trains in each direction.

Lánzhōu seat/hard sleeper ¥54/130, four hours

Xī'ān hard/soft seat ¥51/78, five hours

ℹ Getting Around

Taxis shuttle passengers between Qínzhōu (from both the city bus station 200m south of Tiānshuǐ Dàjiǔdiàn (p852) hotel and also from the long-distance bus station) and the train station in Màijī Qū. It costs ¥10 per person (¥45 for the whole taxi). Alternatively, take the much slower bus 1 or 6 (¥3, 40 minutes).

Around Tiānshuǐ

Màijī Shān — 麦积山

Set among wild and lush green hills southeast of Tiānshuǐ, the riveting grottoes of Màijī Shān (Haystack Mountain) hold some of China's most famous Buddhist rock carvings and externally are far more captivating than the Mògāo Caves.

◉ Sights

Màijī Shān — CAVE, BUDDHIST

(admission ¥70; ⏱ 8am-6pm) The cliff sides of Màijī Shān are riddled with niches and statues carved principally during the Northern Wei and Zhou dynasties (AD 386–581). Within the hard-to-miss Sui-dynasty trinity of Buddha and bodhisattvas is the largest statue on the mountain: the cave's central effigy of Buddha tops out at 15.7m. When the statue was restored three decades ago, a handwritten copy of the *Sutra of Golden Light* was discovered within the Buddha's fan.

Vertigo-inducing catwalks and steep spiral stairways cling to the cliff face, affording close-ups of the art. It's not certain just how the artists managed to clamber so high; one theory is that they created piles from blocks of wood reaching to the top of the mountain before moving down, gradually removing them as they descended.

A considerable amount of pigment still clings to many of the statues – a lot of which are actually made of clay rather than hewn from rock – although you frequently have to climb up steps to peer at them through tight mesh grills with little natural illumination. Much, though, is clearly visible and most of the more impressive sculptures decorate the upper walkways, especially at cave 4.

The entire undertaking is rounded off with a crescent of food stalls selling delicious spicy cold noodle dishes as well as teas and soft drinks.

An English-speaking guide charges ¥70 for the day. It's possible to view normally closed caves (such as cave 133) for an extra fee of ¥500 per group.

The admission ticket includes entry to **Ruiying Monastery** (瑞应寺; Ruìyìng Sì), at the base of the mountain, which acts as a small museum of selected statues. Across from the monastery is the start of a trail to a **botanic garden** (*zhíwùyuán;* admission free with ticket), which allows for a shortcut back to the entrance gate through the forest.

You can also climb **Xiāngjí Shān** (香积山). For the trailhead, head back towards the food stall area you passed on the way in and look for a sign down a side road to the left.

🛏 Sleeping

There are several places where you can spend the night, including cabins within the botanic gardens at the **Hotel Arboretum** (植物园山庄, Zhíwùyuán Shānzhuāng; ☑0938 223 1025; zwyszhotel@126.com; Màijī Arboretum; cabins ¥386). There are also simple **guesthouses** (¥40 to ¥50) in the village about 1km before the entrance gate. Just wander in and your intentions will be clear.

ℹ Getting There & Away

Green bus 34 (¥5, 40 minutes) leaves every 15 minutes from in front of the train station in Tiānshuǐ. The first bus leaves at 6.30am and the last returns around 6pm. The bus may drop you at the crossroads, 5km before the site, from where a taxi van will cost ¥5 per seat to the ticket office.

Bus 5 leaves from the bus terminal just south of Tiānshuǐ Dàjiǔdiàn (p852) in Tiānshuǐ at 8.30am and returns at 2.30pm. Taxis wait for passengers (per person ¥30) at the same location most of the morning.

From the ticket office at Màijī Shān you can either walk the last 2km to 3km to the caves or take the **tour buggy** (关关车; guānguān chē).

Píngliáng 平凉

☑ 0933 / POP 106,800

A booming Chinese mid-sized town, Píngliáng is a logical base for visits to the nearby holy mountain of Kōngtóng Shān. The train station is in the northeastern part of town and the main bus station in the far western part. Xi Dajie is the main street in town and where you'll find hotels, restaurants and banks.

◎ Sights

Kōngtóng Shān
TAOIST TEMPLE
(崆峒山; admission ¥120; ⊙7am-5pm) Kōngtóng Shān, 11km west of Píngliáng, is one of the 12 principal peaks in the Taoist universe. It was first mentioned by the philosopher Zhuangzi (399–295 BC), and illustrious visitors have included none other than the Yellow Emperor. Numerous paths lead over the hilltop past dozens of picturesque (though entirely restored) temples to the summit at over 2100m. While the mountain is an enchanting place to hike, those looking for genuine historical artefacts or ambience will be disappointed.

From the north gate visitor centre (pick up a free map here to orientate yourself) catch a bus to Zhōngtái (¥32) or Xiàngshān (¥48), both essentially small visitor areas on the mountain with paths radiating out to lookouts and temples.

A taxi from Píngliáng will cost ¥30, or you can catch bus 16 (¥1) on Xi Dajie and then transfer to bus 13 (¥2) when you reach Kongtong Dadao. Bus 13 drops you off right in front of the main visitor centre before continuing on to the East Gate. At the end of your visit you can walk down from Zhōngtái to the East Gate and catch bus 13 back to town.

🛌 Sleeping & Eating

Just around the corner from the Hóngyùn Bīnguǎn hotel, look for the Sìzhōng Alley market (Sìzhōng Xiàng shìchǎng). There are numerous restaurants here, and more food stalls serving noodles, spicy hotpot and barbecued meats, as well as fresh fruit.

Hóngyùn Bīnguǎn   HOTEL $

(鸿运宾馆; ☑ 0933 822 6399; 128 Xi Dajie; 西大街128号; d/tw without bathroom ¥128/158, tw ¥188; ❄ @) The hotel has a friendly guesthouse atmosphere and surprisingly pleasant rooms reached by a very narrow staircase. All rooms have computers and broadband internet, and there are discounts of up to 30%.

Píngliáng Bīnguǎn   HOTEL $$$

(平凉宾馆; ☑ 0933 821 9485; 86 Xi Dajie; 西大街86号; tw ¥588; ❄ @) The top hotel in town is just off the main road in a large complex. Expect discounts up to 40%.

ℹ Getting There & Away

BUS

The following services depart from Píngliáng's main bus station, in the western part of town on Lai Yuan Lu:

Gùyuán ¥24, 1½ hours, frequent

Lánzhōu ¥105, five hours, hourly (6.30am to 5.30pm)

Tiānshuǐ ¥65, seven hours, one daily (9am)

Xī'ān ¥88, six hours, every 40 minutes (6.20am to 6pm)

For Tiānshuǐ there are more frequent departures from the east bus station (qìchē dōngzhàn).

TRAIN

It's better to take a bus to Xī'ān as trains either leave or arrive at very inconvenient hours. There's one sleeper train daily to Lánzhōu (hard/soft sleeper ¥99/155, 11 hours) leaving at 9.37pm.

Bus 1 (¥2) runs from the train station to Xi Dajie. A taxi costs ¥10. From Xi Dajie to the bus station costs ¥4 or take bus 16 (¥1).

Níngxià

POP 6.4 MILLION

Best Historic Sites

➡ Western Xia Tombs (p860)

➡ Hèlán Mountain rock carvings (p860)

➡ Xūmí Shān (p864)

➡ Shuǐ Dòng Gōu (p861)

Best Temples

➡ Qīngzhēn Dà Sì (p864)

➡ Gāo Temple (p862)

➡ Guǎngzōng Sì (p862)

➡ Yánfú Sì (p861)

Why Go?

With its raw landscape of dusty plains and stark mountains, sliced in two by the Yellow River (Huáng Hé), there is a distinct *Grapes of Wrath* feel to Níngxià (宁夏). Outside the cities, it's a timeless landscape where farmers till the yellow earth just like their ancestors did.

Yet Níngxià was once the frontline between the empires of the Mongols and the Han Chinese and there is a host of historic sites here, ranging from little-seen Buddhist statues to the royal tombs of long-past dynasties, as well as ancient rock carvings that predate any emperor. And as the homeland of the Muslim Hui ethnic minority, Níngxià is culturally unique, too.

Then there's the chance to camp out under the desert sky, or float down the Yellow River on a traditional raft. But best of all, Níngxià sees few foreign visitors so it seems like you have the place all to yourself.

When to Go
Yínchuān

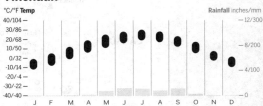

Jun Warm, dry nights will give you a thirst for some local nightlife and Níngxià wine.

Oct It's cooling down and time to play Lawrence of Arabia in the little-visited Tengger Desert.

Nov The Yellow River festival in Yínchuān features concerts and folk dancing.

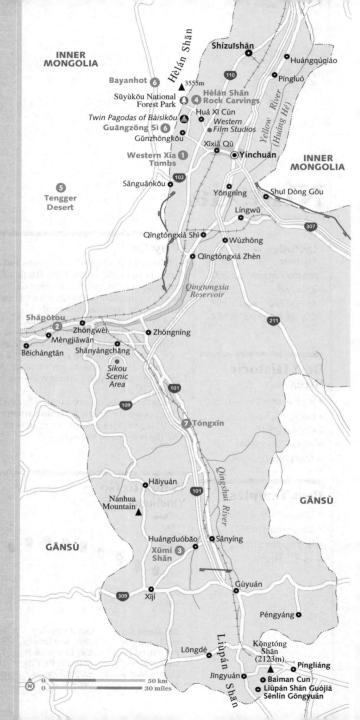

Níngxià Highlights

1 Visit the imperial **Western Xia Tombs** (p860) outside Yínchuān, a rare reminder of this long-extinct culture

2 Raft down the Yellow River or slide down the sand dunes at desert playground **Shāpōtóu** (p863)

3 Explore the little-seen Buddhist grottoes with hundreds of statues at **Xūmí Shān** (p864)

4 Check out the utterly unique rock carvings at **Hèlán Shān** (p860), which date back thousands of years

5 Hop on a camel and trek into the **Tengger Desert** (p864) for an overnight stay

6 Investigate Mongol culture at lonely sites around **Bayanhot** (p861), **Guǎngzōng Sì** (p862) and **Yánfú Sì** (p861)

7 Get way off the beaten track at Tóngxīn's marvellous Ming-era **Great Mosque** (p864)

History

Níngxià had been on the periphery of Chinese empires ever since the Qín dynasty, but it took centre stage in the 10th century AD when the Tangut people declared the establishment of the Xixia (Western Xia) empire in the face of Song opposition. The empire was composed of modern-day Gānsù, Níngxià, Shaanxi and western Inner Mongolia, but it soon collapsed in the face of Mongol might.

The Mongol retreat in the 14th century left a void that was filled by both Muslim traders from the west and Chinese farmers from the east. Tensions between the two resulted in Níngxià being caught up in the great Muslim Rebellion that convulsed northwest China in the mid-19th century.

Once part of Gānsù, Níngxià is China's smallest province, although technically it is an autonomous region for the Muslim Hui ethnic minority, who make up one-third of the population, rather than an official province. It remains one of the poorest areas of China, with a sharp economic divide between the more fertile, Han Chinese–dominated north and the parched, sparsely populated south.

Climate

Part of the Loess Plateau, Níngxià is composed primarily of arid mountain ranges and highlands. Summer temperatures soar during the day, and precipitation is generally no more than a fond memory. Winters are long and often freezing; spring is lovely, though blustery.

Language

Níngxià's dialect is grouped together with the northwestern dialects of Gānsù and Qīnghǎi, an umbrella group known to linguists as Lanyin Mandarin.

❶ Getting There & Around

Níngxià's capital, Yínchuān, is the only viable flight hub, but Níngxià is so small you can drive across it in a few hours. Buses go everywhere, sometimes slowly; trains connect major cities.

Yínchuān 银川

☑ 0951 / POP 750,000

In the sun-parched land that is Níngxià, Yínchuān has managed to thrive. The Tangut founders chose this spot wisely as their capital, planting the city between a source of water (the Yellow River) and a natural barrier from the Gobi Desert (the Hèlán Shān mountains).

Modern-day Yínchuān is predominantly Han, although its many mosques reveal its status as the capital of the Hui peoples' homeland. But the most interesting sights, the Western Xia Tombs and Hèlán Shān to the west of the city, predate both the Han and the Hui. Yínchuān is also a handy jumping-off point for longer trips to western Inner Mongolia.

◉ Sights

Yínchuān is divided into three parts. Xīxià Qū (西夏区, New City), the new industrialised section, is on the western outskirts. Jīnfèng Qū (金凤区) is the central district (the train station is on Jīnfèng's western edge). Xìngqìng Qū (兴庆区, Old City) is 12km east of the train station and has most of the town's sights and hotels.

Níngxià Museum MUSEUM
(宁夏博物馆, Níngxià Bówùguǎn; Renmin Guangchang; ⊙9am-5pm Tue-Sun) FREE Located halfway between the new and old cities, this cavernous, well-mounted museum contains an extensive collection of rock art, Silk Road–era pottery and ancient Korans as well as the requisite hall of communist propaganda and Mao fun facts. It's a good starting point if you want to learn something of Hui culture. Bus 102 from the southern bus terminal (南门汽车站, nánmén qìchēzhàn) passes nearby.

Chéngtiānsì Tǎ PAGODA
(承天寺塔; Jinning Nanjie; admission ¥18; ⊙9am-5pm, to 5.30pm summer) The most impressive site in Xìngqìng Qū – climb the 13 storeys of steep, narrow stairs for 360-degree views of Yínchuān. The pagoda is also known as Xī

PRICE INDICATORS

The following price indicators are used in this chapter:

Sleeping

$ less than ¥250

$$ ¥250 to ¥400

$$$ more than ¥400

Eating

$ less than ¥30

$$ ¥30 to ¥50

$$$ more than ¥50

Yínchuān

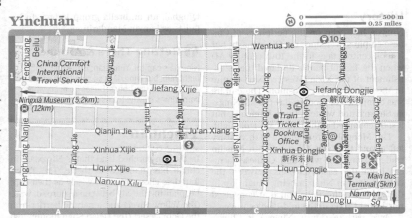

Yínchuān

Tǎ (西塔, West Pagoda) and dates back almost 1000 years to the Western Xià dynasty, though it has been rebuilt several times since.

🛏 Sleeping

There's no shortage of places to stay in Xìngqìng Qū, but the accommodation is a mostly uninspired mix of chain hotels and overpriced, old-school two- and three-star joints. The only hostel in Yínchuān is in the industrial Xīxià Qū. But if you're willing to splash out, then the quality of hotels improves dramatically.

7 Days Inn Gǔlóu BUSINESS HOTEL **$**
(7天连锁酒店鼓楼, 7 Tiān Liánsuǒ Jiǔdiàn Gǔlóu; ☑0951 561 2999; 74 Gulou Nanjie, 鼓楼南街74号; d ¥188; ➠✱@⏾) Its name may sound like a convenience store, and while there is

a franchise feel to the shrink-wrapped towels, flat-screens and Ikea-esque beds in this hotel's compact, bright rooms, the cleanliness, friendly staff and convenient position near the **Drum Tower** (银川鼓楼; Yínchuān Gǔlóu; Jiefang Dongjie; 解放东街) make this a comfortable modern choice. Follow the blue '7' logos down a passageway off the plaza of Gulou Nanjie.

Hanting Express HOTEL **$$**
(汉庭酒店玉皇阁南街店, Hàntíng Jiǔdiàn Yù huánggé Nánjiēdiàn; ☑0951 765 3888; 192 Liqun Dongjie, 利群东街192号; d/tw incl breakfast ¥210/259; ✱⏾) Modern means leatherette bathroom walls, it seems, but this clean chain hotel also made the compact rooms feel spacious and bright. Light(less) sleepers can nab windowless chambers at a 15% discount.

Níngfēng Bīnguǎn HOTEL **$$$**
(宁丰宾馆; ☑609 0222; www.ningfenghotel.com; 6 Jiefang Dongjie, 解放东街6号; d & tw ¥688, discounts of 20%; ✱@⏾) A solid choice which is as comfortable as many more expensive hotels in Yínchuān and better located. Rooms are big and well organised, and the bathrooms are nice and up to date. There's a Chinese restaurant on-site and a few of the helpful staff can speak some English. Call ahead as reception are sometimes reluctant to take foreigners.

🍴 Eating & Drinking

Like the rest of northwest China, noodles are a staple here. Every restaurant serves them and in many places in Níngxià they will be all you can find to eat.

★ Xiānhè Lóu CHINESE $

(仙鹤楼; 204 Xinhua Dongjie; dishes from ¥12; ⊙ 24hr) You can't go wrong at this landmark restaurant which never closes and caters for both big spenders and those on a budget. You could splash out on the pricey fish dishes or the great *kǎoyángpái* (烤羊排; barbecued ribs) from the picture menu, but you can also get a huge plate of beef noodles for ¥12.

The production line of *shuǐjiǎo* (boiled ravioli-style dumplings), a house speciality, is on display. A half *jīn* (Chinese weight, about 600g; ¥30) is normally enough for two people. There are another two branches around the corner on **Zhongshan Nanjie** (仙鹤楼; 118 Zhongshan Nanjie; dishes ¥12-22), the smallest shutting at 9.30pm.

Dà Mǎ Jiǎozi Guǎn DUMPLINGS $

(大妈饺子馆; 32 Jiefang Dongjie; dumplings from ¥15; ⊙ 11am-10.30pm) Popular joint dedicated to Chinese dumplings. They come by the *jīn,* but you can order a half or quarter *jīn,* and there are all sorts of beef, prawn and vegie options. There are plenty of cold dishes, soups and meat and fish dishes available, too, as well as the inevitable noodle choices. Picture menu.

Bái Gōng DIM SUM $$

(白宫; 82 Yuhuange Nanjie, 玉皇阁南街82号; dim sum from ¥15; ⊙ 24hr) Waiters here push around carts piled with all forms of delicious steamed dumplings and buns to point to, as well as more esoteric nibbles such as spicy chicken feet. The carts offer good variety for solo travellers, but as usual with dim sum, you'll find yourself ordering a few to satisfy your appetite. Look for two massive crayfish on the wall outside.

Liángyuán Jiǔbā BAR

(银川缘酒吧; ☑ 138 9517 1102; 127 Wenhua Dongjie, 文化东街127号; bottle of wine ¥98-220; ⊙ 6pm-late) Try Níngxià's distinctively light, herbaceous wine *pútaojiǔ* with live jazz or Tibetan music at this bar, a five-minute walk north of the Drum Tower.

ℹ Information

Bank of China (中国银行, Zhōngguó Yínháng; 170 Jiefang Xijie; ⊙ 8am-noon & 2.30-6pm) You can change travellers cheques and use the 24-hour ATM at this main branch. Other branches change cash only.

China Comfort International Travel Service (CCT, 康辉旅游, Kāng Huī Lǚyóu; ☑ 504 5678; www.chinasilkroadtour.com; 317 Jiefang Xijie; ⊙ 8.30am-noon & 2.30-6pm Mon-Fri) Organ-

ises desert trips, rafting and permits for Éjìnà Qí (Inner Mongolia). It's located 2km west along a road running from the Drum Tower to just before the Fenghuangjie intersection.

China Post (中国邮政, Zhōngguó Yóuzhèng; cnr Jiefang Xijie & Minzu Beijie; ⊙ 9am-5pm Mon-Fri)

Internet Cafe (网吧, wǎngbā; Chaoyang Xiang; per hr ¥2-3; ⊙ 24hr) On the left-hand side of the road as you walk south from Jiefang Dongjie and on the 2nd floor. A big sign outside says 'Internet Cafe Animation.'

Public Security Bureau (PSB, 公安局, Gōng'ānjú; 472 Beijing Donglu; ⊙ 8.30am-noon & 2.30-6.30pm Mon-Fri) For visa extensions. It's on a busy intersection near a hospital, park and schools. Take bus 3 from the Drum Tower.

ℹ Getting There & Away

AIR

Yínchuān Hedong International Airport (银川河东国际机场, Yínchuān Hédōng Guójì Jīchǎng) is located by the Yellow River, 24km southeast of the Drum Tower and Xìngqìng Qū. Flights connect Yínchuān with Běijīng (¥1090), Chéngdū (¥1110), Guǎngzhōu (¥1320), Shànghǎi (¥900), Ürümqi (¥1080) and Xī'ān (¥360). Buy tickets at www.ctrip.com or www.elong.net.

BUS

The main, **southern bus terminal** (南门汽车站, nánmén qìchēzhàn) is 5km south of Nanmen Sq on the road to Zhōngwèi.

Departures from the southern bus terminal run frequently to Bayanhot, Gùyuán and Zhōngwèi as well as:

Lánzhōu ¥140, six hours, two daily (7.20am and 3.40pm)

Xī'ān ¥181, eight to 10 hours, five daily (8.30am to 6.30pm)

Yán'ān ¥136, eight to nine hours, five daily (8am to 5.30pm)

If you're heading north to Inner Mongolia, you need the **northern (tourism) bus station** (北门车站, běimén chēzhàn), in an area full of hostels and cheap restaurants. Bus 316 (¥1) trundles between it and the main bus station.

From the southern terminal the express buses (*kuàikè*) to Zhōngwèi and Gùyuán are quicker than local buses that stop at every village on the way.

TRAIN

Yínchuān is on the Lánzhōu–Běijīng railway line, which runs via Hohhot (11 hours) and Dàtóng (13½ hours) before reaching Běijīng (21 hours). If you're heading for Lánzhōu (hard/soft sleeper ¥131/195, eight hours), the handy overnight K915 train leaves at 10.40pm. For Xī'ān, try train 2653 (hard/soft sleeper ¥195/302, 15½ hours) leaving at 5.06pm.

THE HUI

The Hui (回族) are perhaps China's most unusual ethnic minority; they are the only people to be designated as one solely because of their religious beliefs. The Hui don't have their own language, speaking only Mandarin, and are scattered throughout every province of the country with nearly 80% of the 10 million–odd Hui living outside their official homeland.

Their origins date back more than 1000 years to the time of the Silk Road, when trade thrived between China and the Middle East and Central Asia. Arab traders intermarried with the local women and now most Hui are ethnically indistinguishable from the Han Chinese. What marks them out is their adherence to Islam.

Most Hui men wear white skullcaps, while many women don headscarves. The more educated can read and speak Arabic, a result of studying the Koran in its original language. For many young Hui, learning Arabic is the path to a coveted job as a translator for the Chinese companies on the east coast doing business in the Middle East.

Although the Hui can be found all over China, they are most numerous in the northwest provinces of Gānsù, Níngxià and Shaanxi.

The train station is in Xīxià Qū, about 12km west of the Xìngqìng Qū centre. Book sleeper tickets well in advance. There's a **train ticket booking office** (代售火车票, dàishòu huǒchēpiào; 15 Gongnong Xiang, 工农巷15号; ⊘9am-noon & 2-5pm) near the Bell Tower.

❶ Getting Around

The airport is 25km from the Xìngqìng Qū (Old City) centre; buses (¥20, 30 minutes, hourly, 6am to 6pm) leave to/from in front of the Civil Aviation Administration of China office on Changcheng Donglu, just south of Nanmen Sq. A taxi to/from the airport costs around ¥60.

Between 6am and 11.30pm bus 1 (¥1) runs from the southern bus terminal (from the bus shelter in the middle of the road) to Nanmen Sq (10 minutes) in Xingqìng Qū, along Jiefang Jie and then on to the train station in Xīxià Qū (40 to 50 minutes). Taxis cost ¥7 for the first 3km. A taxi between the train station and Xìngqìng Qū costs ¥20 to ¥30.

Around Yínchuān

Western Xia Tombs 西夏王陵

The **Western Xia Tombs** (Xīxià Wánglíng; admission ¥60; ⊘8am-5.30pm, to 6pm summer), which look like giant beehives, are Níngxià's most famous sight. The first tombs were built a millennium ago by Li Yuanhao, the founder of the Western Xia dynasty. There are nine imperial tombs, plus 200 lesser tombs, in an area of 50 sq km – there are electric carts if you're not up for walking. The one you'll see is Li Yuanhao's, a 23m-tall tomb originally constructed as an octagonal seven-storey wooden pagoda. All that

remains is the large earthen core. Permits, usually organised through local tour operators, are required to visit other tombs in the area.

The examples of Buddhist art in the good site museum (⊘8am-5.30pm) offer a rare glimpse into the ephemeral Western Xia culture, and point to clear artistic influences from neighbouring Tibet and Central Asia. There are also many fascinating artefacts excavated from Li Yuanhao's tomb.

The tombs are 33km west of Yínchuān. A return taxi costs around ¥150 (including waiting time). From the South Gate, you could take bus 2 to its terminus in Xīxià Qū and then take a cheaper taxi (¥25 each way) from there. Yínchuān's southern bus terminal has a bus (¥8, 20 minutes, every two hours) to the tombs. The site is also on the road towards Bayanhot, if you are headed that way.

Hèlán Shān 贺兰山

The rugged Hèlán mountains have long proved an effective barrier against both nomadic invaders and the harsh Gobi winds. They were the preferred burial site for Xixia monarchs, and the foothills are today peppered with graves and honorific temples.

❍ Sights

Rock Carvings ARCHAEOLOGICAL SITE
(贺兰山岩画, Hèlánshān Yánhuà; admission ¥70; ⊘8am-6.30pm) By far the most significant sight in Hèlán Shān are the ancient rock carvings, thought to date back 10,000 years. There are more than 2000 pictographs depicting animals, hunting scenes and faces,

including one (so local guides like to claim) of an alien, and they are the last remnants of the early nomadic tribes who lived in the steppes north of China.

The ticket price includes entry to the world's only **museum** dedicated to ancient rock art and a ride in a golf cart to the valley containing the rock carvings. Don't miss the image of the Rastafarian-like sun god (climb the steps up the hill on the far side of the valley).

Twin Pagodas of Bàisìkǒu   PAGODA
(拜寺口双塔, Bàisìkǒu Shuāngtǎ; admission ¥40; ⏰8am-6pm) About 10km west of the Hèlán Shān rock carvings are these pagodas. You can't climb them, but they're an impressive sight against the backdrop of the barren mountains: 13 and 14 storeys high and decorated with intricate animal faces and Buddha statuettes.

Sūyùkǒu National Forest Park   PARK
(苏峪口国家森林公园, Sūyùkǒu Guójiā Sēnlín Gōngyuán; admission ¥60; ⏰7am-5pm) This park is a good place to start exploring the Hèlán mountains. You can hike up the trails from the car park or take the cable car (up/down ¥50/30) straight up to cool pine-covered hills.

Western Film Studios   FILM LOCATION
(镇北堡西部影城, Zhènběibǎo Xībù Yǐngchéng; admission ¥80; ⏰8am-6pm) This film studio is where the famed Chinese movie *Red Sorghum* was shot, as well as countless other films and TV shows. Hugely popular with Chinese tour groups, who swarm all over it in the summer, it's fun to explore the fake fortress and recreations of old Ming and Qing streets. To get here, take bus 17 (¥5) from the Yínchuān train station.

🛈 Getting There & Away

The only way to get around the Hèlán Shān sites is by taxi. The cheapest way to do it is to take bus 17 from the Yínchuān train station to the Western Film Studios (¥5) and then hire a taxi (¥100) from there. Alternatively, you can hire a minibus from the train station for ¥200 return to do the loop of the sights. You could combine that with a visit to the Western Xia Tombs for around ¥300.

Shuǐ Dòng Gōu   水洞沟

The archaeological site of **Shuǐ Dòng Gōu**, 25km east of Yínchuān, right on the border with Inner Mongolia, has been turned into something of an adventure theme park. The site is divided into two parts; the first is a **museum** that resembles Jabba the Hut's bunker and which contains the Palaeolithic-era relics first uncovered here in 1923.

From there, it's a golf cart ride to an unrestored section of the Great Wall dating back to the Ming dynasty. Then it's a walk, boat trip, donkey- and camel-cart ride to a **fortress** with an elaborate network of underground tunnels once used by Chinese soldiers defending the Wall. The renovated tunnels include trap doors, false passages and booby traps.

The catch is that the admission price to Shuǐ Dòng Gōu only lets you into the site itself. Everything else – the museum, fort and all transport – costs extra, making this an expensive day out. Unless you fancy an 8km walk around the complex, the cheapest way to do it is to buy the through ticket (通票, *tōngpiào*) for ¥130. Standard admission costs ¥60.

Buses from Yínchuān's southern bus terminal, starting at 8.20am, run past Shuǐ Dòng Gōu (¥10, 40 minutes, five daily). To return, wait by the highway and flag down any passing Yínchuān-bound bus.

Bayanhot   阿拉善左旗

Bayanhot (known to the Chinese as Ālāshàn Zuǒqí) is not actually in Níngxià; it's across the border in Inner Mongolia. But the most convenient way to access Bayanhot is from Yínchuān, and a visit here is a good introduction to both Mongol culture and the vast deserts and high blue skies of far western Inner Mongolia.

The original Mongol town was centred on the small 18th-century temple **Yánfú Sì** (延福寺; admission ¥5; ⏰8am-noon & 3-6pm). Completed in 1742, it once housed 200 lamas; around 30 are resident here now.

Next door is the local museum **Ālāshàn Bówùguǎn** (阿拉善博物馆; admission ¥40; ⏰9am-5.30pm), the former home of the local prince, the Alashan Qin Wang. A well-restored, Qing-era complex of buildings and courtyards, there are photos of the last prince (1903–68) and his family, plus some of their personal effects.

Bayanhot means 'Rich City' in Mongolian and there's a thriving jade trade here. Numerous shops deal in it and there's a small market in front of the museum. Bargain hard if you're in a buying mood.

Frequent buses depart from Yínchuān's southern bus terminal for Bayanhot (¥30, two to three hours) between 8am and 6pm (stopping off at the Western Xia Tombs). If you want to travel further west into Inner Mongolia from Bayanhot there are two buses a day to Éjìnà Qí (¥104, eight hours) at 8am and 8.20am. One daily bus goes to Ālàshàn Yòuqí (¥121, six hours) at 7.10am. Note: you need a permit to travel to Éjìnà Qí, which can be arranged by travel agents in Yínchuān.

Around Bayanhot

Guǎngzōng Sì
MONASTERY

(广宗寺; admission ¥80; ⊙8am-6pm) Once one of the most magnificent monasteries in Inner Mongolia, Guǎngzōng Sì has a stunning setting in the mountains 38km south of Bayanhot. At its height, some 2000 monks lived here. So important was the monastery that the main prayer hall, Gandan Danjaling Sum, contains the remains of the sixth Dalai Lama inside the golden stupa that dominates it.

Tragically, the monastery was demolished during the Cultural Revolution; a 1957 photo in the main prayer hall gives you an idea of how big it once was. The temples have since been rebuilt, but in the last couple of years a hotel, yurt restaurants and a supremely tacky shopping street have been added to the complex to entice domestic tour groups here.

There are good walking trails in the mountains behind the complex; take the path to the right of the main temple and follow it for one hour to a grassy plateau with fantastic views.

From Bayanhot, a taxi to the monastery and then back to the highway (where you can flag down any Yínchuān-bound bus) is ¥120. On your way back to Yínchuān, look out for the crumbling, yet still mighty, remains of the Great Wall at **Sānguānkǒu** (三关口). Some sections are up to 10m high and 3m wide.

Zhōngwèi 中卫

☑ 0955 / POP 1 MILLION

With its wide streets and relaxed feel, Zhōngwèi easily wins the prize for Níngxià's best-looking and friendliest city. It's an ideal base for a trip up the Yellow River or further afield into the Tengger Desert.

◉ Sights

Gāo Temple
TEMPLE

(高庙, Gāo Miào; Gulou Beijie; admission ¥30; ⊙7.30am-7pm) One of the more extraordinary temples you'll find in China, this eclectic shrine has at various times catered to the needs of Buddhism, Confucianism and Taoism. It's still a funky mishmash of architectural styles, but the revitalised Buddhist deities have muscled out the original Taoists and Confucians.

The real oddity here is the former **bomb shelter**, built beneath the temple during the Cultural Revolution, which has been converted into a Buddhist hell-haunted house. The eerie, dimly lit tunnels contain numerous scenes of the damned having their tongues cut out, being sawed in half or stoked in the fires of hell, while their screams echo all around. Great stuff.

🛏 Sleeping

A number of hotels in Zhōngwèi won't accept foreigners; those listed here do.

★ North by Northwest Hostel
HOSTEL $

(西北偏北青年旅舍, Xīběi Piānběi Qīngniánlǚshè; ☑ 0955 763 5060; 453190353@qq.com; 87 Xinglong Beijie, 兴隆北街87号; dm ¥40-50, d/tr ¥150/180; ❄ 🛜) It may be Zhōngwèi's only hostel but budget travellers are spoiled with some of the softest beds in Níngxià in spacious clean rooms. The murals, mosaic-like washbasins and homemade Zhōngwèi postcards amp up the art-school vibe. The jovial young staff are extremely helpful, have a go with English and offer Shāpōtóu and desert tours.

Zhōnghuī Shāngwù Bīnguǎn
HOTEL $

(中辉商务宾馆; ☑ 701 0808; 61 Changcheng Dongjie, 长城东街61号; d & tw ¥98-148; ❄ @) The rooms have seen some wear and tear and could be cleaner, but the price is great, the staff amenable and the location very convenient. The more expensive rooms come with computers.

Zhōngwèi Dàjiǔdiàn
HOTEL $$

(中卫大酒店; ☑ 702 5555; 66 Gulou Beijie, 鼓楼北街66号; d & tw ¥368; ❄ @) Big, surprisingly comfortable rooms with decent-sized beds and modern showers are on offer here. Discounts available outside peak season.

🍴 Eating & Drinking

On summer nights, with the lit-up **Drum Tower** (中卫鼓楼; Zhōngwèi Gǔlóu) acting as a beacon, locals eat and drink alfresco at numerous locations around the centre of town.

Zhōngwèi Night Market
MARKET $

(中卫夜市, Zhōngwèi Yèshì; off Xinglong Nanjie; dishes ¥7-20) A Dante's Inferno of flaming woks and grills, the night market is made up of countless stalls in the alleys running left off Xinglong Nanjie (which is lined with Chinese-style bars). There are tonnes of cheap eats. Two favourites to check out are *ròujiāmó* (肉夹馍; fried pork or beef stuffed in bread, sometimes with green peppers and cumin) and *shāguō* (砂锅; mini hotpot).

Hóng Yùn Lái Hàn Cāntīng   CHINESE **$**
(鸿运来汉餐厅; 52 Changcheng Xijie; dishes from ¥13; ⊙9am-9.30pm) Solid restaurant serving up northern Chinese classics as well as solo-diner friendly claypots of *bāozǎifàn* (煲仔饭; meat/veg with spicy peppers on rice). Large picture menu.

ⓘ Information

Bank of China (中国银行, Zhōngguó Yínháng; cnr Gulou Beijie & Gulou Dongjie; ⊙9am-5pm) One of many around town.

China Post (中国邮政, Zhōngguó Yóuzhèng; Gulou Xijie)

Internet Cafe (网吧, wǎngbā; 121 Changcheng Dongjie; per hr ¥2.50; ⊙9am-1am) Dark and smoky and filled with gamers.

Níngxià Desert Travel Service (宁夏沙漠旅行社, Níngxià Shāmò Lǚxíngshè; ☑702 7776, 186 0955 9777; www.nxdesert.com) Professional outfit for camel and rafting trips. A five-night desert camping trip starts at ¥1480. Contact the English-speaking manager, Billy.

Public Security Bureau (PSB, 公安局, Gōng'ānjú; ☑706 0597; Silou Dong Nanjie; ⊙8.30am-noon & 2.30-5pm) For visa extensions you have to go to Yínchuān. About 4km south of the Drum Tower (p862).

ⓘ Getting There & Away

BUS

The **long-distance bus station** (长途汽车站, chángtú qìchēzhàn) is 2.5km east of the Drum Tower, along Gulou Dongjie. Take bus 1 or a taxi (¥7, 10 minutes). Destinations include the following:

Gùyuán ¥70, four hours, two daily (10am and 2.30pm); express bus (快车, kuàichē)

Tóngxīn ¥26, 2½ hours, five daily (from 9am)

Yínchuān ¥53, 2½ hours, half-hourly (6.30am to 6pm); express bus

Buses to Xī'ān (¥180, eight hours, 6pm) run every other day from in front of the train station. There's also a night bus to Lánzhōu (¥80, four hours, one daily), which departs from the Drum Tower at 10pm.

TRAIN

You can reach Yínchuān in 2½ hours (¥25), though you'll be dropped off closer to the city

centre in Yínchuān if you take the bus. It's 5½ hours to Lánzhōu (hard seat/hard sleeper ¥45/89) and 12½ hours to Xī'ān (hard/soft sleeper ¥156/245). For Gùyuán (¥33, 3½ hours) take the Xī'ān train.

Around Zhōngwèi

Shāpótóu   沙坡头

The desert playground of **Shāpótóu** (沙坡头; admission ¥100; ⊙7.30am-6.30pm), 17km west of Zhōngwèi, lies on the fringes of the Tengger Desert at the dramatic convergence of sand dunes, the Yellow River and lush farmlands. It's based around the Shāpótóu Desert Research Centre, which was founded in 1956 to battle the ever-worsening problem of desertification in China's northwest.

These days, though, Shāpótóu is almost an amusement park. You can zipline (¥80)

Zhōngwèi

◉ **Sights**
1 Gāo Temple	A1
2 Zhōngwèi Drum Tower	B2

🛏 **Sleeping**
3 North by Northwest Hostel	A1
4 Zhōnghuī Shāngwù Bīnguǎn	B1
5 Zhōngwèi Dàjiǔdiàn	B1

✕ **Eating**
6 Hóng Yùn Lái Hàn Cāntīng	A1
7 Zhōngwèi Night Market	A2

🍷 **Drinking & Nightlife**
Rhent Bar	(see 3)

TÓNGXĪN

South of Zhōngwèi, the Han Chinese–dominated cities of northern Níngxià give way to the Hui heartland. Journeying here takes you deep into rural Níngxià, through villages of mud-brick houses where the minarets of the numerous mosques tower over endless cornfields.

Of all the mosques in Níngxià, the most hallowed is **Qīngzhēn Dà Sì** (清真大寺, Great Mosque; admission ¥15) in Tóngxīn (同心). Dating back to the 14th century (although the present mosque was built in 1573 and then renovated in 1791), it was the only one of Níngxià's 1000-odd mosques to avoid the ravages of the Cultural Revolution. As such, it's a near-perfect example of Ming- and Qing-era temple architecture. Not until you get up close and notice the crescents that top the pagoda roofs does it become apparent that it's a mosque.

Unsurprisingly, Tóngxīn has a very strong Muslim feel. There are always students in residence at the mosque training to be imams and they will greet you with a *salaam alaikum* and show you around. Tóngxīn is also one of the few places in China outside of southern Xīnjiāng where you'll see women in veils and covered from head to toe in black.

Qīngzhēn Dà Sì is on the south side of town, a ¥5 taxi ride from the bus station on Jingping Jie. There are frequent express buses between Tóngxīn and Yínchuān (¥52, three hours), making a long day trip possible. The last bus back to Yínchuān leaves at 4pm. You could also visit from Zhōngwèi (¥26, 2½ hours), or stop for a couple of hours if you are heading further south to Gùyuán (¥26, two hours). If you get stuck here, try the **Huí Chūn Bīnguǎn** (回春宾馆; ☑0953-803 1888; d¥138; 寒) opposite the bus station.

or hang-glide (¥100) on a wire across the Yellow River or go sand-sledding (¥30) or bungee jumping (¥160).

It's also a good place to raft the churning Yellow River. The traditional mode of transport on the river for centuries was the *yángpí fázi* (leather raft), made from sheep or cattle skins soaked in oil and brine and then inflated. From Shāpōtóu you can roar upstream on a speedboat and return on a traditional raft. Prices range from ¥80 to ¥240, depending on how far you go. You can also combine the boat/raft ride with a camel ride (¥110).

Shāpō Shānzhuāng (沙坡山庄; ☑0955-768 9073; r¥288; ☺Apr-Oct) is a basic but comfortable hotel near the dunes. Meals are available.

Buses (¥5, 45 minutes) run between Zhōngwèi and Shāpōtóu from 7.30am to 6.30pm. You can pick them up on Changcheng Xijie about 200m past the Gāo Temple on the opposite side of the road. Taxis cost ¥30 each way.

Tengger Desert 腾格里沙漠

If you fancy playing Lawrence of Arabia, make a trip out to the Tengger Desert (Ténggélǐ Shāmò), a mystical landscape of shifting sand dunes and the occasional herd of two-humped camels. Shāpōtóu lies on the southern fringe, but it's definitely worth heading deeper into the desert to avoid the crowds. The sun is fierce out here, so you'll need a

hat, sunglasses and plenty of water. Nights are cool, so bring a warm layer.

Níngxià Desert Travel Service (p863) in Zhōngwèi offers overnight camel treks through the desert, with a visit to the Great Wall by car, for ¥500 per person per day for a group of four. The price includes transport, food and guide. Ask your guide to bring along a sand sled for a sunset surfing session. Drinking beers around the campfire under a starry sky tops off the experience. The desert trek can be combined with a rafting trip down the Yellow River.

Gùyuán & Around 固原

☑0954

An expanding but still small and very new city, Gùyuán makes a convenient base for exploring little-visited southern Níngxià. Few foreigners make it down here, so expect some attention from the overwhelmingly Hui locals. Make sure to bring cash, too; precious few ATMs in this part of the world accept foreign cards.

◉ Sights & Activities

Xūmí Shān CAVES

(须弥山; admission ¥50; ☺8am-5pm) These Buddhist grottoes (Xūmí is the Chinese transliteration of the Sanskrit *sumeru*, or Buddhist paradise) some 50km northwest of Gùyuán are southern Níngxià's must-see sight. Cut into the five adjacent sandstone hills are 132 caves housing more than 300 Buddhist statues dating back 1400 years, from the Northern Wei to the Sui and Tang dynasties.

Cave 5 contains the largest statue, a colossal Maitreya (future Buddha), standing 20.6m high. Further uphill, the finest statues are protected by the Yuánguāng Temples (caves 45 and 46; 6th century) and Xiàng-gúo (cave 51; 7th century), where you can walk around the interior and examine the artwork up close – amazingly, the paint on several of the statues is still visible in places.

To reach the caves, take a bus from Gùyuán to Sānyíng (三营; ¥7, one hour). They depart from Wenhua Xilu, by the two big hospitals opposite the night market. From Sānyíng you'll have to hire a taxi for the 40km return trip (¥100 including waiting time) to Xūmí Shān.

Liùpán Shān Guójiā Sēnlín Gōngyuán   PARK

(六盘山国家森林公园, Liùpán Mountain National Forest Park; admission ¥65; ⏱7am-6pm) Those on the trail of Genghis Khan will want to visit southern Níngxià's Liùpán Shān, where some believe the great man died in 1227. Legend has it that he fell ill and came here to ingest medicinal plants native to the area, but perished on its slopes (though it's much more likely he died elsewhere). The mountain is now a protected area.

A walking trail leads 3km up a side valley to a waterfall. About 5km further up the main valley is a clearing with some stone troughs and tables that locals say was used by the Mongols during their stay.

To get here, take a bus from Gùyuán's main bus station to Jīngyuán (泾源; ¥16, one hour) and then hire a taxi for the final 18km to the reserve (¥80 return). A return taxi from Gùyuán will cost ¥200.

Gùyuán Museum   MUSEUM

(固原博物馆, Gùyuán Bówùguǎn; 133 Xicheng Jie, 西城路133号; admission ¥20; ⏱9am-5.30pm Tue-Sun, to 6.30pm summer) For such an out-of-the-way place, Gùyuán's museum is rather good, with Neolithic-era artefacts, Tangut ceramics and some fine figurines from the Northern Wei dynasty. Decent English captions, too.

🛏 Sleeping & Eating

Liùpánshān Bīnguǎn   HOTEL $

(六盘山宾馆; ☎0954 202 1666; 35 Zhongshan Nanjie, 中山南街35号; d & tw ¥200; ❋@) The rooms at this long-standing hotel look their age these days, but they are quiet and it still makes a decent base. Foreigners will be directed to the rear annexe, where there's also a restaurant. Discounts of 30%.

Délóng Business Hotel   HOTEL $$

(德龙商务酒店, Délóng Shāngwù Jiǔdiàn; ☎0954 286 3918; Wenhua Xilu, 文化西路; tw incl breakfast ¥268; ❋@) Friendly, helpful staff and good-sized rooms with modern bathrooms make this the pick of the hotels along Wenhua Xilu. Discounts of 40% are common.

Night Market   MARKET $

(小吃城, Xiǎochī Chéng; dishes from ¥11) This alley of food stalls runs till very late and specialises in delicious shāguō (砂锅, mini hotpot), as well as shāokǎo (barbecue) and noodles. Dishes are on display, so you can pick and choose. It's down a covered arcade off Wenhua Xilu, directly opposite two big hospitals.

ℹ Getting There & Away

BUS

The long-distance bus station is about 4km west of central Gùyuán's hotels and museum. A taxi cost ¥5. There are frequent buses to Tóngxīn, Xī'ān and Yínchuān, as well as the following:

Lánzhōu ¥95, nine hours, one daily (8am)

Tiānshuǐ ¥65, seven hours, one daily (6.30am)

Zhōngwèi ¥70, 2½ hours, two daily (10.10am and 3pm)

TRAIN

Gùyuán is on the Zhōngwèi–Bǎojī railway line. Sleeper tickets are near impossible to get and the majority of trains depart in the middle of the night. To get to the train station, take bus 1 or a taxi (¥5).

Lánzhōu hard sleeper ¥89, 9½ hours, one daily (10.53pm)

Xī'ān hard/soft sleeper ¥151/213, seven to eight hours, four daily

Yínchuān seat/hard sleeper ¥65/152, six hours, four daily (1.14am to 1.27pm)

Inner Mongolia

POP 24.7 MILLION

Best Natural Wonders

➡ Hūlúnbèi'ěr Grasslands (p877)

➡ Badain Jaran Desert (p876)

➡ Hūlún Lake (p878)

Best Temples

➡ Wǔdāng Lamasery (p874)

➡ Wǔtǎ Pagoda (p869)

➡ Dà Zhào (p869)

Why Go?

Mongolia. The word alone stirs up visions of nomadic herders, thundering horses and, of course, the warrior-emperor Genghis Khan. The Mongols conquered half the known world in the 13th century and while their empire is long gone, visitors are still drawn to this land wrapped up in both myth and legend.

Travellers heading north of the Great Wall might half expect to see the Mongol hordes galloping through the vast grasslands. The reality is quite different: 21st-century Inner Mongolia (内蒙古; Nèi Měnggǔ) is a wholly different place from Mongolia itself. The more-visited south of the province is industrialised, prosperous and very much within the realm of China's modern economic miracle. The Mongolia of your dreams exists off the tourist route, amid the shimmering sand dunes of the Badain Jaran Desert or the vast grasslands in the north. Some effort is required to reach these areas, but the spectacular scenery makes it worthwhile.

When to Go
Hohhot

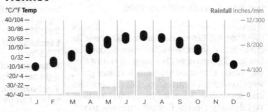

May Good weather and shoulder season equals good value.	**Jul** Hohhot and other regions host the annual Naadam festival.	**Aug & Sep** The best time to see the grasslands and ride Mongolia's famed horses.

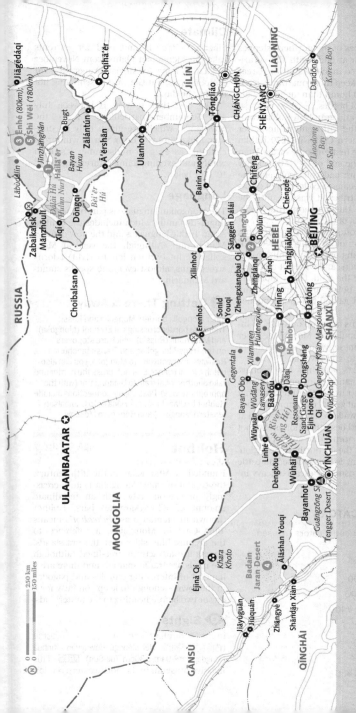

Inner Mongolia Highlights

1 Saddle up and go for a horse ride around the glorious Hūlúnbèi'ěr grasslands near **Hǎilā'ěr** (p874)

2 Wander amid the ancient walls of **Shàngdū** (p872) and contemplate the lost greatness of Kublai Khan's pleasure dome

3 Find some peace and sample the local milk and produce at the laid-back farming town of **Ēnhé** (p877)

4 Mount a camel and set off across the dunes of the **Badain Jaran Desert** (p876)

5 Mingle with the Chinese-speaking ethnic Russians at the unique village of **Shì Wěi** (p877) near the Russian border

6 Listen to the groaning chants of Mongolian monks at the colourful monasteries of **Dà Zhào** (p869) and **Xīlìtú Zhào** (p869) in Hohhot

History

The nomadic tribes of the northern steppes have always been at odds with the agrarian Han Chinese, so much so that the Great Wall was built to keep them out. But it acted more like a speed bump than an actual barrier to the Mongol hordes.

Genghis Khan and grandson Kublai rumbled through in the 13th century, and after conquering southern China in 1279 Kublai Khan became the first emperor of the Yuan dynasty. But by the end of the 14th century the Mongol empire had collapsed, and the Mongols again became a collection of disorganised roaming tribes. It was not until the 18th century that the Qing emperors finally gained full control of the region.

A divide-and-conquer policy by the Qing led to the creation of an 'Inner' and 'Outer' Mongolia. The Qing opened up Inner Mongolia to Han farmers, and waves of migrants came to cultivate the land. Outer Mongolia was spared this policy and, with backing from the USSR, it gained full independence in 1921.

Now Mongolians make up only 15% of Inner Mongolia's population. Most of the other 85% are Han Chinese, with a smattering of Hui, Manchu, Daur and Ewenki.

Inner Mongolia's economy has boomed in recent years thanks to extensive mining of both coal and rare earth minerals. That growth has come at great environmental cost. The mines have swallowed up pastureland at alarming rates and desertification is the root cause of the dust storms that envelop Běijīng each spring. Only the far north of the region, where the economy is largely based on cattle ranching and tourism, has escaped heavy industrialisation.

PRICE INDICATORS

The following price indicators are used in this chapter:

Sleeping

$ less than ¥200

$$ ¥200 to ¥400

$$$ more than ¥400

Eating

$ less than ¥30

$$ ¥30 to ¥50

$$$ more than ¥50

Climate

Siberian blizzards and cold air currents rake the Mongolian plains from November to March. June to August brings pleasant temperatures, but the west is scorching hot during the day.

The best time to visit is between July and September, particularly to see the grasslands, which are green only in summer. Make sure you bring warm, windproof clothing, as even in midsummer it's often windy, and evening temperatures can dip to 10°C or below.

Language

The Mongolian language is part of the Altaic linguistic family, which includes the Central Asian Turkic languages and the now defunct Manchurian. Although the vertical Mongolian script (written left to right) adorns street signs, almost everyone speaks standard Mandarin.

ℹ Getting There & Away

Inner Mongolia borders Mongolia and Russia. There are border crossings at Erenhot (Mongolia) and Mǎnzhōulǐ (Russia), which are stopovers on the Trans-Mongolian and Trans-Manchurian Railways, respectively. To Mongolia, you can also catch a local train to Erenhot, cross the border and take another local train to Ulaanbaatar (with the appropriate visa). Possible air connections include Hohhot to Ulaanbaatar or Hǎilā'ěr to Choibalsan (eastern Mongolia) and Hohhot to Moscow.

Hohhot 呼和浩特

☑ 0471 / POP 2.86 MILLION

Founded by Altan Khan in the 16th century, the capital of Inner Mongolia is an increasingly prosperous city with an inordinate amount of KTV (karaoke) bars. Hohhot (known in Mandarin as *Hūhéhàotè*) means 'Blue City' in Mongolian, a reference to the arching blue skies over the grasslands. Streets are attractively tree-lined (although the roads are traffic-snarled) and there are a handful of interesting temples and pagodas in the town – enough to keep you busy for a day or two before heading to the hinterlands.

◉ Sights

Inner Mongolia Museum MUSEUM
(内蒙古博物院, Nèi Měnggǔ Bówùyuàn; Xinhua Dongdajie; ◉ 9am-5.30pm Tue-Sun) FREE This massive museum in the northeastern section

Hohhot

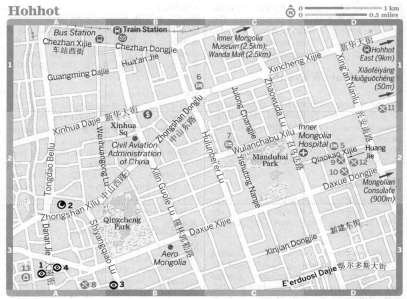

Hohhot

of town has a distinctive sloping roof supposed to resemble the vast steppes of Mongolia. It's one of the better provincial museums, with everything from dinosaurs and Genghis Khan to space-age rockets. Take bus 3 from Xinhua Dajie or pay ¥14 for a cab.

Wǔtǎ Pagoda PAGODA

(五塔寺, Wǔtǎ Sì; Wutasi Houjie; admission ¥35; ◷8am-6pm) This striking, Indian-influenced, five-tiered pagoda was completed in 1732. Its main claim to fame is the Mongolian star chart around the back, though the engraving of the Diamond Sutra (in Sanskrit, Tibetan and Mongolian), extending around the entire base of the structure, is in much better condition. Bus 1 runs by the pagoda.

Dà Zhào MONASTERY

(大召; Danan Jie; admission ¥35; ◷8am-7pm) Dà Zhào is a large, well-maintained lamasery (monastery for lamas) that is still used as a temple. In the sacred main prayer hall you may come upon groups of Mongol monks chanting and praying (usually at 9am).

Xílìtú Zhào MONASTERY

(席力图召; Danan Jie; admission ¥30; ◷7.30am-6.30pm) Across from the Dà Zhào temple is this simple, peaceful monastery, the purported stomping ground of Hohhot's 11th Living Buddha (he actually works elsewhere). Monks chant at 9am and 3pm.

Great Mosque MOSQUE

(清真大寺, Qīngzhēn Dàsì; 28 Tongdao Beilu) North of the old town is the Great Mosque.

Built in the Chinese style, it dates from the Qing dynasty but has been modernised. You can look around as long as you don't enter the prayer hall. The main street, with plenty of food stalls, is worth wandering around.

✨ Festivals & Events

Naadam
CULTURAL, SPORTS

The week-long summer festival known as Naadam features traditional Mongolian sports such as archery, wrestling and horse racing. It takes place at Gegentala and at various grassland areas in early July. Book local tours at your accommodation.

🛏 Sleeping

There are plenty of options in Hohhot from no-name guesthouses near the train station to the Shangri-la. Check www.ctrip.com for last-minute deals.

Āndá Guesthouse
HOSTEL $

(安达旅馆, Āndá Lǚguǎn; ☑159 475 19807, 691 8039; andaguesthouse@hotmail.com; Qiaokao Xijie, 桥靠西街; dm/d with shared bath ¥60/180; @ 🛜) Backpackers love its friendly, English-speaking Mongolian staff and cosy atmosphere. The Āndá has compact dorms and decent-sized basic doubles. The bathrooms especially could be cleaner, but there's a small lounge, kitchen facilities and a cute courtyard. The staff are eager to show off Mongolian culture and organise trips to the grasslands, as well as to the Kubuqi Desert and Naadam.

Finding the place can be difficult; call ahead and get a pick-up from the train station. Otherwise take bus 2, 37 or 61 to the Inner Mongolia Hospital (内蒙古医院大楼A座; Nèi Měnggǔ Yīyuàn Dàlóu A Zuò), then walk west for six minutes on Qiaokao Xijie. It's down an unmarked alley almost opposite the northern end of Huang Jie. Look for the blue sign. A taxi costs ¥11.

A YURT BY ANY OTHER NAME...

'Yurt', the common name for traditional Mongolian tents, is a Turkish word. The Mongolian word is ger, and the Chinese call them 'Měnggǔ bāo' – literally 'Mongolian buns' – perhaps because the white structures with their conical tops resemble puffy steamed breads.

Jīnjiāng Inn
HOTEL $$

(锦江之星旅馆, Jīnjiāng Zhīxīng Lǚguǎn; ☑666 8111; www.jinjianginns.com; 61 Xinhua Dajie, 新华大街61号; d ¥249; ❋ @ 🛜) Big branch of the ultra-efficient chain hotel that has spotless, if somewhat bland, rooms that come with free broadband access.

Nèi Měnggǔ Fàndiàn
HOTEL $$$

(内蒙古饭店, Inner Mongolia Hotel; ☑693 8888; www.nmghotel.com; Wulanchabu Xilu, 乌兰察布西路; r from ¥1480; ❋ @ 🛜 🏊) Despite competition from upmarket Western chains, this 14-storey high-rise is one of Hohhot's best, featuring fine renovated rooms with big comfy beds, a pool and health centre. You can dine Mongolian-style in concrete yurts out back. Some staff speak English. 60% discounts outside the peak summer season.

🍴 Eating & Drinking

Mongolia's notable culinary contribution is huǒguō (火锅; hotpot), a refined version, so the story goes, of the stew originally cooked in soldiers' helmets. Yángròu (羊肉; mutton), miàn (面; noodles), dòufu (豆腐; tofu), mógu (蘑菇; mushrooms) and other vegies are added to the bubbling cauldron.

For an excellent selection of Mongolian and Chinese restaurants, head down to Huang Jie (黄街; Yellow Street), which is lined with about 40 small eateries. There are a few Mongolian music bars nearby; ask at Āndá Guesthouse for the latest hotspot. There are also food options galore at the new Wanda Mall (万达广场, Wàndá Guángchǎng; Xinhua Dongdajie; dishes from ¥15) and along the main shopping strips of Zhongshan Xilu near the junction of Xilin Guole Lu.

⭐ Gǔtāng Qīngchéng Héle Miànguǎn
NOODLES $

(骨汤倾诚饸饹面馆; Wutasi Nanjie; noodles ¥10-11; ⏱24hr) The massive bowls of buckwheat noodles (荞面, qiáomiàn) and unlimited servings of cold Chinese vegie dishes by the counter can sate any hunger pangs you might have. There's also cheap beer and hunks of pork on bone (猪棒骨, zhū bànggǔ, ¥13) to gorge on if the noodles fail to do the trick.

Wūzhūmùqìn Nǎicháguǎn Sì Fēndiàn
MONGOLIAN $

(乌珠穆沁奶茶馆四分店; Huang Jie; meals from Y20; ⏱7am-midnight) This small restaurant serves Mongol 'soul food', including juicy jiǎozi (蒙古饺子; dumplings), makhtai shul (肉汤; meat soup) and suutai tsai (奶茶;

BORDER CROSSING: GETTING TO MONGOLIA

Two direct trains run between Běijīng and Ulaanbaatar (hard/soft sleeper ¥216/336, 30 hours), the Mongolian capital, on Monday and Friday at 8.05am. The same train stops in Erenhot (二连浩特; Èrliánhàotè; hard seat/hard sleeper ¥55/114, 13 hours), at the Mongolian border. Erenhot is listed on Chinese train timetables as Èrlián (二连).

There are also six daily buses from Hohhot to Erenhot (¥95, six hours), leaving between 8am and 1.30pm; buses are more practical than the train. From Erenhot you can catch a jeep across the border (about ¥50) and continue to Ulaanbaatar on the daily 5.50pm local train. A train also runs from Hohhot to Ulaanbaatar on Monday and Friday, leaving at 10.50pm and taking 30 hours.

Air China has several daily flights from Hohhot to Ulaanbaatar (via Běijīng) from ¥2000. Book online at www.ctrip.com. **Aero Mongolia** (空蒙古, Kōng Měnggǔ; ☎138 4818 7711; www.aeromongolia.mn; 36 Daxue Xijie) flies from Hohhot to Ulaanbaatar on Monday, Wednesday and Friday from ¥1800. Flight schedules change in winter.

If you need a visa, head for the Mongolian consulate (p997) in Hohhot. The 30-day visa costs ¥260 and takes four days to process. A rush visa (¥495) can be obtained the following day. US citizens do not need a visa to visit Mongolia. To find the consulate, travel east on Daxue Dongjie, turn left on Dongying Nanjie and look for the consulate 200m on the left. Go early.

There is also a consulate in **Erenhot** (蒙古领事馆, Měnggǔ Lǐngshìguǎn; Youyi Lu; ⊙9am-noon & 3-5pm Mon-Fri). To find the consulate from the bus station, walk half a block east to the T-junction and head left. Walk north along this road (Youyi Lu) for 10 minutes until you see the red, blue and yellow Mongolian flags on your left. A 30-day rush tourist visa (¥495) can be obtained the next day.

---

salty milk tea), along with hunks of lamb on the bone and beef (served by the *jīn*).

Nana's Cafe INTERNATIONAL, MONGOLIAN **$$**
(Huang Jie; dishes from ¥30; ⊙10.30am-10pm) Head through a blue wooden door up to the second level for this cute cafe serving pasta, dumplings and a range of Western dishes. Pair your meal with coffee, beer or salty Mongolian milk tea.

Xīnjiāng Hóngliǔ Zhuāngyuán XINJIANG **$$**
(新疆红柳庄园; Huang Jie; meals from ¥35; ⊙11.30am-2am) With an outdoor area that's busy until the wee hours and smoke billowing off the giant grill, this place specialises in Uighur cuisine from the far western province of Xīnjiāng. The chunky and succulent lamb kebabs (¥8) – nothing like the scrawny, fatty ones sold by street vendors – are especially good. Picture menu.

Xiǎoféiyáng
Huǒguōchéng MONGOLIAN, HOTPOT **$$$**
(小肥羊火锅城, Little Fat Sheep Hotpot City; ☎490 1998; www.littlesheep.com; 80 Wulanchabu Donglu; hotpot dishes from ¥15; ⊙11am-1.30am) Giant branch of the popular and reliable Inner Mongolian chain serving Mongolia's

most famous culinary export. Decent cuts of lamb and beef, a wide choice of fresh vegies and mushrooms and a fun atmosphere. There's a picture menu to help you make your choices.

🛍 Shopping

Souvenir Shops SOUVENIRS
(表记店铺; Biǎojì Diànpù) Opposite Dà Zhào (p869) monastery, this Qing-era street is packed with souvenir stalls selling fake Mongolian tat, jade, Buddhist and Mao memorabilia. South of Dà Zhào is a kitschy open-air shopping plaza done up as a *hútòng* (narrow alley), with stores selling antiques, old books and the usual Mao memorabilia.

ℹ Information

Bank of China (中国银行, Zhōngguó Yínháng; Xinhua Dajie) Has a 24-hour ATM available.
China Post (中国邮政; Zhōngguó Yóuzhèng; Chezhan Dongjie)
Public Security Bureau (PSB, 公安局, Gōng'ānjú; Chileichuan Dajie, 敕勒川大街; ⊙8.30am-noon & 2.30-5pm Mon-Fri) For visa extensions and other enquiries. The foreign-affairs bureau is to the left of the main building, outside the gated compound.

ⓘ Getting There & Away

AIR

Daily flight destinations (routes are reduced in winter) include Běijīng (¥500), Xī'ān (¥800), Hǎilā'ěr (¥1300), Mǎnzhōulǐ (¥1000), and Shànghǎi (¥1350). Book flights on www.elong. net or www.ctrip.com.

BUS

Hohhot's main bus station (长途汽车站, chángtú qìchēzhàn) is next door to the train station.

Bǎotóu ¥40, two hours, every 30 minutes (7am to 7pm)

Běijīng ¥150, six to eight hours, 8.30am, 10.10am, 10.30am, 1.30pm, 3.50pm

Dàtóng ¥65, four hours, hourly (6.30am to 7pm)

Dōngshèng ¥65, three hours, every 30 minutes (6.30am to 7pm)

Erenhot (Èrlián) ¥95, five hours, 7.50am, 8.20am, 9.20am, 12.50pm and 1.30pm

TRAIN

Sleeper tickets are hard to come by in July and August; hotel travel desks can book them for a ¥30 commission. From Hohhot, trains go to the following:

Bǎotóu ¥25, two hours, 16 daily

Běijīng seat/hard sleeper ¥90/167, 10 hours, 13 daily

Dàtóng seat ¥44, four hours, nine daily

Xilinhot seat/hard sleeper ¥92/174, 10 hours, 8.50pm

Yínchuān seat/hard sleeper ¥82/163, 10 hours, three daily

ⓘ Getting Around

Useful bus routes include bus 1, which runs from the train station to the old part of the city past Zhongshan Xilu, and bus 33, which runs east on Xinhua Dajie from the train station. Tickets are ¥1.

Hohhot's airport is 15km east of the city. The airport bus (¥10) leaves from **Civil Aviation Administration of China** (中国民航公司, CAAC, Zhōngguó Mínháng Gōngsī; ☑ 696 4103; Xilin Guole Lu). A taxi will cost ¥50 (flag fall ¥6).

Around Hohhot

In the middle of the fields, 7km east of the airport (about 22km from Hohhot), is Bái Tǎ (白塔, White Pagoda; admission ¥35), a striking seven-storey octagonal tower built during the Liao dynasty. A steep, double-barrelled staircase leads to a small shrine room at the top. Few travellers come here, so you will feel like you have the place to yourself. A taxi from Hohhot will cost around ¥70 return.

About 110km north of Hohhot is the grassland area of Xīlāmùrén (希拉穆仁, Xīlāmùrén), with dozens of faux concrete yurt camps that cater mainly to the Chinese market. Nearby mining operations have accelerated infrastructure development, so don't come this way if you are looking for a true wilderness experience.

For a more authentic Mongolian grassland experience, Āndá Guesthouse (p870) in Hohhot will set you up at the home of a local family where you get to pick your own dried cow dung to light a campfire. Day trips start from ¥290 (including one meal) or ¥390 for an overnight trip (including three meals). Horse riding is an extra ¥100 per hour. The guesthouse also offers multiday tours which cover Bái Tǎ, Wǔdāng Lamasery and the Kùbùqí desert. They were planning to open up a new Mongolian homestay in the very un-touristy Sonid Youqi, so ask.

Shàngdū (Xanadu)　上都

Explorer Marco Polo made it his final stop and poet Samuel Taylor Coleridge immortalised it in Western minds as the ultimate pleasure palace. Today Xanadu, or Shàngdū (元上都遗址, Yuán Shàngdū yízhǐ; admission ¥30; ⊙ 7am-6pm), is little more than a vast prairie with vague remnants of once mighty walls, but it is still a legendary destination thanks to its glory days as one of the most storied cities on earth.

Conceived by Kublai Khan, grandson of Genghis and the first Yuan emperor, Shàngdū's lifespan as the summer capital was relatively brief. Construction of the city started in 1252 and lasted four years, but it was overrun and destroyed by Ming forces in 1369.

Listed as a World Heritage Site by Unesco in June 2012, Shàngdū actually consisted of three distinct cities: the outer city, the imperial city and the palace city. All that is visible now are the outer and inner walls. From the ticket yurt, it's about 1.5km to the outer walls (a golf buggy will take you for ¥10 or rent a bicycle for ¥10). From there, you can walk another 500m to the inner ramparts. Paths through the wildflower-covered grassland that has swallowed up the city offer the chance for pleasant strolls and reflective musings on the vagaries of history.

The gateway to Shàngdū is Lánqí. The town's Xanadu Museum (上都博物馆, Shàngdū Bówùguǎn; admission ¥20; ⊙ 8am-5pm Tue-Sun) is worth visiting for the scale models

LOCAL KNOWLEDGE

ZHAMSU: A GRASSLANDS LIFE

Mongolian Zhamsu, now 52, has spent his entire life living in the grasslands of Xīlāmùrén.

What was your life like growing up? My parents were nomad herders. We lived in a *ger* (yurt). We had more than 300 sheep, 10 cows and 10 horses. I started to help herding when I was seven. Life was hard, but it was less complicated.

How different are the grasslands now? There are more people and fewer animals. The government has banned herding in our area until 2016 to protect the grasslands. So now I live in a house and our *ger* is for tourists to stay in. I still have 20 sheep, but only for the guests to eat, and a few horses for people to ride.

Is Mongolian culture still strong in Inner Mongolia? Not really. Fewer children speak Mongolian now and many young people move to the cities. They speak Mandarin and accept Chinese culture because they think that will lead to a better life. It's only in the grasslands that you can experience traditional Mongolian culture.

Will you ever move to the city? No, I can't imagine how I'd survive. I feel comfortable on the grasslands. I've lived with animals every day for the last 50 years. How could I live without them?

that give a good impression of the sheer ambition of Shàngdū, as well as for relics from the site, including ceramics and statues.

🛏 Sleeping & Eating

Shàngdū's status as a World Heritage site means Lánqí's hotels are overpriced (but expect big discounts outside the peak summer season). Next to the bus station, **188 Liánsuǒ Bīnguǎn** (188 连锁宾馆; ☑0479-423 9188; Jinlianchuan Dajie; r ¥188-588; ❈@) is a good option. On Shangdu Dajie, you'll also find restaurants and a branch of the ICBC bank with an ATM that takes foreign cards.

ℹ Getting There & Away

Although Shàngdū signifies distant wonders in the Western imagination, in truth it's not that isolated (275km northwest of Běijīng). But it does feel remote, partly because of the huge empty prairie it sits in, and also because getting here requires some effort. Hohhot's bus station has buses to Lánqí (蓝旗, ¥132, six to seven hours, 7am and 2pm). From Lánqí it's about a 20km taxi ride (¥150 return) to Shàngdū. Buses return to Hohhot at 7am and 12.30pm.

Bāotóu 包头

Unlovely but booming Bāotóu sprawls across more than 20km of dusty landscape, much of it industrialised and polluted. However, if you're heading to the Wǔdāng Lamasery and Genghis Khan's Mausoleum, you'll likely have to pass through and maybe stop a night.

The older eastern district (Dōnghé) is a convenient place to stay; if you're arriving by train make sure to get off at the Bāotóu East Railway Station (包头东站; Bāotóu Dōngzhàn) and not the west station. The modern western district (Kūnqū) is 25km away and where most residents now work and stay.

🛏 Sleeping & Eating

Head to Nanmenwai Dajie for a selection of hotels, restaurants and banks within walking distance of the East Bāotóu train station and a short hop in a cab (¥7) from the east bus station.

Xīhú Fàndiàn HOTEL $$
(西湖饭店, West Lake Hotel; ☑414 4444; 10 Nanmenwai Dajie, 南门外大街10号; d ¥288; ❈@) A five-minute walk from the train station, this friendly place has plenty of clean, comfortable rooms with modern bathrooms. Expect discounts of 30% to 40%. The hotel was under renovation at the time of research but should be open by the time you read this. Otherwise, several other hotels are located along the same street.

ℹ Getting There & Away

AIR
Flights connect Bāotóu with Běijīng (¥700). Buy tickets at www.ctrip.net. The airport is 2km south of Bāotóu East Railway Station. A taxi there is ¥15, but ¥30 in the other direction.

BUS
When arriving in Bāotóu, ask if the bus stops at Dōnghé or Kūnqū. If it's the latter, you will need to

get off in between and take a bus (K10, ¥2.50) or a taxi (¥35) to get to the eastern Dōnghé district.

Dōngshèng ¥34, two hours, every 30 minutes (6.30am to 6.30pm)

Hohhot ¥40, three hours, every 30 minutes (6.30am to 7.30pm)

Yán'ān (Shaanxi) ¥156, eight hours, 3pm

Yúlín (Shaanxi) ¥92, five hours, eight daily (6.30am to 4.30pm)

TRAIN

Frequent trains between Hohhot and Bāotóu (¥25, two hours) stop at both the east and west stations. The following trains depart from the east station.

Běijīng hard/soft sleeper ¥175/264, 8½ to 13 hours, 10 daily

Lánzhōu hard/soft sleeper ¥223/345, 17 hours, three daily

Tàiyuán hard/soft sleeper ¥184/284, nine to 12½ hours, three daily

Yínchuān hard/soft sleeper ¥142/213, seven hours, four daily

Wǔdāng Lamasery 五当召

Lying on the pilgrim route from Tibet to Outer Mongolia, this handsome, Tibetan-style monastery (五当召, Wǔdāng Zhào; admission ¥45; ☉ 8.30am-4.30pm) saw considerable foot traffic from the time of its establishment in 1749. At its height it was the largest monastery in Inner Mongolia, housing 1200 monks belonging to the Gelugpa sect of Tibetan Buddhism. Around 60 monks are resident here these days, but the monastery's numerous outlying buildings, now occupied by local villagers, are a reminder of how important Wǔdāng once was. Climb the steps leading up the hill opposite the car park for views of the complex and across the prayer-flag-draped landscape. There's a little compound beside the public toilet offering basic beds (¥50, no showers) and home-cooked meals if you wish to stay the night.

The monastery is 67km northeast of Bāotóu. A direct bus (¥20, 1½ hours) departs from the bus parking lot in front of Bāotóu East Railway Station at 9am and 3.20pm. Buses return at 7am and 1pm. Alternatively, bus 7 (¥10, one hour), from the same parking lot, goes to Shíguǎi (石拐), 40km from Bāotóu. From Shíguǎi you can hire a taxi to the monastery (one-way/return ¥50/100).

Genghis Khan Mausoleum

Located 130km south of Bāotóu in the middle of absolutely nowhere is the **Genghis Khan Mausoleum** (成吉思汗陵园, Chéngjí Sīhàn Língyuán; admission ¥120, with museum entry ¥150; ☉ 8am-6pm), China's tribute to the great Mongol warlord. Unfortunately, old Genghis was not buried here. Instead, the mausoleum's existence is justified by an old Mongol tradition of worshipping Genghis Khan's personal effects, including his saddle, bow and other items. Kublai Khan established the cult and handed over care for the objects to the Darhats, a Mongol clan. Darhat elders kept the relics inside eight white tents, which could be moved in times of warfare.

In the early 1950s, the government decided to build a permanent site for the relics and constructed this impressive triple-domed building. By then, most of the relics had been lost or stolen (everything you'll see here is a replica). But even today, some of the guards at the site still claim descent from the Darhat clan. The ¥150 ticket includes entry to a museum with information on Genghis and Monglian culture.

ⓘ Getting There & Away

From Bāotóu there are hourly buses (¥41, two hours, 6.10am to 2.40pm) to Chénglíng (成陵). You'll then have to catch a taxi (¥15) the final 7km to the mausoleum.

To move on, take a cab back to a small tourist village (with shops, hotels and restaurants) to flag down any Dōngshèng-bound bus at the roundabout. Buses should pass by regularly till about 4pm. From Dōngshèng (东胜) you can connect to Hohhot (¥65, four hours, hourly) and other regional destinations.

At the roundabout, there are also share taxis to Ejin Horo Qi (¥15 per person, 伊金霍洛旗; Yījīn Huòluò Qí), known as 'Yī Qí', where you can get a bus to Hohhot (¥70, 4½ hours, last bus 3pm).

Hǎilā'ěr 海拉尔

☑ 0470 / POP 350,000

Hǎilā'ěr is the largest city in northern Inner Mongolia and a busy, ordinary place. Surrounding it are the Hūlúnbèi'ěr Grasslands, a vast expanse of prairie that begins just outside the city and rolls northwards towards the Russian and Mongolian borders, seemingly forever. Superbly lush in July and August, the grasslands are a fantastic sight and *the* place in Inner Mongolia to saddle up a horse.

In the immediate area around Hǎilā'ěr are several touristy yurt camps where you can eat, listen to traditional music and sometimes stay the night. Although they're not places where Mongolians actually live, you can still learn a bit about Mongolian culture, and the wide-open grasslands are a splendid setting. For a more authentic (and far more rustic) experience, you need to travel further away, although staying with local families in the grasslands is not easy to organise unless you speak a bit of Mandarin (or Mongolian).

Hǎilā'ěr's main square is on Zhongyang Dajie, near Xingan Lu. Hotels and services are conveniently located near the main square. Buxing Jie, a pedestrian street just off Zhongyang Dajie, contains a few souvenir shops run by Mongolians. Just past Buxing Jie is a re-creation of a Qing-dynasty *hútòng*, completed in 2010.

◎ Sights

Ewenki Museum   MUSEUM
(鄂温克博物馆, Èwēnkè Bówùguǎn; ◎8.30am-noon & 2.30-5.30pm) FREE Roughly 20,000 Ewenki people live in northern Inner Mongolia, most in the Hūlúnbèi'ěr Grasslands surrounding Hǎilā'ěr. You can glimpse some of their history and culture at this modern museum. The Ewenki have traditionally been herders, hunters and farmers; they are one of the few peoples in China to raise reindeer.

The museum is on the southeastern edge of town. Regular minibuses (¥4, 15 minutes) run here from Buxing Jie beside the Busen shopping centre.

Underground Fortress   FORTRESS
(海拉尔要塞遗址, Hǎilā'ěr Yàosài Yízhǐ; admission ¥60; ◎8.30am-6pm) In the mid-1930s, during the Japanese occupation of Manchuria, this network of tunnels was constructed by the Japanese army in the grasslands north of Hǎilā'ěr. The site now contains a museum, a monument and old tanks and artillery guns to climb on. Inside the freezing, spooky tunnels you can peek into 'rooms' where soldiers bunked and a hospital was located.

The site is 4km northwest of the train station; you'll need an hour to see everything. A taxi between the tunnels and the town centre costs about ¥40. If you want the taxi to wait, then a round trip will be around ¥100. Alternatively, the tunnels are on the road to Jīnzhànghàn, so you might negotiate a stop here en route.

> **GENGHIS' GRAVE**
>
> The great Genghis left stern instructions that his burial place be kept secret. Legend has it that the slaves who built his tomb were massacred afterwards by soldiers, who were then subsequently killed themselves to prevent anyone knowing the location of his grave. Archaeologists hunting for Genghis' final resting place have been further hampered by a reputed curse that has supposedly struck some down. Most historians assume that after his death (and no one knows where that occurred) in 1227, Genghis' body was taken back to Mongolia and buried near his birthplace in Khentii Aimag close to the Onon River.

★☆ Festivals & Events

Naadam   CULTURAL, SPORTS
The Hǎilā'ěr Naadam (sports festival) is held annually in July on the grasslands just north of town. You'll see plenty of wrestling, horse racing and archery. The city is flooded with tour groups at this time, making it difficult to find a room. Hotel prices double during this time.

🛏 Sleeping & Eating

Hǎilā'ěr has a mostly undistinguished, overpriced selection of hotels. Touts at the train station can lead you to rooms (with computers, shared baths) for ¥40 to ¥80.

On summer nights, Buxing Jie and the surrounding alleys become a hub of outdoor *shāokǎo* (barbecue) places that are good for a beer and meeting the locals.

Bèi'ěr Dàjiǔdiàn   HOTEL $$
(贝尔大酒店, Bei'er Hotel; ☑835 8455; 36 Zhongyang Dajie, 中央大街36号; d incl breakfast ¥880 & 980; ❋@) With a large bright lobby, welcoming staff and well-maintained rooms, this is the number-one midrange choice in town. It's advisable to book ahead here, especially in July and August. Discounts knock rooms down to ¥240 and ¥380.

Jīnchuān Dòuhuāzhuāng   HOTPOT $$$
(金川豆花庄; ☑834 6555; Xi Dajie; 2 people per ¥75; ◎10am-11pm) Big and bustling hotpot favourite with the locals; you can choose from a wide selection of meat, seafood and veggie options, as well as opting to make your broth less or more spicy. No English or

picture menu, but the waitresses will help you out. It's on the corner of Xi Dajie and Bei Xiejie, close to Zhongyang Dajie.

ℹ️ Information

Bank of China (中国银行, Zhōngguó Yínháng; cnr Xingan Donglu & Zhongyang Dajie) Next door to Bèi'ĕr Dàjiŭdiàn in the centre of town.

Public Security Bureau (PSB, Gōng'ānjú; Alihe Lu) Opposite CITS in the Hédōng district on the east side of the river.

ℹ️ Getting There & Away

AIR

Hăilă'ĕr's small airport has direct daily flights to Bĕijīng (¥1150, two hours), Hohhot (¥1150, 2¼ hours) and Shanghai (¥1550, 3½ hours). Go to www.elong.net or www.ctrip.com to book flights.

Hunnu Air (☎ +976 7000 1111; www.hunnuair. com) This Mongolian airline flies to Ulaanbaatar (from ¥900) in Mongolia every Wednesday and Saturday. Book tickets online.

BUS

The new **long-distance bus station** (长途车站, chángtú chēzhàn) in the Hédōng district has buses to the following:

Lābùdálín ¥38, two hours, half hourly, 6.40am to 5.30pm

Mănzhōulĭ ¥47, three hours, hourly, 8am to 5pm

TRAIN

Ten daily trains go to Mănzhōulĭ (¥29, two to three hours). There are also daily trains between Hăilă'ĕr and Hā'ĕrbīn (hard/soft sleeper ¥188/284, 11 hours), Qíqíhā'ĕr (seat/hard sleeper ¥63/128, eight hours) and Bĕijīng (hard/soft sleeper ¥423/645, 29 hours).

WORTH A TRIP

INNER MONGOLIA'S FAR WEST

The golden deserts, shimmering lakes and ruined cities of western Inner Mongolia are fantastic places for adventures far from the beaten track. Visiting them, though, requires some logistical help.

One destination is **Khara Khoto** (Black City; 黑城, Hēichéng; admission ¥10; ⊗8am-7pm), a ruined Tangut city built in 1032 and captured by Genghis Khan in 1226 (his last great battle). Khara Khoto continued to thrive under Mongol occupation, but in 1372 an upstart Ming battalion starved the city of its water source, killing everyone inside. Six hundred years of dust storms nearly buried the city, until the Russian explorer PK Kozlov excavated and mapped the site, and recovered hundreds of Tangut-era texts (kept at the Institute of Oriental Manuscripts in St Petersburg). Located about 25km southeast of Éjìnà Qí (额济纳旗), the allure here is the remoteness of the site and surrounding natural beauty. A great time to visit is late September to early October when the poplar trees are changing colours; but be warned that every hotel room in Éjìnà Qí will be booked out at this time.

The second tourist drawcard in these parts is the remote but stunning **Badain Jaran Desert** (巴丹吉林沙漠, Bādānjílín Shāmò), a mysterious landscape of desert lakes, Buddhist temples and towering dunes. The dunes here are the tallest in the world, some topping 380m (the same height, incredibly, as the Empire State Building). The closest town in the region, Ālāshàn Yòuqí (阿拉善右旗), is a 30-minute drive from the dunes. **Badanjilin Travel Service** (巴丹吉林旅行社, Bādānjílín Lǚxíngshè; ☎0483-602 4888; www.badanjilin.net), in town, organises camel treks (from ¥120 per hour) and tours with English-speaking guides from ¥1000. It can also organise a car to Khara Khoto for ¥1600 return. Chéngdū-based **Navo Tours** (☎028-8611 7722; www.navo-tour.com) runs 4WD tours here (three days of which is in the desert) starting from Lánzhōu with English-speaking guides.

This part of Inner Mongolia is highly militarised (China's space city is nearby) and travel permits are required for the road between Jiŭquán and Éjìnà Qí, as well as Khara Khoto itself and the Badain Jaran Desert. Travel agents need at least three days to organise the necessary permits.

The closest rail links are Jiŭquán and Zhāngyè in Gānsù province. However, public transport between Gānsù and Inner Mongolia is limited. A daily bus travels between Ālāshàn Yòuqí and Shāndān Xiàn (山丹县), but the best connections start with other Inner Mongolian towns such as Bayanhot. There are daily buses from Bayanhot to both Éjìnà Qí and Ālāshàn Yòuqí.

The train station is in the northwestern part of town. A taxi to the city-centre is ¥7.

ℹ Getting Around

Airport buses (¥5) connect to all flights and depart from the train station roughly 1½ hours before departure. A taxi to the airport from town costs ¥30.

Buses 1, 3, 7 and 9 run from the train station to Bèi'ěr Dàjiǔdiàn. Bus 18 runs from Hédōng new bus station to the train station while taxis charge ¥12. Taxi fares start at ¥6.

Around Hǎilā'ěr

North of Hǎilā'ěr are few permanent settlements, just the yurts of herders with their flocks of sheep and cows and strings of Mongolian ponies set in some of the greenest grasslands you will ever see. Closer to the Russian border, the rolling prairie becomes more wooded, as spindly white pine trees appear. Bring along binoculars if you want to have a closer look at the Russian villages across the border.

If you speak Chinese, you can hire a private car for ¥500 per day to take in the sights around Hǎilā'ěr. Contact Mr Liu (刘师父, Liú Shīfù, ☎ 159 4775 3673). During busier seasons, he can find Chinese travellers to carpool (拼车, pīnchē) with. He has set itineraries that covers Ēnhé, Shì Wěi and Mǎnzhōulǐ.

Jīnzhànghàn Grasslands 金帐汗草原

Set along a winding river about 40km north of Hǎilā'ěr, this grassland camp (金帐汗草原; Jīnzhànghàn Cǎoyuán; ☎ 133 2700 0919; ☉ Jun–early Oct) has a spectacular setting, even if it is designed for tourists. You can pass an hour or so looking around and sipping milk tea, spend the day horse riding (per hour ¥200) or hiking, or come for an evening of dinner, singing and dancing.

If you want to stay the night, you can sleep in one of the yurts (per person ¥100). There's no indoor plumbing, but there is a toilet hut. To get here, you'll have to hire a taxi from Hǎilā'ěr (about ¥300 return) or join one of the Chinese group tours (sign up at your hotel or at the booth at the Hǎilā'ěr train station).

About 2km before the main camp there are a couple of unsigned family-run camps. Prices for food, accommodation and horse rental are about half what you pay at Jīn-

zhànghàn, but they are rather less organised. To skip the tourist-run camps, push further north through the grasslands towards Ēnhé and Shì Wěi.

Ēnhé 恩和

The township of Ēnhé, located 70km north of Lābùdálín en route to Shì Wěi, is one of the area's unsung villages brimming with atmosphere. Surrounded by hills and acres of lush grass, the village has only just opened to tourism and there's still a very low-key vibe here. Many residents are of Chinese-Russian origin; some could easily pass for Russians. Here, herders milk their cows outside their properties when they aren't taking them out to pasture. Sample boiled milk at your accommodation.

You can ride a horse for ¥60 (a bargain in Inner Mongolia!), hire a bicycle (¥10 per hour) or go for hikes. The mosquitoes are killer in summer so bring plenty of repellent.

🛏 Sleeping

★ Ēnhé Grasslands
International Hostel   HOSTEL $
(呼伦贝尔恩和牧场国际青年旅舍, Hūlúnbèi'ěr Ēnhé Mùchǎng Guójì Qīngnián Lǔshě; ☎ 0470-694 2277; hulunbuiryha@126.com; dm ¥45, d & tw ¥120; 🖥) Rooms at this hostel on the edge of town are housed in comfortable wooden cabins but the best aspect of this hostel is the cozy hall with killer views out to the hill-ringed grasslands. It's a great place to have a beer or meal (dishes from ¥16) and to meet Chinese travellers.

ℹ Getting There & Away

To get here from Hǎilā'ěr, travel to Lābùdálín (拉布达林; ¥38, two hours, half hourly, 6.40am to 5.30pm). From Lābùdálín (sometimes called É'ěrgǔnà) there are two daily direct buses (¥27, two hours) at 12.10am and 2.30pm. Buses return to Lābùdálín at 8.30am and 9.30am. The Shì Wěi-bound buses also stop on the main road leading to Ēnhé where it's a 1.5km walk into town. You can flag onward buses to Shì Wěi from the main road at around 11.15am and 5.15pm.

Shì Wěi 室韦

A small Russian-style village of log cabins located right on the É'ěrgǔnà River, which marks the border with Russia, Shì Wěi is deep within the glorious grasslands. Shì Wěi itself has been discovered by the domestic tourist hordes and is no longer the backwater it once was, although very few foreigners make it up here. But it's still fun to ride a horse along the riverbank (¥40 per half hour), while gazing at the Russian village on the opposite bank. Look for wooden stages on both sides of the river: each country used to host performances for their neighbours!

For a closer look at Russia, you can also walk to the **Friendship Bridge** (友谊桥, Yǒuyì Qiáo; ¥20; ⊙8am-5pm). Chinese tourists pose for photos at the foot of the bridge connecting the two countries before wandering down to a hut to buy Russian chocolate and souvenirs. Taxis can take you to **Línjiāng** (临江) – a less touristy border village with a lovely natural setting – for ¥100 return. You can also find accommodation in Línjiāng but will need to head back to Shì Wěi if you want to get the bus back to Lābùdálín.

🛏 Sleeping & Eating

In Shì Wěi, families have turned their homes into guesthouses and/or restaurants. You can find rooms from ¥100 to ¥300. Come evening, barbecue stalls set up along the main drag and in most of the adjacent lanes.

Zhuóyāzhījiā GUESTHOUSE $
(卓雅之家; ☑150 4701 7557; d & tw ¥100) Neat doubles and courtyard river views can be had for ¥100 at Zhuóyāzhījiā. From the bus drop-off, walk ahead towards the town square and turn left on the last lane. The house is 100m to the right.

ℹ Getting There & Away

From Hǎilā'ěr, travel to Lābùdálín (拉布达林; ¥38, two hours, half hourly, 6.40am to 5.30pm). From Lābùdálín there are two daily direct buses (¥44, four hours) at 9.30am and 3.30pm. Buses return to Lābùdálín at 8am and 1pm but do buy your ticket in advance.

Mǎnzhōulǐ　　満洲里

☑0470 / POP 300,000

This laissez-faire border city, where the Trans-Siberian Railway crosses from China to Russia, is a pastel-painted boomtown of shops, hotels and restaurants catering to the Russian market. Unless you look Asian, expect shopkeepers to greet you in Russian. Mǎnzhōulǐ is modernising at lightning speed, but a few Russian-style log houses still line Yidao Jie.

Mǎnzhōulǐ is small enough to get around on foot. From the train station to the town centre, it's a 10-minute walk. Turn right immediately as you exit the station, then right again to cross the footbridge. You'll come off the bridge near the corner of Yidao Jie and Zhongsu Lu.

⊙ Sights

Hūlún Lake LAKE
(呼伦湖; Hūlún Hú; admission ¥30) One of the largest lakes in China, Hūlún Lake is called Dalai Nuur (Ocean Lake) in Mongolian. It unexpectedly pops out of the grasslands like an enormous inland sea. You can hire a horse (¥100 per 30 minutes) or a quad bike (¥100 per 20 minutes), take a boat ride (¥10 per 20 minutes) or simply stroll along the rocky lakeshore.

The only way to get to Hūlún Hú, 39km southeast of Mǎnzhōulǐ, is to hire a taxi. Expect to pay about ¥200 return, including a visit to the nearby Russian Doll Park.

Russian Doll Park PARK
(套娃广场, Tàowá Guǎngchǎng; ⊙8am-6pm)
FREE This bizarre park is filled with giant Russian *matryoshka* dolls, many with portraits of famous historical figures, from Albert Einstein to Michael Jordan. The largest doll is a Russian-style restaurant. Next to the park is a **museum** (admission ¥20) of Russian art. Bus 6 (¥1.50) runs along Liudao Jie past the bus station and the doll park before terminating at the Russian border area, **Guómén** (国门).

🛏 Sleeping

There are a huge number of hotels and guesthouses in Mǎnzhōulǐ. There are Chinese and Russian signs – гостиница (pronounced 'gastinitsa') is the Russian word for 'hotel'.

Fēngzéyuán Lǚdiàn GUESTHOUSE $
(丰泽源旅店; ☑225 4099, 139 4709 3443; Yidao Jie, 一道街; tw ¥200; @ 🛜) Located inside a restored Russian log cabin (painted yellow and green), this friendly (and cheap, for Mǎnzhōulǐ) guesthouse has large, clean rooms. Coming off the pedestrian bridge from the train station, it's the first building in front of you, next to the statue of Zhou Enlai. Prices fall to ¥50 in low season.

Shangri-La HOTEL $$$
(香格里拉大酒店, Xiānggélǐlā Dàjiǔdiàn; ☑396 8888; www.shangri-la.com; 99 Liudao Jie, 六道街 99号; d¥1388, ste¥4588; ⊖ ❄ @ 🛜 ⊗) Nothing indicates Mǎnzhōulǐ's soaring status more than this outpost of the Shangri-La chain;

it's surely the most remote of its hotels in China if not Asia! The very comfortable rooms offer views over the surrounding grasslands, and there are Chinese and Russian restaurants, a swimming pool and a spa. The efficient staff will drum up someone who can speak English.

✗ Eating

There are plenty of restaurants (*pectopah* in Russian) in town.

Bèijiā'ěr Hú Xī Cāntīng RUSSIAN $$
(贝加尔湖西餐厅; 23 Zhongsu Lu, near Wudao Jie; 中苏路23号; dishes from ¥28; ⊘24hr) The name of the restaurant translates as 'Lake Baikal Western Restaurant', giving some indication of its target audience. Rub shoulders with Russians who come for robust Chinese-style Russian dishes such as borscht and steaks set to a Russian soundtrack. The set meals (from ¥60) let you sample the best dishes and are great paired with cold draft beer. Picture menu available.

Huāyàng Jiǎozi DUMPLINGS $
(花样饺子; Yidao Jie; 一道街; dumplings from ¥13; ⊘10am-10pm) This popular eatery opposite Fēngzéyuán Lǚdiàn serves up all manner of dumplings and cold beer. There's a picture menu on the wall detailing a huge variety of Chinese dishes if you are tired of dumplings.

ⓘ Information

Industrial and Commercial Bank of China (ICBC; 工商银行; Gōngshāng Yínháng; cnr Yidao Jie & Zhongsu Jie)

China International Travel Service (CITS, 中国国际旅行社, Zhōngguó Guójì Lǚxíngshè; ✆622 8319; 35 Erdao Jie; ⊘8-11.30am & 2-4pm Mon-Fri) Sells train tickets for Chinese

ⓘ BORDER CROSSING: GETTING TO RUSSIA

Buses to Zabaikalsk (后贝加尔, *Hòubèijiā'ěr*, ¥92, five hours), over the Russian border, depart eight times daily between 7.40am and 1.30pm from Mǎnzhōulǐ's bus station, but they tend to be much slower than a private car (the Chinese traders on your bus will take ages to get through customs). In Mǎnzhōulǐ you could ask around for a ride from a Russian trader (Russians get through faster). Otherwise, take a taxi to the border (¥40), 9km from town, and get a ride across from there with a Russian driver.

cities and one-day tours (¥270) to the local sights. Located on the 1st floor of Guójì Fàndiàn (International Hotel).

China Post (中国邮政, Zhōngguó Yóuzhèng; cnr Haiguan Jie & Sidao Jie)

Public Security Bureau (PSB, 公安局, Gōng'ānjú; cnr Sandao Jie & Shulin Lu)

ⓘ Getting There & Around

Mǎnzhōulǐ has a small airport on the edge of town; a taxi to the airport will take about 15 minutes (¥40). There are daily flights to Běijīng (¥1250, 2¼ hours) and, in summer, to Hohhot (¥1250, 2½ hours).

You can reach Mǎnzhōulǐ by train from Hǎilā'ěr (¥26, 2½ hours), Hā'ěrbīn (hard/soft sleeper ¥230/348, 12 to 16 hours) or Qíqíhā'ěr (hard/soft sleeper ¥180/265, 11 hours).

There are 10 buses a day to Hǎilā'ěr (¥47, three hours, 6.30am to 5.30pm) from the main bus station on Wudao Jie. Taxis charge ¥10 for most trips around town.

Qīnghǎi

POP 5.7 MILLION

Best Monasteries & Temples

➡ Kumbum Monastery (p889)

➡ Yòuníng Monastery (p889)

➡ Lóngwù Sì (p890)

➡ Princess Wencheng Temple (p894)

Best Natural Sights

➡ Kanbula National Park (p892)

➡ Mt Amnye Machen (p892)

➡ Mèngdá Nature Reserve (p891)

➡ Zhālíng and Èlíng Lakes (p894)

➡ Nangchen County (p895)

Why Go?

Big, bold and beautifully barren, Qīnghǎi (青海), larger than any country in the EU, occupies a vast swathe of the northeastern chunk of the Tibetan Plateau. In fact, as far as Tibetans are concerned, this is Amdo, one of old Tibet's three traditional provinces. Much of what you'll experience here will feel more Tibetan than Chinese; there are monasteries galore, yaks by the hundred and nomads camped out across high-altitude grasslands.

Rough-and-ready, Qīnghǎi is classic off-the-beaten-track territory, often with a last-frontier feel to it. Travelling here can be both inconvenient and uncomfortable, though China's rapid development plans have begun to touch the province, with huge highways and new rail lines under construction.

Despite that, Qīnghǎi still delivers a heavy dose of solitude among middle-of-nowhere high-plateau vistas, Martian-like red mountains and encounters with remote communities of China's ethnic minorities.

When to Go
Xīníng

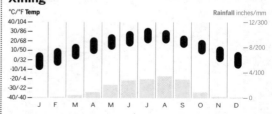

Jan & Feb Tibetan New Year (Losar), with lots of pilgrims and celebrations at monasteries.

Jul & Aug Grasslands at their greenest; landscape dotted with nomad tents.

Sep Safest and most comfortable time for hiking around Mt Amnye Machen.

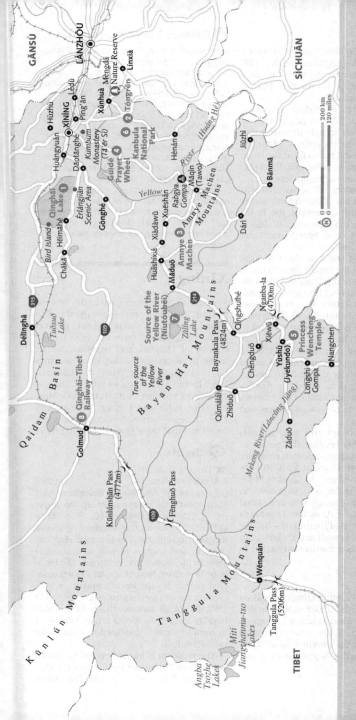

Qīnghǎi Highlights

1 Birdwatch on the shores of **Qīnghǎi Lake** (p888), the largest in China

2 Buy a Tibetan *thangka* straight from the artist's easel in **Tóngrén** (p890)

3 Trek on **Mt Amnye Machen** (p892), eastern Tibet's most sacred mountain

4 Turn the world's largest prayer wheel near the walled Old Town of **Guìdé** (p892)

5 Sidestep the web of prayer flags on a hike around the hills beside **Princess Wencheng Temple** (p894)

6 Hike among the Martian-

like red mountains of **Kanbula National Park** (p889)

7 Venture across the Qīnghǎi–Tibet plateau to the **source of the Yellow River** (p894)

8 Take one of the world's great train rides, the **Qīnghǎi–Tibet Railway** (p888)) to Lhasa, at Xīníng or Golmud

History

The northern Silk Road passed through what is now Qīnghǎi province, and in 121 BC the Han dynasty established a military base near modern Xīníng to counter Tibetan raids on trading caravans.

During the Yarlung dynasty, a time of great expansion of Tibetan power and influence, Qīnghǎi was brought directly under Lhasa's control. After the collapse of the dynasty in AD 842, local rulers filled the ensuing power vacuum, some nominally acting as vassals of Song dynasty emperors.

In the 13th century all of Qīnghǎi was incorporated into the Yuan empire under Genghis Khan. During this time, the Tǔ began to move into the area around Hùzhù, followed a century or so later by the Salar Muslims into Xúnhuà.

After the fall of the Yuan dynasty, local Mongol rulers and the Dalai Lamas in Lhasa wrestled for power. The Qing emperors restored the region to full Chinese control, setting it up as a prefecture with more or less the same boundaries as today. As in the past, however, they left administrative control in the hands of local elites.

Qīnghǎi became a province of China in 1928 during the republican era, though at the time it was under the de facto control of the Muslim Ma clan. When the People's Republic of China was established in 1949, Qīnghǎi retained its provincial borders and capital city, Xīníng.

In the late 1950s an area near Qīnghǎi Lake (Qīnghǎi Hú) became the centre of China's nuclear-weapons research program. During the next 40 years, at least 30 tests were held at a secret base, the Qīnghǎi Mine.

In April 2010, Yùshù, a Tibetan town in remote southwest Qīnghǎi, was devastated by a 7.1-magnitude earthquake. Thousands died – some say tens of thousands – but the rebuilding effort was swift and Yùshù's main centre reopened as a tourist destination in early 2014.

Language

Most of the population in Qīnghǎi speaks a northwestern Chinese dialect similar to that spoken in Gānsù. Most Tibetans here speak the Amdo dialect. You'll have no trouble travelling around the province using Mandarin, though English is less common outside of Xīníng.

ℹ️ Getting There & Around

Most people arrive by train, usually into Xīníng, but after that train lines are limited, so long-distance buses are the best way to get around. In more remote areas you'll often have no option but to hire a private car and driver. Off-the-beaten-track overland routes include south into Sìchuān, at Aba or Shíqú, and north into Gānsù or Xīnjiāng from Golmud (be aware that foreigners travelling this way often need a special permit). Routes southwest into Tibet are even more remote and are often closed to foreigners altogether, and some areas north of Qīnghǎi Lake have been closed to foreigners for years.

As with everything in China, things change rapidly and areas that may be open to travellers one week could be closed or require permits the next. It's always best to check around once you arrive before heading to a new destination, just to be sure.

Xīníng 西宁

📶 0971 / POP 2.2 MILLION

Situated on the eastern edge of the Tibetan Plateau, this lively provincial capital makes a good base from which to dive into the surrounding sights and on to the more remote regions of Qīnghǎi and beyond. Though many travellers use Xīníng as a jumping-off or landing point from the Qīnghǎi-Tibet Railway, it's also a wonderful place to explore the province's varied cultures – Muslim (Huí, Salar and Uighur), Tibetan and Han Chinese – especially the dynamite culinary mix that these groups bring together.

◎ Sights

★ Tibetan Culture & Medicine Museum MUSEUM

(藏文化博物馆; Zàng Wénhuà Bówùguǎn; 📶 531 7881; www.tibetanculturemuseum.org; 36 Jing'er Rd; 经二路36号; admission ¥60; ⊗ 9am-6pm; 🚌 1) Exhibitions at this excellent museum focus on traditional Tibetan medicine, astronomy and science, as well as traditional Tibetan life, homes and costumes. The highlight is a 618m-long *thangka* (Tibetan sacred art) scroll – the world's longest – which charts most of Tibetan history. Completed in 1997, it's not an ancient relic, but it is unbelievably long. It took 400 artists four years to complete and is displayed in a maze-like exhibition hall.

The museum is located on the far northwest side of Xīníng, not too far from Qīnghǎi University. Bus 1 (¥1) goes here from Dong

Dajie (about a 30-minute ride). A taxi costs about ¥15 from the centre.

Dongguan Grand Mosque MOSQUE

(清真大寺, Qīngzhēn Dàsì; 25 Dongguan Dajie; 东关大街25号; admission ¥25; ⊙7am-8pm) About one-third of Xīníng's population is Muslim and there are more than 80 mosques across the city. But this is the big one. In fact, it's one of the largest mosques in China. Friday lunchtime prayers regularly attract 50,000 worshippers who spill out onto the streets before and afterwards. And during Ramadan as many as 300,000 come here to pray. The mosque was first built during the late 14th century and has since been restored.

It's worth visiting in early evening when the whole building is lit up with flashing neon lights. Non-Muslims can't enter the main prayer hall but can stroll around the grounds.

Qīnghǎi Provincial Museum MUSEUM

(青海省博物馆; Qīnghǎi Shěng Bówùguǎn; ☑611 1164; Xinning Sq, 58 Xiguan Dajie, 新宁广场西关大街58号; ⊙9am-4.30pm Mon-Sat; ☐22, 41) **FREE** At the east end of Xīníng Sq, the provincial museum looks like an ominous government building from afar, but once inside, three galleries offer a sophisticated presentation of local history and artefacts, ranging from 5000-year-old pottery recovered from excavations in Qīnghǎi to paintings and Tibetan carpets. You'll be asked to show a passport and sign in before entering.

Inside the museum, bypass the displays of overpriced goods and head upstairs to the two main galleries. On the right, you'll find one exhibit chock full of ancient artifacts – the abundant collection of ancient pottery pieces are particularly interesting. The left-hand gallery contains a collection of local cultural artefacts, including some examples of traditional Qīnghǎi costumes and utensils. The third exhibition showcasing Tibetan carpets is on the ground floor.

Buses go from Xīníng's main drag, Dong Dajie. Alight at Xīnníng Guǎngchǎng Nán (新宁广场南).

City Wall RUIN

(城墙; Chéngqiáng; Kunlun Zhonglu, 昆仑中路) **FREE** One or two isolated sections of Xīníng's old city wall still remain, the most accessible being this short stretch within a park on Kunlun Zhonglu. The wall was originally built in 1385, but different portions were erected, repaired or left to crumble over subsequent centuries. The wall's remains, an

overgrown dirt embankment, aren't all that impressive; however, the tiered pathways that wind through the park make for a nice stroll in good weather.

Běichán Sì BUDDHIST TEMPLE

(北禅寺; ⊙8am-4pm) **FREE** The temple at the foot of a barren hillside on Xīníng's north side is nothing special, but halfway up the steep climb to the top you pass cave temples and shrines that are thought to be 1700 years old. A pagoda, and great views of the city, await you at the top.

The easiest way to get there is to take a ¥6 taxi.

Nánchán Sì BUDDHIST TEMPLE

(南禅寺; 93 Nanshan Lu, 南山路93号) Stood atop Phoenix Mountain, this Buddhist temple is the southern counterpart to Běichán Sì, overlooking Xīníng from the south. The temple was built during the Northern Song dynasty (960–1127) and is the oldest Chan (Chinese Zen) Buddhist temple in Qīnghǎi province. Worth a walk up for incredible views of the city.

🛏 Sleeping

★Mandala International Youth Hostel HOSTEL **$**

(☑522 9053; www.mandalaxining.com; 41 Nanxiaojie, Ningzhiyuan, Qingyafu 2E, 宁智院南小街41号; dm ¥35-60, d ¥50-75; @🛜) Far and away the best place to stay in Xīníng, this guesthouse sits quietly behind the city's Grand Mosque. Bright, spotless dorms and privates are available, each with colourful Tibetan motifs hand-painted on the walls. Shared bathrooms are clean and modern (ours had

QĪNGHǍI XĪNÍNG

Xíning

Tibetan Culture & Medicine Museum (7.5km)

Shengli Lu 胜利路

Xining Road Passenger Transport Terminal (2.5km)

Qinghai Provincial Museum (1.5km)

Huanghe Lu 黄河路

Quyuan Lu 曲苑路

Beichan Si (2km)

Datong Ji

Changliang Lu 长亮路

Central Square

Beer Gardens

Yi'guan Dajie 西关大街

Xi Dajie 西大街

Wenmiao Sq 文庙广场

Xiao Xinjie 小心街

13

4

Dong Dajie 东大街

Bei Dajie 北大街

Mojia Jie 莫家街

9 Snow Lion Tours

15

7

Nanguan Jie 南关街

Nanchuan West Road Passenger Transport Terminal (1.5km)

Shared Taxis to Guidé

Shared Taxis to Kumbum Monastery

Kunlun Zhonglu 昆仑中路

Nanshan Lu 南山路

Qinghai Red Cross Hospital

Nan Dajie 南大街

Jiancai Xiang 建材巷

Tibetan Connections

1

5

Huayuan Lu 花园路

11 12

Xiadu Dajie 夏都大街

Ledu Lu 乐都路

14

Nanxiaojie 南小街

8

6

Zhongnanguan Jie

Dongguan Dajie 东关大街

2 10

Qiyi Lu 七一街

Gonghe Lu 共和路

Wuyi Lu 五一路

Binhe Nanlu 滨河南路

Qilian Lu 祁连路

Xining West (10km)

Xining Railway Station

Huzhu Lu

16

Jianguo Lu 建国路

Bayi Lu 八一路

Bayi Road (500m); CAAC office (1.5km)

Scale: 0 — 500 m / 0 — 0.25 miles

Xīníng

a bathtub), there's fast wi-fi and the downstairs bar/TV room has a great atmosphere.

The Tibetan manager, Westin, speaks excellent English and can offer lots of advice about travelling in the surrounding areas, as well as helping book private cars for day excursions and pointing you in the right direction for exploring Tibetan culture in Xīníng. Prices go up by about ¥20 in summer. Cash only.

Qīnghǎi Sāngzhū Youth Hostel HOSTEL $
(青海桑珠国际青年旅舍; Qīnghǎi Sāngzhū Guójì Qīngnián Lǚshè; ☑359 4118; 94 Huzhu Zhonglu, 互助中路94号; dm ¥40-55, d ¥90; @⊚; ☐32, 33) This spacious hostel has a big lounge decorated with Tibetan artwork and the rooms have comfortable beds. English is spoken and there's traveller information posted on the walls. It's a few kilometres west of town, however, so you'll need to take a bus or taxi to get anywhere.

Lete Youth Hostel HOSTEL $
(理体青年旅舍, Lǐtǐ Qīngnián Lǚshè; ☑820 2080; 16th fl, Bldg 5, International Village Apartments, 2-32 Jiancai Xiang, 建材巷国际村公寓5号楼16层; dm ¥45-55, d without/with bathroom ¥70/140; @⊚) Located in a somewhat unsightly high-rise building, this backpacker joint has a cafe-bar, wide-screen TVs, laundry, kitchen and a small terrace with nice views of the city. Rooms are spacious, though travellers have reported the shared bathrooms could use some sprucing up. Staff members speak English and the travel agency Tibetan Connections (p887) is two floors up.

Sanwant Hotel Xining HOTEL $$$
(西宁神旺大酒店, Xīníng Shénwàng Dà Jiǔdiàn; ☑820 1111; http://sanwant-xining.hotel.com.tw; 79 Changjiang Lu, 长江路79号; s/d ¥650/770;

P✳@⊚) If you're looking to splash out a little, this international hotel does the trick, with sparkling clean rooms, English-speaking staff and a tour desk that can arrange excursions in the area.

Rooms are of an international standard, with ensuite bathrooms (and tubs), though like many international hotels in this part of China, the decor is a bit dated. There's free wi-fi and a big breakfast with a few Western dishes. It's a good option for those stopping over in Xīníng on either side of the Qīnghǎi–Tibet Railway.

Jǐnjiāng Inn HOTEL $$$
(锦江之星; Jǐnjiāng Zhīxīng; ☑492 5666; www.jinjianginns.com; 30 Dong Dajie; 东大街30号; d incl breakfast ¥239; ✳@) This reliable chain hotel is in the heart of Xīníng and has clean rooms and a helpful staff. There are a couple of other locations around town, including one on Nanxiaojie. Book well in advance in summer.

 Eating

Xīníng has a great range of food, especially Tibetan and Hui Muslim cuisines. For Muslim food head to Dongguan Dajie, near the Grand Mosque (p883), or the northern stretch of Nanxiaojie.

ⓘ FULL HOUSE

Scoring a hotel room in Xīníng during the summer months can be surprisingly difficult, especially for foreigners as there are only a few places that will accept them. Book your room or dorm bed as early as possible, preferably one week in advance.

QĪNGHǍI EATS

Qīnghǎi's cuisine is unlike that of any other place in China. Influenced by its mix of ethnic populations – Muslim (Huí, Salar and Uighur), Tibetan and Han Chinese – the food you'll eat here is hearty fare with an emphasis on breads, dumplings and lots of lamb. The following are Qīnghǎi staples. To sample, head to the Mǎzhōng Snack Centre in Xīníng, where all the options are laid out for the taking.

Miànpiàn (面片) Literally translated as 'noodle slices', this dish consists of small, flat squares of noodles cooked in a light broth or oil with greens, fresh tomato and sometimes egg. This is a favourite local snack and you'll see small restaurants all over the province with blinking signs boasting the Chinese characters for *miànpiàn*.

Kǎobǐng (烤饼) These thick pancakes are baked and then further roasted over coal fire and lightly dusted with spicy chilli powder, garlic salt and spices. Order in Muslim restaurants or procure from street vendors, who roast them over coal after dark.

Mómo (馍馍) Tibetan-style dumplings similar to Chinese *bāozi* (steamed meat buns), typically filled with a savoury lamb meatball and served with spiced chilli oil. An alternate version is served in hot broth.

Máoniú suānnǎi (牦牛酸奶, yak milk yoghurt) Whether love or hate, visitors usually have a strong reaction to this Tibetan-style yoghurt made from yak's milk. Shops and vendors all over Qīnghǎi sell small portions in plastic cups, usually served with a sprinkling of rock sugar to balance the tartness. If you enjoy the taste, it's a wonderfully fresh dessert or snack. Locals also claim it helps combat altitude sickness.

For snacks, try one of the cheap barbecue places (烧烤, *shāokǎo*) on Xiao Xinjie that stay open until the early hours.

Mǎzhōng Snack Centre
HAWKER $

(中华名小吃--马忠美食城; Zhōnghuá Míng Xiǎochī–Mǎzhōng Měi Shíchéng; 11-16 Mojia Jie; 莫家街11-16号; noodles ¥12, dishes ¥25) Small stalls selling local and regional specialities line this indoor food court, from Tibetan *mómo* (馍馍; dumplings) to *miànpiàn* (面片; flat noodle pieces) and *chǎodāo xiāomiàn* (炒刀削面; stir-fried spicy noodles). This is an easy option for a cheap, fresh fill-up, especially for those with limited Mandarin skills, as pointing or grab-and-go are the order of the day.

Zhènyà Niúròu Miàn
NOODLES $

(震亚牛肉面; 24 Dongguan Dajie,; 东关大街24号; noodles ¥8-12; ⏰9am-10pm) Join the local Muslim population for their noodle fix at this busy place by the Grand Mosque. There's no menu, but the order of the day is *gān bànmiàn* (干拌面; mince beef noodles; ¥12), which is served swiftly with a side of *suān tāng* (酸汤; black pepper soup) and eaten with a liberal dose of the house chilli oil.

It also does a mean *niúròu miàn* (牛肉面, beef noodles; ¥10). Wash it all down with bottomless cups of dark, flavoursome wheat tea; serve yourself from the hot water basins near the door.

★ Amdo Nomad
Homestyle Restaurant
TIBETAN $$$

(安多藏族牧民人家餐厅; Ānduō Zángzú Mùmín Rénjiā Cāntīng; 22nd fl, Yidan Yuan, Nanxiaojie; 南小街璟城商务宾馆后院一单元22楼; dishes ¥50-70) You might wonder if you're in hipster country as you ascend to the 22nd floor of this residential tower block just off Nanxiaojie. But a door opens and you walk in to a secret Tibetan wonderland: yak hides adorn warm brown walls, and family-style Tibetan meals are served at low tables where you're seated cross-legged.

Food here is authentically Amdo Tibetan. Be sure to sample the *tǔdòu* (土豆, spicy potatoes), *mómo* (馍馍, dumplings) and *miànpiàn* (面片, flat noodle pieces), and finish it off with some *máoniú suānnǎi* (牦牛酸奶, Tibetan yak milk yoghurt). Private rooms and balcony tables have unbeatable views of the city and nearby Nán'guān Mosque lit up in the evening.

It's a bit tough to find. From Nanxiaojie, turn west onto Zhongnanguan Jie and right (north) onto an unmarked road leading out to Dongguan Dajie. Take a swift left into a gated car park for the large high-rise building and enter an unmarked door to the left. Proceed up the grotty elevator to the 22nd floor.

Drinking & Nightlife

Open-air beer gardens line both sides of the Nánchuān River between Kunlun Zhonglu and Xiguan Jie, most of which are open from the afternoon onwards serving big bottles of local beer and snacks.

For a more mellow evening, there is a growing set of cafes, music bars and pubs along Xiadu Dajie between Nanxiao Jie and Huayuan Nanjie.

Xīníng Bar Street
BAR STREET

(酒吧街; jiǔ bā jiē; Wenhua St; 文化街; beer from ¥6) Traditionally Xīníng's nightlife has centred around its so-called bar street: three floors of bars, cafes and restaurants (typically with loud music and neon lights) set around Wenmiao Sq (文庙广场, Wénmiào Guǎngchǎng) off Wenhua Jie.

Greenhouse
CAFE

(古林房咖啡; Gǔlínfáng Kāfēi; ☏820 2710; www.greenhousecoffee.cn; 222-22 Xiadu Dajie, 夏都大街222-22号; coffee from ¥28; ⏰7:30am-11.30pm; 🖥) Rustic split-level wood interior with smoothies and the best coffee in town. Also has a basic menu of pastries and sandwiches. Mellow music selection, too.

Bill's Place
BAR

(火柴人, Huǒchái Rén; ☏824 2626; 222-42 Xiadu Dajie, 夏都大街222-42号; 🖥) This friendly bar/restaurant pulls in Xīníng's expat crowd for good reason. The staff speak decent English and they offer a menu of Western dishes (mains ¥45 to ¥75) like pasta, pizza, salads and a few Mexican items. The real draw is the bar, however, which is one of the few places in the city that mixes cocktails – the margaritas (¥45) are a house speciality. It also has a selection of foreign and Chinese beer and wine.

Shopping

Amdo Café
HANDICRAFTS

(安多咖啡, Ānduō Kāfēiwū; ☏821 3127; 19 Ledu Lu, 乐都路19号; ⏰9am-8pm Mon-Sat; 🖥) Profits from the lovely handmade Tibetan gifts (from ¥30) sold here go back to the local craftswomen. There's also decent coffee (from ¥20).

Xīníng Tibetan Market
MARKET

(西藏市场, Xīzàng Shìchǎng; Xiǎoshāngpǐn Shìchǎng; Huzhu Lu; 互助路小商品市场; ⏰9am-5pm) The four floors of this market are chock-full of Tibetan goods and you'll see groups of monks stopping in to stock up on various Buddhist knicknacks and attire. A few shops specialise in Tibetan Buddhist music (and instruments), and there are numerous places to score a statue of a Buddha or bodhisattva or a string of prayer flags to bring home.

Shuǐjīng Xiàng Market
MARKET

(水井巷商场, Shuǐjīng Xiàng Shāngchǎng; ⏰9am-6pm) This arcade-style market has a double row of shops selling everything from fruit and spices to Tibetan bags and scarves. It's a good place to score a cheap souvenir or some breakfast items. Runs north–south between Xi Dajie and Nanguan Jie.

🛈 Information

Bank of China (中国银行; Zhōngguó Yínháng; 22 Dong Dajie; 东大街22号; ⏰9am-5pm Mon-Fri, 10am-4pm Sat & Sun) Has a number of large branches around town that exchange cash and travellers cheques and have foreign-friendly ATMs.

ICBC ATM (工商银行; Gōngshāng Yínháng; 55 Nanxiaojie; 南小街55号) Has ATMs that accept foreign cards.

Post Office (中国邮政, Zhōngguó Yóuzhèng; cnr Xi Dajie & Nan Dajie, 西大街南大街的路口; ⏰8.30am-6pm)

Public Security Bureau (PSB; 公安局; Gōng'ānjú; 35 Bei Dajie; 北大街35号; ⏰8.30-11.30am & 2.30-5.30pm Mon-Fri) Can extend visas.

Qīnghǎi Red Cross Hospital (青海红十字医院, Qīnghǎi Hóngshízì Yīyuàn; ☏824 7545; Nan Dajie) English-speaking doctors available. Outpatients (门诊部, ménzhěn bù) has a 24-hour pharmacy (药店, yàodiàn).

Snow Lion Tours (☏816 3350; www.snowliontours.com; Cheng Lin Mansion, Office 1212, 7 Dong Dajie; 东大街7号, 成林大厦) Run by a knowledgable English-speaking Tibetan guy; arranges treks, camping with nomads and Tibet permits. The office is located in the same building as the Chéng Lín Hotel.

Tibetan Connections (☏135 1973 7734; www.tibetanconnections.com; 16th fl, Bldg 5, International Village Apartments, 2-32 Jiancai Xiang) This friendly tour company focuses on remoter parts of Amdo and Kham but can arrange trips into Tibet. Prices may be a little higher than local travel agencies but staff speak English and are good to deal with. The agency is located in Lete Youth Hostel (p885).

ⓘ Getting There & Away

AIR

Flights include Běijīng (¥1450), Chéngdū (¥990), Shànghǎi (¥940), Yùshù (¥1280), Golmud (¥1330) and Xī'ān (¥650). There are no direct flights to Lhasa; you must fly via Chéngdū.

The **Civil Aviation Administration of China** (CAAC; 中国民航; Zhōngguó Mínháng; ☐ 813 3333; 32 Bayi Xilu; ☉ 8.30am-5.30pm) has a booking office on Bayi Lu near the long-distance bus station.

BUS

Xīníng's main Jianguo Rd bus station (车站, chēzhàn) closed in 2013 as part of the rebuilding work on the city's main railway station. Buses for most towns in Qīnghǎi and neighbouring provinces currently leave from one of three stations: Bayi Road bus station, **Xinning Road Passenger Transport Terminal** (新宁路客运站; Xīnníng Lù Kèyùn Zhàn; Xinning Lu, 新宁路) and **Nanchuan West Road Passenger Transport Terminal** (南川西路客运站; Nánchuān Xīlù Kèyùn Zhàn; 4 Nanchuan Xilu, 南川西路4号).

Buses to Golmud take around 12 hours, and sleepers to Yùshù can take up to 17 hours.

MINIVAN & SHARED TAXI

Minivans and shared cars depart to some of the same destinations reached by bus. They leave when full so you won't know how long you have to wait around, but once they go the trip will be shorter than the bus ride. These vehicles typically leave between 8am and 2pm.

You can score a ride to Tóngrén (¥70) from the corner of Bayi Lu and Delingha Lu. For Guìdé (¥70), head to the northern side of the intersection on Kunlun Zhonglu (near the bridge).

TRAIN

After being closed for reconstruction for several years, Xīníng Railway Station (火车站, Huǒchē Zhàn) reopened in September 2015, with new high-speed rail services passing through here between Lánzhōu in Gānsù province and Ürümqi in Xīnjiāng. Regional trains also start/stop at Xīníng West Railway Station (西火车站, Xī Huǒchē Zhàn), about 10km west of the city centre.

Lhasa-bound trains pass through Xīníng (hard/soft sleeper ¥500/800, 22 hours) on their way towards the now world-famous Qīnghǎi–Tibet Railway stretch of China's rail network, but the K9801 actually starts here so is usually easier to get tickets for. Make sure to have all your Tibet papers in order.

Other destinations from Xīníng:

Běijīng Sleeper ¥500, 22 to 24 hours

Chéngdū Sleeper ¥400, 25 hours

Golmud Seat/sleeper ¥105/250, eight to 11 hours

Lánzhōu Seat ¥40, 2½ hours

Xī'ān Seat/sleeper ¥120/300, 10 to 14 hours

ⓘ Getting Around

The airport is 27km east of the city. Shuttle buses (¥21, 30 minutes) leave from the CAAC office on Bayi Lu.

City buses cost ¥1 per ride. A handy route is bus 1, which runs from **Bayi Road Bus Station** (八一路汽车站; Bāyī Lù Qìchē Zhàn; cnr Bayi Lu & Huangzhong Lu, 八一路和湟中路路口) along Dongguan Dajie before heading north nearby the Tibetan Culture Museum, a 45-minute ride. Taxis are ¥6 for the first 3km and ¥1.20 per kilometre thereafter.

Around Xīníng

Qīnghǎi Lake

China's largest lake, Qīnghǎi Lake (青海湖; Qīnghǎi Hú; Lake Kokonor; elevation 3600m) has become a huge draw for large tour groups but views of the lake backdropped by mountains still make the trek out worthwhile.

◉ Sights

Bird Island   ISLAND
(鸟岛; Niǎo Dǎo; admission ¥115) This island on China's largest lake (now in fact a peninsula) is the breeding ground for thousands of wild geese, gulls, cormorants, sandpipers, extremely rare black-necked cranes and other bird species. Perhaps the most interesting are the bar-headed geese that migrate over the Himalayas to spend winter on the Indian plains, and have been spotted flying at altitudes of 10,000m.

The island is located on the western side of the lake, about 300km from Xīníng. The best time to visit is from March to early June, when migratory birds have stopped over to nest.

Èrlángjiàn Scenic Area   LAKE
(青海湖二郎剑景区; Qīnghǎi Hú Èrlángjiàn Jǐngū; admission ¥100) The closest Qīnghǎi Lake tourist spot to Xīníng, this site 150km west of town consists of a Chinese-style sightseeing village backing on to the shores of the lake. A long pier allows you to walk out over the calm waters, and on a clear day there are glorious views of the surrounding mountains, as well as the ruin of the **Torpedo Launch**

Experiment Base, China's first torpedo testing site, set up in the 1960s. Though far from the most scenic spot in the area, if you're pressed for time, this is the best way to catch a glimpse of Qīnghǎi Lake without shelling out too much money or doing an overnight.

There are a number of ways to move around the site, including a trolley bus (¥10) that leaves from the main entrance and carries you down to the lake shore. It's an easy 10-minute walk, though, and there are also bicycles for hire (¥15 per hour), which makes for the most pleasant way to explore the area.

Dedicated buses depart regularly from Xīníng's Bayi Road Bus Station and cost ¥37 each way. Don't forget to purchase a ticket for your return journey at the Èrlángjiàn ticket window.

🛏 Sleeping

Niǎo Dǎo Bīnguǎn   HOTEL $$$
(鸟岛宾馆; ☑0970-865 5098; r incl breakfast from ¥380) This hotel offers no-fills accommodation with basic amenities, but is the closest to Bird Island. The hotel is located on the western side of Qīnghǎi Lake in Xiànggōng Village (向公村, Xiànggōng Cūn). You are still 16km from the island here, but you should be able to hire a taxi (¥70 return).

ℹ Getting There & Away

The best way to see the sights here is by hiring a private car and driver (¥500 per day). Alternately, all-inclusive overnights and multiday trips can be organised through travel agencies in Xīníng, including Tibetan Connections (p887). Touts abound at every bus station in Xīníng; bargain hard and you could score a great deal on a shared taxi.

Kumbum Monastery (Tǎ'ěr Sì) 塔尔寺

One of the great monasteries of the Gelugpa (Yellow Hat) sect of Tibetan Buddhism, **Kumbum Monastery** (admission ¥80; ⊙8.30am-6pm) was built in 1577 on hallowed ground – the birthplace of Tsongkhapa, founder of the sect.

It's of enormous historical significance, and hundreds of monks still live here but, perhaps because it's such a big tourist draw for this part of Qīnghǎi, the atmosphere can at times feel a bit overrun. The artwork and architecture, however, remain impressive.

Nine temples are open, each with its own characteristics. The most important is the **Grand Hall of Golden Tiles** (大金瓦殿,

---

WORTH A TRIP

KANBULA NATIONAL PARK

The desert scenery outside of Tóngrén comes to a pinnacle in **Kanbula National Park** (坎布拉国家森林公园; Kǎnbùlā Guójiā Sēnlín Gōngyuán; admission ¥100) where flaming red mountains meet the turquoise waters of a reservoir created by the damming of the Yellow River. A nervous-sweat-inducing road snakes up through the park's peaks, past sleepy Tibetan villages and colourful prayer flags waving high on the wind.

It's best to hire a private driver to bring you here from either Tóngrén (¥300 per day) or Xīníng (¥700 per day) to fully experience the park, including plenty of photo stops and a chance to explore the villages. The drive from Xīníng also passes over dusky 3980m peaks.

Dàjīnwǎ Diàn), where an 11m-high *chörten* (stupa) marks the spot of Tsongkhapa's birth. You'll see pilgrims walking circuits of the building and prostrating outside the entrance. Also worth seeking out is the **Yak Butter Scripture Temple** (酥油画馆, Sūyóuhuà Guǎn), which houses sculptures of human figures, animals and landscapes carved out of yak butter.

Kumbum is located 27km from Xīníng in the town of Huángzhōng. Buses (¥11, 45 minutes) leave every six minutes from Xinning Road Passenger Transport Terminal, starting at 7am. Get off at the last stop and walk up the hill to the monastery. The last bus back is at 7pm.

Yòuníng Monastery   佑宁寺

Well known throughout the Tibetan world, this 17th-century hillside **monastery** (Yòuníng Sì) in the Hùzhù Tǔzú (互助土族) Autonomous County is considered one of the greats of the Gelugpa order. The monastery lies at the edge of a forested valley, and many chapels perch wondrously on the sides of a cliff face. Give yourself a couple of hours to explore the entire picturesque area.

Famous for its academies of medicine and astrology, its scholars and its tulku (living Buddhas), Yòuníng Monastery (*Rgolung* in Tibetan) was instrumental in solidifying Gelugpa dominance over the Amdo region. The monastery was founded by the Mongolian 4th Dalai Lama, and over time became a religious centre for the local Tǔ (themselves a distant Mongolian people). At its height, over 7000 monks resided here; these days there are probably less than 200, all of whom are Tǔ.

There are a couple of ways to reach the monastery. Buses to Píng'ān (¥8, 40 minutes) go from Xīníng's Bayi Road Bus Station (p888). From there, you'll need to hire a taxi (one way/return ¥70/100, 30 minutes). Alternately, if you have a group, you could hire a private car or taxi (return ¥400) from Xīníng. The monastery is about 25km north of Píng'ān.

Tóngrén (Repkong) 同仁

☑ 0973

For several centuries now, the villages outside the monastery town of Tóngrén (Repkong in Tibetan) have been famous for producing some of the Tibetan world's best *thangkas* and painted statues, so much so that an entire school of Tibetan art is named after the town. Visiting Wútún Sì monastery not only gives you a chance to meet the artists, but also to purchase a painting or two, fresh off the easel.

Tóngrén is set on the slopes of the wide and fertile Gu-chu river valley. The local populace is a mix of Tibetans and Tǔ. The valley and surrounding hills are easily explored on foot.

◉ Sights

Lóngwù Sì   MONASTERY
(隆务寺; Rongwo Gonchen Gompa; Dehelong Nanlu; 德合隆南路; admission ¥60) Tóngrén's main monastery is a huge and rambling maze of renovated chapels and monks' residences, dating from 1301. It's well worth a wander, and you'll need one or two hours to see everything. Your ticket includes entry into six main halls, although you may be able to take a peek inside others too.

There are more than 500 resident monks and every day dozens of them go into the courtyard outside the **Hall of Bodhisattva Manjusri** (文殊殿; Wénshū Diàn) to take part in animated, hand-clapping debates. There's a map in English on a wooden board just inside the main gate.

Wútún Sì   MONASTERY
(吾屯寺; admission ¥30) This complex of two monasteries is the place to head if you're interested in Tibetan art. The **Upper (Yango)**

Monastery (吾屯上寺; Wútún Shàngsì) is closest to Tóngrén, while the **Lower (Mango) Monastery** (吾屯下寺; Wútún Xiàsì) is larger and may offer the chance to see monks painting. The monks will show you around and you can usually ask to see a showroom or workshop. The resident artists are no amateurs – commissions for their *thangka* paintings come in all the way from Lhasa, and prices aren't cheap.

Artwork is usually of an exceptionally high quality, but expect to pay hundreds of rénmínbì for the smallest painting, thousands for a poster-sized one and tens or even hundreds of thousands for the largest pieces. There are a handful of showrooms outside the Lower Monastery where you can browse and buy.

The Lower Monastery is easily recognisable by eight large *chörten* out front. While there, check out the 100-year-old **Jampa Lhakhang** (Jampa Temple) and the new chapels dedicated to Chenresig and Tsongkhapa.

The Upper Monastery includes a massive modern *chörten* as well as the old *dukhang* (assembly hall) and the new chapel dedicated to Maitreya (Shampa in Amdo dialect). The interior murals here (painted by local artists) are superb.

To get here, take a minibus (¥2 per seat) from the intersection just uphill from Tóngrén bus station ticket office. The 6.5km walk back takes around an hour, or hail a minibus on its way back to town.

🛏 Sleeping & Eating

★ **Rebgong Norbang Travel Inn**   HOTEL $$
(热贡诺尔邦旅游客栈, Règòng Nuò'ěrbāng Lǚyóu Kèzhàn; ☑ 8726999, 8726555; Xuelian Donglu; 雪莲东路; d/ste ¥140/400; 🅿 @ 🛜) This clean spot is one of the most modern hotels in Tóngrén and offers fantastic value. Most floors have spacious, clean Western-style rooms, but pay a little extra to stay on the floor with rooms in traditional Tibetan style, which have huge wooden beds, books on Tibetan Buddhism and sparkling ensuite bathrooms.

Règòng Sìhéjí Bīnguǎn   HOTEL $$
(热贡四合吉宾馆; ☑ 879 7988; 14 Dehelong Nanlu, 德合隆南路14号; d from ¥160) This hotel has a colourful lobby that leads up through gold hallways to bright and clean rooms with flat-screen TVs and well-maintained bathrooms. It's wellplaced on Tóngrén's main road about 200m before Lóngwù Sì.

XÚNHUÀ

A nice side trip from Tóngrén is to Xúnhuà (循化), a tidy town in the Xúnhuà Salar Autonomous County, about 75km northeast of Tóngrén. The Salar Muslims have their origins in Samarkand and speak an isolated Turkic language, giving the region a Central Asian feel (and cuisine).

Mèngdá Nature Reserve (孟达国家自然保护区; Mèngdá Guójiā Zìrán Bǎohùqū; admission ¥70; ⊙8am-6pm) This nature reserve is home to a tiny lake that is sacred for both Salar Muslims and Tibetan Buddhists, and is much hyped locally. The road to the reserve – which follows the coppery-green Yellow River as it cuts its way through a fantastically scenic gorge of rust-red cliffs – is worth the trip alone. You'll find stunning photo opportunities around every turn. From the main gate of the reserve you can ride horses (¥50, 30 minutes) to the lake or take a gas-powered buggy (free) to a small parking area, then walk the rest of the way. To get to the reserve you'll need to hire a taxi from outside Xúnhuà bus station. Expect to pay at least ¥200 return, including waiting time.

Jiāotōng Bīnguǎn (交通宾馆; ☑0972-881 2615; d/tw ¥160/240) This inn beside Xúnhuà's bus station has comfortable rooms often discounted to less than ¥100.

Homely Teahouse TIBETAN $
(温馨茶艺; Wēnxīn Cháyì; Dehelong Nanlu; 德合隆南路; dishes ¥8-14; ⊙8am-midnight) This authentic Tibetan restaurant – with a yak skull hanging on the wall and plastic flowers throughout – serves *mómo,* yoghurt and noodle soup and a range of beers and teas. It's located in a cosy two-storey wood-panelled building with excellent views of the valley.

ℹ Information

China Construction Bank ATM (建设银行; Jiànshè Yínháng; 47 Zhongshan Lu; 中山路47号) Foreign-card friendly.

ℹ Getting There & Around

The scenery on the road from Xīníng is awesome as it follows a tributary of the Yellow River through steep-sided gorges, but the way out to Xiàhé is even better, passing dramatic red rock scenery and the impressive Gartse Gompa, where local Tibetan herders board the bus to sell fresh yoghurt. For Xiàhé and Línxià, try to buy your ticket one day in advance.

Guìdé 贵德
☑0974

As the Yellow River (黄河; Huáng Hé) flows down from the Tibetan Plateau it makes a series of sharp bends, powering its way past ancient Guìdé. Sitting on the riverbank here at sunset, with a beer in hand, is a great way to end the day. The *gǔchéng* (古城; old town), still largely enclosed within its crumbling 10m-high mud walls, also makes for a

pleasant stroll and is a good base for your stay. But changes are afoot. The government has begun to knock down many buildings in the old town with a plan to redevelop the place into a major tourist attraction, complete with five-star hotels and a golf course. Get here soon before it's discovered by the masses.

◎ Sights & Activities

★**Guìdé National Geological Park** PARK
(贵德国家地质公园; Guìdé Guójiā Dìzhì Gōngyuán; 101 Provincial Rd, 省道101; admission ¥80; ☑11) In the stunning multicoloured clay scenery of Dānxiá Canyon (丹霞峡谷; Dānxiá Xiágǔ), this geopark offers walking trails in among red and orange hills that have eroded into other-wordly shapes. Set against the contrasting blue Qīnghǎi skies and teal waters of the Yellow River, this is a lovely spot to spend an afternoon wandering and taking photos, or exploring the peculiar geology of this part of the Tibetan Plateau.

Signs and maps in English and well-kept paths allow for easy access to the geological formations and make this an easy walk rather than a backcountry hike. The park is located about 20km north of Guìdé. A taxi will cost around ¥50.

Yùhuáng Pavilion CONFUCIAN TEMPLE
(玉皇阁; Yùhuáng Gé; 5 Beida Jie, 北大街5号; admission ¥60; ⊙8.30am-6pm) The focal point of Guìdé's old town is this small temple complex, built in 1592. It includes a three-storey pagoda, which can be climbed for good views, and a **Confucius Temple** (文庙; Wén Miào).

HIKING ON SACRED MT AMNYE MACHEN

The 6282m peak of Machen Kangri, or Mt Amnye Machen (阿尼玛卿, Ānímǎqīng), is Amdo's most sacred mountain – it's eastern Tibet's equivalent to Mt Kailash in western Tibet. Tibetan pilgrims travel for weeks to circumambulate the peak, believing it to be home to the protector deity Machen Pomra. The circuit's sacred geography and wild mountain scenery make it a fantastic, though adventurous, trekking destination.

The full circuit takes around 11 days (including transport to/from Xīníng), though tourists often limit themselves to a half circuit. Several monasteries lie alongside the route.

With almost all of the route above 4000m, and the highest pass hitting 4600m, it's essential to acclimatise before setting off, preferably by spending a night or two at nearby Mǎqìn (玛沁; Tawo; 3760m). You can make a good excursion 70km north of town to Rabgya Gompa (拉加寺; Lājiā Sì), an important branch of Tibet's Sera Monastery. The best months to trek are May to October, though be prepared for snow early and late in the season.

Since local public transport is almost nonexistent, most trekkers go on an organised tour. Expect to pay around US$140 per person per day, all-inclusive.

If you do want to try venturying out on your own, take the bus to Huāshíxiá (花石峡) and then hitch or hire a shared minivan (¥300 to ¥400 per person) to Xiàdàwǔ (下大吾). In Xiàdàwǔ the starting point for the *kora* (holy hike) path is at Guru Gompa (格日寺, Gérì Sì), and from here follow the road east. After three days the road peters out near Xuěshān (雪山), from where you can hitch a ride to Mǎqìn. If you intend to continue past Xuěshān you'll need to ask a local to show you the *kora* path. In Xiàdàwǔ, a guide costs ¥120 to ¥150 per day, and it's about the same price for a packhorse or yak.

China Fortune Wheel
RELIGIOUS SITE

(中华福运轮, Zhōnghuá Fúyùnlún; Nanbinhe Lu, 南滨河路; admission ¥80) This enormous, gold-plated Tibetan prayer wheel is turned with the aid of rushing water from the Yellow River. The prayer wheel is 27m tall, 10m in diameter and weighs 200 tonnes, earning it a spot in the *Guinness World Records* as the world's largest prayer wheel.

Inside the wheel are 200 copies of the Kangyur text, and the base contains a large prayer hall. Near the wheel is a museum of Tibetan artefacts.

The wheel is located in a dedicated park along the Yellow River, which can be reached by following Huanghe Nanlu behind Yùhuáng Pavilion and turning left at the large suspension bridge. Alternately, a mototaxi from Nan Dajie costs ¥10.

Zhācāng Hot Springs
HOT SPRINGS

Guìdé's hot springs (扎仓温泉, Zhācāng Wēnquán), known locally as *rèshuǐ gōu* (热水沟), are a 13km-drive from town past some mightily impressive barren scenery. Here you can join the local Tibetans for a free outdoor bath. There are several guesthouses nearby where you can enter the pools for a fee of ¥20. Naked bathing is common. Don't expect any infrastructure.

🛏 Sleeping & Eating

Guìdé is a busy town and the government's plans to turn it into a tourism centre mean there is already plenty of accommodation and eating options, with more being built all the time. There are lots of bright, clean restaurants along Bei Dajie near Yùhuáng Pavilion, many with atmospheric pavement tables, perfect for munching some *liángmiàn* (凉面; cold noodles with chilli, vinegar and chives) and sipping a cold beer.

Qīnghǎi Guìdé Hot Spring Hotel
HOTEL $$

(温泉宾馆; Wēnquán Bīnguǎn; ☑ 855 3534; 355 Yingbin Lu; 迎宾路355号; d/ste ¥200/550; ✳@⌧) This upmarket option is starting to show its age, but it is still a decent choice for foreigners, with a heated pool, spa and pleasant garden grounds, as well as 24-hour hot water. It should be noted that there are no hot springs on-site.

Jīnhéyuán International Hotel
HOTEL $$$

(金河源国际酒店; Jīnhéyuán Guójì Jiǔdiàn; 33 Yingbin Xilu; 迎宾西路33号; d/ste ¥420/700; P✳@⌢) This sparkling Western-style hotel offers all the standard amenities in bright, spacious rooms decorated to as high a standard as you'll find in this region, with prices to match. There's a breakfast buffet on the 2nd floor and staff speak limited English.

ⓘ Information

There are *wǎngbā* (网吧; internet cafes) on Yingbingo Xilu and Bei Dajie.

China Construction Bank ATM (建设银行, Jiànshè Yínháng; 14 Yingbin Xilu, 迎宾西路) Accepts foreign cards.

ⓘ Getting There & Around

There are regular buses to Xīníng (¥26, two hours) and several other destinations around Qīnghǎi.

The old town is 1.5km from the bus station. Turn left out of the station on Yingbin Xilu, then left again along Nan Dajie and past the old town gate to arrive at Bei Dajie. Three-wheel motorised rickshaws ply the streets of Guìdé. Most short trips cost ¥5 to ¥10.

Yùshù (Jyekundo)　玉树

☑ 0976 / POP 380,000

Until the spring of 2010, Yùshù (Jyekundo is the name of the town itself while Yùshù is the prefecture) and its surrounding areas gained notoriety as one of Qīnghǎi's best adventure-travel destinations. All that changed on 14 April 2010, when a 7.1-magnitude earthquake devastated the town, killing 2698 people (although some believe the true figure across the whole region to be more like 20,000).

After the earthquake most of Jyekundo's buildings were pulled down and an army of construction workers arrived to rebuild the city. Locals were housed in government-issued blue tents, giving the place the look and feel of a refugee camp (and a very dusty, noisy one at that).

In early 2014 the government officially declared Yùshù reopened for tourism. A shiny new town centre built in Tibetan-style architecture (with a modern Chinese twist) replaced the tent village, while a monument shaped like a crumbling building stands as a reminder of the town's painful recent history.

◉ Sights & Activities

Jyekundo Dondrubling Monastery　MONASTERY
(嘎结古寺, Gájié Gǔsì) **FREE** First built in 1398, the Jyekundo Dondrubling Monastery suffered heavy damage from the 2010 earthquake (the main prayer hall was completely destroyed and a number of resident monks were killed). At the time of writing, it was still being rebuilt, albeit with concrete and other modern materials, and probably won't

be completed for a few more years. It's dramatically located on a ridge perched above town. It takes about 20 minutes to walk the 1.5km from town via the atmospheric **mani lhakhang** (chapel containing a large prayer wheel), or a taxi costs around ¥30.

Seng-ze Gyanak Mani Wall　BUDDHIST
(新寨嘉那嘛呢石堆; Xīnzhài Jiānà Mání Shíduī; Xīnzhài Village) **FREE** Completely rebuilt after suffering extensive damage in the 2010 earthquake, this site is thought to be the world's largest *mani* wall (piles of stones with Buddhist mantras carved or painted on them). Founded in 1715, the *mani* consists of an estimated 2.5 billion mantras, piled one on top of the other over hundreds of square metres. It's an astonishing sight that grows more and more marvellous as you circumambulate the wall with the pilgrims. Be sure to turn the dozens of prayer wheels, and head into the pile itself for a moment of quiet reflection.

In addition to the patchwork of *mani* stone piles outside, the rebuild includes a series of stone paths outside the main pile, as well as stone benches.

🎿 Festivals & Events

Horse Festival　CULTURAL
(Yùshù Sàimǎ Jié; 玉树赛马节) Yùshù's spectacular three-day horse festival (late July) features traditional horse and yak races, Tibetan wrestling, archery, shooting and dance. The festival hasn't been regularly held since the earthquake, but did make a comeback in 2014. Double-check the latest before you make this part of your itinerary.

🛏 Sleeping & Eating

After the 2010 earthquake, many hotels in Yùshù were badly damaged or destroyed. Many have since been rebuilt, but prices can be shockingly high for this remote part of China and facilities are still sometimes lacking in amenities, including 24-hour hot water or wi-fi.

Pearl Business Hotel　HOTEL **$$**
(明珠商务宾馆, Míngzhū Shāngwù Bīnguǎn; ☑ 881 1177; 33 Qionglong Lu; 琼龙路33号; d ¥280) This spiffy hotel has an intimate feel with all the regular amenities and bright, clean bathrooms. There's 24-hour hot water and rooms come with hairdryers and high-speed broadband connection. Prices are negotiable so ask to see a room first.

THE SOURCE OF THE YELLOW RIVER

Set in stunning, barren, high-plateau scenery, Zhǎlíng & Èlíng Lakes (扎陵湖和鄂陵湖, Zhǎlíng Hú Hé Èlíng Hú) purportedly host the source of the Yellow River (黄河源头, Huánghé yuántóu), China's most revered waterway. The scenery around the two lakes here, and en route, is awesome. While here you might spot animals including fox, marmot, eagle, antelope and, of course, plenty of yaks.

Note, the widely accepted source of the Yellow River, which is marked by an engraved stone tablet, is actually just the most accessible of a number of sources. Locals refer to it as *niútóubēi* (牛头碑). If you want to get to the very-hard-to-find true source of the Yellow River you'll need a two-day round trip from Mǎduō (玛多; sleeping in the 4WD) and it will cost around ¥3000 per vehicle, assuming you can find a driver willing to take you.

There's nowhere to stay or eat, so most people visit the lake as a day trip from the two-street town of Mǎduō. From Mǎduō, SUVs take you to the lake and back (¥1000 per vehicle; three hours one way). It is possible to camp here in the summer but you'll need to be completely self-sufficient.

Remember this area, including Mǎduō (4260m), is over 4000m high so altitude sickness is a real risk. Consider coming from Yùshù (3680m) rather than Xīníng (2275m) so you don't have to ascend too much in one go.

Kham Inn HOTEL $$$

(康巴驿站; Kāngbā Yìzhàn; ☐881 6111; Middle of Qionglong Lu; 琼龙路中段; d ¥428) Regarded as one of the best hotels in Yùshù, this gleaming place has spotless rooms with TVs, internet, 24-hour hot water, and hairdryers. Bathrooms are big and bright and even the carpets are superclean.

Gǎnggā Rìwú Zàngcān TIBETAN $$

(岗嘎日吾藏餐; Minzhu Lu, west of People's Bank; 民主路中段, 人民银行往西米; meals ¥40-50; ⏰10am-9.30pm) This local restaurant is regarded as the best Tibetan place in Jyekundo. The traditional decor complements the local dishes, which are flavourful and beautifully presented. It's a great option for those wanting to try traditional Tibetan food.

❶ Getting There & Away

AIR

Yùshù Bātáng Airport is 25km south of town. There are daily flights to Xīníng (¥1920), with continuing service to Xī'ān.

BUS

Yùshù's rebuilt **long-distance bus terminal** (玉树长途客运站; Yùshù chángtú kèyùn zhàn; Xihang Lu; 西航路) opened in September 2014 in combination with a new stretch of highway connecting it to Xīníng (¥191) and reducing travel time to just 10 to 13 hours. The terminal also serves Chéngdū with one departure daily, and Chóngqìng. Buses for other parts of Qīnghǎi go from the Provincial Bus Station (省汽车站临

时点, Shěng Qìchē Zhàn Línshí Diǎn) in Dōngfēng village.

Long-distance minibuses depart from outside the long-distance bus terminal bound for Nangchen (¥60, four to five hours), leaving only when full. Vehicles also depart when full for Gānzī (¥180, 13 hours) in Sìchuān from another minivan stand located on Qionglong Lu (琼龙路).

❶ Getting Around

Local bus routes 2, 3 and 4 (¥1) connect the main areas of town via three stations: Zhā Xīkē (扎西科), Fó Xuéyuàn (佛学院) and Xī Háng (西杭). You need to hail the bus for it to stop, and be aware they run very infrequently. Taxis are prevalent and fares start at ¥10, rising steeply if you head anywhere out of town. A taxi to the airport is ¥50.

Around Yùshù

Princess Wencheng Temple 文成公主庙

This **temple** (Wénchéng Gōngzhǔ Miào) is dedicated to the Tang-dynasty Chinese Princess Wencheng, who was instrumental in converting her husband and Tibetan king, Songtsen Gampo, to Buddhism in the 7th century. The temple marks the spot where the princess (and possibly the king) paused for a month en route from Xī'ān to Lhasa.

Said to be the oldest Buddhist temple in Qīnghǎi, the inner chapel has a rock carving (supposedly self-arising) of Vairocana

(Nampa Namse in Tibetan), the Buddha of primordial wisdom, which allegedly dates from the 8th century. To the left is a statue of King Songtsen Gampo.

The temple, which suffered minor damage from the Yùshù earthquake, is small, and few linger in it for long, but do allow time to explore the nearby hills. Here a sprawling spider's web of blue, red, yellow, white and pink prayer flags runs up the slopes, down the slopes and over the ravine, covering every inch of land, and is one of the most extraordinary sights imaginable.

A steep trail, a popular *kora* (route for pilgrims), ascends from the end of the row of eight *chörtens* to the left of the temple. At the end of the trail head up the grassy side valley for some great hiking and stunning open views.

It's located 20km south of Yùshù. Minibuses (¥20 one-way) depart from outside the long-distance bus terminal in Yùshù, or a taxi costs about ¥80 return.

Nangchen 囊谦

📞 0976 / ELEV 3680M

The scenic county of Nangchen (Nángqiān), a former Tibetan kingdom, is the end of the line for most travellers. Further south of here is the Qīnghǎi–Tibet border, with roads to Riwoche and Chamdo, but any attempt to go here without the proper permits (and guide and driver) will land you in hot water.

Most visit just for the drive from Yùshù to the little county capital of Sharda (Xiāngdá Zhèn; 香达镇; 3550m). Several monasteries are scattered about town.

◉ Sights

Sajiya Gompa　　　BUDDHIST TEMPLE

(萨迦寺; Sàjiā Sì) The most recognisable of the Buddhist monasteries scattered around Sharda, this *gompa* is perched on a hill above town like an old manor. You can hike even further up the hill behind the *gompa* for excellent views of the valley.

Jiaba Gompa　　　BUDDHIST TEMPLE

(加巴寺; Jiābā Sì) This *gompa* in the centre of Sharda is where Tibetans, young and old, appear each morning to turn prayer wheels and circumambulate the temple.

Gar Gompa　　　BUDDHIST TEMPLE

(尕尔寺; Gǎ'ěr Sì) Nestled on the ridge of a forested mountain about 70km south of Sharda is this *gompa*. Wildlife is prevalent in the area, including blue sheep and monkeys. It's a popular spot for birdwatchers. A taxi from Sharda costs about ¥500 return.

🛏 Sleeping & Eating

Nangchen Oriental Hotel　　　HOTEL $

(东方宾馆; Dōngfāng Bīnguǎn; 📞 152 9702 5483; d ¥150) With clean bathrooms and hot showers, this hotel has bright rooms with fresh linens and heating in the winter. At the time of writing the owners were planning to install internet in the rooms.

Zhēngqì Niúròu Miàn Guǎn　　　NOODLES $

(蒸汽牛肉面馆; dishes ¥10; ⊙9am-9pm) A popular and cheap place for Muslim-style noodles. Try the *zhá jiàng miàn* (炸酱面), a dish consisting of hearty meat noodles topped with mince beef. There are two locations, one near the Oriental Hotel and another near the town's main bus station.

QĪNGHǍI AROUND YÙSHÙ

MONASTERIES AROUND YÙSHÙ

The road from Yùshù to Xiēwǔ is dotted with monasteries set among beautiful landscapes, perfect for hiking. Minivans ply the route between Yùshù and Xiēwǔ, from where you should be able to get onward transport to Shíqú.

Sebda Gompa (赛巴寺; Sàibā Sì) The main assembly hall at this monastery is impressive, but most surprising is the chapel featuring a huge 18m statue of Guru Rinpoche, with smaller statues of his various manifestations on either side.

Ethnographic Museum (人种学博物馆; Rénzhǒngxué Bówùguǎn; admission ¥10) This small museum has some offbeat gems like traditional Tibetan clothing, swords and stuffed animals. If you have more time you can explore the ruins of the old monastery on the ridge behind the adjacent *gompa* or do some great hiking in the valley opposite.

Drogon Gompa (歇武寺; Xiēwǔ Sì) This Sakyapa-school temple includes the scary *gönkhang* (protector chapel). Set atop a hill, it is adorned with snarling stuffed wolves and Tantric masks. Only men may enter this chapel.

ℹ Information

There are several internet cafes on Xingfu Lu, reached by walking through the alley next to a bank. You can also use wi-fi at some of the hotels in town.

Agricultural Bank of China (农业银行; Nóngyè Yínháng; Xingfu Lu; 幸福路) Not all foreign cards work here, so don't count on getting cash if you're relying on ATMs.

ℹ Getting There & Away

From Sharda bus station on the main road, one daily bus goes to Xīníng (¥264, 20 to 24 hours) departing at 10am. Book at least one day in advance.

For Yùshù (¥60, three to five hours) most locals travel by shared taxi, which assemble on the main road near the hotels. Major road construction was ongoing at the time of research.

Golmud　格尔木

☑ 0979

For three decades Golmud faithfully served overlanders as the last jumping-off point before Lhasa. Bedraggled backpackers hung around the city's truck depot trying to negotiate a lift to the 'Roof of the World.' But since the completion of the Qīnghǎi–Tibet Railway, this lonesome backwater has become even less important, as most Tibet travellers board the train elsewhere and blow right through town. Today it's mostly of use to travellers trying to get between Lhasa and Dūnhuáng (in Gānsù) or Huátǔgōu (en route to Xīnjiāng).

🛏 Sleeping & Eating

There are a few decent hotel options if you get stuck here for the night, though most travellers are just transiting through.

Both Bayi Lu and Kunlun Lu are lined with restaurants.

Dōngfāng Hotel　　　　HOTEL $
(东方宾馆, Dōngfāng Bīnguǎn; ☑ 841 0011; 7 Bayi Lu; 八一中路7号; d ¥100-128, ste ¥260) This centrally located hotel has clean and tidy standard rooms that come equipped with an ADSL cable for laptops. Deluxe rooms come with floor-to-ceiling windows overlooking Hédōng Market (河东市场; Hédōng Shìchǎng).

Ālán Cāntīng　　　　MUSLIM $
(阿兰餐厅; 48-1 Bayi Lu; 八一中路48-1号; dishes ¥5-48, noodles ¥9; ☑ 8.30am-9pm) Serves several types of Muslim-style noodles, including *gānbàn miàn* (干拌面; spaghetti-style noodles with meat sauce) and *niúròu miàn* (牛肉面; beef noodles). Other dishes are available from a separate photo menu.

ℹ Getting There & Away

Note that if you are heading for Dūnhuáng you'll need a special permit (旅行证, *lǚxíng zhèng*; ¥50) when boarding the bus. Permits are available from the **Public Security Bureau** (PSB; 公安局, Gōng'ānjú; 6 Chaidamu Lu; ☑ 8am-noon & 2.30-5pm Mon-Fri). The PSB can also extend visas. We've also heard reports that the PSB only allows tourists to stay one night in Golmud.

There are buses to a number of destinations in Qīnghǎi and neighbouring provinces from Golmud's **main bus station** (格尔木长途车站, Gé'ěrmù Chángtú Chēzhàn; ☑ 845 3688; 23 Jianyuan Lu, 江源南路23号), including Dūnhuáng (¥102, seven to eight hours), Huátǔgōu (¥104, six hours) and Xīníng (¥160, 12 to 14 hours). There is also a sleeper bus to Charklik (Ruòqiāng; ¥224, 10 hours).

Trains to Lhasa (¥368, 15 hours) tend to depart from **Golmud Railway Station** (格尔木火车站; Gé'ěrmù Huǒchē Zhàn; ☑ 722 2222; Yingbin Lu; 迎宾路) late in the evening or at night; you'll need your Tibet permit to be in order to board. Other destinations include Xīníng (¥191, 10 hours) and Dūnhuáng (¥116, 10 hours).

ℹ Information

Bank of China (中国银行; Zhōngguó Yínháng; cnr Kunlun Lu & Chaidamu Lu; ☑ 9am-5pm Mon-Fri, 10am-4.30pm Sat & Sun) Changes travellers cheques and cash. Foreign-friendly ATM.

CAAC (机场售票处; Jīchǎng Shòupiàochù; ☑ 24hr booking line 842 3333; ☑ 8.30am-6pm) Can help book onward flights.

China International Travel Service (CITS, 中国国际旅行社; Zhōngguó Guójì Lǚxíngshè; ☑ 849 6275; 4th fl, 60 Bayi Zhonglu; 八一中路60号4层; ☑ 8.30am-6pm Mon-Fri) The only place in town that can arrange Tibet permits, though they can only be procured as part of a group tour. Look for the characters 中国旅游 (Zhōngguó Lǚyóu, China Travel).

Tibet

POP 3 MILLION

Best Monasteries

➡ Drepung (p905)

➡ Ganden (p911)

➡ Samye (p911)

➡ Sakya (p916)

Best Views

➡ Everest's north face from
Rongphu Monastery (p917)

➡ Nam-tso from Tashi Dor
(p911)

➡ Yamdrok-tso from the
Kamba-la (p912)

➡ Samye Monastery from
Hepo Ri (p911)

Why Go?

For centuries exotic Tibet has captured the imagination of spiritual seekers, mountain adventurers and intrepid travellers. For modern travellers the 'roof of the world' continues to promise breathtaking high-altitude scenery, awe-inspiring monasteries, epic trans-Himalayan road trips and a unique Buddhist culture that remains vibrant even after half a century of assault and repression.

Perhaps the true highlight of Tibet, though, is the Tibetan people, from crimson-robed monks to wild-haired pilgrims, whose colour, good humour and religious devotion are what makes travelling across the plateau such a profound joy.

Tibet is changing at a pace unmatched even in China. The political tensions of recent years have resulted in strict travel restrictions on foreigners throughout the autonomous region, limiting travel to pre-arranged group tours. Despite all this, the magic of old Tibet is still there – you just to have to work a bit harder to find it these days.

When to Go
Lhasa

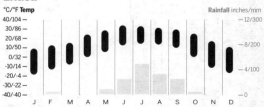

Mar This politically sensitive month brings closures and permit problems; avoid.

May–Sep High season: warm weather, some rain in July/August, and good hiking.

Apr & mid-Oct–Nov A good time to visit, with fewer crowds and warm days.

Tibet Highlights

1 Rub shoulders with Tibetan pilgrims in the holy city of **Lhasa** (p902)

2 Wonder at the murals of angels and demons in the 108 chapels of the

Gyantse Kumbum (p913), an architectural wonder

3 Erase the sins of a lifetime on the three-day pilgrim circuit around sacred **Mt Kailash** (p920)

4 Rouse yourself from a yak-wool tent or monastery guesthouse to catch sunrise at **Everest Base Camp** (p917)

5 Ride the planet's highest rails across the roof of the

world on the **Qinghǎi–Tibet Railway** (p909) to Lhasa

6 Explore the mandala-shaped chapels and stupas at **Samye Monastery** (p911), Tibet's first monastery

7 Hire a vehicle for the week-long trip along the **Friendship Highway** (p912) from Lhasa to Kathmandu, one of Asia's great road trips

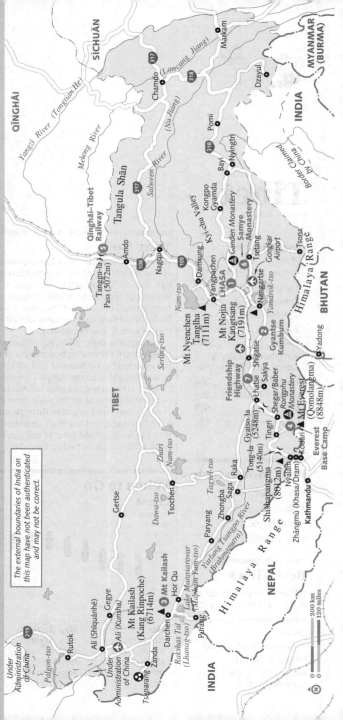

The external boundaries of India on this map have not been authenticated and may not be correct.

History

Recorded Tibetan history began in the 7th century AD, when the Tibetan armies began to assemble a great empire. Under King Songtsen Gampo, the Tibetans occupied Nepal and collected tribute from parts of Yúnnán. Shortly afterwards the Tibetan armies moved north and took control of the Silk Road and the great trade centre of Kashgar, even sacking the imperial Chinese city of Cháng'ān (present-day Xī'ān).

Tibetan expansion came to an abrupt halt in 842 with the assassination of anti-Buddhist King Langdarma; the region subsequently broke into independent feuding principalities. The increasing influence of Buddhism ensured that the Tibetan armies would never again leave their high plateau.

By the 7th century, Buddhism had spread through Tibet, though it had taken on a unique form, as it adopted many of the rituals of Bön (the indigenous pre-Buddhist belief system of Tibet). The prayer flags, pilgrimage circuits and sacred landscapes you'll see across modern Tibet all have their roots in the animist religion of Bön.

From the 13th century, power politics began to play an increasing role in religion. In 1641 the Gelugpa ('Yellow Hat' order) used the support of Mongol troops to crush the Sakyapa, their rivals. It was also during this time of partisan struggle that the Gelugpa leader adopted the title of Dalai Lama (Ocean of Wisdom), given to him by the Mongols. From here on out, religion and politics in Tibet became inextricably entwined and both were presided over by the Dalai Lama.

With the fall of the Qing dynasty in 1911, Tibet entered a period of de facto independence that was to last until 1950. In this year a resurgent communist China invaded Tibet, claiming it was 'liberating' over one million Tibetans from feudal serfdom and bringing it back into the fold of the motherland.

Increasing popular unrest in response to Chinese land reform resulted in a full-blown revolt in 1959, which was crushed by the People's Liberation Army (PLA). Amid popular rumours of a Chinese plot to kidnap him, the Dalai Lama fled to India. He was followed by an exodus of 80,000 of Tibet's best and brightest, who now represent the Tibetan government-in-exile from Dharamsala, India.

The Dalai Lama, who has referred to China's policies on migration as 'cultural genocide', is resigned to pushing for autonomy rather than independence, though even that concession has borne little fruit. The Chinese for their part seem to be waiting for him to die, positioning themselves to control the future politics of reincarnation. The Dalai Lama's tireless insistence on a non-violent solution to the Tibet problem led to him winning the Nobel Peace Prize in 1989, but despite global sympathy for the Tibetan cause, few nations are willing to raise the issue and place new business deals with China's rising economic superpower at risk.

The Chinese are truly baffled by what they perceive as the continuing ingratitude of the Tibetans. They claim that Tibet pre-1950 was a place of abject poverty and feudal exploitation. China, they say, has brought roads, schools, hospitals, airports, factories and rising incomes.

Many Tibetans, however, cannot forgive the destruction in the 1950s and 1960s of hundreds of monasteries and shrines, the restrictions on religious expression, the continued heavy military presence, economic exploitation and their obvious second-class status within their own land. Riots and protests in the spring of 2008 brought this simmering dissatisfaction out into the open, as Lhasa erupted into full-scale riots and protests spread to other Tibetan areas in Gānsù, Sìchuān and Qīnghǎi provinces. The Chinese response was predictable: arrest, imprisonment and an increased police presence in many monasteries. The increasing desperation felt by many Tibetans has led to a spate of self-immolations by Tibetans across the region, including two in Lhasa's Barkhor Circuit in 2012. At the time of writing, riot police armed with fire extinguishers patrolled much of Lhasa's old town.

As immigration and breakneck modernisation continue, the government is gambling that economic advances will diffuse the Tibetans' religious and political aspirations. It's a policy that has so far been successful in the rest of China. Whether it will work in Tibet remains to be seen.

Climate

Most of Tibet is a high-altitude desert plateau at more than 4000m. Days in summer (June to September) are warm, sunny and generally dry but temperatures drop quickly after dark. It's always cool above 4000m and often freezing at night, though thanks to the Himalayan rain shadow there is surprisingly little snow in the 'Land of Snows'. Sunlight is very strong at these altitudes, so bring plenty of high-factor sunscreen and lip balm.

TIBET HISTORY

TIBET TRAVEL RESTRICTIONS

Troubled Tibet is essentially part of China, yet in many ways separate from it. Travel regulations here are much more restrictive than the rest of the nation; tourists currently need to arrange a guided tour in order to visit any place in the Tibetan Autonomous Region (TAR).

Authorities would say this is for tourists' protection, though it has more to do with economic interests and foreigners' tendency to sympathise with the Tibetan cause and bear witness to political tensions. If you want to explore Tibetan areas independently by foot or public transport, you are currently better off heading to the Tibetan areas of Sìchuān and Qīnghǎi.

Travel regulations are in constant flux in Tibet and travel infrastructure is changing at head-spinning speed. Be sure to check current regulations with travel companies and check the designated Tibet branch of the Lonely Planet Thorn Tree (www.lonelyplanet. com/thorntree). Tibet can completely close to foreigners without warning, as it did for several months in 2012. Western Tibet was closed for most of 2014.

At the time of research:

➡ Foreign travellers need a Tibet Tourism Bureau (TTB) permit to get into Tibet and an Alien Travel Permit (and other permits) to travel outside Lhasa.

➡ To get these permits you need to prebook an itinerary, a guide for your entire stay and transport for outside Lhasa with an agency, before travelling to Tibet.

➡ To get on a plane or train to Lhasa you generally need to show your TTB permit. For the plane you need the original, so your agency will courier that to you at an address in China (normally a hostel). A printout/copy is currently acceptable for the train.

➡ You don't need to book transport for your time in Lhasa, but you do need to visit the main monasteries with a guide.

➡ For travel outside Lhasa you will need to prearrange transport hire. You cannot travel outside Lhasa independently and cannot take public transport.

➡ Most agencies charge around ¥200 per person for permits, ¥250 per day for a guide and anywhere from US$100 to US$150 per day for 4WD hire (not per person). Many agencies let you book your own accommodation.

➡ Agencies can only apply for permits 15 days before departure, so there is invariably a last-minute rush to get permits posted to you in time. This obviously complicates booking flight and train tickets; we recommend buying travel insurance and booking a fully refundable ticket if possible.

➡ Travel from Nepal to Tibet brings its own complications, since foreigners can only travel on a group visa (a separate piece of paper), which is only valid for up to three weeks and is almost impossible to extend. If you already have a Chinese visa in your passport it will be cancelled. Group visas in Kathmandu cost US$58 and take 10 days, or you can pay US$118 for express service. US citizens pay a hefty surcharge.

Language

Most urban Tibetans speak Mandarin in addition to Tibetan. Even in the countryside you can get by with basic Mandarin in most restaurants and hotels, since they are normally run by Mandarin-speaking Han or Hui Chinese. That said, Tibetans are extremely pleased when foreign visitors at least greet them in Tibetan, so it's well worth learning a few phrases (see p1023).

ⓘ Getting There & Away

NEPAL ROUTE

The 865km road connecting Lhasa with Kathmandu is known as the Friendship Hwy. Currently the only means of transport for foreigners is a rented vehicle.

When travelling from Nepal to Lhasa, foreigners generally arrange transport and permits through agencies in Kathmandu. Be careful with whom you organise your trip – the vast majority of complaints about Tibet that we receive have been about trips from Kathmandu. If you don't want to organise your own trip, the most common option is a seven-day overland tour to Lhasa, returning by flight to Kathmandu (US$420-620, three weekly).

If you join a fixed-departure tour you will likely end up with travellers from other companies. Accommodation en route is pretty simple. Most agencies advertising in Thamel are agents only; they don't actually run the trips and so will probably just shrug if there's a complaint.

The companies listed here can arrange tours and permits for Tibet and are used to dealing with individual travellers. See www.tibetgreenmap.com for other responsible Tibetan tour operators.

Lhasa

Explore Tibet (☏0891-632 9441, mobile 158 8909 0408; www.tibetexploretour.com; 4-5 House, Namsel No 3, Doudi Rd) Contact Jamphel.

Namchen Tours (☏634 5009; www.tibetnamchen.com) At Barkhor Namchen Guest House. Contact Dhoko.

Road to Tibet (☏133 0898 1522; www.roadtotibet.com) Contact Woeser Phel.

Shigatse Travels (Map p904; ☏633 0489; www.shigatsetravels.com; Yak Hotel, 100 Beijing Donglu) Top-end tours from a large agency that uses European trip managers.

Spinn Café (Map p904; ☏136 5952 3997; www.cafespinn.com; 135 Beijing Donglu) Contact Kong or Pazu.

Tibet Highland Tours (Map p904; ☏139 0898 5060, 634 8144; www.tibethighlandtours.com; Zangyiyuan Lu) Contact Tenzin or Dechen.

Tibetan Guide (☏635 1657, mobile 136 2898 0074; www.tibetanguide.com) Contact Mima Dhondup.

Other Cities in China

Leo Hostel (☏10-8660 8923; www.leohostel.com; 52 Dazhalan Xijie, Qiánmén, Běijīng) Popular backpacker hostel that books tours through an agency in Tibet.

Mix Hostel (☏028-8322 2271; www.mixhostel.com; 23 Renjiawan, Xinghui Xilu, Chéngdū) Popular backpacker hostel.

Snow Lion Tours (☏971-816 3350, 134 3932 9243; www.snowliontours.com; Office 1212, Chenglin Mansion, 7 Dongdajie Lu, Xīníng) Contact Wangden Tsering.

Tibetan Connections (Map p884; ☏135 1973 7734; www.tibetanconnections.com; 16th fl, Bldg 5, International Village Apartments, 2-32 Jiancai Xiang) This friendly tour company focuses on remoter parts of Amdo and Kham but can arrange trips into Tibet. Prices may be a little higher than local travel agencies but staff speak English and are good to deal with.

Travel Wild Tibet (☏0971-6313 188, mobile 139 9712 4471; www.travelwildtibet.com; Qinghai International Business Centre, 12th fl, 37 Kunlun Zhonglu, Xīníng) Contact Tashi Phuntsok.

Whatever you do, when coming from Nepal do not underestimate the sudden rise in elevation; altitude sickness is very common. It is especially not recommended to visit Everest Base Camp within a few days of leaving Kathmandu. Heading to Nepal, you will arrange 4WD hire as part of your Tibet tour.

Better agencies in Kathmandu include the following:

Adventure Greenhill (☏01-4700803; www.advgreenhill.com; Thamel) Travel and trekking agency that can book overland trips to Tibet.

Eco Trek (☏01-4423207; www.ecotrek.com.np; Thamel) Seven-day overland trips, plus tours to Kailash, the latter in conjunction with Indian pilgrim groups.

Royal Mount Trekking (☏01-4241452; www.royaltibet.com; Durbar Marg)

Tashi Delek Nepal Treks & Expeditions (☏01-4410746; www.tibettour.travel; Thamel)

QĪNGHǍI ROUTE

Now that the railway connects Lhasa with Qīnghǎi, there is no reason to suffer the long ride on the sleeper bus from Golmud. It is much harder to get train tickets to Lhasa than from Lhasa, so flying in and taking a train out makes sense.

OTHER ROUTES

Between Lhasa and Sìchuān, Yúnnán and Xīnjiāng provinces are some of the wildest, highest and most remote routes in the world. The bad news is that for the last few years permits have been impossible to obtain for overland routes from Sìchuān and Yúnnán through eastern Tibet. Even if the region reopens you will have to sign on to an organised trip to secure permits.

ⓘ Getting Around

Foreigners travel around Tibet in rented 4WDs. Public buses outside Lhasa are off limits to foreigners and bus stations won't sell you a ticket.

Overland cycling routes are possible, but currently expensive, as you still need a guide and transport, even if you're not travelling in it! For experienced cyclists, the Lhasa–Kathmandu trip is one of the world's great rides.

LHASA ལྷ་ས་ 拉萨

☎ 089 / POP 400,000 / ELEV 3650M

Lhasa is the traditional, political, and spiritual centre of the Tibetan world. Despite uncompromising Chinese-led modernisation, Tibet's premodern and sacred heritage survives in the form of the grand Potala Palace (former seat of the Dalai Lama); the ancient Jokhang Temple (Tibet's first and most holy); the great monastic towns of Sera, Drepung and Ganden; and the city's countless other smaller temples, hermitages, caves, sacred rocks, pilgrim paths and prayer-flag-bedecked hilltops.

Lhasa is a comfortable travellers' destination these days. There are dozens of good budget and midrange hotels and no shortage of excellent inexpensive restaurants. Lhasa is also currently the only place in Tibet where you have a certain freedom to explore without your guide, plus it's cheaper here than the rest of Tibet because you don't need to hire transport.

Lhasa divides clearly into a sprawling Chinese section to the west and a much smaller but infinitely more interesting Tibetan old town in the east, centred on the wonderful Barkhor area. For the last couple of years the oppressive military patrols, riot squads and undercover police in the Barkhor region have lent the old town an atmosphere of occupation.

◉ Sights & Activities

In addition to the main sights and activities listed here, Lhasa's old town is well worth exploring for its backstreet temples, booming craft shops and interesting Muslim neighbourhood.

★ Barkhor PILGRIM CIRCUIT

(བར་བསྐོར་, 八廓, Bākuò; Map p904) FREE It's impossible not to be swept up in the wondrous tide of humanity that is the Barkhor, a *kora* (pilgrim circuit) that winds clockwise around the periphery of the Jokhang Temple. You'll swear it possesses some spiritual centrifugal force, as every time you approach within 50m, you somehow get sucked right in and gladly wind up making the whole circuit again! It's the perfect place to start your explorations of Lhasa, and the last spot you'll want to see before you bid the city farewell.

★ Jokhang Temple BUDDHIST TEMPLE

(ཇོ་ཁང་, 大昭寺, Dàzhāo Sì; Map p904; admission ¥85; ◉ 8.30-6pm, most chapels closed after noon) The 1300-year-old Jokhang Temple is the spiritual heart of Tibet: the continuous waves of awestruck pilgrims prostrating themselves outside are testament to its timeless allure. The central golden Buddha here is the most revered in all of Tibet.

The Jokhang was originally built to house an image of Buddha brought to Tibet by King Songtsen Gampo's Nepalese wife. However, another image, the Jowa Sakyamuni, was later moved here by the king's other wife (the Chinese Princess Wencheng), and it is this image that gives the Jokhang both its name and spiritual potency: Jokhang means 'chapel of the Jowo'.

The two-storeyed Jokhang is best visited in the morning, though the crowds of yak-butter-spooning pilgrims can be thick. Access is possible in the afternoon through

---

ALTITUDE SICKNESS

Altitude sickness (or acute mountain sickness, AMS; p1021) is a life-threatening condition that you should take seriously in Tibet. While medicines such as Diamox can help deal with mild symptoms, the number one rule to follow is to rise in altitude gradually.

Most people experience only minor symptoms (headaches, breathlessness) when flying in to Lhasa (3600m), as long as they take things easy for their first couple of days. The key is to ascend gradually, preferably less than 400m per day. Spend up to a week in and around Lhasa before heading to higher elevations like Nam-tso or Western Tibet, and don't even think about heading straight to Everest Base Camp (5150m) from Kathmandu (1300m): you need *at least* two or three nights along the way, in places such as Nyalam (3750m) and Tingri (4250m).

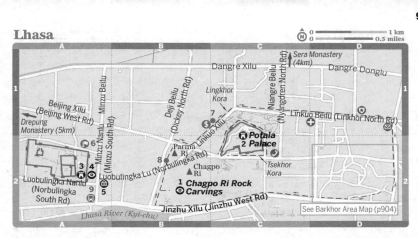

Lhasa

a side entrance but only the ground floor chapels can be viewed (and then only through a grill) and there are no pilgrims.

⭐ **Potala Palace** PALACE
(ᠽᠠᠷᠠᠷ, 布达拉宫, Bùdálā Gōng; Map p903; admission May-Oct ¥200, Nov-Apr ¥100; ◎9.30am-3pm before 1 May, 9am-3.30pm after 1 May, interior chapels close 4.30pm) The magnificent Potala Palace, once the seat of the Tibetan government and the winter residence of the Dalai Lamas, is Lhasa's cardinal landmark. Your first sight of its towering, fortress-like walls is a moment you'll remember for years. An architectural wonder even by modern standards, the palace rises 13 storeys from 130m-high Marpo Ri (Red Hill) and contains more than a thousand rooms. Pilgrims and tourists alike shuffle open-mouthed through the three storeys, trying to take in the dozens of magnificent chapels, golden stupas and prayer halls.

The first recorded use of the site dates from the 7th century AD, when King Songtsen Gampo built a palace here. Construction of the present structure began during the reign of the fifth Dalai Lama in 1645 and took divisions of labourers and artisans more than 50 years to complete. It is impressive enough to have caused Zhou Enlai to send his own troops to protect it from the Red Guards during the Cultural Revolution.

The layout of the Potala Palace includes the rooftop **White Palace** (the eastern part of the building), used for the living quarters of the Dalai Lama, and the central **Red Palace**, used for religious functions. The most stunning chapels of the Red Palace house the jewel-bedecked golden *chörten* (Tibetan stupa) tombs of several previous Dalai La-

Lhasa

◎ Top Sights
1 Chagpo Ri Rock Carvings	B2
2 Potala Palace	C2

◎ Sights
3 Norbulingka	A2
4 Norbulingka Ticket Office	A2
5 Tibet Museum	A2

ⓘ Information
6 Nepalese Consulate-General	A2
7 Wind Horse Adventure	C1

ⓘ Transport
8 City Train Ticket Office	B2
9 Western Bus Station	A2

mas. The apartments of the 13th and 14th Dalai Lamas, in the White Palace, offer a more personal insight into life in the palace. Grand aesthetics and history aside, however, one can't help noticing that today it is essentially an empty shell, notably missing its main occupant, the Dalai Lama, and a cavernous memorial to what once was.

Tickets for the Potala are limited. The day before you wish to visit, you or your guide should take your passport to the ticket booth just inside the far southwest exit (yes, exit), where you will receive a free ticket voucher with a time stamped on it.

The next day, be at the south entrance 30 minutes before the time on the voucher (tour groups use the southeast entrance). After a security check, follow the other visitors to the stairs up into the palace. Halfway up you'll pass the actual ticket booth, where you'll buy

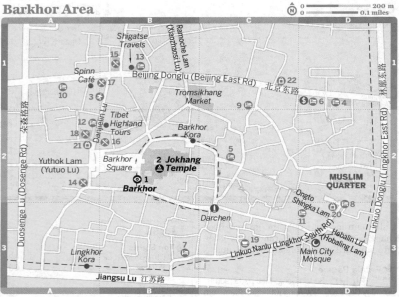

your ticket. Note that if you arrive later than the time on your voucher (or if you forget your voucher) you can be refused a ticket. Photography isn't allowed inside the chapels.

Sera Monastery
BUDDHIST, MONASTERY

(སེ་ར་དགོན་པ, 色拉寺, Sèlā Sì; admission ¥50; ☉9am-5pm) About 5km north of Lhasa, Sera was founded in 1419 by a disciple of Tsongkhapa as one of Lhasa's two great Gelugpa monasteries. About 600 monks are now in residence, down from an original population of around 5000. The half-dozen main colleges feature spectacular prayer halls and chapels. Equally interesting is the monk debating that takes place from 3pm to 5pm in a garden near the assembly hall. Don't miss the fine hour-long *kora* path around the exterior of the monastery.

From Sera Monastery it's possible to take a taxi northwest for a couple of kilometres to little-visited Pabonka Monastery. Built in the 7th century by King Songtsen Gampo, this is one of the most ancient Buddhist sites in the Lhasa region.

A taxi to Sera costs around ¥15 from the old town.

Drepung Monastery   BUDDHIST, MONASTERY
(འབྲས་སྤུངས, 哲蚌寺, Zhébàng Sì; admission ¥50; ☺9.30am-5.30pm, smaller chapels close at 2pm) Along with Sera and Ganden Monasteries, Drepung functioned as one of the three 'pillars of the Tibetan state' and this one was purportedly the largest monastery in the world, with around 7000 resident monks at its peak. Drepung means 'rice heap', a reference to the white buildings dotting the hillside. The 1½-hour-long kora around the 15th-century monastery, 8km west of Lhasa, is among the highlights of a trip to Tibet.

The kings of Tsang and the Mongols savaged the place regularly, though, oddly, the Red Guards pretty much left it alone during the Cultural Revolution. With concerted rebuilding, Drepung once again resembles a monastic village and around 600 monks reside here. At lunchtime you can see the novices bringing in buckets of tsampa and yak-butter tea. In the afternoons you can often see Tibetan-style religious debating (lots of hand slapping and gesticulating). The best way to visit the monastery is to follow the pilgrim groups or the yellow signs.

Nearby Nechung Monastery, a 10-minute walk downhill, was once the home of the Tibetan state oracle and is worth a visit for its bloodcurdling murals.

Bus 25 (¥2) runs from Beijing Donglu to the foot of the Drepung hill, from where minivans (¥3) run up to the monastery. A taxi from the Barkhor area is around ¥30. There is a ¥10 to ¥20 charge per chapel for photography.

★Chagpo Ri Rock Carvings   HISTORIC SITE
(药王山; Yàowáng Shān; Map p903; Deji Zhonglu; admission ¥10; ☺dawn-dusk) This hidden corner of Lhasa features over 5000 painted rock carvings that were created on the back side of Chagpo Ri over the course of a millennium. Throughout the day pilgrims perform full body prostrations in front of the images, while stonecarvers at the far end of the courtyard contribute to a large chörten built entirely of the carvers' mani stones. The best way to visit the area is as part of the Lingkhor pilgrim route.

LHASA'S PILGRIM CIRCUITS

Lhasa's four main koras (pilgrim circuits) are well worth walking, especially during the Saga Dawa festival, when the distinction between tourist and pilgrim can become very fine. Remember always to proceed clockwise.

Nangkhor Encircles the inner precincts of the Jokhang.

Barkhor Traces the outskirts of the Jokhang.

Lingkhor You can join the 8km-long circuit anywhere, but the most interesting section is from the southeastern old town to the Potala Palace.

Potala Kora (Tsekhor) An almost continuous circuit of prayer wheels, chörtens (Tibetan stupas), rock paintings and chapels encircles the Potala Palace. Stop for sweet tea en route at the charming teahouse by the three white chörtens on the northwest corner.

Norbulingka   PALACE
(ནོར་བུ་གླིང་ཀ, 罗布林卡, Luóbùlínkǎ; Map p903; Minzu Lu; admission ¥60; ☺9am-6pm) About 3km west of the Potala Palace is the Norbulingka, the former summer residence of the Dalai Lama. The pleasant park contains several palaces and chapels, the highlight of which is the New Summer Palace (Takten Migyü Podrang), built by the current (14th) Dalai Lama. It's debatable whether it's worth the entry fee.

Tibet Museum   MUSEUM
(རྒྱལ་ཡོངས་སྐུ་འདྲ, 西藏博物馆, Xīzàng Bówùguǎn; Map p903; Minzu Nanlu; ☺10am-5pm Tue-Sun) FREE This museum has some interesting displays, if you can filter out the Chinese propaganda. Starting with the prehistory of Tibet, the multiple halls cover everything from weapons and musical instruments, to folk handicrafts and fine ancient thangkas (Tibetan sacred art). Look for the 18th-century golden urn (exhibit No 310) used by the Chinese to recognise their version of the Panchen Lama. A useful handheld audio self-touring device (¥5) is available with a deposit.

Tenzin Blind Massage Centre   MASSAGE
(Map p904; ✆135 4901 5532; Danjielin Lu; ☺9.30am-11pm) There's no better way to

TIBET LHASA

ℹ️ VISITING MONASTERIES & TEMPLES

Most monasteries and temples extend a warm welcome to foreign guests. Please maintain this good faith by observing the following courtesies:

➡ Always circumambulate monasteries, chapels and other religious objects clockwise, thus keeping shrines and *chörtens* (Tibetan stupas) to your right.

➡ Don't touch or remove anything on an altar and don't take prayer flags or *mani* (prayer) stones.

➡ Don't take photos during a prayer meeting. At other times always ask permission to take a photo, especially when using a flash. The larger monasteries charge photography fees. If a monk stops you from taking a photograph there's no point getting angry – you don't know what pressures they may be under.

➡ Don't wear shorts or short skirts in a monastery, and take your hat off when you go into a chapel.

➡ Don't smoke in a monastery.

➡ If you have a guide, try to ensure that he or she is Tibetan, as Chinese guides invariably know little about Tibetan Buddhism or monastery history.

➡ Be aware that women are generally not allowed in protector chapels (*gönkhang*).

recover from an overland trip than with a massage from this graduate of the Braille Without Borders organisation (www.braille-withoutborders.org). Choose between hour-long Chinese (¥100 per hour) or Tibetan oil massage (¥150), the former clothed, the latter naked (don't be self-conscious, they're blind).

✨ Festivals & Events

Tibetan festivals are held according to the Tibetan lunar calendar, which usually lags at least a month behind the West's Gregorian calendar. The following is a brief selection of Lhasa's major festivals. Most are also celebrated elsewhere in Tibet.

Losar Festival   RELIGIOUS
New year celebration take place in the first week of the first lunar month (February), with performances of Tibetan opera, prayer ceremonies at the Jokhang and Nechung Monastery, and the streets are thronged with Tibetans dressed in their finest.

Saga Dawa   RELIGIOUS
The 15th day (full moon) of the fourth lunar month (May/June) sees huge numbers of pilgrims walking the Lingkhor pilgrim circuit.

Worship of the Buddha   RELIGIOUS
During the second week of the fifth lunar month (June), the parks of Lhasa, in particular the Norbulingka, are crowded with picnickers.

Drepung Festival   RELIGIOUS
The 30th day of the sixth lunar month (July) is celebrated with the displaying at dawn of a huge *thangka* at Drepung Monastery. Lamas and monks perform opera in the main courtyard.

Shötun Festival   RELIGIOUS
The first week of the seventh lunar month (August) sees the unveiling of a giant *thangka* at Drepung Monastery, then moves down to Sera and down to the Norbulingka for performances of *lhamo* (Tibetan opera) and some epic picnics.

Palden Lhamo   RELIGIOUS
The 15th day of the 10th lunar month (normally November) has a procession around the Barkhor circuit bearing Palden Lhamo, protective deity of the Jokhang Temple.

Tsongkhapa Festival   RELIGIOUS
Much respect is shown to Tsongkhapa, the founder of the Gelugpa order, on the anniversary of his death on the 25th of the 10th lunar month (December). Check for processions and monk dances at the monasteries at Ganden, Sera and Drepung.

🛏️ Sleeping

Lhasa has a good range of accommodation for all budgets. Rates depend on visitor numbers but generally peak in July and August (reservations recommended), with discounts of at least 20% at other times.

Banak Shol
HOTEL $

(八郎学宾馆, Bālángxué Bīnguǎn; Map p904; ☑ 632 3829; 8 Beijing Donglu; dm ¥50, d/tr without bathroom ¥100/150, d with bathroom ¥230; ☎) It's a mixed picture at this old backpacker stalwart. The newest triple rooms without bathroom are spacious, fresh and carpeted and the shared shower blocks are sparkling. Unfortunately the older roadside doubles and singles are still small, noisy and overpriced. The recently renovated standard rooms with bathroom are normally the cheapest such options in town.

Rama Kharpo Hotel
HOTEL $

(热玛嘎布宾馆; Map p904; ☑ 634 6963; www.lhasabarkhor.com; 15 Ongto Shingka Lam; dm ¥40, d/tr incl breakfast ¥180/260; ✳☎) Named the 'White Goat' after the legendary founder of the city, this easily-missed lodge is hidden deep in the old town near the Muslim quarter. Both dorm and en-suite rooms are comfortable (though check for barking dogs) and the dark but pleasant cafe is a great meeting place. Bathrooms are en suite but simple. Vehicles can't reach this part of the old town.

Barkhor Namchen House
GUESTHOUSE $

(八廓龙乾家庭旅馆, Bākuò Lóngqián Jiātíng Lǚguǎn; Map p904; ☑ 679 0125; www.tibetnamchen.com; 2 Barkhor North St; dm/d with shared bathroom ¥40/100; @☎) This small backstreet Tibetan-style guesthouse is a good budget choice. The old-town location just off the Barkhor is near perfect, the staff are friendly, and the (squat) bathrooms and hot showers are super-clean. Rooms are fairly small with hard beds and some have limited natural light (ask for an upper-floor room) but you can head to the rooftop for fine views.

★ Kyichu Hotel
HOTEL $$

(吉曲饭店, Jíqǔ Fàndiàn; Map p904; ☑ 633 1541; www.kyichuhotel.com; 18 Beijing Donglu; r standard/deluxe from ¥400/500; ✳@☎) The renovated Kyichu is a friendly and well-run choice that's very popular with repeat travellers to Tibet. Rooms are comfortable and pleasant, with wooden floors, Tibetan carpets and private bathrooms, but the real selling points are the location, the excellent service and – that rarest of Lhasa commodities – a peaceful garden courtyard (with espresso coffee). Reservations recommended.

Yak Hotel
HOTEL $$

(亚宾馆, Yà Bīnguǎn; Map p904; ☑ 630 0195; 100 Beijing Donglu; dm ¥50, d ¥450-650, r VIP ¥880; ✳@☎) The ever-popular Yak has matured in recent years from backpacker hang-out to tour-group favourite, eschewing the cramped dorm rooms (there are three left) for a range of comfortable en-suite rooms. Reservations are recommended. The 5th-floor breakfast bar offers great views of the Potala. Discounts of 30% are standard.

Heritage Hotel
HOTEL $$

(古艺酒店, Gǔyì Jiǔdiàn; Map p904; ☑ 691 1333; heritagehotel@hotmail.com; 11 Chaktsalgang Lu; r ¥300-420; ✳☎) Set inside the artsy courtyard holding the Dropenling (p908) craft centre, the friendly Heritage offers 21 stylish rooms featuring stone-walled showers, wooden floors and Tibetan wall hangings. The old-town location is atmospheric if you don't mind a 10-minute walk to most restaurants.

Gorkha Hotel
HOTEL $$

(郭尔喀饭店, Guò'ěrkā Fàndiàn; Map p904; ☑ 634 7000; gorkhahotel@yahoo.com; 47 Linkuo Nanlu, 林廓南路45号; r/ste ¥380/450; @) This atmospheric Nepali-Tibetan venture is a nice blend of cultures, from the Tibetan-style architecture to the Nepali-style restaurant on the roof. The creaking back block housed the Nepali consulate in the 1950s. Other rooms vary considerably, with some dark and small and others modern, so take a look at a few.

House of Shambhala
BOUTIQUE HOTEL $$$

(桑玛拉宫, Zhuōmǎlā Gōng; Map p904; ☑ 632 6533; www.shambhalaserai.com; 7 Jiri Erxiang, 吉日二巷7号; d incl breakfast ¥675-1015; ⊘ closed mid-Jan to end Apr; @) Hidden in the old town in a historic Tibetan building, the romantic, boutique-style Shambhala mixes the earthy charm of the old town with a great rooftop lounge and spa treatments, making it perfect for couples who prefer atmosphere over mod-cons. The nine rooms, decorated in natural wood and slate with antique Tibetan furniture, vary only in size.

✗ Eating

The staple diet in Tibet is *tsampa* (porridge of roasted barley flour) and *bö cha* (yak-butter tea). Tibetans mix the two in their hands to create doughlike balls. *Momos* (dumplings filled with vegetables or yak meat) and *thugpa* (noodles with meat) are also local comfort food. Variations include *thenthuk* (fried noodle squares) as well as *shemdre* (rice, potato and yak-meat curry). See Eating Tibetan (p752) for Chinese and Tibetan script for Tibetan dishes.

Lhasa is filled with restaurants serving a range of excellent Nepalese, Chinese, Tibetan and Western dishes. Unless noted otherwise, the places listed here are open for breakfast, lunch and dinner.

Tashi I
INTERNATIONAL $

(Map p904; cnr Danjielin Lu & Beijing Donglu; dishes ¥12-35; ⏰8am-10pm; 🖉) Old Lhasa hands like this unpretentious place for its mellow vibe, cheerful service, cheap prices and great location. The food can be hit and miss but there are plenty of breakfast and vegetarian options. Try the *bobis* (chapati-like unleavened bread), which come with seasoned cream cheese and fried vegetables or meat, or some fried apple *momos*.

Woeser Zedroe
Tibetan Restaurant
TIBETAN $

(光明泽缀藏餐馆, Guāngmíng Zézhuì Zàng Cānguǎn; Map p904; Danjielin Lu; mains ¥10-30) This is where visiting and local Tibetans come to fill up after a visit to the Jokhang. Add some pleasant traditional seating and a perfect location to the Tibetan vibe and it's a logical lunch stop. The *momos* are recommended, especially the fried yak meat or cheese varieties. Skip the boiled yak hooves and the phenomenally expensive dishes made with cordyceps.

Pentoc Tibetan Restaurant
TIBETAN $

(Map p904; 📱135 1890 0942; dishes ¥10-20; ⏰8.30am-9pm) Charming English-speaking Pentoc runs this local teahouse restaurant after working in Tashi I for many years. Authentically Tibetan, the simple menu includes breakfasts, and Pentoc's is a good place to try home-made Tibetan standards such as *momos* and *shemdre* (rice, potato and yak meat), plus butter tea, *chang* and even *dal bhat*. It's 20m down an alleyway off Beijing Donglu, on the left.

★Snowland Restaurant
INTERNATIONAL $$

(雪域餐厅, Xuěyù Cāntīng; Map p904; 📱633 7323; 8 Danjielin Lu; dishes ¥25-45; ⏰10am-10pm) This old-timer has a new location but is still an extremely popular place that serves a mix of excellent Continental and Nepali food in very civilised surroundings. The Indian dishes are particularly good, especially the tasty chicken butter masala and giant naan breads. The cakes are the best in town; give the lemon pie our fond regards.

★New Mandala Restaurant
NEPALI $$

(新满斋餐厅, Xīnmǎnzhāi Cāntīng; Map p904; 📱634 2235; west of Barkhor Sq; dishes ¥20-45; ⏰8am-10pm) This Nepali-run restaurant is definitely a winner for its fine views over the Barkhor, either from the mural-filled 2nd floor or the sunny rooftop. The excellent Nepali *thali* (set meal) is a great choice, or try a chicken sizzler. The owner runs the Tashi restaurants in Shigatse and Tsetang.

🍷 Drinking

Tibetans consume large quantities of *chang* (a tangy alcoholic drink derived from fermented barley) and *bö cha* (butter tea). The other major beverage is *cha ngamo* (sweet milky tea). Hole-in-the-wall Tibetan teahouses can be found all over the old town.

★Ani Sangkhung
Nunnery Teahouse
TEAHOUSE

(Map p904; 29 Linkuo Nanlu; tea ¥3-8; ⏰8am-5pm) If you're exploring the old town and need a break, make a beeline for this bustling teahouse in the courtyard of Lhasa's most important (and most politically active) nunnery. The nuns do a great job and the location is superb. Most of the customers these days are Chinese backpackers.

Summit Café
CAFE

(顶峰咖啡店, Dǐngfēng Kāfēidiàn; Map p904; www.thetibetsummitcafe.com; 1 Danjielin Lu; coffee ¥20-30, snacks ¥15-50; ⏰8am-9.30pm; 📶) With authentic espresso coffee and smoothies, free wi-fi and melt-in-your-mouth cheesecakes, this coffeehouse is mocha-flavoured nirvana. It's in the courtyard of the Shangbala Hotel (香巴拉酒店, Xiāngbālā Jiǔdiàn; Map p904; 📱632 3888; www.tibetshangbalahotel.com; ❋📶), a stone's throw from the Jokhang, with less-useful branches around town.

🛍 Shopping

Whether it's prayer wheels, *thangkas,* sun-hats or imported muesli, you shouldn't have a problem finding it in Lhasa. The old town is especially good for buying spiritual souvenirs and pilgrim accessories, with stalls selling prayer flags, amulets, turquoise jewellery, Tibetan boots, cowboy hats, yak butter and juniper incense. Most of this stuff is mass-produced in Nepal. Bargain hard.

★Dropenling
HANDICRAFTS

(Map p904; 📱633 0898; www.tibetcraft.com; 11 Chaktsalgang Lam; ⏰10am-8pm) 🖉 This impressive nonprofit enterprise aims to bolster traditional Tibetan handicrafts in the face of rising Chinese and Nepali imports. There are two shops; a main showroom in the old town and a smaller but more convenient branch (Map p904; ☑632 2443; Danjielin Lu; ☉10am-7pm) next to Lhasa Kitchen restaurant. Ask about the 90-minute artisan walking tour of Lhasa's old town (¥150 minimum for up to five people).

Outlook Outdoor Equipment

OUTDOOR EQUIPMENT

(Kàn Fēngyún Biànhuàn Yuǎnjǐng; Map p904; ☑633 8990; 11 Beijing Donglu) This reliable trekking shop has Western-quality sleeping bags (¥350 to ¥600), Gore-Tex jackets and tents, plus hard-to-find imported knick-knacks like altimeters, trekking socks and Primus cook sets. Gear is also available for rent.

ⓘ Information

EMBASSIES

Nepalese Consulate-General (尼泊尔领事馆, Níbó'ěr Lǐngshìguǎn; Map p903; ☑0891 681 3965; www.nepalembassy.org.cn; 13 Luobulingka Beilu; ☉10am-noon Mon-Fri) Issues visas in 24 hours. The current fee for a 15-/30-/90-day visa is ¥175/280/700. Bring a visa photo. Chinese tourists have to get their visas here; foreigners will find it easier to obtain visas on the spot at Kodari, the Nepalese border town.

INTERNET ACCESS

The Summit Café (p908), Rama Kharpo (p907) and Kyichu Hotel (p907) offer the most convenient free wi-fi for patrons. Public internet cafes currently require you to present a Chinese ID card.

MEDICAL SERVICES

120 Emergency Centre (急救中心, Jíjiù Zhōngxīn; Map p903; ☑633 2462; 16 Linkuo Beilu) Part of People's Hospital. Consultations cost around ¥150.

Tibet Military Hospital (西藏军区总医院, Xīzàng Jūnqū Zǒngyīyuàn; ☑625 3120; Niangre Beilu) Travellers who have received medical attention confirm that this place is the best option (if you have an option).

THE WORLD'S HIGHEST TRAIN RIDE

Since starting in 2006 the Qīnghǎi–Tibet Railway has been the world's highest train ride. With track topping the 5072m Tanggu-la pass and with 80% of the Golmud to Lhasa stretch above 4000m, the railway is an impressive piece of engineering. Its 160km of bridges and elevated track were built over permafrost, so sections of cooling pipes were inserted to help keep the boggy ground frozen in summer. The cost? A cool US$4.1 billion, not including the 2014 extension to Shigatse. While the Chinese are rightfully proud of this engineering marvel; many Tibetans aren't quite so sure. The railway brings cheaper (Chinese-made) goods and greater economic growth to the Tibetan Autonomous Region (TAR), but it also fuels Han migration, delivering one million passengers to Lhasa every year. What the line does best is staple Tibet ever more firmly to the rest of China.

At the time of writing, foreigners needed a copy of their Tibet Tourism Bureau (TTB) permit to buy a ticket. On board passengers have access to piped-in oxygen, although the cabins are not actually pressurised. Soft-sleeper berths come with TVs, and speakers in each cabin make periodic travel announcements about sights along the way. Schedules are designed to let passengers take in the best scenery during daylight hours.

Train departure times and fares to Lhasa (hard sleeper/soft sleeper, lower berth) from the following cities are listed below, but are subject to change. Note that tickets can be very hard to get in July and August, when many agencies impose a surcharge of around ¥200 to get tickets to Lhasa. Check www.chinatibettrain.com for the latest schedules. Services run daily unless noted:

Běijīng West (T27), ¥763/1186, 44 hours, departure 8.09pm

Chéngdū (T22/23), ¥709/1101, 44 hours, every other day, 9pm

Chóngqìng (T222/3), ¥751/1166, 44 hours, every other day, 7.55pm

Guǎngzhōu (T264/5), ¥919/1528, 56 hours, 12.19pm

Lánzhōu (K917), ¥550/852, 27 hours, 12.05pm

Shànghǎi (T164/5), ¥842/1311, 48 hours, 7.52pm

Xīníng (K917, K9801), ¥511/794, 27 hours, 3.05pm

MONEY

Bank of China (Main Office) (中国银行, Zhōngguó Yínháng; Map p903; Linkuo Xilu; ⊙ 9am-1pm & 3.30-6.30pm Mon-Fri, 10.30am-4pm Sat & Sun) West of the Potala, this is the only place to arrange a credit-card advance (3% commission) or a bank transfer. Take a number as you walk in the door. The ATMs outside the building are open 24 hours.

Bank of China (Branch) (中国银行, Zhōngguó Yínháng; Map p904; Beijing Donglu; 10am-4.30pm Mon-Fri, 11am-3.30pm Sat & Sun) The most conveniently located bank changes cash and travellers cheques without fuss. The currency exchange machine and ATMs dispense cash 24 hours a day. It's just west of the Banak Shol Hotel.

POST

China Post (中国邮政, Zhōngguó Yóuzhèng; Map p903; Beijing Donglu; ⊙ 9am-8pm) Buy stamps from the counter in the far-left corner. It's east of the Potala Palace.

PUBLIC SECURITY BUREAU

Lhasa City PSB (PSB, 拉萨市公安局, Lāsà Shì Gōng'ānjú; Map p903; ☑ 624 8154; 17 Linkuo Beilu; ⊙ 9am-12.30pm & 3.30-6pm Mon-Fri) Visa extensions of up to a week are rarely given; if they are it's only a day or two before your visa expires and only through your tour agency.

TELEPHONE

China Mobile (中国移动通信, Zhōngguó Yídòng Tōngxìn; Map p903; Beijing Donglu; ⊙ 9am-6pm Mon-Sat) This is the best place to get a local SIM card for your mobile phone. Choose from data, calls or a mixture of both. It's a fairly complicated procedure and you'll likely need a local ID card so go with your guide. Expect to pay around ¥100 for a month of data.

ⓘ Getting There & Away

AIR

It's possible to buy flights to Lhasa on some online sites, though others (like www.ctrip.com and www.elong.net) won't sell tickets to foreigners. Most airline offices won't sell you a ticket to Lhasa without a permit.

Leaving Lhasa is a lot simpler, as tickets can be purchased (and changed) without hassle from the **Civil Aviation Administration of China** (CAAC, 中国民航, Zhōngguó Mínháng; ☑ 682 5430; 1 Niangre Lu; ⊙ 9am-7pm). Credit cards are not accepted. Flight connections continue to all major destinations in China. Note that most tickets are often discounted by up to 30%, especially to Chéngdū and Chóngqìng.

Flights to/from Lhasa include the following destinations:

Ali ¥2570, three weekly
Běijīng ¥2600, daily
Chéngdū ¥1670, many daily
Chóngqìng ¥1800, daily
Guǎngzhōu ¥2670, daily
Kathmandu ¥4685, three weekly
Kūnmíng ¥2130, daily
Lánzhōu ¥1730, three weekly
Shànghǎi Pǔdōng (via Xī'ān or Chóngqìng) ¥2930, daily
Xī'ān ¥1820, daily
Xīníng ¥1780, daily
Zhōngdiàn (Shangri-la) ¥1550, daily (summer only)

BUS

Foreigners are currently not allowed to travel around Tibet by public transport and so the bus station will not sell you a ticket. Should this change, there are buses from the long-distance station to Shigatse, Gyantse and beyond.

TRAIN

You can buy train tickets up to 18 days in advance at the Lhasa **train station ticket office** (⊙ 7am-10pm) on the southwest edge of town or at the central **city ticket office** (火车票代售处, Huǒchēpiào Dàishòuchù; Map p903; 19 Deji Zhonglu; commission ¥5; ⊙ 8am-5.30pm). Trains to Lhasa arrive in the evening. Departures from Lhasa include the following (all are daily unless noted).

Běijīng West (T28), 1.45pm
Chéngdū (T24), every other day, 7.57am
Chóngqìng (T224), every other day, 12.45pm
Guǎngzhōu (T266), 12.05pm
Lánzhōu (K918), 8.20am
Shànghǎi (T166), 11.25am
Xīníng (K918, K9802), 8.20am

ⓘ Getting Around

TO/FROM THE AIRPORT

Gongkar airport is 65km south of Lhasa. Almost all tourists are picked up by their guide as part of their tour.

Airport buses (¥25, 60 minutes) leave up to 10 times a day between 7.30am and 1.30pm from in front of the CAAC building. The bus is free if you purchased your air ticket at the CAAC office.

A taxi to the airport costs between ¥150 and ¥200.

BICYCLE

A good option for getting around Lhasa once you have acclimatised is to hire a bike. The **Dōngcuò International Youth Hostel** (东措国际青年旅馆, Dōngcuò Guójì Qīngnián Lǔshè; Map p904; ☑ 627 3388; www.yhalasa.com; 10 Beijing Donglu) rents mountain bikes for ¥30 per day with a ¥200 deposit.

BUS

Buses (¥2) travel frequently between Běijīng Donglu and western Lhasa.

TAXI

Taxis charge ¥10 to almost anywhere within the city. Few Chinese drivers know the Tibetan names for even the major sites. Bicycle rickshaws should charge around ¥5 for short trips but require some extended haggling *before* you set off.

AROUND LHASA

Ganden Monastery དགའ་ལྡན་ 甘丹寺

Ganden Monastery BUDDHIST, MONASTERY
(Gāndān Sì; admission ¥50; ☉ dawn-dusk) About 40km east of Lhasa, this monastery, founded in 1417 by Tsongkhapa, was the first Gelugpa monastery. Still the order's heart and soul, it's the one out-of-Lhasa sight to choose if your time is limited. Two *koras* offer astounding views over the braided Kyi-chu Valley and you'll probably meet more pilgrims here than anywhere else. Some 400 monks now study in Ganden and extensive reconstruction has been under way for some time now, alongside a strong police presence.

Nam-tso གནམ་མཚོ་ 纳木错

The waters of sacred **Nam-tso** (Nàmùcuò; admission May-Oct ¥120, Nov-Apr ¥60) shimmer with an almost transcendent turquoise, framed by strings of prayer flags and snow-capped mountain peaks. Geographically part of the Changtang Plateau, the huge lake is bordered to the north by the Tánggǔlā Shān range and to the southeast by 7111m Nyenchen Tanglha peak.

Most travellers head for **Tashi Dor Monastery** in the southeastern corner of the lake. There are some fine walks up to the summits of the twin hills, as well as a short but pilgrim-packed *kora*. The scenery is breathtaking but so is the altitude: at 4730m it's 1100m higher than Lhasa. Do not rush here but instead count on a week in Lhasa at the minimum to avoid acute mountain sickness (AMS).

🛏 Sleeping & Eating

Half a dozen charmless metal guesthouses offer food and accommodation between April and October; the best options are the **Holy Lake Namtso Guesthouse** (神湖纳木措客栈, Shénhú Nàmùcuò Kèzhàn; ☏ 0891-611 0388; dm/d ¥60/150-280; @🛜) or **Namtso Sheep Hotel** (羊宾馆, Yáng Bīnguǎn; ☏ 139 0890 0990; dm ¥40-80, r ¥160-260; 🛜). Bedding is provided but nights here can be very cold. The paucity of toilets and lack of running water are an E. coli outbreak waiting to happen.

ℹ Getting There & Away

Nam-tso is 195km north of Lhasa, a four-hour paved drive over the 5190m Largen-la (la means 'pass'). It's much better to visit as an overnight, rather than a day trip. Even if independent travel returns, there is no public transport to the lake.

Samye Monastery བསམ་ཡས་ དགོན་ 桑耶寺

About 170km southeast of Lhasa, set amongst dramatic sand dunes on the north bank of the Yarlung Tsangpo (Brahmaputra) River is **Samye Monastery** (Sāngyē Sì), the first monastery in Tibet. Founded in AD 775 by King Trisong Detsen, Samye is famed not just for its pivotal role in the introduction of Buddhism to Tibet, but its unique mandala design: the main hall, or **Ütse** (admission ¥40; ☉ 8am-5.30pm), represents Mt Meru, the centre of the universe, while the outer temples represent the oceans, continents, subcontinents and other features of the Buddhist cosmology.

🛏 Sleeping & Eating

The **Samye Monastery Guesthouse** (桑耶寺宾馆, Sāngyésì Bīnguǎn; ☏ 783 6666; d without bathroom ¥140, d/tr ¥220/280), outside the northeast corner of the monastery walls has the best ensuite doubles in town and clean and fresh triples without a shower. The **Friendship Snowland Restaurant** (雪域同胞旅馆, Xuěyù Tóngbāo Lǚguǎn, Gangjong Pönda Sarkhang; meals ¥14-40; ☉ 8am-midnight), outside the east gate, serves good Chinese and Tibetan dishes, banana pancakes and milky tea in a cosy Tibetan atmosphere. Dorm rooms (¥50) with real mattresses (not foam) are available upstairs. There are several other decent accommodation options next door.

ℹ Getting There & Away

If you are heading to Everest Base Camp or the Nepal border, a visit here will only add one day to your itinerary. You may have to detour briefly to the nearby town of Tsetang (泽当; Zédāng) for your guide to pick up a required travel permit. One good option is to take the paved road to Samye via Tsetang and then return via the less-visited north bank road and interesting Dorje Drak Monastery.

THE FRIENDSHIP HIGHWAY

The 865km route between Kathmandu and Lhasa, known as the Friendship Hwy, offers without a doubt one of the world's great overland routes. At times sublime, at times unnerving, at times headache-inducing (the highest point is the Gyatso-la pass at 5100m), it's the yellow-brick road of Tibet, leading to some of the most magical destinations on the plateau.

For the sake of simplicity, we've included the side route from Lhasa to Shigatse via Yamdrok-tso and Gyantse in this section. This is the route most travellers take between the two towns and it's by far the more scenic and attraction-packed.

Yamdrok-Tso ཡར་འབྲོག་མཚོ 羊卓雍错

On the direct road between Gyantse and Lhasa, you'll probably catch your first sight of coiling Yamdrok-tso (Yángzhuó Yōngcuò; admission ¥40) from the summit of the Kamba-la pass (4794m). The lake lies several hundred metres below the road, and in clear weather is a fabulous shade of deep turquoise. Far in the northwest distance is the huge massif of Mt Nojin Kangtsang (7191m).

The small town of Nangartse along the way is essentially a lunch stop, with popular buffets (¥35 to ¥40) at the Lhasa and Yak restaurants, and most people overnight in Gyantse. A 15-minute drive from Nangartse brings you to Samding Monastery (桑丁寺, Sāngdīng Sì; admission ¥20), a charming place with scenic views of the surrounding plain and lakes from the simple but pleasant monastery guesthouse (桑丁寺招待所, Sāngdīng Sì Zhāodàisuǒ; ☑139 8993 3664; dm ¥40).

From Nangartse to Gyantse you cross the 5050m Karo-la, site of the highest battle in British imperial history during the Younghusband invasion of 1903–04, where glaciers spill off the side peaks beside a popular viewpoint (admission ¥50). Avoid the ridiculous 'admission fee' by stopping further below the pass.

Gyantse རྒྱལ་རྩེ 江孜

☑ 0892 / ELEV 3980M

The traditional town of Gyantse (Jiāngzī) is famed for its monumental nine-tiered *chörten*, long considered one of Tibet's architectural wonders. Historically, the town was at the centre of a thriving trans-Himalayan wood and wool trade, and Gyantse carpets were considered the best in Tibet. These days, Gyantse remains one of the less Chinese-influenced settlements, and wandering the backstreets around the monastery affords a rare picture of traditional urban Tibetan life.

◉ Sights & Activities

Gyangtse hosts the colourful Dhama Festival from 20 to 23 June, featuring traditional Tibetan games such as horse-racing, archery, yak-racing and tug-of-war.

GANDEN TO SAMYE HIKE

One of the most popular treks in Tibet is the four- to five-day hike from Ganden Monastery to Samye Monastery, an 80km wilderness walk connecting two of Tibet's most important monasteries. It begins less than 50km from Lhasa and takes you over the high passes of the Shuga-la (5250m) and Chitu-la (5100m). Along the way are subalpine lakes, dwarf forests and meadows, all at high altitude, so it shouldn't be underestimated.

The situation for getting permits for hiking is the same as for normal travel in Tibet. Some agencies will let you arrange your own ad hoc trek (ie horse or yak hire and food), as long as you take a guide and arrange transport to and from the trailheads; others require a fully supported trek. Wind Horse Adventure (Map p903; ☑683 3009; www.windhorsetibet.com; B32 Shenzheng Huayuan, Sera Beilu) in Lhasa is one of the most professional trekking agencies in Lhasa, though it's not the cheapest. For further details of this trek and others in the Everest, Tsurphu, Shalu and Kailash regions, see the trekking chapter of Lonely Planet's *Tibet* guide.

Pelkhor Chöde Monastery
BUDDHIST, MONASTERY

(白居寺, Báijū Sì; admission ¥60; ⊙9am-6.30pm, some chapels closed 1-3pm) The high red-walled compound in the far north of town houses Pelkor Chöde Monastery, founded in 1418. The main assembly hall is the main attraction but there are several other chapels to see. There's a small but visible population of 80 monks and a steady stream of prostrating, praying, donation-offering pilgrims doing the rounds almost any time of the day.

Gyantse Dzong
FORT

(☑817 2116; admission ¥30; ⊙9.30am-6.30pm) The main reason to make the 20-minute climb to the top of the Gyantse Dzong is for the fabulous views of the Pelkor Chöde Monastery and Gyantse's whitewashed old town below. Entry to the *dzong* is via a gate just north of the main roundabout. Vehicles can drive about halfway to the top.

🛏 Sleeping

Gyantse is a popular stop for 4WD tours and has a decent range of accommodation and food along north–south Yingxiong Nanlu.

★ Yeti Hotel
HOTEL $$

(雅迪花园酒店, Yǎdí Huāyuán Jiǔdiàn; ☑817 5555; www.yetihoteltibet.com; 11 Weiguo Lu; d incl breakfast ¥320; ❈@🛜) The revamped three-star Yeti is easily the best midrange option in Gyantse, offering 24-hour hot water, clean carpeted rooms, quality mattresses and reliable wi-fi, so make sure you reserve in advance. The cafe and excellent lobby restaurant serve everything from yak steak to pizza, alongside one of Tibet's best buffet breakfasts. The manager has plans to open a four-star boutique hotel in 2016.

Jiànzàng Hotel
HOTEL $$

(建藏饭店, Jiànzàng Fàndiàn; ☑817 3720; jian-zanghotel@yahoo.com.cn; 14 Yingxiong Nanlu, 英雄南路14号; q per bed ¥50-70, d ¥260; 🛜) The Jiànzàng, with English-speaking staff, offers rooms in a quiet new courtyard block with en suite rooms and 24-hour hot water. If pressed, staff will also show you the quad rooms with showers down the hall. The hotel is popular with 4WD groups and the 2nd-floor Tibetan-style restaurant is a cosy option for breakfast or a cup of tea.

DON'T MISS

GYANTSE KUMBUM

Commissioned by a Gyantse prince in 1427 and sitting inside the Pelkor Chöde complex, the **Gyantse Kumbum** (ཀུན་སྦྱིན་གཞུ, 江孜千佛塔, Jiāngzī Qiānfótǎ; admission incl in entry to Pelkor Chöde) is the town's foremost attraction. The 32m-high chörten, with its white layers trimmed with decorative stripes and its crown-like golden dome, is awe-inspiring. But the inside is no less impressive, and in what seems an endless series of tiny chapels you'll find painting after exquisite painting (*kumbum* means '100,000 images').

🍴 Eating

Tashi Restaurant
NEPALI, INTERNATIONAL $$

(扎西餐厅, Zhāxī Cāntīng; Yingxiong Nanlu; mains ¥30-40; ⊙7.30am-11pm) This Nepali-run place (a branch of Tashi in Shigatse) whips up tasty and filling Indian fare. It also has the usual range of Western breakfasts, Italian and Chinese food. The decor is Tibetan but the Indian movies and Nepali music give it a sub-continental vibe.

Gyantse Kitchen
TIBETAN $$

(江孜厨房, Jiāngzī Chúfáng; Shanghai Zhonglu; dishes ¥30-40; ⊙7am-midnight) This local favourite serves Western, Tibetan and Indian favourites, from chicken sizzlers to breakfast pancakes, plus unique fusion dishes such as yak pizza. The friendly owner, who may join you for a drink, donates a portion of his income to support poor families in Gyantse.

ℹ Getting There & Away

Most people overnight in Gyantse as part of a trip to the Nepal border, Mt Everest, or out west to Mt Kailash. It's only 90km (1½ hours' drive) on to Shigatse.

Shigatse
གཞིས་ཀ་རྩེ 日喀则

☑0892 / POP 80,000 / ELEV 3850M

Shigatse (Rìkāzé) is the second-largest city in Tibet, and like Lhasa has two distinct faces: a Tibetan one and a Chinese one. The Tibetan section, running northeast of the high-walled Tashilhunpo Monastery, is filled with whitewashed compounds, dusty

Shigatse

Shigatse

alleys and prayer-wheel-spinning pilgrims. The modern Chinese section has all the charm of a shopping mall but is where you'll find most restaurants and hotels and other life-support systems. The new airport and train connection to Lhasa looks set to boost Shigatse's economy further.

History

As the traditional capital of the central Tsang region, Shigatse was long a rival with Lhasa for political control of the country. The Tsang kings and later governors exercised their power from the imposing heights of the (recently rebuilt) Shigatse Dzong. Since the time of the Mongol sponsorship of the Gelugpa order, Shigatse has been the seat of the Panchen Lamas, the second-highest-ranking lamas in Tibet. Their centre was and remains the Tashilhunpo Monastery.

⊙ Sights

Tashilhunpo Monastery BUDDHIST, MONASTERY
(བཀྲ་ཤིས་ལྷུན་པོ་, 扎什伦布寺, Zhāshílúnbù Sì; admission ¥80; ⊗9am-7pm) One of the few monasteries in Tibet to weather the stormy seas of the Cultural Revolution, Tashilhunpo remains relatively unscathed. It is a real pleasure to explore the busy cobbled lanes twisting around the aged buildings. Covering 70,000 sq metres, the monastery is now the largest functioning religious institution in Tibet and one of its great monastic sights. The huge golden statue of the Future Buddha is the largest gilded statue in the world.

🛏 Sleeping

★ Gang Gyan Orchard Hotel HOTEL $
(日喀则刚坚宾馆, Rìkāzé Gāngjiān Bīnguǎn; ☑882 0777; 77 Zhufeng Lu; dm ¥50, d with bathroom ¥180; ❄ �🛜) Right next to the carpet factory is this well-run hotel offering modern, recently renovated Western-style rooms with comfortable beds and clean bathrooms with hot water. Each room has its own wifi router. Dorm rooms give access to shared hot showers. Best of all is the location, less than 100m from the entrance of the Tashilhunpo Monastery and next to Shigatse's best restaurants.

Tsampa Hotel HOTEL $$
(臧巴大酒店, Zàngbā Dàjiǔdiàn; ☑866 7888; 9 Renbu Lu; d/tr ¥280/350; ❄ 🛜) This three-star Tibetan place opened in 2012 and is a good choice. The rooms are fresh, modern and carpeted with modern bathrooms and lots of Tibetan touches, including a good Tibetan restaurant.

Gesar Hotel HOTEL $$$
(格萨尔酒店, Gésà'ěr Jiǔdiàn; ☑880 0088; Longjiang Lu; r standard/deluxe ¥380/500; ❄ @ 🛜) This new four-star giant has clean and modern rooms, each decorated with its own thangka of Gesar Ling, and a pleasant rooftop teahouse, though the location in the southwestern suburbs is a bit of a drag. The deluxe rooms are huge but the glass-walled bathrooms won't work unless you and your room mate are very close friends.

Tashi Chotar Hotel HOTEL $$$
(扎西曲塔大酒店, Zhāxī Qūtǎ Dàjiǔdiàn; ☑883 0111; www.zxqthotel.com; 2 Xueqiang Lu; d/tr ¥780/980; ❄ @ 🛜) A new and comfortable four-star place with Tibetan decor, internet cables, nice modern bathrooms and a good central location. Single rooms come with a computer. Rates include breakfast and can dip as low as ¥350 for a double.

🍴 Eating

★ Tibet Family Restaurant TIBETAN $
(丰盛餐厅, Fēngshèng Cāntīng; Phuntsho Serzikhang; dishes ¥15-30; ⊗8am-10pm) This teahouse-style Tibetan place is our favourite for its excellent food, nice outdoor seating and friendly clientele of locals. It also boasts the perfect people-watching location, right at the end of the monastery *kora*. The food runs from simple and fresh vegetable options to more adventurous yak-meat dishes, all great value.

★ Third Eye Restaurant NEPALI $$
(雪莲餐厅, Xuělián Cāntīng; ☑883 8898; Zhufeng Lu; dishes ¥35-50; ⊗9am-10pm) A Nepali-run place that is popular with both locals and tourists. Watch as locals sip *thugpa* (noodles) while travellers treat their taste buds to the city's best Indian curries. It's upstairs, next to the Gang Gyan Shigatse Orchard Hotel.

★ Wordo Kitchen TIBETAN $$
(吾尔朵厨房, Wú'ěrduǒ Chúfáng; ☑882 3994; Zhade Donglu; mains ¥15-70) For something a bit special, head out to this stylish restaurant and museum in the southeast of town. The pleasant Tibetan seating is decorated with old prayer wheels and yak butter pots. Ask for Kelsang to explain the Tibetan menu and make sure you head upstairs to the **museum** (☑139 8992 0067; Wordo Kitchen, Zhade Donglu; admission ¥20, for restaurant customers ¥15; ⊗9.30am-11pm) before or after dinner. Dishes range from curried potatoes to more ambitious braised yak ribs.

Songtsen Tibetan Restaurant INTERNATIONAL $$
(松赞西藏餐厅, Sōngzàn Xīzàng Cāntīng; Buxing Jie; dishes ¥30-45; ⊗9am-10pm) Popular Nepali-style place that serves hearty breakfasts, yak burgers and curries to Land Cruiser groups. It has a great location on the 'pedestrian-only' street, offering good views of the pilgrims ambling past.

🔒 Shopping

The **Tibetan market** (Bangjiakong Lu) in front of the Tenzin Hotel is a good place to pick up souvenirs such as prayer wheels, rosaries and *thangkas*. There are also dozens of souvenir and craft shops along the pedestrian-only street (Buxing Jie). Bargain hard.

Tibet Gang Gyen Carpet Factory CARPETS (西藏刚坚地毯厂, Xīzàng Gāngjiān Dìtǎn Chǎng; www.tibetgang-gyencarpet.com; 9 Zhufeng Lu; ⊙9am-1pm & 3-7pm Mon-Sat) Beside the Gang Gyen Orchard Hotel, 100m down a side alley, this workshop hires and trains impoverished women to weave high quality wool carpets. Upon arrival you'll be directed to the workshop, where you can watch the 80 or so women work on the carpets, singing as they weave, dye, trim and spin; you're free to take photos.

ℹ️ Information

Bank of China (branch) (中国银行, Zhōngguó Yínháng; Zhufeng Lu; ⊙9am-6pm Mon-Sat, 10am-4pm Sun) A short walk from the Gang Gyen Orchard Hotel, this useful branch changes travellers cheques and cash and has a 24-hour ATM outside.

China Post (中国邮政, Zhōngguó Yóuzhèng; cnr Shandong Lu & Zhufeng Lu) It's possible to send international letters and postcards from here, but not international parcels.

Public Security Bureau (公安局, PSB, Gōng'ānjú; ☑882 2240; Jilin Nanlu; ⊙9.30am-12.30pm & 3.30-6.30pm Mon-Fri, 9.30am-2pm Sat & Sun) Your guide will likely have to stop here for half an hour to register and/or pick up an alien's travel permit for the Friendship Hwy or western Tibet. It's in the southeastern suburbs, near the Gesar Hotel.

ℹ️ Getting There & Around

Foreigners are currently not allowed to take any of the plentiful transport to Lhasa (five hours), Gyantse (1½ hours), Saga, Sakya, Lhatse and various other points along the Friendship Hwy.

Shigatse's new airport, 50km east of the city has a twice-weekly service to Chēngdū (¥1880). The train line extension from Lhasa was inaugurated in late 2014.

A taxi anywhere in Shigatse costs ¥10.

Sakya ষ་শ্ব 萨迦

☑0892 / ELEV 4280M

In the 13th century, the monastic town of Sakya (Sàjiā) emerged as an important cen-

tre of scholarship. Less than a century later the Sakya lamas, with Mongol military support, became the short-lived rulers of all Tibet. Still today the local colouring of buildings – ash grey with red and white vertical stripes – symbolises both the Rigsum Gonpo (the trinity of Bodhisattvas) and Sakya authority. For travellers the magnificent, brooding monastery, the visiting bands of pilgrims and the surrounding traditional village make Sakya a real highlight. It's one of our favourites and well worth an overnight stop.

⊙ Sights

★ **Sakya Monastery** BUDDHIST, MONASTERY (admission ¥45; ⊙9am-6pm) The immense, grey, thick-walled southern monastery is one of Tibet's most impressive constructed sights, and one of the largest monasteries. Established in 1268, it was designed defensively, with watchtowers on each corner of its high walls. Inside, the dimly lit hall exudes a sanctity and is on a scale that few others can rival. As usual, morning is the best time to visit as more chapels are open.

🛏️ Sleeping & Eating

Manasarovar Sakya Hotel HOTEL $$ (神湖萨迦宾馆, Shénhú Sàjiā Bīnguǎn; ☑824 2555; 1 Gesang Xilu; d/tr ¥200/280) The renovated rooms at this modern hotel are spacious and comfortable, with hot-water bathrooms and electric blankets, making it the best value in town.

Sakya Monastery Restaurant TIBETAN $ (萨迦寺餐厅, Sàjiā Sì Cāntīng; dishes ¥7-15; ⊙8am-9pm) This Tibetan joint is owned by the monastery and serves fried rice, *thugpa* (noodles), dumplings and lashings of milk tea. It's cosy and always full of characters.

Sakya Farmer's Taste Restaurant TIBETAN $ (萨迦农民美食厅, Sàjiā Nóngmín Měishítīng; ☑824 2221; dishes ¥10-35) Looking over the main street, this Tibetan place has a cosy atmosphere amid Tibetan decor. The green-jacketed waiters are friendly and will help explain the various Tibetan dishes available.

ℹ️ Getting There & Away

Sakya is 25km off the Friendship Hwy. Most people stay overnight at Sakya en route to the Everest region.

Rongphu Monastery & Everest Base Camp

རོང་ཕོ་ཆེ་དགོན་པ་ རྫ་རི་གླང་མའི་གཞས་ཞིག
绒布寺、珠峰

Before heading to the Nepal border, many travellers make the diversion to iconic **Everest Base Camp** (EBC; 5150m). The clear vistas (if you are lucky) of Everest's sheer North Face are far superior to anything you'll see in Nepal. Everest is known locally as Qomolangma (also spelt Chomolungma), or as Zhūfēng in Chinese. Because EBC is a prime target for political protests, the Chinese army maintains a strong presence up here.

Vehicles can drive on a gravel road to **Rongphu Monastery** (admission ¥25), at 5000m reputedly the highest in the world, and then proceed just a few kilometres more to a ramshackle collection of nomad tents set near a China Post kiosk (the highest post office in the world). From here it's a one-hour walk (recommended if you aren't suffering from the altitude) or shuttle-bus ride (¥25) up a winding dirt road to EBC. Tourists are not allowed to visit the expedition tents of actual base camp.

EBC is about 90km off the Friendship Hwy over the 5050m Pang-la. Before you set off you'll have to stop in Baber (new Tingri), or old Tingri if coming from Nepal, to pay the Qomolongma National Park entrance fee of ¥400 vehicle and ¥180 per person. Clarify in advance with your agency who pays what here.

If you are headed from Everest to the Nepal border, note that the dirt road to Tingri via Zombuk village and the Lamna-la offers a handy shortcut.

🛏 Sleeping

Rongphu Monastery
Guesthouse   GUESTHOUSE $
(绒布寺招待所, Róngbù Sì Zhāodàisuǒ; ☎136 2892 1359; dm ¥60, tw without bathroom ¥200) The monastery-run guesthouse at Rongphu is probably the most comfortable place to stay at Everest. The private rooms with proper beds tend to be warmer than the tent camp and there's certainly more privacy. The best value is a bed in a four-bed room. All rooms share the pit toilets. Come the evenings everyone huddles around the yak dung stove in the cosy restaurant (dishes ¥25 to ¥40).

Tent Camp   TENTS $
(dm ¥60; ☉end Mar–mid-Oct) The main alternative to staying at Rongphu is this motley collection of yak-hair tents. Don't expect much privacy: tents sleep six people (your host and perhaps one or two of their relatives will be sharing the space with you) in an open area around the central stove. Even with the fire going it's still bloody cold. Simple meals (¥25) and drinks are available.

Kangjong Hotel   HOTEL $$
(雪域宾馆, Xuěyù Bīnguǎn; ☎139 8992 3995; Baber; d with bathroom ¥220-280, d without bathroom ¥80; ☎) The new blocks have good quality carpeted rooms, clean bathrooms and hot water. Rooms in the older block above the road, with toilets down the hall (no showers), are dim and scruffy. The attached restaurant (dishes ¥20 to ¥50) is a good place to kick back with your guide over a thermos of sweet tea. The hotel is in the middle of town at the crossroads to Shegar.

Tingri to Zhāngmù ཏིང་རི་ འབྲོག 樟木 定日

The huddle of mudbrick buildings that comprises the old village of **Tingri** (Dìngrì; 4250m) now spreads about a kilometre down the Friendship Hwy. The views of the towering Himalayan peaks of Mt Everest (8848m) and Cho Oyu (8153m) across the sweeping plain make up for the truckstop feel.

Ruins on the hill overlooking Tingri are all that remain of the **Tingri Dzong**. This fort was destroyed in a late-18th-century Nepalese invasion. Many more ruins on the plains between Shegar and Nyalam shared the same history.

There are several Tibetan guesthouses and restaurants on the main highway, including the **Héhū Bīnguǎn** (合呼宾馆; ☎136 4892 2335; dm ¥50-80, d with bathroom ¥260), a good place in the centre with good mattresses in the pricier dorms and rooms with hot water bathrooms, plus the best restaurant in town.

From Tingri down to Zhāngmù on the Nepal border is an easy half-day's drive of just under 200km. If you are coming the other way you should break the trip into two days to aid acclimatisation. The highest point along the paved road is the Tong-la pass (5140m), 95km from Tingri, from where you can see a horizon of 8000m Himalayan peaks.

The one-street town of **Nyalam** (Nièlāmù) is about 30km from the Nepal border and a usual staging spot for 4WD trips from Nepal. The **Nyalam Nga-Dhon Guesthouse** (聂拉木阿顿旅馆, Nièlāmù Ā dùn Lǚguǎn; ☑ 827 2113; 2 Chongdui Lu; d without bathroom ¥100, d with bathroom ¥200-300) in the centre offers the best range of rooms, while the new **Shishapangma Hotel International** (☑ 136 5892 8053; r with shared bathroom ¥250-400, d ¥350, ste ¥600-700) is the most luxurious hotel this side of Shigatse. Nyalam's accommodation can get booked out with Indian groups returning from Kailash.

After Nyalam, the road drops like a stone into a lush, deep forested gorge (trees!) lined with spectacular waterfalls, many of which are hundreds of metres high. You can feel the syrupy air getting thicker as you descend towards the subcontinent.

Zhāngmù ঈ嘞অ 樟木

☑ 0892 / ELEV 2250M

The frenetic border town of Zhāngmù (Khasa in Nepalese, Dram in Tibetan) hangs from the forested slopes above the tortuous final kilometres of the Friendship Hwy. The smells of curry and incense float in the air, and the babbling sound of fast-flowing streams cuts through the piercing squeals of Tata truck brakes. After time on the barren high plateau, it's an assault on the senses and a sign that the fabulous chaos of the subcontinent is just a stone's throw away.

🛏 Sleeping & Eating

Sherpa Hotel HOTEL **$$**
(夏尔巴酒店, Xià'ěrbā Jiǔdiàn; ☑ 874 2098; d without/with bathroom ¥120/230; ☎) The pink-painted rooms are clean (if a little small) at this friendly hotel, and hot water is available most of the time in the simple bathrooms. Back rooms are bright and sunny with valley views.

Property Hotel HOTEL **$$**
(财缘宾馆, Cáiyuán Bīnguǎn; ☑ 874 5888; d ¥360; ⓟ✳☎) Midrange Land Cruiser groups like this modern, new place for its clean, good quality (but smallish) rooms, en-suite bathrooms and decent breakfasts.

ⓘ Information

Bank of China (中国银行, Zhōngguó Yínháng; ⊙9.30am-1pm & 3.30-6pm Mon-Fri, 11am-2pm Sat & Sun) This branch at the top end of town will change cash and travellers cheques into yuán and also yuán into dollars, euros or pounds, but doesn't deal in Nepali rupees. The ATM accepts Mastercard, Maestro, Cirrus, Visa and Plus cards.

WESTERN TIBET

Tibet's far wild west, known in Tibetan as Ngari, has few permanent settlers, but is nevertheless a lodestone to a billion pilgrims from three major religions (Buddhism, Hinduism and Jainism). They are drawn to the twin spiritual power places of Mt Kailash and Lake Manasarovar, two of the most legendary and far-flung destinations in the world.

Ngari is a huge, expansive realm of salt lakes, Martian-style deserts, grassy steppes and snowcapped mountains. It's a mesmerising landscape, but also intensely remote: a few tents and herds of yaks may be all the signs of human existence one comes across in half a day's drive. As ever, the transport infrastructure is changing fast. The recent paving of the southern road to Kailash has made the weeklong drive from Lhasa a lot more comfortable and it's now even possible to fly back from Ali.

TIBET ZHĀNGMÙ

BORDER CROSSING: GETTING TO NEPAL

Your transport will take you 8km down switchbacks to **Chinese immigration** (⊙10am-5.30pm, sometimes closed 1.30-3.30pm) next to the Friendship Bridge and Nepal border post at Kodari. If for some reason you don't have transport, orange and blue taxis run this stretch for ¥10 per person.

At **Nepali immigration** (⊙8.30am-4pm) in Kodari, you can get a visa for the same price as in Lhasa (US$25/40/100 for a 15-/30-/90-day visa, or the equivalent in rupees). If you don't have a passport photo you'll be charged an extra US$5. Nepal is 2¼ hours behind Chinese time.

There are four daily buses to Kathmandu – the last bus at 1.30pm is express – or take a bus to Barabise (three hours, last bus 5pm) and change. The easier option is to share a private vehicle with other travellers (Rs 4500 per car, or Rs 1500 per seat; four hours). You'll struggle to find a driver after 5pm.

Warm clothes are essential on any trip to the region, even in summer, and a sleeping bag is recommended. The three-day *kora* around Mt Kailash can be done without a tent but bringing one will give you added flexibility and comfort.

Accommodation along the way ranges from basic guesthouses to chilly hotel rooms. Few have attached bathrooms but most towns have at least one public bathhouse. Most towns now have well-stocked supermarkets, internet cafes and Chinese restaurants, though it's still worth bringing along a few treats, such as peanuts, chocolate bars and dehydrated food from home.

The only places to change money in Ngari are banks in Ali, and it's much easier to change US dollars as cash rather than travellers cheques. It's best just to bring what you expect to spend in rénmínbì.

When to Go

May, June and from mid-September to early October are probably the best times for travel in the region. The summer months of July and August see the bulk of the rain, though it's still very limited. The Drölma-la pass on the Mt Kailash *kora* is usually blocked with snow from late October or early November until early April. The festival of Saga Dawa during May or June brings hundreds of pilgrims and tourists to the mountain.

Permits

You'll need a fistful of permits to visit Ngari: a TTB permit, Alien Travel Permit, military permit, foreign affairs permit etc. The travel agency that organises your 4WD trip will need at least two weeks to arrange these.

ⓘ Getting There & Away

Four-wheel-drive trips to Mt Kailash require a minimum 14 days. Add on three days to explore the Guge Kingdom at Tsaparang. One good option is to exit at Zhāngmù, detouring from Saga to the Friendship Hwy via the beautiful lake of Peiku-tso. For details of the remoter and longer return route via the northern highway, see Lonely Planet's *Tibet* guide.

Lhatse to Kailash

From Lhasa most travellers take the faster, direct southern route to Ngari. It's a two- or three-day trip along the paved Friendship Hwy to the town of Lhatse (拉孜; Lāzī), where there are several hotels, including the

---

WORTH A TRIP

THE LOST KINGDOM OF GUGE

One worthwhile detour from Darchen is to the surreal ruins of the Guge Kingdom at Tsaparang (Gǔgé Gǔchéng; joint admission ticket with Thöling ¥200, optional guide per person ¥10). The ruins, which seem to grow like a honeycomb out of the barren hills, were once the centre of one of Tibet's most prosperous kingdoms. The tunnels and caves are great fun to explore and the chapels offer superb examples of Kashmiri-influenced mural art. A trip here will add three days to your itinerary, but is worth it to see some outstanding scenery and one of Asia's little-known wonders.

From Darchen it's a day's drive to Zanda (札达; Zhádá), the nearest town to Tsaparang (18km away), and home to spectacular Thöling Monastery.

---

friendly budget **Lhatse Tibetan Farmers Hotel** (拉孜农民旅馆, Lāzī Nóngmín Lǚguǎn; ☎832 2333; dm ¥25-45, d without/with bathroom ¥260/90), and the excellent new midrange **Dewang Manor** (德望庄园, Déwàng Zhuāngyuán; ☎139 8902 7775; d ¥250; ❋ ⓢ).

Turning off the Friendship Hwy just after Lhatse, Hwy 219 continues on a mostly paved road to the hamlet of Raka, near where the lesser-travelled northern route branches north. There are simple guesthouses in Raka but most groups continue 60km west to the larger military town of Saga (萨嘎; Sàgá), which has internet cafes and hot public showers. The Saga Hotel (萨嘎宾馆, Sàgá Bīnguǎn; ☎0892-820 2888; d with bathroom ¥380-420; ❋ @) is at the town crossroads and has hot showers and Western bathrooms, or try the budget-option Ālǐ Zhāodàisuǒ (阿里招待所, Ālǐ Zhāodàisuǒ; tr per bed ¥70) across the road.

It's possible to reach Darchen in one long day (490km) from Saga, though many groups split the scenic ride into two days. This also helps with the acclimatisation process. After Lhatse the altitude never drops below 4000m. There are simple guesthouses in both old Zhongba and grubby Paryang (帕羊; Pàyáng). From Paryang to Hor Qu is 200km.

In Hor Qu (霍尔; Huò'ěr), 44km before Mt Kailash, you now have to park your vehicle and take a mandatory 'eco bus' (¥150) on to Darchen (for Mt Kailash) or Lake Manasarovar.

TIBET LHATSE TO KAILASH

Mt Kailash

གངས་རིན་པོ་ཆེ 冈仁波斋峰

Known in Tibetan as Kang Rinpoche, or 'Precious Jewel of Snow', the hulking pyramidal-shaped Mt Kailash (Gāng Rénbōzhāi Fēng; 6714m) seldom needs to be pointed out to travellers: it just dominates the landscape. For Buddhists, Kailash is the abode of Demchok, a wrathful manifestation of Sakyamuni. For Hindus it is the domain of Shiva, the Destroyer and Transformer.

It's not hard to see why Kailash became associated long ago with the myth of a great mountain. More surprising is that this mountain was said to be the source of the four major rivers of South Asia: and most astonishing that the legends are more or less true. The drainage system around Kailash and Lake Manasarovar is in fact the source of the Karnali (a major tributary of the Ganges), the Brahmaputra, Indus and Sutlej Rivers. A visit to Kailash puts you squarely in one of the geographical and spiritual centres of the world.

Activities

Many pilgrims are often happy enough just to gaze at the southern face of Kailash (scarred in such a way that it resembles a swastika – a Buddhist and Hindu symbol of spiritual strength). But for Tibetans and most foreign travellers the purpose of coming here is to complete a *kora* around the mountain.

The *kora* begins in grubby **Darchen** (塔尔钦; Tǎ'ěrqīn; 4560m), and takes (on average) three days to complete (though most Tibetans do it in one 15-hour day). The *kora* is not a climb to the top, but a walk around the central peak. The highest point is the 5630m Drölma-la pass, though no point is below 4600m.

The first day is a 20km walk (six to seven hours) from Darchen to Dira-puk Monastery. The ascent is minimal, which allows you to take your time and enjoy the otherworldly landscape of the Lha-chu river valley. The second day is the hardest, as it involves the ascent to the Drölma-la pass, the steep descent down the pass to the Lham-chu Khir river valley, and hike to the Zutul-puk Monastery. Expect to take eight hours to complete this 18km stretch. The final day is a simple 14km (three hours) walk back to Darchen. Fit walkers can cover the *kora* in two days if they wish, especially as jeep tracks are nibbling away at the beginning and end of the walk.

Any reasonably fit and acclimatised person should be able to complete the three-day walk, but come prepared with warm, waterproof clothing and equipment. Local guides and porters are available in Darchen for ¥150 a day. Larger groups often hire yaks to carry their supplies.

Your guide will register your group with the **PSB** (PSB, 公安局, Gōng'ānjú) in Darchen. There is a ¥150 Kailash entry fee.

🛏 Sleeping & Eating

At the end of each day's walk there is dormitory accommodation (¥60-70) at the local monasteries or in a nearby guesthouse, though it's advisable to carry a tent if walking during July and August or the popular Saga Dawa festival. Instant noodles, tea and beer are available at nomad tents along the way, but bring hot drinks and snacks with you.

Most travellers spend a night in Darchen before the *kora*. Many guesthouses offer basic accommodation (no running water, outdoor pit toilets) and there is now at least one three-star hotel (with wi-fi!). There are a couple of supermarkets, a public shower and patchy internet access.

Pilgrim Hotel (朝圣宾馆, Cháoshèng Bīnguǎn; ☎ 298 0833; dm ¥60) donates part of its profits to local monasteries; otherwise choose the **Lhasa Holyland Guesthouse** (拉萨圣地康桑旅馆, Lāsà Shèngdì Kāngsāng Lǚguǎn; ☎ 139 8907 0818; d ¥70-80) or the cosy **Sun & Moon Guesthouse** (Ninda Dronkhang, 日月宾馆, Rìyuè Bīnguǎn; ☎ 260 7102; q per bed ¥60) located next to the Tibet Medical and Astrological Institute (Menkhang).

Lake Manasarovar

མཚོ་མ་ཕམ 玛旁雄错

After their *kora,* most travellers head to Lake Manasarovar (Mǎpáng Xióngcuò) or Mapham Yum-tso (Victorious Lake) to rest and gaze at the sapphire-blue waters and perfect snowcapped mountain backdrop. The lake is the most venerated in Tibet and has its own five-day *kora,* accessible by jeep track. The admission fee is ¥150.

Picturesque **Chiu village**, site of Chiu Monastery, overlooks the northwestern shore of the lake, and here you'll find a half-dozen identical friendly **guesthouses** (dm ¥50-60), some right down at the water's edge. Basic meals are available. To get to the lake you may have to park at Hor Qu and take the mandatory 'eco' bus (¥150).

Understand China

China Today

A highly idiosyncratic mix of can-do entrepreneurs, inward-looking Buddhists, textbook Marxists, overnight millionaires, the out-of-pocket, leather-faced farmers, unflagging migrant workers and round-the-clock McJobbers, China today is as multifaceted as its challenges are diverse. From the outside, China's autocratic decision-making may suggest national uniformity, but things are actually more in a state of controlled, and not so controlled, chaos.

Best in Print

Country Driving: A Chinese Road Trip (Peter Hessler) Hessler's amusing and insightful journey at the wheel around the highways and byways of China.

Tiger Head, Snake Tails (Jonathan Fenby) Compelling account of contemporary China's myriad challenges and contradictions.

Diary of a Madman & Other Stories (Lu Xun) Astonishing tales from the father of modern Chinese fiction.

Best on Film

Still Life (Jia Zhangke; 2005) Bleak and hauntingly beautiful portrayal of a family devastated by the construction of the Three Gorges Dam.

Raise the Red Lantern (Zhang Yimou; 1991) Exquisitely fashioned tragedy from the sumptuous palette of the Fifth Generation.

In the Mood for Love (Wong Kar-Wai; 2000) Seductive, stylishly costumed and slow-burning Hong Kong romance.

New Superpower or the Next Japan?

Tipped to overtake the US economy sometime before 2020, China can readily seem to be assuming the mantle of superpower. The rash of books trumpeting China's ascendancy echoes the glut of titles in the late 1980s that celebrated the rise of its island neighbour. While the Chinese economy effortlessly streaked past Japan's in 2010 and today gradually fills the United States' rearview mirror, the unstoppable juggernaut of the Chinese economy could be hitting some hefty potholes, if not nearing the end of the road. Some financial analysts foresee China slewing into a long era of stagnation similar to that which depressed Japan after its asset bubble burst in the early 1990s. A combination of bad debt accumulation, imbalanced growth, downward property prices, a burdensome overcapacity and overdependence on exports could commence a persistent squeeze to the brakes on economic growth. Resolving bad debt and sorting out the shaky banking sector and the deeply undercapitalised financial system may be central to any long-term resolution but a real estate slump could limit options, while inequality in China remains among the most severe in the world.

To Boldly Go

In December 2013, the Chang'e 3 probe landed on the surface of the moon, marking the first lunar landing since 1976. Carrying the Yutu (Jade Rabbit) lunar rover, the mission also marked China's coming of age as a space power. Since the 1960s, moon landings have been a superpower hallmark: China's foray into the ether is as much about national standing as it is about scientific research. Rivalries notwithstanding – India's unmanned Mars probe achieved Martian orbit in 2014 – China wants to show the world it has both the ambition and the sophistication to pull a (jade) rabbit from its hat. The space program also casts China as an exploratory power that is willing to take risks, in an arena littered with noble failures. China also has a working space station – the Tiangong-1, a precursor to a much larger station in the pipeline – and plans to put a man on the moon and a rover on Mars (despite a Chinese probe to the Red Planet ending in failure in 2011).

Troubled Waters & Restive Borderlands

China's dazzling economic trajectory over the last two decades has been watched with awe by the West and increasing unease by the Middle Kingdom's neighbours. By virtue of its sheer size and population, a dominant China has been ruffling some East Asian feathers. A growing – and seemingly intractable – spat over the contested and uninhabited Diaoyu Islands (Senkaku Islands to the Japanese) has soured relations between China and Japan. Close to shipping lanes, surrounded by well-stocked fishing grounds and near to the Chunxiao gas field, the islands have aggravated Chinese and Japanese nationalism and overseen a growing mutual antipathy. Occasionally violent anti-Japanese protests in China have been the result. A festering dispute has also seen growing tensions between China and Vietnam, the Philippines and other nations over the control of waters, islands, reefs, atolls and rocky outcrops in the South China Sea. While keeping an eye on maritime issues, at home President Xi Jinping has to deal with growing unrest in Xīnjiāng province, which has led to terror attacks in both Yúnnán and in front of the Gate of Heavenly Peace in Běijīng, as well as a spate of brazen bombings and attacks in Xīnjiāng itself. The increasing Uighur disquiet has prompted an increasingly harsh security clampdown from Běijīng, which may threaten to inflame sentiments further.

POPULATION: **1.35 BILLION**

GDP (PPP): **$13.39 TRILLION**

GDP PER CAPITA: **$9800**

LABOUR FORCE:
797.6 MILLION

UNEMPLOYMENT: **4.1%**

HIGHEST POINT:
MT EVEREST (8848M)

if China were 100 people

92 would be Han Chinese
8 would be ethnic minorities, eg Zhuang, Manchu, Uighur etc

belief systems
(% of population)

70 Atheist   22 Buddhist

4 Christian   1-2 Taoist   1-2 Muslim

population per sq km

BĚIJĪNG   KŪNMÍNG   SHÀNGHǍI

≈ 300 people

History

The epic sweep of China's history paints a perhaps deceptive impression of prolonged epochs of peace occasionally convulsed by break-up, internecine division or external attack. Yet for much of its history China has been in conflict either internally or with outsiders. Although China's size and shape has also continuously changed – from tiny beginnings by the Yellow River (Huáng Hé) to the subcontinent of today – an uninterrupted thread of history runs from its earliest roots to the full flowering of Chinese civilisation. Powerful bonds tie the Chinese of today with their ancestors of 5000 or 6000 years ago, creating the longest-lasting complex civilisation on earth.

From Oracle Bones to Confucius

Evidence from Han tombs suggests that a popular item of cuisine was a thick vegetable and meat stew, and that flavour enhancers such as soy sauce and honey were also used.

The earliest 'Chinese' dynasty, the Shang, was long considered apocryphal. However, archaeological evidence – cattle bones and turtle shells in Hénán covered in mysterious scratches, recognised by a scholar as an early form of Chinese writing – proved that a society known as the Shang developed in central China from around 1766 BC. The area it controlled was tiny – perhaps 200km across – but Chinese historians have argued that the Shang was the first Chinese dynasty. By using Chinese writing on 'oracle bones', the dynasty marked its connection with the Chinese civilisation of the present day.

Sometime between 1050 and 1045 BC, a neighbouring group known as the Zhou conquered Shang territory. The Zhou was one of many states competing for power in the next few hundred years but developments during this period created some of the key sources of Chinese culture that would last till the present day. A constant theme of the first millennium BC was conflict, particularly the periods known as the 'Spring and Autumn' (722–481 BC) and 'Warring States' (475–221 BC).

The Chinese world in the 5th century BC was both warlike and intellectually fertile, in a way similar to ancient Greece during the same period. From this disorder emerged the thinking of Confucius (551–479 BC), whose system of thought and ethics underpinned Chinese culture for 2500 years. A wandering teacher, Confucius dispensed lessons in personal behaviour and statecraft, advocating an ordered and ethical socie-

TIMELINE	c 4000 BC	2698 BC	c 1700 BC
	The first known settlements appear along the Yellow River (Huáng Hé). The river remains a central cultural reference point for the Chinese throughout history.	The possibly mythological Battle of Banquan is fought between the Yellow Emperor (Huangdi) and the Flame Emperor (Yandi), marking the first known battle in Chinese history.	Craftsmen of the Shang dynasty master the production of bronzeware (in the form of ritual vessels) in one of the first examples of multiple production in history.

ty obedient towards hierarchies and inclined towards ritual. Confucius' desire for an ordered and ethical world was a far cry from the warfare of his times.

Early Empires

The Warring States period ended decisively in 221 BC. The Qin kingdom conquered other states in the central Chinese region and Qin Shi Huang proclaimed himself emperor. The first in a line of dynastic rulers that would last until 1912, later histories portrayed Qin Shi Huang as particularly cruel and tyrannical, but the distinction is dubious: the ensuing Han dynasty (206 BC–AD 220) adopted many of the short-lived Qin's practices of government.

Qin Shi Huang oversaw vast public works projects, including walls built by some 300,000 men, connecting defences into what would become the Great Wall. He unified the currency, measurements and written language, providing the basis for a cohesive state.

Establishing a trend that would echo through Chinese history, a peasant, Liu Bang (256–195 BC), rose up and conquered China, founding the Han dynasty. The dynasty is so important that the name Hàn (汉; 漢) still refers to ethnic Chinese and their language (汉语; Hànyǔ; 'language of the Han'). Critical to the centralisation of power, Emperor Wu (140–87 BC) institutionalised Confucian norms in government. Promoting merit as well as order, he was the first leader to experiment with examinations for entry into the bureaucracy, but his dynasty was plagued by economic troubles, as estate owners controlled more and more land. Indeed, the issue of land ownership would be a constant problem throughout Chinese history to today. Endemic economic problems and the inability to exercise control over a growing empire, coupled with social unrest that

So far, some 7000 soldiers in the famous Terracotta Army have been found near Xī'ān. The great tomb of the first emperor still remains unexcavated, although it is thought to have been looted soon after it was built.

ANCIENT ICONS

Tick off the most iconic sights dating from the very birth of the Chinese nation through the nation's imperial heydays.

The Terracotta Warriors (p377) Silent and awe-inspiring emissaries from the dawn of China's imperial past.

The Great Wall (p114) Snaking across north China, mounting peaks, plunging into valleys and collapsing splendidly into ruin.

The Forbidden City (p59) Ornate and privileged bastion of the Ming and Qing dynasty emperors at the heart of Běijīng.

Mògāo Caves (p823) China's most splendid collection of Buddhist art.

---

c 600 BC	551 BC	486 BC	214 BC
Laotzu (Laozi), founder of Taoism, is supposedly born. The folk religion of Taoism goes on to coexist with later introductions such as Buddhism, a reflection of Chinese religion's syncretic, rather than exclusive, nature.	The birth of Confucius, whose ideas, collected in *The Analects*, of an ethical, ordered society that operated through hierarchy and self-development would dominate Chinese culture until the early 20th century.	Work begins on the earliest section of the Grand Canal, connecting the Yangzi River and Huai River in today's Jiāngsū province.	Emperor Qin indentures thousands of labourers to link existing city walls into one Great Wall, made of tamped earth. The stone-clad bastion dates from the Ming dynasty.

Toilet paper was first used in China as early as the 6th century AD, when it was employed by the wealthy and privileged for sanitary purposes.

included an uprising by Taoists (known as the Yellow Turbans) led to the collapse and downfall of the Han. Upheaval would become a constant refrain in later Chinese dynasties.

Han trade along the Silk Road demonstrated clearly that China was fundamentally a Eurasian power in its relations with neighbouring peoples. To the north, the Xiongnu (a name given to various nomadic tribes of Central Asia) posed the greatest threat to China. Diplomatic links were also formed with Central Asian tribes, and the great Chinese explorer Zhang Qian provided the authorities with information on the possibilities of trade and alliances in northern India. During the same period, Chinese influence percolated into areas that would later become known as Vietnam and Korea.

Disunity Restored

Between the early 3rd and late 6th centuries AD, north China witnessed a succession of rival kingdoms vying for power while a potent division formed between north and south. Riven by warfare, the north succumbed to non-Chinese rule, most successfully by the northern Wei dynasty (386–534), founded by the Tuoba, a northern people who embraced Buddhism and left behind some of China's finest Buddhist art, including the famous caves outside Dūnhuáng. A succession of rival regimes followed until nobleman Yang Jian (d 604) reunified China under the fleeting Sui dynasty (581–618). His son Sui Yangdi contributed greatly to the unification of south and north through construction of the Grand Canal, which was later extended and remained China's most important communication route between south and north until the late 19th cen-

---

RUINS

Many of China's historical artefacts may be in a state of perpetual ruin, but some vestiges get top-billing:

Ruins of the Church of St Paul in Macau (p529) China's most sublime architectural wreck.

Jiànkòu Great Wall (后箭扣长城, Hòu Jiànkòu Chángchéng; admission ¥20) No other section of the Great Wall does the tumble-down look in such dramatic fashion.

Great Fountain Ruins (p89) Sublime tangle of Jesuit-designed stonework in the Summer Palace.

Xanadu (p872) A vivid imagination is required to conjure up impressions of Kublai Khan's pleasure palace.

Ming City Wall Ruins Park (p78) Běijīng's last section of Ming city wall.

---

210 BC	109 BC	c 100 BC	c 100 BC
The Terracotta Army, consisting of 8000 sculptures of soldiers and hundreds of chariots and cavalry, is buried in Emporer Qin Shi Huang's mausoleum near Xī'ān.	Sima Qian completes *Records of the Grand Historian*, a groundbreaking historical account of ancient China covering 2500 years starting from the reign of the Yellow Emperor.	The Silk Road between China and the Middle East takes Chinese goods to places as far flung as Rome.	Buddhism first arrives in China from India. This religious system ends up thoroughly assimilated into Chinese culture and is now more powerful in China than in its country of origin.

tury. After instigating three unsuccessful incursions onto Korean soil, resulting in disastrous military setbacks, Sui Yangdi faced revolt and was assassinated in 618 by one of his high officials.

The Tang: China Looks West

Tang rule (618–907) was an outward-looking time, when China embraced the culture of its neighbours – marriage to Central Asian people or wearing Indian-influenced clothes was part of the era's cosmopolitan élan – and distant nations that reached China via the Silk Road. The Chinese nostalgically regard the Tang as their cultural zenith and Chinatowns around the world are called Tángrénjiē (Tang People Streets) to this day. The output of the Tang poets is still regarded as China's finest, as is Tang sculpture, while its legal code became a standard for the whole East Asian region.

The Tang was founded by the Sui general Li Yuan, his achievements consolidated by his son Taizong (r 626–49). Cháng'ān (modern Xī'ān) became the world's most dazzling capital, with its own cosmopolitan foreign quarter, a population of a million, a market where merchants from as far away as Persia mingled with locals, and an astonishing city wall that eventually enveloped 83 sq km. The city exemplified the Tang devotion to Buddhism, with some 91 temples recorded in the city in 722, but a tolerance of, and even absorption with, foreign cultures allowed alien faiths a foothold, including Nestorian Christianity, Manichaeism, Islam, Judaism and Zoroastrianism.

Taizong was succeeded by a unique figure: Chinese history's sole reigning woman emperor, Wu Zetian (r 690–705). Under her leadership the empire reached its greatest extent, spreading well north of the Great Wall and far west into inner Asia. Her strong promotion of Buddhism, however, alienated her from the Confucian officials and in 705 she was forced to abdicate in favour of Xuanzong, who would preside over the greatest disaster in the Tang's history: the rebellion of An Lushan.

Xuanzong appointed minorities from the frontiers as generals, in the belief that they were so far removed from the political system and society that they would not harbour ideas of rebellion. Nevertheless, it was An Lushan, a general of Sogdian-Turkic parentage, who took advantage of his command in north China to make a bid for imperial power. The fighting lasted from 755 to 763, and although An Lushan was defeated, the Tang's control over China was destroyed forever. It had ceded huge amounts of military and tax-collecting power to provincial leaders to enable them to defeat the rebels, and in doing so dissipated its own power. A permanent change in the relationship between the government and the provinces formed; prior to 755, the government had an idea of who

HISTORY THE TANG: CHINA LOOKS WEST

BUDDHIST STATUES

The features of the largest Buddhist statue in the Ancestor Worshipping Cave at the Lóngmén Caves outside Luòyáng are supposedly based on Tang female emperor Wu Zetian, a famous champion of Buddhism.

AD 118	755–763	874	c 1000
Tomb image of a man pushing a wheelbarrow is painted at Chengdu, marking what is thought to be the first known mention of the wheelbarrow in history.	An Lushan rebels against the Tang court. Although his rebellion is subdued, the court cedes immense military and fiscal power to provincial leaders, a recurring problem through Chinese history.	The Huang Chao rebellion breaks out, which will help reduce the Tang empire to chaos and lead to the fall of the capital in 907.	The major premodern inventions – paper, printing, gunpowder, the compass – are commonly used in China. The economy begins to commercialise and create a countrywide market system.

The Tang saw the first major rise to power of eunuchs. Often from ethnic minority groups, they were brought to the capital and given positions within the imperial palace. In many dynasties they had real influence.

owned what land throughout the empire, but after that date the central government's control was permanently weakened. Even today, the dilemma has not been fully resolved.

In its last century, the Tang withdrew from its former openness, turning more strongly to Confucianism, while Buddhism was outlawed by Emperor Wuzong from 842 to 845. The ban was later modified, but Buddhism never regained its previous power and prestige. The Tang decline was a descent into imperial frailty, growing insurgencies, upheaval and chaos.

The Song: Conflict & Prosperity

Further disunity – the fragmentary-sounding Five Dynasties or Ten Kingdoms period – followed the fall of the Tang until the northern Song dynasty (960–1127) was established. The Song dynasty existed in a state of constant conflict with its northern neighbours. The northern Song was a rather small empire coexisting with the non-Chinese Liao dynasty (which controlled a belt of Chinese territory south of the Great Wall that then marked China's northern border) and less happily with the western Xia, another non-Chinese power that pressed hard on the northwestern provinces. In 1126 the Song lost its capital, Kāifēng, to a third non-Chinese people, the Jurchen (previously an ally against the Liao). The Song was driven to its southern capital of Hángzhōu for the period of the southern Song (1127–1279), yet the period was culturally rich and economically prosperous.

The full institution of a system of examinations for entry into the Chinese bureaucracy was brought to fruition during the Song. At a time when brute force decided who was in control in much of medieval Eu-

---

OLD TOWNS & VILLAGES 古镇

For strong shades of historic China, make a beeline for the following *gǔzhèn* (old towns):

Píngyáo (p358) The best preserved of China's ancient walled towns.

Fènghuáng (p478) Exquisite riverside setting, pagodas, temples, covered bridges and an ancient city wall.

Hóngcūn (p395) Gorgeous Huīzhōu village embedded in the lovely south Ānhuī countryside.

Tiánluókēng Tǔlóu Cluster (p292) Overnight in a photogenic Hakka roundhouse.

Shāxī (p677) Flee modern China along Yúnnán's ancient Tea-Horse Rd.

Zhènyuǎn (p641) Slot into low gear and admire the peaks, temples and age-old alleys of this riverside Guìzhōu town.

1024	1215	1286	1298–99
The Song dynasty issues the first unified form of paper currency based on a pre-existing system that merchants used to trade paper receipts in place of heavy coins.	Genghis Khan conquers Běijīng as part of his creation of a massive Eurasian empire under Mongol rule. The Mongols overstretch themselves, however, and neglect good governance.	The Grand Canal is extended to Běijīng. Over time, the canal becomes a major artery for the transport of grain, salt and other important commodities between north and south China.	Marco Polo pens his famous account of his travels to China. Inconsistencies in his story have led some scholars to doubt whether he ever went to China at all.

DIRTY FOREIGN MUD

Although trade in opium had been banned in China by imperial decree at the end of the 18th century, the *cohong* (local merchants' guild) in Guǎngzhōu helped ensure that the trade continued, and fortunes were amassed on both sides. When the British East India Company lost its monopoly on China trade in 1834, imports of the drug increased to 40,000 chests a year.

In 1839, the Qing government sent Imperial Commissioner Lin Zexu to stamp out the opium trade once and for all. Lin successfully blockaded the British in Guǎngzhōu and publicly burned the 'foreign mud' in Hǔmén. Furious, the British sent an expeditionary force of 4000 men from the Royal Navy to exact reparations and secure favourable trade arrangements.

What would become known as the First Opium War began in June 1840 when British forces besieged Guǎngzhōu and forced the Chinese to cede five ports to the British. With the strategic city of Nanking (Nánjīng) under immediate threat, the Chinese were forced to accept Britain's terms in the Treaty of Nanking.

The treaty abolished the monopoly system of trade, opened the 'treaty ports' to British residents and foreign trade, exempted British nationals from all Chinese laws and ceded the island of Hong Kong to the British 'in perpetuity'. The treaty, signed in August 1842, set the scope and character of the unequal relationship between China and the West for the next half-century.

rope, young Chinese men sat tests on the Confucian classics, obtaining office if successful (most were not). The system was heavily biased towards the rich, but was remarkable in its rationalisation of authority, and lasted for centuries. The classical texts set for the examinations became central to the transmission of a sense of elite Chinese culture, even though in later centuries the system's rigidity failed to adapt to social and intellectual change.

China's economy prospered during the Song rule, as cash crops and handicraft products became far more central to the economy, and a genuinely China-wide market emerged, which would become even stronger during the Ming and Qing dynasties. Under the Song the sciences and arts also flourished, with intellectual and technical advances across many disciplines. Kāifēng emerged as an eminent centre of politics, commerce and culture.

The cultural quirk of foot binding appears to have emerged during the Song dynasty. It is still unknown how the custom of binding up a girl's feet in cloths so that they would never grow larger than the size of a fist began, yet for much of the next few centuries, it became a Chinese social norm.

Qing emperor Kangxi sponsored a vast encyclopaedia of Chinese culture, which is still read by scholars today.

1368	1406	1557	c 1600
Zhu Yuanzhang founds the Ming dynasty and tries to impose a rigid Confucian social order on the entire population. However, China is now too commercialised for the policy to work.	Ming Emperor Yongle begins construction of the 800 buildings of the Forbidden City. This complex, along with much of the Great Wall, shows the style and size of late-imperial architecture.	The Portuguese establish a permanent trade base in Macau, the first of the European outposts that will eventually lead to imperialist dominance of China until the mid-19th century.	The period of China's dominance as the world's greatest economy begins to end. By 1800 European economies are industrialising and clearly dominant.

Mongols to Ming

Two Nestorian monks smuggled silkworms out of China in 550 AD, disclosing the method of silk production to the outside world.

The fall of the Song reinforced notions of China's Eurasian location and growing external threats. Genghis Khan (1167–1227) was beginning his rise to power, turning his gaze on China; he took Běijīng in 1215, destroying and rebuilding it; his successors seized Hángzhōu, the southern Song capital, in 1276. The court fled and, in 1279, southern Song resistance finally crumbled. Kublai Khan, grandson of Genghis, now reigned over all of China as emperor of the Yuan dynasty. Under Kublai, the entire population was divided into categories of Han, Mongol and foreigner, with the top administrative posts reserved for Mongols, even though the examination system was revived in 1315. The latter decision unexpectedly strengthened the role of local landed elites: since elite Chinese could not advance in the bureaucracy, they decided to spend more time tending their large estates instead. Another innovation was the introduction of paper money, although overprinting created a problem with inflation.

The Mongols ultimately proved less adept at governance than warfare, their empire succumbing to rebellion and eventual vanquishment within a century. Ruling as Ming emperor Hongwu, Zhu Yuanzhang established his capital in Nánjīng, but by the early 15th century the court had begun to move back to Běijīng, where a hugely ambitious reconstruction project was inaugurated by Emperor Yongle (r 1403–24), building the Forbidden City and devising the layout of the city we see today.

Although the Ming tried to impose a traditional social structure in which people stuck to hereditary occupations, the era was in fact one of great commercial growth and social change. Women became subject to stricter social norms (for instance, widow remarriage was frowned upon); but female literacy also grew. Publishing, via woodblock technology, burgeoned and the novel appeared.

Emperor Yongle, having usurped power from his nephew, was keen to establish his own legitimacy. In 1405 he launched the first of seven great

HISTORY BOOKS

➡ *The City of Heavenly Tranquillity: Beijing in the History of China* (Jasper Becker; 2009) Becker's authoritative and heartbreaking rendering of Běijīng's transformation from magnificent Ming capital to communist–capitalist hybrid.

➡ *The Penguin History of Modern China: The Fall and Rise of a Great Power 1850–2008* (Jonathan Fenby; 2008) Highly readable account of the paroxysms of modern Chinese history.

➡ *China, A History* (John Key; 2008) An accessible and well-written journey through Middle Kingdom history.

1644	1689	1793	1823
Běijīng falls to peasant rebel Li Zicheng and the last Ming emperor Chongzhen hangs himself in Jīngshān Park; the Qing dynasty is established.	The Treaty of Nerchinsk is signed, delineating the border between China and Russia: this is the first modern border agreement in Chinese history, as well as the longest lasting.	British diplomat Lord Macartney visits Běijīng with British industrial products, but is told by the Qianlong emperor that China has no need of his products.	The British are swapping roughly 7000 chests of opium annually – with about 140 pounds of opium per chest, enough to supply one million addicts – compared with 1000 chests in 1773.

maritime expeditions. Led by the eunuch general Zheng He (1371–1433), the fleet consisted of more than 60 large vessels and 255 smaller ones, carrying nearly 28,000 men. The fourth and fifth expeditions departed in 1413 and 1417, and travelled as far as the present Middle East. The great achievement of these voyages was to bring tribute missions to the capital, including two embassies from Egypt. Yet ultimately, they were a dead end, motivated by Yongle's vanity to outdo his father, not for the purpose of conquest or the establishment of a settled trade network. The emperors who succeeded Yongle had little interest in continuing the voyages, and China dropped anchor on its global maritime explorations.

The Great Wall was re-engineered and clad in brick while ships also arrived from Europe, presaging an overseas threat that would develop from entirely different directions. Traders were quickly followed by missionaries, and the Jesuits, led by the formidable Matteo Ricci, made their way inland and established a presence at court. Ricci learned fluent Chinese and spent years agonising over how Christian tenets could be made attractive in a Confucian society with distinctive norms. The Portuguese presence linked China directly to trade with the New World, which had opened up in the 16th century. New crops, such as potatoes, maize, cotton and tobacco, were introduced, further stimulating the commercial economy. Merchants often lived opulent lives, building fine private gardens (as in Sūzhōu) and buying delicate flowers and fruits.

The Ming was eventually undermined by internal power struggles. Natural disasters, including drought and famine, combined with a menace from the north: the Manchu, a nomadic warlike people, who saw the turmoil within China and invaded.

The Qing: The Path to Dynastic Dissolution

After conquering just a small part of China and assuming control in the disarray, the Manchu named their new dynasty the Qing (1644–1911). Once ensconced in the (now torched) Forbidden City, the Manchu realised they needed to adapt their nomadic way of life to suit the agricultural civilisation of China. Threats from inner Asia were neutralised by incorporating the Qing homeland of Manchuria into the empire, as well as that of the Mongols, whom they had subordinated. Like the Mongols before them, the conquering Manchu found themselves in charge of a civilisation whose government they had defeated, but whose cultural power far exceeded their own. The result was quite contradictory: on the one hand, Qing rulers took great pains to win the allegiance of high officials and cultural figures by displaying a familiarity and respect for traditional Chinese culture; on the other hand, the Manchu rulers made

PING PONG

Ping pong (*pīngpāngqiú*) may be China's national sport (*guóqiú*), but it was invented as an after-dinner game by British Victorians who named it *wiff-waff* and first used a ball made from champagne corks.

1839	1842	1856	1882
The Qing official Lin Zexu demands that British traders at Guǎngzhōu hand over 20,000 chests of opium, leading the British to provoke the First Opium War in retaliation.	The Treaty of Nánjīng concludes the First Opium War. China is forced to hand over Hong Kong Island to the British and open up five Chinese ports to foreign trade.	Hong Xiuquan claims to be Jesus' younger brother and starts the Taiping uprising. With the Nian and Muslim uprisings, the Taiping greatly undermines the authority of the Qing dynasty.	Shànghǎi is electrified by the British-founded Shanghai Electric Company. The first electricity-producing plant generates 654kw and the Bund is illuminated by electric light the following year.

strong efforts to remain distinct. They enforced strict rules of social separation between the Han and Manchu, and tried to maintain – not always very successfully – a culture that reminded the Manchu of their nomadic warrior past. The Qing flourished most greatly under three emperors who ruled for a total of 135 years: Kangxi, Yongzheng and Qianlong.

Much of the map of China that we know today derives from the Qing period. Territorial expansion and expeditions to regions of Central Asia spread Chinese power and culture further than ever. The expansion of the 18th century was fuelled by economic and social changes. The discovery of the New World by Europeans in the 15th century led to a new global market in American food crops, such as chillies and sweet potatoes, allowing food crops to be grown in more barren regions, where wheat and rice had not flourished. In the 18th century, the Chinese population doubled from around 150 million to 300 million people.

Historians now take very seriously the idea that in the 18th century China was among the most advanced economies in the world. The impact of imperialism would help commence China's slide down the table, but the seeds of decay had been sown long before the Opium Wars of the 1840s. Put simply, as China's size expanded, its state remained too small. China's dynasty failed to expand the size of government to cope with the new realities of a larger China.

The first railroad in China was the Woosung Railway, which opened in 1876, running between Shànghǎi and Wusong; it operated for less than a year before being dismantled and shipped to Taiwan.

War & Reform

For the Manchu, the single most devastating incident was not either of the Opium Wars, but the far more destructive anti-Qing Taiping Rebellion of 1850–64, an insurgency motivated partly by a foreign credo (Christianity). Established by Hakka leader Hong Xiuquan, the Heavenly Kingdom of Great Peace (Taiping Tianguo) banned opium and intermingling between the sexes, made moves to redistribute property

HISTORIC CITIES

At the centre of things, China's cities have seen dynasties rise, topple and fall, leaving them littered with dynastic vestiges and age-old artefacts.

Běijīng (p54) Heritage, history and imperial grandeur, with the Great Wall to boot.

Xī'ān (p368) The granddaddy of China's old towns, enclosed by an intact Ming-dynasty wall with the Terracotta Warriors in the suburbs.

Hángzhōu (p260) Possibly China's best-looking city, with oodles of charm and an abundance of lakeside history.

Nánjīng (p233) Supreme city walls and imposing imperial Ming vestiges.

1898	1898	1900	1904–05
Emperor Guangxu permits major reforms, including new rights for women, but is thwarted by the Dowager Empress Cixi, who has many reformers arrested and executed.	The New Territories adjoining Kowloon in Hong Kong are leased to the British for 99 years, eventually returning, along with the rest of Hong Kong, in 1997.	The Hanlin Academy in Běijīng – centre of Chinese learning and literature – is accidentally torched by Chinese troops during the Boxer Rebellion, destroying its priceless collection of books.	The Russo–Japanese War is fought entirely on Chinese territory. The victory of Japan is the first triumph by an Asian power over a European one.

and was fiercely anti-Manchu. The Qing eventually reconquered the Taiping capital at Nánjīng, but upwards of 20 million Chinese died in the uprising.

The events that finally toppled the dynasty, however, came in rapid succession. Foreign imperialist incursions continued and Western powers nibbled away at China's coastline; Shànghǎi, Qīngdǎo, Tiānjīn, Gǔlàng Yǔ, Shàntóu, Yāntái, Wēihǎi, Níngbō and Běihǎi would all either fall under semicolonial rule or enclose foreign concessions. Hong Kong was a British colony and Macau was administered by the Portuguese. Attempts at self-strengthening – involving attempts to produce armaments and Western-style military technology – were dealt a brutal blow by the Sino-Japanese War of 1894–95. Fought over control of Korea, it ended with the humiliating destruction of the new Qing navy. Not only was Chinese influence in Korea lost, but Taiwan was ceded to Japan.

Japan itself was a powerful Asian example of reform. In 1868 Japan's rulers, unnerved by ever-greater foreign encroachment, had overthrown the centuries-old system of the Shōgun, who acted as regent for the emperor. An all-out program of modernisation, including a new army, constitution, educational system and railway network was launched, all of which gave Chinese reformers a lot to ponder.

One of the boldest proposals for change, which drew heavily on the Japanese model, was the program put forward in 1898 by reformers, including the political thinker Kang Youwei (1858–1927). However, in September 1898 the reforms were abruptly halted, as the Dowager Empress Cixi, fearful of a coup, placed the emperor under house arrest and executed several of the leading advocates of change. Two years later, Cixi made a decision that helped to seal the Qing's fate. In 1900 north China was convulsed by attacks from a group of peasant rebels whose martial arts techniques led them to be labelled the Boxers, and who sought to expel foreigners and kill Chinese Christian converts. In a major misjudgment, the dynasty declared its support for the Boxers in June. Eventually, a multinational foreign army forced its way into China and defeated the uprising, which had besieged the foreign Legation Quarter in Běijīng. The imperial powers then demanded huge financial reparations from the Qing. In 1902 the dynasty reacted by implementing the Xinzheng (New Governance) reforms. This set of reforms, now half-forgotten in contemporary China, looks remarkably progressive, even set against the standards of the present day.

The Cantonese revolutionary Sun Yatsen (1866–1925) remains one of the few modern historical figures respected in both China and Taiwan. Sun and his Revolutionary League made multiple attempts to undermine Qing rule in the late 19th century, raising sponsorship and support from a wide-ranging combination of the Chinese diaspora, the newly

In the 18th century, the Chinese used an early form of vaccination against smallpox that required not an injection, but instead the blowing of serum up the patient's nose.

1905	1908	1911	1912
Major reforms in the late Qing dynasty include the abolition of the 1000-year-long tradition of examinations in the Confucian classics to enter the Chinese bureaucracy.	Two-year-old Puyi ascends the throne as China's last emperor. Local elites and new classes such as businessmen no longer support the dynasty, leading to its ultimate downfall.	Revolution spreads across China as local governments withdraw support for the dynasty, and instead support a republic under the presidency of Sun Yatsen (fundraising in the US at the time).	Yuan Shikai, leader of China's most powerful regional army, goes to the Qing court to announce that the game is up: on 12 February the last emperor, six-year-old Puyi, abdicates.

emergent middle class, and traditional secret societies. In practice, his own attempts to end Qing rule were unsuccessful, but his reputation as a patriotic figure dedicated to a modern republic gained him high prestige among many of the emerging middle-class elites in China, though much less among the key military leaders.

The end of the Qing dynasty arrived swiftly. Throughout China's southwest, popular resentment against the dynasty had been fuelled by reports that railway rights in the region were being sold to foreigners. A local uprising in the city of Wǔhàn in October 1911 was discovered early, leading the rebels to take over command in the city and hastily declare independence from the Qing dynasty. Within a space of days, then weeks, most of China's provinces did likewise. Provincial assemblies across China declared themselves in favour of a republic, with Sun Yatsen (who was not even in China at the time) as their candidate for president.

The Republic: Instability & Ideas

The Republic of China lasted less than 40 years on the mainland (1912–1949) and continues to be regarded as a dark chapter in modern Chinese history, when the country was under threat from what many described as 'imperialism from without and warlordism from within'. Yet there was also breathing room for new ideas and culture. In terms of freedom of speech and cultural production, the republic was a far richer time than any subsequent era in Chinese history. Yet the period was certainly marked by repeated disasters, similar to the almost contemporaneous Weimar Republic in Germany.

Sun Yatsen returned to China and only briefly served as president, before having to make way for militarist leader Yuan Shikai. In 1912 China held its first general election, and it was Sun's newly established Kuomintang (Nationalist; Guómíndǎng, literally 'Party of the National People') that emerged as the largest grouping. Parliamentary democracy did not last long, as the Kuomintang itself was outlawed by Yuan, and Sun had to flee into exile in Japan. However, after Yuan's death in 1916, the country split into rival regions ruled by militarist warlord-leaders. Supposedly 'national' governments in Běijīng often controlled only parts of northern or eastern China and had no real claim to control over the rest of the country. Also, in reality, the foreign powers still had control over much of China's domestic and international situation. Britain, France, the US and the other Western powers showed little desire to lose those rights, such as extraterritoriality and tariff control.

Shànghǎi became the focal point for the contradictions of Chinese modernity. By the early 20th century, Shànghǎi was a wonder not just of China, but of the world, with skyscrapers, art deco apartment blocks, neon lights, women (and men) in outrageous new fashions, and a

DIAMOND SUTRA

A Chinese wood-block-printed copy of the *Diamond Sutra*, kept in the British Library, is the earliest dated printed book, created in 868. Visit the library website to turn the pages of the sutra online (www.bl.uk/onlinegallery/sacredtexts/diamondsutra.html).

1915	1916	1925	1926
Japan makes the '21 demands', which would give it massive political, economic and trading rights in parts of China. Europe's attention is distracted by WWI.	Yuan Shikai tries to declare himself emperor. He is forced to withdraw and remain president, but dies of uremia later that year. China splits into areas ruled by rival militarists.	The shooting of striking factory workers on 30 May in Shànghǎi by foreign-controlled police inflames nationalist passions, giving hope to the Kuomintang party, now regrouping in Guǎngzhōu.	The Northern Expedition: Kuomintang and communists unite under Soviet advice to bring together China by force, then establish a Kuomintang government.

vibrant, commercially minded, take-no-prisoners atmosphere. The racism that accompanied imperialism was visible every day, as Europeans kept themselves separate from the Chinese. Yet the glamour of modernity was undeniable too, as workers flocked from rural areas to make a living in the city, and Chinese intellectuals sought out French fashion, British architecture and American movies. In the prewar period, Shànghǎi had more millionaires than anywhere else in China, yet its inequalities and squalor also inspired the first congress of the Chinese Communist Party (CCP).

The militarist government that held power in Běijīng in 1917 provided 96,000 Chinese who served on the Western Front in Europe, not as soldiers but digging trenches and doing hard manual labour. This involvement in WWI led to one of the most important events in China's modern history: the student demonstrations of 4 May 1919.

Double-dealing by the Western Allies and Chinese politicians who had made secret deals with Japan led to an unwelcome discovery for the Chinese diplomats at the Paris Peace Conference in 1919. Germany had been defeated, but its Chinese territories – such as Qīngdǎo – were not to be returned to China; they would instead go to Japan. Five days later, on 4 May 1919, some 3000 students gathered in central Běijīng, in front of the Gate of Heavenly Peace, and then marched to the house of a Chinese government minister closely associated with Japan. Once there, they broke in and destroyed the house. Over in a few hours, the event immediately found a place in modern Chinese folklore.

The student demonstration came to symbolise a much wider shift in Chinese society and politics. The May Fourth Movement, as it became

The oldest surviving brick pagoda in China is the Sōngyuè Pagoda, on Sōng Shān in Hénán province, dating to the early sixth century.

HISTORY THE REPUBLIC: INSTABILITY & IDEAS

FOREIGN CONCESSIONS & COLONIES

China's coastline is dotted with a string of foreign concession towns that ooze charm and a sensation of 19th- and early-20th-century grandeur.

French Concession, Shànghǎi (p198) Shànghǎi's most stylish concession goes to the French.

Gǔlàng Yǔ, Xiàmén (p289) Thoroughly charming colonial remains on a beautiful island setting.

Qīngdǎo (p170) Wander the German district for cobbled streets and Teutonic architecture.

Hong Kong (p489) Outstanding ex-colonial cachet on the Guǎngdōng coast.

Macau (p528) An unforgettable cocktail of Cantonese and Portuguese flavour.

Shāmiàn Island (p553) Gentrified and leafy lozenge of Guǎngzhōu sand, decorated with a handsome crop of buildings and streets.

1927	1930s	1930	1931
The Kuomintang leader Chiang Kaishek turns on the communists in Shànghǎi and Guǎngzhōu, having thousands killed and forcing the communists to turn to a rural-based strategy.	Cosmopolitan Shànghǎi is the world's fifth-largest city (the largest in the Far East), supporting a polyglot population of four million people.	Chiang's Kuomintang government achieves 'tariff autonomy': for the first time in nearly 90 years, China regains the power to tax imports freely, an essential part of fiscal stability.	Japan invades Manchuria (northeast China), provoking an international crisis and forcing Chiang to consider anti-Japanese, as well as anti-communist, strategies.

Paul French's *Midnight in Peking* (2012) is a gripping true-crime murder mystery examining the death of Pamela Werner in 1937 Peking.

known, was associated closely with the New Culture, underpinned by the electrifying ideas of 'Mr Science' and 'Mr Democracy'. In literature, a May Fourth generation of authors wrote works attacking the Confucianism that they felt had brought China to its current crisis, and explored new issues of sexuality and self-development. The CCP, later mastermind of the world's largest peasant revolution, was created in the intellectual turmoil of the movement, many of its founding figures associated with Peking University, such as Chen Duxiu (dean of humanities), Li Dazhao (head librarian) and the young Mao Zedong, a mere library assistant.

The Northern Expedition

After years of vainly seeking international support for his cause, Sun Yatsen found allies in the newly formed Soviet Russia. The Soviets ordered the fledgling CCP to ally itself with the much larger 'bourgeois' party, the Kuomintang. Their alliance was attractive to Sun: the Soviets would provide political training, military assistance and finance. From their base in Guǎngzhōu, the Kuomintang and CCP trained together from 1923, in preparation for their mission to reunite China.

Sun died of cancer in 1925. The succession battle in the party coincided with a surge in antiforeign feeling that accompanied the May Thirtieth Incident when 13 labour demonstrators were killed by British police in Shànghǎi on 30 May 1925. Under Soviet advice, the Kuomintang and CCP prepared for their 'Northern Expedition', the big 1926 push north that was supposed to finally unite China. In 1926–27, the Soviet-trained National Revolutionary Army made its way slowly north, fighting, bribing or persuading its opponents into accepting Kuomintang control. The most powerful military figure turned out to be an officer from Zhèjiāng named Chiang Kaishek (1887–1975). Trained in Moscow, Chiang moved steadily forward and finally captured the great prize, Shànghǎi, in March 1927. However, a horrific surprise was in store for his communist allies.

HISTORY MUSEUMS

Hong Kong Museum of History (p501) One of the former British territory's best museums: a colourful narrative supported by imaginative displays.

Shànghǎi History Museum (p203) Excellent chronicle of Shànghǎi's colourful journey from 'Little Sūzhōu' to 'Whore of the Orient' and beyond.

Macau Museum (p533) The ex-Portuguese territory's fascinating history brought vividly to life.

Shaanxi History Museum (p371) Eye-opening and informative chronicle of ancient Chang'an.

1932	1935	1937	1938
War breaks out in the streets of Shànghǎi in February and March, a sign that conflict between the two great powers of East Asia, China and Japan, may soon be coming.	Mao Zedong begins his rise to paramount power at the conference at Zūnyì, held in the middle of the Long March to the northwest, on the run from the Kuomintang.	The Japanese and Chinese clash at Wanping, near Běijīng, on 7 July, sparking the conflict that the Chinese call the 'War of Resistance', which only ends in 1945.	Former prime minister Wang Jingwei announces he has gone over to Japan. He later inaugurates a 'restored' Kuomintang government, with Japan holding the whip hand over government.

The Soviet advisers had not impressed Chiang and he was increasingly convinced that the communists aimed to use their cooperation with the Kuomintang to seize control themselves. Instead, Chiang struck first. Using local thugs and soldiers, Chiang organised a lightning strike by rounding up CCP activists and union leaders in Shànghǎi and killing thousands of them.

Kuomintang Rule

Chiang Kaishek's Kuomintang government officially came to power in 1928 through a combination of military force and popular support. Marked by corruption, it suppressed political dissent with great ruthlessness. Yet Chiang's government also kick-started a major industrialisation effort, greatly augmented China's transport infrastructure and successfully renegotiated what many Chinese called 'unequal treaties' with Western powers. In its first two years, the Kuomintang doubled the length of highways in China and increased the number of students studying engineering. The government never really controlled more than a few (very important) provinces in the east, however, and China remained significantly disunited. Regional militarists continued to control much of western China; the Japanese invaded and occupied Manchuria in 1931; and the communists re-established themselves in the northwest.

In 1934 Chiang Kaishek launched his own ideological counterargument to communism: the New Life Movement. This was supposed to be a complete spiritual renewal of the nation, through a modernised version of traditional Confucian values, such as propriety, righteousness and loyalty. The New Life Movement demanded that the renewed citizens of the nation must wear frugal but clean clothes, consume products made in China rather than seek luxurious foreign goods, and behave in a hygienic manner. Yet Chiang's ideology never had much success. Against a background of massive agricultural and fiscal crisis, prescriptions about what to wear and how to behave lacked popular appeal.

The new policies did relatively little to change the everyday life for the population in the countryside, where more than 80% of China's people lived. Some rural reforms were undertaken, including the establishment of rural cooperatives, but their effects were small. The Nationalist Party also found itself unable to collect taxes in an honest and transparent fashion.

The Long March

The communists had not stood still and after Chiang's treachery, most of what remained of the CCP fled to the countryside. A major centre of activity was the communist stronghold in impoverished Jiāngxī province, where the party began to try out systems of government that would

CHIANG KAISHEK

Chiang Kaishek's New Life Movement and the Chinese Communist Party ideology were attempts to mobilise society through renewal of the individual. But only the communists advocated class war.

1939	1941	1941	1943
On 3–4 May Japanese carpet bombing devastates the temporary Chinese capital of Chóngqìng. From 1938 to 1943, Chóngqìng is one of the world's most heavily bombed cities.	In the base area at Yán'ān (Shaanxi), the 'Rectification' program begins, remoulding the Communist Party into an ideology shaped principally by Mao Zedong.	The Japanese attack the US at Pearl Harbor. China becomes a formal ally of the US, USSR and Britain in WWII, but is treated as a secondary partner at best.	Chiang Kaishek negotiates an agreement with the Allies that, when Japan is defeated, Western imperial privileges in China will end forever, marking the twilight of Western imperialist power in China.

Traditionally the dragon (*lóng*) was associated with the emperor and the male principle while the phoenix (*fènghuáng*) was a symbol of the empress and the female principle.

eventually bring them to power. However, by 1934, Chiang's previously ineffective 'extermination campaigns' were making the CCP's position in Jiāngxī untenable, as the Red Army found itself increasingly encircled by Nationalist troops. The CCP commenced its Long March, travelling over 6400km. Four thousand of the original 80,000 communists who set out eventually arrived, exhausted, in Shaanxi (Shǎnxī) province in the northwest, far out of the reach of the Kuomintang. It seemed possible that within a matter of months, however, Chiang would attack again and wipe them out.

The approach of war saved the CCP. There was growing public discontent at Chiang Kaishek's seeming unwillingness to fight the Japanese. In fact, this perception was unfair. The Kuomintang had undertaken retraining of key regiments in the army under German advice, and also started to plan for a wartime economy from 1931, spurred on by the Japanese invasion of Manchuria. However, events came to a head in December 1936, when the Chinese militarist leader of Manchuria (General Zhang Xueliang) and the CCP kidnapped Chiang. As a condition of his release, Chiang agreed to an openly declared United Front: the Kuomintang and communists would put aside their differences and join forces against Japan.

War & the Kuomintang

China's status as a major participant in WWII is often overlooked or forgotten in the West. The Japanese invasion of China, which began in 1937, was merciless, with the notorious Nánjīng Massacre (also known as the Rape of Nánjīng), just one of a series of war crimes committed by the Japanese Army during its conquest of eastern China. The government had to operate in exile from the far southwestern hinterland of China, as its area of greatest strength and prosperity, China's eastern seaboard, was lost to Japanese occupation.

In China itself, it is now acknowledged that both the Kuomintang and the communists had important roles to play in defeating Japan. Chiang, not Mao, was the internationally acknowledged leader of China during this period, and despite his government's multitude flaws, he maintained resistance to the end. However, his government was also increasingly trapped, having retreated to Sìchuān province and a temporary capital at Chóngqìng. Safe from land attack by Japan, the city still found itself under siege, subjected to some of the heaviest bombing in the war. From 1940, supply routes were cut off as the road to Burma was closed by Britain, under pressure from Japan, and Vichy France closed connections to Vietnam. Although the US and Britain brought China on board as an ally against Japan after Pearl Harbor on 7 December 1941, the Allied 'Europe First' strategy meant that China was always treated as a second-

Ding Ling's novel *The Sun Shines on the Sanggan River* (1948) gives a graphic account of the violence, as well as the joy, that greeted land reform (ie redistribution) in China in the early 1950s.

1946	1949	1950	1957
Communists and the Kuomintang fail to form a coalition government, plunging China back into civil war. Communist organisation, morale and ideology all prove key to the communist victory.	Mao Zedong stands on top of the Gate of Heavenly Peace in Běijīng on 1 October, and announces the formation of the PRC, saying 'The Chinese people have stood up'.	China joins the Korean War, helping Mao to consolidate his regime with mass campaigns that inspire (or terrify) the population.	There is a brief period of liberalisation under the 'Hundred Flowers Movement'. However, criticisms of the regime lead Mao to crack down and imprison or exile thousands of dissidents.

ary theatre of war. Chiang Kaishek's corruption and leadership qualities were heavily criticised, and while these accusations were not groundless, without Chinese Kuomintang armies (which kept one million Japanese troops bogged down in China for eight years), the Allies' war in the Pacific would have been far harder. The communists had an important role as guerrilla fighters, but did far less fighting in battle than the Kuomintang.

The real winners from WWII, however, were the communists. They undertook important guerrilla campaigns against the Japanese across northern and eastern China, but the really key changes were taking place in the bleak, dusty hill country centred on the small town of Yán'ān, capital of the CCP's largest stronghold. The 'Yán'ān way' that developed in those years solidified many CCP policies: land reform involving redistribution of land to the peasants, lower taxes, a self-sufficient economy, ideological education and, underpinning it all, the CCP's military force, the Red Army. By the end of the war with Japan, the communist areas had expanded massively, with some 900,000 troops in the Red Army, and party membership at a new high of 1.2 million.

Above all, the war with Japan had helped the communists come back from the brink of the disaster they had faced at the end of the Long March. The Kuomintang and communists then plunged into civil war in 1946 and after three long years the CCP won. On 1 October 1949 in Běijīng, Mao declared the establishment of the People's Republic of China.

Chiang Kaishek fled to the island of Formosa (Taiwan), which China had regained from Japan after WWII. He took with him China's gold reserves and the remains of his air force and navy, and set up the Republic of China (ROC), naming his new capital Taipei (台北, Táiběi).

Mao's China

Mao's China desired, above all, to exercise ideological control over its population. It called itself 'New China', with the idea that the whole citizenry, down to the remotest peasants, should find a role in the new politics and society. The success of Mao's military and political tactics also meant that the country was, for the first time since the 19th century, united under a strong central government.

Most Westerners – and Western influences – were swiftly removed from the country. The US refused to recognise the new state at all. However, China had decided, in Mao's phrase, to 'lean to one side' and ally itself with the Soviet Union in the still-emerging Cold War. The 1950s marked the high point of Soviet influence on Chinese politics and culture. However, the decade also saw rising tension between the Chinese and the Soviets, fuelled in part by Khrushchev's condemnation of Stalin (which Mao took, in part, as a criticism of his own cult of personality). Sino–Soviet differences were aggravated with the withdrawal of Soviet

MAO ZEDONG

Mao Zedong is one of the most intriguing figures of 20th-century history. Philip Short's *Mao: A Life* (1999), in English, is the most detailed and thoughtful recent account of his life.

1958	1962	1966	1972
The Taiwan Straits Crisis. Mao's government fires missiles near islands under the control of Taiwan in an attempt to prevent rapprochement between the US and USSR in the Cold War.	The Great Leap Forward causes mass starvation. Politburo members Liu Shaoqi and Deng Xiaoping reintroduce limited market reforms, which lead to their condemnation during the Cultural Revolution.	The Cultural Revolution breaks out, and Red Guards demonstrate in cities across China. The movement is marked by violence as a catalyst for transforming society.	US President Richard Nixon visits China, marking a major rapprochement during the Cold War, and the start of full diplomatic relations between the two countries.

technical assistance from China, and reached a peak with intense border clashes during 1969. Relations remained frosty until the 1980s.

Mao's experiences had convinced him that only violent change could shake up the relationship between landlords and their tenants, or capitalists and their employees, in a China that was still highly traditional. The first year of the regime saw some 40% of the land redistributed to poor peasants. At the same time, some one million or so people condemned as 'landlords' were persecuted and killed. The joy of liberation was real for many Chinese, but campaigns of terror were also real and the early 1950s was no golden age.

As relations with the Soviets broke down in the mid-1950s, the CCP leaders' thoughts turned to economic self-sufficiency. Mao, supported by Politburo colleagues, proposed the policy known as the Great Leap Forward (Dàyuèjìn), a highly ambitious plan to harness the power of socialist economics to boost production of steel, coal and electricity. Agriculture was to reach an ever-higher level of collectivisation. Family structures were broken up as communal dining halls were established: people were urged to eat their fill, as the new agricultural methods would ensure plenty for all, year after year.

However, the Great Leap Forward was a horrific failure. Its lack of economic realism caused a massive famine and at least 20 million deaths; historian Frank Dikötter posits a much larger minimum figure of 45 million deaths in his *Mao's Great Famine* (2010). Yet the return to a semi-market economy in 1962, after the Leap had comprehensively ended, did not dampen Mao's enthusiasm for revolutionary renewal. This led to the last and most fanatical of the campaigns that marked Mao's China: the Cultural Revolution of 1966–76.

During the Cultural Revolution, some 2.2 billion Chairman Mao badges were cast. Read *Mao's Last Revolution* (2006), by Roderick MacFarquhar and Michael Schoenhals, for the history; see Zhang Yimou's film *To Live* (1994) to understand the emotions.

Cultural Revolution

Mao had become increasingly concerned that post-Leap China was slipping into 'economism' – a complacent satisfaction with rising standards of living that would blunt people's revolutionary fervour. Mao was particularly concerned that the young generation might grow up with a dimmed spirit of revolution. For these reasons, Mao decided upon a massive campaign of ideological renewal, in which he would attack his own party.

Still the dominant figure in the CCP, Mao used his prestige to undermine his own colleagues. In the summer of 1966, prominent posters in large, handwritten characters appeared at prominent sites, including Peking University, demanding that figures such as Liu Shaoqi (president of the PRC) and Deng Xiaoping (senior Politburo member) must be condemned as 'takers of the capitalist road'. Top leaders suddenly disappeared from sight, only to be replaced by unknowns, such as Mao's

1973	1976	1980	1987
Deng Xiaoping returns to power as deputy premier. The modernising faction in the party fights with the Gang of Four, who support the continuing Cultural Revolution.	Mao Zedong dies, aged 83. The Gang of Four are arrested by his successor and put on trial, where they are blamed for all the disasters of the Cultural Revolution.	The one-child policy is enforced. The state adopts it as a means of reducing the population, but at the same time imposes unprecedented control over the personal liberty of women.	*The Last Emperor*, filmed in the Forbidden City, collects an Oscar for Best Picture, and marks a new openness in China towards the outside world.

wife Jiang Qing and her associates, later dubbed the 'Gang of Four'. Meanwhile, an all-pervasive cult of Mao's personality took over. One million youths at a time, known as Red Guards, would flock to hear Mao in Tiān'ānmén Sq. Posters and pictures of Mao were everywhere. The Red Guards were not ashamed to admit that their tactics were violent. Immense violence permeated throughout society: teachers, intellectuals and landlords were killed in their thousands.

While Mao initiated and supported the Cultural Revolution, it was also genuinely popular among many young people (who had less to lose). However, police authority effectively disappeared, creative activity came to a virtual standstill and academic research was grounded.

The Cultural Revolution could not last. Worried by the increasing violence, the army forced the Red Guards off the streets in 1969. The early 1970s saw a remarkable rapprochement between the US and China: the former was desperate to extricate itself from the quagmire of the Vietnam War; the latter terrified of an attack from the now-hostile USSR. Secretive diplomatic manoeuvres led, eventually, to the official visit of US President Richard Nixon to China in 1972, which began the reopening of China to the West. Slowly, the Cultural Revolution began to cool down, but its brutal legacy survives today. Many of those guilty of murder and violence re-entered society with little or no judgment while today's CCP discourages open analysis and debate of the 'decade of chaos'.

Reform

Mao died in 1976, to be succeeded by the little-known Hua Guofeng (1921–2008). Within two years, Hua had been outmanoeuvred by the greatest survivor of 20th-century Chinese politics, Deng Xiaoping. Deng had been purged twice during the Cultural Revolution, but after Mao's death he was able to reach supreme leadership in the CCP with a radical program. In particular, Deng recognised that the Cultural Revolution had been highly damaging economically to China. Deng enlisted a policy slogan originally invented by Mao's pragmatic prime minister, Zhou Enlai – the 'Four Modernisations'. The party's task would be to set China on the right path in four areas: agriculture, industry, national defence, and science and technology.

To make this policy work, many of the assumptions of the Mao era were abandoned. The first highly symbolic move of the 'reform era' (as the post-1978 period is known) was the breaking down of the collective farms. Farmers were able to sell a proportion of their crops on the free market, and urban and rural areas were also encouraged to establish small local enterprises. 'To get rich is glorious,' Deng declared, adding, 'it doesn't matter if some areas get rich first'. As part of this encouragement of entrepreneurship, Deng designated four areas on China's coast as

The Soviets withdrew all assistance from the PRC in 1960, leaving the great bridge across the Yangzi River at Nánjīng half-built. It became a point of pride for Chinese engineers to finish the job without foreign help.

1988	1989	1997	2001
The daring series *River Elegy (Héshāng)* is broadcast on national TV. It's a devastating indictment of dictatorship and Mao's rule in particular, and is banned in China after 1989.	Hundreds of civilians are killed by Chinese troops in the streets around Tiān'ānmén Sq. No official reassessment has been made, but rumours persist of deep internal conflict within the party.	Hong Kong is returned to the People's Republic of China. Widespread fears that China will interfere directly in its government prove wrong, but its politics become more sensitive to Běijīng.	China joins the World Trade Organization, giving it a seat at the top table that decides global norms on economics and finance.

One product of the new freedom of the 1980s was a revived Chinese film industry. *Red Sorghum*, the first film directed by Zhang Yimou, was a searingly erotic film of a type that had not been seen since 1949.

Special Economic Zones (SEZs), which would be particularly attractive to foreign investors.

Politics was kept on a much shorter rein than the economy, however. Deng was relaxed about a certain amount of ideological impurity, but some other members of the leadership were concerned by the materialism in reform-era China. They supported campaigns of 'antispiritual pollution', in which influences from the capitalist world were condemned. Yet inevitably the overall movement seemed to be towards a freer and market-oriented society.

The new freedoms that the urban middle classes enjoyed created the appetite for more. After student protests demanding further opening up of the party in 1985–86, the prime minister (and relative liberal) Hu Yaobang was forced to resign in 1987 and take responsibility for allowing social forces to get out of control. He was replaced as general secretary by Zhao Ziyang, who was more conservative politically, although an economic reformer. In April 1989 Hu Yaobang died, and students around China used the occasion of his death to organise protests against the continuing role of the CCP in public life. At Peking University, the breeding ground of the May Fourth demonstrations of 1919, students declared the need for 'science and democracy', the modernising watchwords of 80 years earlier, to be revived.

In spring 1989 Tiān'ānmén Sq was the scene of an unprecedented demonstration. At its height, nearly a million Chinese workers and students, in a rare cross-class alliance, filled the space in front of the Gate of Heavenly Peace, with the CCP profoundly embarrassed to have the world's media record such events. By June 1989 the numbers in the square had dwindled to only thousands, but those who remained showed no signs of moving. Martial law was imposed and on the night of 3 June and early hours of 4 June, tanks and armoured personnel carriers were sent in. The death toll in Běijīng has never been officially confirmed, but it seems likely to have been in the high hundreds or even more. Hundreds of people associated with the movement were arrested, imprisoned or forced to flee to the West.

For some three years, China's politics were almost frozen, but in 1992 Deng, the man who had sent in the tanks, made his last grand public gesture. That year, he undertook what Chinese political insiders called his 'southern tour' (*nánxún*). By visiting Shēnzhèn, Deng indicated that the economic policies of reform were not going to be abandoned. The massive growth rates that the Chinese economy has posted ever since have justified his decision. Deng also made another significant choice: grooming Jiang Zemin – the mayor of Shànghǎi, who had peacefully dissolved demonstrations in Shànghǎi in a way that the authorities in

2002	2004	2006	2008
An outbreak of the Severe Acute Respiratory Syndrome (SARS) in Guǎngdōng province and Hong Kong causes 774 deaths and nearly brings Hong Kong's economy to its knees.	The world's first commercially operating Maglev train begins scorching a trail across Shànghǎi's Pǔdōng District, reaching a top speed of 431km per hour.	The Three Gorges Dam is completed. Significant parts of the landscape of western China are lost beneath the waters, but energy is also provided for the expanding Chinese economy.	Běijīng hosts the 2008 Summer Olympic Games and Paralympics. The Games go smoothly and are widely considered to be a great success in burnishing China's image overseas.

Běijīng had not – as his successor by appointing him as general secretary of the party in 1989.

Deng died in 1997, the same year that Hong Kong returned to China under a 'one country, two systems' agreement with the UK, which would maintain the ex-British colony's independence in all aspects except defense and foreign affairs for the next 50 years. Macau followed suit two years later. Faced with a multitude of social problems brought on by inequalities spawned by the Deng years, President Jiang Zemin, with Zhu Rongji as premier, sought to bring economic stability to China while strengthening the centralised power of the state and putting off much-needed political reforms. Faced with a protest of up to 10,000 Falun Gong adherents outside Běijīng's Zhōngnánhǎi in April 1999, Jiang branded the movement a cult and sought its eradication in China through imprisonment and detention, backed up by a draconian propaganda campaign.

21st-Century China

Jiang Zemin was succeeded in 2002 by President Hu Jintao, who made further efforts to tame growing regional inequality and the poverty scarring rural areas. China's lopsided development continued, however, despite an ambitious program to develop the western regions. By 2009, an in-flow of US$325 billion had dramatically boosted GDP per capita in the western regions, but a colossal prosperity gap survived, and significant environmental challenges – from desertification to water shortages to soil erosion – persisted.

The question of political reform found itself shelved, partly because economic growth was bringing prosperity to so many, albeit unevenly. Property prices – especially in the richer eastern coastal provinces – were rocketing and the export- and investment-driven economy was thriving. For the first decade of the 21st century was marked by spectacular riches for some – the number of dollar billionaires doubled in just two years – and property prices began moving dramatically beyond the reach of the less fortunate. This period coincided with the greatest migration of workers to the cities the world has ever seen.

China responded to the credit crunch of 2007 and the downturn in Western economies with a stimulus package of US$586 billion between 2008 and 2009. Property and infrastructure construction enjoyed spectacular growth, buffering China from the worst effects of the downturn, but the export sector contracted as demand dried up overseas. A barrage of restrictions on buying second properties attempted to flush speculators from the market and tame price rises. These policies partially worked, but millions of flats across China lay empty – bought by investors happy to see prices rise – and entire ghost towns (such as Ordos in

BAN ZHAO

Ban Zhao was the most famous female scholar in early China. Dating from the late 1st century AD, her work *Lessons for Women* advocated chastity and modesty as favoured female qualities.

2008	2008	2009	2010
Violent riots in Lhasa, Tibet, again put the uneasy region centre stage. Protests spread to other Tibetan areas in Gānsù, Sìchuān and Qīnghǎi provinces.	A huge 8.0 magnitude earthquake convulses Sìchuān province, leaving 87,000 dead or missing and rendering millions homeless.	July riots in Ürümqi leave hundreds dead as inter-ethnic violence flares between Uighurs and Han Chinese. Běijīng floods the region with soldiers and implements a 10-month internet blackout.	A huge 7.1-magnitude earthquake in the Qīnghǎi region of the far west flattens the remote town of Yùshù in April, killing thousands.

Inner Mongolia, built on the back of the coal rush) had already risen from the ground.

Vice-president from 2008, Xi Jinping replaced Hu Jintao as president in 2013. Pledging to root out corruption, Xi has also sought to instigate reforms, including a relaxation of the one-child policy and the abolition of the *láojiào* (re-education through labour) system. These reforms, however, were matched by a growing zeal for internet and social media controls and a domestic security budget that sucked in more capital than national defense.

Xi Jinping inherited a China that was a tremendous success story, but one that remained beset with problems. Despite resilient and ambitious planning (massive expansion of the high-speed rail network, a space program setting itself bold targets, some of the world's tallest buildings), the Chinese economy was still fundamentally imbalanced. Skewed towards the export industry and high-investment projects, growth needed to derive more from domestic demand to create sustainability, a challenge that his predecessor had left on the back burner but which requires Xi's increasing attention today.

2011	2012	2013	2013
Two high-speed trains collide in July near Wēnzhōu in Zhèjiāng province, killing 40 people, the first fatal high-speed rail crash in China.	After the heaviest rainfall in 60 years, Běijīng is inundated with epic summer floods; 77 people are killed by the floodwaters and 65,000 evacuated.	In December, the total length of China's national high-speed rail network reaches a staggering 10,000km, the world's longest.	China's lunar lander Chang'e 3 touches down on the moon in December; it's the first spacecraft to soft-land on the moon since 1976.

People of China

Despite being the world's most populous nation – the stamping ground of roughly one-fifth of humanity – China is often regarded as being largely homogenous, at least from a remote Western perspective. This is probably because Han Chinese, the majority ethnic type in this energetic and bustling nation, constitute over nine-tenths of the population. But like Chinese cuisine, and of course the nation's mystifying linguistic Babel, you only have to cover a bit more mileage and turn a few extra corners to come face-to-face with a surprising hodgepodge of ethnicities.

Ethnicity

Han Chinese

Han Chinese (汉族; Hànzú), the predominant clan among China's 56th recognised ethnic group, make up the lion's share of China's people, 92% of the total figure. When we think of China – from its writing system to its visual arts, calligraphy, history, literature, language and politics – we tend to associate it with Han culture.

The Han Chinese are distributed throughout China but are predominantly concentrated along the Yellow River, Yangzi River and Pearl River basins. Taking their name from the Han dynasty, the Han Chinese themselves are not markedly homogenous. China was ruled by non-Han Altaic (Turk, Tungusic or Mongolian) invaders for long periods, most demonstrably during the Yuan dynasty (Mongols) and the long Qing dynasty (Manchu), but also under the Jin, the Liao and other eras. This Altaic influence is more evident in northern Chinese with their larger and broader frames and rounder faces, compared to their slighter and thinner southern Han Chinese counterparts, who are physically more similar to the Southeast Asian type. Shànghǎi Chinese for example are notably more southern in appearance; with their rounder faces, Běijīng Chinese are quite typically northern Chinese. With mass migration to the cities from rural areas and the increased frequency of marriage between Chinese from different parts of the land, these physical differences are likely to diminish slightly over time.

The Han Chinese display further stark differences in their rich panoply of dialects, which fragments China into a frequently baffling linguistic mosaic, although the promotion of Mandarin (汉语; Hànyǔ – or 'language of the Han') has blurred this considerably. The common written form of Chinese using characters (汉字; Hànzi – or 'characters of the Han'), however, binds all dialects together.

Overseas Chinese frequently refer to people of Chinese blood from China or abroad as Huárén (华人, 'people of China'). Conversely, foreigners may be quaintly called *yángrén* (洋人; 'people of the ocean') or not as quaintly – down south – as *guǐlǎo* ('foreign devils').

China has almost 90 cities with populations of five to 10 million people and more than 170 cities with between one and five million people.

The Non-Han Chinese

A glance at the map of China reveals that the core heartland regions of Han China are central fragments of modern-day China's huge expanse. The colossal regions of Tibet, Qīnghǎi, Xīnjiāng, Inner Mongolia and the three provinces of the northeast (Manchuria – Hēilóngjiāng, Jílín and

Liáoníng) are all historically non-Han regions, some areas of which remain essentially non-Han today.

Many of these regions are peopled by some of the remaining 8% of the population: China's 55 other ethnic minorities, known collectively as *shǎoshù mínzú* (少数民族; minority nationals). The largest minority groups in China include the Zhuang (壮族), Manchu (满族; Mǎnzú), Miao (苗族), Uighur (维吾尔族; Wéiwú'ěr zú), Yi (彝族), Tujia (土家族), Tibetan (藏族; Zàngzú), Hui (回族), Mongolian (蒙古族; Ménggǔ zú), Buyi (布依族), Dong (侗族), Yao (瑶族), Korean (朝鲜族; Cháoxiǎn zú), Bai (白族), Hani (哈尼族), Li (黎族), Kazak (哈萨克族; Hāsàkè zú) and Dai (傣族). Population sizes differ dramatically, from the sizeable Zhuang in Guǎngxī to small numbers of Menba (门巴族) in Tibet. Ethnic labelling can be quite fluid: the roundhouse-building Hakka (客家; Kèjiā) were once regarded as a separate minority, but are today considered Han Chinese. Ethnic groups also tell us a lot about the historic movement of peoples around China: the Bonan minority, found in small numbers in a few counties of Qīnghǎi and Gānsù, are largely Muslim but show marked Tibetan influence and are said to be descended from Mongol troops once stationed in Qīnghǎi during the Yuan dynasty.

China's minorities tend to cluster along border regions, in the northwest, the west, the southwest, the north and northeast of China, but are also distributed throughout the country. Some groups are found in just one area (such as the Hani in Yúnnán); others, such as the Muslim Hui, live all over China.

Wedged into the southwest corner of China between Tibet, Myanmar (Burma), Vietnam and Laos, fecund Yúnnán province alone is home to more than 20 ethnic groups, making it one of the most ethnically diverse provinces in the country.

Despite Manchu culture once ruling over China during the Qing dynasty (1644–1911), possibly fewer than 50 native speakers of the Manchu language survive today, although the closely related Xibo language is spoken by around 20,000 descendants of Xibo tribes resettled in Xīnjiāng in China's northwest in the 18th century.

The Chinese Character

Shaped by Confucian principles, the Chinese are thoughtful and discreet, subtle but also pragmatic. Conservative and rather introverted, they favour dark clothing over bright or loud colours, while their body language is usually reserved and undemonstrative, yet attentive.

The Chinese can be both delightful and mystifyingly contradictory. One moment they will give their seat to an elderly person on the bus or help someone who is lost, and the next moment they will entirely ignore an old lady who has been knocked over by a motorbike.

Particularly diligent, the Chinese are inured to the kind of hours that may prompt a workers' insurrection elsewhere. This is partly due to a traditional culture of hard work but is also a response to the absence of

China is the world's fastest growing market for luxury goods, and Chinese shoppers spend an average of £3500 per visit to Harrods, the famous London department store. Furthermore, 25% of worldwide Bentley sales in 2013 went to China.

The Naxi created a written language more than 1000 years ago using an extraordinary system of pictographs – the only hieroglyphic language still in use today.

CHINA DEMOGRAPHICS

➡ Population: 1.35 billion

➡ Birth rate: 12.25 births per thousand people

➡ People over 65: 9.4%

➡ Urbanisation rate: 2.85%

➡ Male to female ratio: 1.17 : 1 (under 15s)

➡ Life expectancy: 75 years

CHINA'S 'ONE-CHILD POLICY'

The 'one-child policy' (actually a misnomer) was railroaded into effect in 1979 in a bid to keep China's population to one billion by the year 2000 (a target it failed to meet); the latest government estimate claims the population will peak at 1.5 billion in 2033. The policy was harshly implemented at first, but rural revolt led to a softer stance; nonetheless, it generated much bad feeling between local officials and the rural population.

All non-Han minorities are exempt from the one-child policy; Han Chinese parents who were both single children could have a second child and in a new policy initiative from 2013, this has been expanded to include couples, if at least one of them is a single child. Rural families are allowed to have two children if the first child is a girl, but some have upwards of three or four kids. Additional children often result in fines and families having to shoulder the cost of education themselves, without government assistance. Official stated policy opposes forced abortion or sterilisation, but allegations of coercion continue as local officials strive to meet population targets. In 2014, the film director Zhang Yimou was fined US$1.2m for breaking the one-child policy.

Families who abided by the one-child policy often went to extreme lengths to ensure their child was male, with female infanticide, sex-selective abortion and abandonment becoming commonplace. In parts of China, this resulted in a serious imbalance of the sexes – in 2010, 118 boys were born for every 100 girls. In some provinces the imbalance has been even higher. By 2020, potentially around 35 million Chinese men may be unable to find spouses.

Another consequence of the one-child policy was a rapidly ageing population, with over a quarter of the populace predicted to be over the age of 65 by 2050.

As women can have a second child abroad, this also led to large numbers of mainland women giving birth in Hong Kong (where the child also qualified for Hong Kong citizenship). The Hong Kong government has used new legislation to curb this phenomenon, dubbed 'birth tourism', as government figures revealed that almost half of babies born in the territory in 2010 were born to mainland parents. In 2013, the Hong Kong government prohibited mainland women from visiting Hong Kong to give birth, unless their husband is from the territory.

---

social-security safety nets and an anxiety regarding economic and political uncertainties. The Chinese impressively save much of what they earn, emphasising the virtue of prudence. Despite this restraint, however, wastefulness can be breathtaking when 'face' is involved: mountains of food are often left on restaurant dining tables, particularly if important guests are present.

Chinese people are deeply generous. Don't be surprised if a person you have just met on a train invites you for a meal in the dining carriage; they will almost certainly insist on paying, grabbing the bill from the waitress at blinding speed and tenaciously resisting your attempts to pay.

The Chinese are also an exceptionally dignified people. They are proud of their civilisation and history, their written language and their inventions and achievements. This pride rarely comes across as arrogance, however, and can be streaked with a lack of self-assurance. The Chinese may, for example, be very gratified by China's newfound world status, but may squirm at the mention of food safety.

The modern Chinese character has been shaped by recent political realities, and while Chinese people have always been reserved and circumspect, in today's China they can appear even more prudent. Impressive mental gymnastics are performed to detour contentious domestic political issues, which can make the mainland Chinese appear complicated, despite their reputation for being straightforward.

For an idea of local urban salaries, a chef or waitress in a Shànghǎi restaurant can stand to earn between ¥2300 and ¥3000 (about US$360 to US$475) per month.

Women in China
Equality & Emancipation

Growing up in a Confucian culture, women in China traditionally encountered great prejudice and acquired a far lowlier social status to men. The most notorious expression of female subservience was foot-binding, which became a widespread practice in the Song dynasty. Female resistance to male dominated society could sometimes seek inventive solutions, however: discouraged from reading and writing, women in Jiāngyǒng county (Húnán) once used their own invented syllabic script (partly based on Chinese) called *nǔshū* (女书) to write letters to each other (which men found incomprehensible).

Women in today's China officially share complete equality with men; however, as with other nations that profess sexual equality, the reality is often far different. Chinese women do not enjoy strong political representation and the Chinese Communist Party remains a largely patriarchal organisation. Iconic political leaders from the early days of the Chinese Communist Party were men and the influential echelons of the party persist as a largely male domain. Only a handful of the great scientists celebrated in a long photographic mural at Shànghǎi's Science and Technology Museum are women.

After 1949, the Communist Party tried to outlaw old customs and put women on equal footing with men. It abolished arranged marriages and encouraged women to get an education and join the workforce. Women were allowed to keep their maiden name upon marriage and leave their property to their children. In its quest for equality during this period however, the Communist Party seemed to 'desexualise' women, fashioning instead a kind of idealised worker-mother-peasant paradigm.

David Eimer's *The Emperor Far Away: Travels at the Edge of China* (2014) is a riveting journey through China's periphery, from the deserts of Xīnjiāng and the mountains of Tibet, to the tropical jungles of Xīshuāngbǎnnà and the frozen wastes of far northern Heīlóngjiāng.

Chinese Women Today

High-profile, successful Chinese women are very much in the public eye, but the relative lack of career opportunities for females in other fields also suggests a continuing bias against women in employment.

Women's improved social status today has meant that more women are putting off marriage until their late 20s or early 30s, choosing instead to focus on education and career opportunities. This has been enhanced by the rapid rise in house prices, further encouraging women to leave marriage (and having children) till a later age. Premarital sex and cohabitation before marriage are increasingly common in larger cities and lack the stigma they had several years ago.

Some Chinese women are making strong efforts to protect the rights of women in China, receiving international attention in the process. In 2010 the Simone de Beauvoir prize for women's freedom was awarded to Guo Jianmei, a Chinese lawyer and human rights activist, and filmmaker and professor Ai Xiaoming. Guo Jianmei also received the International Women of Courage Award in 2011.

In a sign of growing confidence among the female workforce, a young Běijīng woman won the first ever gender discrimination lawsuit in China in 2014.

Rural Women in China

A strong rural–urban divide exists. Urban women are far more optimistic and freer, while women from rural areas, where traditional beliefs are at their strongest, fight an uphill battle against discrimination. Rural Chinese mores are heavily biased against females, where a marked preference for baby boys exists. China's women are more likely to commit suicide than men (in the West it is the other way around), while the suicide rate for rural Chinese women is around five times the urban rate.

Religion & Philosophy

Despite the seemingly pragmatic nature of its people, ideas have always possessed an extraordinary potency in China. The Taiping Rebellion fused Christianity with revolutionary principles of social organisation, almost sweeping away the Qing dynasty in the process and leaving 20 million dead in its horrifying 20-year spasm. The momentary incandescence of the Boxer Rebellion drew upon a volatile cocktail of martial-arts practices and superstition, blended with xenophobia, while the chaos of the Cultural Revolution is a further suggestion of what may happen in China when ideas assume the full supremacy they seek.

Religion Today

The Chinese Communist Party (CCP) today remains fearful of ideas and beliefs that challenge its authority. Proselytising is not permitted, religious organisation is regulated and monitored, while organisations such as Falun Gong can be banned outright. Despite these constraints, worship and religious practice is generally permitted and China's spiritual world provides a vivid and colourful backdrop to contemporary Chinese life.

China has always had a pluralistic religious culture, and although statistics in China are a slippery fish, an estimated 400 million Chinese today adhere to a particular faith. The CCP made strident efforts after 1949 to supplant religious worship with the secular philosophy of communism, but since the abandonment of principles of Marxist–Leninist collectivism, this policy has significantly waned.

Religion is enjoying an upswing as people return to faith for spiritual solace at a time of great change, dislocation and uncertainty. The hopeless, poor and destitute may turn to worship as they feel abandoned by communism and the safety nets it once assured. Yet the educated and prosperous are similarly turning to religious belief for a sense of guidance and direction in a land many Chinese suspect has become morally bereft.

Religious belief in China has traditionally been marked by tolerance. Although the faiths are quite distinct, some convergence exists between Buddhism, Taoism and Confucianism, and you may discover shrines where all three faiths are worshipped. Guanyin, the Buddhist Goddess of Mercy, finds her equivalent in Tianhou (Mazu), the Taoist goddess and protector of fisher folk, and the two goddesses can seem almost interchangeable. Other symbioses exist: elements of Taoism and Buddhism can be discerned in the thinking of some Chinese Christians, while the Virgin Mary finds a familiar toehold in the Chinese psyche owing to her physical similarity with Guanyin.

China's oldest surviving Buddhist temple is the White Horse Temple in Luòyáng; other more ancient Buddhist temples may well have existed but have since vanished.

Buddhism

Although not an indigenous faith, Buddhism (佛教; Fójiào) is the religion most deeply associated with China and Tibet. Although Buddhism's authority has long ebbed, the faith still exercises a powerful sway over China's spiritual inclinations. Many Chinese may not be regular temple-goers but they harbour an interest in Buddhism; they may merely be 'cultural Buddhists', with a strong affection for Buddhist civilisation.

Chinese towns with any history usually have several Buddhist temples, but the number is well down on pre-1949 figures. The small Héběi town of Zhèngdìng, for example, has four Buddhist temples, but at one time had eight. Běijīng once had hundreds, compared to the 20 or so you can find today.

Some of China's greatest surviving artistic achievements are Buddhist in inspiration. The largest and most ancient repository of Chinese, Central Asian and Tibetan Buddhist artwork can be found at the Mogao Caves in Gānsù, while the carved Buddhist caves at both Lóngmén and Yúngāng are spectacular pieces of religious and creative heritage. To witness Buddhism at its most devout, consider a trip to Tibet.

Origins

Founded in ancient India around the 5th century BC, Buddhism teaches that all of life is suffering, and that the cause of this anguish is desire, itself rooted in sensation and attachment. Suffering can only be overcome by following the eightfold path, a set of guidelines for moral behaviour, meditation and wisdom. Those who have freed themselves from suffering and the wheel of rebirth are said to have attained nirvana or enlightenment. The term Buddha generally refers to the historical founder of Buddhism, Siddhartha Gautama, but is also sometimes used to denote those who have achieved enlightenment.

Siddhartha Gautama left no writings; the sutras that make up the Buddhist canon were compiled many years after his death.

Buddhism in China

Like other faiths such as Christianity, Nestorianism, Islam and Judaism, Buddhism originally reached China via the Silk Road. The earliest recorded Buddhist temple in China proper dates back to the 1st century AD, but it was not until the 4th century, when a period of warlordism coupled with nomadic invasions plunged the country into disarray, that Buddhism gained mass appeal. Buddhism's sudden growth during this period is often attributed to its sophisticated ideas concerning the afterlife (such as karma and reincarnation), a dimension unaddressed by either Confucianism or Taoism. At a time when existence was especially precarious, spiritual transcendence was understandably popular.

As Buddhism converged with Taoist philosophy (through terminology used in translation) and popular religion (through practice), it went on to develop into something distinct from the original Indian tradition. The most famous example is the esoteric Chan school (Zen in Japanese), which originated sometime in the 5th or 6th century, and focused on

Beyond Tibet, China has four sacred Buddhist mountains, each one the home of a specific Bodhisattva. The two most famous mountains are Wǔtái Shān and Éméi Shān, respectively ruled over by Wenshu and Puxiang.

FALUN GONG

Falun Gong – a practice that merges elements of qìgōng-style regulated breathing and standing exercises with Buddhist teachings, fashioning a quasi-religious creed in the process – literally means 'Practice of the Dharma Wheel'. Riding a wave of interest in qìgōng systems in the 1990s, Falun Gong claimed as many as 100 million adherents in China by 1999. The technique was banned in the same year after over 10,000 practitioners stood in silent protest outside Zhōngnánhǎi in Běijīng, following protests in Tiānjīn when a local magazine published an article critical of Falun Gong. The authorities had been unnerved by the movement's audacity and organisational depth, construing Falun Gong as a threat to the primacy of the CCP. The movement was branded a cult (xiéjiao) and a robust, media-wide propaganda campaign was launched against practitioners, forcing many to undergo 're-education' in prison and labour camps. After the ban, the authorities treated Falun Gong believers harshly and reports surfaced of adherents dying in custody. Falun Gong remains an outlawed movement in China to this day.

GUANYIN 观音

The boundlessly compassionate countenance of Guanyin, the Buddhist Goddess of Mercy, can be encountered in temples across China. The goddess (more strictly a Bodhisattva or a Buddha-to-be) goes under a variety of aliases: Guanshiyin (literally 'Observing the Cries of the World') is her formal name, but she is also called Guanzizai, Guanyin Dashi and Guanyin Pusa, or, in Sanskrit, Avalokiteshvara. Known as Kannon in Japan, Guanyam in Cantonese and Quan Am in Vietnam, Guanyin shoulders the grief of the world and dispenses mercy and compassion. Christians will note a semblance to the Virgin Mary in the aura surrounding the goddess, which at least partially explains why Christianity has found a slot in the Chinese consciousness.

In Tibetan Buddhism, her earthly presence manifests itself in the Dalai Lama, and her home is the Potala Palace in Lhasa. In China, her abode is the island of Pǔtuóshān in Zhèjiāng province, the first two syllables of which derive from the name of her palace in Lhasa.

In temples throughout China, Guanyin is often found at the very rear of the main hall, facing north (most of the other divinities, apart from Weituo, face south). She typically has her own little shrine and stands on the head of a big fish, holding a lotus in her hand. On other occasions, she has her own hall, often towards the rear of the temple.

The goddess (who in earlier dynasties appeared to be male rather than female) is often surrounded by little effigies of the luóhàn (or arhat; those freed from the cycle of rebirth), who scamper about; the Guānyīn Pavilion outside Dàlǐ is a good example of this. Guanyin also appears in a variety of forms, often with just two arms, but sometimes in multi-armed form (as at the Pǔníng Temple in Chéngdé). The 11-faced Guanyin, the fierce horse-head Guanyin, the Songzi Guanyin (literally 'Offering Son Guanyin') and the Dripping Water Guanyin are just some of her myriad manifestations. She has traditionally been a favourite subject for déhuà (white-glazed porcelain) figures, which are typically very elegant.

attaining enlightenment through meditation. Chan was novel not only in its unorthodox teaching methods, but also because it made enlightenment possible for laypeople outside the monastic system. It rose to prominence during the Tang and Song dynasties, after which the centre of practice moved to Japan. Other major Buddhist sects in China include Tiantai (based on the teachings of the Lotus Sutra) and Pure Land, a faith-based teaching that requires simple devotion, such as reciting the Amitabha Buddha's name, in order to gain rebirth in paradise. Today, Pure Land Buddhism is the most common.

Buddhist Schools

Regardless of its various forms, most Buddhism in China belongs to the Mahayana school, which holds that since all existence is one, the fate of the individual is linked to the fate of others. Thus, Bodhisattvas – those who have already achieved enlightenment but have chosen to remain on earth – continue to work for the liberation of all other sentient beings. The most popular Bodhisattva in China is Guanyin, the Goddess of Mercy.

Ethnic Tibetans and Mongols within China practise a unique form of Mahayana Buddhism known as Tibetan or Tantric Buddhism (Lǎma Jiào). Tibetan Buddhism, sometimes called Vajrayana or 'thunderbolt vehicle', has been practised since the early 7th century AD and is influenced by Tibet's pre-Buddhist Bon religion, which relied on priests or shamans to placate spirits, gods and demons. Generally speaking, it is much more mystical than other forms of Buddhism, relying heavily on mudras (ritual postures), mantras (sacred speech), yantras (sacred art) and secret initiation rites. Priests called lamas are believed to be reincarnations of highly evolved beings; the Dalai Lama is the supreme patriarch of Tibetan Buddhism.

Believing he was the son of God and brother of Jesus Christ, Hakka rebel Hong Xiuquan led the bloody and tumultuous pseudo-Christian Taiping Rebellion against the Qing dynasty from 1856 to 1864.

Taoism

A home-grown philosophy-cum-religion, Taoism (道教; Dàojiào) is also perhaps the hardest of all China's faiths to grasp. Controversial, paradoxical, and – like the Tao itself – impossible to pin down, it is a natural counterpoint to rigid Confucianist order and responsibility.

Taoism predates Buddhism in China and much of its religious culture connects to a distant animism and shamanism, despite the purity of its philosophical school. In its earliest and simplest form, Taoism draws from *The Classic of the Way and Its Power* (Taote Jing; Dàodé Jīng), penned by the sagacious Laotzu (Laozi; c 580–500 BC) who left his writings with the gatekeeper of a pass as he headed west on the back of an ox. Some Chinese believe his wanderings took him to a distant land in the west where he became Buddha.

The Classic of the Way and Its Power is a work of astonishing insight and sublime beauty. Devoid of a god-like being or deity, Laotzu's writings instead endeavour to address the unknowable and indescribable principle of the universe, which he calls Dao (*dào*; 道), or 'the Way'. Dao is the way or method by which the universe operates, so it can be understood to be a universal or cosmic principle.

The opening lines of *The Classic of the Way and Its Power* confess, however, that the treatise may fail in its task: 道可道非常道, 名可名非常名 ('The way that can be spoken of is not the real way, the name that can be named is not the true name'). Despite this disclaimer, the 5000-character book, completed in terse classical Chinese, somehow communicates the nebulous power and authority of 'the Way'. The book remains the seminal text of Taoism, and Taoist purists see little need to look beyond its revelations.

One of Taoism's most beguiling precepts, *wúwéi* (inaction) champions the allowing of things to naturally occur without interference. The principle is enthusiastically pursued by students of Taiji Quan, Wuji Quan and other soft martial arts who seek to equal nothingness in their bid to lead an opponent to defeat himself.

The Chinese verb for 'to know' is *zhīdào* (知道), literally 'know the *dào*' or 'to know the way', indicating a possible Taoist etymology.

Confucianism

The very core of Chinese society for the past two millennia, Confucianism (儒家思想; Rújiā Sīxiǎng) is a humanist philosophy that strives for social harmony and the common good. In China, its influence can be seen in everything from the emphasis on education and respect for elders to the patriarchal role of the government.

Confucianism is based upon the teachings of Confucius (Kǒngzǐ), a 6th-century-BC philosopher who lived during a period of constant warfare and social upheaval. While Confucianism has changed considerably throughout the centuries, some of the principal ideas remained the same – namely an emphasis on five basic hierarchical relationships: father–son, ruler–subject, husband–wife, elder–younger and friend–friend. Confucius believed that if each individual carried out his or her proper role in society (ie, a son served his father respectfully while a father provided for his son, a subject served his ruler respectfully while a ruler provided for his subject, and so on) social order could be achieved. Confucius' disciples later gathered his ideas in the form of short aphorisms and conversations, forming the work known as *The Analects* (Lúnyǔ).

Early Confucian philosophy was further developed by Mencius (Mèngzǐ) and Xunzi, both of whom provided a theoretical and practical foundation for many of Confucius' moral concepts. In the 2nd century BC, Confucianism became the official ideology of the Han dynasty, thereby gaining mainstream acceptance for the first time. This was of major importance and resulted in the formation of an educated elite that served

Confucius Institutes around the world aim to promote Chinese language and culture internationally, while simultaneously developing its economic and cultural influences abroad.

NATIONALISM

In today's China, '-isms' (主义; zhǔyì or 'doctrines') are often frowned upon. Any zhǔyì may suggest a personal focus that the CCP would prefer people channel into hard work instead. 'Intellectualism' is suspect as it may clash with political taboos. 'Idealism' is non-pragmatic and potentially destructive, as Maoism showed.

Many argue that China's one-party state has reduced thinking across the spectrum via propaganda and censorship, dumbing down, and an educational system that emphasises patriotic education. This has, however, helped spawn another '-ism': nationalism.

Nationalism is not restricted to Chinese youth but it is this generation – with no experience of the Cultural Revolution's terrifying excesses – which most closely identifies with its message. The fènqīng (angry youth) have been swept along with China's rise; while they are no lovers of the CCP, they yearn for a stronger China that can stand up to 'foreign interference' and dictate its own terms.

The CCP actively encourages strong patriotism, but is nervous about its transformation into aggressive nationalism and the potential for disturbance. Much nationalism in the PRC has little to do with the CCP but everything to do with China; while the CCP has struggled at length to identify itself with China's civilisation and core values, it has been only partially successful. With China's tendency to get quickly swept along by passions, nationalism is an often unseen but quite potent force, most visibly flaring up into the periodic anti-Japanese demonstrations that can convulse large towns and cities.

both the government as bureaucrats and the common people as exemplars of moral action. During the rule of the Tang dynasty an official examination system was created, which, in theory, made the imperial government a true meritocracy. However, this also contributed to an ossification of Confucianism, as the ideology grew increasingly mired in the weight of its own tradition, focusing exclusively on a core set of texts.

Nonetheless, influential figures sporadically reinterpreted the philosophy – in particular Zhu Xi (1130–1200), who brought in elements of Buddhism and Taoism to create Neo Confucianism (Lǐxué or Dàoxué) – and it remained a dominant social force up until the 1911 Revolution toppled the imperial bureaucracy. In the 20th century, intellectuals decried Confucian thought as an obstacle to modernisation and Mao further levelled the sage in his denunciation of 'the Four Olds'. But feudal faults notwithstanding, Confucius' social ethics recently resurfaced in government propaganda where they lent authority to the leadership's emphasis on 'harmony' (héxié).

Christianity

The explosion of interest in Christianity (基督教; Jīdūjiào) in China over recent years is unprecedented except for the wholesale conversions that accompanied the tumultuous rebellion of the pseudo-Christian Taiping in the 19th century.

Christianity first arrived in China with the Nestorians, a sect from ancient Persia that split with the Byzantine Church in 431 AD and arrived in China via the Silk Road in the 7th century. A celebrated tablet – the Nestorian Tablet – in Xī'ān records their arrival. Much later, in the 16th century, the Jesuits arrived and were popular figures at the imperial court, although they made few converts.

Large numbers of Catholic and Protestant missionaries established themselves in the 19th century, but left after the establishment of the People's Republic of China in 1949. One such missionary, James Hudson Taylor from Barnsley in England, immersed himself in Chinese culture and is credited with helping to convert 18,000 Chinese Christians and building 600 churches during his 50 years in 19th-century China.

An inspiring read, *God is Red: The Secret Story of How Christianity Survived and Flourished in Communist China* (2011), by Liao Yiwu, himself not a Christian, relates his encounters with Christians in contemporary China, set against a background of persecution and surging growth for the faith.

In today's China, Christianity is a burgeoning faith perhaps uniquely placed to expand due to its industrious work ethic, associations with first-world nations and its emphasis on human rights and charitable work.

Some estimates point to as many as 100 million Christians in China. However, the exact population is hard to calculate as many groups – outside the four official Christian organisations – lead a strict underground existence (in what are called 'house churches') out of fear of a political clampdown.

In signs of greater official unease at the spread of Christianity, authorities in Wēnzhōu – a city in Zhèjiāng province known as 'China's Jerusalem' – demolished churches, threatened others with demolition and removed large crosses from some church spires in 2014. Officials argued they were enforcing building laws but Christian locals saw the moves as a deliberate attempt to undermine their faith. Běijīng has also recently ratcheted up efforts to suppress fringe Christian groups such as the Church of Almighty God, an apocalyptic church that was designated a cult. Over a thousand members of the Church of Almighty God were arrested over a three-month period in 2014.

> During the Cultural Revolution, many Christian churches around China served as warehouses or factories, and were gradually rehabilitated in the 1980s.

Islam

Islam (伊斯兰教; Yīsīlán Jiào) in China dates to the 7th century, when it was first brought to China by Arab and Persian traders along the Silk Road. Later, during the Mongol Yuan dynasty, maritime trade increased, bringing new waves of merchants to China's coastal regions, particularly the port cities of Guǎngzhōu and Quánzhōu. The descendants of these groups – now scattered across the country – gradually integrated into Han culture, and are today distinguished primarily by their religion. In Chinese, they are referred to as the Hui.

Other Muslim groups include the Uighurs, Kazaks, Kyrgyz, Tajiks and Uzbeks, who live principally in the border areas of the northwest. It is estimated that 1.5% to 3% of Chinese today are Muslim.

Communism & Maoism

Ironically (or perhaps intentionally), Mao Zedong, while struggling to uproot feudal superstition and religious belief, sprung to godlike status in China via a personality cult. In the China of today, Mao retains a semi-deified aura.

Communism sits awkwardly with the economic trajectory of China over the past 30 years. Once a philosophy forged in the white-hot crucible of civil war, revolution and the patriotic fervour to create a nation free from foreign interference, communism had largely run its credible course by the 1960s. By the death of Mao Zedong in 1976, the political philosophy had repeatedly brought the nation to catastrophe, with the Hundred Flowers Movement, the Great Leap Forward and the disastrous violence of the Cultural Revolution.

> Kāifēng in Hénán province is home to the largest community of Jews in China. The religious beliefs and customs of Judaism (犹太教; Yóutài Jiào) have died out, yet the descendants of the original Jews still consider themselves Jewish.

Communism remains the official guiding principle of the CCP. However, young communist aspirants are far less likely to be ideologues than pragmatists seeking to advance within the party structure. In real terms, many argue that communism has become an adjunct to the survival of the CCP.

Chinese Communism owes something to Confucianism. Confucius' philosophy embraces the affairs of man and human society and the relationship between rulers and the ruled, rather than the supernatural world. Establishing a rigid framework for human conduct, the culture of Confucianism was easily requisitioned by communists seeking to establish authority over society.

With the collapse of the Soviet Union in 1989, Běijīng became aware of the dangers of popular power and sought to maintain the coherence and strength of the state. This has meant that the CCP still seeks to impose itself firmly on the consciousness of Chinese people through patriotic education, propaganda, censorship, nationalism and the building of a strong nation.

Communism also has considerable nostalgic value for elderly Chinese who bemoan the loss of values in modern-day China and pine for the days when they felt more secure and society was more egalitarian. Chairman Mao's portrait still hangs in abundance across China, from drum towers in Guǎngxī province to restaurants in Běijīng, testament to a generation of Chinese who still revere the communist leader. Until his spectacular fall from power in 2012, Chinese politician and Chóngqìng party chief Bo Xilai launched popular Maoist-style 'red culture' campaigns in Chóngqìng, which included the singing of revolutionary songs and the mass-texting of quotes from Mao's *Little Red Book*.

Animism

A small percentage of China's population is animist, a primordial religious belief akin to shamanism. Animists see the world as a living being, with rocks, trees, mountains and people all containing spirits that need to live in harmony. If this harmony is disrupted, restoration of this balance is attempted by a shaman who is empowered to mediate between the human and spirit world. Animism is most widely believed by minority groups and exists in a multitude of forms, some of which have been influenced by Buddhism and other religions.

The death of a young toddler, who was run over twice and ignored by nearly 20 passers-by in Fóshān in 2011, prompted a passionate debate about morals in modern Chinese society.

Chinese Cuisine

Cooking plays a central role in both Chinese society and the national psyche. When Chinese people meet, a common greeting is *'Nǐ chīfàn le ma?'* ('Have you eaten yet?'). Work, play, romance, business and family all revolve around food. Catalysts for all manner of enjoyment, meals are occasions for pleasure and entertainment, to clinch deals, strike up new friendships and rekindle old ones. To fully explore this tasty domain on home soil, all you need is a visa, a pair of chopsticks, an explorative palate and a passion for the unusual and unexpected.

Real Chinese Food

Because the nation so skilfully exported its cuisine abroad, your very first impressions of China were probably via your taste buds. Chinatowns the world over teem with the aromas of Chinese cuisine, ferried overseas by China's versatile and hard-working cooks. Sunday sees flocks of diners filling Chinatowns to 'yum cha' and feast on dim sum. Chinese food is indeed a wholesome and succulent point of contact between an immigrant Chinese population and everyone else.

But what you see – and taste – abroad is usually just a wafer-thin slice of a very hefty and wholesome pie. Chinese cuisine in the West is lifted from the cookbook of an emigrant community that mainly originated from China's southern seaboard. In a similar vein, the sing-song melodies of Cantonese were the most familiar of China's languages in Chinatowns, even though the dialect finds little traction in China beyond Hong Kong, Macau, Guǎngdōng, parts of Guǎngxī and KTV parlours nationwide. So although you may be hard pressed to avoid dim sum and *cha siu* in your local Chinatown, finding more 'obscure' specialities from elsewhere in China may still be a challenge, or an expensive proposition. The 'Peking duck' at your local restaurant, for example, may be at best a distant relative of the fowl fired up over fruit-tree wood in the ovens of Běijīng *kǎoyādiàn* (Peking duck restaurants).

To get an idea of the size of its diverse menu, remember that China is not that much smaller than Europe. Just as Europe is a patchwork of different nation states, languages, cultural traditions and climates, China is also a smorgasbord of dialects, languages, ethnic minorities and extreme geographic and climatic differences, despite the common Han Chinese cultural glue.

The sheer size of the land, the strength of local culture and differences in geography and altitude mean there can be little in common between the cuisines of Xīnjiāng and Tibet, even though they are adjacent to each other. Following your nose (and palate) around China is one of the exciting ways to journey the land, so pack a sense of culinary adventure along with your travelling boots!

Regional Cooking

The evolution of China's wide-ranging regional cuisines has been influenced by the climate, the distribution of crop and animal varieties, the type of terrain, proximity to the sea and the influence of neighbouring nations and the import of ingredients and aromas. Naturally seafood is prevalent in coastal regions of China, while in Inner Mongolia and Xīnjiāng there is a dependence on meat such as beef and lamb.

Another crucial ingredient is history. The flight of the Song court south of the Cháng Jiāng (Yangzi River) from northern Jurchen invaders in the 12th century helped develop China's major regional cuisines. This process was further influenced by urbanisation, itself made possible by the commercialisation of agriculture and food distribution, which saw the restaurant industry emerge and the further consolidation of regional schools. Further impetus came from the merchants and bureaucrats who travelled the land, and from improved communications, such as the Grand Canal.

Many Chinese regions lay claim to their own culinary conventions, which may overlap and cross-pollinate each other. The cooking traditions of China's ethnic minorities aside, Han cooking has traditionally been divided into eight schools (中华八大菜系; zhōnghuá bādàcàixì): Chuān (川; Sìchuān cuisine); Huī (徽; Ānhuī cuisine), Lǔ (鲁; Shāndōng cuisine), Mǐn (闽; Fújiàn cuisine), Sū (苏; Jiāngsū cuisine), Xiāng (湘; Húnán cuisine), Yuè (粤; Cantonese/Guǎngdōng cuisine), Zhè (浙; Zhèjiāng cuisine). Although each school is independent and well defined, it is possible to group these eight culinary traditions into northern, southern, western and eastern cooking.

A common philosophy lies at the heart of Chinese cooking, whatever the school. Most vegetables and fruits are yīn foods, generally moist and soft, possessing a cooling effect while nurturing the feminine aspect. Yáng foods – fried, spicy or with red meat – are warming and nourish the masculine side. Any meal should harmonise flavours and achieve a balance between cooling and warming foods.

TRAVEL YOUR TASTE BUDS

China is such a gourmand's paradise you won't know when to stop. In the north, fill up on a tasty dish of wontons (húndún) stuffed with juicy leeks and minced pork, or Mongolian hotpot (Ménggǔ huǒguō), a hearty brew of mutton, onions and cabbage.

Chefs from China's arid northwest can slide a bowl of noodles topped with sliced donkey meat (lǘròu huáng miàn) under your nose or pop sizzling lamb kebabs (kǎo yángròu) between your fingers. Stop by Xī'ān for warming servings of mutton broth and shredded flat bread (yángròu pàomó). A dish of Lánzhōu hand-pulled noodles (lā miàn) is a meal in itself.

In case you're pining for something sweet, head to Shànghǎi for delicious honey-smoked carp (mìzhī xūnyú) where you can also dine on more savoury helpings of steaming xiǎolóngbāo dumplings, which require considerable dexterity to consume without meat juices jetting to all compass points.

Cleanse your palate with a glass of heady Shàoxīng yellow wine (Shàoxīng huángjiǔ) or the more delicate flavours of Dragonwell tea (lóngjǐng chá). It may not exactly give you wings, but a dose of Huángshān braised pigeon (Huángshān dùngē) will definitely give you the stamina to clamber up the misty inclines of Huángshān.

Some like it hot, and little comes hotter than the fiery flavours of Sìchuān. Begin with mouth-numbing mapo tofu (mápó dòufu), followed by the celebrated spicy chicken with peanuts (gōngbǎo jīdīng). If the smoke isn't now coming out of your ears, fish smothered in chilli (shuǐzhǔ yú) should have you breathing fire. Alternatively, test your mettle with a volcanic Chóngqìng hotpot.

In the south, relax with morning dim sum in Guǎngzhōu or a bowl of Cantonese snake soup (shé gēng) in one of the city's boisterous night markets. While in Macau, taste the Macanese dish porco à alentejana, a mouthwatering casserole of pork and clams.

Northern Cooking

With Shāndōng (鲁菜; *lǔcài*) – the oldest of the eight regional schools of cooking – at its heart, northern cooking also embraces Běijīng, northeastern (Manchurian) and Shānxī cuisine, creating the most time-honoured and most central form of Chinese cooking.

In the dry north Chinese wheat belt an accent falls on millet, sorghum, maize, barley and wheat rather than rice (which requires lush irrigation by water to cultivate). Particularly well suited to the harsh and hardy winter climate, northern cooking is rich and wholesome (northerners partially attribute their taller size, compared to southern Chinese, to its effects). Filling breads, such as *mántou* (馒头) or *bǐng* (饼; flat breads), are steamed, baked or fried while noodles may form the basis of any northern meal (although the ubiquitous availability of rice means it can always be found). Northern cuisine is frequently quite salty, and appetising dumplings (饺子; *jiǎozi*) are widely eaten, usually boiled and sometimes fried.

As Běijīng was the principal capital through the Yuan, Ming and Qing dynasties, Imperial cooking is a chief characteristic of the northern school. Peking duck is Běijīng's signature dish, served with typical northern ingredients – pancakes, spring onions and fermented bean paste. You can find it all over China, but it's only true to form in the capital, roasted in ovens fired up with fruit-tree wood.

With China ruled from 1644 to 1911 by non-Han Manchurians, the influence of northeast cuisine *(dōngběi cài)* has naturally permeated northern cooking, dispensing a legacy of rich and hearty stews, dense breads, preserved foods and dumplings.

Meat roasting is also more common in the north than in other parts of China. Meats in northern China are braised until falling off the bone, or slathered with spices and barbecued until smoky. Pungent garlic, chives and spring onions are used with abandon and also employed raw. Also from the northwest is the Muslim Uighur cuisine.

The nomadic and carnivorous diet of the Mongolians also infiltrates northern cooking, most noticeably in the Mongolian hotpot and the Mongolian barbecue. Milk from nomadic herds of cattle, goats and horses has also crept into northern cuisine, as yoghurts *(suānnǎi)* for example.

Hallmark northern dishes:

PINYIN	SCRIPT	ENGLISH
Běijīng kǎoyā	北京烤鸭	Peking duck
jiāo zhá yángròu	焦炸羊肉	deep-fried mutton
jiǎozi	饺子	dumplings
mántou	馒头	steamed buns
qīng xiāng shāo jī	清香烧鸡	chicken wrapped in lotus leaf
ròu bāozi	肉包子	steamed meat buns
sān měi dòufu	三美豆腐	sliced bean curd with Chinese cabbage
shuàn yángròu	涮羊肉	lamb hotpot
sì xǐ wánzi	四喜丸子	steamed and fried pork, shrimp and bamboo shoot balls
yuán bào lǐ jí	芫爆里脊	stir-fried pork tenderloin with coriander
zào liū sān bái	糟溜三白	stir-fried chicken, fish and bamboo shoots

To turn your hand to Chinese cooking while travelling, popular classes can be joined in Běijīng, Shànghǎi and other towns in China. Check under Courses in the destination chapters for listings.

Western Cooking

The cuisine of landlocked western China, a region heavily dappled with ethnic shades and contrasting cultures, welcomes the diner to the more scarlet end of the culinary spectrum. The trademark ingredient of the western school is the fiercely hot red chilli, a potent firecracker of a herb that floods dishes with an all-pervading spiciness. Aniseed, coriander, garlic and peppercorns are thrown in for good measure to add extra pungency and bite.

The standout cuisine of the western school is fiery Sìchuān (川菜; *chuāncài*), one of China's eight regional cooking styles, renowned for its eye-watering peppery aromas. One of the herbs that differentiates Sìchuān cooking from other spicy cuisines is the use of 'flower pepper' *(huājiāo)*, a numbing peppercorn-like herb that floods the mouth with an anaesthetising fragrance in a culinary effect termed *málà* (numb and hot). A Sìchuān dish you can find cooked up by chefs across China is the delicious sour cabbage fish soup (酸菜鱼; *suāncàiyú*; wholesome fish chunks in a spicy broth). The Chóngqìng hotpot is a force to be reckoned with but must be approached with a stiff upper lip (and copious amounts of liquid refreshment). If you want a hotpot pitched between spicy and mild, select a *yuanyang* hotpot *(yuānyāng huǒguō)*, a vessel divided yin-yang style into two different compartments for two different soup bases.

Sìchuān restaurants are everywhere in China, swarming around train stations, squeezed away down food streets or squished into street markets with wobbly stools and rickety tables parked out front.

Another of China's eight regional schools of cooking, dishes from Húnán (湘菜; *xiāngcài*) are similarly pungent, with a heavy reliance on chilli. Unlike Sìchuān food, flower pepper is not employed and instead spicy flavours are often sharper, fiercer and more to the fore. Meat, particularly in Húnán, is marinated, pickled or otherwise processed before cooking, which is generally by stir- or flash-frying.

Cuisine in Tibet includes *tsampa* (porridge of roasted barley flour), *bö cha* (yak-butter tea), *momos* (dumplings filled with vegetables or yak meat), *thugpa* (noodles with meat), *thenthuk* (fried noodle squares) as well as *shemdre* (rice, potato and yak-meat curry).

Western-school dishes:

Spanish traders in the early Qing dynasty first introduced red chilli pepper to China. Not only a spice, chillies are also a rich source of vitamins A and C.

PINYIN	SCRIPT	ENGLISH
bàngbàng jī	棒棒鸡	shredded chicken in a hot pepper and sesame sauce
Chóngqìng huǒguō	重庆火锅	Chóngqìng hotpot
dāndan miàn	担担面	spicy noodles
gānshāo yán lǐ	干烧岩鲤	stewed carp with ham and hot and sweet sauce
huíguō ròu	回锅肉	boiled and stir-fried pork with salty and hot sauce
málà dòufu	麻辣豆腐	spicy tofu
Máoshì Hóngshaōròu	毛氏红烧肉	Mao family braised pork
shuǐ zhǔ niúròu	水煮牛肉	spicy fried and boiled beef
shuǐzhǔyú	水煮鱼	fried and boiled fish, garlic sprouts and celery
suāncàiyú	酸菜鱼	sour cabbage fish soup
yú xiāng ròusī	鱼香肉丝	fish-flavour pork strips
zhàcài ròusī	榨菜肉丝	stir-fried pork or beef tenderloin with tuber mustard

Southern Cooking

The southern Chinese – particularly the Cantonese – historically spear-headed successive waves of immigration overseas, leaving aromatic constellations of Chinatowns around the world. Consequently, Westerners most often associate this school of cooking with China.

Typified by Cantonese (粤菜; *yuècài*) cooking, southern cooking lacks the richness and saltiness of northern cooking and instead coaxes more subtle aromas to the surface. The Cantonese astutely believe that good cooking does not require much flavouring, for it is the *xiān* (natural freshness) of the ingredients that marks a truly high-grade dish. Hence the near obsessive attention paid to the freshness of ingredients in southern cuisine.

The hallmark Cantonese dish is dim sum (点心; Mandarin: *diǎnxīn*). Yum cha (literally 'drink tea'), another name for dim sum dining, in Guǎngzhōu and Hong Kong can be enjoyed on any day of the week. Dishes, often in steamers, are wheeled around on trolleys so you can see what you want to order. Well-known dim sum dishes include *guōtiē* (a kind of fried dumpling), *shāomài* (a kind of open pork dumpling), *chāshāobāo* (pork-filled bun) and *chūnjuǎn* (spring rolls). The extravagantly named *fèngzhuǎ* (phoenix claw) is the name for the ever-popular steamed chicken's feet. *Xiǎolóngbāo* (steamed dumplings) are often sold in dim sum restaurants, but are traditionally from Shànghǎi.

Local esteem for Cantonese food is evident in a popular Chinese saying: 'Be born in Sūzhōu, live in Hángzhōu, eat in Guǎngzhōu and die in Líuzhōu'. (Sūzhōu was famed for its good-looking people, Hángzhōu was a lovely place to live in, Guǎngzhōu was the best place to eat while Liǔzhōu was famed for the wood of its coffins!)

Fújiàn (闽菜; *mǐncài*) cuisine is another important southern cooking style, with its emphasis on light flavours and, due to the province's proximity to the East China Sea, seafood.

Hakka cuisine, from the disparate and migratory Hakka people (Kèjiāzú), is another feature of southern Chinese cooking, as is the food of Cháozhōu in eastern Guǎngdōng.

Rice is the primary staple of southern cuisine. Sparkling paddy fields glitter across the south; the humid climate, plentiful rainfall and well-irrigated land means that rice has been farmed here since the Chinese first populated the region during the Han dynasty (206 BC–AD 220).

Southern-school dishes:

Organic (*yǒujī*) food is experiencing considerable growth and popularity in China, partly as a result of concerns about food safety but also as a reflection of growing incomes.

PINYIN	SCRIPT	ENGLISH
bái zhuó xiā	白灼虾	blanched prawns with shredded scallions
dōngjiāng yánjú jī	东江盐焗鸡	salt-baked chicken
gālí jī	咖喱鸡	curried chicken
háoyóu niúròu	蚝油牛肉	beef with oyster sauce
kǎo rǔzhū	烤乳猪	crispy suckling pig
mì zhī chāshāo	密汁叉烧	roast pork with honey
shé ròu	蛇肉	snake
tángcù lǐjī/gǔlǎo ròu	糖醋里脊/咕老肉	sweet and sour pork fillets
tángcù páigǔ	糖醋排骨	sweet and sour spare ribs

Eastern Cooking

The eastern school of Chinese cuisine derives from a fertile region of China, slashed by waterways and canals, glistening with lakes, fringed by a long coastline and nourished by a subtropical climate. Jiāngsū province itself is the home of Jiāngsū (苏菜; *sūcài*) cuisine – one of the core regions of the eastern school – and is famed as the 'Land of Fish and Rice', a tribute to its abundance of food and produce. The region was also historically prosperous and in today's export-oriented economy, the eastern provinces are among China's wealthiest. This combination of riches and bountiful food created a culture of epicurism and gastronomic enjoyment.

South of Jiāngsū, Zhèjiāng (浙菜; *zhècài*) cuisine is another cornerstone of Eastern cooking. The Song dynasty saw the blossoming of the restaurant industry here; in Hángzhōu, the southern Song-dynasty capital, restaurants and teahouses accounted for two-thirds of the city's business during a splendidly rich cultural era. At this time, one of Hángzhōu's most famous dishes, *dōngpō ròu* (named after the celebrated poet and governor of Hángzhōu, Su Dongpo), achieved fame.

Generally more oily and sweeter than other Chinese schools, the eastern school revels in fish and seafood, reflecting its geographical proximity to major rivers and the sea. Fish is usually *qīngzhēng* (清蒸; steamed) but can be stir-fried, pan-fried or grilled. Hairy crabs (*dàxháxiè*) are a Shànghǎi speciality between October and December. Eaten with soy, ginger and vinegar and downed with warm Shàoxīng wine, the best crabs come from Yangcheng Lake. The crab is believed to increase the body's *yīn* (coldness), so *yáng* (warmth) is added by imbibing lukewarm rice wine with it. It is also usual to eat male and female crabs together.

As with Cantonese food, freshness is a key ingredient in the cuisine, and sauces and seasonings are only employed to augment essential flavours. Stir-frying and steaming are also used, the latter with Shànghǎi's famous *xiǎolóngbāo,* steamer buns filled with nuggets of pork or crab swimming in a scalding meat broth. Learning how to devour these carefully without the meat juice squirting everywhere and scalding the roof of your mouth (or blinding your neighbour) requires some – quite enjoyable – practice.

With a lightness of flavour, Ānhuī (徽菜; *huīcài*) cuisine – one of China's eight principle culinary traditions and firmly in the eastern cooking sphere – puts less emphasis on seafood. Braising and stewing of vegetables and wildlife from its mountainous habitats is a pronounced feature of this regional cuisine.

China's best soy sauce is also produced in the eastern provinces, and the technique of braising meat using soy sauce, sugar and spices was perfected here. Meat cooked in this manner takes on a dark mauve hue auspiciously described as 'red', a colour associated with good fortune.

Famous dishes from the eastern school:

PINYIN	SCRIPT	ENGLISH
gōngbào jīdīng	宫爆鸡丁	spicy chicken with peanuts; kung pao chicken
háoyóu niúròu	蚝油牛肉	beef with oyster sauce
hóngshāo páigǔ	红烧排骨	red-braised spare ribs
hóngshāo qiézi	红烧茄子	red-cooked aubergine
hóngshāo yú	红烧鱼	red-braised fish
huǒguō	火锅	hotpot
húntùn tāng	馄饨汤	wonton soup
jiācháng dòufu	家常豆腐	'homestyle' tofu
jiǎozi	饺子	dumplings
jīdànmiàn	鸡蛋面	noodles and egg
qīngjiāo ròupiàn	青椒肉片	pork and green peppers
shāguō dòufu	沙锅豆腐	bean curd casserole

CHINESE CUISINE REGIONAL COOKING

Streets around China reek with the powerful and popular aromas of stinky tofu (*chòu dòufu*), a form of fermented tofu with an aroma pitched somewhere between unwashed socks and rotting vegetation.

PINYIN	SCRIPT	ENGLISH
suānlàtāng	酸辣汤	hot and sour soup
tiěbǎn niúròu	铁板牛肉	sizzling beef platter
xīhóngshì chǎojīdàn	西红柿炒鸡蛋	fried egg and tomato
xīhóngshì jīdàntāng	西红柿鸡蛋汤	egg and tomato soup
xīhóngshì niúròu	西红柿牛肉	beef and tomato
yúxiāng qiézi	鱼香茄子	fish-flavoured aubergine

Home-Style Dishes

Besides China's regional cuisines, there is a tasty variety of *jiāchángcài* (home-style) dishes you will see all over the land, cooked up in restaurants and along food streets.

Notable *jiāchángcài* dishes:

PINYIN	SCRIPT	ENGLISH
jiāng cōng chǎo xiè	姜葱炒蟹	stir-fried crab with ginger and scallions
mìzhī xūnyú	蜜汁熏鱼	honey-smoked carp
níng shì shànyú	宁式鳝鱼	stir-fried eel with onion
qiézhī yúkuài	茄汁鱼块	fish fillet in tomato sauce
qīng zhēng guìyú	清蒸鳜鱼	steamed Mandarin fish
sōngzǐ guìyú	松子鳜鱼	Mandarin fish with pine nuts
suānlà yóuyú	酸辣鱿鱼	hot and sour squid
xiǎolóngbāo	小笼包	steamer buns
yóubào xiārén	油爆虾仁	fried shrimp
zhá hēi lǐyú	炸黑鲤鱼	fried black carp
zhá yúwán	炸鱼丸	fish balls

Dining Ins & Outs

Chinese Restaurants

Chinese eateries come in every conceivable shape, size and type: from shabby, hole-in-the-wall noodle outfits with flimsy PVC furniture, blaring TV sets and well-worn plastic menus to gilded banquet-style restaurants where elegant cheongsam-clad waitresses show you to your seat, straighten your chopsticks and bring you a warm hand towel and a gold-embossed wine list.

In between are legions of very serviceable midrange restaurants serving cuisine from across China.

As dining in China is such a big, sociable and often ostentatious affair, many Chinese banqueting-style restaurants have huge round tables, thousand-candle-power electric lights and precious little sense of intimacy or romance. Over-attentive and ever-present staff can add to the discomfort for foreigners.

Dining Times

The Chinese eat early. Lunch usually commences from around 11.30am, either self-cooked or a takeaway at home, or in a street-side restaurant. Dinner kicks off from around 6pm. Reflecting these dining times, some restaurants open at around 11am to close for an afternoon break at about 2.30pm before opening again around 5pm and closing in the late evening.

Menus

In Běijīng, Shànghǎi and other large cities, you may be proudly presented with an English menu (英文菜谱; *Yīngwén càipǔ*). In smaller towns and out in the sticks, don't expect anything other than a Chinese-language menu and a hovering waitress with no English-language skills. The best is undoubtedly the ever-handy photo menu. If you like the look of what other diners are eating, just point (我要那个; *wǒ yào nèi gè;* 'I want that' – a very handy phrase). Alternatively, pop into the kitchen and point out what you would like to eat.

Desserts & Sweets

The Chinese do not generally eat dessert, but fruit – typically watermelon (*xīguā*) or oranges (*chéng*) – often concludes a meal. Ice cream can be ordered in some places, but in general sweet desserts (*tiánpǐn*) are consumed as snacks and are seldom available in restaurants.

Table Manners

Chinese meal times are generally relaxed affairs with no strict rules of etiquette. Meals can commence in a Confucian vein before spiralling into total Taoist mayhem, fuelled by incessant toasts with *báijiǔ* (a white spirit) or beer and furious smoking by the men.

Meals typically unfold with one person ordering on behalf of a group. When a group dines, a selection of dishes is ordered for everyone to share rather than individual diners ordering a dish just for themselves. As they arrive, dishes are placed communally in the centre of the table or on a lazy Susan, which may be revolved by the host so that the principal guest gets first choice of whatever dish arrives. Soup may appear midway through the meal or at the end. Rice often arrives at the end of the meal; if you would like it earlier, just ask.

It is good form to fill your neighbours' tea cups or beer glasses when they are empty. To serve yourself tea or any other drink without serving others first is bad form, and appreciation to the pourer is indicated by gently tapping the middle finger on the table.

When your teapot needs a refill, signal this to the waiter by simply taking the lid off the pot.

It's best to wait until someone announces a toast before drinking your beer; if you want to get a quick shot in, propose a toast to the host. The Chinese do in fact toast each other much more than in the West, often each time they drink. A formal toast is conducted by raising your glass in both hands in the direction of the toastee and crying out *gānbēi*, literally 'dry the glass', which is the cue to drain your glass in one hit. This can be quite a challenge if your drink is 65% *báijiǔ*, and your glass is rapidly refilled to the meniscus after you drain it, in preparation for the next toast.

Smokers can light up during the meal, unless they are in the no-smoking area of a restaurant. Depending on the restaurant, smokers may smoke through the entire meal. If you are a smoker, ensure you hand around your cigarettes to others as that is standard procedure.

Don't use your chopsticks to point at people or gesticulate with them and never stick your chopsticks upright in bowls of rice (it's a portent of death).

Last but not least, never insist on paying for the bill if someone else is tenaciously determined to pay – usually the person who invited you to dinner. By all means offer, but then raise your hands in mock surrender when resistance is met; to pay for a meal when another person is determined to pay is to make them lose face.

Chinese toothpick etiquette is similar to that found in other Asian nations: one hand excavates with the toothpick, while the other hand shields the mouth.

Chinese diners will often slurp their noodles quite noisily, which is not considered impolite.

CHINESE CUISINE DINING INS & OUTS

You will be charged for a wrapped-up hand-cleaning wipe if you open it at your restaurant table; if you don't use it, it should not appear on your bill.

It is quite common for banquets and dinners in China to finish abruptly, as everyone stands up and walks away in unison with little delay.

TIPPING

Tipping is never done at cheap restaurants in mainland China. Smart, international restaurants will encourage tipping but it is not obligatory and it's uncertain whether waiting staff receive their tips at the end of the night. Hotel restaurants automatically add a 15% service charge and some high-end restaurants may do the same.

Street Food

Snacking your way around China is a fine way to sample the different flavours of the land while on the move. Most towns have a street market or a night market (夜市; *yèshì*) for good-value snacks and meals so you can either take away or park yourself on a wobbly stool and grab a beer. Street markets such as Kāifēng's boisterous night market abound with choices you may not find in restaurants. Vocal vendors will be forcing their tasty creations on you but you can also see what people are buying and what's being cooked up, so all you have to do is join the queue and point.

Eating with Kids

Similar to travelling with children in China, dining out with kids can be a challenge. Budget eateries won't have kids' menus; nor will they have booster seats. Smarter restaurants may supply these but it can be touch and go. In large cities you will be able to find more restaurants switched on to the needs of families, especially Western restaurants that may have a play area, kids' menu, activities, booster seats and other paraphernalia.

Vegetarianism

If you'd rather chew on a legume than a leg of lamb, it can be hard going trying to find truly vegetarian dishes. China's history of famine and poverty means the consumption of meat has always been a sign of status, and is symbolic of health and wealth. Eating meat is also considered to enhance male virility, so vegetarian men raise eyebrows. Partly because of this, there is virtually no vegetarian movement in China, although Chinese people may forgo meat for Buddhist reasons. For the same reasons, they may avoid meat on certain days of the month but remain carnivorous at other times.

Search on www. bbcgoodfood.com for a mouth-watering selection of Chinese recipes and full instructions on throwing together some classic and lesser-known dishes from around China.

You will find that vegetables are often fried in animal-based oils, while vegetable soups are often made with chicken or beef stock, so simply choosing vegetable items on the menu is ineffective. In Běijīng and Shànghǎi you will, however, find a generous crop of vegetarian restaurants to choose from alongside outfits such as Element Fresh, which has a decent range of healthy vegetarian options.

Out of the large cities, your best bet may be to head to a sizeable active Buddhist temple or monastery, where Buddhist vegetarian restaurants are often open to the public. Buddhist vegetarian food typically consists of 'mock meat' dishes created from tofu, wheat gluten, potato and other vegetables. Some of the dishes are almost works of art, with vegetarian ingredients sculpted to look like spare ribs or fried chicken. Sometimes the chefs go to great lengths to create 'bones' from carrots and lotus roots.

If you want to say 'I am a vegetarian' in Chinese, the phrase to use is *wǒ chī sù* (我吃素).

Breakfast

Breakfast in China is generally light, simple and over and done with quickly. The meal may merely consist of a bowl of rice porridge (粥; *zhōu*) or its watery cousin, rice gruel (稀饭; *xīfàn*). Pickles, boiled eggs, steamed buns, fried peanuts and deep-fried dough sticks (油条; *yóutiáo*) are also popular, washed down with warm soybean milk. Breakfast at your Chinese hotel may consist of some or all of these. Coffee is rarely drunk at breakfast time, unless the family is modern, urban and middle class, but it's easy to find in cafes, especially in large towns. Sliced bread (面包; *miànbāo*) was once rare but is increasingly common, as is butter (黄油; *huángyóu*).

Tea

An old Chinese saying identifies tea as one of the seven basic necessities of life, along with firewood, oil, rice, salt, soy sauce and vinegar. The Chinese were the first to cultivate tea, and the art of brewing and drinking it has been popular since Tang times (AD 618–907).

China has three main types of tea: green tea *(lü chá)*, black tea *(hóng chá)* and *wūlóng* (a semifermented tea, halfway between black and green tea). In addition, there are other variations, including jasmine *(cháshuǐ)* and chrysanthemum *(júhuā chá)*. Some famous regional teas of China are Fújiàn's *tiě guānyīn, pú'ěrh* from Yúnnán and Zhèjiāng's *lóngjǐng* tea. Eight-treasure tea *(bābǎo chá)* consists of rock sugar, dates, nuts and tea combined in a cup; it makes a delicious treat. Tea is to the Chinese what fine wine is to the French: a beloved beverage savoured for its fine aroma, distinctive flavour and pleasing aftertaste.

Alcoholic Drinks

Beer

If tea is the most popular drink in China, then beer (啤酒; *píjiǔ*) is surely second. Many towns and cities have their own brewery and label, although a remarkable feat of socialist standardisation ensures a striking similarity in flavour and strength. You can drink bathtubs of the stuff and still navigate a straight line. If you want your beer cold, ask for *liáng de* (凉的), and if you want it truly arctic, call for *bīngzhèn de* (冰镇的).

The best-known beer is Tsingtao, made with Láo Shān mineral water, which lends it a sparkling quality. It's originally a German beer since the town of Qīngdǎo (formerly spelled 'Tsingtao') was once a German concession and the Chinese inherited the brewery, which dates to 1903, along with Bavarian beer-making ways.

Several foreign beers are also brewed in China and there's a growing market for craft brews in the wealthier cities. If you crave variety, many of the bars we list should have a selection of foreign imported beers; prices will be high, however.

Wine

Surging demand for imported wines saw China and Hong Kong emerge as the world's largest consumer of Bordeaux wines in 2011. Expensive French reds *(hóngjiǔ)* are treasured in a fashionable market that was only finding its feet a mere 15 years ago. Wine has become the drink of choice among an increasingly sophisticated business class eager to appear discerning and flamboyant. Unfortunately this also means you can pay way over the odds at restaurants in Shànghǎi or Běijīng for imported wines. White wine consumption is increasingly associated with female drinkers in China.

China has also cultivated vines and produced wine for an estimated 4000 years, and Chinese wines are generally cheaper than imports from abroad. The provinces of Xīnjiāng and Níngxià in the distant northwest of China are famous for their vineyards.

Traditionally one of the seven necessities of daily life in China, tea was once employed as a form of currency in the Middle Kingdom.

The world's fifth-largest producer of wine in 2010, China became the world's largest market for red wine in 2013.

CHINESE CUISINE DINING INS & OUTS

THE EAST IS RED (WINE)

Wine is hot in China. A bottle of red has become a status symbol for a mushrooming Chinese middle class. In fact, in 2013 China became the world's largest red wine consumer, overtaking France and Italy by glugging (or at least purchasing) 155 million cases of the stuff. Population helps and consumption per capita is still lower than in Europe, but red wine sales managed to triple from 1997 to 2013.

Most wine that is drunk in China is red wine produced in China itself, in Níngxià. In 2012 the wine produced here was worth over 2 billion rénmínbì. International names such as LVMH (of Moët fame) and Pernod Ricard (which owns Australia's Jacob's Creek wines) have taken leases on the Níngxià government-owned land to produce vineyards for local wines.

Since the late '90s the local government has been pumping water into the slopes of the Hèlán Shān mountains, which stand against the Gobi Desert. By the end of 2013 the transformed, fertile soil was feeding 58,000 acres of vines and China became the world's fifth largest wine producer. It's still early days, however – the vines are young, difficult to keep protected from Hèlán Shān's fluctuating temperatures and propagation standards are low.

Níngxià wine may not yet have the same full flavours of its European cousins, but domestically, the region is esteemed for its Merlot, Cabernet Sauvignon and 'Chinese Cabernet' Gernischt grape varieties. The Níngxià government has its sight on expanding to over 1000 wineries by 2024. Enough time to get the notes right and to make Níngxià a name that rolls off the tongue as smoothly as Bordeaux, Beaujolais and Burgundy when singing the praises of red wine.

Try Níngxià's distinctively light, herbaceous wine *pútaojiǔ* with live jazz or Tibetan music in Yínchuān at Liángyuán Jiǔbā (p859), a five-minute walk north of the Drum Tower (p858). In Zhōngwèi, uncork a bottle of red in a cosy booth at the two-level **Rhent Bar** (瑞德酒吧; Ruìdé Jiǔbā; ☑0955 701 9208; Xinlong Beijie; bottle of wine ¥80-200; ☺9am-late).

Spirits

The word 'wine' gets rather loosely translated – many Chinese 'wines' are in fact spirits. Maotai, a favourite of Chinese drinkers, is a very expensive spirit called *báijiǔ* made from sorghum (a type of millet) and used for toasts at banquets. The cheap alternative is Erguotou, distilled in Běijīng but available all over China; look out for the Red Star (Hongxing) brand. *Báijiǔ* ranges across the alcohol spectrum from milder forms to around 65% proof. Milder rice wine is intended mainly for cooking rather than drinking but can be drunk warm like sake.

Arts & Architecture

China is custodian of one of the world's richest cultural and artistic legacies. Until the 20th century, China's arts were deeply conservative and resistant to change, but revolutions in technique and content over the last century fashioned a dramatic transformation. Despite this evolution, China's arts – whatever the period – remain bound by a common aesthetic that taps into the very soul and lifeblood of the nation.

Aesthetics

In reflection of the Chinese character, Chinese aesthetics have traditionally been marked by restraint and understatement, a preference for oblique references over direct explanation, vagueness in place of specificity and an avoidance of the obvious in place of a fondness for the veiled and subtle. Traditional Chinese aesthetics sought to cultivate a more reserved artistic impulse, principles that compellingly find their way into virtually every Chinese art form, from painting to sculpture, ceramics, calligraphy, film, poetry, literature and beyond.

As one of the central strands of the world's oldest civilisation, China's aesthetic traditions are tightly woven into Chinese cultural identity. For millennia, Chinese aesthetics were highly traditionalist and, despite coming under the influence of occupiers from the Mongols to the Europeans, defiantly conservative. It was not until the fall of the Qing dynasty in 1911 and the appearance of the New Culture Movement that China's great artistic traditions began to rapidly transform. In literature the stranglehold of classical Chinese loosened to allow breathing space for *báihuà* (colloquial Chinese) and a progressive new aesthetic began to flower, ultimately leading to revolutions in all of the arts, from poetry to painting, theatre and music.

It is hard to square China's great aesthetic traditions with the devastation inflicted upon them since 1949. Confucius advocated the edifying role of music and poetry in shaping human lives, but 5th-century philosopher Mozi was less enamoured with them, seeing music and other arts as extravagant and wasteful. The communists took this a stage further, enlisting the arts as props in their propaganda campaigns, and permitting the vandalism and destruction of much traditional architecture and heritage. Many of China's traditional skills (such as martial arts lineages) and crafts either died out or went into decline during the Cultural Revolution. Many of the arts have yet to recover fully from this deterioration, even though opening up and reform prompted a vast influx of foreign artistic concepts.

Major art festivals include Běijīng's 798 International Art Festival, China International Gallery Exposition and Běijīng Biennale, the Shànghǎi Biennale, Guǎngzhōu Triennial and Hong Kong's one-day Clockenflap festival.

Calligraphy

Although calligraphy (书法; *shūfǎ*) has a place among most languages that employ alphabets, the art of calligraphy in China is taken to unusual heights of intricacy and beauty. Although Chinese calligraphy is beautiful in its own right, the complex infatuation Chinese people have for their written language helps elucidate their great respect for the art of calligraphy.

To understand how perfectly suited written Chinese is for calligraphy, it is vital to grasp how written Chinese works. A word in English represents a sound alone; a written character in Chinese combines both sound and a picture. Indeed, the sound element of a Chinese character – when present – is often auxiliary to the presentation of a visual image, even if abstract.

Furthermore, although some Chinese characters were simplified in the 1950s as part of a literacy drive, most characters have remained unchanged for thousands of years. As characters are essentially images, they inadequately reflect changes in spoken Chinese over time. A phonetic written language such as English can alter over the centuries to reflect changes in the sound of the language. Being pictographic, Chinese cannot easily do this, so while the spoken language has transformed over the centuries, the written language has remained more static.

> The most abstract calligraphic form is grass or cursive script (cǎoshū), a highly fluid style of penmanship which even Chinese people have difficulty reading.

This helps explain why Chinese calligraphy is the trickiest of China's arts to comprehend for Western visitors, unless they have a sound understanding of written Chinese. The beauty of a Chinese character may be partially appreciated by a Western audience, but for a full understanding it is also essential to understand the meaning of the character in context.

There are five main calligraphic scripts – seal script, clerical script, semicursive script, cursive script and standard script – each of which reflects the style of writing of a specific era. Seal script, the oldest and most complex, was the official writing system during the Qin dynasty and has been employed ever since in the carving of the seals and name chops (stamps carved from stone) that are used to stamp documents. Expert calligraphers have a preference for using full-form characters (fántǐzì) rather than their simplified variants (jiǎntǐzì).

Painting

Traditional Painting

Unlike Chinese calligraphy, no 'insider' knowledge is required for a full appreciation of traditional Chinese painting. Despite its symbolism, obscure references and occasionally abstruse philosophical allusions, Chinese painting is highly accessible. For this reason, traditional Chinese

---

BEST ART MUSEUMS & GALLERIES

Shànghǎi Museum (p191) An outstanding collection of traditional Chinese art and antiquities.

Poly Art Museum (p70) Inspiring displays of traditional bronzes and Buddhist statues.

Rockbund Art Museum (p190) Forward-thinking museum of contemporary art, just off the Bund.

Hong Kong Museum of Art (p503) First-rate display of antiquities, paintings, calligraphy and contemporary Hong Kong art.

M50 (p199) Contemporary art in a converted Shànghǎi industrial zone.

798 Art District (p83) Běijīng's premier art zone, housed in a former electronics factory.

Propaganda Poster Art Centre (p198) Shànghǎi treasure trove of propaganda art from the communist golden age.

AFA (Art for All Society) (p536) Nonprofit gallery promoting the best in contemporary Macau art.

ShanghART (p199) Impressive warehouse-sized Shànghǎi gallery dedicated to contemporary Chinese artists.

paintings – especially landscapes – have long been treasured in the West for their beauty.

As described in Xie He's 6th century AD treatise, the *Six Principles of Painting,* the chief aim of Chinese painting is to capture the innate essence or spirit *(qì)* of a subject and endow it with vitality. The brush line, varying in thickness and tone, was the second principle (referred to as the 'bone method') and is the defining technique of Chinese painting. Traditionally, it was imagined that brushwork quality could reveal the artist's moral character. As a general rule, painters were less concerned with achieving outward resemblance (that was the third principle) than with conveying intrinsic qualities.

Early painters dwelled on the human figure and moral teachings, while also conjuring up scenes from everyday life. By the time of the Tang dynasty, a new genre, known as landscape painting, had begun to flower. Reaching full bloom during the Song and Yuan dynasties, landscape painting meditated on the surrounding environment. Towering mountains, ethereal mists, open spaces, trees and rivers, and light and dark were all exquisitely presented in ink washes on silk. Landscape paintings attempted to capture the metaphysical and the absolute, drawing the viewer into a particular realm where the philosophies of Taoism and Buddhism found expression. Humanity is typically a small and almost insignificant subtext to the performance. The dream-like painting sought to draw the viewer in rather than impose itself on them.

On a technical level, the success of landscapes depended on the artists' skill in capturing light and atmosphere. Blank, open spaces devoid of colour create light-filled voids, contrasting with the darkness of mountain folds, filling the painting with *qì* and vaporous vitality. Specific emotions are not aroused but instead nebulous sensations permeate. Painting and classical poetry often went hand in hand, best exemplified by the work of Tang-dynasty poet-artist Wang Wei (699–759).

The five fundamental brushstrokes necessary to master calligraphy can be found in the character 永, which means eternal or forever.

ARTS & ARCHITECTURE PAINTING

Modern Art

Socialist-Realism

After 1949, classical Chinese techniques were abandoned and foreign artistic techniques imported wholesale. Washes on silk were replaced with oil on canvas and China's traditional obsession with the mysterious and ineffable made way for concrete attention to detail and realism.

By 1970 Chinese artists had aspired to master the skills of socialist-realism, a vibrant communist-endorsed style that drew from European neoclassical art, the lifelike canvases of Jacques-Louis David and the output of Soviet Union painters. Saturated with political symbolism and propaganda, the blunt artistic style was produced on an industrial scale.

The entire trajectory of Chinese painting – which had evolved in glacial increments over the centuries – had been redirected virtually overnight. Vaporous landscapes were substituted with hard-edged panoramas. Traditional Taoist and Buddhist philosophy was overturned and humans became the master of nature. Dreamy vistas were out; smoke stacks, red tractors and muscled peasants were in.

Propaganda Art

Another art form that found a fertile environment during the Mao era was the propaganda poster. Mass-produced from the 1950s onwards and replicated in their thousands through tourist markets across China today, the colourful Chinese propaganda poster was a further instrument of social control in a nation where aesthetics had become subservient to communist orthodoxy.

With a prolific range of themes from chubby, well-fed Chinese babies to the Korean War, the virtues of physical education, the suppression of counter-revolutionary activity and paeans to the achievements of the Great Leap Forward or China as an earthly paradise, propaganda posters were ubiquitous. The golden age of poster production ran through to the 1980s, only declining during Deng Xiaoping's tenure and the opening up of China to the West.

The success of visual propaganda lay in its appeal to a large body of illiterate or semiliterate peasants. The idealism, revolutionary romanticism and vivid colouring of Chinese propaganda art brought hope and vibrancy to a time that was actually often colourless and drab, while adding certainty to an era of great hardship and struggle.

Post-Mao

It was only with the death of Mao Zedong in September 1976 that the shadow of the Cultural Revolution – when Chinese aesthetics were conditioned by the threat of violence – began its retreat and the individual artistic temperament was allowed to thrive afresh.

Painters such as Luo Zhongli employed the realist techniques gleaned from China's art academies to depict the harsh realities etched in the faces of contemporary peasants. Others escaped the suffocating confines of socialist realism to navigate new horizons. A voracious appetite for Western art brought with it fresh concepts and ideas, while the ambiguity of exact meaning in the fine arts offered a degree of protection from state censors.

One group of artists, the Stars, found retrospective inspiration in Picasso and German Expressionism. The ephemeral group had a lasting impact on the development of Chinese art in the 1980s and 1990s, paving the way for the New Wave movement that emerged in 1985. New Wave artists were greatly influenced by Western art, especially the iconoclastic Marcel Duchamp. In true nihilist style, the New Wave artist Huang Yongping destroyed his works at exhibitions, in an effort to escape from the notion of 'art'. Political realities became instant subject matter as performance artists wrapped themselves in plastic or tape to symbolise the repressive realities of modern-day China.

Beyond Tiān'ānmén

The Tiān'ānmén Square protests in 1989 fostered a deep-seated cynicism that permeated artworks with loss, loneliness and social isolation. An exodus of artists to the West commenced. This period also coincided with an upsurge in the art market as investors increasingly turned to artworks, and money began to slosh about.

Much post-1989 Chinese art dwelled obsessively on contemporary socioeconomic realities, with consumer culture, materialism, urbanisation and social change a repetitive focus. More universal themes became apparent, however, as the art scene matured. Meanwhile, many artists who left China in the 1990s have returned, setting up private studios and galleries. Government censorship remains, but artists are branching out into other areas and moving away from overtly political content and China-specific concerns.

Cynical realists Fang Lijun and Yue Minjun fashioned grotesque portraits that conveyed hollowness and mock joviality, tinged with despair. Born in the late 1950s, Wang Guangyi took pop art as a template for his ironic pieces, fused with propaganda art techniques from the Cultural Revolution.

Born just before the Cultural Revolution in 1964 and heavily influenced by German expressionism, Zeng Fanzhi explored the notions

Discovered by amateur astronomer William Kwong Yu Yeung in 2001, the main belt asteroid 83598 Aiweiwei was named after Chinese artist Ai Weiwei in 2001.

In 2011 an ink and brush painting by artist Qi Baishi (1864–1957) sold for ¥425 million (US$65 million) at auction.

of alienation and isolation – themes commonly explored by Chinese artists during this period – in his *Mask* series from the 1990s. Introspection is a hallmark of Zeng's oeuvre. In 2008 Christie's in Hong Kong sold Zeng Fanzhi's painting *Mask Series 1996 No. 6* (featuring masked members of China's communist youth organisation, the Young Pioneers) for US$9.7 million, which is the highest price paid for a contemporary Chinese artwork.

Also born in the early 1960s, Zhang Dali is another artist who gave expression to social change and the gulf between rich and poor, especially the circumstances of the immigrant worker underclass in Běijīng.

Contemporary Directions

Most artists of note and aspiration gravitate to Běijīng (or Shànghǎi perhaps) to work. Today's China provides a huge wellspring of subject matter for artists, tempered by the reality of political censorship and the constraints of taboo. Themes that may appear tame in the West can assume a special power and volatility in China, so works may rely upon their context for potency and effect.

Ai Weiwei, who enjoys great international fame partly due to his disobedient stand, best exemplifies the dangerous overlap between artistic self-expression, dissent and conflict with the authorities. Arrested in 2011 and charged with tax evasion, Ai Weiwei gained further publicity for his temporary *Sunflower Seeds* exhibition at the Tate Modern in London.

Working collaboratively as Birdhead, Shànghǎi analog photographers Ji Weiyu and Song Tao record the social dynamics and architectural habitat of their home city in thoughtful compositions. Běijīng-born Ma Qiusha works in video, photography, painting and installations on themes of a deeply personal nature. In her video work *From No.4 Pingyuanli to No.4 Tianqiaobeili*, the artist removes a bloody razor blade from her mouth after narrating her experiences as a young artist in China. Born in 1982, Ran Huang works largely in film but also across a spectrum of media, conveying themes of absurdity, the irrational and conceptual. Shànghǎi artist Shi Zhiying explores ideas of a more traditional hue in her sublime oil paint depictions on large canvases of landscapes and religious and cultural objects. Also from Shànghǎi, Xu Zhen works with provocative images to unsettle and challenge the viewer. Xu's *Fearless* (2012), a large mixed-media work on canvas, is a powerful maelstrom of symbolism and the fragments of cultural identity. Xīnjiāng-born Zhao Zhao – once an assistant to Ai Weiwei – communicates provocative sentiments in his work. In an interview with *Der Spiegel*, Zhao Zhao observed: 'There are lines that you can't cross in this state. I try to resist being tamed as an artist.'

Ceramics

China's very first vessels – dating back more than 8000 years – were simple handcrafted earthenware pottery, primarily used for religious purposes. The invention of the pottery wheel during the late Neolithic period, however, led to a dramatic technological and artistic leap.

Over the centuries, Chinese potters perfected their craft, introducing many new exciting styles and techniques. The spellbinding artwork of the Terracotta Warriors in Xī'ān reveals a highly developed level of technical skill achieved by Qin-dynasty craftsmen. Periods of artistic evolution, during the cosmopolitan Tang dynasty, for example, prompted further stylistic advances. The Tang dynasty 'three-colour ware' is a much admired type of ceramic from this period, noted for its vivid yellow, green and white glaze. Demand for lovely blue-green celadons grew in countries as distant as Egypt and Persia.

A dark and Gothic image in the West, the bat is commonly used in Chinese porcelain, wood designs, textiles and artwork as it is considered a good luck omen.

DEA / G. DAGLI ORTI / GETTY IMAGES ©

Poet Li Bai depicted on a Qing-dynasty plate

The Yuan dynasty saw the first development of China's standout 'blue and white' *(qīnghuā)* porcelain. Cobalt blue paint from Persia was applied as an underglaze directly to white porcelain with a brush, the vessel then covered with another transparent glaze and fired. This technique was perfected during the Ming Dynasty and such ceramics became hugely popular all over the world, eventually acquiring the name 'China-ware', whether produced in China or not.

Although many kilns were established over China, the most famous was at Jīngdézhèn in Jiāngxī province, where royal porcelain was fired.

During the Qing dynasty, porcelain techniques were further refined and developed, showing superb craftsmanship and ingenuity. British and European consumers dominated the export market, displaying an insatiable appetite for Chinese vases and bowls decorated with flowers and landscapes. Stunning monochromatic ware is another hallmark of the Qing, especially the ox-blood vases, imperial yellow bowls and enamel-decorated porcelain. The Qing is also notable for its elaborate and highly decorative wares.

In 2010 a Qing-dynasty Chinese vase sold for £53.1 million after being discovered in the attic of a house in northwest London and put up for auction.

Jīngdézhèn remains an excellent place to visit ceramic workshops and purchase various types of ceramic wares, from Mao statues to traditional glazed urns. The Shànghǎi Museum has a premier collection of porcelain, while several independent retailers in Běijīng, Shànghǎi and Hong Kong also sell more modish and creative pieces. Spin (p225), in particular, sells a highly creative selection of contemporary ceramic designs.

Sculpture

The earliest sculpture in China dates to the Zhou and Shang dynasties, when small clay and wooden figures were commonly placed in tombs to protect the dead and guide them on their way to heaven.

With the arrival of Buddhism, sculpture turned towards spiritual figures and themes, with sculptors frequently enrolled in huge carving projects for the worship of Sakyamuni. Influences also arrived along the Silk Road from abroad, bringing styles from as far afield as Greece and Persia, via India. The magnificent Buddhist caves at Yúngāng in Shānxī province date back to the 5th century and betray a noticeable Indian influence.

Chisellers also began work on the Lóngmén Caves in Hénán province at the end of the 5th century. The earliest effigies are similar in style to those at Yúngāng, revealing further Indian influences and more other-worldliness in their facial expressions. Later cave sculptures at Lóngmén were completed during the Tang dynasty and reveal a more Chinese style.

The most superlative examples are at the Mògāo Caves at Dūnhuáng in Gānsù province, where well-preserved Indian and Central Asian–style sculptures, particularly of the Tang dynasty, carry overtly Chinese characteristics – many statues feature long, fluid bodies and have warmer, more refined facial features.

The Shànghǎi Museum has a splendid collection of Buddhist sculpture, as does Capital Museum and the Poly Art Museum, both in Běijīng.

Beyond China's grottoes, other mesmerising Chinese sculpture hides away in temples across China. The colossal statue of Guanyin in Pǔníng Temple in Chéngdé is a staggering sight, carved from five different types of wood and towering over 22m in height. Shuānglín Temple outside Píngyáo in Shānxī province is famed for its painted statues from the Song and Yuan dynasties.

The *I Ching* (*Yìjīng*; Book of Changes) is the oldest Chinese text and is used for divination. It is comprised of 64 hexagrams, composed of broken and continuous lines, that represent a balance of opposites (yin and yang), the inevitability of change and the evolution of events.

Literature

Classical Novels

Until the early 20th century, classical literature (古文; *gǔwén*) had been the principal form of writing in China for thousands of years. A breed of purely literary writing, classical Chinese employed a stripped-down form of written Chinese that did not reflect the way people actually spoke or thought. Its grammar differed from the syntax of spoken Chinese and it employed numerous obscure Chinese characters.

Classical Chinese maintained divisions between educated and uneducated Chinese, putting literature beyond the reach of the common person and fashioning a cliquey lingua franca for Confucian officials and scholars.

Classical novels evolved from the popular folk tales and dramas that entertained the lower classes. During the Ming dynasty they were penned in a semivernacular (or 'vulgar') language, and are often irreverently funny and full of action-packed fights.

Probably the best-known novel outside China is *Journey to the West* (Xīyóu Jì) – more commonly known as *Monkey*. Written in the 16th century, it follows the misadventures of a cowardly Buddhist monk (Tripitaka; a stand-in for the real-life pilgrim Xuan Zang) and his companions – a rebellious monkey, lecherous pig-man and exiled monster-immortal – on a pilgrimage to India. In 2007 a Chinese director collaborated with Damon Albarn, of the virtual band Gorillaz, to transform the story into a circus opera that has played to considerable international acclaim.

The 14th-century novel *The Water Margin/Outlaws of the Marsh/All Men are Brothers* (Shuǐhǔ Zhuàn) is, on the surface, an excellent tale of honourable bandits and corrupt officials along the lines of Robin Hood. On a deeper level, though, it is a reminder to Confucian officials of their right to rebel when faced with a morally suspect government (at least one emperor officially banned it).

Published by the Chinese University of Hong Kong Research Centre for Translation, *Renditions* is an excellent journal of Chinese literature in English translation, covering works from classical Chinese to modern writing.

ARTS & ARCHITECTURE LITERATURE

Modern Literature

Early 20th Century

Classical Chinese maintained its authority over literary minds until the early 20th century, when it came under the influence of the West.

Torch-bearing author Lu Xun wrote his short story *Diary of a Madman* in 1918. It was revolutionary stuff. Apart from the opening paragraph, Lu's seminal and shocking fable is written in colloquial Chinese.

For Lu Xun to write his short story in colloquial Chinese was explosive, as readers were finally able to read language as it was spoken. *Diary of a Madman* is a haunting and unsettling work, and from this moment on, mainstream Chinese literature would be written as it was thought and spoken: Chinese writing had been instantly revolutionised.

Other notable contemporaries of Lu Xun include Ba Jin (*Family;* 1931), Mao Dun (*Midnight;* 1933), Lao She (*Rickshaw Boy/Camel Xiangzi;* 1936) and the modernist playwright Cao Yu (*Thunderstorm*). Lu Xun and Ba Jin translated a great deal of foreign literature into Chinese.

Contemporary Writing

The Book and the Sword by Jin Yong/Louis Cha (2004) is China's most celebrated martial-arts novelist's first book. The martial-arts genre (*wǔxiá xiǎoshuō*) is a direct descendant of the classical novel.

A growing number of contemporary voices have been translated into English, but far more exist in Chinese only. The provocative Nobel Prize–winning Mo Yan (*Life and Death are Wearing Me Out;* 2008), Yu Hua (*To Live;* 1992) and Su Tong (*Rice;* 1995) have written momentous historical novels set in the 20th century; all are excellent, though their raw, harrowing subject matter is not for the faint of heart.

Zhu Wen mocks the get-rich movement in his brilliantly funny short stories, published in English as *I Love Dollars and Other Stories of China* (2007). It's a vivid and comic portrayal of the absurdities of everyday China.

'Hooligan author' Wang Shuo (*Please Don't Call Me Human;* 2000) is one of China's best-selling authors with his political satires and convincing depictions of urban slackers. Alai (*Red Poppies;* 2002), an ethnic Tibetan, made waves by writing in Chinese about early-20th-century Tibetan Sìchuān – whatever your politics, it's both insightful and a page-turner. Refused entry into China, exiled author Ma Jian writes more politically critical work; his 2001 novel *Red Dust* was a Kerouacian tale of wandering China as a spiritual pollutant in the 1980s. Banned in China, his 2008 novel *Beijing Coma* is set against the Tiān'ānmén demonstrations of 1989, and their aftermath. China's most renowned dissident writer, Gao Xingjian, won the Nobel Prize for Literature in 2000 for his novel *Soul Mountain,* an account of his travels along the Yangzi after being misdiagnosed with lung cancer. All of his work has been banned in the PRC since 1989.

Controversial blogger Han Han (http://blog.sina.com.cn/twocold) catapulted himself into the literary spotlight with his novel *Triple Door,* a searing critique of China's educational system. His successful 2010 road-trip novel *1988: I Want to Talk with the World* only served to expand his already massive fan base and establish himself as a spokesman of a generation.

Candy (2003) by Mian Mian is a hip take on modern Shànghǎi life, penned by a former heroin addict musing on complicated sexual affairs, suicide and drug addiction in Shēnzhèn and Shànghǎi. It's applauded for its urban underground tone, but is sensational for its framing of post-adolescent themes in contemporary China. *Years of Red Dust: Stories of Shanghai* (2010) by Qiu Xiaolong contains 23 short stories in the context of momentous historic events affecting the city and the inhabitants of Red Dust Lane.

In his novel *Banished,* poet, essayist, short-story writer and blogger Han Dong reaches to his own experiences during the Cultural Revolution for inspiration. Winner of the Man Asian Literary Prize in 2010, Bi Feiyu's *Three Sisters* is a poignant tale of rural China during the political chaos of the early 1970s. In *Northern Girls,* Sheng Keyi illuminates the prejudices and bigotries of modern Chinese society in her story of a Chinese girl arriving as an immigrant worker in Shēnzhèn. *The Fat Years* (2009) by Chan Koonchung is a science fiction novel set in a near-future totalitarian China where the month of February 2011 has gone missing from official records.

For a taste of contemporary Chinese short-story writing with both English and Chinese, buy a copy of *Short Stories in Chinese: New Penguin Parallel Text* (2012). *The Picador Book of Contemporary Chinese Fiction* (2006) brings together a range of different contemporary voices and themes into one accessible book.

Wolf Totem (2009), by Jiang Rong, is an astonishing look at life on the grasslands of Inner Mongolia during the Cultural Revolution and the impact of modern culture on an ancient way of life.

Film

Early Cinema

The moving image in the Middle Kingdom dates to 1896, when Spaniard Galen Bocca unveiled a film projector and blew the socks off wide-eyed crowds in a Shànghǎi teahouse. Shànghǎi's cosmopolitan verve and exotic looks would make it the capital of China's film industry, but China's very first movie – *Conquering Jun Mountain* (an excerpt from a piece of Běijīng opera) – was actually filmed in Běijīng in 1905.

Shànghǎi opened its first cinema in 1908. In those days, cinema owners would cannily run the film for a few minutes, stop it and collect money from the audience before allowing the film to continue. The golden age of Shànghǎi film-making came in the 1930s when the city had over 140 film companies. Its apogee arrived in 1937 with the release of *Street Angel,* a powerful drama about two sisters who flee the Japanese in northeast China and end up as prostitutes in Shànghǎi; and *Crossroads,* a clever comedy about four unemployed graduates. Japanese control of China eventually brought the industry to a standstill and sent many film-makers packing.

Communist Decline

China's film industry was stymied after the Communist Revolution, which sent film-makers scurrying to Hong Kong and Taiwan, where they played key roles in building up the local film industries that flourished there. Cinematic production in China was co-opted to glorify communism and generate patriotic propaganda. The days of the Cultural Revolution (1966–76) were particularly dark. Between 1966 and 1972, just eight movies were made on the mainland, as the film industry was effectively shut down.

Resurgence

It wasn't until two years after the death of Mao Zedong, in September 1978, that China's premier film school – the Běijīng Film Academy – reopened. Its first intake of students included Zhang Yimou, Chen Kaige and Tian Zhuangzhuang, who are considered masterminds of the celebrated 'Fifth Generation'.

The cinematic output of the Fifth Generation signalled an escape from the dour, colourless and proletarian Mao era, and a second glittering golden age of Chinese film-making arrived in the 1980s and 1990s with their lush and lavish tragedies. A bleak but beautifully shot tale of a Chinese Communist Party cadre who travels to a remote village in Shaanxi province to collect folk songs, Chen Kaige's *Yellow Earth* aroused little interest in China but proved a sensation when released in the West in 1985.

It was followed by Zhang's *Red Sorghum,* which introduced Gong Li and Jiang Wen to the world. Gong became the poster girl of Chinese cinema in the 1990s and the first international movie star to emerge from the mainland. Jiang, the Marlon Brando of Chinese film, has proved both a durable leading man and an innovative, controversial director of award-winning films such as *In the Heat of the Sun* and *Devils on the Doorstep.*

Rich, seminal works such as *Farewell My Concubine* (1993; Chen Kaige) and *Raise the Red Lantern* (1991; Zhang Yimou) were garlanded with praise, receiving standing ovations and winning major film awards. Their directors were the darlings of Cannes; Western cinema-goers were entranced. Many Chinese cinema-goers also admired their artistry, but some saw Fifth Generation output as pandering to the Western market.

In 1993 Tian Zhuangzhuang made his brilliant film *The Blue Kite.* A heartbreaking account of the life of one Běijīng family during the Cultural Revolution, it so enraged the censors that Tian was banned from making films for a decade.

Each generation charts its own course and the ensuing Sixth Generation – graduating from the Běijīng Film Academy post-Tiān'ānmén Square protests – was no different.

Sixth Generation film directors eschewed the luxurious beauty of their forebears, and sought to capture the angst and grit of modern urban Chinese life. Their independent, low-budget works put an entirely different and more cynical spin on mainland Chinese film-making, but their darker subject matter and harsh film style (frequently in black and white) left many Western viewers cold.

Independent film-making found an influential precedent with Zhang Yuan's 1990 debut *Mama.* Zhang is also acclaimed for his candid and gritty documentary-style *Beijing Bastards* (1993).

Meanwhile, *The Days,* directed by Wang Xiaoshui, follows a couple drifting apart in the wake of the Tiān'ānmén Square protests. Wang also directed the excellent *Beijing Bicycle* (2001), inspired by De Sica's *Bicycle Thieves.*

The 2010 remake of *The Karate Kid,* starring Jackie Chan, is set in Běijīng and authentically conveys the city despite having nothing to do with karate.

Contemporary Film

Jia Zhangke has emerged as the most acclaimed of China's new filmmakers. His meditative and compassionate look at the social impact of the construction of the Three Gorges Dam on local people, *Still Life* (2006), scooped the Golden Lion at the 2006 Venice Film Festival. His other films include the celebrated *24 City* (2008) and *A Touch of Sin* (2013).

Controversial Sixth Generation director Lou Ye has a prolific and notable portfolio of sensual and atmospheric films. The tragic, noirish experience of *Suzhou River* (2000) is perhaps his best-known work, but *Summer Palace* (2006), *Spring Fever* (2009) and the violent *Mystery* (2014) have maintained his reputation as an *enfant terrible* of China's censorship-laden film industry.

The Hong Kong director Wong Kar-wai is particularly notable for seductively filmed classics such as *In the Mood for Love* (2000) and *2046* (2004).

Historical *wuxia* (martial arts) cinema is enduringly popular in China and typified much film-making in the noughties, with larger-than-life films like *Hero* (2002; Zhang Yimou), *House of Flying Daggers* (2004; Zhang Yimou) and *The Banquet* (2006; Feng Xiaogang) leading the way. Epic historical war dramas such as *Red Cliff* (2008 and 2009; John Woo) and *The Warlords* (2007; Peter Chan) belong to a similar genre.

Chinese Opera

Contemporary Chinese opera, of which the most famous is Běijīng opera (京剧; *Jīngjù*), has a continuous history of some 900 years. Evolving from a convergence of comic and ballad traditions in the Northern Song period, Chinese opera brought together a disparate range of forms: acrobatics, martial arts, poetic arias and stylised dance.

Operas were usually performed by travelling troupes who had a low social status in traditional Chinese society. Chinese law forbade mixed-sex performances, forcing actors to act out roles of the opposite sex. Opera troupes were frequently associated with homosexuality in the public imagination, contributing further to their lowly social status.

Formerly, opera was performed mostly on open-air stages in markets, streets, teahouses or temple courtyards. The shrill singing and loud percussion were designed to be heard over the public throng, prompting American writer PJ O'Rourke to say it was 'as if a truck full of wind chimes collided with a stack of empty oil drums during a birdcall contest'.

Opera performances usually take place on a bare stage, with the actors taking on stylised stock characters who are instantly recognisable to the audience. Most stories are derived from classical literature and Chinese mythology, and tell of disasters, natural calamities, intrigues or rebellions.

As well as Běijīng opera, other famous Chinese operatic traditions include Cantonese opera, Kunqu (from the Jiāngnán region), Min opera (from Fújiàn) and Shànghǎi opera.

Architecture

Traditional Architecture

Four principal styles governed traditional Chinese architecture: imperial, religious, residential and recreational. The imperial style was naturally the most grandiose, overseeing the design of buildings employed by successive dynastic rulers; the religious style was employed for the construction of temples, monasteries and pagodas; while the residential and recreational style took care of the design of houses and private gardens.

Whatever the style, Chinese buildings traditionally followed a similar basic ground plan, consisting of a symmetrical layout oriented around a central axis – ideally running north–south to conform with basic feng shui (*fēngshuǐ*) dictates and to maximise sunshine – with an enclosed courtyard (*yuàn*) flanked by buildings on all sides.

For a taste of Kazakh folk music from northwest Xinjiang province, listen to *Eagle*, by Mamer, an intriguing collection of songs described as 'Chinagrass' by their composer.

ARTS & ARCHITECTURE CHINESE OPERA

Xīnjiāng-born Wang Shu, architect of the distinctive Níngbō Museum, won the coveted Pritzker Architecture Prize in 2012.

BATTLE OF THE BUDDHAS

China's largest ancient Buddha gazes out over the confluence of the waters of the Dàdù River and the Mín River at Lèshān in Sìchuān. When the even bigger Buddha at Bamyan in Afghanistan was demolished by the Taliban, the Lèshān Buddha enjoyed instantaneous promotion to the top spot as the world's largest. The Buddha in the Great Buddha Temple at Zhāngyè in Gānsù province may not take it lying down, though: he is China's largest 'housed reclining Buddha'. Chinese children once climbed inside him to scamper about within his cavernous tummy.

Lounging around in second place is the reclining Buddha in the Mògāo Caves, China's second largest. The vast reclining Buddha at Lèshān is a whopping 170m long and the world's largest 'alfresco' reclining Buddha. Bristling with limbs, the Thousand Arm Guanyin statue in the Pǔníng Temple's Mahayana Hall in Chéngdé also stands up to be counted: she's the largest wooden statue in China (and possibly the world). Not to be outdone, Hong Kong fights for its niche with the Tian Tan Buddha Statue, the world's 'largest outdoor seated bronze Buddha statue'.

CHINESE GARDENS

Classical Chinese gardens can be an acquired taste: there are no lawns, few flowering plants, and misshapen, huge rocks are strewn about. Yet a stroll in Shànghǎi's Yùyuán Gardens (and the gardens of Sūzhōu) is a walk through many different facets of Chinese civilisation, and this is what makes them so unique. Architecture, philosophy, art and literature all converge, and a background in some basics of Chinese culture helps to fully appreciate garden design.

The Chinese for 'landscape' is *shānshuǐ* (山水), literally 'mountain-water'. Mountains and rivers constitute a large part of China's geography, and are fundamental to Chinese life, philosophy, religion and art. So the central part of any garden landscape is a pond surrounded by rock formations. This also reflects the influence of Taoist thought. Contrary to geometrically designed formal European gardens, where humans saw themselves as masters, Chinese gardens seek to create a microcosm of the natural world through an asymmetrical layout of streams, hills, plants and pavilions (they symbolise humanity's place in the universe – never in the centre, just a part of the whole).

Plants are chosen as much for their symbolic meaning as their beauty (the pine for longevity, the peony for nobility) while the use of undulating 'dragon walls' brings good fortune. The names of gardens and halls are often literary allusions to ideals expressed in classical poetry. Painting, too, goes hand in hand with gardening, its aesthetics reproduced in gardens through the use of carefully placed windows and doors that frame a particular view. The central precept of *fēngshuǐ* (literally 'wind water') is also paramount, so rockeries and ponds are deliberately arranged to maximise positive *qì* (energy).

Finally, it's worth remembering that gardens in China have always been lived in. Generally part of a residence, they weren't so much contemplative (as in Japan) as they were a backdrop for everyday life: family gatherings, late-night drinking parties, discussions of philosophy, art and politics – it's the people who spent their leisure hours there who ultimately gave the gardens their unique spirit.

In many aspects, imperial palaces are glorified courtyard homes (south-facing, a sequence of courtyards, side halls and perhaps a garden at the rear) completed on a different scale. Apart from the size, the main dissimilarity would be guard towers on the walls and possibly a moat, imperial yellow roof tiles, ornate dragon carvings (signifying the emperor), the repetitive use of the number nine and the presence of temples.

Religious Architecture

Chinese Buddhist, Taoist and Confucian temples tend to follow a strict, schematic pattern. All temples are laid out on a north–south axis in a series of halls, with the main door of each hall facing south.

With their sequence of halls and buildings interspersed with breezy open-air courtyards, Chinese temples are very different from Christian churches. The roofless courtyards allow the weather to permeate within the temple and permits *qì* (气; spirit) to circulate, dispersing stale air and allowing incense to be burned.

Buddhist Temples

Once you have cracked the logic of Buddhist temples, you can discover how most temples conform to a pattern. The first hall and portal to the temple is generally the Hall of Heavenly Kings, where a sedentary, central statue of the tubby Bodhisattva Maitreya is flanked by the ferocious Four Heavenly Kings. Behind is the first courtyard, where the Drum Tower and Bell Tower may rise to the east and west, and smoking braziers may be positioned.

The main hall is often the Great Treasure Hall sheltering glittering statues of the past, present and future Buddhas, seated in a row. This is the main focal point for worshippers at the temple. On the east and west interior wall of the hall are often 18 *luóhàn* (arhat – a Buddhist who has achieved enlightenment) in two lines, either as statues or paintings. In some temples, they gather in a throng of 500, housed in a separate hall. A statue of Guanyin (the Goddess of Mercy) frequently stands at the rear of the main hall, facing north, atop a fish's head or a rocky outcrop. The goddess may also have her own hall and occasionally presents herself with a huge fan of arms, in her 'Thousand Arm' incarnation – the awesome effigy of Guanyin in the Mahayana Hall at Pǔníng Temple in Chéngdé is the supreme example.

The rear hall may be where the sutras (Buddhist scriptures) were once stored, in which case it will be called the Sutra Storing Building. A pagoda may rise above the main halls or may be the only surviving fragment of an otherwise destroyed temple. Conceived to house the remains of Buddha and later other Buddhist relics, pagodas also contained sutras, religious artefacts and documents.

Taoist Temples

Taoist shrines are more nether-worldly than Buddhist shrines, although the basic layout echoes Buddhist temples. They are decorated with a distinct set of motifs, including the *bāguà* (eight trigrams) formations, reflected in eight-sided pavilions and halls, and the Taiji yin-yang *(yīnyáng)* diagram. Effigies of Laotzu, the Jade Emperor and other characters popularly associated with Taoist myth, such as the Eight Immortals and the God of Wealth, are customary.

Taoist door gods, similar to those in Buddhist temples, often guard temple entrances; the main hall is usually called the Hall of the Three Clear Ones, devoted to a triumvirate of Taoist deities.

Taoist monks (and nuns) are easily distinguished from their shaven-headed Buddhist confrères by their long hair, twisted into topknots, straight trousers and squarish jackets.

Confucian Temples

Confucian temples bristle with steles celebrating local scholars, some supported on the backs of *bìxì* (mythical tortoise-looking dragons). A statue of Kongzi (Confucius) usually resides in the main hall, overseeing rows of musical instruments and flanked by disciples. A mythical animal, the *qílín* (a statue exists at the Summer Palace in Běijīng), is commonly seen. The *qílín* was a chimera that only appeared on earth in times of harmony. The largest Confucian temple in China is at Qūfù in Shāndōng, Confucius' birthplace.

ART DECO IN SHÀNGHĂI

Fans of art deco must visit Shànghǎi. The reign of art deco is one of the city's architectural high-water marks and the city boasts more art deco buildings than any other city, from the drawing boards of the French firm Leonard, Veysseyre and Kruze, and others. Largely emptied of foreigners in 1949, Shànghǎi mostly kept its historic villas and buildings intact, including its fabulous art deco monuments. The Peace Hotel, Bank of China building, Cathay Theatre, Green House, Paramount Ballroom, Broadway Mansions, Liza Building, Savoy Apartments, Picardie Apartments and Majestic Theatre are all art deco gems. For a comprehensive low-down on the style, hunt down a copy of *Shanghai Art Deco* by Deke Erh and Tess Johnston.

Modern Architecture

Architecturally speaking, anything goes in today's China. You only have to look at the Pǔdōng skyline to discover a melange of competing designs, some dramatic, inspiring and novel, others rash. The display represents a nation brimming over with confidence, zeal and money.

If modern architecture in China is regarded as anything post-1949, then China has ridden a roller-coaster ride of styles and fashions. In Běijīng, stand between the Great Hall of the People (1959) and the National Centre for the Performing Arts (2008) and weigh up how far China travelled in 50 years. Interestingly, neither building has clear Chinese motifs. The same applies to the form of Běijīng's CCTV Building, where a continuous loop through horizontal and vertical planes required some audacious engineering.

The coastal areas are an architect's dreamland – no design is too outrageous, zoning laws have been scrapped, and the labour force is large and inexpensive. Planning permission can be simple to arrange – often all it requires is sufficient *guānxī* (connections). Even the once cash-strapped interior provinces are getting in on the act. The planned Sky City in the Húnán capital of Chángshā will be the world's tallest building, if built. Broad Sustainable Building, the company aiming to erect it, says the job can be completed in just 90 days, although the go-ahead was still awaiting government approval at the time of writing. Opening in Chéngdū in 2013, the staggeringly large New Century Global Center is the world's largest freestanding building: big enough to swallow up 20 Sydney Opera Houses!

Many of the top names in international architecture – IM Pei, Rem Koolhaas, Norman Foster, Kengo Kuma, Jean-Marie Charpentier, Herzog & de Meuron – have all designed at least one building in China in the past decade. Other impressive examples of modern architecture include the National Stadium (aka the 'Bird's Nest'), the National Aquatics Center (aka the 'Water Cube') and Běijīng South train station, all in Běijīng; and the art deco–esque Jīnmào Tower, the towering Shànghǎi World Financial Center, Tomorrow Square and the Shànghǎi Tower in Shànghǎi. In Hong Kong, the glittering 2 International Finance Center on Hong Kong Island and the International Commerce Center in Kowloon are each prodigious examples of modern skyscraper architecture.

China's Landscapes

The Land

The world's third-largest country – on a par size-wise with the USA – China swallows up an immense 9.5 million sq km, only surpassed in area by Russia and Canada. Straddling natural environments as diverse as subarctic tundra in the north and tropical rainforests in the south, this massive land embraces the world's highest mountain range and one of its hottest deserts in the west, to the steamy, typhoon-lashed coastline of the South China Sea. Fragmenting this epic landscape is a colossal web of waterways, including one of the world's mightiest rivers, the Yangzi (长江; Cháng Jiāng).

Mountains

China has a largely mountainous and hilly topography, commencing in precipitous fashion in the vast and sparsely populated Qīnghǎi–Tibetan plateau in the west and levelling out gradually towards the fertile, well-watered, populous and wealthy provinces of eastern China.

This mountainous disposition sculpts so many of China's scenic highlights, from the glittering Dragon's Backbone Rice Terraces of Guǎngxī to the incomparable stature of Mt Everest, the stunning beauty of Jiǔzhàigōu National Park in Sìchuān, the ethereal peaks of misty Huángshān in Ānhuī, the vertiginous inclines of Huà Shān in Shaanxi (Shǎnxī), the sublime karst geology of Yángshuò in Guǎngxī and the volcanic drama of Heaven Lake in Jílín.

Averaging 4500m above sea level, the Qīnghǎi–Tibetan region's highest peaks thrust up into the Himalayan mountain range along its southern rim. The Himalayas, on average about 6000m above sea level, include 40 peaks rising dizzyingly to 7000m or more. Also known as the planet's 'third pole', this is where the world's highest peak, Mt Everest – called Zhūmùlǎngmǎfēng by the Chinese – thrusts up jaggedly from the Tibet–Nepal border.

This vast high-altitude region (Tibet alone constitutes one-eighth of China's landmass) is home to an astonishing 37,000 glaciers, the third-largest mass of ice on the planet after the Arctic and Antarctic. This enormous body of frozen water ensures that the Qīnghǎi–Tibetan region is the source of many of China's largest rivers, including the Yellow (Huáng Hé), Mekong (Láncāng Jiāng), and Salween (Nù Jiāng) and, of course, the mighty Yangzi, all of whose headwaters are fed by snowmelt from here. Global warming, however, is inevitably eating into this glacial volume, although experts argue over how quickly they are melting.

This mountain geology further corrugates the rest of China, continuously rippling the land into spectacular ranges. There's the breathtaking 2500km-long Kunlun range, the mighty Karakoram mountains on the

The dawn redwood (Metasequoia), a towering (growing up to 200ft) and elegant fine-needled deciduous Chinese tree, dates to the Jurassic era. Once considered long extinct, a single example was discovered in 1941 in a Sichuan village, followed three years later by the discovery of further trees.

border with Pakistan, the Tiān Shān range in Xīnjiāng, the Tanggula range on the Qīnghǎi–Tibetan plateau, the Qinling mountains and the Greater Khingan range (Daxingan Ling) in the northeast.

Deserts

China contains head-spinningly huge – and growing – desert regions that occupy almost one-fifth of the country's landmass, largely in its mighty northwest. These are inhospitably sandy and rocky expanses where summers are staggeringly hot and winters bone-numbingly cold, but as destinations, the visuals can be sublime. North towards Kazakhstan and Kyrgyzstan, from the plateaus of Tibet and Qīnghǎi, is Xīnjiāng's Tarim Basin, the largest inland basin in the world. This is the location of the mercilessly thirsty Taklamakan Desert – China's largest desert and the world's second largest mass of sand after the Sahara Desert. Many visitors to Xīnjiāng will experience this huge expanse during their travels or can arrange camel-trekking tours and expeditions through its vast sand dunes. China's biggest shifting salt lake, Lop Nur (the site of China's nuclear bomb tests) is also here.

The Silk Road into China steered its epic course through this entire region, ferrying caravans of camels laden with merchandise, languages, philosophies, customs and peoples from the far-flung lands of the Middle East. The harsh environment shares many topographical features in common with the neighbouring nations of Afghanistan, Kyrgyzstan and Kazakhstan, and is almost the exact opposite of China's lush and well-watered southern provinces. But despite the scorching aridity of China's northwestern desert regions, their mountains (the mighty Tiān Shān, Altai, Pamir and Kunlun ranges) contain vast supplies of water, largely in the form of snow and ice.

Northeast of the Tarim Basin is Ürümqi, the world's furthest city from the sea. The Tarim Basin is bordered to the north by the lofty Tiān Shān

SOUTH–NORTH WATER DIVERSION PROJECT

Water is the lifeblood of economic and agricultural growth, but as China only has around 7% of the world's water resources (with almost 20% of its population), the liquid is an increasingly precious resource.

A region of low rainfall, North China faces a worsening water crisis. Farmers are draining aquifers that have taken thousands of years to accumulate, while industry in China uses three to 10 times more water per unit of production than developed nations. Meanwhile, water usage in large cities such as Běijīng and Tiānjīn continues to climb as migrants flood in from rural areas.

To combat the water crisis, the CCP embarked on the construction of the US$62 billion South–North Water Diversion Project, a vast network of pumping stations, canals and aqueducts (as well as a tunnel under the Yellow River) lashing north and south via three routes. The ambition is to divert 3.8 million Olympic swimming pools' worth of water yearly from the Yangzi River to the parched regions of China's north. The first stage began operating in 2013 and water was due to begin flowing along the second stage the following year.

There are concerns, however, that pollution in the Yangzi River waters will become progressively concentrated as water is extracted, while Yangzi cities such as Nánjīng and Wǔhàn are increasingly uneasy that they will be left with a water shortfall. Alarm has also arisen at the pollution in channels – including the Grand Canal, which links Hángzhōu with north China – earmarked to take the diverted waters. There are worries that these polluted reaches are almost untreatable, making elements of the project unviable.

Critics also argue that the project, which will involve the mass relocation of hundreds of thousands of people, will not address the fundamental issue of China's water woes – the absence of policies for the sustainable use of water as a precious resource.

range – home to the glittering mountain lake of Tiān Chí – and to the west by the mighty Pamirs, which border Pakistan. Also in Xīnjiāng is China's hot spot, the Turpan Basin. Known as the 'Oasis of Fire' and 'China's Death Valley', it gets into the record books as China's lowest-lying region and the world's second-deepest depression after the Dead Sea in Israel.

China's most famous desert is, of course, the Gobi, although most of it lies outside the country's borders. In little-visited Western Inner Mongolia, the awesome Badain Jaran Desert offers travellers spectacular journeys among remote desert lakes and colossal sand dunes up to 380m in height; further west lie the famous grasslands and steppes of Inner Mongolia.

Rivers

At about 5460km long and the second-longest river in China, the Yellow River (黄河; Huánghé) is touted as the birthplace of Chinese civilisation and has been fundamental in the development of Chinese society. The mythical architect of China's rivers, the Great Yu, apocryphally noted 'Whoever controls the Yellow River controls China'. From its source in Qīnghǎi, the river runs through North China, meandering past or near many famous towns, including Lánzhōu, Yínchuān, Bāotóu, Hánchéng, Jìnchéng, Lùoyáng, Zhèngzhōu, Kāifēng and Jǐ'nán in Shāndōng, before exiting China north of Dōngyíng (although the watercourse often runs dry nowadays before it reaches the sea).

The Yangzi (the 'Long River'), is one of the longest rivers in the world (and China's longest). Its watershed of almost 2 million sq km – 20% of China's land mass – supports 400 million people. Dropping from its source high on the Tibetan plateau, it runs for 6300km to the sea, of which the last few hundred kilometres are across virtually flat alluvial plains. In the course of its sweeping journey, the river (and its tributaries) fashions many of China's scenic spectacles, including Tiger Leaping Gorge and the Three Gorges, and cuts through a string of huge and historic cities, including Chóngqìng, Wǔhàn and Nánjīng, before surging into the East China Sea north of Shànghǎi. As a transport route, the river is limited, but the Three Gorges cruise is China's most celebrated river journey. The waterborne journey along the Lí River, between Guìlín and Yángshuò in Guǎngxī, is China's other major riverine experience.

Fields & Agriculture

China's hills and mountains may surround travellers with a dramatic backdrop, but they are a massive agricultural headache for farmers. Small plots of land are eked out in patchworks of land squashed between hillsides or rescued from mountain cliffs and ravines, in the demanding effort to feed 20% of the world's population with just 10% of its arable land.

Astonishingly, only 15% of China's land can be cultivated so hillside gradients and inclines are valiantly levelled off, wherever possible, into bands of productive terraced fields. Stunning examples of rice terraces – beautiful in the right light – can be admired at the Yuányáng Rice Terraces in Yúnnán and the Dragon's Backbone Rice Terraces in Guǎngxī.

Wildlife

China's vast size, diverse topography and climatic disparities support an astonishing range of habitats for animal life. The Tibetan plateau alone is the habitat of over 500 species of birds, while half of the animal species in the northern hemisphere exist in China.

It is unlikely you will see many of these creatures in their natural habitat unless you are a specialist, or have a lot of time, patience, persistence, determination and luck. If you go looking for large animals in the wild on the off chance, the likelihood of glimpsing one is virtually nil. But there are plenty of pristine reserves within relatively easy reach of

The World Health Organization estimates that air pollution causes more than 650,000 fatal illnesses per year in China, while more than 95,000 die annually from consuming polluted drinking water.

travellers' destinations such as Chéngdū and Xī'ān and even if you don't get the chance to see animals, the scenery is terrific. Try Yàdīng Nature Reserve in Sìchuān, Mèngdá Nature Reserve in Qīnghǎi, Sānchàhé Nature Reserve in Yúnnán, Fànjìngshān in Guìzhōu, Shénnóngjià in Húběi, Wǔzhīshān in Hǎinán, Kanas Lake Nature Reserve in Xīnjiāng and Chángbái Shān, China's largest nature reserve, in Jílín.

Mammals

China's towering mountain ranges form natural refuges for wildlife, many of which are now protected in parks and reserves that have escaped the depredations of loggers and dam-builders. The barren high plains of the Tibetan plateau are home to several large animals, such as the *chiru* (Tibetan antelope), Tibetan wild ass, wild sheep and goats, and wolves. In theory, many of these animals are protected, but in practice poaching and hunting still threaten their survival.

The beautiful and retiring snow leopard, which normally inhabits the highest parts of the most remote mountain ranges, sports a luxuriant coat of fur against the cold. It preys on mammals as large as mountain goats, but is unfortunately persecuted for allegedly killing livestock.

The Himalayan foothills of western Sìchuān support the greatest diversity of mammals in China. Aside from giant pandas, other mammals found in this region include the panda's small cousin – the raccoon-like red panda – as well as Asiatic black bears and leopards. Among the grazers are golden takin, a large goatlike antelope with a yellowish coat and a reputation for being cantankerous, argali sheep and various deer species, including the diminutive mouse deer.

The sparsely populated northeastern provinces abutting Siberia are inhabited by reindeer, moose, bears, sables and Manchurian tigers.

Overall, China is unusually well endowed with big and small cats. The world's largest tiger, the Manchurian Tiger (Dōngběihǔ) – also known as the Siberian Tiger – only numbers a few hundred in the wild, its remote habitat being one of its principal saviours. Three species of leopard can be found, including the beautiful clouded leopard of tropical rainforests, plus several species of small cat, such as the Asiatic golden cat and a rare endemic species, the Chinese mountain cat.

Rainforests are famous for their diversity of wildlife, and the tropical south of Yúnnán province, particularly the area around Xīshuāngbǎnnà, is one of the richest in China. These forests support Indo-Chinese tigers and herds of Asiatic elephants.

The wild mammals you are most likely to see are several species of monkey. The large and precocious Père David's macaque is common at Éméi Shān in Sìchuān, where bands often intimidate people into handing over their picnics; macaques can also be seen on Hǎinán's Monkey Island. Several other monkey species are rare and endangered, including the beautiful golden monkey of Fànjìngshān and the snub-nosed monkey of the Yúnnán rainforests. But by far the most endangered is the Hǎinán gibbon, numbering just a few dozen individuals on Hǎinán island, thanks to massive forest clearance.

The giant panda (*xióngmāo* – literally 'bear cat') is western Sìchuān's most famous denizen, but the animal's solitary nature makes it elusive for observation in the wild, and even today, after decades of intensive research and total protection in dedicated reserves, sightings are rare. A notoriously fickle breeder (the female is only on heat for a handful of days each spring), there are approximately 1600 pandas in the Chinese wilds according to World Wildlife Fund. Interestingly, the panda has the digestive tract of a carnivore (like other bears), but has become accustomed to exclusively eating bamboo shoots and leaves. However, the panda's digestive tract is unable to efficiently break down plant matter so the

Chángqīng Nature Reserve in Shaanxi province is well worth a visit for its relatively unspoilt montane forest and the chance to see giant pandas in the wild. Find out more at www.cqpanda.com.

mammal needs to consume huge amounts to compensate and spends much of its time eating, clearing one area of bamboo before moving on to another region. The easiest way to see pandas outside of zoos is at the Giant Panda Breeding Research Base, just outside Chéngdū or at the Yǎ'ān Bìfēngxiá Panda Base, also in Sìchuān.

Birds

Most of the wildlife you'll see in China will be birds, and with more than 1300 species recorded, including about 100 endemic or near-endemic species, China offers some fantastic birdwatching opportunities. Spring is usually the best time, when deciduous foliage buds, migrants return from their wintering grounds and nesting gets into full swing. **BirdLife International** (www.birdlife.org/regional/asia), the worldwide bird conservation organisation, recognises 12 Endemic Bird Areas (EBAs) in China, nine of which are wholly within the country and three of which are shared with neighbouring countries.

Although the range of birds is huge, China is a centre of endemicity for several species and these are usually the ones that visiting birders will seek out. Most famous are the pheasant family, of which China boasts 62 species, including many endemic or near-endemic species.

Other families well represented in China include the laughing thrushes, with 36 species; parrotbills, which are almost confined to China and its near neighbours; and many members of the jay family. The crested ibis is a pinkish bird that feeds on invertebrates in the rice paddies, and was once found from central China to Japan.

Among China's more famous large birds are cranes, and nine of the world's 14 species have been recorded here. In Jiāngxī province, on the lower Yangzi, a vast series of shallow lakes and lagoons was formed by stranded overflow from Yangzi flooding. The largest of these is Póyáng Lake, although it is only a few metres deep and drains during winter. Vast numbers of waterfowl and other birds inhabit these swamps year-round, including ducks, geese, herons and egrets. Although it is difficult to reach, and infrastructure for birdwatchers is practically nonexistent, birders are increasingly drawn to the area in winter, when many of the lakes dry up and attract flocks of up to five crane species, including the endangered, pure white Siberian crane.

Recommended destinations include Zhālóng Nature Reserve, one of several vast wetlands in Hēilóngjiāng province. Visit in summer to see breeding storks, cranes and flocks of wildfowl before they fly south for the winter. Běidàihé, on the coast of the Bohai Sea, is well known for migratory birds. Other breeding grounds and wetlands include Qīnghǎi Hú in Qīnghǎi, Cǎohǎi Lake in Guìzhōu, Jiǔzhàigōu in Sìchuān and Mai Po Marsh in Hong Kong. For the latter, the **Hong Kong Bird Watching Society** (www.hkbws.org.hk) organises regular outings and publishes a newsletter in English.

Most birdwatchers and bird tours head straight for Sìchuān, which offers superb birding at sites such as Wòlóng. Here, several spectacular pheasants, including golden, blood and kalij pheasants, live on the steep forested hillsides surrounding the main road. As the road climbs up, higher-altitude species such as eared pheasants and the spectacular Chinese monal may be seen. Alpine meadows host smaller birds, and the rocky scree slopes at the pass hold partridges, the beautiful grandala and the mighty lammergeier (bearded vulture), with a 2m wingspan.

Parts of China are now well-established on the itineraries of global ecotour companies. **Bird Tour Asia** (www.birdtourasia.com) has popular tours to Sìchuān, Tibet, Qīnghǎi and southeast China, as well as providing custom tours. The **China Bird Watching Network** (www.chinabirdnet. org) has useful links to birdwatching societies across China.

In 2010, six of China's *dānxiá* (eroded reddish sandstone rock), karst-like geological formations, were included in Unesco's World Heritage List. The list includes Chìshuǐ in Guìzhōu province. The rocks can also be seen outside Zhāngyè in Gānsù.

Plants

China is home to more than 32,000 species of seed plant and 2500 species of forest tree, plus an extraordinary plant diversity that includes some famous 'living fossils' – a diversity so great that Jílín province in the semifrigid north and Hǎinán province in the tropical south share few plant species.

Apart from rice, the plant probably most often associated with China and Chinese culture is bamboo, of which China boasts some 300 species. Bamboos grow in many parts of China, but bamboo forests were once so extensive that they enabled the evolution of the giant panda, which eats virtually nothing else, and a suite of small mammals, birds and insects that live in bamboo thickets. Most of these useful species are found in the subtropical areas south of the Yangzi, and the best surviving thickets are in southwestern provinces such as Sìchuān.

Many plants commonly cultivated in Western gardens today originated in China, among them the ginkgo tree, a famous 'living fossil' whose unmistakable imprint has been found in 270 million-year-old rocks.

Deciduous forests cover mid-altitudes in the mountains, and are characterised by oaks, hemlocks and aspens, with a leafy understorey that springs to life after the winter snows have melted. Among the more famous blooms of the understorey are rhododendrons and azaleas, and many species of each grow naturally in China's mountain ranges. Best viewed in spring, some species flower right through summer; one of the best places to see them is at Sìchuān's Wòlóng Nature Reserve. All of the nature reserves mentioned under Wildlife earlier are also excellent places for botanical exploration.

A growing number of international wildlife travel outfits arrange botanical expeditions to China, including UK-based **Naturetrek** (www.naturetrek.co.uk), which arranges tours to Yúnnán and Sìchuān.

Endangered Species

Almost every large mammal you can think of in China has crept onto the endangered species list, as well as many of the so-called 'lower' animals and plants. The snow leopard, Indo-Chinese tiger, chiru antelope, crested ibis, Asiatic elephant, red-crowned crane and black-crowned crane are all endangered.

Deforestation, pollution, hunting and trapping for fur, body parts and sport are all culprits. The Convention on International Trade in Endangered Species of Wild Fauna and Flora (CITES) records legal trade in live reptiles and parrots, and high numbers of reptile and wildcat skins. The number of such products collected or sold unofficially is anyone's guess.

Despite the threats, a number of rare animal species cling to survival in the wild. Notable among them are the Chinese alligator in Ānhuī, the giant salamander in the fast-running waters of the Yangzi and Yellow Rivers, the Yangzi River dolphin in the lower and middle reaches of the river (although there have been no sightings since 2002), and the pink dolphin of the Hong Kong islands of Sha Chau and Lung Kwu Chau. The giant panda is confined to the fauna-rich valleys and ranges of Sìchuān.

Intensive monoculture farmland cultivation, the reclaiming of wetlands, river damming, industrial and rural waste, and desertification are reducing unprotected forest areas and making the survival of many of these species increasingly precarious. Although there are laws against killing or capturing rare wildlife, their struggle for survival is further complicated as many remain on the most-wanted lists for traditional Chinese medicine and dinner delicacies.

One of the aims of the Three Gorges Dam is to help prevent flooding on the Yangzi River. The river has caused hundreds of catastrophic floods, including the disastrous inundation of 1931, in which an estimated 145,000 died.

The Environment

China may be vast, but with two-thirds of the land either mountain, desert or uncultivable, the remaining third is overwhelmed by the people of the world's most populous nation. In 2011, for the first time in its history, China's city dwellers outnumbered rural residents, with an urbanisation rate set to increase to 65% by 2050. The speed of development – and the sheer volume of poured concrete – is staggering. During the next 15 years, China is expected to build urban areas equal to 10 times the size of New York City.

Beyond urban areas, deforestation and overgrazing have accelerated the desertification of vast areas of China, particularly in the western provinces. Deserts now cover almost one-fifth of the country and China's dustbowl is the world's largest, swallowing up 200 sq km of arable land every month.

A Greener China?

China is painfully aware of its accelerated desertification, growing water shortages, shrinking glaciers, acidic rain, contaminated rivers, caustic urban air and polluted soil. The government is keenly committed, on a policy level, to the development of greener and cleaner energy sources. China's leaders are also seeking to devise a more sustainable and less wasteful economic model for the nation's future development.

There is evidence of ambitious and bold thinking: in 2010 China announced it would pour billions into developing electric and hybrid vehicles; Běijīng committed itself to overtaking Europe in renewable energy investment by 2020; wind farm construction (in Gānsù, for example) continues apace; and China leads the world in production of solar cells. It aims to reduce energy use per unit of GDP by more than 15% before 2015.

Public protests – sometimes violent – against polluting industries have proliferated in recent years across China and have scored a number of notable victories, including the 2012 demonstrations in Shífāng (Sìchuān), which led to the cancellation of a planned US$1.6 billion copper smelting facility. A 2013 survey in China revealed that 78% of people would demonstrate if polluting industries were constructed near their homes. Much of the agitation is the result of health concerns, since cancer is now the leading cause of death in China and up to 650,000 people die prematurely every year because of atmospheric pollution.

One of China's main energy quandaries is coal. Coal is cheap, easy to extract and remains China's primary energy source, accounting for almost 70% of power requirements.

China has earmarked a staggering US$140 billion for an ambitious program of wind farms; ranging from Xīnjiāng province to Jiāngsū province in the east, the huge wind farms are due for completion in 2020.

In 2010 China overtook the USA as the world's largest energy consumer; in the same year the nation replaced Japan as the world's second-largest economy and is tipped to overtake the USA by 2020 (some say by 2016).

TOP BOOKS ON CHINA'S ENVIRONMENT

➡ *When a Billion Chinese Jump* (2010) Jonathan Watts' sober and engaging study of China's environmental issues.

➡ *China's Environmental Challenges* (2012) Judith Shapiro's excellent primer for understanding China's manifold environmental problems.

➡ *The River Runs Black: The Environmental Challenge to China's Future* (2010; 2nd edition) Elizabeth Economy's frightening look at the unhappy marriage between breakneck economic production and environmental degradation.

➡ *The China Price: The True Cost of Chinese Competitive Advantage* (2008) Alexandra Harney's telling glimpse behind the figures of China's economic rise.

➡ *China's Water Crisis* (2004) Ma Jun rolls up his sleeves to examine the sources of China's water woes.

Martial Arts of China

Unlike Western fighting arts such as Savate, kickboxing, boxing and wrestling, Chinese martial arts are deeply impregnated with religious and philosophical values. And, some might add, a morsel or two of magic. Many eminent exponents of *gōngfū* (功夫) – better known in the West as kung fu – were devout monks or religious recluses who drew inspiration from Buddhism and Taoism and sought a mystical communion with the natural world. Their arts were not leisurely pursuits but were closely entangled with the meaning and purpose of their lives.

Styles & Schools

China lays claim to a bewildering range of martial arts styles, from the flamboyant and showy, inspired by the movements of animals or insects (such as Praying Mantis Boxing) to schools more empirically built upon the science of human movement (such as Wing Chun). On the outer fringes are the esoteric arts, abounding with metaphysical feats, arcane practices and closely guarded techniques.

Many fighting styles were once secretively handed down for generations within families and it is only relatively recently that outsiders have been accepted as students. Some schools, especially the more obscure one, have been driven to extinction partly due to their exclusivity.

Some styles also found themselves divided into competing factions, each laying claim to the original teachings and techniques. Such styles may exist in a state of schism; other styles have become part of the mainstream. Wing Chun in particular has become globally recognised, largely due to its associations with Bruce Lee.

Unlike Korean and Japanese arts such as Taekwondo or Karate-do, there is frequently no international regulatory body that oversees the syllabus, tournaments or grading requirements for China's individual martial arts. Consequently, students of China's myriad martial arts may be rather unsure of what level they have attained. It is often down to the individual teacher to decide what to teach students, and how quickly.

Praying Mantis master Fan Yook Tung once killed two stampeding bulls with an iron-palm technique.

Hard School

Although there is considerable blurring between the two camps, Chinese martial arts are often distinguished between hard and soft schools. Typically aligned with Buddhism, the hard or 'external' (外家; *wàijiā*) school tends to be more vigorous, athletic and concerned with the development of power. Many of these styles are related to Shàolín Boxing and the Shàolín Temple in Hénán province.

Shàolín Boxing is forever associated with Bodhidharma (p415), an ascetic Indian Buddhist monk who visited the Shàolín Temple and added a series of breathing and physical exercises to the Shàolín monk's sedentary meditations. The Shàolín monk's legendary endeavours and fearsome physical skills became known throughout China and beyond. Famous external schools include Báiméi Quán (White Eyebrow Boxing) and Cháng Quán (Long Boxing).

Soft School

Usually inspired by Taoism, the soft or 'internal' Chinese school (内家; *nèijiā*) develops pliancy and softness as a weapon against hard force. Taichi (Tàijí Quán) is the best known soft school, famed for its slow and lithe movements and an emphasis on cultivating *qì* (energy). Attacks are met with yielding movements that smother the attacking force and lead the aggressor off balance. The road to Taichi mastery is a long and difficult one, involving a re-education of physical movement and suppression of one's instinct to tense up when threatened. Other soft schools include the circular moves of Bāguà Zhǎng and the linear boxing patterns of Xíngyì Quán, based on five basic punches – each linked to one of the five elements of Chinese philosophy – and the movements of 12 animals.

Forms

Most students of Chinese martial arts – hard or soft – learn forms (套路; *tàolù*), a series of movements linked together into a pattern, which embody the principal punches and kicks of the style. In essence, forms are unwritten compendiums of the style, to ensure passage from one generation to the next. The number and complexity of forms varies from style to style: taichi may only have one form, although it may be very lengthy (the long form of the Yang style takes around 20 minutes to perform). Five Ancestors Boxing has dozens of forms, while Wing Chun only has three empty-hand forms.

Several Chinese styles of *gōngfū* include drunken sets, where the student mimics the supple movements of an inebriate.

Qìgōng

Closely linked to both the hard and especially the soft martial-arts schools is the practice of *qìgōng*, a technique for cultivating and circulating *qì* around the body. *Qì* can be developed for use in fighting to protect the body, as a source of power or for curative and health-giving purposes.

Qì can be developed in a number of ways – by standing still in fixed postures or with gentle exercises, meditation and measured breathing techniques. Taichi itself is a moving form of *qìgōng* cultivation while at the harder end of the spectrum a host of *qìgōng* exercises aim to make specific parts of the body impervious to attack.

Bāguà Zhǎng

One of the more esoteric and obscure of the soft Taoist martial arts, Bāguà Zhǎng (八卦掌; Eight Trigram Boxing, also known as Pa-kua) is also one of the most intriguing. The Bāguà Zhǎng student wheels around in a circle, rapidly changing direction and speed, occasionally thrusting out a palm strike.

Bāguà Zhǎng draws its inspiration from the trigrams (an arrangement of three broken and unbroken lines) of the classic *Book of Changes*

MARTIAL ARTS OF CHINA BĀGUÀ ZHǍNG

COURSES, BOOKS & FILMS

Often misinterpreted, *gōngfū* teaches an approach to life that stresses patience, endurance, magnanimity and humility. Courses can be found in abundance across China, from Běijīng, Hong Kong, Shànghǎi, Wǔdāng Shān in Húběi to the Shàolín Temple in Hénán.

John F Gilbey's *The Way of a Warrior* is a tongue-in-cheek, expertly written and riveting account of the Oriental fighting arts. *Meditations on Violence: A Comparison of Martial Arts Training & Real World Violence* by Sgt Rory Miller is a graphic, illuminating and down-to-earth book on violence and its consequences.

For metaphysical pointers, soft-school adherents can dip into Laotzu's terse but inspiring *The Classic of the Way and Its Power*. For spectacular (if implausible) Wing Chun moves and mayhem, watch *Ip Man* (2008), starring the indefatigable Donnie Yen.

(Yìjīng or I Ching), the ancient oracle used for divination. The trigrams are typically arranged in circular form and it is this pattern that is traced out by the Bāguà Zhǎng exponent. Training commences by just walking the circle so the student gradually becomes infused with its patterns and rhythms.

A hallmark of the style is the exclusive use of the palm, not the fist, as the principal weapon. This may seem curious and perhaps even ineffectual, but in fact the palm can transmit a lot of power – consider a thrusting palm strike to the chin, for example. The palm is also better protected than the fist as it is cushioned by muscle. The fist also has to transfer its power through a multitude of bones that need to be correctly aligned to avoid damage while the palm sits at the end of the wrist. Consider hitting a brick wall as hard as you can with your palm, and then imagine doing it with your fist!.

The student must become proficient in the subterfuge, evasion, speed and unpredictability that are hallmarks of Bāguà Zhǎng. Force is generally not met with force, but deflected by the circular movements cultivated in students through their meditations upon the circle. Circular forms – arcing, twisting, twining and spinning – are the mainstay of all movements, radiating from the waist.

Despite being dated by historians to the 19th century, Bāguà Zhǎng is quite probably a very ancient art. Beneath the Taoist overlay, the movements and patterns of the art suggest a possibly animistic or shamanistic origin, which gives the art its timeless rhythms.

Wing Chun

Conceived by Ng Mui, a Buddhist nun from the Shàolín Temple, who taught her skills to a young girl called Wing Chun (詠春; Yǒng Chūn), this is a fast and dynamic system of fighting that promises quick results for novices. Wing Chun was the style that taught Bruce Lee how to move and, although he ultimately moved away from it to develop his own style, Wing Chun had an enormous influence on the Hong Kong fighter and actor.

Wing Chun emphasises speed over strength and evasion, rapid strikes and low kicks are its hallmark techniques. Forms are simple and direct, dispensing with the pretty flourishes that clutter other styles.

The art can perhaps best be described as scientific. There are none of the animal forms that make other styles so exciting and mysterious. Instead, Wing Chun is built around its centre line theory, which draws an imaginary line down the human body and centres all attacks and blocks along that line. The line runs through the sensitive regions: eyes, nose, mouth, throat, heart, solar plexus and groin and any blow on these points is debilitating and dangerous.

The three empty-hand forms – which look bizarre to non-initiates – train arm and leg movements that both attack and defend this line. None of the blocks stray beyond the width of the shoulders, as this is the limit of possible attacks, and punches follow the same theory. Punches are delivered with great speed in a straight line, along the shortest distance between puncher and punched. All of this gives Wing Chun its distinctive simplicity.

A two-person training routine called *chi sau* (sticky hands) teaches the student how to be soft and relaxed in response to attacks, as pliancy generates more speed. Weapons in the Wing Chun arsenal include the lethal twin Wing Chun butterfly knives and an extremely long pole, which requires considerable strength to handle with skill.

Iron Shirt (*tiěshān*) is an external *gōngfū qìgōng* training exercise that circulates and concentrates the *qì* in certain areas to protect the body from impacts during a fight.

Zhang Sanfeng, the founder of taichi, was supposedly able to walk more than 1000 *li* (around 350 miles) a day; others say he lived for more than 200 years!

Survival Guide

Directory A–Z

Accommodation

From rustic homesteads, homestays, enterprising youth hostels, student dormitories, guesthouses, courtyard lodgings, snappy boutique hotels and elegant historic residences to metallic five-star towers and converted art deco apartment blocks, China's accommodation choice is impressive (on a national level). The choice varies enormously, however, between regions and cities. Top-tier draws such as Běijīng, Shànghǎi, Hángzhōu and Hong Kong sport a rich variety of accommodation options but other towns can have a poor supply, despite being inundated with visitors. Rural destinations are largely a patchwork of homesteads and hostels, with the occasional boutique-style choice in big ticket villages.

Rooms & Prices

Accommodation is divided by price category, identified by the symbols $ (budget), $$ (midrange) or $$$ (top end); accommodation prices vary across China, so one region's budget breakdown may differ from another. We list the rack rate, which generally reflects the most you are ever expected to pay. However, at most times of the year discounts are in effect which can range from 10% to 60% (see boxed text on p994).

Rooms come with private bathroom or shower room, unless otherwise stated. Rooms are generally easy to procure, but phone ahead to reserve a room in popular tourist towns (such as Hángzhōu), especially for weekend visits.

Most rooms in China fall into the following categories:

Double rooms (双人房、标准间; *shuāng rén fáng* or *biāozhǔn jiān*) In most cases, these are twins, ie with two beds.

One-bed rooms/single (单间; *dānjiān*) This is usually a room with one double-sized bed.

Large-bed rooms (大床房; *dàchuáng fáng*) Larger than a one-bed room, with a big double bed.

Suites (套房; *tàofáng*) Available at most midrange and top-end hotels.

Dorms (多人房; *duōrénfáng*) Usually, but not always, available at youth hostels (and at a few hotels).

Business rooms (商务房; *shāngwù fáng*) Usually equipped with computers.

Restrictions

The majority of hotels in China still do not have the authorisation to accept foreigners. This can be a source of frustration when you find yourself steered towards pricier midrange and top-end lodgings. All hotels we list accept foreign guests. To see if a hotel accepts foreign guests, ask: *zhègè bīnguǎn shōu wàiguórén ma?* (这个宾馆收外国人吗?).

Booking

Booking online can help you secure a room and obtain a good price, but remember you should be able to bargain down the price of your room at hotel reception (except at youth hostels and the cheapest hotels) or over the phone. To secure accommodation, always plan ahead and book your room in advance during the high season. Airports at major cities often have hotel-booking counters that offer discounted rates.

Ctrip (☑400 619 9999; www.english.ctrip.com) Excellent hotel booking, air and train ticketing website, with English helpline. Useful app available.

Elong (☑400 617 1717, 24hr customer support 010-8457

BOOK YOUR STAY ONLINE

For more accommodation reviews by Lonely Planet authors, check out http://lonelyplanet.com/China/hotels. You'll find independent reviews, as well as recommendations on the best places to stay. Best of all, you can book online.

PRACTICALITIES

➡ There are three types of plugs – three-pronged angled pins, two flat pins or two narrow round pins. Electricity is 220V, 50 cycles AC.

➡ The standard English-language newspaper is the (censored) *China Daily* (www. chinadaily.com.cn). China's largest circulation Chinese-language daily is the *People's Daily* (Rénmín Rìbào). It has an English-language edition on http://english.peopledaily. com.cn. Imported English-language newspapers can be bought from five-star hotel bookshops.

➡ Listen to the BBC World Service or Voice of America; however, the websites can be jammed. Chinese Central TV (CCTV) has an English-language channel – CCTV9. Your hotel may have ESPN, Star Sports, CNN or BBC News 24.

➡ China officially subscribes to the international metric system, but you will encounter the ancient Chinese weights and measures system that features the *liǎng* (两; tael; 50g) and the *jīn* (斤; catty; 0.5kg). There are 10 *liǎng* to the *jīn*.

7827; www.elong.net) Hotel and air ticket booking, with English helpline.

Travel Zen (☏400 720 3355; www.travelzen.com) Air tickets and hotel bookings. English helpline.

Checking In & Out

At check-in you will need your passport; a registration form will ask what type of visa you have. For most travellers, the visa is L (travel visa). A deposit (押金; *yājīn*) is required at most hotels; this will be paid either with cash or by providing your credit-card details. International credit cards are generally only accepted at midrange hotels or chain express hotels and top-end accommodation; always have cash in case. If your deposit is paid in cash, you will be given a receipt and the deposit will be returned to you when you check out.

You usually have to check out by noon. If you check out between noon and 6pm you will be charged 50% of the room price; after 6pm you have to pay for another full night.

Camping

There are few places where you can legally camp and as most of China's flat land is put to agricultural use, you will largely be limited to re-mote, hilly regions. Camping is more feasible in wilder and less populated parts of west China. In certain destinations with camping possibilities, travel agencies and hotels will arrange overnight camping trips or multiday treks, in which case camping equipment will be supplied. Camping on the Great Wall is technically illegal, however the watchtowers are often used for pitching tents or rolling out a sleeping bag as long as you clean up after yourself and take care of the Wall.

Courtyard Hotels

Largely confined to Běijīng, courtyard hotels have rapidly mushroomed. Arranged around traditional *sìhéyuàn* (courtyards), rooms are on ground level. Courtyard hotels are charming and romantic, but are often expensive and rooms are small, in keeping with the dimensions of courtyard residences. Facilities will be limited so don't expect a swimming pool, gym or subterranean garage.

Budget Business Chain Hotels

Dotted around much of China, budget business chain hotels can sometimes be a decent alternative to old-school two- and three-star hotels, with rooms around the ¥180 to ¥300 mark. In recent years, however, their once-pristine facilities have sometimes come to resemble the threadbare clunkers they aimed to replace. Still, their sheer ubiquitousness means you can usually find accommodation (but look at the rooms first). They often have membership or loyalty schemes which make rooms cheaper. Chains include:

Home Inn (☏400 820 3333; www.homeinns.com) Includes the Motel 168 chain.

Jinjiang Inn (☏400 820 9999; www.jinjianginns.com)

Guesthouses

The cheapest of the cheap are China's ubiquitous guesthouses (招待所; *zhāodàisuǒ*). Often found clustered near train or bus stations but also dotted around cities and towns, not all guesthouses accept foreigners, and Chinese skills may be crucial in securing a room. Rooms (doubles, twins, triples, quads) are primitive and grey, with tiled floors and possibly a shower room or shabby bathroom; showers may be communal.

Other terms for guesthouses:

➡ 旅店 (*lǚdiàn*)

➡ 旅馆 (*lǚguǎn*)

➡ 有房 means 'rooms available'

➡ 今日有房 'rooms available today'

➡ 住宿 (zhùsù; 'accommodation').

Homesteads

In more rural destinations, small towns and villages, you should be able to find a homestead (农家; nóngjiā) with a small number of rooms in the region of ¥50 (bargaining is possible); you will not need to register. The owner will be more than happy to cook up meals for you as well. Showers and toilets are generally communal.

Hostels

If you're looking for efficiently run budget accommodation, turn to China's youth hostel sector. **Hostelling International** (☏020-8751 3731; www.yhachina.com) hostels are generally well run; other private youth hostels scattered around China are unaffiliated and standards at these may be variable. Book ahead in popular towns as rooms can go fast.

Superb for meeting like-minded travellers, youth hostels are typically staffed by youthful English-speakers who are also well informed on local sightseeing and transport. The foreigner-friendly vibe in youth hostels stands in marked contrast to many Chinese hotels. Double rooms in youth hostels are frequently better than mid-range equivalents, often just as comfortable and better located, and they may be cheaper (but not always). Many offer wi-fi, while most have at least one internet terminal (free, free for 30 minutes or roughly ¥5 to ¥10 per hour). Laundry, book-lending, kitchen facilities, bike rental, lockers, noticeboard, bar and cafe should all be available, and possibly a pool, ping pong, DVDs, PlayStation and other forms of entertainment. Soap, shower gel and toothpaste are generally not provided, although you can purchase them at reception.

Dorms usually cost between ¥40 and ¥55 (discounts of around ¥5 for members). They typically come with bunk beds but may have standard beds. Most dorms won't have en-suite showers, though some do; they should have air-con. Many hostels also have doubles, singles, twins and maybe even family rooms; prices vary but are often around ¥150 to ¥250 for a double, again with discounts for members. Hostels can arrange ticketing or help you book a room in another affiliated youth hostel. Book ahead (online if possible) as rooms are frequently booked out, especially at weekends or the busy holiday periods. In popular destinations, hostels may charge elevated rates on Friday and Saturday.

Hotels

Hotels vary wildly in quality within the same budget bracket. The star rating system employed in China can also be misleading: hotels may be awarded four or five stars when they are patently a star lower in ranking. The best rule of thumb is to choose the newest hotel in each category as renovations can be rare. Deficiencies may not be immediately apparent, so explore and inspect the overall quality of the hotel; viewing the room up front pays dividends.

China has few independent hotels of real distinction, so it's generally advisable to select chain hotels that offer a proven standard of international excellence. Shangri-La, Marriott, Hilton, St Regis, Ritz-Carlton, Marco Polo and Hyatt all have a presence in China and can generally be relied upon for high standards of service and comfort.

Note the following:

➡ English skills are often poor, even in some five-star hotels.

➡ Most rooms are twins rather than doubles, so be clear if you specifically want a double.

➡ Virtually all hotel rooms, whatever the price bracket, will have air-conditioning and a TV.

➡ Very cheap rooms may have neither telephone nor internet access.

➡ Wi-fi is increasingly common in hostels and midrange and top-end hotels (but might be only in the lobby).

➡ Late-night telephone calls or calling cards from 'masseurs' and prostitutes are still common in budget and lower midrange hotels.

➡ All hotel rooms are subject to a 10% or 15% service charge.

HOTEL DISCOUNTS

Always ignore the rack rate and ask for the discounted price or bargain for a room, as discounts usually apply everywhere but youth hostels (except for hostel members) and the cheapest accommodation; you can do this in person at reception, or book online. Apart from during the busy holiday periods (the end of April and first few days of May, the first week of October and Chinese New Year), rooms should be priced well below the rack rate and are rarely booked out. In some towns (such as Hángzhōu), there may be a pricier weekend rate (Friday and Saturday). Discounts of 10% to 60% off the tariff rate (30% is typical) are the norm, available by simply asking at reception, by phoning in advance to reserve a room, or by booking online at **Ctrip** (http://english.ctrip.com).

➡ Practically all hotels will change money for guests, and most midrange and top-end hotels accept credit cards.

➡ A Western breakfast may be available, certainly at four-star establishments.

➡ The Chinese method of designating floors is the same as that used in the USA, but different from, say, that used in Australia. What would be the ground floor in Australia is the 1st floor in China, the 1st is the 2nd, and so on.

In Chinese, hotels are called:

➡ bīnguǎn (宾馆)

➡ dàfàndiàn (大饭店)

➡ dàjiǔdiàn (大酒店)

➡ fàndiàn (饭店)

➡ jiǔdiàn (酒店).

Temples & Monasteries

Some temples and monasteries (especially on China's sacred mountains) provide accommodation. They are cheap but ascetic, and may not have running water or electricity.

Activities

Grab copies of expat magazines in Běijīng, Hong Kong, Guǎngzhōu and Shànghǎi for information on activities such as golf, running, horse riding, cycling, football, cricket, hiking and trekking, swimming, ice skating, skiing, skateboarding, waterskiing and rock climbing.

Children

More comfortable in the large cities of Hong Kong, Běijīng and Shànghǎi, children are likely to feel out of place in smaller towns and in the wilds. With the exception of Hǎinán, China is not famous for its beaches. Ask a doctor specialising in travel medicine for information on recommended immunisations for your child.

Practicalities

➡ Baby food, nappies and milk powder: widely available in supermarkets.

➡ Restaurants: few have baby chairs.

➡ Train travel: children shorter than 1.4m can get a hard sleeper for 75% of the full price or a half-price hard seat. Children shorter than 1.1m ride free, but you have to hold them the entire journey.

➡ Air travel: infants under the age of two fly for 10% of the full airfare, while children between the ages of two and 11 pay half the full price for domestic flights and 75% of the adult price for international flights.

➡ Sights and museums: many have children's admission prices, for children under 1.1m or 1.3m in height.

➡ Always ensure your child carries ID in case they get lost.

Customs Regulations

Chinese customs generally pay tourists little attention. 'Green channels' and 'red channels' at the airport are clearly marked. You are not allowed to import or export illegal drugs, or animals and plants (including seeds). Pirated DVDs and CDs are illegal exports from China – if found they will be confiscated. You can take Chinese medicine up to a value of ¥300 when you depart China.

Duty free, you're allowed to import the following:

➡ 400 cigarettes or the equivalent in tobacco products

➡ 1.5L of alcohol

➡ 50g of gold or silver.

Other considerations:

➡ Importation of fresh fruit and cold cuts is prohibited.

➡ There are no restrictions on foreign currency (but declare any cash exceeding US$5000 or its equivalent in another currency).

Objects considered antiques require a certificate and a red seal to clear customs when leaving China. Anything made before 1949 is considered an antique, and if it was made before 1795 it cannot legally be taken out of the country. To get the proper certificate and red seal, your antiques must be inspected by the **State Administration of Cultural Heritage** (Guójiā Wénwù Jú; 010-5679 2211; www.sach.gov.cn; 83 Beiheyan Dajie) in Běijīng.

Discount Cards

Seniors over the age of 65 are frequently eligible for discounts and 70-and-overs get free admission, so make sure you take your passport when visiting sights as proof of age.

An **International Student Identity Card** (ISIC; www. isic.org; €12) can net students half-price discounts at many sights (but you may have to insist).

DIRECTORY A–Z ELECTRICITY

Electricity

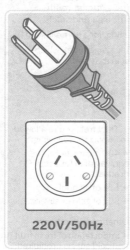

220V/50Hz

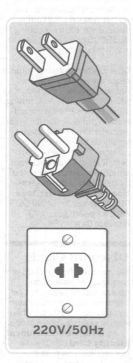

220V/50Hz

Embassies & Consulates

Embassies

Embassies are located in Běijīng, with consulates scattered around the country. There are three main embassy areas in Běijīng: Jiànguóménwài, Sānlǐtún and Liàngmǎqiáo. Embassies are open from 9am to noon and 1.30pm to 4pm Monday to Friday, but visa departments are often only open in the morning. For visas, you need to phone to make an appointment.

Australian Embassy (☑010-5140 4111; www.china. embassy.gov.au; 21 Dongzhimenwai Dajie)

Canadian Embassy (☑010-5139 4000; www. canadainternational.gc.ca; 19 Dongzhimenwai Dajie)

French Embassy (☑010-8531 2000; www.amba-france-cn.org; 60 Tianze Lu)

German Embassy (☑010-8532 9000; www.china.diplo. de; 17 Dongzhimenwai Dajie, 东直门外大街17号)

Indian Embassy (印度大使馆, Yìndù Dàshǐguǎn; ☑010-8531 2500; www.indianembassy.org.cn; 5 Liangmaqiao Beijie, 亮马桥北街5号)

Irish Embassy (☑010-8531 6200; www.embassyofireland. cn; 3 Ritan Donglu)

Japanese Embassy (日本大使馆, Rìběn Dàshǐguǎn; ☑8531 9800; www.cn.emb-japan.go.jp; 1 Liangmaqiaodong Jie, 亮马桥东街1号)

Kazakhstan Embassy (☑010-6532 6182; 9 Sanlitun Dongliujie)

Kyrgyzstan Embassy (☑010-6468-1297; www.kyrgyzstanembassy.net; 18 Xiaoyun Lu, 10/11 H District, King's Garden Villas; ⊙applications 9am-11am Mon, Wed & Fri)

Laotian Embassy (老挝大使馆, Lǎowō Dàshǐguǎn; ☑010-6532 1224; 11 Sanlitun Dongsijie, 三里屯东二街11号)

Mongolian Embassy (蒙古大使馆, Ménggǔ Dàshǐguǎn;

☑010-6532 1203; 2 Xiushui Beijie) There is a separate visa section (☑010-6532 6512; ⊙9-11am Mon-Fri).

Myanmar Embassy (☑010-6532-0359; www.myanmarembassy.com/chinese; 6 Dongzhimenwai Dajie)

Nepalese Embassy (尼泊尔大使馆, Níbó'ěr Dàshǐguǎn; ☑010-6532 1795; www. nepalembassy.org.cn; 1 Sanlitun Xiliujie, 三里屯西六街1号)

Netherlands Embassy (☑010-8532 0200; www. hollandinchina.org; 4 Liangmahe Nanlu)

New Zealand Embassy (☑010-8531 2700; www.nzembassy.com/china; 3 Sanlitun Dongsan Jie)

North Korean Embassy (☑010-6532 1186; 11 Ritan Beilu)

Pakistan Embassy (☑010-6523 3504; www.pakbj.org.pk; 1 Dongzhimenwai Dajie)

Russian Embassy (俄罗斯大使馆, Èluósī Dàshǐguǎn; ☑010-6532 1381; www. russia.org.cn; 4 Dongzhimen Beizhongjie, 东直门内大街东直门北中街4号, off Dongzhimennei Dajie)

South Korean Embassy (南韩大使馆, Nánhán Dàshǐguǎn; ☑010-8531 0700; 20 Dongfang Donglu, 东方东路20号)

Thai Embassy (泰国大使馆, Tàiguó Dàshǐguǎn; ☑6532 1749; www.thaiembassy.org; 40 Guanghua Lu, 光华路40号)

UK Embassy (☑010-5192 4000; www.gov.uk/government/world/china; 11 Guanghua Lu)

US Embassy (☑010-8531 3000; http://beijing.usembassy-china.org.cn; 55 Anjialou Lu) Hong Kong (☑852-2523 9011; 26 Garden Rd, Central)

Vietnamese Embassy (越南大使馆, Yuènán Dàshǐguǎn; ☑010-6532 1155; http:// vnemba.org.cn; 32 Guanghua Lu, 光华路32号)

Consulates

CHÉNGDŪ

France (☎028-6666 6060; 30th fl, Times Plaza, 2 Zongfu Lu), Shěnyáng (☎024-2319 0000; 34 Nanshisan Weilu)
Germany (☎028-8528 0800; 25th fl, Western Tower, 19 Renmin Nanlu 4th Section)
Pakistan (☎028-8526 8316; Ste 2306, One Aerospace Center, No. 7, Xinguanghua Jie)
US (☎028-8558 3992; 4 Lingshiguan Lu)

CHÓNGQÌNG

Canada (☎023-6373 8007; Suite 1705, 17th fl, Metropolitan Tower, 68 Zourong Lu)
UK (☎023-6369 1500; Suite 2801, 28th fl, Metropolitan Tower, 68 Zourong Lu)

ERENHOT

Mongolia (☎151-6497-1992; Youyi Lu; ⊙9am-noon & 3-5pm Mon-Fri)

KŪNMÍNG

Laos (☎0871-316 8916; Ground fl, Kūnmíng Diplomat Compound, 6800 Caiyun Beilu)
Myanmar (缅甸领事馆; ☎0871 6816 2810; www.mcgkunming.org; 99 Yingbin Lu, Guāndù District Consular Zone; 官渡区昆明外国领事区迎宾路99号(世纪金源大酒店旁); ⊙9am-noon Mon-Fri)

GUǍNGZHŌU

Australia (☎020-3814 0111; 12th fl, Development Centre, 3 Linjiang Dadao)
Canada (☎020-8611 6100; Room 801, China Hotel Office Tower, Liuhua Lu)
France (☎020-2829 2000; Room 810, 8th fl, Main Tower, Guǎngzhōu International Hotel, 339 Huanshi Donglu)
Germany (☎020-8313 0000; 14th fl, Main Tower, Yuèhǎi Tiānhé Bldg, 208 Tianhe Lu)
Netherlands (☎020-3813 2200; http://china.nlembassy.org; Teem Tower, 208 Tianhe Lu)
New Zealand (☎020-8667 0253; Room 1055, China Hotel Office Tower, Liuhua Lu)
UK (☎020-8314 3000; 2nd fl, Main Tower, Guǎngdōng

International Hotel, 339 Huanshi Donglu)
US (☎020-3814 5000; Huaxia Lu, Zhujiang New Town, Tianhe District)

HOHHOT

Mongolia (蒙古领事馆, Měnggǔ Lǐngshìguǎn; 5 Dongying Nanjie, 东影南街5号; ⊙9am-noon Mon, Tue & Thu)

HONG KONG

Australia (☎852-2827 8881; 23rd fl, Harbour Centre, 25 Harbour Rd, Wan Chai)
Canada (☎852-3719 4700; 5th fl, Tower 3, Exchange Square, 8 Connaught Place, Central)
France (☎852-3752 9900; 26th fl, Tower II, Admiralty Centre, 18 Harcourt Rd, Admiralty)
Germany (☎852-2105 8777; 21st fl, United Centre, 95 Queensway, Admiralty)
India (☎852-3970 9900; www.cgihk.gov.in; Unit A, 16th fl, United Centre, 95 Queensway, Admiralty)
Ireland (☎852-2527 4897; 1408 Two Pacific Pl, 88 Queensway, Admiralty)
Japan (☎852-2522 1184; www.hk.emb-japan.go.jp; 46-47th fl, One Exchange Sq, 8 Connaught Pl, Central)
Laos (☎852-2544 1186; 14th fl, Arion Commercial Centre, 2-12 Queen's Rd West, Sheung Wan)
Nepal (☎852-2369 7813; www.nepalconsulatehk.org; 715 China Aerospace Tower, Concordia Plaza, 1 Science Museum Rd, Tsim Sha Tsui)
Netherlands ☎852-2599 9200; Room 2402B, 24th fl Great Eagle Centre, 23 Harbour Road, Wan Chai)
New Zealand (☎2525 5044; Room 6501, 65th fl, Central Plaza, 18 Harbour Rd, Wan Chai)
UK (☎852-2901 3000; 1 Supreme Court Rd, Admiralty)
Vietnam (☎852-2591 4510; vnconsul@netvigator.com; 15th fl, Great Smart Tower, 230 Wan Chai Rd, Wan Chai)

JĪNGHÓNG

Laos (老挝领事馆; Lǎowō Lǐngshìguǎn ;☎221 9355; 2/F, Bldg 2, Gaozhuang Xishuangjing, Xuanwei Dadao; 宣慰大

道，告庄西双景综合楼2楼; ⊙8.30-11.30am & 2.30-4.30pm Mon-Fri)

KŪNMÍNG

Thailand (泰国大使馆, Tàiguó Dàshǐguǎn; ☎6532 1749; www.thaiembassy.org; 40 Guanghua Lu, 光华路40号)
Vietnam (☎0871-352 2669; 507, Hongta Mansion, 155 Beijing Lu)

LHASA

Nepal (☎0891-681 3965; 13 Norbulingka Beilu; ⊙10am-noon Mon-Fri)

QĪNGDǍO

Japan (☎0532-8090 0001; 59 Xianggang Donglu)
South Korea (☎0532-8897 6001; 101 Xianggang Donglu)

SHÀNGHǍI

Australia (澳大利亚领事馆, Àodàlìyà Lǐngshìguǎn; ☎021-2215 5200; www.shanghai.china.embassy.gov.au; 22nd fl, CITIC Sq, 1168 West Nanjing Rd; 南京西路1168号22楼; ⊙8.30am-5pm Mon-Fri)
Canada (加拿大领事馆; Jiānádà Lǐngshìguǎn; ☎021-3279 2800; www.shanghai.gc.ca; 8th fl, 1788 West Nanjing Rd; 南京西路1788号8楼; ⊙8.30am-noon & 1-5pm)
France (法国领事馆; Fǎguó Lǐngshìguǎn;☎021-6010 6300; www.consulfrance-shanghai.org; 8th fl, Bldg A, Soho Zhongshan Plaza, 1055 West Zhongshan Rd; 中山西路1055号中山广场A座18楼; ⊙8.15am-12.15pm Mon, 8.45am-12.15pm Tue-Fri)
Germany (德国领事馆; Déguó Lǐngshìguǎn; ☎021-3401 0106; www.shanghai.diplo.de; 181 Yongfu Rd; 永福路181号)
India (☎021-6275 8881; 1008 Shànghǎi International Trade Centre, 2201 West Yan'an Rd)
Ireland (爱尔兰领事馆; Ài'ěrlán Lǐngshìguǎn; ☎021-6010 1360; www.embassyofireland.cn; 700a Shànghǎi Centre, 1376 West Nanjing Rd; 南京西路1376号700a室; ⊙9.30am-12.30pm & 2-5.30pm)
Japan (日本领事馆; Rìběn Lǐngshìguǎn;☎021-5257 4766; www.shanghai.cn.emb-japan.go.jp;

8 Wanshan Rd; 万山路8号; ◎9am-12.30pm & 1.30-5.30pm Mon-Fri)

Nepal (✆021-6272 0259; 16a, 669 West Beijing Rd)

Netherlands (荷兰领事馆; Hélán Lǐngshìguǎn; ✆021-2208 7288; www.hollandinchina. org; 10th fl, Tower B, Dawning Center, 500 Hongbaoshi Rd; 红宝石路500号东银中心东塔10楼; ◎9am-noon & 1-5.30pm Mon-Fri)

New Zealand (新西兰领事馆; Xīnxīlán Lǐngshìguǎn; ✆021-5407 5858; www.nzembassy. com; Room 1605-1607A, 16th fl, The Centre, 989 Changle Rd; 长乐路989号1605-1607A室; ◎8.30am-5pm Mon-Fri)

Thailand (泰王国领事馆; Tàiwángguó Lǐngshìguǎn; ✆021-6288 3030; www.thaishanghai. com; 15th fl, 567 Weihai Rd; 威海路567号15楼; ◎visa office 9.30-11.30am Mon-Fri)

UK (英国领事馆; Yīngguó Lǐngshìguǎn; ✆021-3279 2000; http://ukinchina.fco.gov.uk; Room 319, 3rd fl, Shànghǎi Centre, 1376 West Nanjing Rd; 南京西路1376号301室; ◎8.30am-5.30pm Mon-Fri)

US (美国领事馆; Měiguó Lǐngshìguǎn; ✆after-hour emergency for US citizens 021-3217 4650; http://shanghai.usembassy-china.org.cn; 8th fl, Westgate Tower, 1038 West Nanjing Rd; 南京西路1038号8楼; ◎8.15-11.30am & 1.30-3.30pm Mon-Fri)

SHĚNYÁNG

North Korea (✆024-8685 2742; 37 Beiling Dajie)

South Korea (✆024-2385 3388; 37 Nanshisan Weilu)

US (✆024-2322 1198; 52 Shisi Weilu)

ŪRÜMQI

Kazakhstan (✆0991-369 1444; Hāsàkèsītǎn Lǐngshìguǎn; 216 Kunming Lu; ◎9am-1pm Mon-Fri)

Kyrgyzstan (38 Hetan Beilu; ◎noon-2pm Mon-Fri)

WǓHÀN

France (✆027-6579 7900; Rooms 1701-1708, New World International Trade Center, 568 Jianshe dadao)

Gay & Lesbian Travellers

Greater tolerance exists in the big cities than in the more conservative countryside, but even in urban areas, gay and lesbian visitors should be quite discreet. You will often see Chinese same-sex friends holding hands or putting their arms around each other, but this usually has no sexual connotation.

Spartacus International Gay Guide (Bruno Gmunder Verlag; www.spartacusworld. com/en) Best-selling guide for gay travellers; also available as an iPhone App.

Utopia (www.utopia-asia.com/tipschin.htm) Tips on travelling in China and a complete listing of gay bars nationwide.

Insurance

Carefully consider a travel-insurance policy to cover theft, loss, trip cancellation and medical eventualities. Travel agents can sort this out for you, although it is often cheaper to find good deals with an insurer online or with a broker. Worldwide travel insurance is available at www.lonelyplanet.com/travel-insurance. You can buy, extend and claim online anytime – even if you're already on the road.

Some policies specifically exclude 'dangerous activities' such as scuba diving, skiing and even trekking. Check that the policy covers ambulances or an emergency flight home.

Paying for your airline ticket with a credit card often provides limited travel accident insurance – ask your credit-card company what it's prepared to cover.

You may prefer a policy that pays doctors or hospitals directly rather than reimbursing you for expenditures after the fact. If you have to claim later, ensure you keep all documentation.

Internet Access

Wi-fi accessibility in hotels, cafes, restaurants and bars is generally good. The best option is to bring a wi-fi equipped smartphone, tablet or laptop or use your hotel computer or broadband internet connection.

The Chinese authorities remain mistrustful of the internet, and censorship is heavy-handed. Around 10% of websites are blocked; sites like Google may be slow, while social-networking sites such as Facebook and Twitter are blocked (as is YouTube). Gmail is often inaccessible, as is Google Drive, so plan ahead. Newspapers such as the New York Times are also blocked, as is Bloomberg. Users can get around blocked websites by using a VPN (Virtual Private Network) service such as **Astrill** (www.astrill.com).

Many internet cafes only accept customers with Chinese ID, barring foreigners. In large cities and towns, the area around the train station generally has internet cafes.

The internet icon (@) in hotel reviews indicates the presence of an internet cafe or a terminal where you can get online; wi-fi areas are indicated with a wi-fi icon (📶).

Language Courses

Learning Chinese in China is big business. Weigh up fees and syllabus carefully and check online reviews – some schools are pricey and may use teaching methods unsuited to Westerners. Consider where you would like to study: the Běijīng accent and setting has obvious cachet, but a course in a setting such as Yángshuò can be delightful.

Legal Matters

China does not officially recognise dual nationality or the foreign citizenship of children born in China if one of the parents is a PRC national. If you have Chinese and another nationality you may, in theory, not be allowed to visit China on your foreign passport. In practice, Chinese authorities are not switched on enough to know if you own two passports, and should accept you on a foreign passport. Dual-nationality citizens who enter China on a Chinese passport are subject to Chinese laws and are legally not allowed consular help. If over 16 years of age, carry your passport with you at all times as a form of ID.

Gambling is officially illegal in mainland China. Distributing religious material is also illegal in mainland China.

China takes a particularly dim view of opium and all its derivatives; trafficking in more than 50g of heroin can lead to the death penalty. Foreign-passport holders have been executed in China for drug offences. The Chinese criminal justice system does not ensure a fair trial and defendants are not presumed innocent until proven guilty. If arrested, most foreign citizens have the right to contact their embassy.

Anyone under the age of 18 is considered a minor; the minimum age for driving a car is 18. The age of consent in China is 14; in Hong Kong and Macau it is 16. The age of consent for marriage is 22 for men and 20 for women. There is no minimum age restricting the consumption of alcohol or use of cigarettes.

Money

The Chinese currency is the rénmínbì (RMB), or 'people's money'. The basic unit of RMB is the yuán (元; ¥), which is divided into 10 jiǎo (角), which is again divided into 10 fēn (分). Colloquially, the yuán is referred to as kuài and jiǎo as máo (毛). The fēn has so little value these days that it is rarely used.

The Bank of China issues RMB bills in denominations of ¥1, ¥2, ¥5, ¥10, ¥20, ¥50 and ¥100. Coins come in denominations of ¥1, 5 jiǎo, 1 jiǎo and 5 fēn . Paper versions of the coins remain in circulation.

Hong Kong's currency is the Hong Kong dollar (HK$). The Hong Kong dollar is divided into 100 cents. Bills are issued in denominations of HK$10, HK$20, HK$50, HK$100, HK$500 and HK$1000. Copper coins are worth 50c, 20c and 10c, while the $5, $2 and $1 coins are silver and the $10 coin is nickel and bronze. The Hong Kong dollar is pegged to the US dollar at a rate of US$1 to HK$7.80, though it is allowed to fluctuate a little.

Macau's currency is the pataca (MOP$), which is divided into 100 avos. Bills are issued in denominations of MOP$10, MOP$20, MOP$50, MOP$100, MOP$500 and MOP$1000. There are copper coins worth 10, 20 and 50 avos and silver-coloured MOP$1, MOP$2, MOP$5 and MOP$10 coins. The pataca is pegged to the Hong Kong dollar at a rate of MOP$103.20 to HK$100. In effect, the two currencies are interchangeable and Hong Kong dollars, including coins, are accepted in Macau. Chinese rénmínbì is also accepted in many places in Macau at one-to-one. You can't spend patacas anywhere else, however, so use them before you leave Macau. Prices quoted are in yuán unless otherwise stated.

ATMs

Bank of China and the Industrial & Commercial Bank of China (ICBC) 24-hour ATMs are plentiful, and you can use Visa, MasterCard, Cirrus, Maestro Plus and American Express to withdraw cash. All ATMs accepting international cards have dual-language ability. The network is largely found in sizeable towns and cities. If you plan on staying in China for a few weeks or more, it is advisable to open an account at a bank with a nationwide network of ATMs, such as the Bank of China or ICBC (Industrial and Commercial Bank of China). HSBC and Citibank ATMs are available in larger cities. Keep your ATM receipts so you can exchange your yuán when you leave China.

The exchange rate on ATM withdrawals is similar to that for credit cards, but there is a maximum daily withdrawal amount. Note that banks can charge a withdrawal fee for using the ATM network of another bank, so check with your bank before travelling.

To have money wired from abroad, visit Western Union or Moneygram (www.moneygram.com).

Credit Cards

In large tourist towns, credit cards are relatively straightforward to use, but don't expect to be able to use them everywhere, and always carry enough cash; the exception is in Hong Kong, where international credit cards are accepted almost everywhere (although some shops may try to add a surcharge to offset the commission charged by credit companies, which can range from 2.5% to 7%). Check to see if your credit card company charges a foreign transaction fee (usually between 1% and 3%) for purchases in China.

Where they are accepted, credit cards often deliver a slightly better exchange rate than banks. Money can also be withdrawn at certain ATMs in large cities on credit cards such as Visa, MasterCard and Amex.

Moneychangers

It's best to wait till you reach China to exchange money as the exchange rate will be better. Foreign currency and travellers cheques can be changed at border crossings, international airports, branches of the Bank of China, tourist hotels and some large department stores;

hours of operation for foreign-exchange counters are 8am to 7pm (later at hotels). Top-end hotels will generally change money for hotel guests only. The official rate is given almost everywhere and the exchange charge is standardised, so there is little need to shop around for the best deal.

Australian, Canadian, US, UK, Hong Kong and Japanese currencies and the euro can be changed in China. In some backwaters, it may be hard to change lesser-known currencies; US dollars are still the easiest to change. Lhasa has ATM-style currency exchange machines that can change cash in several currencies into rénmínbì 24 hours a day, with your passport.

Keep at least a few of your exchange receipts. You will need them if you want to exchange any remaining RMB you have at the end of your trip.

Tipping

Almost no one in China (including Hong Kong and Macau) asks for tips. Tipping used to be refused in restaurants, but nowadays many midrange and top-end eateries include their own (often huge) service charge; cheap restaurants do not expect a tip. Taxi drivers throughout China do not ask for or expect tips.

Travellers Cheques

With the prevalence of ATMs across China, travellers cheques are not as useful as they once were and cannot be used everywhere, so always ensure you carry enough ready cash. You should have no problem cashing travellers cheques at tourist hotels, but they are of little use in budget hotels and restaurants. Most hotels will only cash the cheques of guests. If cashing them at banks, aim for larger banks such as the Bank of China or ICBC.

Stick to the major companies such as Thomas Cook, Amex and Visa. In big cities travellers cheques are accepted in almost any currency, but in smaller destinations, it's best to stick to big currencies such as US dollars or UK pounds. Keep your exchange receipts so you can change your money back to its original currency when you leave.

Opening Hours

China officially has a five-day working week. Saturday and Sunday are public holidays.

➡ Banks, offices and government departments open Monday to Friday (roughly 9am until 5pm or 6pm), possibly closing for two hours in the middle of the day; many banks are also open Saturday and maybe Sunday.

➡ Post offices are generally open seven days a week.

➡ Museums generally stay open on weekends and may shut for one day during the week.

➡ Travel agencies and foreign-exchange counters in tourist hotels are usually open seven days a week.

➡ Department stores, shopping malls and shops are open daily from 10am to 10pm.

➡ Internet cafes are typically open 24 hours, but some open at 8am and close at midnight.

➡ Restaurants open from around 10.30am to 11pm; some shut at around 2pm and reopen at 5pm or 6pm.

➡ Bars open in the late afternoon, shutting around midnight or later.

Passports

You must have a passport (护照; hùzhào) on you at all times; it is the most basic travel document and all hotels will insist on seeing it for check-in. It is now mandatory to present your passport when buying train tickets; you will also need it for using internet cafes that accept foreigners.

The Chinese government requires that your passport be valid for at least six months after the expiry date of your visa. You'll need at least one entire blank page in your passport for the visa.

Take an ID card with your photo in case you lose your passport and make photocopies of your passport: your embassy may need these before issuing a new one. You must report the loss to the local Public Security Bureau (PSB), who will issue you with a 'Statement of Loss of Passport'.

Long-stay visitors should register their passport with their embassy.

Post

The international postal service is generally efficient, and airmail letters and postcards will probably take between five and 10 days to reach their destinations. Domestic post is swift – perhaps one or two days from Guǎngzhōu to Běijīng. Intracity post may be delivered the same day it's sent.

China Post operates an express mail service (EMS) that is fast, reliable and ensures that the package is sent by registered post. Not all branches of China Post have EMS.

Major tourist hotels have branch post offices where you can send letters, packets and parcels. Even at cheap hotels you can usually post letters from the front desk. Larger parcels may need to be sent from the town's main post office.

In major cities, private carriers such as **United Parcel Service** (☑800 820 8388; www.ups.com), **DHL** (Dūnháo; ☑800 810 8000; www.cn.dhl. com), **Federal Express** (Liánbāng Kuàidì; ☑800 988 1888;

http://fedex.com/cn) and **TNT Skypak** (☑800 820 9868; www.tnt.com/express/zh_cn) have a pick-up service as well as drop-off centres; call their offices for details.

If you are sending items abroad, take them unpacked with you to the post office to be inspected; an appropriate box or envelope will be found for you. Most post offices offer materials for packaging (including padded envelopes, boxes and heavy brown paper), for which you'll be charged. Don't take your own packaging as it will probably be refused.

Public Holidays

The People's Republic of China has a number of national holidays. Some of the following are nominal holidays that do not result in leave. It's not a great idea to arrive in China or go travelling during the big holiday periods as hotels prices reach their maximum and transport can become tricky.

New Year's Day 1 January

Chinese New Year 19 February 2015, 8 February 2016, 28 January 2017; a week-long holiday for most.

International Women's Day 8 March

Tomb Sweeping Festival First weekend in April; a popular three-day holiday period.

International Labour Day 1 May; for many it's a three-day holiday.

Youth Day 4 May

International Children's Day 1 June

Dragon Boat Festival 20 June 2015, 9 June 2016, 30 May 2017.

Birthday of the Chinese Communist Party 1 July

Anniversary of the Founding of the People's Liberation Army 1 August

Mid-Autumn Festival 27 September 2015, 15 September 2016, 4 October 2017.

National Day 1 October; the big one, a week-long holiday.

GOVERNMENT TRAVEL ADVICE

The following government websites offer travel advisories and information on current hot spots.

Australian Department of Foreign Affairs & Trade (☑1300 139 281; www.smarttraveller.gov.au)

British Foreign & Commonwealth Office (☑0845-850-2829; www.gov.uk/foreign-travel-advice)

Canadian Department of Foreign Affairs & International Trade (☑800-267 6788; http://travel.gc.ca/travelling/advisories)

US State Department (☑888-407 4747; http://travel.state.gov)

Safe Travel

Crime

Travellers are more often the victims of petty economic crime, such as theft, than serious crime. Foreigners are natural targets for pickpockets and thieves – keep your wits about you and make it difficult for thieves to get at your belongings.

High-risk areas in China are train and bus stations, city and long-distance buses (especially sleeper buses), hard-seat train carriages and public toilets.

Women should avoid travelling solo. Even in Běijīng, single women taking taxis have been taken to remote areas and robbed by taxi drivers.

LOSS REPORTS

If something of yours is stolen, report it immediately to the nearest Foreign Affairs Branch of the Public Security Bureau (PSB; 公安局; Gōng'ānjú). Staff will ask you to fill in a loss report before investigating the case.

A loss report is crucial so you can claim compensation if you have travel insurance. Be prepared to spend many hours, perhaps even several days, organising it. Make a copy of your passport in case of loss or theft.

Scams

Con artists are widespread. Well-dressed girls flock along Shànghǎi's East Nanjing Rd, the Bund and Běijīng's Wangfujing Dajie, asking single men to photograph them on their mobile phones before dragging them to expensive cafes or Chinese teahouses, leaving them to foot monstrous bills. 'Poor' art students haunt similar neighbourhoods, press-ganging foreigners into art exhibitions where they are coerced into buying trashy art.

Taxi scams at Běijīng's Capital Airport are legendary; always join the queue at the taxi rank and insist that the taxi driver uses the meter. Try to avoid pedicabs and motorised three wheelers wherever possible; we receive a litany of complaints against pedicab drivers who originally agree on a price and then insist on an alternative figure (sometimes 10 times the sum) once you arrive at the destination.

Be alert at all times if you decide to change money or buy tickets (such as train tickets) on the black market, which we can't recommend.

Always be alert when buying unpriced goods (which is a lot of the time): foreigners are frequently ripped off. Always examine your restaurant bill carefully for hidden extras and, if paying by credit card, ensure there are no extra charges.

Transport

Traffic accidents are the major cause of death in China for people aged between 15 and 45, and the World Health Organization (WHO) estimates there are 600 traffic deaths per day. On long-distance buses, you may find there are no seatbelts, or the seatbelts are virtually unusable through neglect, or inextricably stuffed beneath the seat. Outside of the big cities, taxis are unlikely to have rear seatbelts fitted.

Your greatest danger in China will almost certainly be crossing the road, so develop 360-degree vision and a sixth sense. Crossing only when it is safe to do so could perch you at the side of the road in perpetuity, but don't imitate the local tendency to cross without looking. Note that cars frequently turn on red lights in China, so the green 'walk now' man does not mean it is safe to cross.

Telephone

Mobile Phones

A mobile phone should be the first choice for calls, but ensure your mobile is unlocked for use in China if taking your own. If you have the right phone (eg Blackberry, iPhone, Android), **Skype** (www.skype.com) and **Viber** (www.viber.com) can make calls either very cheap or free with wi-fi access. Also consider buying a data SIM card in China for constant network access away from wi-fi hotspots; plans start at under ¥70 for 300mb of data, 50 minutes of China calls, and around 240 free local SMS per month. If buying 3G SIM cards, China Unicom offers almost twice as much data as China Mobile. China Mobile or China Unicom outlets can sell you a standard SIM card (note that numbers with eights in them are more expensive, numbers with fours are cheaper), which cost from ¥60 to ¥100 and include ¥50 of credit. When this runs out, top up by buying a credit-charging card (*chōngzhí kǎ*) from outlets. Cards are also available from newspaper kiosks and shops displaying the China Mobile sign.

Buying a mobile phone in China is also an option as they are generally inexpensive. Make sure the phone uses W-CDMA, which works on China Unicom and most carriers around the world, and not TD-SCDMA, which works only on China Mobile and not international carriers. Cafes, restaurants and bars in larger towns and cities are frequently wi-fi enabled. Consider investing in a USB portable power bank for charging your phone and other devices while on the road.

Landlines

If making a domestic call, look out for very cheap public phones at newspaper stands (报刊亭; *bàokāntíng*) and hole-in-the-wall shops (小卖部; *xiǎomàibù*); you make your call and then pay the owner. Domestic and international long-distance phone calls can also be made from main telecommunications offices and 'phone bars' (话吧; *huàbà*). Cardless international calls are expensive and it's far cheaper to use an internet phone (IP) card. Public telephone booths are rarely used now in China but may serve as wi-fi hot spots (as in Shànghǎi).

Phonecards

Beyond Skype or Viber, using an IP card on your mobile or a landline phone is much cheaper than calling direct,

VISA TYPES

There are 12 categories of visas (for most travellers, an L visa will be issued).

TYPE	ENGLISH NAME	CHINESE NAME
C	flight attendant	*chéngwù* 乘务
D	resident	*dìngjū* 定居
F	business or student	*fǎngwèn* 访问
G	transit	*guòjìng* 过境
L	travel	*lǚxíng* 旅行
Z	working	*gōngzuò* 工作
M	commercial and trade	*màoyì* 贸易
Q1/Q2	family visits more/less than six months	*qīnshǔ1* 亲属1/ *qīnshǔ2* 亲属2
R	talents/needed skills	*réncái* 人才
S1/S2	Visits to foreign relatives/privates (more/less than six months)	*sīrén1* 私人1/ *sīrén2* 私人2
J1/J2	journalist (more/less than six months)	*jìzhě1* 记者1/ *jìzhě2* 记者2
X1/X2	student (more/less than six months)	*xuéxí1* 学习1/ *xuéxí2* 学习2

but the latter can be hard to find outside the big cities. You dial a local number, punch in your account number, followed by a pin number and finally the number you wish to call. English-language service is usually available. Some IP cards can only be used locally, while others can be used nationwide, while still others are no good for international calls, so it is important to buy the right card (and check the expiry date).

Visas

Applying for Visas
FOR CHINA

Apart from visa-free visits to Hong Kong and Macau and useful 72-hour visa-free transit stays (for visitors from 51 nations) to Běijīng, Shànghǎi, Guǎngzhōu, Xī'ān, Guìlín, Chéngdū, Chóngqìng, Dàlián and Shěnyáng (although you won't be permitted to leave transit cities during your three-day stay), you will need a visa to visit China. Citizens from Japan, Singapore, Brunei, San Marino, Mauritius, the Seychelles and the Bahamas do not require a visa to visit China. There remain a few restricted areas in China that require an additional permit from the PSB. Permits are also required for travel to Tibet, a region that the authorities can suddenly bar foreigners from entering.

Your passport must be valid for at least six months after the expiry date of your visa (nine months for a double-entry visa) and you'll need at least one entire blank page in your passport for the visa. For children under the age of 18, a parent must sign the application form on their behalf.

At the time of writing, the visa application process had become more rigorous and applicants were required to provide the following:

➡ a copy of flight confirmation showing onward/return travel

➡ for double-entry visas, flight confirmation showing all dates of entry and exit

➡ if staying at a hotel in China, confirmation from the hotel (this can be cancelled later if you stay elsewhere)

➡ if staying with friends or relatives, a copy of the information page of their passport, a copy of their China visa and a letter of invitation from them.

At the time of writing, prices for a standard single-entry 30-day visa were as follows:

➡ UK£30 for UK citizens

➡ US$140 for US citizens

➡ US$30 for citizens of other nations.

Double-entry visas:

➡ UK£45 for UK citizens

➡ US$140 for US citizens

➡ US$45 for all other nationals.

Six-month multiple-entry visas:

➡ UK£90 for UK citizens

➡ US$140 for US citizens

➡ US$60 for all other nationals.

A standard 30-day single-entry visa can be issued in four to five working days. In many countries, the visa service has been outsourced from the Chinese embassy to a **Chinese Visa Application Service Centre** (www.visaforchina.org), which levies an extra administration fee. In the case of the UK, a single-entry visa costs UK£30, but the standard administration charge

levied by the centre is an additional UK£36 (three-day express UK£48, postal service UK£54). In some countries, such as the UK, France, the US and Canada, there is more than one service centre nationwide. Visa Application Service Centres are open Monday to Friday.

A standard 30-day visa is activated on the date you enter China, and must be used within three months of the date of issue. Sixty-day and 90-day travel visas are harder to get. To stay longer, you can extend your visa in China.

Visa applications require a completed application form (available from the embassy, visa application service centre or downloaded from its website) and at least one photo (normally 51mm x 51mm). You generally pay for your visa when you collect it. A visa mailed to you will take up to three weeks. In the US and Canada, mailed visa applications have to go via a visa agent, at extra cost. In the US, many people use the **China Visa Service Center** (☑in the US 800 799 6560; www.mychinavisa.com), which offers prompt service. The procedure takes around 10 to 14 days. **CIBT** (www.uk.cibt.com) offers a global network and a fast and efficient turnaround.

Hong Kong is a good place to pick up a China visa. **China Travel Service** (CTS; 广州中国旅行社; Zhōngguó Lǚxíngshè) will be able to obtain one for you, or you can apply directly to the **Visa Office**

of the People's Republic of China (852-3413 2300; www.fmcoprc.gov.hk/eng; 3rd & 4th fl, China Resources Building, 26 Harbour Rd, Wan Chai; 9am-noon & 2-5pm Mon-Fri).

Be aware that American and UK passport holders must pay considerably more for their visas. You must supply two photos. Prices for China visas in Hong Kong are as follows:

Standard visa One-/two-/three-day processing time HK$500/400/200

Double-entry visa One-/two-/three-day processing time HK$600/500/300

Multiple-entry six-month visa One-/two-/three-day processing time HK$800/700/500

Multiple-entry one-, two- or three-year visa One-/two-/three-day processing time HK$1100/1000/800.

You can buy a five-day, Shēnzhèn-only visa (¥160 for most nationalities, ¥469 for Brits; cash only) at the Luóhú border (Lo Wu; 9am to 10.30pm), **Huánggăng** (9am-1pm & 2.30-5pm) and **Shékŏu** (8.45am-12.30pm & 2.30-5.30pm). US citizens must buy a visa in advance in Macau or Hong Kong.

Three-day visas are also available at the **Macau–Zhūhăi border** (¥168 for most nationalities, ¥469 for British, US citizens excluded; 8.30am to 12.15pm, 1pm to 6.15pm and 7pm to 10.30pm). US citizens have to buy a visa in advance in Macau or Hong Kong.

When asked about your itinerary on the application form, list standard tourist destinations; if you are considering going to Tibet or western Xīnjiāng, just leave it off the form. The list you give is not binding. Those working in media or journalism may want to profess a different occupation; otherwise, a visa may be refused or a shorter length of stay than that requested may be granted.

FOR HONG KONG

At the time of writing, most visitors to Hong Kong, including citizens of the EU, Australia, New Zealand, the USA and Canada, could enter and stay for 90 days without a visa. British passport holders get 180 days, while South Africans are allowed to stay 30 days visa-free. If you visit Hong Kong from China, you will need a double-entry, multiple-entry or new visa to re-enter China.

FOR MACAU

Most travellers, including citizens of the EU, Australia, New Zealand, the USA, Canada and South Africa, can enter Macau without a visa for between 30 and 90 days. British passport holders get 180 days. Most other nationalities can get a 30-day visa on arrival, which will cost MOP$100/50/200 per adult/child under 12/family. If you're visiting Macau from China and plan to re-enter China, you will need to be on a multiple- or double-entry visa.

Visa Extensions
FOR CHINA

The Foreign Affairs Branch of the local PSB deals with visa extensions.

First-time extensions of 30 days are usually easy to obtain on single-entry tourist visas; a further extension of a month may be possible, but you may only get another week. Travellers report generous extensions in provincial towns, but don't bank on this. Popping across to Hong Kong to apply for a new tourist visa is another option.

Extensions to single-entry visas vary in price, depending on your nationality. At the time of writing, US travellers paid ¥185, Canadians ¥165, UK citizens ¥160 and Australians ¥100. Expect to wait up to five days for your visa extension to be processed.

The penalty for overstaying your visa in China is up to ¥500 per day. Some travellers have reported having

trouble with officials who read the 'valid until' date on their visa incorrectly. For a one-month travel (L) visa, the 'valid until' date is the date by which you must enter the country (within three months of the date the visa was issued), not the date upon which your visa expires.

FOR HONG KONG

For tourist-visa extensions, inquire at the **Hong Kong Immigration Department** (852-2852 3047; www.immd. gov.hk; 2nd fl, Immigration Tower, 7 Gloucester Rd, Wan Chai; 8.45am-4.30pm Mon-Fri, 9-11.30am Sat). Extensions (HK$160) are not readily granted unless there are extenuating circumstances such as illness.

FOR MACAU

If your visa expires, you can obtain a single one-month extension from the **Macau Immigration Department** (853-2872 5488; Ground fl, Travessa da Amizade; 9am-5pm Mon-Fri).

Residence Permits

The 'green card' is a residence permit, issued to long-term foreign residents in China. Besides needing all the right paperwork, you must also pass a health exam, for which there is a charge. Green cards are valid for five or 10 years. If you lose your card, there's a hefty fee to have it replaced.

Volunteering

Large numbers of Westerners work in China with international development charities such as **VSO** (www. vso.org.uk).

Joy in Action (JIA; www. joyinaction.org) Establishes work camps in places in need in south China.

World Teach (www.world-teach.org) Volunteer teachers.

VSO (www.vso.org.uk) Provides useful experience and the chance to learn Chinese.

Transport

GETTING THERE & AWAY

Flights, cars and tours can be booked online at www.lonelyplanet.com/bookings.

Entering China

No particular difficulties exist for travellers entering China. Chinese immigration officers are scrupulous and highly bureaucratic, but not overly officious. The main requirements are a passport that's valid for travel for six months after the expiry date of your visa, and a visa (see p1003). Travellers arriving in China will receive a health declaration form and an arrivals form to complete.

Air

Airports

Hong Kong, Běijīng and Shànghǎi are China's principal international air gateways; Báiyún International Airport in Guǎngzhōu is of lesser, but growing, importance.

Báiyún International Airport (白云国际机场; Báiyún Guójì Jīchǎng; ☑020-3606 6999; www.baiyunairport.com) In Guǎngzhōu; receiving an increasing number of international flights.

Capital Airport (PEK, Shǒudū Jīchǎng; ☑96158; http://en.bcia.com.cn) Běijīng's international airport; three terminals.

Hong Kong International Airport (HKG; ☑2181 8888; www.hkairport.com) The futuristic passenger terminal consists of eight levels, with check-in on level seven, departures on level six and arrivals on level five. Outlets (including bank branches, moneychangers and five ATMs) total 150, and there are more than 30 cafes, restaurants and bars, and more than 280 check-in counters. Designed by British architect Sir Norman Foster, the airport was the world's largest civil engineering project when it opened in mid-1998, and is on Chek Lap Kok, a largely man-made island off the northern coast of Lantau. It is connected to the mainland by several spans. Among them is the 2.2km-long Tsing Ma Bridge, which is one of the world's largest suspension bridges and is capable of supporting both road and rail transport, including the 34km-long Airport Express high-speed train from Hong Kong Island to Chek Lap Kok via Kowloon.

Hóngqiáo Airport (Hóngqiáo Jīchǎng; ☑3659, 021-6268 8899) In Shànghǎi's west; domestic flights, some international connections.

Pǔdōng International Airport (Pǔdōng Guójì Jīchǎng; ☑021-96990) In Shànghǎi's east; international flights.

Airlines Flying to/ from China

The following list comprises the main airlines flying into Běijīng, Hong Kong, Shànghǎi, Guǎngzhōu and Macau.

Aeroflot Russian Airlines (www.aeroflot.ru)

Air Canada (www.aircanada.ca)

Air China (www.airchina.com)

Air France (www.airfrance.com)

Air Macau (www.airmacau.com.mo)

Air New Zealand (www.airnewzealand.com)

AirAsia (www.airasia.com)

Alitalia (www.alitalia.com)

All Nippon Airways (www.ana.co.jp) Flies to numerous other cities in China.

American Airlines (www.aa.com)

Asiana Airlines (www.flyasiana.com) Also flies to numerous other cities in China.

British Airways (www.britishairways.com)

Cathay Pacific (www.cathaypacific.com)

China Airlines (www.china-airlines.com) Direct flights from Taiwan to numerous other cities in China.

China Eastern Airlines (www.ce-air.com)

China Southern Airlines (www.cs-air.com)

Dragonair (www.dragonair.com)

Emirates Airline (www.emirates.com)

Garuda Indonesia (www.garuda-indonesia.com)

Hong Kong Airlines (www.hkairlines.com)

Japan Airlines (www.jal.com) Also flies to numerous other cities in China.

KLM (www.klm.nl)

Korean Air (www.koreanair.com) Also flies to Qīngdǎo and Shěnyáng.

Lao Airlines (⌨in Guǎngzhōu 020-83884085, in Kūnmíng 0871-6312 5748; www.laoairlines.com) Flights to Jǐnghóng, Kūnmíng and Guǎngzhōu.

Lufthansa Airlines (www.lufthansa.com)

Malaysia Airlines (www.malaysiaairlines.com)

MIAT Mongolian Airlines (www.miat.com)

Nepal Airlines (www.nepalairlines.com.np)

Pakistan International Airlines (www.piac.com.pk)

Philippine Airlines (www.philippineairlines.com)

Qantas Airways (www.qantas.com.au)

Scandinavian Airlines (www.sas.dk)

Silk Air (www.silkair.com)

Singapore Airlines (www.singaporeair.com)

Swiss International Airlines (www.swiss.com)

Thai Airways International (www.thaiairways.com)

Tiger Airways (www.tigerairways.com)

United Airlines (www.ual.com)

Uzbekistan Airways

Vietnam Airlines (www.vietnamair.com.vn)

Virgin Atlantic (www.virgin-atlantic.com)

Tickets

The cheapest tickets to Hong Kong and China exist on price comparison websites or in discount agencies in Chinatowns around the world. Budget and student-travel agents offer cheap tickets, but the real bargains are with agents that deal with the Chinese, who regularly return home. Airfares to China peak between June and September.

The cheapest flights to China are with airlines requiring a stopover at the home airport, such as Air France to Běijīng via Paris, or Malaysia Airlines to Běijīng via Kuala Lumpur.

The best direct ticket deals are available from China's international carriers, such as China Eastern Airlines, Air China or China Southern Airlines.

Firms such as **STA Travel** (www.statravel.co.uk) have offices worldwide and offer competitive prices to most destinations. Beyond internet travel websites – **Expedia** (www.expedia.com) and **Travelocity** (www.travelocity.com) for example – flight comparison websites weigh up the best prices from airline websites, travel agents, search engines and other online sources and are highly versatile, but tend to quote similar fares. They include the following:

Fly.com (www.fly.com)

Kayak (www.kayak.com)

Momondo (www.momondo.com)

Travelsupermarket (www.travelsupermarket.com)

Skyscanner (www.skyscanner.net)

Land

China shares borders with Afghanistan, Bhutan, India, Kazakhstan, Kyrgyzstan, Laos, Mongolia, Myanmar (Burma), Nepal, North Korea, Pakistan, Russia, Tajikistan and Vietnam; the borders with Afghanistan, Bhutan and India are closed. There are also official border crossings between China and its special administrative regions, Hong Kong and Macau.

Lonely Planet *China* guides may be confiscated by officials, primarily at the Vietnam–China border.

Kazakhstan

Border crossings from Ürümqi to Kazakhstan (see p799) are via border posts at Korgas, Ālāshànkǒu, Tǎchéng and Jímùnǎi. Ensure you have a valid Kazakhstan visa (obtainable, at the time of writing, in Ürümqi, or from Běijīng) or China visa.

Apart from Ālāshànkǒu, which links China and Kazakhstan via train, all other border crossings are by bus; you can generally get a bike over, however. Two trains weekly (32 hours) run between Ürümqi and Almaty, and one train per week runs to Astana.

Remember that borders open and close frequently due to changes in government policy; additionally, many are only open when the weather permits. It's always best to check with the **Public Security Bureau** (PSB; Gōng'ānjú) in Ürümqi for the official line.

CLIMATE CHANGE & TRAVEL

Every form of transport that relies on carbon-based fuel generates CO_2, the main cause of human-induced climate change. Modern travel is dependent on aeroplanes, which might use less fuel per kilometre per person than most cars but travel much greater distances. The altitude at which aircraft emit gases (including CO_2) and particles also contributes to their climate change impact. Many websites offer 'carbon calculators' that allow people to estimate the carbon emissions generated by their journey and, for those who wish to do so, to offset the impact of the greenhouse gases emitted with contributions to portfolios of climate-friendly initiatives throughout the world. Lonely Planet offsets the carbon footprint of all staff and author travel.

Kyrgyzstan

There are two routes between China and Kyrgyzstan: one between Kashgar and Osh, via the Irkeshtam Pass; and one between Kashgar and Bishkek, via the dramatic 3752m Torugart Pass. See Getting to Kyrgyzstan, p813.

Laos

From the Měnglà district in China's southern Yúnnán province, you can enter Laos via Boten in Luang Nam Tha province (from Móhān on the China side), while a daily bus runs between Vientiane and Kūnmíng and also from Jǐnghóng to Luang Nam Tha in Laos.

On-the-spot visas for Laos are available at the border; the price of whcdepends on your nationality (although you cannot get a China visa here). See Getting to Laos, p661.

Mongolia

From Běijīng, the Trans-Mongolian Railway trains and the K23 train run to Ulaanbaatar. There are also trains and regular buses between Hohhot and the border town of Erenhot (Èrlián). Mongolian visas on the Chinese side can be acquired in Běijīng, Hohhot or Erenhot. See Getting to Mongolia, p871.

Myanmar (Burma)

The famous Burma Road runs from Kūnmíng in Yúnnán province to the Burmese city of Lashio. The road is open to travellers carrying permits for the region north of Lashio, although you can legally cross the border in only one direction – from the Chinese side (Jiěgào) into Myanmar; however, at the time of writing the border was not open to foreign travellers and flying in from Kūnmíng was the only option. Myanmar visas can only be arranged in Kūnmíng or Běijīng. See Getting to Myanmar, p706.

Nepal

The 865km road connecting Lhasa with Kathmandu is known as the Friendship Highway, currently only traversable by rented vehicle (for foreign travellers). It's a spectacular trip across the Tibetan plateau, the highest point being Gyatso-la Pass (5248m).

Visas for Nepal can be obtained in Lhasa, or at the border at Kodari.

When travelling from Nepal to Tibet, foreigners still have to arrange transport through tour agencies in Kathmandu. Access to Tibet can, however, be restricted for months at a time without warning. See Getting to Nepal p918.

North Korea

Visas for North Korea are not especially hard to arrange although it is not possible to travel independently so you will need to be on a pre-planned tour. Those interested in travelling to North Korea on tours from Běijīng should contact Nicholas Bonner or Simon Cockerell at **Koryo Tours** (☑ 010-6416 7544; www.koryogroup.com; 27 Beisanlitun Nan, Běijīng).

Four international express trains (K27 and K28) run between Běijīng train station and Pyongyang.

See also p112.

Pakistan

The exciting trip on the Karakoram Hwy, said to be the world's highest public international highway, is an excellent way to get to or from Chinese Central Asia. There are buses from Kashgar for the two-day trip to the Pakistani town of Sost via Tashkurgan when the pass is open. Pakistani visas are no longer available to tourists on arrival (and visas are difficult to get in Běijīng), so the safest option is to arrive in China with a visa obtained in your home country. Check the current situation as this could change. See Getting to Pakistan, p813.

Russia

The train from Hā'ěrbīn East to Vladivostok is no longer running but you could take the train to Suífēnhé and take an onward connection there.

The Trans-Mongolian (via Erenhot) and Trans-Manchurian (via Hā'ěrbīn) branches of the Trans-Siberian Railway run from Běijīng to Moscow. There are also border crossings 9km from Mǎnzhōulǐ and at Hēihé. See Getting to Russia p340.

Tajikistan

At the time of writing, the Qolma (Kulma) Pass, linking Kashgar with Murghab, was not yet open to foreign travellers. See Getting to Tajikistan, p813.

Vietnam

Visas are unobtainable at border crossings; Vietnam visas can be acquired in Běijīng, Kūnmíng, Hong Kong and Nánníng. Chinese visas can be obtained in Hanoi. See Getting to Vietnam, p661.

INTERNATIONAL TRAIN ROUTES

In addition to the Trans-Siberian and Trans-Mongolian rail services, the following routes can be travelled by train:

➡ Hung Hom station in Kowloon (Jiǔlóng; Hong Kong; www.mtr.com.hk) to Guǎngzhōu, Shànghǎi, Běijīng

➡ Pyongyang (North Korea) to Běijīng

➡ Almaty (Kazakhstan) to Ürümqi

➡ Astana (Kazakhstan) to Ürümqi

➡ Běijīng to Ulaanbaatar

➡ Běijīng to Hanoi

FRIENDSHIP PASS

China's busiest border with Vietnam is at the obscure Vietnamese town of Dong Dang, 164km northeast of Hanoi. The closest Chinese town to the border is Píngxiáng in Guǎngxī province, about 10km north of the actual border gate.

Seven Hanoi-bound buses run from Nánníng via the Friendship Pass; twice-weekly trains (T5 and T6) connect Běijīng and Hanoi (via Nánníng) while a daily train (T8701 and T8702) links Hanoi with Nánníng (see p622).

HÉKǑU

The Hékǒu–Lao Cai border crossing is 468km from Kūnmíng and 294km from Hanoi. At the time of writing, the only way to reach Vietnam via Hékǒu was by bus from Kūnmíng.

MONG CAI

A third, but little-known border crossing is at Mong Cai in the northeast corner of Vietnam, just opposite the Chinese city of Dōngxīng and around 200km south of Nánníng.

River

At the time of writing, fast ferries from Jǐnghóng in Yúnnán to Chiang Saen in Thailand had been suspended.

Sea

Japan

There are weekly ferries between Osaka and Kōbe and Shànghǎi. There are also twice-weekly boats from Qīngdǎo to Shimonoseki. The weekly ferry from the Tiānjīn International Cruise Home Port to Kōbe (神户; Shénhù) had been suspended indefinitely at the time of writing.

Check in two hours before departure for international sailings. See also Getting to Japan p227.

South Korea

International ferries connect the South Korean port of Incheon with Wēihǎi, Qīngdǎo, Yāntái, Dàlián and Dāndōng. The ferry to Incheon from the Tiānjīn International Cruise Home Port was suspended at the time of research, but should be up and running again.

Tickets can be bought cheaply at the pier, or from **China International Travel Service** (CITS; Zhōngguó Guójì Lǚxíngshè) for a very steep premium.

Taiwan

Daily ferries ply the route between Xiàmén and Kinmen Island in Taiwan, from where you can fly to other major cities in Taiwan. You can also catch a ferry from Fúzhōu's Máwěi ferry terminal to Taiwan's archipelago of Matzu, from where there are boats to Keelung and flights to other cities in Taiwan. See also Getting to Taiwan, p289.

GETTING AROUND

Air

Despite being a land of vast distances, it's quite straightforward to navigate your way terrestrially around China by rail and bus if you have time.

China's air network is extensive and growing. The civil aviation fleet is expected to triple in size over the next two decades, up to 70 new airports were planned for construction by 2015 alone, and 100 more were to be expanded or upgraded. Air safety and quality have improved considerably, but the speed of change generates its own problems: a serious shortage of qualified personnel to fly planes means China needed a reported 18,000 new pilots by 2015. When deciding between flying and using high-speed rail, note that flight delays in China are the worst in the world, according to travel industry monitor FlightStats (while trains almost always leave on time).

Sea Routes

Shuttle buses usually run from **Civil Aviation Administration of China** (CAAC; Zhōngguó Mínháng) offices in towns and cities throughout China to the airport, often via other stops. For domestic flights, arrive at the airport one hour before departure.

Remember to keep your baggage receipt label on your ticket as you will need to show it when you collect your luggage. Planes vary in style and comfort. You may get a hot meal, or just a small piece of cake and an airline souvenir. On-board announcements are delivered in Chinese and English.

Airlines in China

The CAAC is the civil aviation authority for numerous airlines. Some listed here also have subsidiary airlines. Not all Chinese airline websites have English-language capability.

Air China (☑in China 95583; www.airchina.com.cn)

Chengdu Airlines (☑in Chengdu 028-6666 8888; www.chengduair.cc)

China Eastern Airlines (☑in Shànghǎi 95530; www.ceair.com)

China Southern Airlines (☑in Guǎngzhōu 4006 695 539; www.csair.com/en) Serves a web of air routes, including Běijīng, Shànghǎi, Xī'ān and Tiānjīn.

Hainan Airlines (☑in Hǎinán 950718; www.hnair.com)

Shandong Airlines (☑400-60-96777; www.shandongair.com.cn)

Shanghai Airlines (☑in Shànghǎi 95530; www.ceair.com) Owned by China Eastern Airlines.

Shenzhen Airlines (☑in Shēnzhèn 95080; www.shenzhenair.com)

Sichuan Airlines (☑in Chéngdū 4008 300 999; www.scal.com.cn)

Spring Airlines (☑in Shàng-hǎi 95524; www.china-sss.com) Has connections between Shànghǎi and tourist destinations such as Qīngdǎo, Guìlín, Xiàmén and Sānyà.

Tianjin Airlines (☑in Tiānjīn 950710; www.tianjin-air.com)

Tibet Airlines (☑4008 0891 88; www.tibetairlines.com.cn; ⊘7am-9pm) Domestic connections all over China from Lhasa.

Tickets

Except during major festivals and holidays, tickets are easy to purchase, with an oversupply of airline seats. Purchase tickets from branches of the CAAC nationwide, airline offices, travel agents or the travel desk of your hotel; travel agents will usually offer a better discount than airline offices. Discounts are common, except when flying into large cities such as Shànghǎi and Běijīng on the weekend, when the full fare can be the norm. Fares are calculated according to one-way travel, with return tickets simply costing twice the single fare. If flying from Hong Kong or Macau to mainland China, note that these are classified as international flights; it is much cheaper to travel overland into Shēnzhèn, Zhūhǎi or Guǎngzhōu and fly from there.

You can use credit cards at most CAAC offices and travel agents. Departure tax is included in the ticket price.

Ctrip (☑400 619 9999; www.english.ctrip.com) Excellent hotel booking, air and train ticketing website, with English helpline. Useful app available.

Elong (☑400 617 1717, 24hr customer support 010-8467 7827; www.elong.net) Hotel and air ticket booking, with English helpline.

Travel Zen (☑400 720 3355; www.travelzen.com) Air tickets and hotel bookings. English helpline.

Bicycle

Bikes (自行车; zìxíngchē) are an excellent method for getting around China's cities and tourist sights. They can also be invaluable for exploring the countryside and surrounding towns such as Yángshuò.

Hire

Hángzhōu has the world's largest bicycle sharing network with docking stations dotted around the town, however its success (and foreigner-friendly ease of use) has only been fitfully replicated elsewhere in China. Generally, the best places to try are youth hostels that rent out bicycles, as do many hotels, although the latter are more expensive.

Bikes can be hired by the day or by the hour and it is also possible to hire for more than one day. Rental rates vary depending on where you find yourself, but rates start from around ¥10 to ¥15 per day in cities such as Běijīng.

Touring

Cycling through China allows you to go when you want, to see what you want and at your own pace. It can also be an extremely cheap, as well as a highly authentic, way to see the land.

You will have virtually unlimited freedom of movement but, considering the size of China, you will need to combine your cycling days with trips by train, bus, boat, taxi or even planes, especially if you want to avoid particularly steep regions, or areas where the roads are poor or the climate is cold.

A basic packing list for cyclists includes a good bicycle-repair kit, sunscreen and other sun protection, waterproofs, fluorescent strips and camping equipment. Ensure you have adequate clothing, as many routes will be taking you to considerable altitude. Road maps in Chinese are essential for asking locals for directions.

BikeChina (www.bikechina.com) arranges tours and is a good source of information for cyclists coming to China.

Boat

Boat services within China are limited, especially with the growth of high-speed rail and expressways. They're most common in coastal areas, where you are likely to use a boat to reach offshore islands such as Pǔtuóshān or Hǎinán, or the islands off Hong Kong. The Yāntái–Dàlián ferry will probably survive because it saves hundreds of kilometres of overland travel, although a super-long undersea tunnel (p183) is on the drawing board. There's also a ferry every other evening to Dàlián from the **Tiānjīn International Cruise Home Port** (天津国际游轮母港; Tiānjīn Guójì Yóulún Mǔgǎng; ☑022 2560 4137).

The best-known river trip is the three-day boat ride along the Yangzi (Cháng Jiāng) from Chóngqìng to Yíchāng. The Lí River (Lí Jiāng) boat trip from Guìlín to Yángshuò is a popular tourist ride.

Hong Kong employs an out-and-out navy of vessels that connects with the territory's myriad islands, and a number of boats run between the territory and other parts of China, including Macau, Zhūhǎi, Shékǒu (for Shēnzhèn) and Zhōngshān.

Bus

Long-distance bus (长途公共汽车; chángtú gōnggòng qìchē) services are extensive and reach places you cannot reach by train; with the increasing number of intercity highways, journeys are getting quicker.

Buses & Stations

Routes between large cities sport larger, cleaner and more comfortable fleets of private buses, some equipped with toilets and hostesses handing out snacks and mineral water; shorter and more far-flung routes still rely on rattling minibuses into which as many fares as possible are crammed. Buses often wait until they fill up before leaving, or (exasperatingly) trawl the streets looking for fares.

Sleeper buses (卧铺客车; wòpù kèchē) ply popular long-haul routes, costing around double the price of a normal bus service. Bunks can be short, however, and there have been several fatal fires in recent years.

Bus journey times should be used as a rough guide only. You can estimate times for bus journeys on nonhighway routes by calculating the distance against a speed of 25km per hour.

All cities and most towns have one or more long-distance bus station (长途汽车站; chángtú qìchēzhàn), generally located in relation to the direction the bus heads in. In many cities, the train station forecourt doubles as a bus station.

Tickets

Tickets are getting more expensive as fuel prices increase, but are cheaper and easier to get than train tickets; turn up at the bus station and buy your ticket there and then. The earlier you buy, the closer to the front of the bus you will sit, although you may not be able to buy tickets prior to your day of travel. At the time of writing, ID was required for the purchase of bus tickets in restive Xīnjiāng.

Tickets can be hard to procure during national holiday periods.

Dangers & Annoyances

Breakdowns can be a hassle, and some rural roads and provincial routes (especially in the southwest, Tibet and the northwest) remain in bad condition. Precipitous drops, pot holes, dangerous road surfaces and reckless drivers mean accidents remain common. Long-distance journeys can also be cramped and noisy, with Hong Kong films and cacophonous karaoke looped on overhead TVs. Drivers continuously lean on the horn (taking an MP3 player is crucial for one's sanity). Note the following when travelling by bus:

➡ Seat belts are a rarity in many provinces.

➡ Take plenty of warm clothes on buses to high-altitude destinations in winter. A bus breakdown in frozen conditions can prove lethal for those unprepared.

➡ Take a lot of extra water on routes across areas such as the Taklamakan Desert.

Car & Motorcycle

Hiring a car in China has always been complicated or impossible for foreign visitors and in mainland China is currently limited to Běijīng and Shànghǎi, cities that both have frequently gridlocked roads. Throw in the dangers, complexity of Chinese roads for first-time users, and the costs of driving in China and it makes more sense to use the subway/metro system and taxis, both of which are cheap and efficient in Běijīng and Shànghǎi. Hiring a car with a driver from your hotel is possible, but it's generally far cheaper and more convenient to hire a taxi for the day instead.

Driving Licence

To drive in Hong Kong and Macau, you will need an International Driving Permit. Foreigners can drive motorcycles if they are residents in China and have an official Chinese motorcycle licence. International driving permits are generally not accepted in China.

Hire

Běijīng Capital Airport has a **Vehicle Administration Office** (车管所, chēguǎnsuǒ; ☑6453 0010; 1st fl, Terminal 3; ⊙9am-6pm) where you can have a temporary three-month driving licence issued (an international driver's licence is insufficient). This will involve checking your driving licence and a simple medical exam (including an eyesight test). You will need this licence before you can hire a car from **Hertz** (☑400-888-1336; www.hertzchina.com), which has branches at Capital Airport. Check out the **Hertz office** (☑021-6085 1900; Terminal 2; ⊙8am-8pm Mon-Fri & 9am-6pm Sat-Sun) at Shànghǎi's Pǔdōng International Airport for how to obtain a temporary licence in Shànghǎi. There are also branches in both central Běijīng and Shànghǎi. Hire cars from Hertz start from ¥230 per day (up to 150km per day; ¥20,000 deposit). **Avis** (☑400 882 1119) also has a growing network around China, with car rental starting from ¥200 per day (¥5000 deposit).

Road Rules

Cars in China drive on the right-hand side of the road. Even skilled drivers will be unprepared for China's roads: in the cities, cars lunge from all angles and chaos abounds.

Train

For information on travelling by train, see the China by Train chapter, p1012.

Local Transport

Long-distance transport in China is good, but local transport is less efficient, except for cities with metro systems. The choice of local transport is diverse and vehicles can be slow and overburdened, and the network confusing for visitors. Hiring a car is often impractical, while hiring a bike can be inadequate. Unless the town is small, walking is often too tiring. On the plus side, local transport is cheap, taxis are usually ubiquitous and affordable, and metro systems continue to rapidly expand in large tourist towns.

Bus

With extensive networks, buses are an excellent way to get around town, but foreign travellers rarely use them. Ascending a bus, point to your destination on a map and the conductor (seated near the door) will sell you the right ticket. The conductor will usually tell you where to disembark, provided they remember. In conductor-less buses, you put money in a slot near the driver as you embark.

➡ Fares are very cheap (usually ¥1 to ¥2) but buses may be packed.

➡ In cities such as Běijīng, Shànghǎi and Hong Kong, a locally purchased transport card can be used on the buses.

➡ Navigation is tricky for non-Chinese speakers as bus routes at bus stops are generally listed in Chinese, without Pinyin.

➡ In Běijīng and Shànghǎi and other large tourist towns, stops will be announced in English.

Subway, Metro & Light Rail

Going underground or using light rail is fast, efficient and cheap; most networks are either very new or relatively recent and can be found in a rapidly growing number of cities, including Běijīng, Shànghǎi, Sūzhōu, Xī'ān, Hángzhōu, Tiānjīn, Chéngdū, Shēnzhèn, Wǔhàn, Kūnmíng, Chóngqìng and Hong Kong.

Taxi

Taxis (出租汽车; *chūzū qìchē*) are cheap and easy to find. Taxi rates per kilometre are clearly marked on a sticker on the rear side window of the taxi; flag fall varies from city to city, and depends upon the size and quality of the vehicle.

Most taxis have meters but they may only be switched on in larger towns and cities. If the meter is not used (on an excursion out of town, for example, or when hiring a taxi for the day or half-day), negotiate a price before you set off and write the fare down. If you want the meter used, ask for *dǎbiǎo* (打表). Also ask for a receipt (发票; *fāpiào*); if you leave something in the taxi, the taxi number is printed on the receipt so it can be located. Note the following:

➡ Congregation points include train and long-distance bus stations, but usually you can just flag taxis down.

➡ Taxi drivers rarely speak any English so have your destination written down in characters.

➡ If you have communication problems, consider using your mobile to phone your hotel for staff to interpret.

➡ You can hire taxis on a daily or half-day basis, often at reasonable rates (always bargain).

➡ To use the same driver again, ask for his or her card (名片; *míngpiàn*).

➡ In many provinces, taxis often cover long-distance bus routes. They generally charge around 30% to 50% more but are much faster. You need to wait for four passengers.

Other Local Transport

A variety of ramshackle transport options exist across China; always agree on a price in advance (preferably have it written down).

➡ Motor pedicabs are enclosed three-wheeled vehicles (often the same price as taxis).

➡ Pedicabs are pedal-powered versions of motor pedicabs.

➡ Motorbike riders also offer lifts in some towns for what should be half the price of a regular taxi. You must wear a helmet – the driver will provide one.

China by Train

Trains are the best way to travel long distance around China in reasonable speed and comfort. They are also adventurous, exciting, fun, practical and efficient, and ticket prices are reasonable to boot. Colossal investment over recent years has put high-speed rail at the heart of China's rapid modernisation drive. You really don't have to be a trainspotter to find China's railways a riveting subculture and you get to meet the Chinese people at their most relaxed and sociable.

The Chinese Train Network

One of the world's most extensive rail networks, passenger railways penetrate every province in China and high-speed connections are suddenly everywhere. In line with China's frantic economic development and the pressures of transporting 1.4 billion people across the world's third-largest nation, expansion of China's rail network over the past decade has been mind-boggling.

The network currently totals over 103,000km in length. You can climb aboard a train in Běijīng or Shànghǎi and alight in Tibet's capital (although ticket scarcity for trains into Lhasa means it's easier to fly in and take the train out). Lines are poking further into Tibet, with a line to Shigatse opening in 2014. In China, thousands of miles of track are laid every year and new express trains have been zipping across the land since 2007, shrinking once daunting distances. State-of-the-art train stations are ceaselessly appearing, many to serve high-speed links.

With the advent of high-speed D, G and C class express trains, getting between major cities is increasingly a breeze (albeit far more expensive than regular fast trains). High-speed rail has put the squeeze on numerous domestic air routes and the punctuality of trains sees far fewer delays than airports. A high-speed link connected Běijīng and Xī'ān in 2014. The Lánzhōu–Ürümqi high-speed link should be up and running by the time you read this; there is even talk of extending this through Kyrgyzstan, Tajikistan, Uzbekistan, Turkmenistan, Iran and Turkey to Bulgaria. Down south, China is also planning a high-speed link from Kūnmíng in Yúnnán to Singapore, via Laos, Thailand and Malaysia.

Train Types

Chinese train numbers are usually (but not always) prefixed by a letter, designating the category of train.

The fastest, most luxurious and expensive intercity trains are the streamlined, high-speed C, D and G trains, which rapidly shuttle between major cities.

D class trains were the first high-speed trains to appear and breathlessly glide around China at high speed, offering substantial comfort and regular services. D-class temperature-regulated 1st-class carriages have mobile and laptop chargers, seats are two abreast with ample legroom and TV sets. Second-class carriages have five seats in two rows. G class trains are faster than D class trains, but have limited luggage space.

REGULAR TRAINS

TYPE	PINYIN	CHINESE	TOP SPEED (KM/H)
Z class (express)	zhídá	直达	160
T class	tèkuài	特快	140
K class	kuàisù	快速	120

HIGH-SPEED TRAINS

TYPE	PINYIN	CHINESE	TOP SPEED (KM/H)
C class	Chéngjì	城际	350
D class	Dòngchē	动车	250
G class	Gāotiě	高铁	350

Less fast express classes include the overnight Z class trains, while further down the pecking order are older and more basic T and K class trains.

Tickets

It is possible to upgrade (补票; bǔpiào) your ticket once aboard your train. If you have a standing ticket, for example, find the conductor and upgrade to a hard seat, soft seat or hard sleeper (if there are any available).

Soft Sleeper

Soft sleepers are a very comfortable way to travel and work perfectly as mobile hotels; tickets cost much more than hard-class tickets and often sell out, however, so book early. Soft sleepers vary between trains and the best are on the more recent D and Z class trains. All Z class trains are soft-sleeper trains, with very comfortable, up-to-date berths. A few T class trains also offer two-berth compartments, with their own toilet. Tickets on upper berths are slightly cheaper than lower berths. Expect to share with total strangers. If you are asleep, an attendant will wake you to prepare you to disembark so you will have plenty of time to ready your things. Available on some lines, two-bed deluxe soft sleepers usually have a toilet and sink. VIP sleepers, essentially three-bed compartments that one person can book in its entirety, are available on the Kūnmíng–Lìjiāng route.

Soft sleeper carriages contain the following:

➡ four air-conditioned bunks (upper and lower) in a closed compartment

➡ bedding on each berth and a lockable door to the carriage corridor

➡ meals, flat-screen TVs and power sockets on some routes

➡ a small table and stowing space for your bags

➡ a hot-water flask, filled by an attendant (one per compartment).

Hard Sleeper

Hard sleepers are available on slower and less modern T, K and N class trains, as well as trains without a letter prefix. As with soft sleeper, they serve very nicely as an overnight hotel.

There is a small price difference between the numbered berths, with the lowest bunk (下铺; xiàpù) the most expensive and the highest bunk (上铺; shàngpù) the cheapest. The middle bunk (中铺; zhōngpù) is good, as all and sundry invade the lower berth to use it as a seat during the day, while the top one has little headroom and puts you near the speakers. As with soft sleepers, an attendant will wake you well in advance of your station.

Hard-sleeper tickets are the most difficult of all to buy; you almost always need to buy these a few days in advance. Expect:

➡ doorless compartments with half a dozen bunks in three tiers

➡ sheets, pillows and blankets on each berth

➡ a no-smoking policy

➡ lights and speakers out at around 10pm

➡ a hot-water flask, filled by an attendant (one per compartment)

➡ trolleys passing by selling food and drink

➡ a rack above the windows for stowing your baggage.

Seats

Soft-seat class is more comfortable but not nearly as common as hard-seat class. First-class (一等; yīděng) and 2nd-class (二等; èrděng) soft seats are available in D, C and G class high-speed trains. G class trains also offer business class and/or VIP seats, which include a hot meal and added comfort.

First-class comes with TVs, mobile phone and laptop charging points, and seats arranged two abreast.

Second-class soft seats are also very comfortable; staff are very courteous throughout. Overcrowding is not permitted and power points are available. On older trains, soft-seat carriages are often double-decker, and are not as plush as the faster and more modern high-speed express trains.

Hard-seat class is not available on the faster and plusher C, D and G class trains, and is only found on T and K class trains, and trains without a number prefix; a handful of Z class trains have hard seat. Hard-seat class generally has padded seats, but it's hard on your sanity; often unclean and noisy, and painful on the long haul.

Since hard seat is the only class most locals can afford, it's packed to the gills.

You should get a ticket with an assigned seat

TRAVELLING THE TRANS-SIBERIAN RAILWAY

Rolling out of Europe and into Asia, through eight time zones and over 9289km of taiga, steppe and desert, the Trans-Siberian Railway and its connecting routes constitute one of the most famous and most romantic of the world's great train journeys.

There are, in fact, three railways. The 'true' Trans-Siberian line runs from Moscow to Vladivostok. But the routes traditionally referred to as the Trans-Siberian Railway are the two branches that veer off the main line in eastern Siberia for Běijīng.

Since the first option excludes China, most readers of this book will be choosing between the Trans-Mongolian and the Trans-Manchurian railway lines. The Trans-Mongolian route (Běijīng to Moscow, 7865km) is faster, but requires an additional visa and another border crossing – on the plus side, you also get to see some of the Mongolian countryside. The Trans-Manchurian route is longer (Běijīng to Moscow, 9025km).

See Lonely Planet's *Trans-Siberian Railway* for further details.

Trans-Mongolian Railway

Trains offer deluxe two-berth compartments (with shared shower), 1st-class four-berth compartments and 2nd-class four-berth compartments. Tickets for 2nd class/1st class/deluxe cost from around ¥3496/5114/5064 to Moscow, ¥1222/1723/1883 to Ulaanbaatar and ¥2559/3734/4052 to Novosibirsk. Ticket prices are cheaper if you travel in a group. The K23 service departs on Sunday (2nd/1st class ¥1259/1849, 11.22am, 30 hours) and terminates at Ulaanbaatar on Monday.

➡ From Běijīng: train K3 leaves Běijīng Train Station on its five-day journey to Moscow at 11.22am every Tuesday, passing through Dàtóng, Ulaanbaatar and Novosibirsk, arriving in Moscow the following Monday at 1.58pm.

number; if seats have sold out, ask for a standing ticket, which gets you on the train, where you may find a seat or can upgrade; otherwise you will have to stand in the carriage or between carriages (with the smokers).

Hard-seat sections on newer trains are air-conditioned and less crowded.

Buying Tickets

The Achilles heel of China's overburdened rail system, buying tickets can be a pain.

Most tickets are one way only, with prices calculated per kilometre and adjustments made depending on the class of train, availability of air-con, type of sleeper and bunk positioning.

Some tips on buying train tickets:

➡ Never aim to get a sleeper ticket on the day of travel – plan and purchase ahead.

➡ Most tickets can be booked 18 days in advance of your departure date when booking in person at ticket offices, and 20 days when booking online.

➡ Buying tickets for hard-seat carriages at short notice is usually no hassle, but it may be a standing ticket rather than a numbered seat.

➡ You can only buy tickets with cash or bank cards

that are part of the Chinese UnionPay network.

➡ You will need your passport when buying a ticket (the number is printed on your ticket) at all train ticket offices.

➡ All automated ticket machines (eg at Shànghǎi Train Station) require Chinese ID (ie your passport will not work); you will need to queue at the ticket window.

➡ As with air travel, buying tickets around the Chinese New Year, 1 May and 1 October holiday periods can be very hard.

TRAIN TICKETS

TICKET TYPE	PINYIN	CHINESE
soft sleeper	*ruǎnwò*	软卧
hard sleeper	*yìngwò*	硬卧
soft seat	*ruǎnzuò*	软座
hard seat	*yìngzuò*	硬座
standing ticket	*wúzuò* or *zhànpiào*	无座\站票

➡ From Moscow: train K4 leaves at 9.35pm on Tuesday, arriving in Běijīng Train Station the following Monday at 2.04pm. Departure and arrival times may fluctuate slightly.

Trans-Manchurian Railway

Trains have 1st-class two-berth compartments and 2nd-class four-berth compartments; prices are similar to those on the Trans-Mongolian Railway.

➡ From Běijīng: train K19 departs Běijīng Train Station at 11pm on Saturday arriving in Moscow (via Manzhōulǐ) the following Friday at 5.58pm.

➡ From Moscow: train K20 leaves Moscow at 11.58pm on Saturday, arriving at Běijīng Train Station the following Friday at 5.32am. Departure and arrival times may fluctuate slightly.

Visas

Travellers will need Russian and Mongolian visas for the Trans-Mongolian Railway, as well as a Chinese visa. These can often be arranged along with your ticket by travel agents such as China International Travel Service (CITS).

Buying Tickets

Book well in advance (especially in summer); in Běijīng tickets can be conveniently purchased and booked in advance in central Běijīng from **CITS** (Zhōngguó Guójì Lǚxíngshè; www. cits.net; ☑010-6512 0507; Běijīng International Hotel, 9 Jianguomen Neidajie), for a ¥50 mark-up. Tickets can also be booked with a mark-up through **China DIY Travel** (www.china-diy-travel. com; Commission $10 per ticket).

➡ Tickets on many routes (such as to Lhasa) can be very hard to get in July and August; consider flying to distant destinations.

➡ Expect to queue for up to half an hour or more for a train ticket at the station; ticket offices outside of the station are often less busy.

➡ Avoid black market tickets: your passport number must be on the ticket.

➡ Refunds for lost train tickets are arduous and involve purchasing a new ticket and getting a refund at the other end once it has been proved no one occupied your seat.

➡ If you miss your D or G class train, you will be allowed to take the next available train on the same day only, at no charge. For all other trains, your ticket is forfeited (unless your connecting train was late).

Ticket Offices & Buying Online

Ticket offices (售票厅; shòupiàotīng) at train stations are usually to one side of the main train station entrance. Automated ticket machines operate on some routes but never accept foreign passports as ID. At large stations there should be a window manned by someone with basic English skills.

Alternatively, independent train ticket offices usually exist elsewhere in town where tickets can be purchased for a ¥5 commission without the same kind of queues; we've listed these where possible. Larger post offices may also sell train tickets. Your hotel will also be able to rustle up a ticket for you for a commission, and so can a travel agent.

You can buy tickets online at www.12306.cn but the website is Chinese-language only and you will need a Chinese bankcard. It's cheaper to buy your ticket at the station, but tickets can be bought online at the follow-ing (China DIY Travel is the cheapest):

China DIY Travel (www.china-diy-travel.com; Commission $10 per ticket)

CTrip (☑400 619 9999; www. english.ctrip.com)

China Trip Advisor (www. chinatripadvisor.com)

For trains from Hong Kong to Shànghǎi, Guǎngzhōu or Běijīng, tickets can be ordered online at no mark-up from **KCRC** (www.mtr.com.hk), however for Běijīng or Shànghǎi a faster alternative is the high-speed trains from Shēnzhèn to Shànghǎi (D train) and Běijīng (G train), which take around 10 hours compared to 20 to 24 hours for departures from Hong Kong.

You can also find English-language train timetables on these websites.

To get a refund (退票; tuìpiào) on an unused ticket, windows exist at large train stations where you can get from 80% to 95% of your ticket value back, depending on how many days prior to the departure date you cancel.

CHINA TRAIN ROUTES

ROUTE	DURATION	FARE (SEAT/SLEEPER)
Běijīng West–Xī'ān North	5½-6hr	2nd/1st ¥515/824
Běijīng West–Guìlín	10½hr	2nd/1st class ¥806/1249
Běijīng–Dàtóng	6½hr	hard seat/sleeper ¥54/104
Běijīng South–Hángzhōu	5hr	2nd/1st class ¥540/909
Běijīng West–Kūnmíng	33hr	hard seat/sleeper ¥317/555
Běijīng West–Lhasa	43hr	hard/soft sleeper ¥742/1186
Běijīng South–Qīngdǎo	4½hr	2nd/1st class ¥314/474
Běijīng South–Shànghǎi Hóngqiáo	5½hr	2nd/1st class ¥553/933
Běijīng South–Tiānjīn	33min	2nd/1st class ¥54/65
Shànghǎi Hóngqiáo–Hángzhōu	1hr	2nd/1st class ¥77/123
Shànghǎi Hóngqiáo–Shēnzhèn North	8½hr	hard seat/sleeper ¥478/593
Shànghǎi–Lhasa	48hr	hard seat/sleeper ¥402/817
Shànghǎi Hóngqiáo–Nánjīng South	1½hr	2nd/1st class ¥134/229
Shànghǎi Hóngqiáo–Wǔhàn	6hr	2nd/1st class ¥302/428
Shànghǎi Hóngqiáo–Xiàmén North	8hr	2nd/1st class ¥328/413
Shànghǎi–Xī'ān North	10½hr	2nd class seat/soft sleeper ¥338/834
Píngyáo–Xī'ān North	2hr	2nd/1st class ¥150/187
Shēnzhèn–Guìilín	13½hr	hard seat/sleeper ¥128/230
Kūnmíng–Lìjiāng	7-10hr	hard/soft sleeper ¥147/226
Kūnmíng–Chéngdū	17hr	hard seat/sleeper ¥138/246
Kūnmíng-Guìlín	18-22hr	hard seat/sleeper ¥152/270
Ürümqi–Kashgar	24hr	hard/soft sleeper ¥190/339
Wǔhàn–Guǎngzhōu South	4hr	2nd/1st class ¥463/738
Xī'ān North–Luòyáng Lóngmén	2hr	2nd/1st class ¥174/279
Běijīng West–Píngyáo	4hr	2nd/1st class ¥225/322

Train Travel

Trains are generally highly punctual in China and are usually a safe way to travel. Train stations are often conveniently close to the centre of town. On entering a large old-style station (such as Běijīng West Train Station), you will have to find the correct waiting room number, displayed on an illuminated screen as you walk in. Modern stations (such as Shànghǎi Hóngqiáo Train Station) are more straightforward and intelligently designed, without waiting rooms; instead your platform number will appear on the screen.

Trolleys of food and drink are wheeled along carriages during the trip, but prices are high and the selection is limited. You can also load up on mineral water and snacks at stations, where hawkers sell items from platform stalls. Long-distance trains should have a canteen carriage (餐厅车厢; cāntīng chēxiāng); they are sometimes open through the night.

In each class of sleeper, linen is clean and changed for each journey; beds are generally bedbug-free.

If taking a sleeper train, you will generally be required to exchange your paper ticket for a plastic or metal card with your bunk number on it. The conductor then knows when you are due to disembark, and will awake you in time to return your ticket to you.

Internet Resources

The Man in Seat 61 (www.seat61.com/China.htm)
Travel China Guide (www.travelchinaguide.com)
China Tibet Train (www.chinatibettrain.com)

Health

China is a reasonably healthy country to travel in, but some health issues should be noted. Pre-existing medical conditions and accidental injury (especially traffic accidents) account for most life-threatening problems, but becoming ill in some way is not unusual. Outside of the major cities, medical care is often inadequate, and food and waterborne diseases are common. Malaria is still present in some parts of the country, and altitude sickness can be a problem, particularly in Tibet.

In case of accident or illness, it's best just to get a taxi and go to hospital directly.

The following advice is a general guide only and does not replace the advice of a doctor trained in travel medicine.

BEFORE YOU GO

➡ Pack medications in their original, clearly labelled containers.

➡ If you take any regular medication, bring double your needs in case of loss or theft.

➡ Take a signed and dated letter from your physician describing your medical conditions and medications (using generic names).

➡ If carrying syringes or needles, ensure you have a physician's letter documenting their medical necessity.

➡ If you have a heart condition, bring a copy of your ECG taken just prior to travelling.

➡ Get your teeth checked before you travel.

➡ If you wear glasses, take a spare pair and your prescription.

In China you can buy some medications over the counter without a doctor's prescription, but not all, and in general it is not advisable to buy medications locally without a doctor's advice. Fake medications and poorly stored or out-of-date drugs are also common, so try to take your own.

Insurance

➡ Even if you are fit and healthy, don't travel without health insurance – accidents happen.

➡ Declare any existing medical conditions you have (the insurance company *will* check if your problem is pre-existing and will not cover you if it is undeclared).

➡ You may require extra cover for adventure activities such as rock climbing or skiing.

➡ If you're uninsured, emergency evacuation is expensive; bills of more than US$100,000 are not uncommon.

➡ Ensure you keep all documentation related to any medical expenses you incur.

Vaccinations

Specialised travel-medicine clinics stock all available vaccines and can give specific recommendations for your trip. The doctors will consider your vaccination history, the length of your trip, activities you may undertake and underlying medical conditions, such as pregnancy.

➡ Visit a doctor six to eight weeks before departure, as most vaccines don't produce immunity until at least two weeks after they're given.

➡ Ask your doctor for an International Certificate of Vaccination (otherwise known as the 'yellow booklet'), listing all vaccinations received.

➡ The only vaccine required by international regulations is yellow fever. Proof of vaccination against yellow fever is only required if you have visited a country in the yellow-fever zone within the six days prior to entering China. If you are travelling to China directly from South America or Africa, check with a travel clinic as to whether you need a yellow-fever vaccination.

Medical Checklist

Recommended items for a personal medical kit:

➡ Antibacterial cream, eg mucipirocin

➡ Antibiotics for diarrhoea, including norfloxacin, ciprofloxacin or azithromycin for bacterial diarrhoea; or tinidazole for giardia or amoebic dysentery

➡ Antibiotics for skin infections, eg amoxicillin/clavulanate or cephalexin

➡ Antifungal cream, eg clotrimazole

➡ Antihistamine, eg cetrizine for daytime and promethazine for night-time

➡ Anti-inflammatory, eg ibuprofen

➡ Antiseptic, eg Betadine

➡ Antispasmodic for stomach cramps, eg Buscopan

➡ Decongestant, eg pseudoephedrine

➡ Diamox if going to high altitudes

➡ Elastoplasts, bandages, gauze, thermometer (but

RECOMMENDED VACCINATIONS

The World Health Organization (WHO) recommends the following vaccinations for travellers to China:

Adult diphtheria and tetanus (ADT) Single booster recommended if you've not received one in the previous 10 years. Side effects include a sore arm and fever. An ADT vaccine that immunises against pertussis (whooping cough) is also available and may be recommended by your doctor.

Hepatitis A Provides almost 100% protection for up to a year; a booster after 12 months provides at least another 20 years' protection. Mild side effects such as a headache and sore arm occur in 5% to 10% of people.

Hepatitis B Now considered routine for most travellers. Given as three shots over six months; a rapid schedule is also available. There is also a combined vaccination with hepatitis A. Side effects are mild and uncommon, usually a headache and sore arm. Lifetime protection results in 95% of people.

Measles, mumps and rubella (MMR) Two doses of MMR is recommended unless you have had the diseases. Occasionally a rash and a flu-like illness can develop a week after receiving the vaccine. Many adults under 40 require a booster.

Typhoid Recommended unless your trip is less than a week. The vaccine offers around 70% protection, lasts for two to three years and comes as a single shot. Tablets are also available; however, the injection is usually recommended as it has fewer side effects. A sore arm and fever may occur. A vaccine combining hepatitis A and typhoid in a single shot is now available.

Varicella If you haven't had chickenpox, discuss this vaccination with your doctor.

The following immunisations are recommended for travellers spending more than one month in the country or those at special risk:

Influenza A single shot lasts one year and is recommended for those over 65 years of age or with underlying medical conditions such as heart or lung disease.

Japanese B encephalitis A series of three injections with a booster after two years. Recommended if spending more than one month in rural areas in the summer months, or more than three months in the country.

Pneumonia A single injection with a booster after five years is recommended for all travellers over 65 years of age or with underlying medical conditions that compromise immunity, such as heart or lung disease, cancer or HIV.

Rabies Three injections in all. A booster after one year will then provide 10 years' protection. Side effects are rare – occasionally a headache and sore arm.

Tuberculosis A complex issue. High-risk adult long-term travellers are usually recommended to have a TB skin test before and after travel, rather than vaccination. Only one vaccine is given in a lifetime. Children under five spending more than three months in China should be vaccinated.

Pregnant women and children should receive advice from a doctor who specialises in travel medicine.

not mercury), sterile needles and syringes, safety pins and tweezers

➜ Indigestion tablets, such as Quick-Eze or Mylanta

➜ Insect repellent containing DEET

➜ Iodine tablets to purify water (unless you're pregnant or have a thyroid problem)

➜ Laxative, eg coloxyl

➜ Oral-rehydration solution (eg Gastrolyte) for diarrhoea, diarrhoea 'stopper' (eg loperamide) and antinausea medication (eg prochlorperazine)

➜ Paracetamol

➜ Permethrin to impregnate clothing and mosquito nets

➜ Steroid cream for rashes, eg 1% to 2% hydrocortisone

➜ Sunscreen

➜ Thrush (vaginal yeast infection) treatment, eg clotrimazole pessaries or Diflucan tablet

➜ Urinary infection treatment, eg Ural

Websites

Centers for Disease Control & Prevention (www.cdc.gov)

Lonely Planet (www.lonelyplanet.com)

MD Travel Health (www.mdtravelhealth.com) Provides complete travel-health recommendations for every country; updated daily.

World Health Organization (www.who.int/ith) Publishes the excellent *International Travel & Health*, revised annually and available online.

Further Reading

➜ *Healthy Travel – Asia & India* (Lonely Planet) Handy pocket size, packed with useful information.

➜ *Traveller's Health* by Dr Richard Dawood.

➜ *Travelling Well* (www.travellingwell.com.au) by Dr Deborah Mills.

IN CHINA

Availability of Health Care

Good clinics catering to travellers can be found in major cities. They are more expensive than local facilities but you may feel more comfortable dealing with a Western-trained doctor who speaks your language. These clinics usually have a good understanding of the best local hospital facilities and close contacts with insurance companies should you need evacuation.

If you think you may have a serious disease, especially malaria, do not waste time – get to the nearest quality facility. To find the nearest reliable medical facility, contact your insurance company or your embassy. Hospitals are listed in the Information sections in cities and towns throughout the guide.

Infectious Diseases

Dengue

This mosquito-borne disease occurs in some parts of southern China. There is no vaccine so avoid mosquito bites. The dengue-carrying mosquito bites day and

night; so use insect-avoidance measures at all times. Symptoms include high fever, severe headache and body ache. Some people develop a rash and diarrhoea. There is no specific treatment – just rest and paracetamol. Do not take aspirin.

Hepatitis A

A problem throughout China, this food-and-waterborne virus infects the liver, causing jaundice (yellow skin and eyes), nausea and lethargy. There is no specific treatment for hepatitis A; you just need to allow time for the liver to heal. All travellers to China should be vaccinated.

Hepatitis B

The only sexually transmitted disease that can be prevented by vaccination, hepatitis B is spread by contact with infected body fluids. The long-term consequences can include liver cancer and cirrhosis. All travellers to China should be vaccinated.

Japanese B Encephalitis

A rare disease in travellers; however, vaccination is recommended if you're in rural areas for more than a month during summer, or if spending more than three months in the country. No treatment is available; one-third of infected people die, another third suffer permanent brain damage.

Malaria

Malaria has been nearly eradicated in China; it is not generally a risk for visitors to the cities and most tourist areas. It is found mainly in rural areas in the southwestern region bordering Myanmar, Laos and Vietnam, principally Hǎinán, Yúnnán and Guǎngxī. More limited risk exists in the remote rural areas of Fújiàn, Guǎngdōng, Guìzhōu and Sìchuān. Generally, medication is only advised if you are visiting rural Hǎinán, Yúnnán or Guǎngxī.

To prevent malaria:

➡ Avoid mosquitoes and take antimalarial medications (most people who catch malaria are taking inadequate or no antimalarial medication).

➡ Use an insect repellent containing DEET on exposed skin (natural repellents such as citronella can be effective, but require more frequent application than products containing DEET).

➡ Sleep under a mosquito net impregnated with permethrin.

➡ Choose accommodation with screens and fans (if it's not air-conditioned).

➡ Impregnate clothing with permethrin in high-risk areas.

➡ Wear long sleeves and trousers in light colours.

➡ Use mosquito coils.

➡ Spray your room with insect repellent before going out for your evening meal.

Rabies

An increasingly common problem in China, this fatal disease is spread by the bite or lick of an infected animal, most commonly a dog. Seek medical advice immediately after any animal bite and commence postexposure treatment. The pretravel vaccination means the post-bite treatment is greatly simplified.

If an animal bites you:

➡ Gently wash the wound with soap and water, and apply an iodine-based antiseptic.

➡ If you are not prevaccinated, you will need to receive rabies immunoglobulin as soon as possible, followed by a series of five vaccines over the next month. Those who have been prevaccinated require only two shots of vaccine after a bite.

➡ Contact your insurance company to locate the nearest clinic stocking rabies immunoglobulin and vaccine. Immunoglobulin is often unavailable outside of major centres, but it's crucial that you get to a clinic that has immunoglobulin as soon as possible if you have had a bite that has broken the skin.

Schistosomiasis (Bilharzia)

This disease occurs in the central Yangzi River (Cháng Jiāng) basin, carried in water by minute worms that infect certain varieties of freshwater snail found in rivers, streams, lakes and, particularly, behind dams. The infection often causes no symptoms until the disease is well established (several months to years after exposure); any resulting damage to internal organs is irreversible. Effective treatment is available.

➡ Avoid swimming or bathing in fresh water where bilharzia is present.

➡ A blood test is the most reliable way to diagnose the disease, but the test will not show positive until weeks after exposure.

Typhoid

Typhoid is a serious bacterial infection spread via food and water. Symptoms include headaches, a high and slowly progressive fever, perhaps accompanied by a dry cough and stomach pain. Vaccination is not 100% effective, so still be careful about what you eat and drink. All travellers spending more than a week in China should be vaccinated.

Traveller's Diarrhoea

Between 30% and 50% of visitors will suffer from traveller's diarrhoea within two weeks of starting their trip. In most cases, the ailment

---

DRINKING WATER

Follow these tips to avoid becoming ill.

➡ Never drink tap water.

➡ Bottled water is generally safe – check the seal is intact at purchase.

➡ Avoid ice.

➡ Avoid fresh juices – they may have been watered down.

➡ Boiling water is the most efficient method of purifying it.

➡ The best chemical purifier is iodine. It should not be used by pregnant women or those with thyroid problems.

➡ Water filters should also filter out viruses. Ensure your filter has a chemical barrier such as iodine and a pore size of less than 4 microns.

is caused by bacteria and responds promptly to treatment with antibiotics.

Treatment consists of staying hydrated; rehydration solutions such as Gastrolyte are best. Antibiotics such as norfloxacin, ciprofloxacin or azithromycin will kill the bacteria quickly. Loperamide is just a 'stopper' and doesn't cure the problem; it can be helpful, however, for long bus rides. Don't take loperamide if you have a fever, or blood in your stools. Seek medical attention if you do not respond to an appropriate antibiotic.

➡ Eat only at busy restaurants with a high turnover of customers.

➡ Eat only freshly cooked food.

➡ Avoid food that has been sitting around in buffets.

➡ Peel all fruit, cook vegetables and soak salads in iodine water for at least 20 minutes.

➡ Drink only bottled mineral water.

Amoebic Dysentery

Amoebic dysentery is actually rare in travellers and is over-diagnosed. Symptoms are similar to bacterial diarrhoea – fever, bloody diarrhoea and generally feeling unwell. Always seek reliable medical care if you have blood in your diarrhoea. Treatment involves two drugs: tinidazole or metronidazole to kill the parasite in your gut, and then a second drug to kill the cysts. If amoebic dysentery is left untreated, complications such as liver or gut abscesses can occur.

Giardiasis

Giardiasis is a parasite relatively common in travellers. Symptoms include nausea, bloating, excess gas, fatigue and intermittent diarrhoea. 'Eggy' burps are often attributed solely to giardia, but are not specific to the parasite. Giardiasis will eventually go away if left untreated, but this can take months. The treatment of choice is tinidazole, with metronidazole a second option.

Intestinal Worms

These parasites are most common in rural, tropical areas. Some may be ingested in food such as undercooked meat (eg tapeworms) and some enter through your skin (eg hookworms). Consider having a stool test when you return home.

Environmental Hazards

Air Pollution

Air pollution is a significant and worsening problem in many Chinese cities. People with underlying respiratory conditions should seek advice from their doctor prior to travel to ensure they have adequate medications in case their condition worsens. Take treatments such as throat lozenges, and cough and cold tablets.

Altitude Sickness

There are bus journeys in Tibet, Qīnghǎi and Xīnjiāng where the road goes above 5000m. Acclimatising to such extreme elevations takes several weeks at least, but most travellers come up from sea level very fast – a bad move! Acute mountain sickness (AMS) results from a rapid ascent to altitudes above 2700m. It usually commences within 24 to 48 hours of arriving at altitude, and symptoms include headache, nausea, fatigue and loss of appetite (feeling much like a hangover).

If you have altitude sickness, the cardinal rule is that you must not go higher as you are sure to get sicker and could develop one of the more severe and potentially deadly forms of the disease: high-altitude pulmonary oedema (HAPE) and high-altitude cerebral oedema (HACE). Both are medical emergencies and, as there are no rescue facilities similar to those in the Nepal Himalaya, prevention is the best policy.

AMS can be prevented by 'graded ascent'; it is recommended that once you are above 3000m you ascend a maximum of 300m daily with an extra rest day every 1000m. You can also use a medication called Diamox as a prevention or treatment for AMS, but you should discuss this first with a doctor experienced in altitude medicine. Diamox should not be taken by people with a sulphur drug allergy.

If you have altitude sickness, rest where you are for a day or two until your symptoms resolve. You can then carry on, but ensure you follow the graded-ascent guidelines. If symptoms get worse, descend immediately before you are faced with a life-threatening situation. There is no way of predicting who will suffer from AMS, but certain factors predispose you to it: rapid ascent, carrying a heavy load, and having a seemingly minor illness such as a chest infection or diarrhoea. Make sure you drink at least 3L of noncaffeinated drinks daily to stay well hydrated.

Heat Exhaustion

Dehydration or salt deficiency can cause heat exhaustion. Take time to acclimatise to high temperatures, drink sufficient liquids and avoid physically demanding activity.

Salt deficiency is characterised by fatigue, lethargy, headaches, giddiness and muscle cramps; salt tablets may help, but adding extra salt to your food is better.

Hypothermia

Be particularly aware of the dangers of trekking at high altitudes or simply taking a long bus trip over mountains. In Tibet it can go from being mildly warm to blisteringly cold in minutes – blizzards can appear from nowhere.

Progress from very cold to dangerously cold can be rapid due to a combination of wind, wet clothing, fatigue and hunger, even if the air temperature is above freezing. Dress in layers; silk, wool and some artificial fibres are all good insulating materials. A hat is important, as a lot of heat is lost through the head. A strong, waterproof outer layer (and a space blanket for emergencies) is essential. Carry basic supplies, including food containing simple sugars, and fluid to drink.

Symptoms of hypothermia are exhaustion, numb skin (particularly the toes and fingers), shivering, slurred speech, irrational or violent behaviour, lethargy, stumbling, dizzy spells, muscle cramps and violent bursts of energy.

To treat mild hypothermia, first get the person out of the wind and/or rain, remove their clothing if it's wet, and replace it with dry, warm clothing. Give them hot liquids – not alcohol – and high-calorie, easily digestible food. Early recognition and treatment of mild hypothermia is the only way to prevent severe hypothermia, a critical condition that requires medical attention.

Insect Bites & Stings

Bedbugs don't carry disease but their bites are very itchy. Treat the itch with an antihistamine.

Lice inhabit various parts of the human body, most commonly the head and pubic areas. Transmission is via close contact with an affected person. Lice can be difficult to treat, but electric lice combs/detectors can be effective (pick one up before travelling); otherwise you may need numerous applications of an antilice shampoo such as permethrin. Pubic lice (crab lice) are usually contracted from sexual contact.

Ticks are contracted by walking in rural areas, and are commonly found behind the ears, on the belly and in armpits. If you have had a tick bite and experience symptoms such as a rash, fever or muscle aches, see a doctor. Doxycycline prevents some tick-borne diseases.

Women's Health

Pregnant women should receive specialised advice before travelling. The ideal time to travel is in the second trimester (between 14 and 28 weeks), when the risk of pregnancy-related problems is at its lowest and pregnant women generally feel at their best. During the first trimester, miscarriage is a risk; in the third trimester, complications such as premature labour and high blood pressure are possible. Travel with a companion and carry a list of quality medical facilities for your destination, ensuring you continue your standard antenatal care at these facilities. Avoid rural areas with poor transport and medical facilities. Above all, ensure travel insurance covers all pregnancy-related possibilities, including premature labour.

Malaria is a high-risk disease in pregnancy. The World Health Organization recommends that pregnant women do not travel to areas with chloroquine-resistant malaria.

Traveller's diarrhoea can quickly lead to dehydration and result in inadequate blood flow to the placenta. Many drugs used to treat various diarrhoea bugs are not recommended in pregnancy. Azithromycin is considered safe.

Heat, humidity and antibiotics can all contribute to thrush. Treatment is with antifungal creams and pessaries such as clotrimazole. A practical alternative is a single tablet of fluconazole (Diflucan). Urinary tract infections can be precipitated by dehydration or long bus journeys without toilet stops; bring suitable antibiotics.

Supplies of sanitary products may not be readily available in rural areas. Birth-control options may be limited, so bring adequate supplies of your own form of contraception.

Traditional Chinese Medicine

Traditional Chinese Medicine (TCM) views the human body as an energy system in which the basic substances of qì (气; vital energy), jīng (精; essence), xuè (血; blood) and tǐyè (体液; body fluids, blood and other organic fluids) function. The concept of yīn (阴) and yáng (阳) is fundamental to the system. Disharmony between yīn and yáng or within the basic substances may be a result of internal causes (emotions), external causes (climatic conditions) or miscellaneous causes (work, exercise, stress etc). Treatment includes acupuncture, massage, herbs, diet and qì gōng (气功), which seeks to bring these elements back into balance. Treatments can be particularly useful for treating chronic diseases and ailments such as fatigue, arthritis, irritable bowel syndrome and some chronic skin conditions.

Be aware that 'natural' does not always mean 'safe'; there can be drug interactions between herbal and Western medicines. If using both systems, ensure you inform both practitioners of what the other has prescribed.

Language

Discounting its many ethnic minority languages, China has eight major dialect groups: Pǔtōnghuà (Mandarin), Yue (Cantonese), Wu (Shanghainese), Minbei (Fuzhou), Minnan (Hokkien-Taiwanese), Xiang, Gan and Hakka. These dialects also divide into subdialects.

It's the language spoken in Běijīng which is considered the official language of China. It's usually referred to as Mandarin, but the Chinese themselves call it Pǔtōnghuà (meaning 'common speech'). Pǔtōnghuà is variously referred to as Hànyǔ (the Han language), Guóyǔ (the national language) or Zhōngwén or Zhōngguóhuà (Chinese). With the exception of the western and southernmost provinces, most of the population speaks Mandarin (although it may be spoken there with a regional accent). In this chapter, we have included Mandarin, Cantonese, Tibetan, Uighur and Mongolian.

MANDARIN

Writing

Chinese is often referred to as a language of pictographs. Many of the basic Chinese characters are in fact highly stylised pictures of what they represent, but around 90% are compounds of a 'meaning' element and a 'sound' element.

A well-educated, contemporary Chinese person might use between 6000 and 8000 characters. To read a Chinese newspaper you need to know 2000 to 3000 characters, but 1200 to 1500 would be enough to get the gist.

Theoretically, all Chinese dialects share the same written system. In practice, Cantonese adds about 3000 specialised characters of its own and many of the dialects don't have a written form at all.

WANT MORE?
For in-depth language information and handy phrases, check out Lonely Planet's *China Phrasebook*. You'll find it at **shop.lonelyplanet.com**

Pinyin & Pronunciation

In 1958 the Chinese adopted Pinyin, a system of writing their language using the Roman alphabet. The original idea was to eventually do away with Chinese characters. However, tradition dies hard, and the idea was abandoned.

Pinyin is often used on shop fronts, street signs and advertising billboards. Don't expect all Chinese people to be able to use Pinyin, however. In the countryside and the smaller towns you may not see a single Pinyin sign anywhere, so unless you speak and read Chinese you'll need a phrasebook with Chinese characters.

Below we've provided Pinyin alongside the Mandarin script.

Vowels

a	as in 'father'
ai	as in 'aisle'
ao	as the 'ow' in 'cow'
e	as in 'her' (without 'r' sound)
ei	as in 'weigh'
i	as the 'ee' in 'meet' (or like a light 'r' as in 'Grrr!' after c, ch, r, s, sh, z or zh)
ian	as the word 'yen'
ie	as the English word 'yeah'
o	as in 'or' (without 'r' sound)
ou	as the 'oa' in 'boat'
u	as in 'flute'
ui	as the word 'way'
uo	like a 'w' followed by 'o'
yu/ü	like 'ee' with lips pursed

Consonants

c	as the 'ts' in 'bits'
ch	as in 'chop', but with the tongue curled up and back
h	as in 'hay', but articulated from further back in the throat
q	as the 'ch' in 'cheese'
sh	as in 'ship', but with the tongue curled up and back
x	as the 'sh' in 'ship'
z	as the 'ds' in 'suds'
zh	as the 'j' in 'judge' but with the tongue curled up and back

The only consonants that occur at the end of a syllable are n, ng and r.

In Pinyin, apostrophes are occasionally used to separate syllables in order to prevent ambiguity, eg the word píng'ān can be written with an apostrophe after the 'g' to prevent it being pronounced as pín'gǎn.

Tones

Mandarin is a language with a large number of words with the same pronunciation but a different meaning. What distinguishes these homophones (as these words are called) is their 'tonal' quality – the raising and the lowering of pitch on certain syllables. Mandarin has four tones – high, rising, falling-rising and falling, plus a fifth 'neutral' tone that you can all but ignore. Tones are important for distinguishing meaning of words – eg the word ma has four different meanings according to tone, as shown below. Tones are indicated in Pinyin by the following accent marks on vowels:

high tone	mā (mother)
rising tone	má (hemp, numb)
falling-rising tone	mǎ (horse)
falling tone	mà (scold, swear)

Basics

When asking a question it is polite to start with qǐng wèn – literally, 'May I ask?'.

Hello.	你好。	Nǐhǎo.
Goodbye.	再见。	Zàijiàn.
How are you?	你好吗？	Nǐhǎo ma?
Fine. And you?	好。你呢？	Hǎo. Nǐ ne?
Excuse me.		
(to get attention)	劳驾。	Láojià.
(to get past)	借光。	Jièguāng.
Sorry.	对不起。	Duìbùqǐ.
Yes./No.	是。/不是。	Shì./Bùshì.
Please ...	请……	Qǐng ...
Thank you.	谢谢你。	Xièxie nǐ.
You're welcome.	不客气。	Bù kèqi.
What's your name?		
你叫什么名字？		Nǐ jiào shénme míngzi?
My name is ...		
我叫……		Wǒ jiào ...
Do you speak English?		
你会说英文吗？		Nǐ huìshuō Yīngwén ma?
I don't understand.		
我不明白。		Wǒ bù míngbái.

KEY PATTERNS – MANDARIN

To get by in Mandarin, mix and match these simple patterns with words of your choice:

How much is (the deposit)?
(押金)多少？ (Yājīn) duōshǎo?

Do you have (a room)?
有没有(房)？ Yǒuméiyǒu (fáng)?

Is there (heating)?
有(暖气)吗？ Yóu (nuǎnqì) ma?

I'd like (that one).
我要(那个)。 Wǒ yào (nàge).

Please give me (the menu).
请给我(菜单)。 Qǐng gěiwǒ (càidān).

Can I (sit here)?
我能(坐这儿)吗？ Wǒ néng (zuòzhèr) ma?

I need (a can opener).
我想要(一个 Wǒ xiǎngyào (yīge
开罐器)。 kāiguàn qì).

Do we need (a guide)?
需要(向导)吗？ Xūyào (xiàngdǎo) ma?

I have (a reservation).
我有(预订)。 Wǒ yǒu (yùdìng).

I'm (a doctor).
我(是医生)。 Wǒ (shì yīshēng).

Accommodation

Do you have a single/double room?
有没有(单人/ Yǒuméiyǒu (dānrén/
套)房？ tào) fáng?

How much is it per night/person?
每天/人多少钱？ Měi tiān/rén duōshǎo qián?

campsite	露营地	lùyíngdì
guesthouse	宾馆	bīnguǎn
hostel	招待所	zhāodàisuǒ
hotel	酒店	jiǔdiàn
reception	总台	zǒng tái
air-con	空调	kōngtiáo
bathroom	浴室	yùshì
blanket	被子	bèizi
bed	床	chuáng
cot	张婴儿床	zhāng yīng'ér chuáng
hair dryer	吹风机	chuīfēngjī
safe	保险箱	bǎoxiǎnxiāng
sheet	床单	chuángdān
towel	毛巾	máojīn
window	窗	chuāng

SIGNS – MANDARIN

入口	Rùkǒu	Entrance
出口	Chūkǒu	Exit
问讯处	Wènxùnchù	Information
开	Kāi	Open
关	Guān	Closed
禁止	Jìnzhǐ	Prohibited
厕所	Cèsuǒ	Toilets
男	Nán	Men
女	Nǚ	Women

Directions

Where's (a bank)?
(银行) 在哪儿?   (Yínháng) zài nǎr?

What's the address?
地址在哪儿?   Dìzhǐ zài nǎr?

Could you write the address, please?
能不能请你   Néngbunéng qǐng nǐ
把地址写下来?   bǎ dìzhǐ xiě xiàlái?

Can you show me where it is on the map?
请帮我找它在   Qǐng bāngwǒ zhǎo tā zài
地图上的位置。   dìtú shàng de wèizhi.

Go straight ahead.
一直走。   Yīzhí zǒu.

Turn left.
左转。   Zuǒ zhuǎn.

Turn right.
右转。   Yòu zhuǎn.

at the traffic lights	在红绿灯	zài hónglǜdēng
behind	背面	bèimiàn
far	远	yuǎn
in front of ...	……的前面	... de qiánmian
near	近	jìn
next to	旁边	pángbiān
on the corner	拐角	guǎijiǎo
opposite	对面	duìmiàn

Eating & Drinking

What would you recommend?
有什么菜可以   Yǒu shénme cài kěyǐ
推荐的?   tuījiàn de?

What's in that dish?
这道菜用什么   Zhèdào cài yòng shénme
东西做的?   dōngxi zuòde?

That was delicious.
真好吃。   Zhēn hǎochī.

The bill, please!
买单!   Mǎidān!

Cheers!	干杯!	Gānbēi!
I'd like to reserve a table for ...	我想预订一张……的桌子。	Wǒ xiǎng yùdìng yīzhāng ... de zhuōzi.
(eight) o'clock	（八）点钟	(bā) diǎn zhōng
(two) people	（两个）人	(liǎngge) rén

I don't eat ...	我不吃……	Wǒ bùchī ...
fish	鱼	yú
nuts	果仁	guǒrén
poultry	家禽	jiāqín
red meat	牛羊肉	niúyángròu

Key Words

appetisers	凉菜	liángcài
bar	酒吧	jiǔbā
bottle	瓶子	píngzi
bowl	碗	wǎn
breakfast	早饭	zǎofàn
cafe	咖啡屋	kāfēiwū
chidren's menu	儿童菜单	értóng càidān
(too) cold	（太）凉	(tài) liáng
dinner	晚饭	wǎnfàn
dish (food)	盘	pán
food	食品	shípǐn
fork	叉子	chāzi
glass	杯子	bēizi
halal	清真	qīngzhēn
highchair	高凳	gāodèng
hot (warm)	热	rè
knife	刀	dāo
kosher	犹太	yóutài
local specialties	地方小吃	dìfāng xiǎochī
lunch	午饭	wǔfàn
main courses	主菜	zhǔ cài
market	菜市	càishì
menu (in English)	（英文）菜单	(Yīngwén) càidān
plate	碟子	diézi
restaurant	餐馆	cānguǎn
(too) spicy	（太）辣	(tài) là
spoon	勺	sháo
vegetarian food	素食食品	sùshí shípǐn

Meat & Fish

beef	牛肉	niúròu
chicken	鸡肉	jīròu
duck	鸭	yā

fish	鱼	yú
lamb	羊肉	yángròu
pork	猪肉	zhūròu
seafood	海鲜	hǎixiān

Fruit & Vegetables

apple	苹果	píngguǒ
banana	香蕉	xiāngjiāo
bok choy	小白菜	xiǎo báicài
carrot	胡萝卜	húluóbo
celery	芹菜	qíncài
cucumber	黄瓜	huángguā
'dragon eyes'	龙眼	lóngyǎn
fruit	水果	shuǐguǒ
grape	葡萄	pútáo
green beans	扁豆	biǎndòu
guava	石榴	shíliu
lychee	荔枝	lìzhī
mango	芒果	mángguǒ
mushroom	蘑菇	mógū
onion	洋葱	yáng cōng
orange	橙子	chéngzi
pear	梨	lí
pineapple	凤梨	fènglí
plum	梅子	méizi
potato	土豆	tǔdòu
radish	萝卜	luóbo
spring onion	小葱	xiǎo cōng
sweet potato	地瓜	dìguā
vegetable	蔬菜	shūcài
watermelon	西瓜	xīguā

Other

bread	面包	miànbāo
butter	黄油	huángyóu
egg	蛋	dàn
herbs/spices	香料	xiāngliào
pepper	胡椒粉	hújiāo fěn

salt	盐	yán
soy sauce	酱油	jiàngyóu
sugar	砂糖	shātáng
tofu	豆腐	dòufu
vinegar	醋	cù
vegetable oil	菜油	càiyóu

Drinks

beer	啤酒	píjiǔ
Chinese spirits	白酒	báijiǔ
coffee	咖啡	kāfēi
(orange) juice	(橙)汁	(chéng) zhī
milk	牛奶	niúnǎi
mineral water	矿泉水	kuàngquán shuǐ
red wine	红葡萄酒	hóng pútáo jiǔ
rice wine	米酒	mǐjiǔ
soft drink	汽水	qìshuǐ
tea	茶	chá
(boiled) water	(开)水	(kāi) shuǐ
white wine	白葡萄酒	bái pútáo jiǔ
yoghurt	酸奶	suānnǎi

Emergencies

Help!	救命！	Jiùmìng!
I'm lost.	我迷路了。	Wǒ mílù le.
Go away!	走开！	Zǒukāi!
There's been an accident. 出事了。		Chūshì le.
Call a doctor! 请叫医生来！		Qǐng jiào yīshēng lái!
Call the police! 请叫警察！		Qǐng jiào jǐngchá!
I'm ill. 我生病了。		Wǒ shēngbìng le.
It hurts here. 这里痛。		Zhèlǐ tòng.
Where are the toilets? 厕所在哪儿？		Cèsuǒ zài nǎr?

Question Words – Mandarin

How?	怎么？	Zěnme?
What?	什么？	Shénme?
When?	什么时候	Shénme shíhòu?
Where?	哪儿	Nǎr?
Which?	哪个	Nǎge?
Who?	谁？	Shuí?
Why?	为什么？	Wèishénme?

Shopping & Services

I'd like to buy ... 我想买……		Wǒ xiǎng mǎi ...
I'm just looking. 我先看看。		Wǒ xiān kànkan.
Can I look at it? 我能看看吗？		Wǒ néng kànkan ma?
I don't like it. 我不喜欢。		Wǒ bù xǐhuan.

Numbers – Mandarin

1	一	yī
2	二/两	èr/liǎng
3	三	sān
4	四	sì
5	五	wǔ
6	六	liù
7	七	qī
8	八	bā
9	九	jiǔ
10	十	shí
20	二十	èrshí
30	三十	sānshí
40	四十	sìshí
50	五十	wǔshí
60	六十	liùshí
70	七十	qīshí
80	八十	bāshí
90	九十	jiǔshí
100	一百	yībǎi
1000	一千	yīqiān

How much is it?
多少钱？   Duōshǎo qián?

That's too expensive.
太贵了。   Tàiguì le.

Can you lower the price?
能便宜一点吗？   Néng piányi yīdiǎn ma?

There's a mistake in the bill.
帐单上   Zhàngdān shàng
有问题。   yǒu wèntí.

ATM	自动取款机	zìdòng qǔkuǎn jī
credit card	信用卡	xìnyòng kǎ
internet cafe	网吧	wǎngbā
post office	邮局	yóujú
tourist office	旅行店	lǚxíng diàn

Time & Dates

What time is it?
现在几点钟？   Xiànzài jǐdiǎn zhōng?

It's (10) o'clock.
(十)点钟。   (Shí) diǎn zhōng.

Half past (10).
(十)点三十分。   (Shí) diǎn sānshífēn.

morning	早上	zǎoshang
afternoon	下午	xiàwǔ
evening	晚上	wǎnshàng

yesterday	昨天	zuótiān
today	今天	jīntiān
tomorrow	明天	míngtiān

Monday	星期一	xīngqī yī
Tuesday	星期二	xīngqī èr
Wednesday	星期三	xīngqī sān
Thursday	星期四	xīngqī sì
Friday	星期五	xīngqī wǔ
Saturday	星期六	xīngqī liù
Sunday	星期天	xīngqī tiān

January	一月	yīyuè
February	二月	èryuè
March	三月	sānyuè
April	四月	sìyuè
May	五月	wǔyuè
June	六月	liùyuè
July	七月	qīyuè
August	八月	bāyuè
September	九月	jiǔyuè
October	十月	shíyuè
November	十一月	shíyīyuè
December	十二月	shí'èryuè

Transport
Public Transport

boat	船	chuán
bus (city)	大巴	dàbā
bus (intercity)	长途车	chángtú chē
plane	飞机	fēijī
taxi	出租车	chūzū chē
train	火车	huǒchē
tram	电车	diànchē

I want to go to ...
我要去……   Wǒ yào qù ...

Does it stop at (Hāěrbīn)?
在(哈尔滨)能下   Zài (Hā'ěrbīn) néng xià
车吗？   chē ma?

At what time does it leave?
几点钟出发？   Jǐdiǎnzhōng chūfā?

At what time does it get to (Hángzhōu)?
几点钟到   Jǐdiǎnzhōng dào
(杭州)？   (Hángzhōu)?

Can you tell me when we get to (Hángzhōu)?
到了(杭州)   Dàole (Hángzhōu)
请叫我, 好吗？   qǐng jiào wǒ, hǎoma?

I want to get off here.
我想这儿下车。   Wǒ xiǎng zhèr xiàchē.

When's the ... (bus)?	······ (车) 几点走?	... (chē) jǐdiǎn zǒu?
first	首趟	Shǒutàng
last	末趟	Mòtàng
next	下一趟	Xià yītàng
A ... ticket to (Dàlián).	一张到 （大连）的 ······票。	Yīzhāng dào (Dàlián) de ... piào.
1st-class	头等	tóuděng
2nd-class	二等	èrděng
one-way	单程	dānchéng
return	双程	shuāngchéng
aisle seat	走廊的 座位	zǒuláng de zuòwèi
cancelled	取消	qǔxiāo
delayed	晚点	wǎndiǎn
platform	站台	zhàntái
ticket office	售票处	shòupiàochù
timetable	时刻表	shíkè biǎo
train station	火车站	huǒchēzhàn
window seat	窗户的 座位	chuānghu de zuòwèi

Driving & Cycling

bicycle pump	打气筒	dǎqìtóng
child seat	婴儿座	yīng'érzuò
diesel	柴油	cháiyóu
helmet	头盔	tóukuī
mechanic	机修工	jīxiūgōng
petrol	汽油	qìyóu
service station	加油站	jiāyóu zhàn
I'd like to hire a ...	我要租 一辆······	Wǒ yào zū yīliàng ...
4WD	四轮驱动	sìlún qūdòng
bicycle	自行车	zìxíngchē
car	汽车	qìchē
motorcycle	摩托车	mótuochē

Does this road lead to ...?
这条路到······吗? Zhè tiáo lù dào ... ma?

How long can I park here?
这儿可以停多久? Zhèr kěyǐ tíng duōjiǔ?

The car has broken down (at ...).
汽车是（在······）坏的。 Qìchē shì (zài ...) huài de.

I have a flat tyre.
轮胎瘪了。 Lúntāi biě le.

I've run out of petrol.
没有汽油了。 Méiyou qìyóu le.

CANTONESE

Cantonese is the most widely used Chinese language in Hong Kong, Macau, Guǎngdōng, parts of Guǎngxī and the surrounding region. Cantonese speakers use Chinese characters, but pronounce many of them differently from a Mandarin speaker. Also, Cantonese adds about 3000 characters of its own to the character set. Several systems of Romanisation for Cantonese script exist, and no single one has emerged as an official standard. In this chapter we use Lonely Planet's pronunciation guide, designed for maximum accuracy with minimum complexity.

Pronunciation

In Cantonese, the ng sound can appear at the start of a word. Words ending with the consonant sounds p, t, and k are clipped. Many speakers, particularly young people, replace the n with an l at the start of a word – eg náy (you) often sounds like láy. Where relevant, our pronunciation guide reflects this change.

The vowels are pronounced as follows: a as the 'u' in 'but', ai as in 'aisle' (short), au as the 'ou' in 'out', ay as in 'pay', eu as in the 'er' in 'fern', eui as eu followed by i, ew as in 'blew' (short, with lips tightened), i as the 'ee' in 'deep', iu as the 'yu' in 'yuletide', o as in 'go', oy as in 'boy', u as in 'put', ui as in French oui.

Tones in Cantonese fall on vowels (a, e, i, o, u) and on n. The same word pronounced with different tones can have a different meaning, eg gwàt (dig up) vs gwàt (bones). There are six tones, divided into high- and low-pitch groups. High-pitch tones involve tightening the vocal muscles to get a higher note, while lower-pitch tones are made by relaxing the vocal chords to get a lower note. Tones are indicated with the following accent marks: à (high), á (high rising), à̠ (low falling), á̠ (low rising), a̠ (low), a (level – no accent mark).

Basics

Hello.	哈佬 。	hàa·ló
Goodbye.	再見 。	joy·gin
How are you?	你幾好 啊嗎?	láy gáy hó à maa
Fine.	幾好 。	gáy hó
Excuse me.	對唔住 。	deui·ǹg·jew
Sorry.	對唔住 。	deui·ǹg·jew
Yes./No.	係 。/不係	hai/ǹg·hai
Please ...	唔該······	ǹg·gòy ...
Thank you.	多謝 。	dàw·je

What's your name?
你叫乜嘢名? láy giu màt·yé méng aa

My name is ...
我叫⋯⋯　　　ngáw giu ...

Do you speak English?
你識唔識講　　láy sìk·ńg·sìk gáwng
英文啊？　　　yìng·mán aa

I don't understand.
我唔明 。　　　ngáw ǹg mìng

Accommodation

campsite	營地	yìng·day
guesthouse	賓館	bàn·gún
hostel	招待所	jiù·doy·sáw
hotel	酒店	jáu·dim

Do you have a ... room?	有冇⋯⋯房？	yáu·mó ... fàwng
double	雙人	sèung·yàn
single	單人	dàan·yàn

How much is it per ...?	一⋯⋯幾多錢？	yàt ... gáy·dàw chín
night	晚	máan
person	個人	gaw yàn

Directions

Where's ...?　⋯⋯喺邊度？　... hái bìn·do
What's the address?　地址係？　day·jí hai

left	左邊	jáw·bìn
on the corner	十字路口	sap·ji·lo·háu
right	右邊	yau·bìn
straight ahead	前面	chìn·mìn
traffic lights	紅綠燈	hùng·luk·dàng

Eating & Drinking

What would you recommend?
有乜野好介紹？　yáu màt·yé hó gaai·siu

That was delicious.
真好味 。　　jàn hó·may

I'd like the bill, please.
唔該我要埋單 。　ǹg·gòy ngáw yiu màai·dàan

Cheers!
乾杯！　　gàwn·bui

I'd like to book a table for ...	我想訂張檯，⋯⋯嘅 。	ngáw séung deng jèung tóy ... ge
(eight) o'clock	(八)點鐘	(bàat) dím·jùng
(two) people	(兩)位	(léung) ái

Numbers – Cantonese

1	一	yàt
2	二	yi
3	三	sàam
4	四	say
5	五	ńg
6	六	luk
7	七	chàt
8	八	baat
9	九	gáu
10	十	sap
20	二十	yi·sap
30	三十	sàam·sap
40	四十	say·sap
50	五十	ńg·sap
60	六十	luk·sap
70	七十	chàt·sap
80	八十	baat·sap
90	九十	gáu·sap
100	一百	yàt·baak
1000	一千	yàt·chìn

bar	酒吧	jáu·bàa
bottle	樽	jèun
breakfast	早餐	jó·chàan
cafe	咖啡屋	gaa·fè·ngùk
dinner	晚飯	máan·faan
fork	叉	chàa
glass	杯	bui
knife	刀	dò
lunch	午餐	ńg·chàan
market	街市 (HK)	gàai·sí
	市場 (China)	sí·chèung
plate	碟	díp
restaurant	酒樓	jáu·làu
spoon	羹	gàng

Emergencies

Help!　救命！　gau·meng
I'm lost.　我蕩失路 。　ngáw dawng·sàk·lo
Go away!　走開！　jáu·hòy

Call a doctor!
快啲叫醫生！　faai·dì giu yì·sàng

Call the police!
快啲叫警察！　faai·dì giu gíng·chaat

I'm sick.
我病咗 。　ngáw beng·jáw

Shopping & Services

I'd like to buy ...
我想買······ ngáw séung máai ...

How much is it?
幾多錢? gáy·dàw chín

That's too expensive.
太貴啦。 taai gwai laa

There's a mistake in the bill.
帳單錯咗。 jeung·dàan chaw jáw

internet cafe	網吧	máwng·bàa
post office	郵局	yàu·gúk
tourist office	旅行社	léui·hàng·sé

Time & Dates

What time is it?	而家 幾點鐘?	yi·gàa gáy·dím·jùng
It's (10) o'clock.	(十)點鐘。	(sap)·dím·jùng
Half past (10).	(十)點半。	(sap)·dím bun

morning	朝早	jiù·jó
afternoon	下晝	haa·jau
evening	夜晚	ye·máan
yesterday	寢日	kàm·yat
today	今日	gàm·yat
tomorrow	听日	tìng·yat

Transport

boat	船	sèwn
bus	巴士 (HK)	bàa·sí
	公共	gùng·gung
	汽車 (China)	hay·chè
train	火車	fáw·chè

A ... ticket to (Panyu).	一張去 (番禺)嘅 ······飛。	yàt jèung heui (pùn·yèw) ge ... fày
1st-class	頭等	tàu·dáng
2nd-class	二等	yi·dáng
one-way	單程	dàan·chìng
return	雙程	sèung·chìng

At what time does it leave?
幾點鐘出發? gáy·dím jùng chèut·faa

Does it stop at ...?
會唔會喺······停呀? wuí·ng·wuí hái ... tìng aa

At what time does it get to ...?
幾點鐘到······? gáy·dím jùng do ...

TIBETAN

Tibetan is spoken by around six million people, mainly in Tibet. In urban areas almost all Tibetans also speak Mandarin.

Most sounds in Tibetan are similar to those found in English, so if you read our coloured pronunciation guides as if they were English, you'll be understood. Note that â is pronounced as the 'a' in 'ago', ö as the 'er' in 'her', and ü as the 'u' in 'flute' but with a raised tongue. A vowel followed by n, m or ng indicates a nasalised sound (pronounced 'through the nose'). A consonant followed by h is aspirated (accompanied by a puff of air).

There are no direct equivalents of English 'yes' and 'no' in Tibetan. Although it may not be completely correct, you'll be understood if you use la ong for 'yes' and la men for 'no'.

Hello.	བཀྲ་ཤིས་བདེ་ལེགས།	ta·shi de·lek
Goodbye.		
(if staying)	ག་ལེར་ཕེབས།	ka·lee pay
(if leaving)	ག་ལེར་བཞུགས།	ka·lee shu
Excuse me.	དགོངས་དག	gong·da
Sorry.	དགོངས་དག	gong·da
Please.	ཐུགས་རྗེ་གནང་སིག	tu·jay·sig
Thank you.	ཐུགས་རྗེ་ཆེ།	tu·jay·chay

How are you?
ཁྱེད་རང་སྐུ་གཟུགས་ བདེ་པོ་ཡིན་པས། kay·râng ku·su de·po yin·bay

Fine. And you?
བདེ་པོ་ཡིན། ཁྱེད་རང་ཡང་ སྐུ་གཟུགས་བདེ་པོ་ཡིན་པས། de·bo·yin kay·râng·yâng ku·su de·po yin·bay

What's your name?
ཁྱེད་རང་གི་མཚན་ལ་ ག་རེ་རེད། kay·râng·gi tsen·lâ kâ·ray·ray

My name is ...
ངའི་མིང་ལ་ ... རེད། ngay·ming·la ... ray

Do you speak English?
ཁྱེད་རང་དབྱིན་ཇི་སྐད་ ཤེས་ཀྱི་ཡོད་པས། kay·râng in·ji·kay shing·gi yö·bay

I don't understand.
ཧ་གོ་མ་སོང་། ha ko ma·song

How much is it?
གོང་ག་ཚོད་རེད། gong kâ·tsay ray

Where is ...?
... ག་བར་ཡོད་རེད། ... ka·bah yö·ray

UIGHUR

Uighur is spoken all over Xīnjiāng. In China, Uighur is written in Arabic script. The phrases in this chapter reflect the Kashgar dialect.

In our pronunciation guides, stressed syllables are indicated with italics. Most consonant sounds in Uighur are the same as in English, though note that h is pronounced with a puff of air. The vowels are pronounced as follows: a as in 'hat', aa as the 'a' in 'father', ee as in 'sleep' (produced back in the throat), o as in 'go', ö as the 'e' in 'her' (pronounced with rounded lips), u as in 'put', and ü as the 'i' in 'bit' (with the lips rounded and pushed forward). Stressed syllables are in italics.

Basics

Hello.	ئەسسالامۇ	as·saa·laa·mu
	ئەلەيكۇم.	a·lay·kom
Goodbye.	خەير ـ خوش.	hayr·hosh
Excuse me.	كۆرۈوۈچەك گە	ka·chü·rüng ga
	قانداق	kaan·daak
	باردۇ؟	baar·i·du
Sorry.	كۆرۈوۈچەك.	ka·chü·rüng
Yes.	ھەئە.	ee·a·a
No.	ياق.	yaak
Please.	مەرھەممەت.	ma·ree·am·mat
Thank you.	رەخمەت سىزگە.	rah·mat siz·ga
How are you?		
	قانداق	kaan·daak
	ئەھۋالىڭىز؟	a·ee·vaa·li·ngiz
Fine. And you?		
	ياخشى، سىزچۇ؟	yaah·shi siz·chu
What's your name?		
	سىزنىڭ	siz·ning
	ئىسمىڭىز نىمە؟	is·mi·ngiz ni·ma
My name is ...		
	مىنىڭ ئىسمىم ...	mi·ning is·mim ...
Do you speak English?		
	سىز ئىنگگىلىزچە	siz ing·gi·lis·ka
	بىلەمسىز؟	bi·lam·siz
I don't understand.		
	چۈشەنمەيدىم.	man chu·shan·mi·dim
How much is it?		
	قانچە پۇل؟	kaan·cha pool
Where is ...?		
	... نەدە؟	... na·da

MONGOLIAN

Mongolian has an estimated 10 million speakers. The standard Mongolian in the Inner Mongolia Autonomous Region of China is based on the Chahar dialect and written using a cursive script in vertical lines (ie from top to bottom), read from left to right. So if you want to ask a local to read the script in this section, just turn the book 90 degrees clockwise. Our coloured pronunciation guides, however, should simply be read the same way you read English.

Most consonant sounds in Mongolian are the same as in English, though note that r in Mongolian is a hard, trilled sound, kh is a throaty sound like the 'ch' in the Scottish *loch*, and z is pronounced as the 'ds' in 'lads'. As for the vowels, ē is pronounced as in 'there', ô as in 'alone', ö as 'e' with rounded lips, öö as a slightly longer ö, u as in 'cut' and ŭ as in 'good'.

In the pronunciation guides, stressed syllables are in italics.

Basics

Hello.	sēn bēn nô
Goodbye.	ba·yur·tē
Excuse me./Sorry.	ôch·lē·rē
Yes.	teem
No.	oo·gway
Thank you.	ba·yur·laa
How are you?	sēn bēn nô
Fine. And you?	sēn sēn
	sēn nô
What's your name?	tan·nē al·dur
My name is ...	min·nee nur ...
Do you speak English?	ta ang·gul hul
	mu·tun nô
I don't understand.	bee oil·og·sun·gway
How much is it?	hut·tee jôs vē
Where's ...?	... haa bēkh vē

GLOSSARY

apsara – Buddhist celestial being

arhat – Buddhist, especially a monk, who has achieved enlightenment and passes to nirvana at death

běi – north; the other points of the compass are *dōng* (east), *nán* (south) and *xī* (west)

biānjiè – border

biéshù – villa

bīnguǎn – hotel

bìxì – mythical tortoiselike dragon

Bodhisattva – one who is worthy of nirvana and remains on earth to help others attain enlightenment

Bon – pre-Buddhist indigenous faith of Tibet

bówùguǎn – museum

CAAC – Civil Aviation Administration of China

cadre – Chinese government bureaucrat

cāntīng – restaurant

cǎoyuán – grasslands

CCP – Chinese Communist Party

chau – land mass

chéngshì – city

chí – lake, pool

chop – carved name seal that acts as a signature

chörten – Tibetan *stupa*

CITS – China International Travel Service

cūn – village

dàdào – boulevard

dàfàndiàn – large hotel

dàjiē – avenue

dàjiǔdiàn – large hotel

dǎo – island

dàpùbù – large waterfall

dàqiáo – large bridge

dàshà – hotel, building

dàxué – university

déhuà – white-glazed porcelain

dìtiě – subway

dōng – east; the other points of the compass are *běi* (north), *nán* (south) and *xī* (west)

dòng – cave

dòngwùyuán – zoo

fàndiàn – hotel, restaurant

fēng – peak

fēngjǐngqū – scenic area

gé – pavilion, temple

gompa – monastery

gōng – palace

gōngyuán – park

gōu – gorge, valley

guān – pass

gùjū – house, home, residence

hǎi – sea

hǎitān – beach

Hakka – Chinese ethnic group

Han – China's main ethnic group

hé – river

hú – lake

huáqiáo – overseas Chinese

Hui – ethnic Chinese Muslims

huǒchēzhàn – train station

huǒshān – volcano

hútòng – a narrow alleyway

jiāng – river

jiǎo – unit of *renminbi;* 10 jiǎo equals 1 *yuán*

jiàotáng – church

jīchǎng – airport

jiē – street

jié – festival

jīn – unit of weight; 1 *jīn* equals 600g

jīngjù – Beijing opera

jìniànbēi – memorial

jìniànguǎn – memorial hall

jiǔdiàn – hotel

jū – residence, home

junk – originally referred to Chinese fishing and war vessels with square sails; now applies to various types of boating craft

kang – raised sleeping platform

KCR – Kowloon–Canton Railway

kora – pilgrim circuit

Kuomintang – Chiang Kaishek's Nationalist Party; now one of Taiwan's major political parties

lama – a Buddhist priest of the Tantric or Lamaist school; a title bestowed on monks of particularly high spiritual attainment

lǐlòng – Shànghǎi alleyway

lín – forest

líng – tomb

lìshǐ – history

lóu – tower

LRT – Light Rail Transit

lù – road

lǚguǎn – guesthouse

luóhàn – Buddhist, especially a monk, who has achieved enlightenment and passes to nirvana at death; see also *arhat*

mahjong – popular Chinese game for four people; played with engraved tiles

mǎtou – dock

mén – gate

ménpiào – entrance ticket

Miao – ethnic group living in Guìzhōu

miào – temple

MTR – Mass Transit Railway

mù – tomb

nán – south; the other points of the compass are *běi* (north), *dōng* (east) and *xī* (west)

páilou – decorative archway

pinyin – the official system for transliterating Chinese script into roman characters

PLA – People's Liberation Army

Politburo – the 25-member supreme policy-making authority of the Chinese Communist Party
PRC – People's Republic of China
PSB – Public Security Bureau; the arm of the police force set up to deal with foreigners
pùbù – waterfall

qì – life force
qiáo – bridge
qìchēzhàn – bus station

rénmín – people, people's
renminbi – literally 'people's money'; the formal name for the currency of China, the basic unit of which is the yuán; shortened to RMB

sampan – small motorised launch
sānlún mótuōchē – motor tricycle
sānlúnchē – pedal-powered tricycle

SAR – Special Administrative Region
sēnlín – forest
shān – mountain
shāngdiàn – shop, store
shěng – province, provincial
shì – city
shí – rock
shìchǎng – market
shíkū – grotto
shíkùmén – literally 'stone-gate house'; type of 19th-century Shànghǎi residence
shòupiàochù – ticket office
shuǐkù – reservoir
sì – temple, monastery
sìhéyuàn – traditional courtyard house
stupa – usually used as reliquaries for the cremated remains of important lamas

tǎ – pagoda
thangka – Tibetan sacred art
tíng – pavilion

wān – bay
wǎngbā – internet café
wēnquán – hot springs

xī – west; the other points of the compass are dōng (east), běi (north) and nán (south)
xī – small stream, brook
xiá – gorge
xiàn – county
xuěshān – snow mountain
yá – cliff
yán – rock or crag
yóujú – post office
yuán – basic unit of renminbi
yuán – garden

zhào – lamasery
zhāodàisuǒ – guesthouse
zhíwùyuán – botanic gardens
zhōng – middle
Zhōngguó – China
zìrán bǎohùqū – nature reserve

Behind the Scenes

SEND US YOUR FEEDBACK

We love to hear from travellers – your comments keep us on our toes and help make our books better. Our well-travelled team reads every word on what you loved or loathed about this book. Although we cannot reply individually to your submissions, we always guarantee that your feedback goes straight to the appropriate authors, in time for the next edition. Each person who sends us information is thanked in the next edition – the most useful submissions are rewarded with a selection of digital PDF chapters.

Visit **lonelyplanet.com/contact** to submit your updates and suggestions or to ask for help. Our award-winning website also features inspirational travel stories, news and discussions.

Note: We may edit, reproduce and incorporate your comments in Lonely Planet products such as guidebooks, websites and digital products, so let us know if you don't want your comments reproduced or your name acknowledged. For a copy of our privacy policy visit lonelyplanet.com/privacy.

OUR READERS

Many thanks to the travellers who used the last edition and wrote to us with helpful hints, useful advice and interesting anecdotes:

A Aizad Azmi, Alex Jones, Alicia León, Andrea McCracken, Andreas Eirich, Anthamatten Raphael, Antonio Holl **B** Barbara Eisenlauer, Ben Leeuwenburgh , Benedict Tan Jee Chiok, Brian Stepanek **C** Cale Lawlor, Caroline Stephan , Cassandra Hoover, Chris Beggs, Clayton Debattista, Colin Forsyth, Colm Faherty, Cornelis Oudemans **D** Daniel Rubinstein, Deanna Gorham, Dora Müller **E** Elvis Anber, Erica Riordan, Eveline van Gerrevink **F** Fabian Heller **G** Gesa Schwantes, Gillian Davies, Giraudet Jean-Francois **H** Haim Kallai, Harald Groven, Helen Xie, Jakob Hwollander **I** Iris Chen **J** Jack Cartier, Jackson Howard, James Timmis, Jean-Pierre De Montigny, Jenny Ward, Jeroen van Dijk, Jessica Faust, Joeri Vanvaerenbergh, Johanna Sell, John Mandeville, Jon Christo **K** Kai Eggers, Karleen Gribble, Katie Dimmery, Katju Aro, Keimpe Veldboom, Kevin Reitz, Kieran James, Kimberly Asal **L** Laura Chovet, Laura Plunkett, Lisa Mittmann, Lorin Veltkamp, Luke Lorenc **M** Margit Burmeister, Mark Mamin, Martin Woodford, Matt Colautti, Matt Livesey, Matthew Downey, Max Osterhaus, Melisa Baldwick, Melissa Flanagan **N** Nick Speyer, Nina Hall **P** Peter Jones, Petra O'Neill, Pheng Taing **R** Rafael Moreno Ripoll & Clara Murueta-Goyena, Ralpha Jacobson, Richard Whitener, Richard Armitage, Ron Crawford, Ron Perrier, Roseline Olabode **S** Sabrina Cheng, Sander Bovee, Scott Trudell, Sheryl Tapp, Shohei Takashiro, Simon Maria Zumkeller, Steven Quinn, Stijn Kuipers, Susana Fueyo **T** Tobias Müller, Tom Ferguson **V** Valentina Jofre, Valerie van der Burg, Maarten van Luijn **W** William Barnard, William Clements **X** Xuess Wee **Y** Yonatan levin, Yvonne Beaudry

AUTHOR THANKS

Damian Harper

Thanks to Dai Min, Dai Lu, Alvin and Chengyuan, Edward Li, John Zhang, Jimmy Gu and Liu Meina. Much gratitude also to Jiale and Jiafu for everything, as always, plus immense gratitude to the people of China for making this nation such a joy to explore.

Piera Chen

A warm thank you to Alvin Tse, Jackal Tam, and Jose Alfredo Lau do Rosario for their assistance and generosity. Thanks also to all the Guǎngxī and Guǎngdōng folks who enriched my chapters with their wisdom and humour, in particular, Wendy Luo, my only Zhuàng friend in Hong Kong, and Ms Lì, for her fantastic accounts of Yáo folktales. As always, lots of love to my husband, Sze Pang-cheung, and daughter Clio, who add sparkle to all my journeys.

Chung Wah Chow

A big *xièxiè* to my dear friend Cui Qun, commissioning editor of Lonely Planet's domestic Chinese guide *Fújiàn*, for her invaluable insider knowledge of the region and for putting me up in her nice home in Amoy. My biggest thank you, as always, goes to my parents and to my beloved Haider Kikabhoy for all your love, help and inspiration.

Megan Eaves

Big thanks to Liu Weijia and Li Xiaojian for their Qīnghǎi advice, Wu Liang for her help on Yùshù, the great meal and lifelong friendship, and the lovely people of Qīnghǎi I met along the way. David, Nóirín and Tom, thanks for supporting me with a loose rein; and my darling husband, Bill, for his unrelenting endurance of my China obsession.

David Eimer

Special gratitude goes to Annie and Angelina in Chóngqìng and Emi and Joy in Yúnnán. Thanks to Damian Harper for his support and patience, as well as to Megan Eaves and Julie Sheridan at Lonely Planet. As ever, thanks to the many people who provided tips along the way, whether knowingly or unwittingly.

Tienlon Ho

Thanks so much to Damian, Megan, Dianne, Daniel and the Lonely Planet team. Thank you Drolma (Amelia) Koknor, Laura Zhou, Martin Ding, Cao Lijuan, Andy Danzhen, Kris Rubesh, Luoqing Lan, Kevin Liu, Angie Wong, Zhongqiang Wu, Lang Ge, Chen Shifu, Klaus Wang, and Kieran Fitzgerald for sharing your unique insights. Thank you Fu Qin for your energy, and Ajue Wang for your infinite resourcefulness. Thank you 高文慧 for always seeing, 何坤 for always remembering, and Jon for digging with me.

Robert Kelly

Tania Simonetti, desert flower, big love to you for sharing your knowledge of Islam and for pushing me to read all those books on cave art. Cash Huang, you pulled through in time as I knew you would. Lele and Ping, love you guys for your endless support. Finally, thanks to Megan Eaves who I assume knows what she did.

Shawn Low

As always thanks to the DE, Megan, for steadying the China ship. Your knowledge of China is invaluable. Cheers also to CA, Damian (yet another one done and dusted!). Thanks to the LP crew who are working on this: eds, cartos, BDs etc. I've been behind the scenes and know how hard you all work. Thanks also to new friends and old friends on the ground: too numerous to list but I promise to buy you all beers when our paths cross again. Otherwise, we'll catch up on WeChat!

Emily Matchar

Thanks to the entire LP team. Thanks to Marie Kobler and Tim Bonebrake for their excellent Lamma suggestions, and to Michael Johnson for his helpful restaurant advice. Thanks to my friends and especially to my husband, Jamin Asay, for being so willing to help me try out restaurants and bars across Hong Kong and Hainan.

Bradley Mayhew

Thanks to Kelsang at the Yeti Hotel in Gyantse for showing me that city's tourism plans. A big personal thanks to first-rate guide Tenzin Gelek and driver Nordrup, to Big Tenzin and Aja at Highland Tours and to Andre, Alyson and Wanda for their fine company on the road. Cheers to Robert and John for their fine contributions. Love as always to Kelli for doing without me for way too long this year.

Daniel McCrohan

Thanks to porcelain expert Sue Ainsworth for her help in Jǐngdézhèn, to hat enthusiast Kim Greening for museum tips in Běijīng, and to my dear aunt, Pat Rose, for road-testing my research during her latest trip to China. Thanks too, to Mike Freundlich and Jessica Farmer for inspiration in Húnán and to my colleague David Eimer for all his work on the Běijīng chapter. As ever, all my love to Taotao and the kids (我爱你们), and to all my family back in the UK.

Phillip Tang

La neta, gracias gracias gracias to Ernesto and Vek for keeping home, home while I was on the other side of the world. To Lisa, Geraldine, Anna and Waimei for keeping me sane from afar with the magic of the right words (and emoji) at the right time. Thanks to the one French, Chilean, German, three Australian and many Chinese travellers I met on the Silk Road who made me feel less like a camel-less nomad.

ACKNOWLEDGMENTS

Climate map data adapted from Peel MC, Finlayson BL & McMahon TA (2007) 'Updated World Map of the Köppen-Geiger Climate Classification', *Hydrology and Earth System Sciences*, 11, 1633–44.

Cover photograph: The Great Wall, View Stock/Getty Images
Illustrations: pp62-3 and pp196-7 by Michael Weldon.

THIS BOOK

This 14th edition of Lonely Planet's *China* guidebook was researched and written by Damian Harper, Piera Chen, Chung Wah Chow, Megan Eaves, David Eimer, Tienlon Ho, Robert Kelly, Shawn Low, Emily Matchar, Bradley Mayhew, Daniel McCrohan, Dai Min and Phillip Tang. This guidebook was produced by the following:

Destination Editor
Megan Eaves

Commissioning Editor
Joe Bindloss

Senior Cartographer
David Kemp

Product Editor Anne Mason

Book Designers
Jennifer Mullins, Jessica Rose, Wibowo Rusli

Assisting Editors Judith Bamber, Michelle Bennett, Elin Berglund, Peter Cruttenden, Andrea Dobbin, Paul Hardy, Victoria Harrison, Kate James, Gabrielle Innes, Andi Jones, Elizabeth Jones, Anne Mulvaney, Katie O'Connell, Lauren O'Connell, Charlotte Orr, Susan Paterson, Christopher Pitts, Erin Richards, Sally Schafer, Luna Soo, Gabrielle Stefanos, Ross Taylor, Jeanette Wall

Assisting Cartographers
Julie Dodkins, Michael Garrett, Mark Griffiths, Gabriel Lindquist, Diana Von Holdt

Cover Researcher
Naomi Parker

Thanks to Sasha Baskett, Daniel Corbett, Penny Cordner, Helvi Cranfield, Brendan Dempsey, Ryan Evans, Anna Harris, Asha Ioculari, Claire Murphy, Claire Naylor, Karyn Noble, Averil Robertson, Dianne Schallmeiner, Eleanor Simpson, Josh Summers, Samantha Tyson, Lauren Wellicome

Index

Map Legend

Sights

- Beach
- Bird Sanctuary
- Buddhist
- Castle/Palace
- Christian
- Confucian
- Hindu
- Islamic
- Jain
- Jewish
- Monument
- Museum/Gallery/Historic Building
- Ruin
- Shinto
- Sikh
- Taoist
- Winery/Vineyard
- Zoo/Wildlife Sanctuary
- Other Sight

Activities, Courses & Tours

- Bodysurfing
- Diving
- Canoeing/Kayaking
- Course/Tour
- Sento Hot Baths/Onsen
- Skiing
- Snorkelling
- Surfing
- Swimming/Pool
- Walking
- Windsurfing
- Other Activity

Sleeping

- Sleeping
- Camping

Eating

- Eating

Drinking & Nightlife

- Drinking & Nightlife
- Cafe

Entertainment

- Entertainment

Shopping

- Shopping

Information

- Bank
- Embassy/Consulate
- Hospital/Medical
- Internet
- Police
- Post Office
- Telephone
- Toilet
- Tourist Information
- Other Information

Geographic

- Beach
- Hut/Shelter
- Lighthouse
- Lookout
- Mountain/Volcano
- Oasis
- Park
- Pass
- Picnic Area
- Waterfall

Population

- Capital (National)
- Capital (State/Province)
- City/Large Town
- Town/Village

Transport

- Airport
- Border crossing
- Bus
- Cable car/Funicular
- Cycling
- Ferry
- Metro station
- Monorail
- Parking
- Petrol station
- Subway station
- Taxi
- Train station/Railway
- Tram
- Underground station
- Other Transport

Routes

- Tollway
- Freeway
- Primary
- Secondary
- Tertiary
- Lane
- Unsealed road
- Road under construction
- Plaza/Mall
- Steps
- Tunnel
- Pedestrian overpass
- Walking Tour
- Walking Tour detour
- Path/Walking Trail

Boundaries

- International
- State/Province
- Disputed
- Regional/Suburb
- Marine Park
- Cliff
- Wall

Hydrography

- River, Creek
- Intermittent River
- Canal
- Water
- Dry/Salt/Intermittent Lake
- Reef

Areas

- Airport/Runway
- Beach/Desert
- Cemetery (Christian)
- Cemetery (Other)
- Glacier
- Mudflat
- Park/Forest
- Sight (Building)
- Sportsground
- Swamp/Mangrove

Note: Not all symbols displayed above appear on the maps in this book

Dai Min (Daisy Harper)

Ānhuī, Hénán, Húběi, Jiāngsū, Shànghǎi, Zhèjiāng Dai Min grew up in beer-making Qīngdǎo (Tsingtao) on the Shāndōng coast before hopping on the train north to university in Běijīng to read English. She moved to the UK in the 1990s, then to Shànghǎi for two years in the mid-noughties, living on the gritty cusp of the French Concession and, for a while, in West Shànghǎi. Regularly returning to visit her family in China, Dai Min has contributed to several editions of Lonely Planet's *China* and also works as a freelance English–Chinese translator (and multitasking mum).

Phillip Tang

Gānsù, Níngxià, Shaanxi (Shǎnxī) Phillip first visited China in 1998 to put to use his Chinese degree and love of potent cigarettes. He is fascinated with China for the way it transforms itself. His return trips over the years can be signposted through witnessing VCD stores morph into DVD parlours and then mobile-phone emporiums. Phillip lives between Mexico City, London and Sydney. He no longer smokes. Find Phillip's China photos on Instagram @mrtangtangtang, tweets @philliptang and more tips on the Middle Kingdom and elsewhere at http://philliptang.co.uk.